Almanac

By the Editors of Sports Illustrated

Sports Illustrated 2006 Almanac

First Edition. ISBN 1-932994-40-8

SPORTS ILLUSTRATED Executive Editor: Rob Fleder
SPORTS ILLUSTRATED Director, New Product Development: Bruce Kaufman

Sports Illustrated 2006 Almanac was prepared by
TPG Sports, Bishop Publishing, of White Plains, N.Y.

Editorial Director: Morin Bishop   Art Director: Barbara Chilenskas
Senior Editor: Reed Richardson   Photo Editor: John Blackmar
Associate Editor: Chris Freeburn   Editorial Intern: Cameron Berns

Cover photography credits:
Peyton Manning: John Biever
Alex Rodriguez: John Iacono
Lance Armstrong: Joel Saget/Agence France Presse
Shaquille O'Neal: Bob Rosato

Back cover photography credits (left to right):
Matt Leinart: Bob Rosato
Roger Federer: Manny Millan
Danica Patrick: Donald Miralle/Getty Images
Spine photography credit: Al Tielemans
Title page photography credit: John Biever

TIME INC. HOME ENTERTAINMENT

Publisher . . . . Richard Fraiman
Executive Director, Marketing Services . . . . Carol Pittard
Director, Retail & Special Sales . . . . : . . . . Tom Mifsud
Marketing Director, Branded Businesses . . . . Swati Rao
Director, New Product Development . . . . Peter Harper
Financial Director . . . . Steven Sandonato
Prepress Manager . . . . Emily Rabin
Book Production Manager . . . . Jonathan Polsky
Marketing Manager . . . . Kristin Rivela
Associate Prepress Manager . . . . Anne-Michelle Gallero
Assistant Marketing Manager . . . . Calandria Wells

Special thanks: Bozena Bannett, Alexandra Bliss, Glenn Buonocore, Suzanne Janso, Robert Marasco, Brooke McGuire, Chavaughn Raines, Ilene Schreider, Adriana Tierno, Britney Williams

We welcome your comments and suggestions about Sports Illustrated Books. Please write to us at: Sports Illustrated Books, Attention: Book Editors, PO Box 11016, Des Moines, IA 50336-1016

If you would like to order any of our hardcover Collector's Edition books, please call us at 1-800-327-6388. (Monday through Friday, 7:00 a.m.- 8:00 p.m. or Saturday, 7:00 a.m.- 6:00 p.m. Central Time).

CONTENTS

In compiling the *Sports Illustrated 2006 Almanac*, the editors would like to extend their grat itude to the media relations offices of the following organizations for their help in providing information and materials relating to their sports: Major League Baseball; the Canadian Football League; the National Football League; the National Collegiate Athletic Associa tion; the National Basketball Association; the National Hockey League; the Association of Tennis Professionals; the Women's Tennis Association; the U.S. Tennis Association; the U.S. Golf Association; the Ladies Professional Golf Association; the Professional Golfer Association; National Thoroughbred Racing Association; the U.S. Trotting Association the Breeders' Cup; Churchill Downs; the New York Racing Association, Inc.; the Jockey' Guild, Inc.; Championship Auto Racing Teams; the National Hot Rod Association; the International Motor Sports Association; the National Association for Stock Car Auto Rac ing; the Professional Bowlers Association; the Ladies Professional Bowlers Tour; the Unit ed Soccer Leagues; Major League Soccer; the Women's United Soccer Association; the *Fédération Internationale de Football Association*; the U.S. Soccer Federation; the U.S Olympic Committee; USA Track & Field; U.S. Swimming; U.S. Diving; U.S. Skiing; U.S Figure Skating Association; the U.S. Chess Federation; U.S. Curling; the Iditarod Trai Committee; the International Game Fish Association; the USA Gymnastics; U.S. Handbal Association; the Lacrosse Foundation; the American Power Boat Association; the Unlimit ed Hydroplane Racing Association; the Professional Rodeo Cowboys Association; U.S Rowing; the American Amateur Softball Association; the U.S. Speed Skating ; U.S. Rugby Football Union; USA Triathlon; the National Archery Association; USA Wrestling; the U.S. Squash Racquets Association; the U.S. Polo Association; ABC Sports; and the U.S Volleyball Association.

The following sources were consulted in gathering information:

Baseball *The Baseball Encyclopedia*, Macmillan Publishing Co., 1990; *Total Baseball* Viking Penguin, 1995; *Baseballistics*, St. Martin's Press, 1990; *The Book of Baseba Records*, Seymour Siwoff, publisher, 1991; *The Complete Baseball Record Book*, The Sport ing News Publishing Co., 1992; *The Sporting News Baseball Guide*, The Sporting New Publishing Co., 1996; *The Sporting News Official Baseball Register*, The Sporting News Pub lishing Co., 1996; *National League Green Book—1994*, The Sporting News Publishing Co 1993; *American League Red Book—1994*, The Sporting News Publishing Co., 1993; *Th Scouting Report: 1996*, Harper Perennial, 1996.

Pro Football *The Official 1997 National Football League Record & Fact Book*, Th National Football League, 1997; *The Official National Football League Encyclopedia*, Nev American Library, 1990; *The Sporting News Football Guide*, The Sporting News Publishin Co., 1996; *The Sporting News Football Register*, The Sporting News Publishing Co., 199(*The 1993 National Football League Record & Fact Book*, Workman Publishing, 1993; *Th Football Encyclopedia*, David Neft and Richard Cohen, St. Martin's Press, 1991.

College Football *1997 NCAA Football*, The National Collegiate Athletic Association, 1997

Pro Basketball *The Official NBA Basketball Encyclopedia*, Villard Books, 1994; *Th Sporting News Official NBA Guide*, The Sporting News Publishing Co., 1996; *The Sportir News Official NBA Register*, The Sporting News Publishing Co., 1996.

College Basketball *1997 NCAA Basketball*, The National Collegiate Athletic Association 1996.

Hockey   *The National Hockey League Official Guide & Record Book 1997–98*, The National Hockey League, 1997; *The Sporting News Complete Hockey Book,* The Sporting News Publishing Co., 1993; *The Complete Encyclopedia of Hockey,* Visible Ink Press, 1993.

Tennis   *1997 Official USTA Tennis Yearbook*, H.O. Zimman, Inc., 1997; *IBM/ATP Tour 1997 Player Guide*, Association of Tennis Professionals, 1997; *1997 Corel WTA Tour Media Guide*, Corel WTA Tour, 1997.

Golf   *PGA Tour Book 1997*, PGA Tour Creative Services, 1997; *LPGA 1997 Player Guide*, LPGA Communications Department, 1997; *Senior PGA Tour Book 1997*, PGA Tour Creative Services, 1997; *USGA Yearbook 1997*, U.S. Golf Association, 1997.

Boxing   *The Ring 1986–87 Record Book and Boxing Encyclopedia*, The Ring Publishing Corp., 1987. *Computer Boxing Update*, Ralph Citro, Inc., 1992; Bob Yalen, boxing statistician.

Horse Racing   *The American Racing Manual 1994*, Daily Racing Form, Inc., 1994; *1994 Directory and Record Book*, The Thoroughbred Racing Association, 1994; *The Trotting and Pacing Guide 1994*, United States Trotting Association, 1994; *Breeders' Cup 1993 Statistics*, Breeders' Cup Limited, 1993; *NYRA Media Guide 1993*, The New York Racing Association, 1994; *The 120th Kentucky Derby Media Guide, 1994*, Churchill Downs Public Relations Dept., 1994; *The 120th Preakness Press Guide, 1994*, Maryland Jockey Club, 1994; *Harness Racing News,* Harness Racing Communications.

Motor Sports   *The Official NASCAR Yearbook and Press Guide 1997*, UMI Publications, Inc., 1997; *1994 Indianapolis 500 Media Fact Book*, Indy 500 Publications, 1994; *IMSA Yearbook 1995 Season Review*, International Motor Sports Association, 1995; *1994 Winston Drag Racing Series Media Guide*, Sports Marketing Enterprises, 1994.

Bowling   *1994 Professional Bowlers Association Press, Radio and Television Guide*, Professional Bowlers Association, Inc., 1994; *The Professional Women's Bowling Association Tour Guide 1997*.

Soccer   *Rothmans Football Yearbook 1993–94*, Headline Book Publishing, 1993; *American Professional Soccer League 1992 Media Guide*, APSL Media Relations Department, 1992; The *European Football Yearbook*, Facer Publications Limited, 1988; *Soccer America,* Burling Communications; Dan Goldstein, editor of *Football Europe.*

NCAA Sports   *1997–98 National Collegiate Championships*, The National Collegiate Athletic Association, 1998; *1993–94 National Directory of College Athletics,* Collegiate Directories Inc., 1993.

Olympics   *The Complete Book of the Olympics*, Little, Brown and Co., 1991; *The Complete Book of the Summer Olympics,* Little, Brown and Co., 1996.

Track and Field   *American Athletics Annual 1996*, The Athletics Congress/USA, 1996.

Swimming   *6th World Swimming Championships Media Guide*, The World Swimming Championships Organizing Committee, 1991.

Skiing   *U.S. Ski Team 1994 Media Guide / USSA Directory*, U.S. Ski Association, 1993; *Ski Racing Annual Competition Guide 1993–94*, Ski Racing International, 1993; *Ski Magazine's Encyclopedia of Skiing*, Harper & Row, 1974; *Caffe Lavazza Ski World Cup Press Kit*, Biorama, 1991.

The Year In Sports

The taint of steroids was felt throughout the sports world in 2005

The Return of Team Chemistry

From the Super Bowl to the World Series, 2005 taught sports fans that individual superstars may be flashier, but only teams win championships

BY HANK HERSCH

H E HAD PLAYED IN FOUR PRO Bowls over nine NFL seasons, but New Orleans Saints wide receiver Joe Horn was best known nationally for one thing: the $30,000 cell phone call. To celebrate his touchdown against the New York Giants in 2003, he whipped a cellie from a hiding place in a Superdome goalpost pad and pretended to jabber away. Horn's self-conscious display earned him a $30,000 fine from the league and condemnation from columnists across the country.

But then came September, when Hurricane Katrina's 140-mph winds and torrential rains ripped the roof off the Superdome and flooded New Orleans, causing billions of dollars in damages and leaving thousands dead along the Gulf Coast. In the wake of the worst natural disaster in U.S. history, Horn showed his more appealing side to the pundits: Whether raising funds around the country or lifting spirits in New Orleans, he stepped forward as an NFL player committed to more than the game. The Saints would have to decamp to San Antonio and play the season away from home. But because of their struggles they were soon embraced as America's new team. "Everybody is on the same page now—to do everything we can to help the survivors, and to play for each other," Horn said. "Football ain't nothin compared to somebody who lost a loved one or doesn't have a house to go back to."

People can change; perceptions can change; perspectives can change. Sports in 2005 provided abundant examples of each

First baseman Rafael Palmeiro entered the Baltimore Orioles' season with Hall of Fame credentials: 551 home runs and 1,825 RBIs over 18 seasons. He further burnished his image in a March appearance before a Senate subcommittee investigating performance-enhancing drug abuse. In a tone more strident than that of slugger Sammy Sosa and in language less evasive than Mark McGwire's, Palmeiro with a wag of his finger denied that he had ever taken steroids. But in August, three weeks after he pulled out of a slump to

In a season where a steroids scandal called into question baseball's power-hungry past, the "smart ball" White Sox won the World Series with speed, pitching, and strategy

become the fourth major-league player ever to accrue 500 homers and 3,000 hits, Palmeiro began serving a 10-day suspension for testing positive, reportedly for the anabolic steroid stanozolol.

Soon, he was wearing ear plugs to block out the fans' catcalls; then he was blaming his positive test on a shot given him by teammate Miguel Tejada; finally, the Orioles gave him his release. "Raffy's season went from such a high," said Baltimore general manager Jim Beattie, "to one of the worst things that you could do." Despite the specter of steroid abuse—and the almost season-long absence of one prime suspect, Barry Bonds, who, because of a balky right knee, finished 47 homers short of Hank Aaron's all-time record of 755—baseball set an attendance mark, with an total turnout of more than 74.9 million fans. After tight division and wild-card races in both leagues, the Chicago White Sox swept their way to the World Series, the South Siders' first Series win since 1917, breaking major league base-ball's second-oldest championship drought. In doing so, they earned the envy of their cross-town rivals, the North Side's Cubs, who still hold the ignominious distinction of having gone the longest—since 1908—without wining a World Series.

A cloud of scandal—albeit a far less substantial one—also darkened the culmination of Lance Armstrong's brilliant cycling career. In August, shortly after he had broken his own record with a seventh Tour de France victory, the French sports daily *L'Equipe* reported that in winning the 1999

Lance Armstrong just kept rolling along, winning an unprecedented seventh straight Tour de France in July 2005.

SCOTT AUDETTE/AP

Tour, Armstrong had used erythropoietin (EPO) to boost production of oxygen-carrying blood cells. No matter that both an A and a B sample must come back positive under the World Anti-Doping Agency guidelines (just the leftover B was tested); or that obtaining confidential information to match the samples constituted an egregious breach of security; or that Armstrong had a right to be present when the samples were opened. "It's a setup," said Armstrong, who instead of basking in the glow of his unprecedented accomplishments found himself under investigation by the International Cycling Union.

No sport experienced more Katrina-like tumult than hockey. In 2004-05, the NHL became the first league to cancel an entire season because of a labor dispute. After a 301-day lockout by owners, who claimed they lost $224 million in '03-04, players agreed to a $39 million per team salary cap, under which they would receive 54% of league revenues (down from roughly 75%) and no one player would command more than 20% of his team's payroll. The result: Small-market teams became big buyers in

The NHL's 301-day lockout prevented reigning Stanley Cup champs Tampa Bay from defending their title.

the free-agent free-for-all, with one in four players switching uniforms. All that change, plus a flurry of new rules designed to create higher scoring and a more wide-open game—among them smaller goalie gear, larger offensive zones, two-line passes and shootouts to settle ties—left the NHL feeling suddenly hopeful. Said Edmonton Oilers general manager Kevin Lowe of the player movement, "The league could have [spent] $ 10 million on a marketing campaign and not achieved what that did in generating interest."

Before the Indianapolis 500 in May, 23-year-old Danica Patrick of Roscoe, Ill., had driven in only four IRL races and was only known outside motor sports circles for her provocative photos in FHM. "I don't feel insecure about being a girlie," she said. Perhaps that's because she had so many things to feel secure about—especially after qualifying fourth for the 500 (average speed: 227.004 mph) and being the first woman to lead the race. Despite stalling coming out of the pits on Lap 78 and a spinout after a restart on Lap 155 that busted the nose cone and front wing of her Rahal Letterman Racing Panoz-Honda, Patrick held the lead at Indy for 19 laps and was running first with seven to go.

But British driver Dan Wheldon roared out of Indy's deepest field in 20 years to overtake Patrick, who ran low on fuel and finished fourth. Her bold run prompted a 40% leap in the overnight Nielsen ratings from the 500 in 2004 and encouraged more serious discussions between the IRL and rival CART (now the Champ Car circuit) to heal the feud that's decimated open-wheel racing. Who knew a 5'1", 100-pound "girlie" could make such huge waves? Patrick, for one, saying, "I'm going to go out there and prove to you time and again that I belong here, that I will race up front, and that I'm a great driver and not just driving for a great team."

Patrick wasn't the only woman athlete who demonstrated the benefits of crossing over. At the Banquet Open in Wyoming, Mich., Liz Johnson didn't merely become the first woman bowler to advance to the round of 32 in a PBA Tour event—she reached the final, reaping a $20,000 runner-up check and some much-needed attention for her sport.

With 300-plus yard drives and a golf swing considered by some experts as elegant as any in the world, Michelle Wie announced in October that she was turning pro at age 16. While she planned to play in selected LPGA events—no one under 18 can obtain a Tour card—it was largely Wie's potential to keep up with the men that earned her instant endorsements deal from Nike and Sony worth some $10 million.

Since 1997, precious few people in the golf world could utter the term "major championship" without mentioning Tiger Woods in the same sentence. Then came a 34-month stretch in which Woods got married, donated $5 million to build an eponymous learning center in Southern California, bought a 155-foot yacht, changed equipment, revamped his swing—and failed to win any of the 10 majors played. The sport seemed upside down without Tiger on top. He began setting it aright at the Masters in April, blowing a lead with a bogey-bogey finish but rallying to defeat Chris DiMarco on the first playoff hole with an 18-foot birdie putt. Woods had won his fourth green jacket before turning 30; two months later, he won his second claret jug—and 10th major, second only to Jack Nicklaus's 18—with a dominant, five-stroke victory in the British Open at St. Andrews.

Remember when college basketball coach Roy Williams couldn't—all together now—"win the big one"? All those All-Americans at Kansas and all those No.1 rankings had netted him so much acclaim that his failure to earn a title had become increasingly conspicuous. But in his 17th NCAA season, his fifth Final Four, his third championship game and his second year at North Carolina, Williams finally did what he hadn't, leading his alma mater past Illinois 75--70. "I'm not really that much better [as] a coach now than I was about three hours ago," he said to the press afterward, echoing the words uttered by his mentor, Dean Smith, after Smith's title breakthrough with UNC in 1982. Better to attribute Williams's validating victory to the Tar Heels' hulk of a power forward, Sean May, who celebrated his 21st birthday with 26 points and 10 rebounds in the finale.

With his floppy hair, flat-out style and All-Star bona fides, Steve Nash had developed a strong NBA following over the years as a Dallas Mavericks' point guard. But in the off-season he signed with the Phoenix Suns, whose coach, Mike D'Antoni, wanted to run, run and run some more. Suddenly, Nash gained rock-star status for what he did with the rock: setting up teammates with no-look passes, finishing baskets with rococo flourishes, dribbling at warp speed while somehow licking his hands between bounces. With the precocious help of a ferocious center, 22-year-old Amaré Stoudemire, Nash led the league's highest-scoring team (110.4 points per game) to a 33-win turnaround while becoming the third-lowest scoring MVP (15.5 points per game) in NBA history.

Tim Duncan (r.) and rising star Manu Ginobli (l.) led the San Antonio to another NBA title.

Most important, Nash and the fast-breaking Suns were, well, fun. "Guys like to play this way," said D'Antoni, who was named Coach of the Year. "When they're getting 36, 40 points a game it's"—he mimicked a player rubbing his hands in glee—"'When are we going to play again?'"

The NBA desperately needed its bright spots after the dark cloud that descended over the first month of the season. In one of the ugliest scenes in the history of sports, members of the Indiana Pacers engaged in a full-scale, twelve-minute brawl in the stands at The Palace at Auburn Hills after a Detroit Pistons fan threw a cup of beer on supine forward Ron Artest late in a Nov. 19 game. "An unprecedented fiasco," NBA Commissioner David Stern called it. Artest, All-Star forward Jermaine O'Neal and swingman Stephen Jackson would serve combined suspensions of 128 games—including the balance of the season for Artest, the most severe penalty ever served for a fight.

By June, though, the San Antonio Spurs had helped restore some semblance of order; the well-knit—and well-behaved—team led by unflappable power forward Tim

Duncan knocked off reigning champion Detroit in a seven-game Finals. Indeed, the Spurs' march to their second title in three seasons was one of the few ways in which 2005 was—ho hum—just a normal year. Take the NFL, in which Indianapolis Colts quarterback Peyton Manning again put up spectacular numbers (this time throwing 49 touchdown passes to break Dan Marino's 20-year-old record of 48) only to lose in the playoffs (again) to the New England Patriots and QB Tom Brady (this time 20-3 in the AFC divisional playoffs).

The Philadelphia Eagles did provide

Despite some vicious NFL competition, Patriots QB Tom Brady led New England to its third Super Bowl title in four years.

some spice by acquiring the flamboyant wide receiver Terrell Owens, and after losses in three straight NFC title games, he helped quarterback Donovan McNabb reach his first Super Bowl. Owens, returning just 6 1/2 weeks after surgery on his right ankle, was brilliant at Super Bowl XXXIX in Jacksonville, making nine catches for 122 yards. But unsung Patriots wide receiver Deion Branch (who had a record-tying 11 catches for 133 yards) outshone Owens in New England's 24-21 victory—a gritty, clutch performance reminiscent of the Pats' wins in XXXVI and XXXVIII. "It's awesome to see a guy like Deion win [the game's MVP award]," said Brady (23 of 33, 236 yards, two touchdowns), a two-tome honoree. "The guy has

Matt Leinart rebuffed the lure of the NFL and decided to come back for his senior season as quarterback of the USC Trojans.

done everything he can for this team, and this is a team full of guys who cheer for one another. The MVP is nice, but that's not why you play. I'm playing for that diamond ring that's as big as a belt buckle."

Anyone scanning the horizon for the next Brady—tough, gifted and California cool—would do well to start at USC. After piloting the 13–1 Trojans to a share of the national title with LSU in 2003, quarterback Matt Leinart took things a step farther in '04, guiding unbeaten USC to the championship outright and copping the Heisman Trophy. Leinart denuded a potent Oklahoma defense 55-19 in the Orange Bowl, completing 13 of 23 passes for four touchdowns and no interceptions...in the first half. Then he did something really special: He spurned the NFL's millions and returned for his senior season. "Being here with my friends and teammates [is] ultimately more satisfying and will make me happier than any amount of money," Leinart said. "Being in college is the best time of my life." Now that's *cool*.

Late October- November 2004

CLARENCE TABB, JR./THE DETROIT NEWS/AP

NOV 19 A major player-fan brawl erupts at a Pacers-Pistons game after a cup hurled by a spectator drenched Pacer Ron Artest, who promptly stormed into the stands to confront the fan he suspected of throwing the cup. The melee, described by **NBA** commissioner Davd Stern as a "fiasco" resulted in the suspension of three players, including Artest.

THEY SAID IT

Juan Rincon: Twins pitcher, after giving up four runs in a third of an inning in Minnesota's 6-5 loss to the Yankees in Game 4 of the AL Division Series: "Nobody wants to be in my pants right now."

THIS MONTH'S SIGN OF THE
APOCALYPSE

A deep sea diver ended an attempt at a world record descent when he discovered the skeleton of a competitor.

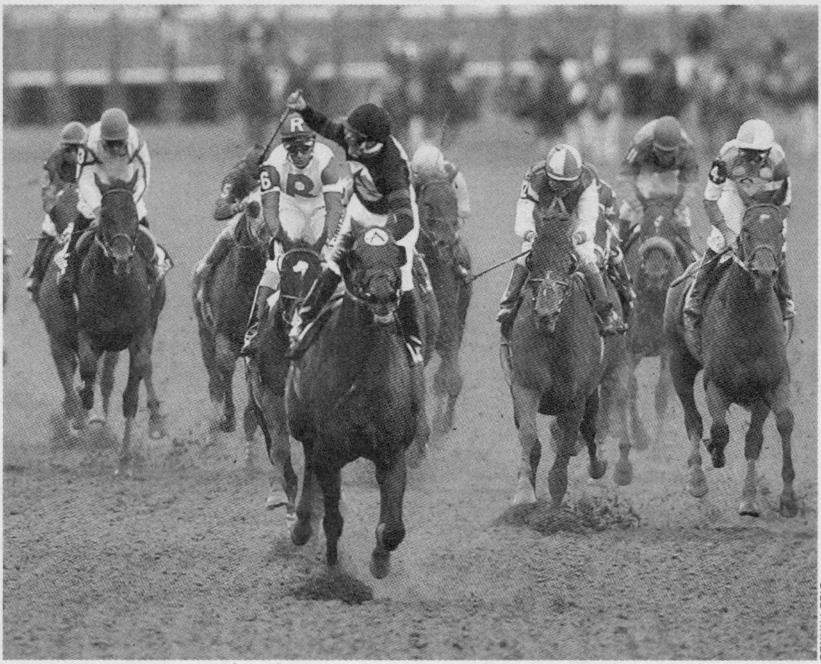

BILL FRAKES

NOV 19 Ghostzapper, ridden by Javier Castellano, breezes past Roses in May and Pleasantly Plump to capture the Breeders' Cup by three lenghts.

NOV 22 Kurt Busch wins the inaugural NEXTEL CUP.

BOB ROSATO/SPORTS ILLUSTRATED

GO FIGURE

700 Career wins by Boston College hockey coach Jerry York, the third NCAA coach to reach the milestone

266 Consecutive boys' cross country dual meet victories - dating back to 1974 - by Christian Brothers Academy in Lincroft, N.J., a national high school record.

$400,000 Bonus pocketed by Red Sox righthander Curt Schilling for finishing second in AL Cy Young voting.

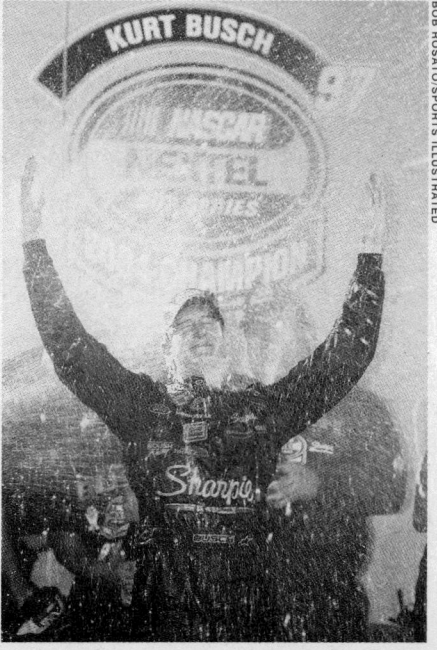

December 2004

DEC 13 Reggie Bush (5) somersaults as USC pushed past UCLA to secure an Orange Bowl berth.

THIS MONTH'S SIGN OF THE
APOCALYPSE

Police in Wales had to use pepper spray to break up a brawl among charity race runners in Santa suits.

THEY SAID IT

Morgan Shepherd: NASCAR driver, on why the NBA brawl couldn't happen in his sport: "None of our fans would ever let go of a beer for any reason, much less throw it at somebody."

MARCELO DEL POZO/REUTERS

DEC 15 Rafael Nadal celebrates both during and after his win over Andy Roddick, which helped Spain to a 3-2 victory over the U.S. in the Davis Cup Final.

JEFF ZELEVANSKY/REUTERS

DEC 20 After throwing for 2,990 yards with 28 touchdowns, USC's Matt Leinart wins the Heisman Trophy, winning five of the six voting regions.

GO FIGURE

12 Snow scrapers distributed to Lions rookies by coach Steve Mariucci , part of his effort to help them adjust to NFL - and Detroit - life.

23 Percentage of Americans who described themselves as hockey fans in a Gallup poll, ranking hockey 10th among 11 sports, behind figure skating and above pro wrestling.

$1.265 million Winning bid in the auction for the Louisville Slugger Babe Ruth used to hit the first home run at Yankee Stadium, the most ever paid for a bat.

January 2005

GO FIGURE

100 Percentage increase for the 2005 Kentucky Derby purse, which was raised from $1 million in '04 to $2 million.

$1,800 Amount David and Victoria Beckham paid a butler to help unwrap their family's Chrismas gifts.

$100,000 Amount donated by Major League baseball to President Bush's inauguration.

THEY SAID IT

Anteus Irbe: Latvian-born Hurricanes goalie, on the NHL owners' negotiating tactics: "They take a shove-it-up-your-throat kind of approach."

JAN 1 Texas QB Vince Young dives past Michigan defenders for one of his four TD runs in the Rose Bowl in Pasadena. Dusty Magnum hit a 37-yard field goal as time expired to clinch the Longhorns' 38-37 win.

RICHARD MACKSON

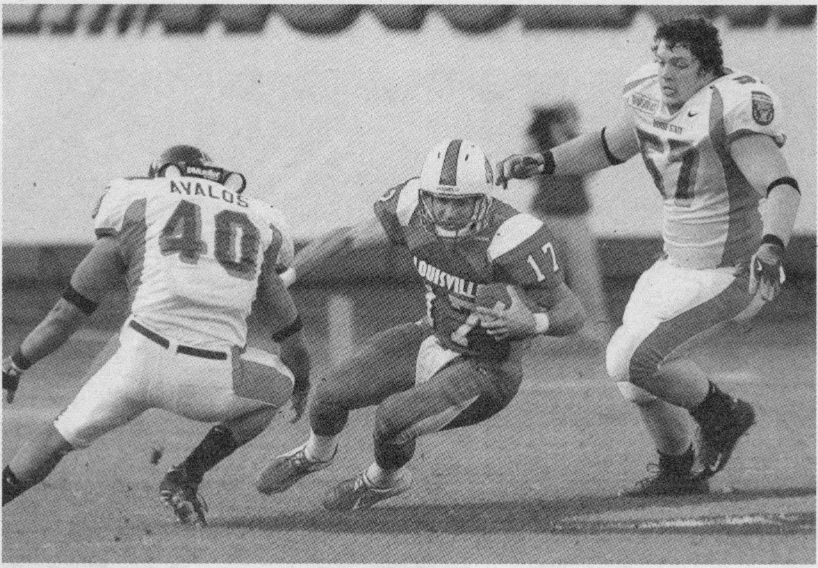

JOE MURPHY/WIREIMAGE.COM

CORINNE DUBREUIL/CAMELEON/ABACA

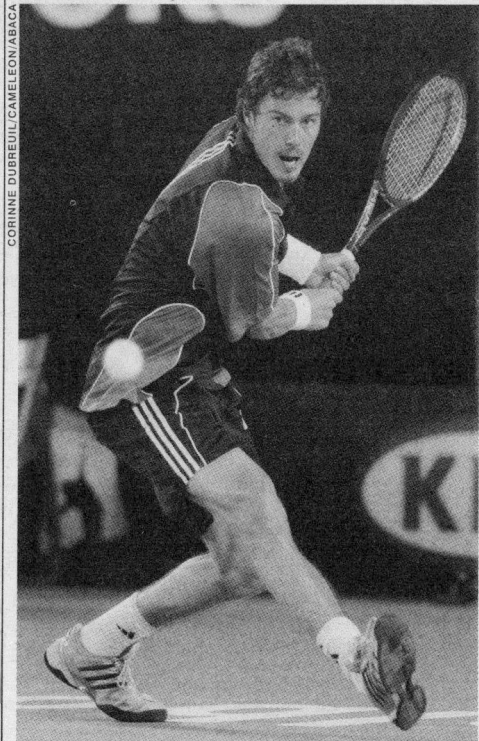

JAN 4 Louisville QB Stefan LeFors scrambles from Boise State tacklers at the Liberty Bowl in Memphis. LeFors, and his Boise State counterpart, Jared Zabransky, led the nation's two most potent offenses to a combined 848 yards. Louisville won 44-40.

THIS MONTH'S SIGN OF THE

APOCALYPSE

An Illinois high school basketball coach was fired for drawing up a play that had a player throw a ball at a heckler.

JAN 30 Marat Safin ended Lleyton Hewitt's hopes of becoming the first homegrown men's champion at the Australian Open since 1976, defeating Hewitt on four sets.

PETER READ MILLER/SPORTS ILLUSTRATED

THEY SAID IT

David Baker: 6'9", 400-pound Arena Football League commissioner on what he hears when he steps on his audio scale: "Come back when you're not in your car."

FEB 6 Running back Corey Dillon fights his way to pay dirt, scoring a touchdown for New England in the fourth quarter of Super Bowl XXXIX. Adam Vinatieri later kicked the 22-yard field goal that would prove to be the Patriot's winning margin in their 24-21 victory over the Philadelphia Eagles.

FRED VUICH/SPORTS ILLUSTRATED

THIS MONTH'S SIGN OF THE
APOCALYPSE

An Oklahoma state senator wants to legalize a form of cockfighting in which the birds wear tiny boxing gloves.

FEB 6 Bode Miller rides down Bormio's Stelvio downhill course to a historic one-two finish (with Daron Rahlves) for the U.S. at the Alpine World Ski Championship in Italy. Miller would end up the first American in 22 years to win the overall World Cup.

FEB 20 Jeff Gordon fought off a hard-charging Dale Earnhardt Jr. to win his third Daytona 500.

GO FIGURE

71½ Days it took British sailor Ellen MacArthur to circumnavigate the globe, a world record for a solo around-the-world trip.

$32,783 Amount Jose Canseco reportedly owed Massachusetts for income taxes he incurred while playing for the Red Sox in 1995 and '96.

$40,000 Asking price of the 2000 World Series ring that Canseco is selling on his web site.

March 2005

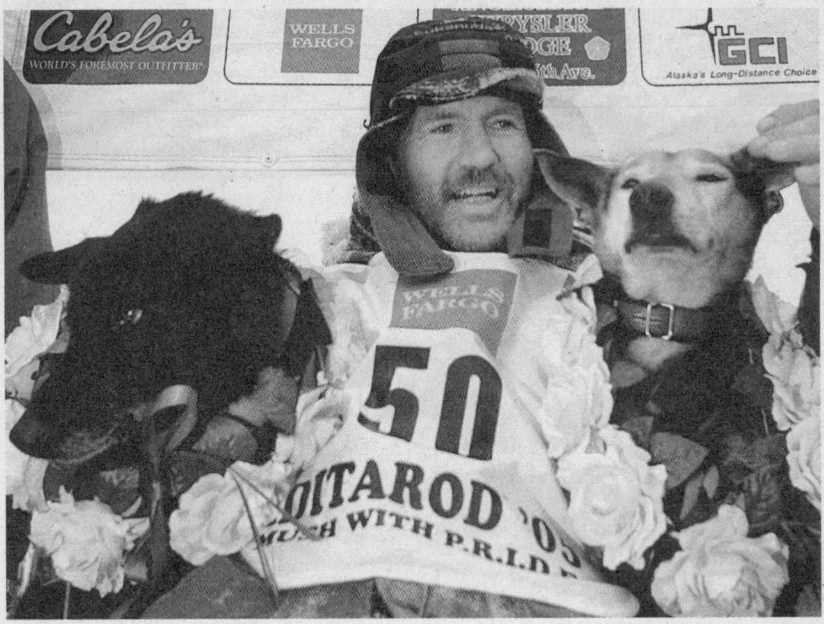

GRILLO / AP

MARCH 16
Norwegian Robert Sorlie wins the 1,161-mile Iditarod Race for the second time. .

MARCH 17 Six and a half years after the home run race between Sosa and McGwire, they and others testified before Congress on steroid use in professional baseball.

GERALD HERBERT / AP

MARCH 19 Though buffeted by Oklahoma University players, Utah's Andrew Bogut (in red, reaching for the ball) dished out seven assists in the Utes' 67-58 win over No.3 OU. When the wave of NCAA basketball opening round upsets was over, only eight of the top 16 seeds remained, the fewest after the tournament's first two rounds since 2000.

GO FIGURE

7 Times that Tiger Woods has played as a professional in the Nissan Open, the only pro-tournament he has entered at least five times without winning.

22 Percentage of boaters who said in a national online survey that their vessels were harder to name than their children or pets.

42 Programs in the NCAA basketball tournament that had graduation rates below 50% in 2004.

THIS MONTH'S SIGN OF THE
APOCALYPSE

A former high school track coach in Oregon was disciplined for allegedly licking blood from an athlete's injury.

April 2005

JOHN W. McDONOUGH

APRIL 4 UNC Tarheels defeat Illinois 75-70 to claim their fourth NCAA basketball championship, the first championship for head coach Roy Williams. Carolina's Sean May is named the tournament's most outstanding player.

APRIL 4 The 2005 major league baseball season kicks off under the glare of the burgeoning steroid scandal, and the hype of the game's greatest rivalry, as the Yankees routed the Red Sox 9-2 in their season opener at Yankee Stadium.

CHUCK SOLOMON

GO FIGURE

73 Days it took Frances Maud Fonteroy to row 4,960 miles from Peru to French Polynesia, making her the first woman to row solo across the Pacific Ocean.

$183,688
Value of the cash and prizes (including a Cadillac XLR convertible, a motor home, and a sailboat) won by Sheena Lindholm, a freshman softball player at Eastern Oregon on *The Price Is Right,* a record haul for the show.

27.5 million Number of hot dogs expected to be eaten at major league stadiums in 2005, according to the National Hot Dog and Sausage Council.

APRIL 10 Tiger Woods outshoots Chris DiMarco in a sudden death playoff to win his fourth green jacket at the Masters at Augusta.

THEY SAID IT

Pete Sampras: Former tennis star, on how he's spent his time since retiring in 2003: "I've been playing a ton of golf. And my wife is pregnant, so I've done a little bit of that."

THIS MONTH'S SIGN OF THE APOCALYPSE

Rockies pitcher Darren Oliver had to leave a spring training game because he was swarmed by bees attracted to the coconut oil in his hair gel.

THEY SAID IT

Drew Gooden: Cavaliers foward, on the ups and downs of his three year NBA career: "I've had to overcome a lot of diversity."

MAY 7 Giacomo (left), a 50-I shot on a five-race winless streak, emerged from obscurity - and from far off the pace - to win the Kentucky Derby.

MAY 12 American businessman and Tampa Bay Buccaneers owner, Malcolm Glazer buys a controlling interest in UK football powerhouse Manchester United, to the consternation of many English fans.

MAY 29 British driver Dan Wheldon speeds to victory at the 89th Indianapolis 500; his win is almost overshadowed by Danica Patrick's highest-ever finish for a female driver in the race's history.

GO FIGURE

41 Years late that the Canadian hockey players will get their 1964 World Championship bronze medals; due to a tiebreaker mix-up, Czechoslovakia, which had the same record as Canada had been the sole team to receive the medal.

$30,637,531 Luxury tax the Yankees are projected to owe on their 2005 payroll of $204.6 million, a record.

$103,325,510 Amount wagered on the 2005 Kentucky Derby, on- and off-track, the first time a U.S. horserace had more than $100 million in bets.

June 2005

BILL FRAKES/SPORTS ILLUSTRATED

DAVID BERGMAN

JUNE 11 Afleet Alex out-paces Kentucky Derby winner Giacomo to win the Belmont Stakes.

JUNE 12 Annika Sorenstam wins her third LPGA Championship, becoming the first woman to win the first two major tournaments of the year since 1986.

MITCHELL LAYTON/GETTY IMAGES

GO **FIGURE**

35 Round in which the Rockies mistakenly drafted pitcher Timothy Brewer, 17, in the Major League entry draft; Brewer, who is from the island of St. Thomas, is in 11th grade and wasn't eligible for the draft.

$996,000 Winning bid for the 1919 bill of sale that sent Red Sox pitcher Babe Ruth to the Yankees.

$415,000 Amount ex-NFL linebacker Bill Romanowski agreed to pay former Raiders teammate Marcus Williams to settle litigation stemming from a 2003 incident in which Romanowski punched Williams in the face, breaking his eye socket and ending his career.

JUNE 11 Mike Tyson quits his fight with little-known Irishman Kevin McBride after getting knocked down in the sixth round. After the fight, Tyson announces his retirement from boxing.

THE YEAR IN SPORTS   33

July 2005

GO FIGURE

4 Hours per day the Indonesian government ordered TV stations to go off the air to conserve energy; only broadcasts of European soccer games are exempt from the blackout.

646 Weight, in pounds, of a nine-foot catfish caught in Thailand's Mekong River; it's believed to be the largest freshwater fish ever caught.

100 to 1 Odds placed by British bookmakers on English tennis pro Tim Henman's two-year-old daughter, Rose, someday winning Wimbledon.

JULY 3 Venus Williams celebrates after defeating top ranked Lindsay Davenport to win her third Wimbledon singles title.

JULY 23 After 48 years, 162 majors, 18 wins and 19 seconds, legendary golfer Jack Nicklaus ends his professional career with one last appearance at the British Open on the Old Course at St. Andrews.

ROBERT LABERGE/GETTY IMAGES

THIS MONTH'S SIGN OF THE
APOCALYPSE

JULY 24 Lance Armstrong wins his seventh straight Tour de France, once again setting a new record for both consecutive Tour triumphs and total Tour victories.

A New York City high school teacher lost his job for using sick days to wrestle professionally as Matt Stryker.

August 2005

BRIAN BAHR/GETTY IMAGE

AUG 3 Philadelphia Flyers G.M. Bob Clarke signs celebrated center Peter Forsberg to a two-year deal worth $11.5 million, leaving the Flyers still $2 million under the salary cap.

THEY SAID IT

Mike Cameron: Mets outfielder, dismissing the problems caused by the sun at Shea Stadium: "The sun has been there 500, 600 years."

AUG 15 Phil Mickelson hits his best-ever tee shot and birdied the 72nd hole to win the PGA Championship at Baltusrol, his second major win.

GO FIGURE

69 Age of Frank Amonte Sr., who became the oldest U.S. jockey to win a thoroughbred race when he rode Evas Boy to victor at Suffolk Downs on August 10.

$373.71 Amount Mike Tyson was fined for riding a Jet Ski without a helmet and too close to shore off Capri.

$17.5 million Amount lost by British bookmakers on Tiger Woods's win at the British Open, a record hit for the bookies.

AUG 16 Justin Gatlin (below, center) wins the 100-meter title at the Word Outdoor Track and Field Championship in Helsinki. Gatlin's .17 second margin of victory was the biggest in meet history.

THIS MONTH'S SIGN OF THE APOCALYPSE

Five teams were denied entry to Scotland for the Homeless World Cup of Soccer because they were too poor.

August 2005 (Cont.)

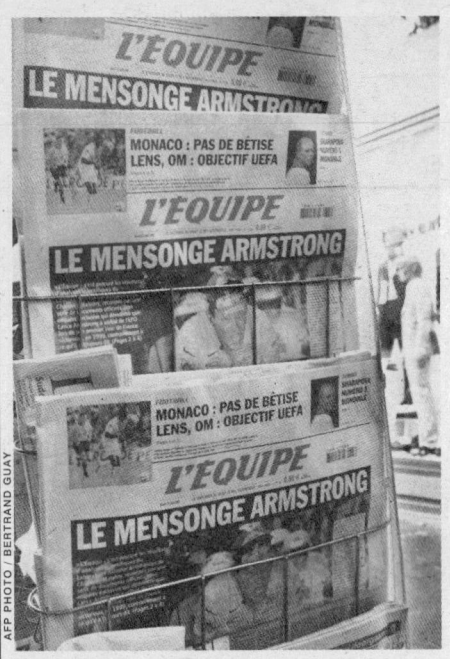

AFP PHOTO / BERTRAND GUAY

AUG 23 French newspaper *L'Equipe* accuses Lance Armstrong of doping in 1999 based on unofficial tests of six year-old partial urine samples. Armstrong denies accusations.

AUG 28 Michael Memea, from Ewa Beach, HI, set off a celebration at home plate with his walk-off solo homer in the Little League World Series Championship. Michael's team, the US Champions, representing the Northwest, beat the Caribbean League champion Willemstad, Curacao, 7-6.

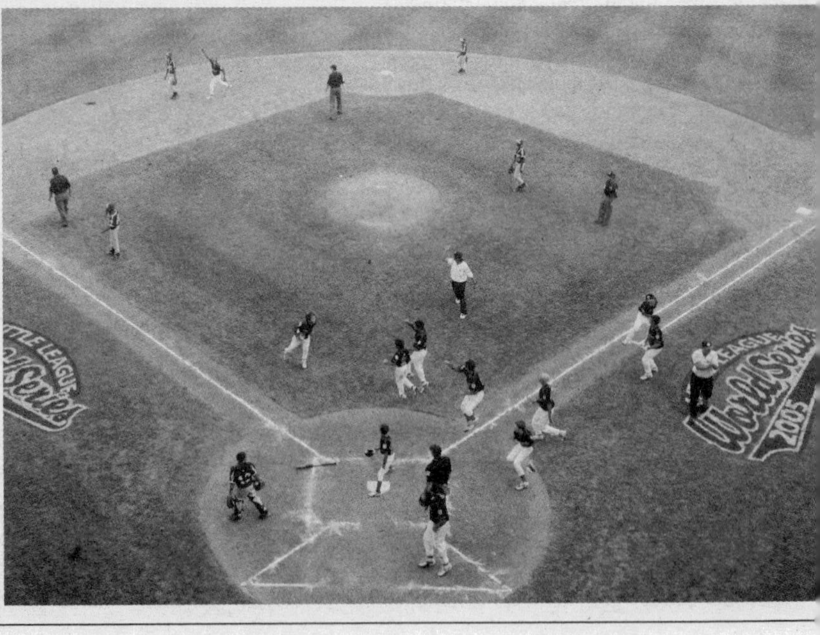

DAVID BERGMAN

JOEL AUERBACH-US PRESSWIRE

GO FIGURE

2 Credits needed in 2005 by USC quarterback and fifth-year senior Matt Leinart to get his sociology degree; he took once class, ballroom dancing, during his final semester.

$40,000 Value of the platinum and diamond earings Serena Williams wore during her first round US Open win over Yung-Jan Chan of Tiawan.

$21,700 Chan's career earnings.

AUG 31 Jeremy Hermida becomes only the second player to hit a grand slam in his first big league at bat. The other player was the Phillies' "Frosty" Bill Duggleby in 1898.

September 2005

MICHAEL C. HEBERT

SEPT 11 Deuce McAllister's power running game and 2 TDs led the Hurricane Katrina-displaced New Orleans Saints to a 23-20 victory over the Carolina Panthers in their season opener.

GO FIGURE

31 Age of Jets punter Ben Graham, the oldest rookie ever to play in the NFL on opening day.

41.6 Graham's net punting average, second best in the NFC through the first three weeks of the season.

10,000 Liters of free beer that a German brewery will pour for supporters of soccer team Hamburg SV: the beermaker promised a party for fans of the first team to beat defending Bundesliga champ Bayern Munich, which lost 2-0 to Hamburg SV.

SEPT 3 Goalkeeper Kasey Keller (18) and the U.S. soccer team celebrate in Columbus, OH, after clinching a berth in the 2006 World Cup with a 2-0 thumping of archrival Mexico.

MANNY MILLAN

SEPT 11 Roger Federer defeats Andre Agassi to win his second straight US Open title, becoming the first man to win both Wimbledon and the US Open two years in a row since Don Budge in 1937-38.

THEY SAID IT

Bill Parcells, Cowboys coach on rookie defensive end and Alabama native Demarcus Ware: "That kid grew up so far out in the country, he had to go toward town to hunt."

October 2005

DARREN CARROLL

OCT 8 Seventeen year-old hockey phenomenon Sidney Crosby delights a standing-room only crowd in his Penguins home debut with his first goal and two assists for his first multipoint game. He had a team-high five points through the first three games.

OCT 5 Golfer Michelle Wie turns pro just before her sixteenth birthday, signing $10 million worth of endorsement deals with Sony and Nike.

DAVID E. KLUTHO

OCT 20 Astros defeat Cardinals 5-1 to win the National League Championship and move on to play the White Sox in the World Series.

GO FIGURE

450 Length in feet of a red-and-white Liverpool scarf knitted by Christina Brockway, an 83-year-old fan of the soccer team who began working on it in 2001.

1,387 Penalties called through the first six weeks of the NFL season, putting the league on pace for 4,081 this year.

3,570 NFL single-season record for penalties, set in 2004.

Late October 2004

THEY SAID IT

Bill Snyder, Kansas State football coach, after the Wildcats' ugly 12-3 win over Kansas: "I think we have great character. We're just not very good."

OCT 27 Catcher A.J. Pierzynski and relief pitcher Bobby Jenks celebrate after the White Sox win Game 4, sweeping the Houston Astros in Chicago's first World Series appearance since 1917.

The World Series
champion
Chicago White Sox

Baseball

New Sox, Same Sweep

One year after the Red Sox exorcised the "Curse," the White Sox swept away Chicago's 88-year old World Series drought in dramatic fashion

BY MARK BECHTEL

THE RECIPE FOR MAJOR LEAGUE success in the early 21st century is shaping up: embrace both a curse and your inner goofball. It worked for the Red Sox in 2004, when the self-described "idiots" won their first World Series since 1918 and finally put to rest talk of the Curse of the Bambino. In '05 it was the White Sox's turn. Playing under manager Ozzie Guillen, a Venezuelan with a Midas touch whose press conferences routinely left writers scratching their heads and English professors wincing. (During the World Series, he explained his style by saying, "I don't do anything the way anyone else has ever done them before, but that's okay because I don't think anyone else has ever done things the way I do them either.") The Sox were a loose, ragtag group that brought a title to Chicago's South Side for the first time since 1917—in just the team's second Fall Classic appearance since the infamous Black Sox threw the 1919 series.

Chicago's run to the title was at times overshadowed by off-the-field stories. As Spring Training camps opened, former slugger Jose Canseco released a book, Juiced, which detailed his steroid use and named several players he said took performance enhancing drugs, including Sammy Sosa, Mark McGwire and Rafael Palmeiro. The charges couldn't have come at a worse time. Steroids had already become a hot button issue during the offseason, when leaked grand jury testimony had implicated several players, including Jason Giambi and Barry Bonds, with using them. (Bonds's personal trainer, Greg Anderson, was one of the subjects of an ongoing federal investigation. In July, he pleaded guilty to a charge of conspiracy to distribute steroids and a count of money laundering. In October, he was sentenced to three months in prison and three months of house arrest.)

Canseco's claims and the grand jury reports didn't go over well with fans or with the government. In March, Congressional hearings into baseball's steroid policy were convened. Canseco testified, as did Palmeiro, whose vehement denial— punctuated with a jab of his index finger at the panel—was the hearing's indelible image. Palmeiro's perfor-

A noticeably leaner Jason Giambi struggled early on, but then surged lated in the season, winning the AL Comeback award.

mance so impressed the legislators that they asked him to join a congressional task force. "When he was asked to join the committee, it was almost like Congress said, 'We want you here and you're the type of person we want on our task force,'" said Fernando Cuza, Palmeiro's agent.

Alas, the goodwill didn't last long. In August, a couple weeks after he got his 3,000th career hit to become just the third player in major league history to amass 3,000 hits and 500 homers, Palmeiro was suspended for a positive steroids test. (He was one of 11 players suspended for 10 days under baseball's new more stringent drug testing program.) When he returned to the field he was booed mercilessly—so bad, in fact, that he began wearing earplugs. Palmeiro had just two hits in 26 at bats after his suspension, and the team sent him home to Texas to recuperate from injuries to his left ankle and right knee. He never returned to the team. "Everything just kind of crumbled, unexpectedly really," Palmeiro said. "I never expected that anything would happen to me, not at this stage of my career anyway."

Ironically, Canseco, who was vilified for trying to make a few bucks off of the steroids controversy when Juiced was released, emerged as one of the most credible figures from the hearings. Even though Palmeiro's failed test came after his appearance, it still called into question the veracity of his testimony. The two other big-name sluggers to testify were Sosa and McGwire. Sosa, who often conferred with his lawyer as if he suddenly didn't understand English, had little to say. McGwire refused to answer any questions about steroids use, saying repeatedly he wasn't there to "talk about the past."

One beleaguered player who was not called to testify was Jason Giambi. Over the winter, the San Francisco Chronicle reported that he had admitted to the grand jury investigating BALCO that he had used steroids and human growth hormone. He apologized the Yankees fans—without specifying exactly what he was apologizing for—and proceeded to play horribly for the first three months of the season. He was hitting .200 as late as mid-May, and at the end off June he had five homers, 22 RBIs and 11 extra base hits. Things were so bad that manager Joe Torre and GM Brian Cashman suggested that he accept a demotion to the minors to work on his swing.

Giambi wasn't the only Yankee to struggle early. Newly acquired starters Jaret Wright and Carl Pavano battled ineffectiveness and injuries, as did Kevin Brown. Cashman did his best to swing a deal for a starter (he eventually landed Shawn Chacon at the trading deadline), and vowed in May, "If I have to, I'll go down to Triple A and get arms there." He did, bringing up Chien-Ming Wang and Aaron Small, and the new faces stabilized the rotation. (Small, a 33-year-old journeyman, went 10-0.) In July, Giambi snapped out of his funk thanks to hitting coach Don Mattingly and old friend McGwire, who TiVoed most of Giambi's games and called him to tell him that he had been standing too close to the plate. In the last three months of the season, he hit 27 homers and knocked in 65 runs, easily winning the AL Comeback Player of the Year award.

The rejuvenated Yanks eventually caught and passed the Red Sox, who had pitching problems of their own. The Boston bullpen was so bad that when closer Keith Foulke went on the DL (mercifully, some Sox fans might argue, considering that his ERA hovered around 6.00 most of the year), his job was given to 2004 World Series hero Curt Schilling. That move by manager Terry Francona raised the ire of outfielder Johnny Damon, who told the Boston Globe, "You've got a lot of upset people in here. I don't think he's ready to be our closer. Mike Timlin deserves to be it. The whole team wants Timlin, and if not Timlin, [Bronson] Arroyo."

It was a surprising turn of events. During Boston's 2004 title run, the chemistry in the clubhouse—which was filled with strong, idiosyncratic personalities—was perfect. Everything they did worked out in the end. In 2005, the team with the perfect karma was the White Sox. Guillen's crew burst out of the blocks, beating up on the two teams most picked to win the AL Central. Chicago took four of six from Cleveland and four of five from Minnesota en route to a 16-4 start that had them four games up before April was over.

Chicago did it with outstanding starting pitching and timely hitting. (Only Paul Konerko had more than 90 RBIs for the Sox.) Mark Buehrle was spectacular, Freddy Garcia was solid, Jose Contreras found consistency and Jon Garland won a career-high 18 games, chopping nearly a run and a half from his ERA. He attributed his improvement to Guillen, who let the 26-year-old pitch himself out of jams. "Ozzie's definitely shown faith in me," Garland said. "He's let me find out a lot about myself by giving me my chances. It's fun playing for him. It's almost like having another rowdy player on the team who keeps everybody going. He makes you laugh."

Rowdy is right. Guillen backed down from no one in his second season on the bench. He took a shot at Rangers manager Buck Showalter, referring to him sarcastically as "the guy who invented baseball." He ripped departed outfielder Magglio Ordonez, who had accused him of meddling in his negotiations to remain with the White Sox and said Guillen was the "enemy." Guillen responded with an expletive-laden tirade, including insults ("He's a piece of [bleep]Æ), threats ("He knows I can [bleep] him over in a lot of ways") and disses ("Who the [bleep] is Magglio Ordonez?"). Guillen also took a shot at another ex-Sox slugger, noting that Carlos Lee, who was traded to Milwaukee, tried to break up a critical double play against the Twins in 2004 "as if his wife was turning [it]." Guillen didn't hold his tongue when it came to his own players, either. He skewered Frank Thomas and Damaso Marte for having bad attitudes, and even tweaked vets Buehrle, Garland, Konerko and Joe Crede for having been selfish in years past.

Selfishness wasn't a problem this year. Guillen coaxed the most out of a couple of castoffs who were just happy to have a

Ozzie Guillen's unorthodox managerial style helped rehabilitate many players that other teams had given up on.

chance to prove they could make it in the bigs. After the White Sox held off a late-season rally by the Indians, they took on the Red Sox in the division series. The heroes of that sweep were Contreras, who won Game 1, and closer Bobby Jenks, who saved Games 2 and 3. Contreras came to the team at the trading deadline in 2004 after the Yankees gave up on him. Jenks came off the waiver wire after the Angels released him. "Sometimes people just need to be in a new environment," White Sox general manager Kenny Williams said. "We did our homework on them and thought they would be fits personality-wise. Talent has never been a question. Now they're in the right fit, with the right manager, the right coaching staff, the right city."

The National League's division races could be summed up in two words: ho hum. The Braves won the East—for the 14th consecutive season—despite a host of injuries.

The Cardinals won the Central by 11 games, though the race was never that close. The only drama was in the West, where the pressing question was whether or not the Padres, who were in first place from May 26 on, would be the first team to win a division with a losing record. San Diego clinched with four games left, when they were 79–79. "The important thing is to get into the playoffs," said utility player Robert Fick, "but you don't want to go into the playoffs with people thinking you're a loser." The Padres avoided history; they won three of their last four to finish 82–80.

The wild card race was a different story. What was a four-team race for much of the season was narrowed down to two by the final week: the Astros and the Phillies. Houston, like the Yankees, had won just 11 of its first 30 games, and at one point the Astros were 15 games under .500. But they bounced back and for the second straight year they wrapped up a postseason berth on the season's final day, beating the Cubs 6–4 as Roy Oswalt won his 20th game. "That's the Astros' way," second baseman Craig Biggio said of his team's penchant for drama. "The only way we know how to get it done."

The drama of the regular season had nothing on what awaited Houston in the playoffs. Leading the Braves two games to one in their division series, the Astros fell behind by five runs in Game 4. But Lance Berkman hit a grand slam in the eighth and Brad Ausmus homered in the ninth to tie the game. Then the bullpens took over. The game stayed 6–6 until the 18th inning, when Chris Burke hit a walk-off, series-winning homer to left. (Amazingly, the same fan who caught Berkman's homer, a 25-year old construction company comptroller named Shaun Dean,

JOHN BIEVER

pitched Mark Mulder in Game 6 after the series shifted back to St Louis, holding the Cards to three hits in seven innings, and Houston was in its first World Series.

The Astros continued their run of amazing postseason games in their Fall Classic with the White Sox. After losing Game 1, Houston scored two in the ninth off of Jenks to tie Game 2—only to lose in the bottom of the ninth on a walkoff home run by Scott Podsednik, who had been homerless in the regular season. That sent the series back to Houston with the Astros in desperate need of a win to stanch the bleeding. They had plenty of chances to claw back into the series in Game 3. After blowing a 4–0 lead, Houston needed a Jason Lane double in the eighth inning to tie the game at 5. In the ninth, the Astros had runners at first and third with one out but couldn't score. They got a leadoff walk in the tenth, a walk and hit batsman in the 11th, and another leadoff walk in the 13th. But they never got a timely hit, and the Sox finally ended the game—which lasted a World Series record five hours and 41 minutes—on a Geoff Blum home run in the 14th.

Houston's inability to figure out the White Sox staff carried over into Game 4. Freddy Garcia threw seven shutout innings and Jermaine Dye singled home the game's only run, giving Chicago the title it had waited so long for. ""A lot of people have waited a long time for this moment, and I'm happy that we were able to give it to them," said Guillen. "I didn't come here for the glamor, I didn't come here for the money. I came here to win."

caught Burke's.) By the time the longest game in postseason history was over, Astros manager Phil Garner had used 23 of his 25 players, including Roger Clemens, who came on in relief for the first time since 1984 and picked up the win. Six players were used at more than one position, including Ausmus, who yo-yoed between two. Said third baseman Morgan Ensberg, "Catcher, first base, back to catcher—it was like a schoolyard game." A very long schoolyard game. "By the 16th I was slaphappy," Ensberg said. "I was walking around the dugout asking people to hit me, and finally [shortstop] Adam Everett slapped me in the face."

That put Houston into the NLCS against the Cardinals. With the Astros one strike away from wrapping up the series at home, Albert Pujols hit a mammoth three-run home run off of closer Brad Lidge to give St. Louis a 5–4 win and—seemingly—take the wind out of Houston's sails. But Roy Oswalt out-

FOR THE RECORD·2005

Final Standings

National League

EASTERN DIVISION

Team	Won	Lost	Pct	GB	Home	Away
Atlanta	90	72	.556	--	53-8	37-44
Philadelphia	88	74	.543	2	46-35	42-39
NY Mets	83	79	.512	7	48-33	35-46
Florida	83	79	.512	7	45-36	38-43

CENTRAL DIVISION

Team	Won	Lost	Pct	GB	Home	Away
St. Louis	100	62	.617	--	50-31	50-31
†Houston	89	73	.549	11	53-28	36-45
Milwaukee	81	81	.500	19	46-35	35-46
Chicago	79	83	.488	21	38-43	41-40
Cincinnati	73	89	.451	27	42-39	31-50
Pittsburgh	67	95	.414	33	34-47	33-48

WESTERN DIVISION

Team	Won	Lost	Pct	GB	Home	Away
San Diego	82	80	.506	--	46-35	6-45
Arizona	77	85	.475	5	36-45	41-40
San Francisco	75	87	.463	7	37-44	38-43
LA Dodgers	71	91	.438	11	40-41	31-50
Colorado	67	95	.414	15	40-41	27-54

†Wild-card team.

American League

EASTERN DIVISION

Team	Won	Lost	Pct	GB	Home	Away
NY Yankees	95	67	.586	--	53-28	42-39
†Boston	95	67	.586	--	54-27	41-40
Toronto	80	82	.494	15	43-38	37-44
Baltimore	74	88	.457	21	36-45	38-43
Tampa Bay	67	95	.414	28	40-41	27-54

CENTRAL DIVISION

Team	Won	Lost	Pct	GB	Home	Away
Chicago	99	63	.611	--	47-34	52-29
Cleveland	93	69	.574	6	43-38	50-31
Minnesota	83	79	.512	16	45-36	38-43
Detroit	71	91	.438	28	39-42	32-49
Kansas City	56	106	.346	43	34-47	2-59

WESTERN DIVISION

Team	Won	Lost	Pct	GB	Home	Away
LA Angels	95	67	.586	--	49-32	46-35
Oakland	88	74	.543	7	43-38	43-38
Texas	79	83	.488	16	44-37	35-46
Seattle	69	93	.426	26	39-42	30-51

2005 Playoffs

National League Division Playoffs

Oct 5 ....Houston 10 at Atlanta 5
Oct 6 ....Houston 1 at Atlanta 7
Oct 8 .... Atlanta 3 at Houston 7
Oct 9 ....Atlanta 6 at Houston 7

(Houston won series 4–1)

Oct 4 ....San Diego 5 at St. Louis 8
Oct 6 ....San Diego 2 at St. Louis 6
Oct 8 ....St Louis 7 at San Diego 4

(St.Louis won the series 3–0)

National League Championship Series

Oct 12 ....Houston 3 at St. Louis 5
Oct 13 ....Houston 4 at St. Louis 1
Oct 15 ....St. Louis 3 at Houston 4
Oct 16 ....St. Louis 1 at Houston 2
Oct 17 ....St Louis 5 at Houston 4
Oct 19 ....Houston 5 at St. Louis 1

(Houston won series 4–2)

GAME 1

											R	H	E
Houston	0	0	0	0	0	0	2	0	1	**3**	**7**	**0**
St. Louis	2	1	0	0	2	0	0	0	x	**5**	**8**	**1**

W—StL: Carpenter **L**— Hou: Pettite. **LOB**—Hou: 6; StL: 4 **2B**—Hou: Beckman **3B**—StL: Walker. **HR**—Hou: Burke; StL: Sanders. **S**— Hou: Pettitte; Isringhausen; StL Carpenter **GIDP**— Hou: Berkman, StL; Sanders; Molina. **T**—2:29 **A**—52,332.

Recap: After Houston centerfielder Carlos Beltran hit a two-run homer to deep right in the visiting half of the first, St. Louis's Albert Pujols answered right back with a two-run shot of his own, serving notice that St. Louis's lineup could stand toe-to-toe, and then some, with Houston's sluggers. The teams traded blows until the sixth, when St. Louis broke the game open with six runs, three of them on a double by Jim Edmonds. Woody Williams went six innings for the win, giving up four runs on four hits, and striking out five.

GAME 2

											R	H	E
Houston	0	1	0	0	1	0	0	2	0	**4**	**11**	**1**
St. Louis	0	0	0	0	0	1	0	0	0	**1**	**6**	**0**

W—Oswalt **L**—Mulder **SV**—Lidge.
E—Hou: Ensberg. **LOB**—Hou: 7; StL: 8. **2B**—Hou: Berkman; Ausmus StL: Molina. **HR** StL: Pujols. **S**—Hou: Oswalt. **SB**—Hou: Ausmus: **CS**—Hou: Taveras. **T**—3:03. **A**—52,358.

Recap: The Astros' prize late-season pickup, Carlos Beltran, reprised his Game 1 performance, blasting a home run in the first inning, and Houston took a 3–0 lead into the fifth. But St. Louis again countered with firepower of its own, getting homers from Larry Walker and Scott Rolen to take a 4–3 lead in the home half. And after Morgan Ensberg tied it for Houston with an RBI single in the seventh, Albert Pujols and Scott Rolen went deep in the eighth to seal it for the Cardinals.

National League Championship Series (Cont.)

GAME 3

Houston	0	0	0	2	0	2	0	0	X	4	11	0
St. Louis	0	0	0	1	1	0	0	1	3	7	1	

W—Clemens. **L**—Morris. **SV**—Lidge.
LOB—StL: 7; Hou: 8. **2B**—StL: Mabry; Hou: Lamb, Everett. **HR**—Hou: Lamb. **SF**: StL: Eckstein, Walker. **SB**—StL: Edmonds. **T**—3:00. **A**—42,823.

Recap: Mike Lamb hit a two-run homer and scored the go-ahead run in the sixth inning off Morris and scored on Jason Lane's single a batter later to make it 3-2. "Mike Lamb has had my number," Morris said. "He came up, and I made a mistake with the cutter, and he hit it for the double. I was trying to go in on him, and he slapped it to right. There's your 3-2 ballgame." Hector Luna replaced Nunez at third and immediately committed a throwing error, allowing Lane to score. Roger Clemens (2-1) yielded two runs and six hits in six innings, throwing 62 of 97 pitches for strikes. The Cardinals got consecutive singles against Clemens to open the fifth and the sixth, but managed one run in each inning on sacrifice flies from David Eckstein and Walker. Morris (1-1) allowed four runs - three earned - and eight hits in 5 1/3 innings.

GAME 4

Houston	0	0	0	1	0	0	1	0	X	2	6	0
St. Louis	0	0	0	1	0	0	0	0	0	1	5	1

W—Qualls. **L**—Marquis. **SV**—Lidge.
LOB—StL: 5; Hou: 11. **2B**—StL: Edmonds **HR**—Hou: Lane. **SF**: StL: Pujols; Hou: Ensberg. **GIDP**—StL: Edmonds, Mabry. **SAC**—Hou: Biggio. **T**—3:11. **A**—43,010.

Recap: With the score tied at 1-1 in the seventh, the Astros took advantage of some shaky play from reliever Jason Marquis to push across the go-ahead run. The righthander, who went 4-0 as a starter vs. Houston this season, issued a leadoff walk to pinch hitter Orlando. St. Louis threatened to send the game into extra innings against Lidge in the ninth. Pujols and Walker opened the frame with consecutive singles to put runners on the corners. Reggie Sanders followed with a slow grounder to third base, but Ensberg was able to throw out Pujols at the plate. John Mabry then hit a weak ground ball to second baseman Eric Bruntlett , who quickly fired to Adam Everett at second base to get Sanders. The shortstop's relay throw to first baseman Lance Berkman just beat Mabry to end the game.

GAME 5

St. Louis	0	0	2	0	0	0	0	0	3	5	9	1
Houston	0	1	0	0	0	0	3	0	0	4	9	2

W—Isringhausen. **L**—Lidge. **LOB**—StL: 8; Hou: 7.
2B—StL: Molina; Hou: Ausmus. **HR**—StL: Pujols; Hou: Berkman. **SAC**—Hou: Burke, Pettitte. **HBP**—Hou: Eckstein, Lane. **T**—3:19. **A**—43,470.

Recap: Pujols hit a go-ahead three-run homer off Lidge with two outs in the top of the ninth inning as the Cardinals staged a season-saving rally. Houston starter Andy Pettitte opened the game by hitting Eckstein with a pitch and walking Edmonds. The Cardinals failed to take advantage as Pettitte retired Pujols, Reggie Sanders and Larry Walker to end the threat. Pettitte nearly escaped a similar jam two innings later. Eckstein and Edmonds hit consecutive singles to put runners on the corners before Pettitte struck out Pujols and Sanders. However, Walker drew a walk to load the bases and Mark Grudzielanek followed with a bloop single to right-center field, plating Eckstein and Edmonds for a 2-1 lead. Pettitte, who lost Game One, allowed two runs and seven hits in 6 1/3 innings. Carpenter yielded four runs - three earned - and nine hits in seven frames.

GAME 6

Houston	0	0	2	1	0	1	1	0	0	5	11	0
St. Louis	0	0	0	1	0	0	0	0	1	4	1	

W—Oswalt. **L**—Mulder. **LOB**—Hou: 7; StL: 6. **2B**—StL: Walker. **HR**—Hou: Lane. **SAC**—Hou: Taveras, Everett, Oswalt. **SF**—StL: Rodriguez. **HBP**—Hou: Eckstein, Grudzielanek. **T**—2:53. **A**—52,438.

Recap: Working off an overpowering fastball that routinely registered 95 miles per hour, Roy Oswalt yielded a run and three hits. After Molina's single put runners on first and second with none out, Abraham Nunez hit a ball that bounced off Oswalt. He picked it up and, from his knees, threw toward second base. Umpire Greg Gibson ruled that Houston shortstop Adam Everett , who had to come off the bag toward first base to take the throw, had successfully tagged Molina before he got to the base. Replays clearly showed Molina was not tagged. John Rodriguez followed with a sacrifice fly to short center field before Oswalt struck out David Eckstein to end the rally.

American League Division Playoffs

Oct. 4 -- Boston 2 at Chicago 14
Oct. 5 -- Boston 4 at Chicago 5
Oct. 7 -- Chicago 5 at Boston 3
(Chicago won series 3-0)

Oct. 4 -- New York 4 at Los Angeles 2
Oct. 5 -- New York 3 at Los Angeles 5
Oct. 7 -- Los Angeles 11 at New York 7
Oct. 9 -- Los Angeles 2 at New York 3
Oct. 10 --New York 3 at Los Angeles 5
(New York won series 3-1)

American League Championship Series

Oct 11 ....Los Angeles 3 at Chicago 2
Oct 12 ....Los Angeles 1 at Chicago 2
Oct 14 ....Chicago 5 at Los Angeles 2

Oct 15 ....Chicago 8 at Los Angeles 2
Oct 16 ....Chicago 6 at Los Angeles 3
(Chicago won series 4-1)

GAME 1

Los Angeles	0	1	2	0	0	0	0	0	0	3	7	1
Chicago	0	0	1	1	0	0	0	0	0	2	7	0

W—Byrd. **L**—Contreras. **SV**—Rodriguez.
LOB—LA 4, Chi 6. **HR**—LA: Anderson; Chi: Crede.
SAC—LA: Figgins. **SB**—LA: Figgins, Erstad. **HBP**—Chi: Rowand. **T**—2:47. **A**—40,659.

Recap: Paul Byrd yielded two runs and five hits. He walked and struck out one, delivered strikes on 47 of 73 pitches and only allowed two runners to reach second base.   The crafty righthander departed after hitting Aaron Rowand to lead off the seventh, but Scot Shields entered and retired the side. The Angels scored two runs for a 3-0 lead in the third. The White Sox responded on Joe Crede 's solo homer to left field in the third, his third in 10 career at-bats against Byrd, and a two-out RBI single by A.J. Pierzynski in an eight-pitch at-bat in the fourth to cut the deficit to 3-2.

GAME 2

Chicago	1	0	0	0	0	0	0	0	1	2	7	1
Los Angeles	0	0	0	0	1	0	0	0	0	1	5	3

W—Buehrle. **L**—Escobar. **LOB**—Chi: 7; LA: 4. **2B**—Chi: Rowand, Crede; LA: Cabrera. **HR**—LA: Quinlan. **GIDP**—LA: Guerrero, Kennedy. **HBP**—LA: Molina; Chi: Iguchi **SB**—Chi: Ozuna. **T**—2:34. **A**—41,013.

Recap: Mark Buehrle pitched a five-hitter and plate umpire Doug Eddings made a controversial call on what appeared to be the final out of the ninth inning before Joe Crede 's game-winning RBI double lifted the White Sox to a 2-1 series evening win.   Starting his third inning of relief, Kelvim Escobar (1-1) retired the first two batters in the bottom of the ninth and struck out A.J. Pierzynski to apparently send the game into extra innings.   But Eddings ruled that the low pitch hit the ground before going into the glove of catcher Josh Paul, who already had rolled the ball back to the mound and was running toward the dugout, and Pierzynski alertly ran to first base to extend the inning. After a lengthy argument, pinch runner Pablo Ozuna stole second without a throw and Crede followed with a drive off the left field fence, allowing Ozuna to score easily.

GAME 3

Chicago	3	0	1	0	1	0	0	0	0	5	11	0
Los Angeles	0	0	0	0	0	2	0	0	0	2	4	0

W—Garland. **L**—Lackey.
LOB—Chi: 6; LA: 1. **2B**—Chi: Iguchi; LA: Erstad.
HR—Chi: Konerko; LA: Cabrera **SAC**—Chi: Iguchi
GIDP—Chi: Rowand; LA: Guerrero. **T**—2:42. **A**—44,725.

Recap: Jon Garland tossed a four-hitter and Paul Konerko homered and drove in three runs in the Chicago White Sox 5-2 victory.   Garland walked leadoff hitter Chone Figgins in the first inning but yielded just two singles, a double and a two-run homer by Orlando Cabrera thereafter while tying a season high with seven strikeouts and throwing 81 of 114 pitches for strikes. Anaheim hit just eight balls out of the infield and stranded just one baserunner. Garland allowed just two balls to reach the outfield until Adam Kennedy blooped a one-out single to left in the sixth. Cabrera then deposited a 2-2 fastball over the left field wall for his first career

GAME 3 *(Cont.)*

postseason homer. However, Chicago and Konerko already had gotten to Anaheim starter John Lackey (0-1) for five runs.

GAME 4

Chicago	3	0	1	1	1	0	0	2	0	8	8	1
Los Angeles	0	1	0	1	0	0	0	0	0	2	6	1

W—Garcia. **L**—Santana.
LOB—Chi: 5; LA: 4 **2B**—Chi: Rowand; LA: Kotchman. **3B**—Chi: Podsednik. **HR**—Chi: Konerko, Pierzynski. **GIDP**—NY: Jeter, Cairo; Bos: Mintkiewicz. **GIDP**—Chi: LA: Finley. **SB**—Chi: Podsednik. **HBD**—Chi: Iguchi. **T**—2:46. **A**—44,857.

Recap: Freddy Garcia pitched Chicago's third consecutive complete game, a six-hitter. He walked one and struck out five.   Konerko belted a 3-2 slider from rookie Ervin Santana (1-1) over the left field fence with two runners on in the opening frame. After getting a run back in the second on Bengie Molina's single that scored Darin Erstad and put runners on the corners with one out, Steve Finley grounded into a double play. However, his bat came in contact with Pierzynski's glove, meaning Finley should have been awarded first base on catcher's interference, which would have loaded the bases with one out. Instead, the Angels were out of the inning. Garcia got the leadoff hitter in every inning but the eighth and threw 74 of 116 pitches for strikes. Santana was tagged for six runs - five earned - and three hits in 4 1/3 innings. He walked three and struck out two.

GAME 5

Chicago	0	1	0	0	1	0	1	1	2	6	8	1
Los Angeles	0	0	1	0	2	0	0	0	0	3	5	2	**1**

W—Contreras. **L**—Escobar.
LOB—Chi: 9; LA: 4. **2B**—Chi: Dye, Konerko, Rowand, Uribe; LA: Figgins, Rivera. **HR**—Chi: Crede. **SAC**—Chi: Pierzynski; LA: Figgins. **SF**—Chi: Rowand, Crede; LA; Anderson **SB**—Chi: Podsednik. **T**—3:11. **A**—44,712.

Recap: Joe Crede drove in three runs, including the go-ahead run in the eighth inning, and Jose Contreras pitched Chicago's fourth consecutive complete game to end the series.   In the eighth, Pierzynski hit a comebacker that bounced off Escobar and rolled toward the first base line. The reliever picked up the ball and attempted to tag Pierzynski with his glove, but was holding the ball in his bare right hand.   First base umpire Randy Marsh initially called Pierzynski out, but the umpires conferred and changed the call, prompting Anaheim manager Mike Scioscia to come out and voice his displeasure to no avail.   In the ninth, the White Sox added some insurance with an RBI double by ALCS MVP Paul Konerko and a sacrifice fly by Rowand. Contreras (2-1), who is 10-1 in his last 11 starts, yielded three runs and five hits

Oct 22 ....Houston 3 at Chicago 5
Oct 23 ....Houston 6 at Chicago 7

Oct 25 ....Chicago 7 at Houston 5
Oct 26 ....Chicago 1 at Houston 0

(Chicago won series 4–0)

GAME 1

Chicago	1	2	0	1	0	0	0	1	x	5	10	0
Houston	0	1	2	0	0	0	0	0	0	3	7	1

W—Contreras. **L**—Rodriguez.
LOB—Chi: 9, Hou: 6. **2B**—Chi: Uribe; Hou: Taveras 2, Berkman **3B**—Chi: Podsednik **HR**—Chi: Dye, Crede; Hou: Lamb. **SAC**—Chi: Everett; Hou: Taveras. **SB**—Chi: Podsednik, Pierzynski; Hou: Burke **GIDP**—Chi: Iguchi, Pierzynski; Hou: Lane. **HBP**—Hou: Bagwell, Ausmus. **T**—3:13. **A**—41,206.

Recap: Jermaine Dye opened the scoring in the first with a drive over the right field. Chicago took a 3-1 edge in the second on an RBI groundout by A.J. Pierzynski and Juan Uribe 's two-out RBI double. Joe Crede's fourth-inning homer against Wandy Rodriguez (0-1) snapped a 3-3 tie. Jose Contreras departed after yielding Willy Taveras' second double of the game to open the frame. The lefthanded Cotts entered and allowed a single to Lance Berkman before striking out Ensberg and Mike Lamb. Jenks struck out Jeff Bagwell with a fastball that registered 99 miles per hour. After Scott Podsednik tripled in an insurance run in the bottom of the eighth, Jenks struck out two in a perfect ninth for the save.

GAME 2

Chicago	0	2	0	0	0	0	4	0	1	7	12	0
Houston	0	1	1	0	2	0	0	0	2	6	9	0

W—Cotts. **L**—Linge. **LOB**—Chi: 5; Hou: 4. **2B**—Chi: Rowand, Uribe 3; Hou: Berkman 2, Ausmus. **3B**—Hou: Taveras. **HR**—Chi: Podsednik, Konerko; Hou: Ensberg **SB**—Chi: Uribe; Hou: Lane. **HBP**—Chi: Dye. **T**—3:11. **A**—41,432.

Recap: Before the seventh, it looked like the Astros were on their way to evening the series. Lance Berkman had driven in three runs and Andy Pettitte limited the White Sox to two runs and eight hits in six innings as Houston built a 4-2 lead. Scott Podsednik homered off Brad Lidge in the bottom of the ninth inning to give the Chicago White Sox a 7-6 victory over the Houston Astros and a commanding two games to none World Series lead. But Dan Wheeler loaded the bases and, with two outs, Konerko hit his fifth postseason homer on the first pitch from Qualls, who had retired 18 of the previous 19 batters he faced.Rookie closer Bobby Jenks yielded a leadoff single to Jeff Bagwell in the ninth and a four-pitch walk to Chris Burke one out later. Both runners advanced on Brad Ausmus' check-swing grounder before pinch hitter Jose Vizcaino lined the first pitch to left field for a two-run single, with Burke beating Podsednik's weak throw to the plate and sliding around the tag of catcher A.J. Pierzynski.

GAME 3

Chicago	0	0	0	0	5	0	0	0	0	0	0	0	0	2	7 14 3
Houston	1	0	2	1	0	0	0	1	0	0	0	0	0	0	5 8 1

W—Marte. **L**—Atascio. **SV**—**Buehrle.**
LOB—Chi: 15; Hou: 15. **2B**—Chi: Konerko, Pierzynski; Hou: Biggio, Lane. **HR**—Chi: Blum, Crede; Hou: Lane. **GIDP**—Chi: Podsednik, Dye, Konerko; Hou: Ensberg, Ausmus. **SB**—Chi: Podsednik, Harris; Hou: Burke. **HBP**—Chi: Crede. **T**—5:41. **A**—42,848.

Recap: Geoff Blum belted a home run in the top of the 14th inning as the White Sox took a commanding three games to none lead in the World Series with the longest game in the history of the Fall Classic. Picked up at the July trade deadline, Blum lined a 2-0 fastball from Ezequiel Astacio (0-1), the seventh pitcher used by Houston, into the right field seats to snap a 5-5 tie. Blum hit just .200 with one homer in 95 at-bats with the White Sox during the regular season and had just one previous at-bat in the playoffs. After Blum's blast, Astacio yielded a pair of infield singles before walking Juan Uribe and Chris Widger to force in another run. With a runner on second, Ausmus reached on shortstop Uribe's error with two outs in the bottom of the 14th, but Game Two starter Mark Buehrle came on and got Adam Everett to pop out for his first career save. Game time easily surpassed the previous mark of 4:51 in Game One of the 2000 World Series between the New York Yankees and Mets. It also matched Game Two of the 1916 World Series between the Boston Red Sox and Brooklyn Robins as the longest Fall Classic contest in terms of innings.

GAME 4

Chicago	0	0	0	0	0	0	0	1	0	1	8	0
Houston	0	0	0	0	0	0	0	0	0	0	5	0

W—Lowe. **L**—Marquis. **SV**—Foulke.
LOB—Chi: 7; Hou: 9. **2B**—Chi: Dye, Crede, Pierzynksi; Hou: Lamb. **3B**—Chi: Podsednik 2. **GIDP**—Hou: Everett. **S**—Chi: Podsednik. **SB**—Hou: Taveras, Berkman. **T**—3:20. **A**—42,936.

Recap: Winner Freddy Garcia and Houston's Brandon Backe pitched shutout ball for seven innings, with Backe allowing four hits and Garcia five. They each struck out seven. Brad Lidge, Houston's closer, came in to start the eighth, and Chicago sent up Willie Harris to bat for Garcia. Harris lined a single to left leading off, Scott Podsednik bunted a difficult high pitch in front of the plate and the speedy Harris took second on the sacrifice. Carl Everett pinch hit for Tadahito Iguchi and grounded to second, moving Harris to third. Jermaine Dye, grounded a single up the middle, which brought Harris home from third. After Chicago wasted a leadoff double by Pierzynski in the ninth, Jason Lane lofted a 3-2 pitch off Bobby Jenks into short center for a single leading off the bottom half. Orlando Palmeiro pinch hit, and grounded to Uribe at shortstop for the final out, with Paul Konerko gloving the ball a half-step before Palmeiro landed on the bag.

2005 World Series Composite Box Score

BATTING	AB	R	H	HR	RBI	Avg
CHICAGO						
Podsednik	21	2	6	1	2	.286
Iguchi	18	2	3	0	1	.167
Crede	17	2	5	2	3	.294
Rowand	17	2	5	0	0	.294
Uribe	16	2	4	0	2	.250
Konerko	16	1	4	1	4	.250
Dye	16	3	7	1	3	.438
Pierzynski	15	3	4	0	3	.267
Everett	9	1	4	0	0	.444
Widger	1	0	0	0	1	.000
Blum	1	1	1	1	1	1.000
Harris	1	1	1	0	0	1.000
Perez	1	0	0	0	0	.000
Pitchers	5	0	0	0	0	.000
Totals	154	20	44	6	20	.204

PITCHING	G	IP	H	BB	SO	ERA
Buehrle	2	7.1	7	0	6	4.91
Garcia	1	7	4	3	7	0.00
Contreras	1	7	6	0	2	3.86
Garland	1	7	7	2	4	2.57
Jenks)	4	5	3	2	2	3.60
Politte	3	2.1	0	2	2	3.86
Marte	1	1.2	0	2	3	0.00
Cotts	4	1.1	1	4	2	0.00
Hernandez	1	1.0	0	4	2	0.00
Vizcaino	1	1.0	0	4	2	0.00
Totals	4	39.5	28	23	37	1.88

(Chicago won series 4–1)

BATTING	AB	R	H	HR	RBI	Avg
HOUSTON						
Biggio	18	3	4	0	1	.222
Ensberg	18	2	2	1	2	.111
Lane	18	1	4	1	2	.222
Ausmus	16	1	4	0	0	.250
Taveras	15	2	5	0	0	.333
Everett	15	2	1	0	0	.067
Berkman	13	0	5	0	6	.385
Lamb	10	1	2	1	1	.200
Bagwell	8	1	1	0	0	.125
Burke	5	1	0	0	0	.000
Palmeiro	2	0	0	0	0	.000
Vizcaino	2	0	1	0	2	.500
Bruntlett	0	0	0	0	0	.000
Pitchers	3	0	0	0	0	.000
Totals	143	14	29	3	14	.101

PITCHING	G	IP	H	BB	SO	ERA
Backe	1	7.0	5	0	7	0.00
Pettitte	1	6.0	8	0	4	3.00
Oswalt	1	6.0	8	5	3	7.50
Qualls	3	5.1	3	2	5	1.69
Lidge	3	3.2	4	0	6	4.91
Rodriguez	2	3.2	4	5	2	2.45
Clemens	1	2.0	4	0	1	13.50
Springer	2	2.0	2	0	1	4.50
Wheeler	2	2.0	2	1	1	13.50
Gallo	2	1.0	0	0	0	0.00
Totals	4	37.5	40	13	32	4.64

2005 Individual Leaders

National League Batting

BATTING AVERAGE

Derrek Lee, Chi	335
Albert Pujols, StL	330
Miguel Cabrera, Fla	323
Todd Helton, Col	320
Sean Casey, Cin	312
Chad Tracy, Ari	308
Matt Holliday, Col	307
David Wright, NYM	306
Brady Clark, Mil	306
Jason Bay, Pit	306

HITS

Derrek Lee, Chi	199
Miguel Cabrera, Fla	198
Jimmy Rollins, Phi	196
Albert Pujols, StL	195
José Reyes, NYM	190
David Eckstein, StL	185
Jason Bay, Pit	183
Brady Clark, Mil	183
Juan Pierre, Fla	181
David Wright, NYM	176

DOUBLES

Derrek Lee, Chi	50
Todd Helton, Col	45
Marcus Giles, Atl	45
Jason Bay, Pit	44
Miguel Cabrera, Fla	43
Joe Randa, SD	43

TRIPLES

José Reyes, NYM	17
Juan Pierre, Fla	13
Rafael Furcal, Atl	11
Jimmy Rollins, Phi	11
Dave Roberts, SD	10
Brian Giles, SD	8

HOME RUNS

Andruw Jones, Atl	51
Derrek Lee, Chi	46
Albert Pujols, StL	41
Adam Dunn, Cin	40
Troy Glaus, Ari	37
Morgan Ensberg, Hou	36
Ken Griffey Jr., Cin	35
Cliff Floyd, NYM	34
Miguel Cabrera, Fla	33
Carlos Delgado, Fla	33

RUNS SCORED

Albert Pujols, Stl	129
Derrek Lee, Chi	120
Jimmy Rollins, Phi	115
Jason Bay, Pit	110
Adam Dunn, Cin	107
Miguel Cabrera, Fla	106
Bobby Abreu, Phi	104
Marcus Giles, Atl	104
Rafael Furcal, Atl	100
Jeff Kent, LAD	100
José Reyes, NYM	99

STOLEN BASES

José Reyes, NYM	60
Juan Pierre, Fla	57
Rafael Furcal, Atl	46
Jimmy Rollins, Phi	41
Ryan Freel, Cin	36

RUNS BATTED IN

Andruw Jones, Atl	128
Pat Burrell, Phi	117
Albert Pujols, StL	117
Miguel Cabrera, Fla	116
Carlos Delgado, Fla	115
Carlos Lee, Mil	114
Derrek Lee, Chi	107
Chase Utley, Phi	105
Jeff Kent, LAD	105
Bobby Abreu, Phi	102

SLUGGING PERCENTAGE

Derrek Lee, Chi	662
Albert Pujols, StL	609
Carlos Delgado, Fla	582
Ken Griffey Jr., Cin	576
Andruw Jones, Atl	575

National League Batting *(Cont.)*

ON-BASE PERCENTAGE

Todd Helton, Col 445
Albert Pujols, StL....................430
Brian Giles, SD.......................423
Derrek Lee, Chi 418
Lance Berkman, Hou 411

BASES ON BALLS

Brian Giles, SD.......................119
Bobby Abreu, Phi....................117
Adam Dunn, Cin 114
Todd Helton, Col 106
Pat Burrell, Phi 99

National League Pitching

EARNED RUN AVERAGE

Roger Clemens, Hou 1.87
Andy Pettitte, Hou 2.39
Dontrelle Willis, Fla................2.63
Pedro Martínez, NYM.............2.82
Chris Carpenter, StL 2.83
Jake Peavy, SD......................2.88
Roy Oswalt, Hou 2.94
John Smoltz, Atl 3.06
John Patterson, Was 3.13
Carlos Zambrano, Chi............3.26

SAVES

Chad Cordero, Was 47
Trevor Hoffman, SD 43
Brad Lidge, Hou 42
Todd Jones, Fla 40
Derrick Turnbow, Mil................39
Jason Isringhausen, StL 39
Billy Wagner, Phi......................38
Ryan Dempster, Chi.................33
Brian Fuentes, Col 31

WINS

Dontrelle Willis, Fla...................22
Chris Carpenter, StL 21
Roy Oswalt, Hou 20
Chris Capuano, Mil 18
Andy Pettitte, Hou 17
Jon Lieber, Phi 17

Two tied with 16.

GAMES PITCHED

Scott Eyre, SF 86
Duaner Sánchez, LAD 79
Gary Majewski, WAS................79
Salomón Torres, Pit 78
Brian Fuentes, Col 78

INNINGS PITCHED

Liván Hernández, Was.............246
Roy Oswalt, Hou 241
Chris Carpenter, StL 241
Dontrelle Willis, Fla.................236
John Smoltz, Atl 229

STRIKEOUTS

Jake Peavy, SD......................216
Chris Carpenter, StL 213
Pedro Martínez, NYM.............208
Brett Myers, Phi......................208
Doug Davis, Mil.......................208
Carlos Zambrano, Chi.............202
A.J. Burnett, Fla 198
Javier Vázquez, Ari 192
Mark Prior, Chi 188

COMPLETE GAMES

Dontrelle Willis, Fla....................7
Chris Carpenter, StL 7
Roy Oswalt, Hou 4
A.J. Burnett, Fla 4
Pedro Martínez, NYM..................4

SHUTOUTS

Dontrelle Willis, Fla.....................5
Chris Carpenter, StL 4
Jake Peavy, SD...........................3

American League Batting

BATTING AVERAGE

IMichael Young, Tex 331
Álex Rodríguez, NYY 321
Vladimir Guerrero, LAA...........317
Johnny Damon, Bos 316
Brian Roberts, Bal...................314
Derek Jeter, NYY 309
Hideki Matsui, NYY 305
Víctor Martínez, Cle 305
Travis Hafner, Cle 305
Miguel Tejada, Bal 304
Ichiro Suzuki, Sea 303

HITS

Michael Young, Tex 221
Ichiro Suzuki, Sea 206
Derek Jeter, NYY 202
Miguel Tejada, Bal...................199
Johnny Damon, Bos 197
Álex Rodríguez, NYY 194
Mark Teixeira, Tex 194
Carl Crawford, TB 194
Hideki Matsui, NYY 192
Chone Figgins, LAA.................186
Grady Sizemore, Cle 185

DOUBLES

Miguel Tejada, Bal....................50
Hideki Matsui, NYY 45
Brian Roberts, Bal....................45
Alfonso Soriano, Tex................43
Travis Hafner, Cle 42
Coco Crisp, Cle 42

TRIPLES

Carl Crawford, TB 15
Ichiro Suzuki, Sea 12
Grady Sizemore, Cle 11
Chone Figgins, LAA.................10
Brandon Inge, Det 9

HOME RUNS

Álex Rodríguez, NYY 48
David Ortiz, Box.......................47
Manny Ramírez, Bos................45
Mark Teixeira, Tex 43
Paul Konerko, Chi 40
Richie Sexson, Sea..................39
Alfonso Soriano, Tex................36
Gary Sheffield, NYY 34
Travis Hafner, Cle 33

RUNS SCORED

Álex Rodríguez, NYY 124
Derek Jeter, NYY 122
David Ortiz, Bos.......................119
Johnny Damon, Bos 119
Michael Young, Tex 114
Chone Figgins, LAA.................113
Manny Ramírez, Bos................112
Mark Teixeira, Tex 112

STOLEN BASES

Chone Figgins, LAA...................62
Scott Podsednik, Chi 59
Carl Crawford, TB 46
Julio Lugo, TB..........................39
Ichiro Suzuki, Sea 33

RUNS BATTED IN

David Ortiz, Bos.......................148
Manny Ramírez, Bos................144
Mark Teixeira, Tex 144
Álex Rodríguez, NYY 130
Gary Sheffield, NYY 123

RUNS BATTED IN *(CONT.)*

Richie Sexson, Sea..................121
Jorge Cantú, TB.......................117
Hideki Matsui, NYY 116
Vladimir Guerrero, LAA............108
Travis Hafner, Cle 108

SLUGGING PERCENTAGE

Álex Rodríguez, NYY 610
David Ortiz, Bos.......................604
Travis Hafner, Cle 595
Manny Ramírez, Bos................594
Mark Teixeira, Tex 575

ON-BASE PERCENTAGE

Jason Giambi, NYY..................440
Álex Rodríguez, NYY. 421
Travis Hafner, Cle 408
David Ortiz, Bos.......................397
Vladimir Guerrero, LAA............394

BASES ON BALLS

Jason Giambi, NYY..................108
David Ortiz, Bos.......................102
Álex Rodríguez, NYY 91
Richie Sexson, Sea 89
Paul Konerko, Chi 81

American League Pitching

EARNED RUN AVERAGE

Kevin Millwood, Cle 2.86
Johan Santana, Min 2.87
Mark Buehrle, Chi 3.12
Jarrod Washburn, LAA 3.20
John Lackey, LAA.................3.44
Carlos Silva, Min 3.44
Kenny Rogers, Tex 3.46
Bartolo Colón, LAA 3.48
Jon Garland, Chi..................3.50
Joe Blanton, Oak 3.53

SAVES

Francisco Rodríguez, LAA 45 .....
Bob Wickman, Cle 45
Joe Nathan, Min....................43
Mariano Rivera, NYY..............43
Danys Báez, TB 41
Francisco Cordero, Tex 37
Eddie Guardado, Sea.............36
B.J. Ryan, Bal 36
Dustin Hermanson, Chi...........34
Miguel Batista Tor..................34
Huston Street, Oak 23

WINS

Bartolo Colón, LAA 21
Jon Garland, Chi.....................18
Cliff Lee, Cle 18
Randy Johnson, NYY...............17
Johan Santana, Min 16
Tim Wakefield, Bos 16
Mark Buehrle, Chi 16

Nine tied with 14.

GAMES PITCHED

Paul Quantrill, NY...................86
Tom Gordon, NY 80
Octavio Dotel, Oak 77
Juan Rincon, Minn 77
B.J. Ryan, Balt 76
Mike Timlin, Bos 76

SHUTOUTS

Jon Garland, Chi......................3
Mike Mussina, NYY 2
Roy Halladay, Tor 2
Johan Santana, Min 2

STRIKEOUTS

Johan Santana, Min 238
Randy Johnson, NYY.............211
John Lackey, LAA..................199
Scott Kazmir, TB 174
Barry Zito, Oak......................171
Danny Haren, Oak 163
C.C. Sabathia, Cle 161
Bartolo Colón, LAA 157
Daniel Cabrera, Bal 157
José Contreras, Chi...............149

INNINGS PITCHED

Mark Buehrle, Chi 236.2
Johan Santana, Min 231.2
Barry Zito, Oak....................228.1
Freddy García, Chi 228.0
Randy Johnson, NYY...........225.2

COMPLETE GAMES

Roy Halladay, Tor 5
Randy Johnson, NYY................4
Jeremy Bonderman, Det...........4

Six tied with 3.

2005 Team Statistics

National League

TEAM BATTING	G	AB	R	H	2B	3B	HR	TB	RBI	BA	OBP	SLG	OPS
Florida Marlins	162	5502	717	1499	306	32	128	2253	678	.272	.339	.409	.748
Chicago Cubs	162	5584	703	1506	323	23	194	2457	674	.270	.324	.440	.764
St. Louis Cardinal	162	5538	805	1494	287	26	170	2343	757	.270	.339	.423	.762
Philadelphia Phillies	162	5542	807	1494	282	35	167	2347	760	.270	348	.423	.772
Colorado Rockies	162	5542	740	1477	280	34	150	2275	704	.267	.333	.411	.744
Atlanta Braves	162	5486	769	1453	308	37	184	2387	733	.265	.333	.435	.768
Cincinnati Reds	163	5565	820	1453	335	15	222	2484	784	.261	.339	.446	.785
San Francisco Giants	162	5462	649	1427	299	26	128	2162	617	.261	.319	.396	.714
Pittsburgh Pirates	162	5573	680	1445	292	38	139	2230	656	.259	.322	.400	.723
Milwaukee Brewers	162	5448	726	1413	327	19	175	2303	689	.259	.331	.423	.754
New York Mets	162	5505	722	1421	279	32	175	2289	683	.258	.322	.416	.738
San Diego Padres	162	5502	684	1416	269	39	130	2153	655	.257	.333	.391	.724
Arizona	162	5550	696	1419	291	27	191	2337	670	.256	.332	.421	.754
Huston Astros	163	5462	693	1400	281	32	161	2228	654	.256	.322	.408	.730
L.A. Dodgers	162	5433	685	1374	284	21	149	2147	653	.253	.326	.395	.721
Washington	162	5426	639	1367	311	32	117	2093	615	.252	.322	.386	.708

TEAM PITCHING	GP	W	L	SV	SVO	CG	SO	R	ERA	IP	Ks	BB
St. Louis Cardinal	162	100	62	48	65	15	14	634	3.49	1445.2	974	443
Houston Astros	163	89	73	45	58	6	11	609	3.51	1443.0	1164	440
New York Mets	162	83	79	38	59	8	11	648	3.76	1435.2	1012	491
Washington	162	81	81	51	69	4	9	673	3.87	1458.0	997	539
Milwaukee Brewers	162	81	81	46	67	7	6	697	3.97	1438.0	1173	569
Atlanta Braves	162	90	72	38	62	8	12	674	3.98	1443.2	929	520
San Diego Padres	162	82	80	45	65	4	8	726	4.13	1455.1	1133	503
Florida Marlins	162	83	79	42	60	-14	15	732	4.16	1442.1	1125	563
Chicago Cubs	161	79	83	39	58	8	10	714	4.19	1440.0	1256	576
Phildelphia Phillies	161	88	74	40	63	4	6	726	4.21	1435.0	1159	487
San Francisco	162	75	87	46	74	4	8	745	4.33	1444.1	972	592
L.A. Dodgers	162	71	91	40	59	6	9	755	4.38	1427.0	1004	471
Pittsburgh Pirates	162	67	95	35	47	4	14	769	4.42	1436.0	958	612
Arizona	162	77	85	45	62	6	10	856	4.84	1456.1	1038	537
Colorado Rockies	162	67	95	37	63	4	4	862	5.13	1418.2	981	604
Cincinnati Reds	163	73	89	31	47	2	1	889	5.15	1433.0	955	492

Note: OPS is on-base percentage plus slugging percentage.

2005 Team Statistics

American League

TEAM BATTING	G	AB	R	H	2B	3B	HR	TB	RBI	BA	OBP	SLG	OPS
Boston Red Sox	162	5626	910	1579	339	21	199	2557	863	.281	.357	.454	.811
New York Yankees	162	5624	886	1152	259	16	229	2530	847	.276	.355	.450	.805
Tampa Bay Devil Rays	162	5552	750	1519	289	40	157	2359	717	.274	.329	.425	.754
Detroit Tigers	162	5602	723	1521	283	45	168	2398	678	.272	.321	.428	.750
Cleveland Indians	162	5609	790	1522	337	30	207	2540	760	.271	.334	.453	.787
Los Angeles Angels	162	5617	760	517	278	30	147	2296	724	.270	.325	.409	.734
Baltimore Orioles	162	5551	729	1492	296	27	189	2409	700	.269	.327	.434	.761
Texas Ranger	162	5716	865	1528	311	29	260	2677	834	.267	.329	.468	.798
Toronto Blue Jays	162	5581	775	1480	307	39	136	2273	735	.265	.331	.407	.738
Kansas City Royals	162	5496	700	1443	289	34	126	2178	651	.263	.320	.396	.716
Oakland Athletics	162	5627	772	1476	310	20	155	2291	739	.262	.330	.407	.737
Chicago White Sox	162	5529	741	1450	253	23	200	2349	713	.262	.322	.425	.747
Minnesota Twins	162	5564	688	1441	269	32	134	2176	644	.259	.323	.391	.714
Seattle Mariners	162	5507	699	1408	289	34	130	2155	657	.256	.317	.391	.709

TEAM PITCHING	GP	W	L	SV	SVO	CG	SO	R	ERA	IP	Ks	BB
Cleveland Indians	162	93	69	51	66	6	10	642	3.61	1452.21	1050	413
Chicago White Sox	162	99	63	54	73	9	10	645	3.61	1475.2	1040	459
Los Angeles Angels	162	95	67	54	71	7	11	643	3.68	1464.1	1126	443
Oakland	162	88	74	38	56	9	12	658	3.69	1450.1	1075	504
Minnesota Twins	162	83	79	44	60	9	8	662	3.71	1464.1	965	348
Toronto Blue Jays	162	80	82	35	56	9	8	705	4.06	1447.0	958	444
Seattle Mariners	162	69	93	39	59	6	7	751	4.49	1427.2	892	496
Detroit Tigers	162	71	91	37	57	7	2	787	4.51	1435.2	907	461
New York Yankees	162	95	67	46	67	8	14	789	4.52	1430.2	985	463
Baltimore Orioles	162	74	88	38	57	2	9	800	4.56	1427.2	1052	580
Boston Red Sox	162	95	67	38	57	6	8	805	4.74	1429.0	959	440
Texas Rangers	162	79	83	46	68	2	6	858	4.96	1440.0	932	522
Tampa Bay	162	67	95	43	69	1	4	936	5.39	1421.2	949	615
Kansas City Royals	162	56	106	25	43	4	4	935	5.49	1413.1	924	580

Note: OPS is on-base percentage plus slugging percentage.

National League Team-by-Team Statistical Leaders

Arizona Diamondbacks

BATTING	G	AB	R	H	2B	3B	HR	RBI	TB	BB	SO	SB	OBP	SLG	BA
Shawn Green	158	581	87	166	37	4	22	73	277	62	95	8	.355	.477	.286
Luis Gonzalez	155	579	90	157	37	0	24	79	266	78	9	4	.366	459	.271
Craig Counsell	150	578	85	148	34	4	9	42	217	78	69	26	.350	.375	.256
Troy Glaus	149	538	78	139	29	1	37	97	281	84	145	4	.363	.522	.258
Royce Clayton	143	522	59	141	28	4	2	44	183	38	105	13	.320	.351	.270
Chad Tracy	145	503	73	155	34	4	27	72	278	35	78	3	.359	.553	.308
Tony Clark	130	349	47	106	22	2	30	87	222	37	88	0	.366	.636	.304
Alex Cintron	122	330	36	90	19	2	8	48	137	12	33	1	.298	.415	.273
Chris Snyder	115	326	24	66	14	0	6	28	98	40	87	0	.297	.301	.202
Quinton McCracken	134	215	23	51	4	3	1	13	64	23	35	4	.313	.298	.237
Luis Terrero	88	161	23	37	6	1	4	20	57	14	40	3	.313	.354	.230
Kelly Stinnett	59	129	15	32	4	0	6	12	54	12	23	0	.317	.419	.248
Conor Jackson	40	85	8	17	3	0	2	8	26	12	14	0	.303	.306	.200
Koyie Hill	34	78	6	17	5	0	0	6	22	11	12	0	.308	.282	.218

PITCHING	GP	GS	W–L	SV	SHO	R	ERA	IP	Ks	BB
Brandon Webb`	33	33	14-12	0	0	98	3.54	229.0	172	59
Javier Vazquez	33	33	11-15	0	1	112	4.42	215.2	192	46
Brad Hasley	28	28	8-12	0	0	101	4.61	160.0	82	39
Claudio Vargas	25	23	9-9	0	0	81	5.24	132.1	95	47
Shawn Estes	21	21	7-8	0	0	70	4.80	123.2	63	45
Russ Ortiz	22	22	5-11	0	0	92	6.89	115.0	46	65
Lance Cormier	67	0	7-3	0	0	50	5.11	79.1	63	43
Jose Valverde	61	0	3-4	15	0	19	2.44	66.1	75	20
Mike Koplove	44	0	2-1	0	0	31	5.07	49.2	28	20
Tim Worrell	51	0	1-2	1	0	30	4.07	48.2	39	12
Brian Bruney	47	0	1-3	12	0	39	7.43	46.0	51	35
Mike Gosling	13	5	0-3	0	0	20	4.45	32.1	14	19
Greg Aquino	35	0	0-1	1	0	29	7.76	31.1	34	17
Brandon Medders	27	0	4-1	0	0	6	1.78	30.1	31	11
Brandon Lyon	32	0	0-2	14	0	25	6.44	29.1	17	10

Atlanta Braves

BATTING	G	AB	R	H	2B	3B	HR	RBI	TB	BB	SO	SB	OBP	SLG	BA
Rafael Furcal	154	616	100	175	31	11	12	58	264	62	78	46	.348	.429	.284
Andruw Jones	160	586	95	154	24	3	51	128	337	64	112	5	.347	.575	.263
Marcus Giles	152	577	104	168	45	4	15	63	266	64	108	16	.365	.461	.291
Adam LoRoche	141	451	53	117	28	0	20	78	205	39	87	0	.320	.455	.259
Chipper Jones	109	358	66	106	30	0	21	72	199	72	56	5	.412	.556	.296
Johnny Estrada	105	357	31	93	26	0	4	39	131	20	38	0	.303	.367	.261
Ryan Langerhans	128	326	48	87	22	3	8	42	139	37	75	0	.348	.426	.267
Todd Hollandsworth	131	303	26	74	17	2	6	36	113	23	66	4	.298	.373	.244
Kelly Johnson	87	290	46	70	12	3	9	40	115	40	75	2	.334	.397	.241
Jeff Francoeur	70	257	41	77	20	1	14	45	141	11	58	3	.336	.435	.300
Wilson Betemit	115	246	36	75	12	4	4	20	107	22	55	1	.359	.549	.305
Julio Franco	108	233	30	64	12	1	9	42	105	27	57	4	.348	.451	.275
Brian Jordan	76	231	25	57	8	2	3	24	78	14	46	2	:295	.338	.247
Brian McCann	59	180	20	50	7	0	5	23	72	18	26	1	.345	400.	.278
Pete Orr	112.	150	32	45	8	1	1	8	58	6	23	7	.331	.387	.300
Raul Mondesi	41	142	17	30	7	1	4	17	51	12	35	0	.271	.359	.211

PITCHING	GP	GS	W–L	SV	SHO	R	ERA	IP	Ks	BB
John Smoltz	33	33	14-7	0	1	83	3.06	229.2	169	53
Horacio Ramirez	33	32	11-9	0	1	108	4.63	202.1	.80	67
Tim Hudson	29	29	14-9	0	0	79	3.52	192.0	115	65
Jorge Sosa	44	20	13-3	0	0	42	2.55	134.0	85	64
John Thomas	17	17	4-6	0	0	52	4.47	98.2	61	28
Kyle Davies	21	14	7-6	0	0	51	4.93	87.2	62	49
Chris Reitsma	76	0	3-6	15	0	32	3.93	73.1	42	14
Mike Hampton	12	12	5-3	0	1	28	3.50	69.1	27	· 18
Jim Brower	69	0	3-3	1	0	36	5.37	60.1	53	32
Dan Kolb	65	0	3-8	11	0	39	5.93	57.2	39	29
Adam Bernero	36	0	4-3	0	0	35	6.51	47.0	37	12
Roman Colon	23	4	1-5	0	0	28	5.28	44.1	30	14
Blaine Boyer	43	0	4-2	0	0	13	3.11	37.2	33	17
John Foster	62	0	4-2	1	0	17	4.15	34.2	32	19
Kyle Farnsworth	26	0	0-0	10	0	6	1.98	27.1	32	7

Chicago Cubs

BATTING	G	AB	R	H	2B	3B	HR	RBI	TB	BB	SO	SB	OBP	SLG	BA
Jeromy Burnitz	160	605	84	156	31	2	24	87	263	57	109	15	.322	.435	.258
Derek Lee	158	594	120	199	50	3	46	107	393	85	109	15	.418	.662	.335
Neifi Perez	154	572	59	157	33	1	9	54	219	18	47	8	.298	.383	.274
Aramis Ramirez	123	463	72	140	30	0	31	92	263	35	60	0	.358	.568	.302
Matt Lawton	120	452	61	121	30	1	11	49	186	62	69	17	.366	.412	.268
Corey Patterson	126	451	47	97	15	3	13	34	157	23	118	15	.254	.348	.215
Michael Barrett	133	424	48	117	32	3	16	61	203	40	61	0	.345	.479	.276
Todd Walker	110	397	50	121	25	3	12	40	188	31	40	1	.355	.474	.305
Jerry Hairston	114	380	51	99	25	2	4	30	140	31	46	8	.336	.368	.261
Nomar Garciaparra	62	230	28	65	12	0	9	30	104	12	24	0	.320	.452	.283
Jose Macias	112	177	15	45	8	0	1	13	56	6	24	4	.274	.316	.254

PITCHING	GP	GS	W–L	SV	SHO	R	ERA	IP	Ks	BB
Greg Maddux	35	35	13-15	0	0	112	4.24	25.0	136	36
Carlos Zambrano	33	33	14-6	0	0	88	3.26	223.1	202 ·	86
Mark Prior	27	27	11-7	0	0	73	3.67	166.2	88	59
Glendon Rusch	46	19	9-8	0	1	79	4.52	145.1	111	53
Jerome Williams	22	20	6-10	0	0	62	4.26	122.2	70	49
Ryan Dempster	63	6	5-3	33	0	35	3.13	92.0	89	49
Michael Wuertz	75	0	6-2	0	0	36	3.81	5.2	89	40
Kerry Wood	21	10	3-4	0	0	32	4.23	66.0	77	26
Sergio Mitre	21	7	2-5	0	1	37	5.37	60.1	37	23
Roberto Novoa	49	0	4-5	0	0	22	4.43	44.2	47	25
Will Ohman	69	0	2-2	0	0	14	2.91	43.1	45	24

Cincinnati Reds

BATTING	G	AB	R	H	2B	3B	HR	RBI	TB	BB	SO	SB	OBP	SLG	BA
Felipe Lopez	148	580	97	169	34	5	23	85	282	57	111	15	.352	.486	.291
Adam Dunn	160	543	107	134	35	2	40	101	293	114	168	4	.387	.540	.247
Sean Casey	37	529	75	165	32	0	9	58	224	48	48	2	.371	.423	.312
Ken Griffey	128	491	85	148	30	0	35	92	283	54	93	0	.369	.576	.301
Rich Aurilia	114	426	61	120	23	2	14	68	189	37	67	2	.338	.444	.282
Austin Kearns	112	387	62	93	26	1	18	67	175	48	107	0	.333	.452	.240
Ryan Freel	103	369	69	100	19	3	4	21	137	51	59	36	.371	.371	.271
Jason LaRue	110	361	38	94	27	0	14	60	163	41	101	0	.355	.452	.260
Wily Mo Pena	99	311	42	79	17	0	19	51	153	20	116	2	.304	.492	.254
Javier Valentin	76	221	36	62	11	0	14	50	115	30	37	0	.362	.520	.281
Edwin Encarnacion	69	211	25	49	16	0	9	31	92	20	60	3	.308	.436	.232
Jacob Cruz	110	127	12	30	10	0	4	18	52	16	46	0	.324	.409	.236
D'Angelo Jimenez	35	105	14	24	7	0	0	5	31	14	23	2	.319	.295	.229

PITCHING	GP	GS	W–L	SV	SHO	R	ERA	IP	Ks	BB
Aaron Harang	32	32	11-13	0	0	93	3.83	211.2	163	51
Eric Milton	34	34	8-15	0	0	141	6.47	186.1	123	52
Ramon Ortiz	30	30	9-11	0	0	110	5.36	171.1	96	51
Brandon Claussen	29	29	10-11	0	0	89	4.21	166.2	121	57
Matt Belisle	60	5	4-8	1	0	49	4.41	85.2	59	26
Luke Hudson	19	16	6-9	0	0	62	6.38	84.2	53	50
David Weathers	73	0	7-4	15	0	36	3.94	77.2	61	29
Kent Mercker	78	0	3-1	4	0	27	3.65	61.2	45	19
Todd Coffey	57	0	4-1	1	0	33	4.50	58.0	26	11
Randy Keisler	24	4	2-1	0	0	45	6.27	56.0	43	28
Paul Wilson	9	9	1-5	0	0	41	7.77	46.1	30	17

Colorado Rockies

BATTING	G	AB	R	H	2B	3B	HR	RBI	TB	BB	SO	SB	OBP	SLG	BA
Garrett Atkins	138	519	62	149	31	1	13	89	221	45	72	0	.347	.426	.287
Todd Helton	144	509	92	163	45	2	20	79	272	106	80	3	.445	.534	.320
Matt Holiday	125	479	68	147	24	7	19	87	242	36	79	14	.361	.505	.307
Luis Gonzalez	128	404	51	118	25	0	9	44	170	20	63	3	.333	.421	.292
Cory Sullivan	139	378	64	111	15	4	4	30	146	28	83	12	.343	.386	.294
Clint Barmes	81	350	55	101	19	1	10	46	152	16	36	6	.330	.434	.289
Aaron Miles	99	324	37	91	13	3	2	28	115	8	38	4	.306	.355	.281
Brad Hawpe	101	305	38	80	10	3	9	47	123	43	70	2	.350	.403	.262
Duston Mohr	98	266	34	57	10	3	17	38	124	23	94	1	.280	.466	.214
JD Closser	92	237	31	52	12	2	7	27	89	32	48	1	.314	.376	.219
Danny Ardoin	80	210	28	48	10	0	6	22	76	20	69	1	.320	.362	.229
Desi Relaford	73	210	24	47	13	2	1	16	67	22	42	3	.308	.319	.224
Omar Quintanilla	39	128	16	28	1	1	0	7	31	9	15	2	.270	.242	.219
Todd Greene	38	126	10	32	4	0	7	23	57	7	21	0	.299	.452	.254
Jorge Piedra	61	112	19	35	8	1	6	16	63	10	15	2	.371	.563	.313

PITCHING	GP	GS	W–L	SV	SHO	R	ERA	IP	Ks	BB
Jeff Francis	33	33	14-12	0	0	119	5.68	183.2	128	70
Jamey Wright	34	27	8-16	0	0	119	5.46	171.1	101	81
Byung-Hyun Kim	40	22	5-12	0	0	82	4.86	148.0	115	71
Jason Jennings	20	20	6-9	0	0	73	5.02	122.0	75	62
Joe Kennedy	16	16	4-8	0	0	81	7.04	92.0	52	44
Aaron Cook	13	13	7-2	0	0	38	3.67	83.1	24	16
Sunny Kim	24	10	6-3	0	1	46	4.90	82.2	55	21
Brian Fuentes	78	0	2-5	31	0	25	2.91	74.1	91	34
Shawn Chacon	13	12	1-7	0	0	33	4.09	72.2	39	36
Jose Acevedo	36	5	2-4	1	0	48	6.47	64.0	31	16
Mike DeJean	66	0	5-4	0	0	33	4.48	62.1	52	30
Marcos Carvajal	39	0	0-2	0	0	30	5.09	53.0	47	21
David Cortes	50	0	2-0	2	0	24	4.10	52.2	36	10

Florida Marlins

BATTING	G	AB	R	H	2B	3B	HR	RBI	TB	BB	SO	SB	OBP	SLG	BA
Juan Pierre	162	656	96	181	19	13	2	47	232	46	45	57	.326	.354	.276
Miguel Cabrera	158	613	106	198	43	2	33	116	344	64	125	1	.385	.561	.323
Carlos Delgado	144	521	81	157	41	3	33	115	303	72	121	0	.399	.582	.301
Juan Encarnacion	141	506	59	145	27	3	16	76	226	41	104	6	.349	.447	.287
Mike Lowell	150	500	56	118	36	1	8	58	180	46	58	4	.298	.360	.236
Paul Lo Duca	132	445	45	126	23	1	6	57	169	34	31	4	.334	.380	.283
Luis Castillo	122	439	72	132	12	4	4	30	164	65	32	10	.391	.374	.301
Alex Gonzalez	130	435	45	115	30	0	5	45	160	31	81	5	.319	.368	.264
Jeff Connie	131	335	42	102	20	2	3	33	135	.38	58	2	.374	.403	.304

Florida Marlins *(Cont.)*

BATTING	G	AB	R	H	2B	3B	HR	RBI	TB	BB	SO	SB	OBP	SLG	BA
Damion Easley	102	267	37	64	19	1	9	30	112	26	47	4	.312	.419	.240
Matt Treanor	58	134	10	27	8	0	0	13	35	16	28	0	.301	.261	.201
Dontrelle Willis	39	92	14	24	4	0	1	11	31	3	13	0	.289	.337	.261
Chris Aquila	65	78	11	19	3	0	0	4	22	3	19	0	.272	.282	.244
Lenny Harris	83	70	5	22	4	0	1	13	29	7	11	0	.385	.414	.314

PITCHING	GP	GS	W-L	SV	SHO	R	ERA	IP	Ks	BB
Dontrelle Willis	34	34	22-10	0	5	79	2.63	236.1	170	55
A.J. Brunett	32	32	12-12	0	2	97	3.44	209.0	198	79
Josh Beckett	29	29	15-8	0	1	75	3.37	178.2	166	58
Brian Moehler	37	25	6-12	0	0	82	4.55	158.1	95	42
Al Leiter	17	16	3-7	0	0	61	6.64	80.0	52	60
Jason Vargas	17	13	5-5	0	0	34	4.03	73.2	59	31
Todd Jones	68	0	1-5	40	0	19	2.10	73.0	62	14
Guillermo Mota	56	0	2-2	2	0	38	4.70	67.0	60	32
Ismael Valdez	14	7	2-2	0	0	32	5.33	50.2	27	22
Jim Mecir	52	0	1-4	0	0	17	3.12	43.1	34	17

Houston Astros

BATTING	G	AB	R	H	2B	3B	HR	RBI	TB	BB	SO	SB	OBP	SLG	BA
Willy Taveras	152	592	82	172	13	4	3	29	202	25	103	34	.325	.341	.291
Craig Biggio	155	590	94	156	40	1	26	69	276	37	90	11	.325	.468	.264
Adam Everett	152	549	58	136	27	2	11	54	200	26	103	21	.290	.364	.248
Morgan Ensberg	150	526	86	149	30	3	36	101	293	85	119	6	.388	.557	.283
Jason Lane	145	517	65	138	34	4	26	78	258	32	105	6	.316	.499	.267
Lance Berkman	132	468	76	137	34	1	24	82	245	91	72	4	.411	.524	.293
Brad Ausmus	134	387	35	100	19	0	3	47	128	51	48	5	.351	.331	.258
Mike Lamb	125	322	41	76	13	5	12	53	135	22	65	1	.284	.419	.236
Chris Burke	108	318	49	79	19	2	5	26	117	23	62	11	.309	.368	.248
Orlando Palmeiro	114	204	22	58	17	2	3	20	88	15	23	3	.341	.431	.284
Jose Vizcaino	98	187	15	46	10	2	1	23	63	15	40	2	.299	.337	.246
Eric Bruntlett	91	109	19	24	5	2	4	14	45	10	25	7	.292	.413	.220
Jeff Bagwell	39	100	11	25	4	0	3	19	38	18	21	0	.358	.380	.250
Raul Chavez	37	99	6	17	3	0	2	6	26	4	18	1	.210	.263	.172

PITCHING	GP	GS	W-L	SV	SHO	R	ERA	IP	Ks	BB
Roy Oswalt	35	35	20-12	0	1	85	2.94	241.2	184	48
Andy Pettite	33	33	17-9	0	0	66	2.39	222.1	171	41
Roger Clemens	32	32	13-8	0	0	51	1.87	211.1	185	62
Brandon Backe	26	25	10-8	0	0	82	4.76	149.1	97	67
Wandy Rodriguez	25	22	10-10	0	0	82	5.53	128.2	80	53
Ezequiel Astacio	22	14	3-6	0	0	56	5.67	81.0	66	25
Chad Qualls	77	0	6-4	0	0	33	3.28	79.2	60	23
Dan Wheeler	71	0	2-3	0	0	18	2.21	73.1	69	19
Brad Lidge	70	0	4-4	0	0	18	2.29	70.2	103	23
Russ Springer	62	0	4-4	0	0	31	4.73	59.0	54	21

Los Angeles Dodgers

BATTING	G	AB	R	H	2B	3B	HR	RBI	TB	BB	SO	SB	OBP	SLG	BA
Jeff Kent	149	553	100	160	36	0	29	105	283	72	85	6	.377	.512	.289
Ceszar Izturis	106	444	48	114	19	2	2	31	143	25	51	8	.302	.322	.257
Jason Phillips	121	399	38	95	20	0	10	55	145	25	50	0	.287	.363	.28
Oscar Robles	110	364	44	99	18	1	5	34	134	31	33	0	.332	.368	.272
Jose Cruz	111	358	46	90	23	2	18	50	171	65	97	0	.366	.478	.251
Jayson Werth	102	337	46	79	22	2	7	43	126	48	114	11	.338	.374	.234
Hee-Seop Choi	133	320	40	81	15	2	15	42	145	34	80	1	.336	.453	.53
Olmedo Saenz	109	319	39	84	24	0	15	63	153	27	63	0	.325	.480	.263
Milton Bradley	75	283	49	82	14	1	13	38	137	25	47	6	.350	.484	.290
Jason Repko	129	276	43	61	15	3	8	20	106	16	80	5	.281	.384	.21
Antonio Perez	98	259	28	77	13	2	3	23	103	21	61	11	.360	.398	.29
J.D. Drew	72	252	48	72	12	1	15	36	131	51	50	1	.412	.520	.286
Mike Edwards	88	239	23	59	9	2	3	15	81	16	34	1	.300	.339	.247
Ricky Ledee	102	237	31	66	16	1	7	39	105	20	55	0	.335	.443	.278
Dioner Navarro	50	176	21	48	9	0	3	14	66	20	21	0	.354	.375	.273
Jose Valentin	56	147	17	25	4	2	2	14	39	31	38	3	.326	.265	.170

PITCHING	GP	GS	W-L	SV	SHO	R	ERA	IP	Ks	BB
Jeff Weaver	34	34	14-11	0	2	111	4.22	224.0	157	43
Derek Lowe	35	35	12-15	0	2	113	3.61	222.0	146	55
Brad Penny	29	29	7-9	0	0	78	3.90	175.1	122	41

Los Angeles Dodgers (*Cont.*)

PITCHING	GP	GS	W–L	SV	SHO	R	ERA	IP	Ks	BB
D.J. Houlton	35	19	6-9	0	0	79	5.16	129.0	90	52
Odalis Perez	19	19	7-8	0	0	59	4.56	108.2	74	28
Duaner Sanchez	79	0	4-7	8	0	36	3.73	82.0	71	36
Giovanni Carrara	72	0	7-4	0	0	35	3.93	75.2	56	38
Yhency Brazoban	74	0	4-10	21	0	46	5.33	72.2	61	32
Elmer Dessens	28	7	1-2	0	0	30	3.56	65.2	37	19
Scott Erickson	19	8	1-4	0	0	37	6.02	55.1	15	25
Steve Schmoll	48	0	2-2	3	0	29	5.01	46.2	29	22

Milwaukee Brewers

BATTING	G	AB	R	H	2B	3B	HR	RBI	TB	BB	SO	SB	OBP	SLG	BA
Carlos Lee	162	618	85	164	41	6	32	114	301	57	87	13	.324	.487	.265
Brady Clark	145	599	94	183	31	1	13	53	255	47	55	10	.372	.426	.306
Geoff Jenkins	148	538	87	157	42	1	25	86	276	56	138	0	.375	.513	.292
Lyle Overbay	158	537	80	148	34	1	19	72	241	78	98	1	.367	.449	.276
Bill Hall	146	501	69	146	39	6	17	62	248	39	103	18	.342	.495	.291
Damian Miller	114	385	50	105	25	1	17	43	159	37	94	0	.340	.413	.273
J.J Hardy	124	372	46	92	22	1	9	50	143	44	48	0	.327	.384	.247
Rickie Weeks	96	360	56	86	13	2	9	42	142	40	96	15	.333	.394	.239
Russell Branyan	85	202	23	52	11	0	13	31	99	39	80	1	.378	.490	.257
Chad Moeller	66	199	23	41	9	1	12	23	73	13	48	0	.257	.367	.206
Jeff Cirillo	77	185	29	52	15	0	7	23	79	23	22	4	.373	.427	.281
Wes Helms	95	168	18	50	13	1	4	24	77	14	30	0	.356	.458	.298
Chris Magruder	101	138	16	28	9	0	4	13	43	7	33	3	.265	.312	.203

PITCHING	GP	GS	W–L	SV	2SHO	R	ERA	IP	Ks	BB
Doug Davis	35	35	11-11	0	1	103	3.84	222.2	208	93
Chris Capuano	35	35	18-12	0	0	105	3.99	219.0	176	91
Tomo Ohka	32	29	11-9	0	0	88	4.04	180.1	98	55
Ben Sheets	22	22	10-9	0	0	66	3.33	156.2	141	25
Victor Santos	29	24	4-13	0	0	87	4.57	141.2	89	60
Derrick Turnbow	69	0	7-1	39	0	15	1.74	67.1	64	24
Wes Obermueller	23	8	1-4	0	0	41	5.26	65.0	33	36
Gary Glover	15	11	5-4	0	0	41	5.57	64.2	58	20
Matt Wise	49	0	4-4	1	0	25	3.36	64.1	62	25
Rick Helling	15	7	3-1	0	0	13	2.39	49.0	42	18
Jorge De La Rosa	38	0	2-2	0	0	23	4.46	42.1	42	38
Julio Santana	41	0	3-5	1	0	21	4.50	42.0	49	19
Ricky Bottalico	40	0	2-2	2	0	24	4.54	41.2	29	19

Montreal Expos

BATTING	G	AB	R	H	2B	3B	HR	RBI	TB	BB	SO	SB	OBP	SLG	BA
Tony Batista	157	606	76	146	30	2	32	110	276	26	78	14	.272	.455	.241
Brad Wilkerson	160	572	112	146	39	2	32	67	285	106	152	13	.374	.498	.255
Endy Chavez	132	502	65	139	20	6	5	34	186	30	40	32	.318	.371	.277
Brian Schneider	135	436	40	112	20	3	12	49	174	42	63	0	.325	.399	.257
Jose Vidro	110	412	51	121	24	0	14	60	187	49	43	3	.367	.454	.294
Terrmel Sledge	133	398	45	107	20	6	15	62	184	40	66	3	.336	.462	.269
Juan Rivera	134	391	48	120	24	1	12	49	182	34	45	6	.364	.465	.307
Orlando Cabrera	103	390	41	96	19	2	4	31	131	28	31	12	.298	.336	.246
Nick Johnson	73	251	35	63	16	0	7	33	100	40	58	6	.359	.398	.251
Jamey Carroll	102	218	36	63	14	2	0	16	81	32	21	5	.378	.372	.289
E Diaz	55	139	9	31	6	1	1	11	42	11	10	2	.293	.302	.223
C Everett	39	127	8	32	10	0	2	14	48	8	19	0	.319	.378	.252
Maicer Izturis	32	107	10	22	5	2	1	4	34	10	20	4	.286	.318	.206

PITCHING	GP	GS	W–L	SV	SHO	R	ERA	IP	Ks	BB
Livan Hernandez	35	35	11–15	0	2	105	3.60	255.0	186	83
Sun-Woo Kim	43	17	4-6	0	0	80	4.58	135.2	87	55
Claudio Vargas	45	14	5-5	0	0	75	5.25	118.1	89	64
Zach Day	19	19	5-10	0	1	53	3.93	116.2	61	45
John Patterson	19	19	4-7	0	0	58	5.03	98.1	99	46
Luis Ayala	81	0	6-12	2	0	30	2.69	90.1	63	15
Tomo Ohka	15	15	3-7	0	0	40	3.40	84.2	38	20
Chad Cordero	69	0	7-3	14	0	28	2.94	82.2	83	43
Rocky Biddle	47	9	4-8	11	0	69	6.92	78.0	51	31
Tony Armas	16	16	2-4	0	0	41	4.88	72.0	54	45
T.J. Tucker	54	1	4-2	0	0	28	3.72	67.2	44	17
Scott Downs	12	12	3-6	0	1	47	5.14	63.0	38	23
Francis Beltran	45	0	2-2	1	0	31	5.47	49.1	48	27
Joe Horgan	47	0	4-1	2	0	18	3.15	40.0	30	22

New York Mets

BATTING	G	AB	R	H	2B	3B	HR	RBI	TB	BB	SO	SB	OBP	SLG	BA
Jose Reyes	161	696	99	190	24	17	7	58	269	27	78	60	.300	.386	.273
Carlos Beltran	151	582	83	155	34	2	16	78	241	56	96	17	.330	.414	.266
David Wright	160	575	99	176	42	1	27	102	301	72	113	17	.388	.523	.306
Cliff Floyd	150	550	85	150	22	2	34	98	278	63	98	12	.358	.505	.273
Mike Piazza	113	398	41	100	23	0	19	62	180	41	67	0	.326	.452	.251
Miguel Cairo	100	327	31	82	18	0	2	19	106	19	31	13	.296	.324	.251
Mike Cameron	76	308	47	84	23	2	12	39	147	29	85	13	.342	.477	.273
Victor Diaz	89	280	41	72	17	3	12	38	131	30	82	6	.329	.468	.257
Doug Mientkiewicz	87	275	36	66	13	0	11	29	112	32	39	0	.322	.407	.240
Kazuo Matsui	87	267	31	68	9	4	3	24	94	14	43	6	.300	.352	.255
Marlon Anderson	123	235	31	62	9	0	7	19	92	18	45	6	.316	.391	.264
Ramon Castro	99	209	26	51	16	0	8	41	91	25	58	1	.321	.435	.244
Chris Woodward	81	173	16	49	10	0	3	18	68	13	46	0	.337	.393	.283
Jose Offerman	86	105	11	24	3	1	2	13	35	11	17	0	.308	.333	.229
Mike Jacobs	30	100	19	31	7	0	11	23	71	10	22	0	.375	.710	.310

PITCHING	GP	GS	W–L	SV	SHO	R	ERA	IP	Ks	BB
Pedro Martinez	31	31	15-8	0	1	69	2.82	217.0	208	47
Tom Glavine	33	33	13-13	0	1	88	3.53	211.1	105	61
Kris Benson	28	28	10-8	0	0	86	4.13	174.1	95	49
Victor Zambrano	31	27	7-12	0	0	85	4.17	166.1	112	77
Aaron Heilman	53	7	5-3	5	1	40	3.17	108.0	106	37
Kazuhisa Ishi	19	16	3-9	0	0	59	5.14	91.0	53	49
Jae Seo	14	14	8-2	0	0	26	2.59	90.1	59	16
Roberto Hernandez	67	0	8-6	4	0	20	2.58	69.2	61	28
Braden Looper	60	0	4-7	28	0	31	3.94	59.1	27	22
Heath Bell	42	0	1-3	0	0	30	5.59	46.2	43	12
Danny Graves	40	0	1-1	10	0	35	6.52	38.2	20	20
Steve Trachsel	6	6	1-4	0	0	20	4.14	37.0	24	12
Juan Padilla	24	0	3-1	1	0	7	1.49	36.1	17	13

Philadelphia Phillies

BATTING	G	AB	R	H	2B	3B	HR	RBI	TB	BB	SO	SB	OBP	SLG	BA
Jimmy Rollins	158	677	115	196	38	11	12	54	292	41	71	41	.338	.431	.290
Bobby Abreu	162	588	104	168	37	1	24	102	279	31	134	31	.405	.474	.286
Pat Burrell	154	562	78	158	27	1	32	117	283	0	160	0	.389	.504	.281
David Bell	150	557	53	138	31	1	10	61	201	0	69	0	.310	.361	.248
Chase Utley	147	543	93	158	39	6	28	105	293	16	109	16	.376	.540	.291
Mike Lieberthal	118	392	48	103	25	0	12	47	164	0	35	0	.336	.418	.263
Kenny Lofton	110	367	67	123	15	5	2	36	154	22	41	22	.392	.420	.335
Ryan Howard	88	312	52	90	17	2	22	63	177	0	100	0	.356	.567	.288
Jason Michaels	105	289	54	88	16	2	4	31	120	3	45	3	.399	.415	.304
Michael Tucker	126	268	35	64	16	1	5	36	97	4	52	4	.318	.362	.239
Jim Thome	59	193	26	40	7	0	7	30	68	0	59	0	.360	.352	.207
Todd Pratt	60	175	17	44	4	0	7	23	69	0	50	0	.332	.394	.251
Tomas Perez	94	159	17	37	7	0	4	22	44	1	27	1	.289	.277	.233
Placido Polanco	43	158	26	50	7	0	3	20	66	0	9	0	.376	.418	.316
Endy chavez	98	116	19	25	4	3	0	11	35	2	14	2	.260	.302	.216

PITCHING	GP	GS	W–L	SV	SHO	R	ERA	IP	Ks	BB
Jon Lieber	35	35	17-13	0	0	107	4.20	18.1	149	41
Brett Myers	34	34	13-8	0	0	94	3.72	215.1	208	8
Cory Lidle	31	31	13-11	0	0	105	4.53	184.2	121	40
Vincente Padilla	27	27	9-12	0	0	79	4.71	147.0	103	74
Ryan Madison	78	0	6-5	0	0	44	4.14	87.0	79	25
Robinson Tejada	26	13	4-3	0	0	36	3.57	85.2	72	51
Randy Wolf	13	13	6-4	0	0	40	4.39	80.0	61	26
Billy Wagner	75	0	4-3	38	0	17	1.51	77.2	87	20
Aaron Fultz	62	0	4-0	0	0	21	2.24	72.1	54	23
Geoff Geary	40	0	2-1	0	0	29	3.72	58.0	42	21
Uqueth Urbina	56	0	4-3	1	0	25	4.13	52.1	66	25
Rheal Cormier	57	0	4-2	0	0	33	5.89	47.1	34	16

Pittsburgh Pirates

BATTING	G	AB	R	H	2B	3B	HR	RBI	TB	BB	SO	SB	OBP	SLG	BA
Jason Bay	162	599	110	183	4	6	32	101	335	95	142	21	.402	.559	.306
Jack Wilson	158	587	60	151	24	7	8	52	213	31	58	7	.299	.363	.257
Rob Mackowiak	142	463	57	126	21	3	9	58	180	43	100	8	.337	.389	.272
Freddy Sanchez	132	453	54	132	26	4	5	35	181	27	36	2	.336	.400	.291
Daryle Ward	133	407	46	106	21	1	12	63	165	37	60	0	.318	.405	.260
Jose Castillo	101	370	49	99	16	3	11	53	154	23	59	2	.307	.416	.268

Pittsburgh Pirates (Cont.)

BATTING	G	AB	R	H	2B	3B	HR	RBI	TB	BB	SO	SB	OBP	SLG	BA
Tike Redman	135	319	33	80	12	4	2	26	106	19	27	4	.292	.332	.251
Humberto Cota	93	297	29	72	20	1	7	43	115	17	80	0	.285	.387	.242
Ryan Doumit	75	231	25	59	13	1	6	35	92	11	48	2	.324	.398	.255
Craig Wilson	59	197	23	52	14	1	5	22	83	30	69	3	.387	.421	.264
Brad Eldred	55	190	23	42	9	0	12	27	87	13	77	1	.279	.458	.221
Ty Wigginton	57	155	20	40	9	1	7	25	72	14	30	0	.324	.465	.258
Chris Duffy	39	126	22	43	4	2	1	9	54	7	22	2	.385	.429	.341
Michael Restovich	66	115	15	27	5	1	3	8	43	11	29	0	.305	.374	.235

PITCHING	GP	GS	W–L	SV	SHO	R	ERA	IP	Ks	BB
Kip Wells	33	33	8-18	0	1	116	5.09	182.0	132	99
Mark Redman	30	30	5-15	0	1	100	4.90	178.1	101	56
Josh Fogg	34	28	6-11	0	0	106	5.05	169.1	85	53
Dave Williams	25	25	10-11	0	1	74	4.41	138.2	88	58
Oliver Perez	20	20	7-5	0	0	68	5.85	103.0	97	70
Salomon Torres	78	0	5-5	3	0	34	2.76	94.2	55	36
Zach Duke	14	14	8-2	0	0	20	1.81	84.2	58	23
Ryan Vogelsong	44	0	2-2	0	0	43	4.43	81.1	52	40
Rick White	71	0	4-7	2	0	39	3.72	75.0	40	29
Brian Meadows	65	0	3-1	0	0	42	4.58	74.2	44	21
Jose Mesa	55	0	2-8	27	0	30	4.76	56.2	37	26

St. Louis Cardinals

BATTING	G	AB	R	H	2B	3B	HR	RBI	TB	BB	SO	SB	OBP	SLG	BA
David Eckstein	158	630	90	185	26	7	8	61	249	58	44	11	.363	.395	.294
Albert Pujols	161	591	129	195	38	2	41	117	360	97	65	16	.430	.609	.330
Mark Grudzielanek	137	528	64	155	30	3	8	59	215	26	81	8	.334	.407	.94
Jim Edmonds	142	467	88	123	37	1	29	89	249	91	139	5	.385	.533	.263
Abraham Nunez	139	421	64	120	13	2	5	44	152	37	63	0	.343	.361	.285
So Taguchi	143	396	45	114	21	2	8	53	163	20	62	11	.322	.412	.288
Yadier Molina	114	385	36	97	15	1	8	49	138	23	30	2	.295	.358	.252
Larry Walker	100	315	66	91	20	1	15	52	158	41	64	2	.384	.502	.289
Reggie Sanders	93	295	49	80	14	2	21	54	161	28	75	14	.340	.546	.271
John Mabry	112	246	26	59	15	1	8	32	100	20	63	0	.295	.407	.240
Scott Rolen	56	196	28	46	12	1	5	28	75	25	28	1	.323	.383	.235
John Rodriguez	56	149	15	44	6	0	5	24	65	19	45	2	.382	.436	.295
Hector Luna	64	137	26	39	10	2	1	18	56	9	25	10	.344	.409	.285
Einar Diaz	58	130	14	27	6	0	1	17	36	5	12	0	.248	.277	.208
Scott Seabol	59	105	11	23	5	0	1	10	31	8	23	0	.272	.295	.219

PITCHING	GP	GS	W–L	SV	SHO	R	ERA	IP	Ks	BB
Chris Carpenter	33	33	21-5	0	4	82	2.83	241.2	213	51
Jason Marquis	33	32	13-14	0	1	110	4.13	207.0	100	69
Mark Mulder	32	32	16-8	0	2	90	3.64	205.0	111	70
Jeff Suppan	32	32	16-10	0	0	93	3.57	194.1	114	63
Matt Morris	32	31	14-10	0	0	101	4.11	192.2	117	37
Julian Tavarez	74	0	2-3	4	0	28	3.43	65.2	47	19
Anthony Reyes	65	0	4-2	3	0	15	2.15	62.2	67	20
Jason Isringhausen	63	0	1-2	39	0	14	2.14	59.0	51	27
Brad Thompson	40	0	4-0	1	0	22	2.95	55.0	29	15
Randy Flores	50	0	3-1	1	0	22	3.46	41.2	43	13
Ray King	77	0	4-4	0	0	17	3.38	40.0	23	16

San Diego Padres

BATTING	G	AB	R	H	2B	3B	HR	RBI	TB	BB	SO	SB	OBP	SLG	BA
Joe Randa	150	555	71	153	43	2	17	68	251	47	81	0	.335	.452	.276
Brian Giles	158	545	92	164	38	8	15	83	263	119	64	13	.423	.483	.301
Ryan Klesko	137	443	61	110	19	1	18	58	185	75	80	3	.358	.418	.248
Khalil Green	121	436	51	109	30	2	15	70	188	25	93	5	.296	.431	.250
Dave Roberts	115	411	65	113	19	10	8	38	176	53	59	23	.356	.428	.275
Mark Loretta	105	404	54	113	16	1	3	38	140	45	34	8	.360	.347	.280
Ramon Hernandez	99	369	36	107	19	2	12	58	166	18	40	1	.322	.450	.290
Xavier Nady	124	326	40	85	15	2	13	43	143	2	67	2	.321	.439	.261
Sean Burroughs	93	284	20	71	7	2	1	17	85	24	41	4	.318	.299	.250
Phil Nevin	73	281	31	72	11	1	9	47	112	19	67	1	.301	.399	.256
Damian Jackson	118	275	44	70	9	0	5	23	94	30	45	15	.335	.342	.255
Robert Fick	93	230	25	61	10	2	3	30	84	26	33	0	.340	.365	.265
Geoff Blum	78	224	26	54	13	1	5	22	84	24	28	3	.321	.375	.241
Mark Sweeney	135	221	31	65	12	1	8	40	103	40	58	4	395	.466	.294

San Diego Padres *(Cont.)*

PITCHING	GP	GS	W–L	SV	SHO	R	ERA	IP	Ks	BB
Jake Peavy	30	30	13-7	0	3	70	2.88	203.0	216	50
Brian Lawrence	33	33	7-15	0	0	106	4.83	195.2	109	57
Woody Williams	28	28	9-12	0	0	92	4.85	159.2	106	51
Adam Eaton	24	24	11-5	0	0	70	4.27	128.2	100	44
Tim Stauffer	15	15	3-6	0	0	50	5.33	81.0	49	29
Scott Linebrink	73	73	8-1	1	0	17	1.83	73.2	70	23
Akinori Otsuka	66	66	2-8	1	0	28	3.59	62.2	60	34
Rudy Seanez	57	57	7-1	0	0	19	2.69	60.1	84	22
Pedro Astacio	12	12	4-2	0	0	21	3.17	59.2	33	26
Darrell May	22	22	1-3	0	0	38	5.61	59.1	32	20
Chris Hammond	55	55	5-1	0	0	25	3.84	58.2	34	14
Trevor Hoffman	60	60	1-6	43	0	23	2.97	57.2	54	12

San Francisco Giants

BATTING	G	AB	R	H	2B	3B	HR	RBI	TB	BB	SO	SB	OBP	SLG	BA
Pedro Feliz	156	569	69	142	30	4	20	81	240	38	102	0	.295	.422	.250
Omar Vizquel	152	568	66	154	28	4	45	199	56	58	24	10	.341	.350	.271
Ray Durham	142	497	67	144	33	0	12	62	213	48	59	6	.356	.429	.290
Mike Matheny	134	443	42	107	34	0	13	59	180	29	91	0	.295	.406	.242
Moises Alou	123	427	67	137	21	3	19	63	221	56	43	5	.400	.518	.321
Edgardo Alfonzo	109	368	36	102	17	1	2	43	127	27	34	2	.327	.345	.277
J.T. Snow	117	367	40	101	17	2	4	40	134	32	61	1	.343	.365	.275
Jason Ellison	131	352	49	93	18	2	4	24	127	24	44	14	.316	.361	.264
Lance Niekro	113	278	32	70	16	3	12	46	128	17	53	0	.295	.460	.252
Randy Winn	58	231	9	83	22	5	14	26	157	11	38	7	.391	.680	.359
Todd Linden	60	171	20	37	8	0	4	13	57	10	54	3	.280	.333	.216
Marquis Grissom	44	137	8	29	4	0	2	15	39	7	18	1	.248	.285	.212

PITCHING	GP	GS	W–L	SV	SHO	R	ERA	IP	Ks	BB
Noah Lowry	33	33	13-13	0	0	92	3.78	204.2	172	76
Brett Tomko	33	30	8-15	1	0	99	4.48	1902.	114	57
Jason Schmidt	29	29	12-7	0	0	90	4.40	172.0	165	85
Brad Hennessey	21	21	5-8	0	0	63	4.64	118.1	64	52
Kirk Rueter	20	18	2-7	0	0	78	5.95	107.1	25	47
Jeff Fassero	48	6	4-7	0	0	48	4.05	91.0	60	31
Scott Eyre	86	0	2-2	0	0	21	2.63	68.1	65	26
Tyler Walker	67	0	6-4	23	0	31	4.23	61.2	54	27
Kevin Correia	16	11	2-5	0	0	31	4.63	58.1	44	31
LaTroy Hawkins	66	0	2-8	6	0	27	3.83	56.1	43	24
Matt Cain	7	7	2-1	0	0	12	2.33	46.1	30	19
Armando Benitez	30	0	2-3	19	0	17	4.50	30.0	23	16

Washington Nationals

BATTING	G	AB	R	H	2B	3B	HR	RBI	TB	BB	SO	SB	OBP	SLG	BA
Brad Wilkerson	148	565	76	140	42	7	11	57	229	84	147	8	.351	.405	.248
Jose Guillen	148	551	81	156	32	2	24	76	264	31	102	1	.338	.479	.283
Pat Wilson	139	520	73	135	29	2	25	90	243	45	148	6	.325	.467	.260
Vinny Castilla	142	494	53	125	36	1	12	66	199	43	82	4	.319	.403	.253
C Guzman	142	456	39	100	19	6	4	31	143	25	76	7	.260	.314	.219
Nick Johnson	131	453	66	131	35	3	15	74	217	80	87	3	.408	.479	.289
Brian Schneider	116	369	38	99	20	1	10	44	151	29	48	1	.330	.409	.268
Jose Vidro	87	309	38	85	21	2	7	32	131	31	30	0	.339	.424	.275
Jamey Carroll	113	30	44	76	8	1	0	22	86	34	55	3	.333	.284	.251
Ryan Church	102	268	41	77	15	3	9	42	125	24	70	3	.353	.466	.287
Deivi Cruz	0	260	28	69	11	1	5	20	97	11	34	0	.298	.373	.265
Junior Spivey	77	59	37	60	15	1	7	21	98	29	83	9	.315	.378	.232
Marlon Byrd	79	229	20	61	15	2	2	26	86	19	50	5	.323	.76	.266
Gary Bennett	68	199	11	44	7	0	1	21	54	21	37	0	.298	.271	.221
Carlos Baerga	93	158	18	40	7	0	2	19	53	7	17	0	.318	.335	.253

PITCHING	GP	GS	W–L	SV	SHO	R	ERA	IP	Ks	BB
Livan Hernandez	35	35	15-10	0	2	116	3.98	246.1	147	84
Esteban Loaiza	34	34	12-10	0	0	93	3.77	217.0	173	55
John Patterson	31	31	9-7	0	2	71	3.13	198.1	185	65
Tony Armas	19	19	7-7	0	0	57	4.97	101.1	59	54
Hector Carrasco	64	5	5-4	2	0	23	2.04	88.1	75	38
Gary Majewski	79	0	4-4	1	0	32	2.93	86.0	50	37
Chad Cordero	74	0	2-4	47	0	24	1.82	74.1	61	17
Luis Ayala	68	0	8-7	1	0	23	2.66	71.0	40	14
Ryan Drese	11	11	3-6	0	0	38	4.98	59.2	26	22

Baltimore Orioles

BATTING

	G	AB	R	H	2B	3B	HR	RBI	TB	BB	SO	SB	OBP	SLG	BA
Miguel Tejada	162	654	89	199	50	5	26	98	337	40	83	5	.349	.515	.304
Melvin Mora	149	593	86	168	30	1	27	88	281	50	112	7	.348	.474	.283
Brian Roberts	143	561	92	176	45	7	18	73	289	67	83	27	.387	.515	.314
Jay Gibbons	139	488	72	135	33	1	26	79	252	28	56	0	.317	.516	.277
Javy Lopez	103	395	47	110	24	2	15	49	181	819	68	0	.322	.458	.278
Luis Matos	121	389	53	109	20	1	4	32	145	45	58	17	.340	.373	.280
Sammy Sosa	102	380	39	84	15	0	14	45	143	27	84	1	.295	.376	.221
Rafael Palmeiro	110	369	47	98	13	3	18	60	165	39	43	2	.339	.447	.266
Eric Byrnes	111	359	47	83	22	2	10	35	141	43	60	5	.295	.393	.231
B.J. Surhoff	91	303	30	78	11	0	5	34	108	25	32	0	.282	.356	.257
Chris Gomez	89	219	27	61	11	0	1	18	75	11	17	2	.359	.342	.279
David Newhan	96	218	31	44	9	1	5	21	68	27	45	9	.279	.312	.202
Larry Bigbie	67	206	22	51	9	0	5	21	77	22	49	3	.314	.374	.248
Sal Fasano	64	160	25	40	3	2	11	20	76	9	41	0	.310	.475	.250
Eli Marrero	54	138	19	25	7	0	7	19	57	11	38	1	.239	.413	.181
Geronimo Gil	64	125	7	24	3	1	4	17	39	5	23	0	.220	.312	.192

PITCHING

	GP	GS	W–L	SV	SHO	R	ERA	IP	Ks	BB
Rodrigo Lopez	35	35	15-12	0	0	126	4.90	209.1	118	63
Bruce Chen	34	32	13-10	0	0	94	3.83	197.1	133	63
Daniel Cabrera	29	29	10-13	0	0	92	4.52	161.1	157	87
Erik Bedard	24	24	6–8	0	0	66	4.00	141.2	125	57
Sidney Ponson	23	23	7-11	0	0	97	6.21	130.1	68	48
Todd Williams	72	0	5-5	1	0	34	3.30	76.1	38	26
Jorge Julio	67	0	3-5	0	0	50	5.90	71.2	58	24
B.J. Ryan	69	0	1-4	36	0	20	2.43	70.1	100	26
Steve Kline	67	0	2-4	0	0	34	4:28	61.0	36	30
James Baldwin	28	0	0-2	1	0	28	3.81	56.2	29	16
Chris Ray	41	0	1-3	0	0	15	2.66	40.2	43	18
John Maine	10	8	2-3	0	0	30	6.30	40.0	24	24
Hayden Penn	8	8	3-2	0	0	30	6.34	38.1	18	21
Steve Reed	30	0	1-2	0	0	24	6.61	32.2	15	11
Eric DuBose	15	3	2-3	0	0	21	5.52	29.1	17	19

Boston Red Sox

BATTING

	G	AB	R	H	2B	3B	HR	RBI	TB	BB	SO	SB	OBP	SLG	BA
Johnny Damon	150	624	117	197	35	6	10	75	274	53	69	18	.366	.439	.316
Edgar Renteria	153	623	100	172	36	4	8	70	240	55	100	9	.335	.385	.276
David Ortiz	159	601	119	180	40	1	47	148	363	102	124	1	.397	.604	.300
Manny Ramirez	152	554	112	162	30	1	45	144	329	80	119	1	.388	.594	.292
Bill Mueller	150	519	69	153	34	3	10	62	223	59	74	0	.369	.430	.295
Jason Varitek	133	470	70	132	30	1	22	70	230	62	117	2	.366	.489	.281
Kevin Millar	134	449	57	122	28	1	9	50	179	54	74	0	.355	.399	.272
Trot Nixon	124	408	64	112	29	1	13	67	182	53	59	2	.357	.446	.275
Tony Graffanino	110	379	68	117	17	3	7	38	161	31	51	7	.366	.425	.309
Alex Cora	96	250	25	58	8	4	3	24	83	11	30	7	.275	.332	.232
John Olerud	87	173	18	50	7	0	7	37	78	16	20	0	.344	.451	.289
Doug Mirabelli	50	136	16	31	7	0	6	18	56	14	48	2	.309	.412	.228
Gabe Kapler	36	97	15	24	7	0	1	9	34	3	15	1	.282	.351	.247
Kevin Youkilis	44	79	11	22	7	0	1	9	32	14	19	0	.400	.405	.278
Roberto Petagine	18	32	4	9	2	0	1	9	14	4	5	0	.361	.438	.281
Adam Hyzdu	12	16	1	4	1	0	0	0	5	2	3	0	.333	.313	.250

PITCHING

	GP	GS	W–L	SV	SHO	R	ERA	IP	Ks	BB
Tim Wakefield	33	33	16-12	0	0	113	4.15	225.1	151	68
Bronso Arroyo	35	32	14-10	0	0	116	4.51	205.1	100	54
Matt Clement	32	32	13-6	0	0	102	4.57	191.0	146	68
David Wells	30	30	15-7	0	0	95	4.45	184.0	107	21
Curt Schilling	32	11	8-8	9	0	59	5.69	93.1	87	22
Wade Miller	16	16	4-4	0	0	53	4.95	80.1	64	47
Mike Timlin	81	0	7-3	13	0	23	2.24	56.0	59	20
Jeremi Gonzalez	28	3	2-1	0	0	39	6.11	45.2	28	16
Keith Foulke	43	0	5-5	15	0	30	5.91	43.2	34	18
John Halama	30	1	1-1	0	0	33	6.18	37.1	26	9
Mike Myers	65	0	3-1	0	0	14	3.13	34.0	21	13
Jonathan Papelbon	17	3	3-1	0	0	11	2.65	26.1	34	17
Matt Mantei	34	0	1-0	0	0	20	6.49	26.1	22	24
Chad Bradford	31	0	2-1	0	0	10	3.86	23.1	10	4

Chicago White Sox

BATTING	G	AB	R	H	2B	3B	HR	RBI	TB	BB	SO	SB	OBP	SLG	BA
Aaron Rowand	157	578	77	156	30	5	13	69	235	32	116	16	.329	.407	.270
Paul Konerko	158	575	98	163	24	0	40	100	307	81	109	0	.375	.534	.283
Jermaine Dye	145	529	74	145	29	2	31	86	271	39	99	4	.333	.512	.274
Tadahito Iguchi	135	511	74	142	25	6	15	71	224	47	114	15	.342	.438	.278
Scott Podsednik	129	507	80	147	28	1	0	25	177	47	75	59	.351	.349	.290
Carl Everett	135	490	58	123	17	2	23	87	213	42	99	4	.311	.435	.251
Juan Uribe	146	481	58	121	23	3	16	71	198	34	77	4	.301	.412	.252
A. J. Pierzynski	128	460	61	118	21	0	18	56	193	23	60	0	.08	.420	.257
Joe Crede	132	432	54	109	21	0	22	62	196	25	66	1	.303	.454	.252
Pablo Ozuna	70	203	27	56	7	2	0	11	67	7	26	14	.313	.330	.276
Timo Perez	76	179	13	39	8	0	2	15	53	12	25	2	.266	.296	.218
Chris Widger	45	141	18	34	8	0	4	11	54	10	22	0	.296	.383	.241
Willie Harris	56	121	17	31	2	1	1	8	38	13	25	10	.333	.314	.256
Frank Thomas	34	105	19	23	3	0	12	26	62	16	31	0	.315	.590	.219
Geoff Blum	31	95	6	19	2	1	1	3	26	4	15	0	.232	.274	.200

PITCHING	GP	GS	W–L	SV	SHO	R	ERA	IP	Ks	BB
Mark Buehrle	33	33	16-8	0	1	99	3.12	236.2	149	40
Freddy Garcia	33	33	14-8	0	0	102	3.87	228.0	146	60
Jon Garland	32	32	18-10	0	3	93	3.50	221.0	115	47
Jose Contreras	32	32	15-7	0	0	91	3.61	204.2	154	75
Orlando Hernandez	24	22	9-9	1	0	77	5.12	128.1	91	50
Luis Vizcaino	65	0	6-5	0	0	30	3.73	70.0	43	29
Cliff Politte	68	0	7-1	1	0	15	2.00	67.1	57	21
Brando McCarthy	12	10	3-2	0	0	30	4.03	67.0	48	17
Neal Cotts	69	0	4-0	0	0	13	1.94	60.1	58	29
Dustin Hermanson	57	0	2-4	34	0	13	2.04	57.1	33	17
Damaso Marte	66	0	3-4	4	0	19	3.77	45.1	54	33
Bobby Jenks	32	0	1-1	6	0	12	2.75	39.1	50	15
Shingo Takatsu	31	0	1-2	8	0	19	5.97	28.2	32	16

Cleveland Indians

BATTING	G	AB	R	H	2B	3B	HR	RBI	TB	BB	SO	SB	OBP	SLG	BA
Grady Sizemore	158	640	111	185	37	11	22	81	310	52	132	22	.348	.484	.289
Coco Crisp	145	594	86	178	42	4	16	69	276	44	81	15	.345	.465	.300
Victor Marinez	147	547	73	167	33	0	20	80	260	63	78	0	.378	.475	.305
Ronnie Belliard	145	536	71	152	36	1	17	78	241	35	72	2	.325	.450	.284
Casey Blake	147	523	72	126	32	1	23	58	229	43	116	4	.308	.438	.241
Aaron Boone	143	511	61	124	19	1	16	60	193	35	92	9	.299	.378	.243
Jhonny Peralta	141	504	82	147	35	4	24	78	262	58	128	0	.366	.520	.292
Travis Hafner	137	486	94	148	42	0	33	108	289	79	123	0	.408	.595	.305
Ben Broussard	142	466	59	119	30	5	19	68	216	32	98	2	.307	.464	.255
Jose Hernandez	84	234	28	54	7	0	6	31	79	14	60	1	.277	.338	.231
Jofy Gerut	44	138	12	38	9	1	1	12	52	18	14	1	.357	.377	.275
Ramon Vazquez	39	85	7	18	5	0	0	5	23	5	17	0	.256	.271	.212
Josh Bard	34	83	6	16	4	0	1	9	23	9	11	0	.266	.277	.193

PITCHING	GP	GS	W–L	SV	SHO	R	ERA	IP	Ks	BB
Jake Westbrook	34	34	15-15	0	0	121	4.49	210.2	119	56
Cliff Lee	32	32	18-5	0	0	91	3.79	202.0	143	52
C.C. Sabathia	31	31	15-10	0	0	92	4.03	196.2	161	62
Kevin Millwood	30	30	9-11	0	0	72	2.86	192.0	146	52
Scott Elarton	31	31	11-9	0	0	100	4.61	181.2	103	48
Sean Douglass	18	16	5-5	0	0	57	5.56	87.1	55	33
Bob Howry	79	0	7-4	3	0	23	2.47	73.0	48	16
David Riske	58	0	3-4	1	0	28	3.10	72.2	48	15
Rafael Betancourt	54	0	4-3	1	0	23	2.79	67.2	73	17
Bob Wickman	64	0	0-4	45	0	17	2.47	62.0	41	21
Arthur Rhodes	47	0	3-1	0	0	13	2.08	43.1	43	12
Jason Davis	11	4	4-2	0	0	22	4.69	40.1	32	20
Scott Sauerback	58	0	1-0	0	0	18	4.04	35.2	35	16
Fernando Cabrera	15	0	2-1	0	0	17	1.47	30.2	29	11

Detroit Tigers

BATTING	G	AB	R	H	2B	3B	HR	RBI	TB	BB	SO	SB	OBP	SLG	BA
Brandon Inge	160	616	75	161	31	9	16	72	258	63	140	7	.330	.419	.261
Craig Monroe	157	567	69	157	30	3	20	89	253	40	95	8	.322	.446	.277
Ivan Rodriguez	129	504	71	139	33	5	14	50	224	11	93	7	.290	.444	.276
Dimitri Young	126	469	61	127	25	3	21	72	221	29	100	1	.325	.471	.271
Omar Infante	121	406	36	90	28	2	9	43	149	16	73	8	.254	.367	.222
Chris Shelton	107	388	61	116	22	3	18	59	198	34	87	0	.360	.510	.299
Rondell White	97	374	49	117	24	3	12	53	183	17	48	1	.348	.489	.313
Placido Polanco	86	343	58	116	20	2	6	36	158	21	16	4	.386	.461	.338
Carlos Guillen	87	334	48	107	15	4	5	23	145	24	45	2	.368	.434	.320
Nook Logan	129	322	47	83	12	5	1	17	108	21	52	23	.305	.335	.258
Magglio Ordonez	82	305	38	92	17	0	8	46	133	30	35	0	.359	.436	.302
Carlos Pena	79	260	37	61	9	0	18	44	124	31	95	0	.325	.477	.235
John McDonald	68	166	18	46	6	1	0	16	54	11	24	6	.326	.325	.277
Curtis Granderson	47	162	18	44	6	3	8	20	80	10	43	1	.314	.494	.272
Vance Wilson	61	152	18	30	4	0	3	19	43	11	26	0	.275	.283	.197
Marcus Thames	38	107	11	21	2	0	7	16	44	9	38	0	.263	.411	.196

PITCHING	GP	GS	W–L	SV	SHO	R	ERA	IP	Ks	BB
Jason Johnson	33	33	8-13	0	0	117	4.54	210.0	93	49
Mike Maroth	34	34	14-14	0	0	123	4.74	209.0	115	51
Nate Robertson	32	32	7-16	0	0	113	4.48	196.2	122	65
Jeremy Bonderman	29	29	14-13	0	0	101	4.57	189.0	145	57
Chris Spurling	56	0	3-4	0	0	30	3.44	70.2	26	22
Franklyn German	58	0	4-0	1	0	26	3.66	59.0	38	34
Wilfredo Ledezma	10	10	2-4	0	0	46	7.07	49.2	30	24
Jamie Walker	66	0	4-3	0	0	22	3.70	48.2	30	13
Fernando Rodney	39	0	2-3	9	0	14	2.86	44.0	42	17
Kyle Farnsworth	46	0	1-1	6	0	12	2.32	42.2	55	20
Matt Ginter	14	1	0-1	0	0	25	6.17	35.0	15	9
Craig Dingman	34	0	2-3	4	0	14	3.66	32.0	24	9
Uqueth Urbina	25	0	1-3	9	0	9	2.63	27.1	31	14
Roman Colon	12	3	1-1	0	0	18	6.12	25.0	17	7
Troy Percival	26	0	1-3	8	0	16	5.76	25.0	20	11

Kansas City Royals

BATTING	G	AB	R	H	2B	3B	HR	RBI	TB	BB	SO	SB	OBP	SLG	BA
Angel Berroa	159	608	68	164	21	5	11	55	228	18	108	7	.305	.375	.270
Emil Brown	150	545	75	156	31	5	17	86	248	48	108	10	.349	.455	.286
Mike Sweeney	121	466	63	140	39	0	21	83	242	33	61	0	.348	.519	.300
David DeJesus	122	461	69	135	31	6	9	56	205	42	76	5	.359	.445	.293
Terrence Long	137	455	62	127	21	3	6	53	172	30	56	3	.321	.378	.279
Mark Teahen	130	447	60	110	29	4	7	55	168	40	107	7	.309	.376	.246
John Buck	118	401	40	97	21	1	12	47	156	23	94	2	.287	.389	.242
Matt Stairs	127	396	55	109	26	1	13	66	176	60	69	1	.373	.444	.275
Ruben Gotay	85	279	31	63	14	2	5	27	96	22	51	2	.287	.344	.226
Joe McEwing	83	180	16	43	7	0	1	6	53	6	35	4	.263	.294	.239
Chip Ambres	53	145	25	35	8	0	4	9	55	16	32	3	.323	.379	.241
Aaron Guiel	33	109	18	32	5	0	4	7	49	6	21	1	.355	.450	.294
Matt Diaz	34	89	7	25	2	1	1	9	36	4	15	0	.323	.404	.281
Shane Costa	27	81	13	19	2	0	2	7	27	5	11	0	.287	.333	.235

PITCHING	GP	GS	W–L	SV	SHO	R	ERA	IP	Ks	BB
Zack Greinke	33	33	5-17	0	0	125	5.80	183.0	114	53
Jose Lima	32	32	5-16	0	0	140	6.99	168.2	80	61
Runelvys Hernandez	29	29	8-14	0	0	101	5.52	159.2	88	70
Mike Wood	47	10	5-8	2	0	66	4.46	115.0	60	52
D.J. Carrasco	21	20	6-8	0	0	67	4.79	114.2	49	51
Andrew Cisco	67	0	2-5	0	0	27	3.11	75.1	76	42
J.P. Howell	15	15	3-5	0	0	55	6.19	72.2	54	39
Mike MacDougal	68	0	5-6	21	0	32	3.33	70.1	72	24
Ambriorix Burgos	59	0	3-5	2	0	29	3.98	63.1	65	31
Jimmy Goble	28	4	1-1	0	0	34	5.70	53.2	38	30
Leo Nunez	41	0	3-2	0	0	45	7.55	53.2	32	18
Jeremy Affeldt	49	0	0-2	1	0	35	5.26	49.2	39	29

Los Angeles Angels of Anaheim

BATTING	G	AB	R	H	2B	3B	HR	RBI	TB	BB	SO	SB	OBP	SLG	BA
Chone Figgins	158	642	113	186	25	10	8	57	255	64	101	62	.352	.397	.290
Darin Erstad	152	605	85	164	33	3	7	65	224	47	108	10	.324	.370	.271
Garret Anderson	142	575	68	163	34	1	17	96	250	23	84	1	.308	.435	.283
Orlando Cabrera	141	540	70	139	28	3	8	57	197	38	50	21	.309	.365	.257
Vladimir Guerrero	140	517	95	164	29	2	32	107	293	60	48	13	.393	.567	.317
Adam Kennedy	129	416	49	125	23	0	2	37	154	29	64	19	.354	.370	.300
Bengie Molina	119	410	45	121	17	0	15	69	183	27	41	0	.336	.446	.295
Steve Finley	112	406	41	90	20	3	12	54	152	26	71	8	.271	.374	.222
Juan Rivera	106	350	46	95	17	1	15	59	159	23	44	1	.316	.454	.271
Jeff DaVanon	108	225	42	52	10	1	2	15	70	39	44	11	.347	.311	.231
Dallas McPherson	61	205	29	50	14	2	8	26	92	14	64	3	.295	.449	.244
Maicer Izturis	77	191	18	47	8	4	1	15	66	17	21	9	.306	.46	.246
Jose Molina	74	184	14	42	4	0	6	-25	64	13	41	2	.286	.348	.228
Robb Quinlan	54	134	17	31	8	0	5	14	54	7	26	0	.273	.403	.231
Casey Kotchman	47	126	16	35	5	0	7	22	61	15	18	1	.352	.484	.278

PITCHING	GP	GS	W–L	SV	SHO	R	ERA	IP	Ks	BB
Bartolo Colon	33	33	21-8	0	0	93	3.48	222.2	157	43
John Lackey	33	33	14-5	0	0	85	3.44	209.0	199	71
Paul Byrd	31	31	12-11	0	1	95	3.74	204.1	102	28
Jarrod Washburn	29	29	8-8	0	1	66	3.20	177.1	94	51
Ervin Santana	23	23	12-8	0	1	73	4.65	133.2	99	47
Scot Shields	78	0	10-11	7	0	33	2.75	91.2	98	37
Francisco Rodriguez	66	0	2-5	45	0	20	2.67	67.1	91	32
Esteban Yan	49	0	1-1	0	0	36	4.59	66.2	45	30
Brendan Donnelly	65	0	9-3	0	0	30	3.72	65.1	53	19
Kevin Gregg	33	2	1-2	0	0	37	5.04	64.1	52	29
Kelvim Escobar	16	7	3-2	1	0	21	3.02	59.2	63	21

Minnesota Twins

BATTING	G	AB	R	H	2B	3B	HR	RBI	TB	BB	SO	SB	OBP	SLG	BA
Shannon Stewart	132	551	69	151	27	3	10	56	214	34	73	7	.323	.388	.274
Jacque Jones	142	523	74	130	22	4	23	73	229	51	120	13	.319	.438	.249
Lew Ford	147	522	70	138	30	4	7	53	197	45	85	13	.338	.377	.264
Justin Morneau	141	490	62	117	23	4	22	79	214	44	94	0	.304	.437	.239
Joe Mauer	131	489	61	144	26	2	9	55	201	61	64	13	.372	.411	.294
Michael Cuddyer	126	422	55	111	25	3	12	42	178	41	93	3	.330	.422	.263
Nick Punto	112	394	45	94	18	4	4	26	132	36	86	13	.301	.335	.239
Torii Hunter	98	372	63	100	24	1	14	56	168	34	65	23	.337	.452	.269
Bret Boone	88	326	33	72	15	3	7	37	114	28	65	4	.290	.350	.221
Matthew LeCroy	101	304	33	79	5	0	17	50	135	41	85	0	.354	.444	.260
Juan Castro	97	272	27	70	18	1	5	33	105	9	39	0	.279	.386	.257
Jason Bartlett	74	224	33	54	10	1	3	16	75	21	37	4	.316	.335	.241
Luis Rodriguez	79	175	21	47	10	2	2	20	67	18	23	2	.335	.383	.269
Terry Tiffee	54	150	9	31	8	1	1	15	44	8	15	1	.245	.293	.207
Mike Redmond	45	148	17	46	9	0	1	26	58	6	14	0	.350	.392	.311
Luis Rivas	59	136	21	35	3	1	1	12	43	9	17	4	.311	.316	.257
Michael Ryan	57	117	7	27	5	0	2	13	38	9	22	1	.283	.325	.231

PITCHING	GP	GS	W–L	SV	SHO	R	ERA	IP	Ks	BB
Johan Santana	33	33	16-7	0	2	77	2.87	231.2	238	45
Brad Radke	31	21	9-12	0	1	98	4.04	200.2	117	23
Carlos Silva	27	27	9-8	0	0	83	3.44	188.1	71	9
Kyle Lohse	31	30	9-13	0	0	85	4.18	178.2	86	44
Joe Mays	31	26	6-10	0	1	109	5.65	156.0	59	41
Jesse Crain	75	0	12-5	1	0	28	2.71	79.2	25	29
Juan Rincon	75	0	6-6	0	0	26	2.45	77.0	84	30
Matt Guerrier	43	0	0-3	0	0	29	3.39	71.2	46	24
Joe Nathan	69	0	7-4	43	0	22	2.70	70.0	94	22
Terry Mulholland	49	0	0-2	0	0	30	4.27	59.0	18	17
J.C. Romero	68	0	4-3	0	0	26	3.47	57.0	48	39
Scott Baker	10	9	3-3	0	0	21	3.35	53.2	32	14

New York Yankees

BATTING	G	AB	R	H	2B	3B	HR	RBI	TB	BB	SO	SB	OBP	SLG	BA
Derek Jeter	159	654	122	202	25	5	19	70	294	77	117	14	.389	.450	.309
Hideki Matsui	162	629	108	192	45	3	23	116	312	63	78	2	.367	.496	.305
Alex Rodriguez	162	605	124	194	29	1	48	130	369	91	139	21	.421	.610	321
Gary Sheffield	154	584	104	170	27	0	34	123	299	78	76	10	.379	.512	.291
Robinson Cano	148	522	78	155	34	4	14	62	239	16	68	1	.320	.458	.297
Bernie Williams	137	485	53	121	19	1	12	64	178	53	75	1	.321	.367	.249
Jorge Pasada	127	474	67	124	23	0	19	71	204	66	94	1	.352	.430	.262
Jason Giambi	122	417	74	113	14	0	32	87	223	108	109	0	.440	.535	.271
Tony Womack	107	329	46	82	8	1	30	15	92	12	49	27	.276	.280	.249
Tino Martinez	83	303	43	73	9	0	17	49	133	38	54	2	.328	.439	.241
Mark Bellhorn	80	300	43	63	20	0	8	30	107	52	112	3	.324	.357	.210
Ruben Sierra	106	170	14	39	12	0	4	29	63	9	41	0	.265	.371	.229
John Flaherty	93	127	10	21	5	0	2	11	32	6	26	0	.206	.252	.165
Bubba Crosby	47	98	15	27	0	1	0	6	32	4	14	4	.304	.327	.276

PITCHING	GP	GS	W–L	SV	SHO	R	ERA	IP	Ks	BB
Randy Johnson	34	34	17-8	0	0	102	3.79	225.2	211	47
Mike Mussina	30	30	13-8	0	2	93	4.41	179.2	142	47
Chien-Ming Wang	18	17	8-5	0	0	58	4.02	116.1	47	32
Hideo Nomo	19	19	5-8	0	0	82	7.24	100.2	59	51
Carl Pavano	17	17	4-6	0	1	66	4.77	100.0	56	18
Tom Gordon	79	0	5-4	2	0	25	2.57	80.2	69	29
Shawn Chacon	14	12	7-3	0	0	26	2.85	79.0	40	30
Mariano Rivera	71	0	7-4	43	0	18	1.38	78.1	80	18
Tanyon Sturtze	64	1	5-3	1	0	43	4.73	78.0	45	27
Aaron Small	15	9	10-0	0	1	27	3.20	76.0	37	24
Kevin Brown	13	13	4-7	0	0	57	6.50	73.1	50	19
Jaret Wright	13	13	5-5	0	0	51	6.08	63.2	34	32
Al Leiter	16	10	4-5	0	0	42	5.49	62.1	45	38
Alan Embree	67	0	2-5	1	0	47	7.62	52.0	38	14
Scott Proctor	29	1	1-0	0	0	32	6.04	44.2	36	17

Oakland Athletics

BATTING	G	AB	R	H	2B	3B	HR	RBI	TB	BB	SO	SB	OBP	SLG	BA
Erick Chavez	160	625	92	168	40	1	27	101	291	58	129	6	.329	.466	.269
Jason Kendall	150	601	70	163	28	1	0	53	193	50	39	8	.345	.321	.271
Mark Kotsay	139	582	75	163	35	1	15	82	245	40	51	5	.325	.421	.280
Scott Hatteberg	134	464	52	119	19	0	7	59	159	51	54	0	.334	.343	.256
Nick Swisher	131	462	66	109	32	1	21	74	206	55	110	0	.322	.446	.236
Mark Ellis	122	434	76	137	21	5	13	52	207	44	51	1	.384	.477	.316
Jay Payton	124	408	62	109	16	1	18	63	181	24	47	0	.306	.444	.267
Marco Scutaro	118	381	48	94	22	3	9	37	149	36	48	5	.310	.391	.247
Bobby Kielty	116	377	55	99	20	0	10	57	149	50	67	3	.350	.395	.263
Dan Johnson	109	375	54	103	21	0	15	58	169	50	52	0	.355	.451	.275
Bobby Crosby	84	333	66	92	25	4	9	38	152	35	54	0	.346	.456	.276
Erubiel Durazo	41	152	15	36	6	1	4	16	56	14	24	1	.305	.368	.237
Keith Ginter	51	137	12	22	5	0	3	25	36	13	25	0	.234	.263	.161
Alberto Castillo	35	101	13	21	5	1	1	14	31	12	22	1	.289	.307	.208
Adam Melhuse	39	97	11	24	7	0	2	12	37	5	28	0	.284	.381	.247

PITCHING	GP	GS	W–L	SV	SHO	R	ERA	IP	Ks	BB
Barry Zito	35	35	14-13	0	0	106	3.86	228.1	171	89
Danny Haren	34	34	14-12	0	0	101	3.73	217.0	163	53
Joe Blanton	33	33	12-12	0	0	86	3.53	201.1	116	67
Kirk Saarlos	29	27	10-9	0	1	75	4.17	159.2	53	54
Rich Harden	22	19	10-5	0	0	42	2.53	128.0	121	43
Justin Duchscherer	65	0	7-4	5	0	25	2.21	85.2	85	19
Huston Street	67	0	5-1	23	0	17	1.72	78.1	72	26
Joe Kennedy	19	8	4-5	0	0	33	4.45	60.2	45	20
Keiichi Yabu	40	0	4-0	1	0	34	4.50	58.0	44	26
Kiko Calero	58	0	4-1	1	0	20	3.23	55.2	52	18
Ricardo Rincon	67	0	1-1	0	0	19	4.34	37.1	27	20
Juan Cruz	28	0	0-3	0	0	33	7.44	32.2	34	22

Seattle Mariners

BATTING	G	AB	R	H	2B	3B	HR	RBI	TB	BB	SO	SB	OBP	SLG	BA
Ichiro Suzuki	162	679	111	206	21	12	15	68	296	48	66	33	.350	.436	.303
Raul Ibanez	162	614	92	172	32	2	20	89	268	71	99	9	.355	.436	.280
Adrian Beltre	156	603	69	154	36	1	19	87	249	38	108	3	.303	.413	.255
Richie Sexson	156	558	99	147	36	1	39	121	302	89	167	1	.369	.541	.263
Jeremy Reed	141	488	61	124	33	3	3	45	172	48	74	12	.322	.352	.254
Randy Winn	102	386	46	106	25	1	6	37	151	37	53	12	.342	.391	.275
Willie Bloomquist	82	249	27	64	15	2	0	22	83	11	38	14	.289	.333	.257
Mike Morse	72	230	27	64	10	1	3	23	85	18	50	3	.349	.370	.256
Yuniesky Betancourt	60	211	24	54	11	5	1	15	78	11	24	1	.296	.370	.256
Jose Lopez	54	190	18	47	19	0	2	25	72	6	25	4	.282	.379	.247
Miguel Olivo	54	152	14	23	4	0	5	18	42	4	49	1	.172	.276	.151
Greg Dobbs	59	142	8	35	7	1	1	20	47	9	25	1	.288	.331	.246
Wilson Valdez	42	126	9	25	5	1	0	8	32	6	25	2	.235	.254	.198
Pat Borders	39	117	12	23	5	0	1	7	31	4	22	0	.228	.265	.197
Yorvit Torrealba	42	108	14	26	4	0	2	8	36	7	25	0	.293	.333	.241

PITCHING	GP	GS	W–L	SV	SHO	R	ERA	IP	Ks	BB
Jamie Moyer	32	32	13-7	0	0	99	4.28	200.0	102	52
Ryan Franklin	32	30	8-15	0	1	110	5.10	190.2	93	62
Joel Pineiro	30	30	7-11	0	0	118	5.62	189.0	107	56
Gil Meche	29	26	10-8	0	0	92	5.09	143.1	83	72
Julio Mateo	55	1	3-6	0	0	32	3.06	88.1	52	17
Felix Hernandez	12	12	4-4	0	0	26	2.67	84.1	77	23
Shigetoshi Hasegawa	46	0	1-3	0	0	31	4.19	66.2	30	16
J.J. Putz	64	0	6-5	1	0	27	3.60	60.0	45	23
Matt Thornton	55	0	0-4	0	0	33	5.21	57.0	57	42
Eddie Guardado	58	0	2-3	36	0	23	2.72	56.1	48	15
Jeff Harris	11	8	2-5	0	0	27	4.19	53.2	25	20
RonVillone	52	0	2-3	1	0	14	2.45	40.1	41	23
Jeff Nelson	49	0	1-3	1	0	17	3.93	36.2	34	22
George Sherrill	29	0	4-3	0	0	12	5.21	19.0	24	7

Tampa Bay Devil Rays

BATTING	G	AB	R	H	2B	3B	HR	RBI	TB	BB	SO	SB	OBP	SLG	BA
Carl Crawford	156	644	101	194	33	15	15	81	302	27	84	46	.331	.469	.301
Julio Lugo	158	616	89	182	36	6	6	57	248	61	72	39	.362	.403	.295
Jorge Cantu	150	598	73	171	40	1	28	117	297	19	83	1	.311	.497	.286
Aubrey Huff	154	575	70	150	26	2	22	92	246	49	88	8	.321	.428	.261
Toby Hall	135	432	28	124	20	0	5	48	159	16	39	0	.315	.368	.287
Travis Lee	129	404	54	110	22	2	12	49	172	35	66	7	.331	.426	.272
Alex Gonzalez	109	349	47	94	20	1	9	38	143	26	74	2	.323	.410	.269
Jonny Gomes	101	348	61	98	13	6	21	54	186	39	113	4	.372	.534	.282
Damon Hollins	120	342	44	85	17	1	13	46	143	23	63	8	.296	.418	.249
Nick Green	111	318	53	76	15	2	5	29	110	33	86	3	.329	.346	.239
Joey Gathright	76	203	29	56	7	3	0	13	69	10	39	20	.316	.340	.276
Eduardo Perez	77	161	23	41	6	0	11	28	80	26	30	0	.368	.497	.255
Josh Phelps	47	158	21	42	10	0	5	26	67	12	48	0	.328	.424	.266
Alex Sanchez	43	133	28	46	8	1	2	13	62	7	25	6	.373	.466	.346

PITCHING	GP	GS	W–L	SV	SHO	R	ERA	IP	Ks	BB
Scott Kazmir	32	32	10-9	0	0	90	3.77	186.0	174	100
Mark Hendrickson	31	31	11-8	0	0	126	5.90	178.1	89	49
Casey Fossum	36	25	8-12	0	0	100	4.92	162.2	128	60
Doug Waechter	29	25	5-12	0	0	109	5.62	157.0	87	38
Seth McClung	34	17	7-11	0	0	85	6.59	109.1	92	62
Travis Harper	52	0	4-6	0	0	57	6.75	73.1	40	24
Danys Baez	67	0	5-4	41	0	27	2.86	72.1	51	30
Dewon Brazelton	20	8	1-8	0	0	65	7.61	71.0	43	60
Lance Carter	39	0	1-2	1	0	31	4.89	57.0	22	15
Chad Orvella	37	0	3-3	1	0	26	3.60	50.0	43	23
Jesus Colome	36	0	2-3	0	0	29	4.57	45.1	28	18
Trever Miller	61	0	2-2	0	0	23	4.06	44.1	35	29
Joe Borowski	32	0	1-5	0	0	15	3.82	35.1	16	11

American League Team-by-Team Statistical Leaders *(Cont.)*

Texas Rangers

BATTING	G	AB	R	H	2B	3B	HR	RBI	TB	BB	SO	SB	OBP	SLG	BA
Michael Young	159	668	114	221	40	5	24	91	343	58	91	5	.385	.513	.331
Hank Blalock	161	647	80	170	34	0	25	92	279	51	132	1	.318	.431	.263
Mark Teixeira	162	644	112	194	41	3	43	144	370	72	124	4	.379	.575	.301
Alfonso Soriano	156	637	102	171	43	2	36	104	326	33	125	30	.309	.512	.268
Kevin Mench	150	557	71	147	33	3	25	73	261	50	68	4	.328	.469	.264
Gary Matthew	131	475	72	121	25	5	17	55	207	47	90	9	.320	.436	.255
David Dellucci	128	435	97	109	17	5	29	65	223	76	121	5	.367	.513	.251
Rod Barajas	120	410	53	104	24	0	21	60	191	26	70	0	.306	.466	.254
Richard Hidalgo	88	308	43	68	12	0	16	43	128	26	74	1	.289	.416	.221
Layne Nix	63	229	28	55	12	3	6	32	91	9	45	2	.267	.397	.240
Adrian Gonzalez	43	150	17	34	7	1	6	17	61	10	37	0	.272	.407	.227
Mark DeRosa	66	148	26	36	5	0	8	20	65	16	35	1	.325	.439	.243
Sandy Alomar	46	128	11	35	7	0	0	14	42	5	12	0	.306	.328	.273
Phil Nevin	29	99	15	18	5	0	3	8	32	8	30	2	.250	.323	.182

PITCHING	GP	GS	W–L	SV	SHO	R	ERA	IP	Ks	BB
Kenny Rogers	30	30	14-8	0	1	86	3.46	195.1	87	53
Chris Young	31	31	12-7	0	0	84	4.26	164.2	137	45
Aaron Sele	21	21	6-12	0	1	76	5.66	116.0	53	41
Chan Ho Park	20	20	8-5	0	0	70	5.66	109.2	80	54
Kameron Loe	48	8	9-6	1	0	43	3.42	92.0	45	31
Joaquin Benoit	32	9	4-4	0	0	39	3.72	87.0	78	38
John Wasdin	31	6	3-2	4	0	37	4.28	75.2	44	20
Doug Brocail	61	0	5-3	1	0	48	5.52	73.1	61	34
Juan Dominquez	22	10	4-6	0	0	37	4.22	70.1	45	25
Ryan Drese	12	12	4-6	0	0	52	6.46	69.2	20	24
Francisco Cordero	69	0	3-1	37	0	28	3.39	69.0	79	30
Pedro Astacio	12	12	2-8	0	0	45	6.04	67.0	45	11
Ricardo Rodriguez	12	10	2-3	0	0	39	5.53	57.0	24	17
Brian Shouse	64	0	3-2	0	0	37	5.23	53.1	35	18
C.J. Wilson	24	6	1-7	1	0	39	6.94	48.0	30	18
Ron Mahay	30	0	0-2	1	0	28	6.81	35.2	30	16

Toronto Blue Jays

BATTING	G	AB	R	H	2B	3B	HR	RBI	TB	BB	SO	SB	OBP	SLG	BA
Vernon Wells	156	620	78	167	30	3	28	97	287	47	86	8	.320	.463	.269
Shea Hillenbrand	152	594	91	173	36	2	18	82	267	26	79	5	.343	.449	.291
Russ Adams	139	481	68	123	27	5	8	63	184	50	57	11	.325	.383	.256
Alex Rios	146	481	71	126	23	6	10	59	191	28	101	14	.306	.397	.262
Eric Hinske	147	477	79	125	31	2	15	68	205	46	121	4	.333	.430	.262
Orlando Hudson	131	461	62	125	25	5	10	63	190	30	65	7	.315	.412	.271
Gregg Zaun	133	434	61	109	18	1	11	61	162	73	70	2	.355	.373	.251
Frank Catalanotto	130	419	56	126	29	5	8	59	189	37	53	0	.367	.451	.301
Reed Johnson	142	398	55	107	21	6	8	58	164	22	82	5	.332	.412	.269
Aaron Hill	105	361	49	99	25	3	3	40	139	34	41	2	.342	.385	.274
Corey Koskie	97	354	49	88	20	0	11	36	141	44	90	4	.37	.398	.249
Frank Menechino	70	148	22	32	7	0	4	13	51	25	33	0	.352	.345	.216
Gabe Gross	40	92	11	23	4	1	1	7	32	10	21	1	.324	.348	.250
Ken Huckaby	35	87	8	18	4	0	0	6	22	5	19	0	.250	.253	.207

PITCHING	GP	GS	W–L	SV	SHO	R	ERA	IP	Ks	BB
Josh Towers	33	33	13-12	0	1	101	3.71	208.2	112	29
Gustavo Chacin	34	34	13-9	0	0	93	3.72	203.0	121	70
Roy Halladay	19	19	12-4	0	2	39	2.41	141.2	108	18
Dave Bush	25	24	5-11	0	0	73	4.49	136.1	75	29
Ted Lilly	25	25	10-11	0	0	79	5.56	126.1	96	58
Scott Downs	26	13	4-3	0	0	49	4.31	94.0	75	34
Pete Walker	41	4	6-6	2	0	33	3.54	84.0	43	33
Miguel Batista	71	0	5-8	31	0	39	4.10	74.2	54	27
Jason Frasor	67	0	3-5	1	0	31	3.25	74.2	62	28
Vinnie Chulk	62	0	0-1	0	0	33	3.88	72.0	39	26
Justin Speier	65	0	3-2	0	0	20	2.57	66.2	56	15
Scott Schoeneweis	80	0	3-4	1	0	23	3.32	57.0	43	25
Dustin McGowan	13	7	1-3	0	0	34	6.35	45.1	34	17

The World Series

Results

1903	Boston (A) 5, Pittsburgh (N) 3	1955	Brooklyn (N) 4, New York (A) 3
1904	No series	1956	New York (A) 4, Brooklyn (N) 3
1905	New York (N) 4, Philadelphia (A) 1	1957	Milwaukee (N) 4, New York (A) 3
1906	Chicago (A) 4, Chicago (N) 2	1958	New York (A) 4, Milwaukee (N) 3
1907	Chicago (N) 4, Detroit (A) 0; 1 tie	1959	Los Angeles (N) 4, Chicago (A) 2
1908	Chicago (N) 4, Detroit (A) 1	1960	Pittsburgh (N) 4, New York (A) 3
1909	Pittsburgh (N) 4, Detroit (A) 3	1961	New York (A) 4, Cincinnati (N) 1
1910	Philadelphia (A) 4, Chicago (N) 1	1962	New York (A) 4, San Francisco (N) 3
1911	Philadelphia (A) 4, New York (N) 2	1963	Los Angeles (N) 4, New York (A) 0
1912	Boston (A) 4, New York (N) 3; 1 tie	1964	St. Louis (N) 4, New York (A) 3
1913	Philadelphia (A) 4, New York (N) 1	1965	Los Angeles (N) 4, Minnesota (A) 3
1914	Boston (N) 4, Philadelphia (A) 0	1966	Baltimore (A) 4, Los Angeles (N) 0
1915	Boston (A) 4, Philadelphia (N) 1	1967	St. Louis (N) 4, Boston (A) 3
1916	Boston (A) 4, Brooklyn (N) 1	1968	Detroit (A) 4, St. Louis (N) 3
1917	Chicago (A) 4, New York (N) 2	1969	New York (N) 4, Baltimore (A) 1
1918	Boston (A) 4, Chicago (N) 2	1970	Baltimore (A) 4, Cincinnati (N) 1
1919	Cincinnati (N) 5, Chicago (A) 3	1971	Pittsburgh (N) 4, Baltimore (A) 3
1920	Cleveland (A) 5, Brooklyn (N) 2	1972	Oakland (A) 4, Cincinnati (N) 3
1921	New York (N) 5, New York (A) 3	1973	Oakland (A) 4, New York (N) 3
1922	New York (N) 4, New York (A) 0; 1 tie	1974	Oakland (A) 4, Los Angeles (N) 1
1923	New York (A) 4, New York (N) 2	1975	Cincinnati (N) 4, Boston (A) 3
1924	Washington (A) 4, New York (N) 3	1976	Cincinnati (N) 4, New York (A) 0
1925	Pittsburgh (N) 4, Washington (A) 3	1977	New York (A) 4, Los Angeles (N) 2
1926	St. Louis (N) 4, New York (A) 3	1978	New York (A) 4, Los Angeles (N) 2
1927	New York (A) 4, Pittsburgh (N) 0	1979	Pittsburgh (N) 4, Baltimore (A) 3
1928	New York (A) 4, St. Louis (N) 0	1980	Philadelphia (N) 4, Kansas City (A) 2
1929	Philadelphia (A) 4, Chicago (N) 1	1981	Los Angeles (N) 4, New York (A) 2
1930	Philadelphia (A) 4, St. Louis (N) 2	1982	St. Louis (N) 4, Milwaukee (A) 3
1931	St. Louis (N) 4, Philadelphia (A) 3	1983	Baltimore (A) 4, Philadelphia (N) 1
1932	New York (A) 4, Chicago (N) 0	1984	Detroit (A) 4, San Diego (N) 1
1933	New York (N) 4, Washington (A) 1	1985	Kansas City (A) 4, St. Louis (N) 3
1934	St. Louis (N) 4, Detroit (A) 3	1986	New York (N) 4, Boston (A) 3
1935	Detroit (A) 4, Chicago (N) 2	1987	Minnesota (A) 4, St. Louis (N) 3
1936	New York (A) 4, New York (N) 2	1988	Los Angeles (N) 4, Oakland (A) 1
1937	New York (A) 4, New York (N) 1	1989	Oakland (A) 4, San Francisco (N) 0
1938	New York (A) 4, Chicago (N) 0	1990	Cincinnati (N) 4, Oakland (A) 0
1939	New York (A) 4, Cincinnati (N) 0	1991	Minnesota (A) 4, Atlanta (N) 3
1940	Cincinnati (N) 4, Detroit (A) 3	1992	Toronto (A) 4, Atlanta (N) 2
1941	New York (A) 4, Brooklyn (N) 1	1993	Toronto (A) 4, Philadelphia (N) 2
1942	St. Louis (N) 4, New York (A) 1	1994	Series canceled due to players' strike.
1943	New York (A) 4, St. Louis (N) 1	1995	Atlanta (N) 4, Cleveland (A) 2
1944	St. Louis (N) 4, St. Louis (A) 2	1996	New York (A) 4, Atlanta (N) 2
1945	Detroit (A) 4, Chicago (N) 3	1997	Florida (N) 4, Cleveland (A) 3
1946	St. Louis (N) 4, Boston (A) 3	1998	New York (A) 4, San Diego (N) 0
1947	New York (A) 4, Brooklyn (N) 3	1999	New York (A) 4, Atlanta (N) 0
1948	Cleveland (A) 4, Boston (N) 2	2000	New York (A) 4 , New York (N) 1
1949	New York (A) 4, Brooklyn (N) 1	2001	Arizona (N) 4, New York (A) 3
1950	New York (A) 4, Philadelphia (N) 0	2002	Anaheim (A) 4, San Francisco (N) 3
1951	New York (A) 4, New York (N) 2	2003	Florida (N) 4, New York (A) 2
1952	New York (A) 4, Brooklyn (N) 3	2004	Boston (A) 4, St. Louis (N) 0
1953	New York (A) 4, Brooklyn (N) 2	2005	Chicago (A) 4, Houston (N) 0
1954	New York (N) 4, Cleveland (A) 0		

Most Valuable Players

1955	Johnny Podres, Bklyn
1956	Don Larsen, NY (A)
1957	Lew Burdette, Mil
1958	Bob Turley, NY (A)
1959	Larry Sherry, LA
1960	Bobby Richardson, NY (A)
1961	Whitey Ford, NY (A)
1962	Ralph Terry, NY (A)
1963	Sandy Koufax, LA
1964	Bob Gibson, StL
1965	Sandy Koufax, LA
1966	Frank Robinson, Balt
1967	Bob Gibson, StL
1968	Mickey Lolich, Det
1969	Donn Clendenon, NY (N)
1970	Brooks Robinson, Balt
1971	Roberto Clemente, Pitt
1972	Gene Tenace, Oak
1973	Reggie Jackson, Oak
1974	Rollie Fingers, Oak
1975	Pete Rose, Cin
1976	Johnny Bench, Cin
1977	Reggie Jackson, NY (A)
1978	Bucky Dent, NY (A)
1979	Willie Stargell, Pitt
1980	Mike Schmidt, Phil
1981	Ron Cey, LA; Steve Yeager, LA; Pedro Guerrero, LA
1982	Darrell Porter, StL
1983	Rick Dempsey, Balt
1984	Alan Trammell, Det
1985	Bret Saberhagen, KC
1986	Ray Knight, NY (N)
1987	Frank Viola, Minn
1988	Orel Hershiser, LA
1989	Dave Stewart, Oak
1990	Jose Rijo, Cin
1991	Jack Morris, Minn
1992	Pat Borders, Tor
1993	Paul Molitor, Tor
1994	Series canceled due to strike.
1995	Tom Glavine, Atl
1996	John Wetteland, NY (A)
1997	Livan Hernandez, Fla
1998	Scott Brosius, NY (A)
1999	Mariano Rivera, NY (A)
2000	Derek Jeter, NY (A)
2001	Randy Johnson, Ariz; Curt Schilling, Ariz
2002	Troy Glaus, Ana
2003	Josh Beckett, Fla
2004	Manny Ramirez, Bos
2005	Jermaine Dye, Chi

Career Batting Leaders (Minimum 40 at bats)

GAMES

Yogi Berra	75
Mickey Mantle	65
Elston Howard	54
Hank Bauer	53
Gil McDougald	53
Phil Rizzuto	52
Joe DiMaggio	51
Frankie Frisch	50
Pee Wee Reese	44
Roger Maris	41
Babe Ruth	41

AT BATS

Yogi Berra	259
Mickey Mantle	230
Joe DiMaggio	199
Frankie Frisch	197
Gil McDougald	190
Hank Bauer	188
Phil Rizzuto	183
Elston Howard	171
Pee Wee Reese	169
Roger Maris	152

HITS

Yogi Berra	71
Mickey Mantle	59
Frankie Frisch	58
Joe DiMaggio	54
Pee Wee Reese	46
Hank Bauer	46
Phil Rizzuto	45
Gil McDougald	45
Lou Gehrig	43
Eddie Collins	42
Babe Ruth	42
Elston Howard	42

BATTING AVERAGE

Bobby Brown	.439
Paul Molitor	.418
Pepper Martin	.418
Hal McRae	.400
Lou Brock	.391
Marquis Grissom	.390
Thurman Munson	.373
George Brett	.373
Pat Borders	.372
Hank Aaron	.364

HOME RUNS

Mickey Mantle	18
Babe Ruth	15
Yogi Berra	12
Duke Snider	11
Reggie Jackson	10
Lou Gehrig	10
Frank Robinson	8
Bill Skowron	8
Joe DiMaggio	8
Goose Goslin	7
Hank Bauer	7
Gil McDougald	7

RUNS BATTED IN

Mickey Mantle	40
Yogi Berra	39
Lou Gehrig	35
Babe Ruth	33
Joe DiMaggio	30
Bill Skowron	29
Duke Snider	26
Reggie Jackson	24
Bill Dickey	24
Hank Bauer	24
Gil McDougald	24

RUNS

Mickey Mantle	42
Yogi Berra	41
Babe Ruth	37
Lou Gehrig	30
Joe DiMaggio	27
Derek Jeter	27
Roger Maris	26
Elston Howard	25
Gil McDougald	23
Jackie Robinson	22

STOLEN BASES

Lou Brock	14
Eddie Collins	14
Frank Chance	10
Davey Lopes	10
Phil Rizzuto	10
Honus Wagner	9
Frankie Frisch	9
Johnny Evers	8
Kenny Lofton	8
Roberto Alomar	7
Joe Tinker	7
Pepper Martin	7
Joe Morgan	7
Rickey Henderson	7

Career Batting Leaders (Cont.)

TOTAL BASES

Mickey Mantle	123
Yogi Berra	117
Babe Ruth	96
Lou Gehrig	87
Joe DiMaggio	84
Duke Snider	79
Hank Bauer	75
Reggie Jackson	74
Frankie Frisch	74
Gil McDougald	72

SLUGGING AVERAGE

Reggie Jackson	.755
Babe Ruth	.744
Lou Gehrig	.731
Bobby Brown	.707
Lenny Dykstra	.700
Al Simmons	.658
Lou Brock	.655
Pepper Martin	.636
Paul Molitor	.636
Joe Harris	.625

STRIKEOUTS

Mickey Mantle	54
Elston Howard	37
Duke Snider	33
Derek Jeter	33
Babe Ruth	30
David Justice	30
Gil McDougald	29
Bill Skowron	26
Bernie Williams	26
Hank Bauer	25
Reggie Jackson	24
Bob Meusel	24
Jorge Posada	24

Career Pitching Leaders

GAMES

Whitey Ford	22
Mariano Rivera	20
Mike Stanton	19
Jeff Nelson	16
Rollie Fingers	16
Allie Reynolds	15
Bob Turley	15
Clay Carroll	14
Clem Labine	13
Mark Wohlers	13

LOSSES

Whitey Ford	8
Eddie Plank	5
Schoolboy Rowe	5
Joe Bush	5
Rube Marquard	5
Christy Mathewson	5
Andy Pettite	5

COMPLETE GAMES

Christy Mathewson	10
Chief Bender	9
Bob Gibson	8
Red Ruffing	7
Whitey Ford	7
George Mullin	6
Eddie Plank	6
Art Nehf	6
Waite Hoyt	6

INNINGS PITCHED

Whitey Ford	146
Christy Mathewson	101⅔
Red Ruffing	85⅔
Chief Bender	85
Waite Hoyt	83⅔
Bob Gibson	81
Art Nehf	79
Allie Reynolds	77
Jim Palmer	65
Catfish Hunter	63

SAVES

Mariano Rivera	9
Rollie Fingers	6
Allie Reynolds	4
Johnny Murphy	4
John Wetteland	4
Robb Nen	4

STRIKEOUTS

Whitey Ford	94
Bob Gibson	92
Allie Reynolds	62
Sandy Koufax	61
Red Ruffing	61
Chief Bender	59
George Earnshaw	56
John Smoltz	52
Waite Hoyt	49
Christy Mathewson	48
Roger Clemens	48

*EARNED RUN AVERAGE

Jack Billingham	0.35
Harry Brecheen	0.83
Babe Ruth	0.87
Sherry Smith	0.89
Sandy Koufax	0.95
Hippo Vaughn	1.00
Monte Pearson	1.01
Christy Mathewson	1.06
Mariano Rivera	1.16
Babe Adams	1.29

WINS

Whitey Ford	10
Bob Gibson	7
Red Ruffing	7
Allie Reynolds	7
Lefty Gomez	6
Chief Bender	6
Waite Hoyt	6
Jack Coombs	5
Three Finger Brown	5
Herb Pennock	5
Christy Mathewson	5
Vic Raschi	5
Catfish Hunter	5

BASES ON BALLS

Whitey Ford	34
Allie Reynolds	32
Art Nehf	32
Jim Palmer	31
Bob Turley	29
Paul Derringer	27
Red Ruffing	27
Don Gullett	26
Burleigh Grimes	26
Vic Raschi	25

SHUTOUTS

Christy Mathewson	4
Three Finger Brown	3
Whitey Ford	3
Bill Hallahan	2
Lew Burdette	2
Bill Dinneen	2
Sandy Koufax	2
Allie Reynolds	2
Art Nehf	2
Bob Gibson	2

*Minimum 25 innings pitched.

Alltime Team Rankings (by championships)

Team	W	L	Appearances	Pct.	Most Recent	Last Championship
New York Yankees	26	13	39	.666	2003	2000
Phil/KC/Oakland Athletics	9	5	14	.643	1990	1989
St. Louis Cardinals	9	7	16	.563	2004	1982
Brooklyn/LA Dodgers	6	12	18	.333	1988	1988
Boston Red Sox	6	4	10	.600	2004	2004
Pittsburgh Pirates	5	2	7	.714	1979	1979
Cincinnati Reds	5	4	9	.556	1990	1990
New York/San Francisco Giants	5	12	17	.294	2002	1954
Detroit Tigers	4	5	9	.444	1984	1984
Washington/Minnesota Twins	3	3	6	.500	1991	1991
St. Louis/Baltimore Orioles	3	4	7	.429	1983	1983
Boston/Milwaukee/Atlanta Braves	3	6	9	.333	1999	1995
Florida Marlins	2	0	2	1.000	2003	2003
Toronto Blue Jays	2	0	2	1.000	1993	1993
New York Mets	2	2	4	.500	2000	1986
Chicago White Sox	3	2	5	.600	2005	2005
Cleveland Indians	2	3	5	.400	1997	1948
Chicago Cubs	2	8	10	.200	1945	1908
Anaheim Angels	1	0	1	1.000	2002	2002
Arizona Diamondbacks	1	0	1	1.000	2001	2001
Kansas City Royals	1	1	2	.500	1985	1985
Philadelphia Phillies	1	4	5	.200	1993	1980
Houston Astros	0	1	1	.000	2005	—
San Diego Padres	0	2	2	.000	1998	—
Seattle/Milwaukee Brewers	0	1	1	.000	1982	—

League Championship Series

National League

1969	New York (E) 3, Atlanta (W) 0
1970	Cincinnati (W) 3, Pittsburgh (E) 0
1971	Pittsburgh (E) 3, San Francisco (W) 1
1972	Cincinnati (W) 3, Pittsburgh (E) 2
1973	New York (E) 3, Cincinnati (W) 2
1974	Los Angeles (W) 3, Pittsburgh (E) 1
1975	Cincinnati (W) 3, Pittsburgh (E) 0
1976	Cincinnati (W) 3, Philadelphia (E) 0
1977	Los Angeles (W) 3, Philadelphia (E) 1
1978	Los Angeles (W) 3, Philadelphia (E) 1
1979	Pittsburgh (E) 3, Cincinnati (W) 0
1980	Philadelphia (E) 3, Houston (W) 2
1981	Los Angeles (W) 3, Montreal (E) 2
1982	St. Louis (E) 3, Atlanta (W) 0
1983	Philadelphia (E) 3, Los Angeles (W) 1
1984	San Diego (W) 3, Chicago (E) 2
1985	St. Louis (E) 4, Los Angeles (W) 2
1986	New York (E) 4, Houston (W) 2
1987	St. Louis (E) 4, San Francisco (W) 3
1988	Los Angeles (W) 4, New York (E) 3
1989	San Francisco (W) 4, Chicago (E) 1
1990	Cincinnati (W) 4, Pittsburgh (E) 2
1991	Atlanta (W) 4, Pittsburgh (E) 3
1992	Atlanta (W) 4, Pittsburgh (E) 3
1993	Philadelphia (E) 4, Atlanta (W) 2
1994	Playoffs canceled due to players' strike.
1995	Atlanta (E) 4, Cincinnati (C) 0
1996	Atlanta (E) 4, St. Louis (C) 3
1997	Florida (wc) 4, Atlanta (E) 2
1998	San Diego (W) 4, Atlanta (E) 2
1999	Atlanta (E) 4, New York (wc) 2
2000	New York (wc) 4, St. Louis (C) 1
2001	Arizona (W) 4, Atlanta (E) 1
2002	San Francisco (wc) 4, St. Louis (C) 1
2003	Florida (wc) 4, Chicago (C) 3
2004	St. Louis (C) 4, Houston (wc) 3
2005	Houston (wc) 4, St. Louis (C) 2

American League

1969	Baltimore (E) 3, Minnesota (W) 0
1970	Baltimore (E) 3, Minnesota (W) 0
1971	Baltimore (E) 3, Oakland (W) 0
1972	Oakland (W) 3, Detroit (E) 2
1973	Oakland (W) 3, Baltimore (E) 2
1974	Oakland (W) 3, Baltimore (E) 1
1975	Boston (E) 3, Oakland (W) 0
1976	New York (E) 3, Kansas City (W) 2
1977	New York (E) 3, Kansas City (W) 2
1978	New York (E) 3, Kansas City (W) 1
1979	Baltimore (E) 3, California (W) 1
1980	Kansas City (W) 3, New York (E) 0
1981	New York (E) 3, Oakland (W) 0
1982	Milwaukee (E) 3, California (W) 2
1983	Baltimore (E) 3, Chicago (W) 1
1984	Detroit (E) 3, Kansas City (W) 0
1985	Kansas City (W) 4, Toronto (E) 3
1986	Boston (E) 4, California (W) 3
1987	Minnesota (W) 4, Detroit (E) 1
1988	Oakland (W) 4, Boston (E) 0
1989	Oakland (W) 4, Toronto (E) 1
1990	Oakland (W) 4, Boston (E) 0
1991	Minnesota (W) 4, Toronto (E) 1
1992	Toronto (E) 4, Oakland (W) 2
1993	Toronto (E) 4, Chicago (W) 2
1994	Playoffs canceled due to players' strike
1995	Cleveland (C) 4, Seattle (W) 2
1996	New York (E) 4, Baltimore (wc) 1
1997	Cleveland (C) 4, Baltimore (E) 2
1998	New York (E) 4, Cleveland (C) 2
1999	New York (E) 4, Boston (wc) 1
2000	New York (E) 4, Seattle (wc) 2
2001	New York (E) 4, Seattle (W) 1
2002	Anaheim (wc) 4, Minnesota (C) 1
2003	New York (E) 4, Boston (wc) 3
2004	Boston (wc) 4, New York (E) 3
2005	Chicago (C) 4, Los Angeles (W) 1

NLCS Most Valuable Player

1977 ....Dusty Baker, LA	1987 ....Jeffrey Leonard, SF	1997 ....Livan Hernandez, Fla
1978 ....Steve Garvey, LA	1988 ....Orel Hershiser, LA	1998 ....Sterling Hitchcock, SD
1979 ....Willie Stargell, Pitt	1989 ....Will Clark, SF	1999 ....Eddie Perez, Atl
1980 ....Manny Trillo, Phil	1990 ....R. Myers/R. Dibble, Cin	2000 ....Mike Hampton, NY
1981 ....Burt Hooton, LA	1991 ....Steve Avery, Atl	2001 ....Craig Counsell, Ariz
1982 ....Darrell Porter, StL	1992 ....John Smoltz, Atl	2002 ....Benito Santiago, SF
1983 ....Gary Matthews, Phil	1993 ....Curt Schilling, Phil	2003 ....Ivan Rodriguez, Fla
1984 ....Steve Garvey, SD	1994 ....Playoffs canceled	2004 ....Albert Pujols, StL
1985 ....Ozzie Smith, StL	1995 ....Mike Devereaux, Atl	2005 ....Roy Oswalt, Hou
1986 ....Mike Scott, Hou	1996 ....Javier Lopez, Atl	

ALCS Most Valuable Player

1980 ....Frank White, KC	1989 ....Rickey Henderson, Oak	1998 ....David Wells, NY
1981 ....Graig Nettles, NY	1990 ....Dave Stewart, Oak	1999 ....Orlando Hernandez, NY
1982 ....Fred Lynn, Calif	1991 ....Kirby Puckett, Minn	2000 ....David Justice, NY
1983 ....Mike Boddicker, Balt	1992 ....Roberto Alomar, Tor	2001 ....Andy Pettitte, NY
1984 ....Kirk Gibson, Det	1993 ....Dave Stewart, Tor	2002 ....Adam Kennedy, Ana
1985 ....George Brett, KC	1994 ....Playoffs canceled	2003 ....Mariano Rivera, NY
1986 ....Marty Barrett, Bos	1995 ....Orel Hershiser, Clev	2004 ....David Ortiz, Bos
1987 ....Gary Gaetti, Minn	1996 ....Bernie Williams, NY	2005 ....Paul Korenko, Chi
1988 ....Dennis Eckersley, Oak	1997 ....Marquis Grissom, Clev	

Divisional Playoffs

National League

1995 ....Atlanta (E) 3, Colorado (wc) 1	
	Cincinnati (C) 3, Los Angeles (W) 0
1996 ....St. Louis (C) 3, San Diego (W) 0	
	Atlanta (E) 3, Los Angeles (wc) 0
1997 ....Atlanta (E) 3, Houston (C) 0	
	Florida (wc) 3, San Francisco (W) 0
1998 ....San Diego (W) 3, Houston (C) 1	
	Atlanta (E) 3, Chicago (wc) 0
1999 ....Atlanta (E) 3, Houston (C) 1	
	New York (wc) 3, Arizona (W) 1
2000 ....St. Louis (C) 3, Atlanta (E) 0	
	New York (E) 3, San Francisco (W) 1
2001 ....Atlanta (E) 3, Houston (C) 0	
	Arizona (W) 3, St. Louis (wc) 2
2002 ....St. Louis (C) 3, Arizona (W) 0	
	San Francisco (wc) 3, Atlanta (E) 2
2003 ....Chicago (C) 3, Atlanta (E) 2	
	Florida (wc) 3, San Francisco (W) 1
2004 ....St. Louis (C) 3, Los Angeles (W) 1	
	Houston (wc) 3, Atlanta (E) 2
2005 ....Houston (wc) 3, Atlanta (e) 1	
	St. Louis (wc) 3, San Diego (w) 1

American League

1995 ....Cleveland (C) 3, Boston (E) 0	
	Seattle (W) 3, New York (wc) 2
1996 ....Baltimore (wc) 3, Cleveland (C) 1	
	New York (E) 3, Texas (W) 1
1997 ....Baltimore (E) 3, Seattle (W) 1	
	Cleveland (C) 3, New York (wc) 2
1998 ....New York (E) 3, Texas (W) 0	
	Cleveland (C) 3, Boston (wc) 1
1999 ....New York (E) 3, Texas (W) 1	
	Boston (wc) 3, Cleveland (C) 2
2000 ....New York (E) 3, Oakland (W) 2	
	Seattle (wc) 3, Chicago (C) 0
2001 ....Seattle (W) 3, Cleveland (wc) 2	
	New York (E) 3, Oakland (wc) 2
2002 ....Minnesota (C) 3, Oakland (W) 2	
	Anaheim (wc) 3, New York (E) 1
2003 ....New York (E) 3, Minnesota (C) 1	
	Boston (wc) 3, Oakland (W) 2
2004 ....New York (E) 3, Minnesota (C) 1	
	Boston (wc) 3 Anaheim (W) 0
2005 ....Los Angeles (w) 3, New York (e) 2	
	Chicago (cw) 3, Boston (e) 0

The All-Star Game

Results

Date	Winner	Score	Site	Date	Winner	Score	Site
7-6-33	American	4–2	Comiskey Park, Chi	7-14-53	National	5–1	Crosley Field, Cin
7-10-34	American	9–7	Polo Grounds, NY	7-13-54	American	11–9	Municipal Stadium, Clev
7-8-35	American	4–1	Municipal Stadium, Clev	7-12-55	National	6–5	County Stadium, Mil
7-7-36	National	4–3	Braves Field, Bos	7-10-56	National	7–3	Griffith Stadium, Wash
7-7-37	American	8–3	Griffith Stadium, Wash	7-9-57	American	6–5	Busch Stadium, StL
7-6-38	National	4–1	Crosley Field, Cin	7-8-58	American	4–3	Memorial Stadium, Balt
7-11-39	American	3–1	Yankee Stadium, NY	7-7-59	National	5–4	Forbes Field, Pitt
7-10-40	National	4–0	Sportsman's Park, StL	8-3-59	American	5–3	Memorial Coliseum, LA
7-8-41	American	7–5	Briggs Stadium, Det	7-11-60	National	5–3	Municipal Stadium, KC
7-6-42	American	3–1	Polo Grounds, NY	7-13-60	National	6–0	Yankee Stadium, NY
7-13-43	American	5–3	Shibe Park, Phil	7-11-61	National	5–4	Candlestick Park, SF
7-11-44	National	7–1	Forbes Field, Pitt	7-31-61	Tie*	1–1	Fenway Park, Bos
1945	No game due to wartime travel restrictions.			7-10-62	National	3–1	D.C. Stadium, Wash
7-9-46	American	12–0	Fenway Park, Bos	7-30-62	American	9–4	Wrigley Field, Chi
7-8-47	American	2–1	Wrigley Field, Chi	7-9-63	National	5–3	Municipal Stadium, Clev
7-13-48	American	5–2	Sportsman's Park, StL	7-7-64	National	7–4	Shea Stadium, NY
7-12-49	American	11–7	Ebbets Field, Bklyn	7-13-65	National	6–5	Metro. Stadium, Minn
7-11-50	National	4–3	Comiskey Park, Chi	7-12-66	National	2–1	Busch Stadium, StL
7-10-51	National	8–3	Briggs Stadium, Det	7-11-67	National	2–1	Anaheim Stadium, Cal
7-8-52	National	3–2	Shibe Park, Phil	7-9-68	National	1–0	Astrodome, Hou

*Game called because of rain after nine innings.

Results (Cont.)

Date	Winner	Score	Site	Date	Winner	Score	Site
7-23-69	National	9–3	R.F.K. Stadium, Wash.	7-12-88	American	2–1	Riverfront Stadium, Cin
7-14-70	National	5–4	Riverfront Stadium, Cin	7-11-89	American	5–3	Anaheim Stadium, Cal
7-13-71	American	6–4	Tiger Stadium, Det	7-10-90	American	2–0	Wrigley Field, Chi
7-25-72	National	4–3	Atlanta Stadium, Atl	7-9-91	American	4–2	SkyDome, Tor
7-24-73	National	7–1	Royals Stadium, KC	7-14-92	American	13–6	Jack Murphy Stadium, SD
7-23-74	National	7–2	Three Rivers Stadium, Pitt	7-13-93	American	9–3	Camden Yards, Balt
7-15-75	National	6–3	County Stadium, Mil	7-12-94	National	8–7	Three Rivers Stadium, Pitt
7-13-76	National	7–1	Veterans Stadium, Phil	7-11-95	National	3–2	The Ballpark in
7-19-77	National	7–5	Yankee Stadium, NY				Arlington, Tex
7-11-78	National	7–3	Jack Murphy Stadium, SD	7-9-96	National	6–0	Veterans Stadium, Phil
7-17-79	National	7–6	Kingdome, Sea	7-8-97	American	3–1	Jacobs Field, Clev
7-8-80	National	4–2	Dodger Stadium, LA	7-7-98	American	13–8	Coors Field, Col
8-9-81	National	5–4	Municipal Stadium, Clev	7-13-99	American	4–1	Fenway Park, Bos
7-13-82	National	4–1	Olympic Stadium, Mtl	7-11-00	American	6–3	Turner Field, Atl
7-6-83	American	13–3	Comiskey Park, Chi	7-10-01	American	4–1	Safeco Field, Sea
7-10-84	National	3–1	Candlestick Park, SF	7-9-02	Tie (11 inn)	7–7	Miller Park, Milwaukee
7-16-85	National	6–1	Metrodome, Minn	7-15-03	American	7–6	Comiskey Park, Chicago
7-15-86	American	3–2	Astrodome, Hou	7-13-04	American	9–4	Minute Maid Park, Hou
7-14-87	National	2–0	Oakland Coliseum, Oak	7-12-05	American	7-5	Comerica Park, Det

Most Valuable Players

1962	Maury Wills, LA	NL	1976	George Foster, Cin	NL	1992	Ken Griffey Jr., Sea	AL
	Leon Wagner, LA	AL	1977	Don Sutton, LA	NL	1993	Kirby Puckett, Minn	AL
1963	Willie Mays, SF	NL	1978	Steve Garvey, LA	NL	1994	Fred McGriff, Atl	NL
1964	Johnny Callison, Phil	NL	1979	Dave Parker, Pitt	NL	1995	Jeff Conine, Fla	NL
1965	Juan Marichal, SF	NL	1980	Ken Griffey, Cin	NL	1996	Mike Piazza, LA	NL
1966	Brooks Robinson, Balt	AL	1981	Gary Carter, Mtl	NL	1997	Sandy Alomar, Clev	AL
1967	Tony Perez, Cin	NL	1982	Dave Concepcion, Cin	NL	1998	Roberto Alomar, Balt	AL
1968	Willie Mays, SF	NL	1983	Fred Lynn, Calif	AL	1999	Pedro Martinez, Bos	AL
1969	Willie McCovey, SF	NL	1984	Gary Carter, Mtl	NL	2000	Derek Jeter, NY	AL
1970	Carl Yastrzemski, Bos	AL	1985	LaMarr Hoyt, SD	NL	2001	Cal Ripken Jr., Balt	AL
1971	Frank Robinson, Balt	AL	1986	Roger Clemens, Bos	AL	2002	None selected	
1972	Joe Morgan, Cin	NL	1987	Tim Raines, Mtl	NL	2003	Garret Anderson, Ana	AL
1973	Bobby Bonds, SF	NL	1988	Terry Steinbach, Oak	AL	2004	Alfonso Soriano, Tex	AL
1974	Steve Garvey, LA	NL	1989	Bo Jackson, KC	AL	2005	Miguel Tejada, Balt	AL
1975	Bill Madlock, Chi	NL	1990	Julio Franco, Tex	AL			
	Jon Matlack, NY	NL	1991	Cal Ripken Jr., Balt	AL			

The Regular Season

Most Valuable Players

NATIONAL LEAGUE

Year	Name and Team	Position	Noteworthy
1911	Wildfire Schulte, Chi	Outfield	21 HR†, 121 RBI†, .300
1912	*Larry Doyle, NY	Second base	10 HR, 90 RBI, .330
1913	Jake Daubert, Bklyn	First base	52 RBI, .350†
1914	*Johnny Evers, Bos	Second base	FA .976†, .279
1915–23	No selection		
1924	Dazzy Vance, StL	Pitcher	28†–6, 2.16 ERA†, 262 K†
1925	Rogers Hornsby, StL	Second base, Manager	39 HR†, 143 RBI†, .403†
1926	*Bob O'Farrell, StL	Catcher	7 HR, 68 RBI, .293
1927	*Paul Waner, Pitt	Outfield	237 hits†, 131 RBI†, .380†
1928	*Jim Bottomley, StL	First base	31 HR†, 136 RBI†, .325
1929	*Rogers Hornsby, Chi	Second base	39 HR, 149 RBI, 156 runs†, .380
1930	No selection		
1931	*Frankie Frisch, StL	Second base	4 HR, 82 RBI, 28 SB†, .311
1932	Chuck Klein, Phil	Outfield	38 HR†, 137 RBI, 226 hits†, .348
1933	*Carl Hubbell, NY	Pitcher	23†–12, 1.66 ERA†, 10 SO†
1934	*Dizzy Dean, StL	Pitcher	30†–7, 2.66 ERA, 195 K†
1935	*Gabby Hartnett, Chi	Catcher	13 HR, 91 RBI, .344
1936	*Carl Hubbell, NY	Pitcher	26†–6, 2.31 ERA†
1937	Joe Medwick, StL	Outfield	31 HR‡, 154 RBI†, 111 runs†, .374†
1938	Ernie Lombardi, Cin	Catcher	19 HR, 95 RBI, .342†
1939	*Bucky Walters, Cin	Pitcher	27†–11, 2.29 ERA†, 137 K‡
1940	*Frank McCormick, Cin	First base	19 HR, 127 RBI, 191 hits†, .309
1941	*Dolph Camilli, Bklyn	First base	34 HR†, 120 RBI†, .285

*Played for pennant or, after 1968, division winner. †Led league. ‡Tied for league lead.

Most Valuable Players (Cont.)
NATIONAL LEAGUE (Cont.)

Year	Name and Team	Position	Noteworthy
1942	*Mort Cooper, StL	Pitcher	22†–7, 1.78 ERA†, 10 SO†
1943	*Stan Musial, StL	Outfield	13 HR, 81 RBI, 220 hits†, .357†
1944	*Marty Marion, StL	Shortstop	FA .972†, 63 RBI
1945	*Phil Cavarretta, Chi	First base	6 HR, 97 RBI, .355†
1946	*Stan Musial, StL	First base, Outfield	103 RBI, 124 runs†, 228 hits†, .365†
1947	Bob Elliott, Bos	Third base	22 HR, 113 RBI, .317
1948	Stan Musial, StL	Outfield	39 HR, 131 RBI†, .376†
1949	*Jackie Robinson, Bklyn	Second base	16 HR, 124 RBI, 37 SB†, .342†
1950	*Jim Konstanty, Phil	Pitcher	16–7, 22 saves†, 2.66 ERA
1951	Roy Campanella, Bklyn	Catcher	33 HR, 108 RBI, .325
1952	Hank Sauer, Chi	Outfield	37 HR‡, 121 RBI†, .270
1953	*Roy Campanella, Bklyn	Catcher	41 HR, 142 RBI†, .312
1954	*Willie Mays, NY	Outfield	41 HR, 110 RBI, 13 3B†, .345†
1955	*Roy Campanella, Bklyn	Catcher	32 HR, 107 RBI, .318
1956	*Don Newcombe, Bklyn	Pitcher	27†–7, 3.06 ERA
1957	*Hank Aaron, Mil	Outfield	44 HR†, 132 RBI†, .322
1958	Ernie Banks, Chi	Shortstop	47 HR†, 129 RBI†, .313
1959	Ernie Banks, Chi	Shortstop	45 HR, 143 RBI†, .304
1960	*Dick Groat, Pitt	Shortstop	2 HR, 50 RBI, .325†
1961	*Frank Robinson, Cin	Outfield	37 HR, 124 RBI, .323
1962	Maury Wills, LA	Shortstop	104 SB†, 208 hits, .299, GG
1963	*Sandy Koufax, LA	Pitcher	25‡–5, 1.88 ERA†, 306 K†
1964	*Ken Boyer, StL	Third Base	24 HR, 119 RBI†, .295
1965	Willie Mays, SF	Outfield	52 HR†, 112 RBI, .317, GG
1966	Roberto Clemente, Pitt	Outfield	29 HR, 119 RBI, 202 hits, .317, GG
1967	*Orlando Cepeda, StL	First base	25 HR, 111 RBI†, .325
1968	*Bob Gibson, StL	Pitcher	22–9, 1.12 ERA†, 268 K†, 13 SO†, GG
1969	Willie McCovey, SF	First base	45 HR†, 126 RBI†, .320
1970	*Johnny Bench, Cin	Catcher	45 HR†, 148 RBI†, .293, GG
1971	Joe Torre, StL	Third base	24 HR, 137 RBI†, .363†
1972	*Johnny Bench, Cin	Catcher	40 HR†, 125 RBI†, .270, GG
1973	*Pete Rose, Cin	Outfield	5 HR, 64 RBI, .338†, 230 hits†
1974	*Steve Garvey, LA	First base	21 HR, 111 RBI, 200 hits, .312, GG
1975	*Joe Morgan, Cin	Second base	17 HR, 94 RBI, 67 SB, .327, GG
1976	*Joe Morgan, Cin	Second base	27 HR, 111 RBI, 60 SB, .320, GG
1977	George Foster, Cin	Outfield	52 HR†, 149 RBI†, .320
1978	Dave Parker, Pitt	Outfield	30 HR, 117 RBI, .334†, GG
1979	Keith Hernandez, StL	First base	11 HR, 105 RBI, 210 hits, .344†, GG
	*Willie Stargell, Pitt	First base	32 HR, 82 RBI, .281
1980	*Mike Schmidt, Phil	Third base	48 HR†, 121 RBI†, .286, GG
1981	Mike Schmidt, Phil	Third base	31 HR†, 91 RBI†, 78 runs†, .316, GG
1982	*Dale Murphy, Atl	Outfield	36 HR, 109 RBI‡, .281, GG
1983	Dale Murphy, Atl	Outfield	36 HR, 121 RBI†, .302, GG
1984	*Ryne Sandberg, Chi	Second base	19 HR, 84 RBI, 114 runs†, .314, GG
1985	*Willie McGee, StL	Outfield	10 HR, 82 RBI, 18 3B†, .353†, GG
1986	Mike Schmidt, Phil	Third base	37 HR†, 119 RBI†, .290, GG
1987	Andre Dawson, Chi	Outfield	49 HR†, 137 RBI†, .287, GG
1988	*Kirk Gibson, LA	Outfield	25 HR, 76 RBI, 106 runs, .290
1989	*Kevin Mitchell, SF	Outfield	47 HR†, 125 RBI†, .291
1990	*Barry Bonds, Pitt	Outfield	33 HR, 114 RBI, .301
1991	*Terry Pendleton, Atl	Third base	23 HR, 86 RBI, .319†
1992	Barry Bonds, Pitt	Outfield	34 HR, 103 RBI, .311
1993	Barry Bonds, SF	Outfield	46 HR†, 123 RBI†, .336
1994	Jeff Bagwell, Hou	First base	39 HR, 116 RBI†, .368
1995	*Barry Larkin, Cin	Shortstop	15 HR, 66 RBI, 51 SB, .319
1996	*Ken Caminiti, SD	Third base	40 HR, 130 RBI, .326
1997	Larry Walker, Col	Outfield	49 HR†, 130 RBI, .452 OBA†, .366, GG
1998	Sammy Sosa, Chi	Outfield	66 HR, 158 RBI†, 134 runs†, 416 TB†, .308
1999	*Chipper Jones, Atl	Third Base	45 HR, 110 RBI, 116 runs, .319
2000	*Jeff Kent, SF	Second Base	33 HR, 125 RBI, 114 runs, .334
2001	Barry Bonds, SF	Outfield	73 HR†, 137 RBI. 177 BB†, .328, .863 SLG†
2002	Barry Bonds, SF	Outfield	46 HR, 110 RBI, .582 OBP†, .370
2003	Barry Bonds, SF	Outfield	45 HR, .341 avg, .529 OBP†, .749 SLG†
2004	Barry Bonds, SF	Outfield	45HR, 101 RBI, .609 OBP, .812 SLG

*Played for pennant or, after 1968, division winner. †Led league. ‡Tied for league lead.

Most Valuable Players (Cont.)

AMERICAN LEAGUE

Year	Name and Team	Position	Noteworthy
1911	Ty Cobb, Det	Outfield	8 HR, 144 RBI†, 24 3B†, .420†
1912	*Tris Speaker, Bos	Outfield	10 HR‡, 98 RBI, 53 2B†, .383
1913	Walter Johnson, Wash	Pitcher	36†–7, 1.09 ERA†, 11 SO†, 243 K†
1914	*Eddie Collins, Phil	Second base	2 HR, 85 RBI, 122 runs†, .344
1915–21	No selection		
1922	George Sisler, StL	First base	8 HR, 105 RBI, 246 hits†, .420†
1923	*Babe Ruth, NY	Outfield	41 HR‡, 131 RBI‡, .393
1924	*Walter Johnson, Wash	Pitcher	23†–7, 2.72 ERA†, 158 K†
1925	*Roger Peckinpaugh, Wash	Shortstop	4 HR, 64 RBI, .294
1926	George Burns, Clev	First base	114 RBI, 216 hits†, 64 2B†, .358
1927	*Lou Gehrig, NY	First base	47 HR, 175 RBI†, 52 2B†, .373
1928	Mickey Cochrane, Phil	Catcher	10 HR, 57 RBI, .293
1929	No selection		
1930	No selection		
1931	*Lefty Grove, Phil	Pitcher	31†–4, 2.06 ERA†, 175 K†
1932	Jimmie Foxx, Phil	First base	58 HR‡, 169 RBI‡, 151 runs†, .364
1933	Jimmie Foxx, Phil	First base	48 HR‡, 163 RBI‡, .356†
1934	*Mickey Cochrane, Det	Catcher	2 HR, 76 RBI, .320
1935	*Hank Greenberg, Det	First base	36 HR‡, 170 RBI‡, 203 hits, .328
1936	*Lou Gehrig, NY	First base	49 HR‡, 152 RBI, 167 runs†, .354
1937	Charlie Gehringer, Det	Second base	14 HR, 96 RBI, 133 runs, .371†
1938	Jimmie Foxx, Bos	First base	50 HR, 175 RBI†, .349†
1939	*Joe DiMaggio, NY	Outfield	30 HR, 126 RBI, .381†
1940	*Hank Greenberg, Det	Outfield	41 HR†, 150 RBI†, 50 2B†, .340
1941	*Joe DiMaggio, NY	Outfield	30 HR, 125 RBI†, .357
1942	*Joe Gordon, NY	Second base	18 HR, 103 RBI, .322
1943	*Spud Chandler, NY	Pitcher	20†–4, 1.64 ERA†, 5 SO‡
1944	Hal Newhouser, Det	Pitcher	29†–9, 2.22 ERA†, 187 K†
1945	*Hal Newhouser, Det	Pitcher	25†–9, 1.81 ERA†, 8 SO†, 212 K†
1946	*Ted Williams, Bos	Outfield	38 HR, 123 RBI, 142 runs†, .342
1947	*Joe DiMaggio, NY	Outfield	20 HR, 97 RBI, .315
1948	*Lou Boudreau, Clev	Shortstop	18 HR, 106 RBI, .355
1949	Ted Williams, Bos	Outfield	43 HR†, 159 RBI‡, 150 runs†, .343
1950	*Phil Rizzuto, NY	Shortstop	125 runs, 200 hits, .324
1951	*Yogi Berra, NY	Catcher	27 HR, 88 RBI, .294
1952	Bobby Shantz, Phil	Pitcher	24†–7, 2.48 ERA
1953	Al Rosen, Clev	Third base	43 HR†, 145 RBI†, 115 runs†, .336
1954	Yogi Berra, NY	Catcher	22 HR, 125 RBI, .307
1955	*Yogi Berra, NY	Catcher	27 HR, 108 RBI, .272
1956	*Mickey Mantle, NY	Outfield	52 HR†, 130 RBI†, 132 runs†, .353†
1957	*Mickey Mantle, NY	Outfield	34 HR, 94 RBI, 121 runs†, .365
1958	Jackie Jensen, Bos	Outfield	35 HR, 122 RBI†, .286
1959	*Nellie Fox, Chi	Second base	2 HR, 70 RBI, .306, GG
1960	*Roger Maris, NY	Outfield	39 HR, 112 RBI†, .283, GG
1961	*Roger Maris, NY	Outfield	61 HR†, 142 RBI†, .269
1962	*Mickey Mantle, NY	Outfield	30 HR, 89 RBI, .321, GG
1963	*Elston Howard, NY	Catcher	28 HR, 85 RBI, .287, GG
1964	Brooks Robinson, Balt	Third base	28 HR, 118 RBI†, .317, GG
1965	*Zoilo Versalles, Minn	Shortstop	126 runs†, 45 2B†, 12 3B‡, GG
1966	*Frank Robinson, Balt	Outfield	49 HR†, 122 RBI†, 122 runs†, .316†
1967	*Carl Yastrzemski, Bos	Outfield	44 HR†, 121 RBI†, 112 runs†, .326†, GG
1968	*Denny McLain, Det	Pitcher	31†–6, 1.96 ERA, 280 K
1969	*Harmon Killebrew, Minn	Third base, First base	49 HR†, 140 RBI†, .276
1970	*Boog Powell, Balt	First base	35 HR, 114 RBI, .297
1971	*Vida Blue, Oak	Pitcher	24–8, 1.82 ERA†, 8 SO†, 301 K
1972	Dick Allen, Chi	First base	37 HR†, 113 RBI†, .308
1973	*Reggie Jackson, Oak	Outfield	32 HR†, 117 RBI†, 99 runs†, .293
1974	Jeff Burroughs, Tex	Outfield	25 HR, 118 RBI†, .301
1975	*Fred Lynn, Bos	Outfield	21 HR, 105 RBI, 103 runs†, .331, GG
1976	*Thurman Munson, NY	Catcher	17 HR, 105 RBI, .302
1977	Rod Carew, Minn	First base	100 RBI, 128 runs†, 239 hits†, .388†
1978	Jim Rice, Bos	Outfield, DH	46 HR†, 139 RBI†, 213 hits†, .315
1979	*Don Baylor, Calif	Outfield, DH	36 HR, 139 RBI†, 120 runs†, .296
1980	*George Brett, KC	Third base	24 HR, 118 RBI, .390†
1981	*Rollie Fingers, Mil	Pitcher	6–3, 28 saves†, 1.04 ERA
1982	*Robin Yount, Mil	Shortstop	29 HR, 114 RBI, 210 hits†, .331, GG

Most Valuable Players *(Cont.)*
AMERICAN LEAGUE *(Cont.)*

Year	Name and Team	Position	Noteworthy
1983	.*Cal Ripken Jr., Balt	Shortstop	27 HR, 102 RBI, 121 runs†, 211 hits†, .318
1984	.*Willie Hernandez, Det	Pitcher	9–3, 32 saves, 1.92 ERA
1985	.Don Mattingly, NY	First base	35 HR, 145 RBI†, 48 2B†, .324, GG
1986	.*Roger Clemens, Bos	Pitcher	24†–4, 2.48 ERA†, 238 K
1987	.George Bell, Tor	Outfield	47 HR, 134 RBI†, .308
1988	.*Jose Canseco, Oak	Outfield	42 HR†, 124 RBI†, 40 SB, .307
1989	.Robin Yount, Mil	Outfield	21 HR, 103 RBI, 101 runs, .318
1990	.*Rickey Henderson, Oak	Outfield	28 HR, 119 runs†, 65 SB†, .325
1991	.Cal Ripken Jr., Balt	Shortstop	34 HR, 114 RBI, .323
1992	.Dennis Eckersley, Oak	Pitcher	7–1, 1.91 ERA, 51 saves
1993	.Frank Thomas, Chi	First base	41 HR, 128 RBI, .317
1994	.Frank Thomas, Chi	First base	38 HR, 101 RBI, .353
1995	.*Mo Vaughn, Bos	First base	39 HR, 126 RBI, .300
1996	.*Juan Gonzalez, Tex	Outfield	47 HR, 144 RBI, .314
1997	.*Ken Griffey Jr., Sea	Outfield	56 HR†, 125 runs†, 393 TB†, 147 RBI†, .304
1998	.*Juan Gonzalez, Tex	Outfield	45 HR, 157 RBI†, 50 2B†, .318
1999	.*Ivan Rodriguez, Tex	Catcher	35 HR, 113 RBI, 116 runs, .332, GG
2000	.*Jason Giambi, Oak	First Base	43 HR, 137 RBI, .333
2001	.Ichiro Suzuki, Sea	Outfield	.350†, 242 H†, 127 R, 56 SB†
2002	.*Miguel Tejada, Oak	Shortstop	34 HR, 131 RBI, .308
2003	.Alex Rodriguez, Tex	Shortstop	47 HR†, 118 RBI, .600 SLG†
2004	.Vladamir Guerrero, Ana	Outfield	39 HR, 126 RBI, .598 SLG

*Played for pennant or, after 1968, division winner. †Led league. ‡Tied for league lead.

Notes: 2B=doubles; 3B=triples; FA=fielding average; GG=won Gold Glove, award begun in 1957; K=strikeouts; O=shutouts; SB=stolen bases; TB=total bases.

Rookies of the Year

NATIONAL LEAGUE

1947*	Jackie Robinson, Bklyn (1B)
1948*	Alvin Dark, Bos (SS)
1949	Don Newcombe, Bklyn (P)
1950	Sam Jethroe, Bos (OF)
1951	Willie Mays, NY (OF)
1952	Joe Black, Bklyn (P)
1953	Junior Gilliam, Bklyn (2B)
1954	Wally Moon, StL (OF)
1955	Bill Virdon, StL (OF)
1956	Frank Robinson, Cin (OF)
1957	Jack Sanford, Phil (P)
1958	Orlando Cepeda, SF (1B)
1959	Willie McCovey, SF (1B)
1960	Frank Howard, LA (OF)
1961	Billy Williams, Chi (OF)
1962	Ken Hubbs, Chi (2B)
1963	Pete Rose, Cin (2B)
1964	Dick Allen, Phil (3B)
1965	Jim Lefebvre, LA (2B)
1966	Tommy Helms, Cin (2B)
1967	Tom Seaver, NY (P)
1968	Johnny Bench, Cin (C)
1969	Ted Sizemore, LA (2B)
1970	Carl Morton, Mtl(P)
1971	Earl Williams, Atl (C)
1972	Jon Matlack, NY (P)
1973	Gary Matthews, SF (OF)
1974	Bake McBride, StL (OF)
1975	John Montefusco, SF (P)
1976	Pat Zachry, Cin (P)
	Butch Metzger, SD (P)
1977	Andre Dawson, Mtl (OF)
1978	Bob Horner, Atl (3B)
1979	Rick Sutcliffe, LA (P)
1980	Steve Howe, LA (P)
1981	Fernando Valenzuela, LA (P)
1982	Steve Sax, LA (2B)
1983	Darryl Strawberry, NY (OF)
1984	Dwight Gooden, NY (P)

AMERICAN LEAGUE

1949	Roy Sievers, StL (OF)
1950	Walt Dropo, Bos (1B)
1951	Gil McDougald, NY (3B)
1952	Harry Byrd, Phil (P)
1953	Harvey Kuenn, Det (SS)
1954	Bob Grim, NY (P)
1955	Herb Score, Clev (P)
1956	Luis Aparicio, Chi (SS)
1957	Tony Kubek, NY (OF, SS)
1958	Albie Pearson, Wash (OF)
1959	Bob Allison, Wash (OF)
1960	Ron Hansen, Balt (SS)
1961	Don Schwall, Bos (P)
1962	Tom Tresh, NY (SS)
1963	Gary Peters, Chi (P)
1964	Tony Oliva, Minn (OF)
1965	Curt Blefary, Balt (OF)
1966	Tommie Agee, Chi (OF)
1967	Rod Carew, Minn (2B)
1968	Stan Bahnsen, NY (P)
1969	Lou Piniella, KC (OF)
1970	Thurman Munson, NY (C)
1971	Chris Chambliss, Clev (1B)
1972	Carlton Fisk, Bos (C)
1973	Al Bumbry, Balt (OF)
1974	Mike Hargrove, Tex (1B)
1975	Fred Lynn, Bos (OF)
1976	Mark Fidrych, Det (P)
1977	Eddie Murray, Balt (DH)
1978	Lou Whitaker, Det (2B)
1979	Alfredo Griffin, Tor (SS)
	John Castino, Minn (3B)
1980	Joe Charboneau, Clev (OF)
1981	Dave Righetti, NY (P)
1982	Cal Ripken Jr., Balt (SS)
1983	Ron Kittle, Chi (OF)
1984	Alvin Davis, Sea (1B)

*Just one selection for both leagues.

Rookies of the Year *(Cont.)*

NATIONAL LEAGUE *(Cont.)*	AMERICAN LEAGUE *(Cont.)*
1985 ....Vince Coleman, StL (OF)	1985 ....Ozzie Guillen, Chi (SS)
1986 ....Todd Worrell, StL (P)	1986 ....Jose Canseco, Oak (OF)
1987 ....Benito Santiago, SD (C)	1987 ....Mark McGwire, Oak (1B)
1988 ....Chris Sabo, Cin (3B)	1988 ....Walt Weiss, Oak (SS)
1989 ....Jerome Walton, Chi (OF)	1989 ....Gregg Olson, Balt (P)
1990 ....Dave Justice, Atl (OF)	1990 ....Sandy Alomar Jr, Clev (C)
1991 ....Jeff Bagwell, Hou (3B)	1991 ....Chuck Knoblauch, Minn (2B)
1992 ....Eric Karros, LA (1B)	1992 ....Pat Listach, Mil (SS)
1993 ....Mike Piazza, LA (C)	1993 ....Tim Salmon, Calif (OF)
1994 ....Raul Mondesi, LA (OF)	1994 ....Bob Hamelin, KC (DH)
1995 ....Hideo Nomo, LA (P)	1995 ....Marty Cordova, Minn (OF)
1996 ....Todd Hollandsworth, LA (OF)	1996 ....Derek Jeter, NY (SS)
1997 ....Scott Rolen, Phil (3B)	1997 ....Nomar Garciaparra, Bos (SS)
1998 ....Kerry Wood, Chi (P)	1998 ....Ben Grieve, Oak (OF)
1999 ....Scott Williamson, Cin (P)	1999 ....Carlos Beltran, KC (OF)
2000 ....Rafael Furcal, Atl (SS)	2000 ....Kazuhiro Sasaki, Sea (P)
2001 ....Albert Pujols, StL (OF)	2001 ....Ichiro Suzuki, Sea (OF)
2002 ....Jason Jennings, Col (P)	2002 ....Eric Hinske, Tor (3B)
2003 ....Dontrelle Willis, Fla (P)	2003 ....Angel Berroa, KC (SS)
2004 ....Jason Bay, Pit (OF)	2004 ....Bobby Crosby, Oak (SS)

Cy Young Award

Year	W–L	Sv	ERA	Year	W–L	Sv	ERA
1956.....*Don Newcombe, Bklyn (NL)	27–7	0	3.06	1962.....Don Drysdale, LA (NL)	25–9	1	2.83
1957.....Warren Spahn, Mil (NL)	21–11	3	2.69	1963.....*Sandy Koufax, LA (NL)	25–5	0	1.88
1958.....Bob Turley, NY (AL)	21–7	1	2.97	1964.....Dean Chance, LA (AL)	20–9	4	1.65
1959.....Early Wynn, Chi (AL)	22–10	0	3.17	1965.....Sandy Koufax, LA (NL)	26–8	2	2.04
1960.....Vernon Law, Pitt (NL)	20–9	0	3.08	1966.....Sandy Koufax, LA (NL)	27–9	0	1.73
1961.....Whitey Ford, NY (AL)	25–4	0	3.21				

NATIONAL LEAGUE

Year	W–L	Sv	ERA
1967 ......Mike McCormick, SF	22–10	0	2.85
1968 ......*Bob Gibson, StL	22–9	0	1.12
1969 ......Tom Seaver, NY	25–7	0	2.21
1970 ......Bob Gibson, StL	23–7	0	3.12
1971 ......Ferguson Jenkins, Chi	24–13	0	2.77
1972 ......Steve Carlton, Phil	27–10	0	1.97
1973 ......Tom Seaver, NY	19–10	0	2.08
1974 ......Mike Marshall, LA	15–12	21	2.42
1975 ......Tom Seaver, NY	22–9	0	2.38
1976 ......Randy Jones, SD	22–14	0	2.74
1977 ......Steve Carlton, Phil	23–10	0	2.64
1978 ......Gaylord Perry, SD	21–6	0	2.72
1979 ......Bruce Sutter, Chi	6–6	37	2.23
1980 ......Steve Carlton, Phil	24–9	0	2.34
1981 ......Fernando Valenzuela, LA	13–7	0	2.48
1982 ......Steve Carlton, Phil	23–11	0	3.10
1983 ......John Denny, Phil	19–6	0	2.37
1984 ......†Rick Sutcliffe, Chi	16–1	0	2.69
1985 ......Dwight Gooden, NY	24–4	0	1.53
1986 ......Mike Scott, Hou	18–10	0	2.22
1987 ......Steve Bedrosian, Phil	5–3	40	2.83
1988 ......Orel Hershiser, LA	23–8	1	2.26
1989 ......Mark Davis, SD	4–3	44	1.85
1990 ......Doug Drabek, Pitt	22–6	0	2.76
1991 ......Tom Glavine, Atl	20–11	0	2.55
1992 ......Greg Maddux, Chi	20–11	0	2.18
1993 ......Greg Maddux, Atl	20–10	0	2.36
1994 ......Greg Maddux, Atl	16–6	0	1.56
1995 ......Greg Maddux, Atl	19–2	0	1.63
1996 ......John Smoltz, Atl	24–8	0	2.94
1997 ......Pedro Martinez, Mtl	17–8	0	1.90
1998 ......Tom Glavine, Atl	20–6	0	2.47
1999 ......Randy Johnson, Ariz	17–9	0	2.48
2000 ......Randy Johnson, Ariz	19–7	0	2.64
2001 ......Randy Johnson, Ariz	21–6	0	2.49
2002 ......Randy Johnson, Ariz	24–5	0	2.32
2003 ......Eric Gagne, LA	2–3	55	1.20
2004 ......Roger Clemens, Hou	18–4	0	2.98

AMERICAN LEAGUE

Year	W–L	Sv	ERA
1967 ......Jim Lonborg, Bos	22–9	0	3.16
1968 ......*Denny McLain, Det	31–6	0	1.96
1969 ......Denny McLain, Det	24–9	0	2.80
............Mike Cuellar, Balt	23–11	0	2.38
1970 ......Jim Perry, Minn	24–12	0	3.03
1971 ......*Vida Blue, Oak	24–8	0	1.82
1972 ......Gaylord Perry, Clev	24–16	1	1.92
1973 ......Jim Palmer, Balt	22–9	1	2.40
1974 ......Catfish Hunter, Oak	25–12	0	2.49
1975 ......Jim Palmer, Balt	23–11	1	2.09
1976 ......Jim Palmer, Balt	22–13	0	2.51
1977 ......Sparky Lyle, NY	13–5	26	2.17
1978 ......Ron Guidry, NY	25–3	0	1.74
1979 ......Mike Flanagan, Balt	23–9	0	3.08
1980 ......Steve Stone, Balt	25–7	0	3.23
1981 ......*Rollie Fingers, Mil	6–3	28	1.04
1982 ......Pete Vuckovich, Mil	18–6	0	3.34
1983 ......LaMarr Hoyt, Chi	24–10	0	3.66
1984 ......*Willie Hernandez, Det	9–3	32	1.92
1985 ......Bret Saberhagen, KC	20–6	0	2.87
1986 ......*Roger Clemens, Bos	24–4	0	2.48
1987 ......Roger Clemens, Bos	20–9	0	2.97
1988 ......Frank Viola, Minn	24–7	0	2.64
1989 ......Bret Saberhagen, KC	23–6	0	2.16
1990 ......Bob Welch, Oak	27–6	0	2.95
1991 ......Roger Clemens, Bos	18–10	0	2.62
1992 ......*Dennis Eckersley, Oak	7–1	51	1.91
1993 ......Jack McDowell, Chi	22–10	0	3.37
1994 ......David Cone, KC	16–4	0	2.94
1995 ......Randy Johnson, Sea	18–2	0	2.48
1996 ......Pat Hentgen, Tor	20–10	0	3.22
1997 ......Roger Clemens, Tor	21–7	0	2.05
1998 ......Roger Clemens, Tor	20–6	0	2.65
1999 ......Pedro Martinez, Bos	23–4	0	1.55
2000 ......Pedro Martinez, Bos	18–6	0	1.74
2001 ......Roger Clemens, NY	20–3	0	3.51
2002 ......Barry Zito, Oak	23–5	0	2.75
2003 ......Roy Halladay, Tor	22–7	0	3.25
2004 ......Johan Santana, Min	20–6	0	2.61

*Won the MVP and Cy Young awards in the same season.
†NL games only. Sutcliffe pitched 15 games with Cleveland before being traded to the Cubs.

Career Individual Batting

GAMES

Pete Rose	3562
Carl Yastrzemski	3308
Hank Aaron	3298
Rickey Henderson	3081
Ty Cobb	3034
Stan Musial	3026
Eddie Murray	3026
Cal Ripken Jr.	3001
Willie Mays	2992
Dave Winfield	2973
Rusty Staub	2951
Brooks Robinson	2896
Robin Yount	2856
Al Kaline	2834
*Rafael Palmeiro	2831
Harold Baines	2830
Eddie Collins	2826
Reggie Jackson	2820
Frank Robinson	2808
Honus Wagner	2792

AT BATS

Pete Rose	14053
Hank Aaron	12364
Carl Yastrzemski	11988
Cal Ripken Jr.	11551
Ty Cobb	11429
Eddie Murray	11336
Robin Yount	11008
Dave Winfield	11003
Stan Musial	10972
Rickey Henderson	10961
Willie Mays	10881
Paul Molitor	10835
Brooks Robinson	10654
*Rafael Palmeiro	10472
Honus Wagner	10430
George Brett	10349
Lou Brock	10332
Cap Anson	10278
Luis Aparicio	10230
Tris Speaker	10208

HOME RUNS

Hank Aaron	755
Babe Ruth	714
*Barry Bonds	708
Willie Mays	660
*Sammy Sosa	588
Frank Robinson	586
Mark McGwire	583
Harmon Killebrew	573
*Rafael Palmeiro	569
Reggie Jackson	563
Mike Schmidt	548
*Ken Griffey Jr.	536
Mickey Mantle	536
Jimmie Foxx	534
Ted Williams	521
Willie McCovey	521
Eddie Mathews	512
Ernie Banks	512
Mel Ott	511
Eddie Murray	504

* Active in 2005.

HITS

Pete Rose	4256
Ty Cobb	4189
Hank Aaron	3771
Stan Musial	3630
Tris Speaker	3515
Carl Yastrzemski	3419
Cap Anson	3418
Honus Wagner	3415
Paul Molitor	3319
Eddie Collins	3313
Willie Mays	3283
Eddie Murray	3255
Nap Lajoie	3251
Cal Ripken Jr.	3184
George Brett	3154
Paul Waner	3152
Robin Yount	3142
Tony Gwynn	3141
Dave Winfield	3110
Rickey Henderson	3055

BATTING AVERAGE (5,000 AB)

Ty Cobb	.367
Rogers Hornsby	.358
Ed Delahanty	.346
Tris Speaker	.345
Ted Williams	.344
Billy Hamilton	.344
Dan Brouthers	.342
Jesse Burkett	.342
Babe Ruth	.342
Harry Heilmann	.342
Willie Keeler	.341
Bill Terry	.341
George Sisler	.340
Lou Gehrig	.340
Jesse Burkett	.338
Tony Gwynn	.338
Nap Lajoie	.338
Al Simmons	.334
Paul Waner	.333
Eddie Collins	.333

RUNS

Rickey Henderson	2295
Ty Cobb	2246
Babe Ruth	2174
Hank Aaron	2174
Pete Rose	2165
*Barry Bonds	2078
Willie Mays	2062
Cap Anson	1996
Stan Musial	1949
Lou Gehrig	1888
Tris Speaker	1882
Mel Ott	1859
Frank Robinson	1829
Eddie Collins	1821
Carl Yastrzemski	1816
Ted Williams	1798
Paul Molitor	1782
Charlie Gehringer	1774
Jimmie Foxx	1751
Honus Wagner	1736

DOUBLES

Tris Speaker	792
Pete Rose	746
Stan Musial	725
Ty Cobb	724
George Brett	665
Nap Lajoie	657
Carl Yastrzemski	646
Honus Wagner	640
Hank Aaron	624
Paul Molitor	605
Paul Waner	605
*Craig Biggio	604
Cal Ripken Jr.	603
*Rafael Palmeiro	572
Robin Yount	585
Cap Anson	581
Wade Boggs	578
Charlie Gehringer	574
*Barry Bonds	564
Eddie Murray	560

TRIPLES

Sam Crawford	309
Ty Cobb	295
Honus Wagner	252
Jake Beckley	243
Roger Connor	233
Tris Speaker	222
Fred Clarke	220
Dan Brouthers	205
Joe Kelley	194
Paul Waner	191
Bid McPhee	188
Eddie Collins	187
Ed Delahanty	185
Sam Rice	184
Jesse Burkett	182
Edd Roush	182
Ed Konetchy	182
Buck Ewing	178
Rabbit Maranville	177
Stan Musial	177

BASES ON BALLS

*Barry Bonds	2311
Rickey Henderson	2190
Babe Ruth	2062
Ted Williams	2021
Joe Morgan	1865
Carl Yastrzemski	1845
Mickey Mantle	1733
Mel Ott	1708
Eddie Yost	1614
Darrell Evans	1605
Stan Musial	1599
Pete Rose	1566
Harmon Killebrew	1559
Lou Gehrig	1508
Mike Schmidt	1507
Eddie Collins	1499
*Frank Thomas	1466
Willie Mays	1464
Jimmie Foxx	1452
Eddie Mathews	1444

Career Individual Batting (Cont.)

RUNS BATTED IN

Hank Aaron	2297
Babe Ruth	2213
Cap Anson	2076
Lou Gehrig	1995
Stan Musial	1951
Ty Cobb	1937
Jimmie Foxx	1922
Eddie Murray	1917
Willie Mays	1903
Mel Ott	1860
*Barry Bonds	1853
Carl Yastrzemski	1844
Ted Williams	1839
*Rafael Palmeiro	1835
Dave Winfield	1833
Al Simmons	1827
Frank Robinson	1812
Honus Wagner	1732
Reggie Jackson	1702
Cal Ripken Jr.	1695

STOLEN BASES

Rickey Henderson	1406
Lou Brock	938
Billy Hamilton	912
Ty Cobb	892
Tim Raines	808
Vince Coleman	752
Eddie Collins	744
Arlie Latham	739
Max Carey	738
Honus Wagner	722
Joe Morgan	689
Willie Wilson	668
Tom Brown	657
Bert Campaneris	649
Otis Nixon	620
George Davis	616
Dummy Hoy	594
Maury Wills	586
George Van Haltren	583
Ozzie Smith	580

TOTAL BASES

Hank Aaron	6856
Stan Musial	6134
Willie Mays	6066
Ty Cobb	5854
Babe Ruth	5793
Pete Rose	5752
*Barry Bonds	5584
Carl Yastrzemski	5539
Eddie Murray	5397
*Rafael Palmeiro	5388
Frank Robinson	5373
Dave Winfield	5221
Cal Ripken Jr.	5168
Tris Speaker	5101
Lou Gehrig	5060
George Brett	5044
Mel Ott	5041
Jimmie Foxx	4956
Ted Williams	4884
Honus Wagner	4862

SLUGGING AVERAGE (5,000 AB)

Babe Ruth	.690
Ted Williams	.634
Lou Gehrig	.632
*Barry Bonds	.611
Jimmie Foxx	.609
Hank Greenberg	.605
*Manny Ramirez	.599
Mark McGwire	.588
Joe DiMaggio	.579
Rogers Hornsby	.577
*Alex Rodriguez	.577
*Frank Thomas	.568
*Larry Walker	.565
Albert Belle	.564
Johnny Mize	.562
*Jim Thome	.569
*Juan Gonzalez	.561
*Ken Griffey Jr.	.561
Stan Musial	.559
Carlos Delgado	.559

ON-BASE PERCENTAGE (5,000 AB)

Ted Williams	.483
Babe Ruth	.474
Billy Hamilton	.455
Lou Gehrig	.447
*Barry Bonds	.443
Rogers Hornsby	.434
Ty Cobb	.433
*Frank Thomas	.429
Tris Speaker	.428
Jimmie Foxx	.428
Eddie Collins	.424
Dan Brouthers	.423
Mickey Mantle	.420
Mickey Cochrane	.419
*Edgar Martinez	.418
Stan Musial	.418
Cupid Childs	.416
Jesse Burkett	.415
Wade Boggs	.415
Mel Ott	.414

STRIKEOUTS

Reggie Jackson	2597
*Sammy Sosa	2194
Andres Galarraga	2003
Jose Canseco	1942
Willie Stargell	1936
Mike Schmidt	1883
*Fred McGriff	1882
Tony Perez	1867
Dave Kingman	1816
*Jim Thome	1762
Bobby Bonds	1757
Dale Murphy	1748
Lou Brock	1730
Mickey Mantle	1710
Harmon Killebrew	1699
Chili Davis	1698
Dwight Evans	1697
Rickey Henderson	1694
Dave Winfield	1686
Gary Gaetti	1602

*Active in 2005.

The 30–30 Club (30 HR, 30 SB in single season)

Year		HR	SB	Year		HR	SB
1922	Kenny Williams, StL	39	37	1995	Sammy Sosa, ChiC	36	34
1956	Willie Mays, NYG	36	40	1996	Barry Bonds, SF	42	40
1957	Willie Mays, NYG	35	38	1996	Ellis Burks, Col	40	32
1963	Hank Aaron, Mil	44	31	1996	Barry Larkin, Cin	33	36
1969	Bobby Bonds, SF	32	45	1996	Dante Bichette, Col	31	31
1970	Tommy Harper, Mil	31	38	1997	Larry Walker, Col	49	33
1973	Bobby Bonds, SF	39	43	1997	Jeff Bagwell, Hou	43	31
1975	Bobby Bonds, NYY	32	30	1997	Raul Mondesi, LA	30	32
1977	Bobby Bonds, Cal	37	41	1997	Barry Bonds, SF	40	37
1978	Bobby Bonds, Chi/Tex	31	43	1998	Alex Rodriguez, Sea	42	46
1983	Dale Murphy, Atl	36	30	1998	Shawn Green, Tor	35	35
1987	Joe Carter, Clev	32	31	1999	Jeff Bagwell, Hou	42	30
1987	Eric Davis, Cin	37	50	1999	Raul Mondesi, LA	33	36
1987	Darryl Strawberry, NYM	39	36	2000	Preston Wilson, Fla	31	36
1987	Howard Johnson, NYM	36	32	2001	Vladimir Guerrero, Mtl	34	37
1988	Jose Canseco, Oak	42	40	2001	Jose Cruz Jr., Tor	34	32
1989	Howard Johnson, NYM	36	41	2001	Bobby Abreu, Phil	31	36
1990	Ron Gant, Atl	32	33	2002	Alfonso Soriano, NYY	39	41
1990	Barry Bonds, Pitt	33	52	2002	Vladimir Guerrero, Mtl	39	40
1991	Ron Gant, Atl	32	34	2003	Alfonso Soriano, NYY	38	35
1991	Howard Johnson, NYM	38	30	2004	Carlos Beltran, KC/Hou	38	42
1992	Barry Bonds, Pitt	34	39	2004	Bobby Abreu, Phil	30	40
1993	Sammy Sosa, ChiC	33	36	2005	Alfonso Soriano, Tex	36	30
1995	Barry Bonds, SF	33	31				

Career Individual Pitching

GAMES

Jesse Orosco	1252
*John Franco	1119
Dennis Eckersley	1071
Hoyt Wilhelm	1070
Dan Plesac	1064
Kent Tekulve	1050
*Mike Stanton	1027
Lee Smith	1022
*Mike Jackson	1005
Goose Gossage	1002
Lindy McDaniel	987
Rollie Fingers	944
Gene Garber	931
Cy Young	906
Sparky Lyle	899
Jim Kaat	898
M. Timlin	893
Paul Assenmacher	884
Jeff Reardon	880
Don McMahon	874

INNINGS PITCHED

Cy Young	7356⅔
Pud Galvin	5941⅓
Walter Johnson	5914⅔
Phil Niekro	5404⅓
Nolan Ryan	5386
Gaylord Perry	5350⅓
Don Sutton	5282⅓
Warren Spahn	5243⅔
Steve Carlton	5217⅓
Grover Alexander	5190
Kid Nichols	5056⅔
Tim Keefe	5047⅓
Bert Blyleven	4970
Bobby Mathews	4956
Mickey Welch	4802
Tom Seaver	4782⅔
Christy Mathewson	4780⅔
Tommy John	4710⅓
*Riberto Clemens	4704⅓
Robin Roberts	4688⅔

WINS

Cy Young	511
Walter Johnson	417
Grover Alexander	373
Christy Mathewson	373
Pud Galvin	365
Warren Spahn	363
Kid Nichols	361
Tim Keefe	342
*Roger Clemens	341
Steve Carlton	329
John Clarkson	328
Eddie Plank	326
Nolan Ryan	324
Don Sutton	324
*Greg Maddux	318
Phil Niekro	318
Gaylord Perry	314
Tom Seaver	311
Charley Radbourn	309
Mickey Welch	307

LOSSES

Cy Young	316
Pud Galvin	310
Nolan Ryan	292
Walter Johnson	279
Phil Niekro	274
Gaylord Perry	265
Don Sutton	256
Jack Powell	254
Eppa Rixey	251
Bert Blyleven	250
Bobby Mathews	248
Robin Roberts	245
Warren Spahn	245
Steve Carlton	244
Early Wynn	244
Jim Kaat	237
Frank Tanana	236
Gus Weyhing	232
Tommy John	231
Bob Friend	230
Ted Lyons	230

WINNING PERCENTAGE**

Al Spalding	.796
Spud Chandler	.717
*Pedro Martinez	.705
Whitey Ford	.690
Dave Foutz	.690
Bob Caruthers	.688
Don Gullett	.686
Lefty Grove	.680
Joe Wood	.671
Vic Raschi	.667
*Roger Clemens	.667
Larry Corcoran	.665
Christy Mathewson	.665
Sam Leever	.660
*Randy Johnson	.658
Sal Maglie	.658
Dick McBride	.656
Sandy Koufax	.655
*Andy Pettitte	.654
Johnny Allen	.654

SAVES

Lee Smith	478
*Trevor Hoffman	436
*John Franco	424
Dennis Eckersley	390
*Mariano Rivera	379
Jeff Reardon	367
Randy Myers	347
Rollie Fingers	341
John Wetteland	330
*Roberto Hernandez	324
*Troy Percival	316
Rick Aguilera	324
*Jose Mesa	319
Robb Nen	314
Tom Henke	311
Goose Gossage	310
Jeff Montgomery	304
Doug Jones	303
Bruce Sutter	300
*Rod Beck	286

EARNED RUN AVERAGE (2,000 IP)

Ed Walsh	1.82
Addie Joss	1.89
Al Spalding	2.04
Three Finger Brown	2.06
John Ward	2.10
Christy Mathewson	2.13
Tommy Bond	2.14
Rube Waddell	2.16
Walter Johnson	2.17
Ed Reulbach	2.28
Will White	2.28
Eddie Plank	2.35
Larry Corcoran	2.36
Eddie Cicotte	2.38
Candy Cummings	2.39
Doc White	2.39
Nap Rucker	2.42
George Bradley	2.43
Jim McCormick	2.43
Chief Bender	2.46

SHUTOUTS

Walter Johnson	110
Grover Alexander	90
Christy Mathewson	79
Cy Young	76
Eddie Plank	69
Warren Spahn	63
Nolan Ryan	61
Tom Seaver	61
Bert Blyleven	60
Don Sutton	58
Pud Galvin	57
Ed Walsh	57
Bob Gibson	56
Three Finger Brown	55
Steve Carlton	55
Jim Palmer	53
Gaylord Perry	53
Juan Marichal	52
Rube Waddell	50
Vic Willis	50

COMPLETE GAMES

Cy Young	749
Pud Galvin	639
Tim Keefe	554
Walter Johnson	531
Kid Nichols	531
Mickey Welch	525
Bobby Mathews	525
Charley Radbourn	489
John Clarkson	485
Tony Mullane	468
Jim McCormick	466
Gus Weyhing	448
Grover Alexander	437
Christy Mathewson	434
Jack Powell	422
Eddie Plank	410
Will White	394
Amos Rusie	392
Vic Willis	388
Tommy Bond	386

* Active in 2005.   ** Minumum 100 victories.

Career Individual Pitching (Cont.)

STRIKEOUTS		BASES ON BALLS	
Nolan Ryan	5714	Nolan Ryan	2795
*Roger Clemens	4502	Steve Carlton	1833
*Randy Johnson	4372	Phil Niekro	1809
Steve Carlton	4136	Early Wynn	1775
Bert Blyleven	3701	Bob Feller	1764
Tom Seaver	3640	Bobo Newsom	1732
Don Sutton	3574	Amos Rusie	1707
Gaylord Perry	3534	Charlie Hough	1665
Walter Johnson	3509	Gus Weyhing	1566
Phil Niekro	3342	Red Ruffing	1541
Ferguson Jenkins	3192	*Roger Clemens	1520
Bob Gibson	3117	Bump Hadley	1442
*Greg Maddux	3052	Warren Spahn	1434
*Pedro Martinez	2861	Earl Whitehill	1431
Jim Bunning	2855	Tony Mullane	1408
Mickey Lolich	2832	Sad Sam Jones	1396
*Curt Schilling	2832	Jack Morris	1390
Cy Young	2803	Tom Seaver	1390
Frank Tanana	2773	Gaylord Perry	1379
David Cone	2668	Bobby Witt	1375

Alltime Winningest Managers

CAREER

	W	L	Pct	Yrs		W	L	Pct	Yrs
Connie Mack	3755	3967	.486	53	Gene Mauch	1907	2044	.483	26
John McGraw	2810	1987	.586	33	Bill McKechnie	1904	1737	.523	25
Sparky Anderson	2238	1855	.547	26	*Joe Torre	1882	1681	.532	24
*Tony LaRussa	2221	1896	.536	27	Ralph Houk	1627	1539	.514	20
Bucky Harris	2168	2228	.493	29	Fred Clarke	1609	1189	.575	19
Joe McCarthy	2155	1346	.616	24	Dick Williams	1592	1474	.519	21
Walter Alston	2063	1634	.558	23	Tommy Lasorda	1589	1434	.526	20
Leo Durocher	2015	1717	.540	24	Earl Weaver	1506	1080	.582	17
*Bobby Cox	2004	1534	.566	23	Clark Griffith	1491	1367	.522	20
Casey Stengel	1942	1868	.510	25	*Lou Pinella	1540	1441	.523	19

REGULAR SEASON

	W	L	Pct	Yrs		W	L	Pct	Yrs
Connie Mack	3731	3948	.486	53	Gene Mauch	1902	2037	.483	26
John McGraw	2784	1959	.587	33	Bill McKechnie	1896	1723	.524	25
*Tony La Russa	2214	1908	.534	27	*Joe Torre	1876	1637	.532	24
Sparky Anderson	2194	1834	.545	26	Ralph Houk	1619	1531	.514	20
Bucky Harris	2157	2218	.493	29	Fred Clarke	1602	1181	.576	19
Joe McCarthy	2125	1333	.615	24	Dick Williams	1571	1451	.520	21
*Bobby Cox	2092	1603	.567	24	Tommy Lasorda	1558	1404	.526	20
Walter Alston	2040	1613	.558	23	*Lou Piniella	1519	1420	.523	19
Leo Durocher	2008	1709	.540	24	Clark Griffith	1491	1367	.522	20
Casey Stengel	1905	1842	.508	25	Earl Weaver	1480	1060	.583	17

WORLD SERIES

	W	L	T	Pct	App	WS		W	L	T	Pct	App	WS
Casey Stengel	37	26	0	.587	10	7	Bucky Harris	11	10	0	.524	3	2
Joe McCarthy	30	13	0	.698	9	7	Billy Southworth	11	11	0	.500	4	2
John McGraw	26	28	2	.482	9	2	Earl Weaver	11	13	0	.458	4	1
Connie Mack	24	19	0	.558	8	5	*Bobby Cox	11	18	0	.379	5	1
*Joe Torre	21	11	0	.657	6	4	Whitey Herzog	10	11	0	.476	3	1
Walter Alston	20	20	0	.500	7	4	Bill Carrigan	8	2	0	.800	2	2
Miller Huggins	18	15	1	.544	6	3	Cito Gaston	8	4	0	.667	2	2
Sparky Anderson	16	12	0	.571	5	3	Danny Murtaugh	8	6	0	.571	2	2
Tommy Lasorda	12	11	0	.522	4	2	Tom Kelly	8	6	0	.571	2	2
Dick Williams	12	14	0	.462	4	2	Ralph Houk	8	8	0	.500	3	2
Frank Chance	11	9	1	.548	4	2	Bill McKechnie	8	14	0	.364	4	2

*Active in 2005.

Individual Batting (Single Season)

HITS

Ichiro Suzuki, 2004 262
George Sisler, 1920 257
Lefty O'Doul, 1929 254
Bill Terry, 1930 254
Al Simmons, 1925 253
Rogers Hornsby, 1922.........250
Chuck Klein, 1930 250
Ty Cobb, 1911 248
George Sisler, 1922 246
Ichiro Suzuki, 2001 242

BATTING AVERAGE

Hugh Duffy, 1894 .... .440
Tip O'Neill, 1887 .... .435
Ross Barnes, 1876 429
Nap Lajoie, 1901 .... .426
Willie Keeler, 1897 .... .424
Rogers Hornsby, 1924 ..... .424
George Sisler, 1922 .... .420
Ty Cobb, 1911 .... .420
Fred Dunlap, 1884 .... .412
Ed Delahanty, 1899 .... .410

DOUBLES

Earl Webb, 1931 67
George Burns, 1926 64
Joe Medwick, 1936...............64
Hank Greenberg, 1934.........63
Paul Waner, 1932 62
Charlie Gehringer, 1936 60
Tris Speaker, 1923...............59
Chuck Klein, 1930 59
Todd Helton, 2000 59
Billy Herman, 1936 57
Billy Herman, 1935 57
Carlos Delgado, 2000...........57

TOTAL BASES

Babe Ruth, 1921 457
Rogers Hornsby, 1922.........450
Lou Gehrig, 1927.................447
Chuck Klein, 1930 445
Jimmie Foxx, 1932...............438
Stan Musial, 1948 429
Sammy Sosa, 2001 425
Hack Wilson, 1930...............423
Chuck Klein, 1932 420
Luis Gonzalez, 2001 419
Lou Gehrig, 1930.................419

TRIPLES

Chief Wilson, 1912................36
Dave Orr, 1886 31
Heinie Reitz, 1894................31
Perry Werden, 1893..............29
Harry Davis, 1897 28
George Davis, 1893..............27
Sam Thompson, 1894...........27
Jimmy Williams, 1899 27
John Reilly, 1890 26
George Treadway, 1894........26
Joe Jackson, 1912................26
Sam Crawford, 1914.............26
Kiki Cuyler, 1925..................26

HOME RUNS

Barry Bonds, 2001................73
Mark McGwire, 1998 70
Sammy Sosa, 1998...............66
Mark McGwire, 1999 65
Sammy Sosa, 2001...............64
Sammy Sosa, 1999...............63
Roger Maris, 1961 61
Babe Ruth, 1927...................60
Babe Ruth, 1921 59
Jimmie Foxx, 1932................58
Hank Greenberg, 1938.........58
Mark McGwire, 1997 58

RUNS BATTED IN

Hack Wilson, 1930................190
Lou Gehrig, 1931 184
Hank Greenberg, 1937.........183
Lou Gehrig, 1927 175
Jimmie Foxx, 1938................175
Lou Gehrig, 1930.................174
Babe Ruth, 1921 171
Chuck Klein, 1930 170
Hank Greenberg, 1935.........170
Jimmie Foxx, 1932................169

STRIKEOUTS

Adam Dunn, 2004.................195
Bobby Bonds, 1970..............189
Jose Hernandez, 2002 188
Bobby Bonds, 1969..............187
Preston Wilson, 2000...........187
Rob Deer, 1987 186
Jose Hernandez, 2001 185
Jim Thome, 2001 185
Pete Incaviglia, 1986............185
Cecil Fielder, 1990...............182
Jim Thome, 2003 182

RUNS

Billy Hamilton, 1894 192
Tom Brown, 1891 177
Babe Ruth, 1921 177
Tip O'Neill, 1887 167
Lou Gehrig, 1936.................167
Billy Hamilton, 1895.............166
Willie Keeler, 1894 165
Joe Kelley, 1894 165
Arlie Latham, 1887...............163
Babe Ruth, 1928...................163
Lou Gehrig, 1931.................163

STOLEN BASES

Hugh Nicol, 1887 138
Rickey Henderson, 1982 130
Arlie Latham, 1887...............129
Lou Brock, 1974 118
Charlie Comiskey, 1887.......117
John Ward, 1887 111
Billy Hamilton, 1889.............111
Billy Hamilton, 1891.............111
Vince Coleman, 1985 110
Arlie Latham, 1888...............109
Vince Coleman, 1987 109

BASES ON BALLS

Barry Bonds, 2004................232
Barry Bonds, 2002................198
Barry Bonds, 2001................177
Babe Ruth, 1923...................170
Ted Williams, 1947 162
Ted Williams, 1949 162
Mark McGwire, 1998 162
Ted Williams, 1946 156
Eddie Yost, 1956 151
Jeff Bagwell, 1999 149
Eddie Joost, 1949................149

SLUGGING AVERAGE

Barry Bonds, 2001.............. .863
Babe Ruth, 1920...................847
Babe Ruth, 1921 846
Barry Bonds, 2004.............. .812
Barry Bonds, 2002................799
Babe Ruth, 1927...................772
Lou Gehrig, 1927.................765
Babe Ruth, 1923...................764
Rogers Hornsby, 1925........ .756
Mark McGwire, 1998 .... .752

Individual Pitching (Single Season)

GAMES

Mike Marshall, 1974............106
Kent Tekulve, 1979 94
Mike Marshall, 1973..............92
Kent Tekulve, 1978...............91
Wayne Granger, 1969 90
Mike Marshall, 1979..............90
Kent Tekulve, 1987...............90
Steve Kline, 2001...................89
Mark Eichhorn, 1987..............89
Paul Quantrill, 2003...............89
Jim Brower, 2004....................89

GAMES STARTED

Will White, 1879 75
Jim Galvin, 1883......................75
Jim McCormick, 1880.............74
Charley Radbourn, 1884 73
Guy Hecker, 1884...................73
Jim Galvin, 1884.....................72
John Clarkson, 1889...............72
Bill Hutchison, 1892...............71
John Clarkson, 1885...............70
Matt Kilroy, 1887.....................69

INNINGS PITCHED

Will White, 1878 ....680.0
Charley Radbourn, 1884....678.2
Guy Hecker, 1884...............670.2
Jim McCormick, 1880.........657.2
Jim Galvin, 1883 ....656.1
Jim Galvin, 1884 ....636.1
Charley Radbourn, 1883....632.1
Bill Hutchison, 1892...........627.0
John Clarkson, 1885...........623.0
Jim Devlin, 1876 ....622.0

WINS

Charley Radbourn, 1884 59
John Clarkson, 1885...............53
Guy Hecker, 1884...................52
John Clarkson, 1889...............49
Charley Radbourn, 1883 48
Charlie Buffinton, 1884 48
Al Spalding, 1876 47
John.Ward, 1879 47
Jim Galvin, 1883.....................46
Jim Galvin, 1884.....................46
Matt Kilroy, 1887....................46

LOSSES

John Coleman, 1883..............48
Will White, 1880 42
Larry McKeon, 1884 41
George Bradley, 1879 40
Jim McCormick, 1879.............40
Henry Porter, 1888.................37
Kid Carsey, 1891 37
George Cobb, 1892................37
Stump Weidman, 1886 36
Bill Hutchison, 1892...............36

WINNING PERCENTAGE

Roy Face, 1959.....................947
Johnny Allen, 1937................938
Greg Maddux, 1995..............905
Randy Johnson, 1995.........900
Ron Guidry, 1978..................893
Freddie Fitzsimmons, 1940...889
Lefty Grove, 1931 886
Bob Stanley, 1978 882
Preacher Roe, 1951.............880
Fred Goldsmith, 1880........875
Tom Seaver, 1981..............875

SAVES

Bobby Thigpen, 1990............57
John Smoltz, 2002.................55
Eric Gagne, 2003...................55
Mariano Rivera, 2004.............53
Randy Myers, 1993................53
Trevor Hoffman, 1998............53
Eric Gagne, 2002...................52
Dennis Eckersley, 1992.........51
Rod Beck, 1998......................51
Mariano Rivera, 2001.............50
Francisco Cordero, 2004.......49

EARNED RUN AVERAGE

Tim Keefe, 1880..................0.86
Dutch Leonard, 1914...........0.96
Three Finger Brown, 1906....1.04
Bob Gibson, 1968.................1.12
Christy Mathewson, 1909 ...1.14
Walter Johnson, 1913.........1.14
Jack Pfiester, 1907 ....1.15
Addie Joss, 1908.................1.16
Carl Lundgren, 1907...........1.17
Denny Driscoll, 1882 ....1.21

SHUTOUTS

George Bradley, 1876 16
Grover Alexander, 1916 16
Jack Coombs, 1910...............13
Bob Gibson, 1968..................13
Jim Galvin, 1884 12
Ed Morris, 1886 12
Grover Alexander, 1915 12
Tommy Bond, 1879 11
Charley Radbourn, 1884 11
Dave Foutz, 1886...................11
Christy Mathewson, 1908 11
Ed Walsh, 1908......................11
Walter Johnson, 1913............11
Sandy Koufax, 1963 11
Dean Chance, 1964...............11

COMPLETE GAMES

Will White, 1879 75
Charley Radbourn, 1884 73
Jim McCormick, 1880.............72
Jim Galvin, 1883......................72
Guy Hecker, 1884...................72
Jim Galvin, 1884.....................71
Tim Keefe, 1883......................68
John Clarkson, 1885...............68
John Clarkson, 1889...............68
Bill Hutchison, 1892...............67

STRIKEOUTS

Matt Kilroy, 1886...................513
Toad Ramsey, 1886..............499
Hugh Daily, 1884 483
Dupee Shaw, 1884 451
Charley Radbourn, 1884 441
Charlie Buffinton, 1884 417
Guy Hecker, 1884.................385
Nolan Ryan, 1973 383
Sandy Koufax, 1965 382
Bill Sweeney, 1884 374

BASES ON BALLS

Amos Rusie, 1890.................289
Mark Baldwin, 1889...............274
Amos Rusie, 1892.................267
Amos Rusie, 1891.................262
Mark Baldwin, 1890...............249
Jack Stivetts, 1891.,..............232
Mark Baldwin, 1891...............227
Phil Knell, 1891.....................226
Bob Barr, 1890 219
Amos Rusie 1893.................218

Manager of the Year

NATIONAL LEAGUE	AMERICAN LEAGUE
1983 ....Tommy Lasorda, LA	1983 ....Tony La Russa, Chi
1984 ....Jim Frey, Chi	1984 ....Sparky Anderson, Det
1985 ....Whitey Herzog, StL	1985 ....Bobby Cox, Tor
1986 ....Hal Lanier, Hou	1986 ....John McNamara, Bos
1987 ....Buck Rodgers, Mtl	1987 ....Sparky Anderson, Det
1988 ....Tommy Lasorda, LA	1988 ....Tony La Russa, Oak
1989 ....Don Zimmer, Chi	1989 ....Frank Robinson, Balt
1990 ....Jim Leyland, Pitt	1990 ....Jeff Torborg, Chi
1991 ....Bobby Cox, Atl	1991 ....Tom Kelly, Minn
1992 ....Jim Leyland, Pitt	1992 ....Tony La Russa, Oak
1993 ....Dusty Baker, SF	1993 ....Gene Lamont, Chi
1994 ....Felipe Alou, Mtl	1994 ....Buck Showalter, NY
1995 ....Don Baylor, Col	1995 ....Lou Piniella, Sea
1996 ....Bruce Bochy, SD	1996 ....Joe Torre, NY/Johnny Oates, Tex
1997 ....Dusty Baker, SF	1997 ....Davey Johnson, Balt
1998 ....Larry Dierker, Hou	1998 ....Joe Torre, NY
1999 ....Jack McKeon, Cin	1999 ....Jimy Williams, Bos
2000 ....Dusty Baker, SF	2000 ....Jerry Manuel, Chi
2001 ....Larry Bowa, Phil	2001 ....Lou Piniella, Sea
2002 ....Tony La Russa, StL	2002 ....Mike Scioscia, Ana
2003 ....Jack McKeon, Fla	2003 ....Tony Pena, KC
2004 ....Bobby Cox, Atl	2004 ....Buck Showalter, Tex

Individual Batting (Single Game)

MOST RUNS

7 ....Guy Hecker, Lou   Aug 15, 1886

MOST HITS

7 ....Wilbert Robinson, Balt   June 10, 1892
      Rennie Stennett, Pitt   Sept 16, 1975

MOST HOME RUNS

4 ....Bobby Lowe, Bos (N)	May 30, 1894
Ed Delahanty, Phil	July 13, 1896
Lou Gehrig, NY (A)	June 3, 1932
Gil Hodges, Bklyn	Aug 31, 1950
Joe Adcock, Mil (N)	July 31, 1954
Rocky Colavito, Clev	June 10, 1959
Willie Mays, SF	April 30, 1961
Mike Schmidt, Phil	April 17, 1976
Bob Horner, Atl	July 6, 1986
Mark Whiten, StL	Sept 7, 1993
Mike Cameron, Sea	May 2, 2002
Shawn Green, LA	May 23, 2002
Carlos Delgado, Tor	Sept 25, 2003

MOST GRAND SLAMS

2 ....Tony Lazzeri, NY (A)	May 24, 1936
Jim Tabor, Bos (A)	July 4, 1939
Rudy York, Bos (A)	July 27, 1946
Jim Gentile, Balt	May 9, 1961
Tony Cloninger, Atl	July 3, 1966
Jim Northrup, Det	June 24, 1968
Frank Robinson, Balt	June 26, 1970
Robin Ventura, Chi (A)	Sept 4, 1995
Chris Hoiles, Balt	Aug 14, 1998
Fernando Tatis, StL	Apr 23, 1999
N. Garciaparra, Bos	May 10, 1999
Bill Mueller, Bos	July 29, 2003

MOST RBIs

12 .....Jim Bottomley, StL	Sept 16, 1924
Mark Whiten, StL	Sept 7, 1993

Individual Batting (Single Inning)

MOST RUNS

3 ....Tommy Burns, Chi (N) Sept 6, 1883, 7th inning
      Ned Williamson, Chi (N) Sept 6, 1883, 7th inning
      Sammy White, Bos (A)   June 18, 1953, 7th inning

MOST RBIs

8 ....Fernando Tatis, StL   Apr 23, 1999, 3rd inning

MOST HITS

3 ....Tommy Burns, Chi (N) Sept 6, 1883, 7th inning
      Fred Pfeiffer, Chi (N)   Sept 6, 1883, 7th inning
      Ned Williamson, Chi (N) Sept 6, 1883, 7th inning
      Gene Stephens, Bos (A) June 18, 1953, 7th inning

Note: All single-game hitting records for a nine-inning game.

Individual Pitching (Single Game)

MOST INNINGS PITCHED

26 .....Leon Cadore, Bklyn   May 1, 1920, tie 1–1
      Joe Oeschger, Bos (N)   May 1, 1920, tie 1–1

MOST RUNS ALLOWED

24 .....Al Travers, Det   May 18, 1912

MOST HITS ALLOWED

36 .....Jack Wadsworth, Lou   Aug 17, 1894

MOST STRIKEOUTS

20 .....Roger Clemens, Bos   April 29, 1986
20 .....Roger Clemens, Bos   Sept 18, 1996
20 .....Kerry Wood, Chi (N)   May 6, 1998
20 .....Randy Johnson, Ariz   May 8, 2001

MOST WALKS ALLOWED

16 .....Bill George, NY (N)   May 30, 1887
     George Van Haltren,   June 27, 1887
     Chi (N)
     Henry Gruber, Clev   Apr 19, 1890
     Bruno Haas, Phil (A)   June 2, 1915

MOST WILD PITCHES

6 .......J.R. Richard, Hou   April 10, 1979
     Phil Niekro, Atl   Aug 14, 1979
     Bill Gullickson, Mtl   April 10, 1982

Individual Pitching (Single Inning)

MOST RUNS ALLOWED

13 .....Lefty O'Doul, Bos (A)   July 7, 1923

MOST WALKS ALLOWED

8 ....Dolly Gray, Wash   Aug 28, 1909

MOST WILD PITCHES

4 ....Walter Johnson, Wash   Sept 21, 1914
     Phil Niekro, Atl   Aug 14, 1979
     Kevin Gregg, Ana   July 25, 2004

Miscellaneous

LONGEST GAME, BY INNINGS

26 .....Brooklyn 1, Boston 1   May 1, 1920

LONGEST NINE-INNING GAME, BY TIME

4:27...Los Angeles 11, San Francisco 10 Oct 5, 2001

Baseball Hall of Fame

Players

	Position	Career	Selected
Hank Aaron	OF	1954–76	1982
Grover Alexander	P	1911–30	1938
Cap Anson	1B	1876–97	1939
Luis Aparicio	SS	1956–73	1984
Luke Appling	SS	1930–50	1964
Richie Ashburn	OF	1948–62	1995
Earl Averill	OF	1929–41	1975
Frank Baker	3B	1908–22	1955
Dave Bancroft	SS	1915–30	1971
Ernie Banks	SS-1B	1953–71	1977
Jake Beckley	1B	1888–1907	1971
Cool Papa Bell*	OF		1974
Johnny Bench	C	1967–83	1989
Chief Bender	P	1903–25	1953
Yogi Berra	C	1946–65	1972
Wade Boggs	3B	1982–99	2005
Jim Bottomley	1B	1922–37	1974
Lou Boudreau	SS	1938–52	1970
Roger Bresnahan	C	1897–1915	1945
George Brett	3B	1973–93	1999
Lou Brock	OF	1961–79	1985
Dan Brouthers	1B	1879–1904	1945
Three Finger Brown	P	1903–16	1949
Jim Bunning	P	1955–71	1996
Jesse Burkett	OF	1890–1905	1946
Roy Campanella	C	1948–57	1969
Rod Carew	1B-2B	1967–85	1991
Max Carey	OF	1910–29	1961
Steve Carlton	P	1965–88	1994
Gary Carter	C	1974–92	2003
Orlando Cepeda	1B	1958–74	1999
Frank Chance	1B	1898–1914	1946
Oscar Charleston*	OF		1976
Jack Chesbro	P	1899–1909	1946
Fred Clarke	OF	1894–1915	1945
John Clarkson	P	1882–94	1963
Roberto Clemente	OF	1955–72	1973
Ty Cobb	OF	1905–28	1936
Mickey Cochrane	C	1925–37	1947
Eddie Collins	2B	1906–30	1939
Jimmy Collins	3B	1895–1908	1945
Earle Combs	OF	1924–35	1970
Roger Connor	1B	1880–97	1976
Stan Coveleski	P	1912–28	1969
Sam Crawford	OF	1899–1917	1957
Joe Cronin	SS	1926–45	1956
Candy Cummings	P	1872–77	1939
Kiki Cuyler	OF	1921–38	1968
Ray Dandridge*	3B		1987
George Davis	SS	1890–1909	1998
Leon Day*	P		1995
Dizzy Dean	P	1930–47	1953
Ed Delahanty	OF	1888–1903	1945
Bill Dickey	C	1928–46	1954
Martin Dihigo*	P-OF		1977
Joe DiMaggio	OF	1936–51	1955
Larry Doby	OF	1947–59	1998
Bobby Doerr	2B	1937–51	1986

Note: Career dates indicate first and last appearances in the majors.
*Elected on the basis of his career in the Negro leagues.

Players *(Cont.)*

	Position	Career	Selected
Don Drysdale	P	1956–69	1984
Hugh Duffy	OF	1888–1906	1945
Dennis Eckersley	P	1975–98	2004
Johnny Evers	2B	1902–29	1939
Buck Ewing	C	1880–97	1946
Red Faber	P	1914–33	1964
Bob Feller	P	1936–56	1962
Rick Ferrell	C	1929–47	1984
Rollie Fingers	P	1968–85	1992
Carlton Fisk	C	1969–93	2000
Elmer Flick	OF	1898–1910	1963
Whitey Ford	P	1950–67	1974
Bill Foster*	P		1996
Nellie Fox	2B	1947–65	1997
Jimmie Foxx	1B	1925–45	1951
Frankie Frisch	2B	1919–37	1947
Pud Galvin	P	1879–92	1965
Lou Gehrig	1B	1923–39	1939
Charlie Gehringer	2B	1924–42	1949
Bob Gibson	P	1959–75	1981
Josh Gibson*	C		1972
Lefty Gomez	P	1930–43	1972
Goose Goslin	OF	1921–38	1968
Hank Greenberg	1B	1930–47	1956
Burleigh Grimes	P	1916–34	1964
Lefty Grove	P	1925–41	1947
Chick Hafey	OF	1924–37	1971
Jesse Haines	P	1918–37	1970
Billy Hamilton	OF	1888–1901	1961
Gabby Hartnett	C	1922–41	1955
Harry Heilmann	OF	1914–32	1952
Billy Herman	2B	1931–47	1975
Harry Hooper	OF	1909–25	1971
Rogers Hornsby	2B	1915–37	1942
Waite Hoyt	P	1918–38	1969
Carl Hubbell	P	1928–43	1947
Catfish Hunter	P	1965–79	1987
Monte Irvin*	OF	1949–56	1973
Reggie Jackson	OF	1967–87	1993
Travis Jackson	SS	1922–36	1982
Ferguson Jenkins	P	1965–83	1991
Hugh Jennings	SS	1891–1918	1945
Judy Johnson*	3B		1975
Walter Johnson	P	1907–27	1936
Addie Joss	P	1902–10	1978
Al Kaline	OF	1953–74	1980
Tim Keefe	P	1880–93	1964
Willie Keeler	OF	1892–1910	1939
George Kell	3B	1943–57	1983
Joe Kelley	OF	1891–1908	1971
George Kelly	1B	1915–32	1973
King Kelly	C	1878–93	1945
Harmon Killebrew	1B-3B	1954–75	1984
Ralph Kiner	OF	1946–55	1975
Chuck Klein	OF	1928–44	1980
Sandy Koufax	P	1955–66	1972
Nap Lajoie	2B	1896–1916	1937
Tony Lazzeri	2B	1926–39	1991
Bob Lemon	P	1941–58	1976
Buck Leonard*	1B		1977
Fred Lindstrom	3B	1924–36	1976
Pop Lloyd*	SS-1B		1977
Ernie Lombardi	C	1931–47	1986
Ted Lyons	P	1923–46	1955
Mickey Mantle	OF	1951–68	1974
Heinie Manush	OF	1923–39	1964
Rabbit Maranville	SS-2B	1912–35	1954
Juan Marichal	P	1960–75	1983
Rube Marquard	P	1908–25	1971
Eddie Mathews	3B	1952–68	1978
Christy Mathewson	P	1900–16	1936
Willie Mays	OF	1951–73	1979
Bill Mazeroski	2B	1956–72	2001
Tommy McCarthy	OF	1884–96	1946
Willie McCovey	1B	1959–80	1986
Joe McGinnity	P	1899–1908	1946
Bid McPhee	2B	1882–99	2000
Joe Medwick	OF	1932–48	1968
Johnny Mize	1B	1936–53	1981
Paul Molitor	3B	1978–98	2004
Joe Morgan	2B	1963–84	1990
Eddie Murray	1B	1977–97	2003
Stan Musial	OF-1B	1941–63	1969
Hal Newhouser	P	1939–55	1992
Kid Nichols	P	1890–1906	1949
Phil Niekro	P	1964–87	1997
Jim O'Rourke	OF	1876–1904	1945
Mel Ott	OF	1926–47	1951
Satchel Paige*	P	1948–65	1971
Jim Palmer	P	1965–84	1990
Herb Pennock	P	1912–34	1948
Tony Perez	1B	1964–86	2000
Gaylord Perry	P	1962–83	1991
Eddie Plank	P	1901–17	1946
Kirby Puckett	OF	1984–95	2001
Charley Radbourn	P	1880–91	1939
Pee Wee Reese	SS	1940–58	1984
Sam Rice	OF	1915–35	1963
Eppa Rixey	P	1912–33	1963
Phil Rizzuto	SS	1941–56	1994
Robin Roberts	P	1948–66	1976
Brooks Robinson	3B	1955–77	1983
Frank Robinson	OF	1956–76	1982
Jackie Robinson	2B	1947–56	1962
Joe (Bullet) Rogan*	P		1998
Edd Roush	OF	1913–31	1962
Red Ruffing	P	1924–47	1967
Amos Rusie	P	1889–1901	1977
Babe Ruth	OF	1914–35	1936
Nolan Ryan	P	1966–93	1999
Ryne Sandberg	2B	1981-97	2005
Ray Schalk	C	1912–29	1955
Mike Schmidt	3B	1972–89	1995
Red Schoendienst	2B	1945–63	1989
Tom Seaver	P	1967–86	1992
Joe Sewell	SS	1920–33	1977
Al Simmons	OF	1924–44	1953
George Sisler	1B	1915–30	1939
Enos Slaughter	OF	1938–59	1985
Hilton Smith*	P		2001
Ozzie Smith	SS	1978–96	2002
Duke Snider	OF	1947–64	1980
Warren Spahn	P	1942–65	1973
Al Spalding	P	1871–78	1939
Tris Speaker	OF	1907–28	1937
Willie Stargell	OF-1B	1962–82	1988
Turkey Stearns*	CF		2000
Don Sutton	P	1966–88	1998
Bill Terry	1B	1923–36	1954
Sam Thompson	OF	1885–1906	1974

*Elected on the basis of his career in the Negro leagues.

Players *(Cont.)*

	Position	Career	Selected
Joe Tinker	SS	1902–16	1946
Pie Traynor	3B	1920–37	1948
Dazzy Vance	P	1915–35	1955
Arky Vaughan	SS	1932–48	1985
Rube Waddell	P	1897–1910	1946
Honus Wagner	SS	1897–1917	1936
Bobby Wallace	SS	1894–1918	1953
Ed Walsh	P	1904–17	1946
Lloyd Waner	OF	1927–45	1967
Paul Waner	OF	1926–45	1952
John Ward	2B-P	1878–94	1964
Mickey Welch	P	1880–92	1973
Willie Wells*	SS	1924–49	1997
Zach Wheat	OF	1909–27	1959
Hoyt Wilhelm	P	1952–72	1985
Billy Williams	OF	1959–76	1987
Ted Williams	OF	1939–60	1966
Vic Willis	P	1898–1910	1995
Hack Wilson	OF	1923–34	1979
Dave Winfield	OF	1973–95	2001
Early Wynn	P	1939–63	1972
Carl Yastrzemski	OF	1961–83	1989
Cy Young	P	1890–1911	1937
Ross Youngs	OF	1917–26	1972
Robin Yount	SS	1974–93	1999

Pioneers/Executives

	Selected
Ed Barrow (manager-executive)	1953
Morgan Bulkeley (executive)	1937
Alexander Cartwright (executive)	1938
Henry Chadwick (writer-executive)	1938
Happy Chandler (commissioner)	1982
Charles Comiskey (manager-executive)	1939
Rube Foster (player-manager-executive)	1981
Ford Frick (commissioner-executive)	1970
Warren Giles (executive)	1979
Will Harridge (executive)	1972
William Hulbert (executive)	1995
Ban Johnson (executive)	1937
Kenesaw M. Landis (commissioner)	1944
Larry MacPhail (executive)	1978
Lee MacPhail Jr. (executive)	1998
Branch Rickey (manager-executive)	1967
Al Spalding (player-executive)	1939
Bill Veeck (owner)	1991
George Weiss (executive)	1971
George Wright (player-manager)	1937
Harry Wright (player-manager-executive)	1953
Tom Yawkey (executive)	1980

Umpires

	Selected
Al Barlick	1989
Nestor Chylak	1999
Jocko Conlan	1974
Tom Connolly	1953
Billy Evans	1973
Cal Hubbard	1976
Bill Klem	1953
Bill McGowan	1992

Managers

	Managed	Selected
Walt Alston	1954–76	1983
Sparky Anderson	1970–94	2000
Leo Durocher	1939–73	1994
Clark Griffith	1901–20	1946
Bucky Harris	1924–56	1975
Ned Hanlon	1899–1907	1996
Miller Huggins	1913–29	1964
Tommy Lasorda	1977–96	1997
Al Lopez	1951–69	1977
Connie Mack	1894–1950	1937
Joe McCarthy	1926–50	1957
John McGraw	1899–1932	1937
Bill McKechnie	1915–46	1962
Wilbert Robinson	1902–31	1945
Frank Selee	1890–1905	1999
Casey Stengel	1934–65	1966
Earl Weaver	1968–82, 85–86	1996

*Elected on the basis of his career in the Negro leagues.

Notable Achievements

No-Hit Games, Nine Innings or More

NATIONAL LEAGUE

Pitcher and Game

1876	July 15	George Bradley, StL vs Hart 2–0
1880	June 12	John Richmond, Wor vs Clev 1–0 (perfect game)
	June 17	Monte Ward, Prov vs Buff 5–0 (perfect game)
	Aug 19	Larry Corcoran, Chi vs Bos 6–0
	Aug 20	Pud Galvin, Buff vs Wor 1–0

Pitcher and Game

1882	Sept 20	Larry Corcoran, Chi vs Wor 5–0
	Sept 22	Tim Lovett, Bklyn vs NY 4–0
1883	July 25	Hoss Radbourn, Prov vs Clev 8–0
	Sept 13	Hugh Daily, Clev vs Phil 1–0
1884	June 27	Larry Corcoran, Chi vs Prov 6–0
	Aug 4	Pud Galvin, Buff vs Det 18–0
1885	July 27	John Clarkson, Chi vs Prov 4–0
	Aug 29	Charles Ferguson, Phil vs Prov 1–0

No-Hit Games, Nine Innings or More *(Cont.)*

NATIONAL LEAGUE *(Cont.)*

Date	Pitcher and Game	Date	Pitcher and Game
1891......July 31	Amos Rusie, NY vs Bklyn 6–0	1956......May 12	Carl Erskine, Bklyn vs NY 3–0
June 22	Tom Lovett, Bklyn vs NY 4–0	Sept 25	Sal Maglie, Bklyn vs Phil 5–0
1892......Aug 6	Jack Stivetts, Bos vs Bklyn 11–0	1959......May 26	Harvey Haddix, Pitt vs Mil 0–1
Aug 22	Alex Sanders, Lou vs Balt 6–2		(hit in 13th; lost in 13th)
1892......Oct 15	Bumpus Jones, Cin vs Pitt 7–1	1960......May 15	Don Cardwell, Chi vs StL 4–0
	(first major league game)	Aug 18	Lew Burdette, Mil vs Phil 1–0
1893......Aug 16	Bill Hawke, Balt vs Wash 5–0	Sept 16	Warren Spahn, Mil vs Phil 4–0
1897......Sept 18	Cy Young, Clev vs Cin 6–0	1961......Apr 28	Warren Spahn, Mil vs SF 1–0
1898......Apr 22	Ted Breitenstein, Cin vs Pitt 11–0	1962......June 30	Sandy Koufax, LA vs NY 5–0
Apr 22	Jim Hughes, Balt vs Bos 8–0	1963......May 11	Sandy Koufax, LA vs SF 8–0
July 8	Frank Donahue, Phil vs Bos 5–0	May 17	Don Nottebart, Hou vs Phil 4–1
Aug 21	Walter Thornton, Chi vs Bklyn 2–0	June 15	Juan Marichal, SF vs Hou 1–0
1899......May 25	Deacon Phillippe, Lou vs NY 7–0	1964......Apr 23	Ken Johnson, Hou vs Cin 0–1
Aug 7	Vic Willis, Bos vs Wash 7–1	June 4	Sandy Koufax, LA vs Phil 3–0
1900......July 12	Noodles Hahn, Cin vs Phil 4–0	June 21	Jim Bunning, Phil vs NY 6–0
1901......July 15	Christy Mathewson, NY vs StL 5–0		(perfect game)
1903......Sept 18	Chick Fraser, Phil vs Chi 10–0	1965......June 14	Jim Maloney, Cin vs NY 0–1
1904......June 11	Bob Wicker, Chi at NY 1–0 (hit in		(hit in 11th; lost in 11th)
	10th; won in 12th)	Aug 19	Jim Maloney, Cin vs Chi 1–0
1905......June 13	Christy Mathewson, NY vs Chi 1–0		(10 innings)
1906......May 1	John Lush, Phil vs Bklyn 6–0	Sept 9	Sandy Koufax, LA vs Chi 1–0
July 20	Mal Eason, Bklyn vs StL 2–0		(perfect game)
1906......Aug 1	Harry McIntire, Bklyn vs Pitt 0–1	1967......June 18	Don Wilson, Hou vs Atl 2–0
	(hit in 11th; lost in 13th)	1968......July 29	George Culver, Cin vs Phil 6–1
1907......May 8	Frank Pfeffer, Bos vs Cin 6–0	Sept 17	Gaylord Perry, SF vs StL 1–0
Sept 20	Nick Maddox, Pitt vs Bklyn 2–1	Sept 18	Ray Washburn, StL vs SF 2–0
1908......July 4	George Wiltse, NY vs Phil 1–0	1969......Apr 17	Bill Stoneman, Mtl vs Phil 7–0
	(10 innings)	Apr 30	Jim Maloney, Cin vs Hou 10–0
Sept 5	Nap Rucker, Bklyn vs Bos 6–0	May 1	Don Wilson, Hou vs Cin 4–0
1909......Apr 15	Leon Ames, NY vs Bklyn 0–3	Aug 19	Ken Holtzman, Chi vs Atl 3–0
	(hit in 10th; lost in 13th)	Sept 20	Bob Moose, Pitt vs NY 4–0
1912......Sept 6	Jeff Tesreau, NY vs Phil 3–0	1970......June 12	Dock Ellis, Pitt vs SD 2–0
1914......Sept 9	George Davis, Bos vs Phil 7–0	July 20	Bill Singer, LA vs Phil 5–0
1915......Apr 15	Rube Marquard, NY vs Bklyn 2–0	1971......June 3	Ken Holtzman, Chi vs Cin 1–0
Aug 31	Jimmy Lavender, Chi vs NY 2–0	June 23	Rick Wise, Phil vs Cin 4–0
1916......June 16	Tom Hughes, Bos vs Pitt 2–0	Aug 14	Bob Gibson, StL vs Pitt 11–0
1917......May 2	Jim Vaughn, Chi vs Cin 0–1	1972......Apr 16	Burt Hooton, Chi vs Phil 4–0
	(hit in 10th; lost in 10th)	Sept 2	Milt Pappas, Chi vs SD 8–0
May 2	Fred Toney, Cin vs Chi 1–0	Oct 2	Bill Stoneman, Mtl vs NY 7–0
	(10 innings)	1973......Aug 5	Phil Niekro, Atl vs SD 9–0
1919......May 11	Hod Eller, Cin vs StL 6–0	1975......Aug 24	Ed Halicki, SF vs NY 6–0
1922......May 7	Jesse Barnes, NY vs Phil 6–0	1976......July 9	Larry Dierker, Hou vs Mtl 6–0
1924......July 17	Jesse Haines, StL vs Bos 5–0	Aug 9	John Candelaria, Pitt vs LA 2–0
1925......Sept 13	Dazzy Vance, Bklyn vs Phil 10–1	Sept 29	John Montefusco, SF vs Atl 9–0
1929......May 8	Carl Hubbell, NY vs Pitt 11–0	1978......Apr 16	Bob Forsch, StL vs Phil 5–0
1934......Sept 21	Paul Dean, StL vs Bklyn 3–0	June 16	Tom Seaver, Cin vs StL 4–0
1938......June 11	Johnny Vander Meer, Cin vs Bos 3–0	1979......Apr 7	Ken Forsch, Hou vs Atl 6–0
June 15	Johnny Vander Meer, Cin vs Bklyn 6–0	1980......June 27	Jerry Reuss, LA vs SF 8–0
1940......Apr 30	Tex Carleton, Bklyn vs Cin, 3–0	1981......May 10	Charlie Lea, Mtl vs SF 4–0
1941......Aug 30	Lon Warneke, StL vs Cin 2–0	Sept 26	Nolan Ryan, Hou vs LA 5–0
1944......Apr 27	Jim Tobin, Bos vs Bklyn 2–0	1983......Sept 26	Bob Forsch, StL vs Mtl 3–0
May 15	Clyde Shoun, Cin vs Bos 1–0	1986......Sept 25	Mike Scott, Hou vs SF 2–0
1946......Apr 23	Ed Head, Bklyn vs Bos 5–0	1988......Sept 16	Tom Browning, Cin vs LA 1–0
1947......June 18	Ewell Blackwell, Cin vs Bos 6–0		(perfect game)
1948......Sept 9	Rex Barney, Bklyn vs NY 2–0	1990 ......June 29	Fernando Valenzuela, LA vs StL 6–0
1950......Aug 11	Vern Bickford, Bos vs Bklyn 7–0	1990......Aug 15	Terry Mulholland, Phil vs SF 6–0
1951......May 6	Cliff Chambers, Pitt vs Bos 3–0		
1952......June 19	Carl Erskine, Bklyn vs Chi 5–0		
1954......June 12	Jim Wilson, Mil vs Phil 2–0		
1955......May 12	Sam Jones, Chi vs Pitt 4–0		

Note: Includes the games struck from the official record book on Sept. 4, 1991, when baseball's committee on statistical accuracy voted to define no-hitters as games of nine innings or more that end with a team getting no hits.

No-Hit Games, Nine Innings or More (Cont.)
NATIONAL LEAGUE (Cont.)

Date	Pitcher and Game	Date	Pitcher and Game
1991......May 23	Tommy Greene, Phil vs Mtl 2–0	1996......May 11	Al Leiter, Fla vs Col 11–0
July 26	Mark Gardner, Mtl vs LA 0–1	Sept 17	Hideo Nomo, LA vs Col 9–0
	(hit in 10th, lost in 10th)	1997......June 10	Kevin Brown, Fla vs SF 9–0
July 28	Dennis Martinez, Mtl vs LA 2–0	July 12	Francisco Cordova (9) and
	(perfect game)		Ricardo Rincon (1), Pitt vs Col 3–0
Sept 11	Kent Mercker (6), Mark Wohlers (2),	1999......June 25	Jose Jimenez, StL vs Ariz 1–0
	and Alejandro Pena (1), Atl vs SD 1–0	2001......May 12	A.J. Burnett, Fla vs SD 3–0
1992......Aug 17	Kevin Gross, LA vs SF 2–0	Sept 3	Bud Smith, StL vs SD 4–0
1993......Sept 8	Darryl Kile, Hou vs NY 7–1	2003......June 11	R. Oswalt (1), P. Munro (2.2), K.
1994......Apr 8	Kent Mercker, Atl vs LA 6–0		Saarloos (1.1), B. Lidge (2), O. Dotel
1995......June 3	Pedro Martinez, Mtl vs SD 1–0		(1), B. Wagner (1), Hou vs NYY 8–0
	(perfect through nine, hit in 10th)	April 27	Kevin Millwood, Phil vs SF 1–0
July 14	Ramon Martinez, LA vs Fla 7–0	2004......May 18	Randy Johnson, Ariz vs Atl 2–0
			(perfect game)

AMERICAN LEAGUE

Date	Pitcher and Game	Date	Pitcher and Game
1901......May 9	Earl Moore, Clev vs Chi 2–4	1934......Sept 18	Bobo Newsom, StL vs Bos 1–2
	(hit in 10th; lost in 10th)		(hit in 10th; lost in 10th)
1902......Sept 20	Jimmy Callahan, Chi vs Det 3–0	1935......Aug 31	Vern Kennedy, Chi vs Clev 5–0
1904......May 5	Cy Young, Bos vs Phil 3–0	1937......June 1	Bill Dietrich, Chi vs StL 8–0
	(perfect game)	1938......Aug 27	Mtle Pearson, NY vs Clev 13–0
Aug 17	Jesse Tannehill, Bos vs Chi 6–0	1940......Apr 16	Bob Feller, Chi vs Chi 1–0
1905......July 22	Weldon Henley, Phil vs StL 6–0		(opening day)
Sept 6	Frank Smith, Chi vs Det 15–0	1945......Sept 9	Dick Fowler, Phil vs StL 1–0
Sept 27	Bill Dinneen, Bos vs Chi 2–0	1946......Apr 30	Bob Feller, Clev vs NY 1–0
1908......June 30	Cy Young, Bos vs NY 8–0	1947......July 10	Don Black, Clev vs Phil 3–0
Sept 18	Bob Rhoades, Clev vs Bos 2–1	Sep 3	Bill McCahan, Phil vs Wash 3–0
Sept 20	Frank Smith, Chi vs Phil 1–0	1948......June 30	Bob Lemon, Clev vs Det 2–0
1908......Oct 2	Addie Joss, Clev vs Chi 1–0	1951......July 1	Bob Feller, Clev vs Det 2–1
	(perfect game)	July 12	Allie Reynolds, NY vs Clev 1–0
1910......Apr 20	Addie Joss, Clev vs Chi 1–0	Sept 28	Allie Reynolds, NY vs Bos 8–0
May 12	Chief Bender, Phil vs Clev 4–0	1952......May 15	Virgil Trucks, Det vs Wash 1–0
Aug 30	Tom Hughes, NY vs Clev 0–5	Aug 25	Virgil Trucks, Det vs NY 1–0
	(hit in 10th; lost in 11th)	1953......May 6	Bobo Holloman, StL vs Phil 6–0
1911......July 29	Joe Wood, Bos vs StL 5–0		(first major league start)
Aug 27	Ed Walsh, Chi vs Bos 5–0	1956......July 14	Mel Parnell, Bos vs Chi 4–0
1912......July 4	George Mullin, Det vs StL 7–0	1966......Oct 8	Don Larsen, NY (A) vs Bklyn (N)
Aug 30	Earl Hamilton, StL vs Det 5–1		2–0 (World Series) (perfect game)
1914......May 14	Jim Scott, Chi vs Wash 0–1	1957......Aug 20	Bob Keegan, Chi vs Wash 6–0
	(hit in 10th; lost in 10th)	1958......July 20	Jim Bunning, Det vs Bos 3–0
May 31	Joe Benz, Chi vs Clev 6–1	Sept 20	Hoyt Wilhelm, Balt vs NY 1–0
1916......June 21	George Foster, Bos vs NY 2–0	1962......May 5	Bo Belinsky, LA vs Balt 2–0
Aug 26	Joe Bush, Phil vs Clev 5–0	June 26	Earl Wilson, Bos vs LA 2–0
Aug 30	Dutch Leonard, Bos vs StL 4–0	Aug 1	Bill Monbouquette, Bos vs Chi 1–0
1917......Apr 14	Ed Cicotte, Chi vs StL 11–0	Aug 26	Jack Kralick, Minn vs KC 1–0
Apr 24	George Mogridge, NY vs Bos 2–1	1965......Sept 16	Dave Morehead, Bos vs Clev 2–0
May 5	Ernie Koob, StL vs Chi 1–0	1966......June 10	Sonny Siebert, Clev vs Wash 2–0
May 6	Bob Groom, StL vs Chi 3–0	1967......Apr 30	Steve Barber (8⅔) and Stu Miller (⅓),
June 23	Ernie Shore, Bos vs Wash 4–0		Balt vs Det 1–2
	(perfect game)	Aug 25	Dean Chance, Minn vs Clev 2–1
1918......June 3	Dutch Leonard, Bos vs Det 5–0	Sept 10	Joel Horlen, Chi vs Det 6–0
1919......Sept 10	Ray Caldwell, Clev vs NY 3–0	1968......Apr 27	Tom Phoebus, Balt vs Bos 6–0
1920......July 1	Walter Johnson, Wash vs Bos 1–0	May 8	Catfish Hunter, Oak vs Minn 4–0
1922......Apr 30	Charlie Robertson, Chi vs Det 2–0		(perfect game)
	(perfect game)	1969......Aug 13	Jim Palmer, Balt vs Oak 8–0
1923......Sept 4	Sam Jones, NY vs Phil 2–0	1970......July 3	Clyde Wright, Cal vs Oak 4–0
Sept 7	Howard Ehmke, Bos vs Phil 4–0	Sept 21	Vida Blue, Oak vs Minn 6–0
1926......Aug 21	Ted Lyons, Chi vs Bos 6–0		
1931......Apr 29	Wes Ferrell, Clev vs StL 9–0		
Aug 8	Bob Burke, Wash vs Bos 5–0		

No-Hit Games, Nine Innings or More *(Cont.)*

AMERICAN LEAGUE *(Cont.)*

1973	Apr 27	Steve Busby, KC vs Det 3–0
	May 15	Nolan Ryan, Cal vs KC 3–0
	July 15	Nolan Ryan, Cal vs Det 6–0
	July 30	Jim Bibby, Tex vs Oak 6–0
1974	June 19	Steve Busby, KC vs Mil 2–0
	July 19	Dick Bosman, Clev vs Oak 4–0
	Sept 28	Nolan Ryan, Cal vs Minn 4–0
1975	June 1	Nolan Ryan, Cal vs Balt 1–0
	Sept 28	Vida Blue (5), Glenn Abbott and Paul Lindblad (1), Rollie Fingers (2), Oak vs Cal 5–0
1976	July 28	John Odom (5) and Francisco Barrios (4), Chi vs Oak 2–1
1977	May 14	Jim Colborn, KC vs Tex 6–0
	May 30	Dennis Eckersley, Clev vs Cal 1–0
	Sept 22	Bert Blyleven, Tex vs Cal 6–0
1981	May 15	Len Barker, Clev vs Tor 3–0 (perfect game)
1983	July 4	Dave Righetti, NY vs Bos 4–0
	Sept 29	Mike Warren, Oak vs Chi 3–0
1984	Apr 7	Jack Morris, Det vs Chi 4–0
	Sept 30	Mike Witt, Cal vs Tex 1–0 (perfect game)
1986	Sept 19	Joe Cowley, Chi vs Cal 7–1
1987	Apr 15	Juan Nieves, Mil vs Balt 7–0
1990	Apr 11	Mark Langston (7), Mike Witt (2), Cal vs Sea 1–0
	June 2	Randy Johnson, Sea vs Det 2–0
	June 11	Nolan Ryan, Tex vs Oak 5–0
	June 29	Dave Stewart, Oak vs Tor 5–0
1990	July 1	Andy Hawkins, NY vs Chi 0–4 (pitched eight of nine–innning game)
	Sept 2	Dave Stieb, Tor vs Clev 3–0
1991	May 1	Nolan Ryan, Tex vs Tor 3–0
	July 13	Bob Milacki (6), Mike Flanagan (1), Mark Williamson (1), and Gregg Olson (1), Balt vs Oak 2–0
	Aug 11	Wilson Alvarez, Chi vs Balt 7–0
	Aug 26	Bret Saberhagen, KC vs Chi 7–0
1993	Apr 22	Chris Bosio, Sea vs Bos 7–0
	Sept 4	Jim Abbott, NY vs Clev 4–0
1994	Apr 27	Scott Erickson, Minn vs Mil 6–0
	July 28	Kenny Rogers, Texas vs Cal 4–0 (perfect game)
1996	May 14	Dwight Gooden, NY vs Sea 2–0
1998	May 17	David Wells, NY vs Minn 4–0 (perfect game)
1999	July 18	David Cone, NY vs Mtl 6–0 (perfect game)
	Sept 11	Eric Milton, Minn vs Ana 7–0
2001	Apr 4	Hideo Nomo, Bos vs Balt 3–0
2002	Apr 27	Derek Lowe, Bos vs TB 10–0

Longest Hitting Streaks

NATIONAL LEAGUE

Player and Team	Year	G
Willie Keeler, Balt	1897	44
Pete Rose, Cin	1978	44
Bill Dahlen, Chi	1894	42
Tommy Holmes, Bos	1945	37
Billy Hamilton, Phil	1894	36
Jimmy Rollins, Phil	2005	36
Luis Castillo, Fla	2002	35
Fred Clarke, Lou	1895	35
Benito Santiago, SD	1987	34
George Davis, NY	1893	33
Rogers Hornsby, StL	1922	32

AMERICAN LEAGUE

Player and Team	Year	G
Joe DiMaggio, NY	1941	56
George Sisler, StL	1922	41
Ty Cobb, Det	1911	40
Paul Molitor, Mil	1987	39
Ty Cobb, Det	1917	35
Ty Cobb, Det	1912	34
George Sisler, StL	1925	34
John Stone, Det	1930	34
George McQuinn, StL	1938	34
Dom DiMaggio, Bos	1949	34

Triple Crown Hitters

NATIONAL LEAGUE

Player and Team	Year	HR	RBI	BA
Paul Hines, Prov	1878	4	50	.358
Hugh Duffy, Bos	1894	18	145	.438
Heinie Zimmerman*, Chi	1912	14	103	.372
Rogers Hornsby, StL	1922	42	152	.401
	1925	39	143	.403
Chuck Klein, Phil	1933	28	120	.368
Joe Medwick, StL	1937	31	154	.374

*Zimmerman ranked first in RBIs as calculated by Ernie Lanigan, but only third as calculated by Information Concepts Inc.

AMERICAN LEAGUE

Player and Team	Year	HR	RBI	BA
Nap Lajoie, Phil	1901	14	125	.422
Ty Cobb, Det	1909	9	115	.377
Jimmie Foxx, Phil	1933	48	163	.356
Lou Gehrig, NY	1934	49	165	.363
Ted Williams, Bos	1942	36	137	.356
	1947	32	114	.343
Mickey Mantle, NY	1956	52	130	.353
Frank Robinson, Balt	1966	49	122	.316
Carl Yastrzemski, Bos	1967	44	121	.326

Triple Crown Pitchers

NATIONAL LEAGUE

Player and Team	Year	W	L	SO	ERA
Tommy Bond, Bos	1877	40	17	170	2.11
Hoss Radbourn, Prov	1884	60	12	441	1.38
Tim Keefe, NY	1888	35	12	333	1.74
John Clarkson, Bos	1889	49	19	284	2.73
Amos Rusie, NY	1894	36	13	195	2.78
Christy Mathewson, NY	1905	31	8	206	1.27
	1908	37	11	259	1.43
Grover Alexander, Phil	1915	31	10	241	1.22
	1916	33	12	167	1.55
	1917	30	13	201	1.86
Hippo Vaughn, Chi	1918	22	10	148	1.74
Grover Alexander, Chi	1920	27	14	173	1.91
Dazzy Vance, Bklyn	1924	28	6	262	2.16
Bucky Walters, Cin	1939	27	11	137	2.29
Sandy Koufax, LA	1963	25	5	306	1.88
	1965	26	8	382	2.04
	1966	27	9	317	1.73
Steve Carlton, Phil	1972	27	10	310	1.97
Dwight Gooden, NY	1985	24	4	268	1.53
Randy Johnson, Ariz	2002	24	5	334	2.32

AMERICAN LEAGUE

Player and Team	Year	W	L	SO	ERA
Cy Young, Bos	1901	33	10	158	1.62
Rube Waddell, Phil	1905	26	11	287	1.48
Walter Johnson, Wash	1913	36	7	303	1.09
	1918	23	13	162	1.27
	1924	23	7	158	2.72
Lefty Grove, Phil	1930	28	5	209	2.54
	1931	31	4	175	2.06
Lefty Gomez, NY	1934	26	5	158	2.33
	1937	21	11	194	2.33
Hal Newhouser, Det	1945	25	9	212	1.81
Roger Clemens, Tor	1997	21	7	292	2.05
	1998	20	6	271	2.64
Pedro Martinez, Bos	1999	23	4	313	2.07

Consecutive Games Played, 500 or More Games

Cal Ripken Jr.	2,632	Sandy Alomar Sr.	648
Lou Gehrig	2,130	Eddie Brown	618
Everett Scott	1,307	Miguel Tejada	599
Steve Garvey	1,207	Roy McMillan	585
Billy Williams	1,117	George Pinckney	577
Joe Sewell	1,103	Steve Brodie	574
Stan Musial	895	Aaron Ward	565
Eddie Yost	829	Alex Rodriguez	546
Gus Suhr	822	Candy LaChance	540
Nellie Fox	798	Buck Freeman	535
Pete Rose	745	Fred Luderus	533
Dale Murphy	740	Clyde Milan	511
Richie Ashburn	730	Charlie Gehringer	511
Ernie Banks	717	Vada Pinson	508
Pete Rose	678	Tony Cuccinello	504
Earl Averill	673	Charlie Gehringer	504
Frank McCormick	652	Omar Moreno	503

Unassisted Triple Plays

Player and Team	Date	Pos	Opp	Opp Batter
Neal Ball, Clev	7-19-09	SS	Bos	Amby McConnell
Bill Wambsganss, Clev	10-10-20	2B	Bklyn	Clarence Mitchell
George Burns, Bos	9-14-23	1B	Clev	Frank Brower
Ernie Padgett, Bos	10-6-23	SS	Phil	Walter Holke
Glenn Wright, Pitt	5-7-25	SS	StL	Jim Bottomley
Jimmy Cooney, Chi	5-30-27	SS	Pitt	Paul Waner
Johnny Neun, Det	5-31-27	1B	Clev	Homer Summa
Ron Hansen, Wash	7-30-68	SS	Clev	Joe Azcue
Mickey Morandini, Phil	9-20-92	2B	Pitt	Jeff King
John Valentin, Bos	7-15-94	SS	Minn	Marc Newfield
Randy Velarde, Oak	5-29-00	2B	NYY	Shane Spencer
Rafael Furcal, Atl	8-10-03	SS	StL	Woody Williams

Pennant Winners

Year	Team	Manager	W	L	Pct	GA
1900	Brooklyn	Ned Hanlon	82	54	.603	4½
1901	Pittsburgh	Fred Clarke	90	49	.647	7½
1902	Pittsburgh	Fred Clarke	103	36	.741	27½
1903	Pittsburgh	Fred Clarke	91	49	.650	6½
1904	New York	John McGraw	106	47	.693	13
1905	New York	John McGraw	105	48	.686	9
1906	Chicago	Frank Chance	116	36	.763	20
1907	Chicago	Frank Chance	107	45	.704	17
1908	Chicago	Frank Chance	99	55	.643	1
1909	Pittsburgh	Fred Clarke	110	42	.724	6½
1910	Chicago	Frank Chance	104	50	.675	13
1911	New York	John McGraw	99	54	.647	7½
1912	New York	John McGraw	103	48	.682	10
1913	New York	John McGraw	101	51	.664	12½
1914	Boston	George Stallings	94	59	.614	10½
1915	Philadelphia	Pat Moran	90	62	.592	7
1916	Brooklyn	Wilbert Robinson	94	60	.610	2½
1917	New York	John McGraw	98	56	.636	10
1918	Chicago	Fred Mitchell	84	45	.651	10½
1919	Cincinnati	Pat Moran	96	44	.686	9
1920	Brooklyn	Wilbert Robinson	93	61	.604	7
1921	New York	John McGraw	94	59	.614	4
1922	New York	John McGraw	93	61	.604	7
1923	New York	John McGraw	95	58	.621	4½
1924	New York	John McGraw	93	60	.608	1½
1925	Pittsburgh	Bill McKechnie	95	58	.621	8½
1926	St. Louis	Rogers Hornsby	89	65	.578	2
1927	Pittsburgh	Donie Bush	94	60	.610	1½
1928	St. Louis	Bill McKechnie	95	59	.617	2
1929	Chicago	Joe McCarthy	98	54	.645	10½
1930	St. Louis	Gabby Street	92	62	.597	2
1931	St. Louis	Gabby Street	101	53	.656	13
1932	Chicago	Charlie Grimm	90	64	.584	4
1933	New York	Bill Terry	91	61	.599	5
1934	St. Louis	Frankie Frisch	95	58	.621	2
1935	Chicago	Charlie Grimm	100	54	.649	4
1936	New York	Bill Terry	92	62	.597	5
1937	New York	Bill Terry	95	57	.625	3
1938	Chicago	Gabby Hartnett	89	63	.586	2
1939	Cincinnati	Bill McKechnie	97	57	.630	4½
1940	Cincinnati	Bill McKechnie	100	53	.654	12
1941	Brooklyn	Leo Durocher	100	54	.649	2½
1942	St. Louis	Billy Southworth	106	48	.688	2
1943	St. Louis	Billy Southworth	105	49	.682	18
1944	St. Louis	Billy Southworth	105	49	.682	14½
1945	Chicago	Charlie Grimm	98	56	.636	3
1946	St. Louis*	Eddie Dyer	98	58	.628	2
1947	Brooklyn	Burt Shotton	94	60	.610	5
1948	Boston	Billy Southworth	91	62	.595	6½
1949	Brooklyn	Burt Shotton	97	57	.630	1
1950	Philadelphia	Eddie Sawyer	91	63	.591	2
1951	New York†	Leo Durocher	98	59	.624	1
1952	Brooklyn	Chuck Dressen	96	57	.627	4½
1953	Brooklyn	Chuck Dressen	105	49	.682	13
1954	New York	Leo Durocher	97	57	.630	5
1955	Brooklyn	Walt Alston	98	55	.641	13½
1956	Brooklyn	Walt Alston	93	61	.604	1
1957	Milwaukee	Fred Haney	95	59	.617	8
1958	Milwaukee	Fred Haney	92	62	.597	8
1959	Los Angeles‡	Walt Alston	88	68	.564	2
1960	Pittsburgh	Danny Murtaugh	95	59	.617	7
1961	Cincinnati	Fred Hutchinson	93	61	.604	4
1962	San Francisco#	Al Dark	103	62	.624	1
1963	Los Angeles	Walt Alston	99	63	.611	6
1964	St. Louis	Johnny Keane	93	69	.574	1
1965	Los Angeles	Walt Alston	97	65	.599	2

Pennant Winners (Cont.)

Year	Team	Manager	W	L	Pct	GA
1966	Los Angeles	Walt Alston	95	67	.586	1½
†1967	St. Louis	Red Schoendienst	101	60	.627	10½
1968	St. Louis	Red Schoendienst	97	65	.599	9
1969	New York (E)††	Gil Hodges	100	62	.617	8
1970	Cincinnati (W)††	Sparky Anderson	102	60	.630	14½
1971	Pittsburgh (E)††	Danny Murtaugh	97	65	.599	7
1972	Cincinnati (W)††	Sparky Anderson	95	59	.617	10½
1973	New York (E)††	Yogi Berra	82	79	.509	1½
1974	Los Angeles (W)††	Walt Alston	102	60	.630	4
1975	Cincinnati (W)††	Sparky Anderson	108	54	.667	20
1976	Cincinnati (W)††	Sparky Anderson	102	60	.630	10
1977	Los Angeles (W)††	Tommy Lasorda	98	64	.605	10
1978	Los Angeles (W)††	Tommy Lasorda	95	67	.586	2½
1979	Pittsburgh (E)††	Chuck Tanner	98	64	.605	2
1980	Philadelphia (E)††	Dallas Green	91	71	.562	1
1981	Los Angeles (W)††	Tommy Lasorda	63	47	.573	**
1982	St. Louis (E)††	Whitey Herzog	92	70	.568	3
1983	Philadelphia (E)††	Pat Corrales/ Paul Owens	90	72	.556	6
1984	San Diego (W)††	Dick Williams	92	70	.568	12
1985	St. Louis (E)††	Whitey Herzog	101	61	.623	3
1986	New York (E)††	Dave Johnson	108	54	.667	21½
1987	St. Louis (E)††	Whitey Herzog	95	67	.586	3
1988	Los Angeles (W)††	Tommy Lasorda	94	67	.584	7
1989	San Francisco (W)††	Roger Craig	92	70	.568	3
1990	Cincinnati (W)††	Lou Piniella	91	71	.562	5
1991	Atlanta (W)††	Bobby Cox	94	68	.580	1
1992	Atlanta (W)††	Bobby Cox	98	64	.605	8
1993	Philadelphia (E)††	Jim Fregosi	97	65	.599	3
1994	Season ended Aug. 11 due to players' strike.					
1995	Atlanta (E)††	Bobby Cox	90	54	.625	21
1996	Atlanta (E)††	Bobby Cox	96	66	.593	8
1997	Florida (wc)††	Jim Leyland	92	70	.568	-9
1998	San Diego (W)††	Bruce Bochy	98	64	.605	9½
1999	Atlanta (E)††	Bobby Cox	103	59	.636	6½
2000	New York (wc)††	Bobby Valentine	94	68	.580	-6½
2001	Arizona (W)††	Bob Brenly	92	70	.568	2
2002	San Francisco (wc)††	Dusty Baker	95	66	.590	-2½
2003	Florida (wc)††	Jack McKeon	91	71	.562	-10
2004	St. Louis (C)††	Tony La Russa	105	57	.648	13
2005	Houston (wc)††	Phil Garner	89	73	.549	-11

*Defeated Brooklyn, two games to none, in playoff for pennant. †Defeated Brooklyn, two games to one, in playoff for pennant. ‡Defeated Milwaukee, two games to none, in playoff for pennant. #Defeated Los Angeles, two games to one, in playoff for pennant. ††Won Championship Series. **First half 36–21; second half 27–26, in season split by strike; defeated Houston in playoff for Western Division title.

THEY SAID IT

Chuck Lamar, Devil Rays G.M., on the state of his team: "The only thing that keeps this organization from being recognized as one of the finest in baseball is wins and losses at the major league level."

Leading Batsmen

Year	Player and Team	BA	Year	Player and Team	BA
1900	Honus Wagner, Pitt	.381	1953	Carl Furillo, Bklyn	.344
1901	Jesse Burkett, StL	.382	1954	Willie Mays, NY	.345
1902	Ginger Beaumtl, Pitt	.357	1955	Richie Ashburn, Phil	.338
1903	Honus Wagner, Pitt	.355	1956	Hank Aaron, Mil	.328
1904	Honus Wagner, Pitt	.349	1957	Stan Musial, StL	.351
1905	Cy Seymour, Cin	.377	1958	Richie Ashburn, Phil	.350
1906	Honus Wagner, Pitt	.339	1959	Hank Aaron, Mil	.355
1907	Honus Wagner, Pitt	.350	1960	Dick Groat, Pitt	.325
1908	Honus Wagner, Pitt	.354	1961	Roberto Clemente, Pitt	.351
1909	Honus Wagner, Pitt	.339	1962	Tommy Davis, LA	.346
1910	Sherry Magee, Phil	.331	1963	Tommy Davis, LA	.326
1911	Honus Wagner, Pitt	.334	1964	Roberto Clemente, Pitt	.339
1912	Heinie Zimmerman, Chi	.372	1965	Roberto Clemente, Pitt	.329
1913	Jake Daubert, Bklyn	.350	1966	Matty Alou, Pitt	.342
1914	Jake Daubert, Bklyn	.329	1967	Roberto Clemente, Pitt	.357
1915	Larry Doyle, NY	.320	1968	Pete Rose, Cin	.335
1916	Hal Chase, Cin	.339	1969	Pete Rose, Cin	.348
1917	Edd Roush, Cin	.341	1970	Rico Carty, Atl	.366
1918	Zach Wheat, Bklyn	.335	1971	Joe Torre, StL	.363
1919	Edd Roush, Cin	.321	1972	Billy Williams, Chi	.333
1920	Rogers Hornsby, StL	.370	1973	Pete Rose, Cin	.338
1921	Rogers Hornsby, StL	.397	1974	Ralph Garr, Atl	.353
1922	Rogers Hornsby, StL	.401	1975	Bill Madlock, Chi	.354
1923	Rogers Hornsby, StL	.384	1976	Bill Madlock, Chi	.339
1924	Rogers Hornsby, StL	.424	1977	Dave Parker, Pitt	.338
1925	Rogers Hornsby, StL	.403	1978	Dave Parker, Pitt	.334
1926	Bubbles Hargrave, Cin	.353	1979	Keith Hernandez, StL	.344
1927	Paul Waner, Pitt	.380	1980	Bill Buckner, Chi	.324
1928	Rogers Hornsby, Bos	.387	1981	Bill Madlock, Pitt	.341
1929	Lefty O'Doul, Phil	.398	1982	Al Oliver, Mtl	.331
1930	Bill Terry, NY	.401	1983	Bill Madlock, Pitt	.323
1931	Chick Hafey, StL	.349	1984	Tony Gwynn, SD	.351
1932	Lefty O'Doul, Bklyn	.368	1985	Willie McGee, StL	.353
1933	Chuck Klein, Phil	.368	1986	Tim Raines, Mtl	.334
1934	Paul Waner, Pitt	.362	1987	Tony Gwynn, SD	.370
1935	Arky Vaughan, Pitt	.385	1988	Tony Gwynn, SD	.313
1936	Paul Waner, Pitt	.373	1989	Tony Gwynn, SD	.336
1937	Joe Medwick, StL	.374	1990	Willie McGee, StL	.335
1938	Ernie Lombardi, Cin	.342	1991	Terry Pendleton, Atl	.319
1939	Johnny Mize, StL	.349	1992	Gary Sheffield, SD	.330
1940	Debs Garms, Pitt	.355	1993	Andres Galarraga, Col	.370
1941	Pete Reiser, Bklyn	.343	1994	Tony Gwynn, SD	.394
1942	Ernie Lombardi, Bos	.330	1995	Tony Gwynn, SD	.368
1943	Stan Musial, StL	.357	1996	Tony Gwynn, SD	.353
1944	Dixie Walker, Bklyn	.357	1997	Tony Gwynn, SD	.372
1945	Phil Cavarretta, Chi	.355	1998	Larry Walker, Col	.363
1946	Stan Musial, StL	.365	1999	Larry Walker, Col	.379
1947	Harry Walker, StL-Phil	.363	2000	Todd Helton, Col	.372
1948	Stan Musial, StL	.376	2001	Larry Walker, Col	.350
1949	Jackie Robinson, Bklyn	.342	2002	Barry Bonds, SF	.370
1950	Stan Musial, StL	.346	2003	Albert Pujols, StL	.359
1951	Stan Musial, StL	.355	2004	Barry Bonds, SF	.362
1952	Stan Musial, StL	.336	2005	Derrek Lee, Chi	.335

Leaders in Runs Scored

Year	Player and Team	Runs	Year	Player and Team	Runs
1900	Roy Thomas, Phil	131	1953	Duke Snider, Bklyn	132
1901	Jesse Burkett, StL	139	1954	Stan Musial, StL	120
1902	Honus Wagner, Pitt	105		Duke Snider, Bklyn	120
1903	Ginger Beaumont, Pitt	137	1955	Duke Snider, Bklyn	126
1904	George Browne, NY	99	1956	Frank Robinson, Cin	122
1905	Mike Donlin, NY	124	1957	Hank Aaron, Mil	118
1906	Honus Wagner, Pitt	103	1958	Willie Mays, SF	121
	Frank Chance, Chi	103	1959	Vada Pinson, Cin	131
1907	Spike Shannon, NY	104	1960	Bill Bruton, Mil	112
1908	Fred Tenney, NY	101	1961	Willie Mays, SF	129
1909	Tommy Leach, Pitt	126	1962	Frank Robinson, Cin	134
1910	Sherry Magee, Phil	110	1963	Hank Aaron, Mil	121
1911	Jimmy Sheckard, Chi	121	1964	Dick Allen, Phil	125
1912	Bob Bescher, Cin	120	1965	Tommy Harper, Cin	126
1913	Tommy Leach, Chi	99	1966	Felipe Alou, Atl	122
	Max Carey, Pitt	99	1967	Hank Aaron, Atl	113
1914	George Burns, NY	100		Lou Brock, StL	113
1915	Gavvy Cravath, Phil	89	1968	Glenn Beckert, Chi	98
1916	George Burns, NY	105	1969	Bobby Bonds, SF	120
1917	George Burns, NY	103		Pete Rose, Cin	120
1918	Heinie Groh, Cin	88	1970	Billy Williams, Chi	137
1919	George Burns, NY	86	1971	Lou Brock, StL	126
1920	George Burns, NY	115	1972	Joe Morgan, Cin	122
1921	Rogers Hornsby, StL	131	1973	Bobby Bonds, SF	131
1922	Rogers Hornsby, StL	141	1974	Pete Rose, Cin	110
1923	Ross Youngs, NY	121	1975	Pete Rose, Cin	112
1924	Frankie Frisch, NY	121	1976	Pete Rose, Cin	130
	Rogers Hornsby, StL	121	1977	George Foster, Cin	124
1925	Kiki Cuyler, Pitt	144	1978	Ivan DeJesus, Chi	104
1926	Kiki Cuyler, Pitt	113	1979	Keith Hernandez, StL	116
1927	Lloyd Waner, Pitt	133	1980	Keith Hernandez, StL	111
	Rogers Hornsby, NY	133	1981	Mike Schmidt, Phil	78
1928	Paul Waner, Pitt	142	1982	Lonnie Smith, StL	120
1929	Rogers Hornsby, Chi	156	1983	Tim Raines, Mtl	133
1930	Chuck Klein, Phil	158	1984	Ryne Sandberg, Chi	114
1931	Bill Terry, NY	121	1985	Dale Murphy, Atl	118
	Chuck Klein, Phil	121	1986	Von Hayes, Phil	107
1932	Chuck Klein, Phil	152		Tony Gwynn, SD	107
1933	Pepper Martin, StL	122	1987	Tim Raines, Mtl	123
1934	Paul Waner, Pitt	122	1988	Brett Butler, SF	109
1935	Augie Galan, Chi	133	1989	Howard Johnson, NY	104
1936	Arky Vaughan, Pitt	122		Will Clark, SF	104
1937	Joe Medwick, StL	111		Ryne Sandberg, Chi	104
1938	Mel Ott, NY	116	1990	Ryne Sandberg, Chi	116
1939	Billy Werber, Cin	115	1991	Brett Butler, LA	112
1940	Arky Vaughan, Pitt	113	1992	Barry Bonds, Pitt	109
1941	Pete Reiser, Bklyn	117	1993	Lenny Dykstra, Phil	143
1942	Mel Ott, NY	118	1994	Jeff Bagwell, Hou	104
1943	Arky Vaughan, Bklyn	112	1995	Craig Biggio, Hou	123
1944	Bill Nicholson, Chi	116	1996	Ellis Burks, Col	142
1945	Eddie Stanky, Bklyn	128	1997	Craig Biggio, Hou	146
1946	Stan Musial, StL	124	1998	Sammy Sosa, Chi	134
1947	Johnny Mize, NY	137	1999	Jeff Bagwell, Hou	143
1948	Stan Musial, StL	135	2000	Jeff Bagwell, Hou	152
1949	Pee Wee Reese, Bklyn	132	2001	Sammy Sosa, Chi	146
1950	Earl Torgeson, Bos	120	2002	Sammy Sosa, Chi	122
1951	Stan Musial, StL	124	2003	Albert Pujols, StL	137
	Ralph Kiner, Pitt	124	2004	Albert Pujols, StL	133
1952	Stan Musial, StL	105	2005	Albert Pujols, StL	129
	Solly Hemus, StL	105			

Leaders in Hits

Year	Player and Team	Hits	Year	Player and Team	Hits
1900	Willie Keeler, Bklyn	208	1955	Ted Kluszewski, Cin	192
1901	Jesse Burkett, StL	228	1956	Hank Aaron, Mil	200
1902	Ginger Beaumont, Pitt	194	1957	Red Schoendienst, NY-Mil	200
1903	Ginger Beaumont, Pitt	209	1958	Richie Ashburn, Phil	215
1904	Ginger Beaumont, Pitt	185	1959	Hank Aaron, Mil	223
1905	Cy Seymour, Cin	219	1960	Willie Mays, SF	190
1906	Harry Steinfeldt, Chi	176	1961	Vada Pinson, Cin	208
1907	Ginger Beaumont, Bos	187	1962	Tommy Davis, LA	230
1908	Honus Wagner, Pitt	201	1963	Vada Pinson, Cin	204
1909	Larry Doyle, NY	172	1964	Roberto Clemente, Pitt	211
1910	Honus Wagner, Pitt	178		Curt Flood, StL	211
	Bobby Byrne, Pitt	178	1965	Pete Rose, Cin	209
1911	Doc Miller, Bos	192	1966	Felipe Alou, Atl	218
1912	Heinie Zimmerman, Chi	207	1967	Roberto Clemente, Pitt	209
1913	Gavvy Cravath, Phil	179	1968	Felipe Alou, Atl	210
1914	Sherry Magee, Phil	171		Pete Rose, Cin	210
1915	Larry Doyle, NY	189	1969	Matty Alou, Pitt	231
1916	Hal Chase, Cin	184	1970	Pete Rose, Cin	205
1917	Heinie Groh, Cin	182		Billy Williams, Chi	205
1918	Charlie Hollocher, Chi	161	1971	Joe Torre, StL	230
1919	Ivy Olson, Bklyn	164	1972	Pete Rose, Cin	198
1920	Rogers Hornsby, StL	218	1973	Pete Rose, Cin	230
1921	Rogers Hornsby, StL	235	1974	Ralph Garr, Atl	214
1922	Rogers Hornsby, StL	250	1975	Dave Cash, Phil	213
1923	Frankie Frisch, NY	223	1976	Pete Rose, Cin	215
1924	Rogers Hornsby, StL	227	1977	Dave Parker, Pitt	215
1925	Jim Bottomley, StL	227	1978	Steve Garvey, LA	202
1926	Eddie Brown, Bos	201	1979	Garry Templeton, StL	211
1927	Paul Waner, Pitt	237	1980	Steve Garvey, LA	200
1928	Freddy Lindstrom, NY	231	1981	Pete Rose, Phil	140
1929	Lefty O'Doul, Phil	254	1982	Al Oliver, Mtl	204
1930	Bill Terry, NY	254	1983	Jose Cruz, Hou	189
1931	Lloyd Waner, Pitt	214		Andre Dawson, Mtl	189
1932	Chuck Klein, Phil	226	1984	Tony Gwynn, SD	213
1933	Chuck Klein, Phil	223	1985	Willie McGee, StL	216
1934	Paul Waner, Pitt	217	1986	Tony Gwynn, SD	211
1935	Billy Herman, Chi	227	1987	Tony Gwynn, SD	218
1936	Joe Medwick, StL	223	1988	Andres Galarraga, Mtl	184
1937	Joe Medwick, StL	237	1989	Tony Gwynn, SD	203
1938	Frank McCormick, Cin	209	1990	Brett Butler, SF	192
1939	Frank McCormick, Cin	209		Lenny Dykstra, Phil	192
1940	Stan Hack, Chi	191	1991	Terry Pendleton, Atl	187
	Frank McCormick, Cin	191	1992	Terry Pendleton, Atl	199
1941	Stan Hack, Chi	186		Andy Van Slyke, Pitt	199
1942	Enos Slaughter, StL	188	1993	Lenny Dykstra, Phil	194
1943	Stan Musial, StL	220	1994	Tony Gwynn, SD	165
1944	Stan Musial, StL	197	1995	Dante Bichette, Col	197
	Phil Cavarretta, Chi	197		Tony Gwynn, SD	197
1945	Tommy Holmes, Bos	224	1996	Lance Johnson, NY	227
1946	Stan Musial, StL	228	1997	Tony Gwynn, SD	220
1947	Tommy Holmes, Bos	191	1998	Dante Bichette, Col	219
1948	Stan Musial, StL	230	1999	Luis Gonzalez, Ariz	206
1949	Stan Musial, StL	207	2000	Todd Helton, Col	216
1950	Duke Snider, Bklyn	199	2001	Rich Aurilia, SF	206
1951	Richie Ashburn, Phil	221	2002	Vladimir Guerrero	206
1952	Stan Musial, StL	194	2003	Albert Pujols, StL	212
1953	Richie Ashburn, Phil	205	2004	Juan Pierre, Fla	221
1954	Don Mueller, NY	212	2005	Derrek Lee, Chi	199

Home Run Leaders

Year	Player and Team	HR	Year	Player and Team	HR
1900	Herman Long, Bos	12	1950	Ralph Kiner, Pitt	47
1901	Sam Crawford, Cin	16	1951	Ralph Kiner, Pitt	42
1902	Tommy Leach, Pitt	6	1952	Ralph Kiner, Pitt	37
1903	Jimmy Sheckard, Bklyn	9		Hank Sauer, Chi	37
1904	Harry Lumley, Bklyn	9	1953	Eddie Mathews, Mil	47
1905	Fred Odwell, Cin	9	1954	Ted Kluszewski, Cin	49
1906	Tim Jordan, Bklyn	12	1955	Willie Mays, NY	51
1907	Dave Brain, Bos	10	1956	Duke Snider, Bklyn	43
1908	Tim Jordan, Bklyn	12	1957	Hank Aaron, Mil	44
1909	Red Murray, NY	7	1958	Ernie Banks, Chi	47
1910	Fred Beck, Bos	10	1959	Eddie Mathews, Mil	46
	Wildfire Schulte, Chi	10	1960	Ernie Banks, Chi	41
1911	Wildfire Schulte, Chi	21	1961	Orlando Cepeda, SF	46
1912	Heinie Zimmerman, Chi	14	1962	Willie Mays, SF	49
1913	Gavvy Cravath, Phil	19	1963	Hank Aaron, Mil	44
1914	Gavvy Cravath, Phil	19		Willie McCovey, SF	44
1915	Gavvy Cravath, Phil	24	1964	Willie Mays, SF	47
1916	Dave Robertson, NY	12	1965	Willie Mays, SF	52
	Cy Williams, Chi	12	1966	Hank Aaron, Atl	44
1917	Dave Robertson, NY	12	1967	Hank Aaron, Atl	39
	Gavvy Cravath, Phil	12	1968	Willie McCovey, SF	36
1918	Gavvy Cravath, Phil	8	1969	Willie McCovey, SF	45
1919	Gavvy Cravath, Phil	12	1970	Johnny Bench, Cin	45
1920	Cy Williams, Phil	15	1971	Willie Stargell, Pitt	48
1921	George Kelly, NY	23	1972	Johnny Bench, Cin	40
1922	Rogers Hornsby, StL	42	1973	Willie Stargell, Pitt	44
1923	Cy Williams, Phil	41	1974	Mike Schmidt, Phil	36
1924	Jack Fournier, Bklyn	27	1975	Mike Schmidt, Phil	38
1925	Rogers Hornsby, StL	39	1976	Mike Schmidt, Phil	38
1926	Hack Wilson, Chi	21	1977	George Foster, Cin	52
1927	Hack Wilson, Chi	30	1978	George Foster, Cin	40
	Cy Williams, Phil	30	1979	Dave Kingman, Chi	48
1928	Hack Wilson, Chi	31	1980	Mike Schmidt, Phil	48
	Jim Bottomley, StL	31	1981	Mike Schmidt, Phil	31
1929	Chuck Klein, Phil	43	1982	Dave Kingman, NY	37
1930	Hack Wilson, Chi	56	1983	Mike Schmidt, Phil	40
1931	Chuck Klein, Phil	31	1984	Dale Murphy, Atl	36
1932	Chuck Klein, Phil	38		Mike Schmidt, Phil	36
	Mel Ott, NY	38	1985	Dale Murphy, Atl	37
1933	Chuck Klein, Phil	28	1986	Mike Schmidt, Phil	37
1934	Ripper Collins, StL	35	1987	Andre Dawson, Chi	49
	Mel Ott, NY	35	1988	Darryl Strawberry, NY	39
1935	Wally Berger, Bos	34	1989	Kevin Mitchell, SF	47
1936	Mel Ott, NY	33	1990	Ryne Sandberg, Chi	40
1937	Mel Ott, NY	31	1991	Howard Johnson, NY	38
	Joe Medwick, StL	31	1992	Fred McGriff, SD	35
1938	Mel Ott, NY	36	1993	Barry Bonds, SF	46
1939	Johnny Mize, StL	28	1994	Matt Williams, SF	43
1940	Johnny Mize, StL	43	1995	Dante Bichette, Col	40
1941	Dolph Camilli, Bklyn	34	1996	Andres Galarraga, Col	47
1942	Mel Ott, NY	30	1997	Larry Walker, Col	49
1943	Bill Nicholson, Chi	29	1998	Mark McGwire, StL	70
1944	Bill Nicholson, Chi	33	1999	Mark McGwire, StL	65
1945	Tommy Holmes, Bos	28	2000	Sammy Sosa, Chi	50
1946	Ralph Kiner, Pitt	23	2001	Barry Bonds, SF	73
1947	Ralph Kiner, Pitt	51	2002	Sammy Sosa, Chi	49
	Johnny Mize, NY	51	2003	Jim Thome, Phil	47
1948	Ralph Kiner, Pitt	40	2004	Adrian Beltre, LA	48
	Johnny Mize, NY	40	2005	Andruw Jones, Atl	51
1949	Ralph Kiner, Pitt	54			

Runs Batted In Leaders

Year	Player and Team	RBI	Year	Player and Team	RBI
1900	Elmer Flick, Phil	110	1953	Roy Campanella, Bklyn	142
1901	Honus Wagner, Pitt	126	1954	Ted Kluszewski, Cin	141
1902	Honus Wagner, Pitt	91	1955	Duke Snider, Bklyn	136
1903	Sam Mertes, NY	104	1956	Stan Musial, StL	109
1904	Bill Dahlen, NY	80	1957	Hank Aaron, Mil	132
1905	Cy Seymour, Cin	121	1958	Ernie Banks, Chi	129
1906	Jim Nealon, Pitt	83	1959	Ernie Banks, Chi	143
	Harry Steinfeldt, Chi	83	1960	Hank Aaron, Mil	126
1907	Sherry Magee, Phil	85	1961	Orlando Cepeda, SF	142
1908	Honus Wagner, Pitt	109	1962	Tommy Davis, LA	153
1909	Honus Wagner, Pitt	100	1963	Hank Aaron, Mil	130
1910	Sherry Magee, Phil	123	1964	Ken Boyer, StL	119
1911	Wildfire Schulte, Chi	121	1965	Deron Johnson, Cin	130
1912	Heinie Zimmerman, Chi	103	1966	Hank Aaron, Atl	127
1913	Gavvy Cravath, Phil	128	1967	Orlando Cepeda, StL	111
1914	Sherry Magee, Phil	103	1968	Willie McCovey, SF	105
1915	Gavvy Cravath, Phil	115	1969	Willie McCovey, SF	126
1916	Heinie Zimmerman, Chi-NY	83	1970	Johnny Bench, Cin	148
1917	Heinie Zimmerman, NY	102	1971	Joe Torre, StL	137
1918	Sherry Magee, Phil	76	1972	Johnny Bench, Cin	125
1919	Hi Myers, Bklyn	73	1973	Willie Stargell, Pitt	119
1920	George Kelly, NY	94	1974	Johnny Bench, Cin	129
	Rogers Hornsby, StL	94	1975	Greg Luzinski, Phil	120
1921	Rogers Hornsby, StL	126	1976	George Foster, Cin	121
1922	Rogers Hornsby, StL	152	1977	George Foster, Cin	149
1923	Irish Meusel, NY	125	1978	George Foster, Cin	120
1924	George Kelly, NY	136	1979	Dave Winfield, SD	118
1925	Rogers Hornsby, StL	143	1980	Mike Schmidt, Phil	121
1926	Jim Bottomley, StL	120	1981	Mike Schmidt, Phil	91
1927	Paul Waner, Pitt	131	1982	Dale Murphy, Atl	109
1928	Jim Bottomley, StL	136		Al Oliver, Mtl	109
1929	Hack Wilson, Chi	159	1983	Dale Murphy, Atl	121
1930	Hack Wilson, Chi	190	1984	Gary Carter, Mtl	106
1931	Chuck Klein, Phil	121		Mike Schmidt, Phil	106
1932	Don Hurst, Phil	143	1985	Dave Parker, Cin	125
1933	Chuck Klein, Phil	120	1986	Mike Schmidt, Phil	119
1934	Mel Ott, NY	135	1987	Andre Dawson, Chi	137
1935	Wally Berger, Bos	130	1988	Will Clark, SF	109
1936	Joe Medwick, StL	138	1989	Kevin Mitchell, SF	125
1937	Joe Medwick, StL	154	1990	Matt Williams, SF	122
1938	Joe Medwick, StL	122	1991	Howard Johnson, NY	117
1939	Frank McCormick, Cin	128	1992	Darren Daulton, Phil	109
1940	Johnny Mize, StL	137	1993	Barry Bonds, SF	123
1941	Dolph Camilli, Bklyn	120	1994	Jeff Bagwell, Hou	116
1942	Johnny Mize, NY	110	1995	Dante Bichette, Col	128
1943	Bill Nicholson, Chi	128	1996	Andres Galarraga, Col	150
1944	Bill Nicholson, Chi	122	1997	Andres Galarraga, Col	140
1945	Dixie Walker, Bklyn	124	1998	Sammy Sosa, Chi	158
1946	Enos Slaughter, StL	130	1999	Mark McGwire, StL	147
1947	Johnny Mize, NY	138	2000	Todd Helton, Col	147
1948	Stan Musial, StL	131	2001	Sammy Sosa, Chi	160
1949	Ralph Kiner, Pitt	127	2002	Lance Berkman, Hou	128
1950	Del Ennis, Phil	126	2003	Preston Wilson, Col	141
1951	Monte Irvin, NY	121	2004	Vinny Castilla, Col	131
1952	Hank Sauer, Chi	121	2005	Andruw Jones, Atl	128

Leading Base Stealers

Year	Player and Team	SB	Year	Player and Team	SB
1900	George Van Haltren, NY	45	1951	Sam Jethroe, Bos	35
	Patsy Donovan, StL	45	1952	Pee Wee Reese, Bklyn	30
1901	Honus Wagner, Pitt	48	1953	Bill Bruton, Mil	26
1902	Honus Wagner, Pitt	43	1954	Bill Bruton, Mil	34
1903	Jimmy Sheckard, Bklyn	67	1955	Bill Bruton, Mil	35
	Frank Chance, Chi	67	1956	Willie Mays, NY	40
1904	Honus Wagner, Pitt	53	1957	Willie Mays, NY	38
1905	Billy Maloney, Chi	59	1958	Willie Mays, SF	31
	Art Devlin, NY	59	1959	Willie Mays, SF	27
1906	Frank Chance, Chi	57	1960	Maury Wills, LA	50
1907	Honus Wagner, Pitt	61	1961	Maury Wills, LA	35
1908	Honus Wagner, Pitt	53	1962	Maury Wills, LA	104
1909	Bob Bescher, Cin	54	1963	Maury Wills, LA	40
1910	Bob Bescher, Cin	70	1964	Maury Wills, LA	53
1911	Bob Bescher, Cin	80	1965	Maury Wills, LA	94
1912	Bob Bescher, Cin	67	1966	Lou Brock, StL	74
1913	Max Carey, Pitt	61	1967	Lou Brock, StL	52
1914	George Burns, NY	62	1968	Lou Brock, StL	62
1915	Max Carey, Pitt	36	1969	Lou Brock, StL	53
1916	Max Carey, Pitt	63	1970	Bobby Tolan, Cin	57
1917	Max Carey, Pitt	46	1971	Lou Brock, StL	64
1918	Max Carey, Pitt	58	1972	Lou Brock, StL	63
1919	George Burns, NY	40	1973	Lou Brock, StL	70
1920	Max Carey, Pitt	52	1974	Lou Brock, StL	118
1921	Frankie Frisch, NY	49	1975	Davey Lopes, LA	77
1922	Max Carey, Pitt	51	1976	Davey Lopes, LA	63
1923	Max Carey, Pitt	51	1977	Frank Taveras, Pitt	70
1924	Max Carey, Pitt	49	1978	Omar Moreno, Pitt	71
1925	Max Carey, Pitt	46	1979	Omar Moreno, Pitt	77
1926	Kiki Cuyler, Pitt	35	1980	Ron LeFlore, Mtl	97
1927	Frankie Frisch, StL	48	1981	Tim Raines, Mtl	71
1928	Kiki Cuyler, Chi	37	1982	Tim Raines, Mtl	78
1929	Kiki Cuyler, Chi	43	1983	Tim Raines, Mtl	90
1930	Kiki Cuyler, Chi	37	1984	Tim Raines, Mtl	75
1931	Frankie Frisch, StL	28	1985	Vince Coleman, StL	110
1932	Chuck Klein, Phil	20	1986	Vince Coleman, StL	107
1933	Pepper Martin, StL	26	1987	Vince Coleman, StL	109
1934	Pepper Martin, StL	23	1988	Vince Coleman, StL	81
1935	Augie Galan, Chi	22	1989	Vince Coleman, StL	65
1936	Pepper Martin, StL	23	1990	Vince Coleman, StL	77
1937	Augie Galan, Chi	23	1991	Marquis Grissom, Mtl	76
1938	Stan Hack, Chi	16	1992	Marquis Grissom, Mtl	78
1939	Stan Hack, Chi	17	1993	Chuck Carr, Fla	58
	Lee Handley, Pitt	17	1994	Craig Biggio, Hou	39
1940	Lonny Frey, Cin	22	1995	Quilvio Veras, Fla	56
1941	Danny Murtaugh, Phil	18	1996	Eric Young, Col	53
1942	Pete Reiser, Bklyn	20	1997	Tony Womack, Pitt	60
1943	Arky Vaughan, Bklyn	20	1998	Tony Womack, Pitt	58
1944	Johnny Barrett, Pitt	28	1999	Tony Womack, Ariz	72
1945	Red Schoendienst, StL	26	2000	Luis Castillo, Fla	62
1946	Pete Reiser, Bklyn	34	2001	Juan Pierre, Col	46
1947	Jackie Robinson, Bklyn	29	2002	Luis Castillo, Fla	48
1948	Richie Ashburn, Phil	32	2003	Juan Pierre, Fla	65
1949	Jackie Robinson, Bklyn	37	2004	Scott Podsednik, Mil	70
1950	Sam Jethroe, Bos	35	2005	José Reyes, NY	60

Leading Pitchers—Winning Percentage

Year	Pitcher and Team	W	L	Pct	Year	Pitcher and Team	W	L	Pct
1900	Jesse Tannehill, Pitt	20	6	.769	1954	Johnny Antonelli, NY	21	7	.750
1901	Jack Chesbro, Pitt	21	10	.677	1955	Don Newcombe, Bklyn	20	5	.800
1902	Jack Chesbro, Pitt	28	6	.824	1956	Don Newcombe, Bklyn	27	7	.794
1903	Sam Leever, Pitt	25	7	.781	1957	Bob Buhl, Mil	18	7	.720
1904	Joe McGinnity, NY	35	8	.814	1958	Warren Spahn, Mil	22	11	.667
1905	Sam Leever, Pitt	20	5	.800		Lew Burdette, Mil	20	10	.667
1906	Ed Reulbach, Chi	19	4	.826	1959	Roy Face, Pitt	18	1	.947
1907	Ed Reulbach, Chi	17	4	.810	1960	Ernie Broglio, StL	21	9	.700
1908	Ed Reulbach, Chi	24	7	.774	1961	Johnny Podres, LA	18	5	.783
1909	Christy Mathewson, NY	25	6	.806	1962	Bob Purkey, Cin	23	5	.821
	Howie Camnitz, Pitt	25	6	.806	1963	Ron Perranoski, LA	16	3	.842
1910	King Cole, Chi	20	4	.833	1964	Sandy Koufax, LA	19	5	.792
1911	Rube Marquard, NY	24	7	.774	1965	Sandy Koufax, LA	26	8	.765
1912	Claude Hendrix, Pitt	24	9	.727	1966	Juan Marichal, SF	25	6	.806
1913	Bert Humphries, Chi	16	4	.800	1967	Dick Hughes, StL	16	6	.727
1914	Bill James, Bos	26	7	.788	1968	Steve Blass, Pitt	18	6	.750
1915	Grover Alexander, Phil	31	10	.756	1969	Tom Seaver, NY	25	7	.781
1916	Tom Hughes, Bos	16	3	.842	1970	Bob Gibson, StL	23	7	.767
1917	Ferdie Schupp, NY	21	7	.750	1971	Don Gullett, Cin	16	6	.727
1918	Claude Hendrix, Chi	19	7	.731	1972	Gary Nolan, Cin	15	5	.750
1919	Dutch Ruether, Cin	19	6	.760	1973	Tommy John, LA	16	7	.696
1920	Burleigh Grimes, Bklyn	23	11	.676	1974	Andy Messersmith, LA	20	6	.769
1921	Bill Doak, StL	15	6	.714	1975	Don Gullett, Cin	15	4	.789
1922	Pete Donohue, Cin	18	9	.667	1976	Steve Carlton, Phil	20	7	.741
1923	Dolf Luque, Cin	27	8	.771	1977	John Candelaria, Pitt	20	5	.800
1924	Emil Yde, Pitt	16	3	.842	1978	Gaylord Perry, SD	21	6	.778
1925	Bill Sherdel, StL	15	6	.714	1979	Tom Seaver, Cin	16	6	.727
1926	Ray Kremer, Pitt	20	6	.769	1980	Jim Bibby, Pitt	19	6	.760
1927	Larry Benton, Bos-NY	17	7	.708	1981*	Tom Seaver, Cin	14	2	.875
1928	Larry Benton, NY	25	9	.735	1982	Phil Niekro, Atl	17	4	.810
1929	Charlie Root, Chi	19	6	.760	1983	John Denny, Phil	19	6	.760
1930	Freddie Fitzsimmons, NY	19	7	.731	1984	Rick Sutcliffe, Chi	16	1	.941
1931	Paul Derringer, StL	18	8	.692	1985	Orel Hershiser, LA	19	3	.864
1932	Lon Warneke, Chi	22	6	.786	1986	Bob Ojeda, NY	18	5	.783
1933	Ben Cantwell, Bos	20	10	.667	1987	Dwight Gooden, NY	15	7	.682
1934	Dizzy Dean, StL	30	7	.811	1988	David Cone, NY	20	3	.870
1935	Bill Lee, Chi	20	6	.769	1989	Mike Bielecki, Chi	18	7	.720
1936	Carl Hubbell, NY	26	6	.813	1990	Doug Drabeck, Pitt	22	6	.786
1937	Carl Hubbell, NY	22	8	.733	1991	John Smiley, Pitt	20	8	.714
1938	Bill Lee, Chi	22	9	.710		Jose Rijo, Cin	15	6	.714
1939	Paul Derringer, Cin	25	7	.781	1992	Bob Tewksbury, StL	16	5	.762
1940	Freddie Fitzsimmons, Bklyn	16	2	.889	1993	Tom Glavine, Atl	22	6	.786
1941	Elmer Riddle, Cin	19	4	.826	1994	Ken Hill, Mtl	16	5	.762
1942	Larry French, Bklyn	15	4	.789	1995	Greg Maddux, Atl	19	2	.905
1943	Mort Cooper, StL	21	8	.724	1996	John Smoltz, Atl	24	8	.750
1944	Ted Wilks, StL	17	4	.810	1997	Denny Neagle, Atl	20	5	.800
1945	Harry Brecheen, StL	15	4	.789	1998	John Smoltz, Atl	17	3	.850
1946	Murray Dickson, StL	15	6	.714	1999	Mike Hampton, Hou	22	4	.846
1947	Larry Jansen, NY	21	5	.808	2000	Randy Johnson, Ariz	19	7	.730
1948	Harry Brecheen, StL	20	7	.741	2001	Curt Schilling, Ariz	22	6	.786
1949	Preacher Roe, Bklyn	15	6	.714	2002	Randy Johnson, Ariz	24	5	.828
1950	Sal Maglie, NY	18	4	.818	2003	Jason Schmidt, SF	17	5	.773
1951	Preacher Roe, Bklyn	22	3	.880	2004	Roger Clemens, Hou	18	4	.818
1952	Hoyt Wilhelm, NY	15	3	.833	2005	Chris Carpenter, StL	21	5	.808
1953	Carl Erskine, Bklyn	20	6	.769					

*1981 percentages based on 10 or more victories. Note: Percentages based on 15 or more victories in all other years.

Leading Pitchers—Earned Run Average

Year	Player and Team	ERA	Year	Player and Team	ERA
1900	Rube Waddell, Pitt	2.37	1953	Warren Spahn, Mil	2.10
1901	Jesse Tannehill, Pitt	2.18	1954	Johnny Antonelli, NY	2.29
1902	Jack Taylor, Chi	1.33	1955	Bob Friend, Pitt	2.84
1903	Sam Leever, Pitt	2.06	1956	Lew Burdette, Mil	2.71
1904	Joe McGinnity, NY	1.61	1957	Johnny Podres, Bklyn	2.66
1905	Christy Mathewson, NY	1.27	1958	Stu Miller, SF	2.47
1906	Three Finger Brown, Chi	1.04	1959	Sam Jones, SF	2.82
1907	Jack Pfiester, Chi	1.15	1960	Mike McCormick, SF	2.70
1908	Christy Mathewson, NY	1.43	1961	Warren Spahn, Mil	3.01
1909	Christy Mathewson, NY	1.14	1962	Sandy Koufax, LA	2.54
1910	George McQuillan, Phil	1.60	1963	Sandy Koufax, LA	1.88
1911	Christy Mathewson, NY	1.99	1964	Sandy Koufax, LA	1.74
1912	Jeff Tesreau, NY	1.96	1965	Sandy Koufax, LA	2.04
1913	Christy Mathewson, NY	2.06	1966	Sandy Koufax, LA	1.73
1914	Bill Doak, StL	1.72	1967	Phil Niekro, Atl	1.87
1915	Grover Alexander, Phil	1.22	1968	Bob Gibson, StL	1.12
1916	Grover Alexander, Phil	1.55	1969	Juan Marichal, SF	2.10
1917	Grover Alexander, Phil	1.83	1970	Tom Seaver, NY	2.81
1918	Hippo Vaughn, Chi	1.74	1971	Tom Seaver, NY	1.76
1919	Grover Alexander, Chi	1.72	1972	Steve Carlton, Phil	1.98
1920	Grover Alexander, Chi	1.91	1973	Tom Seaver, NY	2.08
1921	Bill Doak, StL	2.58	1974	Buzz Capra, Atl	2.28
1922	Rosy Ryan, NY	3.00	1975	Randy Jones, SD	2.24
1923	Dolf Luque, Cin	1.93	1976	John Denny, StL	2.52
1924	Dazzy Vance, Bklyn	2.16	1977	John Candelaria, Pitt	2.34
1925	Dolf Luque, Cin	2.63	1978	Craig Swan, NY	2.43
1926	Ray Kremer, Pitt	2.61	1979	J.R. Richard, Hou	2.71
1927	Ray Kremer, Pitt	2.47	1980	Don Sutton, LA	2.21
1928	Dazzy Vance, Bklyn	2.09	1981	Nolan Ryan, Hou	1.69
1929	Bill Walker, NY	3.08	1982	Steve Rogers, Mtl	2.40
1930	Dazzy Vance, Bklyn	2.61	1983	Atlee Hammaker, SF	2.25
1931	Bill Walker, NY	2.26	1984	Alejandro Pena, LA	2.48
1932	Lon Warneke, Chi	2.37	1985	Dwight Gooden, NY	1.53
1933	Carl Hubbell, NY	1.66	1986	Mike Scott, Hou	2.22
1934	Carl Hubbell, NY	2.30	1987	Nolan Ryan, Hou	2.76
1935	Cy Blanton, Pitt	2.59	1988	Joe Magrane, StL	2.18
1936	Carl Hubbell, NY	2.31	1989	Scott Garrelts, SF	2.28
1937	Jim Turner, Bos	2.38	1990	Danny Darwin, Hou	2.21
1938	Bill Lee, Chi	2.66	1991	Dennis Martinez, Mtl	2.39
1939	Bucky Walters, Cin	2.29	1992	Bill Swift, SF	2.08
1940	Bucky Walters, Cin	2.48	1993	Greg Maddux, Atl	2.36
1941	Elmer Riddle, Cin	2.24	1994	Greg Maddux, Atl	1.56
1942	Mort Cooper, StL	1.77	1995	Greg Maddux, Atl	1.63
1943	Howie Pollet, StL	1.75	1996	Kevin Brown, Fla	1.89
1944	Ed Heusser, Cin	2.38	1997	Pedro Martinez, Mtl	1.90
1945	Hank Borowy, Chi	2.14	1998	Greg Maddux, Atl	1.98
1946	Howie Pollet, StL	2.10	1999	Randy Johnson, Ariz	2.48
1947	Warren Spahn, Bos	2.33	2000	Kevin Brown, LA	2.58
1948	Harry Brecheen, StL	2.24	2001	Randy Johnson, Ariz	2.49
1949	Dave Koslo, NY	2.50	2002	Randy Johnson, Ariz	2.32
1950	Jim Hearn, StL-NY	2.49	2003	Jason Schmidt, SF	2.34
1951	Chet Nichols, Bos	2.88	2004	Jake Peavy, SD	2.27
1952	Hoyt Wilhelm, NY	2.43	2005	Roger Clemens, Hou	1.87

Note: Based on 10 complete games through 1950, then 154 innings until National League expanded in 1962, when it became 162 innings. In strike-shortened 1981, one inning per game required.

Leading Pitchers—Strikeouts

Year	Player and Team	SO	Year	Player and Team	SO
1900	Rube Waddell, Pitt	133	1952	Warren Spahn, Bos	183
1901	Noodles Hahn, Cin	233	1953	Robin Roberts, Phil	198
1902	Vic Willis, Bos	226	1954	Robin Roberts, Phil	185
1903	Christy Mathewson, NY	267	1955	Sam Jones, Chi	198
1904	Christy Mathewson, NY	212	1956	Sam Jones, Chi	176
1905	Christy Mathewson, NY	206	1957	Jack Sanford, Phil	188
1906	Fred Beebe, Chi-StL	171	1958	Sam Jones, StL	225
1907	Christy Mathewson, NY	178	1959	Don Drysdale, LA	242
1908	Christy Mathewson, NY	259	1960	Don Drysdale, LA	246
1909	Orval Overall, Chi	205	1961	Sandy Koufax, LA	269
1910	Christy Mathewson, NY	190	1962	Don Drysdale, LA	232
1911	Rube Marquard, NY	237	1963	Sandy Koufax, LA	306
1912	Grover Alexander, Phil	195	1964	Bob Veale, Pitt	250
1913	Tom Seaton, Phil	168	1965	Sandy Koufax, LA	382
1914	Grover Alexander, Phil	214	1966	Sandy Koufax, LA	317
1915	Grover Alexander, Phil	241	1967	Jim Bunning, Phil	253
1916	Grover Alexander, Phil	167	1968	Bob Gibson, StL	268
1917	Grover Alexander, Phil	200	1969	Ferguson Jenkins, Chi	273
1918	Hippo Vaughn, Chi	148	1970	Tom Seaver, NY	283
1919	Hippo Vaughn, Chi	141	1971	Tom Seaver, NY	289
1920	Grover Alexander, Chi	173	1972	Steve Carlton, Phil	310
1921	Burleigh Grimes, Bklyn	136	1973	Tom Seaver, NY	251
1922	Dazzy Vance, Bklyn	134	1974	Steve Carlton, Phil	240
1923	Dazzy Vance, Bklyn	197	1975	Tom Seaver, NY	243
1924	Dazzy Vance, Bklyn	262	1976	Tom Seaver, NY	235
1925	Dazzy Vance, Bklyn	221	1977	Phil Niekro, Atl	262
1926	Dazzy Vance, Bklyn	140	1978	J.R. Richard, Hou	303
1927	Dazzy Vance, Bklyn	184	1979	J.R. Richard, Hou	313
1928	Dazzy Vance, Bklyn	200	1980	Steve Carlton, Phil	286
1929	Pat Malone, Chi	166	1981	Fernando Valenzuela, LA	180
1930	Bill Hallahan, StL	177	1982	Steve Carlton, Phil	286
1931	Bill Hallahan, StL	159	1983	Steve Carlton, Phil	275
1932	Dizzy Dean, StL	191	1984	Dwight Gooden, NY	276
1933	Dizzy Dean, StL	199	1985	Dwight Gooden, NY	268
1934	Dizzy Dean, StL	195	1986	Mike Scott, Hou	306
1935	Dizzy Dean, StL	182	1987	Nolan Ryan, Hou	270
1936	Van Lingle Mungo, Bklyn	238	1988	Nolan Ryan, Hou	228
1937	Carl Hubbell, NY	159	1989	Jose DeLeon, StL	201
1938	Clay Bryant, Chi	135	1990	David Cone, NY	233
1939	Claude Passeau, Phil-Chi	137	1991	David Cone, NY	241
	Bucky Walters, Cin	137	1992	John Smoltz, Atl	215
1940	Kirby Higbe, Phil	137	1993	Jose Rijo, Cin	227
1941	Johnny Vander Meer, Cin	202	1994	Andy Benes, SD	189
1942	Johnny Vander Meer, Cin	186	1995	Hideo Nomo, LA	236
1943	Johnny Vander Meer, Cin	174	1996	John Smoltz, Atl	276
1944	Bill Voiselle, NY	161	1997	Curt Schilling, Phil	319
1945	Preacher Roe, Pitt	148	1998	Curt Schilling, Phil	300
1946	Johnny Schmitz, Chi	135	1999	Randy Johnson, Ariz	364
1947	Ewell Blackwell, Cin	193	2000	Randy Johnson, Ariz	347
1948	Harry Brecheen, StL	149	2001	Randy Johnson, Ariz	372
1949	Warren Spahn, Bos	151	2002	Randy Johnson, Ariz	334
1950	Warren Spahn, Bos	191	2003	Kerry Wood, Chi	266
1951	Warren Spahn, Bos	164	2004	Randy Johnson, Ariz	290
	Don Newcombe, Bklyn	164	2005	Jake Peavy, SD	216

Leading Pitchers—Saves

Year	Player and Team	SV	Year	Player and Team	SV
1947	Hugh Casey, Bklyn	18	1976	Rawly Eastwick, Cin	26
1948	Harry Gumpert, Cin	17	1977	Rollie Fingers, SD	35
1949	Ted Wilks, StL	9	1978	Rollie Fingers, SD	37
1950	Jim Konstanty, Phil	22	1979	Bruce Sutter, Chi	37
1951	Ted Wilks, StL, Pitt	13	1980	Bruce Sutter, Chi	28
1952	Al Brazle, StL	16	1981	Bruce Sutter, StL	25
1953	Al Brazle, StL	18	1982	Bruce Sutter, StL	36
1954	Jim Hughes, Bklyn	24	1983	Lee Smith, Chi	29
1955	Jack Meyer, Phil	16	1984	Bruce Sutter, StL	45
1956	Clem Labine, Bklyn	19	1985	Jeff Reardon, Mtl	41
1957	Clem Labine, Bklyn	17	1986	Todd Worrell, StL	36
1958	Roy Face, Pitt	20	1987	Steve Bedrosian, Phil	40
1959	Lindy McDaniel, StL	15	1988	John Franco, Cin	39
	Don McMahon, Mil	15	1989	Mark Davis, SD	44
1960	Lindy McDaniel, StL	26	1990	John Franco, NY	33
1961	Stu Miller, SF	17	1991	Lee Smith, StL	47
	Roy Face, Pitt	17	1992	Lee Smith, StL	42
1962	Roy Face, Pitt	28	1993	Randy Myers, Chi	53
1963	Lindy McDaniel, Chi	22	1994	John Franco, NY	30
1964	Hal Woodeshick, Hou	23	1995	Randy Myers, Chi	38
1965	Ted Abernathy, Chi	31	1996	Jeff Brantley, Cin	44
1966	Phil Regan, LA	21		Todd Worrell, LA	44
1967	Ted Abernathy, Cin	28	1997	Jeff Shaw, Cin	42
1968	Phil Regan, Chi, LA	25	1998	Trevor Hoffman, SD	53
1969	Fred Gladding, Hou	29	1999	Ugueth Urbina, Mtl	41
1970	Wayne Granger, Cin	35	2000	Antonio Alfonseca, Fla	45
1971	Dave Giusti, Pitt	30	2001	Robb Nen, SF	45
1972	Clay Carroll, Cin	37	2002	John Smoltz, Atl	55
1973	Mike Marshall, Mtl	13	2003	Eric Gagne, LA	55
1974	Mike Marshall, LA	21	2004	Armando Benitez, Fla	47
1975	Al Hrabosky, StL	22		Jason Isringhausen, StL	47
	Rawly Eastwick, Cin	22	2005	Chad Cordero, Wash	47

American League

Pennant Winners

Year	Team	Manager	W	L	Pct	GA
1901	Chicago	Clark Griffith	83	53	.610	4
1902	Philadelphia	Connie Mack	83	53	.610	5
1903	Boston	Jimmy Collins	91	47	.659	14½
1904	Boston	Jimmy Collins	95	59	.617	1½
1905	Philadelphia	Connie Mack	92	56	.622	2
1906	Chicago	Fielder Jones	93	58	.616	3
1907	Detroit	Hughie Jennings	92	58	.613	1½
1908	Detroit	Hughie Jennings	90	63	.588	½
1909	Detroit	Hughie Jennings	98	54	.645	3½
1910	Philadelphia	Connie Mack	102	48	.680	14½
1911	Philadelphia	Connie Mack	101	50	.669	13½
1912	Boston	Jake Stahl	105	47	.691	14
1913	Philadelphia	Connie Mack	96	57	.627	6½
1914	Philadelphia	Connie Mack	99	53	.651	8½
1915	Boston	Bill Carrigan	101	50	.669	2½
1916	Boston	Bill Carrigan	91	63	.591	2
1917	Chicago	Pants Rowland	100	54	.649	9
1918	Boston	Ed Barrow	75	51	.595	2½
1919	Chicago	Kid Gleason	88	52	.629	3½
1920	Cleveland	Tris Speaker	98	56	.636	2
1921	New York	Miller Huggins	98	55	.641	4½
1922	New York	Miller Huggins	94	60	.610	1
1923	New York	Miller Huggins	98	54	.645	16
1924	Washington	Bucky Harris	92	62	.597	2
1925	Washington	Bucky Harris	96	55	.636	8½
1926	New York	Miller Huggins	91	63	.591	3

Pennant Winners

Year	Team	Manager	W	L	Pct	GA
1927	New York	Miller Huggins	110	44	.714	19
1928	New York	Miller Huggins	101	53	.656	2½
1929	Philadelphia	Connie Mack	104	46	.693	18
1930	Philadelphia	Connie Mack	102	52	.662	8
1931	Philadelphia	Connie Mack	107	45	.704	13½
1932	New York	Joe McCarthy	107	47	.695	13
1933	Washington	Joe Cronin	99	53	.651	7
1934	Detroit	Mickey Cochrane	101	53	.656	7
1935	Detroit	Mickey Cochrane	93	58	.616	3
1936	New York	Joe McCarthy	102	51	.667	19½
1937	New York	Joe McCarthy	102	52	.662	13
1938	New York	Joe McCarthy	99	53	.651	9½
1939	New York	Joe McCarthy	106	45	.702	17
1940	Detroit	Del Baker	90	64	.584	1
1941	New York	Joe McCarthy	101	53	.656	17
1942	New York	Joe McCarthy	103	51	.669	9
1943	New York	Joe McCarthy	98	56	.636	13½
1944	St. Louis	Luke Sewell	89	65	.578	1
1945	Detroit	Steve O'Neill	88	65	.575	1½
1946	Boston	Joe Cronin	104	50	.675	12
1947	New York	Bucky Harris	97	57	.630	12
1948	Cleveland†	Lou Boudreau	97	58	.626	1
1949	New York	Casey Stengel	97	57	.630	1
1950	New York	Casey Stengel	98	56	.636	3
1951	New York	Casey Stengel	98	56	.636	5
1952	New York	Casey Stengel	95	59	.617	2
1953	New York	Casey Stengel	99	52	.656	8½
1954	Cleveland	Al Lopez	111	43	.721	8
1955	New York	Casey Stengel	96	58	.623	3
1956	New York	Casey Stengel	97	57	.630	9
1957	New York	Casey Stengel	98	56	.636	8
1958	New York	Casey Stengel	92	62	.597	10
1959	Chicago	Al Lopez	94	60	.610	5
1960	New York	Casey Stengel	97	57	.630	8
1961	New York	Ralph Houk	109	53	.673	8
1962	New York	Ralph Houk	96	66	.593	5
1963	New York	Ralph Houk	104	57	.646	10½
1964	New York	Yogi Berra	99	63	.611	1
1965	Minnesota	Sam Mele	102	60	.630	7
1966	Baltimore	Hank Bauer	97	63	.606	9
1967	Boston	Dick Williams	92	70	.568	1
1968	Detroit	Mayo Smith	103	59	.636	12
1969	Baltimore (E)‡	Earl Weaver	109	53	.673	19
1970	Baltimore (E)‡	Earl Weaver	108	54	.667	15
1971	Baltimore (E)‡	Earl Weaver	101	57	.639	12
1972	Oakland (W)‡	Dick Williams	93	62	.600	5½
1973	Oakland (W)‡	Dick Williams	94	68	.580	6
1974	Oakland (W)‡	Al Dark	90	72	.556	5
1975	Boston (E)‡	Darrell Johnson	95	65	.594	4½
1976	New York (E)‡	Billy Martin	97	62	.610	10½
1977	New York (E)‡	Billy Martin	100	62	.617	2½
1978	New York (E)†‡	Billy Martin, Bob Lemon	100	63	.613	1
1979	Baltimore (E)‡	Earl Weaver	102	57	.642	8
1980	Kansas City (W)‡	Jim Frey	97	65	.599	14
1981	New York (E)‡	Gene Michael/Bob Lemon	59	48	.551	#
1982	Milwaukee (E)‡	Buck Rodgers, Harvey Kuenn	95	67	.586	1
1983	Baltimore (E)‡	Joe Altobelli	98	64	.605	6
1984	Detroit (E)‡	Sparky Anderson	104	58	.642	15
1985	Kansas City (W)‡	Dick Howser	91	71	.562	1
1986	Boston (E)‡	John McNamara	95	66	.590	5½
1987	Minnesota (W)‡	Tom Kelly	85	77	.525	2
1988	Oakland (W)‡	Tony La Russa	104	58	.642	13
1989	Oakland (W)‡	Tony La Russa	99	63	.611	7
1990	Oakland (W)‡	Tony La Russa	103	59	.636	9

Pennant Winners *(Cont.)*

Year	Team	Manager	W	L	Pct	GA
1991	Minnesota (W)‡	Tom Kelly	95	67	.586	8
1992	Toronto‡	Cito Gaston	96	66	.593	4
1993	Toronto‡	Cito Gaston	95	67	.586	7
1994	Season ended Aug. 11 due to players' strike.					
1995	Cleveland (C)‡	Mike Hargrove	100	44	.694	30
1996	New York (E)‡	Joe Torre	92	70	.568	4
1997	Cleveland (C)‡	Mike Hargrove	86	75	.534	6
1998	New York (E)‡	Joe Torre	114	48	.704	22
1999	New York (E)‡	Joe Torre	98	64	.605	4
2000	New York (E)‡	Joe Torre	87	74	.540	2½
2001	New York (E)‡	Joe Torre	95	65	.594	13½
2002	Anaheim (wc)‡	Mike Scioscia	99	63	.611	-4
2003	New York (E)‡	Joe Torre	101	61	.623	6
2004	Boston (wc)‡	Terry Francona	98	64	.605	-3
2005	Chicago (C)‡	Ozzie Guillen	99	63	.611	6

†Defeated Boston in one-game playoff. ‡Won championship series.

#First half 34–22; second half 25–26, in season split by strike; defeated Milwaukee in playoff for Eastern Divison title.

Leading Batsmen

Year	Player and Team	BA	Year	Player and Team	BA
1901	Nap Lajoie, Phil	.422	1945	Snuffy Stirnweiss, NY	.309
1902	Ed Delahanty, Wash	.376	1946	Mickey Vernon, Wash	.353
1903	Nap Lajoie, Clev	.355	1947	Ted Williams, Bos	.343
1904	Nap Lajoie, Clev	.381	1948	Ted Williams, Bos	.369
1905	Elmer Flick, Clev	.306	1949	George Kell, Det	.343
1906	George Stone, StL	.358	1950	Billy Goodman, Bos	.354
1907	Ty Cobb, Det	.350	1951	Ferris Fain, Phil	.344
1908	Ty Cobb, Det	.324	1952	Ferris Fain, Phil	.327
1909	Ty Cobb, Det	.377	1953	Mickey Vernon, Wash	.337
1910	Nap Lajoie, Clev*	.383	1954	Bobby Avila, Clev	.341
1911	Ty Cobb, Det	.420	1955	Al Kaline, Det	.340
1912	Ty Cobb, Det	.410	1956	Mickey Mantle, NY	.353
1913	Ty Cobb, Det	.390	1957	Ted Williams, Bos	.388
1914	Ty Cobb, Det	.368	1958	Ted Williams, Bos	.328
1915	Ty Cobb, Det	.369	1959	Harvey Kuenn, Det	.353
1916	Tris Speaker, Clev	.386	1960	Pete Runnels, Bos	.320
1917	Ty Cobb, Det	.383	1961	Norm Cash, Det	.361
1918	Ty Cobb, Det	.382	1962	Pete Runnels, Bos	.326
1919	Ty Cobb, Det	.384	1963	Carl Yastrzemski, Bos	.321
1920	George Sisler, StL	.407	1964	Tony Oliva, Minn	.323
1921	Harry Heilmann, Det	.394	1965	Tony Oliva, Minn	.321
1922	George Sisler, StL	.420	1966	Frank Robinson, Balt	.316
1923	Harry Heilmann, Det	.403	1967	Carl Yastrzemski, Bos	.326
1924	Babe Ruth, NY	.378	1968	Carl Yastrzemski, Bos	.301
1925	Harry Heilmann, Det	.393	1969	Rod Carew, Minn	.332
1926	Heinie Manush, Det	.378	1970	Alex Johnson, Cal	.329
1927	Harry Heilmann, Det	.398	1971	Tony Oliva, Minn	.337
1928	Goose Goslin, Wash	.379	1972	Rod Carew, Minn	.318
1929	Lew Fonseca, Clev	.369	1973	Rod Carew, Minn	.350
1930	Al Simmons, Phil	.381	1974	Rod Carew, Minn	.364
1931	Al Simmons, Phil	.390	1975	Rod Carew, Minn	.359
1932	Dale Alexander, Det-Bos	.367	1976	George Brett, KC	.333
1933	Jimmie Foxx, Phil	.356	1977	Rod Carew, Minn	.388
1934	Lou Gehrig, NY	.363	1978	Rod Carew, Minn	.333
1935	Buddy Myer, Wash	.349	1979	Fred Lynn, Bos	.333
1936	Luke Appling, Chi	.388	1980	George Brett, KC	.390
1937	Charlie Gehringer, Det	.371	1981	Carney Lansford, Bos	.336
1938	Jimmie Foxx, Bos	.349	1982	Willie Wilson, KC	.332
1939	Joe DiMaggio, NY	.381	1983	Wade Boggs, Bos	.361
1940	Joe DiMaggio, NY	.352	1984	Don Mattingly, NY	.343
1941	Ted Williams, Bos	.406	1985	Wade Boggs, Bos	.368
1942	Ted Williams, Bos	.356	1986	Wade Boggs, Bos	.357
1943	Luke Appling, Chi	.328	1987	Wade Boggs, Bos	.363
1944	Lou Boudreau, Clev	.327	1988	Wade Boggs, Bos	.366

*League president Ban Johnson declared Ty Cobb batting champion with a .385 average, beating Lajoie's .384. However, subsequent research has led to the revision of Lajoie's average to .383 and Cobb's to .382.

Leading Batsmen (Cont.)

Year	Player and Team	BA	Year	Player and Team	BA
1989	Kirby Puckett, Minn	.339	1998	Bernie Williams, NY	.339
1990	George Brett, KC	.329	1999	Nomar Garciaparra, Bos	.357
1991	Julio Franco, Tex	.341	2000	Nomar Garciaparra, Bos	.372
1992	Edgar Martinez, Sea	.343	2001	Ichiro Suzuki, Sea	.350
1993	John Olerud, Tor	.363	2002	Manny Ramirez, Bos	.349
1994	Paul O'Neill, NY	.359	2003	Bill Mueller, Bos	.326
1995	Edgar Martinez, Sea	.356	2004	Ichiro Suzuki, Sea	.372
1996	Alex Rodriguez, Sea	.358	2005	Michael Young, Tex	.331
1997	Frank Thomas, Chi	.347			

Leaders in Runs Scored

Year	Player and Team	Runs	Year	Player and Team	Runs
1901	Nap Lajoie, Phil	145	1952	Larry Doby, Clev	104
1902	Dave Fultz, Phil	110	1953	Al Rosen, Clev	115
1903	Patsy Dougherty, Bos	108	1954	Mickey Mantle, NY	129
1904	Patsy Dougherty, Bos-NY	113	1955	Al Smith, Clev	123
1905	Harry Davis, Phil	92	1956	Mickey Mantle, NY	132
1906	Elmer Flick, Clev	98	1957	Mickey Mantle, NY	121
1907	Sam Crawford, Det	102	1958	Mickey Mantle, NY	127
1908	Matty McIntyre, Det	105	1959	Eddie Yost, Det	115
1909	Ty Cobb, Det	116	1960	Mickey Mantle, NY	119
1910	Ty Cobb, Det	106	1961	Mickey Mantle, NY	132
1911	Ty Cobb, Det	147		Roger Maris, NY	132
1912	Eddie Collins, Phil	137	1962	Albie Pearson, LA	115
1913	Eddie Collins, Phil	125	1963	Bob Allison, Minn	99
1914	Eddie Collins, Phil	122	1964	Tony Oliva, Minn	109
1915	Ty Cobb, Det	144	1965	Zoilo Versalles, Minn	126
1916	Ty Cobb, Det	113	1966	Frank Robinson, Balt	122
1917	Donie Bush, Det	112	1967	Carl Yastrzemski, Bos	112
1918	Ray Chapman, Clev	84	1968	Dick McAuliffe, Det	95
1919	Babe Ruth, Bos	103	1969	Reggie Jackson, Oak	123
1920	Babe Ruth, NY	158	1970	Carl Yastrzemski, Bos	125
1921	Babe Ruth, NY	177	1971	Don Buford, Balt	99
1922	George Sisler, StL	134	1972	Bobby Murcer, NY	102
1923	Babe Ruth, NY	151	1973	Reggie Jackson, Oak	99
1924	Babe Ruth, NY	143	1974	Carl Yastrzemski, Bos	93
1925	Johnny Mostil, Chi	135	1975	Fred Lynn, Bos	103
1926	Babe Ruth, NY	139	1976	Roy White, NY	104
1927	Babe Ruth, NY	158	1977	Rod Carew, Minn	128
1928	Babe Ruth, NY	163	1978	Ron LeFlore, Det	126
1929	Charlie Gehringer, Det	131	1979	Don Baylor, Cal	120
1930	Al Simmons, Phil	152	1980	Willie Wilson, KC	133
1931	Lou Gehrig, NY	163	1981	Rickey Henderson, Oak	89
1932	Jimmie Foxx, Phil	151	1982	Paul Molitor, Mil	136
1933	Lou Gehrig, NY	138	1983	Cal Ripken, Balt	121
1934	Charlie Gehringer, Det	134	1984	Dwight Evans, Bos	121
1935	Lou Gehrig, NY	125	1985	Rickey Henderson, NY	146
1936	Lou Gehrig, NY	167	1986	Rickey Henderson, NY	130
1937	Joe DiMaggio, NY	151	1987	Paul Molitor, Mil	114
1938	Hank Greenberg, Det	144	1988	Wade Boggs, Bos	128
1939	Red Rolfe, NY	139	1989	Rickey Henderson, NY-Oak	113
1940	Ted Williams, Bos	134		Wade Boggs, Bos	113
1941	Ted Williams, Bos	135	1990	Rickey Henderson, Oak	119
1942	Ted Williams, Bos	141	1991	Paul Molitor, Mil	133
1943	George Case, Wash	102	1992	Tony Phillips, Det	114
1944	Snuffy Stirnweiss, NY	125	1993	Rafael Palmeiro, Tex	124
1945	Snuffy Stirnweiss, NY	107	1994	Frank Thomas, Chi	106
1946	Ted Williams, Bos	142	1995	Albert Belle, Clev	121
1947	Ted Williams, Bos	125		Edgar Martinez, Sea	121
1948	Tommy Henrich, NY	138	1996	Alex Rodriguez, Sea	141
1949	Ted Williams, Bos	150	1997	Ken Griffey Jr., Sea	125
1950	Dom DiMaggio, Bos	131	1998	Derek Jeter, NY	127
1951	Dom DiMaggio, Bos	113	1999	Roberto Alomar, Clev	138

Leaders in Runs Scored (Cont.)

Year	Player and Team	Runs	Year	Player and Team	Runs
2000	Johnny Damon, KC	136	2003	Alex Rodriguez, Tex	124
2001	Alex Rodriguez, Tex	133	2004	Vladimir Guerrero, Ana	124
2002	Alfonso Soriano, NY	128	2005	Alex Rodriguez, NY	124

Leaders in Hits

Year	Player and Team	Hits	Year	Player and Team	Hits
1901	Nap Lajoie, Phil	229	1952	Nellie Fox, Chi	192
1902	Piano Legs Hickman, Bos-Clev	194	1953	Harvey Kuenn, Det	209
1903	Patsy Dougherty, Bos	195	1954	Nellie Fox, Chi	201
1904	Nap Lajoie, Clev	211		Harvey Kuenn, Det	201
1905	George Stone, StL	187	1955	Al Kaline, Det	200
1906	Nap Lajoie, Clev	214	1956	Harvey Kuenn, Det	196
1907	Ty Cobb, Det	212	1957	Nellie Fox, Chi	196
1908	Ty Cobb, Det	188	1958	Nellie Fox, Chi	187
1909	Ty Cobb, Det	216	1959	Harvey Kuenn, Det	198
1910	Nap Lajoie, Clev	227	1960	Minnie Minoso, Chi	184
1911	Ty Cobb, Det	248	1961	Norm Cash, Det	193
1912	Ty Cobb, Det	227	1962	Bobby Richardson, NY	209
1913	Joe Jackson, Clev	197	1963	Carl Yastrzemski, Bos	183
1914	Tris Speaker, Bos	193	1964	Tony Oliva, Minn	217
1915	Ty Cobb, Det	208	1965	Tony Oliva, Minn	185
1916	Tris Speaker, Clev	211	1966	Tony Oliva, Minn	191
1917	Ty Cobb, Det	225	1967	Carl Yastrzemski, Bos	189
1918	George Burns, Phil	178	1968	Bert Campaneris, Oak	177
1919	Ty Cobb, Det	191	1969	Tony Oliva, Minn	197
	Bobby Veach, Det	191	1970	Tony Oliva, Minn	204
1920	George Sisler, StL	257	1971	Cesar Tovar, Minn	204
1921	Harry Heilmann, Det	237	1972	Joe Rudi, Oak	181
1922	George Sisler, StL	246	1973	Rod Carew, Minn	203
1923	Charlie Jamieson, Clev	222	1974	Rod Carew, Minn	218
1924	Sam Rice, Wash	216	1975	George Brett, KC	195
1925	Al Simmons, Phil	253	1976	George Brett, KC	215
1926	George Burns, Clev	216	1977	Rod Carew, Minn	239
	Sam Rice, Wash	216	1978	Jim Rice, Bos	213
1927	Earle Combs, NY	231	1979	George Brett, KC	212
1928	Heinie Manush, StL	241	1980	Willie Wilson, KC	230
1929	Dale Alexander, Det	215	1981	Rickey Henderson, Oak	135
	Charlie Gehringer, Det	215	1982	Robin Yount, Mil	210
1930	Johnny Hodapp, Clev	225	1983	Cal Ripken Jr., Balt	211
1931	Lou Gehrig, NY	211	1984	Don Mattingly, NY	207
1932	Al Simmons, Phil	216	1985	Wade Boggs, Bos	240
1933	Heinie Manush, Wash	221	1986	Don Mattingly, NY	238
1934	Charlie Gehringer, Det	214	1987	Kirby Puckett, Minn	207
1935	Joe Vosmik, Clev	216		Kevin Seitzer, KC	207
1936	Earl Averill, Clev	232	1988	Kirby Puckett, Minn	234
1937	Beau Bell, StL	218	1989	Kirby Puckett, Minn	215
1938	Joe Vosmik, Bos	201	1990	Rafael Palmeiro, Tex	191
1939	Red Rolfe, NY	213	1991	Paul Molitor, Mil	216
1940	Rip Radcliff, StL	200	1992	Kirby Puckett, Minn	210
	Barney McCosky, Det	200	1993	Paul Molitor, Tor	211
	Doc Cramer, Bos	200	1994	Kenny Lofton, Clev	160
1941	Cecil Travis, Wash	218	1995	Lance Johnson, Chi	186
1942	Johnny Pesky, Bos	205	1996	Paul Molitor, Minn	225
1943	Dick Wakefield, Det	200	1997	Nomar Garciaparra, Bos	209
1944	Snuffy Stirnweiss, NY	205	1998	Alex Rodriguez, Sea	213
1945	Snuffy Stirnweiss, NY	195	1999	Derek Jeter, NY	219
1946	Johnny Pesky, Bos	208	2000	Darin Erstad, Ana	240
1947	Johnny Pesky, Bos	207	2001	Ichiro Suzuki, Sea	242
1948	Bob Dillinger, StL	207	2002	Alfonso Soriano, NY	209
1949	Dale Mitchell, Clev	203	2003	Vernon Wells, Tor	215
1950	George Kell, Det	218	2004	Ichiro Suzuki, Sea	262
1951	George Kell, Det	191	2005	Michael Young, Tex	221

Home Run Leaders

Year	Player and Team	HR	Year	Player and Team	HR
1901	Nap Lajoie, Phil	13	1962	Harmon Killebrew, Minn	48
1902	Socks Seybold, Phil	16	1963	Harmon Killebrew, Minn	45
1903	Buck Freeman, Bos	13	1964	Harmon Killebrew, Minn	49
1904	Harry Davis, Phil	10	1965	Tony Conigliaro, Bos	32
1905	Harry Davis, Phil	8	1966	Frank Robinson, Balt	49
1906	Harry Davis, Phil	12	1967	Harmon Killebrew, Minn	44
1907	Harry Davis, Phil	8		Carl Yastrzemski, Bos	44
1908	Sam Crawford, Det	7	1968	Frank Howard, Wash	44
1909	Ty Cobb, Det	9	1969	Harmon Killebrew, Minn	49
1910	Jake Stahl, Bos	10	1970	Frank Howard, Wash	44
1911	Frank Baker, Phil	9	1971	Bill Melton, Chi	33
1912	Frank Baker, Phil	10	1972	Dick Allen, Chi	37
	Tris Speaker, Bos	10	1973	Reggie Jackson, Oak	32
1913	Frank Baker, Phil	13	1974	Dick Allen, Chi	32
1914	Frank Baker, Phil	9	1975	Reggie Jackson, Oak	36
1915	Braggo Roth, Chi-Clev	7		George Scott, Mil	36
1916	Wally Pipp, NY	12	1976	Graig Nettles, NY	32
1917	Wally Pipp, NY	9	1977	Jim Rice, Bos	39
1918	Babe Ruth, Bos	11	1978	Jim Rice, Bos	46
	Tilly Walker, Phil	11	1979	Gorman Thomas, Mil	45
1919	Babe Ruth, Bos	29	1980	Reggie Jackson, NY	41
1920	Babe Ruth, NY	54		Ben Oglivie, Mil	41
1921	Babe Ruth, NY	59	1981	Tony Armas, Oak	22
1922	Ken Williams, StL	39	1981	Dwight Evans, Bos	22
1923	Babe Ruth, NY	41		Bobby Grich, Cal	22
1924	Babe Ruth, NY	46		Eddie Murray, Balt	22
1925	Bob Meusel, NY	33	1982	Reggie Jackson, Cal	39
1926	Babe Ruth, NY	47		Gorman Thomas, Mil	39
1927	Babe Ruth, NY	60	1983	Jim Rice, Bos	39
1928	Babe Ruth, NY	54	1984	Tony Armas, Bos	43
1929	Babe Ruth, NY	46	1985	Darrell Evans, Det	40
1930	Babe Ruth, NY	49	1986	Jesse Barfield, Tor	40
1931	Babe Ruth/ Lou Gehrig NY	46	1987	Mark McGwire, Oak	49
1932	Jimmie Foxx, Phil	58	1988	Jose Canseco, Oak	42
1933	Jimmie Foxx, Phil	48	1989	Fred McGriff, Tor	36
1934	Lou Gehrig, NY	49	1990	Cecil Fielder, Det	51
1935	Jimmie Foxx, Phil	36	1991	Jose Canseco, Oak	44
	Hank Greenberg, Det	36		Cecil Fielder, Det	44
1936	Lou Gehrig, NY	49	1992	Juan Gonzalez, Tex	43
1937	Joe DiMaggio, NY	46	1993	Juan Gonzalez, Tex	46
1938	Hank Greenberg, Det	58	1994	Ken Griffey Jr., Sea	40
1939	Jimmie Foxx, Bos	35	1995	Albert Belle, Clev	50
1940	Hank Greenberg, Det	41	1996	Mark McGwire, Oak	52
1941	Ted Williams, Bos	37	1997	Ken Griffey Jr., Sea	56
1942	Ted Williams, Bos	36	1998	Ken Griffey Jr., Sea	56
1943	Rudy York, Det	34	1999	Ken Griffey Jr., Sea	48
1944	Nick Etten, NY	22	2000	Troy Glaus, Ana	47
1945	Vern Stephens, StL	24	2001	Alex Rodriguez, Tex	52
1946	Hank Greenberg, Det	44	2002	Alex Rodriguez, Tex	57
1947	Ted Williams, Bos	32	2003	Alex Rodriguez, Tex	47
1948	Joe DiMaggio, NY	39	2004	Manny Ramirez, Bos	43
1949	Ted Williams, Bos	43	2005	Alex Rodriguez, NY	48
1950	Al Rosen, Clev	37			
1951	Gus Zernial, Chi-Phil	33			
1952	Larry Doby, Clev	32			
1953	Al Rosen, Clev	43			
1954	Larry Doby, Clev	32			
1955	Mickey Mantle, NY	37			
1956	Mickey Mantle, NY	52			
1957	Roy Sievers, Wash	42			
1958	Mickey Mantle, NY	42			
1959	Rocky Colavito, Clev	42			
	Harmon Killebrew, Wash	42			
1960	Mickey Mantle, NY	40			
1961	Roger Maris, NY	61			

YET ANOTHER SIGN OF THE APOCALYPSE

Rockies pitcher Darren Oliver had to leave a spring training game because he was swarmed by bees attracted to the coconut oil in his hair gel.

Runs Batted In Leaders

Year	Player and Team	RBI	Year	Player and Team	RBI
1907	Ty Cobb, Det	116	1956	Mickey Mantle, NY	130
1908	Ty Cobb, Det	108	1957	Roy Sievers, Wash	114
1909	Ty Cobb, Det	107	1958	Jackie Jensen, Bos	122
1910	Sam Crawford, Det	120	1959	Jackie Jensen, Bos	112
1911	Ty Cobb, Det	144	1960	Roger Maris, NY	112
1912	Frank Baker, Phil	133	1961	Roger Maris, NY	142
1913	Frank Baker, Phil	126	1962	Harmon Killebrew, Minn	126
1914	Sam Crawford, Det	104	1963	Dick Stuart, Bos	118
1915	Sam Crawford, Det	112	1964	Brooks Robinson, Balt	118
	Bobby Veach, Det	112	1965	Rocky Colavito, Clev	108
1916	Del Pratt, StL	103	1966	Frank Robinson, Balt	122
1917	Bobby Veach, Det	103	1967	Carl Yastrzemski, Bos	121
1918	Bobby Veach, Det	78	1968	Ken Harrelson, Bos	109
1919	Babe Ruth, Bos	114	1969	Harmon Killebrew, Minn	140
1920	Babe Ruth, NY	137	1970	Frank Howard, Wash	126
1921	Babe Ruth, NY	171	1971	Harmon Killebrew, Minn	119
1922	Ken Williams, StL	155	1972	Dick Allen, Chi	113
1923	Babe Ruth, NY	131	1973	Reggie Jackson, Oak	117
1924	Goose Goslin, Wash	129	1974	Jeff Burroughs, Tex	118
1925	Bob Meusel, NY	138	1975	George Scott, Mil	109
1926	Babe Ruth, NY	145	1976	Lee May, Balt	109
1927	Lou Gehrig, NY	175	1977	Larry Hisle, Minn	119
1928	Babe Ruth/ Lou Gehrig, NY	142	1978	Jim Rice, Bos	139
1929	Al Simmons, Phil	157	1979	Don Baylor, Cal	139
1930	Lou Gehrig, NY	174	1980	Cecil Cooper, Mil	122
1931	Lou Gehrig, NY	184	1981	Eddie Murray, Balt	78
1932	Jimmie Foxx, Phil	169	1982	Hal McRae, KC	133
1933	Jimmie Foxx, Phil	163	1983	Cecil Cooper, Mil	126
1934	Lou Gehrig, NY	165		Jim Rice, Bos	126
1935	Hank Greenberg, Det	170	1984	Tony Armas, Bos	123
1936	Hal Trosky, Clev	162	1985	Don Mattingly, NY	145
1937	Hank Greenberg, Det	183	1986	Joe Carter, Clev	121
1938	Jimmie Foxx, Bos	175	1987	George Bell, Tor	134
1939	Ted Williams, Bos	145	1988	Jose Canseco, Oak	124
1940	Hank Greenberg, Det	150	1989	Ruben Sierra, Tex	119
1941	Joe DiMaggio, NY	125	1990	Cecil Fielder, Det	132
1942	Ted Williams, Bos	137	1991	Cecil Fielder, Det	133
1943	Rudy York, Det	118	1992	Cecil Fielder, Det	124
1944	Vern Stephens, StL	109	1993	Albert Belle, Clev	129
1945	Nick Etten, NY	111	1994	Kirby Puckett, Minn	112
1946	Hank Greenberg, Det	127	1995	Albert Belle, Clev	126
1947	Ted Williams, Bos	114		Mo Vaughn, Bos	126
1948	Joe DiMaggio, NY	155	1996	Albert Belle, Clev	148
1949	Ted Williams, Bos	159	1997	Ken Griffey Jr., Sea	147
	Vern Stephens, Bos	159	1998	Juan Gonzales, Tex	157
1950	Walt Dropo, Bos	144	1999	Manny Ramirez, Clev	165
	Vern Stephens, Bos	144	2000	Edgar Martinez, Sea	145
1951	Gus Zernial, Chi-Phil	129	2001	Bret Boone, Sea	141
1952	Al Rosen, Clev	105	2002	Alex Rodriguez, Tex	142
1953	Al Rosen, Clev	145	2003	Carlos Delgado, Tor	145
1954	Larry Doby, Clev	126	2004	Miguel Tejada, Balt	150
1955	Ray Boone, Det	116	2005	David Ortiz, Bos	148
	Jackie Jensen, Bos	116			

Note: Runs Batted In not compiled before 1907; officially adopted in 1920.

Leading Base Stealers

Year	Player and Team	SB	Year	Player and Team	SB
1901	Frank Isbell, Chi	48	1908	Patsy Dougherty, Chi	47
1902	Topsy Hartsel, Phil	54	1909	Ty Cobb, Det	76
1903	Harry Bay, Clev	46	1910	Eddie Collins, Phil	81
1904	Elmer Flick, Clev	42	1911	Ty Cobb, Det	83
	Harry Bay, Clev	42	1912	Clyde Milan, Wash	88
1905	Danny Hoffman, Phil	46	1913	Clyde Milan, Wash	75
1906	Elmer Flick, Clev	39	1914	Fritz Maisel, NY	74
	John Anderson, Wash	39	1915	Ty Cobb, Det	96
1907	Ty Cobb, Det	49	1916	Ty Cobb, Det	68

Leading Base Stealers (Cont.)

Year	Player and Team	SB	Year	Player and Team	SB
1917	Ty Cobb, Det	55	1961	Luis Aparicio, Chi	53
1918	George Sisler, StL	45	1962	Luis Aparicio, Chi	31
1919	Eddie Collins, Chi	33	1963	Luis Aparicio, Balt	40
1920	Sam Rice, Wash	63	1964	Luis Aparicio, Balt	57
1921	George Sisler, StL	35	1965	Bert Campaneris, KC	51
1922	George Sisler, StL	51	1966	Bert Campaneris, KC	52
1923	Eddie Collins, Chi	49	1967	Bert Campaneris, KC	55
1924	Eddie Collins, Chi	42	1968	Bert Campaneris, Oak	62
1925	John Mostil, Chi	43	1969	Tommy Harper, Sea	73
1926	John Mostil, Chi	35	1970	Bert Campaneris, Oak	42
1927	George Sisler, StL	27	1971	Amos Otis, KC	52
1928	Buddy Myer, Bos	30	1972	Bert Campaneris, Oak	52
1929	Charlie Gehringer, Det	27	1973	Tommy Harper, Bos	54
1930	Marty McManus, Det	23	1974	Bill North, Oak	54
1931	Ben Chapman, NY	61	1975	Mickey Rivers, Cal	70
1932	Ben Chapman, NY	38	1976	Bill North, Oak	75
1933	Ben Chapman, NY	27	1977	Freddie Patek, KC	53
1934	Bill Werber, Bos	40	1978	Ron LeFlore, Det	68
1935	Bill Werber, Bos	29	1979	Willie Wilson, KC	83
1936	Lyn Lary, StL	37	1980	Rickey Henderson, Oak	100
1937	Bill Werber, Phil	35	1981	Rickey Henderson, Oak	56
	Ben Chapman, Wash-Bos	35	1982	Rickey Henderson, Oak	130
1938	Frank Crosetti, NY	27	1983	Rickey Henderson, Oak	108
1939	George Case, Wash	51	1984	Rickey Henderson, Oak	66
1940	George Case, Wash	35	1985	Rickey Henderson, NY	80
1941	George Case, Wash	33	1986	Rickey Henderson, NY	87
1942	George Case, Wash	44	1987	Harold Reynolds, Sea	60
1943	George Case, Wash	61	1988	Rickey Henderson, NY	93
1944	Snuffy Stirnweiss, NY	55	1989	Rickey Henderson, NY-Oak	77
1945	Snuffy Stirnweiss, NY	33	1990	Rickey Henderson, Oak	65
1946	George Case, Clev	28	1991	Rickey Henderson, Oak	58
1947	Bob Dillinger, StL	34	1992	Kenny Lofton, Clev	66
1948	Bob Dillinger, StL	28	1993	Kenny Lofton, Clev	70
1949	Bob Dillinger, StL	20	1994	Kenny Lofton, Clev	60
1950	Dom DiMaggio, Bos	15	1995	Kenny Lofton, Clev	54
1951	Minnie Minoso, Clev-Chi	31	1996	Kenny Lofton, Clev	75
1952	Minnie Minoso, Chi	22	1997	Brian Hunter, Det	74
1953	Minnie Minoso, Chi	25	1998	Rickey Henderson, Oak	66
1954	Jackie Jensen, Bos	22	1999	Brian Hunter, Sea	44
1955	Jim Rivera, Chi	25	2000	Johnny Damon, KC	46
1956	Luis Aparicio, Chi	21	2001	Ichiro Suzuki, Sea	56
1957	Luis Aparicio, Chi	28	2002	Alfonso Soriano, NY	41
1958	Luis Aparicio, Chi	29	2003	Carl Crawford, TB	55
1959	Luis Aparicio, Chi	56	2004	Carl Crawford, TB	59
1960	Luis Aparicio, Chi	51	2005	Chone Figgins, LA	62

Leading Pitchers—Winning Percentage

Year	Pitcher and Team	W	L	Pct	Year	Pitcher and Team	W	L	Pct
1901	Clark Griffith, Chi	24	7	.774	1920	Jim Bagby, Clev	31	12	.721
1902	Bill Bernhard, Phil-Clev	18	5	.783	1921	Carl Mays, NY	27	9	.750
1903	Earl Moore, Clev	22	7	.759	1922	Joe Bush, NY	26	7	.788
1904	Jack Chesbro, NY	41	12	.774	1923	Herb Pennock, NY	19	6	.760
1905	Jess Tannehill, Bos	22	9	.710	1924	Walter Johnson, Wash	23	7	.767
1906	Eddie Plank, Phil	19	6	.760	1925	Stan Coveleski, Wash	20	5	.800
1907	Wild Bill Donovan, Det	25	4	.862	1926	George Uhle, Clev	27	11	.711
1908	Ed Walsh, Chi	40	15	.727	1927	Waite Hoyt, NY	22	7	.759
1909	George Mullin, Det	29	8	.784	1928	General Crowder, StL	21	5	.808
1910	Chief Bender, Phil	23	5	.821	1929	Lefty Grove, Phil	20	6	.769
1911	Chief Bender, Phil	17	5	.773	1930	Lefty Grove, Phil	28	5	.848
1912	Smoky Joe Wood, Bos	34	5	.872	1931	Lefty Grove, Phil	31	4	.886
1913	Walter Johnson, Wash	36	7	.837	1932	Johnny Allen, NY	17	4	.810
1914	Chief Bender, Phil	17	3	.850	1933	Lefty Grove, Phil	24	8	.750
1915	Smoky Joe Wood, Bos	15	5	.750	1934	Lefty Gomez, NY	26	5	.839
1916	Eddie Cicotte, Chi	15	7	.682	1935	Eldon Auker, Det	18	7	.720
1917	Reb Russell, Chi	15	5	.750	1936	Monte Pearson, NY	19	7	.731
1918	Sad Sam Jones, Bos	16	5	.762	1937	Johnny Allen, Clev	15	1	.938
1919	Eddie Cicotte, Chi	29	7	.806	1938	Red Ruffing, NY	21	7	.750

Leading Pitchers—Winning Percentage (Cont.)

Year	Pitcher and Team	W	L	Pct	Year	Pitcher and Team	W	L	Pct
1939	Lefty Grove, Bos	15	4	.789	1973	Catfish Hunter, Oak	21	5	.808
1940	Schoolboy Rowe, Det	16	3	.842	1974	Mike Cuellar, Balt	22	10	.688
1941	Lefty Gomez, NY	15	5	.750	1975	Mike Torrez, Balt	20	9	.690
1942	Ernie Bonham, NY	21	5	.808	1976	Bill Campbell, Minn	17	5	.773
1943	Spud Chandler, NY	20	4	.833	1977	Paul Splittorff, KC	16	6	.727
1944	Tex Hughson, Bos	18	5	.783	1978	Ron Guidry, NY	25	3	.893
1945	Hal Newhouser, Det	25	9	.735	1979	Mike Caldwell, Mil	16	6	.727
1946	Boo Ferriss, Bos	25	6	.806	1980	Steve Stone, Balt	25	7	.781
1947	Allie Reynolds, NY	19	8	.704	1981*	Pete Vuckovich, Mil	14	4	.778
1948	Jack Kramer, Bos	18	5	.783	1982	Pete Vuckovich, Mil	18	6	.750
1949	Ellis Kinder, Bos	23	6	.793		Jim Palmer, Balt	15	5	.750
1950	Vic Raschi, NY	21	8	.724	1983	Richard Dotson, Chi	22	7	.759
1951	Bob Feller, Clev	22	8	.733	1984	Doyle Alexander, Tor	17	6	.739
1952	Bobby Shantz, Phil	24	7	.774	1985	Ron Guidry, NY	22	6	.786
1953	Ed Lopat, NY	16	4	.800	1986	Roger Clemens, Bos	24	4	.857
1954	Sandy Consuegra, Chi	16	3	.842	1987	Roger Clemens, Bos	20	9	.690
1955	Tommy Byrne, NY	16	5	.762	1988	Frank Viola, Minn	24	7	.774
1956	Whitey Ford, NY	19	6	.760	1989	Bret Saberhagen, KC	23	6	.793
1957	Dick Donovan, Chi	16	6	.727	1990	Bob Welch, Oak	27	6	.818
	Tom Sturdivant, NY	16	6	.727	1991	Scott Erickson, Minn	20	8	.714
1958	Bob Turley, NY	21	7	.750	1992	Mike Mussina, Balt	18	5	.783
1959	Bob Shaw, Chi	18	6	.750	1993	Jimmy Key, NY	18	6	.750
1960	Jim Perry, Clev	18	10	.643	1994	Jimmy Key, NY	17	4	.810
1961	Whitey Ford, NY	25	4	.862	1995	Randy Johnson, Sea	18	2	.900
1962	Ray Herbert, Chi	20	9	.690	1996	Charles Nagy, Clev	17	5	.773
1963	Whitey Ford, NY	24	7	.774	1997	Randy Johnson, Sea	20	4	.833
1964	Wally Bunker, Balt	19	5	.792	1998	David Wells, NY	18	4	.818
1965	Mudcat Grant, Minn	21	7	.750	1999	Pedro Martinez, Bos	23	4	.852
1966	Sonny Siebert, Clev	16	8	.667	2000	Tim Hudson, Oak	20	6	.769
1967	Joel Horlen, Chi	19	7	.731	2001	Roger Clemens, NY	20	3	.870
1968	Denny McLain, Det	31	6	.838	2002	Pedro Martinez, Bos	20	4	.833
1969	Jim Palmer, Balt	16	4	.800	2003	Roy Halladay, Tor	22	7	.759
1970	Mike Cuellar, Balt	24	8	.750	2004	Curt Schilling, Bos	21	6	.778
1971	Dave McNally, Balt	21	5	.808	2005	Cliff Lee, Cle	18	5	.783
1972	Catfish Hunter, Oak	21	7	.750					

*1981 percentages based on 10 or more victories. Note: Percentages based on 15 or more victories in all other years.

Leading Pitchers—Earned Run Average

Year	Player and Team	ERA	Year	Player and Team	ERA
1913	Walter Johnson, Wash	1.14	1942	Ted Lyons, Chi	2.10
1914	Dutch Leonard, Bos	1.01	1943	Spud Chandler, NY	1.64
1915	Smoky Joe Wood, Bos	1.49	1944	Dizzy Trout, Det	2.12
1916	Babe Ruth, Bos	1.75	1945	Hal Newhouser, Det	1.81
1917	Eddie Cicotte, Chi	1.53	1946	Hal Newhouser, Det	1.94
1918	Walter Johnson, Wash	1.27	1947	Spud Chandler, NY	2.46
1919	Walter Johnson, Wash	1.49	1948	Gene Bearden, Clev	2.43
1920	Bob Shawkey, NY	2.46	1949	Mel Parnell, Bos	2.78
1921	Red Faber, Chi	2.47	1950	Early Wynn, Clev	3.20
1922	Red Faber, Chi	2.80	1951	Saul Rogovin, Det-Chi	2.78
1923	Stan Coveleski, Clev	2.76	1952	Allie Reynolds, NY	2.07
1924	Walter Johnson, Wash	2.72	1953	Ed Lopat, NY	2.43
1925	Stan Coveleski, Wash	2.84	1954	Mike Garcia, Clev	2.64
1926	Lefty Grove, Phil	2.51	1955	Billy Pierce, Chi	1.97
1927	Wilcy Moore, NY#	2.28	1956	Whitey Ford, NY	2.47
1928	Garland Braxton, Wash	2.52	1957	Bobby Shantz, NY	2.45
1929	Lefty Grove, Phil	2.81	1958	Whitey aFord, NY	2.01
1930	Lefty Grove, Phil	2.54	1959	Hoyt Wilhelm, Balt	2.19
1931	Lefty Grove, Phil	2.06	1960	Frank Baumann, Chi	2.68
1932	Lefty Grove, Phil	2.84	1961	Dick Donovan, Wash	2.40
1933	Monte Pearson, Clev	2.33	1962	Hank Aguirre, Det	2.21
1934	Lefty Gomez, NY	2.33	1963	Gary Peters, Chi	2.33
1935	Lefty Grove, Bos	2.70	1964	Dean Chance, LA	1.65
1936	Lefty Grove, Bos	2.81	1965	Sam McDowell, Clev	2.18
1937	Lefty Gomez, NY	2.33	1966	Gary Peters, Chi	1.98
1938	Lefty Grove, Bos	3.07	1967	Joe Horlen, Chi	2.06
1939	Lefty Grove, Bos	2.54	1968	Luis Tiant, Clev	1.60
1940	Bob Feller, Clev†	2.62	1969	Dick Bosman, Wash	2.19
1941	Thornton Lee, Chi	2.37	1970	Diego Segui, Oak	2.56

Leading Pitchers—Earned Run Average (Cont.)

Year	Player and Team	ERA	Year	Player and Team	ERA
1971	Vida Blue, Oak	1.82	1989	Bret Saberhagen, KC	2.16
1972	Luis Tiant, Bos	1.91	1990	Roger Clemens, Bos	1.93
1973	Jim Palmer, Balt	2.40	1991	Roger Clemens, Bos	2.62
1974	Catfish Hunter, Oak	2.49	1992	Roger Clemens, Bos	2.41
1975	Jim Palmer, Balt	2.09	1993	Kevin Appier, KC	2.56
1976	Mark Fidrych, Det	2.34	1994	Steve Ontiveros, Oak	2.65
1977	Frank Tanana, Cal	2.54	1995	Randy Johnson, Sea	2.48
1978	Ron Guidry, NY	1.74	1996	Juan Guzman, Tor	2.93
1979	Ron Guidry, NY	2.78	1997	Roger Clemens, Tor	2.05
1980	Rudy May, NY	2.47	1998	Roger Clemens, Tor	2.64
1981	Steve McCatty, Oak	2.32	1999	Pedro Martinez, Bos	2.07
1982	Rick Sutcliffe, Clev	2.96	2000	Pedro Martinez, Bos	1.74
1983	Rick Honeycutt, Tex	2.42	2001	Freddy Garcia, Sea	3.05
1984	Mike Boddicker, Balt	2.79	2002	Pedro Martinez, Bos	2.26
1985	Dave Stieb, Tor	2.48	2003	Pedro Martinez, Bos	2.22
1986	Roger Clemens, Bos	2.48	2004	Johan Santana, Minn	2.61
1987	Jimmy Key, Tor	2.76	2005	Kevin Millwood, Cle	2.86
1988	Allan Anderson, Minn	2.45			

Note: Based on 10 complete games through 1950, then 154 innings until the American League expanded in 1961, when it became 162 innings. In strike-shortened 1981, one inning per game required. Earned runs not tabulated in American League prior to 1913.

#Wilcy Moore pitched only six complete games—he started 12—in 1927 but was recognized as leader because of 213 innings pitched. †Ernie Bonham, New York, had 1.91 ERA and 10 complete games in 1940 but appeared in only 12 games and 99 innings, and Bob Feller was recognized as leader.

Leading Pitchers—Strikeouts

Year	Player and Team	SO	Year	Player and Team	SO
1901	Cy Young, Bos	159	1940	Bob Feller, Clev	261
1902	Rube Waddell, Phil	210	1941	Bob Feller, Clev	260
1903	Rube Waddell, Phil	301	1942	Bobo Newsom, Wash	
1904	Rube Waddell, Phil	349		Tex Hughson, Bos	113
1905	Rube Waddell, Phil	286	1943	Allie Reynolds, Clev	151
1906	Rube Waddell, Phil	203	1944	Hal Newhouser, Det	187
1907	Rube Waddell, Phil	226	1945	Hal Newhouser, Det	212
1908	Ed Walsh, Chi	269	1946	Bob Feller, Clev	348
1909	Frank Smith, Chi	177	1947	Bob Feller, Clev	196
1910	Walter Johnson, Wash	313	1948	Bob Feller, Clev	164
1911	Ed Walsh, Chi	255	1949	Virgil Trucks, Det	153
1912	Walter Johnson, Wash	303	1950	Bob Lemon, Clev	170
1913	Walter Johnson, Wash	243	1951	Vic Raschi, NY	164
1914	Walter Johnson, Wash	225	1952	Allie Reynolds, NY	160
1915	Walter Johnson, Wash	203	1953	Billy Pierce, Chi	186
1916	Walter Johnson, Wash	228	1954	Bob Turley, Balt	185
1917	Walter Johnson, Wash	188	1955	Herb Score, Clev	245
1918	Walter Johnson, Wash	162	1956	Herb Score, Clev	263
1919	Walter Johnson, Wash	147	1957	Early Wynn, Clev	184
1920	Stan Coveleski, Clev	133	1958	Early Wynn, Chi	179
1921	Walter Johnson, Wash	143	1959	Jim Bunning, Det	201
1922	Urban Shocker, StL	149	1960	Jim Bunning, Det	201
1923	Walter Johnson, Wash	130	1961	Camilo Pascual, Minn	221
1924	Walter Johnson, Wash	158	1962	Camilo Pascual, Minn	206
1925	Lefty Grove, Phil	116	1963	Camilo Pascual, Minn	202
1926	Lefty Grove, Phil	194	1964	Al Downing, NY	217
1927	Lefty Grove, Phil	174	1965	Sam McDowell, Clev	325
1928	Lefty Grove, Phil	183	1966	Sam McDowell, Clev	225
1929	Lefty Grove, Phil	170	1967	Jim Lonborg, Bos	246
1930	Lefty Grove, Phil	209	1968	Sam McDowell, Clev	283
1931	Lefty Grove, Phil	175	1969	Sam McDowell, Clev	279
1932	Red Ruffing, NY	190	1970	Sam McDowell, Clev	304
1933	Lefty Gomez, NY	163	1971	Mickey Lolich, Det	308
1934	Lefty Gomez, NY	158	1972	Nolan Ryan, Cal	329
1935	Tommy Bridges, Det	163	1973	Nolan Ryan, Cal	383
1936	Tommy Bridges, Det	175	1974	Nolan Ryan, Cal	367
1937	Lefty Gomez, NY	194	1975	Frank Tanana, Cal	269
1938	Bob Feller, Clev	240	1976	Nolan Ryan, Cal	327
1939	Bob Feller, Clev	246	1977	Nolan Ryan, Cal	341

Leading Pitchers—Strikeouts *(Cont.)*

Year	Player and Team	SO	Year	Player and Team	SO
1978	Nolan Ryan, Cal	260	1992	Randy Johnson, Sea	241
1979	Nolan Ryan, Cal	223	1993	Randy Johnson, Sea	308
1980	Len Barker, Clev	187	1994	Randy Johnson, Sea	204
1981	Len Barker, Clev	127	1995	Randy Johnson, Sea	294
1982	Floyd Bannister, Sea	209	1996	Roger Clemens, Bos	257
1983	Jack Morris, Det	232	1997	Roger Clemens, Tor	292
1984	Mark Langston, Sea	204	1998	Roger Clemens, Tor	271
1985	Bert Blyleven, Clev-Minn	206	1999	Pedro Martinez, Bos	313
1986	Mark Langston, Sea	245	2000	Pedro Martinez, Bos	284
1987	Mark Langston, Sea	262	2001	Hideo Nomo, Bos	220
1988	Roger Clemens, Bos	291	2002	Pedro Martinez, Bos	239
1989	Nolan Ryan, Tex	301	2003	Esteban Loaiza, Chi	207
1990	Nolan Ryan, Tex	232	2004	Johan Santana, Minn	265
1991	Roger Clemens, Bos	241	2005	Johan Santana, Minn	238

Leading Pitchers—Saves

Year	Player and Team	SV	Year	Player and Team	SV
1947	Joe Page, NY	17	1977	Bill Campbell, Bos	31
1948	Russ Christopher, Clev	17	1978	Goose Gossage, NY	27
1949	Joe Page, NY	29	1979	Mike Marshall, Minn	32
1950	Mickey Harris, Wash	15	1980	Dan Quisenberry, KC	33
1951	Ellis Kinder, Bos	14	1981	Rollie Fingers, Mil	28
1952	Harry Dorish, Chi	11	1982	Dan Quisenberry, KC	35
1953	Ellis Kinder, Bos	27	1983	Dan Quisenberry, KC	35
1954	Johnny Sain, NY	22	1984	Dan Quisenberry, KC	44
1955	Ray Narleski, Clev	19	1985	Dan Quisenberry, KC	37
1956	George Zuverink, Bal	16	1986	Dave Righetti, NY	46
1957	Bob Grim, NY	19	1987	Tom Henke, Tor	34
1958	Ryne Duren, NY	20	1988	Dennis Eckersley, Oak	45
1959	Turk Lown, Chi	15	1989	Jeff Russell, Tex	38
1960	Mike Fornieles, Bos	14	1990	Bobby Thigpen, Chi	57
	Johnny Klippstein, Clev	14	1991	Bryan Harvey, Cal	46
1961	Luis Arroyo, NY	29	1992	Dennis Eckersley, Oak	51
1962	Dick Radatz, Bos	24	1993	Jeff Montgomery, KC	45
1963	Stu Miller, Bal	27		Duane Ward, Tor	45
1964	Dick Radatz, Bos	29	1994	Lee Smith, Bal	33
1965	Ron Kline, Wash	29	1995	Jose Mesa, Clev	46
1966	Jack Aker, KC	32	1996	John Wetteland, NY	43
1967	Minnie Rojas, Cal	27	1997	Randy Myers, Balt	45
1968	Al Worthington, Minn	18	1998	Tom Gordon, Bos	46
1969	Ron Perranoski, Minn	31	1999	Mariano Rivera, NY	45
1970	Ron Perranoski, Minn	34	2000	Todd Jones, Det	42
1971	Ken Sanders, Mil	31	2001	Mariano Rivera, NY	50
1972	Sparky Lyle, NY	35	2002	Eddie Guardado, Minn	45
1973	John Hiller, Det	38	2003	Keith Foulke, Oak	43
1974	Terry Forster, Chi	24	2004	Mariano Rivera, NY	53
1975	Goose Gossage, Chi	26	2005	Francisco Rodriguez, LA	45
1976	Sparky Lyle, NY	23		Bob Wickman, Cle	45

The Commissioners of Baseball

Kenesaw Mountain Landis	Elected Nov. 12, 1920. Served until his death on Nov. 25, 1944.
Happy Chandler	Elected April 24, 1945. Served until July 15, 1951.
Ford Frick	Elected Sept. 20, 1951. Served until Nov. 16, 1965.
William Eckert	Elected Nov. 17, 1965. Served until Dec. 20, 1968.
Bowie Kuhn	Elected Feb. 8, 1969. Served until Sept. 30, 1984.
Peter Ueberroth	Elected March 3, 1984. Took office Oct. 1, 1984. Served through March 31, 1989.
A. Bartlett Giamatti	Elected Sept. 8, 1988. Took office April 1, 1989. Served until his death on Sept. 1, 1989.
Francis Vincent Jr.	Appointed Acting Commissioner Sept. 2, 1989. Elected Commissioner Sept. 13, 1989. Served through Sept. 7, 1992.
Allan H. (Bud) Selig	Elected chairman of the executive council and given the powers of interim commissioner on Sept. 9, 1992. Unanimously elected Commissioner July 9, 1998.

Pro Football

DAMIAN STROHMEYER

Tom Brady of the
Super Bowl champion
New England Patriots

Dynastic Journey

As resilient as ever, the Patriots outlasted both old and new foes to win their third Super Bowl in four years

BY HANK HERSCH

One after another, they were revealed to be mere pretenders to the throne: the MVP who broke one of the league's most hallowed records, the Rookie of the Year who had never tasted defeat in 14 starts, the Campbell's Soup pitchman from Philly who struck as much fear with his legs as with his arm. It didn't matter to the reigning king that he lay in a hotel bed shivering with a sore throat and a 103-degree fever on the eve of the AFC championship game; he didn't care that the Super Bowl MVP trophy wound up in the hands of his receiver rather than in his right arm. Just as he had a year earlier, quarterback Tom Brady guided the New England Patriots to the NFL title, leaving his peers in the dust and his teammates in awe.

"What can you say about him? He's amazing," said New England linebacker Ted Johnson during the Pats' playoff run. "He's a winner with such poise and calmness, he almost makes it look effortless."

The same could be said of Brady's cohorts, who, with a 24-21 victory over the Philadelphia Eagles at Super Bowl XXXIX in Jacksonville, claimed the Vince Lombardi Trophy for the third time in four seasons. Though the Pittsburgh Steelers and San Francisco 49ers won four championships in short spans (six and nine years, respectively), New England's run in a time of hard salary caps and rampant turnover may stand out as more impressive. Each title-winning season coach Bill Belichick began with at least 10 starters who hadn't been in the lineup on the previous opening day; in 2004 alone, the Patriots replaced their running back, the fullback, a wideout, three offensive linemen, the tight end, two defensive linemen, two linebackers and the free safety.

"We don't play to make the highlight shows," said Pro Bowl linebacker Tedy Bruschi. "Watch how we celebrate–with our teammates. Always. You play the game to be on a team like this."

Head coach Bill Belichick has a perfect 9–0 playoff record with the Patriots.

2003, he chose to retire at the age of 27 and spent the next four months visiting Japan, Jamaica, Australia and Thailand. While in Thailand, he had second thoughts about quitting in his prime, but said "after two days of hearing all that noise about whether I'd come back or not, I was like, There's no way in hell I'm playing." The decision cost him: an arbitrator ruled that Williams had to repay his former team $8.6 million in bonus money. (The case is tk koming after Williams decided in the off-season to return and suit up for new coach Nick Saban.) It cost the Dolphins as well; they tied for the second-worst record (4-12) after the Niners' 2-14.

Some seemingly happy reunions didn't work out, either. After not playing since December 2000, 37-year-old Deion Sanders made a comeback as a nickelback with the Ravens, but despite three interceptions in nine games couldn't help Baltimore reach the playoffs. Nor did the return of Joe Gibbs to the Washington Redskins' sideline pay immediate dividends. He had retired after the 1992 season with three Super Bowl rings and the highest winning percentage (.683) among coaches with at least 125 victories, then became a Winston Cup-winning NASCAR owner. But the chance to resuscitate the Skins lured him back. "I feel this is where the Lord wants me to be," said Gibbs in October. "If I get kicked around this time, it's for a reason." These were the reasons for Washington's 6-10 mark: abysmal play by Gibbs's hand-

With Brady at the helm, the reconfigured Patriots didn't merely win it all–they ran off the longest winning streak in the NFL's 85-year history. Before bowing to the Steelers 34-20 in Week 8, they rolled up 21 straight victories dating back to Oct. 5, 2003, topping the run of 18 by the 1972 and '73 Miami Dolphins, the 1989 and '90 Niners and the 1997 and '98 Denver Broncos. "Think how long it's been since we lost," said team owner Bob Kraft after win No. 19, a 24-10 knockout of Miami. "Britney Spears has been married twice since then."

The NFL also saw its share of divorces during that record run, perhaps the ugliest being running back Ricky Williams's break from the Dolphins. After rushing for 1,352 yards on a league-leading 392 carries in

picked quarterback, Mark Brunell, and a rushing attack that averaged only 3.7 yards per carry.

Some comebacks, however, yielded happier results. Michael Vick had missed most of the Atlanta Falcons' 2003 season with a broken fibula; he returned to a new coach (rookie Jim Mora) and a new scheme (similar to the West Coast offense, with short, timing-based passes designed to increase accuracy). Vick was merely spectacular, passing for 2,313 yards—and completing a career-best 56.4%—and rushing for 902 more.

Chargers quarterback Drew Brees had been healthy in '03-he just wasn't effective enough to stay in the lineup. Following San Diego's 1-7 start he was benched for five games, and he finished with more picks (15) than touchdown passes (11). But in 2004, Brees reversed not only his own fortunes (27 TD's, seven INT's) but also his team's: The Chargers went 12-4 after going 4-12. He had help from emerging star Antonio Gates, who had 81 receptions and 13 touchdowns, which tied the NFL record for a tight end. The 6'4", 260-pound Gates never played college football, instead becoming an honorable mention All-America basketball player at Kent State in 2002-03. A future with the Lakers or Knicks, however, seemed unlikely. "When there are more NFL scouts at your game than NBA scouts," says Gates, "you get the message."

Despite that attention Gates went undrafted and the Chargers signed him as a free agent. Proving once again that, when it comes to evaluating future NFL talent...well, the term crapshoot comes to mind. Brady had been a sixth-round selection out of Michigan in 2000. With the No. 1 pick in '04, the New York Giants chose Mississippi quarterback Eli Manning. With the No. 4 pick, the Chargers selected North Carolina State quarterback Philip Rivers. With the No. 11 pick, Pittsburgh chose Miami of Ohio quarterback Ben Roethlisberger.

And the 11th would be first. While Rivers rode the bench behind Brees and Manning became a starter late in the season, Roethlisberger took over in Week 2, after Tommy

After an injury-plagued 2003, Michael Vick and the Falcons came back strong.

Maddox tore a tendon in his throwing elbow. He seized the opportunity with the alacrity of Britney Spears's second spouse. Within a couple of months, the 6'5", 242-pounder was so successful that had a hoagie named after him at a Pittsburgh deli: the $7 Roethlisburger (beef, sausage, scrambled eggs and American cheese). In his fifth start, he helped end the Patriots' unbeaten streak, completing 18 of 24 passes for 196 yards and two touchdowns. At season's end, Big Ben not only ranked fifth in passer rating but he had also led Pittsburgh to the league's best mark (15-1) while setting a record for consecutive wins by a rookie QB: 14. The previous standard: six. Said Belichick, "There have been a lot of quarterbacks who have played 10 years and don't do as good a job."

In almost any other season, Roethlisberger would have been the hottest topic in

Quarterback Drew Brees led the resurgent Chargers back to the post-season for the first time in 10 years.

ning had risen above the rest. With 49 touchdown tosses he broke Dan Marino's 20-year-old record of 48; with a passer rating of 121.1, he shattered Steve Young's 10-year-old mark of 112.8. His receivers did the unprecedented: Reggie Wayne, Marvin Harrison and Brandon Stokley each surpassed 1,000 yards and snagged double-digit TD's. The 28-year-old Manning had more scoring passes than all but five teams had total touchdowns; he had more TD's by the season's halfway mark than all but Culpepper threw during the entire year. "To do the things Peyton's been doing week in and week out, it's kind of like when a Bob Dylan song comes along," said Colts owner Jim Irsay. "You don't see something like that very often."

Though Manning won the MVP trophy, Brady had the hardware he coveted most, and he set out to get it in the postseason. In a 49-24 wild-card victory over the Denver Broncos, he threw for 458 yards, with Wayne on the receiving end for 221. That set up a showdown with the Patriots, who had stymied Manning's Colts five straight times. Make that six—with free safety Rodney Harrison and his mates executing yet another prescient defensive scheme from Belichick, Manning completed no pass longer than 18 yards in a 20-3 defeat.

Nor was Big Ben up to toppling New England. The Steelers' punishing ground game had set the tone in their October meeting; this time, at a frozen Heinz Field with the AFC championship on the line, Brady wouldn't be denied. Despite subsisting on a diet of IV fluids the night before to battle his illness, he completed 14 of 21 passes for 207 yards and two TD's in a 41-27 victory.

In the NFC, Favre and Culpepper faced off in one wild-card bout. After dropping a pair of decisions to the Packers during the

signal calling. But his competition in 2004 was scorching. First came the Minnesota Vikings' Daunte Culpepper, who cooled after a red-hot start—through Week 7 he had completed 73.3% of his passes—but still threw for a league-leading 4,717 yards. Then attention shifted to 35-year-old Brett Favre, who rallied the Green Bay Packers to the playoffs after a 1-4 start despite a series of personal tragedies: his father's recent passing, his brother-in-law's death in an ATV accident and his wife's learning she had breast cancer. Along the way, Favre's record streak of starts under center reached 207, outstripping the next longest by 91 games. "Every week I say, 'I can't believe I made another game,'" he said. "Guys are falling all around me, guys in great shape. Even I have to admit I'm fortunate."

But by the end of the 2004 regular season, the Indianapolis Colts' Peyton Man-

regular season, Vikings coach Mike Tice was one loss from unemployment. But with Culpepper throwing four touchdowns and Favre four interceptions, Minnesota prevailed easily, 31-17. Vikings receiving star Randy Moss had a pair of TD's but he made more news for what he did after one of them: He ran to the goalpost, simulated pulling his pants down and stuck his rear out at the Green Bay fans. For Moss's faux moon, the NFL fined him $10,000.

Philadelphia dispatched Moss and the Vikes the following week 27-14, but that was no surprise: Behind quarterback Donovan McNabb, the Eagles had reached the previous three NFC title games, hosting each one. Unfortunately, they had failed to win any of the three. Philly's challenge this time: stop the multifaceted Vick and Atlanta's top-ranked ground game, and score without All-Pro wide receiver Terrell Owens, who was sidelined after undergoing surgery in December for a fractured right

QB Donovan McNabb finally led the Eagles to the Super Bowl after three years of falling one win short.

fibula and torn ligaments in his ankle.

Facing down 26-mph winds, McNabb converted half of his team's 14 third downs and threw for a pair of scores. The Eagles D boxed in Vick, holding him without a rushing attempt for the final 47 minutes. With the 27-10 victory, Philadelphia advanced to its first Super Bowl in 24 years. Only the Patriots stood in the way of their first NFL championship since 1949.

To keep McNabb from running outside or throwing inside, New England junked its 3-4 set for a 4-3, with veteran linebacker Willie McGinest moving to pass-rushing end. While that defense proved effective in some ways—McNabb had zero rushing yards and the Pats sacked him four times—it did little to solve the problems created by Owens, who, without medical clearance, returned to make nine catches for 122 yards.

With Philly up 7-0 in the second quarter, Brady went to work, connecting for TD's with wideout David Givens and Mike Vrabel, a linebacker moonlighting as a tight end. When McNabb answered to tie the score at 14–all, Brady took New England on a nine-play, 66-yard drive, completing four of four passes, the last of which was a two-yard touchdown to running back Corey Dillon with 13:44 left in the game. On the Patriots' next drive, Brady threw a 19-yard pass to receiver Deion Branch that helped set up an Adam Vinatieri field goal to make it 24-14. The spectacular catch also helped Branch (133 yards on a record-tying 11 receptions) snag the Super Bowl MVP award.

McNabb cut the margin to three with 1:48 remaining, but the Eagles could draw no closer. The Patriots were going out the way they came in: on top. "This is a team full of guys who cheer for one another," Brady said. "The MVP is nice, but that's not why you play. I'm playing for that diamond ring."

FOR THE RECORD · 2004 – 2005

2004 NFL Final Standings

American Football Conference

EAST DIVISION

	W	L	T	Pct	Pts	OP
New England	14	2	0	.875	437	260
*NY Jets	10	6	0	.625	333	261
Buffalo	9	7	0	.563	395	284
Miami	4	12	0	.250	275	354

NORTH DIVISION

	W	L	T	Pct	Pts	OP
Pittsburgh	15	1	0	.938	372	251
Baltimore	9	7	0	.563	317	268
Cincinnati	8	8	0	.500	374	372
Cleveland	4	12	0	.250	276	390

SOUTH DIVISION

	W	L	T	Pct	Pts	OP
Indianapolis	12	4	0	.750	522	351
Jacksonville	9	7	0	.563	261	280
Houston	7	9	0	.438	309	339
Tennessee	5	11	0	.313	344	439

WEST DIVISION

	W	L	T	Pct	Pts	OP
San Diego	12	4	0	.750	446	313
*Denver	10	6	0	.625	381	304
Kansas City	7	9	0	.438	483	435
Oakland	5	11	0	.313	320	442

* Wild-card team.

National Football Conference

EAST DIVISION

	W	L	T	Pct	Pts	OP
Philadelphia	13	3	0	.813	386	260
NY Giants	6	10	0	.375	303	347
Dallas	6	10	0	.375	303	347
Washington	6	10	0	.375	240	265

NORTH DIVISION

	W	L	T	Pct	Pts	OP
Green Bay	10	6	0	.625	424	380
†Minnesota	8	8	0	.500	405	395
Detroit	6	10	0	.375	296	350
Chicago	5	11	0	.313	231	331

SOUTH DIVISION

	W	L	T	Pct	Pts	OP
Atlanta	11	5	0	.688	340	337
New Orleans	8	8	0	.500	348	405
Carolina	7	9	0	.438	355	339
Tampa Bay	5	11	0	.313	301	304

WEST DIVISION

	W	L	T	Pct	Pts	OP
Seattle	9	7	0	.563	371	373
†St. Louis	8	8	0	.500	319	392
Arizona	6	10	0	.375	284	322
San Francisco	2	14	0	.125	259	452

† Wild-card team.

2004–05 NFL Playoffs

AFC FIRST ROUND	AFC DIVISIONAL PLAYOFF	AFC CHAMPIONSHIP	NFC CHAMPIONSHIP	NFC DIVISIONAL PLAYOFF	NFC FIRST ROUND

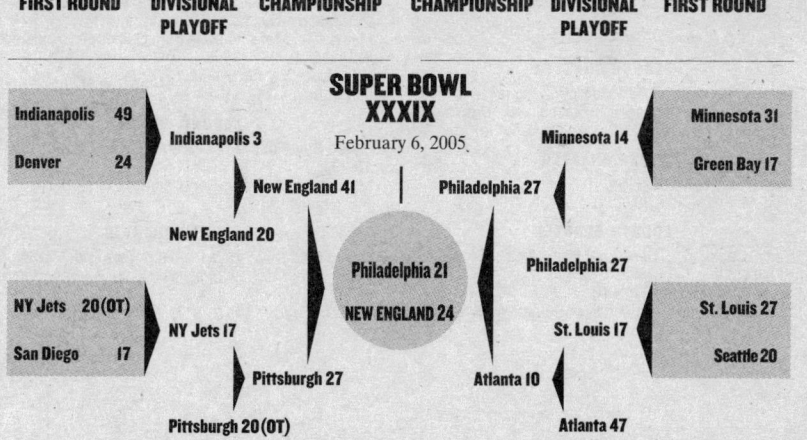

SUPER BOWL XXXIX
February 6, 2005

Indianapolis 49 / Denver 24
Indianapolis 3
New England 41
New England 20
NY Jets 20 (OT) / San Diego 17
NY Jets 17
Pittsburgh 27
Pittsburgh 20 (OT)

Philadelphia 21
NEW ENGLAND 24

Minnesota 14
Philadelphia 27
Philadelphia 27
St. Louis 17
Atlanta 10
Atlanta 47

Minnesota 31 / Green Bay 17
St. Louis 27 / Seattle 20

NFL Playoff Box Scores

AFC Wild-card Games

Denver	0	3	14	7—24
Indianapolis	14	21	0	14—49

FIRST QUARTER

Indianapolis: Mungro 2 pass from Manning (Vanderjagt kick), 7:27.

Indianapolis : James 1 run (Vanderjagt kick), 0:53.

SECOND QUARTER

Indianapolis: Clark 19 pass from Manning (Vanderjagt kick), 8:13.

Denver: FG Elam 33, 5:29.

Indianapolis: Wayne 35 pass from Manning (Vanderjagt kick), 4:49.

Indianapolis: Manning 1 run (Vanderjagt kick), 0:18.

THIRD QUARTER

Denver: Smith 9 pass from Plummer (Elam kick), 9:14.

Denver: Putzier 35 pass from Plummer (Elam kick), 1:21.

FOURTH QUARTER

Indianapolis : Wayne 43 pass from Manning (Vanderjagt kick), 13:26.   TK

Denver: Bell 1 run (Elam kick), 7:57.

Indianapolis: Rhodes 2 run (Vanderjagt kick), 2:08.

A: 56,609; 3:06.

NY Jets	0	7	10	0	3—20
San Diego	0	7	0	10	0—17

SECOND QUARTER

San Diego: McCardell 26 pass from Brees (Kaeding kick), 9:46.

NY Jets: Becht 13 pass from Pennington (Brien kick), 3:30.

THIRD QUARTER

NY Jets: Moss 47 pass from Pennington (Brien kick), 11:00.

NY Jets: FG Brien 42, 1:52.

FOURTH QUARTER

San Diego: FG Kaeding 35, 10:54.

San Diego: Gates 1 pass from Brees (Kaeding kick), 0:16.

OVERTIME

NY Jets: FG Brien 28, 0:08.

A: 67,536; 3:49.

NFC Wild-card Games

St. Louis	7	7	3	10—27
Seattle	3	7	3	7—20

FIRST QUARTER

St. Louis: Holt 15 pass from Bulger (Wilkins kick), 11:36.

Seattle: FG Brown 47, 2:08.

SECOND QUARTER

St. Louis: Faulk 1 run (Wilkins kick), 13:50.

Seattle: Engram 19 pass from Hasselbeck (Brown kick), 8:23.

THIRD QUARTER

Seattle: FG Brown 30, 8:54.

Stl Louis: FG Wilkins 38, 2:38.

FOURTH QUARTER

Seattle: Jackson 23 pass from Hasselbeck (Brown kick), 14:30.

St. Louis: FG Wilkins 27, 8:10.

St. Louis: Cleeland 17 pass from Bulger (Wilkins kick), 2:20.

A: 65,397; 3:17.

Minnesota	17	7	0	7—31
Green Bay	3	7	0	7—17

FIRST QUARTER

Minnesota: Williams 68 pass from Culpepper (Andersen kick), 13:40.

Minnesota: Moss 20 pass from Culpepper (Andersen kick), 10:00.

Minnesota: FG Andersen 35, 6:48.

Green Bay: FG Longwell 43, 2:47.

SECOND QUARTER

Green Bay: Franks 4 pass from Favre (Longwell kick), 10:30.

Minnesota: Burleson 19 pass from Culpepper (Andersen kick), 6:40.

FOURTH QUARTER

Green Bay: Davenport 1 run (Longwell kick), 13:45.

Minnesota: Moss 34 pass from Culpepper (Andersen kick), 10:26.

A: 71,075; 3:00.

AFC Divisional Games

| NY Jets | 0 | 10 | 7 | 0 | 0—17 |
| Pittsburgh | 10 | 0 | 0 | 7 | 3—20 |

| Indianapolis | 0 | 3 | 0 | 0— 3 |
| Kansas City | 0 | 6 | 7 | 7—20 |

FIRST QUARTER
Pittsburgh: FG Reed 45, 5:40.
Pittsburgh: Bettis 3 run (Reed kick), 2:34.

SECOND QUARTER
NY Jets: FG Brien 42, 11:00.
NY Jets: Moss 75 punt return (Brien kick), 3:17.

THIRD QUARTER
NY Jets: Tongue int 86 pass from Roethlisberger (Brien kick), 4:09.

FOURTH QUARTER
Pittsburgh: Ward 4 pass from Roethlisberger (Reed kick), 6:30.

OVERTIME
Pittsburgh: FG Reed 33, 4:01.

A: 64,915; 3:25.

SECOND QUARTER
New England: FG Vinatieri 24, 11:05.
New England: FG Vinatieri 31, 8:41.
Indianapolis: FG Vanderjagt 23, 0:02.

THIRD QUARTER
New England: Givens 5 pass from Brady (Vinatieri kick), 1:38.

FOURTH QUARTER
New England: Brady 1 run (Vinatieri kick), 7:21.

A: 68,756; 2:55.

NFC Divisional Games

| St. Louis | 7 | 10 | 0 | 0—17 |
| Atlanta | 14 | 14 | 10 | 9—47 |

| Minnesota | 0 | 7 | 0 | 7—14 |
| Philadelphia | 7 | 14 | 0 | 6—27 |

FIRST QUARTER
Atlanta: Crumper 18 pass from Vick (Feely kick), 12:10.
St. Louis: Curtis 57 pass from Bulger (Wilkins kick), 9:25.
Atlanta: Dunn 62 run (Feely kick), 8:05.

SECOND QUARTER
Atlanta: Dunn 19 run (Feely kick), 10:20.
St. Louis: Holt 28 pass from Bulger (Wilkins kick), 5:40.
Atlanta: Rossum 68 punt return (Feely kick), 1:18.
St. Louis: FG Wilkins 55, 0:02.

THIRD QUARTER
Atlanta: Price 6 pass from Vick (Feely kick), 10:33.
Atlanta: FG Feely 38, 6:15.

FOURTH QUARTER
Atlanta: Safety, Bulger sacked in end zone, 12:10.
Atlanta: Duckett 4 run (Feely kick), 2:00.

A: 70,709; 2:59.

FIRST QUARTER
Philadelphia: Mitchell 2 pass from McNab (Akers kick), 6:22.

SECOND QUARTER
Philadelphia: Westbrook 7 pass from McNabb (Akers kick), 14:40.
Minnesota: Culpepper 7 run (Andersen kick), 11:09.
Philadelphia: Mitchell TK fumble recovery, ran into end zone(Akers kick), 10:15.

OVERTIME
Philadelphia: FG Akers 21, 13:22.
Philadelphia: FG Akers 23, 6:53.
Minnesota: Robinson 32 pass from Culpepper (Andersen kick), 2:09.

A: 67,742; 3:14.

AFC Championship

New England	10	14	7	10—41
Pittsburgh	3	0	14	10—27

FIRST QUARTER

New England: FG Vinatieri 48, 11:24.
New England: Branch 60 pass from Brady (Vinatieri kick), 6:58.
Pittsburgh: FG Reed 43, 1:26.

SECOND QUARTER

New England: Givens 9 pass from Brady (Vinatieri kick), 7:20.
New England: Harrison 87 interception return (Vinatieri kick), 2:40.

THIRD QUARTER

Pittsburgh: Bettis 5 run (Reed kick), 11:05.
New England: Dillon 25 run (Vinatieri kick), 7:49.
Pittsburgh: Ward 30 pass from Roethlisberger (Reed kick), 2:45.

FOURTH QUARTER

Pittsburgh: FG Reed 20, 13:45.
New England: FG Vinatieri 31, 8:06.
New England: Branch 23 run (Vinatieri kick), 2:35.
Pittsburgh: Burress 7 pass Roethlisberger (Reed kick), 0:56.

A: 65,242; T: 3:09.

NFC Championship

Atlanta	0	10	0	0—10
Philadelphia	7	7	6	7—27

FIRST QUARTER

Philadelphia: Leven 4 run (Akers kick), 4:35.

SECOND QUARTER

Atlanta: FG Feely 23, 10:30.
Philadelphia: Lewis 3 pass from McNabb (Akers kick), 5:21.
Atlanta: Dunn 10 run (Feely kick), 2:08.

THIRD QUARTER

Philadelphia: FG Akers 31, 9:00.
Philadelphia: FG Akers 34, 2:37.

FOURTH QUARTER

Philadelphia: Lewis 2 pass from McNabb (Akers kick), 3:48.

A: 67,717; T:3:00.

New England	0	7	7	10—24
Philadelphia	0	7	7	7—21

SECOND QUARTER

Philadelphia: Smith 6 pass from McNabb (Akers kick), 10:02. **Philadelphia 7–0.**

New England: Givens 4 pass from Brady (Vinatieri kick), 1:24. **7–7.**

THIRD QUARTER

New England: Vrabel 2 pass from Brady (Vinatieri kick), 11:05. **New England 14–7.**
Philadelphia: Westbrook 10 pass from McNabb (Akers kick), 3:44. **14–14.**

FOURTH QUARTER

New England: Dillon 2 run (Vinatieri kick), 13:52. **New England 21–14.**

New England: FG Vinatieri 22, 9:21. **New England 24–14.**

Philadelphia: Lewis 30 pass from McNabb (Akers kick). **New England 24-21.**

A: 78,125; T: 3:38.

Team Statistics

	New England	Philadelphia
FIRST DOWNS	21	24
Rushing	6	4
Passing	14	18
Penalty	1	2
THIRD DOWN EFF.	4–12	9–16
FOURTH DOWN EFF	0–0	0–0
TOTAL NET YARDS	331	369
Total plays	63	72
Avg gain	5.3	5.1
NET YARDS RUSHING	112	45
Rushes	28	17
Avg per rush	4.0	2.6
NET YARDS PASSING	219	324
Completed–Att.	23–33	30–51
Yards per pass	6.3	5.9
Sacked–yards lost	17	33
Had intercepted	0	3
PUNTS–Avg.	7–45.1	3–42.8
PENALTIES–Yds.	7–47	3–35
FUMBLES–Lost	1–1	2–1

Passing

NEW ENGLAND

	Comp	Att	Yds	Int	TD
Brady	23	33	236	0	2

PHILADELPHIA

	Comp	Att	Yds	Int	TD
McNabb	30	51	357	3	3

Rushing

NEW ENGLAND

	No.	Yds	Lg	TD
Dillon	18	75	25	1
Faulk	8	38	12	0

PHILADELPHIA

	No.	Yds	Lg	TD
Westbrook	15	44	22	0
Levens	1	1	1	0

Receiving

NEW ENGLAND

	No.	Yds	Lg	TD
Branch	11	133	27	0
Dillon	3	31	16	0
Faulk	2	27	14	0
Givens	3	19	13	1
Brown	2	17	12	0
Graham	1	7	7	0
Vrabel	1	2	2	1

PHILADELPHIA

	No.	Yds	Lg	TD
Owens	9	122	36	0
Pinkston	4	82	40	0
Westbrook	7	60	15	1
Lewis	4	53	30	1
Smith	4	27	9	1
Mitchell	1	11	11	0
Parry	1	2	2	0

Defense

NEW ENGLAND

	Tck	Ast	Int	Sack
Gay	11	0	0	0
Harrison	7	0	2	1
Bruschi	6	1	1	1
Samuel	4	0	0	0
Phifer	3	0	0	0
Vrabel	2	2	0	1
Johnson	2	1	0	0
Seymour	2	0	0	1
McGinest	2	0	0	0
Reid	2	0	0	0
Wilson	1	0	0	0
Warren	1	0	0	0
Traylor	1	0	0	0
Poteat	1	0	0	0
Colvin	1	0	0	0

PHILADELPHIA

	Tck	Ast	Int	Sack
Lewis	5	1	0	0
Adams	4	1	0	0
Dawkins	4	1	0	0
Ware	4	0	0	0
Trotter	4	0	0	0
Burgess	3	1	0	1
Brown	3	1	0	0
Walker	2	1	0	0
Sheppard	2	1	1	1
Rayburn	2	0	0	0
Hood	2	0	0	0
Jones	2	0	0	0
Simonequ	2	0	0	0
Reese	2	0	0	0
Thomas	1	2	0	0
Kearse	1	1	0	0
Simon	1	0	0	0

Player	Position
Peyton Manning, Indianapolis	Quarterback
Curtis Martin, NY Jets	Running Back
LaDainian Tomlinson, San Diego	Running Back
William Henderson, Green Bay	Running Back
Antonio Gates, San Diego	Tight End
Terrell Owens, Philadelphia	Wide Receiver
Muhsin Muhammad, Carolina	Wide Receiver
Walter Jones, Seattle	Tackle
Willie Anderson, Cincinnati	Tackle
William Roaf, Kansas City	Tackle
Alan Faneca, Pittsburgh	Guard
Brian Waters, Kansas City	Guard
Jeff Hartings, Pittsburgh	Center

DEFENSE

Player	Position
Dwight Freeney, Indianapolis	Defensive End
Julius Peppers, Carolina	Defensive End
Kevin Williams, Minnesota	Defensive Tackle
Richard Seymour, New England	Defensive Tackle
Takeo Spikes, Buffalo	Linebacker
Derrick Brooks, Tampa Bay	Linebacker
James Farrior, Pittsburgh	Linebacker
Ray Lewis, Baltimore	Linebacker
Ronde Barber, Tampa Bay	Cornerback
Champ Bailey, Denver	Cornerback
Lito Sheppard, Philadelphia	Cornerback
Ed Reed, Baltimore	Safety
Brian Dawkins, Philadelphia	Safety

SPECIALISTS

Player	Position
Adam Vinatieri, New England	Kicker
Shane Lechler, Oakland	Punter
Eddie Drummond, Detroit	Kick Returner

2004 AFC Team-by-Team Results

BALTIMORE RAVENS (9–7)

3	at Cleveland	20
30	PITTSBURGH	13
23	at Cincinnati	9
24	KANSAS CITY	27
17	at Washington	10
20	BUFFALO	6
10	at Philadelphia	15
27	CLEVELAND	13
20	at NY Jets	17
30	DALLAS	10
3	at New England	24
26	CINCINNATI	27
37	NY GIANTS	14
10	at Indianapolis	20
7	at Pittsburgh	20
30	MIAMI	23
317		**268**

BUFFALO BILLS (9–7)

10	JACKSONVILLE	13
10	at Oakland	13
17	NEW ENGLAND	31
14	at NY JETS	16
20	MIAMI	13
6	at Baltimore	20
38	ARIZONA	14
22	NY JETS	17
6	at New England	29
37	ST. LOUIS	17
38	at Seattle	9
42	at Miami	32
37	CLEVELAND	7
33	at Cincinnati	17
41	at San Francisco	7
24	PITTSBURGH	29
395		**284**

CINCINNATI BENGALS (8–8)

24	at NY Jets	31
16	MIAMI	13
9	BALTIMORE	23
17	at Pittsburgh	28
17	at Cleveland	34
23	DENVER	10
20	at Tennessee	27
26	DALLAS	3
17	at Washington	10
14	PITTSBURGH	19
58	CLEVELAND	48
27	at Baltimore	26
28	at New England	35
17	BUFFALO	33
23	NY GIANTS	22
38	at Philadelphia	10
374		**372**

CLEVELAND BROWNS (4–12)

20	BALTIMORE	3	7	NY JETS	10
12	at Dallas	19	48	at Cincinnati	58
10	at NY Giants	27	15	NEW ENGLAND	42
17	WASHINGTON	13	7	at Buffalo	37
23	at Pittsburgh	34	0	SAN DIEGO	21
34	CINCINNATI	17	7	at Miami	10
31	PHILADELPHIA	34	22	at Houston	14
13	at Baltimore	27	**276**		**390**
10	PITTSBURGH	24			

DENVER BRONCOS (10–6)

34	KANSAS CITY	24
6	at Jacksonville	7
23	SAN DIEGO	13
16	at Tampa Bay	13
20	CAROLINA	17
31	at Oakland	3
10	at Cincinnati	23
28	ATLANTA	41
31	HOUSTON	13
34	at New Orleans	13
24	OAKLAND	25
17	at San Diego	20
20	MIAMI	17
17	at Kansas City	45
37	at Tennessee	16
33	INDIANAPOLIS	14
381		**304**

HOUSTON TEXANS (7–9)

20	SAN DIEGO	27
16	at Detroit	28
24	at Kansas City	21
30	OAKLAND	17
28	MINNESOTA	34
20	at Tennessee	10
20	JACKSONVILLE	6
13	at Denver	31
14	at Indianapolis	49
13	GREEN BAY	16
31	TENNESSEE	21
7	at NY Jets	29
14	INDIANAPOLIS	23
24	at Chicago	5
21	at Jacksonville	0
14	CLEVELAND	22
309		**339**

INDIANAPOLIS COLTS (12–4)

24	at New England	27
31	at Tennessee	17
45	GREEN BAY	31
24	at Jacksonville	17
35	OAKLAND	14
24	JACKSONVILLE	27
35	at Kansas City	45
31	MINNESOTA	28
49	HOUSTON	14
41	at Chicago	10
41	at Detroit	9
51	TENNESSEE	24
23	at Houston	14
20	BALTIMORE	10
34	SAN DIEGO	31
14	at Denver	33
522		**351**

JACKSONVILLE JAGUARS (9–7)

13	at Buffalo	10
7	DENVER	6
15	at Tennessee	12
17	INDIANAPOLIS	24
21	at San Diego	34
22	KANSAS CITY	16
27	at Indianapolis	24
6	at Houston	20
23	DETROIT	17
15	TENNESSEE	18
16	at Minnesota	27
16	PITTSBURGH	17
22	CHICAGO	3
28	at Green Bay	25
0	HOUSTON	21
13	at Oakland	6
261		**280**

KANSAS CITY CHIEFS (7–9)

24	at Denver	34
17	CAROLINA	28
21	HOUSTON	24
27	at Baltimore	24
16	at Jacksonville	22
56	ATLANTA	10
45	INDIANAPOLIS	35
31	at Tampa Bay	34
20	at New Orleans	27
19	NEW ENGLAND	27
31	SAN DIEGO	34
34	at Oakland	27
49	at Tennessee	38
45	DEN VER	17
31	OAKLAND	30
17	at San Diego	24
483		**435**

MIAMI DOLPHINS (4–12)

7	TENNESSEE	17
13	at Cincinnati	16
3	PITTSBURGH	13
9	NY JETS	17
10	at New England	24
13	at Buffalo	20
31	ST. LOUIS	14
14	at NY Jets	41
23	ARIZONA	24
17	at Seattle	24
24	at San Francisco	17
32	BUFFALO	42
17	at Denver	20
29	NEW ENGLAND	28
10	CLEVELAND	7
23	at Baltimore	30
275		**354**

NEW ENGLAND PATRIOTS (14–2)

27	INDIANAPOLIS	24
23	at Arizona	12
31	at Buffalo	17
24	MIAMI	10
30	SEATTLE	20
13	NY JETS	7
20	at Pittsburgh	34
40	at St. Louis	22
29	BUFFALO	6
27	at Kansas City	19
24	BALTIMORE	3
42	at Cleveland	15
35	CINCINNATI	28
28	at Miami	29
23	at NY Jets	7
21	SAN FRANCISCO	7
437		**260**

NEW YORK JETS (10–6)

131	CINCINNATI	24
34	at San Diego	2
17	at Miami	9
16	BUFFALO	14
22	SAN FRANCISCO	14
7	at New England	13
41	MIAMI	14
17	at Buffalo	22
17	BALTIMORE	20
10	at Cleveland	7
13	at Arizona	3
29	HOUSTON	7
6	at Pittsburgh	17
37	SEATTLE	14
7	NEW ENGLAND	23
29	at St. Louis	32
333		**261**

OAKLAND RAIDERS (5–11)

21	at Pittsburgh	24
13	BUFFALO	10
30	TAMPA BAY	20
17	at Houston	30
14	at Indianapolis	35
3	DENVER	31
26	NEW ORLEANS	31
14	at San Diego	42
27	at Carolina	24
17	SAN DIEGO	23
25	at Denver	24
27	KANSAS CITY	34
10	at Atlanta	35
40	TENNESSEE	35
30	at Kansas City	31
6	JACKSONVILLE	13
320		**442**

PITTSBURGH STEELERS (15–1)

24	OAKLAND	21
13	at Baltimore	30
13	at Miami	3
28	CINCINNATI	17
34	CLEVELAND	23
24	at Dallas	20
34	NEW ENGLAND	20
27	PHILADELPHIA	3
24	at Cleveland	10
19	at Cincinnati	14
16	WASHNGTON	7
17	at Jacksonville	16
17	NY JETS	6
33	at NY Giants	30
20	BALTIMORE	7
29	at Buffalo	24
372		**251**

SAN DIEGO CHARGERS (12–4)

27	at Houston	20
28	NY JETS	34
13	at Denver	23
38	TENNESSEE	17
34	JACKSONVILLE	21
20	at Atlanta	21
17	at Carolina	6
42	OAKLAND	14
43	NEW ORLEANS	17
23	at Oakland	17
34	at Kansas City	31
20	DENVER	17
31	TAMPA BAY	24
21	at Cleveland	0
31	at Indianapolis	34
24	KANSAS CITY	17
446		**313**

TENNESSEE TITANS (5–11)

17	at Miami	7
17	INDIANAPOLIS	31
12	JACKSONVILLE	15
17	at San Diego	38
48	at Green Bay	27
10	HOUSTON	20
3	at Minnesota	20
27	CINCINNATI	20
17	CHICAGO	19
18	at Jacksonville	15
21	at Houston	31
24	at Indianapolis	54
38	KANSAS CITY	49
35	at Oakland	40
16	DENVER	37
24	DETROIT	19
344		**440**

ARIZONA CARDINALS (6–10)

10	at St. Louis	17
12	NEW ENGLAND	23
3	at Atlanta	6
34	NEW ORLEANS	10
28	at San Francisco	31
25	SEATTLE	17
14	at Buffalo	38
24	at Miami	23
17	NY GIANTS	14
10	at Carolina	35
3	NY JETS	13
12	at Detroit	26
28	SAN FRANCISCO	31
31	ST. LOUIS	7
21	at Seattle	24
12	TAMPA BAY	7
284		**322**

ATLANTA FALCONS (11–5)

21	at San Francisco	19
34	ST. LOUIS	17
6	ARIZONA	3
27	at Carolina	10
10	DETROIT	17
21	SAN DIEGO	20
10	at Kansas City	56
41	at Denver	28
24	TAMPA BAY	14
14	at NY Giants	10
24	NEW ORLEANS	21
0	at Tampa Bay	27
35	OAKLAND	10
34	CAROLINA	31
13	at New Orleans	26
26	at Seattle	28
340		**337**

CAROLINA PANTHERS (7–9)

14	GREEN BAY	24
28	at Kansas City	17
10	ATLANTA	27
17	at Denver	20
8	at Philadelphia	30
6	SAN DIEGO	17
17	at Seattle	23
24	OAKLAND	27
37	at San Francisco	27
35	ARIZONA	10
21	TAMPA BAY	14
32	at New Orleans	21
20	ST. LOUIS	7
31	at Atlanta	34
37	at Tampa Bay	20
18	NEW ORLEANS	21
355		**339**

CHICAGO BEARS (5–11)

16	DETROIT	20
21	at Green Bay	10
22	at Minnesota	27
9	PHILADELPHIA	19
10	WASHINGTON	13
7	at Tampa Bay	19
23	SAN FRANCISCO	13
28	at NY Giants	21
19	at Tennessee	17
10	INDIANAPOLIS	41
7	at Dallas	21
24	MINNESOTA	14
3	at Jacksonville	22
5	HOUSTON	24
13	at Detroit	19
14	GREEN BAY	31
231		**331**

DALLAS COWBOYS (6–10)

17	at Minnesota	35
19	CLEVELAND	12
21	at Washington	18
10	NY GIANTS	26
20	PITTSBURGH	24
20	at Green Bay	41
31	DETROIT	21
3	at Cincinnati	26
21	PHILADELPHIA	49
10	at Baltimore	30
21	CHICAGO	7
43	at Seattle	39
13	NEW ORLEANS	27
7	at Philadelphia	12
13	WASHINGTON	10
24	at NY Giants	28
293		**405**

DETROIT LIONS (6–10)

20	at Chicago	16
28	HOUSTON	16
13	PHILADELPHIA	30
17	at Atlanta	10
10	GREEN BAY	38
28	at NY Giants	13
21	at Dallas	31
10	WASHINGTON	17
17	at Jacksonville	23
19	at Minnesota	22
9	INDIANAPOLIS	41
26	ARIZONA	12
13	at Green Bay	16
27	MINNESOTA	28
19	CHICAGO	13
19	at Tennessee	24
296		**350**

GREEN BAY PACKERS (10–6)

24	at Carolina	14
10	CHICAGO	21
31	at Indianapolis	45
7	NY GIANTS	14
27	TENNESSEE	48
38	at Detroit	10
41	DALLAS	20
28	at Washington	14
34	MINNESOTA	31
16	at Houston	13
45	ST. LOUIS	17
17	at Philadelphia	47
16	DETROIT	13
25	JACKSONVILLE	8
34	at Minnesota	31
31	at Chicago	14
424		**380**

MINNESOTA VIKINGS (8–8)

35	DALLAS	17
16	at Philadelphia	27
27	CHICAGO	22
34	at Houston	28
38	at New Orleans	31
20	TENNESSEE	3
13	NY GIANTS	34
28	at Indianapolis	31
31	at Green Bay	34
22	DETROIT	19
27	JACKSONVILLE	16
14	at Chicago	24
23	SEATTLE	27
28	at Detroit	27
31	GREEN BAY	34
18	at Washington	21
405		**395**

NEW ORLEANS SAINTS (8–8)

7	SEATTLE	21
30	SAN FRANCISCO	27
28	at St. Louis	25
10	at Arizona	34
17	TAMPA BAY	20
31	MINNESOTA	38
31	at Oakland	26
17	at San Diego	43
27	KANSAS CITY	20
13	DENVER	34
21	at Atlanta	24
21	CAROLINA	32
27	at Dallas	13
21	at Tampa Bay	17
26	ATLANTA	13
21	at Carolina	18
348		**405**

NEW YORK GIANTS (6–10)

17	at Philadelphia	31
20	WASHINGTON	14
27	CLEVELAND	10
14	at Green Bay	7
26	at Dallas	10
13	DETROIT	28
34	at Minnesota	13
21	CHICAGO	28
14	at Arizona	17
10	ATLANTA	14
6	PHILADELPHIA	27
7	at Washington	31
14	at Baltimore	37
30	PITTSBURGH	33
22	at Cincinnati	23
28	DALLAS	24
303		**347**

PHILADELPHIA EAGLES (13–3)

31	NY GIANTS	17
27	MINNESOTA	16
30	at Detroit	13
19	at Chicago	9
30	CAROLINA	8
34	at Cleveland	31
15	BALTIMORE	10
3	at Pittsburgh	27
49	at Dallas	21
28	WASHINGTON	6
27	at NY Giants	6
47	GREEN BAY	17
17	at Washington	14
12	DALLAS	7
7	at St. Louis	20
10	CINCINNATI	38
386		**260**

ST. LOUIS RAMS (8–8)

17	ARIZONA	10
17	at Atlanta	34
25	NEW ORLEANS	28
24	at San Francisco	14
33	at Seattle	27
28	TAMPA BAY	21
14	at Miami	31
22	NEW ENGLAND	40
23	SEATTLE	12
17	at Buffalo	37
17	at Green Bay	45
16	SAN FRANCISCO	6
7	at Carolina	20
7	at Arizona	31
20	PHILADELPHIA	7
32	NY JETS	29
319		**392**

SAN FRANCISCO 49ERS (2–14)

19	ATLANTA	21
27	at New Orleans	30
0	at Seattle	34
14	ST. LOUIS	24
31	ARIZONA	28
14	at NY Jets	22
13	at Chicago	23
27	SEATTLE	42
27	CAROLINA	37
3	at Tampa Bay	35
17	MIAMI	24
6	at St. Louis	16
31	at Arizona	28
16	WASHINGTON	26
7	BUFFALO	41
7	at New England	21
259		**452**

SEATTLE SEAHAWKS (9–7)

21	at New Orleans	7
10	at Tampa Bay	6
34	SAN FRANCISCO	0
27	ST. LOUIS	33
20	at New England	30
17	at Arizona	25
23	CAROLINA	17
42	at San Francisco	27
12	at St. Louis	23
24	MIAMI	17
9	BUFFALO	38
39	DALLAS	43
27	at Minnesota	23
14	at NY Jets	37
24	ARIZONA	21
28	ATLANTA	26
371		**373**

TAMPA BAY BUCCANEERS (5–11)

10	at Washington	16
6	SEATTLE	10
20	at Oakland	30
13	DENVER	16
20	at New Orleans	17
21	at St. Louis	28
19	CHICAGO	7
34	KANSAS CITY	31
14	at Atlanta	24
35	SAN FRANCISCO	3
14	at Carolina	21
27	ATLANTA	0
24	at San Diego	31
17	NEW ORLEANS	21
20	CAROLINA	37
7	at Arizona	12
301		**304**

WASHINGTON REDSKINS (6–10)

16	TAMPA BAY	10
14	at NY Giants	20
18	DALLAS	21
13	at Cleveland	17
10	BALTIMORE	17
13	at Chicago	10
14	GREEN BAY	28
17	at Detroit	10
10	CINCINNATI	17
6	at Philadelphia	28
7	at Pittsburgh	16
31	NY GIANTS	7
14	PHILADELPHIA	17
26	at San Francisco	16
10	at Dallas	13
21	MINNESOTA	18
240		**265**

American Football Conference

Scoring

TOUCHDOWNS	TD	Rush	Rec	Ret	2PT	Pts	KICKING	PAT	FG	Pts
Tomlinson, SD	18	17	1	0	0	108	Vinatieri, NE	48	31	141
Harrison, Ind	15	0	15	0	0	90	Elam, Den	42	29	129
Holmes, Kan	15	14	1	0	0	90	Reed, Pitt	40	28	124
Martin, NYJ	14	12	2	0	0	84	Graham, Cin	41	27	122
Davis, Hou	14	13	1	0	0	84	Vanderjagt, Ind	59	20	119
Dillon, NE	13	12	1	0	1	80	Stover, Balt	30	29	117
Bettis, Pitt	13	13	0	0	0	78	Lindell, Buff	45	24	117
McGahee, Buff	13	13	0	0	0	78	Kaeding, SD	54	20	114
Gates, SD	13	0	13	0	0	78	Tynes, Kan	58	17	109
							Janikowski, Oak	31	25	106

Two tied with 12.

Passing

	Att	Comp	Yds	TD	Int	Lg	Rating Pts
Manning, Ind	497	336	4557	49	10	80	121.1
Brees, SD	400	262	3159	27	7	79	104.8
Roethlisberger, Pitt	295	196	2621	17	11	58	98.1
Green, Kan	556	369	4591	27	17	70	95.2
Brady, NE	474	288	3692	28	14	50	92.6
Pennington, NYJ	370	242	2673	16	9	48	91.0
Volek, Tenn	357	218	2486	18	10	48	87.1
Plummer, Den	521	303	4089	27	20	85	84.5
Carr, Hou	466	285	3531	16	14	69	83.5
Leftwich, Jac	441	267	2941	15	10	65	82.2

Pass Receiving

RECEPTIONS	No.	Yds	Avg	Lg	TD	YARDS	Yds	No.	Avg	Lg	TD
Gonzalez, Kan	102	1258	12.3	32	7	Johnson, Cin	1274	95	13.4	53	9
Mason, Tenn	96	1168	12.2	37	7	Gonzalez, Kan	1258	102	12.3	32	7
Johnson, Cin	95	1274	13.4	53	9	Bennett, Tenn	1247	80	15.6	48	11
Moulds, Buff	88	1043	11.9	49	5	Wayne, Ind	1210	77	15.7	71	12
Harrison, Ind	86	1113	12.9	59	15	Smith, Jac	1172	74	15.8	65	6
Gates, SD	81	964	11.9	72	13	Mason, Tenn	1168	96	12.2	37	7
Bennett, Tenn	80	1247	15.6	48	11	Smith, Den	1144	79	14.5	85	7
Ward, Pitt	80	1004	12.6	58	4	Johnson, Hou	1142	79	14.5	54	6
Smith, Den	79	1144	14.5	85	7	Harrison, Ind	1113	86	12.9	59	15
Johnson, Hou	79	1142	14.5	54	6	Kennison, Kan	1086	62	17.5	70	8

Rushing

	Att	Yds	Avg	Lg	TD
Martin, NYJ	371	1697	4.6	25	12
Dillon, NE	345	1635	4.7	44	12
James, Ind	334	1548	4.6	40	9
Johnson, Cin	361	1454	4.0	52	12
Tomlinson, SD	339	1335	3.9	42	17
Droughns, Den	275	1240	4.5	51	6
Taylor, Jac	260	1224	4.7	46	2
Davis, Hou	302	1188	3.9	44	13
McGahee, Buff	284	1128	4.0	41	13
Brown, Tenn	220	1067	4.9	52	6

Interceptions

	No.	Yds	Lg	TD
Reed, Balt	9	358	106	1
James, Cin	8	66	23	0
Robinson, Hou	6	146	61	0
Dyson, Tenn	6	135	44	0
Clements, Buff	6	77	35	1

Sacks

Freeney, Ind	16
Ellis, NYJ	11
Suggs, Bal	10.5
Hayward, Den	10.5
Mathis, Ind	10.5
Foley, SD	10

American Football Conference (Cont.)

Punting

	No.	Yds	Avg	Net Avg	TB	In 20	Lg	Blk	Ret	Ret Avg
Lechler, Oak	73	3409	46.7	41.0	14	22	67	0	35	11.8
Smith, Ind	54	2443	45.2	37.9	3	21	62	0	29	13.6
Moorman, Buff	77	3325	43.2	39.1	9	17	80	0	37	8.5
Scifres, SD	69	2974	43.1	40.7	8	29	60	0	23	7.1
Gardocki, Pitt	67	2879	43.0	40.7	6	24	61	0	34	7.4

Punt Returns

	No.	Yds	Avg	Lg	TD
Northcutt, Cle	36	432	12.0	44	0
Welker, Mia/SD	43	464	10.8	71	0
Sams, Balt	55	575	10.5	78	2
Smith, Den	22	223	10.1	30	0
Hall, Kan	23	232	10.1	46	0

Kickoff Returns

	No.	Yds	Avg	Lg	TD
McGee, Buff	52	1370	26.3	104	3
Hall, Kan	68	1718	25.3	97	2
Randle, Pitt	21	527	25.1	41	0
Johnson, NE	41	1016	24.8	93	1
Rhodes, Ind	48	1188	24.8	88	1

National Football Conference

Scoring

TOUCHDOWNS	TD	Rush	Rec	Ret	2PT	Pts
Alexander, Sea	20	16	4	0	0	120
Muhammad, Car	16	0	16	0	0	96
Barber, NYG	15	13	2	0	0	90
Owens, Phil	14	0	14	0	0	84
Moss, Minn	13	0	13	0	0	78
Walker, GB	12	0	12	0	0	72
Horn, NO	11	0	11	0	1	68
Burleson, Minn	10	0	9	1	1	62
Pittman, TB	10	7	3	0	0	60
Holt, StL	10	0	10	0	0	60

KICKING	PAT	FG	Pts
Akers, Phil	41	27	122
Longwell, GB	48	24	120
Brown, Sea	40	23	109
Carney, NO	38	22	104
Hanson, Det	28	24	100
Andersen, Minn	45	18	99
Christie, NYG	33	22	99
Rackers, Ariz	28	22	94
Feely, Atl	40	18	94
Cundiff, Dall	31	20	91

Passing

	Att	Comp	Yds	TD	Int	Lg	Rating Pts
Culpepper, Minn	548	379	4717	39	11	82	110.9
McNabb, Phil	469	300	3875	31	8	80	104.7
Griese, TB	336	233	2632	20	12	68	97.5
Bulger, StL	485	321	3964	21	14	56	93.7
Favre, GB	540	346	4088	30	17	79	92.4
Delhomme, Car	533	310	3886	29	15	63	87.3
Warner, NYG	277	174	2054	6	4	62	86.5
Hasselbeck, Sea	474	279	3385	22	15	60	83.1
Brooks, NO	542	309	3810	21	16	57	79.5

Two tied with 78.1.

Pass Receiving

RECEPTIONS	No.	Yds	Avg	Lg	TD
Horn, NO	94	1399	14.9	57	11
Holt, StL	94	1372	14.6	75	10
Muhammad, Car	93	1405	15.1	51	16
Coles, Wash	90	950	10.6	45	1
Walker, GB	89	1382	15.5	79	12
Bruce, StL	89	1292	14.5	56	6
Jackson, Sea	87	1199	13.8	56	7
Witten, Dall	87	980	11.3	42	6
Driver, GB	84	1208	14.4	50	9
Johnson, SF	82	825	10.1	25	2

YARDS	Yds	No.	Avg	Lg	TD
Muhammad, Car	1405	93	15.1	51	16
Horn, NO	1399	94	14.9	57	11
Walker, GB	1382	89	15.5	79	12
Holt, StL	1372	94	14.6	75	10
Bruce, StL	1292	89	14.5	56	6
Driver, GB	1208	84	14.4	50	9
Owens, Phil	1200	77	15.6	59	14
Jackson, Sea	1199	87	13.8	56	7
Clayton, TB	1193	80	14.9	75	7
Burleson, Minn	1006	68	14.8	68	9

National Football Conference (Cont.)

Rushing

	Att	Yds	Avg	Lg	TD
Alexander, Sea	353	1696	4.8	44	16
Barber, NYG	322	1518	4.7	72	13
Portis, Wash	343	1315	3.8	64	5
Green, GB	259	1163	4.5	90	7
Jones, Det	241	1133	4.7	74	5
Dunn, Atl	265	1106	4.2	60	9
McAllister, NO	269	1074	4.0	71	9
Jones, Chi	240	948	4.0	54	7
Smith, Ariz	267	937	3.5	29	9
Pittman, TB	219	926	4.2	78	7

Interceptions

	No.	Yds	Lg	TD
Lucas, Sea	6	46	25	1
Gamble, Car	6	15	13	0

Seven tied with 5.

Sacks

Berry, Ariz	14.5
Gbaja-Biamila, GB	13.5
Kerney, Atl	13
Williams, Minn	12
Ricke, TB	12

Punting

	No.	Yds	Avg	Net Avg	TB	In 20	Lg	Blk	Ret	Ret Avg
Tupa, Wash	103	4544	44.1	37.1	8	30	61	1	65	11.2
Sauerbrun, Car	76	3351	44.1	40.1	8	25	65	1	38	8.0
Berger, NO	85	3704	43.6	39.9	4	28	63	0	43	7.2
Landeta, StL	40	1733	43.3	34.0	3	9	63	0	24	15.5
Player, Ariz	98	4230	43.2	38.2	7	32	57	1	56	8.7

Punt Returns

	No.	Yds	Avg	Lg	TD
Drummond, Det	24	316	13.2	83	2
Rossum, Atl	37	457	12.4	75	1
Lewis, NO	34	385	11.2	53	0
McQuarters, Chi	44	435	9.9	75	1
Frazier, Dal	24	229	9.5	55	0

Kickoff Returns

	No.	Yds	Avg	Lg	TD
Ponder, NYG	36	967	26.9	91	1
Drummond, Det	41	1092	26.6	99	2
Cox, TB	33	866	26.2	59	0
Ferguson, GB	21	526	25.0	71	0
Robertson, SFO/Car	31	740	23.9	49	0

2004 NFL Team Leaders

AFC Total Offense

	Total Plays	Yds/ Game	Yds/ Play	F Dwns/ Game	Time of Poss
Kansas City	1089	418.4	6.1	24.9	32:14
Indianapolis	968	404.7	6.7	23.7	28:40
Denver	1070	395.8	5.9	21.9	32:38
New England	1035	357.6	5.5	21.5	31:22
San Diego	996	346.4	5.6	20.5	31:30
Tennessee	1053	342.9	5.2	19.2	31:40
NY Jets	996	339.9	5.5	19.6	31:51
Pittsburgh	1012	324.0	5.1	19.4	34:00
Oakland	939	322.1	5.5	17.2	26:47
Cincinnati	1004	321.2	5.1	17.9	29:20
Houston	1001	320.5	5.1	18.8	29:59
Jacksonville	991	313.1	5.1	17.4	30:28
Buffalo	982	293.2	4.8	16.9	30:21
Cleveland	921	280.1	4.9	15.3	28:03
Miami	1022	275.2	4.3	16.7	28:20
Baltimore	991	273.4	4.4	16.2	29:36

AFC Total Defense

	Opp Total Plays	Opp Yds/ Game	Opp Yds/ Play	Opp T of Poss
Pittsburgh	882	258.4	4.7	26:01
Buffalo	978	264.2	4.3	29:39
Denver	918	278.7	4.9	27:23
Baltimore	1009	300.2	4.8	30:24
NY Jets	966	304.9	5.0	28:09
Miami	1009	305.9	4.9	31:40
New England	988	310.8	5.0	28:38
Jacksonville	972	320.9	5.3	29:32
Cleveland	1024	325.9	5.1	31:57
San Diego	991	335.0	5.4	28:30
Cincinnati	1031	335.3	5.2	30:40
Houston	971	341.1	5.6	30:01
Tennessee	977	357.8	5.9	28:20
Indianapolis	1042	370.6	5.7	31:20
Oakland	1072	371.0	5.5	33:13
Kansas City	960	377.3	6.3	27:46

NFC Total Offense

	Total Plays	Yds/ Game	Yds/ Play	F Dwns/ Game	Time of Poss
Green Bay	1053	397.3	6.0	22.1	30:28
Minnesota	985	396.2	6.4	21.9	30:02
St. Louis	1011	367.3	5.8	20.1	31:05
Seattle	1034	352.1	5.4	20.0	29:00
Philadelphia	960	351.1	5.9	18.8	28:26
Carolina	991	326.6	5.3	19.2	29:56
Dallas	1004	324.8	5.2	18.5	30:37
New Orleans	989	324.6	5.3	18.2	28:18
Atlanta	969	317.8	5.2	17.8	29:10
Tampa Bay	949	310.2	5.2	16.9	29:43
NY Giants	951	295.1	5.0	17.6	28:52
Detroit	949	293.9	4.9	16.4	28:03
San Francisco	1026	286.6	4.5	17.5	29:00
Arizona	1047	284.4	4.3	17.5	30:53
Washington	1023	274.8	4.3	16.8	31:19
Chicago	967	238.5	3.9	14.4	28:20

NFC Total Defense

	Opp Total Plays	Opp Yds/ Game	Opp Yds/ Play	Opp T of Poss
Washington	974	267.6	4.4	28:41
Tampa Bay	961	284.5	4.7	30:17
Philadelphia	1039	319.7	4.9	31:34
Arizona	993	321.3	5.2	29:07
NY Giants	1005	324.2	5.2	31:08
Atlanta	999	325.4	5.2	30:50
Dallas	960	330.3	5.5	29:23
St. Louis	1006	334.6	5.3	28:55
Carolina	1021	336.4	5.3	30:04
Chicago	1046	336.9	5.2	31:40
Detroit	1071	337.6	5.0	31:57
San Francisco	1014	342.6	5.4	31:00
Green Bay	967	346.3	5.7	29:32
Seattle	1047	351.3	5.4	31:00
Minnesota	1018	368.9	5.8	29:58
New Orleans	1067	383.8	5.8	31:42

Takeaways/Giveaways

American Football Conference

	Takeaways Int	Takeaways Fum	Takeaways Total	Giveaways Int	Giveaways Fum	Giveaways Total	Net Diff
Indianapolis	18	17	35	9	6	15	20
NY Jets	17	13	30	9	4	13	17
San Diego	18	10	28	6	9	15	13
Pittsburgh	17	11	28	10	6	16	12
New England	18	12	30	9	11	20	10
Baltimore	17	12	29	10	12	22	7
Buffalo	19	13	32	16	9	25	7
Jacksonville	11	11	22	9	8	17	5
Houston	19	6	25	12	10	22	3
Cincinnati	16	14	30	21	9	30	0
Kansas City	11	7	18	12	9	21	-3
Tennessee	16	10	26	17	12	29	-3
Cleveland	15	10	25	17	17	34	-9
Denver	10	7	17	19	8	27	-10
Oakland	7	7	14	18	12	30	-16
Miami	9	8	17	23	13	36	-19

National Football Conference

	Takeaways Int	Takeaways Fum	Takeaways Total	Giveaways Int	Giveaways Fum	Giveaways Total	Net Diff
Carolina	24	11	35	15	8	23	12
Philadelphia	17	10	27	8	8	16	11
Seattle	20	12	32	16	9	25	7
Detroit	14	9	23	11	6	17	6
Atlanta	16	13	29	13	13	26	3
New Orleans	11	15	26	14	10	24	2
NY Giants	12	12	24	11	11	22	2
Washington	17	7	24	14	8	22	2
Arizona	12	13	25	15	11	26	-1
Minnesota	9	10	19	12	9	21	-2
Tampa Bay	15	11	26	14	14	28	-2
Chicago	16	12	28	15	20	35	-7
Green Bay	7	7	14	18	10	28	-14
Dallas	10	8	18	21	12	33	-15
San Francisco	8	9	17	18	16	34	-17
St. Louis	6	8	14	20	15	35	-21

THEY SAID IT

Darnell Jackson, Seahawks wide receiver, on how his focus changes once the regular season starts: "Now it's more about crossing the i's and dotting the t's."

Baltimore Ravens

SCORING

	TD						
	Rush	Rec	Ret	PAT	FG	S	Pts
Stover	0	0	0	30/30	29/32	0	117
J. Lewis	7	0	0	0	0	0	42
Moore	0	4	0	0	0	0	26
Heap	0	3	0	0	0	0	18
Sams	1	0	2	0	0	0	18

RUSHING

	No.	Yds	Avg	Lg	TD
J. Lewis	235	1006	4.3	75	7
C. Taylor	160	714	4.5	47	2

PASSING

	Att	Comp	Pct Comp	Yds	Avg Gain	TD	Int	Rating Pts
Boller	224	116	51.8	1260	5.63	7	9	62.4

RECEIVING

	No.	Yds	Avg	Lg	TD
K. Johnson	35	373	10.7	35	1
T. Taylor	34	421	12.4	47	0
C. Taylor	30	185	6.1	23	0
Heap	27	303	11.2	37	3
Hymes	26	323	12.4	57	2
Wilcox	25	219	8.8	20	1

INTERCEPTIONS: Reed, 9

PUNTING

	No.	Yds	Avg	Net Avg	TB	In 20	Lg	Blk
Zastudil	73	2948	40.4	37.9	12	26	61	TK

SACKS: Suggs, 10.5

Buffalo Bills

SCORING

	TD						
	Rush	Rec	Ret	PAT	FG	S	Pts
Lindell	0	0	0	45/45	24/28	0	117
McGahee	13	0	0	0	0	0	78
Evans	0	9	0	0	0	0	54

RUSHING

	No.	Yds	Avg	Lg	TD
McGahee	284	1128	4.0	41	13
Henry	94	326	3.5	19	0

PASSING

	Att	Comp	Pct Comp	Yds	Avg Gain	TD	Int	Rating Pts
Bledsoe	450	256	56.9	2932	6.52	20	16	76.6

RECEIVING

	No.	Yds	Avg	Lg	TD
Moulds	88	1043	11.9	49	5
Evans	48	843	17.6	69	9
McGahee	22	169	7.7	16	0
Campbell	17	203	11.9	27	5
Shelton	17	114	6.7	24	0
Reed	16	153	9.6	20	0

INTERCEPTIONS: Clements, 6

PUNTING

	No.	Yds	Avg	Net Avg	TB	In 20	Lg	Blk
Moorman	85	3788	44.6	37.1	3	20	71	TK

SACKS: Schobel, 8.0

Cincinnati Bengals

SCORING

	TD						
	Rush	Rec	Ret	PAT	FG	S	Pts
Graham	0	0	0	41/41	27/31	0	122
R. Johnson	12	0	0	0	0	0	72
C. Johnson	0	9	0	0	0	0	54
Houshmandzadeh	0	4	0	0	0	0	24
Schobel	0	4	0	0	0	0	24
Washington	0	3	0	0	0	0	18

RUSHING

	No.	Yds	Avg	Lg	TD
R. Johnson	361	1454	4.0	52	12
Watson	26	161	6.2	25	0
Palmer	18	47	2.6	14	1

PASSING

	Att	Comp	Pct Comp	Yds	Avg Gain	TD	Int	Rating Pts
Palmer	432	263	60.9	2897	6.71	18	18	77.3

RECEIVING

	No.	Yds	Avg	Lg	TD
C. Johnson	95	1274	13.4	53	9
Houshmandzadeh	73	978	13.4	62	4
Washington	31	378	12.2	28	3
Watson	25	171	6.8	21	1
Schobel	21	201	9.6	76	4

INTERCEPTIONS: James, 8

PUNTING

	No.	Yds	Avg	Net Avg	TB	In 20	Lg	Blk
Larson	83	3499	42.2	37.6	7	21	66	TK

SACKS: Smith, 8

Cleveland Browns

SCORING

	TD						
	Rush	Rec	Ret	PAT	FG	S	Pts
Dawson	0	0	0	28/28	24/29	0	100
Heiden	0	5	0	0	0	0	32
Shea	0	4	0	0	0	0	24
Bryant	0	4	0	0	0	0	24
Morgan	0	3	0	0	0	0	18
Suggs	2	1	0	0	0	0	18

RUSHING

	No.	Yds	Avg	Lg	TD
Suggs	199	744	3.7	39	2
Green	163	585	3.6	46	2
Garcia	35	169	4.8	21	2

PASSING

	Att	Comp	Pct Comp	Yds	Avg Gain	TD	Int	Rating Pts
Garcia	252	144	57.1	1731	6.87	10	9	76.7
Holcomb	87	59	67.8	737	8.47	7	5	96.8
McCown	98	48	49.0	608	6.2	4	7	52.6

RECEIVING

	No.	Yds	Avg	Lg	TD
Northcutt	55	806	14.7	58	2
Bryant	42	546	13.0	55	4
Heiden	28	287	10.3	30	5
Shea	26	252	9.7	35	4
Suggs	20	178	8.9	59	1

INTERCEPTIONS: Henry, 4

PUNTING

	No.	Yds	Avg	Net Avg	TB	In 20	Lg	Blk
Frost	85	3404	40	36.4	4	24	54	TK

SACKS: Ekuban, 8

Denver Broncos

SCORING	Rush	TD Rec	Ret	PAT	FG	S	Pts
Elam	0	0	0	42/42	29/34	0	129
Droughns	6	2	0	0	0	0	48
Smith	0	7	0	0	0	0	42
Lelie	0	7	0	0	0	0	42
Hape	0	4	0	0	0	0	24

Two tied with 18.

RUSHING	No.	Yds	Avg	Lg	TD
Droughns	275	1240	4.5	51	6
Bell	75	396	5.3	29	3
Griffin	85	311	3.7	47	2
Plummer	62	202	3.3	22	1

PASSING	Att	Comp	Pct Comp	Yds	Avg Gain	TD	Int	Rating Pts
Plummer	521	303	58.2	4089	7.85	27	20	84.5

RECEIVING	No.	Yds	Avg	Lg	TD
Smith	79	1144	14.5	85	7
Lelie	54	1084	20.1	58	7
Putzier	36	572	15.9	39	2
Droughns	32	241	7.5	23	2
Watts	31	385	12.4	28	1

INTERCEPTIONS: Bailey, 3

PUNTING	No.	Yds	Avg	Net Avg	TB	In 20	Lg	Blk
Knorr	54	2243	41.5	37.1	6	12	66	TK

SACKS: Hayward, 10.5

Indianapolis Colts

SCORING	Rush	TD Rec	Ret	PAT	FG	S	Pts
Vanderjagt	0	0	0	59/60	20/25	0	119
Harrison	0	15	0	0	0	0	90
Wayne	0	12	0	0	0	0	72
Stokley	0	10	0	0	0	0	60
James	9	0	0	0	0	0	56
Pollard	0	6	0	0	0	0	36

RUSHING	No.	Yds	Avg	Lg	TD
James	334	1548	4.6	40	9
Rhodes	53	254	4.8	55	1
Manning	25	38	1.5	19	0

PASSING	Att	Comp	Pct Comp	Yds	Avg Gain	TD	Int	Rating Pts
Manning	497	336	67.6	4557	9.17	49	10	121.1

RECEIVING	No.	Yds	Avg	Lg	TD
Harrison	86	1113	12.9	59	15
Wayne	77	1210	15.7	71	12
Stokley	68	1077	15.8	69	10
James	51	483	9.5	56	0
Pollard	29	309	10.7	31	6
Clark	25	423	16.9	80	5

INTERCEPTIONS: David, 4

PUNTING	No.	Yds	Avg	Net Avg	TB	In 20	Lg	Blk
H. Smith	54	2443	45.2	37.9	3	21	62	TK

SACKS: Freeney, 16

Houston Texans

SCORING	Rush	TD Rec	Ret	PAT	FG	S	Pts
K. Brown	0	0	0	34/34	17/21	0	85
D. Davis	13	1	0	0	0	0	84
Johnson	0	6	0	0	0	0	36
Wells	3	2	0	0	0	0	32
Bradford	0	3	0	0	0	0	18

RUSHING	No.	Yds	Avg	Lg	TD
D. Davis	302	1188	3.9	44	13
Carr	73	299	4.1	24	0
Wells	82	299	3.6	14	3

PASSING	Att	Comp	Pct Comp	Yds	Avg Gain	TD	Int	Rating Pts
Carr	466	285	61.2	3531	7.58	16	14	83.5

RECEIVING	No.	Yds	Avg	Lg	TD
Johnson	79	1142	14.5	54	6
D. Davis	68	588	8.6	38	1
Gaffney	41	632	15.4	69	2
Armstrong	29	415	14.3	44	1
Bradford	27	399	14.8	47	3

INTERCEPTIONS: Robinson, 6

PUNTING	No.	Yds	Avg	Net Avg	TB	In 20	Lg	Blk
Stanley	73	3009	41.2	37.6	7	19	57	TK

SACKS: Wong, 5.5

Jacksonville Jaguars

SCORING	Rush	TD Rec	Ret	PAT	FG	S	Pts
Scobee	0	0	0	21/21	24/31	0	93
J. Smith	0	6	0	0	0	0	36
F. Taylor	2	1	0	0	0	0	18
G. Jones	0	2	0	0	0	0	18

RUSHING	No.	Yds	Avg	Lg	TD
F. Taylor	260	1224	4.7	46	2
Toefield	51	169	3.3	16	0
G. Jones	62	162	2.6	12	3

PASSING	Att	Comp	Pct Comp	Yds	Avg Gain	TD	Int	Rating Pts
Leftwich	441	261	60.5	2941	6.67	15	10	82.2

RECEIVING	No.	Yds	Avg	Lg	TD
J. Smith	74	1172	15.8	65	6
T. Edwards	50	533	10.7	36	1
F. Taylor	36	345	9.6	64	1
Toefield	28	151	5.4	16	1
Williams	27	268	9.9	26	1

INTERCEPTIONS: Darius and Mathis, 5

PUNTING	No.	Yds	Avg	Net Avg	TB	In 20	Lg	Blk
Hanson	84	3592	42.8	37.7	9	28	69	TK

SACKS: Henderson, 6.5

Kansas City Chiefs

SCORING

	TD						
SCORING	Rush	Rec	Ret	PAT	FG	S	Pts
Tynes	0	0	0	58/60	17/23	0	109
Holmes	14	1	0	0	0	0	90
Johnson	9	2	0	0	0	0	66
Blaylock	8	1	0	0	0	0	54
Kennison	0	8	0	0	0	0	50
Gonzalez	0	7	0	0	0	0	42

RUSHING	No.	Yds	Avg	Lg	TD
Holmes	196	892	4.6	33	14
Johnson	120	581	4.8	46	9
Blaylock	118	539	4.6	24	8

PASSING	Att	Comp	Pct Comp	Yds	Avg Gain	TD	Int	Rating Pts
Green	556	369	66.4	4591	.26	27	17	95.2

RECEIVING	No.	Yds	Avg	Lg	TD
Gonzalez	102	1258	12.3	32	7
Kennison	62	1086	17.5	70	8
Morton	55	795	14.5	52	3
Blaylock	25	246	9.8	30	1
Hall	25	230	9.2	22	0

INTERCEPTIONS: Wesley and Warfield, 4

PUNTING	No.	Yds	Avg	Net Avg	TB	In 20	Lg	Blk
Cheek	42	1643	39.1	34.4	6	8	55	TK

SACKS: Allen, 9

New England Patriots

	TD						
SCORING	Rush	Rec	Ret	PAT	FG	S	Pts
Vinatieri	0	0	0	48/48	31/33	0	141
Dillon	12	1	0	0	0	0	80
Patten	0	7	0	0	0	0	42
Graham	0	7	0	0	0	0	42
Branch	0	4	0	0	0	0	24

Two tied with 18.

RUSHING	No.	Yds	Avg	Lg	TD
Dillon	345	1635	4.7	44	12
Faulk	54	255	4.7	20	2
Pass	39	141	3.6	19	0

PASSING	Att	Comp	Pct Comp	Yds	Avg Gain	TD	Int	Rating Pts
Brady	474	288	60.8	3692	7.79	28	14	92.6

RECEIVING	No.	Yds	Avg	Lg	TD
Givens	56	874	15.6	50	3
Patten	44	800	18.2	48	7
Branch	35	454	13.0	26	4
Graham	30	364	12.1	48	7
Pass	28	215	7.7	22	0
Faulk	26	248	9.5	31	1

INTERCEPTIONS: Wilson, 4

PUNTING	No.	Yds	Avg	Net Avg	TB	In 20	Lg	Blk
Miller	56	2350	42	35.4	5	19	69	TK

SACKS: McGinest, 9.5

Miami Dolphins

	TD						
SCORING	Rush	Rec	Ret	PAT	FG	S	Pts
Mare	0	0	0	18/18	12/16	0	54
Chambers	0	7	0	0	0	0	44
Morris	6	0	0	0	0	0	36
McMichael	0	4	0	0	0	0	26
Thompson	0	4	0	0	0	0	24
Minor	3	0	0	0	0	0	18

RUSHING	No.	Yds	Avg	Lg	TD
Morris	132	523	4.0	35	6
Minor	109	388	3.6	34	3

PASSING	Att	Comp	Pct Comp	Yds	Avg Gain	TD	Int	Rating Pts
Feeley	356	191	53.7	1893	5.32	11	15	61.7
Fiedler	190	101	53.2	1186	6.24	7	8	67.1

RECEIVING	No.	Yds	Avg	Lg	TD
McMichael	73	791	10.8	42	4
Chambers	69	898	13.0	76	7
Booker	50	638	12.8	45	1
Thompson	23	359	15.6	36	4
Morris	22	124	5.6	24	0

INTERCEPTIONS: Freeman, Knight, and Surtai, 7

PUNTING	No.	Yds	Avg	Net Avg	TB	In 20	Lg	Blk
Turk	98	4088	41.7	39.3	10	29	67	TK

SACKS: Taylor, 9.5

New York Jets

	TD						
SCORING	Rush	Rec	Ret	PAT	FG	S	Pts
Brien	0	0	0	33/34	24/29	0	105
Martin	12	2	0	0	0	0	84
Moss	0	5	0	0	0	0	30
McCareins	0	4	0	0	0	0	24
Baker	0	4	0	0	0	0	24

RUSHING	No.	Yds	Avg	Lg	TD
Martin	371	1697	4.6	25	12
Jordan	93	479	5.2	33	2
Pennington	34	126	3.7	16	1

PASSING	Att	Comp	Pct Comp	Yds	Avg Gain	TD	Int	Rating Pts
Pennington	370	242	65.4	2673	7.22	16	9	91.0

RECEIVING	No.	Yds	Avg	Lg	TD
McCareins	56	770	13.8	43	4
Moss	45	838	18.6	69	5
Sowell	45	342	7.6	34	1
Martin	41	245	6.2	22	2
Chrebet	31	397	12.8	35	1
Baker	18	182	10.1	23	4

INTERCEPTIONS: Coleman, 4

PUNTING	No.	Yds	Avg	Net Avg	TB	In 20	Lg	Blk
Gowin	80	3057	38.2	35.5	8	22	58	TK

SACKS: Ellis, 11

Oakland Raiders

SCORING

	TD Rush	Rec	Ret	PAT	FG	S	Pts
Janikowski	0	0	0	31/32	25/28	0	106
Porter	0	9	0	0	0	0	54
Curry	0	6	0	0	0	0	36
Wheatley	4	0	0	0	0	0	24
Zereoue	3	0	0	0	0	0	18

RUSHING

	No.	Yds	Avg	Lg	TD
Zereoue	112	425	3.8	55	3
Wheatley	85	327	3.8	60	4
Crockett	49	232	4.7	47	2
Fargas	35	126	3.6	15	1

PASSING

	Att	Comp	Pct Comp	Yds	Avg Gain	TD	Int	Rating Pts
Collins	513	289	56.3	3495	6.81	21	20	74.8

RECEIVING

	No.	Yds	Avg	Lg	TD
Porter	64	998	15.6	52	9
Curry	50	679	13.6	63	6
Gabriel	33	551	16.7	58	2
Jolley	27	313	11.6	34	2
Zereoue	39	284	7.3	13	0
Redmond	32	233	7.3	22	0

INTERCEPTIONS: Buchanon, 3

PUNTING

	No.	Yds	Avg	Net Avg	TB	In 20	Lg	Blk
Lechler	73	3409	46.7	41.2	14	22	67	TK

SACKS: Kelly, 4

Pittsburgh Steelers

SCORING

	TD Rush	Rec	Ret	PAT	FG	S	Pts
Reed	0	0	0	40/40	28/33	0	124
Bettis	13	0	0	0	0	0	78
Ward	1	4	0	0	0	0	30
Burress	0	5	0	0	0	0	30
Tuman	0	3	0	0	0	0	18
Randle El	0	3	0	0	0	0	18

RUSHING

	No.	Yds	Avg	Lg	TD
Bettis	250	941	3.8	29	13
Staley	192	830	4.3	38	1
Haynes	55	272	4.9	18	0
Parker	32	186	5.8	58	0
Roethlisberger	56	144	2.6	20	1

PASSING

	Att	Comp	Pct Comp	Yds	Avg Gain	TD	Int	Rating Pts
Roethlisberger	295	196	66.4	2621	8.89	17	11	98.1

RECEIVING

	No.	Yds	Avg	Lg	TD
Ward	80	1004	12.6	58	4
Burress	35	698	19.9	48	5
Randle El	43	601	14.0	39	3
Haynes	18	142	7.9	26	2

INTERCEPTIONS: Polamalu, 5

PUNTING

	No.	Yds	Avg	Net Avg	TB	In 20	Lg	Blk
Miller	84	3521	41.9	36.0	8	27	72	1

SACKS: Smith, 8

San Diego Chargers

SCORING

	TD Rush	Rec	Ret	PAT	FG	S	Pts
Kaeding	0	0	0	54/55	20/25	0	114
Tomlinson	17	1	0	0	0	0	108
Gates	0	13	0	0	0	0	78
Parker	0	4	0	0	0	0	24
Caldwell	0	3	0	0	0	0	18
Chatman	3	0	0	0	0	0	18

RUSHING

	No.	Yds	Avg	Lg	TD
Tomlinson	339	1335	3.9	42	17
Chatman	65	392	6.0	52	3
Turner	20	104	5.2	30	0
Brees	53	85	1.6	22	2

PASSING

	Att	Comp	Pct Comp	Yds	Avg Gain	TD	Int	Rating Pts
Brees	400	262	65.5	3159	7.9	27	7	104.8

RECEIVING

	No.	Yds	Avg	Lg	TD
Gates	81	964	11.9	72	13
Parker	47	690	14.7	79	4
Tomlinson	53	441	8.3	74	1
McCardell	31	393	12.7	31	1
Caldwell	18	310	17.2	58	3

INTERCEPTIONS: Edwards, 5

PUNTING

	No.	Yds	Avg	Net Avg	TB	In 20	Lg	Blk
Scifres	69	2974	43.1	40.7	8	29	60	TK

SACKS: Foley, 10

Tennessee Titans

SCORING

	TD Rush	Rec	Ret	PAT	FG	S	Pts
Anderson	0	0	0	37/37	17/22	0	88
Bennett	0	11	0	0	0	0	66
Mason	0	7	0	0	0	0	42
Brown	6	0	0	0	0	0	36
Smith	4	0	0	0	0	0	24
Kinney	0	3	0	0	0	0	18

RUSHING

	No.	Yds	Avg	Lg	TD
Brown	220	1067	4.9	52	6
Smith	137	509	3.7	43	4
McNair	23	128	5.6	23	1

PASSING

	Att	Comp	Pct Comp	Yds	Avg Gain	TD	Int	Rating Pts
Volek	357	218	61.1	2486	6.96	18	10	87.1
McNair	215	129	60.0	1343	6.25	8	9	73.1

RECEIVING

	No.	Yds	Avg	Lg	TD
Mason	96	1168	12.2	37	7
Bennett	80	1247	15.6	48	11
Troupe	33	329	10.0	33	1
Kinney	25	193	7.7	21	3
Meier	25	127	5.1	29	2
Smith	22	169	7.7	31	0
Fleming	19	164	8.6	37	2

INTERCEPTIONS: Dyson, 6

PUNTING

	No.	Yds	Avg	Net Avg	TB	In 20	Lg	Blk
Hentrich	73	3117	42.7	40.2	8	20	64	TK

SACKS: Carter, 6

Arizona Cardinals

SCORING	Rush	TD Rec	Ret	PAT	FG	S	Pts
Rackers	0	0	0	28/28	22/29	0	94
E. Smith	9	0	0	0	0	0	54
Fitzgerald	0	8	0	0	0	0	48
Ayanbadejo	3	1	0	0	0	0	24

RUSHING	No.	Yds	Avg	Lg	TD
E. Smith	267	937	3.5	29	9
Hambrick	63	283	4.5	62	1
Avanbadejo	30	122	4.1	23	3
McCown	25	112	3.1	12	2
Scobey	27	89	3.3	10	0

PASSING	Att	Comp	Pct Comp	Yds	Avg Gain	TD	Int	Rating Pts
McCown	408	233	57.1	2511	6.15	11	10	74.1

RECEIVING	No.	Yds	Avg	Lg	TD
Fitzgerald	58	780	13.4	48	8
Boldin	56	623	11.1	31	1
Johnson	49	537	11.0	40	1
Jones	45	426	9.5	40	2
Ayanbadejo	19	171	9.0	21	1

INTERCEPTIONS: Macklin, 4

PUNTING	No.	Yds	Avg	Net Avg	TB	In 20	Lg	Blk
Player	98	4230	43.2	38.2	7	32	57	TK

SACKS: Berry, 14.5

Carolina Panthers

SCORING	Rush	TD Rec	Ret	PAT	FG	S	Pts
Muhammad	0	16	0	0	0	0	96
Kasay	0	0	0	27/28	19/22	0	84
Goings	6	1	0	0	0	0	42
Colbert	0	5	0	0	0	0	32
Mangum	0	3	0	0	0	0	18

RUSHING	No.	Yds	Avg	Lg	TD
Goings	217	821	3.8	57	6
Foster	59	255	4.3	71	2
Hoover	68	246	3.6	16	0

PASSING	Att	Comp	Pct Comp	Yds	Avg Gain	TD	Int	Rating Pts
Delhomme	533	310	58.2	3886	7.29	29	15	87.3

RECEIVING	No.	Yds	Avg	Lg	TD
Muhammad	93	1405	15.1	51	16
Colbert	47	754	16.0	63	5
Goings	45	394	8.8	37	1
Proehl	34	497	14.6	34	0
Mangum	34	323	9.5	26	3

INTERCEPTIONS: Gamble, 6

PUNTING	No.	Yds	Avg	Net Avg	TB	In 20	Lg	Blk
Sauerbrun	76	3351	44.1	40.1	8	25	65	TK

SACKS: Peppers, 11

Atlanta Falcons

SCORING	Rush	TD Rec	Ret	PAT	FG	S	Pts
Feeely	0	0	0	40/40	18/23	0	94
Dunn	9	0	0	0	0	0	54
Duckett	8	0	0	0	0	0	48
Crumpler	0	6	0	0	0	0	36
Price	0	3	0	0	0	0	18
Vick	3	0	0	0	0	0	18

RUSHING	No.	Yds	Avg	Lg	TD
Dunn	265	1106	4.2	60	9
Vick	120	902	7.5	58	3
Duckett	104	509	4.9	35	8

PASSING	Att	Comp	Pct Comp	Yds	Avg Gain	TD	Int	Rating Pts
Vick	321	181	56.4	2313	7.21	14	12	78.1

RECEIVING	No.	Yds	Avg	Lg	TD
Crumpler	48	774	16.1	49	6
Price	45	575	12.8	50	3
White	30	370	12.3	54	2
Dunn	29	293	10.1	59	0
Finneran	23	258	11.2	26	2
Griffith	22	220	10.0	62	1

INTERCEPTIONS: Beasley, 4

PUNTING	No.	Yds	Avg	Net Avg	TB	In 20	Lg	Blk
Mohr	76	3082	40.6	38.8	7	19	56	BK

SACKS: Kerney, 13

Chicago Bears

SCORING	Rush	TD Rec	Ret	PAT	FG	S	Pts
Edinger	0	0	0	22/22	15/24	0	67
Jones	7	0	0	0	0	0	42

Five tied with 12.

RUSHING	No.	Yds	Avg	Lg	TD
Jones	240	948	4.0	54	7
Thomas	122	404	3.3	41	2

PASSING	Att	Comp	Pct Comp	Yds	Avg Gain	TD	Int	Rating Pts
Hutchinson	161	92	57.1	903	5.61	4	3	73.6
Grossman	84	47	56.0	607	7.23	1	3	67.9
Quinn	98	51	52.0	413	4.21	1	3	53.7
Krenzel	127	59	46.5	718	5.65	3	6	52.5

RECEIVING	No.	Yds	Avg	Lg	TD
Jones	56	427	7.6	45	0
Terrell	42	699	16.6	63	1
Wade	42	481	11.5	40	0
Clark	24	282	11.8	31	1
Thomas	17	132	7.8	30	0

INTERCEPTIONS: Vasher, 5

PUNTING	No.	Yds	Avg	Net Avg	TB	In 20	Lg	Blk
Maynard	108	4638	42.9	39.6	5	34	58	TK

SACKS: Brown, 6

Dallas Cowboys

SCORING

SCORING	Rush	TD Rec	Ret	PAT	FG	S	Pts
Cundiff	0	0	0	31/31	20/26	0	91
Jones	7	0	0	0	0		42
Witten	0	6	0	0	0	0	38
Johnson	0	6	0	0	0	0	36
George	4	0	0	0	0		24

Two tied with 12.

RUSHING

RUSHING	No.	Yds	Avg	Lg	TD
Jones	197	819	4.2	53	7
George	132	432	3.3	24	4
Anderson	57	246	4.3	27	1

PASSING

PASSING	Att	Comp	Pct Comp	Yds	Avg Gain	TD	Int	Rating Pts
Testaverde	495	297	60.0	3532	7.14	17	20	76.4

RECEIVING

RECEIVING	No.	Yds	Avg	Lg	TD
Witen	87	980	11.3	42	6
Johnson	70	981	14.0	39	6
Anderson	26	207	8.0	28	0
Glenn	24	400	16.7	48	2
Morgan	22	260	11.8	53	0

INTERCEPTIONS: Newman, 4

PUNTING

PUNTING	No.	Yds	Avg	Net Avg	TB	In 20	Lg	Blk
McBriar	75	3182	42.4	37.0	7	22	68	TK

SACKS: Ellis, 9

Detroit Lions

SCORING

SCORING	Rush	TD Rec	Ret	PAT	FG	S	Pts
Hanson	0	0	0	28/28	24/28	0	100
Williams	0	8	0	0	0		48
Jones	5	1	0	0	0		36
Drummond	0	0	4	0	0		24
Schlesinger	0	3	0	0	0		18
Hakim	0	3	0	0	0		18

RUSHING

RUSHING	No.	Yds	Avg	Lg	TD
Jones	241	1133	4.7	74	5
Bryson	50	264	4.3	28	0
Harrington	48	175	3.6	17	0
Pinner	57	174	3.1	14	2

PASSING

PASSING	Att	Comp	Pct Comp	Yds	Avg Gain	TD	Int	Rating Pts
Harrington	489	274	56.3	3047	6.23	19	12	77.5

RECEIVING

RECEIVING	No.	Yds	Avg	Lg	TD
Williams	54	817	15.1	46	8
Bryson	44	322	7.3	30	0
Alexander	41	377	9.2	30	1
Hakim	31	533	17.2	39	3

INTERCEPTIONS: Bly, 4

PUNTING

PUNTING	No.	Yds	Avg	Net Avg	TB	In 20	Lg	Blk
Harris	92	3765	40.9	36.1	7	32	60	TK

SACKS: Hall, 11.5

Green Bay Packers

SCORING

SCORING	Rush	TD Rec	Ret	PAT	FG	S	Pts
Longwell	0	0	0	48/48	24/28	0	120
Walker	0	12	0	0	0		72
Driver	0	9	0	0	0		56
Green	7	1	0	0	0		48
Franks	0	7	0	0	0		42

Two tied with 18.

RUSHING

RUSHING	No.	Yds	Avg	Lg	TD
Green	259	1163	4.5	90	7
Davenport	71	359	5.1	40	2
Fisher	65	224	3.4	24	0

PASSING

PASSING	Att	Comp	Pct Comp	Yds	Avg Gain	TD	Int	Rating Pts
Favre	540	346	64.1	4088	7.57	30	17	92.4

RECEIVING

RECEIVING	No.	Yds	Avg	Lg	TD
Walker	89	1382	15.5	79	12
Driver	84	1208	14.4	50	9
Fisher	38	277	7.3	25	2
Green	40	275	6.9	48	1
Franks	34	361	10.6	29	7
Henderson	34	239	7.0	38	3

INTERCEPTIONS: Sharper, 4

PUNTING

PUNTING	No.	Yds	Avg	Net Avg	TB	In 20	Lg	Blk
Barker	66	2644	40.1	35.5	7	24.2	64	TK

SACKS: Gbaja-Biamila, 13.5

Minnesota Vikings

SCORING

SCORING	Rush	TD Rec	Ret	PAT	FG	S	Pts
Andersen	0	13	0	45/48	18/22	0	99
Moss	0	9	1	0	0		78
Burleson	0	8	0	0	0		62
Robinson	2	2	0	0	0		48
O. Smith	3	1	0	0	0		26

Two tied with 24.

RUSHING

RUSHING	No.	Yds	Avg	Lg	TD
O Smith	124	544	4.4	38	2
Culpepper	88	406	4.6	16	2
Moore	65	379	5.8	33	0
Bennett	70	276	3.9	25	1

PASSING

PASSING	Att	Comp	Pct Comp	Yds	Avg Gain	TD	Int	Rating Pts
Culpepper	548	379	69.2	4717	8.61	39	11	110.9

RECEIVING

RECEIVING	No.	Yds	Avg	Lg	TD
Burleson	68	1006	14.8	68	9
Moss	49	767	15.7	82	13
Wiggins	71	705	9.9	39	4
Robinson	47	657	14.0	50	8
O. Smith	36	394	10.9	63	2

INTERCEPTIONS: Winfield, 3

PUNTING

PUNTING	No.	Yds	Avg	Net Avg	TB	In 20	Lg	Blk
Bennett	57	2240	39.3	36.3	3	18	61	TK

SACKS: K. Williams, 12

New Orleans Saints

SCORING

	Rush	TD Rec	Ret	PAT	FG	S	Pts
Carney	0	0	0	38/38	22/27	0	104
Horn	0	11	0	0	0	0	68
McAlliser	9	0	0	0	0	0	54
Stallworth	0	5	0	0	0	0	30
Brooks	4	0	0	0	0	0	24
Stecker	2	0	1	0	0	0	18

RUSHING

	No.	Yds	Avg	Lg	TD
McAllister	269	1074	4.0	71	9
Stecker	58	244	4.2	42	2
Brooks	58	173	3.0	15	4

PASSING

	Att	Comp	Pct Comp	Yds	Avg Gain	TD	Int	Rating Pts
Brooks	542	309	57.0	3810	7.03	21	16	79.5

RECEIVING

	No.	Yds	Avg	Lg	TD
Horn	94	1399	14.9	57	11
Stallworth	58	767	13.2	45	5
Pathon	34	581	17.1	38	1
McAllister	34	228	6.7	20	0
Williams	33	362	11.0	22	2

INTERCEPTIONS: McKenzie, 5

PUNTING

	No.	Yds	Avg	Net Avg	TB	In 20	Lg	Blk
Berger	85	3704	43.6	39.9	4	28	63	TK

SACKS: Howard, 11

New York Giants

SCORING

	Rush	TD Rec	Ret	PAT	FG	S	Pts
Christie	0	0	0	33/33	22/28	0	99
Barber	13	2	0	0	0	0	90
Shockey	0	6	0	0	0	0	36
Cloud	3	0	0	0	0	0	18

Ten tied with 6.

RUSHING

	No.	Yds	Avg	Lg	TD
Barber	322	1518	4.7	72	13
Dayne	52	179	3.4	15	1

PASSING

	Att	Comp	Pct Comp	Yds	Avg Gain	TD	Int	Rating Pts
Warner	277	174	62.8	2054	7.42	6	4	86.5
Manning	197	95	48.2	1043	5.29	6	9	55.4

RECEIVING

	No.	Yds	Avg	Lg	TD
Shockey	61	666	10.9	38	6
Barber	52	578	11.1	62	2
Tommer	51	747	14.6	48	0
Hilliard	49	437	8.9	43	0

INTERCEPTIONS: Alexander and Wilson, 3

PUNTING

	No.	Yds	Avg	Net Avg	TB	In 20	Lg	Blk
Feagles	74	3069	41.5	36.7	4	23	55	TK

SACKS: Umenyiora, 7

Philadelphia Eagles

SCORING

	Rush	TD Rec	Ret	PAT	FG	S	Pts
Akers	0	0	0	41/42	27/32	0	122
Owens	0	14	0	0	0	0	84
Westbrook	3	6	0	0	0	0	54
L.J. Smith	0	5	0	0	0	0	30
Levens	4	0	0	0	0	0	24

Two tied with 18.

RUSHING

	No.	Yds	Avg	Lg	TD
Westbrook	177	812	4.6	50	3
Levens	94	410	4.4	45	4
McNabb	41	220	5.4	28	3

PASSING

	Att	Comp	Pct Comp	Yds	Avg Gain	TD	Int	Rating Pts
McNabb	469	300	64.0	3875	8.26	31	8	104.7

RECEIVING

	No.	Yds	Avg	Lg	TD
Owens	77	1200	15.6	59	14
Westbrook	73	703	9.6	50	6
Pinkston	36	676	18.8	80	1
L.J. Smith	34	377	11.1	31	5
C. Lewis	29	267	9.2	21	3

INTERCEPTIONS: Sheppard, 5

PUNTING

	No.	Yds	Avg	Net Avg	TB	In 20	Lg	Blk
Johnson	72	3032	42.1	39.0	6	20	62	TK

SACKS: Kearse, 7.5

St. Louis Rams

SCORING

	Rush	TD Rec	Ret	PAT	FG	S	Pts
Wilkins	0	0	0	32/32	19/24	0	89
Holt	0	10	0	0	0	0	60
Bruce	0	6	0	0	0	0	36
Faulk	3	1	0	0	0	0	28
Jackson	4	0	0	0	0	0	26

Two tied with 18.

RUSHING

	No.	Yds	Avg	Lg	TD
Faulk	195	774	4.0	40	3
Jackson	134	673	5.0	48	4

PASSING

	Att	Comp	Pct Comp	Yds	Avg Gain	TD	Int	Rating Pts
Bulger	45	321	66.2	3964	8.17	21	14	93.7

RECEIVING

	No.	Yds	Avg	Lg	TD
Holt	94	1372	14.6	75	10
Bruce	89	1292	14.5	56	6
Faulk	50	310	6.2	25	1
McDonald	37	494	13.4	52	3
Curtis	32	421	13.2	41	2

INTERCEPTIONS: Butler, 5

PUNTING

	No.	Yds	Avg	Net Avg	TB	In 20	Lg	Blk
Landeta	40	1733	43.3	34.0	3	9	63	TK
Stemke	28	1115	39.8	38.3	3	12	56	TK

SACKS: Fisher, 8.5

San Francisco 49ers

SCORING
		TD					
SCORING	Rush	Rec	Ret	PAT	FG	S	Pts
Peterson	0	0	0	23/23	18/22	0	77
Barlow	7	0	0	0	0	0	42
Lloyd	0	6	0	0	0	0	38
Conway	0	3	0	0	0	0	20
Wilson	0	3	0	0	0	0	18

RUSHING
RUSHING	No.	Yds	Avg	Lg	TD
Barlow	244	822	3.4	60	7
Hicks	96	362	3.8	35	2
Jackson	26	101	3.9	13	0

PASSING
PASSING	Att	Comp	Pct Comp	Yds	Avg Gain	TD	Int	Rating Pts
Rattay	325	198	60.9	2169	6.67	10	10	78.1
Dorsey	226	123	54.4	1231	5.45	6	9	62.4

RECEIVING
RECEIVING	No.	Yds	Avg	Lg	TD
Johnson	82	825	10.1	25	2
Wilson	47	641	13.6	39	3
Lloyd	43	565	13.1	52	6
Conway	38	403	10.6	37	3
Barlow	35	212	6.1	15	0

INTERCEPTIONS: Parrish, 4

PUNTING
PUNTING	No.	Yds	Avg	Net Avg	TB	In 20	Lg	Blk
Lee	96	3990	41.6	36.9	8	25	81	TK

SACKS: Engelberger, 6

Seattle Seahawks

SCORING
		TD					
SCORING	Rush	Rec	Ret	PAT	FG	S	Pts
Alexander	16	4	0	0	0	0	120
Brown	0	0	0	40/40	23/25	0	109
Jackson	0	7	0	0	0	0	44
Stevens	0	3	0	0	0	0	20
Rice	0	3	0	0	0	0	18

RUSHING
RUSHING	No.	Yds	Avg	Lg	TD
Alexander	353	1696	4.8	44	16
Strong	36	131	3.6	11	0
Morris	30	126	4.2	12	0

PASSING
PASSING	Att	Comp	Pct Comp	Yds	Avg Gain	TD	Int	Rating Pts
Hasselbeck	474	279	58.9	3382	7.14	22	15	83.1

RECEIVING
RECEIVING	No.	Yds	Avg	Lg	TD
Jackson	87	1199	13.8	56	7
Engram	36	499	13.9	60	2
Robinson	31	495	16.0	33	2
Stevens	31	349	11.3	32	3
Rice	25	362	14.5	56	3

INTERCEPTIONS: Lucas, 6

PUNTING
PUNTING	No.	Yds	Avg	Net Avg	TB	In 20	Lg	Blk
Rouen	26	1093	42	38.5	1	10	60	TK
Jones	26	988	38	35.0	2	6	51	TK
Walter	24	920	38.3	35.3	1	4	50	TK

SACKS: Okeafor, 8.5

Tampa Bay Buccaneers

SCORING
		TD					
SCORING	Rush	Rec	Ret	PAT	FG	S	Pts
Pittman	7	3	0	0	0	0	60
Gramatia	0	0	0	21/22	11/19	0	54
Clayton	0	7	0	0	0	0	42
Galloway	0	5	1	0	0	0	36
Taylor	0	0	0	11/11	4/5	0	23
Dilger	0	3	0	0	0	0	20

RUSHING
RUSHING	No.	Yds	Avg	Lg	TD
Pittman	219	926	4.2	78	7
Alstott	67	230	3.4	32	2
Garner	30	111	3.7	25	0

PASSING
PASSING	Att	Comp	Pct Comp	Yds	Avg Gain	TD	Int	Rating Pts
Griese	336	233	69.3	2632	7.83	20	12	97.5
Johnson	103	65	63.1	574	6.54	3	3	79.5

RECEIVING
RECEIVING	No.	Yds	Avg	Lg	TD
Clayton	80	1193	14.9	75	7
Pittman	41	391	9.5	68	3
Dilger	39	345	8.8	45	3
Galloway	33	416	12.6	36	5
Alstott	29	202	7.0	20	0
Jurevicius	27	333	12.3	42	2

INTERCEPTIONS: Kelly, 4

PUNTING
PUNTING	No.	Yds	Avg	Net Avg	TB	In 20	Lg	Blk
Bidwell	82	3472	42.3	38.9	7	23	60	TK

SACKS: Rice, 12

Washington Redskins

SCORING
		TD					
SCORING	Rush	Rec	Ret	PAT	FG	S	Pts
Portis	5	2	0	0	0	0	42
Hall	0	0	0	13/13	8/11	0	37
Cooley	0	6	0	0	0	0	36
Gardner	0	5	0	0	0	0	30
Royal	0	4	0	0	0	0	24
Kimrin	0	0	0	6/6	6/10	0	24

RUSHING
RUSHING	No.	Yds	Avg	Lg	TD
Portis	343	1315	3.8	64	5
Betts	90	371	4.1	27	1

PASSING
PASSING	Att	Comp	Pct Comp	Yds	Avg Gain	TD	Int	Rating Pts
Ramsey	272	169	62.1	1665	6.12	10	11	74.8
Brunell	237	118	49.8	1194	5.04	7	6	63.9

RECEIVING
RECEIVING	No.	Yds	Avg	Lg	TD
Coles	90	950	10.6	45	1
Gardner	51	650	12.7	51	5
Portis	40	235	5.9	18	2
Cooley	37	314	8.5	31	6

INTERCEPTIONS: Springs, 5

PUNTING
PUNTING	No.	Yds	Avg	Net Avg	TB	In 20	Lg	Blk
Tupa	103	4544	44.1	37.1	8	30	61	TK

SACKS: Griffin and Springs, 6

2005 NFL Draft

First two rounds of the 69th annual NFL Draft, held April 25–26 in New York City.

First Round

Team	Selection	Position
1. San Francisco	Alex Smith, Utah	QB
2. Miami	Ronnie Brown, Auburn	RB
3. Cleveland	Braylon Edwards, Michigan	WR
4. Chicago	Cedric Benson, Texas	RB
5. Tampa Bay	Carnell Williams, Auburn	RB
6. Tennessee	Adam Jones, West Virginia	CB
7. Minnesota (from Oakland)	Troy Williamson, South Carolina	WR
8. Arizona	Antrel Rolle, Miami (FL)	CB
9. Washington	Carlos Rogers, Auburn	CB
10. Detroit	Mike Williams, USC	WR
11. Dallas	Demarcus Ware, Troy State	DE
12. San Diego (from NY Giants)	Shawne Merriman, Maryland	OLB
13. New Orleans (from Houston)	Jammal Brown, Oklahoma	OT
14. Carolina	Thomas Davis, Georgia	S
15. Kansas City	Derrick Johnson, Texas	OLB
16. Houston (from New Orleans)	Travis Johnson, Florida State	DT
17. Cincinnati	David Pollack, Georgia	DE
18. Minnesota	Eramus James, Wisconson	DE
19. St. Louis	Alex Barron, Florida State	OT
20. Dallas (from Buffalo)	Marcus Spears, Louisiana State	DE
21. Jacksonville	Matt Jones, Arkansas	WR
22. Baltimore	Mark Clayton, Oklahoma	WR
23. Oakland (from Seattle)	Fabian Washington, Nebraska	WR
24. Green Bay	Aarn Rodgers, California	QB
25. Washington (from Denver)	Jason Campbell, Auburn	QB
26. Seattle (from NY Jets through Oakland)	Chris Spencer, Mississippi	C
27. Atlanta	Roddy White, Alabama-Birmingham	WR
28. San Diego	Luis Castillo, Northwestern	DT
29. Indianapolis	Marlin Jackson, Michigan	CB
30. Pittsburgh	Heath Miller, Virginia	TE
31. Philadelphia	Mike Patterson, USC	DT
32. New England	Logan Mankins, Fresno State	OG

Second Round

Team	Selection	Position
33. San Francisco	David Bass, Michigan	C
34. Cleveland	Brodney Pool, Oklahoma	S
35. Philadelphia	Reggie Brown, Georgia	WR
36. Tampa Bay	Barrett Ruud, Nebraska	ILB
37. Detroit (from Tennessee)	Shaun Cody, USC	DT
38. Oakland	Stanford Routt, Houston	CB
39. Chicago	Mark Bradley, Oklahoma	WR
40. New Orleans (from Washington)	Josh Bullocks, Nebraska	S
41. Tennessee (from Detroit)	Michael Roos, Eastern Washington	OT
42. Dallas	Kevin Burnett, Tennessee	OLB
43. NY Giants	Corey Webster, Louisiana State	CB
44. Arizona	JJ Arrington, California	RB
45. Seattle (from Carolina)	Lofa Tatupu, USC	ILB
46. Miami (from Kansas City)	Matt Roth, Iowa	DE
47. NY Jets (from Oakland)	Mike Nugent, Ohio State	PK
48. Cincinnati	Odeli Thurman, Georgia	ILB
49. Minnesota	Marcus Johnson, Mississippi	OT
50. St. Louis	Ronald Bartell Jr., Howard	CB
51. Green Bay (from New Orleans)	Nick Collins, Bethune-Cookman	CB
52. Jacksonville	Khalif Barnes, Washington	OT
53. Baltimore	Dan Cody, Oklahoma	DE
54. Carolina (from Seattle)	Eric Shelton, Louisville	RB
55. Buffalo	Roscoe Parrish, Miami (FL)	WR
56. Denver	Darrent Williams, Oklahoma State	CB
57. NY Jets	Justin Miller, Clemson	CB
58. Green Bay	Terrence Murphy, Texas A&M	WR
59. Atlanta	Jonathan Babineaux, Iowa	DT
60. Indianapolis	Kelvin Hayden, Illinois	CB
61. San Diego	Vincent Jackson, Northern Colorado	WR
62. Pittsburgh	Bryant McFadden, Florida State	CB
63. Philadelphia	Matt McCoy, San Diego State	OLB
64. Baltimore (from New England)	Adam Terry, Syracuse	OT

Final Standings

	W	L	T	Pct	Pts	OP
Berlin*	7	3	0	.700	241	191
Amsterdam*	6	4	0	.600	265	207
Cologne	6	4	0	.600	188	212
Hamburg	5	5	0	.500	213	196
Frankfurt	3	7	0	.300	163	246
Rhein	3	7	0	.300	203	224

*Clinched World Bowl 2005 berth.

2005 World Bowl

June 11, 2005, in Düsseldorf, Germany

Amsterdam Admirals	7	10	7	3—27
Berlin Thunder	0	7	0	14—21

FIRST QUARTER
Amsterdam: R.Martin 22 yd. pass from K.Kittner (C.Snyder kick) 10:08

SECOND QUARTER
Amsterdam: M.Gomez 12 yd. pass from K.Kittner (C.Snyder kick), 11:57
Amsterdam: C.Snyder 32 yd. Field Goal, 7:00
A.Boone 10 yd. pass from D.Ragone (K.Miller kick), 0:33.

THIRD QUARTER
Amsterdam: Smith 18 yd. run (C.Snyder kick), 9:46

FOURTH QUARTER
Berlin: Flowers 10 yd. pass from D.Ragone (K.Miller kick), 13:41
Amsterdam: C.Snyder 28 yard field goal, 9:13.
Berlin: R.Redd 10 yd. pass from D.Ragone (K.Miller kick), 4:55

A: 35,134. T: 3:59.

NFL Europe Individual Leaders

PASSING

	Att	Comp	Pct Comp	Yds	Avg Gain	TD	Pct TD	Int	Pct Int	Lg	Rating Pts
Ragone, Ber	251	158	62.9%	1,746	6.96	13	5.2%	2	0.8	70t	97.5
Eakin, Fra	180	105	58.3%	1,299	7.22	11	6.1%	5	2.8	38	89.6
McBrien, Rhe	217	116	53.5%	1,722	7.94	13	6.0%	12	5.5	73t	76.6
C.Bramlet, Ham	212	131	61.8%	1,463	6.90	7	3.3%	10	4.7	40t	73.7
Thompson, Col	234	126	53.8%	1,561	6.67	8	3.4%	10	4.3	75	68.3

RECEIVING

RECEPTIONS	No.	Yds	Avg	Lg	TD	YARDS	Yds	No.	Avg	Lg	TD
Boone, Ber	43	582	13.5	47	5	Martin, Ams	679	37	18.4	60t	12
Collins, Ham	42	458	10.9	24	0	Boone, Ber	582	43	13.5	47	5
Martin, Ams	37	679	18.4	60t	12	Jennings, Ber	546	33	16.5	70t	4
McCready, Ham	37	474	12.8	35	1	James, Rhe	515	29	17.8	73t	5
Anelli, Fra	36	395	11.0	28	3	McCready, Ham	474	37	12.8	35	1

RUSHING

	Att	Yds	Avg	Lg	TD
Smith, Rhe	223	1,026	4.6	59	5
Chapman, Col	126	718	5.7	42t	5
Smith, Ams	147	711	4.8	56t	2
Payton, Ams	104	578	5.6	53	7
Galloway, Fra	141	516	3.7	31	1

Other Statistical Leaders

Points (TDs)	Martin, Ams	72
Points (Kicking)	France, Ham	71
Yards from Scrimmage	Smith, Rhe	1,111
Interceptions	Tucker, Ams	5
Sacks	White, Col.	7
Punting Avg	Dorsch, Rhe	42.5
Punt Return Avg	Amundson, Ham	11.0
Kickoff Return Avg	Brightful, Fra	27.4

THEY SAID IT

Ike Taylor, Steelers backup cornerback, after being given the chance to start in one of the team's exhibition games: "You only get a once-in-a-lifetime chance so many times."

2004 Canadian Football League

EASTERN DIVISION

	W	L	T	Pts	PF	PA
†Montreal	14	4	0	28	584	371
*Toronto	10	7	1	21	422	414
*Hamilton	9	8	1	19	455	542
Ottawa	5	13	0	19	481	560

WESTERN DIVISION

	W	L	T	Pts	PF	PA
†*British Columbia	13	5	0	26	584	436
*Edmonton	9	9	0	18	532	472
*Saskatchewan	9	9	0	18	476	444
Winnipeg	7	11	0	14	448	507
Calgary	4	14	0	8	396	552

†Clinched division title.

*Clinched playoff berth.

2004 Playoff Results

FIRST ROUND

TORONTO 24, Hamilton 6
Saskatchewan 14, EDMONTON 6

SEMI-FINALS

Toronto 26, MONTREAL 18,
B.C. 27, Saskatchewan 25

Home team in caps.

2004 Grey Cup Championship

Nov. 21, 2004, at Ottawa

Toronto Argonauts	0	17	7	3—27
British Columbia Lions	7	3	3	6—19

A: 51,242.

THEY SAID IT

Jim Bates, Dolphins interim coach, on how his new gig is different from his last head coaching job with the USFL San Antonio Gunslingers in 1985: "I know I'm going to get paid this time.

The Super Bowl

Results

	Date	Winner (Share)	Loser (Share)	Score	Site (Attendance)
I	1-15-67	Green Bay ($15,000)	Kansas City ($7,500)	35–10	Los Angeles (61,946)
II	1-14-68	Green Bay ($15,000)	Oakland ($7,500)	33–14	Miami (75,546)
III	1-12-69	NY Jets ($15,000)	Baltimore ($7,500)	16–7	Miami (75,389)
IV	1-11-70	Kansas City ($15,000)	Minnesota ($7,500)	23–7	New Orleans (80,562)
V	1-17-71	Baltimore ($15,000)	Dallas ($7,500)	16–13	Miami (79,204)
VI	1-16-72	Dallas ($15,000)	Miami ($7,500)	24–3	New Orleans (81,023)
VII	1-14-73	Miami ($15,000)	Washington ($7,500)	14–7	Los Angeles (90,182)
VIII	1-13-74	Miami ($15,000)	Minnesota ($7,500)	24–7	Houston (71,882)
IX	1-12-75	Pittsburgh ($15,000)	Minnesota ($7,500)	16–6	New Orleans (80,997)
X	1-18-76	Pittsburgh ($15,000)	Dallas ($7,500)	21–17	Miami (80,187)
XI	1-9-77	Oakland ($15,000)	Minnesota ($7,500)	32–14	Pasadena (103,438)
XII	1-15-78	Dallas ($18,000)	Denver ($9,000)	27–10	New Orleans (75,583)
XIII	1-21-79	Pittsburgh ($18,000)	Dallas ($9,000)	35–31	Miami (79,484)
XIV	1-20-80	Pittsburgh ($18,000)	Los Angeles ($9,000)	31–19	Pasadena (103,985)
XV	1-25-81	Oakland ($18,000)	Philadelphia ($9,000)	27–10	New Orleans (76,135)
XVI	1-24-82	San Francisco ($18,000)	Cincinnati ($9,000)	26–21	Pontiac, MI (81,270)
XVII	1-30-83	Washington ($36,000)	Miami ($18,000)	27–17	Pasadena (103,667)
XVIII	1-22-84	LA Raiders ($36,000)	Washington ($18,000)	38–9	Tampa (72,920)
XIX	1-20-85	San Francisco ($36,000)	Miami ($18,000)	38–16	Stanford (84,059)
XX	1-26-86	Chicago ($36,000)	New England ($18,000)	46–10	New Orleans (73,818)
XXI	1-25-87	NY Giants ($36,000)	Denver ($18,000)	39–20	Pasadena (101,063)
XXII	1-31-88	Washington ($36,000)	Denver ($18,000)	42–10	San Diego (73,302)
XXIII	1-22-89	San Francisco ($36,000)	Cincinnati ($18,000)	20–16	Miami (75,129)
XXIV	1-28-90	San Francisco ($36,000)	Denver ($18,000)	55–10	New Orleans (72,919)
XXV	1-27-91	NY Giants ($36,000)	Buffalo ($18,000)	20–19	Tampa (73,813)
XXVI	1-26-92	Washington ($36,000)	Buffalo ($18,000)	37–24	Minneapolis (63,130)
XXVII	1-31-93	Dallas ($36,000)	Buffalo ($18,000)	52–17	Pasadena (98,374)
XXVIII	1-30-94	Dallas ($38,000)	Buffalo ($23,500)	30–13	Atlanta (72,817)
XXIX	1-29-95	San Francisco ($42,000)	San Diego ($26,000)	49–26	Miami (74,107)
XXX	1-28-96	Dallas ($42,000)	Pittsburgh ($27,000)	27–17	Tempe, AZ (76,347)
XXXI	1-26-97	Green Bay ($48,000)	New England ($29,000)	35–21	New Orleans (72,301)
XXXII	1-25-98	Denver ($48,000)	Green Bay ($27,500)	31–24	San Diego (68,912)
XXXIII	1-31-99	Denver ($53,000)	Atlanta ($32,500)	34–19	Miami (74,803)
XXXIV	1-30-00	St. Louis ($58,000)	Tennessee ($33,000)	23–16	Atlanta (72,625)
XXXV	1-28-01	Baltimore ($58,000)	NY Giants ($34,500)	34–7	Tampa (71,921)
XXXVI	2-3-02	New England ($63,000)	St. Louis ($34,500)	20–17	New Orleans (72,922)
XXXVII	1-26-03	Tampa Bay ($64,000)	Oakland ($35,000)	48–21	San Diego (67,603)
XXXVIII	2-1-04	New England ($64,000)	Carolina ($35,000)	32–29	Houston (71,525)
XXXIX	2-6-05	New England (68,000)	Philadelphia (36,500)	24–21	Jacksonville (78,125)

Most Valuable Players

Super Bowl	Player/ Team	Position
I	Bart Starr, GB	QB
II	Bart Starr, GB	QB
III	Joe Namath, NYJ	QB
IV	Len Dawson, KC	QB
V	Chuck Howley, Dall	LB
VI	Roger Staubach, Dall	QB
VII	Jake Scott, Mia	S
VIII	Larry Csonka, Mia	RB
IX	Franco Harris, Pitt	RB
X	Lynn Swann, Pitt	WR
XI	Fred Biletnikoff, Oak	WR
XII	Randy White, Dall	DT
	Harvey Martin, Dall	DE
XIII	Terry Bradshaw, Pitt	QB
XIV	Terry Bradshaw, Pitt	QB
XV	Jim Plunkett, Oak	QB
XVI	Joe Montana, SF	QB
XVII	John Riggins, Wash	RB
XVIII	Marcus Allen, Rai	RB
XIX	Joe Montana, SF	QB
XX	Richard Dent, Chi	DE
XXI	Phil Simms, NYG	QB
XXII	Doug Williams, Wash	QB
XXIII	Jerry Rice, SF	WR
XXIV	Joe Montana, SF	QB
XXV	Ottis Anderson, NYG	RB
XXVI	Mark Rypien, Wash	QB
XXVII	Troy Aikman, Dall	QB
XXVIII	Emmitt Smith, Dall	RB
XXIX	Steve Young, SF	QB
XXX	Larry Brown, Dall	DB
XXXI	Desmond Howard, GB	KR
XXXII	Terrell Davis, Den	RB
XXXIII	John Elway, Den	QB
XXXIV	Kurt Warner, StL	QB
XXXV	Ray Lewis, Balt	LB
XXXVI	Tom Brady, NE	QB
XXXVII	Dexter Jackson, TB	S
XXXVIII	Tom Brady, NE	QB
XXXIX	Deion Branch, NE	WR

Composite Standings

	W	L	Pct	Pts	Opp Pts
San Francisco 49ers	5	0	1.000	188	89
Baltimore Ravens	1	0	1.000	34	7
Chicago Bears	1	0	1.000	46	10
New York Jets	1	0	1.000	16	7
Tampa Bay Buccaneers	1	0	1.000	48	21
Pittsburgh Steelers	4	1	.800	120	100
Green Bay Packers	3	1	.750	127	76
Oakland/LA Raiders	3	2	.600	132	114
New York Giants	2	1	.667	66	73
Dallas Cowboys	5	3	.625	221	132
Washington Redskins	3	2	.600	122	103
New England Patriots	3	2	.600	107	148
Baltimore Colts	1	1	.500	23	29
Kansas City Chiefs	1	1	.500	33	42
Miami Dolphins	2	3	.400	74	103
Denver Broncos	2	4	.333	115	206
Los Angeles/St. Louis Rams	1	2	.333	59	67
Carolina Panthers	0	1	.000	29	32
San Diego Chargers	0	1	.000	26	49
Atlanta Falcons	0	1	.000	19	34
Tennesse Titans	0	1	.000	16	23
Philadelphia Eagles	0	2	.000	31	51
Cincinnati Bengals	0	2	.000	37	46
Buffalo Bills	0	4	.000	73	139
Minnesota Vikings	0	4	.000	34	95

Career Leaders

Passing

	GP	Att	Comp	Pct Comp	Yds	Avg Gain	TD	Pct TD	Int	Pct Int	Lg	Rating Pts
Joe Montana, SF	4	122	83	68.0	1142	9.36	11	9.0	0	0.0	44	127.8
Jim Plunkett, Rai	2	46	29	63.0	433	9.41	4	8.7	0	0.0	t80	122.8
Terry Bradshaw, Pitt	4	84	49	58.3	932	11.10	9	10.7	4	4.8	t75	112.8
Troy Aikman, Dall	3	80	56	70.0	689	8.61	5	6.3	1	1.3	t56	111.9
Bart Starr, GB	2	47	29	61.7	452	9.62	3	6.4	1	2.1	t62	106.0
Tom Brady, NE	3	108	71	65.7	735	6.81	6	5.5	1	0.9	52	99.9
Brett Favre, GB	2	69	39	56.5	502	7.28	5	7.2	1	1.4	t81	97.7
Roger Staubach, Dall	4	98	61	62.2	734	7.49	8	8.2	4	4.1	t45	95.4
Kurt Warner, StL	2	89	52	58.4	779	8.75	3	3.4	1	1.1	t73	93.8
Len Dawson, KC	2	44	28	63.6	353	8.02	2	4.5	2	4.5	t46	84.8

Note: Minimum 40 attempts.

Rushing

	GP	Yds	Att	Avg	Lg	TD
Franco Harris, Pitt	4	354	101	3.5	25	4
Larry Csonka, Mia	3	297	57	5.2	9	2
Emmitt Smith, Dall	3	289	70	4.1	38	5
Terrell Davis, Den	2	259	75	4.1	15	3
John Riggins, Wash	2	230	64	3.6	43	2
Timmy Smith, Wash	1	204	22	9.3	58	2
Thurman Thomas, Buff	4	204	52	3.9	31	4
Roger Craig, SF	3	198	52	3.8	18	2
Marcus Allen, Rai	1	191	20	9.6	t74	2
Antowain Smith, NE	2	175	44	4.0	17	2

Receiving

	GP	No.	Yds	Avg	Lg	TD
Jerry Rice, SF	4	33	589	17.9	t48	8
Andre Reed, Buff	4	27	323	11.9	40	0
Deion Branch, NE	2	21	286	13.1	52	1
Roger Craig, SF	3	20	212	10.6	40	2
Thurman Thomas, Buff	4	20	144	7.2	24	0
Jay Novacek, Dall	3	17	178	10.5	23	2
Lynn Swann, Pitt	4	16	364	22.8	t64	3
Michael Irvin, Dall	3	16	256	16.0	25	2
Chuck Foreman, Minn	3	15	139	9.3	26	0
Cliff Branch, Rai	3	14	181	12.9	50	3

Single-Game Leaders

Scoring

	Pts
Roger Craig: XIX, San Francisco vs Miami (1 R, 2 P)	18
Jerry Rice: XXIV, San Francisco vs Denver (3 P); XXIX, SF vs San Diego (3 P)	18
Ricky Watters: XXIX, San Francisco vs San Diego (1 R, 2 P)	18
Terrell Davis: XXXII, Denver vs Green Bay (3 R)	18

Rushing Yards

	Yds
Timmy Smith: XXII, Washington vs Denver	204
Marcus Allen: XVIII, LA Raiders vs Washington	191
John Riggins: XVII, Washington vs Miami	166
Franco Harris: IX, Pittsburgh vs Minnesota	158
Terrell Davis: XXXII, Denver vs Green Bay	157
Larry Csonka: VIII, Miami vs Minnesota	145
Clarence Davis: XI, Oakland vs Minnesota	137
Thurman Thomas: XXV, Buffalo vs NY Giants	135
Emmitt Smith: XXVIII, Dallas vs Buffalo	132
Michael Pittman: XXXVII, Tampa Bay vs Oakland	124

Receptions

	No.
Dan Ross: XVI, Cincinnati vs San Francisco	11
Jerry Rice: XXIII, San Francisco vs Cincinnati	11
Deion Branch: XXXIX, New England vs Phila.	11
Tony Nathan: XIX, Miami vs San Francisco	10
Jerry Rice: XXIX, San Francisco vs San Diego	10
Andre Hastings: XXX, Pittsburgh vs Dallas	10
Deion Branch: XXXVIII, New England vs Carolina	10
Ricky Sanders: XXII, Washington vs Denver	9
Antonio Freeman: XXXII, Green Bay vs Denver	9
Seven tied with eight.	

Touchdown Passes

	No.
Steve Young: XXIX, San Francisco vs San Diego	6
Joe Montana: XXIV, San Francisco vs Denver	5
Terry Bradshaw: XIII, Pittsburgh vs Dallas	4
Doug Williams: XXII, Washington vs Denver	4
Troy Aikman: XXVII, Dallas vs Buffalo	4
Seven tied with three.	

Passing Yards

	Yds
Kurt Warner: XXXIV, St. Louis vs Tennessee	414
Kurt Warner: XXXVI, St. Louis vs New England	365
Joe Montana: XXIII, San Francisco vs Cincinnati	357
Tom Brady: XXXVIII, New England vs. Carolina	354
Doug Williams: XXII, Washington vs Denver	340
John Elway: XXXIII, Denver vs Atlanta	336
Joe Montana: XIX, San Francisco vs Miami	331
Steve Young: XXIX, San Francisco vs San Diego	325
Jake Delhomme: XXXVIII Carolina vs New England	323
Terry Bradshaw: XIII, Pittsburgh vs Dallas	318
Dan Marino: XIX, Miami vs San Francisco	318

Receiving Yards

	Yds
Jerry Rice: XXIII, San Francisco vs Cincinnati	215
Ricky Sanders: XXII, Washington vs Denver	193
Isaac Bruce: XXXIV, St. Louis vs Tennessee	162
Lynn Swann: X, Pittsburgh vs Dallas	161
Andre Reed: XXVII, Buffalo vs Dallas	152
Rod Smith: XXXIII, Denver vs Atlanta	152
Jerry Rice: XXIX, San Francisco vs San Diego	149
Jerry Rice: XXIV, San Francisco vs Denver	148
Deion Branch: XXXVIII, New England vs Carolina	143
Max McGee: I, Green Bay vs Kansas City	138

NFL Playoff History

1933

NFL championship	Chicago Bears 23, NY Giants 21

1934

NFL championship	NY Giants 30, Chicago Bears 13

1935

NFL championship	Detroit 26, NY Giants 7

1936

NFL championship	Green Bay 21, Boston 6

1937

NFL championship	Washington 28, Chicago Bears 21

1938

NFL championship	NY Giants 23, Green Bay 17

1939

NFL championship	Green Bay 27, NY Giants 0

1940

NFL championship	Chicago Bears 73, Washington 0

1941

W. div. playoff	Chicago Bears 33, Green Bay 14
NFL championship	Chicago Bears 37, NY Giants 9

1942

NFL championship	Washington 14, Chicago Bears 6

1943

E. div. playoff	Washington 28, NY Giants 0
NFL championship	Chicago Bears 41, Washington 21

1944

NFL championship	Green Bay 14, NY Giants 7

1945

NFL championship	Cleveland 15, Washington 14

1946

NFL championship	Chicago Bears 24, NY Giants 14

1947

E. div. playoff	Philadelphia 21, Pittsburgh 0
NFL championship	Chi Cardinals 28, Philadelphia 21

1948

NFL championship	Philadelphia 7, Chi Cardinals 0

1949

NFL championship	Philadelphia 14, Los Angeles 0

1950

Am. Conf. playoff	Cleveland 8, NY Giants 3
Nat. Conf. playoff	Los Angeles 24, Chicago Bears 14
NFL championship	Cleveland 30, Los Angeles 28

1951

NFL championship	Los Angeles 24, Cleveland 17

1952

Nat. Conf. playoff	Detroit 31, Los Angeles 21
NFL championship	Detroit 17, Cleveland 7

1953

NFL championship	Detroit 17, Cleveland 16

1954

NFL championship	Cleveland 56, Detroit 10

1955

NFL championship	Cleveland 38, Los Angeles 14

1956

NFL championship	NY Giants 47, Chicago Bears 7

1957

W. Conf. playoff	Detroit 31, San Francisco 27
NFL championship	Detroit 59, Cleveland 14

1958

E. Conf. playoff	NY Giants 10, Cleveland 0
NFL championship	Baltimore 23, NY Giants 17

1959

NFL championship	Baltimore 31, NY Giants 16

1960

NFL championship	Philadelphia 17, Green Bay 13
AFL championship	Houston 24, LA Chargers 16

1961

NFL championship	Green Bay 37, NY Giants 0
AFL championship	Houston 10, San Diego 3

1962

NFL championship	Green Bay 16, NY Giants 7
AFL championship	Dallas Texans 20, Houston 17

1963

NFL championship	Chicago 14, NY Giants 10
AFL E. div. playoff	Boston 26, Buffalo 8
AFL championship	San Diego 51, Boston 10

1964

NFL championship	Cleveland 27, Baltimore 0
AFL championship	Buffalo 20, San Diego 7

1965

NFL W. Conf. playoff	Green Bay 13, Baltimore 10
NFL championship	Green Bay 23, Cleveland 12
AFL championship	Buffalo 23, San Diego 0

1966

NFL championship	Green Bay 34, Dallas 27
AFL championship	Kansas City 31, Buffalo 7

1967

NFL E. Conf. championship	Dallas 52, Cleveland 14
NFL W. Conf. championship	Green Bay 28, Los Angeles 7
NFL championship	Green Bay 21, Dallas 17
AFL championship	Oakland 40, Houston 7

1968

NFL E. Conf. championship	Cleveland 31, Dallas 20
NFL W. Conf. championship	Baltimore 24, Minnesota 14
NFL championship	Baltimore 34, Cleveland 0

1968 *(Cont.)*

AFL W. div. playoff	Oakland 41, Kansas City 6
AFL championship	NY Jets 27, Oakland 23

1969

NFL E. Conf. championship	Cleveland 38, Dallas 14
NFL W. Conf. championship	Minnesota 23, Los Angeles 20
NFL championship	Minnesota 27, Cleveland 7
AFL div. playoffs	Kansas City 13, NY Jets 6
	Oakland 56, Houston 7
AFL championship	Kansas City 17, Oakland 7

1970

AFC div. playoffs	Baltimore 17, Cincinnati 0
	Oakland 21, Miami 14
AFC championship	Baltimore 27, Oakland 17
NFC div. playoffs	Dallas 5, Detroit 0
	San Francisco 17, Minnesota 14
NFC championship	Dallas 17, San Francisco 10

1971

AFC div. playoffs	Miami 27, Kansas City 24
	Baltimore 20, Cleveland 3
AFC championship	Miami 21, Baltimore 0
NFC div. playoffs	Dallas 20, Minnesota 12
	San Francisco 24, Washington 20
NFC championship	Dallas 14, San Francisco 3

1972

AFC div. playoffs	Pittsburgh 13, Oakland 7
	Miami 20, Cleveland 14
AFC championship	Miami 21, Pittsburgh 17
NFC div. playoffs	Dallas 30, San Francisco 28
	Washington 16, Green Bay 3
NFC championship	Washington 26, Dallas 3

1973

AFC div. playoffs	Oakland 33, Pittsburgh 14
	Miami 34, Cincinnati 16
AFC championship	Miami 27, Oakland 10
NFC div. playoffs	Minnesota 27, Washington 20
	Dallas 27, Los Angeles 16
NFC championship	Minnesota 27, Dallas 10

1974

AFC div. playoffs	Oakland 28, Miami 26
	Pittsburgh 32, Buffalo 14
AFC championship	Pittsburgh 24, Oakland 13
NFC div. playoffs	Minnesota 30, St Louis 14
	Los Angeles 19, Washington 10
NFC championship	Minnesota 14, Los Angeles 10

1975

AFC div. playoffs	Pittsburgh 28, Baltimore 10
	Oakland 31, Cincinnati 28
AFC championship	Pittsburgh 16, Oakland 10
NFC div. playoffs	Los Angeles 35, St Louis 23
	Dallas 17, Minnesota 14
NFC championship	Dallas 37, Los Angeles 7

1976

AFC div. playoffs	Oakland 24, New England 21
	Pittsburgh 40, Baltimore 14
AFC championship	Oakland 24, Pittsburgh 7
NFC div. playoffs	Minnesota 35, Washington 20
	Los Angeles 14, Dallas 12
NFC championship	Minnesota 24, Los Angeles 13

1977

AFC div. playoffs	Denver 34, Pittsburgh 21
	Oakland 37, Baltimore 31
AFC championship	Denver 20, Oakland 17
NFC div. playoffs	Dallas 37, Chicago 7
	Minnesota 14, Los Angeles 7
NFC championship	Dallas 23, Minnesota 6

1978

AFC 1st-rd. playoff	Houston 17, Miami 9
AFC div. playoffs	Houston 31, New England 14
	Pittsburgh 33, Denver 10
AFC championship	Pittsburgh 34, Houston 5
NFC 1st-rd. playoff	Atlanta 14, Philadelphia 13
NFC div. playoffs	Dallas 27, Atlanta 20
	Los Angeles 34, Minnesota 10
NFC championship	Dallas 28, Los Angeles 0

1979

AFC 1st-rd. playoff	Houston 13, Denver 7
AFC div. playoffs	Houston 17, San Diego 14
	Pittsburgh 34, Miami 14
AFC championship	Pittsburgh 27, Houston 13
NFC 1st-rd. playoff	Philadelphia 27, Chicago 17
NFC div. playoffs	Tampa Bay 24, Philadelphia 17
	Los Angeles 21, Dallas 19
NFC championship	Los Angeles 9, Tampa Bay 0

1980

AFC 1st-rd. playoff	Oakland 27, Houston 7
AFC div. playoffs	San Diego 20, Buffalo 14
	Oakland 14, Cleveland 12
AFC championship	Oakland 34, San Diego 27
NFC 1st-rd. playoff	Dallas 34, Los Angeles 13
NFC div. playoffs	Philadelphia 31, Minnesota 16
	Dallas 30, Atlanta 27
NFC championship	Philadelphia 20, Dallas 7

1981

AFC 1st-rd. playoff	Buffalo 31, NY Jets 27
AFC div. playoffs	San Diego 41, Miami 38
	Cincinnati 28, Buffalo 21
AFC championship	Cincinnati 27, San Diego 7
NFC 1st-rd. playoff	NY Giants 27, Philadelphia 21
NFC div. playoffs	Dallas 38, Tampa Bay 0
	San Francisco 38, NY Giants 24
NFC championship	San Francisco 28, Dallas 27

1982

AFC 1st-rd. playoffs	Miami 28, New England 13
	LA Raiders 27, Cleveland 10
	NY Jets 44, Cincinnati 17
	San Diego 31, Pittsburgh 28
AFC div. playoffs	NY Jets 17, LA Raiders 14
	Miami 34, San Diego 13
AFC championship	Miami 14, NY Jets 0
NFC 1st-rd. playoffs	Washington 31, Detroit 7
	Green Bay 41, St Louis 16
	Minnesota 30, Atlanta 24
	Dallas 30, Tampa Bay 17
NFC div. playoffs	Washington 21, Minnesota 7
	Dallas 37, Green Bay 26
NFC championship	Washington 31, Dallas 17

1983

AFC 1st-rd. playoff	Seattle 31, Denver 7
AFC div. playoffs	Seattle 27, Miami 20
	LA Raiders 38, Pittsburgh 10
AFC championship	LA Raiders 30, Seattle 14
NFC 1st-rd. playoff	LA Rams 24, Dallas 17
NFC div. playoffs	San Francisco 24, Detroit 23
	Washington 51, LA Rams 7
NFC championship	Washington 24, San Francisco 21

1984

AFC 1st-rd. playoff	Seattle 13, LA Raiders 7
AFC div. playoffs	Miami 31, Seattle 10
	Pittsburgh 24, Denver 17
AFC championship	Miami 45, Pittsburgh 28
NFC 1st-rd. playoff	NY Giants 16, LA Rams 13
NFC div. playoffs	San Francisco 21, NY Giants 10
	Chicago 23, Washington 19
NFC championship	San Francisco 23, Chicago 0

1985

AFC 1st-rd. playoff	New England 26, NY Jets 14
AFC div. playoffs	Miami 24, Cleveland 21
	New England 27, LA Raiders 20
AFC championship	New England 31, Miami 14
NFC 1st-rd. playoff	NY Giants 17, San Francisco 3
NFC div. playoffs	LA Rams 20, Dallas 0
	Chicago 21, NY Giants 0
NFC championship	Chicago 24, LA Rams 0

1986

AFC 1st-rd. playoff	NY Jets 35, Kansas City 15
AFC div. playoffs	Cleveland 23, NY Jets 20
	Denver 22, New England 17
AFC championship	Denver 23, Cleveland 20
NFC 1st-rd. playoff	Washington 19, LA Rams 7
NFC div playoffs	Washington 27, Chicago 13
	NY Giants 49, San Francisco 3
NFC championship	NY Giants 17, Washington 0

1987

AFC 1st-rd. playoff	Houston 23, Seattle 20
AFC div. playoffs	Cleveland 38, Indianapolis 21
	Denver 34, Houston 10
AFC championship	Denver 38, Cleveland 33
NFC 1st-rd. playoff	Minnesota 44, New Orleans 10
NFC div playoffs	Minnesota 36, San Francisco 24
	Washington 21, Chicago 17
NFC championship	Washington 17, Minnesota 10

1988

AFC 1st-rd. playoff	Houston 24, Cleveland 23
AFC div. playoffs	Cincinnati 21, Seattle 13
	Buffalo 17, Houston 10
AFC championship	Cincinnati 21, Buffalo 10
NFC 1st-rd. playoff	Minnesota 28, LA Rams 17
NFC div. playoffs	Chicago 20, Philadelphia 12
	San Francisco 34, Minnesota 9
NFC championship	San Francisco 28, Chicago 3

1989

AFC 1st-rd. playoff	Pittsburgh 26, Houston 23
AFC div. playoffs	Cleveland 34, Buffalo 30
	Denver 24, Pittsburgh 23
AFC championship	Denver 37, Cleveland 21
NFC 1st-rd. playoff	LA Rams 21, Philadelphia 7
NFC div. playoffs	LA Rams 19, NY Giants 13
	San Francisco 41, Minnesota 13
NFC championship	San Francisco 30, LA Rams 3

1990

AFC 1st-rd. playoffs	Miami 17, Kansas City 16
	Cincinnati 41, Houston 14
AFC div. playoffs	Buffalo 44, Miami 34
	LA Raiders 20, Cincinnati 10
AFC championship	Buffalo 51, LA Raiders 3
NFC 1st-rd. playoffs	Chicago 16, New Orleans 6
NFC 1st-rd playoffs	Washington 20, Philadelphia 6
NFC div. playoffs	NY Giants 31, Chicago 3
	San Francisco 28, Washington 10
NFC championship	NY Giants 15, San Francisco 13

1991

AFC 1st-rd. playoffs	Houston 17, NY Jets 10
	Kansas City 10, LA Raiders 6
AFC div. playoffs	Denver 26, Houston 24
	Buffalo 37, Kansas City 14
AFC championship	Buffalo 10, Denver 7
NFC 1st-rd. playoffs	Atlanta 27, New Orleans 20
	Dallas 17, Chicago 13
NFC div. playoffs	Washington 24, Atlanta 7
	Detroit 38, Dallas 6
NFC championship	Washington 41, Detroit 10

1992

AFC 1st-rd. playoffs	San Diego 17, Kansas City 0
	Buffalo 41, Houston 38 (OT)
AFC div. playoffs	Buffalo 24, Pittsburgh 3
	Miami 31, San Diego 0
AFC championship	Buffalo 29, Miami 10
NFC 1st-rd. playoffs	Washington 24, Minnesota 7
	Philadelphia 36, New Orleans 20
NFC div. playoffs	San Francisco 20, Washington 13
	Dallas 34, Philadelphia 10
NFC championship	Dallas 30, San Francisco 20

1993

AFC 1st-rd. playoffs	LA Raiders 42, Denver 24
	Kansas City 27, Pittsburgh 24 (OT)
AFC div. playoffs	Buffalo 29, LA Raiders 23
	Kansas City 28, Houston 20
AFC championship	Buffalo 30, Kansas City 13
NFC 1st-rd. playoffs	NY Giants 17, Minnesota 10
	Green Bay 28, Detroit 24
NFC div. playoffs	San Francisco 44, NY Giants 3
	Dallas 27, Green Bay 17
NFC championship	Dallas 38, San Francisco 21

1994

AFC 1st-rd. playoffs	Miami 27, Kansas City 17
	Cleveland 20, New England 13
AFC div. playoffs	San Diego 22, Miami 21
	Pittsburgh 29, Cleveland 9
AFC championship	San Diego 17, Pittsburgh 13
NFC 1st-rd. playoffs	Green Bay 16, Detroit 12
	Chicago 35, Minnesota 18
NFC div. playoffs	Dallas 35, Green Bay 9
	San Francisco 44, Chicago 15
NFC championship	San Francisco 38, Dallas 28

1995

AFC 1st-rd. playoffs	Buffalo 37, Miami 22
	Indianapolis 35, San Diego 20
AFC div. playoffs	Pittsburgh 40, Buffalo 21
	Indianapolis 10, Kansas City 7
AFC championship	Pittsburgh 20, Indianapolis 16
NFC 1st-rd. playoffs	Philadelphia 58, Detroit 37
	Green Bay 37, Atlanta 20
NFC div. playoffs	Dallas 30, Philadelphia 11
	Green Bay 27, San Francisco 17
NFC championship	Dallas 38, Green Bay 27

1996

AFC 1st-rd. playoffs	Jacksonville 30, Buffalo 27
	Pittsburgh 42, Indianapolis 14
AFC div. playoffs	Jacksonville 30, Denver 27
	New England 28, Pittsburgh 3
AFC championship	New England 20, Jacksonville 6
NFC 1st-rd. playoffs	Dallas 40, Minnesota 15
	San Francisco 14, Philadelphia 0
NFC div. playoffs	Green Bay 35, San Francisco 14
	Carolina 26, Dallas 17
NFC championship	Green Bay 30, Carolina 13

1997

AFC 1st-rd. playoffs	Denver 42, Jacksonville 17
	New England 17, Miami 3
AFC div. playoffs	Denver 14, Kansas City 0
	Pittsburgh 7, New England 6
AFC championship	Denver 24, Pittsburgh 21

1997 *(Cont.)*

NFC 1st-rd. playoffs	Minnesota 23, NY Giants 22
	Tampa Bay 20, Detroit 10
NFC div. playoffs	Green Bay 21, Tampa Bay 7
	San Francisco 38, Minnesota 22
NFC championship	Green Bay 23, San Francisco 10

1998

AFC 1st-rd. playoffs	Miami 24, Buffalo 17
	Jacksonville 25, New England 10
AFC div. playoffs	Denver 38, Miami 3
	NY Jets 34, Jacksonville 24
AFC championship	Denver 23, NY Jets 10
NFC 1st-rd. playoffs	Arizona 20, Dallas 7
	San Francisco 30, Green Bay 27
NFC div. playoffs	Atlanta 20, San Francisco 18
	Minnesota 41, Arizona 21
NFC championship	Atlanta 30, Minnesota 27 (ot)

1999

AFC 1st-rd. playoffs	Tennessee 22, Buffalo 16
	Miami 20, Seattle 17
AFC div. playoffs	Jacksonville 62, Miami 7
	Tennessee 19, Indianapolis 16
AFC championship	Tennessee 33, Jacksonville 14
NFC 1st-rd. playoffs	Washington 27, Detroit 13
	Minnesota 27, Dallas 10
NFC div. playoffs	Tampa Bay 14, Washington 13
	St Louis 49, Minnesota 37
NFC championship	St Louis 11, Tampa Bay 6

2000

AFC 1st-rd. playoffs	Baltimore 21, Denver 3
	Miami 23, Indianapolis 17 (ot)
AFC div. playoffs	Baltimore 24, Tennessee 10
	Oakland 27, Miami 0
AFC championship	Baltimore 16, Oakland 3
NFC 1st-rd. playoffs	New Orleans 31, St. Louis 28
	Philadelphia 21, Tampa Bay 3
NFC div. playoffs	NY Giants 20, Philadelphia 10
	Minnesota 34, New Orleans 16
NFC championship	NY Giants 41, Minnesota 0

2001

AFC 1st-rd. playoffs	Oakland 38, NY Jets 24
	Baltimore 20, Miami 3
AFC div. playoffs	New England 16, Oakland 13(ot)
	Pittsburgh 27, Baltimore 10
AFC championship	New England 24, Pittsburgh 17
NFC 1st-rd. playoffs	Philadelphia 31, Tampa Bay 9
	Green Bay 25, San Francisco 15
NFC div. playoffs	Philadelphia 33, Chicago 19
	St. Louis 45, Green Bay 17
NFC championship	St. Louis 29, Philadelphia 24

2002

AFC 1st-rd. playoffs	NY Jets 41, Indianapolis 0
	Pittsburgh 36, Cleveland 33
AFC div. playoffs	Tennessee 34, Pittsburgh 31 (ot)
	Oakland 30, NY Jets 10
AFC championship	Oakland 41, Tennessee 24
NFC 1st-rd. playoffs	Atlanta 27, Green Bay 7
	San Francisco 39, NY Giants 38
NFC div. playoffs	Philadelphia 20, Atlanta 6
	Tampa Bay 31, San Francisco 6
NFC championship	Tampa Bay 27, Philadelphia 10

2003

AFC 1st-rd. playoffs	Tennessee 20, Baltimore 17
	Indianapolis 41, Denver 10
AFC div. playoffs	New England 17, Tennessee 14
	Indianapolis 38, Kansas City 31
AFC championship	New England 24, Indianapolis 14
NFC 1st-rd. playoffs	Carolina 29, Dallas 10
	Green Bay 33, Seattle 27 (ot)
NFC div. playoffs	Carolina 29, St. Louis 23
	Philadelphia 20, Green Bay 17 (ot)
NFC championship	Carolina 14, Philadelphia 3

2004

AFC 1st-rd. playoffs	Denver 24, Indianapolis 49	NFC 1st-rd. playoffs	Minnesota 31, Green Bay 17
	NY Jets 20, San Diego 17		St. Louis 27, Seattle 20
AFC div. playoffs	New England 20, Indianapolis 3	NFC div. playoffs	Atlanta 47, St. Louis 17
	Pittsburgh 20, NY Jets 17		Philadelphia 27, Minnesota 14
AFC championship	New England 41, Pittsburgh 27	NFC championship	Philadelphia 27, Atlanta 10

Alltime NFL Individual Statistical Leaders

Career Leaders

Scoring

	Yrs	TD	FG	PAT	Pts
†Gary Anderson	23	0	538	820	2,434
†Morten Andersen	23	0	520	798	2,358
George Blanda	26	9	335	943	2,002
Norm Johnson	18	0	366	638	1,736
Nick Lowery	18	0	383	562	1,711
Jan Stenerud	19	0	373	580	1,699
Eddie Murray	19	0	352	539	1,594
Al Del Greco	17	0	347	543	1,584
†John Carney	16	0	370	446	1,556
†Matt Stover	16	0	351	433	1,486
†Steve Christie	14	0	336	468	1,476
Pat Leahy	18	0	304	558	1,470
†Jason Elam	13	0	323	497	1,466
Jim Turner	16	1	304	521	1,439
Matt Bahr	17	0	300	522	1,422

Rushing

	Yrs	Att	Yds	Avg	Lg	TD
†Emmitt Smith	15	4,409	18,355	4.2	75	164
Walter Payton	13	3,838	16,726	4.4	76	110
Barry Sanders	10	3,062	15,269	5.0	85	99
†Curtis Martin	9	3,367	13,495	4.0	70	85
†Jerome Bettis	11	3,369	13,294	3.9	71	82
Eric Dickerson	11	2,996	13,259	4.4	85	90
Tony Dorsett	12	2,936	12,739	4.3	99	77
Jim Brown	9	2,359	12,312	5.2	80	106
Marcus Allen	16	3,022	12,243	4.1	61	123
Franco Harris	13	2,949	12,120	4.1	75	91
Thurman Thomas	13	2,877	12,074	4.2	80	66
†Marshall Faulk	11	2,783	12,064	4.3	71	100
John Riggins	14	2,916	11,352	3.9	66	104
O.J. Simpson	11	2,404	11,236	4.7	94	61
Ricky Watters	9	2,550	10,325	4.1	57	77

Touchdowns

	Yrs	Rush	Rec	Ret	Total TD
†Jerry Rice	20	10	197	1	208
†Emmitt Smith	15	164	11	0	175
Marcus Allen	16	123	21	1	145
†Marshall Faulk	11	100	36	0	136
Cris Carter	15	0	130	1	131
Jim Brown	9	106	20	0	126
Walter Payton	13	110	15	0	125

	Yrs	Rush	Rec	Ret	Total TD
John Riggins	14	104	12	0	116
Lenny Moore	12	63	48	2	113
Barry Sanders	10	99	10	0	109
Don Hutson	11	3	99	3	105
†Tim Brown	17	1	100	4	105
Steve Largent	14	1	100	0	101
Franco Harris	13	91	9	0	100
†Terrell Owens	10	2	98	0	100

Combined Yards Gained

	Yrs	Total	Rush	Rec	Int Ret	Punt Ret	Kickoff Ret	Fum Ret
†Jerry Rice	20	23,546	645	22,895	0	0	6	0
Brian Mitchell	14	23,330	1,967	2,336	0	4,999	14,014	14
Walter Payton	13	21,803	16,726	4,538	0	0	539	0
†Emmitt Smith	15	21,564	18,355	3,224	0	0	0	-15
†Tim Brown	17	19,682	190	14,734	0	3,320	1,235	3
†Marshall Faulk	11	18,607	11,987	6,584	0	0	18	18
Barry Sanders	10	18,308	15,269	2,921	0	0	118	0
Herschel Walker	12	18,168	8,225	4,859	0	0	5,084	0
Marcus Allen	16	17,648	13,366	5,411	0	0	0	-6
Eric Metcalf	13	17,230	2,392	5,572	0	3,453	5,813	0
†Curtis Martin	10	16,568	11,669	3,211	0	0	0	-9
Thurman Thomas	13	16,532	12,074	4,458	0	0	0	0
Tony Dorsett	12	16,326	12,739	3,554	0	0	0	33

† Active in 2004.

Career Leaders (Cont.)

Passing

PASSING EFFICIENCY*

	Yrs	Att	Comp	Pct Comp	Yds	Avg Gain	TD	Pct TD	Int	Pct Int	Rating Pts
Steve Young	15	4,149	2,667	64.3	33,124	7.9	232	5.6	107	2.6	96.8
†Kurt Warner	6	2,066	1,359	65.8	17,197	8.3	109	5.3	71	3.4	94.9
Joe Montana	15	5,391	3,409	63.2	40,551	7.5	273	5.1	139	2.6	92.3
†Peyton Manning	8	3,967	2,517	63.4	30,046	7.6	218	5.4	122	3.1	92.0
†Daunte Culpepper	6	2,490	1,603	64.4	19,367	7.8	132	5.3	82	3.2	92.1
†Trent Green	12	2,920	1,761	60.3	22,265	7.6	134	4.5	83	2.8	87.6
†Tom Brady	5	2,141	1,321	61.7	14,873	6.9	100	4.7	54	2.5	87.5
†Jeff Garcia	6	2,612	1,593	61.0	18,139	6.9	123	4.7	65	2.5	87.2
†Brett Favre	14	7,116	4,379	61.5	50,472	7.1	381	5.4	233	3.3	87.1
Dan Marino	17	8,358	4,967	59.4	61,361	7.3	420	5.0	252	3.0	86.4
†Brian Griese	7	2,221	1,402	63.1	15,696	7.1	100	4.2	74	3.3	85.3
†Rich Gannon	18	4,206	2,533	60.2	28,743	6.8	180	4.3	104	2.3	84.7
Donovan McNabb	7	2,712	1,584	58.4	17,890	6.6	126	4.6	59	2.2	84.7
Jim Kelly	11	4,779	2,874	60.1	35,467	7.4	237	5.0	175	3.7	84.4
Matt Hassleback	7	1,854	1,109	59.8	13,235	7.1	76	4.1	50	2.3	84.1
†Brad Johnson	13	3,504	2,166	61.8	23,913	6.8	143	4.1	98	2.8	84.0
†Mark Brunell	12	3,928	2,342	59.6	27,348	7.0	153	3.9	93	2.4	83.9
Roger Staubach	11	2,958	1,685	57.0	22,700	7.67	153	5.2	109	3.7	83.4
†Steve McNair	10	3,496	2,074	59.3	24,655	7.1	144	4.1	95	2.7	83.3
Neil Lomax	8	3,153	1,817	57.6	22,771	7.22	136	4.3	90	2.9	82.7

*1,500 or more attempts. The passer ratings are based on performance standards established for completion percentage, interception percentage, touchdown percentage and average gain. Passers are allocated points according to how their marks compare with those standards.

YARDS

	Yrs	Att	Comp	Pct Comp	Yds
Dan Marino	17	8,358	4,967	59.4	61,361
John Elway	16	7,250	4,123	56.9	51,475
†Brett Favre	14	7,116	4,379	61.5	50,472
Warren Moon	17	6,823	3,988	58.5	49,325
Fran Tarkenton	18	6,467	3,686	57.0	47,003
†Vinny Testaverde	17	5,925	3,334	56.3	44,475
Dan Fouts	15	5,604	3,297	58.8	43,040
†Drew Bledsoe	12	6,147	3,512	57.1	40,658
Joe Montana	15	5,391	3,409	63.2	40,551
Johnny Unitas	18	5,186	2,830	54.6	40,239
Dave Krieg	19	5,311	3,105	58.5	38,147

	Yrs	Att	Comp	Pct Comp	Yds
Boomer Esiason	14	5,205	2,969	57.0	37,920
Jim Kelly	11	4,779	2,874	60.1	35,467
Jim Everett	12	4,923	2,841	57.7	34,837
Jim Hart	19	5,076	2,593	51.1	34,665
Steve DeBerg	17	4,746	2,924	61.6	34,241
John Hadl	16	4,687	2,363	50.4	33,503
Phil Simms	14	4,647	2,576	55.4	33,462
Steve Young	15	4,149	2,667	64.3	33,124
Troy Aikman	12	4,715	2,898	61.5	32,942

TOUCHDOWNS

	No.
Dan Marino	420
†Brett Favre	379
Fran Tarkenton	342
John Elway	300
Warren Moon	291
Johnny Unitas	290
Joe Montana	273
†Vinny Testaverde	273
Dave Krieg	261
Sonny Jurgensen	255
Dan Fouts	254

	No.
Boomer Esiason	247
John Hadl	244
Len Dawson	239
Jim Kelly	237
George Blanda	236
Steve Young	232
†Drew Bledsoe	225
†Peyton Manning	218
John Brodie	214
Terry Bradshaw	212
Y.A. Tittle	212

	No.
Jim Hart	209
Randall Cunningham	207
Jim Everett	203
Phil Simms	199
Ken Anderson	197
Joe Ferguson	196
Bobby Layne	196
Norm Snead	196

† Active in 2004.

Career Leaders (Cont.)

Receiving

RECEPTIONS

	Yrs	No.	Yds	Avg	Lg	TD		Yrs	No.	Yds	Avg	Lg	TD
†Jerry Rice	20	1,549	22,895	14.8	96	197	†Jimmy Smith	11	804	11,484	14.3	75	64
Cris Carter	16	1,101	13,899	12.6	80	130	†Isaac Bruce	11	786	11,889	15.1	80	75
†Tim Brown	17	1,094	14,934	13.7	80	100	†Keenan McCardell	13	772	10,020	13.0	76	57
Andre Reed	16	951	13,198	13.9	83	87	James Lofton	16	764	14,004	18.3	80	75
Art Monk	16	940	12,721	13.5	79	68	Michael Irvin	12	750	11,904	15.9	87	65
†Marvin Harrison	9	860	11,343	13.2	79	99	Charlie Joiner	18	750	12,146	16.2	87	65
Irving Fryar	17	851	12,785	15.0	80	84	Andre Rison	12	743	10,205	13.7	80	84
†Larry Centers	14	827	6,797	8.2	54	28	Rod Smith	10	734	10,025	13.7	85	60
Steve Largent	14	819	13,089	16.0	74	100	Marshall Faulk	11	729	6,627	9.1	85	36
†Shannon Sharpe	15	815	10,060	12.3	82	62	Gary Clarke	11	699	10,856	15.5	84	65
Henry Ellard	16	814	13,777	16.9	81	65	Terrance Mathis	13	689	8,809	12.8	81	63

YARDS

†Jerry Rice	22,895	Irving Fryar	12,785	†Marvin Harrison	11,290
†Tim Brown	14,934	Art Monk	12,721	Gary Clark	10,856
James Lofton	14,004	Charlie Joiner	12,146	Stanley Morgan	10,716
Cris Carter	13,899	Michael Irvin	11,904	Harold Jackson	10,372
Henry Ellard	13,777	†Isaac Bruce	11,878	Lance Alworth	10,266
Andre Reed	13,198	Don Maynard	11,834	Andre Rison	10,205
Steve Largent	13,089	†Jimmy Smith	11,394		

Sacks

†Bruce Smith	200.0	Chris Doleman	150.5
Reggie White	198.0	†John Randle	137.5
Kevin Greene	160.0	Richard Dent	137.5

Note: Officially compiled since 1982.

Interceptions

	Yrs	No.	Yds	Avg	Lg	TD
Paul Krause	16	81	1185	14.6	81	3
Emlen Tunnell	14	79	1282	16.2	55	4
†Rod Woodson	17	71	1483	20.9	98	17
Dick (Night Train) Lane	14	68	1207	17.8	80	5
Ken Riley	15	65	596	9.2	66	5

Punt Returns

	Yrs	No.	Yds	Avg	Lg	TD
George McAfee	8	112	1431	12.8	74	2
Jack Christiansen	8	85	1084	12.8	89	8
Claude Gibson	5	110	1381	12.6	85	3
Bill Dudley	9	124	1515	12.2	96	3
Rick Upchurch	9	248	3008	12.1	92	8
Desmond Howard	11	244	2895	11.9	95	8

Note: 75 or more returns.

Punting

	Yrs	No.	Yds	Avg	Lg	Blk
†Shane Lechler	6	378	17,330	45.8	73	2
Sammy Baugh	16	338	15,245	45.1	85	9
Tommy Davis	11	511	22,833	44.7	82	2
Yale Lary	11	503	22,279	44.3	74	4
†Todd Sauerbrun	11	771	33,948	44.0	73	6

Note: 250 or more punts.

Kickoff Returns

	Yrs	No.	Yds	Avg	Lg	TD
Gale Sayers	7	91	2781	30.6	103	6
Lynn Chandnois	7	92	2720	29.6	93	3
Abe Woodson	9	193	5538	28.7	105	5
Claude (Buddy) Young	6	90	2514	27.9	104	2
Travis Williams	5	102	2801	27.5	105	6

Note: 75 or more returns.

† Active in 2004.

Single-Season Leaders
Scoring

POINTS

	Year	TD	PAT	FG	Pts
Paul Hornung, GB	1960	15	41	15	176
Gary Anderson, Minn	1998	0	59	35	164
Jeff Wilkins, StL	2003	0	46	39	163
Priest Holmes, KC	2003	27	0	0	162
Mark Moseley, Wash	1983	0	62	33	161
Mike Vanderjagt, Ind	2003	0	46	37	157
Marshall Faulk, StL	2000	26	0	0	156
Gino Cappelletti, Bos	1964	7	38	25	155
Emmitt Smith, Dall	1995	25	0	0	150
Chip Lohmiller, Wash	1991	0	56	31	149

Note: Cappelletti's total includes a two-point conversion.

TOUCHDOWNS

	Year	Rush	Rec	Ret	Total
Priest Holmes, KC	2003	27	0	0	27
Marshall Faulk, StL	2000	18	8	0	26
Emmitt Smith, Dall	1995	25	0	0	25
John Riggins, Wash	1983	24	0	0	24
Priest Holmes, KC	2002	21	3	0	24
O.J. Simpson, Buff	1975	16	7	0	23
Jerry Rice, SF	1987	1	22	0	23
Terrell Davis, Den	1998	21	2	0	23

FIELD GOALS

	Year	Att	No.
Olindo Mare, Mia	1999	46	39
Jeff Wilkins, StL	2003	42	39
John Kasay, Car	1996	45	37
Mike Vanderjagt, Ind	2003	37	37
Cary Blanchard, Ind	1996	40	36
Al Del Greco, Tenn	1998	39	36

Rushing

YARDS GAINED

	Year	Att	Yds	Avg
Eric Dickerson, LA Rams	1984	379	2105	5.6
Jamal Lewis, Balt	2003	387	2066	5.3
Barry Sanders, Det	1997	335	2053	6.1
Terrell Davis, Den	1998	392	2008	5.1
O.J. Simpson, Buff	1973	332	2003	6.0
Earl Campbell, Hou	1980	373	1934	5.2
Jim Brown, Clev	1963	291	1883	6.4
Ahman Green, GB	2003	355	1883	5.3
Barry Sanders, Det	1994	331	1883	5.7
Ricky Williams, Mia	2002	383	1853	4.8

AVERAGE GAIN

	Year	Avg
Beattie Feathers, Chi	1934	8.44
Randall Cunningham, Phil	1990	7.98
Michael Vick, Atl	2002	6.88
Bobby Douglass, Chi	1972	6.87

Minimum 100 attempts.

TOUCHDOWNS

	Year	No.
Priest Holmes, KC	2003	27
Emmitt Smith, Dall	1995	25
John Riggins, Wash	1983	24
Priest Holmes, KC	2002	24
Emmitt Smith, Dall	1994	21
Joe Morris, NYG	1985	21
Terry Allen, Wash	1996	21
Terrell Davis, Den	1998	21

Passing

YARDS GAINED

	Year	Att	Comp	Pct	Yds
Dan Marino, Mia	1984	564	362	64.2	5084
Kurt Warner, StL	2001	546	375	68.7	4830
Dan Fouts, SD	1981	609	360	59.1	4802
Dan Marino, Mia	1986	623	378	60.7	4746
Dan Fouts, SD	1980	589	348	59.1	4715
Warren Moon, Hou	1991	655	404	61.7	4690
Warren Moon, Hou	1990	584	362	62.0	4689
Rich Gannon, Oak	2002	618	418	67.6	4689
Neil Lomax, StL Cards	1984	560	345	61.6	4614
Peyton Manning, Ind.	2004	497	336	67.6	4557
Drew Bledsoe, NE	1994	691	400	57.9	4555

PASSER RATING

	Year	Rat.
Steve Young, SF	1994	112.8
Joe Montana, SF	1989	112.4
Milt Plum, Clev	1960	110.4
Sammy Baugh, Wash	1945	109.9
Kurt Warner, Rams	1999	109.2

TOUCHDOWNS

	Year	No.
Peyton Manning, Ind.	2004	49
Dan Marino, Mia	1984	48
Dan Marino, Mia	1986	44
Kurt Warner, StL	1999	41
Brett Favre, GB	1995	38

Four tied with 36.

Single-Season Leaders *(Cont.)*
Receiving

RECEPTIONS

	Year	No.	Yds
Marvin Harrison, Ind	2002	143	1722
Herman Moore, Det	1995	123	1686
Cris Carter, Minn	1994	122	1256
Jerry Rice, SF	1995	122	1848
Cris Carter, Minn	1995	122	1371
Isaac Bruce, Rams	1995	119	1781
Torry Holt, StL	2003	117	1696
Jimmy Smith, Jax	1999	116	1636
Marvin Harrison, Ind	1999	115	1663
Rod Smith, Den	2001	113	1343

YARDS GAINED

	Year	Yds
Jerry Rice, SF	1995	1848
Isaac Bruce, Rams	1995	1781
Charley Hennigan, Hou	1961	1746
Marvin Harrison, Ind	2002	1722
Torry Holt, StL	2003	1696

TOUCHDOWNS

	Year	No.
Jerry Rice, SF	1987	22
Mark Clayton, Mia	1984	18
Sterling Sharpe, GB	1994	18

Seven tied with 17.

All-Purpose Yards

	Year	Run	Rec	Ret	Total
Michael Lewis, NO	2002	15	200	2432	2647
Lionel James, SD	1985	516	1027	992	2535
Terry Metcalf, StL Cards	1975	816	378	1268	2462
Mack Herron, NE	1974	824	474	1146	2444
Gale Sayers, Chi	1966	1231	447	762	2440
Marshall Faulk, Rams	1999	1381	1048	0	2429
Timmy Brown, Phil	1963	841	487	1100	2428
Barry Sanders, Det	1997	2053	305	0	2358
Tim Brown, Rai	1988	50	725	1542	2317
Marcus Allen, Rai	1985	1759	555	-6	2308
Timmy Brown, Phil	1962	545	849	912	2306
Edgerrin James, Ind	2000	1709	594	0	2303

Punting

	Year	No.	Yds	Avg
Sammy Baugh, Wash	1940	35	1799	51.4
Yale Lary, Det	1963	35	1713	48.9
Sammy Baugh, Wash	1941	30	1462	48.7
Yale Lary, Det	1961	52	2516	48.4
Sammy Baugh, Wash	1942	37	1783	48.2

Sacks

	Year	No.
Michael Strahan, NYG	2001	22.5
Mark Gastineau, NYJ	1984	22
Reggie White, Phil	1987	21
Chris Doleman, Minn	1989	21
Lawrence Taylor, NYG	1986	20.5

Interceptions

	Year	No.
Dick (Night Train) Lane, Rams	1952	14
Dan Sandifer, Wash	1948	13
Spec Sanders, NY Yanks	1950	13
Lester Hayes, Oak	1980	13

Nine tied with 12.

Kickoff Returns

	Year	Avg
Travis Williams, GB	1967	41.1
Gale Sayers, Chi	1967	37.7
Ollie Matson, Chi Cards	1958	35.5
Jim Duncan, Balt Colts	1970	35.4
Lynn Chandnois, Pitt	1952	35.2

Punt Returns

	Year	Avg
Herb Rich, Balt Colts	1950	23.0
Jack Christiansen, Det	1952	21.5
Dick Christy, NY Titans	1961	21.3
Bob Hayes, Dall	1968	20.8

Single-Game Leaders
Scoring

POINTS

	Date	Pts
Ernie Nevers, Chi Cards vs Chi	11-28-29	40
Dub Jones, Clev vs Chi	11-25-51	36
Gale Sayers, Chi vs SF	12-12-65	36
Paul Hornung, GB vs Balt Colts	10-8-61	33

On Thanksgiving Day, 1929, Nevers scored all the Cardinals' points on six rushing TDs and four PATs. The Cards defeated Red Grange and the Bears, 40–6. Jones and Sayers each rushed for four touchdowns and scored two more on returns in their teams' victories. Hornung scored four touchdowns and kicked 6 PATs and a field goal in a 45-7 win over the Colts.

FIELD GOALS

	Date	No.
Jim Bakken, StL Cards vs Pitt	9-24-67	7
Rich Karlis, Minn vs Rams	11-5-89	7
Chris Boniol, Dall vs GB	11-18-96	7
Billy Cundiff, Dall vs NYG	9-15-03	7

Bakken was 7 for 9; Cundiff was 7 for 8; and Karlis and Boniol 7 for 7.

Single-Game Leaders *(Cont.)*

Scoring *(Cont.)*

TOUCHDOWNS

	Date	No.
Ernie Nevers, Chi Cards vs Chi	11-28-29	6
Dub Jones, Clev vs Chi	11-25-51	6
Gale Sayers, Chi vs SF	12-12-65	6
Bob Shaw, Chi Cards vs Balt Colts	10-2-50	5
Jim Brown, Clev vs Balt Colts	11-1-59	5
Abner Haynes, Dall Texans vs Oak	11-26-61	5
Billy Cannon, Hou vs NY Titans	12-10-61	5
Cookie Gilchrist, Buff vs NYJ	12-8-63	5
Paul Hornung, GB vs Balt Colts	12-12-65	5
Kellen Winslow, SD vs Oak	11-22-81	5
Jerry Rice, SF vs Atl	10-14-90	5
James Stewart, Jax vs Phil	10-12-97	5
Shaun Alexander, Sea vs Minn	9-29-02	5

Rushing

YARDS GAINED

	Date	Yds
Jamal Lewis, Balt vs Clev	9-14-03	295
Corey Dillon, Cin vs Den	10-22-00	278
Walter Payton, Chi vs Minn	11-20-77	275
O.J. Simpson, Buff vs Det	11-25-76	273
Shaun Alexander, Sea vs Oak	11-11-01	266

CARRIES

	Date	No.
Jamie Morris, Wash vs Cin	12-17-88	45
Butch Woolfolk, NYG vs Phil	11-20-83	43
James Wilder, TB vs GB	9-30-84	43
Rudi Johnson, Cin vs Hou	11-9-03	43
James Wilder, TB vs Pitt	10-30-83	42
Terrell Davis, Den vs Buff	10-26-97	42
Ricky Williams, Mia vs Buff	9-21-03	42

TOUCHDOWNS

	Date	No.
Ernie Nevers, Chi Cards vs Chi	11-28-29	6
Jim Brown, Clev vs Balt Colts	11-1-59	5
Cookie Gilchrist, Buff vs NYJ	12-8-63	5
James Stewart, Jax vs Phil	10-12-97	5

Passing

YARDS GAINED

	Date	Yds
N. Van Brocklin, Rams vs NY Yanks	9-28-51	554
Warren Moon, Hou vs KC	12-16-90	527
Boomer Esiason, Ariz vs Wash	11-10-96	522
Dan Marino, Mia vs NYJ	10-23-88	521
Phil Simms, NYG vs Cin	10-13-85	513

COMPLETIONS

	Date	No.
Drew Bledsoe, NE vs Minn	11-13-94	45
Rich Gannon, Oak vs Pitt	9-15-02	43
Richard Todd, NYJ vs SF	9-21-80	42
Vinny Testaverde, NYJ vs Sea	12-6-98	42
Warren Moon, Hou vs Dall	11-10-91	41
Ken Anderson, Cin vs SD	12-20-82	40
Phil Simms, NYG vs Cin	10-13-85	40
Brad Johnson, TB vs Chi	11-18-01	40

TOUCHDOWNS

	Date	No.
Sid Luckman, Chi vs NYG	11-14-43	7
Adrian Burk, Phil vs Wash	10-17-54	7
George Blanda, Hou vs NY Titans	11-19-61	7
Y. A. Tittle, NYG vs Wash	10-28-62	7
Joe Kapp, Minn vs Balt Colts	9-28-69	7

Receiving

YARDS GAINED

	Date	Yds
Flipper Anderson, Rams vs NO	11-26-89	336
Stephone Paige, KC vs SD	12-22-85	309
Jim Benton, Clev vs Det	11-22-45	303
Cloyce Box, Det vs Balt Colts	12-3-50	302
Jimmy Smith, Jax vs Balt Ravens	9-10-00	291

RECEPTIONS

	Date	No.
Terrell Owens, SF vs Chi	12-17-00	20
Tom Fears, Rams vs GB	12-3-50	18
Clark Gaines, NYJ vs SF	9-21-80	17
Sonny Randle, StL Cards vs NYG	11-4-62	16
Jerry Rice, SF vs Rams	11-20-94	16
Keenan McCardell, Jax vs Rams	10-20-96	16
Troy Brown, NE vs KC	9-22-02	16

Five tied with 15.

Single-Game Leaders *(Cont.)*
Receiving *(Cont.)*
TOUCHDOWNS

	Date	No.
Bob Shaw, Chi Cards vs Balt Colts	10-2-50	5
Kellen Winslow, SD vs Oak	11-22-81	5
Jerry Rice, SF vs Atl	10-14-90	5

All-Purpose Yards

	Date	Yds
Glyn Milburn, Den vs Sea	12-10-95	404
Billy Cannon, Hou vs NY Titans	12-10-61	373
Tyrone Hughes, NO vs LA Rams	10-23-94	347
Lionel James, SD vs LA Rai	11-10-85	345
Timmy Brown, Phil vs StL Cards	12-16-62	341

Longest Plays

RUSHING	Opponent	Year	Yds
Tony Dorsett, Dall	Minn	1983	99
Ahman Green, GB	Den	2003	98
Andy Uram, GB	Chi Cards	1939	97
Bob Gage, Pitt	Chi	1949	97
Jim Spavital, Balt Colts	GB	1950	96
Bob Hoernschemeyer, Det	NY Yanks	1950	96
Garrison Hearst, SF	NYJ	1998	96
Corey Dillon, Cin	Det	2001	96

PASSING	Opponent	Year	Yds
Frank Filchock to Andy Farkas, Wash	Pitt	1939	99
George Izo to Bobby Mitchell, Wash	Clev	1963	99
Karl Sweetan to Pat Studstill, Det	Balt Colts	1966	99
Sonny Jurgensen to Gerry Allen, Wash	Chi	1968	99
Jim Plunkett to Cliff Branch, LA Rai	Wash	1983	99
Ron Jaworski to Mike Quick, Phil	Atl	1985	99
Stan Humphries to Tony Martin, SD	Sea	1994	99
Brett Favre to Robert Brooks, GB	Chi	1995	99
Trent Green to Marc Boerigter, KC	SD	2002	99

FIELD GOALS	Opponent	Year	Yds
Tom Dempsey, NO	Det	1970	63
Jason Elam, Den	Jax	1998	63
Steve Cox, Clev	Cin	1984	60
Morten Andersen, NO	Chi	1991	60

PUNTS	Opponent	Year	Yds
Steve O'Neal, NYJ	Den	1969	98
Joe Lintzenich, Chi	NYG	1931	94
Shawn McCarthy, NE	Buff	1991	93
Randall Cunningham, Phil	NYG	1989	91

INTERCEPTION RETURNS	Opponent	Year	Yds
Vencie Glenn, SD	Den	1987	103
Louis Oliver, Mia	Buff	1992	103
Seven players tied at 102.			

KICKOFF RETURNS	Opponent	Year	Yds
Al Carmichael, GB	Chi	1956	106
Noland Smith, KC	Den	1967	106
Roy Green, StL Cards	Dall	1979	106

PUNT RETURNS	Opponent	Year	Yds
Robert Bailey, LA Rams	NO	1994	103
Gil LeFebvre, Cin	Brooklyn	1933	98
Charlie West, Minn	Wash	1968	98
Dennis Morgan, Dall	StL Cards	1974	98
Terance Mathis, NYJ	Dall	1990	98

YET ANOTHER SIGN OF THE APOCALYPSE

Bengals wide receiver Chad Johnson asked fans for donations to help pay for a celebration fine he was planning to incur.

Rushing

Year	Player, Team	Att	Yards	Avg	TD	Year	Player, Team	Att	Yards	Avg	TD
1932	Cliff Battles, Bos	148	576	3.9	3	1972	O.J. Simpson, Buff, AFC	292	1251	4.3	6
1933	Jim Musick, Bos	173	809	4.7	5		Larry Brown, Wash, NFC	285	1216	4.3	8
1934	Beattie Feathers, Chi	101	1004	9.9	8	1973	O.J. Simpson, Buff, AFC	332	2003	6.0	12
1935	Doug Russell, Chi Cards	140	499	3.6	0		John Brockington, GB, NFC	265	1144	4.3	3
1936	Alphonse Leemans, NY	206	830	4.0	2	1974	Otis Armstrong, Den, AFC	263	1407	5.3	9
1937	Cliff Battles, Wash	216	874	4.0	5		Lawrence McCutcheon, LA, NFC	236	1109	4.7	3
1938	Byron White, Pitt	152	567	3.7	4	1975	O.J. Simpson, Buff, AFC	329	1817	5.5	16
1939	Bill Osmanski, Chi	121	699	5.8	7		Jim Otis, StL, NFC	269	1076	4.0	5
1940	Byron White, Det	146	514	3.5	5	1976	O.J. Simpson, Buff, AFC	290	1503	5.2	8
1941	Clarence Manders, Bklyn	111	486	4.4	5		Walter Payton, Chi, NFC	311	1390	4.5	13
1942	Bill Dudley, Pitt	162	696	4.3	5	1977	Walter Payton, Chi, NFC	339	1852	5.5	14
1943	Bill Paschal, NY	147	572	3.9	10		Mark van Eeghen, Oak, AFC	324	1273	3.9	7
1944	Bill Paschal, NY	196	737	3.8	9	1978	Earl Campbell, Hou, AFC	302	1450	4.8	13
1945	Steve Van Buren, Phil	143	832	5.8	15		Walter Payton, Chi, NFC	333	1395	4.2	11
1946	Bill Dudley, Pitt	146	604	4.1	3	1979	Earl Campbell, Hou, AFC	368	1697	4.6	19
1947	Steve Van Buren, Phil	217	1008	4.6	13		Walter Payton, Chi, NFC	369	1610	4.4	14
1948	Steve Van Buren, Phil	201	945	4.7	10	1980	Earl Campbell, Hou, AFC	373	1934	5.2	13
1949	Steve Van Buren, Phil	263	1146	4.4	11		Walter Payton, Chi, NFC	317	1460	4.6	6
1950	Marion Motley, Clev	140	810	5.8	3	1981	George Rogers, NO, NFC	378	1674	4.4	13
1951	Eddie Price, NY	271	971	3.6	7		Earl Campbell, Hou, AFC	361	1376	3.8	10
1952	Dan Towler, LA	156	894	5.7	10	1982	Freeman McNeil, NY Jets, AFC	151	786	5.2	6
1953	Joe Perry, SF	192	1018	5.3	10		Tony Dorsett, Dall, NFC	177	745	4.2	5
1954	Joe Perry, SF	173	1049	6.1	8	1983	Eric Dickerson, LA Rams, NFC	390	1808	4.6	18
1955	Alan Ameche, Balt	213	961	4.5	9		Curt Warner, Sea, AFC	335	1449	4.3	13
1956	Rick Casares, Chi	234	1126	4.8	12	1984	Eric Dickerson, LA Rams, NFC	379	2105	5.6	14
1957	Jim Brown, Clev	202	942	4.7	9		Earnest Jackson, SD, AFC	296	1179	4.0	8
1958	Jim Brown, Clev	257	1527	5.9	17	1985	Marcus Allen, LA Raiders, AFC	380	1759	4.6	11
1959	Jim Brown, Clev	290	1329	4.6	14		Gerald Riggs, Atl, NFC	397	1719	4.3	10
1960	Jim Brown, Clev, NFL	215	1257	5.8	9	1986	Eric Dickerson, LA Rams, NFC	404	1821	4.5	11
	Abner Haynes, Dall Texans, AFL	156	875	5.6	9		Curt Warner, Sea, AFC	319	1481	4.6	13
1961	Jim Brown, Clev, NFL	305	1408	4.6	8	1987	Charles White, LA Rams, NFC	324	1374	4.2	11
	Billy Cannon, Hou, AFL	200	948	4.7	6		Eric Dickerson, Ind, AFC	223	1011	4.5	5
1962	Jim Taylor, GB, NFL	272	1474	5.4	19	1988	Eric Dickerson, Ind, AFC	388	1659	4.3	14
	Cookie Gilchrist, Buff, AFL	214	1096	5.1	13		Herschel Walker, Dall, NFC	361	1514	4.2	5
1963	Jim Brown, Clev, NFL	291	1863	6.4	12	1989	Christian Okoye, KC, AFC	370	1480	4.0	12
	Clem Daniels, Oak, AFL	215	1099	5.1	3		Barry Sanders, Det, NFC	280	1470	5.3	14
1964	Jim Brown, Clev, NFL	280	1446	5.2	7	1990	Barry Sanders, Det, NFC	255	1304	5.1	13
	Cookie Gilchrist, Buff, AFL	230	981	4.3	6		Thurman Thomas, Buff, AFC	271	1297	4.8	11
1965	Jim Brown, Clev, NFL	289	1544	5.3	17	1991	Emmitt Smith, Dall, NFC	365	1563	4.3	12
	Paul Lowe, SD, AFL	222	1121	5.0	7		Thurman Thomas, Buff, AFC	288	1407	4.9	7
1966	Jim Nance, Bos, AFL	299	1458	4.9	11	1992	Emmitt Smith, Dall, NFC	373	1713	4.6	18
	Gale Sayers, Chi, NFL	229	1231	5.4	8		Barry Foster, Pitt, AFC	390	1690	4.3	11
1967	Jim Nance, Bos, AFL	269	1216	4.5	7	1993	Emmitt Smith, Dall, NFC	283	1486	5.3	9
	Leroy Kelly, Clev, NFL	235	1205	5.1	11		T. Thomas, Buff, AFC	355	1315	3.7	6
1968	Leroy Kelly, Clev, NFL	248	1239	5.0	16	1994	Barry Sanders, Det, NFC	331	1883	5.7	7
	Paul Robinson, Cin, AFL	238	1023	4.3	8		Chris Warren, Sea, AFC	333	1545	4.6	9
1969	Gale Sayers, Chi, NFL	236	1032	4.4	8						
	Dickie Post, SD, AFL	182	873	4.8	6						
1970	Larry Brown, Wash, NFC	237	1125	4.7	5						
	Floyd Little, Den, AFC	209	901	4.3	3						
1971	Floyd Little, Den, AFC	284	1133	4.0	6						
	John Brockington, GB, NFC	216	1105	5.1	4						

Rushing *(Cont.)*

Year	Player, Team	Att	Yards	Avg	TD
1995	Emmitt Smith, Dall, NFC	377	1773	4.7	25
	Curtis Martin, NE, AFC	368	1487	4.0	14
1996	Barry Sanders, Det, NFC	307	1553	5.1	11
	Terrell Davis, Den, AFC	345	1538	4.5	13
1997	Barry Sanders, Det, NFC	335	2053	6.1	11
	Terrell Davis, Den, AFC	369	1730	4.7	15
1998	Terrell Davis, Den, AFC	392	2008	5.1	21
	Jamal Anderson, Atl, NFC	410	1846	4.5	14
1999	Edgerrin James, Ind, AFC	369	1553	4.2	13
	Stephen Davis, Wash, NFC	290	1405	4.8	17
2000	Edgerrin James, Ind, AFC	387	1709	4.4	13
	Robert Smith, Minn, NFC	295	1521	5.2	7
2001	Priest Holmes, Kan, AFC	327	1555	4.8	8
	Stephen Davis, Wash, NFC	356	1432	4.0	5
2002	Ricky Williams, Mia, AFC	383	1853	4.8	16
	Deuce McAllister, NO, NFC	325	1388	4.3	13
2003	Jamal Lewis, Balt, AFC	387	2066	5.3	14
	Ahman Green, GB, NFC	355	1883	5.3	15
2004	Curtis Martin, NY Jets, AFC	371	1,697	4.6	12
	Shaun Alexander, Seattle, NFC	353	1,696	4.8	16

Passing*

Year	Player, Team	Att	Comp	Yards	TD	Int
1932	Arnie Herber, GB	101	37	639	9	9
1933	Harry Newman, NY	136	53	973	11	17
1934	Arnie Herber, GB	115	42	799	8	12
1935	Ed Danowski, NY	113	57	794	10	9
1936	Arnie Herber, GB	173	77	1239	11	13
1937	Sammy Baugh, Wash	171	81	1127	8	14
1938	Ed Danowski, NY	129	70	848	7	8
1939	Parker Hall, Clev	208	106	1227	9	13
1940	Sammy Baugh, Wash	177	111	1367	12	10
1941	Cecil Isbell, GB	206	117	1479	15	11
1942	Cecil Isbell, GB	268	146	2021	24	14
1943	Sammy Baugh, Wash	239	133	1754	23	19
1944	Frank Filchock, Wash	147	84	1139	13	9
1945	Sammy Baugh, Wash	182	128	1669	11	4
	Sid Luckman, Chi	217	117	1725	14	10
1946	Bob Waterfield, LA	251	127	1747	18	17
1947	Sammy Baugh, Wash	354	210	2938	25	15
1948	Tommy Thompson, Phil	246	141	1965	25	11
1949	Sammy Baugh, Wash	255	145	1903	18	14
1950	Norm Van Brocklin, LA	233	127	2061	18	14
1951	Bob Waterfield, LA	176	88	1566	13	10
1952	Norm Van Brocklin, LA	205	113	1736	14	17
1953	Otto Graham, Clev	258	167	2722	11	9
1954	Norm Van Brocklin, LA	260	139	2637	13	21
1955	Otto Graham, Clev	185	98	1721	15	8
1956	Ed Brown, Chi	168	96	1667	11	12
1957	Tommy O'Connell, Clev	110	63	1229	9	8
1958	Eddie LeBaron, Wash	145	79	1365	11	10
1959	Charlie Conerly, NY	194	113	1706	14	4
1960	Milt Plum, Clev	250	151	2297	21	5
	Jack Kemp, LA, AFL	406	211	3018	20	25
1961	George Blanda, Hou, AFL	362	187	3330	36	22
	Milt Plum, Clev, NFL	302	177	2416	18	10
1962	Len Dawson, Dall, AFL	310	189	2759	29	17
	Bart Starr, GB, NFL	285	178	2438	12	9
1963	Y.A. Tittle, NY, NFL	367	221	3145	36	14
	Tobin Rote, SD, AFL	286	170	2510	20	17
1964	Len Dawson, KC, AFL	354	199	2879	30	18
	Bart Starr, GB, NFL	272	163	2144	15	4
1965	Rudy Bukich, Chi, NFL	312	176	2641	20	9
	John Hadl, SD, AFL	348	174	2798	20	21
1966	Bart Starr, GB, NFL	251	156	2257	14	3
	Len Dawson, KC, AFL	284	159	2527	26	10
1967	Sonny Jurgensen, Wash, NFL	508	288	3747	31	16
	Daryle Lamonica, Oakland, AFL	425	220	3228	30	20
1968	Len Dawson, KC, AFL	224	131	2109	17	9
	Earl Morrall, Balt, NFL	317	182	2909	26	17
1969	S. Jurgensen, Wash, NFL	442	274	3102	22	15
	Greg Cook, Cin, AFL	197	106	1854	15	11
1970	John Brodie, SF, NFC	378	223	2941	24	10
	Daryle Lamonica, Oak, AFC	356	179	2516	22	15
1971	Roger Staubach, Dall, NFC	211	126	1882	15	4
	Bob Griese, Mia, AFC	263	145	2089	19	9
1972	Norm Snead, NY, NFC	325	196	2307	17	12
	Earl Morrall, Mia, AFC	150	83	1360	11	7
1973	Roger Staubach, Dall, NFC	286	179	2428	23	15
	Ken Stabler, Oak, AFC	260	163	1997	14	10
1974	Ken Anderson, Cin, AFC	328	213	2667	18	10
	Sonny Jurgensen, Wash, NFC	167	107	1185	11	5
1975	Ken Anderson, Cin, AFC	377	228	3169	21	11
	Fran Tarkenton, Minn, NFC	425	273	2994	25	13
1976	Ken Stabler, Oak, AFC	291	194	2737	27	17
	James Harris, LA, NFC	158	91	1460	8	6
1977	Bob Griese, Mia, AFC	307	180	2252	22	13
	Roger Staubach, Dall, NFC	361	210	2620	18	9
1978	Roger Staubach, Dall, NFC	413	231	3190	25	16
	Terry Bradshaw, Pitt, AFC	368	207	2915	28	20
1979	Roger Staubach, Dall, NFC	461	267	3586	27	11
	Dan Fouts, SD, AFC	530	332	4082	24	24
1980	Brian Sipe, Clev, AFC	554	337	4132	30	14
	Ron Jaworski, Phi, NFC	451	257	3529	27	12
1981	Ken Anderson, Cin, AFC	479	300	3754	29	10
	Joe Montana, SF, NFC	488	311	3565	19	12
1982	Ken Anderson, Cin, AFC	309	218	2495	12	9
	Joe Theismann, Wash, NFC	252	161	2033	13	9
1983	Steve Bartkowski, Atl, NFC	432	274	3167	22	5
	Dan Marino, Mia AFC	296	173	2210	20	6
1984	Dan Marino, Mia, AFC	564	362	5084	48	17
	Joe Montana, SF, NFC	432	279	3630	28	10
1985	Ken O'Brien, NY, AFC	488	297	3888	25	8
	Joe Montana, SF, NFC	494	303	3653	27	13
1986	Tommy Kramer, Minn, NFC	372	208	3000	24	10
	Dan Marino, Mia, AFC	623	378	4746	44	23
1987	Joe Montana, SF, NFC	398	266	3054	31	13
	Bernie Kosar, Clev, AFC	389	241	3033	22	9

Passing *(Cont.)*

Year	Player, Team	Att	Comp	Yards	TD	Int
1988	Boomer Esiason, Cin, AFC	388	223	3572	28	14
	Wade Wilson, Minn, NFC	332	204	2746	15	9
1989	Joe Montana, SF, NFC	386	271	3521	26	8
	Boomer Esiason, Cin, AFC	455	258	3525	28	11
1990	Jim Kelly, Buffalo, AFC	346	219	2829	24	9
	Phil Simms, NY, NFC	311	184	2284	15	4
1991	Steve Young, SF, NFC	279	180	2517	17	8
	Jim Kelly, Buff, AFC	474	304	3844	33	17
1992	Steve Young, SF, NFC	402	268	3465	25	7
	Warren Moon, Hou, AFC	346	224	2521	18	12
1993	Steve Young, SF, NFC	462	314	4023	29	16
	John Elway, Den, AFC	551	348	4030	25	10
1994	Steve Young, SF, NFC	461	324	3969	35	10
	Dan Marino, Mia, AFC	615	385	4453	30	17
1995	Brett Favre, GB, NFC	570	359	4413	38	13
	Jeff Blake, Cin, AFC	567	326	3822	28	17
1996	Vinny Testaverde, Balt, AFC	549	325	4177	33	19
	Brett Favre, GB, NFC	543	325	3899	39	13
1997	Steve Young, SF, NFC	356	241	3029	19	6
	Mark Brunell, Jax, AFC	435	264	3281	18	7
1998	Randall Cunningham, Minn, NFC	425	259	3704	34	10
	Vinny Testaverde, NYJ, AFC	421	259	3256	29	7
1999	Kurt Warner, StL, NFC	499	325	4353	41	13
	Peyton Manning, Ind, AFC	533	331	4135	26	15
2000	Trent Green, StL, NFC	240	145	2063	16	5
	Brian Griese, Den, AFC	336	216	2688	19	4
2001	Kurt Warner, StL, NFC	546	375	4830	36	22
	Rich Gannon, Oak, AFC	549	361	3828	27	9
2002	Brad Johnson, TB, NFC	451	281	3049	22	6
	Chad Pennington, NYJ, AFC	399	275	3120	22	6
2003	Steve McNair, Tenn, AFC	400	250	3215	24	7
	Daunte Culpepper, Minn, NFC	454	295	3479	25	11
2004	Peyton Manning, Ind, AFC	497	336	4,557	49	10

*Since 1973, the annual passing leaders have been determined by a passer rating system that compares individual performances to a fixed performance standard.

Pass Receiving*

Year	Player, Team	No.	Yds	Avg	TD
1932	Ray Flaherty, NY	21	350	16.7	3
1933	John Kelly, Brooklyn	22	246	11.2	3
1934	Joe Carter, Phil	16	238	14.9	4
	Morris Badgro, NY	16	206	12.9	1
1935	Tod Goodwin, NY	26	432	16.6	4
1936	Don Hutson, GB	34	536	15.8	8
1937	Don Hutson, GB	41	552	13.5	7
1938	Gaynell Tinsley, Chi Cards	41	516	12.6	1
1939	Don Hutson, GB	34	846	24.9	6
1940	Don Looney, Phil	58	707	12.2	4
1941	Don Hutson, GB	58	738	12.7	10
1942	Don Hutson, GB	74	1211	16.4	17
1943	Don Hutson, GB	47	776	16.5	11
1944	Don Hutson, GB	58	866	14.9	9
1945	Don Hutson, GB	47	834	17.7	9
1946	Jim Benton, LA	63	981	15.6	6
1947	Jim Keane, Chi	64	910	14.2	10
1948	Tom Fears, LA	51	698	13.7	4
1949	Tom Fears, LA	77	1013	13.2	9
1950	Tom Fears, LA	84	1116	13.3	7
1951	Elroy Hirsch, LA	66	1495	22.7	17
1952	Mac Speedie, Clev	62	911	14.7	5
1953	Pete Pihos, Phil	63	1049	16.7	10
1954	Pete Pihos, Phil	60	872	14.5	10
	Billy Wilson, SF	60	830	13.8	5
1955	Pete Pihos, Phil	62	864	13.9	7
1956	Billy Wilson, SF	60	889	14.8	5
1957	Billy Wilson, SF	52	757	14.6	6
1958	Raymond Berry, Balt	56	794	14.2	9
	Pete Retzlaff, Phil	56	766	13.7	2
1959	Raymond Berry, Balt	66	959	14.5	14
1960	Lionel Taylor, Den, AFL	92	1235	13.4	12
	Raymond Berry, Balt, NFL	74	1298	17.5	10
1961	Lionel Taylor, Den, AFL	100	1176	11.8	4
	Jim Phillips, LA, NFL	78	1092	14.0	5
1962	Lionel Taylor, Den, AFL	77	908	11.8	4
	Bobby Mitchell, Wash, NFL	72	1384	19.2	11
1963	Lionel Taylor, Den, AFL	78	1101	14.1	10
	Bobby Joe Conrad, St. Louis, NFL	73	967	13.2	10
1964	Charley Hennigan, Houston, AFL	101	1546	15.3	8
	Johnny Morris, Chi, NFL	93	1200	12.9	10
1965	Lionel Taylor, Den, AFL	85	1131	13.3	6
	Dave Parks, SF, NFL	80	1344	16.8	12
1966	Lance Alworth, SD, AFL	73	1383	18.9	13
	Charley Taylor, Wash, NFL	72	1119	15.5	12
1967	George Sauer, NY, AFL	75	1189	15.9	6
	Charley Taylor, Wash, NFL	70	990	14.1	9
1968	Clifton McNeil, SF, NFL	71	994	14.0	7
	Lance Alworth, SD, AFL	68	1312	19.3	10
1969	Dan Abramowicz, NO, NFL	73	1015	13.9	7
	Lance Alworth, SD, AFL	64	1003	15.7	4
1970	Dick Gordon, Chi, NFC	71	1026	14.5	13
	Marlin Briscoe, Buff, AFC	57	1036	18.2	8
1971	Fred Biletnikoff, Oak, AFC	61	929	15.2	9
	Bob Tucker, NY, NFC	59	791	13.4	4
1972	Harold Jackson, Phil, NFC	62	1048	16.9	4
	Fred Biletnikoff, Oak, AFC	58	802	13.8	4
1973	Harold Carmichael, Phil, NFC	67	1116	16.7	9
	Fred Willis, Hou, AFC	57	371	6.5	1
1974	Lydell Mitchell, Balt, AFC	72	544	7.6	2
	Charles Young, Phil, NFC	63	696	11.0	3

*Most catches.

Pass Receiving (Cont.)

Year	Player, Team	No.	Yds	Avg	TD
1975	Chuck Foreman, Minn, NFC	73	691	9.5	9
	Reggie Rucker, Clev, AFC	60	770	12.8	3
	Lydell Mitchell, Balt, AFC	60	544	9.1	4
1976	MacArthur Lane, KC, AFC	66	686	10.4	1
	Drew Pearson, Dall, NFC	58	806	13.9	6
1977	Lydell Mitchell, Balt, AFC	71	620	8.7	4
	Ahmad Rashad, Minn, NFC	51	681	13.4	2
1978	Rickey Young, Minn, NFC	88	704	8.0	5
	Steve Largent, Sea, AFC	71	1168	16.5	8
1979	Joe Washington, Balt, AFC	82	750	9.1	3
	Ahmad Rashad, Minn, NFC	80	1156	14.5	9
1980	Kellen Winslow, SD, AFC	89	1290	14.5	9
	Earl Cooper, SF, NFC	83	567	6.8	4
1981	Kellen Winslow, SD, AFC	88	1075	12.2	10
	Dwight Clark, SF, NFC	85	1105	13.0	4
1982	Dwight Clark, SF, NFC	60	913	15.2	5
	Kellen Winslow, SD, AFC	54	721	13.4	6
1983	Todd Christensen, LA, AFC	92	1247	13.6	12
	Roy Green, StL, NFC	78	1227	15.7	14
	Charlie Brown, Wash, NFC	78	1225	15.7	8
	Earnest Gray, NY, NFC	78	1139	14.6	5
1984	Art Monk, Wash, NFC	106	1372	12.9	7
	Ozzie Newsome, Clev, AFC	89	1001	11.2	5
1985	Roger Craig, SF, NFC	92	1016	11.0	6
	Lionel James, SD, AFC	86	1027	11.9	6
1986	Todd Christensen, LA Rai, AFC	95	1153	12.1	8
	Jerry Rice, SF, NFC	86	1570	18.3	15
1987	J.T. Smith, StL Card, NFC	91	1117	12.3	8
	Al Toon, NY, AFC	68	976	14.4	5
1988	Al Toon, NY, AFC	93	1067	11.5	5
	Henry Ellard, LA Rams, NFC	86	1414	16.4	10
1989	Sterling Sharpe, GB, NFC	90	1423	15.8	12
	Andre Reed, Buff, AFC	88	1312	14.9	9
1990	Jerry Rice, SF, NFC	100	1502	15.0	13
	Haywood Jeffires, Hou, AFC	74	1048	14.2	8
	Drew Hill, Hou, AFC	74	1019	13.8	5
1991	Haywood Jeffires, Hou, AFC	100	1181	11.8	7
	Michael Irvin, Dall, NFC	93	1523	16.4	8
1992	Sterling Sharpe, GB, NFC	108	1461	13.5	13
	Haywood Jeffires, Hou, AFC	90	913	10.1	9
1993	Sterling Sharpe, GB, NFC	112	1274	11.4	11
	Reggie Langhorne, Ind, AFC	85	1038	12.2	3
1994	Cris Carter, Minn, NFC	122	1256	10.3	7
	Ben Coates, NE, AFC	96	1174	12.2	7
1995	Herman Moore, Det, NFC	123	1686	13.7	14
	Carl Pickens, Cin, AFC	99	1234	12.5	17
1996	Jerry Rice, SF, NFC	108	1254	11.6	8
	Carl Pickens, Cin, AFC	100	1180	11.8	12
1997	Herman Moore, Det, NFC	104	1293	12.4	8
	Tim Brown, Oak, AFC	104	1408	13.5	5
1998	Frank Sanders, Ariz, NFC	89	1145	12.9	3
	O.J. McDuffie, Mia, AFC	90	1050	11.7	7
1999	Mushin Muhammad, Car, NFC	96	1253	13.1	8
	Jimmy Smith, Jax, AFC	116	1636	14.1	6
2000	Mushin Muhammad, Car, NFC	102	1183	11.6	6
	Marvin Harrison, Ind, AFC	102	1413	13.9	14
2001	Rod Smith, Den, AFC	113	1343	11.9	11
	Keyshawn Johnson, TB, NFC	106	1266	11.9	1
2002	Marvin Harrison, Ind, AFC	143	1722	12.0	11
	Randy Moss, Minn, NFC	106	1347	12.7	7
2003	LaDainian Tomlinson, SD, AFC	100	725	7.3	4
	Torry Holt, StL, NFC	117	1696	14.5	12
2004	Tony Gonzalez, KC, AFC	102	1,258	12.3	7
	Joe Horn, NO, NFC	94	1,399	14.9	11

YET ANOTHER SIGN OF THE APOCALYPSE

Titans running back Eddie George issued press credentials to his bachelor party.

Scoring

Year	Player, Team	TD	FG	PAT	TP	Year	Player, Team	TD	FG	PAT	TP
1932	Earl Clark, Portsmouth	6	3	10	55	1977	Errol Mann, Oak, AFC	0	20	39	99
1933	Ken Strong, NY	6	5	13	64		Walter Payton, Chi, NFC	16	0	0	96
	Glenn Presnell, Ports	6	6	10	64	1978	Frank Corral, LA, NFC	0	29	31	118
1934	Jack Manders, Chi	3	10	31	79		Pat Leahy, NY, AFC	0	22	41	107
1935	Earl Clark, Det	6	1	16	55	1979	John Smith, NE, AFC	0	23	46	115
1936	Earl Clark, Det	7	4	19	73		Mark Moseley, Wash, NFC	0	25	39	114
1937	Jack Manders, Chi	5	18	15	69	1980	John Smith, NE, AFC	0	26	51	129
1938	Clarke Hinkle, GB	7	3	7	58		Ed Murray, Det, NFC	0	27	35	116
1939	Andy Farkas, Wash	11	0	2	68	1981	Ed Murray, Det, NFC	0	25	46	121
1940	Don Hutson, GB	7	0	15	57		Rafael Septien, Dall, NFC	0	27	40	121
1941	Don Hutson, GB	12	1	20	95		Jim Breech, Cin, AFC	0	22	49	115
1942	Don Hutson, GB	17	1	33	138		Nick Lowery, KC, AFC	0	26	37	115
1943	Don Hutson, GB	12	3	36	117	1982	Marcus Allen, LA, AFC	14	0	0	84
1944	Don Hutson, GB	9	0	31	85		Wendell Tyler, LA, NFC	13	0	0	78
1945	Steve Van Buren, Phil	18	0	2	110	1983	Mark Moseley, Wash, NFC	0	33	62	161
1946	Ted Fritsch, GB	10	9	13	100		Gary Anderson, Pitt, AFC	0	27	38	119
1947	Pat Harder, Chicago Cards	7	7	39	102	1984	Ray Wersching, SF, NFC	0	25	56	131
1948	Pat Harder, Chicago Cards	6	7	53	110,		Gary Anderson, Pitt, AFC	0	24	45	117
1949	Pat Harder, Chicago Cards	8	3	45	102	1985	Kevin Butler, Chi, NFC	0	31	51	144
	Gene Roberts, NY	17	0	0	102		Gary Anderson, Pitt, AFC	0	33	40	139
1950	Doak Walker, Det	11	8	38	128	1986	Tony Franklin, NE, AFC	0	32	44	140
1951	Elroy Hirsch, LA	17	0	0	102		Kevin Butler, Chi, NFC	0	28	36	120
1952	Gordy Soltau, SF	7	6	34	94	1987	Jerry Rice, SF, NFC	23	0	0	138
1953	Gordy Soltau, SF	6	10	48	114		Jim Breech, Cin, AFC	0	24	25	97
1954	Bobby Walston, Phil	11	4	36	114	1988	Scott Norwood, Buff, AFC	0	32	33	129
1955	Doak Walker, Det	7	9	27	96		Mike Cofer, SF, NFC	0	27	40	121
1956	Bobby Layne, Det	5	12	33	99	1989	Mike Cofer, SF, NFC	0	29	49	136
1957	Sam Baker, Wash	1	14	29	77		David Treadwell, Den, AFC	0	27	39	120
	Lou Groza, Clev	0	15	32	77	1990	Nick Lowery, KC, AFC	0	34	37	139
1958	Jim Brown, Clev	18	0	0	108		Chip Lohmiller, Wash, NFC	0	30	41	131
1959	Paul Hornung, GB	7	7	31	94	1991	Chip Lohmiller, Wash, NFC	0	31	56	149
1960	Paul Hornung, GB, NFL	15	15	41	176		Pete Stoyanovich, Mia, AFC	0	31	28	121
	Gene Mingo, Den, AFL	6	18	33	123	1992	Pete Stoyanovich, Mia, AFC	0	30	34	124
1961	Gino Cappelletti, Bos, AFL	8	17	48	147		Morten Anderson, NO, NFC	0	29	33	120
	Paul Hornung, GB, NFL	10	15	41	146		Chip Lohmiller, Wash, NFC	0	30	30	120
1962	Gene Mingo, Den, AFL	4	27	32	137	1993	Jeff Jaeger, Rai, AFC	0	35	27	132
	Jim Taylor, GB, NFL	19	0	0	114		Jason Hanson, Det, NFC	0	34	28	130
1963	Gino Cappelletti, Bos, AFL	2	22	35	113	1994	John Carney, SD, AFC	0	34	33	135
	Don Chandler, NY, NFL	0	18	52	106		Fuad Reveiz, Minn, NFC	0	34	30	132
1964	Gino Cappelletti, Bos, AFL	7	25	36	155		Emmitt Smith, Dall, NFC	22	0	0	132
	Lenny Moore, Balt, NFL	20	0	0	120	1995	Emmitt Smith, Dall, NFC	25	0	0	150
1965	Gale Sayers, Chi, NFL	22	0	0	132		Norm Johnson, Pitt, AFC	0	34	39	141
	Gino Cappelletti, Bos, AFL	9	17	27	132	1996	John Kasay, Car, NFC	0	37	34	145
1966	Gino Cappelletti, Bos, AFL	6	16	35	119		Cary Blanchard, Ind, AFC	0	36	27	135
	Bruce Gossett, LA, NFL	0	28	29	113	1997	Richie Cunningham,				
1967	Jim Bakken, StL, NFL	0	27	36	117		Dall, NFC	0	34	24	126
	George Blanda, Oak, AFL	0	20	56	116		Mike Hollis, Jax, AFC	0	41	31	134
1968	Jim Turner, NY, AFL	0	34	43	145	1998	Gary Anderson, Minn, NFC	0	35	59	164
	Leroy Kelly, Clev, NFL	20	0	0	120		Steve Christie, Buff, AFC	0	33	41	140
1969	Jim Turner, NY, AFL	0	32	33	129	1999	Jeff Wilkins, StL, NFC	0	20	28	124
	Fred Cox, Minn, NFL	0	26	43	121		Mike Vanderjagt, Ind, AFC	0	34	38	145
1970	Fred Cox, Minn, NFC	0	30	35	125	2000	Marshall Faulk, StL, NFC	26	0	0	156
	Jan Stenerud, KC, AFC	0	30	26	116		Matt Stover, Balt, AFC	0	35	30	135
1971	Garo Yepremian, Mia, AFC	0	28	33	117	2001	Marshall Faulk, StL, NFC	21	0	2	128
	Curt Knight, Wash, NFC	0	29	27	114		Mike Vanderjagt, Ind, AFC	0	28	41	125
1972	Chester Marcol, GB, NFC	0	33	29	128	2002	Jay Feely, Atl, NFC	0	32	43	138
	Bobby Howfield, NY AFC	0	27	40	121		Priest Holmes, KC, AFC	24	0	0	144
1973	David Ray, LA, NFC	0	30	40	130	2003	Jeff Wilkins StL, NFC	0	39	46	163
	Roy Gerela, Pitt, AFC	0	29	36	123		Priest Holmes, KC, AFC	27	0	0	162
1974	Chester Marcol, GB, NFC	0	25	19	94	2004	Adam Vinatieri, NE, AFC	0	31	48	141
	Roy Gerela, Pitt, AFC	0	20	33	93		David Akers, Phil, NFC	0	27	41	122
1975	O.J. Simpson, Buff, AFC	23	0	0	138						
	Chuck Foreman, Minn, NFC	22	0	0	132						
1976	Toni Linhart, Balt, AFC	0	20	49	109						
	Mark Moseley, Wash, NFC	0	22	31	97						

Pro Bowl Alltime Results

Date	Result
1-15-39	NY Giants 13, Pro All-Stars 10
1-14-40	Green Bay 16, NFL All-Stars 7
12-29-40	Chi Bears 28, NFL All-Stars 14
1-4-42	Chi Bears 35, NFL All-Stars 24
12-27-42	NFL All-Stars 17, Washington 14
1-14-51	A. Conf. 28, N. Conf. 27
1-12-52	N. Conf. 30, A. Conf. 13
1-10-53	N. Conf. 27, A. Conf. 7
1-17-54	East 20, West 9
1-16-55	West 26, East 19
1-15-56	East 31, West 30
1-13-57	West 19, East 10
1-12-58	West 26, East 7
1-11-59	East 28, West 21
1-17-60	West 38, East 21
1-15-61	West 35, East 31
1-7-62	AFL West 47, East 27
1-14-62	NFL West 31, East 30
1-13-63	AFL West 21, East 14
1-13-63	NFL East 30, West 20
1-12-64	NFL West 31, East 17
1-19-64	AFL West 27, East 24
1-10-65	NFL West 34, East 14
1-16-65	AFL West 38, East 14
1-15-66	AFL All-Stars 30, Buffalo 19
1-15-66	NFL East 36, West 7
1-21-67	AFL East 30, West 23
1-22-67	NFL East 20, West 10
1-21-68	AFL East 25, West 24
1-21-68	NFL West 38, East 20
1-19-69	AFL West 38, East 25
1-19-69	NFL West 10, East 7
1-17-70	AFL West 26, East 3
1-18-70	NFL West 16, East 13
1-24-71	NFC 27, AFC 6
1-23-72	AFC 26, NFC 13
1-21-73	AFC 33, NFC 28
1-20-74	AFC 15, NFC 13
1-20-75	NFC 17, AFC 10
1-26-76	NFC 23, AFC 20
1-17-77	AFC 24, NFC 14
1-23-78	NFC 14, AFC 13
1-29-79	NFC 13, AFC 7
1-27-80	NFC 37, AFC 27
2-1-81	NFC 21, AFC 7
1-31-82	AFC 16, NFC 13
2-6-83	NFC 20, AFC 19
1-29-84	NFC 45, AFC 3
1-27-85	AFC 22, NFC 14
2-2-86	NFC 28, AFC 24
2-1-87	AFC 10, NFC 6
2-7-88	AFC 15, NFC 6
1-29-89	NFC 34, AFC 3
2-4-90	NFC 27, AFC 21
2-3-91	AFC 23, NFC 21
2-2-92	NFC 21, AFC 15
2-7-93	AFC 23, NFC 20
2-6-94	NFC 17, AFC 3
2-5-95	AFC 41, NFC 13
2-4-96	NFC 20, AFC 13
2-2-97	AFC 26, NFC 23
2-1-98	AFC 29, NFC 24
2-7-99	AFC 23, NFC 10
2-6-00	NFC 51, AFC 31
2-4-01	AFC 38, NFC 17
2-9-02	AFC 38, NFC 30
2-2-03	AFC 45, NFC 20
2-8-04	NFC 55, AFC 52
2-13-05	AFC 38, NFC 27

Chicago All-Star Game* Results

Date	Result (Attendance)
8-31-34	Chi Bears 0, All-Stars 0 (79,432)
8-29-35	Chi Bears 5, All-Stars 0 (77,450)
9-3-36	All-Stars 7, Detroit 7 (76,000)
9-1-37	All-Stars 6, Green Bay 0 (84,560)
8-31-38	All-Stars 28, Washington 16 (74,250)
8-30-39	NY Giants 9, All-Stars 0 (81,456)
8-29-40	Green Bay 45, All-Stars 28 (84,567)
8-28-41	Chi Bears 37, All-Stars 13 (98,203)
8-28-42	Chi Bears 21, All-Stars 0 (101,100)
8-25-43	All-Stars 27, Washington 7 (48,471)
8-30-44	Chi Bears 24, All-Stars 21 (48,769)
8-30-45	Green Bay 19, All-Stars 7 (92,753)
8-23-46	All-Stars 16, Los Angeles 0 (97,380)
8-22-47	All-Stars 16, Chi Bears 0 (105,840)
8-20-48	Chi Cardinals 28, All-Stars 0 (101,220)
8-12-49	Philadelphia 38, All-Stars 0 (93,780)
8-11-50	All-Stars 17, Philadelphia 7 (88,885)
8-17-51	Cleveland 33, All-Stars 0 (92,180)
8-15-52	Los Angeles 10, All-Stars 7 (88,316)
8-14-53	Detroit 24, All-Stars 10 (93,818)
8-13-54	Detroit 31, All-Stars 6 (93,470)
8-12-55	All-Stars 30, Cleveland 27 (75,000)
8-10-56	Cleveland 26, All-Stars 0 (75,000)
8-9-57	NY Giants 22, All-Stars 12 (75,000)
8-15-58	All-Stars 35, Detroit 19 (70,000)
8-14-59	Baltimore 29, All-Stars 0 (70,000)
8-12-60	Baltimore 32, All-Stars 7 (70,000)
8-4-61	Philadelphia 28, All-Stars 14 (66,000)
8-3-62	Green Bay 42, All-Stars 20 (65,000)
8-2-63	All-Stars 20, Green Bay 17 (65,000)
8-7-64	Chicago 28, All-Stars 17 (65,000)
8-6-65	Cleveland 24, All-Stars 16 (68,000)
8-5-66	Green Bay 38, All-Stars 0 (72,000)
8-4-67	Green Bay 27, All-Stars 0 (70,934)
8-2-68	Green Bay 34, All-Stars 17 (69,917)
8-1-69	NY Jets 26, All-Stars 24 (74,208)
7-31-70	Kansas City 24, All-Stars 3 (69,940)
7-30-71	Baltimore 24, All-Stars 17 (52,289)
7-28-72	Dallas 20, All-Stars 7 (54,162)
7-27-73	Miami 14, All-Stars 3 (54,103)
1974	No game
8-1-75	Pittsburgh 21, All-Stars 14 (54,103)
7-23-76	Pittsburgh 24, All-Stars 0 (52,895)

*Discontinued.

YET ANOTHER SIGN OF THE APOCALYPSE

Cheerleaders in Michigan helped police track down a hit-and-run suspect by turning his license plate number into a cheer.

Alltime Winningest NFL Coaches

Most Career Wins

Coach	Yrs	Teams	Regular Season				Career			
			W	L	T	Pct	W	L	T	Pct
Don Shula	33	Colts, Dolphins	328	156	6	.676	347	173	6	.665
George Halas	40	Bears	318	148	31	.671	324	151	31	.671
Tom Landry	29	Cowboys	250	162	6	.605	270	178	6	.601
Curly Lambeau	33	Packers, Cardinals, Redskins	226	132	22	.624	229	134	22	.623
Paul Brown	25	Browns, Bengals	213	104	9	.667	222	112	9	.660
Chuck Noll	23	Steelers	193	148	1	.566	209	156	1	.572
†Dan Reeves	23	Broncos, Giants, Falcons	190	165	2	.535	201	174	2	.536
Chuck Knox	22	Rams, Bills, Seahawks	186	147	1	.558	193	158	1	.550
†M. Schottenheimer	19	Browns, Chiefs, Redskins, Chargers	177	117	1	.602	182	129	1	.585
Bud Grant	18	Vikings	158	96	5	.620	168	108	5	.607
†Bill Parcells	17	Giants, Patriots, Jets, Cowboys	154	116	1	.570	165	123	1	.573
Marv Levy	17	Chiefs, Bills	143	112	0	.561	154	120	0	.562
Steve Owen	23	Giants	151	100	17	.595	153	108	17	.581
†Joe Gibbs	13	Redskins	130	70	0	.650	146	75	0	.661
†Bill Cowher	13	Steelers	130	77	1	.627	138	86	1	.616
Hank Stram	17	Chiefs, Saints	131	97	10	.571	136	100	10	.573
Weeb Ewbank	20	Colts, Jets	130	129	7	.502	134	130	7	.507
†Mike Holmgren	13	Packers, Seahawks	125	83	0	.601	134	91	0	.596
Mike Ditka	14	Bears, Saints	121	95	0	.560	127	101	0	.557
Jim Mora	15	Saints, Colts	125	106	0	.541	125	112	0	.527

†Active in 2004.

Top Winning Percentages

	W	L	T	Pct		W	L	T	Pct
Vince Lombardi	105	35	6	.750	Don Shula	347	173	6	.665
John Madden	112	39	7	.731	George Seifert	124	67	0	.649
George Allen	118	54	5	.681	Curly Lambeau	229	134	22	.623
†Joe Gibbs	146	75	0	.674	Bill Walsh	102	63	1	.617
George Halas	324	151	31	.671	†Paul Brown	170	108	6	.609

Note: Minimum 100 victories.

†Active in 2004.

Alltime Number-One Draft Choices

Year	Team	Selection	Position
1936	Philadelphia	Jay Berwanger, Chicago	HB
1937	Philadelphia	Sam Francis, Nebraska	FB
1938	Cleveland	Corbett Davis, Indiana	FB
1939	Chicago Cardinals	Ki Aldrich, Texas Christian	C
1940	Chicago Cardinals	George Cafego, Tennessee	HB
1941	Chicago Bears	Tom Harmon, Michigan	HB
1942	Pittsburgh	Bill Dudley, Virginia	HB
1943	Detroit	Frank Sinkwich, Georgia	HB
1944	Boston	Angelo Bertelli, Notre Dame	QB
1945	Chicago Cardinals	Charley Trippi, Georgia	HB
1946	Boston	Frank Dancewicz, Notre Dame	QB
1947	Chicago Bears	Bob Fenimore, Oklahoma A&M	HB
1948	Washington	Harry Gilmer, Alabama	QB
1949	Philadelphia	Chuck Bednarik, Pennsylvania	C
1950	Detroit	Leon Hart, Notre Dame	E
1951	New York Giants	Kyle Rote, Southern Methodist	HB
1952	Los Angeles	Bill Wade, Vanderbilt	QB
1953	San Francisco	Harry Babcock, Georgia	E
1954	Cleveland	Bobby Garrett, Stanford	QB
1955	Baltimore	George Shaw, Oregon	QB
1956	Pittsburgh	Gary Glick, Colorado A&M	DB
1957	Green Bay	Paul Hornung, Notre Dame	HB
1958	Chicago Cardinals	King Hill, Rice	QB
1959	Green Bay	Randy Duncan, Iowa	QB
1960	Los Angeles	Billy Cannon, Louisiana St	RB
1961	Minnesota	Tommy Mason, Tulane	RB
	Buffalo (AFL)	Ken Rice, Auburn	G

Year	Team	Player	Pos
1962	Washington	Ernie Davis, Syracuse	RB
	Oakland (AFL)	Roman Gabriel, N Carolina St	QB
1963	LA Rams	Terry Baker, Oregon St	QB
	Kansas City (AFL)	Buck Buchanan, Grambling	DT
1964	San Francisco	Dave Parks, Texas Tech	E
	Boston (AFL)	Jack Concannon, Boston College	QB
1965	NY Giants	Tucker Frederickson, Auburn	RB
	Houston (AFL)	Lawrence Elkins, Baylor	E
1966	Atlanta	Tommy Nobis, Texas	LB
	Miami (AFL)	Jim Grabowski, Illinois	RB
1967	Baltimore	Bubba Smith, Michigan St	DT
1968	Minnesota	Ron Yary, Southern California	T
1969	Buffalo (AFL)	O.J. Simpson, Southern California	RB
1970	Pittsburgh	Terry Bradshaw, Louisiana Tech	QB
1971	New England	Jim Plunkett, Stanford	QB
1972	Buffalo	Walt Patulski, Notre Dame	DE
1973	Houston	John Matuszak, Tampa	DE
1974	Dallas	Ed Jones, Tennessee St	DE
1975	Atlanta	Steve Bartkowski, California	QB
1976	Tampa Bay	Lee Roy Selmon, Oklahoma	DE
1977	Tampa Bay	Ricky Bell, Southern California	RB
1978	Houston	Earl Campbell, Texas	RB
1979	Buffalo	Tom Cousineau, Ohio St	LB
1980	Detroit	Billy Sims, Oklahoma	RB
1981	New Orleans	George Rogers, South Carolina	RB
1982	New England	Kenneth Sims, Texas	DT
1983	Baltimore	John Elway, Stanford	QB
1984	New England	Irving Fryar, Nebraska	WR
1985	Buffalo	Bruce Smith, Virginia Tech	DE
1986	Tampa Bay	Bo Jackson, Auburn	RB
1987	Tampa Bay	Vinny Testaverde, Miami (FL)	QB
1988	Atlanta	Aundray Bruce, Auburn	LB
1989	Dallas	Troy Aikman, UCLA	QB
1990	Indianapolis	Jeff George, Illinois	QB
1991	Dallas	Russell Maryland, Miami (FL)	DT
1992	Indianapolis	Steve Emtman, Washington	DT
1993	New England	Drew Bledsoe, Washington St	QB
1994	Cincinnati	Dan Wilkinson, Ohio St	DT
1995	Cincinnati	Ki-Jana Carter, Penn St	RB
1996	New York Jets	Keyshawn Johnson, Southern California	WR
1997	St Louis	Orlando Pace, Ohio St	OT
1998	Indianapolis	Peyton Manning, Tennessee	QB
1999	Cleveland	Tim Couch, Kentucky	QB
2000	Cleveland	Courtney Brown, Penn St	DE
2001	Atlanta	Michael Vick, Virginia Tech	QB
2002	Houston	David Carr, Fresno St	QB
2003	Cincinnati	Carson Palmer, Southern California	QB
2004	San Diego	Eli Manning, Mississippi	QB
2005	San Francisco	Alex Smith, Utah	QB

From 1947 through 1958, the first selection in the draft was a bonus pick, awarded to the winner of a random draw. That club, in turn, forfeited its last-round draft choice. The winner of the bonus choice was eliminated from future draws. The system was abolished after 1958, by which time all clubs had received a bonus choice.

Members of the Pro Football Hall of Fame

Herb Adderley	Fred Biletnikoff	Dave Casper
George Allen	George Blanda	Guy Chamberlin
Marcus Allen	Mel Blount	Jack Christiansen
Lance Alworth	Terry Bradshaw	Earl (Dutch) Clark
Doug Atkins	Bob (the Boomer) Brown	George Connor
Morris (Red) Badgro	Jim Brown	Jimmy Conzelman
Lem Barney	Paul Brown	Lou Creekmur
Cliff Battles	Roosevelt Brown	Larry Csonka
Sammy Baugh	Willie Brown	Al Davis
Chuck Bednarik	Buck Buchanan	Willie Davis
Bert Bell	Nick Buoniconti	Len Dawson
Bobby Bell	Dick Butkus	Joe DeLamielleure
Raymond Berry	Earl Campbell	Eric Dickerson
Elvin Bethea	Tony Canadeo	Dan Dierdorf
Charles W. Bidwill Sr.	Joe Carr	Mike Ditka

Art Donovan
Tony Dorsett
John (Paddy) Driscoll
Bill Dudley
Albert Glen (Turk) Edwards
Carl Eller
John Elway
Weeb Ewbank
Tom Fears
Jim Finks
Ray Flaherty
Len Ford
Dan Fortmann
Dan Fouts
Benny Friedman
Frank Gatski
Bill George
Joe Gibbs
Frank Gifford
Sid Gillman
Otto Graham
Harold (Red) Grange
Bud Grant
Joe Greene
Forrest Gregg
Bob Griese
Lou Groza
Joe Guyon
George Halas
Jack Ham
Dan Hampton
John Hannah
Franco Harris
Mike Haynes
Ed Healey
Mel Hein
Ted Hendricks
Wilbur (Pete) Henry
Arnie Herber
Bill Hewitt
Clarke Hinkle
Elroy (Crazylegs) Hirsch
Paul Hornung
Ken Houston
Cal Hubbard
Sam Huff
Lamar Hunt
Don Hutson
Jimmy Johnson
John Henry Johnson
Charlie Joiner
David (Deacon) Jones
Stan Jones
Henry Jordan
Sonny Jurgensen
Jim Kelly
Leroy Kelly
Walt Kiesling
Frank (Bruiser) Kinard
Paul Krause
Earl (Curly) Lambeau
Jack Lambert

Tom Landry
Dick (Night Train) Lane
Jim Langer
Willie Lanier
Steve Largent
Yale Lary
Dante Lavelli
Bobby Layne
Alphonse (Tuffy) Leemans
Marv Levy
Bob Lilly
Larry Little
James Lofton
Vince Lombardi
Howie Long
Ronnie Lott
Sid Luckman
William Roy (Link) Lyman
Tom Mack
John Mackey
Tim Mara
Wellington Mara
Gino Marchetti
Dan Marino
George Preston Marshall
Ollie Matson
Don Maynard
George McAfee
Mike McCormack
Tommy McDonald
Hugh McElhenny
Johnny (Blood) McNally
Mike Michalske
Wayne Millner
Bobby Mitchell
Ron Mix
Joe Montana
Lenny Moore
Marion Motley
Mike Munchak
Anthony Munoz
George Musso
Bronko Nagurski
Joe Namath
Earle (Greasy) Neale
Ernie Nevers
Ozzie Newsome
Ray Nitschke
Chuck Noll
Leo Nomellini
Merlin Olsen
Jim Otto
Steve Owen
Alan Page
Clarence (Ace) Parker
Jim Parker
Walter Payton
Joe Perry
Pete Pihos
Fritz Pollard
Hugh (Shorty) Ray
Dan Reeves
Mel Renfro

John Riggins
Jim Ringo
Andy Robustelli
Art Rooney
Dan Rooney
Pete Rozelle
Bob St. Clair
Barry Sanders
Gale Sayers
Joe Schmidt
Tex Schramm
Lee Roy Selmon
Billy Shaw
Art Shell
Don Shula
O.J. Simpson
Mike Singletary
Jackie Slater
Jackie Smith
John Stallworth
Bart Starr
Roger Staubach
Ernie Stautner
Jan Stenerud
Dwight Stephenson
Hank Stram
Ken Strong
Joe Stydahar
Lynn Swann
Fran Tarkenton
Charley Taylor
Jim Taylor
Lawrence Taylor
Jim Thorpe
Y.A. Tittle
George Trafton
Charley Trippi
Emlen Tunnell
Clyde (Bulldog) Turner
Johnny Unitas
Gene Upshaw
Norm Van Brocklin
Steve Van Buren
Doak Walker
Bill Walsh
Paul Warfield
Bob Waterfield
Mike Webster
Arnie Weinmeister
Randy White
Dave Wilcox
Bill Willis
Larry Wilson
Kellen Winslow
Alex Wojciechowicz
Willie Wood
Ron Yary
Steve Young
Jack Youngblood

Champions of Other Leagues

Canadian Football League Grey Cup

Year	Results	Site	Attendance
1909	U of Toronto 26, Parkdale 6	Toronto	3,807
1910	U of Toronto 16, Hamilton Tigers 7	Hamilton	12,000
1911	U of Toronto 14, Toronto 7	Toronto	13,687
1912	Hamilton Alerts 11, Toronto 4	Hamilton	5,337
1913	Hamilton Tigers 44, Parkdale 2	Hamilton	2,100
1914	Toronto 14, U of Toronto 2	Toronto	10,500
1915	Hamilton Tigers 13, Toronto RAA 7	Toronto	2,808
1916–19	No game	—	—
1920	U of Toronto 16, Toronto 3	Toronto	10,088
1921	Toronto 23, Edmonton 0	Toronto	9,558
1922	Queen's U 13, Edmonton 1	Kingston	4,700
1923	Queen's U 54, Regina 0	Toronto	8,629
1924	Queen's U 11, Balmy Beach 3	Toronto	5,978
1925	Ottawa Senators 24, Winnipeg 1	Ottawa	6,900
1926	Ottawa Senators 10, Toronto U 7	Toronto	8,276
1927	Balmy Beach 9, Hamilton Tigers 6	Toronto	13,676
1928	Hamilton Tigers 30, Regina 0	Hamilton	4,767
1929	Hamilton Tigers 14, Regina 3	Hamilton	1,906
1930	Balmy Beach 11, Regina 6	Toronto	3,914
1931	Montreal AAA 22, Regina 0	Montreal	5,112
1932	Hamilton Tigers 25, Regina 6	Hamilton	4,806
1933	Toronto 4, Sarnia 3	Sarnia	2,751
1934	Sarnia 20, Regina 12	Toronto	8,900
1935	Winnipeg 18, Hamilton Tigers 12	Hamilton	6,405
1936	Sarnia 26, Ottawa RR 20	Toronto	5,883
1937	Toronto 4, Winnipeg 3	Toronto	11,522
1938	Toronto 30, Winnipeg 7	Toronto	18,778
1939	Winnipeg 8, Ottawa 7	Ottawa	11,738
1940	Ottawa 12, Balmy Beach 5	Ottawa	1,700
1940	Ottawa 8, Balmy Beach 2	Toronto	4,998
1941	Winnipeg 18, Ottawa 16	Toronto	19,065
1942	Toronto RCAF 8, Winnipeg RCAF 5	Toronto	12,455
1943	Hamilton F Wild 23, Winnipeg RCAF 14	Toronto	16,423
1944	Montreal St H-D Navy 7, Hamilton F Wild 6	Hamilton	3,871
1945	Toronto 35, Winnipeg 0	Toronto	18,660
1946	Toronto 28, Winnipeg 6	Toronto	18,960
1947	Toronto 10, Winnipeg 9	Toronto	18,885
1948	Calgary 12, Ottawa 7	Toronto	20,013
1949	Montreal Als 28, Calgary 15	Toronto	20,087
1950	Toronto 13, Winnipeg 0	Toronto	27,101
1951	Ottawa 21, Saskatchewan 14	Toronto	27,341
1952	Toronto 21, Edmonton 11	Toronto	27,391
1953	Hamilton Ticats 12, Winnipeg 6	Toronto	27,313
1954	Edmonton 26, Montreal 25	Toronto	27,321
1955	Edmonton 34, Montreal 19	Vancouver	39,417
1956	Edmonton 50, Montreal 27	Toronto	27,425
1957	Hamilton 32, Winnipeg 7	Toronto	27,051
1958	Winnipeg 35, Hamilton 28	Vancouver	36,567
1959	Winnipeg 21, Hamilton 7	Toronto	33,133
1960	Ottawa 16, Edmonton 6	Vancouver	38,102
1961	Winnipeg 21, Hamilton 14	Toronto	32,651
1962	Winnipeg 28, Hamilton 27	Toronto	32,655
1963	Hamilton 21, British Columbia 10	Vancouver	36,545
1964	British Columbia 34, Hamilton 24	Toronto	32,655
1965	Hamilton 22, Winnipeg 16	Toronto	32,655
1966	Saskatchewan 29, Ottawa 14	Vancouver	36,553
1967	Hamilton 24, Saskatchewan 1	Ottawa	31,358
1968	Ottawa 24, Calgary 21	Toronto	32,655
1969	Ottawa 29, Saskatchewan 11	Montreal	33,172
1970	Montreal 23, Calgary 10	Toronto	32,669
1971	Calgary 14, Toronto 11	Vancouver	34,484
1972	Hamilton 13, Saskatchewan 10	Hamilton	33,993
1973	Ottawa 22, Edmonton 18	Toronto	36,653
1974	Montreal 20, Edmonton 7	Vancouver	34,450
1975	Edmonton 9, Montreal 8	Calgary	32,454

Canadian Football League Grey Cup (Cont.)

Year	Results	Site	Attendance
1976	Ottawa 23, Saskatchewan 20	Toronto	53,467
1977	Montreal 41, Edmonton 6	Montreal	68,318
1978	Edmonton 20, Montreal 13	Toronto	54,695
1979	Edmonton 17, Montreal 9	Montreal	65,113
1980	Edmonton 48, Hamilton 10	Toronto	54,661
1981	Edmonton 26, Ottawa 23	Montreal	52,478
1982	Edmonton 32, Toronto 16	Toronto	54,741
1983	Toronto 18, British Columbia 17	Vancouver	59,345
1984	Winnipeg 47, Hamilton 17	Edmonton	60,081
1985	British Columbia 37, Hamilton 24	Montreal	56,723
1986	Hamilton 39, Edmonton 15	Vancouver	59,621
1987	Edmonton 38, Toronto 36	Vancouver	59,478
1988	Winnipeg 22, British Columbia 21	Ottawa	50,604
1989	Saskatchewan 43, Hamilton 40	Toronto	54,088
1990	Winnipeg 50, Edmonton 11	Vancouver	46,968
1991	Toronto 36, Calgary 21	Winnipeg	51,985
1992	Calgary 24, Winnipeg 10	Toronto	45,863
1993	Edmonton 33, Winnipeg 23	Calgary	50,035
1994	British Columbia 26, Baltimore 23	Vancouver	55,097
1995	Baltimore 37, Calgary 20	Regina, Saskatchewan	52,564
1996	Toronto 43, Edmonton 37	Hamilton, Ontario	38,595
1997	Toronto 47, Saskatchewan 23	Edmonton	60,431
1998	Calgary 26, Hamilton 24	Winnipeg	34,157
1999	Hamilton 32, Calgary 21	Vancouver	45,118
2000	British Columbia 28, Montreal 26	Calgary	43,822
2001	Calgary 27, Winnipeg 19	Montreal	65,255
2002	Montreal 25, Edmonton 16	Edmonton	62,531
2003	Edmonton 34, Montreal 22	Regina, Saskatchewan	50,909
2004	Toronto 27, British Columbia 19	Ottawa	51,242

In 1909, Earl Grey, the Governor-General of Canada, donated a trophy for the Rugby Football Championship of Canada. The trophy, which subsequently became known as the Grey Cup, was originally open only to teams registered with the Canada Rugby Union. Since 1954, it has been awarded to the winner of the Canadian Football League's championship game.

AMERICAN FOOTBALL LEAGUE I

Year	Champion	Record
1926	Philadelphia Quakers	7-2

AMERICAN FOOTBALL LEAGUE II

Year	Champion	Record
1936	Boston Shamrocks	8-3
1937	LA Bulldogs	8-0

AMERICAN FOOTBALL LEAGUE III

Year	Champion	Record
1940	Columbus Bullies	8-1-1
1941	Columbus Bullies	5-1-2

ALL-AMERICAN FOOTBALL CONFERENCE

Year	Championship Game
1946	Cleveland 14, NY Yankees 9
1947	Cleveland 14, NY Yankees 3
1948	Cleveland 49, Buffalo 7
1949	Cleveland 21, San Francisco 7

WORLD FOOTBALL LEAGUE

Year	World Bowl Championship
1974	Birmingham 22, Florida 21
1975	Disbanded midseason

UNITED STATES FOOTBALL LEAGUE

Year	Championship Game
1983	Michigan 24, Philadelphia 22
1984	Philadelphia 23, Arizona 3
1985	Baltimore 28, Oakland 24

NFL EUROPE

Year	Champion	Record
1991	London	9-1-0
1992	Sacramento	8-2-0
1995	Frankfurt	6-4-0
1996	Scotland	7-3-0
1997	Barcelona	5-5-0
1998	Rhein	7-3-0
1999	Frankfurt	6-4-0
2000	Rhein	7-3-0
2001	Berlin	6-4-0
2002	Berlin	6-4-0
2003	Frankfurt	6-4-0
2004	Berlin	9-1-0
2005	Amsterdam	6-4-0

Known as World League of American Football until 1998.

2004 Heisman Trophy winner Matt Leinart led USC to its second-straight national championship.

College Football

Coast to Coast

USC lived up to enormous expectations by going undefeated and winning its second-straight title at Miami's Orange Bowl

BY B.J. SCHECTER

SC coach Pete Carroll is 53 going on 25. He lives every day like a kid on Christmas morning and puts the "E" in enthusiastic. He has been known to play pickup basketball with his players and toss the football around with them before and after games. At one practice, he even played the role of scout team quarterback in a live goal-line drill, leaping over a pair of 270-pound linemen into the end zone—all of this without wearing pads or a helmet. Carroll's rah-rah act didn't fly in the NFL—he was fired after short stints as head coach of the Jets and the Patriots—but his method and his sharp mind have helped take the Trojans back to the top of the college football world.

Before Carroll was hired in December, 2000, USC was mired in mediocrity. It hadn't won a national title in 24 years and recruits were fleeing the Los Angeles area faster than a Big Mac in front of Kirstie Alley. To try to bring USC back to where it was in its heyday—between 1972 and 1979 the Trojans finished No. 1 or No. 2 five times—Carroll used his high-energy approach to renew excitement about football at the school. He tirelessly talked up his program, speaking to recruits more like they were his best friends and telling anyone who would listen about his vision of how to make USC a power again. "This is what SC can be," he said, "as dominant as parity will allow. Ain't no SCs in the NFL."

The commitments started rolling in, practice was fun again and the Trojans played harder and harder for Carroll. He started freshmen right away and confidence began to build; underachievers started to overachieve, lo and behold, USC started winning....and winning....and winning. The Trojans won a co-national title in 2003 with LSU, despite the convoluted BCS computer inexplicably leaving them out of the national championship game even though they were ranked No. 1. But instead of complaining and losing focus after getting shut out of the national championship game, Carroll took the news in stride and in California-like fashion said, in effect, whatever. Carroll

Carroll's intensity and dogged preparation helped USC to victory in the Orange Bowl.

knew that if his team just worried about winning they would get their due and by dominating Michigan in the Rose Bowl, they did.

USC entered the 2004 season as the unanimous favorite to repeat and quickly proved it could play the role of the hunted. Despite losing star receivers Mike Williams (who was denied eligibility by the NCAA when he tried to return after declaring for the NFL draft) and Keary Colbert (whose eligibility expired), they still had plenty of offensive firepower in quarterback Matt Leinart and all-purpose threat Reggie Bush. After early scares against Stanford and Cal, the Trojans kicked into high gear, never losing their No. 1 ranking and earning the right to defend their national title in the Orange Bowl. (This year, it was undefeated Auburn who was left out of the BCS championship game; more on that later).

All season USC and Oklahoma were on a crash course for on e another, and despite all the carping from fans and pundits about the BCS, this was the game most everyone

wanted to see. After a disappointing 2003 season, which ended with ugly losses in the Big 12 and national championship games, Oklahoma dominated opponents and appeared to have the weapons on both sides of the ball to match USC. Oft-injured quarterback Jason White was granted a sixth year of eligibility and was eager to show he was the player who won the Heisman and not the one who sputtered in the Sooners' final two losses. Oklahoma's offensive line and defense were as strong as ever and the Sooners added an x-factor that they had sorely lacked: a phenomenal freshman running back named Adrian Peterson.

The consensus high school player of the year in 2003, Peterson lived up to the considerable hype and provided a much-needed boost to the Sooners' rushing attack. Nicknamed "A.D." as a child for his ability to play sports all day, Peterson ran through opponents and around them, drawing comparisons to Eric Dickerson. In his first 12 games, he rushed for 1,843 yards, scored 15 touchdowns and nearly became the first freshman ever to win the Heisman Trophy (he finished second in the voting). Because of Peterson's legs and White's arm, this Oklahoma team was thought by many to be better than the one that won the national championship in 2000.

Though Auburn and Utah also finished the regular season undefeated (can you say playoff?), few disputed that USC and Oklahoma deserved to play for the national title. The similarities between the two storied programs were staggering. USC had won 10 national titles, Oklahoma seven; both teams were extremely well-coached, possessed high-powered offenses, stout defenses and were statistically identical in nearly every category. USC entered the Orange Bowl as a 1 1/2-point favorite in what was billed as the Game of the Century. As things turned out, it wasn't even the Game of the Week.

In a stunning annihilation, USC dominated Oklahoma in every facet of the game, rolling up 525 yards of offense, holding Peterson to 82 meaningless yards, forcing five turnovers and cruising to a 55-19 victory. Leinart, who threw for 322 yards and five touchdowns (four in the first half), had so much time in the pocket it seemed like he was wearing his red practice jersey and playing against a scout team defense that was prohibited from hitting him.

Trojans' Leinart was obviously well prepared and attacked the Sooners defense with precision. Sooners freshman corner Marcus Walker—only 5'8"— became a frequent victim of Leinart's accuracy. Forced to cover the 6'3" Dwayne Jarrett, Walker was clearly outmatched, giving up five catches for 115 yards and a touchdown. Similarly, the Trojans never allowed Oklahoma's offense to gain momentum. With a dominating defensive line led by Shaun Cody and a swarming group of linebackers bolstered by Lofa Tatupu, USC knew Oklahoma's plays better than the Sooners did. Said Cody of Tatupu, "You should have seen him back there, calling out their plays—

'Left! Right! Screen!' It was like he was in their huddle."

When the Trojans gathered at midfield after the game, they raised their helmets in jubilation knowing that they had won 22 straight games, back-to-back national titles and had laid the groundwork for what could be a dynasty. And with just six senior starters next year, including Leinart, who made a surprise annuncement a week after the game that he would return for his final season, the Trojans' run isn't likely to end any time soon.

"We have structured our program to be able to carry on with the losses that occur, whether it was Carson Palmer or Troy Polamulu or the five running backs we lost a couple of years ago or Mike Williams or Keary Colbert or whatever," said Carroll. "As long as I can hang in there, I can keep it together …I think we're a program on the move. I think we're coming up, and we've got a very good football team and we've got a lot of high hopes for sustaining over a long haul. The big 'D' word. I think anybody that makes that statement is like people talking in the third person."

By season's end many people were talking about Auburn, which made a statement by finishing 13-0, bolstering the case for a playoff. In 2003, the Tigers were picked as the preseason No. 1 by a few national publications, but they couldn't handle the pressure and finished 8-5. Coach Tommy Tuberville nearly got fired and not much was expected of Auburn entering this season. The Tigers weren't ranked in the Top 10 at the start of the season, but with 13 returning starters, including the nation's best backfield in Carnell (Cadillac) Williams, Ronnie Brown and quarterback Jason Campbell, they had plenty of talent to make a run. After a 10-9 victory over defending national champ LSU in September, the Tigers took off.

Remarkably, they ran the table in the rugged SEC—perennially considered by many to be the toughest conference in the nation—and finished the regular season 12-0. Though Auburn got shut out of the Orange Bowl, the Tigers had an outside shot at a co-championship if they could dominate

Auburn running backs Carnell (Cadillac) Williams (l.) and Ronnie Brown proved to be a potent combiantion in the Tiger backfield.

Virginia Tech in the Sugar Bowl. But not many teams dominate the Hokies (USC struggled against Tech in a season-opening 24-13 victory) and though Auburn won 16-13, it wasn't enough to convince the Associated Press voters to rank the Tigers No. 1. Still, there was little doubt Auburn had a championship season.

"I know we're national champions," said Campbell. "We're 13-0. We beat four Top 10 teams [more than any other team in the country]. Really, I don't care what anybody says. We're national champions."

Utah didn't win the national championship, but the Utes had plenty to celebrate. Not only did they finish undefeated, but they also crashed the BCS party. Never before had a team outside the six major conferences played in a BCS Bowl game, but from the start of the season the Utes proved that they were no mid-major. Using an innovative, wide-open spread-option attack, coach Urban Meyer's high-flying team thrashed Texas A&M of the Big 12, Arizona of the

Pac-10 and North Carolina of the ACC to earn an invitation to the Fiesta Bowl. There, Utah manhandled Pittsburgh 35-7 leaving many observers wondering if a Utah-Auburn matchup would have been more exciting.

Meyer constantly pushed the envelope with his offensive schemes, a process he had been developing for years during his stops as assistant coach at Ohio State and Notre Dame. "He was constantly coming up with ideas of how to spread the ball," said Utes offensive coordinator Mike Sanford, who was on the Irish staff with Meyer. "We'd put together entire game plans that just wouldn't fly in the offense Notre Dame was running."

That same offensive philosophy, however, took off at Utah. With an athletic quarterback who could run and pass in Alex Smith, the Utes averaged 46.3 points and 502.7 yards per game. When it clicked, which was usually, opponents had no way to stop it. Meyer, who was 22-2 in two years at Utah, was such a hot commodity that Notre Dame and Florida started jockeying over his services before Utah had played its bowl game. In one circus-like week in December, Notre Dame fired coach Tyrone Willingham, figur-

AL. TIELEMANS

mony turned out to be a pairs competition as two Sooners, two Trojans and Utah quarterback Alex Smith (interestingly, Smith and Bush were high school teammates) were named finalists. The award went to Leinart, but Peterson was probably the best player and lost votes to White.

What would a season be without a BCS controversy to end the year? Entering the final week of the regular season, Cal was ahead of Texas in the polls and in the BCS. But Longhorns coach Mack Brown thought his team deserved to go to a BCS bowl and started lobbying coaches and members of the AP. And despite the fact that Cal beat Southern Miss on the road in its season-finale, Texas jumped over them to earn a berth in the Rose Bowl, while the Bears were relegated to the Holiday Bowl. Texas did beat Michigan in a thrilling Rose Bowl, but the flap over the poll flip-flop was one of the major reasons why the AP decided to remove its poll from the BCS.

There were plenty of other changes—most notably coaches. And while many were fired and others retired, the biggest move was Steve Spurrier replacing Lou Holtz at South Carolina. After spurning a return to Florida, Spurrier brought his fun-and-gun offense to the Gamecocks, meaning the SEC just got a lot more interesting.

It might take a few years for Spurrier to turn South Carolina into a national championship contender, but if the 'ol ball coach wants to win right away he might want to follow Pete Carroll's blueprint: recruit, recruit, recruit and play your players right away. With a core of young talent and another stellar recruiting class, USC continues to be the gold standard of programs. Yes, USC is back, and as long as Carroll is roaming the sidelines—enthusiasm bursting out of his body—the Trojans will hold their rightful place on top of the college football world.

ing that they could land Meyer. But the Gators interviewed Meyer the same day and convinced him to come to Gainesville, leaving Notre Dame in the lurch. (The Irish eventually hired New England Patriots offensive coordinator Charlie Weis, but he didn't start until February, after helping the Pats win their second straight Super Bowl).

Oklahoma's Jason White didn't win his second straight Heisman Trophy, but he came close. After a dreadful end to the 2003 season in which he won the award, White found all the motivation he needed to come back whenever he went out in public. "I'd be walking in the mall, and someone would make a comment," said White. "'Give back the Heisman,' that sort of thing. You hear something like that when you're with your family, it's embarrassing."

White did nothing to embarrass himself in 2004, however, and he combined with Adrian Peterson to form one of the best 1-2 punches in the nation. Only problem was, USC had a quarterback/running back combination just as dangerous in Matt Leinart and Reggie Bush. And the Heisman Trophy cere-

Final Polls

Associated Press

		Record	Pts	SI Preseason Head Coach	Rank
1.	USC (62)	13-0	1622	Pete Carroll	1
2.	Auburn (3)	13-0	1559	Tommy Tuberville	13
3.	Oklahoma	12-1	1454	Bob Stoops	2
4.	Utah	12-0	1438	Kyle Whittingham	19
5.	Texas	11-1	1391	Mack Brown	7
6.	Louisville	11-1	1261	Bobby Petrino	34
7.	Georgia	10-2	1204	Mark Richt	4
8.	Iowa	10-2	1111	Kirk Ferentz	15
9.	California	10-2	1060	Jeff Tedford	22
10.	Virginia Tech	10-3	996	Frank Beamer	38
11.	Miami	9-3	917	Larry Coker	5
12.	Boise State	11-1	888	Dan Hawkins	44
13.	Tennessee	10-3	868	Phillip Fulmer	11
13.	Michigan	9-3	842	Lloyd Carr	12
15.	Florida State	9-3	754	Bobby Bowden	9
16.	LSU	9-3	711	Les Miles	3
17.	Wisconsin	9-3	482	Barry Alvarez	26
18.	Texas Tech	8-4	476	Mike Leach	39
18.	Arizona State	9-3	463	Dirk Koetter	51
20.	Ohio State	8-4	423	Jim Tressel	8
21.	Boston College	9-3	314	Tom O'Brien	29
22.	Fresno State	9-3	203	Pat Hill	40
23.	Virginia	8-4	157	Al Groh	31
24.	Navy	10-2	126	Paul Johnson	67
25.	Pittsburgh	8-4	99	Dave Wannstedt	56

USA Today/ESPN

		Pts	SI Preseason Rank			Pts	SI Preseason Rank
1.	USC (61)	1525	1	13.	Boise State	792	44
2.	Auburn	1460	13	14.	Florida State	776	9
3.	Oklahoma	1366	2	15.	Tennessee	771	11
4.	Texas	1324	7	16.	LSU	693	3
5.	Utah	1300	19	17.	Texas Tech	478	39
6.	Georgia	1191	4	18.	Wisconsin	449	26
7.	Louisville	1166	34	19.	Ohio State	430	8
8.	Iowa	1022	15	20.	Arizona State	377	51
9.	California	937	22	21.	Boston College	245	29
10.	Virginia Tech	906	38	22.	Fresno State	206	40
11.	Miami	903	5	23.	Virginia	157	31
12.	Michigan	802	12	24.	Navy	129	67
				25.	Florida	101	6

Note: Voted by a panel of 60 Div. I-A head coaches; 25 points for 1st, 24 for 2nd, etc.(1st place votes in parentheses).

Bowls and Playoffs

NCAA Division I-A Bowl Results

Note: As voted by a panel of 72 sportswriters and broadcasters following bowl games (1sotes in parentheses).

Date	Bowl	Result	Payout/Team ($)	Attendance
12-14-04	New Orleans	Southern Miss 31, North Texas 10	750,000	27,253
12-21-04	Champs Sports	Georgia Tech 51, Syracuse 14	750,000	28,237
12-22-04	GMAC	Bowling Green 52, Memphis 35	750,000	29,500
12-23-04	Fort Worth	Cincinati 32,Marshall 14	750,000	27,902
12-23-04	Las Vegas	Wyoming 24, UCLA 21	800,000	29,062
12-24-04	Hawaii	Hawaii 59, UAB 40	750,000	39,754
12-27-04	Motor City	Connecticut 39,, Toledo 10	800,000	52,552
12-27-04	MPC Computers	Fresno State 37, Virginia 34 [OT]	750,000	28,516
12-28-04	Independence	Iowa State 17, Miami(OH) 13	1.2 million	43,000
12-28-04	Insight	Oregon State 38, Notre Dame 21	750,000	45,917

NCAA Division I-A Bowl Results (Cont.)

Date	Bowl	Result	Payout/Team($)	Attendance
12-29-04	Houston	Colorado 33, UTEP 28	1.0 million	27,235
12-29-04	Alamo	Ohio State 33, Oklahoma State 7	1.45 million	65,265
12-30-04	Holiday	Texas Tech 45, California 31	2 million	63,711
12-30-04	Silicon Valley	Northern Illinois 34, Troy 21	750,000	21,456
12-30-04	Continental Tire	Boston College 37, Noth Carolina 24	750,000	70,412
12-30-04	Emerald	Navy 34, New Mexico 19	825,000	30,563
12-31-04	Liberty	Louisville 44, Boise State 40	1.35 million	58,355
12-31-04	Peach	Miami (FL) 27, Florida 10	2.3 million	69,322
12-31-04	Music City	Minesota 20, Alabama 16	950,000	66,089
12-31-04	Sun	Arizona State 27, Purdue 23	1.45 million	51,288
1-1-05	Rose	Texas 38, Michigan 37	14 million	93,468
1-1-05	Fiesta	Utah 35, Pittsburgh 7	14 million	73,519
1-1-05	Gator	Florida State 30, West Virginia 18	1.825 million	70,112
1-1-05	Capitol One	Iowa 30, LSU 25	5.125 million	70,229
1-1-05	Cotton	Tennessee 38, Texas A&M 7	3 million	75,704
1-1-05	Outback	Georgia 24, Wisconson 21	2.65 million	62,414
1-3-05	Sugar	Auburn 16, Virginia Tech 13	14 million	77,349
1-4-05	Orange	USC 55, Oklahoma 19	14 million	77,912

NCAA Division I-AA Championship Box Score

James Madison	0	10	14	7 —31
Montana	7	0	14	0- —21

FIRST QUARTER

Mon: Heidelberger 3 pass from Ochs (Snyder kick), 10:08.

SECOND QUARTER

JM: Rabil 28 kick, 8:54.
JM: Fenner 1 run (Rabil kick), 0:16.

THIRD QUARTER

JM: Rascati 11 run (Rabil kick), 11:54.
Mon: Segars 17 pass from Ochs (Snyder kick), 8:51.
Mon: Walden 8 pass from Ochs (Snyder Kick), 7:29
JM: Fenner 1 run (Rabil kick) 3:25

FOURTH QUARTER

JM: Rascati 6 run (Rabil kick), 8:00.

	JAMES MADISON	MONTANA
First downs	32	21
Rushes–yards	61–314	23–44
Passing yards	132	371
Comp/Att/Int	13-18-0	29-38-1
Punts	2–41.5	1–35.0
Fumbles-lost	2–1	1–0
Penalties-yards	6-55	9–70
Time of possession	36:13	23:47

Att: 16,771.

Small College Championship Summaries

NCAA DIVISION II

First round: LI-Cw Post 3, West Chester 35; N Dakota 20, St. Cloud St. 17; Midwest. St. 33, Colorado Mines 52; Catawba 20, Arkansas Tech 24; Edinboro 47, Bentley 44; Grand Val. St. 16, Winona St. 13; SE Okl. St. 30, Tex. A&M King. 40; Fayetteville St. 14, Carson -Newman 35
Second Round: Grnd Val. St. 10, Northwood 7; West Chester 33, Shippensburg 28; N Dakota 20, MIchigan Tech 3; Arkansas Tech 24, Albany St. 42; Texas A&M King. 14, NW Miss. St. 34;Edinboro 32 East Strdsbrg 36; Colorado Mines 35, Pittsburg St. 70; Carson-Newman 12, Valdosta St. 38
Quarterfinals: NW Miss St. 36, Pittsburg St. 50; Grand Val. St. 15, N Dakota 19; West Chester 48, East Strdsbrg 38; Valdosta St. 38, Albany St. 24
Semifinals: N Dakota 19, Pittsburg St. 31; West Chester 21, Valdosta St. 45

Championship: 12-11-04

Pittsburg St.	0	17	9	10—31
Valdosta St.	14	3	7	7—36

NCAA DIVISION III

First round: St. Norbert 23, Wis.-La Crosse 37; Curry 16, Hobart 35; Mary Hardin- Baylor 32, Trinity(TX) 13; Mt. St. Joseph 7, Wheaton 31; Shenandoah 17, Deleware Valley 21; Aurora 34, Wooster 41; Wartburg 14, Concordia-Moor. 28; St. John Fisher 31, Muhlenberg 3; Wash & Jeff. 55; Carthage 31, Alma 28; Chris. Newport 35, Sal. St. 24; Willamette 14, Occidental 28
Second Round: Wis.-La Crosse 14, Lifield 52; Hobart 14, Rowan 45; Mary Hardin-Baylor 42, Hardin Simmons 28; Wheaton 6, Mount Union 27; Occidental 42, Concordia- Moor. 40; St. John Fisher 20, Del. Valley 26; Chris. BNewport 14, Wash. & Jeff. 24; Carthage 14, Wooster 7
Quarterfinals: Occidental 27, Lifield 56; Mary Hardin-Baylor 52, Wash & Jeff. 16; Del. Valley 7, Rowan 56; Carthage 20, Mount Union 38
Semifinals: Mary Hardin-Baylor 38, Mount Union 35; Lifield 52, Rowan 0

Championship: 12-18-04

Linfield	7	14	0	7—28
Mary Hardin-Baylor	7	6	0	8—21

NAIA CHAMPIONSHIP

12-18-04 Savannah, TN

Carroll	0	6	0	9—15
St. Francis	7	0	0	6—13

Awards

Heisman Memorial Trophy

Player, School	Class	Pos	1st	2nd	3rd	Total
Matt Leinart, USC	Jr	QB	267	211	102	1,325
Adrian Peterson, Oklahoma	So	RB	154	180	175	997
Jason White, Oklahoma	Sr	QB	171	149	146	957
Alex Smith, Utah	Jr	QB	· 98	112	117	635
Reggie Bush, USC	Jr	RB	118	80	83	597

Note: Former Heisman winners and the media vote, with ballots allowing for three names (3 points for 1st, 2 for 2nd, 1 for 3rd).

Other Awards

Maxwell Award (Player) ....Jason White, Oklahoma, QB
Sporting News Player of the Year ....Alex Smith, Utah, QB
Walter Camp Player of the Year ....Matt Leinart, USC, QB
Chuck Bednarik Award (Defense) ....David Pollack, Georgia, LB
Vince Lombardi/Rotary Award (Lineman/LB) ....David Pollack, Georgia ,LB
Outland Trophy (Interior Lineman) ....Jammal Brown,Oklahoma, OT
Davey O'Brien Award (QB) ....Jason White, Oklahoma, QB
Unitas Golden Arm Award (Senior QB) ....Jason White, Oklahoma, QB
Doak Walker Award (RB) ....Cedric Benson, Texas, RB
Biletnikoff Award (WR)..Braylon Edwards, Michigan,WR
Butkus Award (Linebacker) ....Derrick Johnson, Texas, LB
Jim Thorpe Award (Defensive Back).........................Carlos Rogers, Auburn, DB
Associated Press Player of the Year ....Matt Leinart, USC, QB
Walter Payton Award (Div I-AA Player).........Lang Campbell, William & Mary, QB
Harlon Hill Trophy (Div II Player) ....Chad Friehauf, Colorado Mlnes, QB
Gagliardi Trophy (Div III Player) ....Rocky Myers, Wesley (Del.), SS

Coaches' Awards

Walter Camp Award ....Tommy Tuberville, Auburn
Eddie Robinson Award (Div I-AA) ....Urban Meyer, Utah
Bobby Dodd Award..Paul Johnson, Navy
Bear Bryant Award ....Tommy Tuberville, Auburn

AFCA COACHES OF THE YEAR

Division I-A ....Tommy Tuberville, Auburn
Division I-AA...Mickey Matthews, James Madison
Division II...Chris Hatcher, Valdosta State
Division III..Jay Locey, Linfield

Football Writers Association of America All-America Team

OFFENSE

QB........Alex Smith, Utah, Jr
RB .......J.J. Arrington, California, Sr
RB ....Adrain Peterson, Oklahoma, Fr
WR ......Braylon Edwards, Michigan, Sr
WR ......Taylor Stubblefield, Purdue, Sr
TE ....Heath Miller, Virginia, Jr
OL ....David Baas, Michigan, Sr
OL ....Jammal Brown, Oklahoma, Sr
OL ....Alex Barron, Florida State, Sr
OL ....Chris Kemoeatu, Utah, Jr
C ....Greg Eslinger, Minesota, Jr
K ....Mike Nugent, Ohio State, Sr
KR ....Reggie BUsh, USC, So

DEFENSE

DL ....Dan Cody, Oklahoma, Sr
DL ....Shaun Cody, USC, Sr
DL ....Jonathan Goddard, Marshall, Sr
DL ....Erasmus James, Wisconsin, Sr
DL ....David Pollack, Georgia, Sr
LB ....Michael Boley, Southern Miss, Sr
LB ....Derrick Johnson, Texas, Sr
DB........Carlos Rogers, Auburn, Sr
DB........Antrel Rolle, Miami, Sr
DB........Ernest Shazor, Michigan, Sr
DB........Marlon Jackson, Michigan Sr
P ....Brandon Fields, Michigan State, So

Division I-A

ATLANTIC COAST CONFERENCE

	Conference		Full Season		
	W	L	W	L	Pct
Virginia Tech	7	1	10	3	.769
Florida St.	6	2	9	3	.750
Miami	5	3	9	3	.750
Virginia	5	3	8	4	.667
North Carolina	5	3	6	6	.500
Georgia Tech	4	4	7	5	.583
Clemson	4	4	6	5	.545
N.C. State	3	5	5	6	.455
Maryland	3	5	5	6	.455
Wake Forest	1	7	4	7	.364
Duke	1	7	2	9	.182

BIG EAST CONFERENCE

	Conference		Full Season		
	W	L	W	L	Pct
Boston College	4	2	9	3	.750
Pittsburgh	4	2	8	4	.667
West Virginia	4	2	8	4	.667
Syracuse	4	2	6	6	.500
Connecticut	3	3	8	4	.667
Rutgers	1	5	4	7	.364
Temple	1	5	2	9	.182

BIG TEN CONFERENCE

	Conference		Full Season		
	W	L	W	L	Pct
Iowa	7	1	10	2	.833
Michigan	7	1	9	3	.750
Wisconson	6	2	9	3	.750
Northwestern	5	3	6	6	.500
Ohio State	4	4	8	4	.667
Purdue	4	4	7	5	.583
Michigan St.	4	4	5	7	.417
Minesota	3	5	7	5	.583
Penn St	2	6	4	7	.364
Illinois	1	7	3	8	.273
Indiana	1	7	3	8	.273

BIG 12 CONFERENCE

	Conference		Full Season		
NORTH	W	L	W	L	Pct
Colorado	4	4	8	5	.615
Iowa St.	4	4	7	5	.583
Missouri	3	5	5	6	.455
Nebraska	3	5	5	6	.455
Kansas	2	6	4	7	.364
Kansas St.	2	6	4	7	.364
SOUTH					
Oklahoma	8	0	12	1	.923
Texas	7	1	11	1	.917
Texas Tech	5	3	8	4	.750
Texas A&M	5	3	7	5	.583
Oklahoma St.	4	4	7	5	.583
Baylor	1	7	3	8	.273

Division I-A (Cont.)

CONFERENCE USA

	Conference		Full Season		
	W	L	W	L	Pct
Louisville	8	0	11	1	.917
Memphis	5	3	8	4	.667
UAB	5	3	7	5	.583
Cincinnati	5	3	7	5	.583
Southern Miss.	5	3	7	5	.583
TCU	3	5	5	6	.455
Tulane	3	5	5	6	.455
South Floridai	3	5	4	7	.364
Houston	3	5	3	8	.273
Army	2	6	2	9	.182
East Carolina	2	6	2	9	.182

MID-AMERICAN ATHLETIC CONFERENCE

	Conference		Full Season		
EAST	W	L	W	L	Pct
Miami (OH)	7	1	8	5	.615
Akron	6	2	6	5	.545
Marshall	6	2	6	6	.500
Kent St	4	4	5	6	.455
Ohio	2	6	4	7	.364
Buffalo	2	6	2	9	.182
Central Florida	0	8	0	11	.000
WEST					
Northern Illinois	7	1	9	3	.750
Toledo	7	1	9	4	.692
Bowling Green	6	2	9	3	.750
Eastern Michigan	4	4	4	7	.364
Central Michigan	3	5	4	7	.364
Ball State	2	6	2	9	.182
Western Michigan	0	8	1	10	.091

MOUNTAIN WEST CONFERENCE

	Conference		Full Season		
	W	L	W	L	Pct
Utah	7	0	12	0	1.000
New Mexico	5	5	7	5	.583
BYU	4	6	5	6	.455
Wyoming	3	5	7	5	.583
Air Force	3	6	5	6	.455
Colorado St.	3	7	4	7	.364
San Diego St.	2	7	4	7	.364
UNLV	1	9	2	9	.182

PACIFIC 10 CONFERENCE

	Conference		Full Season		
	W	L	W	L	Pct
Southern California	8	0	13	0	1.000
California	7	1	10	2	.833
Arizona St.	5	3	9	3	.750
Oregon St.	5	3	7	5	.583
UCLA	4	4	6	6	.500
Oregon	4	4	5	6	.455
Washington State	3	5	5	6	.455
Stanford	2	6	4	7	.364
Arizona	2	6	3	8	.273
Washington	0	8	1	10	.091

Division I-A (Cont.)

SOUTHEASTERN CONFERENCE

	Conference		Full Season		
EAST	W	L	W	L	Pct
Tennessee	7	1	10	3	.769
Georgia	6	2	10	2	.833
Florida	4	4	7	5	.583
S Carolina	4	4	6	5	.545
Kentucky	1	7	2	9	.182
Vanderbilt	1	7	2	9	.182
WEST					
Auburn	8	0	13	0	1.000
LSU	6	2	9	3	.750
Alabama	3	5	6	6	.500
Arkansas	3	5	5	6	.455
Mississippi	3	5	4	7	.364
Mississippi St.	2	6	3	8	.273

SUN BELT CONFERENCE

	Conference		Full Season		
	W	L	W	L	Pct
N Texas	7	0	7	5	.583
Troy	5	2	7	5	.583
New Mexico State	4	3	5	6	.455
Louisiana Monroe	4	3	5	6	.455
Middle Tenn. St.	4	4	5	6	.455
Arkansas St.	3	4	3	8	.273
Utah St	2	5	4	7	.364
La Lafayette	2	5	3	8	.273
Idaho	2	5	3	9	.250

WESTERN ATHLETIC CONFERENCE

	Conference		Full Season		
	W	L	W	L	Pct
Boise St.	8	0	11	1	.917
UTEP	6	2	8	4	.667
Fresno State	5	3	9	3	.750
Louisiana Tech	5	3	6	6	.500
Hawaii	4	4	8	5	.615
Nevada	3	5	5	7	.417
Tulsa	3	5	4	8	.333
SMU	3	5	3	8	.273
Rice	2	6	3	8	.273
San Jose St.	1	7	2	9	.182

INDEPENDENTS

	Full Season		
	W	L	Pct
Navy	10	2	.833
Notre Dame	6	6	.500

Division I-AA
ATLANTIC 10 CONFERENCE

	Conference		Full Season		
	W	L	W	L	Pct
New Hampshire	6	2	10	3	.769
Massachusetts	4	4	6	5	.545
Northeastern	4	4	5	6	.455
Maine	3	5	5	6	.455
Hofstra	3	5	5	6	.455
Rhode Island	2	6	4	7	.364
James Madison	7	1	13	2	.867
William & Mary	7	1	11	3	.786
Delaware	7	1	9	4	.692
Villanova	3	5	6	5	.545
Richmond	2	6	3	8	.273
Towson	0	8	3	8	.273

Division I-AA *(Cont.)*

BIG SKY CONFERENCE

	Conference		Full Season		
	W	L	W	L	Pct
Montana	6	1	12	3	.800
Eastern Washington	6	1	9	4	.692
Portland St.	4	3	7	4	.636
Montana St.	4	3	6	5	.545
Northern Arizona	3	4	4	7	.364
Sacramento St	2	5	3	8	.273
Idaho State	2	5	3	8	.273
Weber State	1	6	1	10	.091

BIG SOUTH CONFERENCE

	Conference		Full Season		
	W	L	W	L	Pct
Coastal Carolina	4	0	10	1	.909
Liberty	3	1	6	5	.545
Gardner Webb	2	2	5	6	.455
Charleston Southern	1	3	5	5	.500
VMI	0	4	0	11	.000

GATEWAY COLLEGIATE ATHLETIC CONFERENCE

	Conference		Full Season		
	W	L	W	L	Pct
Southern Illinois	7	0	10	2	.833
Western Kentucky	6	1	9	3	.750
Northern Iowa	5	2	7	4	.636
SW Missouri St	3	4	6	5	.545
Western Illinois	2	5	4	7	.364
Youngstown St.	2	5	4	7	.364
Illinois St.	2	5	4	7	.364
Indiana St	1	6	4	7	.364

IVY LEAGUE

	Conference		Full Season		
	W	L	W	L	Pct
Harvard	7	0	10	0	1.000
Pennsylvania	6	1	8	2	.800
Cornell	4	3	4	6	.400
Brown	3	4	6	4	.600
Yale	3	4	5	5	.500
Princeton	3	4	5	5	.500
Columbia	1	6	1	9	.100
Dartmouth	1	6	1	9	.100

METRO ATLANTIC ATHLETIC CONFERENCE

	Conference		Full Season		
	W	L	W	L	Pct
Duquesne	4	0	7	3	.700
Marist	3	1	3	6	.333
St. Peter's	1	3	3	7	.300
La Salle	1	3	3	7	.300
Iona	1	3	2	8	.200

Division I-AA (Cont.)

MID-EASTERN ATHLETIC CONFERENCE

	Conference		Full Season		
	W	L	W	L	Pct
Hampton	6	1	10	2	.833
S Carolina St.	6	1	9	2	.818
Bethune Cookman	4	3	6	4	.600
Deleware St.	4	3	4	7	.364
Howard	3	4	6	5	.545
Morgan St.	3	4	5	6	.455
N Carolina A&T	1	6	3	8	.273
Norfolk St.	1	6	1	8	.111
Florida A&M	0	0	3	8	.273

NORTHEAST CONFERENCE

	Conference		Full Season		
	W	L	W	L	Pct
Monmouth (NJ)	6	1	10	1	.909
Central Conn	6	1	8	2	.800
Albany	4	3	4	7	.364
Sacred Heart	3	4	6	4	.600
Wagner	3	4	6	5	.545
Robert Morris	3	4	6	5	.545
Stony Brook	2	5	3	7	.300
St. Francis (PA)	1	6	3	8	.273

OHIO VALLEY CONFERENCE

	Conference		Full Season		
	W	L	W	L	Pct
Jacksonville St	7	1	9	2	.818
Murray St.	6	2	7	4	.636
Eastern Kentucky	6	2	6	5	.545
Eastern Illinois	4	4	5	6	.455
Tennessee Tech	3	4	6	5	.545
Samford	3	5	4	7	.364
SE Missouri State	3	5	3	8	.273
Tennessee State	2	5	4	7	.364
Tennessee Martin	1	7	2	9	.182

PATRIOT LEAGUE

	Conference		Full Season		
	W	L	W	L	Pct
Lehigh	5	1	9	3	.750
Lafayette	5	1	8	4	.667
Bucknell	4	2	7	4	.636
Colgate	4	2	7	4	.636
Fordham	2	4	5	6	.455
Holy Cross	1	5	3	8	.273
Georgetown	0	6	3	8	.273

PIONEER LEAGUE

	Conference		Full Season		
NORTH	W	L	W	L	Pct
Drake	4	0	10	2	.833
San Diego	3	1	7	4	.636
Dayton	2	2	7	3	.700
Valparaiso	1	3	5	6	.455
Butler	0	4	1	10	.091
SOUTH					
Morehead St	2	1	6	6	.500
Jacksonville	2	1	3	7	.300
Davidson	1	2	2	7	.222
Austin Peay	1	2	2	9	.182

Division I-AA (Cont.)

SOUTHERN CONFERENCE

	Conference		Full Season		
	W	L	W	L	Pct
Furman	6	1	10	3	.769
Georgia Southern	6	1	9	3	.750
Wofford	4	3	8	3	.727
Appalachian St.	4	3	6	5	.545
Western Carolina	2	5	4	7	.364
The Citadel	2	5	3	7	.300
Elon University	2	5	3	8	.273
UT-Chattanooga	2	5	2	9	.182

SOUTHLAND CONFERENCE

	Conference		Full Season		
	W	L	W	L	Pct
Sam Houston St	4	1	11	3	.786
Northwestern St	4	1	8	4	.667
Texas State	3	2	5	6	.455
Nicholls St.	2	3	5	5	.500
Stephen F. Austin	1	4	6	5	.545
McNeese State	1	4	4	7	.364

SOUTHWESTERN ATHLETIC CONFERENCE

	Conference		Full Season		
EASTERN	W	L	W	L	Pct
Alabama State	6	1	10	2	.833
Alabama A&M	5	2	7	4	.636
Alcorn St.	4	3	7	4	.636
Jackson St	3	4	4	7	.364
Mississippi Valley St	1	6	3	8	.273
WESTERN8					
Southern	6	1	8	4	.667
Arkansas Pine Bluff	5	2	6	3	.667
Grambling	3	4	6	5	.545
Prairie View	1	6	3	8	.273
Texas Southern	0	7	0	11	.000

INDEPENDENTS

	Full Season		
	W	L	Pct
Cal Poly	9	2	.818
Florida Atlantic	9	3	.750
SE Louisiana	7	4	.636
Southern Utah	6	5	.545
Florida International	3	7	.300
Savannah St	2	8	.200
Northern Colorado	2	9	.182

Division I-A

SCORING

	Class	GP	TD	XP	FG	Pts	Pts/Game
Tyler Jones, Boise St.	Sr	12	0	69	24	141	11.75
DeAngelo Williams	Jr	12	23	0	0	138	11.50
Garrett Wolfe, Northern Ill.	So	11	21	0	0	126	11.45
P.J. Pope, Bowling Green	Jr	12	21	0	0	126	10.50
Jamario Thomas, North Texas	Fr	10	17	0	0	102	10.20
Chad Owens, Hawaii	Sr	13	22	0	0	132	10.15
Eric Shelton, Louisville	Jr	12	20	0	0	120	10.00
Cedric Benson, Texas	Sr	12	20	0	0	120	10.00
Ryan Moats, Louisiana Tech	Jr	12	19	0	0	114	9.50
Carlton Jones, Army	Jr	11	17	0	0	104	9.45

FIELD GOALS

	Class	GP	FGA	FG	Pct	FG/Game
Mike Nugent, Ohio St.	Sr	12	27	24	.889	2.00
Tyler Jones, Boise St.	Sr	12	27	24	.889	2.00
Andrew Wellock, Eastern Michigan	So	11	23	21	.913	1.91
David Rayner, Michigan St.	Sr	12	31	22	.710	1.83
Jonathan Nichols, Mississippi	Sr	11	27	20	.741	1.82

TOTAL OFFENSE

			Rushing		Passing		Total Offense		
	Class	GP	Car	Net	Att	Yds	Yds	Yds/Play	Yds/Game
Sonny Cumbie, Texas Tech	Sr	12	52	-167	642	4742	4575	6.59	381.3
Omar Jacobs, Bowling Green	So	12	95	300	462	4002	4302	7.72	358.5
Timmy Chang, Hawaii	Sr	13	37	15	602	4258	4273	6.69	328.7
Joshua Cribbs, Kent St.	Sr	10	170	893	335	2215	3108	6.15	310.8
Alex Smith, Utah	Jr	12	135	631	317	2952	3583	7.93	298.6
Matt Bohnet, Eastern Mich.	Jr	11	100	424	434	2807	3231	6.05	293.7
Reggie McNeal, Texas A&M	Jr	12	151	718	344	2791	3509	7.09	292.4
Kyle Orton, Purdue	Sr	11	80	112	389	3090	3202	6.83	291.1
Derek Anderson, Oregon St.	Sr	12	75	-152	515	3615	3463	5.87	288.6
Bruce Gradkowski, Toledo	Jr	13	91	191	399	3518	3709	7.57	285.3

RUSHING

	Class	GP	Car	Yds	TD	Avg	Yds/Game
Jamario Thomas, North Texas	Fr	10	285	1801	17	6.32	180.10
J.J. Arrington, California	Sr	12	289	2018	15	6.98	168.17
DeAngelo Williams, Memphis	Jr	12	313	1948	22	6.22	162.33
Cedric Benson, Texas	Sr	12	326	1834	19	5.63	152.83
Garrett Wolfe, Northern Ill.	So	11	256	1656	18	6.47	150.55
Adrian Peterson, Oklahoma	Fr	13	339	1925	15	5.68	148.08
Ryan Moats, Louisiana Tech	Jr	12	288	1774	18	6.16	147.83
Vernand Morency, Oklahoma St.	Jr	11	258	1474	12	5.71	134.00
Andre Hall, South Fla.	Jr	11	210	1357	11	6.46	123.36
Michael Hart, Michigan	Fr	12	282	1455	9	5.16	121.25

PASSING EFFICIENCY

	Class	GP	Att	Comp	Pct Comp	Yds	Yds/Att	TD	Int	Rating Pts
Stefan Lefors, Louisville	Sr	12	257	189	73.54	2596	10.10	20	3	181.7
Alex Smith, Utah	Jr	12	317	214	67.51	2952	9.31	32	4	176.5
Jason Cambell, Auburn	Sr	13	270	188	69.63	2700	10.00	20	7	172.9
Omar Jacobs, Bowling Green	So	12	462	309	66.88	4002	8.66	41	4	167.2
Bruce Gradkowski, Toledoi	Jr	13	399	280	70.18	3518	8.82	27	8	162.6
Jason White, Oklahoma	Sr	13	390	255	65.38	3205	8.22	35	9	159.4
Matt Leinhart, Southern California	Jr	13	412	269	65.29	3322	8.06	33	6	156.5
Aaron Rodgers, California	Jr	12	316	209	66.14	.2566	8.12	24	8	154.3
Lester Ricard, Tulane	So	9	231	143	61.90	1881	8.14	21	9	152.5
Kyle Orton, Purdue	Sr	11	389	236	60.67	3090	7.94	31	5	151.1

Note: Minimum 15 attempts per game.

Division I-A *(Cont.)*

RECEPTIONS PER GAME

	Class	GP	No.	Yds	TD	R/Game
Dante Ridgeway, Ball St.	Jr	11	105	1399	8	9.55
Braylon Edwards, Michigan	Sr	12	97	1330	15	8.08
Bobby Bernal-Wood, Idaho	Sr	12	96	938	3	8.00
Chad Owens, Hawaii	Sr	13	102	1290	17	7.85
Eric Deslauriers, Eastern Michigan	Jr	11	84	1257	13	7.64

RECEIVING YARDS PER GAME

	Class	GP	No.	Yds	TD	Yds/Game
Dante Ridgeway, Ball St.	Jr	11	105	1399	8	127.18
Roddy White, UAB	Sr	12	71	1452	14	121.00
Mike Hass, Oregon St.	Jr	12	86	1379	7	114.92
Eric Deslauriers, Eastern Michigan	Jr	11	84	1257	13	114.27
Braylon Edwards, Michigan	Sr	12	97	1330	15	110.83

ALL-PURPOSE RUNNERS

	Class	GP	Rush	Rec	PR	KOR	Yds	Yds/Game
DeAngelo Williams, Memphis	So	11	1430	384	0	299	2113	192.09
Darren Sproles, Kansas St.	Jr	15	1986	287	190	272	2735	182.33
Jerry Seymour, Central Michigan	Fr	9	1117	103	0	330	1550	172.22
Howard Jackson, Texas–El Paso	Jr	13	1146	391	0	609	2146	165.08
Michael Turner, Northern Illinois	Sr	12	1648	230	0	58	1936	161.33

INTERCEPTIONS

	Class	GP	No.	Int/Game
Chris Harris, La-Monroe	Sr	11	7	.64
Charles Gordon, Kansas	So	11	7	.64
Ko Simpson, South Carolina	Fr	11	6	.55
Brandon Payne, New Mexico	Sr	12	6	.50
Morgan Scalley, Utah	Sr	12	6	.50

PUNTING

	Class	No.	Avg
Brandon Fields, Michigan St.	Jr	50	47.88
John Torp, Colorado	Jr	72	46.54
Daniel Sepulveda, Baylor	So	62	45.97
Steve Weatherford, Illinois	Jr	57	45.42
Matt Payne, Brigam Young	Sr	62	45.29

Note: Minimum of 3.6 per game.

PUNT RETURNS

	Class	No.	Yds	TD	Avg
Ted Ginn Jr., Ohio St.	Fr	15	384	4	25.60
Kevin Robinson, Utah St.	Fr	17	382	2	22.47
Darrell Blackmon, N:C. State	Fr	12	214	1	17.83
Travis Williams, East Caro.	Fr	20	354	1	17.70
Domenik Hixon, Akron	Jr	16	275	1	17.19

Note: Minimum 1.2 per game.

KICKOFF RETURNS

	Class	No.	Yds	TD	Avg
Justin Miller, Clemson	Jr	20	661	2	33.05
Larry Taylor, Connecticut	Fr	12	376	1	31.33
Ashlan Davis, Tulsa	Jr	37	1131	5	30.57
Lance Bennett, Indiana	So	20	599	1	29.95
John Eubanks, Southern Miss.	Jr	21	618	1	29.43

Note: Minimum of 1.2 per game.

Division I-A Team Single-Game Highs

RUSHING AND PASSING

Rushing and passing yards: 548—Brett Basanez, Northwestern, QB, Sept 2, 2004 (vs. TCU)
Rushing and passing plays: 77—Brad Smith, Missouri, QB, Oct 30, 2004 (vs. Nebraska)
Rushing plays: 43—Garrett Wolfe, Northern Ill., RB, Nov 20, 2004 (vs Eastern Mich.)
Net rushing yards: 338—Kay-Jay Harris, West Virginia, RB, Sept 4, 2004 (vs East Caro.)
Passes attempted: 69—Sonny Cumbie, Texas Tech, QB, Sept 11, 2004 (vs New Mexico)
Passes completed: 44—Sonny Cumbie, Texas Tech, QB, Sept 11, 2004 (vs New Mexico)
Passing yards: 522—Kyle Orton, Purdue, QB, Nov 20, 2004 (vs Indiana)

RECEIVING AND RETURNS

Passes caught: Three tied with 15.
Receiving yards: 293—Mike Hass, Oregon State, WR, Sept 10, 2004 (vs Boise St.)
Punt returnyards:
Kickoff return yards: 206—Justin Miller, Clemson, Sept 25, 2004 (vs Florida St.)

Division I-AA

SCORING

	Class	GP	TD	XP	FG	Pts	Pts/Game
Chaz Williams, Ga. Southern	Sr	12	25	0	0	152	12.67
Clifton Dawson, Harvard	So	10	18	0	0	108	10.80
Oscar Bonds, Jacksonville St.	Sr	11	19	0	0	114	10.36
Evan Harney, San Diego	Jr	11	19	0	0	114	10.36
Nick Hartigan, Brown	Jr	10	17	0	0	102	10.20

FIELD GOALS

	Class	GP	FGA	FG	Pct	FG/Game
Joe Johnson, Weber St.	Jr	11	22	17	.773	1.55
Kyle Hooper, Indiana St.	So	11	20	16	.800	1.45
Brian Wingert, Northern Iowa	So	10	18	14	.778	1.40
John Scifres, Southwest Mo. St.	Jr	11	15	15	1.000	1.36
Chris Onorato, Hofstra	Sr	11	20	15	.750	1.36

TOTAL OFFENSE

			Rushing		Passing		Total Offense		
	Class	GP	Car	Net	Att	Yds	Yds	Yds/Play	Yds/Game
Martin Hankins, Southeast. La.	So	11	56	-19	540	4240	4221	7.08	383.7
Travis Lulay, Montana St.	Jr	11	112	371	490	3485	3856	6.41	350.5
Richie Williams, Appalachian St.	Jr	10	137	284	350	3109	3393	6.97	339.3
Ramon Nelson, Samford	Sr	11	167	799	461	2807	3606	5.74	327.8
Dustin Long, Sam Houston St.	Sr	14	45	-12	531	4588	4576	7.94	326.9

RUSHING

	Class	GP	Car	Yds	Avg	TD	Yds/Game
Charles Anthony, Tennessee St.	Sr	11	306	1739	5.68	14	158.09
Sean Mayers, St Peter's	Jr	10	270	1546	5.73	8	154.60
Ed Pricolo, Sacred Heart	Jr	9	209	1339	6.41	14	148.78
Jason Jackson, Morgan St.	Jr	9	202	1191	5.90	9	132.33
Clifton dawson, Harvard	So	10	248	1302	5.25	17	130.20

PASSING EFFICIENCY

					Pct				Rating	
	Class	GP	Att	Comp	Comp	Yds	Yds/Att	TD	Int	Pts
Erik Meyer, Eastern Wash.	Jr	13	382	259	67.80	3707	9.70	31	9	171.4
Joel Sambursky, Southern Ill.	Jr	12	234	142	60.68	2224	9.50	19	5	163.0
Eric Sanders, Northern Iowa	Fr	9	150	95	63.33	1307	8.71	15	5	162.9
Craig Ochs, Montana	Sr	15	450	309	68.67	3807	8.46	33	8	160.4
Lang Campbell, William & Mary	Sr	14	455	298	65.49	3988	8.76	30	5	158.7

Note: Minimum 15 attempts per game. D

RECEPTIONS PER GAME

	Class	GP	No.	Yds	TD	R/G
DaVon Fowlkes, App. St.	Sr	11	103	1618	14	9.36
Ralph Plumb, Yale	Sr	10	79	939	5	7.90
Felton Huggins, S. Eas La.	Jr	11	84	1313	13	7.64
Luke Palko, St. Francis	So	11	82	679	2	7.45
A.J. Smith, South. Utah	Sr	11	79	730	4	7.18

RECEIVING YARDS PER GAME

	Class	GP	No.	Yds	TD	Yds/G
DaVon Fowlkes, App. St.	Sr	11	103	1618	14	147.09
David Ball, New Hamp.	So	12	86	1504	17	125.33
Felton Huggins, S. Eas La.	Jr	11	84	1313	13	119.36
Dominique Thompson,	Sr	14	79	1585	9	113.21
Eric Kimble, East. Wash.	Jr	13	83	1453	19	111.77

INTERCEPTIONS

	Class	GP	No.	Yds	TD	Int/G
Ahmad Treaudo, South U.	Sr	11	9	166	1	.82
Shannon James, Mass.	Jr	11	8	110	0	.73
Thaddeus Kornegay, Ford.	Sr	11	8	103	0	.73
Onsha Whitaker, Murr. St.	Sr	10	7	-1	0	.70
Allante Harrison, Towson	Jr	11	7	128	2	.64

PUNTING

	Class	No.	Avg
Paul Ernster, Northern Ariz.	Sr	55	5.00
David Simonhoff, S. East Mo. St.	So	69	6.27
Ryan Hoffman, Illinois St.	Jr	55	5.00
Brian Claybourn, Western Ky.	Sr	46	3.83
Mike Mellow, Maine	Sr	64	5.82

Division I-AA (Cont)

ALL-PURPOSE RUNNERS

	Class	GP	Rush	Rec	PR	KOR	Yds	Yds/Game
DaVon Fowlkes, Appalachian St.	Sr	11	82	1618	194	419	2313	210.27
John Leverett, Davidson	Sr	9	1084	144	0	534	1762	195.78
Charles Anthony, Tennessee St.	Sr	11	1739	318	0	0	2057	187.00
Darell Jones, Cal Poly	Sr	11	53	1118	403	285	1859	169.00
Robert Carr, Yale	Sr	10	1185	15	0	489	1689	168.90

Division II

SCORING

	Class	GP	TD	XP	FG	Pts	Pts/Game
Danny Woodhead, Chadron St.	Fr	10	27	0	0	162	16.2
Derrick Ross, Tarleton St.	Jr	10	22	0	0	134	13.4
Dallas Mall, Bentley	Sr	10	21	0	0	126	12.6
Rj Rollins, Minn.-Crookston	Jr	10	17	15	2	123	12.3
Derrick Wimbush, Fort Valley St.	Sr	11	22	0	0	134	12.2

FIELD GOALS

	Class	GP	FGA	FG	Pct	FG/Game
Justin Gray, Emporia St.	Sr	11	26	20	.769	1.8
Ha'a Bento, Tex. A&M-Commerce	Jr	10	26	18	.692	1.8
Will Rhody, Valdosta St.	Sr	14	23	22	.957	1.6
Jeff Glas, North Dakota	Jr	14	34	21	.618	1.5
A.J. Haglund, Central Okla.	Sr	10	18	15	.833	1.5

TOTAL OFFENSE

	Class	GP	Yds	Yds/Game
Chad Friehauf, Colorado Mines	Sr	13	5363	412.5
Jimmy Terwilliger, East Stroudsburg	So	12	4292	357.7
Scott Eyster, Delta St.	So	10	3563	356.3
Derek Maupin, West Texas A&M	Sr	10	3511	351.1
Cory Allred, Ark-Monticello	Sr	11	3721	338.3

RUSHING

	Class	GP	Car	Yds	TD	Yds/Game
Danny Woodhead, Chadron St.	Fr	10	284	1840	25	184.0
Antoine Bagwell, California (Pa)	Jr	10	246	1765	20	176.5
Derrick Wimbush, Fort Valley St.	Sr	11	247	1840	22	167.3
Derrick Ross, Tarleton St.	Jr	10	254	1560	22	156.0
Rj Rollins, Minn.-Crookston	Jr	10	270	1551	17	155.1

PASSING EFFICIENCY

	Class	GP	Att	Comp	TD	Int	Rating Pts
Jimmy Terwilliger, East Strodsburg	So	So	362	222	33	11	174.1
Chad Friehauf, Colorado Mines	Sr	Sr	516	384	39	11	170.7
Scott Eyster, Delta St.	So	So	371	229	28	7	159.1
Kevin Weidl, Indiana(Pa)	Jr	Jr	198	113	18	11	152.9
Robert Findora, West Chester	Sr	Sr	355	201	30	20	152.3

RECEPTIONS PER GAME

	Class	GP	No.	Yds	TD	Rec/G
J.J. Richard, Emporia St.	Jr	11	97	1166		8.8
Dustin Creager, Hmbldt St.	Sr	10	88	1036		8.8
Elfren Quiles, Merrimack	Fr	10	88	1406		8.8
Zach Edwards, Cen. Okla.	So	10	79	1230		7.9
Dallas Mall, Bentley	Sr	10	79	1114		7.9

RECEIVING YARDS PER GAME

	Class	GP	No.	Yds	TD	ds/G
Elfren Quiles, Merrimack	Fr	10	88	1406	14	140.6
Chris Samp, Winona St.	Sr	12	78	1587	22	132.3
Nate Washington, Tiffin	Sr	11	69	1428	16	129.8
Zach Edwards, Cent Okla.	So	10	79	1230	8	123.0
Tim Strenfel, East Strdsbrg	Jr	12	69	1388	11	115.7

Division II *(Cont.)*

INTERCEPTIONS

	Class	GP	No.	Yds	Int/ Game
Howard Williams, Jr., Eliz Cty St.	Sr	10	10	174	1.0
Matt Crispell, East Stroudsburg	Jr	12	10	110	0.8
Jonathan Lyles, Newberry	Sr	11	8	32	0.7
Michael Wiggins, East Strdsbrg	So	11	8	117	0.7

Two tied at 0.70

PUNTING

	Class	No.	Avg
Jeff Williams, Adams St.	Jr	71	48.0
Jeff Carpenter, West Ga.	Jr	40	43.8
Michael Koenen, Western Wash.	Sr	37	43.5
Neal Bainbridge, South Dakota St.	So	58	43.1
Jim Schuler, Mercyhurst	Sr	84	42.8

Note: Minimum 3.6 per game.

Division III

SCORING

	Class	GP	TD	XP	FG	Pts	Pts/Game
Tony Sutton, Wooster	Sr	12	33	0	0	198	16.5
Lance Moore, Hardin-Simmons	Sr	11	27	0	0	164	14.9
Casey Meehan, St. Norbert	Jr	11	25	0	0	152	13.8
Neil Suckow, Coe	Fr	10	23	0	0	138	13.8
Richie McNally, Wooster	Sr	12	11	66	10	162	13.5

FIELD GOALS

	Class	GP	FGA	FG	Pct	FG/Game
Lucas Raschke, Wis.-Oshkosh	Fr	10	21	19	.905	1.9
Will Bean, St. John Fisher	Sr	11	22	18	.818	1.6
Michael Chaulk, Wis-Whitewater	Jr	10	22	14	.636	1.4
John Sims, Otterbein	Sr	10	18	14	.778	1.4

Four tied with 1.3.

TOTAL OFFENSE

	Class	GP	Yds	Yds/Game
Adam King, Howard Payne	Sr	10	3680	368.0
Brett Elliot, Lifield	Jr	13	4663	358.7
John Port, Albright	Sr	11	3766	342.4
Brett Borchart, Wis-Stevens Pt.	So	10	3245	324.5

RUSHING

	Class	GP	Car	Yds	TD	Yds/Game
Tony Sutton, Wooster	Sr	12	352	2240	31	186.7
Mark Robinson, St. John Fisher	So	12	386	2194	22	182.8
Phil Porta, Bethel(Minn.)	So	10	303	1736	14	173.6
Brett Trichilo, Wilkes	Sr	10	299	1685	21	168.5
Chris Jacoubs, Moravian	So	11	342	1789	16	162.6

PASSING EFFICIENCY

	Class	GP	Att	Comp	Pct Comp	Yds	TD	Int	Rating Pts
Brett Elliot, Linfield	Jr	13	437	290	66.36	4595	61	11	195.7
Zac Bruney, Mount Zion	Sr	13	270	170	62.96	2662	31	9	177.0
Chris Edwards, Wash. & Jeff.	Jr	13	357	231	64.71	3307	38	10	172.0
Mitch Tanney, Monmouth(Ill.)	Jr	10	212	122	57.55	1952	24	3	169.4
Jordan Neal, Hardin-Simmons	Jr	11	283	188	66.43	2686	24	12	165.7
Dan DesPlaines, Trinity(Tex.)	Sr	11	311	198	63.67	2967	25	9	164.5

Note: Minimum 15 attempts per game.

RECEPTIONS PER GAME

	Class	GP	No.	Yds	TD	Rec/Game
Nick Cushman, Albright	Sr	11	101	1682	17	9.2
Brad Musso, Wheaton(Ill.)	Sr	11	98	1293	9	8.9
Anthony Ballerino, MacMurray	Sr	10	85	1074	11	8.5
Tyke Spencer, North Central(Ill.)	Jr	10	80	1306	13	8.0

2004 NCAA Individual Leaders (Cont.)

Division III (Cont.)

RECEIVING YARDS PER GAME

	Class	GP	No.	Yds	TD	Yds/Game
Nick Cushman, Albright	Sr	11	101	1682	17	152.9
Tyke Spencer, North Central (Ill.)	Jr	10	80	1306	13	130.6
Tom Cleaver, Middlebury	Sr	8	62	943	5	117.9
Brad Musso, Wheaton(Ill.)	Sr	11	98	1293	9	117.5
John Harris, North Park	Jr	10	76	1172	10	117.2

INTERCEPTIONS

	Class	GP	No.	Yds	Int/G
Joe Diekevers, Hope	Jr	10	9	37	0.9
David Garcia, Texas Lutheran	Jr	10	9	121	0.9
Dan Mckeown, Adrian	Jr	10	9	93	0.9
Brett Bueltel,Rose-Hulman	So	10	8	26	0.8
Jeff McLaren, Wslyn(Conn)	Jr	8	6	27	0.8

PUNTING

	Class	No.	Avg
Kevin Soflkiancs, Baldwin-Wallace	Fr	10	42.7
Christian Adams, Guilford	Sr	10	41.2
Willie Thompson, Illinois Col.	Sr	10	41.2
Chris Kemmerer, Buena Vista	So	10	41.1
Dan Eggertsson, Frank. & Marsh.	Sr	11	40.7

Note: Minimum 3.6 per game.

2004 NCAA Division I-A Team Leaders

Offense

SCORING

	GP	Pts	Avg
Louisville	12	597	49.75
Boise St.	12	587	48.92
Utah	12	544	45.33
Bowling Green	12	532	44.33
Fresno St.	12	482	40.17
Southern California	13	496	38.15
California	12	441	36.75
Texas Tech	12	434	36.17
Hawaii	13	467	35.92
Memphis	12	430	35.83

RUSHING

	GP	Car	Yds	Avg	TD	Yds/Game
Rice	11	688	3372	4.90	30	306.55
Texas	12	615	3590	5.84	41	299.17
Navy	12	689	3474	5.04	36	289.50
Air Force	11	648	3051	4.71	32	277.36
Minesota	12	572	3082	5.39	29	256.83
California	12	509	3081	6.05	30	256.75
West Virginia	12	590	3034	5.14	23	252.83
Louisville	12	534	3005	5.63	47	250.42
Virginia	12	550	2914	5.30	34	242.83
Michigan St.	12	500	2862	5.72	22	238.50

TOTAL OFFENSE

	GP	Plays	Yds	Avg	TD	Yds/Game
Louisville	12	893	6468	7.24	80	539.00
Bowling Green	12	904	6076	6.72	69	506.33
Utah	12	869	5997	6.90	75	499.75
Boise St.	12	951	5912	6.22	74	492.67
California	12	840	5909	7.03	59	492.42
Texas Tech	12	944	5900	6.25	59	491.67
Texas	12	890	5573	6.26	55	464.42
Oklahoma	13	971	6007	6.19	61	462.08
Memphis	12	903	5524	6.12	53	460.33
Michigan St.	12	899	5520	6.14	41	460.00

Go Figure

49 - *Years since a Big Ten team last scored exactly four points in a game, as Penn State did in a 6–4 loss to Iowa in 2004.*

Offense (Cont.)

PASSING

	GP	Att	Comp	Int	Pct Comp	Yds	Yds/att	TD
TexasTech	12	651	426	18	65.44	4796	7.37	34
Hawaii	13	636	370	18	58.18	4402	6.92	38
Bowling Green	12	472	313	4	66.31	4057	8.60	41
Purdue	12	486	297	8	61.11	3854	7.93	38
Arizona St.	12	502	289	10	57.57	3808	7.59	35
Rutgers	11	473	303	20	64.06	3416	7.22	19
Oregon St.	12	532	287	17	53.95	3706	6.97	29
Toledo	13	449	308	10	68.60	3879	8.64	28
Louisville	12	359	256	5	71.31	3463	9.65	27
Connecticut	12	464	292	15	62.93	3376	7.28	23

Single-Game Highs

Points Scored: 70—Texas Tech, Sept 18, 2004 (vs TCU).
Net Rushing Yards: 570—Rice, Oct 2, 2004 (vs San Jose St.)
Passing Yards: 590—Purdue, Nov 20, 2004 (vs Indiana)
Rushing and Passing Yards: 763—Purdue, Nov 20, 2004 (vs Indiana)
Fewest Rushing and Passing Yards Allowed: 46—Oklahoma, Dec 4, 2004 (vs. Colorado)

Defense

SCORING

	GP	Pts	Avg
Auburn	13	147	11.3
Virginia Tech	13	167	12.8
Southern California	13	169	13.0
Florida S.t	12	169	14.1
Penn St.	11	168	15.3
Wisconsin	12	185	15.4
Alabama	12	189	15.8
California	12	192	16.0
Georgia	12	198	16.5
Troy	12	200	16.7

TOTAL DEFENSE

	GP	Plays	Yds	Avg	Yds/Game
North Carolina St.	11	701	2435	3.47	221.36
Alabama	12	726	2946	4.06	245.50
LSU	12	743	3083	4.15	256.92
Virginia Tech	13	794	3484	4.39	268.00
Auburn	13	780	3609	4.63	277.62
Southern Cal.	13	851	3631	4.27	279.31
Florida St.	12	798	3406	4.27	283.83
Georgia	12	747	3467	4.64	288.92
Wisconson	12	756	3495	4.62	291.25
Penn St.	11	753	3207	4.26	291.55

RUSHING

	GP	Car	Yds	Avg	TD	Yds/Game
Southern Cal.	13	394	1032	2.62	5	79.4
California	12	368	990	2.69	7	82.5
Florida St.	12	418	997	2.39	5	83.1
Notre Dame	12	399	1058	2.65	6	88.2
Iowa	12	392	1110	2.83	8	92.5
Oklahoma	13	402	1230	3.06	10	94.6
LSU	12	410	1197	2.92	7	99.8
Troy	12	444	1211	2.73	12	100.9
North Carolina St.	11	429	1126	2.62	6	102.4
Boise St.	12	373	1247	3.34	17	103.9

TURNOVER MARGIN

		Turnovers Gained			Turnovers Lost			Margi
	GP	Fum	Int	Total	Fum	Int	Total	Game
Southern Cal.	13	16	22	38	12	7	19	1.46
Oklahoma St.	12	15	11	26	4	5	9	1.42
Bowling Green	12	11	14	25	6	4	10	1.25
Utah	12	13	16	29	9	5	14	1.25
Miami(Fla)	12	14	13	27	7	6	13	1.17
Iowa	12	15	17	32	5	14	19	1.08
Pittsburgh	12	9	17	26	6	7	13	1.08
North Texas	12	12	14	26	9	4	13	1.08
Virginia Tech	13	13	19	32	10	9	19	1.00
Louisville	12	10	17	27	11	5	16	.92

Four tied with 0.85.

PASSING EFFICIENCY

	GP	Att	Comp	Yds	Pct Comp	Yds/Att	TD	Pct TD	Int	Pct Int	Rating Pts
North Carolina St.	11	272	118	1309	43.38	4.81	12	4.41	9	3.31	91.77
Alabama	12	242	105	1357	43.39	5.61	9	3.72	12	4.96	92.86
Fresno St.	12	362	185	2097	51.10	5.79	9	2.49	16	4.42	99.12
Penn St.	11	310	175	1785	56.45	5.76	5	1.61	16	5.16	99.87
Wisconsin	12	369	180	2007	48.78	5.44	13	3.52	11	2.98	100.15
Troy	12	406	217	2521	53.45	6.21	9	2.22	25	6.16	100.56
Virginia Tech	13	332	180	1986	54.22	5.98	8	2.41	19	5.72	100.95
Oregon St.	12	424	186	2352	43.87	5.55	25	5.90	19	4.48	100.99
Southern California	13	457	246	2599	53.83	5.69	13	2.84	22	4.81	101.33
LSU	12	333	160	1886	48.05	5.66	16	4.80	14	4.20	103.02

National Champions

Year	Champion	Record	Bowl Game	Head Coach
1883	Yale	8-0-0	No bowl	Ray Tompkins (Captain)
1884	Yale	9-0-0	No bowl	Eugene L. Richards (Captain)
1885	Princeton	9-0-0	No bowl	Charles DeCamp (Captain)
1886	Yale	9-0-1	No bowl	Robert N. Corwin (Captain)
1887	Yale	9-0-0	No bowl	Harry W. Beecher (Captain)
1888	Yale	13-0-0	No bowl	Walter Camp
1889	Princeton	10-0-0	No bowl	Edgar Poe (Captain)
1890	Harvard	11-0-0	No bowl	George A. Stewart/George C. Adams
1891	Yale	13-0-0	No bowl	Walter Camp
1892	Yale	13-0-0	No bowl	Walter Camp
1893	Princeton	11-0-0	No bowl	Tom Trenchard (Captain)
1894	Yale	16-0-0	No bowl	William C. Rhodes
1895	Pennsylvania	14-0-0	No bowl	George Woodruff
1896	Princeton	10-0-1	No bowl	Garrett Cochran
1897	Pennsylvania	15-0-0	No bowl	George Woodruff
1898	Harvard	11-0-0	No bowl	W. Cameron Forbes
1899	Harvard	10-0-1	No bowl	Benjamin H. Dibblee
1900	Yale	12-0-0	No bowl	Malcolm McBride
1901	Michigan	11-0-0	Won Rose	Fielding Yost
1902	Michigan	11-0-0	No bowl	Fielding Yost
1903	Princeton	11-0-0	No bowl	Art Hillebrand
1904	Pennsylvania	12-0-0	No bowl	Carl Williams
1905	Chicago	11-0-0	No bowl	Amos Alonzo Stagg
1906	Princeton	9-0-1	No bowl	Bill Roper
1907	Yale	9-0-1	No bowl	Bill Knox
1908	Pennsylvania	11-0-1	No bowl	Sol Metzger
1909	Yale	10-0-0	No bowl	Howard Jones
1910	Harvard	8-0-1	No bowl	Percy Houghton
1911	Princeton	8-0-2	No bowl	Bill Roper
1912	Harvard	9-0-0	No bowl	Percy Houghton
1913	Harvard	9-0-0	No bowl	Percy Houghton
1914	Army	9-0-0	No bowl	Charley Daly
1915	Cornell	9-0-0	No bowl	Al Sharpe
1916	Pittsburgh	8-0-0	No bowl	Pop Warner
1917	Georgia Tech	9-0-0	No bowl	John Heisman
1918	Pittsburgh	4-1-0	No bowl	Pop Warner
1919	Harvard	9-0-1	Won Rose	Bob Fisher
1920	California	9-0-0	Won Rose	Andy Smith
1921	Cornell	8-0-0	No bowl	Gil Dobie
1922	Cornell	8-0-0	No bowl	Gil Dobie
1923	Illinois	8-0-0	No bowl	Bob Zuppke
1924	Notre Dame	10-0-0	Won Rose	Knute Rockne
1925	Alabama (H)	10-0-0	Won Rose	Wallace Wade
	Dartmouth (D)	8-0-0	No bowl	Jesse Hawley
1926	Alabama (H)	9-0-1	Tied Rose	Wallace Wade
	Stanford (D)(H)	10-0-1	Tied Rose	Pop Warner
1927	Illinois	7-0-1	No bowl	Bob Zuppke
1928	Georgia Tech (H)	10-0-0	Won Rose	Bill Alexander
	Southern Cal (D)	9-0-1	No bowl	Howard Jones
1929	Notre Dame	9-0-0	No bowl	Knute Rockne
1930	Notre Dame	10-0-0	No bowl	Knute Rockne
1931	Southern Cal	10-1-0	Won Rose	Howard Jones
1932	Southern Cal (H)	10-0-0	Won Rose	Howard Jones
	Michigan (D)	8-0-0	No bowl	Harry Kipke
1933	Michigan	7-0-1	No bowl	Harry Kipke
1934	Minnesota	8-0-0	No bowl	Bernie Bierman
1935	Minnesota (H)	8-0-0	No bowl	Bernie Bierman
	Southern Methodist (D)	12-1-0	Lost Rose	Matty Bell
1936	Minnesota	7-1-0	No bowl	Bernie Bierman
1937	Pittsburgh	9-0-1	No bowl	Jock Sutherland
1938	Texas Christian (AP)	11-0-0	Won Sugar	Dutch Meyer
	Notre Dame (D)	8-1-0	No bowl	Elmer Layden
1939	Southern Cal (D)	8-0-2	Won Rose	Howard Jones
	Texas A&M (AP)	11-0-0	Won Sugar	Homer Norton
1940	Minnesota	8-0-0	No bowl	Bernie Bierman
1941	Minnesota	8-0-0	No bowl	Bernie Bierman
1942	Ohio St	9-1-0	No bowl	Paul Brown

Year	Champion	Record	Bowl Game	Head Coach
1943	Notre Dame	9-1-0	No bowl	Frank Leahy
1944	Army	9-0-0	No bowl	Red Blaik
1945	Army	9-0-0	No bowl	Red Blaik
1946	Notre Dame	8-0-1	No bowl	Frank Leahy
1947	Notre Dame	9-0-0	No bowl	Frank Leahy
	Michigan*	10-0-0	Won Rose	Fritz Crisler
1948	Michigan	9-0-0	No bowl	Bennie Oosterbaan
1949	Notre Dame	10-0-0	No bowl	Frank Leahy
1950	Oklahoma	10-1-0	Lost Sugar	Bud Wilkinson
1951	Tennessee	10-1-0	Lost Sugar	Bob Neyland
1952	Michigan St	9-0-0	No bowl	Biggie Munn
1953	Maryland	10-1-0	Lost Orange	Jim Tatum
1954	Ohio St	10-0-0	Won Rose	Woody Hayes
	UCLA (UPI)	9-0-0	No bowl	Red Sanders
1955	Oklahoma	11-0-0	Won Orange	Bud Wilkinson
1956	Oklahoma	10-0-0	No bowl	Bud Wilkinson
1957	Auburn	10-0-0	No bowl	Shug Jordan
	Ohio St (UPI)	9-1-0	Won Rose	Woody Hayes
1958	Louisiana St	11-0-0	Won Sugar	Paul Dietzel
1959	Syracuse	11-0-0	Won Cotton	Ben Schwartzwalder
1960	Minnesota	8-2-0	Lost Rose	Murray Warmath
1961	Alabama	11-0-0	Won Sugar	Bear Bryant
1962	Southern Cal	11-0-0	Won Rose	John McKay
1963	Texas	11-0-0	Won Cotton	Darrell Royal
1964	Alabama	10-1-0	Lost Orange	Bear Bryant
1965	Alabama	9-1-1	Won Orange	Bear Bryant
	Michigan St (UPI)	10-1-0	Lost Rose	Duffy Daugherty
1966	Notre Dame	9-0-1	No bowl	Ara Parseghian
1967	Southern Cal	10-1-0	Won Rose	John McKay
1968	Ohio St	10-0-0	Won Rose	Woody Hayes
1969	Texas	11-0-0	Won Cotton	Darrell Royal
1970	Nebraska	11-0-1	Won Orange	Bob Devaney
	Texas (UPI)	10-1-0	Lost Cotton	Darrell Royal
1971	Nebraska	13-0-0	Won Orange	Bob Devaney
1972	Southern Cal	12-0-0	Won Rose	John McKay
1973	Notre Dame	11-0-0	Won Sugar	Ara Parseghian
	Alabama (UPI)	11-1-0	Lost Sugar	Bear Bryant
1974	Oklahoma	11-0-0	No bowl	Barry Switzer
	Southern Cal (UPI)	10-1-1	Won Rose	John McKay
1975	Oklahoma	11-1-0	Won Orange	Barry Switzer
1976	Pittsburgh	12-0-0	Won Sugar	Johnny Majors
1977	Notre Dame	11-1-0	Won Cotton	Dan Devine
1978	Alabama	11-1-0	Won Sugar	Bear Bryant
	Southern Cal (UPI)	12-1-0	Won Rose	John Robinson
1979	Alabama	12-0-0	Won Sugar	Bear Bryant
1980	Georgia	12-0-0	Won Sugar	Vince Dooley
1981	Clemson	12-0-0	Won Orange	Danny Ford
1982	Penn St	11-1-0	Won Sugar	Joe Paterno
1983	Miami (FL)	11-1-0	Won Orange	Howard Schnellenberger
1984	Brigham Young	13-0-0	Won Holiday	LaVell Edwards
1985	Oklahoma	11-1-0	Won Orange	Barry Switzer
1986	Penn St	12-0-0	Won Fiesta	Joe Paterno
1987	Miami (FL)	12-0-0	Won Orange	Jimmy Johnson
1988	Notre Dame	12-0-0	Won Fiesta	Lou Holtz
1989	Miami (FL)	11-1-0	Won Sugar	Dennis Erickson
1990	Colorado	11-1-1	Won Orange	Bill McCartney
	Georgia Tech (UPI)	11-0-1	Won Citrus	Bobby Ross
1991	Miami (FL)	12-0-0	Won Orange	Dennis Erickson
	Washington (CNN)	12-0-0	Won Rose	Don James
1992	Alabama	13-0-0	Won Sugar	Gene Stallings
1993	Florida St	12-1-0	Won Orange	Bobby Bowden
1994	Nebraska	13-0-0	Won Orange	Tom Osborne
1995	Nebraska	12-0-0	Won Fiesta	Tom Osborne
†1996	Florida	12-1	Won Sugar	Steve Spurrier
1997	Michigan	12-0	Won Rose	Lloyd Carr
	Nebraska (ESPN)	13-0	Won Orange	Tom Osborne
1998	Tennessee	13-0	Won Fiesta	Phillip Fulmer
1999	Florida St	12-0	Won Sugar	Bobby Bowden
2000	Oklahoma	13-0	Won Orange	Bob Stoops
2001	Miami (FL)	12-0	Won Rose	Larry Coker

National Champions *(Cont.)*

Year	Champion	Record	Bowl Game	Head Coach
2002	Ohio St	14–0	Won Fiesta	Jim Tressel
2003	Louisiana St	13–1	Won Sugar	Nick Saban
	Southern California	12–1	Won Rose	Pete Carroll
2004	Southern California	13-0	Won Orange	Pete Carroll

*The AP, which had voted Notre Dame No. 1, took a second vote, giving the national title to Michigan after its 49–0 win over Southern Cal in the Rose Bowl.   Note: Selectors: Helms Athletic Foundation (H) 1883–1935, The Dickinson System (D) 1924–40, The Associated Press (AP) 1936–present, United Press International (UPI) 1958–90, *USA Today*/CNN (CNN)

Results of Major Bowl Games

Rose Bowl

1-1-02	Michigan 49, Stanford 0
1-1-16	Washington St 14, Brown 0
1-1-17	Oregon 14, Pennsylvania 0
1-1-18	Mare Island 14, Camp Lewis 7
1-1-19	Great Lakes 17, Mare Island 0
1-1-20	Harvard 7, Oregon 6
1-1-21	California 28, Ohio St 0
1-2-22	Washington & Jefferson 0, California 0
1-1-23	Southern Cal 14, Penn St 3
1-1-24	Navy 14, Washington 14
1-1-25	Notre Dame 27, Stanford 10
1-1-26	Alabama 20, Washington 19
1-1-27	Alabama 7, Stanford 7
1-2-28	Stanford 7, Pittsburgh 6
1-1-29	Georgia Tech 8, California 7
1-1-30	Southern Cal 47, Pittsburgh 14
1-1-31	Alabama 24, Washington St 0
1-1-32	Southern Cal 21, Tulane 12
1-2-33	Southern Cal 35, Pittsburgh 0
1-1-34	Columbia 7, Stanford 0
1-1-35	Alabama 29, Stanford 13
1-1-36	Stanford 7, Southern Methodist 0
1-1-37	Pittsburgh 21, Washington 0
1-1-38	California 13, Alabama 0
1-2-39	Southern Cal 7, Duke 3
1-1-40	Southern Cal 14, Tennessee 0
1-1-41	Stanford 21, Nebraska 13
1-1-42	Oregon St 20, Duke 16
1-1-43	Georgia 9, UCLA 0
1-1-44	Southern Cal 29, Washington 0
1-1-45	Southern Cal 25, Tennessee 0
1-1-46	Alabama 34, Southern Cal 14
1-1-47	Illinois 45, UCLA 14
1-1-48	Michigan 49, Southern Cal 0
1-1-49	Northwestern 20, California 14
1-2-50	Ohio St 17, California 14
1-1-51	Michigan 14, California 6
1-1-52	Illinois 40, Stanford 7
1-1-53	Southern Cal 7, Wisconsin 0
1-1-54	Michigan St 28, UCLA 20
1-1-55	Ohio St 20, Southern Cal 7
1-2-56	Michigan 17, UCLA 14
1-1-57	Iowa 35, Oregon St 19
1-1-58	Ohio St 10, Oregon 7
1-1-59	Iowa 38, California 12
1-1-60	Washington 44, Wisconsin 8
1-2-61	Washington 17, Minnesota 7
1-1-62	Minnesota 21, UCLA 3
1-1-63	Southern Cal 42, Wisconsin 37
1-1-64	Illinois 17, Washington 7
1-1-65	Michigan 34, Oregon St 7
1-1-66	UCLA 14, Michigan St 12

1-2-67	Purdue 14, Southern Cal 13
1-1-68	Southern Cal 14, Indiana 3
1-1-69	Ohio St 27, Southern Cal 16
1-1-70	Southern Cal 10, Michigan 3
1-1-71	Stanford 27, Ohio St 17
1-1-72	Stanford 13, Michigan 12
1-1-73	Southern Cal 42, Ohio St 17
1-1-74	Ohio St 42, Southern Cal 21
1-1-75	Southern Cal 18, Ohio St 17
1-1-76	UCLA 23, Ohio St 10
1-1-77	Southern Cal 14, Michigan 6
1-2-78	Washington 27, Michigan 20
1-1-79	Southern Cal 17, Michigan 10
1-1-80	Southern Cal 17, Ohio St 16
1-1-81	Michigan 23, Washington 6
1-1-82	Washington 28, Iowa 0
1-1-83	UCLA 24, Michigan 14
1-2-84	UCLA 45, Illinois 9
1-1-85	Southern Cal 20, Ohio St 17
1-1-86	UCLA 45, Iowa 28
1-1-87	Arizona St 22, Michigan 15
1-1-88	Michigan St 20, Southern Cal 17
1-2-89	Michigan 22, Southern Cal 14
1-1-90	Southern Cal 17, Michigan 10
1-1-91	Washington 46, Iowa 34
1-1-92	Washington 34, Michigan 14
1-1-93	Michigan 38, Washington 31
1-1-94	Wisconsin 21, UCLA 16
1-2-95	Penn St 38, Oregon 20
1-1-96	Southern Cal 41, Northwestern 32
1-1-97	Ohio St 20, Arizona St 17
1-1-98	Michigan 21, Washington St 16
1-1-99	Wisconsin 38, UCLA 31
1-1-2000	Wisconsin 17, Stanford 9
1-1-2001	Washington 34, Purdue 24
1-3-2002	Miami 37, Nebraska 14
1-1-2003	Oklahoma 34, Washington St 14
1-1-2004	Southern Cal 28, Michigan 14
1-1-2005	Texas 38, Michigan 37

City: Pasadena. Stadium: Rose Bowl, capacity 96,576.
Playing Sites: Tournament Park (1902, 1916–22), Rose Bowl (1923–41, since 1943), Duke Stadium, Durham, NC (1942).

Orange Bowl

1-1-35	Bucknell 26, Miami (FL) 0
1-1-36	Catholic 20, Mississippi 19
1-1-37	Duquesne 13, Mississippi St 12
1-1-38	Auburn 6, Michigan St 0
1-2-39	Tennessee 17, Oklahoma 0
1-1-40	Georgia Tech 21, Missouri 7

Note: The Fiesta, Orange, Rose and Sugar Bowls constitute the Bowl Alliance, formed in 1995. The Alliance holds eight berths: one each for the champions of the ACC, Big 10, Big 12, Big East, Pac 10 and SEC, and two at-large, reserved for any Division I-A team with at least nine wins and ranked in the top 12 of the BCS rankings. Of the eight teams, the two highest-ranked go to the Fiesta Bowl in 2003, and the Sugar Bowl in 2004. Once these four BCS matches have been set conferences may place the remaining qualified teams in the other bowls. Teams that have won at least six games against Division I-A teams qualify.

Orange Bowl *(Cont.)*

1-1-41 ....Mississippi St 14, Georgetown 7
1-1-42 ....Georgia 40, Texas Christian 26
1-1-43 ....Alabama 37, Boston College 21
1-1-44 ....Louisiana St 19, Texas A&M 14
1-1-45 ....Tulsa 26, Georgia Tech 12
1-1-46 ....Miami (FL) 13, Holy Cross 6
1-1-47 ....Rice 8, Tennessee 0
1-1-48 ....Georgia Tech 20, Kansas 14
1-1-49 ....Texas 41, Georgia 28
1-2-50 ....Santa Clara 21, Kentucky 13
1-1-51 ....Clemson 15, Miami (FL) 14
1-1-52 ....Georgia Tech 17, Baylor 14
1-1-53 ....Alabama 61, Syracuse 6
1-1-54 ....Oklahoma 7, Maryland 0
1-1-55 ....Duke 34, Nebraska 7
1-2-56 ....Oklahoma 20, Maryland 6
1-1-57 ....Colorado 27, Clemson 21
1-1-58 ....Oklahoma 48, Duke 21
1-1-59 ....Oklahoma 21, Syracuse 6
1-1-60 ....Georgia 14, Missouri 0
1-2-61 ....Missouri 21, Navy 14
1-1-62 ....Louisiana St 25, Colorado 7
1-1-63 ....Alabama 17, Oklahoma 0
1-1-64 ....Nebraska 13, Auburn 7
1-1-65 ....Texas 21, Alabama 17
1-1-66 ....Alabama 39, Nebraska 28
1-2-67 ....Florida 27, Georgia Tech 12
1-1-68 ....Oklahoma 26, Tennessee 24
1-1-69 ....Penn St 15, Kansas 14
1-1-70 ....Penn St 10, Missouri 3
1-1-71 ....Nebraska 17, Louisiana St 12
1-1-72 ....Nebraska 38, Alabama 6
1-1-73 ....Nebraska 40, Notre Dame 6
1-1-74 ....Penn St 16, Louisiana St 9
1-1-75 ....Notre Dame 13, Alabama 11
1-1-76 ....Oklahoma 14, Michigan 6
1-1-77 ....Ohio St 27, Colorado 10
1-2-78 ....Arkansas 31, Oklahoma 6
1-1-79 ....Oklahoma 31, Nebraska 24
1-1-80 ....Oklahoma 24, Florida St 7
1-1-81 ....Oklahoma 18, Florida St 17
1-1-82 ....Clemson 22, Nebraska 15
1-1-83 ....Nebraska 21, Louisiana St 20
1-2-84 ....Miami (FL) 31, Nebraska 30
1-1-85 ....Washington 28, Oklahoma 17
1-1-86 ....Oklahoma 25, Penn St 10
1-1-87 ....Oklahoma 42, Arkansas 8
1-1-88 ....Miami (FL) 20, Oklahoma 14
1-2-89 ....Miami (FL) 23, Nebraska 3
1-1-90 ....Notre Dame 21, Colorado 6
1-1-91 ....Colorado 10, Notre Dame 9
1-1-92 ....Miami (FL) 22, Nebraska 0
1-1-93 ....Florida St 27, Nebraska 14
1-1-94 ....Florida St 18, Nebraska 16
1-1-95 ....Nebraska 24, Miami (FL) 17
1-1-96 ....Florida St 31, Notre Dame 26
12-31-96 ....Nebraska 41, Virginia Tech 21
1-2-98 ....Nebraska 42, Tennessee 17
1-2-99 ....Florida 31, Syracuse 10
1-1-00 ....Michigan 35, Alabama 34 (ot)
1-3-01 ....Oklahoma 13, Florida St 2
1-2-02 ....Florida 56, Maryland 23
1-2-03 ....Southern Cal 38, Iowa 17
1-1-04 ....Miami (FL) 16, Florida St 15
1-4-05 ....Southern Cal 55, Oklahoma 19

City: Miami. Stadium: Pro Player Stadium, capacity 75,192.
Playing Sites: Orange Bowl (1935–96), Pro Player Stadium
(since 1996).

Sugar Bowl

1-1-35 ....Tulane 20, Temple 14
1-1-36 ....Texas Christian 3, Louisiana St 2
1-1-37 ....Santa Clara 21, Louisiana St 14
1-1-38 ....Santa Clara 6, Louisiana St 0
1-2-39 ....Texas Christian 15, Carnegie Tech 7
1-1-40 ....Texas A&M 14, Tulane 13
1-1-41 ....Boston Col 19, Tennessee 13
1-1-42 ....Fordham 2, Missouri 0
1-1-43 ....Tennessee 14, Tulsa 7
1-1-44 ....Georgia Tech 20, Tulsa 18
1-1-45 ....Duke 29, Alabama 26
1-1-46 ....Oklahoma St 33, St. Mary's (CA) 13
1-1-47 ....Georgia 20, N Carolina 10
1-1-48 ....Texas 27, Alabama 7
1-1-49 ....Oklahoma 14, N Carolina 6
1-2-50 ....Oklahoma 35, Louisiana St 0
1-1-51 ....Kentucky 13, Oklahoma 7
1-1-52 ....Maryland 28, Tennessee 13
1-1-53 ....Georgia Tech 24, Mississippi 7
1-1-54 ....Georgia Tech 42, W Virginia 19
1-1-55 ....Navy 21, Mississippi 0
1-2-56 ....Georgia Tech 7, Pittsburgh 0
1-1-57 ....Baylor 13, Tennessee 7
1-1-58 ....Mississippi 39, Texas 7
1-1-59 ....Louisiana St 7, Clemson 0
1-1-60 ....Mississippi 21, Louisiana St 0
1-2-61 ....Mississippi 14, Rice 6
1-1-62 ....Alabama 10, Arkansas 3
1-1-63 ....Mississippi 17, Arkansas 13
1-1-64 ....Alabama 12, Mississippi 7
1-1-65 ....Louisiana St 13, Syracuse 10
1-1-66 ....Missouri 20, Florida 18
1-2-67 ....Alabama 34, Nebraska 7
1-1-68 ....Louisiana St 20, Wyoming 13
1-1-69 ....Arkansas 16, Georgia 2
1-1-70 ....Mississippi 27, Arkansas 22
1-1-71 ....Tennessee 34, Air Force 13
1-1-72 ....Oklahoma 40, Auburn 22
12-31-72 ....Oklahoma 14, Penn St 0
12-31-73 ....Notre Dame 24, Alabama 23
12-31-74 ....Nebraska 13, Florida 10
12-31-75 ....Alabama 13, Penn St 6
1-1-77 ....Pittsburgh 27, Georgia 3
1-2-78 ....Alabama 35, Ohio St 6
1-1-79 ....Alabama 14, Penn St 7
1-1-80 ....Alabama 24, Arkansas 9
1-1-81 ....Georgia 17, Notre Dame 10
1-1-82 ....Pittsburgh 24, Georgia 20
1-1-83 ....Penn St 27, Georgia 23
1-2-84 ....Auburn 9, Michigan 7
1-1-85 ....Nebraska 28, Louisiana St 10
1-1-86 ....Tennessee 35, Miami (FL) 7
1-1-87 ....Nebraska 30, Louisiana St 15
1-1-88 ....Syracuse 16, Auburn 16
1-2-89 ....Florida St 13, Auburn 7
1-1-90 ....Miami (FL) 33, Alabama 25
1-1-91 ....Tennessee 23, Virginia 22
1-1-92 ....Notre Dame 39, Florida 28
1-1-93 ....Alabama 34, Miami (FL) 13
1-1-94 ....Florida 41, West Virginia 7
1-2-95 ....Florida St 23, Florida 17
12-31-95 ....Virginia Tech 28, Texas 10
1-2-97 ....Florida 52, Florida St 20
1-1-98 ....Florida St 31, Ohio St 14
1-1-99 ....Ohio St 24, Texas A&M 14
1-4-00 ....Florida St 46, Virginia Tech 29
1-2-01 ....Miami (FL) 37, Florida 20
1-1-02 ....Louisiana St 47, Illinois 34
1-1-03 ....Georgia 26, Florida St 13
1-4-04 ....Louisiana St 21, Oklahoma 14

Sugar Bowl (Cont.)

1-3-05 ....Auburn 16, Virginia Tech 13

City: New Orleans. Stadium: Louisiana Superdome, capacity 76,791. Playing Sites: Tulane Stadium (1935–74), Louisiana Superdome (since 1975).

Cotton Bowl

1-1-37 ....Texas Christian 16, Marquette 6
1-1-38 ....Rice 28, Colorado 14
1-2-39 ....St. Mary's (CA) 20, Texas Tech 13
1-1-40 ....Clemson 6, Boston Col 3
1-1-41 ....Texas A&M 13, Fordham 12
1-1-42 ....Alabama 29, Texas A&M 21
1-1-43 ....Texas 14, Georgia Tech 7
1-1-44 ....Texas 7, Randolph Field 7
1-1-45 ....Oklahoma St 34, Texas Christian 0
1-1-46 ....Texas 40, Missouri 27
1-1-47 ....Arkansas 0, Louisiana St 0
1-1-48 ....Southern Methodist 13, Penn St 13
1-1-49 ....Southern Methodist 21, Oregon 13
1-2-50 ....Rice 27, N Carolina 13
1-1-51 ....Tennessee 20, Texas 14
1-1-52 ....Kentucky 20, Texas Christian 7
1-1-53 ....Texas 16, Tennessee 0
1-1-54 ....Rice 28, Alabama 6
1-1-55 ....Georgia Tech 14, Arkansas 6
1-2-56 ....Mississippi 14, Texas Christian 13
1-1-57 ....Texas Christian 28, Syracuse 27
1-1-58 ....Navy 20, Rice 7
1-1-59 ....Texas Christian 0, Air Force 0
1-1-60 ....Syracuse 23, Texas 14
1-2-61 ....Duke 7, Arkansas 6
1-1-62 ....Texas 12, Mississippi 7
1-1-63 ....Louisiana St 13, Texas 0
1-1-64 ....Texas 28, Navy 6
1-1-65 ....Arkansas 10, Nebraska 7
1-1-66 ....Louisiana St 14, Arkansas 7
12-31-66 ....Georgia 24, Southern Methodist 9
1-1-68 ....Texas A&M 20, Alabama 16
1-1-69 ....Texas 36, Tennessee 13
1-1-70 ....Texas 21, Notre Dame 17
1-1-71 ....Notre Dame 24, Texas 11
1-1-72 ....Penn St 30, Texas 6
1-1-73 ....Texas 17, Alabama 13
1-1-74 ....Nebraska 19, Texas 3
1-1-75 ....Penn St 41, Baylor 20
1-1-76 ....Arkansas 31, Georgia 10
1-1-77 ....Houston 30, Maryland 21
1-2-78 ....Notre Dame 38, Texas 10
1-1-79 ....Notre Dame 35, Houston 34
1-1-80 ....Houston 17, Nebraska 14
1-1-81 ....Alabama 30, Baylor 2
1-1-82 ....Texas 14, Alabama 12
1-1-83 ....SMU 7, Pittsburgh 3
1-2-84 ....Georgia 10, Texas 9
1-1-85 ....Boston Col 45, Houston 28
1-1-86 ....Texas A&M 36, Auburn 16
1-1-87 ....Ohio St 28, Texas A&M 12
1-1-88 ....Texas A&M 35, Notre Dame 10
1-2-89 ....UCLA 17, Arkansas 3
1-1-90 ....Tennessee 31, Arkansas 27
1-1-91 ....Miami (FL) 46, Texas 3
1-1-92 ....Florida St 10, Texas A&M 2
1-1-93 ....Notre Dame 28, Texas A&M 3
1-1-94 ....Notre Dame 24, Texas A&M 21
1-2-95 ....Southern Cal 55, Texas Tech 14
1-1-96 ....Colorado 38, Oregon 6
1-1-97 ....Brigham Young 19, Kansas St 15
1-1-98 ....UCLA 29, Texas A&M 23
1-1-99 ....Texas 38, Mississippi St 11
1-1-00 ....Arkansas 27, Texas 6

Cotton Bowl (Cont.)

1-1-01 ....Kansas St 35, Tennessee 21
1-1-02 ....Oklahoma 10, Arkansas 3
1-1-03 ....Texas 35, Louisiana St 20
1-2-04 ....Mississippi 31, Oklahoma St 28
1-1-05 ....Tennessee 38, Texas A&M 7

City: Dallas. Stadium: Cotton Bowl, capacity 68,252.

Sun Bowl

1-1-36 ....Hardin-Simmons 14, New Mexico St 14
1-1-37 ....Hardin-Simmons 34, UTEP 6
1-1-38 ....W Virginia 7, Texas Tech 6
1-2-39 ....Utah 26, New Mexico 0
1-1-40 ....Catholic 0, Arizona St 0
1-1-41 ....Case Reserve 26, Arizona St 13
1-1-42 ....Tulsa 6, Texas Tech 0
1-1-43 ....2nd Air Force 13, Hardin-Simmons 7
1-1-44 ....Southwestern (TX) 7, New Mexico 0
1-1-45 ....Southwestern (TX) 35, New Mexico 0
1-1-46 ....New Mexico 34, Denver 24
1-1-47 ....Cincinnati 18, Virginia Tech 6
1-1-48 ....Miami (OH) 13, Texas Tech 12
1-1-49 ....W Virginia 21, UTEP 12
1-2-50 ....UTEP 33, Georgetown 20
1-1-51 ....W Texas St 14, Cincinnati 13
1-1-52 ....Texas Tech 25, Pacific 14
1-1-53 ....Pacific 26, Southern Miss 14
1-1-54 ....UTEP 37, Southern Miss 14
1-1-55 ....UTEP 47, Florida St 20
1-1-56 ....Wyoming 21, Texas Tech 14
1-1-57 ....George Washington 13, UTEP 0
1-1-58 ....Louisville 34, Drake 20
12-31-58 ....Wyoming 14, Hardin-Simmons 6
12-31-59 ....New Mexico St 28, N Texas 8
12-31-60 ....New Mexico St 20, Utah St 13
12-30-61 ....Villanova 17, Wichita St 9
12-31-62 ....W Texas St 15, Ohio 14
12-31-63 ....Oregon 21, Southern Methodist 14
12-26-64 ....Georgia 7, Texas Tech 0
12-31-65 ....UTEP 13, Texas Christian 12
12-24-66 ....Wyoming 28, Florida St 20
12-30-67 ....UTEP 14, Mississippi 7
12-28-68 ....Auburn 34, Arizona 10
12-20-69 ....Nebraska 45, Georgia 6
12-19-70 ....Georgia Tech 17, Texas Tech 9
12-18-71 ....Louisiana St 33, Iowa St 15
12-30-72 ....N Carolina 32, Texas Tech 28
12-29-73 ....Missouri 34, Auburn 17
12-28-74 ....Mississippi St 26, N Carolina 24
12-26-75 ....Pittsburgh 33, Kansas 19
1-2-77 ....Texas A&M 37, Florida 14
12-31-77 ....Stanford 24, Louisiana St 14
12-23-78 ....Texas 42, Maryland 0
12-22-79 ....Washington 14, Texas 7
12-27-80 ....Nebraska 31, Mississippi St 17
12-26-81 ....Oklahoma 40, Houston 14
12-25-82 ....N Carolina 26, Texas 10
12-24-83 ....Alabama 28, Southern Methodist 7
12-22-84 ....Maryland 28, Tennessee 27
12-28-85 ....Georgia 13, Arizona 13
12-25-86 ....Alabama 28, Washington 6
12-25-87 ....Oklahoma St 35, W Virginia 33
12-24-88 ....Alabama 29, Army 28
12-30-89 ....Pittsburgh 31, Texas A&M 28
12-31-90 ....Michigan St 17, Southern Cal 16
12-31-91 ....UCLA 6, Illinois 3
12-31-92 ....Baylor 20, Arizona 15
12-24-93 ....Oklahoma 41, Texas Tech 10
12-30-94 ....Texas 35, N Carolina 31
12-29-95 ....Iowa 38, Washington 18
12-31-96 ....Stanford 38, Michigan St 0

Sun Bowl (Cont.)

12-31-97 ....Arizona St 17, Iowa 7
12-31-98 ....Texas Christian 28, Southern Cal 19
12-31-99 ....Oregon 24, Minnesota 20
12-29-00 ....Wisconsin 21, UCLA 20
12-31-01 ....Washington St 33, Purdue 27
12-31-02 ....Purdue 34, Washington 24
12-31-03 ....Minnesota 31, Oregon 30
12-31-04 ....Arizona State 27, Purdue 23

City: El Paso. Stadium: Sun Bowl, capacity 51,270.

Name Changes: Sun Bowl (1936–86; 94–), John Hancock Sun Bowl (1987–88), John Hancock Bowl (1989–93).

Playing Sites: Kidd Field (1936–62), Sun Bowl (since 1963).

Gator Bowl

1-1-46 ....Wake Forest 26, S Carolina 14
1-1-47 ....Oklahoma 34, N Carolina St 13
1-1-48 ....Maryland 20, Georgia 20
1-1-49 ....Clemson 24, Missouri 23
1-2-50 ....Maryland 20, Missouri 7
1-1-51 ....Wyoming 20, Washington & Lee 7
1-1-52 ....Miami (FL) 14, Clemson 0
1-1-53 ....Florida 14, Tulsa 13
1-1-54 ....Texas Tech 35, Auburn 13
12-31-54 ....Auburn 33, Baylor 13
12-31-55 ....Vanderbilt 25, Auburn 13
12-29-56 ....Georgia Tech 21, Pittsburgh 14
12-28-57 ....Tennessee 3, Texas A&M 0
12-27-58 ....Mississippi 7, Florida 3
1-2-60 ....Arkansas 14, Georgia Tech 7
12-31-60 ....Florida 13, Baylor 12
12-30-61 ....Penn St 30, Georgia Tech 15
12-29-62 ....Florida 17, Penn St 7
12-28-63 ....N Carolina 35, Air Force 0
1-2-65 ....Florida St 36, Oklahoma 19
12-31-65 ....Georgia Tech 31, Texas Tech 21
12-31-66 ....Tennessee 18, Syracuse 12
12-30-67 ....Penn St 17, Florida St 17
12-28-68 ....Missouri 35, Alabama 10
12-27-69 ....Florida 14, Tennessee 13
1-2-71 ....Auburn 35, Mississippi 28
12-31-71 ....Georgia 7, N Carolina 3
12-30-72 ....Auburn 24, Colorado 3
12-29-73 ....Texas Tech 28, Tennessee 19
12-30-74 ....Auburn 27, Texas 3
12-29-75 ....Maryland 13, Florida 0
12-27-76 ....Notre Dame 20, Penn St 9
12-30-77 ....Pittsburgh 34, Clemson 3
12-29-78 ....Clemson 17, Ohio St 15
12-28-79 ....N Carolina 17, Michigan 15
12-29-80 ....Pittsburgh 37, S Carolina 9
12-28-81 ....N Carolina 31, Arkansas 27
12-30-82 ....Florida St 31, W Virginia 12
12-30-83 ....Florida 14, Iowa 6
12-28-84 ....Oklahoma 21, S Carolina 14
12-30-85 ....Florida St 34, Oklahoma St 23
12-27-86 ....Clemson 27, Stanford 21
12-31-87 ....Louisiana St 30, S Carolina 13
1-1-89 ....Georgia 34, Michigan St 27
12-30-89 ....Clemson 27, W Virginia 7
1-1-91 ....Michigan 35, Mississippi 3
12-29-91 ....Oklahoma 48, Virginia 14
12-31-92 ....Florida 27, N Carolina St 10
12-31-93 ....Alabama 24, North Carolina 10
12-30-94 ....Tennessee 45, Virginia Tech 23
1-1-96 ....Syracuse 41, Clemson 0
1-1-97 ....N Carolina 20, W Virginia 13
1-1-98 ....N Carolina 42, Virginia Tech 3
1-1-99 ....Georgia Tech 35, Notre Dame 28
1-1-00 ....Miami 27, Georgia Tech 13
1-1-01 ....Virginia Tech 41, Clemson 20

Gator Bowl (Cont.)

1-1-02 ....Florida St 30, Virginia Tech 17
1-1-03 ....N Carolina St 28, Notre Dame 6
1-1-04 ....Maryland 41, W Virginia 7
1-1-05 ....Florida State 30, West Virginia 18

City: Jacksonville, FL. Stadium: Alltel Stadium, capacity 76,976.

Florida Citrus Bowl

1-1-47 ....Catawba 31, Maryville (TN) 6
1-1-48 ....Catawba 7, Marshall 0
1-1-49 ....Murray St 21, Sul Ross St 21
1-2-50 ....St. Vincent 7, Emory & Henry 6
1-1-51 ....Morris Harvey 35, Emory & Henry 14
1-1-52 ....Stetson 35, Arkansas St 20
1-1-53 ....E Texas St 33, Tennessee Tech 0
1-1-54 ....E Texas St 7, Arkansas St 7
1-1-55 ....NE-Omaha 7, Eastern Kentucky 6
1-2-56 ....Juniata 6, Missouri Valley 6
1-1-57 ....W Texas St 20, Southern Miss 13
1-1-58 ....E Texas St 10, Southern Miss 9
12-27-58 ....E Texas St 26, Missouri Valley 7
1-1-60 ....Middle Tennessee St 21, Presbyterian 12
12-30-60 ....Citadel 27, Tennessee Tech 0
12-29-61 ....Lamar 21, Middle Tennessee St 14
12-22-62 ....Houston 49, Miami (OH) 21
12-28-63 ....Western Kentucky 27, Coast Guard 0
12-12-64 ....E Carolina 14, Massachusetts 13
12-11-65 ....E Carolina 31, Maine 0
12-10-66 ....Morgan St 14, W Chester 6
12-16-67 ....TN-Martin 25, W Chester 8
12-27-68 ....Richmond 49, Ohio 42
12-26-69 ....Toledo 56, Davidson 33
12-28-70 ....Toledo 40, William & Mary 12
12-28-71 ....Toledo 28, Richmond 3
12-29-72 ....Tampa 21, Kent St 18
12-22-73 ....Miami (OH) 16, Florida 7
12-21-74 ....Miami (OH) 21, Georgia 10
12-20-75 ....Miami (OH) 20, S Carolina 7
12-18-76 ....Oklahoma St 49, Brigham Young 21
12-23-77 ....Florida St 40, Texas Tech 17
12-23-78 ....N Carolina St 30, Pittsburgh 17
12-22-79 ....Louisiana St 34, Wake Forest 10
12-20-80 ....Florida 35, Maryland 20
12-19-81 ....Missouri 19, Southern Miss 17
12-18-82 ....Auburn 33, Boston Col 26
12-17-83 ....Tennessee 30, Maryland 23
12-22-84 ....Georgia 17, Florida St 17
12-28-85 ....Ohio St 10, Brigham Young 7
1-1-87 ....Auburn 16, Southern Cal 7
1-1-88 ....Clemson 35, Penn St 10
1-2-89 ....Clemson 13, Oklahoma 6
1-1-90 ....Illinois 31, Virginia 21
1-1-91 ....Georgia Tech 45, Nebraska 21
1-1-92 ....California 37, Clemson 13
1-1-93 ....Georgia 21, Ohio State 14
1-1-94 ....Penn State 31, Tennessee 13
1-2-95 ....Alabama 24, Ohio St 17
1-1-96 ....Tennessee 20, Ohio St 14
1-1-97 ....Tennessee 48, Northwestern 28
1-1-98 ....Florida 21, Penn St 6
1-1-99 ....Michigan 45, Arkansas 31
1-1-00 ....Michigan St 37, Florida 34
1-1-01 ....Michigan 31, Auburn 28
1-1-02 ....Tennessee 45, Michigan 17
1-1-03 ....Auburn 13, Penn St 9
1-1-04 ....Georgia 34, Purdue 27 (OT)
1-1-05 ....Iowa 30, LSU 25

City: Orlando, FL. Stadium: Florida Citrus Bowl, capacity 70,000. Name Change: Tangerine Bowl (1947–82).
Playing Sites: Tangerine Bowl (1947–72, 1974–82); Florida Field, Gainesville (1973); Orlando Stadium/Florida Citrus Bowl-Orlando (since 1983).

Liberty Bowl

12-19-59 ....Penn St 7, Alabama 0
12-17-60 ....Penn St 41, Oregon 12
12-16-61 ....Syracuse 15, Miami (FL) 14
12-15-62 ....Oregon St 6, Villanova 0
12-21-63 ....Mississippi St 16, N Carolina St 12
12-19-64 ....Utah 32, W Virginia 6
12-18-65 ....Mississippi 13, Auburn 7
12-10-66 ....Miami (FL) 14, Virginia Tech 7
12-16-67 ....N Carolina St 14, Georgia 7
12-14-68 ....Mississippi 34, Virginia Tech 17
12-13-69 ....Colorado 47, Alabama 33
12-12-70 ....Tulane 17, Colorado 3
12-20-71 ....Tennessee 14, Arkansas 13
12-18-72 ....Georgia Tech 31, Iowa St 30
12-17-73 ....N Carolina St 31, Kansas 18
12-16-74 ....Tennessee 7, Maryland 3
12-22-75 ....Southern Cal 20, Texas A&M 0
12-20-76 ....Alabama 36, UCLA 6
12-19-77 ....Nebraska 21, N Carolina 17
12-23-78 ....Missouri 20, Louisiana St 15
12-22-79 ....Penn St 9, Tulane 6
12-27-80 ....Purdue 28, Missouri 25
12-30-81 ....Ohio St 31, Navy 28
12-29-82 ....Alabama 21, Illinois 15
12-29-83 ....Notre Dame 19, Boston Col 18
12-27-84 ....Auburn 21, Arkansas 15
12-27-85 ....Baylor 21, Louisiana St 7
12-29-86 ....Tennessee 21, Minnesota 14
12-29-87 ....Georgia 20, Arkansas 17
12-28-88 ....Indiana 34, S Carolina 10
12-28-89 ....Mississippi 42, Air Force 29
12-27-90 ....Air Force 23, Ohio St 11
12-29-91 ....Air Force 38, Mississippi St 15
12-31-92 ....Mississippi 13, Air Force 0
12-28-93 ....Louisville 18, Michigan St 7
12-31-94 ....Illinois 30, E Carolina 0
12-30-95 ....East Carolina 19, Stanford 13
12-27-96 ....Syracuse 30, Houston 17
12-31-97 ....Southern Miss 41, Pittsburgh 7
12-31-98 ....Tulane 41, Brigham Young 27
12-31-99 ....Southern Miss 23, Colorado St 17
12-29-01 ....Colorado St 22, Louisville 17
12-31-01 ....Louisville 28, Brigham Young 10
12-31-02 ....Texas Christian 17, Colorado St 3
12-31-03 ....Utah 17, Southern Mississippi 0
12-31-04 ....Louisville 44, Boise State 40

City: Memphis (since 1965). Stadium: Liberty Bowl Memorial Stadium, capacity 62,921.
Playing Sites: Philadelphia (Municipal Stadium, 1959–63), Atlantic City (Convention Center, 1964).

Bluebonnet Bowl

12-19-59 ....Clemson 23, Texas Christian 7
12-17-60 ....Texas 3, Alabama 3
12-16-61 ....Kansas 33, Rice 7
12-22-62 ....Missouri 14, Georgia Tech 10
12-21-63 ....Baylor 14, LSU 7
12-19-64 ....Tulsa 14, Mississippi 7
12-18-65 ....Tennessee 27, Tulsa 6
12-17-66 ....Texas 19, Mississippi 0
12-23-67 ....Colorado 31, Miami (FL) 21
12-31-68 ....Southern Methodist 28, Oklahoma 27
12-31-69 ....Houston 36, Auburn 7
12-31-70 ....Alabama 24, Oklahoma 24
12-31-71 ....Colorado 29, Houston 17
12-30-72 ....Tennessee 24, Louisiana St 17
12-29-73 ....Houston 47, Tulane 7
12-23-74 ....N Carolina St 31, Houston 31
12-27-75 ....Texas 38, Colorado 21
12-31-76 ....Nebraska 27, Texas Tech 24
12-31-77 ....Southern Cal 47, Texas A&M 28
12-31-78 ....Stanford 25, Georgia 22

Bluebonnet Bowl *(Cont.)*

12-31-79 ....Purdue 27, Tennessee 22
12-31-80 ....N Carolina 16, Texas 7
12-31-81 ....Michigan 33, UCLA 14
12-31-82 ....Arkansas 28, Florida 24
12-31-83 ....Oklahoma St 24, Baylor 14
12-31-84 ....W Virginia 31, Texas Christian 14
12-31-85 ....Air Force 24, Texas 16
12-31-86 ....Baylor 21, Colorado 9
12-31-87 ....Texas 32, Pittsburgh 27

City: Houston. Playing sites: Rice Stadium (1959–67; 1985–86), Astrodome (1968–84, 1987).
Name change: Astro-Bluebonnet Bowl (1968–76). Bowl was discontinued after 1987.

Peach Bowl

12-30-68 ....Louisiana St 31, Florida St 27
12-30-69 ....W Virginia 14, S Carolina 3
12-30-70 ....Arizona St 48, N Carolina 26
12-30-71 ....Mississippi 41, Georgia Tech 18
12-29-72 ....N Carolina St 49, W Virginia 13
12-28-73 ....Georgia 17, Maryland 16
12-28-74 ....Vanderbilt 6, Texas Tech 6
12-31-75 ....W Virginia 13, N Carolina St 10
12-31-76 ....Kentucky 21, N Carolina 0
12-31-77 ....N Carolina St 24, Iowa St 14
12-25-78 ....Purdue 41, Georgia Tech 21
12-31-79 ....Baylor 24, Clemson 18
1-2-81 ....Miami (FL) 20, Virginia Tech 10
12-31-81 ....W Virginia 26, Florida 6
12-31-82 ....Iowa 28, Tennessee 22
12-30-83 ....Florida St 28, N Carolina 3
12-31-84 ....Virginia 27, Purdue 24
12-31-85 ....Army 31, Illinois 29
12-31-86 ....Virginia Tech 25, N Carolina St 24
1-2-88 ....Tennessee 27, Indiana 22
12-31-88 ....N Carolina St 28, Iowa 23
12-30-89 ....Syracuse 19, Georgia 18
12-29-90 ....Auburn 27, Indiana 23
1-1-92 ....E Carolina 37, N Carolina St 34
1-2-93 ....N Carolina 21, Mississippi St 17
12-31-93 ....Clemson 14, Kentucky 13
1-1-95 ....N Carolina St 28, Mississippi St 24
12-30-95 ....Virginia 34, Georgia 27
12-28-96 ....Louisiana St 10, Clemson 7
1-2-98 ....Auburn 21, Clemson 17
12-31-98 ....Georgia 35, Virginia 33
12-30-99 ....Mississippi St 17, Clemson 7
12-29-00 ....Louisiana St 28, Georgia Tech 14
12-31-01 ....N Carolina 16, Auburn 10
12-31-02 ....Maryland 30, Tennessee 3
1-2-04 ....Clemson 27, Tennessee 14
12-31-04 ....Miami(Fl) 27, Florida 10

City: Atlanta. Stadium: Georgia Dome, capacity 71,500.
Playing Sites: Grant Field (1968–70), Atlanta–Fulton County Stadium (1971–92), Georgia Dome (since 1993).

Fiesta Bowl

12-27-71 ....Arizona St 45, Florida St 38
12-23-72 ....Arizona St 49, Missouri 35
12-21-73 ....Arizona St 28, Pittsburgh 7
12-28-74 ....Oklahoma St 16, Brigham Young 6
12-26-75 ....Arizona St 17, Nebraska 14
12-25-76 ....Oklahoma 41, Wyoming 7
12-25-77 ....Penn St 42, Arizona St 30
12-25-78 ....Arkansas 10, UCLA 10
12-25-79 ....Pittsburgh 16, Arizona 10
12-26-80 ....Penn St 31, Ohio St 19
1-1-82 ....Penn St 26, Southern Cal 10
1-1-83 ....Arizona St 32, Oklahoma 21
1-2-84 ....Ohio St 28, Pittsburgh 23

Fiesta Bowl *(Cont.)*

1-1-85 ....UCLA 39, Miami (FL) 37
1-1-86 ....Michigan 27, Nebraska 23
1-2-87 ....Penn St 14, Miami (FL) 10
1-1-88 ....Florida St 31, Nebraska 28
1-2-89 ....Notre Dame 34, W Virginia 21
1-1-90 ....Florida St 41, Nebraska 17
1-1-91 ....Louisville 34, Alabama 7
1-1-92 ....Penn St 42, Tennessee 17
1-1-93 ....Syracuse 26, Colorado 22
1-1-94 ....Arizona 29, Miami (FL) 0
1-2-95 ....Colorado 41, Notre Dame 24
1-2-96 ....Nebraska 62, Florida 24
1-1-97 ....Penn St 38, Texas 15
12-31-97 ....Kansas St 35, Syracuse 18
1-4-99 ....Tennessee 23, Florida St 16
1-2-00 ....Nebraska 31, Tennessee 21
1-1-01 ....Oregon St 41, Notre Dame 9
1-1-02 ....Oregon 38, Colorado 16
1-3-03 ....Ohio St 31, Miami (FL) 24 [2 OT]
1-2-04 ....Ohio St 35, Kansas St 28
1-1-05 ....Utah 35, Pittsburgh 7

City: Tempe, AZ. Stadium: Sun Devil Stadium, capacity 73,471.

Independence Bowl

12-13-76 ....McNeese St 20, Tulsa 16
12-17-77 ....Louisiana Tech 24, Louisville 14
12-16-78 ....E Carolina 35, Louisiana Tech 13
12-15-79 ....Syracuse 31, McNeese St 7
12-13-80 ....Southern Miss 16, McNeese St 14
12-12-81 ....Texas A&M 33, Oklahoma St 16
12-11-82 ....Wisconsin 14, Kansas St 3
12-10-83 ....Air Force 9, Mississippi 3
12-15-84 ....Air Force 23, Virginia Tech 7
12-21-85 ....Minnesota 20, Clemson 13
12-20-86 ....Mississippi 20, Texas Tech 17
12-19-87 ....Washington 24, Tulane 12
12-23-88 ....Southern Miss 38, UTEP 18
12-16-89 ....Oregon 27, Tulsa 24
12-15-90 ....Louisiana Tech 34, Maryland 34
12-29-91 ....Georgia 24, Arkansas 15
12-31-92 ....Wake Forest 39, Oregon 35
12-31-93 ....Virginia Tech 45, Indiana 20
12-28-94 ....Virginia 20, Texas Christian 10
12-29-95 ....Louisiana St 45, Michigan St 26
12-31-96 ....Auburn 32, Army 29
12-28-97 ....Louisiana St 27, Notre Dame 9
12-31-98 ....Mississippi 35, Texas Tech 18
12-31-99 ....Mississippi 27, Oklahoma 25
12-31-00 ....Mississippi St 43, Texas A&M 41
12-27-01 ....Alabama 14, Iowa St 13
12-27-02 ....Mississippi 27, Nebraska 23
12-31-03 ....Arkansas 27, Missouri 14
12-28-04 ....Iowa State 17, Miami(OH) 13

City: Shreveport, LA. Stadium: Independence Stadium, capacity 50,459.

All-American Bowl

12-22-77 ....Maryland 17, Minnesota 7
12-20-78 ....Texas A&M 28, Iowa St 12
12-29-79 ....Missouri 24, S Carolina 14
12-27-80 ....Arkansas 34, Tulane 15
12-31-81 ....Mississippi St 10, Kansas 0
12-31-82 ....Air Force 36, Vanderbilt 28
12-22-83 ....W Virginia 20, Kentucky 16
12-29-84 ....Kentucky 20, Wisconsin 19
12-31-85 ....Georgia Tech 17, Michigan St 14
12-31-86 ....Florida St 27, Indiana 13
12-22-87 ....Virginia 22, Brigham Young 16

12-29-88 ....Florida 14, Illinois 10
12-28-89 ....Texas Tech 49, Duke 21
12-28-90 ....N Carolina St 31, Southern Miss. 27

City: Birmingham, AL. Stadium: Legion Field.
Name Change: Hall of Fame Classic (1977–84). Bowl was discontinued after 1990.

Holiday Bowl

12-22-78 ....Navy 23, Brigham Young 16
12-21-79 ....Indiana 38, Brigham Young 37
12-19-80 ....Brigham Young 46, SMU 45
12-18-81 ....Brigham Young 38, Washington St 36
12-17-82 ....Ohio St 47, Brigham Young 17
12-23-83 ....Brigham Young 21, Missouri 17
12-21-84 ....Brigham Young 24, Michigan 17
12-22-85 ....Arkansas 18, Arizona St 17
12-30-86 ....Iowa 39, San Diego St 38
12-30-87 ....Iowa 20, Wyoming 19
12-30-88 ....Oklahoma St 62, Wyoming 14
12-29-89 ....Penn St 50, Brigham Young 39
12-29-90 ....Texas A&M 65, Brigham Young 14
12-30-91 ....Iowa 13, Brigham Young 13
12-30-92 ....Hawaii 27, Illinois 17
12-30-93 ....Ohio St 28, Brigham Young 21
12-30-94 ....Michigan 24, Colorado St 14
12-29-95 ....Kansas St 54, Colorado St 21
12-30-96 ....Colorado 33, Washington 21
12-29-97 ....Colorado St 35, Missouri 24
12-30-98 ....Arizona 23, Nebraska 20
12-29-99 ....Kansas St 24, Washington 20
12-29-00 ....Oregon 35, Texas 30
12-28-01 ....Texas 47, Washington 43
12-27-02 ....Kansas St 34, Arizona St 27
12-30-03 ....Washington St 28, Texas 20
12-30-04 ....Texas Tech 45, California 31

City: San Diego. Stadium: Qualcomm Stadium, capacity 70,000.

Las Vegas Bowl

12-19-81 ....Toledo 27, San Jose St 25
12-18-82 ....Fresno St 29, Bowling Green 28
12-17-83 ....Northern Illinois 20, Cal St–Fullerton 13
12-15-84 ....UNLV 30, Toledo 13*
12-14-85 ....Fresno St 51, Bowling Green 7
12-13-86 ....San Jose St 37, Miami (OH) 7
12-12-87 ....Eastern Michigan 30, San Jose St 27
12-10-88 ....Fresno St 35, Western Michigan 30
12-9-89 ....Fresno St 27, Ball St 6
12-8-90 ....San Jose St 48, Central Michigan 24
12-14-91 ....Bowling Green 28, Fresno St 21
12-18-92 ....Bowling Green 35, Nevada 34
12-17-93 ....Utah St 42, Ball St 33
12-15-94 ....UNLV 52, Central Michigan 24
12-14-95 ....Toledo 40, Nevada 37
12-19-96 ....Nevada 18, Ball St 15
12-19-97 ....Oregon 41, Air Force 13
12-19-98 ....N Carolina 20, San Diego St 13
12-18-99 ....Utah 17, Fresno St 16
12-21-00 ....UNLV 31, Arkansas 14
12-25-01 ....Utah 10, Southern Cal 6
12-25-02 ....UCLA 27, New Mexico 13
12-24-03 ....Oregon St 55, New Mexico 14
12-23-04 ....Wyoming 24, UCLA, 21

* Toledo won later by forfeit. City: Las Vegas (since 1992). Stadium: Sam Boyd Silver Bowl Stadium, capacity 40,0.

Name change: California Bowl (1981–91).

Playing sites: Fresno, CA (Bulldog Stadium, 1981–91), Las Vegas.

Aloha Bowl

12-25-82	Washington 21, Maryland 20
12-26-83	Penn St 13, Washington 10
12-29-84	Southern Methodist 27, Notre Dame 20
12-28-85	Alabama 24, Southern Cal 3
12-27-86	Arizona 30, N Carolina 21
12-25-87	UCLA 20, Florida 16
12-25-88	Washington St 24, Houston 22
12-25-89	Michigan St 33, Hawaii 13
12-25-90	Syracuse 28, Arizona 0
12-25-91	Georgia Tech 18, Stanford 17
12-25-92	Kansas 23, Brigham Young 20
12-25-93	Colorado 41, Fresno St 30
12-25-94	Boston College 12, Kansas St 7
12-25-95	Kansas 51, UCLA 30
12-25-96	Navy 42, California 38
12-25-97	Washington 51, Michigan St 23
12-25-98	Colorado 51, Oregon 43
12-25-99	Wake Forest 23, Arizona St 3
12-25-00	Boston College 31, Arizona St 17

City: Honolulu. Stadium: Aloha Stadium. Bowl was discontinued after 2000.

Freedom Bowl

12-16-84	Iowa 55, Texas 17
12-30-85	Washington 20, Colorado 17
12-30-86	UCLA 31, Brigham Young 10
12-30-87	Arizona St 33, Air Force 28
12-29-88	Brigham Young 20, Colorado 17
12-30-89	Washington 34, Florida 7
12-29-90	Colorado St 32, Oregon 31
12-30-91	Tulsa 28, San Diego St 17
12-29-92	Fresno St 24, Southern Cal 7
12-30-93	Southern Cal 28, Utah 21
12-29-94	Utah 16, Arizona 13

City: Anaheim. Stadium: Anaheim Stadium. Bowl was discontinued after 1994.

Outback Bowl

12-23-86	Boston College 27, Georgia 24
1-2-88	Michigan 28, Alabama 24
1-2-89	Syracuse 23, Louisiana St 10
1-1-90	Auburn 31, Ohio St 14
1-1-91	Clemson 30, Illinois 0
1-1-92	Syracuse 24, Ohio St 17
1-1-93	Tennessee 38, Boston College 23
1-1-94	Michigan 42, N Carolina St 7
1-2-95	Wisconsin 34, Duke 20
1-1-96	Penn St 43, Auburn 14
1-1-97	Alabama 17, Michigan 14
1-1-98	Georgia 33, Wisconsin 6
1-1-99	Penn St 26, Kentucky 14
1-1-00	Georgia 28, Purdue 25
1-1-01	S Carolina 24, Ohio St 7
1-1-02	S Carolina 31, Ohio St 28
1-1-03	Michigan 38, Florida 30
1-1-04	Iowa 37, Florida 17
1-1-05	Georgia 24, Wisconsin 21

City: Tampa. Stadium: Raymond James Stadium, capacity 75,000. Name change: Hall of Fame Bowl (1986–95).

Insight.com Bowl

12-31-89	Arizona 17, N Carolina St 10
12-31-90	California 17, Wyoming 15
12-31-91	Indiana 24, Baylor 0
12-29-92	Washington St 31, Utah 28
12-29-93	Kansas St 52, Wyoming 17
12-29-94	Brigham Young 31, Oklahoma 6
12-27-95	Texas Tech 55, Air Force 41
12-27-96	Wisconsin 38, Utah 10
12-27-97	Arizona 20, New Mexico 14
12-26-98	Missouri 34, W Virginia 31
12-31-99	Colorado 62, Boston College 28
12-28-00	Iowa St 37, Pittsburgh 29
12-29-01	Syracuse 26, Kansas St 3
12-26-02	Pittsburgh 38, Oregon St 13
12-26-03	California 52, Virginia Tech 49
12-28-04	Oregon State 38, Notre Dame 21

City: Tucson. Stadium: Arizona Stadium, capacity 55,883. Name change: Copper Bowl 1989–97.

Tangerine Bowl

12-28-90	Florida St 24, Penn St 17
12-28-91	Alabama 30, Colorado 25
1-1-93	Stanford 24, Penn St 3
1-1-94	Boston College 31, Virginia 13
1-2-95	S Carolina 24, W Virginia 21
12-30-95	N Carolina 20, Arkansas 10
12-27-96	Miami (FL) 31, Virginia 21
12-29-97	Georgia Tech 35, W Virginia 30
12-29-98	Miami (FL) 46, N Carolina St 23
12-30-99	Illinois 62, Virginia 21
12-28-00	N Carolina St 38, Minnesota 30
12-20-01	Pittsburgh 34, N Carolina St 19
12-23-02	Texas Tech 55, Clemson 15
12-22-03	N Carolina St 56, Kansas 26

City: Miami. Stadium: Pro Player Stadium, capacity 75,192. Name change: Blockbuster Bowl (1990–93), Carquest Bowl (1994–97), Micron PC Bowl (1998–00).

Alamo Bowl

12-31-93	California 37, Iowa 3
12-31-94	Washington St 10, Baylor 3
12-28-95	Texas A&M 22, Michigan 20
12-29-96	Iowa 27, Texas Tech 0
12-30-97	Purdue 33, Oklahoma St 20
12-29-98	Purdue 37, Kansas St 34
12-28-99	Penn St 24, Texas A&M 0
12-30-00	Nebraska 66, Northwestern 17
12-29-01	Iowa 16, Texas Tech 13
12-28-02	Wisconsin 31, Colorado 28 (OT)
12-29-03	Nebraska 17, Michigan St 3
12-29-04	Ohio State 33, Oklahoma State 7

City: San Antonio, TX. Stadium: Alamodome, capaciity 67,000.

1936

		Record	Coach
1.	Minnesota	7-1-0	Bernie Bierman
2.	Louisiana St	9-0-1	Bernie Moore
3.	Pittsburgh	7-1-1	Jack Sutherland
4.	Alabama	8-0-1	Frank Thomas
5.	Washington	7-1-1	Jimmy Phelan
6.	Santa Clara	7-1-0	Buck Shaw
7.	Northwestern	7-1-0	Pappy Waldorf
8.	Notre Dame	6-2-1	Elmer Layden
9.	Nebraska	7-2-0	Dana X. Bible
10.	Pennsylvania	7-1-0	Harvey Harman
11.	Duke	9-1-0	Wallace Wade
12.	Yale	7-1-0	Ducky Pond
13.	Dartmouth	7-1-1	Red Blaik
14.	Duquesne	7-2-0	John Smith
15.	Fordham	5-1-2	Jim Crowley
16.	Texas Christian	8-2-2	Dutch Meyer
17.	Tennessee	6-2-2	Bob Neyland
18.	Arkansas	7-3-0	Fred Thomsen
19.	Navy	6-3-0	Tom Hamilton
20.	Marquette	7-1-0	Frank Murray

1937

		Record	Coach
1.	Pittsburgh	9-0-1	Jack Sutherland
2.	California	9-0-1	Stub Allison
3.	Fordham	7-0-1	Jim Crowley
4.	Alabama	9-0-0	Frank Thomas
5.	Minnesota	6-2-0	Bernie Bierman
6.	Villanova	8-0-1	Clipper Smith
7.	Dartmouth	7-0-2	Red Blaik
8.	Louisiana St	9-1-0	Bernie Moore
9.	Notre Dame	6-2-1	Elmer Layden
	Santa Clara	8-0-0	Buck Shaw
11.	Nebraska	6-1-2	Biff Jones
12.	Yale	6-1-1	Ducky Pond
13.	Ohio St	6-2-0	Francis Schmidt
14.	Holy Cross	8-0-2	Eddie Anderson
	Arkansas	6-2-2	Fred Thomsen
16.	Texas Christian	4-2-2	Dutch Meyer
17.	Colorado	8-0-0	Bunnie Oakes
18.	Rice	5-3-2	Jimmy Kitts
19.	N Carolina	7-1-1	Ray Wolf
20.	Duke	7-2-1	Wallace Wade

1938

		Record	Coach
1.	Texas Christian	10-0-0	Dutch Meyer
2.	Tennessee	10-0-0	Bob Neyland
3.	Duke	9-0-0	Wallace Wade
4.	Oklahoma	10-0-0	Tom Stidham
5.	#Notre Dame	8-1-0	Elmer Layden
6.	Carnegie Tech	7-1-0	Bill Kern
7.	Southern Cal	8-2-0	Howard Jones
8.	Pittsburgh	8-2-0	Jack Sutherland
9.	Holy Cross	8-1-0	Eddie Anderson
10.	Minnesota	6-2-0	Bernie Bierman
11.	Texas Tech	10-0-0	Pete Cawthon
12.	Cornell	5-1-1	Carl Snavely
13.	Alabama	7-1-1	Frank Thomas
14.	California	10-1-0	Stub Allison
15.	Fordham	6-1-2	Jim Crowley
16.	Michigan	6-1-1	Fritz Crisler
17.	Northwestern	4-2-2	Pappy Waldorf
18.	Villanova	8-0-1	Clipper Smith
19.	Tulane	7-2-1	Red Dawson
20.	Dartmouth	7-2-0	Red Blaik

#Selected No. 1 by the Dickinson System.

1939

		Record	Coach
1.	Texas A&M	10-0-0	Homer Norton
2.	Tennessee	10-0-0	Bob Neyland
3.	#Southern Cal	7-0-2	Howard Jones
4.	Cornell	8-0-0	Carl Snavely
5.	Tulane	8-0-1	Red Dawson
6.	Missouri	8-1-0	Don Faurot
7.	UCLA	6-0-4	Babe Horrell
8.	Duke	8-1-0	Wallace Wade
9.	Iowa	6-1-1	Eddie Anderson
10.	Duquesne	8-0-1	Buff Donelli
11.	Boston College	9-1-0	Frank Leahy
12.	Clemson	8-1-0	Jess Neely
13.	Notre Dame	7-2-0	Elmer Layden
14.	Santa Clara	5-1-3	Buck Shaw
15.	Ohio St	6-2-0	Francis Schmidt
16.	Georgia Tech	7-2-0	Bill Alexander
17.	Fordham	6-2-0	Jim Crowley
18.	Nebraska	7-1-1	Biff Jones
19.	Oklahoma	6-2-1	Tom Stidham
20.	Michigan	6-2-0	Fritz Crisler

#Selected No. 1 by the Dickinson System.

1940

		Record	Coach
1.	Minnesota	8-0-0	Bernie Bierman
2.	Stanford	9-0-0	C. Shaughnessy
3.	Michigan	7-1-0	Fritz Crisler
4.	Tennessee	10-0-0	Bob Neyland
5.	Boston College	10-0-0	Frank Leahy
6.	Texas A&M	8-1-0	Homer Norton
7.	Nebraska	8-1-0	Biff Jones
8.	Northwestern	6-2-0	Pappy Waldorf
9.	Mississippi St	9-0-1	Allyn McKeen
10.	Washington	7-2-0	Jimmy Phelan
11.	Santa Clara	6-1-1	Buck Shaw
12.	Fordham	7-1-0	Jim Crowley
13.	Georgetown	8-1-0	Jack Hagerty
14.	Pennsylvania	6-1-1	George Munger
15.	Cornell	6-2-0	Carl Snavely
16.	SMU	8-1-1	Matty Bell
17.	Hard.-Simmons	9-0-0	Abe Woodson
18.	Duke	7-2-0	Wallace Wade
19.	Lafayette	9-0-0	Hooks Mylin
20.	—		

Only 19 teams selected.

1941

		Record	Coach
1.	Minnesota	8-0-0	Bernie Bierman
2.	Duke	9-0-0	Wallace Wade
3.	Notre Dame	8-0-1	Frank Leahy
4.	Texas	8-1-1	Dana X. Bible
5.	Michigan	6-1-1	Fritz Crisler
6.	Fordham	7-1-0	Jim Crowley
7.	Missouri	8-1-0	Don Faurot
8.	Duquesne	8-0-0	Buff Donelli
9.	Texas A&M	9-1-0	Homer Norton
10.	Navy	7-1-1	Swede Larson
11.	Northwestern	5-3-0	Pappy Waldorf
12.	Oregon St	7-2-0	Lon Stiner
13.	Ohio St	6-1-1	Paul Brown
14.	Georgia	8-1-1	Wally Butts
15.	Pennsylvania	7-1-1	George Munger
16.	Mississippi St	8-1-1	Allyn McKeen
17.	Mississippi	6-2-1	Harry Mehre
18.	Tennessee	8-2-0	John Barnhill

1941 (CONT.)

	Record	Coach
19. Washington St	6-4-0	Babe Hollingbery
20. Alabama	8-2-0	Frank Thomas

1942

	Record	Coach
1. Ohio St	9-1-0	Paul Brown
2. Georgia	10-1-0	Wally Butts
3. Wisconsin	8-1-1	H. Stuhldreher
4. Tulsa	10-0-0	Henry Frnka
5. Georgia Tech	9-1-0	Bill Alexander
6. Notre Dame	7-2-2	Frank Leahy
7. Tennessee	8-1-1	John Barnhill
8. Boston College	8-1-0	Denny Myers
9. Michigan	7-3-0	Fritz Crisler
10. Alabama	7-3-0	Frank Thomas
11. Texas	8-2-0	Dana X. Bible
12. Stanford	6-4-0	Marchie Schwartz
13. UCLA	7-3-0	Babe Horrell
14. William & Mary	9-1-1	Carl Voyles
15. Santa Clara	7-2-0	Buck Shaw
16. Auburn	6-4-1	Jack Meagher
17. Washington St	6-2-2	Babe Hollingbery
18. Mississippi St	8-2-0	Allyn McKeen
19. Minnesota	5-4-0	George Hauser
Holy Cross	5-4-1	Ank Scanlon
Penn St	6-1-1	Bob Higgins

1943

	Record	Coach
1. Notre Dame	9-1-0	Frank Leahy
2. Iowa Pre-Flight	9-1-0	Don Faurot
3. Michigan	8-1-0	Fritz Crisler
4. Navy	8-1-0	Billick Whelchel
5. Purdue	9-0-0	Elmer Burnham
6. Great Lakes	10-2-0	Tony Hinkle
7. Duke	8-1-0	Eddie Cameron
8. Del Monte P-F	7-1-0	Bill Kern
9. Northwestern	6-2-0	Pappy Waldorf
10. March Field	9-1-0	Paul Schissler
11. Army	7-2-1	Red Blaik
12. Washington	4-0-0	Ralph Welch
13. Georgia Tech	7-3-0	Bill Alexander
14. Texas	7-1-0	Dana X. Bible
15. Tulsa	6-0-1	Henry Frnka
16. Dartmouth	6-1-0	Earl Brown
17. Bainbridge NTS	7-0-0	Joe Maniaci
18. Colorado College	7-0-0	Hal White
19. Pacific	7-2-0	Amos A. Stagg
20. Pennsylvania	6-2-1	George Munger

1944

	Record	Coach
1. Army	9-0-0	Red Blaik
2. Ohio St	9-0-0	Carroll Widdoes
3. Randolph Field	11-0-0	Frank Tritico
4. Navy	6-3-0	Oscar Hagberg
5. Bainbridge NTS	9-0-0	Joe Maniaci
6. Iowa Pre-Flight	10-1-0	Jack Meagher
7. Southern Cal	7-0-2	Jeff Cravath
8. Michigan	8-2-0	Fritz Crisler
9. Notre Dame	8-2-0	Ed McKeever
10. March Field	7-1-2	Paul Schissler
11. Duke	5-4-0	Eddie Cameron
12. Tennessee	8-0-1	John Barnhill
13. Georgia Tech	8-2-0	Bill Alexander
Norman P-F	6-0-0	John Gregg
15. Illinois	5-4-1	Ray Eliot
16. El Toro Marines	8-1-0	Dick Hanley
17. Great Lakes	9-2-1	Paul Brown
18. Fort Pierce	9-0-0	Hamp Pool
19. St. Mary's P-F	4-4-0	Jules Sikes
20. 2nd Air Force	7-2-1	Bill Reese

1945

	Record	Coach
1. Army	9-0-0	Red Blaik
2. Alabama	9-0-0	Frank Thomas
3. Navy	7-1-1	Oscar Hagberg
4. Indiana	9-0-1	Bo McMillan
5. Oklahoma A&M	8-0-0	Jim Lookabaugh
6. Michigan	7-3-0	Fritz Crisler
7. St. Mary's (CA)	7-1-0	Jimmy Phelan
8. Pennsylvania	6-2-0	George Munger
9. Notre Dame	7-2-1	Hugh Devore
10. Texas	9-1-0	Dana X. Bible
11. Southern Cal	7-3-0	Jeff Cravath
12. Ohio St	7-2-0	Carroll Widdoes
13. Duke	6-2-0	Eddie Cameron
14. Tennessee	8-1-0	John Barnhill
15. Louisiana St	7-2-0	Bernie Moore
16. Holy Cross	8-1-0	John DeGrosa
17. Tulsa	8-2-0	Henry Frnka
18. Georgia	8-2-0	Wally Butts
19. Wake Forest	4-3-1	Peahead Walker
20. Columbia	8-1-0	Lou Little

1946

	Record	Coach
1. Notre Dame	8-0-1	Frank Leahy
2. Army	9-0-1	Red Blaik
3. Georgia	10-0-0	Wally Butts
4. UCLA	10-0-0	B. LaBrucherie
5. Illinois	7-2-0	Ray Eliot
6. Michigan	6-2-1	Fritz Crisler
7. Tennessee	9-1-0	Bob Neyland
8. Louisiana St	9-1-0	Bernie Moore
9. N Carolina	8-1-1	Carl Snavely
10. Rice	8-2-0	Jess Neely
11. Georgia Tech	8-2-0	Bobby Dodd
12. Yale	7-1-1	Howard Odell
13. Pennsylvania	6-2-0	George Munger
14. Oklahoma	7-3-0	Jim Tatum
15. Texas	8-2-0	Dana X. Bible
16. Arkansas	6-3-1	John Barnhill
17. Tulsa	9-1-0	J.O. Brothers
18. N Carolina St	8-2-0	Beattie Feathers
19. Delaware	9-0-0	Bill Murray
20. Indiana	6-3-0	Bo McMillan

1947

	Record	Coach
1. Notre Dame	9-0-0	Frank Leahy
2. #Michigan	9-0-0	Fritz Crisler
3. SMU	9-0-1	Matty Bell
4. Penn St	9-0-0	Bob Higgins
5. Texas	9-1-0	Blair Cherry
6. Alabama	8-2-0	Red Drew
7. Pennsylvania	7-0-1	George Munger

Note: Except where indicated with an asterisk, the polls from 1936 through 1964 were taken before the bowl games and those from 1965 through the present were taken after the bowl games.

1947 (CONT.)

		Record	Coach
8.	Southern Cal	7-1-1	Jeff Cravath
9.	N Carolina	8-2-0	Carl Snavely
10.	Georgia Tech	9-1-0	Bobby Dodd
11.	Army	5-2-2	Red Blaik
12.	Kansas	8-0-2	George Sauer
13.	Mississippi	8-2-0	Johnny Vaught
14.	William & Mary	9-1-0	Rube McCray
15.	California	9-1-0	Pappy Waldorf
16.	Oklahoma	7-2-1	Bud Wilkinson
17.	N Carolina St	5-3-1	Beattie Feathers
18.	Rice	6-3-1	Jess Neely
19.	Duke	4-3-2	Wallace Wade
20.	Columbia	7-2-0	Lou Little

#The AP, which had voted Notre Dame No. 1 before the bowl games, took a second vote, giving the title to Michigan after its 49–0 win over Southern Cal in the Rose Bowl.

1948

		Record	Coach
1.	Michigan	9-0-0	Bennie Oosterbaan
2.	Notre Dame	9-0-1	Frank Leahy
3.	N Carolina	9-0-1	Carl Snavely
4.	California	10-0-0	Pappy Waldorf
5.	Oklahoma	9-1-0	Bud Wilkinson
6.	Army	8-0-1	Red Blaik
7.	Northwestern	7-2-0	Bob Voigts
8.	Georgia	9-1-0	Wally Butts
9.	Oregon	9-1-0	Jim Aiken
10.	SMU	8-1-1	Matty Bell
11.	Clemson	10-0-0	Frank Howard
12.	Vanderbilt	8-2-1	Red Sanders
13.	Tulane	9-1-0	Henry Frnka
14.	Michigan St	6-2-2	Biggie Munn
15.	Mississippi	8-1-0	Johnny Vaught
16.	Minnesota	7-2-0	Bernie Bierman
17.	William & Mary	6-2-2	Rube McCray
18.	Penn St	7-1-1	Bob Higgins
19.	Cornell	8-1-0	Lefty James
20.	Wake Forest	6-3-0	Peahead Walker

1949

		Record	Coach
1.	Notre Dame	10-0-0	Frank Leahy
2.	Oklahoma	10-0-0	Bud Wilkinson
3.	California	10-0-0	Pappy Waldorf
4.	Army	9-0-0	Red Blaik
5.	Rice	9-1-0	Jess Neely
6.	Ohio St	6-1-2	Wes Fesler
7.	Michigan	6-2-1	Bennie Oosterbaan
8.	Minnesota	7-2-0	Bernie Bierman
9.	Louisiana St	8-2-0	Gaynell Tinsley
10.	Pacific	11-0-0	Larry Siemering
11.	Kentucky	9-2-0	Bear Bryant
12.	Cornell	8-1-0	Lefty James
13.	Villanova	8-1-0	Jim Leonard
14.	Maryland	8-1-0	Jim Tatum
15.	Santa Clara	7-2-1	Len Casanova
16.	N Carolina	7-3-0	Carl Snavely
17.	Tennessee	7-2-1	Bob Neyland
18.	Princeton	6-3-0	Charlie Caldwell
19.	Michigan St	6-3-0	Biggie Munn
20.	Missouri	7-3-0	Don Faurot
	Baylor	8-2-0	Bob Woodruff

1950

		Record	Coach
1.	Oklahoma	10-0-0	Bud Wilkinson
2.	Army	8-1-0	Red Blaik
3.	Texas	9-1-0	Blair Cherry
4.	Tennessee	10-1-0	Bob Neyland
5.	California	9-0-1	Pappy Waldorf
6.	Princeton	9-0-0	Charlie Caldwell
7.	Kentucky	10-1-0	Bear Bryant
8.	Michigan St	8-1-0	Biggie Munn
9.	Michigan	5-3-1	Bennie Oosterhaan
10.	Clemson	8-0-1	Frank Howard
11.	Washington	8-2-0	Howard Odell
12.	Wyoming	9-0-0	Bowden Wyatt
13.	Illinois	7-2-0	Ray Eliot
14.	Ohio St	6-3-0	Wes Fesler
15.	Miami (FL)	9-0-1	Andy Gustafson
16.	Alabama	9-2-0	Red Drew
17.	Nebraska	6-2-1	Bill Glassford
18.	Washington & Lee	8-2-0	George Barclay
19.	Tulsa	9-1-1	J.O. Brothers
20.	Tulane	6-2-1	Henry Frnka

1951

		Record	Coach
1.	Tennessee	10-0-0	Bob Neyland
2.	Michigan St	9-0-0	Biggie Munn
3.	Maryland	9-0-0	Jim Tatum
4.	Illinois	8-0-1	Ray Eliot
5.	Georgia Tech	10-0-1	Bobby Dodd
6.	Princeton	9-0-0	Charlie Caldwell
7.	Stanford	9-1-0	Chuck Taylor
8.	Wisconsin	7-1-1	Ivy Williamson
9.	Baylor	8-1-1	George Sauer
10.	Oklahoma	8-2-0	Bud Wilkinson
11.	Texas Christian	6-4-0	Dutch Meyer
12.	California	8-2-0	Pappy Waldorf
13.	Virginia	8-1-0	Art Guepe
14.	San Francisco	9-0-0	Joe Kuharich
15.	Kentucky	7-4-0	Bear Bryant
16.	Boston University	6-4-0	Buff Donelli
17.	UCLA	5-3-1	Red Sanders
18.	Washington St	7-3-0	Forest Evashevski
19.	Holy Cross	8-2-0	Eddie Anderson
20.	Clemson	7-2-0	Frank Howard

1952

		Record	Coach
1.	Michigan St	9-0-0	Biggie Munn
2.	Georgia Tech	11-0-0	Bobby Dodd
3.	Notre Dame	7-2-1	Frank Leahy
4.	Oklahoma	8-1-1	Bud Wilkinson
5.	Southern Cal	9-1-0	Jess Hill
6.	UCLA	8-1-0	Red Sanders
7.	Mississippi	8-0-2	Johnny Vaught
8.	Tennessee	8-1-1	Bob Neyland
9.	Alabama	9-2-0	Red Drew
10.	Texas	8-2-0	Ed Price
11.	Wisconsin	6-2-1	Ivy Williamson
12.	Tulsa	8-1-1	J.O. Brothers
13.	Maryland	7-2-0	Jim Tatum
14.	Syracuse	7-2-0	Ben Schwartzwalder
15.	Florida	7-3-0	Bob Woodruff
16.	Duke	8-2-0	Bill Murray
17.	Ohio St	6-3-0	Woody Hayes
18.	Purdue	4-3-2	Stu Holcomb
19.	Princeton	8-1-0	Charlie Caldwell
20.	Kentucky	5-4-2	Bear Bryant

1953

		Record	Coach
1.	Maryland	10-0-0	Jim Tatum
2.	Notre Dame	9-0-1	Frank Leahy
3.	Michigan St	8-1-0	Biggie Munn
4.	Oklahoma	8-1-1	Bud Wilkinson
5.	UCLA	8-1-0	Red Sanders
6.	Rice	8-2-0	Jess Neely
7.	Illinois	7-1-1	Ray Eliot
8.	Georgia Tech	8-2-1	Bobby Dodd
9.	Iowa	5-3-1	Forest Evashevski
10.	W Virginia	8-1-0	Art Lewis
11.	Texas	7-3-0	Ed Price
12.	Texas Tech	10-1-0	DeWitt Weaver
13.	Alabama	6-2-3	Red Drew
14.	Army	7-1-1	Red Blaik
15.	Wisconsin	6-2-1	Ivy Williamson
16.	Kentucky	7-2-1	Bear Bryant
17.	Auburn	7-2-1	Shug Jordan
18.	Duke	7-2-1	Bill Murray
19.	Stanford	6-3-1	Chuck Taylor
20.	Michigan	6-3-0	Bennie Oosterbaan

1954

		Record	Coach
1.	Ohio St	9-0-0	Woody Hayes
2.	#UCLA	9-0-0	Red Sanders
3.	Oklahoma	10-0-0	Bud Wilkinson
4.	Notre Dame	9-1-0	Terry Brennan
5.	Navy	7-2-0	Eddie Erdelatz
6.	Mississippi	9-1-0	Johnny Vaught
7.	Army	7-2-0	Red Blaik
8.	Maryland	7-2-1	Jim Tatum
9.	Wisconsin	7-2-0	Ivy Williamson
10.	Arkansas	8-2-0	Bowden Wyatth
11.	Miami (FL)	8-1-0	Andy Gustafson
12.	W Virginia	8-1-0	Art Lewis
13.	Auburn	7-3-0	Shug Jordan
14.	Duke	7-2-1	Bill Murray
15.	Michigan	6-3-0	Bennie Oosterbaan
16.	Virginia Tech	8-0-1	Frank Moseley
17.	Southern Cal	8-3-0	Jess Hill
18.	Baylor	7-3-0	George Sauer
19.	Rice	7-3-0	Jess Neely
20.	Penn St	7-2-0	Rip Engle

#Selected No. 1 by UP.

1955

		Record	Coach
1.	Oklahoma	10-0-0	Bud Wilkinson
2.	Michigan St	8-1-0	Duffy Daugherty
3.	Maryland	10-0-0	Jim Tatum
4.	UCLA	9-1-0	Red Sanders
5.	Ohio St	7-2-0	Woody Hayes
6.	Texas Christian	9-1-0	Abe Martin
7.	Georgia Tech	8-1-1	Bobby Dodd
8.	Auburn	8-1-1	Shug Jordan
9.	Notre Dame	8-2-0	Terry Brennan
10.	Mississippi	9-1-0	Johnny Vaught
11.	Pittsburgh	7-3-0	John Michelosen
12.	Michigan	7-2-0	Bennie Oosterbaan
13.	Southern Cal	6-4-0	Jess Hill
14.	Miami (FL)	6-3-0	Andy Gustafson
15.	Miami (OH)	9-0-0	Ara Parseghian
16.	Stanford	6-3-1	Chuck Taylor
17.	Texas A&M	7-2-1	Bear Bryant
18.	Navy	6-2-1	Eddie Erdelatz
19.	W Virginia	8-2-0	Art Lewis
20.	Army	6-3-0	Red Blaik

1956

		Record	Coach
1.	Oklahoma	10-0-0	Bud Wilkinson
2.	Tennessee	10-0-0	Bowden Wyatt
3.	Iowa	8-1-0	Forest Evashevski
4.	Georgia Tech	9-1-0	Bobby Dodd
5.	Texas A&M	9-0-1	Bear Bryant
6.	Miami (FL)	8-1-1	Andy Gustafson
7.	Michigan	7-2-0	Bennie Oosterbaan
8.	Syracuse	7-1-0	Ben Schwartzwalder
9.	Michigan St	7-2-0	Duffy Daugherty
10.	Oregon St	7-2-1	Tommy Prothro
11.	Baylor	8-2-0	Sam Boyd
12.	Minnesota	6-1-2	Murray Warmath
13.	Pittsburgh	7-2-1	John Michelosen
14.	Texas Christian	7-3-0	Abe Martin
15.	Ohio St	6-3-0	Woody Hayes
16.	Navy	6-1-2	Eddie Erdelatz
17.	Geo Washington	7-1-1	Gene Sherman
18.	Southern Cal	8-2-0	Jess Hill
19.	Clemson	7-1-2	Frank Howard
20.	Colorado	7-2-1	Dallas Ward
	Penn St	6-2-1	Rip Engle

1957

		Record	Coach
1.	Auburn	10-0-0	Shug Jordan
2.	#Ohio St	8-1-0	Woody Hayes
3.	Michigan St	8-1-0	Duffy Daugherty
4.	Oklahoma	9-1-0	Bud Wilkinson
5.	Navy	8-1-1	Eddie Erdelatz
6.	Iowa	7-1-1	Forest Evashevski
7.	Mississippi	8-1-1	Johnny Vaught
8.	Rice	7-3-0	Jess Neely
9.	Texas A&M	8-2-0	Bear Bryant
10.	Notre Dame	7-3-0	Terry Brennan
11.	Texas	6-3-1	Darrell Royal
12.	Arizona St	10-0-0	Dan Devine
13.	Tennessee	7-3-0	Bowden Wyatt
14.	Mississippi St	6-2-1	Wade Walker
15.	N Carolina St	7-1-2	Earle Edwards
16.	Duke	6-2-2	Bill Murray
17.	Florida	6-2-1	Bob Woodruff
18.	Army	7-2-0	Red Blaik
19.	Wisconsin	6-3-0	Milt Brunt
20.	VMI	9-0-1	John McKenna

#Selected No. 1 by UP.

1958

		Record	Coach
1.	Louisiana St	10-0-0	Paul Dietzel
2.	Iowa	7-1-1	Forest Evashevski
3.	Army	8-0-1	Red Blaik
4.	Auburn	9-0-1	Shug Jordan
5.	Oklahoma	9-1-0	Bud Wilkinson
6.	Air Force	9-0-1	Ben Martin
7.	Wisconsin	7-1-1	Milt Bruhn
8.	Ohio St	6-1-2	Woody Hayes
9.	Syracuse	8-1-0	Ben Schwartzwalder
10.	Texas Christian	8-2-0	Abe Martin
11.	Mississippi	8-2-0	Johnny Vaught
12.	Clemson	8-2-0	Frank Howard
13.	Purdue	6-1-2	Jack Mollenkopf
14.	Florida	6-3-1	Bob Woodruff
15.	S Carolina	7-3-0	Warren Giese
16.	California	7-3-0	Pete Elliott
17.	Notre Dame	6-4-0	Terry Brennan
18.	SMU	6-4-0	Bill Meek
19.	Oklahoma St	7-3-0	Cliff Speegle
20.	Rutgers	8-1-0	John Stiegman

1959

		Record	Coach
1.	Syracuse	10-0-0	Ben Schwartzwalder
2.	Mississippi	9-1-0	Johnny Vaught
3.	Louisiana St	9-1-0	Paul Dietzel
4.	Texas	9-1-0	Darrell Royal
5.	Georgia	9-1-0	Wally Butts
6.	Wisconsin	7-2-0	Milt Bruhn
7.	Texas Christian	8-2-0	Abe Martin
8.	Washington	9-1-0	Jim Owens
9.	Arkansas	8-2-0	Frank Broyles
10.	Alabama	7-1-2	Bear Bryant
11.	Clemson	8-2-0	Frank Howard
12.	Penn St	8-2-0	Rip Engle
13.	Illinois	5-3-1	Ray Eliot
14.	Southern Cal	8-2-0	Don Clark
15.	Oklahoma	7-3-0	Bud Wilkinson
16.	Wyoming	9-1-0	Bob Devaney
17.	Notre Dame	5-5-0	Joe Kuharich
18.	Missouri	6-4-0	Dan Devine
19.	Florida	5-4-1	Bob Woodruff
20.	Pittsburgh	6-4-0	John Michelosen

1960

		Record	Coach
1.	Minnesota	8-1-0	Murray Warmath
2.	Mississippi	9-0-1	Johnny Vaught
3.	Iowa	8-1-0	Forest Evashevski
4.	Navy	9-1-0	Wayne Hardin
5.	Missouri	9-1-0	Dan Devine
6.	Washington	9-1-0	Jim Owens
7.	Arkansas	8-2-0	Frank Broyles
8.	Ohio St	7-2-0	Woody Hayes
9.	Alabama	8-1-1	Bear Bryant
10.	Duke	7-3-0	Bill Murray
11.	Kansas	7-2-1	Jack Mitchell
12.	Baylor	8-2-0	John Bridgers
13.	Auburn	8-2-0	Shug Jordan
14.	Yale	9-0-0	Jordan Oliver
15.	Michigan St	6-2-1	Duffy Daugherty
16.	Penn St	6-3-0	Rip Engle
17.	New Mexico St	10-0-0	Warren Woodson
18.	Florida	8-2-0	Ray Graves
19.	Syracuse	7-2-0	Ben Schwartzwalder
	Purdue	4-4-1	Jack Mollenkopf

1961

		Record	Coach
1.	Alabama	10-0-0	Bear Bryant
2.	Ohio St	8-0-1	Woody Hayes
3.	Texas	9-1-0	Darrell Royal
4.	Louisiana St	9-1-0	Paul Dietzel
5.	Mississippi	9-1-0	Johnny Vaught
6.	Minnesota	7-2-0	Murray Warmath
7.	Colorado	9-1-0	Sonny Grandelius
8.	Michigan St	7-2-0	Duffy Daugherty
9.	Arkansas	8-2-0	Frank Broyles
10.	Utah St	9-0-1	John Ralston
11.	Missouri	7-2-1	Dan Devine
12.	Purdue	6-3-0	Jack Mollenkopf
13.	Georgia Tech	7-3-0	Bobby Dodd
14.	Syracuse	7-3-0	Ben Schwartzwalder
15.	Rutgers	9-0-0	John Bateman
16.	UCLA	7-3-0	Bill Barnes
17.	Rice	7-3-0	Jess Neely
	Penn St	7-3-0	Rip Engle
	Arizona	8-1-1	Jim LaRue
20.	Duke	7-3-0	Bill Murray

1962

		Record	Coach
1.	Southern Cal	10-0-0	John McKay
2.	Wisconsin	8-1-0	Milt Bruhn
3.	Mississippi	9-0-0	Johnny Vaught
4.	Texas	9-0-1	Darrell Royal
5.	Alabama	9-1-0	Bear Bryant
6.	Arkansas	9-1-0	Frank Broyles
7.	Louisiana St	8-1-1	Charlie McClendon
8.	Oklahoma	8-2-0	Bud Wilkinson
9.	Penn St	9-1-0	Rip Engle
10.	Minnesota	6-2-1	Murray Warmath

11–20: UPI

11.	Georgia Tech	7-2-1	Bobby Dodd
12.	Missouri	7-1-2	Dan Devine
13.	Ohio St	6-3-0	Woody Hayes
14.	Duke	8-2-0	Bill Murray
	Washington	7-1-2	Jim Owens
16.	Northwestern	7-2-0	Ara Parseghian
	Oregon St	8-2-0	Tommy Prothro
18.	Arizona St	7-2-1	Frank Kush
	Miami (FL)	7-3-0	Andy Gustafson
	Illinois	2-7-0	Pete Elliott

1963

		Record	Coach
1.	Texas	10-0-0	Darrell Royal
2.	Navy	9-1-0	Wayne Hardin
3.	Illinois	7-1-1	Pete Elliott
4.	Pittsburgh	9-1-0	John Michelosen
5.	Auburn	9-1-0	Shug Jordan
6.	Nebraska	9-1-0	Bob Devaney
7.	Mississippi	7-0-2	Johnny Vaught
8.	Alabama	8-2-0	Bear Bryant
9.	Oklahoma	8-2-0	Bud Wilkinson
10.	Michigan St	6-2-1	Duffy Daugherty

11–20: UPI

11.	Mississippi St	6-2-2	Paul Davis
12.	Syracuse	8-2-0	Ben Schwartzwalder
13.	Arizona St	8-1-0	Frank Kush
14.	Memphis St	9-0-1	Billy J. Murphy
15.	Washington	6-4-0	Jim Owens
16.	Penn St	7-3-0	Rip Engle
	Southern Cal	7-3-0	John McKay
	Missouri	7-3-0	Dan Devine
19.	N Carolina	8-2-0	Jim Hickey
20.	Baylor	7-3-0	John Bridgers

1964

		Record	Coach
1.	Alabama	10-0-0	Bear Bryant
2.	Arkansas	10-0-0	Frank Broyles
3.	Notre Dame	9-1-0	Ara Parseghian
4.	Michigan	8-1-0	Bump Elliott
5.	Texas	9-1-0	Darrell Royal
6.	Nebraska	9-1-0	Bob Devaney
7.	Louisiana St	7-2-1	Charlie McClendon
8.	Oregon St	8-2-0	Tommy Prothro
9.	Ohio St	7-2-0	Woody Hayes
10.	Southern Cal	7-3-0	John McKay

11–20: UPI

11.	Florida St	8-1-1	Bill Peterson
12.	Syracuse	7-3-0	Ben Schwartzwalder
13.	Princeton	9-0-0	Dick Colman
14.	Penn St	6-4-0	Rip Engle
	Utah	8-2-0	Ray Nagel
16.	Illinois	6-3-0	Pete Elliott
	New Mexico	9-2-0	Bill Weeks
18.	Tulsa	8-2-0	Glenn Dobbs
19.	Missouri	6-3-1	Dan Devine

1964 (CONT.)

		Record	Coach
20.	Mississippi	5-4-1	Johnny Vaught
	Michigan St	4-5-1	Duffy Daugherty

1965

		Record	Coach
1.	Alabama	9-1-1	Bear Bryant
2.	#Michigan St	10-1-0	Duffy Daugherty
3.	Arkansas	10-1-0	Frank Broyles
4.	UCLA	8-2-1	Tommy Prothro
5.	Nebraska	10-1-0	Bob Devaney
6.	Missouri	8-2-1	Dan Devine
7.	Tennessee	8-1-2	Doug Dickey
8.	Louisiana St	8-3-0	Charlie McClendon
9.	Notre Dame	7-2-1	Ara Parseghian
10.	Southern Cal	7-2-1	John McKay
11–20: UPI			
11.	Texas Tech	8-2-0	J.T. King
12.	Ohio St	7-2-0	Woody Hayes
13.	Florida	7-3-0	Ray Graves
14.	Purdue	7-2-1	Jack Mollenkopf
15.	Georgia	6-4-0	Vince Dooley
16.	Tulsa	8-2-0	Glenn Dobbs
17.	Mississippi	6-4-0	Johnny Vaught
18.	Kentucky	6-4-0	Charlie Bradshaw
19	Syracuse	7-3-0	Ben Schwartzwalder
20.	Colorado	6-2-2	Eddie Crowder

#Selected No. 1 by UPI.

1966*

		Record	Coach
1.	Notre Dame	9-0-1	Ara Parseghian
2.	Michigan St	9-0-1	Duffy Daugherty
3.	Alabama	10-0-0	Bear Bryant
4.	Georgia	9-1-0	Vince Dooley
5.	UCLA	9-1-0	Tommy Prothro
6.	Nebraska	9-1-0	Bob Devaney
7.	Purdue	8-2-0	Jack Mollenkopf
8.	Georgia Tech	9-1-0	Bobby Dodd
9.	Miami (FL)	7-2-1	Charlie Tate
10.	SMU	8-2-0	Hayden Fry
11–20: UPI			
11.	Florida	8-2-0	Ray Graves
12.	Mississippi	8-2-0	Johnny Vaught
13.	Arkansas	8-2-0	Frank Broyles
14.	Tennessee	7-3-0	Doug Dickey
15.	Wyoming	9-1-0	Lloyd Eaton
16.	Syracuse	8-2-0	Ben Schwartzwalder
17.	Houston	8-2-0	Bill Yeoman
18.	Southern Cal	7-3-0	John McKay
19.	Oregon St	7-3-0	Dee Andros
20.	Virginia Tech	8-1-1	Jerry Claiborne

1967*

		Record	Coach
1.	Southern Cal	9-1-0	John McKay
2.	Tennessee	9-1-0	Doug Dickey
3.	Oklahoma	9-1-0	Chuck Fairbanks
4.	Indiana	9-1-0	John Pont
5.	Notre Dame	8-2-0	Ara Parseghian
6.	Wyoming	10-0-0	Lloyd Eaton
7.	Oregon St	7-2-1	Dee Andros
8.	Alabama	8-1-1	Bear Bryant

9.	Purdue	8-2-0	Jack Mollenkopf
10.	Penn St	8-2-0	Joe Paterno
11–20: UPI†			
11.	UCLA	7-2-0	Tommy Prothro
12.	Syracuse	8-2-0	Ben Schwartzwalder
13.	Colorado	8-2-0	Eddie Crowder
14.	Minnesota	8-2-0	Murray Warmath
15.	Florida St	7-2-1	Bill Peterson
16.	Miami (FL)	7-3-0	Charlie Tate
17.	N Carolina St	8-2-0	Earle Edwards
18.	Georgia	7-3-0	Vince Dooley
19.	Houston	9-2-0	Bill Yeoman
20.	Arizona St	8-2-0	Frank Kush

†UPI ranked Penn St 11th and did not rank Alabama, which was on probation.

1968

		Record	Coach
1.	Ohio St	10-0-0	Woody Hayes
2.	Penn St	11-0-0	Joe Paterno
3.	Texas	9-1-1	Darrell Royal
4.	Southern Cal	9-1-1	John McKay
5.	Notre Dame	7-2-1	Ara Parseghian
6.	Arkansas	10-1-0	Frank Broyles
7.	Kansas	9-2-0	Pepper Rodgers
8.	Georgia	8-1-2	Vince Dooley
9.	Missouri	8-3-0	Dan Devine
10.	Purdue	8-2-0	Jack Mollenkopf
11.	Oklahoma	7-4-0	Chuck Fairbanks
12.	Michigan	8-2-0	Bump Elliott
13.	Tennessee	8-2-1	Doug Dickey
14.	SMU	8-3-0	Hayden Fry
15.	Oregon St	7-3-0	Dee Andros
16.	Auburn	7-4-0	Shug Jordan
17.	Alabama	8-3-0	Bear Bryant
18.	Houston	6-2-2	Bill Yeoman
19.	Louisiana St	8-3-0	Charlie McClendon
20.	Ohio	10-1-0	Bill Hess

1969

		Record	Coach
1.	Texas	11-0-0	Darrell Royal
2.	Penn St	11-0-0	Joe Paterno
3.	Southern Cal	10-0-1	John McKay
4.	Ohio St	8-1-0	Woody Hayes
5.	Notre Dame	8-2-1	Ara Parseghian
6.	Missouri	9-2-0	Dan Devine
7.	Arkansas	9-2-0	Frank Broyles
8.	Mississippi	8-3-0	Johnny Vaught
9.	Michigan	8-3-0	Bo Schembechler
10.	Louisiana St	9-1-0	Charlie McClendon
11.	Nebraska	9-2-0	Bob Devaney
12.	Houston	9-2-0	Bill Yeoman
13.	UCLA	8-1-1	Tommy Prothro
14.	Florida	9-1-1	Ray Graves
15.	Tennessee	9-2-0	Doug Dickey
16.	Colorado	8-3-0	Eddie Crowder
17.	W Virginia	10-0-1	Jim Carlen
18.	Purdue	8-2-0	Jack Mollenkopf
19.	Stanford	7-2-1	John Ralston
20.	Auburn	8-3-0	Shug Jordan

1970

		Record	Coach
1.	Nebraska	11-0-1	Bob Devaney
2.	Notre Dame	10-1-0	Ara Parseghian
3.	#Texas	10-1-0	Darrell Royal
4.	Tennessee	11-0-1	Bill Battle

Note: Except where indicated with an asterisk, the polls from 1936 through 1964 were taken before the bowl games and those from 1965 through the present were taken after the bowl games. Additionally, the AP ranked only ten teams in its polls from 1962–67; positions 11–20 from those years are from the UPI poll.

1970 (CONT.)

		Record	Coach
5.	Ohio St	9-1-0	Woody Hayes
6.	Arizona St	11-0-0	Frank Kush
7.	Louisiana St	9-3-0	Charlie McClendon
8.	Stanford	9-3-0	John Ralston
9.	Michigan	9-1-0	Bo Schembechler
10.	Auburn	9-2-0	Shug Jordan
11.	Arkansas	9-2-0	Frank Broyles
12.	Toledo	12-0-0	Frank Lauterbur
13.	Georgia Tech	9-3-0	Bud Carson
14.	Dartmouth	9-0-0	Bob Blackman
15.	Southern Cal	6-4-1	John McKay
16.	Air Force	9-3-0	Ben Martin
17.	Tulane	8-4-0	Jim Pittman
18.	Penn St	7-3-0	Joe Paterno
19.	Houston	8-3-0	Bill Yeoman
20.	Oklahoma	7-4-1	Chuck Fairbanks
	Mississippi	7-4-0	Johnny Vaught

#Selected No. 1 by UPI.

1971

		Record	Coach
1.	Nebraska	13-0-0	Bob Devaney
2.	Oklahoma	11-1-0	Chuck Fairbanks
3.	Colorado	10-2-0	Eddie Crowder
4.	Alabama	11-1-0	Bear Bryant
5.	Penn St	11-1-0	Joe Paterno
6.	Michigan	11-1-0	Bo Schembechler
7.	Georgia	11-1-0	Vince Dooley
8.	Arizona St	11-1-0	Frank Kush
9.	Tennessee	10-2-0	Bill Battle
10.	Stanford	9-3-0	John Ralston
11.	Louisiana St	9-3-0	Charlie McClendon
12.	Auburn	9-2-0	Shug Jordan
13.	Notre Dame	8-2-0	Ara Parseghian
14.	Toledo	12-0-0	John Murphy
15.	Mississippi	10-2-0	Billy Kinard
16.	Arkansas	8-3-1	Frank Broyles
17.	Houston	9-3-0	Bill Yeoman
18.	Texas	8-3-0	Darrell Royal
19.	Washington	8-3-0	Jim Owens
20.	Southern Cal	6-4-1	John McKay

1972

		Record	Coach
1.	Southern Cal	12-0-0	John McKay
2.	Oklahoma	11-1-0	Chuck Fairbanks
3.	Texas	10-1-0	Darrell Royal
4.	Nebraska	9-2-1	Bob Devaney
5.	Auburn	10-1-0	Shug Jordan
6.	Michigan	10-1-0	Bo Schembechler
7.	Alabama	10-2-0	Bear Bryant
8.	Tennessee	10-2-0	Bill Battle
9.	Ohio St	9-2-0	Woody Hayes
10.	Penn St	10-2-0	Joe Paterno
11.	Louisiana St	9-2-1	Charlie McClendon
12.	N Carolina	11-1-0	Bill Dooley
13.	Arizona St	10-2-0	Frank Kush
14.	Notre Dame	8-3-0	Ara Parseghian
15.	UCLA	8-3-0	Pepper Rodgers
16.	Colorado	8-4-0	Eddie Crowder
17.	N Carolina St	8-3-1	Lou Holtz
18.	Louisville	9-1-0	Lee Corso
19.	Washington St	7-4-0	Jim Sweeney
20.	Georgia Tech	7-4-1	Bill Fulch

1973

		Record	Coach
1.	Notre Dame	11-0-0	Ara Parseghian
2.	Ohio St	10-0-1	Woody Hayes
3.	Oklahoma	10-0-1	Barry Switzer
4.	#Alabama	11-1-0	Bear Bryant
5.	Penn St	12-0-0	Joe Paterno
6.	Michigan	10-0-1	Bo Schembechler
7.	Nebraska	9-2-1	Tom Osborne
8.	Southern Cal	9-2-1	John McKay
9.	Arizona St	11-1-0	Frank Kush
	Houston	11-1-0	Bill Yeoman
11.	Texas Tech	11-1-0	Jim Carlen
12.	UCLA	9-2-0	Pepper Rodgers
13.	Louisiana St	9-3-0	Charlie McClendon
14.	Texas	8-3-0	Darrell Royal
15.	Miami (OH)	11-0-0	Bill Mallory
16.	N Carolina St	9-3-0	Lou Holtz
17.	Missouri	8-4-0	Al Onofrio
18.	Kansas	7-4-1	Don Fambrough
19.	Tennessee	8-4-0	Bill Battle
20.	Maryland	8-4-0	Jerry Claiborne
	Tulane	9-3-0	Bennie Ellender

#Selected No. 1 by UPI.

1974

		Record	Coach
1.	Oklahoma	11-0-0	Barry Switzer
2.	#Southern Cal	10-1-1	John McKay
3.	Michigan	10-1-0	Bo Schembechler
4.	Ohio St	10-2-0	Woody Hayes
5.	Alabama	11-1-0	Bear Bryant
6.	Notre Dame	10-2-0	Ara Parseghian
7.	Penn St	10-2-0	Joe Paterno
8.	Auburn	10-2-0	Shug Jordan
9.	Nebraska	9-3-0	Tom Osborne
10.	Miami (OH)	10-0-1	Dick Crum
11.	N Carolina St	9-2-1	Lou Holtz
12.	Michigan St	7-3-1	Denny Stolz
13.	Maryland	8-4-0	Jerry Claiborne
14.	Baylor	8-4-0	Grant Teaff
15.	Florida	8-4-0	Doug Dickey
16.	Texas A&M	8-3-0	Emory Ballard
17.	Mississippi St	9-3-0	Bob Tyler
	Texas	8-4-0	Darrell Royal
19.	Houston	8-3-1	Bill Yeoman
20.	Tennessee	7-3-2	Bill Battle

#Selected No. 1 by UPI

1975

		Record	Coach
1.	Oklahoma	11-1-0	Barry Switzer
2.	Arizona St	12-0-0	Frank Kush
3.	Alabama	11-1-0	Bear Bryant
4.	Ohio St	11-1-0	Woody Hayes
5.	UCLA	9-2-1	Dick Vermeil
6.	Texas	10-2-0	Darrell Royal
7.	Arkansas	10-2-0	Frank Broyles
8.	Michigan	8-2-2	Bo Schembechler
9.	Nebraska	10-2-0	Tom Osborne
10.	Penn St	9-3-0	Joe Paterno
11.	Texas A&M	10-2-0	Emory Bellard
12.	Miami (OH)	11-1-0	Dick Crum
13.	Maryland	9-2-1	Jerry Claiborne
14.	California	8-3-0	Mike White
15.	Pittsburgh	8-4-0	Johnny Majors
16.	Colorado	9-3-0	Bill Mallory
17.	Southern Cal	8-4-0	John McKay
18.	Arizona	9-2-0	Jim Young
19.	Georgia	9-3-0	Vince Dooley
20.	W Virginia	9-3-0	Bobby Bowden

1976

		Record	Coach
1.	Pittsburgh	12-0-0	Johnny Majors
2.	Southern Cal	11-1-0	John Robinson
3.	Michigan	10-2-0	Bo Schembechler
4.	Houston	10-2-0	Bill Yeoman
5.	Oklahoma	9-2-1	Barry Switzer
6.	Ohio St	9-2-1	Woody Hayes
7.	Texas A&M	10-2-0	Emory Bellard
8.	Maryland	11-1-0	Jerry Claiborne
9.	Nebraska	9-3-1	Tom Osborne
10.	Georgia	10-2-0	Vince Dooley
11.	Alabama	9-3-0	Bear Bryant
12.	Notre Dame	9-3-0	Dan Devine
13.	Texas Tech	10-2-0	Steve Sloan
14.	Oklahoma St	9-3-0	Jim Stanley
15.	UCLA	9-2-1	Terry Donahue
16.	Colorado	8-4-0	Bill Mallory
17.	Rutgers	11-0-0	Frank Burns
18.	Kentucky	9-3-0	Fran Curci
19.	Iowa St	8-3-0	Earle Bruce
20.	Mississippi St	9-2-0	Bob Tyler

1977

		Record	Coach
1.	Notre Dame	11-1-0	Dan Devine
2.	Alabama	11-1-0	Bear Bryant
3.	Arkansas	11-1-0	Lou Holtz
4.	Texas	11-1-0	Fred Akers
5.	Penn St	11-1-0	Joe Paterno
6.	Kentucky	10-1-0	Fran Curci
7.	Oklahoma	10-2-0	Barry Switzer
8.	Pittsburgh	9-2-1	Jackie Sherrill
9.	Michigan	10-2-0	Bo Schembechler
10.	Washington	10-2-0	Don James
11.	Ohio St	9-3-0	Woody Hayes
12.	Nebraska	9-3-0	Tom Osborne
13.	Southern Cal	8-4-0	John Robinson
14.	Florida St	10-2-0	Bobby Bowden
15.	Stanford	9-3-0	Bill Walsh
16.	San Diego St	10-1-0	Claude Gilbert
17.	N Carolina	8-3-1	Bill Dooley
18.	Arizona St	9-3-0	Frank Kush
19.	Clemson	8-3-1	Charley Pell
20.	Brigham Young	9-2-0	LaVell Edwards

1978

		Record	Coach
1.	Alabama	11-1-0	Bear Bryant
2.	#Southern Cal	12-1-0	John Robinson
3.	Oklahoma	11-1-0	Barry Switzer
4.	Penn St	11-1-0	Joe Paterno
5.	Michigan	10-2-0	Bo Schembechler
6.	Clemson	11-1-0	Charley Pell
7.	Notre Dame	9-3-0	Dan Devine
8.	Nebraska	9-3-0	Tom Osborne
9.	Texas	9-3-0	Fred Akers
10.	Houston	9-3-0	Bill Yeoman
11.	Arkansas	9-2-1	Lou Holtz
12.	Michigan St	8-3-0	Darryl Rogers
13.	Purdue	9-2-1	Jim Young
14.	UCLA	8-3-1	Terry Donahue
15.	Missouri	8-4-0	Warren Powers
16.	Georgia	9-2-1	Vince Dooley
17.	Stanford	8-4-0	Bill Walsh
18.	N Carolina	9-3-0	Bo Rein
19.	Texas A&M	8-4-0	Emory Bellard (4–2) Tom Wilson (4–2)
20.	Maryland	9-3-0	Jerry Claiborne

#Selected No. 1 by UPI.

1979

		Record	Coach
1.	Alabama	12-0-0	Bear Bryant
2.	Southern Cal	11-0-1	John Robinson
3.	Oklahoma	11-1-0	Barry Switzer
4.	Ohio St	11-1-0	Earle Bruce
5.	Houston	11-1-0	Bill Yeoman
6.	Florida St	11-1-0	Bobby Bowden
7.	Pittsburgh	11-1-0	Jackie Sherrill
8.	Arkansas	10-2-0	Lou Holtz
9.	Nebraska	10-2-0	Tom Osborne
10.	Purdue	10-2-0	Jim Young
11.	Washington	10-1-0	Don James
12.	Texas	9-3-0	Fred Akers
13.	Brigham Young	11-1-0	LaVell Edwards
14.	Baylor	8-4-0	Grant Teaff
15.	N Carolina	8-3-1	Dick Crum
16.	Auburn	8-3-0	Doug Barfield
17.	Temple	10-2-0	Wayne Hardin
18.	Michigan	8-4-0	Bo Schembechler
19.	Indiana	8-4-0	Lee Corso
20.	Penn St	8-4-0	Joe Paterno

1980

		Record	Coach
1.	Georgia	12-0-0	Vince Dooley
2.	Pittsburgh	11-1-0	Jackie Sherrill
3.	Oklahoma	10-2-0	Barry Switzer
4.	Michigan	10-2-0	Bo Schembechler
5.	Florida St	10-2-0	Bobby Bowden
6.	Alabama	10-2-0	Bear Bryant
7.	Nebraska	10-2-0	Tom Osborne
8.	Penn St	10-2-0	Joe Paterno
9.	Notre Dame	9-2-1	Dan Devine
10.	N Carolina	11-1-0	Dick Crum
11.	Southern Cal	8-2-1	John Robinson
12.	Brigham Young	12-1-0	LaVell Edwards
13.	UCLA	9-2-0	Terry Donahue
14.	Baylor	10-2-0	Grant Teaff
15.	Ohio St	9-3-0	Earle Bruce
16.	Washington	9-3-0	Don James
17.	Purdue	9-3-0	Jim Young
18.	Miami (FL)	9-3-0	H. Schnellenberger
19.	Mississippi St	9-3-0	Emory Bellard
20.	SMU	8-4-0	Ron Meyer

1981

		Record	Coach
1.	Clemson	12-0-0	Danny Ford
2.	Texas	10-1-1	Fred Akers
3.	Penn St	10-2-0	Joe Paterno
4.	Pittsburgh	11-1-0	Jackie Sherrill
5.	SMU	10-1-0	Ron Meyer
6.	Georgia	10-2-0	Vince Dooley
7.	Alabama	9-2-1	Bear Bryant
8.	Miami (FL)	9-2-0	H. Schnellenberger
9.	N Carolina	10-2-0	Dick Crum
10.	Washington	10-2-0	Don James
11.	Nebraska	9-3-0	Tom Osborne
12.	Michigan	9-3-0	Bo Schembechler
13.	Brigham Young	11-2-0	LaVell Edwards
14.	Southern Cal	9-3-0	John Robinson
15.	Ohio St	9-3-0	Earle Bruce
16.	Arizona St	9-2-0	Darryl Rogers
17.	W Virginia	9-3-0	Don Nehlen
18.	Iowa	8-4-0	Hayden Fry
19.	Missouri	8-4-0	Warren Powers
20.	Oklahoma	7-4-1	Barry Switzer

1982

		Record	Coach
1.	Penn St.	11-1-0	Joe Paterno
2.	SMU	11-0-1	Bobby Collins
3.	Nebraska	12-1-0	Tom Osborne
4.	Georgia	11-1-0	Vince Dooley
5.	UCLA	10-1-1	Terry Donahue
6.	Arizona St.	10-2-0	Darryl Rogers
7.	Washington	10-2-0	Don James
8.	Clemson	9-1-1	Danny Ford
9.	Arkansas	9-2-1	Lou Holtz
10.	Pittsburgh	9-3-0	Foge Fazio
11.	Louisiana St	8-3-1	Jerry Stovall
12.	Ohio St	9-3-0	Earle Bruce
13.	Florida St	9-3-0	Bobby Bowden
14.	Auburn	9-3-0	Pat Dye
15.	Southern Cal	8-3-0	John Robinson
16.	Oklahoma	8-4-0	Barry Switzer
17.	Texas	9-3-0	Fred Akers
18.	N Carolina	8-4-0	Dick Crum
19.	W Virginia	9-3-0	Don Nehlen
20.	Maryland	8-4-0	Bobby Ross

1983

		Record	Coach
1.	Miami (FL)	11-1-0	H. Schnellenberger
2.	Nebraska	12-1-0	Tom Osborne
3.	Auburn	11-1-0	Pat Dye
4.	Georgia	10-1-1	Vince Dooley
5.	Texas	11-1-0	Fred Akers
6.	Florida	9-2-1	Charlie Pell
7.	Brigham Young	11-1-0	LaVell Edwards
8.	Michigan	9-3-0	Bo Schembechler
9.	Ohio St	9-3-0	Earle Bruce
10.	Illinois	10-2-0	Mike White
11.	Clemson	9-1-1	Danny Ford
12.	SMU	10-2-0	Bobby Collins
13.	Air Force	10-2-0	Ken Hatfield
14.	Iowa	9-3-0	Hayden Fry
15.	Alabama	8-4-0	Ray Perkins
16.	W Virginia	9-3-0	Don Nehlen
17.	UCLA	7-4-1	Terry Donahue
18.	Pittsburgh	8-3-1	Foge Fazio
19.	Boston College	9-3-0	Jack Bicknell
20.	E Carolina	8-3-0	Ed Emory

1984

		Record	Coach
1.	Brigham Young	13-0-0	LaVell Edwards
2.	Washington	11-1-0	Don James
3.	Florida	9-1-1	Chas Pell (0-1-1)
			Galen Hall (9-0)
4.	Nebraska	10-2-0	Tom Osborne
5.	Boston College	10-2-0	Jack Bicknell
6.	Oklahoma	9-2-1	Barry Switzer
7.	Oklahoma St	10-2-0	Pat Jones
8.	SMU	10-2-0	Bobby Collins
9.	UCLA	9-3-0	Terry Donahue
10.	Southern Cal	10-3-0	Ted Tollner
11.	S Carolina	10-2-0	Joe Morrison
12.	Maryland	9-3-0	Bobby Ross
13.	Ohio St	9-3-0	Earle Bruce
14.	Auburn	9-4-0	Pat Dye
15.	Louisiana St	8-3-1	Bill Arnsparger
16.	Iowa	8-4-1	Hayden Fry
17.	Florida St	7-3-2	Bobby Bowden
18.	Miami (FL)	8-5-0	Jimmy Johnson
19.	Kentucky	9-3-0	Jerry Claiborne
20.	Virginia	8-2-2	George Welsh

1985

		Record	Coach
1.	Oklahoma	11-1-0	Barry Switzer
2.	Michigan	10-1-1	Bo Schembechler
3.	Penn St.	11-1-0	Joe Paterno
4.	Tennessee	9-1-2	Johnny Majors
5.	Florida	9-1-1	Galen Hall
6.	Texas A&M	10-2-0	Jackie Sherrill
7.	UCLA	9-2-1	Terry Donahue
8.	Air Force	12-1-0	Fisher DeBerry
9.	Miami (FL)	10-2-0	Jimmy Johnson
10.	Iowa	10-2-0	Hayden Fry
11.	Nebraska	9-3-0	Tom Osborne
12.	Arkansas	10-2-0	Ken Hatfield
13.	Alabama	9-2-1	Ray Perkins
14.	Ohio St	9-3-0	Earle Bruce
15.	Florida St	9-3-0	Bobby Bowden
16.	Brigham Young	11-3-0	LaVell Edwards
17.	Baylor	9-3-0	Grant Teaff
18.	Maryland	9-3-0	Bobby Ross
19.	Georgia Tech.	9-2-1	Bill Curry
20.	Louisiana St	9-2-1	Bill Arnsparger

1986

		Record	Coach
1.	Penn St.	12-0-0	Joe Paterno
2.	Miami (FL)	11-1-0	Jimmy Johnson
3.	Oklahoma	11-1-0	Barry Switzer
4.	Arizona St.	10-1-1	John Cooper
5.	Nebraska	10-2-0	Tom Osborne
6.	Auburn	10-2-0	Pat Dye
7.	Ohio St	10-3-0	Earle Bruce
8.	Michigan	11-2-0	Bo Schembechler
9.	Alabama	10-3-0	Ray Perkins
10.	Louisiana St	9-3-0	Bill Arnsparger
11.	Arizona	9-3-0	Larry Smith
12.	Baylor	9-3-0	Grant Teaff
13.	Texas A&M	9-3-0	Jackie Sherrill
14.	UCLA	8-3-1	Terry Donahue
15.	Arkansas	9-3-0	Ken Hatfield
16.	Iowa	9-3-0	Hayden Fry
17.	Clemson	8-2-2	Danny Ford
18.	Washington	8-3-1	Don James
19.	Boston College	9-3-0	Jack Bicknell
20.	Virginia Tech.	9-2-1	Bill Dooley

1987

		Record	Coach
1.	Miami (FL)	12-0-0	Jimmy Johnson
2.	Florida St	11-1-0	Bobby Bowden
3.	Oklahoma	11-1-0	Barry Switzer
4.	Syracuse	11-0-1	Dick MacPherson
5.	Louisiana St	10-1-1	Mike Archer
6.	Nebraska	10-2-0	Tom Osborne
7.	Auburn	9-1-2	Pat Dye
8.	Michigan St	9-2-1	George Perles
9.	UCLA	10-2-0	Terry Donahue
10.	Texas A&M	10-2-0	Jackie Sherrill
11.	Oklahoma St	10-2-0	Pat Jones
12.	Clemson	10-2-0	Danny Ford
13.	Georgia	9-3-0	Vince Dooley
14.	Tennessee	10-2-1	Johnny Majors
15.	S Carolina	8-4-0	Joe Morrison
16.	Iowa	10-3-0	Hayden Fry
17.	Notre Dame	8-4-0	Lou Holtz
18.	Southern Cal	8-4-0	Larry Smith
19.	Michigan	8-4-0	Bo Schembechler
20.	Arizona St.	7-4-1	John Cooper

1988

		Record	Coach
1.	Notre Dame	12-0-0	Lou Holtz
2.	Miami (FL)	11-1-0	Jimmy Johnson
3.	Florida St	11-1-0	Bobby Bowden
4.	Michigan	9-2-1	Bo Schembechler
5.	W Virginia	11-1-0	Don Nehlen
6.	UCLA	10-2-0	Terry Donahue
7.	Southern Cal	10-2-0	Larry Smith
8.	Auburn	10-2-0	Pat Dye
9.	Clemson	10-2-0	Danny Ford
10.	Nebraska	11-2-0	Tom Osborne
11.	Oklahoma St	10-2-0	Pat Jones
12.	Arkansas	10-2-0	Ken Hatfield
13.	Syracuse	10-2-0	Dick MacPherson
14.	Oklahoma	9-3-0	Barry Switzer
15.	Georgia	9-3-0	Vince Dooley
16.	Washington St	9-3-0	Dennis Erickson
17.	Alabama	9-3-0	Bill Curry
18.	Houston	9-3-0	Jack Pardee
19.	Louisiana St	8-4-0	Mike Archer
20.	Indiana	8-3-1	Bill Mallor

†1989

		Record	Coach
1.	Miami (FL)	11-1-0	Dennis Erickson
2.	Notre Dame	12-1-0	Lou Holtz
3.	Florida St	10-2-0	Bobby Bowden
4.	Colorado	11-1-0	Bill McCartney
5.	Tennessee	11-1-0	Johnny Majors
6.	Auburn	10-2-0	Pat Dye
7.	Michigan	10-2-0	Bo Schembechler
8.	Southern Cal	9-2-1	Larry Smith
9.	Alabama	10-2-0	Bill Curry
10.	Illinois	10-2-0	John Mackovic
11.	Nebraska	10-2-0	Tom Osborne
12.	Clemson	10-2-0	Danny Ford
13.	Arkansas	10-2-0	Ken Hatfield
14.	Houston	9-2-0	Jack Pardee
15.	Penn St	8-3-1	Joe Paterno
16.	Michigan St	8-4-0	George Perles
17.	Pittsburgh	8-3-1	Mike Gottfried
18.	Virginia	10-3-0	George Welsh
19.	Texas Tech	9-3-0	Spike Dykes
20.	Texas A&M	8-4-0	R.C. Slocum
21.	W Virginia	8-3-1	Don Nehlen
22.	Brigham Young	10-3-0	LaVell Edwards
23.	Washington	8-4-0	Don James
24.	Ohio St	8-4-0	John Cooper
25.	Arizona	8-4-0	Dick Tomey

1990

		Record	Coach
1.	Colorado	11-1-1	Bill McCartney
2.	#Ga. Tech (UPI)	11-0-1	Bobby Ross
3.	Miami (FL)	10-2-0	Dennis Erickson
4.	Florida St	10-2-0	Bobby Bowden
5.	Washington	10-2-0	Don James
6.	Notre Dame	9-3-0	Lou Holtz
7.	Michigan	9-3-0	Gary Moeller
8.	Tennessee	9-2-2	Johnny Majors
9.	Clemson	10-2-0	Ken Hatfield
10.	Houston	10-1-0	John Jenkins
11.	Penn St	9-3-0	Joe Paterno
12.	Texas	10-2-0	David McWilliams
13.	Florida	9-2-0	Steve Spurrier
14.	Louisville	10-1-1	H. Schnellenberger
15.	Texas A&M	9-3-1	R.C. Slocum
16.	Michigan St	8-3-1	George Perles

		Record	Coach
17.	Oklahoma	8-3-0	Gary Gibbs
18.	Iowa	8-4-0	Hayden Fry
19.	Auburn	8-3-1	Pat Dye
20.	Southern Cal	8-4-1	Larry Smith
21.	Mississippi	9-3-0	Billy Brewer
22.	Brigham Young	10-3-0	LaVell Edwards
23.	Virginia	8-4-0	George Wells
24.	Nebraska	9-3-0	Tom Osborne
25.	Illinois	8-4-0	John Mackovic

1991

		Record	Coach
1.	Miami (FL)	12-0-0	Dennis Erickson
2.	#Washington	12-0-0	Don James
3.	Penn St	11-2-0	Joe Paterno
4.	Florida St	11-2-0	Bobby Bowden
5.	Alabama	11-1-0	Gene Stallings
6.	Michigan	10-2-0	Gary Moeller
7.	Florida	10-2-0	Steve Spurrier
8.	California	10-2-0	Bruce Snyder
9.	E Carolina	11-1-0	Bill Lewis
10.	Iowa	10-1-1	Hayden Fry
11.	Syracuse	10-2-0	Paul Pasqualoni
12.	Texas A&M	10-2-0	R.C. Slocum
13.	Notre Dame	10-3-0	Lou Holtz
14.	Tennessee	9-3-0	Johnny Majors
15.	Nebraska	9-2-1	Tom Osborne
16.	Oklahoma	9-3-0	Gary Gibbs
17.	Georgia	9-3-0	Ray Goff
18.	Clemson	9-2-1	Ken Hatfield
19.	UCLA	9-3-0	Terry Donahue
20.	Colorado	8-3-1	Bill McCartney
21.	Tulsa	10-2-0	David Rader
22.	Stanford	8-4-0	Dennis Green
23.	Brigham Young	8-3-2	LaVell Edwards
24.	N Carolina St	9-3-0	Dick Sheridan
25.	Air Force	10-3-0	Fisher DeBerry

#Selected No. 1 by *USA Today*/ CNN.

1992

		Record	Coach
1.	Alabama	13-0-0	Gene Stallings
2.	Florida St	11-1-0	Bobby Bowden
3.	Miami	11-1-0	Dennis Erickson
4.	Notre Dame	10-1-1	Lou Holtz
5.	Michigan	9-0-3	Gary Moeller
6.	Syracuse	10-2-0	Paul Pasqualoni
7.	Texas A&M	12-1-0	R.C. Slocum
8.	Georgia	10-2-0	Ray Goff
9.	Stanford	10-3-0	Bill Walsh
10.	Florida	9-4-0	Steve Spurrier
11.	Washington	9-3-0	Don James
12.	Tennessee	9-3-0	Johnny Majors
13.	Colorado	9-2-1	Bill McCartney
14.	Nebraska	9-3-0	Tom Osborne
15.	Washington St	9-3-0	Mike Price
16.	Mississippi	9-3-0	Billy Brewer
17.	N Carolina St	9-3-1	Dick Sheridan
18.	Ohio St	8-3-1	John Cooper
19.	N Carolina	9-3-0	Mack Brown
20.	Hawaii	11-2-0	Bob Wagner
21.	Boston College	8-3-1	Tom Coughlin
22.	Kansas	8-4-0	Glen Mason
23.	Mississippi St	7-5-0	Jackie Sherrill
24.	Fresno St	9-4-0	Jim Sweeney
25.	Wake Forest	8-4-0	Bill Dooley

1993

		Record	Coach
1.	Florida St	12-1-0	Bobby Bowden
2.	Notre Dame	11-1-0	Lou Holtz
3.	Nebraska	11-1-0	Tom Osborne
4.	Auburn	11-0-0	Terry Bowden
5.	Florida	11-2-0	Steve Spurrier

1993 *(Cont.)*

		Record	Coach
6.	Wisconsin	10-1-1	Barry Alvarez
7.	W Virginia	11-1-0	Don Nehlen
8.	Penn St.	10-2-0	Joe Paterno
9.	Texas A&M	10-2-0	R.C. Slocum
10.	Arizona	10-2-0	Dick Tomey
11.	Ohio St	10-1-1	John Cooper
12.	Tennessee	9-2-1	Phil Fulmer
13.	Boston College	9-3-0	Tom Coughlin
14.	Alabama	9-3-1	Gene Stallings
15.	Miami	9-3-0	Dennis Erickson
16.	Colorado	8-3-1	Bill McCartney
17.	Oklahoma	9-3-0	Gary Gibbs
18.	UCLA	8-4-0	Terry Donahue
19.	N Carolina	10-3-0	Mack Brown
20.	Kansas St	9-2-1	Bill Snyder
21.	Michigan	8-4-0	Gary Moeller
22.	Virginia Tech	9-3-0	Frank Beamer
23.	Clemson	9-3-0	Ken Hatfield
24.	Louisville	9-3-0	H. Schnellenberger
25.	California	9-4-0	Keith Gilbertson

1994

		Record	Coach
1.	Nebraska	13-0-0	Tom Osborne
2.	Penn St.	12-0-0	Joe Paterno
3.	Colorado	11-1-0	Bill McCartney
4.	Florida St	10-1-1	Bobby Bowden
5.	Alabama	12-1-0	Gene Stallings
6.	Miami (FL)	10-2-0	Dennis Erickson
7.	Florida	10-2-1	Steve Spurrier
8.	Texas A&M	10-0-1	R.C. Slocum
9.	Auburn	9-1-1	Terry Bowden
10.	Utah	10-2-0	Ron McBride
11.	Oregon	9-4-0	Rich Brooks
12.	Michigan	8-4-0	Gary Moeller
13.	Southern Cal	8-3-1	John Robinson
14.	Ohio St	9-4-0	John Cooper
15.	Virginia	9-3-0	George Welsh
16.	Colorado St	10-2-0	Sonny Lubick
17.	N Carolina St	9-3-0	Mike O'Cain
18.	Brigham Young	10-3-0	LaVell Edwards
19.	Kansas St	9-3-0	Bill Snyder
20.	Arizona	8-4-0	Dick Tomey
21.	Washington St	8-4-0	Mike Price
22.	Tennessee	8-4-0	Phillip Fulmer
23.	Boston College	7-4-1	Dan Henning
24.	Mississippi St	8-4-0	Jackie Sherrill
25.	Texas	8-4-0	John Mackovic

1995

		Record	Coach
1.	Nebraska	12-0-0	Tom Osborne
2.	Florida	12-1-0	Steve Spurrier
3.	Tennessee	11-1-0	Phillip Fulmer
4.	Florida St	10-2-0	Bobby Bowden
5.	Colorado	10-2-0	Rick Neuheisel
6.	Ohio St	11-2-0	John Cooper
7.	Kansas St	10-2-0	Bill Snyder
8.	Northwestern	10-2-0	Gary Barnett
9.	Kansas	10-2-0	Glen Mason
10.	Virginia Tech	10-2-0	Frank Beamer
11.	Notre Dame	9-3-0	Lou Holtz
12.	Southern Cal	9-2-1	John Robinson
13.	Penn St.	9-3-0	Joe Paterno
14.	Texas	10-2-1	John Mackovic
15.	Texas A&M	9-3-0	S.C. Slocum
16.	Virginia	9-4-0	George Welsh
17.	Michigan	9-4-0	Lloyd Carr
18.	Oregon	9-3-0	Mike Bellotti
19.	Syracuse	9-3-0	Paul Pasqualoni
20.	Miami (FL)	8-3-0	Butch Davis

21.	Alabama	8-3-0	Gene Stallings
22.	Auburn	8-4-0	Terry Bowden
23.	Texas Tech	9-3-0	Spike Dykes
24.	Toledo	11-0-1	Gary Pinkel
25.	Iowa	8-4-0	Hayden Fry

1996

		Record*	Coach
1.	Florida	12-1	Steve Spurrier
2.	Ohio St	11-1	John Cooper
3.	Florida St	11-1	Bobby Bowden
4.	Arizona St	11-1	Bruce Snyder
5.	Brigham Young	14-1	LaVell Edwards
6.	Nebraska	11-2	Tom Osborne
7.	Penn St	11-2	Joe Paterno
8.	Colorado	10-2	Rick Neuheisel
9.	Tennessee	10-2	Phillip Fulmer
10.	N Carolina	10-2	Mack Brown
11.	Alabama	10-3	Gene Stallings
12.	Louisiana St	10-2	Gerry DiNardo
13.	Virginia Tech	10-2	Frank Beamer
14.	Miami (FL)	9-3	Butch Davis
15.	Northwestern	9-3	Gary Barnett
16.	Washington	9-3	Jim Lambright
17.	Kansas St	9-3	Bill Snyder
18.	Iowa	9-3	Hayden Fry
19.	Notre Dame	8-3	Lou Holtz
20.	Michigan	8-4	Lloyd Carr
21.	Syracuse	9-3	Paul Pasqualoni
22.	Wyoming	10-2	Joe Tiller
23.	Texas	8-5	John Mackovic
24.	Auburn	8-4	Terry Bowden
25.	Army	10-2	Bob Sutton

1997

		Record	Coach
1.	Michigan	12-0	Lloyd Carr
2.	Nebraska	13-0	Tom Osborne
3.	Florida St	11-1	Bobby Bowden
4.	Florida	10-2	Steve Spurrier
5.	UCLA	10-2	Bob Toledo
6.	N Carolina	11-1	Mack Brown
7.	Tennessee	11-2	Phillip Fulmer
8.	Kansas St	11-1	Bill Snyder
9.	Washington St	10-2	Mike Price
10.	Georgia	10-2	Jim Donnan
11.	Auburn	10-3	Terry Bowden
12.	Ohio St	10-3	John Cooper
13.	Louisiana St	9-3	Gerry DiNardo
14.	Arizona St	8-3	Bruce Snyder
15.	Purdue	9-3	Joe Tiller
16.	Penn St	9-3	Joe Paterno
17.	Colorado St	11-2	Sonny Lubick
18.	Washington	8-4	Jim Lambright
19.	Southern Mississippi	9-3	Jeff Bower
20.	Texas A&M	9-4	R. C. Slocum
21.	Syracuse	9-4	Paul Pasqualoni
22.	Mississippi	8-4	Tommy Tuberville
23.	Missouri	7-5	Larry Smith
24.	Oklahoma St	8-4	Bob Simmons
25.	Georgia Tech	7-5	George O'Leary

1998

		Record	Coach
1.	Tennessee	13-0	Phillip Fulmer
2.	Ohio St	11-1	John Cooper
3.	Florida St	11-2	Bobby Bowden
4.	Arizona	12-1	Dick Tomey
5.	Florida	10-2	Steve Spurrier
6.	Wisconsin	11-1	Barry Alvarez
7.	Tulane	12-0	Tommy Bowden
8.	UCLA	10-2	Bob Toledo
9.	Georgia Tech	10-2	George O'Leary

1998

		Record	Coach
10.	Kansas St	11–2	Bill Snyder
11.	Texas A&M	11–3	R.C. Slocum
12.	Michigan	10–3	Lloyd Carr
13.	Air Force	12–1	Fisher DeBerry
14.	Georgia	9–3	Jim Donnan
15.	Texas	9–3	Mack Brown
16.	Arkansas	9–3	Houston Nutt
17.	Penn St	9–3	Joe Paterno
18.	Virginia	9–3	George Welsh
19.	Nebraska	9–4	Frank Solich
20.	Miami (FL)	9–3	Butch Davis
21.	Missouri	8–4	Larry Smith
22.	Notre Dame	9–3	Bob Davie
23.	Virginia Tech	9–3	Frank Beamer
24.	Purdue	9–4	Joe Tiller
25.	Syracuse	8–4	Paul Pasqualoni

1999

		Record	Coach
1.	Florida St	12–0	Bobby Bowden
2.	Virginia Tech	11–1	Frank Beamer
3.	Nebraska	12–1	Frank Solich
4.	Wisconsin	10–2	Barry Alvarez
5.	Michigan	10–2	Lloyd Carr
6.	Kansas St	11–1	Bill Snyder
7.	Michigan St	10–2	Nick Saban
8.	Alabama	10–3	Mike DuBose
9.	Tennessee	9–3	Phillip Fulmer
10.	Marshall	13–0	Bob Pruett
11.	Penn St	10–3	Joe Paterno
12.	Florida	9–4	Steve Spurrier
13.	Mississippi St	10–2	Jackie Sherrill
14.	Southern Miss	9–3	Jeff Bower
15.	Miami (FL)	9–4	Butch Davis
16.	Georgia	8–4	Jim Donnan
17.	Arkansas	8–4	Houston Nutt
18.	Minnesota	8–4	Glen Mason
19.	Oregon	9–3	Mike Bellotti
20.	Georgia Tech	8–4	Goerge O'Leary
21.	Texas	9–5	Mack Brown
22.	Mississippi	8–4	David Cutcliffe
23.	Texas A&M	8–4	R.C. Slocum
24.	Illinois	8–4	Ron Turner
25.	Purdue	7–5	Joe Tiller

2000

		Record	Coach
1.	Oklahoma	13–0	Bob Stoops
2.	Miami (FL)	11–1	Butch Davis
3.	Washington	11–1	Rick Neuheisel
4.	Oregon St	11–1	Dennis Erickson
5.	Florida St	11–2	Bobby Bowden
6.	Virginia Tech	11–1	Frank Beamer
7.	Oregon	10–2	Mike Belotti
8.	Nebraska	10–2	Frank Solich
9.	Kansas St	11–3	Bill Snyder
10.	Florida	10–3	Steve Spurrier
11.	Michigan	9–3	Lloyd Carr
12.	Texas	9–3	Mack Brown
13.	Purdue	8–4	Joe Tiller
14.	Colorado St	10–2	Sonny Lubeck
15.	Notre Dame	9–3	Bob Davie
16.	Clemson	9–3	Tommy Bowden
17.	Georgia Tech	9–3	George O'Leary

18.	Auburn	9–4	Tommy Tuberville
19.	S Carolina	8–4	Lou Holtz
20.	Georgia	8–4	Jim Donnan
21.	Texas Christian	10–2	Dennis Franchione
22.	Louisiana State	8–4	Nick Saban
23.	Wisconsin	9–4	Barry Alvarez
24.	Mississippi St	8–4	Jackie Sherrill
25.	Iowa St	9–3	Dan McCarney

2001

		Record	Coach
1.	Miami (FL)	12–0	Larry Coker
2.	Oregon	11–1	Mike Belotti
3.	Florida	10–2	Steve Spurrier
4.	Tennessee	11–2	Phillip Fulmer
5.	Texas	11–2	Mack Brown
6.	Oklahoma	11–2	Bob Stoops
7.	Louisiana St	10–3	Nick Saban
8.	Nebraska	11–2	Frank Solich
9.	Colorado	10–3	Gary Barnett
10.	Washington St	10–2	Mike Price
11.	Maryland	10–2	Ralph Friedgen
12.	Illinois	10–2	Ron Turner
13.	S Carolina	9–3	Lou Holtz
14.	Syracuse	10–3	Paul Pasqualoni
15.	Florida St	8–4	Bobby Bowden
16.	Stanford	9–3	Tyrone Willingham
17.	Louisville	11–2	John Smith
18.	Virginia Tech	8–4	Frank Beamer
19.	Washington	8–4	Rick Neuheisel
20.	Michigan	8–4	Lloyd Carr
21.	Boston College	8–4	Tom O'Brien
22.	Georgia	8–4	Mark Richt
23.	Toledo	10–2	Tom Amstutz
24.	Georgia Tech	8–5	George O'Leary
25.	Brigham Young	12–2	Gary Crowton

2002

		Record	Coach
1.	Ohio St	14–0	Jim Tressel
2.	Miami (FL)	12–1	Larry Coker
3.	Georgia	13–1	Mark Richt
4.	Southern Cal	11–2	Pete Carroll
5.	Oklahoma	12–2	Bob Stoops
6.	Texas	11–2	Mack Brown
7.	Kansas St	11–2	Bill Snyder
8.	Iowa	11–2	Kirk Ferentz
9.	Michigan	10–3	Lloyd Carr
10.	Washington St	10–3	Mike Price
11.	Alabama	10–3	Dennis Franchione
12.	N Carolina St	11–3	Chuck Amato
13.	Maryland	11–3	Ralph Friedgen
14.	Auburn	9–4	Tommy Tuberville
15.	Boise St	12–1	Dan Hawkins
16.	Penn St	9–4	Joe Paterno
17.	Notre Dame	10–3	Tyrone Willingham
18.	Virginia Tech	10–4	Frank Beamer
19.	Pittsburgh	9–4	Walt Harris
20.	Colorado	9–5	Gary Barnett
21.	Florida St	9–5	Bobby Bowden
22.	Viriginia	9–5	Al Groh
23.	Texas Christian	10–2	Gary Patterson
24.	Marshall	11–2	Bob Pruett
25.	W Virginia	9–4	Rich Rodriguez

†In 1989 the AP expanded its final poll to 25 teams.
*In 1996 the NCAA introduced overtime to break ties.

2003

		Record	Coach
1.	Southern Cal	12–1	Pete Carroll
2.	Louisiana St*	13–1	Nick Saban
3.	Oklahoma	12–2	Bob Stoops
4.	Ohio St	11–2	Jim Tressel
5.	Miami (FL)	11–2	Larry Coker
6.	Michigan	10–3	Lloyd Carr
7.	Georgia	11–3	Mark Richt
8.	Iowa	10–3	Kirk Ferentz
9.	Washington St	10–3	Bill Doba
10.	Miami (OH)	13–1	Terry Hoeppner
11.	Florida St	10–3	Bobby Bowden
12.	Texas	10–3	Mack Brown
13.	Kansas St	11–4	Bill Snyder
	Mississippi	10–3	David Cutcliffe
15.	Tennessee	10–3	Phillip Fulmer
16.	Boise St	13–1	Dan Hawkins
17.	Maryland	10–3	Ralph Friedgen
18.	Nebraska	10–3	Frank Solich/Bo Pelini
	Purdue	9–4	Joe Tiller
20.	Minnesota	10–3	Glen Mason
21.	Utah	10–2	Urban Meyer
22.	Clemson	9–4	Tommy Bowden
23.	Bowling Green	11–3	Gregg Brandon
24.	Florida	8–5	Ron Zook
25.	Texas Christian	11–2	Gary Patterson

*Ranked No. 1 in *USAToday*/ESPN Poll.

2004

		Record	Coach
1.	USC	13-0	Pete Carrol
2.	Auburn	13-0	Tommy Tuberville
3.	Oklahoma	12-1	Bob Stoops
4.	Utah	12-0	Kyle Whittingham
5.	Texas	11-1	Mack Brown
6.	Louisville	11-1	Bobby Petrino
7.	Georgia	10-2	Mark Richt
8.	Iowa	10-2	Kirk Ferentz
9.	California	10-2	Jeff Tedford
10.	Virginia Tech	10-3	Frank Beamer
11.	Miami	9-3	Larry Coker
12.	Tennessee	10-3	Phillip Fulmer
13.	Michigan	9-3	Lloyd Carr
14.	Florida	8-5	Ron Zook
15.	Michigan	9-3	Lloyd Carr
16.	LSU	9-3	Les Miles
17.	Wisconson	9-3	Barry Alvarez
18.	Texas Tech	8-4	Mike Leach
19.	Arizona State	9-3	Dirk Koetter
20.	Ohio State	8-4	Jim Tressel
21.	Boston College	9-3	Tom O'Brien
22.	Fresno State	9-3	Pat Hill
23.	Virginia	8-4	Al Groh
24.	Navy	10-2	Paul Johnson
25.	Pittsburgh	8-4	Walt Harris

*Ranked No. 1 in *USAToday*/ESPN Poll.

THEY SAID IT

Lou Holtz, South Carolina football coach, on the one writer who voted the Gamecocks No. 1 in the SEC preseason poll: "He probably voted in crayon."

NCAA Divisional Championships

Division I-AA

Year	Winner	Runner-Up	Score
1978	Florida A&M	Massachusetts	35–28
1979	Eastern Kentucky	Lehigh	30–7
1980	Boise St	Eastern Kentucky	31–29
1981	Idaho St	Eastern Kentucky	34–23
1982	Eastern Kentucky	Delaware	17–14
1983	Southern Illinois	Western Carolina	43–7
1984	Montana St	Louisiana Tech	19–6
1985	Georgia Southern	Furman	44–42
1986	Georgia Southern	Arkansas St	48–21
1987	NE Louisiana	Marshall	43–42
1988	Furman	Georgia Southern	17–12
1989	Georgia Southern	Stephen F. Austin St	37–34
1990	Georgia Southern	NV-Reno	36–13
1991	Youngstown St	Marshall	25–17
1992	Marshall	Youngstown St	31–28
1993	Youngstown St	Marshall	17–5
1994	Youngstown St	Boise St	28–14
1995	Montana	Marshall	22–20
1996	Marshall	Montana	49–29
1997	Youngstown St	McNesse St	10–9
1998	Massachusetts	Georgia Southern	55–43
1999	Georgia Southern	Youngstown St	59–24
2000	Georgia Southern	Montana	27–25
2001	Montana	Furman	13–6
2002	Western Kentucky	McNeese St	34–14
2003	Delaware	Colgate	40–0
2004	James Madison	Montana	31–21

Division II

Year	Winner	Runner-Up	Score
1973	Louisiana Tech	Western Kentucky	34–0
1974	Central Michigan	Delaware	54–14
1975	Northern Michigan	Western Kentucky	16–14
1976	Montana St	Akron	24–13
1977	Lehigh	Jacksonville St	33–0
1978	Eastern Illinois	Delaware	10–9
1979	Delaware	Youngstown St	38–21
1980	Cal Poly SLO	Eastern Illinois	21–13
1981	SW Texas St	N Dakota St	42–13
1982	SW Texas St	UC–Davis	34–9
1983	N Dakota St	Central St (OH)	41–21
1984	Troy St	N Dakota St	18–17
1985	N Dakota St	N Alabama	35–7
1986	N Dakota St	S Dakota	27–7
1987	Troy St	Portland St	31–17
1988	N Dakota St	Portland St	35–21
1989	Mississippi College	Jacksonville St	3–0
1990	N Dakota St	Indiana (PA)	51–11
1991	Pittsburg St	Jacksonville St	23–6
1992	Jacksonville St	Pittsburg St	17–13
1993	N Alabama	Indiana (PA)	41–34
1994	N Alabama	Texas A&M–Kingsville	16–10
1995	N Alabama	Pittsburg St	27–7
1996	Northern Colorado	Carson-Newman	23–14
1997	Northern Colorado	New Haven	51–0
1998	NW Missouri St	Carson-Newman	24–6
1999	NW Missouri St	Carson-Newman	58–52 (OT)
2000	Delta St	Bloomsburg	63–34
2001	Grand Valley St	N Dakota	17–14
2002	Grand Valley St	Valdosta St	31–24
2003	Grand Valley St	N Dakota	10–3
2004	Valdosta State	Pittsburg State	36-31

Division III

Year	Winner	Runner-Up	Score
1973	Wittenberg	Juniata	41–0
1974	Central (IA)	Ithaca	10–8
1975	Wittenberg	Ithaca	28–0
1976	St. John's (MN)	Towson St	31–28
1977	Widener	Wabash	39–36
1978	Baldwin-Wallace	Wittenberg	24–10
1979	Ithaca	Wittenberg	14–10
1980	Dayton	Ithaca	63–0
1981	Widener	Dayton	17–10
1982	W Georgia	Augustana (IL)	14–0
1983	Augustana (IL)	Union (NY)	21–17
1984	Augustana (IL)	Central (IA)	21–12

Division III (Cont.)

Year	Winner	Runner-Up	Score
1985	Augustana (IL)	Ithaca	20–7
1986	Augustana (IL)	Salisbury St	31–3
1987	Wagner	Dayton	19–3
1988	Ithaca	Central (IA)	39–24
1989	Dayton	Union (NY)	17–7
1990	Allegheny	Lycoming	21–14 (OT)
1991	Ithaca	Dayton	34–20
1992	WI-LaCrosse	Washington & Jefferson	16–12
1993	Mount Union	Rowan	34–24
1994	Albion	Washington & Jefferson	38–15
1995	WI-LaCrosse	Rowan	36–7
1996	Mount Union	Rowan	56–24
1997	Mount Union	Lycoming	61–12
1998	Mount Union	Rowan	44–24
1999	Pacific Lutheran	Rowan	42–13
2000	Mount Union	St. John's	10–7
2001	Mount Union	Bridgewater	30–27
2002	Mount Union	Trinity (TX)	48–7
2003	St. John's (MN)	Mount Union	24–6
2004	Linfield	Mary Hardin-Baylor	28-21

NAIA Divisional Championships

Division I

Year	Winner	Runner-Up	Score
1956	St. Joseph's (IN)/ Montana St		0–0
1957	Pittsburg St (KS)	Hillsdale (MI)	27–26
1958	NE Oklahoma	Northern Arizona	19–13
1959	Texas A&I	Lenoir-Rhyne (NC)	20–7
1960	Lenoir-Rhyne (NC)	Humboldt St (CA)	15–14
1961	Pittsburg St (KS)	Linfield (OR)	12–7
1962	Central St (OK)	Lenoir-Rhyne (NC)	28–13
1963	St. John's (MN)	Prairie View (TX)	33–27
1964	Concordia-Moorhead/ Sam Houston		7–7
1965	St. John's (MN)	Linfield (OR)	33–0
1966	Waynesburg (PA)	WI-Whitewater	42–21
1967	Fairmont St (WV)	Eastern Washington	28–21
1968	Troy St (MI)	Texas A&I	43–35
1969	Texas A&I	Concordia-Moorhead (MN)	32–7
1970	Texas A&I	Wofford (SC)	48–7
1971	Livingston (AL)	Arkansas Tech	14–12
1972	E Texas St	Carson-Newman (TN)	21–18
1973	Abilene Christian	Elon (NC)	42–14
1974	Texas A&I	Henderson St (AR)	34–23
1975	Texas A&I	Salem (WV)	37–0
1976	Texas A&I	Central Arkansas	26–0
1977	Abilene Christian	SW Oklahoma	24–7
1978	Angelo St (TX)	Elon (NC)	34–14
1979	Texas A&I	Central St (OK)	20–14
1980	Elon (NC)	NE Oklahoma	17–10
1981	Elon (NC)	Pittsburg St	3–0
1982	Central St (OK)	Mesa (CO)	14–11
1983	Carson-Newman (TN)	Mesa (CO)	36–28
1984	Carson-Newman (TN)/Central Arkansas		19–19
1985	Central Arkansas/ Hillsdale (MI)		10–10
1986	Carson-Newman (TN)	Cameron (OK)	17–0
1987	Cameron (OK)	Carson-Newman (TN)	30–2
1988	Carson-Newman (TN)	Adams St (CO)	56–21
1989	Carson-Newman (TN)	Emporia St (KS)	34–20
1990	Central St (OH)	Mesa St (CO)	38–16
1991	Central Arkansas	Central St (OH)	19–16
1992	Central St (OH)	Gardner-Webb (NC)	19–16
1993	E Central (OK)	Glenville St (WV)	49–35
1994	Northeastern St (OK)	Arkansas–Pine Bluff	13–12
1995	Central St (OH)	Northeastern St (OK)	37–7
1996	SW Oklahoma St	Montana Tech	33–31
1997	Findlay (OH)	Willamette (OR)	14–7
1998	Azusa Pacific	Olivet Nazarene	17–14
1999	Northwestern Oklahoma St	Georgetown (KY)	34–26
2000	Georgetown (KY)	Northwestern Oklahoma St	20–0
2001	Georgetown (KY)	Sioux Falls	49–27
2002	Carroll (MN)	Georgetown (KY)	28–7
2003	Carroll (MN)	Northwestern Oklahoma St	41–28
2004	Carroll(MN)	St. Francis	15-13

Division II†

Year	Winner	Runner-Up	Score
1970	Westminster (PA)	Anderson (IN)	21–16
1971	California Lutheran	Westminster (PA)	30–14
1972	Missouri Southern	Northwestern (IA)	21–14
1973	Northwestern (IA)	Glenville St (WV)	10–3
1974	Texas Lutheran	Missouri Valley	42–0
1975	Texas Lutheran	California Lutheran	34–8
1976	Westminster (PA)	Redlands (CA)	20–13
1977	Westminster (PA)	California Lutheran	17–9
1978	Concordia-Moorhead (MN)	Findlay (OH)	7–0
1979	Findlay (OH)	Northwestern (IA)	51–6
1980	Pacific Lutheran	Wilmington (OH)	38–10
1981	Austin Coll./ Conc.-Moorhead (MN)		24–24
1982	Linfield (OR)	William Jewell (MO)	33–15
1983	Northwestern (IA)	Pacific Lutheran	25–21
1984	Linfield (OR)	Northwestern (IA)	33–22
1985	WI-La Crosse	Pacific Lutheran	24–7
1986	Linfield (OR)	Baker (KS)	17–0
1987	Pacific Lutheran	WI-Stevens Point*	16–16
1988	Westminster (PA)	WI-La Crosse	21–14
1989	Westminster (PA)	WI-La Crosse	51–30
1990	Peru St (NE)	Westminster (PA)	17–7
1991	Georgetown (KY)	Pacific Lutheran	28–20
1992	Findlay (OH)	Linfield (OR)	26–13
1993	Pacific Lutheran (WA)	Westminster (PA)	50–20
1994	Westminster (PA)	Pacific Lutheran	27–7
1995	Findlay (OH)	Central Washington	21–21
1996	Sioux Falls (SD)	Western Washington	47–25

*Forfeited 1987 season due to use of an ineligible player.   †In 1997 the NAIA consolidated its two divisions into one.

Awards

Heisman Memorial Trophy

Awarded to the best college player by the Downtown Athletic Club of New York City. The trophy is named after John W. Heisman, who coached Georgia Tech to the national championship in 1917 and later served as DAC athletic director.

Year	Winner, College, Position	Winner's Season Statistics	Runner-Up, College
1935	Jay Berwanger, Chicago, HB	Rush: 119 Yds: 577 TD: 6	Monk Meyer, Army
1936	Larry Kelley, Yale, E	Rec: 17 Yds: 372 TD: 6	Sam Francis, Nebraska
1937	Clint Frank, Yale, HB	Rush: 157 Yds: 667 TD: 11	Byron White, Colorado
1938	†Davey O'Brien, Texas Christian, QB	Att/Comp: 194/110 Yds: 1733 TD: 19	Marshall Goldberg, Pittsburgh
1939	Nile Kinnick, Iowa, HB	Rush: 106 Yds: 374 TD: 5	Tom Harmon, Michigan
1940	Tom Harmon, Michigan, HB	Rush: 191 Yds: 852 TD: 16	John Kimbrough, Texas A&M
1941	†Bruce Smith, Minnesota, HB	Rush: 98 Yds: 480 TD: 6	Angelo Bertelli, Notre Dame
1942	Frank Sinkwich, Georgia, HB	Att/Comp: 166/84 Yds: 1392 TD: 10	Paul Governali, Columbia
1943	Angelo Bertelli, Notre Dame, QB	Att/Comp: 36/25 Yds: 511 TD: 10	Bob Odell, Pennsylvania
1944	Les Horvath, Ohio State, QB	Rush: 163 Yds: 924 TD: 12	Glenn Davis, Army
1945	*†Doc Blanchard, Army, FB	Rush: 101 Yds: 718 TD: 13	Glenn Davis, Army
1946	Glenn Davis, Army, HB	Rush: 123 Yds: 712 TD: 7	Charley Trippi, Georgia
1947	†John Lujack, Notre Dame, QB	Att/Comp: 109/61 Yds: 777 TD: 9	Bob Chappius, Michigan
1948	*Doak Walker, Southern Methodist, HB	Rush: 108 Yds: 532 TD: 8	Charlie Justice, N Carolina
1949	†Leon Hart, Notre Dame, E	Rec: 19 Yds: 257 TD: 5	Charlie Justice, N Carolina
1950	*Vic Janowicz, Ohio St, HB	Att/Comp: 77/32 Yds: 561 TD: 12	Kyle Rote, Southern Methodist
1951	Dick Kazmaier, Princeton, HB	Rush: 149 Yds: 861 TD: 9	Hank Lauricella, Tennessee
1952	Billy Vessels, Oklahoma, HB	Rush: 167 Yds: 1072 TD: 17	Jack Scarbath, Maryland
1953	John Lattner, Notre Dame, HB	Rush: 134 Yds: 651 TD: 6	Paul Giel, Minnesota
1954	Alan Ameche, Wisconsin, FB	Rush: 146 Yds: 641 TD: 9	Kurt Burris, Oklahoma
1955	Howard Cassady, Ohio St, HB	Rush: 161 Yds: 958 TD: 15	Jim Swink, Texas Christian
1956	Paul Hornung, Notre Dame, QB	Att/Comp: 111/59 Yds: 917 TD: 3	Johnny Majors, Tennessee
1957	John David Crow, Texas A&M, HB	Rush: 129 Yds: 562 TD: 10	Alex Karras, Iowa
1958	Pete Dawkins, Army, HB	Rush: 78 Yds: 428 TD: 6	Randy Duncan, Iowa
1959	Billy Cannon, Louisiana St, HB	Rush: 139 Yds: 598 TD: 6	Rich Lucas, Penn St
1960	Joe Bellino, Navy, HB	Rush: 168 Yds: 834 TD: 18	Tom Brown, Minnesota

Heisman Memorial Trophy (Cont.)

Year	Winner, College, Position	Winner's Season Statistics	Runner-Up, College
1961	Ernie Davis, Syracuse, HB	Rush: 150 Yds: 823 TD: 15	Bob Ferguson, Ohio St
1962	Terry Baker, Oregon St, QB	Att/Comp: 203/112 Yds: 1738 TD: 15	Jerry Stovall, Louisiana St
1963	*Roger Staubach, Navy, QB	Att/Comp: 161/107 Yds: 1474 TD: 7	Billy Lothridge, Georgia Tech
1964	John Huarte, Notre Dame, QB	Att/Comp: 205/114 Yds: 2062 TD: 16	Jerry Rhome, Tulsa
1965	Mike Garrett, Southern Cal, HB	Rush: 267 Yds: 1440 TD: 16	Howard Twilley, Tulsa
1966	Steve Spurrier, Florida, QB	Att/Comp: 291/179 Yds: 2012 TD: 16	Bob Griese, Purdue
1967	Gary Beban, UCLA, QB	Att/Comp: 156/87 Yds: 1359 TD: 8	O.J. Simpson, Southern Cal
1968	O.J. Simpson, Southern Cal, HB	Rush: 383 Yds: 1880 TD: 23	Leroy Keyes, Purdue
1969	Steve Owens, Oklahoma, FB	Rush: 358 Yds: 1523 TD: 23	Mike Phipps, Purdue
1970	Jim Plunkett, Stanford, QB	Att/Comp: 358/191 Yds: 2715 TD: 18	Joe Theismann, Notre Dame
1971	Pat Sullivan, Auburn, QB	Att/Comp: 281/162 Yds: 2012; 20 TD	Ed Marinaro, Cornell
1972	Johnny Rodgers, Nebraska, FL	Rec: 55 Yds: 942 TD: 17	Greg Pruitt, Oklahoma
1973	John Cappelletti, Penn St, HB	Rush: 286 Yds: 1522 TD: 17	John Hicks, Ohio St
1974	*Archie Griffin, Ohio St, HB	Rush: 256 Yds: 1695 TD: 12	Anthony Davis, Southern Cal
1975	Archie Griffin, Ohio St, HB	Rush: 262 Yds: 1450 TD: 4	Chuck Muncie, California
1976	†Tony Dorsett, Pittsburgh, HB	Rush: 370 Yds: 2150 TD: 23	Ricky Bell, Southern Cal
1977	Earl Campbell, Texas, FB	Rush: 267 Yds: 1744 TD: 19	Terry Miller, Oklahoma St
1978	*Billy Sims, Oklahoma, HB	Rush: 231 Yds: 1762 TD: 20	Chuck Fusina, Penn St
1979	Charles White, Southern Cal, HB	Rush: 332 Yds: 1803 TD: 19	Billy Sims, Oklahoma
1980	George Rogers, S Carolina, HB	Rush: 324 Yds: 1894 TD: 14	Hugh Green, Pittsburgh
1981	Marcus Allen, Southern Cal, HB	Rush: 433 Yds: 2427 TD: 23	Herschel Walker, Georgia
1982	*Herschel Walker, Georgia, HB	Rush: 335 Yds: 1752 TD: 17	John Elway, Stanford
1983	Mike Rozier, Nebraska, HB	Rush: 275 Yds: 2148 TD: 29	Steve Young, Brigham Young
1984	Doug Flutie, Boston College, QB	Att/Comp: 396/233 Yds: 3454 TD: 27	Keith Byars, Ohio St
1985	Bo Jackson, Auburn, HB	Rush: 278 Yds: 1786 TD: 17	Chuck Long, Iowa
1986	Vinny Testaverde, Miami (FL), QB	Att/Comp: 276/175 Yds: 2557 TD: 26	Paul Palmer, Temple
1987	Tim Brown, Notre Dame, WR	Rec: 39 Yds: 846 TD: 7	Don McPherson, Syracuse
1988	*Barry Sanders, Oklahoma St, RB	Rush: 344 Yds: 2628 TD: 39	Rodney Peete, Southern Cal
1989	*Andre Ware, Houston, QB	Att/Comp: 578/365 Yds: 4699 TD: 46	Anthony Thompson, Indiana
1990	*Ty Detmer, Brigham Young, QB	Att/Comp: 562/361 Yds: 5188 TD: 41	Raghib Ismail, Notre Dame
1991	*Desmond Howard, Michigan, WR	Rec: 61 Yds: 950 TD: 23	Casey Weldon, Florida St
1992	Gino Torretta, Miami (FL), QB	Att/Comp: 402/228 Yds: 3060 TD: 19	Marshall Faulk, San Diego St
1993	†Charlie Ward, Florida St, QB	Att/Comp: 380/264 Yds: 3032 TD: 27	Heath Shuler, Tennessee
1994	Rashaan Salaam, Colorado, RB	Rush: 298 Yds: 2055 TD: 24	Ki-Jana Carter, Penn St
1995	Eddie George, Ohio State, RB	Rush: 303 Yds: 1826 TD: 23	Tommie Frazier, Nebraska
1996	†Danny Wuerffel, Florida, QB	Att/Comp: 360/207 Yds: 3625 TD: 39	Troy Davis, Iowa St
1997	†Charles Woodson, Michigan, CB/WR	7 interceptions; Rec: 11 Yds: 231 TD: 4	Peyton Manning, Tennessee
1998	Ricky Williams, Texas, RB	Rush: 361 Yds: 2124 TD: 28	Michael Bishop, Kansas St
1999	Ron Dayne, Wisconsin, RB	Rush: 303 Yds: 1834 TD: 19	Joe Hamilton, Georgia Tech
2000	Chris Weinke, Florida St, QB	Att/Comp: 431/266 Yds: 4167 TD: 33	Josh Heupel, Oklahoma
2001	Eric Crouch, Nebraska, QB	Att/Comp: 189/105 Yds: 1510 TD: 7; Rush: 1115 Yds, 18 TD	Rex Grossman, Florida
2002	Carson Palmer, Southern Cal, QB	Att/Comp: 450/228 Yds: 3639 TD: 32	Brad Banks, Iowa
2003	Jason White, Oklahoma, QB	Pct. Comp: 64; 3744 Yds; TD: 40	Larry Fitzgerald, Pittsburgh
2004	Matt Leinart, Southern Cal, QB	Att/Comp: 269/412 Yds: 2990 TD: 28	Adrian Peterson, Oklahoma

*Juniors (all others seniors).   †Winners who played for national championship teams the same year.

Note: Former Heisman winners and national media cast votes, with ballots allowing for three names (3 points for first, 2 for second and 1 for third).

Maxwell Award

Given to the nation's outstanding college football player by the Maxwell Football Club of Philadelphia.

Year	Player, College, Position	Year	Player, College, Position
1937	Clint Frank, Yale, HB	1971	Ed Marinaro, Cornell, RB
1938	Davey O'Brien, Texas Christian, QB	1972	Brad Van Pelt, Michigan St, DB
1939	Nile Kinnick, Iowa, HB	1973	John Cappelletti, Penn St, RB
1940	Tom Harmon, Michigan, HB	1974	Steve Joachim, Temple, QB
1941	Bill Dudley, Virginia, HB	1975	Archie Griffin, Ohio St, RB
1942	Paul Governali, Columbia, QB	1976	Tony Dorsett, Pittsburgh, RB
1943	Bob Odell, Pennsylvania, HB	1977	Ross Browner, Notre Dame, DE
1944	Glenn Davis, Army, HB	1978	Chuck Fusina, Penn St, QB
1945	Doc Blanchard, Army, FB	1979	Charles White, Southern Cal, RB
1946	Charley Trippi, Georgia, HB	1980	Hugh Green, Pittsburgh, DE
1947	Doak Walker, Southern Meth, HB	1981	Marcus Allen, Southern Cal, RB
1948	Chuck Bednarik, Pennsylvania, C	1982	Herschel Walker, Georgia, RB
1949	Leon Hart, Notre Dame, E	1983	Mike Rozier, Nebraska, RB
1950	Reds Bagnell, Pennsylvania, HB	1984	Doug Flutie, Boston College, QB
1951	Dick Kazmaier, Princeton, HB	1985	Chuck Long, Iowa, QB
1952	John Lattner, Notre Dame, HB	1986	Vinny Testaverde, Miami (FL), QB
1953	John Lattner, Notre Dame, HB	1987	Don McPherson, Syracuse, QB
1954	Ron Beagle, Navy, E	1988	Barry Sanders, Oklahoma St, RB
1955	Howard Cassady, Ohio St, HB	1989	Anthony Thompson, Indiana, RB
1956	Tommy McDonald, Oklahoma, HB	1990	Ty Detmer, Brigham Young, QB
1957	Bob Reifsnyder, Navy, T	1991	Desmond Howard, Michigan, WR
1958	Pete Dawkins, Army, HB	1992	Gino Torretta, Miami (FL), QB
1959	Rich Lucas, Penn St, QB	1993	Charlie Ward, Florida St, QB
1960	Joe Bellino, Navy, HB	1994	Kerry Collins, Penn St, QB
1961	Bob Ferguson, Ohio St, FB	1995	Eddie George, Ohio St, RB
1962	Terry Baker, Oregon St, QB	1996	Danny Wuerffel, Florida, QB
1963	Roger Staubach, Navy, QB	1997	Peyton Manning, Tennessee, QB
1964	Glenn Ressler, Penn St, C	1998	Ricky Williams, Texas, RB
1965	Tommy Nobis, Texas, LB	1999	Ron Dayne, Wisconsin, RB
1966	Jim Lynch, Notre Dame, LB	2000	Drew Brees, Purdue, QB
1967	Gary Beban, UCLA, QB	2001	Ken Dorsey, Miami (FL), QB
1968	O.J. Simpson, Southern Cal, RB	2002	Larry Johnson, Penn St, RB
1969	Mike Reid, Penn St, DT	2003	Eli Manning, Mississippi, QB
1970	Jim Plunkett, Stanford, QB	2004	Jason White, Oklahoma, QB

Davey O'Brien National Quarterback Award

Given to the top quarterback in the nation by the Davey O'Brien Educational and Charitable Trust of Fort Worth. Named for Texas Christian Hall of Fame quarterback Davey O'Brien (1936–38).

Year	Player, College	Year	Player, College
1981	Jim McMahon, Brigham Young	1993	Charlie Ward, Florida St
1982	Todd Blackledge, Penn St	1994	Kerry Collins, Penn St
1983	Steve Young, Brigham Young	1995	Danny Wuerffel, Florida
1984	Doug Flutie, Boston College	1996	Danny Wuerffel, Florida
1985	Chuck Long, Iowa	1997	Peyton Manning, Tennessee
1986	Vinny Testaverde, Miami (FL)	1998	Michael Bishop, Kansas St
1987	Don McPherson, Syracuse	1999	Joe Hamilton, Georgia Tech
1988	Troy Aikman, UCLA	2000	Chris Weinke, Florida St
1989	Andre Ware, Houston	2001	Eric Crouch, Nebraska
1990	Ty Detmer, Brigham Young	2002	Brad Banks, Iowa
1991	Ty Detmer, Brigham Young	2003	Jason White, Oklahoma
1992	Gino Torretta, Miami (FL)	2004	Jason White, Oklahoma

Note: Originally honored the outstanding football player in the Southwest as follows: 1977—Earl Campbell, Texas, RB; 1978—Billy Sims, Oklahoma, RB; 1979—Mike Singletary, Baylor, LB; 1980—Mike Singletary, Baylor, LB.

Vince Lombardi/Rotary Award

Given to the outstanding college lineman of the year, the award is sponsored by the Rotary Club of Houston.

Year	Player, College, Position	Year	Player, College, Position
1970	Jim Stillwagon, Ohio St, MG	1985	Tony Casillas, Oklahoma, NG
1971	Walt Patulski, Notre Dame, DE	1986	Cornelius Bennett, Alabama, LB
1972	Rich Glover, Nebraska, MG	1987	Chris Spielman, Ohio St, LB
1973	John Hicks, Ohio St, OT	1988	Tracy Rocker, Auburn, DT
1974	Randy White, Maryland, DT	1989	Percy Snow, Michigan St, LB
1975	Lee Roy Selmon, Oklahoma, DT	1990	Chris Zorich, Notre Dame, NG
1976	Wilson Whitley, Houston, DT	1991	Steve Emtman, Washington, DT
1977	Ross Browner, Notre Dame, DE	1992	Marvin Jones, Florida St, LB
1978	Bruce Clark, Penn St, DT	1993	Aaron Taylor, Notre Dame, OT
1979	Brad Budde, Southern Cal, G	1994	Warren Sapp, Miami (FL), DT
1980	Hugh Green, Pittsburgh, DE	1995	Orlando Pace, Ohio St, OT
1981	Kenneth Sims, Texas, DT	1996	Orlando Pace, Ohio St, OT
1982	Dave Rimington, Nebraska, C	1997	Grant Wistrom, Nebraska, DE
1983	Dean Steinkuhler, Nebraska, G	1998	Dat Nguyen, Texas A&M, LB
1984	Tony Degrate, Texas, DT	1999	Corey Moore, Virginia Tech, DE

Lombardi Award (Cont.)

Year	Player, College, Position
2000	Jamal Reynolds, Florida St, DE
2001	Julius Peppers, N Carolina, DE
2002	Terrell Suggs, Arizona St, DL

Year	Player, College, Position
2003	Tommie Harris, Oklahoma, DT
2004	David Pollack, Georgia

Outland Trophy

Given to the outstanding interior lineman, selected by the Football Writers Association of America.

Year	Player, College, Position
1946	George Connor, Notre Dame, T
1947	Joe Steffy, Army, G
1948	Bill Fischer, Notre Dame, G
1949	Ed Bagdon, Michigan St, G
1950	Bob Gain, Kentucky, T
1951	Jim Weatherall, Oklahoma, T
1952	Dick Modzelewski, Maryland, T
1953	J.D. Roberts, Oklahoma, G
1954	Bill Brooks, Arkansas, G
1955	Calvin Jones, Iowa, G
1956	Jim Parker, Ohio St, G
1957	Alex Karras, Iowa, T
1958	Zeke Smith, Auburn, G
1959	Mike McGee, Duke, T
1960	Tom Brown, Minnesota, G
1961	Merlin Olsen, Utah St, T
1962	Bobby Bell, Minnesota, T
1963	Scott Appleton, Texas, T
1964	Steve DeLong, Tennessee, T
1965	Tommy Nobis, Texas, G
1966	Loyd Phillips, Arkansas, T
1967	Ron Yary, Southern Cal, T
1968	Bill Stanfill, Georgia, T
1969	Mike Reid, Penn St, DT
1970	Jim Stillwagon, Ohio St, MG
1971	Larry Jacobson, Nebraska, DT
1972	Rich Glover, Nebraska, MG
1973	John Hicks, Ohio St, OT
1974	Randy White, Maryland, DE
1975	Lee Roy Selmon, Oklahoma, DT

Year	Player, College, Position
1976	Ross Browner, Notre Dame, DE
1977	Brad Shearer, Texas, DT
1978	Greg Roberts, Oklahoma, G
1979	Jim Ritcher, N Carolina St, C
1980	Mark May, Pittsburgh, OT
1981	Dave Rimington, Nebraska, C
1982	Dave Rimington, Nebraska, C
1983	Dean Steinkuhler, Nebraska, G
1984	Bruce Smith, Virginia Tech, DT
1985	Mike Ruth, Boston College, NG
1986	Jason Buck, Brigham Young, DT
1987	Chad Hennings, Air Force, DT
1988	Tracy Rocker, Auburn, DT
1989	Mohammed Elewonibi, Brigham Young, G
1990	Russell Maryland, Miami (FL), DT
1991	Steve Emtman, Washington, DT
1992	Will Shields, Nebraska, G
1993	Rob Waldrop, Arizona, NG
1994	Zach Wiegert, Nebraska, G
1995	Jonathan Ogden, UCLA, OT
1996	Orlando Pace, Ohio St, OT
1997	Aaron Taylor, Nebraska, G
1998	Kris Farris, UCLA, OL
1999	Chris Samuels, Alabama, OL
2000	John Henderson, Tennessee, DT
2001	Bryant McKinnie, Miami (FL), OT
2002	Rien Long, Washington St, DL
2003	Robert Gallery, Iowa, OT
2004	Jammal Brown, Oklahoma, OT

Butkus Award

Given to the top collegiate linebacker, the award was established by the Downtown Athletic Club of Orlando and named for college Hall of Famer Dick Butkus of Illinois.

Year	Player, College
1985	Brian Bosworth, Oklahoma
1986	Brian Bosworth, Oklahoma
1987	Paul McGowan, Florida St
1988	Derrick Thomas, Alabama
1989	Percy Snow, Michigan St
1990	Alfred Williams, Colorado
1991	Erick Anderson, Michigan
1992	Marvin Jones, Florida St
1993	Trev Alberts, Nebraska
1994	Dana Howard, Illinois

Year	Player, College
1995	Kevin Hardy, Illinois
1996	Matt Russell, Colorado
1997	Andy Katzenmoyer, Ohio St
1998	Chris Claiborne, Southern Cal
1999	LaVar Arrington, Penn St
2000	Dan Morgan, Miami (FL)
2001	Rocky Calmus, Oklahoma
2002	E.J. Henderson, Maryland
2003	Teddy Lehman, Oklahoma
2004	Derrick Johnson, Texas

Jim Thorpe Award

Given to the best defensive back of the year, the award is presented by the Jim Thorpe Athletic Club of Oklahoma City.

Year	Player, College
1986	Thomas Everett, Baylor
1987	Bennie Blades, Miami (FL)
	Rickey Dixon, Oklahoma
1988	Deion Sanders, Florida St
1989	Mark Carrier, Southern Cal
1990	Darryl Lewis, Arizona
1991	Terrell Buckley, Florida St
1992	Deon Figures, Colorado
1993	Antonio Langham, Alabama
1994	Chris Hudson, Colorado

Year	Player, College
1995	Greg Myers, Colorado St
1996	Lawrence Wright, Florida
1997	Charles Woodson, Michigan
1998	Antoine Winfield, Ohio St
1999	Tyrone Carter, Minnesota
2000	Jamar Fletcher, Wisconsin
2001	Roy Williams, Oklahoma
2002	Terence Newman, Kansas St
2003	Derrick Strait, Oklahoma
2004	Carlos Rogers, Auburn

Walter Payton Player of the Year Award

Given to the top Division I-AA player as voted by Division I-AA sports information directors. Sponsored by Sports Network.

Year	Player, College, Position
1987	Kenny Gamble, Colgate, RB
1988	Dave Meggett, Towson St, RB
1989	John Friesz, Idaho, QB
1990	Walter Dean, Grambling, RB
1991	Jamie Martin, Weber St, QB
1992	Michael Payton, Marshall, QB
1993	Doug Nussmeier, Idaho, QB
1994	Steve McNair, Alcorn St, QB
1995	Dave Dickenson, Montana, QB
1996	Archie Amerson, Northern Arizona, RB
1997	Brian Finneran, Villanova, WR
1998	Jerry Azumah, New Hampshire, RB
1999	Adrian Peterson, Georgia Southern, RB
2000	Louis Ivory, Furman, RB
2001	Brian Westbrook, Villanova, RB
2002	Tony Romo, Eastern Ilinois, QB
2003	Jamaal Branch, Colgate, RB
2004	Lang Campbell, William & Mary, QB

NCAA Division I-A Individual Records

Career

SCORING

Most Points Scored: 468—Travis Prentice, Miami (OH), 1996–99
Most Points Scored per Game: 12.1—Marshall Faulk, San Diego St, 1991–93
Most Touchdowns Scored: 73—Travis Prentice, Miami (OH), 1996–99
Most Touchdowns Scored per Game: 2.0—Marshall Faulk, San Diego St, 1991–93
Most Touchdowns Scored, Rushing: 73—Travis Prentice, Miami (OH), 1996–99
Most Touchdowns Scored, Passing: 121—Ty Detmer, Brigham Young, 1988–91
Most Touchdowns Scored, Receiving: 50—Troy Edwards, Louisiana Tech, 1996–98
Most Touchdowns Scored, Interception Returns: 5—Ken Thomas, San Jose St, 1979–82; Jackie Walker, Tennessee, 1969–71; Deltha O'Neal, California, 1996–99
Most Touchdowns Scored, Punt Returns: 8—Wes Walker, Texas Tech, 2000–03; Antonio Perkings, Oklahoma, 2001–04
Most Touchdowns Scored, Kickoff Returns: 6—Anthony Davis, Southern Cal, 1972–74

TOTAL OFFENSE

Most Plays: 2,587—Timmy Chang, Hawaii, 2000–04
Most Plays per Game: 50.1—Timmy Chang, Hawaii, 2000–04
Most Yards Gained: 16,910—Timmy Chang, Hawaii, 2000–04 (17,072 passing, -162 rushing)
Most Yards Gained per Game: 382.4—Tim Rattay, Louisiana Tech, 1997–99
Most 300+ Yard Games: 33 —Ty Detmer, Brigham Young, 1988–91

RUSHING

Most Rushes: 1,215—Steve Bartalo, Colorado St, 1983–86 (4813 yds)
Most Rushes per Game: 34.0—Ed Marinaro, Cornell, 1969–71
Most Yards Gained: 6,397—Ron Dayne, Wisconsin, 1996–99
Most Yards Gained per Game: 174.6—Ed Marinaro, Cornell, 1969–71

RUSHING (CONT.)

Most 100+ Yard Games: 33—Tony Dorsett, Pittsburgh, 1973–76; Archie Griffin, Ohio St, 1972–75
Most 200+ Yard Games: 11—Marcus Allen, Southern Cal, 1978–81; Ricky Williams, Texas, 1995–98; Ron Dayne, Wisconsin, 1996–99

PASSING

Highest Passing Efficiency Rating: 168.4—Ryan Dinwiddie, Boise St, 2000–03 (992 attempts, 622 completions, 82 touchdown passes, 21 interceptions, 9,819 yards)
Most Passes Attempted: 2,436—Timmy Chang, Hawaii, 2000–04
Most Passes Attempted per Game: 47.0—Tim Rattay, Louisiana Tech, 1997–99
Most Passes Completed: 1,388—Timmy Chang, Hawaii, 2000–04
Most Passes Completed per Game: 30.8—Tim Rattay, Louisiana Tech, 1997–99
*Highest Completion Percentage: 67.1—Tim Couch, Kentucky, 1996–98
Most Yards Gained: 17,072—Timmy Chang, Hawaii, 2000–04
Most Yards Gained per Game: 386.2—Tim Rattay, Louisiana Tech, 1997–99

*Minimum 1,000 attempts.

RECEIVING

Most Passes Caught: 316—Taylor Stubblefield, Purdue, 2001–04
Most Passes Caught per Game: 10.5—Emmanuel Hazard, Houston, 1989–90
Most Yards Gained: 5,005—Trevor Insley, Nevada, 1996–99
Most Yards Gained per Game: 140.9—Alex Van Dyke, Nevada, 1994–95
Highest Average Gain per Reception: 25.7—Wesley Walker, California, 1973–75

Career *(Cont.)*

ALL-PURPOSE RUNNING

Most Plays: 1,347—Steve Bartalo, Colorado St, 1983-86 (1,215 rushes, 132 receptions)

Most Yards Gained: 7,206—Ricky Williams, Texas, 1995–98 (6,279 rushing, 927 receiving)

Most Yards Gained per Game: 237.8—Ryan Benjamin, Pacific, 1990–92

Highest Average Gain per Play: 17.4—Anthony Carter, Michigan, 1979–82

INTERCEPTIONS

Most Passes Intercepted: 29—Al Brosky, Illinois, 1950–52

Most Passes Intercepted per Game: 1.1—Al Brosky, Illinois, 1950–52

Most Yards on Interception Returns: 501— Terrell Buckley, Florida St, 1989–91

Highest Average Gain per Interception: 26.5— Tom Pridemore, W Virginia, 1975–77

SPECIAL TEAMS

Highest Punt Return Average: 23.6—Jack Mitchell, Oklahoma, 1946–48

Highest Kickoff Return Average: 36.2—Forrest Hall, San Francisco, 1946–47

Highest Average Yards per Punt: 46.3—Todd Sauerbrun, W Virginia, 1991–94

Note: 150–249 punts.

Single Season

SCORING

Most Points Scored: 234—Barry Sanders, Oklahoma St, 1988

Most Points Scored per Game: 21.3—Barry Sanders, Oklahoma St, 1988

Most Touchdowns Scored: 39—Barry Sanders, Oklahoma St, 1988

Most Touchdowns Scored, Rushing: 37— Barry Sanders, Oklahoma St, 1988

Most Touchdowns Scored, Passing: 54— David Klingler, Houston, 1990

Most Touchdowns Scored, Receiving: 27— Troy Edwards, Louisiana Tech, 1998

Most Touchdowns Scored, Interception Returns: 4—Deltha O'Neal, California, 1999

Most Touchdowns Scored, Punt Returns: 5—Chad Owens, Hawaii, 2004

Most Touchdowns Scored, Kickoff Returns: 5—Ashlan Davis, Tulsa, 2004

TOTAL OFFENSE

Most Plays: 814—Kliff Kingsbury, Texas Tech, 2002

Most Yards Gained: 5,976—B.J. Symons, Texas Tech, 2003

Most Yards Gained per Game: 474.6—David Klingler, Houston, 1990

Most 300+ Yard Games: 12—Ty Detmer, Brigham Young, 1990

RUSHING

Most Rushes: 403—Marcus Allen, Southern Cal, 1981

Most Rushes per Game: 39.6—Ed Marinaro, Cornell, 1971

Most Yards Gained: 2,628—Barry Sanders, Oklahoma St, 1988

Most Yards Gained per Game: 238.9—Barry Sanders, Oklahoma St, 1988

Most 100+ Yard Games: 12—Quentin Griffin, Oklahoma, 2002

PASSING

Highest Passing Efficiency Rating: 183.3— Shaun King, Tulane, 1998 (328 attempts, 223 completions, 6 interceptions, 3,232 yards, 36 TD passes)

Most Passes Attempted: 719—B.J. Symons, Texas Tech, 2003

Most Passes Attempted per Game: 58.5— David Klingler, Houston, 1990

Most Passes Completed: 479—Kliff Kingsbury, Texas Tech, 2002

Most Passes Completed per Game: 36.4—Tim Couch, Kentucky, 1998

Highest Completion Percentage: 73.6— Daunte Culpepper, Central Florida, 1998

Most Yards Gained: 5,833—B.J. Symons, Texas Tech, 2003

Most Yards Gained per Game: 467.3—David Klingler, Houston, 1990

RECEIVING

Most Passes Caught: 142—Emmanuel Hazard, Houston, 1989

Most Passes Caught per Game: 13.4—Howard Twilley, Tulsa, 1965

Most Yards Gained: 2,060—Trevor Insley, Nevada, 1999

Most Yards Gained per Game: 187.3—Trevor Insley, Nevada, 1999

Highest Average Gain per Reception: 27.9— Elmo Wright, Houston, 1968 (min. 30 receptions)

ALL-PURPOSE RUNNING

Most Plays: 432—Marcus Allen, Southern Cal, 1981

Most Yards Gained: 3,250—Barry Sanders, Oklahoma St, 1988

Most Yards Gained per Game: 295.5—Barry Sanders, Oklahoma St, 1988

Highest Average Gain per Play: 18.5—Henry Bailey, UNLV, 1992

Single Season (Cont.)

INTERCEPTIONS

Most Passes Intercepted: 14 — Al Worley, Washington, 1968
Most Yards on Interception Returns: 302 — Charles Phillips, Southern Cal, 1974
Highest Average Gain per Interception: 50.6 — Norm Thompson, Utah, 1969

SPECIAL TEAMS

Highest Punt Return Average: 25.9 — Bill Blackstock, Tennessee, 1951
Highest Kickoff Return Average: 40.1 — Paul Allen, Brigham Young, 1961
Highest Average Yards per Punt: 50.3 — Chad Kessler, Louisiana St, 1997

Single Game

SCORING

Most Points Scored: 48—Howard Griffith, Illinois, 1990 (vs Southern Illinois)
Most Field Goals: 7—Dale Klein, Nebraska, 1985 (vs Missouri); Mike Prindle, Western Michigan, 1984 (vs Marshall)
Most Extra Points (Kick): 13—Derek Mahoney, Fresno St, 1991 (vs New Mexico); Terry Leiweke, Houston, 1968 (vs Tulsa)
Most Extra Points (2-Pts): 6—Jim Pilot, New Mexico St, 1961 (vs Hardin-Simmons)

TOTAL OFFENSE

Most Yards Gained: 732—David Klingler, Houston, 1990 (vs Arizona St)

RUSHING

Most Yards Gained: 406—LaDainian Tomlinson, Texas Christian, 1999 (vs UTEP)
Most Touchdowns Rushed: 8—Howard Griffith, Illinois, 1990 (vs Southern Illinois)

PASSING

Most Passes Completed: 55—Rusty LaRue, Wake Forest, 1995 (vs Duke); Drew Brees, Purdue, 1998 (vs Wisconsin)
Most Yards Gained: 716—David Klingler, Houston, 1990 (vs Arizona St)
Most Touchdown Passes: 11—David Klingler, Houston, 1990 [vs Eastern Washington (I-AA)]

RECEIVING

Most Passes Caught: 23—Randy Gatewood, UNLV, 1994 (vs Idaho)
Most Yards Gained: 405—Troy Edwards, Louisiana Tech, 1998 (vs Nebraska)
Most Touchdown Catches: 7—Rashaun Woods, Oklahoma St, 2003 (vs Southern Methodist)

NCAA Division I-AA Individual Records

Career

SCORING

Most Points Scored: 544—Brian Westbrook, Villanova, 1998-01
Most Touchdowns Scored: 89—Brian Westbrook, Villanova, 1998-01
Most Touchdowns Scored, Rushing: 84—Adrian Peterson, Georgia Southern, 1998-01
Most Touchdowns Scored, Passing: 139—Willie Totten, Mississippi Valley, 1982-85
Most Touchdowns Scored, Receiving: 50—Jerry Rice, Mississippi Valley, 1981-84

RUSHING

Most Rushes: 1,124—Charles Roberts, Cal St-Sacramento, 1997-00
Most Rushes per Game: 38.2—Arnold Mickens, Butler, 1994-95
Most Yards Gained: 6,559—Adrian Peterson, Georgia Southern, 1998-01
Most Yards Gained per Game: 190.7—Arnold Mickens, Butler, 1994-95

PASSING

Highest Passing Efficiency Rating: 170.8—Shawn Knight, William & Mary, 1991-94
Most Passes Attempted: 1,680—Marcus Brady, Cal St—Northridge, 1998-01; Steve McNair, Alcorn St, 1991-94
Most Passes Completed: 1,039—Marcus Brady, Cal St—Northridge, 1998-01
Most Passes Completed per Game: 26.5—Chris Sanders, Chattanooga, 1999-00
Highest Completion Percentage: 67.3—Dave Dickenson, Montana, 1992-95
Most Yards Gained: 14,496—Steve McNair, Alcorn St, 1991-94
Most Yards Gained per Game: 350.0—Neil Lomax, Portland St, 1978-80

RECEIVING

Most Passes Caught: 317—Jacquay Nunnally, Florida A&M, 1997-00
Most Yards Gained: 4,693—Jerry Rice, Mississippi Valley, 1981-84
Most Yards Gained per Game: 119.1—Tramon Douglas, Grambling, 2002-03
Highest Average Gain per Reception: 24.3—John Taylor, Delaware St, 1982-85

Single Season

SCORING

Most Points Scored: 176—Brian Westbrook, Villanova, 2001
Most Touchdowns Scored: 29—Adrian Peterson, Georgia Southern, 1999; Brian Westbrook, Villanova, 2001
Most Touchdowns Scored, Rushing: 29—Jamaal Branch, Colgate, 2003
Most Touchdowns Scored, Passing: 56—Willie Totten, Mississippi Valley, 1984
Most Touchdowns Scored, Receiving: 27—Jerry Rice, Mississippi Valley, 1984

RUSHING

Most Rushes: 450—Jamaal Branch, Colgate, 2003
Most Rushes per Game: 40.9—Arnold Mickens, Butler, 1994
Most Yards Gained: 2,326—Jamaal Branch, Colgate, 2003
Most Yards Gained per Game: 225.5—Arnold Mickens, Butler, 1994

PASSING

Highest Passing Efficiency Rating: 204.6—Shawn Knight, William & Mary, 1993
Most Passes Attempted: 592—Martin Hankins, Southeastern La. 2003
Most Passes Completed: 405—Brett Gordon, Villanova, 2002
Most Passes Completed per Game: 32.4—Willie Totten, Mississippi Valley, 1984
Highest Completion Percentage: 70.6—Giovanni Carmazzi, Hofstra, 1997
Most Yards Gained: 4,863—Steve McNair, Alcorn St, 1994
Most Yards Gained per Game: 455.7—Willie Totten, Mississippi Valley, 1984

RECEIVING

Most Passes Caught: 120—Stephen Campbell, Brown, 2000
Most Yards Gained: 1,712—Eddie Conti, Delaware, 1998
Most Yards Gained per Game: 168.2—Jerry Rice, Mississippi Valley, 1984
Highest Average Gain per Reception: 28.9—Mikhael Ricks, Stephen F. Austin, 1997; (min. 35 receptions)

Single Game

SCORING

Most Points Scored: 42—Jesse Burton, McNeese St, 1998 (vs Southern Utah); Archie Amerson, Northern Arizona, 1996 (vs Weber St)
Most Field Goals: 8—Goran Lingmerth, Northern Arizona, 1986 (vs Idaho)

RUSHING

Most Yards Gained: 437—Maurice Hicks, N Carolina A&T, 2001 (vs Morgan St)
Most Touchdowns Rushed: 7—Archie Amerson, Northern Arizona, 1996 (vs Weber St)

PASSING

Most Passes Completed: 50—Martin Hankins, Southeastern La., 2004. (vs. Jacksonville) Cal St–Northridge, 1995 (vs St. Mary's [CA])
Most Yards Gained: 624—Jamie Martin, Weber St, 1991 (vs Idaho St)
Most Touchdown Passes: 9—Willie Totten, Mississippi Valley, 1984 (vs Kentucky St)

RECEIVING

Most Passes Caught: 24—Chas Gessner, Brown, 2002, (vs Rhode Island); Jerry Rice, Mississippi Valley, 1983 (vs Southern–BR)
Most Yards Gained: 376—Kassim Osgood, Cal Poly, 2000 (vs Northern Iowa)
Most Touchdown Catches: 6—Cos DeMatteo, Chattanooga, 2000 (vs Mississippi Valley)

NCAA Division II Individual Records

Career

SCORING

Most Points Scored: 570—Ian Smart, C.W. Post, 1999–2002
Most Touchdowns Scored: 95—Ian Smart, C.W. Post, 1999–2002
Most Touchdowns Scored, Rushing: 94—Ian Smart, C.W. Post, 1999–2002
Most Touchdowns Scored, Passing: 121—Marc Eddy, Bentley, 2001–04
Most Touchdowns Scored, Receiving: 78—Dallas Mall, Bentley, 2001–04

RUSHING

Most Rushes: 1,131—Josh Ranek, S Dakota St, 1997–01
Most Rushes per Game: 29.8—Bernie Peeters, Luther, 1968–71
Most Yards Gained: 6,958—Brian Shay, Emporia St, 1995–98
Most Yards Gained per Game: 183.4—Anthony Gray, Western NM, 1997–98

Career *(Cont.)*

PASSING

Highest Passing Efficiency Rating: 190.8—Dusty Bonner, Valdosta St, 2000–01
Most Passes Attempted: 1,898—Andrew Webb, Fort Lewis, 2000–03
Most Passes Completed: 1,007—Andrew Webb, Fort Lewis, 2000–03
Most Passes Completed per Game: 25.7—Chris Hatcher, Valdosta St, 1991–94
Highest Completion Percentage: 72.7—Dusty Bonner, Valdosta St, 2000–01
Most Yards Gained: 11,742—Andrew Webb, Fort Lewis, 2000–03
Most Yards Gained per Game: 323.7—Dusty Bonner, Valdosta St, 2000–01

RECEIVING

Most Passes Caught: 323—Clarence Coleman, Ferris St, 1998–01
Most Yards Gained: 4,983—Clarence Coleman, Ferris St, 1998–01
Most Yards Gained per Game: 160.8—Chris George, Glenville St, 1993–94
Highest Average Gain per Reception: 23.2—Romar Crenshaw, Southeastern Okla., 2000–03

Single Season

SCORING

Most Points Scored: 212—David Kircus, Grand Valley St, 2002
Most Touchdowns Scored: 35—David Kircus, Grand Valley St, 2002
Most Touchdowns Scored, Rushing: 33—Ian Smart, C.W. Post, 2001
Most Touchdowns Scored, Passing: 54—Dusty Bonner, Valdosta St, 2000
Most Touchdowns Scored, Receiving: 35—David Kircus, Grand Valley St, 2002

RUSHING

Most Rushes: 385—Joe Gough, Wayne St (MI), 1994
Most Rushes per Game: 38.6—Mark Perkins, Hobart, 1968
Most Yards Gained: 2,653—Kavin Gailliard, American International, 1999
Most Yards Gained per Game: 222.0—Anthony Gray, Western New Mexico, 1997

PASSING

Highest Passing Efficiency Rating: 221.63—Curt Anes, Grand Valley St, 2001
Most Passes Attempted: 559—Andrew Webb, Fort Lewis 2001
Most Passes Completed: 384—Chad Friehauf, Colorado Mines 2004
Most Passes Completed per Game: 32.4—Lance Funderburk, Valdosta St, 1995
Highest Completion Percentage: 74.7—Chris Hatcher, Valdosta St, 1994
Most Yards Gained: 4,646—Chad Friehauf, Colorado Mines 2004
Most Yards Gained per Game: 393.4—Grady Benton, W Texas A&M, 1994

RECEIVING

Most Passes Caught: 119—Brad Bailey, W Texas A&M, 1994
Most Yards Gained: 1,876—Chris George, Glenville St, 1993
Most Yards Gained per Game: 187.6—Chris George, Glenville St, 1993
Highest Average Gain per Reception: 32.5—Tyrone Johnson, Western St, 1991 (min. 30 receptions)

Single Game

SCORING

Most Points Scored: 48—Paul Zaeske, N Park, 1968 (vs N Central); Junior Wolf, Panhandle St, 1958 (vs St. Mary [KS])
Most Field Goals: 6—Steve Huff, Central Missouri St, 1985 (vs SE Missouri St); Austin Wellock, Ashland, 2002 (vs. Wayne St)

RUSHING

Most Yards Gained: 410—Andrew Terry, Ferris St, 2004 (vs Findlay)
Most Touchdowns Rushed: 8—Junior Wolf, Panhandle St, 1958 (vs St. Mary [KS])

PASSING

Most Passes Completed: 76—Jarrod DeGeorgia, Wayne St (NE),1996 (vs Drake)
Most Yards Gained: 645—Matt Kohn, Indianapolis, 2003 (vs Michigan Tech)
Most Touchdowns Passed: 10—Bruce Swanson, N Park, 1968 (vs N Central)

RECEIVING

Most Passes Caught: 23—Chris George, Glenville St, 1994 (vs WV Wesleyan); Barry Wagner, Alabama A&M, 1989 (vs Clark Atlanta)
Most Yards Gained: 401—Kevin Ingram, W Chester, 1998 (vs Clarion)
Most Touchdown Catches: 8—Paul Zaeske, N Park, 1968 (vs N Central)

Career

SCORING

Most Points Scored: 562—R.J. Bowers, Grove City, 1997–00
Most Touchdowns Scored: 92—R.J. Bowers, Grove City, 1997–00
Most Touchdowns Scored, Rushing: 91—R.J. Bowers, Grove City, 1997–00
Most Touchdowns Scored, Passing: 148—Justin Peery, Westminster (MO), 1996–99
Most Touchdowns Scored, Receiving: 75—Scott Pingel, Westminster (MO), 1996–99

RUSHING

Most Rushes: 1,190—Steve Tardif, Maine Maritime, 1996–99
Most Rushes per Game: 32.7—Chris Sizemore, Bridgewater (VA), 1972–74
Most Yards Gained: 7,353—R.J. Bowers, Grove City, 1997–00
Most Yards Gained per Game: 187.1—Tony Sutton, Wooster, 2002–04

PASSING

Highest Passing Efficiency Rating: 194.2—Bill Borchert, Mount Union, 1994–97
Most Passes Attempted: 1,696—Kirk Baumgartner, WI-Stevens Point, 1986–89
Most Passes Completed: 1,012—Justin Peery, Westminster (MO), 1996–99
Most Passes Completed per Game: 25.9—Justin Peery, Westminster (MO), 1996–99
Highest Completion Percentage: 67.0—Gary Smeck, Mount Union, 1997–00
Most Yards Gained: 13,262—Justin Peery, Westminster (MO), 1996–99
Most Yards Gained per Game: 340.1—Justin Peery, Westminster (MO), 1996–99

RECEIVING

Most Passes Caught: 436—Scott Pingel, Westminster (MO), 1996–99
Most Yards Gained: 6,108—Scott Pingel, Westminster (MO), 1996–99
Most Yards Gained per Game: 156.6—Scott Pingel, Westminster (MO), 1996–99
Highest Average Gain per Reception: 23.4—Michael Coleman, Widener, 1998–2001

Single Season

SCORING

Most Points Scored: 248—Dan Pugh, Mount Union, 2002
Most Points Scored per Game: 20.8—James Regan, Pomona-Pitzer, 1997
Most Touchdowns Scored: 41—Dan Pugh Mount Union, 2002
Most Touchdowns Scored, Rushing: 35—Dan Pugh, Mount Union, 2002
Most Touchdowns Scored, Passing: 61—Brett Elliott, Linfield, 2004
Most Touchdowns Scored, Receiving: 26—Scott Pingel, Westminster (MO), 1998

RUSHING

Most Rushes: 463—Dante Washington, Carthage, 2004
Most Rushes per Game: 38.0—Mike Birosak, Dickinson, 1989
Most Yards Gained: 2,385—Dante Brown, Marietta, 1996

PASSING

Highest Passing Efficiency Rating: 225.0—Mike Simpson, Eureka, 1994
Most Passes Attempted: 575—Brett Dietz, Hanover, 2003
Most Passes Completed: 360—Brett Dietz, Hanover, 2003
Most Passes Completed per Game: 32.9—Justin Peery, Westminster (MO), 1999
Highest Completion Percentage: 72.9—Jim Ballard, Mount Union, 1993
Most Yards Gained: 4,595—Brett Elliott, Linfield, 2004
Most Yards Gained per Game: 450.1—Justin Peery, Westminster (MO), 1998

RECEIVING

Most Passes Caught: 136—Scott Pingel, Westminster (MO), 1999
Most Yards Gained: 2,157—Scott Pingel, Westminster, (MO), 1998
Most Yards Gained per Game: 215.7—Scott Pingel, Westminster, (MO), 1998
Highest Average Gain per Reception: 26.9—

Single Game

SCORING

Most Field Goals: 6—Jim Hever, Rhodes, 1984 (vs Millsaps)

PASSING

Most Passes Completed: 51—Scott Kello, Sul Ross St, 2002 (vs Howard Payne)
Most Yards Gained: 731—Zamir Amin, Menlo, 2000 (vs California Lutheran)
Most Touchdown Passes: 9—Joe Zarlinga, Ohio Northern, 1998 (vs Capital)

RUSHING

Most Yards Gained: 441—Dante Brown, Marietta, 1996 (vs Baldwin-Wallace)
Most Touchdowns Rushed: 8—Carey Bender, Coe, 1994 (vs Beloit)

RECEIVING

Most Passes Caught: 23—Sean Munroe, Mass-Boston, 1992 (vs Mass-Maritime)
Most Yards Gained: 418—Lewis Howes, Principia, 2002 (vs Martin Luther)
Most Touchdown Catches: 7—Matt Perceval, Wesleyan (CT), 1998 (vs Middlebury)

Career

Scoring

POINTS (KICKERS)

	Years	Pts
Roman Anderson, Houston	1988–91	423
Billy Bennett, Georgia	2000–03	409
Carlos Huerta, Miami (FL)	1988–91	397
Jason Elam, Hawaii	1988–92	395
Derek Schmidt, Florida St	1984–87	393

POINTS (NON-KICKERS)

	Years	Pts
Travis Prentice, Miami (OH)	1996–99	468
Ricky Williams, Texas	1995–98	452
Brock Forsey, Boise St	1999–02	408
Cedric Benson, Texas	2001–04	404
Anthony Thompson, Indiana	1986–89	394
Ron Dayne, Wisconsin	1996–99	378

POINTS PER GAME (NON-KICKERS)

	Years	Pts/Game
Marshall Faulk, San Diego St	1991–93	12.1
Ed Marinaro, Cornell	1969–71	11.8
Bill Burnett, Arkansas	1968–70	11.3
Steve Owens, Oklahoma	1967–69	11.2
Eddie Talboom, Wyoming	1948–50	10.8

Total Offense

YARDS GAINED

	Years	Yds
Timmy Chang	2000–04	16,910
Ty Detmer, Brigham Young	1988–91	14,665
Philip Rivers, N Carolina St	2000–03	13,582
Luke McCown, Louisiana Tech	2000–03	12,731
Tim Rattay, Louisiana Tech	1997–99	12,618

YARDS PER GAME

	Years	Yds/Game
Tim Rattay, Louisiana Tech	1997–99	382.4
Chris Vargas, Nevada	1992–93	320.9
Timmy Chang	2000–04	319.1
Ty Detmer, Brigham Young	1988–91	318.8
Daunte Culpepper, Central Florida	1996–98	313.5

Rushing

YARDS GAINED

	Years	Yds
Ron Dayne, Wisconsin	1996–99	6,397
Ricky Williams, Texas	1995–98	6,279
Tony Dorsett, Pittsburgh	1973–76	6,082
Charles White, Southern Cal	1976–79	5,598
Travis Prentice, Miami (OH)	1996–99	5,596

YARDS PER GAME

	Years	Yds/Game
Ed Marinaro, Cornell	1969–71	174.6
O.J. Simpson, Southern Cal	1967–68	164.4
Herschel Walker, Georgia	1980–82	159.4
LeShon Johnson, Northern Illinois	1992–93	150.6
Ron Dayne, Wisconsin	1996–99	148.8

TOUCHDOWNS RUSHING

	Years	TD
Travis Prentice, Miami (OH)	1996–99	73
Ricky Williams, Texas	1995–98	72
Anthony Thompson, Indiana	1986–89	64
Cedric Benson	2001–04	64
Ron Dayne, Wisconsin	1996–99	63
Eric Crouch, Nebraska	1998–01	59

Passing

PASSING EFFICIENCY

	Years	Rating
Ryan Dinwiddie, Boise St	2000–03	168.4
Danny Wuerffel, Florida	1993–96	163.6
Ty Detmer, Brigham Young	1988–91	162.7
Steve Sarkisian, Brigham Young	1995–96	162.0
Billy Blanton, San Diego St	1993–96	157.1

Note: Minimum 500 completions.

YARDS GAINED

	Years	Yds
Timmy Chang, Hawaii	2000–03	17,072
Ty Detmer, Brigham Young	1988–91	15,031
Philip Rivers, N Carolina St	2000–03	13,484
Tim Rattay, Louisiana Tech	1997–99	12,746
Luke McCown, Louisiana Tech	2000–03	12,666

COMPLETIONS

	Years	Comp
Timmy Chang, Hawaii	2000–03	1,388
Kliff Kingsbury, Texas Tech	1999–02	1,231
Philip Rivers, N Carolina St	2000–03	1,147
Luke McCown, Louisiana Tech	2000–03	1,063
Chris Redman, Louisville	1996–99	1,031
Tim Rattay, Louisiana Tech	1997–99	1,015

TOUCHDOWNS PASSING

	Years	TD
Ty Detmer, Brigham Young	1988–91	121
Timmy Chang, Hawaii	2000–04	117
Tim Rattay, Louisiana Tech	1997–99	115
Danny Wuerffel, Florida	1993–96	114
Chad Pennington, Marshall	1997–99	100
Kliff Kingsbury, Texas Tech	1999–02	95
Philip Rivers, N Carolina St	2000–03	95

Receiving

CATCHES

	Years	No.
Taylor Stubblefield, Purdue	2001–04	316
Josh Davis, Marshall	2001–04	306
Arnold Jackson, Louisville	1997–00	300
Trevor Insley, Nevada	1996–99	298
Geoff Noisy, Nevada	1995–98	295
Rashaun Woods, Oklahoma St	2000–03	293

CATCHES PER GAME

	Years	No./Game
Emmanuel Hazard, Houston	1989–90	10.5
Alex Van Dyke, Nevada	1994–95	10.3
Howard Twilley, Tulsa	1963–65	10.0
Jason Phillips, Houston	1987–88	9.4
Troy Edwards, Louisiana Tech	1996–98	8.2
Bryan Reeves, Nevada	1992–93	8.2

YARDS GAINED

	Years	Yds
Trevor Insley, Nevada	1996–99	5,005
Marcus Harris, Wyoming	1993–96	4,518
Rashaun Woods, Oklahoma St	2000–03	4,412
Ryan Yarborough, Wyoming	1990–93	4,357
Troy Edwards, Louisiana Tech	1996–98	4,352

TOUCHDOWN CATCHES

	Years	TD
Troy Edwards, Louisiana Tech	1996–98	50
Darius Watts, Marshall	2000–03	47
Aaron Turner, Pacific	1989–92	43
Ryan Yarborough, Wyoming	1990–93	42
Rashaun Woods, Oklahoma St	2000–03	42
Braylon Edwards, Michigan	2001–04	39
Marcus Harris, Wyoming	1993–96	38
Clarkston Hines, Duke	1986–89	38

Career *(Cont.)*

All-Purpose Running

YARDS GAINED	Years	Yds
Ricky Williams, Texas	1996–98	7,206
Napoleon McCallum, Navy	1981–85	7,172
Darrin Nelson, Stanford	1977–78, 80–81	6,885
Kevin Faulk, Louisiana St	1995–98	6,833
Darren Sproles, Kansas State	2001–04	4,979

YARDS PER GAME	Years	Yds/Game
Ryan Benjamin, Pacific	1990–92	237.8
Sheldon Canley, San Jose St	1988–90	205.8
Howard Stevens, Louisville	1971–72	193.7
O.J. Simpson, Southern Cal	1967–68	192.9
Alex Van Dyke, Nevada	1994–95	188.5

THEY SAID IT

"Maurice Weeks, Virginia safety, after returning a kickoff 100 yards against North Carolina: "That was just instinct. Kind of like running from the cops".

Interceptions

PLAYER/SCHOOL	Years	Int
Al Brosky, Illinois	1950–52	29
John Provost, Holy Cross	1972–74	27
Martin Bayless, Bowling Green	1980–83	27
Tom Curtis, Michigan	1967–69	25
Tony Thurman, Boston Col	1981–84	25
Tracy Saul, Texas Tech	1989–92	25

Punting Average

PLAYER/SCHOOL	Years	Avg
Todd Sauerbrun, W Virginia	1991–94	46.3
Reggie Roby, Iowa	1979–82	45.6
Greg Montgomery, Michigan St	1985–87	45.4
Tom Tupa, Ohio St	1984–87	45.2
Barry Helton, Colorado	1984–87	44.9

Note: 150–249 punts.

Punt Return Average

PLAYER/SCHOOL	Years	Avg
Jack Mitchell, Oklahoma	1946–48	23.6
Gene Gibson, Cincinnati	1949–50	20.5
Eddie Macon, Pacific	1949–51	18.9
Jackie Robinson, UCLA	1939–40	18.8
Dan Shelton, Illinois	2001–04	17.9
Bobby Dillon, Texas	1949–51	17.7
Mike Fuller, Auburn	1972–74	17.7

Note: At least 30 returns.

Kickoff Return Average

PLAYER/SCHOOL	Years	Avg
Anthony Davis, Southern Cal	1972–74	35.1
Eric Booth, Southern Miss	1994–97	32.4
Overton Curtis, Utah St	1957–58	31.0
Fred Montgomery, New Mexico St	1991–92	30.5
Altie Taylor, Utah St	1966–68	29.3

Note: At least 30 returns.

Single Season

Scoring

POINTS	Year	Pts
Barry Sanders, Oklahoma St	1988	234
Brock Forsey, Boise St	2002	192
Troy Edwards, Louisiana Tech	1998	186
Mike Rozier, Nebraska	1983	174
Lydell Mitchell, Penn St	1971	174

FIELD GOALS	Year	FG
Billy Bennett, Georgia	2003	31
John Lee, UCLA	1984	29
Paul Woodside, W Virginia	1982	28
Luis Zendejas, Arizona St	1983	28
Nick Browne, Texas Christian	2003	28

Three tied with 27.

All-Purpose Running

YARDS GAINED	Year	Yds
Barry Sanders, Oklahoma St	1988	3,250
Ryan Benjamin, Pacific	1991	2,995
Troy Edwards, Louisiana Tech	1998	2,784
Darren Sproles, Kansas St	2003	2,735
Mike Pringle, Fullerton St	1989	2,690

All-Purpose Running *(Cont.)*

YARDS PER GAME	Year	Yds/Game
Barry Sanders, Oklahoma St	1988	295.5
Ryan Benjamin, Pacific	1991	249.6
Byron (Whizzer) White, Colorado	1937	246.3
Mike Pringle, Fullerton St	1989	244.6
Paul Palmer, Temple	1986	239.4

Total Offense

YARDS GAINED	Year	Yds
B.J. Symons, Texas Tech	2003	5,976
David Klingler, Houston	1990	5,221
Ty Detmer, Brigham Young	1990	5,022
Kliff Kingsbury, Texas Tech	2002	4,903
Tim Rattay, Louisiana Tech	1998	4,840

YARDS PER GAME	Year	Yds/Game
David Klingler, Houston	1990	474.6
B.J. Symons, Texas Tech	2003	459.7
Andre Ware, Houston	1989	423.7
Ty Detmer, Brigham Young	1990	418.5
Tim Rattay, Louisiana Tech	1998	403.3

Single Season *(Cont.)*

Rushing

YARDS GAINED

	Year	Yds
Barry Sanders, Oklahoma St	1988	2,628
Marcus Allen, Southern Cal	1981	2,342
Troy Davis, Iowa St	1996	2,185
LaDainian Tomlinson, Texas Christian	2000	2,158
Mike Rozier, Nebraska	1983	2,148

YARDS PER GAME

	Year	Yds/Game
Barry Sanders, Oklahoma St	1988	238.9
Marcus Allen, Southern Cal	1981	212.9
Ed Marinaro, Cornell	1971	209.0
Troy Davis, Iowa St	1996	198.6
LaDainian Tomlinson, Texas Christian	2000	196.2

TOUCHDOWNS RUSHING

	Year	TD
Barry Sanders, Oklahoma St	1988	37
Mike Rozier, Nebraska	1983	29
Willis McGahee, Miami (FL)	2002	28
Ricky Williams, Texas	1998	27
Lee Suggs, Virginia Tech	2000	27
Brock Forsey, Boise St	2002	26

Passing

PASSING EFFICIENCY

	Year	Rating
Shaun King, Tulane	1998	183.3
Stefan Lefors, Louisville	2004	181.7
Michael Vick, Virginia Tech	1999	180.4
Danny Wuerffel, Florida	1995	178.4
Jim McMahon, Brigham Young	1980	176.9

YARDS GAINED

	Year	Yds
B.J. Symons, Texas Tech	2003	5,833
Ty Detmer, Brigham Young	1990	5,188
David Klingler, Houston	1990	5,140
Kliff Kingsbury, Texas Tech	2002	5,017
Tim Rattay, Louisiana Tech	1998	4,943

COMPLETIONS

	Year	Att	Comp
Kliff Kingsbury, Texas Tech	2002	712	479
B.J. Symons, Texas Tech	2003	719	470
Sony cumbie, Texas Tech	2004	642	421
Tim Couch, Kentucky	1998	553	400
Tim Rattay, Louisiana Tech	1998	559	380

Passing *(Cont.)*

TOUCHDOWNS PASSING

	Year	TD
David Klingler, Houston	1990	54
B.J. Symons, Texas Tech	2003	52
Jim McMahon, Brigham Young	1980	47
Andre Ware, Houston	1989	46
Tim Rattay, Louisiana Tech	1998	46

Receiving

CATCHES

	Year	GP	No.
Emmanuel Hazard, Houston	1989	11	142
Troy Edwards, Louisiana Tech	1998	12	140
Nate Burleson, Nevada	2002	12	138
Howard Twilley, Tulsa	1965	10	134
Trevor Insley, Nevada	1999	11	134

CATCHES PER GAME

	Year	No.	No./Game
Howard Twilley, Tulsa	1965	134	13.4
Emmanuel Hazard, Houston	1989	142	12.9
Trevor Insley, Nevada	1999	134	12.2
Troy Edwards, Louisiana Tech	1998	140	11.7
Alex Van Dyke, Nevada	1995	129	11.7

YARDS GAINED

	Year	Yds
Trevor Insley, Nevada	1999	2,060
Troy Edwards, Louisiana Tech	1998	1,996
Alex Van Dyke, Nevada	1995	1,854
J.R. Tolver, San Diego St	2002	1,785
Howard Twilley, Tulsa	1965	1,779

TOUCHDOWN CATCHES

	Year	TD
Troy Edwards, Louisiana Tech	1998	27
Randy Moss, Marshall	1997	25
Emmanuel Hazard, Houston	1989	22
Larry Fitzgerald, Pittsburgh	2003	22
Desmond Howard, Michigan	1991	19
Ashley Lelie, Hawaii	2001	19

Single Game

Scoring

POINTS

	Opponent	Year	Pts
Howard Griffith, Illinois	Southern Illinois	1990	48
Marshall Faulk, San Diego St	Pacific	1991	44
Jim Brown, Syracuse	Colgate	1956	43
Showboat Boykin, Mississippi	Mississippi St	1951	42
Fred Wendt, UTEP*	New Mexico St	1948	42
Rashaun Woods, Oklahoma St	SMU	2003	42

*UTEP was Texas Mines in 1948.

FIELD GOALS

	Opponent	Year	FG
Dale Klein, Nebraska	Missouri	1985	7
Mike Prindle, Western Michigan	Marshall	1984	7

Note: 14 tied with 6.

Klein's distances were 32-22-43-44-29-43-43. Prindle's distances were 32-44-42-23-48-41-27.

Single Game *(Cont.)*

Total Offense

YARDS GAINED	Opponent	Year	Yds
David Klingler, Houston	Arizona St	1990	732
Matt Vogler, TCU	Houston	1990	696
B.J. Symons, Texas Tech	Mississippi	2003	681
Brian Lindgren, Idaho	Middle Tenn St	2001	657
David Klingler, Houston	Texas Christian	1990	625
Scott Mitchell, Utah	Air Force	1988	625

Passing

YARDS GAINED	Opponent	Year	Yds
David Klingler, Houston	Arizona St	1990	716
Matt Vogler, TCU	Houston	1990	690
B.J. Symons, Texas Tech	Mississippi	2003	661
Brian Lindgren, Idaho	Middle Tenn St	2001	637
Scott Mitchell, Utah	Air Force	1988	631

COMPLETIONS	Opponent	Year	Comp
Drew Brees, Purdue	Wisconsin	1998	55
Rusty LaRue, Wake Forest	Duke	1995	55
Rusty LaRue, Wake Forest	NC St	1995	50
Brian Lindgren, Idaho	Middle Tenn St	2001	49
Kliff Kingsbury, Texas Tech	Missouri	2002	49
Kliff Kingsbury, Texas Tech	Texas A&M	2002	49
Bruce Gradkowski, Toledo	Pittsburgh	2003	49

TOUCHDOWNS PASSING	Opponent	Year	TD
David Klingler, Houston	E Wash	1990	11

Note: Klingler's TD passes were 5-48-29-7-3-7-40-10-7-8-51.

Rushing

YARDS GAINED	Opponent	Year	Yds
LaDainian Tomlinson, Texas Christian	UTEP	1999	406
Tony Sands, Kansas	Missouri	1991	396
Marshall Faulk, San Diego St	Pacific	1991	386
Troy Davis, Iowa St	Missouri	1996	378
Anthony Thompson, Indiana	Wisconsin	1989	377
Robbie Mixon, Central Michigan	Eastern Mich	2002	377

TOUCHDOWNS RUSHING	Opponent	Year	TD
Howard Griffith, Illinois	Southern Illinois	1990	8

Note: Griffith's TD runs were 5-51-7-41-5-18-5-3.

Receiving

CATCHES	Opponent	Year	No.
Randy Gatewood, UNLV	Idaho	1994	23
Jay Miller, Brigham Young	New Mexico	1973	22
Troy Edwards, La. Tech	Nebraska	1998	21
Chris Daniels, Purdue	Michigan St	1999	21
Rick Eber, Tulsa	Idaho St	1967	20
Kenny Christian, Eastern Michigan	Temple	2000	20

YARDS GAINED	Opponent	Year	Yds
Troy Edwards, Louisiana Tech	Nebraska	1998	405
Randy Gatewood, UNLV	Idaho	1994	363
Chuck Hughes, UTEP*	N Texas St	1965	349
Nate Burleson, Nevada	San Jose St	2001	326
Rick Eber, Tulsa	Idaho St	1967	322

*UTEP was Texas Western in 1965.

TOUCHDOWN CATCHES	Opponent	Year	TD
Rashaun Woods, Okl. St	SMU	2003	7
Tim Delaney, San Diego St	New Mex. St	1969	6

Longest Plays (since 1941)

PASSING	Opponent	Year	Yds
Fred Owens to Jack Ford, Portland	St. Mary's (CA)	1947	99
Bo Burris to Warren McVea, Houston	Washington St	1966	99
Colin Clapton to Eddie Jenkins, Holy Cross	Boston U	1970	99
Terry Peel to Robert Ford, Houston	Syracuse	1970	99
Terry Peel to Robert Ford, Houston	San Diego St	1972	99
Cris Collinsworth to Derrick Gaffney, Florida	Rice	1977	99
Scott Ankrom to James Maness, Texas Christian	Rice	1984	99
Gino Toretta to Horace Copeland, Miami (FL)	Arkansas	1991	99
John Paci to Thomas Lewis, Indiana	Penn St	1993	99
Troy DeGar to Wes Caswell, Tulsa	Oklahoma	1996	99
Drew Brees to Vinny Sutherland, Purdue	Northwestern	1999	99
Dan Urban to Justin McCariens, Northern Illinois	Ball St	2000	99
Jason Johnson to Brandon Marshall, Arizona	Idaho	2001	99
Dondrial Pinkins to Troy Williamson, S Carolina	Virginia	2003	99

RUSHING	Opponent	Year	Yd
Gale Sayers, Kansas	Nebraska	1963	99
Max Anderson, Arizona St	Wyoming	1967	99
Ralph Thompson, W Texas St	Wichita St	1970	99
Kelsey Finch, Tennessee	Florida	1977	99
Eric Vann, Kansas	Oklahoma	1997	99

FIELD GOALS	Opponent	Year	Yds
Steve Little, Arkansas	Texas	1977	67
Russell Erxleben, Texas	Rice	1977	67
Joe Williams, Wichita St	Southern IL	1978	67
Martin Gramatica, Kansas St	Northern IL	1998	65
Tony Franklin, Texas A&M	Baylor	1976	65

PUNTS	Opponent	Year	Yds
Pat Brady, Nevada*	Loyola (CA)	1950	99
George O'Brien, Wisconsin	Iowa	1952	96
John Hadl, Kansas	Oklahoma	1959	94
Carl Knox, Texas Christian	Oklahoma St	1947	94
Preston Johnson, SMU	Pittsburgh	1940	94

*Nevada was Nevada-Reno in 1950.

DIVISION I-A WINNINGEST TEAMS

Alltime Winning Percentage

	Yrs	W	L	T	Pct	GP	Bowl Record
Michigan	125	842	275	36	.746	1,153	17-17-0
Notre Dame	116	802	263	42	.743	1,107	13-12-0
Oklahoma	110	749	285	53	.713	1,087	22-13-1
Texas	112	787	310	33	.711	1,130	20-21-2
Alabama	110	764	299	43	.710	1,106	29-19-3
Ohio St.	115	764	298	53	.709	1,115	16-19-0
Nebraska	115	786	317	40	.705	1,143	21-21-0
Tennessee	108	746	306	53	.699	1,105	23-21-0
Southern Cal	112	720	297	54	.697	1,071	27-15-0
Penn St.	118	760	338	41	.685	1,139	23-12-2
Boise St.	37	295	136	2	.684	433	4-0-0
Florida St.	58	428	200	17	.677	645	18-12-2
Georgia	111	683	372	54	.640	1,109	21-15-3
Miami (OH)	116	632	348	44	.639	1,024	6-2-0
Miami (FL)	78	516	288	19	.639	823	16-12-0
Louisiana St	111	658	372	47	.633	1,077	17-17-1
Washington	115	669	363	50	.631	1,052	14-14-1
South Florida	8	55	33	0	.625	88	
Auburn	112	647	379	47	.625	1,073	16-12-2
Arizona St	92	516	313	24	.619	853	10-8-1
Florida	98	597	364	40	.616	1,001	13-17-0
Colorado	115	643	396	36	.615	1,075	11-14-0
Central Michigan	104	526	333	36	.608	895	0-2-0
Texas A&M	110	634	409	48	.603	1,091	13-14-0
Syracuse	115	664	434	49	.600	1,147	

Note: Includes bowl games.

Alltime Victories

Michigan	842	Georgia	683	Pittsburgh	628
Notre Dame	802	Syracuse	664	Army	624
Texas	787	Louisiana St	658	Arkansas	624
Nebraska	786	Auburn	647	N Carolina	619
Alabama	764	Colorado	643	Minnesota	619
Ohio St	764	Washington	639	Virginia Tech	615
Penn St.	760	Texas A&M	634	Clemson	600
Oklahoma	749	Miami (OH)	632	Navy	599
Tennessee	746	W Virginia	631	Florida	597
Southern Cal	720	Georgia Tech	630	Mississippi	587

NUMBER ONE VS NUMBER TWO

The No. 1 and No. 2 teams, according to the Associated Press Poll, have met 33 times, including 13 bowl games, since the poll's inception in 1936. The No. 1 teams have a 20-11-2 record in these matchups. Notre Dame (4-3-2) has played in nine of the games.

Date	Results	Stadium
10-9-43	No. 1 Notre Dame 35, No. 2 Michigan 12	Michigan (Ann Arbor)
11-20-43	No. 1 Notre Dame 14, No. 2 Iowa Pre-Flight 13	Notre Dame (South Bend)
12-2-44	No. 1 Army 23, No. 2 Navy 7	Municipal (Baltimore)
11-10-45	No. 1 Army 48, No. 2 Notre Dame 0	Yankee (New York)
12-1-45	No. 1 Army 32, No. 2 Navy 13	Municipal (Philadelphia)
11-9-46	No. 1 Army 0, No. 2 Notre Dame 0	Yankee (New York)
1-1-63	No. 1 Southern Cal 42, No. 2 Wisconsin 37 (Rose Bowl)	Rose Bowl (Pasadena)
10-12-63	No. 2 Texas 28, No. 1 Oklahoma 7	Cotton Bowl (Dallas)
1-1-64	No. 1 Texas 28, No. 2 Navy 6 (Cotton Bowl)	Cotton Bowl (Dallas)
11-19-66	No. 1 Notre Dame 10, No. 2 Michigan St 10	Spartan (E Lansing)
9-28-68	No. 1 Purdue 37, No. 2 Notre Dame 22	Notre Dame (South Bend)
1-1-69	No. 1 Ohio St 27, No. 2 Southern Cal 16 (Rose Bowl)	Rose Bowl (Pasadena)
12-6-69	No. 1 Texas 15, No. 2 Arkansas 14	Razorback (Fayetteville)
11-25-71	No. 1 Nebraska 35, No. 2 Oklahoma 31	Owen Field (Norman)
1-1-72	No. 1 Nebraska 38, No. 2 Alabama 6 (Orange Bowl)	Orange Bowl (Miami)
1-1-79	No. 2 Alabama 14, No. 1 Penn St 7 (Sugar Bowl)	Sugar Bowl (New Orleans)
9-26-81	No. 1 Southern Cal 28, No. 2 Oklahoma 24	Coliseum (Los Angeles)
1-1-83	No. 2 Penn St 27, No. 1 Georgia 23 (Sugar Bowl)	Sugar Bowl (New Orleans)

NUMBER ONE VS NUMBER TWO *(Cont.)*

Date	Results	Stadium
10-19-85	No. 1 Iowa 12, No. 2 Michigan 10	Kinnick (Iowa City)
9-27-86	No. 2 Miami (FL) 28, No. 1 Oklahoma 16	Orange Bowl (Miami)
1-2-87	No. 2 Penn St 14, No. 1 Miami (FL) 10 (Fiesta Bowl)	Sun Devil (Tempe)
11-21-87	No. 2 Oklahoma 17, No. 1 Nebraska 7	Memorial (Lincoln)
1-1-88	No. 2 Miami (FL) 20, No. 1 Oklahoma 14 (Orange Bowl)	Orange Bowl (Miami)
11-26-88	No. 1 Notre Dame 27, No. 2 Southern Cal 10	Coliseum (Los Angeles)
9-16-89	No. 1 Notre Dame 24, No. 2 Michigan 19	Michigan (Ann Arbor)
11-16-91	No. 2 Miami (FL) 17, No. 1 Florida St 16	Campbell (Tallahassee)
1-1-93	No. 2 Alabama 34, No. 1 Miami (FL) 13 (Sugar Bowl)	Superdome (New Orleans)
11-13-93	No. 2 Notre Dame 31, No. 1 Florida St 24	Notre Dame (South Bend)
1-1-94	No. 1 Florida St 18, No. 2 Nebraska 16 (Orange Bowl)	Orange Bowl (Miami)
1-2-96	No. 1 Nebraska 62, No. 2 Florida 24 (Fiesta Bowl)	Sun Devil (Tempe)
11-30-96	No. 2 Florida St 24, No. 1 Florida 21	Campbell (Tallahassee)
1-4-99	No. 1 Tennessee 23, No. 2 Florida St 16 (Fiesta Bowl)	Sun Devil (Tempe)
1-4-00	No. 1 Florida St 46, No. 2 Virginia Tech 29 (Sugar Bowl)	Superdome (New Orleans)
1-3-03	No. 2 Ohio St 31, Miami (FL) 24 [2OT] (Fiesta Bowl)	Sun Devil (Tempe)
1-4-05	No. 2 Oklahoma 19, Southern Cal 55 (Orange Bowl)	Pro Player Stadium (Miami)

LONGEST DIVISION I-A WINNING STREAKS

Wins	Team	Yrs	Ended by	Score
47	Oklahoma	1953–57	Notre Dame	7–0
39	Washington	1908–14	Oregon St	0–0
37	Yale	1890–93	Princeton	6–0
37	Yale	1887–89	Princeton	10–0
35	Toledo	1969–71	Tampa	21–0
34	Miami	2000–03	Ohio St	31–24 (2ot)
34	Pennsylvania	1894–96	Lafayette	6–4
31	Oklahoma	1948–50	Kentucky	13–7
31	Pittsburgh	1914–18	Cleveland Naval Reserve	10–9
31	Pennsylvania	1896–98	Harvard	10–0
30	Texas	1968–70	Notre Dame	24–11

LONGEST DIVISION I-A UNBEATEN STREAKS

No.	W	T	Team	Yrs	Ended by	Score
63	59	4	Washington	1907–17	California	27–0
56	55	1	Michigan	1901–05	Chicago	2–0
50	46	4	California	1920–25	Olympic Club	15–0
48	47	1	Oklahoma	1953–57	Notre Dame	7–0
48	47	1	Yale	1885–89	Princeton	10–0
47	42	5	Yale	1879–85	Princeton	6–5
44	42	2	Yale	1894–96	Princeton	24–6
42	39	3	Yale	1904–08	Harvard	4–0
39	37	2	Notre Dame	1946–50	Purdue	28–14
37	36	1	Oklahoma	1972–75	Kansas	23–3
37	37	0	Yale	1890–93	Princeton	6–0
35	35	0	Toledo	1969–71	Tampa	21–0
35	34	1	Minnesota	1903–05	Wisconsin	16–12
34	34	0	Miami	2000–03	Ohio St	31–24 (2ot)
34	33	1	Nebraska	1912–16	Kansas	7–3
34	34	0	Pennsylvania	1894–96	Lafayette	6–4
34	32	2	Princeton	1884–87	Harvard	12–0
34	29	5	Princeton	1877–82	Harvard	1–0
33	30	3	Tennessee	1926–30	Alabama	18–6
33	31	2	Georgia Tech	1914–18	Pittsburgh	32–0
33	30	3	Harvard	1911–15	Cornell	10–0
32	31	1	Nebraska	1969–71	UCLA	20–17
32	30	2	Army	1944–47	Columbia	21–20
32	31	1	Harvard	1898–1900	Yale	28–0
31	30	1	Penn St	1967–70	Colorado	41–13
31	30	1	San Diego St	1967–70	Long Beach St	27–11
31	29	2	Georgia Tech	1950–53	Notre Dame	27–14
31	31	0	Oklahoma	1948–50	Kentucky	13–7
31	31	0	Pittsburgh	1914–18	Cleveland Naval	10–9
31	31	0	Pennsylvania	1896–98	Harvard	10–0

Note: Includes bowl games.

LONGEST DIVISION I-A LOSING STREAKS

Losses		Seasons	Ended Against	Score
34	Northwestern	1979–82	Northern Illinois	31–6
28	Virginia	1958–61	William & Mary	21–6
28	Kansas St	1945–48	Arkansas St	37–6
27	New Mexico St	1988–90	Cal St–Fullerton	43–9
27	Eastern Michigan	1980–82	Kent St	9–7

MOST-PLAYED DIVISION I-A RIVALRIES

GP	Opponents (Series Leader Listed First)	Record	First Game
114	Minnesota–Wisconsin	59-47-8	1890
113	Missouri–Kansas	52-52-9	1891
111	Nebraska-Kansas	87-21-3	1892
111	Texas–Texas A&M	72-34-5	1894
109	Miami (OH)–Cincinnati	58-44-7	1888
109	N Carolina–Virginia	†56-49-4	1892
108	Auburn–Georgia	52-48-8	1892
108	Oregon–Oregon St	54-44-10	1894
107	Purdue–Indiana	66-35-6	1891
107	Stanford–California	54-42-11	1892
105	Army–Navy	49-49-7	1890
104	Baylor–Texas Christian*	49-47-7	1899
103	Utah–Utah St	72-28-4	1892

GP	Opponents (Series Leader Listed First)	Record	First Game
102	Clemson–S Carolina	62-36-4	1896
102	Kansas–Kansas St	62-35-5	1902
101	Mississippi–Miss St	58-37-6	1901
101	N Carolina–Wake Forest	67-32-2	1897
100	Tennessee–Kentucky	68-23-9	1893
99	Georgia–Georgia Tech	56-38-5	1893
99	Nebraska–Iowa St	81-16-2	1896
99	Texas–Oklahoma	55-39-5	1900
99	Oklahoma–Oklahoma St	76-16-7	1904

*Have not met since 1995.

†Disputed series record: Virginia claims N Carolina leads series 55-49-4 based on a forfeited game in 1956.

NCAA Coaches' Records

ALLTIME WINNINGEST DIVISION I-A COACHES

Coach (Alma Mater)	Colleges Coached	Yrs	W	L	T	Pct
Knute Rockne (Notre Dame '14)†	Notre Dame 1918–30	13	105	12	5	.881
Frank W. Leahy (Notre Dame '31)†	Boston Col 1939–40; Notre Dame 1941–43, 1946–53	13	107	13	9	.864
George W. Woodruff (Yale 1889)†	Pennsylvania 1892–01; Illinois 1903; Carlisle 1905	12	142	25	2	.846
Barry Switzer (Arkansas '60)	Oklahoma 1973–88	16	157	29	4	.837
Tom Osborne (Hastings '59)†	Nebraska 1973–98	25	255	49	3	.836
Percy D. Haughton (Harvard 1899)†	Cornell 1899–1900; Harvard 1908–16; Columbia 1923–24	13	96	17	6	.832
Bob Neyland (Army '16)†	Tennessee 1926–34, 1936–40, 1946–52	21	173	31	12	.829
Fielding Yost (W Virginia 1895)†	Ohio Wesleyan 1897; Nebraska 1898; Kansas 1899; Stanford 1900; Michigan 1901–23, 1925–26	29	196	36	12	.828
Bud Wilkinson (Minnesota '37)†	Oklahoma 1947–63	17	145	29	4	.826
Jock Sutherland (Pittsburgh '18)†	Lafayette 1919–23; Pittsburgh 1924–38	20	144	28	14	.812
Bob Devaney (Alma, MI '39)†	Wyoming 1957–61; Nebraska 1962–72	16	136	30	7	.806
*Phillip Fulmer (Tennessee '71)	Tennessee 1992–	12	113	28	0	.801
Frank W. Thomas (Notre Dame '23)†	Tenn.-Chattanooga 1925–28; Alabama 1931–42, 1944–46	19	141	33	9	.795
Henry L. Williams (Yale 1891)†	Army 1891; Minnesota 1900–21	23	141	34	12	.786
Gil Dobie (Minnesota '02)†	N Dakota St 1906–07; Washington 1908-16; Navy 1917–19; Cornell 1920–35; Boston College 1936–38	33	180	45	15	.781
Bear Bryant (Alabama '36)†	Maryland 1945; Kentucky 1946–53; Texas A&M 1954–57, Alabama 1958–82	38	323	85	17	.780

*Active in 2003. †Hall of Fame member.

Note: Minimum 10 years as head coach at Division I institutions; record at four-year colleges only; bowl games included; ranked by percentage, ties computed as half won, half lost.

ALLTIME WINNINGEST DIVISION I-A COACHES *(Cont.)*

By Victories

	Yrs	W	L	T	Pct		Yrs	W	L	T	Pct
*Bobby Bowden	39	351	102	4	.773	Bo Schembechler	27	234	65	8	.775
*Joe Paterno	39	343	116	3	.746	Hayden Fry	37	232	178	10	.564
Paul (Bear) Bryant	38	323	85	17	.780	Jess Neely	40	207	176	-19	.539
Glenn (Pop) Warner	44	319	106	32	.733	Warren Woodson	31	203	95	14	.673
Amos Alonzo Stagg	57	314	199	35	.605	Don Nehlen	30	202	128	8	.609
LaVell Edwards	29	257	100	3	.718	Vince Dooley	25	201	77	10	.715
Tom Osborne	25	255	49	3	.836	Eddie Anderson	39	201	128	15	.606
*Lou Holtz	33	243	132	7	.651	*Active in 2004.					
Woody Hayes	33	238	72	10	.759						

Most Bowl Victories

	W	L	T		W	L	T
*Joe Paterno	20	10	1	Barry Switzer	8	5	0
*Bobby Bowden	19	8	1	*Jackie Sherrill	8	6	0
Paul (Bear) Bryant	15	12	2	Darrell Royal	8	7	1
Jim Wacker	13	2	0	Vince Dooley	8	10	2
*Lou Holtz	12	8	2	Pat Dye	7	2	1
Tom Osborne	12	13	0	Bob Devaney	7	3	0
Don James	10	5	0	Dan Devine	7	3	0
John Vaught	10	8	0	Earle Bruce	7	5	0
Bobby Dodd	9	4	0	Charlie McClendon	7	6	0
Johnny Majors	9	7	0	Hayden Fry	7	9	1
*John Robinson	8	1	0	LaVell Edwards	7	14	1
Terry Donahue	8	4	1	*Active in 2003.			

WINNINGEST ACTIVE DIVISION I-A COACHES
By Percentage

						Bowls		
Coach, College	Yrs	W	L	T	Pct#	W	L	T
Bob Stoops, Oklahoma	6	67	12	0	.848	3	3	0
Phillip Fulmer, Tennessee	13	123	31	0	.799	7	6	0
Steve Spurrier	15	142	40	2	.777	6	6	0
Bobby Bowden, Florida St	39	351	102	4	.773	19	8	1
Lloyd Carr, Michigan	9	86	26	0	.768	5	4	0
Frank Solich, Ohio	6	58	198	0	.753	2	3	0
Joe Paterno, Penn St	39	343	116	3	.746	20	10	1
Bill Snyder, Kansas St	16	131	62	1	.678	6	5	0
Terry Hoeppner, Indiana	6	48	25	0	.658	1	1	0
Dennis Franchione, Texas A&M	22	166	86	2	.657	4	2	0
Gary Patterson, TCU	5	32	17	0	.653	1	3	0
Tommy Bowden, Clemson	7	56	28	0	.667	2	3	0

#Bowl games included in overall record. Ties computed as half win, half loss.

Note: Minimum five years as Division I-A head coach; record at four-year colleges only.

Go Figure

0 - *Football losses suffered by NAIA school Ohio Dominican, according to the UNDEFEATED SINCE 1911 T-shirts the school sold in 2004.*

0 - *Games played by Ohio Dominican before 2004, which fielded its first football team in the 93-year history of the school last fall.*

WINNINGEST ACTIVE DIVISION I-A COACHES (Cont.)

By Victories

Bobby Bowden, Florida St	351	Fisher DeBerry, Air Force	161
Joe Paterno, Penn St	343	Dick Tomey, San Jose St.	158
Frank Beamer, Viginia Tech	177	Mack Brown, Texas	156
Ken Hatfield, Rice	167	Steve Spurrier, South Carolina	142
Dennis Franchione, Texas A&M	166	Mike Price, UTEP	137

WINNINGEST ACTIVE DIVISION I-AA COACHES

By Percentage

Coach, College	Yrs	W	L	T	Pct*
Mike Kelly, Dayton	23	215	43	1	.827
Al Bagnoli, Pennsylvania	22	173	51	0	.773
Pete Richardson, Southern	16	138	48	1	.736
Dick Biddle, Colgate	8	69	27	0	.710
Joe Taylor, Hampton	21	160	68	4	.707
Tommy Tate, McNeese St.	5	43	19	0	.694
Kevin Higgins, Citadel	7	56	25	1	.689
Walt Hameline, Wagner	24	169	181	1	.675
Alvin Wyatt Sr., Bethune-Cookman	7	54	25	0	.674
Joe Walton, Robert Morris	11	73	37	1	.662

*Playoff games included.

Note: Minimum five years as a Division I-A and/or Division I-AA head coach; record at four-year colleges only.

By Victories

Mike Kelly, Dayton	215	Walt Hameline, Wagner	169
Bob Ford, Albany St.	205	Andy Talley, Villanova	162
Al Bagnoli, Pennsylvania	180	Rob Ash, Drake	161
Joe Taylor, Hampton	172	Jerry Moore, Appalachian St.	155
Jimmye Laycock, William & Mary	170	Pete Richardson, Southern U.	146

WINNINGEST ACTIVE DIVISION II COACHES

By Percentage

Coach, College	Yrs	W	L	T	Pct*
Chris Hackler, Valdosta St	5	59	7	0	.894
Chuck Broyles, Pittsburg St (KS)	15	154	30	2	.833
Bryan Collins, C.W. Post	7	63	14	0	.818
Ken Sparks, Carson-Newman	25	242	57	2	.807
Bill Zwaan, West Chester	7	65	18	0	.783
Peter Yetten, Bentley	17	126	43	1	.744
John Luckhardt, California (PA)	20	152	53	2	.739
Dale Lennon, N Dakota	8	71	26	0	.732
Richard Cundiff, Tex. A&M-Kingsville	5	43	6	0	.729
Frank Cignetti, Indiana (PA)	23	193	73	1	.725

*Ties computed as half win, half loss. Playoff games included.

Note: Minimum five years as a college head coach; record at four-year colleges only.

By Victories

Ken Sparks, Carson-Newman	242	John Luckhardt, California (PA)	152
Frank Cignetti, Indiana (PA)	191	Monte Cater, Shepherd	147
Dennis Douds, E Stroudsburg	188	Danny Hale, Bloomsburg	135
Mel Tjeerdsma, NW Missouri St	166	Peter Yetten, Bentley	126
Chuck Broyles, Pittsburg St.	154	George Mihalik, Slippery Rock	115

WINNINGEST ACTIVE DIVISION III
By Percentage

Coach, College	Yrs	W	L	T	Pct*
Larry Kehres, Mount Union	19	217	19	3	.914
Joe Fincham, Wittenberg	9	88	14	0	.863
Jim Purtill, St. Norbert	6	56	9	0	.862
Rick Willis, Wartburg	8	72	14	0	.837
Jay Locey, Linfield	9	74	17	0	.813
Chris Creighton, Wabash	6	65	17	0	.793
John Gagliardi, St. John's (MN)	56	421	117	11	.777
Dick Farley, Williams	17	114	19	3	.849
Charles Priore, Trinity (Conn.)	5	31	9	0	.775
Jimmie Keeling, Hardin-Simmons	15	127	37	0	.774
Dean Paul, Ohio Northern	6	48	14	0	.774

*Ties computed as half won, half lost. Playoff games included.

Note: Minimum five years as a college head coach; record at four-year colleges only.

By Victories

John Gagliardi, St John's (MN)	421	Rick Giancola, Montclair St	152
Frank Girardi, Lycoming	244	Bob Bierie, Loras	144
Larry Kehres, Mount Union	217	Barry Streeter, Gettysburg	133
Eric Hamilton, College of New Jersey	172	Rich Lockner, Carnegie Mellon	132
Wayne Perry, Hanover	164	Michael DeLong, Springfield	132

NAIA Coaches' Records

WINNINGEST ACTIVE NAIA COACHES
By Percentage

Coach, College	Yrs	W	L	T	Pct*
Bill Cronin, Georgetown (KY)	8	85	14	0	.859
Mike Van Diest, Carroll (MT)	6	64	16	0	.800
Hank Biesiot, Dickinson St (ND)	29	212	72	1	.746
Peter Shinnick, Azusa Pacific (CA)	5	47	17	0	.734
Carl Poelker, McKendree (IL)	23	157	65	1	.706
Orv Otten, Northwestern (IA)	10	71	35	0	.670
Geno DeMarco, Geneva (PA)	12	83	44	0	.654
Todd Sturdy, St. Ambrose (TX)	10	67	36	0	.650
Vic Wallace, Lambuth (TN)	23	160	86	4	.648
Paul Troth, Missouri Valley	8	55	31	0	.640
Kevin Donley, St. Francis (IN)	26	180	104	1	.633

*Playoff games included.

Note: Minimum five years as a collegiate head coach and includes record against four-year institutions only.

By Victories

Hank Biesiot, Dickinson St (ND)	212	Fran Schwenk, Doane (NE)	116
Kevin Donley, St. Francis (IN)	180	Bob Green, Montana Tech	106
Vic Wallace, Lambuth (TN)	160	Merle Masoholder, Central Methodist (MO)	94
Carl Poelker, McKendree (IL)	157	Courtney Meyer, Concordia (NE)	94
Jim Dennison, Walsh (OH)	151	Dave Dallas, Kansas Wesleyan	89

Tim Duncan
of the NBA champion
San Antonio Spurs

Pro Basketball

JOHN W. McDONOUGH

Fighting For Respect?

After an ugly, early-season brawl, the NBA found its offensive flair, but defense still ruled as San Antonio beat Detroit in a Final featuring the league's two stingiest teams.

BY STEPHEN CANNELLA

The Earth did not go spinning out of its orbit after the events of Nov. 19, 2004, a date that will live in infamy for NBA lovers (yes, they're out there) and haters alike. The league did not collapse; there was no fan boycott. In fact, apart from some stricter crowd-control measures—beer cups shrank, arena security staffs grew—very little changed in the wake of the much-publicized brawl between visiting Indiana Pacers players and fans at the Palace at Auburn Hills, home of the defending champion Detroit Pistons. Fans everywhere kept on booing and heckling and cursing. Players continued to taunt and preen. And the NBA staggered on as a league more likely to make headlines with off-court controversy than on-court drama.

Yet there's no denying that the "Malice at the Palace," which erupted when Indiana forward Ron Artest vaulted several rows into the stands to exact revenge after being hit by a beer-filled cup hurled by a fan, was a watershed moment for the NBA and the entire sports culture. Commissioner David Stern called the beyond-ugly incident an "unprecedented fiasco" and "a humiliation for everyone associated with the NBA." For days, replays of the mayhem clogged not only the sports networks but news channels, morning shows and pundit gabfests as well. Over and over, America watched Artest and teammate Stephen Jackson throw punches at fans behind the Pacers' bench, with patrons swinging back. The out-of-control Artest, along with teammate Jermaine O'Neal, also duked it out with a handful of fans who later rushed the court. Chaos reigned for 10 minutes and, after the game was called with 45.9 seconds remaining, Palace fans bombarded the Pacers with cups and food as the team bolted from the court.

The social contract between athletes and spectators had been tested before, but never had it been so severely breached. Stern acted quickly and harshly, suspending Artest for the remainder of the season, the longest non-drug related ban in league history. Jackson (30 games) and O'Neal (25) were

"The Malice at the Palace" cast the NBA in an unflattering light.

also suspended. Detroit's Ben Wallace, who precipitated the incident with a hard foul on Artest that caused both benches to clear, was banned for six games. That wasn't the only fallout: There were criminal investigations and civil suits filed by fans, as well as revocations of some spectators' season tickets by the Pistons. Stern tightened security in all 30 NBA arenas, issued new guidelines for the sale of alcohol and published a fan code of conduct in an effort to make civility a standard part of the NBA experience.

The nastiest fan-player violence in U.S. sports history was so unsettling that Clemson football coach Tommy Bowden cited the near-riot as a root cause of a pregame dust-up between the Tigers and South Carolina the following day. "[Players] watched that basketball fiasco on TV," he said. "And that's on 24 hours a day, every major news program... and they watched it, watched it, watched it."

Most of America did as well, which is more than can be said about what should have been the must-see moments of the 2004–05 season. Ratings for ABC's broadcast of the NBA Finals—the San Antonio Spurs beat the Pistons in seven games—declined by 29% from the previous year and were the second-lowest for the event since it moved to prime time in 1982. In terms of capturing a wide audience, the Finals suffered from the matchup of two franchises steeped in fundamentals and the fine art of team defense. The Spurs were a sublime collection of international talent—at any

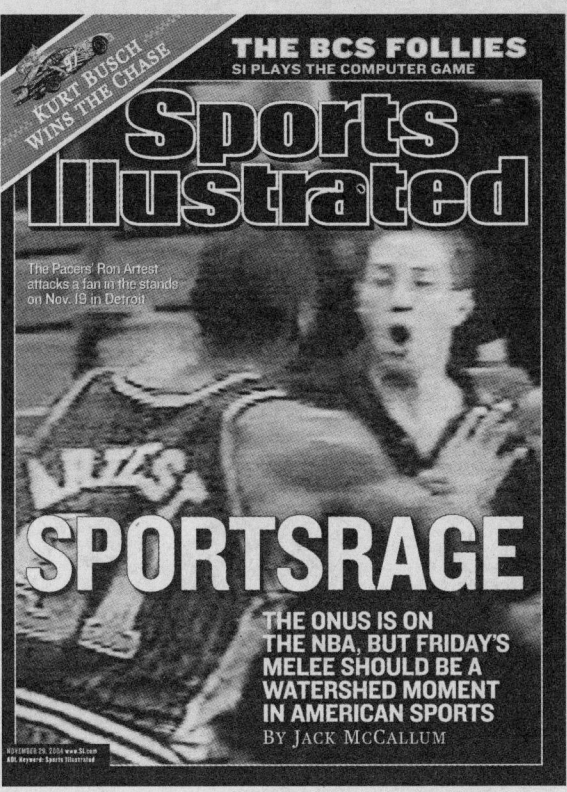

THE BCS FOLLIES
SI PLAYS THE COMPUTER GAME

KURT BUSCH WINS THE CHASE

Sports Illustrated

The Pacers' Ron Artest attacks a fan in the stands on Nov. 19 in Detroit

SPORTSRAGE

THE ONUS IS ON THE NBA, BUT FRIDAY'S MELEE SHOULD BE A WATERSHED MOMENT IN AMERICAN SPORTS
BY JACK McCALLUM

given moment their lineup might feature natives of the U.S, France, Argentina, Slovenia and the U.S. Virgin Islands—led by laconic center Tim Duncan, who won his third Finals MVP award. But stylistically, they and the Pistons were teams designed to stir the heart of basketball purists, students of the X's and O's of textbook hoops. The lack of colorful star power (read: no Shaquille O'Neal) caused most viewers to yawn and reach for the remote.

It didn't help that the series began with four blowouts—two by each team, with a 21-point average margin of victory—and was overshadowed by some juicy NBA soap operas. There was the constant speculation about the future of Pistons coach Larry Brown, who, despite reaching the Finals for the second straight year, was squabbling with ownership and was rumored to be looking ahead to the next

Steve Nash's run-and-gun offensive style rejuvenated the Suns and earned him league MVP honors

JOHN W. McDONOUGH

ily to feed," and Artest's request for a month off during the season so he could promote an R&B album produced by his upstart record label, TruWarier.

That's unfortunate because, in many ways, the NBA was as entertaining on the court as it's been since Michael Jordan retired. Along with the leagues' move to a six-division format, the 2004 trade that sent Shaquille O'Neal from the Lakers to the Miami Heat drastically altered the standings. The Heat, winners of 42 games in 2003–04, instantly became the best team in the Eastern Conference during the regular season with a 59-23 record. After going to the Finals in four of the past five years, the Shaq-less and Jackson-less Lakers missed the playoffs and sank into a last-place tie with the Golden State Warriors in the Pacific Division.

The Pacific was won by the Phoenix Suns, a non-playoff team in 2004 that cruised to a league-best 62-20 record built on what Timberwolves general manager Kevin McHale called "blitzkrieg basketball": a running, gunning, fast-breaking style that took a defense-oriented league by storm. Led by magical guard Steve, who was named the league's MVP, the Suns averaged 110.4 points per game, more than any team since 1994–95. They averaged more three-pointers per game (9.7) than any team in history, and their relentless fast break was the highest-octane offense the league had seen since the Showtime Lakers of the 1980s. The Suns were at the vanguard of a league-wide offensive renaissance. Six different teams averaged at least 100 points (only two averaged triple figures in 2003–04), while the number of squads that scored fewer than 90 points per game dropped from five in

stop in his itinerant career. There was the announcement between Games 2 and 3 that Phil Jackson would return to coach the Los Angeles Lakers in 2005–06 after a yearlong hiatus. (Never mind that Jackson had ripped Lakers star Kobe Bryant in a tell-all 2004 best-seller titled, ahem, "The Last Season.") And, with the league's collective bargaining agreement about to expire and labor and management engaged in more saber-rattling than meaningful negotiation, there was the very real prospect of a July 1 lockout.

It should have been no surprise, then, that the season would be eclipsed by off-court storylines. Before the Palace slugfest the two biggest stories had been Minnesota Timberwolves guard Latrell Sprewell (2004–05 salary: $14.6 million) complaining about his contract by saying he had "a fam-

'03–04 to one in '04–05. This ignominious honor fell to the New Orleans Hornets, whose offense couldn't even outscore the expansion Charlotte Bobcats'.

The scoring bubble burst in the playoffs, however. The high-flying Suns were defeated in five games in the Western Conference finals by San Antonio, the stylistic yin to Phoenix's yang. The Spurs, who won the Southwest Division with a 59-23 record, were the league's stingiest team during the regular season, allowing just 88.4 points per game, and they bottled up Nash and his mates with little difficulty. The Pistons took a harder road to the Finals, outlasting the Heat—who were without the injured Shaq and rising star Dwayne Wade for part of the series—in seven hard-fought games.

The Spurs and Pistons stayed true to their defensive leanings early in the Finals—some might say too true, as the first four games were an even exchange of blowouts by the home team. Spirited San Antonio guard Manu Ginobili, who established himself as one of the league's most reliable and entertaining scorers during the season, did most of the heavy lifting as San Antonio won Games 1 and 2. The Pistons used their lockdown defense to even the series, holding the Spurs to 79 and 71 points in Games 3 and 4. As far drama, well, there was little. In the four games, the winning team outscored the loser by a combined 101-59 in the fourth quarter.

Things got more interesting in Game 5 at the Palace, thanks mainly to Spurs backup forward Robert Horry, who again demonstrated why he's known around the league as "Big Shot Rob." No active player has a longer resume of clutch postseason shots than Horry, a veteran of five NBA championship teams. He came to San Antonio's rescue late in the third period of a taut game, nailing his first basket with nine seconds remaining. Including that shot Horry proceed to pump in 21 points, 15 of them on three-pointers, in a little over 17 minutes on the floor, single-handedly keeping the Spurs alive in a game that went into overtime tied at 89. He buried his last six shots, a scintillating performance that included a rim-rattling lefthanded dunk and then the dagger, a rainmaking three with 5.8 seconds left in OT. That shot gave the Spurs a 96-95 win and a 3-2 lead in the series and capped one of the most brilliant performances in Finals history. "If fans couldn't appreciate that," said San Antonio guard Brent Barry, "they'll never appreciate anything about this game."

The Pistons, led by Richard Hamilton's 23 points and 21 from point guard Chauncey Billups, rebounded for a 95-86 win in Game 6 in San Antonio, but they fell short of a repeat championship in a wildly entertaining Game 7. Detroit led 39-38 at halftime, but their advantage evaporated when Duncan took over in the third period. The poker-faced Duncan had actually been a disappointment for much of the series. But he turned in a virtuoso performance in Game 5 (26 points, 19 rebounds) and put together his finest quarter of the series in the third period of Game 7, scoring 12 points and grabbing six rebounds. That surge put the Spurs in control of the game—they won 81-74—and locked up the MVP trophy for Duncan. The award just as easily could have gone to Ginobili, who was San Antonio's best player in Games 1 and 2 and in the fourth quarter of the clincher. He also set up Horry's heroic shot in Game 5 with a heads-up pass out of a double team. "Manu is unbelievable," Duncan said after Game 7. "I don't think we've even scratched the surface with him."

With their third championship in seven years and second in the past three, the Spurs presented themselves as candidates to be the league's next dynasty. But if the Pistons return to the Finals in 2006, it won't be under Brown's guidance. Brown negotiated a buyout of his contract from Detroit, freeing him to pursue other jobs or, perhaps, rest after a year full of health challenges. He missed 17 games after a hip operation that led to problems with his bladder, and he underwent his third surgery in nine months shortly after the Finals ended.

Still, within a week, the most nomadic of coaches was angling to run the team he followed while growing up on Long Island, the

Pistons coach Larry Brown led his team back to the Finals, but only weeks later, he accepted the Knicks' head coaching job.

New York Knicks. The deal, which earlier in the year Brown had called his "dream job," was finalized in late July, when he signed a five-year contract worth more than $50 million to replace Herb Williams. (Brown was the Knicks' fourth coach in less than a year, while New York was the eighth stop in Brown's NBA career.) His rebuilding job was arguably more daunting than the one facing the Lakers' Jackson, who had to patch relations with Bryant before facing life in L.A. without Shaq for the first time.

As beneficial as having the league's two most-celebrated coaches in the two biggest media markets would be, the best news of the off-season came in late June when the owners and the players' staved off a work stoppage by settling on a new collective bargaining agreement. The new labor deal raised the league's minimum age to 19 and banned players from playing until a year after their high classes had graduated. The new rule meant the days of players jumping from high school to the pros—as Cleveland Cavaliers star LeBron James did in 2003—were over. The rule didn't affect the 2005 draftees, who were led by 20-year-old Utah center Andrew Bogut, an Australian native who was taken by the Milwaukee Bucks with the top pick. In fact, each of the first five players chosen were collegians—a reversal from 2004, when a record eight prep players were chosen in the first round.

Those players would be part of a pivotal era for the NBA, which lost another signature star—the Pacers' Reggie Miller—to retirement. The league must prove that the Palace brouhaha was an isolated incident, not a bubbling-over of deep-seated tensions between the league's fans and its players. The litmus test might be the 2005–06 return of Artest, who will surely be treated as NBA enemy No. 1 wherever he travels with his Indiana teammates. That could be the rarest of NBA storylines: one the entire sports world is sure to follow.

FOR THE RECORD • 2004 – 2005

NBA Final Standings

Eastern Conference
ATLANTIC DIVISION

Team	W	L	Pct	GB
Boston	45	37	.549	—
Philadelphia	43	39	.524	2
New Jersey	42	40	.512	3
Toronto	33	49	.402	12
New York	33	49	.402	12

Western Conference
NORTHWEST DIVISION

Team	W	L	Pct	GB
Seattle	52	30	.634	—
Denver	49	33	.598	3
Minnesota	44	38	.537	8
Portland	27	55	.329	25
Utah	26	56	.317	26

CENTRAL DIVISION

Team	W	L	Pct	GB
Detroit	54	28	.659	—
Chicago	47	35	.573	7
Indiana	44	38	.537	10
Cleveland	42	40	.512	12
Milwaukee	30	52	.366	24

PACIFIC DIVISION

Team	W	L	Pct	GB
Phoenix	62	20	.756	—
Sacramento	50	32	.610	12
L.A. Clippers	37	45	.451	25
L.A. Lakers	34	48	.415	28
Golden State	34	48	.415	28

SOUTHEAST DIVISION

Team	W	L	Pct	GB
Miami	59	23	.720	—
Washington	45	37	.549	14
Orlando	36	46	.439	23
Charlotte	18	64	.220	41
Atlanta	13	69	.159	46

SOUTHWEST DIVISION

Team	W	L	Pct	GB
San Antonio	59	23	.720	—
Dallas	58	24	.707	1
Houston	51	31	.622	8
Memphis	45	37	.549	14
New Orleans	18	64	.220	41

2005 NBA Playoffs

EASTERN CONFERENCE

1st ROUND	SEMIFINALS	FINALS

Washington
Chicago
→ Washington (4-2)
→ Miami (4-0)
Miami
New Jersey
→ Miami (4-0)
Detroit (4-3)

Detroit
Philadelphia
→ Detroit (4-1)
→ Detroit (4-2)
Indiana
Boston
→ Indiana (4-3)

NBA FINALS

SAN ANTONIO (4-3)

WESTERN CONFERENCE

FINALS	SEMIFINALS	1st ROUND

Phoenix (4-0)
Phoenix (4-2)
Dallas (4-3)

San Antonio (4-1)
Seattle (4-1)
San Antonio (4-2)
San Antonio (4-1)

Phoenix
Memphis
Dallas
Houston
Seattle
Sacramento
Denver
San Antonio

2005 NBA Playoff Results

Eastern Conference First Round

Game 1	New Jersey 98	at Miami	116
Game 2	New Jersey 87	at Miami	104
Game 3	Miami 108	at New Jersey	105
Game 4	Miami 110	at New Jersey	97

Miami won series 4–0.

Game 1	Philadelphia 85	at Detroit	106
Game 2	Philadelphia 84	at Detroit	99
Game 3	Detroit 104	at Philadelphia	115
Game 4	Detroit 97	at Philadelphia	92
Game 5	Philadelphia 78	at Detroit	88

Detroit won series 4–1.

Game 1	Washington 94	at Chicago	103
Game 2	Washington 103	at Chicago	113
Game 3	Chicago 99	at Washington	117
Game 4	Chicago 99	at Washington	106
Game 5	Washington 112	at Chicago	110
Game 6	Chicago 91	at Washington	94

Washington won series 4–2.

Game 1	Indiana 82	at Boston	102
Game 2	Indiana 82	at Boston	79
Game 3	Boston 76	at Indiana	99
Game 4	Boston 110	at Indiana	79
Game 5	Indiana 90	at Boston	85
Game 6	Boston 92	at Indiana	89
Game 7	Indiana 97	at Boston	70

Indiana won series 4–3.

Western Conference First Round

Game 1	Memphis 103	at Phoenix	114
Game 2	Memphis 103	at Phoenix	108
Game 3	Phoenix 110	at Memphis	90
Game 4	Phoenix 123	at Memphis	115

Phoenix won series 4–0.

Game 1	Denver 93	at San Antonio	87
Game 2	Denver 76	at San Antonio	104
Game 3	San Antonio 86	at Denver	78
Game 4	San Antonio 126	at Denver	115
Game 5	Denver 89	at San Antonio	99

San Antonio won series 4–1.

Game 1	Sacramento 82	at Seattle	87
Game 2	Sacramento 93	at Seattle	105
Game 3	Seattle 104	at Sacramento	116
Game 4	Seattle 115	at Sacramento	102
Game 5	Sacramento 118	at Seattle	122

Seattle won series 4–1.

Game 1	Houston 98	at Dallas	86
Game 2	Houston 113	at Dallas	111
Game 3	Dallas 106	at Houston	102
Game 4	Dallas 97	at Houston	93
Game 5	Houston 100	at Dallas	103
Game 6	Dallas 83	at Houston	101
Game 7	Houston 76	at Dallas	116

Dallas won series 4–3.

Eastern Conference Semifinals

Game 1	Washington 86	at Miami	105
Game 2	Washington 102	at Miami	108
Game 3	Miami 102	at Washington	95
Game 4	Miami 99	at Washington	95

Miami won series 4–0.

Game 1	Indiana 81	at Detroit	96
Game 2	Indiana 92	at Detroit	83
Game 3	Detroit 74	at Indiana	79
Game 4	Detroit 89	at Indiana	76
Game 5	Indiana 67	at Detroit	86
Game 6	Detroit 88	at Indiana	79

Detroit won series 4–2.

Western Conference Semifinals

Game 1	Dallas 102	at Phoenix	127
Game 2	Dallas 108	at Phoenix	106
Game 3	Phoenix 119	at Dallas	102
Game 4	Phoenix 109	at Dallas	119
Game 5	Dallas 108	at Phoenix	114
Game 6	Phoenix 130	at Dallas	126

Phoenix won series 4–2.

Game 1	Seattle 81	at San Antonio	103
Game 2	Seattle 91	at San Antonio	108
Game 3	San Antonio 91	at Seattle	92
Game 4	San Antonio 89	at Seattle	101
Game 5	Seattle 90	at San Antonio	103
Game 6	San Antonio 98	at Seattle	96

San Antonio won series 4–2.

Eastern Conference Finals

Game 1	Detroit 90	at Miami	81
Game 2	Detroit 86	at Miami	92
Game 3	Miami 113	at Detroit	204
Game 4	Miami 96	at Detroit	106
Game 5	Detroit 76	at Miami	88
Game 6	Miami 66	at Detroit	91
Game 7	Detroit 88	at Miami	82

Detroit won series 4–3.

Western Conference Finals

Game 1	San Antonio 121	at Phoenix	114
Game 2	San Antonio 111	at Phoenix	108
Game 3	Phoenix 92	at San Antonio	102
Game 4	Phoenix 111	at San Antonio	106
Game 5	San Antonio 101	at Phoenix	95

San Antonio won series 4–1.

Finals

Game 1	Detroit 69	at San Antonio	84
Game 2	Detroit 76	at San Antonio	97
Game 3	San Antonio 79	at Detroit	96
Game 4	San Antonio 71	at Detroit	102
Game 5	Detroit 95	at San Antonio	96*
Game 6	San Antonio 86	at Detroit	95
Game 7	Detroit 74	at San Antonio	81

San Antonio won series 4–3.

* Overtime.

NBA Finals Composite Box Score

SAN ANTONIO SPURS

Player	GP	Mpg	FG%	3FG%	FT%	Rebounds Off	Rebounds Total	Apg	Spg	Bpg	To	Ppg
Tim Duncan	7	40.7	.419	.000	.667	4.70	14.10	2.1	.43	2.14	2.43	20.6
Manu Ginobili	7	36.0	.494	.387	.854	1.10	5.90	4.0	1.29	.14	3.29	18.
Tony Parker	7	38.1	.458	.143	.438	.30	2.40	3.4	.29	.14	3.14	13.9
Robert Horry	7	28.6	.444	.484	.733	1.90	4.90	2.1	1.00	.71	1.14	10.6
Bruce Bowen	7	38.7	.380	.448	.667	.10	2.70	2.0	.57	.71	1.57	7.9
Nazr Mohammed	7	22.6	.433	.000	.727	2.90	6.00	.0	.29	.86	.71	4.9
Brent Barry	7	20.6	.407	.375	.800	.40	2.10	1.6	.57	.29	1.14	4.6
Beno Udrih	5	8.8	.364	.500	1.000	.40	1.00	.8	.20	.00	1.60	2.4
Devin Brown	6	5.8	.273	.500	.571	.20	1.00	.5	.00	.00	.17	1.8
Glenn Robinson	3	4.7	.200	.000	.000	.00	1.00	.0	.00	1.00	.33	.7
Rasho Nesterovic	4	6.5	.500	.000	.000	.80	2.00	.3	.00	.25	.25	.5
Tony Massenburg	3	3.0	.000	.000	.000	.00	1.00	.0	.00	.00	.00	.0
Avg	**7**	**243.6**	**.429**	**.398**	**.698**	**12.3**	**41.7**	**16.4**	**4.6**	**5.6**	**15.7**	**84.9**

DETROIT PISTONS

Player	GP	Mpg	FG%	3FG%	FT%	Rebounds Off	Rebounds Total	Apg	Spg	Bpg	To	Ppg
Chauncey Billups	7	40.1	.434	.297	.909	1.30	5.00	6.3	1.00	.14	1.29	20.4
Richard Hamilton	7	42.0	.386	.167	.750	1.30	5.30	2.6	.57	.14	2.00	16.7
Rasheed Wallace	7	32.7	.438	.294	.250	1.90	5.60	1.9	2.00	2.43	1.00	10.9
Ben Wallace	7	40.0	.569	.000	.429	3.90	10.30	1.0	1.71	3.00	1.00	10.7
Antonio McDyess	7	21.9	.508	.000	.556	2.60	7.30	1.0	.86	1.14	1.43	10.1
Tayshaun Prince	7	39.1	.382	.111	.857	1.70	4.90	2.6	1.43	.57	1.14	10.1
Lindsey Hunter	7	19.7	.381	.000	.875	.70	1.90	2.7	1.29	.14	.57	5.6
Carlos Arroyo	5	6.0	.500	.000	.500	.00	.20	.6	.20	.00	.40	2.2
Darvin Ham	5	2.0	.333	.000	.000	.00	.70	.0	.00	.00	.00	.7
Darko Milicic	3	2.2	.500	.000	.000	.60	.60	.0	.00	.00	.00	.4
Ronald Dupree	5	1.6	.000	.000	.000	.00	.00	.0	.00	.00	.00	.0
Elden Campbell	1	1.0	.000	.000	.000	.00	.00	.0	.00	.00	.00	.0
Avg	7	243.6	.434	.240	.738	13.7	41.0	18.6	9.0	7.6	9.9	86.7

NBA Finals Box Scores

Game 1

DETROIT 69

Player	Min	FG M-A	FT M-A	Reb O-T	A	PF	S	TO	TP
C. Billups	43	9-16	6-6	0-4	6	1	4	1	25
R. Hamilton	39	7-21	0-1	1-1	1	2	0	2	14
R. Wallace	33	2-5	0-0	3-7	1	4	2	1	4
T. Prince	32	4-12	3-4	2-5	4	2	1	3	11
B. Wallace	39	3-6	1-2	2-8	1	3	2	1	7
A. McDyess	23	1-8	0-1	1-7	0	2	1	1	2
L. Hunter	16	1-5	0-0	2-3	1	3	1	2	2
C. Arroyo	13	1-3	0-0	0-0	1	2	1	1	2
D. Ham	1	1-1	0-0	0-0	0	0	0	0	2
R. Dupree	1	0-0	0-0	0-0	0	0	0	0	0
Totals	240	29-77	10-14	11-35	15	19	12	12	69

Percentages: FG—.377, FT—.714. 3-pt goals: 1–6, .167 (Billups 1–4, Hamilton 0-1, Hunter 0-1). Team rebounds: 7. Blocked shots: 10 (R. Wallace 6, B. Wallace 3, Billups 1).

SAN ANTONIO 84

Player	Min	FG M-A	FT M-A	Reb O-T	A	PF	S	TO	TP
T. Parker	41	7-17	1-2	1-4	3	1	0	4	15
M. Ginobili	39	10-16	4-4	3-9	2	3	1	4	26
T. Duncan	41	10-22	4-5	6-17	2	2	0	3	24
B. Bowen	35	0-6	0-0	0-2	2	4	0	1	0
N. Mohammed	26	4-8	2-2	4-7	0	1	1	0	10
R. Horry	28	2-6	1-2	0-3	3	2	1	0	7
B. Barry	10	0-1	0-0	0-1	0	4	0	1	0
B. Udrih	7	0-0	0-0	1-1	0	0	0	1	0
D. Brown	6	0-1	0-0	0-2	0	0	1	0	0
G. Robinson	6	1-2	0-0	0-3	0	0	0	0	2
R. Nesterovic	1	0-0	0-0	0-0	0	0	0	0	0
Totals	240	34-79	12-15	15-49	12	17	17	15	84

Percentages: FG—.430, FT—.800. 3-pt goals: 4–13, .308 (Parker 0-1, Ginobili 2-4, Bowen 0-3, Horry 2-4, Barry 0-1). Team rebounds: 9. Blocked shots: 8 (Duncan 2, Bowen 1, Mohammed 2, Robinson 3).

A: 18,797. Officials: Callahan, Garretson, Javie.

Game 2

DETROIT 76

Player	Min	FG M-A	FT M-A	Reb O-T	A	PF	S	TO	TP
C. Billups	40	6-14	1-1	1-5	3	3	0	4	13
R. Hamilton	35	5-15	4-5	2-7	3	4	1	0	14
T. Prince	33	1-7	1-1	1-3	0	4	0	1	3

SAN ANTONIO 97

Player	Min	FG M-A	FT M-A	Reb O-T	A	PF	S	TO	TP
M. Ginobili	32	6-8	11-13	1-3	7	3	3	3	27
T. Parker	28	6-9	0-1	0-1	2	5	0	0	12
T. Duncan	37	5-10	8-9	3-11	1	2	0	2	18

Game 2, (cont.)

Player	Min	FG M-A	FT M-A	Reb O-T	A	PF	S	TO	TP
R. Wallace	33	5-12	1-2	3-8	4	5	2	1	11
B. Wallace..	33	4-6	1-3	4-8	2	3	0	3	9
L. Hunter....	24	3-7	1-2	2-4	3	1	1	1	7
A. McDyess..	24	7-14	1-2	3-7	2	4	1	2	15
C. Arroyo...	8	2-3	0-0	0-1	0	1	0	1	4
D. Ham	4	0-1	0-0	2-2	0	0	0	0	0
D. Milicic......	3	0-1	0-0	0-0	0	0	0	0	0
R. Dupree ...	3	0-2	0-0	0-0	0	0	0	0	0
Totals........	240	33-82	10-16	18-45	17	25	5	13	76

Percentages: FG—.402, FT—.625. 3-pt goals: 0-6 .000 (Billups 0-3, Hunter 0-1, R. Wallace 0-2). Team rebounds:8. Blocked shots: 2 (Prince 1, B. Wallace 1).

Player	Min	FG M-A	FT M-A	Reb O-T	A	PF	S	TO	TP
B. Bowen ...	36	5-13	1-2	0-3	1	3	1	1	15
N. Mohammed	25	1-2	4-5	3-5	0	2	0	2	6
R. Horry	28	4-10	2-2	1-6	5	2	4	2	12
B. Barry......	26	0-3	0-0	0-1	5	1	2	2	0
B. Udrih	18	2-4	2-2	0-2	2	0	1	2	7
G. Robinson.	3	0-1	0-0	0-0	0	0	0	1	0
R. Nesterovic .	3	0-0	0-0	1-3	0	0	0	0	0
Totals........	240	29-62	28-34	9-36	23	19	11	15	97

Percentages: FG—.468, FT—.824. 3-pt goals: 11-24, .458 (Ginobili 4-5, Parker 0-1, Bowen 4-8, Horry 2-6, Barry 0-1, Udrih 1-1). Team rebounds: 5. Blocked shots: 7(Duncan 4, Mohammed 2, Horry 1).
A: 18,797. Officials: Crawford, Fryer, Nies.

Game 3

SAN ANTONIO 79

Player	Min	FG M-A	FT M-A	Reb O-T	A	PF	S	TO	TP
T. Parker...	40	8-16	5-8	0-2	4	4	2	4	21
M. Ginobili .	29	2-6	2-2	0-4	0	4	0	6	7
B. Bowen ...	42	4-8	1-2	0-0	2	4	2	1	13
T. Duncan ..	38	5-15	4-4	3-10	4	3	3	2	14
N. Moham..	18	2-4	0-0	3-7	0	3	0	1	4
R,. Horry ...	30	2-7	1-2	1-5	2	0	0	0	6
B. Barry	21	4-5	0-0	0-4	1	1	0	1	10
R. Nesterovic.	8	1-2	0-0	2-3	1	1	0	0	2
B. Udrih	7	0-0	0-0	1-2	2	1	0	3	0
G. Robinson.	5	0-2	0-0	0-0	0	0	0	0	0
D. Brown	2	1-2	0-0	0-0	0	0	0	0	2
Totals........	240	29-67	13-20	10-37	16	21	7	18	79

Percentages: FG—.433, FT—.650. 3-pt goals: 8-17, .471 (Parker 0-2, Ginobili 1-5, Bowen 4-6, Horry 1-3, Barry 2-2, Robinson 0-1). Team rebounds:8. Blocked shots: 3 (Bowen, Duncan, Horry).

DETROIT 96

Player	Min	FG M-A	FT M-A	Reb O-T	A	PF	S	TO	TP
R. Hamilton..	43	11-23	2-3	1-3	4	5	2	3	24
C. Billups ...	37	6-12	5-7	2-6	7	5	0	1	20
T. Prince.....	40	4-10	4-4	0-6	5	0	1	2	12
R. Wallace..	37	4-13	0-0	3-7	1	3	1	3	8
B. Wallace..	39	7-10	1-2	6-11	1	2	3	1	15
L. Hunter....	21	1-6	1-1	0-1	4	2	2	0	3
A. McDyess..	19	6-9	0-0	4-9	0	1	3	1	12
D. Ham	1	0-0	0-0	1-1	0	0	0	0	0
C. Arroyo...	1	1-1	0-0	0-0	0	0	0	0	2
D. Milicic...	1	0-1	0-0	0-0	0	0	0	0	0
R. Dupree ..	1	0-0	0-0	0-0	0	0	0	0	0
Totals........	240	40-85	13-17	17-44	22	18	12	11	96

Percentages: FG—.471, FT—.765. 3-pt goals: 3-14, .214 (Hamilton 0-1, Billups 3-7, Hunter 0-2, R. Wallace 0-4). Team rebounds: 5. Blocked shots: 10 (B. Wallace 5, McDyess, Hunter 1, Prince 1, R. Wallace 1). Officials: Crawford, Delaney, Salvatore.

Game 4

SAN ANTONIO 71

Player	Min	FG M-A	FT M-A	Reb O-T	A	PF	S	TO	TP
T. Parker.....	37	6-13	0-2	0-4	4	2	0	3	12
M. Ginobili .	32	4-9	3-4	0-4	3	3	1	2	12
T. Duncan ..	39	5-17	6-9	3-16	2	2	0	3	16
B. Bowen ...	33	2-3	2-2	1-3	4	4	0	3	6
N. Moham..	17	2-6	0-0	3-5	0	2	0	1	4
D. Brown ...	20	2-8	3-5	1-3	2	1	0	0	8
R. Horry ...	20	2-6	0-0	3-4	0	1	0	1	5
R. Nesterovic	14	0-0	0-2	0-2	0	1	0	0	0
B. Udrih ...	11	2-5	0-0	0-0	0	2	0	2	5
B. Barry......	11	1-2	0-0	1-1	0	2	0	1	3
T. Massenburg	6	0-1	0-0	0-2	0	1	0	0	0
Totals........	240	26-70	14-24	12-44	15	21	1	17	71

Percentages: FG—.371, FT—.583. 3-pt goals: 5-15, .333 (Parker 0-1, Ginobili 1-5, Brown 1-2, Horry 1-3, Udrih 1-2, Barry 1-2). Team rebounds: 10. Blocked shots: 9 (Duncan 3, Bowen 2, Parker, Ginobili, Horry, Nesterovic).

DETROIT 102

Player	Min	FG M-A	FT M-A	Reb O-T	A	PF	S	TO	TP
C. Billups ...	38	5-14	7-7	0-5	7	1	2	1	17
R. Hamilton..	38	4-16	4-4	2-9	4	4	1	1	12
T. Prince.....	36	6-14	1-1	2-2	1	2	2	0	13
R. Wallace..	33	6-10	0-1	2-8	2	3	2	0	14
B. Wallace..	39	5-11	1-4	5-13	1	3	3	0	11
L. Hunter....	22	7-10	3-3	0-1	5	4	2	0	17
A. McDyess..	19	6-11	1-1	2-7	1	4	1	1	13
C. Arroyo...	7	1-3	1-2	0-0	2	0	0	0	3
D. Ham	4	0-0	0-0	0-0	1	0	0	0	0
D. Milicic..	2	1-1	0-0	0-2	0	0	0	0	2
R. Dupree ..	2	0-0	0-0	0-0	0	0	0	0	0
Totals	240	41-90	18-23	13-47	23	22	13	3	102

Percentages: FG—.456, FT—.783. 3-pt goals: 2-9, .222 (Billups 0-4, Hamilton 0-1, Prince 0-2, R. Wallace 2-2,). Team rebounds: 7. Blocked shots: 6 (B. Wallace 3, R. Wallace 2, McDyess). A: 22,076. Officials: Bavetta, DeRosa, Rush.

Game 5

SAN ANTONIO 96 (OT)

Player	Min	FG M-A	FT M-A	Reb O-T	A	PF	S	TO	TP
T. Parker.....	45	7-15	0-0	1-2	3	4	0	6	14
M. Ginobili .	44	5-16	5-5	3-6	9	4	1	2	15
T.Duncan....	48	11-24	4-11	8-19	2	3	0	2	26

DETROIT 95

Player	Min	FG M-A	FT M-A	Reb O-T	A	PF	S	TO	TP
Hamilton....	49	7-15	1-2	1-4	2	5	0	5	15
Billups........	44	11-26	10-11	3-5	7	2	0	1	34
Prince.........	48	5-10	0-0	3-9	3	3	3	1	10

Game 5 (cont.)

Player	Min	FG M-A	FT M-A	Reb O-T	A	PF	S	TO	TP
B. Bowen ...	44	4-8	0-0	0-5	3	4	1	3	10
N. Moham..	26	3-4	0-0	1-3	0	3	1	0	6
R. Horry	32	7-12	2-3	5-7	2	5	0	3	21
B. Barry.....	22	1-3	0-0	1-2	0	3	0	0	3
D. Brown......	4	0-0	1-2	0-1	1	0	0	0	1
Totals........	265	38-82	12-21	19-45	20	26	3	16	96

Percentages: FG—.463, FT—.571. 3-pt goals: 8-20, .400 (Parker 0-3, Ginobili 0-4, Bowen 2-5, Horry 5-6, Barry 1-2). Team rebounds: 7. Blocked shots: 3, (Duncan 2, Barry).

Player	Min	FG M-A	FT M-A	Reb O-T	A	PF	S	TO	TP
R. Wallace..	41	6-15	0-0	1-5	1	5	3	0	12
B. Wallace..	48	4-9	5-6	5-12	1	1	0	2	13
Hunter........	18	0-3	2-2	0-1	2	1	1	1	2
McDyess....	17	4-6	1-2	3-6	1	3	0	1	9
Totals.............	265	37-84	19-23	16-42	17	20	7	11	95

Percentages: FG—.440, FT—..826. 3-pt goals: 2-9, .222 (Billups 2-7, Prince 0-1, Hunter.0-1). Team rebounds: 10. Blocked shots: 11 (R. Wallace 4, B. Wallace 4, McDyess 2, Prince).
A: 22,076. Officials: Callahan, Garretson, Javie.

Game 6

DETROIT 95

Player	Min	FG M-A	FT M-A	Reb O-T	A	PF	S	TO	TP
Hamilton.....	49	7-15	1-2	1-4	2	5	0	5	15
Billups........	44	11-26	10-11	3-5	7	2	0	1	34
Prince........	48	5-10	0-0	3-9	3	3	3	1	10
R. Wallace..	41	6-15	0-0	1-5	1	5	3	0	12
B. Wallace..	48	4-9	5-6	5-12	1	1	0	2	13
Hunter........	18	0-3	2-2	0-1	2	1	1	1	2
McDyess....	17	4-6	1-2	3-6	1	3	0	1	9
Totals.............	265	37-84	19-23	16-42	17	20	7	11	95

Percentages: FG—.440, FT—..826. 3-pt goals: 2-9, .222 (Billups 2-7, Prince 0-1, Hunter 0-1). Team rebounds: 10. Blocked shots: 11 (R. Wallace 4, B. Wallace 4, McDyess 2, Prince).

SAN ANTONIO 86

Player	Min	FG M-A	FT M-A	Reb O-T	A	PF	S	TO	TP
T. Parker.....	45	7-15	0-0	1-2	3	4	0	6	14
M. Ginobili.	44	5-16	5-5	3-6	9	4	1	2	15
T.Duncan....	48	11-24	4-11	8-19	2	3	0	2	26
B. Bowen ...	44	4-8	0-0	0-5	3	4	1	3	10
N. Moham. .	26	3-4	0-0	1-3	0	3	1	0	6
R. Horry	32	7-12	2-3	5-7	2	5	0	3	21
B. Barry......	22	1-3	0-0	1-2	0	3	0	0	3
D. Brown......	4	0-0	1-2	0-1	1	0	0	0	1
Totals.............	265	38-82	12-21	19-45	20	26	3	16	96

Percentages: FG—.463, FT—..571. 3-pt goals: 8-20, .400 (Parker 0-3, Ginobili 0-4, Bowen 2-5, Horry 5-6, Barry 1-2). Team rebounds: 7. Blocked shots: 3 (Duncan 2, Barry).
A: 22,076. Officials: Callahan, Garretson, Javie.

Game 7

SAN ANTONIO 81

Player	Min	FG M-A	FT M-A	Reb O-T	A	PF	S	TO	TP
T. Parker.....	38	3-11	1-2	0-2	3	4	0	1	8
M. Ginobili.	35	8-13	5-5	0-5	4	3	1	3	23
T.Duncan....	42	10-27	5-6	5-11	3	2	0	5	25
B. Bowen ...	41	2-4	0-0	0-4	1	5	0	1	5
N. Moham. .	22	0-3	0-0	1-7	0	3	0	0	0
R. Horry	32	4-7	5-6	2-5	1	1	1	1	15
B. Barry......	29	2-3	0-0	0-4	2	2	2	2	5
D. Brown......	1	0-0	1-0	0-0	0	0	0	0	0
Totals........	265	38-82	12-21	19-45	20	26	3	16	96

Percentages: FG—.463, FT—..571. 3-pt goals: 8-20, .400 (Parker 0-3, Ginobili 0-4, Bowen 2-5, Horry 5-6, Barry 1-2). Team rebounds: 7. Blocked shots: 3 (Duncan 2, Barry).

DETROIT 74

Player	Min	FG M-A	FT M-A	Reb O-T	A	PF	S	TO	TP
Hamilton.....	46	6-18	3-4	1-8	1	3	0	1	15
Billups........	40	3-8	7-8	1-4	8	4	1	1	13
Prince........	41	4-13	0-0	1-2	1	1	2	1	9
R. Wallace..	28	5-10	0-0	0-1	1	5	2	1	11
B. Wallace..	38	6-10	0-2	2-11	1	5	2	0	12
Hunter........	21	2-8	0-0	0-1	2	2	1	0	4
McDyess....	23	5-7	0-0	3-7	2	4	0	2	10
Totals.............	240	31-74	10-14	8-34	17	24	8	6	74

Percentages: FG—.440, FT—..826. 3-pt goals: 2-9, .222 (Billups 2-7, Prince 0-1, Hunter 0-1). Team rebounds: 10. Blocked shots: 11 (R. Wallace 4, B. Wallace 4, McDyess 2, Prince).
A: 22,076. Officials: Callahan, Garretson, Javie.

All-NBA Teams

FIRST TEAM	SECOND TEAM	THIRD TEAM
F Tim Duncan, San Antonio	F LeBron James, Cleveland	F Tracy McGrady, Houston
F Dirk Nowitzki, Dallas	F Kevin Garrett, Minnesota	F Shawn Marion, Phoenix
C Shaquille O'Neal, Miami	C Amar Stoudemire, Phoenix	C Ben Wallace, Detroit
G Allen Iverson, Philadelphia	G Dwyane Wadd, Miami	G Kobe Bryant, LA Lakers
G Steve Nash, Phoenix	G Ray Allen, Seattle	G Gilbert Arenas, Washington

All-Defensive Team

FIRST TEAM	SECOND TEAM
C Ben Wallace, Detroit	F Tayshaun Prince, Detroit
F Kevin Garnett, Minnesota	C Marcus Camby, Denver
G Bruce Bowen, San Antonio	G Chauncey Billups, Detroit
F Tim Duncan, San Antonio	F Andrei Kirilenko, Utah
G Larry Hughes, Washington	G Jason Kidd, New Jersey

All-Rookie Teams

FIRST TEAM	SECOND TEAM
Emeka Okafor, Charlotte	Nenad Krstic, New Jersey
Dwight Howard, Orlando	Josh Smith, Atlanta
Ben Gordon, Chicago	Josh Childress, Atlanta
Andre Iguodala, Philadelphia	Jameer Nelson, Orlando
Luol Deng, Chicago	Al Jefferson, Boston

NBA Individual Leaders

Scoring

	GP	Pts	Avg
Allen Iverson, Phil	75	2,302	30.7
Kobe Bryant, LAL	66	1,819	27.6
LeBron James, Clev	80	2,175	27.2
Dirk Nowitzki, Dall	78	2,032	26.1
Amare Stoudemire, Phoe	80	2,080	26.0
Tracy McGrady, Hou	78	2,003	25.7
Gilbert Arenas, Wash	80	2,038	25.5
Vince Carter, NJ	77	1,886	24.5
Dwyane Wade, Mia	77	1,854	24.1
Ray Allen, Sea	78	1,867	23.9

Rebounds

	GP	Reb	Avg
Kevin Garnett, Minn	82	1,108	13.5
Ben Wallace, Det	74	902	12.2
Shawn Marion, Phoe	81	915	11.3
Emeka Okafor, Char	73	795	10.9
Troy Murphy, GS	70	756	10.8
Shaquille O'Neal, Mia	73	760	10.4
Kurt Thomas, NY	80	831	10.4
Dwight Howard, Orl	82	823	10.0
Dirk Nowitzki, Dall	78	757	9.7
Tyson Chandler, Chi	80	775	9.7

Assists

	GP	Assists	Avg
Steve Nash, Phoe	75	861	11.5
Brevin Knight, Charl	66	591	9.0
Jason Kidd, NJ	66	545	8.3
Stephon Marbury, NY	82	668	8.1
Allen Iverson, Phil	75	596	7.9
LeBron James, Clev	80	577	7.2
Steve Francis, Orl	78	547	7.0
Andre Miller, Den	82	569	6.9
Mike Bibby, Sac	80	541	6.8
Dwyane Wade, Mia	77	520	6.8

Field-Goal Percentage

	FGA	FGM	Pct
Shaquille O'Neal, LAL	1,095	658	.601
Amare Stoudemire, Phoe	1,336	747	.559
Yao Ming, Hou	975	538	.552
Udonis Haslem, Mia	641	346	.540
Eddy Curry, Chi	730	393	.538
Ruben Patterson, Port	601	319	.531
Mark Blount, Bos	618	327	.529
Brad Miller, Sac	609	319	.524
Carlos Boozer, Utah	693	361	.521
Dwight Howard, Orl	677	352	.520

Free-Throw Percentage

	FTA	FTM	Pct
Reggie Miller, Ind	268	250	.933
Earl Boykins, Den	303	279	.921
Peja Stojakovic, Sac	275	253	.920
Damon Stoudamire, Port	199	182	.915
Chauncey Billups, Det	382	343	.898
Steve Nash, Phoe	238	211	.887
Luke Ridnour, Sea	180	159	.883
Ray Allen, Sea	428	378	.883
Austin Croshere, Ind	256	226	.883
Danny Fortson. Sea	258	227	.880

Three-Point Field-Goal Percentage

	3FGM	3FGA	Pct
Fred Hoiberg, Minn	70	145	.483
Joe Johnson, Phoe	177	370	.478
Cuttino Mobley, Sac	150	342	.439
Mike Miller, Mem	140	323	.433
Damon Jones, Mia	225	521	.432
Steve Nash, Phoe	94	218	.431
Jon Barry, Hou	71	165	.430
Chauncy Billups, Det	165	387	.426
Eric Platkowski, Chi	57	134	.425
Jason Terry, Dall	103	245	.420

Steals

	GP	Steals	Avg
Larry Hughes, Wash	61	176	2.89
Allen Iverson, Phil	75	180	2.40
LeBron James, Clev	80	177	2.21
Shawn Marion, Phoe	81	163	2.01
Brevin Knight, Char	66	131	1.98
Gilbert Arenas, Wash	80	139	1.74
Tracy McGrady, Hou	78	135	1.73
Andre Iguodala, Phil	82	138	1.68
Gerald Wallace, Char	70	117	1.67
Paul Pierce, Bos	82	133	1.62

Blocked Shots

	GP	BS	Avg
Andrei Kirilenko, Utah	41	136	3.32
Marcus Camby, Den	66	199	3.02
Tim Duncan, SA	66	174	2.64
Theo Ratliff, Port	63	158	2.51
Ben Wallace, Det	74	176	2.38
Shaquille O'Neal, Mia	73	171	2.34
Joel Przybilla, Port	76	163	2.14
Zadrunas Ilgauskas, Clev	78	165	2.12
Elton Brand, LAC	81	169	2.09
Adonal Foyle, GS	78	159	2.04

NBA Team Statistics

Offense

Team	FG Pct	3FG Pct	FT Pct	Rebound Avg Off	Total	A	TO	Stl	Scoring Avg
Phoenix	47.7	39.3	74.8	11.8	44.1	23.5	13.4	7.0	110.4
Sacramento	45.9	37.4	78.7	12.5	42.4	24.5	12.6	8.2	103.7
Dallas	45.7	36.4	13.8	12.1	42.9	19.6	12.8	8.6	102.5
Miami	48.6	37.7	67.2	10.8	43.0	21.8	13.3	6.4	101.5
Boston	46.8	34.9	76.4	11.1	40.8	22.1	15.6	8.1	101.3
Washington	43.7	34.3	72.5	13.8	42.8	19.1	13.8	8.7	100.5
Toronto	44.4	38.5	77.4	10.3	40.1	20.4	12.6	7.6	99.7
Denver	45.9	34.0	76.3	11.8	42.0	23.9	14.4	9.1	99.5
Orlando	45.4	34.9	75.9	12.7	43.7	19.3	15.6	7.7	99.5
Philadelphia	43.7	34.8	78.9	11.1	42.0	20.7	15.2	9.2	99.1
Seattle	44.4	36.5	79.0	12.7	40.9	18.1	12.7	6.7	98.9
Golden St	43.0	35.2	72.2	13.0	42.7	22.1	13.1	7.8	98.7
LA Lakers	43.7	35.5	77.7	12.5	43.2	20.4	13.7	6.2	98.7
New York	45.1	35.6	76.7	11.8	41.0	20.3	13.9	7.7	97.3
Milwaukee	45.0	35.1	77.2	12.0	41.3	21.0	13.3	6.5	97.2
Minnesota	45.9	34.5	79.6	11.5	43.0	23.4	12.6	5.6	96.8
Cleveland	44.7	33.2	75.2	13.6	42.3	22.6	13.1	8.0	96.5
San Antonio	45.3	36.3	72.4	12.0	42.4	21.6	13.0	7.5	96.2
LA Clippers	45.9	34.5	77.8	12.0	41.9	23.2	14.8	7.3	95.7
Houston	44.3	36.4	78.1	10.7	42.3	21.1	13.1	6.9	95.1
Chicago	43.2	35.7	75.0	12.2	43.8	21.3	16.1	7.0	94.5
Charlotte	43.2	36.3	70.9	13.2	41.7	21.9	13.9	8.5	94.3
Memphis	44.7	35.7	75.4	10.8	41.9	20.9	14.0	8.5	93.4
Detroit	44.4	34.5	73.9	12.9	43.4	21.8	13.1	7.0	93.3
Indiana	43.2	34.4	79.2	10.6	40.1	18.2	13.4	7.9	93.0
Utah	44.9	32.8	75.7	12.8	40.1	22.3	14.9	6.6	93.0
Portland	45.1	36.2	72.5	11.8	41.1	21.0	15.1	7.1	92.9
Atlanta	44.1	31.2	71.1	13.4	41.9	19.7	15.3	7.7	92.7
New Jersey	42.9	36.2	76.3	10.4	39.5	21.6	13.4	7.9	91.4
New Orleans	41.5	31.5	76.6	12.4	40.2	21.0	13.9	6.7	88.4

Defense (Opponent's Statistics)

Team	FG Pct	3FG Pct	FT Pct	Rebound Avg. Off	Total	A	TO	Stl	Scoring Avg
San Antonio	42.6	36.7	76.8	10.9	40.2	16.9	14.5	7.2	88.4
Detroit	43.0	33.8	75.1	11.3	39.6	19.7	13.1	7.4	89.5
Houston	42.3	33.8	74.2	10.9	40.7	20.7	12.5	7.4	91.0
Memphis	43.2	35.1	77.1	12.1	41.2	19.9	15.0	7.5	91.1
Indiana	44.0	36.5	74.3	11.9	41.3	18.8	13.4	6.7	92.2
New Jersey	43.9	36.8	74.4	10.7	41.2	20.3	15.1	7.3	92.9
Chicago	42.2	33.4	74.4	11.9	42.7	20.9	14.9	8.4	93.4
Miami	42.7	34.8	76.0	11.2	40.5	19.8	12.4	7.5	95.0
Minnesota	43.8	36.3	75.2	12.6	41.4	21.7	11.1	6.6	95.3
New Orleans	45.2	36.7	77.5	11.6	41.9	21.2	13.5	7.7	95.5
Cleveland	45.2	37.6	75.0	11.4	39.8	21.2	14.1	6.7	95.7
LA Clippers	44.4	36.8	76.2	12.0	39.5	21.1	12.8	7.8	96.5
Seattle	45.9	35.7	74.9	11.3	37.9	20.7	12.8	6.2	96.6
Dallas	43.8	33.0	75.4	13.1	43.2	20.9	14.7	7.1	96.8
Portland	44.7	34.3	75.5	14.0	42.2	23.5	12.6	8.5	96.9
Utah	45.8	37.5	76.4	10.5	37.7	19.4	14.0	7.9	97.3
Denver	44.7	34.5	74.6	11.9	41.7	21.7	15.7	7.8	97.5
New York	46.5	36.4	75.6	11.8	41.7	20.7	14.1	7.3	99.7
Philadelphia	44.3	36.2	76.7	11.6	44.1	22.9	16.4	8.3	99.8
Milwaukee	46.4	34.3	77.1	11.4	40.8	23.8	12.8	7.5	100.2
Charlotte	46.3	36.1	76.7	11.7	43.2	21.6	15.2	7.6	100.2
Boston	44.4	35.6	75.3	12.7	42.3	22.7	14.8	8.7	100.4
Washington	45.9	36.4	76.2	12.4	43.0	23.0	15.1	7.2	100.8
Golden State	45.8	36.3	74.5	12.9	46.7	22.7	14.6	7.0	100.9
Toronto	46.7	35.6	74.4	12.1	45.3	22.1	13.9	6.2	101.4
Sacramento	45.9	35.7	73.8	13.4	44.3	21.5	14.2	7.6	101.6
LA Lakers	45.3	36.1	78.0	12.5	42.4	24.4	11.2	7.7	101.7
Orlando	45.1	34.3	75.4	12.5	42.1	21.3	13.9	8.5	101.8
Atlanta	47.6	37.9	77.0	11.0	41.3	22.0	14.3	8.7	102.5
Phoenix	44.5	33.5	74.4	15.0	46.1	21.2	13.2	7.7	103.3

NBA Team-by-Team Statistical Leaders

Atlanta Hawks

Player	GP	MPG	FG%	3Pt%	FT%	OFF	DEF	Total	APG	SPG	BPG	TO	PF	PPG
Al Harrington	66	38.6	.459	.216	.672	2.20	4.80	7.00	3.2	1.29	.24	3.09	3.80	17.5
Tyronn Lue	70	.7	.451	.355	.861	.20	1.90	2.10	4.6	.47	.00	1.50	2.40	11.2
Tony Delk	56	23.9	.416	.356	.757	.50	1.80	2.30	1.9	.84	.05	.96	2.20	11.9
Josh Childress	80	.7	.470	.232	.823	2.40	3.60	6.00	1.9	.93	.44	1.33	2.30	10.1
Josh Smith	74	27.7	.455	.174	.688	2.00	4.20	6.20	1.7	.80	1.95	1.82	2.10	9.7
Predrag Drobnjak	71	20.2	.438	.352	.800	1.00	2.30	3.40	.7	.59	.34	1.10	1.90	8.4
Tom Gugliotta	47	20.6	.411	.308	.767	1.20	2.90	4.10	1.4	.87	.36	1.21	2.20	5.1
Jason Collier	70	.5	.463	.429	.676	1.20	1.40	2.60	.3	.21	.19	.90	2.10	5.7
Obinna Ekezie	42	17.4	.434	.000	.774	1.60	2.60	4.30	.3	.52	.29	1.07	3.10	5.5
Boris Diaw	66	.2	.422	.180	.740	.80	1.80	2.60	2.3	.56	.27	1.32	1.90	4.8
Royal Ivey	62	13.0	.429	.333	.701	.30	1.00	1.40	1.7	.63	.11	.94	2.30	3.5
Donta Smith	38	11.4	.389	.273	.688	.50	.90	1.40	1.0	.61	.13	.66	1.30	3.3
Kevin Willis	29	11.9	.389	.000	.739	1.00	1.60	2.60	.3	.28	.24	.52	1.80	3.0
Michael Stewart	12	12.1	.524	.000	.429	1.80	1.60	3.30	.4	.50	.42	.50	2.70	2.1
Hawks	**82**	**242.1**	**.441**	**.312**	**.711**	**13.4**	**28.5**	**41.9**	**19.7**	**7.7**	**4.2**	**16.1**	**24.5**	**92.7**
Opponents	**82**	**242.7**	**.476**	**.379**	**.770**	**11.0**	**30.3**	**41.3**	**22.0**	**8.7**	**5.9**	**14.8**	**21.7**	**102.5**

Boston Celtics

Player	GP	MPG	FG%	3Pt%	FT%	OFF	DEF	Total	APG	SPG	BPG	TO	PF	PPG
Paul Pierce	82	36.1	.455	.370	.822	1.00	5.60	6.60	4.2	1.62	.48	2.80	3.10	21.6
Antoine Walker	77	38.4	.422	.323	.539	2.40	6.70	9.00	3.4	1.16	.75	3.29	2.80	19.1
Ricky Davis	82	32.9	.462	.339	.815	.80	2.20	3.00	3.0	1.09	.33	2.50	2.10	16.0
Gary Payton	77	33.0	.468	.326	.761	.60	2.40	3.10	6.1	1.14	.16	1.92	1.60	11.3
Raef LaFrentz	80	27.5	.496	.364	.811	1.90	5.00	6.90	1.2	.53	1.24	.88	3.30	11.1
Mark Blount	82	26.0	.529	.000	.713	1.70	3.10	4.80	1.6	.40	.78	1.93	2.80	9.4
Al Jefferson	71	14.8	.528	.000	.630	1.70	2.70	4.40	.3	.31	.77	.93	2.70	6.7
Tony Allen	77	16.4	.475	.387	.731	1.10	1.80	2.90	.8	.99	.31	1.00	2.00	6.4
Marcus Banks	81	14.1	.402	.356	.742	.40	1.20	1.60	1.9	.78	.16	.98	1.80	4.6
Delonte West	39	13.0	.426	.358	.704	.40	1.30	1.70	1.4	.54	.21	.62	1.80	4.5
Kendrick Perkins	60	9.1	.471	.000	.638	.90	2.10	2.90	.4	.15	.62	.72	1.60	2.5
Justin Reed	23	5.3	.517	.000	.733	.30	.30	.70	.4	.13	.04	.22	.50	1.8
Celtics	**82**	**242.4**	**.468**	**.349**	**.764**	**11.1**	**29.7**	**40.8**	**22.1**	**8.1**	**5.2**	**15.8**	**24.4**	**101.3**
Opponents	**82**	**242.4**	**.444**	**.356**	**.753**	**12.7**	**29.6**	**42.3**	**22.7**	**8.7**	**4.9**	**15.6**	**23.6**	**100.4**

Chicago Bulls

Player	GP	MPG	FG%	3Pt%	FT%	OFF	DEF	Total	APG	SPG	BPG	TO	PF	PPG
Eddy Curry	63	28.7	.538	.000	.720	1.80	3.50	5.40	.6	.33	.92	2.59	3.20	16.1
Kirk Hinrich	77	36.4	.397	.355	.792	.40	3.50	3.90	6.4	1.58	.27	2.29	3.20	15.7
Ben Gordon	82	24.4	.411	.405	.863	.70	2.00	2.60	2.0	.65	.12	2.27	2.70	15.1
Luol Deng	61	27.3	.434	.265	.741	1.50	3.80	5.30	2.2	.79	.44	1.93	1.60	11.7
Andres Nocioni	81	23.4	.401	.258	.766	9.0	3.90	4.80	1.5	.46	.42	1.67	2.60	8.4
Tyson Chandler	80	27.4	.494	.000	.673	3.30	6.40	9.70	.8	.86	1.76	1.48	3.40	8.0
Othella Harrington	70	18.2	.512	.000	.718	1.50	2.70	4.20	.8	.34	.26	1.20	2.70	8.0
Antonio Davis	72	25.6	.461	.000	.757	2.10	3.80	5.90	1.1	.38	.57	1.33	2.00	7.0
Jannero Pargo	32	14.2	.385	.348	.739	.40	1.10	1.50	2.4	.50	.03	1.41	1.70	6.4
Chris Duhon	82	26.5	.352	.355	.731	.30	2.30	2.60	4.9	1.00	.04	1.45	2.50	5.9
Eric Piatkowski	68	12.4	.430	.425	.804	.20	.90	1.20	.8	.43	.01	.54	1.00	4.8
Laurence Funderburke	2	10.5	.500	.000	.600	.50	1.00	1.50	.0	.00	.00	.00	1.00	4.5
Adrian Griffin	69	9.7	.360	.222	.750	.80	1.40	2.10	.8	.62	.06	.43	1.10	2.2
Jared Reiner	19	6.9	.333	.000	.250	.70	1.30	2.00	.1	.16	.37	.47	1.80	1.1
Frank Williams	9	7.9	.150	.000	.000	.20	.40	.70	1.2	.22	.33	.33	1.00	.7
Bulls	**82**	**241.8**	**.432**	**.357**	**.750**	**12.2**	**31.6**	**43.8**	**21.3**	**7.0**	**4.5**	**16.7**	**24.7**	**89.7**
Opponents	**82**	**241.8**	**.422**	**.334**	**.744**	**11.9**	**30.8**	**42.7**	**20.9**	**8.4**	**5.3**	**15.5**	**23.3**	**93.4**

Cleveland Cavaliers

Player	GP	MPG	Field Goals		FT%	Rebounds			APG	SPG	BPG	TO	PF	PPG
			FG%	3Pt%		OFF	DEF	Total						
LeBron James	80	42.4	.472	.351	.750	1.40	6.00	7.40	7.2	2.21	.65	3.28	1.80	27.2
Z. Ilgauskas	78	33.5	.468	.286	.799	3.80	4.80	8.60	1.3	.68	2.12	2.45	4.00	16.9
Drew Gooden	82	30.8	.492	.179	.810	2.50	6.70	9.20	1.6	.94	.93	1.62	2.80	14.4
Jeff McInnis	76	34.9	.412	.345	.813	.40	1.60	2.10	5.1	.74	.01	1.54	2.30	12.8
Ira Newbie	74	24.8	.429	.358	.797	1.10	1.90	3.00	1.2	.68	.24	.82	1.90	5.9
Robert Traylor	74	17.9	.444	.000	.539	1.80	2.60	4.50	.8	.73	.68	.99	2.90	5.5
A. Varejao	54	16.0	.513	.000	.535	2.00	2.70	4.80	.5	.76	.70	.48	2.30	4.9
A. Pavlovic	65	13.3	.435	.385	.688	.20	.90	1.10	.8	.45	.06	.72	1.90	4.8
Lucious Harris	73	15.5	.395	.323	.812	.50	1.10	1.70	.7	.37	.08	.40	.90	4.3
Eric Snow	81	22.8	.382	.289	.738	.50	1.50	1.90	3.9	.83	.20	1.10	2.30	4.0
Dajuan Wagner	11	9.3	.327	.192	.750	.00	.20	.20	1.2	.45	.00	.82	1.40	4.0
Jiri Welsch	71	18.5	.402	.309	.763	.40	2.00	2.40	1.5	.62	.07	1.03	1.70	6.5
Luke Jackson	10	4.3	.370	.667	.833	.20	.40	.60	.3	.00	.00	.20	.40	2.9
Cavaliers	**82**	**242.1**	**.447**	**.332**	**.752**	**13.6**	**28.7**	**42.3**	**22.6**	**8.0**	**5.6**	**13.9**	**22.6**	**96.5**
Opponents	**82**	**242.1**	**.452**	**.376**	**.750**	**11.4**	**28.3**	**39.8**	**21.2**	**6.7**	**5.1**	**14.8**	**21.6**	**95.7**

Dallas Mavericks

Player	GP	MPG	Field Goals		FT%	Rebounds			APG	SPG	BPG	TO	PF	PPG
			FG%	3Pt%		OFF	DEF	Total						
Dirk Nowitzki	78	38.7	.459	.399	.869	1.20	8.50	9.70	3.1	1.24	1.53	2.26	2.80	26.1
Michael Finley	64	36.8	.427	.407	.831	.70	3.40	4.10	2.6	.75	.28	.94	1.90	15.7
J. Stackhouse	56	28.9	.414	.267	.849	.70	2.60	3.30	2.3	.95	.18	1.89	1.90	14.9
Josh Howard	76	32.2	.475	.296	.733	2.20	4.10	6.40	1.4	1.53	.64	1.61	2.80	12.6
Jason Terry	80	30.0	.501	.420	.844	.50	1.90	2.40	5.4	1.36	.19	1.84	2.20	12.4
Keith Van Horn	62	24.2	.456	.380	.815	1.40	3.30	4.70	1.2	.58	.34	1.31	2.70	11.2
Erick Dampier	59	27.3	.550	.000	.605	3.10	5.40	8.50	.9	.25	1.36	1.73	3.50	9.2
Marquis Daniels	60	23.5	.437	.200	.737	1.50	2.20	3.60	2.1	1.38	.23	1.43	2.10	9.1
Devin Harris	76	15.4	.429	.336	.757	.40	1.00	1.30	2.2	1.01	.25	1.08	1.80	5.7
Alan Henderson	52	15.6	.494	.000	.583	2.10	2.30	4.50	.3	.46	.42	.69	2.00	3.5
Shawn Bradley	77	11.5	.452	.000	.683	.90	1.90	2.80	.2	.32	.82	.43	2.00	2.7
D. Armstrong	66	15.0	.321	.252	.853	.50	1.20	1.70	2.7	.68	.12	1.02	1.40	4.0
D. Illunga-Mbenga	15	3.9	.429	.000	.750	.20	.30	.50	.0	.00	.33	.33	.90	1.0
Mavericks	**82**	**240.6**	**.457**	**.364**	**.789**	**12.1**	**30.9**	**42.9**	**19.6**	**8.6**	**5.6**	**13.4**	**22.3**	**102.5**
Opponents	**82**	**240.6**	**.438**	**.330**	**.754**	**13.1**	**30.1**	**43.2**	**20.9**	**7.1**	**4.9**	**15.6**	**23.2**	**96.8**

Denver Nuggets

Player	GP	MPG	Field Goals		FT%	Rebounds			APG	SPG	BPG	TO	PF	PPG
			FG%	3Pt%		OFF	DEF	Total						
Carmelo Anthony	75	34.8	.431	.266	.796	1.90	3.80	5.70	2.6	.91	.40	2.99	3.10	20.8
Kenyon Martin	70	32.5	.490	.000	.646	2.10	5.20	7.30	2.4	1.43	1.11	2.13	3.30	15.5
Andre Miller	82	34.8	.477	.154	.838	1.20	2.90	4.10	6.9	1.48	.10	2.68	2.50	13.6
Earl Boykins	82	26.4	.413	.337	.921	.50	1.30	1.70	4.5	.95	.15	1.48	1.50	12.4
Marcus Camby	66	30.5	.465	.000	.723	2.00	8.00	10.00	2.3	.92	3.02	1.56	2.70	10.3
Voshon Lenard	3	18.0	.385	.333	.625	.00	2.00	2.00	.3	.33	.00	.67	.70	9.7
Nené	55	23.9	.503	.000	.660	1.90	4.00	5.90	1.5	.91	.87	1.71	3.00	9.6
Wesley Person	41	16.3	.473	.461	.692	.10	2.40	2.40	1.1	.52	.16	.40	1.00	8.1
DeMarr Johnson	71	17.4	.499	.358	.792	.60	1.50	2.10	1.1	.61	.25	.92	2.00	7.1
Eduardo Najera	68	17.4	.450	.286	.637	1.50	2.10	3.60	1.0	.60	.35	.90	2.20	5.2
Greg Buckner	70	21.7	.528	.405	.778	.90	2.00	3.00	1.9	1.07	.09	.70	2.40	6.2
Bryon Russell	70	14.0	.377	.376	.792	.70	1.70	2.50	1.0	.63	.16	.50	1.90	4.4
Francisco Elson	67	14.0	.468	.333	.570	.90	2.10	3.00	.5	.51	.61	.60	1.90	3.7
Luis Flores	16	4.8	.483	.500	1.000	.10	.10	.20	.7	.13	.00	.69	.60	2.2
Mark Pope	9	3.0	.333	.000	.000	.60	.30	.90	.1	.11	.22	.11	.60	.4
Nuggets	**82**	**240.9**	**.459**	**.340**	**.763**	**11.8**	**30.2**	**42.0**	**23.9**	**9.2**	**6.0**	**14.9**	**22.9**	**99.5**
Opponents	**82**	**240.9**	**.447**	**.345**	**.746**	**11.9**	**29.8**	**41.7**	**21.7**	**7.8**	**5.6**	**16.4**	**23.9**	**97.5**

Detroit Pistons

Player	GP	MPG	Field Goals		FT%	Rebounds			APG	SPG	BPG	TO	PF	PPG
			FG%	3Pt%		OFF	DEF	Total						
Richard Hamilton...76		38.5	.440	.305	.858	1.00	2.90	3.90	4.9	1.01	.17	2.86	3.10	18.7
Chauncy Billups 80		35.8	.442	.426	.898	.60	2.80	3.40	5.8	1.01	.11	2.25	2.40	16.5
Tayshaun Prince....82		37.1	.487	.341	.807	1.60	3.70	5.30	3.0	.68	.87	1.65	2.00	14.7
Rasheed Wallace .79		34.0	.440	.318	.697	2.20	5.90	8.20	1.8	.82	1.46	1.61	3.00	14.5
Ben Wallace.........74		36.1	.453	.111	.428	3.90	8.20	12.20	1.7	1.43	2.38	1.11	2.10	9.7
A. McDyess.........77		23.3	.513	.000	.656	2.30	4.00	6.30	.9	.60	.68	1.21	2.60	9.6
Carlos Arroyo........70		10.7	.389	.267	.799	.40	1.10	1.50	4.0	.63	.06	1.53	2.00	6.6
Carlos Delfino 30		15.3	.359	.257	.575	.40	1.40	1.80	1.3	.73	.20	.77	1.50	3.9
Lindsey Hunter.....76		15.1	.358	.274	.793	.50	1.10	1.60	1.7	.89	.17	.89	1.60	3.8
Ronald Dupree.....47		10.0	.480	.500	.617	.70	1.30	2.00	.5	.15	.21	.47	1.30	3.2
Elden Campbell ...40		9.8	.317	.000	.764	.70	1.60	2.30	.5	.20	.18	.73	1.40	3.0
Horace Jenkins ...15		6.9	.333	.000	.923	.20	.40	.60	.6	.33	.07	.47	.40	2.8
Darko Milicic 37		6.9	.329	.000	.708	.10	1.10	1.20	.2	.05	.46	.43	.80	1.8
Derrick Coleman 5		10.0	.214	.000	1.000	.60	2.40	3.00	.0	.00	.00	.40	1.20	1.8
Pistons.............82		**243.4**	**.444**	**.345**	**.739**	**12.9**	**30.6**	**43.4**	**21.8**	**7.0**	**6.1**	**13.8**	**20.0**	**93.3**
Opponents 82		**243.4**	**.430**	**.338**	**.751**	**11.3**	**28.3**	**39.6**	**19.7**	**7.4**	**4.5**	**13.8**	**22.6**	**89.5**

Golden State Warriors

Player	GP	MPG	Field Goals		FT%	Rebounds			APG	SPG	BPG	TO	PF	PPG
			FG%	3Pt%		OFF	DEF	Total						
J. Richardson 72		37.8	.446	.338	.693	1.70	4.20	5.90	3.9	1.46	.44	2.35	2.20	21.7
Baron Davis.........46		34.4	.387	.333	.761	.70	3.10	3.80	7.9	1.76	.30	2.85	2.70	19.2
Troy-Murphy 70		33.9	.414	.399	.730	3.60	7.20	10.80	1.4	.76	.47	1.54	2.70	15.4
Mike Dunleavy 79		32.5	.451	.388	.779	1.20	4.30	5.50	2.6	1.00	.33	1.67	2.50	13.4
Derek Fisher.........74		30.0	.393	.371	.862	.50	2.40	2.90	4.1	1.03	.05	1.74	2.40	11.9
Mickael Pietrus.....67		22.0	.427	.344	.698	1.00	1.90	2.80	1.2	.69	.27	1.37	2.10	9.5
Z. Cabarkapa.......40		11.9	.486	.361	.815	.90	1.70	2.60	.6	.25	.13	.75	1.50	6.0
Adonal Foyle 78		21.8	.502	.000	.556	2.10	3.40	5.50	.7	.33	2.04	.74	2.60	4.5
Calbert Cheaney...55		17.3	.426	.000	.649	.60	1.70	2.30	1.2	.31	.27	.64	1.70	4.5
Rodney White 58		11.7	.419	.400	.614	.40	1.10	1.50	.8	.55	.19	.64	1.10	5.1
Andris Biedrins ...30		12.8	.577	.000	.475	1.60	2.40	3.90	.4	.40	.80	.40	2.90	3.6
Ansu Sesay 16		8.0	.405	.250	.542	1.10	1.30	2.40	.8	.13	.19	.50	1.00	3.1
N. Tskitishvili.........35		6.3	.297	.118	.571	.30	.80	1.20	.3	.23	.31	.54	.90	1.4
Warriors 82		**242.7**	**.430**	**.352**	**.722**	**13.0**	**29.7**	**42.7**	**22.1**	**7.8**	**5.1**	**13.6**	**22.4**	**98.7**
Opponents 82		**242.7**	**.458**	**.363**	**.745**	**12.9**	**33.8**	**46.7**	**22.7**	**7.0**	**5.1**	**15.3**	**21.7**	**100.9**

Houston Rockets

Player	GP	MPG	Field Goals		FT%	Rebounds			APG	SPG	BPG	TO	PF	PPG
			FG%	3Pt%		OFF	DEF	Total						
Tracy McGrady 78		40.8	.431	.326	.774	.90	5.30	6.20	5.7	1.73	.67	2.58	2.10	25.7
Yao Ming 80		30:6	.552	.000	.783	2.60	5.80	8.40	.8	.43	2.00	2.45	3.70	18.3
Mike James 74		25.1	.441	.386	.752	.50	2.30	2.80	3.6	.88	.08	1.43	2.40	11.8
David Wesley 80		34.7	.398	.375	.857	.50	2.40	2.90	3.3	1.20	.11	1.41	2.70	11.9
Bob Sura 61		31.5	.427	.355	.750	1.30	4.20	5.50	5.2	1.07	.11	2.41	2.80	10.3
Juwan Howard 61		26.6	.451	.000	.843	2.10	3.60	5.70	1.5	.52	.08	1.30	2.30	9.6
Jon Barry.............69		21.8	.438	.430	.873	.40	1.90	2.30	2.4	.87	.13	.97	1.40	6.6
Charlie Ward 14		25.7	.312	.314	.846	.40	2.40	2.80	3.1	1.07	.00	1.29	1.60	5.4
Scott Padgett 66		14.3	.421	.397	.725	.70	2.10	2.80	.8	.50	.15	.45	1.80	4.2
D. Mutombo 80		15.2	.498	.000	.741	1.90	3.50	5.30	.1	.20	1.26	.64	1.70	4.0
C. Weatherspoon .40		13.1	.412	.000	.829	.90	2.20	3.10	.4	.23	.15	.38	1.90	3.1
Rod Strickland 16		12.3	.209	.500	.900	.20	1.50	1.70	2.4	.19	.13	1.00	.90	1.8
Ryan Bowen.........66		9.2	.423	.500	.667	.30	.80	1.20	.3	.35	.08	.11	.90	1.7
Moochie Norris.....38		9.5	.321	.000	.833	.30	.90	1.20	1.0	.47	.05	.71	1.20	2.4
Vin Baker 27		7.6	.310	.000	.529	.60	.80	1.40	.4	.07	.15	.63	1.40	1.3
Rockets 82		**242.1**	**.443**	**.364**	**.781**	**10.7**	**31.7**	**42.4**	**21.1**	**6.9**	**4.6**	**13.8**	**22.0**	**95.1**
Opponents 82		**242.1**	**.423**	**.338**	**.742**	**10.9**	**29.8**	**40.7**	**20.7**	**7.4**	**4.1**	**13.3**	**21.6**	**91.0**

Indiana Pacers

Player	GP	MPG	FG%	3Pt%	FT%	OFF	DEF	Total	APG	SPG	BPG	TO	PF	PPG
Ron Artest 7		41.6	.496	.412	9.22	1.10	5.30	6.40	3.1	1.71	.86	2.43	3.90	24.6
Jermaine O'Neal ...44		34.8	.452	.167	.754	1.90	6.90	8.80	1.9	.57	2.00	2.98	3.90	24.3
Stephen Jackson..51		35.4	.403	.360	.830	.90	4.00	4.90	2.3	1.25	.27	2.41	3.00	18.7
Jamaal Tinsley 40		32.5	.418	.372	.744	.70	3.40	4.00	6.4	2.03	.30	3.35	2.80	15.4
Reggie Miller........66		31.9	.437	.322	.933	.30	2.10	2.40	2.2	.76	.08	1.17	1.70	14.8
Fred Jones 77		29.5	.425	.380	.850	.40	2.70	3.10	2.5	.79	.40	1.48	2.20	10.6
Austin Croshere ...73		25.0	.378	.259	.883	1.40	3.70	5.10	1.3	.66	.23	1.42	2.10	8.9
Anthony Johnson ...63		27.7	.445	.380	.752	.50	2.30	2.80	4.8	.94	.24	1.52	2.30	8.4
Jeff Foster 61		26.1	.519	.000	.634	3.40	5.70	9.00	.7	.75	.20	.90	3.00	7.0
Dale Davis 61		21.4	.479	.000	.606	2.50	3.70	6.10	.8	.52	1.07	.70	2.70	4.7
David Harrison 43		17.7	.576	.000	.571	1.10	2.00	3.10	.3	.37	1.28	1.23	3.10	6.1
Jonathan Bender ...7		13.3	.400	.200	.500	.70	1.30	2.00	.6	.14	.29	1.43	1.30	5.1
James Jones 75		17.7	.396	.398	.855	.50	1.80	2.30	.8	.41	.37	.57	1.60	4.9
Scot Pollard..........49		17.7	.473	.000	.673	1.70	2.40	4.20	.4	.61	.49	.63	2.50	3.9
Eddie Gill 73		14.0	.335	.308	.877	.20	1.30	1.50	1.1	.81	.07	.82	1.40	3.7
Michael Curry 18		13.8	.448	.000	.500	.40	1.10	1.50	.8	.28	.22	.28	2.20	1.7
Pacers...............82		**242.7**	**.432**	**.344**	**.792**	**10.6**	**29.5**	**40.1**	**18.2**	**7.5**	**4.4**	**14.3**	**23.0**	**93.0**
Opponents 82		**242.7**	**.440**	**.365**	**.743**	**11.9**	**29.5**	**41.3**	**18.8**	**6.7**	**4.8**	**13.9**	**23.0**	**92.2**

Los Angeles Clippers

Player	GP	MPG	FG%	3Pt%	FT%	OFF	DEF	Total	APG	SPG	BPG	TO	PF	PPG
Corey Maggette ...66		36.9	.431	.304	.857	1.10	4.90	6.00	3.4	1.06	.12	2.95	2.90	22.2
Elton Brand 81		37.0	.503	.000	.752	3.70	5.90	9.50	2.6	.77	2.09	2.26	3.00	20.0
Bobby Simmons...75		37.3	.466	.435	.846	1.70	4.20	5.90	2.7	1.41	.21	1.80	3.00	16.4
Marko Jaric 50		33.1	.414	.371	.720	.40	2.80	3.20	6.1	1.68	.34	1.96	2.10	9.9
Chris Kaman 63		25.9	.497	.000	.661	2.10	4.60	6.70	1.2	.41	1.08	1.83	2.90	9.1
Chris Wilcox.........54		18.6	.514	.000	.611	1.20	3.10	4.20	.7	.48	.44	1.43	2.40	7.9
Shawn Livingston ..30		27.1	.414	.000	.746	.70	2.20	3.00	5.0	1.07	.37	2.50	2.70	7.4
Kerry Kittles..........11		22.1	.384	.333	.600	.10	2.80	2.90	1.8	.73	.27	.64	1.10	6.3
Zeljko Rebraca.....58		16.0	.568	.000	.859	.80	2.30	3.20	.4	.22	.69	.84	2.20	5.8
Rick Brunson........80		24.3	.376	.369	.770	.30	2.10	2.30	5.1	1.03	.09	1.56	1.30	5.5
Mikki Moore..........74		15.9	.502	.000	.787	1.30	2.00	3.30	.6	.26	.43	.85	2.30	5.4
Quinton Ross 78		21.3	.432	.250	.673	.80	1.90	2.70	1.4	.65	.28	.69	2.10	5.1
Darrick Martin 11		17.3	.320	.278	.625	.30	.60	.90	2.5	.55	.00	.55	1.70	3.8
Lionel Chalmers ..36		12.0	.336	.245	.625	.10	.80	.90	1.4	.36	.00	.75	1.50	2.0
Kenny Anderson ..43		17.3	.423	.462	.730	.60	1.50	2.00	2.4	.77	.00	1.14	2.00	4.7
Mamadou N'diaye.11		6.5	.400	.000	.571	.80	1.60	1.60	.1	.09	.45	.00	1.80	1.8
Clippers 82		**244.3**	**.459**	**.345**	**.778**	**12.0**	**29.9**	**41.9**	**23.2**	**7.3**	**5.2**	**15.7**	**22.2**	**95.7**
Opponents 82		**244.3**	**.444**	**.368**	**.762**	**12.0**	**27.5**	**39.5**	**21.1**	**7.8**	**4.8**	**13.7**	**23.6**	**96.5**

Los Angeles Lakers

Player	GP	MPG	FG%	3Pt%	FT%	OFF	DEF	Total	APG	SPG	BPG	TO	PF	PPG
Kobe Bryant.........66		40.7	.433	.339	.816	1.40	4.50	5.90	6.0	1.30	.80	4.09	2.60	27.6
Caron Butler........77		35.7	.445	.304	.862	1.90	3.90	5.80	1.9	1.43	.30	1.62	2.80	15.5
Lamar Odom 64		36.3	.473	.308	.695	2.10	8.10	10.20	3.7	.66	1.02	2.52	3.30	15.2
Chucky Atkins 82		35.4	.426	.387	.803	.40	2.00	2.40	4.4	.89	.02	1.84	2.20	13.6
Chris Mihm..........75		24.9	.507	.000	.678	2.60	4.10	6.70	.7	.19	1.44	1.47	3.20	9.8
Jumaine Jones.....76		24.1	.432	.391	.733	1.40	3.80	5.20	.9	.58	.32	.64	2.20	7.6
Devean George ...15		20.4	.356	.362	.750	.90	2.70	3.50	.9	.53	.13	.80	2.10	7.3
Brian Cook 72		15.1	.417	.392	.757	.90	2.10	3.00	.5	.32	.36	.40	1.90	6.4
Tierre Brown........76		14.0	.356	.361	.787	.30	.90	1.20	2.0	.42	.01	.97	.80	4.4
Brian Grant..........69		16.5	.493	.000	.722	1.50	2.30	3.70	.5	.33	.33	.62	2.50	3.8
S. Medvedenko 43		9.8	.455	.000	.821	.70	1.10	1.80	.3	.21	.05	.30	1.50	3.8
Luke Walton 61		12.6	.411	.262	.708	.90	1.40	2.30	1.5	.43	.18	.95	1.10	3.2
Sasha Vujacic 35		11.5	.282	.270	.947	.40	1.40	1.80	1.5	.34	.06	.43	1.20	2.9
Tony Bobbitt 2		6.0	.400	.500	.000	.00	1.50	1.50	.0	.00	.00	.00	.50	2.5
Vlade Divac 15		8.7	.419	.000	.667	1.20	.90	2.10	1.3	.27	.07	.93	1.70	2.3
Lakers...............82		**241.2**	**.437**	**.355**	**.777**	**12.5**	**30.6**	**43.2**	**20.4**	**6.2**	**4.2**	**14.3**	**21.9**	**98.7**
Opponents 82		**241.2**	**.453**	**.361**	**.780**	**12.5**	**29.9**	**42.4**	**24.4**	**7.6**	**5.1**	**11.8**	**22.1**	**101.7**

Memphis Grizzlies

Player	GP	MPG	FG%	3Pt%	FT%	OFF	DEF	Total	APG	SPG	BPG	TO	PF	PPG
Pau Gasol	56	32.0	51.4	16.7	76.8	2.3	5.0	7.3	2.4	0.7	1.7	2.5	2.6	17.8
Mike Miller	76	30.0	50.5	43.3	72.0	0.5	3.5	4.0	2.9	0.7	0.3	1.7	2.6	13.7
Bonzi Wells	69	21.6	44.1	34.6	75.0	0.7	2.6	3.3	1.2	1.2	0.4	1.3	2.4	10.3
Stromile Swift	60	21.3	44.9	0.0	75.8	1.5	3.0	4.6	0.7	.07	1.5	1.5	3.0	10.1
Jason Williams	71	27.5	41.3	32.4	79.2	0.3	1.5	1.7	5.6	1.1	0.1	1.8	1.3	10.1
Shane Battier	80	31.5	44.2	39.6	79.0	2.0	3.2	5.2	1.6	1.1	1.0	0.9	2.5	9.9
Lorenzen Wright	80	28.6	46.9	0.0	66.2	2.2	5.5	7.7	1.1	0.7	0.9	1.3	3.1	9.6
Brian Cardinal	58	24.7	37.0	35.2	87.3	1.1	2.8	3.9	2.0	1.5	0.3	1.4	3.0	9.0
Lames Posey	50	27.6	35.7	30.9	86.5	0.9	3.5	4.4	1.8	1.0	0.5	1.4	2.7	8.1
Earl Watson	80	22.6	42.6	31.9	65.9	0.4	1.6	2.1	4.5	1.0	0.2	2.1	2.3	7.7
Dahntay Jones	52	12.5	43.7	38.3	68.8	0.2	1.1	1.3	0.4	0.3	0.2	0.6	1.6	4.5
Antonio Burks	24	9.1	46.7	27.3	73.7	0.0	0.5	0.5	1.2	0.5	0.0	0.5	1.0	3.0
Ryan Humphrey	35	9.1	40.8	0.0	48.7	1.4	1.1	2.5	0.2	0.3	0.0	0.7	1.0	2.9
Jake Tsakalidis	31	9.0	50.0	0.0	77.8	0.7	1.1	1.8	0.3	0.1	0.5	0.4	1.4	2.5
Grizzlies	82	240.3	.447	.357	.754	10.8	28.1	39.0	20.9	8.5	5.8	14.6	23.3	93.4
Opponents	82	240.3	.432	.351	.771	12.1	29.1	41.2	19.9	7.5	5.8	15.9	22.6	91.1

Miami Heat

Player	GP	MPG	FG%	3Pt%	FT%	OFF	DEF	Total	APG	SPG	BPG	TO	PF	PPG
Dwyane Wade	77	38.6	.478	.289	.762	1.40	3.70	5.20	6.8	1.57	1.06	4.17	3.00	24.1
Shaquille O'Neal	73	34.1	.601	.000	.461	3.50	6.90	10.40	2.7	.49	2.34	2.78	3.60	22.9
Eddie Jones	80	35.5	.428	.372	.806	.50	4.60	5.10	2.7	1.08	.48	1.24	3.10	12.7
Damon Jones	80	31.4	.456	.432	.791	.20	2.60	2.80	4.3	.54	.06	1.20	1.50	11.6
Udonis Haslem	80	33.4	.540	.000	.791	3.00	6.10	9.10	1.4	.79	.51	1.41	3.30	10.9
Rasual Butler	65	18.5	.399	.373	.771	.20	2.10	2.30	1.0	.28	.45	.57	1.60	6.5
C. Laettner	49	15.1	.582	.143	.763	.70	1.90	2.70	.8	.65	.31	.59	1.60	5.3
Keyon Dooling	74	16.0	.403	.253	.780	.10	1.10	1.20	1.8	.53	.15	.88	1.60	5.2
Alonzo Mourning	37	19.0	.472	.000	.582	1.40	3.90	5.40	.5	.22	2.00	1.54	2.20	7.6
Michael Doleac	41	14.7	.447	.000	.610	.90	2.30	3.20	.6	.29	.28	.45	2.00	4.0
S. Anderson	66	17.7	.452	.172	.818	.60	2.30	2.90	1.1	.61	.21	.76	2.10	3.9
Qyntel Woods	3	13.3	.417	.000	.000	.70	1.30	2.00	.0	1.33	.00	.67	2.00	3.3
Dorell Wright	3	9.0	.273	.000	1.000	.00	.30	.30	1.0	1.33	.00	1.00	.70	2.3
Wang Zhizhi	20	4.6	.472	.667	.583	.30	.60	.90	.3	.15	.10	.25	.50	2.2
Steve Smith	50	15.0	.411	.390	.863	.30	1.00	1.30	1.4	.28	.14	.54	1.60	6.3
Heat	82	243.7	.486	.377	.672	10.8	32.2	43.0	21.8	6.4	5.8	13.7	22.1	101.5
Opponents	82	243.7	.427	.348	.760	11.2	29.2	40.5	19.8	7.4	3.2	13.2	24.6	95.0

Milwaukee Bucks

Player	GP	MPG	FG%	3Pt%	FT%	OFF	DEF	Total	APG	SPG	BPG	TO	PF	PPG
Michael Redd	75	38.0	.441	.355	.854	1.00	3.20	4.20	2.3	.84	.11	1.77	2.00	23.0
Desmond Mason	80	36.2	.443	.125	.802	1.10	2.80	3.90	2.7	.73	.34	2.05	2.50	17.2
Joe Smith	74	30.6	.514	.000	.768	2.40	4.90	7.30	.9	.58	.51	1.07	3.00	11.0
Maurice Williams	80	28.2	.438	.323	.850	.60	2.40	3.10	6.1	.93	.14	2.45	2.80	10.2
Dan Gadzuric	81	22.0	.539	.000	.538	3.20	5.10	8.30	.4	.58	1.31	1.00	2.80	7.3
A. Goldwire	33	16.3	.419	.400	.839	.30	1.50	1.80	2.4	.45	.00	.45	1.00	5.2
Marcus Fizer	54	16.7	.455	.000	.680	.50	2.70	3.20	1.2	.46	.24	1.17	1.80	6.2
Zaza Pachulia	74	18.9	.452	.000	.746	1.80	3.30	5.10	.8	.59	.46	.95	2.20	6.2
Kendall Gill	14	20.3	.400	.333	.900	.80	1.90	2.60	1.9	1.00	.29	.64	2.60	6.1
Toni Kukoc	53	20.7	.410	.362	.721	.60	2.40	3.00	3.0	.74	.25	1.21	1.30	5.6
Erick Strickland	62	16.4	.375	.253	.813	.20	1.50	1.70	1.9	.48	.02	1.03	1.70	4.9
Calvin Booth	51	8.8	.454	.000	.813	.60	1.50	2.10	.2	.29	.55	.31	1.50	2.4
Daniel Santiago	11	9.5	.333	.000	.727	.50	1.20	1.70	.1	.27	.36	.36	2.50	2.0
Reese Gaines	21	8.9	.340	.286	.750	.00	.60	.70	.3	.24	.05	.33	.80	2.0
Bucks	82	241.2	.450	.351	.772	12.0	29.3	41.3	21.0	6.4	3.5	13.8	21.9	97.2
Opponents	82	241.2	.464	.343	.771	11.4	29.4	40.8	23.8	7.4	4.5	13.0	23.8	100.2

Minnesota Timberwolves

Player	GP	MPG	Field Goals		FT%	Rebounds			APG	SPG	BPG	TO	PF	PPG
			FG%	3Pt%		OFF	DEF	Total						
Kevin Garnett	82	38.1	.502	.240	.811	3.00	10.50	13.50	5.7	1.48	1:37	2.71	2.50	22.2
Wally Szczerbiak	81	31.6	.506	.373	.855	1.00	2.70	3.70	2.4	.49	.20	1.63	2.20	15.5
Ndudi Ebi	2	27.0	.524	.000	.556	3.00	5.00	8.00	.5	.50	.50	1.50	3.50	13.5
Sam Cassell	59	25.8	.464	.262	.865	.40	2.20	2.70	5.1	.61	.24	1.85	2.70	13.5
Latrell Sprewell	80	30.6	.414	.327	.830	.80	2.40	3.20	2.2	.66	.26	1.59	1.60	12.8
Troy Hudson	79	21.9	.401	.345	.778	.20	1.10	1.30	3.6	.34	.08	1.43	1.50	8.7
Eddie Griffin	70	21.3	.387	.328	.718	1.80	4.60	6.50	.8	.33	1.69	.79	1.70	7.5
Trenton Hassell	82	25.2	.474	.091	.789	1.00	1.70	2.70	1.6	.37	.37	.78	2.40	6.6
M. Olowokandi	62	19.6	.456	.000	.667	1.70	3.50	5.20	.5	.24	.90	1.10	3.10	5.9
Fred Hoiberg	76	16.7	.489	.483	.873	.40	2.00	2.40	1.1	.66	.20	.26	1.40	5.8
Anthony Carter	66	11.2	.407	.118	.686	.20	.90	1.00	2.4	.53	.27	.94	1.30	2.7
John Thomas	44	11.8	.488	.000	.587	.90	1.30	2.20	.4	.34	.30	.41	1.90	2.5
Mark Madsen	41	14.7	.515	.000	.500	1.50	1.60	3.10	.4	.17	.34	.59	2.50	2.1
Ervin Johnson	46	8.9	.519	1.000	.640	.90	1.50	2.50	.1	.15	.28	.39	1.90	1.6
Timberwolves	**82**	**240.9**	**.459**	**.345**	**.796**	**11.5**	**31.5**	**43.0**	**23.4**	**5.6**	**5.4**	**13.2**	**21.6**	**96.8**
Opponents	**82**	**240.9**	**.438**	**.363**	**.752**	**12.6**	**28.8**	**41.4**	**21.7**	**6.6**	**3.9**	**11.7**	**29.9**	**95.3**

New Jersey Nets

Player	GP	MPG	Field Goals		FT%	Rebounds			APG	SPG	BPG	TO	PF	PPG
			FG%	3Pt%		OFF	DEF	Total						
Vince Carter	77	36.7	.452	.406	.798	1.40	3.80	5.20	4.2	1.42	.62	2.18	3.20	24.5
R. Jefferson	33	41.1	.422	.337	.844	1.50	5.80	7.30	4.0	1.00	.52	4.00	3.30	22.2
Jason Kidd	66	36.9	.398	.360	.740	1.40	6.00	7.40	8.3	1.86	.14	2.53	1.70	14.4
Nenad Krstic	75	26.2	.493	.000	.725	2.10	3.20	5.30	1.0	.43	.84	1.49	3.70	10.0
Ron Mercer	18	21.7	.411	.000	.700	.50	1.70	2.20	1.1	.89	.11	.78	1.10	7.6
Rodney Buford	64	20.5	.382	.315	.822	.30	1.20	1.40	1.0	.63	.06	.55	1.60	7.0
Travis Best	76	19.2	.420	.306	.885	1.90	4.20	6.10	1.9	.87	.12	.88	1.90	6.8
Jason Collins	80	31.8	.412	.333	.656	1.50	3.00	4.50	1.3	.89	.89	1.14	4.00	6.4
Brian Scalabrine	54	21.6	.398	.324	.768	1.80	3.30	5.10	1.6	.63	.33	1.22	2.10	6.3
Clifford Robinson	71	23.8	.386	.247	.639	.80	2.20	2.90	1.5	.87	.75	.93	2.50	7.5
Jacque Vaughn	71	19.9	.449	.333	.835	.20	1.30	1.50	1.9	.58	.01	.87	1.90	5.3
Zoran Planinic	43	12.0	.448	.375	.697	.40	1.20	1.60	1.0	.58	.00	.95	1.80	5.0
Jabari Smith	45	14.4	.419	.500	.745	.60	1.80	2.50	.8	.56	.31	.87	2.30	3.7
Billy Thomas	25	14.2	.362	.304	.778	.30	1.20	1.40	.7	.56	.04	.36	1.20	3.7
Donnell Harvey	3	5.3	1.000	.000	1.000	.70	1.70	2.30	.3	.33	.33	.33	.70	2.7
Kaniel Dickens	11	5.5	.286	.333	1.000	.30	.50	180	.1	.18	.09	.18	.50	1.2
Awvee Storey	9	3.6	.300	.500	.500	.40	.10	.60	.1	.00	.00	.00	.30	.9
Nets	**82**	**242.7**	**.429**	**.362**	**.763**	**10.4**	**29.1**	**39.5**	**21.6**	**7.9**	**3.8**	**14.2**	**24.2**	**91.4**
Opponents	**82**	**242.7**	**.439**	**.368**	**.744**	**10.7**	**30.5**	**41.2**	**20.3**	**7.3**	**4.9**	**15.6**	**22.9**	**92.9**

New Orleans Hornets

Player	GP	MPG	Field Goals		FT%	Rebounds			APG	SPG	BPG	TO	PF	PPG
			FG%	3Pt%		OFF	DEF	Total						
Lee Nailon	68	29.7	.478	.000	.806	1.90	2.50	4.40	1.6	.53	.24	1.62	2.80	14.2
Dan Dickau	71	29.4	.405	.347	.833	.50	2.10	2.50	4.9	1.07	.06	2.04	2.80	12.5
Jamaal Magloire	23	30.6	.432	.000	.602	3.40	5.50	8.90	1.3	.35	1.00	2.57	3.20	11.7
P.J. Brown	82	34.4	.446	.000	.864	3.20	5.70	9.00	2.2	.90	.61	1.23	2.80	10.8
J.R. Smith	76	24.5	.394	.288	.689	.50	1.50	2.00	1.9	.72	.14	1.43	1.80	10.3
Bostjian Nachbar	71	18.9	.392	.383	.689	.30	2.20	2.60	1.0	.41	.23	1.03	2.60	7.0
Chris Anderson	67	21.3	.534	.000	.689	2.00	4.10	6.10	1.1	.21	1.49	.96	2.10	7.7
Casey Jacobsen	84	21.4	.404	.373	.786	.40	1.60	2.00	1.3	.39	.10	.85	1.20	6.5
Speedy Claxton	62	30.1	.421	.180	.736	.60	2.40	3.00	6.0	1.76	.13	1.92	3.00	11.5
David West	30	18.4	.436	.400	.680	1.30	3.00	4.30	.8	.40	.53	1.23	2.10	6.2
J. Harrington	29	19.0	.360	.316	.829	.40	1.70	2.20	2.1	.86	.17	1.41	2.50	5.6
Alex Garcia	8	18.3	.346	.278	.750	.90	1.00	1.90	2.3	.50	.13	1.00	1.90	5.5
Jackson Vroman	46	15.3	.412	.000	.640	1.40	2.40	3.80	.9	.54	.41	1.39	2.30	4.6
Matt Freije	23	19.2	.291	.259	.625	.70	2.00	2.70	.9	.57	.09	.74	1.70	4.0
George Lynch	44	21.2	.360	.297	.739	1.30	2.70	4.00	2.0	.73	.27	1.30	1.90	3.7
Maciej Lampe	37	10.3	.371	.500	.682	.60	1.80	2.40	.3	.14	.19	.46	1.40	3.1
Hornets	**82**	**243.0**	**.415**	**.315**	**.766**	**12.4**	**27.8**	**40.2**	**21.0**	**6.7**	**3.8**	**14.8**	**23.0**	**88.4**
Opponents	**82**	**243.0**	**.452**	**.367**	**.775**	**11.5**	**30.3**	**41.9**	**21.2**	**7.7**	**5.5**	**14.2**	**21.1**	**95.5**

New York Knicks

Player	GP	MPG	FG%	3Pt%	FT%	OFF	DEF	Total	APG	SPG	BPG	TO	PF	PPG
			Field Goals			Rebounds								
Stephon Marbury...82	82	40.0	.462	.354	.834	.60	2.40	3.00	8.1	1.49	.07	2.84	2.30	21.7
Jamal Crawford....70	70	38.4	.398	.361	.843	.50	2.40	2.90	4.3	1.31	.27	2.11	1.90	17.7
Tim Thomas 71	71	27.3	.439	.409	.786	.60	2.70	3.30	1.5	.58	.24	1.59	3.10	12.0
Allan Houston.......20	20	26.6	.415	.388	.837	.20	1.00	1.20	2.1	.40	.10	1.05	2.00	11.9
Kurt Thomas 80	80	35.7	.471	.500	.786	2.10	8.30	10.40	2.0	.88	.99	1.24	3.90	11.5
Mike Sweetney 77	77	19.6	.531	.000	.749	2.20	3.20	5.40	.6	.35	.36	1.40	2.90	8.4
Malik Rose 76	76	19.4	.449	.100	.737	1.70	2.80	4.50	.8	.61	.21	1.34	2.70	7.0
A. Hardaway 37	37	24.2	.423	.300	.739	.50	1.90	2.40	2.0	.76	.08	1.35	2.10	7.3
Maurice Taylor......65	65	20.6	.455	.333	.612	1.00	2.90	4.00	1.0	.42	.31	1.45	2.80	7.3
Trevor Ariza 80	80	17.3	.442	.231	.695	1.10	1.90	3.00	1.1	.88	.23	.91	1.90	5.9
Jerome Williams .79	79	15.3	.502	.000	.669	1.50	2.10	3.60	.5	.70	.13	.82	2.00	4.5
Jackie Butler 3	3	1.7	1.000	.000	1.000	.00	.00	.00	.0	.33	.00	.33	.00	3.3
J. Jackson..........21	21	11.0	.515	.000	.615	.10	1.00	1.10	1.1	.33	.05	.48	1.20	2.0
Jamison Brewer ..18	18	10.3	.297	.200	.462	.30	.90	1.20	.7	.44	.06	.72	.60	1.7
Bruno Sundov 21	21	3.5	.297	.333	1.000	.30	.30	.60	.1	.10	.10	.29	.80	1.2
Knicks...............82	82	242.4	.451	.356	.767	11.8	29.2	41.0	20.3	7.7	3.2	14.7	23.7	97.3
Opponents 82	82	242.4	.465	.364	.756	11.8	29.9	41.7	20.7	7.3	4.7	14.6	21.2	99.7

Orlando Magic

Player	GP	MPG	FG%	3Pt%	FT%	OFF	DEF	Total	APG	SPG	BPG	TO	PF	PPG
			Field Goals			Rebounds								
Steve Francis 78	78	38.2	.423	.299	.823	1.60	4.20	5.80	7.0	1.44	.36	4.06	3.50	21.3
Grant Hill 67	67	34.9	.509	.231	.821	1.10	3.60	4.70	3.3	1.45	.42	2.40	2.10	19.7
Hedo Turkoglu.....67	67	26.2	.419	.380	.836	.90	2.60	3.50	2.3	.61	.27	1.78	2.10	14.0
Dwight Howard...82	82	32.6	.520	.000	.671	3.50	6.50	10.00	.9	.94	1.66	2.01	2.80	12.0
Jameer Nelson.....79	79	20.4	.455	.312	.682	.70	1.80	2.40	3.0	.99	.04	1.48	2.50	8.7
D. Stevenson......55	55	19.8	.408	.373	.554	.70	1.20	1.90	1.3	.29	.16	1.04	1.30	7.8
Kelvin Cato 62	62	24.6	.539	.000	.783	1.60	5.10	6.70	.6	.89	1.32	1.03	2.70	7.0
Doug Christie 52	52	29.3	.392	.242	.897	.70	2.70	3.40	3.8	1.54	.35	2.00	2.00	6.6
Andre Barrett.......38	38	12.7	.363	.269	.737	.30	.80	1.10	1.8	.50	.03	.71	1.30	3.1
Tony Battie 81	81	23.4	.460	.000	.723	1.30	4.20	5.60	.5	.37	1.00	1.00	3.00	4.9
Pat Garrity 71	71	13.5	.402	.333	.879	.30	1.50	1.70	.4	.27	.13	.42	1.50	4.6
Stacey Augmon ...55	55	12.1	.407	.000	.740	.80	1.00	1.80	.7	.42	.15	.56	1.50	3.5
Brandon Hunter ...31	31	7.2	.507	.000	.538	.80	1.40	2.20	.1	.13	.23	.71	1.40	3.1
Mario Kasun.........45	45	7.9	.480	.000	.558	1.20	1.70	2.80	.2	.18	.29	.58	1.90	2.6
Mark Jones 10	10	11.6	.290	.000	.500	.60	.70	1.30	.6	.50	.20	.30	1.60	2.3
A. DeClercq 8	8	6.1	.444	.000	.333	.90	.40	1.30	.0	.25	.00	.13	1.80	1.1
Magic 82	82	240.3	.454	.349	.759	12.7	31.0	43.7	19.3	7.7	5.4	16.1	23.6	99.5
Opponents 82	82	240.3	.451	.343	.754	12.5	29.6	42.1	21.3	8.5	4.3	14.5	23.4	101.8

Philadelphia 76ers

Player	GP	MPG	FG%	3Pt%	FT%	OFF	DEF	Total	APG	SPG	BPG	TO	PF	PPG
			Field Goals			Rebounds								
Allen Iverson 75	75	42.3	.424	.308	.835	.70	3.30	4.00	7.9	2.40	.12	4.59	1.90	30.7
Chris Webber.......67	67	35.4	.433	.341	.794	1.90	7.20	9.10	4.7	1.40	.79	2.72	3.20	19.5
Marc Jackson.......81	81	24.4	.465	.000	.828	2.30	2.70	5.00	1.0	.40	.22	1.62	2.10	12.0
Kyle Korver 82	82	32.5	.418	.405	.854	.50	4.10	4.60	2.2	1.26	.40	1.29	3.20	11.5
Andre Iguodala ...82	82	32.8	.493	.331	.743	1.10	4.60	5.70	3.0	1.68	.59	1.70	2.50	9.0
S. Dalembert 72	72	24.8	.524	.000	.601	2.60	4.90	7.50	.5	.64	1.68	1.58	3.30	8.2
Willie Green.........57	57	18.7	.366	.286	.776	.40	1.90	2.30	1.8	.60	.11	1.32	2.10	7.7
Rodney Rogers 58	58	23.6	.382	.286	.743	1.10	3.20	4.20	1.5	.71	.34	1.48	3.00	7.7
John Salmons 58	58	17.1	.405	.341	.729	.20	1.90	2.10	2.0	.69	.22	.88	1.60	4.1
Josh Davis 42	42	7.8	.378	.358	.824	.70	1.20	1.90	.3	.19	.10	.36	1.10	2.8
Aaron McKie 68	68	16.4	.430	.323	.625	.30	2.20	2.50	1.5	.71	.25	.46	1.70	2.2
Michael Bradley ...18	18	6.6	.625	.000	.375	.40	1.10	1.60	.3	.06	.11	.28	.70	1.8
Kendrick Brown......8	8	6.9	.333	.000	.800	.10	1.30	1.40	.5	.38	.13	.63	.50	1.5
Kevin Ollie 26	26	6.1	.355	.000	.667	.10	.60	.70	.7	.19	.00	.23	.60	1.1
76ers...............82	82	242.1	.437	.348	.789	11.1	30.9	42.0	20.9	9.2	3.9	15.5	22.9	99.1
Opponents 82	82	242.1	.443	.362	.767	11.6	32.5	44.1	22.9	8.3	4.7	17.0	23.5	99.9

Phoenix Suns

Player	GP	MPG	FG%	3Pt%	FT%	OFF	DEF	Total	APG	SPG	BPG	TO	PF	PPG
			Field Goals			Rebounds								
A. Stoudemire 80	80	36.1	.559	.188	.733	2.70	6.20	8.90	1.6	.96	1.63	2.36	3.50	26.0
Shawn Marion 81	81	38.6	.476	.334	.833	2.90	8.40	11.30	1.9	2.01	1.47	1.54	2.50	19.4
Joe Johnson......82	82	39.5	.461	.478	.750	1.50	3.70	5.10	3.5	.99	.29	1.80	2.00	17.1
Steve Nash...........75	75	34.3	.502	.431	.887	.80	2.60	3.30	11.5	.99	.08	3.27	1.80	15.5
Q. Richardson 79	79	35.9	.389	.358	.739	1.20	4.90	6.10	2.0	1.22	.34	1.29	2.50	14.9
Jim Jackson 64	64	31.0	.426	.414	.931	.50	3.70	4.20	2.9	.55	.08	1.80	2.40	10.5
Leandro Barbosa ..63	63	17.3	.475	.467	.797	.50	1.60	2.10	2.0	.48	.11	1.38	2.00	7.0
Steven Hunter 76	76	13.8	.614	.000	.479	1.30	1.70	3.00	.2	.05	1.34	.58	1.70	4.6
Walter McCarty ...72	72	12.6	.404	.355	.517	.40	1.50	1.90	.5	.35	.21	.50	2.00	3.6
Smush Parker 16	16	9.0	.419	.231	.692	.30	.50	.80	.9	.31	.00	1.19	1.00	3.0
Jake Voskuhl 38	38	9.5	.458	.000	.684	.80	1.60	2.40	.4	.11	.29	.53	1.60	2.1
Yuta Tabuse 4	4	4.3	.167	1.000	1.000	.50	.50	1.00	.8	.00	.00	.25	.30	1.8
Paul Shirley 9	9	3.3	.455	.000	.500	.10	.10	.20	.3	.00	.00	.11	.30	1.3
Bo Outlaw 39	39	5.5	.353	.000	.556	.40	.90	1.40	.3	.15	.31	.21	.70	.7
Suns 82	82	241.2	.477	.393	.748	11.8	32.3	44.1	23.5	7.0	5.5	13.7	19.1	110.4
Opponents 82	82	241.2	.445	.335	.744	15.0	31.1	46.1	21.2	7.6	4.2	13.8	21.3	103.3

Portland Trail Blazers

Player	GP	MPG	FG%	3Pt%	FT%	OFF	DEF	Total	APG	SPG	BPG	TO	PF	PPG
			Field Goals			Rebounds								
Zach Randolph 46	46	34.8	.448	.000	.815	3.10	6.50	9.60	1.9	.74	.37	2.43	2.40	18.9
S. Abdur-Rahim....54	54	34.6	.503	.385	.866	2.30	5.00	7.30	2.1	.91	.48	2.17	2.80	16.8
D. Stoudamire 81	81	34.1	.392	.369	.915	.70	3.10	3.80	5.7	1.06	.02	2.02	2.00	15.8
Darius Miles 63	63	27.0	.482	.348	.600	1.10	3.60	4.70	2.0	1.19	1.24	2.49	3.00	12.8
Ruben Patterson ..70	70	28.0	.531	.080	.599	1.80	2.10	3.90	2.0	1.51	.30	2.04	2.30	11.6
Nick Van Exel 53	53	30.5	.381	.389	.784	.40	2.70	3.00	4.3	.83	.00	1.74	1.30	11.1
D. Anderson 47	47	26.4	.389	.384	.805	.50	2.20	2.70	3.0	.77	.09	1.49	1.90	9.2
S. Telfair 68	68	19.6	.393	.246	.789	.10	1.40	1.50	3.3	.51.	.06	1.84	1.80	6.8
Joel Przybilla 76	76	24.4	.598	.000	.517	2.30	5.40	7.70	1.0	.32	2.14	1.29	3.10	6.4
Travis Outlaw 59	59	13.4	.498	.400	.653	.70	1.40	2.10	.6	.51	.68	.66	1.30	5.4
Theo Ratliff 63	63	27.5	.447	.000	.692	1.80	3.50	5.30	.5	.37	2.51	.89	2.90	4.8
Viktor Khryapa 32	32	16.3	.435	.364	.548	.90	2.50	3.40	.8	.63	.56	1.03	2.50	4.2
Richie Frahm 43	43	11.6	.400	.388	.840	.40	1.00	1.40	.7	.35	.09	.33	.80	3.8
Ha Seung-Jin 19	19	5.5	.435	.000	.545	.30	.60	.90	.1	.05	.26	.63	1.10	1.4
Geno Carlisle 6	6	2.7	.667	.000	.667	.20	.00	.20	.2	.00	.00	.17	.20	1.3
Maurice Baker........5	5	3.8	.000	.000	.000	.20	.20	.40	.2	.20	.00	.20	.60	.0
Trail Blazers 82	82	240.6	.451	.362	.725	11.8	29.3	41.1	21.0	7.1	6.6	16.0	20.8	92.9
Opponents 82	82	240.6	.447	.343	.755	14.0	28.2	42.2	23.5	8.5	5.0	13.4	20.4	96.9

Sacramento Kings

Player	GP	MPG	FG%	3Pt%	FT%	OFF	DEF	Total	APG	SPG	BPG	TO	PF	PPG
			Field Goals			Rebounds								
P. Stojakovic 66	66	38.4	.444	.402	.920	.90	3.40	4.30	2.1	1.20	.18	1.55	2.40	20.1
Mike Bibby 80	80	38.6	.443	.360	.775	1.00	3.20	4.20	6.8	1.55	.38	2.54	2.40	19.6
Cuttino Mobley`......66	66	36.2	.438	.439	.820	.70	2.80	3.50	2.8	1.12	.45	2.02	2.30	17.2
Brad Miller 56	56	37.3	.524	.263	.812	2.50	6.80	9.30	3.9	1.23	1.21	1.46	3.20	15.6
Kenny Thomas 73	73	29.7	.470	.200	.762	2.50	4.80	7.30	2.1	.92	.23	1.79	3.10	12.4
Bobby Jackson 25	25	21.4	.427	.344	.862	.90	2.50	3.40	2.4	.56	.08	1.12	2.30	12.0
C. Williamson 72	72	21.2	.473	.000	.799	1.40	2.20	3.60	1.1	.53	.21	1.19	3.00	10.3
Darius Songaila....81	81	20.6	.527	.000	.847	1.50	2.70	4.20	1.4	.63	.22	.86	2.50	7.5
Brian Skinner 49	49	19.2	.507	.000	.357	2.20	3.50	5.70	.9	.63	1.00	.82	2.10	4.8
Maurice Evans 65	65	19.0	.442	.329	.756	1.40	1.70	3.10	.7	.57	.12	.52	1.60	6.4
Eddie House 68	68	13.1	.451	.454	.852	.20	1.00	1.20	1.4	.65	.09	.51	1.00	5.8
Kevin Martin 45	45	10.1	.385	.200	.655	.60	.60	1.30	.5	.36	.07	.53	.80	2.9
Greg Ostertag 56	56	9.9	.440	.000	.342	1.00	2.00	3.00	.7	.13	.71	.43	1.60	1.6
Eric Daniels 21	21	3.4	.333	.500	.000	.30	.50	.90	.2	.10	.00	.29	.30	.6
Kings..................82	82	242.1	.459	.374	.787	12.5	39.9	42.4	24.5	8.2	3.8	13.1	20.5	103.7
Opponents 82	82	242.1	.459	.357	.738	13.4	30.9	44.3	21.5	7.6	4.4	14.7	21.5	101.6

San Antonio Spurs

Player	GP	MPG	Field Goals		FT%	Rebounds			APG	SPG	BPG	TO	PF	PPG
			FG%	3Pt%		OFF	DEF	Total						
Tim Duncan 66		33.4	.496	.333	.670	3.10	8.00	11.10	2.7	.68	2.64	1.92	2.20	20.3
Tony Parker 80		34.2	.482	.276	.650	.60	3.10	3.70	6.1	1.23	.05	2.69	2.10	16.6
Manu Ginobili 74		29.6	.471	.376	.803	1.00	3.40	4.40	3.9	1.61	.36	2.32	2.60	16.0
Glenn Robinson 9		17.4	.442	.333	.800	.40	2.20	2.70	.9	.44	.33	.78	2.10	10.0
Bruce Bowen 82		32.0	.420	.403	.634	.60	2.90	3.50	1.5	.67	.48	.70	2.10	8.2
Brent Barry 81		21.5	.423	.357	.837	.40	2.00	2.30	2.2	.48	.25	.79	1.50	7.4
Devin Brown........67		18.5	.423	.372	.792	.60	2.10	2.60	1.4	.58	.18	.79	1.20	7.4
N. Mohammed 77		25.1	.480	.000	.674	3.20	4.40	7.60	.4	.75	1.12	1.40	3.10	9.5
Robert Horry 75		18.6	.419	.370	.789	1.20	2.40	3.60	1.1	.89	.80	.92	1.80	6.0
Beno Udrih..........80		14.4	.444	.4088	.753	.20	.80	1.00	1.9	.51	.13	.96	1.20	5.9
R. Nesterovic 70		25.5	.460	.000	.467	2.60	3.90	6.60	1.0	.44	1.67	1.04	3.00	5.9
Dion Glover 7		9.7	.364	.125	.800	.40	1.10	1.60	.6	.43	.43	.29	1.30	3.6
Sean Marks 23		10.6	.338	.000	.786	.80	1.70	2.40	.3	.13	.48	.61	1.30	3.3
T. Massenburg ...61		11.5	.407	.000	.762	.90	1.80	2.70	.2	.30	.33	.66	2.00	3.2
Mike Wilks 48		5.8	.416	.313	.750	.10	.40	.50	.7	.29	.02	.29	.50	1.7
Linton Johnson III...2		7.5	.000	.000	.500	.00	1.50	1.50	.0	.50	.00	.50	.50	.0
Spurs.................82		**241.5**	**.453**	**.363**	**.724**	**12.0**	**30.4**	**42.4**	**21.6**	**7.5**	**6.6**	**13.7**	**20.9**	**96.2**
Opponents 82		**241.5**	**.426**	**.367**	**.768**	**10.9**	**39.3**	**40.2**	**16.9**	**7.2**	**5.1**	**15.1**	**23.1**	**88.4**

Seattle SuperSonics

Player	GP	MPG	Field Goals		FT%	Rebounds			APG	SPG	BPG	TO	PF	PPG
			FG%	3Pt%		OFF	DEF	Total						
Ray Allen 78		39.3	.428	.376	.883	1.00	3.40	4.40	3.7	1.08	.06	2.19	2.10	23.9
Rashard Lewis 71		38.0	.462	.400	.777	1.50	3.90	5.50	1.3	1.06	.87	1.73	2.20	20.5
V. Radmanovic 63		29.5	.409	.389	.786	.80	3.80	24.60	1.4	.90	.49	1.27	2.70	11.8
Antonio Daniels....75		27.0	.438	.297	.816	.30	2.00	2.30	4.1	.68	.04	1.04	1.00	11.2
Luke Ridnour.......82		31.4	.405	.376	.883	.70	1.80	2.50	5.9	1.15	.28	1.82	2.30	10.0
Danny Fortson......62		16.9	.522	.000	.880	2.50	3.10	5.60	.1	.24	.11	1.47	4.30	7.5
Ronald Murray 49		18.0	.361	.253	.738	.30	1.70	2.00	1.3	.61	.22	1.16	1.20	7.0
Damien Wilkens ...29		17.9	.435	.271	.618	1.00	1.30	2.30	.9	.76	.34	.55	1.90	6.3
Nick Collison 82		17.0	.537	.000	.703	1.90	2.70	4.60	.4	.41	.61	.76	3.10	5.6
Reggie Evans:......79		23.8	.476	.000	.534	3.20	6.10	9.30	.7	.73	.19	1.32	2.60	4.9
Jerome James......80		16.6	.509	.000	.723	1.00	2.00	3.00	.2	.29	1.39	1.10	3.50	4.9
V. Potapenko 33		10.2	.517	.000	.871	.90	1.50	2.40	.3	.21	.09	.36	1.60	3.5
Robert Swift.........16		4.5	.455	.000	.556	.10	.30	.30	.1	.06	.44	.25	1.00	.9
Mateen Cleaves ...14		4.6	.357	.000	.750	.10	.30	.40	.5	.14	.00	.14	.10	.9
Sonics 82		**240.9**	**.444**	**.365**	**.790**	**12.7**	**28.2**	**40.9**	**18.1**	**6.7**	**4.1**	**13.6**	**23.7**	**98.9**
Opponents 82		**240.9**	**.459**	**.357**	**.749**	**11.3**	**26.5**	**37.9**	**20.7**	**6.2**	**4.8**	**13.2**	**23.8**	**96.6**

Toronto Raptors

Player	GP	MPG	Field Goals		FT%	Rebounds			APG	SPG	BPG	TO	PF	PPG
			FG%	3Pt%		OFF	DEF	Total						
Jalen Rose 81		33.5	.455	.394	.854	.50	2.90	3.40	2.6	.78	.12	2.22	2.30	18.5
Chris Bosh 81		37.2	.471	.300	.760	2.40	6.50	8.90	1.9	.94	1.40	2.31	2.80	16.8
Rafer Alston 80		34.0	.414	.357	.740	.50	3.00	3.50	6.4	148	.09	2.13	2.70	14.2
Morris Peterson....82		30.6	.420	.385	.832	.90	3.30	4.10	2.1	1.11	.22	1.13	2.70	12.5
Donyell Marshall ..65		25.3	.443	.416	.791	1.50	5.10	6.60	1.2	.88	.71	.65	2.10	11.5
Eric Williams........55		24.0	.430	.384	.696	.80	2.30	3.10	1.7	.69	.07	1.09	2.70	7.7
Matt Bonner 82		18.9	.533	.424	.789	1.30	2.20	3.50	.6	.48	.23	.49	2.70	7.2
Lamond Murray ...62		14.8	.426	.438	.763	.70	1.90	2.60	.8	.52	.26	.87	1.40	6.0
Milt Palacio.........80		19.2	.446	.167	.742	.30	1.40	1.70	3.5	.60	.16	1.30	1.60	5.8
Omar Cook...........5		14.8	.417	.000	.500	.40	1.00	1.40	4.4	1.20	.20	1.20	1.20	4.6
Loren Woods........45		15.8	.433	.000	.576	1.80	3.10	4.90	.4	.18	.87	.82	1.70	3.9
Rafael Araujo 59		12.5	.434	.333	.782	1.00	2.10	3.10	.3	.36	.14	.88	2.70	3.3
Pape Sow 27		9.4	.397	.000	.593	.70	1.40	2.10	.1	.44	.15	.37	1.70	2.3
Aaron Williams 42		7.5	.460	.000	.882	.40	1.00	1.40	.2	.12	.19	.40	1.70	1.7
Raptors 82		**241.5**	**.444**	**.385**	**.774**	**10.3**	**29.8**	**40.1**	**20.4**	**7.6**	**3.9**	**13.3**	**22.9**	**99.7**
Opponents 82		**241.5**	**.467**	**.356**	**.744**	**12.1**	**33.2**	**45.3**	**22.1**	**6.2**	**4.4**	**14.4**	**21.9**	**101.4**

Utah Jazz

Player	GP	MPG	FG%	3Pt%	FT%	OFF	DEF	Total	APG	SPG	BPG	TO	PF	PPG
Carlos Boozer	51	34.7	.521	.000	.698	2.80	6.20	9.00	2.8	.80	.47	2.69	3.50	17.8
Andrei Kirilenko	41	32.9	.493	.299	.784	2.20	4.00	6.20	3.2	1.63	3.32	2.20	2.50	15.6
Matt Harpring	78	33.1	.489	.209	.778	2.50	3.60	6.20	1.8	.90	.21	1.71	3.20	14.0
Mehmet Okur	82	28.1	.468	.270	.850	2.40	5.10	7.50	2.0	.39	.43	1.72	2.80	12.9
Raja Bell	63	28.4	.454	.403	.747	.80	2.40	3.20	1.4	.70	.13	1.25	3.30	12.3
Gordan Giricek	81	20.5	.448	.362	.810	.30	1.90	2.20	1.7	.57	.14	1.11	1.90	8.8
Keith McLeod	53	26.1	.350	.250	.767	.40	1.80	2.10	4.5	1.19	.23	1.87	2.60	7.8
Howard Eisley	74	19.3	.398	.262	.795	.20	1.00	1.20	3.4	.61	.12	1.50	2.10	5.6
Raul Lopez	31	16.7	.422	.444	.818	.20	1.00	1.30	4.0	.71	.10	1.52	2.50	5.2
Kirk Snyder	68	13.3	.372	.353	.667	.70	1.00	1.80	.5	.38	.28	.85	1.70	5.0
Ben Handlogten	21	14.1	.518	.000	.529	1.10	2.00	3.10	.6	.33	.24	.86	2.60	4.5
Jarron Collins	50	19.2	.414	.000	.697	1.10	2.10	3.30	1.2	.22	.12	.68	2.90	4.3
Kris Humphries	67	13.0	.404	.333	.436	1.10	1.90	2.90	.6	.37	.27	.78	1.40	4.1
R. Livingston	17	13.4	.423	.625	.882	.20	.50	.70	2.6	.71	.12	.82	1.60	3.8
Curtis Borchardt	67	12.8	.430	.000	.732	1.30	2.10	3.30	.7	.15	.48	.78	2.40	3.0
Jazz	**82**	**241.2**	**.449**	**.328**	**.757**	**12.8**	**27.4**	**40.1**	**22.3**	**6.6**	**4.6**	**15.8**	**26.7**	**93.0**
Opponents	**82**	**241.2**	**.458**	**.375**	**.764**	**10.5**	**27.2**	**37.2**	**19.4**	**7.9**	**5.8**	**14.4**	**25.1**	**97.3**

Washington Wizards

Player	GP	MPG	FG%	3Pt%	FT%	OFF	DEF	Total	APG	SPG	BPG	TO	PF	PPG
Gilbert Arenas	80	40.9	.431	.365	.814	1.00	3.70	4.70	5.1	1.74	.29	3.03	3.10	25.5
Larry Hughes	61	38.7	.430	.282	.777	1.20	5.00	6.30	4.7	2.89	.30	2.51	2.80	22.0
Antawn Jamison	68	38.3	.437	.341	.760	2.40	5.30	7.60	2.3	.81	.24	1.74	2.20	19.6
Jarvis Hayes	54	28.9	.389	.341	.839	.80	3.40	4.20	1.7	.91	.17	1.15	2.00	10.2
B. Haywood	68	27.4	.560	.000	.609	3.00	3.90	6.80	.8	.76	1.68	1.41	3.20	9.4
Juan Dixon	63	16.7	.416	.327	.897	.50	1.40	1.90	1.8	.68	.06	1.08	1.60	8.0
Etan Thomas	47	20.8	.502	.000	.528	1.80	3.40	5.20	.4	.36	1.09	1.06	2.80	7.1
Kwame Brown	42	21.6	.460	.000	.574	1.70	3.20	4.90	.9	.60	.36	1.60	2.70	7.0
Jared Jeffries	77	26.1	.468	.314	.584	2.00	2.90	4.90	2.0	.86	.45	1.48	2.70	6.8
Steve Blake	44	14.7	.328	.387	.805	.40	1.20	1.60	1.6	.30	.00	.89	1.10	4.3
Damone Brown	14	10.9	.371	.364	.444	.70	1.30	2.00	1.0	.07	.43	1.07	1.20	3.9
Anthony Peeler	40	13.2	.373	.385	.889	.40	1.30	1.60	1.4	.45	.05	.70	1.00	3.8
Laron Profit	42	10.2	.438	.286	.640	.60	1.20	1.80	.9	.38	.12	.64	1.00	3.2
Peter Ramos	6	3.3	.500	.000	.500	.20	.50	.70	.0	.00	.17	.50	.70	1.8
Samaki Walker	14	9.6	.355	.000	.667	.60	.70	1.30	.3	.21	.50	.57	1.80	1.7
Michael Ruffin	79	16.0	.414	.000	.433	2.00	2.20	4.20	.8	.54	.52	.56	2.40	1.4
Wizards	**82**	**241.8**	**.437**	**.343**	**.725**	**13.8**	**29.0**	**42.8**	**19.1**	**8.7**	**4.2**	**14.3**	**22.0**	**100.5**
Opponents	**82**	**241.8**	**.459**	**.364**	**.762**	**12.4**	**30.6**	**43.0**	**23.0**	**7.2**	**5.0**	**15.9**	**24.3**	**100.8**

Charlotte Bobcats

Player	GP	MPG	FG%	3Pt%	FT%	OFF	DEF	Total	APG	SPG	BPG	TO	PF	PPG
Emeka Okafor	73	35.6	.447	.000	.609	3.80	7.10	10.90	.9	.85	1.71	1.71	2.90	15.1
Primoz Brezec	72	31.6	.512	.000	.745	3.10	4.20	7.40	1.2	.46	.76	1.47	2.50	13.0
Kareem Rush	48	20.2	.387	.372	.771	.40	1.40	1.90	1.4	.42	.15	.98	1.50	8.4
Gerald Wallace	70	30.7	.449	.274	.661	1.70	3.80	5.50	2.0	1.67	1.30	2.27	2.60	11.1
Brevin Knight	66	29.5	.422	.150	.852	.30	2.30	2.60	9.0	1.98	.08	2.23	2.90	10.1
Keith Bogans	74	24.2	.381	.329	.727	1.00	2.00	3.10	1.8	.92	.11	1.65	2.30	9.6
Jason Hart	74	25.5	.449	.368	.785	.20	2.50	2.70	5.0	1.34	.19	1.38	2.30	9.5
Matt Carroll	25	17.2	.389	.333	.855	.50	1.90	2.40	.7	.68	.08	1.00	1.50	9.0
Jason Kapono	81	18.4	.401	.412	.524	.40	1.60	2.00	.8	.49	.07	.57	1.60	8.5
Melvin Ely	79	20.9	.432	.000	.575	1.80	2.30	4.10	1.0	.41	.87	1.46	2.50	7.3
Malik Allen	36	14.4	.475	.000	.929	1.10	1.60	2.80	.5	.25	.61	.50	1.50	5.4
Tamar Slay	8	9.8	.333	.167	.000	.80	1.00	1.80	.4	.63	.00	1.00	2.50	3.5
Jamal Sampson	23	14.3	.452	.000	.590	1.60	3.70	5.30	.3	.17	.74	.74	2.30	3.4
Theron Smith	33	15.5	.324	.250	.875	1.20	2.30	3.50	.8	.18	.12	.82	1.80	3.2
Cory Alexander	16	12.6	.327	.421	.750	.50	1.30	1.80	2.3	.56	.06	1.19	1.80	3.1
B. Robinson	31	10.6	.444	.375	.692	.50	1.10	1.50	1.0	.35	.13	.65	1.40	3.0
Jahidi White	17	7.9	.452	.000	.350	.60	1.40	2.00	.1	.12	.71	.65	1.80	2.5
Wizards	**82**	**242.4**	**.432**	**.363**	**.709**	**13.2**	**28.5**	**41.7**	**21.9**	**8.5**	**5.4**	**14.5**	**23.1**	**94.3**
Opponents	**82**	**242.4**	**.463**	**.361**	**.767**	**11.7**	**31.5**	**43.2**	**21.6**	**7.6**	**5.4**	**15.8**	**22.7**	**100.2**

2005 NBA Draft

The 2005 NBA Draft was held on June 24 in New York City.

First Round

1. Andrew Bogut, Milwaukee
2. Marvin Williams, Atlanta
3. Deron Williams, Utah
4. Chris Paul, New Orleans
5. Raymond Felton, Charlotte
6. Martell Webster, Portland
7. Charlie Villanueva, Toronto
8. Channing Frye, New York
9. Ike Diogu, Golden State
10. Andrew Bynum, LA Lakers
11. Fran Vazquez, Orlando
12. Yaroslav Korolev, LA Clippers
13. Sean May, Charlotte
14. Rashad McCants, Minnesota
15. Antoine Wright, New Jersey
16. Joey Graham, Toronto
17. Danny Grange, Indiana
18. Gerald Green, Boston
19. Hakim Warrick, Memphis
20. Julius Hodge, Denver
21. Nate Robinson, Phoenix (from New York)
22. Jarrett Jack, Denver (from Portland)
23. Francisco Garcia, Sacramento
24. Luther Head, Houston
25. Johan Petro, Seattle
26. Jason Maxiell., Detroit
27. Linas Kleiza, Portland (from Denver)
28. Ian Mahinmi, San Antonio
29. Wayne Simien, Miami
30. David Lee, New York

Second Round

31. Salim Stoudamire, Atlanta
32. Daniel Ewing, LA Clippers
33. Brandon Bass, New Orleans
34. C.J. Miles, Utah
35. Ricky Sanchez, Portland (from Denver)
36. Ersan Ilyasova, Milwaukee
37. Ronny Turiaf, LA Lakers
38. Travis Diener, Orlando
39. Von Wafer, LA Lakers
40. Monta Ellis, Golden State
41. Roko Ujic, Toronto
42. Chris Taft, Golden State
43. Mile Ilic, New Jersey
44. Martynas Andriuskevcius, Orlando (from Clev)
45. Louis Williams, Philadelphia
46. Erazem Lorbek, Indiana
47. Bracey Wright, Minnesota
48. Mickael Gelabale, Seattle
49. Andre Blatche, Washington
50. Ryan Gomes, Boston
51. Robert Whaley, Utah
52. Axel Hervelle, Denver
53. Orien Green, Boston
54. Dijon Thompson, New York (from Phoenix)
55. Lawrence Roberts, Seattle (from Memphis)
56. Amir Johnson, Detroit
57. Marcin Gortat, Phoenix (from Orlando)
58. Uros Slokar, Toronto
59. Cenk Akyol, Atlanta
60. Alex Acker, Atlanta

Women's National Basketball Association

2005 Final Standings

EASTERN CONFERENCE

Team	W	L	Pct	GB
†Connecticut	26	8	.765	—
*Indiana	21	13	.618	5
*New York	18	16	.529	8
*Detroit	16	18	.471	10
Washington	16	18	.471	10
Charlotte	6	28	.176	20

†Clinched conference title.   *Clinched playoff berth.

WESTERN CONFERENCE

Team	W	L	Pct	GB
*Sacramento	25	9	.735	—
*Seattle	20	14	.588	5
*Houston	19	15	.559	6
*Los Angeles	17	17	.500	8
Phoenix	16	18	.471	9
Minnesota	14	20	.412	11
San Antonio	7	27	.206	18

2005 Playoffs

FIRST ROUND

EASTERN CONFERENCE

Game 1......Indiana 63   at New York 51
Game 2......New York 50   at Indiana 58
        Indiana won series 2–0.

Game 1......Connecticut 73   at Detroit 62
Game 2......Detroit 67   at Connecticut 75
        Connecticut won series 2–0.

WESTERN CONFERENCE

Game 1......Seattle 75   at Houston 67
Game 2......Houston 67   at Seattle 64
Game 3......Houston 75   at Seattle 58
        Houston won series 2–1.

Game 1......Sacramento 75   at Los Angeles 72
Game 3......Sacramento 81   at Los Angeles 63
        Sacramento won series 2–0.

EASTERN CONFERENCE FINALS

Game 1......Connecticut 73   at Indiana 68
Game 2......Indiana 67   at Connecticut 77
        Connecticut won series 2–0.

WESTERN CONFERENCE FINALS

Game 1......Sacramento 73   at Houston 69
Game 2......Houston 65   at Sacramento 74
        Sacramento won series 2–0.

WNBA FINALS

Game 1...........Sacramento 69   at Connecticut 65
Game 2...........Sacramento 70   at Connecticut 77 (OT)
Game 3...........Connecticut 55   at Sacramento 66
Game 4...........Connecticut 59   at Sacramento 62

        Sacramento won series 3–1.

FOR THE RECORD·Year by Year

NBA Champions

Season	Winner	Series	Runner-Up	Winning Coach	Finals MVP
1946–47	Philadelphia	4–1	Chicago	Eddie Gottlieb	—
1947–48	Baltimore	4–2	Philadelphia	Buddy Jeannette	—
1948–49	Minneapolis	4–2	Washington	John Kundla	—
1949–50	Minneapolis	4–2	Syracuse	John Kundla	—
1950–51	Rochester	4–3	New York	Les Harrison	—
1951–52	Minneapolis	4–3	New York	John Kundla	—
1952–53	Minneapolis	4–1	New York	John Kundla	—
1953–54	Minneapolis	4–3	Syracuse	John Kundla	—
1954–55	Syracuse	4–3	Ft Wayne	Al Cervi	—
1955–56	Philadelphia	4–1	Ft Wayne	George Senesky	—
1956–57	Boston	4–3	St Louis	Red Auerbach	—
1957–58	St Louis	4–2	Boston	Alex Hannum	—
1958–59	Boston	4–0	Minneapolis	Red Auerbach	—
1959–60	Boston	4–3	St Louis	Red Auerbach	—
1960–61	Boston	4–1	St Louis	Red Auerbach	—
1961–62	Boston	4–3	LA Lakers	Red Auerbach	—
1962–63	Boston	4–2	LA Lakers	Red Auerbach	—
1963–64	Boston	4–1	San Francisco	Red Auerbach	—
1964–65	Boston	4–1	LA Lakers	Red Auerbach	—
1965–66	Boston	4–3	LA Lakers	Red Auerbach	—
1966–67	Philadelphia	4–2	San Francisco	Alex Hannum	—
1967–68	Boston	4–2	LA Lakers	Bill Russell	—
1968–69	Boston	4–3	LA Lakers	Bill Russell	Jerry West, LA
1969–70	New York	4–3	LA Lakers	Red Holzman	Willis Reed, NY
1970–71	Milwaukee	4–0	Baltimore	Larry Costello	Kareem Abdul-Jabbar, Mil
1971–72	LA Lakers	4–1	New York	Bill Sharman	Wilt Chamberlain, LA
1972–73	New York	4–1	LA Lakers	Red Holzman	Willis Reed, NY
1973–74	Boston	4–3	Milwaukee	Tommy Heinsohn	John Havlicek, Bos
1974–75	Golden State	4–0	Washington	Al Attles	Rick Barry, GS
1975–76	Boston	4–2	Phoenix	Tommy Heinsohn	JoJo White, Bos
1976–77	Portland	4–2	Philadelphia	Jack Ramsay	Bill Walton, Port
1977–78	Washington	4–3	Seattle	Dick Motta	Wes Unseld, Wash
1978–79	Seattle	4–1	Washington	Lenny Wilkens	Dennis Johnson, Sea
1979–80	LA Lakers	4–2	Philadelphia	Paul Westhead	Magic Johnson, LA
1980–81	Boston	4–2	Houston	Bill Fitch	Cedric Maxwell, Bos
1981–82	LA Lakers	4–2	Philadelphia	Pat Riley	Magic Johnson, LA
1982–83	Philadelphia	4–0	LA Lakers	Billy Cunningham	Moses Malone, Phil
1983–84	Boston	4–3	LA Lakers	K.C. Jones	Larry Bird, Bos
1984–85	LA Lakers	4–2	Boston	Pat Riley	Kareem Abdul-Jabbar, LA
1985–86	Boston	4–2	Houston	K.C. Jones	Larry Bird, Bos
1986–87	LA Lakers	4–2	Boston	Pat Riley	Magic Johnson, LA
1987–88	LA Lakers	4–3	Detroit	Pat Riley	James Worthy, LA
1988–89	Detroit	4–0	LA Lakers	Chuck Daly	Joe Dumars, Det
1989–90	Detroit	4–1	Portland	Chuck Daly	Isiah Thomas, Det
1990–91	Chicago	4–1	LA Lakers	Phil Jackson	Michael Jordan, Chi
1991–92	Chicago	4–2	Portland	Phil Jackson	Michael Jordan, Chi
1992–93	Chicago	4–2	Phoenix	Phil Jackson	Michael Jordan, Chi
1993–94	Houston	4–3	New York	Rudy Tomjanovich	Hakeem Olajuwon, Hou
1994–95	Houston	4–0	Orlando	Rudy Tomjanovich	Hakeem Olajuwon, Hou
1995–96	Chicago	4–2	Seattle	Phil Jackson	Michael Jordan, Chi
1996–97	Chicago	4–2	Utah	Phil Jackson	Michael Jordan, Chi
1997–98	Chicago	4–2	Utah	Phil Jackson	Michael Jordan, Chi
1993–99	San Antonio	4–1	New York	Gregg Popovich	Tim Duncan, SA
1999–00	LA Lakers	4–2	Indiana	Phil Jackson	Shaquille O'Neal, LA
2000–01	LA Lakers	4–1	Philadelphia	Phil Jackson	Shaquille O'Neal, LA
2001–02	LA Lakers	4–0	New Jersey	Phil Jackson	Shaquille O'Neal, LA
2002–03	San Antonio	4–2	New Jersey	Gregg Popovich	Tim Duncan, SA
2003–04	Detroit	4–1	LA Lakers	Larry Brown	Chauncey Billups, Det
2004–05	San Antonio	4–3	Detroit	Gregg Popovich	Tim Duncan, SA

Most Valuable Player: Maurice Podoloff Trophy

Season	Player, Team	GP	Field Goals		3-Pt FG		Free Throws		Rebounds		A	Stl	BS	Avg
			FGM	Pct	FGM	Pct	FTM	Pct	Off	Total				
1955–56	Bob Pettit, StL	72	646	42.9	–	–	557	73.6	–	1,164	189	–	–	25.7
1956–57	Bob Cousy, Bos	64	478	37.8	–	–	363	82.1	–	309	478	–	–	20.6
1957–58	Bill Russell, Bos	69	456	44.2	–	–	230	51.9	–	1,564	202	–	–	16.6
1958–59	Bob Pettit, StL	72	719	43.8	–	–	667	75.9	–	1,182	221	–	–	29.2
1959–60	Wilt Chamberlain, Phil	72	1,065	46.1	–	–	577	58.2	–	1,941	168	–	–	37.6
1960–61	Bill Russell, Bos	78	532	42.6	–	–	258	55.0	–	1,868	264	–	–	16.9
1961–62	Bill Russell, Bos	76	575	45.7	–	–	286	59.5	–	1,891	341	–	–	18.9
1962–63	Bill Russell, Bos	78	511	43.2	–	–	287	55.5	–	1,843	348	–	–	16.8
1963–64	Oscar Robertson, Cin	79	840	48.3	–	–	800	85.3	–	783	868	–	–	31.4
1964–65	Bill Russell, Bos	78	429	43.8	–	–	244	57.3	–	1,878	410	–	–	14.1
1965–66	Wilt Chamberlain, Phil	79	1,074	54.0	–	–	501	51.3	–	1,943	414	–	–	33.5
1966–67	Wilt Chamberlain, Phil	81	785	68.3	–	–	386	44.1	–	1,957	630	–	–	24.1
1967–68	Wilt Chamberlain, Phil	82	819	59.5	–	–	354	38.0	–	1,952	702	–	–	24.3
1968–69	Wes Unseld, Balt	82	427	47.6	–	–	277	60.5	–	1,491	213	–	–	13.8
1969–70	Willis Reed, NY	81	702	50.7	–	–	351	75.6	–	1,126	161	–	–	21.7
1970–71	Kareem Abdul-Jabbar, Mil	82	1,063	57.7	–	–	470	69.0	–	1,311	272	–	–	31.7
1971–72	Kareem Abdul-Jabbar, Mil	81	1,159	57.4	–	–	504	68.9	–	1,346	370	–	–	34.8
1972–73	Dave Cowens, Bos	82	740	45.2	–	–	204	77.9	–	1,329	333	–	–	20.5
1973–74	Kareem Abdul-Jabbar, Mil	81	948	53.9	–	–	295	70.2	287	1,178	386	112	283	27.0
1974–75	Bob McAdoo, Buff	82	1,095	51.2	–	–	641	80.5	307	1,155	179	92	174	34.5
1975–76	Kareem Abdul-Jabbar, LA	82	914	52.9	–	–	447	70.3	272	1,383	413	119	338	37.7
1976–77	Kareem Abdul-Jabbar, LA	82	888	57.9	–	–	376	70.1	266	1,090	319	101	261	26.2
1977–78	Bill Walton, Port	58	460	52.2	–	–	177	72.0	118	766	291	60	146	18.9
1978–79	Moses Malone, Hou	82	716	54.0	–	–	599	73.9	587	1,444	147	79	119	24.8
1979–80	Kareem Abdul-Jabbar, LA	82	835	60.4	0	00.0	364	76.5	190	886	371	81	280	24.8
1980–81	Julius Erving, Phil	82	794	52.1	4	22.2	422	78.7	244	657	364	173	147	24.6
1981–82	Moses Malone, Hou	81	945	51.9	0	00.0	630	76.2	558	1,188	142	76	125	31.1
1982–83	Moses Malone, Phil	78	654	50.1	0	00.0	600	76.1	445	1,194	101	89	157	24.5
1983–84	Larry Bird, Bos	79	758	49.2	18	24.7	374	88.8	181	796	520	144	69	24.2
1984–85	Larry Bird, Bos	80	918	52.2	56	42.7	403	88.2	164	842	531	129	98	28.7
1985–86	Larry Bird, Bos	82	796	49.6	82	42.3	441	89.6	190	805	557	166	51	25.8
1986–87	Magic Johnson, LA Lakers	80	683	52.2	8	20.5	535	84.8	122	504	977	138	36	23.9
1987–88	Michael Jordan, Chi	82	1,069	53.5	7	13.2	723	84.1	139	449	485	259	131	35.0
1988–89	Magic Johnson, LA Lakers	77	579	50.9	59	31.4	513	91.1	111	607	988	138	22	22.5
1989–90	Magic Johnson, LA Lakers	79	546	48.0	106	38.4	567	89.0	128	522	907	132	34	22.3
1990–91	Michael Jordan, Chi	82	990	53.9	29	31.2	571	85.1	118	492	453	223	83	31.5
1991–92	Michael Jordan, Chi	80	943	51.9	27	27.0	491	83.2	91	511	489	182	75	30.1
1992–93	Charles Barkley, Phoe	76	716	52.0	67	30.5	445	76.5	237	928	385	119	74	25.6
1993–94	Hakeem Olajuwon, Hou	80	894	52.8	8	42.1	388	71.6	229	955	287	128	297	27.3
1994–95	David Robinson, SA	81	788	53.0	6	30.0	656	77.4	234	877	236	134	262	27.6
1995–96	Michael Jordan, Chi	82	916	49.5	111	42.7	548	83.4	148	543	352	180	42	30.4
1996–97	Karl Malone, Utah	82	864	55.0	0	00.0	521	75.5	193	809	368	113	48	27.4
1997–98	Michael Jordan, Chi	82	881	46.5	30	23.8	565	78.4	130	475	283	141	45	28.7
1998–99	Karl Malone, Utah	49	393	49.3	0	00.0	378	78.8	107	463	201	62	28	23.8
1999–00	Shaquille O'Neal, LA Lakers	79	956	57.4	0	00.0	432	52.4	336	1078	299	36	239	29.7
2000–01	Allen Iverson, Phil	71	762	42.0	98	32.0	585	81.4	50	273	325	78	20	31.1
2001–02	Tim Duncan, SA	82	764	50.8	1	10.0	560	79.9	268	1042	307	61	203	25.5
2002–03	Tim Duncan, SA	81	714	51.3	6	27.3	450	71.0	260	1045	316	55	237	23.3
2003–04	Kevin Garnett, Minn	82	804	49.9	11	25.6	368	79.1	245	1139	409	120	178	24.2
2003–04	Steve Nash, Phoe	75	430	50.2	94	43.1	211	88.7	80	330	861	74	6	26.0

Coach of the Year: Arnold (Red) Auerbach Trophy

1962–63...Harry Gallatin, StL	1977–78...Hubie Brown, Atl	1992–93...Pat Riley, NY
1963–64...Alex Hannum, SF	1978–79...Cotton Fitzsimmons, KC	1993–94...Lenny Wilkens, Atl
1964–65...Red Auerbach, Bos	1979–80...Bill Fitch, Bos	1994–95...Del Harris, LA Lakers
1965–66...Dolph Schayes, Phil	1980–81...Jack McKinney, Ind	1995–96...Phil Jackson, Chi
1966–67...Johnny Kerr, Chi	1981–82...Gene Shue, Wash	1996–97...Pat Riley, Mia
1967–68...Richie Guerin, StL	1982–83...Don Nelson, Mil	1997–98...Larry Bird, Ind
1968–69...Gene Shue, Balt	1983–84...Frank Layden, Utah	1998–99...Mike Dunleavy, Port
1969–70...Red Holzman, NY	1984–85...Don Nelson, Mil	1999–00...Glenn (Doc) Rivers, Orl
1970–71...Dick Motta, Chi	1985–86...Mike Fratello, Atl	2000–01...Larry Brown, Phil
1971–72...Bill Sharman, LA	1986–87...Mike Schuler, Port	2001–02...Rick Carlisle, Det
1972–73...Tom Heinsohn, Bos	1987–88...Doug Moe, Den	2002–03...Gregg Popovich, SA
1973–74...Ray Scott, Det	1988–89 Cotton Fitzsimmons, Phoe	2003–04...Hubie Brown, Mem
1974–75...Phil Johnson, KC-Oma	1989–90...Pat Riley, LA Lakers	2004–05...Mike D'Antoni, Phoe
1975–76...Bill Fitch, Clev	1990–91...Don Chaney, Hou	
1976–77...Tom Nissalke, Hou	1991–92...Don Nelson, GS	

Note: Award named after Auerbach in 1986.

Rookie of the Year: Eddie Gottlieb Trophy

1952-53 ....Don Meineke, FW
1953-54 ....Ray Felix, Balt
1954-55 ....Bob Pettit, Mil
1955-56 ....Maurice Stokes, Roch
1956-57 ....Tom Heinsohn, Bos
1957-58 ....Woody Sauldsberry, Phil
1958-59 ....Elgin Baylor, Minn
1959-60 ....Wilt Chamberlain, Phil
1960-61 ....Oscar Robertson, Cin
1961-62 ....Walt Bellamy, Chi
1962-63 ....Terry Dischinger, Chi
1963-64 ....Jerry Lucas, Cin
1964-65 ....Willis Reed, NY
1965-66 ....Rick Barry, SF
1966-67 ....Dave Bing, Det
1967-68 ....Earl Monroe, Balt
1968-69 ....Wes Unseld, Balt
1969-70 ....K. Abdul-Jabbar, Mil
1970-71 ....Dave Cowens, Bos

Geoff Petrie, Port
1971-72 ....Sidney Wicks, Port
1972-73 ....Bob McAdoo, Buff
1973-74 ....Ernie DiGregorio, Buff
1974-75 ....Keith Wilkes, GS
1975-76 ....Alvan Adams, Phoe
1976-77 ....Adrian Dantley, Buff
1977-78 ....Walter Davis, Phoe
1978-79 ....Phil Ford, KC
1979-80 ....Larry Bird, Bos
1980-81 ....Darrell Griffith, Utah
1981-82 ....Buck Williams, NJ
1982-83 ....Terry Cummings, SD
1983-84 ....Ralph Sampson, Hou
1984-85 ....Michael Jordan, Chi
1985-86 ....Patrick Ewing, NY
1986-87 ....Chuck Person, Ind
1987-88 ....Mark Jackson, NY
1988-89 ....Mitch Richmond, GS

1989-90 ....David Robinson, SA
1990-91 ....Derrick Coleman, NJ
1991-92 ....Larry Johnson, Char
1992-93 ....Shaquille O'Neal, Orl
1993-94 ....Chris Webber, GS
1994-95 ....J. Kidd, Dall/G. Hill, Det
1995-96 ....Damon Stoudamire, Tor
1996-97 ....Allen Iverson, Phil
1997-98 ....Tim Duncan, SA
1998-99 ....Vince Carter, Tor
1999-00 ....Steve Francis, Hou
Elton Brand, Chi
2000-01 ....Mike Miller, Orl
2001-02 ....Pau Gasol, Mem
2002-03 ....Amare Stoudemire, Phoe
2003-04 ....LeBron James, Clev
2004-05 ....Emeka Okafor, Char

Defensive Player of the Year

1982-83 ...Sidney Moncrief, Mil
1983-84 ...Sidney Moncrief, Mil
1984-85 ...Mark Eaton, Utah
1985-86 ...Alvin Robertson, SA
1986-87 ...Michael Cooper, Lakers
1987-88 ...Michael Jordan, Chi
1988-89 ...Mark Eaton, Utah
1989-90 ...Dennis Rodman, Det

1990-91 ...Dennis Rodman, Det
1991-92 ...David Robinson, SA
1992-93 ...Hakeem Olajuwon, Hou
1993-94 ...Hakeem Olajuwon, Hou
1994-95 ...Dikembe Mutombo, Den
1995-96 ...Gary Payton, Sea
1996-97 ...Dikembe Mutombo, Den
1997-98 ...Dikembe Mutombo, Atl

1998-99 ...Alonzo Mourning, Mia
1999-00 ...Alonzo Mourning, Mia
2000-01 ...Dikembe Mutombo, Phil
2001-02 ...Ben Wallace, Det
2002-03 ...Ben Wallace, Det
2003-04 ...Ron Artest, Ind
2004-05 ...Ben Wallace, Det

Sixth Man Award

1982-83 ...Bobby Jones, Phil
1983-84 ...Kevin McHale, Bos
1984-85 ...Kevin McHale, Bos
1985-86 ...Bill Walton, Bos
1986-87 ...Ricky Pierce, Mil
1987-88 ...Roy Tarpley, Dall
1988-89 ...Eddie Johnson, Phoe
1989-90 ...Ricky Pierce, Mil

1990-91 ...Detlef Schrempf, Ind
1991-92 ...Detlef Schrempf, Ind
1992-93 ...Cliff Robinson, Port
1993-94 ...Dell Curry, Char
1994-95 ...Anthony Mason, NY
1995-96 ...Tony Kukoc, Chi
1996-97 ...John Starks, NY
1997-98 ...Danny Manning, Phoe

1998-99 ...Darrell Armstrong, Orl
1999-00 ...Rodney Rogers, Phoe
2000-01 ...Aaron McKie, Phil
2001-02 ...Corliss Williamson, Det
2002-03 ...Bobby Jackson, Sac
2003-04 ...Antawn Jamison, Dall
2004-05 ...Ben Gordon, Chi

J. Walter Kennedy Citizenship Award

1974-75 ...Wes Unseld, Wash
1975-76 ...Slick Watts, Sea
1976-77 ...Dave Bing, Wash
1977-78 ...Bob Lanier, Det
1978-79 ...Calvin Murphy, Hou
1979-80 ...Austin Carr, Clev
1980-81 ...Mike Glenn, NY
1981-82 ...Kent Benson, Det
1982-83 ...Julius Erving, Phil
1983-84 ...Frank Layden, Utah
1984-85 ...Dan Issel, Den

1985-86 ...Michael Cooper, Lakers
Rory Sparrow, NY
1986-87 ...Isiah Thomas, Det
1987-88 ...Alex English, Den
1988-89 ...Thurl Bailey, Utah
1989-90 ...Glenn Rivers, Atl
1990-91 ...Kevin Johnson, Phoe
1991-92 ...Magic Johnson, Lakers
1992-93 ...Terry Porter, Port
1993-94 ...Joe Dumars, Det
1994-95 ...Joe O'Toole, Atl

1995-96 ...Chris Dudley, Port
1996-97 ...P.J. Brown, Mia
1997-98 ...Steve Smith, Atl
1998-99 ...Brian Grant, Port
1999-00 ...Vlade Divac, Sac
2000-01 ...Dikembe Mutombo, Phil
2001-02 ...Alonzo Mourning, Mia
2002-03 ...David Robinson, SA
2003-04 ...Reggie Miller, Ind
2004-05 ...Eric Snow, Clev

Most Improved Player

1985-86 ...Alvin Robertson, SA
1986-87 ...Dale Ellis, Sea
1987-88 ...Kevin Duckworth, Port
1988-89 ...Kevin Johnson, Phoe
1989-90 ...Rony Seikaly, Mia
1990-91 ...Scott Skiles, Orl
1991-92 ...Pervis Ellison, Wash

1992-93 ...Chris Jackson, Den
1993-94 ...Don MacLean, Wash
1994-95 ...Dana Barros, Phil
1995-96 ......Gheorghe Muresan, Wash
1996-97 ...Isaac Austin, Mia
1997-98 ...Alan Henderson, Atl
1998-99 ...Darrell Armstrong, Orl

1999-00 ...Jalen Rose, Ind
2000-01 ...Tracy McGrady, Orl
2001-02 ...Jermaine O'Neal, Ind
2002-03 ...Gilbert Arenas, GS
2003-04 ...Zach Randolph, Port
2004-05 ...Bobby Simmons, LA Clippers

Executive of the Year

1972-73 ...Joe Axelson, KC-Oma
1973-74 ...Eddie Donovan, Buff
1974-75 ...Dick Vertlieb, GS
1975-76 ...Jerry Colangelo, Phoe
1976-77 ...Ray Patterson, Hou
1977-78 ...Angelo Drossos, SA
1978-79 ...Bob Ferry, Wash
1979-80 ...Red Auerbach, Bos
1980-81 ...Jerry Colangelo, Phoe
1981-82 ...Bob Ferry, Wash
1982-83 ...Zollie Volchok, Sea

1983-84...Frank Layden, Utah
1984-85...Vince Boryla, Den
1985-86...Stan Kasten, Atl
1986-87...Stan Kasten, Atl
1987-88...Jerry Krause, Chi
1988-89...Jerry Colangelo, Phoe
1989-90...Bob Bass, SA
1990-91...Bucky Buckwalter, Port
1991-92...Wayne Embry, Clev
1992-93...Jerry Colangelo, Phoe
1993-94...Bob Whitsitt, Sea

1994-95...Jerry West, LA Lakers
1995-96...Jerry Krause, Chi
1996-97...Bob Bass, Char
1997-98...Wayne Embry, Clev
1998-99...Geoff Petrie, Sac
1999-00...John Gabriel, Orl
2000-01...Geoff Petrie, Sac
2001-02...Rod Thorn, NJ
2002-03...Joe Dumars, Det
2003-04...Jerry West, Mem
2004-05...Bryan Colangelo, Phoe

Scoring

MOST POINTS, CAREER

	Pts	Avg
Kareem Abdul-Jabbar	38,387	24.6
Karl Malone	36,928	25.0
Michael Jordan	32,292	30.1
Wilt Chamberlain	31,419	30.1
Moses Malone	27,409	20.6
Elvin Hayes	27,313	21.0
Hakeem Olajuwon	26,946	21.8
Oscar Robertson	26,710	25.7
Dominique Wilkins	26,669	24.8
John Havlicek	26,395	20.8

MOST POINTS, SEASON

Wilt Chamberlain, Phil	4,029	1961–62
Wilt Chamberlain, SF	3,586	1962–63
Michael Jordan, Chi	3,041	1986–87
Wilt Chamberlain, Phil	3,033	1960–61
Wilt Chamberlain, SF	2,948	1963–64
Michael Jordan, Chi	2,868	1987–88
Bob McAdoo, Buff	2,831	1974–75
Rick Barry, SF	2,775	1966–67
Michael Jordan, Chi	2,753	1989–90
Elgin Baylor, LA	2,719	1962–63

HIGHEST SCORING AVERAGE, CAREER

Michael Jordan	30.1	1,072 games
Wilt Chamberlain	30.1	1,045 games
Allen Iverson	27.4	610 games
Elgin Baylor	27.4	846 games
Jerry West	27.0	932 games
Shaquille O'Neal	26.7	882 games
Bob Pettit	26.4	792 games
George Gervin	26.2	791 games
Oscar Robertson	25.7	1,040 games

Note: Minimum 400 games.

HIGHEST SCORING AVERAGE, SEASON

Wilt Chamberlain, Phil	50.4	1961–62
Wilt Chamberlain, SF	44.8	1962–63
Wilt Chamberlain, Phil	38.4	1960–61
Wilt Chamberlain, Phil	37.6	1959–60
Michael Jordan, Chi	37.1	1986–87
Wilt Chamberlain, SF	36.9	1963–64
Rick Barry, SF	35.6	1966–67
Michael Jordan, Chi	35.0	1987–88
Elgin Baylor, LA	34.8	1960–61

Note: Minimum 70 games.

MOST POINTS, GAME

	Player, Team	Opp	Date
100	Wilt Chamberlain, Phil	NY	3/2/62
78	Wilt Chamberlain, Phil	LA	12/8/61
73	Wilt Chamberlain, Phil	Chi	1/13/62
73	Wilt Chamberlain, SF	NY	11/16/62
73	David Thompson, Den	Det	4/9/78
72	Wilt Chamberlain, SF	LA	11/3/62
71	David Robinson, SA	LAC	4/24/94
71	Elgin Baylor, LA	NY	11/15/60
70	Wilt Chamberlain, SF	Syr	3/10/63
69	Michael Jordan, Chi	Clev	3/28/90

Field-Goal Percentage

Highest FG Percentage, Career: .599—Artis Gilmore

Highest FG Percentage, Season: .727—Wilt Chamberlain, LA Lakers, 1972–73 (426/586)

Free Throws

HIGHEST FREE-THROW PERCENTAGE, CAREER

Mark Price	.904
Rick Barry	.900
Steve Nash	.892
Calvin Murphy	.892
Peja Stojakovic	.890

Note: Minimum 1200 free throws made.

HIGHEST FREE-THROW PERCENTAGE, SEASON

Calvin Murphy, Hou	.958	1980–81
Mahmoud Abdul-Rauf, Den	.956	1993–94
Jeff Hornacek, Utah	.950	1999–00
Mark Price, Clev	.948	1992–93
Mark Price, Clev	.947	1991–92

MOST FREE THROWS MADE, CAREER

	No.	Yrs	Pct
Karl Malone	9,787	19	.742
Moses Malone	8,531	19	.769
Oscar Robertson	7,694	14	.838
Michael Jordan	7,327	15	.835
Jerry West	7,160	14	.814

Three-Point Field Goals

Most Three-Point Field-Goals, Career: 2,560— Reggie Miller

Highest Three-Point Field-Goal Percentage, Career: .454—Steve Kerr

Most Three-Point Field Goals, Season: .267— Dennis Scott, Orl, 1995–96

Highest Three-Point Field-Goal Percentage, Season: .524—Steve Kerr, Chi, 1994–95

Most Three-Point Field Goals, Game: 12—Kobe Bryant, LA Lakers vs Seattle, 1/7/03

Note: First year of shot: 1979–80.

Steals

Most Steals, Career: 3,265—John Stockton

Most Steals, Season: 301—Alvin Robertson, San Antonio, 1985–86

Most Steals, Game: 11—Kendall Gill, New Jersey vs Miami, 4/3/99; Larry Kenon, San Antonio vs Kansas City, 12/26/76

Rebounds

MOST REBOUNDS, CAREER

	No.	Yrs	Avg
Wilt Chamberlain	23,924	14	22.9
Bill Russell	21,620	13	22.5
Kareem Abdul-Jabbar	17,440	20	11.4
Elvin Hayes	16,279	16	12.5
Moses Malone	16,212	19	12.2
Karl Malone	14,968	19	10.1
Robert Parish	14,715	21	9.1
Nate Thurmond	14,464	14	15.0
Walt Bellamy	14,241	14	13.7
Wes Unseld	13,769	13	14.0

Rebounds *(Cont.)*

MOST REBOUNDS, SEASON

Wilt Chamberlain, Phil	2,149	1960–61
Wilt Chamberlain, Phil	2,052	1961–62
Wilt Chamberlain, Phil	1,957	1966–67
Wilt Chamberlain, Phil	1,952	1967–68
Wilt Chamberlain, SF	1,946	1962–63
Wilt Chamberlain, Phil	1,943	1965–66
Wilt Chamberlain, Phil	1,941	1959–60
Bill Russell, Bos	1,930	1963–64
Bill Russell, Bos	1,878	1964–65
Bill Russell, Bos	1,868	1960–61

MOST REBOUNDS, GAME

	Player, Team	Opp	Date
55	Wilt Chamberlain, Phil	Bos	11/24/60
51	Bill Russell, Bos	Syr	2/5/60
49	Bill Russell, Bos	Phil	11/16/57
49	Bill Russell, Bos	Det	3/11/65
45	Wilt Chamberlain, Phil	Syr	2/6/60
45	Wilt Chamberlain, Phil	LA	1/21/61

Assists

MOST ASSISTS, CAREER

John Stockton	15,806
Mark Jackson	10,334
Magic Johnson	10,141
Oscar Robertson	9,887
Isiah Thomas	9,061

Assists *(Cont.)*

MOST ASSISTS, SEASON

John Stockton, Utah	1,164	1990–91
John Stockton, Utah	1,134	1989–90
John Stockton, Utah	1,128	1987–88
John Stockton, Utah	1,126	1991–92
Isiah Thomas, Det	1,123	1984–85

MOST ASSISTS, GAME: 30—Scott Skiles, Orlando vs Denver, 12/30/90

Blocked Shots

MOST BLOCKED SHOTS, CAREER

Hakeem Olajuwon	3,830
Kareem Abdul-Jabbar	3,189
Dikembe Mutombo	3,089
Mark Eaton	3,064
David Robinson	2,954

MOST BLOCKED SHOTS, SEASON

Mark Eaton, Utah	456	1984–85
Manute Bol, Wash	397	1985–86
Elmore Smith, LA	393	1973–74

MOST BLOCKED SHOTS, GAME: 17—Elmore Smith, LA Lakers vs Portland, 10/28/73

NBA Alltime Playoff Leaders

Scoring

MOST POINTS, CAREER

	Pts	Yrs	Avg
Michael Jordan	5,987	13	33.4
Kareem Abdul-Jabbar	5,762	18	24.3
Karl Malone	4,761	19	24.7
Jerry West	4,457	13	29.1
Shaquille O'Neal	4,294	11	27.2
Larry Bird	3,897	12	23.8
John Havlicek	3,776	13	22.0
Hakeem Olajuwon	3,755	15	25.9
Magic Johnson	3,701	13	19.5
Scottie Pippen	3,642	15	17.7

*HIGHEST SCORING AVERAGE, CAREER

	Avg	Games
Michael Jordan	33.4	179
Allen Iverson	30.6	57
Jerry West	29.1	153
Shaquille O'Neal	27.2	158
Elgin Baylor	27.0	134
George Gervin	27.0	59
Hakeem Olajuwon	25.9	145
Dirk Nowitzki	25.6	40
Bob Pettit	25.5	88
Dominique Wilkins	25.4	55

*Minimum of 25 games.

Scoring *(Cont.)*

MOST POINTS, GAME

	Player, Team	Opp	Date
†63	Michael Jordan, Chi	Bos	4/20/86
61	Elgin Baylor, LA	Bos	4/14/62
56	Wilt Chamberlain, Phil	Syr	3/22/62
56	Michael Jordan, Chi	Mia	4/29/92
56	Charles Barkley, Phoe	GS	5/4/94
55	Rick Barry, SF	Phil	4/18/67
55	Michael Jordan, Chi	Clev	5/1/88
55	Michael Jordan, Chi	Phoe	4/16/95
55	Michael Jordan, Chi	Wash	4/27/97

†Double overtime game.

Rebounds

MOST REBOUNDS, CAREER

	No.	Yrs	Avg
Bill Russell	4,104	13	24.9
Wilt Chamberlain	3,913	13	24.5
Kareem Abdul-Jabbar	2,481	18	10.5
Karl Malone	2,062	19	10.7
Shaquille O'Neal	2,040	11	12.9

MOST REBOUNDS, GAME

	Player, Team	Opp	Date
41	Wilt Chamberlain, Phil	Bos	4/5/67
40	Bill Russell, Bos	Phil	3/23/58
40	Bill Russell, Bos	StL	3/29/60
*40	Bill Russell, Bos	LA	4/18/62

Three tied at 39.
*Overtime game.

Assists

MOST ASSISTS, CAREER

	No.	Games
Magic Johnson	2,346	190
John Stockton	1,839	182
Larry Bird	1,062	164
Scottie Pippen	1,035	204
Michael Jordan	1,022	179

MOST ASSISTS, GAME

	Player, Team	Opp	Date
24	Magic Johnson, LAL	Pho	5/15/84
24	John Stockton, Utah	LAL	5/17/88
23	Magic Johnson, LAL	Port	5/3/85
22	Doc Rivers, Atl	Bos	5/16/88
Four tied at 21.			

Games played

Kareem Abdul-Jabbar	237
Scottie Pippen	204
Danny Ainge	193
Karl Malone	193
Magic Johnson	190

Appearances

John Stockton	19
Karl Malone	19
Kareem Abdul-Jabbar	18
Robert Parish	16
Dolph Schayes	15
Clyde Drexler	15
Tree Rollins	15
Jerome Kersey	15
Hakeem Olajuwon	15

NBA Season Leaders

Scoring

1946–47	Joe Fulks, Phil	1389	1975–76	Bob McAdoo, Buff	31.1
1947–48	Max Zaslofsky, Chi	1007	1976–77	Pete Maravich, NO	31.1
1948–49	George Mikan, Minn	1698	1977–78	George Gervin, SA	27.2
1949–50	George Mikan, Minn	1865	1978–79	George Gervin, SA	29.6
1950–51	George Mikan, Minn	1932	1979–80	George Gervin, SA	33.1
1951–52	Paul Arizin, Phil	1674	1980–81	Adrian Dantley, Utah	30.7
1952–53	Neil Johnston, Phil	1564	1981–82	George Gervin, SA	32.3
1953–54	Neil Johnston, Phil	1759	1982–83	Alex English, Den	28.4
1954–55	Neil Johnston, Phil	1631	1983–84	Adrian Dantley, Utah	30.6
1955–56	Bob Pettit, StL	1849	1984–85	Bernard King, NY	32.9
1956–57	Paul Arizin, Phil	1817	1985–86	Dominique Wilkins, Atl	30.3
1957–58	George Yardley, Det	2001	1986–87	Michael Jordan, Chi	37.1
1958–59	Bob Pettit, StL	2105	1987–88	Michael Jordan, Chi	35.0
1959–60	Wilt Chamberlain, Phil	2707	1988–89	Michael Jordan, Chi	32.5
1960–61	Wilt Chamberlain, Phil	3033	1989–90	Michael Jordan, Chi	33.6
1961–62	Wilt Chamberlain, Phil	4029	1990–91	Michael Jordan, Chi	31.5
1962–63	Wilt Chamberlain, SF	3586	1991–92	Michael Jordan, Chi	30.1
1963–64	Wilt Chamberlain, SF	2948	1992–93	Michael Jordan, Chi	32.6
1964–65	Wilt Chamberlain, SF-Phil	2534	1993–94	David Robinson, SA	29.8
1965–66	Wilt Chamberlain, Phil	2649	1994–95	Shaquille O'Neal, Orl	29.3
1966–67	Rick Barry, SF	2775	1995–96	Michael Jordan, Chi	30.4
1967–68	Dave Bing, Det	2142	1996–97	Michael Jordan, Chi	29.6
1968–69	Elvin Hayes, SD	2327	1997–98	Michael Jordan, Chi	28.7
1969–70	Jerry West, LA	*31.2	1998–99	Allen Iverson, Phil	26.8
1970–71	Kareem Abdul-Jabbar, Mil	31.7	1999–00	Shaquille O'Neal, LA Lakers	29.7
1971–72	Kareem Abdul-Jabbar, Mil	34.8	2000–01	Allen Iverson, Phil	31.1
1972–73	Nate Archibald, KC-Oma	34.0	2001–02	Allen Iverson, Phil	31.4
1973–74	Bob McAdoo, Buff	30.6	2002–03	Tracy McGrady, Orl	32.1
1974–75	Bob McAdoo, Buff	34.5	2003–04	Tracy McGrady, Orl	28.0
			2004–05	Allen Iverson, Phil	30.7

*Based on per game average since 1969–70.

Rebounding

1950–51	Dolph Schayes, Syr	1080	1963–64	Bill Russell, Bos	1930
1951–52	Larry Foust, FW	880	1964–65	Bill Russell, Bos	1878
	Mel Hutchins, Mil	880	1965–66	Wilt Chamberlain, Phil	1943
1952–53	George Mikan, Minn	1007	1966–67	Wilt Chamberlain, Phil	1957
1953–54	Harry Gallatin, NY	1098	1967–68	Wilt Chamberlain, Phil	1952
1954–55	Neil Johnston, Phil	1085	1968–69	Wilt Chamberlain, LA	1712
1955–56	Bob Pettit, StL	1164	1969–70	Elvin Hayes, SD	*16.9
1956–57	Maurice Stokes, Roch	1256	1970–71	Wilt Chamberlain, LA	18.2
1957–58	Bill Russell, Bos	1564	1971–72	Wilt Chamberlain, LA	19.2
1958–59	Bill Russell, Bos	1612	1972–73	Wilt Chamberlain, LA	18.6
1959–60	Wilt Chamberlain, Phil	1941	1973–74	Elvin Hayes, Capital	18.1
1960–61	Wilt Chamberlain, Phil	2149	1974–75	Wes Unseld, Wash	14.8
1961–62	Wilt Chamberlain, Phil	2052	1975–76	Kareem Abdul-Jabbar, LA	16.9
1962–63	Wilt Chamberlain, SF	1946	1976–77	Bill Walton, Port	14.4

Rebounding *(Cont.)*

1977–78	Len Robinson, NO	15.7	1991–92	Dennis Rodman, Det	18.7
1978–79	Moses Malone, Hou	17.6	1992–93	Dennis Rodman, Det	18.3
1979–80	Swen Nater, SD	15.0	1993–94	Dennis Rodman, SA	17.3
1980–81	Moses Malone, Hou	14.8	1994–95	Dennis Rodman, SA	16.8
1981–82	Moses Malone, Hou	14.7	1995–96	Dennis Rodman, Chi	14.9
1982–83	Moses Malone, Phil	15.3	1996–97	Dennis Rodman, Chi	16.1
1983–84	Moses Malone, Phil	13.4	1997–98	Dennis Rodman, Chi	15.0
1984–85	Moses Malone, Phil	13.1	1998–99	Chris Webber, Sac	13.0
1985–86	Bill Laimbeer, Det	13.1	1999–00	Dikembe Mutombo, Atl	14.1
1986–87	Charles Barkley, Phil	14.6	2000–01	Dikembe Mutombo, Atl	13.5
1987–88	Michael Cage, LA Clippers	13.0	2001–02	Ben Wallace, Det	13.0
1988–89	Hakeem Olajuwon, Hou	13.5	2002–03	Ben Wallace, Det	15.4
1989–90	Hakeem Olajuwon, Hou	14.0	2003–04	Kevin Garnett, Minn	13.9
1990–91	David Robinson, SA	13.0	2004–05	Kevin Garnett, Minn	13.5

*Based on per game average since 1969–70.

Assists

1946–47	Ernie Calverly, Prov	202	1975–76	Don Watts, Sea	8.1
1947–48	Howie Dallmar, Phil	120	1976–77	Don Buse, Ind	8.5
1948–49	Bob Davies, Roch	321	1977–78	Kevin Porter, NJ-Det	10.2
1949–50	Dick McGuire, NY	386	1978–79	Kevin Porter, Det	13.4
1950–51	Andy Phillip, Phil	414	1979–80	Micheal Richardson, NY	10.1
1951–52	Andy Phillip, Phil	539	1980–81	Kevin Porter, Wash	9.1
1952–53	Bob Cousy, Bos	547	1981–82	Johnny Moore, SA	9.6
1953–54	Bob Cousy, Bos	578	1982–83	Magic Johnson, LA	10.5
1954–55	Bob Cousy, Bos	557	1983–84	Magic Johnson, LA	13.1
1955–56	Bob Cousy, Bos	642	1984–85	Isiah Thomas, Det	13.9
1956–57	Bob Cousy, Bos	478	1985–86	Magic Johnson, LA Lakers	12.6
1957–58	Bob Cousy, Bos	463	1986–87	Magic Johnson, LA Lakers	12.2
1958–59	Bob Cousy, Bos	557	1987–88	John Stockton, Utah	13.8
1959–60	Bob Cousy, Bos	715	1988–89	John Stockton, Utah	13.6
1960–61	Oscar Robertson, Cin	690	1989–90	John Stockton, Utah	14.5
1961–62	Oscar Robertson, Cin	899	1990–91	John Stockton, Utah	14.2
1962–63	Guy Rodgers, SF	825	1991–92	John Stockton, Utah	13.7
1963–64	Oscar Robertson, Cin	868	1992–93	John Stockton, Utah	12.0
1964–65	Oscar Robertson, Cin	861	1993–94	John Stockton, Utah	12.6
1965–66	Oscar Robertson, Cin	847	1994–95	John Stockton, Utah	12.3
1966–67	Guy Rodgers, Chi	908	1995–96	John Stockton, Utah	11.2
1967–68	Wilt Chamberlain, Phil	702	1996–97	Mark Jackson, Ind	11.4
1968–69	Oscar Robertson, Cin	772	1997–98	Rod Strickland, Wash	10.1
1969–70	Len Wilkens, Sea	*9.1	1998–99	Jason Kidd, Phoe	10.8
1970–71	Norm Van Lier, Cin	10.1	1999–00	Jason Kidd, Phoe	10.1
1971–72	Jerry West, LA	9.7	2000–01	Jason Kidd, Phoe	9.8
1972–73	Nate Archibald, KC-Oma	11.4	2001–02	Andre Miller, Clev	10.9
1973–74	Ernie DiGregorio, Buff	8.2	2002–03	Jason Kidd, NJ	8.9
1974–75	Kevin Porter, Wash	8.0	2003–04	Jason Kidd, NJ	9.2
			2004–05	Steve Nash, Phoe	11.5

*Based on per game average since 1969–70.

Field-Goal Percentage

1946–47	Bob Feerick, Wash	40.1	1968–69	Wilt Chamberlain, LA	58.3
1947–48	Bob Feerick, Wash	34.0	1969–70	Johnny Green, Cin	55.9
1948–49	Arnie Risen, Roch	42.3	1970–71	Johnny Green, Cin	58.7
1949–50	Alex Groza, Ind	47.8	1971–72	Wilt Chamberlain, LA	64.9
1950–51	Alex Groza, Ind	47.0	1972–73	Wilt Chamberlain, LA	72.7
1951–52	Paul Arizin, Phil	44.8	1973–74	Bob McAdoo, Buff	54.7
1952–53	Neil Johnston, Phil	45.2	1974–75	Don Nelson, Bos	53.9
1953–54	Ed Macauley, Bos	48.6	1975–76	Wes Unseld, Wash	56.1
1954–55	Larry Foust, FW	48.7	1976–77	Kareem Abdul-Jabbar, LA	57.9
1955–56	Neil Johnston, Phil	45.7	1977–78	Bobby Jones, Den	57.8
1956–57	Neil Johnston, Phil	44.7	1978–79	Cedric Maxwell, Bos	58.4
1957–58	Jack Twyman, Cin	45.2	1979–80	Cedric Maxwell, Bos	60.9
1958–59	Ken Sears, NY	49.0	1980–81	Artis Gilmore, Chi	67.0
1959–60	Ken Sears, NY	47.7	1981–82	Artis Gilmore, Chi	65.2
1960–61	Wilt Chamberlain, Phil	50.9	1982–83	Artis Gilmore, SA	62.6
1961–62	Walt Bellamy, Chi	51.9	1983–84	Artis Gilmore, SA	63.1
1962–63	Wilt Chamberlain, SF	52.8	1984–85	James Donaldson, LA Clippers	63.7
1963–64	Jerry Lucas, Cin	52.7	1985–86	Steve Johnson, SA	63.2
1964–65	Wilt Chamberlain, SF-Phil	51.0	1986–87	Kevin McHale, Bos	60.4
1965–66	Wilt Chamberlain, Phil	54.0	1987–88	Kevin McHale, Bos	60.4
1966–67	Wilt Chamberlain, Phil	68.3	1988–89	Dennis Rodman, Det	59.5
1967–68	Wilt Chamberlain, Phil	59.5	1989–90	Mark West, Phoe	62.5

Field-Goal Percentage (Cont.)

1990–91	Buck Williams, Port	60.2
1991–92	Buck Williams, Port	60.4
1992–93	Cedric Ceballos, Phoe	57.6
1993–94	Shaquille O'Neal, Orl	59.9
1994–95	Chris Gatling, GS	63.3
1995–96	Gheorghe Muresan, Wash	58.4
1996–97	Gheorghe Muresan, Wash	60.4
1997–98	Shaquille O'Neal, LA Lakers	58.4
1998–99	Shaquille O'Neal, LA Lakers	57.6
1999–00	Shaquille O'Neal, LA Lakers	57.4
2000–01	Shaquille O'Neal, LA Lakers	57.2
2001–02	Shaquille O'Neal, LA Lakers	57.9
2002–03	Eddy Curry, Chi	58.5
2003–04	Shaquille O'Neal, LA Lakers	58.4
2004–05	Shaquille O'Neal, Mia	60.1

Free-Throw Percentage

1946–47	Fred Scolari, Wash	81.1
1947–48	Bob Feerick, Wash	78.8
1948–49	Bob Feerick, Wash	85.9
1949–50	Max Zaslofsky, Chi	84.3
1950–51	Joe Fulks, Phil	85.5
1951–52	Bob Wanzer, Roch	90.4
1952–53	Bill Sharman, Bos	85.0
1953–54	Bill Sharman, Bos	84.4
1954–55	Bill Sharman, Bos	89.7
1955–56	Bill Sharman, Bos	86.7
1956–57	Bill Sharman, Bos	90.5
1957–58	Dolph Schayes, Syr	90.4
1958–59	Bill Sharman, Bos	93.2
1959–60	Dolph Schayes, Syr	89.2
1960–61	Bill Sharman, Bos	92.1
1961–62	Dolph Schayes, Syr	89.6
1962–63	Larry Costello, Syr	88.1
1963–64	Oscar Robertson, Cin	85.3
1964–65	Larry Costello, Phil	87.7
1965–66	Larry Siegfried, Bos	88.1
1966–67	Adrian Smith, Cin	90.3
1967–68	Oscar Robertson, Cin	87.3
1968–69	Larry Siegfried, Bos	86.4
1969–70	Flynn Robinson, Mil	89.8
1970–71	Chet Walker, Chi	85.9
1971–72	Jack Marin, Balt	89.4
1972–73	Rick Barry, GS	90.2
1973–74	Ernie DiGregorio, Buff	90.2
1974–75	Rick Barry, GS	90.4
1975–76	Rick Barry, GS	92.3
1976–77	Ernie DiGregorio, Buff	94.5
1977–78	Rick Barry, GS	92.4
1978–79	Rick Barry, Hou	94.7
1979–80	Rick Barry, Hou	93.5
1980–81	Calvin Murphy, Hou	95.8
1981–82	Kyle Macy, Phoe	89.9
1982–83	Calvin Murphy, Hou	92.0
1983–84	Larry Bird, Bos	88.8
1984–85	Kyle Macy, Phoe	90.7
1985–86	Larry Bird, Bos	89.6
1986–87	Larry Bird, Bos	91.0
1987–88	Jack Sikma, Mil	92.2
1988–89	Magic Johnson, LA Lakers	91.1
1989–90	Larry Bird, Bos	93.0
1990–91	Reggie Miller, Ind	91.8
1991–92	Mark Price, Clev	94.7
1992–93	Mark Price, Clev	94.8
1993–94	Mahmoud Abdul-Rauf, Den	95.6
1994–95	Spud Webb, Sac	93.4
1995–96	Mahmoud Abdul-Rauf, Den	93.0
1996–97	Mark Price, GS	90.6
1997–98	Chris Mullin, Ind	93.9
1998–99	Reggie Miller, Ind	91.5
1999–00	Jeff Hornacek, Utah	95.0
2000–01	Reggie Miller, Ind	92.8
2001–02	Reggie Miller, Ind	91.1
2002–03	Allan Houston, NY	91.9
2003–04	Peja Stojakovic, Sac	92.7
2004–05	Reggie Miller, Ind	93.3

Three-Point Field-Goal Percentage

1979–80	Fred Brown, Sea	44.3
1980–81	Brian Taylor, SD	38.3
1981–82	Campy Russell, NY	43.9
1982–83	Mike Dunleavy, SA	34.5
1983–84	Darrell Griffith, Utah	36.1
1984–85	Byron Scott, LA Lakers	43.3
1985–86	Craig Hodges, Mil	45.1
1986–87	Kiki Vandeweghe, Por	48.1
1987–88	Craig Hodges, Mil-Phoe	49.1
1988–89	Jon Sundvold, Mia	52.2
1989–90	Steve Kerr, Clev	50.7
1990–91	Jim Les, Sac	46.1
1991–92	Dana Barros, Sea	44.6
1992–93	B.J. Armstrong, Chi	45.3
1993–94	Tracy Murray, Por	45.9
1994–95	Steve Kerr, Chi	52.4
1995–96	Tim Legler, Wash	52.2
1996–97	Kevin Gamble, Sac	48.2
1997–98	Dale Ellis, Sea	46.0
1998–99	Dell Curry, Char	47.6
1999–00	Hubert Davis, Dall	49.1
2000–01	Brent Barry, Sea	47.6
2001–02	Steve Smith, SA	47.2
2002–03	Bruce Bowen, SA	44.1
2003–04	Anthony Peeler, Sac	48.2
2004–05	Fred Hoiberg, Minn	49.6

Steals

1973–74	Larry Steele, Por	2.68
1974–75	Rick Barry, GS	2.85
1975–76	Don Watts, Sea	3.18
1976–77	Don Buse, Ind	3.47
1977–78	Ron Lee, Phoe	2.74
1978–79	M.L. Carr, Det	2.46
1979–80	Micheal Richardson, NY	3.23
1980–81	Magic Johnson, LA	3.43
1981–82	Magic Johnson, LA	2.67
1982–83	Micheal Richardson, GS-NJ	2.84
1983–84	Rickey Green, Utah	2.65
1984–85	Micheal Richardson, NJ	2.96
1985–86	Alvin Robertson, SA	3.67
1986–87	Alvin Robertson, SA	3.21
1987–88	Michael Jordan, Chi	3.16
1988–89	John Stockton, Utah	3.21
1989–90	Michael Jordan, Chi	2.77
1990–91	Alvin Robertson, Mil	3.04
1991–92	John Stockton, Utah	2.98
1992–93	Michael Jordan, Chi	2.83
1993–94	Nate McMillan, Sea	2.96
1994–95	Scottie Pippen, Chi	2.94
1995–96	Gary Payton, Sea	2.85
1996–97	Mookie Blaylock, Atl	2.72
1997–98	Mookie Blaylock, Atl	2.6
1998–99	Kendall Gill, NJ	2.68
1999–00	Eddie Jones, Char	2.67
2000–01	Allen Iverson, Phil	2.5
2001–02	Allen Iverson, Phil	2.80
2002–03	Allen Iverson, Phil	2.74
2003–04	Baron Davis, NO	2.36
2004–05	Larry Hughes, Wash	2.89

Blocked Shots

1973–74	Elmore Smith, LA	4.85	1989–90	Hakeem Olajuwon, Hou	4.59
1974–75	Kareem Abdul-Jabbar, Mil	3.26	1990–91	Hakeem Olajuwon, Hou	3.95
1975–76	Kareem Abdul-Jabbar, LA	4.12	1991–92	David Robinson, SA	4.49
1976–77	Bill Walton, Port	3.25	1992–93	Hakeem Olajuwon, Hou	4.17
1977–78	George Johnson, NJ	3.38	1993–94	Dikembe Mutombo, Den	4.10
1978–79	Kareem Abdul-Jabbar, LA	3.95	1994–95	Dikembe Mutombo, Den	3.91
1979–80	Kareem Abdul-Jabbar, LA	3.41	1995–96	Dikembe Mutombo, Den	4.49
1980–81	George Johnson, SA	3.39	1996–97	Shawn Bradley, NJ	3.40
1981–82	George Johnson, SA	3.12	1997–98	Marcus Camby, Tor	3.65
1982–83	Wayne Rollins, Atl	4.29	1998–99	Alonzo Mourning, Mia	3.91
1983–84	Mark Eaton, Utah	4.28	1999–00	Alonzo Mourning, Mia	3.72
1984–85	Mark Eaton, Utah	5.56	2000–01	Theo Ratliff, Phil/Atl	3.74
1985–86	Manute Bol, Wash	4.96	2001–02	Ben Wallace, Det	3.48
1986–87	Mark Eaton, Utah	4.06	2002–03	Theo Ratliff, Atl	3.23
1987–88	Mark Eaton, Utah	3.71	2003–04	Theo Ratliff, Port	3.61
1988–89	Manute Bol, GS	4.31	2004–05	Andrei Kirilenko, Utah	3.32

NBA All-Star Game Results

Year	Result	Site	Winning Coach	Most Valuable Player
1951	East 111, West 94	Boston	Joe Lapchick	Ed Macauley, Bos
1952	East 108, West 91	Boston	Al Cervi	Paul Arizin, Phil
1953	West 79, East 75	Ft Wayne	John Kundla	George Mikan, Minn
1954	East 98, West 93 (OT)	New York	Joe Lapchick	Bob Cousy, Bos
1955	East 100, West 91	New York	Al Cervi	Bill Sharman, Bos
1956	West 108, East 94	Rochester	Charley Eckman	Bob Pettit, StL
1957	East 109, West 97	Boston	Red Auerbach	Bob Cousy, Bos
1958	East 130, West 118	St Louis	Red Auerbach	Bob Pettit, StL
1959	West 124, East 108	Detroit	Ed Macauley	B. Pettit, StL/E. Baylor, Minn
1960	East 125, West 115	Philadelphia	Red Auerbach	Wilt Chamberlain, Phil
1961	West 153, East 131	Syracuse	Paul Seymour	Oscar Robertson, Cin
1962	West 150, East 130	St Louis	Fred Schaus	Bob Pettit, StL
1963	East 115, West 108	Los Angeles	Red Auerbach	Bill Russell, Bos
1964	East 111, West 107	Boston	Red Auerbach	Oscar Robertson, Cin
1965	East 124, West 123	St Louis	Red Auerbach	Jerry Lucas, Cin
1966	East 137, West 94	Cincinnati	Red Auerbach	Adrian Smith, Cin
1967	West 135, East 120	San Francisco	Fred Schaus	Rick Barry, SF
1968	East 144, West 124	New York	Alex Hannum	Hal Greer, Phil
1969	East 123, West 112	Baltimore	Gene Shue	Oscar Robertson, Cin
1970	East 142, West 135	Philadelphia	Red Holzman	Willis Reed, NY
1971	West 108, East 107	San Diego	Larry Costello	Lenny Wilkens, Sea
1972	West 112, East 110	Los Angeles	Bill Sharman	Jerry West, LA
1973	East 104, West 84	Chicago	Tom Heinsohn	Dave Cowens, Bos
1974	West 134, East 123	Seattle	Larry Costello	Bob Lanier, Det
1975	East 108, West 102	Phoenix	K.C. Jones	Walt Frazier, NY
1976	East 123, West 109	Philadelphia	Tom Heinsohn	Dave Bing, Wash
1977	West 125, East 124	Milwaukee	Larry Brown	Julius Erving, Phil
1978	East 133, West 125	Atlanta	Billy Cunningham	Randy Smith, Buff
1979	West 134, East 129	Detroit	Lenny Wilkens	David Thompson, Den
1980	East 144, West 135 (OT)	Washington	Billy Cunningham	George Gervin, SA
1981	East 123, West 120	Cleveland	Billy Cunningham	Nate Archibald, Bos
1982	East 120, West 118	New Jersey	Bill Fitch	Larry Bird, Bos
1983	East 132, West 123	Los Angeles	Billy Cunningham	Julius Erving, Phil
1984	East 154, West 145 (OT)	Denver	K.C. Jones	Isiah Thomas, Det
1985	West 140, East 129	Indiana	Pat Riley	Ralph Sampson, Hou
1986	East 139, West 132	Dallas	K.C. Jones	Isiah Thomas, Det
1987	West 154, East 149 (OT)	Seattle	Pat Riley	Tom Chambers, Sea
1988	East 138, West 133	Chicago	Mike Fratello	Michael Jordan, Chi
1989	West 143, East 134	Houston	Pat Riley	Karl Malone, Utah
1990	East 130, West 113	Miami	Chuck Daly	Magic Johnson, LA Lakers
1991	East 116, West 114	Charlotte	Chris Ford	Charles Barkley, Phil
1992	West 153, East 113	Orlando	Don Nelson	Magic Johnson, LA Lakers
1993	West 135, East 132	Salt Lake City	Paul Westphal	K. Malone/ J. Stockton, Utah
1994	East 127, West 118	Minneapolis	Lenny Wilkens	Scottie Pippen, Chi
1995	West 139, East 112	Phoenix	Paul Westphal	Mitch Richmond, Sac
1996	East 129, West 118	San Antonio	Phil Jackson	Michael Jordan, Chi
1997	East 132, West 120	Cleveland	Doug Collins	Glen Rice, Char
1998	East 135, West 114	New York	Larry Bird	Michael Jordan, Chi
1999	Cancelled due to lockout.			
2000	West 137, East 126	Oakland	Phil Jackson	O'Neal, Lakers/T. Duncan,SA
2001	East 111, West 110	Washington	Larry Brown	Allen Iverson, Phil
2002	West 135, East 120	Philadelphia	Don Nelson	Kobe Bryant, LA Lakers
2003	West 155, East 145 (2OT)	Atlanta	Rick Adelman	Kevin Garnett, Minn
2004	West 136, East 132	Los Angeles	Flip Saunders	Shaquille O'Neal, LA Lakers
2005	East 125, West 115	Denver	Stan Van Gundy	Allen Iverson, Phil

Members of the Basketball Hall of Fame

Contributors

Senda Abbott (1984)
Forest C. (Phog) Allen (1959)
Clair F. Bee (1967)
Danny Biasone (2000)
Hubie Brown (2005)
Walter A. Brown (1965)
John W. Bunn (1964)
Jerry Colangelo (2004)
Bob Douglas (1971)
Al Duer (1981)
Wayne Embry (1999)
Clifford Fagan (1983)
Harry A. Fisher (1973)
Larry Fleisher (1991)
Edward Gottlieb (1971)
Luther H. Gulick (1959)
Lester Harrison (1979)
Chick Hearn (2003)

Ferenc Hepp (1980)
Edward J. Hickox (1959)
Paul D. (Tony) Hinkle (1965)
Ned Irish (1964)
R. William Jones (1964)
J. Walter Kennedy (1980)
Meadowlark Lemon (2003)
Emil S. Liston (1974)
Earl Lloyd (2003)
John B. McLendon (1978)
Bill Mokray (1965)
Ralph Morgan (1959)
Frank Morgenweck (1962)
James Naismith (1959)
Peter F. Newell (1978)
C.M. Newton (2000)
John J. O'Brien (1961)
Larry O'Brien (1991)

Harold G. Olsen (1959)
Maurice Podoloff (1973)
H. V. Porter (1960)
William A. Reid (1963)
Elmer Ripley (1972)
Lynn W. St. John (1962)
Abe Saperstein (1970)
Arthur A. Schabinger (1961)
Amos Alonzo Stagg (1959)
Boris Stankovic (1991)
Edward Steitz (1983)
Chuck Taylor (1968)
Oswald Tower (1959)
Arthur L. Trester (1961)
Clifford Wells (1971)
Lou Wilke (1982)
Fred Zollner (1999)

Players

Kareem Abdul-Jabbar (1995)
Nate (Tiny) Archibald (1991)
Paul J. Arizin (1977)
Thomas B. Barlow (1980)
Rick Barry (1987)
Elgin Baylor (1976)
John Beckman (1972)
Walt Bellamy (1993)
Sergei Belov (1992)
Dave Bing (1990)
Larry Bird (1998)
Carol Blazejowski (1994)
Bennie Borgmann (1961)
Bill Bradley (1982)
Joseph Brennan (1974)
Al Cervi (1984)
Wilt Chamberlain (1978)
Charles (Tarzan) Cooper (1976)
Kresimir Cosic (1996)
Bob Cousy (1970)
Dave Cowens (1991)
Joan Crawford (1997)
Billy Cunningham (1986)
Denise Curry (1997)
Drazen Dalipagic (2004)
Bob Davies (1969)
Forrest S. DeBernardi (1961)
Dave DeBusschere (1982)
H.G. (Dutch) Dehnert (1968)
Anne Donovan (1995)
Clyde Drexler (2004)
Paul Endacott (1971)
Alex English (1997)
Julius Erving (1993)
Harold (Bud) Foster (1964)
Walter (Clyde) Frazier (1987)
Max (Marty) Friedman (1971)
Joe Fulks (1977)
Lauren (Laddie) Gale (1976)
Harry (the Horse) Gallatin (1991)
William Gates (1989)
George Gervin (1996)
Tom Gola (1975)
Gail Goodrich (1996)

Hal Greer (1981)
Robert (Ace) Gruenig (1963)
Clifford O. Hagan (1977)
Victor Hanson (1960)
John Havlicek (1983)
Connie Hawkins (1992)
Elvin Hayes (1990)
Marques Haynes (1998)
Tom Heinsohn (1986)
Nat Holman (1964)
Robert J. Houbregs (1987)
Bailey Howell (1997)
Chuck Hyatt (1959)
Dan Issel (1993)
Harry (Buddy) Jeannette (1994)
Earvin (Magic) Johnson (2002)
William C. Johnson (1976)
D. Neil Johnston (1990)
K.C. Jones (1989)
Sam Jones (1983)
Edward (Moose) Krause (1975)
Bob Kurland (1961)
Bob Lanier (1992)
Joe Lapchick (1966)
Nancy Lieberman-Cline (1996)
Clyde Lovellette (1988)
Jerry Lucas (1979)
Angelo (Hank) Luisetti (1959)
C. Edward Macauley (1960)
Moses Malone (2001)
Peter P. Maravich (1987)
Hortencia Marcari (2005)
Slater Martin (1981)
Bob McAdoo (2000)
Branch McCracken (1960)
Jack McCracken (1962)
Bobby McDermott (1988)
Dick McGuire (1993)
Kevin McHale (1999)
Dino Meneghin (2003)
Ann Meyers (1993)
George L. Mikan (1959)
Vern Mikkelsen (1995)
Cheryl Miller (1995)

Earl Monroe (1990)
Calvin Murphy (1993)
Charles (Stretch) Murphy (1960)
H. O. (Pat) Page (1962)
Robert Parish (2003)
Drazen Petrovic (2002)
Bob Pettit (1970)
Andy Phillip (1961)
Jim Pollard (1977)
Frank Ramsey (1981)
Willis Reed (1981)
Arnie Risen (1998)
Oscar Robertson (1979)
John S. Roosma (1961)
Bill Russell (1974)
John (Honey) Russell (1964)
Adolph Schayes (1972)
Ernest J. Schmidt (1973)
John J. Schommer (1959)
Barney Sedran (1962)
Uljana Semjonova (1993)
Bill Sharman (1975)
Christian Steinmetz (1961)
Lusia Harris Stewart (1992)
Maurice Stokes (2004)
Isiah Thomas (2000)
David Thompson (1996)
John A. (Cat) Thompson (1962)
Nate Thurmond (1984)
Jack Twyman (1982)
Wes Unseld (1988)
Robert (Fuzzy) Vandivier (1974)
Edward A. Wachter (1961)
Bill Walton (1993)
Robert F. Wanzer (1987)
Jerry West (1979)
Nera White (1992)
Lenny Wilkens (1989)
Lynette Woodard (2004)
John R. Wooden (1960)
James Worthy (2003)
George (Bird) Yardley (1996)

Coaches

Harold Anderson (1984)
Red Auerbach (1968)
Leon Barmore (2003)
Sam Barry (1978)
Ernest A. Blood (1960)
Jim Boeheim (2005)
Larry Brown (2002)

Jim Calhoun (2005)
Howard G. Cann (1967)
H. Clifford Carlson (1959)
Lou Carnesecca (1992)
Ben Carnevale (1969)
Pete Carril (1997)
Everett Case (1981)

John Chaney (2001)
Jody Conradt (1998)
Denny Crum (1994)
Chuck Daly (1994)
Everett S. Dean (1966)
Antonio Diaz-Miguel (1997)
Edgar A. Diddle (1971)

Note: Year of election in parentheses.

Coaches *(Cont.)*

Bruce Drake (1972)
Clarence Gaines (1981)
Jack Gardner (1983)
Amory T. (Slats) Gill (1967)
Aleksandr Gomelsky (1995)
Sue Gunter (2005)
Alex Hannum (1998)
Marv Harshman (1984)
Don Haskins (1997)
Edgar S. Hickey (1978)
Howard A. Hobson (1965)
Red Holzman (1986)
Hank Iba (1968)
Alvin F. (Doggie) Julian (1967)
Frank W. Keaney (1960)
George E. Keogan (1961)
Bob Knight (1991)

Mike Krzyzewski (2001)
John Kundla (1995)
Ward L. Lambert (1960)
Harry Litwack (1975)
Kenneth D. Loeffler (1964)
A.C. (Dutch) Lonborg (1972)
Arad A. McCutchan (1980)
Al McGuire (1992)
Frank McGuire (1976)
Walter E. Meanwell (1959)
Raymond J. Meyer (1978)
Ralph Miller (1988)
Billie Moore (1999)
Aleksandar Nikolic (1998)
Lute Olson (2002
Jack Ramsay (1992)
Cesare Rubini (1994)

Adolph F. Rupp (1968)
Leonard D. Sachs (1961)
Bill Sharman (2004)
Everett F. Shelton (1979)
Dean Smith (1982)
Pat Summitt (2000)
Fred R. Taylor (1985)
Bertha Teague (1984)
John Thompson (1999)
Margaret Wade (1984)
Stanley H. Watts (1985)
Lenny Wilkens (1998)
John R. Wooden (1972)
Morgan Wooten (2000)
Phil Woolpert (1992)
Kay Yow (2002)

Referees

James E. Enright (1978)
George T. Hepbron (1960)
George Hoyt (1961)
Matthew P. Kennedy (1959)
Lloyd Leith (1982)
Zigmund J. Mihalik (1985)

John P. Nucatola (1977)
Ernest C. Quigley (1961)
J. Dallas Shirley (1979)
Earl Strom (1995)
David Tobey (1961)
David H. Walsh (1961)

Teams

Buffalo Germans (1961)
First Team (1959)
Harlem Globetrotters (2002)
Original Celtics (1959)
Renaissance (1963)

ABA Champions

Year	Champion	Series	Runner-up	Winning Coach
1968	Pittsburgh Pipers	4–3	New Orleans Bucs	Vince Cazetta
1969	Oakland Oaks	4–1	Indiana Pacers	Alex Hannum
1970	Indiana Pacers	4–2	Los Angeles Stars	Bob Leonard
1971	Utah Stars	4–3	Kentucky Colonels	Bill Sharman
1972	Indiana Pacers	4–2	New York Nets	Bob Leonard
1973	Indiana Pacers	4–3	Kentucky Colonels	Bob Leonard
1974	New York Nets	4–1	Utah Stars	Kevin Loughery
1975	Kentucky Colonels	4–1	Indiana Pacers	Hubie Brown
1976	New York Nets	4–2	Denver Nuggets	Kevin Loughery

ABA Postseason Awards

Most Valuable Player

1967–68	Connie Hawkins, Pitt
1968–69	Mel Daniels, Ind
1969–70	Spencer Haywood, Den
1970–71	Mel Daniels, Ind
1971–72	Artis Gilmore, Ken
1972–73	Billy Cunningham, Car
1973–74	Julius Erving, NY
1974–75	Julius Erving, NY
	George McGinnis, Ind
1975–76	Julius Erving, NY

Rookie of the Year

1967–68	Mel Daniels, Minn
1968–69	Warren Armstrong, Oak
1969–70	Spencer Haywood, Den
1970–71	Charlie Scott, Vir
	Dan Issel, Ken
1971–72	Artis Gilmore, Ken
1972–73	Brian Taylor, NY
1973–74	Swen Nater, SA
1974–75	Marvin Barnes, StL
1975–76	David Thompson, Den

Coach of the Year

1967–68	Vince Cazetta, Pitt
1968–69	Alex Hannum, Oak
1969–70	Bill Sharman, LA
	Joe Belmont, Den
1970–71	Al Bianchi, Vir
1971–72	Tom Nissalke, Dall
1972–73	Larry Brown, Car
1973–74	Babe McCarthy, Ken
	Joe Mullaney, Utah
1974–75	Larry Brown, Den
1975–76	Larry Brown, Den

ABA Season Leaders

Scoring

		GP	Pts	Avg
1967–68	Connie Hawkins, Pitt	70	1875	26.8
1968–69	Rick Barry, Oak	35	1190	34.0
1969–70	Spencer Haywood, Den	84	2519	30.0
1970–71	Dan Issel, Ken	83	2480	29.4
1971–72	Charlie Scott, Vir	73	2524	34.6
1972–73	Julius Erving, Vir	71	2268	31.9
1973–74	Julius Erving, NY	84	2299	27.4
1974–75	George McGinnis, Ind	79	2353	29.8
1975–76	Julius Erving, NY	84	2462	29.3

Assists

1967–68	Larry Brown, NO	6.5
1968–69	Larry Brown, Oak	7.1
1969–70	Larry Brown, Wash	7.1
1970–71	Bill Melchionni, NY	8.3
1971–72	Bill Melchionni, NY	8.4
1972–73	Bill Melchionni, NY	7.5
1973–74	Al Smith, Den	8.2
1974–75	Mack Calvin, Den	7.7
1975–76	Don Buse, Ind	8.2

Rebounds

1967–68	Mel Daniels, Minn	15.6
1968–69	Mel Daniels, Ind	16.5
1969–70	Spencer Haywood, Den	19.5
1970–71	Mel Daniels, Ind	18.0
1971–72	Artis Gilmore, Ken	17.8
1972–73	Artis Gilmore, Ken	17.5
1973–74	Artis Gilmore, Ken	18.3
1974–75	Swen Nater, SA	16.4
1975–76	Artis Gilmore, Ken	15.5

Steals

1973–74	Ted McClain, Car	2.98
1974–75	Brian Taylor, NY	2.80
1975–76	Don Buse, Ind	4.12

Blocked Shots

1973–74	Caldwell Jones, SD	4.00
1974–75	Caldwell Jones, SD	3.24
1975–76	Billy Paultz, SA	3.05

World Championship of Basketball

Year	Winner	Runner-Up	Score	Site
1950	Argentina	United States	†	Rio de Janeiro
1954	United States	Brazil	†	Rio de Janeiro
1959	Brazil	United States	†	Santiago, Chile
1963	Brazil	Yugoslavia	†	Rio de Janeiro
1967	Soviet Union	Yugoslavia	†	Montevideo, Uruguay
1970	Yugoslavia	Brazil	†	Ljubljana, Yugoslavia
1974	Soviet Union	Yugoslavia	†	San Juan
1978	Yugoslavia	Soviet Union	82–81 (OT)	Manila
1982	Soviet Union	United States	95–94	Cali, Colombia
1986	United States	Soviet Union	87–85	Madrid
1990	Yugoslavia	Soviet Union	92–75	Buenos Aires
1994*	United States	Russia	137–91	Toronto
1998	Yugoslavia	Russia	64–62	Athens
2002	Yugoslavia	Argentina	84–77 (OT)	Indianapolis

*U.S. professionals began competing in 1994. In 1998, a labor dispute resulted in a boycott of the World Championship by NBA stars; the U.S. roster was filled by members of the CBA and European professional leagues and college players.
†Result determined by overall record in final round of competition.

THEY SAID IT

Jeanie Buss, Lakers vice president, on the strained relationship between her father, Lakers owner Jerry Buss, and her boyfriend, former coach Phil Jackson: "I'm now the national spokesperson for not mixing business and pleasure."

College Basketball

Sean May powered
North Carolina to its
fourth national
championship.

Power Surge

At the end of a topsy-turvy tournament, UNC outmuscled favorite Illinois to win the title and restore the grandeur to Tar Heel basketball

BY B.J. SCHECTER

SEAN MAY LAY ON THE FLOOR OF the Edward Jones Dome, exhausted and out of breath. All around him his teammates were celebrating, cutting down the nets, whooping it up on the court and gesturing to the droves of North Carolina fans in the stands who were cheering their every move. The Tar Heels had just defeated top-ranked Illinois, 75-70, to win the national title thanks to the dominance of May, and now the junior center just needed to catch his breath. "What's this, my big man is tired?" Carolina coach Roy Williams said to May, who looked up and smiled. "Yeah, coach," May answered, "that was a tough one. I just need to lay down for a few minutes."

If anyone had earned the right to sprawl out on the game's biggest stage, it was May. The 6'9", 260-pound junior center continually killed gritty Illinois with his wide body, heart and determination, scoring a game-high 26 points (on 10 of 11 shooting) and grabbing 10 rebounds. At the Tar Heels' team meal before the game, several of May's teammates came up to him and said, "I hope you're hungry

because we're going to be feeding you all night." May wasn't exactly sure what they meant at first, but once the game started May began to have a feast in the post, overpowering every Illinois defender who stood in his way.

It was just the type of performance that Illinois coaches gravely feared. As the Illini coaches watched game film of North Carolina in room 815 of the Marriott in downtown St. Louis two nights before the final, a flurry of May highlights were played over and over again. "He's a man, he's a beast," said Illinois coach Bruce Weber as he rewound the tape and shook his head. "We've got to get to May in the first 10 seconds. We have to post trap him. I'm not saying he's not going to score after that but we have to get a body on him early and push him off the block. That's the key." Instead, May was the one doing the pushing on the block and when he got the ball in the low post he wouldn't be denied.

May had extra motivation coming into the championship game. All year, he had heard that North Carolina had the talent but not the heart to win the title. And in

the two days leading up to the final the media kept pushing the theme that Carolina had the most talent but Illinois was the better team. May wasn't buying any of it. Back in the preseason, Williams wrote a series of dates on a board in the Tar Heels' locker room. One was April 4, the date of the national championship game. It was also—unbeknownst to anyone on the team at the time—May's 21st birthday. When he saw April 4 on the board, May grew excited and said: "Coach, I promise you it's going to be a very special day."

And it was. On the afternoon of the final, May watched a video of the 1976 final, in which May's father, Scott, helped Indiana cap off a perfect season with a national championship. Sean had often watched the clips of the '76 Hoosiers for inspiration, but as North Carolina was warming up before the title game, May was

UNC coach Roy Williams finally achieved the title victory that had eluded him at Kansas.

caught off guard when the Jumbotron played a clip of his father embracing teammate Quinn Buckner after Indiana's victory. "I froze," said May. "That really pumped me up. It gave me goose bumps."

North Carolina would need everything May had to hold off Illinois, which was in the midst of a dream season and entered the game 37-1. The Tar Heels built a 13-point lead at the half, bolstered by May and enigmatic guard Rashad McCants, who scored all 14 of his points in the first 20 minutes. But Illinois came roaring back, and after the Illini tied the game at 70 on a Luthar Head three-pointer with just over two minutes remaining, the roof of the Edwards Jones Dome—which was filled with a sea of orange—nearly came off.

However, Carolina never lost its cool. After McCants threw up a wild shot in the lane, fantastic freshman Marvin Williams followed it up with a tip-in to give the Tar Heels a 72-70 advantage. (Williams was a perfect example of the Tar Heels' wealth of talent. He didn't even start, yet was the second overall pick in the NBA draft less than three months later.)

It was a lead North Carolina would never relinquish. Illinois had two final chances to tie or take the lead. On their second attempt, Head got the ball after his own missed three-point attempt and drove through the lane, attempting to dish it off to teammate Jack Ingram, who was standing outside the arc. But Carolina point guard Raymond Felton stepped into the passing lane, stole the ball and was fouled with 31 seconds left (he hit one of two free throws). The cold-blooded steal took all of the wind out of Illinois. "That steal was the key to the game," said May. "After that, we could see the doubt in their eyes."

When the final buzzer sounded, May skipped around the floor and pumped his fists as confetti rained down. Coach Williams raised his hands in the air, caught his breath and looked up to the private box where his mentor Dean Smith and North Carolina alum Michael Jordan were sitting. Then, unexpectedly, Williams sprinted off the court and took off down a tunnel after Weber. When he caught up with the Illinois coach he tried to console him, telling Weber that he had been on the losing end many times before and that he felt for him. When Williams returned to the floor, he told anyone who would listen that he was happy for his kids—a couple of whom had lived through a 20-loss season three years earlier—and that he wasn't a better coach than three hours before. But in a sense he was. Williams joined an elite fraternity and brought a storied program back to glory in the process.

North Carolina may have won the national title, but the regular season belonged to Illinois. On December 1, the Illini announced themselves as the team to beat by crushing then-No. 1 Wake Forest, 91-73. They wouldn't relinquish the top spot until losing to the Tar Heels. With a high-powered three-guard offense led by the efficient Deron Williams and the dynamic Dee Brown, Illinois ran, shot and passed teams out of the gym. The Illini nearly went undefeated in the regular season, losing only at Ohio State, 65-64, in early March and entered the NCAA tournament as the overwhelming favorite.

"I haven't seen a team in 10 to 12 years swing the ball as quickly and efficiently as they do," said Gonzaga coach Mark Few after his Zags were trounced by the Illini, 89-72, in November. "If you're not playing against them, it's a joy to watch because it's how basketball should be played."

Illinois' dream season nearly ended in the Chicago Regional final against Arizona. With the Illini trailing by 15 points and only four minutes remaining, Williams got in his teammates' faces and pleaded with them to keep fighting. Illinois began pressing, Williams hit three-pointer after three-pointer and Illinois forced an overtime. And then another. Somehow Illinois came away with a 90-89 victory that Weber called "a miracle." Said Williams afterward, "I didn't want to go down without a fight."

Many mid-major schools carried the same motto into the NCAA tournament, which made the early-rounds the most thrilling and bracket-busting in years. Every year there are Cinderellas and head-scratching upsets that could only happen, say, one out of 100 times, but this year was ridiculous. How else do you explain little Vermont knocking off Big East tournament champion Syracuse, 60-57, on senior guard T.J. Sorrentine's 26-foot prayer in the closing seconds? Or Bucknell's 64-63 shocker over Kansas on Chris McNaughton's jump-hook over Jayhawks' All-American Wayne Simien with 10.5 seconds remaining? Perhaps most surprising of all was 12th-seeded Wisconsin-Milwaukee, which gave the big boys fits with its 1-2-1-1 zone press and sent No. 5 seed Alabama and No. 5 Boston College packing. When the dust cleared, just eight of the top 16 seeds remained.

BILL FRAKES

ing and hitting three-pointers to match West Virginia. The Cardinals sent the game into over-time, where they pre-vailed, 93-85.

Overtime quickly became the theme of the regional finals as three of the four games needed to go beyond regulation for the first time in history of the NCAA tournament. The comebacks of Illinois and Louisville were indeed thrilling, but the wildest one of all was the Kentucky-Michigan State game in the Austin Regional final. Michigan State, which had eliminated top-seeded Duke in the regional semifinal, held a three-point lead in the final seconds when Kentucky frantically tried to tie it.

The excitement didn't stop after the early rounds. Like a fine wine, this tournament only got better with age. As March Madness reached the regional finals all of the little guys had gone home except West Virginia, which was on the NCAA bubble before making a run to the final of the Big East tournament. The sharp-shooting Mountaineers received an early scare against Creighton, but then kicked it into high gear, knocking off top-seeded Wake Forest and Texas Tech. Then, in the Albuquerque Regional final, West Virginia opened up a 20-point first-half lead against Louisville and looked like it was headed to its first Final Four since Jerry West was the team's star in the late 1950s. But at halftime, Cardinals coach Rick Pitino scrapped his gameplan and Louisville began press-

After missing a few three-point attempts, Patrick Sparks got the ball at the top of the key, leaned in and put up a shot. The ball bounced around the rim four times before falling in, tying the game. Or so Kentucky thought. Sparks' foot appeared as if it may have been on the line, which would have made the shot a two instead of a three and the game would have been over. Officials looked at the shot at every angle for five minutes before ruling it a three. It was the right call and the game continued, lasting into double overtime before Michigan State prevailed, 94-88.

The Michigan State women also had quite a season, rallying from a 16-point deficit to beat Tennessee and gain a shot at the national title. There, the Spartans met upstart Baylor, which had come back from

MANNY MILLAN

one of the game's most respected coaches, however. Temple's John Chaney has long been an advocate for his players and has railed numerous times against NCAA rules that he said hurt players coming from difficult circumstances. He's blunt, often funny and hard, yet likeable. But he crossed the line before, during and after a late-season game with Big Five rival St. Joseph's. Prior to the game, Chaney complained that St. Joe's had set too many illegal screens and threatened to send in "one of my goons" if such infractions were not called. Sure enough, early in Temple's 63-56 loss, Chaney sent in rarely used 6'8", 250-pound Nehemiah Ingram, who committed five fouls in a matter of minutes. On the final one, Ingram threw St. Joe's forward John Bryant to the ground, causing Bryant to leave the game, writhing in pain, holding his right arm.

Chaney showed little remorse when questioned about the incident after the game, saying, in effect, I told you so. It was only after it was discovered that Bryant had suffered a fractured arm that Chaney expressed any regret. He served a self-imposed three-game suspension and then didn't coach the Owls in the Atlantic-10 tournament. He personally apologized to Bryant and his family and offered to pay their medical bills. Good gestures all, but the damage was already done. Chaney was given a second chance by the university and kept his job, but a foolish decision seriously affected his legacy.

The legacy of North Carolina coach Roy Williams will now include a national championship. Maligned at Kansas for his inability to win the big one, Williams will be viewed as a savior in Chapel Hill for bringing the Tar Heels back to prominence. Next season may be a rebuilding one after his top four players—Sean May, Rashad McCants, Raymond Felton and Marvin Williams—left school early for the NBA draft, but that doesn't matter. Coach Williams and North Carolina finished on top.

18 down to beat LSU in the other semifinal. On paper, it was a classic matchup of two teams who could really shoot and run. But led by Sophia Young and the deadly three-point shooting of Emily Niemann (5 of 7 from beyond the arc), Baylor took control from the opening tip and cruised to an 84-62 victory.

It was a remarkable transformation for Baylor and coach Kim Mulkey-Robinson. When Mulkey-Robinson, a former Louisiana Tech point guard and assistant, arrived in Waco in 2000, the Bears had just come off a 7-20 season and had never made the NCAA tournament. But Mulkey-Robinson sold her players on her high-energy, running-and-gunning system, set her sights on the top and quickly turned Baylor into a national power. "Every year, we've been getting closer and now we have it all," said Baylor senior center Steffanie Blackmon. "It takes something special to get to where we are now."

The fantastic men's NCAA tournament was preceded by an ugly incident involving

NCAA Championship Game Box Score

North Carolina 75

	Min	FG M–A	FT M–A	Reb O–T	A	PF	TP
J. Williams	22	3-6	0-0	1-5	0	1	9
R. McCants	31	6-15	0-0	1-2	1	0	14
S. May	34	10-11	6-8	2-10	2	1	26
R. Felton	35	4-9	5-6	0-3	7	4	17
J. Manuel	18	0-1	0-2	0-3	2	4	0
M. Scott	13	0-2	0-0	0-2	0	0	0
R. Terry	2	0-0	0-0	0-0	0	0	0
Q. Thomas	1	0-0	0-0	0-1	0	1	0
M. Williams	24	4-8	0-1	3-5	0	2	8
D. Noel	20	0-0	1-2	1-3	0	0	1
Totals		27-52	12-19	8-34	12	13	75

Percentages: FG-.519, FT-.632. 3-Point Goals: 9-16,.563 (M. Scott 0-1, J. Williams 3-4, R. Felton 4-5, R. McCants 2-5, M. Williams 0-1). Team Rebounds: 34. Blocked Shots: 2 (J. Williams , S. May 1). Turnovers: 10 (J. Manuel 2, R. Felton 2, S. May 1, R McCants 2, Q Thomas 1, M Williams 0-1). Steals: 4 (J. Williams 1, R. Felton, R. McCants 1).

Halftime: Connecticut 41, Gergia Tech 26.

A: 44,468.

Illinois 70

	Min	FG M–A	FT M–A	Reb O–T	A	PF	TP
J. Augustine	9	0-3	0-0	1-2	0	5	0
R. Powell Jr	38	4-10	0-0	8-14	1	2	9
L. Head	37	8-21	0-0	1-5	3	1	21
D. Williams	40	7-16	0-2	0-4	7	4	17
D. Brown	38	4-10	2-2	0-4	7	1	12
R. McBride	2	0-0	0-0	0-0	0	0	0
W. Carter	5	0-1	0-0	1-1	0	1	0
N. Smith	1	0-0	0-0	0-0	0	0	0
J. Ingram	30	4-9	2-2	5-7	0	4	11
Totals		27-70	4-6	16-37	18	18	70

Percentages: FG-.386, FT-.667. 3-Point Goals:12-40, .300 (J. Ingram 1-3, L. Head 5-16, R. Powell 1-2, D Brown 2-8, D Williams 3-10, W Carter 0-1). Team Rebounds: 37. Blocked Shots: 1 (L. Head 1). Turnovers: 8 (L. Head 4, R. Powell 2, J Augustine 1, D Williams 1). Steals: 8 (L. Head 2, R. Powell 1, D. Brown 3, D. Williams 1; W. Carter).

Officials: Ed Corbett, John Cahill, Verne Harris

Final AP Top 25

National Invitation Tournament Scores

Opening round: Davidson 77, Virginia Commonwealth 62; CS Fullerton 85, Oregon State 83; Southwest Missouri State 105, Rice 82; San Francisco 69, Denver 67; Western Kentucky 88, Kent State 80 OT; Wichita State 85, Houston 69; Buffalo 81, Drexel 76 OT; Saint Joseph's 53, Hofstra 44

First round: Western Michigan 54, Marquette 40; Holy Cross 78, Notre Dame 73; South Carlina 69, Miami 63; Virginia Tech 60, Temple 50; DePaul 75, Missouri 70; Texas Christian 60, Miami(Ohio) 58; Georgetown 64, Boston U. 34; Vanderbilt 67, Indiana 60; Texas A&M 82, Clemson 74; Maryland 85, Oral Roberts 72; Memphis 90, Northeastern 65; UNLV 89, Arizona State 78; CS Fullerton 85, San Francisco 69; Saint Joseph's 55, Buffalo 50; Davidson 82, Southwest Missouri State 71; Wichita State 84, Western Kentucky 81

Second round: Memphis 83, Virginia Tech 62; Texas A&M 75, DePaul 72; Texas Christian 78, Western Michigan 76 OT; Saint Joseph's 68, Holy Cross 60; Vanderbilt 65, Wichita State 63; Georgetown 74, CS Fullerton 57; South Carolina 77, UNLV 66; Maryland 78, Davidson 63

Quarterfinals: Saint Joseph's 58, Texas A&M 51; Memphis 81, Vanderbilt 68; South Carolina 69, Georgetown 66; Maryland 85, Texas Christian 73

Semifinals: Saint Joseph's 70, Memphis 58; South Carolina 75, Maryland 67

Championship Game: South Carolina 60, Saint Joseph's 57

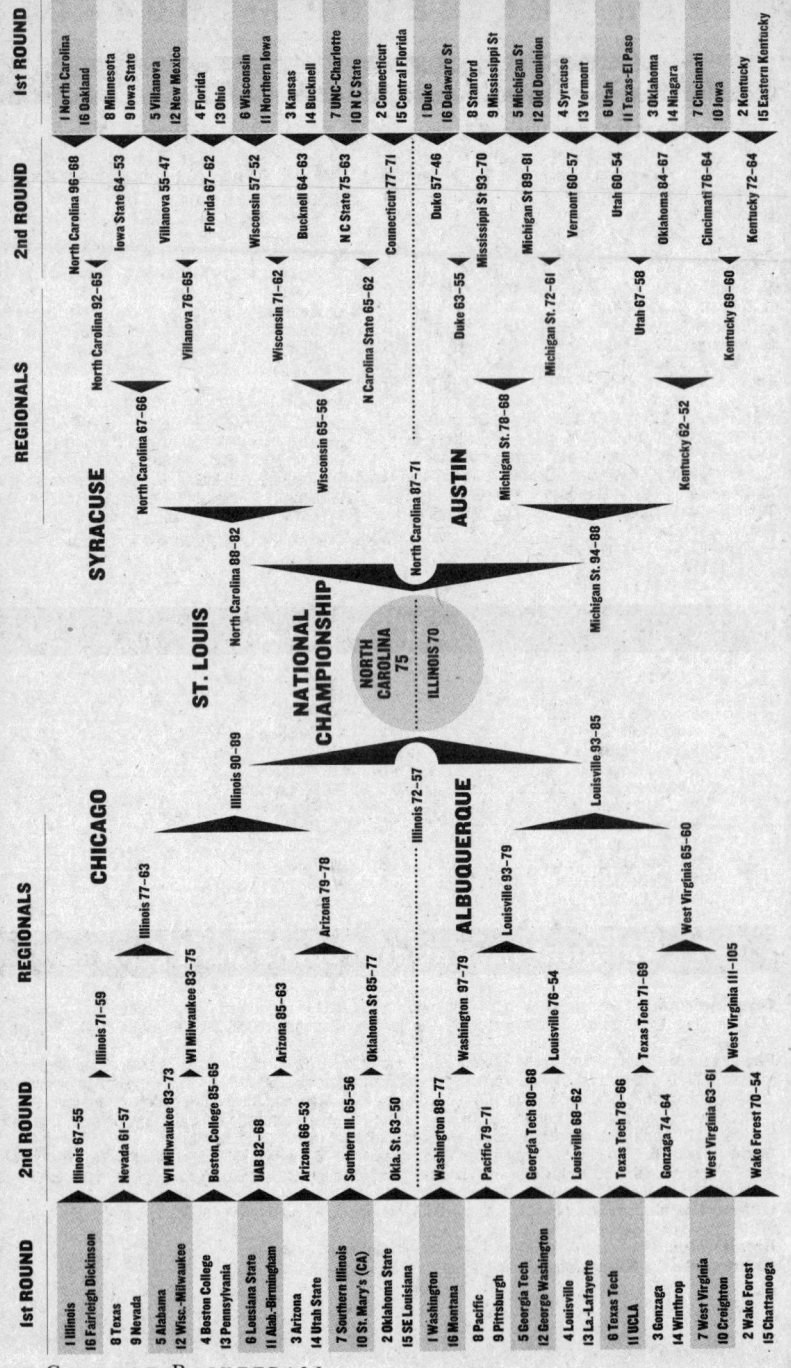

America East

	Conference			All Games		
	W	L	Pct	W	L	Pct
Vermont	17	2	.895	23	6	.793
Northeastern	15	3	.833	21	8	.724
Boston U.	14	4	.778	20	8	.714
Albany (NY)	9	9	.500	13	15	.464
Maine	8	10	.444	14	15	.483
Binghamton	8	11	.421	12	17	.414
Stony Brook	6	12	.333	12	17	.414
UMBC	5	13	.278	11	18	.379
New Hampshire	5	13	.278	9	19	.321
Hartford	4	14	.222	8	20	.286

Atlantic Coast

	Conference			All Games		
	W	L	Pct	W	L	Pct
North Carolina	14	2	.875	26	3	.897
Wake Forest	13	3	.813	26	4	.867
Duke	11	5	.688	22	5	.815
Georgia Tech	8	8	.500	17	10	.630
Virginia Tech	8	8	.500	15	12	.556
Maryland	7	9	.438	16	11	.593
Miami (FLA)	7	9	.438	16	11	.593
No Carolina St	7	9	.438	17	12	.586
Clemson	5	11	313	15	14	.517
Virginia	4	12	.250	13	14	.481
Florida St	4	12	.250	12	18	.400

Atlantic Sun

	Conference			All Games		
	W	L	Pct	W	L	Pct
Central Florida	13	7	.650	23	8	.742
Gardner Webb	13	7	.650	18	11	.621
Belmont	12	8	.600	14	16	.467
Lipscomb	11	9	.550	16	12	.571
Mercer	11	9	.550	16	12	.571
Jacksonville	11	9	.550	16	13	.552
Georgia	11	9	.550	14	15	.483
Troy St	10	10	.500	12	18	.400
Florida Atlantic	10	10	.500	10	17	.370
Stetson	8	12	.400	10	17	.370
Campbell	0	20	.000	2	25	.074

Atlantic 10

	Conference			All Games		
EAST	W	L	Pct	W	L	Pct
St Joseph's	14	2	.875	17	10	.630
Temple	11	5	.688	15	12	.556
Massachusetts	9	7	.563	16	11	.593
Fordham	8	8	.500	12	1	.444
Rhode Island	4	12	.250	6	21	.222
St Bonaventure	1	15	.063	2	25	.074
WEST						
George Washington	11	5	.688	19	7	.731
Dayton	10	6	.625	17	10	.630
Xavier	10	6	.625	16	11	.593
Richmond	8	8	.500	13	14	.481
Duquesne	5	11	.313	8	21	.276
La Salle	5	11	.313	9	18	.333

Big East

	Conference			All Games		
EAST	W	L	Pct	W	L	Pct
Boston College	13	3	.813	24	3	.889
Connecticut	13	3	.813	21	6	.778
Syracuse	11	5	.688	24	6	.800
Villanova	11	5	.688	21	6	.778
Pittsburgh	10	6	.625	20	7	.741
Notre Dame	9	7	.563	17	10	.630
West Virginia	8	8	.500	18	9	.667
Georgetown	8	8	.500	16	11	.593
Providence	4	12	.250	14	16	.467
Seton Hall	4	12	.250	12	15	.444
St John's	3	13	188	9	18	.333
Rutgers	2	14	.125	9	18	.333

Big Sky

	Conference			All Games		
	W	L	Pct	W	L	Pct
Portland St	11	3	.786	19	8	.704
Montana	9	5	.643	15	12	.556
Montana St	9	5	.643	14	13	.519
Sacramento St	8	6	.571	12	15	.444
Weber St	7	7	.500	12	15	.444
Eastern Washington	5	9	.357	8	19	.296
Northern Arizona	4	10	.286	11	17	.393
Idaho St	3	11	.214	9	18	.333

Big South

	Conference			All Games		
	W	L	Pct	W	L	Pct
Winthrop	15	1	.938	24	5	.828
Liberty	11	5	.688	13	14	.481
UNC-Asheville	8	8	.500	11	16	.407
Birm'ham Southern	7	9	.438	15	13	.536
Radford	7	9	.438	12	15	.444
High Point	7	9	.438	12	17	.414
Charleston Southern	7	9	.438	11	16	.407
Coastal Carolina	7	9	.438	10	17	.370
VMI	3	13	.188	9	18	.333

Big 10

	Conference			All Games		
	W	L	Pct	W	L	Pct
Illinois	15	1	.938	29	1	.937
Michigan St	13	3	.813	22	5	815
Wisconsin	11	5	.688	20	7	.741
Minnesota	10	6	.625	20	9	.690
Indiana	10	6	.625	15	12	.556
Ohio State	8	8	.500	19	11	.633
Iowa	7	9	.438	19	10	.655
Northwestern	6	10	.375	14	15	.483
Michigan	4	12	.250	13	17	.433
Purdue	3	13	.188	7	20	.259
Penn St	1	15	.063	7	22	.241

Note: Standings based on regular-season conference play only; overall records include all tournament play.

Big 12

	Conference			All Games		
	W	L	Pct	W	L	Pct
Kansas	12	4	.750	22	5	.815
Oklahoma	12	4	.750	23	6	.793
Oklahoma St	11	5	.688	21	6	.778
Texas Tech	10	6	.625	18	9	.667
Texas	9	7	.563	20	9	.690
Iowa St	9	7	.563	17	10	.630
Texas A&M	9	8	.500	19	8	.704
Nebraska	7	9	.438	14	13	.519
Missouri	7	9	.438	15	15	.500
Kansas St	6	10	.376	16	10	.593
Colorado	4	12	.250	13	15	.464
Baylor	1	15	.063	9	18	.333

Big West

	Conference			All Games		
	W	L	Pct	W	L	Pct
Pacific	17	0	1.000	24	2	.923
Utah St	13	5	.722	22	7	.759
Cal St Northridge	12	5	.706	17	11	.607
Cal St Fullerton	11	6	.647	17	9	.654
UC Irvine	7	10	.412	14	12	.538
Santa Barbara	7	10	.412	10	16	.385
Long Beach St	6	11	.353	9	19	.321
Idaho	6	12	.355	8	21	.276
UC Riverside	4	13	.235	9	18	.333
Cal Poly	3	14	.176	5	21	.192

Colonial

	Conference			All Games		
	W	L	Pct	W	L	Pct
Old Dominion	15	3	.833	25	5	.833
UNC-Wilmington	13	5	.722	18	9	.667
Va. Commonwealth	13	5	.722	17	11	.607
Hofstra	12	6	.667	20	7	.741
Drexel	12	6	.667	17	10	.630
George Mason	10	8	.556	16	12	.571
Delaware	7	11	.389	10	19	.345
William & Mary	3	15	.167	7	20	.259
James Madison	3	15	.167	6	21	.222
Towson	2	16	.111	5	23	.179

Conference USA

	Conference			All Games		
	W	L	Pct	W	L	Pct
Louisville	14	2	.875	26	14	.867
Charlotte	12	4	.750	21	6	.778
Cincinnati	12	4	.750	24	6	.800
UAB	10	6	.625	20	9	.690
Depaul	10	6	.625	18	9	.667
Houston	9	7	.563	18	12	.600
Memphis	9	7	.563	16	14	.533
Texas Christian	8	8	.500	18	12	.600
Marquette	7	9	.438	19	10	.655
Saint Louis	6	10	.375	9	20	.310
S Florida	5	11	.313	12	15	.444
Tulane	4	12	.250	10	17	.370
E Carolina	4	12	.250	9	19	.321
Southern Miss	2	14	.125	11	17	.393

Horizon League

	Conference			All Games		
	W	L	Pct	W	L	Pct
WI-Milwaukee	14	2	.875	22	5	.815
WI-Green Bay	10	6	.625	17	10	.630
Detroit	9	7	.563	12	15	.444
IL-Chicago	8	8	.500	14	13	.519
Wright St	8	8	.500	14	14	.500
Loyola Chicago	8	8	.500	11	16	.407
Butler	7	9	.438	13	14	.481
Cleveland St	6	10	.375	9	16	.360
Youngstown St	2	14	.125	5	22	.185

Ivy League

	Conference			All Games		
	W	L	Pct	W	L	Pct
Pennsylvania	13	1	.929	20	8	.714
Cornell	8	6	.571	13	14	.481
Harvard	7	7	.500	12	15	.444
Yale	7	7	.500	11	16	.407
Dartmouth	7	7	.500	10	17	.370
Princeton	6	8	.429	15	13	.536
Brown	5	9	.357	12	16	.429
Columbia	3	11	.214	12	15	.444

Metro Atlantic

	Conference			All Games		
	W	L	Pct	W	L	Pct
Niagara	13	5	.722	18	9	.667
Rider	13	5	.722	17	10	.630
Fairfield	11	7	.611	14	14	.500
St Peter's	10	8	.556	15	12	.556
Iona	9	9	.500	13	15	.464
Manhattan	9	9	.500	14	13	.519
Marist	8	10	.444	11	16	.407
Canisius	8	10	.444	10	17	.370
Loyola (MD)	5	13	.278	6	21	.222
Siena	4	14	.222	6	23	.207

Mid-American

	Conference			All Games		
EAST	W	L	Pct	W	L	Pct
Miami (OH)	12	6	.667	18	9	.667
Ohio	11	6	.647	17	9	.654
Buffalo	11	7	.611	19	8	.704
Akron	11	7	.611	18	9	.667
Kent State	10	7	.588	18	11	.621
Marshall	3	15	.167	6	21	.222
WEST						
Western Michigan	11	7	.833	18	11	.621
Toledo	11	7	.667	12	12	.571
Bowling Green	10	8	.444	17	10	.630
Ball St	10	8	.556	15	12	.556
Northern Illinois	7	11	.278	11	16	.407
Eastern Michigan	5	13	.389	12	17	.414
Central Michigan	4	14	.111	10	17	.370

Mid-Continent

	Conference			All Games		
	W	L	Pct	W	L	Pct
Oral Roberts	12	3	.800	22	6	.786
MO-Kansas City	11	4	.733	15	11	.577
Valparaiso	10	5	.667	15	14	.517
Indiana-Purdue	9	6	.600	15	14	.577
Chicago St	7	8	.467	8	17	.320
Western Illinois	6	9	.400	10	16	.385
Oakland	6	9	.400	8	18	.308
Southern Utah	6	10	.375	13	14	.481
Centenary	1	14	.067	3	23	.115

Mid-Eastern Athletic

	Conference			All Games		
	W	L	Pct	W	L	Pct
Delaware St	14	4	.778	16	13	.552
Coppin St	13	4	.765	13	13	.500
Hampton	13	5	.722	15	12	.556
S Carolina St	11	7	.611	18	11	.621
Norfolk St	11	7	.611	13	13	.500
Morgan St	10	7	.588	12	15	.444
Florida A&M	10	8	.556	13	14	.481
Bethune Cookman	8	10	.444	12	16	.429
N Carolina A&T	5	13	.278	6	23	.207
Howard	3	16	.111	5	22	.185
MD-Eastern Shore	1	17	.056	2	25	.074

Missouri Valley

	Conference			All Games		
	W	L	Pct	W	L	Pct
Southern Illinois	15	3	.833	25	6	.806
Wichita St	12	6	.667	19	8	.704
Northern Iowa	11	7	.611	21	9	.700
Creighton	11	7	.611	20	10	.667
SW Missouri St	10	8	.556	16	11	.593
Illinois St	8	10	.444	17	12	.586
Drake	7	11	.389	12	15	.444
Bradley	6	12	.333	13	14	.481
Evansville	5	13	.278	11	16	.407
Indiana St	5	13	.278	10	19	.345

Mountain West

	Conference			All Games		
	W	L	Pct	W	L	Pct
Utah	13	1	.929	25	4	.862
New Mexico	9	4	.692	22	16	.786
Air Force	9	5	.643	18	11	.621
Wyoming	7	7	.500	15	12	.556
Nevada–Las Vegas	6	7	.462	14	12	.538
San Diego St	4	10	.286	10	17	.370
Colorado St	3	10	.231	11	15	.423
Brigham Young	3	10	.231	9	19	.321

Northeast

	Conference			All Games		
	W	L	Pct	W	L	Pct
Monmouth (NJ)	14	4	.778	15	12	.556
Fairleigh Dickinson	13	5	.722	17	12	.586
Robert Morris	11	7	.611	14	14	.500
St Francis (PA)	10	8	.556	15	12	.556
LIU-Brooklyn	10	8	.556	13	14	.481
Wagner	10	8	.556	11	16	.407
St Francis (NY)	9	9	.500	13	14	.481
Central Conn	8	10	.444	12	15	.444
Quinnipiac	6	12	.333	10	17	.370
Mt St Mary's	5	13	.278	7	20	.259
Sacred Heart	3	15	.167	4	23	.148

Ohio Valley

	Conference			All Games		
	W	L	Pct	W	L	Pct
Tennessee Tech	12	4	.750	17	10	.630
Eastern Ky	11	5	.568	19	18	.704
Murray St	11	5	.688	17	10	.630
Samford	10	6	.625	15	12	.556
SE Missouri St	9	7	.563	14	13	.519
Tennessee St	9	7	.563	14	16	.467
Austin Peay	9	7	.563	11	18	.379
Eastern Illinois	7	9	.438	12	15	.444
Morehead St	5	11	.313	11	16	.407
Tennessee-Martin	3	13	.188	6	21	.222
Jacksonville St	2	14	.125	7	22	.241

Pac 10

	Conference			All Games		
	W	L	Pct	W	L	Pct
Arizona	15	3	.833	25	5	.833
Washington	14	4	.778	24	5	.828
Stanford	11	7	.611	17	11	.607
UCLA	11	7	.611	18	9	.667
Oregon St	8	10	.444	16	13	.552
Washington St	7	11	.389	12	15	.444
Arizona St	7	11	.389	18	12	.600
Oregon	6	12	.333	14	13	.519
California	6	12	.333	13	15	.464
Southern Cal	5	13	.278	12	17	.414

Patriot League

	Conference			All Games		
	W	L	Pct	W	L	Pct
EAST						
Holy Cross	13	1	.929	22	5	.815
Bucknell	10	4	.714	19	9	.679
American	8	6	.571	15	11	.577
Lehigh	7	7	.500	13	14	.481
Colgate	7	7	.500	12	15	.444
Lafayette	5	9	.357	9	18	.333
Navy	5	9	.357	9	18	.333
Army	1	13	.071	3	23	.115

Southeastern

EAST	Conference W	L	Pct	All Games W	L	Pct
Kentucky	14	2	.875	23	4	.852
Florida	12	4	.750	20	7	.741
Vanderbilt	8	8	.500	18	12	.600
S Carolina	7	9	.438	15	12	.556
Tennessee	6	10	.375	13	16	.448
Georgia	2	14	.125	8	19	.296
WEST						
Alabama	12	4	.750	23	6	.793
Louisiana St	12	4	.750	19	8	.704
Mississippi St	9	7	.563	21	9	.700
Arkansas	6	10	.375	18	11	.621
Auburn	4	12	.250	13	16	.448
Mississippi	4	12	.250	13	16	.448

Southern

NORTH	Conference W	L	Pct	All Games W	L	Pct
Chattanooga	10	6	.625	17	10	.630
Appalachian St	9	7	.563	16	11	.593
UNC-Greensboro	9	7	.563	16	11	.593
Elon	5	11	.313	7	22	.241
E Tennessee St	4	12	.250	9	18	.333
Western Carolina	3	13	.188	8	21	.276
WEST						
Davidson	16	0	1.000	20	7	.741
Charleston	10	6	.625	18	9	.667
Georgia Southern	10	6	.625	17	12	.586
Furman	9	7	.563	16	12	.571
Wofford	7	9	.438	14	13	.519
The Citadel	4	12	.250	12	15	.444

Southland

	Conference W	L	Pct	All Games W	L	Pct
Northwestern St	13	3	.813	19	11	.633
SE Louisiana	13	3	.813	21	8	.724
Sam Houston St	11	5	.688	17	11	.607
Texas–San Antonio	9	6	.600	14	12	.538
Lamar	9	7	.563	17	10	.630
McNeese St	8	8	.500	13	14	.481
Texas St	8	8	.500	14	13	.519
Texas Arlington	7	9	.438	13	14	.481
S.F. Austin	6	10	.375	12	15	.444
Louisiana-Monroe	2	13	.133	8	18	.308
Nicholls St	1	15	.063	6	21	.222

Southwestern Athletic

	Conference W	L	Pct	All Games W	L	Pct
Alabama A&M	12	6	.667	15	13	.536
Alabama St	11	7	.611	13	14	.481
Grambling	11	7	.611	14	11	.560
Jackson St	11	7	.611	15	15	.500
Miss. Valley St	11	7	.611	13	14	.481
Southern	10	8	.556	13	14	.481
Alcorn St	6	12	.333	7	22	.241
AR–Pine Bluff	6	12	.333	8	19	.296
Prairie View	6	12	.333	6	21	.222
Texas Southern	6	12	.333	8	18	.308

Sun Belt

EAST	Conference W	L	Pct	All Games W	L	Pct
AR–Little Rock	10	4	.714	18	9	.667
Western Kentucky	9	5	.643	20	7	.741
Middle Tennessee St	7	7	.500	18	11	.621
Arkansas St	7	7	.500	15	12	.556
Florida Int'l	4	10	.286	12	16	.407
WEST						
Denver	12	3	.800	18	9	.667
Louisiana-Lafayette	11	4	.733	17	10	.630
New Orleans	7	8	.467	13	16	.448
N Texas	6	9	.400	14	13	.519
S Alabama	6	9	.400	10	17	.370
New Mexico St	1	14	.067	6	23	.207

West Coast

	Conference W	L	Pct	All Games W	L	Pct
Gonzaga	12	2	.857	23	4	.852
St Mary's (CA)	11	3	.786	24	7	.774
San Diego	7	7	.500	15	12	.556
Santa Clara	7	7	.500	14	15	.483
San Francisco	6	8	.429	15	12	.556
Pepperdine	6	8	.429	16	13	.552
Portland	4	10	.286	15	14	.517
Loyola Marymount	3	11	.214	11	16	.407

Western Athletic

	Conference W	L	Pct	All Games W	L	Pct
Nevada	16	2	.889	24	5	.828
Texas–El Paso	14	4	.778	24	7	.774
Rice	12	6	.667	18	10	.643
Fresno St	9	9	.500	15	13	.536
Louisiana Tech	9	9	.500	14	14	.500
Southern Methodist	9	9	.500	14	13	.519
Hawaii	7	11	.389	15	12	.556
Boise St	6	12	.333	13	17	.433
Tulsa	5	13	.278	9	19	.321
San Jose St	3	15	.167	6	22	.214

Independents

	All Games W	L	Pct
TX A&M–Corpus Christi	20	8	.714
Utah Valley State	16	12	.571
TX–Pan American	12	16	.428
Cal Davis	11	17	.392
Northern Colorado	8	21	.276
IU–PU Fort Wayne	7	22	.241
Savannah St	0	28	.000

Scoring

	Class	GP	FG	3FG	FT	Pts	Avg
Keydren Clark, St. Peter's	Jr.	28	230	109	152	721	25.8
Taylor Coppenrath, Vermont	Sr.	31	271	9	226	777	25.1
Juan Mendez, Niagra	Sr.	30	221	39	224	705	23.5
Rob Monroe, Quinnipiac	Sr.	26	173	72	171	589	22.7
Bo McCalebb, New Orleans	So.	30	261	25	132	679	22.6
Ike Diogu, Arizona St	Jr.	32	229	18	248	724	22.6
Tim Smith, East Tenn. St	Jr.	29	245	59	96	645	22.2
Jose Juan Barea, Northeatern	Jr.	30	233	68	131	665	22.2
J.J. Redick, Duke	Jr.	33	202	121	196	721	21.8
Ryan Gomes, Providence	Sr.	31	247	52	124	670	21.6
Darshan Luckey, St. Francis(Pa.)	Jr.	28	212	39	139	602	21.5
Hakim Warrick, Syracuse	Sr.	34	253	9	211	726	21.4
Daryll Hill, St. John's(N.Y.)	So.	27	201	51	107	560	20.7
Nick Fazekas, Nevada	So.	32	223	33	183	662	20.7
Michael Harris, Rice	Sr.	31	240	7	152	639	20.6
Seamus Boxley, Portland St.	Sr.	28	205	13	153	576	20.6
Omar Thomas, UTEP	Sr.	35	248	13	207	716	20.5
Paul Millsap, Louisiana Tech	So.	29	225	0	143	593	20.4
Andrew Bogut, Utah	So.	35	281	9	144	715	20.4
Wayne Simien, Kansas	Sr.	26	191	4	142	528	20.3
Steven Smith, La Salle	Jr.	29	206	34	142	588	20.3
Dainmon Gonner, Southeast Mo. St.	Sr.	27	195	41	116	547	20.3
Tiras Wade, La- Lafayette	Jr.	31	215	77	121	628	20.3
Elton Nesbitt, Ga. Southern	Jr.	31	193	92	147	625	20.2
Maurice Bailey, Sacred Heart	Sr.	27	174	40	154	542	20.1

FIELD-GOAL PERCENTAGE

	Class	GP	FG	FGA	Pct
Bruce Brown Hampton	Jr	30	178	269	66.2
Nate Harris, Utah St.	Jr	32	172	264	65.2
Eric Williams, Wake Forest	Jr	33	201	319	63.0
Chad McKnight, Morehead St.	Sr	27	155	246	63.0
Aaron Andrews, Morgan St.	Sr	28	140	224	62.5
Michael Haney, Eastern Ky.	Sr	31	174	279	62.4
Kyle Hines, UNC Greensboro	Fr	30	175	282	62.1
Andrew Bogut, Utah	So	35	281	453	62.0
Carl Landry, Purdue	Jr	25	160	259	61.8
Quincy Davis, Tulne	Jr	28	153	250	61.2

Note: Minimum 5 made per game.

FREE-THROW PERCENTAGE

	Class	GP	FT	FTA	Pct
Blake Ahearn, SW Mo. St	So	32	90	95	94.7
J.J. Redick, Duke	Jr	33	196	209	93.8
Vince Greene, Illinois St.	Sr	30	81	88	92.0
Salim Stoudamire, Arziona	Sr	36	122	134	91.0
Jamaal Hilliard, Lafayette	So	28	91	100	91.0
Chris McCray, Maryland	Jr	31	102	113	90.3
Derek Raivio, Gonzaga	So	31	102	113	90.3
Anthony Roberson, Florida	Jr	32	81	90	90.0
David Doubley, Pacific	Sr	31	94	105	89.5
Jerry Johnson, Rider	Sr	30	107	120	89.2

Note: Minimum 2.5 made per game.

REBOUNDS

	Class	GP	Reb	Avg
Paul Millsap, Louisiana Tech	So	29	360	12.4
Andrew Bogut, Utah	So	35	427	12.2
Lance Allred, Weber St.	Sr	29	348	12.0
Michael Harris, Rice	Sr	31	363	11.7
Dwayne Jones, St. Joseph's	Jr	36	418	11.6
Shelden Williams, Duke.	Jr	33	369	11.2
Wayne Simien, Kansas	Sr	26	287	11.0
Lawrence Roberts, Mississippi St.	Sr	32	351	11.0
Sean May, North Carolina	Jr	37	397	10.7
Juan Mendez, Niagra	Sr	30	319	10.6

ASSISTS

	Class	GP	A	Avg
Damitrius Coleman, Mercer	Jr	28	224	8.0
Will Funn, Portland St.	Sr	28	224	8.0
Marcus Williams, Connecticut	So	31	243	7.8
Walker Russell, Jacksonville St	Jr	29	211	7.3
Jose Juan Barea, Northeastern	Jr	30	218	7.3
Aaron Miles, Kansas	Sr	30	216	7.2
Filiberto Rivera, UTEP	Sr	32	229	7.2
Javier Mendiburu, Wis.-Green Bay	Sr	26	184	7.1
Garrett Farha, St. Francis (Pa.)	Jr	28	194	6.9
Raymond Felton, North Carolina	Jr	36	249	6.9

*Includes games played in tournaments.

NCAA Men's Division I Individual Leaders (Cont.)

THREE-POINT FIELD-GOAL PERCENTAGE

	Class	GP	FG	FGA	Avg
Salim Stoudamire, Arizona	Sr	36	120	238	50.4
Will Whittington, Marist	So	28	97	197	49.2
Dennis Trammell, Ball St.	Sr	23	59	122	48.4
Chris Lofton, Tennessee	Fr	31	93	200	46.5
Drake Diener, DePaul	Sr	31	85	184	46.2
Steve Novak, Marquette	Jr	31	89	193	46.1
John Reimold, Bowlig Green	Sr	29	79	173	45.7
Troy DeVries, New Mexico	Sr	33	93	206	45.1
Taquan Dean, Louisville	Jr	37	122	273	44.7
J. Robert Merritt, Samford	Jr	28	85	193	44.0

Note: Minimum 2.5 made per game.

BLOCKED SHOTS

	Class	GP	BS	Avg
Deng Gai, Fairfield	Sr	30	165	5.5
Shawn James, Northeastern	Fr	25	136	5.4
Shelden Williams, Duke	Jr	33	122	3.7
Kyle Hines, UNC Greensboro	Fr	30	106	3.5
Dwayne Jones, St. Joseph's	Jr	36	109	3.0
Yemi Nicholson, Denver	Jr	31	92	3.0
Chaz Crawford, Drexel	So	29	86	3.0
Anthony King, Miami(Fla.)	So	29	86	3.0
Ronald Alexander, Mississippi Val.	Jr	28	82	2.9
Josh Boone, Connecticut	So	31	90	2.9

THREE-POINT FIELD GOALS MADE PER GAME

	Class	GP	FG	Avg
Brendan Plavich, Charlotte	Sr	29	114	3.9
Keydren Clark, St. Peter's	Jr	28	109	3.9
Pat Carroll, St. Joseph's	Sr	35	135	3.9
T.J Sorrentine, Vermont	Sr	31	116	3.7
J.J Redick, Duke	Jr	33	121	3.7
Will Whittington, Marist	So	28	97	3.5
Jerry Johnson, Rider	Sr	30	102	3.4
Ed McCants, Wis-Milwaukee	Sr	32	107	3.3
Salim Stoudamire, Arizona	Sr	36	120	3.3
Taquan Dean, Louisville	Jr	37	122	3.3

STEALS

	Class	GP	S	Avg
Obie Trotter, A&M	Jr	32	125	3.9
Chakowby Hicks, Norfolk St.	Sr	27	91	3.4
Keydren Clark, St. Peter's	Jr	28	93	3.3
Hosea Butler Mississippi Val.	Sr	28	91	3.3
Eddie Basden, Charlotte	Sr	29	93	3.2
Ibrahim Jaaber, Penn	So	29	85	2.9
DaShawn Freeman,Sacramento S	Jr	28	82	2.9
Kevin Hamilton, Holy Cross	Jr	32	92	2.9
Damitrius Coleman, Mercer	Jr	28	80	2.9
Mardy Collins, Temple	Jr	30	85	2.8

Single-Game Highs

POINTS

45 .....Joe Knight, Lehigh, March 30, 2005 (vs Colgate)
43 .....Elton Nesbitt, Ga. Southern, January 17, 2005 (vs Chattanooga)
43 .....Keydren Clark, St. Peter's, Dec. 30, 2004 (vs. Coll. of Charleston)

REBOUNDS

25 .....Paul Millsap, Louisiana Tech, February 27, 2005 (vs Boise St.)
24 .....Sean May, North Carolina, March 6, 2005 (vs. Duke)
24 .....Michael Harris, Rice, February 27, 2005 (vs Hawaii)

ASSISTS

18 .....Filiberto Rivera, UTEP, February 25, 2005 (vs Louisiana Tech)
18......Ronald Steele, Alabama, December 1, 2004 (vs East Tenn. St.)
16 .....Jonathan Bluitt, Oral Roberts, January 20, 2005 (vs Oakland)
15 .....Rodney Billups, Denver, February 5, 2005 (vs La.-Lafayette)

THREE POINT FIELD GOALS

11 ....Elton Nesbitt, Ga. Southern, January 17,2005 (vs Chattanooga)
10 .....Joe Knight, Lehigh, March 4, 2005 (vs Colgate)
10 .....Elton Nesbitt, Ga. Southern, February 14, 2005 (vs. The Citadel)
Five tied with 9

STEALS

10 .....Doron Perkins, Santa Clara, February 24, 2005 (vs San Diego)
10 .....Louis Ford, Howard, December 6, 2004 (vs. Md.-East. Shore)
9 ....Obie Trotter, Alabama A&M, March 5, 2005 (vs. Jackson St)
9 ....Bryan Hopkins, Southern Methodist, Feb.10, 2005 (vs. San Jose St)
9 ....Mardy Collins, Temple, November 27, 2004 (vs. South Carolina)
Nine tied with 8

BLOCKED SHOTS

13......Deng Gai, Fairfield, January 22, 2005(vs Siena)
13 .....Anthony King, Miami(Fla.), November 29, 2004(vs. Fla. Atlantic)
11 .....Shawn James, Northeastern, Dec. 30, 2004 & Feb. 27, 2005
       (vs.Albany(N.Y.) & Iona, respectively)
11 .....Mustafa Al-Sayyad, Fresno St, February 19, 2005 (vs. Buffalo)

Four tied with 10

NCAA Men's Division I Team Leaders

SCORING OFFENSE

	GP	W	L	Pts	Avg
North Carolina	37	33	4	3257	88.0
Washington	35	29	6	3026	86.5
Wake Forest	33	27	6	2801	84.9
Niagra	30	20	10	2537	84.6
Maryland	32	19	13	2620	81.9
Ga. Southern	31	18	13	2506	80.8
Louisville	38	33	5	3066	80.7
Lamar	29	18	11	2338	80.6
Mercer	28	16	12	2242	80.1
Arizona	37	30	7	2948	79.7

SCORING DEFENSE

	GP	W	L	Pts	Avg
Air Force	30	18	12	1629	54.3
Princeton	28	15	13	1521	54.3
Boston U	29	20	9	1616	55.7
Southeastern La.	33	24	9	1842	55.8
Holy Cross	32	25	7	1817	56.8
Washington St.	28	12	16	1594	56.9
Utah	35	29	6	2005	57.3
Utah St.	32	24	8	1848	57.8
St. Joseph's.	36	24	12	2110	58.6
Bucknell	33	23	10	1946	59.0
UNC Wilmington	30	15	15	1787	59.6

SCORING MARGIN

	Off	Def	Mar
North Carolina	88.0	70.3	17.8
Louisville	80.7	64.1	16.6
Illinois	77.0	61.1	15.9
Utah St.	72.3	57.8	14.6
Oklahoma St.	78.3	65.2	13.1
Florida	76.2	63.1	13.1
Michigan St.	78.5	65.4	13.1
Duke	78.2	65.2	13.0
Washington	86.5	74.2	12.3
Oklahoma	75.2	63.3	11.9

FIELD-GOAL PERCENTAGE

	FG	FGA	Pct
Utah St.	851	1621	52.5
Utah	837	1628	51.4
Samford	616	1224	50.3
Gonzaga	856	1702	50.3
North Carolina	1128	2260	49.9
Oklahoma St.	911	1833	49.7
Pacific	794	1598	49.7
Tex. A&M-Corp. Chris	768	1553	49.5
New Mexico	855	1733	49.3
Portland St.	708	1440	49.2

FIELD-GOAL PERCENTAGE DEFENSE

	FG	FGA	Pct
Boston U	588	1584	37.1
Cincinnati	749	2008	37.3
Connecticut	761	2011	37.8
Memphis	827	2155	38.4
Kansas	663	1712	38.7
Nevada	727	1872	38.8
Holy Cross	604	1554	38.9
Louisville	823	2116	38.9
Sam Houston St.	676	1738	38.9
Syracuse	760	1950	39.0

FREE-THROW PERCENTAGE

	FT	FTA	Pct
UTEP.	606	765	79.2
Oklahoma St.	521	668	78.0
Michigan St.	543	699	77.7
Arizona	541	697	77.6
Monmouth	420	545	77.1
Army	296	385	76.9
Duquesne	360	471	76.4
Morehead St.	386	507	76.1
Niagra	601	791	76.0
Texas Tech	526	696	75.6

THREE-POINT FIELD GOALS MADE PER GAME

	GP	FG	Avg
Troy.	30	338	11.3
Belmont	30	292	9.7
Louisville	38	361	9.5
Vanderbilt	34	322	9.5
Furman	29	267	9.2
West Virginia	35	319	9.1
Niagara	30	270	9.0
Davidson	32	286	8.9
Air Force	30	266	8.9
Georgia St.	29	257	8.9

REBOUNDING MARGIN

	GP	REB	Opp REB	Margin /G
Connecticut	31	1412	1062	11.3
Chattanooga	31	1284	948	10.8
Utah	35	1194	827	10.5
Pittsburgh	29	1103	855	8.6
Mississippi St.	34	1389	1101	8.5
Gonzaga	31	1191	943	8.0
Nevada	32	1270	1026	7.6
North Carolina	37	1499	1222	7.5
Wake Forest	33	1315	1081	7.1
Niagara	30	1222	1014	6.9

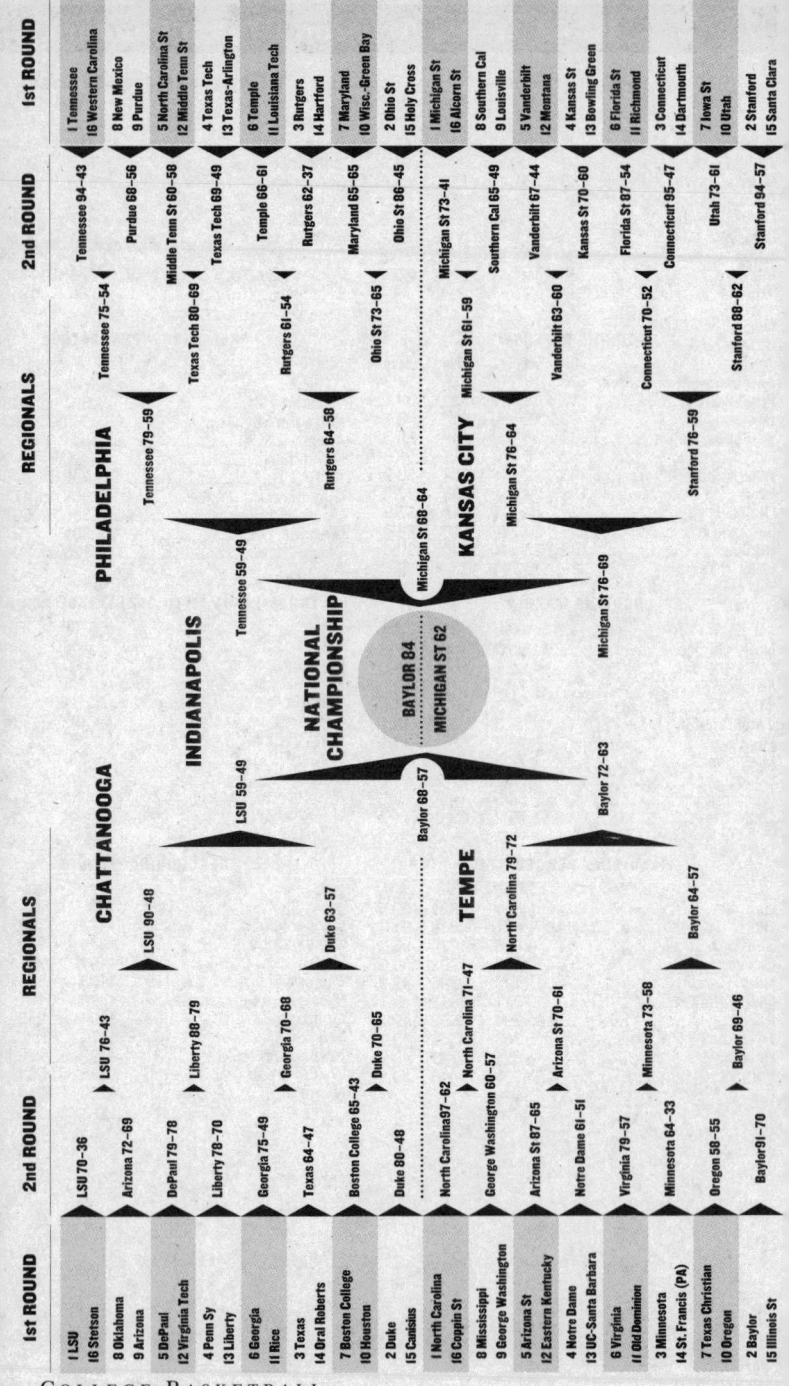

2005 NCAA Basketball Women's Division I Tournament

1st ROUND

1 LSU
16 Stetson
8 Oklahoma
9 Arizona
5 DePaul
12 Virginia Tech
4 Penn St
13 Liberty
6 Georgia
11 Rice
3 Texas
14 Oral Roberts
7 Boston College
10 Houston
2 Duke
15 Canisius

1 North Carolina
16 Coppin St
8 Mississippi
9 George Washington
5 Arizona St
12 Eastern Kentucky
4 Notre Dame
13 UC-Santa Barbara
6 Virginia
11 Old Dominion
3 Minnesota
14 St. Francis (PA)
7 Oregon
10 Oregon
2 Baylor
15 Illinois St

2nd ROUND

LSU 70–36
Arizona 72–69
DePaul 79–78
Liberty 78–70
Georgia 75–49
Texas 64–47
Boston College 65–43
Duke 80–48

North Carolina 97–62
George Washington 60–57
Arizona St 87–65
Notre Dame 61–51
Virginia 79–57
Minnesota 64–33
Oregon 58–55
Baylor 91–70

REGIONALS — CHATTANOOGA / TEMPE

LSU 76–43
Liberty 88–79
Georgia 70–68
Duke 70–65

North Carolina 71–47
Arizona St 70–61
Minnesota 73–58
Baylor 69–46

LSU 90–48
Duke 63–57

North Carolina 79–72
Baylor 64–57

LSU 59–49
Baylor 72–63

Baylor 68–57

REGIONALS — PHILADELPHIA / KANSAS CITY

Tennessee 75–54
Middle Tenn St 60–58
Rutgers 61–54
Ohio St 73–65

Michigan St 61–59
Vanderbilt 63–60
Connecticut 70–52
Stanford 88–62

Tennessee 79–59
Rutgers 64–58

Michigan St 76–64
Stanford 76–59

Tennessee 59–49
Michigan St 76–69

Michigan St 68–64

2nd ROUND

Tennessee 94–43
Purdue 68–56
Texas Tech 80–69
Temple 66–61
Rutgers 62–37
Maryland 65–65
Ohio St 86–45

Michigan St 73–41
Southern Cal 65–49
Vanderbilt 67–44
Kansas St 70–60
Florida St 97–54
Connecticut 95–47
Utah 73–61
Stanford 94–57

1st ROUND

1 Tennessee
16 Western Carolina
8 New Mexico
9 Purdue
5 North Carolina St
12 Middle Tenn St
4 Texas Tech
13 Texas-Arlington
6 Temple
11 Louisiana Tech
3 Rutgers
14 Hartford
7 Maryland
10 Wisc.-Green Bay
2 Ohio St
15 Holy Cross

1 Michigan St
16 Alcorn St
8 Southern Cal
9 Louisville
5 Vanderbilt
12 Montana
4 Kansas St
13 Bowling Green
6 Florida St
11 Richmond
3 Connecticut
14 Dartmouth
7 Iowa St
10 Utah
2 Stanford
15 Santa Clara

NATIONAL CHAMPIONSHIP

BAYLOR 84
MICHIGAN ST 62

INDIANAPOLIS

NCAA WOMEN'S CHAMPIONSHIP GAME BOX SCORE

Baylor 84

	Min	FG M-A	FT M-A	Reb O-T	A	PF	TP
S. Young	36	10-19	6-9	4-9	4	1	26
A Wabara	10	0-1	0-0	0-2	1	1	0
A. Blackmon	35	8-19	6-8	2-7	1	2	22
C. Whitaker	32	0-2	0-1	3-5	6	1	0
C. Scott	18	3-3	0-0	1-4	3	0	7
C. Fox	2	0-0	0-0	0-2	0	0	0
L. Wyatt	20	3-5	2-4	1-6	0	4	8
A. Tisdale	8	0-2	2-2	0-0	1	2	2
E. Niemann	33	6-10	2-2	1-3	1	1	19
Totals	200	30-61	18-26	12-38	17	12	84

Percentages: FG—.492, FT—.692, 3-pt goals: 6–12, .500 (A Wabara 0-1, C Scott 1-1, . Wyatt 0-1, A Tisdale 0-1, E Niemann 5-8). Team rebounds: 7. Blocked shots: 0. Turnovers: 12 (S Young 3, S Blackmon 2, C Scott 2, A Tisdale 2, C Whitaekr, A Wabara, L Wyatt). Steals: 8 (C Whitaker 2, A Wabara 2, S Blackmon, C Ononiwu, E Niemann, C Scott).

Halftime: Connecticut 30, Tennessee 24.
A: 18,211. Officials: Mattingly, Kantner, Enterline.

Michigan State 62

	Min	FG M-A	FT M-A	Reb O-T	A	PF	TP
L. Shimek	37	3-6	0-0	0-5	2	3	7
K. Roehrig	30	3-8	2-2	0-5	0	3	8
K.Haynie	37	7-14	3-5	0-1	5	4	17
L. Bowen	37	5-14	8-10	1-3	1	0	20
V. Lucas-Perry	25	3-6	0-0	0-2	0	3	7
R. Haynes	19	0-3	1-2	0-2	1	2	1
M. Dwyer	1	0-0	0-0	1-1	0	0	0
M. Small	1	0-0	0-0	0-0	0	0	0
K. Grantham	3	0-0	0-0	0-0	0	2	0
L.Hall	9	1-2	0-0	0-1	0	2	2
Totals	200	22-53	14-19	2-20	9	19	62

Percentages: FG—.415, FT—.737. 3-pt goals: 4–18, .222 (L Shimek 1-2, K Haynie 0-3, L Bowen 2-9, V Lucas-Perry 1-3, R Haynes 0-1). Team rebounds: 2. Blocked shots: 5 (K Roehrig 3, L Shimek, L Hall). Turnovers: 12 (L Shmiek 4, L Bowen 2, R Haynes 2, K Haynie, M Dwyer, V Lucas-Perry, K Roehrig). Steals: 8 (K Haynie 5, L Bowen 2, V Lucas-Perry)

NCAA Women's Division I Individual Leaders

SCORING

Player and Team	Class	GP	TFG	3FG	FT	Pts	Avg
Tan White, Mississippi St	Sr	29	241	61	138	681	23.5
Emily Faurholt, Idaho	Jr	30	241	46	169	697	23.2
Tori Talbert, Texas St	Sr	25	208	0	144	560	22.4
Tamara James, Miami(Fla.)	Jr	29	242	39	124	647	22.3
Beth Swink, St Francis(Pa.)	Sr	31	255	1	177	688	22.2
Rolanda Monroe, Southern U	Jr	30	219	67	135	640	21.3
Kendra Wecker, Kansas St.	Sr	29	240	40	89	609	21.0
Reka Cserny, Harvard	Sr	27	192	26	154	564	20.9
Tara Boothe, Xavier	Jr	32	254	30	121	659	20.6
Seimone Augustus, LSU	Jr	36	303	5	113	724	20.1
Sugiery Monsac, Robrt Morris	Jr	30	218	15	151	602	20.1
Jenni Lingor, Southwest Mo. St.	Sr	33	217	83	143	660	20.0
Sandora Irvin, TCU	Sr	33	237	24	159	657	19.9
Tiffani Mayes, East Tenn. St.	Sr	29	219	2	131	571	19.7
Emily Christian, Tennessee Tech	Jr	29	209	11	137	566	19.5

Boy Band Bearcat Booster

How does a Cincinnati sports fan vent if he's married to someone who probably doesn't know a Bearcat from a Burberry scarf? If you're Nick Lachey you fire off a 672-word column to your old hometown paper. The Newlyweds star, who studied sports medicine at Miami (Ohio), was made a "contributor" by The Cincinnati Enquirer, which ran his piece on May 30. Lachey argued that embattled Bearcats basketball coach Bob Huggins "deserves to go out on his own terms."

NCAA Women's Division I Individual Leaders (Cont.)

FIELD-GOAL PERCENTAGE

Player and Team	Class	GP	FG	FGA	Pct
Katie Feenstra, Liberty ....Sr		32	230	343	67.1
Amber Jackson, San Jose St. ...Fr		30	05	311	65.9
Ashley Earley, Vanderbilt ....Sr		32	240	375	64.0
Latoya Davis, Texas Tech ....Jr		31	157	256	61.3
Becky O'Neil, Weber St. ....So		29	145	237	61.2
Crystal Kelly, Western Ky. ....Fr		30	214	350	61.1
Brooke Smith, Stanford.............So		35	199	326	61.0
Tiffany Mor, Wis -Green Bay .....Sr		31	203	333	61.0
Erlana Larkins, North Carolina...Fr		34	181	297	60.9
Khara Smith, Depaul.................Jr		31	232	386	60.1

Note: Minimum 5 made per game.

REBOUNDS

Player and Team	Class	GP	Reb	Avg
Sancho Lyttle, Houston ....Sr		30	362	12.1
Sandora Irvin, TCU ....Sr		33	390	11.8
Nakeya Downing, SE La. ....Sr		27	318	11.8
Khara Smith, DePaul ....Jr		31	364	11.7
Sugiery Monsac, Robert Morris......Jr		30	348	11.6
Kemie Nkele, UC Riverside...........Fr		28	321	11.5
Evena Morency, SC St. ....Sr		29	321	11.1
Kristy Brown, Stetson ....Sr		31	334	10.8
Jen Perugini, Youngstown St. ....Sr		27	288	10.7
Jennifer Fleischer, Penn...............Jr		27	287	10.6

FREE-THROW PERCENTAGE

Player and Team	Class	GP	FT	FTA	Pct
Kristin Iwanaga, California ....Sr		29	85	91	93.4
Nefertiti Walker, Stetson ....Jr		31	80	87	92.0
Melissa Yeagley, Iona ....Jr		26	83	92	90.2
Megan duffy, Notre Dame ....Jr		33	137	153	89.5
Tynisha Alexander, Tenn Tech .Sr		29	109	122	89.3
Katie Gearlds, Purdue...............So		30	81	91	89.0
Kate Endress, Ball St ....Sr		29	86	97	88.7
Nicole Lauden, Auburn.............Sr		29	85	97	87.6
Leilani Mitchell, Idaho ....So		30	168	192	87.5
Jess Strom, Penn St. ....Sr		29	129	148	87.2

Note: Minimum 2.5 made per game.

ASSISTS

Player and Team	Class	GP	A	Avg
Yolanda paige, West Virginia...........Sr		34	297	8.7
Temeka Johnson, LSU.....................Sr		36	278	7.7
Erin Grant, Texas Tech.....................Jr		31	218	7.0
Corrie Mizusawa, Oregon ....Sr		30	209	7.0
Anesia Smith, Maryland...................Sr		32	214	6.7
Shona Thorburn, Utah.....................Sr		34	221	6.5
Carolyn Kieger, Marquette ....Jr		30	185	6.2
Erica McGlaston, San Jose St.........Sr		30	185	6.2
Shannon Mathews, Gonzaga...........Sr		32	197	6.2
Anedra Gilmore, South Fla..............Sr		31	190	6.1

THREE-POINT FIELD-GOAL PERCENTAGE

Player and Team	Class	GP	FG	FGA	Pct
K.C. Cowgill, S.W Mo. St...........Sr		33	74	139	53.2
Ashley Cazee, Eastern Ky.........Fr		28	56	113	49.6
Matea Pender, UMBC ....Jr		28	62	127	48.8
Jill Marano, La Salle ....Sr		28	57	123	46.3
Kate Endress, Ball St. ....Sr		29	70	152	46.1
Allie Quigley, DePaul ....Fr		31	79	173	45.7
Meg Bulger, West Virginia ....So		34	88	197	44.7
Caity Matter, Ohio St.................Sr		35	73	164	44.5
Lisa Verhoff, Indiana St. ....Jr		32	68	155	43.9
Jayme Wilson, Oakland.............Jr		29	62	142	43.7

Note: Minimum 2.0 made per game.

BLOCKED SHOTS

Player and Team	Class	GP	BS	Avg
Marita Payne, Auburn ....Jr		28	141	5.0
Ashley Sparkman, NW St. ....Sr		27	132	4.9
Sandora Irvin, TCU ....Sr		33	150	4.5
Cassie Hager, Northern Iowa ....Jr		31	135	4.4
Brooke McAfee, IUPUI....................Jr		28	105	3.8
Alison Bales, Duke.........................So		36	134	3.4
zane Teilane, Western Ill................Jr		28	96	3.4
Jessica Davenport, Ohio St. ....So		35	116	3.3
Kemie Nkele,UC Riverside.............Fr		28	92	3.3
Cisti Greenwalt, Texas Tech..........Sr		32	105	3.3

NCAA Men's Division II Individual Leaders

SCORING

Player and Team	Class	GP	TFG	3FG	FT	Pts	Avg
David Logan, Indianapolis.......................................Sr		29	291	121	126	829	28.6
Yandel Brown, Columbus St. ....Sr		32	298	148	148	892	27.9
Lewis Muse, Concord ....Sr		27	287	0	146	720	26.7
Hakim Rasul, Abilene Christian...............................Jr		25	246	8	149	649	26.0
Brad Oleson, Alas. Fairbanks ....Sr		30	241	94	157	733	24.4
Rodney Mayes, West Va. Tech...............................Sr		27	224	12	177	637	23.6
Stacey Moragne, Mass-Lowell................................Jr		28	239	38	120	636	22.7
Tayron Thomas, Phililedphia U. ....Jr		29	240	37	140	657	22.7
Robert epps, St. Thomas Aquinas.........................Sr		30	229	6	208	672	22.4
Justice Graham, Glenville St....................................Sr		28	212	38	162	624	22.3

REBOUNDS

Player and Team	Class	GP	Reb	Avg
Ramel Allen, Bridgeport	Sr	30	423	14.1
Jakim Donaldson, Edinboro	Sr	31	406	13.1
Jayson Williams, Lane	Sr	32	389	12.2
Letheal Cook, Bowie St.	Sr	29	347	12.0
Kevin Johnson, Humboldt St.	So	27	309	11.4
Justin James, Midwestern St.	Sr	29	324	11.2
Osvaldo Haynes, Anderson (S.C.)	Sr	28	305	10.9
Robert Hamilton, Tex. A&M-King.	Sr	28	303	10.8
Joseph King, Miles	Sr	27	289	10.7
John Sullivan, New Haven	Jr	29	309	10.7

ASSISTS

Player and Team	Class	GP	A	Avg
Darnell Miller, West Ga.	Sr	28	219	7.8
Darnell Evans, Wayne St. (Mich)	Sr	31	232	7.5
Tim Haley, Cal St. Chico	Sr	27	202	7.5
Mark Borders, Tampa	Jr	29	213	7.3
Christopher Dunn, West V.A St.	Jr	29	200	6.9
Dennis Springs, Ferris St.	Jr	31	213	6.9
Zack Whiting, Chaminade	So	27	183	6.8
Chris Kozole, Holy Family	Jr	30	195	6.5
Donald Sexton, Tusculum	Jr	29	185	6.4
Adam Lubbehusen, Oakland City	Sr	31	197	6.4

FIELD-GOAL PERCENTAGE

Player and Team	Class	GP	FG	FGA	Pct
Callistus Eziukwu, Grnd Vlly St	Fr	28	157	213	73.7
Jonathan Martin, Crsn-Nwmn	Sr	25	144	209	68.9
Marc Milbourne Swan, NJIT	So	28	155	236	65.7
Jordan roth, Quincy	Jr	29	152	236	64.4
Jeremiah Tinch, Mars Hill	Sr	30	176	274	64.2
Brian Robinson, Assumption	Sr	27	177	277	63.9
Turner Trofholz, South Dakota	Jr	33	272	428	63.6
Randy Holbrook, Southern Ind.	Sr	29	170	271	62.7
Ash Cannan, Colo. Christian	Sr	28	161	257	62.6
Rone Smith, Arkansas Tech	Jr	27	186	297	62.6

Note: Minimum 5 made per game.

FREE-THROW PERCENTAGE

Player and Team	Class	GP	FT	FTA	Pct
Luqman Jaaber, VA Union	Sr	34	125	139	89.9
Jason Smith, Ala-Huntsville	So	27	87	98	88.8
Josh Mueller, South Dakota	Sr	33	146	265	88.5
Carlton Epps, Ferris St.	Sr	31	98	111	88.3
Dustin Bremerman, Seat. Pac.	So	29	80	91	87.9
Bill Johnson, Slippery Rock	Jr	27	115	131	87.8
Karim Telfer, Augusta St.	Jr	30	139	159	87.4
Douglas Tshomba, Tusculum	Jr	29	76	87	87.4
Brad Oleson, Alas. Fairbanks	Sr	30	157	180	87.2
Micheal Hicks, Central Mo. St.	Jr	31	136	156	87.2

Note: Minimum 2.5 made per game.

NCAA Women's Division II Individual Leaders

SCORING

Player and Team	Class	GP	TFG	3FG	FT	Pts	Avg
Candice Allen, Cal Poly Pomona	Sr	26	247	47	186	727	28.0
Lauren Meyer, Georgian Court	Sr	27	218	6	208	650	24.1
Katie McElree, Cal St. Bakersfield	Jr	28	257	44	98	656	23.4
Cassie King, N.C. Central	So	29	264	2	134	664	22.9
LaShonda Chiles, Anderson(S.C)	So	36	286	90	160	822	22.8
Allyson Hardy, Bowie St.	Sr	25	197	39	136	569	22.8
Kristen Gattuso, Fairmont St.	Sr	32	248	104	127	727	22.7
Erika Quigley, St. Cloud St.	So	33	297	1	153	748	22.7
Carone Harris, Central Ark.	Sr	35	238	85	229	790	22.6
Melissa Patterson, Pitt.-Johnstown	Sr	27	202	53	146	603	22.3

REBOUNDS

Player and Team	Class	GP	Reb	Avg
Celeste Trahan, Elizabeth City St.	Fr	29	398	13.7
Rachill Robinson, Bowie St.	Sr	28	349	12.5
Keauna Vinson, Barton	So	22	271	12.3
Erika Quigley, St. Cloud St.	So	33	400	12.1
Elfreda Reid, Lincoln (Mo.)	Sr	26	310	11.9
Shonda Holder, Queens (N.Y.)	Sr	27	321	11.9
Francis Carvajal, West Va. Wslyn	Sr	28	329	11.8
Lucresua West, Fla. Southern	Sr	23	268	11.7
Sidney Thomas, Fairmont St.	Jr	31	357	11.5
Kim Rowley, Goldey-Beacom	So	23	260	11.3

ASSISTS

Player and Team	Class	GP	A	Avg
Kim Abts, Cal St. Chico	Sr	30	290	9.7
Jen Gwin, Gannon	Sr	30	255	8.5
Nicole Woods, Belmont Abbey	Jr	30	243	8.1
Callie iorfido, Edinboro	Jr	28	225	8.0
Lisa perry, West Liberty St.	Fr	27	199	7.4
Princess Wimsatt, Bellarmine	Sr	30	213	7.1
Meghan Wolster, South Dakota	Jr	20	196	6.5
Natassia Boucicault, Shaw	Jr	34	215	6.3
Amanda Davidson, Indianpolis	Sr	31	194	6.3
Michelle Brown, Emporia St.	Sr	33	200	6.1

NCAA Women's Division II Individual Leaders (Cont.)

FIELD-GOAL PERCENTAGE

Player and Team	Class	GP	FG	FGA	Pct
Sammy Kromm, Wis- Parkside	.Sr	32	215	332	64.8
Becky Marquardt-King, Lk. Sup.	Jr	29	168	261	64.4
Ashley Langen, North Dakota	...Fr	31	202	332	60.8
Shevon Gibbons, Bentley	.........Sr	36	229	378	60.6
Sephanie Ponds, Anderson(SC)	So	36	258	426	60.6
Lucresia West, Fla. Southern	....Sr	23	204	340	60.0
Jessica Fesenmaier, M.N St. M	So	31	166	283	58.7
Ashley Gronewoller, C.O. Mines	Jr	28	144	247	58.3
Ashlee Gustin, Fort Hayes St.	...So	29	152	263	57.8
Selma Barbosa, Mo. West. St.	..Sr	29	202	351	57.5

Note: Minimum 5 made per game.

FREE-THROW PERCENTAGE

Player and Team	Class	GP	FT	FTA	Pct
Adrienne Taalak, Alas. Frbnks	Sr	23	93	101	92.1
Donna Iohery, Molloy	Jr	26	109	122	89.3
Amanda Newton, Drury	Jr	31	125	140	89.3
Laura Parker, Lees-McRae	Jr	28	82	92	89.1
Karyn Creager, Northern Ky.	So	28	77	87	88.5
Whitney VanBrocklin, NW Nzrn	Jr	27	83	94	88.3
Hannah Stolba, Minn St. Mnkt	Sr	27	70	80	87.5
Eva Vodrazkova, Augusta St.	Jr	25	70	80	87.5
Kristi Ferris, Mars Hill	Jr	28	101	116	87.1
Lauren meyer, Georgian Court	Sr	27	208	239	87.0

Note: Minimum 2.5 made per game.

NCAA Men's Division III Individual Leaders

SCORING

Player and Team	Class	GP	TFG	3FG	FT	Pts	Avg
Tim Russell, Albertus Magnus	.....................Sr	25	292	74	161	819	32.8
Nick Pelotte, Plymouth St.	.....................Sr	29	262	81	211	816	28.1
Jeremy Coleman, Phila. Bible	.....................Sr	30	324	21	173	842	28.1
Jarett Kearse, Lincoln (Pa.)	.....................Sr	22	203	105	97	608	27.6
Kyle Myrick, Lincoln (Pa)	.....................Jr	27	280	19	132	711	26.3
Michael Reich, Colorado Col.	.....................Sr	23	182	39	189	592	25.7
Nick Thomas, Dubuque	.....................So	25	199	79	164	641	25.6
Cedric Isom, East Tex. Baptist	.....................Jr	25	233	41	96	603	24.1
Santo Provenzano, Hood	.....................So	25	206	5	179	596	23.8
Chris Hendershot, FDU-Florham	.....................Sr	25	204	7	175	590	23.6

REBOUNDS

Player and Team	Class	GP	Reb	Avg
Anthony Fitzgerald,Villa Julie	..........Jr	28	369	13.2
Jeremy Coleman, Phila. Bible	........Sr	30	391	13.0
Ifesinachi Anosike, Salem St	...........Sr	29	371	12.8
Tim Troy, Utica	...............Sr	25	310	12.4
Badou Gaye, Gwynedd-Mercy	......Sr	27	331	12.3
Sekani Francis, Lehman	.................Fr	27	327	12.1
Seth Hauben, Rochester	.................Sr	30	363	12.1
John Smith, Staten Island	.............Sr	29	346	11.9
Isaac Rosefelt, St. Thomas(Minn.)	.So	26	306	11.8
Shacun Malave, City Tech	..............Sr	25	290	11.6

ASSISTS

Player and Team	Class	GP	A	Avg
John Ancrum, Elma	.........................So	29	245	8.4
Mike McGarvey, Ursinus	.................Jr	28	212	7.6
Kenny Wood, Villa Julie	...................Sr	28	205	7.3
Jake Green, Piedmont	....................Fr	26	185	7.1
Brian Adamczyk, Bridgewater St.	...Sr	26	180	6.9
Keith Darden, Concordia-Austin	.....Sr	25	170	6.8
Blake Brookman, Chris. Newport	...Sr	26	175	6.7
David Shepherd, Tufts	....................So	26	174	6.7
Kevin Christensen, Wis. Lutheran	...Sr	27	179	6.6
Chris Alesi, Baruch	........................Sr	25	161	6.4B

FIELD-GOAL PERCENTAGE

Player and Team	Class	GP	FG	FGA	Pct
Brandon King, Rowan	...............Sr	26	141	196	71.9
Ryan Hodges, Cal Lutheran	.....Sr	23	187	273	68.5
Philip Hawley, Randolph-Macon	So	27	159	237	67.1
Brice Assie, Western Conn. St.	..Sr	29	225	339	66.4
Ifesinachi Anosike, Salem St.	.....Sr	29	148	225	65.8
Robert Cates, Southwestern	.....Jr	27	141	215	65.6
Jajcen Harris, Lake Erie	...........So	27	150	234	64.1
Badou Gaye, Gwynedd-Mercy	..Sr	27	218	343	63.6
Evan Arnold, Illinois Col.	...........Sr	23	123	194	63.4
Franklyn Beckford, Lake Forest	..Jr	24	120	190	63.2

Note: Minimum 5 made per game.

FREE-THROW PERCENTAGE

Player and Team	Class	GP	FT	FTA	Pct
Hans Hoeg, Wis.-River Falls	....So	25	113	121	93.4
Casey Meador, Louisiana Col.	...Jr	24	74	81	91.4
Eric Dickenson, Oglethorpe	.....So	24	143	157	91.1
Kent Raymond, Wheaton (Ill.)	...Fr	26	98	108	90.7
Adam Rich, Thomas	.....................Jr	26	70	78	89.7
Nick Bennett, Wis.-Stev. Pnt.	....Sr	32	110	123	89.4
Dan Thomas, Pitt.- Bradford	...So	25	84	94	89.4
Kevin Christensen, Wis. Luth.	...Sr	27	125	140	89.3
Greg Badenhop, Ohio Northern	So	26	102	115	88.7
Aubrey Shelton, Puget Sound	...Sr	26	94	106	88.7

Note: Minimum 2.5 made per game.

SCORING

Player and Team	Class	GP	TFG	3FG	FT	Pts	Avg
Camille Manning, City Tech	Sr	24	194	68	166	622	25.9
Stephanie Cleary, Ithaca	Sr	29	227	54	154	662	22.8
Sharon Billips, Farmingdale	Sr	29	252	34	110	648	22.3
Ashley Edwards, Concordia-Austin	Sr	26	266	59	178	569	21.9
Sarah DeLuca, Gordon	Sr	28	225	20	138	608	21.7
Leigh Sulkowski, Wash. & Jeff.	Jr	23	190	40	78	498	21.7
DeeDee Arnall, Pacific (Ore.)	Jr	25	199	0	133	531	21.2
Shayla Bell, John Carroll	Jr	25	182	17	117	498	19.9
Acasha Gordon, Staten Island	So	29	218	61	74	571	19.7
Chelsea Lutha, Widener	Jr	27	180	8	159	527	19.5

REBOUNDS

Player and Team	Class	GP	Reb	Avg
Chari' Cooper, Kean	Fr	24	368	15.3
Jacclyn Rock, Staten Island	Sr	29	415	14.3
Cheyenne Noble, Wentworth Inst.	So	25	334	13.4
Kim, Enoch, Greensboro	Fr	22	285	13.0
Tarn Udall, Colorado Col.	Fr	25	322	12.9
Lauren Dodrill, Frank & Marsh	Sr	25	316	12.6
Cassie Womack, Shenandoah	So	25	312	12.5
Jaime Wiliams, Immaculata	Sr	20	249	12.5
Amanda Chapin, Westfield St.	Jr	23	284	12.3
Jocelyn McNair, Becker	So	25	306	12.2

FIELD-GOAL PERCENTAGE

Player and Team	Class	GP	FG	FGA	Pct
Vanessa Wyffels, Willamette	Fr	24	173	233	74.2
Kim Sheets, Webster	Jr	28	157	248	63.3
Karalyn Dehn, Ripon	Jr	27	168	266	63.2
Hannah Stubbs, Wslyn (CT)	Jr	27	187	299	62.5
Lisa Winkle, Calvin	So	30	205	342	59.9
Ashley Riley, Kalamazoo	Sr	26	141	237	59.5
Debbie Bruen, Mary Wash.	So	29	155	262	59.2
Lisa Martinez, Mary Hardin	Jr	25	171	290	59.0
Danielle Holbrook, Otterbein	Sr	27	176	304	57.9
Kristen Benjamin, Thiel	Sr	26	174	302	57.6

Note: Minimum 5 made per game.

ASSISTS

Player and Team	Class	GP	A	Avg
Tara Toland, Ferrum	Sr	26	193	7.4
Mandy Pearson, Concordia-M'head	Sr	24	175	7.3
Marissa Coop, LeTourneau	Jr	25	178	7.1
Symbri Tuttle, McMurry	So	24	166	6.9
Tiffany Trent, Cazenovia	Sr	22	139	6.3
Kristen McDonald, Calvin	Sr	30	185	6.2
Kira Peterson, Coast Guard	Sr	26	160	6.2
Nicole Stefanski, Staten Island	Fr	29	172	5.9
Marisa Clark, Medaille	Fr	27	155	5.7
Sarah Dorman, Keuka	So	24	137	5.7

FREE-THROW PERCENTAGE

Player and Team	Class	GP	FT	FTA	Pct
Kari Simpson, Me.-Farmington	So	28	95	106	89.6
Kelly Turner, Pacific Lutheran	Jr	25	76	85	89.4
Ashley Edwards, Cncrd-Austin	Sr	26	178	200	89.0
Alison Kessler, St. Ma. (Ind.)	Fr	26	89	100	89.0
Colleen Hession, Williams	Jr	26	84	95	88.4
Nya Geschke, Wis.-White.	Sr	26	92	105	87.6
Heather Kessler, York(Pa.)	Sr	26	92	105	87.6
Jacey Brooks, Buffalo St.	Jr	26	107	123	87.0
K.J. Krasco, Colby-Sawyer	Jr	29	103	119	86.6
Marissa Coop, LeTourneau	Jr	25	87	101	86.1

Note: Minimum 2.5 made per game.

FOR THE RECORD·Year by Year

NCAA Men's Division I Championship Results

NCAA Final Four Results

Year	Winner	Score	Runner-up	Third Place	Fourth Place	Winning Coach
1939	Oregon	46–33	Ohio St	*Oklahoma	*Villanova	Howard Hobson
1940	Indiana	60–42	Kansas	*Duquesne	*Southern Cal	Branch McCracken
1941	Wisconsin	39–34	Washington St	*Pittsburgh	*Arkansas	Harold Foster
1942	Stanford	53–38	Dartmouth	*Colorado	*Kentucky	Everett Dean
1943	Wyoming	46–34	Georgetown	*Texas	*DePaul	Everett Shelton
1944	Utah	42–40 (OT)	Dartmouth	*Iowa St	*Ohio St	Vadal Peterson
1945	Oklahoma St	49–45	NYU	*Arkansas	*Ohio St	Hank Iba
1946	Oklahoma St	43–40	N Carolina	Ohio St	California	Hank Iba
1947	Holy Cross	58–47	Oklahoma	Texas	CCNY	Alvin Julian
1948	Kentucky	58–42	Baylor	Holy Cross	Kansas St	Adolph Rupp
1949	Kentucky	46–36	Oklahoma St	Illinois	Oregon St	Adolph Rupp
1950	CCNY	71–68	Bradley	N Carolina St	Baylor	Nat Holman
1951	Kentucky	68–58	Kansas St	Illinois	Oklahoma St	Adolph Rupp
1952	Kansas	80–63	St. John's (NY)	Illinois	Santa Clara	Forrest Allen
1953	Indiana	69–68	Kansas	Washington	Louisiana St	Branch McCracken
1954	La Salle	92–76	Bradley	Penn St	Southern Cal	Kenneth Loeffler
1955	San Francisco	77–63	La Salle	Colorado	Iowa	Phil Woolpert
1956	San Francisco	83–71	Iowa	Temple	Southern Meth	Phil Woolpert
1957	N Carolina	54–53 (3OT)	Kansas	San Francisco	Michigan St	Frank McGuire
1958	Kentucky	84–72	Seattle	Temple	Kansas St	Adolph Rupp
1959	California	71–70	W Virginia	Cincinnati	Louisville	Pete Newell
1960	Ohio St	75–55	California	Cincinnati	NYU	Fred Taylor
1961	Cincinnati	70–65 (OT)	Ohio St	Vacated‡	Utah	Edwin Jucker
1962	Cincinnati	71–59	Ohio St	Wake Forest	UCLA	Edwin Jucker
1963	Loyola (IL)	60–58 (OT)	Cincinnati	Duke	Oregon St	George Ireland
1964	UCLA	98–83	Duke	Michigan	Kansas St	John Wooden
1965	UCLA	91–80	Michigan	Princeton	Wichita St	John Wooden
1966	UTEP	72–65	Kentucky	Duke	Utah	Don Haskins
1967	UCLA	79–64	Dayton	Houston	N Carolina	John Wooden
1968	UCLA	78–55	N Carolina	Ohio St	Houston	John Wooden
1969	UCLA	92–72	Purdue	Drake	N Carolina	John Wooden
1970	UCLA	80–69	Jacksonville	New Mexico St	St. Bonaventure	John Wooden
1971	UCLA	68–62	Vacated‡	Vacated‡	Kansas	John Wooden
1972	UCLA	81–76	Florida St	N Carolina	Louisville	John Wooden
1973	UCLA	87–66	Memphis St	Indiana	Providence	John Wooden
1974	N Carolina St	76–64	Marquette	UCLA	Kansas	Norm Sloan
1975	UCLA	92–85	Kentucky	Louisville	Syracuse	John Wooden
1976	Indiana	86–68	Michigan	UCLA	Rutgers	Bob Knight
1977	Marquette	67–59	N Carolina	UNLV	NC-Charlotte	Al McGuire
1978	Kentucky	94–88	Duke	Arkansas	Notre Dame	Joe Hall
1979	Michigan St	75–64	Indiana St	DePaul	Penn	Jud Heathcote
1980	Louisville	59–54	Vacated‡	Purdue	Iowa	Denny Crum
1981	Indiana	63–50	N Carolina	Virginia	Louisiana St	Bob Knight
1982	N Carolina	63–62	Georgetown	*Houston	*Louisville	Dean Smith
1983	N Carolina St	54–52	Houston	*Georgia	*Louisville	Jim Valvano
1984	Georgetown	84–75	Houston	*Kentucky	*Virginia	John Thompson
1985	Villanova	66–64	Georgetown	St. John's (NY)	Vacated‡	Rollie Massimino
1986	Louisville	72–69	Duke	*Kansas	*Louisiana St	Denny Crum
1987	Indiana	74–73	Syracuse	*UNLV	*Providence	Bob Knight
1988	Kansas	83–79	Oklahoma	*Arizona	*Duke	Larry Brown
1989	Michigan	80–79 (OT)	Seton Hall	*Duke	*Illinois	Steve Fisher
1990	UNLV	103–73	Duke	*Arkansas	*Georgia Tech	Jerry Tarkanian
1991	Duke	72–65	Kansas	*UNLV	*N Carolina	Mike Krzyzewski
1992	Duke	71–51	Michigan	*Cincinnati	*Indiana	Mike Krzyzewski
1993	N Carolina	77–71	Michigan	*Kansas	*Kentucky	Dean Smith
1994	Arkansas	76–72	Duke	*Arizona	*Florida	Nolan Richardson
1995	UCLA	89–78	Arkansas	*N Carolina	*Oklahoma St	Jim Harrick
1996	Kentucky	76–67	Syracuse	Vacated‡	Mississippi St	Rick Pitino
1997	Arizona	84–79 (OT)	Kentucky	*Minnesota	*N Carolina	Lute Olson
1998	Kentucky	78–69	Utah	*Stanford	*N Carolina	Tubby Smith
1999	Connecticut	77–74	Duke	*Michigan St	*Ohio St	Jim Calhoun
2000	Michigan St	89–76	Florida	*Wisconsin	*N Carolina	Tom Izzo
2001	Duke	82–72	Arizona	*Maryland	*Michigan St	Mike Krzyzewski
2002	Maryland	64–52	Indiana	*Kansas	*Oklahoma	Gary Williams
2003	Syracuse	81–78	Kansas	*Marquette	*Texas	Jim Boeheim
2004	Connecticut	82–73	Georgia Tech	*Oklahoma St	*Duke	Jim Calhoun
2005	North Carolina	75-70	Illinois	*Louisville	*Michigan St	Roy Williams

*Tied for third place. ‡Student-athletes representing St. Joseph's (PA) in 1961, Villanova in 1971, Western Kentucky in 1971, UCLA in 1980, Memphis State in 1985 and Massachusetts in 1996 were declared ineligible subsequent to the tournament. Under NCAA rules, the teams' and ineligible student-athletes' records were deleted, and the teams' places in the standings were vacated.

NCAA Final Four MVPs

Year	Winner, School	GP	Field Goals FGM	Field Goals Pct	3-Pt FG FGA	3-Pt FG FGM	Free Throws FTM	Free Throws Pct	Reb	A	Stl	BS	Avg
1939	None selected												
1940	Marv Huffman, Indiana	2	7	—	—	—	4	—	—	—	—	—	9.0
1941	John Kotz, Wisconsin	2	8	—	—	—	6	—	—	—	—	—	11.0
1942	Howard Dallmar, Stanford	2	8	—	—	—	4	66.7	—	—	—	—	10.0
1943	Ken Sailors, Wyoming	2	10	—	—	—	8	72.7	—	—	—	—	14.0
1944	Arnie Ferrin, Utah	2	11	—	—	—	6	—	—	—	—	—	14.0
1945	Bob Kurland, Oklahoma St	2	16	—	—	—	5	—	—	—	—	—	18.5
1946	Bob Kurland, Oklahoma St	2	21	—	—	—	10	66.7	—	—	—	—	26.0
1947	George Kaftan, Holy Cross	2	18	—	—	—	12	70.6	—	—	—	—	24.0
1948	Alex Groza, Kentucky	2	16	—	—	—	5	—	—	—	—	—	18.5
1949	Alex Groza, Kentucky	2	19	—	—	—	14	—	—	—	—	—	26.0
1950	Irwin Dambrot, CCNY	2	12	42.9	—	—	4	50.0	—	—	—	—	14.0
1951	None selected												
1952	Clyde Lovellette, Kansas	2	24	—	—	—	18	—	—	—	—	—	33.0
1953	*B.H. Horn, Kansas	2	17	—	—	—	17	—	—	—	—	—	25.5
1954	Tom Gola, La Salle	2	12	—	—	—	14	—	—	—	—	—	19.0
1955	*Bill Russell, San Francisco	2	19	—	—	—	9	—	—	—	—	—	23.5
1956	*Hal Lear, Temple	2	32	—	—	—	16	—	—	—	—	—	40.0
1957	*Wilt Chamberlain, Kansas	2	18	51.4	—	—	19	70.4	25	—	—	—	32.5
1958	*Elgin Baylor, Seattle	2	18	34.0	—	—	12	75.0	41	—	—	—	24.0
1959	*Jerry West, West Virginia	2	22	66.7	—	—	22	68.8	25	—	—	—	33.0
1960	Jerry Lucas, Ohio State	2	16	66.7	—	—	3	100.0	23	—	—	—	17.5
1961	*Jerry Lucas, Ohio State	2	20	71.4	—	—	16	94.1	25	—	—	—	28.0
1962	Paul Hogue, Cincinnati	2	23	63.9	—	—	12	63.2	38	—	—	—	29.0
1963	Art Heyman, Duke	2	18	41.0	—	—	15	68.2	19	—	—	—	25.5
1964	Walt Hazzard, UCLA	2	11	55.0	—	—	8	66.7	10	—	—	—	15.0
1965	*Bill Bradley, Princeton	2	34	63.0	—	—	19	95.0	24	—	—	—	43.5
1966	*Jerry Chambers, Utah	2	25	53.2	—	—	20	83.3	35	—	—	—	35.0
1967	Lew Alcindor, UCLA	2	14	60.9	—	—	11	45.8	38	—	—	—	19.5
1968	Lew Alcindor, UCLA	2	22	62.9	—	—	9	90.0	34	—	—	—	26.5
1969	Lew Alcindor, UCLA	2	23	67.7	—	—	16	64.0	41	—	—	—	31.0
1970	Sidney Wicks, UCLA	2	15	71.4	—	—	9	60.0	34	—	—	—	19.5
1971	*†Howard Porter, Villanova	2	20	48.8	—	—	7	77.8	24	—	—	—	23.5
1972	Bill Walton, UCLA	2	20	69.0	—	—	17	73.9	41	—	—	—	28.5
1973	Bill Walton, UCLA	2	28	82.4	—	—	2	40.0	30	—	—	—	29.0
1974	David Thompson, NC State	2	19	51.4	—	—	11	78.6	17	—	—	—	24.5
1975	Richard Washington, UCLA	2	23	54.8	—	—	8	72.7	20	—	—	—	27.0
1976	Kent Benson, Indiana	2	17	50.0	—	—	7	63.6	18	—	—	—	20.5
1977	Butch Lee, Marquette	2	11	34.4	—	—	8	100.0	6	2	1	1	15.0
1978	Jack Givens, Kentucky	2	28	65.1	—	—	8	66.7	17	4	1	3	32.0
1979	Earvin Johnson, Michigan St	2	17	68.0	—	—	19	86.4	17	3	0	2	26.5
1980	Darrell Griffith, Louisville	2	23	62.2	—	—	11	68.8	7	15	0	2	28.5
1981	Isiah Thomas, Indiana	2	14	56.0	—	—	9	81.8	4	9	3	4	18.5
1982	James Worthy, N Carolina	2	20	74.1	—	—	2	28.6	8	9	0	4	21.0
1983	*Akeem Olajuwon, Houston	2	16	55.2	—	—	9	64.3	40	3	2	5	20.5
1984	Patrick Ewing, Georgetown	2	8	57.1	—	—	2	100.0	18	1	1	15	9.0
1985	Ed Pinckney, Villanova	2	8	57.1	—	—	12	75.0	15	6	3	0	14.0
1986	Pervis Ellison, Louisville	2	15	60.0	—	—	6	75.0	24	2	3	1	18.0
1987	Keith Smart, Indiana	2	14	63.6	1	0	7	77.8	7	7	0	2	17.5
1988	Danny Manning, Kansas	2	25	55.6	1	0	6	66.7	17	4	8	9	28.0
1989	Glen Rice, Michigan	2	24	49.0	16	7	4	100.0	16	1	0	3	29.5
1990	Anderson Hunt, UNLV	2	19	61.3	16	9	2	50.0	4	9	1	1	24.5
1991	Christian Laettner, Duke	2	12	54.5	1	1	21	91.3	17	2	1	2	23.0
1992	Bobby Hurley, Duke	2	10	41.7	12	7	8	80.0	3	11	0	3	17.5
1993	Donald Williams, N Carolina	2	15	65.2	14	10	10	100.0	4	2	2	0	25.0
1994	Corliss Williamson, Arkansas	2	21	50.0	0	0	10	71.4	21	8	4	3	26.0
1995	Ed O'Bannon, UCLA	2	16	45.7	8	3	10	76.9	25	3	7	1	22.5
1996	Tony Delk, Kentucky	2	15	41.7	16	8	6	54.6	9	2	3	2	22.0
1997	Miles Simon, Arizona	2	17	45.9	10	3	17	77.3	8	6	0	1	27.0
1998	Jeff Sheppard, Kentucky	2	16	55.2	10	4	7	77.8	10	7	4	0	21.5
1999	Richard Hamilton, Connecticut	2	20	51.3	7	3	8	72.7	12	4	2	1	25.5
2000	Mateen Cleaves, Michigan St	2	8	44.4	4	3	10	83.3	6	5	2	0	14.5
2001	Shane Battier, Duke	2	13	50.0	12	5	12	70.6	19	8	2	6	21.5
2002	Juan Dixon, Maryland	2	16	59.3	15	7	12	80.0	8	5	7	0	25.5
2003	Carmelo Anthony, Syracuse	2	19	54.3	6	9	9	81.1	24	8	4	0	26.5
2004	Emeka Okafor, Connecticut	2	17	65.4	0	0	8	53.3	22	2	1	4	21.0
2005	Sean May, North Carolina	2	19	65.5	0	0	10	71.4	17	5	1	2	24.0

*Not a member of the championship-winning team.   †Record later vacated.

Best NCAA Tournament Single-Game Scoring Performances

Player and Team	Year	Round	FG	3FG	FT	TP
Austin Carr, Notre Dame vs Ohio	1970	1st	25	—	11	61
Bill Bradley, Princeton vs Wichita St	1965	C*	22	—	14	58
Oscar Robertson, Cincinnati vs Arkansas	1958	C	21	—	14	56
Austin Carr, Notre Dame vs Kentucky	1970	2nd	22	—	8	52
Austin Carr, Notre Dame vs Texas Christian	1971	1st	20	—	12	52
David Robinson, Navy vs Michigan	1987	1st	22	0	6	50
Elvin Hayes, Houston vs Loyola (IL)	1968	1st	20	—	9	49
Hal Lear, Temple vs SMU	1956	C*	17	—	14	48
Austin Carr, Notre Dame vs Houston	1971	C	17	—	13	47
Dave Corzine, DePaul vs Louisville	1978	2nd	18	—	10	46

C=regional third place; C*=third-place game.

NIT Championship Results

Year	Winner	Score	Runner-up	Year	Winner	Score	Runner-up
1938	Temple	60–36	Colorado	1972	Maryland	100–69	Niagara
1939	Long Island U	44–32	Loyola (IL)	1973	Virginia Tech	92–91 (OT)	Notre Dame
1940	Colorado	51–40	Duquesne	1974	Purdue	97–81	Utah
1941	Long Island U	56–42	Ohio U	1975	Princeton	80–69	Providence
1942	W Virginia	47–45	W Kentucky	1976	Kentucky	71–67	NC-Charlotte
1943	St. John's (NY)	48–27	Toledo	1977	St. Bonaventure	94–91	Houston
1944	St. John's (NY)	47–39	DePaul	1978	Texas	101–93	N Carolina St
1945	DePaul	71–54	Bowling Green	1979	Indiana	53–52	Purdue
1946	Kentucky	46–45	Rhode Island	1980	Virginia	58–55	Minnesota
1947	Utah	49–45	Kentucky	1981	Tulsa	86–84 (OT)	Syracuse
1948	St. Louis	65–52	NYU	1982	Bradley	67–58	Purdue
1949	San Francisco	48–47	Loyola (IL)	1983	Fresno St	69–60	DePaul
1950	CCNY	69–61	Bradley	1984	Michigan	83–63	Notre Dame
1951	BYU	62–43	Dayton	1985	UCLA	65–62	Indiana
1952	La Salle	75–64	Dayton	1986	Ohio St	73–63	Wyoming
1953	Seton Hall	58–46	St. John's (NY)	1987	Southern Miss	84–80	La Salle
1954	Holy Cross	71–62	Duquesne	1988	Connecticut	72–67	Ohio St
1955	Duquesne	70–58	Dayton	1989	St. John's (NY)	73–65	St. Louis
1956	Louisville	93–80	Dayton	1990	Vanderbilt	74–72	St. Louis
1957	Bradley	84–83	Memphis St	1991	Stanford	78–72	Oklahoma
1958	Xavier (OH)	78–74 (OT)	Dayton	1992	Virginia	81–76	Notre Dame
1959	St. John's (NY)	76–71 (OT)	Bradley	1993	Minnesota	62–61	Georgetown
1960	Bradley	88–72	Providence	1994	Villanova	80–73	Vanderbilt
1961	Providence	62–59	St. Louis	1995	Virginia Tech	65–64 (OT)	Marquette
1962	Dayton	73–67	St. John's (NY)	1996	Nebraska	60–56	St. Joseph's
1963	Providence	81–66	Canisius	1997	Michigan	82–73	Florida St
1964	Bradley	86–54	New Mexico	1998	Minnesota	79–72	Penn St
1965	St. John's (NY)	55–51	Villanova	1999	California	61–60	Clemson
1966	BYU	97–84	NYU	2000	Wake Forest	71–61	Notre Dame
1967	Southern Illinois	71–56	Marquette	2001	Tulsa	79–60	Alabama
1968	Dayton	61–48	Kansas	2002	Memphis	72–62	S Carolina
1969	Temple	89–76	Boston College	2003	St. John's	70–67	Georgetown
1970	Marquette	65–53	St. John's (NY)	2004	Michigan	62–55	Rutgers
1971	N Carolina	84–66	Georgia Tech	2005	South Carolina	60–57	Saint Joseph's

NCAA Men's Division I Season Leaders

Scoring Average

Year	Player and Team	Ht	Class	GP	FG	3FG	FT	Pts	Avg
1948	Murray Wier, Iowa	5-9	Sr	19	152	—	95	399	21.0
1949	Tony Lavelli, Yale	6-3	Sr	30	228	—	215	671	22.4
1950	Paul Arizin, Villanova	6-3	Sr	29	260	—	215	735	25.3
1951	Bill Mlkvy, Temple	6-4	Sr	25	303	—	125	731	29.2
1952	Clyde Lovellette, Kansas	6-9	Sr	28	315	—	165	795	28.4
1953	Frank Selvy, Furman	6-3	Jr	25	272	—	194	738	29.5
1954	Frank Selvy, Furman	6-3	Sr	29	427	—	355	1209	41.7
1955	Darrell Floyd, Furman	6-1	Jr	25	344	—	209	897	35.9
1956	Darrell Floyd, Furman	6-1	Sr	28	339	—	268	946	33.8
1957	Grady Wallace, S Carolina	6-4	Sr	29	336	—	234	906	31.2
1958	Oscar Robertson, Cincinnati	6-5	So	28	352	—	280	984	35.1
1959	Oscar Robertson, Cincinnati	6-5	Jr	30	331	—	316	978	32.6
1960	Oscar Robertson, Cincinnati	6-5	Sr	30	369	—	273	1011	33.7
1961	Frank Burgess, Gonzaga	6-1	Sr	26	304	—	234	842	32.4
1962	Billy McGill, Utah	6-9	Sr	26	394	—	221	1009	38.8
1963	Nick Werkman, Seton Hall	6-3	Jr	22	221	—	208	650	29.5
1964	Howard Komives, Bowling Green	6-1	Sr	23	292	—	260	844	36.7

Scoring Average (Cont.)

Year	Player and Team	Ht	Class	GP	FG	3FG	FT	Pts	Avg
1965	Rick Barry, Miami (FL)	6-7	Sr	26	340	—	293	973	37.4
1966	Dave Schellhase, Purdue	6-4	Sr	24	284	—	213	781	32.5
1967	Jim Walker, Providence	6-3	Sr	28	323	—	205	851	30.4
1968	Pete Maravich, Louisiana St	6-5	So	26	432	—	274	1138	43.8
1969	Pete Maravich, Louisiana St	6-5	Jr	26	433	—	282	1148	44.2
1970	Pete Maravich, Louisiana St	6-5	Sr	31	522	—	337	1381	44.5
1971	Johnny Neumann, Mississippi	6-6	So	23	366	—	191	923	40.1
1972	Dwight Lamar, Southwestern Louisiana	6-1	Jr	29	429	—	196	1054	36.3
1973	William Averitt, Pepperdine	6-1	Sr	25	352	—	144	848	33.9
1974	Larry Fogle, Canisius	6-5	So	25	326	—	183	835	33.4
1975	Bob McCurdy, Richmond	6-7	Sr	26	321	—	213	855	32.9
1976	Marshall Rodgers, TX-Pan American	6-2	Sr	25	361	—	197	919	36.8
1977	Freeman Williams, Portland St	6-4	Jr	26	417	—	176	1010	38.8
1978	Freeman Williams, Portland St	6-4	Sr	27	410	—	149	969	35.9
1979	Lawrence Butler, Idaho St	6-3	Sr	27	310	—	192	812	30.1
1980	Tony Murphy, Southern-BR	6-3	Sr	29	377	—	178	932	32.1
1981	Zam Fredrick, S Carolina	6-2	Sr	27	300	—	181	781	28.9
1982	Harry Kelly, Texas Southern	6-7	Jr	29	336	—	190	862	29.7
1983	Harry Kelly, Texas Southern	6-7	Sr	29	333	—	169	835	28.8
1984	Joe Jakubick, Akron	6-5	Sr	27	304	—	206	814	30.1
1985	Xavier McDaniel, Wichita St	6-8	Sr	31	351	—	142	844	27.2
1986	Terrance Bailey, Wagner	6-2	Jr	29	321	—	212	854	29.4
1987	Kevin Houston, Army	5-11	Sr	29	311	63	268	953	32.9
1988	Hersey Hawkins, Bradley	6-3	Sr	31	377	87	284	1125	36.3
1989	Hank Gathers, Loyola Marymount	6-7	Jr	31	419	0	177	1015	32.7
1990	Bo Kimble, Loyola Marymount	6-5	Sr	32	404	92	231	1131	35.3
1991	Kevin Bradshaw, U.S. Int'l	6-6	Sr	28	358	60	278	1054	37.6
1992	Brett Roberts, Morehead St	6-8	Sr	29	278	66	193	815	28.1
1993	Greg Guy, TX-Pan American	6-1	Jr	19	189	67	111	556	29.3
1994	Glenn Robinson, Purdue	6-8	Jr	34	368	79	215	1030	30.3
1995	Kurt Thomas, Texas Christian	6-9	Sr	27	288	3	202	781	28.9
1996	Kevin Granger, Texas Southern	6-3	Sr	24	194	30	230	648	27.0
1997	Charles Jones, LIU-Brooklyn	6-3	Jr	30	338	109	118	903	30.1
1998	Charles Jones, LIU-Brooklyn	6-3	Sr	30	326	116	101	869	29.0
1999	Alvin Young, Niagara	6-3	Sr	29	253	65	157	728	25.1
2000	Courtney Alexander, Fresno St	6-6	Sr	27	252	58	107	669	24.8
2001	Ronnie McCollum, Centenary	6-4	Sr	27	244	85	214	787	29.1
2002	Jason Conley, Virginia Military	6-5	Fr	28	285	79	171	820	29.3
2003	Ruben Douglas, New Mexico	6-5	Sr	28	218	94	253	783	28.0
2004	Keydren Clark, St. Peter's	5-8	So	29	233	112	197	775	26.7
2005	Keydren Clark, St. Peter's	5-9	Jr	28	230	109	152	721	25.8

Rebounds

Year	Player and Team	Ht	Class	GP	Reb	Avg
1951	Ernie Beck, Pennsylvania	6-4	So	27	556	20.6
1952	Bill Hannon, Army	6-3	So	17	355	20.9
1953	Ed Conlin, Fordham	6-5	So	26	612	23.5
1954	Art Quimby, Connecticut	6-5	Jr	26	588	22.6
1955	Charlie Slack, Marshall	6-5	Jr	21	538	25.6
1956	Joe Holup, George Washington	6-6	Sr	26	604	†.256
1957	Elgin Baylor, Seattle	6-6	Jr	25	508	†.235
1958	Alex Ellis, Niagara	6-5	Sr	25	536	†.262
1959	Leroy Wright, Pacific	6-8	Jr	26	652	†.238
1960	Leroy Wright, Pacific	6-8	Sr	17	380	†.234
1961	Jerry Lucas, Ohio St	6-8	Jr	27	470	†.198
1962	Jerry Lucas, Ohio St	6-8	Sr	28	499	†.211
1963	Paul Silas, Creighton	6-7	Sr	27	557	20.6
1964	Bob Pelkington, Xavier (OH)	6-7	Sr	26	567	21.8
1965	Toby Kimball, Connecticut	6-8	Sr	23	483	21.0
1966	Jim Ware, Oklahoma City	6-8	Sr	29	607	20.9
1967	Dick Cunningham, Murray St	6-10	Jr	22	479	21.8
1968	Neal Walk, Florida	6-10	Jr	25	494	19.8
1969	Spencer Haywood, Detroit	6-8	So	22	472	21.5
1970	Artis Gilmore, Jacksonville	7-2	Jr	28	621	22.2
1971	Artis Gilmore, Jacksonville	7-2	Sr	26	603	23.2
1972	Kermit Washington, American	6-8	Jr	23	455	19.8
1973	Kermit Washington, American	6-8	Sr	22	439	20.0
1974	Marvin Barnes, Providence	6-9	Sr	32	597	18.7
1975	John Irving, Hofstra	6-9	So	21	323	15.4
1976	Sam Pellom, Buffalo	6-8	So	26	420	16.2
1977	Glenn Mosley, Seton Hall	6-8	Sr	29	473	16.3
1978	Ken Williams, N Texas St	6-7	Sr	28	411	14.7
1979	Monti Davis, Tennessee St	6-7	Jr	26	421	16.2
1980	Larry Smith, Alcorn St	6-8	Sr	26	392	15.1
1981	Darryl Watson, Miss Valley	6-7	Sr	27	379	14.0

Rebounds (Cont.)

Year	Player and Team	Ht	Class	GP	Reb	Avg
1982	LaSalle Thompson, Texas	6-10	Jr	27	365	13.5
1983	Xavier McDaniel, Wichita St	6-7	So	28	403	14.4
1984	Akeem Olajuwon, Houston	7-0	Jr	37	500	13.5
1985	Xavier McDaniel, Wichita St	6-8	Sr	31	460	14.8
1986	David Robinson, Navy	6-11	Jr	35	455	13.0
1987	Jerome Lane, Pittsburgh	6-6	So	33	444	13.5
1988	Kenny Miller, Loyola (IL)	6-9	Fr	29	395	13.6
1989	Hank Gathers, Loyola (CA)	6-7	Jr	31	426	13.7
1990	Anthony Bonner, St. Louis	6-8	Sr	33	456	13.8
1991	Shaquille O'Neal, Louisiana St	7-1	So	28	411	14.7
1992	Popeye Jones, Murray St	6-8	Sr	30	431	14.4
1993	Warren Kidd, Middle Tenn St	6-9	Sr	26	386	14.8
1994	Jerome Lambert, Baylor	6-8	Jr	24	355	14.8
1995	Kurt Thomas, Texas Christian	6-9	Sr	27	393	14.6
1996	Marcus Mann, Mississippi Valley	6-8	Sr	29	394	13.6
1997	Tim Duncan, Wake Forest	6-11	Sr	31	457	14.7
1998	Ryan Perryman, Dayton	6-7	Sr	33	412	12.5
1999	Ian McGinnis, Dartmouth	6-8	So	26	317	12.2
2000	Darren Phillips, Fairfield	6-7	Sr	29	405	14.0
2001	Chris Marcus, Western Kentucky	7-1	Jr	31	374	12.1
2002	Jeremy Bishop, Quinnipiac	6-6	Jr	29	347	12.0
2003	Brandon Hunter, Ohio	6-7	Sr	30	378	12.6
2004	Paul Millsap, Louisiana Tech	6-7	Fr	30	374	12.5
2005	Paul Millsap, Louisiana Tech	6-8	So	29	360	12.4

†From 1956–1962, title was based on highest individual recoveries out of total by both teams in all games.

Assists

Year	Player and Team	Class	GP	A	Avg
1984	Craig Lathen, IL-Chicago	Jr	29	274	9.45
1985	Rob Weingard, Hofstra	Sr	24	228	9.50
1986	Mark Jackson, St. John's (NY)	Jr	36	328	9.11
1987	Avery Johnson, Southern-BR	Jr	31	333	10.74
1988	Avery Johnson, Southern-BR	Sr	30	399	13.30
1989	Glenn Williams, Holy Cross	Sr	28	278	9.93
1990	Todd Lehmann, Drexel	Sr	28	260	9.29
1991	Chris Corchiani, N Carolina St	Sr	31	299	9.65
1992	Van Usher, Tennessee Tech	Sr	29	254	8.76
1993	Sam Crawford, New Mex St	Sr	34	310	9.12
1994	Jason Kidd, California	So	30	272	9.06
1995	Nelson Haggerty, Baylor	Sr	28	284	10.10
1996	Raimonds Miglinieks, UC-Irvine	Sr	27	230	8.52
1997	Kenny Mitchell, Dartmouth	Sr	26	203	7.81
1998	Ahlon Lewis, Arizona St	Sr	32	294	9.19
1999	Doug Gottlieb, Oklahoma St	Jr	34	299	8.79
2000	Mark Dickel, UNLV	Sr	31	280	9.03
2001	Markus Carr, Cal St-Northridge	Jr	32	286	8.94
2002	T.J. Ford, Texas	Fr	33	273	8.27
2003	Martell Bailey, IL-Chicago	Jr	30	244	8.13
2004	Greg Davis, Troy St	Sr	31	256	-8.26
2005	Damitrius Coleman, Mercer	Jr	28	224	8.00
	Will Funn, Portland St	Sr	28	224	8.00

Blocked Shots

Year	Player and Team	Class	GP	BS	Avg
1986	David Robinson, Navy	Jr	35	207	5.91
1987	David Robinson, Navy	Sr	32	144	4.50
1988	Rodney Blake, St. Joseph's (PA)	Sr	29	116	4.00
1989	Alonzo Mourning, Georgetown	Fr	34	169	4.97
1990	Kenny Green, Rhode Island	Sr	26	124	4.77
1991	Shawn Bradley, Brigham Young	Fr	34	177	5.21
1992	Shaquille O'Neal, Louisiana St	Jr	30	157	5.23
1993	Theo Ratliff, Wyoming	Jr	28	124	4.43
1994	Grady Livingston, Howard	Jr	26	115	4.42
1995	Keith Closs, Central Conn St	Fr	26	139	5.35
1996	Keith Closs, Central Conn St	So	28	178	6.36
1997	Adonal Foyle, Colgate	Jr	28	180	6.43
1998	Jerome James, Florida A&M	Sr	27	125	4.63
1999	Tarvis Williams, Hampton	Jr	27	135	5.00
2000	Ken Johnson, Ohio St	Sr	30	161	5.37
2001	Tarvis Williams, Hampton	Sr	32	147	4.59
2002	Wojciech Myrda, LA-Monroe	Sr	32	172	5.38
2003	Emeka Okafor, Connecticut	So	33	156	4.73
2004	Anwar Ferguson, Houston	Sr	27	111	4.11
2005	Deng Gai, Fairfield	Sr	30	165	5.50

Steals

Year	Player and Team	Class	GP	S	Avg
1986	Darron Brittman, Chicago St	Sr	28	139	4.96
1987	Tony Fairley, Charleston Sou	Sr	28	114	4.07
1988	Aldwin Ware, Florida A&M	Sr	29	142	4.90
1989	Kenny Robertson, Cleveland St	Jr	28	111	3.96
1990	Ronn McMahon, E Washington	Sr	29	130	4.48
1991	Van Usher, Tennessee Tech	Jr	28	104	3.71
1992	Victor Snipes, NE Illinois	So	25	86	3.44
1993	Jason Kidd, California	Fr	29	110	3.80
1994	Shawn Griggs, SW Louisiana	Sr	30	120	4.00
1995	Roderick Anderson, Texas	Sr	30	101	3.37
1996	Pointer Williams, McNeese St	Sr	27	118	4.37
1997	Joel Hoover, MD-Eastern Shore	Fr	28	90	3.21
1998	Bonzi Wells, Ball St	Sr	29	103	3.55
1999	Shawnta Rogers, George Wash	Sr	29	103	3.55
2000	Carl Williams, Liberty	Sr	28	107	3.82
2001	Greedy Daniels, Texas Christian	Jr	25	108	4.32
2002	Desmond Cambridge, AL A&M	Sr	29	160	5.52
2003	Alexis McMillan, Stetson	Sr	22	87	3.95
2004	Marques Green, St. Bonaventure	Sr	27	107	3.96
2005	Obie Trotter, Alabama A&M	Jr	32	125	3.91

Single Game Records

SCORING HIGHS VS DIVISION I OPPONENT

Pts	Player and Team vs Opponent	Date
72	Kevin Bradshaw, U.S. Int'l vs Loyola Marymount	1-5-91
69	Pete Maravich, Louisiana St vs Alabama	2-7-70
68	Calvin Murphy, Niagara vs Syracuse	12-7-68
66	Jay Handlan, Washington & Lee vs Furman	2-17-51
66	Pete Maravich, Louisiana St vs Tulane	2-10-69
66	Anthony Roberts, Oral Roberts vs N Carolina A&T	2-19-77
65	Anthony Roberts, Oral Roberts vs Oregon	3-9-77
65	Scott Haffner, Evansville vs Dayton	2-18-89
64	Pete Maravich, Louisiana St vs Kentucky	2-21-70
63	Johnny Neumann, Mississippi vs Louisiana St	1-30-71
63	Hersey Hawkins, Bradley vs Detroit	2-22-88

SCORING HIGHS VS NON-DIVISION I OPPONENT

Pts	Player and Team vs Opponent	Date
100	Frank Selvy, Furman vs Newberry	2-13-54
85	Paul Arizin, Villanova vs Philadelphia NAMC	2-12-49
81	Freeman Williams, Portland St vs Rocky Mountain	2-3-78
73	Bill Mlkvy, Temple vs Wilkes	3-3-51
71	Freeman Williams, Portland St vs Southern Oregon	2-9-77

REBOUNDING HIGHS ALL-TIME

Reb	Player and Team vs Opponent	Date
51	Bill Chambers, William & Mary vs Virginia	2-14-53
43	Charlie Slack, Marshall vs Morris Harvey	1-12-54
42	Tom Heinsohn, Holy Cross vs Boston College	3-1-55
40	Art Quimby, Connecticut vs Boston U	1-11-55
39	Maurice Stokes, St. Francis (PA) vs John Carroll	1-28-55
39	Dave DeBusschere, Detroit vs Central Michigan	1-30-60
39	Keith Swagerty, Pacific vs UC-Santa Barbara	3-5-65

REBOUNDING HIGHS SINCE 1973*

Reb	Player and Team vs Opponent	Date
35	Larry Abney, Fresno St vs Southern Methodist	2-17-00
34	David Vaughn, Oral Roberts vs Brandeis	1-8-73
32	Jervaughn Scales, Southern-BR vs Grambling	2-7-94
32	Durand Macklin, Louisiana St vs Tulane	11-26-76
31	Jim Bradley, Northern Illinois vs WI-Milwaukee	2-19-73
31	Calvin Natt, NE Louisiana vs Georgia Southern	12-29-76

ASSISTS

A	Player and Team vs Opponent	Date
22	Tony Fairley, Baptist vs Armstrong St	2-9-87
22	Avery Johnson, Southern-BR vs Texas Southern	1-25-88
22	Sherman Douglas, Syracuse vs Providence	1-28-89
21	Mark Wade, UNLV vs Navy	12-29-86

Single Game Records *(Cont.)*

21	Kelvin Scarborough, New Mexico vs Hawaii	2-13-87
21	Anthony Manuel, Bradley vs UC-Irvine	12-19-87
21	Avery Johnson, Southern-BR vs Alabama St	1-16-88

STEALS

S	Player and Team vs Opponent	Date
13	Mookie Blaylock, Oklahoma vs Centenary	12-12-87
13	Mookie Blaylock, Oklahoma vs Loyola Marymount	12-17-88
12	Kenny Robertson, Cleveland St vs Wagner	12-3-88
12	Terry Evans, Oklahoma vs Florida A&M	1-27-93
12	Richard Duncan, Middle Tenn St vs Eastern Kentucky	2-20-99
12	Greedy Daniels, Texas Christian vs AR–Pine Bluff	12-30-00
12	Jehiel Lewis, Navy vs Bucknell	1-12-02

BLOCKED SHOTS

BS	Player and Team vs Opponent	Date
14	David Robinson, Navy vs NC–Wilmington	1-4-86
14	Shawn Bradley, Brigham Young vs Eastern Kentucky	12-7-90
14	Roy Rogers, Alabama vs Georgia	2-10-96
14	Loren Woods, Arizona vs Oregon	2-3-00

Eight tied with 13

Single Season Records

POINTS

Player and Team	Year	GP	FG	3FG	FT	Pts
Pete Maravich, Louisiana St	1970	31	522	—	337	1381
Elvin Hayes, Houston	1968	33	519	—	176	1214
Frank Selvy, Furman	1954	29	427	—	355	1209
Pete Maravich, Louisiana St	1969	26	433	—	282	1148
Pete Maravich, Louisiana St	1968	26	432	—	274	1138
Bo Kimble, Loyola Marymount	1990	32	404	92	231	1131
Hersey Hawkins, Bradley	1988	31	377	87	284	1125
Austin Carr, Notre Dame	1970	29	444	—	218	1106
Austin Carr, Notre Dame	1971	29	430	—	241	1101
Otis Birdsong, Houston	1977	36	452	—	186	1090

SCORING AVERAGE

Player and Team	Year	GP	FG	3FG	FT	Pts	Avg
Pete Maravich, Louisiana St	1970	31	522		337	1381	44.5
Pete Maravich, Louisiana St	1969	26	433		282	1148	44.2
Pete Maravich, Louisiana St	1968	26	432		274	1138	43.8
Frank Selvy, Furman	1954	29	427		355	1209	41.7
Johnny Neumann, Mississippi	1971	23	366		191	923	40.1
Freeman Williams, Portland St	1977	26	417		176	1010	38.8
Billy McGill, Utah	1962	26	394		221	1009	38.8
Calvin Murphy, Niagara	1968	24	337		242	916	38.2
Austin Carr, Notre Dame	1970	29	444		218	1106	38.1
Austin Carr, Notre Dame	1971	29	430		241	1101	38.0

REBOUNDS

Player and Team	Year	GP	Reb	Player and Team	Year	GP	Reb
Walt Dukes, Seton Hall	1953	33	734	Artis Gilmore, Jacksonville	1970	28	621
Leroy Wright, Pacific	1959	26	652	Tom Gola, La Salle	1955	31	618
Tom Gola, La Salle	1954	30	652	Ed Conlin, Fordham	1953	26	612
Charlie Tyra, Louisville	1956	29	645	Art Quimby, Connecticut	1955	25	611
Paul Silas, Creighton	1964	29	631	Bill Russell, San Francisco	1956	29	609
Elvin Hayes, Houston	1968	33	624	Jim Ware, Oklahoma City	1966	29	607

REBOUND AVERAGE ALL-TIME

Player and Team	Year	GP	Reb	Avg
Charlie Slack, Marshall	1955	21	538	25.6
Leroy Wright, Pacific	1959	26	652	25.1
Art Quimby, Connecticut	1955	25	611	24.4
Charlie Slack, Marshall	1956	22	520	23.6
Ed Conlin, Fordham	1953	26	612	23.5

REBOUND AVERAGE SINCE 1973*

Player and Team	Year	GP	Reb	Avg
Kermit Washington, American	1973	22	439	20.0
Marvin Barnes, Providence	1973	30	571	19.0
Marvin Barnes, Providence	1974	32	597	18.7
Pete Padgett, NV-Reno	1973	26	462	17.8
Jim Bradley, Northern Illinois	1973	24	426	17.8

*Freshmen became eligible for varsity play in 1973.

Single Season Records *(Cont.)*

ASSISTS

Player and Team	Year	GP	A	Player and Team	Year	GP	A
Mark Wade, UNLV	1987	38	406	Sherman Douglas, Syracuse	1989	38	326
Avery Johnson, Southern-BR	1988	30	399	Sam Crawford, New Mex. St	1993	34	310
Anthony Manuel, Bradley	1988	31	373	Greg Anthony, UNLV	1991	35	310
Avery Johnson, Southern-BR	1987	31	333	Reid Gettys, Houston	1984	37	309
Mark Jackson, St. John's (NY)	1986	32	328	Carl Golston, Loyola (IL)	1985	33	305

ASSIST AVERAGE

Player and Team	Year	GP	A	Avg	Player and Team	Year	GP	A	Avg
Avery Johnson, Southern-BR	1988	30	399	13.3	Chris Corchiani, N Carolina St	1991	31	299	9.6
Anthony Manuel, Bradley	1988	31	373	12.0	Tony Fairley, Charleston So.*	1987	28	270	9.6
Avery Johnson, Southern-BR	1987	31	333	10.7	Tyrone Bogues, Wake Forest	1987	29	276	9.5
Mark Wade, UNLV	1987	38	406	10.7	Ron Weingard, Hofstra	1985	24	228	9.5
Nelson Haggerty, Baylor	1995	28	284	10.1	Craig Neal, Georgia Tech	1988	32	303	9.5
Glenn Williams, Holy Cross	1989	28	278	9.9	*Formerly Baptist.				

FIELD-GOAL PERCENTAGE

Player and Team	Year	GP	FG	FGA	Pct
Steve Johnson, Oregon St	1981	28	235	315	74.6
Dwayne Davis, Florida	1989	33	179	248	72.2
Keith Walker, Utica	1985	27	154	216	71.3
Steve Johnson, Oregon St	1980	30	211	297	71.0
Adam Mark, Belmont	2002	26	150	212	70.8
Oliver Miller, Arkansas	1991	38	254	361	70.4
Alan Williams, Princeton	1987	25	163	232	70.3
Mark McNamara, California	1982	27	231	329	70.2
Warren Kidd, Middle Tennessee St	1991	30	173	247	70.0
Pete Freeman, Akron	1991	28	175	250	70.0

Based on qualifiers for annual championship.

FREE-THROW PERCENTAGE

Player and Team	Year	GP	FT	FTA	Pct
Blake Ahearn SW Mo. St*	2004	33	117	120	97.5
Craig Collins, Penn St	1985	27	94	98	95.9
J.J. Redick, Duke	2004	37	143	150	95.3
Steve Drabyn, Belmont	2003	29	78	82	95.1
Rod Foster, UCLA	1982	27	95	100	95.0
Clay McKnight, Pacific	2000	24	74	78	94.9
Matt Logie, Lehigh	2003	28	91	96	94.8
Blake Ahearn, Missouri State	2005	32	90	95	94.7
Danny Basile, Marist	1994	27	84	89	94.4
Carlos Gibson, Marshall	1978	28	84	89	94.4
Jim Barton, Dartmouth	1986	26	65	69	94.2

*Southwest Missouri State changed name to Missouri State after 2004–05 season

Based on qualifiers for annual championship.

THREE-POINT FIELD-GOAL PERCENTAGE

Player and Team	Year	GP	3FG	3FGA	Pct
Glenn Tropf, Holy Cross	1988	29	52	82	63.4
Sean Wightman, Western Michigan	1992	30	48	76	63.2
Keith Jennings, E Tennessee St	1991	33	84	142	59.2
Dave Calloway, Monmouth (NJ)	1989	28	48	82	58.5
Steve Kerr, Arizona	1988	38	114	199	57.3
Reginald Jones, Prairie View	1987	28	64	112	57.1
Jim Cantamessa, Siena	1998	29	66	117	56.4
Joel Tribelhorn, Colorado St	1989	33	76	135	56.3
Mike Joseph, Bucknell	1988	28	65	116	56.0
Brian Jackson, Evansville	1995	27	53	95	55.8

Based on qualifiers for annual championship.

Single Season Records *(Cont.)*

STEALS

Player and Team	Year	GP	S
Desmond Cambridge, Alabama A&M	2002	29	160
Mookie Blaylock, Oklahoma	1988	39	150
Aldwin Ware, Florida A&M	1988	29	142
Darron Brittman, Chicago St	1986	28	139
John Linehan, Providence	2002	31	139

BLOCKED SHOTS

Player and Team	Year	GP	BS
David Robinson, Navy	1986	35	207
Adonal Foyle, Colgate	1997	28	180
Keith Closs, Central Conn St	1996	28	178
Shawn Bradley, BYU	1991	34	177
Wojiech Myrda, LA–Monroe	2002	32	172

STEAL AVERAGE

Player and Team	Year	GP	S	Avg
D. Cambridge, Alabama A&M	2002	29	160	5.52
Darron Brittman, Chicago St	1986	28	139	4.96
Aldwin Ware, Florida A&M	1988	29	142	4.90
John Linehan, Providence	2002	31	139	4.48
Ronn McMahon, E Washington	1990	29	130	4.48

BLOCKED-SHOT AVERAGE

Player and Team	Year	GP	BS	Avg
Adonal Foyle, Colgate	1997	28	180	6.43
Keith Closs, Central Conn St	1996	28	178	6.36
David Robinson, Navy	1986	35	207	5.91
Adonal Foyle, Colgate	1996	29	165	5.69
Deng Gai, Fairfield	2005	30	165	5.50

Career Records

POINTS

Player and Team	Ht	Final Year	GP	FG	3FG*	FT	Pts
Pete Maravich, Louisiana St	6-5	1970	83	1387	—	893	3667
Freeman Williams, Portland St	6-4	1978	106	1369	—	511	3249
Lionel Simmons, La Salle	6-7	1990	131	1244	56	673	3217
Alphonso Ford, Mississippi Valley	6-2	1993	109	1121	333	590	3165
Harry Kelly, Texas Southern	6-7	1983	110	1234	—	598	3066
Hersey Hawkins, Bradley	6-3	1988	125	1100	118	690	3008
Oscar Robertson, Cincinnati	6-5	1960	88	1052	—	869	2973
Danny Manning, Kansas	6-10	1988	147	1216	10	509	2951
Alfredrick Hughes, Loyola (IL)	6-5	1985	120	1226	—	462	2914
Elvin Hayes, Houston	6-8	1968	93	1215	—	454	2884
Larry Bird, Indiana St	6-9	1979	94	1154	—	542	2850
Otis Birdsong, Houston	6-4	1977	116	1176	—	480	2832
Kevin Bradshaw, Bethune-Cookman, U.S. Int'l	6-6	1991	111	1027	132	618	2804
Allan Houston, Tennessee	6-6	1993	128	902	346	651	2801
Hank Gathers, Southern Cal, Loyola Marymount	6-7	1990	117	1127	0	469	2723
Reggie Lewis, Northeastern	6-7	1987	122	1043	30 (1)	592	2708
Daren Queenan, Lehigh	6-5	1988	118	1024	29	626	2703
Byron Larkin, Xavier (OH)	6-3	1988	121	1022	51	601	2696
David Robinson, Navy	7-1	1987	127	1032	1	604	2669
Wayman Tisdale, Oklahoma	6-9	1985	104	1077	—	507	2661

*Listed is the number of three-pointers scored since it became the national rule in 1987; the number in the parentheses is number scored prior to 1987—these counted as three points in the game but counted as two-pointers in the national rankings. The three-pointers in the parentheses are not included in total points.

SCORING AVERAGE

Player and Team	Final Year	GP	FG	FT	Pts	Avg
Pete Maravich, Louisiana St	1968	83	1387	893	3667	44.2
Austin Carr, Notre Dame	1971	74	1017	526	2560	34.6
Oscar Robertson, Cincinnati	1960	88	1052	869	2973	33.8
Calvin Murphy, Niagara	1970	77	947	654	2548	33.1
Dwight Lamar, Southwestern Louisiana	1973	57	768	326	1862	32.7
Frank Selvy, Furman	1954	78	922	694	2538	32.5
Rick Mount, Purdue	1970	72	910	503	2323	32.3
Darrell Floyd, Furman	1956	71	868	545	2281	32.1
Nick Werkman, Seton Hall	1964	71	812	649	2273	32.0
Willie Humes, Idaho St	1971	48	565	380	1510	31.5
William Averitt, Pepperdine	1973	49	615	311	1541	31.4
Elgin Baylor, Coll. of Idaho, Seattle	1958	80	956	588	2500	31.3
Elvin Hayes, Houston	1968	93	1215	454	2884	31.0
Freeman Williams, Portland St	1978	106	1369	511	3249	30.7
Larry Bird, Indiana St	1979	94	1154	542	2850	30.3

Career Records *(Cont.)*

REBOUNDS ALL-TIME

Player and Team	Final Year	GP	Reb
Tom Gola, La Salle	1955	118	2201
Joe Holup, George Washington	1956	104	2030
Charlie Slack, Marshall	1956	88	1916
Ed Conlin, Fordham	1955	102	1884
Dickie Hemric, Wake Forest	1955	104	1802

REBOUNDS SINCE 1973*

Player and Team	Final Year	GP	Reb
Tim Duncan, Wake Forest	1997	128	1570
Derrick Coleman, Syracuse	1990	143	1537
Malik Rose, Drexel	1996	120	1514
Ralph Sampson, Virginia	1983	132	1511
Pete Padgett, NV-Reno	1976	104	1464

ASSISTS

Player and Team	Final Year	GP	A
Bobby Hurley, Duke	1993	140	1076
Chris Corchiani, N Carolina St	1991	124	1038
Ed Cota, N Carolina	2000	138	1030
Keith Jennings, E Tennessee St	1991	127	983
Steve Blake, Maryland	2003	138	972

FIELD-GOAL PERCENTAGE

Player and Team	Final Year	FG	FGA	Pct
Steve Johnson, Oregon St	1981	828	1222	67.8
Michael Bradley, Kentucky/Villanova	2001	441	651	67.7
Murray Brown, Florida St	1980	566	847	66.8
Lee Campbell, SW Missouri St	1990	411	618	66.5
Warren Kidd, Middle Tennessee St	1993	496	747	66.4

Note: Minimum 400 field goals and 4 FG made per game.

FREE-THROW PERCENTAGE

Player and Team	Final Year	FT	FTA	Pct
Gary Buchanan, Villanova	2003	324	355	91.3
Greg Starrick, Kentucky; Southern Illinois	1972	341	375	90.9
Jack Moore, Nebraska	1982	446	495	90.1
Steve Henson, Kansas St	1990	361	401	90.0
Steve Alford, Indiana	1987	535	596	89.8

Note: Minimum 300 free throws made.

*Freshmen became eligible for varsity play in 1973.

THEY SAID IT

Chattanooga women's basketball coach Wes Moore comparing his team with No. 1 Tennessee: "Their freshmen were high school McDonald's All-Americans; our freshmen ate at McDonalds in high school."

Career Records (Cont.)

THREE-POINT FIELD GOALS MADE

Player and Team	Final Year	GP	3FG
Curtis Staples, Virginia	1998	122	413
Keith Veney, Lamar; Marshall	1997	111	409
Doug Day, Radford	1993	117	401
Michael Watson, MO–Kansas City	2004	117	391
Ronnie Schmitz, MO–Kansas City	1993	112	378

THREE-POINT FIELD-GOAL PERCENTAGE

Player and Team	Final Year	3FG	3FGA	Pct
Tony Bennett, WI–Green Bay	1992	290	584	49.7
David Olson, Eastern Illinois	1992	262	562	46.6
Ross Land, Northern Arizona	2000	308	664	46.4
Dan Dickau, Washington/Gonzaga	2002	215	465	46.2
Sean Jackson, Ohio/Princeton	1992	243	528	46.0

Note: Minimum 200 3-point field goals and 2.0 3FG/G.

STEALS

Player and Team	Final Year	GP	S
John Linehan, Providence	2002	122	385
Eric Murdock, Providence	1991	117	376
Pepe Sanchez, Temple	2000	116	365
Cookie Belcher, Nebraska	2001	131	353
Kevin Braswell, Georgetown	2002	128	349

BLOCKED SHOTS

Player and Team	Final Year	GP	BS
Wojciech Myrda, Louisiana-Monroe	2002	115	535
Adonal Foyle, Colgate	1997	87	492
Tim Duncan, Wake Forest	1997	128	481
Alonzo Mourning, Georgetown	1992	120	453
Tarvis Williams, Hampton	2001	114	452

NCAA Men's Division I Team Leaders

Division I Team Alltime Wins

Team	First Year	Yrs	W	L	T
Kentucky	1903	102	1904	583	1
N Carolina	1911	95	1860	681	0
Kansas	1899	107	1848	769	0
Duke	1906	100	1764	787	0
St. John's (NY)	1908	98	1677	802	0
Syracuse	1901	104	1657	759	0
Temple	1895	109	1639	.902	0
Pennsylvania	1897	105	1592	892	2
Indiana	1901	105	1570	853	0
Notre Dame	1898	100	1565	863	1
UCLA	1920	86	1549	700	0
Oregon St	1902	104	1546	1098	0
Utah	1909	97	1570	799	0
Princeton	1901	105	1510	917	0
Purdue	1897	107	1470	863	0
Washington	1896	103	1463	992	0

Note: Minimum of 25 years in Division I.

Division I Alltime Winning Percentage

Team	First Year	Yrs	W	L	T	Pct
Kentucky	1903	102	1904	583	1	.765
N Carolina	1911	95	1860	681	0	.732
UNLV	1959	47	963	390	0	.712
Kansas	1899	107	1848	769	0	.706
Duke	1906	100	1764	787	0	.691
UCLA	1920	86	1549	700	0	.689
Syracuse	1901	104	1657	759	0	.686
St. John's (NY)	1908	98	1677	802	0	.676
Western Kentucky	1915	86	1503	745	0	.669
Utah	1909	98	1570	799	0	.663
Illinois	1906	100	1520	805	0	.654
Louisville	1912	91	1484	793	0	.652
Arizona	1905	100	1488	805	1	.649
Indiana	1901	105	1570	853	0	.648
Arkansas	1924	82	1407	770	0	.646
Temple	1895	109	1639	902	0	.645
Notre Dame	1898	100	1565	863	1	.645

NCAA Men's Division I Winning Streaks

Longest—Full Season

Team	Games	Years	Ended by
UCLA	88	1971–74	Notre Dame (71–70)
San Francisco	60	1955–57	Illinois (62–33)
UCLA	47	1966–68	Houston (71–69)
UNLV	45	1990–91	Duke (79–77)
Texas	44	1913–17	Rice (24–18)
Seton Hall	43	1939–41	LIU-Brooklyn (49–26)
LIU-Brooklyn	43	1935–37	Stanford (45–31)
UCLA	41	1968–69	Southern Cal (46–44)
Marquette	39	1970–71	Ohio St (60–59)
Cincinnati	37	1962–63	Wichita St (65–64)
N Carolina	37	1957–58	W Virginia (75–64)

Longest—Regular Season

Team	Games	Years	Ended by
UCLA	76	1971–74	Notre Dame (71–70)
Indiana	57	1975–77	Toledo (59–57)
Marquette	56	1970–72	Detroit (70–49)
Kentucky	54	1952–55	Georgia Tech (59–58)
San Francisco	51	1955–57	Illinois (62–33)
Pennsylvania	48	1970–72	Temple (57–52)
Ohio State	47	1960–62	Wisconsin (86–67)
Texas	44	1913–17	Rice (24–18)
UCLA	43	1966–68	Houston (71–69)
LIU-Brooklyn	43	1935–37	Stanford (45–31)
Seton Hall	42	1939–41	LIU-Brooklyn (49–26)

Longest—Home Court

Team	Games	Years	Team	Games	Years
Kentucky	129	1943–55	Lamar	80	1978–84
St. Bonaventure	99	1948–61	Long Beach St	75	1968–74
UCLA	98	1970–76	UNLV	72	1974–78
Cincinnati	86	1957–64	Arizona	71	1987–92
Marquette	81	1967–73	Cincinnati	68	1972–78
Arizona	81	1945–51	Western Kentucky	67	1949–55

NCAA Men's Division I Winningest Coaches

Active Coaches*

WINS

Coach and Team	W
Bob Knight, Texas Tech	854
Lou Henson, New Mexico St	779
Eddie Sutton, Oklahoma St	781
Lute Olson, Arizona	740
John Chaney, Temple	724
Mike Krzyzewski, Duke	721
Jim Boeheim, Syracuse	703
Jim Calhoun, Connecticut	703
Hugh Durham, Jacksonville	633
Billy Tubbs, Lamar	624
Tom Davis, Drake	569

Note: Minimum 5 years as a Division I head coach; includes record at 4-year colleges only.
*Active in 2004–05.

WINNING PERCENTAGE

Coach and Team	Yrs	W	L	Pct
Mark Few, Gonzaga	6	159	37	.811
Roy Williams, N Carolina	17	470	116	.802
Bo Ryan, Wisconsinc	21	476	140	.773
Mike Krzyzewski, Duke	30	721	246	.746
Jim Boeheim, Syracuse	29	703	241	.745
Lute Olson, Arizona	31	710	250	.740
Tubby Smith, Kentucky	14	343	120	.741
Bob Huggins, Cincinnati	24	567	199	.740
Rick Pitino, Louisville	19	449	159	.738
Bruce Weber, Illinois	7	166	63	.725
Eddie Sutton, Oklahoma St	35	781	299	.723

Note: Minimum 5 years as a Division I head coach; includes record at 4-year colleges only.
*Active in 2004–05.

Alltime Winningest Men's Division I Coaches

	W
Dean Smith (N Carolina)	879
Adolph Rupp (Kentucky)	876
Bob Knight (Army, Indiana, Texas Tech)	854
Jim Phelan (Mt. St. Mary's)	830
Lefty Driesell (Davidson, Maryland, James Madison, Georgia St)	786
Eddie Sutton (Creighton, Arkansas, Kentucky, Oklahoma St)	781
Jerry Tarkanian (Long Beach St, UNLV, Fresno St)	778
Lou Henson (Hardin-Simmons, New Mexico St, Illinois, New Mexico St)	779
Hank Iba (NW Missouri St, Colorado, Oklahoma St)	764
Ed Diddle (Western Kentucky)	759
Phog Allen (Baker, Kansas, Haskell, Central Missouri St, Kansas)	746
Lute Olson (Long Beach St, Iowas, Arizona)	740
Jerry Tarkanian (Long Beach St, UNLV, Fresno St)	729
Norm Stewart (Northern Iowa, Missouri)	728
John Chaney (Cheyney St, Temple)	724
Ray Meyer (DePaul)	724
Mike Krzyzewsk (Army, Duke)	721
Don Haskins (UTEP)	719

Note: Minimum 10 head coaching seasons in Division I.

Alltime Winningest Men's Division I Coaches *(Cont.)*
WINNING PERCENTAGE

Coach (Team, Years)	Yrs	W	L	Pct
Clair Bee (Rider 29–31, LIU-Brooklyn 32–45, 46–51)	21	412	87	.826
Adolph Rupp (Kentucky 31–72)	41	876	190	.822
John Wooden (Indiana St 47–48, UCLA 49–75)	29	664	162	.804
Roy Williams (Kansas 89–2003, N Carolina 2003–)	17	470	116	.802
John Kresse (Charleston 80–02)	23	560	143	.797
Ralph Jones (Butler, Wabash, Purdue, Illinois)	17	194	51	.792
Francis Schmidt (Tulsa, Arkansas, TCU)	17	258	72	.782
Jerry Tarkanian (Long Beach St 69–73, UNLV 74–92, Fresno St 95–02)	31	729	201	.784
Dean Smith (N Carolina 62–97)	36	879	254	.776
George Keogan (St. Louis 16, Allegheny 19, Valparaiso 20–21, Notre Dame 24–43)	27	414	127	.765
Jack Ramsay (St. Joseph's [PA] 56–66)	11	231	71	.765
Frank Keaney (Rhode Island 21–48)	28	401	124	.764
Vic Bubas (Duke 60–69)	10	213	67	.761
Harry Fisher (Columbia 07–16, Army 22–23, 25)	16	189	60	.759
Fred Bennon (Brigham Young 09–10, Utah 11-14, Montana St 15-19	11	95	32	.748
Charles (Chick) Davies (Duquesne 25–43, 47–48)	21	314	106	.748
Ray Mears (Wittenberg 57–62, Tennessee 63–77)	21	399	135	.747
Edward McNIchol (Penn 21-30)	10	186	63	.747
Mike Krzyzewski (Army 76–80, Duke 81–)	30	721	246	.746
Jim Boeheim (Syracuse 77–)	29	703	241	.746
Lute Olson (Long Beach St 73–74, Iowa 74–83, Arizona 83–)	32	740	256	.743

Note: Minimum 10 head coaching seasons in Division I.

NCAA Women's Division I Championship Results

Year	Winner	Score	Runner-up	Winning Coach
1982	Louisiana Tech	76–62	Cheyney	Sonja Hogg
1983	Southern Cal	69–67	Louisiana Tech	Linda Sharp
1984	Southern Cal	72–61.	Tennessee	Linda Sharp
1985	Old Dominion	70–65	Georgia	Marianne Stanley
1986	Texas	97–81	Southern Cal	Jody Conradt
1987	Tennessee	67–44	Louisiana Tech	Pat Summitt
1988	Louisiana Tech	56–54	Auburn	Leon Barmore
1989	Tennessee	76–60	Auburn	Pat Summitt
1990	Stanford	88–81	Auburn	Tara VanDerveer
1991	Tennessee	70–67 (OT)	Virginia	Pat Summitt
1992	Stanford	78–62	Western Kentucky	Tara VanDerveer
1993	Texas Tech	84–82	Ohio State	Marsha Sharp
1994	N Carolina	60–59	Louisiana Tech	Sylvia Hatchell
1995	Connecticut	70–64	Tennessee	Geno Auriemma
1996	Tennessee	83–65	Georgia	Pat Summitt
1997	Tennessee	68–59	Old Dominion	Pat Summitt
1998	Tennessee	93–75	Louisiana Tech	Pat Summitt
1999	Purdue	62–45	Duke	Carolyn Peck
2000	Connecticut	71–52	Tennessee	Geno Auriemma
2001	Notre Dame	68–66	Purdue	Muffet McGraw
2002	Connecticut	82–70	Oklahoma	Geno Auriemma
2003	Connecticut	73–68	Tennessee	Geno Auriemma
2004	Connecticut	70–61	Tennessee	Geno Auriemma
2005	Baylor	84–62	Michigan St.	Kim Mulkey-Robinson

NCAA Women's Division I Alltime Individual Leaders

Single-Game Records
SCORING HIGHS

Pts	Player and Team vs Opponent	Year
60	Cindy Brown, Long Beach St vs San Jose St	1987
58	Kim Perrot, SW Louisiana vs SE Louisiana	1990
58	Lorri Bauman, Drake vs SW Missouri St	1984
56	Jackie Stiles, SW Missouri St vs Evansville	2000
55	Patricia Hoskins, Mississippi Valley vs Southern-BR	1989
55	Patricia Hoskins, Mississippi Valley vs Alabama St	1989
54	Anjinea Hopson, Grambling vs Jackson St	1994
54	Mary Lowry, Baylor vs Texas	1994
54	Wanda Ford, Drake vs SW Missouri St	1986

Three tied with 53.

Single-Game Records *(Cont.)*
REBOUNDS

Reb	Player and Team vs Opponent	Year
40	Deborah Temple, Delta St vs AL-Birmingham	1983
37	Rosina Pearson, Bethune-Cookman vs Florida Memorial	1985
33	Maureen Formico, Pepperdine vs Loyola (CA)	1985
31	Darlene Beale, Howard vs S Carolina St	1987
30	Cindy Bonforte, Wagner vs Queens (NY)	1983
30	Kayone Hankins, New Orleans vs. Nicholls St	1994
30	Wanda Ford, Drake vs Eastern Illinois	1985
30	Jennifer Butler, Massachusetts vs Florida	2003

Three tied with 29.

ASSISTS

A	Player and Team vs Opponent	Year
23	Michelle Burden, Kent St vs Ball St	1991
22	Shawn Monday, Tennessee Tech vs Morehead St	1988
22	Veronica Pettry, Loyola (IL) vs Detroit	1989
22	Tine Freil, Pacific vs Wichita St	1991
21	Tine Freil, Pacific vs Fresno St	1992
21	Amy Bauer, Wisconsin vs Detroit	1989
21	Neacole Hall, Alabama St vs Southern-BR	1989

Six tied with 20.

Single Season Records
POINTS

Player and Team	Year	GP	FG	3FG	FT	Pts
Jackie Stiles, SW Missouri St*	2001	35	365	65	267	1062
Cindy Brown, Long Beach St	1987	35	362	—	250	974
Genia Miller, Cal St-Fullerton	1991	33	376	0	217	969
Sheryl Swoopes, Texas Tech	1993	34	356	32	211	955
Andrea Congreaves, Mercer	1992	28	353	77	142	925
Wanda Ford, Drake	1986	30	390	—	139	919
Chamique Holdsclaw, Tennessee	1998	39	370	9	166	915
Barbara Kennedy, Clemson	1982	31	392	—	124	908
Patricia Hoskins, Mississippi Valley	1989	27	345	13	205	908
LaTaunya Pollard, Long Beach St	1983	31	376	—	155	907

*school changed name to Missouri State after 2004–05 season

SEASON SCORING AVERAGE

Player and Team	Year	GP	FG	3FG	FT	Pts	Avg
Patricia Hoskins, Mississippi Valley	1989	27	345	13	205	908	33.6
Andrea Congreaves, Mercer	1992	28	353	77	142	925	33.0
Deborah Temple, Delta St	1984	28	373	—	127	873	31.2
Andrea Congreaves, Mercer	1993	26	302	51	150	805	31.0
Wanda Ford, Drake	1986	30	390	—	139	919	30.6
Anucha Browne, Northwestern	1985	28	341	—	173	855	30.5
LeChandra LeDay, Grambling	1988	28	334	36	146	850	30.4
Jackie Stiles, SW MIssouri St	2001	35	365	65	267	1062	30.3
Kim Perrot, Southwestern Louisiana	1990	28	308	95	128	839	30.0
Tina Hutchinson, San Diego St	1984	30	383	—	132	898	29.9
Jan Jensen, Drake	1991	30	358	6	166	888	29.6
Genia Miller, Cal St-Fullerton	1991	33	376	0	217	969	29.4
Barbara Kennedy, Clemson	1982	31	392	—	124	908	29.3
LaTaunya Pollard, Long Beach St	1983	31	376	—	155	907	29.3
Lisa McMullen, Alabama St	1991	28	285	126	119	815	29.1

Single Season Records (Cont.)

REBOUNDS

Player and Team	Year	GP	Reb	Player and Team	Year	GP	Reb
Wanda Ford, Drake	1985	30	534	R. Pearson, Beth.-Cookman	1985	26	480
Wanda Ford, Drake	1986	30	506	Patricia Hoskins, Miss Valley	1987	28	476
Anne Donovan, Old Dominion	1983	35	504	Cheryl Miller, Southern Cal	1985	30	474
Darlene Jones, Miss Valley	1983	31	487	Darlene Beale, Howard	1987	29	459
Melanie Simpson, Okla. City	1982	37	481	Olivia Bradley, W Virginia	1985	30	458

REBOUND AVERAGE

Player and Team	Year	GP	Reb	Avg
Rosina Pearson, Bethune-Cookman	1985	26	480	18.5
Wanda Ford, Drake	1985	30	534	17.8
Katie Beck, E Tennessee St	1988	25	441	17.6
DeShawne Blocker, E Tennessee St	1994	26	450	17.3
Patricia Hoskins, Mississippi Valley	1987	28	476	17.0
Wanda Ford, Drake	1986	30	506	16.9
Patricia Hoskins, Mississippi Valley	1989	27	440	16.3
Joy Kellogg, Oklahoma City	1984	23	373	16.2
Deborah Mitchell, Mississippi Coll.	1983	28	447	16.0
Cheryl Miller, Southern California	1985	30	474	15.8

FIELD-GOAL PERCENTAGE

Player and Team	Year	GP	FG	FGA	Pct
Myndee Larsen, Southern Utah	1998	28	249	344	72.4
Chantelle Anderson, Vanderbilt	2001	34	292	404	72.3
Deneka Knowles, Southeastern La.	1996	26	199	276	72.1
Barbara Farris, Tulane	1998	27	151	210	71.9
Renay Adams, Tennessee Tech	1991	30	185	258	71.7
Regina Days, Georgia Southern	1986	27	234	332	70.5
Kim Wood, WI-Green Bay	1994	27	188	271	69.4
Kelly Lyons, Old Dominion	1990	31	308	444	69.4
Alisha Hill, Howard	1995	28	194	281	69.0
Ruth Riley, Notre Dame	1999	31	198	290	68.3

Based on qualifiers for annual championship.

FREE-THROW PERCENTAGE

Player and Team	Year	GP	FT	FTA	Pct
Shanna Zolman, Tennessee	2004	35	88	92	95.7
Ginny Doyle, Richmond	1992	29	96	101	95.0
Jill Marano, La Salle	2003	29	88	93	94.6
Sue Bird, Connecticut	2002	39	98	104	94.2
Paula Corder-King, SE Missouri St	1999	28	111	118	94.1
Kandi Brown, Morehead St	2003	28	104	111	93.7
Linda Cyborski, Delaware	1991	29	74	79	93.7
Kandi Brown, Morehead St	2002	29	74	79	93.7
Kristin Iwanaga, California	2005	29	85	91	93.4
Paula Corder-King, SE Missouri St	2000	27	69	74	93.2

Based on qualifiers for annual championship.

Career Records
POINTS

Player and Team	Yrs	GP	Pts
Jackie Stiles, SW Missouri St*	1997–01	129	3393
Patricia Hoskins, Mississippi Valley	1985–89	110	3122
Lorri Bauman, Drake	1981–84	120	3115
Chamique Holdsclaw, Tennessee	1995–99	148	3025
Cheryl Miller, Southern Cal	1983–86	128	3018
Cindy Blodgett, Maine	1994–98	118	3005
Valorie Whiteside, Appalachian St	1984–88	116	2944
Joyce Walker, Louisiana St	1981–84	117	2906
Sandra Hodge, New Orleans	1981–84	107	2860
Andrea Congreaves, Mercer	1989–93	108	2796

SCORING AVERAGE

Player and Team	Yrs	GP	FG	3FG	FT	Pts	Avg
Patricia Hoskins, Mississippi Valley	1985–89	110	1196	24	706	3122	28.4
Sandra Hodge, New Orleans	1981–84	107	1194	—	472	2860	26.7
Jackie Stiles, SW Missouri St*	1997–01	129	1160	221	852	3393	26.3
Lorri Bauman, Drake	1981–84	120	1104	—	907	3115	26.0
Andrea Congreaves, Mercer	1989–93	108	1107	153	429	2796	25.9
Cindy Blodgett, Maine	1994–98	118	1055	219	676	3005	25.5
Valorie Whiteside, Appalachian St	1984–88	116	1153	0	638	2944	25.4
Joyce Walker, Louisiana St	1981–84	117	1259	—	388	2906	24.8
Tarcha Hollis, Grambling	1988–91	85	904	3	247	2058	24.2
Korie Hlede, Duquesne	1994–98	109	1045	162	379	2631	24.1

*school changed name to Missouri State after 2004–05 season

NCAA Men's Division II Championship Results

Year	Winner	Score	Runner-up	Third Place	Fourth Place
1957	Wheaton (IL)	89–65	Kentucky Wesleyan	Mount St Mary's (MD)	Cal St-Los Angeles
1958	S Dakota	75–53	St. Michael's	Evansville	Wheaton (IL)
1959	Evansville	83–67	SW Missouri St	N Carolina A&T	Cal St-Los Angeles
1960	Evansville	90–69	Chapman	Kentucky Wesleyan	Cornell College
1961	Wittenberg	42–38	SE Missouri St	S Dakota St	Mount St Mary's (MD)
1962	Mount St Mary's (MD)	58–57 (OT)	Cal St-Sacramento	Southern Illinois	Nebraska Wesleyan
1963	S Dakota St	44–42	Wittenberg	Oglethorpe	Southern Illinois
1964	Evansville	72–59	Akron	N Carolina A&T	Northern Iowa
1965	Evansville	85–82 (OT)	Southern Illinois	N Dakota	St Michael's
1966	Kentucky Wesleyan	54–51	Southern Illinois	Akron	N Dakota
1967	Winston-Salem	77–74	SW Missouri St	Kentucky Wesleyan	Illinois St
1968	Kentucky Wesleyan	63–52	Indiana St	Trinity (TX)	Ashland
1969	Kentucky Wesleyan	75–71	SW Missouri St	†Vacated	Ashland
1970	Philadelphia Textile	76–65	Tennessee St	UC-Riverside	Buffalo St
1971	Evansville	97–82	Old Dominion	†Vacated	Kentucky Wesleyan
1972	Roanoke	84–72	Akron	Tennessee St	Eastern Mich
1973	Kentucky Wesleyan	78–76 (OT)	Tennessee St	Assumption	Brockport St
1974	Morgan St	67–52	SW Missouri St	Assumption	New Orleans
1975	Old Dominion	76–74	New Orleans	Assumption	TN-Chattanooga
1976	Puget Sound	83–74	TN-Chattanooga	Eastern Illinois	Old Dominion
1977	TN-Chattanooga	71–62	Randolph-Macon	N Alabama	Sacred Heart
1978	Cheyney	47–40	WI-Green Bay	Eastern Illinois	Central Florida
1979	N Alabama	64–50	WI-Green Bay	Cheyney	Bridgeport
1980	Virginia Union	80–74	New York Tech	Florida Southern	N Alabama
1981	Florida Southern	73–68	Mount St Mary's (MD)	Cal Poly-SLO	WI-Green Bay
1982	District of Columbia	73–63	Florida Southern	Kentucky Wesleyan	Cal St-Bakersfield
1983	Wright St	92–73	District of Columbia	*Cal St-Bakersfield	*Morningside
1984	Central Missouri St	81–77	St. Augustine's	*Kentucky Wesleyan	*N Alabama
1985	Jacksonville St	74–73	S Dakota St	*Kentucky Wesleyan	*Mount St. Mary's (MD)
1986	Sacred Heart	93–87	SE Missouri St	*Cheyney	*Florida Southern
1987	Kentucky Wesleyan	92–74	Gannon	*Delta St	*Eastern Montana
1988	Lowell	75–72	AK-Anchorage	Florida Southern	Troy St
1989	N Carolina Central	73–46	SE Missouri St	UC-Riverside	Jacksonville St
1990	Kentucky Wesleyan	93–79	Cal St-Bakersfield	N Dakota	Morehouse
1991	N Alabama	79–72	Bridgeport (CT)	*Cal St-Bakersfield	*Virginia Union
1992	Virginia Union	100–75	Bridgeport (CT)	*Cal St-Bakersfield	*California (PA)
1993	Cal St-Bakersfield	85–72	Troy St (AL)	*New Hampshire Coll	*Wayne St (MI)

*Indicates tied for third. †Student-athletes representing American International in 1969 and Southwestern Louisiana in 1971 were declared ineligible subsequent to the tournament. Under NCAA rules, the teams' and ineligible student-athletes' records were deleted, and the teams' places in the final standings were vacated.

NCAA Men's Division II Championship Results (Cont.)

Year	Winner	Score	Runner-up	Third Place	Fourth Place
1994	Cal St-Bakersfield	92–86	Southern Indiana	*New Hampshire Coll	*Washburn
1995	Southern Indiana	71–63	UC–Riverside	*Norfolk St	*Indiana (PA)
1996	Fort Hays St	70–63	Northern Kentucky	*California (PA)	*Virginia Union
1997	Cal St-Bakersfield	57–56	Northern Kentucky	*Lynn	*Salem-Teikyo
1998	UC-Davis	83–77	Kentucky Wesleyan	*St. Rose	*Virginia Union
1999	Kentucky Wesleyan	75–60	Metropolitan St	*Truman St	*Florida Southern
2000	Metropolitan St	97–79	Kentucky Wesleyan	*Missouri Southern	*Seattle Pacific
2001	Kentucky Wesleyan	72–63	Washburn	*Western Washington	*Tampa
2002	Metropolitan St	80–72	Kentucky Wesleyan	*Shaw	*Indiana (PA)
2003	Northeastern St (OK)	75–64	vacated	*Bowie St	*Queens (NC)
2004	Kennesaw St	84–59	Southern Indiana	*Humboldt St	*Metropolitan St
2005	Virginia Union	63–58	Bryant	*Lynn	*Tarleton St

*tied for third place

NCAA Men's Division II Alltime Individual Leaders

SINGLE-GAME SCORING HIGHS

Pts	Player and Team vs Opponent	Date
113	Bevo Francis, Rio Grande vs Hillsdale	1954
84	Bevo Francis, Rio Grande vs Alliance	1954
82	Bevo Francis, Rio Grande vs Bluffton	1954
80	Paul Crissman, Southern Cal Col vs Pacific Christian	1966
77	William English, Winston-Salem vs Fayetteville St	1968

Single Season Records

SCORING AVERAGE

Player and Team	Year	GP	FG	FT	Pts	Avg
Bevo Francis, Rio Grande	1954	27	444	367	1255	46.5
Earl Glass, Mississippi Industrial	1963	19	322	171	815	42.9
Earl Monroe, Winston-Salem	1967	32	509	311	1329	41.5
John Rinka, Kenyon	1970	23	354	234	942	41.0
Willie Shaw, Lane	1964	18	303	121	727	40.4

REBOUND AVERAGE

Player and Team	Year	GP	Reb	Avg
Tom Hart, Middlebury	1956	21	620	29.5
Tom Hart, Middlebury	1955	22	649	29.5
Frank Stronczek, American Int'l	1966	26	717	27.6
R.C. Owens, College of Idaho	1954	25	677	27.1
Maurice Stokes, St Francis (PA)	1954	26	689	26.5

ASSISTS

Player and Team	Year	GP	A
Steve Ray, Bridgeport	1989	32	400
Steve Ray, Bridgeport	1990	33	385
Tony Smith, Pfeiffer	1992	35	349
Jim Ferrer, Bentley	1989	31	309
Rob Paternostro, New Hamp. Coll.	1995	33	309

ASSIST AVERAGE

Player and Team	Year	GP	A	Avg
Steve Ray, Bridgeport	1989	32	400	12.5
Steve Ray, Bridgeport	1990	33	385	11.7
Demetri Beekman, Assumption	1993	23	264	11.5
Ernest Jenkins, NM Highlands	1995	27	291	10.8
Brian Gregory, Oakland	1989	28	300	10.7

FIELD-GOAL PERCENTAGE

Player and Team	Year	Pct
Todd Linder, Tampa	1987	75.2
Maurice Stafford, N Alabama	1984	75.0
Matthew Cornegay, Tuskegee	1982	74.8
Callistus Eziukwu, Grand Valley St	2005	73.7
Brian Moten, W Georgia	1992	73.4

FREE-THROW PERCENTAGE

Player and Team	Year	Pct
Paul Cluxton, Northern Kentucky	1997	100.0
Tomas Rimkus, Pace	1997	95.6
C.J. Cowgill, Chaminade	2001	95.0
Billy Newton, Morgan St	1976	94.4
Kent Andrews, McNeese St	1968	94.4

Career Records

POINTS

Player and Team	Yrs	Pts
Travis Grant, Kentucky St	1969–72	4045
Bob Hopkins, Grambling	1953–56	3759
Tony Smith, Pfeiffer	1989–92	3350
Earnest Lee, Clark Atlanta	1984–87	3298
Joe Miller, Alderson-Broaddus	1954–57	3294

Career Records (Cont.)

CAREER SCORING AVERAGE

Player and Team	Yrs	GP	Pts	Avg
Travis Grant, Kentucky St	1969–72	121	4045	33.4
John Rinka, Kenyon	1967–70	99	3251	32.8
Florindo Vieira, Quinnipiac	1954–57	69	2263	32.8
Willie Shaw, Lane	1961–64	76	2379	31.3
Mike Davis, Virginia Union	1966–69	89	2758	31.0

REBOUND AVERAGE

Player and Team	Yrs	GP	Reb	Avg
Tom Hart, Middlebury	1953, 55–56	63	1738	27.6
Maurice Stokes, St. Francis (PA)	1953–55	72	1812	25.2
Frank Stronczek, American Int'l	1965–67	62	1549	25.0
Bill Thieben, Hofstra	1954–56	76	1837	24.2
Hank Brown, Lowell Tech	1965–67	49	1129	23.0

ASSISTS

Player and Team	Yrs	A
Demetri Beekman, Assumption	1990–93	1044
Adam Kaufman, Edinboro	1998–01	936
Rob Paternostro, New Hamp. Coll.	1992–95	919
Tony Smith, Pfeiffer	1989–92	828
Jamie Stevens, Montana St-Billings	1996–99	805

ASSIST AVERAGE

Player and Team	Yrs	GP	A	Avg
Steve Ray, Bridgeport	1989–90	65	785	12.1
Demetri Beekman, Assumption	1990–93	119	1044	8.8
Ernest Jenkins, NM Highlands	1992–95	84	699	8.3
Adam Kaufman, Edinboro	1998–01	116	936	8.1
Mark Benson, Texas A&I	1989–91	86	674	7.8

Note: Minimum 550 Assists.

FIELD-GOAL PERCENTAGE

Player and Team	Yrs	Pct
Todd Linder, Tampa	1984–87	70.8
Tom Schurfranz, Bellarmine	1989–92	70.2
Chad Scott, California (PA)	1991–94	70.0
Ed Phillips, Alabama, A&M	1968–71	68.9
Ulysses Hackett, SC-Spartanburg	1990–92	67.9

Note: Minimum 400 FGM.

FREE-THROW PERCENTAGE

Player and Team	Yrs	Pct
Paul Cluxton, Northern Kentucky	1994–97	93.5
Kent Andrews, McNeese St	1967–69	91.6
Jon Hagen, Minn St-Mankato	1963–65	90.0
Dave Reynolds, Davis & Elkins	1986–89	89.3
Michael Shue, Lock Haven	1994–97	88.5

Note: Minimum 250 FTM.

NCAA Men's Division III Championship Results

Year	Winner	Score	Runner-up	Third Place	Fourth Place
1975	LeMoyne-Owen	57–54	Glassboro St	Augustana (IL)	Brockport St
1976	Scranton	60–57	Wittenberg	Augustana (IL)	Plattsburgh St
1977	Wittenberg	79–66	Oneonta St	Scranton	Hamline
1978	North Park	69–57	Widener	Albion	Stony Brook
1979	North Park	66–62	Potsdam St	Franklin & Marshall	Centre
1980	North Park	83–76	Upsala	Wittenberg	Longwood
1981	Potsdam St	67–65 (OT)	Augustana (IL)	Ursinus	Otterbein
1982	Wabash	83–62	Potsdam St	Brooklyn	Cal St-Stanislaus
1983	Scranton	64–63	Wittenberg	Roanoke	WI–Whitewater
1984	WI–Whitewater	103–86	Clark (MA)	DePauw	Upsala
1985	North Park	72–71	Potsdam St	Nebraska Wesleyan	Widener
1986	Potsdam St	76–73	LeMoyne-Owen	Nebraska Wesleyan	Jersey City St
1987	North Park	106–100	Clark (MA)	Wittenberg	Stockton St
1988	Ohio Wesleyan	92–70	Scranton	Nebraska Wesleyan	Hartwick
1989	WI–Whitewater	94–86	Trenton St	Southern Maine	Centre
1990	Rochester	43–42	DePauw	Washington (MD)	Calvin
1991	WI–Platteville	81–74	Franklin & Marshall	Otterbein	Ramapo (NJ)
1992	Calvin	62–49	Rochester	WI–Platteville	Jersey City St
1993	Ohio Northern	71–68	Augustana	Mass–Dartmouth	Rowan
1994	Lebanon Valley Coll	66–59 (OT)	New York University	Wittenberg	St Thomas (MN)
1995	WI–Platteville	69–55	Manchester	Rowan	Trinity (CT)
1996	Rowan	100–93	Hope (MI)	Illinois Wesleyan	Franklin & Marshall
1997	Illinois Wesleyan	89–86	Nebraska Wesleyan	Williams	Alvernia
1998	WI–Platteville	69–56	Hope (MI)	Williams	Wilkes
1999	WI–Platteville	76–75 (2 OT)	Hampden-Sydney	William Paterson	Connecticut Coll.
2000	Calvin	79–74	WI–Eau Claire	Salem St	Franklin & Marshall
2001	Catholic	76–62	William Paterson	*Illinois Wesleyan	*Ohio Northern
2002	Otterbein	102–83	Elizabethtown	Carthage	Rochester
2003	Williams	67–65	Gustavus Adolphus	Wooster	Hampden Sydney
2004	WI–Stevens Point	84–82	Williams	John Carroll	Amherst
2005	WI–Stevens Point	73–49	Rochester	Calvin	York

NCAA Men's Division III Alltime Individual Leaders

SINGLE-GAME SCORING HIGHS

Pts	Player and Team vs Opponent	Year
77	Jeff Clement, Grinnell vs Illinois College	1998
69	Steve Diekmann, Grinnell vs Simpson	1995
64	Tim Russell, Albertus Magnus	2005
63	Ryan Hodges, Cal-Lutheran	2005
63	Joe DeRoche, Thomas vs St. Joseph's (ME)	1988
62	Nick Pelotte, Plymouth St	2005
62	Shannon Lilly, Bishop vs Southwest Assembly of God	1983
61	Steve Honderd, Calvin vs Kalamazoo	1993
61	Dana Wilson, Husson vs Ricker	1974

Single Season Records

SCORING AVERAGE

Player and Team	Year	GP	FG	FT	Pts	Avg
Steve Diekmann, Grinnell	1995	20	223	162	745	37.3
Rickey Sutton, Lyndon St	1976	14	207	93	507	36.2
Shannon Lilly, Bishop	1983	26	345	218	908	34.9
Dana Wilson, Husson	1974	20	288	122	698	34.9
Rickey Sutton, Lyndon St	1977	16	223	112	558	34.9

REBOUND AVERAGE

Player and Team	Year	GP	Reb	Avg
Joe Manley, Bowie St	1976	29	579	20.0
Fred Petty, New Hampshire College	1974	22	436	19.8
Larry Williams, Pratt	1977	24	457	19.0
Charles Greer, Thomas	1977	17	318	18.7
Larry Parker, Plattsburgh St	1975	23	430	18.7

ASSISTS

Player and Team	Year	GP	A
Robert James, Kean	1989	29	391
Tennyson Whitted, Ramapo	2002	29	319
Ricky Spicer, WI-Whitewater	1989	31	295
Joe Marcotte, New Jersey Tech	1995	30	292
Andre Bolton, Chris. Newport	1996	30	289

ASSIST AVERAGE

Player and Team	Year	GP	A	Avg
Robert James, Kean	1989	29	391	13.5
Albert Kirchner, Mt. St. Vincent	1990	24	267	11.1
Tennyson Whitted, Ramapo	2002	29	319	11.0
Ron Torgalski, Hamilton	1989	26	275	10.6
Louis Adams, Rust	1989	22	227	10.3

FIELD-GOAL PERCENTAGE

Player and Team	Year	Pct
Travis Weiss, St. John's (MN)	1994	76.6
Pete Metzelaars, Wabash	1982	75.3
Tony Rychlec, Mass. Maritime	1981	74.9
Tony Rychlec, Mass. Maritime	1982	73.1
Russ Newnan, Menlo	1991	73.0

FREE-THROW PERCENTAGE

Player and Team	Year	Pct
Korey Coon, IL Wesleyan	2000	96.3
Chanse Young, Manchester	1998	95.6
Andy Enfield, Johns Hopkins	1991	95.3
Nick Wilkins, Coe	2003	95.7
Chris Carideo, Widener	1992	95.2

Career Records

POINTS

Player and Team	Yrs	Pts
Andre Foreman, Salisbury St	1989–92	2940
Willie Chandler, Misericordia	2000–03	2898
Lamont Strothers, Chris. Newport	1988–91	2709
Matt Hancock, Colby	1987–90	2678
Scott Fitch, Geneseo St	1990–94	2634

SCORING AVERAGE

Player and Team	Yrs	GP	Avg
Dwain Govan, Bishop	1974–75	55	32.8
Dave Russell, Shepherd	1974–75	60	30.6
Rickey Sutton, Lyndon St	1976–79	80	29.7
John Atkins, Knoxville	1976–78	70	28.7
Steve Petnik, Windham	1974–77	76	27.6

REBOUND AVERAGE

Player and Team	Yrs	GP	Reb	Avg
Larry Parker, Plattsburgh St	1975–78	85	1482	17.4
Charles Greer, Thomas	1975–77	58	926	16.0
Willie Parr, LeMoyne-Owen	1974–76	76	1182	15.6
Michael Smith, Hamilton	1989–92	107	1632	15.2
Dave Kufeld, Yeshiva	1977–80	81	1222	15.1

ASSIST AVERAGE

Player and Team	Yrs	Avg
Phil Dixon, Shenandoah	1993–96	8.6
Tennyson Whitted, Ramapo	2000–03	8.5
Steve Artis, Chris. Newport	1990–93	8.1
David Genovese, Mt. St. Vincent	1992–95	7.5
Kevin Root, Eureka	1989–91	7.1

Hockey

Pittsburgh Pengions owner/player Mario Lemieux with his team's No. I draft pick, Sidney Crosby

A Season On Ice

A frustrating lockout was resolved only after the NHL missed an entire year. Now the question is: "Can hockey come back?"

BY B.J. SCHECTER

WHEN WE LAST LEFT THE National Hockey League, Commissioner Gary Bettman was beaming. He had just handed Lord Stanley's Cup to Tampa Bay Lightning captain Dave Andreychuk, prompting a packed crowd at the Ice Palace to cheer wildly as the 40-year-old veteran tearfully skated around the ice. The Lightning had just beaten the Calgary Flames in a thrilling seven-game series to cap another exhilarating postseason, a new breakout star had emerged in Flames forward Jarome Iginla and, for a brief moment, all of hockey's problems—the low scoring, the poor television ratings and an impending labor dispute—were put aside.

Unfortunately, the NHL's brief moment in the sun wouldn't last long. Shortly after the Stanley Cup Finals ended, the bickering between the league and the Players' Union over the Collective Bargaining Agreement, which was set to expire on Sept. 15, began and neither side seemed willing to move an inch. Bettman insisted

that there would be no hockey until the players agreed to a modified economic system directly linking revenues to players' salaries. The league, claiming that salaries currently ate up nearly three-quarters of its revenue, warned that it could not survive unless salaries were scaled back at least 20% from their current level. The union, for its part, said it would not consider anything resembling a salary cap. The NHL countered by saying that if no agreement were reached the players would be locked out; as spring turned to summer, the two sides began to drift further apart.

Sure enough, on Sept. 15, Bettman announced that the owners were locking the players out, citing $1.8 billion in losses over the last decade. And to make matters worse, both sides said they were prepared to sit out a year or more. It was the second work stoppage in 10 years for the NHL—the owners locked out the players for 103 days in the 1994-95 season before reaching a deal and playing a shortened 48-game schedule.

"The owners recognize there is no choice," Bettman said. "This industry is sick. The players are really bearing the risk of this work stoppage. This union doesn't seem to care about the problems, the game or the fans. To use a hockey term, they are instigating a fight. This union's leadership negotiates by confrontation. We are hurting. We need help. No league would do what we're doing if we were not suffering."

The league may have been suffering, but the American public didn't seem to care. Seen as a niche sport in the U.S., hockey's popularity had been dwindling for several years and the NHL was forced to sign a new television deal (agreed upon before the lockout) for significantly less money than the previous one. As the months passed with no deal, the NFL, the NBA and college basketball picked up steam and, not surprisingly, hockey wasn't missed. "In Anaheim people would come up to be in restaurants and ask how my year was going," said former Mighty Ducks star Paul Kariya. "I had to tell them we weren't playing."

NHL Commissioner Gary Bettman and the owners still got most of what they wanted in the new Collective Bargaining Agreement.

A Gallup Poll of sports fans taken in mid-January revealed that half of the respondents wouldn't be "disappointed at all" if there were no season. And even more shocking was that Canadians didn't seem to be yearning for hockey either. A similar poll in Canada showed that 77% of Canadians didn't miss the NHL. While many people predicted that Canada would fall into a depression without professional hockey, they simply went on with their lives. If die-hard hockey fans didn't give a hoot than who would? Ken Dryden, Canada's Minister of Social Development, who also won six Stanley Cups as a goalie with the Canadiens, went so far as to say that perhaps the NHL was "more of a habit than a passion."

Neither side seemed to worry about the public's lack of interest, however. News of failed labor talks barely registered a blip on the radar screen. After all, how many times can you report that no progress has been made? The league insisted that when the economic system was fixed the product would be better than ever. In order to help increase scoring, the league decreased the size of goalie's pads and shifted each net back two feet. And there would be no more ties; instead those games would be decided by a shootout. What's more, new camera angles would be used in NBC's broadcasts, showcasing the hard-hitting, up-and-down action not seen before on American television, and teams would wear new spiffy uniforms. Good changes all, but they did little good without a season.

trying to forge an economic system when one side doesn't have a handle on the economics might have been an impossible task."

Bob Goodenow, the union's executive director, insisted that the players weren't at fault, saying his side had worked hard to get a deal, but the league wouldn't work with them. "Keep one thing clear: The players never asked for more money," said Goodenow. "At some point concessions end, and they ended here today. It's unfortunate that during the negotiations the league tried to paint the players as very greedy. This is not about greed. It's about a fair deal."

In December, there was a brief glimmer of hope when the union proposed a 24% rollback in salaries, a major concession. It was the first significant step in the negotiations and brought the two sides back to the table, but when they got there, they reverted back to form. The league, offering no concessions and still insisting on a hard salary cap, quickly infuriated the Union and negotiations stalled. When the talks broke off, the season was all but dead.

Finally, on Feb. 16, Bettman stood in front of a throng of reporters at a Manhattan hotel and officially cancelled the season. This marked the first time a professional sport in North America lost a full season to a labor dispute. "This is a sad regrettable day that all of us wish could have been avoided," said Bettman. "Everyone associated with the National Hockey League owes our fans an apology for the situation in which we find ourselves. We are truly sorry."

Immediately, the blame game began. "My biggest regret in this whole process is that we never could get the union to look at the books and understand exactly what our economics were," said Bettman. "In retrospect,

The biggest losers in the deal, however, were neither the owners nor the players. Rather, it was teams' support staffs and local businesses in and around the 30 NHL arenas that were the hardest hit, especially in small-market hockey hotbeds like Buffalo, Montreal, and Ottawa. Without hockey games to bring in fans and fill the registers, these two groups shared a similar financial fate—losing both money and jobs. Facing few alternatives, it was these people who bore the brunt of the lockout's effects.

The NHL players, though, had options and some 300 of them left to play in Europe. Others went to Russia to play or returned to their native countries. Owners still made piles of money in their other businesses—some even claimed they were losing less money with their teams not playing—but the little man suffered.

One might think that hockey would have learned from Major League Baseball's mistakes. When in 1994, a mid-summer strike cancelled the remainder of the season. Not until four years later, when a thrilling home run race between Mark McGwire and

Sammy Sosa captivated the nation, did the fans finally come back. And this was America's pastime, a sport that many Americans grew up watching and adoring. How long would it take hockey to recover?

"I think this is going to throw hockey into the Dark Ages," said Detroit Red Wings center Kris Draper. "For a sport struggling to find its identity in a lot of markets, to walk away for a year and a half, two years, and think you'll start right back as a major sport, that's impossible."

Two days after the season was cancelled, word leaked out that the union would have accepted a salary cap if it were $49 million. The league, which held firm at $42.5 million, said they might have settled at $45 million. Suddenly, a deal seemed possible and in a last ditch effort, both sides agreed to meet one final time in New York City. Even before the meeting, rumors began to fly: The Hockey News reported that an agreement had been reached in principle and ESPN reported that a deal was imminent. The NHL even brought in Wayne Gretzky and Mario Lemieux to help expedite a deal.

But the excitement quickly fizzled once the two sides reached the bargaining table. Before the salary cap figure could be negotiated, the union asked if the cap would be fixed throughout the term of the agreement. Bettman said it would, but the union wanted the number to go up as revenue went up. Neither side would budge and after a 6 1/2 hour meeting, the season was officially dead with no hope of resuscitation. "There was a misconception that the two sides were close," said Trevor Linden, the NHL Players Association president. "I think it was crystal clear from our standpoint we weren't, and that was evident today." Added agent Don Meehan in an interview with Canada's TSN network: "I think we continue to be embarrassed in this industry."

The labor strife not only affected the current players, but also the league's future stars. With no Collective Bargaining Agreement in place by the end of March, the NHL cancelled the draft, which would have been held in June, putting on hold the professional debut of Sidney Crosby. The 17-year-old Canadian was widely regarded as the No. 1 pick and a star the league desperately needed.

If you looked hard enough you could find pretty good hockey, but unfortunately, you often had to go to places like Siberia to find it. Some of the best players in the world, including Vincent Lecavalier, Brad Richards and Jaromir Jagr, played in the Russian Superleague, while the NHL's other stars scattered in leagues across the globe. They all came together in May at the World Championships in Vienna, where Jagr led the Czech Republic to the title with a 3-0 win over Canada in the final.

It was an exciting tournament, and a good distraction from the NHL labor mess, but it didn't bring the league and the union any closer. However, as summer began, the deep freeze between the two sides started to thaw. They began talking regularly, often spending 15-hour days together ironing out the details, even spending July 4th negotiating the terms of a new Collective Bargaining Agreement. Finally, after a 301-day lockout, the two sides reached a deal on July 13. The new agreement included a 24% rollback in salaries (which the Union offered back in December) and a $39 million salary cap that would be linked to league revenues. Also, salaries can't exceed 54% of league-wide revenues, but if revenues increase then the cap can rise as well. High-paid stars were hurt almost immediately with teams buying out their contracts at a fraction of their value, but younger players benefited as the minimum salary rose from $185,000 to $450,000.

Neither side claimed victory, but it was clear that the league had won. From the beginning, they had insisted on a salary cap and a system linked to league-wide revenues and, in the end, both of their goals were achieved. "I think this will turn out to be a wonderful agreement for the players, a wonderful agreement for the game, a wonderful agreement for our fans," said Bettman. "It's the type of agreement that we think a professional sports league like ours can thrive under for everyone's benefit, because we are true economic partners, true partners in the game, sharing fairly. And that's always been our goal and objective."

In a move that injected some excitement back into the NHL, the Phoenix Coyotes named Hall-of-Famer Wayne Gretzky their new head coach in August.

After both sides approved the deal, their common objective became moving forward and winning the fans back. With the new rules passed to liven up the game and increase scoring, the NHL was off to a good start. However, given the dwindling popularity of the game and fans disenchantment with the labor strife it may take several years before the NHL becomes more than a blip on the radar screen of professional sports.

The good news is that the agreement opened the door for phenom Sidney Crosby to join the league. Widely regarded as the next Wayne Gretzky (even by Gretzky himself), the 17-year-old forward is the young, marketable star the NHL has sorely lacked over the last several years. When the Pittsburgh Penguins won the draft lottery it was a foregone conclusion that Crosby would be the No. 1 pick and a week later, he was.

But even budding young stars like Crosby may not compel people to watch. With all the changes on and off the ice it might take a while before fans recognize the game. "There has never been anything like this in any sport at any time," said agent Don Meehan. "A new landscape, a new CBA, and when the players report to training camp, they will have to absorb some new rules. This will be chaotic."

Chaotic, indeed. Hockey may be back, but it may take some time before it becomes relevant again.

2004 NHL Final Standings

Eastern Conference

NORTHEAST DIVISION

	GP	W	L	T	OTL	Pts	GF	GA
Boston	82	41	19	15	7	104	209	188
Toronto	82	45	24	10	3	103	242	204
Ottawa	82	43	23	10	6	102	262	189
Montreal	82	41	30	7	4	93	208	192
Buffalo	82	37	34	7	4	85	220	221

ATLANTIC DIVISION

	GP	W	L	T	OTL	Pts	GF	GA
Philadelphia	82	40	21	15	6	101	229	186
New Jersey	82	43	25	12	2	100	213	164
NY Islanders	82	38	29	11	4	91	237	210
NY Rangers	82	27	40	7	8	69	206	250
Pittsburgh	82	23	47	8	4	58	190	303

SOUTHEAST DIVISION

	GP	W	L	T	OTL	Pts	GF	GA
Tampa Bay	82	48	21	11	6	106	245	192
Atlanta	82	33	37	8	4	78	214	243
Carolina	82	28	34	14	6	76	172	209
Florida	82	28	35	15	4	75	188	221
Washington	82	23	46	10	3	59	186	253

Western Conference

CENTRAL DIVISION

	GP	W	L	T	OTL	Pts	GF	GA
Detroit	82	48	21	11	2	109	255	189
St. Louis	82	39	30	11	2	91	191	198
Nashville	82	38	29	11	4	91	216	217
Columbus	82	25	45	8	4	62	177	238
Chicago	82	20	43	11	8	59	188	259

NORTHWEST DIVISION

	GP	W	L	T	OTL	Pts	GF	GA
Vancouver	82	43	24	10	5	101	235	194
Colorado	82	40	22	13	7	100	236	198
Calgary	82	42	30	7	3	94	200	176
Edmonton	82	36	29	12	5	89	221	208
Minnesota	82	30	29	20	3	83	188	183

PACIFIC DIVISION

	GP	W	L	T	OTL	Pts	GF	GA
San Jose	82	43	21	12	6	104	219	183
Dallas	82	41	26	13	2	97	194	175
Los Angeles	82	28	29	16	9	81	205	217
Anaheim	82	29	35	10	8	76	184	213
Phoenix	82	22	36	18	6	68	188	245

OTL=overtime loss; worth 1 pt.

2004 Stanley Cup Playoffs

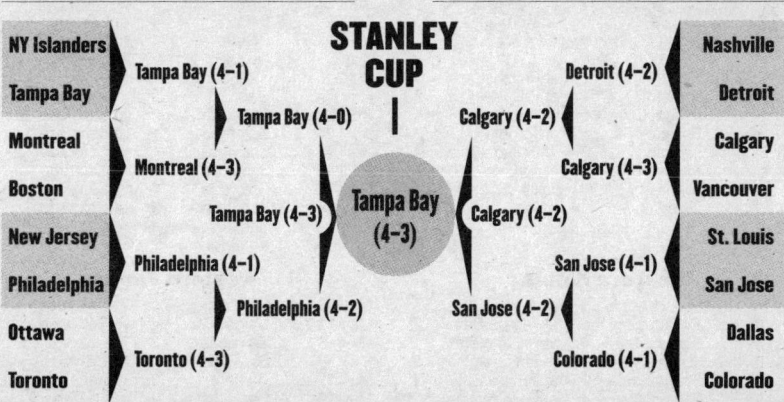

EASTERN CONFERENCE
QUARTERFINALS · SEMIFINALS · CONFERENCE FINAL

WESTERN CONFERENCE
CONFERENCE FINAL · SEMIFINALS · QUARTERFINALS

NY Islanders
Tampa Bay

Montreal
Boston

New Jersey
Philadelphia

Ottawa
Toronto

Tampa Bay (4–1)
Tampa Bay (4–0)
Montreal (4–3)
Tampa Bay (4–3)
Philadelphia (4–1)
Philadelphia (4–2)
Toronto (4–3)

STANLEY CUP

Tampa Bay (4–3)

Calgary (4–2)
Calgary (4–3)
Calgary (4–2)
San Jose (4–1)
San Jose (4–2)
Colorado (4–1)

Detroit (4–2)

Nashville
Detroit

Calgary
Vancouver

St. Louis
San Jose

Dallas
Colorado

Stanley Cup Playoff Results

Conference Quarterfinals

EASTERN CONFERENCE

April 8	NY Islanders 0	at Tampa Bay	3
April 10	NY Islanders 3	at Tampa Bay	0
April 12	Tampa Bay 3	at NY Islanders	0
April 14	Tampa Bay 3	at NY Islanders	0
April 16	NY Islanders 2	at Tampa Bay	3*

Tampa Bay won series 4–1.

Conference Quarterfinals (Cont.)

EASTERN CONFERENCE (Cont.)

April 7	Montreal	0	at Boston	3	April 15	Montreal	5	at Boston	1
April 9	Montreal	1	at Boston	2*	April 17	Boston	2	at Montreal	5
April 11	Boston	2	at Montreal	3	April 19	Montreal	2	at Boston	0
Aoril 13	Boston	4	at Montreal	3†		Montreal won series 4–3.			

April 8	New Jersey	2	at Philadelphia	3	April 8	Ottawa	4	at Toronto	2
April 10	New Jersey	2	at Philadelphia	3	April 10	Ottawa	0	at Toronto	2
April 12	Philadelphia	2	at New Jersey	4	April 12	Toronto	2	at Ottawa	0
April 14	Philadelphia	3	at New Jersey	0	April 14	Toronto	1	at Ottawa	4
April 17	New Jersey	1	at Philadelphia	3	April 16	Ottawa	0	at Toronto	2
	Philadelphia won series 4–1.				April 18	Toronto	1	at Ottawa	2†
					April 20	Ottawa	1	at Toronto	4
						Toronto won series 4–3.			

WESTERN CONFERENCE

April 7	Nashville	1	at Detroit	3	April 7	Calgary	3	at Vancouver	5
April 10	Nashville	1	at Detroit	2	April 9	Calgary	2	at Vancouver	1
April 11	Detroit	1	at Nashville	3	April 11	Vancouver	2	at Calgary	1
April 13	Detroit	0	at Nashville	3	April 13	Vancouver	0	at Calgary	4
April 15	Nashville	1	at Detroit	4	April 15	Calgary	2	at Vancouver	1
April 17	Detroit	2	at Nashville	0	April 17	Vancouver	5	at Calgary	4*
	Detroit won series 4–2.				April 19	Calgary	3	at Vancouver	2*
April 8	St. Louis	0	at San Jose	1*		Calgary won series 4–3.			
April 10	St. Louis	1	at San Jose	3	April 7	Dallas	1	at Colorado	3
April 12	San Jose	1	at St. Louis	4	April 9	Dallas	2	at Colorado	5
April 13	San Jose	4	at St. Louis	3	April 12	Colorado	3	at Dallas	4*
April 15	St. Louis	1	at San Jose	3	April 14	Colorado	3	at Dallas	2†
	San Jose won series 4–1.				April 17	Dallas	1	at Colorado	5
						Colorado won series 4–1.			

Conference Semifinals

EASTERN CONFERENCE

April 23	Montreal	0	at Tampa Bay	4	April 22	Calgary	2	at Detroit	1*
April 25	Montreal	1	at Tampa Bay	3	April 24	Calgary	2	at Detroit	5
April 27	Tampa Bay	4	at Montreal	3*	April 27	Detroit	2	at Calgary	3
April 29	Tampa Bay	3	at Montreal	1	April 29	Detroit	4	at Calgary	2
	Tampa Bay won series 4–0.				May 1	Calgary	1	at Detroit	0
					May 3	Detroit	0	at Calgary	1
April 22	Toronto	1	at Philadelphia	3		Calgary won series 4–2.			
April 25	Toronto	1	at Philadelphia	2					
April 28	Philadelphia	1	at Toronto	4	April 22	Colorado	2	at San Jose	5
April 30	Philadelphia	1	at Toronto	3	April 24	Colorado	1	at San Jose	4
May 2	Toronto	2	at Philadelphia	7	April 26	San Jose	1	at Colorado	0
May 4	Philadelphia	3	at Toronto	2*	April 28	San Jose	0	at Colorado	1*
	Philadelphia won series 4–2.				May 1	Colorado	2	at San Jose	1*
					May 4	San Jose	1	at Colorado	1
						San Jose won series 4–2.			

Eastern Finals

May 8	Philadelphia	1	at Tampa Bay	3
May 10	Philadelphia	6	at Tampa Bay	2
May 13	Tampa Bay	4	at Philadelphia	1
May 15	Tampa Bay	2	at Philadelphia	3
May 18	Philadelphia	2	at Tampa Bay	4
May 20	Tampa Bay	4	at Philadelphia	5*
May 22	Philadelphia	1	at Tampa Bay	2
	Tampa Bay won series 4–3.			

Western Finals

May 9	Calgary	4	at San Jose	3*
May 11	Calgary	4	at San Jose	1
May 13	San Jose	3	at Calgary	0
May 16	San Jose	4	at Calgary	2
May 17	Calgary	3	at San Jose	0
May 19	San Jose	1	at Calgary	3
	Calgary won series 4–2.			

Stanley Cup Finals

May 25	Calgary	4	at Tampa Bay	1	June 3	Calgary	3	at Tampa Bay	2*
May 27	Calgary	1	at Tampa Bay	4	June 5	Tampa Bay	3	at Calgary	2†
May 29	Tampa Bay	0	at Calgary	3	June 7	Calgary	1	at Tampa Bay	2
May 31	Tampa Bay	1	at Calgary	0		Tampa Bay won series 4–3.			

*Overtime game. †Double overtime game.

Stanley Cup Championship Box Scores

Game 1

Calgary 1   2   1—4
Tampa Bay.......0   0   1—1

FIRST PERIOD

Scoring: 1, Calgary, Martin Gelinas 7 (Craig Conroy, Andrew Ference), 3:02. Penalties: S Yelle, Cgy (int), 11:32; P Kubina, TB (holding), 18:52.

SECOND PERIOD

Scoring: 2, Calgary, Jarome Iginla 11 (shorthanded) (Unassisted), 15:21. 3, Calgary, Stephane Yelle 3 (Unassisted), 18:08. Penalties: R Regehr, Cgy (holding), 9:22; A Ference, Cgy (hooking), 14:48.

THIRD PERIOD

Scoring: 4, Tampa Bay, Martin St. Louis 6 (power play) (Brad Richards, Dan Boyle), 4:13. 5, Calgary, Chris Simon 4 (power play) (Oleg Saprykin, Robyn

THIRD PERIOD (CONT.)

Regehr), 19:40. Penalties: V Nieminen, Cgy (roughing), 3:05; S Donovan, Cgy (roughing), 4:30; C Stillman, TB (roughing), 4:30; A Roy, TB (roughing), 4:30; O Saprykin, Cgy (unsportsmanlike cond), 7:55; R Fedotenko, TB (roughing), 17:50; M St. Louis, TB (high sticking), 19:06.

Shots on goal: CGY 5-10-4—19; TB 10-8-6—24

Power-play opportunities: CGY:1 of 4, TB 1 of 5.

Goalies: Cgy, Miikka Kiprusoff (24 shots, 23 saves). TB, Nikolai Khabibulin (19 shots, 15 saves).

Referees: McCreary, Walkom. Linesmen: Murphy, Driscoll. A: 21,674.

Game 2

Calgary 0   0   1—1
Tampa Bay.......1   0   3—4

FIRST PERIOD

Scoring: 1, Tampa Bay, Ruslan Fedotenko 10 (Jassen Cullimore, Vincent Lecavalier), 7:10. Penalties: A Roy, TB (interference), 2:00; D Afanasenkov, TB (boarding), 7:58; D Lowry, Cgy (obstruction hooking), 10:21; V Lecavalier, Tam (high sticking), 13:33; S Donovan, Cgy (holding), 15:04; Bench, Tam (too many men; served by D Afanasenkov), 16:59.

SECOND PERIOD

Scoring: None. Penalties: F Modin, Tam (obstr hooking), 0:53; O Saprykin, Cgy (goalie interference), 19:22.

THIRD PERIOD

Scoring: 2, Tampa Bay, Brad Richards 9 (Dave Andreychuk, Martin St. Louis), 2:51. 3, Tampa Bay, Dan Boyle 2 (Brad Richards, Fredrik Modin), 4:00. 4, Tampa Bay, Martin St. Louis 7 (power play) (Vincent Lecavalier, Dave Andreychuk), 5:58. 5, Calgary, Ville Nieminen 4 (power play) (Shean Donovan, Robyn Regehr), 12:21. Penalties: S Yelle, Cgy (cross

THIRD PERIOD (CONT.)

checking), 0:37; C Kobasew, Cgy (roughing), 5:50; C Clark, Cgy (roughing), 5:50; B Richards, TB (roughing), 5:50; C Stillman, Tam (major fighting), 5:50; D Boyle, TB (roughing), 5:50; C Simon, Cgy (cross checking), 5:50; A Ference, Cgy (unsportsmanlike cond, fighting major), 5:50; A Roy, TB (major fighting), 8:31; C Dingman, Tam (double minor roughing, misconduct, game misconduct), 8:31; C Simon, Cgy (instigator, fighting major, misconduct), 8:31; T Taylor, Tam (holding), 10:35; C Kobasew, Cgy (interference), 14:27; R Regehr, Cgy (holding), 15:13; M Gelinas, Cgy (cross checking, game misconduct), 19:48; C Kobasew, Cgy (misconduct), 20:00; P Kubina, Tam (misconduct), 20:00.

Shots on goal: Cgy 6-9-4—19; TB 8-10-13—31

Power-play opportunities: CGY 1 of 7, TB 1 of 9.

Goalies : Cgy, Miikka Kiprusoff (31 shots, 27 saves). TB, Nikolai Khabibulin (19 shots, 18 saves).

Referees: Watson, Walkom. Linesmen: Murphy, Scapinello. A: 22,222.

Game 3

Tampa Bay.......0   0   0—0
Calgary 0   2   1—3

FIRST PERIOD

Scoring: None. Penalties: M Gelinas, Cgy (elbowing), 0:21; B Lukowich, Tam (cross checking), 3:50; V Lecavalier, Tam (major fighting), 6:17; J Iginla, Cgy (major fighting), 6:17; C Clark, Cgy (tripping), 7:10; D Boyle, Tam (hooking), 9:36; M Gelinas, Cgy (holding stick), 17:03.

SECOND PERIOD

Scoring: 1, Calgary, Chris Simon 5 (power play) (Jarome Iginla, Jordan Leopold), 13:53. 2, Calgary, Shean Donovan 5 (Unassisted), 17:09. Penalties: B Lukowich, Tam (slashing), 13:03.

THIRD PERIOD

Scoring: 3, Calgary, Jarome Iginla 12 (power play) (Robyn Regehr, Chris Simon), 18:28. Penalties: S Donovan, Cgy (holding), 4:05; C Sarich, Tam (slashing), 17:23; C Sarich, TB (misconduct), 19:16.

Shots on goal: TB 5-6-10—21; Cgy 2-12-4 —18

Power-play opportunities: TB 0 of 4, Cgy 2 of 4.

Goalies : Tampa Bay, Nikolai Khabibulin (18 shots, 15 saves). Cgy Miikka Kiprusoff (21 shots, 21 saves).

Referees: McCreary, Fraser. Linesmen: Wheler, Driscoll. A: 19,221.

Game 4

Tampa Bay.......1   0   0—1
Calgary 0   0   0—0

FIRST PERIOD

Scoring: 1, Tampa Bay, Brad Richards 10 (power play) (Dave Andreychuk, Dan Boyle), 2:48. Penalties: C Clark, Cgy (cross checking), 1:52; M Commodore, Cgy (holding), 1:52; V Lecavalier, TB (tripping), 7:50; D Afanasenkov, Tam (elbowing), 12:52; C Kobasew, Cgy (holding), 16:40.

SECOND PERIOD

Scoring: None. Penalties: K Oliwa, Cgy (holding), 5:07.

THIRD PERIOD

Scoring: None. Penalties: V Nieminen, Cgy (major boarding, game misconduct), 15:47.

Shots on goal: TB 12-7-5—24; Cgy 12-5-12—29.

Power-play opportunities: TB 1 of 5, Cgy 0 of 2.

Goalies : TB, N. Khabibulin (29 shots, 29 saves). Cgy, M. Kiprusoff (24 shots, 23 saves). Referees: Watson, Fraser. Linesmen: Murphy, Wheler. A: 19,221.

Stanley Cup Championship Box Scores (Cont.)

Game 5

Calgary 1	1	0	1	—3
Tampa Bay 1	0	1	0	—2

FIRST PERIOD
Scoring: 1, Calgary, Martin Gelinas 8 (power play) (Toni Lydman, Steve Montador) 2:13. 2, Tampa Bay, Martin St. Louis 8 (Martin Cibak, Chris Dingman),19:26. Penalties: F Modin, TB (high sticking), 1:43; D Lowry, Cgy (interference), 8:41; A Roy, TB (roughing), 13:18.

SECOND PERIOD
Scoring: 3, Calgary, Jarome Iginla 13 (Unassisted), 5:10.

THIRD PERIOD
Scoring: 4, Tampa Bay, Fredrik Modin 8 (power play) (Brad Richards, Dave Andreychuk)0:37. Penalties: R Warrener, Cgy (holding stick), 0:31.

OVERTIME
Scoring: 5, Calgary, Oleg Saprykin 3 (Jarome Iginla, Marcus Nilson),14:40.

Shots on goal: Cgy 11-14-4-7—36; TB 9-3-8-8—28
Power-play Opportunities: Cgy 1 of 2, TB 1 of 2.
Goalies : Cgy, Miikka Kiprusoff (28 shots, 26 saves).
Tampa Bay, Nikolai Khabibulin (36 shots, 33 saves).
Referees: Bill McCreary, Stephen Walkom. Linesmen: Ray Scapinello, Scott Driscoll. A: 22,426.

Game 6

Tampa Bay 0	2	0	0	1—3
Calgary 0	2	0	0	0—2

FIRST PERIOD
Scoring: None. Penalties: D Andreychuk, Tam (elbowing), 11:59; A Ference, Cgy (hooking), 11:59; C Sarich, Tam (interference), 16:34; R Fedotenko, Tam (interference), 19:01.

SECOND PERIOD
Scoring: 1, Tampa Bay, Brad Richards 11 (power play) (Martin St. Louis, Ruslan Fedotenko) 4:17. 2, Calgary, Chris Clark 3 (Stephane Yelle, Ville Nieminen), 9:05. 3, Tampa Bay, Brad Richards 12 (power play) (Unassisted)10:52. 4, Calgary, Marcus Nilson 4 (Oleg Saprykin, Andrew Ference),17:49. Penalties: J Leopold, Cgy (interference), 2:34; C Conroy, Cgy (obstruction hooking), 9:25.

THIRD PERIOD
Scoring: None. Penalties: C Conroy, Cgy (hooking), 0:45; C Simon, Cgy (cross checking), 8:38; J Cullimore, Tam (interference), 11:18.

OVERTIME
Scoring: None. Penalties: None.

SECOND OVERTIME
Scoring: 5, Tampa Bay, Martin St. Louis 9 (Tim Taylor, Jassen Cullimore),0:33.

Shots on goal: TB 6-5-7-7-2—27; Cgy 6-13-7-7-0—33
Power-play opportunities: TB 2 of 4, Cgy 0 of 3.
Goalies : TB, Nikolai Khabibulin (33 shots, 31 saves). Cgy, Miikka Kiprusoff (27 shots, 24 saves).
Referees: McCreary, Walkom. Linesmen: Wheler, Scapinello. A: 19,221.

Game 7

Calgary 0	0	1	—1
Tampa Bay 1	1	0	—2

FIRST PERIOD
Scoring: 1, Tampa Bay, Ruslan Fedotenko 11 (power play) (Brad Richards, Fredrik Modin), 13:31. Penalties: M Nilson, Cgy (slashing), 1:10; O Saprykin, Cgy (tripping), 11:59; J Cullimore, TB (int.), 19:42.

SECOND PERIOD
Scoring: 2, Tampa Bay, Ruslan Fedotenko 12 (Vincent Lecavalier, Cory Stillman), 14:38. Penalties: M Gelinas, Cgy (boarding), 4:16; C Clark, Cgy (tripping), 18:46.

THIRD PERIOD
Scoring: 3, Calgary, Craig Conroy 6 (power play) (Jordan Leopold), 9:21. Penalties: N Pratt, Tam (interference), 8:50; A Ference, Cgy (charging), 18:59; D Andreychuk, Tam (tripping), 19:37.

Shots on goal: Cgy 3-4 -10—17; TB 6-4-5—15
Power-play opportunities: Cgy 1 of 2, TB 1 of 5.
Goalies : Calgary, Miikka Kiprusoff (15 shots, 13 saves). Tampa Bay, Nikolai Khabibulin (17 shots, 16 saves).
Referees: McCreary, Fraser. Linesmen: Murphy, Wheler. A: 22,717.

Individual Playoff Leaders

Scoring

POINTS

Player and Team	GP	G	A	Pts	+/–	PM
Brad Richards, TB 23	12	14	26	5	4
Martin St, Louis, TB 23	9	15	24	6	14
Jarome Iginla, Cgy 26	13	9	22	13	45
Fredrik Modin, TB 23	8	11	19	7	10
Craig Conroy, Cgy 26	6	11	17	12	12
Vincent Lecavalier, TB ...23	9	7	16	-2	25
Keith Primeau, Phil 18	9	7	16	11	22
Martin Gelinas, Cgy.......26	8	7	15	10	35
Alexei Zhamnov, Phil 18	4	10	14	-1	8
Ruslan Fedotenko, TB ...22	12	2	14	0	14

Player and Team	GP	G	A	Pts	+/–	PM
V. Damphousse, SJ 17	7	7	14	0	20
Dave Andreychuk, TB ...23	1	13	14	-2	14
Jeremy Roenick, Phil......18	4	9	13	4	8
Patrick Marleau, SJ 17	8	4	12	0	8
Joe Sakic, Col 11	7	5	12	0	8
Marcus Nilson, Cgy.........26	4	7	11	0	12
Peter Forsberg, Col.........11	4	7	11	6	12
Saku Koivu, Mtl...........11	3	8	11	1	10

GOALS

Player and Team	GP	G
Jarome Iginla, Cgy	26	13
Brad Richards, TB	23	12
Ruslan Fedotenko, TB	22	12
Martin St. Louis, TB	23	9
Vincent Lacavalier, TB	23	9
Keith Primeau, Phil	18	9

GAME-WINNING GOALS

Player and Team	GP	GW
Brad Richards, TB	23	7

Six tied with 3.

POWER PLAY GOALS

Player and Team	GP	PP
Brad Richards, TB	23	7
Ruslan Fedotenko, TB	22	5
Jaromė Iginla, Cgy	26	4
Patrick Marleau, SJ	17	4
Chris Simon, Cgy	16	4

SHORT-HANDED GOALS

Player and Team	GP	SH
Jarome Iginla, Cgy	26	2
Keith Primeau, Phil	18	2

ASSISTS

Player and Team	GP	A
Martin St. Louis, TB	23	15
Brad Richards, TB	23	14
Dave Andreychuk, TB	23	13
Fredrik Modin, TB	23	11
Craig Conroy, Cgy	26	11

PLUS/MINUS

Player and Team	GP	+/–
Jarome Iginla, Cgy	26	13
Craig Conroy, Cgy	26	12
Keith Primeau, Phil	18	11
Martin Gelinas, Cgy	26	10
Simon Gagne, Phil	18	10

Goaltending (Minimum 420 minutes)

GOALS AGAINST AVERAGE

Player and Team	GP	W - L -T	Avg
Curtis Joseph, Det	9	4- 4- 0	1.39
N. Khabibulin, TB	23	16- 7- 0	1.71
Evgeni Nabokov, SJ	17	10- 7- 0	1.71
Miikka Kiprusoff, Cgy	26	15-11- 0	1.85
David Aebischer, Col	11	6- 5- 0	2.08

SAVE PERCENTAGE

Player and Team	GP	W-L-T	GAA	GA	SV	SV%	SA
Curtis Joseph, Det	9	4-4-0	1.39	12	185	.939	197
E. Nabokov, SJ	17	10-7-0	1.71	30	431	.935	461
N. Khabibulin, TB	23	16-7-0	1.71	40	558	.933	598
Ed Belfour, Tor	13	6-7-0	2.09	27	352	.929	379
M. Kiprusoff, Cgy	26	15-11-0	1.85	51	659	.928	710

NHL Awards

Award	Player and Team
Hart Trophy (MVP)	Martin St. Louis, TB
Calder Trophy (top rookie)	Andrew Raycroft, Bos
Vezina Trophy (top goaltender)	Martin Brodeur, NJ
Norris Trophy (top defenseman)	Scott Niedermayer, NJ
Lady Byng Trophy (for gentlemanly play)	Brad Richards, TB
Adams Award (top coach)	John Tortorella, TB

Award	Player and Team
Selke Trophy (top defensive forward)	Kris Draper, Det
Jennings Trophy (goaltender on club allowing fewest goals)	Martin Brodeur, NJ
Conn Smythe Trophy (playoff MVP)	Brad Richards, TB

Individual Regular Season Leaders

Scoring

POINTS

Player and Team	GP	G	A	Pts	+/–	PM
Martin St. Louis, TB	82	38	56	94	35	24
Ilya Kovalchuk, Atl	81	41	46	87	-10	63
Joe Sakic, Col	81	33	54	87	11	42
Markus Naslund, Van	78	35	49	84	24	58
Marian Hossa, Ott	81	36	46	82	4	46
Patrik Elias, NJ	82	38	43	81	26	44
Daniel Alfredsson, Ott	77	32	48	80	12	24
Cory Stillman, TB	81	25	55	80	18	36
Robert Lang, Det	69	30	49	79	4	24
Alex Tanguay, Col	69	25	54	79	30	42

Player and Team	GP	G	A	Pts	+/–	PM
Brad Richards, TB	82	26	53	79	14	12
Mats Sundin, Tor	81	31	44	75	11	52
Mark Recchi, Phil	82	26	49	75	18	47
Milan Hejduk, Col	82	35	40	75	19	20
Jaromir Jagr, NYR	77	31	43	74	-5	38
Jarome Iginla, Cgy	81	41	32	73	21	84
Joe Thornton, Bos	77	23	50	73	18	98
Steve Sullivan, Nash	80	24	49	73	1	48
Keith Tkachuk, StL	75	33	38	71	8	83
Scott Gomez, NJ	80	14	56	70	18	70

GOALS

Player and Team	GP	G
Jarome Iginla, Cgy	81	41
Rick Nash, Clb	80	41
Ilya Kovalchuk, Atl	81	41
Martin St. Louis, TB	82	38
Patrik Elias, NJ	82	38

POWER PLAY GOALS

Player and Team	GP	PP
Rick Nash, Clb	80	19
Keith Tkachuk, StL	75	18
Milan Hejduk, Col	82	16
Ilya Kovalchuk, Atl	81	16

GAME-WINNING GOALS

Player and Team	GP	GW
Mats Sundin, Tor	81	10
Bill Guerin, Dal	82	10
Jarome Iginla, Cgy	81	10
Richard Zednik, Mon	81	9
Glen Murray, Bos	81	9
Patrik Elias, NJ	82	9
J. Cheechoo, SJ	81	9

SHORT-HANDED GOALS

Player and Team	GP	SHG
Martin St. Louis, TB	82	8
Kris Draper, Det	67	5
Kevyn Adams, Car	73	5

ASSISTS

Player and Team	GP	A
Scott Gomez, NJ	80	56
Martin St. Louis, TB	82	56
Cory Stillman, TB	81	55
Alex Tanguay, Col	69	54
Joe Sakic, Col	81	54
Brad Richards, TB	82	53

PLUS/MINUS

Player and Team	GP	+/–
Martin St. Louis, TB	82	35
Marek Malik, Van	78	35
Zdeno Chara, Ott	79	33
Fredrik Modin, TB	82	31
Nils Ekman, SJ	82	30
Alex Tanguay, Col	69	30

Goaltending
(Minimum 25 games)

GOALS AGAINST AVERAGE

Player and Team	GP	W-L-T	GAA	TGA
Miikka Kiprusoff, Cgy ...38		24-10-4	1.70	65
Dwayne Roloson, Minn..48		19-18-11	1.88	89
Marty Turco, Dall..........73		37-21-13	1.98	144
Martin Brodeur, NJ 75		38-26-11	2.03	154
Robert Esche, Phil 40		21-11-7	2.04	79

SAVE PERCENTAGE

Player and Team	GP	W-L-T	GA	SA	Pct
Miikka Kiprusoff, Cgy...38		24-10-4	65	966	.933
D. Roloson, Minn.........48		19-18-11	89	1323	.933
Roberto Luongo, Fla ..72		25-33-14	172	2475	.931
Vesa Toskala, SJ 28		12-8-4	53	760	.930
A. Raycroft, Bos 57		29-18-9	117	1586	.926

WINS

Player and Team	GP	GAA	W	L	T
Martin Brodeur, NJ 75		2.03	38	26	11
Marty Turco, Dall 73		1.98	37	21	13
Tomas Vokoun, Nash...........73		2.53	34	29	10
Ed Belfour, Tor 59		2.13	34	19	6
Jose Theodore, Mtl 67		2.27	33	28	5
Dan Cloutier, Van 60		2.27	33	21	6

SHUTOUTS

Player and Team	GP	W	L	T	SO
Martin Brodeur, NJ 75		38	26	11	11
Ed Belfour, Tor 59		34	19	6	10
Evgeni Nabokov, SJ 59		31	19	8	9
Marty Turco, Dall 73		37	21	13	9
Roberto Luongo, Fla 72		25	33	14	7

NHL Team-by-Team Statistical Leaders

Anaheim Mighty Ducks
SCORING

Player	GP	G	A	Pts	+/–	PM
Sergei Fedorov, C........80		31	34	65	-5	2
Vaclav Prospal, LW 82		19	35	54	-9	54
Petr Sykora, RW..........81		23	29	52	-9	34
Steve Rucchin, C..........82		20	23	43	-14	12
Joffrey Lupul, C............75		13	21	34	-6	28
Andy McDonald, LW....79		9	21	30	-13	24
Rob Niedermayer, C 55		12	16	28	-6	34
Niclas Havelid, D 79		6	20	26	-28	28
Samuel Pahlsson, C.....82		8	14	22	-2	52
Stanislav Chistov, LW....56		2	16	18	-16	26
Jason Krog, LW 80		6	12	18	-4	16
Vitaly Vishnevski, D.......73		6	10	16	0	51
Sandis Ozolinsh, D 36		5	11	16	-7	24
Ruslan Salei, D 82		4	11	15	-1	110
Martin Skoula, D 21		2	7	9	3	2
Todd Simpson, D 46		4	3	7	-6	105
Keith Carney, D............69		2	5	7	-5	42
Chris Kunitz, LW 21		0	6	6	1	12
Kurt Sauer, D...............55		1	4	5	-8	32
Lance Ward, D..............46		0	4	4	-1	94
Mike Leclerc, LW 10		1	3	4	-1	4
Cam Severson, LW 31		3	0	3	-3	50
Garrett Burnett, LW 39		1	2	3	0	184
Craig Johnson, LW 39		1	2	3	-4	14
Tony Martensson, C........6		1	1	2	-2	0
Mikael Holmqvist, C......21		2	0	2	-6	25
Petr Schastlivy, LW........22		2	0	2	-3	4
JS Giguere, G 55		0	2	2	0	4

GOALTENDING

Player	GP	Mins	W	L	T	Avg	SO
J.S. Giguere........55		3210	17	31	6	2.62	3
Martin Gerber 32		1698	11	12	4	2.26	2
Ilya Bryzgalov.......1		60	1	0	0	1.98	0

Atlanta Thrashers
SCORING

Player	GP	G	A	Pts	+/–	PM
Ilya Kovalchuk, LW 81		41	46	87	-10	63
S. McEachern, RW 82		17	38	55	5	76
Marc Savard, C............45		19	33	52	-8	85
Slava Kozlov, LW 76		20	32	52	-12	74
Patrik Stefan, C............82		14	26	40	-7	26
Randy Robitaille, C.......69		11	26	37	-12	20
R. Petrovicky, RW 78		16	15	31	-9	123
Frantisek Kaberle, D......67		3	26	29	2	30
Dany Heatley, RW........31		13	12	25	-8	18
Serge Aubin, LW..........66		10	15	25	0	73
Jeff Cowan, LW............58		9	15	24	2	68
Andy Sutton, D 65		8	13	21	0	94
Daniel Tjarnqvist, D......68		5	15	20	-4	20
J.P. Vigier, RW............70		10	8	18	-18	22
Garnet Exelby, D 71		1	9	10	-10	134
Ivan Majesky, D............63		3	7	10	-7	76
Yannick Tremblay, D......38		2	8	10	-13	13
Chris Tamer, D..............38		2	5	7	-9	55
J.L. Grand-Pierre, RW....27		2	2	4	-7	26
Shawn Heins, D...........17		0	4	4	-1	16
Ben Simon, C...............52		3	0	3	-10	2
Tommi Santala, C.........33		1	2	3	-7	22
Zdenek Blatny, LW.......16		3	0	3	0	6
Francis Lessard, RW......62		1	1	2	-5	181
Pasi Nurminen, G 64		2	2	0	0	35
Kyle Rossiter, D 2		0	1	1	1	0
Derek MacKenzie, C ...12		0	1	1	0	10
Kamil Piros, RW 14		0	1	1	-3	4

GOALTENDING

Player	GP	Mins	W	L	T	Avg	SO
Pasi Nurminen 64		3738	25	30	7	2.78	3
Kari Lehtonen 4		240	4	0	0	1.25	1
Byron Dafoe........16		973	4	11	1	3.15	0

Boston Bruins
SCORING

Player	GP	G	A	Pts	+/–	PM
Joe Thornton, C	77	23	50	73	18	98
Glen Murray, RW	81	32	28	60	17	56
Brian Rolston, C	82	19	29	48	9	40
Mike Knuble, RW	82	21	25	46	19	32
S. Samsonov, LW	58	17	23	40	12	4
Patrice Bergeron, C	71	16	23	39	5	22
Nick Boynton, D	81	6	24	30	17	98
Dan McGillis, D	80	5	23	28	-1	65
Martin Lapointe, RW	78	15	10	25	-5	67
P.J. Axelsson, LW	68	6	14	20	2	42
Jiri Slegr, D	36	4	15	19	5	27
Travis Green, C	64	11	5	16	-6	67
Jeff Jillson, D	50	4	10	14	-1	35
Michael Nylander, C	15	1	11	12	3	14
Sean O'Donnell, D	82	1	10	11	10	110
Ted Donato, LW	63	6	5	11	2	18
Hal Gill, D	82	2	7	9	16	99
Sergei Gonchar, D	15	4	5	9	6	12
Rob Zamuner, LW	57	4	5	9	3	16
Shaone Morrisonn, D	30	1	7	8	10	10
Ian Moran, D	35	1	4	5	3	28
Michal Grosek, LW	33	3	2	5	1	33
Sandy McCarthy, RW	37	3	1	4	0	28
Craig MacDonald, C	18	0	3	3	0	8
Andy Hilbert, C	18	2	0	2	1	9
Carl Corazzini, C	12	2	0	2	2	0
Andrew Raycroft, G	57	0	2	2	0	0
Sergei Zinovjev, C	10	0	1	1	1	2
Doug Doull, LW	35	0	1	1	2	132

GOALTENDING

Player	GP	Mins	W	L	T	Avg	SO
Andrew Raycroft	57	3420	29	18	9	2.05	3
Felix Potvin	28	1605	12	8	6	2.50	4

Buffalo Sabres
SCORING

Player	GP	G	A	Pts	+/–	PM
Daniel Briere, C	82	28	37	65	-7	70
Miroslav Satan, RW	82	29	28	57	-15	30
Chris Drury, C	76	18	35	53	8	68
J.P. Dumont, RW	77	22	31	53	-9	40
Jochen Hecht, LW	64	15	37	52	17	49
Dmitri Kalinin, D	77	10	24	34	0	42
M. Afinogenov, RW	73	17	14	31	-4	57
Alexei Zhitnik, D	68	4	24	28	-13	102
Ales Kotalik, RW	62	15	11	26	-1	41
Curtis Brown, C	68	9	12	21	2	30
Taylor Pyatt, LW	63	8	12	20	-7	25
Adam Mair, C	81	6	14	20	-3	146
Derek Roy, C	49	9	10	19	-8	12
Chris Taylor, C	54	6	6	12	-2	22
Rory Fitzpatrick, D	60	4	7	11	-5	44
James Patrick, D	55	4	7	11	11	12
Brian Campbell, D	53	3	8	11	-8	12
Henrik Tallinder, D	72	1	9	10	5	26
Milan Bartovic, RW	23	1	8	9	1	18
Mike Grier, RW	14	1	8	9	10	4
Andy Delmore, D	37	2	5	7	-5	29
Jay McKee, D	43	2	3	5	6	41
Jeff Jillson, D	14	0	3	3	-3	19
Eric Boulton, LW	44	1	2	3	-2	110
Jason Botterill, LW	19	2	1	3	0	14
Andrew Peters, LW	42	2	0	2	-3	151
Brad Brown, D	13	0	2	2	3	12
Martin Biron, G	52	0	2	2	0	10
Mika Noronen, G	35	1	0	1	0	0

GOALTENDING

Player	GP	Mins	W	L	T	Avg	SO
Martin Biron	52	2972	26	18	5	2.52	2
Mika Noronen	35	1796	11	17	2	2.57	2
Ryan Miller	3	178	0	3	0	5.06	0

Calgary Flames
SCORING

Player	GP	G	A	Pts	+/–	PM
Jarome Iginla, RW	81	41	32	73	21	84
Craig Conroy, C	63	8	39	47	13	44
Shean Donovan, RW	82	18	24	42	14	72
Martin Gelinas, LW	76	17	18	35	10	70
Jordan Leopold, D	82	9	24	33	8	24
D. McAmmond, C	64	17	13	30	9	18
Steve Reinprecht, C	44	7	22	29	1	4
M. Lombardi, C	79	16	13	29	4	32
Oleg Saprykin, LW	69	12	17	29	1	41
Chris Clark, RW	82	10	15	25	-3	106
Toni Lydman, D	67	4	16	20	6	30
Robyn Regehr, D	82	4	14	18	14	74
Stephane Yelle, C	53	4	13	17	1	24
Chuck Kobasew, RW	70	6	11	17	-12	51
Rhett Warrener, D	77	3	14	17	8	97
Andrew Ference, D	72	4	12	16	5	53

SCORING (CONT.)

Player	GP	G	A	Pts	+/–	PM
Denis Gauthier, D	80	1	15	16	4	113
Ville Nieminen, LW	19	3	5	8	6	18
Josh Green, LW	36	2	4	6	-3	24
Marcus Nilson, LW	14	5	0	5	3	14
Chris Simon, LW	13	3	2	5	1	25
Krzysztof Oliwa, LW	65	3	2	5	-8	247

GOALTENDING

Player	GP	Mins	W	L	T	Avg	SO
Miikka Kiprusoff	38	2301	24	10	4	1.70	4
J. McLennan	26	1446	12	9	3	2.20	4
Roman Turek	18	1031	6	11	0	2.33	3
Dany Sabourin	4	169	0	3	0	3.56	0

Carolina Hurricanes
SCORING

Player	GP	G	A	Pts	+/–	PM
Josef Vasicek, C	82	19	26	45	-3	60
Erik Cole, LW	80	18	24	42	-4	93
Sean Hill, D	80	13	26	39	-2	84
Rod Brind'Amour, C	78	12	26	38	0	28
Jeff O'Neill, RW	67	14	20	34	-12	607
Eric Staal, C	81	11	20	31	-6	40
Ron Francis, C	68	10	20	30	-12	14
Radim Vrbata, RW	80	12	13	25	-10	24
Bret Hedican, D	81	7	17	24	-10	64
Kevyn Adams, C	73	10	12	22	6	43
Justin Williams, RW	32	5	13	18	2	32
Craig Adams, RW	80	7	10	17	-5	69
Danny Markov, D	44	4	10	14	-6	37
Marty Murray, C	66	5	7	12	6	8
Niclas Wallin, D	57	3	7	10	-8	51
Aaron Ward, D	49	3	5	8	1	37
Pavel Brendl, RW	18	5	3	8	0	8
Jesse Boulerice, RW	76	6	1	7	-5	127
Glen Wesley, D	74	0	6	6	18	32
Ryan Bayda, LW	44	3	3	6	-14	22
Bob Boughner, D	43	0	5	5	-9	80
J. Svoboda, RW	33	3	1	4	3	6

GOALTENDING

Player	GP	Mins	W	L	T	Avg	SO
Kevin Weekes	66	3765	23	30	11	2.33	6
Arturs Irbe	10	564	5	2	1	2.45	0
Jamie Storr	14	660	0	8	2	2.91	0

Colorado Avalanche
SCORING

Player	GP	G	A	Pts	+/–	PM
Joe Sakic, C	81	33	54	87	11	2
Alex Tanguay, LW	69	25	54	79	30	42
Milan Hejduk, RW	82	35	40	75	19	20
Peter Forsberg, C	39	18	37	55	16	30
Rob Blake, D	74	13	33	46	6	61
S. Konowalchuk, LW	76	19	20	39	2	70
Paul Kariya, LW	51	11	25	36	-5	22
John-Michael Liles, D	79	10	24	34	7	28
Teemu Selanne, RW	78	16	16	32	2	32
Adam Foote, D	73	8	22	30	13	87
Derek Morris, D	69	6	22	28	4	47
Martin Skoula, D	58	2	14	16	2	30
Karlis Skrastins, D	82	5	8	13	18	26
Steve Moore, C	57	5	7	12	-5	37
Andrei Nikolishin, C	49	5	7	12	3	24
Dan Hinote, RW	59	4	7	11	-6	57
Matthew Barnaby, RW	13	4	5	9	3	37
Travis Brigley, LW	36	3	4	7	0	10
Cody McCormick, C	44	2	3	5	-4	73
Brad Larsen, LW	26	2	2	4	2	11
Peter Worrell, LW	49	3	1	4	2	179
D. Hendrickson, C	20	1	3	4	-8	6
Jim Cummins, RW	55	1	2	3	-5	147

GOALTENDING

Player	GP	Mins	W	L	T	Avg	SO
David Aebischer	62	3703	32	19	9	2.09	4
Philippe Sauve	17	986	7	7	3	3.04	0
Tommy Salo	5	304	1	3	1	2.37	0

Chicago Blackhawks
SCORING

Player	GP	G	A	Pts	+/–	PM
Tyler Arnason, C	82	22	33	55	-13	16
Bryan Berard, D	58	13	34	47	-24	53
Mark Bell, LW	82	21	24	45	-14	106
Tuomo Ruutu, C	82	23	21	44	-31	58
Steve Sullivan, RW	56	15	28	43	-7	36
Kyle Calder, LW	66	21	18	39	-18	29
Brett McLean, C	76	11	20	31	-11	54
Nathan Dempsey, D	58	8	17	25	-5	30
Alexei Zhamnov, C	23	6	12	18	-8	14
Scott Nichol, C	75	7	11	18	-16	145
Igor Korolev, C	62	3	10	13	-15	22
Ville Nieminen, LW	60	2	11	13	-15	40
S. Robidas, D	45	2	10	12	6	33
Jim Vandermeer, D	23	2	10	12	-6	58
Eric Daze, LW	19	4	7	11	-7	0
Deron Quint, D	51	4	7	11	-26	18
Igor Radulov, LW	36	4	7	11	-2	18
Mikhail Yakubov, C	30	1	7	8	-12	8
A. Karpovtsev, D	24	0	7	7	-17	14
Travis Moen, LW	82	4	2	6	-17	142
Burke Henry, D	23	2	4	6	0	24
VandenBussche, RW	65	4	1	5	-10	120

GOALTENDING

Player	GP	Mins	W	L	T	Avg	SO
Craig Anderson	21	1205	6	14	0	2.84	1
Michael Leighton	34	1988	6	18	8	2.99	2
Jocelyn Thibault	14	821	5	7	2	2.85	1
Steve Passmore	9	478	2	6	0	2.89	0
Adam Munro	7	426	1	5	1	3.66	0

Columbus Blue Jackets
SCORING

Player	GP	G	A	Pts	+/–	PM
Rick Nash, LW	80	41	16	57	-35	87
David Vyborny, RW	82	22	31	53	-26	40
Todd Marchant, C	77	9	25	34	-17	34
Nikolai Zherdev, RW	57	13	21	34	-11	54
Trevor Letowski, RW	73	15	17	32	-12	16
Geoff Sanderson, LW	67	13	16	29	-9	34
Anders Eriksson, D	66	7	20	27	-6	18
Andrew Cassels, C	58	6	20	26	-24	26
Manny Malhotra, C	56	12	13	25	-5	24
Jaroslav Spacek, D	58	5	17	22	-13	45
Tyler Wright, RW	68	9	9	18	-19	63
Darryl Sydor, D	49	2	13	15	-19	26
Rostislav Klesla, D	47	2	11	13	-16	27
Lasse Pirjeta, C	57	2	8	10	-6	20
Derrick Walser, D	27	1	8	9	-6	22
Aaron Johnson, D	29	2	6	8	-2	32
Alexander Svitov, C	29	2	6	8	-8	16
Duvie Westcott, D	34	0	7	7	-15	39
Luke Richardson, D	64	1	5	6	-11	48
Jody Shelley, LW	76	3	3	6	-10	228
Scott Lachance, D	77	0	4	4	-23	44
Mark Hartigan, C	9	1	3	4	-2	6
Espen Knutsen, C	14	0	4	4	-5	2
Kent McDonell, RW	29	1	2	3	-7	36
Tim Jackman, RW	19	1	2	3	-7	16
David Ling, RW	50	1	2	3	-3	98

GOALTENDING

Player	GP	Mins	W	L	T	Avg	SO
Marc Denis	66	3796	21	36	7	2.56	5
Fred Brathwaite	21	1050	4	11	1	3.37	0
Pascal Leclaire	2	119	0	2	0	3.52	0

Dallas Stars

SCORING

Player	GP	G	A	Pts	+/-	PM
Bill Guerin, RW	82	34	35	69	14	109
Jason Arnott, C	73	21	36	57	23	66
Brenden Morrow, LW	81	25	24	49	10	121
Mike Modano, C	76	14	30	44	-21	46
Sergei Zubov, D	77	7	35	42	0	20
Pierre Turgeon, C	76	15	25	40	17	20
Stu Barnes, C	77	11	18	29	7	18
Jere Lehtinen, RW	58	13	13	26	0	20
Philippe Boucher, D	70	8	16	24	15	64
Rob DiMaio, RW	69	9	15	24	2	52
R. Matvichuk, D	75	1	20	21	0	36
Teppo Numminen, D	62	3	14	17	-5	18
Scott Young, RW	53	8	8	16	-15	14
Steve Ott, C	73	2	10	12	-2	152
David Oliver, RW	36	7	5	12	6	12
Don Sweeney, D	63	0	11	11	22	18
Shayne Corson, LW	17	5	5	10	12	29
Valeri Bure, RW	13	2	5	7	3	6
Trevor Daley, D	27	1	5	6	-6	14
Jon Klemm, D	58	2	4	6	10	24
Niko Kapanen, C	67	1	5	6	-15	16
Aaron Downey, RW	37	1	1	2	2	77

GOALTENDING

Player	GP	Mins	W	L	T	Avg	SO
Marty Turco	73	4359	37	21	13	1.98	9
Ron Tugnutt	11	548	3	7	0	2.41	1
Dan Ellis	1	60	1	0	0	3.00	0

Detroit Red Wings

SCORING

Player	GP	G	A	Pts	+/-	PM
Brett Hull, RW	81	25	43	68	-4	2
Pavel Datsyuk, C	75	30	38	68	-2	35
B Shanahan, LW	82	25	28	53	15	117
Steve Yzerman, C	75	18	33	51	10	46
Mathieu Schneider, D	78	14	32	46	22	56
Ray Whitney, LW	67	14	29	43	7	22
Henrik Zetterberg, LW	61	15	28	43	15	14
Kris Draper, C	67	24	16	40	22	31
Nicklas Lidstrom, D	81	10	28	38	19	18
Kirk Maltby, LW	79	14	19	33	24	80
Tomas Holmstrom, LW	67	15	15	30	8	38
Steve Thomas, RW	44	10	12	22	8	25
Chris Chelios, D	69	2	19	21	12	61
Jiri Fischer, D	81	4	15	19	0	75
Jason Woolley, D	55	4	15	19	19	28
Boyd Devereaux, C	61	6	9	15	-1	20
Jason Williams, C	49	6	7	13	1	15
Mathieu Dandenault, D	65	3	9	12	9	40
Mark Mowers, RW	52	3	8	11	3	4
Darren McCarty, RW	43	6	5	11	2	50
Jamie Rivers, D	50	3	4	7	9	41
Niklas Kronwall, D	20	1	4	5	5	16
Robert Lang, C	6	1	4	5	2	0
Derian Hatcher, D	15	0	4	4	4	8
Jiri Hudler, C	12	1	2	3	-1	10
Dominik Hasek, G	14	0	2	2	0	2

GOALTENDING

Player	GP	Mins	W	L	T	Avg	SO
Manny Legace	41	2325	23	10	5	2.12	3
Curtis Joseph	31	1708	16	10	3	2.39	2
Dominik Hasek	14	817	8	3	2	2.20	2
Marc Lamothe	2	125	1	0	1	1.45	0

Edmonton Oilers

SCORING

Player	GP	G	A	Pts	+/-	PM
Ryan Smyth, LW	82	23	36	59	11	70
Radek Dvorak, RW	78	15	35	50	18	26
Mike York, C	61	16	26	42	18	15
Shawn Horcoff, C	80	15	25	40	0	73
Ales Hemsky, RW	71	12	22	34	-7	14
Raffi Torres, LW	80	20	14	34	12	65
Ethan Moreau, LW	81	20	12	32	7	96
F. Pisani, RW	76	16	14	30	14	46
Steve Staios, D	82	6	22	28	17	8
M.A. Bergeron, D	54	9	17	26	13	26
Eric Brewer, D	77	7	18	25	-6	67
Cory Cross, D	68	7	14	21	9	56
Jarret Stoll, C	68	10	11	21	8	42
Jason Smith, D	68	7	12	19	13	98
Igor Ulanov, D	42	5	13	18	19	28
Adam Oates, C	60	2	16	18	0	8
Brad Isbister, LW	51	10	8	18	-2	54
G. Laraque, RW	66	6	11	17	7	99
Petr Nedved, C	16	5	10	15	1	4
Jason Chimera, LW	60	4	8	12	-1	57
Marty Reasoner, C	17	2	6	8	5	10
Scott Ferguson, D	52	1	5	6	-5	80
Alexei Semenov, D	46	2	3	5	8	32

GOALTENDING

Player	GP	Mins	W	L	T	Avg	SO
Ty Conklin	38	2086	17	14	4	2.42	1
Tommy Salo	44	2487	17	18	6	2.58	3
Jussi Markkanen	7	394	2	2	2	1.83	0
S. Valiquette	1	14	0	0	0	8.65	0

Florida Panthers
SCORING

Player	GP	G	A	Pts	+/–	PM
Olli Jokinen, C	82	26	32	58	-16	81
Valeri Bure, RW	55	20	25	45	0	20
Mike Van Ryn, D	79	13	24	37	-16	52
Kristian Huselius, LW	76	10	21	31	-6	24
Stephen Weiss, C	50	12	17	29	-10	10
Viktor Kozlov, RW	48	11	16	27	-4	16
Juraj Kolnik, RW	53	14	11	25	-7	14
Niklas Hagman, LW	75	10	13	23	-5	22
Nathan Horton, C	55	14	8	22	-5	57
Jay Bouwmeester, D	61	2	18	20	-15	30
Matt Cullen, C	56	6	13	19	-2	24
Marcus Nilson, LW	69	6	13	19	-9	26
Lyle Odelein, D	82	4	12	16	-7	88
Pavel Trnka, D	67	3	13	16	2	51
Donald Audette, RW	28	6	7	13	-9	22
Mathieu Biron, D	57	3	10	13	-13	51
Byron Ritchie, C	50	5	6	11	-10	84
M. Samuelsson, RW	37	3	6	9	0	35
Vaclav Nedorost, C	32	4	3	7	-6	12
Lukas Krajicek, D	18	1	6	7	-2	12
Andreas Lilja, D	79	3	4	7	-8	90
Branislav Mezei, D	45	0	7	7	-4	80
Eric Beaudoin, LW	30	2	4	6	-6	12
I. Novoseltsev, RW	17	1	4	5	-6	8

GOALTENDING

Player	GP	Mins	W	L	T	Avg	SO
Roberto Luongo	72	4252	25	33	14	2.43	7
Steve Shields	16	732	3	6	1	3.44	0

Los Angeles Kings
SCORING

Player	GP	G	A	Pts	+/–	PM
Luc Robitaille, LW	80	22	29	51	4	56
A. Frolov, LW	77	24	24	48	8	24
Trent Klatt, RW	82	17	26	43	2	46
Zigmund Palffy, RW	35	16	25	41	18	12
Jozef Stumpel, C	64	8	29	37	5	16
Derek Armstrong, C	57	14	21	35	4	33
Eric Belanger, C	81	13	20	33	-16	44
Jaroslav Modry, D	79	5	27	32	11	44
L. Visnovsky, D	58	8	21	29	8	26
Sean Avery, C	76	9	19	28	2	261
Joe Corvo, D	72	8	17	25	7	36
Ian Laperriere, RW	62	10	12	22	-4	58
M. Cammalleri, C	31	9	6	15	1	20
Martin Straka, C	32	6	8	14	-9	4
Mattias Norstrom, D	74	1	13	14	-3	44
Jon Sim, LW	48	6	7	13	0	27
Scott Barney, RW	19	5	6	11	3	4
Esa Pirnes, C	57	3	8	11	-9	12
Brad Chartrand, C	53	3	4	7	-3	30
Nathan Dempsey, D	17	4	3	7	-7	2
Tim Gleason, D	47	0	7	7	1	21
Jason Holland, D	52	3	3	6	5	24
John Tripp, RW	34	1	5	6	-4	33
Tomas Zizka, D	15	2	3	5	-4	12

GOALTENDING

Player	GP	Mins	W	L	T	Avg	SO
R. Cechmanek	49	2701	18	21	6	2.51	5
Cristobal Huet	41	2199	10	16	10	2.43	3
Milan Hnilicka	2	80	0	1	0	3.76	0

Minnesota Wild
SCORING

Player	GP	G	A	Pts	+/–	PM
A. Daigle, RW	78	20	31	51	-4	14
A. Brunette, LW	82	15	34	49	3	12
M. Gaborik, RW	65	18	22	40	10	20
Sergei Zholtok, C	59	13	16	29	4	19
Pascal Dupuis, LW	59	11	15	26	5	20
Antti Laaksonen, LW	77	12	14	26	0	20
Richard Park, RW	73	13	12	25	0	28
Wes Walz, C	57	12	13	25	5	32
Jim Dowd, C	55	4	20	24	6	38
Filip Kuba, D	77	5	19	24	-7	28
P.M. Bouchard, LW	61	4	18	22	-7	22
Marc Chouinard, C	45	11	10	21	4	17
Andrei Zyuzin, D	65	8	13	21	4	48
Jason Wiemer, C	62	7	11	18	-6	106
Nick Schultz, D	79	6	10	16	12	16
Willie Mitchell, D	70	1	13	14	12	83
S. Veilleux, LW	19	2	8	10	0	20
Rickard Wallin, C	15	5	4	9	1	14
C. Brandner, LW	35	4	5	9	-2	8
Matt Johnson, LW	57	7	1	8	4	177
Eric Chouinard, RW	31	3	4	7	-7	6
Brent Burns, RW	36	1	5	6	-10	12
Alex Henry, D	71	2	4	6	4	106
Jason Marshall, D	12	1	4	5	-1	18

GOALTENDING

Player	GP	Mins	W	L	T	Avg	SO
D. Roloson	48	2847	19	18	11	1.88	5
M.Fernandez	37	2166	11	14	9	2.49	2

Montreal Canadiens
SCORING

Player	GP	G	A	Pts	+/–	PM
Mike Ribeiro, LW	81	20	45	65	15	34
Michael Ryder, RW	81	25	38	63	10	26
Saku Koivu, C	68	14	41	55	-5	52
Richard Zednik, RW	81	26	24	50	5	63
Sheldon Souray, D	63	15	20	35	4	104
Yanic Perreault, C	69	16	15	31	-10	40
Patrice Brisebois, D	71	4	27	31	17	22
Jan Bulis, C	72	13	17	30	-8	30
Andrei Markov, D	69	6	22	28	-2	20
Pierre Dagenais, LW	50	17	10	27	15	24
Niklas Sundstrom, RW	66	8	12	20	3	18
Francis Bouillon, D	73	2	16	18	1	70
Joe Juneau, C	70	5	10	15	-4	20
Steve Begin, C	52	10	5	15	6	41
Craig Rivet, D	80	4	8	12	-1	98
Jason Ward, RW	53	5	7	12	3	21
Andreas Dackell, RW	60	4	8	12	8	10
Stephane Quintal, D	73	3	5	8	10	82
Donald Audette, RW	23	3	5	8	-4	16
Jim Dowd, C	14	3	2	5	6	6
Chad Kilger, LW	36	2	2	4	2	14
Mike Komisarek, D	46	0	4	4	4	34
Jose Theodore, G	67	0	3	3	0	4
Alexei Kovalev, RW	12	1	2	3	-4	12
Darren Langdon, LW	64	0	3	3	-2	135

GOALTENDING

Player	GP	Mins	W	L	T	Avg	SO
Jose Theodore	67	3961	33	28	5	2.27	6
Mathieu Garon	19	1003	8	6	2	2.27	0

Nashville Predators

SCORING

Player	GP	G	A	Pts	+/-	PM
Scott Walker, RW	75	25	42	67	4	94
Marek Zidlicky, D	82	14	39	53	-16	82
Martin Erat, LW	76	16	33	49	10	38
David Legwand, C	82	18	29	47	9	46
Kimmo Timonen, D	77	12	32	44	-7	52
Vladimir Orszagh, RW	82	16	21	37	-4	74
Scott Hartnell, LW	59	18	15	33	-5	87
Greg Johnson, C	82	14	18	32	-21	33
Steve Sullivan, RW	24	9	21	30	8	12
A. Johansson, LW	47	12	15	27	-2	26
Adam Hall, RW	79	13	14	27	-8	37
Dan Hamhuis, D	80	7	19	26	-12	57
Denis Arkhipov, C	72	9	12	21	-2	22
Rem Murray, C	39	8	9	17	-1	12
Jason York, D	67	2	13	15	-4	64
Mark Eaton, D	75	4	9	13	16	26
J. Stevenson, LW	53	5	4	9	-2	103
A.Hutchinson, D	18	4	4	8	1	4
Jordin Tootoo, RW	70	4	4	8	-6	137
Jim McKenzie, LW	61	1	3	4	-13	88
Wyatt Smith, C	18	3	1	4	2	2
Jamie Allison, D	47	0	3	3	-7	76
Robert Schnabel, D	20	0	3	3	6	34

GOALTENDING

Player	GP	Mins	W	L	T	Avg	SO
Tomas Vokoun	73	4221	34	29	10	2.53	3
Chris Mason	17	744	4	4	1	2.18	1

New York Islanders

SCORING

Player	GP	G	A	Pts	+/-	PM
Trent Hunter, RW	77	25	26	51	23	16
Oleg Kvasha, LW	81	15	36	51	4	48
M. Czerkawski, RW	81	25	24	49	8	16
Jason Blake, LW	75	22	25	47	11	56
Adrian Aucoin, D	81	13	31	44	29	54
Michael Peca, C	76	11	29	40	17	71
Mark Parrish, RW	59	24	11	35	8	18
Alexei Yashin, C	47	15	19	34	-1	10
Shawn Bates, LW	69	9	23	32	-8	46
Kenny Jonsson, D	79	5	24	29	25	22
Roman Hamrlik, D	81	7	22	29	2	68
Janne Niinimaa, D	82	9	19	28	12	64
Dave Scatchard, C	61	9	16	25	12	78
Arron Asham, RW	79	12	12	24	-12	92
Cliff Ronning, C	40	9	15	24	3	2
M. Weinhandl, RW	55	8	12	20	9	26
Justin Papineau, C	64	8	5	13	4	8
Eric Cairns, D	72	2	6	8	-5	189
Radek Martinek, D	47	4	3	7	-9	43
Sven Butenschon, D	41	1	6	7	-3	30
Justin Mapletoft, C	27	1	4	5	-1	6

GOALTENDING

Player	GP	Mins	W	L	T	Avg	SO
Rick DiPietro	50	2844	23	18	5	2.36	5
Garth Snow	39	2015	14	15	5	2.80	1
W. Dubielewicz	2	105	1	0	1	1.72	0

New Jersey Devils

SCORING

Player	GP	G	A	Pts	+/-	PM
Patrik Elias, LW	82	38	43	81	26	44
Scott Gomez, C	80	14	56	70	18	70
Scott Niedermayer, D	81	14	40	54	20	44
Jeff Friesen, LW	81	17	20	37	8	26
Brian Rafalski, D	69	6	30	36	6	24
John Madden, C	80	12	23	35	7	22
Sergei Brylin, C	82	14	19	33	10	20
Brian Gionta, RW	75	21	8	29	19	36
T. Stevenson, RW	61	14	13	27	0	76
Jay Pandolfo, LW	82	13	13	26	5	14
J.Langenbrunner, RW	53	10	16	26	9	43
Paul Martin, D	70	6	18	24	12	4
Grant Marshall, RW	65	8	7	15	-9	67
Colin White, D	75	2	11	13	10	96
Erik Rasmussen, C	69	7	6	13	5	41
Scott Stevens, D	38	3	9	12	3	22
Igor Larionov, C	49	1	10	11	3	20
Michael Rupp, RW	51	6	5	11	-1	41
Jan Hrdina, C	13	1	6	7	4	10
Viktor Kozlov, RW	11	2	4	6	0	2
C. Berglund, LW	23	2	3	5	-4	4
David Hale, D	65	0	4	4	12	72
Tommy Albelin, D	45	1	3	4	7	4

GOALTENDING

Player	GP	Mins	W	L	T	Avg	SO
Martin Brodeur	75	4555	38	26	11	2.03	11
S. Clemmensen	4	238	3	1	0	1.01	2
Corey Schwab	3	187	2	0	1	0.64	1

New York Rangers

SCORING

Player	GP	G	A	Pts	+/-	PM
Bobby Holik, C	82	25	31	56	4	96
Mark Messier, C	76	18	25	43	3	42
Alexei Kovalev, RW	66	13	29	42	-5	54
Martin Rucinsky, LW	69	13	29	42	13	62
Brian Leetch, D	57	13	23	36	-5	24
Matthew Barnaby, RW	69	12	20	32	15	120
Eric Lindros, C	39	10	22	32	7	60
Petr Nedved, C	65	14	17	31	-9	42
Jaromir Jagr, RW	31	15	14	29	-1	12
Jan Hlavac, LW	72	5	21	26	-8	16
Tom Poti, D	67	10	14	24	-1	47
Chris Simon, LW	65	14	9	23	14	225
Vladimir Malakhov, D	56	3	15	18	-5	53
Anson Carter, RW	43	10	7	17	-12	14
Boris Mironov, D	75	3	13	16	1	86\
Greg de Vries, D	53	3	12	15	12	37
Darius Kasparaitis, D	44	1	9	10	11	48
Jamie Lundmark, C	56	2	8	10	-8	33
Joel Bouchard, D	28	1	7	8	2	10
Dan LaCouture, LW	59	5	2	7	-13	82
Fedor Tyutin, D	25	2	5	7	-4	14
Jed Ortmeyer, RW	58	2	4	6	-10	16
Jozef Balej, RW	13	1	4	5	0	4
Josh Green, LW	14	3	2	5	0	8

GOALTENDING

Player	GP	Mins	W	L	T	Avg	SO
Mike Dunham	57	3148	16	30	6	3.03	2
Jussi Markkanen	26	1244	8	12	1	2.56	2
Jason Labarbera	4	198	1	2	0	4.84	0
S. Valiquette	2	120	1	1	0	3.00	0
Jamie McLennan	4	244	1	3	0	2.96	0

Ottawa Senators

SCORING

Player	GP	G	A	Pts	+/–	PM
Marian Hossa, RW	81	36	46	82	4	46
Daniel Alfredsson, RW	77	32	48	80	12	24
Martin Havlat, RW	68	31	37	68	12	46
Jason Spezza, C	78	22	33	55	22	71
Bryan Smolinski, C	80	19	27	46	22	49
Radek Bonk, C	66	12	32	44	2	66
Wade Redden, D	81	17	26	43	21	65
Zdeno Chara, D	79	16	25	41	33	147
Peter Schaefer, LW	81	15	24	39	22	26
Todd White, C	53	9	20	29	12	22
Chris Phillips, D	82	7	16	23	15	46
Josh Langfeld, RW	38	7	10	17	6	16
Karel Rachunek, D	60	1	16	17	17	29
Chris Neil, RW	82	8	8	16	13	194
Antoine Vermette, LW	57	7	7	14	5	16
Peter Bondra, RW	23	5	9	14	1	16
Shaun Van Allen, C	73	2	10	12	6	80
Vaclav Varada, LW	30	5	5	10	2	26
Mike Fisher, C	24	4	6	10	-3	39
Brian Pothier, D	55	2	6	8	6	24
Petr Schastlivy, LW	43	2	4	6	-1	14
Curtis Leschyshyn, D	56	1	4	5	13	16
Shane Hnidy, D	37	0	5	5	2	72

GOALTENDING

Player	GP	Mins	W	L	T	Avg	SO
Patrick Lalime	57	3324	25	23	7	2.29	5
Martin Prusek	29	1528	16	6	3	2.12	3
Ray Emery	3	126	2	0	0	2.38	0

Philadelphia Flyers

SCORING

Player	GP	G	A	Pts	+/–	PM
Mark Recchi, LW	82	26	49	75	18	47
Michal Handzus, C	82	20	38	58	18	82
John LeClair, LW	75	23	32	55	20	51
Tony Amonte, RW	80	20	33	53	13	38
Jeremy Roenick, C	62	19	28	47	1	62
Simon Gagne, LW	80	24	21	45	12	29
Kim Johnsson, D	80	13	29	42	16	26
Sami Kapanen, RW	74	12	18	30	9	14
Joni Pitkanen, D	71	8	19	27	15	44
Justin Williams, RW	47	6	20	26	10	32
Keith Primeau, C	54	7	15	22	11	80
Alexei Zhamnov, C	20	5	13	18	7	14
M. Ragnarsson, D	70	7	9	16	12	58
Radovan Somik, LW	53	4	10	14	-2	17
Donald Brashear, LW	64	6	7	13	-1	212
Eric Desjardins, D	48	1	11	12	11	28
Chris Therien, D	56	1	9	10	2	50
Mike Comrie, C	21	4	5	9	2	12
Eric Weinrich, D	54	2	7	9	11	32
B. Radivojevic, RW	24	1	8	9	0	36
Claude Lapointe, C	42	5	3	8	2	32
Patrick Sharp, C	41	5	2	7	-3	55

GOALTENDING

Player	GP	Mins	W	L	T	Avg	SO
Robert Esche	40	2322	21	11	7	2.04	3
Jeff Hackett	27	1630	10	10	6	2.39	3
Sean Burke	15	825	6	5	2	2.55	1
Antero Niittymaki	3	180	3	0	0	1.00	0

Phoenix Coyotes

SCORING

Player	GP	G	A	Pts	+/–	PM
Shane Doan, LW	79	27	41	68	-11	47
Ladislav Nagy, LW	55	24	28	52	11	46
Daymond Langkow, C	81	21	31	52	4	40
Paul Mara, D	81	6	36	42	-11	48
Chris Gratton, C	68	11	18	29	-19	93
Jan Hrdina, C	55	11	15	26	-10	30
Brian Savage, LW	61	12	13	25	-5	36
B. Radivojevic, RW	53	9	14	23	-5	36
Radoslav Suchy, D	82	7	14	21	1	8
Cale Hulse, D	82	3	17	20	-4	123
Jeff Taffe, C	59	8	10	18	-8	20
Daniel Cleary, RW	68	6	11	17	-8	42
Mike Comrie, C	28	8	7	15	-8	16
Mike Sillinger, C	60	8	6	14	-14	54
Fredrik Sjostrom, RW	57	7	6	13	-7	22
David Tanabe, D	45	5	7	12	4	22
Krystofer Kolanos, C	41	4	6	10	-9	24
Mike Johnson, RW	11	1	9	10	-1	10
Tyson Nash, LW	69	3	5	8	-6	110
Ossi Vaananen, D	67	2	4	6	-10	87
Brad Ference, D	63	0	5	5	-19	103
Landon Wilson, RW	35	1	3	4	-3	16
Derek Morris, D	14	0	4	4	-5	2

GOALTENDING

Player	GP	Mins	W	L	T	Avg	SO
Sean Burke	32	1795	10	15	5	2.81	1
Brian Boucher	40	2364	10	19	10	2.74	5
J.M. Pelletier	4	175	1	1	0	4.12	0
Brent Johnson	8	486	1	6	1	2.59	0
Zac Bierk	4	190	0	1	2	3.79	0

Pittsburgh Penguins

SCORING

Player	GP	G	A	Pts	+/-	PM
Dick Tarnstrom, D	80	16	36	52	-37	38
Aleksey Morozov, RW	75	16	34	50	-24	24
Ryan Malone, LW	81	22	21	43	-23	64
Milan Kraft, C	66	19	21	40	-22	18
Rico Fata, RW	73	16	18	34	-46	54
Konstantin Koltsov, LW	82	9	20	29	-30	30
Ric Jackman, D	25	7	17	24	-5	14
Tomas Surovy, LW	47	11	12	23	-8	16
Tom Kostopoulos, RW	60	9	13	22	-14	67
Drake Berehowsky,D	47	5	16	21	-16	50
Brian Holzinger, C	61	6	15	21	-27	38
Mike Eastwood, C	82	4	15	19	-18	40
Matt Bradley, RW	82	7	9	16	-27	65
Martin Strbak, D	44	3	11	14	-11	38
Lasse Pirjeta, C	13	6	6	12	3	0
Martin Straka, C	22	4	8	12	-16	16
Eric Meloche, RW	25	3	7	10	-6	20
Brooks Orpik, D	79	1	9	10	-36	127
Marc Bergevin, D	52	1	8	9	-8	27
Mario Lemieux, C	10	1	8	9	-2	6
Josef Melichar, D	82	3	5	8	-17	62
Patrick Boileau, D	16	3	4	7	-16	8
Landon Wilson, RW	19	5	1	6	0	31
Jon Sim, LW	15	2	3	5	-4	6
Ramzi Abid, LW	16	3	2	5	-5	27
Dan Focht, D	52	2	3	5	-23	105
Kelly Buchberger, C	71	1	3	4	-19	109

Player	GP	Mins	W	L	T	Avg	SO
Sebastien Caron	40	2213	9	24	5	3.74	1
J.S. Aubin	22	1067	7	9	0	2.98	1
M.A. Fleury	21	1154	4	14	3	3.64	1
Andy Chiodo	8	486	3	4	1	3.46	0
Martin Brochu	1	33	0	0	0	1.84	0

St. Louis Blues

SCORING

Player	GP	G	A	Pts	+/-	PM
Keith Tkachuk, LW	75	33	38	71	8	83
Doug Weight, C	75	14	51	65	-3	37
Pavol Demitra, C	68	23	35	58	1	18
Chris Pronger, D	80	14	40	54	-1	88
Dallas Drake, RW	79	13	22	35	10	65
Scott Mellanby, RW	68	14	17	31	-7	76
Petr Cajanek, C	70	12	14	26	12	16
Mark Rycroft, RW	71	9	12	21	2	32
Christian Backman, D	66	5	13	18	3	16
Eric Nickulas, RW	44	7	11	18	-2	44
Mike Danton, C	68	7	5	12	-8	141
Ryan Johnson, C	69	4	7	11	-2	8
Jamal Mayers, RW	80	6	5	11	-19	91
Eric Boguniecki, RW	27	6	4	10	-1	20
Mike Sillinger, C	16	5	5	10	4	14
A. Khavanov, D	48	3	7	10	2	18
Eric Weinrich, D	26	2	8	10	1	14
Bryce Salvador, D	69	3	5	8	-4	47
Brian Savage, LW	13	4	3	7	-3	2
Murray Baron, D	80	1	5	6	-6	61
Pascal Rheaume, C	25	1	3	4	-3	4
Peter Sejna, LW	20	2	2	4	-9	4
Jeff Heerema, RW	22	1	2	3	-5	4
Barret Jackman, D	15	1	2	3	-1	41

GOALTENDING

Player	GP	Mins	W	L	T	Avg	SO
Chris Osgood	67	3861	31	25	8	2.24	3
Reinhard Divis	13	629	4	4	2	2.76	0
Brent Johnson	10	493	4	3	1	2.43	1

San Jose Sharks

SCORING

Player	GP	G	A	Pts	+/-	PM
Patrick Marleau, C	80	28	29	57	-5	24
Nils Ekman, LW	82	22	33	55	30	34
Alyn McCauley, C	82	20	27	47	23	28
J. Cheechoo, RW	81	28	19	47	5	33
Marco Sturm, LW	64	21	20	41	0	36
V. Damphousse, C	82	12	29	41	-5	66
Brad Stuart, D	77	9	30	39	9	34
Alex Korolyuk, LW	63	19	18	37	20	18
Wayne Primeau, C	72	9	20	29	4	90
Scott Thornton, LW	80	13	14	27	-6	84
Mike Ricci, C	71	7	19	26	8	40
Niko Dimitrakos, RW	68	9	15	24	6	49
Kyle McLaren, D	64	2	22	24	10	60
Scott Hannan, D	82	6	15	21	10	48
Mike Rathje, D	80	2	17	19	18	46
Tom Preissing, D	69	2	17	19	8	12
Christian Ehrhoff, D	41	1	11	12	4	14
Todd Harvey, RW	47	4	5	9	3	38
Scott Parker, RW	50	1	3	4	0	101
Mark Smith, C	36	1	3	4	-5	72
Curtis Brown, C	12	2	2	4	1	6
Rob Davison, D	55	0	3	3	-3	92

GOALTENDING

Player	GP	Mins	W	L	T	Avg	SO
Evgeni Nabokov	59	3456	31	19	8	2.21	9
Vesa Toskala	28	1541	12	8	4	2.06	1

Tampa Bay Lightning

SCORING

Player	GP	G	A	Pts	+/-	PM
Martin St. Louis, RW	82	38	56	94	35	24
Cory Stillman, LW	81	25	55	80	18	36
Brad Richards, C	82	26	53	79	14	12
Vincent Lecavalier, C	81	32	34	66	23	52
Fredrik Modin, LW	82	29	28	57	31	32
Dan Boyle, D	78	9	30	39	23	60
Ruslan Fedotenko, RW	77	17	22	39	14	30
Dave Andreychuk, LW	82	21	18	39	-9	42
Pavel Kubina, D	81	17	18	35	9	85
Tim Taylor, C	82	7	15	22	-5	25
Cory Sarich, D	82	3	16	19	5	89
Brad Lukowich, D	79	5	14	19	29	24
D. Afanasenkov, LW	71	6	10	16	-4	12
Ben Clymer, RW	66	2	8	10	5	50
Martin Cibak, C	63	2	7	9	-1	30
Darryl Sydor, D	31	1	6	7	3	6
Jassen Cullimore, D	79	2	5	7	8	58
Shane Willis, RW	12	0	6	6	1	2
Chris Dingman, LW	74	1	5	6	-9	140
Nolan Pratt, D	58	1	3	4	11	42

GOALTENDING

Player	GP	Mins	W	L	T	Avg	SO
N. Khabibulin	55	3274	28	19	7	2.33	3
John Grahame	29	1688	18	9	1	2.06	1

Toronto Maple Leafs

SCORING

Player	GP	G	A	Pts	+/-	PM
Mats Sundin, C	81	31	44	75	11	52
Bryan McCabe, D	75	16	37	53	22	86
Joe Nieuwendyk, C	64	22	28	50	7	26
Gary Roberts, LW	72	28	20	48	9	84
Owen Nolan, RW	65	19	29	48	4	110
Darcy Tucker, RW	64	21	11	32	4	68
Nik Antropov, C	62	13	18	31	7	62
Tomas Kaberle, D	71	3	28	31	16	18
Robert Reichel, C	69	11	19	30	2	30
A. Mogilny, RW	37	8	22	30	9	12
Ken Klee, D	66	4	25	29	-1	36
A Ponikarovsky, LW	73	9	19	28	14	44
Matthew Stajan, C	69	14	13	27	7	22
Mikael Renberg,RW	59	12	13	25	-1	50
Tie Domi, RW	80	7	13	20	-2	208
Karel Pilar, D	50	2	17	19	2	22
Tom Fitzgerald, RW	69	7	10	17	-2	52
Brian Leetch, D	15	2	13	15	11	10
Ron Francis, C	12	3	7	10	3	0
Aki Berg, D	79	2	7	9	-1	40
Ric Jackman, D	29	2	4	6	-11	13
Calle Johansson, D	8	0	6	6	5	0
Bryan Marchment, D	75	1	3	4	4	106
Harold Druken, C	9	0	4	4	4	2

GOALTENDING

Player	GP	Mins	W	L	T	Avg	SO
Ed Belfour	59	3444	34	19	6	2.13	10
Trevor Kidd	15	883	6	5	2	3.26	1
Mikael Tellqvist	11	647	5	3	2	2.87	0

Vancouver Canucks

SCORING

Player	GP	G	A	Pts	+/-	PM
Markus Naslund, LW	78	35	49	84	24	58
Todd Bertuzzi, RW	69	17	43	60	21	122
Brendan Morrison, C	82	22	38	60	16	50
Daniel Sedin, LW	82	18	36	54	18	18
Brent Sopel, D	80	10	32	42	11	36
Henrik Sedin, C	76	11	31	42	23	32
Trevor Linden, C	82	14	22	36	-6	26
Mattias Ohlund, D	82	14	20	34	14	73
Sami Salo, D	74	7	19	26	8	22
Ed Jovanovski, D	56	7	16	23	2	64
Matt Cooke, C	53	11	12	23	5	73
Jason King, RW	47	12	9	21	0	8
Marek Malik, D	78	3	16	19	35	45
Artem Chubarov, C	65	12	7	19	1	14
Mike Keane, LW	64	8	9	17	7	20
Magnus Arvedson, LW	41	8	7	15	7	12
Jarkko Ruutu, LW	71	6	8	14	-13	133
Brad May, LW	70	5	6	11	-2	137
Geoff Sanderson, LW	13	3	4	7	-1	4
Bryan Allen, D	74	2	5	7	-10	94
Jiri Slegr, D	16	2	5	7	6	8
Ryan Kesler, C	28	2	3	5	-2	16
Nolan Baumgartner, D	9	0	3	3	3	2
Tyler Bouck, RW	18	1	2	3	-4	23
Martin Rucinsky, LW	13	1	2	3	2	10

GOALTENDING

layer	GP	Mins	W	L	T	Avg	SO
Dan Cloutier	60	3539	33	21	6	2.27	5
Johan Hedberg	21	1098	8	6	2	2.51	3
Alexander Auld	6	349	2	2	2	2.06	0

Washington Capitals

SCORING

Player	GP	G	A	Pts	+/-	PM
Robert Lang, C	63	29	45	74	2	24
Sergei Gonchar, D	56	7	42	49	-20	44
Jeff Halpern, C	79	19	27	46	-21	56
Jaromir Jagr, RW	46	16	29	45	-4	26
Peter Bondra, RW	54	21	14	35	-17	22
Kip Miller, LW	66	9	22	31	-10	8
Dainius Zubrus, RW	54	12	15	27	-16	38
Alexander Semin, LW	52	10	12	22	-2	36
Mike Grier, RW	68	8	12	20	-19	32
Brian Willsie, RW	49	10	5	15	-7	18
Josef Boumedienne, D	37	2	12	14	-10	30
Brendan Witt, D	72	2	10	12	-22	123
Matt Pettinger, LW	71	7	5	12	-9	37
Joel Kwiatkowski, D	80	6	6	12	-28	89
Jason Doig, D	65	2	9	11	-12	105
Trent Whitfield, C	44	6	5	11	-2	14
Anson Carter, RW	19	5	5	10	2	6
Bates Battaglia, LW	66	4	6	10	-23	38
Boyd Gordon, RW	41	1	5	6	-9	8
Craig Johnson, LW	15	0	6	6	-6	8
Rick Berry, D	65	0	6	6	-5	108
Stephen Peat, RW	64	5	0	5	-10	90

GOALTENDING

Player	GP	Mins	W	L	T	Avg	SO
Olaf Kolzig	63	3738	19	35	9	2.89	2
Maxime Ouellet	6	365	2	3	1	3.12	1
Rastislav Stana	6	211	1	2	0	3.12	0
Matt Yeats	5	258	1	3	0	3.03	0
S. Charpentier	7	369	0	6	0	3.41	0

2005 NHL Draft

First Round

The opening round of the 2005 NHL draft was held on July 30 in Ottawa, Ontario, Canada..

Team	Selection	Position	Team	Selection	Position
1.....Pittsburgh	Sidney Crosby	C	16...Atlanta	Alex Bourret	F
2.....Anaheim	Bobby Ryan	F	17...Phoenix	Martin Hanzal	C
3.....Carolina	Jack Johnson	D	18...Nashville	Ryan Parent	D
4.....Minnesota	Benoit Pouliout	F	19...Detroit	Jakub Kindl	D
5.....Montreal	Carey Price	G	20...Florida	Kenndal McArdle	F
6.....Columbus	Gilbert Brule	C	21...Toronto	Tuukka Rask	G
7.....Chicago	Jack Skille	F	22...Boston	Matt Lashoff	D
8.....San Jose	Devin Setoguchi	F	23...New Jersey	Nicklas Bergfors	F
9.....Ottawa	Brian Lee	D	24...St. Louis	T. J. Oshie	C
10...Vancouver	Luc Bourdon	D	25...Edmonton	Andrew Cogliano	C
11...Los Angeles	Anze Kopitar	C	26...Calgary	Matt Pelech	D
12...N.Y. Rangers	Marc Staal	D	27...Washington	Joe Finley	D
13...Buffalo	Marek Zagrapan	C	28...Dallas	Matt Niskanen	D
14...Washington	Sasha Pokulok	D	29...Philadelphia	Steve Downie	F
15...NY Islanders	Ryan O'Meara	C	30...Tampa Bay	Vladimir Mihalik	D

FOR THE RECORD · Year by Year

The Stanley Cup

Awarded annually to the team that wins the NHL's best-of-seven final-round playoffs. The Stanley Cup is the oldest trophy competed for by professional athletes in North America. It was donated in 1893 by Frederick Arthur, Lord Stanley of Preston.

Results

1892–93.....Montreal A.A.A.	1900–01.....Winnipeg Victorias	1907–08.....Montreal Wanderers
1893–94.....Montreal A.A.A.	1901–02.....Winnipeg Victorias (Jan)	1908–09.....Ottawa Senators
1894–95.....Montreal Victorias	1901–02.....Montreal A.A.A. (Mar)	1909–10.....Montreal Wanderers
1895–96.....Winnipeg Victorias (Feb)	1902–03.....Montreal A.A.A. (Feb)	1910–11.....Ottawa Senators
1895–96.....Montreal Victorias (Dec)	1902–03.....Ottawa Silver Seven (Mar)	1911–12.....Quebec Bulldogs
1896–97.....Montreal Victorias	1903–04.....Ottawa Silver Seven	1912–13.....Quebec Bulldogs
1897–98.....Montreal Victorias	1904–05.....Ottawa Silver Seven	1913–14.....Toronto Blueshirts
1898–99.....Montreal Victorias (Feb)	1905–06.....Ottawa Silver Seven (Mar)	1914–15.....Vancouver Millionaires
1898–99.....Montreal Shamrocks (Mar)	1905–06.....Montreal Wanderers (Mar)	1915–16.....Montreal Canadiens
1899–1900...Montreal Shamrocks	1906–07.....Kenora Thistles (Jan)	1916–17.....Seattle Metropolitans
	1906–07.....Montreal Wanderers (Mar)	

NHL WINNERS AND FINALISTS

Season	Champion	Finalist	GP in Final
1917–18	Toronto Arenas	Vancouver Millionaires	5
1918–19	No decision*	No decision*	5
1919–20	Ottawa Senators	Seattle Metropolitans	5
1920–21	Ottawa Senators	Vancouver Millionaires	5
1921–22	Toronto St. Pats	Vancouver Millionaires	5
1922–23	Ottawa Senators	Vancouver Maroons, Edmonton Eskimos	2, 4
1923–24	Montreal Canadiens	Vancouver Maroons, Calgary Tigers	2, 2
1924–25	Victoria Cougars	Montreal Canadiens	4
1925–26	Montreal Maroons	Victoria Cougars	4
1926–27	Ottawa Senators	Boston Bruins	4
1927–28	New York Rangers	Montreal Maroons	5
1928–29	Boston Bruins	New York Rangers	2
1929–30	Montreal Canadiens	Boston Bruins	2
1930–31	Montreal Canadiens	Chicago Blackhawks	5
1931–32	Toronto Maple Leafs	New York Rangers	3
1932–33	New York Rangers	Toronto Maple Leafs	4
1933–34	Chicago Blackhawks	Detroit Red Wings	4
1934–35	Montreal Maroons	Toronto Maple Leafs	3

NHL WINNERS AND FINALISTS (CONT.)

Season	Champion	Finalist	GP in Final
1935–36	Detroit Red Wings	Toronto Maple Leafs	4
1936–37	Detroit Red Wings	New York Rangers	5
1937–38	Chicago Blackhawks	Toronto Maple Leafs	4
1938–39	Boston Bruins	Toronto Maple Leafs	5
1939–40	New York Rangers	Toronto Maple Leafs	6
1940–41	Boston Bruins	Detroit Red Wings	4
1941–42	Toronto Maple Leafs	Detroit Red Wings	7
1942–43	Detroit Red Wings	Boston Bruins	4
1943–44	Montreal Canadiens	Chicago Blackhawks	4
1944–45	Toronto Maple Leafs	Detroit Red Wings	7
1945–46	Montreal Canadiens	Boston Bruins	5
1946–47	Toronto Maple Leafs	Montreal Canadiens	6
1947–48	Toronto Maple Leafs	Detroit Red Wings	4
1948–49	Toronto Maple Leafs	Detroit Red Wings	4
1949–50	Detroit Red Wings	New York Rangers	7
1950–51	Toronto Maple Leafs	Montreal Canadiens	5
1951–52	Detroit Red Wings	Montreal Canadiens	4
1952–53	Montreal Canadiens	Boston Bruins	5
1953–54	Detroit Red Wings	Montreal Canadiens	7
1954–55	Detroit Red Wings	Montreal Canadiens	7
1955–56	Montreal Canadiens	Detroit Red Wings	5
1956–57	Montreal Canadiens	Boston Bruins	5
1957–58	Montreal Canadiens	Boston Bruins	6
1958–59	Montreal Canadiens	Toronto Maple Leafs	5
1959–60	Montreal Canadiens	Toronto Maple Leafs	4
1960–61	Chicago Blackhawks	Detroit Red Wings	6
1961–62	Toronto Maple Leafs	Chicago Blackhawks	6
1962–63	Toronto Maple Leafs	Detroit Red Wings	5
1963–64	Toronto Maple Leafs	Detroit Red Wings	7
1964–65	Montreal Canadiens	Chicago Blackhawks	7
1965–66	Montreal Canadiens	Detroit Red Wings	6
1966–67	Toronto Maple Leafs	Montreal Canadiens	6
1967–68	Montreal Canadiens	St. Louis Blues	4
1968–69	Montreal Canadiens	St. Louis Blues	4
1969–70	Boston Bruins	St. Louis Blues	4
1970–71	Montreal Canadiens	Chicago Blackhawks	7
1971–72	Boston Bruins	New York Rangers	6
1972–73	Montreal Canadiens	Chicago Blackhawks	6
1973–74	Philadelphia Flyers	Boston Bruins	6
1974–75	Philadelphia Flyers	Buffalo Sabres	6
1975–76	Montreal Canadiens	Philadelphia Flyers	4
1976–77	Montreal Canadiens	Boston Bruins	4
1977–78	Montreal Canadiens	Boston Bruins	6
1978–79	Montreal Canadiens	New York Rangers	5
1979–80	New York Islanders	Philadelphia Flyers	6
1980–81	New York Islanders	Minnesota North Stars	5
1981–82	New York Islanders	Vancouver Canucks	4
1982–83	New York Islanders	Edmonton Oilers	4
1983–84	Edmonton Oilers	New York Islanders	5
1984–85	Edmonton Oilers	Philadelphia Flyers	5
1985–86	Montreal Canadiens	Calgary Flames	6
1986–87	Edmonton Oilers	Philadelphia Flyers	7
1987–88	Edmonton Oilers	Boston Bruins	4
1988–89	Calgary Flames	Montreal Canadiens	6
1989–90	Edmonton Oilers	Boston Bruins	5
1990–91	Pittsburgh Penguins	Minnesota North Stars	6
1991–92	Pittsburgh Penguins	Chicago Blackhawks	4
1992–93	Montreal Canadiens	Los Angeles Kings	5
1993–94	New York Rangers	Vancouver Canucks	7
1994–95	New Jersey Devils	Detroit Red Wings	4
1995–96	Colorado Avalanche	Florida Panthers	4
1996–97	Detroit Red Wings	Philadelphia Flyers	4
1997–98	Detroit Red Wings	Washington Capitals	4
1998–99	Dallas Stars	Buffalo Sabres	6
1999–2000	New Jersey Devils	Dallas Stars	6

NHL WINNERS AND FINALISTS *(CONT.)*

Season	Champion	Finalist	GP in Final
2000–01	Colorado Avalanche	New Jersey Devils	7
2001–02	Detroit Red Wings	Carolina Hurricanes	5
2002–03	New Jersey Devils	Anaheim Mighty Ducks	7
2003–04	Tampa Bay	Calgary	7
2004-05	No Stanley Cup was awarded due to season lockout		

*In 1919 the Montreal Canadiens traveled to meet Seattle, the PCHL champions. After 5 games had been played—the teams were tied at 2 wins and 1 tie—the series was called off by the local Department of Health because of the influenza epidemic and the death of Canadiens defenseman Joe Hall from influenza.

Conn Smythe Trophy

Awarded to the Most Valuable Player of the Stanley Cup playoffs, as selected by the Professional Hockey Writers Association. The trophy is named after the former coach, general manager, president and owner of the Toronto Maple Leafs.

1965	Jean Beliveau, Mtl	1986	Patrick Roy, Mtl
1966	Roger Crozier, Det	1987	Ron Hextall, Phil
1967	Dave Keon, Tor	1988	Wayne Gretzky, Edm
1968	Glenn Hall, StL	1989	Al MacInnis, Cgy
1969	Serge Savard, Mtl	1990	Bill Ranford, Edm
1970	Bobby Orr, Bos	1991	Mario Lemieux, Pitt
1971	Ken Dryden, Mtl	1992	Mario Lemieux, Pitt
1972	Bobby Orr, Bos	1993	Patrick Roy, Mtl
1973	Yvan Cournoyer, Mtl	1994	Brian Leetch, NYR
1974	Bernie Parent, Phil	1995	Claude Lemieux, NJ
1975	Bernie Parent, Phil	1996	Joe Sakic, Col
1976	Reggie Leach, Phil	1997	Mike Vernon, Det
1977	Guy Lafleur, Mtl	1998	Steve Yzerman, Det
1978	Larry Robinson, Mtl	1999	Joe Nieuwendyk, Dall
1979	Bob Gainey, Mtl	2000	Scott Stevens, NJ
1980	Bryan Trottier, NYI	2001	Patrick Roy, Col
1981	Butch Goring, NYI	2002	Nicklas Lidstrom, Det
1982	Mike Bossy, NYI	2003	J.-S. Giguere, Ana
1983	Bill Smith, NYI	2004	Brad Richards, TB
1984	Mark Messier, Edm	2005	No Award--No Season
1985	Wayne Gretzky, Edm		

Alltime Stanley Cup Playoff Leaders
Points

	Yrs	GP	G	A	Pts		Yrs	GP	G	A	Pts
Wayne Gretzky, four teams	16	208	122	260	382	Denis Savard, Chi, Mtl	16	169	66	109	175
*Mark Messier, Edm, Van, NYR	18	236	109	186	295	*Mario Lemieux, Pitt	8	107	76	96	172
Jari Kurri, four teams	15	200	106	127	233	Denis Potvin, NYI	14	185	56	108	164
Glenn Anderson, four teams	15	225	93	121	214	*Sergei Fedorov, Det, Ana	13	162	50	113	163
Paul Coffey, six teams	16	198	59	137	196	Mike Bossy, NYI	10	129	85	75	160
*Brett Hull, four teams	19	202	103	87	190	Gordie Howe, Det, Hart	20	157	68	92	160
Doug Gilmour, seven teams	18	182	60	128	188	Bobby Smith, Minn, Mtl	13	184	64	96	160
Bryan Trottier, NYI, Pitt	17	221	71	113	184	*Al MacInnis, Cgy, StL	19	177	39	121	160
*Steve Yzerman, Det	19	192	70	111	181	*Claude Lemieux, six teams	17	233	80	77	157
Ray Bourque, Bos, Col	21	214	41	139	180						
Jean Beliveau, Mtl	17	162	79	97	176						

*Active in 2003–04 season.

Goals

	Yrs	GP	G
Wayne Gretzky, four teams	17	208	122
*Mark Messier, Edm, NYR	18	236	109
Jari Kurri, five teams	15	200	106
*Brett Hull, Cgy, StL, Dall, Det	19	202	103
Glenn Anderson, four teams	15	225	93
Mike Bossy, NYI	10	129	85
Maurice Richard, Mtl	15	133	82
*Claude Lemieux, six teams	17	233	80
Jean Beliveau, Mtl	17	162	79
*Joe Sakic, Col	11	153	78

*Active in 2003–04.

Assists

	Yrs	GP	A
Wayne Gretzky, four teams	17	208	260
*Mark Messier, Edm, NYR	18	236	186
Ray Bourque, Bos, Col	21	214	139
Paul Coffey, six teams	16	198	137
Doug Gilmour, seven teams	18	182	128
Jari Kurri, five teams	15	196	127
Glenn Anderson, four teams	15	225	121
*Al MacInnis, Cgy, StL	19	177	121
Larry Robinson, Mtl, LA	20	227	116
Larry Murphy, six teams	15	215	115

*Active in 2003–04.

Alltime Stanley Cup Playoff Goaltending Leaders

WINS	W	L	Pct		SHUTOUTS	GP	W	SO
Patrick Roy, Mtl, Col	151	94	.616		Patrick Roy, Mtl, Col	247	151	23
Grant Fuhr, five teams	92	50	.648		*Martin Brodeur, NJ	144	84	20
Billy Smith, LA, NYI	88	36	.710		*Curtis Joseph, four teams	133	62	16
*Martin Brodeur, NJ	84	60	.583		Clint Benedict, Ott, Mtl M	48	25	15
*Ed Belfour, four teams	88	68	.564		*Ed Belfour, four teams	161	88	14
Ken Dryden, Mtl	80	32	.714		Jacques Plante, five teams	112	71	14
Mike Vernon, four teams	77	56	.579		**GOALS AGAINST AVG**			**Avg**
Jacques Plante, five teams	71	37	.657		*Martin Brodeur, NJ			1.87
Andy Moog, four teams	68	57	.544		George Hainsworth, Mtl, Tor			1.93
*Curtis Joseph, four teams	62	66	.484		Turk Broda, Tor			1.98
					*Dominik Hasek, Chi, Buff, Det			2.03
*Active in 2003–04.					*Ed Belfour, four teams			2.17

Note: At least 50 games played.
*Active in 2003–04.

Alltime Stanley Cup Playoff Wins

TEAM	W	L	Pct		TEAM	W	L	Pct
Montreal	391	262	.599		Buffalo	99	110	.474
Detroit	257	236	.521		Calgary*	84	98	.462
Toronto	251	269	.483		Washington	69	85	.448
Boston	242	264	.478		Vancouver	66	89	.426
Chicago	188	218	.463		Los Angeles	65	101	.392
NY Rangers	183	195	.484		San Jose	39	45	.464
Philadelphia	178	161	.525		Carolina§	35	49	.417
St. Louis	138	165	.455		Ottawa	31	38	.449
Dallas#	137	137	.500		Phoenix††	28	63	.308
Edmonton	135	90	.600		Tampa Bay	23	17	.575
NY Islanders	131	102	.562		Anaheim	19	17	.528
Colorado**	122	102	.545		Florida	13	18	.419
Pittsburgh	109	99	.524		Minnesota	8	10	.444
New Jersey†	107	86	.549		Nashville	2	4	.333

*Atlanta Flames 1972–80. †Colorado Rockies 1976–82. #Minnesota North Stars 1967–93. **Quebec Nordiques 1979–95. ††Winnipeg Jets 1979–96. §Hartford Whalers 1979–97. Note: Teams ranked by playoff victories.

Stanley Cup Playoff Coaching Records

Coach	Team	Yrs	Series	Series W	Series L	Games	Games W	Games L	T	Cups	Pct
†Glen Sather	Edm	10	27	21	6	*126	89	37	0	4	.706
Toe Blake	Mtl	13	23	18	5	119	82	37	0	8	.689
Scott Bowman	Five teams	28	68	49	19	353	223	130	0	9	.632
Bob Hartley	Col	4	13	10	3	80	49	31	0	1	.613
Hap Day	Tor	9	14	10	4	80	49	31	0	5	.613
Al Arbour	StL, NYI	16	42	30	12	209	123	86	0	4	.589
†Ken Hitchcock	Dall, Phil	7	19	13	6	111	64	47	0	1	.577
Mike Keenan	five teams	11	28	18	10	160	91	69	0	1	.569
Fred Shero	Phil, NYR	8	21	15	6	108	61	47	0	2	.565
†Jacques Lemaire	Mtl, NJ, Minn	7	18	12	6	101	57	44	0	1	.564

*Does not include suspended game, May 24, 1988. †Active in 2003–04.
Note: Coaches ranked by winning percentage. Minimum: 65 games.

The 10 Longest Overtime Games

Date	Result	OT	Scorer	Series	Series Winner
3-24-36	Det 1 vs Mtl M 0	116:30	Mud Bruneteau	SF	Det
4-3-33	Tor 1 vs Bos 0	104:46	Ken Doraty	SF	Tor
5-4-00	Phil 2 vs Pitt 1	92:01	Keith Primeau	CSF	Phil
4-24-03	Ana 4 vs Dall 3	80:48	Petr Sykora	CSF	Ana
4-24-96	Pitt 3 vs Wash 2	79:15	Petr Nedved	CQF	Pitt
3-23-43	Tor 3 vs Det 2	70:18	Jack McLean	SF	Det
3-28-30	Mtl 2 vs NYR 1	68:52	Gus Rivers	SF	Mtl
4-18-87	NYI 3 vs Wash 2	68:47	Pat LaFontaine	DSF	NYI
4-27-94	Buff 1 vs NJ 0	65:43	Dave Hannan	CQF	NJ
3-27-51	Mtl 3 vs Det 2	61:09	Maurice Richard	SF	Mtl

Hart Memorial Trophy

Awarded annually "to the player adjudged to be the most valuable to his team." The original trophy was donated by Dr. David A. Hart, father of Cecil Hart, former manager-coach of the Montreal Canadiens. In the 1980s Wayne Gretzky won the award nine times.

Year	Winner	Key Statistics	Runner-Up
1924	Frank Nighbor, Ott	10 goals, 3 assists in 20 games	Sprague Cleghorn, Mtl
1925	Billy Burch, Ham	20 goals, 4 assists in 27 games	Howie Morenz, Mtl
1926	Nels Stewart, Mtl M	42 points in 36 games	Sprague Cleghorn, Mtl
1927	Herb Gardiner, Mtl	12 points in 44 games as defenseman	Bill Cook, NYR
1928	Howie Morenz, Mtl	33 goals, 18 assists	Roy Worters, Pitt
1929	Roy Worters, NYA	1.21 goals against, 13 shutouts	Ace Bailey, Tor
1930	Nels Stewart, Mtl M	39 goals, 16 assists	Lionel Hitchman, Bos
1931	Howie Morenz, Mtl	28 goals, 23 assists	Eddie Shore, Bos
1932	Howie Morenz, Mtl	24 goals, 25 assists	Ching Johnson, NYR
1933	Eddie Shore, Bos	27 assists in 48 games as defenseman	Bill Cook, NYR
1934	Aurel Joliat, Mtl	27 points	Lionel Conacher, Chi
1935	Eddie Shore, Bos	26 assists in 48 games as defenseman	Charlie Conacher, Tor
1936	Eddie Shore, Bos	16 assists in 46 games as defenseman	Hooley Smith, Mtl M
1937	Babe Siebert, Mtl	28 points	Lionel Conacher, Mtl M
1938	Eddie Shore, Bos	17 points in 47 games as defenseman	Paul Thompson, Chi
1939	Toe Blake, Mtl	led NHL in points (47)	Syl Apps, Tor
1940	Ebbie Goodfellow, Det	28 points	Syl Apps, Tor
1941	Bill Cowley, Bos	led NHL in assists (45) and points (62)	Dit Clapper, Bos
1942	Tom Anderson, Bos	41 points	Syl Apps, Tor
1943	Bill Cowley, Bos	led NHL in assists (45)	Doug Bentley, Chi
1944	Babe Pratt, Tor	57 points in 50 games	Bill Cowley, Bos
1945	Elmer Lach, Mtl	led NHL in assists (54) and points (80)	Maurice Richard, Mtl
1946	Max Bentley, Chi	61 points in 47 games	Gaye Stewart, Tor
1947	Maurice Richard, Mtl	led NHL in goals (45); 26 assists	Milt Schmidt, Bos
1948	Buddy O'Connor, NYR	60 points in 60 games	Frank Brimsek, Bos
1949	Sid Abel, Det	28 goals, 26 assists	Bill Durnan, Mtl
1950	Charlie Rayner, NYR	6 shutouts	Ted Kennedy, Tor
1951	Milt Schmidt, Bos	61 points in 62 games	Maurice Richard, Mtl
1952	Gordie Howe, Det	led NHL in goals (47) and points (86)	Elmer Lach, Mtl
1953	Gordie Howe, Det	led NHL in goals (49) and points (95)	Al Rollins, Chi
1954	Al Rollins, Chi	5 shutouts	Red Kelly, Det
1955	Ted Kennedy, Tor	52 points	Harry Lumley, Tor
1956	Jean Beliveau, Mtl	led NHL in goals (47) and points (88)	Tod Sloan, Tor
1957	Gordie Howe, Det	led NHL in goals (44) and points (89)	Jean Beliveau, Mtl
1959	Andy Bathgate, NYR	74 points in 70 games	Gordie Howe, Det
1960	Gordie Howe, Det	45 assists, 73 points	Bobby Hull, Chi
1961	Bernie Geoffrion, Mtl	50 goals, 95 points	Johnny Bower, Tor
1962	Jacques Plante, Mtl	42 wins, 2.37 goals against avg.	Doug Harvey, NYR
1963	Gordie Howe, Det	47 assists, 73 points	Stan Mikita, Chi
1964	Jean Beliveau, Mtl	50 assists, 78 points	Bobby Hull, Chi
1965	Bobby Hull, Chi	39 goals, 32 assists	Norm Ullman, Det
1966	Bobby Hull, Chi	led NHL in goals (54) and points (97)	Jean Beliveau, Mtl
1967	Stan Mikita, Chi	led NHL in assists (62) and points (97)	Ed Giacomin, NYR
1968	Stan Mikita, Chi	40 goals, 47 assists	Jean Beliveau, Mtl
1969	Phil Esposito, Bos	led NHL in assists (77) and points (126)	Jean Beliveau, Mtl
1970	Bobby Orr, Bos	led NHL in assists (87) and points (120)	Tony Esposito, Chi
1971	Bobby Orr, Bos	102 assists, 139 points	Tony Esposito, Chi
1972	Bobby Orr, Bos	80 assists, 117 points	Ken Dryden, Mtl
1973	Bobby Clarke, Phil	67 assists, 104 points	Phil Esposito, Bos
1974	Phil Esposito, Bos	led NHL in goals (68) and points (145)	Bernie Parent, Phil
1975	Bobby Clarke, Phil	89 assists, 116 points	Rogatien Vachon, LA
1976	Bobby Clarke, Phil	89 assists, 119 points	Denis Potvin, NYI
1977	Guy Lafleur, Mtl	led NHL in assists (80) and points (136)	Bobby Clarke, Phil
1978	Guy Lafleur, Mtl	led NHL in goals (60) and points (132)	Bryan Trottier, NYI
1979	Bryan Trottier, NYI	led NHL in assists (87) and points (134)	Guy Lafleur, Mtl
1980	Wayne Gretzky, Edm	51 goals, 86 assists	Marcel Dionne, LA
1981	Wayne Gretzky, Edm	led NHL in assists (109) and points (164)	Mike Liut, StL
1982	Wayne Gretzky, Edm	NHL-record 92 goals and 212 points	Bryan Trottier, NYI
1983	Wayne Gretzky, Edm	led NHL in goals (71) and points (196)	Pete Peeters, Bos
1984	Wayne Gretzky, Edm	led NHL in goals (87) and points (205)	Rod Langway, Wash
1985	Wayne Gretzky, Edm	led NHL in goals (73) and points (208)	Dale Hawerchuk, Winn
1986	Wayne Gretzky, Edm	NHL-record 163 assists and 215 points	Mario Lemieux, Pitt

Hart Memorial Trophy *(Cont.)*

Year	Winner	Key Statistics	Runner-Up
1987	Wayne Gretzky, Edm	led NHL in assists (121) and points (183)	Ray Bourque, Bos
1988	Mario Lemieux, Pitt	led NHL in goals (70) and points (168)	Grant Fuhr, Edm
1989	Wayne Gretzky, LA	114 assists, 168 points	Mario Lemieux, Pitt
1990	Mark Messier, Edm	84 assists, 129 points	Ray Bourque, Bos
1991	Brett Hull, StL	led NHL in goals (86); 131 points	Wayne Gretzky, LA
1992	Mark Messier, NYR	72 assists, 107 points	Patrick Roy, Mtl
1993	Mario Lemieux, Pitt	69 goals, 91 assists in 60 games	Doug Gilmour, Tor
1994	Sergei Fedorov, Det	56 goals, 64 assists	Dominik Hasek, Buff
1995	Eric Lindros, Phil	29 goals, 41 assists in 46 games	Jaromir Jagr, Pitt
1996	Mario Lemieux, Pitt	led NHL in goals (69) and points (161)	Mark Messier, NYR
1997	Dominik Hasek, Buff	5 shutouts, 2.27 goals against avg.	Paul Kariya, Ana
1998	Dominik Hasek, Buff	13 shutouts, 2.09 goals against avg.	Jaromir Jagr, Pitt
1999	Jaromir Jagr, Pitt	44 goals, 127 points	Alexei Yashin, Ott
2000	Chris Pronger, StL	62 points, +52 plus/minus rating	Jaromir Jagr, Pitt
2001	Joe Sakic, Col	118 points, +45 plus/minus rating	Mario Lemieux, Pitt
2002	Jose Theodore, Mtl	2.11 goals against avg./7 shutouts	Jarome Iginla, Cal
2003	Peter Forsberg, Col	77 assists, +52 plus/minus rating	Markus Naslund, Van
2004	Martin St. Louis, TB	94 points, +35 plus/minus rating	Jarome Iginla, Cal
2005	No Award		

Art Ross Trophy

Awarded annually "to the player who leads the league in scoring points at the end of the regular season. The trophy was presented to the NHL in 1947 by Arthur Howie Ross, former manager-coach of the Boston Bruins. The tie-breakers, in order, are as follows: (1) player with most goals, (2) player with fewer games played, (3) player scoring first goal of the season. Bobby Orr is the only defenseman in NHL history to win this trophy, and he won it twice (1970 and 1975).

Year	Winner	Pts	Year	Winner	Pts
1919	Newsy Lalonde, Mtl	44	1957	Gordie Howe, Det	89
1920	Joe Malone, Que	30	1958	Dickie Moore, Mtl	84
1921	Newsy Lalonde, Mtl	48	1959	Dickie Moore, Mtl	96
1922	Punch Broadbent, Ott	41	1960	Bobby Hull, Chi	81
1923	Babe Dye, Tor	46	1961	Bernie Geoffrion, Mtl	95
1924	Cy Denneny, Ott	37	1962	Bobby Hull, Chi	84
1925	Babe Dye, Tor	23	1963	Gordie Howe, Det	86
1926	Nels Stewart, Mtl M	44	1964	Stan Mikita, Chi	89
1927	Bill Cook, NYR	42	1965	Stan Mikita, Chi	87
1928	Howie Morenz, Mtl	37	1966	Bobby Hull, Chi	97
1929	Ace Bailey, Tor	51	1967	Stan Mikita, Chi	97
1930	Cooney Weiland, Bos	32	1968	Stan Mikita, Chi	87
1931	Howie Morenz, Mtl	73	1969	Phil Esposito, Bos	126
1932	Harvey Jackson, Tor	51	1970	Bobby Orr, Bos	120
1933	Bill Cook, NYR	53	1971	Phil Esposito, Bos	152
1934	Charlie Conacher, Tor	50	1972	Phil Esposito, Bos	133
1935	Charlie Conacher, Tor	57	1973	Phil Esposito, Bos	130
1936	Sweeney Schriner, NYA	45	1974	Phil Esposito, Bos	145
1937	Sweeney Schriner, NYA	46	1975	Bobby Orr, Bos	135
1938	Gordie Drillon, Tor	52	1976	Guy Lafleur, Mtl	125
1939	Toe Blake, Mtl	47	1977	Guy Lafleur, Mtl	136
1940	Milt Schmidt, Bos	52	1978	Guy Lafleur, Mtl	132
1941	Bill Cowley, Bos	62	1979	Bryan Trottier, NYI	134
1942	Bryan Hextall, NYR	56	1980	Marcel Dionne, LA	137
1943	Doug Bentley, Chi	73	1981	Wayne Gretzky, Edm	164
1944	Herb Cain, Bos	82	1982	Wayne Gretzky, Edm	212
1945	Elmer Lach, Mtl	80	1983	Wayne Gretzky, Edm	196
1946	Max Bentley, Chi	61	1984	Wayne Gretzky, Edm	205
1947	*Max Bentley, Chi	72	1985	Wayne Gretzky, Edm	208
1948	Elmer Lach, Mtl	61	1986	Wayne Gretzky, Edm	215
1949	Roy Conacher, Chi	68	1987	Wayne Gretzky, Edm	183
1950	Ted Lindsay, Det	78	1988	Mario Lemieux, Pitt	168
1951	Gordie Howe, Det	86	1989	Mario Lemieux, Pitt	199
1952	Gordie Howe, Det	86	1990	Wayne Gretzky, LA	142
1953	Gordie Howe, Det	95	1991	Wayne Gretzky, LA	163
1954	Gordie Howe, Det	81	1992	Mario Lemieux, Pitt	131
1955	Bernie Geoffrion, Mtl	75	1993	Mario Lemieux, Pitt	160
1956	Jean Beliveau, Mtl	88	1994	Wayne Gretzky, LA	130
			1995	Jaromir Jagr, Pitt	70

Art Ross Trophy (Cont.)

Year	Winner	Pts	Year	Winner	Pts
1996	Mario Lemieux, Pitt	161	2001	Jaromir Jagr, Pitt	121
1997	Mario Lemieux, Pitt	122	2002	Jarome Iginla, Cgy	96
1998	Jaromir Jagr, Pitt	102	2003	Peter Forsberg, Col	106
1999	Jaromir Jagr, Pitt	127	2004	Martin St. Louis, TB	94
2000	Jaromir Jagr, Pitt	96	2005	No Award	

Note: Listing includes scoring leaders prior to inception of Art Ross Trophy in 1947–48.

Lady Byng Memorial Trophy

Awarded annually "to the player adjudged to have exhibited the best type of sportsmanship and gentlemanly conduct combined with a high standard of playing ability." Lady Byng, who first presented the trophy in 1925, was the wife of Canada's Governor-General. She donated a second trophy in 1936 after the first was given permanently to Frank Boucher of the New York Rangers, who won it seven times in eight seasons. Stan Mikita, one of the league's most penalized players during his early years in the NHL, won the trophy twice late in his career (1967 and 1968).

1925..........Frank Nighbor, Ott	1952..........Sid Smith, Tor	1979..........Bob MacMillan, Atl
1926..........Frank Nighbor, Ott	1953..........Red Kelly, Det	1980..........Wayne Gretzky, Edm
1927..........Billy Burch, NYA	1954..........Red Kelly, Det	1981..........Rick Kehoe, Pitt
1928..........Frank Boucher, NYR	1955..........Sid Smith, Tor	1982..........Rick Middleton, Bos
1929..........Frank Boucher, NYR	1956..........Earl Reibel, Det	1983..........Mike Bossy, NYI
1930..........Frank Boucher, NYR	1957..........Andy Hebenton, NYR	1984..........Mike Bossy, NYI
1931..........Frank Boucher, NYR	1958..........Camille Henry, NYR	1985..........Jari Kurri, Edm
1932..........Joe Primeau, Tor	1959..........Alex Delvecchio, Det	1986..........Mike Bossy, NYI
1933..........Frank Boucher, NYR	1960..........Don McKenney, Bos	1987..........Joe Mullen, Cgy
1934..........Frank Boucher, NYR	1961..........Red Kelly, Tor	1988..........Mats Naslund, Mtl
1935..........Frank Boucher, NYR	1962..........Dave Keon, Tor	1989..........Joe Mullen, Cgy
1936..........Doc Romnes, Chi	1963..........Dave Keon, Tor	1990..........Brett Hull, StL
1937..........Marty Barry, Det	1964..........Ken Wharram, Chi	1991..........Wayne Gretzky, LA
1938..........Gordie Drillon, Tor	1965..........Bobby Hull, Chi	1992..........Wayne Gretzky, LA
1939..........Clint Smith, NYR	1966..........Alex Delvecchio, Det	1993..........Pierre Turgeon, NYI
1940..........Bobby Bauer, Bos	1967..........Stan Mikita, Chi	1994..........Wayne Gretzky, LA
1941..........Bobby Bauer, Bos	1968..........Stan Mikita, Chi	1995..........Ron Francis, Pitt
1942..........Syl Apps, Tor	1969..........Alex Delvecchio, Det	1996..........Paul Kariya, Ana
1943..........Max Bentley, Chi	1970..........Phil Goyette, StL	1997..........Paul Kariya, Ana
1944..........Clint Smith, Chi	1971..........John Bucyk, Bos	1998..........Ron Francis, Pitt
1945..........Billy Mosienko, Chi	1972..........Jean Ratelle, NYR	1999..........Wayne Gretzky, NYR
1946..........Toe Blake, Mtl	1973..........Gilbert Perreault, Buff	2000..........Pavol Demitra, StL
1947..........Bobby Bauer, Bos	1974..........John Bucyk, Bos	2001..........Joe Sakic, Col
1948..........Buddy O'Connor, NYR	1975..........Marcel Dionne, Det	2002..........Ron Francis, Car
1949..........Bill Quackenbush, Det	1976..........Jean Ratelle, NYR-Bos	2003..........Alexander Mogilny, Det
1950..........Edgar Laprade, NYR	1977..........Marcel Dionne, LA	2004..........Brad Richards, TB
1951..........Red Kelly, Det	1978..........Butch Goring, LA	2005..........No Award

James Norris Memorial Trophy

Awarded annually "to the defense player who demonstrates throughout the season the greatest all-around ability in the position." James Norris was the former owner-president of the Detroit Red Wings. Bobby Orr holds the record for most consecutive times winning the award (eight, 1968–1975).

1954.......Red Kelly, Det	1972.......Bobby Orr, Bos	1990.......Ray Bourque, Bos
1955.......Doug Harvey, Mtl	1973.......Bobby Orr, Bos	1991.......Ray Bourque, Bos
1956.......Doug Harvey, Mtl	1974.......Bobby Orr, Bos	1992.......Brian Leetch, NYR
1957.......Doug Harvey, Mtl	1975.......Bobby Orr, Bos	1993.......Chris Chelios, Chi
1958.......Doug Harvey, Mtl	1976.......Denis Potvin, NYI	1994.......Ray Bourque, Bos
1959.......Tom Johnson, Mtl	1977.......Larry Robinson, Mtl	1995.......Paul Coffey, Det
1960.......Doug Harvey, Mtl	1978.......Denis Potvin, NYI	1996.......Chris Chelios, Chi
1961.......Doug Harvey, Mtl	1979.......Denis Potvin, NYI	1997.......Brian Leetch, NYR
1962.......Doug Harvey, NYR	1980.......Larry Robinson, Mtl	1998.......Rob Blake, LA
1963.......Pierre Pilote, Chi	1981.......Randy Carlyle, Pitt	1999.......Al MacInnis, StL
1964.......Pierre Pilote, Chi	1982.......Doug Wilson, Chi	2000.......Chris Pronger, StL
1965.......Pierre Pilote, Chi	1983.......Rod Langway, Wash	2001.......Nicklas Lidstrom, Det
1966.......Jacques Laperriere, Mtl	1984.......Rod Langway, Wash	2002.......Nicklas Lidstrom, Det
1967.......Harry Howell, NYR	1985.......Paul Coffey, Edm	2003.......Nicklas Lidstrom, Det
1968.......Bobby Orr, Bos	1986.......Paul Coffey, Edm	2004.......Scott Niedermayer, NJ
1969.......Bobby Orr, Bos	1987.......Ray Bourque, Bos	2005.......No Award
1970.......Bobby Orr, Bos	1988.......Ray Bourque, Bos	
1971.......Bobby Orr, Bos	1989.......Chris Chelios, Mtl	

Calder Memorial Trophy

Awarded annually "to the player selected as the most proficient in his first year of competition in the National Hockey League." Frank Calder was a former NHL president. Sergei Makarov, who won the award in 1989–90, was the oldest recipient of the trophy, at 31. Players are no longer eligible for the award if they are 26 or older as of September 15th of the season in question.

1933 ......Carl Voss, Det	1958 ......Frank Mahovlich, Tor	1983 ......Steve Larmer, Chi
1934 ......Russ Blinko, Mtl M	1959 ......Ralph Backstrom, Mtl	1984 ......Tom Barrasso, Buff
1935 ......Dave Schriner, NYA	1960 ......Bill Hay, Chi	1985 ......Mario Lemieux, Pitt
1936 ......Mike Karakas, Chi	1961 ......Dave Keon, Tor	1986 ......Gary Suter, Cgy
1937 ......Syl Apps, Tor	1962 ......Bobby Rousseau, Mtl	1987 ......Luc Robitaille, LA
1938 ......Cully Dahlstrom, Chi	1963 ......Kent Douglas, Tor	1988 ......Joe Nieuwendyk, Cgy
1939 ......Frank Brimsek, Bos	1964 ......Jacques Laperriere, Mtl	1989 ......Brian Leetch, NYR
1940 ......Kilby MacDonald, NYR	1965 ......Roger Crozier, Det	1990 ......Sergei Makarov, Cgy
1941 ......Johnny Quilty, Mtl	1966 ......Brit Selby, Tor	1991 ......Ed Belfour, Chi
1942 ......Grant Warwick, NYR	1967 ......Bobby Orr, Bos	1992 ......Pavel Bure, Van
1943 ......Gaye Stewart, Tor	1968 ......Derek Sanderson, Bos	1993 ......Teemu Selanne, Winn
1944 ......Gus Bodnar, Tor	1969 ......Danny Grant, Minn	1994 ......Martin Brodeur, NJ
1945 ......Frank McCool, Tor	1970 ......Tony Esposito, Chi	1995 ......Peter Forsberg, Que
1946 ......Edgar Laprade, NYR	1971 ......Gilbert Perreault, Buff	1996 ......Daniel Alfredsson, Ott
1947 ......Howie Meeker, Tor	1972 ......Ken Dryden, Mtl	1997 ......Bryan Berard, NYI
1948 ......Jim McFadden, Det	1973 ......Steve Vickers, NYR	1998 ......Sergei Samsonov, Bos
1949 ......Pentti Lund, NYR	1974 ......Denis Potvin, NYI	1999 ......Chris Drury, Col
1950 ......Jack Gelineau, Bos	1975 ......Eric Vail, Atl	2000 ......Scott Gomez, NJ
1951 ......Terry Sawchuk, Det	1976 ......Bryan Trottier, NYI	2001 ......Evgeni Nabakov, SJ
1952 ......Bernie Geoffrion, Mtl	1977 ......Willi Plett, Atl	2002 ......Dany Heatley, Atl
1953 ......Gump Worsley, NYR	1978 ......Mike Bossy, NYI	2003 ......Barret Jackman, StL
1954 ......Camille Henry, NYR	1979 ......Bobby Smith, Minn	2004 ......Andrew Raycroft, Bos
1955 ......Ed Litzenberger, Chi	1980 ......Ray Bourque, Bos	2005 ......No Award
1956 ......Glenn Hall, Det	1981 ......Peter Stastny, Que	
1957 ......Larry Regan, Bos	1982 ......Dale Hawerchuk, Winn	

Vezina Trophy

Awarded annually "to the goalkeeper adjudged to be the best at his position." The trophy is named after Georges Vezina, an outstanding goalie for the Montreal Canadiens who collapsed during a game on November 28, 1925, and died four months later of tuberculosis. The general managers of the NHL teams vote on the award.

1927 ......George Hainsworth, Mtl	1958 ......Jacques Plante, Mtl	1980 ......Bob Sauve, Buff
1928 ......George Hainsworth, Mtl	1959 ......Jacques Plante, Mtl	Don Edwards, Buff
1929 ......George Hainsworth, Mtl	1960 ......Jacques Plante, Mtl	1981 ......Richard Sevigny, Mtl
1930 ......Tiny Thompson, Bos	1961 ......Johnny Bower, Tor	Denis Herron, Mtl
1931 ......Roy Worters, NYA	1962 ......Jacques Plante, Mtl	Michel Larocque, Mtl
1932 ......Charlie Gardiner, Chi	1963 ......Glenn Hall, Chi	1982 ......Billy Smith, NYI
1933 ......Tiny Thompson, Bos	1964 ......Charlie Hodge, Mtl	1983 ......Pete Peeters, Bos
1934 ......Charlie Gardiner, Chi	1965 ......Terry Sawchuk, Tor	1984 ......Tom Barrasso, Buff
1935 ......Lorne Chabot, Chi	Johnny Bower, Tor	1985 ......Pelle Lindbergh, Phil
1936 ......Tiny Thompson, Bos	1966 ......Gump Worsley, Mtl	1986 ......John Vanbiesbrouck,
1937 ......Normie Smith, Det	Charlie Hodge, Mtl	NYR
1938 ......Tiny Thompson, Bos	1967 ......Glenn Hall, Chi	1987 ......Ron Hextall, Phil
1939 ......Frank Brimsek, Bos	Rogie Vachon, Mtl	1988 ......Grant Fuhr, Edm
1940 ......Dave Kerr, NYR	1969 ......Jacques Plante, StL	1989 ......Patrick Roy, Mtl
1941 ......Turk Broda, Tor	Glenn Hall, StL	1990 ......Patrick Roy, Mtl
1942 ......Frank Brimsek, Bos	1970 ......Tony Esposito, Chi	1991 ......Ed Belfour, Chi
1943 ......Johnny Mowers, Det	1971 ......Ed Giacomin, NYR	1992 ......Patrick Roy, Mtl
1944 ......Bill Durnan, Mtl	Gilles Villemure, NYR	1993 ......Ed Belfour, Chi
1945 ......Bill Durnan, Mtl	1972 ......Tony Esposito, Chi	1994 ......Dominik Hasek, Buff
1946 ......Bill Durnan, Mtl	Gary Smith, Chi	1995 ......Dominik Hasek, Buff
1947 ......Bill Durnan, Mtl	1973 ......Ken Dryden, Mtl	1996 ......Jim Carey, Wash
1948 ......Turk Broda, Tor	1974 ......Bernie Parent, Phil	1997 ......Dominik Hasek, Buff
1949 ......Bill Durnan, Mtl	Tony Esposito, Chi	1998 ......Dominik Hasek, Buff
1950 ......Bill Durnan, Mtl	1975 ......Bernie Parent, Phil	1999 ......Dominik Hasek, Buff
1951 ......Al Rollins, Tor	1976 ......Ken Dryden, Mtl	2000 ......Olaf Kolzig, Wash
1952 ......Terry Sawchuk, Det	1977 ......Ken Dryden, Mtl	2001 ......Dominik Hasek, Buff
1953 ......Terry Sawchuk, Det	Michel Larocque, Mtl	2002 ......Jose Theodore, Mtl
1954 ......Harry Lumley, Tor	1978 ......Ken Dryden, Mtl	2003 ......Martin Brodeur, NJ
1955 ......Terry Sawchuk, Det	Michel Larocque, Mtl	2004 ......Martin Brodeur, NJ
1956 ......Jacques Plante, Mtl	1979 ......Ken Dryden, Mtl	2005 ......No Award
1957 ......Jacques Plante, Mtl	Michel Larocque, Mtl	

Selke Trophy

Awarded annually "to the forward who best excels in the defensive aspects of the game." The trophy is named after Frank J. Selke, the architect of the Montreal Canadians dynasty that won five consecutive Stanley Cups in the late '50s. The winner is selected by a vote of the Professional Hockey Writers Association.

1978........Bob Gainey, Mtl	1988........Guy Carbonneau, Mtl	1998........Jere Lehtinen, Dall
1979........Bob Gainey, Mtl	1989........Guy Carbonneau, Mtl	1999........Jere Lehtinen, Dall
1980........Bob Gainey, Mtl	1990........Rick Meagher, StL	2000........Steve Yzerman, Det
1981........Bob Gainey, Mtl	1991........Dirk Graham, Chi	2001........John Madden, NJ
1982........Steve Kasper, Bos	1992........Guy Carbonneau, Mtl	2002........Michael Peca, NYI
1983........Bobby Clarke, Phil	1993........Doug Gilmour, Tor	2003........Jere Lehtinen, Dall
1984........Doug Jarvis, Wash	1994........Sergei Fedorov, Det	2004........Kris Draper, Det
1985........Craig Ramsay, Buff	1995........Ron Francis, Pitt	2005........No Award
1986........Troy Murray, Chi	1996........Sergei Fedorov, Det	
1987........Dave Poulin, Phil	1997........Michael Peca, Buff	

Adams Award

Awarded annually "to the NHL coach adjudged to have contributed the most to his team's success." The trophy is named in honor of Jack Adams, longtime coach and general manager of the Detroit Red Wings. The winner is selected by a vote of the National Hockey League Broadcasters' Association.

1974 .....Fred Shero, Phil	1985 .....Mike Keenan, Phil	1996 .....Scotty Bowman, Det
1975 .....Bob Pulford, LA	1986 .....Glen Sather, Edm	1997 .....Ted Nolan, Buff
1976 ....Don Cherry, Bos	1987 .....Jacques Demers, Det	1998 .....Pat Burns, Bos
1977 .....Scott Bowman, Mtl	1988 .....Jacques Demers, Det	1999 .....Jacques Martin, Ott
1978 ....Bobby Kromm, Det	1989 .....Pat Burns, Mtl	2000 .....Joel Quenneville, StL
1979 .....Al Arbour, NYI	1990 .....Bob Murdoch, Winn	2001 .....Bill Barber, Phil
1980 ....Pat Quinn, Phil	1991 .....Brian Sutter, StL	2002 .....Bob Francis, Phoe
1981 .....Red Berenson, StL	1992 .....Pat Quinn, Van	2003 .....Jacques Lemaire, Minn
1982 .....Tom Watt, Winn	1993 .....Pat Burns, Tor	2004 .....John Tortorella, TB
1983 .....Orval Tessier, Chi	1994 .....Jacques Lemaire, NJ	2005 .....No Award
1984 .....Bryan Murray, Wash	1995 .....Marc Crawford, Que	

THEY SAID IT

*Jeremy Roenick, Flyers center, said
of the players' viewpoint on
the NHL's new Collective
Bargaining Agreement:
"We got our asses kicked."*

Alltime Point Leaders

	Player	Yrs	GP	G	A	Pts	Pts/game
1.	Wayne Gretzky, Edm, LA, StL, NYR	20	1487	894	1963	2857	1.921
2.	*Mark Messier, Edm, NYR, Van	25	1756	694	1193	1887	1.074
3.	Gordie Howe, Det, Hart	26	1767	801	1049	1850	1.047
4.	*Ron Francis, four teams	23	1731	549	1249	1798	1.038
5.	Marcel Dionne, Det, LA, NYR	18	1348	731	1040	1771	1.314
6.	*Steve Yzerman, Det	21	1453	678	1043	1721	1.184
7.	*Mario Lemieux, Pitt	16	889	683	1018	1701	1.913
8.	Phil Esposito, Chi, Bos, NYR	18	1282	717	873	1590	1.240
9.	Ray Bourque, Bos, Col	22	1612	410	1169	1579	.980
10.	Paul Coffey, eight teams	21	1409	396	1135	1531	1.087
11.	Stan Mikita, Chi	22	1394	541	926	1467	1.052
12.	Bryan Trottier, NYI, Pitt	18	1279	524	901	1425	1.114
13.	*Adam Oates, seven teams	19	1337	341	1079	1420	1.062
14.	Doug Gilmour, seven teams	20	1474	450	964	1414	.959
15.	Dale Hawerchuk, Winn, Buff, StL, Phil	16	1188	518	891	1409	1.186

*Active in 2003–04.

Alltime Goal-Scoring Leaders

	Player	Yrs	GP	G	G/game
1.	Wayne Gretzky, Edm, LA, StL, NYR	20	1487	894	.601
2.	Gordie Howe, Det, Hart	26	1767	801	.453
3.	*Brett Hull, Cal, StL, Dall, Det	19	1264	741	.586
4.	Marcel Dionne, Det, LA, NYR	18	1348	731	.542
5.	Phil Esposito, Chi, Bos, NYR	18	1282	717	.559
6.	Mike Gartner, Wash, Minn, NYR, Tor, Phoe	19	1432	708	.494
7.	*Mark Messier, Edm, NYR, Van	25	1756	694	.395
8.	*Mario Lemieux, Pitt	16	889	683	.768
9.	*Steve Yzerman, Det	21	1453	678	.467
10.	*Luc Robitaille, LA, Pitt, NYR, Det	18	1366	653	.478

*Active in 2003–04.

Alltime Assist Leaders

	Player	Yrs	GP	A	A/game
1.	Wayne Gretzky, Edm, LA, StL, NYR	20	1487	1963	1.320
2.	*Ron Francis, Hart, Pitt, Car	23	1731	1249	.721
3.	*Mark Messier, Edm, NYR, Van	25	1756	1193	.679
4.	Ray Bourque, Bos, Col	22	1612	1169	.725
5.	Paul Coffey, eight teams	21	1409	1135	.806
6.	*Adam Oates, seven teams	19	1337	1079	.807
7.	Gordie Howe, Det, Hart	26	1767	1049	.594
8.	*Steve Yzerman, Det	21	1453	1043	.718
9.	Marcel Dionne, Det, LA, NYR	18	1348	1040	.771
10.	*Mario Lemieux, Pitt	16	889	1018	1.145

*Active player in 2003–04.

Alltime Penalty Minutes Leaders

Player		Yrs	GP	PIM	Min/game
1.	Dave Williams, Tor, Van, Det, LA, Hart	14	962	3966	4.12
2.	Dale Hunter, Que, Wash, Col	19	1407	3565	2.53
3.	*Tie Domi, Tor, NYR, Winn	15	943	3406	3.61
4.	Marty McSorley, Pitt, Edm, LA, NYR, SJ, Bos	17	961	3381	3.52
5.	Bob Probert, Det, Chi	16	935	3300	3.53
6.	*Rob Ray, Buff, Ott	15	900	3207	3.56
7.	Craig Berube, Phil, Tor, Cgy, Wash, NYI	17	1054	3149	2.99
8.	Tim Hunter, Cgy, Que, Van, SJ	16	815	3146	3.86
9.	Chris Nilan, Mtl, NYR, Bos	13	688	3043	4.42
10.	Rick Tocchet, Phil, Pitt, LA, Bos, Wash, Phoe	18	1144	2974	2.60

*Active in 2003–04.

Goaltending Records

ALLTIME WIN LEADERS

Goaltender	W	L	T	Pct
Patrick Roy, Mtl, Col	551	315	131	.618
Terry Sawchuk, five teams	447	330	173	.562
*Ed Belfour, Chi, SJ, Dall, Tor	435	281	111	.593
Jacques Plante, five teams	434	246	147	.614
Tony Esposito, Mtl, Chi	423	306	152	.566
Glenn Hall, Det, Chi, StL	407	327	163	.545
*Martin Brodeur, NJ	403	217	105	.628
Grant Fuhr, six teams	403	295	114	.567
*Curtis Joseph, StL, Edm, Tor, Det	396	289	90	.569
Mike Vernon, Cgy, Det, SJ, Fla	385	273	92	.575

*Active in 2003–04.

ACTIVE GOALTENDING LEADERS

Goaltender	W	L	T	Pct
Martin Brodeur, NJ	403	217	105	.628
Chris Osgood, Det, NYI, StL	305	177	66	.617
Ed Belfour, Chi, SJ, Dall, Tor	435	281	111	.593
Dominik Hasek, Chi, Buff, Det	296	192	82	.591
Patrick Lalime, Pitt, Ott	167	112	32	.588
Roman Turek, Dall, StL, Cgy	159	115	43	.569
Curtis Joseph, StL, Edm, Tor, Det	396	289	90	.569
Nikolai Khabibulin, Phoe, TB	209	187	58	.524
Olaf Kolzig, Wash	234	220	63	.514
Felix Potvin, five teams	266	260	85	.505

Note: Ranked by winning percentage; minimum 250 games played. All players active in 2003–04.

ALLTIME SHUTOUT LEADERS

Goaltender	Team	Yrs	GP	SO
Terry Sawchuk	Det, Bos, Tor, LA, NYR	21	971	103
George Hainsworth	Mtl, Tor	11	465	94
Glenn Hall	Det, Chi, StL	18	906	84
Jacques Plante	Mtl, NYR, StL, Tor, Bos	18	837	82
Tiny Thompson	Bos, Det	12	553	81
Alex Connell	Ott, Det, NYA, Mtl M	12	417	81
Tony Esposito	Mtl, Chi	16	886	76
*Martin Brodeur	NJ	12	740	75
*Ed Belfour	Chi, SJ, Dall, Tor	15	856	75
Lorne Chabot	NYR, Tor, Mtl, Chi, Mtl M, NYA	11	411	73

*Active in 2003–04.

ALLTIME GOALS AGAINST AVERAGE LEADERS (PRE-1950)

Goaltender	Team	Yrs	GP	GA	GAA
George Hainsworth	Mtl, Tor	11	465	937	1.91
Alex Connell	Ott, Det, NYA, Mtl M	12	417	830	1.91
Chuck Gardiner	Chi	7	316	664	2.02
Lorne Chabot	NYR, Tor, Mtl, Chi, Mtl M, NYA	11	411	861	2.04
Tiny Thompson	Bos, Det	12	553	1183	2.08

ALLTIME GOALS AGAINST AVERAGE LEADERS (POST-1950)

Goaltender	Team	Yrs	GP	GA	GAA
*Martin Brodeur	NJ	12	740	1573	2.17
*Dominik Hasek	Chi, Buff, Det	13	595	1284	2.23
Ken Dryden	Mtl	8	397	870	2.24
*Roman Turek	Dall, StL, Cgy	8	328	734	2.31
Jacques Plante	Mtl, NYR, StL, Tor, Bos	18	837	1965	2.38

*Active in 2003–04.

Note: Minimum 250 games played. Goals against average equals goals against per 60 minutes played.

Coaching Records

Coach	Team	Seasons	W	L	T	Pct
Scott Bowman............five teams		1967–87, 91–2002	1244	583	314	.654
Toe Blake ....Mtl		1955–68	500	255	159	.634
*Ken Hitchcock..........Dall, Phil		1995–	362	211	94	.613
Fred Shero ....Phil, NYR		1971–81	390	225	119	.612
*Glen Sather................Edm, NYR		1979-89, 93-94, 2003-04	497	310	125	.600
Emile Francis ....NYR, StL		1965–77, 81–83	388	273	117	.574
Billy Reay ....Tor, Chi		1957–59, 63–77	542	385	175	.571
*Marc Crawford..........Que, Col, Van		1994–	369	264	108	.571
*Pat Burns...................Mtl, Tor, Bos, NJ		1988–2001, 2002–	501	359	153	.570
Al Arbour.....................StL, NYI		1970–94	781	577	248	.564
*Pat Quinn...................Phil, LA, Van, Tor		1978–	616	460	157	.563

Note: Minimum 600 regular-season games. Ranked by percentage. *Active in 2003–04.

Messier Bids Farewell

MEMO TO any other NHLers mulling retirement: If you want to get into the Hall of Fame in your first year of eligibility, plan on playing another year. Last week center Ron Francis, 42, called it quits after 23 NHL seasons, bringing to four the number of surefire Hall of Famers who have skated into the sunset since the lockout ended. (Mark Messier, Scott Stevens and Al MacInnis retired earlier this month.) Four is also the maximum number that can be inducted in one year. Consider the class of 2008--the first year this Fab Four will be eligible--booked.

One of the lockout's repercussions is that it deprived fans of a chance to bid these stars a proper farewell. Francis, who played with a gentleman's understated grace, wouldn't have had it any other way. After 10 years with the Whalers (he's the best player in their otherwise barren history), he played in Mario Lemieux's shadow in Pittsburgh, where he won Stanley Cups in 1991 and '92. A decade later he led the Hurricanes' run to the 2002 finals. He finished with 1,249 assists, second only to Wayne Gretzky, and is third in games played (1,731).

In typical fashion, Francis departed not with a glitzy press conference but with a statement posted on the players' association's website. He'll get plenty of attention when the Hall of Fame comes calling.g.

Single-Season Records

Goals

Player	Season	GP	G	Player	Season	GP	G
Wayne Gretzky, Edm	1981–82	80	92	Wayne Gretzky, Edm	1982–83	80	71
Wayne Gretzky, Edm	1983–84	74	87	Brett Hull, StL	1991–92	73	70
Brett Hull, StL	1990–91	78	86	Mario Lemieux, Pitt	1987–88	77	70
Mario Lemieux, Pitt	1988–89	76	85	Bernie Nicholls, LA	1988–89	79	70
Alexander Mogilny, Buff	1992–93	77	76	Mario Lemieux, Pitt	1992–93	60	69
Phil Esposito, Bos	1970–71	78	76	Mario Lemieux, Pitt	1995–96	70	69
Teemu Selanne, Winn	1992–93	84	76	Mike Bossy, NYI	1978–79	80	69
Wayne Gretzky, Edm	1984–85	80	73	Phil Esposito, Bos	1973–74	78	68
Brett Hull, StL	1989–90	80	72	Jari Kurri, Edm	1985–86	78	68
Jari Kurri, Edm	1984–85	73	71	Mike Bossy, NYI	1980–81	79	68

Assists

Player	Season	GP	A	Player	Season	GP	A
Wayne Gretzky, Edm	1985–86	80	163	Wayne Gretzky, LA	1989–90	73	102
Wayne Gretzky, Edm	1984–85	80	135	Bobby Orr, Bos	1970–71	78	102
Wayne Gretzky, Edm	1982–83	80	125	Mario Lemieux, Pitt	1987–88	77	98
Wayne Gretzky, LA	1990–91	78	122	Adam Oates, Bos	1992–93	84	97
Wayne Gretzky, Edm	1986–87	79	121	Doug Gilmour, Tor	1992–93	83	95
Wayne Gretzky, Edm	1981–82	80	120	Pat LaFontaine, Buff	1992–93	84	95
Wayne Gretzky, Edm	1983–84	74	118	Mario Lemieux, Pitt	1985–86	79	93
Mario Lemieux, Pitt	1988–89	76	114	Peter Stastny, Que	1981–82	80	93
Wayne Gretzky, LA	1988–89	78	114	Wayne Gretzky, LA	1993–94	81	92
Wayne Gretzky, Edm	1987–88	64	109	Mario Lemieux, Pitt	1995–96	70	92
Wayne Gretzky, Edm	1980–81	80	109	Ron Francis, Pitt	1995–96	77	92

Points

Player	Season	G	A	Pts	Player	Season	G	A	Pts
Wayne Gretzky, Edm	1985–86	52	163	215	Wayne Gretzky, LA	1990–91	41	122	163
Wayne Gretzky, Edm	1981–82	92	120	212	Mario Lemieux, Pitt	1995–96	69	92	161
Wayne Gretzky, Edm	1984–85	73	135	208	Mario Lemieux, Pitt	1992–93	69	91	160
Wayne Gretzky, Edm	1983–84	87	118	205	Steve Yzerman, Det	1988–89	65	90	155
Mario Lemieux, Pitt	1988–89	85	114	199	Phil Esposito, Bos	1970–71	76	76	152
Wayne Gretzky, Edm	1982–83	71	125	196	Bernie Nicholls, LA	1988–89	70	80	150
Wayne Gretzky, Edm	1986–87	62	121	183	Wayne Gretzky, Edm	1987–88	40	109	149
Mario Lemieux, Pitt	1987–88	70	98	168	Pat LaFontaine, Buff	1992–93	53	95	148
Wayne Gretzky, LA	1988–89	54	114	168	Mike Bossy, NYI	1981–82	64	83	147
Wayne Gretzky, Edm	1980–81	55	109	164	Phil Esposito, Bos	1973–74	68	77	145

Points per Game

Player	Season	GP	Pts	Avg	Player	Season	GP	Pts	Avg
Wayne Gretzky, Edm	1983–84	74	205	2.77	Mario Lemieux, Pitt	1987–88	77	168	2.18
Wayne Gretzky, Edm	1985–86	80	215	2.69	Wayne Gretzky, LA	1988–89	78	168	2.15
Mario Lemieux, Pitt	1992–93	60	160	2.67	Wayne Gretzky, LA	1990–91	78	163	2.09
Wayne Gretzky, Edm	1981–82	80	212	2.65	Mario Lemieux, Pitt	1989–90	59	123	2.08
Mario Lemieux, Pitt	1988–89	76	199	2.62	Wayne Gretzky, Edm	1980–81	80	164	2.05
Wayne Gretzky, Edm	1984–85	80	208	2.60	Mario Lemieux, Pitt	1991–92	64	131	2.05
Wayne Gretzky, Edm	1982–83	80	196	2.45	Bill Cowley, Bos	1943–44	36	71	1.97
Wayne Gretzky, Edm	1987–88	64	149	2.33	Phil Esposito, Bos	1970–71	78	152	1.95
Wayne Gretzky, Edm	1986–87	79	183	2.32	Wayne Gretzky, LA	1989–90	73	142	1.95
Mario Lemieux, Pitt	1995–96	70	161	2.30	Steve Yzerman, Det	1988–89	80	155	1.94

Note: Minimum 50 points in one season.

Goals per Game

Player	Season	GP	G	Avg
Joe Malone, Mtl	1917–18	20	44	2.20
Cy Denneny, Ott	1917–18	22	36	1.64
Newsy Lalonde, Mtl	1917–18	14	23	1.64
Joe Malone, Que	1919–20	24	39	1.63
Newsy Lalonde, Mtl	1919–20	23	36	1.57
Joe Malone, Ham	1920–21	20	30	1.50
Babe Dye, Ham-Tor	1920–21	24	35	1.46
Cy Denneny, Ott	1920–21	24	34	1.42
Reg Noble, Tor	1917–18	20	28	1.40
Newsy Lalonde, Mtl	1920–21	24	33	1.38

Note: Minimum 20 goals in one season.

Assists per Game

Player	Season	GP	A	Avg
Wayne Gretzky, Edm	1985–86	80	163	2.04
Wayne Gretzky, Edm	1987–88	64	109	1.70
Wayne Gretzky, Edm	1984–85	80	135	1.69
Wayne Gretzky, Edm	1983–84	74	118	1.59
Wayne Gretzky, Edm	1982–83	80	125	1.56
Wayne Gretzky, LA	1990–91	78	122	1.56
Wayne Gretzky, Edm	1986–87	79	121	1.53
Mario Lemieux, Pitt	1992–93	60	91	1.52
Wayne Gretzky, Edm	1981–82	80	120	1.50
Mario Lemieux, Pitt	1988–89	76	114	1.50

Note: Minimum 35 assists in one season.

Shutout Leaders

	Season	SO	Length of Schedule
George Hainsworth, Mtl	1928–29	22	44
Alex Connell, Ott	1925–26	15	36
Alex Connell, Ott	1927–28	15	44
Hal Winkler, Bos	1927–28	15	44
Tony Esposito, Chi	1969–70	15	76
George Hainsworth, Mtl	1926–27	14	44
Clint Benedict, Mtl M	1926–27	13	44
Alex Connell, Ott	1926–27	13	44
George Hainsworth, Mtl	1927–28	13	44
John Roach, NYR	1928–29	13	44
Roy Worters, NYA	1928–29	13	44
Harry Lumley, Tor	1953–54	13	70
Dominik Hasek, Buff	1997–98	13	82
Tiny Thompson, Bos	1928–29	12	44
Lorne Chabot, Tor	1928–29	12	44
Chuck Gardiner, Chi	1930–31	12	44
Terry Sawchuk, Det	1951–52	12	70
Terry Sawchuk, Det	1953–54	12	70
Terry Sawchuk, Det	1954–55	12	70
Glenn Hall, Det	1955–56	12	70
Bernie Parent, Phil	1973–74	12	78
Bernie Parent, Phil	1974–75	12	80
Lorne Chabot, NYR	1927–28	11	44
Harry Holmes, Det	1927–28	11	44

	Season	SO	Length of Schedule
Clint Benedict, Mtl M	1928–29	11	44
Joe Miller, Pitt Pirates	1928–29	11	44
Tiny Thompson, Bos	1932–33	11	44
Terry Sawchuk, Det	1950–51	11	70
Dominik Hasek, Buff	2000–01	11	82
Martin Brodeur, NJ	2003–04	11	82
Lorne Chabot, NYR	1926–27	10	44
Roy Worters, Pitt Pirates	1927–28	10	44
Clarence Dolson, Det	1928–29	10	44
John Roach, Det	1932–33	10	48
Chuck Gardiner, Chi	1933–34	10	48
Tiny Thompson, Bos	1935–36	10	48
Frank Brimsek, Bos	1938–39	10	48
Bill Durnan, Mtl	1948–49	10	60
Gerry McNeil, Mtl	1952–53	10	70
Harry Lumley, Tor	1952–53	10	70
Tony Esposito, Chi	1973–74	10	78
Ken Dryden, Mtl	1976–77	10	80
Martin Brodeur, NJ	1996–97	10	82
Martin Brodeur, NJ	1997–98	10	82
Roman Cechmanek, Phil	2000–01	10	82
Byron Dafoe, Bos	1998–99	10	82
Ed Belfour, Tor	2003–04	10	82

Wins

	Season	Record
Bernie Parent, Phil	1973–74	47-13-12
Bernie Parent, Phil	1974–75	44-14-9
Terry Sawchuk, Det	1950–51	44-13-13
Terry Sawchuk, Det	1951–52	44-14-12
Tom Barasso, Pitt	1992–93	43-14-5
Ed Belfour, Chi	1990–91	43-19-7
Martin Brodeur, NJ	1997–98	43-17-8
Martin Brodeur, NJ	1999–00	43-20-8
Jacques Plante, Mtl	1955–56	42-12-10
Jacques Plante, Mtl	1961–62	42-14-14
Ken Dryden, Mtl	1975–76	42-10-8
Mike Richter, NYR	1993–94	42-12-6
Roman Turek, StL	1999–00	42-15-9
Martin Brodeur, NJ	2000–01	42-17-11

Goals Against Average

(PRE-1950)

	Season	GP	GAA
George Hainsworth, Mtl	1928–29	44	0.92
George Hainsworth, Mtl	1927–28	44	1.05
Alex Connell, Ott	1925–26	36	1.12
Tiny Thompson, Bos	1928–29	44	1.18
Roy Worters, NYA	1928–29	38	1.21

(POST-1950)

	Season	GP	GAA
Miika Kiprusoff, Cal	2003–04	38	1.6949
Marty Turco, Dall	2002–03	55	1.7287
Tony Esposito, Chi	1971–72	48	1.7698
Al Rollins, Tor	1950–51	40	1.7744
Ron Tugnutt, Ott	1998–99	43	1.7943

Single-Game Records

Goals

	Date	G
Joe Malone, Que vs Tor	1-31-20	7
Newsy Lalonde, Mtl vs Tor	1-10-20	6
Joe Malone, Que vs Ott	3-10-20	6
Corb Denneny, Tor vs Ham	1-26-21	6
Cy Denneny, Ott vs Ham	3-7-21	6
Syd Howe, Det vs NYR	2-3-44	6
Red Berenson, StL vs Phil	11-7-68	6
Darryl Sittler, Tor vs Bos	2-7-76	6

Assists

	Date	A
Billy Taylor, Det vs Chi	3-16-47	7
Wayne Gretzky, Edm vs Wash	2-15-80	7
Wayne Gretzky, Edm vs Chi	12-11-85	7
Wayne Gretzky, Edm vs Que	2-14-86	7

Note: 24 tied with 6.

Points

	Date	G	A	Pts
Darryl Sittler, Tor vs Bos	2-7-76	6	4	10
Maurice Richard, Mtl vs Det	12-28-44	5	3	8
Bert Olmstead, Mtl vs Chi	1-9-54	4	4	8
Tom Bladon, Phil vs Clev	12-11-77	4	4	8
Bryan Trottier, NYI vs NYR	12-23-78	5	3	8
Peter Stastny, Que vs Wash	2-22-81	4	4	8
Anton Stastny, Que vs Wash	2-22-81	3	5	8
Wayne Gretzky, Edm vs NJ	11-19-83	3	5	8
Wayne Gretzky, Edm vs Minn	1-4-84	4	4	8
Paul Coffey, Edm vs Det	3-14-86	2	6	8
Mario Lemieux, Pitt vs StL	10-15-88	2	6	8
Bernie Nicholls, LA vs Tor	12-1-88	2	6	8
Mario Lemieux, Pitt vs NJ	12-31-88	5	3	8

NHL Season Leaders

Points

eason	Player and Club	Pts	Season	Player and Club	Pts
1917–18	Joe Malone, Mtl	44	1956–57	Gordie Howe, Det	89
1918–19	Newsy Lalonde, Mtl	30	1957–58	Dickie Moore, Mtl	84
1919–20	Joe Malone, Que	48	1958–59	Dickie Moore, Mtl	96
1920–21	Newsy Lalonde, Mtl	41	1959–60	Bobby Hull, Chi	81
1921–22	Punch Broadbent, Ott	46	1960–61	Bernie Geoffrion, Mtl	95
1922–23	Babe Dye, Tor	37	1961–62	Andy Bathgate, NY	84
1923–24	Cy Denneny, Ott	23		Bobby Hull, Chi	84
1924–25	Babe Dye, Tor	44	1962–63	Gordie Howe, Det	86
1925–26	Nels Stewart, Mtl M	42	1963–64	Stan Mikita, Chi	89
1926–27	Bill Cook, NY	37	1964–65	Stan Mikita, Chi	87
1927–28	Howie Morenz, Mtl	51	1965–66	Bobby Hull, Chi	97
1928–29	Ace Bailey, Tor	32	1966–67	Stan Mikita, Chi	97
1929–30	Cooney Weiland, Bos	73	1967–68	Stan Mikita, Chi	87
1930–31	Howie Morenz, Mtl	51	1968–69	Phil Esposito, Bos	126
1931–32	Harvey Jackson, Tor	53	1969–70	Bobby Orr, Bos	120
1932–33	Bill Cook, NY	50	1970–71	Phil Esposito, Bos	152
1933–34	Charlie Conacher, Tor	52	1971–72	Phil Esposito, Bos	133
1934–35	Charlie Conacher, Tor	57	1972–73	Phil Esposito, Bos	130
1935–36	Sweeney Schriner, NYA	45	1973–74	Phil Esposito, Bos	145
1936–37	Sweeney Schriner, NYA	46	1974–75	Bobby Orr, Bos	135
1937–38	Gord Drillon, Tor	52	1975–76	Guy Lafleur, Mtl	125
1938–39	Hector Blake, Mtl	47	1976–77	Guy Lafleur, Mtl	136
1939–40	Milt Schmidt, Bos	52	1977–78	Guy Lafleur, Mtl	132
1940–41	Bill Cowley, Bos	62	1978–79	Bryan Trottier, NYI	134
1941–42	Bryan Hextall, NY	54	1979–80	Marcel Dionne, LA	137
1942–43	Doug Bentley, Chi	73		Wayne Gretzky, Edm	137
1943–44	Herb Cain, Bos	82	1980–81	Wayne Gretzky, Edm	164
1944–45	Elmer Lach, Mtl	80	1981–82	Wayne Gretzky, Edm	212
1945–46	Max Bentley, Chi	61	1982–83	Wayne Gretzky, Edm	196
1946–47	Max Bentley, Chi	72	1983–84	Wayne Gretzky, Edm	205
1947–48	Elmer Lach, Mtl	61	1984–85	Wayne Gretzky, Edm	208
1948–49	Roy Conacher, Chi	68	1985–86	Wayne Gretzky, Edm	215
1949–50	Ted Lindsay, Det	78	1986–87	Wayne Gretzky, Edm	183
1950–51	Gordie Howe, Det	86	1987–88	Mario Lemieux, Pitt	168
1951–52	Gordie Howe, Det	86	1988–89	Mario Lemieux, Pitt	199
1952–53	Gordie Howe, Det	95	1989–90	Wayne Gretzky, LA	142
1953–54	Gordie Howe, Det	81	1990–91	Wayne Gretzky, LA	163
1954–55	Bernie Geoffrion, Mtl	75	1991–92	Mario Lemieux, Pitt	131
1955–56	Jean Beliveau, Mtl	88	1992–93	Mario Lemieux, Pitt	160

Points (Cont.)

Season	Player and Club	Pts	Season	Player and Club	Pts
1993–94	Wayne Gretzky, LA	130	1999–00	Jaromir Jagr, Pitt	96
1994–95	Jaromir Jagr, Pitt	70	2000–01	Jaromir Jagr, Pitt	121
1995–96	Mario Lemieux, Pitt	161	2001–02	Jarome Iginla, Cgy	96
1996–97	Mario Lemieux, Pitt	122	2002–03	Peter Forsberg, Col	106
1997–98	Jaromir Jagr, Pitt	102	2003–04	Martin St. Louis, TB	94
1998–99	Jaromir Jagr, Pitt	127			

Goals

Season	Player and Club	G	Season	Player and Club	G
1917–18	Joe Malone, Mtl	44	1961–62	Bobby Hull, Chi	50
1918–19	Odie Cleghorn, Mtl	23	1962–63	Gordie Howe, Det	38
1919–20	Joe Malone, Que	39	1963–64	Bobby Hull, Chi	43
1920–21	Babe Dye, Ham-Tor	35	1964–65	Norm Ullman, Det	42
1921–22	Punch Broadbent, Ott	32	1965–66	Bobby Hull, Chi	54
1922–23	Babe Dye, Tor	26	1966–67	Bobby Hull, Chi	52
1923–24	Cy Denneny, Ott	22	1967–68	Bobby Hull, Chi	44
1924–25	Babe Dye, Tor	38	1968–69	Bobby Hull, Chi	58
1925–26	Nels Stewart, Mtl	34	1969–70	Phil Esposito, Bos	43
1926–27	Bill Cook, NY	33	1970–71	Phil Esposito, Bos	76
1927–28	Howie Morenz, Mtl	33	1971–72	Phil Esposito, Bos	66
1928–29	Ace Bailey, Tor	22	1972–73	Phil Esposito, Bos	55
1929–30	Cooney Weiland, Bos	43	1973–74	Phil Esposito, Bos	68
1930–31	Bill Cook, NY	30	1974–75	Phil Esposito, Bos	61
1931–32	Charlie Conacher, Tor	34	1975–76	Guy Lafleur, Mtl	56
	Bill Cook, NY	34	1976–77	Steve Shutt, Mtl	60
1932–33	Bill Cook, NY	28	1977–78	Guy Lafleur, Mtl	60
1933–34	Charlie Conacher, Tor	32	1978–79	Mike Bossy, NYI	69
1934–35	Charlie Conacher, Tor	36	1979–80	Charlie Simmer, LA	56
1935–36	Charlie Conacher, Tor	23		Blaine Stoughton, Hart	56
	Bill Thoms, Tor	23	1980–81	Mike Bossy, NYI	68
1936–37	Larry Aurie, Det	23	1981–82	Wayne Gretzky, Edm	92
	Nels Stewart, Bos-NYA	23	1982–83	Wayne Gretzky, Edm	71
1937–38	Gord Drill, Tor	26	1983–84	Wayne Gretzky, Edm	87
1938–39	Roy Conacher, Bos	26	1984–85	Wayne Gretzky, Edm	73
1939–40	Bryan Hextall, NY	24	1985–86	Jari Kurri, Edm	68
1940–41	Bryan Hextall, NY	26	1986–87	Wayne Gretzky, Edm	62
1941–42	Lynn Patrick, NY	32	1987–88	Mario Lemieux, Pitt	70
1942–43	Doug Bentley, Chi	43	1988–89	Mario Lemieux, Pitt	85
1943–44	Doug Bentley, Chi	38	1989–90	Brett Hull, StL	72
1944–45	Maurice Richard, Mtl	50	1990–91	Brett Hull, StL	78
1945–46	Gaye Stewart, Tor	37	1991–92	Brett Hull, StL	70
1946–47	Maurice Richard, Mtl	50	1992–93	Alexander Mogilny, Buff	76
1947–48	Ted Lindsay, Det	33		Teemu Selanne, Winn	76
1948–49	Sid Abel, Det	28	1993–94	Pavel Bure, Van	60
1949–50	Maurice Richard, Mtl	43	1994–95	Peter Bondra, Wash	34
1950–51	Gordie Howe, Det	43	1995–96	Mario Lemieux, Pitt	69
1951–52	Gordie Howe, Det	47	1996–97	Keith Tkachuk, Phoe	52
1952–53	Gordie Howe, Det	49	1997–98	Teemu Selanne, Ana	52
1953–54	Maurice Richard, Mtl	37		Peter Bondra, Wash	52
1954–55	Bernie Geoffrion, Mtl	38	1998–99	Teemu Selanne, Ana	47
	Maurice Richard, Mtl	38	1999–00	Pavel Bure, Fla	58
1955–56	Jean Beliveau, Mtl	47	2000–01	Pavel Bure, Fla	59
1957–58	Dickie Moore, Mtl	36	2001–02	Jarome Iginla, Cgy	52
1956–57	Gordie Howe, Det	44	2002–03	Milan Hejduk, Col	50
1958–59	Jean Beliveau, Mtl	45	2003–04	Jarome Iginla, Cgy	41
1959–60	Bobby Hull, Chi	39		Rick Nash, Clb	41
	Bronco Horvath, Bos	39		Ilya Kovalchuk, Atl	41
1960–61	Bernie Geoffrion, Mtl	50			

Assists

Season	Player and Club	A	Season	Player and Club	A
1917–18	statistic not kept		1964–65	Stan Mikita, Chi	59
1918–19	Newsy Lalonde, Mtl	9	1965–66	Stan Mikita, Chi	48
1919–20	Corbett Denneny, Tor	12		Bobby Rousseau, Mtl	48
1920–21	Louis Berlinquette, Mtl	9		Jean Beliveau, Mtl	48
1921–22	Punch Broadbench, Ott	14	1966–67	Stan Mikita, Chi	62
1922–23	Babe Dye, Tor	11	1967–68	Phil Esposito, Bos	49
1923–24	Billy Boucher, Mtl	6	1968–69	Phil Esposito, Bos	77
1924–25	Cy Denneny, Ott	15	1969–70	Bobby Orr, Bos	87
1925–26	Cy Denneny, Ott	12	1970–71	Bobby Orr, Bos	102
1926–27	Dick Irvin, Chi	18	1971–72	Bobby Orr, Bos	80
1927–28	Howie Morenz, Mtl	18	1972–73	Phil Esposito, Bos	75
1928–29	Frank Boucher, NY	16	1973–74	Bobby Orr, Bos	89
1929–30	Frank Boucher, NY	36	1974–75	Bobby Clarke, Phil	89
1930–31	Joe Primeau, Tor	36		Bobby Orr, Bos	89
1931–32	Joe Primeau, Tor	37	1975–76	Bobby Clarke, Phil	89
1932–33	Frank Boucher, NY	28	1976–77	Guy Lafleur, Mtl	80
1933–34	Joe Primeau, Tor	32	1977–78	Bryan Trottier, NYI	77
1934–35	Art Chapman, NYA	28	1978–79	Bryan Trottier, NYI	87
1935–36	Art Chapman, NYA	28	1979–80	Wayne Gretzky, Edm	86
1936–37	Syl Apps, Tor	29	1980–81	Wayne Gretzky, Edm	109
1937–38	Syl Apps, Tor	29	1981–82	Wayne Gretzky, Edm	120
1938–39	Bill Cowley, Bos	34	1982–83	Wayne Gretzky, Edm	125
1939–40	Milt Schmidt, Bos	30	1983–84	Wayne Gretzky, Edm	118
1940–41	Bill Cowley, Bos	45	1984–85	Wayne Gretzky, Edm	135
1941–42	Phil Watson, NY	37	1985–86	Wayne Gretzky, Edm	163
1942–43	Bill Cowley, Bos	45	1986–87	Wayne Gretzky, Edm	121
1943–44	Clint Smith, Chi	49	1987–88	Wayne Gretzky, Edm	109
1944–45	Elmer Lach, Mtl	54	1988–89	Wayne Gretzky, LA	114
1945–46	Elmer Lach, Mtl	34		Mario Lemieux, Pitt	114
1946–47	Billy Taylor, Det	46	1989–90	Wayne Gretzky, LA	102
1947–48	Doug Bentley, Chi	37	1990–91	Wayne Gretzky, LA	122
1948–49	Doug Bentley, Chi	43	1991–92	Wayne Gretzky, LA	90
1949–50	Ted Lindsay, Det	55	1992–93	Adam Oates, Bos	97
1950–51	Gordie Howe, Det	43	1993–94	Wayne Gretzky, LA	92
	Ted Kennedy, Tor	43	1994–95	Ron Francis, Pitt	48
1951–52	Elmer Lach, Mtl	50	1995–96	Mario Lemieux, Pitt	92
1952–53	Gordie Howe, Det	46		Ron Francis, Pitt	92
1953–54	Gordie Howe, Det	48	1996–97	Mario Lemieux, Pitt	72
1954–55	Bert Olmstead, Mtl	48	1997–98	Jaromir Jagr, Pitt	67
1955–56	Bert Olmstead, Mtl	56		Wayne Gretzky, NYR	67
1956–57	Ted Lindsay, Det	55	1998–99	Jaromir Jagr, Pitt	83
1957–58	Henri Richard, Mtl	52	1999–00	Mark Recchi, Phil	63
1958–59	Dickie Moore, Mtl	55	2000–01	Jaromir Jagr, Pitt	69
1959–60	Bobby Hull, Chi	42		Adam Oates, Wash	69
1960–61	Jean Beliveau, Mtl	58	2001–02	Adam Oates, Wash	57
1961–62	Andy Bathgate, NY	56	2002–03	Peter Forsberg, Col	77
1962–63	Henri Richard, Mtl	50	2003–04	Scott Gomez, NJ	56
1963–64	Andy Bathgate, NY-Tor	58		Martin St. Louis, TB	56

Goals Against Average

Season	Goaltender and Club	GP	Min	GA	SO	Avg
1917–18	Georges Vezina, Mtl	21	1282	84	1	3.93
1918–19	Clint Benedict, Ott	18	1113	53	2	2.86
1919–20	Clint Benedict, Ott	24	1444	64	5	2.66
1920–21	Clint Benedict, Ott	24	1457	75	2	3.09
1921–22	Clint Benedict, Ott	24	1508	84	2	3.34
1922–23	Clint Benedict, Ott	24	1478	54	4	2.19
1923–24	Georges Vezina, Mtl	24	1459	48	3	1.97
1924–25	Georges Vezina, Mtl	30	1860	56	5	1.81
1925–26	Alex Connell, Ott	36	2251	42	15	1.12
1926–27	Clint Benedict, Mtl M	43	2748	65	13	1.42
1927–28	George Hainsworth, Mtl	44	2730	48	13	1.05
1928–29	George Hainsworth, Mtl	44	2800	43	22	0.92
1929–30	Tiny Thompson, Bos	44	2680	98	3	2.19
1930–31	Roy Worters, NYA	44	2760	74	8	1.61
1931–32	Chuck Gardiner, Chi	48	2989	92	4	1.85
1932–33	Tiny Thompson, Bos	48	3000	88	11	1.76
1933–34	Wilf Cude, Det-Mtl	30	1920	47	5	1.47
1934–35	Lorne Chabot, Chi	48	2940	88	8	1.80
1935–36	Tiny Thompson, Bos	48	2930	82	10	1.68
1936–37	Normie Smith, Det	48	2980	102	6	2.05
1937–38	Tiny Thompson, Bos	48	2970	89	7	1.80
1938–39	Frank Brimsek, Bos	43	2610	68	10	1.56
1939–40	Dave Kerr, NYR	48	3000	77	8	1.54
1940–41	Turk Broda, Tor	48	2970	99	5	2.00
1941–42	Frank Brimsek, Bos	47	2930	115	3	2.35
1942–43	Johnny Mowers, Det	50	3010	124	6	2.47
1943–44	Bill Durnan, Mtl	50	3000	109	2	2.18
1944–45	Bill Durnan, Mtl	50	3000	121	1	2.42
1945–46	Bill Durnan, Mtl	40	2400	104	4	2.60
1946–47	Bill Durnan, Mtl	60	3600	138	4	2.30
1947–48	Turk Broda, Tor	60	3600	143	5	2.38
1948–49	Bill Durnan, Mtl	60	3600	126	10	2.10
1949–50	Bill Durnan, Mtl	64	3840	141	8	2.20
1950–51	Al Rollins, Tor	40	2367	70	5	1.77
1951–52	Terry Sawchuk, Det	70	4200	133	12	1.90
1952–53	Terry Sawchuk, Det	63	3780	120	9	1.90
1953–54	Harry Lumley, Tor	69	4140	128	13	1.86
1954–55	Harry Lumley, Tor	69	4140	134	8	1.94
	Terry Sawchuk, Det	68	4060	132	12	1.94
1955–56	Jacques Plante, Mtl	64	3840	119	7	1.86
1956–57	Jacques Plante, Mtl	61	3660	123	9	2.02
1957–58	Jacques Plante, Mtl	57	3386	119	9	2.11
1958–59	Jacques Plante, Mtl	67	4000	144	9	2.16
1959–60	Jacques Plante, Mtl	69	4140	175	3	2.54
1960–61	Johnny Bower, Tor	58	3480	145	2	2.50
1961–62	Jacques Plante, Mtl	70	4200	166	4	2.37
1962–63	Jacques Plante, Mtl	56	3320	138	5	2.49
1963–64	Johnny Bower, Tor	51	3009	106	5	2.11
1964–65	Johnny Bower, Tor	34	2040	81	3	2.38
1965–66	Johnny Bower, Tor	35	1998	75	3	2.25
1966–67	Glenn Hall, Chi	32	1664	66	2	2.38
1967–68	Gump Worsley, Mtl	40	2213	73	6	1.98
1968–69	Jacques Plante, StL	37	2139	70	5	1.96
1969–70	Ernie Wakely, StL	30	1651	58	4	2.11
1970–71	Jacques Plante, Tor	40	2329	73	4	1.88
1971–72	Tony Esposito, Chi	48	2780	82	9	1.77
1972–73	Ken Dryden, Mtl	54	3165	119	6	2.26
1973–74	Bernie Parent, Phil	73	4314	136	12	1.89
1974–75	Bernie Parent, Phil	68	4041	137	12	2.03
1975–76	Ken Dryden, Mtl	62	3580	121	8	2.03
1976–77	Michael Larocque, Mtl	26	1525	53	4	2.09
1977–78	Ken Dryden, Mtl	52	3071	105	5	2.05
1978–79	Ken Dryden, Mtl	47	2814	108	5	2.30
1979–80	Bob Sauve, Buff	32	1880	74	4	2.36
1980–81	Richard Sevigny, Mtl	33	1777	71	2	2.40
1981–82	Denis Herron, Mtl	27	1547	68	3	2.64
1982–83	Pete Peeters, Bos	62	3611	142	8	2.36
1983–84	Pat Riggin, Wash	41	2299	102	4	2.66

Goals Against Average (Cont.)

Season	Goaltender and Club	GP	Min	GA	SO	Avg
1984–85	Tom Barrasso, Buff	54	3248	144	5	2.66
1985–86	Bob Froese, Phil	51	2728	116	5	2.55
1986–87	Brian Hayward, Mtl	37	2178	102	1	2.81
1987–88	Pete Peeters, Wash	35	1896	88	2	2.78
1988–89	Patrick Roy, Mtl	48	2744	113	4	2.47
1989–90	Patrick Roy, Mtl	54	3173	134	3	2.53
	Mike Liut, Hart-Wash	37	2161	91	4	2.53
1990–91	Ed Belfour, Chi	74	4127	170	4	2.47
1991–92	Patrick Roy, Mtl	67	3935	155	5	2.36
1992–93	Felix Potvin, Tor	48	2781	116	2	2.50
1993–94	Dominik Hasek, Buff	58	3358	109	7	1.95
1994–95	Dominik Hasek, Buff	41	2416	85	5	2.11
1995–96	Ron Hextall, Phil	53	3102	112	4	2.17
	Chris Osgood, Det	50	2933	106	5	2.17
1996–97	Martin Brodeur, NJ	67	3838	120	10	1.88
1997–98	Ed Belfour, Dall	61	3581	112	9	1.88
1998–99	Ron Tugnutt, Ott	43	2508	75	3	1.79
1999–00	Brian Boucher, Phil	35	2038	65	4	1.91
2000–01	Marty Turco, Dall	26	1266	40	3	1.90
2001–02	Patrick Roy, Col	63	3774	122	9	1.94
2002–03	Marty Turco, Dall	55	3193	92	7	1.72
2003–04	Miikka Kiprusoff, Cgy	38	2301	65	4	1.70

Penalty Minutes

Season	Player and Club	GP	PIM	Season	Player and Club	GP	PIM
1918–19	Joe Hall, Mtl	17	85	1961–62	Lou Fontinato, Mtl	54	167
1919–20	Cully Wilson, Tor	23	79	1962–63	Howie Young, Det	64	273
1920–21	Bert Corbeau, Mtl	24	86	1963–64	Vic Hadfield, NYR	69	151
1921–22	Sprague Cleghorn, Mtl	24	63	1964–65	Carl Brewer, Tor	70	177
1922–23	Billy Boucher, Mtl	24	52	1965–66	Reggie Fleming, Bos-NYR	69	166
1923–24	Bert Corbeau, Tor	24	55	1966–67	John Ferguson, Mtl	67	177
1924–25	Billy Boucher, Mtl	30	92	1967–68	Barclay Plager, StL	49	153
1925–26	Bert Corbeau, Tor	36	121	1968–69	Forbes Kennedy, Phil-Tor	77	219
1926–27	Nels Stewart, Mtl M	44	133	1969–70	Keith Magnuson, Chi	76	213
1927–28	Eddie Shore, Bos	44	165	1970–71	Keith Magnuson, Chi	76	291
1928–29	Red Dutton, Mtl M	44	139	1971–72	Brian Watson, Pitt	75	212
1929–30	Joe Lamb, Ott	44	119	1972–73	Dave Schultz, Phil	76	259
1930–31	Harvey Rockburn, Det	42	118	1973–74	Dave Schultz, Phil	73	348
1931–32	Red Dutton, NYA	47	107	1974–75	Dave Schultz, Phil	76	472
1932–33	Red Horner, Tor	48	144	1975–76	Steve Durbano, Pitt-KC	69	370
1933–34	Red Horner, Tor	42	126	1976–77	Dave Williams, Tor	77	338
1934–35	Red Horner, Tor	46	125	1977–78	Dave Schultz, LA-Pitt	74	405
1935–36	Red Horner, Tor	43	167	1978–79	Dave Williams, Tor	77	298
1936–37	Red Horner, Tor	48	124	1979–80	Jimmy Mann, Winn	72	287
1937–38	Red Horner, Tor	47	82	1980–81	Dave Williams, Van	77	343
1938–39	Red Horner, Tor	48	85	1981–82	Paul Baxter, Pitt	76	409
1939–40	Red Horner, Tor	30	87	1982–83	Randy Holt, Wash	70	275
1940–41	Jimmy Orlando, Det	48	99	1983–84	Chris Nilan, Mtl	76	338
1941–42	Jimmy Orlando, Det	48	81	1984–85	Chris Nilan, Mtl	77	358
1942–43	Jimmy Orlando, Det	40	89	1985–86	Joey Kocur, Det	59	377
1943–44	Mike McMahon, Mtl	42	98	1986–87	Tim Hunter, Cgy	73	361
1944–45	Pat Egan, Bos	48	86	1987–88	Bob Probert, Det	74	398
1945–46	Jack Stewart, Det	47	73	1988–89	Tim Hunter, Cgy	75	375
1946–47	Gus Mortson, Tor	60	133	1989–90	Basil McRae, Minn	66	351
1947–48	Bill Barilko, Tor	57	147	1990–91	Bob Ray, Buff	66	350
1948–49	Bill Ezinicki, Tor	52	145	1991–92	Mike Peluso, Chi	63	408
1949–50	Bill Ezinicki, Tor	67	144	1992–93	Marty McSorley, LA	81	399
1950–51	Gus Mortson, Tor	60	142	1993–94	Tie Domi, Winn	81	347
1951–52	Gus Kyle, Bos	69	127	1994–95	Enrico Ciccone, TB	41	225
1952–53	Maurice Richard, Mtl	70	112	1995–96	Matthew Barnaby, Buff	73	335
1953–54	Gus Mortson, Chi	68	132	1996–97	Gino Odjick, Van	70	371
1954–55	Fern Flaman, Bos	70	150	1997–98	Donald Brashear, Van	77	372
1955–56	Lou Fontinato, NYR	70	202	1998–99	Rob Ray, Buff	76	261
1956–57	Gus Mortson, Chi	70	147	1999–00	Denny Lambert, Atl	73	219
1957–58	Lou Fontinato, NYR	70	152	2000–01	Matthew Barnaby, TB	76	265
1958–59	Ted Lindsay, Chi	70	184	2001–02	Peter Worrell, Fla	79	354
1959–60	Carl Brewer, Tor	67	150	2002–03	Jody Shelley, Clb	68	249
1960–61	Pierre Pilote, Chi	70	165	2003–04	Sean Avery, LA	76	261

NHL All-Star Game

First played in 1947, this game was scheduled before the start of the regular season and used to match the defending Stanley Cup Champions against a squad made up of the league All-stars from other teams. In 1966 the games were moved to mid-season, although there was no game that year. The format changed to a conference versus conference showdown in 1969.

Results

Year	Site	Score	MVP	Attendance
1947	Toronto	All-Stars 4, Toronto 3	None named	14,169
1948	Chicago	All-Stars 3, Toronto 1	None named	12,794
1949	Toronto	All-Stars 3, Toronto 1	None named	13,541
1950	Detroit	Detroit 7, All-Stars 1	None named	9,166
1951	Toronto	1st team 2, 2nd team 2	None named	11,469
1952	Detroit	1st team 1, 2nd team 1	None named	10,680
1953	Montreal	All-Stars 3, Montreal 1	None named	14,153
1954	Detroit	All-Stars 2, Detroit 2	None named	10,689
1955	Detroit	Detroit 3, All-Stars 1	None named	10,111
1956	Montreal	All-Stars 1, Montreal 1	None named	13,095
1957	Montreal	All-Stars 5, Montreal 3	None named	13,003
1958	Montreal	Montreal 6, All-Stars 3	None named	13,989
1959	Montreal	Montreal 6, All-Stars 1	None named	13,818
1960	Montreal	All-Stars 2, Montreal 1	None named	13,949
1961	Chicago	All-Stars 3, Chicago 1	None named	14,534
1962	Toronto	Toronto 4, All-Stars 1	Eddie Shack, Tor	14,236
1963	Toronto	All-Stars 3, Toronto 3	Frank Mahovlich, Tor	14,034
1964	Toronto	All-Stars 3, Toronto 2	Jean Beliveau, Mtl	14,232
1965	Montreal	All-Stars 5, Montreal 2	Gordie Howe, Det	13,529
1967	Montreal	Montreal 3, All-Stars 0	Henri Richard, Mtl	14,284
1968	Toronto	Toronto 4, All-Stars 3	Bruce Gamble, Tor	15,753
1969	Montreal	East 3, West 3	Frank Mahovlich, Det	16,260
1970	St Louis	East 4, West 1	Bobby Hull, Chi	16,587
1971	Boston	West 2, East 1	Bobby Hull, Chi	14,790
1972	Minnesota	East 3, West 2	Bobby Orr, Bos	15,423
1973	NY Rangers	East 5, West 4	Greg Polis, Pitt	16,986
1974	Chicago	West 6, East 4	Garry Unger, StL	16,426
1975	Montreal	Wales 7, Campbell 1	Syl Apps Jr, Pitt	16,080
1976	Philadelphia	Wales 7, Campbell 5	Pete Mahovlich, Mtl	16,436
1977	Vancouver	Wales 4, Campbell 3	Rick Martin, Buff	15,607
1978	Buffalo	Wales 3, Campbell 2 (OT)	Billy Smith, NYI	16,433
1980	Detroit	Wales 6, Campbell 3	Reg Leach, Phil	21,002
1981	Los Angeles	Campbell 4, Wales 1	Mike Liut, StL	15,761
1982	Washington	Wales 4, Campbell 2	Mike Bossy, NYI	18,130
1983	NY Islanders	Campbell 9, Wales 3	Wayne Gretzky, Edm	15,230
1984	New Jersey	Wales 7, Campbell 6	Don Maloney, NYR	18,939
1985	Calgary	Wales 6, Campbell 4	Mario Lemieux, Pitt	16,825
1986	Hartford	Wales 4, Campbell 3 (OT)	Grant Fuhr, Edm	15,100
1988	St Louis	Wales 6, Campbell 5 (OT)	Mario Lemieux, Pitt	17,878
1989	Edmonton	Campbell 9, Wales 5	Wayne Gretzky, LA	17,503
1990	Pittsburgh	Wales 12, Campbell 7	Mario Lemieux, Pitt	16,236
1991	Chicago	Campbell 11, Wales 5	Vince Damphousse, Tor	18,472
1992	Philadelphia	Campbell 10, Wales 6	Brett Hull, StL	17,380
1993	Montreal	Wales 16, Campbell 6	Mike Gartner, NYR	17,137
1994	NY Rangers	East 9, West 8	Mike Richter, NYR	18,200
1996	Boston	East 5, West 4	Ray Bourque, Bos	17,565
1997	San Jose	East 11, West 7	Mark Recchi, Mtl	17,565
1998	Vancouver	N America 8, World 7	Teemu Selanne, Ana (World)	18,422
1999	Tampa Bay	N America 8, World 6	Wayne Gretzky, NYR (N America)	19,758
2000	Toronto	World 9, N America 4	Pavel Bure, Fla (World)	19,300
2001	Denver	N America 14, World 12	Bill Guerin, Bos (N America)	18,646
2002	Los Angeles	World 8, N America 5	Eric Daze, Chi (N America)	18,118
2003	Sunrise, Fla.	West 6, East 5 (shootout)	Dany Heatley, Atl (East)	19,250
2004	St. Paul, Minn.	East 6, West 4	Joe Sakic, Col (West)	19,434
2005	No game played			

Note: The Challenge Cup, a series between the NHL All-Stars and the Soviet Union, was played instead of the All-Star Game in 1979. Eight years later, Rendez-Vous '87, a two-game series matching the Soviet Union and the NHL All-Stars, replaced the All-Star Game. The 1995 NHL All-Star game was cancelled due to a labor dispute. The 1998 NHL All-Star game, billed as a preview to the 1998 Winter Olympics in Nagano, Japan, matched North Amercian–born All-Stars and All-Stars born elsewhere. In 2005, no game was played due to season-long lockout.

Hockey Hall of Fame

Located in Toronto, the Hockey Hall of Fame was officially opened on August 26, 1961. The current chairman is William C. Hay. There are, at present, 306 members of the Hockey Hall of Fame—209 players, 84 "builders," and 14 on-ice officials. (One member, Alan Eagleson, resigned from the Hall 3-25-98.) To be eligible, player and referee/linesman candidates should have been out of the game for three years, but the Hall's Board of Directors can make exceptions.

Players

Sid Abel (1969)
Jack Adams (1959)
Charles (Syl) Apps (1961)
George Armstrong (1975)
Irvine (Ace) Bailey (1975)
Donald H. (Dan) Bain (1945)
Hobey Baker (1945)
Bill Barber (1990)
Marty Barry (1965)
Andy Bathgate (1978)
Bobby Bauer (1996)
Jean Beliveau (1972)
Clint Benedict (1965)
Douglas Bentley (1964)
Max Bentley (1966)
Hector (Toe) Blake (1966)
Leo Boivin (1986)
Dickie Boon (1952)
Mike Bossy (1991)
Emile (Butch) Bouchard (1966)
Frank Boucher (1958)
George (Buck) Boucher (1960)
Ray Bourque (2004)
Johnny Bower (1976)
Russell Bowie (1945)
Frank Brimsek (1966)
Harry L. (Punch) Broadbent (1962)
Walter (Turk) Broda (1967)
John Bucyk (1981)
Billy Burch (1974)
Harry Cameron (1962)
Gerry Cheevers (1985)
Francis (King) Clancy (1958)
Aubrey (Dit) Clapper (1947)
Bobby Clarke (1987)
Sprague Cleghorn (1958)
Paul Coffey (2004)
Neil Colville (1967)
Charlie Conacher (1961)
Lionel Conacher (1994)
Roy Conacher (1998)
Alex Connell (1958)
Bill Cook (1952)
Fred (Bun) Cook (1995)
Arthur Coulter (1974)
Yvan Cournoyer (1982)
Bill Cowley (1968)
Samuel (Rusty) Crawford (1962)
Jack Darragh (1962)
Allan M. (Scotty) Davidson (1950)
Clarence (Hap) Day (1961)
Alex Delvecchio (1977)
Cy Denneny (1959)
Marcel Dionne (1992)
Gordie Drillon (1975)
Charles Drinkwater (1950)

Ken Dryden (1983)
Woody Dumart (1992)
Thomas Dunderdale (1974)
Bill Durnan (1964)
Mervyn A. (Red) Dutton (1958)
Cecil (Babe) Dye (1970)
Phil Esposito (1984)
Tony Esposito (1988)
Arthur F. Farrell (1965)
Bernie Federko (2002)
Viacheslav Fetisov (2001)
Ferdinand (Fern) Flaman (1990)
Frank Foyston (1958)
Frank Frederickson (1958)
Grant Fuhr (2003)
Bill Gadsby (1970)
Bob Gainey (1992)
Chuck Gardiner (1945)
Herb Gardiner (1958)
Jimmy Gardner (1962)
Mike Gartner (2001)
Bernie (Boom Boom) Geoffrion (1972)
Eddie Gerard (1945)
Ed Giacomin (1987)
Rod Gilbert (1982)
Clark Gilles (2002)
Hamilton (Billy) Gilmour (1962)
Frank (Moose) Goheen (1952)
Ebenezer R. (Ebbie) Goodfellow (1963)
Michel Goulet (1998)
Mike Grant (1950)
Wilfred (Shorty) Green (1962)
Wayne Gretzky (1999)
Si Griffis (1950)
George Hainsworth (1961)
Glenn Hall (1975)
Joe Hall (1961)
Doug Harvey (1973)
Dale Hawerchuk (2001)
George Hay (1958)
William (Riley) Hern (1962)
Bryan Hextall (1969)
Harry (Hap) Holmes (1972)
Tom Hooper (1962)
George (Red) Horner (1965)
Miles (Tim) Horton (1977)
Gordie Howe (1972)
Syd Howe (1965)
Harry Howell (1979)
Bobby Hull (1983)
John (Bouse) Hutton (1962)
Harry M. Hyland (1962)
James (Dick) Irvin (1958)
Harvey (Busher) Jackson (1971)

Ernest (Moose) Johnson (1952)
Ivan (Ching) Johnson (1958)
Tom Johnson (1970)
Aurel Joliat (1947)
Gordon (Duke) Keats (1958)
Leonard (Red) Kelly (1969)
Ted (Teeder) Kennedy (1966)
Dave Keon (1986)
Jari Kurri (2001)
Elmer Lach (1966)
Guy Lafleur (1988)
Pat LaFonaine (2003)
Edouard (Newsy) Lalonde (1950)
Rod Langway (2002)
Jacques Laperriere (1987)
Guy LaPointe (1993)
Edgar Laprade (1993)
Reed Larson (1996)
Jean (Jack) Laviolette (1962)
Hugh Lehman (1958)
Jacques Lemaire (1984)
Mario Lemieux (1997)
Percy LeSueur (1961)
Herbert A. Lewis (1989)
Ted Lindsay (1966)
Harry Lumley (1980)
Lanny McDonald (1992)
Frank McGee (1945)
Billy McGimsie (1962)
George McNamara (1958)
Duncan (Mickey) MacKay (1952)
Frank Mahovlich (1981)
Joe Malone (1950)
Sylvio Mantha (1960)
Jack Marshall (1965)
Fred G. (Steamer) Maxwell (1962)
Stan Mikita (1983)
Dicky Moore (1974)
Patrick (Paddy) Moran (1958)
Howie Morenz (1945)
Billy Mosienko (1965)
Joe Mullen (2000)
Larry Murphy (2004)
Frank Nighbor (1947)
Reg Noble (1962)
Herbert (Buddy) O'Connor (1988)
Harry Oliver (1967)
Bert Olmstead (1985)
Bobby Orr (1979)
Bernie Parent (1984)
Brad Park (1988)
Lester Patrick (1947)
Lynn Patrick (1980)
Gilbert Perreault (1990)
Tommy Phillips (1945)
Pierre Pilote (1975)

Players *(Cont.)*

Didier (Pit) Pitre (1962)
Jacques Plante (1978)
Denis Potvin (1991)
Walter (Babe) Pratt (1966)
Joe Primeau (1963)
Marcel Pronovost (1978)
Bob Pulford (1991)
Harvey Pulford (1945)
Hubert (Bill) Quackenbush (1976)
Frank Rankin (1961)
Jean Ratelle (1985)
Claude (Chuck) Rayner (1973)
Kenneth Reardon (1966)
Henri Richard (1979)
Maurice (Rocket) Richard (1961)
George Richardson (1950)
Gordon Roberts (1971)
Larry Robinson (1995)
Art Ross (1945)
Blair Russel (1965)
Ernest Russell (1965)
Jack Ruttan (1962)
Borje Salming (1996)
Denis Savard (2000)
Serge Savard (1986)
Terry Sawchuk (1971)
Fred Scanlan (1965)
Milt Schmidt (1961)
Dave (Sweeney) Schriner (1962)
Earl Seibert (1963)
Oliver Seibert (1961)
Eddie Shore (1947)
Steve Shutt (1993)
Albert C. (Babe) Siebert (1964)
Harold (Bullet Joe) Simpson (1962)
Daryl Sittler (1989)
Alfred E. Smith (1962)
Billy Smith (1993)
Clint Smith (1991)
Reginald (Hooley) Smith (1972)
Thomas Smith (1973)
Allan Stanley (1981)
Russell (Barney) Stanley (1962)
Peter Stastny (1998)
John (Black Jack) Stewart (1964)
Nels Stewart (1962)
Bruce Stuart (1961)
Hod Stuart (1945)
Frederic (Cyclone) (O.B.E.)
   Taylor (1947)
Cecil R. (Tiny) Thompson (1959)
Vladislav Tretiak (1989)
Harry J. Trihey (1950)
Bryan Trottier (1997)
Norm Ullman (1982)
Georges Vezina (1945)
Jack Walker (1960)
Marty Walsh (1962)
Harry Watson (1994)
Harry E. Watson (1962)

Players *(Cont.)*

Ralph (Cooney) Weiland (1971)
Harry Westwick (1962)
Fred Whitcroft (1962)
Gordon (Phat) Wilson (1962)
Lorne (Gump) Worsley (1980)
Roy Worters (1969)

Builders

Charles Adams (1960)
Weston W. Adams (1972)
Thomas (Frank) Ahearn (1962)
John (Bunny) Ahearne (1977)
Montagu Allan (C.V.O.) (1945)
Keith Allen (1992)
Al Arbour (1996)
Harold Ballard (1977)
David Bauer (1989)
John Bickell (1978)
Scott Bowman (1991)
George V. Brown (1961)
Walter A. Brown (1962)
Frank Buckland (1975)
Walter L. Bush (2000)
Jack Butterfield (1980)
Frank Calder (1947)
Angus D. Campbell (1964)
Clarence Campbell (1966)
Joe Cattarinich (1977)
Bob Cole (1996)
Joseph (Leo) Dandurand (1963)
Francis Dilio (1964)
George S. Dudley (1958)
James A. Dunn (1968)
Robert Alan Eagleson (1989–98*)
Cliff Fletcher (2004)
Sergio Gambucci (1996)
Emile Francis (1982)
Jack Gibson (1976)
Tommy Gorman (1963)
Frank Griffiths (1993)
William Hanley (1986)
Charles Hay (1974)
James C. Hendy (1968)
Foster Hewitt (1965)
William Hewitt (1947)
Fred J. Hume (1962)
Mike Ilitch (2003)
George (Punch) Imlach (1984)
Tommy Ivan (1974)
William M. Jennings (1975)
Bob Johnson (1992)
Gordon W. Juckes (1979)
John Kilpatrick (1960)
Brian Kilrea (2003)
Seymour Knox III (1993)
George Leader (1969)
Robert LeBel (1970)
Thomas F. Lockhart (1965)
Paul Loicq (1961)
Frederic McLaughlin (1963)

Builders *(Cont.)*

John Mariucci (1985)
Frank Mathers (1992)
John (Jake) Milford (1984)
Hartland Molson (1973)
Scotty Morrison (1999)
Mngr. Athol (Pere) Murray (1998)
Roger Neilson (2002)
Francis Nelson (1947)
Bruce A. Norris (1969)
James Norris, Sr. (1958)
James D. Norris (1962)
William M. Northey (1947)
John O'Brien (1962)
Brian O'Neill (1994)
Fred Page (1993)
Craig Patrick (1996)
Frank Patrick (1958)
Allan W. Pickard (1958)
Rudy Pilous (1985)
Norman (Bud) Poile (1990)
Samuel Pollock (1978)
Donat Raymond (1958)
John Robertson (1947)
Claude C. Robinson (1947)
Philip D. Ross (1976)
Gunther Sabetzki (1995)
Glen Sather (1997)
Frank J. Selke (1960)
Harry Sinden (1983)
Frank D. Smith (1962)
Conn Smythe (1958)
Edward M. Snider (1988)
Lord Stanley of Preston (1945)
James T. Sutherland (1947)
Anatoli V. Tarasov (1974)
Bill Torrey (1995)
Lloyd Turner (1958)
William Tutt (1978)
Carl Potter Voss (1974)
Fred C. Waghorn (1961)
Arthur Wirtz (1971)
Bill Wirtz (1976)
John A. Ziegler, Jr. (1987)

Referees/Linesmen

Neil Armstrong (1991)
John Ashley (1981)
William L. Chadwick (1964)
John D'Amico (1993)
Chaucer Elliott (1961)
George Hayes (1988)
Robert W. Hewitson (1963)
Fred J. (Mickey) Ion (1961)
Matt Pavelich (1987)
Mike Rodden (1962)
J. Cooper Smeaton (1961)
Roy (Red) Storey (1967)
Frank Udvari (1973)
Andy van Hellemond (1999)

Note: Year of election to the Hall of Fame is in parentheses after the member's name.
*Eagleson resigned from Hall March 25, 1998.

Tennis

Six-time Grand Slam winner Roger Federer

Greatest Ever?

Amid effusive praise, the unstoppable Roger Federer steamrolled his way to two more Grand Slam titles

BY B.J. SCHECTER

A S HE WALKED OUT TO A BOIS-terous ovation at Arthur Ashe Stadium for perhaps the last time, Andre Agassi did his best to soak it all in. At one point in his career, Agassi was so consumed with winning that the thought of taking the court for a Grand Slam final would make him sick, but this was different. He was older—at 35, Agassi was the oldest man to make the U.S. Open Final in 31 years—and wiser and, most importantly, his priorities had changed. Agassi and his wife Steffi Graf, a former No. 1 player herself, are the proud parents of two children and Agassi was more con-cerned about playtime with his three-year-old son and 23-month-old daughter than his opponent on the other side of the net.

Not that Agassi didn't care. Throughout the U.S. Open he displayed a passion, intensity and will to win that was unmatched by his peers. Agassi's epic, five-set victory over rising American star James Blake in the quarterfinals was the highlight of the tournament and one of the best matches of the year. But to beat Roger Federer, Agassi knew he would need a lot more than passion and willpower; he would need to play the best match of his career.

Federer was not only ranked No. 1 in the world and considered by many to be the greatest player of all-time, but he was also nearly unbeatable in finals, having won 21 straight entering the match. And the Swiss-born Federer wasn't about to help the American reach a fairy tale ending. After dropping the first set, Agassi took control in the second, attacking Federer's serve with vicious returns and controlling rallies by spraying balls all over the court. Agassi won the set 6-3 and used the same approach in the third to break Federer and go up 4-2. Federer was clearly rattled and the pro-Agassi crowd was rocking.

But Federer summoned his inner-cham-pion and broke back to regain the momen-tum. Back on serve that neither man would crack, they went into the third-set tiebreaker like two heavyweight champions going into the final round, matching blow

for blow. In the tiebreaker, Federer delivered the knockout punch by dominating 7-1. Having seized control of the match, Federer cruised in the fourth set, 6-1, to win the Open.

The record will show that Federer beat Agassi for his sixth Grand Slam title, but Agassi was the real winner of the U.S. Open. In May, with his ailing back giving him fits, Agassi lost in the first-round to qualifier Jarkko Nieminen. After deciding not to play in Wimbledon, he even considered retiring, but then he quickly came to the conclusion that he wasn't washed up yet. Agassi called his trainer, Gil Reyes, and said, "I ain't finished. Let's get it right. Let's fix it."

And they did. Agassi worked tirelessly on his fitness and rehabilitating his back for at least one more run, his wife and children never far from his mind. He took solace in the fact that no matter what happened he would always be considered a champion to his wife and children. Agassi also played to the crowd more than ever, was a ham in press conferences and became one of the most well liked players on the tour. Blake, who lost the heartbreaking five-setter, which ended in the wee hours of the morning, went so far as to say, "If I was in the stands, I'd cheer for him too."

That's because Agassi was no longer the wild-haired, rock-the-establishment rebel he was when he first burst onto the scene nearly 20 years ago. He was clearly not the same person who once spit on an umpire in the U.S. Open and skipped Wimbledon because tournament directors wouldn't allow him to wear his colorful shirts. The new Agassi was respectful, somewhat reserved, polished and socially conscious. He teared up during one press conference at the Open when he was asked about the devastation caused by Hurricane Katrina on the Gulf Coast and vowed to do everything he could to help. Shortly thereafter, the USTA gave $500,000 to the Red Cross.

No matter what else Agassi does in his career—if he does anything at all—he will be forever remembered as the people's champion at this U.S. Open. And even if he doesn't win another match, Agassi will always remain No. 1 in his family's eyes. For him, that is more important than anything. "It's not about defining myself by what happens [on the court] anymore," said Agassi. "I pretty much know who I am, and I work on being more of that every day. Having a beautiful family makes any disappointments a bit easier and the good a lot better."

Over the last two years there's been no player better than Federer. With efficient, purposeful ground strokes, deadly return and methodical attacking approach, Federer has no peer. But after losing in the semifinals of the Australian and French, he showed he was human and certainly beatable. At least that's what Andy Roddick thought when he met Federer in the final at Wimbledon. Roddick came into the match confident and playing better than ever with an improved backhand and serve-and-volley game. But he was no match for Federer who had an answer for everything Roddick threw at him and produced an easy 6-3, 6-4, 7-6 victory. "I did everything I could," said Roddick. "I tried going to his forehand and coming in; he passed me. I tried to go to his backhand and come in; he passed me. Tried staying back; he figured out a way to pass me, even though I was at the baseline. It's not like I have a lot of questions."

After his victory at Wimbledon—his third straight—and the win over Agassi, Federer was unquestionably on his way to becoming the best ever in the mind of someone who faced some pretty good players in his day. "He's the best I've ever played against," said Agassi after the U.S. Open. "There's nowhere to go. Other guys you play, there's a safety zone. He plays the game in a special way. I haven't seen it before."

Tennis has never seen anything like the Williams sisters. When they are on their game, there's nobody better, but too often Venus and Serena have been more interested in their clothing lines and acting careers than tennis. But there were more reasons to the Williams sisters' sudden disappearance from the top of the rankings than disenchantment with the game. Both Venus and Serena were plagued with injuries and they were deeply affected by the tragic murder of their oldest sister, Yetunde Price, in September 2003. "To be in the situation I've been placed in for a little over a year, it's not easy to come out and perform your best," said Serena.

Serena summoned her inner strength to win the Australian Open—her first Grand Slam title in more than two years—with a pair of terrific performances in the semis and finals. After dropping the first set to Maria Sharapova in the semis, Serena fought back to win the next two 7-5, 8-6. Then after falling behind 4-1 to Lindsay Davenport in the final, Serena won 12 of the next 15 games to take the title. Venus demonstrated the same fighting sprit to win Wimbledon by refusing to accept defeat. She became the lowest seeded player (No. 14) in the open era to win Wimbledon and was the first woman to twice save championship point and win. How dramatic was Venus' 4-6, 7-6, 9-7 victory over Davenport? She was two points from losing eight times, but fought back in the longest women's final (2 hours, 45 minutes) in Wimbledon history. Afterward, Venus bounced around Centre Court, her infectious smile captivating the capacity crowd at every turn, while Davenport tried to figure out what happened. "She just took it away from me," said a stunned Davenport. "She was … incredible."

The other Grand Slam champions had their moments, but they were short-lived. Marat Safin won the Australian Open, his first Slam in five years, with a dramatic victory over Federer in the semis and then dispatched native son Lleyton Hewitt in the final. But Safin was barely heard of for the rest of the year. Young Spaniard Rafael Nadal became tennis' next big thing after he won the French Open—beating Federer in the semis—but he flamed out in the year's final two Slams. On the women's side, Justine Henin-Hardenne and Kim Clijsters won the French Open and U.S. Open respectively, but while they may be tennis' future stars they lack the flash and marketability of the Williams sisters. With two Slams, Federer was a good as ever and, at 24-years-old, is a threat eclipse Pete Sampras' record of 14 Grand Slam titles if he maintains his dominance. But it was Agassi who gave tennis fans the most to applaud in 2005. Whether or not he ever plays another set, we will always remember his glorious run one summer in Flushing.

FOR THE RECORD·2004-2005

2005 Grand Slam Champions

Australian Open
Men's Singles

	Winner	Runner-up	Score
Quarterfinals	Marat Safin	Dominik Hrbaty	6–2, 6–4, 6–2
	Roger Federer	Andre Agassi	6–3, 6–4, 6–4
	Lleyton Hewitt	David Nalbandian	6–3, 6–2, 1–6, 3–6, 10-8
	Andy Roddick	Nikolay Davydenko	6–3, 7–5, 4–1 ret.
Semifinals	Marat Safin	Roger Federer	5–7, 6–4, 5–7, 7–6(6), 9-7
	Lleyton Hewitt	Andy Roddick	3–6, 7–6(3), 7–6(4), 6-1
Final	Marat Safin	Lleyton Hewitt	1–6, 6-3, 6–4, 6–4

Women's Singles

	Winner	Runner-up	Score
Quarterfinals	Lindsay Davenport	Alicia Molik	6–4, 4–6, 9–7
	Nathalie Dechy	Patty Schnyder	5–7, 6–1, 7–5
	Maria Sharapova	Svetlana Kuznetsova	4–6, 4–6, 6–2
	Serena Williams	Amelie Mauresmo	6–2, 6–2
Semifinals	Lindsay Davenport	Nathalie Dechy	2–6, 7–6 (7–5),6–4
	Serena Williams	Maria Sharapova	2–6, 7–5, 8-6
Final	Serena Williams	Lindsay Davenport	2-6, 6-3, 6-0

Doubles

	Winner	Runner-up	Score
Men's Final	Wayne Black/ Kevin Ullyett	Bob Bryan/ Mike Bryan	6–4, 6–4
Women's Final	Svetlana Kuznetsova/ Alicia Molik	Lindsay Davenport/ Corina Morariu	6–3, 6–4
Mixed Final	Scott Draper/ Samantha Stoser	Kevin Ullyett/ Liezel Huber	6–2, 2–6, 7–6 (10-6)

French Open
Men's Singles

	Winner	Runner-up	Score
Quarterfinals	Roger Federer	Victor. Hanescu	6-2, 7-6, (7-3), 6-3
	Rafael Nadal	David Ferrer	7-5, 6-2, 6-0
	Nikolay Davydenko	Tommy Robredo	3-6, 6-1, 6-2, 4-6, 6-4
	Guillermo Canas	Mariano Puerta.	2-3, 6-3, 6-1, 3-6, 4-6
Semifinals	Rafael Nadal	Roger Federer	3-6, 6-4, 4-6; 3-6
	Mariano Puerta	Nikolay Davydenko	3-6, 7-5, 6-2, 4-6, 4-6
Final	Rafael Nadal	Mariano Puerta	6–7(6), 6–3, 6–1, 7–5

Women's Singles

	Winner	Runner-up	Score
Quarterfinals	Lindsay Davenport	Mary Pierce	3-6, 2-6
	Elena Likhovtseva	Sesil Karatantcheva	2-6, 6-4, 6-4
	Nadia Petrova	Ana Ivanovic	6-2, 6-2
	Justine Henin-Hardenne	Maria Sharapova	6-4, 6-2
Semifinals	Mary Pierce	Elena Likhovtseva	6-1, 6-1
	Justine Henin-Hardenne	Nadia Petrova	6-2, 6-3
Final	Justine Henin-Hardenne	Mary Pierce	6–1, 6–1

French Open *(Cont.)*

Doubles

	Winner	Runner-Up	Score
Men's Final	Max Mirnyi/ Jonas Bjorkman	Mike Bryan/ Bob Bryan	2-6, 6-1, 6-4
Women's Final	Paola Suarez/ Virginia Pascual	Liezel Huber/ Cara Black	6-0, 6-3 4-6, 6-3, 6-3
Mixed Final	Daniela Hantuchova/ Fabrice Santoro	Martina Navratilova/ Leander Paes	3-6, 6-3, 6-2

Wimbledon

Men's Singles

	Winner	Runner-Up	Score
Quarterfinals	Roger Federer	Fernando Gonzalez	7–5, 6–2, 7–6 (7–2)
	Lleyton Hewitt	Feliciano Lopez	7–5, 6–4, 7–6 (7–2)
	Thomas Johansson	David Nalbandian	7–6 (7–5), 6–2, 6–2
	Andy Roddick	Sebastien Grosjean	3–6, 6–2, 6–1, 3–6, 6–3
Semifinals	Roger Federer	Lleyton Hewitt	6–3, 6–4, 7–6 (7–2)
	Andy Roddick	Thomas Johansson	6–7, 6–2, 7–6 (12–10), 7–6 (7–5)
Final	Roger Federer	Andy Roddick	6–2, 7–6 (7–2), 6–4

Women's Singles

	Winner	Runner-Up	Score
Quarterfinals	Lindsay Davenport	Svetlana Kuznetsova	7–6 (7–1), 6–3
	Maria Sharapova	Nadia Petrova	7–6 (8–6), 6–3
	Amelie Mauresmo	Anastasia Myskina	6–3, 6–4
	Venus Williams	Mary Pierce	6–0, 7–6 (12–10)
Semifinals	Venus Williams	Maria Sharapova	7–6 (7–2), 6–1
	Lindsay Davenport	Amelie Mauresmo	6–7, 7–6 (7–4), 6–4
Final	Venus Williams	Lindsay Davenport	4–6, 7–6 (7–2), 9–7

Doubles

	Winner	Runner-Up	Score
Men's Final	Stephen Huss/ Wesley Moodie	Bob Bryan/ Mike Bryan	7–6 (7–4), 6–3, 6–7 (2–7), 6–3
Women's Final	Cara Black/ Liezel Huber	Svetlana Kuznetsova/ Amelie Mauresmo	6–2, 6–1
Mixed Final	Mhesh Bhupathi/ Mary Pierce	Paul Hanley/ Tatiana Perebiynis	6–4, 6–2

U.S. Open

Men's Singles

	WINNER	RUNNER-UP	SCORE
Quarterfinals	Andre Agassi	James Blake	3-6, 3-6, 6-3, 6-3, 7-6, (8-6)
	Robby Ginepri	Guillermo Coria	4-6, 6-1, 7-5, 3-6, 7-5
	Roger Federer	David Nalbandian	6-2, 6-4, 6-4
	Lleyton Hewitt	Jarkko Nieminen	2-6, 6-1, 3-6, 6-3, 6-1
Semifinals	Roger Federer	Lleyton Hewitt	6-3, 7-6, (7-0),4-6, 6-3
	Andre Agassi	Robby Ginepri	6-4, 5-7, 6-3, 4-6, 6-3
Final	Roger Federer	Andre Agassi	6-3, 2-6, 7-6, (7-1), 6-1

U.S. Open (Cont.)
Women's Singles

	Winner	Runner-Up	Score
Quarterfinals	Maria Sharapova	Nadia Petrova	7-5, 4-6, 6-4
	Kim Clijsters	Venus Williams	4-6, 7-5, 6-1
	Elena Dementieva	Lindsay Davenport	6-1, 3-6, 7-6, (8-6)
	Mary Pierce	Amelie Mauresmo	6-4, 6-1
Semifinals	Kim Clijsters	Maria Sharapova	6-2, 6-7, 6-3
	Mary Pierce	Elena Dementieva	3-6, 6-2, 6-2
Final	Kim Clijsters	Mary Pierce	6-3, 6-1

Doubles

	Winner	Runner-Up	Score
Men's Final	Mike Bryan/ Bob Bryan	Max Mirnyi/ Jonas Bjorkman	6-1, 6-4
Women's Final	Lisa Raymond/ Samantha Stosur	Elena Dementieva/ Flavia Penetta	6-2, 5-7, 6-3
Mixed Final	Daniela Huntuchova/ Mahesh Bhupathi	Katrina Srebotnik/ Nenad Zimonjic	6-4, 6-2

Major Tournament Results

Men's Tour (late 2004)

Date	Tournament	Site	Singles Winner	Surface	Prize Money ($)
Oct 10	Lyon Grand Prix	Lyon, France	Robin Soderling	Indoor Carpet	800,000
Oct 24	Madrid Masters	Madrid, Spain	Marat Safin	OutdoorHard	2,250,000
Oct 31	St. Petersberg Open	St. Petersberg Russia	Mikhail Youzhney	Indoor Hard	975,000
Oct 31	Swiss Indoor	Basel, Switzerland	Jiri Novak	Indoora Carpet	1,000,000
Oct 31	Stockholm Opem	Stockholem, Sweden	Thomas Johansson	Indoors Hard	800,000
Nov 7	Paris Masters	Paris,	Marat Safin	Indoors Carpet	2,250,000

Men's Tour (through Oct 3, 2005)

Date	Tournament	Site	Winner	Surface	Prize Money ($)
Jan 8	Qatar Open	Doha, Qatar	Roger Federer	Outdoor Hard	1,000,000
Jan 30	Australian Open	Melbourne	Marat Safin	Outdoor Hard	5,952,601
Feb 13	Marseille Open	Marseille, France	Joachim Johansson	Indoor Hard	585,000
Feb 20	ABM/Amro	Rotterdam,	Roger Federer	Indoor Hard	935,000
Feb 27	Dubai Open	Dubai, UAE	Roger Federer	Outdoor Hard	975,000
Mar 20	Pacific Life Open	Indian Wells, California	Roger Federer	Outdoor Hard	2,725,000
Mar 28	Nasdaq 100O Open	Miami	Roger Federer	Outdoor Hard	3,200,000
Apr 17	Monte Carlo Masters	Monte-Carlo, Monaco	Rafael Nadal Johansson	Outdoor Clay	2,285,000
Apr 24	Open SEAT Godó	Barcelona, Spain	Rafael Nadal	Outdoor Clay	1,040,000
May 1	Estoril Open	Estoril, Portugal	Gaston Gaudio	Outdoor Clay	625,000
May 1	BMW Open	Munich,	David Nalbandian	Outdoor Clay	370,000
May 8	Italian Masters	Rome	Rafael Nadal	Outdoor Clay	2,285,000
May 15	Hamburg Masters	Hamburg Germany	Roger Federer	Outdoor Clay	2,285,000

Men's Tour (through September 19, 2005) (Cont.)

Start Date	Tournament	Site	Winner	Surface	Prize Money
June 5	French Open	Paris	Rafael Nadal	Outdoor Clay	5,900,000
June 12	Gerry Weber Open	Halle, Germany	Roger Federer	Outdoor Grass	800,000
June 19	Ordina Open	'S-Hertog'bosch, Netherlands	Mario Ancic	Outdoor Grass	370,000
July 3	Wimbledon	Wimbledon	Roger Federer	Outdoor Grass	5,750,000
July 24	Mercedes Cup	Stuttgart	Rafael Nadal	Outdoor Clay	720,000
July 31	RCA Championship	Indianapolis	Robby Ginepri	Outdoor Hard	575,000
July 31	Generali Open	Kitzbuhel, Austria	Gaston Gaudio	Outdoor Clay	760,000
Aug 7	Legg Mason Classic	Wash., D.C.	Andy Roddick	Outdoor Hard	575,000
Aug 14	Tennis Masters Series	Montreal	Rafael Nadal	Outdoor Hard	2,200,000
Aug 21	Western & Southern	Cinncinati	Roger Federer	Outdoor Hard	2,200,000
Sept 11	U.S. Open	New York City	Roger Federer	Outdoor Hard	17,700,000
Sept 18	China Open	Beijing	Rafael Nadal	Outdoor Hard	475,000

Women's Tour (Late 2004)

Date	Tournament	Site	Winner	Runner-Up	Score
Sept 22	Sparkassen Cup	Leipzig, Germany	Anastasia Myskina	Justine Henin-Hardenne	3–6, 6–3, 6–3
Sept 29	Ladies Kremlin Cup	Moscow	Anastasia Myskina	Amelie Mauresmo	6–2, 6–4
Sept 29	Japan Open	Tokyo	Maria Sharapova	Aniko Kapros	2–6, 6–2, 7–6 (7-5)
Oct 13	Swisscom Challenge	Zurich	Justine Henin-Hardenne	Jelena Dokic	6–0, 6–4
Oct 20	Generali Ladies Open	Linz, Aust.	Ai Sugiyama	Nadia Petrova	7–5, 6–4
Nov 3	Sanex Championships	Los Angeles	Kim Clijsters	Amelie Mauresmo	6–2, 6–0

Women's Tour (through September 20, 2005)

Start Date	Tournament	Site	Winner	Runner-Up	Score
Jan 15	Medibank Int'l	Sydney	Alicia Molik	Samantha Stosur	6–7, (5-7), 6-4, 7-5
Jan 30	Australian Open	Melbourne	Serena Williams	L. Davenport	2-6, 6-3, 6-0
Feb 6	Pan Pacific Open	Tokyo	Maria Sharapova	L. Davenport	6-1, 6-3, 7-6, (7-5)
Feb 21	Qatar Open	Doha, Qatar	Maria Sharapova	Alicia Molik	4-6, 6-1, 6-4
Mar 19	Pacific Life Open	Indian Wells, California	Kim Clijsters	Lindsay Davenport	6-4, 4-6, 6-2
Apr 3	NASDAQ-100 Open	Miami	Kim Clijsters	Maria Sharapova	6-3, 7-5
Apr 10	Bausch & Lomb Championships	Amelia Island, Florida	Lindsay Davenport	Silvia Farina Elia	7-5, 7-5
Apr 17	Family Circle Cup	Charleston, S Carolina	Justin Henin-Hardenne	Elena Dementieva	7-5, 6-4
May 1	J&S Cup	Warsaw	Justin Henin-Hardenne	Svetlana Kuznetsova	3-6, 6-2, 7-5
May 8	German Open	Berlin	Justin Henin-Hardenne	Nadia Petrova	6-3, 4-6, 6-3
May 15	Italia Masters	Rome	Amelie Mauresmo	Patty Schnyder	2-6, 6-3,6-4
May 21	Int'l de Strasbourg	Strasbourg,Fra	Anabel Medina Garrigues	Marta Domachowska	6-4, 6-3
June 5	French Open	Paris	Juntine Henin-Hardenne	Mary Pierce	6-1, 6-1
June 18	Hastings Direct Int'l Championships	Eastbourne, England	Kim Clijsters	Vera Douchevina	7-5, 6-0
July 2	Wimbledon	Wimbledon	Venus Williams	L. Davenport	4-6, 7-6, (7-4), 9-7
July 31	Bank of the West	Stanford	Kim Clijsters	Venus Williams	7-5, 6-2
Aug 7	Acura Classic	San Diego	Mary Pierce	Ai Sugiyama	6-0, 6-3
Aug 14	JP Morgan Chase Open	Carson, CA	Kim Clijsters	Daniela Hantuchova	6-4, 6-1
Aug 21	Rogers Cup	Toronto	Kim Clijsters	Justine Henin-Hardenne	7-5, 6-1
Aug 27	Pilot Pen Int'l	New Haven,CT	L. Davenport	Amelia Mauresmo	6-4, 6-4
Sept. 11	U.S. Open	New York City	Kim Clijsters	Mary Pierce	6-3, 6-1

2004 Singles Leaders

Men

Rank	Player	Country	Points	Events
2.	......Roger Federer	SUI	6335	20
1.	......Andy Roddick	USA	3655	23
3.	......Lleyton Hewitt	AUS	3590	20
4	......Marat Safin	RUS	3060	24
5.	......Carlos Moya	ESP	2520	23
6	......Tim Henman	GBR	2465	20
7	......Guillermo Coria	ARG	2400	19
8.	......Andre Agassi	USA	2100	19
9.	......David Nalbandian	ARG	1945	19
10	.....Gaston Gaudio	ARG	1920	24

Note: Compiled by the ATP Tour, through 2004 season.

Women

Rank	Player	Country	Points
1.	......Lindsay Davenport	USA	4760
2.	......Amelia Mauresmo	FRA	4546
3.	......Anastasia Myskina	RUS	4012
4.	......Maria Sharapova	RUS	3536
5.	......Svetlana Kuznetsova	RUS	3533
6.	......Elena Dementieva	RUS	3448
7.	......Serena Williams	USA	3128
8.	......Junstine Henin-Hardenne	BEL	2884
9.	......Venus Williams	USA	2400
10.	....Jennifer Capriati	USA	2359

Note: Compiled by the WTA, as of Nov 10, 2004.

Helping Hand

At the 2005 US Open, menswear received almost as much comment as the scores. Rafael Nadal's Aquaman tank top made it respectable for the men's draw to embark on inane discussions about capri pants and skin exposure and fabric swatches. Past US Opens have produced individual disasters (Andre Agassi once showed up as a pirate, in gold earrings, a bandana and sideburns) but Nadal was hardly alone this year: Nearly every court featured some player flashing his manly guns. Once the bastion of guys nicknamed Muslces (Ken Rosewall) or Jimbo (Jimmy Connors), tennis today is all about looking for Himbo. "It's the tipping point," said Billie Jean King, the sport's expert on breaking sexual barriers. "We're much more alike than we used to be. Why not? I love it. I just wish I coud see more of their legs."

National Team Competition

2004 Davis Cup World Group Final

Spain def. U.S. 3–2, Dec 3–5, 2004 in Sevilla
- Moya (Esp) def. Fish (U.S.) 6–4, 6–2, 6–3
- Nadal (Esp) def. Roddick (U.S.) 6–7 (6), 6–2, 7–6 (6), 6–2
- B. Bryan and M. Bryan (U.S.) def. Ferrero and Robredo (Esp) 6–0, 6–3, 6–2
- Moya (Esp) def Roddick (U.S.) 6–2, 7–6 (1), 7–6 (5)
- Fish (U.S.) def. Robredo (Esp) 7–6 (8), 6–2

2005 Davis Cup World Group Tournament

FIRST ROUND

Slovak Republic def. Spain 4–1
Netherlands def. Switzerland 2–3
Australia def. Austria 5–0
Argentina def. Czech Republic 5–0
Russia def. Chile 4–1
France def. Sweden 3–2
Romania def. Belarus 3–2
Croatia def. U.S. 3–2

QUARTERFINAL ROUND

Slovak Republic def. Netherlands 4–1
Argentina def. Australia 4–1
Russia def. France 3–2
Croatia def. Romania 4–1

SEMIFINALS

Slovak Republic def. Argentina 4-1
- Karol Beck (Slo) def. Guillermo Coria (Arg) 7-5, 6-4, 6-4
- David Nalbandian (Arg) def Dominik Hrbaty (Slo) 3-6, 7-5, 7-5, 6-3
- Karol Beck and Michael Mertinak (Slo) def. David Nalbandian and Mariano Puerta (Arg) 7-6, (7-5), 7-5, 7-6, (6-5)
- Dominik Hrbaty (Slo) def. Guillermo Coria (Arg) 7-6, (7-2), 6-2, 6-3
- Karol Kuchera (Slo) def. Mariano Puerta (Arg) 4-6, 6-3, 2-1

Croatia def. Russia, 3-2
- Nikolay Davydenko (Rus) def. Mario Ancic (Cro) 7-5, 6-4, 5-7, 6-4
- Ivan Ljubicic (Cro) def. Mikhail Youzhny (Rus) 3-6, 6-3, 6-4, 4-6, 6-4
- Mario Ancic and Ivan Ljubicic (Cro) def. Igor Andreev and Dmitry Tursonov (Rus) 6-2, 4-6, 7-6, (7-5), 3-6, 6-4
- Ivan Ljubicic (Cro) def. Nikolay Davydenko (Rus) 6-3, 7-6, (7-6), 6-4
- Dmitry Tursunov (Rus) def. Ivo Karlovic (Cro) 6-4, 6-4

FINAL: Slovak Republic versus Croatia to be held Dec. 2-4, 2005.

2004 Federation Cup World Group Tournament

QUARTERFINALS

Russia def. Italy 4-1
USA def. Belgium 5-0
Spain def. Argentina 3-2
France def. Austria 4-1

SEMIFINALS

Russia def. USA 4-1
France def. Spain 3-1

FINALS

Russia def. France 3-2

Note: Finals were held Sept. 17-18, 2004, in Paris.

Grand Slam Tournaments

MEN

Australian Championships

Year	Winner	Finalist	Score
1905	Rodney Heath	A. H. Curtis	4–6, 6–3, 6–4, 6–4
1906	Tony Wilding	H. A. Parker	6–0, 6–4, 6–4
1907	Horace M. Rice	H. A. Parker	6–3, 6–4, 6–4
1908	Fred Alexander	A. W. Dunlop	3–6, 3–6, 6–0, 6–2, 6–3
1909	Tony Wilding	E. F. Parker	6–1, 7–5, 6–2
1910	Rodney Heath	Horace M. Rice	6–4, 6–3, 6–2
1911	Norman Brookes	Horace M. Rice	6–1, 6–2, 6–3
1912	J. Cecil Parke	A. E. Beamish	3–6, 6–3, 1–6, 6–1, 7–5
1913	E. F. Parker	H. A. Parker	2–6, 6–1, 6–2, 6–3
1914	Pat O'Hara Wood	G. L. Patterson	6–4, 6–3, 5–7, 6–1
1915	Francis G. Lowe	Horace M. Rice	4–6, 6–1, 6–1, 6–4
1916–18	No tournament		
1919	A. R. F. Kingscote	E. O. Pockley	6–4, 6–0, 6–3
1920	Pat O'Hara Wood	Ron Thomas	6–3, 4–6, 6–8, 6–1, 6–3
1921	Rhys H. Gemmell	A. Hedeman	7–5, 6–1, 6–4
1922	Pat O'Hara Wood	Gerald Patterson	6–0, 3–6, 3–6, 6–3, 6–2
1923	Pat O'Hara Wood	C. B. St John	6–1, 6–1, 6–3
1924	James Anderson	R. E. Schlesinger	6–3, 6–4, 3–6, 5–7, 6–3
1925	James Anderson	Gerald Patterson	11–9, 2–6, 6–2, 6–3
1926	John Hawkes	J. Willard	6–1, 6–3, 6–1
1927	Gerald Patterson	John Hawkes	3–6, 6–4, 3–6, 18–16, 6–3
1928	Jean Borotra	R. O. Cummings	6–4, 6–1, 4–6, 5–7, 6–3
1929	John C. Gregory	R. E. Schlesinger	6–2, 6–2, 5–7, 7–5
1930	Gar Moon	Harry C. Hopman	6–3, 6–1, 6–3
1931	Jack Crawford	Harry C. Hopman	6–4, 6–2, 2–6, 6–1
1932	Jack Crawford	Harry C. Hopman	4–6, 6–3, 3–6, 6–3, 6–1
1933	Jack Crawford	Keith Gledhill	2–6, 7–5, 6–3, 6–2
1934	Fred Perry	Jack Crawford	6–3, 7–5, 6–1
1935	Jack Crawford	Fred Perry	2–6, 6–4, 6–4, 6–4
1936	Adrian Quist	Jack Crawford	6–2, 6–3, 4–6, 3–6, 9–7
1937	Vivian B. McGrath	John Bromwich	6–3, 1–6, 6–0, 2–6, 6–1
1938	Don Budge	John Bromwich	6–4, 6–2, 6–1
1939	John Bromwich	Adrian Quist	6–4, 6–1, 6–3
1940	Adrian Quist	Jack Crawford	6–3, 6–1, 6–2
1941–45	No tournament		
1946	John Bromwich	Dinny Pails	5–7, 6–3, 7–5, 3–6, 6–2
1947	Dinny Pails	John Bromwich	4–6, 6–4, 3–6, 7–5, 8–6
1948	Adrian Quist	John Bromwich	6–4, 3–6, 6–3, 2–6, 6–3
1949	Frank Sedgman	Ken McGregor	6–3, 6–3, 6–2
1950	Frank Sedgman	Ken McGregor	6–3, 6–4, 4–6, 6–1
1951	Richard Savitt	Ken McGregor	6–3, 2–6, 6–3, 6–1
1952	Ken McGregor	Frank Sedgman	7–5, 12–10, 2–6, 6–2
1953	Ken Rosewall	Mervyn Rose	6–0, 6–3, 6–4
1954	Mervyn Rose	Rex Hartwig	6–2, 0–6, 6–4, 6–2
1955	Ken Rosewall	Lew Hoad	9–7, 6–4, 6–4
1956	Lew Hoad	Ken Rosewall	6–4, 3–6, 6–4, 7–5
1957	Ashley Cooper	Neale Fraser	6–3, 9–11, 6–4, 6–2
1958	Ashley Cooper	Mal Anderson	7–5, 6–3, 6–4
1959	Alex Olmedo	Neale Fraser	6–1, 6–2, 3–6, 6–3
1960	Rod Laver	Neale Fraser	5–7, 3–6, 6–3, 8–6, 8–6
1961	Roy Emerson	Rod Laver	1–6, 6–3, 7–5, 6–4
1962	Rod Laver	Roy Emerson	8–6, 0–6, 6–4, 6–4
1963	Roy Emerson	Ken Fletcher	6–3, 6–3, 6–1
1964	Roy Emerson	Fred Stolle	6–3, 6–4, 6–2
1965	Roy Emerson	Fred Stolle	7–9, 2–6, 6–4, 7–5, 6–1
1966	Roy Emerson	Arthur Ashe	6–4, 6–8, 6–2, 6–3
1967	Roy Emerson	Arthur Ashe	6–4, 6–1, 6–1
1968	Bill Bowrey	Juan Gisbert	7–5, 2–6, 9–7, 6–4
1969*	Rod Laver	Andres Gimeno	6–3, 6–4, 7–5
1970	Arthur Ashe	Dick Crealy	6–4, 9–7, 6–2

*Became Open (amateur and professional) in 1969.

MEN (Cont.)
Australian Championships (Cont.)

Year	Winner	Finalist	Score
1971	Ken Rosewall	Arthur Ashe	6–1, 7–5, 6–3
1972	Ken Rosewall	Mal Anderson	7–6, 6–3, 7–5
1973	John Newcombe	Onny Parun	6–3, 6–7, 7–5, 6–1
1974	Jimmy Connors	Phil Dent	7–6, 6–4, 4–6, 6–3
1975	John Newcombe	Jimmy Connors	7–5, 3–6, 6–4, 7–5
1976	Mark Edmondson	John Newcombe	6–7, 6–3, 7–6, 6–1
1977 (Jan)	Roscoe Tanner	Guillermo Vilas	6–3, 6–3, 6–3
1977 (Dec)	Vitas Gerulaitis	John Lloyd	6–3, 7–6, 5–7, 3–6, 6–2
1978	Guillermo Vilas	John Marks	6–4, 6–4, 3–6, 6–3
1979	Guillermo Vilas	John Sadri	7–6, 6–3, 6–2
1980	Brian Teacher	Kim Warwick	7–5, 7–6, 6–3
1981	Johan Kriek	Steve Denton	6–2, 7–6, 6–7, 6–4
1982	Johan Kriek	Steve Denton	6–3, 6–3, 6–2
1983	Mats Wilander	Ivan Lendl	6–1, 6–4, 6–4
1984	Mats Wilander	Kevin Curren	6–7, 6–4, 7–6, 6–2
1985 (Dec)	Stefan Edberg	Mats Wilander	6–4, 6–3, 6–3
1987 (Jan)	Stefan Edberg	Pat Cash	6–3, 6–4, 3–6, 5–7, 6–3
1988	Mats Wilander	Pat Cash	6–3, 6–7, 3–6, 6–1, 8–6
1989	Ivan Lendl	Miloslav Mecir	6–2, 6–2, 6–2
1990	Ivan Lendl	Stefan Edberg	4–6, 7–6, 5–2, ret.
1991	Boris Becker	Ivan Lendl	1–6, 6–4, 6–4, 6–4
1992	Jim Courier	Stefan Edberg	6–3, 3–6, 6–4, 6–2
1993	Jim Courier	Stefan Edberg	6–2, 6–1, 2–6, 7–5
1994	Pete Sampras	Todd Martin	7–6, 6–4, 6–4
1995	Andre Agassi	Pete Sampras	4–6, 6–1, 7–6, 6–4
1996	Boris Becker	Michael Chang	6–2, 6–4, 2–6, 6–2
1997	Pete Sampras	Carlos Moya	6–2, 6–3, 6–3
1998	Petr Korda	Marcelo Ríos	6–2, 6–2, 6–2
1999	Yevgeny Kafelnikov	Thomas Enqvist	4–6, 6–0, 6–3, 7–6
2000	Andre Agassi	Yevgeny Kafelnikov	3–6, 6–3, 6–2, 6–4
2001	Andre Agassi	Arnaud Clement	6–4, 6–2, 6–2
2002	Thomas Johansson	Marat Safin	3–6, 6–4, 6–4, 7–6 (7-4)
2003	Andre Agassi	Rainer Schuettler	6–2, 6–2, 6–1
2004	Roger Federer	Marat Safin	7–6 (7-3), 6–4, 6–2
2005	Marat Safin	Lleyton Hewitt	1-6, 6-3, 6-4, 6-4

French Championships

Year	Winner	Finalist	Score
1925†	Rene Lacoste	Jean Borotra	7–5, 6–1, 6–4
1926	Henri Cochet	Rene Lacoste	6–2, 6–4, 6–3
1927	Rene Lacoste	Bill Tilden	6–4, 4–6, 5–7, 6–3, 11–9
1928	Henri Cochet	Rene Lacoste	5–7, 6–3, 6–1, 6–3
1929	Rene Lacoste	Jean Borotra	6–3, 2–6, 6–0, 2–6, 8–6
1930	Henri Cochet	Bill Tilden	3–6, 8–6, 6–3, 6–1
1931	Jean Borotra	Claude Boussus	2–6, 6–4, 7–5, 6–4
1932	Henri Cochet	Giorgio de Stefani	6–0, 6–4, 4–6, 6–3
1933	Jack Crawford	Henri Cochet	8–6, 6–1, 6–3
1934	Gottfried von Cramm	Jack Crawford	6–4, 7–9, 3–6, 7–5, 6–3
1935	Fred Perry	Gottfried von Cramm	6–3, 3–6, 6–1, 6–3
1936	Gottfried von Cramm	Fred Perry	6–0, 2–6, 6–2, 2–6, 6–0
1937	Henner Henkel	Henry Austin	6–1, 6–4, 6–3
1938	Don Budge	Roderick Menzel	6–3, 6–2, 6–4
1939	Don McNeill	Bobby Riggs	7–5, 6–0, 6–3
1940	No tournament		
1941‡	Bernard Destremau	n/a	n/a
1942‡	Bernard Destremau	n/a	n/a
1943‡	Yvon Petra	n/a	n/a
1944‡	Yvon Petra	n/a	n/a
1945‡	Yvon Petra	Bernard Destremau	7–5, 6–4, 6–2
1946	Marcel Bernard	Jaroslav Drobny	3–6, 2–6, 6–1, 6–4, 6–3
1947	Joseph Asboth	Eric Sturgess	8–6, 7–5, 6–4
1948	Frank Parker	Jaroslav Drobny	6–4, 7–5, 5–7, 8–6
1949	Frank Parker	Budge Patty	6–3, 1–6, 6–1, 6–4
1950	Budge Patty	Jaroslav Drobny	6–1, 6–2, 3–6, 5–7, 7–5
1951	Jaroslav Drobny	Eric Sturgess	6–3, 6–3, 6–3
1952	Jaroslav Drobny	Frank Sedgman	6–2, 6–0, 3–6, 6–4
1953	Ken Rosewall	Vic Seixas	6–3, 6–4, 1–6, 6–2

MEN *(Cont.)*
French Championships *(Cont.)*

Year	Winner	Finalist	Score
1954	Tony Trabert	Arthur Larsen	6–4, 7–5, 6–1
1955	Tony Trabert	Sven Davidson	2–6, 6–1, 6–4, 6–2
1956	Lew Hoad	Sven Davidson	6–4, 8–6, 6–3
1957	Sven Davidson	Herbie Flam	6–3, 6–4, 6–4
1958	Mervyn Rose	Luis Ayala	6–3, 6–4, 6–4
1959	Nicola Pietrangeli	Ian Vermaak	3–6, 6–3, 6–4, 6–1
1960	Nicola Pietrangeli	Luis Ayala	3–6, 6–3, 6–4, 4–6, 6–3
1961	Manuel Santana	Nicola Pietrangeli	4–6, 6–1, 3–6, 6–0, 6–2
1962	Rod Laver	Roy Emerson	3–6, 2–6, 6–3, 9–7, 6–2
1963	Roy Emerson	Pierre Darmon	3–6, 6–1, 6–4, 6–4
1964	Manuel Santana	Nicola Pietrangeli	6–3, 6–1, 4–6, 7–5
1965	Fred Stolle	Tony Roche	3–6, 6–0, 6–2, 6–3
1966	Tony Roche	Istvan Gulyas	6–1, 6–4, 7–5
1967	Roy Emerson	Tony Roche	6–1, 6–4, 2–6, 6–2
1968*	Ken Rosewall	Rod Laver	6–3, 6–1, 2–6, 6–2
1969	Rod Laver	Ken Rosewall	6–4, 6–3, 6–4
1970	Jan Kodes	Zeljko Franulovic	6–2, 6–4, 6–0
1971	Jan Kodes	Ilie Nastase	8–6, 6–2, 2–6, 7–5
1972	Andres Gimeno	Patrick Proisy	4–6, 6–3, 6–1, 6–1
1973	Ilie Nastase	Nikki Pilic	6–3, 6–3, 6–0
1974	Bjorn Borg	Manuel Orantes	6–7, 6–0, 6–1, 6–1
1975	Bjorn Borg	Guillermo Vilas	6–2, 6–3, 6–4
1976	Adriano Panatta	Harold Solomon	6–1, 6–4, 4–6, 7–6
1977	Guillermo Vilas	Brian Gottfried	6–0, 6–3, 6–0
1978	Bjorn Borg	Guillermo Vilas	6–1, 6–1, 6–3
1979	Bjorn Borg	Victor Pecci	6–3, 6–1, 6–7, 6–4
1980	Bjorn Borg	Vitas Gerulaitis	6–4, 6–1, 6–2
1981	Bjorn Borg	Ivan Lendl	6–1, 4–6, 6–2, 3–6, 6–1
1982	Mats Wilander	Guillermo Vilas	1–6, 7–6, 6–0, 6–4
1983	Yannick Noah	Mats Wilander	6–2, 7–5, 7–6
1984	Ivan Lendl	John McEnroe	3–6, 2–6, 6–4, 7–5, 7–5
1985	Mats Wilander	Ivan Lendl	3–6, 6–4, 6–2, 6–2
1986	Ivan Lendl	Mikael Pernfors	6–3, 6–2, 6–4
1987	Ivan Lendl	Mats Wilander	7–5, 6–2, 3–6, 7–6
1988	Mats Wilander	Henri Leconte	7–5, 6–2, 6–1
1989	Michael Chang	Stefan Edberg	6–1, 3–6, 4–6, 6–4, 6–2
1990	Andres Gomez	Andre Agassi	6–3, 2–6, 6–4, 6–4
1991	Jim Courier	Andre Agassi	3–6, 6–4, 2–6, 6–1, 6–4
1992	Jim Courier	Petr Korda	7–5, 6–2, 6–1
1993	Sergi Bruguera	Jim Courier	6–4, 2–6, 6–2, 3–6, 6–3
1994	Sergi Bruguera	Alberto Berasategui	6–3, 7–5, 2–6, 6–1
1995	Thomas Muster	Michael Chang	7–5, 6–2, 6–4
1996	Yevgeny Kafelnikov	Michael Stich	7–6, 7–5, 7–6
1997	Gustavo Kuerten	Sergi Bruguera	6–3, 6–4, 6–2
1998	Carlos Moya	Alex Corretja	6–3, 7–5, 6–3
1999	Andre Agassi	Andrei Medvedev	1–6, 2–6, 6–4, 6–3, 6–4
2000	Gustavo Kuerten	Magnus Norman	6–2, 6–3, 2–6, 7–6
2001	Gustavo Kuerten	Alex Corretja	6–7, 7–5, 6–2, 6–0
2002	Albert Costa	Juan Carlos Ferrero	6–1, 6–0, 4–6, 6–3
2003	Juan Carlos Ferrero	Martin Verkerk	6–1, 6–3, 6–2
2004	Gaston Gaudio	Guillermo Coria	8–6, 0–6, 3–6, 6–4, 6–1
2005	Rafael Nadal	Mariano Puerta	6–7, 6–3, 6–1,7–5

*Became Open (amateur and professional) in 1968 but closed to contract professionals in 1972.

†1925 was the first year that entries were accepted from all countries.‡From 1941 to 1945 the event was called Tournoi de France and was closed to all foreigners.

Wimbledon Championships

Year	Winner	Finalist	Score
1877	Spencer W. Gore	William C. Marshall	6–1, 6–2, 6–4
1878	P. Frank Hadow	Spencer W. Gore	7–5, 6–1, 9–7
1879	John T. Hartley	V. St Leger Gould	6–2, 6–4, 6–2
1880	John T. Hartley	Herbert F. Lawford	6–0, 6–2, 2–6, 6–3
1881	William Renshaw	John T. Hartley	6–0, 6–2, 6–1
1882	William Renshaw	Ernest Renshaw	6–1, 2–6, 4–6, 6–2, 6–2
1883	William Renshaw	Ernest Renshaw	2–6, 6–3, 6–3, 4–6, 6–3
1884	William Renshaw	Herbert F. Lawford	6–0, 6–4, 9–7

MEN (Cont.)
Wimbledon Championship (Cont.)

Year	Winner	Finalist	Score
1885	William Renshaw	Herbert F. Lawford	7–5, 6–2, 4–6, 7–5
1886	William Renshaw	Herbert F. Lawford	6–0, 5–7, 6–3, 6–4
1887	Herbert F. Lawford	Ernest Renshaw	1–6, 6–3, 3–6, 6–4, 6–4
1888	Ernest Renshaw	Herbert F. Lawford	6–3, 7–5, 6–0
1889	William Renshaw	Ernest Renshaw	6–4, 6–1, 3–6, 6–0
1890	William J. Hamilton	William Renshaw	6–8, 6–2, 3–6, 6–1, 6–1
1891	Wilfred Baddeley	Joshua Pim	6–4, 1–6, 7–5, 6–0
1892	Wilfred Baddeley	Joshua Pim	4–6, 6–3, 6–3, 6–2
1893	Joshua Pim	Wilfred Baddeley	3–6, 6–1, 6–3, 6–2
1894	Joshua Pim	Wilfred Baddeley	10–8, 6–2, 8–6
1895	Wilfred Baddeley	Wilberforce V. Eaves	4–6, 2–6, 8–6, 6–2, 6–3
1896	Harold S. Mahoney	Wilfred Baddeley	6–2, 6–8, 5–7, 8–6, 6–3
1897	Reggie F. Doherty	Harold S. Mahoney	6–4, 6–4, 6–3
1898	Reggie F. Doherty	H. Laurie Doherty	6–3, 6–3, 2–6, 5–7, 6–1
1899	Reggie F. Doherty	Arthur W. Gore	1–6, 4–6, 6–2, 6–3, 6–3
1900	Reggie F. Doherty	Sidney H. Smith	6–8, 6–3, 6–1, 6–2
1901	Arthur W. Gore	Reggie F. Doherty	4–6, 7–5, 6–4, 6–4
1902	H. Laurie Doherty	Arthur W. Gore	6–4, 6–3, 3–6, 6–0
1903	H. Laurie Doherty	Frank L. Riseley	7–5, 6–3, 6–0
1904	H. Laurie Doherty	Frank L. Riseley	6–1, 7–5, 8–6
1905	H. Laurie Doherty	Norman E. Brookes	8–6, 6–2, 6–4
1906	H. Laurie Doherty	Frank L. Riseley	6–4, 4–6, 6–2, 6–3
1907	Norman E. Brookes	Arthur W. Gore	6–4, 6–2, 6–2
1908	Arthur W. Gore	H. Roper Barrett	6–3, 6–2, 4–6, 3–6, 6–4
1909	Arthur W. Gore	M. J. G. Ritchie	6–8, 1–6, 6–2, 6–2, 6–2
1910	Anthony F. Wilding	Arthur W. Gore	6–4, 7–5, 4–6, 6–2
1911	Anthony F. Wilding	H. Roper Barrett	6–4, 4–6, 2–6, 6–2 ret
1912	Anthony F. Wilding	Arthur W. Gore	6–4, 6–4, 4–6, 6–4
1913	Anthony F. Wilding	Maurice E. McLoughlin	8–6, 6–3, 10–8
1914	Norman E. Brookes	Anthony F. Wilding	6–4, 6–4, 7–5
1915–18	No tournament		
1919	Gerald L. Patterson	Norman E. Brookes	6–3, 7–5, 6–2
1920	Bill Tilden	Gerald L. Patterson	2–6, 6–3, 6–2, 6–4
1921	Bill Tilden	Brian I. C. Norton	4–6, 2–6, 6–1, 6–0, 7–5
1922	Gerald L. Patterson	Randolph Lycett	6–3, 6–4, 6–2
1923	Bill Johnston	Francis T. Hunter	6–0, 6–3, 6–1
1924	Jean Borotra	Rene Lacoste	6–1, 3–6, 6–1, 3–6, 6–4
1925	Rene Lacoste	Jean Borotra	6–3, 6–3, 4–6, 8–6
1926	Jean Borotra	Howard Kinsey	8–6, 6–1, 6–3
1927	Henri Cochet	Jean Borotra	4–6, 4–6, 6–3, 6–4, 7–5
1928	Rene Lacoste	Henri Cochet	6–1, 4–6, 6–4, 6–2
1929	Henri Cochet	Jean Borotra	6–4, 6–3, 6–4
1930	Bill Tilden	Wilmer Allison	6–3, 9–7, 6–4
1931	Sidney B. Wood Jr	Francis X. Shields	walkover
1932	Ellsworth Vines	Henry Austin	6–4, 6–2, 6–0
1933	Jack Crawford	Ellsworth Vines	4–6, 11–9, 6–2, 2–6, 6–4
1934	Fred Perry	Jack Crawford	6–3, 6–0, 7–5
1935	Fred Perry	Gottfried von Cramm	6–2, 6–4, 6–4
1936	Fred Perry	Gottfried von Cramm	6–1, 6–1, 6–0
1937	Don Budge	Gottfried von Cramm	6–3, 6–4, 6–2
1938	Don Budge	Henry Austin	6–1, 6–0, 6–3
1939	Bobby Riggs	Elwood Cooke	2–6, 8–6, 3–6, 6–3, 6–2
1940–45	No tournament		
1946	Yvon Petra	Geoff E. Brown	6–2, 6–4, 7–9, 5–7, 6–4
1947	Jack Kramer	Tom P. Brown	6–1, 6–3, 6–2
1948	Bob Falkenburg	John Bromwich	7–5, 0–6, 6–2, 3–6, 7–5
1949	Ted Schroeder	Jaroslav Drobny	3–6, 6–0, 6–3, 4–6, 6–4
1950	Budge Patty	Frank Sedgman	6–1, 8–10, 6–2, 6–3
1951	Dick Savitt	Ken McGregor	6–4, 6–4, 6–4
1952	Frank Sedgman	Jaroslav Drobny	4–6, 6–3, 6–2, 6–3
1953	Vic Seixas	Kurt Nielsen	9–7, 6–3, 6–4
1954	Jaroslav Drobny	Ken Rosewall	13–11, 4–6, 6–2, 9–7
1955	Tony Trabert	Kurt Nielsen	6–3, 7–5, 6–1
1956	Lew Hoad	Ken Rosewall	6–2, 4–6, 7–5, 6–4
1957	Lew Hoad	Ashley Cooper	6–2, 6–1, 6–2
1958	Ashley Cooper	Neale Fraser	3–6, 6–3, 6–4, 13–11
1959	Alex Olmedo	Rod Laver	6–4, 6–3, 6–4

MEN (Cont.)
Wimbledon Championships (Cont.)

Year	Winner	Finalist	Score
1960	Neale Fraser	Rod Laver	6–4, 3–6, 9–7, 7–5
1961	Rod Laver	Chuck McKinley	6–3, 6–1, 6–4
1962	Rod Laver	Martin Mulligan	6–2, 6–2, 6–1
1963	Chuck McKinley	Fred Stolle	9–7, 6–1, 6–4
1964	Roy Emerson	Fred Stolle	6–4, 12–10, 4–6, 6–3
1965	Roy Emerson	Fred Stolle	6–2, 6–4, 6–4
1966	Manuel Santana	Dennis Ralston	6–4, 11–9, 6–4
1967	John Newcombe	Wilhelm Bungert	6–3, 6–1, 6–1
1968*	Rod Laver	Tony Roche	6–3, 6–4, 6–2
1969	Rod Laver	John Newcombe	6–4, 5–7, 6–4, 6–4
1970	John Newcombe	Ken Rosewall	5–7, 6–3, 6–2, 3–6, 6–1
1971	John Newcombe	Stan Smith	6–3, 5–7, 2–6, 6–4, 6–4
1972	Stan Smith	Ilie Nastase	4–6, 6–3, 6–3, 4–6, 7–5
1973	Jan Kodes	Alex Metreveli	6–1, 9–8, 6–3
1974	Jimmy Connors	Ken Rosewall	6–1, 6–1, 6–4
1975	Arthur Ashe	Jimmy Connors	6–1, 6–1, 5–7, 6–4
1976	Bjorn Borg	Ilie Nastase	6–4, 6–2, 9–7
1977	Bjorn Borg	Jimmy Connors	3–6, 6–2, 6–1, 5–7, 6–4
1978	Bjorn Borg	Jimmy Connors	6–2, 6–2, 6–3
1979	Bjorn Borg	Roscoe Tanner	6–7, 6–1, 3–6, 6–3, 6–4
1980	Bjorn Borg	John McEnroe	1–6, 7–5, 6–3, 6–7, 8–6
1981	John McEnroe	Bjorn Borg	4–6, 7–6, 7–6, 6–4
1982	Jimmy Connors	John McEnroe	3–6, 6–3, 6–7, 7–6, 6–4
1983	John McEnroe	Chris Lewis	6–2, 6–2, 6–2
1984	John McEnroe	Jimmy Connors	6–1, 6–1, 6–2
1985	Boris Becker	Kevin Curren	6–3, 6–7, 7–6, 6–4
1986	Boris Becker	Ivan Lendl	6–4, 6–3, 7–5
1987	Pat Cash	Ivan Lendl	7–6, 6–2, 7–5
1988	Stefan Edberg	Boris Becker	4–6, 7–6, 6–4, 6–2
1989	Boris Becker	Stefan Edberg	6–0, 7–6, 6–4
1990	Stefan Edberg	Boris Becker	6–2, 6–2, 3–6, 3–6, 6–4
1991	Michael Stich	Boris Becker	6–4, 7–6, 6–4
1992	Andre Agassi	Goran Ivanisevic	6–7, 6–4, 6–4, 1–6, 6–4
1993	Pete Sampras	Jim Courier	7–6, 7–6, 3–6, 6–3
1994	Pete Sampras	Goran Ivanisevic	7–6, 7–6, 6–0
1995	Pete Sampras	Boris Becker	6–7, 6–2, 6–4, 6–2
1996	Richard Krajicek	MaliVai Washington	6–3, 6–4, 6–3
1997	Pete Sampras	Cedric Pioline	6–4, 6–2, 6–4
1998	Pete Sampras	Goran Ivanisevic	6–7, 7–6, 6–4, 3–6, 6–2
1999	Pete Sampras	Andre Agassi	6–3, 6–4, 7–5
2000	Pete Sampras	Patrick Rafter	6–7, 7–6, 6–4, 6–2
2001	Goran Ivanisevic	Patrick Rafter	6–3, 3–6, 6–3, 2–6, 9–7
2002	Lleyton Hewitt	David Nalbandian	6–1, 6–3, 6–2
2003	Roger Federer	Mark Philippoussis	7–6 (7-5), 6–2, 7–6 (7-3)
2004	Roger Federer	Andy Roddick	4–6, 7–5, 7–6 (7-3), 6–4
2005	Roger Federer	Andy Roddick	6–2, 7–6 (7-2), 6–4

*Became Open (amateur and professional) in 1968 but closed to contract professionals in 1972

Note: Prior to 1922 the tournament was run on a challenge-round system. The previous year's winner "stood out"of an All Comers event, which produced a challenger to play him for the title.

United States Championships

Year	Winner	Finalist	Score
1881	Richard D. Sears	W.E. Glyn	6–0, 6–3, 6–2
1882	Richard D. Sears	C.M. Clark	6–1, 6–4, 6–0
1883	Richard D. Sears	James Dwight	6–2, 6–0, 9–7
1884	Richard D. Sears	H.A. Taylor	6–0, 1–6, 6–0, 6–2
1885	Richard D. Sears	G.M. Brinley	6–3, 4–6, 6–0, 6–3
1886	Richard D. Sears	R.L. Beeckman	4–6, 6–1, 6–3, 6–4
1887	Richard D. Sears	H.W. Slocum Jr	6–1, 6–3, 6–2
1888‡	H. W. Slocum Jr	H.A. Taylor	6–4, 6–1, 6–0
1889	H. W. Slocum Jr	Q.A. Shaw	6–3, 6–1, 4–6, 6–2
1890	Oliver S. Campbell	H.W. Slocum Jr	6–2, 4–6, 6–3, 6–1
1891	Oliver S. Campbell	Clarence Hobart	2–6, 7–5, 7–9, 6–1, 6–2
1892	Oliver S. Campbell	Frederick H. Hovey	7–5, 3–6, 6–3, 7–5
1893‡	Robert D. Wrenn	Frederick H. Hovey	6–4, 3–6, 6–4, 6–4
1894	Robert D. Wrenn	M.F. Goodbody	6–8, 6–1, 6–4, 6–4

MEN *(Cont.)*
United States Championships *(Cont.)*

Year	Winner	Finalist	Score
1895	Frederick H. Hovey	Robert D. Wrenn	6–3, 6–2, 6–4
1896	Robert D. Wrenn	Frederick H. Hovey	7–5, 3–6, 6–0, 1–6, 6–1
1897	Robert D. Wrenn	Wilberforce V. Eaves	4–6, 8–6, 6–3, 2–6, 6–2
1898‡	Malcolm D. Whitman	Dwight F. Davis	3–6, 6–2, 6–2, 6–1
1899	Malcolm D. Whitman	J. Parmly Paret	6–1, 6–2, 3–6, 7–5
1900	Malcolm D. Whitman	William A. Larned	6–4, 1–6, 6–2, 6–2
1901‡	William A. Larned	Beals C. Wright	6–2, 6–8, 6–4, 6–4
1902	William A. Larned	Reggie F. Doherty	4–6, 6–2, 6–4, 8–6
1903	H. Laurie Doherty	William A. Larned	6–0, 6–3, 10–8
1904‡	Holcombe Ward	William J. Clothier	10–8, 6–4, 9–7
1905	Beals C. Wright	Holcombe Ward	6–2, 6–1, 11–9
1906	William J. Clothier	Beals C. Wright	6–3, 6–0, 6–4
1907‡	William A. Larned	Robert LeRoy	6–2, 6–2, 6–4
1908	William A. Larned	Beals C. Wright	6–1, 6–2, 8–6
1909	William A. Larned	William J. Clothier	6–1, 6–2, 5–7, 1–6, 6–1
1910	William A. Larned	Thomas C. Bundy	6–1, 5–7, 6–0, 6–8, 6–1
1911	William A. Larned	Maurice E. McLoughlin	6–4, 6–4, 6–2
1912†	Maurice E. McLoughlin	Bill Johnson	3–6, 2–6, 6–2, 6–4, 6–2
1913	Maurice E. McLoughlin	Richard N. Williams	6–4, 5–7, 6–3, 6–1
1914	Richard N. Williams	Maurice E. McLoughlin	6–3, 8–6, 10–8
1915	Bill Johnston	Maurice E. McLoughlin	1–6, 6–0, 7–5, 10–8
1916	Richard N. Williams	Bill Johnston	4–6, 6–4, 0–6, 6–2, 6–4
1917#	R.L. Murray	N. W. Niles	5–7, 8–6, 6–3, 6–3
1918	R.L. Murray	Bill Tilden	6–3, 6–1, 7–5
1919	Bill Johnston	Bill Tilden	6–4, 6–4, 6–3
1920	Bill Tilden	Bill Johnston	6–1, 1–6, 7–5, 5–7, 6–3
1921	Bill Tilden	Wallace F. Johnson	6–1, 6–3, 6–1
1922	Bill Tilden	Bill Johnston	4–6, 3–6, 6–2, 6–3, 6–4
1923	Bill Tilden	Bill Johnston	6–4, 6–1, 6–4
1924	Bill Tilden	Bill Johnston	6–1, 9–7, 6–2
1925	Bill Tilden	Bill Johnston	4–6, 11–9, 6–3, 4–6, 6–3
1926	Rene Lacoste	Jean Borotra	6–4, 6–0, 6–4
1927	Rene Lacoste	Bill Tilden	11–9, 6–3, 11–9
1928	Henri Cochet	Francis T. Hunter	4–6, 6–4, 3–6, 7–5, 6–3
1929	Bill Tilden	Francis T. Hunter	3–6, 6–3, 4–6, 6–2, 6–4
1930	John H. Doeg	Francis X. Shields	10–8, 1–6, 6–4, 16–14
1931	Ellsworth Vines	George M. Lott Jr	7–9, 6–3, 9–7, 7–5
1932	Ellsworth Vines	Henri Cochet	6–4, 6–4, 6–4
1933	Fred Perry	Jack Crawford	6–3, 11–13, 4–6, 6–0, 6–1
1934	Fred Perry	Wilmer L. Allison	6–4, 6–3, 1–6, 8–6
1935	Wilmer L. Allison	Sidney B. Wood Jr	6–2, 6–2, 6–3
1936	Fred Perry	Don Budge	2–6, 6–2, 8–6, 1–6, 10–8
1937	Don Budge	Gottfried von Cramm	6–1, 7–9, 6–1, 3–6, 6–1
1938	Don Budge	Gene Mako	6–3, 6–8, 6–2, 6–1
1939	Bobby Riggs	Welby Van Horn	6–4, 6–2, 6–4
1940	Don McNeill	Bobby Riggs	4–6, 6–8, 6–3, 6–3, 7–5
1941	Bobby Riggs	Francis Kovacs II	5–7, 6–1, 6–3, 6–3
1942	Ted Schroeder	Frank Parker	8–6, 7–5, 3–6, 4–6, 6–2
1943	Joseph R. Hunt	Jack Kramer	6–3, 6–8, 10–8, 6–0
1944	Frank Parker	William F. Talbert	6–4, 3–6, 6–3, 6–3
1945	Frank Parker	William F. Talbert	14–12, 6–1, 6–2
1946	Jack Kramer	Tom P. Brown	9–7, 6–3, 6–0
1947	Jack Kramer	Frank Parker	4–6, 2–6, 6–1, 6–0, 6–3
1948	Pancho Gonzales	Eric W. Sturgess	6–2, 6–3, 14–12
1949	Pancho Gonzales	Ted Schroeder	16–18, 2–6, 6–1, 6–2, 6–4
1950	Arthur Larsen	Herbie Flam	6–3, 4–6, 5–7, 6–4, 6–3
1951	Frank Sedgman	Vic Seixas	6–4, 6–1, 6–1
1952	Frank Sedgman	Gardnar Mulloy	6–1, 6–2, 6–3
1953	Tony Trabert	Vic Seixas	6–3, 6–2, 6–3
1954	Vic Seixas	Rex Hartwig	3–6, 6–2, 6–4, 6–4
1955	Tony Trabert	Ken Rosewall	9–7, 6–3, 6–3
1956	Ken Rosewall	Lew Hoad	4–6, 6–2, 6–3, 6–3
1957	Mal Anderson	Ashley J. Cooper	10–8, 7–5, 6–4
1958	Ashley J. Cooper	Mal Anderson	6–2, 3–6, 4–6, 10–8, 8–6
1959	Neale Fraser	Alex Olmedo	6–3, 5–7, 6–2, 6–4

MEN (Cont.)
United States Championships (Cont.)

Year	Winner	Finalist	Score
1960	Neale Fraser	Rod Laver	6–4, 6–4, 9–7
1961	Roy Emerson	Rod Laver	7–5, 6–3, 6–2
1962	Rod Laver	Roy Emerson	6–2, 6–4, 5–7, 6–4
1963	Rafael Osuna	Frank Froehling III	7–5, 6–4, 6–2
1964	Roy Emerson	Fred Stolle	6–4, 6–2, 6–4
1965	Manuel Santana	Cliff Drysdale	6–2, 7–9, 7–5, 6–1
1966	Fred Stolle	John Newcombe	4–6, 12–10, 6–3, 6–4
1967	John Newcombe	Clark Graebner	6–4, 6–4, 8–6
1968*	Arthur Ashe	Tom Okker	14–12, 5–7, 6–3, 3–6, 6–3
1968**	Arthur Ashe	Bob Lutz	4–6, 6–3, 8–10, 6–0, 6–4
1969	Rod Laver	Tony Roche	7–9, 6–1, 6–3, 6–2
1969**	Stan Smith	Bob Lutz	9–7, 6–3, 6–1
1970	Ken Rosewall	Tony Roche	2–6, 6–4, 7–6, 6–3
1971	Stan Smith	Jan Kodes	3–6, 6–3, 6–2, 7–6
1972	Ilie Nastase	Arthur Ashe	3–6, 6–3, 6–7, 6–4, 6–3
1973	John Newcombe	Jan Kodes	6–4, 1–6, 4–6, 6–2, 6–3
1974	Jimmy Connors	Ken Rosewall	6–1, 6–0, 6–1
1975	Manuel Orantes	Jimmy Connors	6–4, 6–3, 6–3
1976	Jimmy Connors	Bjorn Borg	6–4, 3–6, 7–6, 6–4
1977	Guillermo Vilas	Jimmy Connors	2–6, 6–3, 7–6, 6–0
1978	Jimmy Connors	Bjorn Borg	6–4, 6–2, 6–2
1979	John McEnroe	Vitas Gerulaitis	7–5, 6–3, 6–3
1980	John McEnroe	Bjorn Borg	7–6, 6–1, 6–7, 5–7, 6–4
1981	John McEnroe	Bjorn Borg	4–6, 6–2, 6–4, 6–3
1982	Jimmy Connors	Ivan Lendl	6–3, 6–2, 4–6, 6–4
1983	Jimmy Connors	Ivan Lendl	6–3, 6–7, 7–5, 6–0
1984	John McEnroe	Ivan Lendl	6–3, 6–4, 6–1
1985	Ivan Lendl	John McEnroe	7–6, 6–3, 6–4
1986	Ivan Lendl	Miloslav Mecir	6–4, 6–2, 6–0
1987	Ivan Lendl	Mats Wilander	6–7, 6–0, 7–6, 6–4
1988	Mats Wilander	Ivan Lendl	6–4, 4–6, 6–3, 5–7, 6–4
1989	Boris Becker	Ivan Lendl	7–6, 1–6, 6–3, 7–6
1990	Pete Sampras	Andre Agassi	6–4, 6–3, 6–2
1991	Stefan Edberg	Jim Courier	6–2, 6–4, 6–0
1992	Stefan Edberg	Pete Sampras	3–6, 6–4, 7–6, 6–2
1993	Pete Sampras	Cedric Pioline	6–4, 6–4, 6–3
1994	Andre Agassi	Michael Stich	6–1, 7–6, 7–5
1995	Pete Sampras	Andre Agassi	6–4, 6–3, 4–6, 7–5
1996	Pete Sampras	Michael Chang	6–1, 6–4, 7–6
1997	Patrick Rafter	Greg Rusedski	6–3, 6–2, 4–6, 7–5
1998	Patrick Rafter	Mark Philippoussis	6–3, 3–6, 6–2, 6–0
1999	Andre Agassi	Todd Martin	6–4, 6–7, 6–7, 6–3, 6–2
2000	Marat Safin	Pete Sampras	6–4, 6–3, 6–3
2001	Lleyton Hewitt	Pete Sampras	7–6, 6–1, 6–1
2002	Pete Sampras	Andre Agassi	6–3, 6–4, 5–7, 6–4
2003	Andy Roddick	Juan Carlos Ferrero	6–3, 7–6 (7-2), 6–3
2004	Roger Federer	Lleyton Hewitt	6–0, 7–6 (7-3), 6–0
2005	Roger Federer	Andre Agassi	6–3, 2–6, (7-1), 6–1

‡No challenge round played.*Became Open (amateur and professional) in 1968.†Challenge round abolished; #National Patriotic Tournament.**Amateur event held.

WOMEN
Australian Championships

Year	Winner	Finalist	Score
1922	Margaret Molesworth	Esna Boyd	6–3, 10–8
1923	Margaret Molesworth	Esna Boyd	6–1, 7–5
1924	Sylvia Lance	Esna Boyd	6–3, 3–6, 6–4
1925	Daphne Akhurst	Esna Boyd	1–6, 8–6, 6–4
1926	Daphne Akhurst	Esna Boyd	6–1, 6–3
1927	Esna Boyd	Sylvia Harper	5–7, 6–1, 6–2
1928	Daphne Akhurst	Esna Boyd	7–5, 6–2
1929	Daphne Akhurst	Louise Bickerton	6–1, 5–7, 6–2
1930	Daphne Akhurst	Sylvia Harper	10–8, 2–6, 7–5
1931	Coral Buttsworth	Margorie Crawford	1–6, 6–3, 6–4
1932	Coral Buttsworth	Kathrine Le Messurier	9–7, 6–4

WOMEN (Cont.)
Australian Championships (Cont.)

Year	Winner	Finalist	Score
1933	Joan Hartigan	Coral Buttsworth	6–4, 6–3
1934	Joan Hartigan	Margaret Molesworth	6–1, 6–4
1935	Dorothy Round	Nancye Wynne Bolton	1–6, 6–1, 6–3
1936	Joan Hartigan	Nancye Wynne Bolton	6–4, 6–4
1937	Nancye Wynne Bolton	Emily Westacott	6–3, 5–7, 6–4
1938	Dorothy Bundy	D. Stevenson	6–3, 6–2
1939	Emily Westacott	Nell Hopman	6–1, 6–2
1940	Nancye Wynne Bolton	Thelma Coyne	5–7, 6–4, 6–0
1941–45	No tournament		
1946	Nancye Wynne Bolton	Joyce Fitch	6–4, 6–4
1947	Nancye Wynne Bolton	Nell Hopman	6–3, 6–2
1948	Nancye Wynne Bolton	Marie Toomey	6–3, 6–1
1949	Doris Hart	Nancye Wynne Bolton	6–3, 6–4
1950	Louise Brough	Doris Hart	6–4, 3–6, 6–4
1951	Nancye Wynne Bolton	Thelma Long	6–1, 7–5
1952	Thelma Long	H. Angwin	6–2, 6–3
1953	Maureen Connolly	Julia Sampson	6–3, 6–2
1954	Thelma Long	J. Staley	6–3, 6–4
1955	Beryl Penrose	Thelma Long	6–4, 6–3
1956	Mary Carter	Thelma Long	3–6, 6–2, 9–7
1957	Shirley Fry	Althea Gibson	6–3, 6–4
1958	Angela Mortimer	Lorraine Coghlan	6–3, 6–4
1959	Mary Carter-Reitano	Renee Schuurman	6–2, 6–3
1960	Margaret Smith	Jan Lehane	7–5, 6–2
1961	Margaret Smith	Jan Lehane	6–1, 6–4
1962	Margaret Smith	Jan Lehane	6–0, 6–2
1963	Margaret Smith	Jan Lehane	6–2, 6–2
1964	Margaret Smith	Lesley Turner	6–3, 6–2
1965	Margaret Smith	Maria Bueno	5–7, 6–4, 5–2 ret.
1966	Margaret Smith	Nancy Richey	Default
1967	Nancy Richey	Lesley Turner	6–1, 6–4
1968	Billie Jean King	Margaret Smith	6–1, 6–2
1969*	Margaret Smith Court	Billie Jean King	6–4, 6–1
1970	Margaret Smith Court	Kerry Melville Reid	6–3, 6–1
1971	Margaret Smith Court	Evonne Goolagong	2–6, 7–6, 7–5
1972	Virginia Wade	Evonne Goolagong	6–4, 6–4
1973	Margaret Smith Court	Evonne Goolagong	6–4, 7–5
1974	Evonne Goolagong	Chris Evert	7–6, 4–6, 6–0
1975	Evonne Goolagong	Martina Navratilova	6–3, 6–2
1976	Evonne Goolagong Cawley	Renata Tomanova	6–2, 6–2
1977 (Jan)	Kerry Melville Reid	Dianne Balestrat	7–5, 6–2
1977 (Dec)	Evonne Goolagong Cawley	Helen Gourlay	6–3, 6–0
1978	Chris O'Neil	Betsy Nagelsen	6–3, 7–6
1979	Barbara Jordan	Sharon Walsh	6–3, 6–3
1980	Hana Mandlikova	Wendy Turnbull	6–0, 7–5
1981	Martina Navratilova	Chris Evert Lloyd	6–7, 6–4, 7–5
1982	Chris Evert Lloyd	Martina Navratilova	6–3, 2–6, 6–3
1983	Martina Navratilova	Kathy Jordan	6–2, 7–6
1984	Chris Evert Lloyd	Helena Sukova	6–7, 6–1, 6–3
1985 (Dec)	Martina Navratilova	Chris Evert Lloyd	6–2, 4–6, 6–2
1987 (Jan)	Hana Mandlikova	Martina Navratilova	7–5, 7–6
1988	Steffi Graf	Chris Evert	6–1, 7–6
1989	Steffi Graf	Helena Sukova	6–4, 6–4
1990	Steffi Graf	Mary Joe Fernandez	6–3, 6–4
1991	Monica Seles	Jana Novotna	5–7, 6–3, 6–1
1992	Monica Seles	Mary Joe Fernandez	6–2, 6–3
1993	Monica Seles	Steffi Graf	4–6, 6–3, 6–2
1994	Steffi Graf	Arantxa Sánchez Vicario	6–0, 6–2
1995	Mary Pierce	Arantxa Sánchez Vicario	6–3, 6–2
1996	Monica Seles	Anke Huber	6–4, 6–1
1997	Martina Hingis	Mary Pierce	6–2, 6–2
1998	Martina Hingis	Conchita Martinez	6–3, 6–3
1999	Martina Hingis	Amelie Mauresmo	6–2, 6–3
2000	Lindsay Davenport	Martina Hingis	6–1, 7–5
2001	Jennifer Capriati	Martina Hingis	6–4, 6–3

WOMEN *(Cont.)*
Australian Championships *(Cont.)*

Year	Winner	Finalist	Score
2002	Jennifer Capriati	Martina Hingis	4–6, 7–6 (9–7), 6–2
2003	Serena Williams	Venus Williams	7–6 (7-4), 3–6, 6–4
2004	Justine Henin-Hardenne	Kim Clijsters	6–3, 4–6, 6–3
2005	Serena Williams	Lindsay Davenport	2–6, 6-3, 6-0

*Became Open (amateur and professional) in 1969.

French Championships

Year	Winner	Finalist	Score
1925†	Suzanne Lenglen	Kathleen McKane	6–1, 6–2
1926	Suzanne Lenglen	Mary K. Browne	6–1, 6–0
1927	Kea Bouman	Irene Peacock	6–2, 6–4
1928	Helen Wills	Eileen Bennett	6–1, 6–2
1929	Helen Wills	Simone Mathieu	6–3, 6–4
1930	Helen Wills Moody	Helen Jacobs	6–2, 6–1
1931	Cilly Aussem	Betty Nuthall	8–6, 6–1
1932	Helen Wills Moody	Simone Mathieu	7–5, 6–1
1933	Margaret Scriven	Simone Mathieu	6–2, 4–6, 6–4
1934	Margaret Scriven	Helen Jacobs	7–5, 4–6, 6–1
1935	Hilde Sperling	Simone Mathieu	6–2, 6–1
1936	Hilde Sperling	Simone Mathieu	6–3, 6–4
1937	Hilde Sperling	Simone Mathieu	6–2, 6–4
1938	Simone Mathieu	Nelly Landry	6–0, 6–3
1939	Simone Mathieu	Jadwiga Jedrzejowska	6–3, 8–6
1940–45	No tournament		
1946	Margaret Osborne	Pauline Betz	1–6, 8–6, 7–5
1947	Patricia Todd	Doris Hart	6–3, 3–6, 6–4
1948	Nelly Landry	Shirley Fry	6–2, 0–6, 6–0
1949	Margaret Osborne duPont	Nelly Adamson	7–5, 6–2
1950	Doris Hart	Patricia Todd	6–4, 4–6, 6–2
1951	Shirley Fry	Doris Hart	6–3, 3–6, 6–3
1952	Doris Hart	Shirley Fry	6–4, 6–4
1953	Maureen Connolly	Doris Hart	6–2, 6–4
1954	Maureen Connolly	Ginette Bucaille	6–4, 6–1
1955	Angela Mortimer	Dorothy Knode	2–6, 7–5, 10–8
1956	Althea Gibson	Angela Mortimer	6–0, 12–10
1957	Shirley Bloomer	Dorothy Knode	6–1, 6–3
1958	Zsuzsi Kormoczi	Shirley Bloomer	6–4, 1–6, 6–2
1959	Christine Truman	Zsuzsi Kormoczi	6–4, 7–5
1960	Darlene Hard	Yola Ramirez	6–3, 6–4
1961	Ann Haydon	Yola Ramirez	6–2, 6–1
1962	Margaret Smith	Lesley Turner	6–3, 3–6, 7–5
1963	Lesley Turner	Ann Haydon Jones	2–6, 6–3, 7–5
1964	Margaret Smith	Maria Bueno	5–7, 6–1, 6–2
1965	Lesley Turner	Margaret Smith	6–3, 6–4
1966	Ann Jones	Nancy Richey	6–3, 6–1
1967	Francoise Durr	Lesley Turner	4–6, 6–3, 6–4
1968*	Nancy Richey	Ann Jones	5–7, 6–4, 6–1
1969	Margaret Smith Court	Ann Jones	6–1, 4–6, 6–3
1970	Margaret Smith Court	Helga Niessen	6–2, 6–4
1971	Evonne Goolagong	Helen Gourlay	6–3, 7–5
1972	Billie Jean King	Evonne Goolagong	6–3, 6–3
1973	Margaret Smith Court	Chris Evert	6–7, 7–6, 6–4
1974	Chris Evert	Olga Morozova	6–1, 6–2
1975	Chris Evert	Martina Navratilova	2–6, 6–2, 6–1
1976	Sue Barker	Renata Tomanova	6–2, 0–6, 6–2
1977	Mima Jausovec	Florenza Mihai	6–2, 6–7, 6–1
1978	Virginia Ruzici	Mima Jausovec	6–2, 6–2
1979	Chris Evert Lloyd	Wendy Turnbull	6–2, 6–0
1980	Chris Evert Lloyd	Virginia Ruzici	6–0, 6–3
1981	Hana Mandlikova	Sylvia Hanika	6–2, 6–4
1982	Martina Navratilova	Andrea Jaeger	7–6, 6–1
1983	Chris Evert Lloyd	Mima Jausovec	6–1, 6–2
1984	Martina Navratilova	Chris Evert Lloyd	6–3, 6–1
1985	Chris Evert Lloyd	Martina Navratilova	6–3, 6–7, 7–5
1986	Chris Evert Lloyd	Martina Navratilova	2–6, 6–3, 6–3

WOMEN *(Cont.)*
French Championships *(Cont.)*

Year	Winner	Finalist	Score
1987	Steffi Graf	Martina Navratilova	6–4, 4–6, 8–6
1988	Steffi Graf	Natalia Zvereva	6–0, 6–0
1989	Arantxa Sánchez Vicario	Steffi Graf	7–6, 3–6, 7–5
1990	Monica Seles	Steffi Graf	7–6, 6–4
1991	Monica Seles	Arantxa Sánchez Vicario	6–3, 6–4
1992	Monica Seles	Steffi Graf	6–2, 3–6, 10–8
1993	Steffi Graf	Mary Joe Fernandez	4–6, 6–2, 6–4
1994	Arantxa Sánchez Vicario	Mary Pierce	6–4, 6–4
1995	Steffi Graf	Arantxa Sánchez Vicario	7–5, 4–6, 6–0
1996	Steffi Graf	Arantxa Sánchez Vicario	6–3, 6–7 (4–7), 10–8
1997	Iva Majoli	Martina Hingis	6–4, 6–2
1998	Arantxa Sánchez Vicario	Monica Seles	7–6 (7–5), 0–6, 6–2
1999	Steffi Graf	Martina Hingis	4–6, 7–5, 6–2
2000	Mary Pierce	Conchita Martinez	6–2, 7–5
2001	Jennifer Capriati	Kim Clijsters	1–6, 6–4, 12–10
2002	Serena Williams	Venus Williams	7–5, 6–3
2003	Justine Henin-Hardenne	Kim Clijsters	6–0, 6–4
2004	Anastasia Myskina	Elena Dementieva	6–1, 6–2
2005	Justine Henin-Hardenne	Mary Pierce	6–1, 6–1

†1925 was the first year that entries were accepted from all countries. *Became Open (amateur and professional) in 1968 but closed to contract professionals in 1972.

Wimbledon Championships

Year	Winner	Finalist	Score
1884	Maud Watson	Lilian Watson	6–8, 6–3, 6–3
1885	Maud Watson	Blanche Bingley	6–1, 7–5
1886	Blanche Bingley	Maud Watson	6–3, 6–3
1887	Charlotte Dod	Blanche Bingley	6–2, 6–0
1888	Charlotte Dod	Blanche Bingley Hillyard	6–3, 6–3
1889	Blanche Bingley Hillyard	n/a	n/a
1890	Lena Rice	n/a	n/a
1891	Charlotte Dod	n/a	n/a
1892	Charlotte Dod	Blanche Bingley Hillyard	6–1, 6–1
1893	Charlotte Dod	Blanche Bingley Hillyard	6–8, 6–1, 6–4
1894	Blanche Bingley Hillyard	n/a	n/a
1895	Charlotte Cooper	n/a	
1896	Charlotte Cooper	Mrs. W. H. Pickering	6–2, 6–3
1897	Blanche Bingley Hillyard	Charlotte Cooper	5–7, 7–5, 6–2
1898	Charlotte Cooper	n/a	n/a
1899	Blanche Bingley Hillyard	Charlotte Cooper	6–2, 6–3
1900	Blanche Bingley Hillyard	Charlotte Cooper	4–6, 6–4, 6–4
1901	Charlotte Cooper Sterry	Blanche Bingley Hillyard	6–2, 6–2
1902	Muriel Robb	Charlotte Cooper Sterry	7–5, 6–1
1903	Dorothea Douglass	n/a	n/a
1904	Dorothea Douglass	Charlotte Cooper Sterry	6–0, 6–3
1905	May Sutton	Dorothea Douglass	6–3, 6–4
1906	Dorothea Douglass	May Sutton	6–3, 9–7
1907	May Sutton	Dorothea Douglass Lambert Chambers	6–1, 6–4
1908	Charlotte Cooper Sterry	n/a	n/a
1909	Dora Boothby	n/a	n/a
1910	Dorothea Douglass Lambert Chambers	Dora Boothby	6–2, 6–2
1911	Dorothea Douglass Lambert Chambers	Dora Boothby	6–0, 6–0
1912	Ethel Larcombe	n/a	n/a
1913	Dorothea Douglass Lambert Chambers		
1914	Dorothea Douglass Lambert Chambers	Ethel Larcombe	7–5, 6–4
1915–18	No tournament		
1919	Suzanne Lenglen	Dorothea Douglass Lambert Chambers	10–8, 4–6, 9–7
1920	Suzanne Lenglen	Dorothea Douglass Lambert Chambers	6–3, 6–0
1921	Suzanne Lenglen	Elizabeth Ryan	6–2, 6–0
1922	Suzanne Lenglen	Molla Mallory	6–2, 6–0

WOMEN *(Cont.)*
Wimbledon Championships *(Cont.)*

Year	Winner	Finalist	Score
1923	Suzanne Lenglen	Kathleen McKane	6–2, 6–2
1924	Kathleen McKane	Helen Wills	4–6, 6–4, 6–2
1925	Suzanne Lenglen	Joan Fry	6–2, 6–0
1926	Kathleen McKane Godfree	Lili de Alvarez	6–2, 4–6, 6–3
1927	Helen Wills	Lili de Alvarez	6–2, 6–4
1928	Helen Wills	Lili de Alvarez	6–2, 6–3
1929	Helen Wills	Helen Jacobs	6–1, 6–2
1930	Helen Wills Moody	Elizabeth Ryan	6–2, 6–2
1931	Cilly Aussem	Hilde Kranwinkel	7–5, 7–5
1932	Helen Wills Moody	Helen Jacobs	6–3, 6–1
1933	Helen Wills Moody	Dorothy Round	6–4, 6–8, 6–3
1934	Dorothy Round	Helen Jacobs	6–2, 5–7, 6–3
1935	Helen Wills Moody	Helen Jacobs	6–3, 3–6, 7–5
1936	Helen Jacobs	Hilde Kranwinkel Sperling	6–2, 4–6, 7–5
1937	Dorothy Round	Jadwiga Jedrzejowska	6–2, 2–6, 7–5
1938	Helen Wills Moody	Helen Jacobs	6–4, 6–0
1939	Alice Marble	Kay Stammers	6–2, 6–0
1940–45	No tournament		
1946	Pauline Betz	Louise Brough	6–2, 6–4
1947	Margaret Osborne	Doris Hart	6–2, 6–4
1948	Louise Brough	Doris Hart	6–3, 8–6
1949	Louise Brough	Margaret Osborne duPont	10–8, 1–6, 10–8
1950	Louise Brough	Margaret Osborne duPont	6–1, 3–6, 6–1
1951	Doris Hart	Shirley Fry	6–1, 6–0
1952	Maureen Connolly	Louise Brough	6–4, 6–3
1953	Maureen Connolly	Doris Hart	8–6, 7–5
1954	Maureen Connolly	Louise Brough	6–2, 7–5
1955	Louise Brough	Beverly Fleitz	7–5, 8–6
1956	Shirley Fry	Angela Buxton	6–3, 6–1
1957	Althea Gibson	Darlene Hard	6–3, 6–2
1958	Althea Gibson	Angela Mortimer	8–6, 6–2
1959	Maria Bueno	Darlene Hard	6–4, 6–3
1960	Maria Bueno	Sandra Reynolds	8–6, 6–0
1961	Angela Mortimer	Christine Truman	4–6, 6–4, 7–5
1962	Karen Hantze Susman	Vera Sukova	6–4, 6–4
1963	Margaret Smith	Billie Jean Moffitt	6–3, 6–4
1964	Maria Bueno	Margaret Smith	6–4, 7–9, 6–3
1965	Margaret Smith	Maria Bueno	6–4, 7–5
1966	Billie Jean King	Maria Bueno	6–3, 3–6, 6–1
1967	Billie Jean King	Ann Haydon Jones	6–3, 6–4
1968*	Billie Jean King	Judy Tegart	9–7, 7–5
1969	Ann Haydon Jones	Billie Jean King	3–6, 6–3, 6–2
1970	Margaret Smith Court	Billie Jean King	14–12, 11–9
1971	Evonne Goolagong	Margaret Smith Court	6–4, 6–1
1972	Billie Jean King	Evonne Goolagong	6–3, 6–3
1973	Billie Jean King	Chris Evert	6–0, 7–5
1974	Chris Evert	Olga Morozova	6–0, 6–4
1975	Billie Jean King	Evonne Goolagong Cawley	6–0, 6–1
1976	Chris Evert	Evonne Goolagong Cawley	6–3, 4–6, 8–6
1977	Virginia Wade	Betty Stove	4–6, 6–3, 6–1
1978	Martina Navratilova	Chris Evert	2–6, 6–4, 7–5
1979	Martina Navratilova	Chris Evert Lloyd	6–4, 6–4
1980	Evonne Goolagong Cawley	Chris Evert Lloyd	6–1, 7–6
1981	Chris Evert Lloyd	Hana Mandlikova	6–2, 6–2
1982	Martina Navratilova	Chris Evert Lloyd	6–1, 3–6, 6–2
1983	Martina Navratilova	Andrea Jaeger	6–0, 6–3
1984	Martina Navratilova	Chris Evert Lloyd	7–6, 6–2
1985	Martina Navratilova	Chris Evert Lloyd	4–6, 6–3, 6–2
1986	Martina Navratilova	Hana Mandlikova	7–6, 6–3
1987	Martina Navratilova	Steffi Graf	7–5, 6–3
1988	Steffi Graf	Martina Navratilova	5–7, 6–2, 6–1
1989	Steffi Graf	Martina Navratilova	6–2, 6–7, 6–1
1990	Martina Navratilova	Zina Garrison	6–4, 6–1
1991	Steffi Graf	Gabriela Sabatini	6–4, 3–6, 8–6
1992	Steffi Graf	Monica Seles	6–2, 6–1

WOMEN *(Cont.)*
Wimbledon Championships *(Cont.)*

Year	Winner	Finalist	Score
1993	Steffi Graf	Jana Novotna	7–6, 1–6, 6–4
1994	Conchita Martinez	Martina Navratilova	6–4, 3–6, 6–3
1995	Steffi Graf	Arantxa Sánchez Vicario	4–6, 6–1, 7–5
1996	Steffi Graf	Arantxa Sánchez Vicario	6–3, 7–5
1997	Martina Hingis	Jana Novotna	2–6, 6–3, 6–3
1998	Jana Novotna	Nathalie Tauziat	6–4, 7–6
1999	Lindsay Davenport	Steffi Graf	6–4, 7–5
2000	Venus Williams	Lindsay Davenport	6–3, 7–6
2001	Venus Williams	Justine Henin	6–1, 3–6, 6–0
2002	Serena Williams	Venus Williams	7–6 (7–4), 6–3
2003	Serena Williams	Venus Williams	4–6, 6–4, 6–2
2004	Maria Sharapova	Serena Williams	6–1, 6–4
2005	Venus Williams	Lindsay Davenport	4-6, 7-6, (7-4), 9-7

*Became Open (amateur and professional) in 1968 but closed to contract professionals in 1972.

Note: Prior to 1922 the tournament was run on a challenge-round system. The previous year's winner "stood out" of an All-Comers event, which produced a challenger to play her for the title.

United States Championships

Year	Winner	Finalist	Score
1887	Ellen Hansell	Laura Knight	6–1, 6–0
1888	Bertha L. Townsend	Ellen Hansell	6–3, 6–5
1889	Bertha L. Townsend	Louise Voorhes	7–5, 6–2
1890	Ellen C. Roosevelt	Bertha L. Townsend	6–2, 6–2
1891	Mabel Cahill	Ellen C. Roosevelt	6–4, 6–1, 4–6, 6–3
1892	Mabel Cahill	Elisabeth Moore	5–7, 6–3, 6–4, 4–6, 6–2
1893	Aline Terry	Alice Schultze	6–1, 6–3
1894	Helen Hellwig	Aline Terry	7–5, 3–6, 6–0, 3–6, 6–3
1895	Juliette Atkinson	Helen Hellwig	6–4, 6–2, 6–1
1896	Elisabeth Moore	Juliette Atkinson	6–4, 4–6, 6–2, 6–2
1897	Juliette Atkinson	Elisabeth Moore	6–3, 6–3, 4–6, 3–6, 6–3
1898	Juliette Atkinson	Marion Jones	6–3, 5–7, 6–4, 2–6, 7–5
1899	Marion Jones	Maud Banks	6–1, 6–1, 7–5
1900	Myrtle McAteer	Edith Parker	6–2, 6–2, 6–0
1901	Elisabeth Moore	Myrtle McAteer	6–4, 3–6, 7–5, 2–6, 6–2
1902**	Marion Jones	Elisabeth Moore	6–1, 1–0, ret.
1903	Elisabeth Moore	Marion Jones	7–5, 8–6
1904	May Sutton	Elisabeth Moore	6–1, 6–2
1905	Elisabeth Moore	Helen Homans	6–4, 5–7, 6–1
1906	Helen Homans	Maud Barger-Wallach	6–4, 6–3
1907	Evelyn Sears	Carrie Neely	6–3, 6–2
1908	Maud Barger–Wallach	Evelyn Sears	6–3, 1–6, 6–3
1909	Hazel Hotchkiss	Maud Barger–Wallach	6–0, 6–1
1910	Hazel Hotchkiss	Louise Hammond	6–4, 6–2
1911	Hazel Hotchkiss	Florence Sutton	8–10, 6–1, 9–7
1912†	Mary K. Browne	Eleanora Sears	6–4, 6–2
1913	Mary K. Browne	Dorothy Green	6–2, 7–5
1914	Mary K. Browne	Marie Wagner	6–2, 1–6, 6–1
1915	Molla Bjurstedt	Hazel Hotchkiss Wightman	4–6, 6–2, 6–0
1916	Molla Bjurstedt	Louise Hammond Raymond	6–0, 6–1
1917‡	Molla Bjurstedt	Marion Vanderhoef	4–6, 6–0, 6–2
1918	Molla Bjurstedt	Eleanor Goss	6–4, 6–3
1919	Hazel Hotchkiss Wightman	Marion Zinderstein	6–1, 6–2
1920	Molla Bjurstedt Mallory	Marion Zinderstein	6–3, 6–1
1921	Molla Bjurstedt Mallory	Mary K. Browne	4–6, 6–4, 6–2
1922	Molla Bjurstedt Mallory	Helen Wills	6–3, 6–1
1923	Helen Wills	Molla Bjurstedt Mallory	6–2, 6–1
1924	Helen Wills	Molla Bjurstedt Mallory	6–1, 6–3
1925	Helen Wills	Kathleen McKane	3–6, 6–0, 6–2
1926	Molla Bjurstedt Mallory	Elizabeth Ryan	4–6, 6–4, 9–7
1927	Helen Wills	Betty Nuthall	6–1, 6–4
1928	Helen Wills	Helen Jacobs	6–2, 6–1
1929	Helen Wills	Phoebe Holcroft Watson	6–4, 6–2
1930	Betty Nuthall	Anna McCune Harper	6–1, 6–4
1931	Helen Wills Moody	Eileen Whitingstall	6–4, 6–1
1932	Helen Jacobs	Carolin Babcock	6–2, 6–2
1933	Helen Jacobs	Helen Wills Moody	8–6, 3–6, 3–0, ret.
1934	Helen Jacobs	Sarah Palfrey	6–1, 6–4
1935	Helen Jacobs	Sarah Palfrey Fabyan	6–2, 6–4

WOMEN *(Cont.)*
United States Championships *(Cont.)*

Year	Winner	Finalist	Score
1936	Alice Marble	Helen Jacobs	4–6, 6–3, 6–2
1937	Anita Lizane	Jadwiga Jedrzejowska	6–4, 6–2
1938	Alice Marble	Nancye Wynne	6–0, 6–3
1939	Alice Marble	Helen Jacobs	6–0, 8–10, 6–4
1940	Alice Marble	Helen Jacobs	6–2, 6–3
1941	Sarah Palfrey Cooke	Pauline Betz	7–5, 6–2
1942	Pauline Betz	Louise Brough	4–6, 6–1, 6–4
1943	Pauline Betz	Louise Brough	6–3, 5–7, 6–3
1944	Pauline Betz	Margaret Osborne	6–3, 8–6
1945	Sarah Palfrey Cooke	Pauline Betz	3–6, 8–6, 6–4
1946	Pauline Betz	Patricia Canning	11–9, 6–3
1947	Louise Brough	Margaret Osborne	8–6, 4–6, 6–1
1948	Margaret Osborne duPont	Louise Brough	4–6, 6–4, 15–13
1949	Margaret Osborne duPont	Doris Hart	6–4, 6–1
1950	Margaret Osborne duPont	Doris Hart	6–4, 6–3
1951	Maureen Connolly	Shirley Fry	6–3, 1–6, 6–4
1952	Maureen Connolly	Doris Hart	6–3, 7–5
1953	Maureen Connolly	Doris Hart	6–2, 6–4
1954	Doris Hart	Louise Brough	6–8, 6–1, 8–6
1955	Doris Hart	Patricia Ward	6–4, 6–2
1956	Shirley Fry	Althea Gibson	6–3, 6–4
1957	Althea Gibson	Louise Brough	6–3, 6–2
1958	Althea Gibson	Darlene Hard	3–6, 6–1, 6–2
1959	Maria Bueno	Christine Truman	6–1, 6–4
1960	Darlene Hard	Maria Bueno	6–4, 10–12, 6–4
1961	Darlene Hard	Ann Haydon	6–3, 6–4
1962	Margaret Smith	Darlene Hard	9–7, 6–4
1963	Maria Bueno	Margaret Smith	7–5, 6–4
1964	Maria Bueno	Carole Graebner	6–1, 6–0
1965	Margaret Smith	Billie Jean Moffitt	8–6, 7–5
1966	Maria Bueno	Nancy Richey	6–3, 6–1
1967	Billie Jean King	Ann Haydon Jones	11–9, 6–4
1968*	Virginia Wade	Billie Jean King	6–4, 6–4
1968#	Margaret Smith Court	Maria Bueno	6–2, 6–2
1969	Margaret Smith Court	Nancy Richey	6–2, 6–2
1969#	Margaret Smith Court	Virginia Wade	4–6, 6–3, 6–0
1970	Margaret Smith Court	Rosie Casals	6–2, 2–6, 6–1
1971	Billie Jean King	Rosie Casals	6–4, 7–6
1972	Billie Jean King	Kerry Melville	6–3, 7–5
1973	Margaret Smith Court	Evonne Goolagong	7–6, 5–7, 6–2
1974	Billie Jean King	Evonne Goolagong	3–6, 6–3, 7–5
1975	Chris Evert	Evonne Goolagong Cawley	5–7, 6–4, 6–2
1976	Chris Evert	Evonne Goolagong Cawley	6–3, 6–0
1977	Chris Evert	Wendy Turnbull	7–6, 6–2
1978	Chris Evert	Pam Shriver	7–6, 6–4
1979	Tracy Austin	Chris Evert Lloyd	6–4, 6–3
1980	Chris Evert Lloyd	Hana Mandlikova	5–7, 6–1, 6–1
1981	Tracy Austin	Martina Navratilova	1–6, 7–6, 7–6
1982	Chris Evert Lloyd	Hana Mandlikova	6–3, 6–1
1983	Martina Navratilova	Chris Evert Lloyd	6–1, 6–3
1984	Martina Navratilova	Chris Evert Lloyd	4–6, 6–4, 6–4
1985	Hana Mandlikova	Martina Navratilova	7–6, 1–6, 7–6
1986	Martina Navratilova	Helena Sukova	6–3, 6–2
1987	Martina Navratilova	Steffi Graf	7–6, 6–1
1988	Steffi Graf	Gabriela Sabatini	6–3, 3–6, 6–1
1989	Steffi Graf	Martina Navratilova	3–6, 6–4, 6–2
1990	Gabriela Sabatini	Steffi Graf	6–2, 7–6
1991	Monica Seles	Martina Narvatilova	7–6, 6–1
1992	Monica Seles	Arantxa Sánchez Vicario	6–3, 6–2
1993	Steffi Graf	Helena Sukova	6–3, 6–3
1994	Arantxa Sánchez Vicario	Steffi Graf	1–6, 7–6, 6–4
1995	Steffi Graf	Monica Seles	7–6, 0–6, 6–3
1996	Steffi Graf	Monica Seles	7–5, 7–4
1997	Martina Hingis	Venus Williams	6–0, 6–4
1998	Lindsay Davenport	Martina Hingis	6–3, 7–5
1999	Serena Williams	Martina Hingis	6–3, 7–6
2000	Venus Williams	Lindsay Davenport	6–4, 7–5
2001	Venus Williams	Serena Williams	6–2, 6–4
2002	Serena Williams	Venus Williams	6–4, 6–3

WOMEN *(Cont.)*
United States Championships *(Cont.)*

Year	Winner	Finalist	Score
2003	Justine Henin-Hardenne	Kim Clijsters	7–5, 6–1
2004	Svetlana Kuznetsova	Elena Dementieva	6–3, 7–5
2005	Kim Clijsters	Mary Pierce	6-3, 6-1

**Five-set final abolished; †Challenge round abolished. *Became Open (amateur and professional) in 1968.
‡National Patriotic Tournament; #Amateur event held.

Singles

Don Budge, 1938
Maureen Connolly, 1953
Rod Laver, 1962, 1969
Margaret Smith Court, 1970
Steffi Graf, 1988

Doubles

Frank Sedgman and Ken McGregor, 1951
Martina Navratilova and Pam Shriver, 1984
Maria Bueno and two partners: Christine Truman
(Australian), Darlene Hard (French, Wimbledon
and U.S. Championships), 1960
Martina Hingis and two partners: Mirjana Lucic
(Australian), Jana Novotna (French, Wimbledon
and U.S. Championships), 1998

Mixed Doubles

Margaret Smith and Ken Fletcher, 1963
Owen Davidson and two partners: Lesley Turner
(Australian), Billie Jean King (French, Wimbledon
and U.S. Championships), 1967

Alltime Grand Slam Champions
MEN

Player	Aus. S-D-M	French S-D-M	Wim. S-D-M	U.S. S-D-M	Total
Roy Emerson	6-3-0	2-6-0	2-3-0	2-4-0	28
John Newcombe	2-5-0	0-3-0	3-6-0	2-3-1	25
Frank Sedgman	2-2-2	0-2-2	1-3-2	2-2-2	22
Bill Tilden	†	0-0-1	3-1-0	7-5-4	21
Rod Laver	3-4-0	2-1-1	4-1-2	2-0-0	20
John Bromwich	2-8-1	0-0-0	0-2-2	0-3-1	19
Jean Borotra	1-1-1	1-5-2	2-3-1	0-0-1	18
Fred Stolle	0-3-1	1-2-0	0-2-3	1-3-2	18
Ken Rosewall	4-3-0	2-2-0	0-2-0	2-2-1	18
Neale Fraser	0-3-1	0-3-0	1-2-0	2-3-3	18
Adrian Quist	3-10-0	0-1-0	0-2-0	0-1-0	17
John McEnroe	0-0-0	0-0-1	3-4-0	4-5-0	17
Jack Crawford	4-4-3	1-1-1	1-1-1	0-0-0	17
Mark Woodforde	0-2-2	0-1-1	0-6-1	0-3-1	17

†Did not compete.

WOMEN

Player	Aus. S-D-M	French S-D-M	Wim. S-D-M	U.S. S-D-M	Total
Margaret Smith Court	11-8-2	5-4-4	3-2-5	5-5-8	62
*Martina Navratilova	3-8-1	2-7-2	9-7-4	4-9-2	58
Billie Jean King	1-0-1	1-1-2	6-10-4	4-5-4	39
Doris Hart	1-1-2	2-5-3	1-4-5	2-4-5	35
Helen Wills Moody	†	4-2-0	8-3-1	7-4-2	31
Louise Brough	1-1-0	0-3-0	4-5-4	1-8-3	30**
Margaret Osborne duPont	†	2-3-0	1-5-1	3-8-6	29**
Elizabeth Ryan	†	0-4-0	0-12-7	0-1-2	26
Steffi Graf	4-0-0	6-0-0	7-1-0	5-0-0	23
Pam Shriver	0-7-0	0-4-1	0-5-0	0-5-0	22
Chris Evert	2-0-0	7-2-0	3-1-0	6-0-0	21
Darlene Hard	†	1-3-2	0-4-3	2-6-0	21
Suzanne Lenglen	†	2-2-2#	6-6-3	0-0-0	21
Nancye Wynne Bolton	6-10-4	0-0-0	0-0-0	0-0-0	20
Maria Bueno	0-1-0	0-1-1	3-5-0	4-4-0	19
Thelma Coyne Long	2-12-4	0-0-1	0-0-0	0-0-0	19

*Active player. †Did not compete. #Suzanne Lenglen also won four singles titles at the French Championships before 1925, when competition was first opened to entries from all nations.**From 1940–45, with competition in the U.S. Championships thinned due to wartime constraints, Louise Brough Clapp also won four doubles titles (1942–45) and one mixed doubles title (1942); and Margaret Osborne duPont won five doubles titles (1941–45) and three mixed doubles titles (1943–45).

Alltime Grand Slam Singles Champions

MEN

Player	Aus.	French	Wim.	U.S.	Total
Pete Sampras	2	0	7	5	14
Roy Emerson	6	2	2	2	12
Bjorn Borg	0	6	5	0	11
Rod Laver	3	2	4	2	11
Bill Tilden	†	0	3	7	10
Jimmy Connors	1	0	2	5	8
Ivan Lendl	2	3	0	3	8
Fred Perry	1	1	3	3	8
Ken Rosewall	4	2	0	2	8
*Andre Agassi	4	1	1	2	8
Henri Cochet	†	4	2	1	7
Rene Lacoste	†	3	2	2	7
Bill Larned	†	†	0	7	7
John McEnroe	0	0	3	4	7
John Newcombe	2	0	3	2	7
Willie Renshaw	†	†	7	†	7
Dick Sears	†	†	0	7	7

*Active player. †Did not compete.

WOMEN

Player	Aus.	French	Wim.	U.S.	Total
Margaret Smith Court	11	5	3	5	24
Steffi Graf	4	6	7	5	22
Helen Wills Moody	†	4	8	7	19
Chris Evert	2	7	3	6	18
Martina Navratilova	3	2	9	4	18
Billie Jean King	1	1	6	4	12
Maureen Connolly	1	2	3	3	9
*Monica Seles	4	3	0	2	9
Suzanne Lenglen	†	2#	6	0	8
Molla Bjurstedt Mallory	†	†	0	8	8
Maria Bueno	0	0	3	4	7
Evonne Goolagong	4	1	2	0	7
Dorothea D.L. Chambers	†	†	7	0	7
*Serena Williams	2	1	2	2	7
Nancye Wynne Bolton	6	0	0	0	6
Louise Brough	1	0	4	1	6
Margaret Osborne duPont	†	2	1	3	6
Doris Hart	1	2	1	2	6
Blanche Bingley Hillyard	†	†	6	†	6

*Active player. †Did not compete.

#Suzanne Lenglen also won four singles titles at the French Championships before 1925, when competition was first opened to entries from all nations.

Davis Cup

the 1898 U.S. Championships. A Davis Cup meeting between two countries is known as a tie and is a three-day event consisting of two singles matches, followed by one doubles match and then two more singles matches. The United States boasts the greatest number of wins (31), followed by Australia (20).

Year	Winner	Finalist	Site	Score
1900	United States	Great Britain	Boston	3–0
1901	No tournament			
1902	United States	Great Britain	New York	3–2
1903	Great Britain	United States	Boston	4–1
1904	Great Britain	Belgium	Wimbledon	5–0
1905	Great Britain	United States	Wimbledon	5–0
1906	Great Britain	United States	Wimbledon	5–0
1907	Australasia	Great Britain	Wimbledon	3–2
1908	Australasia	United States	Melbourne	3–2
1909	Australasia	United States	Sydney	5–0
1910	No tournament			
1911	Australasia	United States	Christchurch, NZ	5–0
1912	Great Britain	Australasia	Melbourne	3–2
1913	United States	Great Britain	Wimbledon	3–2
1914	Australasia	United States	New York	3–2
1915–18	No tournament			
1919	Australasia	Great Britain	Sydney	4–1
1920	United States	Australasia	Auckland, NZ	5–0
1921	United States	Japan	New York	5–0
1922	United States	Australasia	New York	4–1
1923	United States	Australasia	New York	4–1
1924	United States	Australia	Philadelphia	5–0
1925	United States	France	Philadelphia	5–0
1926	United States	France	Philadelphia	4–1
1927	France	United States	Philadelphia	3–2
1928	France	United States	Paris	4–1
1929	France	United States	Paris	3–2
1930	France	United States	Paris	4–1
1931	France	Great Britain	Paris	3–2
1932	France	United States	Paris	3–2
1933	Great Britain	France	Paris	3–2
1934	Great Britain	United States	Wimbledon	4–1
1935	Great Britain	United States	Wimbledon	5–0
1936	Great Britain	Australia	Wimbledon	3–2
1937	United States	Great Britain	Wimbledon	4–1
1938	United States	Australia	Philadelphia	3–2
1939	Australia	United States	Philadelphia	3–2
1940–45	No tournament			
1946	United States	Australia	Melbourne	5–0
1947	United States	Australia	New York	4–1
1948	United States	Australia	New York	5–0
1949	United States	Australia	New York	4–1
1950	Australia	United States	New York	4–1
1951	Australia	United States	Sydney	3–2
1952	Australia	United States	Adelaide	4–1
1953	Australia	United States	Melbourne	3–2
1954	United States	Australia	Sydney	3–2
1955	Australia	United States	New York	5–0
1956	Australia	United States	Adelaide	5–0
1957	Australia	United States	Melbourne	3–2
1958	United States	Australia	Brisbane	3–2
1959	Australia	United States	New York	3–2
1960	Australia	Italy	Sydney	4–1
1961	Australia	Italy	Melbourne	5–0
1962	Australia	Mexico	Brisbane	5–0
1963	United States	Australia	Adelaide	3–2
1964	Australia	United States	Cleveland	3–2
1965	Australia	Spain	Sydney	4–1
1966	Australia	India	Melbourne	4–1
1967	Australia	Spain	Brisbane	4–1
1968	United States	Australia	Adelaide	4–1
1969	United States	Romania	Cleveland	5–0
1970	United States	W Germany	Cleveland	5–0
1971	United States	Romania	Charlotte, NC	3–2
1972	United States	Romania	Bucharest	3–2

Davis Cup (Cont.)

Year	Winner	Finalist	Site	Score
1973	Australia	United States	Cleveland	5–0
1974	South Africa	India	*	walkover
1975	Sweden	Czechoslovakia	Stockholm	3–2
1976	Italy	Chile	Santiago	4–1
1977	Australia	Italy	Sydney	3–1
1978	United States	Great Britain	Palm Springs	4–1
1979	United States	Italy	San Francisco	5–0
1980	Czechoslovakia	Italy	Prague	4–1
1981	United States	Argentina	Cincinnati	3–1
1982	United States	France	Grenoble, France	4–1
1983	Australia	Sweden	Melbourne	3–2
1984	Sweden	United States	Göteborg, Sweden	4–1
1985	Sweden	W Germany	Munich	3–2
1986	Australia	Sweden	Melbourne	3–2
1987	Sweden	India	Göteborg, Sweden	5–0
1988	West Germany	Sweden	Göteborg, Sweden	4–1
1989	West Germany	Sweden	Stuttgart	3–2
1990	United States	Australia	St. Petersburg	3–2
1991	France	United States	Lyon	3–1
1992	United States	Switzerland	Fort Worth, TX	3–1
1993	Germany	Australia	Dusseldorf	4–1
1994	Sweden	Russia	Moscow	4–1
1995	United States	Russia	Moscow	3–2
1996	France	Sweden	Malmö, Sweden	3–2
1997	Sweden	United States	Göteborg, Sweden	5–0
1998	Sweden	Italy	Milan	4–1
1999	Australia	France	Nice, France	3–2
2000	Spain	Australia	Barcelona	3–1
2001	France	Australia	Melbourne	3–2
2002	Russia	France	Paris	3–2
2003	Australia	Spain	Melbourne	3–1
2004	Spain	United States	Seville, Spain	3-2

*India refused to play the final in protest over South Africa's governmental policy of apartheid.
Note: Prior to 1972 the challenge-round system was in effect, with the previous year's winner "standing out" of the competition until the finals. A straight 16-nation tournament has been held since 1981.

Federation Cup

The Federation Cup was started in 1963 by the International Lawn Tennis Federation (now the ITF). Until 1991 all entrants gathered at one site at one time for a tournament that was concluded within one week. Since 1995 the Fed Cup, as it is now called, has been contested in three rounds by a World Group of eight nations. A meeting between two countries now consists of five matches: four singles and one doubles. The United States has the most wins (15), followed by Australia (7).

Year	Winner	Finalist	Site	Score
1963	United States	Australia	London	2–1
1964	Australia	United States	Philadelphia	2–1
1965	Australia	United States	Melbourne	2–1
1966	United States	W Germany	Turin	3–0
1967	United States	Great Britain	W Berlin	2–0
1968	Australia	Netherlands	Paris	3–0
1969	United States	Australia	Athens	2–1
1970	Australia	Great Britain	Freiburg	3–0
1971	Australia	Great Britain	Perth	3–0
1972	South Africa	Great Britain	Johannesburg	2–1
1973	Australia	South Africa	Bad Homburg	3–0
1974	Australia	United States	Naples	2–1
1975	Czechoslovakia	Australia	Aix-en-Provence	3–0
1976	United States	Australia	Philadelphia	2–1
1977	United States	Australia	Eastbourne, G.B.	2–1
1978	United States	Australia	Melbourne	2–1
1979	United States	Australia	Madrid	3–0
1980	United States	Australia	W Berlin	3–0
1981	United States	Great Britain	Nagoya	3–0
1982	United States	W Germany	Santa Clara, CA	3–0
1983	Czechoslovakia	W Germany	Zurich	2–1
1984	Czechoslovakia	Australia	Sao Paulo	2–1
1985	Czechoslovakia	United States	Tokyo	2–1
1986	United States	Czechoslovakia	Prague	3–0
1987	W Germany	United States	Vancouver	2–1

Federation Cup (Cont.)

Year	Winner	Finalist	Site	Score
1988	Czechoslovakia	USSR	Melbourne	2–1
1989	United States	Spain	Tokyo	3–0
1990	United States	USSR	Atlanta	2–1
1991	Spain	United States	Nottingham	2–1
1992	Germany	Spain	Frankfurt	2–1
1993	Spain	Australia	Frankfurt	3–0
1994	Spain	United States	Frankfurt	3–0
1995	Spain	United States	Valencia, Spain	3–2
1996	United States	Spain	Atlantic City	5–0
1997	France	Netherlands	Hertogenbosch, Neth.	4–1
1998	Spain	Switzerland	Geneva	3–2
1999	United States	Russia	Palo Alto, California	4–1
2000	United States	Spain	Las Vegas, Nevada	5–0
2001	Belgium	Russia	Barcelona	2–1
2002	Slovak Republic	Spain	Maspalomas, C. Isles	3–1
2003	France	United States	Moscow	4–1
2004	Russia	France	Moscow	3-2
2005	Russia	France	Paris	3-2

ATP Computer Year-End Top 10

MEN

1973
1. Ilie Nastase
2. John Newcombe
3. Jimmy Connors
4. Tom Okker
5. Stan Smith
6. Ken Rosewall
7. Manuel Orantes
8. Rod Laver
9. Jan Kodes
10. Arthur Ashe

1974
1. Jimmy Connors
2. John Newcombe
3. Bjorn Borg
4. Rod Laver
5. Guillermo Vilas
6. Tom Okker
7. Arthur Ashe
8. Ken Rosewall
9. Stan Smith
10. Ilie Nastase

1975
1. Jimmy Connors
2. Guillermo Vilas
3. Bjorn Borg
4. Arthur Ashe
5. Manuel Orantes
6. Ken Rosewall
7. Ilie Nastase
8. John Alexander
9. Roscoe Tanner
10. Rod Laver

1976
1. Jimmy Connors
2. Bjorn Borg
3. Ilie Nastase
4. Manuel Orantes
5. Raul Ramirez
6. Guillermo Vilas
7. Adriano Panatta
8. Harold Solomon
9. Eddie Dibbs
10. Brian Gottfried

1977
1. Jimmy Connors
2. Guillermo Vilas
3. Bjorn Borg
4. Vitas Gerulaitis
5. Brian Gottfried
6. Eddie Dibbs
7. Manuel Orantes
8. Raul Ramirez
9. Ilie Nastase
10. Dick Stockton

1978
1. Jimmy Connors
2. Bjorn Borg
3. Guillermo Vilas
4. John McEnroe
5. Vitas Gerulaitis
6. Eddie Dibbs
7. Brian Gottfried
8. Raul Ramirez
9. Harold Solomon
10. Corrado Barazzutti

1979
1. Bjorn Borg
2. Jimmy Connors
3. John McEnroe
4. Vitas Gerulaitis
5. Roscoe Tanner
6. Guillermo Vilas
7. Arthur Ashe
8. Harold Solomon
9. Jose Higueras
10. Eddie Dibbs

1980
1. Bjorn Borg
2. John McEnroe
3. Jimmy Connors
4. Gene Mayer
5. Guillermo Vilas
6. Ivan Lendl
7. Harold Solomon
8. Jose–Luis Clerc
9. Vitas Gerulaitis
10. Eliot Teltscher

1981
1. John McEnroe
2. Ivan Lendl
3. Jimmy Connors
4. Bjorn Borg
5. Jose–Luis Clerc
6. Guillermo Vilas
7. Gene Mayer
8. Eliot Teltscher
9. Vitas Gerulaitis
10. Peter McNamara

1982
1. John McEnroe
2. Jimmy Connors
3. Ivan Lendl
4. Guillermo Vilas
5. Vitas Gerulaitis
6. Jose–Luis Clerc
7. Mats Wilander
8. Gene Mayer
9. Yannick Noah
10. Peter McNamara

1983
1. John McEnroe
2. Ivan Lendl
3. Jimmy Connors
4. Mats Wilander
5. Yannick Noah
6. Jimmy Arias
7. Jose Higueras
8. Jose–Luis Clerc
9. Kevin Curren
10. Gene Mayer

ATP Computer Year-End Top 10 (Cont.)
MEN (CONT.)

1984
1 ....John McEnroe
2 ....Jimmy Connors
3 ....Ivan Lendl
4 ....Mats Wilander
5 ....Andres Gomez
6 ....Anders Jarryd
7 ....Henrik Sundstrom
8 ....Pat Cash
9 ....Eliot Teltscher
10 ..Yannick Noah

1985
1 ....Ivan Lendl
2 ....John McEnroe
3 ....Mats Wilander
4 ....Jimmy Connors
5 ....Stefan Edberg
6 ....Boris Becker
7 ....Yannick Noah
8 ....Anders Jarryd
9 ....Miloslav Mecir
10 ..Kevin Curren

1986
1 ....Ivan Lendl
2 ....Boris Becker
3 ....Mats Wilander
4 ....Yannick Noah
5 ....Stefan Edberg
6 ....Henri Leconte
7 ....Joakim Nystrom
8 ....Jimmy Connors
9 ....Miloslav Mecir
10 ..Andres Gomez

1987
1 ....Ivan Lendl
2 ....Stefan Edberg
3 ....Mats Wilander
4 ....Jimmy Connors
5 ....Boris Becker
6 ....Miloslav Mecir
7 ....Pat Cash
8 ....Yannick Noah
9 ....Tim Mayotte
10 ..John McEnroe

1988
1 ....Mats Wilander
2 ....Ivan Lendl
3 ....Andre Agassi
4 ....Boris Becker
5 ....Stefan Edberg
6 ....Kent Carlsson
7 ....Jimmy Connors
8 ....Jakob Hlasek
9 ....Henri Leconte
10 ..Tim Mayotte

1989
1 ....Ivan Lendl
2 ....Boris Becker
3 ....Stefan Edberg
4 ....John McEnroe
5 ....Michael Chang
6 ....Brad Gilbert
7 ....Andre Agassi
8 ....Aaron Krickstein
9 ....Alberto Mancini
10...Jay Berger

1990
1 ....Stefan Edberg
2 ....Boris Becker
3 ....Ivan Lendl
4 ....Andre Agassi
5 ....Pete Sampras
6 ....Andres Gomez
7 ....Thomas Muster
8 ....Emilio Sanchez
9 ....Goran Ivanisevic
10...Brad Gilbert

1991
1 ....Stefan Edberg
2 ....Jim Courier
3 ....Boris Becker
4 ....Michael Stich
5 ....Ivan Lendl
6 ....Pete Sampras
7 ....Guy Forget
8 ....Karel Novacek
9 ....Petr Korda
10...Andre Agassi

1992
1 ....Jim Courier
2 ....Stefan Edberg
3 ....Pete Sampras
4 ....Goran Ivanisevic
5 ....Boris Becker
6 ....Michael Chang
7 ....Petr Korda
8 ....Ivan Lendl
9 ....Andre Agassi
10...Richard Krajicek

1993
1 ....Pete Sampras
2 ....Michael Stich
3 ....Jim Courier
4 ....Sergi Bruguera
5 ....Stefan Edberg
6 ....Andrei Medvedev
7 ....Goran Ivanisevic
8 ....Michael Chang
9 ....Thomas Muster
10...Cedric Pioline

1994
1 ....Pete Sampras
2 ....Andre Agassi
3 ....Boris Becker
4 ....Sergi Bruguera
5 ....Goran Ivanisevic
6 ....Michael Chang
7 ....Stefan Edberg
8 ....Alberto Berasategui
9 ....Michael Stich
10...Todd Martin

1995
1 ....Pete Sampras
2 ....Andre Agassi
3 ....Thomas Muster
4 ....Boris Becker
5 ....Michael Chang
6 ....Yevgeny Kafelnikov
7 ....Thomas Enqvist
8 ....Jim Courier
9 ....Wayne Ferreira
10...Goran Ivanisevic

1996
1 ....Pete Sampras
2 ....Michael Chang
3 ....Yevgeny Kafelnikov
4 ....Goran Ivanisevic
5 ....Thomas Muster
6 ....Boris Becker
7 ....Richard Krajicek
8 ....Andre Agassi
9 ....Thomas Enqvist
10...Wayne Ferreira

1997
1 ....Pete Sampras
2 ....Patrick Rafter
3 ....Michael Chang
4 ....Jonas Bjorkman
5 ....Yevgeny Kafelnikov
6 ....Greg Rusedski
7 ....Carlos Moya
8 ....Sergei Bruguera
9 ....Thomas Muster
10...Marcelo Rios

1998
1 ....Pete Sampras
2 ....Marcelo Rios
3 ....Alex Corretja
4 ....Patrick Rafter
5 ....Carlos Moya
6 ....Andre Agassi
7 ....Tim Henman
8 ....Karol Kucera
9 ..Greg Rusedski
10...Richard Krajicek

ATP Computer Year-End Top 10 *(Cont.)*

MEN *(CONT.)*

1999

1 ....Andre Agassi
2 ...Yevgeny Kafelnikov
3 ...Pete Sampras
4 ....Thomas Enqvist
5 ...Gustavo Kuerten
6 ...Nicolas Kiefer
7 ...Todd Martin
8 ...Nicolas Lapentti
9 ...Marcelo Rios
10 ..Richard Krajicek

2000

1 ....Gustavo Kuerten
2 ...Marat Safin
3 ...Pete Sampras
4 ...Magnus Norman
5 ...Yevgeny Kafelnikov
6 ...Andre Agassi
7 ...Lleyton Hewitt
8 ...Alex Corretja
9 ...Thomas Enqvist
10 ..Tim Henman

2001

1 ....Lleyton Hewitt
2 ....Gustavo Kuerten
3 ....Andre Agassi
4 ....Yevgeny Kafelnikov
5 ....Juan Carlos Ferrero
6 ....Sebastien Grosjean
7 ....Patrick Rafter
8 ....Tommy Haas
9 ....Tim Henman
10 ..Pete Sampras

2002

1 ....Lleyton Hewitt
2 ....Andre Agassi
3 ....Marat Safin
4 ....Juan Carlos Ferrero
5 ....Carlos Moya
6 ....Roger Federer
7 ....Jiri Novak
8 ....Tim Henman
9 ....Albert Costa
10 ..Andy Roddick

2003

1 ....Andy Roddick
2 ....Roger Federer
3 ....Juan Carlos Ferrero
4 ....Andre Agassi
5 ....Guillermo Coria
6 ....Rainer Schuettler
7 ....Carlos Moya
8 ....David Nalbandian
9 ....Mark Philippoussis
10 ..Sebastien Grosjean

2004

1 ....Roger Federer
2 ....Andy Roddick
3 ....Lleyton Hewitt
4 ....Marat Safin
5 ....Carlos Moya
6 ....Tim Henman
7 ....Guillermo Coria
8 ....Andre Agassi
9 ....David Nalbandian
10 ..Gaston Gaudio

WTA Computer Year-End Top 10

WOMEN

1973

1 ....Margaret Smith Court
2 ...Billie Jean King
3 ...Evonne Goolagong
4 ...Chris Evert
5 ...Rosie Casals
6 ...Virginia Wade
7 ...Kerry Reid
8 ...Nancy Gunter
9 ...Julie Heldman
10...Helga Masthoff

1974

1 ....Billie Jean King
2 ...Evonne Goolagong
3 ...Chris Evert
4 ...Virginia Wade
5 ...Julie Heldman
6 ...Rosie Casals
7 ...Kerry Reid
8 ...Olga Morozova
9 ...Lesley Hunt
10...Francoise Durr

1975

1 ....Chris Evert
2 ....Billie Jean King
3 ...Evonne Goolagong Cawley
4 ...Martina Navratilova
5 ...Virginia Wade
6 ...Margaret Smith Court
7 ...Olga Morozova
8 ...Nancy Gunter
9 ...Francoise Durr
10...Rosie Casals

1976

1 ....Chris Evert
2 ....Evonne Goolagong Cawley
3 ....Virginia Wade
4 ....Martina Navratilova
5 ....Sue Barker
6 ....Betty Stove
7 ....Dianne Balestrat
8 ....Mima Jausovec
9 ....Rosie Casals
10 ....Francoise Durr

1977

1 ....Chris Evert
2 ....Billie Jean King
3 ....Martina Navratilova
4 ....Virginia Wade
5 ....Sue Barker
6 ....Rosie Casals
7 ....Betty Stove
8 ....Dianne Balestrat
9 ....Wendy Turnbull
10...Kerry Reid

1978

1 ....Martina Navratilova
2 ....Chris Evert
3 ....Evonne Goolagong Cawley
4 ....Virginia Wade
5 ....Billie Jean King
6 ....Tracy Austin
7 ....Wendy Turnbull
8 ....Kerry Reid
9 ....Betty Stove
10...Dianne Balestrat

1979

1 ....Martina Navratilova
2 ....Chris Evert Lloyd
3 ....Tracy Austin
4 ....Evonne Goolagong Cawley
5 ....Billie Jean King
6 ....Dianne Balestrat
7 ....Wendy Turnbull
8 ....Virginia Wade
9 ....Kerry Reid
10...Sue Barker

1980

1 ....Chris Evert Lloyd
2 ....Tracy Austin
3 ....Martina Navratilova
4 ....Hana Mandlikova
5 ....Evonne Goolagong Cawley
6 ....Billie Jean King
7 ....Andrea Jaeger
8 ....Wendy Turnbull
9 ....Pam Shriver
10...Greer Stevens

1981

1 ....Chris Evert Lloyd
2 ....Tracy Austin
3 ....Martina Navratilova
4 ....Andrea Jaeger
5 ....Hana Mandlikova
6 ....Sylvia Hanika
7 ....Pam Shriver
8 ....Wendy Turnbull
9 ....Bettina Bunge
10...Barbara Potter

1982

1 ....Martina Navratilova
2 ....Chris Evert Lloyd
3 ....Andrea Jaeger
4 ....Tracy Austin
5 ....Wendy Turnbull
6 ....Pam Shriver
7 ....Hana Mandlikova
8 ....Barbara Potter
9 ....Bettina Bunge
10...Sylvia Hanika

1983

1 ....Martina Navratilova
2 ....Chris Evert Lloyd
3 ....Andrea Jaeger
4 ....Pam Shriver
5 ....Sylvia Hanika
6 ....Jo Durie
7 ....Bettina Bunge
8 ....Wendy Turnbull
9 ....Tracy Austin
10...Zina Garrison

1984

1 ....Martina Navratilova
2 ....Chris Evert Lloyd
3 ....Hana Mandlikova
4 ....Pam Shriver
5 ....Wendy Turnbull
6 ....Manuela Maleeva
7 ....Helena Sukova
8 ....Claudia Kohde-Kilsch
9 ....Zina Garrison
10...Kathy Jordan

WTA Computer Year-End Top 10 (Cont.)
WOMEN (CONT.)

1985
1 ....Martina Navratilova
2 ....Chris Evert Lloyd
3 ....Hana Mandlikova
4 ....Pam Shriver
5 ....Claudia Kohde-
         Kilsch
6 ....Steffi Graf
7 ....Manuela Maleeva
8 ....Zina Garrison
9 ....Helena Sukova
10...Bonnie Gadusek

1986
1 ....Martina Navratilova
2 ....Chris Evert Lloyd
3 ....Pam Shriver
4 ....Hana Mandlikova
5 ....Helena Sukova
6 ....Pam Shriver
7 ....Claudia Kohde-
         Kilsch
8 ....Manuela Maleeva
9 ....Kathy Rinaldi
10...Gabriela Sabatini

1987
1 ....Steffi Graf
2 ....Martina Navratilova
3 ....Chris Evert
4 ....Pam Shriver
5 ....Hana Mandlikova
6 ....Gabriela Sabatini
7 ....Helena Sukova
8 ....Manuela Maleeva
9 ....Zina Garrison
10...Claudia Kohde-
         Kilsch

1988
1 ....Steffi Graf
2 ....Martina Navratilova
3 ....Chris Evert
4 ....Gabriela Sabatini
5 ....Pam Shriver
6 ....Manuela Maleeva-
         Fragniere
7 ....Natalia Zvereva
8 ....Helena Sukova
9 ....Zina Garrison
10...Barbara Potter

1989
1 ....Steffi Graf
2 ....Martina Navratilova
3 ....Gabriela Sabatini
4 ....Zina Garrison
5 ....A.S. Vicario
6 ....Monica Seles
7 ....Conchita Martinez
8 ....Helena Sukova
9 ....Manuela Maleeva-
         Fragniere
10...Chris Evert*

1990
1 ....Steffi Graf
2 ....Monica Seles
3 ....Martina Navratilova
4 ....Mary Joe Fernandez
5 ....Gabriela Sabatini
6 ....Katerina Maleeva
7 ....A.S. Vicario
8 ....Jennifer Capriati
9 ....M. Maleeva-Fragniere
10...Zina Garrison

1991
1 ....Monica Seles
2 ....Steffi Graf
3 ....Gabriela Sabatini
4 ....Martina Navratilova
5 ....Arantxa Sánchez
         Vicario
6 ....Jennifer Capriati
7 ....Jana Novotna
8 ....Mary Joe Fernandez
9 ....Conchita Martinez
10...M. Maleeva-Fragniere

1992
1 ....Monica Seles
2 ....Steffi Graf
3 ....Gabriela Sabatini
4 ....Arantxa Sánchez
         Vicario
5 ....Martina Navratilova
6 ....Mary Joe Fernandez
7 ....Jennifer Capriati
8 ....Conchita Martinez
9 ....M. Maleeva-Fragniere
10...Jana Novotna

1993
1 ....Steffi Graf
2 ....Arantxa Sánchez
         Vicario
3 ....Martina Navratilova
4 ....Conchita Martinez
5 ....Gabriela Sabatini
6 ....Jana Novotna
7 ....Mary Joe Fernandez
8 ....Monica Seles
9 ....Jennifer Capriati
10...Anke Huber

1994
1 ....Steffi Graf
2 ....Arantxa Sánchez
         Vicario
3 ....Conchita Martinez
4 ....Jana Novotna
5 ....Mary Pierce
6 ....Lindsay Davenport
7 ....Gabriela Sabatini
8 ....Martina Navratilova
9 ....Kimiko Date
10...Natasha Zvereva

1995
1 ....Steffi Graf (co-No. 1)
1 ....Monica Seles
         (co-No. 1)
2 ....Conchita Martinez
3 ....A. S.Vicario
4 ....Kimiko Date
5 ....Mary Pierce
6 ....Magdalena Maleeva
7 ....Gabriela Sabatini
8 ....Mary Joe Fernandez
9 ....Iva Majoli
10 ..Anke Huber

1996
1 ....Steffi Graf
2 ....Monica Seles
3 ....Jana Novotna
4 ....Lindsay Davenport
5 ....Martina Hingis
6 ....Stephanie de Ville
7 ....Tamarine
         Tanasugarn
8 ....Anke Huber
9 ....Conchita Martinez
10...Julie Halard-
         Decugis

1997
1 ....Martina Hingis
2 ....Jana Novotna
3 ....Lindsay Davenport
4 ....Amanda Coetzer
5 ....Monica Seles
6 ....Iva Majoli
7 ....Mary Pierce
8 ....Irina Spirlea
9 ....Arantxa Sánchez
         Vicario
10...Mary Joe Fernandez

1998
1 ....Lindsay Davenport
2 ....Martina Hingis
3 ....Jana Novotna
4 ....A.S. Vicario
5 ....Venus Williams
6 ....Monica Seles
7 ....Mary Pierce
8 ....Conchita Martinez
9 ....Steffi Graf
10...Nathalie Tauziat

1999
1 ....Martina Hingis
2 ....Lindsay Davenport
3 ....Venus Williams
4 ....Serena Williams
5 ....Mary Pierce
6 ....Monica Seles
7 ....Nathalie Tauziat
8 ....Barbara Schett
9 ....J. Halard-Decugis
10 ..Amelie Mauresmo

2000
1 ....Martina Hingis
2 ....Lindsay Davenport
3 ....Venus Williams
4 ....Monica Seles
5 ....Conchita Martinez
6 ....Serena Williams
7 ....Mary Pierce
8 ....Anna Kournikova
9 ....Arantxa
         Sánchez Vicario
10 ..Nathalie Tauziat

2001
1 ....Lindsay Davenport
2 ....Jennifer Capriati
3 ....Venus Williams
4 ....Martina Hingis
5 ....Kim Clijsters
6 ....Serena Williams
7 ....Justine Henin
8 ....Jelena Dokic
9 ....Amelie Mauresmo
10 ..Monica Seles

2002
1 ....Serena Williams
2 ....Venus Williams
3 ....Jennifer Capriati
4 ....Kim Clijsters
5 ....Justine Henin
6 ....Amelie Mauresmo
7 ....Monica Seles
8 ....Daniela Hantuchova
9 ....Jelena Dokic
10 ..Martina Hingis

2003
1 ....Justine Henin-
         Hardenne
2 ....Kim Clijsters
3 ....Serena Williams
4 ....Amelie Mauresmo
5 ....Lindsay Davenport
6 ....Jennifer Capriati
7 ....Anastasia Myskina
8 ....Elena Dementieva
9 ....Chandra Rubin
10 ..Ai Sugiyama

2004
1 ....Lindsay Davenport
2 ....Amelie Mauresmo
3 ....Anastasia Myskina
4 ....Maria Sharapova
5 ....Svetlana Kuznetsova
6 ....Elena Dementieva
7 ....Serena Williams
8 ....Justine Henin-
         Hardenne
9 ....Venus Williaims
10 ..Jennifer Capriati

*When Chris Evert announced her retirement at the 1989 United States Open, she was ranked fourth in the world. That was her last official series tournament.

Prize Money

Top 25 Men's Career Prize Money Leaders

Note: From arrival of Open tennis in 1968 through September 20, 2005.

	Earnings ($)
Pete Sampras	43,280,489
Andre Agassi	30,509,175
Boris Becker	25,080,956
Yevgeny Kafelnikov	23,883,797
Ivan Lendl	21,262,417
Stefan Edberg	20,630,941
Goran Ivanisevic	19,876,579
Michael Chang	19,145,632
Roger Federer	17,710,198
Lleyton Hewitt	15,147,146
Gustavo Kuerten	14,609,954
Jim Courier	14,033,132
Michael Stich	12,592,483
John McEnroe	12,539,622
Thomas Muster	12,224,410
Sergi Bruguera	11,632,199
Carlos Moya	11,362,175
Patrick Rafter	11,127,058
Jonas Bjorkman	11,115,936
Tim Henman	10,719,782
Petr Korda	10,448,450
Alex Corretja	10,338,209
Thomas Enqvist	10,290,743
Richard Krajicek	10,077,425
Wayne Ferreira	9,969,617

Top 25 Women's Career Prize Money Leaders

Note: From arrival of Open tennis in 1968 through September 20, 2005.

	Earnings ($)
Steffi Graf	21,895,277
Martina Navratilova	21,400,871
Lindsay Davenport	20,651,965
Martina Hingis	18,345,825
Arantxa Sánchez Vicario	16,942,640
Venus Williams	15,998,556
Serena Williams	15,867,287
Monica Seles	14,891,762
Kim Clijsters	12,426,547
Conchita Martinez	11,459,442
Jana Novotna	11,249,284
Jennifer Capriati	10,206,639
Justine Henin-Hardenne	9,360,409
Mary Pierce	8,898,891
Chris Evert	8,896,195
Gabriela Sabatini	8,785,850
Amelie Mauresmo	7,930,555
Natasha Zvereva	7,792,503
Nathalie Tauziat	6,649,907
Helena Sukova	6,391,245
Lisa Raymond	6,023,262
Elena Dementieva	5,768,256
Amanda Coetzer	5,594,821
Ai Sugiyama	5,504,552
Pam Shriver	5,460,566

Ungentlemanly Quarterly?

For those who like to keep abreast of the tennis news: French Open winner Anastasia Myskina filed an $8 million suit against *GQ* claiming the magazine did not prevent topless shots taken of her during a photo session two years ago from being sold to the Russian glossy *Medved*, which featured them in its August 2004 issue. According to the lawsuit, Myskina, 23, never intended for the pictures to be published and that they "are highly embarrassing and have caused Ms. Myskina great emotional distress and economic harm."

Open Era Overall Wins

Men's Career Leaders—Singles Titles Won

The top tournament-winning men from the institution of Open tennis in 1968 through Sept 26, 2005.

	W		W
Jimmy Connors	109	Thomas Muster	44
Ivan Lendl	94	Stefan Edberg	41
John McEnroe	77	Stan Smith	39
Pete Sampras	64	Michael Chang	34
Bjorn Borg	62	Roger Federer	33
Guillermo Vilas	62	Arthur Ashe	33
Andre Agassi	60	Mats Wilander	33
Ilie Nastase	57	John Newcombe	32
Boris Becker	49	Manuel Orantes	32
Rod Laver	47	Ken Rosewall	32
		Tom Okker	31

Women's Career Leaders—Singles Titles Won

The top tournament-winning women from the institution of Open tennis in 1968 through Sept. 26, 2005.

	W		W
Martina Navratilova	167	Helga Masthoff	37
Chris Evert	157	Venus Williams	33
Steffi Graf	107	Conchita Martinez	33
Margaret Smith Court	92	Olga Morozova	31
Evonne Goolagong Cawley	88	Kim Clijsters	29
Billie Jean King	67	Tracy Austin	29
Maria Bueno	63	Arantxa Sánchez Vicario	29
Virginia Wade	55	Hana Mandlikova	27
Monica Seles	53	Gabriela Sabatini	27
Lindsay Davenport	49	Francoise Durr-Browning	26
Martina Hingis	40	Serena Williams	26

Annual ATP/WTA Champions

Men—ATP Tour World Championship

Year	Player	Year	Player
1970	Stan Smith	1987	Ivan Lendl
1971	Ilie Nastase	1988	Boris Becker
1972	Ilie Nastase	1989	Stefan Edberg
1973	Ilie Nastase	1990	Andre Agassi
1974	Guillermo Vilas	1991	Pete Sampras
1975	Ilie Nastase	1992	Boris Becker
1976	Manuel Orantes	1993	Michael Stich
1977	Not held	1994	Pete Sampras
1978	Jimmy Connors	1995	Boris Becker
1979	John McEnroe	1996	Pete Sampras
1980	Bjorn Borg	1997	Pete Sampras
1981	Bjorn Borg	1998	Alex Corretja
1982	Ivan Lendl	1999	Pete Sampras
1983	Ivan Lendl	2000	Gustavo Kuerten
1984	John McEnroe	2001	Lleyton Hewitt
1985	John McEnroe	2002	Lleyton Hewitt
1986 (Jan)	Ivan Lendl	2003	Roger Federer
1986 (Dec)	Ivan Lendl	2004	Roger Federer

Note: Event held twice in 1986. *Since 1984 the final has been best-of-five sets.

Women—WTA Tour Championship

Year	Player	Year	Player
1972	Chris Evert	1988	Gabriela Sabatini
1973	Chris Evert	1989	Steffi Graf
1974	Evonne Goolagong	1990	Monica Seles
1975	Chris Evert	1991	Monica Seles
1976	Evonne Goolagong Cawley	1992	Monica Seles
1977	Chris Evert	1993	Steffi Graf
1978	Martina Navratilova	1994	Gabriela Sabatini
1979	Martina Navratilova	1995	Steffi Graf
1980	Tracy Austin	1996	Steffi Graf
1981	Martina Navratilova	1997	Jana Novotna
1982	Sylvia Hanika	1998	Martina Hingis
1983	Martina Navratilova	1999	Lindsay Davenport
1984*	Martina Navratilova	2000*	Martina Hingis
1985	Martina Navratilova	2001	Serena Williams
1986 (Mar)	Martina Navratilova	2002	Kim Clijsters
1986 (Nov)	Martina Navratilova	2003	Kim Clijsters
1987	Steffi Graf	2004	Maria Sharapova

YET ANOTHER SIGN OF THE APOCALYPSE

*Former tennis star Pat Cash said he was
"50 percent sure" he had an affair with a woman who
claims to have slept with David Beckham.*

Pauline Betz Addie (1965)
George T. Adee (1964)
Fred B. Alexander (1961)
Wilmer L. Allison (1963)
Manuel Alonso (1977)
Malcolm Anderson (2000)
Arthur Ashe (1985)
Juliette Atkinson (1974)
H.W. Bunny Austin (1997)
Tracy Austin (1992)
Lawrence A. Baker Sr. (1975)
Maud Barger–Wallach (1958)
Angela Mortimer Barrett (1993)
Boris Becker (2003)
Karl Behr (1969)
Bjorn Borg (1987)
Jean Borotra (1976)
Lesley Turner Bowrey (1997)
Maureen Connolly Brinker (1968)
John Bromwich (1984)
Norman Everard Brookes (1977)
Mary K. Browne (1957)
Jacques Brugnon (1976)
Butch Buchholz (2005)
J. Donald Budge (1964)
Maria E. Bueno (1978)
May Sutton Bundy (1956)
Mabel E. Cahill (1976)
Rosie Casals (1996)
Oliver S. Campbell (1955)
Malcolm Chace (1961)
Dorothy (Dodo) Cheney (2004)
Dorothea Douglass
   Chambers (1981)
Philippe Chatrier (1992)
Louise Brough Clapp (1967)
Clarence Clark (1983)
Joseph S. Clark (1955)
William J. Clothier (1956)
Henri Cochet (1976)
Arthur W. (Bud) Collins Jr. (1994)
Jimmy Connors (1998)
Ashley Cooper (1991)
Jim Courier (2004)
Margaret Smith Court (1979)
Gottfried von Cramm (1977)
Jack Crawford (1979)
Joseph F. Cullman III (1990)
Allison Danzig (1968)
Sarah Palfrey Danzig (1963)
Herman David (1998)
Dwight F. Davis (1956)

Charlotte Dod (1983)
John H. Doeg (1962)
Lawrence Doherty (1980)
Reginald Doherty (1980)
Jaroslav Drobny (1983)
Margaret Osborne duPont
   (1967)
Francoise Durr (2003)
James Dwight (1955)
Stefan Edberg (2004)
Roy Emerson (1982)
Pierre Etchebaster (1978)
Chris Evert (1995)
Robert Falkenburg (1974)
Neale Fraser (1984)
Shirley Fry-Irvin (1970)
Charles S. Garland (1969)
Althea Gibson (1971)
Kathleen McKane Godfree
   (1978)
Richard A. Gonzales (1968)
Evonne Goolagong Cawley
   (1988)
Steffi Graf (2004)
Bryan M. Grant Jr. (1972)
David Gray (1985)
Clarence Griffin (1970)
King Gustaf V of Sweden
   (1980)
Harold H. Hackett (1961)
Ellen Forde Hansell (1965)
Darlene R. Hard (1973)
Doris J. Hart (1969)
Gladys M. Heldman (1979)
W.E. (Slew) Hester Jr. (1981)
Bob Hewitt (1992)
Lew Hoad (1980)
Harry Hopman (1978)
Fred Hovey (1974)
Joseph R. Hunt (1966)
Lamar Hunt (1993)
Francis T. Hunter (1961)
Helen Hull Jacobs (1962)
William Johnston (1958)
Ann Haydon Jones (1985)
Perry Jones (1970)
Robert Kelleher (2000)
Billie Jean King (1987)
Jan Kodes (1990)
John A. Kramer (1968)
Rene Lacoste (1976)
Al Laney (1979)

William A. Larned (1956)
Arthur D. Larsen (1969)
Rod G. Laver (1981)
Ivan Lendl (2001)
Suzanne Lenglen (1978)
Dorothy Round Little (1986)
George M. Lott Jr. (1964)
Gene Mako (1973)
Molla Bjurstedt Mallory (1958)
Hana Mandlikova (1994)
Alice Marble (1964)
Alastair B. Martin (1973)
Dan Maskell (1996)
William McChesney Martin (1982)
John McEnroe (1999)
Ken McGregor (1999)
Chuck McKinley (1986)
Maurice McLoughlin (1957)
Frew McMillan (1992)
W. Donald McNeill (1965)
Elisabeth H. Moore (1971)
Gardnar Mulloy (1972)
R. Lindley Murray (1958)
Julian S. Myrick (1963)
Ilie Nastase (1991)
Martina Navratilova (2000)
John D. Newcombe (1986)
Arthur C. Nielsen Sr (1971)
Yannick Noah (2005)
Jana Novotna (2005)
Alex Olmedo (1987)
Rafael Osuna (1979)
Mary Ewing Outerbridge (1981)
Frank A. Parker (1966)
Gerald Patterson (1989)
Budge Patty (1977)
Theodore R. Pell (1966)
Fred Perry (1975)
Tom Pettitt (1982)
Nicola Pietrangeli (1986)
Adrian Quist (1984)
Dennis Ralston (1987)
Ernest Renshaw (1983)
William Renshaw (1983)
Vincent Richards (1961)
Nancy Richey (2003)
Bobby Riggs (1967)
Helen Wills Moody Roark
   (1959)
Anthony D. Roche (1986)
Ellen C. Roosevelt (1975)
Mervyn Rose (2001)

Ken Rosewall (1980)
Elizabeth Ryan (1972)
Manuel Santana (1984)
Richard Savitt (1976)
Frederick R. Schroeder (1966)
Eleonora Sears (1968)
Richard D. Sears (1955)
Frank Sedgman (1979)
Pancho Segura (1984)
Vic Seixas Jr. (1971)
Francis X. Shields (1964)
Betty Nuthall Shoemaker (1977)
Pam Shriver (2002)
Henry W. Slocum Jr. (1955)
Stan Smith (1987)

Fred Stolle (1985)
William F. Talbert (1967)
Bill Tilden (1959)
Lance Tingay (1982)
Ted Tinling (1986)
Brian Tobin (2003)
Bertha Townsend Toulmin
  (1974)
Tony Trabert (1970)
James H. Van Alen (1965)
John Van Ryn (1963)
Guillermo Vilas (1991)
Ellsworth Vines (1962)
Virginia Wade (1989)
Marie Wagner (1969)

Holcombe Ward (1956)
Watson Washburn (1965)
Malcolm D. Whitman (1955)
Hazel Hotchkiss Wightman
  (1957)
Mats Wilander (2002)
Anthony Wilding (1978)
Richard Norris Williams II
  (1957)
Major Walter Clopton Wingfield
  (1997)
Sidney B. Wood (1964)
Robert D. Wrenn (1955)
Beals C. Wright (1956)

Note: Years in parentheses are dates of induction.

Super Soph

Liza Wischer, a sophomore at Red River High in Grand Forks, N. Dak., didn't lose a set in the individual tournament as she won the singles title at the North Dakota State Girls Tennis Tournament for the third straight year. She was 26–0 for the season and led the Roughriders to a 14–0 record.

Golf

**2005 Masters
and British Open champion
Tiger Woods**

Back In The Swing

With a retooled swing, Tiger Woods once again dominated, winning two Majors; while 16-year old phenom Michelle Wie turned pro at the end of an amazing year

BY STEPHEN CANNELLA

I F HE HAD CHECKED THE SCORE-card of his life before teeing off for the 2005 Masters, Tiger Woods might have noticed that he had a comfortable lead over most of his competitors, if not the entire human race. Not yet 30, he had already won eight major titles, more than anyone in history except Ben Hogan (9), Gary Player (9), Walter Hagen (11) and Jack Nicklaus (18). True, it had been 34 months since his last major championship, but few would argue that he wasn't the most organically gifted golfer the sport had ever seen. There were also the little matters of his kingly wealth (he takes home upwards of $80 million a year in winnings and endorsement pay) and seemingly storybook domestic life (he married Swedish model Elin Nordegren in October 2004).

Yet when the proceedings were over at Augusta, after Woods had fended off Chris DiMarco in a sudden death playoff to win his fourth green jacket, Tiger acted and sounded like someone who felt he had something to prove before the victory. His celebration on the 18th green after his victorious birdie putt was one of the most emotional of his career. Later he spoke of the "validation" that he felt after winning. To be sure, it was impressive and well-earned victory, one of the hardest-fought of Woods's glorious career. But one suspects he would have kept the respect of the links community even had he lost.

But then 2005 was a year of validation for many in the golf world. Phil Mickelson, who finally won his first major title at the 2004 Masters, took his second in the 2005 PGA Championship at Baltusrol Golf Club in Springfield, N.J. Many players (113, to be precise) have won a single major. The PGA victory placed Mickelson in the far more exclusive club of two-time major winners, confirming his spot in the golf pantheon. Not that a one-hit wonder is someone to sneer at: Many a touring pro would give anything for a major victory, a feeling New Zealand's Michael Campbell knows better than most. After turning pro in 1993, Campbell, 36, spent the next 12 years chas-

Michelle Wie placed 2nd at the LPGA Championship and nearly made the cut at the PGA's John Deere Classic.

ing his golf dreams around the globe on the Australian, Asian and European tours. That effort was validated with an upset win at the 2005 U.S. Open at Pinehurst.

Michelle Wie, the wunderkind of the women's game, was also in search of ways to certify herself as a major player, to prove that the immense hype surrounding her rise through the golf ranks was more than merely that. After turning 16 in October, she turned pro, signed multi-million dollar deals with Nike and Sony, and made it clear that she intends to someday qualify for the men's Tour. Wie's talent (she made the cut in every LPGA event she entered as an amateur) and marketability (a Hawaiian native, she is fluent in Korean and is studying Chinese and Japanese) made her the most anticipated newcomer on the golf stage since Tiger Woods turned pro in 1996.

It's tempting to say that Woods's dominance in 2005—in addition to the Masters, he won the British Open and regained the No. 1 world ranking he had lost to Singh the previous year—was a return to form after a two-year slump. He was 0-for-10 in majors heading into the Masters, and he won just one tournament in 2004. But the golf world actually saw the debut of a new Tiger in 2005, one with a remodeled swing, new equipment—and, if possible, a more complete game.

In March 2004 Woods began working with instructor Hank Haney to build a leaner, more efficient swing, a stroke he slowly honed throughout the year. Then he broke down and finally joined golf's arms race. In recent years drivers with oversized heads and space-age shafts have been de rigueur on the PGA Tour. However Woods, opting for precision over power, continued to play with a relatively small 265cc driver with a 43.5-inch shaft.

Before the 2005 season Woods traded that old school club for a 460cc model with a 45-inch graphite shaft. He also quietly began playing a new ball, a potent four-piece, solid-core model developed for him by Nike. The equipment changes essentially leveled the playing field between Woods and his competitors, many of whom had been able to out-hit him with superior gear. The result: In 2005, Tiger's superior talent again took over. He once more began hitting shots other players could only dream of.

Armed with a new swing and new toys, Woods went to work at the fabled course at Augusta. After an opening-round 74 put him seven strokes behind DiMarco, Woods climbed back into contention and made a spirited rally in a third round pushed to Sunday morning because of rain. He took a three-shot lead into the final 18. Woods had never lost a major when he led after 54 holes, but DiMarco staged a rally of his own in the final round. He and Woods traded birdies after the turn, and Woods clung to a one-stroke lead as they headed for the par-3 16th.

Woods's birdie chip on 16 didn't clinch the tournament—he coughed up a two-stroke lead on the final two holes of regulation play—but it will be remembered as one of the most incredible shots in Masters history. After whacking his tee shot long and to the left of the green, Woods was left with just one play: Pitch onto the dizzyingly steep green above the hole and pray the ball rolled close enough to leave him a makeable par putt. Woods's prayers were answered—and then some. He deftly chipped onto the green, and the ball began a slow, curvy joyride down the slope toward the cup. After pausing at the lip for dramatic effect, the hot new Nike orb tumbled into the hole—and into lore, as one of Woods's most amazing shots. "You expect the unexpected," said DiMarco, "and unfortunately it's not unexpected when he's doing it."

DiMarco surged back to force a playoff, but finally succumbed when Woods birdied the first extra hole. The victory gave Woods, who was in his ninth pro season, nine major titles—one more than Nicklaus had at the same point in his career. A five-stroke victory over Colin Montgomerie at the British Open brought Woods a step closer to Nicklaus's record, and continued a poetic trend: When Nicklaus retires, Woods wins. When Nicklaus played his final U.S. Open, in 2000, Woods won; ditto for Nicklaus's last PGA Championship (2000). Golf's greatest player bid adieu to Augusta and the British Open in 2005, a fitting passing of the torch to the man who will likely supplant him one day.

Woods nearly preceded his British win with a come-from-behind victory at the U.S. Open; tied for seventh at the start of the final round, he finished second, two strokes behind Campbell. The humble New Zealander—he referred to himself during the tournament as "little old me"—was the beneficiary of a startling Sunday collapse by defending champion and third-round leader Retief Goosen. Goosen's short game fell apart on Pinehurst's asphalt-like greens. After a birdie and six pars on the first seven holes of the round, Campbell, who began the day four shots back, found himself leading. He held up under a late rush by Woods and iced the biggest win of his career with a final-round 69. "Deep down inside, I knew that I had it in me to do something special," he said.

His devoted galleries always expect something special from Mickelson, who delivered with a heart-stopping win at the PGA. Mickelson needed a Monday morning birdie on the 72nd hole—rain suspended play on Sunday—after frittering away the three-stroke lead he carried into the final round, but the win nonetheless suggested that, at age 35, his best golf may be ahead of him. "I've only had two [majors] for an hour or two," he said after bringing himself halfway to a career Grand Slam. "But it's a long-term goal to get the other two."

Wie's long-term goals are equally lofty. And why not? Before turning pro, she came close to becoming the youngest player to win the women's U.S. Open; she was tied for the lead after three rounds before shooting a nervous 82 on Sunday. (Her presence on the leaderboard sent final round TV ratings soaring 86% over the previous year's.) In July, at the John Deere Classic, she came within two strokes of becoming the first woman since Babe Zaharias in 1945 to make the cut in a PGA event. Later that month, she reached the quarterfinals of the U.S. Amateur Public Links Championship. But those events were mere stepping stones to someone who yearns to dominate a sport. "I want to make a statement to all women that there are no limitations," Wie said, more than a year before she turned pro. "If I can drive the ball 300 yards, if I can compete against men, if I can make it to the Masters, then maybe I can inspire them to break free in their own lives."

In 2006, we should find out how close Wie is to being the next Tiger Woods. If 2005 is any indication, we should hear plenty from the current version as well.

FOR THE RECORD·2004-2005

Men's Majors

The Masters
Augusta National GC (par 72; 7,270 yds);
Augusta, GA, April 10, 2005

Player	Score	Earnings ($)
Tiger Woods	74-66-65-71--276	1,260,000
Chris DiMarco	67-67-74-68--276	756,000
Retief Goosen	71-75-70-67--283	406,000
Luke Donald	68-77-69-69--283	406,000
Vijay Singh	68-73-71-72--284	237,300
Mike Weir	74-71-68-71--284	237,300
Mark Hensby	69-73-70-72--284	237,300
Rod Pampling	73-71-70-70--284	237,300
Trevor Immelman	73-73-65-73--284	237,300
Phil Mickelson	70-72-69-74--285	189,000
Tim Herron	76-68-70-72--286	168,000
David Howell	72-69-76-69--286	168,000
Tom Lehman	74-74-70-69--287	135,333
Justin Leonard	75-71-70-71--287	135,333
Thomas Levet	71-75-68-73--287	135,333
Ryan Moore*	71-71-75-70--287	
Kirk Triplett	75-68-72-73--288	112,000
Chad Campbell	73-73-67-75--288	112,000
Darren Clarke	72-76-69-71--288	112,000
Bernhard Langer	74-74-70-71--289	84,840
Jeff Maggert	74-74-72-69--289	84,840

*Amateur.
Won playoff.

British Open
St. Andrews GC (par 72; 6,609 yds);
St. Andrews, Scotland, July 17, 2005

Player	Score	Earnings ($)
Tiger Woods	66-67-71-70--274	1,261,584
Colin Montgomerie	71-66-70-72--279	753,446
Fred Couples	68-71-73-68--280	424,909
Jose Maria Olazabal	68-70-68-74--280	424,909
Geoff Ogilvy	71-74-67-69--281	214,060
Bernhard Langer	71-69-70-71--281	214,060
Vijay Singh	69-69-70-71--281	214,060
Michael Campbell	69-72-68-72--281	214,060
Sergio Garcia	70-69-69-73--281	214,060
Retief Goosen	68-73-66-74--281	214,060
Graeme McDowell	69-72-74-67--282	116,959
Nick Faldo	74-69-70-69--282	116,959
Ian Poulter	70-72-71-69--282	116,959
Kenny Perry	71-71-68-72--282	116,959
David Frost	77-65-72-69--283	81,102
Nick O'Hearn	73-69-70-71--283	81,102
Mark Hensby	67-77-69-70--283	81,102
Lloyd Saltman	73-71-68-71--283	81,102
Trevor Immelman	68-70-73-72--283	81,102
John Daly	71-69-70-73--283	81,102
Sean O'Hair	73-67-70-73--283	81,102
Darren Clarke	73-70-67-73--283	81,102

Nine tied at 284.

U.S. Open
Pinehurst #2 GC, (par 70; 7,290 yds);
Pinehurst, NC, June 19, 2005

Player	Score	Earnings ($)
Michael Campbell	71-69-71-69--280	1,170,000
Tiger Woods	70-71-72-69--282	700,000
Sergio Garcia	71-69-75-70--285	320,039
Tim Clark	76-69-70-70--285	320,039
Mark Hensby	71-68-72-74--285	320,039
Rocco Mediate	67-74-74-71--286	187,813
Davis Love III	77-70-70-69--286	187,813
Vijay Singh	70-70-74-72--286	187,813
Nick Price	72-71-72-72--287	150,834
Arron Oberholser	76-67-71-73--287	150,834
Bob Estes	70-73-75-70--288	123,857
Corey Pavin	73-72-70-73--288	123,857
Peter Hedblom	77-66-70-75--288	123,857
Retief Goosen	68-70-69-81--288	123,857
David Toms	70-72-70-77--289	88,120
Fred Couples	71-74-74-70--289	88,120
Stewart Cink	73-74-73-69--289	88,120
Ernie Els	71-76-72-70--289	88,120
Ryuji Imada	77-68-73-71--289	88,120
John Cook	71-76-70-72--289	88,120
Peter Jacobsen	72-73-69-75--289	88,120
K.J. Choi	69-70-74-76-289	88,120

PGA Championship
Baltusrol GC (par 70; 7,392 yds)
Springfield, NJ, August 14, 2005

Player	Score	Earnings ($)
Phil Mickelson	67-65-72-72--276	1,170,000
Steve Elkington	68-70-68-71--277	572,000
Thomas Bjorn	71-71-63-72--277	572,000
Tiger Woods	75-69-66-68--278	286,000
Davis Love III	68-68-68-74--278	286,000
Geoff Ogilvy	69-69-72-69--279	201,500
Michael Campbell	73-68-68-69--279	201,500
Retief Goosen	68-70-69-72--279	201,500
Pat Perez	68-71-67-73--279	201,500
Vijay Singh	70-67-69-74--280	131,800
Ted Purdy	69-75-70-66--280	131,800
David Toms	71-72-69-68--280	131,800
Steve Flesch	70-71-69-70--280	131,800
Dudley Hart	70-73-67-71--280	131,800
Charles Howell III	70-71-68-72--281	102,500
Stuart Appleby	67-70-69-75--281	102,500
Tim Clark	71-73-70-68--282	82,500
Zach Johnson	70-70-73-69--282	82,500
Trevor Immelman	67-72-72-71--282	82,500
Joe Ogilvie	74-68-69-71--282	82,500
Bo Van Pelt	70-70-68-74--282	82,500
Lee Westwood	68-68-71-75--282	82,500

Late 2004 PGA Tour Events

Tournament	Final Round	Winner	Score/ Under Par	Earnings ($)
WCG American Express Champ	Oct 3	Ernie Els	270/–18	1,200,00
Southern Farm Bureau Classic	Oct 3	Fred Funk	266/–22	540,000
Las Vegas Invitational	Oct 10	Andre Stolz	266/–21	720,000
Greater Greensboro Classic	Oct 17	Brent Geiberger	270/–18	828,000
Funai Classic at Walt Disney World	Oct 23	Ryan Palmer	266/–22	756,000
Chrysler Championship	Oct 2	Vijay Singh	266/–18	900,000
The Tour Championship	Nov 6	Retief Goosen	269/–11	1,080,000
WGC World Cup	Nov 20	Paul Casey/Luke Donald	257/–31	700,000 each

2005 PGA Tour Events

Tournament	Final Round	Winner	Score/ Under Par	Earnings ($)
Mercedes Championships	Jan 9	Stuart Appleby	271/–21	1,060,000
Sony Open in Hawaii	Jan 16	Vijay Singh	269/–11	864,000
Buick Invitational	Jan 23	Tiger Woods	272/–16	810,000
Bob Hope Chrysler Classic	Jan 30	Justin Leonard	332/–28	900,000
FBR Open	Feb 6	Phil Mickelson	267/–17	936,000
AT&T Pebble Beach National Pro-Am	Feb 13	Phil Mickelson	269/–19	954,000
Nissan Open	Feb 20	Adam Scott	133/–9	864,000
WGC Match Play Championship	Feb 27	David Toms	6&5	1,200,000
Chrysler Classic of Tucson	Feb 27	Jeff Ogilvy	269/–19	540,000
Ford Championship	Mar 6	Tiger Woods	264/–24	900,000
Honda Classic	Mar 13	Padraig Harrington	274/–14	900,000
Bay Hill Invitational	Mar 20	Kenny Perry	276/–12	900,000
The Players Championship	Mar 27	Fred Funk	279/–9	1,440,000
BellSouth Classic	Apr 3	Phil Mickelson	208/–8	810,000
The Masters	Apr 10	Tiger Woods	276/–12	1,170,000
MCI Heritage	Apr 17	Peter Leonard	277/–7	864,000
Shell Houston Open	Apr 24	Vijay Singh	275/–13	900,000
Zurich Classic of New Orleans	May 1	Tom Petrovic	275/–13	918,000
Wachovia Championship	May 8	Vijay Singh	276/–12	1,080,000
EDS Byron Nelson Classic	May 15	Ted Purdy	265/–15	1,044,000
Bank of America Colonial	May 22	Ken Perry	261/–19	954,000
FedEx St. Jude Classic	May 29	Justin Leonard	266/–14	846,000
Memorial Tournament	June 5	Bart Bryant	272/–16	945,000
Booz Allen Classic	June 12	Sergio Garcia	270/–14	945,000
U.S. Open Championship	June 19	Michael Campbell	280/Even	1,125,000
Barclays Classic	June 26	Padraig Harrington	274/–10	864,000
Cialis Western Open	July 3	Jim Furyk	270/–14	864,000
John Deere Classic	July 10	Sean O'Hair	268/–16	684,000
B.C. Open	July 17	Jason Bohn	264/–24	540,00
British Open	July 17	Tiger Woods	274/–14	1,300,000
U.S. Bank Championship	July 24	Ben Crane	260/–20	630,000
Buick Open	July 31	Vijay Singh	264/–24	810,000
The International	Aug 7	Retief Godson	278/32	900,000
PGA Championship	Aug 14	Vijay Singh*	276/–4	1,125,000
WGC-NEC Invitational	Aug 21	Stewart Cink	269/–11	1,200,000
Reno-Tahoe Open	Aug 21	Vaughn Taylor	278/–10	540,000
Buick Championship	Aug 28	Brad Faxon	266/–14	774,000
Deutsche Bank Championship	Sep 5	Olin Browne	270/–14	990,000
Bell Canadian Open	Sep 11	Mark Calcavecchia	275/-5	756,000
84 Lumber Classic of Pennsylvania	Sep 18	Jason Gore	274/-14	792,000
Valero Texas Open	Sep 25	Robert Gamez	262/-18	630,000

* Won playoff. ‡ Revised Stableford scoring.

Kraft Nabisco Championship

Mission Hills CC; Rancho Mirage, CA
(par 72; 6,535 yds) March 24–27

Player	Score	Earnings ($)
Annika Sorenstam	70-69-66-68—273	270,000
Rosie Jones	69-70-71-71—281	166,003
Laura Diaz	75-69-71-68—283	106,791
Criste Kerr	72-70-70-71—283	106,971
Grace Park	73-68-76-67—284	68,165
Mi Hyun Kim	69-71-72-72—284	68,165
Juli Inkster	70-74-72-69—285	51,350
Lorie Kane	71-76-69-70—286	44,988
Candie Kung	72-73-71-71—287	34,591
Wendy Doolan	74-69-73-71—287	34,591
Dorothy Delasin	71-72-73-71—287	34,591
Beth Daniel	74-72-69-72—287	34,591
Reilley Rankin	73-68-74-72—287	34,591
Michelle Wie*	70-74-73-71—288	
Kim Saiki	74-71-72-73—288	27,175
Brandie Burton	72-71-72-73—288	27,175
Hee-Won Han	76-71-69-73—289	24,267
Natalie Gulbis	73-71-72-73—289	24,267
Shi Hyun Ahn	77-76-71-66—290	21,692
Paula Creamer	74-72-72-72—290	21,692
Young Kim	76-70-70-74—290	21,692

*Amateur.

McDonald's LPGA Championship

Bulle Rock GC; Havre de Grace, MD
(par 72; 6,488 yds) June 9–12

Player	Score	Earnings ($)
Annika Sorenstam	68-67-69-73—277	270,000
Michelle Wie*	69-71-71-69—280	
Paula Creamer	68-73-74-67—282	140,517
Laura Davies	67-70-74-71—282	140,517
Lorean Ochoa	72-72-68-72—284	82,486
Natalie Gulbis	67-71-73-73—284	82,486
Mi Hyun Kim	69-75-74-67—285	43,993
Pat Hurst	72-73-71-69—285	43,993
Gloria Park	71-71-72-71—285	43,993
Carin Koch	74-70-69-72—285	43,993
Moira Dunn	71-68-72-74—285	43,993
Young Kim	73-68-68-76—285	43,993
Candie Kung	72-73-73-68—286	29,303
Juli Inkster	75-71-71-69—286	29,309
Jeong Jang	71-71-69-75—286	29,309
Lindsey Wright	71-72-72-72—287	23,899
Angela Stanford	69-73-73-72—287	23,899
Jennifer Rosales	71-73-69-74—287	23,899
Marisa Baena	70-69-73-75—287	23,899
Karrie Web	74-75-72-67—288	19,797
Beth Bader	72-72-72-72—288	19,797
Laura Diaz	67-72-76-73—288	19,797

*Amateur.

U.S. Women's Open

Cherry Hills CC; Cherry Hills Village, Co
(par 72; 6,481 yds) June 23-26

Player	Score	Earnings ($)
Birdie Kim	74-72-69-72—287	560,000
Brittany Lane*	69-77-72-71—289	
Morgan Pressel*	71-73-70-75—288	
Lorie Kane	74-71-76-69—290	272,723
Natalie Gulbis	70-75-74-71—290	272,723
Lorena Ochoa	74-68-77-72—291	116,310
Karine Icher	69-75-75-72—291	116,310
Candie Kung	73-73-71-74—291	116,310
Young Jo	74-71-70-76—291	116,310
Cristie Kerr	74-71-72-75—292	80,523
Angela Stanford	69-74-73-76—292	80,523
Karen Stupples	75-70-69-78—292	80,523
Soo Yun Kang	74-74-74-71—293	61,402
Meg Mallon	71-74-75-73—293	61,402
Paige MacKenzie*	75-75-69-74—293	
Heather Bowie	77-73-69-74—293	61,402
Tina Barrett	73-74-71-75—293	61,402
Jamie Hullett	75-72-70-76—293	61,402
Leta Lindley	73-76-73-72—294	47,480

Eight players tied at 296.

*Amateur.

Weetabix Women's British Open

Royal Birkdale GC; Southport, England,
(par 72; 6,346 yds) July 28–July 31

Player	Score	Earnings ($)
Jeong Jang	68-66-69-69—272	280,208
Sophie Gustafson	69-73-67-67—276	175,130
Michelle Wie*	75-67-67-69—278	
Young Kim	74-68-67-69—278	122,591
Liselotte Neumann	71-70-68-70—279	81,144
Annika Sorenstam	73-69-66-71—279	81,144
Cristie Kerr	73-66-69-71—279	81,144
Natalie Gulbis	76-70-68-66—280	58,669
Grace Park	77-68-67-68—280	58,669
Louise Stahle*	73-65-73-69—280	
Ai Miyazato	72-73-69-67—281	44,221
Michele Redman	75-71-67-68—281	44,221
Karen Stupples	74-71-65-71—281	44,221
Karrie Webb	75-66-69-71—281	44,221
Becky Morgan	79-66-67-70—282	30,298
Yuri Fudoh	75-69-68-70—282	30,298
Carin Koch	76-68-66-72—282	30,298
Juli Inkster	74-68-68-72—282	30,298
Paula Creamer	75-69-65-73—282	30,298
Pat Hurst	75-65-70-73—283	24,956

*Amateur.

Women's Tour Results

Late 2004 LPGA Tour Events

Tournament	Final Round	Winner	Score/ Under Par	Earnings ($)
Asahi Ryokuken International Champ.	Oct 10	Lisolette Neumann	2743/–15	150,000
Samsung World Championship	Oct 17	Annika Sorenstam	270/-18	206,250
CJ Nine Bridges Classic	Oct 31	Grace Park	200/-16	202,500
Mizuno Classic	Nov 7	Annika Sorenstam	194/-22	150,000
LPGA Tournament of Champions	Nov 14	Heathery Daly-Donofrio	269/19	130,000
ADT Championship	Nov 21	Annika Sorenstam*	275/-13	215,000

2005 LPGA Tour Events

Tournament	Final Round	Winner	Score/ Under Par	Earnings ($)
SBS Open	Feb 26	Jennifer Rosales	208/–8	150,000
MasterCard Classic	Mar 6	Annika Sorenstam	209/–7	180,000
Safeway International	Mar 20	Annika Sorenstam	277/–11	210,000
Kraft Nabisco Championship	Mar 27	Annika Sorenstam	273/–15	270,000
Takefuji Classic	Apr 16	Wendy Ward	200/–16	165,000
Corona Morelia Championship	Apr 24	Carin Koch	279/–9	150,000
Franklin American Mortgage Champ.	May 1	Stacy Prammanasudh	274/–14	150,000
Michelob ULTRA Open.	May 8	Cristie Kerr	276/–8	330,000
Chick-fil-A Charity Championship	May 15	Annika Sorenstam	265/–23	240,000
Sybase Classic	May 22	Paula Creamer	278/–6	187,500
LPGA Corning Classic	May 29	Jimin Kang	273/–15	165,000
ShopRite LPGA Classic	June 5	Annika Sorenstam	196/–17	210,000
McDonald's LPGA Championship	June 12	Annika Sorenstam	277/–11	270,000
Wegman's Rochester LPGA	June 19	Lorena Ochoa	273/–15	225,000
U.S. Women's Open	June 26	Birdie Kim	287/+3	560,000
HSBC Women's World Match Play	July 3	Marisa Baena	1 up	500,000
Jamie Farr Owens Corning	July 10	Heather Bowie	274/–11	180,000
Canadian Women's Open	July 17	Meena Lee	279/–9	195,000
Evian Masters	July 23	Paula Creamer	273/–15	375,880
Weetabix Women's British Open	July 31	Jeong Jang	272/–16	280,208
Safeway Classic	Aug 21	Soo-Yun Kang	201/–15	210,000
Wendy's Chamionship for Children	Aug 28	Cristie Kerr	270/–18	150,000
State Farm Classic	Sep 4	Pat Hurst	271/–17	195,000
John Q. Hammons Hotel Classic	Sep 18	Annika Sorenstam	208/–5	150,000
Office Depot Championship	Oct. 2	Hee-Hon Wan	201/–12	195,000

* Won playoff.

Late 2004 Senior Tour Events

Tournament	Final Round	Winner	Score/Under Par	Earnings ($)
Constellation Energy Classic	Oct 3	Wayne Levi	200/–16	225,000
Administaff Small Business Classic	Oct 10	Larry Nelson	202/–14	240,000
SBC Championship	Oct 17	Mark McNulty	195/–18	225,000
Charles Schwab Cup Championship	Oct 24	Mark McNulty	277/–11	440,000

2005 Senior Tour Events

Tournament	Final Round	Winner	Score/Under Par	Earnings ($)
MasterCard Championship	Jan 23	Dana Quigley	198/–18	250,000
Turtle Bay Championship	Jan 30	Hale Irwin	200/–16	225,000
Wendy's Champions Skins Game	Feb 6	Jack Nicklaus	11 skins	340,000
ACE Group Classic	Feb 20	Mark James	203/–13	240,000
Outback Steakhouse Pro-Am	Feb 27	Hale Irwin	134/–8	240,000
SBC Classic	Mar 13	Des Smyth	211/–5	225,000
Toshiba Senior Classic	Mar 20	Mark Johnson	200/–13	240,000
Liberty Mutual Legends of Golf	April 24	Des Smyth	208/–8	350,000
FedEx Kinko's Classic	May 1	Jim Thorpe	206/–10	240,000
Blue Angels Classic	May 15	Jim Thorpe	194/–16	225,000
Bruno's Memorial Classic	May 22	D.A. Weibring	201/–15	225,000
Senior PGA Championship	May 29	Mike Reid*	280/–8	360,000
Allianz Championship	June 5	Tom Jenkins	204/–9	225,000
Bayer Advantage Classic	June 12	Dana Quigley	133–11	247,500
Bank of America Championship	June 26	Mark McNulty	204/–12	232,500
Commerce Bank Championship	July 3	Ron Streck	197/–16	225,000
Ford Senior Players Championship	July 10	Peter Jacobsen	273/–15	375,000
Senior British Open	July 24	Tom Watson*	280/–4	274,099
U.S. Senior Open	July 31	Allen Doyle	274/–10	470,000
3M Championship	Aug 7	Tom Purtzer	201/–15	262,500
Boeing Greater Seattle Classic	Aug 21	David Eger	199/–17	240,000
Jeld-Wen Tradition	Aug 28	Loren Roberts	273/–15	375,000
First Tee Open at Pebble Beach	Sep 4	Hale Irwin	203/13	300,000
Constellation Energy Classic	Sep 18	Bob Guilder	198/–18	255,000
Georgia-Pacific Grand Champions	Sep 23	Mike McCullough	133/–11	400,000
SAS Championship	Oct 2	Hale Irwin	203/–13	285,000

*Won playoff.

Going to Extremes	Andre Tolme, a 35-year-old civil engineer from New Hampshire, golfed the breath of Mongolia. Traveling by jeep and sleeping in a tent, Tolme and his caddie, a native Mongolian named Khatanbaatar, covered 1,234 miles in a 180 day trek. Tolme, who said he shot a 12,170, or 290 over par, said he did it to raise awareness of extreme golf.

U.S. Amateur Results*

Tournament	Final Round	Winner	Score	Runner-Up
Women's Amateur Public Links	July 16	Eun Jung Lee	37 holes	Tiffany Chudy
Men's Amateur Public Links	July 16	Clay Ogden	1 up	Martin Ureta
Girls' Junior Amateur	July 23	In-Kyung Kim	5 & 4,	In-Bee Park
Boys' Junior Amateur	July 23	Kevin Tway	5 & 3	Brad Johnson
Women's Amateur	Aug 7	Morgan Pressel	9 & 8	Maru Martinez
Men's Amateur	Aug 28	Edoardo Molinari	4 & 3	Dillon Dougherty
Women's Mid-Amateur	Sep 15	Mary Anne Lapointe	1 up	Kerry Postillion

*Results through 10/3/05.

International Results*

Tournament	Final Round	Winner	Score	Runner-Up
The President's Cup	Sept 25	United States	18½ - 15½	International

*Results through 10/3/05.

PGA Tour Final 2004 Money Leaders

Name	Events	Best Finish	Scoring Average*	Money ($)
Vijay Singh	29	1 (9)	69.19	10,905,166
Ernie Els	16	1 (3)	69.69	5,787,225
Phil Mickelson	22	1 (2)	69.63	5,784,823
Tiger Woods	19	1 (1)	69.68	5,365,472
Stewart Clink	28	1 (2)	70.10	4,450,270
Retief Goosen	16	1 (2)	69.58	3,885,573
Adam Scott	16	1 (2)	70.67	3,724,984
Stephen Ames	27	1 (1)	70.08	3,303,205
Sergio Garcia	18	1 (2)	70.56	3,239,215
Davis Love III	24	2 (2)	70.76	3,075,092

*Adjusted for average score of field in each tournament entered.

LPGA Tour Final 2004 Money Leaders

Name	Events	Best Finish	Scoring Average	Money ($)
Annika Sorenstam	18	1 (8)	68.70	2,544.707
Grace Park	24	1 (2)	69.99	1,525,471
Lorena Ochoa	27	1 (2)	70.02	1,450,824
Meg Mallon	21	1 (3)	70.86	1,358,623
Cristie Kerr	24	1 (3)	70.33	1,189,990
Karen Stupples	25	1 (2)	70.65	968,852
Mi Hyun Kim	28	2 (1)	70.48	931,693
Hee-Won Han	28	1 (1)	70.80	840,605
Karrie Webb	22	1 (1)	70.53	748,316
Jennifer Rosales	21	1 (1)	71.18	693,625

Senior Tour Final 2004 Money Leaders

Name	Events	Best Finish	Scoring Average	Money ($)
Craig Stadler	21	1 (5)	69.30	2,306,066
Hale Irwin	23	1 (2)	69.58	2,035,397
Tom Kite	27	1 (1)	69.98	1,831,211
Gil Morgan	26	1 (1)	69.76	1,606,453
Bruce Fleisher	28	1 (2)	70.33	1,537,571
Larry Nelson	25	1 (2)	70.62	1,428,224
Mark McNulty	20	1 (3)	70.03	1,423,048
D.A. Weibring	25	1 (1)	70.28	1,413,795
Jim Thorpe	26	1 (2)	70.44	1,378,343
Allen Doyle	27	1 (1)	70.31	1,298,555

Great Expectations

Michelle Wie missed the cut at the Sony Open in Hawaii. Wie came within a shot of reaching the third round at the 2004 Sony, her PGA Tour debut, and was nine over in her first two rounds, missing the cut by seven strokes. With the largest galleries of the tournamant watching, the Honolulu native was undone by blustery conditions and a second-round thriple boogey on the par-4 6th. "After coming in so close last year, I almost took it for granted that I was going to play better," she said. "I think I tried too hard. Wie has had little time for regrets, however. On the day she turned pro in 2005, she signed more than $10 million worth of endorsement deals.

Men's Golf

THE MAJOR TOURNAMENTS

The Masters

Year	Winner	Score	Runner-Up	Year	Winner	Score	Runner-Up
1934	Horton Smith	284	Craig Wood	1972	Jack Nicklaus	286	Bruce Crampton
1935	Gene Sarazen* (144) (only 36-hole playoff)	282	Craig Wood (149)				Bobby Mitchell Tom Weiskopf
1936	Horton Smith	285	Harry Cooper	1973	Tommy Aaron	283	J.C. Snead
1937	Byron Nelson	283	Ralph Guldahl	1974	Gary Player	278	Tom Weiskopf
1938	Henry Picard	285	Ralph Guldahl Harry Cooper	1975	Jack Nicklaus	276	Dave Stockton Johnny Miller
1939	Ralph Guldahl	279	Sam Snead				Tom Weiskopf
1940	Jimmy Demaret	280	Lloyd Mangrum	1976	Ray Floyd	271	Ben Crenshaw
1941	Craig Wood	280	Byron Nelson	1977	Tom Watson	276	Jack Nicklaus
1942	Byron Nelson* (69)	280	Ben Hogan (70)	1978	Gary Player	277	Hubert Green
1943–45	No tournament						Rod Funseth
1946	Herman Keiser	282	Ben Hogan				Tom Watson
1947	Jimmy Demaret	281	Byron Nelson Frank Stranahan	1979	Fuzzy Zoeller* (4–3)†	280	Ed Sneed (4–4) Tom Watson (4–4)
1948	Claude Harmon	279	Cary Middlecoff	1980	Seve Ballesteros	275	Gibby Gilbert
1949	Sam Snead	282	Johnny Bulla Lloyd Mangrum				Jack Newton Johnny Miller
1950	Jimmy Demaret	283	Jim Ferrier	1981	Tom Watson	280	Jack Nicklaus
1951	Ben Hogan	280	Skee Riegel	1982	Craig Stadler* (4)	284	Dan Pohl (5)
1952	Sam Snead	286	Jack Burke Jr.	1983	Seve Ballesteros	280	Ben Crenshaw
1953	Ben Hogan	274	Ed Oliver Jr.				Tom Kite
1954	Sam Snead* (70)	289	Ben Hogan (71)	1984	Ben Crenshaw	277	Tom Watson
1955	Cary Middlecoff	279	Ben Hogan	1985	Bernhard Langer	282	Curtis Strange
1956	Jack Burke Jr.	289	Ken Venturi				Seve Ballesteros
1957	Doug Ford	282	Sam Snead				Ray Floyd
1958	Arnold Palmer	284	Doug Ford Fred Hawkins	1986	Jack Nicklaus	279	Greg Norman Tom Kite
1959	Art Wall Jr.	284	Cary Middlecoff	1987	Larry Mize* (4–3)	285	Seve Ballesteros (5)
1960	Arnold Palmer	282	Ken Venturi				Greg Norman (4–4)
1961	Gary Player	280	Charles R. Coe Arnold Palmer	1988	Sandy Lyle	281	Mark Calcavecchia
				1989	Nick Faldo* (5–3)	283	Scott Hoch (5–4)
1962	Arnold Palmer* (68)	280	Gary Player (71) D. Finsterwald (77)	1990	Nick Faldo* (4–4)	278	Ray Floyd (4–x)
				1991	Ian Woosnam	277	José María Olazábal
1963	Jack Nicklaus	286	Tony Lema	1992	Fred Couples	275	Ray Floyd
1964	Arnold Palmer	276	Dave Marr Jack Nicklaus	1993	Bernhard Langer	277	Chip Beck
				1994	José María Olazábal	279	Tom Lehman
1965	Jack Nicklaus	271	Arnold Palmer Gary Player	1995	Ben Crenshaw	274	Davis Love III
				1996	Nick Faldo	276	Greg Norman
1966	Jack Nicklaus* (70)	288	Tommy Jacobs (72) Gay Brewer Jr. (78)	1997	Tiger Woods	270	Tom Kite
				1998	Mark O'Meara	279	David Duval
1967	Gay Brewer Jr.	280	Bobby Nichols				Fred Couples
1968	Bob Goalby	277	Roberto DeVicenzo	1999	José María Olazábal	280	Davis Love III
1969	George Archer	281	Billy Casper George Knudson Tom Weiskopf	2000	Vijay Singh	278	Ernie Els
				2001	Tiger Woods	272	David Duval
				2002	Tiger Woods	276	Retief Goosen
				2003	Mike Weir	281	Len Mattiace
1970	Billy Casper* (69)	279	Gene Littler (74)	2004	Phil Mickelson	279	Ernie Els
1971	Charles Coody	279	Johnny Miller Jack Nicklaus	2005	Tiger Woods	276	Chris DiMarco

*Winner in playoff. Playoff scores are in parentheses. †Playoff cut from 18 holes to sudden death.
Note: Played at Augusta National Golf Club, Augusta, GA.

United States Open Championship

Year	Winner	Score	Runner-Up	Site
1895	Horace Rawlins	†173	Willie Dunn	Newport GC, Newport, RI
1896	James Foulis	†152	Horace Rawlins	Shinnecock Hills GC, Southampton, NY
1897	Joe Lloyd	†162	Willie Anderson	Chicago GC, Wheaton, IL
1898	Fred Herd	328	Alex Smith	Myopia Hunt Club, Hamilton, MA
1899	Willie Smith	315	George Low	Baltimore CC, Baltimore
			Val Fitzjohn	
			W.H. Way	
1900	Harry Vardon	313	John H. Taylor	Chicago GC, Wheaton, IL
1901	Willie Anderson* (85)	331	Alex Smith (86)	Myopia Hunt Club, Hamilton, MA
1902	Laurie Auchterlonie	307	Stewart Gardner	Garden City GC, Garden City, NY
1903	Willie Anderson* (82)	307	David Brown (84)	Baltusrol GC, Springfield, NJ
1904	Willie Anderson	303	Gil Nicholls	Glen View Club, Golf, IL
1905	Willie Anderson	314	Alex Smith	Myopia Hunt Club, Hamilton, MA
1906	Alex Smith	295	Willie Smith	Onwentsia Club, Lake Forest, IL
1907	Alex Ross	302	Gil Nicholls	Philadelphia Cricket Club, Chestnut Hill, PA
1908	Fred McLeod* (77)	322	Willie Smith (83)	Myopia Hunt Club, Hamilton, MA
1909	George Sargent	290	Tom McNamara	Englewood GC, Englewood, NJ
1910	Alex Smith* (71)	298	John McDermott (75)	Philadelphia Cricket Club, Chestnut Hill, PA
			Macdonald Smith (77)	
1911	John McDermott* (80)	307	Mike Brady (82)	Chicago GC, Wheaton, IL
			George Simpson (85)	
1912	John McDermott-	294	Tom McNamara	CC of Buffalo, Buffalo
1913	Francis Ouimet* (72)	304	Harry Vardon (77)	The Country Club, Brookline, MA
			Edward Ray (78)	
1914	Walter Hagen	290	Chick Evans	Midlothian CC, Blue Island, IL
1915	Jerry Travers	297	Tom McNamara	Baltusrol GC, Springfield, NJ
1916	Chick Evans	286	Jock Hutchison	Minikahda Club, Minneapolis
1917–18	No tournament			
1919	Walter Hagen* (77)	301	Mike Brady (78)	Brae Burn CC, West Newton, MA
1920	Edward Ray	295	Harry Vardon	Inverness CC, Toledo
			Jack Burke	
			Leo Diegel	
			Jock Hutchison	
1921	Jim Barnes	289	Walter Hagen	Columbia CC, Chevy Chase, MD
			Fred McLeod	
1922	Gene Sarazen	288	John L. Black	Skokie CC, Glencoe, IL
			Bobby Jones	
1923	Bobby Jones* (76)	296	Bobby Cruickshank (78)	Inwood CC, Inwood, NY
1924	Cyril Walker	297	Bobby Jones	Oakland Hills CC, Birmingham, MI
1925	W. MacFarlane* (75–72)	291	Bobby Jones (75–73)	Worcester CC, Worcester, MA
1926	Bobby Jones	293	Joe Turnesa	Scioto CC, Columbus, OH
1927	Tommy Armour* (76)	301	Harry Cooper (79)	Oakmont CC, Oakmont, PA
1928	Johnny Farrell* (143)	294	Bobby Jones (144)	Olympia Fields CC, Matteson, IL
1929	Bobby Jones* (141)	294	Al Espinosa (164)	Winged Foot GC, Mamaroneck, NY
1930	Bobby Jones	287	Macdonald Smith	Interlachen CC, Hopkins, MN
1931	Billy Burke* (149–148)	292	George Von Elm	Inverness Club, Toledo
			(149–149)	
1932	Gene Sarazen	286	Phil Perkins	Fresh Meadows CC, Flushing, NY
			Bobby Cruickshank	
1933	Johnny Goodman	287	Ralph Guldahl	North Shore CC, Glenview, IL
1934	Olin Dutra	293	Gene Sarazen	Merion Cricket Club, Ardmore, PA
1935	Sam Parks Jr.	299	Jimmy Thompson	Oakmont CC, Oakmont, PA
1936	Tony Manero	282	Harry Cooper	Baltusrol GC (Upper Course), Springfield, NJ
1937	Ralph Guldahl	281	Sam Snead	Oakland Hills CC, Birmingham, MI
1938	Ralph Guldahl	284	Dick Metz	Cherry Hills CC, Denver
1939	Byron Nelson* (68–70)	284	Craig Wood (68–73)	Philadelphia CC, Philadelphia
			Denny Shute (76)	
1940	Lawson Little* (70)	287	Gene Sarazen (73)	Canterbury GC, Cleveland
1941	Craig Wood	284	Denny Shute	Colonial Club, Fort Worth
1942–45	No tournament			
1946	Lloyd Mangrum* (72–72)	284	Vic Ghezzi (72–73)	Canterbury GC, Cleveland
			Byron Nelson (72–73)	

United States Open Championship (Cont.)

Year	Winner	Score	Runner-Up	Site
1947	Lew Worsham* (69)	282	Sam Snead (70)	St. Louis CC, Clayton, MO
1948	Ben Hogan	276	Jimmy Demaret	Riviera CC, Los Angeles
1949	Cary Middlecoff	286	Sam Snead Clayton Heafner	Medinah CC, Medinah, IL
1950	Ben Hogan* (69)	287	Lloyd Mangrum (73) George Fazio (75)	Merion GC, Ardmore, PA
1951	Ben Hogan	287	Clayton Heafner	Oakland Hills CC, Birmingham, MI
1952	Julius Boros	281	Ed Oliver	Northwood CC, Dallas
1953	Ben Hogan	283	Sam Snead	Oakmont CC, Oakmont, PA
1954	Ed Furgol	284	Gene Littler	Baltusrol GC (Lower Course), Springfield, NJ
1955	Jack Fleck* (69)	287	Ben Hogan (72)	Olympic Club (Lake Course), San Francisco
1956	Cary Middlecoff	281	Ben Hogan Julius Boros	Oak Hill CC, Rochester, NY
1957	Dick Mayer* (72)	282	Cary Middlecoff (79)	Inverness Club, Toledo
1958	Tommy Bolt	283	Gary Player	Southern Hills CC, Tulsa
1959	Billy Casper	282	Bob Rosburg	Winged Foot GC, Mamaroneck, NY
1960	Arnold Palmer	280	Jack Nicklaus	Cherry Hills CC, Denver
1961	Gene Littler	281	Bob Goalby Doug Sanders	Oakland Hills CC, Birmingham, MI
1962	Jack Nicklaus* (71)	283	Arnold Palmer (74)	Oakmont CC, Oakmont, PA
1963	Julius Boros* (70)	293	Jacky Cupit (73) Arnold Palmer (76)	The Country Club, Brookline, MA
1964	Ken Venturi	278	Tommy Jacobs	Congressional CC, Bethesda, MD
1965	Gary Player* (71)	282	Kel Nagle (74)	Bellerive CC, St. Louis
1966	Billy Casper* (69)	278	Arnold Palmer (73)	Olympic Club (Lake Course), San Francisco
1967	Jack Nicklaus	275	Arnold Palmer	Baltusrol GC (Lower Course), Springfield, NJ
1968	Lee Trevino	275	Jack Nicklaus	Oak Hill CC, Rochester, NY
1969	Orville Moody	281	Deane Beman Al Geiberger Bob Rosburg	Champions GC (Cypress Creek Course), Houston
1970	Tony Jacklin	281	Dave Hill	Hazeltine GC, Chaska, MN
1971	Lee Trevino* (68)	280	Jack Nicklaus (71)	Merion GC (East Course), Ardmore, PA
1972	Jack Nicklaus	290	Bruce Crampton	Pebble Beach GL, Pebble Beach, CA
1973	Johnny Miller	279	John Schlee	Oakmont CC, Oakmont, PA
1974	Hale Irwin	287	Forrest Fezler	Winged Foot GC, Mamaroneck, NY
1975	Lou Graham* (71)	287	John Mahaffey (73)	Medinah CC, Medinah, IL
1976	Jerry Pate	277	Tom Weiskopf Al Geiberger	Atlanta Athletic Club, Duluth, GA
1977	Hubert Green	278	Lou Graham	Southern Hills CC, Tulsa
1978	Andy North	285	Dave Stockton J.C. Snead	Cherry Hills CC, Denver
1979	Hale Irwin	284	Gary Player Jerry Pate	Inverness Club, Toledo
1980	Jack Nicklaus	272	Isao Aoki	Baltusrol GC (Lower Course), Springfield, NJ
1981	David Graham	273	George Burns Bill Rogers	Merion GC, Ardmore, PA
1982	Tom Watson	282	Jack Nicklaus	Pebble Beach GL, Pebble Beach, CA
1983	Larry Nelson	280	Tom Watson	Oakmont CC, Oakmont, PA
1984	Fuzzy Zoeller* (67)	276	Greg Norman (75)	Winged Foot GC, Mamaroneck, NY
1985	Andy North	279	Dave Barr T.C. Chen Denis Watson	Oakland Hills CC, Birmingham, MI
1986	Ray Floyd	279	Lanny Wadkins Chip Beck	Shinnecock Hills GC, Southampton, NY
1987	Scott Simpson	277	Tom Watson	Olympic Club (Lake Course), San Francisco
1988	Curtis Strange* (71)	278	Nick Faldo (75)	The Country Club, Brookline, MA
1989	Curtis Strange	278	Chip Beck Mark McCumber Ian Woosnam	Oak Hill CC, Rochester, NY
1990	Hale Irwin* (74) (3)	280	Mike Donald (74) (4)	Medinah CC, Medinah, IL
1991	Payne Stewart* (75)	282	Scott Simpson (77)	Hazeltine GC, Chaska, MN
1992	Tom Kite	285	Jeff Sluman	Pebble Beach GL, Pebble Beach, CA
1993	Lee Janzen	272	Payne Stewart	Baltusrol GC, Springfield, NJ
1994	Ernie Els*	279	Loren Roberts Colin Montgomerie	Oakmont CC, Oakmont, PA

United States Open Championship (Cont.)

Year	Winner	Score	Runner-Up	Site
1995	Corey Pavin	280	Greg Norman	Shinnecock Hills GC, Southampton, NY
1996	Steve Jones	278	Davis Love III	Oakland Hills CC, Birmingham, MI
			Tom Lehman	
1997	Ernie Els	276	Colin Montgomerie	Congressional CC, Bethesda, MD
1998	Lee Janzen	280	Payne Stewart	The Olympic Club, San Francisco
1999	Payne Stewart	279	Phil Mickelson	Pinehurst Resort and CC, Pinehurst, NC
2000	Tiger Woods	272	Miguel Angel Jiménez	Pebble Beach GL, Pebble Beach, CA
			Ernie Els	
2001	Retief Goosen* (70)	276	Mark Brooks (72)	Southern Hills CC, Tulsa
2002	Tiger Woods	277	Phil Mickelson	Bethpage Black Course, Bethpage, NY
2003	Jim Furyk	272	Stephen Leaney	Olympia Fields CC, Olympia Fields, IL
2004	Retief Goosen	276	Phil Mickelson	Shinnecock Hills GC, Southampton, NY
2005	Michael Campbell	280	Tiger Woods	Pinehurst Resort and CC, Pinehurst, NC

*Winner in playoff. Playoff scores are in parentheses. The 1990 playoff went to one hole of sudden death after an 18-hole playoff. In the 1994 playoff, Montgomerie was eliminated after 18 playoff holes, and Els beat Roberts on the 20th.
†Before 1898, 36 holes. From 1898 on, 72 holes.

British Open

Year	Winner	Score	Runner-Up	Site
1860†	Willie Park	174	Tom Morris Sr.	Prestwick, Scotland
1861‡	Tom Morris Sr.	163	Willie Park	Prestwick, Scotland
1862	Tom Morris Sr.	163	Willie Park	Prestwick, Scotland
1863	Willie Park	168	Tom Morris Sr.	Prestwick, Scotland
1864	Tom Morris, Sr.	160	Andrew Strath	Prestwick, Scotland
1865	Andrew Strath	162	Willie Park	Prestwick, Scotland
1866	Willie Park	169	David Park	Prestwick, Scotland
1867	Tom Morris Sr.	170	Willie Park	Prestwick, Scotland
1868	Tom Morris Jr.	154	Tom Morris Sr.	Prestwick, Scotland
1869	Tom Morris Jr.	157	Tom Morris Sr.	Prestwick, Scotland
1870	Tom Morris Jr.	149	David Strath	Prestwick, Scotland
			Bob Kirk	
1871	No tournament			
1872	Tom Morris Jr.	166	David Strath	Prestwick, Scotland
1873	Tom Kidd	179	Jamie Anderson	St. Andrews, Scotland
1874	Mungo Park	159	No record	Musselburgh, Scotland
1875	Willie Park	166	Bob Martin	Prestwick, Scotland
1876	Bob Martin#	176	David Strath	St. Andrews, Scotland
1877	Jamie Anderson	160	Bob Pringle	Musselburgh, Scotland
1878	Jamie Anderson	157	Robert Kirk	Prestwick, Scotland
1879	Jamie Anderson	169	Andrew Kirkaldy	St. Andrews, Scotland
			James Allan	
1880	Robert Ferguson	162	No record	Musselburgh, Scotland
1881	Robert Ferguson	170	Jamie Anderson	Prestwick, Scotland
1882	Robert Ferguson	171	Willie Fernie	St. Andrews, Scotland
1883	Willie Fernie*	159	Robert Ferguson	Musselburgh, Scotland
1884	Jack Simpson	160	Douglas Rolland	Prestwick, Scotland
			Willie Fernie	
1885	Bob Martin	171	Archie Simpson	St. Andrews, Scotland
1886	David Brown	157	Willie Campbell	Musselburgh, Scotland
1887	Willie Park Jr.	161	Bob Martin	Prestwick, Scotland
1888	Jack Burns	171	Bernard Sayers	St. Andrews, Scotland
			David Anderson	
1889	Willie Park Jr.* (158)	155	Andrew Kirkaldy (163)	Musselburgh, Scotland
1890	John Ball	164	Willie Fernie	Prestwick, Scotland
1891	Hugh Kirkaldy	166	Andrew Kirkaldy	St. Andrews, Scotland
			Willie Fernie	
1892	Harold Hilton	**305	John Ball	Muirfield, Scotland
			Hugh Kirkaldy	
1893	William Auchterlonie	322	John E. Laidlay	Prestwick, Scotland
1894	John H. Taylor	326	Douglas Rolland	Royal St. George's, England
1895	John H. Taylor	322	Alexander Herd	St. Andrews, Scotland
1896	Harry Vardon* (157)	316	John H. Taylor (161)	Muirfield, Scotland
1897	Harold Hilton	314	James Braid	Hoylake, England
1898	Harry Vardon	307	Willie Park Jr.	Prestwick, Scotland
1899	Harry Vardon	310	Jack White	Royal St. George's, England
1900	John H. Taylor	309	Harry Vardon	St. Andrews, Scotland

British Open (Cont.)

Year	Winner	Score	Runner-Up	Site
1901	James Braid	309	Harry Vardon	Muirfield, Scotland
1902	Alexander Herd	307	Harry Vardon	Hoylake, England
1903	Harry Vardon	300	Tom Vardon	Prestwick, Scotland
1904	Jack White	296	John H. Taylor	Royal St. George's, England
1905	James Braid	318	John H. Taylor	St. Andrews, Scotland
			Rolland Jones	
1906	James Braid	300	John H. Taylor	Muirfield, Scotland
1907	Arnaud Massy	312	John H. Taylor	Hoylake, England
1908	James Braid	291	Tom Ball	Prestwick, Scotland
1909	John H. Taylor	295	James Braid	Deal, England
			Tom Ball	
1910	James Braid	299	Alexander Herd	St. Andrews, Scotland
1911	Harry Vardon	303	Arnaud Massy	Royal St. George's, England
1912	Ted Ray	295	Harry Vardon	Muirfield, Scotland
1913	John H. Taylor	304	Ted Ray	Hoylake, England
1914	Harry Vardon	306	John H..Taylor	Prestwick, Scotland
1915–19	No tournament			
1920	George Duncan	303	Alexander Herd	Deal, England
1921	Jock Hutchison* (150)	296	Roger Wethered (159)	St. Andrews, Scotland
1922	Walter Hagen	300	George Duncan	Royal St. George's, England
			Jim Barnes	
1923	Arthur G. Havers	295	Walter Hagen	Troon, Scotland
1924	Walter Hagen	301	Ernest Whitcombe	Hoylake, England
1925	Jim Barnes	300	Archie Compston	Prestwick, Scotland
			Ted Ray	
1926	Bobby Jones	291	Al Watrous	Royal Lytham & St. Annes, England
1927	Bobby Jones	285	Aubrey Boomer	St. Andrews, Scotland
1928	Walter Hagen	292	Gene Sarazen	Royal St. George's, England
1929	Walter Hagen	292	Johnny Farrell	Muirfield, Scotland
1930	Bobby Jones	291	Macdonald Smith	Hoylake, England
			Leo Diegel	
1931	Tommy Armour	296	Jose Jurado	Carnoustie, Scotland
1932	Gene Sarazen	283	Macdonald Smith	Prince's, England
1933	Denny Shute* (149)	292	Craig Wood (154)	St. Andrews, Scotland
1934	Henry Cotton	283	Sidney F. Brews	Royal St. George's, England
1935	Alfred Perry	283	Alfred Padgham	Muirfield, Scotland
1936	Alfred Padgham	287	James Adams	Hoylake, England
1937	Henry Cotton	290	Reginald A. Whitcombe	Carnoustie, Scotland
1938	Reginald A. Whitcombe	295	James Adams	Royal St. George's, England
1939	Richard Burton	290	Johnny Bulla	St. Andrews, Scotland
1940–45	No tournament			
1946	Sam Snead	290	Bobby Locke	St. Andrews, Scotland
			Johnny Bulla	
1947	Fred Daly	293	Reginald W. Horne	Hoylake, England
			Frank Stranahan	
1948	Henry Cotton	294	Fred Daly	Muirfield, Scotland
1949	Bobby Locke* (135)	283	Harry Bradshaw (147)	Royal St. George's, England
1950	Bobby Locke	279	Roberto DeVicenzo	Troon, Scotland
1951	Max Faulkner	285	Tony Cerda	Portrush, Ireland
1952	Bobby Locke	287	Peter Thomson	Royal Lytham & St. Annes, England
1953	Ben Hogan	282	Frank Stranahan	Carnoustie, Scotland
			Dai Rees	
			Peter Thomson	
			Tony Cerda	
1954	Peter Thomson	283	Sidney S. Scott	Royal Birkdale, England
			Dai Rees	
			Bobby Locke	
1955	Peter Thomson	281	John Fallon	St. Andrews, Scotland
1956	Peter Thomson	286	Flory Van Donck	Hoylake, England
1957	Bobby Locke	279	Peter Thomson	St. Andrews, Scotland
1958	Peter Thomson* (139)	278	Dave Thomas (143)	Royal Lytham & St. Annes, England
1959	Gary Player	284	Fred Bullock	Muirfield, Scotland
			Flory Van Donck	
1960	Kel Nagle	278	Arnold Palmer	St. Andrews, Scotland
1961	Arnold Palmer	284	Dai Rees	Royal Birkdale, England
1962	Arnold Palmer	276	Kel Nagle	Troon, Scotland

British Open (Cont.)

Year	Winner	Score	Runner-Up	Site
1963	Bob Charles* (140)	277	Phil Rodgers (148)	Royal Lytham & St. Annes, England
1964	Tony Lema	279	Jack Nicklaus	St. Andrews, Scotland
1965	Peter Thomson	285	Brian Huggett	Southport, England
			Christy O'Connor	
1966	Jack Nicklaus	282	Doug Sanders	Muirfield, Scotland
			Dave Thomas	
1967	Robert DeVicenzo	278	Jack Nicklaus	Hoylake, England
1968	Gary Player	289	Jack Nicklaus	Carnoustie, Scotland
			Bob Charles	
1969	Tony Jacklin	280	Bob Charles	Royal Lytham & St. Annes, England
1970	Jack Nicklaus* (72)	283	Doug Sanders (73)	St. Andrews, Scotland
1971	Lee Trevino	278	Lu Liang Huan	Royal Birkdale, England
1972	Lee Trevino	278	Jack Nicklaus	Muirfield, Scotland
1973	Tom Weiskopf	276	Johnny Miller	Troon, Scotland
1974	Gary Player	282	Peter Oosterhuis	Royal Lytham & St. Annes, England
1975	Tom Watson* (71)	279	Jack Newton (72)	Carnoustie, Scotland
1976	Johnny Miller	279	Jack Nicklaus	Royal Birkdale, England
			Seve Ballesteros	
1977	Tom Watson	268	Jack Nicklaus	Turnberry, Scotland
1978	Jack Nicklaus	281	Ben Crenshaw	St. Andrews, Scotland
			Tom Kite	
			Ray Floyd	
			Simon Owen	
1979	Seve Ballesteros	283	Ben Crenshaw	Royal Lytham & St. Annes, England
			Jack Nicklaus	
1980	Tom Watson	271	Lee Trevino	Muirfield, Scotland
1981	Bill Rogers	276	Bernhard Langer	Royal St. George's, England
1982	Tom Watson	284	Nick Price	Troon, Scotland
			Peter Oosterhuis	
1983	Tom Watson	275	Andy Bean	Royal Birkdale, England
1984	Seve Ballesteros	276	Tom Watson	St. Andrews, Scotland
			Bernhard Langer	
1985	Sandy Lyle	282	Payne Stewart	Royal St. George's, England
1986	Greg Norman	280	Gordon Brand	Turnberry, Scotland
1987	Nick Faldo	279	Paul Azinger	Muirfield, Scotland
			Rodger Davis	
1988	Seve Ballesteros	273	Nick Price	Royal Lytham & St. Annes, England
1989††	Mark Calcavecchia* (4-3-3-3)	275	Wayne Grady (4-4-4-4)	Troon, Scotland
			Greg Norman (3-3-4-x)	
1990	Nick Faldo	270	Payne Stewart	St. Andrews, Scotland
			Mark McNulty	
1991	Ian Baker-Finch	272	Mike Harwood	Royal Birkdale, England
1992	Nick Faldo	272	John Cook	Muirfield, Scotland
1993	Greg Norman	267	Nick Faldo	Royal St. George's, England
1994	Nick Price	268	Jesper Parnevik	Turnberry, Scotland
1995	John Daly* (4-3-4-4)	282	C. Rocca (5-4-7-3)	St. Andrews, Scotland
1996	Tom Lehman	271	Mark McCumber	Royal Lytham & St. Annes, England
			Ernie Els	
1997	Justin Leonard	272	Jesper Parnevik	Troon, Scotland
			Darren Clarke	
1998	Mark O'Meara* (4-4-5-4)	280	Brian Watts (5-4-5-5)	Southport, England
1999	Paul Lawrie* (5-4-3-3)	290	Jean Van de Velde (6-4-3-5)	Carnoustie GC, Carnoustie,
			Justin Leonard (5-4-4-5)	Scotland
2000	Tiger Woods	269	Thomas Bjorn	St. Andrews, Scotland
			Ernie Els	
2001	David Duval	274	Niclas Fasth	Royal Lytham & St. Annes, England
2002	Ernie Els*	278	Stuart Appleby	Muirfield, Scotland
2003	Ben Curtis	283	Vijay Singh	Royal St. George's, England
2004	Todd Hamilton*	274	Ernie Els	Troon, Scotland
2005	Tiger Woods	274	Colin Montgomerie	St. Andrews, Scotland

*Winner in playoff. †The first event was open only to professional golfers.
‡The second annual open was open to amateurs and pros. #Tied, but refused playoff.
**Championship extended from 36 to 72 holes. ††Playoff cut from 18 holes to 4 holes.

PGA Championship

Year	Winner	Score	Runner-Up	Site
1916	Jim Barnes	1 up	Jock Hutchison	Siwanoy CC, Bronxville, NY
1917–18	No tournament			
1919	Jim Barnes	6 & 5	Fred McLeod	Engineers CC, Roslyn, NY
1920	Jock Hutchison	1 up	J. Douglas Edgar	Flossmoor CC, Flossmoor, IL
1921	Walter Hagen	3 & 2	Jim Barnes	Inwood CC, Far Rockaway, NY
1922	Gene Sarazen	4 & 3	Emmet French	Oakmont CC, Oakmont, PA
1923	Gene Sarazen	1 up 38 holes	Walter Hagen	Pelham CC, Pelham, NY
1924	Walter Hagen	2 up	Jim Barnes	French Lick CC, French Lick, IN
1925	Walter Hagen	6 & 5	William Mehlhorn	Olympia Fields CC, Olympia Fields, IL
1926	Walter Hagen	5 & 3	Leo Diegel	Salisbury GC, Westbury, NY
1927	Walter Hagen	1 up	Joe Turnesa	Cedar Crest CC, Dallas
1928	Leo Diegel	6 & 5	Al Espinosa	Five Farms CC, Baltimore
1929	Leo Diegel	6 & 4	Johnny Farrell	Hillcrest CC, Los Angeles
1930	Tommy Armour	1 up	Gene Sarazen	Fresh Meadow CC, Flushing, NY
1931	Tom Creavy	2 & 1	Denny Shute	Wannamoisett CC, Rumford, RI
1932	Olin Dutra	4 & 3	Frank Walsh	Keller GC, St. Paul
1933	Gene Sarazen	5 & 4	Willie Goggin	Blue Mound CC, Milwaukee
1934	Paul Runyan	1 up	Craig Wood	Park CC, Williamsville, NY
1935	Johnny Revolta	5 & 4 38 holes	Tommy Armour	Twin Hills CC, Oklahoma City
1936	Denny Shute	3 & 2	Jimmy Thomson	Pinehurst CC, Pinehurst, NC
1937	Denny Shute	1 up 37 holes	Harold McSpaden	Pittsburgh FC, Aspinwall, PA
1938	Paul Runyan	8 & 7	Sam Snead	Shawnee CC, Shawnee-on-Delaware, PA
1939	Henry Picard	1 up 37 holes	Byron Nelson	Pomonok CC, Flushing, NY
1940	Byron Nelson	1 up	Sam Snead	Hershey CC, Hershey, PA
1941	Vic Ghezzi	1 up 38 holes	Byron Nelson	Cherry Hills CC, Denver
1942	Sam Snead	2 & 1	Jim Turnesa	Seaview CC, Atlantic City
1943	No tournament			
1944	Bob Hamilton	1 up	Byron Nelson	Manito G & CC, Spokane, WA
1945	Byron Nelson	4 & 3	Sam Byrd	Morraine CC, Dayton
1946	Ben Hogan	6 & 4	Ed Oliver	Portland GC, Portland, OR
1947	Jim Ferrier	2 & 1	Chick Harbert	Plum Hollow CC, Detroit
1948	Ben Hogan	7 & 6	Mike Turnesa	Norwood Hills CC, St. Louis
1949	Sam Snead	3 & 2	Johnny Palmer	Hermitage CC, Richmond
1950	Chandler Harper	4 & 3	Henry Williams Jr.	Scioto CC, Columbus, OH
1951	Sam Snead	7 & 6	Walter Burkemo	Oakmont CC, Oakmont, PA
1952	Jim Turnesa	1 up	Chick Harbert	Big Spring CC, Louisville
1953	Walter Burkemo	2 & 1	Felice Torza	Birmingham CC, Birmingham, MI
1954	Chick Harbert	4 & 3	Walter Burkemo	Keller GC, St. Paul
1955	Doug Ford	4 & 3	Cary Middlecoff	Meadowbrook CC, Detroit
1956	Jack Burke	3 & 2	Ted Kroll	Blue Hill CC, Boston
1957	Lionel Hebert	2 & 1	Dow Finsterwald	Miami Valley CC, Dayton
1958	Dow Finsterwald	276	Billy Casper	Llanerch CC, Havertown, PA
1959	Bob Rosburg	277	Jerry Barber Doug Sanders	Minneapolis GC, St. Louis Park, MN
1960	Jay Hebert	281	Jim Ferrier	Firestone CC, Akron
1961	Jerry Barber* (67)	277	Don January (68)	Olympia Fields CC, Olympia Fields, IL
1962	Gary Player	278	Bob Goalby	Aronimink GC, Newton Square, PA
1963	Jack Nicklaus	279	Dave Ragan Jr.	Dallas Athletic Club, Dallas
1964	Bobby Nichols	271	Jack Nicklaus Arnold Palmer	Columbus CC, Columbus, OH
1965	Dave Marr	280	Billy Casper Jack Nicklaus	Laurel Valley CC, Ligonier, PA
1966	Al Geiberger	280	Dudley Wysong	Firestone CC, Akron
1967	Don January* (69)	281	Don Massengale (71)	Columbine CC, Littleton, CO
1968	Julius Boros	281	Bob Charles Arnold Palmer	Pecan Valley CC, San Antonio
1969	Ray Floyd	276	Gary Player	NCR CC, Dayton
1970	Dave Stockton	279	Arnold Palmer Bob Murphy	Southern Hills CC, Tulsa

PGA Championship (Cont.)

Year	Winner	Score	Runner-Up	Site
1971	Jack Nicklaus	281	Billy Casper	PGA Nat'l GC, Palm Beach Gardens, FL
1972	Gary Player	281	Tommy Aaron	Oakland Hills CC, Birmingham, MI
			Jim Jamieson	
1973	Jack Nicklaus	277	Bruce Crampton	Canterbury GC, Cleveland
1974	Lee Trevino	276	Jack Nicklaus	Tanglewood GC, Winston-Salem, NC
1975	Jack Nicklaus	276	Bruce Crampton	Firestone CC, Akron
1976	Dave Stockton	281	Ray Floyd	Congressional CC, Bethesda, MD
			Don January	
1977†	Lanny Wadkins* (4-4-4)	282	Gene Littler (4-4-5)	Pebble Beach GL, Pebble Beach, CA
1978	John Mahaffey* (4–3)	276	Jerry Pate (4–4)	Oakmont CC, Oakmont, PA
			Tom Watson (4–5)	
1979	David Graham* (4-4-2)	272	Ben Crenshaw (4-4-4)	Oakland Hills CC, Birmingham, MI
1980	Jack Nicklaus	274	Andy Bean	Oak Hill CC, Rochester, NY
1981	Larry Nelson	273	Fuzzy Zoeller	Atlanta Athletic Club, Duluth, GA
1982	Raymond Floyd	272	Lanny Wadkins	Southern Hills CC, Tulsa
1983	Hal Sutton	274	Jack Nicklaus	Riviera CC, Pacific Palisades, CA
1984	Lee Trevino	273	Gary Player	Shoal Creek, Birmingham, AL
			Lanny Wadkins	
1985	Hubert Green	278	Lee Trevino	Cherry Hills CC, Denver
1986	Bob Tway	276	Greg Norman	Inverness CC, Toledo
1987	Larry Nelson* (4)	287	Lanny Wadkins (5)	PGA Natl GC, Palm Beach Gardens, FL
1988	Jeff Sluman	272	Paul Azinger	Oak Tree GC, Edmond, OK
1989	Payne Stewart	276	Mike Reid	Kemper Lakes GC, Hawthorn Woods, IL
1990	Wayne Grady	282	Fred Couples	Shoal Creek, Birmingham, AL
1991	John Daly	276	Bruce Lietzke	Crooked Stick GC, Carmel, IN
1992	Nick Price	278	Jim Gallagher Jr.	Bellerive CC, St. Louis
1993	Paul Azinger* (4–4)	272	Greg Norman (4–5)	Inverness CC, Toledo
1994	Nick Price	269	Corey Pavin	Southern Hills CC, Tulsa
1995	Steve Elkington* (3)	267	Colin Montgomerie (4)	Riviera CC, Pacific Palisades, CA
1996	Mark Brooks* (3)	277	Kenny Perry (x)	Valhalla GC, Louisville
1997	Davis Love III	269	Justin Leonard	Winged Foot GC, Mamaroneck, NY
1998	Vijay Singh	271	Steve Stricker	Sahalee CC, Redmond, WA
1999	Tiger Woods	277	Sergio Garcia	Medinah CC, Medinah, IL
2000	Tiger Woods* (3-4-5)	270	Bob May (4-4-x)	Valhalla GC, Louisville
2001	David Toms	265	Phil Mickelson	Atlanta AC, Duluth, GA
2002	Rich Beem	278	Tiger Woods	Hazeltine National GC, Shaska, MN
2003	Shaun Micheel	276	Chad Campbell	Oak Hill CC, Rochester, NY
2004	Vijay Singh*	280	Chris DiMarco	Whistling Straits GC, Kohler, WI
2005	Phil Mickelson	276	Steve Elkington	Baltusrol GC, Springfield, NJ

*Winner in playoff. †Playoff changed from 18 holes to sudden death.

Alltime Major Championship Winners

	Masters	U.S. Open	British Open	PGA Champ.	U.S. Amateur	British Amateur	Total
†Jack Nicklaus	6	4	3	5	2	0	20
Bobby Jones	0	4	3	0	5	1	13
*Tiger Woods	4	2	2	2	3	0	12
Walter Hagen	0	2	4	5	0	0	11
Ben Hogan	2	4	1	2	0	0	9
†Gary Player	3	1	3	2	0	0	9
John Ball	0	0	1	0	0	8	9
†Arnold Palmer	4	1	2	0	1	0	8
†Tom Watson	2	1	5	0	0	0	8
Harold Hilton	0	0	2	0	1	4	7
Gene Sarazen	1	2	1	3	0	0	7
Sam Snead	3	0	1	3	0	0	7
Harry Vardon	0	1	6	0	0	0	7

*Active PGA player. †Active Senior PGA player.

Alltime Multiple Professional Major Winners

MASTERS		U.S. OPEN (Cont.)		BRITISH OPEN (Cont.)		
Jack Nicklaus	6	Hale Irwin	3	J.H. Taylor	5	Tiger Woods 2
Arnold Palmer	4	Julius Boros	2	Peter Thomson	5	
Tiger Woods	4	Billy Casper	2	Tom Watson	5	**PGA CHAMPIONSHIP**
Jimmy Demaret	3	Ernie Els	2	Walter Hagen	4	Walter Hagen 5
Nick Faldo	3	Retief Goosen	2	Bobby Locke	4	Jack Nicklaus 5
Gary Player	3	Ralph Guldahl	2	Tom Morris Sr.	4	Gene Sarazen 3
Sam Snead	3	Walter Hagen	2	Tom Morris Jr.	4	Sam Snead 3
Seve Ballesteros	2	Lee Janzen	2	Willie Park	4	Jim Barnes 2
Ben Crenshaw	2	John McDermott	2	Jamie Anderson	3	Leo Diegel 2
Ben Hogan	2	Cary Middlecoff	2	Seve Ballesteros	3	Raymond Floyd 2
Bernhard Langer	2	Andy North	2	Henry Cotton	3	Ben Hogan 2
Byron Nelson	2	Gene Sarazen	2	Nick Faldo	3	Byron Nelson 2
José María Olazábal	2	Alex Smith	2	Robert Ferguson	3	Larry Nelson 2
Horton Smith	2	Payne Stewart	2	Bobby Jones	3	Gary Player 2
Tom Watson	2	Curtis Strange	2	Jack Nicklaus	3	Paul Runyan 2
		Lee Trevino	2	Gary Player	3	Denny Shute 2
U.S. OPEN		Tiger Woods	2	Harold Hilton	2	Dave Stockton 2
				Bob Martin	2	Lee Trevino 2
Willie Anderson	4	**BRITISH OPEN**		Greg Norman	2	Tiger Woods 2
Ben Hogan	4			Arnold Palmer	2	Vijay Singh 2
Bobby Jones	4	Harry Vardon	6	Willie Park Jr.	2	
Jack Nicklaus	4	James Braid	5	Lee Trevino	2	

THE PGA TOUR

Most Career Wins*

	Wins		Wins		Wins
Sam Snead	82	Billy Casper	51	Tom Watson	39
Jack Nicklaus	73	Tiger Woods	45	Lloyd Mangrum	36
Ben Hogan	64	Walter Hagen	44	Horton Smith	32
Arnold Palmer	62	Cary Middlecoff	40	Harry Cooper	31
Byron Nelson	52	Gene Sarazen	39	Jimmy Demaret	31

* Through 10/3/05

Season Money Leaders

		Earnings ($)			Earnings ($)			Earnings ($)
1934	Paul Runyan	6,767.00	1958	Arnold Palmer	42,607.50	1982	Craig Stadler	446,462.00
1935	Johnny Revolta	9,543.00	1959	Art Wall	53,167.60	1983	Hal Sutton	426,668.00
1936	Horton Smith	7,682.00	1960	Arnold Palmer	75,262.85	1984	Tom Watson	476,260.00
1937	Harry Cooper	14,138.69	1961	Gary Player	64,540.45	1985	Curtis Strange	542,321.00
1938	Sam Snead	19,534.49	1962	Arnold Palmer	81,448.33	1986	Greg Norman	653,296.00
1939	Henry Picard	10,303.00	1963	Arnold Palmer	128,230.00	1987	Curtis Strange	925,941.00
1940	Ben Hogan	10,655.00	1964	Jack Nicklaus	113,284.50	1988	Curtis Strange	1,147,644.00
1941	Ben Hogan	18,358.00	1965	Jack Nicklaus	140,752.14	1989	Tom Kite	1,395,278.00
1942	Ben Hogan	13,143.00	1966	Billy Casper	121,944.92	1990	Greg Norman	1,165,477.00
1943	No statistics compiled		1967	Jack Nicklaus	188,998.08	1991	Corey Pavin	979,430.00
1944	Byron Nelson*	37,967.69	1968	Billy Casper	205,168.67	1992	Fred Couples	1,344,188.00
1945	Byron Nelson*	63,335.66	1969	Frank Beard	164,707.11	1993	Nick Price	1,478,557.00
1946	Ben Hogan	42,556.16	1970	Lee Trevino	157,037.63	1994	Nick Price	1,499,927.00
1947	Jimmy Demaret	27,936.83	1971	Jack Nicklaus	244,490.50	1995	Greg Norman	1,654,959.00
1948	Ben Hogan	32,112.00	1972	Jack Nicklaus	320,542.26	1996	Tom Lehman	1,780,159.00
1949	Sam Snead	31,593.83	1973	Jack Nicklaus	308,362.10	1997	Tiger Woods	2,066,833.00
1950	Sam Snead	35,758.83	1974	Johnny Miller	353,021.59	1998	David Duval	2,591,031.00
1951	Lloyd Mangrum	26,088.83	1975	Jack Nicklaus	298,149.17	1999	Tiger Woods	6,616,585.00
1952	Julius Boros	37,032.97	1976	Jack Nicklaus	266,438.57	2000	Tiger Woods	9,188,321.00
1953	Lew Worsham	34,002.00	1977	Tom Watson	310,653.16	2001	Tiger Woods	5,687,777.00
1954	Bob Toski	65,819.81	1978	Tom Watson	362,428.93	2002	Tiger Woods	6,912,625.00
1955	Julius Boros	63,121.55	1979	Tom Watson	462,636.00	2003	Vijay Singh	7,573,907.00
1956	Ted Kroll	72,835.83	1980	Tom Watson	530,808.33	2004	Vijay singh	10,905,166.00
1957	Dick Mayer	65,835.00	1981	Tom Kite	375,698.84			

* War bonds. Note: Total money listed from 1968 through 1974. Official money listed from 1975 on.

Career Money Leaders*

		Earnings ($)
1	Tiger Woods	$53,755,760
2	Vijay Singh	$44,306,091
3	Phil Mickelson	$35,197,533
4	Davis Love III	$31,304,634
5	Ernie Els	$26,094,175
6	Jim Furyk	$23,308,818
7	David Toms	$22,599,128
8	Nick Price	$20,317,580
9	Justin Leonard	$20,147,023
10	Kenny Perry	$19,335,833
11	Scott Hoch	$18,487,114
12	Fred Couples	$18,241,270
13	Mark Calcavecchia	$18,222,972
14	Fred Funk	$17,628,180
15	Brad Faxon	$17,028,228
16	Chris DiMarco	$17,007,175

		Earnings ($)
17	Tom Lehman	$16,951,359
18	Mike Weir	$16,893,211
19	Jeff Sluman	$16,489,445
20	David Duval	$16,363,979
21	Scott Verplank	$15,659,714
22	Stewart Cink	$15,555,391
23	Hal Sutton	$15,267,685
24	Stuart Appleby	$15,044,638
25	Loren Roberts	$14,692,278
26	Retief Goosen	$14,304,734
27	Jay Haas	$14,276,918
28	Bob Estes	$14,117,230
29	Bob Tway	$14,079,078
30	Greg Norman	$13,963,611
31	Mark O'Meara	$13,878,515
32	Sergio Garcia	$13,781,692
33	John Huston	$13,600,959

		Earnings ($)
34	Paul Azinger	$13,513,261
35	Jeff Maggert	$13,024,848
36	Jerry Kelly	$12,634,738
37	Lee Janzen	$12,492,306
38	Billy Mayfair	$12,435,709
39	Kirk Triplett	$12,430,473
40	Jesper Parnevik	$12,117,480
41	Robert Allenby	$11,936,366
42	Rocco Mediate	$11,905,800
43	Corey Pavin	$11,866,897
44	Payne Stewart	$11,737,008
45	Steve Elkington	$11,672,520
46	John Cook	$11,574,409
47	Tim Herron	$11,422,614
48	Steve Flesch	$11,355,728
49	Steve Lowery	$11,093,792
50	Tom Kite	$11,041,042

*Through 10/3/04.

Year by Year Statistical Leaders

SCORING AVERAGE

1980	Lee Trevino	69.73
1981	Tom Kite	69.80
1982	Tom Kite	70.21
1983	Raymond Floyd	70.61
1984	Calvin Peete	70.56
1985	Don Pooley	70.36
1986	Scott Hoch	70.08
1987	David Frost	70.09
1988	Greg Norman	69.38
1989	Payne Stewart	69.485†
1990	Greg Norman	69.10
1991	Fred Couples	69.59
1992	Fred Couples	69.38
1993	Greg Norman	68.90
1994	Greg Norman	68.81
1995	Greg Norman	69.06
1996	Tom Lehman	69.32
1997	Nick Price	68.98
1998	David Duval	69.13
1999	Tiger Woods	68.43
2000	Tiger Woods	67.79
2001	Tiger Woods	68.81
2002	Tiger Woods	68.13
2003	Tiger Woods	68.41
2004	Vijay Singh	69.19

Note: Scoring average per round, with adjustments made at each round for the field's course scoring average.

DRIVING DISTANCE

		Yds
1980	Dan Pohl	274.3
1981	Dan Pohl	280.1
1982	Bill Calfee	275.3
1983	John McComish	277.4
1984	Bill Glasson	276.5
1985	Andy Bean	278.2
1986	Davis Love III	285.7
1987	John McComish	283.9
1988	Steve Thomas	284.6
1989	Ed Humenik	280.9
1990	Tom Purtzer	279.6
1991	John Daly	288.9
1992	John Daly	283.4
1993	John Daly	288.9

DRIVING DISTANCE (Cont.)

1994	Davis Love III	283.8
1995	John Daly	289.0
1996	John Daly	288.8
1997	John Daly	302.0
1998	John Daly	299.4
1999	John Daly	305.6
2000	John Daly	301.4
2001	John Daly	306.7
2002	John Daly	306.8
2003	Hank Kuehne	321.4
2004	Hank Kuehne	314.4

Note: Average computed by charting distance of two tee shots on a predetermined par-four or par-five hole (one on front nine, one on back nine).

DRIVING ACCURACY

1980	Mike Reid	79.5
1981	Calvin Peete	81.9
1982	Calvin Peete	84.6
1983	Calvin Peete	81.3
1984	Calvin Peete	77.5
1985	Calvin Peete	80.6
1986	Calvin Peete	81.7
1987	Calvin Peete	83.0
1988	Calvin Peete	82.5
1989	Calvin Peete	82.6
1990	Calvin Peete	83.7
1991	Hale Irwin	'78.3
1992	Doug Tewell	82.3
1993	Doug Tewell	82.5
1994	David Edwards	81.6
1995	Fred Funk	81.3
1996	Fred Funk	78.7
1997	Allen Doyle	80.8
1998	Bruce Fleisher	81.4
1999	Fred Funk	80.2
2000	Fred Funk	79.7
2001	Joe Durant	81.1
2002	Fred Funk	81.2
2003	Fred Funk	77.9
2004	Fred Funk	77.2

Note: Percentage of fairways hit on number of par-four and par-five holes played; par-three holes excluded.

GREENS IN REGULATION

1980	Jack Nicklaus	72.1
1981	Calvin Peete	73.1
1982	Calvin Peete	72.4
1983	Calvin Peete	71.4
1984	Andy Bean	72.1
1985	John Mahaffey	71.9
1986	John Mahaffey	72.0
1987	Gil Morgan	73.3
1988	John Adams	73.9
1989	Bruce Lietzke	72.6
1990	Doug Tewell	70.9
1991	Bruce Lietzke	73.3
1992	Tim Simpson	74.0
1993	Fuzzy Zoeller	73.6
1994	Bill Glasson	73.0
1995	Lenny Clements	72.3
1996	Fred Couples	71.8
	Mark O'Meara	71.8
1997	Tom Lehman	72.7
1998	Hal Sutton	71.3
1999	Tiger Woods	71.4
2000	Tiger Woods	75.2
2001	Tom Lehman	74.5
2002	Tiger Woods	74.0
2003	Joe Durant	72.9
2004	Joe Durant	73.3

Note: Average of greens reached in regulation out of total holes played; hole is considered hit in regulation if any part of the ball rests on the putting surface in two shots less than the hole's par—a par-5 hit in two shots is one green in regulation.

PUTTING

1980	Jerry Pate	28.81
1981	Alan Tapie	28.70
1982	Ben Crenshaw	28.65
1983	Morris Hatalsky	27.96
1984	Gary McCord	28.57
1985	Craig Stadler	28.627†
1986	Greg Norman	1.736
1987	Ben Crenshaw	1.743
1988	Don Pooley	1.729
1989	Steve Jones	1.734

† Number had to be carried to extra decimal place to determine winner.

Year by Year Statistical Leaders (Cont.)

PUTTING (Cont.)

1990	Larry Rinker	1.7467†	1995	Jim Furyk	1.708	2000	Brad Faxon	1.704
1991	Jay Don Blake	1.7326†	1996	Brad Faxon	1.709	2001	David Frost	1.708
1992	Mark O'Meara	1.731	1997	Don Pooley	1.718	2002	Bob Heintz	1.682
1993	David Frost	1.739	1998	Rick Fehr	1.722	2003	John Huston	1.713
1994	Loren Roberts	1.737	1999	Brad Faxon	1.723	2004	Stewart Cink	1.723

Note: Average number of putts taken on greens reached in regulation; prior to 1986, based on average number of putts per 18 holes.

SAND SAVES

1980	Bob Eastwood	65.4	1989	Mike Sullivan	66.0	1998	Keith Fergus	71.0
1981	Tom Watson	60.1	1990	Paul Azinger	67.2	1999	Jeff Sluman	67.3
1982	Isao Aoki	60.2	1991	Ben Crenshaw	64.9	2000	Fred Couples	67.0
1983	Isao Aoki	62.3	1992	Mitch Adcock	66.9	2001	Franklin Langham	68.9
1984	Peter Oosterhuis	64.7	1993	Ken Green	64.4	2002	J. Olazabal	64.9
1985	Tom Purtzer	60.8	1994	Corey Pavin	65.4	2003	Stuart Appleby	62.1
1986	Paul Azinger	63.8	1995	Billy Mayfair	68.6	2004	Dan Forsman	62.3
1987	Paul Azinger	63.2	1996	Gary Rusnak	64.0			
1988	Greg Powers	63.5	1997	Bob Estes	70.3			

Note: Percentage of up-and-down efforts from greenside sand traps only—fairway bunkers excluded.

PAR BREAKERS

1980	Tom Watson	.213	1984	Craig Stadler	.220	1988	Ken Green	.236
1981	Bruce Lietzke	.225	1985	Craig Stadler	.218	1989	Greg Norman	.224
1982	Tom Kite	.2154†	1986	Greg Norman	.248	1990	Greg Norman	.219
1983	Tom Watson	.211	1987	Mark Calcavecchia	.221			

Note: Average based on total birdies and eagles scored out of total holes played. Discontinued as an official category after 1990.

EAGLES

1980	Dave Eichelberger	16	1988	Ken Green	21	1997	Tiger Woods	104.1
1981	Bruce Lietzke	12	1989	Lon Hinkle	14	1998	Davis Love III	83.3
1982	Tom Weiskopf	10		Duffy Waldorf	14	1999	Vijay Singh	104.8
	J.C. Snead	10	1990	Paul Azinger	14	2000	Tiger Woods	72.0
	Andy Bean	10	1991	Andy Bean	15	2001	Phil Mickelson	73.8
1983	Chip Beck	15	1992	Dan Forsman	18	2002	John Daly	78.4
1984	Gary Hallberg	15	1993	Davis Love III	15	2003	Tiger Woods	76.5
1985	Larry Rinker	14	1994	Davis Love III	18	2004	Nick Price	90.0
1986	Joey Sindelar	16	1995	Kelly Gibson	16			
1987	Phil Blackmar	20	1996	Tom Watson	97.2			

Note: Total of eagles scored 1980–1995. Since 1996 winner determined by number of holes played per eagle.

BIRDIES

1980	Andy Bean	388	1989	Ted Schulz	415	1998	David Duval	4.29
1981	Vance Heafner	388	1990	Mike Donald	401	1999	Tiger Woods	4.46
1982	Andy Bean	392	1991	Scott Hoch	446	2000	Tiger Woods	4.92
1983	Hal Sutton	399	1992	Jeff Sluman	417	2001	Phil Mickelson	4.49
1984	Mark O'Meara	419	1993	John Huston	426	2002	Tiger Woods	4.47
1985	Joey Sindelar	411	1994	Brad Bryant	397	2003	Vijay Singh	4.41
1986	Joey Sindelar	415	1995	Steve Lowery	410	2004	Vijay Singh	4.40
1987	Dan Forsman	409	1996	Fred Couples	4.20			
1988	Dan Forsman	465	1997	Tiger Woods	4.25			

Note: Total of birdies scored 1980–95. Since 1996, winner determined by average number of birdies per round.

ALL-AROUND

1987	Dan Pohl	170	1993	Gil Morgan	252	1999	Tiger Woods	120
1988	Payne Stewart	170	1994	Bob Estes	227	2000	Tiger Woods	113
1989	Paul Azinger	250	1995	Justin Leonard	323	2001	Phil Mickelson	174
1990	Paul Azinger	162	1996	Fred Couples	214	2002	Phil Mickelson	259
1991	Scott Hoch	283	1997	Bill Glasson	282	2003	Tiger Woods	206
1992	Fred Couples	256	1998	John Huston	151	2004	Jeff Ogilvy	268

Note: Sum of the places of standing from the other statistical categories; the player with the number closest to zero leads.

† Number had to be carried to extra decimal place to determine winner.

PGA Player of the Year Award

1948	Ben Hogan	1967	Jack Nicklaus	1986	Bob Tway
1949	Sam Snead	1968	Not awarded	1987	Paul Azinger
1950	Ben Hogan	1969	Orville Moody	1988	Curtis Strange
1951	Ben Hogan	1970	Billy Casper	1989	Tom Kite
1952	Julius Boros	1971	Lee Trevino	1990	Wayne Levi
1953	Ben Hogan	1972	Jack Nicklaus	1991	Fred Couples
1954	Ed Furgol	1973	Jack Nicklaus	1992	Fred Couples
1955	Doug Ford	1974	Johnny Miller	1993	Nick Price
1956	Jack Burke	1975	Jack Nicklaus	1994	Nick Price
1957	Dick Mayer	1976	Jack Nicklaus	1995	Greg Norman
1958	Dow Finsterwald	1977	Tom Watson	1996	Tom Lehman
1959	Art Wall	1978	Tom Watson	1997	Tiger Woods
1960	Arnold Palmer	1979	Tom Watson	1998	David Duval
1961	Jerry Barber	1980	Tom Watson	1999	Tiger Woods
1962	Arnold Palmer	1981	Bill Rogers	2000	Tiger Woods
1963	Julius Boros	1982	Tom Watson	2001	Tiger Woods
1964	Ken Venturi	1983	Hal Sutton	2002	Tiger Woods
1965	Dave Marr	1984	Tom Watson	2003	Tiger Woods
1966	Billy Casper	1985	Lanny Wadkins	2004	Vijay Singh

Vardon Trophy: Scoring Average

Year	Winner	Avg	Year	Winner	Avg	Year	Winner	Avg
1937	Harry Cooper	*500	1963	Billy Casper	70.58	1984	Calvin Peete	70.56
1938	Sam Snead	520	1964	Arnold Palmer	70.01	1985	Don Pooley	70.36
1939	Byron Nelson	473	1965	Billy Casper	70.85	1986	Scott Hoch	70.08
1940	Ben Hogan	423	1966	Billy Casper	70.27	1987	Don Pohl	70.25
1941	Ben Hogan	494	1967	Arnold Palmer	70.18	1988	Chip Beck	69.46
1942–46	No award		1968	Billy Casper	69.82	1989	Greg Norman	69.49
1947	Jimmy Demaret	69.90	1969	Dave Hill	70.34	1990	Greg Norman	69.10
1948	Ben Hogan	69.30	1970	Lee Trevino	70.64	1991	Fred Couples	69.59
1949	Sam Snead	69.37	1971	Lee Trevino	70.27	1992	Fred Couples	69.38
1950	Sam Snead	69.23	1972	Lee Trevino	70.89	1993	Nick Price	69.11
1951	Lloyd Mangrum	70.05	1973	Bruce Crampton	70.57	1994	Greg Norman	68.81
1952	Jack Burke	70.54	1974	Lee Trevino	70.53	1995	Steve Elkington	69.62
1953	Lloyd Mangrum	70.22	1975	Bruce Crampton	70.51	1996	Tom Lehman	69.32
1954	E.J. Harrison	70.41	1976	Don January	70.56	1997	Nick Price	68.98
1955	Sam Snead	69.86	1977	Tom Watson	70.32	1998	David Duval	69.13
1956	Cary Middlecoff	70.35	1978	Tom Watson	70.16	1999	Tiger Woods	68.43
1957	Dow Finsterwald	70.30	1979	Tom Watson	70.27	2000	Tiger Woods	67.79
1958	Bob Rosburg	70.11	1980	Lee Trevino	69.73	2001	Tiger Woods	68.81
1959	Art Wall	70.35	1981	Tom Kite	69.80	2002	Tiger Woods	68.13
1960	Billy Casper	69.95	1982	Tom Kite	70.21	2003	Tiger Woods	68.41
1961	Arnold Palmer	69.85	1983	Raymond Floyd	70.61	2004	Vijay Singh	68.84
1962	Arnold Palmer	70.27						

*Point system used, 1937–41.

Note: As of 1988, based on minimum of 60 rounds per year. Adjusted for average score of field in tournaments entered.

Alltime PGA Tour Records*

Scoring

90 HOLES

324—(65-61-67-66-65) by Joe Durant, at four courses, La Quinta, CA, to win the 2001 Bob Hope Classic (36 under par).

72 HOLES

254—(64-62-63-65) by Tommy Armour III, at LaCantera GC, San Antonio, TX, to win the 2003 Valero Texas Open (26 under par).

54 HOLES, OPENING ROUNDS

189—(64-62-63) by John Cook, at the TPC at Southwind, Memphis, en route to winning the 1996 St. Jude Classic.

189—(65-60-64) Mark Calcavecchia, at the TPC at Scottsdale, Scottsdale, AZ, en route to winning the 2001 Phoenix Open.

54 HOLES, OPENING ROUNDS (Cont.)

189—(64-62-63) by Tommy Armour III, at LaCantera GC, San Antonio, TX, en route to winning the 2003 Valero Texas Open.

54 HOLES, CONSECUTIVE ROUNDS

189—(63-63-63) by Chandler Harper in the last three rounds to win the 1954 Texas Open at Brackenridge Park GC, San Antonio.

189—(64-62-63) by John Cook, at the TPC at Southwind, Memphis, in the first three rounds en route to winning the 1996 St. Jude Classic.

189—(65-60-64) Mark Calcavecchia, at the TPC at Scottsdale, Scottsdale, AZ, in the first three rounds en route to winning the 2001 Phoenix Open.

Alltime PGA Tour Records (Cont.)*

Scoring (Cont.)

54 HOLES, CONSECUTIVE ROUNDS (Cont.)

189—(64-62-63) by Tommy Armour III, at LaCantera GC, San Antonio, TX, in the first three rounds en route to winning the 2003 Valero Texas Open.

36 HOLES, OPENING ROUNDS

125—(64–61) by Tiger Woods, in the 2000 World Golf Championships/ NEC Invitational, which he won, at Firestone CC, Akron.

125—(65–60) by Mark Calcavecchia, in the 2001 Phoenix Open, which he won, at TPC at Scottsdale, Scottsdale, AZ.

36 HOLES, CONSECUTIVE ROUNDS

125—(64–61) by Gay Brewer, in the middle rounds of the 1967 Pensacola Open, which he won, at Pensacola CC, Pensacola, FL.

125—(63–62) by Ron Streck, in the last two rounds to win the 1978 Texas Open at Oak Hills CC, San Antonio.

125—(62–63) by Blaine McCallister, in the middle two rounds of the 1988 Hardee's Golf Classic, which he won at Oakwood CC, Coal Valley, IL.

125—(62–63) by John Cook, in the middle two rounds of the 1996 St. Jude Classic, which he won at the TPC at Southwind, Memphis.

125—(62–63) by John·Cook, in the fourth and fifth rounds in winning the 1997 Bob Hope Chrysler Classic at Indian Wells CC, Indian Hills, CA.

125—(64–61) by Tiger Woods, in the first two rounds of the 2000 World Golf Championship/ NEC Invitational, which he won, at Firestone CC, Akron.

125—(65–60) by Mark Calcavecchia, in the first two rounds of the 2001 Phoenix Open, which he won, at TPC at Scottsdale, Scottsdale, AZ.

125—(62-63) by Tommy Armour III, in the middle two rounds of the 2003 Valero Texas Open, which he won at LaCantera GC, San Antonio, TX.

18 HOLES

59—by Al Geiberger, at Colonial Country Club, Memphis, in second round in winning the 1977 Memphis Classic.

59—by Chip Beck, at Sunrise Golf Club, Las Vegas, in third round of the 1991 Las Vegas Invitational.

59—by David Duval, on the Palmer Course at PGA West, La Quinta, CA, in the fifth round of the 1999 Bob Hope Chrysler Classic.

9 HOLES

27—by Mike Souchak, at Brackenridge Park GC, San Antonio, on par-35 second nine of first round in the 1955 Texas Open.

27—by Andy North, at En-Joie GC, Endicott, NY, on par-34 second nine of first round in the 1975 BC Open.

27—by Billy Mayfair, at Warwick Hills, Grand Blanc, MI, on par-36 back nine of fourth round, 2001 Buick Open.

MOST CONSECUTIVE ROUNDS UNDER 70

19—Byron Nelson in 1945.

Scoring (Cont.)

MOST BIRDIES IN A ROW

8—Bob Goalby, at Pasadena GC, St. Petersburg, FL, during fourth round in winning the 1961 St Petersburg Open.

8—Fuzzy Zoeller, at Oakwood CC, Coal Valley, IL, during first round of 1976 Quad Cities Open.

8—Dewey Arnette, at Warwick Hills GC, Grand Blanc, MI, during first round of the 1987 Buick Open.

8—Edward Fryatt, at the Blue Course of the Doral Resort and Spa, Miami, during second round of the 2000 Doral-Ryder Open.

MOST BIRDIES IN A ROW TO WIN

5—Jack Nicklaus, to win 1978 Jackie Gleason Inverrary Classic (last 5 holes).

Wins

MOST CONSECUTIVE YEARS WINNING AT LEAST ONE TOURNAMENT

17—Jack Nicklaus, 1962–78.

17—Arnold Palmer, 1955–71.

16—Billy Casper, 1956–71.

MOST CONSECUTIVE WINS

11—Byron Nelson, from Miami Four Ball, March 8–11, 1945, through Canadian Open, August 2–4, 1945.

MOST WINS IN A SINGLE EVENT

8—Sam Snead, Greater Greensboro Open, 1938, 1946, 1949, 1950, 1955, 1956, 1960, and 1965.

MOST CONSECUTIVE WINS IN A SINGLE EVENT

4—Walter Hagen, PGA Championships, 1924–27.

4—Gene Sarazen, Miami Open, 1926, (schedule change) 1928–30.

4—Tiger Woods, Bay Hill Invitational, 2000–03

MOST WINS IN A CALENDAR YEAR

18—Byron Nelson, 1945

MOST YEARS BETWEEN WINS

15 yrs, 5 mos—Butch Baird, 1961–76.

MOST YEARS FROM FIRST WIN TO LAST

28 yrs, 11 mos, 20 days—Raymond Floyd, 1963–92.

YOUNGEST WINNERS

19 yrs, 10 mos—John McDermott, 1911 U.S. Open.

OLDEST WINNER

52 yrs, 10 mos—Sam Snead, 1965 Greater Greensboro Open.

WIDEST WINNING MARGIN: STROKES

16—Bobby Locke, 1948 Chicago Victory National Championship.

*Through 12/31/03.

THE MAJOR TOURNAMENTS

LPGA Championship

Year	Winner	Score	Runner-Up	Site
1955	Beverly Hanson† (4 & 3)	220	Louise Suggs	Orchard Ridge CC, Ft Wayne, IN
1956	Marlene Hagge*	291	Patty Berg	Forest Lake CC, Detroit
1957	Louise Suggs	285	Wiffi Smith	Churchill Valley CC, Pittsburgh
1958	Mickey Wright	288	Fay Crocker	Churchill Valley CC, Pittsburgh
1959	Betsy Rawls	288	Patty Berg	Sheraton Hotel CC, French Lick, IN
1960	Mickey Wright	292	Louise Suggs	Sheraton Hotel CC, French Lick, IN
1961	Mickey Wright	287	Louise Suggs	Stardust CC, Las Vegas
1962	Judy Kimball	282	Shirley Spork	Stardust CC, Las Vegas
1963	Mickey Wright	294	Mary Lena Faulk Mary Mills Louise Suggs	Stardust CC, Las Vegas
1964	Mary Mills	278	Mickey Wright	Stardust CC, Las Vegas
1965	Sandra Haynie	279	Clifford A. Creed	Stardust CC, Las Vegas
1966	Gloria Ehret	282	Mickey Wright	Stardust CC, Las Vegas
1967	Kathy Whitworth	284	Shirley Englehorn	Pleasant Valley CC, Sutton, MA
1968	Sandra Post*	294	Kathy Whitworth (75)	Pleasant Valley CC, Sutton, MA
1969	Betsy Rawls	293	Susie Berning Carol Mann	Concord GC, Kiameshia Lake, NY
1970	Shirley Englehorn*	285	Kathy Whitworth (78)	Pleasant Valley CC, Sutton, MA
1971	Kathy Whitworth	288	Kathy Ahern	Pleasant Valley CC, Sutton, MA
1972	Kathy Ahern	293	Jane Blalock	Pleasant Valley CC, Sutton, MA
1973	Mary Mills	288	Betty Burfeindt	Pleasant Valley CC, Sutton, MA
1974	Sandra Haynie	288	JoAnne Carner	Pleasant Valley CC, Sutton, MA
1975	Kathy Whitworth	288	Sandra Haynie	Pine Ridge GC, Baltimore
1976	Betty Burfeindt	287	Judy Rankin	Pine Ridge GC, Baltimore
1977	Chako Higuchi	279	Pat Bradley Sandra Post Judy Rankin	Bay Tree Golf Plantation, N Myrtle Beach, SC
1978	Nancy Lopez	275	Amy Alcott	Jack Nicklaus GC, Kings Island, OH
1979	Donna Caponi	279	Jerilyn Britz	Jack Nicklaus GC, Kings Island, OH
1980	Sally Little	285	Jane Blalock	Jack Nicklaus GC, Kings Island, OH
1981	Donna Caponi	280	Jerilyn Britz Pat Meyers	Jack Nicklaus GC, Kings Island, OH
1982	Jan Stephenson	279	JoAnne Carner	Jack Nicklaus GC, Kings Island, OH
1983	Patty Sheehan	279	Sandra Haynie	Jack Nicklaus GC, Kings Island, OH
1984	Patty Sheehan	272	Beth Daniel Pat Bradley	Jack Nicklaus GC, Kings Island, OH
1985	Nancy Lopez	273	Alice Miller	Jack Nicklaus GC, Kings Island, OH
1986	Pat Bradley	277	Patty Sheehan	Jack Nicklaus GC, Kings Island, OH
1987	Jane Geddes	275	Betsy King	Jack Nicklaus GC, Kings Island, OH
1988	Sherri Turner	281	Amy Alcott	Jack Nicklaus GC, Kings Island, OH
1989	Nancy Lopez	274	Ayako Okamoto	Jack Nicklaus GC, Kings Island, OH
1990	Beth Daniel	280	Rosie Jones	Bethesda CC, Bethesda, MD
1991	Meg Mallon	274	Pat Bradley Ayako Okamoto	Bethesda CC, Bethesda, MD
1992	Betsy King	267	Karen Noble	Bethesda CC, Bethesda, MD
1993	Patty Sheehan	275	Lauri Merten	Bethesda CC, Bethesda, MD
1994	Laura Davies	279	Alice Ritzman	DuPont CC, Wilmington, DE
1995	Kelly Robbins	274	Laura Davies	DuPont CC, Wilmington, DE
1996	Laura Davies	213†	Julie Piers	DuPont CC, Wilmington, DE
1997	Chris Johnson*	281	Leta Lindley	DuPont CC, Wilmington, DE
1998	Se Ri Pak	273	Donna Andrews	DuPont CC, Wilmington, DE
1999	Juli Inkster	268	Liselotte Neumann	DuPont CC, Wilmington, DE
2000	Juli Inkster*	281	Stefania Croce	DuPont CC, Wilmington, DE
2001	Karrie Webb	270	Laura Diaz	DuPont CC, Wilmington, DE
2002	Se Ri Pak	279	Beth Daniel	DuPont CC, Wilmington, DE
2003	Annika Sorenstam*	278	Grace Park	DuPont CC, Wilmington, DE
2004	Annika Sorenstam	271	Shi Hyun Ahn	DuPont CC, Wilmington, DE
2005	Annika Sorenstam	277	Michelle Wie	Bulle Rock GC, Harve de Grace, MD

*Won playoff. †Won match-play final. #Shortened due to rain.

U.S. Women's Open

Year	Winner	Score	Runner-Up	Site
1946	Patty Berg	5 & 4	Betty Jameson	Spokane CC, Spokane, WA
1947	Betty Jameson	295	Sally Sessions	Starmount Forest CC, Greensboro, NC
			Polly Riley	
1948	Babe Zaharias	300	Betty Hicks	Atlantic City CC, Northfield, NJ
1949	Louise Suggs	291	Babe Zaharias	Prince George's G & CC, Landover, MD
1950	Babe Zaharias	291	Betsy Rawls	Rolling Hills CC, Wichita, KS
1951	Betsy Rawls	293	Louise Suggs	Druid Hills GC, Atlanta
1952	Louise Suggs	284	Marlene Bauer	Bala GC, Philadelphia
			Betty Jameson	
1953	Betsy Rawls* (71)	302	Jackie Pung (77)	CC of Rochester, Rochester, NY
1954	Babe Zaharias	291	Betty Hicks	Salem CC, Peabody, MA
1955	Fay Crocker	299	Mary Lena Faulk	Wichita CC, Wichita, KS
			Louise Suggs	
1956	Kathy Cornelius* (75)	302	Barbara McIntire (82)	Northland CC, Duluth, MN
1957	Betsy Rawls	299	Patty Berg	Winged Foot GC, Mamaroneck, NY
1958	Mickey Wright	290	Louise Suggs	Forest Lake CC, Detroit
1959	Mickey Wright	287	Louise Suggs	Churchill Valley CC, Pittsburgh
1960	Betsy Rawls	292	Joyce Ziske	Worcester CC, Worcester, MA
1961	Mickey Wright	293	Betsy Rawls	Baltusrol GC (Lower Course), Springfield, NJ
1962	Murle Breer	301	Jo Ann Prentice	Dunes GC, Myrtle Beach, SC
			Ruth Jessen	
1963	Mary Mills	289	Sandra Haynie	Kenwood CC, Cincinnati
			Louise Suggs	
1964	Mickey Wright* (70)	290	Ruth Jessen (72)	San Diego CC, Chula Vista, CA
1965	Carol Mann	290	Kathy Cornelius	Atlantic City CC, Northfield, NJ
1966	Sandra Spuzich	297	Carol Mann	Hazeltine Natl GC, Chaska, MN
1967	Catherine LaCoste	294	Susie Berning	Hot Springs GC (Cascades Course),
			Beth Stone	Hot Springs, VA
1968	Susie Berning	289	Mickey Wright	Moslem Springs GC, Fleetwood, PA
1969	Donna Caponi	294	Peggy Wilson	Scenic Hills CC, Pensacola, FL
1970	Donna Caponi	287	Sandra Haynie	Muskogee CC, Muskogee, OK
			Sandra Spuzich	
1971	JoAnne Carner	288	Kathy Whitworth	Kahkwa CC, Erie, PA
1972	Susie Berning	299	Kathy Ahern	Winged Foot GC, Mamaroneck, NY
			Pam Barnett	
			Judy Rankin	
1973	Susie Berning	290	Gloria Ehret	CC of Rochester, Rochester, NY
			Shelley Hamlin	
1974	Sandra Haynie	295	Carol Mann	La Grange CC, La Grange, IL
			Beth Stone	
1975	Sandra Palmer	295	JoAnne Carner	Atlantic City CC, Northfield, NJ
			Sandra Post	
			Nancy Lopez	
1976	JoAnne Carner* (76)	292	Sandra Palmer (78)	Rolling Green CC, Springfield, PA
1977	Hollis Stacy	292	Nancy Lopez	Hazeltine Natl GC, Chaska, MN
1978	Hollis Stacy	289	JoAnne Carner	CC of Indianapolis, Indianapolis
			Sally Little	
1979	Jerilyn Britz	284	Debbie Massey	Brooklawn CC, Fairfield, CT
			Sandra Palmer	
1980	Amy Alcott	280	Hollis Stacy	Richland CC, Nashville
1981	Pat Bradley	279	Beth Daniel	La Grange CC, La Grange, IL
1982	Janet Anderson	283	Beth Daniel	Del Paso CC, Sacramento
			Sandra Haynie	
			Donna White	
			JoAnne Carner	
1983	Jan Stephenson	290	JoAnne Carner	Cedar Ridge CC, Tulsa
			Patty Sheehan	
1984	Hollis Stacy	290	Rosie Jones	Salem CC, Peabody, MA
1985	Kathy Baker	280	Judy Dickinson	Baltusrol GC (Upper Course), Springfield, NJ
1986	Jane Geddes* (71)	287	Sally Little (73)	NCR GC, Dayton
1987	Laura Davies* (71)	285	Ayako Okamoto (73)	Plainfield CC, Plainfield, NJ
			JoAnne Carner (74)	
1988	Liselotte Neumann	277	Patty Sheehan	Baltimore CC, Baltimore
1989	Betsy King	278	Nancy Lopez	Indianwood G & CC, Lake Orion, MI
1990	Betsy King	284	Patty Sheehan	Atlanta Athletic Club, Duluth, GA
1991	Meg Mallon	283	Pat Bradley	Colonial Club, Fort Worth

U.S. Women's Open (Cont.)

Year	Winner	Score	Runner-Up	Site
1992	Patty Sheehan* (72)	280	Juli Inkster	Oakmont CC, Oakmont, PA
1993	Lauri Merten	280	Donna Andrew Helen Alfredsson	Crooked Stick, Carmel, IN
1994	Patty Sheehan	277	Tammie Green	Indianwood G & CC, Lake Orion, MI
1995	Annika Sorenstam	278	Meg Mallon	The Broadmoor GC, Colorado Springs, CO
1996	Annika Sorenstam	272	Kris Tschetter	Pine Needles GC, Southern Pines, NC
1997	Alison Nicholas	274	Nancy Lopez	Pumpkin Ridge GC, North Plains, OR
1998	Se Ri Pak†	290	Jenny Chuasiriporn	Blackwolf Run Golf Resort, Kohler, WI
1999	Juli Inkster	272	Sherri Turner	Old Waverly GC, West Point, MS
2000	Karrie Webb	282	Cristie Kerr/ Meg Mallon	Merit GC, Libertyville, IL
2001	Karrie Webb	273	Se Ri Pak	Pine Needles GC, Southern Pines, NC
2002	Juli Inkster	276	Annika Sorenstam	Prairie Dunes CC, Hutchinson, KS
2003	Hilary Lunke*	283	Kelly Robbins	Pumpkin Ridge GC, North Plains, OR
2004	Meg Mallon	274	Annika Sorenstam	The Orchards GC, South Hadley, MA
2005	Birdie Kim	287	Brittany Lang Morgan Pressel	Cherry Hills CC, Cherry Hills Village, CO

* Winner in playoff. † Winner on second hole of sudden death after 18-hole playoff ended in a tie.

Nabisco Championship

Year	Winner	Score	Runner-Up	Year	Winner	Score	Runner-Up
1972	Jane Blalock	213	Carol Mann				JoAnne Carner
			Judy Rankin	1990	Betsy King	283	Kathy Postlewait
1973	Mickey Wright	284	Joyce Kazmierski				Shirley Furlong
1974	Jo Ann Prentice*	289	Jane Blalock	1991	Amy Alcott	273	Dottie Mochrie
			Sandra Haynie	1992	Dottie Mochrie*	279	Juli Inkster
1975	Sandra Palmer	283	Kathy McMullen	1993	Helen Alfredsson	284	Amy Benz
1976	Judy Rankin	285	Betty Burfeindt				Tina Barrett
1977	Kathy Whitworth	289	JoAnne Carner				Betsy King
			Sally Little	1994	Donna Andrews	276	Laura Davies
1978	Sandra Post*	283	Penny Pulz	1995	Nanci Bowen	285	Susie Redman
1979	Sandra Post	276	Nancy Lopez	1996	Patti Sheehan	281	Kelly Robbins
1980	Donna Caponi	275	Amy Alcott				Meg Mallon
1981	Nancy Lopez	277	Carolyn Hill				Annika Sörenstam
1982	Sally Little	278	Hollis Stacy	1997	Betsy King	276	Kris Tschetter
			Sandra Haynie	1998	Pat Hurst	281	Helen Dobson
1983	Amy Alcott	282	Beth Daniel	1999	Dottie Pepper	269	Meg Mallon
			Kathy Whitworth	2000	Karrie Webb	274	Dottie Pepper
1984	Juli Inkster*	280	Pat Bradley	2001	Annika Sorenstam	281	five players
1985	Alice Miller	275	Jan Stephenson	2002	Annika Sorenstam	280	Liselotte Neumann
1986	Pat Bradley	280	Val Skinner	2003	P. Meunier-Lebouc	281	Annika Sorenstam
1987	Betsy King*	283	Patty Sheehan	2004	Grace Park	277	Aree Song
1988	Amy Alcott	274	Colleen Walker	2005	Anika Sorenstam	273	Rosie Jones
1989	Juli Inkster	279	Tammie Green				

*Winner in sudden-death playoff. Note: Designated fourth major in 1983; played at Mission Hills CC, Rancho Mirage, CA.

du Maurier Classic

Year	Winner	Score	Runner-Up	Site
1973	Jocelyne Bourassa*	214	Sandra Haynie Judy Rankin	Montreal GC, Montreal
1974	Carole Jo Callison	208	JoAnne Carner	Candiac GC, Montreal
1975	JoAnne Carner*	214	Carol Mann	St. George's CC, Toronto
1976	Donna Caponi*	212	Judy Rankin	Cedar Brae G & CC, Toronto
1977	Judy Rankin	214	Pat Meyers Sandra Palmer	Lachute G & CC, Montreal
1978	JoAnne Carner	278	Hollis Stacy	St. George's CC, Toronto
1979	Amy Alcott	285	Nancy Lopez	Richelieu Valley CC, Montreal
1980	Pat Bradley	277	JoAnne Carner	St. George's CC, Toronto
1981	Jan Stephenson	278	Nancy Lopez Pat Bradley	Summerlea CC, Dorion, Quebec
1982	Sandra Haynie	280	Beth Daniel	St. George's CC, Toronto
1983	Hollis Stacy	277	JoAnne Carner Alice Miller	Beaconsfield GC, Montreal
1984	Juli Inkster	279	Ayako Okamoto	St. George's G & CC, Toronto
1985	Pat Bradley	278	Jane Geddes	Beaconsfield CC, Montreal
1986	Pat Bradley*	276	Ayako Okamoto	Board of Trade CC, Toronto
1987	Jody Rosenthal	272	Ayako Okamoto	Islesmere GC, Laval, Quebec
1988	Sally Little	279	Laura Davies	Vancouver GC, Coquitlam, British Columbia
1989	Tammie Green	279	Pat Bradley Betsy King	Beaconsfield GC, Montreal

du Maurier Classic (Cont.)

Year	Winner	Score	Runner-Up	Site
1990	Cathy Johnston	276	Patty Sheehan	Westmount G & CC, Kitchener, Ontario
1991	Nancy Scranton	279	Debbie Massey	Vancouver GC, Coquitlam, British Columbia
1992	Sherri Steinhauer	277	Judy Dickinson	St. Charles CC, Winnipeg, Manitoba
1993	Brandie Burton	277	Betsy King	London Hunt and CC, London, Ontario
1994	Martha Nause	279	Michelle McGann	Ottawa Hunt and GC, Ottawa, Ont.
1995	Jenny Lidback	280	Liselotte Neumann	Beaconsfield GC, Pointe-Claire, Quebec
1996	Laura Davies	277	Nancy Lopez	Edmonton CC, Edmonton, Alberta
			Karrie Webb	
1997	Colleen Walker	278	Liselotte Neumann	Glen Abbey GC, Oakville, Ontario
1998	Brandie Burton	270	Annika Sorenstam	Essex G & CC, Windsor, Ontario
1999	Karrie Webb	277	Laura Davies	Priddis Greens G & CC, Calgary, Alberta
2000	Meg Mallon	282	Rosie Jones	Royal Ottawa GC, Aylmer, Quebec

*Winner in sudden-death playoff. Note: Designated third major in 1979; discontinued in 2001.

Women's British Open

Year	Winner	Score	Runner-Up	Site
2001	Se Ri Pak	277	Mi Hyun Kim	Sunningdale GC, Berkshire, England
2002	Karrie Webb	273	Michelle Ellis	Turnberry GC, Ailsa, Scotland
			Paula Marti	
2003	Annika Sorenstam	278	Se Ri Pak	Royal Lytham & St. Annes, England
2004	Karen Stupples	269	Rachel Teske	Sunningdale GC, Berjshire, England
2005	Jeong Jang	272	Sophie Gustafson	Royal Birkdale CC, Merseyside, England

Note: Designated fourth major in 2001.

Alltime Major Championship Winners

	LPGA	U.S. Open	Nabisco	Brit. Open	‡du Maurier	#Titleholders	†Western	U.S. Am	Brit. Am	Total
Patty Berg	0	1	0	0	0	7	7	1	0	16
Mickey Wright	4	4	0	0	0	2	3	0	0	13
Louise Suggs	1	2	0	0	0	4	4	1	1	13
Babe Zaharias	0	3	0	0	0	3	4	1	1	12
*Juli Inkster	2	2	2	0	1	0	0	3	0	10
Betsy Rawls	2	4	0	0	0	0	2	0	0	8
*JoAnne Carner	0	2	0	0	0	0	0	5	0	7
*Annika Sorenstam	2	2	2	1	0	0	0	0	0	7
Kathy Whitworth	3	0	0	0	0	2	1	0	0	6
Pat Bradley	1	1	1	0	3	0	0	0	0	6
*Patty Sheehan	3	2	1	0	0	0	0	0	0	6
Glenna Vare	0	0	0	0	0	0	0	6	0	6
*Betsy King	1	2	3	0	0	0	0	0	0	6

*Active LPGA player.
#Major from 1937–1972. †Major from 1937–1967. ‡Major from 1979–2000.

Alltime Multiple Professional Major Winners

LPGA

Mickey Wright	4
Nancy Lopez	3
Patty Sheehan	3
Kathy Whitworth	3
Donna Caponi	2
Sandra Haynie	2
Mary Mills	2
Betsy Rawls	2
Laura Davies	2
Juli Inkster	2
Se Ri Pak	2
Annika Sorenstam	2

U.S. OPEN

Betsy Rawls	4
Mickey Wright	4
Susie Maxwell Berning	3

U.S. OPEN (Cont.)

Hollis Stacy	3
Babe Zaharias	3
JoAnne Carner	2
Donna Caponi	2
Betsy King	2
Meg Mallon	2
Patty Sheehan	2
Louise Suggs	2
Annika Sorenstam	2
Karrie Webb	2
Juli Inkster	2

NABISCO/DINAH SHORE

Amy Alcott	3
Betsy King	3
Juli Inkster	2
Annika Sorenstam	2

DU MAURIER

Pat Bradley	3
Brandie Burton	2
JoAnne Carner	2

TITLEHOLDERS

Patty Berg	7
Louise Suggs	4
Babe Zaharias	3
Dorothy Kirby	2
Marilynn Smith	2
Kathy Whitworth	2
Mickey Wright	2

WESTERN OPEN

Patty Berg	7
Louise Suggs	4
Babe Zaharias	4
Mickey Wright	3
June Beebe	2
Opal Hill	2
Betty Jameson	2
Betsy Rawls	2

THE LPGA TOUR

Most Career Wins†

	Wins		Wins		Wins
Kathy Whitworth	88	JoAnne Carner*	43	Pat Bradley	31
Mickey Wright	82	Sandra Haynie	42	Juli Inkster*	30
Annika Sorenstam*	63	Babe Zaharias	41	Karrie Webb*	30
Patty Berg	60	Carol Mann	38	Amy Alcott*	29
Louise Suggs	58	Patty Sheehan*	35	Jane Blalock	29
Betsy Rawls	55	Betsy King*	34	Judy Rankin	26
Nancy Lopez	48	Beth Daniel*	33		

*Active player.

Season Money Leaders

	Earnings ($)		Earnings ($)		Earnings ($)
1950...Babe Zaharias	14,800	1969...Carol Mann	49,152	1987...Ayako Okamoto	466,034
1951...Babe Zaharias	15,087	1970...Kathy Whitworth	30,235	1988...Sherri Turner	350,851
1952...Betsy Rawls	14,505	1971...Kathy Whitworth	41,181	1989...Betsy King	654,132
1953...Louise Suggs	19,816	1972...Kathy Whitworth	65,063	1990...Beth Daniel	863,578
1954...Patty Berg	16,011	1973...Kathy Whitworth	82,864	1991...Pat Bradley	763,118
1955...Patty Berg	16,492	1974...JoAnne Carner	87,094	1992...Dottie Mochrie	693,335
1956...Marlene Hagge	20,235	1975...Sandra Palmer	76,374	1993...Betsy King	595,992
1957...Patty Berg	16,272	1976...Judy Rankin	150,734	1994...Laura Davies	687,201
1958...Beverly Hanson	12,639	1977...Judy Rankin	122,890	1995...Annika Sorenstam	666,533
1959...Betsy Rawls	26,774	1978...Nancy Lopez	189,814	1996...Karrie Webb	1,002,000
1960...Louise Suggs	16,892	1979...Nancy Lopez	197,489	1997...Annika Sorenstam	1,236,789
1961...Mickey Wright	22,236	1980...Beth Daniel	231,000	1998...Annika Sorenstam	1,092,748
1962...Mickey Wright	21,641	1981...Beth Daniel	206,998	1999...Karrie Webb	1,591,959
1963...Mickey Wright	31,269	1982...JoAnne Carner	310,400	2000...Karrie Webb	1,876,853
1964...Mickey Wright	29,800	1983...JoAnne Carner	291,404	2001...Annika Sorenstam	2,105,868
1965...Kathy Whitworth	28,658	1984...Betsy King	266,771	2002...Annika Sorenstam	2,863,904
1966...Kathy Whitworth	33,517	1985...Nancy Lopez	416,472	2003...Annika Sorenstam	2,029,506
1967...Kathy Whitworth	32,937	1986...Pat Bradley	492,021	2004...Annika Sorenstam	2,544,707
1968...Kathy Whitworth	48,379				

Career Money Leaders†

	Earnings ($)		Earnings ($)		Earnings ($)
1. Annika Sorenstam	17,701,781	11. Lorie Kane	6,124,451	20. Sherri Steinhauer	4,501,431
2. Karrie Webb	10,680,412	11. Pat Bradley	5,750,965	21. Michelle Redman	4,409,989
3. Juli Inkster	9,845,671	12. Kelly Robbins	5,716,765	22. Pat Hurst	3,744,958
4. Meg Mallon	8,762,007	13. Patty Sheehan	5,513,409	23. Catriona Matthew	3,489,868
5. Beth Daniel	8,464,679	14. Nancy Lopez	5,320,877	24. Brandie Burton	4,021,171
6. Rosie Jones	8,243,451	15. Liselotte Neumann	5,273,309	25. Tammie Green	4,097,260
7. Se Ri Pak	8,081,987	16. Christie Kerr	5,089,691	26. Jane Geddes	3,805,553
8. Betsy King	7,637,621	17. Mi-Hyun Kim	5,080,730	27. Donna Andrews	3,613,684
9. Laura Davies	7,342,983	18. Grace Park	4,978,394	28. Chris Johnson	3,603,023
10. Dottie Pepper	6,827,284	19. Rachel Hetherington	4,557,362	28. D. Ammaccapane	3,602,500

LPGA Player of the Year

1966	Kathy Whitworth	1979	Nancy Lopez	1992	Dottie Mochrie
1967	Kathy Whitworth	1980	Beth Daniel	1993	Betsy King
1968	Kathy Whitworth	1981	JoAnne Carner	1994	Beth Daniel
1969	Kathy Whitworth	1982	JoAnne Carner	1995	Annika Sörenstam
1970	Sandra Haynie	1983	Patty Sheehan	1996	Laura Davies
1971	Kathy Whitworth	1984	Betsy King	1997	Annika Sorenstam
1972	Kathy Whitworth	1985	Nancy Lopez	1998	Annika Sorenstam
1973	Kathy Whitworth	1986	Pat Bradley	1999	Karrie Webb
1974	JoAnne Carner	1987	Ayako Okamoto	2000	Karrie Webb
1975	Sandra Palmer	1988	Nancy Lopez	2001	Annika Sorenstam
1976	Judy Rankin	1989	Betsy King	2002	Annika Sorenstam
1977	Judy Rankin	1990	Beth Daniel	2003	Annika Sorenstam
1978	Nancy Lopez	1991	Pat Bradley	2004	Annika Sorenstam

†Through 10/3/05.

Vare Trophy: Best Scoring Average*

		Avg			Avg			Avg
1953	Patty Berg	75.00	1971	Kathy Whitworth	72.88	1988	Colleen Walker	71.26
1954	Babe Zaharias	75.48	1972	Kathy Whitworth	72.38	1989	Beth Daniel	70.38
1955	Patty Berg	74.47	1973	Judy Rankin	73.08	1990	Beth Daniel	70.54
1956	Patty Berg	74.57	1974	JoAnne Carner	72.87	1991	Pat Bradley	70.76
1957	Louise Suggs	74.64	1975	JoAnne Carner	72.40	1992	Dottie Mochrie	70.80
1958	Beverly Hanson	74.92	1976	Judy Rankin	72.25	1993	Nancy Lopez	70.83
1959	Betsy Rawls	74.03	1977	Judy Rankin	72.16	1994	Beth Daniel	70.90
1960	Mickey Wright	73.25	1978	Nancy Lopez	71.76	1995	Annika Sorenstam	71.00
1961	Mickey Wright	73.55	1979	Nancy Lopez	71.20	1996	Annika Sorenstam	70.47
1962	Mickey Wright	73.67	1980	Amy Alcott	71.51	1997	Karrie Webb	70.00
1963	Mickey Wright	72.81	1981	JoAnne Carner	71.75	1998	Annika Sorenstam	69.99
1964	Mickey Wright	72.46	1982	JoAnne Carner	71.49	1999	Karrie Webb	69.43
1965	Kathy Whitworth	72.61	1983	JoAnne Carner	71.41	2000	Karrie Webb	70.05
1966	Kathy Whitworth	72.60	1984	Patty Sheehan	71.40	2001	Annika Sorenstam	69.42
1967	Kathy Whitworth	72.74	1985	Nancy Lopez	70.73	2002	Annika Sorenstam	68.70
1968	Carol Mann	72.04	1986	Pat Bradley	71.10	2003	Se Ri Pak	70.03
1969	Kathy Whitworth	72.38	1987	Betsy King	71.14	2004	Grace Park	69.99
1970	Kathy Whitworth	72.26						

Alltime LPGA Tour Records†

Scoring

72 HOLES

259—(65-62-67-65) by Wendy Doolan to win at the Dell Urich GC, Tucson, AZ, in the 2003 Welch's/Fry's Champ. (21 under par).

261—(71-61-63-66) by Se Ri Pak to win at the Highland Meadows CC, Sylvania, OH, in the 1998 Jamie Farr Kroger Classic (23 under par).

261—(65-59-69-68) by Annika Sorenstam to win at the Moon Valley CC, Phoenix, in the 2001 Standard Register PING (27 under par).

54 HOLES

192—(63-63-66) by Annika Sorenstam to win at the Seta GC, Otsu-shi, Shiga, Japan in the 2003 Mizuno Classic (24 under par).

193—(66-61-66) by Karrie Webb to lead at the Walnut Hills CC, East Lansing, MI, in the 2000 Oldsmobile Classic (23 under par).

193—(65-59-69) by Annika Sorenstam to lead at the Moon Valley CC, Phoenix, in the 2001 Standard Register PING (23 under par)

36 HOLES

124—(65-59) by Annika Sorenstam to lead at the Moon Valley CC, Phoenix, in the 2001 Standard Register PING (20 under par).

18 HOLES

59—by Annika Sorenstam at the Moon Valley CC, Phoenix, in the second round in winning the 2001 Standard Register PING (13 under par).

9 HOLES

28—by Mary Beth Zimmerman at Rail GC, 1984 Rail Charity Golf Classic, Springfield, IL (par 36). Zimmerman shot 64.

28—by Pat Bradley at Green Gables CC, Denver, 1984 Columbia Savings Classic (par 35). Bradley shot 65.

28—by Muffin Spencer-Devlin at Knollwood CC, Elmsford, NY, in winning the 1985 MasterCard International Pro-Am (par 35). Spencer-Devlin shot 64.

Scoring (Cont.)

9 HOLES (Cont.)

28—by Peggy Kirsch at Squaw Creek CC, Vienna, OH, in the 1991 Phar-Mor (par 35).

28—by Renee Heiken at Highland Meadows CC, Sylvania, OH, in the 1996 Jamie Farr Kroger Classic (par 34).

28—by Annika Sorenstam at the Moon Valley CC, Phoenix, in the 2001 Standard Register PING (par 36).

28—by Danielle Ammaccapane at Highland Meadows GC, Sylvania, OH, in the 2002 Jamie Farr Kroger Classic (par 34)

28—by Young Kim at Dell Urich GC, Tucson, AZ, in the 2003 Welch's/Fry's Championship (par 35)

28—by Chris Johnson at Highland Meadows GC, Sylvania, OH, in the 2003 Jamie Farr Kroger Classic (par 34)

MOST CONSECUTIVE ROUNDS UNDER 70

11—Annika Sorenstam, in 2002.

MOST BIRDIES IN A ROW

9—Beth Daniel at Onion Creek Club in Austin, in the second round of the 1999 Philips Invitational. Daniel shot 62 (8 under par).

Wins

MOST CONSECUTIVE WINS IN SCHEDULED EVENTS

4—Mickey Wright, in 1962.
4—Mickey Wright, in 1963.
4—Kathy Whitworth, in 1969.
4—Annika Sorenstam in 2001.

MOST CONSECUTIVE WINS IN ENTERED TOURNAMENTS

5—Nancy Lopez, in 1978.

MOST WINS IN A CALENDAR YEAR

13—Mickey Wright, in 1963.

WIDEST WINNING MARGIN, STROKES

14—Louise Suggs, 1949 U.S. Women's Open.
14—Cindy Mackey, 1986 MasterCard Int'l Pro-Am.

†Through 10/3/04. *Must play 70 rounds in order to qualify; Annika Sorenstam compiled an average of 69.02 in 60 rounds in 2003.

U.S. Senior Open

Year	Winner	Score	Runner-Up	Site
1980	Roberto DeVicenzo	285	William C. Campbell	Winged Foot GC, Mamaroneck, NY
1981	Arnold Palmer* (70)	289	Bob Stone (74) Billy Casper (77)	Oakland Hills CC, Birmingham, MI
1982	Miller Barber	282	Gene Littler Dan Sikes, Jr.	Portland GC, Portland, OR
1983	Billy Casper* (75) (3)	288	Rod Funseth (75) (4)	Hazeltine GC, Chaska, MN
1984	Miller Barber	286	Arnold Palmer	Oak Hill CC, Rochester, NY
1985	Miller Barber	285	Roberto DeVicenzo	Edgewood Tahoe GC, Stateline, NV
1986	Dale Douglass	279	Gary Player	Scioto CC, Columbus, OH
1987	Gary Player	270	Doug Sanders	Brooklawn CC, Fairfield, CT
1988	Gary Player* (68)	288	Bob Charles (70)	Medinah CC, Medinah, IL
1989	Orville Moody	279	Frank Beard	Laurel Valley GC, Ligonier, PA
1990	Lee Trevino	275	Jack Nicklaus	Ridgewood CC, Paramus, NJ
1991	Jack Nicklaus (65)	282	Chi Chi Rodriguez (69)	Oakland Hills CC, Birmingham, MI
1992	Larry Laoretti	275	Jim Colbert	Saucon Valley CC, Bethlehem, PA
1993	Jack Nicklaus	278	Tom Weiskopf	Cherry Hills CC, Englewood, CO
1994	Simon Hobday	274	Jim Albus	Pinehurst Resort & CC, Pinehurst, NC
1995	Tom Weiskopf	275	Jack Nicklaus	Congressional CC, Bethesda, MD
1996	Dave Stockton	277	Hale Irwin	Canterbury GC, Beachwood, OH
1997	Graham Marsh	280	Hale Irwin	Olympia Fields CC, Olympia Fields, IL
1998	Hale Irwin	285	Vicente Fernandez	Riviera CC, Pacific Palisades, CA
1999	Dave Eichelberger	281	Ed Dougherty	Des Moines G & CC, Des Moines, IA
2000	Hale Irwin	267	Bruce Fleisher	Saucon Valley CC, Bethlehem, PA
2001	Bruce Fleisher	280	Isao Aoki Gil Morgan	Salem CC, Peabody, MA
2002	Don Pooley*	274	Tom Watson	Caves Valley GC, Owings Mill, MD
2003	Bruce Lietzke	277	Tom Watson	Inverness GC, Toledo, OH
2004	Peter Jacobsen	272	Hale Irwin	Bellerive CC, St. Louis, MO
2005	Allen Doyle	274	D.A. Weibring Loren Roberts	NCR GC, Kettering, OH

*Winner in playoff. Playoff scores are in parentheses. The 1983 playoff went to one hole of sudden death after an 18-hole playoff.

CHAMPIONS TOUR
Season Money Leaders

Year	Winner	Earnings ($)	Year	Winner	Earnings ($)	Year	Winner	Earnings ($)
1980	Don January	44,100	1989	Bob Charles	725,887	1997	Hale Irwin	2,449,420
1981	Miller Barber	83,136	1990	Lee Trevino	1,190,518	1998	Hale Irwin	2,861,945
1982	Miller Barber	106,890	1991	Mike Hill	1,065,657	1999	Bruce Fleisher	2,515,705
1983	Don January	237,571	1992	Lee Trevino	1,027,002	2000	Larry Nelson	2,708,005
1984	Don January	328,597	1993	Dave Stockton	1,175,944	2001	Allen Doyle	2,553,582
1985	Peter Thomson	386,724	1994	Dave Stockton	1,402,519	2002	Hale Irwin	3,028,304
1986	Bruce Crampton	454,299	1995	Jim Colbert	1,444,386	2003	Tom Watson	1,853,108
1987	Chi Chi Rodriguez	509,145	1996	Jim Colbert	1,627,890	2004	Craig Stadler	2,306,066
1988	Bob Charles	533,929						

Career Money Leaders†

	Earnings ($)			Earnings ($)			Earnings ($)
1. Hale Irwin	20,329,465		11. Isao Aoki	8,917,390		21. John Jacobs	7,501,819
2. Gil Morgan	14,249,619		12. Jim Thorpe	8,891,160		22. Tom Kite	7,239,419
3. Bruce Fleisher	11,873,051		13. Raymond Floyd	8,797,506		23. Vicente Fernandez	7,197,427
4. Larry Nelson	11,708,819		14. Jim Dent	8,641,889		24. J.C. Snead	7,145,996
5. Jim Colbert	11,302,900		15. Jay Sigel	8,554,889		25. Doug Tewell	7,145,822
6. Dave Stockton	10,433,865		16. George Archer	8,329,648		26. Bob Murphy	6,997,579
7. Dana Quigley	10,044,993		17. Mike Hill	8,257,545		27. Dale Douglass	6,915,081
8. Allen Doyle	9,838,091		18. Graham Marsh	8,236,554		28. Tom Wargo	6,883,834
9. Lee Trevino	9,758,773		19. Tom Jenkins	7,778,606		29. Jose Maria Canizares	6,745,179
10. Bob Charles	8,951,920		20. Bruce Summerhays	7,681,091		30. John Bland	6,692,468

Most Career Wins†

	Wins		Wins
Hale Irwin	40	Jim Colbert	20
Lee Trevino	29	Bruce Crampton	20
Miller Barber	24	George Archer	19
Bob Charles	23	Gary Player	19
Gil Morgan	23	Bruce Fleisher	18
Don January	22	Mike Hill	18
Chi Chi Rodriguez	22	Larry Nelson	18

†Through 10/3/04.

MAJOR MEN'S AMATEUR CHAMPIONSHIPS

U.S. Amateur

Year	Winner	Score	Runner-Up	Site
1895	Charles B. Macdonald	12 & 11	Charles E. Sands	Newport GC, Newport, RI
1896	H.J. Whigham	8 & 7	J.G Thorp	Shinnecock Hills GC, Southampton, NY
1897	H.J. Whigham	8 & 6	W. Rossiter Betts	Chicago GC, Wheaton, IL
1898	Findlay S. Douglas	5 & 3	Walter B. Smith	Morris County GC, Morristown, NJ
1899	H.M. Harriman	3 & 2	Findlay S. Douglas	Onwentsia Club, Lake Forest, IL
1900	Walter Travis	2 up	Findlay S. Douglas	Garden City GC, Garden City, NY
1901	Walter Travis	5 & 4	Walter E. Egan	CC of Atlantic City, NJ
1902	Louis N. James	4 & 2	Eben M. Byers	Glen View Club, Golf, IL
1903	Walter Travis	5 & 4	Eben M. Byers	Nassau CC, Glen Cove, NY
1904	H. Chandler Egan	8 & 6	Fred Herreshoff	Baltusrol GC, Springfield, NJ
1905	H. Chandler Egan	6 & 5	D.E. Sawyer	Chicago GC, Wheaton, IL
1906	Eben M. Byers	2 up	George S. Lyon	Englewood GC, Englewood, NJ
1907	Jerry Travers	6 & 5	Archibald Graham	Euclid Club, Cleveland, OH
1908	Jerry Travers	8 & 7	Max H. Behr	Garden City GC, Garden City, NY
1909	Robert A. Gardner	4 & 3	H. Chandler Egan	Chicago GC, Wheaton, IL
1910	William C. Fownes Jr.	4 & 3	Warren K. Wood	The Country Club, Brookline, MA
1911	Harold Hilton	1 up	Fred Herreshoff	The Apawamis Club, Rye, NY
1912	Jerry Travers	7 & 6	Charles Evans Jr.	Chicago GC, Wheaton, IL
1913	Jerry Travers	5 & 4	John G. Anderson	Garden City GC, Garden City, NY
1914	Francis Ouimet	6 & 5	Jerry Travers	Ekwanok CC, Manchester, VT
1915	Robert A. Gardner	5 & 4	John G. Anderson	CC of Detroit, Grosse Pt. Farms, MI
1916	Chick Evans	4 & 3	Robert A. Gardner	Merion Cricket Club, Haverford, PA
1917–18	No tournament			
1919	S. Davidson Herron	5 & 4	Bobby Jones	Oakmont CC, Oakmont, PA
1920	Chick Evans	7 & 6	Francis Ouimet	Engineers' CC, Roslyn, NY
1921	Jesse P. Guilford	7 & 6	Robert A. Gardner	St. Louis CC, Clayton, MO
1922	Jess W. Sweetser	3 & 2	Chick Evans	The Country Club, Brookline, MA
1923	Max R. Marston	1 up	Jess W. Sweetser	Flossmoor CC, Flossmoor, IL
1924	Bobby Jones	9 & 8	George Von Elm	Merion Cricket Club, Ardmore, PA
1925	Bobby Jones	8 & 7	Watts Gunn	Oakmont CC, Oakmont, PA
1926	George Von Elm	2 & 1	Bobby Jones	Baltusrol GC, Springfield, NJ
1927	Bobby Jones	8 & 7	Chick Evans	Minikahda Club, Minneapolis
1928	Bobby Jones	10 & 9	T. Phillip Perkins	Brae Burn CC, West Newton, MA
1929	Harrison R. Johnston	4 & 3	Dr. O.F. Willing	Del Monte G & CC, Pebble Beach, CA
1930	Bobby Jones	8 & 7	Eugene V. Homans	Merion Cricket Club, Ardmore, PA
1931	Francis Ouimet	6 & 5	Jack Westland	Beverly CC, Chicago, IL
1932	C. Ross Somerville	2 & 1	John Goodman	Baltimore CC, Timonium, MD
1933	George T. Dunlap Jr.	6 & 5	Max R. Marston	Kenwood CC, Cincinnati, OH
1934	Lawson Little	8 & 7	David Goldman	The Country Club, Brookline, MA
1935	Lawson Little	4 & 2	Walter Emery	The Country Club, Cleveland, OH
1936	John W. Fischer	1 up	Jack McLean	Garden City GC, Garden City, NY
1937	John Goodman	2 up	Raymond E. Billows	Alderwood CC, Portland, OR
1938	William P. Turnesa	8 & 7	B. Patrick Abbott	Oakmont CC, Oakmont, PA
1939	Marvin H. Ward	7 & 5	Raymond E. Billows	North Shore CC, Glenview, IL
1940	Richard D. Chapman	11 & 9	W. McCullough Jr.	Winged Foot GC, Mamaroneck, NY
1941	Marvin H. Ward	4 & 3	B. Patrick Abbott	Omaha Field Club, Omaha, NE
1942–45	No tournament			
1946	Ted Bishop	1 up	Smiley L. Quick	Baltusrol GC, Springfield, NJ
1947	Skee Riegel	2 & 1	John W. Dawson	Del Monte G & CC, Pebble Beach, CA
1948	William P. Turnesa	2 & 1	Raymond E. Billows	Memphis CC, Memphis, TN
1949	Charles R. Coe	11 & 10	Rufus King	Oak Hill CC, Rochester, NY
1950	Sam Urzetta	1 up	Frank Stranahan	Minneapolis GC, Minneapolis, MN
1951	Billy Maxwell	4 & 3	Joseph F. Gagliardi	Saucon Valley CC, Bethlehem, PA
1952	Jack Westland	3 & 2	Al Mengert	Seattle GC, Seattle, WA
1953	Gene Littler	1 up	Dale Morey	Oklahoma City G & CC, Oklahoma City
1954	Arnold Palmer	1 up	Robert Sweeny	CC of Detroit, Grosse Pt. Farms, MI
1955	E. Harvie Ward Jr.	9 & 8	William Hyndman III	CC of Virginia, Richmond, VA
1956	E. Harvie Ward Jr.	5 & 4	Charles Kocsis	Knollwood Club, Lake Forest, IL
1957	Hillman Robbins Jr.	5 & 4	Dr. Frank M. Taylor	The Country Club, Brookline, MA
1958	Charles R. Coe	5 & 4	Tommy Aaron	Olympic Club, San Francisco, CA
1959	Jack Nicklaus	1 up	Charles R. Coe	Broadmoor GC, Colorado Springs, CO
1960	Deane Beman	6 & 4	Robert W. Gardner	St. Louis CC, Clayton, MO
1961	Jack Nicklaus	8 & 6	H. Dudley Wysong	Pebble Beach GL, Pebble Beach, CA

U.S. Amateur (Cont.)

Year	Winner	Score	Runner-Up	Site
1962	Labron E. Harris Jr.	1 up	Downing Gray	Pinehurst CC, Pinehurst, NC
1963	Deane Beman	2 & 1	Richard H. Sikes	Wakonda Club, Des Moines, IA
1964	William C. Campbell	1 up	Edgar M. Tutwiler	Canterbury GC, Cleveland, OH
1965	Robert J. Murphy Jr.	291	Robert B. Dickson	Southern Hills, CC, Tulsa
1966	Gary Cowan	285–75	Deane Beman	Merion GC, Ardmore, PA
1967	Robert B. Dickson	285	Marvin Giles III	Broadmoor GC, Colorado Springs
1968	Bruce Fleisher	284	Marvin Giles III	Scioto CC, Columbus, OH
1969	Steven N. Melnyk	286	Marvin Giles III	Oakmont CC, Oakmont, PA
1970	Lanny Wadkins	279	Tom Kite	Waverley CC, Portland, OR
1971	Gary Cowan	280	Eddie Pearce	Wilmington CC, Wilmington DE
1972	Marvin Giles III	285	two tied	Charlotte CC, Charlotte, NC
1973	Craig Stadler	6 & 5	David Strawn	Inverness Club, Toledo
1974	Jerry Pate	2 & 1	John P. Grace	Ridgewood CC, Ridgewood, NJ
1975	Fred Ridley	2 up	Keith Fergus	CC of Virginia, Richmond
1976	Bill Sander	8 & 6	C. Parker Moore Jr.	Bel Air CC, Los Angeles
1977	John Fought	9 & 8	Doug Fischesser	Aronimink GC, Newton Square, PA
1978	John Cook	5 & 4	Scott Hoch	Plainfield CC, Plainfield, NJ
1979	Mark O'Meara	8 & 7	John Cook	Canterbury GC, Cleveland
1980	Hal Sutton	9 & 8	Bob Lewis	CC of North Carolina, Pinehurst, NC
1981	Nathaniel Crosby	1 up	Brian Lindley	Olympic Club, San Francisco
1982	Jay Sigel	8 & 7	David Tolley	The Country Club, Brookline, MA
1983	Jay Sigel	8 & 7	Chris Perry	North Shore CC, Glenview, IL
1984	Scott Verplank	4 & 3	Sam Randolph	Oak Tree GC, Edmond, OK
1985	Sam Randolph	1 up	Peter Persons	Montclair GC, West Orange, NJ
1986	Buddy Alexander	5 & 3	Chris Kite	Shoal Creek, Shoal Creek, AL
1987	Bill Mayfair	4 & 3	Eric Rebmann	Jupiter Hills Club, Jupiter, FL
1988	Eric Meeks	7 & 6	Danny Yates	Va. Hot Springs G & CC, VA
1989	Chris Patton	3 & 1	Danny Green	Merion GC, Ardmore, PA
1990	Phil Mickelson	5 & 4	Manny Zerman	Cherry Hills CC, Englewood, CO
1991	Mitch Voges	7 & 6	Manny Zerman	The Honors Course, Ooltewah, TN
1992	Justin Leonard	8 & 7	Tom Scherrer	Muirfield Village GC, Dublin, OH
1993	John Harris	5 & 3	Danny Ellis	Champions GC, Houston
1994	Tiger Woods	2 up	Trip Kuehne	TPC-Sawgrass, Ponte Vedre, FL
1995	Tiger Woods	2 up	Buddy Marucci	Newport Country Club, Newport, RI
1996	Tiger Woods	38 holes	Steve Scott	Pumpkin Ridge GC, Cornelius, OR
1997	Matthew Kuchar	2 & 1	Joel Kribel	Cog Hill G & CC, Lemont, IL
1998	Hank Kuehne	2 & 1	Tom McKnight	Oak Hill CC, Rochester, NY
1999	David Gossett	9 & 8	Sung Yoon Kim	Pebble Beach GL, Pebble Beach, CA
2000	Jeff Quinney	39 holes	James Driscoll	Baltusrol GC, Upper Springfield, NJ
2001	Bubba Dickerson	1 up	Robert Hamilton	East Lake GC, Atlanta
2002	Ricky Barnes	2 & 1	Hunter Mahan	Oakland Hills CC, Bloomfield Hills, MI
2003	Nick Flanagan	37 holes	Frank Abbott	East Lake GC, Atlanta
2004	Ryan Moore	2 up	Luke List	Winged Foot GC, Mamaroneck, NY
2005	Edoardo Molinari	4 & 3	Dillon Dougherty	Merion GC, Ardmore, PA

Note: All stroke play from 1965 to 1972.

U.S. Junior Amateur

1948...Dean Lind	1963...Gregg McHatton	1978...Don Hurter	1993...Tiger Woods
1949...Gay Brewer	1964...Johnny Miller	1979...Jack Larkin	1994...Terry Noe
1950...Mason Rudolph	1965...James Masserio	1980...Eric Johnson	1995...D. Scott Hailes
1951...Tommy Jacobs	1966...Gary Sanders	1981...Scott Erickson	1996...Shane McMenamy
1952...Don Bisplinghoff	1967...John Crooks	1982...Rich Marik	1997...Jason Allred
1953...Rex Baxter	1968...Eddie Pearce	1983...Tim Straub	1998...James Oh
1954...Foster Bradley	1969...Aly Trompas	1984...Doug Martin	1999...Hunter Mahan
1955...William Dunn	1970...Gary Koch	1985...Charles Rymer	2000...Matthew Rosenfeld
1956...Harlan Stevenson	1971...Mike Brannan	1986...Brian Montgomery	2001...Henry Liaw
1957...Larry Beck	1972...Bob Byman	1987...Brett Quigley	2002...Charlie Beljan
1958...Buddy Baker	1973...Jack Renner	1988...Jason Widener	2003...Brian Harman
1959...Larry Lee	1974...David Nevatt	1989...David Duval	2004...Sihwan Kim
1960...Bill Tindall	1975...Brett Mullin	1990...Mathew Todd	2005...Kevin Tway
1961...Charles McDowell	1976...Madden Hatcher III	1991...Tiger Woods	
1962...Jim Wiechers	1977...Willie Wood Jr.	1992...Tiger Woods	

Mid-Amateur Championship

1981...Jim Holtgrieve	1987...Jay Sigel	1993...Jeff Thomas	1999...Danny Green
1982...William Hoffer	1988...David Eger	1994...Tim Jackson	2000...Greg Puga
1983...Jay Sigel	1989...James Taylor	1995...Jerry Courville Jr.	2001...Tim Jackson
1984...Mike Podolak	1990...Jim Stuart	1996...John Miller	2002...George Zahringer
1985...Jay Sigel	1991...Jim Stuart	1997...Ken Bakst	2003...Nathan Smith
1986...Bill Loeffler	1992...Danny Yates	1998...John Miller	2004...Austin Eaton III

British Amateur

887	H. G. Hutchinson	1928	T.P. Perkins	1970	M. Bonallack
1888	John Ball	1929	C.J.H. Tolley	1971	Steve Melnyk
1889	J.E. Laidlay	1930	Robert T. Jones Jr	1972	Trevor Homer
1890	John Ball	1931	E. Martin Smith	1973	R. Siderowf
1891	J.E. Laidlay	1932	J. DeForest	1974	Trevor Homer
1892	John Ball	1933	M. Scott	1975	M. Giles
1893	Peter Anderson	1934	W. Lawson Little	1976	R. Siderowf
1894	John Ball	1935	W. Lawson Little	1977	P. McEvoy
1895	L.M.B. Melville	1936	H. Thomson	1978	P. McEvoy
1896	F.G. Tait	1937	R. Sweeney Jr	1979	J. Sigel
1897	A.J.T. Allan	1938	C.R. Yates	1980	D. Evans
1898	F.G. Tait	1939	A.T. Kyle	1981	P. Ploujoux
1899	John Ball	1940–45	not held	1982	M. Thompson
1900	H.H. Hilton	1946	J. Bruen	1983	A. Parkin
1901	H.H. Hilton	1947	Willie D. Turnesa	1984	J.M. Olazabal
1902	C. Hutchings	1948	Frank R. Stranahan	1985	G. McGimpsey
1903	R. Maxwell	1949	S.M. McReady	1986	D. Curry
1904	W.J. Travis	1950	Frank R. Stranahan	1987	P. Mayo
1905	A.G. Barry	1951	Richard D. Chapman	1988	C. Hardin
1906	James Robb	1952	E.H. Ward	1989	S. Dodd
1907	John Ball	1953	J.B. Carr	1990	R. Muntz
1908	E.A. Lassen	1954	D.W. Bachli	1991	G. Wolstenholme
1909	R. Maxwell	1955	J.W. Conrad	1992	S. Dundas
1910	John Ball	1956	J.C. Beharrel	1993	I. Pyman
1911	H.H. Hilton	1957	R. Reid Jack	1994	L. James
1912	John Ball	1958	J.B. Carr	1995	G. Sherry
1913	H.H. Hilton	1959	Deane Beman	1996	W. Bladon
1914	J.L.C. Jenkins	1960	J.B. Carr	1997	C. Watson
1915–19	not held	1961	M. Bonallack	1998	Sergio Garcia
1920	C.J.H. Tolley	1962	R. Davies	1999	Graeme Storm
1921	W.I. Hunter	1963	M. Lunt	2000	Mikko Ilonen
1922	E.W.E. Holderness	1964	C. Clark	2001	Michael Hoey
1923	R.H. Wethered	1965	M. Bonallack	2002	Alejandro Larrazabal
1924	E.W.E. Holderness	1966	C.R. Cole	2003	Gary Wolstenholme
1925	R. Harris	1967	R. Dickson	2004	Stuart Wilson
1926	Jess Sweetser	1968	M. Bonallack	2005	Brian McElhinney
1927	Dr. W. Tweddell	1969	M. Bonallack		

Amateur Public Links

1922	Edmund R. Held	1952	Omer L. Bogan	1980	Jodie Mudd
1923	Richard J. Walsh	1953	Ted Richards Jr	1981	Jodie Mudd
1924	Joseph Coble	1954	Gene Andrews	1982	Billy Tuten
1925	Raymond J. McAuliffe	1955	Sam D. Kocsis	1983	Billy Tuten
1926	Lester Bolstad	1956	James H. Buxbaum	1984	Bill Malley
1927	Carl F. Kauffmann	1957	Don Essig III	1985	Jim Sorenson
1928	Carl F. Kauffmann	1958	Daniel D. Sikes Jr	1986	Bill Mayfair
1929	Carl F. Kauffmann	1959	William A. Wright	1987	Kevin Johnson
1930	Robert E. Wingate	1960	Verne Callison	1988	Ralph Howe III
1931	Charles Ferrera	1961	Richard H. Sikes	1989	Tim Hobby
1932	R.L. Miller	1962	Richard H. Sikes	1990	Michael Combs
1933	Charles Ferrera	1963	Robert Lunn	1991	David Berganio Jr
1934	David A. Mitchell	1964	William McDonald	1992	Warren Schulte
1935	Frank Strafaci	1965	Arne Dokka	1993	David Berganio Jr
1936	B. Patrick Abbott	1966	Lamont Kaser	1994	Guy Yamamoto
1937	Bruce N. McCormick	1967	Verne Callison	1995	Chris Wollmann
1938	Al Leach	1968	Gene Towry	1996	Tim Hogarth
1939	Andrew Szwedko	1969	John M. Jackson Jr	1997	Tim Clark
1940	Robert C. Clark	1970	Robert Risch	1998	Trevor Immelman
1941	William M. Welch Jr	1971	Fred Haney	1999	Hunter Haas
1942–45	not held	1972	Bob Allard	2000	D.J. Trahan
1946	Smiley L. Quick	1973	Stan Stopa	2001	Chez Reavie
1947	Wilfred Crossley	1974	Charles Barenaba	2002	Ryan Moore
1948	Michael R. Ferentz	1975	Randy Barenaba	2003	Brandt Snedeker
1949	Kenneth J. Towns	1976	Eddie Mudd	2004	Ryan Moore
1950	Stanley Bielat	1977	Jerry Vidovic	2005	Clay Ogden
1951	Dave Stanley	1978	Dean Prince		
		1979	Dennis Walsh		

U.S. Senior Golf

1955 ....J. Wood Platt	1972 ....Lewis W. Oehmig	1989 ....Bo Williams
1956 ....Frederick J. Wright	1973 ....William Hyndman III	1990 ....Jackie Cummings
1957 ....J. Clark Espie	1974 ....Dale Morey	1991 ....Bill Bosshard
1958 ....Thomas C. Robbins	1975 ....William F. Colm	1992 ....Clarence Moore
1959 ....J. Clark Espie	1976 ....Lewis W. Oehmig	1993 ....Joe Ungvary
1960 ....Michael Cestone	1977 ....Dale Morey	1994 ....O. Gordon Brewer
1961 ....Dexter H. Daniels	1978 ..........K.K. Compton	1995 ....James Stahl Jr.
1962 ....Merrill L. Carlsmith	1979 ....William C. Campbell	1996 ....O. Gordon Brewer
1963 ....Merrill L. Carlsmith	1980 ....William C. Campbell	1997 ....Cliff Cunningham
1964 ....William D. Higgins	1981 ....Ed Updegraff	1998 ....Bill Shean Jr.
1965 ....Robert B. Kiersky	1982 ....Alton Duhon	1999 ....Bill Ploeger
1966 ....Dexter H. Daniels	1983 ....William Hyndman III	2000 ....Bill Shean Jr.
1967 ....Ray Palmer	1984 ....Bob Rawlins	2001 ....Kemp Richardson
1968 ....Curtis Person Sr.	1985 ....Lewis W. Oehmig	2002 ....Greg Reynolds
1969 ....Curtis Person Sr.	1986 ....Bo Williams	2003 ....Kemp Richardson
1970 ....Gene Andrews	1987 ....John Richardson	2004 ....Mark Bemowski
1971 ....Tom Draper	1988 ....Clarence Moore	

Note: Event is for amateur golfers at least 55 years of age.

MAJOR WOMEN'S AMATEUR CHAMPIONSHIPS

U.S. Women's Amateur

Year	Winner	Score	Runner-Up	Site
1895 ....Mrs. Charles S. Brown		132	Nellie Sargent	Meadow Brook Club, Hempstead, NY
1896 ....Beatrix Hoyt		2 & 1	Mrs. Arthur Turnure	Morris Couty GC, Morristown, NJ
1897 ....Beatrix Hoyt		5 & 4	Nellie Sargent	Essex County Club, Manchester, MA
1898 ....Beatrix Hoyt		5 &3	Maude Wetmore	Ardsley Club, Ardsley-on-Hudson, NY
1899 ....Ruth Underhill		2 & 1	Margaret Fox	Philadelphia CC, Philadelphia, PA
1900 ....Frances C. Griscom		6 & 5	Margaret Curtis	Shinnecock Hills GC, Shinnecock Hills, NY
1901 ....Genevieve Hecker		5 & 3	Lucy Herron	Baltusrol GC, Springfield, NJ
1902 ....Genevieve Hecker		4 & 3	Louisa A. Wells	The Country Club, Brookline, MA
1903 ....Bessie Anthony		7 & 6	J. Anna Carpenter	Chicago GC, Wheaton, IL
1904 ....Georgianna M. Bishop		5 & 3	Mrs. E.F. Sanford	Merion Cricket Club, Haverford, PA
1905 ....Pauline Mackay		1 up	Margaret Curtis	Morris County GC, Convent, NJ
1906 ....Harriot S. Curtis		2 & 1	Mary B. Adams	Brae Burn CC, West Newton, MA
1907 ....Margaret Curtis		7 & 6	Harriot S. Curtis	Midlothian CC, Blue Island, IL
1908 ....Katherine C. Harley		6 & 5	Mrs. T.H. Polhemus	Chevy Chase Club, Chevy Chase, MD
1909 ....Dorothy I. Campbell		3 & 2	Nonna Barlow	Merion Cricket Club, Haverford, PA
1910 ....Dorothy I. Campbell		2 & 1	Mrs. G.M. Martin	Homewood CC, Flossmoor, IL
1911 ....Margaret Curtis		5 & 3	Lillian B. Hyde	Baltusrol GC, Springfield, NJ
1912 ....Margaret Curtis		3 & 2	Nonna Barlow	Essex County Club, Manchester, MA
1913 ....Gladys Ravenscroft		2 up	Marion Hollins	Wilmington CC, Wilmington, DE
1914 ....Katherine Harley		1 up	Elaine V. Rosenthal	Nassau CC, Glen Cove, NY
1915 ....Florence Vanderbeck		3 & 2	Margaret Gavin	Onwentsia Club, Lake Forest, IL
1916 ....Alexa Stirling		2 & 1	Mildred Caverly	Belmont Springs CC, Waverley, MA
1917–18 ....No tournament				
1919 ....Alexa Stirling		6 & 5	Margaret Gavin	Shawnee CC, Shawnee-on-Delaware, PA
1920 ....Alexa Stirling		5 & 4	Dorothy Campbell	Mayfield CC, Cleveland
1921 ....Marion Hollins		5 & 4	Alexa Stirling	Hollywood GC, Deal, NJ
1922 ....Glenna Collett		5 & 4	Margaret Gavin	Greenbriar GC, White Sulphur Springs, WV
1923 ....Edith Cummings		3 & 2	Alexa Stirling	Westchester-Biltmore CC, Rye, NY
1924 ....Dorothy Campbell		7 & 6	Mary K. Browne	Rhode Island CC, Nyatt, RI
1925 ....Glenna Collett		9 & 8	Alexa Stirling	St. Louis CC, Clayton, MO
1926 ....Helen Stetson		3 & 1	Elizabeth Goss	Merion Cricket Club, Ardmore, PA
1927 ....Miriam Burns Horn		5 & 4	Maureen Orcutt	Cherry Valley Club, Garden City, NY
1928 ....Glenna Collett		13 & 12	Virginia Van Wie	Va. Hot Springs G & TC, Hot Springs, VA
1929 ....Glenna Collett		4 & 3	Leona Pressler	Oakland Hills CC, Birmingham, MI
1930 ....Glenna Collett		6 & 5	Virginia Van Wie	Los Angeles CC, Beverly Hills, CA
1931 ....Helen Hicks		2 & 1	Glenna Collet Vare	CC of Buffalo, Williamsville, NY
1932 ....Virginia Van Wie		10 & 8	Glenna Collet Vare	Salem CC, Peabody, MA
1933 ....Virginia Van Wie		4 & 3	Helen Hicks	Exmoor CC, Highland Park, IL
1934 ....Virginia Van Wie		2 & 1	Dorothy Traung	Whitemarsh Valley CC, Chestnut Hill, PA
1935 ....Glenna Collett Vare		3 & 2	Patty Berg	Interlachen CC, Hopkins, MN
1936 ....Pamela Barton		4 & 3	Maureen Orcutt	Canoe Brook CC, Summit, NJ
1937 ....Estelle Lawson		7 & 6	Patty Berg	Memphis CC, Memphis, TN
1938 ....Patty Berg		6 & 5	Estelle Lawson	Westmoreland CC, Wilmette, IL

U.S. Women's Amateur (Cont.)

Year	Winner	Score	Runner-Up	Site
1939	Betty Jameson	3 & 2	Dorothy Kirby	Wee Burn Club, Darien, CT
1940	Betty Jameson	6 & 5	Jane S. Cothran	Del Monte G & CC, Pebble Beach, CA
1941	Elizabeth Hicks	5 & 3	Helen Sigel	The Country Club, Brookline, MA
1942–45	No tournament			
1946	Babe Zaharias	11 & 9	Clara Sherman	Southern Hills CC, Tulsa
1947	Louise Suggs	2 up	Dorothy Kirby	Franklin Hills CC, Franklin, MI
1948	Grace S. Lenczyk	4 & 3	Helen Sigel	Del Monte G & CC, Pebble Beach, CA
1949	Dorothy Porter	3 & 2	Dorothy Kielty	Merion GC, Ardmore, PA
1950	Beverly Hanson	6 & 4	Mae Murray	Atlanta AC, Atlanta
1951	Dorothy Kirby	2 & 1	Claire Doran	Town & CC, St. Paul
1952	Jacqueline Pung	2 & 1	Shirley McFedters	Waverley CC, Portland, OR
1953	Mary Lena Faulk	3 & 2	Polly Riley	Rhode Island CC, West Barrington, RI
1954	Barbara Romack	4 & 2	Mickey Wright	Allegheny CC, Sewickley, PA
1955	Patricia A. Lesser	7 & 6	Jane Nelson	Myers Park CC, Charlotte
1956	Marlene Stewart	2 & 1	JoAnne Gunderson	Meridian Hills CC, Indianapolis
1957	JoAnne Gunderson	8 & 6	Ann Casey Johnstone	Del Paso CC, SacramentoA
1958	Anne Quast	3 & 2	Barbara Romack	Wee Burn CC, Darien, CT
1959	Barbara McIntire	4 & 3	Joanne Goodwin	Congressional CC, Washington, D.C.
1960	JoAnne Gunderson	6 & 5	Jean Ashley	Tulsa CC, Tulsa
1961	Anne Quast Decker	14 & 13	Phyllis Preuss	Tacoma G & CC, Tacoma, WA
1962	JoAnne Gunderson	9 & 8	Anne Baker	CC of Rochester, Rochester, NY
1963	Anne Quast Decker	2 & 1	Peggy Conley	Taconic GC, Williamstown, MA
1964	Barbara McIntire	3 & 2	JoAnne Gunderson	Prairie Dunes CC, Hutchinson, KS
1965	Jean Ashley	5 & 4	Anne Quast Decker	Lakewood CC, Denver
1966	JoAnne Gunderson	1 up	Marlene Stewart Streit	Sewickley Heights GC, Sewickley, PA
1967	Mary Lou Dill	5 & 4	Jean Ashley	Annandale GC, Pasadena
1968	JoAnne Gunderson Carner	5 & 4	Anne Quast Decker	Birmingham CC, Birmingham, MI
1969	Catherine Lacoste	3 & 2	Shelley Hamling	Las Colinas CC, Irving, TX
1970	Martha Wilkinson	3 & 2	Cynthia Hall	Wee Burn CC, Darien, CT
1971	Laura Baugh	1 up	Beth Barry	Atlanta CC, Atlanta
1972	Mary Budke	5 & 4	Cynthia Hill	St. Louis CC, St. Louis
1973	Carol Semple	1 up	Anne Quast Decker	Montclair GC, Montclair, NJ
1974	Cynthia Hill	5 & 4	Carol Semple	Broadmoor GC, Seattle
1975	Beth Daniel	3 & 2	Donna Horton	Brae Burn CC, West Newton, MA
1976	Donna Horton	2 & 1	Marianne Bretton	Del Paso CC, Sacramento
1977	Beth Daniel	3 & 1	Cathy Sherk	Cincinnati CC, Cincinnati
1978	Cathy Sherk	4 & 3	Judith Oliver	Sunnybrook GC, Plymouth Meeting, PA
1979	Carolyn Hill	7 & 6	Patty Sheehan	Memphis CC, Memphis
1980	Juli Inkster	2 up	Patti Rizzo	Prairie Dunes CC, Hutchinson, KS
1981	Juli Inkster	1 up	Lindy Goggin	Waverley CC, Portland, OR
1982	Juli Inkster	4 & 3	Cathy Hanlon	Broadmoor GC, Colorado Springs, CO
1983	Joanne Pacillo	2 & 1	Sally Quinlan	Canoe Brook CC, Summit, NJ
1984	Deb Richard	1 up	Kimberly Williams	Broadmoor GC, Seattle
1985	Michiko Hattori	5 & 4	Cheryl Stacy	Fox Chapel CC, Pittsburgh
1986	Kay Cockerill	9 & 7	Kathleen McCarthy	Pasatiempo GC, Santa Cruz, CA
1987	Kay Cockerill	3 & 2	Tracy Kerdyk	Rhode Island CC, Barrington, RI
1988	Pearl Sinn	6 & 5	Karen Noble	Minikahda Club, Minneapolis
1989	Vicki Goetze	4 & 3	Brandie Burton	Pinehurst CC (No. 2), Pinehurst, NC
1990	Pat Hurst	37 holes	Stephanie Davis	Canoe Brook CC, Summit, NJ
1991	Amy Fruhwirth	5 & 4	Heidi Voorhees	Prairie Dunes CC, Hutchinson, KN
1992	Vicki Goetz	1 up	Annika Sorensteam	Kemper Lakes GC, Hawthorne Hills, IL
1993	Jill McGill	1 up	Sarah Ingram	San Diego CC, Chula Vista, CA
1994	Wendy Ward	2 & 1	Jill McGill	The Homestead, Hot Springs, WV
1995	Kelli Kuehne	4 & 3	Anne-Marie Knight	The Country Club, Brookline, MA
1996	Kelli Kuehne	2 & 1	Marisa Baena	Firethorn GC, Lincoln, NE
1997	Silvia Cavalleri	5 & 4	Robin Burke	Brae Burn CC, West Newton, MA
1998	Grace Park	7 & 6	Jenny Chuasiriporn	Barton Hills CC, Ann Arbor, MI
1999	Dorothy Delasin	4 & 3	Jimin Kang	Biltmore Forest CC, Asheville, NC
2000	Marcy Newton	8 & 7	Laura Myerscough	Waverley CC, Portland, OR
2001	Meredith Duncan	37 holes	Nicole Perrot	Flint Hills GC, Wichita, KA
2002	Becky Lucidi	3 & 2	Brandi Jackson	Sleepy Hollow CC, Scarborough, NY
2003	Virada Nirapathpongporn	2 & 1	Jane Park	Philadelphia CC, Gladwyne, PA
2004	Jane Park	1 up	Amanda McCurdy	Kahkwa Club, Erie, PA
2005	Morgan Pressel	9 & 8	Maru Martinez	Ansley GC, Roswell, GA

U.S. Girls' Junior Amateur

1949 ....Marlene Bauer	1969 ....Hollis Stacy	1989 ....Brandie Burton
1950 ....Patricia Lesser	1970 ....Hollis Stacy	1990 ....Sandrine Mendiburu
1951 ....Arlene Brooks	1971 ....Hollis Stacy	1991 ....Emilee Klein
1952 ....Mickey Wright	1972 ....Nancy Lopez	1992 ....Jamie Koizumi
1953 ....Millie Meyerson	1973 ....Amy Alcott	1993 ....Kellee Booth
1954 ....Margaret Smith	1974 ....Nancy Lopez	1962 ....Maureen Orcutt
1955 ....Carole Jo Kabler	1975 ....Dayna Benson	1963 ....Sis Choate
1956 ....JoAnne Gunderson	1976 ....Pilar Dorado	1994 ....Kelli Kuehne
1957 ....Judy Eller	1977 ....Althea Tome	1995 ....Marcy Newton
1958 ....Judy Eller	1978 ....Lori Castillo	1996 ....Dorothy Delasin
1959 ....Judy Rand	1979 ....Penny Hammel	1997 ....Beth Bauer
1960 ....Carol Sorenson	1980 ....Laurie Rinker	1998 ....Leigh Anne Hardin
1961 ....Mary Lowell	1981 ....Kay Cornelius	1999 ....Aree Wongluekiet
1962 ....Mary Lou Daniel	1982 ....Heather Farr	2000 ....Lisa Ferrero
1963 ....Janis Ferraris	1983 ....Kim Saiki	2001 ....Nicole Perrot
1964 ....Peggy Conley	1984 ....Cathy Mockett	2002 ....In-Bee Park
1965 ....Gail Sykes	1985 ....Dana Lofland	2003 ....Sukjin-Lee Wuesthoff
1966 ....Claudia Mayhew	1986 ....Pat Hurst	2004 ....J. Granada
1967 ....Elizabeth Story	1987 ....Michelle McGann	2005 ....In-Kyung Kim
1968 ....Peggy Harmon	1988 ....Jamille Jose	

Women's British Open Amateur

1893 ....Lady Margaret Scott	1930 ....Miss D. Fishwick	1968 ....B. Varangot
1894 ....Lady Margaret Scott	1931 ....Miss E. Wilson	1975 ....C. Lacoste
1895 ....Lady Margaret Scott	1932 ....Miss E. Wilson	1976 ....D. Oxley
1896 ....Miss Pascoe	1933 ....Miss E. Wilson	1977 ....A. Uzielli
1897 ....Miss E.C. Orr	1934 ....Mrs. A.M. Holm	1978 ....E. Kennedy
1898 ....Miss L. Thomson	1935 ....Miss W. Morgan	1979 ....M. Madill
1899 ....Miss M. Hezlet	1936 ....Miss P. Barton	1980 ....A. Quast
1900 ....Miss Adair	1937 ....Miss J. Anderson	1981 ..............I.C. Robertson
1901 ....Miss Graham	1938 ....Mrs. A.M. Holm	1982 ....K. Douglas
1902 ....Miss M. Hezlet	1939 ....Miss P. Barton	1983 ....J. Thornhill
1903 ....Miss Adair	1940–45 ......not held	1984 ....J. Rosenthal
1904 ....Miss L. Dod	1946 ..............G.W. Hetherington	1985 ....L. Beman
1905 ....Miss B. Thompson	1947 ....B. Zaharias	1986 ....M. McGuire
1906 ....Mrs. Kennon	1948 ....L. Suggs	1987 ....J. Collingham
1907 ....Miss M. Hezlet	1949 ....F. Stephens	1988 ....J. Furby
1908 ....Miss M. Titterton	1950 ....Vicomtesse de Saint	1989 ....H. Dobson
1909 ....Miss D. Campbell	...............................Sauveur	1990 ....J. Hall
1910 ....Miss Grant Suttie	1951 ..............P.J. MacCann	1991 ....V. Michaud
1911 ....Miss D. Campbell	1952 ....M. Paterson	1992 ....P. Pedersen
1912 ....Miss G. Ravenscroft	1953 ....M. Stewart	1993 ....Catriona Lambert
1913 ....Miss M. Dodd	1954 ....F. Stephens	1994 ....Emma Duggleby
1914 ....Miss C. Leitch	1955 ....J. Valentine	1995 ....Julie Hall
1915–19 ......not held	1956 ....M. Smith	1996 ....Kelli Kuehne
1920 ....Miss C. Leitch	1957 ....P. Garvey	1997 ....Alison Rose
1921 ....Miss C. Leitch	1958 ....J. Valentine	1998 ....K. Rostron
1922 ....Miss J. Wethered	1959 ....E. Price	1999 ....Marine Monnet
1923 ....Miss D. Chambers	1960 ....B. McIntyre	2000 ....Rebecca Hudson
1924 ....Miss J. Wethered	1961 ....M. Spearman	2001 ....Rebecca Hudson
1925 ....Miss J. Wethered	1962 ....M. Spearman	2002 ....Rebecca Hudson
1926 ....Miss C. Leitch	1963 ....B. Varangot	2003 ....Elisa Serramia
1927 ....Miss Thion de la	1964 ....C. Sorenson	2004 ....Louise Stahle
...............................Chaume	1965 ....B. Varangot	2005 ....Heather MacRae
1928 ....Miss N. Le Blan	1966 ....E. Chadwick	
1929 ....Miss J. Wethered	1967 ....E. Chadwick	

Women's Amateur Public Links

1977 ....Kelly Fuiks	1986 ....Cindy Schreyer	1996 ....Heather Graff
1978 ....Kelly Fuiks	1987 ....Tracy Kerdyk	1997 ....Jo Jo Robertson
1979 ....Lori Castillo	1988 ....Pearl Sinn	1998 ....Amy Spooner
1980 ....Lori Castillo	1989 ....Pearl Sinn	1999 ....Jody Niemann
1981 ....Mary Enright	1990 ....Cathy Mockett	2000 ....Catherine Cartwright
1982 ....Nancy Taylor	1991 ....Tracy Hanson	2001 ....Candie Kung
1983 ....Kelli Antolock	1992 ....Amy Fruhwirth	2002 ....Annie Thurman
1984 ....Heather Farr	1993 ....Connie Masterson	2003 ....Michelle Wie
1985 ....Danielle	1994 ....Jill McGill	2004 ....Ya-Ni Tseng
...............................Ammaccapane	1995 ....Jo Jo Robertson	2005 ....Eun Jung Lee

U.S. Senior Women's Amateur

1964 ....Loma Smith	1978 ....Alice Dye	1992 ....Rosemary Thompson
1965 ....Loma Smith	1979 ....Alice Dye	1993 ....Anne Sander
1966 ....Maureen Orcutt	1980 ....Dorothy Porter	1994 ....Marlene Streit
1967 ....Marge Mason	1981 ....Dorothy Porter	1995 ....Jean Smith
1968 ....Carolyn Cudone	1982 ....Edean Ihlanfeldt	1996 ....Gayle Borthwick
1969 ....Carolyn Cudone	1983 ....Dorothy Porter	1997 ....Nancy Fitzgerald
1970 ....Carolyn Cudone	1984 ....Constance Guthrie	1998 ....Gayle Borthwick
1971 ....Carolyn Cudone	1985 ....Marlene Streit	1999 ....C. Semple Thompson
1972 ....Carolyn Cudone	1986 ....Connie Guthrie	2000 ....C. Semple Thompson
1973 ....Gwen Hibbs	1987 ....Anne Sander	2001 ....C. Semple Thompson
1974 ....Justine Cushing	1988 ....Lois Hodge	2002 ....C. Semple Thompson
1975 ....Alberta Bower	1989 ....Anne Sander	2003 ....Marlene Streit
1976 ....Cecile H. Maclaurin	1990 ....Anne Sander	2004 ....Carolyn Creekmore
1977 ....Dorothy Porter	1991 ....Phyllis Preuss	

Women's Mid-Amateur Championship

1987 ....Cindy Scholefield	1994 ....Sarah Ingram	2001 ....Laura Shanahan
1988 ....Martha Lang	1995 ....Ellen Port	2002 ....Kathy Hartwiger
1989 ....Robin Weiss	1996 ....Ellen Port	2003 ....Amber Marsh
1990 ....C. Semple Thompson	1997 ....C. Semple Thompson	2004 ....Corey Weworski
1991 ....Sarah LeBrun Ingram	1998 ....Virginia Derby Grimes	2005 ....Mary Anne Lapointe
1992 ....M. Mamey-McInerney	1999 ....Alissa Herron	
1993 ....Sarah Ingram	2000 ....Ellen Port	

International Golf

Ryder Cup Matches

Year	Results	Site
1927	United States 9½, Great Britain 2½	Worcester CC, Worcester, MA
1929	Great Britain 7, United States 5	Moortown GC, Leeds, England
1931	United States 9, Great Britain 3	Scioto CC, Columbus, OH
1933	Great Britain 6½, United States 5½	Southport and Ainsdale Courses, Southport, England
1935	United States 9, Great Britain 3	Ridgewood CC, Ridgewood, NJ
1937	United States 8, Great Britain 4	Southport and Ainsdale Courses, Southport, England
1939–1945	No tournament	
1947	United States 11, Great Britain 1	Portland GC, Portland, OR
1949	United States 7, Great Britain 5	Ganton GC, Scarborough, England
1951	United States 9½, Great Britain 2½	Pinehurst CC, Pinehurst, NC
1953	United States 6½, Great Britain 5½	Wentworth Club, Surrey, England
1955	United States 8, Great Britain 4	Thunderbird Ranch & CC, Palm Springs, CA
1957	Great Britain 7½, United States 4½	Lindrick GC, Yorkshire, England
1959	United States 8½, Great Britain 3½	Eldorado CC, Palm Desert, CA
1961	United States 14½, Great Britain 9½	Royal Lytham & St. Annes GC, St Anne's-on-the-Sea, England
1963	United States 23, Great Britain 9	East Lake CC, Atlanta
1965	United States 19½, Great Britain 12½	Royal Birkdale GC, Southport, England
1967	United States 23½, Great Britain 8½	Champions GC, Houston
1969	United States 16, Great Britain 16	Royal Birkdale GC, Southport, England
1971	United States 18½, Great Britain 13½	Old Warson CC, St. Louis
1973	United States 19, Great Britain 13	Hon Co of Edinburgh Golfers, Muirfield, Scotland
1975	United States 21, Great Britain 11	Laurel Valley GC, Ligonier, PA
1977	United States 12½, Great Britain 7½	Royal Lytham & St. Annes GC, St. Annes-on-the-Sea, Eng.
1979	United States 17, Europe 11	Greenbrier, White Sulphur Springs, WV
1981	United States 18½, Europe 9½	Walton Heath GC, Surrey, England
1983	United States 14½, Europe 13½	PGA National GC, Palm Beach Gardens, FL
1985	Europe 16½, United States 11½	Belfry GC, Sutton Coldfield, England
1987	Europe 15, United States 13	Muirfield GC, Dublin, OH
1989	Europe 14, United States 14	Belfry GC, Sutton Coldfield, England
1991	United States 14½, Europe 13½	Ocean Course, Kiawah Island, SC
1993	United States 15, Europe 13	Belfry GC, Sutton Coldfield, England
1995	Europe 14½, United States 13½	Oak Hill CC, Rochester, NY
1997	Europe 14½, United States 13½	Valderrama GC, Sotogrande, Spain
1999	United States 14½, Europe 13½	The Country Club, Brookline, MA
2002	Europe 15½, Unites States 12½	Belfry GC, Sutton Coldfield, England
2004	Europe 18½, United States 9½	Oakland Hills CC, Bloomfield Hills, MI

Team matches held every odd year between U.S. professionals and those of Great Britain/Europe. Team members selected on basis of finishes in PGA and European tour events. Match in 2001 canceled due to 9/11 terrorist attacks.

Walker Cup Matches

Year	Results	Site
1922	United States 8, Great Britain 4	Nat'l Golf Links of America, Southampton, NY
1923	United States 6, Great Britain 5	St. Andrews, Scotland
1924	United States 9, Great Britain 3	Garden City GC, Garden City, NY
1926	United States 6, Great Britain 5	St. Andrews, Scotland
1928	United States 11, Great Britain 1	Chicago GC, Wheaton, IL
1930	United States 10, Great Britain 2	Royal St. George GC, Sandwich, England
1932	United States 8, Great Britain 1	The Country Club, Brookline, MA
1934	United States 9, Great Britain 2	St. Andrews, Scotland
1936	United States 9, Great Britain 0	Pine Valley GC, Clementon, NJ
1938	Great Britain 7, United States 4	St. Andrews, Scotland
1940–46	No tournament	
1947	United States 8, Great Britain 4	St. Andrews, Scotland
1949	United States 10, Great Britain 2	Winged Foot GC, Mamaroneck, NY
1951	United States 6, Great Britain 3	Birkdale GC, Southport, England
1953	United States 9, Great Britain 3	The Kittansett Club, Marion, MA
1955	United States 10, Great Britain 2	St. Andrews, Scotland
1957	United States 8, Great Britain 3	Minikahda Club, Minneapolis
1959	United States 9, Great Britain 3	Muirfield, Scotland
1961	United States 11, Great Britain 1	Seattle GC, Seattle
1963	United States 12, Great Britain 8	Ailsa Course, Turnberry, Scotland
1965	Great Britain 11, United States 11	Baltimore CC, Five Farms, Baltimore, MD
1967	United States 13, Great Britain 7	Royal St. George's GC, Sandwich, England
1969	United States 10, Great Britain 8	Milwaukee CC, Milwaukee, WI
1971	Great Britain 13, United States 11	St. Andrews, Scotland
1973	United States 14, Great Britain 10	The Country Club, Brookline, MA
1975	United States 15½, Great Britain 8½	St. Andrews, Scotland
1977	United States 16, Great Britain 8	Shinnecock Hills GC, Southampton, NY
1979	United States 15½, Great Britain 8½	Muirfield, Scotland
1981	United States 15, Great Britain 9	Cypress Point Club, Pebble Beach, CA
1983	United States 13½, Great Britain 10½	Royal Liverpool GC, Hoylake, England
1985	United States 13, Great Britain 11	Pine Valley GC, Pine Valley, NJ
1987	United States 16½, Great Britain 7½	Sunningdale GC, Berkshire, England
1989	Great Britain 12½, United States 11½	Peachtree Golf Club, Atlanta
1991	United States 14, Great Britain 10	Portmarnock GC, Dublin, Ireland
1993	United States 19, Great Britain 5	Interlachen CC, Edina, MN
1995	Great Britain/Ireland 14, United States 10	Royal Porthcawl, Porthcawl, Wales
1997	United States 18, Great Britain/Ireland 6	Quaker Ridge GC, Scarsdale, NY
1999	Great Britain/Ireland 15, United States 9	Nairn GC, Nairn, Scotland
2001	Great Britain/Ireland 15, United States 9	Ocean Forest GC, Sea Island, GA
2003	Great Britain/Ireland 12½, United States 11½	Ganton GC, Ganton, England
2005	United States 12½, Great Britain/Ireland 11½	Chicago GC, Wheaton IL

Men's amateur team competition every other year between United States and Great Britain/Ireland. U.S. team members selected by USGA.

Solheim Cup Matches

Year	Results	Site
1990	United States 11½, Europe 4½	Lake Nona GC, Orlando, FL
1992	Europe 11½, United States 6½	Dalmahoy Hotel GC, Edinburgh
1994	United States 13, Europe 7	The Greenbriar, White Sulpher Springs, WV
1996	United States 17, Europe 11	Marriot St Pierre Hotel & CC, Chepstow, Wales
1998	United States 16, Europe 12	Muirfield Village GC, Dublin, OH
2000	Europe 14½, United States, 11½	Loch Lomond GC, Luss, Scotand
2002	United States 15½, Europe 12½	Interlachen CC, Minneapolis, MN
2003	Europe 17½, United States 10½	Barseback G&CC, Malmo, Sweden
2005	United States 15½, Europe 12½	Crooked Stick GC, Carmel IN

Women's team matches held every other year between U.S. professionals and those of Europe. Team members selected on the basis of finishes in LPGA and European tour events.

Curtis Cup Matches

Year	Results	Site
1932	United States 5½, British Isles 3½	Wentworth GC, Wentworth, England
1934	United States 6½, British Isles 2½	Chevy Chase Club, Chevy Chase, MD
1936	United States 4½, British Isles 4½	King's Course, Gleneagles, Scotland
1938	United States 5½, British Isles 3½	Essex CC, Manchester, MA
1940–46	No tournament	
1948	United States 6½, British Isles 2½	Birkdale GC, Southport, England

Curtis Cup Matches *(Cont.)*

Year	Results	Site
	United States 7½, British Isles 1½	CC of Buffalo, Williamsville, NY

Year	Results	Site
1952	British Isles 5, United States 4	Muirfield, Scotland
1954	United States 6, British Isles 3	Merion GC, Ardmore, PA
1956	British Isles 5, United States 4	Prince's GC, Sandwich Bay, England
1958	British Isles 4½, United States 4½	Brae Burn CC, West Newton, Mass.
1960	United States 6½, British Isles 2½	Lindrick GC, Worksop, England
1962	United States 8, British Isles 1	Broadmoor CG, Colorado Springs,CO
1964	United States 10½, British Isles 7½	Royal Porthcawl GC, Porthcawl, South Wales
1966	United States 13, British Isles 5	Va. Hot Springs G & TC, Hot Springs, VA
1968	United States 10½, British Isles 7½	Royal County Down GC, Newcastle, N. Ire.
1970	United States 11½, British Isles 6½	Brae Burn CC, West Newton, MA
1972	United States 10, British Isles 8	Western Gailes, Ayrshire, Scotland
1974	United States 13, British Isles 5	San Francisco GC, San Francisco
1976	United States 11½, British Isles 6½	Royal Lytham & St. Annes GC, England
1978	United States 12, British Isles 6	Apawamis Club, Rye, NY
1980	United States 13, British Isles 5	St. Pierre G & CC, Chepstow, Wales
1982	United States 14½, British Isles 3½	Denver CC, Denver
1984	United States 9½, British Isles 8½	Muirfield, Scotland
1986	British Isles 13, United States 5	Prairie Dunes CC, Hutchinson, KS
1988	British Isles 11, United States 7	Royal St. George's GC, Sandwich, England
1990	United States 14, British Isles 4	Somerset Hills CC, Bernardsville, NJ
1992	Great Britain/Ireland 10, United States 8	Royal Liverpool GC, Hoylake, England
1994	Great Britain/Ireland 9, United States 9	The Honors Course, Ooltewah, TN
1996	Great Britain/Ireland 11½, United States 6½	Killarney Golf & Fishing Club, Killarney, Ireland
1998	United States 10, Great Britain/Ireland 8	The Minikahda Club, Minneapolis
2000	United States 10, Great Britain/Ireland 8	Ganton GC, North Yorkshire, England
2002	United States 11, Great Britain/Ireland 7	Fox Chapel GC, Pittsburgh, PA
2004	United States 10, Great Britain/Ireland 8	Formby GC, Merseyside, England

Women's amateur team competition every other year between the United States and Great Britain/Ireland. U.S. team members selected by USGA.

Presidents Cup Matches

Year	Results	Site
1994	United States 20, International 12	Robert Trent Jones GC, Lake Manassas, VA
1996	United States 16½, International 15½	Robert Trent Jones GC, Lake Manassas, VA
1998	International 20½, United States 11½	Royal Melbourne GC, Melbourne, Australia
2000	United States 21½, International 10½	Robert Trent Jones GC, Lake Manassas, VA
2003	International 17, United States 17	Fan Court Hotel CC, George, South Africa
2005	United States 18½, International 15½	Robert Trent Jones GC, Lake Manassas, VA

A biennial event played in non-Ryder Cup years designed to provide non-European players with international team and match play.

Boxing

Heavyweight champion
John Ruiz absorbs James
Toney's right cross

Name Game

With three different titleholders as well as an interim champion, boxing's heavyweight division is in disarray

BY STEPHEN CANNELLA

QUICK, NAME THE HEAVYWEIGHT champion of the world. Once upon a time, when giants named Ali, Frazier, Foreman and Tyson bestrode the sports landscape, the question would have been a gimme on any current events quiz, a yardstick of basic pop culture literacy. That era has long passed. In 2005 such a simple query would have stumped all but the most dedicated students of the sweet science. Never mind that, depending on how many of the sport's many sanctioning bodies one cared to recognize, as many as four different fighters could lay claim to the mantle of world's top heavyweight. In the Balkanized world of boxing, having so many correct—and, for the most part, uncharismatic—answers to choose from only made guessing the champ's identity more difficult. "Today, I don't know who the champion is," one of the sport's giants, former undisputed titleholder Joe Frazier, said in July. "[The heavyweight] division is crazy, it's running wild."

It was dull as well, mainly because the top fighters in what once was boxing's most glamorous division were for the most part inactive in 2005. After retaining the World Boxing Council (WBC) belt with a December 2004 knockout of Britain's Danny Williams, Vitali Klitschko (35-2, 34 KOs) spent much of the following year dodging a mandatory title defense against Hasim Rahman (40-5, 34 KOs). The 6'7" Ukranian, a multilingual PhD, once seemed heavyweight most likely to become a transcendant figure. He underwent back surgery in April, however, and his image took a severe hit when he postponed scheduled showdowns with Rahman three times. Klitschko's idleness—and his repeated requests to fight someone other than the WBC's top challenger—finally forced the WBC to declare Rahman "interim champion" after he won a decision over No. 2 challenger Monte Barrett in Chicago on Aug. 13.

The WBC also announced it would strip Klitschko of his belt and remove the "interim" tag from Rahman's title if their long-anticipated bout didn't happen by the end of the year, and Klitschko finally agreed to step into the ring in Las Vegas on Nov. 12. There was more on the line than the WBC crown and a $12 million purse: The bout would mark the return of legendary promoter Bob

Lightweights Castillo (l.) and Corrales battled in a fierce fight.

NICK LAHAM/GETTY IMAGES

Arum, who hadn't put on a heavyweight title fight since 1995. Klitschko was the sole top heavyweight not controlled by rival promoter Don King, who backed Rahman and the other three heavyweight titleholders: John Ruiz (World Boxing Association), Chris Byrd (International Boxing Federation) and Lamon Brewster (World Boxing Organization). King had promised to stage a title unification tournament among his fighters. If the underdog Rahman could wrest away the WBC belt, there was the chance that such a tournament could bring much-needed order to the heavyweight ranks.

If it ever became a reality, the event would at least stir fan interest in the heavyweight division, a feat the likely participants were unable pull off individually. IBF champ Byrd (38-2-1) relaxed for most of 2005; his last fight was in November 2004, when he defeated Jameel McCline. (He finally scheduled an October defense against DaVarryl Williamson.) Byrd was a smooth boxer and athletic ring presence, but the lefthander was also a light hitter who kept up a nice-guy persona outside the ring—two traits that limited his marketability. Brewster (32-2), by comparison, kept a busy schedule, holding onto his title with a 53-second knockout of Andrew Golota in Chicago in May and then agreeing to another defense against little-known German contender Luan Krasniqi on Sept. 28 in Hanburg, Germany. (The date would have been the 100th birthday of former champion and German hero Max Schmeling, who died in February.) But Brewster's standing was diminished by the fact that the upstart WBO was the least-regarded of boxing's four sanctioning bodies.

That left Ruiz (41-6-1), who was still in possession of the WBA belt, by default. On April 30 the Bostonian defended the title against aging former middleweight champ James Toney. In his third heavyweight bout

the 36-year-old, 233-pound Toney, who was outweighed by eight pounds, wore down Ruiz in 12 hard-fought but dull rounds at New York's Madison Square Garden and won a close judges' decision. Said the newly-minted titleholder, "I am soon going to be the undisputed champion of hte world."

Immediately after the fight Ruiz, 33, announced his retirement—a decision he reconsidered a few weeks later, when it was revealed that Toney had tested positive for the steroid nandrolone in a postfight urine test. Toney insisted that the failed test was related to a drug he took to treat biceps and triceps injuries, saying, "If the steroids were supposed to make me look bigger or stronger, steroids would be out of business because my body looked terrible that night." Nevertheless, the New York State Athletic Commission suspended him for 90 days and declared the fight a no decision, and the WBA awarded its title back to Ruiz. The fighter known as the Quiet Man quickly came out of his short retirement, and he shed his undemonstrative image as well. "To all of the a------s who want me out of the game," Ruiz said in May, "I'm back!"

A few weeks later a fellow Bostonian, 271-pound pug Kevin McBride, handed Mike Tyson his latest devastating defeat, a seventh-round TKO at the MCI Center in Washington, D.C.. Once the youngest heavyweight champion ever, Tyson, 39, long ago morphed into little more than a pugilistic lounge act. The McBride fight did nothing to reverse that trend: Tyson was called for fouls for trying to break McBride's arm and an intentional head-butt. (McBride said afterward that Tyson also tried to bite one of his nipples.) When the bell rang for the seventh round the battered Tyson slumped on his stool and refused to come out, and afterward he said he was pulling the plug on his 20-year fight career. "I don't have the guts for it," said Tyson, who, despite still being a reported $30 million in debt, added that he wanted to move overseas to do missionary work. "I'm not going to disgrace the sport."

As the heavyweights stumbled and bumbled, two little-known lightweights did the sweet science proud with a fight for the ages. On May 7 WBO champion Diego Corrales met Jose Luis Castillo, the WBC beltholder, in a unification bout in Las Vegas. Their 10-round slugfest was the year's best fight and instantly took a place among the best boxing displays of all time. Over the first nine rounds both fighters launched savage attacks, bombarding each other with body blows and bone-crunching shots to the head, and by the final round Castillo's face was purple and swollen and Corrales could barely see out of his puffy left eye.

Early in the 10th, Castillo sent Corrales to the floor with a crushing left hand; after Corrales wobbled to his feet, an exhausted-looking Castillo again put him on his back with another left. As referee Tony Weeks counted him out, the seemingly spent Corrales spit out his mouthpiece. The ploy forced the official to stop the count so the protective device could be washed off, and during the 28-second delay Corrales underwent an amazing revival. He staggered to his feet and stunned the advancing Castillo with a quick left, then followed the blow with a flurry of punches to Castillo's head. The last was a vicious right that left Castillo in a state of semi-consciousness: He stayed on his feet, but with his face blank and his arms hanging at his sides Weeks stopped the fight. Less than a minute after he appeared to have lost, Corrales was the undisputed lightweight champion. "All I want to do," Corrales said afterward, "is go soak my face."

Castillo instantly called for a rematch. One was quickly scheduled for Oct. 8, and it instantly became the most-anticipated bout of the year. Meanwhile, the stars of two of boxing's marquee names diminished in 2005. Undisputed middleweight champion Bernard Hopkins, 40, lost his crown on July 16, when he dropped a split decision to 26-year-old challenger Jermaine Taylor in Las Vegas. It ended Hopkins's streak of 20 consecutive successful title defenses and was his first loss since 1993.

That defeat came at the hands of Roy Jones Jr., and over the ensuing years he and Hopkins vied for the unofficial title as the sport's best pound-for-pound fighter. But Jones's career appeared to be on the ropes in 2005 as well. Jones was knocked out by light heavyweight Glen Johnson in September 2004, his second straight loss, and the closest he came to the ring for most of 2005 was as a fight analyst for HBO. He finally agreed to an October bout against Antonio Tarver, the rubber match in a trilogy that began in 2003. Six weeks before the fight, however, the WBC recommended that Jones, 36, undergo neurological testing and get medical approval before stepping into the ring because he had suffered knockouts in his two previous bouts.

Otherwise, the most closely-followed fighters of the year were either long-passed former champs or Hollywood creations. In March, Hilary Swank won the Best Actress Academy Award for her portrayal of a female fighter in "Million Dollar Baby." (Director Clint Eastwood was also awarded an Oscar.) "Cinderella Man" was less of a box office success, but it won critical acclaim for its portrayal of Depression-era heavyweight king Jim Braddock, who was played by Russell Crowe. And the Ken Burns documentary Unforgivable Blackness riveted television viewers with the story of Jack Johnson, who overcame prejudice and rival Tommy Burns to become the first African-American heavyweight champ in 1908.

While moviegoers celebrated boxing's past, Nigerian heavyweight Samuel Peter emerged as one of the sport's rising stars. Young (24), powerful, raw and undefeated in his first 24 bouts, Peter was hailed by many as a future champion. After a lackluster year, his rise through the ranks could provide a much-needed jolt of excitement for boxing in 2006.

FOR THE RECORD·2004–2005

Current Champions

Division	Weight Limit	WBA Champion	WBC Champion	IBF Champion
Heavyweight	None	John Ruiz	Vitali Klitschko	Chris Byrd
Cruiserweight	190	Jean-Mark Mormeck	Jean-Mark Mormeck	O'Neil Bell
Light Heavyweight	175	Fabrice Tiozzo	Tomasz Adamek	Clinton Woods
Super Middleweight	168	Mikkel Kessler	Markus Beyer	Jeff Lacy
Middleweight	160	Jermain Taylor	Jermain Taylor	Jermain Taylor
Junior Middleweight	154	Alex Terra Garcia	Ricardo Mayorga	Roman Karmazin
Welterweight	147	Luis Collazo	Zab Judah	Zab Judah
Junior Welterweight	140	Carlos Maussa	Floyd Mayweather	Ricky Hatton
Lightweight	135	Juan Diaz	Diego Corrales	Jesus Chavez
Junior Lightweight	130	Vicente Mosquera	Marco Antonio Barrera	Erik Morales
Featherweight	126	Chris John	In Jin Chi	Juan Manuel Marquez
Junior Featherweight	122	Mahyar Monshipour	Oscar Larios	Israel Vazquez
Bantamweight	118	Wladimir Sidorenko	Hozumi Hasegawa	Rafael Marquez
Junior Bantamweight	115	Jose Martin Castillo	Masamori Tokuyama	Luis Perez
Flyweight	112	Lorenzo Parra	Pongsaklek Wonjongkam	Vic Darchinyan
Junior Flyweight	108	Roberto Vasquez	Brian Viloria	Will Grigsby
Strawweight	105	Yukata Niida	Eagle Akakura	Muhammad Rachman

Note: WBC=World Boxing Council; WBA=World Boxing Association; IBF=International Boxing Federation.
Champions as of October 1, 2005.

Championship and Major Fights of 2004 and 2005

Abbreviations: WBC=World Boxing Council; WBA= World Boxing Association; IBF=International Boxing Federation; KO=knockout; TKO=technical knockout; UD=unanimous decision; SD=split decision; DQ=disqualification; MD=majority decision; TD=technical decision. Bouts from Oct 1, 2003 to Sept 1, 2004.

Heavyweight

Date	Winner	Loser	Result	Title	Site
Nov. 13	John Ruiz	Andrew Golota	UD	WBA	New York City
Nov 13	Chris Byrd	Jameel McCline	SD	IBF	New York City
Dec 11	Vitali Klitschko	Danny Williams	TKO 8	WBC	Las Vegas
April 30	James Toney	John Ruiz	UD	WBA	New York City
Au 13	Hasim Rahman	Monte Barrett	UD	Interim WBC	Chicago

Cruiserweight

Date	Winner	Loser	Result	Title	Site
Jan 21	Enzo MaCarinelli	Rich La Montagne	TKO 4	IBF	Hollywood, FL
April 2	Jean-Marc Mormeck	Wayne Brathwaite	UD	WBC/WBA	Worchester,MA
May 20	O'Neil Bell	Dale Brown	UD	IBF	Hollywood,FL
Aug 26	O'Neil Bell	Sebastian Rothman	KO 2	IBF	Hollywoood,FL

Light Heavyweight

Date	Winner	Loser	Result	Title	Site
Sep 25	Glengoffe Johnson	Roy Jones	KO 9	IBF	Memphis, TN
Feb 6	Glengoffe Johnson	Clinton Woods	UD	IBF	Sheffield, England
Feb 24	Fabrice Tiozzo	Dariusz Michalczewski	TKO 6	WBA	Hamburg,Germany
March 4	Clinton Woods	Rico Hoye	TKO 5	Vacant IBF	Rotherman,England
May 21	Tomasz Adamek	Paul Briggs	MD	Vacant WBC	Chicago
Mar 12	Markus Beyer	Danny Green	MD	WBC	Zwicku, Germany

Super Middleweight

Date	Winner	Loser	Result	Title	Site
Oct 2	Jeff Lacy	Syd Vanderpool	TKO 8	IBF	Las Vegas
Oct 9	Markus Beyer	Cristian Sanavia	KO 6	WBC	Erfurt,Germany
Nov 12	Mikkel Kessler	Manny Siaca	TKO 7	WBA	Copenhagen, Denmark
Dec 4	Jeff Lacy	Omar Sheika	UD	IBF	Las Vegas
Dec 18	Markus Beyer	Yoshmori Nishizawa	UD	WBC	Bayreuth,Germany
March 5	Jeff Key	Rubin Williams	TKO 7	IBF	Las Vegas
June 6	Mikkel Kessler	Anthony Mundine	UD	WBA	Sydney, Australia
Sep 3	Markus Beyer	Omar Sheika	UD	WBC	Berlin,Germany

Middleweight

Date	Winner	Loser	Result	Title	Site
Sep. 18	Bernard Hopkins	Oscar de La Hoya	KO 9	WBC/WBA/IBF	Los Angeles
Feb 19	Bernard Hopkins	Howard Eastman	UD	WBC/WBA	Los Angeles
July 16	Jermaine Taylor	Bernard Hopkins	SD	WBC/WBA	New York City

Junior Middleweight (Super Welterweight)

Date	Winner	Loser	Result	Title	Site
Oct 2	Travis Simms	Branco McKart	UD	WBA	New York City
Oct 2	Kassim Ouma	Verno Phillips	UD	IBF	Las Vegas
Jan 29	Kassim Ouma	Kofi Jantoah	UD	IBF	Atlantic City
May 21	Alejandro Garcia	Roshi Wells	TKO 2	Interim WBA	Chicago
July 14	Roman Karmazin	Kassim Ouma	UD	IBF	Las Vegas
Aug 13	Alejandro	Luca Messi	UD	WBA	Chicago
Aug 13	Ricardo Mayora	Michele Piccirilo	UD	Vacant WBC	Chicago

Welterweight

Date	Winner	Loser	Result	Title	Site
Feb 5	Zab Judah	Cory Spinks	TKO 9	WBC/WBA/IBF	St. Louis
April 2	Luis Collazo	Jose Rivera	SD	WBA	Worcester, MA
May 14	Zab Judah	Cosme Rivera	TKO 3	WBC/WB/IBF	Las Vegas
Aug 13	Luis Collazo	Miguel Gonzalez	TKO 8	WBA	Chicago

Junior Welterweight (Super Lightweight)

Date	Winner	Loser	Result	Title	Site
Oct 23	Vivian Hams	Oktay Urkal	TKO 11	WBA	Berlin, Germany
Nov 6	Kostya Tszyu	Sharmba Mitchell	TKO 3	IBF	Phoenix
Jan 29	Arturo Gatti	James Leija	KO 5	WBC	Atlantic City
Beb 23	Robbie Peden	Nate Campbell	TKO 8	IBF	Melbourne, Australia
June 4	Ricky Hatton	Kostya Tszyo	TKO 11	IBF	Manchester, England
June 11	Carlos Maussu	Vivian Harris	KO 7	WBA	Atlantic City
June 25	Floyd Mayweather	Arturo Gatti	TKO 6	WBC	Atlantic City
Sep 17	Robbie Peden	Nate Campbell	TKO 8	IBF	Melbourne, Australia

Lightweight

Date	Winner	Loser	Result	Title	Site
Nov. 4	Juan Diaz	Julien Lorcy	UD	WBA	San Antonio
Dec 4	Jose Castillo	Joel Casamayor	SD	WBC	Las Vegas
Jan 21	Juan Diaz	Billy Irwin	TKO 9	WBA	Houston, TX
Mar 5	Jose Luis Castillo	Julio Diaz	TKO 10	WBC	Las Vegas
May 7	Diego Corrales	Jose Luis Castillo	TKO 10	WBC	Las Vegas
June 17	Leavander Johnson	Stefano Zoff	TKO 7	Vacant IBF	Milan, Italy
Sep 17	Leavander Johnson	Jesus Chavez	TKO 11	IBF	Las Vegas

Junior Lightweight (Super Featherweight)

Date	Winner	Loser	Result	Title	Site
Nov 27	Marco Barera	Erik Morales	MD	WBC	Las Vegas
April 9	Marco Barrera	Mzonke Fana	KO2	WBC	El Paso, TX
April 30	Yodsanan Nanthachai	Vicente Mosquera	UD	WBA	New York
Sept. 17	Marco Barrera	Robbie Peden	UD	WBC/IBF	Las Vegas

Featherweight

Date	Winner	Loser	Result	Title	Site
Dec 2	Chris John	Jose Cheo Rojas	Draw	WBA	Tenggarong, Indonesia
April 22	Chris John	Derrick Gainer	UD	WBA	Jakarta, Indonesia
May 7	Juan Marquez	Victor Polo	UD	WBA	Las Vegas
Aug 7	Chris John	Tommy Browne	TKO 9	WBA	Penrith, Australia
Aug. 20	Ricardo Juarez	Humberto Soto	UD	Interim WBC	Rosemont, IL

Junior Featherweight (Super Bantamweight)

Date	Winner	Loser	Result	Title	Site
Nov 27	Oscar Larios	Nedal Hussein	UD	WBC	Las Vegas
Feb 10	Oscar Larios	Wayne McCullough	UD	WBC	Lemoore,CA
May 31	Israel Vazquez	Armando Guerrero	UD	IBF	Lynwood, IL
June 25	Mahyar Monshipour	Julio Zarate	TKO 8	WBC	Poiters, France
July 16	Oscar Larios	Wayne McCullough	TKO 10	WBC	Las Vegas

Bantamweight

Date	Winner	Loser	Result	Title	Site
Jan 31	Rafael Marquez	Pete Frissina	TKO 2	IBF	Phoenix
Feb 26	Wladimir Sidorenko	Julio Zarate	UD	Vacant WBA	Hamburg, Germany
April 6	Hozumi Haseguwa	Veerapool Sahaprom	UD	WBC	Tokyo, Japan
May 28	Rafael Marquez	Ricardo Vargas	UD	IBF	Los Angeles
Aug 31	P. Kratigdaenygym	RicardoCorboda	SD	WBA	Bangkok Thailand
Sept. 25	Hozumi Hasegawa	Gerardo Martinez	TKO 7	WBC	Yokohama, Japan

Junior Bantamweight (Super Flyweight)

Date	Winner	Loser	Result	Title	Site
Dec 3	Martin Castillo	Alexander Munoz	UD	WBC	Laredo, TX
Jan 3	Katsuhige Kawashima	Jose Navarro	SD	WBC	Tokyo, Japan
Mar 19	Martin Castillo	Eric Morel	UD	WBA	Las Vegas
Apr 29	Mahyor Monshipur	Shigera Nakazaho	TKO 6	WBA	Marseille, France
Apr 30	Luis Perez	Luis Bolono	TKO 6	IBF	New York City
Jun 6	Martin Castillo	Hideyashu Ishihara	UD	WBA	Nagoya, Japan
Jul 18	Masamori Tokoyama	K. Kawashima	UD	WBC	Osaka, Japan
Jul 30	Jorge Arce	Angel Priolo	TKO 3	WBC	La Paz, Mexico

Flyweight

Date	Winner	Loser	Result	Title	Site
Dec 16	Irene Pacheo	Vic Darchinyan	TKO 11	IBF	Hollywood, FL
Mar 27	Vic Darhinyan	Mzukisi Sikali	TKO 8	IBF	Homebush Bay, Austrailia
Aug. 24	Vic Darchinyan	Jair Jimenez	TKO 5	IBF	Sydney, Austrailia
Sept. 19	Lorenzo Para	Takefmi Sakata	MD	WBA	Tokyo, Japan

Junior Flyweight

Date	Winner	Loser	Result	Title	Site
Dec 28	Israel Vazquez	Artyom Simonyan	TKO 5	IBF	El Cajon, CA
May 14	Will Grisby	Jose Burgos	UD	IBF	Las Vegas

Strawweight (Mini Flyweight)

Date	Winner	Loser	Result	Title	Sit
Dec 18	Jorge Arce	Juan Centeno	TKO 3	WBC	Sinaloa, Mexico
Dec 18	Issac Bustos	Eagle Kyowa	TKO 4	WBC	Tokyo, Japan
Mar 11	Eric Ortiz	Jose Aguire	TKO 7	WBC	Mexico City
Apr 4	Takayma Katsunari	Issac Bustos	UD	WBC	Osaka,Japan
Apr 29	Roberto Vasquez	Beibis Mendoza	TKO 10	Vacant WBA	Fort Amadis, Panama
Aug 6	Eagle Kyowa	Katsunari Takuyama	UD	WBC	Tokyo,Japan
Aug 20	Roberto Vasquez	Jose Aguire	TKO 4	WBA	Fort Amador, Panama
Sept. 25	Yutaka Niida	Eriberto Gejon	SD	WBA	Yokohama, Japan

World Champions

Sanctioning bodies: the National Boxing Association (NBA), the New York State Athletic Commission (NY), the World Boxing Association (WBA), the World Boxing Council (WBC), and the International Boxing Federation (IBF).

Heavyweights
(Weight: Unlimited)

Champion	Reign	Champion	Reign	Champion	Reign
John L. Sullivan*	1885–92	Jimmy Ellis WBA	1968–70	Riddick Bowe*	1992–93
James J. Corbett*	1892–97	Joe Frazier*	1970–73	Evander Holyfield*	1993–94
Bob Fitzsimmons*	1897–99	George Foreman*	1973–74	Michael Moorer*	1994
James J. Jeffries*	1899–05†	Muhammad Ali*	1974–78	George Foreman*	1994–95
Marvin Hart*	1905–06	Leon Spinks*	1978	Oliver McCall WBC	1995
Tommy Burns*	1906–08	Ken Norton WBC	1978	Frank Bruno WBC	1995–96
Jack Johnson*	1908–15	Larry Holmes WBC	1978–80	Bruce Seldon WBA	1995–96
Jess Willard*	1915–19	Muhammad Ali*	1978–79†	Mike Tyson WBA	1996
Jack Dempsey*	1919–26	John Tate WBA	1979–80	Michael Moorer IBF	1996–97
Gene Tunney*	1926–28†	Mike Weaver WBA	1980–82	Shannon Briggs*	1997–98
Max Schmeling*	1930–32	Larry Holmes*	1980–85	Lennox Lewis* WBC	1997–01
Jack Sharkey*	1932–33	Michael Dokes WBA	1982–83	E. Holyfield WBA, IBF	1996–99
Primo Carnera*	1933–34	Gerrie Coetzee WBA	1983–84	Lennox Lewis	1999–01
Max Baer*	1934–35	Tim Witherspoon WBC	1984	E. Holyfield WBA	2000–01
James J. Braddock*	1935–37	Pinklon Thomas WBC	1984–86	John Ruiz WBA	2001–03
Joe Louis*	1937–49†	Greg Page WBA	1984–85	Hasim Rahman* WBC, IBF	
Ezzard Charles*	1949–51	Michael Spinks*	1985–87		2001
Jersey Joe Walcott*	1951–52	Tim Witherspoon WBA	1986	Chris Byrd IBF	2002–
Rocky Marciano*	1952–56†	Trevor Berbick WBC	1986	Roy Jones Jr.. WBA	2003
Floyd Patterson*	1956–59	Mike Tyson WBC	1986–87	Lennox Lewis* WBC	2001–04
Ingemar Johansson*	1959–60	James Smith WBA	1986–87	John Ruiz, WBA	2003–
Floyd Patterson*	1960–62	Tony Tucker IBF	1987	Vitali Klitschko, WBC	2004–
Sonny Liston*	1962–64	Mike Tyson*	1987–90		
Muhammad Ali*	1964–70†	Buster Douglas*	1990		
Ernie Terrell WBA	1965–67	Evander Holyfield*	1990–92		
Joe Frazier* NY	1968–70	Lennox Lewis WBC	1993–95		

Cruiserweights
(Weight Limit: 190 pounds)

CHAMPION	REIGN	Champion	Reign	Champion	Reign
Marvin Camel* WBC	1980	Evander Holyfield*	1988†	A. Washington IBF	1996–97
Carlos De Leon* WBC	1980–82	Toufik Belbouli WBA	1989	Uriah Grant IBF	1997
Ossie Ocasio WBA	1982–84	Robert Daniels WBA	1989–91	Imamu Mayfield IBF	1997–98
S.T. Gordon* WBC	1982–83	Carlos De Leon* WBC	1989–90	Fabrice Tiozzo WBA	1997–00
Carlos De Leon* WBC	1983–85	Glenn McCrory IBF	1989–90	J.C. Gomez* WBC	1998–02†
Marvin Camel IBF	1983–84	Jeff Lampkin IBF	1990	Arthur Williams IBF	1998–99
Lee Roy Murphy IBF	1984–86	M. Duran* WBC	1990–91	Vassiliy Girov* IBF	1999–03
Piet Crous WBA	1984–85	Bobby Czyz WBA	1991–92†	James Toney* IBF	2003
Alfonso Ratliff* WBC	1985	Anaclet Wamba* WBC	1991–95†	Virgil Hill WBA	2000–02
Dwight Braxton WBA	1985–86	James Pritchard IBF	1991	Wayne Braithwaite WBC	2002–05
Bernard Benton* WBC	1985–86	James Warring IBF	1991–92	J.M. Mormeck WBA	2002–
Carlos De Leon* WBC	1986–88	Alfred Cole IBF	1992–96	J.M. Mormeck WBC	2005–
Evander Holyfield* WBA	1986–88	Orlin Norris WBA	1993–95	Kelvin Davis IBF	2004–05
Ricky Parkey IBF	1986–87	Nate Miller WBA	1995–97	O'Neil Bell IBF	2005–
E. Holyfield* WBA, IBF	1987–88	M. Dominguez* WBC	1996–98		

*Lineal champion.
†Champion relinquished title to retire or switch weight classes, or had title stripped by boxing organization.

Light Heavyweights
(Weight Limit: 175 pounds)

Champion	Reign
Jack Root*	1903
George Gardner*	1903
Bob Fitzsimmons*	1903–05
Jack O'Brien*	1905–12†
Jack Dillon*	1914–16
Battling Levinsky*	1916–20
Georges Carpentier*	1920–22
Battling Siki*	1922–23
Mike McTigue*	1923–25
Paul Berlenbach*	1925–26
Jack Delaney*	1926–27†
Jimmy Slattery NBA	1927
Tommy Loughran*	1927–29†
Maxie Rosenbloom*	1930–34
George Nichols NBA	1932
Bob Godwin NBA	1933
Bob Olin*	1934–35
John Henry Lewis*	1935–38†
Melio Bettina	1939
Billy Conn*	1939–40†
Anton Christoforidis	1941
Gus Lesnevich*	1941–48
Freddie Mills*	1948–50
Joey Maxim*	1950–52
Archie Moore*	1952–62†
Harold Johnson NBA	1961
Harold Johnson*	1962–63
Willie Pastrano*	1963–65

Champion	Reign
Jose Torres*	1965–66
Dick Tiger*	1966–68
Bob Foster*	1968–74†
Vicente Rondon WBA	1971–72
John Conteh WBC	1974–77
Victor Galindez* WBA	1974–78
Miguel A. Cuello WBC	1977–78
Mate Parlov WBC	1978
Mike Rossman* WBA	1978–79
Victor Galindez* WBA	1979
Marvin Johnson* WBC	1978–79
M.S. Muhammad* WBC	1979–81
Marvin Johnson WBA	1979–80
E.M. Muhammad* WBA	1980–81
Michael Spinks* WBA	1981–83
Dwight Qawi WBC	1981–83
Michael Spinks*	1983–85†
J. B. Williamson WBC	1985–86
Slobodan Kacar IBF	1985–86
Marvin Johnson* WBA	1986–87
Dennis Andries WBC	1986–87
Bobby Czyz IBF	1986–87
Leslie Stewart WBA	1987
Virgil Hill* WBA	1987–91
Pr Charles Williams IBF	1987–93
Thomas Hearns WBC	1987†
Donny Lalonde WBC	1987–88

Champion	Reign
Sugar Ray Leonard WBC	1988
Dennis Andries WBC	1989
Jeff Harding WBC	1989–90
Dennis Andries WBC	1990–91
Thomas Hearns* WBA	1991–92
Jeff Harding WBC	1991–94
Iran Barkley* WBA	1992
Virgil Hill* WBA	1992–97
Henry Maske IBF	1993–96
Mike McCallum WBC	1994–95
Fabrice Tiozzo WBC	1995–96
D. Michalczewski* IBF	1997†
Roy Jones Jr. WBC, WBA	1997–03
William Guthrie IBF	1997–98
Reggie Johnson IBF	1998–99
Roy Jones Jr.*	1999–03
Bruno Girard WBA	2001–03
Mehdi Sahnoune WBA	2003
Silvio Branco WBA	2003–04
Antonio Tarver WBC, IBF	2003
Roy Jones Jr. WBC	2003
Glencoffe Johnson IBF	2004–05
Fabrice Tiozzo WBA	2004–
Antonio Tarver* WBC	2004–05
Clinton Woods IBF	2005–
Tomasz Adamek WBC	2005–

Super Middleweights
(Weight Limit: 168 pounds)

Champion	Reign
Murray Sutherland* IBF	1984
Chong-Pal Park* IBF	1984–87
Chong-Pal Park* WBA	1987–88
G. Rocchigiani IBF	1988–89
F. Obelmejias* WBA	1988–89
Sugar Ray Leonard WBC	1988–90†
In-Chul Baek* WBA	1989–90
Lindell Holmes IBF	1990–91
Chris Tiozzo* WBA	1990–91
Mauro Galvano WBC	1990–92
Victor Cordova* WBA	1991
Darrin Van Horn IBF	1991–92
Iran Barkley IBF	1992
Nigel Benn WBC	1992–96

Champion	Reign
James Toney IBF	1992–94
Michael Nunn* WBA	1992–94
Steve Little* WBA	1994
Frank Liles* WBA	1994–99
Roy Jones Jr. IBF	1994–96
Thulane Malinga WBC	1996
V. Nardiello WBC	1996
Robin Reid WBC	1996–97
Charles Brewer IBF	1997–98
Thulane Malinga WBC	1997–98
Richie Woodhall WBC	1998–99
Sven Ottke IBF	1998–03
Byron Mitchell* WBA	1999–00
Markus Beyer WBC	1999–00

Champion	Reign
Bruno Girard* WBA	2000–01†
Glenn Catley WBC	2000–01
Eric Lucas WBC	2000–03
Byron Mitchell WBA	2000–03
Sven Ottke WBA	2003†
Anthony Mundine WBA	2003
Markus Beyer WBC	2003–
Sven Ottke, IBF	2003–05
Cristian Sanavia WBC	2004–05
Manny Siaca, WBA	2004–05
Mikkel Kessler WBA	2005–
Jeff Lacy IBF	2005–

*Lineal champion. †Champion retired or relinquished title.

Middleweights
(Weight Limit: 160 pounds)

Champion	Reign
Jack Dempsey*	1884–91
Bob Fitzsimmons*	1891–97†
Kid McCoy*	1897–98
Tommy Ryan*	1898–07†
Stanley Ketchel*	1908
Billy Papke*	1908
Stanley Ketchel*	1908–10†
Frank Klaus*	1913
George Chip*	1913–14
Al McCoy*	1914–17
Mike O'Dowd*	1917–20
Johnny Wilson*	1920–23
Harry Greb*	1923–26
Tiger Flowers*	1926
Mickey Walker*	1926–31†
Gorilla Jones*	1931–32
Marcel Thil*	1932–37
Fred Apostoli*	1937–39
Al Hostak NBA	1938
Solly Krieger NBA	1938–39
Al Hostak NBA	1939–40
Ceferino Garcia*	1939–40
Ken Overlin*	1940–41
Tony Zale NBA	1940–41
Billy Soose*	1941
Tony Zale*	1941–47
Rocky Graziano*	1947–48
Tony Zale*	1948
Marcel Cerdan*	1948–49
Jake La Motta*	1949–51

Champion	Reign
Sugar Ray Robinson*	1951
Randy Turpin*	1951
Sugar Ray Robinson*	1951–52†
Bobo Olson*	1953–55
Sugar Ray Robinson*	1955–57
Gene Fullmer*	1957
Sugar Ray Robinson*	1957
Carmen Basilio*	1957–58
Sugar Ray Robinson*	1958–60
Gene Fullmer NBA	1959–62
Paul Pender*	1960–61
Terry Downes*	1961–62
Paul Pender*	1962–63†
Dick Tiger WBA	1962–63
Dick Tiger*	1963
Joey Giardello*	1963–65
Dick Tiger*	1965–66
Emile Griffith*	1966–67
Nino Benvenuti*	1967
Emile Griffith*	1967–68
Nino Benvenuti*	1968–70
Carlos Monzon*	1970–77†
Rodrigo Valdez WBC	1974–76
Rodrigo Valdez*	1977–78
Hugo Corro*	1978–79
Vito Antuofermo*	1979–80
Alan Minter*	1980
Marvin Hagler*	1980–87
Sugar Ray Leonard*	1987†
Frank Tate IBF	1987–88

Champion	Reign
Sumbu Kalambay WBA	1987–89
Thomas Hearns* WBC	1987–88
Iran Barkley* WBC	1988–89
Michael Nunn IBF	1988–91
Roberto Duran* WBC	1989–90†
Michael Nunn* IBF	1991
Mike McCallum WBA	1989–91
Julian Jackson WBC	1990–93
James Toney* IBF	1991–93†
Reggie Johnson WBA	1992–94
Roy Jones Jr.* IBF	1993–95†
G. McClellan WBC	1993–95†
Jorge Castro WBA	1994–95
Shinji Takehara WBA	1995–96
Jullian Jackson WBC	1995
Quincy Taylor WBC	1995–96
Bernard Hopkins* IBF	1994–
Keith Holmes WBC	1996–98
William Joppy WBA	1996–97
J.C. Green WBA	1997
William Joppy WBA	1998–01
Hassine Cherifi WBC	1998–99
Keith Holmes WBC	1999–00
Felix Trinidad WBA	2001
William Joppy WBA	2001–03
Bernard Hopkins*WBC/IBF	
	2001–05
Bernard Hopkins WBA	2003–05
Jermain Taylor WBA/WBC/IBF	
	2005–

Junior Middleweights
(Weight Limit: 154 pounds)

Champion	Reign
Emile Griffith (EBU)	1962–63
Dennis Moyer*	1962–63
Ralph Dupas*	1963
Sandro Mazzinghi*	1963–65
Nino Benvenuti*	1965–66
Ki-Soo Kim*	1966–68
Sandro Mazzinghi*	1968
Freddie Little*	1969–70
Carmelo Bossi*	1970–71
Koichi Wajima*	1971–74
Oscar Albarado*	1974–75
Koichi Wajima*	1975
Miguel de Oliveira WBC	1975–76
Jae-Do Yuh*	1975–76
Elisha Obed WBC	1975–76
Koichi Wajima*	1976
Jose Duran*	1976
Eckhard Dagge WBC	1976–77
Miguel Angel Castellini*	1976–77
Eddie Gazo*	1977–78
Rocky Mattioli WBC	1977–79
Masashi Kudo*	1978–79
Maurice Hope WBC	1979–81
Ayub Kalule*	1979–81
Wilfred Benitez WBC	1981–82
Sugar Ray Leonard*	1981–82†
Tadashi Mihara WBA	1981–82

Champion	Reign
Davey Moore WBA	1982–83
Thomas Hearns* WBC	1982–84
Roberto Duran WBA	1983–84
Mark Medal IBF	1984
Thomas Hearns*	1984–86†
Mike McCallum* WBA	1984–87†
Carlos Santos IBF	1984–86
Buster Drayton IBF	1986–87
Duane Thomas WBC	1986–87
Matthew Hilton IBF	1987–88
Lupe Aquino WBC	1987
Gianfranco Rosi WBC	1987–88
Julian Jackson WBC	1987–90
Donald Curry WBC	1988–89
Robert Hines IBF	1988–89
Darrin Van Horn IBF	1989
Rene Jacquot WBC	1989
John Mugabi* WBC	1989–90
Gianfranco Rosi IBF	1989–94
Terry Norris* WBC	1990–93
Gilbert Dele WBA	1991
Vinny Pazienza WBA	1991–92
Julio C. Vasquez WBA	1992–95
Simon Brown* WBC	1993–94
Terry Norris* WBC	1994
Luis Santana* WBC	1995–95
Vincent Pettway IBF	1994–95

Champion	Reign
Paul Vaden IBF	1995
Carl Daniels WBA	1995
Terry Norris* WBC	1995–97
Terry Norris* IBF	1995–96†
L. Boudouani WBA	1996–99
Raul Marquez IBF	1997
Keith Mullings* WBC	1997–99
Yori Boy Campas IBF	1997–98
Fernando Vargas IBF	1998–00
F. Javier Castillejo* WBC	1999–01
David Reid WBA	1999–00
Felix Trinidad WBA	2000–01
Felix Trinidad WBA, IBF	2001†
Oscar De La Hoya*	
WBC	2001–03
Fernando Vargas WBA	2001–02
Ronald Wright IBF†	2001–04
Oscar De La Hoya*	
WBC/WBA	2002–03
Shane Mosley* WBC	2003–04
Alejandro Garcia WBA	2003–05
Ronald Wright WBA,	
WBC	2004–05
Verno Phillips IBF	2004–05
Ricardo Mayora WBC	2005–
Alex T. Garcia WBA	2005–
Roman Karmazin IBF	2005–

*Lineal champion.
†Champion relinquished title to retire or switch weight classes, or had title stripped by boxing organization.

Welterweights
(Weight Limit: 147 pounds)

Champion	Reign
Paddy Duffy*	1888–90†
Mysterious Billy Smith*	1892–94
Tommy Ryan*	1894–98†
Mysterious Billy Smith*	1898–1900
Rube Ferns*	1900
Matty Matthews*	1900–01
Rube Ferns*	1901
Joe Walcott*	1901–04
The Dixie Kid*	1904–05†
Honey Mellody*	1906–07
Mike Sullivan*	1907–08†
Jimmy Gardner*	1908†
Jimmy Clabby*	1910–1†
Waldemar Holberg*	1914
Tom McCormick*	1914
Matt Wells*	1914–15
Mike Glover*	1915
Jack Britton*	1915
Ted "Kid" Lewis*	1915–16
Jack Britton*	1916–17
Ted "Kid" Lewis*	1917–19
Jack Britton*	1919–22
Mickey Walker*	1922–26
Pete Latzo*	1926–27
Joe Dundee*	1927–29
Jackie Fields*	1929–30
Young Jack Thompson*	1930
Tommy Freeman*	1930–31
Young Jack Thompson*	1931
Lou Brouillard*	1931–32
Jackie Fields*	1932–33
Young Corbett III*	1933
Jimmy McLarnin*	1933–34
Barney Ross*	1934
Jimmy McLarnin*	1934–35
Barney Ross*	1935–38

Champion	Reign
Henry Armstrong*	1938–40
Fritzie Zivic*	1940–41
Red Cochrane*	1941–46
Marty Servo*	1946
Sugar Ray Robinson*	1946–51†
Johnny Bratton*	1951
Kid Gavilan*	1951–54
Johnny Saxton*	1954–55
Tony DeMarco*	1955
Carmen Basilio*	1955–56
Johnny Saxton*	1956
Carmen Basilio*	1956–57†
Virgil Akins*	1958
Don Jordan*	1958–60
Kid Paret*	1960–61
Emile Griffith*	1961
Kid Paret*	1961–62
Emile Griffith*	1962–63
Luis Rodriguez*	1963
Emile Griffith*	1963–66†
Curtis Cokes*	1966–69
Jose Napoles*	1969–70
Billy Backus*	1970–71
Jose Napoles*	1971–75
Hedgemon Lewis NY	1972–73
Angel Espada WBA	1975–76
John H. Stracey*	1975–76
Carlos Palomino*	1976–79
Pipino Cuevas WBA	1976–80
Wilfredo Benitez*	1979
Sugar Ray Leonard*	1979–80
Roberto Duran*	1980
Thomas Hearns WBA	1980–81
Sugar Ray Leonard*	1980–82†
Donald Curry* WBA	1983–85

Champion	Reign
Milton McCrory WBC	1983–85
Donald Curry*	1985–86
Lloyd Honeyghan*	1986–87
Jorge Vaca* WBC	1987–88
Lloyd Honeyghan* WBC	1988–89
Mark Breland WBA	1987
Marlon Starling WBA	1987–88
Tomas Molinares WBA	1988–89
Simon Brown IBF	1988–91
Mark Breland WBA	1989–90
Marlon Starling* WBC	1989–90
Aaron Davis WBA	1990–91
Maurice Blocker* WBC	1990–91
Meldrick Taylor WBA	1991–92
Simon Brown* WBC	1991
Buddy McGirt* WBC	1991–93
Felix Trinidad IBF	1993–00
Pernell Whitaker* WBC	1993–97
Crisanto Espana WBA	1992–94
Ike Quartey WBA	1994–97†
Oscar De La Hoya* WBC	1997–99
James Page WBA	1998–01
Felix Trinidad* IBF, WBC	1999–00†
Shane Mosley* WBC	2000–02
Andrew Lewis WBA	2001–02
Vernon Forrest IBF	2001
Vernon Forrest* WBC	2001–03
Ricardo Mayorga WBA	2002
Ricardo Mayroga* WBC	2003–
Michele Piccirillo IBF	2002–03
Jose Rivera WBA	2003
Cory Spinks IBF, WBC, WBA	2003–05
Zab Judah WBC/IBF	2005–
Luis Collazo WBA	2005–

Junior Welterweights
(Weight Limit: 140 pounds)

Champion	Reign
Pinkey Mitchell*	1922–25
Red Herring	1925
Mushy Callahan*	1926–30
Jack (Kid) Berg*	1930–31
Tony Canzoneri*	1931–32
Johnny Jadick*	1932–33
Sammy Fuller	1932–33
Battling Shaw*	1933
Tony Canzoneri*	1933
Barney Ross*	1933–35†
Tippy Larkin*	1946
Carlos Ortiz*	1959–60
Duilio Loi*	1960–62
Eddie Perkins*	1962
Duilio Loi*	1962–63†
Roberto Cruz WBA	1963
Eddie Perkins*	1963–65
Carlos Hernandez*	1965–66
Sandro Lopopolo*	1966–67
Paul Fujii*	1967–68
Nicolino Loche*	1968–72
Pedro Adigue WBC	1968–70
Bruno Arcari WBC	1970–74
Alfonso Frazer*	1972
Antonio Cervantes*	1972–76
Perico Fernandez WBC	1974–75
S. Muangsurin WBC	1975–76
Wilfred Benitez*	1976–79†
M. Velasquez WBC	1976

Champion	Reign
S. Muangsurin WBC	1976–78
A. Cervantes WBA	1977–80
Sang-Hyun Kim WBC	1978–80
Saoul Mamby WBC	1980–82
Aaron Pryor* WBA	1980–83
Leroy Haley WBC	1982–83
Aaron Pryor* IBF	1983–85†
Bruce Curry WBC	1983–84
Johnny Bumphus WBA	1984
Bill Costello WBC	1984–85
Gene Hatcher WBA	1984–85
Ubaldo Sacco WBA	1985–86
Lonnie Smith* WBC	1985–86
Patrizio Oliva WBA	1986–87
Gary Hinton IBF	1986
Rene Arredondo* WBC	1986
Tsuyoshi Hamada WBC	1986–87
Joe Louis Manley IBF	1986–87
Terry Marsh IBF	1987
Juan Coggi WBA	1987–90
Rene Arredondo WBC	1987
R. Mayweather* WBC	1987–89
James McGirt IBF	1988
Meldrick Taylor IBF	1988–90
Julio César Chávez* WBC	1989–94
Julio César Chávez* IBF	1990–91
Loreto Garza WBA	1990–91
Juan Coggi WBA	1991
Edwin Rosario WBA	1991–92

Champion	Reign
Rafael Pineda IBF	1991–92
Akinobu Hiranaka WBA	1992
Pernell Whitaker* IBF	1992–93†
Charles Murray IBF	1993–94
Jake Rodriguez IBF	1994–95
Juan Coggi WBA	1993–94
Frankie Randall* WBC	1994
Frankie Randall WBA	1994–96
Juan Coggi WBA	1996
Julio César Chávez* WBC	1994–96
Kostya Tszyu IBF	1995–97
Frankie Randall WBA	1996–97
Oscar De La Hoya* WBC	1996–97†
Khalid Rahilou WBA	1997–98
Vincent Phillips* IBF	1997–99
Sharmba Mitchell WBA	1998–01
Kostya Tszyu WBC	1998–
Terronn Millett* IBF	1999–00
Zab Judah* IBF	2000–01
Kostya Tszyu*† WBA/WBC	2001–03
Kostya Tszyu* IBF	2003–05
Vivian Harris WBA	2003–05
Arturo Gatti WBC	2004–05
F Mayweather* WBC	2005–
Carlos Maussa WBA	2005–
Ricky Hatton IBF	2005–

Lightweights
(Weight Limit: 135 pounds)

Champion	Reign
Jack McAuliffe*	1886–94†
Kid Lavigne*	1896–99
Frank Erne*	1899–1902
Joe Gans*	1902–04
Jimmy Britt*	1904–05
Battling Nelson*	1905–06
Joe Gans*	1906–08
Battling Nelson*	1908–10
Ad Wolgast*	1910–12
Willie Ritchie*	1912–14
Freddie Welsh*	1915–17
Benny Leonard*	1917–25†
Jimmy Goodrich*	1925
Rocky Kansas*	1925–26
Sammy Mandell*	1926–30
Al Singer*	1930
Tony Canzoneri*	1930–33
Barney Ross*	1933–35†
Tony Canzoneri*	1935–36
Lou Ambers*	1936–38
Henry Armstrong*	1938–39
Lou Ambers*	1939–40
Sammy Angott NBA	1940–41
Lew Jenkins*	1940–41
Sammy Angott*	1941–42†
Beau Jack* NY	1942–43
Bob Montgomery* NY	1943
Sammy Angott NBA	1943–44
Beau Jack* NY	1943–44
Bob Montgomery* NY	1944–47
Juan Zurita NBA	1944–45
Ike Williams*	1947–51
James Carter*	1951–52
Lauro Salas*	1952
James Carter*	1952–54
Paddy DeMarco*	1954
James Carter*	1954–55
Wallace Smith*	1955–56
Joe Brown*	1956–62

Champion	Reign
Carlos Ortiz*	1962–65
Ismael Laguna*	1965
Carlos Ortiz*	1965–68
Carlos Teo Cruz*	1968–69
Mando Ramos*	1969–70
Ismael Laguna*	1970
Ken Buchanan*	1970–72
Roberto Duran*	1972–79†
Chango Carmona WBC	1972
Rodolfo Gonzalez WBC	1972–74
Ishimatsu Suzuki WBC	1974–76
Esteban DeJesus WBC	1976–78
Jim Watt WBC*	1979–81
Ernesto Espana WBA	1979–80
Hilmer Kenty WBA	1980–81
Sean O'Grady WBA	1981
Claude Noel WBA	1981
Alexis Arguello* WBC	1981–82†
Arturo Frias WBA	1981–82
Ray Mancini* WBA	1982–84
Alexis Arguello	1982–83
Edwin Rosario WBC	1983–84
Choo Choo Brown IBF	1984
L. Bramble* WBA	1984–86
Jose Luis Ramirez WBC	1984–85
Harry Arroyo IBF	1984–85
Jimmy Paul IBF	1985–86
Hector Camacho WBC	1985–86
Greg Haugen IBF	1986–87
Edwin Rosario* WBA	1986–87
Julio César Chávez* WBA	1987–88
Jose Luis Ramirez WBC	1987–88
Julio César Chávez*	1988–89†
Vinny Pazienza IBF	1987–88
Greg Haugen IBF	1988–89
P. Whitaker* WBC, IBF	1989–90
Edwin Rosario WBA	1989–90

Champion	Reign
Juan Nazario WBA	1990
P. Whitaker* WBA, WBC	1990–92†
Pernell Whitaker* IBF	1991–92†
Julio César Chávez IBF	1990–91
Edwin Rosario WBA	1991–92
Julio César Chávez WBC	1990–92
Miguel Gonzalez WBC	1992–95
Joey Gamache WBA	1992–93
Dingaan Thobela WBA	1993
Fred Pendleton* IBF	1993–94
Orzubek Nazarov WBA	1993–98
Rafael Ruelas* IBF	1994–95
Oscar De La Hoya* IBF	1995†
Phillip Holiday IBF	1995–97
Jean B. Mendy* WBC	1996–97
Steve Johnston* WBC	1997–98
Shane Mosley IBF	1997–99†
Jean B. Mendy WBA	1998–99
Cesar Bazan* WBC	1998–99
Steve Johnston* WBC	1999–00
Julien Lorcy WBA	1999
Stefano Zoff WBA	1999
Paul Spadafora IBF	1999–03
Gilbert Serrano WBA	1999–00
T. Hatakeyama WBA	2000–01
Jose Luis Castillo* WBC	2000–02
Julien Lorcy WBA	2001
Raul Balbi WBA	2001
F. Mayweather* WBC	2002–03
Leonard Dorin WBA	2002–03
Javier Jauregui IBF	2003–04
Julio Diaz IBF	2004–05
Lakva Sim WBA	2004
Juan Diaz WBA	2004–
Jose Luis Castillo WBC	2004–05
Diego Corrales WBC	2005–
Jesus Chavez IBF	2005–

Junior Lightweights
(Weight Limit: 130 pounds)

Champion	Reign
Johnny Dundee*	1921–23
Jack Bernstein*	1923
Johnny Dundee*	1923–24
Steve (Kid) Sullivan*	1924–25
Mike Ballerino*	1925
Tod Morgan*	1925–29
Benny Bass*	1929–31
Kid Chocolate*	1931–33
Frankie Klick*	1933–34†
Sandy Saddler*	1949–50†
Harold Gomes*	1959–60
Gabriel (Flash) Elorde*	1960–67
Yoshiaki Numata*	1967
Hiroshi Kobayashi*	1967–71
Rene Barrientos WBC	1969–70
Yoshiaki Numata WBC	1970–71
Alfredo Marcano*	1971–72
R. Arredondo WBC	1971–74
Ben Villaflor*	1972–73
Kuniaki Shibata*	1973
Ben Villaflor*	1973–76
Kuniaki Shibata WBC	1974–75
Alfredo Escalera WBC	1975–78
Samuel Serrano*	1976–80
Alexis Arguello WBC	1978–80

Champion	Reign
Yasutsune Uehara*	1980–81
Rafael Limon WBC	1980–81
C. Boza-Edwards WBC	1981
Samuel Serrano*	1981–83
R. Navarrete WBC	1981–82
Rafael Limon WBC	1982
Bobby Chacon WBC	1982–83
Roger Mayweather*	1983–84
Hector Camacho WBC	1983–84
Rocky Lockridge*	1984–85
Hwan-Kil Yuh IBF	1984–85
Julio César Chávez WBC	1984–87
Lester Ellis IBF	1985
Wilfredo Gomez*	1985–86
Barry Michael IBF	1985–87
Alfredo Layne* WBA	1986
Brian Mitchell* WBA	1986–91†
Rocky Lockridge IBF	1987–88
Azumah Nelson* WBC	1988–94
Tony Lopez IBF	1988–89
Juan Molina IBF	1989–90
Tony Lopez IBF	1990–91
Joey Gamache WBA	1991
Brian Mitchell IBF	1991
Genaro Hernandez WBA	1991–95
James Leija* WBC	1994

Champion	Reign
Juan Molina IBF	1991–95
Gabriel Ruelas* WBC	1994–95
Eddie Hopson IBF	1995
Tracy Patterson IBF	1995
Azumah Nelson* WBC	1995–97
Choi Yong-Soo WBA	1995–98
Arturo Gatti WBC	1995–98†
Genaro Hernandez* WBC	1997–98
Roberto Garcia IBF	1998–99
Floyd Mayweather* WBC	1998–01†
T. Hatakeyama WBA	1998–99
Lakva Sim WBA	1999
Diego Corrales IBF	1999–01
Jong Kwon Baek WBA	1999–00
Joel Casamayor WBA	2000–02
Steve Forbes IBF	2000–02†
Acelino Freitas* WBA	2002–04
Y. Nantchachai WBA	2002–05
S. Singmanassak WBC	2002–03
Jesus Chavez WBC	2003–04
Carlos Hernandez IBF	2003–04
Erik Morales WBC/IBF	2004–05
Erik Morales IBF	2004–
Marco A. Barrera WBC	2005–
Vicente Mosquera WBA	2005–

Featherweights
(Weight Limit: 126 pounds)

Champion	Reign
Torpedo Billy Murphy*	..1890
Young Griffo*	..1890–92†
George Dixon*	.1892–97
Solly Smith*	.1897–98
Dave Sullivan*	.1898
George Dixon*	.1898–1900
Terry McGovern*	.1900–01
Young Corbett II*	.1901–03†
Abe Attell*	.1903–04
Tommy Sullivan*	.1904–05†
Abe Attell*	.1906–12
Johnny Kilbane*	.1912–23
Eugene Criqui*	.1923
Johnny Dundee*	.1923–24†
"Kid" Kaplan*	.1925–26†
Tony Canzoneri*	.1927–28
Andre Routis*	.1928–29
Battling Battalino*	.1929–32†
Tommy Paul NBA	.1932–33
Kid Chocolate NY	.1932–33†
Freddie Miller NBA	.1933–36
Mike Beloise NY	.1936–37
Petey Sarron NBA	.1936–37
Maurice Holtzer	.1937–38
Henry Armstrong*	.1937–38†
Joey Archibald* NY	.1938–39
Leo Rodak NBA	.1938–39
Joey Archibald	.1939–40
Petey Scalzo NBA	.1940–41
Harry Jeffra*	.1940–41
Joey Archibald*	.1941
Richie Lamos NBA	.1941
Chalky Wright*	.1941–42
Jackie Wilson NBA	.1941–43
Willie Pep*	.1942–48
Jackie Callura NBA	.1943
Phil Terranova NBA	.1943–44
Sal Bartolo NBA	.1944–46

Champion	Reign
Sandy Saddler*	.1948–49
Willie Pep*	.1949–50
Sandy Saddler*	.1950–57†
Kid Bassey*	.1957–59
Davey Moore*	.1959–63
Sugar Ramos*	.1963–64
Vicente Saldivar*	.1964–67†
Paul Rojas WBA	.1968
Jose Legra WBC	.1968–69
Shozo Saijyo WBA	.1968–71
J. Famechon* WBC	.1969–70
Vicente Saldivar* WBC	..1970
Kuniaki Shibata* WBC	.1970–72
Antonio Gomez WBA	.1971–72
C. Sanchez* WBC	.1972
Ernesto Marcel WBA	.1972–74
Jose Legra* WBC	.1972–73
Eder Jofre* WBC	.1973–74†
Ruben Olivares WBA	.1974
Bobby Chacon WBC	.1974–75
Alexis Arguello* WBA	.1974–76†
Ruben Olivares WBA	.1975
Poison Kotey WBC	.1975–76
Danny Lopez* WBC	.1976–80
Rafael Ortega WBA	.1977
Cecilio Lastra WBA	.1977–78
Eusebio Pedroza* WBA	..1978–85
S. Sanchez* WBC	.1980–82†
Juan LaPorte WBC	.1982–84
Wilfredo Gomez WBC	.1984
Min-Keun Oh IBF	.1984–85
Azumah Nelson WBC	.1984–88
Barry McGuigan* WBA	.1985–86
Ki Young Chung IBF	.1985–86
Steve Cruz* WBA	.1986–87
Antonio Rivera IBF	.1986–88
A. Esparragoza* WBA	..1987–91
Calvin Grove IBF	.1988

Champion	Reign
Jorge Paez IBF	.1988–91
Jeff Fenech WBC	.1988–90†
Marcos Villasana WBC	..1990–91
Paul Hodkinson WBC	..1991–93
Troy Dorsey IBF	.1991
Manuel Medina IBF	.1991–93
Yung Kyun Park* WBA	.1991–93
Gregorio Vargas WBC	..1993
Tom Johnson IBF	.1993–97†
Eloy Rojas* WBA	.1993–96
Kevin Kelley WBC	.1993–95
A. Gonzalez WBC	.1995
Manuel Medina WBC	.1995–95
Luisito Espinosa WBC	.1995–99
Wilfredo Vazquez* WBA	..1996–98
Hector Lizarraga IBF	.1997–98
Naseem Hamed* WBA	..1998†
Naseem Hamed*	.1998–01
Freddy Norwood WBA	.1998
Manuel Medina IBF	.1998–99
Antonio Cermeno WBA	..1998–99
Cesar Soto WBC	.1999
Freddy Norwood WBA	.1999–00
Naseem Hamed* WBC	.1999†
Paul Ingle IBF	.1999–00
Guty Espadas WBC	.2000–01
Erik Morales WBC	.2000–02
Derrick Gainer WBA	.2000–03
Mbulelo Botile IBF	.2001
Frankie Toledo IBF	.2001
Manuel Medina IBF	.2001
Marco A. Barrera* WBA/WBC	
	.2001–03
Johnny Tapia IBF	.2002
Marco A. Barrera* WBC	.2002†
Erik Morales WBC	.2002–03
Juan Marquez IBF	.2003–
Chris John WBA	.2005–
In Jin Chi WBC	.2004–

Junior Featherweights
(Weight Limit: 122 pounds)

Champion	Reign
Jack (Kid) Wolfe*	.1922–23
Carl Duane*	.1923–24
Rigoberto Riasco* WBC	.1976
R. Kobayashi* WBC	.1976
Dong-Kyun Yum* WBC	.1976–77
Wilfredo Gomez* WBC	.1977–83†
Soo-Hwan Hong WBA	.1977–78
Ricardo Cardona WBA	.1978–80
Leo Randolph WBA	.1980
Sergio Palma WBA	.1980–82
Leonardo Cruz WBA	.1982–84
Jaime Garza* WBC	.1983
Bobby Berna IBF	.1983–84
Loris Stecca WBA	.1984
Seung-Il Suh IBF	.1984–85
Victor Callejas WBA	.1984–86
Juan Meza* WBC	.1984–85
Ji-Won Kim IBF	.1985–86
Lupe Pintor* WBC	.1985–86
S. Payakaroon* WBC	.1986–87

Champion	Reign
Seung-Hoon Lee IBF	.1987–88
Louie Espinoza WBA	.1987†
Jeff Fenech* WBC	.1987†
Julio Gervacio WBA	.1987–88
Daniel Zaragoza* WBC	.1988–90
Jose Sanabria IBF	.1988–89
B. Pinango WBA	.1988
J.J. Estrada WBA	.1988–89
Fabrice Benichou IBF	.1989–90
Jesus Salud WBA	.1989–90
Welcome Ncita IBF	.1990–92
Paul Banke* WBC	.1990
Luis Mendoza WBA	.1990–91
Raul Perez WBA	.1992
Pedro Decima* WBC	.1990–91
K. Hatanaka* WBC	.1991
Daniel Zaragoza* WBC	.1991–92
Thiery Jacob* WBC	.1992
Tracy Patterson* WBC	.1992–94
Kennedy McKinney IBF	.1993–94

Champion	Reign
Wilfredo Vasquez WBA	..1992–95
Vuyani Bungu IBF	.1994–99†
H. Acero* Sanchez WBC	..1994–95
Antonio Cermeno WBA	.1995–98†
Daniel Zaragoza* WBC	.1995–97
Erik Morales* WBC	.1997–00†
Enrique Sanchez WBA	.1998
Nestor Garza WBA	.1998–00
Benedict Ledwaba IBF	.1999–01
Clarence Adams WBA	.2000–01†
Willie Jorrin WBC	.2000–02
Manny Pacquiao IBF	.2001–04
Yober Ortega WBA	.2001–02
Y. Sithyodthong WBA	.2002
Osamu Sato WBA	.2002
Salim Medjkoune WBA	.2002–03
Mahyar Monshipour WBA	
	.2003–
Oscar Larios WBC	.2002–
Israel Vazquez IBF	.2004–

*Lineal champion.
†Champion relinquished title to retire or switch weight classes, or had title stripped by boxing organization.

Bantamweights
(Weight Limit: 118 pounds)

Champion	Reign	Champion	Reign	Champion	Reign
Spider Kelly	1887	Georgie Pace NBA	1939–40	Gaby Canizales*	1986
Hughey Boyle	1887–88	Lou Salica*	1940–42	Bernardo Pinango*	1986–87†
Spider Kelly	1889	Manuel Ortiz*	1942–47	W. Vasquez WBA	1987–88
Chappie Moran	1889–90	Harold Dade*	1947	Kevin Seabrooks* IBF	1987–88
George Dixon	1890–91	Manuel Ortiz*	1947–50	Kaokor Galaxy WBA	1988
Pedlar Palmer	1895–99	Vic Toweel*	1950–52	Moon Sung-Kil WBA	1988–89
Terry McGovern*	1899–00†	Jimmy Carruthers*	1952–54†	Kaokor Galaxy WBA	1989
Harry Harris	1901	Robert Cohen*	1954–56	Raul Perez WBC	1988–91
Harry Forbes*	1901–03	Paul Macias NBA	1955–57	O. Canizales* IBF	1988–95†
Frankie Neil*	1903–04	Mario D'Agata*	1956–57	Luisito Espinosa WBA	1989–91
Joe Bowker*	1904–05†	Alphonse Halimi*	1957–59	Israel Contreras WBA	1991–92
Jimmy Walsh*	1905–06†	Joe Becerra*	1959–60†	Eddie Cook WBA	1992–93
Owen Moran	1907–08	Eder Jofre*	1961–65	Greg Richardson WBC	1991
Monte Attell	1909–10	Fighting Harada*	1965–68	J. Tatsuyoshi, WBC	1991–92
Frankie Conley	1910–11	Lionel Rose*	1968–69	Victor Rabanales WBC	1992–93
Johnny Coulon*	1910–14	Ruben Olivares*	1969–70	Jung-Il Byun WBC	1993
Kid Williams*	1914–17	Chucho Castillo*	1970–71	Jorge Julio WBA	1993
Kewpie Ertle	1915	Ruben Olivares*	1971–72	Yasuei Yakushiji WBC	1993–95
Pete Herman*	1917–20	Rafael Herrera*	1972	Junior Jones WBA	1994
Joe Lynch*	1920–21	Enrique Pinder*	1972–73	John M. Johnson WBA	1994
Pete Herman*	1921	Romeo Anaya*	1973	D. Chuvatana WBA	1994–95
Johnny Buff*	1921–22	Arnold Taylor*	1973–74	V. Sahaprom* WBA	1995–96
Joe Lynch*	1922–24	Rafael Herrera WBC	1973–74	W. McCullough WBC	1995–96
Abe Goldstein*	1924	Soo-Hwan Hong*	1974–75	Harold Mestre IBF	1995
Cannonball Martin*	1924–25	Rodolfo Martinez WBC	1974–76	Mbulelo Botile IBF	1995–97
Phil Rosenberg*	1925–27†	Alfonso Zamora*	1975–77	Nana Konadu* WBA	1996–98
Bud Taylor NBA	1927–28	Carlos Zarate* WBC	1976–79	S. Singmanassak WBC	1996–97
Bushy Graham NY	1928–29	Jorge Lujan	1977–80	Tim Austin IBF	1997–03
Panama Al Brown*	1929–35	Lupe Pintor* WBC	1979–83†	J.Tatsuyoshi WBC	1997–98
Sixto Escobar NBA	1934–35	Julian Solis	1980	Johnny Tapia * WBA	1998–99
Baltazar Sangchilli*	1935–36	Jeff Chandler*	1980–84	V. Sahaprom* WBC	1998–05
Lou Salica NBA	1935	Albert Davila WBC	1983–85	Paulie Ayala* WBA	1999–01†
Sixto Escobar NBA	1935–36	Richard Sandoval*	1984–86	Eidy Moya WBA	2001–02
Tony Marino*	1936	Satoshi Shingaki IBF	1984–85	Johnny Bredahl WBA	2002–05
Sixto Escobar*	1936–37	Jeff Fenech IBF	1985	Rafael Marquez IBF	2003–
Harry Jeffra*	1937–38	Daniel Zaragoza WBC	1985	H. Hasegawa WBC	2005–
Sixto Escobar*	1938–39†	Miguel Lora WBC	1985–88	W. Sidorenko WBA	2005–

Junior Bantamweights
(Weight Limit: 115 pounds)

Champion	Reign	Champion	Reign	Champion	Reign
Rafael Orono* WBC	1980–81	Ellyas Pical IBF	1987–89	Gerry Penalosa* WBC	1997–98
Chul-Ho Kim* WBC	1981–82	Giberto Roman* WBC	1988–89	Johnny Tapia IBF	1997–99†
Gustavo Ballas WBA	1981	Juan Polo Perez IBF	1989–90	Satoshi Iida WBA	1997–98
Rafael Pedroza WBA	1981–82	Nana Konadu* WBC	1989–90	In-Joo Cho* WBC	1998–00
Jiro Watanabe WBA	1982–84	Sung-Kil Moon* WBC	1990–93	Jesus Rojas WBA	1998–99
Rafael Orono* WBC	1982–83	Robert Quiroga IBF	1990–93	Mark Johnson IBF	1999–00
Payao Poontarat* WBC	1983–84	Julio Borboa IBF	1993–94	Hideki Todaka WBA	1999–00
Joo-Do Chun IBF	1983–85	Katsuya Onizuka WBA	1993–94	Felix Machado IBF	2000–03
Jiro Watanabe*	1984–86	Lee Hyung-Chul WBA	1994–95	M. Tokuyama* WBC	2000–04
Kaosai Galaxy WBA	1984	Jose Luis Bueno* WBC	1993–94	Leo Gamez WBA	2000–01
Ellyas Pica IBF	1985–86	H. Kawashima* WBC	1994–97	Celes Kobayashi WBA	2001–02
Cesar Polanco IBF	1986	Harold Grey IBF	1994–95	Alexander Munoz WBA	2002–05
Gilberto Roman* WBC	1986–87	Alimi Goitia WBA	1995–96	Luis Perez IBF	2003–
Ellyas Pical IBF	1986	Yokthai Sith-Oar WBA	1996–97	KatsushigeKawashima WBC	
Santos Laciar* WBC	1987	Carlos Salazar IBF	1995–96		2004–05
Tae-Il Chang IBF	1987	Harold Grey IBF	1996	M. Tokuyama WBC	2005–
Sugar Rojas* WBC	1987–88	Danny Romero IBF	1996–97	Jose M Castillo WBA	2005–

*Lineal champion.
†Champion relinquished title to retire or switch weight classes, or had title stripped by boxing organization.

Flyweights
(Weight Limit: 112 pounds)

Champion	Reign
Sid Smith*	1913
Bill Ladbury*	1913–14
Percy Jones*	1914†
Joe Symonds*	1914–16
Jimmy Wilde*	1916–23
Pancho Villa*	1923–25†
Fidel La Barba*	1925–27†
Frenchy Belanger* NBA	1927–28
Izzy Schwartz NY	1927–29
Frankie Genaro* NBA	1928–29
Spider Pladner* NBA	1929
Frankie Genaro* NBA	1929–31
Midget Wolgast NY	1930–35
Young Perez* NBA	1931–32
Jackie Brown* NBA	1932–35
Benny Lynch*	1935–38†
Small Montana NY	1935–37
Peter Kane*	1938–43
Little Dado NY	1938–40
Jackie Paterson*	1943–48
Rinty Monaghan*	1948–50†
Terry Allen*	1950
Dado Marino*	1950–52
Yoshio Shirai*	1952–54
Pascual Perez*	1954–60
Pone Kingpetch*	1960–62
Masahiko Harada*	1962–63
Pone Kingpetch*	1963
Hiroyuki Ebihara*	1963–64
Pone Kingpetch*	1964–65
Salvatore Burrini*	1965–66
H. Accavallo WBA	1966–68
Walter McGowan*	1966
Chartchai Chionoi*	1966–69
Efren Torres*	1969–70
Hiroyuki Ebihara WBA	1969
B. Villacampo WBA	1969–70

Champion	Reign
Chartchai Chionoi*	1970
B. Chartvanchai WBA	1970
Masao Ohba WBA	1970–73
Erbito Salavarria*	1970–73†
B. Gonzalez WBA	1972
V. Borkorsor WBC	1972–73†
Venice Borkorsor*	1973†
Chartchai Chionoi WBA	1973–7.4
B. Gonzalez* WBA	1973–74
Shoji Oguma* WBC	1974–75
S. Hanagata WBA	1974–75
Miguel Canto* WBC	1975–79
Erbito Salavarria WBA	1975–76
Alfonso Lopez WBA	1976
G. Espadas WBA	1976–78
B. Gonzalez WBA	1978–79
Chan-Hee Park* WBC	1979–80
Luis Ibarra WBA	1979–80
Tae-Shik Kim WBA	1980
Shoji Oguma* WBC	1980–81
Peter Mathebula WBA	1980–81
Santos Laciar WBA	1981
Antonio Avelar* WBC	1981–82
Luis Ibarra WBA	1981
Juan Herrera WBA	1981–82
P. Cardona* WBC	1982
Santos Laciar WBA	1982–85
Freddie Castillo* WBC	1982
E. Mercedes* WBA	1982–83
Charlie Magri* WBC	1983
Frank Cedeno* WBC	1983–84
Soon-Chun Kwon IBF	1983–85
Koji Kobayashi* WBC	1984
Gabriel Bernal* WBC	1984
Sot Chitalada* WBC	1984–88
Hilario Zapate WBA	1985–87
Chong-Kwan Chung IBF	1985–86

Champion	Reign
Bi-Won Chung IBF	1986
Hi-Sup Shin IBF	1986–87
Dodie Penalosa IBF	1987
Fidel Bassa WBA	1987–89
Choi-Chang Ho IBF	1987–88
Rolando Bohol IBF	1988
Yong-Kang Kim* WBC	1988–89
Duke McKenzie IBF	1988–89
Sot Chitalada* WBC	1989–91
Dave McAuley IBF	1989–92
Jesus Rojas WBA	1989–90
Yul-Woo Lee WBA	1990
L. Tamakuma WBA	1990–91
M. Kittikasem* WBC	1991–92
Yuri Arbachakov* WBC	1992–97
Yong Kang Kim WBA	1991–92
Rodolfo Blanco IBF	1992–93
P. Sithbangprachan IBF	1993–95
David Griman WBA	1992–94
S.S. Ploenchit WBA	1994–96
Francisco Tejedor IBF	1995
Danny Romero IBF	1995–96
Mark Johnson IBF	1996–99†
Jose Bonilla WBA	1996–98
Chatchai Sasakul* WBC	1997–98
Hugo Soto WBA	1998–99
Manny Pacquiao* WBC	1998–99
Leo Gamez WBA	1999
Irene Pacheco IBF	1999–05
S. Pisnurachan WBA	1999–00
M. Sinsurat* WBC	1999–00
Malcolm Tunacao* WBC	2000–01
Eric Morel WBA	2000–03
P. Wonjongkam* WBC	2001–
Lorenzo Parra WBA	2003–
Vic Darchinyan IBF	2005–

Junior Flyweights
(Weight Limit: 108 pounds)

Champion	Reign	Champion	Reign	Champion	Reign
Franco Udella WBC	1975	Francisco Quiroz WBA	1984–85	S. Sor Jaturong WBC, IBF	1995–96
Jaime Rios WBA	1975–76	Joey Olivo WBA	1985	Carlos Murillo WBA	1996
Luis Estaba* WBC	1975–78	Myung-Woo Yuh* WBA	1985–91	Keiji Yamaguchi WBA	1996
Juan Guzman WBA	1976	Jum-Hwan Choi IBF	1986–88	Michael Carbajal IBF	1996–97
Yoko Gushiken WBA	1976–81	Tacy Macalos IBF	1988–89	Saman Jaturong* WBC	1995–99
Freddy Castillo* WBC	1978	German Torres WBC	1988–89	Phichitchor Siriwat WBA	1996–00
Sor Vorasingh* WBC	1978	Yul-Woo Lee WBC	1989	Mauricio Pastrana IBF	1997–98†
Sung-Jun Kim* WBC	1978–80	M. Kittikasem IBF	1989–90	Will Grigsby IBF	1998–99
Shigeo Nakajima* WBC	1980	H. Gonzalez WBC	1989–90	Ricardo Lopez IBF	1999–02
Hilario Zapata* WBC	1980–82	Michael Carbajal IBF	1990–94	Yo-Sam Choi* WBC	1999–02
Pedro Flores WBA	1981	R. Pascua WBC	1990	Beibis Mendoza WBA	2000–01
Hwan-Jin Kim WBA	1981	M. C. Castro WBC	1991	Rosendo Alvarez WBA	2001–05
Katsuo Tokashiki WBA	1981–83	H. Gonzalez WBC	1991–93	Jorge Arce* WBC	2002–05
Amado Urzua* WBC	1982	Hirokia Ioka* WBA	1991–92	Jose Burgos IBF	2003–05
Tadashi Tomori* WBC	1982	Myung-Woo Yuh* WBA	1993†	Brian Viloria WBC	2005–
Hilario Zapata* WBC	1982–83	Michael Carbajal* WBC	1993–94	R Vasquez WBA	2005–
Jung-Koo Chang* WBC	1983–88†	Leo Gamez WBA	1993–95	Will Grigsby IBF	2005–
Lupe Madera WBA	1983–84	H. Gonzalez* WBC, IBF	1994–95		
Dodie Penalosa IBF	1983–86	Choi Hi-Yong WBA	1995–96		

Strawweights
(Weight Limit: 105 pounds)

Champion	Reign	Champion	Reign	Champion	Reign
Kyung-Yun Lee* IBF	1987	Manny Melchor IBF	1992	Keitaro Hoshino WBA	2000–01
Hiroki Ioka* WBC	1987–88	Hideyuki Ohashi WBA	1992–93	Chana Porpaoin WBA	2001
Leo Gamez WBA	1988–89	R.S. Voraphin IBF	1992–96	Roberto Leyva IBF	2001–02
S. Sithnaruepol IBF	1988–89	Chana Porpaoin WBA	1993–95	Yutaka Niida WBA	2001†
N. Kiatwanchai* WBC	1988–89	Rosendo Alvarez WBA	1995–98	Miguel Barrera IBF	2002–03
Bong-Jun Kim WBA	1989–91	R. Sor Vorapin IBF	1996–97	Edgar Cardenas IBF	2003
Nico Thomas IBF	1989	Zolani Petelo* IBF	1997–00†	Noel Arambulet WBA	2002–04
Eric Chavez IBF	1989–90	W. Chor Charoen WBC	1998–00	Daniel Reyes IBF	2003–05
Jum-Hwan Choi* WBC	1989–90	R. Lopez* WBA, WBC	1998–99†	Eagle Akakura WBC	2004–
Hideyuki Ohashi* WBC	1990	Songkram Popaoin WBA	1999	Yukata Niida WBA	2004–
F. Lookmingkwan IBF	1990–92	Noel Arambulet WBA	1999–00	M Rachman IBF	2005–
Ricardo Lopez* WBC	1990–98†	Jose Aguirre* WBC	2000–04		
Hi-Yong Choi WBA	1991–92	Joma Gamboa WBA	2000		

*Lineal champion.

†Champion relinquished title to retire or switch weight classes, or had title stripped by boxing organization.

Boxing Match?

He signed up for NBC's reality boxing show The Contender, but Joey (the Greek God) Gilbert's experience ended up being more like something out of The Bachelor. During the May 24 series finale in Las Vegas, Gilbert, a 165-pounder who was eliminated in the quarterfinals, was introduced by his trainer to former Dallas Cowboys cheerleader Bonnie-Jill Laflin, a TV sports correspondent for KCAL in Los Angeles and the cohost of ESPN2's SpeedWorld. Now, says Laflin, 29, "things are moving really fast." (Read: She took Gilbert, 29, home to L.A. to meet the parents.) Says her smitten slugger "[Executive producer] Sly Stallone told me great things would flow from The Contender--and Bonnie-Jill fits that description completely."

Alltime Career Leaders

Total Bouts

Name	Years Active	Bouts	Name	Years Active	Bouts
Len Wickwar	1928–47	463	Maxie Rosenbloom	1923–39	299
Jack Britton	1905–30	350	Harry Greb	1913–26	298
Johnny Dundee	1910–32	333	Young Stribling	1921–33	286
Billy Bird	1920–48	318	Battling Levinsky	1910–29	282
George Marsden	1928–46	311	Ted (Kid) Lewis	1909–29	279

Note: Based on records in *The Ring Record Book* and *Boxing Encyclopedia.*

Most Knockouts

Name	Years Active	KOs	Name	Years Active	KOs
Archie Moore	1936–63	130	Sandy Saddler	1944–56	103
Young Stribling	1921–33	126	Sam Langford	1902–26	102
Billy Bird	1920–48	125	Henry Armstrong	1931–45	100
George Odwell	1930–45	114	Jimmy Wilde	1911–23	98
Sugar Ray Robinson	1940–65	110	Len Wickwar	1928–47	93

Note: Based on records in *The Ring Record Book* and *Boxing Encyclopedia.*

Million Dollar Maybe

Christy Martin still hasn't seen Million Dollar Baby, but she knows all about Lucia Rijker, who plays the fighter who battles Hilary Swank in the movie's climactic bout. For years after Martin landed on the cover of SI in 1996, Rijker told anyone who'd listen that while Martin--who was managed by Don King--might be the most visible women's boxer around, she, Rijker, was the best. But Martin never fought the former kickboxing champ. At a press conference before Martin's bout with Belinda Laracuente in 2000, Rijker showed up and accused Martin of ducking her. A melee ensued, and Martin suffered a broken bone in her hand, while Rijker was cut under the eye.

Five years later, with women's boxing--and Rijker especially--buoyed by the success of Baby, the two will finally meet in the ring. Martin, 36, and Rijker, 37, will fight on July 30 in Las Vegas for the biggest prize in women's boxing history: $ 1 million. (The loser gets $ 250,000.) The fight will be Martin's first in two years. In 2003 she was noticeably over-matched against Laila Ali and was KO'd in the fourth round. Saying she was "very discouraged with myself and with boxing in general," the West Virginia coal miner's daughter hung up her pink trunks and returned to Orlando, where she manages super middleweight Rowland Bryant. (Bryant, who is trained by Martin's husband, Jim, is 11--0 with six first-round knockouts.) But last summer, while in her hometown of Mullens, W.Va., fans encouraged her to end what she calls her "self-imposed hiatus."

Martin (45-3-2, 31 KOs) will go into the bout as the underdog. Rijker is undefeated in 17 fights, with 14 knockouts, and she'll be trained by Hall of Famer Emanuel Steward, who calls Rijker "the best one-on-one competitive female athlete ever in the history of any sport." Says Martin, "After you've been on top, people want to see you fail. I'm not going to give them that privilege. I have as much determination as I did in '96 to show people I'm still here, and still legitimate."

—Aimee Berg

World Heavyweight Championship Fights

Date	Winner	Wgt	Loser	Wgt	Result	Site
Sept 7, 1892	James J. Corbett*	178	John L. Sullivan	212	KO 21	New Orleans
Jan 25, 1894	James J. Corbett*	184	Charley Mitchell	158	KO 3	Jacksonville
Mar 17, 1897	Bob Fitzsimmons*	167	James J. Corbett	183	KO 14	Carson City, NV
June 9, 1899	James J. Jeffries*	206	Bob Fitzsimmons	167	KO 11	Coney Island, NY
Nov 3, 1899	James J. Jeffries*	215	Tom Sharkey	183	Ref 25	Coney Island, NY
Apr 6, 1900	James J. Jeffries*	n/a	Jack Finnegan	n/a	KO 1	Detroit
May 11, 1900	James J. Jeffries*	218	James J. Corbett	188	KO 23	Coney Island, NY
Nov 15, 1901	James J. Jeffries*	211	Gus Ruhlin	194	TKO 6	San Francisco
July 25, 1902	James J. Jeffries*	219	Bob Fitzsimmons	172	KO 8	San Francisco
Aug 14, 1903	James J. Jeffries*	220	James J. Corbett	190	KO 10	San Francisco
Aug 25, 1904	James J. Jeffries*	219	Jack Munroe	186	TKO 2	San Francisco
July 3, 1905	Marvin Hart*	190	Jack Root	171	KO 12	Reno
Feb 23, 1906	Tommy Burns*	180	Marvin Hart	188	Ref 20	Los Angeles
Oct 2, 1906	Tommy Burns*	n/a	Jim Flynn	n/a	KO 15	Los Angeles
Nov 28, 1906	Tommy Burns*	172	Jack O'Brien	163½	Draw 20	Los Angeles
May 8, 1907	Tommy Burns*	180	Jack O'Brien	167	Ref 20	Los Angeles
Jul 4, 1907	Tommy Burns*	181	Bill Squires	180	KO 1	Colma, CA
Dec 2, 1907	Tommy Burns*	177	Gunner Moir	204	KO 10	London
Feb 10, 1908	Tommy Burns*	n/a	Jack Palmer	n/a	KO 4	London
Mar 17, 1908	Tommy Burns*	n/a	Jem Roche	n/a	KO 1	Dublin
Apr 18, 1908	Tommy Burns*	n/a	Jewey Smith	n/a	KO 5	Paris
June 13, 1908	Tommy Burns*	184	Bill Squires	183	KO 8	Paris
Aug 24, 1908	Tommy Burns*	181	Bill Squires	184	KO 13	Sydney
Sept 2, 1908	Tommy Burns*	183	Bill Lang	187	KO 6	Melbourne
Dec 26, 1908	Jack Johnson*	192	Tommy Burns	168	TKO 14	Sydney
Mar 10, 1909	Jack Johnson*	n/a	Victor McLaglen	n/a	ND 6	Vancouver
May 19, 1909	Jack Johnson*	205	Jack O'Brien	161	ND 6	Philadelphia
June 30, 1909	Jack Johnson*	207	Tony Ross	214	ND 6	Pittsburgh
Sept 9, 1909	Jack Johnson*	209	Al Kaufman	191	ND 10	San Francisco
Oct 16, 1909	Jack Johnson*	205½	Stanley Ketchel	170¼	KO 12	Colma, CA
July 4, 1910	Jack Johnson*	208	James J. Jeffries	227	KO 15	Reno
July 4, 1912	Jack Johnson*	195½	Jim Flynn	175	TKO 9	Las Vegas
Dec 19, 1913	Jack Johnson*	n/a	Jim Johnson	n/a	Draw 10	Paris
June 27, 1914	Jack Johnson*	221	Frank Moran	203	Ref 20	Paris
Apr 5, 1915	Jess Willard*	230	Jack Johnson	205½	KO 26	Havana
Mar 25, 1916	Jess Willard*	225	Frank Moran	203	ND 10	New York City
July 4, 1919	Jack Dempsey*	187	Jess Willard	245	TKO 4	Toledo, OH
Sept 6, 1920	Jack Dempsey*	185	Billy Miske	187	KO 3	Benton Harbor, MI
Dec 14, 1920	Jack Dempsey*	188¼	Bill Brennan	197	KO 12	New York City
July 2, 1921	Jack Dempsey*	188	Georges Carpentier	172	KO 4	Jersey City
July 4, 1923	Jack Dempsey*	188	Tommy Givvons	175½	Ref 15	Shelby, MT
Sept 14, 1923	Jack Dempsey*	192½	Luis Firpo	216½	KO 2	New York City
Sept 23, 1926	Gene Tunney*	189½	Jack Dempsey	190	UD 10	Philadelphia
Sept 22, 1927	Gene Tunney*	189½	Jack Dempsey	192½	UD 10	Chicago
July 26, 1928	Gene Tunney*	192	Tom Heeney	203½	TKO 11	New York City
June 12, 1930	Max Schmeling*	188	Jack Sharkey	197	DQ 4	New York City
July 3, 1931	Max Schmeling*	189	Young Stribling	186½	TKO 15	Cleveland
June 21, 1932	Jack Sharkey*	205	Max Schmeling	188	Split 15	Long Island City
June 29, 1933	Primo Carnera*	260½	Jack Sharkey	201	KO 6	Long Island City
Oct 22, 1933	Primo Carnera*	259½	Paulino Uzcudun	229¼	UD 15	Rome
Mar 1, 1934	Primo Carnera*	270	Tommy Loughran	184	UD 15	Miami
June 14, 1934	Max Baer*	209½	Primo Carnera	263¼	TKO 11	Long Island City
June 13, 1935	James J. Braddock*	193¾	Max Baer	209½	UD 15	Long Island City
June 22, 1937	Joe Louis*	197¼	James J. Braddock	197	KO 8	Chicago
Aug 30, 1937	Joe Louis*	197	Tommy Farr	204¼	UD 15	New York City
Feb 23, 1938	Joe Louis*	200	Nathan Mann	193½	KO 3	New York City
Apr 1, 1938	Joe Louis*	202½	Harry Thomas	196	KO 5	Chicago
June 22, 1938	Joe Louis*	198¼	Max Schmeling	193	KO 1	New York City
Jan 25, 1939	Joe Louis*	200¼	John Henry Lewis	180¾	KO 1	New York City
Apr 17, 1939	Joe Louis*	201¼	Jack Roper	204¾	KO 1	Los Angeles
June 28, 1939	Joe Louis*	200¾	Tony Galento	233¾	TKO 4	New York City
Sept 20, 1939	Joe Louis*	200	Bob Pastor	183	KO 11	Detroit
Feb 9, 1940	Joe Louis*	203	Arturo Godoy	202	Split 15	New York City
Mar 29, 1940	Joe Louis*	201½	Johnny Paychek	187½	KO 2	New York City
June 20, 1940	Joe Louis*	199	Arturo Godoy	201¼	TKO 8	New York City
Dec 16, 1940	Joe Louis*	202¼	Al McCoy	180¾	TKO 6	Boston
Jan 31, 1941	Joe Louis*	202½	Red Burman	188	KO 5	New York City

World Heavyweight Championship Fights (Cont.)

Date	Winner	Wgt	Loser	Wgt	Result	Site
Feb 17, 1941	Joe Louis*	203½	Gus Dorazio	193½	KO 2	Philadelphia
Mar 21, 1941	Joe Louis*	202	Abe Simon	254½	TKO 13	Detroit
Apr 8, 1941	Joe Louis*	203½	Tony Musto	199½	TKO 9	St Louis
May 23, 1941	Joe Louis*	201½	Buddy Baer	237½	DQ 7	Washington, D.C.
June 18, 1941	Joe Louis*	199½	Billy Conn	174	KO 13	New York City
Sept 29, 1941	Joe Louis*	202¼	Lou Nova	202½	TKO 6	New York City
Jan 9, 1942	Joe Louis*	206¾	Buddy Baer	250	KO 1	New York City
Mar 27, 1942	Joe Louis*	207½	Abe Simon	255½	KO 6	New York City
June 9, 1946	Joe Louis*	207	Billy Conn	187	KO 8	New York City
Sept 18, 1946	Joe Louis*	211	Tami Mauriello	198½	KO 1	New York City
Dec 5, 1947	Joe Louis*	211½	Jersey Joe Walcott	194½	Split 15	New York City
June 25, 1948	Joe Louis*	213½	Jersey Joe Walcott	194¾	KO 11	New York City
June 22, 1949	Ezzard Charles*	181¾	Jersey Joe Walcott	195½	UD 15	Chicago
Aug 10, 1949	Ezzard Charles*	180	Gus Lesnevich	182	TKO 8	New York City
Oct 14, 1949	Ezzard Charles*	182	Pat Valentino	188½	KO 8	San Francisco
Aug 15, 1950	Ezzard Charles*	183¼	Freddie Beshore	184½	TKO 14	Buffalo
Sept 27, 1950	Ezzard Charles*	184½	Joe Louis	218	UD 15	New York City
Dec 5, 1950	Ezzard Charles*	185	Nick Barone	178½	KO 11	Cincinnati
Jan 12, 1951	Ezzard Charles*	185	Lee Oma	193	TKO 10	New York City
Mar 7, 1951	Ezzard Charles*	186	Jersey Joe Walcott	193	UD 15	Detroit
May 30, 1951	Ezzard Charles*	182	Joey Maxim	181½	UD 15	Chicago
July 18, 1951	Jersey Joe Walcott*	194	Ezzard Charles	182	KO 7	Pittsburgh
June 5, 1952	Jersey Joe Walcott*	196	Ezzard Charles	191½	UD 15	Philadelphia
Sept 23, 1952	Rocky Marciano*	184	Jersey Joe Walcott	196	KO 13	Philadelphia
May 15, 1953	Rocky Marciano*	184½	Jersey Joe Walcott	197¾	KO 1	Chicago
Sept 24, 1953	Rocky Marciano*	185	Roland LaStarza	184¾	TKO 11	New York City
June 17, 1954	Rocky Marciano*	187½	Ezzard Charles	185½	UD 15	New York City
Sept 17, 1954	Rocky Marciano*	187	Ezzard Charles	192½	KO 8	New York City
May 16, 1955	Rocky Marciano*	189	Don Cockell	205	TKO 9	San Francisco
Sept 21, 1955	Rocky Marciano*	188¼	Archie Moore	188	KO 9	New York City
Nov 30, 1956	Floyd Patterson*	182¼	Archie Moore	187¾	KO 5	Chicago
July 29, 1957	Floyd Patterson*	184	Tommy Jackson	192½	TKO 10	New York City
Aug 22, 1957	Floyd Patterson*	187¼	Pete Rademacher	202	KO 6	Seattle
Aug 18, 1958	Floyd Patterson*	184½	Roy Harris	194	TKO 13	Los Angeles
May 1, 1959	Floyd Patterson*	182½	Brian London	206	KO 11	Indianapolis
June 26, 1959	Ingemar Johansson*	196	Floyd Patterson	182	TKO 3	New York City
June 20, 1960	Floyd Patterson*	190	Ingemar Johansson	194¾	KO 5	New York City
Mar 13, 1961	Floyd Patterson*	194¾	Ingemar Johansson	206½	KO 6	Miami Beach
Dec 4, 1961	Floyd Patterson*	188½	Tom McNeeley	197	KO 4	Toronto
Sept 25, 1962	Sonny Liston*	214	Floyd Patterson	189	KO 1	Chicago
July 22, 1963	Sonny Liston*	215	Floyd Patterson	194½	KO 1	Las Vegas
Feb 25, 1964	Cassius Clay*	210½	Sonny Liston	218	TKO 7	Miami Beach
Mar 5, 1965	Ernie Terrell	199	Eddie Machen	192	UD 15	Chicago
May 25, 1965	Muhammad Ali*	206	Sonny Liston	215¼	KO 1	Lewiston, ME
Nov 1, 1965	Ernie Terrell	206	George Chuvalo	209	UD 15	Toronto
Nov 22, 1965	Muhammad Ali*	210	Floyd Patterson	196¾	TKO 12	Las Vegas
Mar 29, 1966	Muhammad Ali*	214½	George Chuvalo	216	UD 15	Toronto
May 21, 1966	Muhammad Ali*	201½	Henry Cooper	188	TKO 6	London
June 28, 1966	Ernie Terrell	209½	Doug Jones	187½	UD 15	Houston
Aug 6, 1966	Muhammad Ali*	209½	Brian London	201½	KO 3	London
Sept 10, 1966	Muhammad Ali*	203½	Karl Mildenberger	194¼	TKO 12	Frankfurt
Nov 14, 1966	Muhammad Ali*	212¾	Cleveland Williams	210½	TKO 3	Houston
Feb 6, 1967	Muhammad Ali*	212¼	Ernie Terrell	212½	UD 15	Houston
Mar 22, 1967	Muhammad Ali*	211½	Zora Folley	202½	KO 7	New York City
Mar 4, 1968	Joe Frazier	204½	Buster Mathis	243½	TKO 11	New York City
Apr 27, 1968	Jimmy Ellis	197	Jerry Quarry	195	Maj 15	Oakland
June 24, 1968	Joe Frazier NY	203½	Manuel Ramos	208	TKO 2	New York City
Aug 14, 1968	Jimmy Ellis	198	Floyd Patterson	188	Ref 15	Stockholm
Dec 10, 1968	Joe Frazier NY	203	Oscar Bonavena	207	UD 15	Philadelphia
Apr 22, 1969	Joe Frazier NY	204½	Dave Zyglewicz	190½	KO 1	Houston
June 23, 1969	Joe Frazier NY	203½	Jerry Quarry	198½	TKO 8	New York City
Feb 16, 1970	Joe Frazier NY	205	Jimmy Ellis	201	TKO 5	New York City
Nov 18, 1970	Joe Frazier	209	Bob Foster	188	KO 2	Detroit
Mar 8, 1971	Joe Frazier*	205½	Muhammad Ali	215	UD 15	New York City
Jan 15, 1972	Joe Frazier*	215½	Terry Daniels	195	TKO 4	New Orleans
May 26, 1972	Joe Frazier*	217½	Ron Stander	218	TKO 5	Omaha
Jan 22, 1973	George Foreman*	217½	Joe Frazier	214	TKO 2	Kingston, Jam.
Sept 1, 1973	George Foreman*	219½	Jose Roman	196½	KO 1	Tokyo

Date	Winner	Wgt	Loser	Wgt	Result	Site
Mar 26, 1974	George Foreman*	224¼	Ken Norton	212¼	TKO 2	Caracas
Oct 30, 1974	Muhammad Ali*	216½	George Foreman	220	KO 8	Kinshasa, Zaire
Mar 24, 1975	Muhammad Ali*	223½	Chuck Wepner	225	TKO 15	Cleveland
May 16, 1975	Muhammad Ali*	224½	Ron Lyle	219	TKO 11	Las Vegas
July 1, 1975	Muhammad Ali*	224½	Joe Bugner	230	UD 15	Kuala Lumpur, Malay.
Oct 1, 1975	Muhammad Ali*	224½	Joe Frazier	215	TKO 15	Manila
Feb 20, 1976	Muhammad Ali*	226	Jean Pierre Coopman	206	KO 5	San Juan
Apr 30, 1976	Muhammad Ali*	230	Jimmy Young	209	UD 15	Landover, MD
May 24, 1976	Muhammad Ali*	230	Richard Dunn	206½	TKO 5	Munich
Sept 28, 1976	Muhammad Ali*	221	Ken Norton	217½	UD 15	New York City
May 16, 1977	Muhammad Ali*	221¼	Alfredo Evangelista	209¼	UD 15	Landover, MD
Sept 29, 1977	Muhammad Ali*	225	Earnie Shavers	211¼	UD 15	New York City
Feb 15, 1978	Leon Spinks*	197¼	Muhammad Ali	224¼	Split 15	Las Vegas
June 9, 1978	Larry Holmes	209	Ken Norton	220	Split 15	Las Vegas
Sept 15, 1978	Muhammad Ali*	221	Leon Spinks	201	UD 15	New Orleans
Nov 10, 1978	Larry Holmes*	214	Alfredo Evangelista	208¼	KO 7	Las Vegas
Mar 23, 1979	Larry Holmes*	214	Osvaldo Ocasio	207	TKO 7	Las Vegas
June 22, 1979	Larry Holmes*	215	Mike Weaver	202	TKO 12	New York City
Sept 28, 1979	Larry Holmes*	210	Earnie Shavers	211	TKO 11	Las Vegas
Oct 20, 1979	John Tate	240	Gerrie Coetzee	222	UD 15	Pretoria
Feb 3, 1980	Larry Holmes *	213½	Lorenzo Zanon	215	TKO 6	Las Vegas
Mar 31, 1980	Mike Weaver	232	John Tate	232	KO 15	Knoxville
Mar 31, 1980	Larry Holmes*	211	Leroy Jones	254½	TKO 8	Las Vegas
July 7, 1980	Larry Holmes*	214¼	Scott LeDoux	226	TKO 7	Minneapolis
Oct 2, 1980	Larry Holmes*	211¼	Muhammad Ali	217½	TKO 11	Las Vegas
Oct 25, 1980	Mike Weaver	210	Gerrie Coetzee	226½	KO 13	Sun City, S.A.
Apr 11, 1981	Larry Holmes*	215	Trevor Berbick	215½	UD 15	Las Vegas
June 12, 1981	Larry Holmes*	212¼	Leon Spinks	200¼	TKO 3	Detroit
Oct 3, 1981	Mike Weaver	215	James Quick Tillis	209	UD 15	Rosemont, IL
Nov 6, 1981	Larry Holmes*	213¼	Renaldo Snipes	215¾	TKO 11	Pittsburgh
June 11, 1982	Larry Holmes*	212½	Gerry Cooney	225½	TKO 13	Las Vegas
Nov 26, 1982	Larry Holmes*	217½	Tex Cobb	234¼	UD 15	Houston
Dec 10, 1982	Michael Dokes	216	Mike Weaver	209¾	TKO 1	Las Vegas
Mar 27, 1983	Larry Holmes*	221	Lucien Rodriguez	209	UD 12	Scranton, PA
May 20, 1983	Michael Dokes	223	Mike Weaver	218½	Draw 15	Las Vegas
May 20, 1983	Larry Holmes*	213	Tim Witherspoon	219½	Split 12	Las Vegas
Sept 10, 1983	Larry Holmes*	223	Scott Frank	211¼	TKO 5	Atlantic City
Sept 23, 1983	Gerrie Coetzee	215	Michael Dokes	217	KO 10	Richfield, OH
Nov 25, 1983	Larry Holmes*	219	Marvis Frazier	200	TKO 1	Las Vegas
Mar 9, 1984	Tim Witherspoon	220¼	Greg Page	239½	Maj 12	Las Vegas
Aug 31, 1984	Pinklon Thomas	216	Tim Witherspoon	217	Maj 12	Las Vegas
Nov 9, 1984	Larry Holmes* IBF	221½	James Smith	227	TKO 12	Las Vegas
Dec 1, 1984	Greg Page	236½	Gerrie Coetzee	218	KO 8	Sun City, S.A.
Mar 15, 1985	Larry Holmes*	223½	David Bey	233¼	TKO 10	Las Vegas
Apr 29, 1985	Tony Tubbs	229	Greg Page	239½	UD 15	Buffalo
May 20, 1985	Larry Holmes*	224¼	Carl Williams	215	UD 15	Las Vegas
June 15, 1985	Pinklon Thomas	220¼	Mike Weaver	221¼	KO 8	Las Vegas
Sept 21, 1985	Michael Spinks*	200	Larry Holmes	221½	UD 15	Las Vegas
Jan 17, 1986	Tim Witherspoon	227	Tony Tubbs	229	Maj 15	Atlanta
Mar 22, 1986	Trevor Berbick	218½	Pinklon Thomas	222¾	UD 15	Las Vegas
Apr 19, 1986	Michael Spinks*	205	Larry Holmes	223	Split 15	Las Vegas
July 19, 1986	Tim Witherspoon	234¾	Frank Bruno	228	TKO 11	Wembley, Eng.
Sept 6, 1986	Michael Spinks*	201	Steffen Tangstad	214¾	TKO 4	Las Vegas
Nov 22, 1986	Mike Tyson	221¼	Trevor Berbick	218½	TKO 2	Las Vegas
Dec 12, 1986	James Smith	228½	Tim Witherspoon	233½	TKO 1	New York City
Mar 7, 1987	Mike Tyson	219	James Smith	233	UD 12	Las Vegas
May 30, 1987	Mike Tyson	218¾	Pinklon Thomas	217¾	TKO 6	Las Vegas
May 30, 1987	Tony Tucker	222¼	Buster Douglas	227¼	TKO 10	Las Vegas
June 15, 1987	Michael Spinks*	208¾	Gerry Cooney	238	TKO 5	Atlantic City
Aug 1, 1987	Mike Tyson	221	Tony Tucker	221	UD 12	Las Vegas
Oct 16, 1987	Mike Tyson	216	Tyrell Biggs	228¾	TKO 7	Atlantic City
Jan 22, 1988	Mike Tyson	215¾	Larry Holmes	225¾	TKO 4	Atlantic City
Mar 20, 1988	Mike Tyson	216¼	Tony Tubbs	238¼	KO 2	Tokyo
June 27, 1988	Mike Tyson*	218¼	Michael Spinks	212¼	KO 1	Atlantic City
Feb 25, 1989	Mike Tyson*	218	Frank Bruno	228	TKO 5	Las Vegas
July 21, 1989	Mike Tyson*	219¼	Carl Williams	218	TKO 1	Atlantic City

Date	Winner	Wgt	Loser	Wgt	Result	Site
Feb 10, 1990	Buster Douglas*	231½	Mike Tyson	220½	KO 10	Tokyo
Oct 25, 1990	Evander Holyfield*	208	Buster Douglas	246	KO 3	Las Vegas
Apr 19, 1991	Evander Holyfield*	212	George Foreman	257	UD 12	Atlantic City
Nov 23, 1991	Evander Holyfield*	210	Bert Cooper	215	TKO 7	Atlanta
June 19, 1992	Evander Holyfield*	210	Larry Holmes	233	UD 12	Las Vegas
Nov 13, 1992	Riddick Bowe*	235	Evander Holyfield	205	UD 12	Las Vegas
Feb 6, 1993	Riddick Bowe*	243	Michael Dokes	244	KO 1	New York City
May 8, 1993	Lennox Lewis	235	Tony Tucker	235	UD 12	Las Vegas
May 22, 1993	Riddick Bowe*	244	Jesse Ferguson	224	KO 2	Washington, D.C.
Oct 2, 1993	Lennox Lewis	229	Frank Bruno	233	KO 7	London
Nov 6, 1993	Evander Holyfield*	217	Riddick Bowe	246	Split 12	Las Vegas
Apr 22, 1994	Michael Moorer*	214	Evander Holyfield	214	Split 12	Las Vegas
May 6, 1994	Lennox Lewis	235	Phil Jackson	218	TKO 8	Atlantic City
Nov 6, 1994	George Foreman*	250	Michael Moorer	222	KO 10	Las Vegas
Mar 11, 1995	Riddick Bowe	241	Herbie Hide	214	KO 6	Las Vegas
Apr 8, 1995	Oliver McCall	231	Larry Holmes	236	UD 12	Las Vegas
Apr 8, 1995	Bruce Seldon	236	Tony Tucker	243	TKO 7	Las Vegas
Apr 22, 1995	George Foreman*	256	Axel Schulz	221	Split 12	Las Vegas
Jun 17, 1995	Riddick Bowe	243	Jorge Luis Gonzalez	237	KO 6	Las Vegas
Aug 19, 1995	Bruce Seldon	234	Joe Hipp	233	TKO 10	Las Vegas
Sept 2, 1995	Frank Bruno	247¾	Oliver McCall	234¾	UD 12	London
Dec 9, 1995	Frans Botha	237	Axel Shulz	223	Split 12	Stuttgart
Mar 16, 1996	Mike Tyson	220	Frank Bruno	247	TKO 3	Las Vegas
June 22, 1996	Michael Moorer	222¼	Axel Shulz	222¾	Split 12	Dortmund, Ger.
Sept 7, 1996	Mike Tyson	219	Bruce Seldon	229	TKO 1	Las Vegas
Nov 3, 1996	George Foreman*	253	Crawford Grimsley		UD 12	Tokyo
Nov 9, 1996	Evander Holyfied	215	Mike Tyson	222	TKO 11	Las Vegas
Feb 7, 1997	Lennox Lewis	251	Oliver McCall	237	TKO 5	Las Vegas
Apr 26, 1997	George Foreman*	253	Lou Savarese		Split 12	Atlantic City
June 28, 1997	Evander Holyfield	218	Mike Tyson	218	DQ 4	Las Vegas
Oct 4, 1997	Lennox Lewis	244	Andrew Golota	244	TKO 1	Atlantic City
Nov 8, 1997	Evander Holyfield	214	Michael Moorer	223	TKO 8	Las Vegas
Nov 22, 1997	Shannon Briggs*		George Foreman		MD 12	Atlantic City
Mar 28, 1998	Lennox Lewis	243	Shannon Briggs	228	TKO 5	Atlantic City
Mar 13, 1999	Evander Holyfield	215	Lennox Lewis*	246	Draw 12	New York City
Nov 13, 1999	Lennox Lewis*	242	Evander Holyfield	217	UD 12	Las Vegas
Apr 29, 2000	Lennox Lewis*	247	Michael Grant	250	KO 2	New York
July 15, 2000	Lennox Lewis*	250	Frans Botha	236	TKO 2	London
Aug 12, 2000	Evander Holyfield	221	John Ruiz	224	UD 12	Las Vegas
Nov 11, 2000	Lennox Lewis*	249	David Tua	245	UD 12	Las Vegas
Mar 3, 2001	John Ruiz	227	Evander Holyfield	217	UD 12	Las Vegas
Apr 22, 2001	Hasim Rahman*	238	Lennox Lewis	253½	KO 5	Brakpan, S Africa
Nov 17, 2001	Lennox Lewis*	246½	Hasim Rahman	236	KO 4	Las Vegas
Dec 15, 2001	John Ruiz	232	Evander Holyfield	219	Draw 12	Mashantucket, CT
June 8, 2002	Lennox Lewis*	249¼	Mike Tyson	234½	KO 8	Memphis, TN
July 27, 2002	John Ruiz	233	Kirk Johnson	238	DQ 10	Las Vegas
Dec 14, 2002	Chris Byrd	214	Evander Holyfield	220	UD 12	Atlantic City
Mar 1, 2003	Roy Jones Jr.	193	John Ruiz	226	UD 12	Las Vegas
June 21, 2003	Lennox Lewis*	256½	Vitali Klitschko	248	TKO 6	Los Angeles
Sept 20, 2003	Chris Byrd	211½	Fres Oquendo	224	UD 12	Uncasville, CT
April 17, 2004	Chris Byrd	210½	Andrew Golota	237½	Draw 12	New York City
April 17, 2004	John Ruiz	240	Fres Oquendo	225	TKO 11	New York City
April 24, 2004	Vitali Klitschko	245	Corrie Sanders	235	TKO 8	Los Angeles
Nov 13, 2004	John Ruiz	239	Andrew Golota	238	UD	New York City
Nov 13, 2004	Chris Byrd	214	Jameel McCline	270	Split 12	New York City
Dec 11, 2004	Vitali Klitschko	250	Danny Williams	270	TKO 8	Las Vegas
April 30, 2005	James Toney	231	John Ruiz	244	ND	New York City
Aug 13, 2005	Hasim Rahman	236	Monte Barrett	224	UD	Chicago, Illinois

*Lineal champion. KO=knockout; TKO=technical knockout; UD=unanimous decision; Split=split decision; Ref=referee's decision; MD=majority decision; DQ=disqualification; ND=no decision.

Year	Fighter	Year	Fighter	Year	Fighter
1928	Gene Tunney	1935	Barney Ross	1940	Billy Conn
1929	Tommy Loughran	1936	Joe Louis	1941	Joe Louis
1930	Max Schmeling	1937	Henry Armstrong	1942	Ray Robinson
1932	Jack Sharkey	1938	Joe Louis	1943	Fred Apostoli
1934	T. Canzoneri/B. Ross	1939	Joe Louis	1944	Beau Jack

Note: No award in 1933; no fight of the year named until 1945

Year	Fighter	Fight	Winner	Site
1945	Willie Pep	Rocky Graziano–Freddie Cochrane	Rocky Graziano	New York City
1946	Tony Zale	Tony Zale–Rocky Graziano	Tony Zale	New York City
1947	Gus Lesnevich	Rocky Graziano–Tony Zale	Rocky Graziano	Chicago
1948	Ike Williams	Marcel Cerdan–Tony Zale	Marcel Cerdan	Jersey City
1949	Ezzard Charles	Willie Pep–Sandy Saddler	Willie Pep	New York City
1950	Ezzard Charles	Jake LaMotta–Laurent Dauthuille	Jake LaMotta	Detroit
1951	Ray Robinson	Jersey Joe Walcott–Ezzard Charles	Jersey Joe Walcott	Pittsburgh
1952	Rocky Marciano	Rocky Marciano–Jersey Joe Walcott	Rocky Marciano	Philadelphia
1953	Carl Olson	Rocky Marciano–Roland LaStarza	Rocky Marciano	New York City
1954	Rocky Marciano	Rocky Marciano–Ezzard Charles	Rocky Marciano	New York City
1955	Rocky Marciano	Carmen Basilio–Tony DeMarco	Carmen Basilio	Boston
1956	Floyd Patterson	Carmen Basilio–Johnny Saxton	Carmen Basilio	Syracuse
1957	Carmen Basilio	Carmen Basilio–Ray Robinson	Carmen Basilio	New York City
1958	Ingemar Johansson	Ray Robinson–Carmen Basilio	Ray Robinson	Chicago
1959	Ingemar Johansson	Gene Fullmer–Carmen Basilio	Gene Fullmer	San Francisco
1960	Floyd Patterson	Floyd Patterson–Ingemar Johansson	Floyd Patterson	New York City
1961	Joe Brown	Joe Brown–Dave Charnley	Joe Brown	London
1962	Dick Tiger	Joey Giardello–Henry Hank	Joey Giardello	Philadelphia
1963	Cassius Clay	Cassius Clay–Doug Jones	Cassius Clay	New York City
1964	Emile Griffith	Cassius Clay–Sonny Liston	Cassius Clay	Miami Beach
1965	Dick Tiger	Floyd Patterson–George Chuvalo	Floyd Patterson	New York City
1966	No award	Jose Torres–Eddie Cotton *	Jose Torres	Las Vegas
1967	Joe Frazier	Nino Benvenuti–Emile Griffith	Nino Benvenuti	New York City
1968	Nino Benvenuti	Dick Tiger–Frank DePaula	Dick Tiger	New York City
1969	Jose Napoles	Joe Frazier–Jerry Quarry	Joe Frazier	New York City
1970	Joe Frazier	Carlos Monzon–Nino Benvenuti	Carlos Monzon	Rome
1971	Joe Frazier	Joe Frazier–Muhammad Ali	Joe Frazier	New York City
1972	Muhammad Ali Carlos Monzon	Bob Foster–Chris Finnegan	Bob Foster	London
1973	George Foreman	George Foreman–Joe Frazier	George Foreman	Kingston, Jam.
1974	Muhammad Ali	Muhammad Ali–George Foreman	Muhammad Ali	Kinshasa, Zaire
1975	Muhammad Ali	Muhammad Ali–Joe Frazier	Muhammad Ali	Manila
1976	George Foreman	George Foreman–Ron Lyle	George Foreman	Las Vegas
1977	Carlos Zarate	Joe Young–George Foreman	Joe Young	San Juan
1978	Muhammad Ali	Leon Spinks–Muhammad Ali	Leon Spinks	Las Vegas
1979	Ray Leonard	Danny Lopez–Mike Ayala	Danny Lopez	San Antonio
1980	Thomas Hearns	Saad Muhammad–Yaqui Lopez	Saad Muhammad	McAfee, NJ
1981	Ray Leonard Salvador Sanchez	Ray Leonard–Tommy Hearns	Ray Leonard	Las Vegas
1982	Larry Holmes	Bobby Chacon–Rafael Limon	Bobby Chacon	Sacramento
1983	Marvin Hagler	Bobby Chacon–Cornelius Boza-Edwards	Bobby Chacon	Las Vegas
1984	Thomas Hearns	Jose Luis Ramirez–Edwin Rosario	Jose Luis Ramirez	San Juan
1985	Donald Curry Marvin Hagler	Marvin Hagler–Tommy Hearns	Marvin Hagler	Las Vegas
1986	Mike Tyson	Stevie Cruz–Barry McGuigan	Stevie Cruz	Las Vegas
1987	Evander Holyfield	Ray Leonard–Marvin Hagler	Ray Leonard	Las Vegas
1988	Mike Tyson	Tony Lopez–Rocky Lockridge	Tony Lopez	Inglewood, CA
1989	Pernell Whitaker	Roberto Duran–Iran Barkley	Roberto Duran	Atlantic City
1990	Julio César Chávez	Julio César Chávez–Meldrick Taylor	Julio César Chávez	Las Vegas
1991	James Toney	Robert Quiroga–Kid Akeem Anifowoshe	Robert Quiroga	San Antonio
1992	Riddick Bowe	Riddick Bowe–Evander Holyfield	Riddick Bowe	Las Vegas
1993	Michael Carbajal	Michael Carbajal–Humberto Gonzalez	Michael Carbajal	Las Vegas
1994	Roy Jones	Jorge Castro–John David Jackson	Jorge Castro	Monterrey, Mex.
1995	Oscar De La Hoya	Saman Sor Jaturong–Chiquita Gonzalez	Saman Sor Jaturong	Inglewood, CA
1996	Evander Holyfield	Evander Holyfield–Mike Tyson	Evander Holyfield	Las Vegas
1997	Evander Holyfield	Arturo Gatti–Gabriel Ruelas	Arturo Gatti	Atlantic City
1998	Floyd Mayweather	Ivan Robinson–Arturo Gatti	Ivan Robinson	Atlantic City
1999	Paulie Ayala	Paulie Ayala–Johnny Tapia	Paulie Ayala	Las Vegas
2000	Felix Trinidad	Erik Morales–Marco Antonio Barrera	Erik Morales	Las Vegas
2001	Bernard Hopkins	Micky Ward–Emanuel Burton	Micky Ward	Las Vegas

Ring Magazine Fighter of the Year

Year	Fighter	Fight	Winner	Site
2002	Vernon Forrest	Micky Ward–Arturo Gatti	Micky Ward	Uncasville, CT
2003	James Toney	Micky Ward–Arturo Gatti	Arturo Gatti	Atlantic City
2004	Glen Johnson	Marco Antonio Barrera–Erik Morales	Marco Barrera	Las Vegas

U.S. Olympic Gold Medalists

LIGHT FLYWEIGHT

1984 ....Paul Gonzales

FLYWEIGHT

1904 ....George Finnegan
1920 ....Frank Di Gennara
1024 ....Fidel LaBarba
1952 ....Nathan Brooks
1976 ....Leo Randolph
1984 ....Steve McCrory

BANTAMWEIGHT

1904 ....Oliver Kirk
1988 ....Kennedy McKinney

FEATHERWEIGHT

1904 ....Oliver Kirk
1924 ....John Fields
1984 ....Meldrick Taylor

LIGHTWEIGHT

1904 ....Harry Spanger
1920 ....Samuel Mosberg
1968 ....Ronald W. Harris
1976 ....Howard Davis
1984 ....Pernell Whitaker
1992 ....Oscar De La Hoya

LIGHT WELTERWEIGHT

1952 ....Charles Adkins
1972 ....Ray Seales
1976 ....Ray Leonard
1984 ....Jerry Page

WELTERWEIGHT

1904 ....Albert Young
1932 ....Edward Flynn
1984 ....Mark Breland

LIGHT MIDDLEWEIGHT

1960 ....Wilbert McClure
1984 ....Frank Tate
1996 ....David Reid

MIDDLEWEIGHT

1904 ....Charles Mayer
1932 ....Carmen Bath
1952 ....Floyd Patterson
1960 ....Edward Crook
1976 ....Michael Spinks

LIGHT HEAVYWEIGHT

1920 ....Eddie Eagan
1952 ....Norvel Lee
1956 ....James Boyd
1960 ....Cassius Clay
1976 ....Leon Spinks
1988 ....Andrew Maynard
2004 ....Andre Ward

HEAVYWEIGHT

1984 ....Henry Tillman
1988 ....Ray Mercer

SUPER HEAVYWEIGHT

1904 ....Samuel Berger
1952 ....H. Edward Sanders
1956 ....T. Peter
               Rademacher
1964 ....Joe Frazier
1968 ....George Foreman
1984 ....Tyrell Biggs

THEY SAID IT

Don King, boxing promoter, disatisfied with HBO's marketing of the fight between Felix Trinidad and Ricardo Mayorga, says he's going to start his own boxing channel that will feature live fights and tapes of historic bouts. "This isn't a dream," said King. "It's going to happen. I'm not going to be an indentured servant anymore."

Lineal Heavyweight Champions

Champion	Reign	Age*	Career	W-L-D (KO)	Successful Defenses
John L. Sullivan	1885–92	26	1878–92	38-1-3 (33)	0
James J. Corbett	1892–97	26	1884–03	11-4-2 (7)	1
Bob Fitzsimmons	1897–99	33	1880–16	74-8-3 (67)	0
James J. Jeffries†	1899–05	24	1896–10	18-1-2 (15)	7
Marvin Hart	1905–06	28	1899–10	28-7-4 (19)	0
Tommy Burns	1906–08	24	1900–20	46-5-8 (37)	11
Jack Johnson	1908–15	30	1894–28	77-13-14 (48)	9
Jess Willard	1915–19	33	1911–23	23-6-1 (20)	1
Jack Dempsey	1919–26	24	1914–27	60-6-8 (50)	5
Gene Tunney†	1926–28	29	1915–28	61-1-1 (45)	2
Max Schmeling	1930–32	24	1924–48	56-10-4 (39)	1
Jack Sharkey	1932–33	29	1924–36	38-13-3 (14)	0
Primo Carnera	1933–34	26	1928–37	88-14-0 (69)	2
Max Baer	1934–35	25	1929–41	72-12-0 (53)	0
James J. Braddock	1935–37	29	1926–38	51-26-7 (26)	0
Joe Louis†	1937–49	23	1934–51	68-3-0 (54)	25
Ezzard Charles	1949–51	27	1940–59	96-25-1 (59)	8
Jersey Joe Walcott	1951–52	37	1930–53	53-18-1 (33)	1
Rocky Marciano†	1952–56	29	1947–56	49-0-0 (43)	6
Floyd Patterson	1956–59	21	1952–72	55-8-1 (40)	4
Ingemar Johansson	1959–60	26	1952–63	26-2-0 (17)	0
Floyd Patterson	1960–62	25	1952–72	55-8-1 (40)	2
Sonny Liston	1962–64	30	1953–70	50-4-0 (39)	1
Muhammad Ali	1964–71	22	1960–81	56-5-0 (37)	9
Joe Frazier	1971–73	27	1965–81	32-4-1 (27)	2
George Foreman	1973–74	24	1969–97	76-5-0 (68)	2
Muhammad Ali	1974–78	32	1960–81	56-5-0 (37)	10
Leon Spinks	1978	24	1977–95	26-17-3 (14)	0
Muhammad Ali†	1978–79	36	1960–81	56-5-0 (37)	0
Larry Holmes	1980–85	29	1973–	69-6-0 (44)	20
Michael Spinks	1985–88	29	1977–88	32-1-0 (21)	3
Mike Tyson	1988–90	21	1985–	49-4-0 (43)	2
Buster Douglas	1990	29	1981–99	38-6-1 (25)	0
Evander Holyfield	1990–92	28	1984–	38-5-2 (26)	3
Riddick Bowe	1992–93	25	1989–96	40-1-0 (32)	2
Evander Holyfield	1993–94	31	1984–	38-5-2 (26)	0
Michael Moorer	1994	26	1988–97	39-2-0 (31)	0
George Foreman	1994–97	45	1969–97	76-5-0 (68)	3
Shannon Briggs	1997–98	25	1992–00	32-3-1 (25)	0
Lennox Lewis	1998–01	32	1989–2004	40-2-1 (31)	5
Hasim Rahman	2001	28	1994–	35-4-0 (29)	0
Lennox Lewis†	2001–04	36	1989–2004	41-2-1 (32)	2
Chris Byrd	2002–	35	1993–	38-2-1 (20)	3
John Ruiz	2001–03—	31	1992–	38-5-1 (28)	2
Roy Jones, Jr.	2003	34	1989–	49-3-0 (38)	0
John Ruiz	2003—	33	1992–	41-6-1 (28)	2
Vitali Klitschko	2004–	34	1996–	34-2-0 (33)	1

*Age when boxer won world championship.
† Boxer retired or relinquished world title.

Horse Racing

2005 Preakness and Belmont winner Afleet Alex

Stretch Drive

Although Giacomo scored the biggest upset, favorite Afleet Alex ran the most dazzling races

BY STEPHEN CANNELLA

CONFIDENCE COMES EASY IN those warm, pre-summer days before the Kentucky Derby, when the roses are in bloom and hope springs eternal for betting favorites and hopeless longshots alike. It's particularly tempting to croon when your colt has been tabbed as thoroughbred racing's next superhorse, as Bellamy Road was early in 2005. In April, the towering three-year-old, the pride of New York Yankees chieftain George Steinbrenner's stable, blew away the field with a 17 1/2-length victory at the Wood Memorial. While racing fans buzzed, Bellamy Road's handlers drooled. "We're not just thinking about the Kentucky Derby," Edward Sexton, the manager of Steinbrenner's farm in Ocala, Fla., said a few days before the Run for the Roses. "We're thinking about the Triple Crown."

The racing gods have spent the last quarter century puncturing such hubris, however, choosing instead to elevate overlooked horses from obscurity to the winner's circle. Even the most atheistic horseman might admit that divine intervention was the only explanation for why 50-1 longshot Giacomo, not favorite Bellamy Road or any of the other elite horses in one of the deepest Derby fields in memory, ran to glory at Churchill Downs. And what else could have lifted Afleet Alex from his knees after a potentially tragic stumble in the Preakness and guided him to victory? The

talented but undersized colt followed that miraculous finish with a resounding win in the Belmont Stakes. So in the end, it was one tantalizing length, the margin by which Giacomo bested him in the Derby, that separated Afleet Alex from the Triple Crown. Yes, the racing gods can be cruel indeed.

Railbirds must now wonder if their sport will ever again produce a transcendant champion. It was the 27th consecutive year the Triple Crown went unclaimed, the longest drought since Sir Barton hit the first Derby/Preakness/Belmont trifecta in 1919. (Affirmed was the last to do it, in 1978.) With each passing year, the anticipation of another winner grows more fervent. The pressure on favorites like Bellamy Road—who, for the record, finished seventh in the Derby and sat out the rest of the Triple Crown series with a leg injury—weighs more heavily.

Not that there haven't been close calls; in each of the last five Triple Crown seasons a horse has made it two-thirds of the way to glory. No one could have predicted that, on the second Sunday in May, Giacomo would bid to continue that trend. The colt entered the Kentucky Derby with just one win in seven lifetime starts and a 0-3 record in 2005. In the pre-race rush, he was ignored by bettors and media alike, for good reason. The 2005 Derby was the province of celebrity trainers like Nick Zito, who had four quality horses in the field in addition to

50–1 longshot Giacomo (l.) won the 131st Kentucky Derby.

favorite Bellamy Road, and Todd Pletcher, the 2004 Eclipse Award winner as the year's best trainer. By contrast, Giacomo was handled by 59-year-old John Shirreffs, a respected but unremarkable horseman who had been training since 1978. "I never expected to be here," said Shirreffs after Giacomo's win. "Just getting to Kentucky was such a thrill."

Jerry Moss, Giacomo's owner, had an even lower profile in horse circles. From 1962 to '90 Moss and legendary trumpeter Herb Alpert ran A&M Records, presiding over an all-star collection of acts ranging from the Carpenters to Janet Jackson to the Police. In retirement Moss dabbled in the thoroughbred game, and in 2002 he named a newly-dropped colt Giacomo, after the son of former Police frontman Sting. Giacomo ran well as a two-year-old, and despite a poor performance early in 2005 Moss made him his first-ever Derby starter. Something about the horse just felt right to the old music man with an ear for hits. "I don't mind when people don't believe in me," he said before the Derby. "We think Giacomo is going to run the race of his life."

Critics will say that Giacomo didn't win the Derby as much as the rest of the field lost it. Led by the speedy Spanish Chestnut, the field got off to a blistering pace, dashing the first three quarters of a mile in 1:09.59, the second-fastest six-furlong split ever in the Derby. While Bellamy Road and several other horses kept speed, jockey Mike Smith held Giacomo back. With a half mile to go he was 18th—and in perfect position to climb when that fevered pace took its inevitable toll on the rest of the field. After the turn for home, Smith guided Giacomo to a clear lane on the outside, and from there he made a sensational run past a string of

BILL FRAKES

more celebrated—and more fatigued—horses. Before a stunned crowd of 156,435, Giacomo crossed the line half a length ahead of 72-1 shot Closing Argument and a full length past Afleet Alex. At 50-1, he was the longest-paying Derby winner in 92 years. It was a sweet victory for the 39-year-old Smith, who had finished second in the Derby twice before. "You start to get older, and you wonder if you're ever going to get one," he said.

Giacomo's unlikely Triple Crown dreams faded with a respectable third-place finish at Pimlico Race Course in Baltimore two weeks later, but a record Preakness crowd of 115,318 did get to witness one of the most terrifying and spectacular moments in racing history. Afleet Alex, the second betting choice at the Derby, entered as a 3-1 favorite, but as he came off the final turn he trailed 13-1 long shot Scrappy T. Ramon Dominguez, Scrappy T's jockey, could feel Afleet Alex steaming up behind him over his right shoulder so, in a desperate request for speed, he tapped his whip on his mount's left side.

Scrappy T overreacted to the whip, however, and veered to the right—into the path of the speeding Afleet Alex. The horses clipped heels, and for a horrifying moment

Afleet Alex (c.) won the 2005 Preakness Stakes after an incredible recovery.

from modest roots in Philadelphia. Like Funny Cide, he was owned by a conglomerate of five regular guys who found themselves crashing the sport of kings. In 2004, Chuck Zacney, the owner of a medical billing firm, started the partnership and the Philadelphians pooled $100,000, good money for men of middle class means, but a pittance for the ritzy standards of thoroughbred racing. Their first purchase, for the bargain price of $75,000, was Afleet Alex.

Afleet Alex seemed certain to go down. His knees hit the dirt and his nose dropped to within a foot of the track. Jockey Jeremy Rose, at the mercy of gravity and his horse, desperately grabbed hold of Afleet Alex's black mane. "I was scared, and I hang on real good when I'm scared," Rose said. "And Alex, he's so athletic I think he could do a backflip if you asked him to."

A somersault might have been less shocking than his mount's actual response. As the crowd gasped, Afleet Alex popped back up, regained his footing, and blazed past Scrappy T, cruising to a 4 3/4-length win. It was as spine-tingling a moment as most fans will ever see on a racetrack, and perhaps the most improbable victory ever by a pre-race favorite.

Afleet Alex's Preakness triumph torpedoed Triple Crown talk for another year, but it won him a permanent spot in racing lore and validated his reputation as an elite horse. He confirmed that at the Belmont Stakes, where he passed eight horses on the final turn and galloped to an easy seven-length victory. (Giacomo finished seventh.) Interestingly, Afleet Alex's biography combined many elements of the backstories of Funny Cide and Smarty Jones, the horses who preceded him in 2003 and 2004, respectively, as Triple Crown near misses.

Like Smarty Jones, Afleet Alex came

The owners weren't the only beneficiaries of that investment. Zacney and his partners donated a portion of their winnings to Alex's Lemonade Stand, a Philadelphia-based cancer charity named after Alex Scott, an eight-year-old girl who had succumbed to a lifelong battle with neuroblastoma in 2004. "I'm incredibly excited," Alex's mother, Liz Scott, said after Afleet Alex's Preakness win. "And later on, I'm sure I'm going to cry."

After the Belmont, Zacney and friends said they would run Afleet Alex again in 2006, and racing fans salivated at the prospect of a Breeders Cup showdown between Afleet Alex and Ghostzapper, the reigning Horse of the Year. It didn't happen. Ghostzapper, a popular five-year-old and the 2004 Breeders Cup champion, was retired two days after the Belmont with a hairline fracture in his right leg. Afleet Alex had injury problems of his own, undergoing surgery in July to repair an ankle fracture.

In August, Derby favorite Bellamy Road returned after a three-month layoff, finishing second to Flower Alley in the Travers at Saratoga. The race raised hopes that in the Breeders Cup he might fulfill the awesome promise he displayed before the Triple Crown. As for the Triple Crown itself? Expectant race fans would have to wait at least another year.

FOR THE RECORD·2003–2004

THOROUGHBRED RACING

The Triple Crown

131st Kentucky Derby

May 7, 2004. Grade I, 3-year-olds; 10th race, Churchill Downs, Louisville. All 126 lbs. Distance: 1¼ miles. Purse: $2,000,000 guaranteed. Track: Fast. Off: 6:11 p.m. Winner: Giacomo (By Holy Bull out of Set Them Free by stop the Music); Times: 0:22.88, 0:45.38, 1:09.59, 1:35.88, 2:02.75. Won: Driving. Breeder: Mr. & Mr.s J. Moss.

Horse	Finish-PP	Margin	Jockey/Trainer
Giacomo	1–10	½	M. Smith/J. Shirreffs
Closing Argument	2–18	½	C. Velasquez/K. McLaughlin
Afleet Alex	3–12	2½	J. Rose/Tim Ritchey
Don't Get Mad	4–17	2¾	T. Baze/Ronald Ellis
Buzzards Bay	5–20	5½	M. Guidry/Jeff Mullins
Wilko	6–14	no	Corey Nakatani/Craig Dollase
Bellamy Road	7–16	¾	J. Castellano/Nick Zito
Andromeda's Hero	8–2	no	R. Bejarano/Nick Zito
Flower Alley	9–7	head	J. Chavez/Todd Pletcher
High Fly	10–11	nk	Jerry Bailey/Nick Zito
Greeley's Galaxy	11–9	2¼	Kent Desormeaux/Warren Stute
Coin Silver	12–5	1¼	P. Valenzuela/Todd Pletcher
Greater Good	13–8	¾	John McKee/Robert Holthus
Noble Causeway	14–4	2½	Gary Stevens/Nick Zito
Sun King	15–3	4	Edgar Prado/Nick Zito
Spanish Chestnut	16–13	7	J. Bravo/P. Biacone
Sort It Out	17–1	2½	B. Blanc/B. Baffert
Going Wild	18–19	3½	J. Valdivia/Wayne Lukas

130th Preakness Stakes

May 21, 2004. Grade I, 3-year-olds; 12th race, Pimlico Race Course, Baltimore. All 126 lbs. Distance: 1³⁄₁₆ miles; Stakes value: $1,000,000. Track: Fast. Off: 6:21 p.m. Winner: AfleetAlex (By Northern Afleet out of Maggy Hawk by Hawkster); Times: 0:2317, 0:46.07, 1:10.72, 1:36.04, 1:55.04. Won: Driving. Breeder: John Martin Silvertand

Horse	Finish-PP	Margin	Jockey/Trainer
Afleet Alex	1-12	4¾	J. Rose/Tim Ritchey
Scrappy T	2–5	5	Ramon Dominguez/Robert Bailes
Giacomo	3–13	1	M. Smith/J. Shirreffs
Sun King	4–10	1	R. Bejarano/Nick Zito
High Limit	5–11	6¾	Edgar Prado/Robert Frankel
Noble Causeway	6–3	1¼	Gary Stevens/Nick Zito
Greeley's Galaxy	7–4	1	David Flores/Warren Stute
Malibu Moonshine	8–1	6	S. Hamilton/K. Leatherbury
Closing Argument	9–7	2¼	C. Velasquez/K. McLaughlin
High Fly	10–2	5½—	Jerry Bailey/Nick Zito

137th Belmont Stakes

June 11, 2004. Grade I, 3-year-olds; 11th race, Belmont Park, Elmont, NY. All 126 lbs. Distance: 1½ miles. Stakes value: $1,000,000. Track: Fast. Off: 6:48 p.m. Winner: AfleetAlex (By Northern Afleet out of Maggy Hawk by Hawkster); Times: 0:24.47, 48.62, 1:12.92, 1:38.05, 2:04.25, 2:28.75. Won: Driving. Breeder: John Martin Silvertand.

Horse	Finish-PP	Margin	Jockey/Trainer
Afleet Alex	1–9	7	J. Rose/Tim Ritchey
Andromeda's Hero	2–7	6¾	R. Bejarano/Nick Zito
Nolan's Cat	3–1	2¼	N. Arroyo/Dale Romans
Indy Storm	4–10	1	Edgar Prado/Nick Zito
A. P. Arrow	5–3	nk	Jerry Bailey/Wayne Lukas
Chekhov	6–11	½	Gary Stevens/Patrick Biancone
Giacomo	7–5	head	M. Smith/J. Shirreffs
Southern Africa	8–4	4¼	J. Court/M. Puhich
Watchmon	9–6	12	J. Castellano/P. Reynolds

Major Stakes Races

Late 2004

Date	Race	Track	Distance	Winner	Jockey/Trainer	Purse ($)
Sept 6	Pennsylvania Derby	Philadelphia	1⅛ miles	Love of Money	R. Albarado Jr./ R. Dutrow	750,000
Sept 19	Atto Mile S	Woodbine	1 mile	Soaring Free	T. Kabel/ M. Frostad	1,000,000
Sept 25	Super Derby XXIV	Louisiana Downs	1⅛ miles	Fantasticat	G. Melancon/ B. Barnett	500,000
Oct 2	Jockey Club Gold Cup	Belmont Park	1¼ miles	FunnyCide	Jose Santos/ B. Tagg	1,000,000
Oct 2	Hirsch Turf Classic Invitational	Belmont Park	1½ miles	Kitten's Joy	John Velasquez/ D. Romans	750,000
Oct 2	Vosburgh Stakes	Belmont Park	6 furlongs	Pic Central	Victor Espinoza/ P. Lobo	490,000
Oct 2	Flower Bowl Invitational	Belmont	1¼ miles	Riskaverse	C. Velasquez/ P. Kelley	750,000
Oct 2	Yellow Ribbon S	Santa Anita	1¼ miles	Light Jig	Rene Douglas/ R. Frankel	411,800
Oct 2	Hawthorne Gold Cup	Hawthorne	1¼ miles	Freefour--internet	G. Kuntzweiler/ M. Maker	750,000
Oct 2	Goodwood B.C.	Santa Anita	1⅛ miles	Lundy's Liability	David Flores/ R. Frankel	480,000
Oct 2	Indiana B.C. Oaks	Hoosier Park	1 1/16 miles	Day--dreaming	John Velasquez/ C. McGaughey	406,300
Oct 3	Indiana Derby	Hoosier Park	1 1/16 miles	Brass Hat	W. Martinez/ W Bradley	511,300
Oct 8	Darley Alcibiades S	Keeneland	1 1/16 miles	Runway Model	R. Bejarano B. Flint	400,000
Oct 8	Meadowlands B. Cup	Meadowlands	1⅛ miles	Balto Star	J. Velasquez/ T. Peltcher	500,000
Oct 9	Champagne S.	Belmont Park	1 1/16 miles	Proud Accolade	John Velasquez/ T. Pletcher	500,000
Oct 9	Lane's End B. Futurity	Keenland	1 1/16 miles	Consolidator	R. Bejarano/ D.W. Lukas	500,000
Oct 9	Beldame S.	Belmont Park	1⅛ miles	Sightseek	J. Castellano/ R. Frankel	735,000
Oct 9	Frizette	Belmont Park	1 1/16 miles	Balleto	C. Nakatani/ T. Albertrani	500,000
Oct 9	Shaswell Turf Mile	Keenland	1 mile	Nothing to Lose	R. Albarado/ R. Frankel	600,000
OOct 10	Overbrook Spinster S	Keeneland	1⅛ miles	Azeri	Pat Day/ D.W. Lukas	500,000
Oct 10	Winstart Galaxy S	Keeneland	1 3/16 miles	Stay Forever	E. Castro/ M. Wolfson	500,000
Oct 16	Queen Elizabeth II Challenge Cup	Keenland	1½ miles	Ticker Tape	K. Desormeaux/ J. Cassidy	500,000
Oct 25	Pattison Canadian Internattional	WOX	1⅛ miles	Sulamani	L. Dettori/ S. bin Surror	1,500,000
Oct 25	E.P. Taylor S	Woodbine	1¼ miles	Commer--cante	J. Velasquez/ R. Frankel	750,000
Oct 30	Breeders Cup Classic Stakes	Lone Star Park	1¼ mile	Ghost--zapper	J. Castellano/ R. Frankel	3,668,000
Oct 30	Breeders Cup Turf Stakes	Lone Star Park	1½ mile	Better Talk Now	R. Dominguez/ H.G. Motion	1,834,000
Oct 30	Breeders Cup Distaff	Lone Star Park	1⅛ mile	Ashado	J Velazquez/ T. Pletcher	1,834,000
Oct 30	Breeders Cup Mile Stakes	Lone Star Park	1 mile	Singletary	David Flores/ D. Chatlos	$1,680,000
Oct 30	Breeders Cup Juvenile Stakes	Lone Star Park	1 1/16 miles	Wilko	L. Dettori/ J. Noseda	1,375,500
Oct 30	Breeders Cup Juvenile Fillies	Lone Star Park	1 1/16 miles	Sweet Catomine	C. Nakatani/ J. Canani	917,000
Oct 30	Breeders Cup Filly & Mare	Lone Star Park	1⅜ miles	Ouija Board	/K. Fallon E. Dunlop	1, 292,970
Oct 30	Breeders Cup Sprint Stakes	Lone Star Park	6 furlongs	Speightstow	nJohn Velasquez/ T. Pletcher	1,060,000
Nov 26	Clark Handicap	Churchill Downs	1⅛ miles	Saint Liam	Edgar Prado/ R. Dutrow	558,000

Major Stakes Races *(Cont.)*

2004 (through August 22)

Date	Race	Track	Distance	Winner	Jockey/Trainer	Purse ($)
Jan 29	Ocala Sunshine Million C	Gulfstream	1⅛ miles	Music Toujours	J. Sadler/ Jorge Chavez	1,000,000
Jan 29	Sunshine Millions Turf	Santa Anita	1⅛ miles	Star Over the Bay	M. Mitchell/ T Baze	500,000
Jan 29	Sunshine Millions Distaff	Gulfstream	1¹⁄₁₆ miles	Sweet Lips	R. Frankel Rene Douglas	500,000
Jan 29	Sunshine Milions Sprint	Gulfstream	6 furlongs	Red Warrior	J. Garcia/ G. Gomez	500,000
Jan 29	Cloverlead Fm F&S T.S.	Gulfstream	1⅛ miles	Valentine Dancer	C.A. Lewis/ John Court	500,000
Feb 2	Donn Handicap	Gulfstream	1⅛ miles	Saint Liam Image	R. Dutrow Jr./ Edgar Prado	500,000
Mar 5	Santa Anita Handicap	Santa Anita	1¼ miles	Rock Hard Ten	R. Mandella/ Gary Stevens	1,000,000
Mar 12	Louisiana Derby	Fair Grounds	1¹⁄₁₆ miles	High Limit	Robert Frankel/ R. Dominguez	600,000
Mar 12	New Orleans Handicap	Fair Grounds	1⅛ miles	Badge of Silver	Robert Frankel/ Jerry Bailey	500,000
Mar 21	Mervin Muniz Handicap	Fair Grounds Park	1⅛ miles	Rapid Proof	H. Wiggins/ B. Hernandez	500,000
Mar 26	Dubai World Cup	Nad al Sheba	200 m	Roses in May	D. Romans/ J. Velasquez	6,000,000
Mar 26	Dubai Duty Free	Nad al Sheba	1⅛ miles	Elvstroem	T. Basil/ N. Rawiller	2,000,000
Mar 26	Dubai Golden Shaheen	Nad al Sheba	1200 m	Saratoga County	G. Weaver/ J. Castellano	2,000,000
Mar 26	UAE Derby	Nad al Sheba	1800 m	Blues and Royals	S. bin Suroor/ K. McEvoy	2,000,000
Mar 26	Lane's End Stakes	Turfway Park	1⅛ miles	Flower Alley	Todd Pletcher/ J. Chavez	500,000
Apr 2	Florida Derby	Gulfstream	1⅛ miles	High Fly	N. Zito/ Jerry Bailey	1,000,000
Apr 2	Winstar Derby	Sunland Park	1⅛ miles	Thor's Echo	D. O'Neill/ C. Nakatani	500,000
Apr 9	Wood Memorial	Aqueduct	1⅛ miles	Bellamy Road	N. Zito/ J. Castellano	750,000
Apr 9	Santa Anita Derby	Santa Anita	1⅛ miles	Buzzard's/ Bay	J. Mullins/ M Guidry	750,000
Apr 9	Ashland Stakes	Keeneland	1¹⁄₁₆ miles	Sis City	R. Dutrow/ Edgar Prado	500,000
Apr 9	Apple Blossom Handicap	Oaklawn	1¹⁄₁₆ miles	Dream of Summer	J. Garcia/ P. Valenzuela	500,000
Apr 9	Illinois Derby Classic	Hawthorne	1⅛ miles	Greeley's Galaxy	G. Stute/ K. Desormeaux	500,000
Apr 9	Oaklawn Handicap	Oaklawm	1⅛ miles	Grand Reward	D.W. Lucas/ J. McKee	490,000
Apr 9	Toyota Blue Grass	Keeneland	1⅛ miles	Bandini Jones	T. Pletcher/ J. Velasquez	750,000
Apr 16	Arkansas Derby	Belmont Park	1⅛ miles	Afleet Alex	T. Ritchey/ Jeremy Rose	1,000,000
May 6	Kentucky Oaks	Churchill Downs	1⅛ miles	Summerly	S. Asmussen/ Jerry Bailey	554,400
May 7	Kentucky Derby	Churchill Downs	1¼ miles	Giacomo	J. Shirreffs/ Nick Zito	2,399,600
May 7	Woodford Reserve Classic	Churchill Downs	1⅛ miles	America Alive	N. Howard/ R. Albarado	470,400
May 20	Pimlico Special	Pimlico	1⅛ miles	Eddington	M. Hennig/ Eibar Coa	500,000
May 21	Preakness Stakes	Pimlico	1³⁄₁₆ miles	Afleet Alex	T. Ritchey/ J. Rose	1,000,000
May 30	Metropolitan Handicap	Belmont Park	1 mile	Ghostzapper	J. Castellano/ R. Frankel	750,000
May 30	Shoemaker B.C. Mile	Hollywood Park	1mile	Castledale	Rene Douglas/ J. Mullins	369,000
June 11	Belmont Stakes	Afleet Alex	1½ miles	Afleet Alex	J. Rose/ T. Ritchey	1,000,000

Major Stakes Races (Cont.)

2004 (through August 22) (Cont.)

Date	Race	Track	Distance	Winner	Jockey/Trainer	Purse ($)
June 18...	Stephen Foster	Churchill Downs	1⅛ miles	Saint Liam	Edgar Prado/ R. Frankel	828,000
June 26	Irish Derby	Curragh	1½ miless	Hurricane Run	Kieren Fallon/ A. Fabre	1,252,100
June 26...	Queen's Plate Stakes	Woodbine	1¼ miles	Wild Desert	P. Valenzuela/ R. Frankel	812,700
July 2......	Suburban Handicap	Belmont Park	1¼ miles	Offlee Wind Joy	Edgar Prado/ J. Rodriguez	500,000
July 2......	United Nations Stakes	Monmouth Park	1⅜ miles	Better Talk Now	R. Dominguez/ G. Motion	750,000
July 3......	American Oaks	Hollywood	1¼ miles	Cesario	Y. Fukunaga K.Sumii/	750,000
July 9......	Hollywood Gold Cup	Hollywood	1¼ miles	Lava Man	P. Valenzuela/ D. O'Neill	750,000
July 10....	Princess Rooney Handicap	Calder	6 furlongs	Madcap Escapade	Jerry Bailey/ F. Brothers	500,000
July 10....	Smile Sprint Handicap	Calder	6 furlongs	Woke Up Dreamin	M. Smith/ B. Baffert	500,000
July 16....	Delaware Oaks	Delaware Park	1 1/16 miles	R. Lady Joy	L. Lezcano/ K. Ziadie	500,300
July 16....	Virginia Derby	Colonial Downs	1 3/16 miles	English Channel	J. Velasquez/ T. Pletcher	750,000
July 17....	Delaware Handicap	Delaware Park	1¼ miles	Island Sand	Jerry Bailey/ L. Jones	1,001,800
July 23....	Coaching Club American Oaks	Belmont Park	1¼ miles	Smuggler	Edgar Prado/ C. McGaughey	500,000
July 30....	Diana Stakes	Saratoga	1⅛ miles	Sand Springs	J. Velasquez/ W. Mott	500,000
Aug 6 750,000	Whitney Handicap	Saratoga	1⅛ miles	Commentator	N. Zito	G. Stevens/
Aug 7	Haskell Handicap	Monmouth	1⅛ miles	Roman Ruler	J. Bailey/ B. Baffert	1,015,000
Aug 7	Arlington Million	Arlington	1¼ miles	Powerscourt	K. Fallon/ A. O'Brien	1,000,000
Aug 13	Beverly D. Stakes	Arlington	1 3/16 miles	Angara	G. Stevens/ P. Biancone	750,000
Aug 13	Secretariat Stakes	Arlington	1¼ miles	Gun Salute	C.H. Velasquez/ W. Mott	400,000
Aug 13	Sword Dancer Invitational	Saratoga	1½ miles	King's Drama	L. Chavez/ R. Frankel	500,000
Aug 14	Virginia Derby	Mountaineer Park	1⅛ miles	Real Dandy	M. Guidry/ S. Asmussen	750,000
Aug 20	Alabama Stakes	Saratoga	1¼ miles	Sweet Symphony	Jerry Bailey W. Mott	750,000
Aug 21	Pacific Classic	Del Mar	1¼ miles	Borrego	G. Gomez/ B. Greely	1,000,000
Aug 27	Travers Stakes	Saratoga	1¼ miles	Flower Alley	J. Velasquez/ T. Pletcher	1,000,000
Sept 5	Pennsylvania Derby	Philadelphia	1⅛ miles	Sun King	R. Bejarano/ N. Zito	750,000
Sept 24	Hawthorne Gold Cup	Hawthorne	1¼ miles	Super Frolic	V. Espinoza/ V. Cerin	750,000

2004 Statistical Leaders

Horses

Horse	Starts	1st	2nd	3rd	Purses ($)	Horse	Starts	1st	2nd	3rd	Purses ($)
Smarty Jones	7	6	1	0	7,563,535	Southern Image	4	3	1	0	1,612,150
Ghostzapper	4	4	0	0	2,590,000	Better Talk Now	8	2	2	0	1,407,000
Ashado	8	5	2	1	2,259,640	Pleasantly Perfect	4	2	1	1	1,240,000
Roses in May	6	5	1	0	1,723,277	Birdstone	6	3	0	0	1,236,600
Kitten's Joy	8	6	2	0	1,625,796	Singletary	6	3	2	1	1,192,910

Jockeys

Jockey	Mounts	1st	2nd	3rd	Purses ($)	Win Pct	$ Pct*
John Velasquez	1327	335	222	181	22,248,661	.25	.56
Edgar Prado	1445	281	249	204	18,342,106	.19	.51
Victor Espinoza	1336	240	244	185	15,933,757	18	50
Stewart Elliott	1363	262	211	177	14,533,061	.19	.48
Jerry Bailey	641	148	113	99	14,503,844	.23	.56
Javier Castellano	1283	212	204	197	13,038,943	.17	.48
Corey Nakatani	1080	220	194	146	12,466,557	.20	.52
Rafael Bejarano	1922	455	355	280	12,210,087	.24	.57
Ramon Dominguez	1353	383	231	216	11,507,889	.28	.61
Cornelio Velasquez	1593	240	260	241	11,098,689	.15	.47

*Percentage in the Money (1st, 2nd, and 3rd).

Trainers

Trainer	Starts	1st	2nd	3rd	Purses ($)	Win Pct	$ Pct*
Todd Pletcher	948	240	154	125	17,511,923	.25	.55
Robert Frankel	491	135	94	60	15,605,911	.27	.59
Steven Asmussen	2293	555	361	348	14,003,202	.24	.55
John Servis	284	68	38	38	8,922,686	.24	.51
Bob Baffert	562	105	75	74	7,627,913	.19	.45
Richard Dutrow, Jr.	603	166	117	87	7,576,986	.28	.61
Scott Lake	1688	374	297	251	7,420,036	.22	.55
Dale Romans	580	109	87	87	7,081,653	.19	.49
Doug O'Neill	938	170	132	124	7,004,827	.18	.45
Nicholas Zito	452	86	68	52	6,967,792	.19	.46

*Percentage in the Money (1st, 2nd, and 3rd).

Owners

Owner	Starts	1st	2nd	3rd	Purses ($)
Michael Gill	2885	487	432	345	10,835,561
Someday Farm	12	7	2	0	7,584,305
Stronach Stables	507	109	81	74	7,193,867
Kenneth & Sarah Ramsey	361	84	63	42	5,855,964
Sam-Son Farms	260	47	36	38	4,830,939
Eugene & Laura Melnyk	453	93	68	63	4,447,689
Juddmonte Farms, Inc.	113	35	20	7	3,454,794
Gary Tanaka	136	21	22	16	3,112,187
Robert & Beverly Lewis	263	50	41	35	3,069,130
Robert Bone	353	113	66	49	3,015,251

HARNESS RACING

Major Stakes Races

Late 2004

Date	Race	Location	Winner	Driver/Trainer	Purse ($)
Nov 23	BC Two-year-old Filly Trot	Woodbine	Flirtin Miss	John Campbell/ Jim Takter	600,000
Nov 23	BC Two-year-old Filly Pace	Woodbine	Restive Hanover	Andy Miller/ Ervin Miller	610,000
Nov 23	BC Two-year-old Colt Trot	Woodbine	Ken Warkentin	David Miller/ Jim Takter	550,000

Late 2004 (cont)

Date	Race	Location	Winner	Driver/Trainer	Purse ($)
Nov 23	BC Two-year-old Colt Pace	Woodbine	Village Jolt	Ron Pierce/ Ed Hart	700,000
Nov 23	BC Three-year-old Filly Trot	Woodbine	Housethatruthbuilt	Brian Sears/ Trond Smedshammer	530,000
Nov 23	BC Three-year-old Filly Pace	Woodbine	Rainbow Blue	Brian Sears/ George Teague	650,000
Nov 23	BC Three-year-old Colt Trot	Woodbine	Yankee Slide	Brian Sears/ Steve Elliott	530,000
Nov 23	BC Three-year-old Colt Pace	Meadowlands	Western Terror	Ron Pierce/ Brett Pelling	580,000
Dec 4	Goldsmith Maid	Meadowlands	Aeronautess	J. Ingrassia/ F. Ingrassia	211,800
Dec 4	Governor's Cup	Meadowlands	Syncro's Z Tam	P. Lachance/ P. Lachance	237,400
Oct 17	Valley Victory	Meadowlands	Diesel Don	John Campbell/ Chuck Sylvester	228,600
Dec 4	Three Diamonds	Meadowlands	Restive Hanover	Andy Miller/ Erv Miller	200,000

2005 (through September 23)

Date	Race	Location	Winner	Driver/Trainer	Purse ($)
May 28	New Jersey Classic	Meadowlands	Rocknroll Hanover	Brian Sears/ Brett Pelling	500,000
June 18	North America Cup	Woodbine	Rocknroll Hanover	Brian Sears/ Brett Pelling	1,500,000
July 15	Stanley Dancer	Meadowlands	Classic Photo	Ron Pierce/ Ervin Miller	350,000
July 16	Meadowlands Pace	Meadowlands	Rocknroll Hanover	Brian Sears/ Brett Pelling	1,000,000
July 30	Classic Series Trot	Meadowlands	Mr. Muscleman	Ron Pierce/ Noel Dailey	250,000
July 30	Classic Series Pace	Meadowlands	Boulder Creek	Brian Sears/ Mark Silva	250,000
July 30	Classic Series Oaks	Meadowlands	Peaceful Way	Trevor Ritchie/ David Tingley	250,000
July 30	Classic Series Distaff	Meadowlands	Burning Point	Ron Pierce/ Steve Elliott	250,000
Aug 4	Peter Haughton	Meadowlands	Keystone Savage	Brian Sears/ Dane Snyder	460,000
Aug 4	Merrie Annabelle	Meadowlands	Miss Wisconsin	Mike Lachance/ Ron Gurfein	390,000
Aug 5	Woodrow Wilson	Meadowlands	Western Ace	Ron Pierce/ George Teague	375,000
Aug 5	Sweetheart	Meadowlands	Lonesome Day	David Miller/ Ross Croghan	330,000
Aug 6	Hambletonian	Meadowlands	Vivid Photo	Roger Hammer/ Roger Hammer	1,500,000
Sept 22	Little Brown Jug	Delaware, OH	P-Forty-Seven	Dave Palone/ Kelly O'Donnell	570,000

Major Races

The Hambletonian

Raced at The Meadowlands, East Rutherford, NJ, on August 6, 2005

Horse	Driver	PP	¼	½	¾	Stretch	Finish
Vivid Photo	R. Hammer	6	7	7o	6oo	4-1¼	1-2 3/4
Classic Photol	R. Pierce	5	6	6o	4oo	3½	2-2 3/4
Muscle Memory	C. Manzi	1	1	2	2	2½	3-5 1/4
Strong Yankee	B. Sears	3	3	1	1	1½	4-6 1/4
Self Professed	E. Ledford	7	2	3	5	5-3	5-6 3/4
Mr. DreamOm	D. Miller	10	10	10	10	10-7	6-12
Gettindownanddirty	P. MacDonell	9	9	9	9	9-6½	7DH-13
Muscle Bound	M. Lachance	8	8	8o	8o	8-5½	7DH-13
Northern Ensign	J. Campbell	4	5	5o	3o	7-4¾	10P923¾
Racino	G Brennan	2	4	4	7	6x-3½	X9XP10-20

Times: 0:28.2, 0:57.2, 1:26.3, 1:54.1

The Little Brown Jug

Raced at the Delaware County Fairgrounds, in Delaware, OH, on September 22, 2005

Horse	Driver	PP	¼	½	¾	Stretch	Finish
P-Forty-Seven	Palone	1	3	4	3	2-1	1-3/4
Village Jolt	Pierce	2	4	3o	1oo	1-1	2-3/4
Rocknroll Hanover	Sears5	1	1	2	2	3-2	3-3 1/4
Up Front Jerry	Moiseyev	9	6	6	5	4-4	4-4 1/4
Cam's Fool	Campbell	4	7	70	70	5-4 ½	5-6
Up Front Tornado	Ledford	3	5	50	400	6-6½	6-11
Climb The Ladder	Silverman	8	9	8	8	7-8½	7-13
Roddy's Bags Again	Ouellette	7	20	20	60	8-10½	8-18
Dreamfair Kogel	Zeron	6	8	9	9	9-DIS	9-DIS

Time-27.1; 56.4; 1:25.0; 1:54.1

2004 Statistical Leaders

2004 Leading Moneywinners by Age, Sex and Gait

Division	Horse	Starts	1st	2nd	3rd	Earnings ($)
2-Year-Old Pacing Colts	Village Jolt	10	6	2	0	918,577
2-Year-Old Pacing Fillies	Restive Hanover	14	9	3	0	590,607
3-Year-Old Pacing Colts	Times Are A Changin	22	10	6	3	1,175,574
3-Year-Old Pacing Fillies	Rainbow Blue	21	20	0	0	1,195,010
Older Pacing Horses	Royal Mattjesty	29	8	8	5	850,186
Older Pacing Mares	Bunny Hole	17	4	5	2	484,819
2-Year-Old Trotting Colts	Ken Warkentin	9	8	0	1	643,240
2-Year-Old Trotting Fillies	Solveig	12	6	3	0	593,304
3-Year-Old Trotting Colts	Windsong's Legacy	12	9	2	1	1,713,806
3-Year-Old Trotting Fillies	House That Ruth Built	15	11	3	1	848,109
Older Trotting Horses	Mr. Muscleman	14	7	5	0	593,323
Older Trotting Mares	Stroke Play	9	7	1	0	410,936

Drivers

Driver	Earnings ($)	Driver	Earnings ($)
Ronald Pierce	12,327,863	John Campbell	7,240,312
Brian Sears	10,028,306	Luc Ouellette	7,185,998
David Miller	8,493,176	Michel Lachance	6,696,056
Catello Manzi	7,693,362	Chris Christoforou	6,022,677
George Brennan	7,521,453	Paul MacDonell	5,865,450

Not So Sweet Finish

Three year-old filly Sweet Catomine, who had been an expected contender for the 2005 Kentucky Derby, retired suddenly a week before the race. Sweet Catomine had been a favorite in the Santa Anita Derby a month prior, but had come in second. Owner Marty Wygod later revealed that she had bled during he final prerace workout and he had smuggled her out of her barn and placed her in a hyperbaric chamaber at a clinic 140 miles away. Hollywood Park stewards cleared Wygod of any wrongdoing, but he was subsequently sued by a bettor. "I hate ambulance chasers," Wygolds said/.

FOR THE RECORD · Year by Year

THOROUGHBRED RACING

Kentucky Derby

Run at Churchill Downs, Louisville, KY, on the first Saturday in May.

Year	Winner (Margin)	Jockey	Second	Third	Time
1875	Aristides (1)	Oliver Lewis	Volcano	Verdigris	2:37¾
1876	Vagrant (2)	Bobby Swim	Creedmoor	Harry Hill	2:38¼
1877	Baden-Baden (2)	William Walker	Leonard	King William	2:38
1878	Day Star (2)	Jimmie Carter	Himyar	Leveler	2:37¼
1879	Lord Murphy (1)	Charlie Shauer	Falsetto	Strathmore	2:37
1880	Fonso (1)	George Lewis	Kimball	Bancroft	2:37½
1881	Hindoo (4)	Jimmy McLaughin	Lelex	Alfambra	2:40
1882	Apollo (½)	Babe Hurd	Runnymede	Bengal	2:40¼
1883	Leonatus (3)	Billy Donohue	Drake Carter	Lord Raglan	2:43
1884	Buchanan (2)	Isaac Murphy	Loftin	Audrain	2:40¼
1885	Joe Cotton (Neck)	Erskine Henderson	Bersan	Ten Booker	2:37¼
1886	Ben Ali (½)	Paul Duffy	Blue Wing	Free Knight	2:36½
1887	Montrose (2)	Isaac Lewis	Jim Gore	Jacobin	2:39¼
1888	MacBeth II (1)	George Covington	Gallifet	White	2:38¼
1889	Spokane (Nose)	Thomas Kiley	Proctor Knott	Once Again	2:34½
1890	Riley (2)	Isaac Murphy	Bill Letcher	Robespierre	2:45
1891	Kingman (1)	Isaac Murphy	Balgowan	High Tariff	2:52¼
1892	Azra (Nose)	Alonzo Clayton	Huron	Phil Dwyer	2:41½
1893	Lookout (5)	Eddie Kunze	Plutus	Boundless	2:39¼
1894	Chant (2)	Frank Goodale	Pearl Song	Sigurd	2:41
1895	Halma (3)	Soup Perkins	Basso	Laureate	2:37½
1896	Ben Brush (Nose)	Willie Simms	Ben Eder	Semper Ego	2:07¼
1897	Typhoon II (Head)	Buttons Garner	Ornament	Dr. Catlett	2:12½
1898	Plaudit (Neck)	Willie Simms	Lieber Karl	Isabey	2:09
1899	Manuel (2)	Fred Taral	Corsini	Mazo	2:12
1900	Lieut. Gibson (4)	Jimmy Boland	Florizar	Thrive	2:06¼
1901	His Eminence (2)	Jimmy Winkfield	Sannazarro	Driscoll	2:07¾
1902	Alan-a-Dale (Nose)	Jimmy Winkfield	Inventor	The Rival	2:08¾
1903	Judge Himes (¾)	Hal Booker	Early	Bourbon	2:09
1904	Elwood (½)	Frankie Prior	Ed Tierney	Brancas	2:08½
1905	Agile (3)	Jack Martin	Ram's Horn	Layson	2:10¾
1906	Sir Huon (2)	Roscoe Troxler	Lady Navarre	James Reddick	2:08⅕
1907	Pink Star (2)	Andy Minder	Zal	Ovelando	2:12⅗
1908	Stone Street (1)	Arthur Pickens	Sir Cleges	Dunvegan	2:15⅕
1909	Wintergreen (4)	Vincent Powers	Miami	Dr. Barkley	2:08⅕
1910	Donau (½)	Fred Herbert	Joe Morris	Fighting Bob	2:06⅖
1911	Meridian (¾)	George Archibald	Governor Gray	Colston	2:05
1912	Worth (Neck)	Carroll H. Schilling	Duval	Flamma	2:09⅖
1913	Donerail (½)	Roscoe Goose	Ten Point	Gowell	2:04⅘
1914	Old Rosebud (8)	John McCabe	Hodge	Bronzewing	2:03⅖
1915	Regret (2)	Joe Notter	Pebbles	Sharpshooter	2:05⅖
1916	George Smith (Neck)	Johnny Loftus	Star Hawk	Franklin	2:04
1917	Omar Khayyam (2)	Charles Borel	Ticket	Midway	2:04⅗
1918	Exterminator (1)	William Knapp	Escoba	Viva America	2:10⅘
1919	Sir Barton (5)	Johnny Loftus	Billy Kelly	Under Fire	2:09⅘
1920	Paul Jones (Head)	Ted Rice	Upset	On Watch	2:09
1921	Behave Yourself (Head)	Charles Thompson	Black Servant	Prudery	2:04⅕
1922	Morvich (½)	Albert Johnson	Bet Mosie	John Finn	2:04⅗
1923	Zev (1½)	Earl Sande	Martingale	Vigil	2:05⅖
1924	Black Gold (½)	John Mooney	Chilhowee	Beau Butler	2:05⅕
1925	Flying Ebony (1½)	Earl Sande	Captain Hal	Son of John	2:07⅗
1926	Bubbling Over (5)	Albert Johnson	Bagenbaggage	Rock Man	2:03⅗
1927	Whiskery (Head)	Linus McAtee	Osmond	Jock	2:06
1928	Reigh Count (3)	Chick Lang	Misstep	Toro	2:10⅖
1929	Clyde Van Dusen (2)	Linus McAtee	Naishapur	Panchio	2:10⅘
1930	Gallant Fox (2)	Earl Sande	Gallant Knight	Ned O.	2:07⅗
1931	Twenty Grand (4)	Charles Kurtsinger	Sweep All	Mate	2:01⅘
1932	Burgoo King (5)	Eugene James	Economic	Stepenfetchit	2:05⅕
1933	Brokers Tip (Nose)	Don Meade	Head Play	Charley O.	2:06⅘
1934	Cavalcade (2½)	Mack Garner	Discovery	Agrarian	2:04
1935	Omaha (1½)	Willie Saunders	Roman Soldier	Whiskolo	2:05
1936	Bold Venture (Head)	Ira Hanford	Brevity	Indian Broom	2:03⅗

Kentucky Derby *(Cont.)*

Year	Winner (Margin)	Jockey	Second	Third	Time
1937	War Admiral (1¾)	Charles Kurtsinger	Pompoon	Reaping Reward	2:03⅕
1938	Lawrin (1)	Eddie Arcaro	Dauber	Can't Wait	2:04⅘
1939	Johnstown (8)	James Stout	Challedon	Heather Broom	2:03⅗
1940	Gallahadion (1½)	Carroll Bierman	Bimelech	Dit	2:05
1941	Whirlaway (8)	Eddie Arcaro	Staretor	Market Wise	2:01⅖
1942	Shut Out (2½)	Wayne Wright	Alsab	Valdina Orphan	2:04⅖
1943	Count Fleet (3)	John Longden	Blue Swords	Slide Rule	2:04
1944	Pensive (4½)	Conn McCreary	Broadcloth	Stir Up	2:04⅕
1945	Hoop Jr. (6)	Eddie Arcaro	Pot o' Luck	Darby Dieppe	2:07
1946	Assault (8)	Warren Mehrtens	Spy Song	Hampden	2:06⅗
1947	Jet Pilot (Head)	Eric Guerin	Phalanx	Faultless	2:06⅘
1948	Citation (3½)	Eddie Arcaro	Coaltown	My Request	2:05⅖
1949	Ponder (3)	Steve Brooks	Capot	Palestinian	2:04⅕
1950	Middleground (1¼)	William Boland	Hill Prince	Mr. Trouble	2:01⅗
1951	Count Turf (4)	Conn McCreary	Royal Mustang	Ruhe	2:02⅗
1952	Hill Gail (2)	Eddie Arcaro	Sub Fleet	Blue Man	2:01⅗
1953	Dark Star (Head)	Hank Moreno	Native Dancer	Invigorator	2:02
1954	Determine (1½)	Ray York	Hasty Road	Hasseyampa	2:03
1955	Swaps (1½)	Bill Shoemaker	Nashua	Summer Tan	2:01⅘
1956	Needles (¾)	Dave Erb	Fabius	Come On Red	2:03⅖
1957	Iron Liege (Nose)	Bill Hartack	Gallant Man	Round Table	2:02⅕
1958	Tim Tam (½)	Ismael Valenzuela	Lincoln Road	Noureddin	2:05
1959	Tomy Lee (Nose)	Bill Shoemaker	Sword Dancer	First Landing	2:02⅕
1960	Venetian Way (3½)	Bill Hartack	Bally Ache	Victoria Park	2:02⅖
1961	Carry Back (¾)	John Sellers	Crozier	Bass Clef	2:04
1962	Decidedly (2¼)	Bill Hartack	Roman Line	Ridan	2:00⅖
1963	Chateaugay (1¼)	Braulio Baeza	Never Bend	Candy Spots	2:01⅘
1964	Northern Dancer (Neck)	Bill Hartack	Hill Rise	The Scoundrel	2:00
1965	Lucky Debonair (Neck)	Bill Shoemaker	Dapper Dan	Tom Rolfe	2:01⅕
1966	Kauai King (½)	Don Brumfield	Advocator	Blue Skyer	2:02
1967	Proud Clarion (1)	Bobby Ussery	Barbs Delight	Damascus	2:00⅗
1968	Forward Pass (Disq.)	Ismael Valenzuela	Francie's Hat	T.V. Commercial	2:02⅕
1969	Majestic Prince (Neck)	Bill Hartack	Arts and Letters	Dike	2:01⅘
1970	Dust Commander (5)	Mike Manganello	My Dad George	High Echelon	2:03⅖
1971	Canonero II (3¾)	Gustavo Avila	Jim French	Bold Reason	2:03⅕
1972	Riva Ridge (3¼)	Ron Turcotte	No Le Hace	Hold Your Peace	2:01⅘
1973	Secretariat (2½)	Ron Turcotte	Sham	Our Native	1:59⅖
1974	Cannonade (2¼)	Angel Cordero Jr.	Hudson County	Agitate	2:04
1975	Foolish Pleasure (1¾)	Jacinto Vasquez	Avatar	Diabolo	2:02
1976	Bold Forbes (1)	Angel Cordero Jr.	Honest Pleasure	Elocutionist	2:01⅗
1977	Seattle Slew (1¾)	Jean Cruguet	Run Dusty Run	Sanhedrin	2:02⅕
1978	Affirmed (1½)	Steve Cauthen	Alydar	Believe It	2:01⅕
1979	Spectacular Bid (2¾)	Ronald J. Franklin	General Assembly	Golden Act	2:02⅖
1980	Genuine Risk (1)	Jacinto Vasquez	Rumbo	Jaklin Klugman	2:02
1981	Pleasant Colony (¾)	Jorge Velasquez	Woodchopper	Partez	2:02
1982	Gato Del Sol (2½)	Eddie Delahoussaye	Laser Light	Reinvested	2:02⅕
1983	Sunny's Halo (2)	Eddie Delahoussaye	Desert Wine	Caveat	2:02⅕
1984	Swale (3¼)	Laffit Pincay Jr.	Coax Me Chad	At the Threshold	2:02⅖
1985	Spend A Buck (5)	Angel Cordero Jr.	Stephan's Odyssey	Chief's Crown	2:00⅕
1986	Ferdinand (2¼)	Bill Shoemaker	Bold Arrangement	Broad Brush	2:02⅘
1987	Alysheba (¾)	Chris McCarron	Bet Twice	Avies Copy	2:03⅖
1988	Winning Colors (Neck)	Gary Stevens	Forty Niner	Risen Star	2:02⅕
1989	Sunday Silence (2½)	Pat Valenzuela	Easy Goer	Awe Inspiring	2:05
1990	Unbridled (3½)	Craig Perret	Summer Squall	Pleasant Tap	2:02
1991	Strike the Gold (1¾)	Chris Antley	Best Pal	Mane Minister	2:03
1992	Lil E. Tee (1)	Pat Day	Casual Lies	Dance Floor	2:03
1993	Sea Hero (2½)	Jerry Bailey	Prairie Bayou	Wild Gale	2:02⅖
1994	Go for Gin (2½)	Chris McCarron	Strodes Creek	Blumin Affair	2:03⅗
1995	Thunder Gulch (2¼)	Gary Stevens	Tejano Run	Timber Country	2:01⅕
1996	Grindstone (Nose)	Jerry Bailey	Cavonnier	Prince of Thieves	2:01
1997	Silver Charm (Head)	Gary Stevens	Captain Bodgit	Free House	2:02⅖
1998	Real Quiet (½)	Kent Desormeaux	Victory Gallop	Indian Charlie	2:02⅒
1999	Charismatic (Neck)	Chris Antley	Menifee	Cat Thief	2:03⅕
2000	Fusaichi Pegasus (1½)	Kent Desormeaux	Aptitude	Impeachment	2:01.12
2001	Monarchos (4¾)	Jorge Chavez	Invisible Ink	Congaree	1:59.97
2002	War Emblem (4)	Victor Espinoza	Proud Citizen	Perfect Drift	2:01.13
2003	Funny Cide (1¾)	Jose Santos	Empire Maker	Peace Rules	2:01.19
2004	Smarty Jones (2¾)	Stewart Elliott	Lion Heart	Imperialism	2:04.06
2005	Giacomo	Mike Smith	Closing Argument	Afleet Alex	2:02.75

Note: Distance: 1½ miles (1875–95), 1¼ miles (1896–present).

Preakness

Run at Pimlico Race Course, Baltimore, Md., two weeks after the Kentucky Derby.

Year	Winner (Margin)	Jockey	Second	Third	Time
1873	Survivor (10)	G. Barbee	John Boulger	Artist	2:43
1874	Culpepper (¾)	W. Donohue	King Amadeus	Scratch	2:56½
1875	Tom Ochiltree (2)	L. Hughes	Viator	Bay Final	2:43½
1876	Shirley (4)	G. Barbee	Rappahannock	Algerine	2:44¾
1877	Cloverbrook (4)	C. Holloway	Bombast	Lucifer	2:45½
1878	Duke of Magenta (6)	C. Holloway	Bayard	Albert	2:41¾
1879	Harold (3)	L. Hughes	Jericho	Rochester	2:40½
1880	Grenada (¾)	L. Hughes	Oden	Emily F.	2:40½
1881	Saunterer (½)	T. Costello	Compensation	Baltic	2:40½
1882	Vanguard (Neck)	T. Costello	Heck	Col Watson	2:44½
1883*	Jacobus (4)	G. Barbee	Parnell		2:42½
1884*	Knight of Ellerslie (2)	S. Fisher	Welcher		2:39½
1885	Tecumseh (2)	Jim McLaughlin	Wickham	John C.	2:49
1886	The Bard (3)	S. Fisher	Eurus	Elkwood	2:45
1887	Dunboyne (1)	W. Donohue	Mahoney	Raymond	2:39½
1888	Refund (3)	F. Littlefield	Judge Murray	Glendale	2:49
1889*	Buddhist (8)	W. Anderson	Japhet	*	2:17½
1890*	Montague (3)	W. Martin	Philosophy	Barrister	2:36¾
1894	Assignee (3)	Fred Taral	Potentate	Ed Kearney	1:49¼
1895	Belmar (1)	Fred Taral	April Fool	Sue Kittie	1:50½
1896	Margrave (1)	H. Griffin	Hamilton II	Intermission	1:51
1897	Paul Kauvar (1½)	C. Thorpe	Elkins	On Deck	1:51¼
1898	Sly Fox (2)	C. W. Simms	The Huguenot	Nuto	1:49⅗
1899	Half Time (1)	R. Clawson	Filigrane	Lackland	1:47
1900	Hindus (Head)	H. Spencer	Sarmation	Ten Candles	1:48⅖
1901	The Parader (2)	F. Landry	Sadie S.	Dr. Barlow	1:47⅕
1902	Old England (Nose)	L. Jackson	Major Daingerfield	Namtor	1:45⅘
1903	Flocarline (½)	W. Gannon	Mackey Dwyer	Rightful	1:44⅘
1904	Bryn Mawr (1)	E. Hildebrand	Wotan	Dolly Spanker	1:44⅕
1905	Cairngorm (Head)	W. Davis	Kiamesha	Coy Maid	1:45⅘
1906	Whimsical (4)	Walter Miller	Content	Larabie	1:45
1907	Don Enrique (1)	G. Mountain	Ethon	Zambesi	1:45⅖
1908	Royal Tourist (4)	E. Dugan	Live Wire	Robert Cooper	1:46⅖
1909	Effendi (1)	Willie Doyle	Fashion Plate	Hilltop	1:39⅘
1910	Layminster (½)	R. Estep	Dalhousie	Sager	1:40⅗
1911	Watervale (1)	E. Dugan	Zeus	The Nigger	1:51
1912	Colonel Holloway (5)	C. Turner	Bwana Tumbo	Tipsand	1:56⅗
1913	Buskin (Neck)	J. Butwell	Kleburne	Barnegat	1:53⅖
1914	Holiday (¾)	A. Schuttinger	Brave Cunarder	Defendum	1:53⅘
1915	Rhine Maiden (1½)	Douglas Hoffman	Half Rock	Runes	1:58
1916	Damrosch (1½)	Linus McAtee	Greenwood	Achievement	1:54⅘
1917	Kalitan (2)	E. Haynes	Al M. Dick	Kentucky Boy	1:54⅖
1918*	War Cloud (¾)	Johnny Loftus	Sunny Slope	Lanius	1:53⅗
1918*	Jack Hare, Jr (2)	C. Peak	The Porter	Kate Bright	1:53⅖
1919	Sir Barton (4)	Johnny Loftus	Eternal	Sweep On	1:53
1920	Man o' War (1½)	Clarence Kummer	Upset	Wildair	1:51⅗
1921	Broomspun (¾)	F. Coltiletti	Polly Ann	Jeg	1:54⅕
1922	Pillory (Head)	L. Morris	Hea	June Grass	1:51⅗
1923	Vigil (1¼)	B. Marinelli	General Thatcher	Rialto	1:53⅗
1924	Nellie Morse (1½)	J. Merimee	Transmute	Mad Play	1:57⅕
1925	Coventry (4)	Clarence Kummer	Backbone	Almadel	1:59
1926	Display (Head)	J. Maiben	Blondin	Mars	1:59⅘
1927	Bostonian (½)	A. Abel	Sir Harry	Whiskery	2:01⅗
1928	Victorian (Nose)	Sonny Workman	Toro	Solace	2:00⅕
1929	Dr. Freeland (1)	Louis Schaefer	Minotaur	African	2:01⅗
1930	Gallant Fox (¾)	Earl Sande	Crack Brigade	Snowflake	2:00⅗
1931	Mate (1½)	G. Ellis	Twenty Grand	Ladder	1:59
1932	Burgoo King (Head)	E. James	Tick On	Boatswain	1:59⅘
1933	Head Play (4)	Charles Kurtsinger	Ladysman	Utopian	2:02
1934	High Quest (Nose)	R. Jones	Cavalcade	Discovery	1:58⅕
1935	Omaha (6)	Willie Saunders	Firethorn	Psychic Bid	1:58⅖
1936	Bold Venture (Nose)	George Woolf	Granville	Jean Bart	1:59
1937	War Admiral (Head)	Charles Kurtsinger	Pompoon	Flying Scot	1:58⅖
1938	Dauber (7)	M. Peters	Cravat	Menow	1:59⅘
1939	Challedon (1¼)	George Seabo	Gilded Knight	Volitant	1:59⅘
1940	Bimelech (3)	F. A. Smith	Mioland	Gallahadion	1:58⅗
1941	Whirlaway (5½)	Eddie Arcaro	King Cole	Our Boots	1:58⅘

Preakness (Cont.)

Year	Winner (Margin)	Jockey	Second	Third	Time
1942	Alsab (1)	B. James	Requested Sun Again	(dead heat for second)	1:57
1943	Count Fleet (8)	Johnny Longden	Blue Swords	Vincentive	1:57⅖
1944	Pensive (¾)	Conn McCreary	Platter	Stir Up	1:59⅕
1945	Polynesian (2½)	W. D. Wright	Hoop Jr.	Darby Dieppe	1:58⅘
1946	Assault (Neck)	Warren Mehrtens	Lord Boswell	Hampden	2:01⅖
1947	Faultless (1¼)	Doug Dodson	On Trust	Phalanx	1:59
1948	Citation (5½)	Eddie Arcaro	Vulcan's Forge	Boyard	2:02⅖
1949	Capot (Head)	Ted Atkinson	Palestinian	Noble Impulse	1:56
1950	Hill Prince (5)	Eddie Arcaro	Middleground	Dooley	1:59⅕
1951	Bold (7)	Eddie Arcaro	Counterpoint	Alerted	1:56⅖
1952	Blue Man (3½)	Conn McCreary	Jampol	One Count	1:57⅖
1953	Native Dancer (Neck)	Eric Guerin	Jamie K.	Royal Bay Gem	1:57⅘
1954	Hasty Road (Neck)	Johnny Adams	Correlation	Hasseyampa	1:57⅖
1955	Nashua (1)	Eddie Arcaro	Saratoga	Traffic Judge	1:54⅗
1956	Fabius (¾)	Bill Hartack	Needles	No Regrets	1:58⅖
1957	Bold Ruler (2)	Eddie Arcaro	Iron Liege	Inside Tract	1:56⅕
1958	Tim Tam (1½)	I. Valenzuela	Lincoln Road	Gone Fishin'	1:57⅕
1959	Royal Orbit (4)	William Harmatz	Sword Dancer	Dunce	1:57
1960	Bally Ache (4)	Bobby Ussery	Victoria Park	Celtic Ash	1:57⅗
1961	Carry Back (¾)	Johnny Sellers	Globemaster	Crozier	1:57⅗
1962	Greek Money (Nose)	John Rotz	Ridan	Roman Line	1:56⅕
1963	Candy Spots (3½)	Bill Shoemaker	Chateaugay	Never Bend	1:56⅕
1964	Northern Dancer (2¼)	Bill Hartack	The Scoundrel	Hill Rise	1:56⅘
1965	Tom Rolfe (Neck)	Ron Turcotte	Dapper Dan	Hail to All	1:56⅕
1966	Kauai King (1¾)	Don Brumfield	Stupendous	Amberoid	1:55⅖
1967	Damascus (2¼)	Bill Shoemaker	In Reality	Proud Clarion	1:55⅕
1968	Forward Pass (6)	I. Valenzuela	Out of the Way	Nodouble	1:56⅘
1969	Majestic Prince (Head)	Bill Hartack	Arts and Letters	Jay Ray	1:55⅗
1970	Personality (Neck)	Eddie Belmonte	My Dad George	Silent Screen	1:56⅕
1971	Canonero II (1½)	Gustavo Avila	Eastern Fleet	Jim French	1:54
1972	Bee Bee Bee (1¼)	Eldon Nelson	No Le Hace	Key to the Mint	1:55⅗
1973	Secretariat (2½)	Ron Turcotte	Sham	Our Native	1:54⅖
1974	Little Current (7)	Miguel Rivera	Neapolitan Way	Cannonade	1:54⅗
1975	Master Derby (1)	Darrel McHargue	Foolish Pleasure	Diabolo	1:56⅖
1976	Elocutionist (3)	John Lively	Play the Red	Bold Forbes	1:55
1977	Seattle Slew (1½)	Jean Cruguet	Iron Constitution	Run Dusty Run	1:54⅖
1978	Affirmed (Neck)	Steve Cauthen	Alydar	Believe It	1:54⅖
1979	Spectacular Bid (5½)	Ron Franklin	Golden Act	Screen King	1:54⅕
1980	Codex (4¾)	Angel Cordero Jr.	Genuine Risk	Colonel Moran	1:54⅕
1981	Pleasant Colony (1)	Jorge Velasquez	Bold Ego	Paristo	1:54⅗
1982	Aloma's Ruler (½)	Jack Kaenel	Linkage	Cut Away	1:55⅖
1983	Deputed Testamony (2¾)	Donald Miller Jr.	Desert Wine	High Honors	1:55⅖
1984	Gate Dancer (1½)	Angel Cordero Jr.	Play On	Fight Over	1:53⅗
1985	Tank's Prospect (Head)	Pat Day	Chief's Crown	Eternal Prince	1:53⅖
1986	Snow Chief (4)	Alex Solis	Ferdinand	Broad Brush	1:54⅘
1987	Alysheba (½)	Chris McCarron	Bet Twice	Cryptoclearance	1:55⅘
1988	Risen Star (1¼)	E. Delahoussaye	Brian's Time	Winning Colors	1:56⅕
1989	Sunday Silence (Nose)	Pat Valenzuela	Easy Goer	Rock Point	1:53⅘
1990	Summer Squall (2¼)	Pat Day	Unbridled	Mister Frisky	1:53⅗
1991	Hansel (Head)	Jerry Bailey	Corporate Report	Mane Minister	1:54
1992	Pine Bluff (¾)	Chris McCarron	Alydeed	Casual Lies	1:55⅗
1993	Prairie Bayou (½)	Mike Smith	Cherokee Run	El Bakan	1:56⅗
1994	Tabasco Cat (¾)	Pat Day	Go For Gin	Concern	1:56⅖
1995	Timber Country (½)	Pat Day	Oliver's Twist	Thunder Gulch	1:54⅖
1996	Louis Quatorze (3¼)	Pat Day	Skip Away	Editor's Note	1:53⅖
1997	Silver Charm (Head)	Gary Stevens	Free House	Captain Bodgit	1:54⅖
1998	Real Quiet (2¼)	Kent Desormeaux	Victory Gallop	Classic Cat	1:54⅗
1999	Charismatic (1½)	Chris Antley	Menifee	Badge	1:55⅕
2000	Red Bullet (3¾)	Jerry Bailey	Fusaichi Pegasus	Impeachment	1:56.04
2001	Point Given (2¼)	Gary Stevens	A P Valentine	Congaree	1:55.51
2002	War Emblem (¾)	Victor Espinoza	Magic Weisner	Proud Citizen	1:56.36
2003	Funny Cide (9¾)	Jose Santos	Midway Road	Scrimshaw	1:55.61
2004	Smarty Jones (11½)	Stewart Elliott	Rock Hard Ten	Eddington	1:55.59
2005	Afleet Alex	J Rose	Scrappy T	Giacomo	1:55.04

*Preakness was a two-horse race in 1883, '84 and '89. It was not run 1891–1893; and in 1918, it was run in two divisions.

Note: Distance: 1½ miles (1873–88), 1¼ miles (1889), 1½ miles (1890), 1 1/16 miles (1894–1900), 1 mile and 70 yards (1901–1907), 1 1/16 miles (1908), 1 mile (1909–10), 1⅛ miles (1911–24), 1 3/16 miles (1925–present).

Belmont

Run at Belmont Park, Elmont, NY, three weeks after the Preakness Stakes. Held previously at two locations in the Bronx (NY): Jerome Park (1867–1889) and Morris Park (1890–1904).

Year	Winner (Margin)	Jockey	Second	Third	Time
1867	Ruthless (Head)	J. Gilpatrick	De Courcy	Rivoli	3:05
1868	General Duke (2)	R. Swim	Northumberland	Fannie Ludlow	3:02
1869	Fenian (Unknown)	C. Miller	Glenelg	Invercauld	3:04¼
1870	Kingfisher (½)	E. Brown	Foster	Midday	2:59½
1871	Harry Bassett (3)	W. Miller	Stockwood	By-the-Sea	2:56
1872	Joe Daniels (¾)	James Rowe	Meteor	Shylock	2:58¼
1873	Springbok (4)	James Rowe	Count d'Orsay	Strachino	3:01¾
1874	Saxon (Neck)	G. Barbee	Grinstead	Aaron Pennington	2:39½
1875	Calvin (2)	R. Swim	Aristides	Milner	2:40¼
1876	Algerine (Head)	W. Donahue	Fiddlestick	Barricade	2:40½
1877	Cloverbrook (1)	C. Holloway	Loiterer	Baden-Baden	2:46
1878	Duke of Magenta (2)	L. Hughes	Bramble	Sparta	2:43½
1879	Spendthrift (5)	S. Evans	Monitor	Jericho	2:42¾
1880	Grenada (½)	L. Hughes	Ferncliffe	Turenne	2:47
1881	Saunterer (Neck)	T. Costello	Eole	Baltic	2:47
1882	Forester (5)	James McLaughlin	Babcock	Wyoming	2:43
1883	George Kinney (2)	James McLaughlin	Trombone	Renegade	2:42½
1884	Panique (½)	James McLaughlin	Knight of Ellerslie	Himalaya	2:42
1885	Tyrant (3½)	Paul Duffy	St. Augustine	Tecumseh	2:43
1886	Inspector B (1)	James McLaughlin	The Bard	Linden	2:41
1887*	Hanover (28-32)	James McLaughlin	Oneko		2:43½
1888*	Sir Dixon (12)	James McLaughlin	Prince Royal		2:40¼
1889	Eric (Head)	W. Hayward	Diable	Zephyrus	2:47
1890	Burlington (1)	S. Barnes	Devotee	Padishah	2:07¾
1891	Foxford (Neck)	E. Garrison	Montana	Laurestan	2:08¾
1892*	Patron (Unknown)	W. Hayward	Shellbark		2:17
1893	Comanche (Head)	Willie Simms	Dr. Rice	Rainbow	1:53¼
1894	Henry of Navarre (2-4)	Willie Simms	Prig	Assignee	1:56½
1895	Belmar (Head)	Fred Taral	Counter Tenor	Nanki Pooh	2:11½
1896	Hastings (Neck)	H. Griffin	Handspring	Hamilton II	2:24½
1897	Scottish Chieftain (1)	J. Scherrer	On Deck	Octagon	2:23¼
1898	Bowling Brook (8)	P. Littlefield	Previous	Hamburg	2:32
1899	Jean Bereaud (Head)	R. R. Clawson	Half Time	Glengar	2:23
1900	Ildrim (Head)	N. Turner	Petrucio	Missionary	2:21½
1901	Commando (½)	H. Spencer	The Parader	All Green	2:21
1902	Masterman (2)	John Bullmann	Ranald	King Hanover	2:22½
1903	Africander (2)	John Bullmann	Whorler	Red Knight	2:23⅕
1904	Delhi (3½)	George Odom	Graziallo	Rapid Water	2:06⅗
1905	Tanya (1/2)	E. Hildebrand	Blandy	Hot Shot	2:08
1906	Burgomaster (4)	L. Lyne	The Quail	Accountant	2:20
1907	Peter Pan (1)	G. Mountain	Superman	Frank Gill	Unknown
1908	Colin (Head)	Joe Notter	Fair Play	King James	Unknown
1909	Joe Madden (8)	E. Dugan	Wise Mason	Donald MacDonald	2:21⅗
1910*	Sweep (6)	J. Butwell	Duke of Ormonde		2:22
1913	Prince Eugene (½)	Roscoe Troxler	Rock View	Flying Fairy	2:18
1914	Luke McLuke (8)	M. Buxton	Gainer	Charlestonian	2:20
1915	The Finn (4)	G. Byrne	Half Rock	Pebbles	2:18⅖
1916	Friar Rock (3)	E. Haynes	Spur	Churchill	2:22
1917	Hourless (10)	J. Butwell	Skeptic	Wonderful	2:17⅘
1918	Johren (2)	Frank Robinson	War Cloud	Cum Sah	2:20⅖
1919	Sir Barton (5)	Johnny Loftus	Sweep On	Natural Bridge	2:17⅖
1920*	Man o' War (20)	Clarence Kummer	Donnacona		2:14⅕
1921	Grey Lag (3)	Earl Sande	Sporting Blood	Leonardo II	2:16⅘
1922	Pillory (2)	C. H. Miller	Snob II	Hea	2:18⅘
1923	Zev (1½)	Earl Sande	Chickvale	Rialto	2:19
1924	Mad Play (2)	Earl Sande	Mr. Mutt	Modest	2:18⅘
1925	American Flag (8)	Albert Johnson	Dangerous	Swope	2:16⅘
1926	Crusader (1)	Albert Johnson	Espino	Haste	2:32⅕
1927	Chance Shot (1½)	Earl Sande	Bois de Rose	Flambino	2:32⅖
1928	Vito (3)	Clarence Kummer	Genie	Diavolo	2:33⅕
1929	Blue Larkspur (¾)	Mack Garner	African	Jack High	2:32⅘
1930	Gallant Fox (3)	Earl Sande	Whichone	Questionnaire	2:31⅗

Belmont (Cont.)

Year	Winner (Margin)	Jockey	Second	Third	Time
1931	Twenty Grand (10)	Charles Kurtsinger	Sun Meadow	Jamestown	2:29⅗
1932	Faireno (1½)	T. Malley	Osculator	Flag Pole	2:32⅘
1933	Hurryoff (1½)	Mack Garner	Nimbus	Union	2:32⅗
1934	Peace Chance (6)	W. D. Wright	High Quest	Good Goods	2:29⅕
1935	Omaha (1½)	Willie Saunders	Firethorn	Rosemont	2:30⅗
1936	Granville (Nose)	James Stout	Mr. Bones	Hollyrood	2:30
1937	War Admiral (3)	Charles Kurtsinger	Sceneshifter	Vamoose	2:28⅗
1938	Pasteurized (Neck)	James Stout	Dauber	Cravat	2:29⅖
1939	Johnstown (5)	James Stout	Belay	Gilded Knight	2:29⅗
1940	Bimelech (¾)	F. A. Smith	Your Chance	Andy K	2:29⅗
1941	Whirlaway (2½)	Eddie Arcaro	Robert Morris	Yankee Chance	2:31
1942	Shut Out (2)	Eddie Arcaro	Alsab	Lochinvar	2:29⅕
1943	Count Fleet (25)	Johnny Longden	Fairy Manhurst	Deseronto	2:28⅕
1944	Bounding Home (½)	G. L. Smith	Pensive	Bull Dandy	2:32⅕
1945	Pavot (5)	Eddie Arcaro	Wildlife	Jeep	2:30⅕
1946	Assault (3)	Warren Mehrtens	Natchez	Cable	2:30⅘
1947	Phalanx (5)	R. Donoso	Tide Rips	Tailspin	2:29⅖
1948	Citation (8)	Eddie Arcaro	Better Self	Escadru	2:28⅕
1949	Capot (½)	Ted Atkinson	Ponder	Palestinian	2:30⅕
1950	Middleground (1)	William Boland	Lights Up	Mr. Trouble	2:28⅗
1951	Counterpoint (4)	D. Gorman	Battlefield	Battle Morn	2:29
1952	One Count (2½)	Eddie Arcaro	Blue Man	Armageddon	2:30⅕
1953	Native Dancer (Neck)	Eric Guerin	Jamie K.	Royal Bay Gem	2:38⅗
1954	High Gun (Neck)	Eric Guerin	Fisherman	Limelight	2:30⅘
1955	Nashua (9)	Eddie Arcaro	Blazing Count	Portersville	2:29
1956	Needles (Neck)	David Erb	Career Boy	Fabius	2:29⅘
1957	Gallant Man (8)	Bill Shoemaker	Inside Tract	Bold Ruler	2:26⅗
1958	Cavan (6)	Pete Anderson	Tim Tam	Flamingo	2:30⅕
1959	Sword Dancer (¾)	Bill Shoemaker	Bagdad	Royal Orbit	2:28⅖
1960	Celtic Ash (5½)	Bill Hartack	Venetian Way	Disperse	2:29⅗
1961	Sherluck (2¼)	Braulio Baeza	Globemaster	Guadalcanal	2:29⅕
1962	Jaipur (Nose)	Bill Shoemaker	Admiral's Voyage	Crimson Satan	2:28⅘
1963	Chateaugay (2½)	Braulio Baeza	Candy Spots	Choker	2:30⅕
1964	Quadrangle (2)	Manuel Ycaza	Roman Brother	Northern Dancer	2:28⅖
1965	Hail to All (Neck)	John Sellers	Tom Rolfe	First Family	2:28⅖
1966	Amberold (2½)	William Boland	Buffle	Advocator	2:29⅗
1967	Damascus (2½)	Bill Shoemaker	Cool Reception	Gentleman James	2:28⅘
1968	Stage Door Johnny (1¼)	Hellodoro Gustines	Forward Pass	Call Me Prince	2:27⅕
1969	Arts and Letters (5½)	Braulio Baeza	Majestic Prince	Dike	2:28⅘
1970	High Echelon (¾)	John L. Rotz	Needles N Pins	Naskra	2:34
1971	Pass Catcher (¾)	Walter Blum	Jim French	Bold Reason	2:30⅖
1972	Riva Ridge (7)	Ron Turcotte	Ruritania	Cloudy Dawn	2:28
1973	Secretariat (31)	Ron Turcotte	Twice a Prince	My Gallant	2:24
1974	Little Current (7)	Miguel A. Rivera	Jolly Johu	Cannonade	2:29⅕
1975	Avatar (Neck)	Bill Shoemaker	Foolish Pleasure	Master Derby	2:28⅕
1976	Bold Forbes (Neck)	Angel Cordero Jr.	McKenzie Bridge	Great Contractor	2:29
1977	Seattle Slew (4)	Jean Cruguet	Run Dusty Run	Sanhedrin	2:29⅗
1978	Affirmed (Head)	Steve Cauthen	Alydar	Darby Creek Road	2:26⅘
1979	Coastal (3¼)	Ruben Hernandez	Golden Act	Spectacular Bid	2:28⅗
1980	Temperence Hill (2)	Eddie Maple	Genuine Risk	Rockhill Native	2:29⅘
1981	Summing (Neck)	George Martens	Highland Blade	Pleasant Colony	2:29
1982	Conquistador Cielo (14½)	Laffit Pincay, Jr.	Gato Del Sol	Illuminate	2:28⅕
1983	Caveat (3½)	Laffit Pincay Jr.	Slew o'Gold	Barberstown	2:27⅘
1984	Swale (4)	Laffit Pincay Jr.	Pine Circle	Morning Bob	2:27⅕
1985	Creme Fraiche (½)	Eddie Maple	Stephan's Odyssey	Chief's Crown	2:27
1986	Danzig Connection (1¼)	Chris McCarron	Johns Treasure	Ferdinand	2:29⅘
1987	Bet Twice (14)	Craig Perret	Cryptoclearance	Gulch	2:28⅕
1988	Risen Star (14¾)	Eddie Delahoussaye	Kingpost	Brian's Time	2:26⅖
1989	Easy Goer (8)	Pat Day	Sunday Silence	Le Voyageur	2:26
1990	Go and Go (8¼)	Michael Kinane	Thirty Six Red	Baron de Vaux	2:27⅕
1991	Hansel (Head)	Jerry Bailey	Strike the Gold	Mane Minister	2:28
1992	A.P. Indy (¾)	Eddie Delahoussaye	My Memoirs	Pine Bluff	2:26
1993	Colonial Affair (2¼)	Julie Krone	Kissin Kris	Wild Gale	2:29⅘
1994	Tabasco Cat (2)	Pat Day	Go For Gin	Strodes Creek	2:26⅘

Belmont (Cont.)

Year	Winner (Margin)	Jockey	Second	Third	Time
1995	Thunder Gulch (2)	Gary Stevens	Star Standard	Citadeed	2:32
1996	Editor's Note (1)	Rene Douglas	Skip Away	My Flag	2:28⅘
1997	Touch Gold (¾)	Chris McCarron	Silver Charm	Free House	2:28⅘
1998	Victory Gallop (Nose)	Gary Stevens	Real Quiet	Thomas Jo	2:29⅘
1999	Lemon Drop Kid (Head)	Jose Santos	Vision and Verse	Charismatic	2:27⅘
2000	Commendable (1½)	Pat Day	Aptitude	Unshaded	2:31.19
2001	Point Given (12¼)	Gary Stevens	A P Valentine	Monarchos	2:26.56
2002	Sarava (½)	Edgar Prado	Medaglia d'Oro	Sunday Break	2:29.71
2003	Empire Maker (¾)	Jerry Bailey	Ten Most Wanted	Funny Cide	2:28.26
2004	Birdstone (1)	Edgar Prado	Smarty Jones	Royal Assault	2:27.59
2005	Afleet Alex	J Rose	Andromeda's Hero	Nolan's Cat	2:28.75

*Belmont was a two-horse race in 1887, '88, '92, 1910 and '20; and was not held in 1911–1912.

Note: Distance: 1 mile 5 furlongs (1867–89), 1¼ miles (1890–1905), 1⅜ miles (1906–25), 1½ miles (1926–present).

Triple Crown Winners

Year	Horse	Jockey	Owner	Trainer
1919	Sir Barton	John Loftus	J. K. L. Ross	H. G. Bedwell
1930	Gallant Fox	Earle Sande	Belair Stud	James Fitzsimmons
1935	Omaha	William Saunders	Belair Stud	James Fitzsimmons
1937	War Admiral	Charles Kurtsinger	Samuel D. Riddle	George Conway
1941	Whirlaway	Eddie Arcaro	Calumet Farm	Ben Jones
1943	Count Fleet	John Longden	Mrs J. D. Hertz	Don Cameron
1946	Assault	Warren Mehrtens	King Ranch	Max Hirsch
1948	Citation	Eddie Arcaro	Calumet Farm	Jimmy Jones
1973	Secretariat	Ron Turcotte	Meadow Stable	Lucien Laurin
1977	Seattle Slew	Jean Cruguet	Karen L. Taylor	William H. Turner Jr.
1978	Affirmed	Steve Cauthen	Harbor View Farm	Laz Barrera

End of the Day

Thoroughbred racing's all-time leading monet winner, Pat Day, who has amassed a career total of more than $298 million in winning purses arrived at his decision to retire in much the same way he won 8,803 races - he took his time, then he made his move. Day decided to hang up his tack in July 2005 after spending several days alone in a cabin on the Kentucky River. After returning from hip surgery in May, Day ran only a few races and found the thrill of victory diminished. "On the turn for home, most guys break into the clear to make their move, and if you're following them, it can leave you in the clear too," says fellow Hall of Fame jockey Jerry Bailey. "Not Pat. He'd wait so long for a hole that it would only be good for him, not anyone else."

Horse of the Year

Year	Horse	Owner	Trainer	Breeder
1936	Granville	Belair Stud	James Fitzsimmons	Belair Stud
1937	War Admiral	Samuel D. Riddle	George Conway	Mrs. Samuel D. Riddle
1938	Seabiscuit	Charles S. Howard	Tom Smith	Wheatley Stable
1939	Challedon	William L. Brann	Louis J. Schaefer	Branncastle Farm
1940	Challedon	William L. Brann	Louis J. Schaefer	Branncastle Farm
1941	Whirlaway	Calumet Farm	Ben Jones	Calumet Farm
1942	Whirlaway	Calumet Farm	Ben Jones	Calumet Farm
1943	Count Fleet	Mrs. John D. Hertz	Don Cameron	Mrs. John D. Hertz
1944	Twilight Tear	Calumet Farm	Ben Jones	Calumet Farm
1945	Busher	Louis B. Mayer	George Odom	Idle Hour Stock Farm
1946	Assault	King Ranch	Max Hirsch	King Ranch
1947	Armed	Calumet Farm	Jimmy Jones	Calumet Farm
1948	Citation	Calumet Farm	Jimmy Jones	Calumet Farm
1949	Capot	Greentree Stable	John M. Gaver Sr.	Greentree Stable
1950	Hill Prince	C.T. Chenery	Casey Hayes	C.T. Chenery
1951	Counterpoint	C.V. Whitney	Syl Veitch	C.V. Whitney
1952	One Count	Mrs. W. M. Jeffords	O. White	W M. Jeffords
1953	Tom Fool	Greentree Stable	John M. Gaver Sr.	D.A. Headley
1954	Native Dancer	A.G. Vanderbilt	Bill Winfrey	A.G. Vanderbilt
1955	Nashua	Belair Stud	James Fitzsimmons	Belair Stud
1956	Swaps ·	Ellsworth-Galbreath	Mesh Tenney	R. Ellsworth
1957	Bold Ruler	Wheatley Stable	James Fitzsimmons	Wheatley Stable
1958	Round Table	Kerr Stables	Willy Molter	Claiborne Farm
1959	Sword Dancer	Brookmeade Stable	Elliott Burch	Brookmeade Stable
1960	Kelso	Bohemia Stable	C. Hanford	Mrs. R.C. duPont
1961	Kelso	Bohemia Stable	C. Hanford	Mrs. R.C. duPont
1962	Kelso	Bohemia Stable	C. Hanford	Mrs. R.C. duPont
1963	Kelso	Bohemia Stable	C. Hanford	Mrs. R.C. duPont
1964	Kelso	Bohemia Stable	C. Hanford	Mrs. R.C. duPont
1965	Roman Brother	Harbor View Stable	Burley Parke	Ocala Stud
1966	Buckpasser	Ogden Phipps	Eddie Neloy	Ogden Phipps
1967	Damascus	Mrs. E. W. Bancroft	Frank Y. Whiteley Jr.	Mrs. E. W. Bancroft
1968	Dr. Fager	Tartan Stable	John A. Nerud	Tartan Farms
1969	Arts and Letters	Rokeby Stable	Elliott Burch	Paul Mellon
1970	Fort Marcy	Rokeby Stable	Elliott Burch	Paul Mellon
1971	Ack Ack	E.E. Fogelson	Charlie Whittingham	H.F. Guggenheim
1972	Secretariat	Meadow Stable	Lucien Laurin	Meadow Stud
1973	Secretariat	Meadow Stable	Lucien Laurin	Meadow Stud
1974	Forego	Lazy F Ranch	Sherrill W. Ward	Lazy F Ranch
1975	Forego	Lazy F Ranch	Sherrill W. Ward	Lazy F Ranch
1976	Forego	Lazy F Ranch	Frank Y. Whiteley Jr.	Lazy F Ranch
1977	Seattle Slew	Karen L. Taylor	Billy Turner Jr.	B.S. Castleman
1978	Affirmed	Harbor View Farm	Laz Barrera	Harbor View Farm
1979	Affirmed	Harbor View Farm	Laz Barrera	Harbor View Farm
1980	Spectacular Bid	Hawksworth Farm	Bud Delp	Mmes. Gilmore & Jason
1981	John Henry	Dotsam Stable	Ron McAnally and Lefty Nickerson	Golden Chance Farm
1982	Conquistador Cielo	H. de Kwiatkowski	Woody Stephens	L.E. Landoli
1983	All Along	Daniel Wildenstein	P.L. Biancone	Dayton
1984	John Henry	Dotsam Stable	Ron McAnally	Golden Chance Farm
1985	Spend a Buck	Hunter Farm	Cam Gambolati	Irish Hill & R.W. Harper
1986	Lady's Secret	Mr. & Mrs. Eugene Klein	D. Wayne Lukas	R.H. Spreen
1987	Ferdinand	Mrs. H.B. Keck	Charlie Whittingham	H.B. Keck
1988	Alysheba	D. & P. Scharbauer	Jack Van Berg	Preston Madden
1989	Sunday Silence	Gaillard, Hancock, & Whittingham	Charlie Whittingham	Oak Cliff Thoroughbreds
1990	Criminal Type	Calumet Farm	D. Wayne Lukas	Calumet Farm
1991	Black Tie Affair	Jeffrey Sullivan	Ernie Poulos	Stephen D. Peskoff
1992	A.P. Indy	Tomonori Tsurumaki	Neil Drysdale	W.S. Farish & W.S. Kilroy
1993	Kotashaan	La Presle Farm	Richard Mandella	La Presle Farm
1994	Holy Bull	Jimmy Croll	Jimmy Croll	Pelican Stable
1995	Cigar	Allen E. Paulson	William Mott	Allen E. Paulson
1996	Cigar	Allen E. Paulson	William Mott	Allen E. Paulson
1997	Favorite Trick	Joseph LaCombe	William Mott	Mr. & Mrs. M.L. Wood
1998	Skip Away	Carolyn Hine	Hubert Hine	Anna Marie Barnhart
1999	Charismatic	Robert & Beverly Lewis	D. Wayne Lukas	William Farish/Partners

Horse of the Year (Cont.)

Year	Horse	Owner	Trainer	Breeder
2000	Tiznow	Michael Cooper and Cecilia Straub-Rubens	Jay M. Robbins	Cecilia Straub-Rubens
2001	Point Given	The Thoroughbred Corp.	Bob Baffert	The Thoroughbred Corp.
2002	Azeri	Allen Paulson Living Trust	Laura de Seroux	Allen Paulson
2003	Mineshaft	William Farish	Neil Howard	William Farish
2004	Ghostzapper	Frank Stronach	Bobby Frankel	Frank Stronach

Note: From 1936 to 1970, the *Daily Racing Form* annually selected a "Horse of the Year." In 1971 the *Daily Racing Form*, with the Thoroughbred Racing Association and the National Turf Writers Association, jointly created the Eclipse Awards.

Eclipse Award Winners

2-YEAR-OLD COLT	2-YEAR-OLD FILLY	3-YEAR-OLD COLT
1971 Riva Ridge	1971 Numbered Account	1971 Canonero II
1972 Secretariat	1972 La Prevoyante	1972 Key to the Mint
1973 Protagonist	1973 Talking Picture	1973 Secretariat
1974 Foolish Pleasure	1974 Ruffian	1974 Little Currant
1975 Honest Pleasure	1975 Dearly Precious	1975 Wajima
1976 Seattle Slew	1976 Sensational	1976 Bold Forbes
1977 Affirmed	1977 Lakeville Miss	1977 Seattle Slew
1978 Spectacular Bid	1978 Candy Eclair, It's in the Air	1978 Affirmed
1979 Rockhill Native	1979 Smart Angle	1979 Spectacular Bid
1980 Lord Avie	1980 Heavenly Cause	1980 Temperence Hill
1981 Deputy Minister	1981 Before Dawn	1981 Pleasant Colony
1982 Roving Boy	1982 Landaluce	1982 Conquistador Cielo
1983 Devil's Bag	1983 Althea	1983 Slew o' Gold
1984 Chief's Crown	1984 Outstandingly	1984 Swale
1985 Tasso	1985 Family Style	1985 Spend A Buck
1986 Capote	1986 Brave Raj	1986 Snow Chief
1987 Forty Niner	1987 Epitome	1987 Alysheba
1988 Easy Goer	1988 Open Mind	1988 Risen Star
1989 Rhythm	1989 Go for Wand	1989 Sunday Silence
1990 Fly So Free	1990 Meadow Star	1990 Unbridled
1991 Arazi	1991 Pleasant Stage	1991 Hansel
1992 Gilded Time	1992 Eliza	1992 A.P. Indy
1993 Dehere	1993 Phone Chatter	1993 Prairie Bayou
1994 Timber Country	1994 Flanders	1994 Holy Bull
1995 Maria's Mon	1995 Golden Attraction	1995 Thunder Gulch
1996 Boston Harbor	1996 Storm Song	1996 Skip Away
1997 Favorite Trick	1997 Countess Diana	1997 Silver Charm
1998 Answer Lively	1998 Silverbulletday	1998 Real Quiet
1999 Anees	1999 Chilukki	1999 Charismatic
2000 Macho Uno	2000 Caressing	2000 Tiznow
2001 Johannesburg	2001 Tempera	2001 Point Given
2002 Vindication	2002 Storm Flag Flying	2002 War Emblem
2003 Action This Day	2003 Halfbridled	2003 Funny Cide
2004 Declan's Moon	2004 Sweet Catomine	2004 Smarty Jones

CHAMPION TURF HORSE	CHAMPION MALE TURF HORSE (Cont.)	CHAMPION FEMALE TURF HORSE (Cont.)
1971 Run the Gantlet (3)	1991 Tight Spot (4)	1984 Royal Heroine (4)
1972 Cougar II (6)	1992 Sky Classic (5)	1985 Pebbles (4)
1973 Secretariat (3)	1993 Kotashaan (5)	1986 Estrapade (6)
1974 Dahlia (4)	1994 Paradise Creek (5)	1987 Miesque (3)
1975 Snow Knight (4)	1995 Northern Spur (4)	1988 Miesque (4)
1976 Youth (3)	1996 Singspiel (4)	1989 Brown Bess (7)
1977 Johnny D (3)	1997 Chief Bearhart (4)	1990 Laugh and Be Merry (5)
1978 Mac Diarmida (3)	1998 Buck's Boy (5)	1991 Miss Alleged (4)
	1999 Daylami (5)	1992 Flawlessly (4)
CHAMPION MALE TURF HORSE	2000 Kalanisi (4)	1993 Flawlessly (5)
1979 Bowl Game (5)	2001 Fantastic Light (5)	1994 Hatoof (5)
1980 John Henry (5)	2002 High Chaparral (3)	1995 Possibly Perfect (5)
1981 John Henry (6)	2003 High Chaparral (4)	1996 Wandesta (5)
1982 Perrault (4)	2004 Kitten's Joy	1997 Ryafan (3)
1983 John Henry (8)		1998 Fiji (4)
1984 John Henry (9)	**CHAMPION FEMALE TURF HORSE**	1999 Soaring Softly (4)
1985 Cozzene (4)	1979 Trillion (5)	2000 Perfect Sting (4)
1986 Manila (3)	1980 Just a Game II (4)	2001 Banks Hill (3)
1987 Theatrical (5)	1981 De La Rose (3)	2002 Golden Apples (4)
1988 Sunshine Forever (3)	1982 April Run (4)	2003 Islington (4)
1989 Steinlen (6)	1983 All Along (4)	2004 Ouija Board
1990 Itsallgreektome (3)		

Eclipse Award Winners (Cont.)

3-YEAR-OLD FILLY

1971	Turkish Trousers
1972	Susan's Girl
1973	Desert Vixen
1974	Chris Evert
1975	Ruffian
1976	Revidere
1977	Our Mims
1978	Tempest Queen
1979	Davona Dale
1980	Genuine Risk
1981	Wayward Lass
1982	Christmas Past
1983	Heartlight No. One
1984	Life's Magic
1985	Mom's Command
1986	Tiffany Lass
1987	Sacahuista
1988	Winning Colors
1989	Open Mind
1990	Go for Wand
1991	Dance Smartly
1992	Saratoga Dew
1993	Hollywood Wildcat
1994	Heavenly Prize
1995	Serena's Song
1996	Yank's Music
1997	Ajina
1998	Banshee Breeze
1999	Silverbulletday
2000	Surfside
2001	Xtra Heat
2002	Farda Amiga
2003	Bird Town
2004	Ashado

OLDER COLT, HORSE OR GELDING

1971	Ack Ack (5)
1972	Autobiography (4)
1973	Riva Ridge (4)
1974	Forego (4)
1975	Forego (5)
1976	Forego (6)
1977	Forego (7)
1978	Seattle Slew (4)
1979	Affirmed (4)
1980	Spectacular Bid (4)
1981	John Henry (6)
1982	Lemhi Gold (4)
1983	Bates Motel (4)
1984	Slew o'Gold (4)
1985	Vanlandingham (4)
1986	Turkoman (4)
1987	Ferdinand (4)
1988	Alysheba (4)
1989	Blushing John (4)
1990	Criminal Type (5)
1991	Black Tie Affair (5)
1992	Pleasant Tap (5)
1993	Bertrando (4)
1994	The Wicked North (5)
1995	Cigar (5)
1996	Cigar (6)
1997	Skip Away (4)
1998	Skip Away (5)
1999	Victory Gallop (4)
2000	Lemon Drop Kid (4)
2001	Tiznow (4)

Note: Number in parentheses is horse's age.

OLDER COLT, HORSE OR GELDING

2002	Left Bank (5)
2003	Mineshaft (4)
2004	Ghostzapper (4)

OLDER FILLY OR MARE

1971	Shuvee (5)
1972	Typecast (6)
1973	Susan's Girl (4)
1974	Desert Vixen (4)
1975	Susan's Girl (6)
1976	Proud Delta (4)
1977	Cascapedia (4)
1978	Late Bloomer (4)
1979	Waya (5)
1980	Glorious Song (4)
1981	Relaxing (5)
1982	Track Robbery (6)
1983	Ambassador of Luck (4)
1984	Princess Rooney (4)
1985	Life's Magic (4)
1986	Lady's Secret (4)
1987	North Sider (5)
1988	Personal Ensign (4)
1989	Bayakoa (5)
1990	Bayakoa (6)
1991	Queena (5)
1992	Paseana (5)
1993	Paseana (6)
1994	Sky Beauty (4)
1995	Inside Information (4)
1996	Jewel Princess (4)
1997	Hidden Lake (4)
1998	Escena (5)
1999	Beautiful Pleasure (4)
2000	Riboletta (6)
2001	Gourmet Girl (6)
2002	Azeri (4)
2003	Azeri (5)
2004	Azeri (6)

STEEPLECHASE OR HURDLE HORSE

1971	Shadow Brook (7)
1972	Soothsayer (5)
1973	Athenian Idol (5)
1974	Gran Kan (8)
1975	Life's Illusion (4)
1976	Straight & True (6)
1977	Cafe Prince (7)
1978	Cafe Prince (8)
1979	Martie's Anger (4)
1980	Zaccio (4)
1981	Zaccio (5)
1982	Zaccio (6)
1983	Flatterer (4)
1984	Flatterer (5)
1985	Flatterer (6)
1986	Flatterer (7)
1987	Inlander (6)
1988	Jimmy Lorenzo (6)
1989	Highland Bud (4)
1990	Morley Street (7)
1991	Morley Street (8)
1992	Lonesome Glory (4)
1993	Lonesome Glory (5)
1994	Warm Spell (6)
1995	Lonesome Glory (7)
1996	Correggio (5)
1997	Lonesome Glory (9)

STEEPLECHASE OR HURDLE HORSE

1998	Flat Top (5)
1999	Lonesome Glory (11)
2000	All Gong (6)
2001	Pompeyo (7)
2002	Flat Top (9)
2003	McDynamo (6)
2004	Hirapour (8)

SPRINTER

1971	Ack Ack (5)
1972	Chou Croute (4)
1973	Shecky Greene (3)
1974	Forego (4)
1975	Gallant Bob (3)
1976	My Juliet (4)
1977	What a Summer (4)
1978	Dr. Patches (4)
	J.O. Tobin (4)
1979	Star de Naskra (4)
1980	Plugged Nickel (3)
1981	Guilty Conscience (5)
1982	Gold Beauty (3)
1983	Chinook Pass (4)
1984	Eillo (4)
1985	Precisionist (4)
1986	Smile (4)
1987	Groovy (4)
1988	Gulch (4)
1989	Safely Kept (3)
1990	Housebuster (3)
1991	Housebuster (4)
1992	Rubiano (5)
1993	Cardmania (5)
1994	Cherokee Run (4)
1995	Not Surprising (5)
1996	Lit de Justice (6)
1997	Smoke Glacken (3)
1998	Reraise (3)
1999	Artax (4)
2000	Kone Gold (6)
2001	Squirtle Squirt (3)
2002	Orientate (4)
2003	Aldebaran (5)
2004	Speightstown (6)

OUTSTANDING OWNER

1971	Mr. & Mrs. E. E. Fogleson
1974	Dan Lasater
1975	Dan Lasater
1976	Dan Lasater
1977	Maxwell Gluck
1978	Harbor View Farm
1979	Harbor View Farm
1980	Mr. & Mrs. Bertram
1981	Dotsam Stable
1982	Viola Sommer
1983	John Franks
1984	John Franks
1985	Mr. & Mrs. Eugene Klein
1986	Mr. & Mrs. Eugene Klein
1987	Mr. & Mrs. Eugene Klein
1988	Ogden Phipps
1989	Ogden Phipps
1990	Frances Genter
1991	Sam-Son Farm
1992	Juddmonte Farms
1993	John Franks
1994	John Franks

Eclipse Award Winners (Cont.)

1995.....Allen E. Paulson
1996.....Allen E. Paulson
1997.....Carolyn Hine
1998.....Frank Stronach
1999.....Frank Stronach
2000.....Frank Stronach
2001.....Richard Englander
2002.....Richard Englander
2003...Juddmonte Farms
2004 ...Frank Stronach

OUTSTANDING TRAINER

1971.....Charlie Whittingham
1972.....Lucien Laurin
1973.....H. Allen Jerkens
1974.....Sherrill Ward
1975.....Steve DiMauro
1976.....Lazaro Barrera
1977.....Lazaro Barrera
1978.....Lazaro Barrera
1979.....Lazaro Barrera
1980.....Bud Delp
1981.....Ron McAnally
1982.....Charlie Whittingham
1983.....Woody Stephens
1984.....Jack Van Berg
1985.....D. Wayne Lukas
1986.....D. Wayne Lukas
1987.....D. Wayne Lukas
1988.....Claude R. McGaughey III
1989.....Charlie Whittingham
1990.....Carl Nafzger
1991.....Ron McAnally
1992.....Ron McAnally
1993.....Bobby Frankel
1994.....D. Wayne Lukas
1995.....William Mott
1996.....William Mott
1997.....Bob Baffert
1998.....Bob Baffert
1999.....Bob Baffert
2000.....Robert Frankel
2001.....Robert Frankel
2002.....Robert Frankel
2003.....Robert Frankel
2004.....Todd Pletcher

OUTSTANDING JOCKEY

1971.....Laffit Pincay Jr.
1972.....Braulio Baeza
1973.....Laffit Pincay Jr
1974.....Laffit Pincay Jr
1975.....Braulio Baeza
1976.....Sandy Hawley
1977.....Steve Cauthen
1978.....Darrel McHargue
1979.....Laffit Pincay Jr.
1980.....Chris McCarron
1981.....Bill Shoemaker
1982.....Angel Cordero Jr
1983.....Angel Cordero Jr
1984.....Pat Day
1985.....Laffit Pincay Jr
1986.....Pat Day
1987.....Pat Day
1988.....Jose Santos
1989.....Kent Desormeaux
1990.....Craig Perret
1991.....Pat Day
1992.....Kent Desormeaux
1993.....Mike Smith
1994.....Mike Smith
1995.....Jerry Bailey
1996.....Jerry Bailey
1997.....Jerry Bailey
1998.....Gary Stevens
1999.....Jorge Chavez
2000.....Jerry Bailey
2001.....Jerry Bailey
2002.....Jerry Bailey
2003.....Jerry Bailey
2004.....John Velasquez

OUTSTANDING APPRENTICE JOCKEY

1971.....Gene St. Leon
1972.....Thomas Wallis
1973.....Steve Valdez
1974.....Chris McCarron
1975.....Jimmy Edwards
1976.....George Martens
1977.....Steve Cauthen
1978.....Ron Franklin
1979.....Cash Asmussen
1980.....Frank Lovato Jr.
1981.....Richard Migliore
1982.....Alberto Delgado
1983.....Declan Murphy
1984.....Wesley Ward
1985.....Art Madrid Jr.
1986.....Allen Stacy
1987.....Kent Desormeaux
1988.....Steve Capanas
1989.....Michael Luzzi
1990.....Mark Johnston
1991.....Mickey Walls
1992.....Jesus A. Bracho
1993.....Juan Umana
1994.....Dale Beckner
1995.....Ramon Perez
1996.....Neil Pozansky
1997.....Phil Teator
　　　　　Roberto Rosado
1998.....Shaun Bridgmohan
1999.....Ariel Smith
2000.....Tyler Baze
2001.....Jeremy Rose
2002.....Ryan Fogelsonger
2003.....Eddie Castro
2004.....Brian Hernandez

Eclipse Award Winners (Cont.)

OUTSTANDING BREEDER

1974.....John W. Galbreath
1975.....Fred W. Hooper
1976.....Nelson Bunker Hunt
1977.....Edward Plunket Taylor
1978.....Harbor View Farm
1979.....Claiborne Farm
1980.....Mrs. Henry D. Paxson
1981.....Golden Chance Farm
1982.....Fred W. Hooper
1983.....Edward Plunket Taylor
1984.....Claiborne Farm
1985.....Nelson Bunker Hunt
1986.....Paul Mellon
1987.....Nelson Bunker Hunt
1988.....Ogden Phipps
1989.....North Ridge Farm
1990.....Calumet Farm
1991.....John and Betty Mabee
1992.....William S. Farish III
1993.....Allen Paulson
1994.....William T. Young
1995.....Juddmonte Farms
1996.....Fansworth Farms
1997.....Golden Eagle Farm
1998.....John and Betty Mabee

OUTSTANDING BREEDER (Contd)

1999.....William Farish/Partners
2000.....Frank Stronach/Adena
          Springs
2001.....Juddmonte Farms
2002.....Juddmonte Farms
2003.....Juddmonte Farms
2004.....Frank Stronach/Adena
          Springs

AWARD OF MERIT

1976.....Jack J. Dreyfus
1977.....Steve Cauthen
1978.....Ogden Phipps
1979.....Frank E. Kilroe
1980.....John D. Schapiro
1981.....Bill Shoemaker
1984.....John Gaines
1985.....Keene Daingerfield
1986.....Herman Cohen
1987.....J. B. Faulconer
1988.....John Forsythe
1989.....Michael P. Sandler
1991:....Fred W. Hooper
1994.....Alfred G. Vanderbilt
1996.....Allen E. Paulson
2002.....Howard Battle
          Ogden Phipps

SPECIAL AWARD

1971.....Robert J. Kleberg
1974.....Charles Hatton
1976.....Bill Shoemaker
1980.....John T. Landry
          Pierre E. Bellocq (Peb)
1984.....C. V. Whitney
1985.....Arlington Park
1987.....Anheuser-Busch
1988.....Edward J. DeBartolo Sr.
1989.....Richard Duchossois
1994.....John Longden
          Edward Arcaro
1998.....Oak Tree Racing
          Association
2002.....Keeneland Library

Note: Special Award and Award of Merit, for long-term and/or outstanding service to the industry, not presented annually.

Rare Foal

A white throughbred filly was born at Lost Creek Farm, to the amazement of its owners. Called Caramel, the filly was sired by the chestnut Trust N Lock out of the chocolate-colored Deebrand, and becomes only the thirtieth white thoroughbred foal born since 1896 among resigstered thoroughbreads. "When it first happened, we didn't know what to believe," said owner Nancy Mazzoni. We couldn't honestly believe she was legitimate.

Breeders' Cup

Location: Hollywood 1984, '87, '97; Aqueduct 1985; Santa Anita 1986, '93, '03; Churchill Downs 1988, '91, '98,'00; Gulfstream (FL) 1989, '92, '99; Belmont 1990, '95, '01; Woodbine (Toronto) 1996; Arlington 2002.

Juveniles

Year	Winner (Margin)	Jockey	Second	Third	Time
1984	Chief's Crown (¾)	Don MacBeth	Tank's Prospect	Spend a Buck	1:36⅕
1985	Tasso (Nose)	Laffit Pincay Jr.	Storm Cat	Scat Dancer	1:36⅕
1986	Capote (1¼)	Laffit Pincay Jr.	Qualify	Alysheba	1:43⅘
1987	Success Express (1¾)	Jose Santos	Regal Classic	Tejano	1:35⅕
1988	Is It True (1¼)	Laffit Pincay Jr.	Easy Goer	Tagel	1:46⅗
1989	Rhythm (2)	Craig Perret	Grand Canyon	Slavic	1:43⅗
1990	Fly So Free (3)	Jose Santos	Take Me Out	Lost Mountain	1:43⅖
1991	Arazi (4¾)	Pat Valenzuela	Bertrando	Snappy Landing	1:44⅗
1992	Gilded Time (¾)	Chris McCarron	It'sali'lknownfact	River Special	1:43⅖
1993	Brocco (5)	Gary Stevens	Blumin Affair	Tabasco Cat	1:42⅘
1994	Timber Country (½)	Pat Day	Eltish	Tejano Run	1:44⅖
1995	Unbridled's Song (Neck)	Mike Smith	Hennessy	Editor's Note	1:41⅗
1996	Boston Harbor (Neck)	Jerry Bailey	Acceptable	Ordway	1:43⅖
1997	Favorite Trick (5½)	Pat Day	Dawson's Legacy	Nationalore	1:41⅗
1998	Answer Lively (Head)	Jerry Bailey	Aly's Alley	Cat Thief	1:44
1999	Anees (2½)	Gary Stevens	Chief Seattle	High Yield	1:42.29
2000	Macho Uno (Nose)	Jerry Bailey	Point Given	Street Cry	1:42.05
2001	Johannesburg (1¼)	Michael Kinane	Repent	Siphonic	1:42.27
2002	Vindication (2¾)	Mike Smith	Kafwain	Hold That Tiger	1:49.61
2003	Action This Day (2¼)	David Flores	Minister Eric	Chapel Royal	1:43.62
2004	Wilko (¾)	Frankie Dettori	Afleet Alex	Sun King	1:42.09

Note: One mile (1984–85, '87), 1 1/16 miles (1986 and 1988–2001, '03), 1⅛ miles (2002).

Juvenile Fillies

Year	Winner (Margin)	Jockey	Second	Third	Time
1984	Outstandingly*	Walter Guerra	Dusty Heart	Fine Spirit	1:37⅘
1985	Twilight Ridge (1)	Jorge Velasquez	Family Style	Steal a Kiss	1:35⅘
1986	Brave Raj (5½)	Pat Valenzuela	Tappiano	Saros Brig	1:43⅕
1987	Epitome (Nose)	Pat Day	Jeanne Jones	Dream Team	1:36⅖
1988	Open Mind (1¾)	Angel Cordero Jr.	Darby Shuffle	Lea Lucinda	1:46⅗
1989	Go for Wand (2¾)	Randy Romero	Sweet Roberta	Stella Madrid	1:44⅕
1990	Meadow Star (5)	Jose Santos	Private Treasure	Dance Smartly	1:44
1991	Pleasant Stage (Neck)	Eddie Delahoussaye	La Spia	Cadillac Women	1:46⅖
1992	Eliza (1½)	Pat Valenzuela	Educated Risk	Boots 'n Jackie	1:42⅘
1993	Phone Chatter (Head)	Laffit Pincay	Sardula	Heavenly Prize	1:43
1994	Flanders (Head)	Pat Day	Serena's Song	Stormy Blues	1:45⅕
1995	My Flag (½)	Jerry Bailey	Cara Rafaela	Golden Attraction	1:42⅖
1996	Storm Song (4½)	Craig Perret	Love That Jazz	Critical Factor	1:43⅗
1997	Countess Diana (8½)	Shane Sellers	Career Collection	Primaly	1:42⅕
1998	Silverbulletday (½)	Gary Stevens	Excellent Meeting	Three Ring	1:43⅗
1999	Cash Run (1¼)	Jerry Bailey	Chilukki	Surfside	1:43.31
2000	Caressing (½)	John Velazquez	Platinum Tiara	Shes a Devil Due	1:42.72
2001	Tempera (1½)	David Flores	Imperial Gesture	Bella Bellucci	1:41.49
2002	Storm Flag Flying (½)	John Velazquez	Composure	Santa Catarina	1:49.60
2003	Halfbridled (2½)	Julie Krone	Ashado	Victory U.S.A.	1:42.75
2004	Sweet Cantomine(3¾)	Corey Nakatani	Balleto	Runway Model	1:41.65

*In 1984, winner Fran's Valentine dq'd. Note: One mile (1984-85, '87), 1 1/16 miles (1986 and 1988-01, '03), 1⅛ miles (02).

Sprint

Year	Winner (Margin)	Jockey	Second	Third	Time
1984	Eillo (Nose)	Craig Perret	Commemorate	Fighting Fit	1:10⅕
1985	Precisionist (¾)	Chris McCarron	Smile	Mt. Livermore	1:08⅖
1986	Smile (1¼)	Jacinto Vasquez	Pine Tree Lane	Bedside Promise	1:08⅖
1987	Very Subtle (4)	Pat Valenzuela	Groovy	Exclusive Enough	1:08⅘
1988	Gulch (¾)	Angel Cordero Jr	Play the King	Afleet	1:10⅖
1989	Dancing Spree (Neck)	Angel Cordero Jr	Safely Kept	Dispersal	1:09
1990	Safely Kept (Neck)	Craig Perret	Dayjur	Black Tie Affair	1:09⅗
1991	Sheikh Albadou (Neck)	Pat Eddery	Pleasant Tap	Robyn Dancer	1:09⅕
1992	Thirty Slews (Neck)	Eddie Delahoussaye	Meafara	Rubiano	1:08⅕
1993	Cardmania (Neck)	Eddie Delahoussaye	Meafara	Gilded Time	1:08⅗
1994	Cherokee Run (Head)	Mike Smith	Soviet Problem	Cardmania	1:09⅖
1995	Desert Stormer (Neck)	Kent Desormeaux	Mr. Greeley	Lit de Justice	1:09

Breeders' Cup *(Cont.)*

Sprint *(cont.)*

Year	Winner (Margin)	Jockey	Second	Third	Time
1996	Lit de Justice (1¼)	Corey Nakatani	Paying Dues	Honour and Glory	1:08⅗
1997	Elmhurst (½)	Corey Nakatani	Hesabull	Bet on Sunshine	1:08
1998	Reraise (2)	Corey Nakatani	Grand Slam	Kona Gold	1:09
1999	Artax (½)	Jorge Chavez	Kona Gold	Big Jag	1:07.89
2000	Kona Gold (½)	Alex Solis	Honest Lady	Bet on Sunshine	1:07.77
2001	Squirtle Squirt (½)	Jerry Bailey	Xtra Heat	Caller One	1:08.41
2002	Orientate (½)	Jerry Bailey	Thunderello	Crafty C.T.	1:08.89
2003	Cajun Beat (2¼)	Cornelio Velasquez	Bluesthestandard	Shake You Down	1:07.95
2004	Speightstown (1¼)	J. Velasquez	Kela	My Cousin Matt	1:08.11

Note: Six furlongs (since 1984).

Mile

Year	Winner (Margin)	Jockey	Second	Third	Time
1984	Royal Heroine (1½)	Fernando Toro	Star Choice	Cozzene	1:32⅗
1985	Cozzene (2¼)	Walter Guerra	Al Mamoon*	Shadeed	1:35
1986	Last Tycoon (Head)	Yves St-Martin	Palace Music	Fred Astaire	1:35⅕
1987	Miesque (3½)	Freddie Head	Show Dancer	Sonic Lady	1:32⅘
1988	Miesque (4)	Freddie Head	Steinlen	Simply Majestic	1:38⅗
1989	Steinlen (¾)	Jose Santos	Sabona	Most Welcome	1:37⅕
1990	Royal Academy (Neck)	Lester Piggott	Itsallgreektome	Priolo	1:35⅕
1991	Opening Verse (2¼)	Pat Valenzuela	Val de Bois	Star of Cozzene	1:37⅖
1992	Lure (3)	Mike Smith	Paradise Creek	Brief Truce	1:32⅘
1993	Lure (2¼)	Mike Smith	Ski Paradise	Fourstars Allstar	1:33⅖
1994	Barathea (Head)	Frankie Dettori	Johann Quatz	Unfinished Symph	1:34⅖
1995	Ridgewood Pearl (2)	John Murtagh	Fastness	Sayyedati	1:43⅗
1996	Da Hoss (1½)	Gary Stevens	Spinning World	Same Old Wish	1:35⅘
1997	Spinning World (2)	Cash Asmussen	Geri	Decorated Hero	1:32⅘
1998	Da Hoss (Head)	John Velazquez	Hawksley Hill	Labeeb	1:35⅕
1999	Silic (Neck)	Corey Nakatani	Tuzla	Docksider	1:34.26
2000	War Chant (Neck)	Gary Stevens	North East Bound	Dansili	1:34.67
2001	Val Royal (1¾)	Jose Valdivia	Forbidden Apple	Bach	1:32.05
2002	Domedriver (¾)	Thierry Thulliez	Rock of Gibraltar	Good Journey	1:36.92
2003	Six Perfections (¾)	Jerry Bailey	Touch of the Blues	Century City	1:33.86
2004	Singletary (½)	David Flores	Antonius Pius	Six Perfections	1:36.90

*2nd place finisher Palace Music was disqualified for interference and placed 9th.

Distaff

Year	Winner (Margin)	Jockey	Second	Third	Time
1984	Princess Rooney (7)	Eddie Delahoussaye	Life's Magic	Adored	2:02⅖
1985	Life's Magic (6¼)	Angel Cordero Jr.	Lady's Secret	Dontstop Themusic	2:02
1986	Lady's Secret (2½)	Pat Day	Fran's Valentine	Outstandingly	2:01⅕
1987	Sacahuista (2¼)	Randy Romero	Clabber Girl	Oueee Bebe	2:02⅘
1988	Personal Ensign (Nose)	Randy Romero	Winning Colors	Goodbye Halo	1:52
1989	Bayakoa (1½)	Laffit Pincay Jr.	Gorgeous	Open Mind	1:47⅖
1990	Bayakoa (6¾)	Laffit Pincay Jr.	Colonial Waters	Valay Maid	1:49⅕
1991	Dance Smarty (½)	Pat Day	Versailles Treaty	Brought to Mind	1:50⅘
1992	Paseana (4)	Chris McCarron	Versailles Treaty	Magical Maiden	1:48
1993	Hollywood Wildcat (Nose)	Eddie Delahoussaye	Paseana	Re Toss	1:48⅕
1994	One Dreamer (Neck)	Gary Stevens	Heavenly Prize	Miss Dominique	1:50⅗
1995	Inside Information (13½)	Mike Smith	Heavenly Prize	Lakeway	1:46
1996	Jewel Princess (1½)	Corey Nakatani	Serena's Song	Different	1:48⅖
1997	Ajina (2)	Mike Smith	Sharp Cat	Escena	1:47⅕
1998	Escena (Nose)	Gary Stevens	Banshee Breeze	Keeper Hill	1:49⅘
1999	Beautiful Pleasure (¾)	Jorge Chavez	Banshee Breeze	Heritage of Gold	1:47.56
2000	Spain (1½)	Victor Espinoza	Surfside	Heritage of Gold	1:47.66
2001	Unbridled Elaine (head)	Pat Day	Spain	Too Item Limit	1:49.21
2002	Azeri (5)	Mike Smith	Farda Amiga	Imperial Gesture	1:48.64
2003	Adoration (4½)	Pat Valenzuela	Elloluv	Got Koko	1:49.17
2004	Ashado (1¼)	J. Velasquez	Storm Flag Flying	Stellar Jane	1:48.26

Note: 1¼ miles (1984–87), 1⅛ miles (since 1988).

Breeders' Cup *(Cont.)*

Turf

Year	Winner (Margin)	Jockey	Second	Third	Time
1984	Lashkari (Neck)	Yves St. Martin	All Along	Raami	2:25⅕
1985	Pebbles (Neck)	Pat Eddery	Strawberry Rd II	Mourjane	2:27
1986	Manila (Neck)	Jose Santos	Theatrical	Estrapade	2:25⅖
1987	Theatrical (½)	Pat Day	Trempolino	Village Star II	2:24⅖
1988	Great Communicator (½)	Ray Sibille	Sunshine Forever	Indian Skimmer	2:35⅕
1989	Prized (Head)	Eddie Delahoussaye	Sierra Roberta	Star Lift	2:28
1990	In the Wings (½)	Gary Stevens	With Approval	El Senor	2:29⅗
1991	Miss Alleged (2)	Eric Legrix	Itsallgreektome	Quest for Fame	2:30⅘
1992	Fraise (Nose)	Pat Valenzuela	Sky Classic	Quest For Fame	2:24
1993	Kotashaan (½)	Kent Desormeaux	Bien Bien	Luazar	2:25
1994	Tikkanen (1½)	Mike Smith	Hatoof	Paradise Creek	2:26⅖
1995	Northern Spur (Neck)	Chris McCarron	Freedom Cry	Carnegie	2:42
1996	Pilsudski (1¼)	Walter Swinburn	Singspiel	Swain	2:30⅕
1997	Chief Bearhart (¾)	Jose Santos	Borgia	Flag Down	2:23⅘
1998	Buck's Boy (1¼)	Shane Sellers	Yagli	Dushyantor	2:28⅗
1999	Daylami (2½)	Frankie Dettori	Royal Anthem	Buck's Boy	2:24.73
2000	Kalanisi (½)	John Murtagh	Quiet Resolve	John's Call	2:26.96
2001	Fantastic Light (¾)	Frankie Dettori	Milan	Timboroa	2:24.36
2002	High Chaparral (1¼)	Michael Kinane	With Anticipation	Falcon Flight	2:30.14
2003	High Chaparral/Johar	Michael Kinane/Alex Solis		Falbrav	2:24.24
2004	Better Talk Now (1¼)	R. Dominguez	Kitten's Joy	Powerscourt	2:29.15

Note: 1½ miles.

Classic

Year	Winner (Margin)	Jockey	Second	Third	Time
1984	Wild Again (Head)	Pat Day	Slew o' Gold*	Gate Dancer	2:03⅖
1985	Proud Truth (Head)	Jorge Velasquez	Gate Dancer	Turkoman	2:00⅘
1986	Skywalker (1¼)	Laffit Pincay Jr.	Turkoman	Precisionist	2:00⅖
1987	Ferdinand (Nose)	Bill Shoemaker	Alysheba	Judge Angelucci	2:01⅖
1988	Alysheba (Nose)	Chris McCarron	Seeking the Gold	Waquoit	2:04⅘
1989	Sunday Silence (½)	Chris McCarron	Easy Goer	Blushing John	2:00⅕
1990	Unbridled (1)	Pat Day	Ibn Bey	Thirty Six Red	2:02⅕
1991	Black Tie Affair (1¼)	Jerry Bailey	Twilight Agenda	Unbridled	2:02⅘
1992	A.P. Indy (2)	Eddie Delahoussaye	Pleasant Tap	Jolypha	2:00⅕
1993	Arcangues (2)	Jerry Bailey	Bertrando	Kissin Kris	2:00⅘
1994	Concern (Neck)	Jerry Bailey	Tabasco Cat	Dramatic Gold	2:02⅖
1995	Cigar (2½)	Jerry Bailey	L'Carriere	Unaccounted For	1:59⅖
1996	Alphabet Soup (Nose)	Chris McCarron	Louis Quatorze	Cigar	2:01
1997	Skip Away (6)	Mike Smith	Deputy Commander	Dowty	1:59⅕
1998	Awesome Again (¾)	Pat Day	Silver Charm	Swain	2:02
1999	Cat Thief (1¼)	Pat Day	Budroyale	Golden Missile	1:59.52
2000	Tiznow (Neck)	Chris McCarron	Giant's Causeway	Captain Steve	2:00.75
2001	Tiznow (Nose)	Chris McCarron	Sakhee	Albert the Great	2:00.62
2002	Volponi (6½)	Jose Santos	Medaglia d'Oro	Milwaukee Brew	2:01.39
2003	Pleasantly Perfect (1½)	Alex Solis	Medaglia d'Oro	Dynever	1:59.88
2004	Ghostzapper (3)	J. Castellano	Roses in May	Perfectly Pleasant	1:59.02

*2nd place finisher Gate Dancer was disqualified for interference and placed 3rd.

Note: 1¼ miles.

England's Triple Crown Winners

England's Triple Crown consists of the Two Thousand Guineas, held at Newmarket; the Epsom Derby, held at Epsom Downs; and the St. Leger Stakes, held at Doncaster.

Year	Horse	Owner	Year	Horse	Owner
1853	West Australian	Mr. Bowes	1900	Diamond Jubilee	Prince of Wales
1865	Gladiateur	F. DeLagrange	1903	*Rock Sand	J. Miller
1866	Lord Lyon	R. Sutton	1915	Pommern	S. Joel
1886	*Ormonde	Duke of Westminster	1917	Gay Crusader	Mr. Fairie
1891	Common	†F. Johnstone	1918	Gainsborough	Lady James Douglas
1893	Isinglass	H. McCalmont	1935	*Bahram	Aga Khan
1897	Galtee More	J. Gubbins	1970	‡Nijinsky II	C. W. Engelhard
1899	Flying Fox	Duke of Westminster			

*Imported into United States. †Raced in name of Lord Alington in Two Thousand Guineas. ‡Canadian-bred.

Annual Leaders

Horse—Money Won

Year	Horse	Age	Starts	1st	2nd	3rd	Winnings ($)
1919	Sir Barton	3	13	8	3	2	88,250
1920	Man o' War	3	11	11	0	0	166,140
1921	Morvich	2	11	11	0	0	115,234
1922	Pillory	3	7	4	1	1	95,654
1923	Zev	3	14	12	1	0	272,008
1924	Sarzen	3	12	8	1	1	95,640
1925	Pompey	2	10	7	2	0	121,630
1926	Crusader	3	15	9	4	0	166,033
1927	Anita Peabody	2	7	6	0	1	111,905
1928	High Strung	2	6	5	0	0	153,590
1929	Blue Larkspur	3	6	4	1	0	153,450
1930	Gallant Fox	3	10	9	1	0	308,275
1931	Gallant Flight	2	7	7	0	0	219,000
1932	Gusto	3	16	4	3	2	145,940
1933	Singing Wood	2	9	3	2	2	88,050
1934	Cavalcade	3	7	6	1	0	111,235
1935	Omaha	3	9	6	1	2	142,255
1936	Granville	3	11	7	3	0	110,295
1937	Seabiscuit	4	15	11	2	2	168,580
1938	Stagehand	3	15	8	2	3	189,710
1939	Challedon	3	15	9	2	3	184,535
1940	Bimelech	3	7	4	2	1	110,005
1941	Whirlaway	3	20	13	5	2	272,386
1942	Shut Out	3	12	8	2	0	238,872
1943	Count Fleet	3	6	6	0	0	174,055
1944	Pavot	2	8	8	0	0	179,040
1945	Busher	3	13	10	2	1	273,735
1946	Assault	3	15	8	2	3	424,195
1947	Armed	6	17	11	4	1	376,325
1948	Citation	3	20	19	1	0	709,470
1949	Ponder	3	21	9	5	2	321,825
1950	Noor	5	12	7	4	1	346,940
1951	Counterpoint	3	15	7	2	1	250,525
1952	Crafty Admiral	4	16	9	4	1	277,225
1953	Native Dancer	3	10	9	1	0	513,425
1954	Determine	3	15	10	3	2	328,700
1955	Nashua	3	12	10	1	1	752,550
1956	Needles	3	8	4	2	0	440,850
1957	Round Table	3	22	15	1	3	600,383
1958	Round Table	4	20	14	4	0	662,780
1959	Sword Dancer	3	13	8	4	0	537,004
1960	Bally Ache	3	15	10	3	1	445,045
1961	Carry Back	3	16	9	1	3	565,349
1962	Never Bend	2	10	7	1	2	402,969
1963	Candy Spots	3	12	7	2	1	604,481
1964	Gun Bow	4	16	8	4	2	580,100
1965	Buckpasser	2	11	9	1	0	568,096
1966	Buckpasser	3	14	13	1	0	669,078
1967	Damascus	3	16	12	3	1	817,941
1968	Forward Pass	3	13	7	2	0	546,674
1969	Arts and Letters	3	14	8	5	1	555,604
1970	Personality	3	18	8	2	1	444,049
1971	Riva Ridge	2	9	7	0	0	503,263
1972	Droll Role	4	19	7	3	4	471,633
1973	Secretariat	3	12	9	2	1	860,404
1974	Chris Evert	3	8	5	1	2	551,063
1975	Foolish Pleasure	3	11	5	4	1	716,278
1976	Forego	6	8	6	1	1	401,701
1977	Seattle Slew	3	7	6	0	1	641,370
1978	Affirmed	3	11	8	2	0	901,541
1979	Spectacular Bid	3	12	10	1	1	1,279,334
1980	Temperence Hill	3	17	8	3	1	1,130,452
1981	John Henry	6	10	8	0	0	1,798,030
1982	Perrault	5	8	4	1	2	1,197,400
1983	All Along	4	7	4	1	1	2,138,963
1984	Slew o'Gold	4	6	5	1	0	2,627,944
1985	Spend A Buck	3	7	5	1	1	3,552,704

Horse—Money Won *(Cont.)*

Year	Horse	Age	Starts	1st	2nd	3rd	Winnings ($)
1986	Snow Chief	3	9	6	1	1	1,875,200
1987	Alysheba	3	10	3	3	1	2,511,156
1988	Alysheba	4	9	7	1	0	3,808,600
1989	Sunday Silence	3	9	7	2	0	4,578,454
1990	Unbridled	3	11	4	3	2	3,718,149
1991	Dance Smartly	3	8	8	0	0	2,876,821
1992	A.P. Indy	3	7	5	0	1	2,622,560
1993	Kotashaan	3	10	6	3	0	2,619,014
1994	Paradise Creek	5	11	8	2	1	2,610,187
1995	Cigar	5	10	10	0	0	4,819,800
1996	Cigar	6	8	5	2	1	4,910,000
1997	Skip Away	4	11	4	5	2	4,089,000
1998	Silver Charm	4	9	6	2	0	4,696,506
1999	Almutawakel	4	4	1	1	1	3,290,000
2000	Dubai Millennium	4	1	1	0	0	3,600,000
2001	Captain Steve	4	6	2	1	1	4,201,200
2002	War Emblem	4	10	5	0	0	3,455,000
2003	Pleasantly Perfect	5	4	2	0	1	2,470,000
2004	Smarty Jones	3	7	6	1	0	7,563,535

Trainer—Money Won

Year	Trainer	Wins	Winnings ($)	Year	Trainer	Wins	Winnings ($)
1908	James Rowe, Sr.	50	284,335	1957	Jimmy Jones	70	1,150,910
1909	Sam Hildreth	73	123,942	1958	Willie Molter	69	1,116,544
1910	Sam Hildreth	84	148,010	1959	Willie Molter	71	847,290
1911	Sam Hildreth	67	49,418	1960	Hirsch Jacobs	97	748,349
1912	John F. Schorr	63	58,110	1961	Jimmy Jones	62	759,856
1913	James Rowe, Sr.	18	45,936	1962	Mesh Tenney	58	1,099,474
1914	R. C. Benson	45	59,315	1963	Mesh Tenney	40	860,703
1915	James Rowe, Sr.	19	75,596	1964	Bill Winfrey	61	1,350,534
1916	Sam Hildreth	39	70,950	1965	Hirsch Jacobs	91	1,331,628
1917	Sam Hildreth	23	61,698	1966	Eddie Neloy	93	2,456,250
1918	H. Guy Bedwell	53	80,296	1967	Eddie Neloy	72	1,776,089
1919	H. Guy Bedwell	63	208,728	1968	Eddie Neloy	52	1,233,101
1920	L. Feustal	22	186,087	1969	Elliott Burch	26	1,067,936
1921	Sam Hildreth	85	262,768	1970	Charlie Whittingham	82	1,302,354
1922	Sam Hildreth	74	247,014	1971	Charlie Whittingham	77	1,737,115
1923	Sam Hildreth	75	392,124	1972	Charlie Whittingham	79	1,734,020
1924	Sam Hildreth	77	255,608	1973	Charlie Whittingham	85	1,865,385
1925	G. R. Tompkins	30	199,245	1974	Pancho Martin	166	2,408,419
1926	Scott P. Harlan	21	205,681	1975	Charlie Whittingham	93	2,437,244
1927	W. H. Bringloe	63	216,563	1976	Jack Van Berg	496	2,976,196
1928	John F. Schorr	65	258,425	1977	Laz Barrera	127	2,715,848
1929	James Rowe, Jr.	25	314,881	1978	Laz Barrera	100	3,307,164
1930	Sunny Jim Fitzsimmons	47	397,355	1979	Laz Barrera	98	3,608,517
1931	Big Jim Healey	33	297,300	1980	Laz Barrera	99	2,969,151
1932	Sunny Jim Fitzsimmons	68	266,650	1981	Charlie Whittingham	74	3,993,300
1933	Humming Bob Smith	53	135,720	1982	Charlie Whittingham	63	4,587,457
1934	Humming Bob Smith	43	249,938	1983	D. Wayne Lukas	78	4,267,261
1935	Bud Stotler	87	303,005	1984	D. Wayne Lukas	131	5,835,921
1936	Sunny Jim Fitzsimmons	42	193,415	1985	D. Wayne Lukas	218	11,155,188
1937	Robert McGarvey	46	209,925	1986	D. Wayne Lukas	259	12,345,180
1938	Earl Sande	15	226,495	1987	D. Wayne Lukas	343	17,502,110
1939	Sunny Jim Fitzsimmons	45	266,205	1988	D. Wayne Lukas	318	17,842,358
1940	Silent Tom Smith	14	269,200	1989	D. Wayne Lukas	305	16,103,998
1941	Plain Ben Jones	70	475,318	1990	D. Wayne Lukas	267	14,508,871
1942	John M. Gaver Sr.	48	406,547	1991	D. Wayne Lukas	289	15,942,223
1943	Plain Ben Jones	73	267,915	1992	D. Wayne Lukas	230	9,806,436
1944	Plain Ben Jones	60	601,660	1993	Robert Frankel	79	8,883,252
1945	Silent Tom Smith	52	510,655	1994	D. Wayne Lukas	147	9,247,457
1946	Hirsch Jacobs	99	560,077	1995	D. Wayne Lukas	194	12,842,865
1947	Jimmy Jones	85	1,334,805	1996	D. Wayne Lukas	192	15,966,344
1948	Jimmy Jones	81	1,118,670	1997	D. Wayne Lukas	175	10,338,957
1949	Jimmy Jones	76	978,587	1998	Bob Baffert	139	15,000,870
1950	Preston Burch	96	637,754	1999	Bob Baffert	169	16,934,607
1951	John M. Gaver Sr.	42	616,392	2000	Bob Baffert	146	11,831,605
1952	Plain Ben Jones	29	662,137	2001	Bob Baffert	138	16,354,996
1953	Harry Trotsek	54	1,028,873	2002	Robert Frankel	117	17,748,340
1954	Willie Molter	136	1,107,860	2003	Robert Frankel	114	19,143,289
1955	Sunny Jim Fitzsimmons	66	1,270,055	2004	Todd A. Pletcher	240	17,511,923
1956	Willie Molter	142	1,227,402				

Jockey—Money Won

Year	Jockey	Mts	1st	2nd	3rd	Pct	Winnings ($)
1919	John Loftus	177	65	36	24	.37	252,707
1920	Clarence Kummer	353	87	79	48	.25	292,376
1921	Earl Sande	340	112	69	59	.33	263,043
1922	Albert Johnson	297	43	57	40	.14	345,054
1923	Earl Sande	430	122	89	79	.28	569,394
1924	Ivan Parke	844	205	175	121	.24	290,395
1925	Laverne Fator	315	81	54	44	.26	305,775
1926	Laverne Fator	511	143	90	86	.28	361,435
1927	Earl Sande	179	49	33	19	.27	277,877
1928	Pony McAtee	235	55	43	25	.23	301,295
1929	Mack Garner	274	57	39	33	.21	314,975
1930	Sonny Workman	571	152	88	79	.27	420,438
1931	Charles Kurtsinger	519	93	82	79	.18	392,095
1932	Sonny Workman	378	87	48	55	.23	385,070
1933	Robert Jones	471	63	57	70	.13	226,285
1934	Wayne D. Wright	919	174	154	114	.19	287,185
1935	Silvio Coucci	749	141	125	103	.19	319,760
1936	Wayne D. Wright	670	100	102	73	.15	264,000
1937	Charles Kurtsinger	765	120	94	106	.16	384,202
1938	Nick Wall	658	97	94	82	.15	385,161
1939	Basil James	904	191	165	105	.21	353,333
1940	Eddie Arcaro	783	132	143	112	.17	343,661
1941	Don Meade	1,164	210	185	158	.18	398,627
1942	Eddie Arcaro	687	123	97	89	.18	481,949
1943	John Longden	871	173	140	121	.20	573,276
1944	Ted Atkinson	1,539	287	231	213	.19	899,101
1945	John Longden	778	180	112	100	.23	981,977
1946	Ted Atkinson	1,377	233	213	173	.17	1,036,825
1947	Douglas Dodson	646	141	100	75	.22	1,429,949
1948	Eddie Arcaro	726	188	108	98	.26	1,686,230
1949	Steve Brooks	906	209	172	110	.23	1,316,817
1950	Eddie Arcaro	888	195	153	144	.22	1,410,160
1951	Bill Shoemaker	1,161	257	197	161	.22	1,329,890
1952	Eddie Arcaro	807	188	122	109	.23	1,859,591
1953	Bill Shoemaker	1,683	485	302	210	.29	1,784,187
1954	Bill Shoemaker	1,251	380	221	142	.30	1,876,760
1955	Eddie Arcaro	820	158	126	108	.19	1,864,796
1956	Bill Hartack	1,387	347	252	184	.25	2,343,955
1957	Bill Hartack	1,238	341	208	178	.28	3,060,501
1958	Bill Shoemaker	1,133	300	185	137	.26	2,961,693
1959	Bill Shoemaker	1,285	347	230	159	.27	2,843,133
1960	Bill Shoemaker	1,227	274	196	158	.22	2,123,961
1961	Bill Shoemaker	1,256	304	186	175	.24	2,690,819
1962	Bill Shoemaker	1,126	311	156	128	.28	2,916,844
1963	Bill Shoemaker	1,203	271	193	137	.22	2,526,925
1964	Bill Shoemaker	1,056	246	147	133	.23	2,649,553
1965	Braulio Baeza	1,245	270	200	201	.22	2,582,702
1966	Braulio Baeza	1,341	298	222	190	.22	2,951,022
1967	Braulio Baeza	1,064	256	184	127	.24	3,088,888
1968	Braulio Baeza	1,089	201	184	145	.18	2,835,108
1969	Jorge Velasquez	1,442	258	230	204	.18	2,542,315
1970	Laffit Pincay Jr.	1,328	269	208	187	.20	2,626,526
1971	Laffit Pincay Jr.	1,627	380	288	214	.23	3,784,377
1972	Laffit Pincay Jr.	1,388	289	215	205	.21	3,225,827
1973	Laffit Pincay Jr.	1,444	350	254	209	.24	4,093,492
1974	Laffit Pincay Jr.	1,278	341	227	180	.27	4,251,060
1975	Braulio Baeza	1,190	196	208	180	.16	3,674,398
1976	Angel Cordero Jr.	1,534	274	273	235	.18	4,709,500
1977	Steve Cauthen	2,075	487	345	304	.23	6,151,750
1978	Darrel McHargue	1,762	375	294	263	.21	6,188,353
1979	Laffit Pincay Jr.	1,708	420	302	261	.25	8,183,535
1980	Chris McCarron	1,964	405	318	282	.20	7,666,100
1981	Chris McCarron	1,494	326	251	207	.22	8,397,604
1982	Angel Cordero Jr.	1,838	397	338	227	.22	9,702,520
1983	Angel Cordero Jr.	1,792	362	296	237	.20	10,116,807
1984	Chris McCarron	1,565	356	276	218	.23	12,038,213
1985	Laffit Pincay Jr.	1,409	289	246	183	.21	13,415,049
1986	Jose Santos	1,636	329	237	222	.20	11,329,297
1987	Jose Santos	1,639	305	268	208	.19	12,407,355
1988	Jose Santos	1,867	370	287	265	.20	14,877,298

Jockey—Money Won (Cont.)

Year	Jockey	Mts	1st	2nd	3rd	Pct	Winnings ($)
1989	Jose Santos	1,459	285	238	220	.20	13,847,003
1990	Gary Stevens	1,504	283	245	202	.19	13,881,198
1991	Chris McCarron	1,440	265	228	206	.18	14,441,083
1992	Kent Desormeaux	1,568	361	260	208	.23	14,193,006
1993	Mike Smith	1,510	343	235	214	.23	14,008,148
1994	Mike Smith	1,484	317	250	196	.21	15,979,820
1995	Jerry Bailey	1,265	287	193	144	.23	16,308,230
1996	Jerry Bailey	1,187	298	189	165	.25	19,465,376
1997	Jerry Bailey	1,143	272	186	178	.26	18,260,553
1998	Gary Stevens	869	178	145	122	.20	19,358,840
1999	Pat Day	1,265	254	209	209	.20	18,092,845
2000	Pat Day	1,219	267	206	186	.22	17,479,838
2001	Jerry Bailey	912	227	194	137	.25	22,597,720
2002	Jerry Bailey	832	213	139	118	.26	19,271,814
2003	Jerry Bailey	776	206	149	97	.27	23,354,960
2004	John R. Velazquez	1,327	335	222	181	.25	22,248,661

Jockey—Races Won

Year	Jockey	Mts	1st	2nd	3rd	Pct
1895	J. Perkins	762	192	177	129	.25
1896	J. Scherrer	1,093	271	227	172	.24
1897	H. Martin	803	173	152	116	.21
1898	T. Burns	973	277	213	149	.28
1899	T. Burns	1,064	273	173	266	.26
1900	C. Mitchell	874	195	140	139	.23
1901	W. O'Connor	1,047	253	221	192	.24
1902	J. Ranch	1,069	276	205	181	.26
1903	G.C. Fuller	918	229	152	122	.25
1904	E. Hildebrand	1,169	297	230	171	.25
1905	D. Nicol	861	221	143	136	.26
1906	W. Miller	1,384	388	300	199	.28
1907	W. Miller	1,194	334	226	170	.28
1908	V. Powers	1,260	324	204	185	.26
1909	V. Powers	704	173	121	114	.25
1910	G. Garner	947	200	188	153	.20
1911	T. Koerner	813	162	133	112	.20
1912	P. Hill	967	168	141	129	.17
1913	M. Buxton	887	146	131	136	.16
1914	J. McTaggart	787	157	132	106	.20
1915	M. Garner	775	151	118	90	.19
1916	F. Robinson	791	178	131	124	.23
1917	W. Crump	803	151	140	101	.19
1918	F. Robinson	864	185	140	108	.21
1919	C. Robinson	896	190	140	126	.21
1920	J. Butwell	721	152	129	139	.21
1921	C. Lang	696	135	110	105	.19
1922	M. Fator	859	188	153	116	.22
1923	I. Parke	718	173	105	95	.24
1924	I. Parke	844	205	175	121	.24
1925	A. Mortensen	987	187	145	138	.19
1926	R. Jones	1,172	190	163	152	.16
1927	L. Hardy	1,130	207	192	151	.18
1928	J. Inzelone	1,052	155	152	135	.15
1929	M. Knight	871	149	132	133	.17
1930	H.R. Riley	861	177	145	123	.21
1931	H. Roble	1,174	173	173	155	.15
1932	J. Gilbert	1,050	212	144	160	.20
1933	J. Westrope	1,224	301	235	166	.25
1934	M. Peters	1,045	221	179	147	.21
1935	C. Stevenson	1,099	206	169	146	.19
1936	B. James	1,106	245	195	161	.22
1937	J. Adams	1,265	260	186	177	.21
1938	J. Longden	1,150	236	168	171	.21
1939	D. Meade	1,284	255	221	180	.20
1940	E. Dew	1,377	287	201	180	.21

Jockey—Races Won *(Cont.)*

Year	Jockey	Mts	1st	2nd	3rd	Pct
1941	D. Meade	1,164	210	185	158	.18
1942	J. Adams	1,120	245	185	150	.22
1943	J. Adams	1,069	228	159	171	.21
1944	T. Atkinson	1,539	287	231	213	.19
1945	J.D. Jessop	1,085	290	182	168	.27
1946	T. Atkinson	1,377	233	213	173	.17
1947	J. Longden	1,327	316	250	195	.24
1948	J. Longden	1,197	319	233	161	.27
1949	G. Glisson	1,347	270	217	181	.20
1950	W. Shoemaker	1,640	388	266	230	.24
1951	C. Burr	1,319	310	232	192	.24
1952	A. DeSpirito	1,482	390	247	212	.26
1953	W. Shoemaker	1,683	485	302	210	.29
1954	W. Shoemaker	1,251	380	221	142	.30
1955	W. Hartack	1,702	417	298	215	.25
1956	W. Hartack	1,387	347	252	184	.25
1957	W. Hartack	1,238	341	208	178	.28
1958	W. Shoemaker	1,133	300	185	137	.26
1959	W. Shoemaker	1,285	347	230	159	.27
1960	W. Hartack	1,402	307	247	190	.22
1961	J. Sellers	1,394	328	212	227	.24
1962	R. Ferraro	1,755	352	252	226	.20
1963	W. Blum	1,704	360	286	215	.21
1964	W. Blum	1,577	324	274	170	.21
1965	J. Davidson	1,582	319	228	190	.20
1966	A. Gomez	996	318	173	142	.32
1967	J. Velasquez	1,939	438	315	270	.23
1968	A. Cordero Jr.	1,662	345	278	219	.21
1969	L. Snyder	1,645	352	290	243	.21
1970	S. Hawley	1,908	452	313	265	.24
1971	L Pincay Jr.	1,627	380	288	214	.23
1972	S. Hawley	1,381	367	269	200	.27
1973	S. Hawley	1,925	515	336	292	.27
1974	C.J. McCarron	2,199	546	392	297	.25
1975	C.J. McCarron	2,194	458	389	305	.21
1976	S. Hawley	1,637	413	245	201	.25
1977	S. Cauthen	2,075	487	345	304	.23
1978	E. Delahoussaye	1,666	384	285	238	.23
1979	D. Gall	2,146	479	396	326	.22
1980	C.J. McCarron	1,964	405	318	282	.20
1981	D. Gall	1,917	376	305	297	.20
1982	Pat Day	1,870	399	326	255	.21
1983	Pat Day	1,725	454	321	251	.26
1984	Pat Day	1,694	399	296	259	.24
1985	C.W. Antley	2,335	469	371	288	.20
1986	Pat Day	1,417	429	246	202	.30
1987	Kent Desormeaux	2,207	450	370	294	.28
1988	Kent Desormeaux	1,897	474	295	276	.25
1989	Kent Desormeaux	2,312	598	385	309	.25
1990	Pat Day	1,421	364	265	222	.26
1991	Pat Day	1,405	430	256	213	.31
1992	Russell Baze	1,691	433	296	237	.25
1993	Russell Baze	1,579	410	297	225	.26
1994	Russell Baze	1,588	415	301	266	.26
1995	Russell Baze	1,531	445	310	232	.29
1996	Russell Baze	1,482	415	297	200	.28
1997	Edgar S. Prado	2,037	533	384	308	.26
1998	Edgar S. Prado	1,969	470	377	285	.23
1999	Edgar S. Prado	1,902	402	307	276	.21
2000	Ramon Dominguez	1,586	361	293	238	.23
2001	Ramon Dominguez	1,864	431	368	278	.23
2002	Russell Baze	1,508	431	302	219	.29
2003	Ramon Dominguez	1,627	453	316	252	.28
2004	Rafael Bejarano	1,922	455	355	280	.24

Leading Jockeys—Career Records

Jockey	Years Riding	Mts	1st	2nd	3rd	Win Pct	Winnings ($)
Laffit Pincay Jr. (2003)	39	48,486	9,531	7,784	6,650	.197	236,851,825
Russell Baze	32	41,084	9,108	7,001	5,847	.221	136,719,971
Bill Shoemaker (1990)	42	40,350	8,833	6,136	4,987	.219	123,375,524
Pat Day (2004)	33	40,298	8,803	6,860	5,687	.218	297,912,019
Dave Gall (1999)	41	41,775	7,396	6,525	6,131	.177	24,547,584
Chris McCarron (2002)	28	34,244	7,141	5,670	4,673	.209	264,351,679
Angel Cordero (1992)	31	38,656	7,057	6,136	5,359	.183	164,561,227
Jorge Velasquez (1998)	35	40,852	6,795	6,178	5,755	.166	125,544,379
Sandy Hawley (1998)	31	31,455	6,449	4,825	4,159	.205	88,681,292
Larry Snyder (1994)	35	35,681	6,388	5,030	3,440	.179	47,207,289
Eddie Delahoussaye (2002)	32	39,213	6,384	5,676	5,585	.163	195,881,170
Earlie Fires	41	44,212	6,360	5,454	5,277	.144	83,169,737
Carl Gambardella (1994)	39	39,018	6,349	5,953	5,353	.163	29,389,041
John Longden (1966)	40	32,413	6,032	4,914	4,273	.186	24,665,800
Jerry Bailey	32	30,746	5,869	4,537	3,915	.191	291,028,681
Mario Pino	26	34,578	5,588	5,096	4,761	.162	90,630,277
Edgar Prado	22	28,545	5,473	4,646	4,060	.192	163,100,032
Jacinto Vasquez (1998)	38	37,337	5,228	4,714	4,510	.140	82,754,115
Ron Ardoin (2003)	31	32,335	5,226	4,298	3,793	.162	58,908,059
Anthony Black	29	32,230	4,940	4,268	4,138	.153	56,531,333

Note: Jockeys ranked by wins. Records go through October 2005, and include available statistics for races ridden in foreign countries. Figures in parentheses after jockey's name indicate last year in which he rode.

Leading jockeys courtesy of *National Thoroughbred Racing Association.*

Ticket Tales

Chris Hertzog, a 39-year-old Phoenix firefighter, spent $100 on Kentucky Derby quick picks at the Turf Paradise racetrack. Hertzog thought he had misplaced his winning ticket, worth $864,253, but it was recovered by teller Branda Reagan, 41, to whom Herzog later gave $25,000.

HORSES

Ack Ack (1986, 1966)
Affectionately (1989, 1960)
Affirmed (1980, 1975)
All Along (1990, 1979)
Alsab (1976, 1939)
Alydar (1989, 1975)
Alysheba (1993, 1984)
American Eclipse (1970, 1814)
A.P. Indy (2000, 1989)
Armed (1963, 1941)
Artful (1956, 1902)
Arts and Letters (1994, 1966)
Assault (1964, 1943)
Battleship (1969, 1927)
Bayakoa (1998, 1984)
Bed o' Roses (1976, 1947)
Beldame (1956, 1901)
Ben Brush (1955, 1893)
Bewitch (1977, 1945)
Bimelech (1990, 1937)
Black Gold (1989, 1921)
Black Helen (1991, 1932)
Blue Larkspur (1957, 1926)
Bold 'n Determined (1997, 1977)
Bold Ruler (1973, 1954)
Bon Nouvel (1976, 1960)
Boston (1955, 1833)
Bowl of Flowers (2004, 1988)
Broomstick (1956, 1901)
Buckpasser (1970, 1963)
Busher (1964, 1942)
Bushranger (1967, 1930)
Cafe Prince (1985, 1970)
Carry Back (1975, 1958)
Cavalcade (1993, 1931)
Challedon (1977, 1936)
Chris Evert (1988, 1971)
Cicada (1967, 1959)
Cigar (2002, 1990)
Citation (1959, 1945)
Coaltown (1983, 1945)
Colin (1956, 1905)
Commando (1956, 1898)
Count Fleet (1961, 1940)
Crusader (1995, 1923)
Dahlia (1981, 1970)
Damascus (1974, 1964)
Dance Smartly (2003, 1988)
Dark Mirage (1974, 1965)
Davona Dale (1985, 1976)
Desert Vixen (1979, 1970)
Devil Diver (1980, 1939)
Discovery (1969, 1931)
Domino (1955, 1891)
Dr. Fager (1971, 1964)
Easy Goer (1997, 1986)
Eight Thirty (1994, 1936)

Elkridge (1966, 1938)
Emperor of Norfolk (1988, 1885)
Equipoise (1957, 1928)
Exceller (1999, 1973)
Exterminator (1957, 1915)
Fairmount (1985, 1921)
Fair Play (1956, 1905)
Fashion (1980, 1837)
Firenze (1981, 1884)
Flatterer (1994, 1979)
Flawlessly (2004, 1988)
Foolish Pleasure (1995, 1972)
Forego (1979, 1970)
Fort Marcy (1998, 1964)
Gallant Bloom (1977, 1966)
Gallant Fox (1957, 1927)
Gallant Man (1987, 1954)
Gallorette (1962, 1942)
Gamely (1980, 1964)
Genuine Risk (1986, 1977)
Go For Wand (1996, 1987)
Good and Plenty (1956, 1900)
Grandville (1997, 1933)
Grey Lag (1957, 1918)
Gun Bow (1999, 1960)
Hamburg (1986, 1895)
Hanover (1955, 1884)
Henry of Navarre (1985, 1891)
Hill Prince (1991, 1947)
Hindoo (1955, 1878)
Holy Bull (2001, 1991)
Imp (1965, 1894)
Jay Trump (1971, 1957)
John Henry (1990, 1975)
Johnstown (1992, 1936)
Jolly Roger (1965, 1922)
Kelso (1967, 1957)
Kentucky (1983, 1861)
Kingston (1955, 1884)
Lady's Secret (1992, 1982)
La Prevoyante (1995, 1970)
L'Escargot (1977, 1963)
Lexington (1955, 1850)
Longfellow (1971, 1867)
Luke Blackburn (1956, 1877)
Majestic Prince (1988, 1966)
Man o' War (1957, 1917)
Maskette.(2001, 1908)
Miesque (1999, 1984)
Miss Woodford (1967, 1880)
Myrtlewood (1979, 1932)
Nashua (1965, 1952)
Native Dancer (1963, 1950)
Native Diver (1978, 1959)
Needles (2000, 1953)
Neji (1966, 1950)
Noor (2002, 1945)

Northern Dancer (1976, 1961)
Oedipus (1978, 1946)
Old Rosebud (1968, 1911)
Omaha (1965, 1932)
Pan Zareta (1972, 1910)
Parole (1984, 1873)
Paseana (2001, 1987)
Personal Ensign (1993, 1984)
Peter Pan (1956, 1904)
Precisionist (2003, 1981)
Princess Doreen (1982, 1921)
Princess Rooney (1991, 1980)
Real Delight (1987, 1949)
Regret (1957, 1912)
Reigh Count (1978, 1923)
Riva Ridge (1998, 1969)
Roamer (1981, 1911)
Roseben (1956, 1901)
Round Table (1972, 1954)
Ruffian (1976, 1972)
Ruthless (1975, 1864)
Salvator (1955, 1886)
Sarazen (1957, 1921)
Seabiscuit (1958, 1933)
Searching (1978, 1952)
Seattle Slew (1981, 1974)
Secretariat (1974, 1970)
Serena's Song (2002, 1992)
Shuvee (1975, 1966)
Silver Spoon (1978, 1956)
Sir Archy (1955, 1805)
Sir Barton (1957, 1916)
Skip Away (2004, 1993)
Slew o' Gold (1992, 1980)
Spectacular Bid (1982, 1976)
Stymie (1975, 1941)
Sun Beau (1996, 1925)
Sunday Silence (1996, 1986)
Susan's Girl (1976, 1969)
Swaps (1966, 1952)
Sword Dancer (1977, 1956)
Sysonby (1956, 1902)
Ta Wee (1994, 1967)
Ten Broeck (1982, 1872)
Tim Tam (1985, 1955)
Tom Fool (1960, 1949)
Top Flight (1966, 1929)
Tosmah (1984, 1961)
Twenty Grand (1957, 1928)
Twilight Tear (1963, 1941)
Two Lea (1982, 1946)
War Admiral (1958, 1934)
Whirlaway (1959, 1938)
Whisk Broom II (1979, 1907)
Winning Colors (2000, 1985)
Zaccio (1990, 1976)
Zev (1983, 1920)

Note: Years of election and foaling in parentheses.

HARNESS RACING

Major Races

Hambletonian

Year	Winner	Driver	Year	Winner	Driver
1926	Guy McKinney	Nat Ray	1967	Speedy Streak	Del Cameron
1927	Iosola's Worthy	Marvin Childs	1968	Nevele Pride	Stanley Dancer
1928	Spenser	W. H. Leese	1969	Lindy's Pride	H. Beissinger
1929	Walter Dear	Walter Cox	1970	Timothy T.	J. Simpson Jr.
1930	Hanover's Bertha	Tom Berry	1971	Speedy Crown	H. Beissinger
1931	Calumet Butler	R. D. McMahon	1972	Super Bowl	Stanley Dancer
1932	The Marchioness	William Caton	1973	Flirth	Ralph Baldwin
1933	Mary Reynolds	Ben White	1974	Christopher T.	Bill Haughton
1934	Lord Jim	Doc Parshall	1975	Bonefish	Stanley Dancer
1935	Greyhound	Sep Palin	1976	Steve Lobell	Bill Haughton
1936	Rosalind	Ben White	1977	Green Speed	Bill Haughton
1937	Shirley Hanover	Henry Thomas	1978	Speedy Somolli	H. Beissinger
1938	McLin Hanover	Henry Thomas	1979	Legend Hanover	George Sholty
1939	Peter Astra	Doc Parshall	1980	Burgomeister	Bill Haughton
1940	Spencer Scott	Fred Egan	1981	Shiaway St. Pat	Ray Remmen
1941	Bill Gallon	Lee Smith	1982	Speed Bowl	Tom Haughton
1942	The Ambassador	Ben White	1983	Duenna	Stanley Dancer
1943	Volo Song	Ben White	1984	Historic Freight	Ben Webster
1944	Yankee Maid	Henry Thomas	1985	Prakas	Bill O'Donnell
1945	Titan Hanover	H. Pownall Sr.	1986	Nuclear Kosmos	Ulf Thoresen
1946	Chestertown	Thomas Berry	1987	Mack Lobell	John Campbell
1947	Hoot Mon	Sep Palin	1988	Armbro Goal	John Campbell
1948	Demon Hanover	Harrison Hoyt	1989	Park Ave. Joe/Probe*	R. Waples/B. Fahy
1949	Miss Tilly	Fred Egan	1990	Harmonious	John Campbell
1950	Lusty Song	Del Miller	1991	Giant Victory	Jack Moiseyev
1951	Mainliner	Guy Crippen	1992	Alf Palema	Mickey McNichol
1952	Sharp Note	Bion Shively	1993	American Winner	Ron Pierce
1953	Helicopter	Harry Harvey	1994	Victory Dream	Michel Lachance
1954	Newport Dream	Del Cameron	1995	Tagliabue	John Campbell
1955	Scott Frost	Joe O'Brien	1996	Continentalvictory	Michel Lachance
1956	The Intruder	Ned Bower	1997	Malabar Man	Mal Burroughs
1957	Hickory Smoke	J. Simpson Sr.	1998	Muscles Yankee	John Campbell
1958	Emily's Pride	Flave Nipe	1999	Self Possessed	Michel Lachance
1959	Diller Hanover	Frank Ervin	2000	Yankee Paco	T.J. Ritchie
1960	Blaze Hanover	Joe O'Brien	2001	Scarlet Knight	Stefan Melander
1961	Harlan Dean	James Arthur	2002	Chip Chip Hooray	Eric Ledford
1962	A. C.'s Viking	Sanders Russell	2003	Amigo Hall	Mike Lachance
1963	Speedy Scot	Ralph Baldwin	2004	Windsong's Legacy	T. Smedshammer
1964	Ayres	J. Simpson Sr.	2005	P-Forty-Seven	Dave Palone
1965	Egyptian Candor	Del Cameron			
1966	Kerry Way	Frank Ervin			

*Park Avenue Joe and Probe dead-heated for win. Park Avenue finished first in the summary 2-1-1 to Probe's 1-9-1 finish.
Note: Run at 1 mile since 1947.

Little Brown Jug

Year	Winner	Driver	Year	Winner	Driver
1946	Ensign Hanover	Wayne Smart	1977	Governor Skipper	John Chapman
1947	Forbes Chief	Del Cameron	1978	Happy Escort	William Popfinger
1948	Knight Dream	Frank Safford	1979	Hot Hitter	Herve Filion
1949	Good Time	Frank Ervin	1980	Niatross	Clint Galbraith
1950	Dudley Hanover	Del Miller	1981	Fan Hanover	Glen Garnsey
1951	Tar Heel	Del Cameron	1982	Merger	John Campbell
1952	Meadow Rice	Wayne Smart	1983	Ralph Hanover	Ron Waples
1953	Keystoner	Frank Ervin	1984	Colt Fortysix	Chris Boring
1954	Adios Harry	Morris MacDonald	1985	Nihilator	Bill O'Donnell
1955	Quick Chief	Bill Haughton	1986	Barberry Spur	Bill O'Donnell
1956	Noble Adios	John Simpson Sr.	1987	Jaguar Spur	Dick Stillings
1957	Torpid	John Simpso Sr.	1988	B. J. Scoot	Michel Lachance
1958	Shadow Wave	Joe O'Brien	1989	Goalie Jeff	Michel Lachance
1959	Adios Butler	Clint Hodgins	1990	Beach Towel	Ray Remmen
1960	Bullet Hanover	John Simpson Sr.	1991	Precious Bunny	Jack Moiseye
1961	Henry T. Adios	Stanley Dancer	1992	Fake Left	Ron Waples
1962	Lehigh Hanover	Stanley Dancer	1993	Life Sign	John Campbell
1963	Overtrick	John Patterson	1994	Magical Mike	Michel Lachance
1964	Vicar Hanover	Bill Haughton	1995	Nick's Fantasy	John Campbell
1965	Bret Hanover	Frank Ervin	1996	Armbro Operative	Jack Moiseyev
1966	Romeo Hanover	George Sholty	1997	Western Dreamer	Michel Lachance
1967	Best of All	James Hackett	1998	Shady Character	Ron Pierce
1968	Rum Customer	Bill Haughton	1999	Blissful Hall	Ron Pierce
1969	Laverne Hanover	Bill Haughton	2000	Astreos	Chris Christoforou
1970	Most Happy Fella	Stanley Dancer	2001	Bettor's Delight	Michel Lachance
1971	Nansemond	Herve Filion	2002	Million Dollar Cam	Luc Ouellette
1972	Strike Out	Keith Waples	2003	No Pan Intended	David S. Miller
1973	Melvin's Woe	Joe O'Brien	2004	Timesareachanging	Ron Pierce
1974	Armbro Omaha	Bill Haughton	2005	Vivid Photo	Roger Hammer
1975	Seatrain	Ben Webster			
1976	Keystone Ore	Stanley Dancer			

Border Control

Stewart Elliot, who road Smarty Jones to victory at the 2004 Kentucky Derby and Preakness, was detained by US immigration officials after returning from an overseas trip. Elliott, a Canadian and permanent US resident, had pled guilty to an aggravated assault charge after a 2001 fight at a friend's home. He served a year of probabtion and paid a fine. However, US law permits the deportation of foreigners with felony convictions. Elliot was briefly held by immigration authorities, but was later released.

Breeders' Crown

1984

Div	Winner	Driver
2PC	Dragon's Lair	Jeff Mallet
2PF	Amneris	John Campbell
3PC	Troublemaker	Bill O'Donnell
3PF	Naughty But Nice	Tommy Haughton
2TC	Workaholic	Berndt Lindstedt
2TF	Conifer	George Sholty
3TC	Baltic Speed	Jan Nordin
3TF	Fancy Crown	Bill O'Donnell

1985

Div	Winner	Driver
2PC	Robust Hanover	John Campbell
2PF	Caressable	Herve Filion
3PC	Nihilator	Bill O'Donnell
3PF	Stienam	Buddy Gilmour
2TC	Express Ride	John Campbell
2TF	JEF's Spice	Mickey McNichol
3TC	Prakas	John Campbell
3TF	Armbro Devona	Bill O'Donnell
AP	Division Street	Michel Lachance
AT	Sandy Bowl	John Campbell

1986

Div	Winner	Driver
2PC	Sunset Warrior	Bill Gale
2PF	Halcyon	Ray Remmen
3PC	Masquerade	Richard Silverman
3PF	Glow Softly	Ron Waples
2TC	Mack Lobell	John Campbell
2TF	Super Flora	Ron Waples
3TC	Sugarcane Hanover	Ron Waples
3TF	JEF's Spice	Bill O'Donnell
APM	Samshu Bluegrass	Michel Lachance
ATM	Grades Singing	Herve Filion
APH	Forrest Skipper	Lucien Fontaine
ATH	Nearly Perfect	Mickey McNichol

1987

Div	Winner	Driver
2PC	Camtastic	Bill O'Donnell
2PF	Leah Almahurst	Bill Fahy
3PC	Call For Rain	Clint Galbraith
3PF	Pacific	Tom Harmer
2TC	Defiant One	Howard Beissinger
2TF	Nan's Catch	Berndt Lindstedt
3TC	Mack Lobell	John Campbell
3TF	Armbro Fling	George Sholty
APM	Follow My Star	John Campbell
ATM	Grades Singing	Olle Goop
APH	Armbro Emerson	Walter Whelan
ATH	Sugarcane Hanover	Ron Waples

1988

Div	Winner	Driver
2PC	Kentucky Spur	Dick Stillings
2PF	Central Park West	John Campbell
3PC	Camtastic	Bill O'Donnell
3PF	Sweet Reflection	Bill O'Donnell
2TC	Valley Victory	Bill O'Donnell
2TF	Peace Corps	John Campbell
3TC	Firm Tribute	Mark O'Mara
3TF	Nalda Hanover	Mickey McNichol
APM	Anniecrombie	Dave Magee
ATM	Armbro Flori	Larry Walker
APH	Call For Rain	Clint Galbraith
ATH	Mack Lobell	John Campbell

1989

Div	Winner	Driver
2PC	Till We Meet Again	Mickey McNichol
2PF	Town Pro	Doug Brown
3PC	Goalie Jeff	Michel Lachance
3PF	Cheery Hello	John Campbell
2TC	Royal Troubador	Carl Allen
2TF	Delphi's Lobell	Ron Waples
3TC	Esquire Spur	Dick Stillings
3TF	Pace Corps	John Campbell
APM	Armbro Feather	John Kopas
ATM	Grades Singing	Olle Goop
APH	Matt's Scooter	Michel Lachance
ATH	Delray Lobell	John Campbell

1990

Div	Winner	Driver
2PC	Artsplace	John Campbell
2PF	Miss Easy	John Campbell
3PC	Beach Towel	Ray Remmen
3PF	Town Pro	Doug Brown
2TC	Crysta's Best	Dick Richardson Jr.
2TF	Jean Bi	Jan Nordin
3TC	Embassy Lobell	Michel Lachance
3TF	Me Maggie	Berndt Lindstedt
APM	Caesar's Jackpot	Bill Fahy
ATM	Peace Corps	Stig Johansson
APH	Bay's Fella	Paul MacDonell
ATH	No Sex Please	Ron Waples

1991

Div	Winner	Driver
2PC	Digger Almahurst	Doug Brown
2PF	Hazleton Kay	John Campbell
3PC	Three Wizzards	Bill Gale
3PF	Miss Easy	John Campbell
2TC	King Conch	Bill Gale
2TF	Armbro Keepsake	John Campbell
3TC	Giant Victory	Ron Pierce
3TF	Twelve Speed	Ron Waples
APM	Delinquent Account	Bill O'Donnell
ATM	Me Maggie	Berndt Lindstedt
APH	Camluck	Michel Lachance
ATH	Billyjojimbob	Paul MacDonell

1992

Div	Winner	Driver
2PC	Village Jiffy	Ron Waples
2PF	Immortality	John Campbell
3PC	Kingsbridge	Roger Mayotte
3PF	So Fresh	John Campbell
2TC	Giant Chill	John Patterson Jr.
2TF	Winky's Goal	Cat Manzi
3TC	Baltic Striker	Michel Lachance
3TF	Imperfection	Michel Lachance
APM	Shady Daisy	Ron Pierce
ATM	Peace Corps	Torbjorn Jansson
APH	Artsplace	John Campbell
ATH	No Sex Please	Ron Waples

Note: 2=Two-year-old; T=Trotter; C=Colt; 3=Three-year-old; P=Pacer; F=Filly; A=Aged; H=Horse; M=Mare.

Breeders' Crown (Cont.)

1993

Div	Winner	Driver
2PC	Expensive Scooter	Jack Moiseyev
2PF	Electric Scooter	Mike Lachance
3PC	Life Sign	John Campbell
3PF	Immortality	John Campbell
2TC	Westgate Crown	John Campbell
2TF	Gleam	Jimmy Takter
3TC	Pine Chip	John Campbell
3TF	Expressway Hanover	Per Henriksen
APM	Swing Back	Kelly Sheppard
ATM	Lifetime Dream	Paul MacDonnell
APH	Staying Together	Bill O'Donnell
ATH	Earl	Chris Christoforou Jr.

1994

Div	Winner	Driver
2PC	Jenna's Beach Boy	Bill Fahy
2PF	Yankee Cashmere	Peter Wrenn
3PC	Magical Mike	Michel Lachance
3PF	Hardie Hanover	Tim Twaddle
2TC	Eager Seelster	Teddy Jacobs
2TF	Lookout Victory	John Patterson
3TC	Incredible Abe	Italo Tamborrino
3TF	Imageofa Clear Day	Bill O'Donnell
APM	Shady Daisy	Michel Lachance
ATM	Armbro Keepsake	Stig Johansson
APH	Village Jiffy	Paul MacDonell
ATH	Pine Chip	John Campbell

1995

Div	Winner	Driver
2PC	John Street North	Jack Moiseyev
2PF	Paige Nicole Q	John Campbell
3PC	Jenna's Beach Boy	Bill Fahy
3PF	Headline Hanover	Doug Brown
2TC	Armbro Officer	Steve Condren
2TF	Continentalvictory	Michel Lachance
3TC	Abundance	Bill O'Donnell
3TF	Lookout Victory	Sonny Patterson
APM	Ellamony	Mike Saftic
ATM	CR Kay Suzie	Rod Allen
APH	That'll Be Me	Roger Mayotte
ATH	Panifesto	Luc Ouellette

1996

Div	Winner	Driver
2PC	His Mattjesty	Doug Brown
2PF	Before Sunrise	Steve Condren
3PC	Armbro Operative	Michel Lachance
3PF	Mystical Maddy	Michel Lachance
2TC	Malabar Man	Mal Burroughs
2TF	Armbro Prowess	Jimmy Takter
3TC	Running Sea	Wally Hennessey
3TF	Personal Banner	Peter Wrenn
APM	She's A Great Lady	John Campbell
APH	Jenna's Beach Boy	Bill Fahy
AT	CR Kay Suzie	Rod Allen

1997

Div	Winner	Driver
2PC	Artiscape	Michel Lachance
2PF	Take Flight	Luc Ouellette
3PC	Village Jasper	Paul McDonnell
3PF	Stienam's Place	Jack Moiseyev
2TC	Catch As Catch Can	Wally Hennessey
2TF	My Dolly	Wally Hennessey
3TC	Malabar Man	Malvern Burroughs
3TF	No Nonsense Woman	Jim Doherty
APM	Jay's Table	John Campbell
APH	Red Bow Tie	Luc Ouellette
AT	Moni Maker	Wally Hennessey

1998

Div	Winner	Driver
2PC	Badlands Hanover	Ron Pierce
2PF	Juliet's Fate	George Brennan
3PC	Artiscape	Michel Lachance
3PF	Galleria	George Brennan
2TC	CR Commando	Carl Allen
2TF	Musical Victory	Luc Ouellette
3TC	Muscles Yankee	John Campbell
3TF	Lassie's Goal	Mark O'Mara
APM	Shore By Five	Daniel Dube
APH	Red Bow Tie	Luc Ouellette
AT	Supergrit	Ron Pierce

1999

Div	Winner	Driver
2PC	Tyberwood	Richard Silverman
2PF	Eternal Camnation	Eric Ledford
3PC	Grinfromeartoear	Chris Christoforou
3PF	Odies Fame	David Wall
2TC	Master Lavec	Daniel Daley
2TF	Dream of Joy	James Meittinis
3TC	CR Renegade	Rodney Allen
3TF	Oolong	Ronald Pierce
APM	Shore By Five	Daniel Dube
APH	Red Bow Tie	Luc Ouellette
AT	Supergrit	Ronald Pierce

2000

Div	Winner	Driver
2PC	Bettor's Delight	Michel Lachance
2PF	Lady MacBeach	Luc Ouellette
3PC	Gallo Blue Chip	Daniel Dube
3PF	Popcorn Penny	Ryan Anderson
2TC	Banker Hall	Trevor Ritchie
2TF	Syrinx Hanover	Trevor Ritchie
3TC	Fast Photo	Michel Lachance
3TF	Aviano	Trevor Ritchie
APM	Ron's Girl	Michel Lachance
APH	Western Ideal	Michel Lachance
AT	Magician	David Miller

2001

Div	Winner	Driver
2PC	Western Shooter	John Campbell
2PF	Cam Swifty	Jim Meittinis
3PC	Real Desire	John Campbell
3PF	Bunny Lake	John Stark Jr.
2TC	Duke Of York	Paul MacDonnell
2TF	Cameron Hall	Michel Lachance
3TC	Liberty Balance	Randall Waples
3TF	Syrinx Hanover	John Campbell
APM	Eternal Camnation	Eric Ledford
APH	Goliath Bayama	Sylvain Filion
AT	Varenne	G. Minnucci

2002

Div	Winner	Driver
2PC	Totally Western	Mario Baillargeon
2PF	Armbro Amoretto	Luc Ouellette
3PC	Art Major	John Campbell
3PF	Allamerican Nadia	Chris Christoforou
2TC	Broadway Hall	John Campbell
2TF	Pick Me Up	Luc Ouellette
3TC	Kadabra	David S. Miller
3TF	Cameron Hall	Trevor Ritchie
APM	Molly Can Do It	Jack Moiseyev
APH	Real Desire	John Campbell
AT	Fool's Goal	Jack Moiseyev

Breeders' Crown (Cont.)

	2003			2004	
Div	Winner	Driver	Div	Winner	Driver
2PC	I Am A Fool	Ron Pierce	2PC	Village Jolt	Ron Pierce
2PF	Pans Culottes	Daniel Dube	2PH	Restive Hanover	Andy Miller
3PC	No Pan Intended	David Miller	3PC	Western Terror	Brian Sears
3PF	Burning Point	Kevin Wallis	3PF	Rainbow Blue	Ron Pierce
2TC	Cantab Hall	Michel Lachance	2TC	Ken Warkentin	David Miller
2TF	Forever Starlet	David Miller	2TF	Flirtin Miss	John Campbell
3TC	Mr. Muscleman	Ron Pierce	3TC	Yankee Slide	Brian Sears
3TF	Stroke Play	Brian Sears	3TF	Housethatruthbuilt	Brian Sears
APM	Eternal Camnation	Eric Ledford	APM	Always Cam	David Miller
APH	Art Major	John Campbell	APH	Boulder Creek	Ron Pierce
AT	Fool's Goal	Jack Moiseyev	AT	Ambro Affair	Ron Pierce

Note: 2=Two-year-old; T=Trotter; C=Colt; 3=Three-year-old; P=Pacer; F=Filly; A=Aged; H=Horse; M=Mare.

Triple Crown Winners

Trotting

Trotting's Triple Crown consists of the Hambletonian (first run in 1926), the Kentucky Futurity (first run in 1893) and the Yonkers Trot (known as the Yonkers Futurity when it began in 1955).

Year	Horse	Owner	Breeder	Trainer & Driver
1955	Scott Frost	S.A. Camp Farms	Est of W.N. Reynolds	Joe O'Brien
1963	Speedy Scot	Castleton Farms	Castleton Farms	Ralph Baldwin
1964	Ayres	Charlotte Sheppard	Charlotte Sheppard	John Simpson Sr
1968	Nevele Pride	Nevele Acres & Lou Resnick	Mr & Mrs E.C. Quin	Stanley Dancer
1969	Lindy's Pride	Lindy Farm	Hanover Shoe Farms	Howard Beissinger
1972	Super Bowl	Rachel Dancer & Rose Hild Breeding Farm	Stoner Creek Stud	Stanley Dancer

Pacing

Pacing's Triple Crown consists of the Cane Pace (called the Cane Futurity when it began in 1955), the Little Brown Jug (first run in 1946) and the Messenger Stakes (first run in 1956).

Year	Horse	Owner	Breeder	Trainer/Driver
1959	Adios Butler	Paige West & Angelo Pellillo	R.C. Carpenter	Paige West/Clint Hodgins
1965	Bret Hanover	Richard Downing	Hanover Shoe Farms	Frank Ervin
1966	Romeo Hanover	Lucky Star Stables & Morton Finder	Hanover Shoe Farms	Jerry Silverman/ William Meyer (Cane) & George Sholty (Jug & Messenger)
1968	Rum Customer	Kennilworth Farms & L. C. Mancuso	Mr. & Mrs. R.C. Larkin	Bill Haughton
1970	Most Happy Fella	Egyptian Acres Stable	Stoner Creek Stud	Stanley Dancer
1980	Niatross	Niagara Acres, C. Galbraith & Niatross Stables	Niagara Acres	Clint Galbraith
1983	Ralph Hanover	Waples Stable, Pointsetta Stable, Grant's Direct Stable & P. J. Baugh	Hanover Shoe Farms	Stew Firlotte/Ron Waples
1997	Western Dreamer	Daniel and Matthew Daly and Patrick Daly Jr.	Kentuckiana Farms	Bill Robinson/Michel Lachance
1999	Blissful Hall	Daniel Plouffe	Walnut Hall Limited	Ben Wallace/Ron Pierce
2003	No Pan Intended	Peter Pan Stables, Inc.	Winbak Farm	Ivan Sugg/David Miller

Awards

Horse of the Year

Year	Horse	Gait	Owner	Year	Horse	Gait	Owner
1947	Victory Song	T	Castleton Farm	1980	Niatross	P	Niatross Syndicate, Niagara Acres, Clint Galbraith
1948	Rodney	T	R.H. Johnston	1981	Fan Hanover	P	Dr. J. Glen Brown
1949	Good Time	P	William Cane	1982	Cam Fella	P	Norm Clements, Norm Faulkner
1950	Proximity	T	Ralph and Gordon Verhurst	1983	Cam Fella	P	JEF's Standardbred, Norm Clements, Norm Faulkner
1951	Pronto Don	T	Hayes Fair Acres Stable				
1952	Good Time	P	William Cane				
1953	Hi Lo's Forbes	P	Mr. and Mrs. Earl Wagner	1984	Fancy Crown	T	Fancy Crown Stable
1954	Stenographer	T	Max Hempt	1985	Nihilator	P	Wall Street-Nihilator Syndicate
1955	Scott Frost	T	S.A. Camp Farms				
1956	Scott Frost	T	S.A. Camp Farms	1986	Forrest Skipper	P	Forrest L. Bartlett
1957	Torpid	P	Sherwood Farm				
1958	Emily's Pride	T	Walnut Hall and Castleton Farms	1987	Mack Lobell	T	One More Time Stable and Fair Wind Farm
1959	Bye Bye Byrd	P	Mr. and Mrs. Rex Larkin	1988	Mack Lobell	T	John Erik Magnusson
1960	Adios Butler	P	Adios Butler Syndicate	1989	Matt's Scooter	P	Gordon and Illa Rumpel, Charles Jurasvinski
1961	Adios Butler	P	Adios Butler Syndicate				
1962	Su Mac Lad	T	I.W. Berkemeyer	1990	Beach Towel	P	Uptown Stables
1963	Speedy Scot	T	Castleton Farm	1991	Precious Bunny	P	R. Peter Heffering
1964	Bret Hanover	P	Richard Downing				
1965	Bret Hanover	P	Richard Downing	1992	Artsplace	P	George Segal
1966	Bret Hanover	P	Richard Downing	1993	Staying Together	P	Robert Hamather
1967	Nevele Pride	T	Nevele Acres				
1968	Nevele Pride	T	Nevele Acres, Louis Resnick	1994	Cam's Card Shark	P	Jeffrey S. Snyder
1969	Nevele Pride	T	Nevele Acres, Louis Resnick	1995	CR Kay Suzie	T	Carl & Rod Allen Stable, Inc.
1970	Fresh Yankee	T	Duncan MacDonald	1996	Continental-victory	T	Continentalvictory Stables
1971	Albatross	P	Albatross Stable	1997	Malabar Man	T	Malvern Burroughs
1972	Albatross	P	Amicable Stable	1998	Moni Maker	T	Moni Maker Stable
1973	Sir Dalrae	P	A La Carte Racing Stable	1999	Moni Maker	T	Moni Maker Stable
1974	Delmonica Hanover	T	Delvin Miller, W. Arnold Hanger	2000	Gallo Blue Chip	P	Dan Gernatt Farms
				2001	Bunny Lake	P	W. Springtime Racing Stable
1975	Savoir	T	Allwood Stable				
1976	Keystone Ore	P	Mr. and Mrs. Stanley Dancer, Rose Hild Farms, Robert Jones	2002	Real Desire	P	Brittany Farms
				2003	No Pan Intended	P	Peter Pan Stables, Inc.
1977	Green Speed	T	Beverly Lloyds	2004	Rainbow Blue	P	George Teague Jr
1978	Abercrombie	P	Shirley Mitchell, L. Keith Bulen				
1979	Niatross	P	Niagara Acres, Clint Galbraith				

Driver of the Year

Year	Driver	Year	Driver	Year	Driver
1968	Stanley Dancer	1980	Ron Waples	1993	Jack Moiseyev
1969	Herve Filion	1981	Herve Filion	1994	Dave Magee
1970	Herve Filion	1982	Bill O'Donnell	1995	Luc Ouellette
1971	Herve Filion	1983	John Campbell	1996	Tony Morgan
1972	Herve Filion	1984	Bill O'Donnell		Luc Ouellette
1973	Herve Filion	1985	Michel Lachance	1997	Tony Morgan
1974	Herve Filion	1986	Michel Lachance	1998	Walter Case Jr.
1975	Joe O'Brien	1987	Michel Lachance	1999	Dave Palone
1976	Herve Filion	1988	John Campbell	2000	Dave Palone
1977	Donald Dancer	1989	Herve Filion	2001	Stephane Bouchard
1978	Carmine Abbatiello	1990	John Campbell	2002	Tony Morgan
	Herve Filion	1991	Walter Case Jr.	2003	Dave Palone
1979	Ron Waples	1992	Walter Case Jr.	2004	Dave Palone

Note: Balloting is conducted by the U.S Trotting Association for the U.S. Harness Writers Association.

Leading Drivers—Money Won

Year	Driver	Winnings ($)	Year	Driver	Winnings ($)
1946	Thomas Berry	121,933	1976	Herve Filion	2,278,634
1947	H.C. Fitzpatrick	133,675	1977	Herve Filion	2,551,058
1948	Ralph Baldwin	153,222	1978	Carmine Abbatiello	3,344,457
1949	Clint Hodgins	184,108	1979	John Campbell	3,308,984
1950	Del Miller	306,813	1980	John Campbell	3,732,306
1951	John Simpson Sr.	333,316	1981	Bill O'Donnell	4,065,608
1952	Bill Haughton	311,728	1982	Bill O'Donnell	5,755,067
1953	Bill Haughton	374,527	1983	John Campbell	6,104,082
1954	Bill Haughton	415,577	1984	Bill O'Donnell	9,059,184
1955	Bill Haughton	599,455	1985	Bill O'Donnell	10,207,372
1956	Bill Haughton	572,945	1986	John Campbell	9,515,055
1957	Bill Haughton	586,950	1987	John Campbell	10,186,495
1958	Bill Haughton	816,659	1988	John Campbell	11,148,565
1959	Bill Haughton	771,435	1989	John Campbell	9,738,450
1960	Del Miller	567,282	1990	John Campbell	11,620,878
1961	Stanley Dancer	674,723	1991	Jack Moiseyev	9,568,468
1962	Stanley Dancer	760,343	1992	John Campbell	8,202,108
1963	Bill Haughton	790,086	1993	John Campbell	9,926,482
1964	Stanley Dancer	1,051,538	1994	John Campbell	9,834,139
1965	Bill Haughton	889,943	1995	John Campbell	9,469,797
1966	Stanley Dancer	1,218,403	1996	Michel Lachance	8,408,231
1967	Bill Haughton	1,305,773	1997	Michel Lachance	9,215,388
1968	Bill Haughton	1,654,463	1998	John Campbell	10,768,771
1969	Del Insko	1,635,463	1999	Luc Ouellette	10,841,495
1970	Herve Filion	1,647,837	2000	John Campbell	11,160,462
1971	Herve Filion	1,915,945	2001	John Campbell	14,184,863
1972	Herve Filion	2,473,265	2002	John Campbell	11,967,597
1973	Herve Filion	2,233,303	2003	David Miller	11,490,590
1974	Herve Filion	3,474,315	2004	Ron Pierce	12,327,863
1975	Carmine Abbatiello	2,275,093			

Motor Sports

Formula One legend Michael Schumacher struggled in 2005

Shifting Gears

New rules hampered F/I legend Schumacher, while Danica Patrick rose to stardom in the IRL

BY MARK BECHTEL

THE INDIANAPOLIS 500 MIGHT have been eclipsed by the Daytona 500 as the biggest race in America, but as far as venues go, no track can hold a candle to the Brickyard for racing drama. Or, in 2005, for bizarre happenings. The 2.5-mile track gave each of the three major circuits— NASCAR, IRL and F/1—its most memorable, compelling moment of the year.

The fun started in May, when, during an otherwise unremarkable walkup to the 89th Indy 500, a rookie began routinely putting up some of the fastest practice times. Nothing out of the ordinary there, until you took a look at the driver. Smaller than most, a little softer around the edges, nice smile and a recent past history that included posing for a laddie mag in a bikini. Danica Patrick, a 23-year-old, was unlike any driver the Brickyard had seen. She wasn't the first woman to try to qualify for the race, but she was the first to unashamedly embrace her sex appeal. And, lest anyone be able to rightfully accuse her of getting by on looks alone, she was the first to have a real chance to drink milk in Victory Lane. "If I'm doing something," she said, "it's because I feel I

can beat everyone; I feel like I can win."

In qualifying, Patrick nearly put her car on the pole. She had been fastest in practice, but she drove too low going into Turn 1 on her first qualifying lap, and her car wobbled. Patrick recovered and ran each of her final three laps faster than pole winner Tony Kanaan's average of 227.566 mph. But since starting positions take all four laps into account, she started fourth. Patrick was livid with herself, staying in her garage stall for half an hour before facing the media. Under Indy's new qualifying format, she could have withdrawn her time and taken another shot at the pole, but Bobby Rahal—who, along with David Letterman, co-owns her car—decided not to risk losing the position. "Bobby told me, 'I've won from where you are,'" said Patrick. "We've got great cars, and we'll just go racing now."

When she did, she backed up her qualifying time—this despite the fact that her qualifying run made her even more of a media darling in the days leading up to the race. "She's not just talented, but she's the best-looking racer we've had as well—not to make the women who went before her mad," said driver Sam Hornish Jr. "She's a

23-year-old Danica Patrick was the first-ever woman to lead the Indy 500 and won the race's Rookie of the Year Award.

very marketable package." Front-page stories were the norm, with NASCAR relegated to the inside. "NASCAR isn't used to being put on the third page of USA Today," Rahal said. "Which means they'll probably be trying to hire Danica away from us." (Fortunately for Rahal, he signed her to a multiyear contract.)

On lap 56, Patrick became the first female to lead a lap at Indy. But, as many first-time drivers do at Indy, she made a few mistakes. She stalled coming out of the pits on lap 78, which dropped her from fourth to 16th. She worked her back to the front before making another small gaffe, one that had dire consequences for two other racers but turned out to be a huge break for Patrick. On a restart on lap 155 she spun out, taking out the cars of Tomas Enge and Thomas Scheckter. She also busted her own nose cone, which sent her back to the pits. There, she got a new nose and fuel. Patrick returned to the track in ninth place with 41 laps left—but, because she had made an extra pit stop, she had a full

tank of gas. When the cars in front of her pitted on lap 172, she stayed out and, to the delight of the crowd, inherited the lead.

Patrick lost the lead to Dan Wheldon on lap 186, then blew by him on a restart three laps later. But the Englishman, who was running on fresher tires, retook the lead with six laps to go. He held on, giving owner Michael Andretti his first Indy 500 win. Patrick, who was running less than full throttle to conserve fuel, wound up fourth.

Her performance launched Patrick into the spotlight, but it was Wheldon, a 27-year-old Englishman, who broke Hornish's IRL single-season victory record by posting five wins, all but locking up the season title.

Racing at the Brickyard went from the sublime to the ridiculous when the F/1 circus rolled into town in June. A set of new rules had been enacted before the season to level the playing field. The most significant: A driver could only use one set of tires during a race—the same set he qualified on. Before the season, Eddie Irvine suggested that five-time defending champ Michael Schumacher would be effected. "Michael has always been very hard on tires," said Irvine. "He just murders them. He won't be able to do that this season, so a lot will depend on how he adapts to the rules and also how good a tire Bridgestone produces for Ferrari."

As it turned out, not a very good one. The early part of the 2005 season showed that Michelin made a much better tire for the new rule. The Ferraris of Schumacher and his teammate, Rubens Barrichello, were running more like Hyundais, with only five podium finishes (and no wins) between them in the nine races before the US Grand Prix. Spain's Fernando Alonso proved to be the man to beat, winning four of the first nine.

The difference in tire performance took on a whole new dimension when the cars arrived at the Brickyard. After Ralf Schumacher crashed in practice in Turn 13, the banked turn, Michelin engineers concluded that the tires they had brought couldn't handle the circuit's banked turn. There was talk of a rules modification and of slowing the cars down before the turn, but in the end, F/1 told the Michelin drivers there would be no concessions. The 14 Michelin cars in the 20-car field responded by pulling into the pits after the parade lap, leaving six cars to run the race. "There was a good chance someone would have been killed if we had raced with those tires," said Nick Fry, the boss of the BAR-Honda team. "This is a black eye for our sport." And Red Bull driver David Coulthard, who did not race, worried, "I hope this doesn't hurt the future of F/1 in the States."

When it comes to the future, no circuit's is as bright as NASCAR's. In their second season under the new Chase for the Nextel Cup playoff system, the stock car guys put on another fantastic show. And the driver who was most dominant heading into the postseason was Tony Stewart, a Hoosier who made a statement when he won the Brickyard 500 in August. Stewart won the series title in 2002, a year in which excitement—and not usually the good kind—followed him just about everywhere he went.

Following the 2004 season, he packed up and left Charlotte, returning home to Columbus, Ind., a sleepy town where, as one of the guys, he could sit at the local Dairy Queen and sip shakes unbothered. "I'm just so much more relaxed now," he said from a swing on the front porch of his small three-bedroom house on a quiet, tree-lined street. "

Content at home, Stewart came alive in the middle part of the 2005 season. He won three of four races heading into the Brickyard, and finally got a win on the legendary track. He celebrated by climbing the catch fence before he collapsed in a mixture of joy and exhaustion on the wall. A few days later he was honored with a parade in Columbus. He followed the win up with another the following week at Watkins Glen, bringing his total to five in seven races and cementing his place atop the standings.

One thing Stewart couldn't do in 2005 was win his first Daytona 500. After leading much of the season-opening race, he finished seventh. Jeff Gordon won the race, outdueling Dale Earnhardt Jr. and giving fans a taste of what they thought might be a great season rivalry between the two stars. But by the time the 10-car field was set, the two were on the outside, Gordon a victim of inconsistency, Earnhardt of team tumult. He started the season with a new crew chief, Pete Rondeau, who came to him from teammate Michael Waltrip's crew. After 11 races, Rondeau was gone. And Earnhardt and Waltrip had a series of scrapes on the track that led Dale Earnhardt Inc. director of competition Tony Eury Sr. to say "I don't know what [Earnhardt's] problem is with Michael, but it will be fixed ... I guarantee it." Earnhardt didn't get much better results with his new crew chief, Steve Hmiel, and was 17th when the Chase field was set.

While the two young guns missed out on the playoffs, two vets showed that the kids' domination of the sport wasn't quite complete. Mark Martin and Rusty Wallace, two forty-somethings at the tail end of their careers, cruised into the Chase. Neither won a race, but both drew upon their experience to stay out of trouble and avoid bad finishes. Their presence in the Chase might have been unexpected, but in 2005, that was par for the course.

Indy Racing League

Indianapolis 500

Results of the 89th running of the Indianapolis 500 and fourth race of the 2005 Indy Racing League season. Held Sunday, May 29, 2005, at the 2.5-mile Indianapolis Motor Speedway in Indianapolis. Distance, 500 miles; starters, 33; time of race, 3 hours, 14 mins., 55.2395 seconds; average speed, 138.518 mph; margin of victory, 0.1559 seconds; caution flags, 8 for 56 laps; lead changes, 17 among nine drivers.

TOP 10 FINISHERS

Pos.	Driver (start pos.)	C/E/T	Qual. Speed	Laps	Status
1	Dan Wheldon (16)	D/H/F	224.308	200	running
2	Vitor Meira (7)	P/H/F	226.848	200	running
3	Bryan Herta (18)	D/H/F	223.972	200	running
4	Danica Patrick (4)	P/H/F	227.004	200	running
5	Buddy Lazier (9)	D/C/F	226.353	200	running
6	Dario Franchitti (6)	D/H/F	226.873	200	running
7	Scott Sharp (3)	P/H/F	227.126	200	running
8	Tony Kanaan (1)	D/H/F	227.566	200	running
9	Helio Castroneves (5)	D/T/F	226.927	199	running
10	Ryan Briscoe (24)	D/T/F	224.080	199	running

2005 Indy Racing League Results (through September 25)

Date	Race	Winner (start pos.)	C/E/T	Qual. Speed
Mar 6	Miami 300	Dan Wheldon (11)	D/H/F	212.768
Mar 19	Phoenix 200	Sam Hornishh Jr. (6)	D/T/F	175.772
Apr 3	Grand Prix of St. Petersburg	Dan Wheldon (9)	D/H/F	101.323
Apr 30	Japan 300	Dan Wheldon (5)	D/H/F	204.227
May 29	Indianapolis 500	Dan Wheldon (16)	D/H/F	224.308
June 11	Texas 500	Tomas Scheckter (1)	D/C/F	213.847
June 25	Richmond 250*	Helio Castroneves (2)	D/T/F	175.797
July 3	Kansas 300	Tony Kanaan (8)	D/H/F	213.411
July 16	Nashville 200	Dario Franchitti(4)	D/H/F	199.089
July 24	Milwaukee 225	Sam Hornish Jr. (1)	D/T/F	170.296
July 31	Michigan 400	Bryan Herta (1)	D/H/F	219.141
Aug 14	Kentucky 300	Scott Sharp(7)	P/H/F	216.993
Aug 21	Pikes Peak 225*	Dan Wheldon (11)	D/H/F	173.660
Sep 11	Chicago 300	Dan Wheldon (5)	D/H/F	215.484
Sept 25	Watkins Glen Int'l	Scott Dixon (4)	P/T/F	133.497

Note: Distances are in miles unless followed by K (kilometers) or * (laps).

2004 Final Championship Standings

Driver	Pts
Tony Kanaan	618
Dan Wheldon	533
Buddy Rice	485
Helio Castroneves	446
Adrian Fernandez	445
Dario Franchitti	409
Sam Hornish Jr	387
Vitor Meira	376
Bryan Herta	362
Scott Dixon	355

Champ Car World Series

2005 Champ Car Series Results (through September 24)

Date	Event	Winner (start pos.)	Car	Avg Speed
April 10	Grand Prix of Long Beach	Sebastian Bourdais (4)	Lola-Ford	89.811
May 22	Grand Prix of Monterrey	Bruno Junqueira (5)	Lola-Ford	77.602
June 4	Milwaukee 250	Paul Tracy (3)	Lola-Ford	130.301
June 19	Grand Prix of Portland	Cristiano da Matta (10)	Lola-Ford	110.898
June 26	Grand Prix of Cleveland	Paul Tracy (3)	Lola-Ford	108.755
July 10	Molson Indy Toronto	Justi Wilson (9)	Lola-Ford	85.296
July 17	Grand Prix of Edmonto	Sebastien Bourdais (10)	Lola-Ford	104.609
July 31	Grand Prix of San Jose	Sebastien Bourdais (1)	Lola-Ford	76.431
Aug 14	Grand Prix of Denver	Sebastien Bourdais (2)	Lola-Ford	87.338
Aug 28	Molson Indy Montreal	Oriol Servia (2)	Lola-Ford	107.746
Sept 24	Las Vegas 400	Sebastien Bourdais (1)	Lola-Ford	172.962

*Series formerly known as CART until 2005 season.

2004 Championship Standings

Driver	Overall	Road	Oval
Sebastien Bourdais	369	334	35
Bruno Junqueira	341	293	48
Patrick Carpentier	266	212	54
Paul Tracy	254	247	7
Mario Dominguez	244	212	32
A.J. Allmendinger	229	188	41
Alex Tagiliani	218	205	13
Jimmy Vasser	201	157	44
Ryan Hunter Reay	199	157	42
Oriol Servia	199	172	27

National Association for Stock Car Auto Racing

Daytona 500

Results of the 46th Daytona 500, the opening round of the 2004 Nextel Cup series. Held Sunday, February 15, 2004, at the 2.5-mile high-banked Daytona International Speedway.

Distance, 500 miles; starters, 43; time of race, 3:11:53; average speed, 156.345 mph; margin of victory, .273 seconds; caution flags, four for 23 laps; lead changes, 28.

TOP 10 FINISHERS

Pos.	Driver (start pos.)	Car	Laps	Winnings ($)
1	Jeff Gordon (15)	Chevrolet	203	1,497,150
2	Kurt Busch (13)	Ford	203	1,106,130
3	Dale Earnhardt Jr (5)	Chevrolet	203	828,796
4	Scott Riggs (12)	Chevrolet	203	643,896
5	Jimmie Johnson (2)	Chevrolet	203	533,579
6	Mark Martin (32)	Ford	203	395,313
7	Tony Stewart (4)	Chevrolet	203	442,610
8	Sterling Marlin (18)	Dodge	203	341,341
9	Kevin Lepage (8)	Dodge	203	307,138
10	Rusty Wallace (36)	Dodge	203	317,646

2004 Nextel Cup* Final Standings

Driver	Pts	Starts	Wins	Top 5	Top 10
Kurt Busch	6506	36	3	10	21
Jimmie Johnson	6498	36	8	20	23
Jeff Gordon	6490	36	5	16	25
Mark Matin	6399	36	1	10	15
Dale Earnhardt Jr	6368	36	6	16	21
Tony Stewart	6326	36	2	10	19
Ryan Newman	6180	36	2	11	14
Matt Kenseth	6069	36	2	8	16
Elliot Sadler	6024	36	2	8	14
Jeremy Mayfield	6000	36	1	5	13

*Series name changed from Winston Cup after 2003 season.

2004 Nextel Cup* Driver Winnings

Driver	Winnings ($)
Kurt Busch	9,677,543
Jimmie Johnson	8,275,721
Jeff Gordon	8,439,382
Mark Martin	5,479,004
Dale Earnhardt Jr	8,913,510
Tony Stewart	7,830,807
Ryan Newman	6,354,256
Matt Kenseth	7,405,309
Elliot Sadler	6,244,954
Jeremy Mayfield	4,919,342

Late 2004 Nextel Cup* Series Results

Date	Track/Distance	Winner (start pos.)	Car	Laps	Winnings ($)
Oct 3	Talladega 500	Dale Earnhardt Jr (10)	Chevrolet	188	305,968
Oct 10	Kansas 400	Joe Nemechek (1)	Chevrolet	267	279,725
Oct 16	Lowe's 500	Jimmie Johnson (9)	Chevrolet	334	191,450
Oct 24	Martinsville 500	Jimmie Johnson (18)	Chevrolet	500	157,440
Oct 31	Atlanta 500	Jimmie Johnson (8)	Chevrolet	325	298,250
Nov 7	Phoenix 500	Dale Earnhardt Jr (14)	Chevrolet	315	274,503
Nov 14	Darlington 500	Jimmie Johnson (4)	Chevrolet	367	269,675
Nov 21	Homestead 400	Greg Biffle (2)	Ford	271	314,850

2005 Nextel Cup Series Results (through October 10)

Date	Track/Distance	Winner (start pos.)	Car	Laps	Winnings ($)
Feb 15	Daytona 500	Jeff Gordon (15)	Chevrolet	203	1,497,150
Feb 27	Fontana 500	Greg Biffle (5)	Ford	250	288,650
Mar 13	Vegas 400	Jimmie Johnson (9)	Chevrolet	267	428,066
Mar 20	Atlanta 500	Carl Edwards (4)	Ford	325	165,450
Apr 3	Bristol 500	Kevin Harvick (13)	Chevrolet	500	189,001
Apr 10	Martinsville 500	Jeff Gordon (16)	Chevrolet	500	186,051
Apr 17	Texas 500	Greg Biffle (5)	Ford	334	522,250
Apr 23	Phoenix 500	Kurt Busch (2)	Ford	312	264,000
May 1	Talladega 500	Jeff Gordon (2)	Chevrolet	194	355,116
May 7	Darlington 500	Greg Biffle(3)	Ford	370	305,975
May 14	Richmond 400	Kasey Kahne(1)	Dodge	400	257,325
May 29	Lowe's 600	Jimmie Johnson (5)	Chevrolet	400	470,091
June 5	Dover 400	Greg Biffle (2)	Ford	400	282,800
June 12	Pocono 500	Carl Edwards (29)	Ford	201	196,150
June 19	Michigan 400	Greg Biffle (25)	Ford	200	171,075
June 26	Infineon 350	Tony Stewart (7)	Chevrolet	110	348,761
July 2	Daytona 400	Tony Stewart (1)	Chevrolet	160	368,261
July 10	Chicagoland 400	Dale Earnhardt Jr(25)	Chevrolet	267	325,033
July 17	New Hampshire 300	Tony Stewart (13)	Chevrolet	300	283,986
July 24	Pocono 500	Kurt Busch (2)	Ford	203	261,275
Aug 7	Indianapolis 400	Tony Stewart (22)	Chevrolet	160	554,661
Aug 14	Watkins Glen	Tony Stewart (1)	Chevrolet	92	269,006
Aug 21	Michigan 400	Jeremy Mayfield (11)	Dodge	200	181,550
Aug 27	Bristol 500	Matt Kenseth (1)	Ford	500	360,536
Sept 4	California 500	Kyle Busch (25)	Chevrolet	254	241,065
Sept 10	Richmond 400	Kurt Busch (5)	Ford	400	242,900
Sept 18	New Hampshire 300	Ryan Newman (13)	Dodge	300	248,866
Sept 25	Dover 400	Jimmie Johnson (5)	Chevrolet	404	296,641
Oct 2	Talladega 500	Dale Jarrett (2)	Ford	190	239,833
Oct 9	Kansas 400	Mark Martin (19)	Ford	267	339,725

*Series name changed from Winston Cup after 2003 season.

Formula One Grand Prix Racing

2005 Formula One Results (through October 17)

Grand Prix	Date	Winner	Car	Laps	Time
Australian	Mar 6	Giancarlo Fisichella	Renault	57	1:24:17.366
Malaysian	Mar 20	Fernando Alonso	Renault	56	1:31:33.736
Bahrain	Apr 3	Fernando Alonso	Renault	57	1:29:18.531
San Marino	Apr 24	Fernando Alonso	Renault	62	1:27:41.921
Spain	May 8	Kimi Räikkönen	McLaren-Mercedes	66	1:27:16.830
Monaco	May 22	Kimi Räikkönen	McLaren-Mercedes	78	1:45:15.556
European	May 29	Fernando Alonso	Renault	59	1:31:46.648
Canadian	June 12	Kimi Räikkönen	McLaren-Mercedes	70	1:32:43.181
United States	June 19	Michael Schumacher	Ferrari	73	1:29:43.181
French	July 3	Fernando Alonso	Renault	70	1:31:22.233
British	July 10	Juan Pablo Montoya	McLaren-Mercedes	60	1:24:29.588
German	July 24	Fernando Alonso	Renault	67	1:26:28.599
Hungarian	July 31	Kimi Räikkönen	McLaren-Mercedes	70	1:37:25.552
Turkish	Aug 21	Kimi Räikkönen	McLaren-Mercedes	58	1:24:34.454
Italian	Sept 4	Juan Pablo Montoya	McLaren-Mercedes	53	1:14:28.659
Belgian	Sep 11	Kimi Räikkönen	McLaren-Mercedes	44	1:30:01.295
Brazilian	Sept 25	Juan Pablo Montoya	McLaren-Mercedes	71	1:29:20.574
Japanese	Oct 9	Kimi Räikkönen	McLaren-Mercedes	53	1:29:02.212
Chinese	Oct 16	Fernando Alonso	Renault	56	1:39:53.618

2004 World Championship Final Standings

Drivers compete in Grand Prix races for the title of World Driving Champion. Below are the top 10 drivers from the 2004 season. Points are awarded for places 1–6 as follows: 10-6-4-3-2-1.

Driver	Country	Team	Pts
Michael Schumacher	Germany	Ferrari	148
Rubens Barrichello	Brazil	Ferrari	114
Jenson Button	England	Honda	85
Fernando Alonso	Spain	Renault	59
Juan Pablo Montoya	Colombia	Williams-BMW	58
Jarno Trulli	Italy	Renault	46
Kimi Räikkönen	Finland	McLaren-Mercedes	45
Takuma Sato	Japan	Honda	34
Ralf Schumacher	Germany	Williams	24
David Coulthard	Scottland	McLaren-Mercedes	24

Professional Sports Car Racing

The 24 Hours of Daytona

Held at the Daytona International Speedway on Feb 5-6, 2005, the 24 Hours of Daytona serves as the opening round of Grand American Road Racing Association's season.

Place	Drivers	Car (Class)	Distance
1	Max Angelelli, Wayne Taylor, Emmanuel Collard	Pontiac Riley	710 laps (119.397mph)
2	Butch Leitzinger, Elliot Forbes Robinson, Jimmie Johnson	Pontiac Crawford	699
3	Andy Wallace, Jan Lammers, Tony Stewart	Pontiac Crawford	699
4	Stefan Johansson, Jamie McMurray, Cort Wagner	Lexus Riley	698
5	Fabrizio Gollin, Matteo Bobbi, Didier Theys	Lexus Doran	697

2005 American Le Mans Series—Prototype Class (through October 10)

Date	Race	Winners	Car
Mar 19	12 Hours of Sebring	J.J. Lehto, M. Werner, T. Kristensen	Audi R8
Apr 15-17	Grand Prix of Atlanta	J.J. Lehto, Marco Werner	Audi R8
May 22	Mid Ohio	Butch Leitzinger, J. Weaver,	Lola EX257/AER
July 4	Grand Prix of New England	J.J. Lehto, Marco Werner	Audi R8
July 17	Grand Prix of Sonoma	Emanuele Pirro, Frank Biela	Audi R8
July 30	Grand Prix of Portland	Frank Biela, Emanuele Pirro	Audi R8
Aug 21	Road America 500	Emanuele Pirro, Frank Biela	Audi R8
Sept 4	Grand Prix of Mosport	James Weaver, Butch Leitzinger	Lola EX257/AER
Oct 1	Petit Le Mans	Emanuele Pirro, Frank Biela	Audi R8

2005 American Le Mans Series—GTS Class (through October 10)

Date	Race	Winners	Car
Mar 19	12 Hours at Sebring	D. Turner, D. Brabham, S. Ortelli	Aston Martin DB9
Apr 15-17	Grand Prix of Atlanta	Ron Fellows, Johnny O'Connell	Corvette C6-R
May 22	Mid Ohio	J. O'Connell, Ron Fellows	Corvette C6-R
July 4	Grand Prix of New England	Oliver Gavin, Olivier Beretta	Corvette C6-R
July 17	Grand Prix of Sonoma	Ron Fellows, Johnny O'Connell	Corvette C6-R
July 30	Grand Prix of Portland	Olivier Beretta, Oliver Gavin	Corvette C6-R
Aug 21	Road America 500	Oliver Gavin, Olivier Beretta	Corvette C6-R
Sept 4	Grand Prix of Mosport	Olivier Beretta, Oliver Gain	Corvette C6-R
Oct 1	Petit Le Mans	Oliver Gavin, Olivier Beretta,	Corvette C6-R

2005 American Le Mans Series—GT Class (through October 10)

Date	Race	Winners	Car
Mar 19	12 Hours at Sebring	J. Bergmeister, P. Long, L. Luhr	Porsche 911 GT3
Apr 15-17	Grand Prix of Atlanta	B. Auberlen, R. Liddell	Panoz EsperanteGT
May 22	Mid Ohio	Timo Bernhard, Romain Dumas	Porsche 911 GT3
July 4	Grand Prix of New England	Romain Dumas, Timo Berhard	Porsche 911 GT3
July 17	Grand Prix of Sonoma	Timo Bernhard, Romain Dumas	Porsche 911 GT3
July 30	Grand Prix of Portland	Romain Dumas, Tim Bernhard	Porsche 911 GT3
Aug 21	Road America 500	J. Bergmeister, Patrick Long	Porsche 911 GT3
Sept 4	Gran Prix of Mosport	J. Bergmeister, Patrick Long	Porsche 911 GT3
Oct 1	Petit Le Mans	Jorg Bergmeister, Patrick Long	Porsche 911 GT3

Professional Sports Car Racing *(Cont.)*

2004 American Le Mans Series Championship Final Standings

PROTOTYPE CLASS	Pts	GTS CLASS	Pts	GT CLASS	Pts
Frank Biela	163	Oliver Gavin	173	Patrick Long	156
Emanuele Pirro	163	Olivier Beretta	173	Jorg Bergmeister	156
Marco Werner	135	Ron Fellows	158	Timo Bernhard	134
J.J. Lehto	135	Johnny O'Connell	158	Romain Dumas	134
Andy Wallace	119	Terry Borcheller	103	Johannes Van Overbeek	101
James Weaver	113	Johnny Mowlem	103	Jon Fogarty	101

24 Hours of Le Mans

Held at Le Mans, France, on June 18-19, 2005, the 24 Hours of Le Mans is the most prestigious international event in endurance racing.

Place	Drivers	Car	Laps
1	J.J. Lehto, Marco Werner, Tom Kristensen	Audi R8	372 (138.930 mph)
2	Emanuel Collard, JC Boullion, E Comas	Pescarolo Judd	368
3	Frank Biela, Emanuele Pirro, Allan McNish	Audi R8	364
4	F Montagny, JM Gounon, Stephane Ortelli	Audi R8	362
5	Oliver Gavin, Olivier Beretta, Jan Magnussen	Corvette C6-R	349

National Hot Rod Association

2005 Results (through October 10)

TOP FUEL

Date	Race, Site	Winner
Feb 10-13	Winternationals, Pomona, CA	Scott Kalitta
Feb 25-27	Kragen Nationals, Phoenix	Tony Schumacher
Mar 17-20	Gatornationals, Gainesville, FL	Doug Kalitta
Apr 8-10	Spring Nationals, Houston	Tony Schumacher
Apr 14-17	Las Vegas Nationals, Las Vegas	Larry Dixon
Apr 29-May 1	Thunder Valley Nationals, Bristol, TN	Doug Kalitta
May 12–15	Southern Nationals, Atlanta	Doug Kalitta
May 19-22	Pontiac Nationals, Columbus, OH	Tony Schumacher
May 26–29	Summer Nationals, Topeka, KS	David Grubnic
June 9–12	Carquest Nationals, Joliet, Ilinois	Scott Kalitta
June 16–19	Super Nationals, Englishtown, NJ	Larry Dixon
June 24–26	Sears Nationals, St. Louis	Brandon Bernstein
July 15-17	Mile High Nationals, Denver	Tony Schumacher
July 22-24	Carquest Nationals, Kent WA	Brandon Bernstein
July 29–July 31	Autolite Nationals, Sonoma, CA	Doug Kalitta
Aug 11–14	Lucas Oil Nationals, Brainerd, MN	Doug Kalitta
Aug 19–21	Mid-South Nationals, Memphis	Rod Fuller
Aug 31–Sept 5	U.S. Nationals, Indianapolis	Larry Dixon
Sept 15-18	Toyo Tires Nationals, Reading, PA	Tony Schumacher
Sept 29-Oct 2	Ameriquest Mortgage Nationals, Joliet, IL	Tony Schumacher
Oct 6-9	O'Reilly Fall Nationals, Ennis, TX	Tony Schumacher

FUNNY CAR

Date	Race, Site	Winner
Feb 10–13	Winternationals, Pomona, CA	Tommy Johnson Jr
Feb 25-27	Kragen Nationals, Phoenix	John Force
Mar 17-20	Gatornationals, Gainesville, FL	Whit Bazemore
Apr 8-10	Spring National, Houston	Rober Hight
Apr 14-17	Las Vegas Nationals, Las Vegas	Whit Bazemore
Apr 29–May 1	Thunder Valley Nationals, Bristol, TN	Gary Scelzi
May 12–15	Southern Nationals, Atlanta	John Force

2005 Results (through October 10) *(Cont.)*

FUNNY CAR *(CONT.)*

Date	Race, Site	Winner
May 19-22	Pontiac Nationals, Columbus, OH	John Force
May 26-29	Summer Nationals, Topeka, KS	John Force
June 9-12	Carquest Nationals, Joliet Ilinois	Gary Scelzi
June 16–19	Super Nationals, Englishtown, NJ	Del Worsham
June 24-26	Sears Nationals, St. Louis	Ron Capps
July 15-17	Mile High Nationals, Denver	Robert Hight
July 22–24	Carquest Nationals, Kent, WA	Eric Medlen
July 29–July 31	Autolite Nationals, Sonoma, CA	Gary Scelzi
Aug 11–14	Lucas Oil Nationals, Brainerd, MN	Eric Medlen
Aug 19-Aug 21	Mid-South Nationals, Memphis	Eric Medlen
Aug 31-Sept 5	U.S. Nationals, Indianapolis	Del Worsham
Sept 15-18	Toyo Tires, Nationals Reading PA	Tony Pedregon
Sept 29-Oct 2	Ameriquest Mortgage Nationals, Joliet, IL	RonCapps
Oct 6-9	O'Reilly Fall Nationals, Ennis, TX	John Force

PRO STOCK

Date	Race, Site	Winner
Feb 10-13	Winternationals, Pomona, CA	Dave Connolly
Feb 25-27	Kragen Nationals, Phoenix	Allen Johnson
Mar 17-20	Gatornationals, Gainesville, FL	Jason Line
Apr 1–4	Spring Nationals, Houston	Warren Johnson
Apr 15–18	Las Vegas Nationals, Las Vegas	Dave Connolly
Apr 29–May 1	Thunder Valley Nationals, Bristol, TN	Mike Romine
May 12–15	Southern Nationals, Atlanta	Greg Anderson
May 19-22	Pontiac Nationals. Columbus, OH	Greg Anderson
May 26-29	Summer Nationals, Topeka, KS	Greg Anderson
June 9-12	Carquest Nationals, Joliet IL	Jason Line
June 16-19	Super National, Englishtown, NJ	Jason Line
June 24-26	Sears Nationals, St Louis	Kurt Johnson
July 15-17	Mile High Nationals, Denver	Warren Johnson
July 22-24	Carquest Nationals, Kent WA	Kurt Johnson
July 29–July 31	Autolite Nationals, Sonoma, CA	Greg Anderson
Aug 11-14	Lucas Oil Nationals, Brainerd, MN	Kurt Johnson
Aug 19–21	Mid-South Nationals, Memphis	Greg Anderson
Aug 31-Sept 5	U.S. Nationals, Indianapolis	Greg Anderson
Sept 15–18	Toyo Tires Nationals, Reading, PA	Greg Anderson
Sept 29-Oct 2	Ameriquest Mortgage Nationals, Joliet, IL	Jason Line
Oct 6-9	O'Reilly Fall Nationals, Ennis, TX	Greg Anderson

2004 NHRA Final Standings

TOP FUEL		FUNNY CAR		PRO STOCK	
Driver	Pts	Driver	Pts	Driver	Pts
Tony Schumacher	1994	John Force	1883	Greg Anderson	2402
Doug Kalitta	1668	Del Worsham	1586	Jason Line	1660
Brandon Bernstein	1531	Gary Scelzi	1565	Dave Connolly	1526
Scott Kalitta	1440	Gary Densham	1405	Larry Morgan	1256
David Grubnic	1368	Eric Medlen	1375	Kurt Johnson	1245

FOR THE RECORD·Year by Year

Indianapolis 500

First held in 1911, the Indianapolis 500—200 laps of the 2.5-mile Indianapolis Motor Speedway Track (called the Brickyard in honor of its original pavement)—grew to become the most famous auto race in the world. Though the Memorial Day weekend event lost participants and prestige in the mid-1990s due to feuding in the world of U.S. open-wheel racing, it annually attracts crowds of over 100,000.

Year	Winner (start pos.)	Chassis-Engine	Avg Speed	Pole Winner	Speed
1911	Ray Harroun (28)	Marmon-Marmon	74.590	Lewis Strang	First entered
1912	Joe Dawson (7)	National-National	78.720	Gil Anderson	First entered
1913	Jules Goux (7)	Peugeot-Peugeot	75.930	Caleb Bragg	Drew pole
1914	Rene Thomas (15)	Delage-Delage	82.470	Jean Chassagne	Drew pole
1915	Ralph DePalma (2)	Mercedes-Mercedes	89.840	Howard Wilcox	98.90
1916	Dario Resta (4)	Peugeot-Peugeot	84.000	John Aitken	96.69
1917–18	No race				
1919	Howard Wilcox (2)	Peugeot-Peugeot	88.050	Rene Thomas	104.78
1920	Gaston Chevrolet (6)	Frontenac-Frontenac	88.620	Ralph DePalma	99.15
1921	Tommy Milton (20)	Frontenac-Frontenac	89.620	Ralph DePalma	100.75
1922	Jimmy Murphy (1)	Duesenberg-Miller	94.480	Jimmy Murphy	100.50
1923	Tommy Milton (1)	Miller-Miller	90.950	Tommy Milton	108.17
1924	L.L. Corum	Duesenberg-Duesenberg	98.230	Jimmy Murphy	108.037
	Joe Boyer (21)				
1925	Peter DePaolo (2)	Duesenberg-Duesenberg	101.130	Leon Duray	113.196
1926	Frank Lockhart (20)	Miller-Miller	95.904	Earl Cooper	111.735
1927	George Souders (22)	Duesenberg-Duesenberg	97.545	Frank Lockhart	120.100
1928	Louis Meyer (13)	Miller-Miller	99.482	Leon Duray	122.391
1929	Ray Keech (6)	Miller-Miller	97.585	Cliff Woodbury	120.599
1930	Billy Arnold (1)	Summers-Miller	100.448	Billy Arnold	113.268
1931	Louis Schneider (13)	Stevens-Miller	96.629	Russ Snowberger	112.796
1932	Fred Frame (27)	Wetteroth-Miller	104.144	Lou Moore	117.363
1933	Louis Meyer (6)	Miller-Miller	104.162	Bill Cummings	118.524
1934	Bill Cummings (10)	Miller-Miller	104.863	Kelly Petillo	119.329
1935	Kelly Petillo (22)	Wetteroth-Offy	106.240	Rex Mays	120.736
1936	Louis Meyer (28)	Stevens-Miller	109.069	Rex Mays	119.664
1937	Wilbur Shaw (2)	Shaw-Offy	113.580	Bill Cummings	123.343
1938	Floyd Roberts (1)	Wetteroth-Miller	117.200	Floyd Roberts	125.681
1939	Wilbur Shaw (3)	Maserati-Maserati	115.035	Jimmy Snyder	130.138
1940	Wilbur Shaw (2)	Maserati-Maserati	114.277	Rex Mays	127.850
1941	Floyd Davis	Wetteroth-Offy	115.117	Mauri Rose	128.691
	Mauri Rose (17)				
1942–45	No race				
1946	George Robson (15)	Adams-Sparks	114.820	Cliff Bergere	126.471
1947	Mauri Rose (3)	Deidt-Offy	116.338	Ted Horn	126.564
1948	Mauri Rose (3)	Deidt-Offy	119.814	Rex Mays	130.577
1949	Bill Holland (4)	Deidt-Offy	121.327	Duke Nalon	132.939
1950	Johnnie Parsons (5)	Kurtis-Offy	124.002	Walt Faulkner	134.343
1951	Lee Wallard (2)	Kurtis-Offy	126.244	Duke Nalon	136.498
1952	Troy Ruttman (7)	Kuzma-Offy	128.922	Fred Agabashian	138.010
1953	Bill Vukovich (1)	KK500A-Offy	128.740	Bill Vukovich	138.392
1954	Bill Vukovich (19)	KK500A-Offy	130.840	Jack McGrath	141.033
1955	Bob Sweikert (14)	KK500C-Offy	128.209	Jerry Hoyt	140.045
1956	Pat Flaherty (1)	Watson-Offy	128.490	Pat Flaherty	145.596
1957	Sam Hanks (13)	Salih-Offy	135.601	Pat O'Connor	143.948
1958	Jim Bryan (7)	Salih-Offy	133.791	Dick Rathmann	145.974
1959	Rodger Ward (6)	Watson-Offy	135.857	Johnny Thomson	145.908
1960	Jim Rathmann (2)	Watson-Offy	138.767	Eddie Sachs	146.592
1961	A.J. Foyt (7)	Trevis-Offy	139.130	Eddie Sachs	147.481
1962	Rodger Ward (2)	Watson-Offy	140.293	Parnelli Jones	150.370
1963	Parnelli Jones (1)	Watson-Offy	143.137	Parnelli Jones	151.153
1964	A.J. Foyt (5)	Watson-Offy	147.350	Jim Clark	158.828
1965	Jim Clark (2)	Lotus-Ford	150.686	A.J. Foyt	161.233
1966	Graham Hill (15)	Lola-Ford	144.317	Mario Andretti	165.899
1967	A.J. Foyt (4)	Coyote-Ford	151.207	Mario Andretti	168.982
1968	Bobby Unser (3)	Eagle-Offy	152.882	Joe Leonard	171.559
1969	Mario Andretti (2)	Hawk-Ford	156.867	A.J. Foyt	170.568
1970	Al Unser (1)	PJ Colt-Ford	155.749	Al Unser	170.221
1971	Al Unser (5)	PJ Colt-Ford	157.735	Peter Revson	178.696
1972	Mark Donohue (3)	McLaren-Offy	162.962	Bobby Unser	195.940
1973	Gordon Johncock (11)	Eagle-Offy	159.036	Johnny Rutherford	198.413
1974	Johnny Rutherford (25)	McLaren-Offy	158.589	A.J. Foyt	191.632

Year	Winner (start pos.)	Chassis-Engine	Avg speed	Pole Winner	Speed
1975	Bobby Unser (3)	Racers Eagle-Offy	149.213	A.J. Foyt	193.976
1976	Johnny Rutherford (1)	McLaren-Offy	148.725	Johnny Rutherford	188.957
1977	A.J. Foyt (4)	Coyote-Ford	161.331	Tom Sneva	198.884
1978	Al Unser (5)	Lola-Cosworth	161.361	Tom Sneva	202.156
1979	Rick Mears (1)	Penske-Cosworth	158.899	Rick Mears	193.736
1980	Johnny Rutherford (1)	Chaparral-Cosworth	142.862	Johnny Rutherford	192.256
1981	Bobby Unser (1)	Penske-Cosworth	139.084	Bobby Unser	200.546
1982	Gordon Johncock (5)	Wildcat-Cosworth	162.026	Rick Mears	207.004
1983	Tom Sneva (4)	March-Cosworth	162.117	Teo Fabi	207.395
1984	Rick Mears (1)	March-Cosworth	163.612	Tom Sneva	210.029
1985	Danny Sullivan (8)	March-Cosworth	152.982	Pancho Carter	212.583
1986	Bobby Rahal (4)	March-Cosworth	170.722	Rick Mears	216.828
1987	Al Unser (20)	March-Cosworth	162.175	Mario Andretti	215.390
1988	Rick Mears (1)	Penske-Chevrolet	144.809	Rick Mears	219.198
1989	Emerson Fittipaldi (3)	Penske-Chevrolet	167.581	Rick Mears	223.885
1990	Arie Luyendyk (3)	Lola-Chevrolet	185.981*	Emerson Fittipaldi	225.301
1991	Rick Mears (1)	Penske-Chevrolet	176.457	Rick Mears	224.113
1992	Al Unser Jr (12)	Galmer-Chevrolet	134.477	Roberto Guerrero	232.482
1993	Emerson Fittipaldi (9)	Penske-Chevrolet	157.207	Arie Luyendyk	223.967
1994	Al Unser Jr (1)	Penske-Mercedes	160.872	Al Unser Jr	228.011
1995	Jacques Villeneuve (5)	Reynard-Ford	153.616	Scott Brayton	231.616
1996	Buddy Lazier (5)	Reynard-Ford	147.956	Tony Stewart	233.100†
1997	Arie Luyendyk (1)	G Force-Oldsmobile	145.827	Arie Luyendyk	231.468
1998	Eddie Cheever (17)	Dallara-Oldsmobile	145.155	Billy Boat	223.503
1999	Kenny Brack (8)	Dallara-Oldsmobile	153.176	Arie Luyendyk	225.179
2000	Juan Montoya (2)	G Force-Oldsmobile	167.607	Greg Ray	223.471
2001	Helio Castroneves (11)	Dallara-Oldsmobile	153.601	Scott Sharp	226.037
2002	Helio Castroneves (13)	Dallara-Chevrolet	166.499	Bruno Junqueira	231.342
2003	Gil de Ferran	Panoz-Toyota	156.291	Helio Castroneves	231.725
2004	Buddy Rice (1)	G Force-Honda	138.518	Buddy Rice	222.024
2005	Dan Wheldon	Dallara-Honda	157.603	Tony Kanaan	227.566

*Track record, winning speed. †Track record, qualifying speed.

Indianapolis 500 Rookie of the Year Award

1952	Art Cross
1953	Jimmy Daywalt
1954	Larry Crockett
1955	Al Herman
1956	Bob Veith
1957	Don Edmunds
1958	George Amick
1959	Bobby Grim
1960	Jim Hurtubise
1961	Parnelli Jones*
	Bobby Marshman
1962	Jimmy McElreath
1963	Jim Clark*
1964	Johnny White
1965	Mario Andretti*
1966	Jackie Stewart
1967	Denis Hulme
1968	Billy Vukovich
1969	Mark Donohue*
1970	Donnie Allison

1971	Denny Zimmerman
1972	Mike Hiss
1973	Graham McRae
1974	Pancho Carter
1975	Bill Puterbaugh
1976	Vern Schuppan
1977	Jerry Sneva
1978	Rick Mears*
	Larry Rice
1979	Howdy Holmes
1980	Tim Richmond
1981	Josele Garza
1982	Jim Hickman
1983	Teo Fabi
1984	Michael Andretti
	Roberto Guerrero
1985	Arie Luyendyk*
1986	Randy Lanier
1987	Fabrizio Barbazza
1988	Billy Vukovich III

1989	Bernard Jourdain
	Scott Pruett
1990	Eddie Cheever*
1991	Jeff Andretti
1992	Lyn St. James
1993	Nigel Mansell
1994	Jacques Villeneuve*
1995	Gil de Ferran
1996	Tony Stewart
1997	Jeff Ward
1998	Steve Knapp
1999	Robby McGehee
2000	Juan Montoya*
2001	Helio Castroneves*
2002	Alex Barron
	Tomas Scheckter
2003	Tora Tagaki
2004	Kosuke Matsuura
2005	Danica Patrick

*Future winner of Indy 500.

Champ Car World Series Champions

From 1909 to 1955, this championship was awarded by the American Automobile Association (AAA), and from 1956 to 1979 by the United States Auto Club (USAC). Since 1979, Championship Auto Racing Teams (CART) has conducted the championship. Known as PPG CART World Series until 1998. Series name changed to Champ Car World Series for 2005 racing season.

Year	Champion	Year	Champion	Year	Champion
1909	George Robertson	1942–45	No racing	1978	Tom Sneva
1910	Ray Harroun	1946	Ted Horn	1979	A.J. Foyt
1911	Ralph Mulford	1947	Ted Horn	1979	Rick Mears
1912	Ralph DePalma	1948	Ted Horn	1980	Johnny Rutherford
1913	Earl Cooper	1949	Johnnie Parsons	1981	Rick Mears
1914	Ralph DePalma	1950	Henry Banks	1982	Rick Mears
1915	Earl Cooper	1951	Tony Bettenhausen	1983	Al Unser
1916	Dario Resta	1952	Chuck Stevenson	1984	Mario Andretti
1917	Earl Cooper	1953	Sam Hanks	1985	Al Unser
1918	Ralph Mulford	1954	Jimmy Bryan	1986	Bobby Rahal
1919	Howard Wilcox	1955	Bob Sweikert	1987	Bobby Rahal
1920	Tommy Milton	1956	Jimmy Bryan	1988	Danny Sullivan
1921	Tommy Milton	1957	Jimmy Bryan	1989	Emerson Fittipaldi
1922	Jimmy Murphy	1958	Tony Bettenhausen	1990	Al Unser Jr.
1923	Eddie Hearne	1959	Rodger Ward	1991	Michael Andretti
1924	Jimmy Murphy	1960	A.J. Foyt	1992	Bobby Rahal
1925	Peter DePaolo	1961	A.J. Foyt	1993	Nigel Mansell
1926	Harry Hartz	1962	Rodger Ward	1994	Al Unser Jr.
1927	Peter DePaolo	1963	A.J. Foyt	1995	Jacques Villeneuve
1928	Louis Meyer	1964	A.J. Foyt	1996	Jimmy Vasser
1929	Louis Meyer	1965	Mario Andretti	1997	Alex Zanardi
1930	Billy Arnold	1966	Mario Andretti	1998	Alex Zanardi
1931	Louis Schneider	1967	A.J. Foyt	1999	Juan Montoya
1932	Bob Carey	1968	Bobby Unser	2000	Gil de Ferran
1933	Louis Meyer	1969	Mario Andretti	2001	Gil de Ferran
1934	Bill Cummings	1970	Al Unser	2002	Cristiano da Matta
1935	Kelly Petillo	1971	Joe Leonard	2003	Paul Tracy
1936	Mauri Rose	1972	Joe Leonard	2004	Sebastian Bourdais
1937	Wilbur Shaw	1973	Roger McCluskey		
1938	Floyd Roberts	1974	Bobby Unser		
1939	Wilbur Shaw	1975	A.J. Foyt		
1940	Rex Mays	1976	Gordon Johncock		
1941	Rex Mays	1977	Tom Sneva		

Alltime Champ Car* Leaders

WINS		POLE POSITIONS	
A.J. Foyt	67	Mario Andretti	67
Mario Andretti	52	A.J. Foyt	53
Michael Andretti	42	Bobby Unser	49
Al Unser	39	Rick Mears	40
Bobby Unser	35	Michael Andretti	32
Al Unser Jr	31	Al Unser	27
†Paul Tracy	30	†Paul Tracy	25
Rick Mears	29	Johnny Rutherford	23
Johnny Rutherford	27	Gordon Johncock	20
Rodger Ward	26	Rex Mays	19
Gordon Johncock	25	Danny Sullivan	19
Bobby Rahal	24	†Sebastien Bourdais	18
Ralph DePalma	24	Bobby Rahal	18
Tommy Milton	23	Emerson Fittipaldi	17
Tony Bettenhausen	22	Gil de Ferran	16
Emerson Fittipaldi	22	Tony Bettenhausen	14
Earl Cooper	20	Juan Montoya	14
Jimmy Bryan	19	Don Branson	14
Jimmy Murphy	19	Tom Sneva	14
Danny Sullivan	17	Parnelli Jones	12
Ralph Mulford	17		

*Series known as CART prior to 2005 season
†Active driver. Note: Leaders through September 2005.

Stock Car Racing's Major Events

In 1985, Winston began offering a $1 million bonus to any driver to win three of the top four NASCAR events in the same season. A fifth event, the Brickyard 400 (in Indianapolis) was added in 1994. As of 1998 the Winston million was awarded to any driver who won three of the five events. The other four races are the richest (Daytona 500), the fastest (Talladega 500), the longest (Charlotte 600) and the oldest (Southern 500 at Darlington). Only five drivers, Lee Roy Yarbrough (1969), David Pearson (1976), Bill Elliott (1985), Dale Jarrett (1996) and Jeff Gordon (1997, '98) have scored the three-track hat trick.

Daytona 500

Year	Driver	Make	Speed	Pole winner	Speed
1959	Lee Petty	Oldsmobile	135.520	Cotton Owens	143.198
1960	Junior Johnson	Chevrolet	124.740	Fireball Roberts	151.556
1961	Marvin Panch	Pontiac	149.601	Fireball Roberts	155.709
1962	Fireball Roberts	Pontiac	152.529	Fireball Roberts	156.995
1963	Tiny Lund	Ford	151.566	Johnny Rutherford	165.183
1964	Richard Petty	Plymouth	154.345	Paul Goldsmith	174.910
1965	Fred Lorenzen	Ford	141.539	Darel Dieringer	171.151
1966	Richard Petty	Plymouth	160.627	Richard Petty	175.165
1967	Mario Andretti	Ford	149.926	Curtis Turner	180.831
1968	Cale Yarborough	Mercury	143.251	Cale Yarborough	189.222
1969	Lee Roy Yarbrough	Ford	157.950	David Pearson	190.029
1970	Pete Hamilton	Plymouth	149.601	Cale Yarborough	194.015
1971	Richard Petty	Plymouth	144.462	A.J. Foyt	182.744
1972	A.J. Foyt	Mercury	161.550	Bobby Isaac	186.632
1973	Richard Petty	Dodge	157.205	Buddy Baker	185.662
1974	Richard Petty	Dodge	140.894	David Pearson	185.017
1975	Benny Parsons	Chevrolet	153.649	Donnie Allison	185.827
1976	David Pearson	Mercury	152.181	A.J. Foyt	185.943
1977	Cale Yarborough	Chevrolet	153.218	Donnie Allison	188.048
1978	Bobby Allison	Ford	159.730	Cale Yarborough	187.536
1979	Richard Petty	Oldsmobile	143.977	Buddy Baker	196.049
1980	Buddy Baker	Oldsmobile	177.602*	A.J. Foyt	195.020
1981	Richard Petty	Buick	169.651	Bobby Allison	194.624
1982	Bobby Allison	Buick	153.991	Benny Parsons	196.317
1983	Cale Yarborough	Pontiac	155.979	Ricky Rudd	198.864
1984	Cale Yarborough	Chevrolet	150.994	Cale Yarborough	201.848
1985	Bill Elliott	Ford	172.265	Bill Elliott	205.114
1986	Geoff Bodine	Chevrolet	148.124	Bill Elliott	205.039
1987	Bill Elliott	Ford	176.263	Bill Elliott	210.364†
1988	Bobby Allison	Buick	137.531	Ken Schrader	193.823
1989	Darrell Waltrip	Chevrolet	148.466	Ken Schrader	196.996
1990	Derrike Cope	Chevrolet	165.761	Ken Schrader	196.515
1991	Ernie Irvan	Chevrolet	148.148	Davey Allison	195.955
1992	Davey Allison	Ford	160.256	Sterling Marlin	192.213
1993	Dale Jarrett	Chevrolet	154.972	Kyle Petty	189.426
1994	Sterling Marlin	Chevrolet	156.931	Loy Allen Jr	190.158
1995	Sterling Marlin	Chevrolet	141.710	Dale Jarrett	193.498
1996	Dale Jarrett	Ford	154.308	Dale Earnhardt	189.510
1997	Jeff Gordon	Chevrolet	148.295	Mike Skinner	189.813
1998	Dale Earnhardt	Chevrolet	172.712	Bobby Labonte	192.415
1999	Jeff Gordon	Chevrolet	161.551	Jeff Gordon	195.067
2000	Dale Jarrett	Ford	155.669	Dale Jarrett	191.091
2001	Michael Waltrip	Chevrolet	161.783	Bill Elliott	183.570
2002	Ward Burton	Dodge	142.971	Jimmie Johnson	185.831
2003	Michael Waltrip	Chevrolet	133.87	Jeff Green	186.606
2004	Dale Earnhardt Jr.	Chevrolet	156.345	Greg Biffle	188.387
2005	Jeff Gordon	Chevrolet	135.173	Dale Jarrett	188.312

*Track record, winning speed. †Track record, qualifying speed. Note: The Daytona 500, held annually in February, now opens the NASCAR season with 200 laps around the high-banked Daytona International Speedway.

Charlotte 600

Year	Winner	Car	Avg Speed	Pole Winner
1960	Joe Lee Johnson	Chevrolet	107.752	Joe Lee Johnson
1961	David Pearson	Pontiac	111.634	Richard Petty
1962	Nelson Stacy	Ford	125.552	Fireball Roberts
1963	Fred Lorenzen	Ford	132.418	Junior Johnson
1964	Jim Paschal	Plymouth	125.772	Junior Johnson
1965	Fred Lorenzen	Ford	121.772	Fred Lorenzen
1966	Marvin Panch	Plymouth	135.042	Paul Goldsmith
1967	Jim Paschal	Plymouth	135.832	Cale Yarborough
1968	Buddy Baker	Dodge	104.207	Donnie Allison
1969	Lee Roy Yarbrough	Mercury	134.631	Donnie Allison
1970	Donnie Allison	Ford	129.680	Bobby Isaac
1971	Bobby Allison	Mercury	140.442	Charlie Glotzbach
1972	Buddy Baker	Dodge	142.255	Bobby Allison
1973	Buddy Baker	Dodge	134.890	Buddy Baker
1974	David Pearson	Mercury	135.720	David Pearson
1975	Richard Petty	Dodge	145.327	David Pearson
1976	David Pearson	Mercury	137.352	David Pearson
1977	Richard Petty	Dodge	137.636	David Pearson
1978	Darrell Waltrip	Chevrolet	138.355	David Pearson
1979	Darrell Waltrip	Chevrolet	136.674	Neil Bonnet
1980	Benny Parsons	Chevrolet	119.265	Cale Yarborough
1981	Bobby Allison	Buick	129.326	Neil Bonnett
1982	Neil Bonnett	Ford	130.508	David Pearson
1983	Neil Bonnett	Chevrolet	140.406	Buddy Baker
1984	Bobby Allison	Buick	129.233	Harry Gant
1985	Darrell Waltrip	Chevrolet	141.807	Bill Elliott
1986	Dale Earnhardt	Chevrolet	140.406	Geoff Bodine
1987	Kyle Petty	Ford	131.483	Bill Elliott
1988	Darrell Waltrip	Chevrolet	124.460	Davey Allison
1989	Darrell Waltrip	Chevrolet	144.077	Alan Kulwicki
1990	Rusty Wallace	Pontiac	137.650	Ken Schrader
1991	Davey Allison	Ford	138.951	Mark Martin
1992	Dale Earnhardt	Chevrolet	132.980	Bill Elliott
1993	Dale Earnhardt	Chevrolet	145.504	Ken Schrader
1994	Jeff Gordon	Chevrolet	139.445	Jeff Gordon
1995	Bobby Labonte	Chevrolet	151.952	Jeff Gordon
1996	Dale Jarrett	Ford	147.581	Jeff Gordon
1997	Jeff Gordon	Chevrolet	136.745	Jeff Gordon
1998	Jeff Gordon	Chevrolet	136.424	Jeff Gordon
1999	Jeff Burton	Ford	151.367	Bobby Labonte
2000	Matt Kenseth	Ford	142.640	Dale Earnhardt Jr
2001	Jeff Burton	Ford	138.107	Ryan Newman
2002	Mark Martin	Ford	137.729	Jimmie Johnson
2003	Jimmie Johnson	Chevrolet	126.198	Ryan Newman
2004	Jimmie Johnson	Chevrolet	142.763	Jimmie Johnson
2005	Jimmie Johnson	Chevrolet	114.698	Ryan Newman

Note: Held at the 1.5-mile high-banked Lowe's Motor Speedway in Charlotte on Memorial Day weekend.

Brickyard 400

Year	Winner	Car	Avg Speed	Pole Winner	Speed
1994	Jeff Gordon	Chevrolet	131.977	Rick Mast	172.414
1995	Dale Earnhardt	Chevrolet	155.206	Jeff Gordon	172.536
1996	Dale Jarrett	Ford	139.508	Jeff Gordon	176.419
1997	Ricky Rudd	Ford	130.814	Ernie Irvan	177.736
1998	Jeff Gordon	Chevrolet	126.772	Ernie Irvan	179.394
1999	Dale Jarrett	Ford	148.194	Jeff Gordon	179.612
2000	Bobby Labonte	Pontiac	155.912	Ricky Rudd	181.068
2001	Jeff Gordon	Chevrolet	130.790	Jimmy Spencer	179.666
2002	Bill Elliott	Dodge	125.033	Tony Stewart	182.960
2003	Kevin Harvick	Chevrolet	134.554	Kevin Harvick	184.343*
2004	Jeff Gordon	Chevrolet	115.037	Casey Mears	186.293*
2005	Tony Stewart	Chevrolet	148.782	Elliot Sadler	184.117

*Track record.

Talladega 500

Year	Winner	Car	Avg Speed	Pole Winner	Speed
1970	Pete Hamilton	Plymouth	152.321	Bobby Isaac	199.658
1971	Donnie Allison	Mercury	147.419	Donnie Allison	185.869
1972	David Pearson	Mercury	134.400	Bobby Isaac	192.428
1973	David Pearson	Mercury	131.956	Buddy Baker	193.435
1974	David Pearson	Mercury	130.220	David Pearson	186.086
1975	Buddy Baker	Ford	144.94	Buddy Baker	189.947
1976	Buddy Baker	Ford	169.887	Dave Marcis	189.197
1977	Darrell Waltrip	Chevrolet	164.887	A.J. Foyt	192.424
1978	Cale Yarborough	Oldsmobile	155.699	Cale Yarborough	191.904
1979	Bobby Allison	Ford	154.770	Darrell Waltrip	195.644
1980	Buddy Baker	Oldsmobile	170.481	David Pearson	197.704
1981	Bobby Allison	Buick	149.376	Bobby Allison	195.864
1982	Darrell Waltrip	Buick	156.697	Benny Parsons	200.176
1983	Richard Petty	Pontiac	135.936	Cale Yarborough	202.650
1984	Cale Yarborough	Chevrolet	172.988	Cale Yarborough	202.692
1985	Bill Elliott	Ford	186.288	Bill Elliott	209.398
1986	Bobby Allison	Buick	157.698	Bill Elliott	212.229
1987	Davey Allison	Ford	154.228	Bill Elliott	221.809
1988	Phil Parsons	Oldsmobile	156.547	Davey Allison	198.969
1989	Davey Allison	Ford	155.869	Mark Martin	193.061
1990	Dale Earnhardt	Chevrolet	159.571	Bill Elliott	199.388
1991	Harry Gant	Oldsmobile	165.620	Ernie Irvan	195.186
1992	Davey Allison	Ford	167.609	Ernie Irvan	192.831
1993	Ernie Irvan	Chevrolet	155.412	Dale Earnhardt	192.355
1994	Dale Earnhardt	Chevrolet	157.478	Ernie Irvan	193.298
1995	Mark Martin	Ford	178.902	Terry Labonte	196.532
1996	Sterling Marlin	Chevrolet	149.999	Ernie Irvan	192.855
1997	Mark Martin	Ford	188.354	John Andretti	193.627
1998	Dale Jarrett	Ford	159.318	Ken Schrader	196.153
1999	Dale Earnhardt	Chevrolet	166.632	Joe Nemechek	198.331
2000	Dale Earnhardt	Chevrolet	165.681	Joe Nemechek	190.279
2001	Dale Earnhardt Jr.	Chevrolet	164.185	Stacy Compton	185.240
2002	Dale Earnhardt Jr.	Chevrolet	183.665	qualifying cancelled	—
2003	Michael Waltrip	Chevrolet	156.045	Elliot Sadler	189.943
2004	Jeff Gordon	Chevrolet	129.396	Ricky Rudd	191.180
2005	Dale Jarrett	Ford	143.818	Elliot Sadler	189.26

Note: Formerly the Winston 500, held at the 2.66-mile Talladega Superspeedway.

Southern 500

Year	Winner	Car	Avg Speed	Pole Winner
1950	Johnny Mantz	Plymouth	76.260	Wally Campbell
1951	Herb Thomas	Hudson	76.900	Marshall Teague
1952	Fonty Flock	Oldsmobile	74.510	Dick Rathman
1953	Buck Baker	Oldsmobile	92.780	Fonty Flock
1954	Herb Thomas	Hudson	94.930	Buck Baker
1955	Herb Thomas	Chevrolet	92.281	Tim Flock
1956	Curtis Turner	Ford	95.067	Buck Baker
1957	Speedy Thompson	Chevrolet	100.100	Paul Goldsmith
1958	Fireball Roberts	Chevrolet	102.590	Fireball Roberts
1959	Jim Reed	Chevrolet	111.836	Fireball Roberts
1960	Buck Baker	Pontiac	105.901	Cotton Owens
1961	Nelson Stacy	Ford	117.880	Fireball Roberts
1962	Larry Frank	Ford	117.965	Fireball Roberts
1963	Fireball Roberts	Ford	129.784	Fireball Roberts
1964	Buck Baker	Dodge	117.757	Richard Petty
1965	Ned Jarrett	Ford	115.924	Junior Johnson
1966	Darel Dieringer	Mercury	114.830	Lee Yarborough
1967	Richard Petty	Plymouth	131.933	David Pearson
1968	Cale Yarborough	Mercury	126.132	Charlie Glotzbach
1969	Lee Roy Yarbrough	Ford	105.612	Cale Yarborough
1970	Buddy Baker	Dodge	128.817	David Pearson
1971	Bobby Allison	Mercury	131.398	Bobby Allison
1972	Bobby Allison	Chevrolet	128.124	David Pearson
1973	Cale Yarborough	Chevrolet	134.033	David Pearson
1974	Cale Yarborough	Chevrolet	111.075	Richard Petty
1975	Bobby Allison	Matador	116.825	David Pearson
1976	David Pearson	Mercury	120.534	David Pearson
1977	David Pearson	Mercury	106.797	Darrell Waltrip
1978	Cale Yarborough	Oldsmobile	116.828	David Pearson
1979	David Pearson	Chevrolet	126.259	Bobby Allison
1980	Terry Labonte	Chevrolet	115.210	Darrell Waltrip
1981	Neil Bonnett	Ford	126.410	Harry Gant
1982	Cale Yarborough	Buick	126.703	David Pearson
1983	Bobby Allison	Buick	123.343	Neil Bonnett
1984	Harry Gant	Chevrolet	128.270	Harry Gant
1985	Bill Elliott	Ford	121.254	Bill Elliott
1986	Tim Richmond	Chevrolet	121.068	Tim Richmond
1987	Dale Earnhardt	Chevrolet	115.520	Davey Allison
1988	Bill Elliott	Ford	128.297	Bill Elliott
1989	Dale Earnhardt	Chevrolet	135.462	Alan Kulwicki
1990	Dale Earnhardt	Chevrolet	123.141	Dale Earnhardt
1991	Harry Gant	Oldsmobile	133.508	Davey Allison
1992	Darrell Waltrip	Chevrolet	129.114	Sterling Marlin
1993	Mark Martin	Ford	137.932	Ken Schrader
1994	Bill Elliott	Ford	127.915	Geoff Bodine
1995	Jeff Gordon	Chevrolet	121.231	John Andretti
1996	Jeff Gordon	Chevrolet	135.757	Dale Jarrett
1997	Jeff Gordon	Chevrolet	121.149	Bobby Labonte
1998	Jeff Gordon	Chevrolet	139.031	Dale Jarrett
1999	Jeff Burton	Ford	100.816	Kenny Irwin
2000	Bobby Labonte	Pontiac	108.275	Jeremy Mayfield
2001	Ward Burton	Dodge	122.773	Kurt Busch
2002	Jeff Gordon	Chevrolet	118.617	Sterling Marlin
2003	Terry Labonte	Chevrolet	120.744	Ryan Newman
2004	Jimmie Johnson	Chevrolet	125.044	Kurt Busch

Note: Held at the 1.366-mile Darlington (S.C.) Raceway on November 14, 2004.

Nextel Cup* NASCAR Champions

Year	Driver	Car	Wins	Poles	Winnings ($)
1949	Red Byron	Oldsmobile	2	1	5,800
1950	Bill Rexford	Oldsmobile	1	0	6,175
1951	Herb Thomas	Hudson	7	4	18,200
1952	Tim Flock	Hudson	8	4	20,210
1953	Herb Thomas	Hudson	11	10	27,300
1954	Lee Petty	Dodge	7	3	26,706
1955	Tim Flock	Chrysler	18	19	33,750
1956	Buck Baker	Chrysler	14	12	29,790
1957	Buck Baker	Chevrolet	10	5	24,712
1958	Lee Petty	Oldsmobile	7	4	20,600
1959	Lee Petty	Plymouth	10	2	45,570
1960	Rex White	Chevrolet	6	3	45,260
1961	Ned Jarrett	Chevrolet	1	4	27,285
1962	Joe Weatherly	Pontiac	9	6	56,110
1963	Joe Weatherly	Mercury	3	6	58,110
1964	Richard Petty	Plymouth	9	8	98,810
1965	Ned Jarrett	Ford	13	9	77,966
1966	David Pearson	Dodge	14	7	59,205
1967	Richard Petty	Plymouth	27	18	130,275
1968	David Pearson	Ford	16	12	118,824
1969	David Pearson	Ford	11	14	183,700
1970	Bobby Isaac	Dodge	11	13	121,470
1971	Richard Petty	Plymouth	21	9	309,225
1972	Richard Petty	Plymouth	8	3	227,015
1973	Benny Parsons	Chevrolet	1	0	114,345
1974	Richard Petty	Dodge	10	7	299,175
1975	Richard Petty	Dodge	13	3	378,865
1976	Cale Yarborough	Chevrolet	9	2	387,173
1977	Cale Yarborough	Chevrolet	9	3	477,499
1978	Cale Yarborough	Oldsmobile	10	8	530,751
1979	Richard Petty	Chevrolet	5	1	531,292
1980	Dale Earnhardt	Chevrolet	5	0	588,926
1981	Darrell Waltrip	Buick	12	11	693,342
1982	Darrell Waltrip	Buick	12	7	873,118
1983	Bobby Allison	Buick	6	0	828,355
1984	Terry Labonte	Chevrolet	2	2	713,010
1985	Darrell Waltrip	Chevrolet	3	4	1,318,735
1986	Dale Earnhardt	Chevrolet	5	1	1,783,880
1987	Dale Earnhardt	Chevrolet	11	1	2,099,243
1988	Bill Elliott	Ford	6	6	1,574,639
1989	Rusty Wallace	Pontiac	6	4	2,247,950
1990	Dale Earnhardt	Chevrolet	9	4	3,083,056
1991	Dale Earnhardt	Chevrolet	4	0	2,396,685
1992	Alan Kulwicki	Ford	2	6	2,322,561
1993	Dale Earnhardt	Chevrolet	6	2	3,353,789
1994	Dale Earnhardt	Chevrolet	4	2	3,400,733
1995	Jeff Gordon	Chevrolet	7	9	4,347,343
1996	Terry Labonte	Chevrolet	2	4	4,030,648
1997	Jeff Gordon	Chevrolet	10	1	4,201,227
1998	Jeff Gordon	Chevrolet	13	7	6,175,867
1999	Dale Jarrett	Ford	4	0	3,608,829
2000	Bobby Labonte	Pontiac	4	2	4,041,750
2001	Jeff Gordon	Chevrolet	6	8	6,649,076
2002	Tony Stewart	Pontiac	3	4	4,695,150
2003	Matt Kenseth	Ford	1	2	4,038,120
2004	Kurt Busch	Chevrolet	3	1	4,200,330

*Series name changed from Winston Cup after 2003 season.

Alltime NASCAR Leaders

WINS		POLE POSITIONS	
Richard Petty	200	Richard Petty	126
David Pearson	105	David Pearson	113
Bobby Allison	84	Cale Yarborough	70
Darrell Waltrip	84	Darrell Waltrip	59
Cale Yarborough	83	Bobby Allison	57
Dale Earnhardt	76	*Bill Elliott	55
*Jeff Gordon	72	*Jeff Gordon	54
*Rusty Wallace	55	Bobby Isaac	51
Lee Petty	54	Junior Johnson	47
Ned Jarrett	50	Buck Baker	44
Junior Johnson	50	*Mark Martin	42
Herb Thomas	48	Buddy Baker	40
Buck Baker	46	Tim Flock	39
*Bill Elliott	44	Herb Thomas	39
Tim Flock	40	Geoff Bodine	37

*Active drivers. Note: NASCAR wins leaders and pole positions leaders through Sept. 28, 2005.

Formula One Grand Prix Racing

World Driving Champions

Year	Winner	Car	Year	Winner	Car
1950	Guiseppe Farina, Italy	Alfa Romeo	1975	Niki Lauda, Austria	Ferrari
1951	Juan-Manuel Fangio, Argentina	Alfa Romeo	1976	James Hunt, Grt Britain	McLaren-Ford
			1977	Niki Lauda, Austria	Ferrari
1952	Alberto Ascari, Italy	Ferrari	1978	Mario Andretti, U.S.	Lotus-Ford
1953	Alberto Ascari, Italy	Ferrari	1979	Jody Scheckter, S Africa	Ferrari
1954	Juan-Manuel Fangio, Argentina	Maserati-Mercedes	1980	Alan Jones, Australia	Williams-Ford
			1981	Nelson Piquet, Brazil	Brabham-Ford
1955	Juan-Manuel Fangio, Argentina	Mercedes	1982	Keke Rosberg, Finland	Williams-Ford
			1983	Nelson Piquet, Brazil	Brabham-BMW
1956	Juan-Manuel Fangio, Argentina	Ferrari	1984	Niki Lauda, Austria	McLaren-Porsche
			1985	Alain Prost, France	McLaren-Porsche
1957	Juan-Manuel Fangio, Argentina	Maserati	1986	Alain Prost, France	McLaren-Porsche
			1987	Nelson Piquet, Brazil	Williams-Honda
1958	Mike Hawthorn, Grt Britain	Ferrari	1988	Ayrton Senna, Brazil	McLaren-Honda
1959	Jack Brabham, Australia	Cooper-Climax	1989	Alain Prost, France	McLaren-Honda
1960	Jack Brabham, Australia	Cooper-Climax	1990	Ayrton Senna, Brazil	McLaren-Honda
1961	Phil Hill, U.S.	Ferrari	1991	Ayrton Senna, Brazil	McLaren-Honda
1962	Graham Hill, Grt Britain	BRM	1992	Nigel Mansell, Grt Britain	Williams-Renault
1963	Jim Clark, Scotland	Lotus-Climax	1993	Alain Prost, France	Williams-Renault
1964	John Surtees, Grt Britain	Ferrari	1994	Michael Schumacher, Ger	Benetton-Ford
1965	Jim Clark, Scotland	Lotus-Climax	1995	Michael Schumacher, Ger	Benetton-Renault
1966	Jack Brabham, Australia	Brabham-Repco	1996	Damon Hill, Grt Britain	Williams-Renault
1967	Denny Hulme, New Zealand	Brabham-Repco	1997	Jacques Villeneuve, Can	Williams-Renault
			1998	Mika Hakkinen, Finland	McLaren-Mercedes
1968	Graham Hill, Grt Britain	Lotus-Ford	1999	Mika Hakkinen, Finland	McLaren-Mercedes
1969	Jackie Stewart, Scotland	Matra-Ford	2000	Michael Schumacher, Ger	Ferrari
1970	Jochen Rindt, Austria*	Lotus-Ford	2001	Michael Schumacher, Ger	Ferrari
1971	Jackie Stewart, Scotland	Tyrell-Ford	2002	Michael Schumacher, Ger	Ferrari
1972	Emerson Fittipaldi, Brazil	Lotus-Ford	2003	Michael Schumacher, Ger	Ferrari
1973	Jackie Stewart, Scotland	Tyrell-Ford	2004	Michael Schumacher, Ger	Ferrari
1974	Emerson Fittipaldi, Brazil	McLaren-Ford			

*The championship was awarded posthumously, after Rindt was killed during practice for the Italian Grand Prix.

Alltime Grand Prix Winners

Driver	Wins	Driver	Wins
*Michael Schumacher, Germany	84	Jim Clark, Great Britain	25
Alain Prost, France	51	Niki Lauda, Austria	25
Ayrton Senna, Brazil	41	Juan Manuel Fangio, Argentina	24
Nigel Mansell, Great Britain	31	Nelson Piquet, Brazil	23
Jackie Stewart, Great Britain	27	Damon Hill, Great Britain	22

*Active driver. Note: Grand Prix winners through Sept. 26, 2005.

Alltime Grand Prix Pole Winners

Driver	Poles	Driver	Poles
Ayrton Senna, Brazil	65	Juan Manuel Fangio, Argentina	29
*Michael Schumacher, Germany	63	Mika Hakkinen, Finland	26
Alain Prost, France	33	Niki Lauda, Austria	24
Jim Clark, Great Britain	33	Nelson Piquet, Brazil	24
Nigel Mansell, Great Britain	32	Damon Hill, Great Britain	20

*Active driver. Note: Pole winners through Sept. 26, 2005.

Professional Sports Car Racing

The 24 Hours of Daytona

Year	Winner	Car	Avg Speed	Distance
1962	Dan Gurney	Lotus 19-Class SP11	104.101 mph	3 hrs (312.42 mi)
1963	Pedro Rodriguez	Ferrari-Class 12	102.074 mph	3 hrs (308.61 mi)
1964	Pedro Rodriguez/Phil Hill	Ferrari 250 LM	98.230 mph	2,000 km
1965	Ken Miles/Lloyd Ruby	Ford	99.944 mph	2,000 km
1966	Ken Miles/Lloyd Ruby	Ford Mark II	108.020 mph	24 hrs (2,570.63 mi)
1967	Lorenzo Bandini/Chris Amon	Ferrari 330 P4	105.688 mph	24 hrs (2,537.46 mi)
1968	Vic Elford/Jochen Neerpasch	Porsche 907	106.697 mph	24 hrs (2,565.69 mi)
1969	Mark Donohue/Chuck Parsons	Chevy Lola	99.268 mph	24 hrs (2,383.75 mi)
1970	Pedro Rodriguez/Leo Kinnunen	Porsche 917	114.866 mph	24 hrs (2,758.44 mi)
1971	Pedro Rodriguez/Jackie Oliver	Porsche 917K	109.203 mph	24 hrs (2,621.28 mi)
1972*	Mario Andretti/Jacky Ickx	Ferrari 312/P	122.573 mph	6 hrs (738.24 mi)
1973	Peter Gregg/Hurley Haywood	Porsche Carrera	106.225 mph	24 hrs (2,552.7 mi)
1974	(No race)			
1975	Peter Gregg/Hurley Haywood	Porsche Carrera	108.531 mph	24 hrs (2,606.04 mi)
1976†	Peter Gregg/Brian Redman/ John Fitzpatrick	BMW CSL	104.040 mph	24 hrs (2,092.8 mi)
1977	John Graves/Hurley Haywood/ Dave Helmick	Porsche Carrera	108.801 mph	24 hrs (2,615 mi)
1978	Rolf Stommelen/ Antoine Hezemans/Peter Gregg	Porsche Turbo	108.743 mph	24 hrs (2,611.2 mi)
1979	Ted Field/Danny Ongais/ Hurley Haywood	Porsche Turbo	109.249 mph	24 hrs (2,626.56 mi)
1980	Volkert Meri/Rolf Stommelen/ Reinhold Joest	Porsche Turbo	114.303 mph	24 hrs
1981	Bob Garretson/Bobby Rahal/ Brian Redman	Porsche Turbo	113.153 mph	24 hrs
1982	John Paul Jr/John Paul Sr/ Rolf Stommelen	Porsche Turbo	114.794 mph	24 hrs
1983	Preston Henn/Bob Wollek/ Claude Ballot-Lena/A.J. Foyt	Porsche Turbo	98.781 mph	24 hrs
1984	Sarel van der Merwe/ Graham Duxbury/Tony Martin	Porsche March	103.119 mph	24 hrs (2,476.8 mi)
1985	A.J. Foyt/Bob Wollek/ Al Unser/Thierry Boutsen	Porsche 962	104.162 mph	24 hrs (2,502.68 mi)
1986	Al Holbert/Derek Bell/Al Unser Jr.	Porsche 962	105.484 mph	24 hrs (2,534.72 mi)
1987	Chip Robinson/Derek Bell/ Al Holbert/Al Unser Jr.	Porsche 962	111.599 mph	24 hrs (2,680.68 mi)
1988	Martin Brundle/John Nielsen/ Raul Boesel	Jaguar XJR-9	107.943 mph	24 hrs (2,591.68 mi)

The 24 Hours of Daytona (Cont.)

Year	Winner	Car	Avg Speed	Distance
1989	John Andretti/Derek Bell/ Bob Wollek	Porsche 962	92.009 mph	24 hrs (2,210.76 mi)
1990	Davy Jones/ Jan Lammers/ Andy Wallace	Jaguar XJR-12	112.857 mph	24 hrs (2,709.16 mi)
1991	Hurley Haywood/ John Winter/ Frank Jelinski/ Henri Pescarolo/ Bob Wollek	Porsche 962C	106.633 mph	24 hrs (2,559.64 mi)
1992	Massahiro Hasemi/ Kazuoyshi Hoshino/ Toshio Suzuki/ Anders Olofsson	Nissan R91CP	112.987 mph	24 hrs (2,712.72 mi)
1993	P.J. Jones/Mark Dismore/ Rocky Moran	Toyota Eagle MK III	103.537 mph	24 hrs (2,484.88 mi)
1994	Paul Gentilozzi/ Scott Pruett/ Butch Leitzinger/ Steve Millen	Nissan 300 ZX	104.80 mph	24 hrs (2,693.67 mi)
1995	Jurgen Lassig/ Christophe Buochut/ Giovanni Lavaggi/ Marco Werner	Porsche Spyder K8	102.28 mph	690 laps (2,456.4 mi)
1996	Wayne Taylor/ Scott Sharp/ Jim Pace	Oldsmobile Mark III	103.32 mph	697 laps (2,481.32 mi)
1997	Elliot Forbes-Robinson/ John Schneider/Rob Dyson/ John Paul Jr/Butch Leitzinger/James Weaver/Andy Wallace	Ford R & S MK III	102.292 mph	690 laps (2,456.4 mi)
1998	Arie Luyendyk/Didier Theys/ Mauro Baldi	Ferrari 333 SP	105.565 mph	711 laps (2,531.16 mi)
1999	Elliott Forbes-Robinson/ Butch Leitzinger/ Andy Wallace	Ford R & S MK III	104.9 mph	708 laps (2,520.48 mi)
2000	Olivier Beretta/Karl Wendlinger/ Dominique Dupuy	Dodge Viper	107.207 mph	723 laps (2,573.88 mi)
2001	Ron Fellows/Chris Kneifel/Franck Freon/Johnny O'Connell	Corvette	97.293 mph	656 laps (2,335.360 mi)
2002	Didier Theys/Fredy Lienhard/ Max Papis/Mauro Baldi	Dallara-Judd (SRP)	106.143 mph	716 laps (2,548.96 mi)
2003	Kevin Buckler/Michael Schrom Timo Bernhard/Jorg Bergmeister	Porsche GT3 RS	114.068† mph	694 laps (2,470.64 mi)
2004	Forest Barber/Terry Borcheller Andy Pilgrim/Christian Fittipaldi	Pontiac Doran	117.651	526 laps (1,872.56 mi)
2005	Wayne Taylor, Max Angelelli, Emmanuel Collard	Pontiac Riley	119.397 mph	710 laps (2,527.60 mi)

*Race shortened due to fuel crisis. †Course lengthened from 3.81 miles to 3.84 miles. † Top speed.

World SportsCar Champions*

Year	Winner	Car	Year	Winner	Car
1978	Peter Gregg	Porsche 935	1989	Geoff Brabham	Nissan GTP
1979	Peter Gregg	Porsche 935	1990	Geoff Brabham	Nissan GTP
1980	John Fitzpatrick	Porsche 935	1991	Geoff Brabham	Nissan NPT
1981	Brian Redman	Chevy Lola	1992	Juan Fangio II	Toyota EGL MKIII
1982	John Paul Jr	Chevy Lola	1993	Juan Fangio II	Toyota EGL MKIII
1983	Al Holbert	Chevy March	1994	Wayne Taylor	Mazda Kudzu
1984	Randy Lanier	Chevy March	1995	Fermin Velez	Ferrari 333 SP
1985	Al Holbert	Porsche 962	1996	Wayne Taylor	Mazda Kudzu
1986	Al Holbert	Porsche 962	1997	Butch Leitzinger	Ford R&S MKIII
1987	Chip Robinson	Porsche 962	1998	Butch Leitzinger	Ford R&S MKIII
1988	Geoff Brabham	Nissan GTP			

Year	Prototype	GTS		GT
1999	Elliott Forbes-Robinson	Olivier Beretta		Cort Wagner
2000	Allan McNish	Olivier Beretta		Sascha Maassen
2001	Emanuele Pirro	Terry Borcheller		Jörg Müller
2002	Tom Kristensen	Ron Fellows		Lucas Luhr
2003	Frank Biela/Marco Werner	Ron Fellows/John O'Connell		Sascha Maassen/L. Luhr
2004	Frank Biela/Emanuele Piroo	Oliver Gavin, Olivier Beretta		Patrick Long/Jorg Bergmeister

*1978–93 champions raced in the GT series, which in 1994 was replaced by the World SportsCar series. Beginning in 1999, racing was reclassified according to the American Le Mans Series. The Series is comprised of two different types of race cars divided into two categories and five separate classes. The Prototype category features open-cockpit prototype World Sports Cars (WSC) and Le Mans Prototypes (LMP), as well as Grand Touring Prototype (GTP) class cars. The Grand Touring category features the Grand Touring S (GTS) class cars, formerly known as GT2, and Grand Touring (GT) cars, formerly known as GT3. Both classes feature purpose-built race cars with an emphasis on spectator car identification.

Alltime SportsCar Leaders

PROTOTYPE WINS (WSC/GTP ERA: 1994–2005)		GTS AND GT WINS (IMSA GT: 1971–1994)	
James Weaver	16	Al Holbert	49
Butch Leitzinger	15	Peter Gregg	41
Frank Biela	15	Hurley Haywood	31
J.J. Lehto	12	Geoff Brabham	26
Emanuele Pirro	10	Parker Johnstone	25
Rinaldo Capello	9	Jim Downing	23
Wayne Taylor	8	Irv Hoerr	23
David Brabham	8	Jack Baldwin	22
Gianpiero Moretti	7	Don Devendorf	22
Allan McNish	6	Bob Earl	22
		Tommy Riggins	22

Seven tied with five.

Note: Leaders through October 1, 2005

24 Hours of Le Mans

Year	Winning Drivers	Car
1923	André Lagache/René Léonard	Chenard & Walker
1924	John Duff/Francis Clement	Bentley
1925	Gérard de Courcelles/André Rossignol	La Lorraine
1926	Robert Bloch/André Rossignol	La Lorraine
1927	J. Dudley Benjafield/Sammy Davis	Bentley
1928	Woolf Barnato/Bernard Rubin	Bentley
1929	Woolf Barnato/Sir Henry Birkin	Bentley Speed 6
1930	Woolf Barnato/Glen Kidston	Bentley Speed 6
1931	Earl Howe/Sir Henry Birkin	Alfa Romeo 8C-2300 sc
1932	Raymond Sommer/Luigi Chinetti	Alfa Romeo 8C-2300 sc
1933	Raymond Sommer/Tazio Nuvolari	Alfa Romeo 8C-2300 sc
1934	Luigi Chinetti/Philippe Etancelin	Alfa Romeo 8C-2300 sc
1935	John Hindmarsh/Louis Fontés	Lagonda M45R
1936	Race cancelled	
1937	Jean-Pierre Wimille/Robert Benoist	Bugatti 57G sc
1938	Eugene Chaboud/Jean Tremoulet	Delahaye 135M
1939	Jean-Pierre Wimille/Pierre Veyron	Bugatti 57G sc
1940–48	Races cancelled	
1949	Luigi Chinetti/Lord Selsdon	Ferrari 166MM
1950	Louis Rosier/Jean-Louis Rosier	Talbot-Lago
1951	Peter Walker/Peter Whitehead	Jaguar C
1952	Hermann Lang/Fritz Reiss	Mercedes-Benz 300 SL
1953	Tony Rolt/Duncan Hamilton	Jaguar C
1954	Froilan Gonzales/Maurice Trintignant	Ferrari 375
1955	Mike Hawthorn/Ivor Bueb	Jaguar D
1956	Ron Flockhart/Ninian Sanderson	Jaguar D
1957	Ron Flockhart/Ivor Bueb	Jaguar D
1958	Olivier Gendebien/Phil Hill	Ferrari 250 TR58
1959	Carroll Shelby/Roy Salvadori	Aston Martin DBR1
1960	Olivier Gendebien/Paul Frère	Ferrari 250 TR59/60
1961	Olivier Gendebien/Phil Hill	Ferrari 250 TR61
1962	Olivier Gendebien/Phil Hill	Ferrari 250P
1963	Lodovico Scarfiotti/Lorenzo Bandini	Ferrari 250P
1964	Jean Guichel/Nino Vaccarella	Ferrari 275P
1965	Jochen Rindt/Masten Gregory	Ferrari 250LM
1966	Chris Amon/Bruce McLaren	Ford Mk2
1967	Dan Gurney/A.J. Foyt	Ford Mk4
1968	Pedro Rodriguez/Lucien Bianchi	Ford GT40
1969	Jacky Ickx/Jackie Oliver	Ford GT40
1970	Hans Herrmann/Richard Attwood	Porsche 917
1971	Helmut Marko/Gijs van Lennep	Porsche 917
1972	Henri Pescarolo/Graham Hill	Matra-Simca MS670
1973	Henri Pescarolo/Gérard Larrousse	Matra-Simca MS670B

Year	Winning Drivers	Car
1974	Henri Pescarolo/Gérard Larrousse	Matra-Simca MS670B
1975	Jacky Ickx/Derek Bell	Mirage-Ford MB
1976	Jacky Ickx/Gijs van Lennep	Porsche 936
1977	Jacky Ickx/Jurgen Barth/Hurley Haywood	Porsche 936
1978	Jean-Pierre Jaussaud/Didier Pironi	Renault-Alpine A442
1979	Klaus Ludwig/Bill Whittington/Don Whittington	Porsche 935
1980	Jean-Pierre Jaussaud/Jean Rondeau	Rondeau-Ford M379B
1981	Jacky Ickx/Derek Bell	Porsche 936-81
1982	Jacky Ickx/Derek Bell	Porsche 956
1983	Vern Schuppan/Hurley Haywood/Al Holbert	Porsche 956-83
1984	Klaus Ludwig/Henri Pescarolo	Porsche 956B
1985	Klaus Ludwig/Paolo Barilla/John Winter	Porsche 956B
1986	Derek Bell/Hans-Joachim Stuck/Al Holbert	Porsche 962C
1987	Derek Bell/Hans-Joachim Stuck/Al Holbert	Porsche 962C
1988	Jan Lammers/Johnny Dumfries/Andy Wallace	Jaguar XJR9LM
1989	Jochen Mass/Manuel Reuter/Stanley Dickens	Sauber-Mercedes C9-88
1990	John Nielsen/Price Cobb/Martin Brundle	TWR Jaguar XJR-12
1991	Volker Weidler/Johnny Herbert/Bertrand Gachof	Mazda 787B
1992	Derek Warwick/Yannick Dalmas/Mark Blundell	Peugeot 905B
1993	Geoff Brabham/Christophe Bouchut/Eric Helary	Peugeot 905
1994	Yannick Dalmas/Hurley Haywood/Mauro Baldi	Porsche 962
1995	Yannick Dalmas/J.J. Lehto/Masanori Sekiya	McLaren BMW
1996	Manuel Reuter/Davy Jones/Alexander Wurz	TWR Porsche
1997	Michele Alboreto/Stefan Johansson/Tom Kristensen	TWR Porsche
1998	Allan McNish/Laurent Aiello/Stephane Ortelli	Porsche GT One
1999	Yannick Dalmas/Joachim Winkelhock/Pierluigi Martini	BMW V12 LMR
2000	Frank Biela/Tom Kristensen/Emanuele Pirro	Audi R8
2001	Frank Biela/Tom Kristensen/Emanuele Pirro	Audi R8
2002	Frank Biela/Tom Kristensen/Emanuele Pirro	Audi R8
2003	Rinaldo Capello/Tom Kristensen/Guy Smith	Bentley EXP Speed 8
2004	Rinaldo Capello/Seiji Ara/Tom Kristensen	Audi R8
2005	J.J. Lehto/Marco Werner/Tom Kristensen	Audi R8

Jeff Gordon's "Ringer"

Driving cars? No problem. "But it takes a while to get used to driving nails," says Jeff Gordon. "Once you get your throw down, though, it becomes a lot of fun." Enough fun that the four-time NASCAR champ got a handful of blisters last week when he joined celebs such as Diddy, Steve Carell, Jerome Bettis and Rudy Giuliani to build 45 houses for a Habitat for Humanity project in New York City's Rockefeller Center. The homes were built in sections that were then loaded onto flatbed trucks and driven to hurricane-damaged neighborhoods on the Gulf Coast. Gordon's girlfriend, model Ingrid Vandebosch (above, with Gordon), was so handy with a hammer that the construction workers on hand called her "Ringer."

—Adam Duerson

Drag Racing: Milestone Performances

Top Fuel
ELAPSED TIME

Time (Sec.)	Driver	Date	Site
9.00	Jack Chrisman	Feb 18, 1961	Pomona, CA
8.97	Jack Chrisman	May 20, 1961	Empona, VA
7.96	Bobby Vodnick	May 16, 1964	Bayview, MD
6.97	Don Johnson	May 7, 1967	Carlsbad, CA
5.97	Mike Snively	Nov 17, 1972	Ontario, CA
5.78	Don Garlits	Nov 18, 1973	Ontario, CA
5.698	Gary Beck	Oct 10, 1975	Ontario, CA
5.573	Gary Beck	Oct 18, 1981	Irvine, CA
5.484	Gary Beck	Sept 6, 1982	Clermont, IN
5.391	Gary Beck	Oct 1, 1983	Fremont, CA
5.280	Darrell Gwynn	Sept 25, 1986	Ennis, TX
5.176	Darrell Gwynn	April 4, 1987	Ennis, TX
5.090	Joe Amato	Oct 1, 1987	Ennis, TX
4.990	Eddie Hill	April 9, 1988	Ennis, TX
4.881	Gary Ormsby	Sept 28, 1990	Topeka, KS
4.799	Cory McClenathan	Sept 19, 1992	Mohnton, PA
4.762	Cory McClenathan	Oct 3, 1993	Topeka, KS
4.690	Michael Brotherton	May 20, 1994	Englishtown, NJ
4.595	Joe Amato	July 5, 1996	Topeka, KS
4.539	Joe Amato	Mar 21, 1998	Baytown, TX
4.525	Gary Scelzi	Oct 23, 1998	Ennis, TX
4.503	Mike Dunn	Feb 5, 1999	Pomona, CA
4.486	Larry Dixon	Apr 9, 1999	Houston
4.480	Gary Scelzi	Oct 31, 1999	Houston
4.477	Kenny Bernstein	June 2, 2001	Joliet, IL
4.441	Tony Schumacher	Oct 4, 2003	Reading, PA
4.437	Tony Schumacher	Oct 1, 2005	Joliet, IL

SPEED

MPH	Driver	Date	Site
180.36	Connie Kalitta	Sept 3, 1962	Indianapolis
190.26	Don Garlits	Sept 21, 1963	East Haddam, CT
201.34	Don Garlits	Aug 1, 1964	Great Meadows, NJ
211.26	Donny Milani	May 15, 1965	Sacramento, CA
223.32	Don Cook	Apr 24, 1965	Fremont, CA
230.17	James Warren	Apr 10, 1967	Fresno, CA
243.24	Don Garlits	Mar 18, 1973	Gainesville, FL
250.69	Don Garlits	Oct 11, 1975	Ontario, CA
260.11	Joe Amato	Mar 18, 1984	Gainesville, FL
272.56	Don Garlits	Mar 23, 1986	Gainesville, FL
282.13	Joe Amato	Sept 5, 1987	Clermont, IN
291.54	Connie Kalitta	Feb 11, 1989	Pomona, CA
301.70	Kenny Bernstein	Mar 20, 1992	Gainesville, FL
311.86	Kenny Bernstein	Oct 30, 1994	Pomona, CA
319.82	Joe Amato	Mar 21, 1998	Baytown, TX
323.50	Joe Amato	May 17, 1998	Englishtown, NJ
326.44	Gary Scelzi	Nov 2, 1998	Houston
326.91	Tony Schumacher	Oct 22, 1999	Dallas
330.55	Mike Dunn	June 2, 2001	Joliet, IL
332.18	Kenny Bernstein	Oct. 7, 2001	Richardson, TX
332.75	Larry Dixon	Apr 3, 2003	Las Vegas
333.41	Brandon Bernstein	May 22, 2004	Joliet, IL
336.15	Tony Schumacher	May 25, 2005	Hebron, OH

Funny Car
ELAPSED TIME

Time (sec.)	Driver	Date	Site
6.92	Leroy Goldstein	Sept 3, 1970	Clermont, IN
5.987	Don Prudhomme	Oct 12, 1975	Ontario, CA
5.868	Raymond Beadle	July 16, 1981	Englishtown, NJ
5.799	Tom Anderson	Sept 3, 1982	Clermont, IN
5.637	Don Prudhomme	Sept 4, 1982	Clermont, IN
5.588	Rick Johnson	Feb 3, 1985	Pomona, CA
5.425	Kenny Bernstein	Sept 26, 1986	Ennis, TX
5.397	Kenny Bernstein	April 5, 1987	Ennis, TX
5.255	Ed McCulloch	April 17, 1988	Ennis, TX
5.193	Don Prudhomme	Mar 2, 1989	Baytown, TX
5.077	Cruz Pedregon	Sept 20, 1992	Mohnton, PA
4.987	Chuck Etcholis	Oct 2, 1993	Topeka, KS
4.819	Cruz Pedregon	Mar 21, 1998	Baytown, TX
4.807	Cruz Pedregon	Nov 1, 1998	Houston
4.788	John Force	Apr 11, 1999	Houston
4.763	John Force	June 2, 2001	Joliet, IL
4.750	William Bazemore	Sept 28, 2001	Joliet, IL
4.731	John Force	Oct. 7, 2001	Yorba Linda, CA
4.713	Whit Bazemore	May 22, 2004	Joliet, IL
4.665	John Force	Oct 3, 2004	Joliet, IL

SPEED

MPH	Driver	Date	Site
200.44	Gene Snow	Aug, 1968	Houston
250.00	Don Prudhomme	May 23, 1982	Baton Rouge
260.11	Kenny Bernstein	Mar 18, 1984	Gainesville, FL
271.41	Kenny Bernstein	Aug 30, 1986	Indianapolis
280.72	Mike Dunn	Oct 2, 1987	Ennis, TX
290.13	Jim White	Oct 11, 1991	Ennis, TX
291.82	Jim White	Oct 25, 1991	Pomona, CA
300.40	Jim Epler	Oct 3, 1993	Topeka, KS
303.64	John Force	Sept 2, 1995	Indianapolis
308.74	John Force	Sept 28, 1997	Topeka, KS
317.46	John Force	Mar 21, 1998	Baytown, TX
323.89	John Force	May 17, 1998	Englishtown, NJ
324.05	John Force	Mar 19, 1999	Gainesville, FL
325.45	William Bazemore	Sept 28, 2001	Joliet, IL
326.87	Gary Densham	Feb. 9, 2002	Bellflower, CA
330.55	Gary Scelzi	May 22, 2004	Joliet, IL
333.58	John Force	Oct 3, 2004	Joliet, IL

Pro Stock
ELAPSED TIME

Time (sec.)	Driver	Date	Site
7.778	Lee Shepherd	Mar 12, 1982	Gainesville, FL
7.655	Lee Shepherd	Oct 1, 1982	Fremont, CA
7.557	Bob Glidden	Feb 2, 1985	Pomona, CA
7.497	Bob Glidden	Sep 13, 1985	Maple Grove, PA
7.377	Bob Glidden	Aug 28, 1986	Clermont, IN
7.294	Frank Sanchez	Oct 7, 1988	Baytown, TX
7.184	Darrell Alderman	Oct 12, 1990	Ennis, TX
7.099	Scott Geoffrion	Sept 19, 1992	Mohnton, PA
6.988	Kurt Johnson	May 20, 1994	Englishtown, NJ
6.873	Warren Johnson	Mar 14, 1998	Gainesville, FL
6.867	Warren Johnson	Oct 23, 1998	Ennis, TX
6.866	Warren Johnson	Mar 19, 1999	Gainesville, FL
6.843	Warren Johnson	Apr 30, 1999	Dinwiddie, VA
6.840	Kurt Johnson	May 1, 1999	Dinwiddie, VA
6.822	Warren Johnson	Oct 23, 1999	Dallas
6.801	Kurt Johnson	Sept 29, 2001	Joliet, IL
6.750	Jeg Coughlin	Oct. 7, 2001	Delaware, OH
6.670	Greg Anderson	May 18, 2003	Englishtown, NJ
6.633	Greg Anderson	March 19, 2005	Gainesville, FL

Pro Stock *(Cont.)*

Time (sec.)	Driver	SPEED Date	Site
181.08	Warren Johnson	Oct 1, 1982	Fremont, CA
190.07	Warren Johnson	Aug 29, 1986	Clermont, IN
191.32	Bob Glidden	Sept 4, 1987	Clermont, IN
192.18	Warren Johnson	Oct 13, 1990	Ennis, TX
193.21	Bob Glidden	July 28, 1991	Sonoma, CA
194.51	Warren Johnson	July 31, 1992	Sonoma, CA
195.99	Warren Johnson	May 21, 1993	Englishtown, NJ
196.24	Warren Johnson	Mar 19, 1993	Gainesville, FL
197.15	Warren Johnson	Apr 23, 1994	Commerce, GA
199.15	Warren Johnson	Mar 10, 1995	Baytown, TX
201.20	Warren Johnson	Mar 14, 1998	Gainesville, FL
201.34	Warren Johnson	Oct 23, 1998	Ennis, TX
201.37	Warren Johnson	Mar 19, 1999	Gainesville, FL
202.24	Warren Johnson	Apr 30,1999	Dinwiddie, VA
202.33	Warren Johnson	Oct 23, 1999	Dallas
202.36	Warren Johnson	Oct 31, 1999	Houston
202.70	Kurt Johnson	Sept 29, 2001	Joliet, IL
204.35	Mark Osborne	Oct. 6, 2001	Abdingdon, VA
207.18	Greg Anderson	May 18, 2003	Englishtown, NJ
208.23	Greg Anderson	March 19, 2005	Gainesville, FL

Alltime Drag Racing Leaders
NHRA CAREER WINS

*John Force	119
*Warren Johnson	94
Bob Glidden	85
*Pat Austin	75
Kenny Bernstein	69
*Frank Manzo	61
Joe Amato	57
*David Rampy	57
Don Prudhomme	49
*Bob Newberry	48

*Active driver. Note: Leaders through September 2005.

Lost in Translation

NASCAR driver Morgan Shepherd doesn't have a full-time sponsor, so he often puts religious messages on his car. At the UAW-DaimlerChrysler 400 in Las Vegas earlier this month, his hood read RACING WITH JESUS. But during driver introductions, guest P.A. man Robin Leach announced Shepherd as the driver of the "Racing with HAY-zeus" Dodge. Said Shepherd of Leach, "I'd love to meet him just so I can say, 'Nice to meet you, Mr. Leak.'"

—*Adam Duerson*

Bowling

Out of Nowhere

In 2005, Patrick Allen emerged as a new powerhouse, while Liz Johnson's success hinted at a co-ed future for the PBA

BY HANK HERSCH

"FOUR YEARS, BABY! FOUR years!"

Patrick Allen wasn't celebrating his election to high office in Yspilanti, Mich., but rather something far more valuable to a 34-year-old journeyman bowler: the quadrennial exemption that comes with winning the PBA Denny's World Championship. In the April 3 final, Allen defeated Chris Loschetter 235–210 the hard way, surviving an open 10th frame to claim $120,000 and the first major title of his six-year career. "That's not the way you want to win a tournament, getting seven and two pins in the 10th," said Allen, of Tarrytown, N.Y. "You want to go up and throw a good shot."

Allen threw more of those than anyone on the Tour, outpolling Tommy Jones for the PBA's highest office: Bowler of the Year. The emergence of the southpaw Allen was the most notable development in an already memorable 2004–05 campaign. Among these highlights were Walter Ray Williams Jr.'s chase for the most career victories, the first title-match appearance by a woman in the Tour's 46-year history, and the ongoing changes to league rules. These largely successful changes included instituting an all-match play bracket format, field exemptions and increased prize money.

Before the season began, Allen could barely finish in the money in a regional event, let alone contend for a major. But a half-hour lesson with Dick Ritger in upstate New York helped straighten him out. After finishing second to Danny Wiseman in the Miller High Life Masters, Allen won his first event of the season—and the second of his career—in January, blowing out Brad Angelo 267–183 in the final of the Dallas Open. In the final of the Birmingham (Ala.) Open a week later, Allen prevailed 218–216 thanks to Mike DeVaney's ringing 10 pin in 10th frame to become the Tour's first back-to-back titlist since Williams in 2000.

Chris Barnes denied Allen a major win at the U.S. Open in North Brunswick, N.J.;

MARVIN FONG/THE PLAIN DEALER

Barnes converted the four pin with his final shot to snap an eight-game losing streak on TV, 213–212. But Allen got even four events later at the World Championship, eliminating Barnes four games to three in the round-of-eight at Eastern Michigan's Convocation Center. He then rolled an 11-strike 279 to dust off Mike Scroggins by 81 pins in the semifinals before edging Loschetter. "Now I have to stay focused and not take anything for granted," Allen said.

His primary competition for Bowler of the Year, 26-year-old Tommy Jones of Greenville, S.C., had won a week earlier at the Banquet Open in Wyoming, Mich. But Jones received less notoriety for his fourth victory of the season than for whom he had beaten: Liz Johnson. Before the PWBA tour folded in the fall of 2003, Johnson had won 11 titles and more than $500,000 over eight seasons. At the Banquet Open, she became the first woman to advance to the round of 32 in a PBA Tour event, downing Barnes, DeVaney, Richard Wolfe and Wes Malott during a 23-game, two-day stretch to reach the final.

"I just had to try [to] be consistent," Johnson told pba.com. "These guys out here can bowl some big games. When you get out there with them, you better put your striking shoes on."

Johnson's run ended against Jones, 219–192, but she picked up a $20,000 runner-up check and a flood of support at Spectrum Lanes. "I have been running on adrenaline and good nerves," she said. "I still can't believe I was a part of this. I don't think I can describe everything that's going on in my head."

The victory ran Jones's record to 8–0 in televised matches in 2004–05, and with 17th- and 16th-place finishes in the final two events, he lifted his season's prize money to $224,130. But Allen's season was slightly better: three victories, a win in one major and a second in two others. His $350,740 in earnings more than doubled his career total; it was also the second highest mark in PBA history, behind Williams's $419,700 in '02—03.

The 45-year-old Williams led the Tour in average for the sixth time, rolling a 227.07. But while he won the fifth event of the season, the Uniroyal Tire Classic, he was shut out the rest of the way, leaving him one career victory short of Earl Anthony's 41. Still, when next season rolls around, you can bet Williams will be aiming to knock down "Square Earl's" record once and for all.

The Majors

MEN

2005 Tournament of Champions

	Games	Total	Earnings ($)
Steve Jaros	2	495	100,000
Norm Duke	2	498	30,100
Randy Pederson	1	255	10,000
Bryan Goebel	1	186	10,000

Playoff Results: Duke def. Pederson 256–255; Jaros def. Goebel 247–186; Jaros def. Duke 248–242.

Held at the Mohegan Sun in Uncasville, CT, April 6-10, 2005.

2005 U.S. Open

	Games	Total	Earnings ($)
Chris Barnes	1	213	100,000
Patrick Allen	2	406	50,000
Mika Koivuniemi	2	407	25,000
Walter Ray Williams, Jr.	1	179	15,000

Playoff Results: Koivuniemi def. Williams 212–179; Allen def Koivuniemi 194–194 (18-17 in sudden death roll-off); Barnes def Allen 213–212.

Held at Miller Park in Milwaukee WI, February 13–20, 2005.

2005 ABC Masters

CHAMPIONSHIP ROUND

Bowler	Games	Total	Earnings ($)
Danny Wiseman	1	268	100,000
Patrick Allen	3	669	50,000
Patrick Healey, Jr.	1	219	25,000
Brian Boghosian	1	153	15,000

Playoff Results: Allen def. Boghosian 238–153; Allen def. Healer Jr. 248–219; Wiseman def. Allen 268–183.

Held at Miller Park in Milwaukee WI, October 24-31, 2004.

2005 PBA World Championship

CHAMPIONSHIP ROUND

Bowler	Games	Total	Earnings ($)
Patrick Allen	2	514	120,000
Chris Loschetter	2	441	50,000
Brian Voss	1	165	20,000
Mike Scroggins	1	198	20,000

Playoff Results: Allen def. Scroggins 279–198; Loschetter def. Voss 231–165; Allen def. Loschetter 235–210.

Held at Eastern Michigan Convocation Center in Ypsilanti, MI, Mar 26-April 3, 2005.

WOMEN

2002 Miller High Life National Players Championship

CHAMPIONSHIP ROUND

Bowler	Games	Total	Earnings ($)
Marianne DiRupo	3	689	13,000
Leanne Barrette	1	158	7,000
Michelle Feldman	1	191	4,600
Kelly Kulick	1	152	4,200
Tammy Turner	1	190	3,700

Playoff Results: DiRupo def. Turner and Kulick, 266–190–152; DiRupo def. Feldman, 243–191; DiRupo def. Barrette 180–158.

Held at Funquest Lanes, Collierville, TN, July 21–25, 2002.

2003 WIBC Queens

CHAMPIONSHIP ROUND

Bowler	Games	Total	Earnings ($)
Wendy Macpherson	1	218	14,000
Kendra Gaines	2	415	11,000
Tish Johnson	2	457	8,500
Robin Romeo	1	218	6,500
Lisa Bishop	1	180	5,500

Playoff Results: Johnson def. Romeo and Bishop 242–218–180; Gaines def. Johnson 222–215; Macpherson def. Gaines 218–193.

Held at the National Bowling Stadium in Reno, NV, April 7–11, 2003.

2003 U.S. Open

CHAMPIONSHIP ROUND

Bowler	Games	Total	Earnings ($)
Kelly Kulick	4	951	30,000
Carolyn Dorin-Ballard	1	195	15,000
Michelle Feldman	1	174	11,000
Wendy Macpherson	1	179	9,000
Leanne Barrette	1	213	7,000

Playoff Results: Kulick def. Barrette 213–213 with rolloff 39–35; Kulick def. Macpherson 221–179; Kulick def. Feldman 256–174; Kulick def. Dorin-Ballard 261–195.

Held in Sterling Heights, MI, May 26–June 1, 2003.

Note: The PWBA suspended operations during the 2003 season.

PBA Tour Results

Men

2004–05 Tour

Date	Event	Winner	Earnings ($)	Runner-Up
Sept 14-20	Japan Cup	Tommy Jones	50,000	Minoru Senden
Oct. 24-31	Miller High Life Master	Danny Wiseman	100,000	Patrick Allen
Nov. 3-7	Chicago Open	Brian Himmler	40,100	Brian Voss
Nov. 10-14	Uniroyal Tire Classic	W. Ray. Williams Jr.	40,000	Doug Kent
Nov. 17- 21	Bowlers Open	Rick Lawrence	40,000	Brad Angelo
Nov. 23-28	Pepsi Open	Jason Hurd	40,000	Mike Edwards
Dec. 1-5	Denver Open	Tommy Jones	40,000	Brian Voss
Dec 8-12	Medford Classic	Mike Wolfe	40,000	Norm Duke
Dec. 15-19	Orange County Classic	Brian Voss	40,000	Michael Machuga
Jan. 5-9	Geico Open	Mika Koivuniemi	40,000	Parker Bohn III
Jan. 12-16	El Paso Classic	Parker BohnIII	40,000	Robert Smith
Jan. 19-23	Dallas Open	Patrick Allen	40,000	Brad Angelo
Jan. 26-30	Brimingham Open	Patrick Allen	40,000	Mike DeVaney
Feb. 2-6	Atlanta Classic	Norm Duke	40,000	Ryan Shafer
Feb. 9-13	Jackson Hewitt Open	Amleto Monacelli	40.100	David Traber
Feb. 13-20	U.S. Open Odor-Eaters	Chris Barnes	100,000	Patrick Allen
Feb. 23-27	Cambridge Credit Classic	Tommy Jones	40,100	Tony Reyes
March 2-6	Baby Ruth Real Deal Classic	Mika Koivuniemi	40,000	Jim Pratt
March 16-20	Banquet Open	Tommy Jones	40,000	Liz Johnson
March 26-April 3	Denny's World Championship	Patrick Allen	120,000	Chris Loschettter
April. 6-10	Dexter Tour. Champions	Steve Jaros	100,000	Norm Duke

2005 Senior Tour

Date	Event	Winner	Earnings ($)	Runner-Up
Apr 16–20	Empire State Open	Henry Gonzalez	8,050	Vince Mazzanti
April 23–27	Clarksville Open	Dale Eagle	8,000	Tom Baker
April 30–May 5	Chillicothe Open	Robert Class	8,000	Gene Stus
May 14–20	Senior U.S. Open	Tom Baker	20,000	Dennis Psaropolous
June 6–10	Senior Tuscon Open	Matt Surina	8,000	Tom Baker
June 11–16	ABC Senior Masters	Vince Mazzanti	20,000	Robert Glass
June 19–23	Northern California Classic	Ross Packard	8,000	Vince Mazzanti
June 26–30	Epicenter Classic	Dale Eagle	8,000	Robert Glass
July 30-Aug.3	Manassas Open	Ray Johnson	8,000	Guppy Troup
Aug 8–11	Lake County Open	Gene Vincent	8,000	Roger LeClair
Aug 13–17	Jackson Open	Charlie Tapp	8,000	Vince Mazzanti

†PWBA Tour Results

2002 Fall Tour

Date	Event	Winner	Earnings ($)	Runner-Up
Sep 15–22	Three Rivers Open	Leanne Barrette	9,000	Marianne DiRupo
Sep 22–26	Burlington Open	Carolyn Dorin-Ballard	9,000	Kendra Gaines
Sep 29–Oct 3	Lady Ebonite Classic	Liz Johnson	12,000	Leanne Barrette
Oct 7–10	Greater Pasadena Open	Tish Johnson	9,000	Liz Johnson
Oct 20–24	Wheelchair Awareness Classic	Tiffany Stanbrough	9,000	Kelly Kulick
Oct 27–Nov 1	Greater San Diego Open	Michelle Feldman	9,000	Wendy Macpherson

2003 Tour

Date	Event	Winner	Earnings ($)	Runner-Up
Nov 3–8	Storm Las Vegas Challenge	Tiffany Stanbrough	12,000	Kendra Gaines
April 7–11	WIBC Queens	Wendy Macpherson	14,000	Kendra Gaines
May 26–Jun 1	U.S. Open	Kelly Kulick	30,000	Carolyn Dorin-Ballard
Jun 5–8	Greater Terre Haute Open	Tiffany Stanbrough	15,000	Lisa Bishop
Jun 11–15	Greater Rockford Classic	Tiffany Stanbrough	15,000	Michelle Feldman
Jun 19–22	Greater Cincinnati Open	Carolyn Dorin-Ballard	15,000	Liz Johnson
Jun 26–29	Greater Harrisburg Open	Dede Davidson	15,000	Cara Honeychurch
July 3–6	Greater Memphis Open	Tennelle Milligan	15,000	Cara Honeychurch
July 9–13	Dallas Open	Michelle Feldman	15,000	Kendra Gaines

Note: Remainder of 2003 tour cancelled.

†Known as LBPT until 1998.

Tour Leaders

PBA: 2004–05

MONEY LEADERS

Name (Titles)	Events	Earnings ($)
Patrick Allen	21	350,740
Tommy Jones	21	224,130
Chris Barnes	21	194,300
Danny Wiseman	21	186,050
Mika Koivuniemi	21	163,800

AVERAGE

Name	Events	Average
Walter Ray Williams Jr	21	227.07
Chris Barnes	21	226.69
Robert Smith	21	224.26
Jason Couch	21	224.03
Mika Koivuniemi	21	223.73

Seniors: 2005

MONEY LEADERS

Name	Events	Earnings ($)
Tom Baker	10	40,050
Robert Glass	11	38,500
Vince Mazzanti Jr.	11	36,600
Dale Eagle	11	28,800
Don Sylvia	11	19,550

AVERAGE

Name	Events	Average
Tom Baker	10	226.97
Robert Glass	11	222.45
Roger Bowker	9	220.47
Dale Eagle	11	219.37
Henry Gonzalez	10	218.84

PWBA: 2002

MONEY LEADERS

Name (Titles)	Tournaments	Earnings ($)
Michelle Feldman (3)	19	82,405
Leanne Barrette (3)	18	72,960
Kim Terrell (1)	19	69,487
Kendra Gaines (1)	19	68,800
Carolyn Dorin-Ballard (2)	19	65,672

AVERAGE

Name	Games	Average
Leanne Barrette	717	216.45
Carolyn Dorin-Ballard	738	215.46
Wendy Macpherson	741	214.39
Michelle Feldman	745	213.93
Kendra Gaines	743	213.93

Men's Majors

BPAA United States Open

Year	Winner	Score	Runner-Up	Site
1942	John Crimmins	265.09–262.33	Joe Norris	Chicago
1943	Connie Schwoegler	not available	Frank Benkovic	Chicago
1944	Ned Day	315.21–298.21	Paul Krumske	Chicago
1945	Buddy Bomar	304.46–296.16	Joe Wilman	Chicago
1946	Joe Wilman	310.27–305.37	Therman Gibson	Chicago
1947	Andy Varipapa	314.16–308.04	Allie Brandt	Chicago
1948	Andy Varipapa	309.23–309.06	Joe Wilman	Chicago
1949	Connie Schwoegler	312.31–307.27	Andy Varipapa	Chicago
1950	Junie McMahon	318.37–307.17	Ralph Smith	Chicago
1951	Dick Hoover	305.29–304.07	Lee Jouglard	Chicago
1952	Junie McMahon	309.29–305.41	Bill Lillard	Chicago
1953	Don Carter	304.17–297.36	Ed Lubanski	Chicago
1954	Don Carter	308.02–307.25	Bill Lillard	Chicago
1955	Steve Nagy	307.17–303.34	Ed Lubanski	Chicago
1956	Bill Lillard	304.30–304.22	Joe Wilman	Chicago
1957	Don Carter	308.49–305.45	Dick Weber	Chicago
1958	Don Carter	311.03–308.09	Buzz Fazio	Minneapolis
1959	Billy Welu	311.48–310.26	Ray Bluth	Buffalo
1960	Harry Smith	312.24–308.12	Bob Chase	Omaha
1961	Bill Tucker	318.49–309.11	Dick Weber	San Bernardino, CA
1962	Dick Weber	299.34–297.38	Roy Lown	Miami Beach
1963	Dick Weber	642–591	Billy Welu	Kansas City, MO
1964	Bob Strampe	714–616	Tommy Tuttle	Dallas
1965	Dick Weber	608–586	Jim St. John	Philadelphia
1966	Dick Weber	684–681	Nelson Burton Jr.	Lansing, MI
1967	Les Schissler	613–610	Pete Tountas	St. Ann, MO
1968	Jim Stefanich	12,401–12,104	Billy Hardwick	Garden City, NY
1969	Billy Hardwick	12,585–11,463	Dick Weber	Miami
1970	Bobby Cooper	12,936–12,307	Billy Hardwick	Northbrook, IL
1971	Mike Limongello	397 (2 games)	Teata Semiz	St. Paul, MN
1972	Don Johnson	233 (1 game)	George Pappas	New York City
1973	Mike McGrath	712 (3 games)	Earl Anthony	New York City
1974	Larry Laub	749 (3 games)	Dave Davis	New York City
1975	Steve Neff	279 (1 game)	Paul Colwell	Grand Prairie, TX
1976	Paul Moser	226 (1 game)	Jim Frazier	Grand Prairie, TX
1977	Johnny Petraglia	279 (1 game)	Bill Spigner	Greensboro, NC
1978	Nelson Burton Jr.	873 (4 games)	Jeff Mattingly	Greensboro, NC
1979	Joe Berardi	445 (2 games)	Earl Anthony	Windsor Locks, CT
1980	Steve Martin	930 (4 games)	Earl Anthony	Windsor Locks, CT
1981	Marshall Holman	684 (3 games)	Mark Roth	Houston
1982	Dave Husted	1011 (4 games)	Gil Sliker	Houston
1983	Gary Dickinson	214 (1 game)	Steve Neff	Oak Lawn, IL
1984	Mark Roth	244 (1 game)	Guppy Troup	Oak Hill, IL
1985	Marshall Holman	233 (1 game)	Wayne Webb	Venice, FL
1986	Steve Cook	467 (2 games)	Frank Ellenburg	Venice, FL
1987	Del Ballard Jr.	525 (2 games)	Pete Weber	Tacoma, WA
1988	Pete Weber	929 (4 games)	Marshall Holman	Atlantic City
1989	Mike Aulby	429 (2 games)	Jim Pencak	Edmond, OK
1990	Ron Palombi Jr.	269 (1 game)	Amleto Monacelli	Indianapolis
1991	Pete Weber	956 (4 games)	Mark Thayer	Indianapolis
1992	Robert Lawrence	667 (3 games)	Scott Devers	Canandaigua, NY
1993	Del Ballard Jr.	505 (2 games)	Walter Ray Williams Jr.	Canandaigua, NY
1994	Justin Hromek	267 (1 game)	Parker Bohn III	Troy, MI
1995	Dave Husted	266 (1 game)	Paul Koehler	Troy, MI
1996	Dave Husted	730 (3 games)	George Brooks	Indianapolis
1998	Walter Ray Williams Jr.	466 (2 games)	Tim Criss	Fairfield, CT
1999	Bob Learn Jr.	231 (1 game)	Jason Couch	Uncasville, CT
2000	Robert Smith	202 (1 game)	Norm Duke	Phoenix
2001	Mika Koivuniemi	247 (1 game)	Patrick Healey Jr	Fountain Valley, CA
2003	Walter Ray Williams Jr.	236 (1 game)	Michael Haugen Jr.	Fountain Valley, CA

Note: From 1942 to 1970, the tournament was called the BPAA All-Star. Peterson scoring was used from 1942 through 1962. Under this system, the winner of an individual match game gets one point, plus one point for each 50 pins knocked down. From 1963 through 1967, a three-game championship was held between the two top qualifiers. From 1968 through 1970 total pinfall determined the winner. From 1971 to the present, five qualifiers compete for the championship.

BPAA United States Open (Cont.)

Year	Winner	Score	Runner-Up	Site
2004	Pete Weber	231 (1 game)	Brian Voss	Fountain Valley, CA
2005	Chris Barnes	213 (1 game)	Patrick Allen	North Brunswick, NJ

Note: From 1942 to 1970, the tournament was called the BPAA All-Star. Peterson scoring was used from 1942 through 1962. Under this system, the winner of an individual match game gets one point, plus one point for each 50 pins knocked down. From 1963 through 1967, a three-game championship was held between the two top qualifiers. From 1968 through 1970 total pinfall determined the winner. From 1971 to the present, five qualifiers compete for the championship.

Touring Players Championship

Year	Winner	Score	Runner-Up	Site
1996	Mike Aulby	268 (1 game)	Parker Bohn III	Harmarville, PA
1997	Steve Hoskins	932 (4 games)	Danny Wiseman	Harmarville, PA
1998	Dennis Horan	481 (2 games)	Parker Bohn III	Akron, OH
1999	Steve Hoskins	503 (2 games)	Parker Bohn III	Akron, OH
2000	Dennis Horan	924 (4 games)	Pete Weber	Akron, OH
2001	Tournament discontinued			

PBA World Championship

Year	Winner	Score	Runner-Up	Site
1960	Don Carter	6512 (30 games)	Ronnie Gaudern	Memphis
1961	Dave Soutar	5792 (27 games)	Morrie Oppenheim	Cleveland
1962	Carmen Salvino	5369 (25 games)	Don Carter	Philadelphia
1963	Billy Hardwick	13,541 (61 games)	Ray Bluth	Long Island, NY
1964	Bob Strampe	13,979 (61 games)	Ray Bluth	Long Island, NY
1965	Dave Davis	13,895 (61 games)	Jerry McCoy	Detroit
1966	Wayne Zahn	14,006 (61 games)	Nelson Burton Jr.	Long Island, NY
1967	Dave Davis	421 (2 games)	Pete Tountas	New York City
1968	Wayne Zahn	14,182 (60 games)	Nelson Burton Jr.	New York City
1969	Mike McGrath	13,670 (60 games)	Bill Allen	Garden City, NY
1970	Mike McGrath	660 (3 games)	Dave Davis	Garden City, NY
1971	Mike Limongello	911 (4 games)	Dave Davis	Paramus, NJ
1972	Johnny Guenther	12,986 (56 games)	Dick Ritger	Rochester, NY
1973	Earl Anthony	212 (1 game)	Sam Flanagan	Oklahoma City
1974	Earl Anthony	218 (1 game)	Mark Roth	Downey, CA
1975	Earl Anthony	245 (1 game)	Jim Frazier	Downey, CA
1976	Paul Colwell	191 (1 game)	Dave Davis	Seattle
1977	Tommy Hudson	206 (1 game)	Jay Robinson	Seattle
1978	Warren Nelson	453 (2 games)	Joseph Groskind	Reno
1979	Mike Aulby	727 (3 games)	Earl Anthony	Las Vegas
1980	Johnny Petraglia	235 (1 game)	Gary Dickinson	Sterling Heights, MI
1981	Earl Anthony	242 (1 game)	Ernie Schlegel	Toledo, OH
1982	Earl Anthony	233 (1 game)	Charlie Tapp	Toledo, OH
1983	Earl Anthony	210 (1 game)	Mike Durbin	Toledo, OH
1984	Bob Chamberlain	961 (4 games)	Dan Eberl	Toledo, OH
1985	Mike Aulby	476 (2 games)	Steve Cook	Toledo, OH
1986	Tom Crites	190 (1 game)	Mike Aulby	Toledo, OH
1987	Randy Pedersen	759 (3 games)	Amleto Monacelli	Toledo, OH
1988	Brian Voss	246 (1 game)	Todd Thompson	Toledo, OH
1989	Pete Weber	221 (1 game)	Dave Ferraro	Toledo, OH
1990	Jim Pencak	900 (4 games)	Chris Warren	Toledo, OH
1991	Mike Miller	450 (2 games)	Norm Duke	Toledo, OH
1992	Eric Forkel	833 (4 games)	Bob Vespi	Toledo, OH
1993	Ron Palombi Jr.	237 (1 game)	Eugene McCune	Toledo, OH
1994	David Traber	196 (1 game)	Dale Traber	Toledo, OH
1995	Scott Alexander	246 (1 game)	Wayne Webb	Toledo, OH
1996	Butch Soper	442 (2 games)	Walter Ray Williams Jr.	Toledo, OH
1997	Rick Steelsmith	888 (4 games)	Brian Voss	Toledo, OH
1998	Pete Weber	277 (1 game)	David Ozio	Toledo, OH
1999	Tim Criss	238 (1 game)	Dave Arnold	Toledo, OH
2000	Norm Duke	492 (2 games)	Jason Couch	Toledo, OH
2001	Walter Ray Williams Jr.	258 (1 game)	Jeff Lizzi	Toledo, OH
2002	Doug Kent	417 (2 games)	Lonnie Waliczek	Toledo, OH
2003	Walter Ray Williams Jr	443 (2 games)	Brian Kretzer	Taylor, MI
2004	Tom Baker	523 (2 games)	Mika Koivuniemi	Ypsilanti, MI
2005	Patrick Allen	235 (1 game)	Chris Loschetter	Ypsilanti, MI

Note: Totals from 1963–66, 1968–69 and 1972 include bonus pins.

Tournament of Champions

Year	Winner	Score	Runner-Up	Site
1965	Billy Hardwick	484 (2 games)	Dick Weber	Akron, OH
1966	Wayne Zahn	595 (3 games)	Dick Weber	Akron, OH
1967	Jim Stefanich	227 (1 game)	Don Johnson	Akron, OH
1968	Dave Davis	213 (1 game)	Don Johnson	Akron, OH
1969	Jim Godman	266 (1 game)	Jim Stefanich	Akron, OH
1970	Don Johnson	299 (1 game)	Dick Ritger	Akron, OH
1971	Johnny Petraglia	245 (1 game)	Don Johnson	Akron, OH
1972	Mike Durbin	775 (3 games)	Tim Harahan	Akron, OH
1973	Jim Godman	451 (2 games)	Barry Asher	Akron, OH
1974	Earl Anthony	679 (3 games)	Johnny Petraglia	Akron, OH
1975	Dave Davis	448 (2 games)	Barry Asher	Akron, OH
1976	Marshall Holman	441 (2 games)	Billy Hardwick	Akron, OH
1977	Mike Berlin	434 (2 games)	Mike Durbin	Akron, OH
1978	Earl Anthony	237 (1 game)	Teata Semiz	Akron, OH
1979	George Pappas	224 (1 game)	Dick Ritger	Akron, OH
1980	Wayne Webb	750 (3 games)	Gary Dickinson	Akron, OH
1981	Steve Cook	287 (1 game)	Pete Couture	Akron, OH
1982	Mike Durbin	448 (2 games)	Steve Cook	Akron, OH
1983	Joe Berardi	865 (4 games)	Henry Gonzalez	Akron, OH
1984	Mike Durbin	950 (4 games)	Mike Aulby	Akron, OH
1985	Mark Williams	616 (3 games)	Bob Handley	Akron, OH
1986	Marshall Holman	233 (1 game)	Mark Baker	Akron, OH
1986	Marshall Holman	233 (1 game)	Mark Baker	Akron, OH
1987	Pete Weber	928 (4 games)	Jim Murtishaw	Akron, OH
1988	Mark Williams	237 (1 game)	Tony Westlake	Fairlawn, OH
1989	Del Ballard Jr.	490 (2 games)	Walter Ray Williams Jr.	Fairlawn, OH
1990	Dave Ferraro	226 (1 game)	Tony Westlake	Fairlawn, OH
1991	David Ozio	476 (2 games)	Amleto Monacelli	Fairlawn, OH
1992	Marc McDowell	471 (2 games)	Don Genalo	Fairlawn, OH
1993	George Branham III	227 (1 game)	Parker Bohn III	Fairlawn, OH
1994	Norm Duke	422 (2 games)	Eric Forkel	Fairlawn, OH
1995	Mike Aulby	502 (2 games)	Bob Spaulding	Lake Zurich, IL
1996	Dave D'Entremont	971 (4 games)	Dave Arnold	Lake Zurich, IL
1997	John Gant	446 (2 games)	Mike Aulby	Reno
1998	Bryan Goebel	245 (1 game)	Steve Hoskins	Overland Park, KS
1999	Jason Couch	427 (2 games)	Chris Barnes	Overland Park, KS
2000	Jason Couch	198 (1 game)	Ryan Shafer	Lake Zurich, IL
2001	Not held			
2002	Jason Couch	478 (2 games)	Ryan Shafer	Uncasville, CT
2003	Patrick Healey Jr	432 (2 games)	Randy Pedersen	Uncasville, CT
2004	Tom Baker	523 (2 games)	Mika Koivuniemi	Ypsilanti, MI
2005	Steve Jaros	248 (1 game)	Norm Duke	Uncasville, CT

ABC Masters Tournament

Year	Winner	Scoring Avg	Runner-Up	Site
1951	Lee Jouglard	201.8	Joe Wilman	St. Paul, MN
1952	Willard Taylor	200.32	Andy Varipapa	Milwaukee
1953	Rudy Habetler	200.13	Ed Brosius	Chicago
1954	Eugene Elkins	205.19	W. Taylor	Seattle
1955	Buzz Fazio	204.13	Joe Kristof	Ft. Wayne, IN
1956	Dick Hoover	209.9	Ray Bluth	Rochester, NY
1957	Dick Hoover	216.39	Bill Lillard	Ft. Worth, TX
1958	Tom Hennessy	209.15	Lou Frantz	Syracuse, NY
1959	Ray Bluth	214.26	Billy Golembiewski	St. Louis
1960	Billy Golembiewski	206.13	Steve Nagy	Toledo, OH
1961	Don Carter	211.18	Dick Hoover	Detroit
1962	Billy Golembiewski	223.12	Ron Winger	Des Moines, IA
1963	Harry Smith	219.3	Bobby Meadows	Buffalo
1964	Billy Welu	227	Harry Smith	Oakland, CA
1965	Billy Welu	202.12	Don Ellis	St. Paul, MN
1966	Bob Strampe	219.80	Al Thompson	Rochester, NY
1967	Lou Scalia	216.9	Bill Johnson	Miami Beach
1968	Pete Tountas	220.15	Buzz Fazio	Cincinnati
1969	Jim Chestney	223.2	Barry Asher	Madison, WI
1970	Don Glover	215.10	Bob Strampe	Knoxville, TN
1971	Jim Godman	229.8	Don Johnson	Detroit
1972	Bill Beach	220.27	Jim Godman	Long Beach, CA
1973	Dave Soutar	218.61	Dick Ritger	Syracuse, NY
1974	Paul Colwell	234.17	Steve Neff	Indianapolis
1975	Eddie Ressler	213.51	Sam Flanagan	Dayton, OH
1976	Nelson Burton Jr.	220.79	Steve Carson	Oklahoma City
1977	Earl Anthony	218.21	Jim Godman	Reno
1978	Frank Ellenburg	200.61	Earl Anthony	St. Louis
1979	Doug Myers	202.9	Bill Spigner	Tampa
1980	Neil Burton	206.69	Mark Roth	Louisville
1981	Randy Lightfoot	218.3	Skip Tucker	Memphis
1982	Joe Berardi	207.12	Ted Hannahs	Baltimore
1983	Mike Lastowski	212.65	Pete Weber	Niagara Falls
1984	Earl Anthony	212.5	Gil Sliker	Reno
1985	Steve Wunderlich	210.4	Tommy Kress	Tulsa
1986	Mark Fahy	206.5	Del Ballard Jr.	Las Vegas
1987	Rick Steelsmith	210.7	Brad Snell	Niagara Falls
1988	Del Ballard Jr.	219.1	Keith Smith	Jacksonville
1989	Mike Aulby	218.5	Mike Edwards	Wichita
1990	Chris Warren	231.6	David Ozio	Reno
1991	Doug Kent	226.8	George Branham III	Toledo, OH
1992	Ken Johnson	230.0	Dave D'Entremont	Corpus Christi, TX
1993	Norm Duke	245.68	Patrick Allen	Tulsa
1994	Steve Fehr	213.09	Steve Anderson	Greenacres, FL
1995	Mike Aulby	230.7	Mark Williams	Reno
1996	Ernie Schlegel	221.2	Mike Aulby	Salt Lake City
1997	Jason Queen	225.5	Eric Forkel	Huntsville, AL
1998	Mike Aulby	224.0	Parker Bohn III	Reno
1999	Brian Boghosian	246.0	Parker Bohn III	Syracuse, NY
2000	Mika Koivuniemi	241.0	Pete Weber	Albuquerque
2001	Parker Bohn III	224.0	Jason Couch	Reno
2002	Brett Wolfe	222.3	Dennis Horan Jr.	Reno
2003	Bryon Smith	236.0	W. R. Williams Jr.	Reno
2004	Walter Ray Williams Jr	252.5	Chris Barnes	Reno
2005	Danny Wiseman	223.7	Patrick Allen	Milwaukee, WI

BPAA United States Open

Year	Winner	Score	Runner-Up	Site
1949	Marion Ladewig	113.26–104.26	Catherine Burling	Chicago
1950	Marion Ladewig	151.46–146.06	Stephanie Balogh	Chicago
1951	Marion Ladewig	159.17–148.03	Sylvia Wene	Chicago
1952	Marion Ladewig	154.39–142.05	Shirley Garms	Chicago
1953	Not held			
1954	Marion Ladewig	148.29–143.01	Sylvia Wene	Chicago
1955	Sylvia Wene	142.30–141.11	Sylvia Fanta	Chicago
1955	Anita Cantaline	144.40–144.13	Doris Porter	Chicago
1956	Marion Ladewig	150.16–145.41	Marge Merrick	Chicago
1957	Not held			
1958	Merle Matthews	145.09–143.14	Marion Ladewig	Minneapolis
1959	Marion Ladewig	149.33–143.00	Donna Zimmerman	Buffalo
1960	Sylvia Wene	144.14–143.26	Marion Ladewig	Omaha
1961	Phyllis Notaro	144.13–143.12	Hope Riccilli	San Bernardino, CA
1962	Shirley Garms	138.44–135.49	Joy Abel	Miami Beach
1963	Marion Ladewig	586–578	Bobbie Shaler	Kansas City, MO
1964	LaVerne Carter	683–609	Evelyn Teal	Dallas
1965	Ann Slattery	597–550	Sandy Hooper	Philadelphia
1966	Joy Abel	593–538	Bette Rockwell	Lansing, MI
1967	Gloria Bouvia	578–516	Shirley Garms	St. Ann, MO
1968	Dotty Fothergill	9,000–8,187	Doris Coburn	Garden City, NY
1969	Dotty Fothergill	8,284–8,258	Kayoka Suda	Miami
1970	Mary Baker	8,730–8,465	Judy Cook	Northbrook, IL
1971	Paula Carter	5,660–5,650	June Llewellyn	Kansas City, MO
1972	Lorrie Nichols	5,272–5,189	Mary Baker	Denver
1973	Millie Martorella	5,553–5,294	Patty Costello	Garden City, NY
1974	Patty Costello	219–216	Betty Morris	Irving, TX
1975	Paula Carter	6,500–6,352	Lorrie Nichols	Toledo, OH
1976	Patty Costello	11,341–11,281	Betty Morris	Tulsa
1977	Betty Morris	10,511–10,358	Virginia Norton	Milwaukee
1978	Donna Adamek	236–202	Vesma Grinfelds	Miami
1979	Diana Silva	11,775–11,718	Bev Ortner	Phoenix
1980	Pat Costello	223–199	Shinobu Saitoh	Rockford, IL
1981	Donna Adamek	201–190	Nikki Gianulias	Rockford, IL
1982	Shinobu Saitoh	12,184–12,028	Robin Romeo	Hendersonville, TN
1983	Dana Miller-Mackie	247–200	Aleta Sill	St. Louis
1984	Karen Ellingsworth	236–217	Lorrie Nichols	St. Louis
1985	Pat Mercatani	214–178	Nikki Gianulias	Topeka, KS
1986	Wendy Macpherson	265–179	Lisa Wagner	Topeka, KS
1987	Carol Norman	206–179	Cindy Coburn	Mentor, OH
1988	Lisa Wagner	226–218	Lorrie Nichols	Winston-Salem, NC
1989	Robin Romeo	187–163	Michelle Mullen	Addison, IL
1990	Dana Miller-Mackie	190–189	Tish Johnson	Dearborn Heights, MI
1991	Anne Marie Duggan	196–185	Leanne Barrette	Fountain Valley, CA
1992	Tish Johnson	216–213	Aleta Sill	Fountain Valley, CA
1993	Dede Davidson	213–194	Dana Miller-Mackie	Garland, TX
1994	Aleta Sill	229–170	Anne Marie Duggan	Wichita
1995	Cheryl Daniels	235–180	Tish Johnson	Blaine, MN
1996	Liz Johnson	265–236	Marianne DiRupo	Indianapolis
1997	No event—tournament rescheduled to April, beginning in 1998.			
1998	Aleta Sill	276–151	Tammy Turner	Milford, CT
1999	Kim Adler	213–195	Lynda Barnes	Uncasville, CT
2000	Tennelle Grijalva	239–155	Kelly Kulick	Phoenix
2001	Kim Terrell	234–220	Wendy Macpherson	Laughlin, NV
2003	Kelly Kulick	261–195	Carolyn Dorin-Ballard	Sterling Heights, MI

Note: From 1942 to 1970, tournament was called the BPAA All-Star. Peterson scoring used from 1949 to '62. Under this system, the winner of an individual match game gets one point, plus one point for each 50 pins. From 1963 to '67, a three-game championship was held between the two top qualifiers. From 1968 to '73, 1975 to '77, 1979 and 1982, total pinfall determined the winner. In the other years, five qualifiers competed in a playoff for the championship, with the final listed above.

AMF Gold Cup *(Discontinued)*

Year	Winner	Score	Runner-Up	Site
1997	Aleta Sill	221–179	C. Gianotti-Block	Richmond, VA
1998	Dana Miller-Mackie	278–170	Dede Davidson	Richmond, VA
1999	Dana Miller-Mackie	236–222	Cara Honeychurch	Richmond, VA

WIBC Queens

ear	Winner	Score	Runner-Up	Site
1961	Janet Harman	794–776	Eula Touchette	Fort Wayne, IN
1962	Dorothy Wilkinson	799–794	Marion Ladewig	Phoenix
1963	Irene Monterosso	852–803	Georgette DeRosa	Memphis
1964	D. D. Jacobson	740–682	Shirley Garms	Minneapolis
1965	Betty Kuczynski	772–739	LaVerne Carter	Portland, OR
1966	Judy Lee	771–742	Nancy Peterson	New Orleans
1967	Millie Ignizio	840–809	Phyllis Massey	Rochester, NY
1968	Phyllis Massey	884–853	Marian Spencer	San Antonio
1969	Ann Feigel	832–765	Millie Ignizio	San Diego
1970	Millie Ignizio	807–797	Joan Holm	Tulsa
1971	Millie Ignizio	809–778	Katherine Brown	Atlanta
1972	Dotty Fothergill	890–841	Maureen Harris	Kansas City, MO
1973	Dotty Fothergill	804–791	Judy Soutar	Las Vegas
1974	Judy Soutar	939–705	Betty Morris	Houston
1975	Cindy Powell	758–674	Patty Costello	Indianapolis
1976	Pam Buckner	214–178	Shirley Sjostrom	Denver
1977	Dana Stewart	175–167	Vesma Grinfelds	Milwaukee
1978	Loa Boxberger	197–176	Cora Fiebig	Miami
1979	Donna Adamek	216–181	Shinobu Saitoh	Tucson
1980	Donna Adamek	213–165	Cheryl Robinson	Seattle
1981	Katsuko Sugimoto	166–158	Virginia Norton	Baltimore
1982	Katsuko Sugimoto	160–137	Nikki Gianulias	St. Louis
1983	Aleta Sill	214–188	Dana Miller-Mackie	Las Vegas
1984	Kazue Inahashi	248–222	Aleta Sill	Niagara Falls
1985	Aleta Sill	279–192	Linda Graham	Toledo, OH
1986	Cora Fiebig	223–177	Barbara Thorberg	Orange County, CA
1987	Cathy Almeida	850–817	Lorrie Nichols	Hartford, CT
1988	Wendy Macpherson	213–199	Leanne Barrette	Reno/Carson City, NV
1989	Carol Gianotti	207–177	Sandra Jo Shiery	Bismarck-Mandan, ND
1990	Patty Ann	207–173	Vesma Grinfelds	Tampa
1991	Dede Davidson	231–159	Jeanne Maiden	Cedar Rapids, IA
1992	Cindy Coburn-Carroll	184–170	Dana Miller-Mackie	Lansing, MI
1993	Jan Schmidt	201–163	Pat Costello	Baton Rouge, LA
1994	Anne Marie Duggan	224–177	Wendy Macpherson-Papanos	Salt Lake City
1995	Sandra Postma	226–187	Carolyn Dorin	Tucson
1996	Lisa Wagner	231–226	Tammy Turner	Buffalo
1997	S.J. Shiery-Odom	209–185	Audry Allen	Reno
1998	Lynda Norry	213–157	Karen Stroud	Davenport, IA
1999	Leanne Barrette	256–174	Dede Davidson	Indianapolis
2000	Wendy Macpherson	227–202	Marianne DiRupo	Reno
2001	Carolyn Dorin-Ballard	213–197	Kelly Kulick	Ft. Lauderdale, FL
2002	Kim Terrell	227–214	Kim Adler	Wauwatosa, WI
2003	Wendy Macpherson	218–193	Kendra Gaines	Reno

Sam's Town Invitational *(Discontinued)*

Year	Winner	Score	Runner-Up	Site
1984	Aleta Sill	238 (1 game)	Cheryl Daniels	Las Vegas
1985	Patty Costello	236 (1 game)	Robin Romeo	Las Vegas
1986	Aleta Sill	238 (1 game)	Dina Wheeler	Las Vegas
1987	Debbie Bennett	880 (4 games)	Lorrie Nichols	Las Vegas
1988	Donna Adamek	634 (3 games)	Robin Romeo	Las Vegas
1989	Tish Johnson	210 (1 game)	Dede Davidson	Las Vegas
1990	Wendy Macpherson	900 (4 games)	Jeanne Maiden	Las Vegas
1991	Lorrie Nichols	469 (2 games)	Dana Miller-Mackie	Las Vegas
1992	Tish Johnson	279 (1 game)	Robin Romeo	Las Vegas
1993	Robin Romeo	194 (1 game)	Tammy Turner	Las Vegas
1994	Tish Johnson	178 (1 game)	Carol Gianotti	Las Vegas
1995	Michelle Mullen	202 (1 game)	Cheryl Daniels	Las Vegas
1996	C. Gianotti-Block	892 (4 games)	Leanne Barrette	Las Vegas
1997	Kim Adler	953 (4 games)	Wendy Macpherson	Las Vegas
1998	Julie Gardner	961 (4 games)	Dede Davidson	Las Vegas
1999	Wendy Macpherson	209 (1 game)	Marianne DiRupo	Las Vegas
2000	Dede Davidson	183 (1 game)	Tiffany Stanbrough	Las Vegas

PWBA Championships *(Discontinued)*

1960...Marion Ladewig	1966...Joy Abel	1972...Patty Costello	1978...Toni Gillard
1961...Shirley Garms	1967...Betty Mivalez	1973...Betty Morris	1979...Cindy Coburn
1962...Stephanie Balogh	1968...Dotty Fothergill	1974...Pat Costello	1980...Donna Adamek
1963...Janet Harman	1969...Dotty Fothergill	1975...Pam Buckner	
1964...Betty Kuczynski	1970...Bobbe North	1976...Patty Costello	
1965...Helen Duval	1971...Patty Costello	1977...Vesma Grinfelds	

THEY SAID IT

Frances Wormser, a 101-year-old baseball fan from Ventura, Calif., on what bowling next to Babe Ruth in the 1940s was like.: "He would take a swig of whiskey before he bowled," she said. "He didn't care about bowling a spare or a strike--he was just interested in winning, and he always won. He was such an ugly man."

Men's Awards

BWAA Bowler of the Year

1942	Johnny Crimmins	1973	Don McCune
1943	Ned Day	1974	Earl Anthony
1944	Ned Day	1975	Earl Anthony
1945	Buddy Bomar	1976	Earl Anthony
1946	Joe Wilman	1977	Mark Roth
1947	Buddy Bomar	1978	Mark Roth
1948	Andy Varipapa	1979	Mark Roth
1949	Connie Schwoegler	1980	Wayne Webb
1950	Junie McMahon	1981	Earl Anthony
1951	Lee Jouglard	1982	Earl Anthony
1952	Steve Nagy	1983	Earl Anthony
1953	Don Carter	1984	Mark Roth
1954	Don Carter	1985	Mike Aulby
1955	Steve Nagy	1986	Walter Ray Williams Jr.
1956	Bill Lillard	1987	Marshall Holman
1957	Don Carter	1988	Brian Voss
1958	Don Carter	1989	Mike Aulby/ Amleto Monacelli*
1959	Ed Lubanski	1990	Amleto Monacelli
1960	Don Carter	1991	David Ozio
1961	Dick Weber	1992	Dave Ferraro
1962	Don Carter	1993	Walter Ray Williams Jr.
1963	Dick Weber	1994	Norm Duke
	Billy Hardwick*	1995	Mike Aulby
1964	Billy Hardwick	1996	Walter Ray Williams Jr.
	Bob Strampe*	1997	Walter Ray Williams Jr.
1965	Dick Weber	1998	Walter Ray Williams Jr.
1966	Wayne Zahn	1999	Parker Bohn III
1967	Dave Davis	2000	Norm Duke
1968	Jim Stefanich	2001	Parker Bohn III
1969	Billy Hardwick	2002	Walter Ray Williams Jr.
1970	Nelson Burton Jr.	2003	Walter Ray Williams Jr.
1971	Don Johnson	2004	Mika Koivuniemi
1972	Don Johnson	2005	Patrick Allen

PBA Bowler of the Year. The PBA began selecting a player of the year in 1963. Its selection has been the same as the BWAA's in all but three years.

Women's Awards

BWAA Bowler of the Year

1948	Val Mikiel	1976	Patty Costello
1949	Val Mikiel	1977	Betty Morris
1950	Marion Ladewig	1978	Donna Adamek
1951	Marion Ladewig	1979	Donna Adamek
1952	Marion Ladewig	1980	Donna Adamek
1953	Marion Ladewig	1981	Donna Adamek
1954	Marion Ladewig	1982	Nikki Gianulias
1955	Marion Ladewig	1983	Lisa Wagner
1956	Sylvia Martin	1984	Aleta Sill
1957	Anita Cantaline	1985	Aleta Sill/Patty Costello*
1958	Marion Ladewig	1986	Lisa Wagner/Jeanne Madden*
1959	Marion Ladewig	1987	Betty Morris
1960	Sylvia Martin	1988	Lisa Wagner
1961	Shirley Garms	1989	Robin Romeo
1962	Shirley Garms	1990	Tish Johnson/Leanne Barrette*
1963	Marion Ladewig	1991	Leanne Barrette
1964	LaVerne Carter	1992	Tish Johnson
1965	Betty Kuczynski	1993	Lisa Wagner
1966	Joy Abel	1994	Anne Marie Duggan
1967	Millie Martorella	1995	Tish Johnson
1968	Dotty Fothergill	1996	Wendy Macpherson
1969	Dotty Fothergill	1997	Wendy Macpherson
1970	Mary Baker	1998	Carol Gianotti-Block
1971	Paula Sperber Carter	1999	Wendy Macpherson
1972	Patty Costello	2000	Wendy Macpherson
1973	Judy Soutar	2001	Carolyn Dorin-Ballard
1974	Betty Morris	2002	Leanne Barrette
1975	Judy Soutar		

*PWBA Bowler of the Year. The PWBA began selecting a player of the year in 1983. Its selection has been the same as the BWAA's in all but three years.

Career Leaders

Earnings

MEN

Walter Ray Williams Jr. $3,369,632
Pete Weber $2,628,518
Parker Bohn III $2,311,864
Mike Aulby $2,097,253
Brian Voss.................................$2,202,197

WOMEN

Wendy Macpherson....................$1,194,535
Aleta Sill $1,071,194
Tish Johnson $1,063,062
Leanne Barrette $1,010,343
Anne Marie Duggan......................$936,421

Titles

MEN

Earl Anthony..41
Walter Ray Williams Jr................................40
Mark Roth..34
Pete Weber 31
Parker Bohn III 30

WOMEN

Lisa Wagner..32
Aleta Sill...31
Leanne Barrette 26
Patty Costello 25
Tish Johnson...25

Note: Leaders through Sept 22, 2005

Can't We All Just Bowl Along?

Bowling apparently wasn't as conducive to diplomacy as Ping-Pong was 33 years ago. In October 2004, Bill O'Reilly refused Al Franken's challenge to go head-to-head as part of the Great American Meetup Bowl. The nationwide kegling event pitted Team Blue (Kerry supporters) against Team Red (Bush backers). "If Kerry and Bush supporters can put aside their differences for a day to compete, well, then, so can Bill O'Reilly and I," said Franken. A spokesman for Fox said, "Bill O'Reilly is not going to respond to anything Al Franken says."

Soccer

Captain Kristine Lilly led the US women's team to an undefeated record in 2005.

Americans Rising

The US women kept on winning despite both player and coach turnover, while a young US men's team played its way into the World Cup

BY HANK HERSCH

IN 2005 HE BECAME INDISPUTABLY the face of U.S. men's soccer-not to mention the legs, the heart and the lungs. A team that had long needed an up-and-comer to lead it found one in 23-year-old forward Landon Donovan, whose behind-the-scenes influence suddenly soared to the high level of his on-field contributions. The result: The Americans marched through World Cup qualifying with more ease than ever, not only clinching a fifth straight berth in the tournament but challenging to become one of the eight top-seeded teams in 2006 as well.

Though 11 players take to the pitch, it's often the sheer will of one or two of them that determines a team's trajectory. Take the U.S. women, who relied on the forceful presence of Abby Wambach up front and, in the midfield, the steel will of captain Kristine Lilly, who closed in on 300 caps. They showed that the squad was ready to move successfully forward after the Mia Hamm Era, leading the

Yanks to their third straight Algarve Cup title-this time without allowing a goal in four matches. The tournament in Portugal marked a flying start for Greg Ryan, the former assistant who was appointed head coach after April Heinrichs's resignation in February.

Or take, most remarkably, Jerzy Dudek and Liverpool, which in May reached the Champions League final in Istanbul-the culmination of Europe's most prestigious club competition. The last time the English side had gained the European Cup, in 1985, had lived in infamy: Its fans started a riot in the stands at Heysel Stadium in Brussels, Belgium, and 39 people were killed. Liverpool was banned from competing on the Continent for six years.

The team's supporters—40,000 strong—were more quiescent in Istanbul, but then at first they had little to get excited about. By halftime, AC Milan had charged ahead 3–0, a seemingly secure cushion for such a defensively stalwart team. But within a

Keeper Jerzy Dudek helped Liverpool complete a stunning comeback against AC Milan in the Champions League final.

15-minute span, Liverpool captain Steven Gerrard headed in a cross, Vladimir Smicer netted a low volley and Xabi Alonso drove home a rebound of his own penalty kick to tie the match.

Then Dudek, Liverpool's top keeper, took over, stoning a running header by the reigning European Footballer of the Year, striker Andriy Shevchenko; scrambling to thwart a Shevchenko follow-up touch from even closer; and, after 30 scoreless minutes of overtime, making a diving save on a penalty kick by Shevchenko to extend the shootout. In one of the most unlikely comebacks in Champions League history, Liverpool prevailed 3-2 on PK's to win its fifth European Cup-as many as every other English side put together. "I don't think anyone has seen a game like that," said Liverpool defender Jamie Carragher. "I cannot believe we just won. People will be talking about that game in 20 or 30 years."

Two other venerable English sides underwent convulsive experiences in '05. Chelsea won its first top-flight title in 50 years-thanks to Portuguese manager José Mourinho; English defender John Terry, the Premier League's player of the year; and, above all, 38-year-old Siberian oil magnate Roman Abramovich, who after buying the team in '03 spent nearly $500 million in transfer fees while running up a Steinbrennerian $220 million payroll. The purchase in May of Manchester United, on the other hand, inspired far less optimism. Believing that 76-year-old Malcolm Glazer, the owner of the NFL's Tampa Bay Buccaneers, would try to curb expenses while raising ticket prices, some Red Devils fans burned Glazer in effigy, compared him with Hitler and vowed to flood the market with forged Man U tickets.

At least American players got a warmer reception overseas. Former Clemson defender Oguchi Onyewu, at 6'4" and 210 pounds, became a bruising fixture on the back line of Standard de Liege in Belgium; midfielder DaMarcus Beasley scored three goals for PSV Eindhoven in Champions League play; and Kasey Keller settled solidly into goal for

**US men's scoring leader
Landon Donovan**

DAVID BERGMAN

Borussia Moenchengladbach (not to mention moved with his family into a German castle). And the exports were especially productive in England, with midfielder Claudio Reyna earning the Premiership's highest rating for his first month's play at Manchester City.

After a second, short stint with Bayer Lerkusen in Germany, Donovan returned in January to play for the Los Angeles Galaxy in MLS and became the most reliable member for an American side that was in peril of missing the Cup. Because of a labor dispute, the U.S. Soccer Federation was poised to bring in replacement players as the last round of qualifying was about to begin. But late one night, Donovan phoned USSF president Bob Contigulia to try to break the impasse. With the players' promising not to strike as talks continued, the first team took the field in Trinidad and Tobago and prevailed 2-1. Then when the negotiations stalled in early June, Donovan buttonholed USSF executive vice president Sunil Gulati on a flight home from Panama; the two hammered out the framework for labor peace through 2010. "These things are always about relationships, and if you create good ones, you can always find middle ground," Donovan told SI's Grant Wahl. "I don't think either side needs to battle for every dollar. If we're going to miss a World Cup based on that, then that's stupid."

By September, Donovan and company were poised to qualify for the Cup with a win over Mexico, a matchup that Donovan relished. Ever since he was caught discreetly relieving himself on a training-field shrub in Guadalajara during the '04 Olympic qualifying tournament—an incident caught on video and replayed endlessly in Mexico—he has been a target of fans south of the border. Their feelings had gotten full voice at Mexico City's Azteca Stadium back in March, when the U.S. had bowed 2-1 in its second match of the final, six-team qualifying round. That victory had run Mexico's record against the Yanks at Azteca to 22-0-1. "I would like to play them anywhere but here," said Donovan, "and I like our chances."

This time, the result couldn't have been more satisfying. With Keller extending his qualifying shutout streak to 507 minutes, and Steve Ralston and Beasley scoring, the U.S. dominated Mexico 2-0. "Here, everyone's interested in baseball and American football," said Mexico coach Ricardo La Volpe, whose team also earned a berth in Germany. "It's easy for them, because they aren't playing under any pressure. My mother, my grandmother or my great grandmother could play for a team like that."

Donovan's feelings about Mexico's plight? "They suck," he said. "I'm so happy."

2004 European Championship

Group Standings

Country	GP	W	L	T	GF	GA	Pts
GROUP A							
*Portugal	3	2	1	0	4	2	6
*Greece	3	1	1	1	4	4	4
Spain	3	1	1	1	2	2	4
Russia	3	1	2	0	2	4	3
GROUP B							
*France	3	2	0	1	7	4	7
*England	3	2	1	0	8	4	6
Croatia	3	0	1	2	4	6	2
Switzerland	3	0	2	1	1	6	1

Country	GP	W	L	T	GF	GA	Pts
GROUP C							
*Sweden	3	1	0	2	8	3	5
*Denmark	3	1	0	2	4	2	5
Italy	3	1	0	2	3	2	5
Bulgaria	3	0	3	0	1	9	0
GROUP D							
*Czech Rep.	3	3	0	0	7	4	9
*Netherlands	3	1	1	1	6	4	4
Germany	3	0	1	2	2	3	2
Latvia	3	0	2	1	1	5	1

*Advanced to second round.

Note: In group play, teams are awarded three points for a victory, one for a tie. The top two in each group advance to the Round of 16. First tiebreaker is head-to-head competition, second is goal differential, third goals scored.

GROUP A	GROUP B	GROUP C	GROUP D
Greece 2, Portugal 1	Switzerland 0, Croatia 0	Denmark 0, Italy 0	Germany 1, Netherlands 1
Spain 1, Russia 0	France 2, England 1	Sweden 5, Bulgaria 0	Czech Rep. 2, Latvia 1
Greece 1, Spain 1	England 3, Switzerland 0	Denmark 2, Bulgaria 0	Latvia 0, Germany 0
Portugal 2, Russia 0	France 2, Croatia 2	Italy 1, Sweden 1	Czech Rep. 3, Neth. 2
Portugal 1, Spain 0	England 4, Croatia 2	Italy 2, Bulgaria 1	Netherlands 3, Latvia 0
Russia 2, Greece 1	France 3, Switzerland 1	Sweden 2, Denmark 2	Czech Rep. 2, Germany 1

Euro 2004—Quarterfinals

EURO 2004 FINAL

Portugal / England	Portugal (2–2)*	
Sweden / Netherlands	Netherlands (0–0)*	
	Portugal (2–1)	Greece (1–0)
	Greece (1–0)	
Greece / France	Greece (1–0)	
Czech Rep. / Denmark	Czech Rep. (3–0)	

*Portugal and the Netherlands advanced on penalties, 6–5 and 5–4, respectively.

2004 Final Standings

EASTERN CONFERENCE								WESTERN CONFERENCE						
Team	GP	W	L	T	Pts	GF	GA	Team	GP	W	L	T	Pts	GF	GA
†*Columbus 30		12	15	13	49	49	32	†*Kansas City ..30		14	9	7	49	38	30
*D.C. United.....30		11	10	9	42	43	42	*Los Angeles....30		11	9	10	43	42	40
*MetroStars 30		11	12	7	40	47	49	*Colorado.........30		10	9	11	41	29	32
*New England ..30		8	13	9	33	42	43	*San Jose.........30		9	10	11	38	41	35
Chicago 30		8	13	9	33	36	44	Dallas...............30		10	14	6	36	34	45

Note: Three points for a win. One point for a tie. †Conference champion. *Qualified for playoffs

SCORING LEADERS

Player, Team	GP	G	A	Pts
Amado Guevara, MetroStars	24	10	10	30
Pat Noonan, NE	29	11	8	30
Brian Ching, SJ	35	12	4	28
Jaime Moreno, DC	27	7	14	28
Eddie Johnson, Dal	26	12	3	27
Josh Wolff, KC	26	10	7	26
Davy Arnaud, KC	30	9	8	25

ASSISTS LEADERS

Player, Team	GP	A
Jaime Moreno, DC	27	11
Jose Cancela, NE	25	10
Landon Donovan, LA	27	10
Simon Elliott, Clb	24	10
Amado Guevara, MetroStars	25	10
Dema Kovalenko, DC	29	10
Ronnie O'Brien, Dal	25	9

GOALS LEADERS

Player, Team	GP	G
Brian Ching, SF	25	12
Eddie Johnson, Dal	26	12
Edson Buddle, Clb	24	11
Pat Noonan, NE	29	11
Damani Ralph, Chi	26	11
Carlos Ruiz, LA	20	11

GOALS-AGAINST-AVERAGE LEADERS

Player, Team	GAA
Nick Rimando, D.C.	1.00
Tone Meola, KC	1.05
Joe Cannon, Col	1.07
Jon Busch, Clb	1.07
Pat Onstad, SJ	1.28
Kevin Hartman, LA	1.32

2004 PLAYOFFS

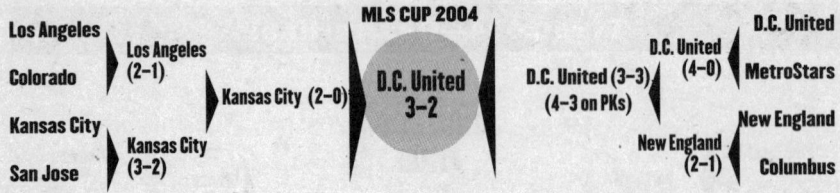

Note: Scores for conference semifinals are two-game aggregates, all others are single games. *Golden-goal overtime.

MLS Cup 2004

CARSON, CALIF., NOVEMBER 14, 2004

D.C. United	3	0—3
Kansas City	1	1—2

Goals: Burciaga Jr. 6; Eskandarian 19; Eskandarian 23; Zotinca 26 (og); Wolff 58.

D.C. United—Rimando, Nelsen, Stewart (Prideaux 82), Eskandarian (Adu 65), Petke, Gomez (Gros 59), Olsen, Carroll, Kovalenko, Namoff, Moreno

Kansas City—Oshoniyi, Garcia, Zavagnin, Burciaga Jr., Gutierrez, Conrad, Jewsbury (Taylor 66), Wolff, Arnaud, Zotinca (Walsh 82), Stephenson (Simutenkov 46)

Att: 25,772

2005 U.S. Men's National Team Results

Date	Opponent	Result	U.S. Goals	Site
Feb. 9	Trin. & Tob.*	2–1 W	Johnson, Lewis	Port of Spain, Trinidad & Tobago
March 27	Mexico*	1-2 L	Lewis	Mexico City, Mexico
March 30	Guatemala*	2-0 W	Johnson, Ralston	Birmingham, Ala.
June 4	Costa Rica*	3-0 W	Donovan (2), McBride	Salt Lake City, Utah
June 8	Panama*	3-0 W	Beasley (2), Vanney	Columbus, Ohio
August 17	Trin. & Tob. *	1-0 W	Donovan, Bocanegra, McBride	Panama City, Panama
Sept. 3	Mexico*	2-1 W	Ralston, Beasley	E. Hartford, Conn.
Sept. 7	Guatemala*	0-0 T	N/A	Guatemala City, Guatemala
Oct. 8	Costa Rica*	0-3 L	N/A	San Jose, Costa Rica
Oct 12	Panama*	2–0 W	Martino, Twellman	Foxboro, Mass.

*CONCACAF World Cup Qualifying game. Record in 2005, through Oct 12: 7-2-1.

2006 Men's World Cup Qualified Teams*

Zone	Country	Date Qualified	Points
Africa	Togo	Oct. 8, 2005	23
Africa	Cote d'Ivoire	Oct. 8, 2005	22
Africa	Angola	Oct. 8, 2005	21
Africa	Ghana	Oct. 8, 2005	21
Africa	Tunisia	Oct. 8, 2005	21
Asia	Japan	June 8, 2005	15
Asia	Saudi Arabia	June 8, 2005	14
Asia	Iran	June 8, 2005	13
Asia	South Korea	June 8, 2005	10
Europe	Germany	Host	N/A
Europe	Ukraine	Sept. 3, 2005	24
Europe	Netherlands	Oct. 8, 2005	32
Europe	Portugal	Oct. 8, 2005	30
Europe	England	Oct. 8, 2005	25
Europe	Ukraine	Oct. 8, 2005	25
Europe	Poland	Oct. 8, 2005	24
Europe	Italy	Oct. 8, 2005	23
Europe	Sweden	Oct. 12, 2005	24
Europe	Serbia and Montenegro	Oct. 12, 2005	22
Europe	France	Oct. 12, 2005	20
North America	United States	Sept. 3, 2005	22
North America	Mexico	Sept. 7, 2005	22
North America	Costa Rica	Oct. 8, 2005	16
South America	Argentina	June 8, 2005	34
South America	Brazil	Sept. 4, 2005	34
South America	Ecuador	Oct. 8, 2005	28
South America	Paraguay	Oct. 8, 2005	28

*as of Oct 12, 2005

2005 U.S. Women's National Team Results

Date	Opponent	Result	U.S. Goals	Site
March 9	France @	1-0 W	Welsch	Ferreiras, Portugal
March 11	Finland @	3-0 W	Welsh (2), Wambach	Guia, Portugal
March 13	Denmark @	4-0 W	Wambach, Welsh, Lilly (2)	Villa Real de San Antonio, Portugal
March 15	Germany @	1-0 W	Welsh	Faro, Portugal
June 26	Canada	2-0 W	Chalupny, Welsh	Virginia Beach, Va.
July 10	Ukraine	7-0 W	Welsh, Lilly, Wagner, Fotopolous (2), Milbrett, O'Reilly	Portland, Ore.
July 24	Iceland	3-0 W	Boxx, Fotopolous (2)	Carson, Calif.

#Four Nations Tournament. * CONCACAF Olympic Qualifying Tournament. @ Algarve Cup. ^ Olympics.
Record in 2005, through Oct 12: 7–0–0.

International Club Competition

Intercontinental Cup

Competition between winners of European Cup and Libertadores Cup.

YOKOHAMA, JAPAN: DECEMBER 12, 2004

FC Porto (Port)	0	0	0—0
Once Caldas (Col)	0	0	0—0

FC Porto won 8–7 on penalty kicks.

Goals: None

Penalthy Shots: FC Porto–Diego scored, Alberto scored, Quaresma scored, Miniche missed, McCarthy scored, Costinha scored, J. Costa scored, R. Costa scored, Emanuel scored;
Once Caldas–Vanegas scored, Alcazar scored, Viafara scored, De Nigris scored, Fabbro missed, Velasquez scored, Diaz scored, Cataño scored, Garcia missed

Att: 45,748.

FC Porto: Baia (Nuno), Seitaridis, Jorge Costa, Emanuel, Ricardo Costa, Costinha, Maniche, Diego, Derlei (Alberto), Fabiano (Quaresma), McCarthy.

Once Caldas: Henao, Garcia, Vanegas, Cambio (Cataño), Rojas, Velasquez, Viafara, Soto (Alcazar) Arango (Diaz) Fabbro, De Nigris

UEFA Cup

Competition between teams other than league champions and cup-winners from UEFA.

LISBON, PORTUGAL: MAY 18, 2005

Sporting CP (Port)	1	0 —1
CSKA Moskva (Rus)	0	3 —3

Goals: Régis 29; Berezoutski 56; Zhirkov 66; Love 75.

Att: 46,500.

Sporting CP: Garica, Tello, Barbosa, Rochemback, Régis (Douala 80) Moutinho (Viana 88), Pinto (Niculae 73) Muniz

CSKA Moskva: Berezoutski, Ignashevich, Zhirkov, Rahimic, Odiah, Carvalho (Semberas 82), Aldonin (Gusev 86), Love, Olic (Krasic 67)

European Cup (Champions League)

League champions of the countries belonging to UEFA (Union of European Football Associations).

GELSENKIRCHEN, GERMANY: MAY 25, 2005

Liverpool (Eng)	3	0 —3
AC Milan (Ita)	0	3 —3

Liverpool won 3–2 on penalty kicks.

Goals: Maldini 1; Crespo 39, 44; Gerrard 54, Smicer 56; Alonso 59

Att: 65,00.

Liverpool: Dudek, Finnan (Hamann 46), Traore, Hyypia, Carragher, Riise, Gerrard, L. Garcia, Alonso, Kewell (Smicer 23), Baros (Cisse 85)

AC Milan: Dida, Cafu, Maldini, Stam, Nesta, Gattuso (R, Costa 112), Seedorf (Serginho 86), Pirlo, Kaka, Shevchenko, Crespo (Tomasson 85)

Libertadores Cup

Competition between champion clubs and runners-up of 10 South American National Associations.

(2ND LEG) SÃO PAULO, BRAZIL: JULY 15, 2005

São Paulo* (Bra)	1	3—4
Atlético Paranaense (Col)	0	0—0

* Two-game aggregate: 5–1;

Goals: Amoroso 16; Fabão 52; Luizão 70; Tardelli 88.

Att: 78,000.

São Paulo: Ceni, Amoroso, Fabão, Cicinho, Mineiro, Josué, Danilo, Junior (Santos) Amoroso (Tardelli), Luizão (Souza).

Atlético Paranaense: Diego, Jancarlos, Danilo, Marcão (Rodrigo), Cocito, Rocha (Bahia), Evandro, Lima (Fernandinho), Aloísio.

2004–2005 Club Champions—Europe

Country	League Champion	League Scoring Leader, Club	Cup Winner
Albania	SK Tirana	Dorian Bylykbashi, Partizani	Teuta Durrës
Andorra	Matecosa UE Sant Julia	n/a	Santa Coloma
Armenia	Pyunik Yerevan	Edgar Manucharian, Pyunik Yerevan	Mika Ashtarak
		Galust Petrosian, Pyunik Yerevan	
Austria	Austria Wien	Christian Mayrleb, Pasching	Austria Wien
Azerbaijan	FK Baki	Zaur Ramazanov, Karvan	FK Baki
Belarus	Shakhtsyor Salihorsk	Alyaksandr Klimenka, Shakhtsyor	MTZ-RIPA Minsk
Belgium	Club Brugge KV	Nenad Jestrovic, RSC Anderlecht	Germinal Beerschot
Bosnia & Herz	Zrinjski Mostar	Zoran Rajovic, Zrinjski Mostar	Sarajevo
Bulgaria	CSKA Sofia	Martin Kamburov, Lokomotiv	Levski Sofia
Croatia	Hajduk Split	Tomislav Erceg, Rijeka	Rijeka
Cyprus	Anorthosis Famagusta	Lukasz Sosin, Apollon	Omonia Nicosia
Czech Republic	AC Sparta Prague	Tomas Jun, AC Sparta Prague	Banik Ostrava
Denmark	Brøndby IF	Steffen Højer, OB	Brøndby IF
England	Chelsea	Thierry Henry, Arsenal	Arsenal
Estonia	Levadia Tallinn*	Vjatseslav Zahhovaiko, Flora*	Levadia Tallinn
Faroe Islands	HB Tórshavn*	Sonni L. Petersen, EB/Streymur*	GI Gøta
Finland	MyPa Anjalankoski	Juho Mäkela, HJK Helsinki	MyPa Anjalankoski*
France	Olympique Lyonnais	Alexander Frei, Rennes	AJ Auxerroise
Georgia	Dinamo Tbilisi	Levani Melkadze, Dinamo Tbilisi	Lokomotivi Tblisi
Germany	Bayern München	Marek Mintal, 1.FC Nürnberg	Bayern München
Greece	Olympiakos Piraeus	Fanis Gekas, Kallithea/Panathinaikos	Olympiakos Piraes
Hungary	Debreceni Vasutas	Tomas Medved, Lombard-Pápa	Matav VC Sopron
Iceland	FH Hafnarfjör	Tryggvi Gudmundsson, FH Hafnarfjör	Valur Rejkavik
Ireland	Shelbourne*	Jason Byrne, Shelbourne	Longford Town*
Israel	Maccabi Haifa	Roberto Colautti, Maccabi Haifa	Maccabi Tel Aviv
Italy	Juventus	Christiano Lucarell, Livorno	Internazionale 1908
Kazakhstan	Kairat Almaty	Ulugbek Bakayev, Tobol*	FK Taraz*
		Arsen Tlekhugov, Kairat Almaty	
Latvia	Liepajas Metalurgs	Alexander Katasonov, Metalurgs	FK Ventspils*
Lithuania	Ekranas Panevezys	Povilas Luksys, Ekranas Panevezys*	FBK Kaunas*
Luxembourg	F 91 Dudelange	n/a	CS Pétange
Macedonia	Rabotniki Skopje	n/a	Bashkimi Kumanovo
Malta	Sliema Wanderers	Andrew Cohen, Hibernians	Birkirkara
Moldova	Sheriff Tiraspol	Catalin Lichioiu, Nistru Otaci	Nistru Otaci
Netherlands	PSV Eindhoven	Dirk Kuijt, Feyenoord	PSV Eindhoven
Northern Ireland	Glentoran Belfast	Chris Morgan, Glentoran Belfast	Portadown
Norway	Rosenborg*	Frode Johnsen, Rosenborg	Brann*
Poland	Wisla Kraków	Tomasz Frankowski, Wisla Kraków	Dyskobolia Groclin
Portugal	SL Benfica	Liedson Muniz, Sporting CP	Vitória FC Setúbal
Romania	Steaua Bucharest	n/a	Dinamo Bucharest
Russia	Lokmotiv Moskva*	Aleksandr Kerzhakov, Zenit*	CSKA Moskva
San Marino	SP Tre Penne	Matteo Pazzaglia, Montevito	Pennarossa
Scotland	Rangers	n/a	Glasgow Celtic
Serbia and Montenegro	Partizan Belgrade	n/a	Zeleznik Belgrade
Slovakia	Artmedia Petrzalka	Filip Sebo, Petrzalka	Dukla Bansk Bystrica
Slovenia	ND Gorica	Kliton Bozgo, Maribor	Publikum Celje
Spain	FC Barcelona	Diego Forlán, Villareal	Real Betis Balompi
Sweden	Malmo FF*	Markus Rosenberg. Halmstads	Djurgårdens IF*
Switzerland	FC Basel	Christian Giménez, FC Basel	FC Zürich
Turkey	Fenerbahçe Istanbul	Fatih Tekke, Trabzonspor	Galatasaray Istanbul
Ukraine	Shakhtar Donetsk	A. Kosyrin, Chornomorets Odesa	Dynamo Kiev
Wales	TNS	Marc Lloyd-Williams, TNS	TNS

Note: Results are from 2005 unless followed by *.

The World Cup

Results

Year	Champion	Score	Runner-Up	Winning Coach
1930	Uruguay	4–2	Argentina	Alberto Supicci
1934	Italy	2–1	Czechoslovakia	Vittorio Pozzo
1938	Italy	4–2	Hungary	Vittorio Pozzo
1950	Uruguay	2–1	Brazil	Juan Lopez
1954	W Germany	3–2	Hungary	Sepp Herberger
1958	Brazil	5–2	Sweden	Vicente Feola
1962	Brazil	3–1	Czechoslovakia	Aymore Moreira
1966	England	4–2	W Germany	Alf Ramsey
1970	Brazil	4–1	Italy	Mario Zagalo
1974	W Germany	2–1	Netherlands	Helmut Schoen
1978	Argentina	3–1	Netherlands	César Menotti
1982	Italy	3–1	W Germany	Enzo Bearzot
1986	Argentina	3–2	W Germany	Carlos Bilardo
1990	W Germany	1–0	Argentina	Franz Beckenbauer
1994	Brazil	0–0 (3–2)	Italy	Carlos Alberto Parreira
1998	France	3–0	Brazil	Aime Jacquet
2002	Brazil	2–0	Germany	Luis Felipe Scolari

Alltime World Cup Participation

Of the 69 nations that have taken part in the World Cup Finals, only Brazil has competed in each of the 17 tournaments held to date. West Germany or an undivided Germany (1934, '38, '94 and '98) has played in 15 World Cups. Ranked by victories.

Nation	Matches	W	T	L	Goals For	Goals Against
Brazil	87	60	14	13	191	82
*Germany	85	50	18	17	176	106
Italy	70	39	17	14	110	67
Argentina	60	30	11	19	102	70
England	50	22	15	13	68	45
France	44	21	7	16	86	61
Spain	45	19	12	14	71	53
Yugoslavia	37	17	6	14	60	46
†Russia	37	17	6	14	64	44
Uruguay	40	15	10	15	65	57
Hungary	32	15	3	14	87	57
Netherlands	31	14	9	8	55	34
Poland	28	14	5	9	42	36
Sweden	41	14	9	18	67	65
Austria	29	12	4	13	42	48
Czechoslovakia	30	11	5	14	44	45
Belgium	36	10	9	17	46	63
Mexico	41	10	11	20	43	79
Romania	21	8	5	8	30	32
Chile	25	7	6	12	31	40
Portugal	12	7	0	5	25	16
Denmark	13	7	2	4	24	18
Switzerland	22	6	3	13	33	51
United States	22	6	2	14	25	45
Paraguay	19	5	7	7	25	34
Turkey	10	5	1	4	20	17
Croatia	9	5	0	4	11	7
Scotland	23	4	7	12	25	41
Peru	15	4	3	8	19	31
Cameroon	17	4	7	6	16	28
Nigeria	11	4	1	6	14	16
Bulgaria	25	3	8	14	22	49
S Korea	21	3	6	12	19	49
Colombia	13	3	2	8	14	23
Northern Ireland	13	3	5	5	13	23
Costa Rica	7	3	1	3	9	12
Wales	5	2	6	1	10	7
Morocco	10	2	4	4	10	13
Senegal	5	2	2	1	7	6
Norway	8	2	3	3	7	8
Saudi Arabia	10	2	1	7	7	25
Algeria	6	2	1	3	6	10
Japan	7	2	1	4	6	7
E Germany	6	2	2	2	5	5
S Africa	6	1	3	2	8	11
N Korea	4	1	1	2	5	9
Tunisia	9	1	3	5	5	11
Cuba	3	1	1	1	5	12
Republic of Ireland	13	1	5	3	4	7
Iran	6	1	1	4	4	12
Jamaica	3	1	0	2	3	9
Ecuador	3	1	0	2	2	4
Israel	3	1	0	2	1	3
Egypt	4	0	2	2	3	6
Honduras	3	0	2	1	2	3
Kuwait	3	0	1	2	2	6
Slovenia	3	0	0	3	2	7
United Arab Emirates	3	0	0	3	2	11
New Zealand	3	0	0	3	2	12
Haiti	3	0	0	3	2	14
Iraq	3	0	0	3	1	4
Bolivia	6	0	1	5	1	20
El Salvador	6	0	0	6	1	22
Australia	3	0	1	2	0	5
Dutch East Indies	1	0	0	1	0	6
Canada	3	0	0	3	0	5
Zaire	3	0	0	3	0	14
Greece	3	0	0	3	0	8
China	3	0	0	3	0	9

*Includes West Germany 1950–90. †Includes USSR 1930–1990.
Note: Matches decided by penalty kicks are shown as drawn games.

World Cup Final Box Scores

URUGUAY 1930

Uruguay	1	3 —4
Argentina	2	0 —2

FIRST HALF

Scoring: 1, Uruguay, Dorado (12); 2, Argentina, Peucelle (20); 3, Argentina, Stabile (37).

SECOND HALF

Scoring: 4, Uruguay, Cea (57); 5, Uruguay, Iriarte (68); 6, Uruguay, Castro (89).

Argentina: Botosso, Della Toree, Paternoster, J. Evaristo, Monti, Suarez, Peucelle, Varallo, Stabile, Ferreira, M. Evaristo.

Uruguay: Ballesteros, Nasazzi, Mascheroni, Andrade, Fernandez, Gestido, Dorado, Scarone, Castro, Cea, Iriarte.

Referee: Langenus (Belgium).

ITALY 1934

Italy	0	1	1 —2
Czechoslovakia	0	1	0 —1

SECOND HALF

Scoring: 1, Czech., Puc (70); 2, Italy, Orsi (80).

OVERTIME

Scoring: 3, Italy, Schiavio (95).

Italy: Combi, Monzeglio, Allemandi, Ferraris Monti, Monti, Bertolini, Guaita, Meazza, Schiavio, Ferrari, Orsi.

Czechoslovakia: Planicka, Zenisek, Ctyroky, Kostalek, Cambal, Cambal, Krcil, Junek, Svoboda, Sobotka, Nejedly, Puc.

Referee: Eklind (Sweden).

FRANCE 1938

Italy	3	1 —4
Hungary	1	1 —2

FIRST HALF

Scoring: 1, Italy, Colaussi (5); 2, Hungary, Titkos (7); 3, Italy, Piola (16); 4, Italy, Piola (35).

SECOND HALF

Scoring: 5, Hungary, Sarosi (70); 6, Italy, Colaussi (82).

Italy: Olivieri, Foni, Rava, Serantoni, Andreolo, Locatelli, Biavati, Meazza, Piola, Ferrari, Colaussi.

Hungary: Szabo, Polger, Biro, Szalay, Szucs, Lazar, Sas, Vincze, Sarosi, Zsengeller, Titkos.

Referee: Capdeville (France).

BRAZIL 1950

Uruguay	0	2 —2
Brazil	0	1 —1

SECOND HALF

Scoring: 1, Brazil, Friaca (47); 2, Uruguay, Schiaffino (66); 3, Uruguay, Ghiggia (79).

Uruguay: Maspoli, Gonzales, Tejera, Gambretta, Varela, Andrade, Ghiggia, Perez, Miguez, Schiffiano, Moran.

Brazil: Barbosa, Augusto, Juvenal, Bauer, Banilo, Bigode, Friaca, Zizinho, Ademir, Jair, Chico.

Referee: Reader (England).

SWITZERLAND 1954

W Germany	2	1 —3
Hungary	2	0 —2

FIRST HALF

Scoring: 1, Hungary, Puskas (6); 2, Hungary, Czibor (8); 3, W Germ., Morlock (10); 4, W Germ., Rahn (18).

SECOND HALF

Scoring: 5, W Germany, Rahn (84).

W Germany: Turek, Posipal, Kohlmeyer, Eckel, Liebrich, Mai, Rahn, Morlock, O.Walter, F. Walter, Schaefer.

Hungary: Grosics, Buzansky, Lantos, Bozsik, Lorant, Zakarias, Czibor, Kocsis, Hidegkuti, Puskas, Toth.

Referee: Ling (England).

SWEDEN 1958

Brazil	2	3 —5
Sweden	1	1 —2

FIRST HALF

Scoring:1, Sweden, Liedholm (3); 2, Brazil, Vava (9); 3, Brazil, Vava (32).

SECOND HALF

Scoring: 4, Brazil, Pelé (55); 5, Brazil, Zagalo (68); 6, Sweden Simonsson (80); 7, Brazil, Pelé (90).

Brazil: Glymar, D. Santos, N. Santos, Zito, Bellini, Orlando, Garrincha, Didi, Vava, Pelé, Zagalo.

Sweden: Svensson, Bergmark, Axbom, Boerjesson, Gustavsson, Parling, Hamrin, Gren, Simonsson, Liedholm, Skoglund.

Referee: Guigue (France).

CHILE 1962

Brazil	1	2 —3
Czechoslovakia	1	0 —1

FIRST HALF

Scoring: 1, Czech., Masopust (15); 2, Brazil, Amarildo (17).

SECOND HALF

Scoring: 3, Brazil, Zito (68); 4, Brazil, Vava (77).

Brazil: Glymar, D. Santos, N. Santos, Zito, Mauro, Zozimo, Garrincha, Didi, Vava, Amarildo, Zagalo.

Czechoslovakia: Schroiff, Tichy, Novak, Pluskal, Popluhar, Masopust, Pospichal, Scherer, Kvasnak, Kadraba, Jelinek.

Referee: Latychev (USSR).

World Cup Final Box Scores *(Cont.)*

ENGLAND 1966

England	1	1	2 —4
W Germany	1	1	0 —2

FIRST HALF

Scoring: 1, W Germany, Haller (12); 2, England, Hurst (18).

SECOND HALF

Scoring: 3, England, Peters (78); 4, W. Germany, Weber (90).

OVERTIME

Scoring: 5, England, Hurst (101); 6, England, Hurst (120).

England: Banks, Cohen, Wilson, Stiles, J. Charlton, Moore, Ball, Hurst, Hunt, R. Charlton, Peters.

W Germany: Tilkowski, Hottges, Schmellinger, Beckenbauer, Schulz, Weber, Held, Haller, Seeler, Overath, Emmerich.

Referee: Dienst (Switzerland).

W GERMANY 1974

W Germany	2	0 —2
Netherlands	1	0 —1

FIRST HALF

Scoring: 1, Netherlands, Neeskens, PK (1); 2, W Germany, Breitner, PK (26); 3, W Germany, Müller (44).

W Germany: Maier, Vogts, Beckenbauer, Schwarzenbeck, Breitner, Hoeness, Bonhof, Overath, Grabowski, Müller, Holzenbein.

Netherlands: Jongbloed, Suurbier, Rijsbergen (de Jong), Haan, Krol, Jansen, Neeskens, van Hanagem, Cruyff, Rensenbrink (van der Kerkhof).

Referee: Taylor (England).

ITALY 1982

Italy	0	3 —3
W Germany	0	1 —1

SECOND HALF

Scoring: 1, Italy, Rossi (57); 2, Italy, Tardelli (68); 3, Italy, Altobelli (81); 4, W Germany, Breitner (83).

Italy: Zoff, Bergomi, Scirea, Collovati, Cabrini, Oriali, Gentile, Tardelli, Conti, Rossi, Graziani (Altobelli, Causio).

W Germany: Schumacher, Kaltz, Stielike, K. Foerster, B. Foerster, Dremmler (Hrubesch), Breitner, Briegel, Rummenigge (Müller), Fischher (Littbarski).

Referee: Coelho (Brazil).

MEXICO 1986 *(Cont.)*

Argentina: Pumpido, Brown, Cuciuffo, Ruggeri, Olarticoecha, Bastista, Giusti, Burruchaga (Trobbiani 90), Enrique, Maradona, Valdona.

W Germany: Schumacher, Jakobs, Forster, Eder, Brehme, Matthaus, Berthold, Magath (Hoeness 62), Briegel, Rummenigge, Allofs (Voller 46).

Referee: Filho (Brazil).

MEXICO 1970

Brazil	1	3 —4
Italy	1	0 —1

FIRST HALF

Scoring: 1, Brazil, Pelé (18); 2, Italy, Boninsegna (32).

SECOND HALF

Scoring: 3, Brazil, Gerson (65); 4, Brazil, Jairzinho (70); 5, Brazil, Alberto (86).

Brazil: Feliz, Alberto, Brito, Wilson, Piazza, Everaldo, Clodoaldo, Gerson, Jairzinho, Tostao, Pelé, Rivelino.

Italy: Albertosi, Burgnich, Cera, Rosato, Facchetti, Bertini (Juliano), Mazzola, De Sisti, Domenghini, Boninsegna (Rivera), Riva.

Referee: Glockner (E Germany).

ARGENTINA 1978

Argentina	1	0	2 —3
Netherlands	0	1	0 —1

FIRST HALF

Scoring: 1, Argentina, Kempes (38).

SECOND HALF

Scoring: 2, Netherlands, Nanninga (81).

OVERTIME

Scoring: 3, Arg., Kempes (104); 4, Arg., Bertoni (114).

Argentina: Fillol, Olguin, Galvan, Passarella, Tarantini, Ardiles (Larrosa), Gallego, Kempes, Bertoni, Luque, Ortiz (Houseman).

Netherlands: Jongbloed, Jansen (Suurbier), Krol, Brandts, Poortvliet, Neeskens, Haan, W. van der Kerkhoff, R. van der Kerkhoff, Rep (Nanninga), Rensenbrink.

Referee: Gonella (Italy).

MEXICO 1986

Argentina	1	2 —3
W Germany	0	2 —2

FIRST HALF

Scoring: 1, Argentina, Brown (22).

SECOND HALF

Scoring: 2, Arg., Valdano (55); 3, W Germ., Rummenigge (73); 4, W Germ., Voller (81); 5, Arg., Burruchaga (83).

ITALY 1990

W Germany	0	1 —1
Argentina	0	0 —0

SECOND HALF

Scoring: 1, W Germany, Brehme, PK (84).

W Germany: Illgner, Brehme, Kohler, Augenthaler, Buchwald, Berthold (Reuter), Littbarski, Haessler, Mattaeus, Voeller, Klinsmann.

Argentina: Goychoechea, Lorenzo, Serrizuela, Sensini, Ruggeri (Monzon), Simon, Basualdo, Burruchag (Calderon), Maradona, Troglio, Dezottir.

Referee: Coelho (Brazil).

World Cup Final Box Scores (Cont.)

UNITED STATES 1994

Italy...................0	0	0——0
Brazil 0	0	0——0

Scoring: None. Shootout goals: Italy—2: Albertini, Evani; Brazil—3: Romario, Branco, Dunga.

Italy: Pagliuca, Benarrivo, Maldini, Baresi, Mussi (Apolloni 35), Albertini, D. Baggio (Evani 95), Berti, Donadoni, Baggio, Massaro.

Brazil: Taffarel, Jorginho (Cafu 21), Branco, Aldair, Santos, Silva, Dunga, Zinho (Viola 106), Mazinho, Bebeto, Romario.

Referee: Puhl (Hungary).

FRANCE 1998

Brazil 0		0——0
France 2		1——3

FIRST HALF

Scoring: 1, France, Zidane (27); 2, France, Zidane (45).

SECOND HALF

Scoring: 3, France, Petit (90).

Brazil: Taffarel, Cafu, Aldair, Baiano, Carlos, Sampaio (Edmundo 74), Dunga, Rivaldo, Leonardo, (Denilson 46), Bebeto, Ronaldo.

France: Barthez, Lizarazu, Desailly, Thuram, Leboeuf, Djorkaeff (Vieira 75) Deschamps, Zidane, Petit, Karembeu (Boghossian 57), Guivarc'h (Dugarry 66).

Referee: Belqola (Morocco).

KOREA/JAPAN 2002

Brazil.........................0	2 —2	
Germany 0	0 —0	

SECOND HALF

Scoring: 1, Brazil, Ronaldo (67); 2, Brazil, Ronaldo (79).

Brazil: Marcos, Cafu, Lucio, Roque Junior, Edmilson, Carlos, Silva, Ronaldo (Denilson, 90), Rivaldo, Ronaldinho (Juninho, 85), Kleberson.

Germany: Kahn, Linke, Ramelow, Neuville, Hamann, Klose (Bierhoff, 74), Jeremies (Asamoah, 77), Bode (Ziege, 84), Schneider, Metzelder, Frings.

Referee: Collina (Italy).

Alltime Leaders

GOALS

Player, Nation	Tournaments	Goals	Player, Nation	Tournaments	Goals
Gerd Müller, W Germany	1970, '74	14	Gary Lineker, England	1986, '90	10
Just Fontaine, France	1958	13	Ademir, Brazil	1950	9
Pelé, Brazil	1958, '62, '66, '70	12	Eusebio, Portugal	1966	9
Ronaldo, Brazil	1998, 2002	12	Jairzinho, Brazil	1970, '74	9
Sandor Kocsis, Hungary	1954	11	Paolo Rossi, Italy	1982, '86	9
Teofilo Cubillas, Peru	1970, '78	10	K.H. Rummenigge, W Ger	1978, '82, '86	9
Gregorz Lato, Poland	1974, '78, '82	10	Uwe Seeler, W Germany	1958, '62, '66, '70	9
Helmut Rahn, W Germany	1954, '58	10	Vava, Brazil	1958, '62	9

LEADING SCORER, CUP BY CUP

Year	Player, Nation	Goals	Year	Player, Nation	Goals
1930	Guillermo Stabile, Argentina	8	1966	Eusebio Ferreira, Portugal	9
1934	Oldrich Nejedly, Czechoslovakia	5	1970	Gerd Müller, W Germany	10
1938	Leonidas da Silva, Brazil	8	1974	Gregorz Lato, Poland	7
1950	Ademir de Menenzes, Brazil	9	1978	Mario Kempes, Argentina	6
1954	Sandor Kocsis, Hungary	11	1982	Paolo Rossi, Italy	6
1958	Just Fontaine, France	13	1986	Gary Lineker, England	6
1962	Florian Albert, Hungary	4	1990	Salvatore Schillaci, Italy	6
	Valentin Ivanov, USSR		1994	Hristo Stoichkov, Bulgaria	6
	Garrincha, Brazil; Vava, Brazil			Oleg Salenko, Russia	
	Drazan Jerkovic, Yugoslavia		1998	Davor Suker, Croatia	6
	Leonel Sanchez, Chile		2002	Ronaldo, Brazil	8

Most Goals, Individual, One Game

Goals	Player, Nation	Score	Date
5	Oleg Salenko, Russia	Russia–Cameroon, 6–1	6-28-94
4	Leonidas, Brazil	Brazil–Poland, 6–5	6-5-38
4	Ernest Willimowski, Poland	Brazil–Poland, 6–5	6-5-38
4	Gustav Wetterström, Sweden	Sweden–Cuba, 8–0	6-12-38
4	Juan Alberto Schiaffino, Uruguay	Uruguay–Bolivia, 8–0	7-2-50
4	Ademir, Brazil	Brazil–Sweden, 7–1	7-9-50
4	Sandor Kocsis, Hungary	Hungary–W Germany, 8–3	6-20-54
4	Just Fontaine, France	France–W Germany, 6–3	6-28-58
4	Eusebio, Portugal	Portugal–N Korea, 5–3	7-23-66
4	Emilio Butragueño, Spain	Spain–Denmark, 5–1	6-18-86

Note: 31 players have scored 32 World Cup hat tricks. Gerd Müller of West Germany is the only man to have two World Cup hat tricks, both in 1970. The last hat tricks were 6-1-02, Miroslav Klose (Ger) vs. Saudi Arabia; 6-21-98, Gabriel Batistuta (Arg) vs. Jamaica; 6-23-90, Tomas Skuhravy (Czech) vs. Costa Rica; and 6-17-90, Michel (Spain) vs. S Korea.

Attendance and Goal Scoring, Year by Year

Year	Site	No. of Games	Goals	Goals/Game	Attendance	Avg Att
1930	Uruguay	18	70	3.89	434,500	24,139
1934	Italy	17	70	4.12	395,000	23,235
1938	France	18	84	4.67	483,000	26,833
1950	Brazil	22	88	4.00	1,337,000	60,773
1954	Switzerland	26	140	5.38	943,000	36,269
1958	Sweden	35	126	3.60	868,000	24,800
1962	Chile	32	89	2.78	776,000	24,250
1966	England	32	89	2.78	1,614,677	50,459
1970	Mexico	32	95	2.97	1,673,975	52,312
1974	W Germany	38	97	2.55	1,774,022	46,685
1978	Argentina	38	102	2.68	1,610,215	42,374
1982	Spain	52	146	2.80	1,856,277	35,698
1986	Mexico	52	132	2.54	2,441,731	46,956
1990	Italy	52	115	2.21	2,514,443	48,354
1994	United States	52	140	2.69	3,567,415	68,604
1998	France	64	171	2.67	2,775,400	43,366
2002	Korea/Japan	64	161	2.52	2,705,216	42,269
Totals		580	1,754	3.02	25,064,655	43,215

The United States in the World Cup

Date	Opponent	Result	Scoring
URUGUAY 1930: FINAL COMPETITION			
7-13-30	Belgium	3–0 W	U.S.: McGhee 2, Patenaude
7-17-30	Paraguay	3–0 W	U.S.: Patenaude 2, Florie
7-26-30	Argentina	1–6 L	Arg.: Monti 2, Scopelli 2, Stabile 2 U.S.: Brown.
ITALY 1934: FINAL COMPETITION			
5-27-34	Italy	1–7 L	U.S.: Donelli Italy: Schiavio 3, Orsi 2, Meazza, Ferrari
BRAZIL 1950: FINAL COMPETITION			
6-25-50	Spain	1–3 L	U.S.: Pariani Spain: Igoa, Basora, Zarra
6-29-50	England	1–0 W	U.S.: Gaetjens.
7-2-50	Chile	2–5 L	U.S.: Wallace, Maca Chile: Robledo, Cremaschi 3, Prieto
ITALY 1990: FINAL COMPETITION			
6-10-90	Czechoslovakia	1–5 L	U.S.: Caligiuri Czech.: Skuhravy 2, Hasek, Bilek, Luhovy
6-14-90	Italy	0–1 L	Italy: Giannini
6-19-90	Austria	1–2 L	U.S.: Murray Austria: Rodax, Ogris

Date	Opponent	Result	Scoring
UNITED STATES 1994: FINAL COMPETITION			
6-18-94	Switzerland	1–1 T	U.S.: Wynalda Switz.: Bregy
6-22-94	Colombia	2–1 W	U.S.: Escobar (own goal), Stewart Colombia: Valencia
6-26-94	Romania	1–0 L	Romania: Petrescu
7-4-94	Brazil	1–0 L	Brazil: Bebeto
FRANCE 1998: FINAL COMPETITION			
6-15-98	Germany	2–0 L	Germany: Möller, Klinsmann
6-21-98	Iran	2–1 L	U.S.: McBride Iran: Estili, Mahdavikia
6-25-98	Yugoslavia	1–0 L	Yugoslavia: Komljenovic
KOREA/JAPAN 2002: FINAL COMPETITION			
6-5-02	Portugal	3–2 W	U.S.: O'Brien, Costa (own goal), McBride Portugal: Beto, Agoos (own goal)
6-10-02	S Korea	1–1 T	U.S.: Mathis S Korea: Ahn
6-14-02	Poland	3–1 L	Poland: Olisadebe, Kryszalowicz, Zewlakow U.S.: Donovan
6-17-02	Mexico	2–0 W	U.S.: McBride, Donovan
6-21-02	Germany	1–0 L	Germany: Ballack

International Competition

European Championship

Official name: the European Football Championship. Held every four years since 1960.

Year	Champion	Score	Runner-up	Year	Champion	Score	Runner-up
1960	USSR	2–1	Yugoslavia	1984	France	2–0	Spain
1964	Spain	2–1	USSR	1988	Holland	2–0	USSR
1968	Italy	2–0	Yugoslavia	1992	Denmark	2–0	Germany
1972	W Germany	3–0	USSR	1996	Germany†	2–1	Czech Republic
1976	Czechoslovakia*	2–2	W Germany	2000	France†	2–1	Italy
1980	W Germany	2–1	Belgium	2004	Greece	1–0	Portugal

*Won on penalty kicks. †Won in sudden-death overtime.

Under-20 World Championship

Year	Host	Champion	Runner-Up
1977	Tunisia	USSR	Mexico
1979	Japan	Argentina	USSR
1981	Australia	W Germany	Qatar
1983	Mexico	Brazil	Argentina
1985	USSR	Brazil	Spain
1987	Chile	Yugoslavia	W Germany
1989	Saudi Arabia	Portugal	Nigeria
1991	Portugal	Portugal	Brazil
1993	Australia	Brazil	Ghana
1995	Qatar	Argentina	Brazil
1997	Malaysia	Argentina	Uruguay
1999	Nigeria	Spain	Japan
2001	Argentina	Argentina	Ghana
2003	UAE	Brazil	Spain
2005	Netherlands	Argentina	Nigeria

Under-17 World Championship

Year	Champion
1985	Nigeria
1987	USSR
1989	Saudi Arabia
1991	Ghana
1993	Nigeria

Under-17 *(Cont.)*

Year	Champion
1995	Ghana
1997	Brazil
1999	Brazil
2001	France
2003	Brazil
2005	Mexico

Pan American Games

Year	Champion
1951	Argentina
1955	Argentina
1959	Argentina
1963	Brazil
1967	Mexico
1971	Argentina
1975	Brazil/Mexico (tie)
1979	Brazil
1983	Uruguay
1987	Brazil
1991	United States
1995	Argentina
1999	Mexico
2003	Argentina

South American Championship (Copa America)

Year	Champion	Host	Year	Champion	Host
1916	Uruguay	Argentina	1953	Paraguay	Peru
1917	Uruguay	Uruguay	1955	Argentina	Chile
1919	Brazil	Brazil	1956	Uruguay	Uruguay
1920	Uruguay	Chile	1957	Argentina	Peru
1921	Argentina	Argentina	1958	Argentina	Argentina
1922	Brazil	Brazil	1959	Uruguay	Ecuador
1923	Uruguay	Uruguay	1963	Bolivia	Bolivia
1924	Uruguay	Uruguay	1967	Uruguay	Uruguay
1925	Argentina	Argentina	1975	Peru	Various sites
1926	Uruguay	Chile	1979	Paraguay	Various sites
1927	Argentina	Peru	1983	Uruguay	Various sites
1929	Argentina	Argentina	1987	Uruguay	Argentina
1935	Uruguay	Peru	1989	Brazil	Brazil
1937	Argentina	Argentina	1990	Brazil	Argentina
1939	Peru	Peru	1991	Argentina	Chile
1941	Argentina	Chile	1993	Argentina	Ecuador
1942	Uruguay	Uruguay	1995	Uruguay	Uruguay
1945	Argentina	Chile	1997	Brazil	Bolivia
1946	Argentina	Argentina	1999	Brazil	Paraguay
1947	Argentina	Ecuador	2001	Colombia	Colombia
1949	Brazil	Brazil	2004	Brazil	Peru

Awards

European Footballer of the Year

Year	Player	Club	Year	Player	Club
1956	Stanley Matthews	Blackpool	1966	Bobby Charlton	Manchester United
1957	Alfredo Di Stefano	Real Madrid	1967	Florian Albert	Ferencvaros
1958	Raymond Kopa	Real Madrid	1968	George Best	Manchester United
1959	Alfredo Di Stefano	Real Madrid	1969	Gianni Rivera	AC Milan
1960	Luis Suarez	Barcelona	1970	Gerd Mueller	Bayern Munich
1961	Omar Sivori	Juventus	1971	Johan Cruyff	Ajax
1962	Josef Masopust	Dukla Prague	1972	Franz Beckenbauer	Bayern Munich
1963	Lev Yashin	Moscow Dynamo	1973	Johan Cruyff	Barcelona
1964	Denis Law	Manchester United	1974	Johan Cruyff	Barcelona
1965	Eusebio	Benfica	1975	Oleg Blokhin	Dynamo Kiev

European Footballer of the Year (Cont.)

Year	Player	Club	Year	Player	Club
1976	Franz Beckenbauer	Bayern Munich	1991	Jean-Pierre Papin	Olympique Marseille
1977	Allan Simonsen	Borussia M'gladbach	1992	Marco Van Basten	AC Milan
1978	Kevin Keegan	SV Hamburg	1993	Roberto Baggio	Juventus
1979	Kevin Keegan	SV Hamburg	1994	Hristo Stoichkov	Barcelona
1980	Karl-Heinz Rummenigge	Bayern Munich	1995	George Weah	AC Milan
1981	Karl-Heinz Rummenigge	Bayern Munich	1996	Matthias Sammer	Borussia Dortmund
1982	Paolo Rossi	Juventus	1997	Ronaldo	Inter Milan
1983	Michel Platini	Juventus	1998	Zinedine Zidane	Juventus
1984	Michel Platini	Juventus	1999	Rivaldo	Barcelona
1985	Michel Platini	Juventus	2000	Luis Figo	Real Madrid
1986	Igor Belanov	Dynamo Kiev	2001	Michael Owen	Liverpool
1987	Ruud Gullit	AC Milan	2002	Ronaldo	Real Madrid
1988	Marco Van Basten	AC Milan	2003	Pavel Nedved	Juventus
1989	Marco Van Basten	AC Milan	2004	Andriy Shevchenko	AC Milan
1990	Lothar Matthaeus	Inter Milan			

African Footballer of the Year

Year	Player	Club	Year	Player	Club
1970	Salif Keita	St. Etienne	1988	Kalusha Bwalya	Cercle Bruges
1971	Ibrahim Sunday	Asante Kotoko	1989	George Weah	Monaco
1972	Chérif Soueymane	Hafia	1990	Roger Milla	St. Denis
1973	Tshimen Bwanga	TP Mazembe	1991	Abedi Pele Ayew	Marseille
1974	Paul Moukila	CARA Brazzaville	1992	Abedi Pele Ayew	Marseille
1975	Ahmed Faras	Mohammedia	1993	Rashidi Yekini	FC Zurich
1976	Roger Milla	Canon Yaounde	1994	George Weah	Paris St. Germain
1977	Tarak Dhiab	Esperance	1995	George Weah	AC Milan
1978	Karim Abdul Razak	Asante Kotoko	1996	Nwankwo Kanu	Inter Milan
1979	Thomas Nkono	Canon Yaounde	1997	Victor Ikpeba	Monaco
1980	Jean Manga Onguene	Canon Yaounde	1998	Mustapha Hadji	Deportivo Coruna
1981	Lakhdar Belloumi	GCR Mascara	1999	Nwankwo Kanu	Arsenal
1982	Thomas Nkono	Espanol	2000	Patrick Mboma	Parma
1983	Mahmoud Al-Khatib	Al Ahli	2001	El Hadji Diouf	Lens
1984	Theophile Abega	Toulouse	2002	El Hadji Diouf	Lens
1985	Mohamed Timoumi	Royal Armed Forces	2003	Samuel Eto'o	Real Mallorca
1986	Badou Ezaki	Real Mallorca	2004	Samuel Eto'o	FC Barcelona
1987	Rabah Madjer	FC Porto			

South American Player of the Year

Year	Player	Club	Year	Player	Club
1971	Tostao	Cruzeiro	1988	Ruben Paz	Racing Buenos Aires
1972	Teofilo Cubillas	Alianza Lima	1989	Bebeto	Vasco da Gama
1973	Pelé	Santos	1990	Raul Amarilla	Olimpia
1974	Elias Figueroa	Internacional	1991	Oscar Ruggeri	Velez Sarsfield
1975	Elias Figueroa	Internacional	1992	Rai	São Paulo
1976	Elias Figueroa	Internacional	1993	Carlos Valderrama	Junior Barranquilla
1977	Zico	Flamengo	1994	Cafu	São Paulo
1978	Mario Kempes	Valencia	1995	Enzo Francescoli	River Plate
1979	Diego Maradona	Argentinos Juniors	1996	Jose-Luis Chilavert	Velez Sarsfield
1980	Diego Maradona	Boca Juniors	1997	Marcelo Salas	River Plate
1981	Zico	Flamengo	1998	Martin Palermo	Boca Juniors
1982	Zico	Flamengo	1999	Javier Saviola	River Plate
1983	Socrates	Corinthians	2000	Romario	Vasco da Gama
1984	Enzo Francescoli	River Plate	2001	Juan Riquelme	Boca Juniors
1985	Julio Cesar Romero	Fluminense	2002	Jose Cardozo	Toluca
1986	Antonio Alzamendi	River Plate	2003	Carlos Tevez	Boca Juniors
1987	Carlos Valderrama	Deportivo Cali	2004	Carlos Tevez	Boca Juniors

International Club Competition

Intercontinental Cup

Competition between winners of European Cup and Libertadores Cup.

1960...Real Madrid, Spain	1964...Inter, Italy	1968...Estudiantes, Argentina
1961...Penarol, Uruguay	1965...Inter, Italy	1969...Milan, Italy
1962...Santos, Brazil	1966...Penarol, Uruguay	1970...Feyenoord, Netherlands
1963...Santos, Brazil	1967...Racing Club, Argentina	1971...Nacional, Uruguay

Intercontinental Cup *(Cont.)*

1972....Ajax Amsterdam, Netherlands	1984...Independiente, Argentina	1996...Juventus, Italy
1973...Independiente, Argentina	1985...Juventus, Italy	1997...Borussia Dortmund, Ger.
1974...Atletico de Madrid, Spain	1986...River Plate, Argentina	1998...Real Madrid, Spain
1975...No tournament	1987...Porto, Portugal	1999...Manchester United, England
1976...Bayern Munich	1988...Nacional, Uruguay	2000...Boca Juniors, Argentina
1977...Boca Juniors, Argentina	1989...Milan, Italy	2001...Bayern Munich, Germany
1978...No tournament	1990...Milan, Italy	2002...Real Madrid, Spain
1979...Olimpia, Paraguay	1991...Red Star Belgrade, Yugos.	2003...Boca Juniors, Argentina
1980...Nacional, Uruguay	1992...São Paulo, Brazil	2004...FC Porto, Portugal
1981...Flamengo, Brazil	1993...São Paulo, Brazil	
1982...Penarol, Uruguay	1994...Velez Sarsfield, Argentina	
1983...Gremio, Brazil	1995...Ajax Amsterdam, Netherlands	

Note: Until 1968 a best-of-three-games format decided the winner. From 1968 to '79: two-game/total-goal format. One-game championship since 1980. The European Cup runner-up substituted for the winner in 1971, 1973, 1974, and 1979.

European Cup (Champions League)

1956...Real Madrid, Spain	1974...Bayern Munich, W Germany	1988...PSV Eindhoven, Netherlands
1957...Real Madrid, Spain		1989...AC Milan, Italy
1958...Real Madrid, Spain	1975...Bayern Munich, W Germany	1990...AC Milan, Italy
1959...Real Madrid, Spain		1991...Red Star Belgrade, Yugoslav.
1960...Real Madrid, Spain	1976...Bayern Munich, W Germany	1992...Barcelona, Spain
1961...Benfica, Portugal		1993...Olympique Marseille, France
1962...Benfica, Portugal	1977...Liverpool, England	1994...AC Milan, Italy
1963...AC Milan, Italy	1978...Liverpool, England	1995...Ajax Amsterdam, Netherlands
1964...Inter-Milan, Italy	1979...Nottingham Forest, England	1996...Juventus, Italy
1965...Inter-Milan, Italy		1997...Borussia Dortmund, Ger.
1966...Real Madrid, Spain	1980...Nottingham Forest, England	1998...Real Madrid, Spain
1967...Celtic, Scotland		1999...Manchester United, England
1968...Manchester United, England	1981...Liverpool, England	
1969...AC Milan, Italy	1982...Aston Villa, England	2000...Real Madrid, Spain
1970...Feyenoord, Netherlands	1983...SV Hamburg, W Germany	2001...Bayern Munich, Germany
1971...Ajax Amsterdam, Netherlands		2002...Real Madrid, Spain
1972...Ajax Amsterdam, Netherlands	1984...Liverpool, England	2003...AC Milan, Italy
1973...Ajax Amsterdam, Netherlands	1985...Juventus, Italy	2004...FC Porto, Portugal
	1986...Steaua Bucharest, Romania	2005...Liverpool, England
	1987...Porto, Portugal	

Note: On four occasions the European Cup winner has refused to play in the Intercontinental Cup and has been replaced by the runner-up: Panathinaikos (Greece) in 1971, Juventus (Italy) in 1973, Atletico Madrid (Spain) in 1974, and Malmo (Sweden) in 1979.

Libertadores Cup

Competition between champion clubs and runners-up of 10 South American National Associations.

1960...Penarol, Uruguay	1976...Cruzeiro, Brazil	1992...São Paulo, Brazil
1961...Penarol, Uruguay	1977...Boca Juniors, Argentina	1993...São Paulo, Brazil
1962...Santos, Brazil	1978...Boca Juniors, Argentina	1994...Velez Sarsfield, Argentina
1963...Santos, Brazil	1979...Olimpia, Paraguay	1995...Gremio, Brazil
1964...Independiente, Argentina	1980...Nacional, Uruguay	1996...River Plate, Argentina
1965...Independiente, Argentina	1981...Flamengo, Brazil	1997...Cruzeiro, Brazil
1966...Penarol, Uruguay	1982...Penarol, Uruguay	1998...Vasco da Gama, Brazil
1967...Racing Club, Argentina	1983...Gremio, Brazil	1999...Palmeiras, Brazil
1968...Estudiantes, Argentina	1984...Independiente, Argentina	2000...Boca Juniors, Argentina
1969...Estudiantes, Argentina	1985...Argentinos Juniors, Arg	2001...Boca Juniors, Argentina
1970...Estudiantes, Argentina	1986...River Plate, Argentina	2002...Olimpia, Paraguay
1971...Nacional, Uruguay	1987...Penarol, Uruguay	2003...Boca Juniors, Argentina
1972...Independiente, Argentina	1988...Nacional, Uruguay	2004...Once Caldas, Colombia
1973...Independiente, Argentina	1989...Atletico Nacional, Colombia	2005...São Paulo, Brazil
1974...Independiente, Argentina	1990...Olimpia, Paraguay	
1975...Independiente, Argentina	1991...Colo Colo, Chile	

UEFA Cup

1958...Barcelona, Spain	1965...Ferencvaros, Hungary	1972...Tottenham Hotspur, England
1959...No tournament	1966...Barcelona, Spain	1973...Liverpool, England
1960...Barcelona, Spain	1967...Dynamo Zagreb, Yugoslav.	1974...Feyenoord, Netherlands
1961...AS Roma, Italy	1968...Leeds United, England	1975...Borussia Monchengladbach, W Germany
1962...Valencia, Spain	1969...Newcastle United, England	
1963...Valencia, Spain	1970...Arsenal, England	1976...Liverpool, England
1964...Real Zaragoza, Spain	1971...Leeds United, England	1977...Juventus, Italy

UEFA Cup (Cont.)

1978...PSV Eindhoven, Netherl.
1979...Borussia Monchengladbach, W Germany
1980...Eintracht Frankfurt, W Germany
1981...Ipswich Town, England
1982...IFK Gothenburg, Sweden
1983...Anderlecht, Belgium
1984...Tottenham Hotspur, England
1985...Real Madrid, Spain
1986...Real Madrid, Spain
1987...IFK Gothenburg, Sweden
1988...Bayer Leverkusen, W Germany
1989...Naples, Italy
1990...Juventus, Italy
1991...Inter-Milan, Italy
1992...Torino, Italy
1993...Juventus, Italy
1994...Internazionale, Italy
1995...Parma, Italy
1996...Bayern Munich, Germany
1997...Schalke 04, Germany
1998...Inter Milan, Italy
1999...Parma, Italy
2000...Galatasaray, Turkey
2001...Liverpool, England
2002...Feyenoord, Netherlands
2003...FC Porto, Portugal
2004...Valencia, Spain
2005...CSKA Moskva, Russia

International Club Competition *(Cont.)*

European Cup-Winners' Cup

1961...AC Fiorentina, Italy
1962...Atletico Madrid, Spain
1963...Tottenham Hotspur, England
1964...Sporting Lisbon, Portugal
1965...West Ham United, England
1966...Borussia Dortmund, W Ger
1967...Bayern Munich, W Germ.
1968...AC Milan, Italy
1969...Slovan Bratislava, Czech.
1970...Manchester City, England
1971...Chelsea, England
1972...Glasgow Rangers, Scotland
1973...AC Milan, Italy
1974...Magdeburg, E Germany
1975...Dynamo Kiev, USSR
1976...Anderlecht, Belgium
1977...SV Hamburg, W Germ.
1978...Anderlecht, Belgium
1979...Barcelona, Spain
1980...Valencia, Spain
1981...Dynamo Tbilisi, USSR
1982...Barcelona, Spain
1983...Aberdeen, Scotland
1984...Juventus, Italy
1985...Everton, England
1986...Dynamo Kiev, USSR
1987...Ajax Amsterdam, Neth.
1988...Mechelen, Belgium
1989...Barcelona, Spain
1990...Sampdoria, Italy
1991...Manchester United, England
1992...Werder Bremen, Germany
1993...Parma, Italy
1994...Arsenal, England
1995...Real Zaragoza, Spain
1996...Paris St. Germain, France
1997...Barcelona, Spain
1998...Chelsea, England
1999...Lazio, Italy

Note: the Cup-Winners Cup was discontinued after 1999.

Major League Soccer

MLS Cup Results

Year	Champion	Score	Runner-up	Regular Season MVP
1996	D.C. United	3–2 (ot)	Los Angeles	Carlos Valderrama, TB
1997	D.C. United	2–1	Colorado	Preki, Kansas City
1998	Chicago	2–0	D.C. United	Marco Etcheverry, D.C.
1999	D.C. United	2–0	Los Angeles	Jason Kreis, Dallas
2000	Kansas City	1–0	Chicago	Tony Meola, Kansas City
2001	San Jose	2–1 (ot)	Los Angeles	Alex Pineda Chacon, Mia
2002	Los Angeles	1–0 (ot)	New England	Carlos Ruiz, Los Angeles
2003	San Jose	4–2	Chicago	Preki, Kansas City
2004	D.C. United	3–2	Kansas City	Amado Guevara, MetroSt

A-League

Year	Champion	Score	Runner-Up	Regular Season MVP
1991	San Francisco	1–3, 2–0 (1–0 on PKs)	Albany	Jean Harbor, Maryland
1992	Colorado	1–0	Tampa Bay	Taifour Diane, Colorado
1993	Colorado	3–1 (OT)	Los Angeles	Taifour Diane, Colorado
1994	Montreal	1–0	Colorado	Paulinho, Los Angeles
1995	Seattle	1–2 (SO), 3–0, 2–1 (SO)	Atlanta	Peter Hattrup, Seattle
1996	Seattle	2–0	Rochester	Wolde Harris, Colorado
1997	Milwaukee	2–1 (SO)	Carolina	Doug Miller, Rochester
1998	Rochester	3–1	Minnesota	Mark Baena, Seattle
1999	Minnesota	2–1	Rochester	John Swallen, Minnesota
2000	Rochester	3–1	Minnesota	Vitalis Takawira, Mil
2001	Rochester	2–0	Vancouver	Paul Conway, Charleston
2002	Milwaukee	2–1 (2 OT)	Richmond	Leighton O'Brien, Seattle
2003	Charleston	3–0	Minnesota	Thiago Martins, Pittsburgh
2004	Montreal	2–0	Seattle	Greg Sutton, Montreal
2005	Seattle	1–1 (4–3 on PKs)	Richmond	Jason Jordan, Vancouver

Woman's United Soccer Association

Founders Cup Results

Year	Champion	Score	Runner-up	Regular Season MVP
2001	Bay Area	3–3 (4–2 PKs)	Atlanta	Tiffeny Milbrett, New York
2002	Carolina	3–2	Washington	Marinette Pichon, Philadelphia
2003	Washington	2–1 (OT)	Atlanta	Maren Meinert, Boston

Note: WUSA suspended operations after the 2003 season.

U.S. Open Cup

Open to all amateur and professional teams in the United States, the annual U.S. Open Cup is the oldest cup competition in the country and among the oldest in the world. The tournament is a single-elimination event running concurrent to the MLS season. The winner advances to the CONCACAF Cup, a tournament of the top club teams from North and Central America and the Caribbean.

Year	Champion	Year	Champion
1914	Brooklyn Field Club (NYC)	1961	Ukrainian Nationals (Philadelphia)
1915	Bethlehem Steel FC (PA)	1962	New York Hungaria (NYC)
1916	Bethlehem Steel FC (PA)	1963	Ukrainian Nationals (Philadelphia)
1917	Fall River Rovers (MA)	1964	Los Angeles Kickers (CA)
1918	Bethlehem Steel FC (PA)	1965	New York Hungaria (NYC)
1919	Bethlehem Steel FC (PA)	1966	Ukrainian Nationals (Philadelphia)
1920	Ben Miller FC (St. Louis)	1967	Greek American AA (NYC)
1921	Robbins Dry Dock FC (Brooklyn)	1968	Greek American AA (NYC)
1922	Scullin Steel FC (St. Louis)	1969	Greek American AA (NYC)
1923	Paterson FC (NJ)	1970	Elizabeth SC (Union, NJ)
1924	Fall River FC (MA)	1971	Hota SC (NYC)
1925	Shawsheen FC (Andover, MA)	1972	Elizabeth SC (Union, NJ)
1926	Bethlehem Steel FC (PA)	1973	Maccabee SC (Los Angeles)
1927	Fall River FC (MA)	1974	Greek American AA (NYC)
1928	New York National FC (NYC)	1975	Maccabee SC (Los Angeles)
1929	Hakoah All Star SC (NYC)	1976	San Francisco AC (CA)
1930	Fall River FC (MA)	1977	Maccabee SC (Los Angeles)
1931	Fall River FC (MA)	1978	Maccabee SC (Los Angeles)
1932	New Bedford FC (MA)	1979	Brooklyn Dodgers SC (NYC)
1933	Stix, Baer and Fuller FC (St. Louis)	1980	NY Pancyprian-Freedoms (NYC)
1934	Stix, Baer and Fuller FC (St. Louis)	1981	Maccabee SC (Los Angeles)
1935	Central Breweries FC (Chicago)	1982	NY Pancyprian-Freedoms (NYC)
1936	German-Americans (Philadelphia)	1983	NY Pancyprian-Freedoms (NYC)
1937	New York American FC (NYC)	1984	AO Krete (NYC)
1938	Sparta A and BA (Chicago)	1985	Greek American AC (San Francisco)
1939	St. Mary's Celtic SC (Brooklyn)	1986	Kutis SC (St. Louis)
1940	—	1987	Club Espana (Washington, D.C.)
1941	Pawtucket FC (RI)	1988	Busch SC (St. Louis)
1942	Gallatin SC (PA)	1989	HRC Kickers (St. Petersburg, FL)
1943	Brooklyn Hispano SC (NYC)	1990	AAC Eagles (Chicago)
1944	Brooklyn Hispano SC (NYC)	1991	Brooklyn Italians SC (East NY)
1945	Brookhattan FC (NYC)	1992	San Jose Oaks (CA)
1946	Chicago Viking FC (IL)	1993	Club Deportivo Mexico (San Francisco)
1947	Ponta Delgada SC (Fall River, MA)	1994	Greek American AC (San Francisco)
1948	Simpkins-Ford SC (St. Louis)	1995	Richmond Kickers (VA)
1949	Morgan SC (PA)	1996	D.C. United (MLS)
1950	Simpkins-Ford SC (St. Louis)	1997	Dallas Burn (MLS)
1951	German Hungarian SC (NYC)	1998	Chicago Fire (MLS)
1952	Harmarville SC (PA)	1999	Rochester Rhinos (A-League)
1953	Falcons SC (Chicago)	2000	Chicago Fire (MLS)
1954	New York Americans (NYC)	2001	Los Angeles Galaxy (MLS)
1955	Eintracht Sport Club (NYC)	2002	Columbus Crew (MLS)
1956	Harmarville SC (PA)	2003	Chicago Fire (MLS)
1957	Kutis SC (St. Louis)	2004	Kansas City Wizards (MLS)
1958	Los Angeles Kickers (CA)	2005	Los Angeles Galaxy (MLS)
1959	McIlvaine Canvasbacks (Los Angeles)		
1960	Ukrainian Nationals (Philadelphia)		

North American Soccer League

Formed in 1968 by the merger of the National Professional Soccer League and the USA League, both of which had begun operations a year earlier. The NPSL's lone champion was the Oakland Clippers. The USA League, which brought entire teams in from Europe, was won in 1967 by the L.A. Wolves, who were the English League's Wolverhampton Wanderers.

Year	Champion	Score	Runner-Up	Regular Season MVP
1968	Atlanta	0–0, 3–0	San Diego	John Kowalik, Chi
1969	Kansas City	No game	Atlanta	Cirilio Fernandez, KC
1970	Rochester	3–0,1–3	Washington	Carlos Metidieri, Roch
1971	Dallas	1–2, 4–1, 2–0	Atlanta	Carlos Metidieri, Roch
1972	New York	2–1	St. Louis	Randy Horton, NY
1973	Philadelphia	2–0	Dallas	Warren Archibald, Mia
1974	Los Angeles	4–3*	Miami	Peter Silvester, Balt
1975	Tampa Bay	2–0	Portland	Steve David, Mia
1976	Toronto	3–0	Minnesota	Pelé, NY
1977	New York	2–1	Seattle	Franz Beckenbauer, NY
1978	New York	3–1	Tampa Bay	Mike Flanagan, NE
1979	Vancouver	2–1	Tampa Bay	Johan Cruyff, LA
1980	New York	3–0	Ft. Lauderdale	Roger Davies, Sea
1981	Chicago	1–0*	New York	Giorgio Chinaglia, NY
1982	New York	1–0	Seattle	Peter Ward, Sea
1983	Tulsa	2–0	Toronto	Roberto Cabanas, NY
1984	Chicago	2–1, 3–2	Toronto	Steve Zungul, SJ

*Shootout.

Championship Format: 1968 and 1970: Two games/total goals. 1971 and 1984: Best-of-three series. 1972–1983: One-game championship. Title in 1969 went to the regular-season champion.

Statistical Leaders

SCORING

Year	Player/Team	Pts	Year	Player/Team	Pts
1968	John Kowalik, Chi	69	1977	Steven David, LA	58
1969	Kaiser Motaung, Atl	36	1978	Giorgio Chinaglia, NY	79
1970	Kirk Apostolidis, Dall	35	1979	Oscar Fabbiani, Tampa Bay	58
1971	Carlos Metidieri, Roch	46	1980	Giorgio Chinaglia, NY	77
1972	Randy Horton, NY	22	1981	Giorgio Chinaglia, NY	74
1973	Kyle Rote, Dall	30	1982	Giorgio Chinaglia, NY	55
1974	Paul Child, San Jose	36	1983	Roberto Cabanas, NY	66
1975	Steven David, Miami	52	1984	Slavisa Zungul, Golden Bay	50
1976	Giorgio Chinaglia, NY	49			

Brandi Gets The Boot

Brandi Chastain may be a step slower than she was in her prime, her footwork less nimble, but the resolve that served her so well over 13 years with the U.S. women's soccer team is undiminished. "No," was Chastain's answer when she was asked on June 22 if she was retired from international competition. Never mind that earlier that day, coach Greg Ryan said he had cut the 36-year-old from the national team. Ryan, who took over as coach two months ago, added, "What I'm looking for in future defenders are qualities that she doesn't possess at this point."

Unlike former teammates Mia Hamm, Julie Foudy and Joy Fawcett, all of whom gracefully stepped aside after the U.S.'s gold medal performance at the 2004 Olympics, Chastain has no desire to retire. But the end of her storied career--three Olympics, three World Cups, one famous shirtless celebration--has been in sight for a while. She briefly lost her starting job to Cat Reddick, 23, in Athens and hasn't played for the national team since last December. Meanwhile Ryan has overhauled half the roster since the conclusion of last year's Olympics. Still, Chastain, who plays for the California Storm of the Women's Premier Soccer League, refused to close the door on her international career. "Giving up is the easiest way," she told the San Francisco Chronicle. "But I don't want the easy way."
—*Mark Bechtel & Stephen Cannella*

NCAA Sports

Men's NCAA Div. I
soccer champions
Indiana University

Show Stoppers

NCAA's soccer, hockey and baseball finals reaffirmed an old adage: Defense wins championships

BY HANK HERSCH

The heroes of the 2004–05 NCAA finals had something in common: Each had the most panoramic view of the action during his team's march to the title. Thanks to the man between the pipes, or in the net, or behind the plate, the more storied programs prevailed in all three finals, proving not merely that defense wins championships—the last line of defense does.

MEN'S SOCCER
After 110 blistering minutes, the Men's College Cup in Carson, Calif., had played to a 1–1 draw and would have to be decided by penalty kicks. Indiana goalkeeper Jay Nolly had been under siege for most of the second half and 20 minutes of overtime, but he stoned the fourth of UC Santa Barbara's five penalty kicks, shot by All-America defender Tony Lochhead. Now he faced down midfielder Nate Boyden with a chance to clinch back-to-back titles for the Hoosiers. "I never really look at the [shooter's] moves," said Nolly, a senior from Lit-

tleton, Colo. "My focus is on the ball. There's a few tendencies that strikers do that give away a few things—how they line up, how they stand. I get a read right away on what I'm going to do and commit fully."

The prolonged showdown at the Home Depot Center only extended a battle between the two sides that had been bitterly joined three months earlier. After the Gauchos defeated Indiana 1–0 in September to snap the champ's 23-game unbeaten streak, first-year Hoosiers coach Mike Freitag assailed UCSB's hard-charging tactics, saying that the Gauchos displayed a "lack of class" and that it was "just a shame that a team like that is ranked number one."

Freitag's barbs hardly fazed UCSB coach Tim Vom Steeg, who over six years had built the program in his own combative image. When he arrived the Gauchos had just completed a 2-17-1 season and had posted only one winning record in eight years. Vom Steeg cut 18 of 24 players, recruited blue-collar bruisers more than willing to tackle and, in 2001, landed blue-chip keeper Dan

On the way to the title, Denver goalie Peter Mannino gave up only 5 goals in his final 6 games.

Kennedy. Net result: The Gauchos finished the regular season with the top ranking and a 17-2-1 mark, reaching their first NCAA finals after two straight tournament appearances.

To win, though, the upstarts would have to dethrone the nation's most successful program. Five-time champion Indiana had barely missed a beat under Freitag, who, after 11 years as an assistant, took over for founding coach Jerry Yeagley. Freitag's troops took the finals lead in the 27th minute, when forward Jacob Peterson poked a looping shot past Kennedy. Nolly preserved that edge until forward Drew McAthy, the Cup's offensive MVP, banged home a rebound with nine minutes left in regulation.

Entering penalty kicks, Vom Steeg replaced the 6'1" Kennedy with 6'3" sophomore Kyle Reynish, who stopped a pair of Indiana attempts. But after UCSB striker Neil Jones put his shot over the crossbar, Nolly thwarted Lochhead by diving right. Then he dived left to stop midfielder Nate Boyden, clinching Indiana's 3–2 triumph on penalties as well as the defensive MVP award. "It feels kind of weird," Freitag said. "As the assistant coach, I'd be running around like crazy. But I'm not overly excited now. It was meant to be, I think."

MEN'S HOCKEY

The feelings in the North Dakota locker room after the championship game ranged from incredulousness to bitterness to shock. It wasn't that the Fighting Sioux had fallen by the lopsided score of 4–1. Or that Denver had prevailed before a near-sellout crowd in Columbus, Ohio, despite starting four freshmen. Or that they had bowed to their Western Collegiate Hockey Associa-

tion rival for the fifth time in a row and in a second straight final.

No, what stunned the UND players were the shots totals: They'd fired 45 on goal to the Pioneers' 24. "I thought we deserved to win that game," said Fighting Sioux defenseman Nick Fuher. "We played hard, we got 45 shots on goal. How do you expect not to win when you get 45 shots on goal?"

The source of Fuher's consternation? One of those Denver freshmen. Two nights after Peter Mannino Jr. stopped 41 Colorado College shots in a 6–2 national semifinal win, he thwarted a career-high 44 to lift the Pioneers to their seventh national championship, second only to Michigan's 9 titles. North Dakota fired 23 shots on Mannino in the third period alone to tie a 50-year-old Frozen Four record, going with a man-advantage for the final two minutes after pulling its goalie.

None of those volleys slipped past Mannino, the son of a produce deliveryman from Farmington Hills, Mich. "He made an awful lot of good saves," said losing coach Dave Hakstol. "That's the one factor you can't control in a hockey game—how the guy wearing the pads at the other end is going to play."

"My team allowed me to see the puck," said Mannino, who surrendered only five

PETER AIKEN/WIREIMAGE.COM

goals in his final six games. "When there were rebounds, they cleaned them right away."

Mannino's classmate Peter Stastny, meanwhile, took care of the offense. The son and namesake of the NHL Hall of Famer, he scored his first goal to snap a 1–1 tie midway through the second period, deflecting a slap shot from the right circle by Kevin Ulanski. "It hit me in the, um, butt," Stastny offered. He gave Denver a 3–1 cushion with a second power-play goal 8:19 into the third, blasting a one-timer past the Fighting Sioux's star goalie, Jordan Parise.

Mannino did the rest. "I didn't really feel any pressure because you dream about being in a situation like this your entire life," he said, "Things just clicked."

BASEBALL

Once more the championship series in Omaha was over, and once more Taylor Teagarden had disappeared. A year earlier, the Texas catcher was on the Longhorn team that failed to show at the second-place trophy presentation following a sweep by Cal State Fullerton. (He said it was a mixup.) And when the 2005 CWS ended, Teagarden was again nowhere to be seen—only this time he was at the bottom of a dogpile at Rosenblatt Stadium field after catching the final strike in a clinching 6–2 victory over Florida. "This is the best thing that ever happened to me," Teagarden said. "This team will be remembered forever. We stamped our name on history today."

The Longhorns' style certainly made a memorable impression. Despite scoring only 24 runs—tying Fullerton for the lowest output by a national champion since 1993—they went 5–0 at Omaha by combining tight defense and timely hitting with overpowering pitching. Their ERA in the CWS was 1.40, and the 1.6 runs they allowed per game was the second-fewest by a titlist since the introduction of aluminum bats in 1974. Much of the credit for the hurlers' success went to Teagarden, a junior who had recovered from a rib cage injury that sidelined him during the Big 12 tournament. "He means so much," said pitching coach Tom Holliday. "When he was healthy our staff took off."

Teagarden set the tone at the plate as well as behind it. After beating Florida 4–2 in the best-of-three series opener, Texas grabbed a 1–0 lead in the second inning of Game 2 after Teagarden's sacrifice bunt—the team's 10th in five games—set up a run-scoring single by third baseman David Maroul. Using small-ball to take an early advantage and ratchet up the pressure is typical of the Longhorns' Augie Garrido. "It's all about momentum," said Garrido, 66, the winningest coach in Division I history.

Maroul, the No. 8 hitter, kept it up, contributing a long ball and four RBIs; he was named Most Outstanding Player after batting .500 in the series. A four-run sixth inning was more than enough offense for sophomore righthander Kyle McCulloch, who struck out eight and allowed two runs in 6 2/3 innings. When Teagarden squeezed the final pitch from junior stopper J. Brent Cox, Texas had its sixth national championship, second only to USC's 12.

"Last year we had the better team," said Teagarden, who like all but one of the Longhorns taking field in the finals, hails from Texas. "I still think that. But it doesn't matter what you think. It's about coming into a situation and performing."

NCAA Team Champions

Fall 2004

			Champion	Runner-Up
Cross-Country	MEN	Division I:	Colorado	Wisconsin
		Division II:	Western State	Adams State
		Division III:	Calvin	North Central College
	WOMEN	Division I:	Colorado	Duke
		Division II:	Adams St	Edinboro
		Division III:	Williams	Middlebury
Field Hockey	WOMEN	Division I:	Wake Forest	Duke
		Division II	Bloomsburg	UMass–Lowell
		Division III:	Salisbury	Middlebury
Football	MEN	Division I-AA:	James Madison	Montana
		Division II:	Valdosta State	Pittsburg State
		Division III:	Linfield College	Mary Hardin -Baylo
Soccer	MEN	Division I:	Indiana	UC–Santa Barbara
		Division II:	Seattle	SIU-Edwardsville
		Division III:	Messiah	UC–Santa Cruz
	WOMEN	Division I:	Notre Dame	UCLA
		Division II:	Metro State	Adelphi
		Division III:	Wheaton	Puget Sound
Volleyball	WOMEN	Division I:	Standford	Minnesota
		Division II:	Barry	Truman State
		Division III:	Juniata	Washington University
Water Polo	MEN		UCLA	Stanford

Oh, they often call me Speedo

A Speedo is a good gag gift, but the Auburn men's swimming team wasn't playing around when they presented one of the itsy-bitsy swimsuits to President George W. Bush at a White House reception for 15 NCAA championship teams. "We think of it as normal, everyday attire," said Auburn captain B.J. Jones, "so we didn't register the comedy until he said, 'I won't be wearing this--in public, that is.'" Bush also got a surfboard (which he dubbed "Surfboard One") from the Pepperdine men's volleyball team and a personalized helmet from the Johns Hopkins lacrosse squad.

—*Adam Duerson*

Winter 2004-2005

			Champion	Runner-Up
Basketball	MEN	Division I:	North Carolina	Illinois
		Division II:	Virginia Union	Bryant
		Division III:	WI-Stevens Point	Rochester
	WOMEN	Division I:	Baylor	Michigan State
		Division II:	Wasburn	Seattle Pacific
		Division III:	Millikin	Randolph-Macon
Fencing			Notre Dame	Ohio State
Gymnastics	MEN		Oklahoma	Ohio State
	WOMEN		Georgia	Alabama
Ice Hockey	MEN	Division I:	Denver	North Dakota
		Division III:	Middlebury	St. Thomas
	WOMEN	Division I:	Harvard	Minnesota
		Division III:	Middlebury	Elmira
Rifle			Army	AK-Fairbanks
Skiing			Denver	Vermont
Swimming and Diving	MEN	Division I:	Auburn	Standford
		Division II:	Drury	CSU–Bakersfield
		Division III:	Kenyon	Emory
	WOMEN	Division I:	Georgia	Auburn
		Division II:	Truman St	Drury
		Division III:	Emory	Kenyon
Wrestling	MEN	Division I:	Oklahoma St	Michigan
		Division II:	Nebraska–Omaha	Augustana
		Division III:	Augsburg	Wartburg
Indoor Track and Field	MEN	Division I:	Arkansas	Wisconsin
		Division II:	Abilene	Adams State
		Division III:	WI-La Crosse	Lincoln University
	WOMEN	Division I:	Tennessee	Florida
		Division II:	St. Augustine	Abilene Christian
		Division III:	WI-Oshkosh	Wartburg

Spring 2005

			Champion	Runner-Up
Baseball		Division I:	Texas	Florida
		Division II:	Mocs	North Florida
		Division III:	WI-Whitewater	Cortland St
Golf	MEN	Division I:	Georgia	Georgia Tech
		Division II:	USC Aiken	Armstrong Atlantic
		Division III:	Guilford College	Redlands
	WOMEN	Division I:	Duke	UCLA
		Division II:	Rollins College	Grand Valley
		Division III	Methodist	Mary Hardin-Baylor
Lacrosse	MEN	Division I:	John Hopkins	Duke
		Division II:	NYIT	Limestone College
		Division III:	Salisbury	Middlebury
	WOMEN	Division I:	Northwestern	Virginia
		Division II	Stonehill	West Chester
		Division III:	College of New Jersey	Salisbury
Rowing	WOMEN	Division I:	California	Virginia
		Division II	Western Washington	Mercyhurst
		Division III:	Ithaca	Smith

Spring 2005 (Cont.)

			Champion	Runner-Up
Softball		Division I:	Michigan	UCLA
		Division II:	Lynn University	Kennesaw State
		Division III:	St. Thomas	Salisbury
Tennis	MEN	Division I:	UCLA	Baylor
		Division II:	W Florida	North Florida
		Division III:	UC Santa Cruz	Middlebury
	WOMEN	Division I:	Stanford	Texas
		Division II:	Armstrong Atlantic	BYU-Hawaii
		Division III:	Emory	Washington & Lee
Outdoor Track and Field	MEN	Division I:	Arkansas	Florida
		Division II:	Abilene Christian	Adams State
		Division III:	Lincoln	WI–La Crosse
	WOMEN	Division I:	Texas	UCLA/South Carolina
		Division II:	Lincoln	Cal State Bakersfield
		Division III:	Wartburg	Calvin/WI-Oshkosh
Volleyball			Pepperdine	UCLA
Water Polo	WOMEN		UCLA	Stanford

NCAA Division I Individual Champions

Fall 2004
Cross Country
MEN

Champion	Runner-Up
Simon Bairu, Wisconsin	Matt Gonzales, New Mexico

WOMEN

Champion	Runner-Up
Shalane Flanagan, N Carolina	Kim Smith, Providence

Winter 2004–2005
Fencing
MEN

	Champion	Runner-Up
Sabre	Sergey Isayenko, St. John's	Patrick Ghattas, Notre Dame
Foil	Boaz Ellis, Ohio St	Gabriel Sinkin, NYU
Épée	Michael Sobieraj, Notre Dame	Marek Petraszek, Wayne St. (MI)

WOMEN

	Champion	Runner-Up
Sabre	Emily Jacobso, Barnard	Mariel Zagunis, Notre Dame
Foil	Emily Cross, Harvard	Alicja Kryczalo, Notre Dame
Épée	Anna Garina, Wayne St	Elizabeth Midgley, Barnard

Gymnastics
MEN

	Champion	Runner-Up
All-around	Luis Vargas, Penn St	Randy Monahan, Ohio St
Vault	Michael Reavis, Iowa	Guillermo Alvarezo, Minnesota
Parallel bars	Justin Springs, Illinois	DJ Bucher, Ohio St
Horizontal bar	Ronald Ferris, Ohio St	Justin Spring, Illinois
		Graham Ackerman, California
Floor exercise	Graham Ackerman, California	Michael McNamara, Iowa
Pommel horse	Luis Vargas, Penn St	Guillermo Alvarezo, Minnesota
Rings	David Henderson, Oklahoma	Brian Lee, Army

Winter 2004-2005 (Cont.)

Gymnastics (Cont.)

WOMEN

	Champion	Runner-Up
All-around	Katie Heenan, Georgia	Kristen Maloney, UCLA
Balance beam	Kristen Maloney, UCLA	Kristen Esposito, Nebraska
Uneven bars	Terin Humphrey, Alabama	Kelsey Ericksen, Georgia
Floor exercise	Courtney Bumpers, N. Carolina	Ashley Miles, Alabama
Vault	Kristen Maloney, UCLA	Janet Anson, Iowa St

Skiing

MEN

	Champion	Runner-Up
Slalom	David Chodounsky, Dartmouth	John Rusten, Middlebury
Giant slalom	Grey Hardy, Vermont	Warner Nickerson, Colby
10-kilometer classic	Rene Reisshauser, Denver	John Stene, Denver
20-kilometer free	Rene Reisshauser, Denver	Erling Christiansen, Colorado

WOMEN

	Champion	Runner-Up
Slalom	Megan Hughes, Middlebury	Tiina Salo, Nevada
Giant slalom	Jamie Kingsbury, Vermont	Abbi B Lathrop, Colby
5-kilometer classic	Mandy Kaempf, AK-Anchorage	Lindsay Williams, Michigan
15-kilometer free	Many Kaempf, AK-Anchorage	Nicole Deyoung, AK-Anchorage

Wrestling

	Champion	Runner-Up
125 lb	Joe Dubuque, Indiana	Kyle Ott, Illinois
133 lb	Travis Lee, Cornell	Shawn Bunch, Edinboro
141 lb	Teyon Ware, Oklahoma	Nate Gallick, Iowa St
149 lb	Zack Esposito, Oklahoma	Phillip Simpson, Army
157 lb	Ryan Bertin, Michigan	Jo Johnson, Iowa
165 lb	Johnny Hendricks, Oklahoma St	Mark Perry, Iowa
174 lb	Chris Pendleton, Oklahoma St	Ben Askren, Missouri
184 lb	Greg Jones, W Virginia	Tyler Baier, Cornell
197 lb	Jake Rosholt, Oklahoma St.	Sean Stander, Northern Iowa
HWT	Steve Moco, Oklahoma	Cole Konrad, Minnesota

Swimming and Diving

MEN

	Champion	Time	Runner-Up	Time
50-yd freestyle	Fred Bousquet, Auburn	18.90**	Duje Draganja, California	19.01
100-yd freestyle	Duje Draganja, California	41.49**	Fred Bousquet, Auburn	42.19
200-yd freestyle	Duje Draganja, California	1:15.78	Ryan Wochomurka, Auburn	1:16
500-yd freestyle	Peter Vanderkaay, Michigan	4:09.82	Tyler Deberry, Arizona	4:14.35
1650-yd freestyle	Larsen Jensen, Southern Cal	14:32.01	PeterVanderkaay, Michigan	14:36.54
100-yd backstroke	Matt Grevers, Northwestern	45.52	Ryan Lochte, Florida	45.65
200-yd backstroke	Ryan Lochete,Florida	1:38.37**	Van Wie Doug, Auburn	1:41.24
100-yd breaststroke	Gary Marshall, Stanford	52.68	Mihaly Flaskay, Southern Cal	52.92
200-yd breaststroke	Vladislav Polyakovi, Alabama	1:53.93	Mike Alexandrov, Northwestern	1:54.04
100-yd butterfly	Duje Draganja, California	45.39	Daniel Ditoro, Texas	46.18
200-yd butterfly	Davis Tarwater, Michigan	1:42.30	Rainer Kendrick, Texas	1:43.97
200- IM	Ryan Lochte, Florida	1:41.71**	Eric Shanteau , Auburn	1:44.15
400-m IM	Ousama Melloui, Southern Cal	3:39.19	Robert Margalis, Georgia	3:39.93

	Champion	Pts	Runner-Up	Pts
1-meter diving	Joona Puhakka, Arizona	421.05	Chris Colwill, Georgia	387.45
3-meter diving	Miguel Velazovez, Miami	211.15	Joona Puhakku, Arizona	205.85
Platform	Matthew Bricker, Auburn	604.35	Steve Segerlin, Auburn	555.65

†World record. #American record. *NCAA record.

Winter 2004-2005(Cont.)
Swimming and Diving (Cont.)

WOMEN

	Champion	Time	Runner-Up	Time
50-yd freestyle	Kara Lynn Joyce, Georgia	21.94	Sarah Wanezek, Texas	22.27
100-yd freestyle	Kara Lynn Joyce, Georgia	53.15	Lacey Nymeyer, Arizona	48.56
200-yd freestyle	Margaret Hoelzer, Auburn	1:44.60	Amanda Weir, Georgia	1:45.07
500-yd freestyle	Emily Mason, Arizona	4:37.11	Caroline Burckle, Florida	4:38.89
1650-yd freestyle	Flavia Rigamonti, SMU	15:46.84	Hayley Peirsol, Auburn	15:52.48
100-yd backstroke	Marshi Smith, Arizona	52.82	Margaret Hoelzer, Auburn	52.99
200-yd backstroke	Kirsty Coventry, Auburn	1.50.54	Margaret Hoelzer, Auburn	1:52.14
100-yd breaststroke	Caroline Bruce, Stanford	1:00.69	Lindsey Ertter, Georgia	59.85
200-yd breaststroke	Caroline Bruce, Stanford	2:08.67	Anne Poleska, Alabama,	2:09.63
100-yd butterfly	Mary Descenza, Georgia	52.11	Whitney Myers, Arizona	52.74
200-yd butterfly	Mary Descenza, Georgia	1:54.19	Emily Mason, Arizona	1:54.79
200-yd IM	Kristy Coventry, Auburn	1:54.37	Whitney Myers, Arizona	1:56.43
400-yd IM	Kristy Coventry, Auburn	4:09.69	Emily Mason, Arizona	4:08.09

	Champion	Pts	Runner-Up	Pts
1-meter diving	Qiong Jie Huang, Hawaii	327.00	Blythe Hartley, Southern Cal	324.00
3-meter diving	Blythe Hartley, Southern Cal	586.15	Nancilea Underwood, Iowa	561.85
Platform	Cassandra Cardinell, Indiana	501.45	Anna Kiess, Houston	478.95

† World record. #American record. *NCAA record.

Indoor Track and Field

MEN

	Champion	Time/Mark	Runner-Up	Time/Mark
60-meter dash	DaBryan Blanton, Oklahoma	6.58	Dusty Stamer, Nebraska	6.62
60-meter hurdles	Antwon Hicks, Mississippi	7.64	Josh Walkerm Florida	7.66
200-meter dash	Wallace Spearmon, Arkansas	20.10	Walter Dix, Florida St	20.37
400-meter dash	Kerron Clement, Florida	44.57	Terry Gatson, Arkansas	45.29
800-meter run	Kevin Hicks, Florida A&M	1:46.97	James Hatch, Arkansas	1:47.40
Mile run	Nick Willis, Michigan	4:00.69	Sean Jefferson, Indiana	4:01.56
3,000-meter run	Chris Solinsky, Wisconsin	7:53.59	Peter Kosgei, Arkansas	7:54.45
5,000-meter run	Ian Dobson, Stanford	13:43.36	Robert Cheseret, Arizona	13:44.51
High jump	Jesse Williams, Southern Cal	2.26m	Dusty Jones, Nebraska	2.23m
Pole vault	Tommy Skipper, Oregon	5.60m	Ray Scotten, Nebraska	5.50m
Long jump	Aarik Wilson, Indiana	8.17m	Trevell Quinley, Arizona St	7.92m
Triple jump	Aarik Wilson, Indiana	16.92m	Rodrigo Mendes, Indiana	16.61m
Shot put	Edis Elkasevic, Auburn	19.69m	Nedzad Mulabegovic, Purdue	19.67m
35-pound wt throw	Spyridon Jullien, Virginia Tech	23.18m	Cory Martin, Auburn	22.16m

WOMEN

	Champion	Time/Mark	Runner-Up	Time/Mark
60-meter dash	Fana Ashby, Auburn	7.18	Toyin Olupona, Tennessee	7.24
60-meter hurdles	Virginia Powell, Southern Cal	7.97	Priscilla Lopes, Nebraska	7.99
200-meter dash	Tremedia Brice, Texas So	22.90	Fana Ashby, Auburn	22.91
400-meter dash	Tiandra Ponteen, Florida	50.91	Hazel Ann Regis, LSU	50.92
800-meter run	Aneita Denton, Arkansa	2:03.65	Neisha Bernard Thomas, LSU	2:03.93
Mile run	Anne Shadle, Nebraska	4:38.23	Shannon Rowbury, Duke	4:39.02
3,000-meter run	Renee Metivier, Colorado	9.22.81	Adriana Pirtea, Texas	9.23.58
5,000-meter run	Ida Nilsson, Arizona	15:50.20	Caroline Bierbaum, Columbia	15:52.53
High jump	Chaunte Howard, Georgia Tech	1.92m	Gaelle Niare, Southern Methodist	1.92m
Pole vault	Amy Linnen, Kansas	4.30m	Kate Soma, Washington	4.30m
Long jump	Tianna Madison, Tennessee	6.78m	Marashevet Hooker, Texas	6.56m
Triple jump	Gisele Oliveira, Clemson	13.76m	Erica McLain, Stanford	13.62m
Shot put	Kimberli Barrett, Miami	18.10m	Michelle Carter, Texas	17.86m
20-pound wt throw	Candice Scott, Florida	24.17m	Loree Smith, Colorado St	22.65m

*NCAA record.

Rifle

	Champion	Pts	Runner-Up	Pts
Smallbore	Matthew Rawlings, AK-Fairbanks	101.5	Jamie Beyerle, AK-Fairbanks	98.5
Air rifle	Beth Tidmore, Memphis	104.2	Andrea Franzen, Nebraska	101.4

*NCAA record.

Spring 2005
Golf

MEN

Champion	Score	Runner-Up	Score
James Lepp, Washington	276	Michael Putnam, Pepperdine	276

WOMEN

Anna Grzebien, Duke	286	Leah Wigger, Virginia	287

Outdoor Track and Field

MEN

	Champion	Mark	Runner-Up	Mark
100-meter dash	Walter Dix, Florida St	10.21	Wes Felix, So. Cal	10.25
200-meter dash	Wallace Spearmon, Arkansas	19.91	Xavier Carter, LSU	20.08
400-meter dash	Darold Williamson, Baylor	44.51	Jamel Ashley, Miss St	44.75
800-meter run	Dmitrijs Milkevics, Nebraska	1:44.74	Kevin Hicks, Florida A&M	1:44.94
1,500-meter run	Leonel Manzano, Texas	3:37.13	Bryan Lindsay, Brigham Young	3:38.31
5,000-meter run	Ryan Hall, Stanford	13:22.32	Ian Dobson, Stanford	13:22.54
10,000-meter run	Robert Cheseret Arizona	28:20.11	Galen Rupp, Oregon	28:23.75
110-meter hurdles	Josh Walker, Florida	13.39	Antwon Hicks, Mississippi	13.42
400-meter hurdles	Kerron Clement, Florida	47.56	Bennie Brazell, LSU	47.67
3,000-m steeple	Mircea Bogdan, Texas	8:27.29	Peter Kosgei, Arkansas	8:29.13
High jump	Jesse Williams, Southern Cal	2.29m	Mickael Hanany, UT-El-Paso	2.26m
Pole vault	Robison Pratt, Brigham Young	5.50m	Brian Mondschein, Virginia Tech	5.40m
Long jump	Fabrice Lapierre, Texas A&M	8.15m	Oliver Koenig, Iowa St	8.00m
Triple jump	Rodrigo Mendes, BYU	17.04m	Allen Simms, USC	17.03m
Shot put	Edis Elkasevi, Auburn	20.88m	Sheldon Battle, Kansas	20.30m
Discus throw	Michael Robertson, Stanford	61.70m	Vikas Gowda, N Carolina	60.08m
Hammer throw	Spyridon Jullien, Virginia Tech	70.43m	Mattias Jons, Boise St	68.87m
Javelin throw	Gabriel Wallin, Boise St	78.76m	Trevor Snyder, Georgia	76.03m
Decathlon	Trey Hardee, Texas	7,881 pts	Mustafa Abdur Rahim, Dartmouth	7,739 pts

WOMEN

	Champion	Mark	Runner-Up	Mark
100-meter dash	Marshevet Hooker, Texas	11.16	Cleo Tyson, Tennessee	11.29
200-meter dash	Sheri Ann Brooks, Fla Intn'l	22.85	Shalonda Solomon, S. Carolina	22.86
400-meter dash	Monique Henderson, UCLA	50.10	Tiandra Ponteen, So Florida	50.83
800-meter run	Aneita Denton, Arkansas	2:02.84	Maggie Vessey, Cal Poly-SLO	2:03.10
1,500-meter run	Anne Shadle, Nebraska	4:11.37	Johanna Nilson, N. Arizona	4:13.36
5,000-meter run	Megan Metcalfe, West Virginia	16:31.88	Sara Bei, Stanford	16:32.42
10,000-meter run	Sara Slattery, Colorado	33:02.21	Caroline Bierbaum, Columbia	33:03.37
100-meter hurdles	Virginia Powell, Southern Cal	12.80	Priscilla Lopes, Nebraska	12.82
400-meter hurdles	Shauna Smith, Wyoming	54.32	Shevon Stoddart, South Carolina	54.47
3,000-m steeple	Victoria Mitchell, Butler	9:54.32	Cassie Hunt, Illinois	9:59.82
High jump	Sharon Day, Cal-Poly SLO	1.93m	Chaunte Howard, Georgia Tech	1.86m
Pole vault	Kate Soma, Washington	4.30m	Shayla Balentine, San Diego	4.30m
Long jump	Tianna Madison, Tennessee	6.66m	Marshevet Hooker, Texas	6.60m
Triple jump	Candice Baucham, UCLA	14.07m	Gisele Oliveira, Clemson	13.73m
Shot put	Kimberli Barrett, Miami	18.20m	Michelle Carter, Texas	17.06m
Discus throw	Beth Mallory, Alabama	59.35m	Rachel Longfors, Florida	57.03m
Hammer throw	Loree Smith, Colorado	68.47m	Jenny Dahlgren, Georgia	66.72m
Javelin throw	Dana Pounds, Air Force	56.48m	Sarah Malone, Oregon	51.61m
Heptathlon	Lela V. Nelson, E. Michigan	5,878 pts	Jessica Stockard, Georgia	5,794 pts

Tennis

MEN

	Champion	Score	Runner-Up
Singles	B. Dorsch, Baylor	6-2, 7-6 (6)	B. Kohloeffel, UCLA
Doubles	Alberto Francis/Kris Kwinta UCLA	7-6 (4), 7-5	Michael Kokta, Lars Poerschke, Baylor

WOMEN

	Champion	Score	Runner-Up
Singles	Zuzana Zemenova, Georgia	7-5, 6-4	Audra Cohen, Northwestern
Doubles	Alice Barnes/Erin Burdette Stanford	6-3, 6-4	Amber Liu/Anne Yelsey Staznford

CHAMPIONSHIP RESULTS

Baseball

DIVISION I

Year	Champion	Coach	Score	Runner-Up	Most Outstanding Player
1947	California*	Clint Evans	8–7	Yale	No award
1948	Southern Cal	Sam Barry	9–2	Yale	No award
1949	Texas*	Bibb Falk	10–3	Wake Forest	Charles Teague, Wake Forest, 2B
1950	Texas	Bibb Falk	3–0	Washington St	Ray VanCleef, Rutgers, CF
1951	Oklahoma*	Jack Baer	3–2	Tennnessee	Sidney Hatfield, Tennessee, P-1B
1952	Holy Cross	Jack Barry	8–4	Missouri	James O'Neill, Holy Cross, P
1953	Michigan	Ray Fisher	7–5	Texas	J.L. Smith, Texas, P
1954	Missouri	John (Hi) Simmons	4–1	Rollins	Tom Yewcic, Michigan St, C
1955	Wake Forest	Taylor Sanford	7–6	Western Michigan	Tom Borland, Oklahoma St, P
1956	Minnesota	Dick Siebert	12–1	Arizona	Jerry Thomas, Minnesota, P
1957	California*	George Wolfman	1–0	Penn St	Cal Emery, Penn St, P-1B
1958	Southern Cal	Rod Dedeaux	8–7†	Missouri	Bill Thom, Southern Cal, P
1959	Oklahoma St	Toby Greene	5–3	Arizona	Jim Dobson, Oklahoma St, 3B
1960	Minnesota	Dick Siebert	2–1‡	Southern Cal	John Erickson, Minnesota, 2B
1961	Southern Cal*	Rod Dedeaux	1–0	Oklahoma St	Littleton Fowler, Oklahoma St, P
1962	Michigan	Don Lund	5–4	Santa Clara	Bob Garibaldi, Santa Clara, P
1963	Southern Cal	Rod Dedeaux	5–2	Arizona	Bud Hollowell, Southern Cal, C
1964	Minnesota	Dick Siebert	5–1	Missouri	Joe Ferris, Maine, P
1965	Arizona St	Bobby Winkles	2–1#	Ohio St	Sal Bando, Arizona St, 3B
1966	Ohio St	Marty Karow	8–2	Oklahoma St	Steve Arlin, Ohio St, P
1967	Arizona St	Bobby Winkles	11–2	Houston	Ron Davini, Arizona St, C
1968	Southern Cal*	Rod Dedeaux	4–3	Southern Illinois	Bill Seinsoth, Southern Cal, 1B
1969	Arizona St	Bobby Winkles	10–1	Tulsa	John Dolinsek, Arizona St, LF
1970	Southern Cal	Rod Dedeaux	2–1	Florida St	Gene Ammann, Florida St, P
1971	Southern Cal	Rod Dedeaux	7–2	Southern Illinois	Jerry Tabb, Tulsa, 1B
1972	Southern Cal	Rod Dedeaux	1–0	Arizona St	Russ McQueen, Southern Cal, P
1973	Southern Cal*	Rod Dedeaux	4–3	Arizona St	Dave Winfield, Minnesota, P-OF
1974	Southern Cal	Rod Dedeaux	7–3	Miami (FL)	George Milke, Southern Cal, P
1975	Texas	Cliff Gustafson	5–1	S Carolina	Mickey Reichenbach, Texas, 1B
1976	Arizona	Jerry Kindall	7–1	Eastern Michigan	Steve Powers, Arizona, P-DH
1977	Arizona St	Jim Brock	2–1	S Carolina	Bob Horner, Arizona St, 3B
1978	Southern Cal*	Rod Dedeaux	10–3	Arizona St	Rod Boxberger, Southern Cal, P
1979	Cal St–Fullerton	Augie Garrido	2–1	Arkansas	Tony Hudson, Cal St–Fullerton, P
1980	Arizona	Jerry Kindall	5–3	Hawaii	Terry Francona, Arizona, LF
1981	Arizona St	Jim Brock	7–4	Oklahoma St	Stan Holmes, Arizona St, LF
1982	Miami (FL)*	Ron Fraser	9–3	Wichita St	Dan Smith, Miami (FL), P
1983	Texas*	Cliff Gustafson	4–3	Alabama	Calvin Schiraldi, Texas, P
1984	Cal St–Fullerton	Augie Garrido	3–1	Texas	John Fishel, Cal St–Fullerton, LF
1985	Miami (FL)	Ron Fraser	10–6	Texas	Greg Ellena, Miami (FL), DH
1986	Arizona	Jerry Kindall	10–2	Florida St	Mike Senne, Arizona, LF
1987	Stanford	Mark Marquess	9–5	Oklahoma St	Paul Carey, Stanford, RF
1988	Stanford	Mark Marquess	9–4	Arizona St	Lee Plemel, Stanford, P
1989	Wichita St	Gene Stephenson	5–3	Texas	Greg Brummett, Wichita St, P
1990	Georgia	Steve Webber	2–1	Oklahoma St	Mike Rebhan, Georgia, P
1991	Louisiana St	Skip Bertman	6–3	Wichita St	Gary Hymel, Louisiana St, C
1992	Pepperdine	Andy Lopez	3–2	Cal St–Fullerton	Phil Nevin, Cal St–Fullerton, 3B
1993	Louisiana St	Skip Bertman	8–0	Wichita St	Todd Walker, Louisiana St, 2B
1994	Oklahoma	Larry Cochell	13–5	Georgia Tech	Chip Glass, Oklahoma, CF
1995	Cal St–Fullerton*	Augie Garrido	11–5	Southern Cal	Mark Kotsay, Cal St–Fullerton, CF-P
1996	Louisiana St*	Skip Bertman	9–8	Miami (FL)	Pat Burrell, Miami (FL), 3B
1997	Louisiana St*	Skip Bertman	13–6	Alabama	Brandon Larson, Louisiana St, SS
1998	Southern Cal	Mike Gillespie	21–14	Arizona St	Wes Rachels, Southern Cal, 2B
1999	Miami (FL)	Jim Morris	6–5	Florida St	Marshall McDougall, FSU 3B/2B
2000	Louisiana St*	Skip Bertman	6–5	Stanford	Trey Hodges, Louisiana St, P
2001	Miami (FL)*	Jim Morris	12–1	Stanford	Charlton Jimerson, Miami (FL), OF
2002	Texas	Augie Garrido	12–6	South Carolina	Huston Street, Texas, P
2003	Rice	Wayne Graham	14–2^	Stanford	John Hudgins, Stanford, P
2004	Cal St–Fullerton	George Horton	3–2^	Texas	Jason Windsor, Cal St–Fullerton
2005	Texas	Augie Garrido	6-2	Florida	David Maroul, Texas

*Undefeated teams in College World Series play. †12 innings. ‡10 innings. #15 innings. ^Score of decisive game of best-of-three series.

Baseball (Cont.)

DIVISION II

Year	Champion	Year	Champion	Year	Champion
1968	Chapman*	1972	Florida Southern	1976	Cal Poly–Pomona
1969	Illinois St*	1973	UC–Irvine*	1977	UC–Riverside
1970	Cal St-Northridge	1974	UC–Irvine	1978	Florida Southern
1971	Florida Southern	1975	Florida Southern	1979	Valdosta St

DIVISION II (Cont.)

Year	Champion	Year	Champion	Year	Champion
1980	Cal Poly–Pomona*	1989	Cal Poly–SLO	1998	Tampa*
1981	Florida Southern*	1990	Jacksonville St	1999	Cal St–Chico
1982	UC–Riverside*	1991	Jacksonville St	2000	SE Oklahoma St
1983	Cal Poly–Pomona*	1992	Tampa*	2001	St. Mary's (TX)
1984	Cal St-Northridge	1993	Tampa	2002	Columbus St
1985	Florida Southern*	1994	Central Missouri St	2003	Central Missouri St
1986	Troy St	1995	Florida Southern*	2004	Kennesaw St
1987	Troy St*	1996	Kennesaw St*	2005	Florida Southern
1988	Florida Southern*	1997	Cal St–Chico*		

DIVISION III

Year	Champion	Year	Champion	Year	Champion
1976	Cal St-Stanislaus	1986	Marietta	1996	William Paterson
1977	Cal St-Stanislaus	1987	Montclair St	1997	Southern Maine
1978	Glassboro St	1988	Ithaca	1998	Eastern Connecticut St
1979	Glassboro St	1989	NC Wesleyan	1999	N Carolina Wesleyan
1980	Ithaca	1990	Eastern Connecticut St	2000	Montclair St
1981	Marietta	1991	Southern Maine	2001	St. Thomas (MN)
1982	Eastern Connecticut St	1992	William Paterson	2002	Eastern Connecticut St
1983	Marietta	1993	Montclair St	2003	Chapman
1984	Ramapo	1994	WI-Oshkosh	2004	WI-Stevens Pt
1985	WI–Oshkosh	1995	La Verne	2005	Wisconsin

*Undefeated teams in final series.

Cross-Country

Men
DIVISION I

Year	Champion	Coach	Pts	Runner-Up	Pts	Individual Champion	Time
1938	Indiana	Earle Hayes	51	Notre Dame	61	Greg Rice, Notre Dame	20:12.9
1939	Michigan St	Lauren Brown	54	Wisconsin	57	Walter Mehl, Wisconsin	20:30.9
1940	Indiana	Earle Hayes	65	Eastern Michigan	68	Gilbert Dodds, Ashland	20:30.2
1941	Rhode Island	Fred Tootell	83	Penn St	110	Fred Wilt, Indiana	20:30.1
1942	Indiana	Earle Hayes	57			Oliver Hunter, Notre Dame	20:18.0
	Penn St	Charles Werner	57				
1943	No meet						
1944	Drake	Bill Easton	25	Notre Dame	64	Fred Feiler, Drake	21:04.2
1945	Drake	Bill Easton	50	Notre Dame	65	Fred Feiler, Drake	21:14.2
1946	Drake	Bill Easton	42	NYU	98	Quentin Brelsford, Ohio Wesleyan	20:22.9
1947	Penn St	Charles Werner	60	Syracuse	72	Jack Milne, North Carolina	20:41.1
1948	Michigan St	Karl Schlademan	41	Wisconsin	69	Robert Black, Rhode Island	19:52.3
1949	Michigan St	Karl Schlademan	59	Syracuse	81	Robert Black, Rhode Island	20:25.7
1950	Penn St	Charles Werner	53	Michigan St	55	Herb Semper Jr, Kansas	20:31.7
1951	Syracuse	Robert Grieve	80	Kansas	118	Herb Semper Jr, Kansas	20:09.5
1952	Michigan St	Karl Schlademan	65	Indiana	68	Charles Capozzoli, Georgetown	19:36.7
1953	Kansas	Bill Easton	70	Indiana	82	Wes Santee, Kansas	19:43.5
1954	Oklahoma St	Ralph Higgins	61	Syracuse	118	Allen Frame, Kansas	19:54.2
1955	Michigan St	Karl Schlademan	46	Kansas	68	Charles Jones, Iowa	19:57.4
1956	Michigan St	Karl Schlademan	28	Kansas	88	Walter McNew, Texas	19:55.7
1957	Notre Dame	Alex Wilson	121	Michigan St	127	Max Truex, Southern Cal	19:12.3
1958	Michigan St	Francis Dittrich	79	Western Michigan	104	Crawford Kennedy, Michigan State	20:07.1
1959	Michigan St	Francis Dittrich	44	Houston	120	Al Lawrence, Houston	20:35.7
1960	Houston	John Morriss	54	Michigan St	80	Al Lawrence, Houston	19:28.2

Men (Cont.)

DIVISION I (Cont.)

Year	Champion	Coach	Pts	Runner-Up	Pts	Individual Champion	Time
1961	Oregon St	Sam Bell	68	San Jose St	82	Dale Story, Oregon St	19:46.6
1962	San Jose St	Dean Miller	58	Villanova	69	Tom O'Hara, Loyola (IL)	19:20.3
1963	San Jose St	Dean Miller	53	Oregon	68	Victor Zwolak, Villanova	19:35.0
1964	W Michigan	George Dales	86	Oregon	116	Elmore Banton, Ohio	20:07.5
1965	W Michigan	George Dales	81	Northwestern	114	John Lawson, Kansas	29:24.0
1966	Villanova	James Elliott	79	Kansas St	155	Gerry Lindgren, Wash St	29:01.4
1967	Villanova	James Elliott	91	Air Force	96	Gerry Lindgren, Wash St	30:45.6
1968	Villanova	James Elliott	78	Stanford	100	Michael Ryan, Air Force	29:16.8
1969	UT–El Paso	Wayne Vandenburg	74	Villanova	88	Gerry Lindgren, Wash St	28:59.2
1970	Villanova	James Elliott	85	Oregon	86	Steve Prefontaine, Oregon	28:00.2
1971	Oregon	Bill Dellinger	83	Washington St	122	Steve Prefontaine, Oregon	29:14.0
1972	Tennessee	Stan Huntsman	134	E Tennessee St	148	Neil Cusack, E Tenn St	28:23.0
1973	Oregon	Bill Dellinger	89	UT–El Paso	157	Steve Prefontaine, Oregon	28:14.0
1974	Oregon	Bill Dellinger	77	Western Kentucky	110	Nick Rose, Western Ky	29:22.0
1975	UT–El Paso	Ted Banks	88	Washington St	92	Craig Virgin, Illinois	28:23.3
1976	UT–El Paso	Ted Banks	62	Oregon	117	Henry Rono, Washington St	28:06.6
1977	Oregon	Bill Dellinger	100	UT–El Paso	105	Henry Rono, Washington St	28:33.5
1978	UT–El Paso	Ted Banks	56	Oregon	72	Alberto Salazar, Oregon	29:29.7
1979	UT–El Paso	Ted Banks	86	Oregon	93	Henry Rono, Washington St	28:19.6
1980	UT–El Paso	Ted Banks	58	Arkansas	152	Suleiman Nyambui, UTEP	29:04.0
1981	UT–El Paso	Ted Banks	17	Providence	109	Mathews Motshwarateu, UTEP	28:45.6
1982	Wisconsin	Dan McClimon	59	Providence	138	Mark Scrutton, Colorado	30:12.6
1983	Vacated			Wisconsin	164	Zakarie Barie, UT–El Paso	29:20.0
1984	Arkansas	John McDonnell	101	Arizona	111	Ed Eyestone, Brigham Young	29:28.8
1985	Wisconsin	Martin Smith	67	Arkansas	104	Timothy Hacker, Wisconsin	29:17.88
1986	Arkansas	John McDonnell	69	Dartmouth	141	Aaron Ramirez, Arizona	30:27.53
1987	Arkansas	John McDonnell	87	Dartmouth	119	Joe Falcon, Arkansas	29:14.97
1988	Wisconsin	Martin Smith	105	Northern Arizona	160	Robert Kennedy, Indiana	29:20.0
1989	Iowa St	Bill Bergan	54	Oregon	72	John Nuttall, Iowa St	29:30.55
1990	Arkansas	John McDonnell	68	Iowa St	96	Jonah Koech, Iowa St	29:05.0
1991	Arkansas	John McDonnell	52	Iowa St	114	Sean Dollman, Western Ky	30:17.1
1992	Arkansas	John McDonnell	46	Wisconsin	87	Bob Kennedy, Indiana	30:15.3
1993	Arkansas	John McDonnell	31	Brigham Young	153	Josephat Kapkory, Wash St	29:32.4
1994	Iowa St	Bill Bergan	65	Colorado	88	Martin Keino, Arizona	30:08.7
1995	Arkansas	John McDonnell	100	Northern Arizona	142	Godfrey Siamusiye, Arkansas	30:09
1996	Stanford	Vin Lananna	46	Arkansas	74	Godfrey Siamusiye, Arkansas	29:49
1997	Stanford	Vin Lananna	53	Arkansas	56	Mebrahtom Keflezighi, UCLA	28:54
1998	Arkansas	John McDonnell	97	Stanford	114	Adam Goucher, Colorado	29:26
1999	Arkansas	John McDonnell	58	Wisconsin	185	David Kimani, S Alabama	30:06.6
2000	Arkansas	John McDonnell	83	Colorado	94	Keith Kelly, Providence	30:14.5
2001	Colorado	Mark Wetmore	90	Stanford	91	Boaz Cheboiywo, E Michigan	28:47
2002	Stanford	Andrew Gerard	47	Wisconsin	107	Jorge Torres, Colorado	29:04.7
2003	Stanford	Andrew Gerard	24	Wisconsin	124	Dathan Ritzenhein, Colorado	29:14.1
2004	Colorado	Mark Wetmore	90	Wisconsin	94	Simon Bairu, Wisconsin	30:37.7

DIVISION II

Year	Champion	Year	Champion	Year	Champion
1958	Northern Illinois	1974	SW Missouri St	1990	Edinboro
1959	S Dakota St	1975	UC–Irvine	1991	UMass–Lowell
1960	Central St (OH)	1976	UC–Irvine	1992	Adams St
1961	Southern Illinois	1977	Eastern Illinois	1993	Adams St
1962	Central St (OH)	1978	Cal Poly–SLO	1994	Adams St
1963	Emporia St	1979	Cal Poly–SLO	1995	Western St
1964	Kentucky St	1980	Humboldt St	1996	S Dakota St
1965	San Diego St	1981	Millersville	1997	S Dakota
1966	San Diego St	1982	Eastern Washington	1998	Adams St
1967	San Diego St	1983	Cal Poly–Pomona	1999	Western St
1968	Eastern Illinois	1984	SE Missouri St	2000	Western St
1969	Eastern Illinois	1985	S Dakota St	2001	Western St
1970	Eastern Michigan	1986	Edinboro	2002	Western St
1971	Cal St–Fullerton	1987	Edinboro	2003	Adams St
1972	N Dakota St	1988	Edinboro/ Mankato St	2004	Western St
1973	S Dakota St	1989	S Dakota St		

Men (Cont.)

DIVISION III

Year	Champion	Year	Champion	Year	Champion
1973	Ashland	1984	St. Thomas (MN)	1995	Williams
1974	Mount Union	1985	Luther	1996	WI–La Crosse
1975	North Central	1986	St. Thomas (MN)	1997	N Central
1976	North Central	1987	N Central	1998	N Central
1977	Occidental	1988	WI–Oshkosh	1999	N Central
1978	N Central	1989	WI–Oshkosh	2000	Calvin
1979	N Central	1990	WI–Oshkosh	2001	WI–La Crosse
1980	Carleton	1991	Rochester	2002	WI–Oshkosh
1981	N Central	1992	N Central	2003	Calvin College
1982	N Central	1993	N Central	2004	Calvin College
1983	Brandeis	1994	Williams		

Women

DIVISION I

Year	Champion	Coach	Pts	Runner-Up	Pts	Individual Champion	Time
1981	Virginia	John Vasvary	36	Oregon	83	Betty Springs, N Carolina St	16:19.0
1982	Virginia	Martin Smith	48	Stanford	91	Lesley Welch, Virginia	16:39.7
1983	Oregon	Tom Heinonen	95	Stanford	98	Betty Springs, N Carolina St	16:30.7
1984	Wisconsin	Peter Tegen	63	Stanford	89	Cathy Branta, Wisconsin	16:15.6
1985	Wisconsin	Peter Tegen	58	Iowa St	98	Suzie Tuffey, N Carolina St	16:22.5
1986	Texas	Terry Crawford	62	Wisconsin	64	Angela Chalmers, N Arizona	16:55.49
1987	Oregon	Tom Heinonen	97	N Carolina St	99	Kimberly Betz, Indiana	16:10.85
1988	Kentucky	Don Weber	75	Oregon	128	Michelle Dekkers, Indiana	16:30.0
1989	Villanova	Marty Stern	99	Kentucky	168	Vicki Huber, Villanova	15:59.86
1990	Villanova	Marty Stern	82	Providence	172	Sonia O'Sullivan, Villanova	16:06.0
1991	Villanova	Marty Stern	85	Arkansas	168	Sonia O'Sullivan, Villanova	16:30.3
1992	Villanova	Marty Stern	123	Arkansas	130	Carole Zajac, Villanova	17:01.9
1993	Villanova	Marty Stern	66	Arkansas	71	Carole Zajac, Villanova	16:40.3
1994	Villanova	John Marshall	75	Michigan	108	Jennifer Rhines, Villanova	16:31.2
1995	Providence	Ray Treacy	88	Colorado	123	Kathy Butler, Wisconsin	16:51
1996	Stanford	Beth Alford-Sullivan	101	Villanova	106	Amy Skieresz, Arizona	17:04
1997	BYU	Patrick Shane	100	Stanford	102	Carrie Tollefson, Villanova	16:58
1998	Villanova	Marcus O'Sullivan	106	Brigham Young	110	Katie McGregor, Michigan	16:47.21
1999	BYU	Patrick Shane	72	Arkansas	125	Erica Palmer, Wisconsin	16:39.50
2000	Colorado	Mark Wetmore	117	Brigham Young	167	Kara Grgas-Wheeler, Colorado	20:30.5
2001	BYU	Patrick Shane	62	N Carolina St	148	Tara Chaplin, Arizona	20:24
2002	BYU	Patrick Shane	85	Stanford	113	Shalane Flanagan	19:36.0
2003	Stanford	Dena Evans	120	Brigham Young	128	Shalane Flanagan	19:30.4
2004	Colorado	Mark Wetmore	63	Duke	144	Kim Smith, Providence	20:08.5

DIVISION II

Year	Champion	Year	Champion	Year	Champion
1981	S Dakota St	1989	Cal Poly–SLO	1997	Adams St
1982	Cal Poly–SLO	1990	Cal Poly–SLO	1998	Adams St
1983	Cal Poly–SLO	1991	Cal Poly–SLO	1999	Adams St
1984	Cal Poly–SLO	1992	Adams St	2000	Western St
1985	Cal Poly–SLO	1993	Adams St	2001	Western St
1986	Cal Poly–SLO	1994	Adams St	2002	Western St
1987	Cal Poly–SLO	1995	Adams St	2003	Adams St
1988	Cal Poly–SLO	1996	Adams St	2004	Adams St

DIVISION III

Year	Champion	Year	Champion	Year	Champion
1981	Central (IA)	1989	Cortland St	1998	Calvin
1982	St. Thomas (MN)	1990	Cortland St	1999	Calvin
1983	WI–La Crosse	1991	WI–Oshkosh	2000	Middlebury
1984	St. Thomas (MN)	1992	Cortland St	2001	Middlebury
1985	Franklin & Marshall	1993	Cortland St	2002	Williams
1986	St. Thomas (MN)	1994	Cortland St	2003	Middlebury
1987	St. Thomas (MN)/ WI–Oshkosh	1995	Cortland St	2004	Williams College
1988	WI–Oshkosh	1996	WI–Oshkosh		
		1997	Cortland St		

Fencing

Men's and Women's Combined
TEAM CHAMPIONS

Year	Champion	Coach	Pts	Runner-Up	Pts
1990	Penn St	Emmanuil Kaidanov	36	Columbia–Barnard	35
1991	Penn St	Emmanuil Kaidanov	4700	Columbia–Barnard	4200
1992	Columbia–Barnard	G. Kolombatovich/A. Kogler	4150	Penn St	3646
1993	Columbia–Barnard	G. Kolombatovich/A. Kogler	4525	Penn St	4500
1994	Notre Dame	Michael DeCicco	4350	Penn St	4075
1995	Penn St	Emmanuil Kaidanov	440	St. John's (NY)	413
1996	Penn St	Emmanuil Kaidanov	1500	Notre Dame	1190
1997	Penn St	Emmanuil Kaidanov	1530	Notre Dame	1470
1998	Penn St	Emmanuil Kaidanov	149	Notre Dame	147
1999	Penn St	Emmanuil Kaidanov	171	Notre Dame	139
2000	Penn St	Emmanuil Kaidanov	175	Notre Dame	171
2001	St. John's (NY)	Yuri Gelman	180	Penn St	172
2002	Penn St	Emmanuil Kaidanov	195	St. John's (NY)	190
2003	Notre Dame	Janusz Bednarski	182	Penn St	179
2004	Ohio St	Vladimir Nazlymov	194	Penn St	160
2005	Notre Dame	Janusz Bednarski	173	Ohio St	171

Men
TEAM CHAMPIONS

Year	Champion	Coach	Pts	Runner-Up	Pts
1941	Northwestern	Henry Zettleman	28½	Illinois	27
1942	Ohio St	Frank Riebel	34	St. John's (NY)	33½
1943–46	No tournament				
1947	NYU	Martinez Castello	72	Chicago	50½
1948	CCNY	James Montague	30	Navy	28
1949	Army/Rutgers	S. Velarde/D. Cetrulo	63		
1950	Navy	Joseph Fiems	67½	NYU/Rutgers	66½
1951	Columbia	Servando Velarde	69	Pennsylvania	64
1952	Columbia	Servando Velarde	71	NYU	69
1953	Pennsylvania	Lajos Csiszar	94	Navy	86
1954	Columbia	Irving DeKoff	61		
	NYU	Hugo Castello	61		
1955	Columbia	Irving DeKoff	62	Cornell	57
1956	Illinois	Maxwell Garret	90	Columbia	88
1957	NYU	Hugo Castello	65	Columbia	64
1958	Illinois	Maxwell Garret	47	Columbia	43
1959	Navy	Andre Deladrier	72	NYU	65
1960	NYU	Hugo Castello	65	Navy	57
1961	NYU	Hugo Castello	79	Princeton	68
1962	Navy	Andre Deladrier	76	NYU	74
1963	Columbia	Irving DeKoff	55	Navy	50
1964	Princeton	Stan Sieja	81	NYU	79
1965	Columbia	Irving DeKoff	76	NYU	74
1966	NYU	Hugo Castello	5–0	Army	5–2
1967	NYU	Hugo Castello	72	Pennsylvania	64
1968	Columbia	Louis Bankuti	92	NYU	87
1969	Pennsylvania	Lajos Csiszar	54	Harvard	43
1970	NYU	Hugo Castello	71	Columbia	63
1971	NYU/Columbia	Hugo Castello/Louis Bankuti	68		
1972	Detroit	Richard Perry	73	NYU	70
1973	NYU	Hugo Castello	76	Pennsylvania	71
1974	NYU	Hugo Castello	92	Wayne St (MI)	87
1975	Wayne St (MI)	Istvan Danosi	89	Cornell	83
1976	NYU	Herbert Cohen	79	Wayne St (MI)	77
1977	Notre Dame	Michael DeCicco	114*	NYU	114
1978	Notre Dame	Michael DeCicco	121	Pennsylvania	110
1979	Wayne St (MI)	Istvan Danosi	119	Notre Dame	108
1980	Wayne St (MI)	Istvan Danosi	111	Pennsylvania/MIT	106
1981	Pennsylvania	Dave Micahnik	113	Wayne St (MI)	111
1982	Wayne St (MI)	Istvan Danosi	85	Clemson	77
1983	Wayne St (MI)	Aladar Kogler	86	Notre Dame	80
1984	Wayne St (MI)	Gil Pezza	69	Penn St	50
1985	Wayne St (MI)	Gil Pezza	141	Notre Dame	140

Men

TEAM CHAMPIONS (CONT.)

1986	Notre Dame	Michael DeCicco	151	Columbia	141
1987	Columbia	George Kolombatovich	86	Pennsylvania	78
1988	Columbia	G. Kolombatovich/A. Kogler	90	Notre Dame	83
1989	Columbia	G. Kolombatovich/A. Kogler	88	Penn St	85

*Tie broken by a fence-off. Note: Beginning in 1990, men's and women's combined teams competed for the national championship. See p. 573.

INDIVIDUAL CHAMPIONS

	Foil	Sabre	Épée
1941	Edward McNamara, Northwestern	William Meyer, Dartmouth	G.H. Boland, Illinois
1942	Byron Kreiger, Wayne St (MI)	Andre Deladrier, St. John's (NY)	Ben Burtt, Ohio St
1943–46	No tournament		
1947	Abraham Balk, NYU	Oscar Parsons, Temple	Abraham Balk, NYU
1948	Albert Axelrod, CCNY	James Day, Navy	William Bryan, Navy
1949	Ralph Tedeschi, Rutgers	Alex Treves, Rutgers	Richard C. Bowman, Army
1950	Robert Nielsen, Columbia	Alex Treves, Rutgers	Thomas Stuart, Navy
1951	Robert Nielsen, Columbia	Chamberless Johnston, Princeton	Daniel Chafetz, Columbia
1952	Harold Goldsmith, CCNY	Frank Zimolzak, Navy	James Wallner, NYU
1953	Ed Nober, Brooklyn	Robert Parmacek, Penn	Jack Tori, Pennsylvania
1954	Robert Goldman, Pennsylvania	Steve Sobel, Columbia	Henry Kolowrat, Princeton
1955	Herman Velasco, Illinois	Barry Pariser, Columbia	Donald Tadrawski, Notre Dame
1956	Ralph DeMarco, Columbia	Gerald Kaufman, Columbia	Kinmont Hoitsma, Princeton
1957	Bruce Davis, Wayne St (MI)	Bernie Balaban, NYU	James Margolis, Columbia
1958	Bruce Davis, Wayne St (MI)	Art Schankin, Illinois	Roland Wommack, Navy
1959	Joe Paletta, Navy	Al Morales, Navy	Roland Wommack, Navy
1960	Gene Glazer, NYU	Mike Desaro, NYU	Gil Eisner, NYU
1961	Herbert Cohen, NYU	Israel Colon, NYU	Jerry Halpern, NYU
1962	Herbert Cohen, NYU	Barton Nisonson, Columbia	Thane Hawkins, Navy
1963	Jay Lustig, Columbia	Bela Szentivanyi, Wayne St (MI)	Larry Crum, Navy
1964	Bill Hicks, Princeton	Craig Bell, Illinois	Paul Pesthy, Rutgers
	Foil	**Sabre**	**Épée**
1965	Joe Nalven, Columbia	Howard Goodman, NYU	Paul Pesthy, Rutgers
1966	Al Davis, NYU	Paul Apostol, NYU	Bernhardt Hermann, Iowa
1967	Mike Gaylor, NYU	Todd Makler, Pennsylvania	George Masin, NYU
1968	Gerard Esponda, San Francisco	Todd Makler, Pennsylvania	Don Sieja, Cornell
1969	Anthony Kestler, Columbia	Norman Braslow, Penn	James Wetzler, Pennsylvania
1970	Walter Krause, NYU	Bruce Soriano, Columbia	John Nadas, Case Reserve
1971	Tyrone Simmons, Detroit	Bruce Soriano, Columbia	George Szunyogh, NYU
1972	Tyrone Simmons, Detroit	Bruce Soriano, Columbia	Ernesto Fernandez, Penn
1973	Brooke Makler, Pennsylvania	Peter Westbrock, NYU	Risto Hurme, NYU
1974	Greg Benko, Wayne St (MI)	Steve Danosi, Wayne St (MI)	Risto Hurme, NYU
1975	Greg Benko, Wayne St (MI)	Yuri Rabinovich, Wayne St (MI)	Risto Hurme, NYU
1976	Greg Benko, Wayne St (MI)	Brian Smith, Columbia	Randy Eggleton, Pennsylvania
1977	Pat Gerard, Notre Dame	Mike Sullivan, Notre Dame	Hans Wieselgren, NYU
1978	Ernest Simon, Wayne St (MI)	Mike Sullivan, Notre Dame	Bjorne Vaggo, Notre Dame
1979	Andrew Bonk, Notre Dame	Yuri Rabinovich, Wayne St (MI)	Carlos Songini, Cleveland St
1980	Ernest Simon, Wayne St (MI)	Paul Friedberg, Pennsylvania	Gil Pezza, Wayne St (MI)
1981	Ernest Simon, Wayne St (MI)	Paul Friedberg, Pennsylvania	Gil Pezza, Wayne St (MI)
1982	Alexander Flom, George Mason	Neil Hick, Wayne St (MI)	Peter Schifrin, San Jose St
1983	Demetrios Valsamis, NYU	John Friedberg, N Carolina	Ola Harstrom, Notre Dame
1984	Charles Higgs-Coulthard, Notre Dame	Michael Lofton, NYU	Ettore Bianchi, Wayne St (MI)
1985	Stephan Chauvel, Wayne St (MI)	Michael Lofton, NYU	Ettore Bianchi, Wayne St (MI)
1986	Adam Feldman, Penn St	Michael Lofton, NYU	Chris O'Loughlin, Pennsylvania
1987	William Mindel, Columbia	Michael Lofton, NYU	James O'Neill, Harvard
1988	Marc Kent, Columbia	Robert Cottingham, Columbia	Jon Normile, Columbia
1989	Edward Mufel, Penn St	Peter Cox, Penn St	Jon Normile, Columbia
1990	Nick Bravin, Stanford	David Mandell, Columbia	Jubba Beshin, Notre Dame
1991	Ben Atkins, Columbia	Vitali Nazlimov, Penn St	Marc Oshima, Columbia
1992	Nick Bravin, Stanford	Tom Strzalkowski, Penn St	Harald Bauder, Wayne St
1993	Nick Bravin, Stanford	Tom Strzalkowski, Penn St	Ben Atkins, Columbia
1994	Kwame van Leeuwen, Harvard	Tom Strzalkowski, Penn St	Harald Winkman, Princeton
1995	Sean McClain, Stanford	Paul Palestis, NYU	Mike Gattner, Lawrence
1996	Thorstein Becker, Wayne St (MI)	Maxim Pekarev, Princeton	Jeremy Kahn, Duke
1997	Cliff Bayer, Pennsylvania	Keith Smart, St. John's (NY)	Alden Clarke, Stanford
1998	Ayo Griffin, Yale	Luke LaValle, Notre Dame	George Hentea, St. John's (NY)

Men (Cont.)
INDIVIDUAL CHAMPIONS (Cont.)

1999 .....Felix Reichling, Stanford	Keeth Smart, St. John's (NY)	Alex Roytblat St. John's (NY)
2000 .....Felix Reichling, Stanford	Gabor Szelle, Notre Dame	Daniel Landgren, Penn St
2001 .....William Jed Dupree, Columbia	Ivan Lee, St. John's (NY)	Soren Thompson, Princeton
2002 .....Nontapat Panchan, Penn St	Ivan Lee, St. John's (NY)	Arpád Horváth, St. John's (NY)
2003 .....Nontapat Panchan, Penn St	Adam Crompton, Ohio St	Weston Kelsey, Air Force
2004 .....Boaz Ellis, Ohio St	Adam Crompton, Ohio St	Arpád Horváth, St. John's (NY)
2005 .....Boaz Ellis, Ohio St	Sergey Isayenko, St. John's	Michal Sobieraj, Notre Dame

Women
TEAM CHAMPIONS

Year	Champion	Coach	Rec	Runner-Up	Rec
1982	Wayne St (MI)	Istvan Danosi	7–0	San Jose St	6–1
1983	Penn St	Beth Alphin	5–0	Wayne St (MI)	3–2
1984	Yale	Henry Harutunian	3–0	Penn St	2–1
1985	Yale	Henry Harutunian	3–0	Pennsylvania	2–1
1986	Pennsylvania	David Micahnik	3–0	Notre Dame	2–1
1987	Notre Dame	Yves Auriol	3–0	Temple	2–1
1988	Wayne St (MI)	Gil Pezza	3–0	Notre Dame	2–1
1989	Wayne St (MI)	Gil Pezza	3–0	Columbia-Barnard	2–1

Note: Beginning in 1990, men's and women's combined teams competed for the national championship. See p. 573.

INDIVIDUAL CHAMPIONS

Foil	Foil (Cont.)	Sabre (Cont.)
1982 ...Joy Ellingson, San Jose St	1997 ...Yelena Kalkina, Ohio St	2005 ....Emily Jacobson, Barnard
1983 ...Jana Angelakis, Penn St	1998 ....F. Zimmermann, Stanford	**Épée**
1984 ...Mary Jane O'Neill, Penn	1999 ...Monique DeBruin, Stanford	1995 ....Tina Loven, St. John's (NY)
1985 ...C. Bilodeaux, Columbia-Barn.	2000 ....Eva Petschnigg, Princeton	1996 ....N. Dygert, St. John's (NY)
1986 ...M. Sullivan, Notre Dame	2001 ...Iris Zimmerman, Stanford	1997 ....Magda Krol, Notre Dame
1987 ...C. Bilodeaux, Columbia-Barn.	2002 ...Alicja Kryczalo, Notre Dame	1998 ....Charlotte Walker, Penn St
1988 ...M. Sullivan, Notre Dame	2003 ...Alicja Kryczalo, Notre Dame	1999 ....F. Zimmermann, Stanford
1989 ...Yasemin Topcu, Wayne St (MI)	2004 ...Alicja Kryczalo, Notre Dame	2000 ....Jessica Burke, Penn St
1990 ...Tzu Moy, Columbia-Barn.	2005 ....Alicja Kryczalo, Notre Dame	2001 ....E. Takács, St. John's (NY)
1991 ...Heidi Piper, Notre Dame	**Sabre**	2002 ....Stephanie Eim, Penn St
1992 ...Olga Cheryak, Penn St	2000 ....Caroline Purcell, MIT	2003 ....Katarzyna Trzopek, Penn St
1993 ...Olga Kalinovskaya, Penn St	2001 ....Sada Jacobson, Yale	2004.....Anna Garina, Wayne St (MI)
1994 ...Olga Kalinovskaya, Penn St	2002 ....Sada Jacobson, Yale	2005.....Anna Garina, Wayne St (MI)
1995 ...Olga Kalinovskaya, Penn St	2003 ....Alexis Jemal, Rutgers	
1996 ....Olga Kalinovskaya, Penn St	2004 ....Valerie Providenza, ND	

Field Hockey

DIVISION I

Year	Champion	Coach	Score	Runner-Up
1981	Connecticut	Diane Wright	4–1	Massachusetts
1982	Old Dominion	Beth Anders	3–2	Connecticut
1983	Old Dominion	Beth Anders	3–1 (3 OT)	Connecticut
1984	Old Dominion	Beth Anders	5–1	Iowa
1985	Connecticut	Diane Wright	3–2	Old Dominion
1986	Iowa	Judith Davidson	2–1 (2 OT)	New Hampshire
1987	Maryland	Sue Tyler	2–1 (OT)	N Carolina
1988	Old Dominion	Beth Anders	2–1	Iowa
1989	N Carolina	Karen Shelton	2–1 (3 OT)*	Old Dominion
1990	Old Dominion	Beth Anders	5–0	N Carolina
1991	Old Dominion	Beth Anders	2–0	N Carolina
1992	Old Dominion	Beth Anders	4–0	Iowa
1993	Maryland	Missy Meharg	2–1 (3 OT)*	N Carolina
1994	James Madison	Christy Morgan	2–1 (3 OT)*	N Carolina
1995	N Carolina	Karen Shelton-Scroggs	5–1	Maryland
1996	N Carolina	Karen Shelton-Scroggs	3–0	Princeton
1997	N Carolina	Karen Shelton	3–2	Old Dominion
1998	Old Dominion	Beth Anders	3–2	Princeton
1999	Maryland	Missy Meharg	2–1	Michigan
2000	Old Dominion	Beth Anders	3–1	N Carolina

DIVISION I (CONT.)

Year	Champion	Coach	Score	Runner-Up
2001	Michigan	Marcia Pankratz	2–0	Maryland
2002	Wake Forest	Jennifer Averill	2–0	Penn St
2003	Wake Forest	Jennifer Averill	3–1	Duke
2004	Wake Forest	Jennifer Averill	3–0	Duke

*Penalty strokes.

DIVISION II *(Discontinued, then renewed)*

Year	Champion	Coach	Score	Runner-Up
1981	Pfeiffer	Ellen Briggs	5–3	Bentley
1982	Lock Haven	Sharon E. Taylor	4–1	Bloomsburg
1983	Bloomsburg	Jan Hutchinson	1–0	Lock Haven
1992	Lock Haven	Sharon E. Taylor	3–1	Bloomsburg
1993	Bloomsburg	Jan Hutchinson	2–1 (2 OT)	Lock Haven
1994	Lock Haven	Sharon E. Taylor	2–1	Bloomsburg
1995	Lock Haven	Sharon E. Taylor	1–0	Bloomsburg
1996	Bloomsburg	Jan Hutchinson	1–0	Lock Haven
1997	Bloomsburg	Jan Hutchinson	2–0	Kutztown
1998	Bloomsburg	Jan Hutchinson	4–3 (OT)	Lock Haven
1999	Bloomsburg	Jan Hutchinson	2–0	Bentley
2000	Lock Haven	Pat Rudy	2–0	Bentley
2001	Bentley	Kell McGowan	4–2	E Stroudsburg
2002	Bloomsburg	Jan Hutchinson	5–0	Bentley
2003	Bloomsburg	Jan Hutchinson	4–1	UMass–Lowell
2004	Bloomsburg	Jan Hutchinson	3–2	Bentley

DIVISION III

Year	Champion	Year	Champion	Year	Champion
1981	Trenton St	1989	Lock Haven	1997	William Smith
1982	Ithaca	1990	Trenton St	1998	Middelbury
1983	Trenton St	1991	Trenton St	1999	College of New Jersey
1984	Bloomsburg	1992	William Smith	2000	William Smith
1985	Trenton St	1993	Cortland St	2001	Cortland St
1986	Salisbury St	1994	Cortland St	2002	Rowan
1987	Bloomsburg	1995	Trenton St	2003	Salisbury
1988	Trenton St	1996	College of New Jersey	2004	Salisbury

Golf

Men

DIVISION I

Results, 1897–1938

Year	Champion	Site	Individual Champion
1897	Yale	Ardsley Casino	Louis Bayard Jr, Princeton
1898	Harvard (spring)		John Reid Jr, Yale
1898	Yale (fall)		James Curtis, Harvard
1899	Harvard		Percy Pyne, Princeton
1900	No tournament		
1901	Harvard	Atlantic City	H. Lindsley, Harvard
1902	Yale (spring)	Garden City	Charles Hitchcock Jr, Yale
1902	Harvard (fall)	Morris County	Chandler Egan, Harvard
1903	Harvard	Garden City	F.O. Reinhart, Princeton
1904	Harvard	Myopia	A.L. White, Harvard
1905	Yale	Garden City	Robert Abbott, Yale
1906	Yale	Garden City	W.E. Clow Jr, Yale
1907	Yale	Nassau	Ellis Knowles, Yale
1908	Yale	Brae Burn	H.H. Wilder, Harvard
1909	Yale	Apawamis	Albert Seckel, Princeton
1910	Yale	Essex County	Robert Hunter, Yale
1911	Yale	Baltusrol	George Stanley, Yale
1912	Yale	Ekwanok	F.C. Davison, Harvard
1913	Yale	Huntingdon Valley	Nathaniel Wheeler, Yale
1914	Princeton	Garden City	Edward Allis, Harvard
1915	Yale	Greenwich	Francis Blossom, Yale

Men
DIVISION I *(Cont.)*
Results, 1897–1938 *(Cont.)*

Year	Champion	Site	Individual Champion
1916 ....Princeton		Oakmont	J.W. Hubbell, Harvard
1917–18 ....No tournament			
1919 ....Princeton		Merion	A.L. Walker Jr, Columbia
1920 ....Princeton		Nassau	Jess Sweetster, Yale
1921 ....Dartmouth		Greenwich	Simpson Dean, Princeton
1922 ....Princeton		Garden City	Pollack Boyd, Dartmouth
1923 ....Princeton		Siwanoy	Dexter Cummings, Yale
1924 ....Yale		Greenwich	Dexter Cummings, Yale
1925 ....Yale		Montclair	Fred Lamprecht, Tulane
1926 ....Yale		Merion	Fred Lamprecht, Tulane
1927 ....Princeton		Garden City	Watts Gunn, Georgia Tech
1928 ....Princeton		Apawamis	Maurice McCarthy, Georgetown
1929 ....Princeton		Hollywood	Tom Aycock, Yale
1930 ....Princeton		Oakmont	G.T. Dunlap Jr, Princeton
1931 ....Yale		Olympia Fields	G.T. Dunlap Jr, Princeton
1932 ....Yale		Hot Springs	J.W. Fischer, Michigan
1933 ....Yale		Buffalo	Walter Emery, Oklahoma
1934 ....Michigan		Cleveland	Charles Yates, Georgia Tech
1935 ....Michigan		Congressional	Ed White, Texas
1936 ....Yale		North Shore	Charles Kocsis, Michigan
1937 ....Princeton		Oakmont	Fred Haas Jr, Louisiana St
1938 ....Stanford		Louisville	John Burke, Georgetown

Results, 1939–2004

Year	Champion (Score)	Coach	Runner-Up (Score)	Host or Site	Individual Champion
1939 ....Stanford (612)	Eddie Twiggs	Northwestern (614)	Wakonda	Vincent D'Antoni, Tulane
			Princeton (614)		
1940 ....Princeton (601)	Walter Bourne		Ekwanok	Dixon Brooke, Virginia
	Louisiana St (601)	Mike Donahue			
1941 ....Stanford (580)	Eddie Twiggs	Louisiana St (599)	Ohio St	Earl Stewart, Louisiana St
1942 ....Louisiana St (590)	Mike Donahue		Notre Dame	Frank Tatum Jr, Stanford
	Stanford (590)	Eddie Twiggs			
1943 ....Yale (614)	William Neale Jr	Michigan (618)	Olympia Fields	Wallace Ulrich, Carleton
1944 ....Notre Dame (311)	George Holderith	Minnesota (312)	Inverness	Louis Lick, Minnesota
1945 ....Ohio St (602)	Robert Kepler	Northwestern (621)	Ohio St	John Lorms, Ohio St
1946 ....Stanford (619)	Eddie Twiggs	Michigan (624)	Princeton	George Hamer, Georgia
1947 ....Louisiana St (606)	T.P. Heard	Duke (614)	Michigan	Dave Barclay, Michigan
1948 ....San Jose St (579)	Wilbur Hubbard	Louisiana St (588)	Stanford	Bob Harris, San Jose St
1949 ....N Texas (590)	Fred Cobb	Purdue (600)	Iowa St	Harvie Ward, N Carolina
			Texas (600)		
1950 ....N Texas (573)	Fred Cobb	Purdue (577)	New Mexico	Fred Wampler, Purdue
1951 ....N Texas (588)	Fred Cobb	Ohio St (589)	Ohio St	Tom Nieporte, Ohio St
1952 ....N Texas (587)	Fred Cobb	Michigan (593)	Purdue	Jim Vickers, Oklahoma
1953 ....Stanford (578)	Charles Finger	N Carolina (580)	Broadmoor	Earl Moeller, Oklahoma St
1954 ....SMU (572)	Graham Ross	N Texas (573)	Houston	Hillman Robbins, Memphis St
1955 ....Louisiana St (574)	Mike Barbato	N Texas (583)	Tennessee	Joe Campbell, Purdue
1956 ....Houston (601)	Dave Williams	N Texas (602)	Ohio St	Rick Jones, Ohio St
			Purdue (602)		
1957 ....Houston (602)	Dave Williams	Stanford (603)	Broadmoor	Rex Baxter Jr., Houston
1958 ....Houston (570)	Dave Williams	Oklahoma St (582)	Williams	Phil Rodgers, Houston
1959 ....Houston (561)	Dave Williams	Purdue (571)	Oregon	Dick Crawford, Houston
1960 ....Houston (603)	Dave Williams	Purdue (607)	Broadmoor	Dick Crawford, Houston
			Oklahoma St (607)		
1961 ....Purdue (584)	Sam Voinoff	Arizona St (595)	Lafayette	Jack Nicklaus, Ohio St
1962 ....Houston (588)	Dave Williams	Oklahoma St (598)	Duke	Kermit Zarley, Houston
1963 ....Oklahoma St (581)	Labron Harris	Houston (582)	Wichita St	R.H. Sikes, Arkansas
1964 ....Houston (580)	Dave Williams	Oklahoma St (587)	Broadmoor	Terry Small, San Jose St
1965 ....Houston (577)	Dave Williams	Cal St–LA (587)	Tennessee	Marty Fleckman, Houston
1966 ....Houston (582)	Dave Williams	San Jose St (586)	Stanford	Bob Murphy, Florida
1967 ....Houston (585)	Dave Williams	Florida (588)	Shawnee, PA	Hale Irwin, Colorado
1968 ....Florida (1154)	Buster Bishop	Houston (1156)	New Mexico St	Grier Jones, Oklahoma St
1969 ....Houston (1223)	Dave Williams	Wake Forest (1232)	Broadmoor	Bob Clark, Cal St–LA
1970 ....Houston (1172)	Dave Williams	Wake Forest (1182)	Ohio St	John Mahaffey, Houston
1971 ....Texas (1144)	George Hannon	Houston (1151)	Arizona	Ben Crenshaw, Texas

Men (Cont.)
DIVISION I (Cont.)
Results, 1939-2004 (Cont.)

Year	Champion (Score)	Coach	Runner-Up (Score)	Host or Site	Individual Champion
1972	Texas (1146)	George Hannon	Houston (1159)	Cape Coral	Ben Crenshaw, Texas
					Tom Kite, Texas
1973	Florida (1149)	Buster Bishop	Oklahoma St (1159)	Oklahoma St	Ben Crenshaw, Texas
1974	Wake Forest (1158)	Jess Haddock	Florida (1160)	San Diego St	Curtis Strange, Wake Forest
1975	Wake Forest (1156)	Jess Haddock	Oklahoma St (1189)	Ohio St	Jay Haas, Wake Forest
1976	Oklahoma St (1166)	Mike Holder	Brigham Young (1173)	New Mexico	Scott Simpson, So Cal
1977	Houston (1197)	Dave Williams	Oklahoma St (1205)	Colgate	Scott Simpson, So Cal
1978	Oklahoma St (1140)	Mike Holder	Georgia (1157)	Oregon	David Edwards, Oklahoma St
1979	Ohio St (1189)	James Brown	Oklahoma St (1191)	Wake Forest	Gary Hallberg, Wake Forest
1980	Oklahoma St (1173)	Mike Holder	Brigham Young (1177)	Ohio St	Jay Don Blake, Utah St
1981	BYU (1161)	Karl Tucker	Oral Roberts (1163)	Stanford	Ron Commans, So Cal
1982	Houston (1141)	Dave Williams	Oklahoma St (1151)	Pinehurst	Billy Ray Brown, Houston
1983	Oklahoma St (1161)	Mike Holder	Texas (1168)	Fresno St	Jim Carter, Arizona St
1984	Houston (1145)	Dave Williams	Oklahoma St (1146)	Houston	John Inman, N Carolina
1985	Houston (1172)	Dave Williams	Oklahoma St (1175)	Florida	Clark Burroughs, Ohio St
1986	Wake Forest (1156)	Jess Haddock	Oklahoma St (1160)	Wake Forest	Scott Verplank, Oklahoma St
1987	Oklahoma St (1160)	Mike Holder	Wake Forest (1176)	Ohio St	Brian Watts, Oklahoma St
1988	UCLA (1176)	Eddie Merrins	UT–El Paso (1179)	Southern Cal	E.J. Pfister, Oklahoma St
			Oklahoma (1179)		
			Oklahoma St (1179)		
1989	Oklahoma (1139)	Gregg Grost	Texas (1158)	Oklahoma	Phil Mickelson, Arizona St
				Oklahoma St	
1990	Arizona St (1155)	Steve Loy	Florida (1157)	Florida	Phil Mickelson, Arizona St
1991	Oklahoma (1161)	Mike Holder	N Carolina (1168)	San Jose St	Warren Schutte, UNLV
1992	Arizona (1129)	Rick LaRose	Arizona St (1136)	New Mexico	Phil Mickelson, Arizona St
1993	Florida (1145)	Buddy Alexander	Georgia Tech (1146)	Kentucky	Todd Demsey, Arizona St
1994	Stanford (1129)	Wally Goodwin	Texas (1133)	McKinney, TX	Justin Leonard, Texas
1995	Oklahoma St* (1156)	Mike Holder	Stanford (1156)	Ohio St	Chip Spratlin, Auburn
1996	Arizona St (1186)	Randy Lein	UNLV (1189)	Chattanooga	Tiger Woods, Stanford
1997	Pepperdine (1148)	John Geiberger	Wake Forest (1151)	Evanston, IL	Charles Warren, Clemson
1998	UNLV (1118)	Dwaine Knight	Clemson (1121)	Albuquerque	James McLean, Minnesota
1999	Georgia (1180)	Chris Haack	Oklahoma St (1183)	Chaska, MN	Donald Luke, Northwestern
2000	Oklahoma St* (1116)	Mike Holder	Georgia Tech (1116)	Opelika, AL	Charles Howell, Oklahoma St
2001	Florida (1126)	Buddy Alexander	Clemson (1144)	Durham, NC	Nick Gilliam, Florida
2002	Minnesota (1134)	Brad James	Georgia Tech	Ohio St	Troy Matteson, Ga. Tech
2003	Clemson (1191)	Larry Penley	Oklahoma St	Oklahoma St	A. Canizares, Arizona St
2004	California (1134)	Steve Desimone	UCLA (1140)	Hot Springs, Va	Ryan Moore, UNLV
2005	Georgia (1135)	Chris Haack	Georgia Tech (1145)	Caves Valley	James Lepp, Washington

*Won sudden death playoff. Notes: Match play, 1897-1964; par-70 tournaments held in 1969, 1973 and 1989; par-71 tournaments held in 1968, 1981 and 1988; all other championships par-72 tournaments. Scores are based on 4 rounds instead of 2 after 1967.

DIVISION II

Year	Champion	Year	Champion	Year	Champion
1963	SW Missouri St	1978	Columbus St	1993	Abilene Christian
1964	Southern Illinois	1979	UC-Davis	1994	Columbus St
1965	Middle Tennessee St	1980	Columbus St	1995	Florida Southern
1966	Cal St–Chico	1981	Florida Southern	1996	Florida Southern
1967	Lamar	1982	Florida Southern	1997	Columbus St
1968	Lamar	1983	SW Texas St	1998	Florida Southern
1969	Cal St–Northridge	1984	Troy St	1999	Florida Southern
1970	Rollins	1985	Florida Southern	2000	Florida Southern
1971	New Orleans	1986	Florida Southern	2001	W Florida
1972	New Orleans	1987	Tampa	2002	Rollins
1973	Cal St–Northridge	1988	Tampa	2003	Francis Marion
1974	Cal St–Northridge	1989	Columbus St	2004	S Carolina–Aiken
1975	UC–Irvine	1990	Florida Southern	2005	W Florida
1976	Troy St	1991	Florida Southern		
1977	Troy St	1992	Columbus St		

Note: Par-71 tournaments held in 1967, 1970, 1976-78, 1985, 1988 and 2001; par-70 tournament held in 1996; all other championships par-72 tournaments.

Men (Cont.)
DIVISION III

Year	Champion	Year	Champion	Year	Champion
1975	Wooster	1986	Cal St–Stanislaus	1997	Methodist (NC)
1976	Cal St–Stanislaus	1987	Cal St–Stanislaus	1998	Methodist (NC)
1977	Cal St–Stanislaus	1988	Cal St–Stanislaus	1999	Methodist (NC)
1978	Cal St–Stanislaus	1989	Cal St–Stanislaus	2000	Greensboro
1979	Cal St–Stanislaus	1990	Methodist (NC)	2001	WI–Eau Claire
1980	Cal St–Stanislaus	1991	Methodist (NC)	2002	Guilford
1981	Cal St–Stanislaus	1992	Methodist (NC)	2003	Averett
1982	Ramapo	1993	UC–San Diego	2004	Gustavus Adolphus
1983	Allegheny	1994	Methodist (NC)	2005	Guilford
1984	Cal St–Stanislaus	1995	Methodist (NC)		
1985	Cal St–Stanislaus	1996	Methodist (NC)		

Note: All championships par-72 except for 1986, 1988 and 2001, which were par-71; fourth round of 1975 championships canceled as a result of bad weather; first round of 1988 championships canceled as a result of rain.

Women
DIVISION I

Year	Champion	Coach	Score	Runner-Up	Score	Individual Champion
1982	Tulsa	Dale McNamara	1191	Texas Christian	1227	Kathy Baker, Tulsa
1983	Texas Christian	Fred Warren	1193	Tulsa	1196	Penny Hammel, Miami (FL)
1984	Miami (FL)	Lela Cannon	1214	Arizona St	1221	Cindy Schreyer, Georgia
1985	Florida	Mimi Ryan	1218	Tulsa	1233	Danielle Ammaccapane, Arizona St
1986	Florida	Mimi Ryan	1180	Miami (FL)	1188	Page Dunlap, Florida
1987	San Jose St	Mark Gale	1187	Furman	1188	Caroline Keggi, New Mexico
1988	Tulsa	Dale McNamara	1175	Georgia/Arizona	1182	Melissa McNamara, Tulsa
1989	San Jose St	Mark Gale	1208	Tulsa	1209	Pat Hurst, San Jose St
1990	Arizona St	Linda Vollstedt	1206	UCLA	1222	Susan Slaughter, Arizona
1991	UCLA*	Jackie Steinmann	1197	San Jose St	1197	Annika Sorenstam, Arizona
1992	San Jose St	Mark Gale	1171	Arizona	1175	Vicki Goetze, Georgia
1993	Arizona St	Linda Vollstedt	1187	Texas	1189	Charlotta Sorenstam, Texas
1994	Arizona St	Linda Vollstedt	1189	Southern Cal	1205	Emilee Klein, Arizona St
1995	Arizona St	Linda Vollstedt	1155	San Jose St	1181	Kristel Mourgue d'Algue, Arizona St
1996	Arizona*	Rick LaRose	1240	San Jose St	1240	Marisa Baena, Arizona
1997	Arizona St	Linda Vollstedt	1178	San Jose St	1180	Heather Bowie, Texas
1998	Arizona St	Linda Vollstedt	1155	Florida	1173	Jennifer Rosales, So Cal
1999	Duke	Dan Brooks	895	Arizona St/Georgia	903	Grace Park, Arizona St
2000	Arizona	Todd McCorkle	1175	Stanford	1196	Jenna Daniels, Arizona
2001	Georgia	Todd McCorkle	1176	Duke	1179	Candy Hannemann, Duke
2002	Duke	Dan Brooks	1164	Arizona/Auburn/Texas	1160	Virada Nirapathpongporn, Duke
2003	Southern Cal	Andrea Gaston	1197	Pepperdine	1212	Mikaela Parmlid, So Cal
2004	UCLA	Carrie Forsyth	1148	Oklahoma St	1151	Sarah Huarte, California
2005	Duke	Dan Brooks	1170	UCLA	1175	Anna Grzebien, Duke

*Won sudden death playoff. Note: Par-74 tournaments held in 1983 and 1988; par-72 tournament held in 1990, 2000 and 2001; all other championships par-73 tournaments.

DIVISIONS II AND III

Year	Champion	Year	Champion
1996	Methodist (NC)	1998	Methodist (NC)
1997	Lynn	1999	Methodist (NC)

DIVISION II

Year	Champion
2000	Florida Southern
2001	Florida Southern
2002	Florida Southern
2003	Rollins (FL)
2004	Rollins (FL)
2005	Rollins (FL)

DIVISION III

Year	Champion
2000	Methodist (NC)
2001	Methodist (NC)
2002	Methodist (NC)
2003	Methodist (NC)
2004	Methodist (NC)
2005	Methodist (NC)

Gymnastics

Men
TEAM CHAMPIONS

Year	Champion	Coach	Pts	Runner-Up	Pts
1938	Chicago	Dan Hoffer	22	Illinois	18
1939	Illinois	Hartley Price	21	Army	17
1940	Illinois	Hartley Price	20	Navy	17
1941	Illinois	Hartley Price	68.5	Minnesota	52.5
1942	Illinois	Hartley Price	39	Penn St	30
1943–47	No tournament				
1948	Penn St	Gene Wettstone	55	Temple	34.5
1949	Temple	Max Younger	28	Minnesota	18
1950	Illinois	Charley Pond	26	Temple	25
1951	Florida St	Hartley Price	26	Illinois/ Southern Cal	23.5
1952	Florida St	Hartley Price	89.5	Southern Cal	75
1953	Penn St	Gene Wettstone	91.5	Illinois	68
1954	Penn St	Gene Wettstone	137	Illinois	68
1955	Illinois	Charley Pond	82	Penn St	69
1956	Illinois	Charley Pond	123.5	Penn St	67.5
1957	Penn St	Gene Wettstone	88.5	Illinois	80
1958	Michigan St	George Szypula	79		
	Illinois	Charley Pond	79		
1959	Penn St	Gene Wettstone	152	Illinois	87.5
1960	Penn St	Gene Wettstone	112.5	Southern Cal	65.5
1961	Penn St	Gene Wettstone	88.5	Southern Illinois	80.5
1962	Southern Cal	Jack Beckner	95.5	Southern Illinois	75
1963	Michigan	Newton Loken	129	Southern Illinois	73
1964	Southern Illinois	Bill Meade	84.5	Southern Cal	69.5
1965	Penn St	Gene Wettstone	68.5	Washington	51.5
1966	Southern Illinois	Bill Meade	187.200	California	185.100
1967	Southern Illinois	Bill Meade	189.550	Michigan	187.400
1968	California	Hal Frey	188.250	Southern Illinois	188.150
1969	Iowa	Mike Jacobson	161.175	Penn St	160.450
	Michigan*	Newton Loken		Colorado St	
1970	Michigan	Newton Loken	164.150	Iowa St	164.050
				New Mexico St	
1971	Iowa St	Ed Gagnier	319.075	Southern Illinois	316.650
1972	Southern Illinois	Bill Meade	315.925	Iowa St	312.325
1973	Iowa St	Ed Gagnier	325.150	Penn St	323.025
1974	Iowa St	Ed Gagnier	326.100	Arizona St	322.050
1975	California	Hal Frey	437.325	Louisiana St	433.700
1976	Penn St	Gene Wettstone	432.075	Louisiana St	425.125
1977	Indiana St	Roger Counsil	434.475		
	Oklahoma	Paul Ziert	434.475		
1978	Oklahoma	Paul Ziert	439.350	Arizona St	437.075
1979	Nebraska	Francis Allen	448.275	Oklahoma	446.625
1980	Nebraska	Francis Allen	563.300	Iowa St	557.650
1981	Nebraska	Francis Allen	284.600	Oklahoma	281.950
1982	Nebraska	Francis Allen	285.500	UCLA	281.050
1983	Nebraska	Francis Allen	287.800	UCLA	283.900
1984	UCLA	Art Shurlock	287.300	Penn St	281.250
1985	Ohio St	Michael Willson	285.350	Nebraska	284.550
1986	Arizona St	Don Robinson	283.900	Nebraska	283.600
1987	UCLA	Art Shurlock	285.300	Nebraska	284.750
1988	Nebraska	Francis Allen	288.150	Illinois	287.150
1989	Illinois	Yoshi Hayasaki	283.400	Nebraska	282.300
1990	Nebraska	Francis Allen	287.400	Minnesota	287.300
1991	Oklahoma	Greg Buwick	288.025	Penn St	285.500
1992	Stanford	Sadao Hamada	289.575	Nebraska	288.950
1993	Stanford	Sadao Hamada	276.500	Nebraska	275.500
1994	Nebraska	Francis Allen	288.250	Stanford	285.925
1995	Stanford	Sadao Hamada	232.400	Nebraska	231.525
1996	Ohio St	Peter Kormann	232.150	California	231.775
1997	California	Barry Weiner	233.825	Oklahoma	232.725
1998	California	Barry Weiner	231.200	Iowa	229.675
1999	Michigan	Kurt Golder	232.550	Ohio St	230.850
2000	Penn St	Randy Jepson	231.975	Michigan	231.850
2001	Ohio St	Miles Avery	218.125	Oklahoma	217.775
2002	Oklahoma	Mark Williams	219.300	Ohio St	218.650
2003	Oklahoma	Mark Williams	222.600	Ohio St	220.700
2004	Penn St	Randy Jepson	223.350	Oklahoma	222.300
2005	Oklahoma	Mark Williams	225.675	Ohio St	225.450

*Trampoline.

Men (Cont.)

INDIVIDUAL CHAMPIONS

ALL-AROUND	HORIZONTAL BAR	PARALLEL BARS
1938.....Joe Giallombardo, Illinois	1938.....Bob Sears, Army	1938.....Erwin Beyer, Chicago
1939.....Joe Giallombardo, Illinois	1939.....Adam Walters, Temple	1939.....Bob Sears, Army
1940.....Joe Giallombardo, Illinois	1940.....Norm Boardman, Temple	1940.....Bob Hanning, Minnesota
Paul Fina, Illinois	1941.....Newt Loken, Minnesota	1941.....Caton Cobb, Illinois
1941.....Courtney Shanken, Chicago	1942.....Norm Boardman, Temple	1942.....Hal Zimmerman, Penn St
1942.....Newt Loken, Minnesota	1948.....Joe Calvetti, Illinois	1948.....Ray Sorenson, Penn St
1948.....Ray Sorenson, Penn St	1949.....Bob Stout, Temple	1949.....Joe Kotys, Kent
1949.....Joe Kotys, Kent	1950.....Joe Kotys, Kent	Mel Stout, Michigan St
1950.....Joe Kotys, Kent	1951.....Bill Roetzheim, Florida St	1950.....Joe Kotys, Kent
1951.....Bill Roetzheim, Florida St	1952.....Charles Simms, So Cal	1951.....Jack Beckner, So Cal
1952.....Jack Beckner, Southern Cal	1953.....Hal Lewis, Navy	1952.....Jack Beckner, So Cal
1953.....Jean Cronstedt, Penn St	1954.....Jean Cronstedt, Penn St	1953.....Jean Cronstedt, Penn St
1954.....Jean Cronstedt, Penn St	1955.....Carlton Rintz, Michigan St	1954.....Jean Cronstedt, Penn St
1955.....Karl Schwenzfeier, Penn St	1956.....Ronnie Amster, Florida St	1955.....Carlton Rintz, Michigan St
1956.....Don Tonry, Illlinois	1957.....Abie Grossfeld, Illinois	1956.....Armando Vega, Penn St
1957.....Armando Vega, Penn St	1958.....Abie Grossfeld, Illinois	1957.....Armando Vega, Penn St
1958.....Abie Grossfeld, Illinois	1959.....Stanley Tarshis, Mich St	1958.....Tad Muzyczko, Mich St
1959.....Armando Vega, Penn St	1960.....Stanley Tarshis, Mich St	1959.....Armando Vega, Penn St
1960.....Jay Werner, Penn St	1961.....Bruno Klaus, Southern Ill	1960.....Robert Lynn, Southern Cal
1961.....Gregor Weiss, Penn St	1962.....Robert Lynn, So Cal	1961.....Fred Tijerina, Southern Ill
1962.....Robert Lynn, Southern Cal	1963.....Gil Larose, Michigan	Jeff Cardinalli, Springfield
1963.....Gil Larose, Michigan	1964.....Ron Barak, Southern Cal	1962.....Robert Lynn, Southern Cal
1964.....Ron Barak, Southern Cal	1965.....Jim Curzi, Michigan St	1963.....Arno Lascari, Michigan
1965.....Mike Jacobson, Penn St	Mike Jacobsen, Penn St	1964.....Ron Barak, Southern Cal
1966.....Steve Cohen, Penn St	1966.....Rusty Rock, Cal St–	1965.....Jim Curzi, Michigan St
1967.....Steve Cohen, Penn St	Northridge	1966.....Jim Curzi, Michigan St
1968.....Makoto Sakamoto, So Cal	1967.....Rich Grigsby, Cal St–	1967.....Makoto Sakamoto, So Cal
1969.....Mauno Nissinen, Wash	Northridge	1968.....Makoto Sakamoto, So Cal
1970.....Yoshi Hayasaki, Wash	1968.....Makoto Sakamoto, So Cal	1969.....Ron Rapper, Michigan
1971.....Yoshi Hayasaki, Wash	1969.....Bob Manna, New Mexico	1970.....Ron Rapper, Michigan
1972.....Steve Hug, Stanford	1970.....Yoshi Hayasaki, Wash	1971.....Brent Simmons, Iowa St
1973.....Steve Hug, Stanford	1971.....Brent Simmons, Iowa St	Tom Dunn, Penn St
Marshall Avener, Penn St	1972.....Tom Lindner, Southern Ill	1972.....Dennis Mazur, Iowa St
1974.....Steve Hug, Stanford	1973.....Jon Aitken, New Mexico	1973.....Steve Hug, Stanford
1975.....Wayne Young, BYU	1974.....Rick Banley, Indiana St	1974.....Steve Hug, Stanford
1976.....Peter Kormann,	1975.....Rich Larsen, Iowa St	1975.....Yoichi Tomita,
Southern Conn St	1976.....Tom Beach, California	Long Beach St
1977.....Kurt Thomas, Indiana St	1977.....John Hart, UCLA	1976.....Gene Whelan, Penn St
1978.....Bart Conner, Oklahoma	1978.....Mel Cooley, Washington	1977.....Kurt Thomas, Indiana St
1979.....Kurt Thomas, Indiana St	1979.....Kurt Thomas, Indiana St	1978.....John Corritore, Michigan
1980.....Jim Hartung, Nebraska	1980.....Philip Cahoy, Nebraska	1979.....Kurt Thomas, Indiana St
1981.....Jim Hartung, Nebraska	1981.....Philip Cahoy, Nebraska	1980.....Philip Cahoy, Nebraska
1982.....Peter Vidmar, UCLA	1982.....Peter Vidmar, UCLA	1981.....Philip Cahoy, Nebraska
1983.....Peter Vidmar, UCLA	1983.....Scott Johnson, Nebraska	Peter Vidmar, UCLA
1984.....Mitch Gaylord, UCLA	1984.....Charles Lakes, Illinois	Jim Hartung, Nebraska
1985.....Wes Suter, Nebraska	1985.....Dan Hayden, Arizona St	1982.....Jim Hartung, Nebraska
1986.....Jon Louis, Stanford	Wes Suter, Nebraska	1983.....Scott Johnson, Nebraska
1987.....Tom Schlesinger, Nebraska	1986.....Dan Hayden, Arizona St	1984.....Tim Daggett, UCLA
1988.....Vacated†	1987.....David Moriel, UCLA	1985.....Dan Hayden, Arizona St
1989.....Patrick Kirsey, Nebraska	1988.....Vacated†	Noah Riskin, Ohio St
1990.....Mike Racanelli, Ohio St	1989.....Vacated†	Seth Riskin, Ohio St
1991.....John Roethlisberger, Minn	1990.....Chris Waller, UCLA	1986.....Dan Hayden, Arizona St
1992.....John Roethlisberger, Minn	1991.....Luis Lopez, New Mexico	1987.....Kevin Davis, Nebraska
1993.....John Roethlisberger, Minn	1992.....Jair Lynch, Stanford	Tom Schlesinger, Nebraska
1994.....Dennis Harrison, Nebraska	1993.....Steve McCain, UCLA	1988.....Kevin Davis, Nebraska
1995.....Richard Grace, Nebraska	1994.....Jim Foody, UCLA	1989.....Vacated†
1996.....Blaine Wilson, Ohio St	1995.....Rick Kieffer, Nebraska	1990.....Patrick Kirksey, Nebraska
1997.....Blaine Wilson, Ohio St	1996.....Carl Imhauser, Temple	1991.....Scott Keswick, UCLA
1998.....Travis Romagnoli, Illinois	1997.....Marshall Nelson, Nebraska	John Roethlisberger, Minn
1999.....Justin Hardabura, Nebraska	1998.....Todd Bishop, Oklahoma	1992.....Dom Minicucci, Temple
2000.....Jamie Natalie, Ohio St	1999.....Todd Bishop, Oklahoma	1993.....Jair Lynch, Stanford
2001.....Jamie Natalie, Ohio St	2000.....Michael Ashe, California	1994.....Richard Grace, Nebraska
2002.....Raj Bhavsar, Ohio St	2001.....Michael Ashe, California	1995.....Richard Grace, Nebraska
2003.....Daniel Furney, Oklahoma	2002.....Daniel Diaz-Luong, Mich.	1996.....Jamie Ellis, Stanford
2004.....Luis Vargas, Penn St	2003.....Linas Gaveika, Iowa	Blaine Wilson, Ohio St
2005.....Luis Vargas, Penn St	2004.....Justin Spring, Illinois	1997.....Marshall Nelson, Nebraska
	2005.....Ronald Ferris, Ohio St	1998.....Marshall Nelson, Nebraska
		1999.....Justin Toman, Michigan

Men (Cont.)

INDIVIDUAL CHAMPIONS (Cont.)

PARALLEL BARS (CONT.)
2000.....Kris Zimmerman, Michigan
         Justin Toman, Michigan
2001 ....Raj Bhavsar, Ohio St
2002 ....Cody Moore, California
2003 ....Daniel Furney, Oklahoma
2004 ....Ramon Jackson, Wm & M
2005 ....Justin Springs, Illinois

VAULT
1938.....Erwin Toman, Chicago
1939.....Marv Forman, Illinois
1940.....Earl Shanken, Chicago
1941.....Earl Shanken, Chicago
1942.....Earl Shanken, Chicago
1948.....Jim Peterson, Minnesota
1962.....Bruno Klaus, Southern Ill
1963.....Gil Larose, Michigan
1964.....Sidney Oglesby, Syracuse
1965.....Dan Millman, California
1966.....Frank Schmitz, S Illinois
1967.....Paul Mayer, S Illinois
1968.....Bruce Colter, Cal St–LA
1969.....Dan Bowles, California
         Jack McCarthy, Illinois
1970.....Doug Boger, Arizona
1971.....Pat Mahoney, Cal St–N'rdge
1972.....Gary Morava, Southern Ill
1973.....John Crosby, S Conn St
1974.....Greg Goodhue, Oklahoma
1975.....Tom Beach, California
1976.....Sam Shaw, Cal St-Fullerton
1977.....Steve Wejmar, Wash
1978.....Ron Galimore, Louisiana St
1979.....Leslie Moore, Oklahoma
1980.....Ron Galimore, Iowa St
1981.....Ron Galimore, Iowa St
1982.....Randall Wickstrom, Cal
         Steve Elliott, Nebraska
1983.....Chris Riegel, Nebraska
         Mark Oates, Oklahoma
1984.....Chris Riegel, Nebraska
1985.....Derrick Cornelius, Cort. St
1986.....Chad Fox, New Mexico
1987.....Chad Fox, New Mexico
1988.....Chad Fox, New Mexico
1989.....Chad Fox, New Mexico
1990.....Brad Hayashi, UCLA
1991.....Adam Carton, Penn St
1992.....Jason Hebert, Syracuse
1993.....Steve Wiegel, N Mexico
1994.....Steve McCain, UCLA
1995.....Ian Bachrach, Stanford
1996.....Jay Thornton, Iowa
1997.....Blaine Wilson, Ohio St
1998.....Travis Romagnoli, Illinois
1999.....Guard Young, BYU
2000.....Guard Young, BYU
2001.....Daren Lynch, Ohio St
2002.....Dan Gill, Stanford
2003.....Andrew DiGiore, Michigan
2004.....Graham Ackerman, Cal
2005.....Michael Reavis, Iowa

POMMEL HORSE
1938.....Erwin Beyer, Chicago
1939.....Erwin Beyer, Chicago
1940.....Harry Koehnemann, Illinois
1941.....Caton Cobb, Illinois
1942.....Caton Cobb, Illinois

POMMEL HORSE (CONT.)
1948.....Steve Greene, Penn St
1949.....Joe Berenato, Temple
1950.....Gene Rabbitt, Syracuse
1951.....Joe Kotys, Kent
1952.....Frank Bare, Illinois
1953.....Carlton Rintz, Michigan St
1954.....Robert Lawrence, Penn St
1955.....Carlton Rintz, Michigan St
1956.....James Brown, Cal St–L.A.
1957.....John Davis, Illinois
1958.....Bill Buck, Iowa
1959.....Art Shurlock, California
1960.....James Fairchild, California
1961.....James Fairchild, California
1962.....Mike Aufrecht, Illinois
1963.....Russ Mills, Yale
1964.....Russ Mills, Yale
1965.....Bob Elsinger, Springfield
1966.....Gary Hoskins, Cal St–L.A.
1967.....Keith McCanless, Iowa
1968.....Jack Ryan, Colorado
1969.....Keith McCanless, Iowa
1970.....Russ Hoffman, Iowa St
         John Russo, Wisconsin
1971.....Russ Hoffman, Iowa St
1972.....Russ Hoffman, Iowa St
1973.....Ed Slezak, Indiana St
1974.....Ted Marcy, Stanford
1975.....Ted Marcy, Stanford
1976.....Ted Marcy, Stanford
1977.....Chuck Walter, New Mexico
1978.....Mike Burke, Northern Ill
1979.....Mike Burke, Northern Ill
1980.....David Stoldt, Illinois
1981.....Mark Bergman, California
         Steve Jennings, New Mexico
1982.....Peter Vidmar, UCLA
         Steve Jennings, New Mexico
1983.....Doug Kieso, Northern Ill
1984.....Tim Daggett, UCLA
1985.....Tony Pineda, UCLA
1986.....Curtis Holdsworth, UCLA
1987.....Li Xiao Ping, Cal St-Fullerton
1988.....Vacated†
         Mark Sohn, Penn St
1989.....Mark Sohn, Penn St
         Chris Waller, UCLA
1990.....Mark Sohn, Penn St
1991.....Mark Sohn, Penn St
1992.....Che Bowers, Nebraska
1993.....John Roethlisberger, Minn
1994.....Jason Bertram, California
1995.....Drew Durbin, Ohio St
1996.....Drew Durbin, Ohio St
1997.....Drew Durbin, Ohio St
1998.....Josh Birckelbaw, California
1999.....Brandon Stefaniak, Penn St
2000.....Brandon Stefaniak, Penn St
         Don Jackson, Iowa
2001.....Clay Strother, Minnesota
2002.....Clay Strother, Minnesota
2003.....Josh Landis, Oklahoma
2004.....Bob Rogers, Illinois
2005 ....Luis Vargas, Penn St

FLOOR EXERCISE
1941.....Lou Fina, Illinois
1953.....Bob Sullivan, Illinois

FLOOR EXERCISE (CONT.)
1954.....Jean Cronstedt, Penn St
1955.....Don Faber, UCLA
1956.....Jamile Ashmore, Florida St
1957.....Norman Marks, Cal St–LA
1958.....Abie Grossfeld, Illinois
1959.....Don Tonry, Illinois
1960.....Ray Hadley, Illinois
1961.....Robert Lynn, Southern Cal
1962.....Robert Lynn, Southern Cal
1963.....Tom Seward, Penn St
         Mike Henderson, Michigan
1964.....Rusty Mitchell, S Illinois
1965.....Frank Schmitz, S Illinois
1966.....Frank Schmitz, S Illinois
1967.....Dave Jacobs, Michigan
1968.....Toby Towson, Michigan St
1969.....Toby Towson, Michigan St
1970.....Tom Proulx, Colorado St
1971.....Stormy Eaton, New Mexico
1972.....Odessa Lovin, Oklahoma
1973.....Odessa Lovin, Oklahoma
1974.....Doug Fitzjarrell, Iowa St
1975.....Kent Brown, Arizona St
1976.....Bob Robbins, Colorado St
1977.....Ron Galimore, Louisiana St
1978.....Curt Austin, Iowa St
1979.....Mike Wilson, Oklahoma
         Bart Conner, Oklahoma
1980.....Steve Elliott, Nebraska
1981.....James Yuhashi, Oregon
1982.....Steve Elliott, Nebraska
1983.....Scott Johnson, Nebraska
         David Branch, Arizona St
         Donnie Hinton, Arizona St
1984.....Kevin Ekburg, Northern Ill
1985.....Wes Suter, Nebraska
1986.....Jerry Burrell, Arizona St
         Brian Ginsberg, UCLA
1987.....Chad Fox, New Mexico
1988.....Chris Wyatt, Temple
1989.....Jody Newman, Arizona St
1990.....Mike Racanelli, Ohio St
1991.....Brad Hayashi, UCLA
1992.....Brian Winkler, Michigan
1993.....Richard Grace, Nebraska
1994.....Mark Booth, Stanford
1995.....Jay Thornton, Iowa
1996.....Ian Bachrach, Stanford
1997.....Jeremy Killen, Oklahoma
1998.....Darin Gerlach, Temple
1999.....Jason Hardabura, Nebraska
2000.....Jamie Natalie, Ohio St
2001.....Clay Strother, Minnesota
2002.....Clay Strother, Minnesota
2003.....Josh Landis, Oklahoma
2004.....Graham Ackerman, Cal
2005.....Graham Ackerman, Cal

RINGS
1959.....Armando Vega, Penn St
1960.....Sam Garcia, Southern Cal
1961.....Fred Orlofsky, Southern Ill
1962.....Dale Cooper, Michigan St
1963.....Dale Cooper, Michigan St
1964.....Chris Evans, Arizona St
1965.....Glenn Gailis, Iowa
1966.....Ed Gunny, Michigan St
1967.....Josh Robison, California

Men (Cont.)

INDIVIDUAL CHAMPIONS (Cont.)

RINGS (CONT.)

1968.....Pat Arnold, Arizona
1969.....Paul Vexler, Penn St
        Ward Maythaler, Iowa St
1970.....Dave Seal, Indiana St
1971.....Charles Ropiequet, S Illinois
1972.....Dave Seal, Indiana St
1973.....Bob Mahorney, Indiana St
1974.....Keith Heaver, Iowa St
1975.....Keith Heaver, Iowa St
1976.....Doug Wood, Iowa St
1977.....Doug Wood, Iowa St
1978.....Scott McEldowney, Oregon
1979.....Kirk Mango, Northern Ill
1980.....Jim Hartung, Nebraska

RINGS (CONT.)

1981.....Jim Hartung, Nebraska
1982.....Jim Hartung, Nebraska
1983.....Alex Schwartz, UCLA
1984.....Tim Daggett, UCLA
1985.....Mark Diab, Iowa St
1986.....Mark Diab, Iowa St
1987.....Paul O'Neill, Hou. Baptist
1988.....Paul O'Neill, New Mexico
1989.....Vacated†
        Paul O'Neill, New Mexico
1990.....Wayne Cowden, Penn St
1991.....Adam Carton, Penn St
1992.....Scott Keswick, UCLA
1993.....Chris LaMorte, N Mexico

RINGS (CONT.)

1994.....Chris LaMorte, N Mexico
1995.....Dave Frank, Temple
1996.....Scott McCall, Will. & Mary
        Blaine Wilson, Ohio St
1997.....Blaine Wilson, Ohio St
1998.....Dan Fink, Oklahoma
1999.....Cortney Bramwell, BYU
2000.....Cortney Bramwell, BYU
2001.....Chris Lakeman, Penn St
2002.....Marshall Erwin, Stanford
2003.....Kevin Tan, Penn St
2004.....Kevin Tan, Penn St
2005.....David Henderson, Okla.

†Championships won by Miguel Rubio (All Around, 1988; Horizontal Bar, 1988–89) and Alfonso Rodriguez (Pommel Horse, 1988; Rings, 1989; Parallel Bars, 1989) were vacated by action of the NCAA Committee on Infractions.

DIVISION II (Discontinued after 1984)

Year	Champion	Coach	Pts	Runner-Up	Pts
1968	Cal St–Northridge	Bill Vincent	179.400	Springfield	178.050
1969	Cal St–Northridge	Bill Vincent	151.800	Southern Connecticut St	145.075
1970	Northwestern Louisiana	Armando Vega	160.250	Southern Connecticut St	159.300
1971	Cal St–Fullerton	Dick Wolfe	158.150	Springfield	156.987
1972	Cal St–Fullerton	Dick Wolfe	160.550	Southern Connecticut St	153.050
1973	Southern Connecticut St	Abe Grossfeld	160.750	Cal St–Northridge	158.700
1974	Cal St–Fullerton	Dick Wolfe	309.800	Southern Connecticut St	309.400
1975	Southern Connecticut St	Abe Grossfeld	411.650	IL–Chicago	398.800
1976	Southern Connecticut St	Abe Grossfeld	419.200	IL–Chicago	388.850
1977	Springfield	Frank Wolcott	395.950	Cal St–Northridge	381.250
1978	IL–Chicago	C. Johnson/A. Gentile	406.850	Cal St–Northridge	400.400
1979	IL–Chicago	Clarence Johnson	418.550	WI–Oshkosh	385.650
1980	WI–Oshkosh	Ken Allen	260.550	Cal St–Chico	256.050
1981	WI–Oshkosh	Ken Allen	209.500	Springfield	201.550
1982	WI–Oshkosh	Ken Allen	216.050	E Stroudsburg	211.200
1983	E Stroudsburg	Bruno Klaus	258.650	WI–Oshkosh	257.850
1984	E Stroudsburg	Bruno Klaus	270.800	Cortland St	246.350

Women

TEAM CHAMPIONS

Year	Champion	Coach	Pts	Runner-Up	Pts
1982	Utah	Greg Marsden	148.60	Cal St–Fullerton	144.10
1983	Utah	Greg Marsden	184.65	Arizona St	183.30
1984	Utah	Greg Marsden	186.05	UCLA	185.55
1985	Utah	Greg Marsden	188.35	Arizona St	186.60
1986	Utah	Greg Marsden	186.95	Arizona St	186.70
1987	Georgia	Suzanne Yoculan	187.90	Utah	187.55
1988	Alabama	Sarah Patterson	190.05	Utah	189.50
1989	Georgia	Suzanne Yoculan	192.65	UCLA	192.60
1990	Utah	Greg Marsden	194.900	Alabama	194.575
1991	Alabama	Sarah Patterson	195.125	Utah	194.375
1992	Utah	Greg Marsden	195.650	Georgia	194.600
1993	Georgia	Suzanne Yoculan	198.000	Alabama	196.825
1994	Utah	Greg Marsden	196.400	Alabama	196.350
1995	Utah	Greg Marsden	196.650	Alabama	196.425
				Michigan	196.425
1996	Alabama	Sarah Patterson	198.025	UCLA	197.475
1997	UCLA	Valorie Kondos	197.150	Arizona St	196.850
1998	Georgia	Suzanne Yoculan	197.725	Florida	196.350
1999	Georgia	Suzanne Yoculan	196.850	Michigan	196.550
2000	UCLA	Valorie Kondos	197.300	Utah	196.875
2001	UCLA	Valorie Kondos	197.575	Georgia	197.400
2002	Alabama	Sarah Patterson	197.575	Georgia	197.250
2003	UCLA	Valorie Kondos Field	197.825	Alabama	197.275
2004	UCLA	Valorie Kondos Field	198.125	Georgia	197.200
2005	Georgia	Suzanne Yoculan	197.825	Alabama	197.400

Women (Cont.)

INDIVIDUAL CHAMPIONS

ALL-AROUND

1982.....Sue Stednitz, Utah
1983.....Megan McCunniff, Utah
1984......Megan McCunniff-Marsden, Utah
1985.......Penney Hauschild, Alabama
1986.......Penney Hauschild, Alabama
Jackie Brummer, Arizona St
1987.....Kelly Garrison-Steves, Oklahoma
1988.....Kelly Garrison-Steves, Okla
1989.....Corrinne Wright, Georgia
1990.....Dee Dee Foster, Alabama
1991.....Hope Spivey, Georgia
1992.....Missy Marlowe, Utah
1993.....Jenny Hansen, Kentucky
1994.....Jenny Hansen, Kentucky
1995.....Jenny Hansen, Kentucky
1996.....Meredith Willard, Alabama
1997.....Kim Arnold, Georgia
1998.....Kim Arnold, Georgia
1999.....Theresa Kulikowski, Utah
2000.....Mohini Bhardwaj, UCLA
Heather Brink, Nebraska
2001....Onnis Willis, UCLA
Elise Ray, Michigan
2002 .....Jamie Dantzscher, UCLA
2003 .....Richelle Simpson, Neb.
2004 .....Jeana Rice, Alabama
2005 ....Katie Heenan, Georgia

VAULT

1982.....Elaine Alfano, Utah
1983.....Elaine Alfano, Utah
1984.....Megan Marsden, Utah
1985.....Elaine Alfano, Utah
1986.....Kim Neal, Arizona St
Pam Loree, Penn St
1987.....Yumi Mordre, Washington
1988.....Jill Andrews, UCLA
1989.....Kim Hamilton, UCLA
1990.....Michele Bryant, Nebraska
1991.....Anna Basaldva, Arizona
1992.....Tammy Marshall, Mass.
Heather Stepp, Georgia
Kristein Kenoyer, Utah
1993.....Heather Stepp, Georgia
1994.....Jenny Hansen, Kentucky
1995.....Jenny Hansen, Kentucky
1996.....Leah Brown, Georgia
1997.....Susan Hines, Florida
1998.....Susan Hines, Florida
1999.....Heidi Moneymaker, UCLA
2000.....Heather Brink, Nebraska
2001.....Cory Fritzinger, Georgia
2002.....Jamie Dantzscher, UCLA

VAULT (Cont.)

2003.....Ashley Miles, Alabama
2004.....Ashley Miles, Alabama
2005.....Kristen Maloney, UCLA

BALANCE BEAM

1982.....Sue Stednitz, Utah
1983.....Julie Goewey, Cal St–Fullerton
1984.....Heidi Anderson, Oregon St
1985.....Lisa Zeis, Arizona St
1986.....Jackie Brummer, Arizona St
1987.....Yumi Mordre, Washington
1988.....Kelly Garrison-Steves, Oklahoma
1989.....Jill Andrews, UCLA
Joy Selig, Oregon St
1990.....Joy Selig, Oregon St
1991.....Missy Marlowe, Utah
1992.....Missy Marlowe, Utah
1992 Dana Dobransky, Alabama
1993.....Dana Dobransky, Alabama
1994.....Jenny Hansen, Kentucky
1995.....Jenny Hansen, Kentucky
1996.....Summer Reid, UUtah
1997.....Summer Reid, Utah
Elizabeth Reid, Arizona St
1998 Larissa Fontaine, Stanford
Susan Hines, Florida
1999.....Theresa Kulikowski, Utah
2000.....Lena Degteva, UCLA
2001.....Theresa Kulikowski, Utah
2002.....Elise Ray, Michigan
2003.....Kate Richardson, UCLA
2004.....Ashley Kelly, Arizona St
2005.....Kristen Maloney, UCLA

FLOOR EXERCISE

1982.....Mary Ayotte-Law, Oregon St
1983.....Kim Neal, Arizona St
1984.....Maria Anz, Florida
1985.....Lisa Mitzel, Utah
1986.....Lisa Zeis, Arizona St
P. Hauschild, Alabama
1987.....Kim Hamilton, UCLA
1988.....Kim Hamilton, UCLA
1989.....Corrinne Wright, Georgia
Kim Hamilton, UCLA
1990.....Joy Selig, Oregon St
1991.....Hope Spivey, Georgia
1992.....Missy Marlowe, Utah
1993.....Heather Stepp, Georgia
Tammy Marshall, Mass.
Amy Durham, Oregon St

FLOOR EXERCISE (Cont.)

1994......Hope Spivey-Sheeley, Georgia
1995.....Jenny Hansen, Kentucky
Stella Umeh, UCLA
Leslie Angeles, Georgia
1996.....Heidi Hornbeek, Arizona
Kim Kelly, Alabama
1997.....Leah Brown, Georgia
1998.....Kim Arnold, Georgia
Jenni Beathard, Georgia
Betsy Hamm, Florida
1999.....Marny Oestreng, Bowl. Green
2000.....Suzanne Sears, Georgia
2001.....Mohini Bhardwaj, UCLA
2002.....Jamie Dantzscher, UCLA
Nicole Arnstad, LSU
2003.....Richelle Simpson, Neb.
2004.....Ashley Miles, Alabama
Courtney Bumpers, UNC
2005.....Courtney Bumpers, UNC

UNEVEN BARS

1982.....Lisa Shirk, Pittsburgh
1983.....Jeri Cameron, Arizona St
1984.....Jackie Brummer, Arizona St
1985.......Penney Hauschild, Alabama
1986.....Lucy Wener, Georgia
1987.....Lucy Wener, Georgia
1988.....Kelly Garrison-Steves, Oklahoma
1989.....Lucy Wener, Georgia
1990.....Marie Roethlisberger, Minnesota
1991.....Kelly Macy, Georgia
1992.....Missy Marlowe, Utah
1993.....Agina Simpkins, Georgia
Beth Wymer, Michigan
1994.....Sandy Woolsey, Utah
Beth Wymer, Michigan
Lori Strong, Georgia
1995.....Beth Wymer, Michigan
1996.....Stephanie Woods, Alabama
1997.....Jenni Beathard, Georgia
1998.....Karin Lichey, Georgia
Stella Umeh, UCLA
1999.....Angie Leionard, Utah
2000.....Mohini Bhardwaj, UCLA
2001.....Yvonne Tousek, UCLA
2002.....Andree' Pickens, Alabama
2003.....Jamie Dantzscher, UCLA
Kate Richardson, UCLA
2004.....Elise Ray, Michigan
2005.....Terin Humphrey, Alabama

Ice Hockey

Men

DIVISION I

Year	Champion	Coach	Score	Runner-Up	Most Outstanding Player
1948	Michigan	Vic Heyliger	8–4	Dartmouth	Joe Riley, Dartmouth, F
1949	Boston College	John Kelley	4–3	Dartmouth	Dick Desmond, Dartmouth, G

Men
DIVISION I

Year	Champion	Coach	Score	Runner-Up	Most Outstanding Player
1950	Colorado College	Cheddy Thompson	13–4	Boston University	Ralph Bevins, Boston University, G
1951	Michigan	Vic Heyliger	7–1	Brown	Ed Whiston, Brown, G
1952	Michigan	Vic Heyliger	4–1	Colorado College	Kenneth Kinsley, Colorado Coll, G
1953	Michigan	Vic Heyliger	7–3	Minnesota	John Matchefts, Michigan, F
1954	Rensselaer	Ned Harkness	5–4 (OT)	Minnesota	Abbie Moore, Rensselaer, F
1955	Michigan	Vic Heyliger	5–3	Colorado College	Philip Hilton, Colorado College, D
1956	Michigan	Vic Heyliger	7–5	Michigan Tech	Lorne Howes, Michigan, G
1957	Colorado College	Thomas Bedecki	13–6	Michigan	Bob McCusker, Colorado Coll, F
1958	Denver	Murray Armstrong	6–2	N Dakota	Murray Massier, Denver, F
1959	N Dakota	Bob May	4–3 (OT)	Michigan St	Reg Morelli, N Dakota, F
1960	Denver	Murray Armstrong	5–3	Michigan Tech	Bob Marquis, Boston University, F
1961	Denver	Murray Armstrong	12–2	St. Lawrence	Barry Urbanski, Boston Univ, G
1962	Michigan Tech	John MacInnes	7–1	Clarkson	Louis Angotti, Michigan Tech, F
1963	N Dakota	Barney Thorndycraft	6–5	Denver	Al McLean, N Dakota, F
1964	Michigan	Allen Renfrew	6–3	Denver	Bob Gray, Michigan, G
1965	Michigan Tech	John MacInnes	8–2	Boston College	Gary Milroy, Michigan Tech, F
1966	Michigan St	Amo Bessone	6–1	Clarkson	Gaye Cooley, Michigan St, G
1967	Cornell	Ned Harkness	4–1	Boston University	Walt Stanowski, Cornell, D
1968	Denver	Murray Armstrong	4–0	N Dakota	Gerry Powers, Denver, G
1969	Denver	Murray Armstrong	4–3	Cornell	Keith Magnuson, Denver, D
1970	Cornell	Ned Harkness	6–4	Clarkson	Daniel Lodboa, Cornell, D
1971	Boston University	Jack Kelley	4–2	Minnesota	Dan Brady, Boston University, G
1972	Boston University	Jack Kelley	4–0	Cornell	Tim Regan, Boston University, G
1973	Wisconsin	Bob Johnson	4–2	Vacated	Dean Talafous, Wisconsin, F
1974	Minnesota	Herb Brooks	4–2	Michigan Tech	Brad Shelstad, Minnesota, G
1975	Michigan Tech	John MacInnes	6–1	Minnesota	Jim Warden, Michigan Tech, G
1976	Minnesota	Herb Brooks	6–4	Michigan Tech	Tom Vanelli, Minnesota, F
1977	Wisconsin	Bob Johnson	6–5 (OT)	Michigan	Julian Baretta, Wisconsin, G
1978	Boston University	Jack Parker	5–3	Boston College	Jack O'Callahan, Boston Univ, D
1979	Minnesota	Herb Brooks	4–3	N Dakota	Steve Janaszak, Minnesota, G
1980	N Dakota	John Gasparini	5–2	Northern Michigan	Doug Smail, N Dakota, F
1981	Wisconsin	Bob Johnson	6–3	Minnesota	Marc Behrend, Wisconsin, G
1982	N Dakota	John Gasparini	5–2	Wisconsin	Phil Sykes, N Dakota, F
1983	Wisconsin	Jeff Sauer	6–2	Harvard	Marc Behrend, Wisconsin, G
1984	Bowling Green	Jerry York	5–4 (OT)	MN–Duluth	Gary Kruzich, Bowling Green, G
1985	Rensselaer	Mike Addesa	2–1	Providence	Chris Terreri, Providence, G
1986	Michigan St	Ron Mason	6–5	Harvard	Mike Donnelly, Michigan St, F
1987	N Dakota	John Gasparini	5–3	Michigan St	Tony Hrkac, N Dakota, F
1988	Lake Superior St	Frank Anzalone	4–3 (OT)	St. Lawrence	Bruce Hoffort, Lake Superior St, G
1989	Harvard	Bill Cleary	4–3 (OT)	Minnesota	Ted Donato, Harvard, F
1990	Wisconsin	Jeff Sauer	7–3	Colgate	Chris Tancill, Wisconsin, F
1991	N Michigan	Rick Comley	8–7 (3OT)	Boston University	Scott Beattie, N Michigan, F
1992	Lake Superior St	Jeff Jackson	4–2	Wisconsin	Paul Constantin, Lake Superior St, F
1993	Maine	Shawn Walsh	5–4	Lake Superior St	Jim Montgomery, Maine, F
1994	Lake Superior St	Jeff Jackson	9–1	Boston University	Sean Tallaire, Lake Superior St, F
1995	Boston University	Jack Parker	6–2	Maine	Chris O'Sullivan, Boston Univ, F
1996	Michigan	Red Berenson	3–2 (OT)	Colorado College	Brendan Morrison, Michigan, F
1997	N Dakota	Dean Blais	6–4	Boston University	Matt Henderson, N Dakota, F
1998	Michigan	Red Berenson	3–2 (OT)	Boston Coll	Marty Turco, Michigan, G
1999	Maine	Shawn Walsh	3–2 (OT)	New Hampshire	Alfie Michaud, Maine, G
2000	N Dakota	Dean Blais	4–2	Boston College	Lee Goren, N Dakota, F
2001	Boston College	Jerry York	3–2 (OT)	N Dakota	Chuck Kobasew, Boston Coll, F
2002	Minnesota	Don Lucia	4–3 (OT)	Maine	Grant Potulny, Minnesota, F
2003	Minnesota	Don Lucia	5–1	New Hampshire	Thomas Vanek, Minnesota, F
2004	Denver	George Gwozdecky	1–0	Maine	Adam Berkhoel, Denver, G
2005	Denver	George Gwozdecky	4–1	North Dakota	Peter Mannino, Denver

DIVISION II (Discontinued)

Year	Champion	Coach	Score	Runner-Up
1978	Merrimack	Thom Lawler	12–2	Lake Forest
1979	Lowell	Bill Riley Jr	6–4	Mankato St
1980	Mankato St	Don Brose	5–2	Elmira
1981	Lowell	Bill Riley Jr	5–4	Plattsburgh St
1982	Lowell	Bill Riley Jr	6–1	Plattsburgh St
1983	RIT	Brian Mason	4–2	Bemidji St
1984	Bemidji St	R.H. (Bob) Peters	14–4*	Merrimack
1993	Bemidji St	R.H. (Bob) Peters	15–6*	Mercyhurst
1994	Bemidji St	R.H. (Bob) Peters	7–6*	AL–Huntsville
1995	Bemidji St	R.H. (Bob) Peters	11–6*	Mercyhurst

Ice Hockey (Cont.)

DIVISION II (Cont.)

Year	Champion	Coach	Score	Runner-Up
1996	AL–Huntsville	Doug Ross	10–1*	Bemidji St
1997	Bemidji St	R.H. (Bob) Peters	7–4*	AL–Huntsville
1998	AL–Huntsville	Doug Ross	11–4*	Bemidji St
1999	St. Michael's (VT)	Lou DiMasi	12–9*	New Hamp. Coll

*Two-game, total-goal series.

DIVISION III

Year	Champion	Coach	Score	Runner-Up
1984	Babson	Bob Riley	8–0	Union (NY)
1985	RIT	Bruce Delventhal	5–1	Bemidji St
1986	Bemidji St	R.H. (Bob) Peters	8–5	Vacated
1987	Vacated			Oswego St
1988	WI–River Falls	Rick Kozuback	7–1, 3–5, 3–0	Elmira
1989	WI–Stevens Point	Mark Mazzoleni	3–3, 3–2	RIT
1990	WI–Stevens Point	Mark Mazzoleni	10–1, 3–6, 1–0	Plattsburgh St
1991	WI–Stevens Point	Mark Mazzoleni	6–2	Mankato St
1992	Plattsburgh St	Bob Emery	7–3	WI–Stevens Point
1993	WI–Stevens Point	Joe Baldarotta	4–3	WI–River Falls
1994	WI–River Falls	Dean Talafous	6–4	WI–Superior
1995	Middlebury	Bill Beaney	1–0	Fredonia St
1996	Middlebury	Bill Beaney	3–2	RIT
1997	Middlebury	Bill Beaney	3–2	WI–Superior
1998	Middlebury	Bill Beaney	2–1	WI–Stevens Point
1999	Middlebury	Bill Beaney	5–0	WI–Superior
2000	Norwich	Michael McShane	2–1	St. Thomas (MN)
2001	Plattsburgh	Bob Emery	6–2	RIT
2002	WI–Superior	Dan Stauber	3–2	Norwich
2003	Norwich	Michael McShane	2–1	Oswego St
2004	Middlebury	Bill Beaney	1–0	St. Norbert
2005	Middlebury	Bill Beaney	5–0	St. Thomas

Women - DIVISION I

Year	Champion	Coach	Score	Runner-Up
2001	Minnesota-Duluth	Shannon Miller	4–2	St. Lawrence
2002	Minnesota-Duluth	Shannon Miller	3–2	Brown
2003	Minnesota-Duluth	Shannon Miller	4–3 (2 OT)	Harvard
2004	Minnesota	Laura Holldorson	6–2	Harvard
2005	Minnesota	Laura Holldorson	4–3	Harvard

Lacrosse

Men - DIVISION I

Year	Champion	Coach	Score	Runner-Up
1971	Cornell	Richie Moran	12–6	Maryland
1972	Virginia	Glenn Thiel	13–12	Johns Hopkins
1973	Maryland	Bud Beardmore	10–9 (2 OT)	Johns Hopkins
1974	Johns Hopkins	Bob Scott	17–12	Maryland
1975	Maryland	Bud Beardmore	20–13	Navy
1976	Cornell	Richie Moran	16–13 (OT)	Maryland
1977	Cornell	Richie Moran	16–8	Johns Hopkins
1978	Johns Hopkins	Henry Ciccarone	13–8	Cornell
1979	Johns Hopkins	Henry Ciccarone	15–9	Maryland
1980	Johns Hopkins	Henry Ciccarone	9–8 (2 OT)	Virginia
1981	N Carolina	Willie Scroggs	14–13	Johns Hopkins
1982	N Carolina	Willie Scroggs	7–5	Johns Hopkins
1983	Syracuse	Roy Simmons Jr	17–16	Johns Hopkins
1984	Johns Hopkins	Don Zimmerman	13–10	Syracuse
1985	Johns Hopkins	Don Zimmerman	11–4	Syracuse
1986	N Carolina	Willie Scroggs	10–9 (OT)	Virginia
1987	Johns Hopkins	Don Zimmerman	11–10	Cornell
1988	Syracuse	Roy Simmons Jr	13–8	Cornell
1989	Syracuse	Roy Simmons Jr	13–12	Johns Hopkins
1990	Syracuse	Roy Simmons Jr	21–9	Loyola (MD)
1991	N Carolina	Dave Klarmann	18–13	Towson St
1992	Princeton	Bill Tierney	10–9	Syracuse
1993	Syracuse	Roy Simmons Jr	13–12	N Carolina
1994	Princeton	Bill Tierney	9–8 (OT)	Virginia
1995	Syracuse	Roy Simmons Jr	13–9	Maryland
1996	Princeton	Bill Tierney	13–12 (OT)	Virginia
1997	Princeton	Bill Tierney	19–7	Maryland
1998	Princeton	Bill Tierney	15–5	Maryland
1999	Virginia	Dom Starsia	12–10	Syracuse
2000	Syracuse	John Desko	13–7	Princeton
2001	Princeton	Bill Tierney	10–9 (OT)	Syracuse

Men (Cont.)

DIVISION I (Cont.)

Year	Champion	Coach	Score	Runner-Up
2002	Syracuse	John Desko	13–12	Princeton
2003	Virginia	Dom Starsia	9–7	Johns Hopkins
2004	Syracuse	John Desko	14–13	Navy
2005	John Hopkins	Dave Pietramala	9–8	Duke

DIVISION II (Discontinued, then renewed)

Year	Champion	Coach	Score	Runner-Up
1974	Towson St	Carl Runk	18–17 (OT)	Hobart
1975	Cortland St	Chuck Winters	12–11	Hobart
1976	Hobart	Jerry Schmidt	18–9	Adelphi
1977	Hobart	Jerry Schmidt	23–13	Washington (MD)
1978	Roanoke	Paul Griffin	14–13	Hobart
1979	Adelphi	Paul Doherty	17–12	MD–Baltimore County
1980	MD–Baltimore County	Dick Watts	23–14	Adelphi
1981	Adelphi	Paul Doherty	17–14	Loyola (MD)
1993	Adelphi	Kevin Sheehan	11–7	LIU–C.W. Post
1994	Springfield	Keith Bugbee	15–12	New York Tech
1995	Adelphi	Sandy Kapatos	12–10	Springfield
1996	LIU–C.W. Post	Tom Postel	15–10	Adelphi
1997	New York Tech	Jack Kaley	18–11	Adelphi
1998	Adelphi	Sandy Kapatos	18–6	LIU–C.W. Post
1999	Adelphi	Sandy Kapatos	11–8	LIU–C.W. Post
2000	Limestone	Mike Cerino	10–9	LIU–C.W. Post
2001	Adelphi	Sandy Kapatos	14–10	Limestone
2002	Limestone	T.W. Johnson	11–9	New York Tech
2003	New York Tech	Jack Kaley	9–4	Limestone
2004	Le Moyne	Dan Sheehan	11–10 (2OT)	Limestone
2005	NYIT	Jack Kalley	14–13	Limestone

DIVISION III

Year	Champion	Coach	Score	Runner-Up
1980	Hobart	Dave Urick	11–8	Cortland St
1981	Hobart	Dave Urick	10–8	Cortland St
1982	Hobart	Dave Urick	9–8 (OT)	Washington (MD)
1983	Hobart	Dave Urick	13–9	Roanoke
1984	Hobart	Dave Urick	12–5	Washington (MD)
1985	Hobart	Dave Urick	15–8	Washington (MD)
1986	Hobart	Dave Urick	13–10	Washington (MD)
1987	Hobart	Dave Urick	9–5	Ohio Wesleyan
1988	Hobart	Dave Urick	18–9	Ohio Wesleyan
1989	Hobart	Dave Urick	11–8	Ohio Wesleyan
1990	Hobart	B.J. O'Hara	18–6	Washington (MD)
1991	Hobart	B.J. O'Hara	12–11	Salisbury St
1992	Nazareth (NY)	Scott Nelson	13–12	Hobart
1993	Hobart	B.J. O'Hara	16–10	Ohio Wesleyan
1994	Salisbury St	Jim Berkman	15–9	Hobart
1995	Salisbury St	Jim Berkman	22–13	Nazareth
1996	Nazareth	Scott Nelson	11–10 (OT)	Washington (MD)
1997	Nazareth	Scott Nelson	15–14 (OT)	Washington (MD)
1998	Washington (MD)	John Haus	16–10	Nazareth
1999	Salisbury St	Jim Berkman	13–6	Middlebury
2000	Middlebury	Erin Quinn	16–12	Salisbury St
2001	Middlebury	Erin Quinn	15–10	Gettysburg
2002	Middlebury	Erin Quinn	14–9	Gettysburg
2003	Salisbury	Jim Berkman	14–13	Middlebury
2004	Salisbury	Jim Berkman	13–9	Nazareth
2005	Salisbury	Jim Berkman	11–10	Middlebury

Women* - DIVISION I

Year	Champion	Coach	Score	Runner-Up
2001	Maryland	Cindy Timchal	14–13 (OT)	Georgetown
2002	Princeton	Chris Sailer	12–7	Georgetown
2003	Princeton	Chris Sailer	8–7 (OT)	Virginia
2004	Virginia	Julie Myers	10–4	Princeton
2005	Northwestern	Kelly Amonte	13–10	Virginia

DIVISION II

Year	Champion	Coach	Score	Runner-Up
2001	LIU–C.W. Post	Karen MacCrate	13–9	W Chester
2002	Westchester	Ginny Martino	11–6	Stonehill
2003	Stonehill	Michael Daly	9–8	Longwood
2004	Adelphi	Jill Lessne	12–11	West Chester
2005	Stonehill	Michael Daly	13–10	West Chester

*Divisions I and II competed for a single championship until 2001.

Women *(Cont.)*
DIVISIONS I AND II

Year	Champion	Coach	Score	Runner-Up
1982	Massachusetts	Pamela Hixon	9–6	Trenton St
1983	Delaware	Janet Smith	10–7	Temple
1984	Temple	Tina Sloan Green	6–4	Maryland
1985	New Hampshire	Marisa Didio	6–5	Maryland
1986	Maryland	Sue Tyler	11–10	Penn St
1987	Penn St	Susan Scheetz	7–6	Temple
1988	Temple	Tina Sloan Green	15–7	Penn St
1989	Penn St	Susan Scheetz	7–6	Harvard
1990	Harvard	Carole Kleinfelder	8–7	Maryland
1991	Virginia	Jane Miller	8–6	Maryland
1992	Maryland	Cindy Timchal	11–10	Harvard
1993	Virginia	Jane Miller	8–6 (OT)	Princeton
1994	Princeton	Chris Sailer	10–7	Virginia
1995	Maryland	Cindy Timchal	13–5	Princeton
1996	Maryland	Cindy Timchal	10–5	Virginia
1997	Maryland	Cindy Timchal	8–7	Loyola (MD)
1998	Maryland	Cindy Timchal	11–5	Virginia
1999	Maryland	Cindy Timchal	16–6	Virginia
2000	Maryland	Cindy Timchal	16–8	Princeton

DIVISION III

Year	Champion	Score	Runner-Up	Year	Champion	Score	Runner-Up
1985	Trenton St	7–4	Ursinus	1995	Trenton St	14–13	William Smith
1986	Ursinus	12–10	Trenton St	1996	Trenton St	15–8	Middlebury
1987	Trenton St	8–7 (ot)	Ursinus	1997	Middlebury	14–9	College of NJ*
1988	Trenton St	14–11	William Smith	1998	Coll of NJ	14–9	Williams
1989	Ursinus	8–6	Trenton St	1999	Middlebury	10–9	Amherst
1990	Ursinus	7–6	St. Lawrence	2000	Coll of NJ	14–8	Williams
1991	Trenton St	7–6	Ursinus	2001	Middlebury	11–10	Amherst
1992	Trenton St	5–3	William Smith	2002	Middlebury	12–6	College of NJ*
1993	Trenton St	10–9	William Smith	2003	Amherst	11–9	Middlebury
1994	Trenton St	29–11	William Smith	2004	Middlebury	13–11 (OT)	College of NJ

*Formerly Trenton St

Rifle

						Individual Champions	
Year	Champion	Coach	Score	Runner-Up	Score	Air Rifle	Smallbore
1980	Tennessee Tech	James Newkirk	6201	W Virginia	6150	Rod Fitz-Randolph, Tennessee Tech	Rod Fitz-Randolph, Tennessee Tech
1981	Tennessee Tech	James Newkirk	6139	W Virginia	6136	John Rost, W Virginia	Kurt Fitz-Randolph, Tennessee Tech
1982	Tennessee Tech	James Newkirk	6138	W Virginia	6136	John Rost, W Virginia	Kurt Fitz-Randolph, Tennessee Tech
1983	W Virginia	Edward Etzel	6166	Tennessee Tech	6148	Ray Slonena, Tennessee Tech	David Johnson, W Virginia
1984	W Virginia	Edward Etzel	6206	E Tennessee St	6142	Pat Spurgin, Murray St	Bob Broughton, W Virginia
1985	Murray St	Elvis Green	6150	W Virginia	6149	Christian Heller, W Virginia	Pat Spurgin, Murray St
1986	W Virginia	Edward Etzel	6229	Murray St	6163	Marianne Wallace, Murray St	Mike Anti, W Virginia
1987	Murray St	Elvis Green	6205	W Virginia	6203	Rob Harbison, TN–Martin	Web Wright, W Virginia
1988	W Virginia	Greg Perrine	6192	Murray St	6183	Deena Wigger, Murray St	Web Wright, W Virginia
1989	W Virginia	Edward Etzel	6234	S Florida	6180	Michelle Scarborough, S Florida	Deb Sinclair, AK–Fairbanks
1990	W Virginia	Marsha Beasley	6205	Navy	6101	Gary Hardy, W Virginia	M. Scarborough, S Florida
1991	W Virginia	Marsha Beasley	6171	AK–Fairbanks	6110	Ann Pfiffner, W Virginia	Soma Dutta, UT–El Paso
1992	W Virginia	Marsha Beasley	6214	AK–Fairbanks	6166	Ann Pfiffner, W Virginia	Tim Manges, W Virginia
1993	W Virginia	Marsha Beasley	6179	AK–Fairbanks	6169	Trevor Gathman, W Virginia	Eric Uptagrafft, W Virginia
1994	AK–Fairbanks	Randy Pitney	6194	W Virginia	6187	Nancy Napolski, Kentucky	Cory Brunetti, AK–Fairbanks
1995	W Virginia	Marsha Beasley	6241	Air Force	6187	Benji Belden, Murray St	Oleg Selezner, AK–Fairbanks
1996	W Virginia	Marsha Beasley	6179	Air Force	6168	T. Gathman, WVa	Joe Johnson, Navy

Rifle (Cont.)

Year	Champion	Coach	Score	Runner-Up	Score	Air Rifle	Smallbore
1997	W Virginia	Marsha Beasley	6223	Kentucky	6175	Marra Hastings, Murray St	Marcos Scrivner, W Virginia
1998	W Virginia	Marsha Beasley	6214	AK–Fairbanks	6175	Emily Caruso, Norwich	Karen Juzinuk, Xavier
1999	AK-Fairbanks	Randy Pitney	6276	Navy	6168	Kelly Mansfield, AK-Fairbanks	Kelly Mansfield, AK–Fairbanks
2000	AK-Fairbanks	Randy Pitney	6285	Xavier	6156	Kelly Mansfield, AK-Fairbanks	Nicole Allaire, Nebraska
2001	AK-Fairbanks	David Johnson	6283	Kentucky	6175	Matthew Emmons, AK-Fairbanks	Matthew Emmons, AK-Fairbanks
2002	AK-Fairbanks	Randy Pitney	6241	Kentucky	6209	Ryan Tanoue, Nevada	Matthew Emmons AK-Fairbanks
2003	AK-Fairbanks	Glenn Dubis	6287	Xavier	6187	Jamie Beyerle, AK-Fairbanks	Matthew Emmons AK-Fairbanks
2004	AK-Fairbanks	Glenn Dubis	6273	Nevada	6185	Morgan Hicks, Murray State	Matthew Rawlings AK–Fairbanks
2005	Army	Ron Wigger	4659	Jacksonville	4658	Beth Tidmore, Murr St	Matthew Rawlings

Skiing

Year	Champion	Coach	Pts	Runner-Up	Pts	Host or Site
1954	Denver	Willy Schaeffler	384.0	Seattle	349.6	NV–Reno
1955	Denver	Willy Schaeffler	567.05	Dartmouth	558.935	Norwich
1956	Denver	Willy Schaeffler	582.01	Dartmouth	541.77	Winter Park
1957	Denver	Willy Schaeffler	577.95	Colorado	545.29	Ogden Snow Basin
1958	Dartmouth	Al Merrill	561.2	Denver	550.6	Dartmouth
1959	Colorado	Bob Beattie	549.4	Denver	543.6	Winter Park
1960	Colorado	Bob Beattie	571.4	Denver	568.6	Bridger Bowl
1961	Denver	Willy Schaeffler	376.19	Middlebury	366.94	Middlebury
1962	Denver	Willy Schaeffler	390.08	Colorado	374.30	Squaw Valley
1963	Denver	Willy Schaeffler	384.6	Colorado	381.6	Solitude
1964	Denver	Willy Schaeffler	370.2	Dartmouth	368.8	Franconia Notch
1965	Denver	Willy Schaeffler	380.5	Utah	378.4	Crystal Mountain
1966	Denver	Willy Schaeffler	381.02	Western Colorado	365.92	Crested Butte
1967	Denver	Willy Schaeffler	376.7	Wyoming	375.9	Sugarloaf Mountain
1968	Wyoming	John Cress	383.9	Denver	376.2	Mount Werner
1969	Denver	Willy Schaeffler	388.6	Dartmouth	372.0	Mount Werner
1970	Denver	Willy Schaeffler	386.6	Dartmouth	378.8	Cannon Mountain
1971	Denver	Peder Pytte	394.7	Colorado	373.1	Terry Peak
1972	Colorado	Bill Marolt	385.3	Denver	380.1	Winter Park
1973	Colorado	Bill Marolt	381.89	Wyoming	377.83	Middlebury
1974	Colorado	Bill Marolt	176	Wyoming	162	Jackson Hole
1975	Colorado	Bill Marolt	183	Vermont	115	Fort Lewis
1976	Colo/Dart	Bill Marolt/Jim Page	112			Bates
1977	Colorado	Bill Marolt	179	Wyoming	154.5	Winter Park
1978	Colorado	Bill Marolt	152.5	Wyoming	121.5	Cannon Mountain
1979	Colorado	Tim Hinderman	153	Utah	130	Steamboat Springs
1980	Vermont	Chip LaCasse	171	Utah	151	Lake Placid and Stowe
1981	Utah	Pat Miller	183	Vermont	172	Park City
1982	Colorado	Tim Hinderman	461	Vermont	436.5	Lake Placid
1983	Utah	Pat Miller	696	Vermont	650	Bozeman
1984	Utah	Pat Miller	750.5	Vermont	684	New Hampshire
1985	Wyoming	Tim Ameel	764	Utah	744	Bozeman
1986	Utah	Pat Miller	612	Vermont	602	Vermont
1987	Utah	Pat Miller	710	Vermont	627	Anchorage
1988	Utah	Pat Miller	651	Vermont	614	Middlebury
1989	Vermont	Chip LaCasse	672	Utah	668	Jackson Hole
1990	Vermont	Chip LaCasse	671	Utah	571	Vermont
1991	Colorado	Richard Rokos	713	Vermont	682	Park City, UT
1992	Vermont	Chip LaCasse	693.5	New Mexico	642.5	New Hampshire
1993	Utah	Pat Miller	783	Vermont	700.5	Steamboat Springs
1994	Vermont	Chip LaCasse	688	Utah	667	Sugarloaf, ME
1995	Colorado	Richard Rokos	720.5	Utah	711	New Hampshire
1996	Utah	Pat Miller	719	Denver	635.5	Montana St
1997	Utah	Pat Miller	686	Vermont	646.5	Vermont
1998	Colorado	Richard Rokos	654	Utah	651.5	Montana St
1999	Colorado	Richard Rokos	650	Denver	636	Bates College
2000	Denver	Kurt Smitz	720	Colorado	621	Park City, UT
2001	Denver	Kurt Smitz	649	Vermont	605	Middlebury, VT
2002	Denver	Kurt Smitz	656	Colorado	612	Anchorage
2003	Utah	Kevin Sweeney	682	Vermont	551	Hanover, NH
2004	New Mexico	George Brooks	623	Utah	581	Donner Summit, CA
2005	Denver	Kurt Smitz	622.5	Vermont	575	Stowe, VT

Soccer

Men
DIVISION I

Year	Champion	Coach	Score	Runner-Up
1959	St. Louis	Bob Guelker	5–2	Bridgeport
1960	St. Louis	Bob Guelker	3–2	Maryland
1961	West Chester	Mel Lorback	2–0	St. Louis
1962	St. Louis	Bob Guelker	4–3	Maryland
1963	St. Louis	Bob Guelker	3–0	Navy
1964	Navy	F.H. Warner	1–0	Michigan St
1965	St. Louis	Bob Guelker	1–0	Michigan St
1966	San Francisco	Steve Negoesco	5–2	LIU–Brooklyn
1967	Michigan St	Gene Kenney	0–0	Game called due to
	St. Louis	Harry Keough		inclement weather
1968	Maryland	Doyle Royal	2–2 (2 OT)	
	Michigan St	Gene Kenney		
1969	St. Louis	Harry Keough	4–0	San Francisco
1970	St. Louis	Harry Keough	1–0	UCLA
1971	Vacated		3–2	St. Louis
1972	St. Louis	Harry Keough	4–2	UCLA
1973	St. Louis	Harry Keough	2–1 (4 OT)	UCLA
1974	Howard	Lincoln Phillips	2–1 (4 OT)	St. Louis
1975	San Francisco	Steve Negoesco	4–0	SIU–Edwardsville
1976	San Francisco	Steve Negoesco	1–0	Indiana
1977	Hartwick	Jim Lennox	2–1	San Francisco
1978	Vacated		2–0	Indiana
1979	SIU–Edwardsville	Bob Guelker	3–2	Clemson
1980	San Francisco	Steve Negoesco	4–3 (OT)	Indiana
1981	Connecticut	Joe Morrone	2–1 (OT)	Alabama A&M
1982	Indiana	Jerry Yeagley	2–1 (8 OT)	Duke
1983	Indiana	Jerry Yeagley	1–0 (2 OT)	Columbia
1984	Clemson	I.M. Ibrahim	2–1	Indiana
1985	UCLA	Sigi Schmid	1–0 (8 OT)	American
1986	Duke	John Rennie	1–0	Akron
1987	Clemson	I.M. Ibrahim	2–0	San Diego St
1988	Indiana	Jerry Yeagley	1–0	Howard
1989	Santa Clara	Steve Sampson	1–1 (2 OT)	
	Virginia	Bruce Arena		
1990	UCLA	Sigi Schmid	1–0 (OT)	Rutgers
1991	Virginia	Bruce Arena	0–0*	Santa Clara
1992	Virginia	Bruce Arena	2–0	San Diego
1993	Virginia	Bruce Arena	2–0	S Carolina
1994	Virginia	Bruce Arena	1–0	Indiana
1995	Wisconsin	Jim Launder	2–0	Duke
1996	St. John's (NY)	Dave Masur	4–1	Florida International
1997	UCLA	Sigi Schmid	2–1	Virginia
1998	Indiana	Jerry Yeagley	3–1	Stanford
1999	Indiana	Jerry Yeagley	1–0	Santa Clara
2000	Connecticut	Ray Reid	2–0	Creighton
2001	N Carolina	Elmar Bolowich	2–0	Indiana
2002	UCLA	Tom Fitzgerald	1–0	Stanford
2003	Indiana	Jerry Yeagley	2–1	St. John's (NY)
2004	Indiana	Jerry Yeagley	1–1 (2 OT 3-2)	UC–Santa Barbara

*Under a rule passed in 1991, the NCAA determined that when a score is tied after regulation and overtime, and the championship is determined by penalty kicks, the official score will be 0–0.

DIVISION II

Year	Champion	Year	Champion	Year	Champion
1972	SIU–Edwardsville	1980	Lock Haven	1988	Florida Tech
1973	MO–St. Louis	1981	Tampa	1989	New Hampshire College
1974	Adelphi	1982	Florida International	1990	Southern Connecticut St
1975	Baltimore	1983	Seattle Pacific	1991	Florida Tech
1976	Loyola (MD)	1984	Florida International	1992	Southern Connecticut St
1977	Alabama A&M	1985	Seattle Pacific	1993	Seattle Pacific
1978	Seattle Pacific	1986	Seattle Pacific	1994	Tampa
1979	Alabama A&M	1987	Southern Connecticut St	1995	Southern Connecticut St

Men (Cont.)

DIVISION II (CONT.)

Year	Champion
1996	Grand Canyon
1997	Cal St-Bakersfield
1998	Southern Connecticut St

Year	Champion
1999	Southern Connecticut St
2000	Cal St-Dominguez Hills
2001	Tampa

Year	Champion
2002	Sonoma St
2003	Lynn
2004	Seattle

Year	Champion
1974	Brockport St
1975	Babson
1976	Brandeis
1977	Lock Haven
1978	Lock Haven
1979	Babson
1980	Babson
1981	Glassboro St
1982	NC–Greensboro
1983	NC–Greensboro
1984	Wheaton (IL)

DIVISION III

Year	Champion
1985	NC–Greensboro
1986	NC–Greensboro
1987	NC–Greensboro
1988	UC–San Diego
1989	Elizabethtown
1990	Glassboro St
1991	UC–San Diego
1992	Kean
1993	UC–San Diego
1994	Bethany (WV)

Year	Champion
1995	Williams
1996	College of New Jersey
1997	Wheaton (IL)
1998	Ohio Wesleyan
1999	St. Lawrence
2000	Messiah
2001	Richard Stockton
2002	Messiah
2003	Trinity (TX)
2004	Messiah

Women

DIVISION I

Year	Champion	Coach	Score	Runner-Up
1982	N Carolina	Anson Dorrance	2–0	Central Florida
1983	N Carolina	Anson Dorrance	4–0	George Mason
1984	N Carolina	Anson Dorrance	2–0	Connecticut
1985	George Mason	Hank Leung	2–0	N Carolina
1986	N Carolina	Anson Dorrance	2–0	Colorado College
1987	N Carolina	Anson Dorrance	1–0	Massachusetts
1988	N Carolina	Anson Dorrance	4–1	N Carolina St
1989	N Carolina	Anson Dorrance	2–0	Colorado College
1990	N Carolina	Anson Dorrance	6–0	Connecticut
1991	N Carolina	Anson Dorrance	3–1	Wisconsin
1992	N Carolina	Anson Dorrance	9–1	Duke
1993	N Carolina	Anson Dorrance	6–0	George Mason
1994	N Carolina	Anson Dorrance	5–0	Notre Dame
1995	Notre Dame	Chris Petrucelli	1–0	Portland
1996	N Carolina	Anson Dorrance	1–0	Notre Dame
1997	N Carolina	Anson Dorrance	2–0	Connecticut
1998	Florida	Becky Burleigh	1–0	N Carolina
1999	N Carolina	Anson Dorrance	2–0	Notre Dame
2000	N Carolina	Anson Dorrance	2–1	UCLA
2001	Santa Clara	Jerry Smith	1–0	N Carolina
2002	Portland	Clive Charles	2–1	Santa Clara
2003	N Carolina	Anson Dorrance	6–0	Connecticut
2004	Norte Dame	Randy Waldrum	1–1(OT 4-3)	UCLA

DIVISION II

Year	Champion
1988	Cal St–Hayward
1989	Barry
1990	Sonoma St
1991	Cal St–Dominguez Hills
1992	Barry
1993	Barry
1994	Franklin Pierce
1995	Franklin Pierce
1996	Franklin Pierce
1997	Franklin Pierce
1998	Lynn
1999	Franklin Pierce
2000	UC-San Diego
2001	UC-San Diego
2002	Christian Brothers
2003	Kennesaw St
2004	Metro St

DIVISION III

Year	Champion
1986	Rochester
1987	Rochester
1988	William Smith
1989	UC–San Diego
1990	Ithaca
1991	Ithaca
1992	Cortland St
1993	Trenton St
1994	Trenton St
1995	UC–San Diego
1996	UC–San Diego
1997	UC–San Diego
1998	Macalester
1999	UC–San Diego
2000	College of New Jersey*
2001	Ohio Wesleyan
2002	Ohio Wesleyan
2003	Oneonta St
2004	Wheaton College

*Formerly Trenton St

Softball

DIVISION I

Year	Champion	Coach	Score	Runner-Up
1982	UCLA*	Sharron Backus	2–0†	Fresno St
1983	Texas A&M	Bob Brock	2–0‡	Cal St–Fullerton
1984	UCLA	Sharron Backus	1–0#	Texas A&M
1985	UCLA	Sharron Backus	2–1**	Nebraska
1986	Cal St–Fullerton*	Judi Garman	3–0	Texas A&M
1987	Texas A&M	Bob Brock	4–1	UCLA
1988	UCLA	Sharron Backus	3–0	Fresno St
1989	UCLA*	Sharron Backus	1–0	Fresno St
1990	UCLA	Sharron Backus	2–0	Fresno St
1991	Arizona	Mike Candrea	5–1	UCLA
1992	UCLA*	Sharron Backus	2–0	Arizona
1993	Arizona	Mike Candrea	1–0	UCLA
1994	Arizona	Mike Candrea	4–0	Cal St–Northridge
1995	Vacated	—		Arizona
1996	Arizona*	Mike Candrea	6–4	Washington
1997	Arizona	Mike Candrea	10–2***	UCLA
1998	Fresno St	Margie Wright	1–0	Arizona
1999	UCLA	Sue Enquist	3–2	Washington
2000	Oklahoma	Patty Gasso	3–1	UCLA
2001	Arizona*	Mike Candrea	1–0	UCLA
2002	California	Diane Ninemire	6–0	Arizona
2003	UCLA	Sue Enquist	1–0**	California
2004	UCLA	Sue Enquist	3–1	California
2005	Michigan	Carol Hutchins	4–1	St. Thomas

*Undefeated teams in final series. †Eight innings. ‡12 innings. #13 innings. **Nine innings. ***Five innings.

DIVISION II

Year	Champion	Year	Champion	Year	Champion
1982	Sam Houston St	1990	Cal St–Bakersfield	1998	California (PA)
1983	Cal St–Northridge	1991	Augustana (SD)	1999	Humboldt St
1984	Cal St–Northridge	1992	Missouri Southern	2000	N Dakota St
1985	Cal St–Northridge	1993	Florida Southern	2001	Nebraska–Omaha
1986	SF Austin St	1994	Merrimack	2002	St. Mary's (IA)
1987	Cal St–Northridge	1995	Kennesaw St	2003	UC Davis
1988	Cal St–Bakersfield	1996	Kennesaw St	2004	Angelo St
1989	Cal St–Bakersfield	1997	California (PA)*	2005	Lynn University

DIVISION III

Year	Champion	Year	Champion	Year	Champion
1982	Sam Houston St	1989	Trenton St*	1998	WI–Stevens Point
1982	Eastern Connecticut St*	1990	Eastern Connecticut St	1999	Simpson (IA)
1983	Trenton St	1991	Central (IA)	2000	St. Mary's
1984	Buena Vista*	1992	Trenton St	2001	Muskingum*
1985	Eastern Connecticut St	1993	Central (IA)	2002	Williams
1986	Eastern Connecticut St	1994	Trenton St	2003	Central (IA)
1987	Trenton St*	1995	Chapman	2004	St. Thomas
1988	Central (IA)	1996	Trenton St*	2005	St. Thomas
		1997	Simpson (IA)*		

*Undefeated teams in final series.

Swimming and Diving

Men
DIVISION I

Year	Champion	Coach	Pts	Runner-Up	Pts
1937	Michigan	Matt Mann	75	Ohio St	39
1938	Michigan	Matt Mann	46	Ohio St	45
1939	Michigan	Matt Mann	65	Ohio St	58
1940	Michigan	Matt Mann	45	Yale	42
1941	Michigan	Matt Mann	61	Yale	58
1942	Yale	Robert J.H. Kiphuth	71	Michigan	39
1943	Ohio St	Mike Peppe	81	Michigan	47
1944	Yale	Robert J.H. Kiphuth	39	Michigan	38
1945	Ohio St	Mike Peppe	56	Michigan	48
1946	Ohio St	Mike Peppe	61	Michigan	37
1947	Ohio St	Mike Peppe	66	Michigan	39
1948	Michigan	Matt Mann	44	Ohio St	41
1949	Ohio St	Mike Peppe	49	Iowa	35
1950	Ohio St	Mike Peppe	64	Yale	43
1951	Yale	Robert J.H. Kiphuth	81	Michigan St	60
1952	Ohio St	Mike Peppe	94	Yale	81
1953	Yale	Robert J.H. Kiphuth	96½	Ohio St	73½
1954	Ohio St	Mike Peppe	94	Michigan	67

Men (Cont.)
DIVISION I (Cont.)

Year	Champion	Coach	Pts	Runner-Up	Pts
1955	Ohio St	Mike Peppe	90	Yale/ Michigan	51
1956	Ohio St	Mike Peppe	68	Yale	54
1957	Michigan	Gus Stager	69	Yale	61
1958	Michigan	Gus Stager	72	Yale	63
1959	Michigan	Gus Stager	137½	Ohio St	44
1960	Southern Cal	Peter Daland	87	Michigan	73
1961	Michigan	Gus Stager	85	Southern Cal	62
1962	Ohio St	Mike Peppe	92	Southern Cal	46
1963	Southern Cal	Peter Daland	81	Yale	77
1964	Southern Cal	Peter Daland	96	Indiana	91
1965	Southern Cal	Peter Daland	285	Indiana	278½
1966	Southern Cal	Peter Daland	302	Indiana	286
1967	Stanford	Jim Gaughran	275	Southern Cal	260
1968	Indiana	James Counsilman	346	Yale	253
1969	Indiana	James Counsilman	427	Southern Cal	306
1970	Indiana	James Counsilman	332	Southern Cal	235
1971	Indiana	James Counsilman	351	Southern Cal	260
1972	Indiana	James Counsilman	390	Southern Cal	371
1973	Indiana	James Counsilman	358	Tennessee	294
1974	Southern Cal	Peter Daland	339	Indiana	338
1975	Southern Cal	Peter Daland	344	Indiana	274
1976	Southern Cal	Peter Daland	398	Tennessee	237
1977	Southern Cal	Peter Daland	385	Alabama	204
1978	Tennessee	Ray Bussard	307	Auburn	185
1979	California	Nort Thornton	287	Southern Cal	227
1980	California	Nort Thornton	234	Texas	220
1981	Texas	Eddie Reese	259	UCLA	189
1982	UCLA	Ron Ballatore	219	Texas	210
1983	Florida	Randy Reese	238	Southern Meth	227
1984	Florida	Randy Reese	287½	Texas	277
1985	Stanford	Skip Kenney	403½	Florida	302
1986	Stanford	Skip Kenney	404	California	335
1987	Stanford	Skip Kenney	374	Southern Cal	296
1988	Texas	Eddie Reese	424	Southern Cal	369½
1989	Texas	Eddie Reese	475	Stanford	396
1990	Texas	Eddie Reese	506	Southern Cal	423
1991	Texas	Eddie Reese	476	Stanford	420
1992	Stanford	Skip Kenney	632	Texas	356
1993	Stanford	Skip Kenney	520½	Michigan	396
1994	Stanford	Skip Kenney	566½	Texas	445
1995	Michigan	Jon Urbanchek	561	Stanford	475
1996	Texas	Eddie Reese	479	Auburn	443½
1997	Auburn	David Marsh	496½	Stanford	340
1998	Stanford	Skip Kenney	594	Auburn	394½
1999	Auburn	David Marsh	467½	Stanford	414½
2000	Texas	Eddie Reese	538	Auburn	385
2001	Texas	Eddie Reese	597½	Stanford	457½
2002	Texas	Eddie Reese	512	Stanford	5011
2003	Auburn	David Marsh	609½	Texas	413
2004	Auburn	David Marsh	634	Stanford	377½
2005	Auburn	David Marsh	491	Stanford	414

DIVISION II

Year	Champion	Year	Champion	Year	Champion
1963	SW Missouri St	1978	Cal St–Northridge	1993	Cal St–Bakersfield
1964	Bucknell	1979	Cal St–Northridge	1994	Oakland (MI)
1965	San Diego St	1980	Oakland (MI)	1995	Oakland (MI)
1966	San Diego St	1981	Cal St–Northridge	1996	Oakland (MI)
1967	UC–Santa Barbara	1982	Cal St–Northridge	1997	Oakland (MI)
1968	Long Beach St	1983	Cal St–Northridge	1998	Cal St–Bakersfield
1969	UC–Irvine	1984	Cal St–Northridge	1999	Drury
1970	UC–Irvine	1985	Cal St–Northridge	2000	Cal St–Bakersfield
1971	UC–Irvine	1986	Cal St–Bakersfield	2001	Cal St–Bakersfield
1972	Eastern Michigan	1987	Cal St–Bakersfield	2002	Cal St–Bakersfield
1973	Cal St–Chico	1988	Cal St–Bakersfield	2003	Drury
1974	Cal St–Chico	1989	Cal St–Bakersfield	2004	Cal St–Bakersfield
1975	Cal St–Northridge	1990	Cal St–Bakersfield	2005	Drury
1976	Cal St–Chico	1991	Cal St–Bakersfield		
1977	Cal St–Northridge	1992	Cal St–Bakersfield		

DIVISION III

Year	Champion	Year	Champion	Year	Champion
1975	Cal St–Chico	1986	Kenyon	1997	Kenyon
1976	St. Lawrence	1987	Kenyon	1998	Kenyon
1977	Johns Hopkins	1988	Kenyon	1999	Kenyon
1978	Johns Hopkins	1989	Kenyon	2000	Kenyon
1979	Johns Hopkins	1990	Kenyon	2001	Kenyon
1980	Kenyon	1991	Kenyon	2002	Kenyon
1981	Kenyon	1992	Kenyon	2003	Kenyon
1982	Kenyon	1993	Kenyon	2004	Kenyon
1983	Kenyon	1994	Kenyon	2005	Kenyon
1984	Kenyon	1995	Kenyon		
1985	Kenyon	1996	Kenyon		

Women

DIVISION I

Year	Champion	Coach	Pts	Runner-Up	Pts
1982	Florida	Randy Reese	505	Stanford	383
1983	Stanford	George Haines	418½	Florida	389½
1984	Texas	Richard Quick	392	Stanford	324
1985	Texas	Richard Quick	643	Florida	400
1986	Texas	Richard Quick	633	Florida	586
1987	Texas	Richard Quick	648½	Stanford	631½
1988	Texas	Richard Quick	661	Florida	542½
1989	Stanford	Richard Quick	610½	Texas	547
1990	Texas	Mark Schubert	632	Stanford	622½
1991	Texas	Mark Schubert	746	Stanford	653
1992	Stanford	Richard Quick	735½	Texas	651
1993	Stanford	Richard Quick	649½	Florida	421
1994	Stanford	Richard Quick	512	Texas	421
1995	Stanford	Richard Quick	497½	Michigan	478½
1996	Stanford	Richard Quick	478	SMU	397
1997	Southern Cal	Mark Schubert	406	Stanford	395
1998	Stanford	Richard Quick	422	Arizona	378
1999	Georgia	Jack Bauerle	504½	Stanford	441
2000	Georgia	Jack Bauerle	490½	Arizona	472
2001	Georgia	Jack Bauerle	389	Stanford	387½
2002	Auburn	David Marsh	474	Georgia	386
2003	Auburn	David Marsh	536	Georgia	373
2004	Auburn	David Marsh	569	Georgia	431
2005	Georgia	Jack Bauerle	609.5	Auburn	492

DIVISION II

Year	Champion	Year	Champion	Year	Champion
1982	Cal St–Northridge	1990	Oakland (MI)	1998	Drury
1983	Clarion	1991	Oakland (MI)	1999	Drury
1984	Clarion	1992	Oakland (MI)	2000	Drury
1985	S Florida	1993	Oakland (MI)	2001	Truman St
1986	Clarion	1994	Oakland (MI)	2002	Truman St
1987	Cal St–Northridge	1995	Air Force	2003	Truman St
1988	Cal St–Northridge	1996	Air Force	2004	Truman St
1989	Cal St–Northridge	1997	Drury	2005	Truman St

DIVISION III

Year	Champion	Year	Champion	Year	Champion
1982	Williams	1990	Kenyon	1998	Kenyon
1983	Williams	1991	Kenyon	1999	Kenyon
1984	Kenyon	1992	Kenyon	2000	Kenyon
1985	Kenyon	1993	Kenyon	2001	Denison
1986	Kenyon	1994	Kenyon	2002	Kenyon
1987	Kenyon	1995	Kenyon	2003	Kenyon
1988	Kenyon	1996	Kenyon	2004	Kenyon
1989	Kenyon	1997	Kenyon	2005	Emory

Tennis

Men

INDIVIDUAL CHAMPIONS 1883–1945

Year	Champion	Year	Champion
1883	Joseph Clark, Harvard (spring)	1914	George Church, Princeton
1883	Howard Taylor, Harvard (fall)	1915	Richard Williams II, Harvard
1884	W.P. Knapp, Yale	1916	G. Colket Caner, Harvard
1885	W.P. Knapp, Yale	1917–18	No tournament
1886	G.M. Brinley, Trinity (CT)	1919	Charles Garland, Yale
1887	P.S. Sears, Harvard	1920	Lascelles Banks, Yale
1888	P.S. Sears, Harvard	1921	Philip Neer, Stanford
1889	R.P. Huntington Jr, Yale	1922	Lucien Williams, Yale
1890	Fred Hovey, Harvard	1923	Carl Fischer, Philadelphia Osteo
1891	Fred Hovey, Harvard	1924	Wallace Scott, Washington
1892	William Larned, Cornell	1925	Edward Chandler, California
1893	Malcolm Chace, Brown	1926	Edward Chandler, UC Berkeley
1894	Malcolm Chace, Yale	1927	Wilmer Allison, Texas
1895	Malcolm Chace, Yale	1928	Julius Seligson, Lehigh
1896	Malcolm Whitman, Harvard	1929	Berkeley Bell, Texas
1897	S.G. Thompson, Princeton	1930	Clifford Sutter, Tulane
1898	Leo Ware, Harvard	1931	Keith Gledhill, Stanford
1899	Dwight Davis, Harvard	1932	Clifford Sutter, Tulane
1900	Raymond Little, Princeton	1933	Jack Tidball, UCLA
1901	Fred Alexander, Princeton	1934	Gene Mako, Southern Cal
1902	William Clothier, Harvard	1935	Wilbur Hess, Rice
1903	E.B. Dewhurst, Pennsylvania	1936	Ernest Sutter, Tulane
1904	Robert LeRoy, Columbia	1937	Ernest Sutter, Tulane
1905	E.B. Dewhurst, Pennsylvania	1938	Frank Guernsey, Rice
1906	Robert LeRoy, Columbia	1939	Frank Guernsey, Rice
1907	G. Peabody Gardner Jr, Harvard	1940	Donald McNeil, Kenyon
1908	Nat Niles, Harvard	1941	Joseph Hunt, Navy
1909	Wallace Johnson, Pennsylvania	1942	Frederick Schroeder Jr, Stanford
1910	R.A. Holden Jr, Yale	1943	Pancho Segura, Miami (FL)
1911	E.H. Whitney, Harvard	1944	Pancho Segura, Miami (FL)
1912	George Church, Princeton	1945	Pancho Segura, Miami (FL)
1913	Richard Williams II, Harvard		

DIVISION I

Year	Champion	Coach	Pts	Runner-Up	Pts	Individual Champion
1946	Southern Cal	William Moyle	9	William & Mary	6	Robert Falkenburg, Southern Cal
1947	William & Mary	Sharvey G. Umbeck	10	Rice	4	Gardner Larned, William & Mary
1948	William & Mary	Sharvey G. Umbeck	6	San Francisco	5	Harry Likas, San Francisco
1949	San Francisco	Norman Brooks	7	Rollins/Tulane/ Washington	4	Jack Tuero, Tulane
1950	UCLA	William Ackerman	11	California/ USC	5	Herbert Flam, UCLA
1951	Southern Cal	Louis Wheeler	9	Cincinnati	7	Tony Trabert, Cincinnati
1952	UCLA	J.D. Morgan	11	California/USC	5	Hugh Stewart, Southern Cal
1953	UCLA	J.D. Morgan	11	California	6	Hamilton Richardson, Tulane
1954	UCLA	J.D. Morgan	15	Southern Cal	10	Hamilton Richardson, Tulane
1955	Southern Cal	George Toley	12	Texas	7	Jose Aguero, Tulane
1956	UCLA	J.D. Morgan	15	Southern Cal	14	Alejandro Olmedo, Southern Cal
1957	Michigan	William Murphy	10	Tulane	9	Barry MacKay, Michigan
1958	Southern Cal	George Toley	13	Stanford	9	Alejandro Olmedo, Southern Cal
1959	Notre Dame	Thomas Fallon	8			Whitney Reed, San Jose St
	Tulane	Emmet Pare	8			
1960	UCLA	J.D. Morgan	18	Southern Cal	8	Larry Nagler, UCLA
1961	UCLA	J.D. Morgan	17	Southern Cal	16	Allen Fox, UCLA
1962	Southern Cal	George Toley	22	UCLA	12	Rafael Osuna, Southern Cal
1963	Southern Cal	George Toley	27	UCLA	19	Dennis Ralston, Southern Cal
1964	Southern Cal	George Toley	26	UCLA	25	Dennis Ralston, Southern Cal
1965	UCLA	J.D. Morgan	31	Miami (FL)	13	Arthur Ashe, UCLA
1966	Southern Cal	George Toley	27	UCLA	23	Charles Pasarell, UCLA
1967	Southern Cal	George Toley	28	UCLA	23	Bob Lutz, Southern Cal
1968	Southern Cal	George Toley	31	Rice	23	Stan Smith, Southern Cal
1969	Southern Cal	George Toley	35	UCLA	23	Joaquin Loyo-Mayo, Southern Cal
1970	UCLA	Glenn Bassett	26	Trinity (TX)	22	Jeff Borowiak, UCLA
				Rice	22	
1971	UCLA	Glenn Bassett	35	Trinity (TX)	27	Jimmy Connors, UCLA
1972	Trinity (TX)	Clarence Mabry	36	Stanford	30	Dick Stockton, Trinity (TX)
1973	Stanford	Dick Gould	33	Southern Cal	28	Alex Mayer, Stanford

Men (Cont.)

DIVISION I (Cont.)

Year	Champion	Coach	Pts	Runner-Up	Pts	Individual Champion
1974	Stanford	Dick Gould	30	Southern Cal	25	John Whitlinger, Stanford
1975	UCLA	Glenn Bassett	27	Miami (FL)	20	Bill Martin, UCLA
1976	Southern Cal	George Toley	21			Bill Scanlon, Trinity (TX)
	UCLA	Glenn Bassett	21			
1977	Stanford	Dick Gould		Trinity (TX)		Matt Mitchell, Stanford
1978	Stanford	Dick Gould		UCLA		John McEnroe, Stanford
1979	UCLA	Glenn Bassett		Trinity (TX)		Kevin Curren, Texas
1980	Stanford	Dick Gould		California		Robert Van't Hof, Southern Cal
1981	Stanford	Dick Gould		UCLA		Tim Mayotte, Stanford
1982	UCLA	Glenn Bassett		Pepperdine		Mike Leach, Michigan
1983	Stanford	Dick Gould		SMU		Greg Holmes, Utah
1984	UCLA	Glenn Bassett		Stanford		Mikael Pernfors, Georgia
1985	Georgia	Dan Magill		UCLA		Mikael Pernfors, Georgia
1986	Stanford	Dick Gould		Pepperdine		Dan Goldie, Stanford
1987	Georgia	Dan Magill		UCLA		Andrew Burrow, Miami (FL)
1988	Stanford	Dick Gould		Louisiana St		Robby Weiss, Pepperdine
1989	Stanford	Dick Gould		Georgia		Donni Leaycraft, Louisiana St
1990	Stanford	Dick Gould		Tennessee		Steve Bryan, Texas
1991	Southern Cal	Dick Leach		Georgia		Jared Palmer, Stanford
1992	Stanford	Dick Gould		Notre Dame		Alex O'Brien, Stanford
1993	Southern Cal	Dick Leach		Georgia		Chris Woodruff, Tennessee
1994	Southern Cal	Dick Leach		Stanford		Mark Merklein, Florida
1995	Stanford	Dick Gould		Mississippi		Sargis Sargsian, Arizona St
1996	Stanford	Dick Gould		UCLA		Cecil Mamiit, Southern Cal
1997	Stanford	Dick Gould		Georgia		Luke Smith, UNLV
1998	Stanford	Dick Gould		Georgia		Bob Bryan, Stanford
1999	Georgia	Manuel Diaz		UCLA		Jeff Morrison, Florida
2000	Stanford	Dick Gould		VA–Commonwealth		Alex Kim, Stanford
2001	Georgia	Manuel Diaz		Tennessee		Matias Boeker, Georgia
2002	Southern Cal	Dick Leach		Georgia		Matias Boeker, Georgia
2003	Illinois	Craig Tiley		Vanderbilt		Amer Delic, Illinois
2004	Baylor	Matt Knoll		UCLA		Benjamin Becker, Baylor
2005	UCLA	Billy Martin		Baylor		Benedikt Dorsch, Baylor

Note: Prior to 1977, individual wins counted in the team's total points. In 1977, a dual-match single-elimination team championship was initiated, eliminating the point system.

DIVISION II

Year	Champion	Year	Champion	Year	Champion
1963	Cal St–LA	1978	SIU–Edwardsville	1993	Lander
1964	Cal St–LA/S Illinois	1979	SIU–Edwardsville	1994	Lander
1965	Cal St–LA	1980	SIU–Edwardsville	1995	Lander
1966	Rollins	1981	SIU–Edwardsville	1996	Lander
1967	Long Beach St	1982	SIU–Edwardsville	1997	Lander
1968	Fresno St	1983	SIU–Edwardsville	1998	Lander
1969	Cal St–Northridge	1984	SIU–Edwardsville	1999	Lander
1970	UC–Irvine	1985	Chapman	2000	Lander
1971	UC–Irvine	1986	Cal-Poly–SLO	2001	Rollins
1972	UC–Irvine/ Rollins	1987	Chapman	2002	BYU-Hawaii
1973	UC–Irvine	1988	Chapman	2003	BYU-Hawaii
1974	San Diego	1989	Hampton	2004	W Florida
1975	UC–Irvine/San Diego	1990	Cal-Poly–SLO	2005	W Florida
1976	Hampton	1991	Rollins		
1977	UC–Irvine	1992	UC–Davis		

DIVISION III

Year	Champion	Year	Champion	Year	Champion
1976	Kalamazoo	1986	Kalamazoo	1997	Washington (MD)
1977	Swarthmore	1987	Kalamazoo	1998	UC–Santa Cruz
1978	Kalamazoo	1988	Washington & Lee	1999	Williams
1979	Redlands	1989	UC–Santa Cruz	2000	Trinity (TX)
1980	Gustavus Adolphus	1990	Swarthmore	2001	Williams
1981	Claremont-M-S/ Swarthmore	1991	Kalamazoo	2002	Williams
1982	Gustavus Adolphus	1992	Kalamazoo	2003	Emory
1983	Redlands	1993	Kalamazoo	2004	Middlebury
1984	Redlands	1994	Washington (MD)	2005	UC–Santa Cruz
1985	Swarthmore	1995	UC–Santa Cruz		
		1996	UC–Santa Cruz		

Women
DIVISION I

Year	Champion	Coach	Runner-Up	Individual Champion
1982	Stanford	Frank Brennan	UCLA	Alycia Moulton, Stanford
1983	Southern Cal	Dave Borelli	Trinity (TX)	Beth Herr, Southern Cal
1984	Stanford	Frank Brennan	Southern Cal	Lisa Spain, Georgia
1985	Southern Cal	Dave Borelli	Miami (FL)	Linda Gates, Stanford
1986	Stanford	Frank Brennan	Southern Cal	Patty Fendick, Stanford
1987	Stanford	Frank Brennan	Georgia	Patty Fendick, Stanford
1988	Stanford	Frank Brennan	Florida	Shaun Stafford, Florida
1989	Stanford	Frank Brennan	UCLA	Sandra Birch, Stanford
1990	Stanford	Frank Brennan	Florida	Debbie Graham, Stanford
1991	Stanford	Frank Brennan	UCLA	Sandra Birch, Stanford
1992	Florida	Andy Brandi	Texas	Lisa Raymond, Florida
1993	Texas	Jeff Moore	Stanford	Lisa Raymond, Florida
1994	Georgia	Jeff Wallace	Stanford	Angela Lettiere, Georgia
1995	Texas	Jeff Moore	Florida	Keri Phebus, UCLA
1996	Florida	Andy Brandi	Stanford	Jill Craybas, Florida
1997	Stanford	Frank Brennan	Florida	Lilia Osterloh, Stanford
1998	Florida	Andy Brandi	Duke	Vanessa Webb, Duke
1999	Stanford	Frank Brennan	Florida	Zuzana Lesenarova, UC–SD
2000	Georgia	Jeff Wallace	Stanford	Laura Granville, Stanford
2001	Stanford	Lele Forood	Vanderbilt	Laura Granville, Stanford
2002	Stanford	Lele Forood	Florida	Bea Bielek, Wake Forest
2003	Florida	Roland Thornqvist	Stanford	Amber Liu, Stanford
2004	Stanford	Lele Forood	UCLA	Amber Liu, Stanford
2005	Stanford	Lele Forood	Texas	Alice Barnes, Stanford

DIVISION II

Year	Champion	Year	Champion	Year	Champion
1982	Cal St–Northridge	1991	Cal Poly–Pomona	1999	BYU–Hawaii
1983	TN–Chattanooga	1992	Cal Poly–Pomona	2000	BYU–Hawaii
1984	TN–Chattanooga	1993	UC–Davis	2001	Lynn
1985	TN–Chattanooga	1994	N Florida	2002	BYU–Hawaii
1986	SIU–Edwardsville	1995	Armstrong St	2003	BYU–Hawaii
1987	SIU–Edwardsville	1996	Armstrong St	2004	BYU–Hawaii
1988	SIU–Edwardsville	1997	Lynn	2005	Armstrong Atlantic
1989	SIU–Edwardsville	1998	Lynn		
1990	UC–Davis				

DIVISION III

Year	Champion	Year	Champion	Year	Champion
1982	Occidental	1990	Gustavus Adolphus	1998	Kenyon
1983	Principia	1991	Mary Washington	1999	Amherst
1984	Davidson	1992	Pomona-Pitzer	2000	Trinity (TX)
1985	UC–San Diego	1993	Kenyon	2001	Williams
1986	Trenton St	1994	UC–San Diego	2002	Williams
1987	UC–San Diego	1995	Kenyon	2003	Emory
1988	Mary Washington	1996	Emory	2004	Emory
1989	UC–San Diego	1997	Kenyon	2005	Emory

Indoor Track and Field

Men
DIVISION I

Year	Champion	Coach	Pts	Runner-Up	Pts
1965	Missouri	Tom Botts	14	Oklahoma St	12
1966	Kansas	Bob Timmons	14	Southern Cal	13
1967	Southern Cal	Vern Wolfe	26	Oklahoma	17
1968	Villanova	Jim Elliott	35	Southern Cal	25
1969	Kansas	Bob Timmons	41½	Villanova	33
1970	Kansas	Bob Timmons	27½	Villanova	26
1971	Villanova	Jim Elliott	22	UT-El Paso	19¼
1972	Southern Cal	Vern Wolfe	19	Bowling Green/ Mich St	18
1973	Manhattan	Fred Dwyer	18	Kansas/Kent St/UTEP	12
1974	UT-El Paso	Ted Banks	19	Colorado	18
1975	UT-El Paso	Ted Banks	36	Kansas	17½
1976	UT-El Paso	Ted Banks	23	Villanova	15
1977	Washington St	John Chaplin	25½	UT-El Paso	25
1978	UT-El Paso	Ted Banks	44	Auburn	38
1979	Villanova	Jim Elliott	52	UT-El Paso	51
1980	UT-El Paso	Ted Banks	76	Villanova	42
1981	UT-El Paso	Ted Banks	76	SMU	51
1982	UT-El Paso	John Wedel	67	Arkansas	30

Men *(Cont.)*
DIVISION I *(Cont.)*

Year	Champion	Coach	Pts	Runner-Up	Pts
1983	SMU	Ted McLaughlin	43	Villanova	32
1984	Arkansas	John McDonnell	38	Washington St	28
1985	Arkansas	John McDonnell	70	Tennessee	29
1986	Arkansas	John McDonnell	49	Villanova	22
1987	Arkansas	John McDonnell	39	SMU	31
1988	Arkansas	John McDonnell	34	Illinois	29
1989	Arkansas	John McDonnell	34	Florida	31
1990	Arkansas	John McDonnell	44	Texas A&M	36
1991	Arkansas	John McDonnell	34	Georgetown	27
1992	Arkansas	John McDonnell	53	Clemson	46
1993	Arkansas	John McDonnell	66	Clemson	30
1994	Arkansas	John McDonnell	83	UT-El Paso	45
1995	Arkansas	John McDonnell	59	GMU/Tennessee	26
1996	George Mason	John Cook	39	Nebraska	31½
1997	Arkansas	John McDonnell	59	Auburn	27
1998	Arkansas	John McDonnell	56	Stanford	36½
1999	Arkansas	John McDonnell	65	Stanford	42½
2000	Arkansas	John McDonnell	69½	Stanford	52
2001	Louisiana St	Pat Henry	34	Texas Christian	33
2002	Tennessee	Bill Webb	62½	Louisiana St	44
2003	Arkansas	John McDonnell	52	Auburn	28
2004	Louisiana St	Pat Henry	45½	Florida	38
2005	Arkansas	John McDonnell	54	Wisconsin	43

DIVISION II

Year	Champion	Year	Champion	Year	Champion
1985	SE Missouri St	1992	St. Augustine's	1999	Abilene Christian
1986	Not held	1993	Abilene Christian	2000	Abilene Christian
1987	St. Augustine's	1994	Abilene Christian	2001	St. Augustine's
1988	Abil. Christian/St. August.	1995	St. Augustine's	2002	Abilene Christian
1989	St. Augustine's	1996	Abilene Christian	2003	Abilene Christian
1990	St. Augustine's	1997	Abilene Christian	2004	Abilene Christian
1991	St. Augustine's	1998	Abilene Christian	2005	Abilene Christian

DIVISION III

Year	Champion	Year	Champion	Year	Champion
1985	St. Thomas (MN)	1992	WI–La Crosse	1999	Lincoln (PA)
1986	Frostburg St	1993	WI–La Crosse	2000	Lincoln (PA)
1987	WI–La Crosse	1994	WI–La Crosse	2001	WI–La Crosse
1988	WI–La Crosse	1995	Lincoln (PA)	2002	WI–La Crosse
1989	N Central	1996	Lincoln (PA)	2003	WI–La Crosse
1990	Lincoln (PA)	1997	WI–La Crosse	2004	WI–La Crosse
1991	WI–La Crosse	1998	Lincoln (PA)	2005	WI–La Crosse

Women
DIVISION I

Year	Champion	Coach	Pts	Runner-Up	Pts
1983	Nebraska	Gary Pepin	47	Tennessee	44
1984	Nebraska	Gary Pepin	59	Tennessee	48
1985	Florida St	Gary Winckler	34	Texas	32
1986	Texas	Terry Crawford	31	Southern Cal	26
1987	Louisiana St	Loren Seagrave	49	Tennessee	30
1988	Texas	Terry Crawford	71	Villanova	52
1989	Louisiana St	Pat Henry	61	Villanova	34
1990	Texas	Terry Crawford	50	Wisconsin	26
1991	Louisiana St	Pat Henry	48	Texas	39
1992	Florida	Bev Kearney	50	Stanford	26
1993	Louisiana St	Pat Henry	49	Wisconsin	44
1994	Louisiana St	Pat Henry	48	Alabama	29
1995	Louisiana St	Pat Henry	40	UCLA	37
1996	Louisiana St	Pat Henry	52	Georgia	34
1997	Louisiana St	Pat Henry	49	Texas/Wisconsin	39
1998	Texas	Bev Kearney	60	Louisiana St	30
1999	Texas	Bev Kearney	61	Louisiana St	57
2000	UCLA	Jeanette Bolden	51	South Carolina	41
2001	UCLA	Jeanette Bolden	53½	South Carolina	40
2002	Louisiana St	Pat Henry	57	Florida	35
2003	Louisiana St	Pat Henry	62	South Carolina/Florida	44
2004	Lousiana St	Pat Henry	52	Florida	51
2005	Tennessee	J.J. Clark	46	Florida	36

Women (Cont.)

DIVISION II

Year	Champion	Year	Champion	Year	Champion
1985	St. Augustine's	1992	Alabama A&M	1999	Abilene Christian
1986	Not held	1993	Abilene Christian	2000	Abilene Christian
1987	St. Augustine's	1994	Abilene Christian	2001	St. Augustine's
1988	Abilene Christian	1995	Abilene Christian	2002	N Dakota St
1989	Abilene Christian	1996	Abilene Christian	2003	St. Augustine's
1990	Abilene Christian	1997	Abilene Christian	2004	Lincoln
1991	Abilene Christian	1998	Abilene Christian	2005	St.Augustine

DIVISION III

Year	Champion	Year	Champion	Year	Champion
1985	MA–Boston	1992	Christopher Newport	1999	Wheaton (MA)
1986	MA–Boston	1993	Lincoln (PA)	2000	Wheaton (MA)
1987	MA–Boston	1994	WI–Oshkosh	2001	Wheaton (MA)
1988	Christopher Newport	1995	WI–Oshkosh	2002	Wheaton (MA)
1989	Christopher Newport	1996	WI–Oshkosh	2003	Wheaton (MA)
1990	Christopher Newport	1997	Christopher Newport	2004	WI–Oshkosh
1991	Cortland St	1998	Christopher Newport	2005	WI–Oshkosh
		Year	Champion		

Outdoor Track and Field

Men

DIVISION I

Year	Champion	Coach	Pts	Runner-Up	Pts
1921	Illinois	Harry Gill	20†	Notre Dame	16†
1922	California	Walter Christie	28†	Penn St	19†
1923	Michigan	Stephen Farrell	29†	Mississippi St	16
1924	No meet				
1925	Stanford*	R.L. Templeton	31†		
1926	Southern Cal*	Dean Cromwell	27†		
1927	Illinois*	Harry Gill	35†		
1928	Stanford	R.L. Templeton	72	Ohio St	31
1929	Ohio St	Frank Castleman	50	Washington	42
1930	Southern Cal	Dean Cromwell	55†	Washington	40
1931	Southern Cal	Dean Cromwell	77†	Ohio St	31†
1932	Indiana	Billy Hayes	56	Ohio St	49†
1933	Louisiana St	Bernie Moore	58	Southern Cal	54
1934	Stanford	R.L. Templeton	63	Southern Cal	54†
1935	Southern Cal	Dean Cromwell	74†	Ohio St	40†
1936	Southern Cal	Dean Cromwell	103†	Ohio St	73
1937	Southern Cal	Dean Cromwell	62	Stanford	50
1938	Southern Cal	Dean Cromwell	67†	Stanford	38
1939	Southern Cal	Dean Cromwell	86	Stanford	44†
1940	Southern Cal	Dean Cromwell	47	Stanford	28†
1941	Southern Cal	Dean Cromwell	81†	Indiana	50
1942	Southern Cal	Dean Cromwell	85†	Ohio St	44†
1943	Southern Cal	Dean Cromwell	46	California	39
1944	Illinois	Leo Johnson	79	Notre Dame	43
1945	Navy	E.J. Thomson	62	Illinois	48†
1946	Illinois	Leo Johnson	78	Southern Cal	42†
1947	Illinois	Leo Johnson	59†	Southern Cal	34†
1948	Minnesota	James Kelly	46	Southern Cal	41†
1949	Southern Cal	Jess Hill	55†	UCLA	31
1950	Southern Cal	Jess Hill	49†	Stanford	28
1951	Southern Cal	Jess Mortenson	56	Cornell	40
1952	Southern Cal	Jess Mortenson	66†	San Jose St	24†
1953	Southern Cal	Jess Mortenson	80	Illinois	41
1954	Southern Cal	Jess Mortenson	66†	Illinois	31†
1955	Southern Cal	Jess Mortenson	42	UCLA	34
1956	UCLA	Elvin Drake	55†	Kansas	51
1957	Villanova	James Elliott	47	California	32
1958	Southern Cal	Jess Mortenson	48†	Kansas	40†
1959	Kansas	Bill Easton	73	San Jose St	48
1960	Kansas	Bill Easton	50	Southern Cal	37
1961	Southern Cal	Jess Mortenson	65	Oregon	47

Men (Cont.)
DIVISION I (Cont.)

Year	Champion	Coach	Pts	Runner-Up	Pts
1962	Oregon	William Bowerman	85	Villanova	40†
1963	Southern Cal	Vern Wolfe	61	Stanford	42
1964	Oregon	William Bowerman	70	San Jose St	40
1965	Oregon	William Bowerman	32		
	Southern Cal	Vern Wolfe	32		
1966	UCLA	Jim Bush	81	Brigham Young	33
1967	Southern Cal	Vern Wolfe	86	Oregon	40
1968	Southern Cal	Vern Wolfe	58	Washington St	57
1969	San Jose St	Bud Winter	48	Kansas	45
1970	Brigham Young	Clarence Robison	35		
	Kansas	Bob Timmons	35		
	Oregon	William Bowerman	35		
1971	UCLA	Jim Bush	52	Southern Cal	41
1972	UCLA	Jim Bush	82	Southern Cal	49
1973	UCLA	Jim Bush	56	Oregon	31
1974	Tennessee	Stan Huntsman	60	UCLA	56
1975	UT-El Paso	Ted Banks	55	UCLA	42
1976	Southern Cal	Vern Wolfe	64	UT-El Paso	44
1977	Arizona St	Senon Castillo	64	UT-El Paso	50
1978	UCLA/UTEP	Jim Bush/Ted Banks	50		
1979	UT-El Paso	Ted Banks	64	Villanova	48
1980	UT-El Paso	Ted Banks	69	UCLA	46
1981	UT-El Paso	Ted Banks	70	SMU	57
1982	UT-El Paso	John Wedel	105	Tennessee	94
1983	Southern Methodist	Ted McLaughlin	104	Tennessee	102
1984	Oregon	Bill Dellinger	113	Washington St	94½
1985	Arkansas	John McDonnell	61	Washington St	46
1986	SMU	Ted McLaughlin	53	Washington St	52
1987	UCLA	Bob Larsen	81	Texas	28
1988	UCLA	Bob Larsen	82	Texas	41
1989	Louisiana St	Pat Henry	53	Texas A&M	51
1990	Louisiana St	Pat Henry	44	Arkansas	36
1991	Tennessee	Doug Brown	51	Washington St	42
1992	Arkansas	John McDonnell	60	Tennessee	46½
1993	Arkansas	John McDonnell	69	LSU/Ohio St	45
1994	Arkansas	John McDonnell	83	UT-El Paso	45
1995	Arkansas	John McDonnell	61½	UCLA	55
1996	Arkansas	John McDonnell	55	George Mason	40
1997	Arkansas	John McDonnell	55	Texas	42½
1998	Arkansas	John McDonnell	58½	Stanford	51
1999	Arkansas	John McDonnell	59	Stanford	52
2000	Stanford	Vin Lananna	72	Arkansas	59
2001	Tennessee	Bill Webb	50	Texas Christian	49
2002	Louisiana St	Pat Henry	64	Tennessee	57
2003	Arkansas	John McDonnell	59	Auburn	50
2004	Arkansas	John McDonnell	65½	Florida	49
2005	Arkansa	John McDonnell	109	Adams State	84

*Unofficial championship. †Fraction of a point.

DIVISION II

Year	Champion	Year	Champion	Year	Champion
1963	MD–Eastern Shore	1977	Cal St–Hayward	1992	St. Augustine's
1964	Fresno St	1978	Cal St–LA	1993	St. Augustine's
1965	San Diego St	1979	Cal Poly–SLO	1994	St. Augustine's
1966	San Diego St	1980	Cal Poly–SLO	1995	St. Augustine's
1967	Long Beach St	1981	Cal Poly–SLO	1996	Abilene Christian
1968	Cal Poly–SLO	1982	Abilene Christian	1997	Abilene Christian
1969	Cal Poly–SLO	1983	Abilene Christian	1998	St. Augustine's
1970	Cal Poly–SLO	1984	Abilene Christian	1999	Abilene Christian
1971	Kentucky St	1985	Abilene Christian	2000	Abilene Christian
1972	Eastern Michigan	1986	Abilene Christian	2001	St. Augustine's
1973	Norfolk St	1987	Abilene Christian	2002	Abilene Christian
1974	Eastern Illinois	1988	Abilene Christian	2003	Abilene Christian
	Norfolk St	1989	St. Augustine's	2004	Abilene Christian
1975	Cal St–Northridge	1990	St. Augustine's	2005	Abilene Christian
1976	UC–Irvine	1991	St. Augustine's		

Men (Cont.)

Year	Champion	Year	Champion	Year	Champion
1974	Ashland	1985	Lincoln (PA)	1996	Lincoln (PA)
1975	Southern–N Orleans	1986	Frostburg St	1997	WI–La Crosse
1976	Southern–N Orleans	1987	Frostburg St	1998	N Central
1977	Southern–N Orleans	1988	WI–La Crosse	1999	Lincoln (PA)
1978	Occidental	1989	N Central	2000	Nebraska Wesleyan
1979	Slippery Rock	1990	Lincoln (PA)	2001	WI–La Crosse
1980	Glassboro St	1991	WI–La Crosse	2002	WI–La Crosse
1981	Glassboro St	1992	WI–La Crosse	2003	WI–La Crosse
1982	Glassboro St	1993	WI–La Crosse	2004	WI–La Crosse
1983	Glassboro St	1994	N Central	2005	Lincoln
1984	Glassboro St	1995	Lincoln (PA)		

Women – DIVISION I

Year	Champion	Coach	Pts	Runner-Up	Pts
1982	UCLA	Scott Chisarn	153	Tennessee	126
1983	UCLA	Scott Chisam	116 /2	Florida St	108
1984	Florida St	Gary Winckler	145	Tennessee	124
1985	Oregon	Tom Heinonen	52	Florida St/LSU	46
1986	Texas	Terry Crawford	65	Alabama	55
1987	Louisiana St	Loren Seagrave	62	Alabama	53
1988	Louisiana St	Loren Seagrave	61	UCLA	58
1989	Louisiana St	Pat Henry	86	UCLA	47
1990	Louisiana St	Pat Henry	53	UCLA	46
1991	Louisiana St	Pat Henry	78	Texas	67
1992	Louisiana St	Pat Henry	87	Florida	81
1993	Louisiana St	Pat Henry	93	Wisconsin	44
1994	Louisiana St	Pat Henry	86	Texas	43
1995	Louisiana St	Pat Henry	69	UCLA	58
1996	Louisiana St	Pat Henry	81	Texas	52
1997	Louisiana St	Pat Henry	63	Texas	62
1998	Texas	Bev Kearney	60	UCLA	55
1999	Texas	Bev Kearney	62	UCLA	60
2000	Louisiana St	Pat Henry	59	Southern Cal	56
2001	Southern Cal	Ron Allice	64	UCLA	55
2002	South Carolina	Curtis Frye	82	UCLA	72
2003	Louisiana St	Pat Henry	64	Texas	50
2004	UCLA	Jeanette Bolden	69	Louisiana St	68
2005	Texas	Bev Kearney	55	Cal State/South Carolina	48

DIVISION II

Year	Champion	Year	Champion	Year	Champion
1982	Cal Poly–SLO	1990	Cal Poly–SLO	1998	Abilene Christian
1983	Cal Poly–SLO	1991	Cal Poly–SLO	1999	Abilene Christian
1984	Cal Poly–SLO	1992	Alabama A&M	2000	St. Augustine's
1985	Abilene Christian	1993	Alabama A&M	2001	St. Augustine's
1986	Abilene Christian	1994	Alabama A&M	2002	St. Augustine's
1987	Abilene Christian	1995	Abilene Christian	2003	Lincoln
1988	Abilene Christian	1996	Abilene Christian	2004	Lincoln
1989	Cal Poly–SLO	1997	St. Augustine's	2005	Lincoln

DIVISION III

Year	Champion	Year	Champion	Year	Champion
1982	Central (IA)	1990	WI–Oshkosh	1998	Chris. Newport
1983	WI–La Crosse	1991	WI–Oshkosh	1999	Lincoln (PA)
1984	WI–La Crosse	1992	Chris. Newport	2000	Lincoln (PA)
1985	Cortland State	1993	Lincoln (PA)	2001	Wheaton (MA)
1986	MA–Boston	1994	Chris. Newport	2002	Wheaton (MA)
1987	Chris. Newport	1995	WI–Oshkosh	2003	Wheaton (MA)
1988	Chris. Newport	1996	WI–Oshkosh	2004	WI–Oshkosh
1989	Chris. Newport	1997	WI–Oshkosh	2005	Wartburg

Volleyball

Men

Year	Champion	Coach	Score	Runner-Up	Most Outstanding Player
1970	UCLA	Al Scates	3–0	Long Beach St	Dane Holtzman, UCLA
1971	UCLA	Al Scates	3–0	UC–Santa Barbara	K. Kilgore, UCLA/T. Bonynge, UCSB
1972	UCLA	Al Scates	3–2	San Diego St	Dick Irvin, UCLA
1973	San Diego St	Jack Henn	3–1	Long Beach St	Duncan McFarland, San Diego St
1974	UCLA	Al Scates	3–2	UC–Santa Barbara	Bob Leonard, UCLA
1975	UCLA	Al Scates	3–1	UC–Santa Barbara	John Bekins, UCLA
1976	UCLA	Al Scates	3–0	Pepperdine	Joe Mika, UCLA

Men (Cont.)

Year	Champion	Coach	Score	Runner-Up	Most Outstanding Player
1977	Southern Cal	Ernie Hix	3–1	Ohio St	Celso Kalache, Southern Cal
1978	Pepperdine	Marv Dunphy	3–2	UCLA	Mike Blanchard, Pepperdine
1979	UCLA	Al Scates	3–1	Southern Cal	Sinjin Smith, UCLA
1980	Southern Cal	Ernie Hix	3–1	UCLA	Dusty Dvorak, Southern Cal
1981	UCLA	Al Scates	3–2	Southern Cal	Karch Kiraly, UCLA
1982	UCLA	Al Scates	3–0	Penn St	Karch Kiraly, UCLA
1983	UCLA	Al Scates	3–0	Pepperdine	Ricci Luyties, UCLA
1984	UCLA	Al Scates	3–1	Pepperdine	Ricci Luyties, UCLA
1985	Pepperdine	Marv Dunphy	3–1	Southern Cal	Bob Ctvrtlik, Pepperdine
1986	Pepperdine	Rod Wilde	3–2	Southern Cal	Steve Friedman, Pepperdine
1987	UCLA	Al Scates	3–0	Southern Cal	Ozzie Volstad, UCLA
1988	Southern Cal	Bob Yoder	3–2	UC–Santa Barbara	Jen-Kai Liu, Southern Cal
1989	UCLA	Al Scates	3–1	Stanford	Matt Sonnichsen, UCLA
1990	Southern Cal	Jim McLaughlin	3–1	Long Beach St	Bryan Ivie, Southern Cal
1991	Long Beach St	Ray Ratelle	3–1	Southern Cal	Brent Hilliard, Long Beach St
1992	Pepperdine	Marv Dunphy	3–0	Stanford	Alon Grinberg, Pepperdine
1993	UCLA	Al Scates	3–0	Cal St–Northridge	Mike Sealy/Jeff Nygaard, UCLA
1994	Penn St	Tom Peterson	3–2	UCLA	Ramon Hernandez, Penn·St
1995	UCLA	Al Scates	3–0	Penn St	Jeff Nygaard, UCLA
1996	UCLA	Al Scates	3–2	Hawaii	Yuval Katz, Hawaii
1997	Stanford	Ruben Nieves	3–2	UCLA	Mike Lambert, Stanford
1998	UCLA	Al Scates	3–2	Pepperdine	George Roumain, Pepperdine
1999	Brigham Young	Carl McGown	3–0	Long Beach St	Ossie Antonetti, Brigham Young
2000	UCLA	Al Scates	3–0	Ohio St	Brandon Taliaferro, UCLA
2001	Brigham Young	Carl McGown	3–0	UCLA	Mike Wall, Brigham Young
2002	Hawaii	Mike Wilton	3–1	Pepperdine	Costas Theochardis, Hawaii
2003	Lewis	Dave Deuser	3–2	Brigham Young	Gustavo Meyer, Lewis
2004	Brigham Young	Tom Peterson	3–2	Long Beach St	Carlos Moreno, Brigham Young
2005	Pepperdine	Marv Dunphy	3–2	UCLA	Sean Rooney, Pepperdine

Women - DIVISION I

Year	Champion	Coach	Score	Runner-Up
1981	Southern Cal	Chuck Erbe	3–2	UCLA
1982	Hawaii	Dave Shoji	3–2	Southern Cal
1983	Hawaii	Dave Shoji	3–0	UCLA
1984	UCLA	Andy Banachowski	3–2	Stanford
1985	Pacific	John Dunning	3–1	Stanford
1986	Pacific	John Dunning	3–0	Nebraska
1987	Hawaii	Dave Shoji	3–1	Stanford
1988	Texas	Mick Haley	3–0	Hawaii
1989	Long Beach St	Brian Gimmillaro	3–0	Nebraska
1990	UCLA	Andy Banachowski	3–0	Pacific
1991	UCLA	Andy Banachowski	3–2	Long Beach St
1992	Stanford	Don Shaw	3–1	UCLA
1993	Long Beach St	Brian Gimmillaro	3–1	Penn St
1994	Stanford	Don Shaw	3–1	UCLA
1995	Nebraska	Terry Pettit	3–1	Texas
1996	Stanford	Don Shaw	3–0	Hawaii
1997	Stanford	Don Shaw	3–2	Penn St
1998	Long Beach St	Brian Gimmillaro	3–2	Penn St
1999	Penn St	Russ Rose	3–0	Stanford
2000	Nebraska	John Cook	3–2	Wisconsin
2001	Stanford	Don Shaw	3–0	Long Beach St
2002	Southern Cal	Mick Haley	3–1	Stanford
2003	Southern Cal	Mick Haley	3–1	Florida
2004	Stanford	Don Shaw	3–0	Minnesota

DIVISION II

Year	Champion	Year	Champion	Year	Champion
1981	Cal St–Sacramento	1989	Cal St–Bakersfield	1997	West Texas A&M
1982	UC–Riverside	1990	West Texas A&M	1998	Hawaii Pacific
1983	Cal St–Northridge	1991	West Texas A&M	1999	BYU–Hawaii
1984	Portland St	1992	Portland St	2000	Hawaii Pacific
1985	Portland St	1993	Northern Michigan	2001	Barry
1986	UC–Riverside	1994	Northern Michigan	2002	BYU–Hawaii
1987	Cal St–Northridge	1995	Barry	2003	N Alabama
1988	Portland St	1996	Nebraska–Omaha	2004	Truman St

DIVISION III

Year	Champion	Year	Champion	Year	Champion	Year	Champion
1981	UC–San Diego	1987	UC–San Diego	1993	Washington (MO)	1999	Central (IA)
1982	La Verne	1988	UC–San Diego	1994	Washington (MO)	2000	Central (IA)
1983	Elmhurst	1989	Washington (MO)	1995	Washington (MO)	2001	La Verne
1984	UC–San Diego	1990	UC–San Diego	1996	Washington (MO)	2002	WI–Whitewater
1985	Elmhurst	1991	Washington (MO)	1997	UC–San Diego	2003	Washington (MO)
1986	UC–San Diego	1992	Washington (MO)	1998	Central (IA)	2004	Juniata

Water Polo

Men

Year	Champion	Coach	Score	Runner-Up
1969	UCLA	Bob Horn	5–2	California
1970	UC–Irvine	Ed Newland	7–6 (3 OT)	UCLA
1971	UCLA	Bob Horn	5–3	San Jose St
1972	UCLA	Bob Horn	10–5	UC–Irvine
1973	California	Pete Cutino	8–4	UC–Irvine
1974	California	Pete Cutino	7–6	UC–Irvine
1975	California	Pete Cutino	9–8	UC–Irvine
1976	Stanford	Art Lambert	13–12	UCLA
1977	California	Pete Cutino	8–6	UC–Irvine
1978	Stanford	Dante Dettamanti	7–6 (3 OT)	California
1979	UC–Santa Barbara	Pete Snyder	11–3	UCLA
1980	Stanford	Dante Dettamanti	8–6	California
1981	Stanford	Dante Dettamanti	17–6	Long Beach St
1982	UC–Irvine	Ed Newland	7–4	Stanford
1983	California	Pete Cutino	10–7	Southern Cal
1984	California	Pete Cutino	9–8	Stanford
1985	Stanford	Dante Dettamanti	12–11 (2 OT)	UC–Irvine
1986	Stanford	Dante Dettamanti	9–6	California
1987	California	Pete Cutino	9–8 (OT)	Southern Cal
1988	California	Pete Cutino	14–11	UCLA
1989	UC–Irvine	Ed Newland	9–8	California
1990	California	Steve Heaston	8–7	Stanford
1991	California	Steve Heaston	7–6	UCLA
1992	California	Steve Heaston	12–11	Stanford
1993	Stanford	Dante Dettamanti	11–9	Southern Cal
1994	Stanford	Dante Dettamanti	14–10	Southern Cal
1995	UCLA	Guy Baker	10–8	California
1996	UCLA	Guy Baker	8–7	Southern Cal
1997	Pepperdine	Terry Schroeder	8–7 (OT)	Southern Cal
1998	Southern Cal	John Williams	9–8 (2 OT)	Stanford
1999	UCLA	Guy Baker	6–5	Stanford
2000	UCLA	Guy Baker/Adam Krikorian	11–2	UC–San Diego
2001	Stanford	Dante Dettamanti	8–5	UCLA
2002	Stanford	John Vargas	7–6	California
2003	Southern Cal	Jovan Vavic	9–7	Stanford
2004	UCLA	Adam Krikorian	10–9	Stanford

Women

Year	Champion	Coach	Score	Runner-Up
2001	UCLA	Adam Krikorian	5–4	Stanford
2002	Stanford	John Tanner	8–4	UCLA
2003	UCLA	Adam Krikorian	4–3	Stanford
2004	Southern Cal	Jovan Vavic	10–8	Loyola-M'mnt
2004	UCLA	Adam Krikorian	3–2	Stanford

Wrestling

DIVISION I

Year	Champion	Coach	Pts	Runner-Up	Pts	Most Outstanding Wrestler
1928	Oklahoma St*	E.C. Gallagher				
1929	Oklahoma St	E.C. Gallagher	26	Michigan	18	
1930	Oklahoma St*	E.C. Gallagher	27	Illinois	14	
1931	Oklahoma St*	E.C. Gallagher		Michigan		
1932	Indiana*	W.H. Thom		Oklahoma St		Edwin Belshaw, Indiana
1933	OK St*/Iowa St*	E. Gallagher/H. Otopalik				A. Kelley, OK St/P. Johnson, Harv
1934	Oklahoma St	E.C. Gallagher	29	Indiana	19	Ben Bishop, Lehigh
1935	Oklahoma St	E.C. Gallagher	36	Oklahoma	18	Ross Flood, Oklahoma St
1936	Oklahoma	Paul Keen	14	Central St/ OK St	10	Wayne Martin, Oklahoma
1937	Oklahoma St	E.C. Gallagher	31	Oklahoma	13	Stanley Henson, Oklahoma St
1938	Oklahoma St	E.C. Gallagher	19	Illinois	15	Joe McDaniels, Oklahoma St
1939	Oklahoma St	E.C. Gallagher	33	Lehigh	12	Dale Hanson, Minnesota
1940	Oklahoma St	E.C. Gallagher	24	Indiana	14	Don Nichols, Michigan
1941	Oklahoma St	Art Griffith	37	Michigan St	26	Al Whitehurst, Oklahoma St
1942	Oklahoma St	Art Griffith	31	Michigan St	26	David Arndt, Oklahoma St
1946	Oklahoma St	Art Griffith	25	Northern Iowa	24	Gerald Leeman, Northern Iowa
1947	Cornell	Paul Scott	32	Northern Iowa	19	William Koll, Northern Iowa
1948	Oklahoma St	Art Griffith	33	Michigan St	28	William Koll, Northern Iowa
1949	Oklahoma St	Art Griffith	32	Northern Iowa	27	Charles Hetrick, Oklahoma St
1950	Northern Iowa	David McCuskey	30	Purdue	16	Anthony Gizoni, Waynesburg
1951	Oklahoma	Port Robertson	24	Oklahoma St	23	Walter Romanowski, Cornell
1952	Oklahoma	Port Robertson	22	Northern Iowa	21	Tommy Evans, Oklahoma
1953	Penn St	Charles Speidel	21	Oklahoma	15	Frank Bettucci, Cornell
1954	Oklahoma St	Art Griffith	32	Pittsburgh	17	Tommy Evans, Oklahoma
1955	Oklahoma St	Art Griffith	40	Penn St	31	Edward Eichelberger, Lehigh

DIVISION I (Cont.)

Year	Champion	Coach	Pts	Runner-Up	Pts	Most Outstanding Wrestler
1956	Oklahoma St	Art Griffith	65	Oklahoma	62	Dan Hodge, Oklahoma
1957	Oklahoma	Port Robertson	73	Pittsburgh	66	Dan Hodge, Oklahoma
1958	Oklahoma St	Myron Roderick	77	Iowa St	62	Dick Delgado, Oklahoma
1959	Oklahoma St	Myron Roderick	73	Iowa St	51	Ron Gray, Iowa St
1960	Oklahoma	Thomas Evans	59	Iowa St	40	Dave Auble, Cornell
1961	Oklahoma St	Myron Roderick	82	Oklahoma	63	E. Gray Simons, Lock Haven
1962	Oklahoma St	Myron Roderick	82	Oklahoma	45	E. Gray Simons, Lock Haven
1963	Oklahoma	Thomas Evans	48	Iowa St	45	Mickey Martin, Oklahoma
1964	Oklahoma St	Myron Roderick	87	Oklahoma	58	Dean Lahr, Colorado
1965	Iowa St	Harold Nichols	87	Oklahoma St	86	Yojiro Uetake, Oklahoma St
1966	Oklahoma St	Myron Roderick	79	Iowa St	70	Yojiro Uetake, Oklahoma St
1967	Michigan St	Grady Peninger	74	Michigan	63	Rich Sanders, Portland St
1968	Oklahoma St	Myron Roderick	81	Iowa St	78	Dwayne Keller, Oklahoma St
1969	Iowa St	Harold Nichols	104	Oklahoma	69	Dan Gable, Iowa St
1970	Iowa St	Harold Nichols	99	Michigan St	84	Larry Owings, Washington
1971	Oklahoma St	Tommy Chesbro	94	Iowa St	66	Darrell Keller, Oklahoma St
1972	Iowa St	Harold Nichols	103	Michigan St	72½	Wade Schalles, Clarion
1973	Iowa St	Harold Nichols	85	Oregon St	72½	Greg Strobel, Oregon St
1974	Oklahoma	Stan Abel	69½	Michigan	67	Floyd Hitchcock, Bloomsburg
1975	Iowa	Gary Kurdelmeier	102	Oklahoma	77	Mike Frick, Lehigh
1976	Iowa	Gary Kurdelmeier	123½	Iowa St	85¾	Chuch Yagla, Iowa
1977	Iowa St	Harold Nichols	95½	Oklahoma St	88¾	Nick Gallo, Hofstra
1978	Iowa	Dan Gable	94½	Iowa St	94	Mark Churella, Michigan
1979	Iowa	Dan Gable	122½	Iowa St	88	Bruce Kinseth, Iowa
1980	Iowa	Dan Gable	110¾	Oklahoma St	87	Howard Harris, Oregon St
1981	Iowa	Dan Gable	129¾	Oklahoma	100¼	Gene Mills, Syracuse
1982	Iowa	Dan Gable	131¾	Iowa St	111	Mark Schultz, Oklahoma
1983	Iowa	Dan Gable	155	Oklahoma St	102	Mike Sheets, Oklahoma St
1984	Iowa	Dan Gable	123¾	Oklahoma St	98	Jim Zalesky, Iowa
1985	Iowa	Dan Gable	145¼	Oklahoma	98½	Barry Davis, Iowa
1986	Iowa	Dan Gable	158	Oklahoma	84¼	Marty Kistler, Iowa
1987	Iowa St	Jim Gibbons	133	Iowa	108	John Smith, Oklahoma St
1988	Arizona St	Bobby Douglas	93	Iowa	85½	Scott Turner, N Carolina St
1989	Oklahoma St	Joe Seay	91¼	Arizona St	70½	Tim Krieger, Iowa St
1990	Oklahoma St	Joe Seay	117¾	Arizona St	104¾	Chris Barnes, Oklahoma St
1991	Iowa	Dan Gable	157	Oklahoma St	108¾	Jeff Prescott, Penn St
1992	Iowa	Dan Gable	149	Oklahoma St	100½	Tom Brands, Iowa
1993	Iowa	Dan Gable	123¾	Penn St	87½	Terry Steiner, Iowa
1994	Oklahoma St	John Smith	94¾	Iowa	76½	Pat Smith, Oklahoma St
1995	Iowa	Dan Gable	134	Oregon St	77½	T.J. Jaworsky, N Carolina
1996	Iowa	Dan Gable	122½	Iowa St	78½	Les Gutches, Oregon St
1997	Iowa	Dan Gable	170	Oklahoma St	113½	Lincoln McIlravy, Iowa
1998	Iowa	Jim Zalesky	115	Minnesota	102	Joe Williams, Iowa
1999	Iowa	Jim Zalesky	100½	Minnesota	98½	Cael Sanderson, Iowa St
2000	Iowa	Jim Zalesky	116	Iowa St	109½	Cael Sanderson, Iowa St
2001	Minnesota	J Robinson	138½	Iowa	125½	Cael Sanderson, Iowa St
2002	Minnesota	J Robinson	126½	Iowa St	104	Cael Sanderson, Iowa St
2003	Oklahoma St	John Smith	143	Minnesota	104½	Eric Larkin, Arizona St
2004	Oklahoma St	John Smith	123½	Iowa	82	Jesse Jantzen, Harvard
2005	Oklahoma	John Smith	150	Michigan	83	Ryan Bertin, Michigan

*Unofficial champions.

DIVISION II

Year	Champion	Year	Champion	Year	Champion
1963	Western St (CO)	1978	Northern Iowa	1992	Central Oklahoma
1964	Western St (CO)	1979	Cal St–Bakersfield	1993	Central Oklahoma
1965	Mankato St	1980	Cal St–Bakersfield	1994	Central Oklahoma
1966	Cal Poly–SLO	1981	Cal St–Bakersfield	1995	Central Oklahoma
1967	Portland St	1982	Cal St–Bakersfield	1996	Pittsburgh–Johnstown
1968	Cal Poly–SLO	1983	Cal St–Bakersfield	1997	San Francisco St
1969	Cal Poly–SLO	1984	SIU–Edwardsville	1998	N Dakota St
1970	Cal Poly–SLO	1985	SIU–Edwardsville	1999	Pittsburgh–Johnstown
1971	Cal Poly–SLO	1986	SIU–Edwardsville	2000	N Dakota St
1972	Cal Poly–SLO	1987	Cal St–Bakersfield	2001	N Dakota St
1973	Cal Poly–SLO	1988	N Dakota St	2002	Central Oklahoma
1974	Cal Poly–SLO	1989	Portland St	2003	Central Oklahoma
1975	Northern Iowa	1990	Portland St	2004	Nebraska–Omaha
1976	Cal St–Bakersfield	1991	Nebraska–Omaha	2005	Omaha
1977	Cal St–Bakersfield				

DIVISION III

Year	Champion	Year	Champion	Year	Champion
1974	Wilkes	1977	Brockport St	1980	Brockport St
1975	John Carroll	1978	Buffalo	1981	Trenton St
1976	Montclair St	1979	Trenton St	1982	Brockport St

Wrestling (Cont.)

Year	Champion	Year	Champion	Year	Champion
1983	Brockport St	1991	Augsburg	1999	Wartburg
1984	Trenton St	1992	Brockport	2000	Augsburg
1985	Trenton St	1993	Augsburg	2001	Augsburg
1986	Montclair St	1994	Ithaca	2002	Augsburg
1987	Trenton St	1995	Augsburg	2003	Wartburg
1988	St. Lawrence	1996	Wartburg	2004	Wartburg
1989	Ithaca	1997	Augsburg	2005	Augsburg
1990	Ithaca	1998	Augsburg		

Individual Championship Records

SWIMMING
Men

Event	Time	Record Holder	Date
50-yard freestyle	18.90	Fred Bousquet, Auburn	3-24-05
100-yard freestyle	41.49	Duje Draganja, California	3-26-05
200-yard freestyle	1:33.03	Matt Biondi, California	4-3-87
500-yard freestyle	4:08.75	Tom Dolan, Michigan	3-23-95
1,650-yard freestyle	14:26.62	Chris Thompson, Michigan	3-24-01
100-yard backstroke	45.25	Neil Walker, Texas	3-28-97
200-yard backstroke	1:38.37	Ryan Lochete, Florida	3-26-05
100-yard breaststroke	52.32	Jeremy Linn, Tennessee	3-28-97
200-yard breaststroke	1:52.62	Brendan Hansen, Texas	3-29-03
100-yard butterfly	45.44	Ian Crocker, Texas	3-29-02
200-yard butterfly	1:41.78	Melvin Stewart, Tennessee	3-30-91
200-yard individual medley	1:41.71	Ryan Lochte, Florida	3-24-05
400-yard individual medley	3:38.18	Tom Dolan, Michigan	3-24-95

Women

Event	Time	Record Holder	Date
50-yard freestyle	21.69	Maritza Correia, Georgia	3-21-02
100-yard freestyle	47.29	Maritza Correia, Georgia	3-22-03
200-yard freestyle	1:43.08	Martina Moravcova, Southern Methodist	3-28-97
500-yard freestyle	4:34.39	Janet Evans, Stanford	3-15-90
1,650-yard freestyle	15:39.14	Janet Evans, Stanford	3-17-90
100-yard backstroke	49.97	Natalie Coughlin, California	3-22-02
200-yard backstroke	1:49.52	Natalie Coughlin, California	3-22-02
100-yard breaststroke	59.05	Kristy Kowal, Georgia	3-20-98
200-yard breaststroke	2:07.36	Tara Kirk, Stanford	3-22-02
100-yard butterfly	50.01	Natalie Coughlin, California	3-22-02
200-yard butterfly	1:53.36	Limin Liu, Nevada	3-20-99
200-yard individual medley	1:53.91	Maggie Bowen, Auburn	3-21-02
400-yard individual medley	4:02.28	Summer Sanders, Stanford	3-20-92

Individual Collegiate Records

INDOOR TRACK AND FIELD
Men

Event	Mark	Record Holder	Date
55-meter dash	6.00	Lee McRae, Pittsburgh	3-14-86
60-meter dash	6.45	Leonard Myles-Mills, Brigham Young	2-20-99
55-meter hurdles	7.07	Allen Johnson, North Carolina	3-13-92
60-meter hurdles	7.47	Reggie Torian, Wsconsin	3-5-99
200-meter dash	20.10	Wallace Spearmon, Arkansas	3-12-05
400-meter dash	44.57	Kerron Clement, Florida	3-12-05
800-meter run	1:44.84	Paul Ereng, Virginia	3-4-89
Mile run	3:55.00	Tony Waldrop, North Carolina	2-17-74
3,000-meter run	7:46.03	Adam Goucher, Colorado	3-14-98
5,000-meter run	13:20.40	Suleiman Nyambui, UT–El Paso	2-6-81
High jump	7 ft 9¼ in	Hollis Conway, SW Louisiana	3-11-89
Pole vault	19 ft 2¼ in	Jacob Davis, Texas	3-6-99
Long jump	28 ft 2¼ in	Miguel Pate, Alabama	3-1-02
Triple jump	57 ft 5 in	Charlie Simpkins, Baptist	1-17-86
Shot put	70 ft 6½ in	Terry Albritton, Stanford	2-4-77
35-pound weight throw	78 ft 6½ in	Tore Johnsen, UT–El Paso	2-25-84

INDOOR TRACK AND FIELD (CONT.)

Women

Event	Mark	Record Holder	Date
55-meter dash	6.56	Gwen Torrence, Georgia	3-14-87
60-meter dash	7.09	Angela Williams, Southern Cal	3-11-01
55-meter hurdles	7.39	Tiffany Lott, Brigham Young	3-7-97
60-meter hurdles	7.90	Perdita Felicien, Illinois	3-8-02
200-meter dash	22.49	Muna Lee, Louisiana St	3-14-03
400-meter dash	51.05	Maicel Malone, Arizona St	3-9-91
800-meter run	2:01.65	Amy Wickus, Wisconsin	2-12-94
Mile run	4:28.31	Vicki Huber, Villanova	2-5-88
3,000-meter run	8:53.54	PattiSue Plumer, Stanford	2-27-83
5,000-meter run	15:17.28	Sonia O'Sullivan, Villanova	1-26-91
High jump	6 ft 5½ in	Four recordholders	—
Pole vault	14 ft 10 ¼ in	Amy Linnen, Arizona	3-13-02
Long jump	22 ft 8 in	Elva Goulbourne, Auburn	2-23-02
Triple jump	46 ft 9 in	Suzette Lee, Louisiana St	3-8-97
Shot put	61 ft 9½ in	Teri Tunks, Southern Methodist	2-28-98
20-pound weight throw	79 ft 3¼ in	Dawn Ellerbe, South Carolina	3-12-05

OUTDOOR TRACK AND FIELD

Men

Event	Mark	Record Holder	Date
100-meter dash	9.92	Ato Bolden, UCLA	6-1-96
200-meter dash	19.86	Justin Gatlin, Tennessee	5-12-02
400-meter dash	44.00	Quincy Watts, Southern Cal	6-6-92
800-meter run	1:44.74	Dmitrijs Milkevics, Nebraska	6-11-05
1,500-meter run	3:35.30	Sydney Maree, Villanova	6-6-81
3,000-meter steeplechase	8:05.40	Henry Rono, Washington St	4-8-78
5,000-meter run	13:08.40	Henry Rono, Washington St	4-8-78
10,000-meter run	27:36.20	Gabriel Kamau, UT–El Paso	4-24-82
110-meter high hurdles	13.00	Renaldo Nehemiah, Maryland	5-6-79
400-meter intermediate hurdles	47.56	Kerron Clement, Florida	6-11-05
High jump	7 ft 9¾ in	Hollis Conway, SW Louisiana	6-3-89
Pole vault	19 ft 7½ in	Lawrence Johnson, Tennessee	5-25-96
Long jump	28 8¼ ft	Erick Walder, Arkansas	4-2-94
Triple jump	57 ft 7¾ in	Keith Connor, Southern Methodist	6-5-82
Shot put	72 ft 2¼ in	John Godina, UCLA	6-3-95
Discus throw	219 ft 6 in	Gábor Máté, Auburn	3-25-00
Hammer throw	268 ft 10 in	Balazs Kiss, Southern Cal	5-19-95
Javelin throw (new javelin)	268 ft 7 in	Esko Mikkola, Arizona	6-3-98
Decathlon	8463 pts	Tom Pappas, Tennessee	3-17/18-99

Women

Event	Mark	Record Holder	Date
100-meter dash	10.78	Dawn Sowell, Louisiana St	6-3-89
200-meter dash	22.04	Dawn Sowell, Louisiana St	6-2-89
400-meter dash	50.10	Monique Henderson, UCLA	6-11-05
800-meter run	1:59.11	Suzy Favor, Wisconsin	6-1-90
1,500-meter run	4:08.26	Suzy Favor, Wisconsin	6-2-90
3,000-meter run	8:47.35	Vicki Huber, Villanova	6-3-88
5,000-meter run	15:23.03	Kathy Hayes, Oregon	5-4-85
10,000-meter run	32:22.97	Carole Zajac, Villanova	4-23-92
100-meter hurdles	12.61	Gail Devers, UCLA	5-21-88
400-meter hurdles	54.54	Ryan Tolbert, Vanderbilt	6-6-97
High jump	6 ft 6 in	Amy Acuff, UCLA	5-19-95
		Kajsa Bergqvist, Southern Methodist	5-22-99
Pole vault	14 ft 10¼ in	Amy Linnen, Arizona	3-9-02
Long jump	22 ft 11¼ in	Jackie Joyner-Kersee, UCLA	5-4-85
Triple jump	46 ft 2in	Candice Bauchman, UCLA	6-11-05
Shot put	62 ft 3¼ in	Meg Ritchie, Arizona	5-7-83
Discus throw	222 ft 5 in	Meg Ritchie, Arizona	4-26-81
Hammer throw	220 ft 6 in	Jamine Moton, Clemson	5-29-02
Javelin throw (new javelin)	197 ft 8 in	Angeliki Tsiolakoudi, UT–El Paso	6-3-00
Heptathlon	6527 pts	Diane Guthrie-Gresham, George Mason	6-2/3-95

Sebastian Coe was a key part of London's successful 2012 bid

Olympics

London Calling

Despite stiff competition from Paris and New York, London won the 2012 Games. But how much will it cost to make it safe?

BY MERRELL NODEN

IF THE EMOTIONAL ROLLERCOASTER ever becomes an Olympic event, there's no doubt where an entire mint's worth of gold medals will have to be awarded retroactively: To the people of London who, within the space of 24 hours went from giddy jubilation at winning the 2012 Games to sickened horror at seeing their city targeted by a team of cold-blooded suicide bombers.

The good news came at lunchtime on July 6 and inspired dancing in the streets. The awful blow arrived the following morning, at the height of the rush hour, when three bombs ripped through the London Underground, and another peeled off the top of a double-decker bus in central London. Fifty-six people died in those four explosions, including the four bombers, all young Muslim men from the northern city of Leeds. London, which has endured its share of terror campaigns in the past, soldiered bravely on, and while it was not clear if the two events were linked as cause and effect, the attack underscored the importance and cost of security for all major events in this post 9-11 world.

Thanks in part to spiraling security costs, the Athens Games of 2004 are now expected to cost $11 billion, twice their original estimate, with security accounting for $1.8 billion of that figure, up from an original estimate of $122 million. This was far from good news. Last year, the Greek government's debt rose to 112% of its GDP. "The country is confronted with a severe fiscal problem," admitted Greek Prime Minister Costas Karamanlis. "Public debt has exceeded even the most pessimistic estimates."

In their $2.375 billion budget, London organizers had allotted $400 million for security, a figure that immediately looked absurdly low in the wake of the following day's events. To help put the increase into perspective, the total cost for security nine years ago at the Atlanta Games was $150 million—and it of course proved to be insufficient when Eric Robert Rudolph's homemade bomb ripped through Olympic

London's subway bombings highlighted the security challenges facing the 2012 Games.

Park in downtown Atlanta, killing one woman and injuring about 100 other people. (In August, Rudolph was given one life sentence for the Olympic bombing and three others for each of the bombings he committed soon afterwards.)

Despite the constant worry about safety now etched in the minds of all in the Olympic movement, 2005 was nevertheless a good year for the Olympics and for the International Olympic Committee, specifically. At the midpoint of IOC President Jacques Rogge's first term, the IOC's finances were extremely strong, with reserves running at $244 million, enough to permit the IOC to survive for four years even if a future Games had to be cancelled. The three cities preparing to host upcoming Games—Turin, Italy; Beijing, China; and Vancouver, Canada—all seemed to be progressing towards the timely completion of facilities, even if the ultimate costs of hosting the Olympics continue to look very different from the original rosy projections: Just days before London was chosen, the Montreal Gazette reported that the costs for the 2010 Winter

Games in Vancouver were already running 40% above initial projections.

It was, of course, a terribly disappointing year for the other cities hoping to host the 2012 Games: Moscow, Madrid, New York, and Paris. While Moscow, which had hosted the Olympics as recently as 1980, was deemed the weakest candidate by most Olympic observers, the other cities were all thought to have at least an outside chance in one of the most wide-open campaigns ever. "I've never seen a contest like it," marveled Kevan Gosper, a veteran IOC member from Australia. "It has got to be the greatest peacetime competition between five of the greatest and most historic cities in history, not just in Olympic history."

The five cities spent a total of $150 million to promote their bids, with New York leading the pack with $35 million. New York organizers hoped that IOC members would overlook their last minute shift of the proposed Olympic stadium from Manhattan to Queens in their quest to make a statement about the Olympics' resilience in the face of terrorism.

The vote, which took place in Singapore, as part of the 117th IOC Session, attracted an incredible array of athletes and politicians, from David Beckham and Muhammad Ali to world leaders like British Prime Minister Tony Blair and French President Jacques Chirac. Mayor Michael Bloomberg of New York and Hillary Clinton, the senator from New York, were also there. There was no shortage of hoopla either; the session included a full military parade, a fly-over, and a 21-gun salute. About 1,500 members of the media, which outnumbered the 115 potential voters by roughly 10 to 1, covered the meeting.

Moscow was eliminated first, to no one's surprise. New York followed, to the surprise of many, then Madrid, which had been the top vote getter in the previous round.

Poor New York never really came close to winning, getting bumped out in just the second round of the IOC's devil-take-the-hindmost voting format. If New York was ever the frontrunner, it was so only for the briefest of moments in 2002, when the United States Olympic Committee picked New York over San Francisco as its candidate for the 2012 Games. With the 9-11 attacks so fresh in everyone's mind, choosing New York seemed like the sort of big affirmative gesture the IOC is always hoping to make.

Unfortunately for New York's chances, its bid depended on building a brand new West Side stadium that would later be used by the New York Jets. Virtually everyone found some fault with the way the deal was to be financed. Some community activists condemned the sweetheart deal the city proposed to give the Jets, while others argued that the congestion would be unbearable and the land was really needed for other uses. In early June, just four weeks before the vote, the New York State Public Authorities Control Board voted against the West Side stadium deal, forcing Doctoroff and his team to scramble madly for a second option. The IOC made special allowances for the plan to include a stadium in Queens, but no one can have thought it boded well to have to perform this last minute juggling.

"I think it confused people," said U.S.O.C. member Jim Easton. "They tried to correct it at the end, but the first impression is the one that people hang with."

If there was a silver lining to this cloud it was that with the 2008 Summer Games in Asia and the 2012 Games in Europe, the U.S. instantly became a favorite to host the 2016 Games, with San Francisco, Washington, D.C., Los Angeles, and Houston all mentioned as possible candidates. Surely New York might join them, having done well in its first attempt? "I just don't know if we will be able to keep those forces in place for another four years," confessed Doctoroff, just days before hearing the bad news.

That left London and Paris. Right up until the moment the final choice was announced, Paris had been considered the clear favorite (SI, for instance, put Paris's chances at 1-2, with London second at 4-1 and New York third at 15-1). Paris had bid twice in the last 20 years. They never really expected to beat Barcelona for the 1992 Games, since the Catalan capital is the hometown of then-IOC chief Juan Antonio Samaranch. They seemed to have been done in four years ago by their own arrogance and ineptitude. This time, however, everyone agreed that the French had their act together; or did they? In a show of either fatuous bravado or oafishness, Chirac even went so far as to bash English food, claiming that it was, along with Finnish food, the worst in Europe. In the end, it was Chirac who ate crow, probably raw, and certainly not flavored with any of those lovely piquant sauces the French so love. The final vote for London was 54-50. Had the French capital been chosen, it would have made Olympic history as the first city to host three Olympics. Now that honor belongs to London, Paris's ancient rival.

The French did not take the news well. "Waterloo again," moaned the headline of one weblog, and the dailies agreed: "France KO'd," declared the front page of France Soir. "Paris has lost and her torturer is London," wrote Le Monde, adding that the loss was a personal setback for the French president. "Jacques Chirac missed a great oppor-

London's initial estimate of $400 million for Olympic security seems destined to grow.

tunity to restore morale to an 'old country' feeling morose and fearful of globalization."

Afterwards, the French hinted darkly that London had won by dirty tricks. Rogge felt compelled to investigate charges that Blair had broken IOC rules by arriving three days before the vote and thus having plenty of time to entertain key IOC members in his hotel suite. Chirac, they whined, had only been able to arrive one day before and so had been at a disadvantage. "Mr. Blair was very successful in selling the idea that members should vote for London," said Rogge. "London won because it was a great bid. Its candidature file was outstanding."

Certainly Blair was one hero of London's great win. In the spring, his Labor Party had won a third election, but before and after his leadership had been under constant assault —even from members of his own party— over his decision to send troops to support George Bush's war in Iraq. Hoping to lend support to the London bid, Blair flew out to Singapore on the

eve of the G8 Summit, which he was to host in Scotland, and set to work in hopes of toppling favored Paris. Blair has said he has no plan to run again, which means he will not be prime minister when the Games actually take place.

The other man to emerge a hero was Sebastian Coe, who of course had already tasted Olympic glory of a different kind, as winner of the 1500 meters at both the 1980 and '84 Games. Lord Coe, as he is now known, joined the London bid team a year before the key vote, and that, as Robert Frost once said, "has made all the difference." With Coe's charisma and energy driving the team, London's chances went from slim to surprisingly strong. "If it hadn't been for him, we'd be holding a press conference in French," said Dick Pound, an IOC member from Canada.

Mindful of how close Athens came to not being ready on time, the London organizing team set to work immediately. "We are going to take all seven years, I can promise you," said Keith Mills, chief executive of the bid team, in a not-so-subtle dig at Athens. They formed the London

British Prime Minister Tony Blair was on hand in Singapore to witness London's victory.

and environmental concerns. The second of those they've worked diligently to rectify. In 2004, the Chinese planted 42.3 million trees in Beijing, and noted with pride the fact that 229 days had good or better air quality. That was two more than the target number, dubbed "Mission Blue Sky." Compared with 1998, when 141 days counted as "highly polluted," there were only 17 such days in Beijing last year.

Organizing Committee for the Olympic Games (LOCOG), and named Coe its chairman and Mills his deputy. A new Olympic lottery is expected to raise 1.5 billion pounds of the 2.375 billion pounds needed. Even after the bombings, the city gave its enthusiastic support to an event which can only make London even more of a target than it already is: In response to London's "Volunteer to Win" campaign, 50,000 volunteers signed up within the first month of the announcement.

At the heart of the London bid is the development of a 500-acre wasteland about three miles east of London's business center, in Stratford. Scarred by junkyards and food processing plants, the area has absorbed "two or three centuries of industrial abuse," said David Stubbs, the environmental manager for the London bid. A considerable effort would have to go into cleaning the area up, which the organizers proposed doing through a $4.2 billion subsidy.

If there is a wildcard in the near future for the IOC, it's Beijing. Smarting from losing the 2000 Games to Sydney, the Chinese worked exceptionally hard to remedy what everyone perceived as its two greatest weaknesses: human rights

No one really questions whether the Chinese leaders will be ready, both on the field of play and as hosts. Nothing is going to be allowed to mar what should be a great coming-out party for a nation that has already arrived in the first years of the 21st century as a major economic superpower. The Chinese government is promising $300,000, land, an apartment and a car for anyone who wins a gold medal. It has announced that its goal is to win 40 gold medals and 110 in all. To ensure success, the leaders of the Chinese Olympic movement have made a pact with Russia to share training and coaching expertise. What's more, crowds in Beijing will be encouraged to cheer for Russians in events that do not have Chinese contenders. That arrangement raised a few eyebrows around the Olympic community.

And so it's on to Turin. The XX Winter Olympic Games begin on February 10 and end on the 26th. That gives the beautiful old baroque city, which was the capital of Italy until 1945, 16 days to show the world its stuff, and everyone expects the usual mix of high drama and poignant heartache.

FOR THE RECORD·2002–2004 Games

2004 Summer Games

TRACK AND FIELD
Men

100 METERS
1. ...Justin Gatlin, United States — 9.85
2. ...Francis Obikwelu, Portugal — 9.86
3. ...Maurice Greene, United States — 9.87

200 METERS
1. ...Shawn Crawford, United States — 19.79
2. ...Bernard Williams, United States — 20.01
3. ...Justin Gatlin, United States — 20.03

400 METERS
1. ...Jeremy Wariner, United States — 44.00
2. ...Otis Harris, United States — 44.16
3. ...Derrick Brew, United States — 44.42

800 METERS
1. ...Yuriy Borzakovskiy, Russia — 1:44.45
2. ...Mbulaeni Mulaudzi, S Africa — 1:44.61
3. ...Wilson Kipketer, Denmark — 1:44.65

1,500 METERS
1. ...Hicham El Guerrouj, Morocco — 3:34.18
2. ...Bernard Lagat, Kenya — 3:34.30
3. ...Rui Silva, Portugal — 3:34.68

5,000 METERS
1. ...Hicham El Guerrouj, Morocco — 13:14.39
2. ...Kenenisa Bekele, Ethiopia — 13:14.59
3. ...Eliud Kipchoge, Kenya — 13:15.10

10,000 METERS
1. ...Kenenisa Bekele, Ethiopia — 27:05.10 OR
2. ...Sileshi Sihine, Ethiopia — 27:09.39
3. ...Zersenay Tadesse, Eritrea — 27:22.57

MARATHON
1. ...Stefano Baldini, Italy — 2:10:55
2. ...Mebrahtom Keflezighi, United States — 2:11:29
3. ...Vanderlei de Lima, Brazil — 2:12:11

110-METER HURDLES
1. ...Xiang Liu, China — 12.91 EWR
2. ...Terrence Trammell, United States — 13.18
3. ...Anier García, Cuba — 13.20

400-METER HURDLES
1. ...Felix Sanchez, Dominican Republic — 47.63
2. ...Danny McFarlane, Jamaica — 48.11
3. ...Naman Keita, France — 48.26

3,000-METER STEEPLECHASE
1. ...Ezekiel Kemboi, Kenya — 8:05.81
2. ...Brimin Kipruto, Kenya — 8:06.11
3. ...Paul Kipsiele Koech, Kenya — 8:06.64

4 X 100-METER RELAY
1. ...Great Britian: (Jason Gardener, Darren Campbell, Marlon Devonish, Mark Lewis Francis) — 38.07
2. ...United States — 38.08
3. ...Nigeria — 38.23

4 X 400-METER RELAY
1. ...United States: (Otis Harris, Derrick Brew, Jeremy Wariner, Darold Williamson) — 2:55.91
2. ...Australia — 3:00.60
3. ...Nigeria — 3:00.90

20-KILOMETER WALK
1. ...Ivano Brugnetti, Italy — 1:19:40
2. ...Francisco Javier Fernandez, Spain — 1:19:45
3. ...Nathan Deakes, Australian — 1:20:02

50-KILOMETER WALK
1. ...Robert Korzeniowski, Poland — 3:38:46
2. ...Denis Nizhegorodov, Russia — 3:42:50
3. ...Aleksey Voyevodin, Russia — 3:43:34

HIGH JUMP
1. ...Stefan Holm, Sweden — 7 ft 8¾ in
2. ...Matthew Hemingway, United States — 7 ft 8 in
3. ...Yaroslav Baba, Czech Republic — 7 ft 8 in

POLE VAULT
1. ...Timothy Mack, United States — 19 ft 6¼ in
2. ...Toby Stevenson, United States — 19 ft 4¼ in
3. ...Giuseppe Gibilisco, Italy — 19 ft 2¼ in

LONG JUMP
1. ...Dwight Phillips, United States — 28 ft 2¼ in
2. ...John Moffitt, United States — 27 ft 9½ in
3. ...Joan Lino Martinez, Spain — 27 ft 3¾ in

TRIPLE JUMP
1. ...Christian Olsson, Sweden — 58 ft 4½ in
2. ...Marian Oprea, Romania — 57 ft 7 in
3. ...Danila Burkenya, Russia — 57 ft 4¼ in

SHOT PUT
1. ...Yuriy Bilonog, Ukraine — 69 ft 5¼ in
2. ...Adam Nelson, United States — 69 ft 5¼ in
3. ...Joachim Olsen, Denmark — 69 ft 1½ in

DISCUS THROW
1. ...Virgilijus Alekna, Lithuania — 229 ft 3 in
2. ...Zoltan Kovago, Hungary — 219 ft 11 in
3. ...Aleksander Tammert, Estonia — 218 ft 8 in

HAMMER THROW
1. ...Adrian Zsolt, Hungary — 272 ft 11 in
2. ...Koji Murofushi, Japan — 272 ft
3. ...Ivan Tikhon, Belarus — 261 ft 10 in

JAVELIN
1. ...Andreas Thorkildsen, Norway — 283 ft 9 in
2. ...Vadims Vasilevskis, Latvia — 278 ft 8 in
3. ...Sergey Makarov, Russia — 278 ft 4 in

DECATHLON
	Pts
1. ...Roman Seberle, Czech Republic	8893 OR
2. ...Bryan Clay, United States	8820
3. ...Dmitriy Karpov, Kazakhstan	8725

Note: OR=Olympic record. WR=world record. EOR=equals Olympic record. EWR=equals world record.

TRACK AND FIELD (Cont.)
Women

100 METERS
1. ...Yuliya Nesterenko, Belarus — 10.93
2. ...Lauryn Williams, United States — 10.96
3. ...Veronica Campbell, Jamaica — 10.97

200 METERS
1. ...Veronica Campbell, Jamaica — 22.05
2. ...Allyson Felix, United States — 22.18
3. ...Debbie Ferguson, Bahamas — 22.30

400 METERS
1. ...Tonique Williams-Darling, Bahamas — 49.41
2. ...Ana Guevara, Mexico — 49.56
3. ...Natalya Antyukh, Russia — 49.89

800 METERS
1. ...Kelly Holmes, Great Britain — 1:56.38
2. ...Hasna Benhassi, Morocco — 1:56.43
3. ...Jolanda Ceplak, Slovenia — 1:56.43

1,500 METERS
1. ...Kelly Holmes, Great Britain — 3:57.90
2. ...Tatyana Tomashova, Russia — 3:58.12
3. ...Maria Cioncan, Romania — 3:58.39

5,000 METERS
1. ...Meseret Defar, Ethiopia — 14:45.65
2. ...Isabella Ochichi, Kenya — 14:48.19
3. ...Tirunesh Dibaba, Ethiopia — 14:51.83

10,000 METERS
1. ...Huina Xing, China — 30:24.36
2. ...Ejegayehu Dibaba, Ethiopia — 30:24.98
3. ...Derartu Tulu, Ethiopia — 30:26.42

MARATHON
1. ...Noguchi Mizuki, Japan — 2:26:20
2. ...Nyambura Wincatherine, Kenya — 2:26:32
3. ...Deena Kastor, United States — 2:27:20

100-METER HURDLES
1. ...Joanna Hayes, United States — 12.37 OR
2. ...Olena Krasovska, Ukraine — 12.45
3. ...Melissa Morrison, United States — 12.56

400-METER HURDLES
1. ...Faní Halkiá, Greece — 52.82
2. ...Ionela Tirlea-Manolache, Romania — 53.38
3. ...Tetiana Tereschuk-Antipova, Ukraine — 53.44

4 X 100-METER RELAY
1. ...Jamaica (T. Lawrence, S. Simpson, Aleen Bailey, Veronica Campbell) — 41.73
2. ...Russia — 42.27
3. ...France — 42.54

4 X 400-METER RELAY
1. ...United States (DeeDee Trotter, Monique Henderson, Sanya Richards, Monique Hennagan) — 3:19.01
2. ...Russia — 3:20.16
3. ...Jamaica — 3:22.00

20-KILOMETER WALK
1. ...Athanasía Tsoumeléka, Greece — 1:29:12
2. ...Olimpiada Ivanova, Russia — 1:29:16
3. ...Jane Saville, Australia — 1:29:25

HIGH JUMP
1. ...Yelena Slesarenko, Russia — 6 ft 9 in
2. ...Hestrie Cloete, S Africa — 6 ft 7½ in
3. ...Vita Styopina, Ukraine — 6 ft 7½ in

POLE VAULT
1. ...Yelena Isinbayeva, Russia — 16 ft 1¼ in WR
2. ...Svetlana Feofanova, Russia — 15 ft 7 in
3. ...Anna Rogowska, Poland — 15 ft 5 in

LONG JUMP
1. ...Tatyana Lebedeva, Russia — 23 ft 2½ in
2. ...Irina Simajina, Russia — 23 ft 1¾ in
3. ...Tatyana Kotova, Russia — 23 ft 1¼ in

TRIPLE JUMP
1. ...Frangoise Mbango Etone, Cameroon — 50 ft 2½ in
2. ...Chrysopigi Devetzi, Greece — 50 ft ½ in
3. ...Tatyana Lebedeva, Russia — 49 ft 8¼ in

SHOT PUT
1. ...Yumileidi Cumba Jay, Cuba — 64 ft 3¼ in
2. ...Nadine Kleinert, Germany — 64 ft 1¾ in
3. ...Svetlana Krivelyova, Russia — 63 ft 11½ in

DISCUS THROW
1. ...Natalya Sadova, Russia — 219 ft 10 in
2. ...Anastasia Kelesidou, Greece — 218 ft 9 in
3. ...Iryna Yatchenko, Belarus — 217 ft 1 in

JAVELIN
1. ...Osleidys Menendez, Cuba — 234 ft 8 in OR
2. ...Steffi Nerius, Germany — 215 ft 11 in
3. ...Mirela Manjani, Greece — 210 ft 11 in

HEPTATHLON — Pts
1. ...Carolina Kluft, Sweden — 6952
2. ...Austra Skujyte, Lithuania — 6435
3. ...Kelly Sotherton, Great Britain — 6424

HAMMER THROW
1. ...Olga Kuzenkova, Russia — 246 ft 1½ in OR
2. ...Yipsi Moreno, Cuba — 240 ft 8¼ in
3. ...Yunaika Crawford, Cuba — 240 ft ½ in

INDIVIDUAL ARCHERY

Men
1. ....Marco Galiazzo, Italy
2. ....Hiroshi Yamamoto, Japan
3. ....Tim Cuddihy, Australia

Women
1. ....Sung Hyun Park, S Korea
2. ....Sung Jin Lee, S Korea
3. ....Alison Williamson, Great Britain

TEAM ARCHERY

Men
1. ....S Korea
2. ....Taiwan
3. ....Ukraine

Women
1. ....S Korea
2. ....China
3. ....Taiwan

Note: OR=Olympic record. WR=world record. EOR=equals Olympic record. EWR=equals world record.

BADMINTON

Men

SINGLES
1. ...Taufik Hidayat, Indonesia
2. ...Seung Mo Shon, S Korea
3. ...Soni Dwi Kuncoro, Indonesia

DOUBLES
1. ...Ha Tae Kwon/ Dong Moon Kim, S Korea
2. ...Dong Soo Lee/ Yoo Yong Sung, S Korea
3. ...Eng Hian/ Limpele Flandy, Indonesia

Women

SINGLES
1. ...Ning Zhang, China
2. ...Mia Audina, Netherlands
3. ...Mi Zhou, China

DOUBLES
1. ...Yang Wei/ Jiewen Zhang, China
2. ...Gao Ling/ Sui Huang, China
3. ...Kyung Min Ra/ Lee Kyung Won, S Korea

MIXED DOUBLES
1. ...Jun Zhang/ Gao Ling, China
2. ...Nathan Robertson/ Gail Emms, Great Britain
3. ...Jens Eriksen/ Schjoldager Mette, Denmark

BASEBALL
1. ...Cuba
2. ...Australia
3. ...Japan

BASKETBALL

Men

Final: Argentina 84, Italy 69
United States (3rd)
Argentina: Juan Sanchez, Emanuel Ginobili, Alejandro Montecchia, Fabricio Oberto, Walter Herrmann, Gabriel Fernandez, Hugo Sconochini, Luis Scola, Leonardo Gutierrez, Andres Nocioni, Carlos Delfino, Ruben Wolkowyski.

Women

Final: United States 74, Australia 63
Russia (3rd)
United States: Shannon Johnson, Dawn Staley, Suzanne Bird, Sheryl Swoopes, Ruth Riley, Lisa Leslie, Tamika Catchings, Tina Thompson, Diana Taurasi, Yolanda Griffith, Katie Smith, Swintayla Cash.

BOXING

LIGHT FLYWEIGHT (106 LB)
1. ...Yan Bhartelemy Varela, Cuba
2. ...Atagun Yal Cinkaya, Turkey
3. ...Shiming Zou, China
3. ...Sergey Kazakov, Russia

FLYWEIGHT (112 LB)
1. ...Yuriokis Gamboa Toledano, Cuba
2. ...Jerome Thomas, France
3. ...Fuad Aslanov, Azerbaijan
3. ...Rustamhodza Rahimov, Germany

BANTAMWEIGHT (119 LB)
1. ...Guillermo Rigondeaux Ortiz, Cuba
2. ...Worapoj Petchkoom, Thailand
3. ...Aghasi Mammadov, Azerbaijan
3. ...Bahodirion Sooltonov, Uzbekistan

FEATHERWEIGHT (125 LB)
1. ...Alexei Tichtchenko, Russia
2. ...Song Guk Kim, N Korea
3. ...Vitali Tajbert, Germany
3. ...Seok Hwan Jo, S Korea

LIGHTWEIGHT (132 LB)
1. ...Mario Kindelan Mesa, Cuba
2. ...Amir Khan, Great Britain
3. ...Serik Yeleuov, Kazakhstan
3. ...Murat Khrachev, Russia

LIGHT WELTERWEIGHT (139 LB)
1. ...Manus Boonjumnong, Thailand
2. ...Yudel Johnson Cedeno, Cuba
3. ...Boris Georgive, Bulgaria
3. ...Ionut Gheorghe, Romania

WELTERWEIGHT (147 LB)
1. ...Bakhtiyar Artayev, Kazakhstan
2. ...Lorenzo Aragon Armenteros, Cuba
3. ...Oleg Saitov, Russia
3. ...Jung Joo Kim, S Korea

MIDDLEWEIGHT (165 LB)
1. ...Gaydarbek Gaydarbekov, Russia
2. ...Gennadiy Golovkin, Kazakhstan
3. ...Suriya Prasathinphimai, Thailand
3. ...Andre Dirrell, United States

LIGHT HEAVYWEIGHT (178 LB)
1. ...Andre Ward, United States
2. ...Magomed Aripgadjiev, Belarus
3. ...Utkirbek Haydarov, Uzbekistan
3. ...Ahmed Ismail, Egypt

HEAVYWEIGHT (201 LB)
1. ...Odlanier Solis Fonte, Cuba
2. ...Viktar Zuyev, Belarus
3. ...Mohamed Elsayed, Egypt
3. ...Naser Al Shami, Syria

SUPERHEAVYWEIGHT (201+ LB)
1. ...Alexander Povetkin, Russia
2. ...Mohamed Aly, Egypt
3. ...Roberto Cammarelle, Italy
3. ...Michel Lopez Nunez, Cuba

CANOE/KAYAK

Men

C-1 FLATWATER 500 METERS
1.	...Andreas Dittmer, Germany	1:46.383
2.	...David Cal, Spain	1:46.723
3.	...Maxim Opalev, Russia	1:47.767

C-1 FLATWATER 1,000 METERS
1.	...David Cal, Spain	3:46.201
2.	...Andreas Dittmer, Germany	3:46.721
3.	...Attila Vajda, Hungary	3:49.025

C-2 FLATWATER 500 METERS
1.	...G. Meng/ W. Yang, China	1:40.278
2.	...I. Blanco/ L. Pajon, Cuba	1:40.350
3.	...A. Kostoglod/ A. Kovalev, Russia	1:40.442

C-2 FLATWATER 1,000 METERS
1.	...C. Gille/ T. Wylenzek, Germany	3:41.802
2.	...A. Kostoglod/ A. Kovalev, Russia	3:42.990
3.	...G. Kolonics/ G. Kozmann, Hungary	3:43.106

C-1 WHITEWATER SLALOM
		Pts
1.	...Tony Estanguet, France	189.16
2.	...Michal Martikan, Slovakia	189.28
3.	...Stefan Pfannmoeller, Germany	191.56

C-2 WHITEWATER SLALOM
		Pts
1.	...Pavel/ Peter Hochschorner, Slovakia	207.16
2.	...M. Becker/ S. Henze, Germany	210.98
3.	...J. Volf/ O. Stepanek, Czech Republic	212.86

K-1 FLATWATER 500 METERS
1.	...Adam Van Koeverden, Canada	1:37.919
2.	...Nathan Baggaley, Australia	1:38.467
3.	...Ian Wynne, Great Britain	1:38.547

K-1 FLATWATER 1,000 METERS
1.	...Eirik Veraas Larsen, Norway	3:25.897
2.	...Ben Fouhy, New Zealand	3:27.413
3.	...Adam Van Koeverden, Canada	3:28.218

Men (Cont.)

K-2 FLATWATER 500 METERS
1.	...R. Rauhe/ T. Wieskoetter, Germany	1:27.040
2.	...C. Robinson/ N. Baggaley, Australia	1:27.920
3.	...R. Piatrushenka/ V. Makhneu, Belarus	1:27.996

K-2 FLATWATER 1,000 METERS
1.	...M. Oscarsson/ H. Nilsson, Sweden	3:18.420
2.	...B. Bonomi/ A. Rossi, Italy	3:19.484
3.	...E.V. Larsen/ N.O. Fjeldheim, Norway	3:19.528

K-4 FLATWATER 1,000 METERS
1.	...Hungary	2:56.919
2.	...Germany	2:58.659
3.	...Slovakia	2:59.314

K-1 WHITEWATER SLALOM
		Pts
1.	...Benoit Peschier, France	187.96
2.	...Campbell Walsh, Great Britain	190.17
3.	...Fabien Lefevre, France	190.99

Women

K-1 FLATWATER 500 METERS
1.	...Natasa Janics, Hungary	1:47.741
2.	...Josefa Idem Guerrini, Italy	1:49.729
3.	...Caroline Brunet, Canada	1:50.601

K-2 FLATWATER 500 METERS
1.	...K. Kovacs/ N. Janics, Hungary	1:38.101
2.	...B. Fischer/ C. Leonhardt, Germany	1:39.533
3.	...A. Pastuszka/ B. Sokoloska, Poland	1:40.077

K-4 FLATWATER 500 METERS
1.	...Germany	1:34.340
2.	...Hungary	1:34.536
3.	...Ukraine	1:36.192

K-1 WHITEWATER SLALOM
		Pts
1.	...Elena Kaliska, Slovakia	210.03
2.	...Rebecca Giddens, United States	214.62
3.	...Helen Reeves, Great Britain	218.77

CYCLING

Men

ROAD RACE
1.	...Paolo Bettini, Italy	5:41:44
2.	...Sergio Paulinho, Portugal	5:41:45
3.	...Axel Merckx, Belgium	5:41:52

INDIVIDUAL TIME TRIAL
1.	...Tyler Hamilton, United States	57:31.74
2.	...Vyatcheslav Ekimov, Russia	57:50.58
3.	...Robert Julich, United States	57:58.19

1KM TIME TRIAL
1.	...Chris Hoy, Great Britain	1:00.711
2.	...Arnaud Tournant, France	1:00.896
3.	...Stefan Nimke, Germany	1:01.186

4,000-METER INDIVIDUAL PURSUIT
1.	...Bradley Wiggins, Great Britain	4:16.304
2.	...Brad McGee, Australia	4:20.436
3.	...Sergi Escobar, Spain	4:17.947

4,000-METER TEAM PURSUIT
1.	...Australia (Graeme Brown, Brett Lancaster, Brad McGee, Luke Roberts)	3:58.233
2.	...Great Britain	4:01.760
3.	...Spain	4:05.523

Men (Cont.)

SPRINT
1.	...Ryan Bayley, Australia	10.743
2.	...Theo Bos, Netherlands	10.710
3.	...Rene Wolff, German	10.612

POINTS RACE
1.	...Mikhail Ignatyev, Russia	93
2.	...Joan Llaneras, Spain	82
3.	...Guido Fulst, Germany	79

KIERIN
1.	...Ryan Bayley, Australia	10.601
2.	...Jose Escuredo, Spain	
3.	...Shane Kelly, Australia	

MADISON
1.	...G. Brown/ S. O'Grady, Australia	22
2.	...F. Marvulli/ B. Risi, Switzerland	15
3.	...R. Hayles/ B. Wiggins, Great Britain	12

OLYMPIC SPRINT
1.	...Germany	43.980
2.	...Japan	44.246
3.	...France	44.359

CYCLING (Cont.)

Women

POINTS RACE
1. ...Olga Slyusareva, Russia — 20
2. ...Belem Guerrero Mendez, Mexico — 14
3. ...Erin Mirabella, United States — 9

SPRINT
1. ...Lori-Ann Muenzer, Canada — 12.140
2. ...Tamilla Abassova, Russia — —
3. ...Anna Meares, Australia — 11.822

INDIVIDUAL TIME TRIAL
1. ...L. Zijlaard-van Moorsel, Netherlands — 31:11.53
2. ...Deirdre Demet-Barry, United States — 31:35.62
3. ...Karin Thuerig, Switzerland — 31:54.89

ROAD RACE
1. ...Sara Carrigan, Australia — 3:24:24
2. ...Judith Arndt, Germany — 3:24:31
3. ...Olga Slyusareva, Russia — 3:25:03

3,000-METER INDIVIDUAL PURSUIT
1. ...Sarah Ulmer, New Zealand — 3:24.537 WR
2. ...Katie Mactier, Australia — 3:27.650
3. ...L. Zijlaard-van Moorsel, Netherlands — 3:27.037

500-M TIME TRIAL
1. ...Anna Meares, Australia — 33.952
2. ...Jiang Yonghua, China — 34.112
3. ...Natallia Tsylinskaya, Belarus — 34.167

DIVING

Men

SPRINGBOARD

	Pts
1. ...Bo Peng, China	787.38
2. ...Alexandre Despatie, Canada	755.97
3. ...Dmitry Sautin, Russia	753.27

PLATFORM

	Pts
1. ...Jia Hu, China	748.08
2. ...Matthew Helm, Australia	730.56
3. ...Liang Tian, China	729.66

Women

SPRINGBOARD

	Pts
1. ...Jingjing Guo, China	633.15
2. ...Minxia Wu, China	612.00
3. ...Yulia Pakhalina, Russia	610.62

PLATFORM

	Pts
1. ...Chantelle Newbery, Australia	590.31
2. ...Lishi Lao, China	576.30
3. ...Loudy Tourky, Australia	561.66

EQUESTRIAN

TEAM EVENTING
1. ...France
2. ...Great Britain
3. ...United States

INDIVIDUAL DRESSAGE — Pts
1. ...Anky van Grunsven, Netherlands — 85.825
2. ...Ulla Salzgeber, Germany — 83.450
3. ...Beatriz Ferrer-Salat, Spain — 79.575

INDIVIDUAL EVENTING — Pts
1. ...Leslie Law, Great Britain — 44.40
2. ...Kim Severson, United States — 45.20
3. ...Philippa Funnell, Great Britain — 46.60

TEAM JUMPING
1. ...Germany
2. ...United States
3. ...Sweden

TEAM DRESSAGE
1. ...Germany
2. ...Spain
3. ...United States

INDIVIDUAL JUMPING — Pts
1. ...Cian O'Connor, Ireland — 4.00
2. ...Rodrigo Pessoa, Brazil — 8.00
3. ...Chris Kappler, United States — 8.00

FENCING

Men

FOIL
1. ...Brice Guyart, France
2. ...Salvatore Sanzo, Italy
3. ...Andrea Cassara, Italy

TEAM FOIL
1. ...Italy
2. ...China
3. ...Russia

SABRE
1. ...Aldo Montano, Italy
2. ...Zsolt Nemcsik, Hungary
3. ...Vladislav Tretiak, Ukraine

TEAM SABRE
1. ...France
2. ...Italy
3. ...Russia

ÉPÉE
1. ...Marcel Fischer, Switzerland
2. ...Lei Wang, China
3. ...Pavel Kolobkov, Russia

TEAM ÉPÉE
1. ...France
2. ...Hungary
3. ...Germany

Women

FOIL
1. ...Valentina Vezzali, Italy
2. ...Giovanna Trillini, Italy
3. ...Sylwia Gruchala, Poland

SABRE
1. ...Mariel Zagunis, United States
2. ...Xue Tan, China
3. ...Sada Jacobson, United States

FENCING (Cont.)

Women (Cont.)

ÉPÉE

1. ....Timea Nagy, Hungary
2. ....Laura Flessel-Colovic, France
3. ....Maureen Nisima, France

TEAM ÉPÉE

1. ....Russia
2. ....Germany
3. ....France

FIELD HOCKEY

Men

1. ....Australia
2. ....Netherlands
3. ....Germany

Women

1. ....Germany
2. ....Netherlands
3. ....Argentina

GYMNASTICS

Men

ALL-AROUND

		Pts
1.	Paul Hamm, United States	57.823
2.	Dae Eun Kim, S Korea	57.811
3.	Tae Young Yang, S Korea	57.774

HORIZONTAL BAR

		Pts
1.	Igor Cassina, Italy	9.812
2.	Paul Hamm, United States	9.812
3.	Isao Yoneda, Japan	9.787

PARALLEL BARS

		Pts
1.	Valeri Goncharov, Ukraine	9.787
2.	Hiroyuki Tomita, Japan	9.775
3.	Xiaopeng Li, China	9.762

VAULT

		Pts
1.	Gervasio Deferr, Spain	9.737
2.	Evgeni Sapronenko, Latvia	9.706
3.	Marian Dragulescu, Romania	9.612

POMMEL HORSE

		Pts
1.	Haibin Teng, China	9.837
2.	Marius Urzica, Romania	9.825
3.	Takehiro Kashima, Japan	9.787

RINGS

		Pts
1.	Dimosthenis Tampakos, Greece	9.862
2.	Jordan Jovtchev, Bulgaria	9.850
3.	Yuri Chechi, Italy	9.812

FLOOR EXERCISE

		Pts
1.	Kyle Shewfelt, Canada	9.787
2.	Marian Dragulescu, Romania	9.787
3.	Jordan Jovtchev, Bulgaria	9.775

TEAM COMBINED EXERCISES

1. ....Japan
2. ....United States
3. ....Romania

Women

ALL-AROUND

		Pts
1.	Carly Patterson, United States	38.387
2.	Svetlana Khorkina, Russia	38.211
3.	Nan Zhang, China	38.049

VAULT

		Pts
1.	Monica Rosu, Romania	9.656
2.	Annia Hatch, United States	9.481
3.	Anna Pavlova, Russia	9.475

UNEVEN BARS

		Pts
1.	Emilie Lepennec, France	9.687
2.	Terin Humphrey, United States	9.662
2.	Courtney Kupets, United States	9.637

BALANCE BEAM

		Pts
1.	Catalina Ponor, Romania	9.787
2.	Carly Patterson, United States	9.775
3.	Alexandra Eremia, Romania	9.700

FLOOR EXERCISE

		Pts
1.	Catalina Ponor, Romania	9.750
2.	Nicoleta Sofronie, Romania	9.562
3.	Patricia Moreno, Spain	9.487

TEAM COMBINED EXERCISES

1. ....Romania
2. ....United States
3. ....Russia

JUDO

Men

EXTRA-LIGHTWEIGHT
1. ....Tadahiro Nomura, Japan
2. ....Nestor Khergiani, Georgia
3. ....Khashbaatar Tsagaanbaatar, Mongolia
3. ....Choi Min-ho, S Korea

HALF-LIGHTWEIGHT
1. ....Masato Uchishiba, Japan
2. ....Jozef Krnac, Slovakia
3. ....Georgi Georgiev, Bulgaria
3. ....Yordanis Arencibia, Cuba

LIGHTWEIGHT
1. ....Won Hee Lee, S Korea
2. ....Vitaliy Makarov, Russia
3. ....Leandro Guilheiro, Brazil
3. ....James Pedro, United States

HALF-MIDDLEWEIGHT
1. ....Ilias Iliadas, Greece
2. ....Roman Gontyuk, Ukraine
3. ....Flavio Canto, Brazil
3. ....Dmitri Nossov, Russia

MIDDLEWEIGHT
1. ....Zurab Zviadauri, Georgia
2. ....Hiroshi Izumi, Japan
3. ....Mark Huizinga, Netherlands
3. ....Khasanbi Taov, Russia

HALF-HEAVYWEIGHT
1. ....Ihar Makarau, Belarus
2. ....Sung Ho Jang, S Korea
3. ....Michael Jurack, Germany
3. ....Ariel Zeevi, Israel

HEAVYWEIGHT
1. ....Keiji Suzuki, Japan
2. ....Tamerlan Tmenov, Russia
3. ....Indrek Pertelson, Estonia
3. ....Dennis Van Der Geest, Netherlands

Women

EXTRA-LIGHTWEIGHT
1. ....Ryoko Tani, Japan
2. ....Frederique Jossinet, France
3. ....Feng Gao, China
3. ....Julia Matijass, Germany

HALF-LIGHTWEIGHT
1. ....Dongmei Xian, China
2. ....Yuki Yokosawa, Japan
3. ....Ilse Heylen, Belgium
3. ....Amarilis Savon, Cuba

LIGHTWEIGHT
1. ....Yvonne Boenisch, Germany
2. ....Sun-Hi Kye, N Korea
3. ....Deborah Gravenstijn, Netherlands
3. ....Yurisleidy Lupetey, Cuba

HALF-MIDDLEWEIGHT
1. ....Ayumi Tanimoto, Japan
2. ....Claudia Heill, Austria
3. ....Urska Zolnir, Slovenia
3. ....Driulys Gonzalez, Cuba

MIDDLEWEIGHT
1. ....Masae Ueno, Japan
2. ....Edith Bosch, Netherlands
3. ....Dongya Qin, China
3. ....Annett Boehm, Germany

HALF-HEAVYWEIGHT
1. ....Noriko Anno, Japan
2. ....Xia Liu, China
3. ....Lucia Morico, Italy
3. ....Yurisel Laborde, Cuba

HEAVYWEIGHT
1. ....Maki Tsukada, Japan
2. ....Daima Mayelis Beltran, Cuba
3. ....Fuming Sun, China
3. ....Tea Donguzashvili, Russia

MODERN PENTATHLON

Men
1. ......Andrey Moiseev, Russia
2. ......Andrejus Zadneprovskis, Lithuania
3. ......Libor Capalini, Czech Republic

Women
1. ......Zsuzsanna Voros, Hungary
2. ......Jelena Rublevska, Latvia
3. ......Georgina Harland, Great Britain

MOUNTAIN BIKING

Men
1. ......Julien Absalon, France   2:15.02
2. ......Jose Antonio Hermida, Spain   2:16.02
3. ......Bart Brentjens, Netherlands   2:17.05

Women
1. ......Gunn-Rita Dahle, Norway   1:56.51
2. ......Marie-Helene Premont, Canada   1:57.50
3. ......Sabine Spitz, Germany   1:59.21

ROWING

Men

SINGLE SCULLS
1. ...Olaf Tufte, Norway   6:49.30
2. ...Jueri Jaanson, Estonia   6:51.42
3. ...Ivo Yanakiev, Bulgaria   6:52.80

DOUBLE SCULLS
1. ...S. Vieilledent/ A. Hardy, France   6:29.00
2. ...L. Spik/ I. Cop, Slovenia   6:31.72
3. ...R. Galtarossa/ A. Sartori, Italy   6:32.93

LIGHTWEIGHT DOUBLE SCULLS
1. ...T. Kucharski/R. Sycz, Poland   6:20.93
2. ...F. Dufour/ P. Touron, France   6:21.46
3. ...V. Polymeros/ N. Skiathitis, Greece   6:23.23

QUADRUPLE SCULLS
1. ...Russia   5:56.85
2. ...Czech Republic   5:57.43
3. ...Ukraine   5:58.87

ROWING (Cont.)

Men (Cont.)

COXLESS PAIR

1. ...D. Jinn/ J. Tomkins, Australia — 6:30.76
2. ...S. Skelin/ N. Skelin, Croatia — 6:32.64
3. ...D. Cech/ R. di Clemente, S Africa — 6:33.40

COXLESS FOUR

1. ...Great Britain — 6:06.98
2. ...Canada — 6:07.06
3. ...Italy — 6:10.41

LIGHTWEIGHT COXLESS FOUR

1. ...Denmark — 6:01.39
2. ...Australia — 6:02.79
3. ...Italy — 6:03.74

EIGHT-OARS

1. ...United States — 5:42.48
2. ...Netherlands — 5:43.75
3. ...Australia — 5:45.38

Women

SINGLE SCULLS

1. ...Katrin Rutschow-Stomporowski, Germany — 7:18.12
2. ...Yekaterina Karsten, Belarus — 7:22.04
3. ...Rumyana Neykova, Bulgaria — 7:23.10

DOUBLE SCULLS

1. ...C. Evers-Swindell/ G. Evers-Swindell, NZ — 7:01.79
2. ...B. Oppelt/ P. Waleska, Germany — 7:02.78
3. ...E. Laverick/ S. Winckless, Great Britain — 7:07.58

LIGHTWEIGHT DOUBLE SCULLS

1. ...C. Burcica/ A. Alupei, Romania — 6:56.05
2. ...D. Reimer/ C. Blasberg, Germany — 6:57.33
3. ...K. van Der Kolk/ M. van Eupen, Neth — 6:58.54

QUADRUPLE SCULLS

1. ...Germany — 6:29.29
2. ...Great Britain — 6:31.26
3. ...Australia — 6:34.73

COXLESS PAIR

1. ...G. Damian/ V. Susanu, Romania — 7:06.55
2. ...K. Grainger/ C. Bishop, Great Britain — 7:08.66
3. ...Y. Bichyk/ N. Helakh, Bulgaria — 7:09.86

EIGHT-OARS

1. ...Romania — 6:17.70
2. ...United States — 6:19.56
3. ...Netherlands — 6:19.85

SHOOTING

Men

RAPID-FIRE PISTOL

	Pts
1. ...Ralf Schumann, Germany	694.9
2. ...Sergei Poliakov, Russia	692.7
3. ...Serguie Alifirenko, Russia	692.3

FREE PISTOL

	Pts
1. ...Mikhail Nestruev, Russia	663.3
2. ...Jong Oh Jin, S Korea	661.5
3. ...Jong Su Kim, N Korea	657.7

AIR PISTOL

	Pts
1. ...Yifu Wang, China	690.0
2. ...Mikhail Nestruev, Russia	689.8
3. ...Vladimir Isakov, Russia	684.3

RUNNING TARGET

	Pts
1. ...Manfred Kurzer, Germany	682.4
2. ...Alexander Blinov, Russia	678.0
3. ...Dimitri Lykin, Russia	677.1

SMALL-BORE RIFLE, THREE-POSITION

	Pts
1. ...Zhanbo Gia, China	1264.5
2. ...Michael Anti, United States	1263.1
3. ...Christian Planer, Austria	1262.8

SMALL-BORE RIFLE, PRONE

	Pts
1. ...Matt Emmons, United States	703.3
2. ...Christian Lusch, Germany	702.2
3. ...Serguei Martynov, Belarus	701.6

AIR RIFLE

	Pts
1. ...Qinan Zhu, China	702.7
2. ...Jie Ling, China	701.3
3. ...Jozef Gonci, Slovakia	697.4

TRAP

	Pts
1. ...Alexei Alipov, Russia	149.0
2. ...Giovanni Pellielo, Italy	146.0
3. ...Adam Vella, Australia	145.0

DOUBLE TRAP

	Pts
1. ...Ahmed Al Maktoum, UAE	189.0
2. ...Rajyavardhan Rathore, India	179.0
3. ...Zheng Wang, China	178.0

SKEET

	Pts
1. ...Andrea Benelli, Italy	149.0
2. ...Marko Kemppainen, Finland	149.0
3. ...Juan Miguel Rodriguez, Cuba	147.0

Women

SPORT PISTOL

	Pts
1. ...Mariya Grozdeva, Bulgaria	688.2
2. ...Lenka Hykova, Czech Republic	687.8
3. ...Irada Ashumova, Azerbaijan	687.3

AIR PISTOL

	Pts
1. ...Olena Kostevych, Ukraine	483.3
2. ...Jasna Sekaric, Serbia & Montenegro	483.3
3. ...Mariya Grozdeva, Bulgaria	482.3

SHOOTING (Cont.)

Women (Cont.)

SMALL-BORE RIFLE, THREE-POSITION

		Pts
1.	Lioubov Galkina, Russia	688.4
2.	Valentina Turisini, Italy	685.9
3.	Chengyi Wang, China	685.4

AIR RIFLE

		Pts
1.	Li Du, China	502.0
2.	Lioubov Galkina, Russia	501.5
3.	Katerina Kurkova, Czech Republic	501.1

DOUBLE TRAP

		Pts
1.	Kimberly Rhode, United States	146.0
2.	Bo Na Lee, S Korea	145.0
3.	E Gao, China	142.0

TRAP

		Pts
1.	Suzanne Balogh, Australia	88.0
2.	Maria Quintanal, Spain	84.0
3.	Bo Na Lee, S Korea	83.0

SKEET

		Pts
1.	Diana Igaly, Hungary	97.0
2.	Ning Wei, China	93.0
3.	Zemfina Meftakhetdinova, Azerbaijan	93.0

SOCCER

Men
1. Argentina
2. Paraguay
3. Italy

Women
1. United States
2. Brazil
3. Germany

SOFTBALL
1. United States
2. Australia
3. Japan

SWIMMING

Men

50-METER FREESTYLE

1.	Gary Hall Jr., United States	21.93
2.	Duje Draganja, Croatia	21.94
3.	Roland Schoeman, S Africa	22.02

100-METER FREESTYLE

1.	Pieter van den Hoogenband, Netherlands	48.17
2.	Roland Schoeman, S Africa	48.23
3.	Ian Thorpe, Australia	48.56

200-METER FREESTYLE

1.	Ian Thorpe, Australia,	1:44.71 OR
2.	Pieter van den Hoogenband, Netherlands	1:45.23
3.	Michael Phelps, United States	1:45.32

400-METER FREESTYLE

1.	Ian Thorpe, Australia	3:43.10
2.	Grant Hackett, Australia	3:43.36
3.	Klete Keller, United States	3:44.11

1,500-METER FREESTYLE

1.	Grant Hackett, Australia	14:43.40 OR
2.	Larsen Jensen, United States	14:45.29
3.	David Davies, Great Britain	14:45.95

100-METER BACKSTROKE

1.	Aaron Peirsol, United States	54.06
2.	Markus Rogan, Austria	54.35
3.	Tomomi Morita, Japan	54.36

200-METER BACKSTROKE

1.	Aaron Peirsol, United States	1:54.95 OR
2.	Markus Rogan, Austria	1:57.35
3.	Razvan Florea, Romania	1:57.56

100-METER BREASTSTROKE

1.	Kosuke Kitajima, Japan	1:00.08
2.	Brendan Hansen, United States	1:00.25
3.	Hugues Duboscq, France	1:00.88

200-METER BREASTSTROKE

1.	Kosuke Kitajima, Japan	2:09.44 OR
2.	Daniel Gyurta, Hungary	2:10.80
3.	Brendan Hansen, United States	2:10.87

100-METER BUTTERFLY

1.	Michael Phelps, United States	51.25 OR
2.	Ian Crocker, United States	51.29
3.	Andriy Serdinov, Ukraine	51.36

200-METER BUTTERFLY

1.	Michael Phelps, United States	1:54.04 OR
2.	Takashi Yamamoto, Japan	1:54.56
3.	Stephen Parry, Great Britain	1:55.52

200-METER INDIVIDUAL MEDLEY

1.	Michael Phelps, United States	1:57.14 OR
2.	Ryan Lochte, United States	1:58.78
3.	George Bovell, Trinidad & Tobago	1:58.80

400-METER INDIVIDUAL MEDLEY

1.	Michael Phelps, United States	4:08.26 WR
2.	Eric Vendt, United States	4:11.81
3.	Laszlo Cseh, Hungary	4:12.15

4 X 100-METER MEDLEY RELAY

1.	United States (Aaron Peirsol, Brendan Hanson, Ian Crocker, Jason Lezak)	3:30.68 WR
2.	Germany	3:33.62
3.	Japan	3:35.22

4 X 100-METER FREESTYLE RELAY

1.	S Africa (Schoeman, Ferns, Townsend, Neethling)	3:13.17 WR
2.	Netherlands	3:14.36
3.	United States	3:14.62

4 X 200-METER FREESTYLE RELAY

1.	United States (Phelps, Lochte, Vanderkaay, Keller)	7:07.33
2.	Australia	7:07.46
3.	Italy	7:11.83

Note: OR=Olympic record. WR=world record. EOR=equals Olympic record. EWR=equals world record.

SWIMMING *(Cont.)*
Women

50-METER FREESTYLE
1. ...Inge de Bruijn, Netherlands — 24.58
2. ...Malia Metella, France — 24.89
3. ...Lisbeth Lenton, Australia — 24.91

100-METER FREESTYLE
1. ...Jodie Henry, Australia — 53.84
2. ...Inge de Bruijn, Netherlands — 54.16
3. ...Natalie Coughlin, United States — 54.40

200-METER FREESTYLE
1. ...Camelia Potec, Romania — 1:58.03
2. ...Federica Pellegrini, Italy — 1:58.22
3. ...Solenne Figues, France — 1:58.45

400-METER FREESTYLE
1. ...Laure Manaudou, France — 4:05.34
2. ...Otylia Jedrzejczak, Poland — 4:05.84
3. ...Kaitlin Sandeno, United States — 4:06.19

800-METER FREESTYLE
1. ...Ai Shibata, Japan — 8:24.54
2. ...Laure Manaudou, France — 8:24.96
3. ...Diana Munz, United States — 8:26.61

100-METER BACKSTROKE
1. ...Natalie Coughlin, United States — 1:00.37
2. ...Kirsty Coventry, Zimbabwe — 1:00.50
3. ...Laure Manaudou, France — 1:00.88

200-METER BACKSTROKE
1. ...Kirsty Coventry, Zimbabwe — 2:09.19
2. ...Stanislava Komarova, Russia — 2:09.72
3. ...Antie Buschschulte, Germany — 2:09.88

100-METER BREASTSTROKE
1. ...Xuejuan Luo, China — 1:06.64
2. ...Brooke Hanson, Australia — 1:07.15
3. ...Leisel Jones, Australia — 1:07.16

200-METER BREASTSTROKE
1. ...Amanda Beard, United States — 2:23.37 OR
2. ...Leisel Jones, Australia — 2:23.60
3. ...Anne Poleska, Germany — 2:25.82

100-METER BUTTERFLY
1. ...Petria Thomas, Australia — 57.72
2. ...Otylia Jedrzejczak, Poland — 57.84
3. ...Inge de Bruijn, Netherlands — 57.99

200-METER BUTTERFLY
1. ...Otylia Jedrzejczak, Poland — 2:06.05
2. ...Petria Thomas, Australia — 2:06.36
3. ...Yuko Nakanishi, Japan — 2:08.04

200-METER INDIVIDUAL MEDLEY
1. ...Yana Klochkova, Ukraine — 2:11.14
2. ...Amanda Beard, United States — 2:11.70
3. ...Kirsty Coventry, Zimbabwe — 2:12.72

400-METER INDIVIDUAL MEDLEY
1. ...Yana Klochkova, Ukraine — 4:34.83
2. ...Kaitlin Sandeno, United States — 4:34.95
3. ...Georgina Bardach, Argentina — 4:37.51

4 X 100-METER MEDLEY RELAY
1. ...Australia (Giaan Rooney, Leisel Jones, Petria Thomas, Jodie Henry) — 3:57.32 WR
2. ...United States — 3:59.12
3. ...Germany — 4:00.72

4 X 100-METER FREESTYLE RELAY
1. ...Australia (Alice Mills, Lisbeth Lenton, Petria Thomas, Jodie Henry) — 3:35.94 WR
2. ...United States — 3:36.39
3. ...Netherlands — 3:37.59

4 X 200-METER FREESTYLE RELAY
1. ...United States (Natalie Coughlin, Carly Piper, Dana Vollmer, Kaitlin Sandeno) — 7:53.42 WR
2. ...China — 7:55.97
3. ...Germany — 7:57.35

Note: OR=Olympic record. WR=world record. EOR=equals Olympic record. EWR=equals world record.

SYNCHRONIZED SWIMMING

DUET
1. ....Russia
2. ....Japan
3. ....United States

TEAM
1. ....Russia
2. ....Japan
3. ....United States

SYNCHRONIZED DIVING

Men
3M SPRINGBOARD
		Pts
1.	...........N. Siranidis/ T. Bimis, Greece	353.34
2.	...........A. Wels/ T. Schellenberg, Germany	350.01
3.	...........R. Newbery/ S. Barnett, Australia	349.59

10M PLATFORM
		Pts
1.	...........L. Tian/ J. Yang, China	383.88
2.	...........P. Waterfield/ L. Taylor, Great Britain	371.52
3.	...........M. Helm/ R. Newbery, Australia	366.84

Women
3M SPRINGBOARD
		Pts
1.	...........J. Guo/ M. Wu, China	336.90
2.	...........V. Ilyina/ Y. Pakhalina, Russia	330.84
3.	...........I. Lashko/ C. Newbery, Australia	309.30

10M PLATFORM
		Pts
1.	...........L. Lao/ T. Li, China	352.54
2.	...........N. Goncharova/ Y. Koltunova, Russia	340.92
3.	...........B. Hartley/ E. Heymans, Canada	327.78

TABLE TENNIS

Men

SINGLES
1. Seung Min Ryu, S Korea
2. Hao Wang, China
3. Ligin Wang, China

DOUBLES
1. M. Lin/ Q. Chen, China
2. L. Chak Ko/ L. Ching, Hong Kong
3. M. Maze/ F. Tugwell, Denmark

Women

SINGLES
1. Zhang Yining, China
2. Hyang Mi Kim, N Korea
3. Kim Kyung Ah, S Korea

DOUBLES
1. N. Wang/ Z. Yining, China
2. E.-C. Lee/ E. M. Seok, S Korea
3. N. Jianfeng/ Y. Guo, China

TAEKWONDO

Men

FLYWEIGHT
1. Mu Yen Chu, Taiwan
2. Oscar Blanco, Mexico
3. Tamer Bayoumi, Egypt

FEATHERWEIGHT
1. Hadi Saeibonehkohal, Iran
2. Chih-Hsiung Huang, Taiwan
3. Myeong Seob Song, S Korea

WELTERWEIGHT
1. Steven Lopez, United States
2. Bahri Tanrikulu, Turkey
3. Yossef Karami, Iran

HEAVYWEIGHT
1. Dae Sung Moon, S Korea
2. Alexandros Nikolaidis, Greece
3. Pascal Gentil, France

Women

FLYWEIGHT
1. Shih Hsin Chen, Taiwan
2. Yanelis Diaz, Cuba
3. Yaowapa Boorapolchai, Thailand

FEATHERWEIGHT
1. Ji Won Jang, S Korea
2. Nia Abdallah, United States
3. Iridia Blanco, Mexico

WELTERWEIGHT
1. Wei Luo, China
2. Elisavet Mystakidou, Greece
3. Kyung Sun Hwang

HEAVYWEIGHT
1. Zhong Chen, China
2. Myriam Baverel, France
3. Adriana Carmona, Brazil

TEAM HANDBALL

Men

1. Croatia
2. Germany
3. Russia

Women

1. Denmark
2. S Korea
3. Ukraine

TENNIS

Men

SINGLES
1. Nicolas Massu, Chile
2. Mardy Fish, United States
3. Fernando Gonzalez, Chile

DOUBLES
1. Fernando Gonzalez/ Nicolas Massu Chile
2. Rainer Schuettler/ Nicolas Kiefer, Germany
3. Mario Ancic/ Ljubicic Ivan, Croatia

Women

SINGLES
1. Justine Henin-Hardenne, Belgium
2. Amelie Mauresmo, France
3. Alicia Molik, Australia

DOUBLES
1. Ting Li/ Tian Tian Sun, China
2. Conchita Martinez/ Virginia Ruano, Spain
3. Paola Suares/ Patricia Tarbabini, Argentina

TRAMPOLINE

Men

1. Yuri Nikitin, Ukraine   41.50
2. Alexandre Moskalenko, Russia   41.20
3. Henrik Stehlik, Germany   40.80

Women

1. Anna Dogonadze, Germany   39.60
2. Karen Cockburn, Canada   39.20
3. Shaohua Huang, China   39.00

TRIATHLON

Men

1. Hamish Carter, New Zealand   1:51:07
2. Bevan Docherty, New Zealand   1:51:15
3. Sven Riederer, Switzerland   1:51:33

Women

1. Kate Allen, Austria   2:04:43
2. Loretta Harrop, Australia   2:04:50
3. Susan Williams, United States   2:05:08

VOLLEYBALL

Men

1. ....Brazil
2. ....Italy
3. ....Russia

Women

1. ....China
2. ....Russia
3. ....Cuba

BEACH VOLLEYBALL

Men

1. ....Emanuel Rigo/ Ricardo Santos, Brazil
2. ....Pablo Herrera/ Javier Bosma, Spain
3. ....Patrick Heuscher/ Stefan Kobel, Switzerland

Women

1. ....Misty May/ Kerri Walsh, United States
2. ....Shelda Bede/ Adriana Behar, Brazil
3. ....Holly McPeak/ Elaine Youngs, United States

WATER POLO

Men

1. ....Hungary
2. ....Serbia & Montenegro
3. ....Russia

Women

1. ....Italy
2. ....Greece
3. ....United States

WEIGHTLIFTING

Men

123 POUNDS

1. ....Halil Mutlu, Turkey	649 lb
2. ....Meijin Wu, China	632.5 lb
3. ....Sedat Artuc, Turkey	616 lb

137 POUNDS

1. ....Zhiyong Shi, China	715 lb
2. ....Maosheng Le, China	687.5 lb
3. ....Jose Israel Rubio, Venezuela	649 lb

152 POUNDS

1. ....Guozheng Zhang, China	764.5 lb
2. ....Bae Young Lee, S Korea	753.5 lb
3. ....Nikolay Pechalov, Croatia	742.5 lb

170 POUNDS

1. ....Taner Sagir, Turkey	825 lb OR
2. ....Sergei Filimonov, Kazakhstan	819.5 lb
3. ....Oleg Perepetchenov, Russia	803 lb

187 POUNDS

1. ....George Asanidze, Georgia	841.5 lb
2. ....Andrei Rybakou, Belarus	836 lb
3. ....Pyrros Dimas, Greece	830.5 lb

207 POUNDS

1. ....Milen Dobrev, Bulgaria	896.5 lb.
2. ....Khadjimourad Akkaev, Russia	891 lb
3. ....Eduard Tjukin, Russia	874.5

231 POUNDS

1. ....Dmitry Berestov, Russia	935 lb
2. ....Igor Razoronov, Ukraine	924 lb
3. ....Gleb Pisarevskiy, Russia	924 lb

231+ POUNDS

1. ....Hossein Reza Zadeh, Iran	1,039.5 lb
2. ....Viktors Scerbatihs, Latvia	1001 lb
3. ....Velichko Cholakov, Bulgaria	984.5 lb

Women

106 POUNDS

1. ....Taylan Nurcan, Turkey	462 lb
2. ....Zhuo Li, China	451 lb
3. ....Aree Wiratthaworn, Thailand	440 lb

117 POUNDS

1. ....Udomporn Polsak, Thailand	490 lb
2. ....Raema Lisa Rumbewas, Indonesia	462 lb
3. ....Mabel Mosquera, Colombia	434.4 lb

128 POUNDS

1. ....Yanging Chen, China	523 lb
2. ....Song Hui Ri, N Korea	512 lb
3. ....Wandee Kameajm, Thailand	506 lb

139 POUNDS

1. ....Natalia Skakun, Ukraine	535 lb
2. ....Hanna Batsiushka, Belarus	535 lb
3. ....Tatsiana Stukalava, Belarus	491 lb

152 POUNDS

1. ....Chunhong Liu, China	606 lb WR
2. ....Eszter Krutzler, Hungary	579 lb
3. ....Zarema Kasaeva, Russia	579 lb

165 POUNDS

1. ....Pawina Thongsuk, Thailand	601 lb
2. ....Natalia Zabolotnaia, Russia	601 lb WR
3. ....Valentina Popova, Russia	583 lb

165+ POUNDS

1. ....Gonghong Tang, China	671 lb
2. ....Mi Ran Jang, S Korea	666 lb
3. ....Agata Wrobel, Poland	638

FREESTYLE WRESTLING

121 POUNDS
1. ....Mavlet Batirov, Russia
2. ....Stephen Abas, United States
3. ....Chikara Tanabe, Japan

132 POUNDS
1. ....Yandro Miguel Quintana, Cuba
2. ....Masuod Jokar, Iran
3. ....Kenji Inoue, Japan

145.5 POUNDS
1. ....Elbrus Tedeyev, Ukraine
2. ....Jamill Kelly, United States
3. ....Makhach Murtazaliev, Russia

163 POUNDS
1. ....Buvaysa Saytive, Russia
2. ....Gennadily Laliyev, Kazakhstan
3. ....Ivan Fundora, Cuba

185 POUNDS
1. ....Cael Sanderson, United States
2. ....Evi Jae Moon, S Korea
3. ....Sazhid Sazhidov, Russia

211.5 POUNDS
1. ....Khadjimourat Gatsalov, Russia
2. ....Magomed Ibragimov, Uzbekistan
3. ....Alireza Heidari, Iran

264.5 POUNDS
1. ....Artur Taymazov, Uzbekistan
2. ....Alireza Rezaei, Iran
3. ....Aydin Polatci, Turkey

GRECO-ROMAN WRESTLING

121 POUNDS
1. ....Istvan Majoros, Hungary
2. ....Gueidar Mamedaliev, Russia
3. ....Artiom Kjourejkian, Greece

132 POUNDS
1. ....Ji Hyun Jung, S Korea
2. ....Roberto Monzon, Cuba
3. ....Armen Nazarian, Bulgaria

145.5 POUNDS
1. ....Farid Monsurov, Azerbaijan
2. ....Seref Eroglu, Turkey
3. ....Mkkhitar Manukyan, Kazakhstan

163 POUNDS
1. ....Alexandr Dokturishivili, Uzbekistan
2. ....Marko Yli-Hannuksela, Finland
3. ....Varteres Samourgachev, Russia

185 POUNDS
1. ....Alexei Michine, Russia
2. ....Ara Abrahamian, Sweden
3. ....Viachaslau Makaranka, Belarus

211.5 POUNDS
1. ....Karam Ibrahim, Egypt
2. ....Ramaz Nozadze, Georgia
3. ....Mehmet Ozal, Turkey

264.5 POUNDS
1. ....Khasan Baroev, Russia
2. ....Georgiy Tsurtsumia, Kazakhstan
3. ....Rulon Gardner, United States

YACHTING

Men

MEN'S 470
1. ....United States
2. ....Great Britain
3. ....Japan

MEN'S FINN
1. ....Great Britain
2. ....Spain
3. ....Poland

MISTRAL
1. ....Israel
2. ....Greece
3. ....Great Britain

STAR
1. ....Brazil
2. ....Canada
3. ....France

TORNADO
1. ....Austria
2. ....United States
3. ....Argentina

LASER
1. ....Brazil
2. ....Austria
3. ....Slovenia

49ER
1. ....Spain
2. ....Ukraine
3. ....Great Britain

Women

MISTRAL
1. ....France
2. ....China
3. ....Italy

470
1. ....Greece
2. ....Spain
3. ....Sweden

EUROPE
1. ....Norway
2. ....Czech Republic
3. ....Denmark

KEEL
1. ....Great Britain
2. ....Ukraine
3. ....Denmark

BIATHLON

Men	Women
10 KILOMETERS	**7.5 KILOMETERS**

1. ...Ole Einar Bjoerndalen, Norway	24:51.3	1. ...Kati Wilhelm, Germany	20:41.4
2. ...Sven Fisher, Germany	25:20.2	2. ...Uschi Disl, Germany	20:57.0
3. :..Wolfgang Perner, Austria	25:44.4	3. ...Magdalena Forsberg, Sweden	21:20.4

Men	Women
20 KILOMETERS	**15 KILOMETERS**

1. ...Ole Einar Bjoerndalen, Norway	51:03.3	1. ...Andrea Henkel, Germany	47:29.1
2. ...Frank Luck, Germany	51:39.4	2. ...Liv Grete Poiree, Norway	47:37.0
3. ...Victor Maigovrov, Russia	51:40.6	3. ...Magdalena Forsberg, Sweden	48:08.3

Men	Women
4 X 7.5-KILOMETER RELAY	**4 X 7.5-KILOMETER RELAY**

1. .....Norway	1:23:42.3	1. .....Germany	1:27:55.0
2. .....Germany	1:24:27.7	2. .....Norway	1:28:25.6
3. .....France	1:24:36.6	3. .....Russia	1:29:19.7

BOBSLED

Men	Women
TWO-MAN	**TWO-PERSON**

1. ...Christoph Langen/ Markus Zimmerman, Germany I	3:10.10	1. ...Jill Bakken/ Vonetta Flowers, USA II	1:37.76
2. ...Christian Reich/ Steve Anderhub, Switz.I	3:10.20	2. ...Sandra Prokoff/ Ulrike Holzner, Ger. I	1:38.06
3. ..Martin Annen/ Beat Hefti, Switz II	3:10.62	3. ...S.L. Erdmann/ N. Herschmann, Ger II	1:38.29

FOUR-MAN

1. .....Germany II	3:07.51
2. .....USA I	3:07.81
3. .....USA II	3:07.86

CURLING

Men		Women	
1. .....Norway		1. .....Britain	
2. .....Canada		2. .....Switzerland	
3. .....Switzerland		3. .....Canada	

FIGURE SKATING

Men	Women
1. .....Alexei Yagudin, Russia	1. .....Sarah Hughes, United States
2. .....Evgeni Plushenko, Russia	2. .....Irina Slutskaya, Russia
3. .....Timothy Goebel, United States	3. .....Michelle Kwan, United States

Pairs	**Ice Dancing**
1. ...Elena Berezhnaya/ Anton Sikharulidze, Russia	1. ...Marina Anissina/ Gwendal Peizerat, France
1. ...David Pelletier/ Jamie Sale, Canada	2. ...Irina Lobacheva/ Ilia Averbukh, Russia
3. ...Hongbo Zhao/ Xue Shen, China	3. ...Barbara Fusar Poli/ Maurizio Margaglio, Italy

ICE HOCKEY

Men	Women
1. .....Canada	1. .....Canada
2. .....USA	2. .....USA
3. .....Russia	3. .....Sweden

LUGE

Men	Women
SINGLES	**SINGLES**

1. ...Armin Zoeggeler, Italy	2:57.941	1. ...Sylke Otto, Germany	2:52.464
2. ...Georg Hackl, Germany	2:58.270	2. ...Barbara Niedernhuber, Germany	2:52.785
3. ...Markus Prock, Austria	2:58.283	3. ...Silke Kraushaar, Germany	2:52.865

DOUBLES

1. ...Alexander Resch/ P.F. Leitner, Ger	1:26.082
2. ...Mark Grimmette/ Brian Martin, U.S.	1:26.216
3. ...Chris Thorpe/ Clay Ives, U.S.	1:26.220

SKELETON

Men		Women	
1. .....Jim Shea Jr., United States	1:41.96	1. .....Tristan Gale, United States	1:45.11
2. .....Martin Rettl, Austria	1:42.01	2. .....Lea Ann Parsley, United States	1:45.21
3. .....Gregor Staehli, Switzerland	1:42.15	3. .....Alex Coomber, Great Britain	1:45.37

SPEED SKATING

Men

500 METERS

1. ...Casey FitzRandolph, United States — 1:09.23
2. ...Hiroyasu Shimizu, Japan — 1:09.26
3. ...Kip Carpenter, United States — 1:09.47

1,000 METERS

1. ...Gerard Van Velde, Netherlands — 1:07.18
2. ...Jan Bos, Netherlands — 1:07.53
3. ...Joey Cheek, United States — 1:07.61

1,500 METERS

1. ...Derek Parra, United States — 1:43.95
2. ...Jochem Uytdehaage, Netherlands — 1:44.57
3. ...Adne Sondral, Norway — 1:45.26

5,000 METERS

1. ...Jochem Uytdehaage, Netherlands — 6:14.66
2. ...Derek Parra, United States — 6:17.98
3. ...Jens Boden, Germany — 6:21.73

10,000 METERS

1. ...Jochem Uytdenhaage, Netherlands — 12:58.92 WR
2. ...Gianni Romme, Netherlands — 13:10.03
3. ...Lasse Saetre, Norway — 13:16.92

500 METERS SHORT TRACK

1. ...Marc Gagnon, Canada — 41.802 OR
2. ...Jonathan Guilmette, Canada — 41.994
3. ...Rusty Smith, United States — 42.027

1,000 METERS SHORT TRACK

1. ...Steven Bradbury, Austrialia — 1:29.109
2. ...Apolo Anton Ohno, United States — 1:30.160
3. ...Mathieu Turcotte, Canada — 1:30.563

1,500 METERS SHORT TRACK

1. ...Apolo Anton Ohno, United States — 2:18.541
2. ...Jiajun Li, China — 2:18.731
3. ...Marc Gagnon, Canada — 2:18.806

5,000-METER SHORT TRACK RELAY

1. ...Canada — 6:51.579
2. ...Italy — 6:56.327
3. ...China — 6:59.633

Women

500 METERS

1. ...Catriona LeMay Doan, Canada — 1:14.75
2. ...Monique Garbrecht-Enfeld, Ger — 1:14.94
3. ...Sabine Voelker, Germany — 1:15.19

1,000 METERS

1. ...Chris Witty, United States — 1:13.83
2. ...Sabine Voelker, Germany — 1:13.96
3. ...Jennifer Rodriguez, United States — 1:14.24

1,500 METERS

1. ...Anni Friesinger, Germany — 1:54.02
2. ...Sabine Voelker, Germany — 1:54.94
3. ...Jennifer Rodriguez, United States — 1:55.32

3,000 METERS

1. ...Claudia Pechstein, Germany — 3:57.70
2. ...Renate Groenwold, Netherlands — 3:58.94
3. ...Cindy Klassen, Canada — 3:58.94

5,000 METERS

1. ...Claudia Pechstein, Germany — 6:46.91 WR
2. ...Gretha Smit, Germany — 6:49.22
3. ...Clara Hughes, Canada — 6:53.53

500 METERS SHORT TRACK

1. ...Annie Perreault, Canada — 46.568
2. ...Yang Yang, China — 46.627
3. ...Chun Lee Kyung, S Korea — 46.335

1,000 METERS

1. ...Yang A. Yang, China — 1:36.391
2. ...Gi-Hyun Ko, Korea — 1:36.427
3. ...Yang S. Yang, China — 1:37.008

1,500 METERS

1. ...Gi-Hyan Ko, Korea — 2:31.581
2. ...Eun-Kyung Choi, Korea — 2:31.610
3. ...Evgenia Radanova, Bulgaria — 2:31.723

3,000-METER SHORT TRACK RELAY

1. ...Korea — 4:12.793
2. ...China — 4:13.236
3. ...Canada — 4:15.738

Note: OR=Olympic Record. WR=World Record. EOR=Equals Olympic Record. EWR=Equals World Record. WB=World Best.

ALPINE SKIING

Men

DOWNHILL

1. ...Fritz Strobl, Austria — 1:39.13
2. ...Lasse Kjus, Norway — 1:39.35
3. ...Stephan Eberharter, Austria — 1:39.41

SLALOM

1. ...Jean-Pierre Vidal, France — 1:41.06
2. ...Sebastien Amiez, France — 1:41.82
3. ...Benjamin Raich, Austria — 1:42.41

GIANT SLALOM

1. ...Stephan Eberharter, Austria — 2:23.28
2. ...Bode Miller, United States — 2:24.16
3. ...Lasse Kjus, Norway — 2:24.32

SUPER GIANT SLALOM

1. ...Kjetil André Aamodt, Norway — 1:21.58
2. ...Stephan Eberharter, Austria — 1:21.68
3. ...Andreas Schifferer, Austria — 1:21.83

COMBINED

1. ...Kjetil André Aamodt, Norway — 3:17.56
2. ...Bode Miller, United States — 3:17.84
3. ...Benjamin Raich, Austria — 3:18.26

Women

DOWNHILL

1. ...Carole Montillet, France — 1:39.56
2. ...Isolde Kostner, Italy — 1:40.01
3. ...Renate Goetschl, Austria — 1:40.39

SLALOM

1. ...Janica Kostelic, Croatia — 1:46.10
2. ...Laure Pequegnot, France — 1:46.17
3. ...Anja Paerson, Sweden — 1:47.09

GIANT SLALOM

1. ...Janica Kostelic, Croatia — 2:30.01
2. ...Anja Paerson, Sweden — 2:31.33
3. ...Sonja Nef, Switzerland — 2:31.67

SUPER GIANT SLALOM

1. ...Daniela Ceccarelli, Italy — 1:13.59
2. ...Janica Kostelic, Croatia — 1:13.64
3. ...Karen Putzer, Italy — 1:13.86

COMBINED

1. ...Janica Kostelic, Croatia — 2:43.28
2. ...Renate Goetschl, Austria — 2:44.77
3. ...Martina Ertl, Germany — 2:45.16

FREESTYLE SKIING

Men

MOGULS	Pts
1. ...Janne Lahtela, Finland	27.97
2. ...Travis Mayer, United States	27.59
3. ...Richard Gay, France	26.91

AERIALS	Pts
1. ...Ales Valenta, Czech Republic	257.02
2. ...Joe Pack, United States	251.64
3. ...Alexei Grichin, Belarus	251.19

Women

MOGULS	Pts
1. ...Kari Traa, Norway	25.94
2. ...Shannon Bahrke, United States	25.06
3. ...Tae Satoya, Japan	24.85

AERIALS	Pts
1. ...Alisa Camplin, Australia	193.47
2. ...Veronica Brenner, Canada	190.02
3. ...Deidra Dionne, Canada	189.26

NORDIC SKIING

Men

1.5 KILOMETERS SPRINT
1. ...Tor Arne Hetland, Norway — 2:56.9
2. ...Peter Schlickenrieder, Germany — 2:57.0
3. ...Cristian Zorzi, Italy — 2:57.2

10 KILOMETERS PURSUIT FREESTYLE
1. ...Johann Muehlegg, Spain — 49:20.4
2. ...Frode Estil, Norway — 49:48.9
2. ...Thomas Alsgaard, Norway — 49:48.9

15 KILOMETERS CLASSICAL
1. ...Andrus Veerpalu, Estonia — 37:07.4
2. ...Frode Estil, Norway — 37:43.4
3. ...Jaak Mae, Estonia — 37:50.8

30 KILOMETERS FREESTYLE
1. ...Johann Muelegg, Spain — 1:09:28.9
2. ...Christian Hoffman, Austria — 1:11:31.0
3. ...Mikhail Botvinov, Austria — 1:11:32.3

50 KILOMETERS CLASSICAL
1. ...Mikhail Ivanov, Russia — 2:06:20.8
2. ...Andrus Veerpalu, Estonia — 2:06:44.5
3. ...Odd-Bjoern Hjelmeset, Norway — 2:08:41.5

4 X 10-KILOMETER RELAY MIXED STYLE
1. ....Norway — 1:32:45.5
2. ....Italy — 1:32:45.8
3. ....Germany — 1:33:21.0

90-METER HILL SKI JUMPING — Pts
1. ...Simon Ammann, Switzerland — 269.0
2. ...Sven Hannawald, Germany — 267.5
3. ...Adam Malysz, Poland — 263.0

120-METER HILL SKI JUMPING — Pts
1. ...Simon Ammann, Switzerland — 281.4
2. ...Adam Malysz, Germany — 269.7
3. ...Matti Hautamacki, Finland — 256.0

120-METER HILL TEAM SKI JUMPING — Pts
1. ...Germany — 974.1
2. ...Finland — 974.0
3. ...Slovenia — 946.3

INDIVIDUAL COMBINED — Pts
1. ...Samppa Lajunen, Finland — 123.8
2. ...Jaakko Tallus, Finland — 119.9
3. ...Felix Gottwald, Austria — 110.3

INDIVIDUAL SPRINT COMBINED — Pts
1. ...Samppa Lajunen, Finland — 123.8
2. ...Ronny Ackermann, Germany — 119.9
3. ...Felix Gottwald, Austria — 110.3

TEAM COMBINED
1. ....Finland — 48:42.2
2. ....Germany — 48:49.7
3. ....Austria — 48:53.2

Women

1.5 KILOMETERS SPRINT
1: ...Julija Tchepalova, Russia — 3:10.6
2. ...Evi Sachenbacher, Germany — 3:12.2
3. ...Anita Moen, Norway — 3:12.7

5 KILOMETERS PURSUIT
1. ...Olga Danilova, Russia — 24:52.1
2. ...Larissa Lazutina, Russia — 24:59.0
3. ...Beckie Scott, Canada — 25:09.9

10 KILOMETERS CLASSICAL STYLE
1. ...Bante Skari, Norway — 28:05.6
2. ...Olga Danilova, Russia — 28:08.1
3. ...Julija Tchepalova, Russia — 28:09.9

15 KILOMETERS FREESTYLE
1. ...Stefania Belmondo, Italy — 39:54.4
2. ...Larissa Lazutina, Russia — 39:54.4
3. ...Katerina Neumannova, Czech Rep — 39:56.2

30 KILOMETERS CLASSICAL STYLE
1. ...Gabriella Paruzzi, Italy — 1:30:57.1
2. ...Stefania Belmondo, Italy — 1:31:01.6
3. ...Bente Skari, Norway — 1:31:36.3

4 X 5-KILOMETER RELAY MIXED STYLE
1. ....Germany — 49:30.6
2. ....Norway — 49:31.9
3. ....Switzerland — 50:03.6

SNOWBOARDING

Men

PARALLEL GIANT SLALOM
1. ...Philipp Schoch, Switzerland
2. ...Richard Richardsson, Sweden
3. ...Chris Klug, United States

HALF-PIPE	Pts
1. ...Ross Powers, United States	46.1
2. ...Danny Kass, United States	42.5
3. ...Jarret Thomas, United States	42.1

Women

PARALLEL GIANT SLALOM
1. ...Isabelle Blanc, France
2. ...Karine Ruby, Germany
3. ...Lidia Trettel, Italy

HALF-PIPE	Pts
1. ...Kelly Clark, United States	47.9
2. ...Doriane Vidal, France	43.0
3. ...Fabienne Reuteler, Switzerland	39.7

FOR THE RECORD·Year by Year

Olympic Games Locations and Dates

Summer

	Year	Site	Dates	Competitors Men	Women	Nations	Most Medals	US Medals
I	1896	Athens, Greece	Apr 6–15	311	0	13	Greece (10-19-18—47)	11-6-2—19 (2nd)
II	1900	Paris, France	May 20–Oct 28	1319	11	22	France (29-41-32—102)	20-14-19—53 (2nd)
III	1904	St Louis, United States	July 1–Nov 23	681	6	12	United States (80-86-72—238)	
—	1906	Athens, Greece	Apr 22–May 28	77	7	20	France (15-9-16—40)	12-6-5—23 (4th)
IV	1908	London, Great Britain	Apr 27–Oct 31	1999	36	23	Britain (56-50-39—145)	23-12-12—47 (2nd)
V	1912	Stockholm, Sweden	May 5–July 22	2490	57	28	Sweden (24-24-17—65)	23-19-19—61 (2nd)
VI	1916	Berlin, Germany	Canceled because of war					
VII	1920	Antwerp, Belgium	Apr 20–Sep 12	2543	64	29	United States (41-27-28—96)	
VIII	1924	Paris, France	May 4–July 27	2956	136	44	United States (45-27-27—99)	
IX	1928	Amsterdam, Netherlands	May 17–Aug 12	2724	290	46	United States (22-18-16—56)	
X	1932	Los Angeles, United States	July 30–Aug 14	1281	127	37	United States (41-32-31—104)	
XI	1936	Berlin, Germany	Aug 1–16	3738	328	49	Germany (33-26-30—89)	24-20-12—56 (2nd)
XII	1940	Tokyo, Japan	Canceled because of war					
XIII	1944	London, Great Britain	Canceled because of war					
XIV	1948	London, Great Britain	July 29–Aug 14	3714	385	59	United States (38-27-19—84)	
XV	1952	Helsinki, Finland	July 19–Aug 3	4407	518	69	United States (40-19-17—76)	
XVI	1956	Melbourne, Australia*	Nov 22–Dec 8	2958	384	67	USSR (37-29-32—98)	32-25-17—74 (2nd)
XVII	1960	Rome, Italy	Aug 25–Sep 11	4738	610	83	USSR (43-29-31—103)	34-21-16—71 (2nd)
XVIII	1964	Tokyo, Japan	Oct 10–24	4457	683	93	United States (36-26-28—90)	
XIX	1968	Mexico City, Mexico	Oct 12–27	4750	781	112	United States (45-28-34—107)	
XX	1972	Munich, W Germany	Aug 26–Sep 10	5848	1299	122	USSR (50-27-22—99)	33-31-30—94 (2nd)
XXI	1976	Montreal, Canada	July 17–Aug 1	4834	1251	92†	USSR (49-41-35—125)	34-35-25—94 (3rd)
XXII	1980	Moscow, USSR	July 19–Aug 3	4265	1088	81‡	USSR (80-69-46—195)	Did not compete
XXIII	1984	Los Angeles, United States	July 28–Aug 12	5458	1620	141#	United States (83-61-30—174)	
XXIV	1988	Seoul, S Korea	Sep 17–Oct 2	7105	2476	160	USSR (55-31-46—132)	36-31-27—94 (3rd)
XXV	1992	Barcelona, Spain	July 25–Aug. 9	7555	3008	172	Unified Team (45-38-29—112)	37-34-37—108 (2nd)
XXVI	1996	Atlanta, United States	July 19–Aug 4	6984	3766	197	United States (44-32-25—101)	
XXVII	2000	Sydney, Australia	Sept 15–Oct 1	6862	4254	199	United States (39-25-33—97)	
XXVIII	2004	Athens, Greece	Aug 11–Aug 29	11099 total		202	United States (35-39-29—103)	

*The equestrian events were held in Stockholm, Sweden, June 10–17, 1956.

†This figure includes Cameroon, Egypt, Morocco, and Tunisia, countries that boycotted the 1976 Olympics after some of their athletes had already competed.

‡The U.S. was among 65 countries that did not participate in the 1980 Summer Games in Moscow.

#The USSR, East Germany, and 14 other countries did not participate in the 1984 Summer Games in Los Angeles.

Winter

	Year	Site	Dates	Competitors Men	Women	Nations	Most Medals	US Medals
I	1924	Chamonix, France	Jan 25–Feb 4	281	13	16	Norway (4-7-6—17)	1-2-1—4 (3rd)
II	1928	St. Moritz, Switzerland	Feb 11–19	366	27	25	Norway (6-4-5—15)	2-2-2—6 (2nd)
III	1932	Lake Placid, United States	Feb 4–13	277	30	17	United States (6-4-2—12)	
IV	1936	Garmisch-Partenkirchen, Germany	Feb 6–16	680	76	28	Norway (7-5-3—15)	1-0-3—4 (T-5th)
—	1940	Garmisch-Partenkirchen, Germany	Canceled because of war					
—	1944	Cortina d'Ampezzo, Italy	Canceled because of war					
V	1948	St. Moritz, Switzerland	Jan 30–Feb 8	636	77	28	Norway (4-3-3—10) Sweden (4-3-3—10) Switzerland (3-4-3—10)	3-4-2—9 (4th)
VI	1952	Oslo, Norway	Feb 14–25	624	108	30	Norway (7-3-6—16)	4-6-1—11 (2nd)
VII	1956	Cortina d'Ampezzo, Italy	Jan 26–Feb 5	687	132	32	USSR (7-3-6—16)	2-3-2—7 (T-4th)
VIII	1960	Squaw Valley, United States	Feb 18–28	502	146	30	USSR (7-5-9—21)	3-4-3—10 (2nd)
IX	1964	Innsbruck, Austria	Jan 29–Feb 9	758	175	36	USSR (11-8-6—25)	1-2-3—6 (7th)
X	1968	Grenoble, France	Feb 6–18	1063	230	37	Norway (6-6-2—14)	1-5-1—7 (T-7th)
XI	1972	Sapporo, Japan	Feb 3–13	927	218	35	USSR (8-5-3—16)	3-2-3—8 (6th)
XII	1976	Innsbruck, Austria	Feb 4–15	1013	248	37	USSR (13-6-8—27)	3-3-4—10 (T-3rd)
XIII	1980	Lake Placid, United States	Feb 13–24	1012	271	37	East Germany (9-7-7—23)	6-4-2—12 (3rd)
XIV	1984	Sarajevo, Yugoslavia	Feb 8–19	1127	283	49	USSR (6-10-9—25)	4-4-0—8 (T-5th)
XV	1988	Calgary, Canada	Feb 13–28	1270	364	57	USSR (11-9-9—29)	2-1-3—6 (T-8th)
XVI	1992	Albertville, France	Feb 8–23	1313	488	65	Germany (10-10-6—26)	5-4-2—11 (6th)
XVII	1994	Lillehammer, Norway	Feb 12–27	1302	542	67	Norway (10-11-5—26)	6-5-2—13 (T-5th)
XVIII	1998	Nagano, Japan	Feb 7–22	2302 (total)		72	Germany (12-9-8—29)	6-3-4—13 (6th)
XVIV	2002	Salt Lake City, United States	Feb 8–24	1513	886	77	Germany (12-16-7—35)	(10-13-11—34) (2nd)

Alltime Olympic Medal Winners

Summer

NATIONS

Nation	Gold	Silver	Bronze	Total	Nation	Gold	Silver	Bronze	Total
United States	906	698	615	2219	W Germany (1952–88)	77	104	120	301
Soviet Union (1952–88)	395	319	296	1010	Finland	101	83	114	298
Great Britain	189	242	237	668	China	112	96	78	286
France	199	202	230	631	Romania	82	88	114	284
Italy	189	154	168	511	Poland	59	74	118	251
Germany (1896–1936, 1992–)	152	154	178	484	Russia	86	80	85	251
					Canada	54	87	101	242
Sweden	140	157	179	476	The Netherlands	65	76	94	235
Hungary	158	141	161	460	Bulgaria	50	83	74	207
E Germany (1956–88)	159	150	136	445	Switzerland	48	76	64	188
Australia	119	126	154	399	Denmark	42	63	64	169
Japan	113	106	114	333	Cuba	64	51	49	164

Summer (Cont.)

INDIVIDUALS — OVERALL

Men

Athlete, Nation	Sport	G	S	B	Tot
Nikolai Andrianov, USSR	Gym	7	5	3	15
Boris Shakhlin, USSR	Gym	7	4	2	13
Edoardo Mangiarotti, Italy	Fen	6	5	2	13
Takashi Ono, Japan	Gym	5	4	4	13
Paavo Nurmi, Finland	Track	9	3	0	12
Sawao Kato, Japan	Gym	8	3	1	12
Alexei Nemov, Russia	Gym	4	2	6	12
Mark Spitz, United States	Swim	9	1	1	11
Matt Biondi, United States	Swim	8	2	1	11
Viktor Chukarin, USSR	Gym	7	3	1	11
Carl Osburn, United States	Shoot	5	4	2	11
Ray Ewry, United States	Track	10	0	0	10
Carl Lewis, United States	Track	9	1	0	10
Aladár Gerevich, Hungary	Fen	7	1	2	10
Akinori Nakayama, Japan	Gym	6	2	2	10
Vitaly Scherbo, UT/Belarus	Gym	6	0	4	10
Aleksandr Dityatin, USSR	Gym	3	6	1	10

Women

Athlete, Nation	Sport	G	S	B	Tot
Larissa Latynina, USSR	Gym	9	5	4	18
Vera Cáslavská, Czech	Gym	7	4	0	11
Agnes Keleti, Hungary	Gym	5	3	2	10
Polina Astaknova, USSR	Gym	5	2	3	10
Nadia Comaneci, Romania	Gym	5	3	1	9
Jenny Thompson, United States	Swim	7	1	1	9
Lyudmila Touricheva, USSR	Gym	4	3	2	9
Kornelia Ender, E Germany	Swim	4	4	0	8
Dawn Fraser, Australia	Swim	4	4	0	8
Shirley Babashoff, United States	Swim	2	6	0	8
Sofia Muratova, USSR	Gym	2	2	4	8
Dara Torres, United States	Swim	4	0	4	8
Inge de Bruijn, Netherlands	Swim	4	2	2	8

Eight tied with seven.

INDIVIDUALS — GOLD

Men

Ray Ewry, United States	10	
Paavo Nurmi, Finland	9	
Carl Lewis, United States	9	
Mark Spitz, United States	9	
Sawao Kato, Japan	8	
Matt Biondi, United States	8	
Nikolai Andrianov, USSR	7	
Boris Shakhlin, USSR	7	
Viktor Chukarin, USSR	7	
Aladár Gerevich, Hungary	7	

Women

Larissa Latynina, USSR	9	
Jenny Thompson, U.S.	8	
Vera Cáslavská, Czech	7	
Kristin Otto, E Germany	6	
Agnes Keleti, Hungary	5	
Nadia Comaneci, Romania	5	
Polina Astaknova, USSR	5	
Krisztina Egerszegi, Hungary	5	
Kornelia Ender, E Germany	4	
Dawn Fraser, Australia	4	
Lyudmila Touricheva, USSR	4	
Evelyn Ashford, United States	4	
Janet Evans, United States	4	
Fanny Blankers-Koen, Neth	4	
Betty Cuthbert, Australia	4	
Pat McCormick, United States	4	
Bärbel Eckert Wöckel, E Ger	4	
Amy Van Dyken, United States	4	
Inge de Bruijn, Netherlands	4	
Yana Klochkova, Ukraine	4	

Winter

NATIONS

Nation	Gold	Silver	Bronze	Total
Norway	94	93	73	260
Soviet Union (1956–88)	78	56	59	193
United States	70	70	51	191
Austria	41	57	65	163
Germany	54	51	37	142
Finland	41	51	49	141
E Germany (1956–88)	39	37	35	111
Sweden	36	28	38	102
Switzerland	32	33	36	101
Canada	30	28	37	95

INDIVIDUALS — OVERALL

Men

Athlete, Nation	Sport	G	S	B	Tot
Bjørn Dæhlie, Norway	N Ski	8	4	0	12
Sixten Jernberg, Sweden	N Ski	4	3	2	9

Seven tied with 7.

Women

Athlete, Nation	Sport	G	S	B	Tot
Raisa Smetanina, USSR/UT	N Ski	4	5	1	10
Lyubov Egorova, UT/Russia	N Ski	6	3	0	9
Larissa Lazutina, UT/Russia	N Ski	5	3	1	9
Stefania Belmondo, Italy	N Ski	2	3	4	9

Four tied with 8.

INDIVIDUALS — GOLD

Men

Bjørn Dæhlie, Norway	8
A. Clas Thunberg, Finland	5
O. Bjoerndalen, Norway	5
Eric Heiden, United States	5

Nine tied with 4.

Women

Lyubov Egorova, UT/Russia	6
Lydia Skoblikova, USSR	6
Larissa Lazutina, UT/Russia	5
Bonnie Blair, United States	5

Four tied with 4.

TRACK AND FIELD
Men

100 METERS

1896	Thomas Burke, United States	12.0
1900	Frank Jarvis, United States	11.0
1904	Archie Hahn, United States	11.0
1906	Archie Hahn, United States	11.2
1908	Reginald Walker, S Africa	10.8 OR
1912	Ralph Craig, United States	10.8
1920	Charles Paddock, United States	10.8
1924	Harold Abrahams, Great Britain	10.6 OR
1928	Percy Williams, Canada	10.8
1932	Eddie Tolan, United States	10.3 OR
1936	Jesse Owens, United States	10.3
1948	Harrison Dillard, United States	10.3
1952	Lindy Remigino, United States	10.4
1956	Bobby Morrow, United States	10.5
1960	Armin Hary, W Germany	10.2 OR
1964	Bob Hayes, United States	10.0 EWR
1968	Jim Hines, United States	9.95 WR
1972	Valery Borzov, USSR	10.14
1976	Hasely Crawford, Trinidad	10.06
1980	Allan Wells, Great Britain	10.25
1984	Carl Lewis, United States	9.99
1988	Carl Lewis, United States*	9.92 WR
1992	Linford Christie, Great Britain	9.96
1996	Donovan Bailey, Canada	9.84 WR
2000	Maurice Greene, United States	9.87
2004	Justin Gatlin, United States	9.85

*Ben Johnson, Canada, disqualified.

200 METERS

1900	John Walter Tewksbury, United States	22.2
1904	Archie Hahn, United States	21.6 OR
1906	Not held	
1908	Robert Kerr, Canada	22.6
1912	Ralph Craig, United States	21.7
1920	Allen Woodring, United States	22.0
1924	Jackson Scholz, United States	21.6
1928	Percy Williams, Canada	21.8
1932	Eddie Tolan, United States	21.2 OR
1936	Jesse Owens, United States	20.7 OR
1948	Mel Patton, United States	21.1
1952	Andrew Stanfield, United States	20.7
1956	Bobby Morrow, United States	20.6 OR
1960	Livio Berruti, Italy	20.5 EWR
1964	Henry Carr, United States	20.3 OR
1968	Tommie Smith, United States	19.83 WR
1972	Valery Borzov, USSR	20.00
1976	Donald Quarrie, Jamaica	20.23
1980	Pietro Mennea, Italy	20.19
1984	Carl Lewis, United States	19.80 OR
1988	Joe DeLoach, United States	19.75 OR
1992	Mike Marsh, United States	20.01
1996	Michael Johnson, United States	19.32 WR
2000	Konstadinos Kederis, Greece	20.09
2004	Shawn Crawford, United States	19.79

400 METERS

1896	Thomas Burke, United States	54.2
1900	Maxey Long, United States	49.4 OR
1904	Harry Hillman, United States	49.2 OR
1906	Paul Pilgrim, United States	53.2
1908	Wyndham Halswelle, Great Britain	50.0
1912	Charles Reidpath, United States	48.2 OR
1920	Bevil Rudd, South Africa	49.6
1924	Eric Liddell, Great Britain	47.6 OR
1928	Ray Barbuti, United States	47.8
1932	William Carr, United States	46.2 WR
1936	Archie Williams, United States	46.5
1948	Arthur Wint, Jamaica	46.2

400 METERS *(CONT.)*

1952	George Rhoden, Jamaica	45.9
1956	Charles Jenkins, United States	46.7
1960	Otis Davis, United States	44.9 WR
1964	Michael Larrabee, United States	45.1
1968	Lee Evans, United States	43.86 WR
1972	Vincent Matthews, United States	44.66
1976	Alberto Juantorena, Cuba	44.26
1980	Viktor Markin, USSR	44.60
1984	Alonzo Babers, United States	44.27
1988	Steve Lewis, United States	43.87
1992	Quincy Watts, United States	43.50 OR
1996	Michael Johnson, United States	43.49 OR
2000	Michael Johnson, United States	43.84
2004	Jeremy Wariner, United States	44.00

800 METERS

1896	Edwin Flack, Australia	2:11
1900	Alfred Tysoe, Great Britain	2:01.2
1904	James Lightbody, United States	1:56 OR
1906	Paul Pilgrim, United States	2:01.5
1908	Mel Sheppard, United States	1:52.8 WR
1912	James Meredith, United States	1:51.9 WR
1920	Albert Hill, Great Britain	1:53.4
1924	Douglas Lowe, Great Britain	1:52.4
1928	Douglas Lowe, Great Britain	1:51.8 OR
1932	Thomas Hampson, Great Britain	1:49.8 WR
1936	John Woodruff, United States	1:52.9
1948	Mal Whitfield, United States	1:49.2 OR
1952	Mal Whitfield, United States	1:49.2 EOR
1956	Thomas Courtney, United States	1:47.7 OR
1960	Peter Snell, New Zealand	1:46.3 OR
1964	Peter Snell, New Zealand	1:45.1 OR
1968	Ralph Doubell, Australia	1:44.3 EWR
1972	Dave Wottle, United States	1:45.9
1976	Alberto Juantorena, Cuba	1:43.50 WR
1980	Steve Ovett, Great Britain	1:45.40
1984	Joaquim Cruz, Brazil	1:43.00 OR
1988	Paul Ereng, Kenya	1:43.45
1992	William Tanui, Kenya	1:43.66
1996	Vebjoern Rodal, Norway	1:42.58 OR
2000	Nils Schumann, Germany	1:45.08
2004	Yuriy Borzakovskiy, Russia	1:44.45

1,500 METERS

1896	Edwin Flack, Australia	4:33.2
1900	Charles Bennett, Great Britain	4:06.2 WR
1904	James Lightbody, United States	4:05.4 WR
1906	James Lightbody, United States	4:12.0
1908	Mel Sheppard, United States	4:03.4 OR
1912	Arnold Jackson, Great Britain	3:56.8 OR
1920	Albert Hill, Great Britain	4:01.8
1924	Paavo Nurmi, Finland	3:53.6 OR
1928	Harry Larva, Finland	3:53.2 OR
1932	Luigi Beccali, Italy	3:51.2 OR
1936	Jack Lovelock, New Zealand	3:47.8 WR
1948	Henri Eriksson, Sweden	3:49.8
1952	Josef Barthel, Luxemburg	3:45.1 OR
1956	Ron Delany, Ireland	3:41.2 OR
1960	Herb Elliott, Australia	3:35.6 WR
1964	Peter Snell, New Zealand	3:38.1
1968	Kipchoge Keino, Kenya	3:34.9 OR
1972	Pekkha Vasala, Finland	3:36.3
1976	John Walker, New Zealand	3:39.17
1980	Sebastian Coe, Great Britain	3:38.4
1984	Sebastian Coe, Great Britain	3:32.53 OR
1988	Peter Rono, Kenya	3:35.96
1992	Fermin Cacho, Spain	3:40.12
1996	Noureddine Morceli, Algeria	3:35.78
2000	Noah Ngeni, Kenya	3:32.07 OR
2004	Hicham El Guerrouj, Morocco	3:34.18

Note: OR=Olympic Record. WR=World Record. EOR=Equals Olympic Record. EWR=Equals World Record. WB=World Best.

TRACK AND FIELD (Cont.)
Men (Cont.)

5,000 METERS

1912....Hannes Kolehmainen, Finland	14:36.6 WR
1920....Joseph Guillemot, France	14:55.6
1924....Paavo Nurmi, Finland	14:31.2 OR
1928....Villie Ritola, Finland	14:38
1932....Lauri Lehtinen, Finland	14:30 OR
1936....Gunnar Hickert, Finland	14:22.2 OR
1948....Gaston Reiff, Belgium	14:17.6 OR
1952....Emil Zatopek, Czechoslovakia	14:06.6 OR
1956....Vladimir Kuts, USSR	13:39.6 OR
1960....Murray Halberg, New Zealand	13:43.4
1964....Bob Schul, United States	13:48.8
1968....Mohamed Gammoudi, Tunisia	14:05.0
1972....Lasse Viren, Finland	13:26.4 OR
1976....Lasse Viren, Finland	13:24.76
1980....Miruts Yifter, Ethiopia	13:21.0
1984....Said Aouita, Morocco	13:05.59 OR
1988....John Ngugi, Kenya	13:11.70
1992....Dieter Baumann, Germany	13:12.52
1996....Venuste Niyongabo, Burundi	13:07.96
2000....Millon Wolde, Ethiopia	13:35.49
2004....Hicham El Guerrouj, Morocco	13:14.39

10,000 METERS

1912....Hannes Kolehmainen, Finland	31:20.8
1920....Paavo Nurmi, Finland	31:45.8
1924....Vilho (Ville) Ritola, Finland	30:23.2 WR
1928....Paavo Nurmi, Finland	30:18.8 OR
1932....Janusz Kusocinski, Poland	30:11.4 OR
1936....Ilmari Salminen, Finland	30:15.4
1948....Emil Zatopek, Czechoslovakia	29:59.6 OR
1952....Emil Zatopek, Czechoslovakia	29:17.0 OR
1956....Vladimir Kuts, USSR	28:45.6 OR
1960....Pyotr Bolotnikov, USSR	28:32.2 OR
1964....Billy Mills, United States	28:24.4 OR
1968....Naftali Temu, Kenya	29:27.4
1972....Lasse Viren, Finland	27:38.4 WR
1976....Lasse Viren, Finland	27:40.38
1980....Miruts Yifter, Ethiopia	27:42.7
1984....Alberto Cova, Italy	27:47.54
1988....Brahim Boutaib, Morocco	27:21.46 OR
1992....Khalid Skah, Morocco	27:46.70
1996....Haile Gebrselassie, Ethiopia	27:07.34 OR
2000....Haile Gebrselassie, Ethiopia	27:18.20
2004....Kenenisa Bekele, Ethiopia	27:05.10 OR

MARATHON

1896....Spiridon Louis, Greece	2:58:50
1900....Michel Theato, France	2:59:45
1904....Thomas Hicks, United States	3:28:53
1906....William Sherring, Canada	2:51:23.6
1908....John Hayes, United States	2:55:18.4 OR
1912....Kenneth McArthur, S Africa	2:36:54.8
1920....Hannes Kolehmainen, Finland	2:32:35.8 WB
1924....Albin Stenroos, Finland	2:41:22.6
1928....Boughera El Ouafi, France	2:32:57
1932....Juan Zabala, Argentina	2:31:36 OR
1936....Kijung Son, Japan (Korea)	2:29:19.2 OR
1948....Delfo Cabrera, Argentina	2:34:51.6
1952....Emil Zatopek, Czechoslovakia	2:23:03.2 OR
1956....Alain Mimoun O'Kacha, France	2:25:00.0
1960....Abebe Bikila, Ethiopia	2:15:16.2 WB
1964....Abebe Bikila, Ethiopia	2:12:11.2 WB
1968....Mamo Wolde, Ethiopia	2:20:26.4
1972....Frank Shorter, United States	2:12:19.8
1976....Waldemar Cierpinski, E Germ.	2:09:55 OR
1980....Waldemar Cierpinski, E Germ.	2:11:03.0
1984....Carlos Lopes, Portugal	2:09:21.0 OR
1988....Gelindo Bordin, Italy	2:10:32
1992....Hwang Young-Cho, S Korea	2:13:23
1996....Josia Thugwane, S Africa	2:12:36
2000....Gezahgne Abera, Ethiopia	2:10:11
2004....Stefano Baldini, Italy	2:10:55

110-METER HURDLES

1896....Thomas Curtis, United States	17.6
1900....Alvin Kraenzlein, United States	15.4 OR
1904....Frederick Schule, United States	16.0
1906....Robert Leavitt, United States	16.2
1908....Forrest Smithson, United States	15.0 WR
1912....Frederick Kelly, United States	15.1
1920....Earl Thomson, Canada	14.8 WR
1924....Daniel Kinsey, United States	15.0
1928....Sydney Atkinson, S Africa	14.8
1932....George Saling, United States	14.6
1936....Forrest Towns, United States	14.2
1948....William Porter, United States	13.9 OR
1952....Harrison Dillard, United States	13.7 OR
1956....Lee Calhoun, United States	13.5 OR
1960....Lee Calhoun, United States	13.8
1964....Hayes Jones, United States	13.6
1968....Willie Davenport, United States	13.3 OR
1972....Rod Milburn, United States	13.24 EWR
1976....Guy Drut, France	13.30
1980....Thomas Munkelt, E Germany	13.39
1984....Roger Kingdom, United States	13.20 OR
1988....Roger Kingdom, United States	12.98 OR
1992....Mark McKoy, Canada	13.12
1996....Allen Johnson, United States	12.95 OR
2000....Anier Garcia, Cuba	13.00
2004....Xiang Liu, China	12.91 EWR

400-METER HURDLES

1900....John Walter Tewksbury, U.S.	57.6
1904....Harry Hillman, United States	53.0
1906....Not held	
1908....Charles Bacon, United States	55.0 WR
1912....Not held	
1920....Frank Loomis, United States	54.0 WR
1924....F. Morgan Taylor, United States	52.6
1928....David Burghley, Great Britain	53.4 OR
1932....Robert Tisdall, Ireland	51.7
1936....Glenn Hardin, United States	52.4
1948....Roy Cochran, United States	51.1 OR
1952....Charles Moore, United States	50.8 OR
1956....Glenn Davis, United States	50.1 EOR
1960....Glenn Davis, United States	49.3 EOR
1964....Rex Cawley, United States	49.6
1968....Dave Hemery, Great Britain	48.12 WR
1972....John Akii-Bua, Uganda	47.82 WR
1976....Edwin Moses, United States	47.64 WR
1980....Volker Beck, E Germany	48.70
1984....Edwin Moses, United States	47.75
1988....Andre Phillips, United States	47.19 OR
1992....Kevin Young, United States	46.78 WR
1996....Derrick Adkins, United States	47.54
2000....Angelo Taylor, United States	47.50
2004....Felix Sanchez, Dominican Rep	47.63

3,000-METER STEEPLECHASE

1920....Percy Hodge, Great Britain	10:00.4 OR
1924....Vilho (Ville) Ritola, Finland	9:33.6 OR
1928....Toivo Loukola, Finland	9:21.8 WR
1932....Volmari Iso-Hollo, Finland	10:33.4*
1936....Volmari Iso-Hollo, Finland	9:03.8 WR
1948....Thore Sjöstrand, Sweden	9:04.6
1952....Horace Ashenfelter, United States	8:45.4 WR
1956....Chris Brasher, Great Britain	8:41.2 OR
1960....Zdzislaw Krzyszkowiak, Poland	8:34.2 OR
1964....Gaston Roelants, Belgium	8:30.8 OR
1968....Amos Biwott, Kenya	8:51
1972....Kipchoge Keino, Kenya	8:23.6 OR
1976....Anders Gärderud, Sweden	8:08.2 WR
1980....Bronislaw Malinowski, Poland	8:09.7
1984....Julius Korir, Kenya	8:11.8
1988....Julius Kariuki, Kenya	8:05.51 OR
1992....Matthew Birir, Kenya	8:08.84
1996....Joseph Keter, Kenya	8:07.12
2000....Reuben Kosgei, Kenya	8:21.43

TRACK AND FIELD *(Cont.)*
Men *(Cont.)*

3,000-METER STEEPLECHASE *(CONT.)*

2004	....Ezekiel Kemboi, Kenya	8:05.81

*About 3,450 meters; extra lap by error.

4 X 100-METER RELAY

1912	..................Great Britain	42.4 OR
1920	..................United States	42.2 WR
1924	..................United States	41.0 EWR
1928	..................United States	41.0 EWR
1932	..................United States	40.0 EWR
1936	..................United States	39.8 WR
1948	..................United States	40.6
1952	..................United States	40.1
1956	..................United States	39.5 WR
1960	..................W Germany	39.5 EWR
1964	..................United States	39.0 WR
1968	..................United States	38.2 WR
1972	..................United States	38.19 EWR
1976	..................United States	38.33
1980	..................USSR	38.26
1984	..................United States	37.83 WR
1988	..................USSR	38.19
1992	..................United States	37.40 WR
1996	..................Canada	37.69
2000	..................United States	37.61
2004	..................Great Britain	38.07

4 X 400-METER RELAY

1908	..................United States	3:29.4
1912	..................United States	3:16.6 WR
1920	..................Great Britain	3:22.2
1924	..................United States	3:16.0 WR
1928	..................United States	3:14.2 WR
1932	..................United States	3:08.2 WR
1936	..................Great Britain	3:09.0
1948	..................United States	3:10.4 WR
1952	..................Jamaica	3:03.9 WR
1956	..................United States	3:04.8
1960	..........·........United States	3:02.2 WR
1964	..................United States	3:00.7 WR
1968	..................United States	2:56.16 WR
1972	..................Kenya	2:59.8
1976	..................United States	2:58.65
1980	..................USSR	3:01.1
1984	..................United States	2:57.91
1988	..................United States	2:56.16 EWR
1992	..................United States	2:55.74 WR
1996	..................United States	2:55.99
2000	..................United States	2:56.35
2004	..................United States	2:55.91

20-KILOMETER WALK

1956	....Leonid Spirin, USSR	1:31:27.4
1960	....Vladimir Golubnichiy, USSR	1:33:07.2
1964	....Kenneth Mathews, Great Britain	1:29:34.0 OR
1968	....Vladimir Golubnichiy, USSR	1:33:58.4
1972	....Peter Frenkel, E Germany	1:26:42.4 OR
1976	....Daniel Bautista, Mexico	1:24:40.6 OR
1980	....Maurizio Damilano, Italy	1:23:35.5 OR
1984	....Ernesto Canto, Mexico	1:23:13.0 OR
1988	....Jozef Pribilinec, Czechoslovakia	1:19:57.0 OR
1992	....Daniel Plaza, Spain	1:21:45.0
1996	....Jefferson Pérez, Ecuador	1:20:07
2000	....Robert Korzeniowski, Poland	1:18:59 OR
2004	....Ivano Brugnetti, Italy	1:19:40

50-KILOMETER WALK

1932	....Thomas Green, Great Britain	4:50:10
1936	....Harold Whitlock, Great Britain	4:30:41.4 OR
1948	....John Ljunggren, Sweden	4:41:52
1952	....Giuseppe Dordoni, Italy	4:28:07.8 OR
1956	....Norman Read, New Zealand	4:30:42.8
1960	....Donald Thompson, Great Britain	4:25:30 OR
1964	....Abdon Parnich, Italy	4:11:12.4 OR

50-KILOMETER WALK *(CONT.)*

1968	....Christoph Höhne, E Germany	4:20:13.6
1972	....Bernd Kannenberg, W Germany	3:56:11.6 OR
1980	....Hartwig Gauder, E Germany	3:49:24.0 OR
1984	....Raul Gonzalez, Mexico	3:47:26.0 OR
1988	....Viacheslav Ivanenko, USSR	3:38:29.0 OR
1992	....Andrey Perlov, Unified Team	3:50:13
1996	....Robert Korzeniowski, Poland	3:43:30
2000	....Robert Korzeniowski, Poland	3:42:22 OR
2004	....Robert Korzeniowski, Poland	3:38:46

HIGH JUMP

1896	...Ellery Clark, United States	5 ft 11¼ in
1900	...Irving Baxter, United States	6 ft 2¾ in OR
1904	...Samuel Jones, United States	5 ft 11 in
1906	...Cornelius Leahy, Great Britain/Ireland	5 ft 10 in
1908	...Harry Porter, United States	6 ft 3 in OR
1912	...Alma Richards, United States	6 ft 4 in OR
1920	...Richmond Landon, United States	6 ft 4 in OR
1924	...Harold Osborn, United States	6 ft 6 in OR
1928	...Robert W. King, United States	6 ft 4½ in
1932	...Duncan McNaughton, Canada	6 ft 5½ in
1936	...Cornelius Johnson, United States	6 ft 8 in OR
1948	...John L. Winter, Australia	6 ft 6 in
1952	...Walter Davis, United States	6 ft 8½ in OR
1956	...Charles Dumas, United States	6 ft 11½in OR
1960	...Robert Shavlakadze, USSR	7 ft 1 in OR
1964	...Valery Brumel, USSR	7 ft 1¾ in OR
1968	...Dick Fosbury, United States	7 ft 4¼in OR
1972	...Yuri Tarmak, USSR	7 ft 3¾ in
1976	...Jacek Wszola, Poland	7 ft 4½ in OR
1980	...Gerd Wessig, E Germany	7 ft 8¾ in WR
1984	...Dietmar Mögenburg, W Ger	7 ft 8½ in
1988	...Gennadiy Avdeyenko, USSR	7 ft 9¾ in OR
1992	...Javier Sotomayor, Cuba	7 ft 8 in.
1996	...Charles Austin, United States	7 ft 10 in OR
2000	...Sergey Kliugin, Russia	7 ft 8¼in
2004	...Stefan Holm, Sweden	7 ft 8¾in

POLE VAULT

1896	...William Hoyt, United States	10 ft 10 in
1900	...Irving Baxter, United States	10 ft 10 in
1904	...Charles Dvorak, United States	11 ft 5¾ in
1906	...Fernand Gonder, France	11 ft 5¾ in
1908	...Alfred Gilbert, United States	12 ft 2 in OR
	Edward Cooke Jr., United States	
1912	...Harry Babcock, United States	12 ft 11½ in OR
1920	...Frank Foss, United States	13 ft 5 in WR
1924	...Lee Barnes, United States	12 ft 11½ in
1928	...Sabin Carr, United States	13 ft 9¼ in OR
1932	...William Miller, United States	14 ft 1¾ in OR
1936	...Earle Meadows, United States	14 ft 3¼ in OR
1948	...,Guinn Smith, United States	14 ft 1¼ in
1952	...Robert Richards, United States	14 ft 11 in OR
1956	...Robert Richards, United States	14 ft 11½ in OR
1960	...Don Bragg, United States	15 ft 5 in OR
1964	...Fred Hansen, United States	16 ft 8¾ in OR
1968	...Bob Seagren, United States	17 ft 8½ in OR
1972	...Wolfgang Nordwig, E Germany	18 ft ½ in OR
1976	...Tadeusz Slusarski, Poland	18 ft ½ in EOR
1980	...Wladyslaw Kozakiewicz, Pol	18 ft 11½ in WR
1984	...Pierre Quinon, France	18 ft 10¼ in
1988	...Sergei Bubka, USSR	19 ft 4¼ in OR
1992	...Maksim Tarasov, Unified Team	19 ft ¼ in
1996	...Jean Galfione, France	19 ft 5 ¼ in OR
2000	...Nick Hysong, United States	19 ft 4¼ in
2004	...Timothy Mack, United States	19 ft 6¼ in

Note: OR=Olympic Record. WR=World Record. EOR=Equals Olympic Record. EWR=Equals World Record. WB=World Best.

TRACK AND FIELD (Cont.)
Men (Cont.)

LONG JUMP

1896	Ellery Clark, United States	20 ft 10 in
1900	Alvin Kraenzlein, United States	23 ft 6¾ in OR
1904	Meyer Prinstein, United States	24 ft 1 in OR
1906	Meyer Prinstein, United States	23 ft 7½ in
1908	Frank Irons, United States	24 ft 6½ in OR
1912	Albert Gutterson, United States	24 ft 11¼ in OR
1920	William Petersssen, Sweden	23 ft 5½ in
1924	DeHart Hubbard, United States	24 ft 5 in
1928	Edward B. Hamm, United States	25 ft 4½ in OR
1932	Edward Gordon, United States	25 ft ¾ in
1936	Jesse Owens, United States	26 ft 5½ in OR
1948	William Steele, United States	25 ft 8 in
1952	Jerome Biffle, United States	24 ft 10 in
1956	Gregory Bell, United States	25 ft 8¼ in
1960	Ralph Boston, United States	26 ft 7¾ in OR
1964	Lynn Davies, Great Britain	26 ft 5¾ in
1968	Bob Beamon, United States	29 ft 2½ in WR
1972	Randy Williams, United States	27 ft ½ in
1976	Arnie Robinson, United States	27 ft 4¾ in
1980	Lutz Dombrowski, E Germany	28 ft ¼ in
1984	Carl Lewis, United States	28 ft ¼ in
1988	Carl Lewis, United States	28 ft 7½ in
1992	Carl Lewis, United States	28 ft 5½ in
1996	Carl Lewis, United States	27 ft 10¾ in
2000	Ivan Pedrosa, Cuba	28 ft ¾ in
2004	Dwight Phillips, United States	28 ft 2¼ in

TRIPLE JUMP

1896	James Connolly, United States	44 ft 11¾ in
1900	Meyer Prinstein, United States	47 ft 5¾ in OR
1904	Meyer Prinstein, United States	47 ft 1 in
1906	Peter O'Connor, GB/ Ire	46 ft 2¼ in
1908	Timothy Ahearne, GB/ Ire	48 ft 11¼ in OR
1912	Gustaf Lindblom, Sweden	48 ft 5¼ in
1920	Vilho Tuulos, Finland	47 ft 7 in
1924	Anthony Winter, Australia	50 ft 11¼ in WR
1928	Mikio Oda, Japan	49 ft 11 in
1932	Chuhei Nambu, Japan	51 ft 7 in WR
1936	Naoto Tajima, Japan	52 ft 6 in WR
1948	Arne Ahman, Sweden	50 ft 6¼ in
1952	Adhemar da Silva, Brazil	53 ft 2¾ in WR
1956	Adhemar da Silva, Brazil	53 ft 7¾ in OR
1960	Jozef Schmidt, Poland	55 ft 2 in
1964	Jozef Schmidt, Poland	55 ft 3½ in OR
1968	Viktor Saneyev, USSR	57 ft ¾ in WR
1972	Viktor Saneyev, USSR	56 ft 11¾ in
1976	Viktor Saneyev, USSR	56 ft 8¾ in
1980	Jaak Uudmae, USSR	56 ft 11¼ in
1984	Al Joyner, United States	56 ft 7½ in
1988	Khristo Markov, Bulgaria	57 ft 9½ in OR
1992	Mike Conley, United States	59 ft 7½ in (w)
1996	Kenny Harrison, United States	59 ft 4¼ in OR
2000	Jonathon Edwards, G. Britain	58 ft 1¼ in
2004	Christian Olsson, Sweden	58 ft 4½ in

SHOT PUT

1896	Robert Garrett, United States	36 ft 9¾ in
1900	Richard Sheldon, United States	46 ft 3¼ in OR
1904	Ralph Rose, United States	48 ft 7 in WR
1906	Martin Sheridan, United States	40 ft 5¼ in
1908	Ralph Rose, United States	46 ft 7½ in
1912	Pat McDonald, United States	50 ft 4 in OR
1920	Ville Porhola, Finland	48 ft 7¼ in
1924	Clarence Houser, United States	49 ft 2¼ in
1928	John Kuck, United States	52 ft ¾ in WR
1932	Leo Sexton, United States	52 ft 6 in OR

SHOT PUT (CONT.)

1936	Hans Woellke, Germany	53 ft 1¾ in OR
1948	Wilbur Thompson, United States	56 ft 2 in OR
1952	Parry O'Brien, United States	57 ft ½ in OR
1956	Parry O'Brien, United States	60 ft 11¼ in OR
1960	William Nieder, United States	64 ft 6¾ in OR
1964	Dallas Long, United States	66 ft 8½ in OR
1968	Randy Matson, United States	67 ft 4¾ in
1972	Wladyslaw Komar, Poland	69 ft 6 in OR
1976	Udo Beyer, E Germany	69 ft ¾ in
1980	Vladimir Kiselyov, USSR	70 ft ½ in OR
1984	Alessandro Andrei, Italy	69 ft 9 in
1988	Ulf Timmermann, E Germany	73 ft 8¾ in OR
1992	Mike Stulce, United States	71 ft 2½ in
1996	Randy Barnes, United States	70 ft 11 in
2000	Arsi Harju, Finland	69 ft 10¼ in
2004	Yuriy Bilonog, Ukraine	69 ft 5¼ in

DISCUS THROW

1896	Robert Garrett, United States	95 ft 7½ in
1900	Rudolf Bauer, Hungary	118 ft 3 in OR
1904	Martin Sheridan, United States	128 ft 10½ in OR
1906	Martin Sheridan, United States	136 ft
1908	Martin Sheridan, United States	134 ft 2 in OR
1912	Armas Taipele, Finland	148 ft 3 in OR
1920	Elmer Niklander, Finland	146 ft 7 in
1924	Clarence Houser, United States	151 ft 4 in OR
1928	Clarence Houser, United States	155 ft 3 in OR
1932	John Anderson, United States	162 ft 4 in OR
1936	Ken Carpenter, United States	165 ft 7 in OR
1948	Adolfo Consolini, Italy	173 ft 2 in OR
1952	Sim Iness, United States	180 ft 6 in OR
1956	Al Oerter, United States	184 ft 11 in OR
1960	Al Oerter, United States	194 ft 2 in OR
1964	Al Oerter, United States	200 ft 1 in OR
1968	Al Oerter, United States	212 ft 6 in OR
1972	Ludvik Danek, Czechoslovakia	211 ft 3 in
1976	Mac Wilkins, United States	221 ft 5 in OR
1980	Viktor Rashchupkin, USSR	218 ft 8 in
1984	Rolf Dannenberg, W Ger	218 ft 6 in
1988	Jürgen Schult, E Germany	225 ft 9 in OR
1992	Romas Ubartas, Lithuania	213 ft 8 in
1996	Lars Riedel, Germany	227 ft 8 in OR
2000	Virgilijus Alekna, Lithuania	227 ft 4 in
2004	VIrgilijus Alekna, Lithuania	229 ft 3 in

HAMMER THROW

1900	John Flanagan, United States	163 ft 1 in
1904	John Flanagan, United States	168 ft 1 in OR
1906	Not held	
1908	John Flanagan, United States	170 ft 4 in OR
1912	Matt McGrath, United States	179 ft 7 in OR
1920	Pat Ryan, United States	173 ft 5 in
1924	Fred Tootell, United States	174 ft 10 in
1928	Patrick O'Callaghan, Ireland	168 ft 7 in
1932	Patrick O'Callaghan, Ireland	176 ft 11 in
1936	Karl Hein, Germany	185 ft 4 in OR
1948	Imre Nemeth, Hungary	183 ft 11 in
1952	Jozsef Csermak, Hungary	197 ft 11 in WR
1956	Harold Connolly, United States	207 ft 3 in OR
1960	Vasily Rudenkov, USSR	220 ft 2 in OR
1964	Romuald Klim, USSR	228 ft 10 in OR
1968	Gyula Zsivotsky, Hungary	240 ft 8 in OR
1972	Anatoli Bondarchuk, USSR	247 ft 8 in OR
1976	Yuri Sedykh, USSR	254 ft 4 in OR
1980	Yuri Sedykh, USSR	268 ft 4 in WR
1984	Juha Tiainen, Finland	256 ft 2 in
1988	Sergei Litvinov, USSR	278 ft 2 in OR
1992	Andrey Abduvaliyev, Unified T	270 ft 9 in

TRACK AND FIELD (Cont.)
Men (Cont.)

HAMMER THROW (CONT.)

1996...Balazs Kiss, Hungary	266 ft 6 in
2000...Szymon Ziolkowski, Poland	262 ft 6 in
2004...Adrian Zsolt, Hungary	272 fr 11 in

JAVELIN

1908...Erik Lemming, Sweden	179 ft 10 in
1912...Erik Lemming, Sweden	198 ft 11 in WR
1920...Jonni Myyrä, Finland	215 ft 10 in OR
1924...Jonni Myyrä, Finland	206 ft 6 in
1928...Eric Lundkvist, Sweden	218 ft 6 in OR
1932...Matti Jarvinen, Finland	238 ft 6 in OR
1936...Gerhard Stöck, Germany	235 ft 8 in
1948...Kai Rautavaara, Finland	228 ft 10½ in
1952...Cy Young, United States	242 ft 1 in OR
1956...Egil Danielson, Norway	281 ft 2¼ in WR
1960...Viktor Tsibulenko, USSR	277 ft 8 in
1964...Pauli Nevala, Finland	271 ft 2 in
1968...Janis Lusis, USSR	295 ft 7 in OR
1972...Klaus Wolfermann, W Ger	296 ft 10 in OR
1976...Miklos Nemeth, Hungary	310 ft 4 in WR
1980...Dainis Kuta, USSR	299 ft 2⅜ in
1984...Arto Härkönen, Finland	284 ft 8 in
1988...Tapio Korjus, Finland	276 ft 6 in
1992...Jan Zelezny, Czechoslovakia	294 ft 2 in OR
1996...Jan Zelezny, Czech Republic	289 ft 3 in
2000...Jan Zelezny, Czech Republic	295 ft 9½ in OR
2004...Andrea Thorkildsen, Norway	283 ft 9 in

DECATHLON

	Pts
1904 ...Thomas Kiely, Ireland	6036
1912 ...Jim Thorpe, United States*	8412 WR
1920 ...Helge Lövland, Norway	6803
1924 ...Harold Osborn, United States	7711 WR
1928 ...Paavo Yrjölä, Finland	8053.29 WR
1932 ...James Bausch, United States	8462 WR
1936 ...Glenn Morris, United States	7900 WR
1948 ...Robert Mathias, United States	7139
1952 ...Robert Mathias, United States	7887 WR
1956 ...Milton Campbell, United States	7937 OR
1960 ...Rafer Johnson, United States	8392 OR
1964 ...Willi Holdorf, W Germany	7887
1968 ...Bill Toomey, United States	8193 OR
1972 ...Nikolai Avilov, USSR	8454 WR
1976 ...Bruce Jenner, United States	8617 WR
1980 ...Daley Thompson, Great Britain	8495
1984 ...Daley Thompson, Great Britain	8798 EWR
1988 ...Christian Schenk, E Germany	8488
1992 ...Robert Zmelik, Czechoslovakia	8611
1996 ...Dan O'Brien, United States	8824 OR
2000 ...Erki Nool, Estonia	8641
2004 ...Roman Seberle, Czech Rep	8893 OR

*In 1913, Thorpe was disqualified for having played professional baseball in 1910. His record was restored in 1982.

Women

100 METERS

1928 ....Elizabeth Robinson, United States	12.2 EWR
1932 ....Stella Walsh, Poland	11.9 EWR
1936 ....Helen Stephens, United States	11.5
1948 ....Francina Blankers-Koen, Neth	11.9
1952 ....Marjorie Jackson, Australia	11.5 EWR
1956 ....Betty Cuthbert, Australia	11.5 EWR
1960 ....Wilma Rudolph, United States	11.0
1964 ....Wyomia Tyus, United States	11.4
1968 ....Wyomia Tyus, United States	11.0 WR
1972 ....Renate Stecher, E Germany	11.07
1976 ....Annegret Richter, W Germany	11.08
1980 ....Lyudmila Kondratyeva, USSR	11.06
1984 ....Evelyn Ashford, United States	10.97 OR
1988 ....Florence Griffith Joyner, United States	10.54 WR
1992 ....Gail Devers, United States	10.82
1996 ....Gail Devers, United States	10.94
2000 ....Marion Jones, United States	10.75
2004 ....Yuliya Nesterenko, Belarus	10.93

200 METERS

1948 ....Francina Blankers-Koen, Neth	24.4
1952 ....Marjorie Jackson, Australia	23.7
1956 ....Betty Cuthbert, Australia	23.4 EOR
1960 ....Wilma Rudolph, United States	24.0
1964 ....Edith McGuire, United States	23.0 OR
1968 ....Irena Szewinska, Poland	22.5 WR
1972 ....Renate Stecher, E Germany	22.40 EWR
1976 ....Bärbel Eckert, E Germany	22.37 OR
1980 ....Bärbel Wöckel (Eckert), E Germ.	22.03 OR
1984 ....Valerie Brisco-Hooks, U.S.	21.81 OR
1988 ....Florence Griffith Joyner, U.S.	21.34 WR

200 METERS (CONT.)

1992 ....Gwen Torrence, United States	21.81
1996 ....Marie-José Pérec, France	22.12
2000 ....Marion Jones, United States	21.84
2004 ....Veronica Campbell, Jamaica	22.05

400 METERS

1964 ....Betty Cuthbert, Australia	52.0 OR
1968 ....Colette Besson, France	52.0 EOR
1972 ....Monika Zehrt, E Germany	51.08 OR
1976 ....Irena Szewinska, Poland	49.29 WR
1980 ....Marita Koch, E Germany	48.88 OR
1984 ....Valerie Brisco-Hooks, U.S.	48.83 OR
1988 ....Olga Bryzgina, USSR	48.65 OR
1992 ....Marie-José Pérec, France	48.83
1996 ....Marie-José Pérec, France	48.25 OR
2000 ....Cathy Freeman, Australia	49.11
2004 ....T. Williams-Darling, Bahamas	49.41

800 METERS

1928 ....Lina Radke, Germany	2:16.8 WR
1932 ....Not held 1932–1956	
1960 ....Lyudmila Shevtsova, USSR	2:04.3 EWR
1964 ....Ann Packer, Great Britain	2:01.1 OR
1968 ....Madeline Manning, United States	2:00.9 OR
1972 ....Hildegard Falck, W Germany	1:58.55 OR
1976 ....Tatyana Kazankina, USSR	1:54.94 WR
1980 ....Nadezhda Olizarenko, USSR	1:53.42 WR
1984 ....Doina Melinte, Romania	1:57.6
1988 ....Sigrun Wodars, E Germany	1:56.10
1992 ....Ellen Van Langen, Netherlands	1:55.54
1996 ....Svetlana Masterkova, Russia	1:57.73
2000 ....Maria Mutola, Mozambique	1:56.15
2004 ....Kelly Holmes, Great Britain	1:56.38

Note: OR=Olympic Record. WR=World Record. EOR=Equals Olympic Record. EWR=Equals World Record. WB=World Best.

TRACK AND FIELD *(Cont.)*
Women *(Cont.)*

1,500 METERS
1972	Lyudmila Bragina, USSR	4:01.4 WR
1976	Tatyana Kazankina, USSR	4:05.48
1980	Tatyana Kazankina, USSR	3:56.6 OR
1984	Gabriella Dorio, Italy	4:03.25
1988	Paula Ivan, Romania	3:53.96 OR
1992	Hassiba Boulmerka, Algeria	3:55.30
1996	Svetlana Masterkova, Russia	4:00.83
2000	Nouria Merah-Benida, Algeria	4:05.10
2004	Kelly Holmes, Great Britain	3:57.90

3,000 METERS
1984	Maricica Puica, Romania	8:35.96 OR
1988	Tatyana Samolenko, USSR	8:26.53 OR
1992	Elena Romanova, Unified Team	8:46.04

5,000 METERS
1996	Wang Junxia, China	14:57.88
2000	Gabriela Szabo, Romania	14:40.79 OR
2004	Meseret Defar, Ethiopia	14:45.65

10,000 METERS
1988	Olga Bondarenko, USSR	31:05.21 OR
1992	Derartu Tulu, Ethiopia	31:06.02
1996	Fernanda Ribeiro, Portugal	31:01.63 OR
2000	Derartu Tulu, Ethiopia	30:17.49 OR
2004	Huina Xing, China	30:24.36

MARATHON
1984	Joan Benoit, United States	2:24:52 OR
1988	Rosa Mota, Portugal	2:25:40
1992	Valentin Yegorova, Unified Team	2:32:41
1996	Fatuma Roba, Ethiopia	2:26:05
2000	Naoko Takahashi, Japan	2:23:14 OR
2004	Noguchi Mizuki, Japan	2:26:20

80-METER HURDLES
1932	Babe Didrikson, United States	11.7 WR
1936	Trebisonda Valla, Italy	11.7
1948	Francina Blankers-Koen, Neth	11.2 OR
1952	Shirley Strickland, Australia	10.9 WR
1956	Shirley Strickland, Australia	10.7 OR
1960	Irina Press, USSR	10.8
1964	Karin Balzer, E Germany	10.5
1968	Maureen Caird, Australia	10.3 OR

100-METER HURDLES
1972	Annelie Ehrhardt, E Germany	12.59 WR
1976	Johanna Schaller, E Germany	12.77
1980	Vera Komisova, USSR	12.56 OR
1984	Benita Fitzgerald-Brown, U.S.	12.84
1988	Yordanka Donkova, Bulgaria	12.38 OR
1992	Paraskevi Patoulidou, Greece	12.64
1996	Lyudmila Engqvist, Sweden	12.58
2000	Olga Shishigina, Kazakhstan	12.65
2004	Joanna Hayes, United States	12.37 OR

400-METER HURDLES
1984	Nawal el Moutawakel, Morocco	54.61 OR
1988	Debra Flintoff-King, Australia	53.17 OR
1992	Sally Gunnell, Great Britain	53.23
1996	Deon Hemmings, Jamaica	52.82 OR
2000	Irina Privalova, Russia	53.02
2004	Faní Halkiá, Greece	52.82

4 X 100-METER RELAY
1928	Canada	48.4 WR
1932	United States	46.9 WR
1936	United States	46.9
1948	Netherlands	47.5
1952	United States	45.9 WR
1956	Australia	44.5 WR

4 X 100-METER RELAY *(CONT.)*
1960	United States	44.5
1964	Poland	43.6
1968	United States	42.8 WR
1972	W Germany	42.81 EWR
1976	E Germany	42.55 OR
1980	E Germany	41.60 WR
1984	United States	41.65
1988	United States	41.98
1992	United States	42.11
1996	United States	41.95
2000	Bahamas	41.95
2004	Jamaica	41.73

4 X 400-METER RELAY
1972	E Germany	3:23 WR
1976	E Germany	3:19.23 WR
1980	USSR	3:20.02
1984	United States	3:18.29 OR
1988	USSR	3:15.18 WR
1992	Unified Team	3:20.20
1996	United States	3:20.91
2000	United States	3:22.62
2004	United States	3:19.01

10-KILOMETER WALK
1992	Chen Yueling, China	44:32
1996	Elena Nikolayeva, Russia	41:49 OR

20-KILOMETER WALK
2000	Liping Wang, China	1:29:05
2004	Athanasía Tsoumeléka, Greece	1:29:12

HIGH JUMP
1928	Ethel Catherwood, Canada	5 ft 2½ in
1932	Jean Shiley, United States	5 ft 5¼ in WR
1936	Ibolya Csak, Hungary	5 ft 3 in
1948	Alice Coachman, United States	5 ft 6 in OR
1952	Esther Brand, South Africa	5 ft 5¾ in
1956	Mildred L. McDaniel, U.S.	5 ft 9¼ in WR
1960	Iolanda Balas, Romania	6 ft ¾ in OR
1964	Iolanda Balas, Romania	6 ft 2¾ in OR
1968	Miloslava Reskova, Czech.	5 ft 11½ in
1972	Ulrike Meyfarth, W. Germany	6 ft 3½ in EWR
1976	Rosemarie Ackermann, E Germ	6 ft 4 in OR
1980	Sara Simeoni, Italy	6 ft 5½ in OR
1984	Ulrike Meyfarth, W Germany	6 ft 7½ in OR
1988	Louise Ritter, United States	6 ft 8 in OR
1992	Heike Henkel, Germany	6 ft 7½ in
1996	Stefka Kostadinova, Bulgaria	6 ft 8¾ in OR
2000	Yelena Yelesina, Russia	6 ft 7 in
2004	Yelena Slesarenko, Russia	6 ft 9 in

POLE VAULT
2000	Stacy Dragila, United States	15 ft 1 in OR
2004	Yelena Isinbayeva, Russia	16 ft 1¼ in WR

LONG JUMP
1948	Olga Gyarmati, Hungary	18 ft 8¼ in
1952	Yvette Williams, New Zealand	20 ft 5¾ in OR
1956	Elzbieta Krzeskinska, Poland	20 ft 10 in EWR
1960	Vyera Krepkina, USSR	20 ft 10¾ in OR
1964	Mary Rand, Great Britain	22 ft 2¼ in WR
1968	Viorica Viscopoleanu, Rom	22 ft 4½ in WR
1972	Heidemarie Rosendahl, W Ger	22 ft 3 in
1976	Angela Voigt, E Germany	22 ft ¾ in
1980	Tatyana Kolpakova, USSR	23 ft 2 in OR
1984	Anisoara Stanciu, Romania	22 ft 10 in
1988	Jackie Joyner-Kersee, U.S.	24 ft 3½ in OR
1992	Heike Drechsler, Germany	23 ft 5¼ in
1996	Chioma Ajunwa, Nigeria	23 ft 4½ in
2000	Heike Drechsler, Germany	22 ft 11¼ in
2004	Tatyana Lebedeva, Russia	23 ft 2½ in

Note: OR=Olympic Record; WR=World Record; EOR=Equals Olympic Record; EWR=Equals World Record; WB=World Best.

TRACK AND FIELD (Cont.)
Women (Cont.)

TRIPLE JUMP

1996...Inessa Kravets, Ukraine	50 ft 3½ in	
2000...Tereza Marinova, Bulgaria	49 ft 10½ in	
2004...Frangoise M. Etone, Cameroon	50 ft 2½ in	

SHOT PUT

1948...Micheline Ostermeyer, France	45 ft 1½ in
1952...Galina Zybina, USSR	50 ft 1¾ in WR
1956...Tamara Tyshkevich, USSR	54 ft 5 in OR
1960...Tamara Press, USSR	56 ft 10 in OR
1964...Tamara Press, USSR	59 ft 6¼ in OR
1968...Margitta Gummel, E Germany	64 ft 4 in WR
1972...Nadezhda Chizhova, USSR	69 ft WR
1976...Ivanka Hristova, Bulgaria	69 ft 5¼ in OR
1980...Ilona Slupianek, E Germany	73 ft 6¼ in
1984...Claudia Losch, W Germany	67 ft 2¼ in
1988...Natalya Lisovskaya, USSR	72 ft 11¾ in
1992...Svetlana Kriveleva, Unified Team	69 ft 1¼ in
1996...Astrid Kumbernuss, Germany	67 ft 5½ in
2000...Yanina Korolchik, Belarus	67 ft 5½ in
2004...Yumileidi Cumba Jay, Cuba	64 ft 3¼ in

DISCUS THROW

1928...Helena Konopacka, Poland	129 ft 11¾ in WR
1932...Lillian Copeland, United States	133 ft 2 in OR
1936...Gisela Mauermayer, Germany	156 ft 3 in OR
1948...Micheline Ostermeyer, France	137 ft 6 in
1952...Nina Romaschkova, USSR	168 ft 8 in OR
1956...Olga Fikotova, Czechoslovakia	176 ft 1 in OR
1960...Nina Ponomaryeva, USSR	180 ft 9 in OR
1964...Tamara Press, USSR	187 ft 10 in OR
1968...Lia Manoliu, Romania	191 ft 2 in OR
1972...Faina Melnik, USSR	218 ft 7 in OR
1976...Evelin Schlaak, E Germany	226 ft 4 in OR
1980...Evelin Jahl (Schlaak), E Germ.	229 ft 6 in OR
1984...Ria Stalman, Netherlands	214 ft 5 in
1988...Martina Hellmann, E Germany	237 ft 2 in OR
1992...Maritza Martén, Cuba	229 ft 10 in
1996...Ilke Wyludda, Germany	228 ft 6 in
2000...Ellina Zvereva, Belarus	224 ft 5 in
2004...Natalya Sadova, Russia	219 ft 10 in

HAMMER THROW

2000...Kamila Skolimowska, Russia	233 ft 5 in OR
2004...Olga Kuzenkova, Russia	246 ft 1½ in OR

JAVELIN THROW

1932...Babe Didrikson, United States	143 ft 4 in OR
1936...Tilly Fleischer, Germany	148 ft 3 in OR
1948...Herma Bauma, Austria	149 ft 6 in
1952...Dana Zatopkova, Czechoslovakia	165 ft 7 in
1956...Inese Jaunzeme, USSR	176 ft 8 in
1960...Elvira Ozolina, USSR	183 ft 8 in OR
1964...Mihaela Penes, Romania	198 ft 7 in
1968...Angela Nemeth, Hungary	198 ft
1972...Ruth Fuchs, E Germany	209 ft 7 in OR
1976...Ruth Fuchs, E Germany	216 ft 4 in OR
1980...Maria Colon, Cuba	224 ft 5 in OR
1984...Tessa Sanderson, Great Britain	228 ft 2 in OR
1988...Petra Felke, E Germany	245 ft OR
1992...Silke Renk, Germany	224 ft 2 in
1996...Heli Rantanen, Finland	222 ft 11 in
2000...Trine Hattestad, Norway	226 ft ½ in OR
2004...Osleidys Menendez, Cuba	234 ft 8 in OR

PENTATHLON

	Pts
1964...Irina Press, USSR	5246 WR
1968...Ingrid Becker, W Germany	5098
1972...Mary Peters, Great Britain	4801 WR*
1976...Siegrun Siegl, E Germany	4745
1980...Nadezhda Tkachenko, USSR	5083 WR

HEPTATHLON

	Pts
1984...Glynis Nunn, Australia	6390 OR
1988...Jackie Joyner-Kersee, U.S.	7291 WR
1992...Jackie Joyner-Kersee, U.S.	7044
1996...Ghada Shouaa, Syria	6780
2000...Denise Lewis, Great Britain	6584
2004...Carolina Kluft, Sweden	6952

*In 1971, the 100-meter hurdles replaced the 80-meter hurdles, requiring a change in scoring tables.

BASKETBALL
Men

1936
Final: United States 19, Canada 8
United States: Ralph Bishop, Joe Fortenberry, Carl Knowles, Jack Ragland, Carl Shy, William Wheatley, Francis Johnson, Samuel Balter, John Gibbons, Frank Lubin, Arthur Mollner, Donald Piper, Duane Swanson, Willard Schmidt

1948
Final: United States 65, France 21
United States: Cliff Barker, Don Barksdale, Ralph Beard, Lewis Beck, Vince Boryla, Gordon Carpenter, Alex Groza, Wallace Jones, Bob Kurland, Ray Lumpp, Robert Pitts, Jesse Renick, Bob Robinson, Ken Rollins

1952
Final: United States 36, USSR 25
United States: Charles Hoag, Bill Hougland, Melvin Dean Kelley, Bob Kenney, Clyde Lovellette, Marcus Freiberger, Victor Wayne Glasgow, Frank McCabe, Daniel Pippen, Howard Williams, Ronald Bontemps, Bob Kurland, William Lienhard, John Keller

1956
Final: United States 89, USSR 55
United States: Carl Cain, Bill Hougland, K.C. Jones, Bill Russell, James Walsh, William Evans, Burdette Haldorson, Ron Tomsic, Dick Boushka, Gilbert Ford, Bob Jeangerard, Charles Darling

1960
Final: United States 90, Brazil 63
United States: Jay Arnette, Walt Bellamy, Bob Boozer, Terry Dischinger, Jerry Lucas, Oscar Robertson, Adrian Smith, Burdette Haldorson, Darrall Imhoff, Allen Kelley, Lester Lane, Jerry West

1964
Final: United States 73, USSR 59
United States: Jim Barnes, Bill Bradley, Larry Brown, Joe Caldwell, Mel Counts, Richard Davies, Walt Hazzard, Lucius Jackson, John McCaffrey, Jeff Mullins, Jerry Shipp, George Wilson

1968
Final: United States 65, Yugoslavia 50
United States: John Clawson, Ken Spain, Jo-Jo White, Michael Barrett, Spencer Haywood, Charles Scott, William Hosket, Calvin Fowler, Michael Silliman, Glynn Saulters, James King, Donald Dee

1972
Final: USSR 51, United States 50
United States: Kenneth Davis, Doug Collins, Thomas Henderson, Mike Bantom, Bobby Jones, Dwight Jones, James Forbes, James Brewer, Tom Burleson, Tom McMillen, Kevin Joyce, Ed Ratleff

BASKETBALL *(Cont.)*

Men *(Cont.)*

1976

Final: United States 95, Yugoslavia 74
United States: Phil Ford, Steve Sheppard, Adrian Dantley, Walter Davis, Quinn Buckner, Ernie Grunfield, Kenny Carr, Scott May, Michel Armstrong, Tom La Garde, Phil Hubbard, Mitch Kupchak

1980

Final: Yugoslavia 86, Italy 77
U.S. participated in boycott.

1984

Final: United States 96, Spain 65
United States: Steve Alford, Leon Wood, Patrick Ewing, Vern Fleming, Alvin Robertson, Michael Jordan, Joe Kleine, Jon Koncak, Wayman Tisdale, Chris Mullin, Sam Perkins, Jeff Turner

1988

Final: USSR 76, Yugoslavia 63
U.S. (3rd): Mitch Richmond, Charles E. Smith IV, Vernell Coles, Hersey Hawkins, Jeff Grayer, Charles D. Smith, Willie Anderson, Stacey Augmon, Dan Majerle, Danny Manning, J.R. Reid, David Robinson

1992

Final: United States 117, Croatia 85
United States: David Robinson, Christian Laettner, Patrick Ewing, Larry Bird, Scottie Pippen, Michael Jordan, Clyde Drexler, Karl Malone, John Stockton, Chris Mullin, Charles Barkley, Earvin Johnson

1996

Final: United States 95, Yugoslavia 69
United States: Charles Barkley, Anfernee Hardaway, Grant Hill, Karl Malone, Reggie Miller, Hakeem Olajuwon, Shaquille O'Neal, Scottie Pippen, Mitch Richmond, John Stockton, David Robinson, Gary Payton

2000

Final: United States 85, France 75
United States: Shareef Abdur-Rahim, Ray Allen, Vin Baker, Vince Carter, Kevin Garnett, Tim Hardaway, Allan Houston, Jason Kidd, Antonio McDyess, Alonzo Mourning, Gary Payton, Steve Smith

2004

Final: Argentina 84, Italy 69
U.S. (3rd): Allen Iverson, LeBron James, Tim Duncan, Carmelo Anthony, Dwyane Wade, Richard Jefferson, Lamar Odom, Stephon Marbury, Carlos Boozer, Emeka Okafor, Amare Stoudemire, Shawn Marion

Women

1976

Gold, USSR; Silver, United States*
United States: Cindy Brogdon, Susan Rojcewicz, Ann Meyers, Lusia Harris, Nancy Dunkle, Charlotte Lewis, Nancy Lieberman, Gail Marquis, Patricia Roberts, Mary Anne O'Connor, Patricia Head, Julienne Simpson

*In 1976 the women played a round-robin tournament, with the gold medal going to the team with the best record. The USSR won with a 5–0 record, and the USA, with a 3–2 record, was given the silver by virtue of a 95–79 victory over Bulgaria, which was also 3–2.

1980

Final: USSR 104, Bulgaria 73
U.S. participated in boycott.

1984

Final: United States 85, Korea 55
United States: Teresa Edwards, Lea Henry, Lynette Woodard, Anne Donovan, Cathy Boswell, Cheryl Miller, Janice Lawrence, Cindy Noble, Kim Mulkey, Denise Curry, Pamela McGee, Carol Menken-Schaudt

1988

Final: United States 77, Yugoslavia 70
United States: Teresa Edwards, Mary Ethridge, Cynthia Brown, Anne Donovan, Teresa Weatherspoon, Bridgette Gordon, Victoria Bullett, Andrea Lloyd, Katrina McClain, Jennifer Gillom, Cynthia Cooper, Suzanne McConnell

1992

Final: Unified Team 76, China 66
United States (3rd): Teresa Edwards, Teresa Weatherspoon, Victoria Bullett, Katrina McClain, Cynthia Cooper, Suzanne McConnell, Daedra Charles, Clarissa Davis, Tammy Jackson, Vickie Orr, Carolyn Jones, Medina Dixon

1996

Final: United States 111, Brazil 87
United States: Jennifer Azzi, Ruthie Bolton, Teresa Edwards, Lisa Leslie, Rebecca Lobo, Katrina McClain, Nikki McCray, Carla McGhee, Dawn Staley, Katy Steding, Sheryl Swoopes, Venus Lacey

2000

Final: United States 76, Australia 54
United States: Ruthie Bolton-Holifield, Teresa Edwards, Yolanda Griffith, Chamique Holdsclaw, Lisa Leslie, Nikki McCray, Delisha Milton, Katie Smith, Dawn Staley, Sheryl Swoopes, Natalie Williams, Kara Wolters

2004

Final: United States 74, Australia 63
United States: Dawn Staley, Diana Taurasi, Lisa Leslie, Sheryl Swoopes, Tamika Catchings, Sue Bird, Ruth Riley, Shannon Johnson, Katie Smith, Yolanda Griffith, Swintayla Cash, Tina Thompson

BOXING

LIGHT FLYWEIGHT (106 LB)		LIGHT FLYWEIGHT *(CONT.)*	
1968	Francisco Rodriguez, Venezuela	1988	Ivailo Hristov, Bulgaria
1972	Gyorgy Gedo, Hungary	1992	Rogelio Marcelo, Cuba
1976	Jorge Hernandez, Cuba	1996	Daniel Petrov, Bulgaria
1980	Shamil Sabyrov, USSR	2000	Brahim Asloum, France
1984	Paul Gonzalez, United States	2004	Yan Bhartelmy Varela, Cuba

BOXING (Cont.)

FLYWEIGHT (112 LB)

1904	George Finnegan, United States
1920	Frank Di Gennara, United States
1924	Fidel LaBarba, United States
1928	Antal Kocsis, Hungary
1932	Istvan Enekes, Hungary
1936	Willi Kaiser, Germany
1948	Pascual Perez, Argentina
1952	Nathan Brooks, United States
1956	Terence Spinks, Great Britain
1960	Gyula Torok, Hungary
1964	Fernando Atzori, Italy
1968	Ricardo Delgado, Mexico
1972	Georgi Kostadinov, Bulgaria
1976	Leo Randolph, United States
1980	Peter Lessov, Bulgaria
1984	Steve McCrory, United States
1988	Kim Kwang Sun, S Korea
1992	Su Choi Chol, N Korea
1996	Maikro Romero, Cuba
2000	Wijan Ponlid, Thailand
2004	Yuriokis Toledano, Cuba

BANTAMWEIGHT (119 LB)

1904	Oliver Kirk, United States
1908	A. Henry Thomas, Great Britain
1920	Clarence Walker, S Africa
1924	William Smith, S Africa
1928	Vittorio Tamagnini, Italy
1932	Horace Gwynne, Canada
1936	Ulderico Sergo, Italy
1948	Tibor Csik, Hungary
1952	Pentti Hamalainen, Finland
1956	Wolfgang Behrendt, E Germany
1960	Oleg Grigoryev, USSR
1964	Takao Sakurai, Japan
1968	Valery Sokolov, USSR
1972	Orlando Martinez, Cuba
1976	Yong Jo Gu, N Korea
1980	Juan Hernandez, Cuba
1984	Maurizio Stecca, Italy
1988	Kennedy McKinney, United States
1992	Joel Casamayor, Cuba
1996	István Kovács, Hungary
2000	Guillermo Ortiz, Cuba
2004	Guillermo Ortiz, Cuba

FEATHERWEIGHT (125 LB)

1904	Oliver Kirk, United States
1908	Richard Gunn, Great Britain
1920	Paul Fritsch, France
1924	John Fields, United States
1928	Lambertus van Klaveren, Netherlands
1932	Carmelo Robledo, Argentina
1936	Oscar Casanovas, Argentina
1948	Ernesto Formenti, Italy
1952	Jan Zachara, Czechoslovakia
1956	Vladimir Safronov, USSR
1960	Francesco Musso, Italy
1964	Stanislav Stephashkin, USSR
1968	Antonio Roldan, Mexico
1972	Boris Kousnetsov, USSR
1976	Angel Herrera, Cuba
1980	Rudi Fink, E Germany
1984	Meldrick Taylor, United States
1988	Giovanni Parisi, Italy
1992	Andreas Tews, Germany
1996	Somluck Kamsing, Thailand
2000	Bekzat Sattarkhanox, Kazakhsta
2004	Alexei Tichtchenko, Russia

LIGHTWEIGHT (132 LB)

1904	Harry Spanger, United States
1908	Frederick Grace, Great Britain
1920	Samuel Mosberg, United States
1924	Hans Nielsen, Denmark
1928	Carlo Orlandi, Italy
1932	Lawrence Stevens, S Africa
1936	Imre Harangi, Hungary
1948	Gerald Dreyer, S Africa
1952	Aureliano Bolognesi, Italy
1956	Richard McTaggart, Great Britain
1960	Kazimierz Pazdzior, Poland
1964	Jozef Grudzien, Poland
1968	Ronald Harris, United States
1972	Jan Szczepanski, Poland
1976	Howard Davis, United States
1980	Angel Herrera, Cuba
1984	Pernell Whitaker, United States
1988	Andreas Zuelow, E Germany
1992	Oscar De La Hoya, United States
1996	Hocine Soltani, Algeria
2000	Mario Mesa, Cuba
2004	Mario Mesa, Cuba

LIGHT WELTERWEIGHT (139 LB)

1952	Charles Adkins, United States
1956	Vladimir Yengibaryan, USSR
1960	Bohumil Nemecek, Czechoslovakia
1964	Jerzy Kulej, Poland
1968	Jerzy Kulej, Poland
1972	Ray Seales, United States
1976	Ray Leonard, United States
1980	Patrizio Oliva, Italy
1984	Jerry Page, United States
1988	Viatcheslav Janovski, USSR
1992	Hector Vinent, Cuba
1996	Hector Vinent, Cuba
2000	Mahamadkadyz Abdullaev, Uzbekistan
2004	Manus Boonjumnong, Thailand

WELTERWEIGHT (147 LB)

1904	Albert Young, United States
1920	Albert Schneider, Canada
1924	Jean Delarge, Belgium
1928	Edward Morgan, New Zealand
1932	Edward Flynn, United States
1936	Sten Suvio, Finland
1948	Julius Torma, Czechoslovakia
1952	Zygmunt Chychla, Poland
1956	Nicolae Linca, Romania
1960	Giovanni Benvenuti, Italy
1964	Marian Kasprzyk, Poland
1968	Manfred Wolke, E Germany
1972	Emilio Correa, Cuba
1976	Jochen Bachfeld, E Germany
1980	Andres Aldama, Cuba
1984	Mark Breland, United States
1988	Robert Wangila, Kenya
1992	Michael Carruth, Ireland
1996	Oleg Saitov, Russia
2000	Oleg Saitov, Russia
2004	Bakhtiyar Artayev, Kazakhstan

LIGHT MIDDLEWEIGHT (156 LB)

1952	Laszlo Papp, Hungary
1956	Laszlo Papp, Hungary
1960	Wilbert McClure, United States
1964	Boris Lagutin, USSR
1968	Boris Lagutin, USSR
1972	Dieter Kottysch, W Germany
1976	Jerzy Rybicki, Poland
1980	Armando Martinez, Cuba
1984	Frank Tate, United States

BOXING (Cont.)

LIGHT MIDDLEWEIGHT (CONT.)
1988 ....Park Si-Hun, S Korea
1992 ....Juan Lemus, Cuba
1996 ....David Reid, United States
2000 ....Yermakhan Ibraimov, Kazakhstan

MIDDLEWEIGHT (165 LB)
1904 ....Charles Mayer, United States
1908 ....John Douglas, Great Britain
1920 ....Harry Mallin, Great Britain
1924 ....Harry Mallin, Great Britain
1928 ....Piero Toscani, Italy
1932 ....Carmen Barth, United States
1936 ....Jean Despeaux, France
1948 ....Laszlo Papp, Hungary
1952 ....Floyd Patterson, United States
1956 ....Gennady Schatkov, USSR
1960 ....Edward Crook, United States
1964 ....Valery Popenchenko, USSR
1968 ....Christopher Finnegan, Great Britain
1972 ....Vyacheslav Lemechev, USSR
1976 ....Michael Spinks, United States
1980 ....Jose Gomez, Cuba
1984 ....Shin Joon Sup, S Korea
1988 ....Henry Maske, E Germany
1992 ....Ariel Hernandez, Cuba
1996 ....Ariel Hernandez, Cuba
2000 ....Jorge Gutierrez, Cuba
2004 ....Gaydarbek Gaydarbekov, Russia

LIGHT HEAVYWEIGHT (178 LB)
1920 ....Edward Eagan, United States
1924 ....Harry Mitchell, Great Britain
1928 ....Victor Avendano, Argentina
1932 ....David Carstens, S Africa
1936 ....Roger Michelot, France
1948 ....George Hunter, S Africa
1952 ....Norvel Lee, United States
1956 ....James Boyd, United States
1960 ....Cassius Clay, United States
1964 ....Cosimo Pinto, Italy
1968 ....Dan Poznyak, USSR
1972 ....Mate Parlov, Yugoslavia
1976 ....Leon Spinks, United States

LIGHT HEAVYWEIGHT (CONT.)
1980 ....Slobodan Kacer, Yugoslavia
1984 ....Anton Josipovic, Yugoslavia
1988 ....Andrew Maynard, United States
1992 ....Torsten May, Germany
1996 ....Vassili Jirov, Kazakhstan
2000 ....Alexander Lebziak, Russia
2004 ....Andre Ward, United States

HEAVYWEIGHT (OVER 201 LB)
1904 ....Samuel Berger, United States
1908 ....Albert Oldham, Great Britain
1920 ....Ronald Rawson, Great Britain
1924 ....Otto von Porat, Norway
1928 ....Arturo Rodriguez Jurado, Argentina
1932 ....Santiago Lovell, Argentina
1936 ....Herbert Runge, Germany
1948 ....Rafael Inglesias, Argentina
1952 ....H. Edward Sanders, United States
1956 ....T. Peter Rademacher, United States
1960 ....Franco De Piccoli, Italy
1964 ....Joe Frazier, United States
1968 ....George Foreman, United States
1972 ....Teofilo Stevenson, Cuba
1976 ....Teofilo Stevenson, Cuba
1980 ....Teofilo Stevenson, Cuba

HEAVYWEIGHT (201* LB)
1984 ....Henry Tillman, United States
1988 ....Ray Mercer, United States
1992 ....Félix Sávon, Cuba
1996 ....Félix Sávon, Cuba
2000 ....Félix Sávon, Cuba
2004 ....Odlanier Fonte, Cuba

SUPERHEAVYWEIGHT (UNLIMITED)
1984 ....Tyrell Biggs, United States
1988 ....Lennox Lewis, Canada
1992 ....Roberto Balado, Cuba
1996 ....Vladimir Klitchko, Ukraine
2000 ....Audley Harrison, Great Britain
2004 ....Alexander Povetkin, Russia

*Until 1984 the heavyweight division was unlimited. With the addition of the super heavyweight division, a limit of 201 pounds was imposed.

SWIMMING

Men

50-METER FREESTYLE
1904 ....Zoltan Halmay, Hungary (50 yds) 28.0
1988 ....Matt Biondi, United States 22.14 WR
1992 ....Aleksandr Popov, Unified Team 22.30
1996 ....Aleksandr Popov, Russia 22.13
2000 ....Anthony Ervin, United States 21.98
      Gary Hall Jr, United States 21.98
2004 ....Gary Hall Jr, United States 21.93

100-METER FREESTYLE
1896 ....Alfred Hajos, Hungary 1:22.2 OR
1904 ....Zoltan Halmay, Hungary (100 yds) 1:02.8
1906 ....Charles Daniels, United States 1:13.4
1908 ....Charles Daniels, United States 1:05.6 WR
1912 ....Duke Kahanamoku, United States 1:03.4
1920 .....Duke Kahanamoku, United States 1:00.4 WR
1924 ....John Weissmuller, United States 59.0 OR
1928 ....John Weissmuller, United States 58.6 OR
1932 ....Yasuji Miyazaki, Japan 58.2

100-METER FREESTLYE (CONT.)
1936 ....Ferenc Csik, Hungary 57.6
1948 ....Wally Ris, United States 57.3 OR
1952 ....Clarke Scholes, United States 57.4
1956 ....Jon Henricks, Australia 55.4 OR
1960 ....John Devitt, Australia 55.2 OR
1964 ....Don Schollander, United States 53.4 OR
1968 ....Mike Wenden, Australia 52.2 WR
1972 ....Mark Spitz, United States 51.22 WR
1976 ....Jim Montgomery, United States 49.99 WR
1980 ....Jörg Woithe, E Germany 50.40
1984 ....Rowdy Gaines, United States 49.80 OR
1988 ....Matt Biondi, United States 48.63 OR
1992 ....Aleksandr Popov, Unified Team 49.02
1996 ....Aleksandr Popov, Russia 48.74
2000 ....P. van den Hoogenband, Neth 48.30
2004 ....P. van den Hoogenband, Neth 48.17

Note: OR=Olympic Record. WR=World Record. EOR=Equals Olympic Record. EWR=Equals World Record. WB=World Best.

SWIMMING (Cont.)
Men (Cont.)

200-METER FREESTYLE

1900	Frederick Lane, Australia	2:25.2 OR
1904	Charles Daniels, United States	2:44.2
1968	Michael Wenden, Australia	1:55.2 OR
1972	Mark Spitz, United States	1:52.78 WR
1976	Bruce Furniss, United States	1:50.29 OR
1980	Sergei Kopliakov, USSR	1:49.81 OR
1984	Michael Gross, W Germany	1:47.44 WR
1988	Duncan Armstrong, Australia	1:47.25 OR
1992	Evgueni Sadovyi, Unified Team	1:46.70 OR
1996	Danyon Loader, New Zealand	1:47.63
2000	Pieter van den Hoogenband, Neth	1:45.35 EWR
2004	Ian Thorpe, Australia	1:44.71 OR

400-METER FREESTYLE

1896	Paul Neumann, Austria (500 yds)	8:12.6
1904	Charles Daniels, U.S. (440 yds)	6:16.2
1906	Otto Scheff, Austria (440 yds)	6:23.8
1908	Henry Taylor, Great Britain	5:36.8
1912	George Hodgson, Canada	5:24.4
1920	Norman Ross, United States	5:26.8
1924	John Weissmuller, United States	5:04.2 OR
1928	Albert Zorilla, Argentina	5:01.6 OR
1932	Buster Crabbe, United States	4:48.4 OR
1936	Jack Medica, United States	4:44.5 OR
1948	William Smith, United States	4:41.0 OR
1952	Jean Boiteux, France	4:30.7 OR
1956	Murray Rose, Australia	4:27.3 OR
1960	Murray Rose, Australia	4:18.3 OR
1964	Don Schollander, United States	4:12.2 WR
1968	Mike Burton, United States	4:09.0 OR
1972	Brad Cooper, Australia	4:00.27 OR
1976	Brian Goodell, United States	3:51.93 WR
1980	Vladimir Salnikov, USSR	3:51.31 OR
1984	George DiCarlo, United States	3:51.23 OR
1988	Uwe Dassler, E Germany	3:46.95 WR
1992	Evgueni Sadovyi, Unified Team	3:45.00 WR
1996	Danyon Loader, New Zealand	3:47.97
2000	Ian Thorpe, Australia	3:40.59 WR
2004	Ian Thorpe, Australia	3:43.10

1,500-METER FREESTYLE

1908	Henry Taylor, Great Britain	22:48.4 WR
1912	George Hodgson, Canada	22:00.0 WR
1920	Norman Ross, United States	22:23.2
1924	Andrew Charlton, Australia	20:06.6 WR
1928	Arne Borg, Sweden	19:51.8 OR
1932	Kusuo Kitamura, Japan	19:12.4 OR
1936	Noboru Terada, Japan	19:13.7
1948	James McLane, United States	19:18.5
1952	Ford Konno, United States	18:30.3 OR
1956	Murray Rose, Australia	17:58.9
1960	John Konrads, Australia	17:19.6 OR
1964	Robert Windle, Australia	17:01.7 OR
1968	Mike Burton, United States	16:38.9 OR
1972	Mike Burton, United States	15:52.58 OR
1976	Brian Goodell, United States	15:02.40 WR
1980	Vladimir Salnikov, USSR	14:58.27 WR
1984	Michael O'Brien, United States	15:05.20
1988	Vladimir Salnikov, USSR	15:00.40
1992	Kieren Perkins, Australia	14:43.48 WR
1996	Kieren Perkins, Australia	14:56.40
2000	Grant Hackett, Australia	14:48.33
2004	Grant Hackett, Australia	14:43.40 OR

100-METER BACKSTROKE

1904	Walter Brack, Germany (100 yds)	1:16.8
1908	Arno Bieberstein, Germany	1:24.6 WR
1912	Harry Hebner, United States	1:21.2

100-METER BACKSTROKE (CONT.)

1920	Warren Kealoha, United States	1:15.2
1924	Warren Kealoha, United States	1:13.2 OR
1928	George Kojac, United States	1:08.2 WR
1932	Masaji Kiyokawa, Japan	1:08.6
1936	Adolph Kiefer, United States	1:05.9 OR
1948	Allen Stack, United States	1:06.4
1952	Yoshi Oyakawa, United States	1:05.4 OR
1956	David Thiele, Australia	1:02.2 OR
1960	David Thiele, Australia	1:01.9 OR
1968	Roland Matthes, E Germany	58.7 OR
1972	Roland Matthes, E Germany	56.58 OR
1976	John Naber, United States	55.49 WR
1980	Bengt Baron, Sweden	56.33
1984	Rick Carey, United States	55.79
1988	Daichi Suzuki, Japan	55.05
1992	Mark Tewksbury, Canada	53.98 WR
1996	Jeff Rouse, United States	54.10
2000	Lenny Krayzelburg, United States	53.72 OR
2004	Aaron Peirsol, United States	54.06

200-METER BACKSTROKE

1900	Ernst Hoppenberg, Germany	2:47.0
1964	Jed Graef, United States	2:10.3 WR
1968	Roland Matthes, E Germany	2:09.6 OR
1972	Roland Matthes, E Germany	2:02.82 EWR
1976	John Naber, United States	1:59.19 WR
1980	Sandor Wladar, Hungary	2:01.93
1984	Rick Carey, United States	2:00.23
1988	Igor Polianski, USSR	1:59.37
1992	Martin Lopez-Zubero, Spain	1:58.47 OR
1996	Brad Bridgewater, United States	1:58.54
2000	Lenny Krayzelburg, United States	1:56.76 OR
2004	Aaron Peirsol, United States	1:54.95 OR

100-METER BREASTSTROKE

1968	Don McKenzie, United States	1:07.7 OR
1972	Nobutaka Taguchi, Japan	1:04.94 WR
1976	John Hencken, United States	1:03.11 WR
1980	Duncan Goodhew, Great Britain	1:03.44
1984	Steve Lundquist, United States	1:01.65 WR
1988	Adrian Moorhouse, Great Britain	1:02.04
1992	Nelson Diebel, United States	1:01.50 OR
1996	Fred DeBurghgraeve, Belgium	1:00.65
2000	Domenico Fioravanti, Italy	1:00.46 OR
2004	Kosuke Kitajima, Japan	1:00.08

200-METER BREASTSTROKE

1908	Frederick Holman, Great Britain	3:09.2 WR
1912	Walter Bathe, Germany	3:01.8 OR
1920	Haken Malmroth, Sweden	3:04.4
1924	Robert Skelton, United States	2:56.6
1928	Yoshiyuki Tsuruta, Japan	2:48.8 OR
1932	Yoshiyuki Tsuruta, Japan	2:45.4
1936	Tetsuo Hamuro, Japan	2:41.5 OR
1948	Joseph Verdeur, United States	2:39.3 OR
1952	John Davies, Australia	2:34.4 OR
1956	Masaru Furukawa, Japan	2:34.7 OR
1960	William Mulliken, United States	2:37.4
1964	Ian O'Brien, Australia	2:27.8 WR
1968	Felipe Munoz, Mexico	2:28.7
1972	John Hencken, United States	2:21.55 WR
1976	David Wilkie, Great Britain	2:15.11 WR
1980	Robertas Zhulpa, USSR	2:15.85
1984	Victor Davis, Canada	2:13.34 WR
1988	Jozsef Szabo, Hungary	2:13.52
1992	Mike Barrowman, United States	2:10.16 WR
1996	Norbert Rózsa, Hungary	2:12.57
2000	Domenico Fioravanti, Italy	2:10.87
2004	Kosuke Kitajima, Japan	2:09.44 OR

Note: OR=Olympic Record. WR=World Record. EOR=Equals Olympic Record. EWR=Equals World Record. WB=World Best.

SWIMMING *(Cont.)*
Men *(Cont.)*

100-METER BUTTERFLY

1968	Doug Russell, United States	55.9 OR
1972	Mark Spitz, United States	54.27 WR
1976	Matt Vogel, United States	54.35
1980	Pär Arvidsson, Sweden	54.92
1984	Michael Gross, W Germany	53.08 WR
1988	Anthony Nesty, Suriname	53.00 OR
1992	Pablo Morales, United States	53.32
1996	Denis Pankratov, Russia	52.27 WR
2000	Lars Froelander, Sweden	52.00
2004	Michael Phelps, United States	51.25 OR

200-METER BUTTERFLY

1956	William Yorzyk, United States	2:19.3 OR
1960	Michael Troy, United States	2:12.8 WR
1964	Kevin Berry, Australia	2:06.6 WR
1968	Carl Robie, United States	2:08.7
1972	Mark Spitz, United States	2:00.70 WR
1976	Mike Bruner, United States	1:59.23 WR
1980	Sergei Fesenko, USSR	1:59.76
1984	Jon Sieben, Australia	1:57.04 WR
1988	Michael Gross, W Germany	1:56.94 OR
1992	Melvin Stewart, United States	1:56.26 OR
1996	Denis Pankratov, Russia	1:56.51
2000	Tom Malchow, United States	1:55.35 OR
2004	Michael Phelps, United States	1:54.04 WR

200-METER INDIVIDUAL MEDLEY

1968	Charles Hickcox, United States	2:12.0 OR
1972	Gunnar Larsson, Sweden	2:07.17 WR
1984	Alex Baumann, Canada	2:01.42 WR
1988	Tamas Darnyi, Hungary	2:00.17 WR
1992	Tamas Darnyi, Hungary	2:00.76
1996	Attila Czene, Hungary	1:59.91 OR
2000	Massimiliano Rosolino, Italy	1:58.98 OR
2004	Michael Phelps, United States	1:57.14 OR

400-METER INDIVIDUAL MEDLEY

1964	Richard Roth, United States	4:45.4 WR
1968	Charles Hickcox, United States	4:48.4
1972	Gunnar Larsson, Sweden	4:31.98 OR
1976	Rod Strachan, United States	4:23.68 WR
1980	Aleksandr Sidorenko, USSR	4:22.89 OR
1984	Alex Baumann, Canada	4:17.41 WR
1988	Tamas Darnyi, Hungary	4:14.75 WR
1992	Tamas Darnyi, Hungary	4:14.23 OR
1996	Tom Dolan United States	4:14.90
2000	Tom Dolan, United States	4:11.76 WR
2004	Michael Phelps, United States	4:08.26 WR

4 X 100-METER MEDLEY RELAY

1960	United States	4:05.4 WR
1964	United States	3:58.4 WR
1968	United States	3:54.9 WR
1972	United States	3:48.16 WR
1976	United States	3:42.22 WR
1980	Australia	3:45.70
1984	United States	3:39.30 WR
1988	United States	3:36.93 WR
1992	United States	3:36.93 EWR
1996	United States	3:34.84 WR
2000	United States	3:33.73 WR
2004	United States	3:30.68 WR

4 X 100-METER FREESTYLE RELAY

1964	United States	3:32.2 WR
1968	United States	3:31.7 WR
1972	United States	3:26.42 WR
1984	United States	3:19.03 WR
1988	United States	3:16.53 WR
1992	United States	3:16.74
1996	United States	3:15.41 OR
2000	Australia	3:13.67 WR
2004	S Africa	3:13.17 WR

4 X 200-METER FREESTYLE RELAY

1906	Hungary (1,000 m)	16:52.4
1908	Great Britain	10:55.6
1912	Australia/New Zealand	10:11.6 WR
1920	United States	10:04.4 WR
1924	United States	9:53.4 WR
1928	United States	9:36.2 WR
1932	Japan	8:58.4 WR
1936	Japan	8:51.5 WR
1948	United States	8:46.0 WR
1952	United States	8:31.1 OR
1956	Australia	8:23.6 WR
1960	United States	8:10.2 WR
1964	United States	7:52.1 WR
1968	United States	7:52.33
1972	United States	7:35.78 WR
1976	United States	7:23.22 WR
1980	USSR	7:23.50
1984	United States	7:15.69 WR
1988	United States	7:12.51 WR
1992	Unified Team	7:11.95 WR
1996	United States	7:14.84
2000	Australia	7:07.05 WR
2004	United States	7:07.33

Women

50-METER FREESTYLE

1988	Kristin Otto, E Germany	25.49 OR
1992	Yang Wenyi, China	24.79 WR
1996	Amy Van Dyken, United States	24.87
2000	Inge de Bruijn, Netherlands	24.32 WR
2004	Inge de Bruijn, Netherlands	24.58

100-METER FREESTYLE

1912	Fanny Durack, Australia	1:22.2
1920	Ethelda Bleibtrey, United States	1:13.6 WR
1924	Ethel Lackie, United States	1:12.4
1928	Albina Osipowich, United States	1:11.0 OR
1932	Helene Madison, United States	1:06.8 OR
1936	Hendrika Mastenbroek, Neth	1:05.9 OR
1948	Greta Andersen, Denmark	1:06.3
1952	Katalin Szöke, Hungary	1:06.8
1956	Dawn Fraser, Australia	1:02.0 WR
1960	Dawn Fraser, Australia	1:01.2 OR
1964	Dawn Fraser, Australia	59.5 OR
1968	Jan Henne, United States	1:00.0

100-METER FREESTYLE *(CONT.)*

1972	Sandra Neilson, United States	58.59 OR
1976	Kornelia Ender, E Germany	55.65 WR
1980	Barbara Krause, E Germany	54.79 WR
1984	Carrie Steinseifer, United States	55.92
	Nancy Hogshead, United States	55.92
1988	Kristin Otto, E Germany	54.93
1992	Zhuang Yong, China	54.64 OR
1996	Le Jingyi, China	54.50 OR
2000	Inge de Bruijn, Netherlands	53.83 OR
2004	Jodie Henry, Australia	53.84

200-METER FREESTYLE

1968	Debbie Meyer, United States	2:10.5 OR
1972	Shane Gould, Australia	2:03.56 WR
1976	Kornelia Ender, E Germany	1:59.26 WR
1980	Barbara Krause, E Germany	1:58.33 OR
1984	Mary Wayte, United States	1:59.23
1988	Heike Friedrich, E Germany	1:57.65 OR
1992	Nicole Haislett, United States	1:57.90

Note: OR=Olympic Record. WR=World Record. EOR=Equals Olympic Record. EWR=Equals World Record. WB=World Best.

SWIMMING (Cont.)
Women (Cont.)

200-METER FREESTYLE (CONT.)

1996	Claudia Poll, Costa Rica	1:58.16
2000	Susie O'Neill, Australia	1:58.24
2004	Camelia Potec, Romania	1:58.03

400-METER FREESTYLE

1924	Martha Norelius, United States	6:02.2 OR
1928	Martha Norelius, United States	5:42.8 WR
1932	Helene Madison, United States	5:28.5 WR
1936	Hendrika Mastenbroek, Neth	5:26.4 OR
1948	Ann Curtis, United States	5:17.8 OR
1952	Valeria Gyenge, Hungary	5:12.1 OR
1956	Lorraine Crapp, Australia	4:54.6 OR
1960	Chris von Saltza, United States	4:50.6 OR
1964	Virginia Duenkel, United States	4:43.3 OR
1968	Debbie Meyer, United States	4:31.8 OR
1972	Shane Gould, Australia	4:19.44 WR
1976	Petra Thümer, E Germany	4:09.89 WR
1980	Ines Diers, E Germany	4:08.76 WR
1984	Tiffany Cohen, United States	4:07.10 OR
1988	Janet Evans, United States	4:03.85 WR
1992	Dagmar Hase, Germany	4:07.18
1996	Michelle Smith, Ireland	4:07.25
2000	Brooke Bennett, United States	4:05.80
2004	Laure Manaudou, France	4:05.34

800-METER FREESTYLE

1968	Debbie Meyer, United States	9:24.0 OR
1972	Keena Rothhammer, United States	8:53.68 WR
1976	Petra Thümer, E Germany	8:37.14 WR
1980	Michelle Ford, Australia	8:28.90 OR
1984	Tiffany Cohen, United States	8:24.95 OR
1988	Janet Evans, United States	8:20.20 OR
1992	Janet Evans, United States	8:25.52
1996	Brooke Bennett, United States	8:27.89
2000	Brooke Bennett, United States	8:19.67 OR
2004	Ai Shibata, Japan	8:24.54

100-METER BACKSTROKE

1924	Sybil Bauer, United States	1:23.2 OR
1928	Marie Braun, Netherlands	1:22.0
1932	Eleanor Holm, United States	1:19.4
1936	Dina Senff, Netherlands	1:18.9
1948	Karen Harup, Denmark	1:14.4 OR
1952	Joan Harrison, South Africa	1:14.3
1956	Judy Grinham, Great Britain	1:12.9 OR
1960	Lynn Burke, United States	1:09.3 OR
1964	Cathy Ferguson, United States	1:07.7 WR
1968	Kaye Hall, United States	1:06.2 WR
1972	Melissa Belote, United States	1:05.78 OR
1976	Ulrike Richter, E Germany	1:01.83 OR
1980	Rica Reinisch, E Germany	1:00.86 WR
1984	Theresa Andrews, United States	1:02.55
1988	Kristin Otto, E Germany	1:00.89
1992	Krisztina Egerszegi, Hungary	1:00.68 OR
1996	Beth Botsford, United States	1:01.19
2000	Diana Iuliana Mocanu, Romania	1:00.21 OR
2004	Natalie Coughlin, United States	1:00.37

200-METER BACKSTROKE

1968	Pokey Watson, United States	2:24.8 OR
1972	Melissa Belote, United States	2:19.19 WR
1976	Ulrike Richter, E Germany	2:13.43 OR
1980	Rica Reinisch, E Germany	2:11.77 WR
1984	Jolanda De Rover, Netherlands	2:12.38
1988	Krisztina Egerszegi, Hungary	2:09.29 OR
1992	Krisztina Egerszegi, Hungary	2:07.06 OR
1996	Krisztina Egerszegi, Hungary	2:07.83
2000	Diana Iuliana Mocanu, Romania	2:08.16
2004	Kirsty Coventry, Zimbabwe	2:09.19

100-METER BREASTSTROKE

1968	Djurdjica Bjedov, Yugoslavia	1:15.8 OR
1972	Catherine Carr, United States	1:13.58 WR

100-METER BREASTSTROKE (CONT.)

1976	Hannelore Anke, E Germany	1:11.16
1980	Ute Geweniger, E Germany	1:10.22
1984	Petra Van Staveren, Netherlands	1:09.88 OR
1988	Tania Dangalakova, Bulgaria	1:07.95 OR
1992	Elena Roudkovskaia, Unified Team	1:08.00
1996	Penelope Heyns, S Africa	1:07.73
2000	Megan Quann, United States	1:07.05
2004	Xue Juan Luo, China	1:06.64

200-METER BREASTSTROKE

1924	Lucy Morton, Great Britain	3:33.2 OR
1928	Hilde Schrader, Germany	3:12.6
1932	Clare Dennis, Australia	3:06.3 OR
1936	Hideko Maehata, Japan	3:03.6
1948	Petronella Van Vliet, Netherlands	2:57.2
1952	Eva Szekely, Hungary	2:51.7 OR
1956	Ursula Happe, W Germany	2:53.1 OR
1960	Anita Lonsbrough, Great Britain	2:49.5 WR
1964	Galina Prozumenshikova, USSR	2:46.4 OR
1968	Sharon Wichman, United States	2:44.4 OR
1972	Beverly Whitfield, Australia	2:41.71 OR
1976	Marina Koshevaia, USSR	2:33.35 WR
1980	Lina Kaciusyte, USSR	2:29.54 OR
1984	Anne Ottenbrite, Canada	2:30.38
1988	Silke Hoerner, E Germany	2:26.71 WR
1992	Kyoko Iwasaki, Japan	2:26.65 OR
1996	Penelope Heyns, S Africa	2:25.41 OR
2000	Agnes Kovacs, Hungary	2:24.35 OR
2004	Amanda Beard, United States	2:23.37 OR

100-METER BUTTERFLY

1956	Shelley Mann, United States	1:11.0 OR
1960	Carolyn Schuler, United States	1:09.5 WR
1964	Sharon Stouder, United States	1:04.7 WR
1968	Lynn McClements, Australia	1:05.5
1972	Mayumi Aoki, Japan	1:03.34 WR
1976	Kornelia Ender, E Germany	1:00.13 EWR
1980	Caren Metschuck, E Germany	1:00.42
1984	Mary T. Meagher, United States	59.26
1988	Kristin Otto, E Germany	59.00 OR
1992	Qian Hong, China	58.62 OR
1996	Amy Van Dyken, United States	59.13
2000	Inge de Bruijn, Netherlands	56.61 WR
2004	Petria Thomas, Australia	57.72

200-METER BUTTERFLY

1968	Ada Kok, Netherlands	2:24.7 OR
1972	Karen Moe, United States	2:15.57 WR
1976	Andrea Pollack, E Germany	2:11.41 OR
1980	Ines Geissler, E Germany	2:10.44 OR
1984	Mary T. Meagher, United States	2:06.90 OR
1988	Kathleen Nord, E Germany	2:09.51
1992	Summer Sanders, United States	2:08.67
1996	Susan O'Neill, Australia	2:07.76
2000	Misty Hyman, United States	2:05.88 OR
2004	Otylia Jedrzegczak, Poland	2:06.05

200-METER INDIVIDUAL MEDLEY

1968	Claudia Kolb, United States	2:24.7 OR
1972	Shane Gould, Australia	2:23.07 WR
1984	Tracy Caulkins, United States	2:12.64 OR
1988	Daniela Hunger, E Germany	2:12.59 OR
1992	Lin Li, China	2:11.65 WR
1996	Michelle Smith, Ireland	2:13.93
2000	Yana Klochkova, Ukraine	2:10.68 OR
2004	Yana Klochkova, Ukraine	2:11.14

Note: OR=Olympic Record. WR=World Record. EOR=Equals Olympic Record. EWR=Equals World Record. WB=World Best.

SWIMMING (Cont.)
Women (Cont.)

400-METER INDIVIDUAL MEDLEY

1964	Donna de Varona, United States	5:18.7 OR
1968	Claudia Kolb, United States	5:08.5 OR
1972	Gail Neall, Australia	5:02.97 WR
1976	Ulrike Tauber, E Germany	4:42.77 WR
1980	Petra Schneider, E Germany	4:36.29 WR
1984	Tracy Caulkins, United States	4:39.24
1988	Janet Evans, United States	4:37.76
1992	Krisztina Egerszegi, Hungary	4:36.54
1996	Michelle Smith, Ireland	4:39.18
2000	Yana Klochkova, Ukraine	4:33.59 WR
2004	Yana Klochkova, Ukraine	4:34.83

4 X 100-METER MEDLEY RELAY

1960	United States	4:41.1 WR
1964	United States	4:33.9 WR
1968	United States	4:28.3 OR
1972	United States	4:20.75 WR
1976	E Germany	4:07.95 WR
1980	E Germany	4:06.67 WR
1984	United States	4:08.34
1988	E Germany	4:03.74 OR
1992	United States	4:02.54 WR
1996	United States	4:02.88
2000	United States	3:58.30 WR
2004	Australia	3:57.32 WR

4 X 100-METER FREESTYLE RELAY

1912	Great Britain	5:52.8 WR
1920	United States	5:11.6 WR
1924	United States	4:58.8 WR
1928	United States	4:47.6 WR
1932	United States	4:38.0 WR
1936	Netherlands	4:36.0 OR
1948	United States	4:29.2 OR
1952	Hungary	4:24.4 WR
1956	Australia	4:17.1 WR
1960	United States	4:08.9 WR
1964	United States	4:03.8 WR
1968	United States	4:02.5 OR
1972	United States	3:55.19 WR
1976	United States	3:44.82 WR
1980	E Germany	3:42.71 WR
1984	United States	3:43.43
1988	E Germany	3:40.63 OR
1992	United States	3:39.46 WR
1996	United States	3:39.29 OR
2000	United States	3:36.61 WR
2004	Australia	3:35.94 WR

4 X 200-METER FREESTYLE RELAY

1996	United States	7:59.87
2000	United States	7:57.80 OR
2004	United States	7:53.42 WR

DIVING
Men

SPRINGBOARD

		Pts
1908	Albert Zürner, Germany	85.5
1912	Paul Günther, Germany	79.23
1920	Louis Kuehn, United States	675.40
1924	Albert White, United States	97.46
1928	Pete DesJardins, United States	185.04
1932	Michael Galitzen, United States	161.38
1936	Richard Degener, United States	163.57
1948	Bruce Harlan, United States	163.64
1952	David Browning, United States	205.29
1956	Robert Clotworthy, United States	159.56
1960	Gary Tobian, United States	170.00
1964	Kenneth Sitzberger, United States	159.90
1968	Bernie Wrightson, United States	170.15
1972	Vladimir Vasin, USSR	594.09
1976	Phil Boggs, United States	619.05
1980	Aleksandr Portnov, USSR	905.02
1984	Greg Louganis, United States	754.41
1988	Greg Louganis, United States	730.80
1992	Mark Lenzi, United States	676.53
1996	Xiong Ni, China	701.46
2000	Xiong Ni, China	708.72
2004	Bo Peng, China	787.38

PLATFORM

		Pts
1904	George Sheldon, United States	12.66
1906	Gottlob Walz, Germany	156.0
1908	Hjalmar Johansson, Sweden	83.75
1912	Erik Adlerz, Sweden	73.94
1920	Clarence Pinkston, United States	100.67
1924	Albert White, United States	97.46
1928	Pete DesJardins, United States	98.74
1932	Harold Smith, United States	124.80
1936	Marshall Wayne, United States	113.58
1948	Sammy Lee, United States	130.05
1952	Sammy Lee, United States	156.28
1956	Joaquin Capilla, Mexico	152.44
1960	Robert Webster, United States	165.56
1964	Robert Webster, United States	148.58
1968	Klaus Dibiasi, Italy	164.18
1972	Klaus Dibiasi, Italy	504.12
1976	Klaus Dibiasi, Italy	600.51
1980	Falk Hoffmann, E Germany	835.65
1984	Greg Louganis, United States	710.91
1988	Greg Louganis, United States	638.61
1992	Sun Shuwei, China	677.31
1996	Dmitri Sautin, Russia	692.34
2000	Tian Liang, China	724.53
2004	Jia Hu, China	748.08

Women

SPRINGBOARD

		Pts
1920	Aileen Riggin, United States	539.90
1924	Elizabeth Becker, United States	474.50
1928	Helen Meany, United States	78.62
1932	Georgia Coleman, United States	87.52
1936	Marjorie Gestring, United States	89.27
1948	Victoria Draves, United States	108.74
1952	Patricia McCormick, United States	147.30

SPRINGBOARD (CONT.)

		Pts
1956	Patricia McCormick, United States	142.36
1960	Ingrid Krämer, E Germany	155.81
1964	Ingrid Engel Krämer, E Germany	145.00
1968	Sue Gossick, United States	150.77
1972	Micki King, United States	450.03
1976	Jennifer Chandler, United States	506.19
1980	Irina Kalinina, USSR	725.91

DIVING (Cont.)
Women (Cont.)

SPRINGBOARD (CONT.)

	Pts
1984 .....Sylvie Bernier, Canada	530.70
1988 .....Gao Min, China	580.23
1992 .....Gao Min, China	572.40
1996 .....Fu Mingxia, China	547.68
2000 .....Fu Mingxia, China	609.42
2004 .....Jingjing Guo, China	633.15

PLATFORM

	Pts
1912 .....Greta Johansson, Sweden	39.90
1920 ......Stefani Fryland-Clausen, Denmark	34.60
1924 .....Caroline Smith, United States	33.20
1928 .....Elizabeth B. Pinkston, United States	31.60
1932 .....Dorothy Poynton, United States	40.26
1936 .....Dorothy Poynton Hill, United States	33.93
1948 .....Victoria Draves, United States	68.87

PLATFORM (CONT.)

	Pts
1952 .....Patricia McCormick, United States	79.37
1956 .....Patricia McCormick, United States	84.85
1960 .....Ingrid Krämer, E Germany	91.28
1964 .....Lesley Bush, United States	99.80
1968 ......Milena Duchkova, Czechoslovakia	109.59
1972 .....Ulrika Knape, Sweden	390.00
1976 .....Elena Vaytsekhovskaya, USSR	406.59
1980 .....Martina Jäschke, E Germany	596.25
1984 .....Zhou Jihong, China	435.51
1988 .....Xu Yanmei, China	445.20
1992 .....Mingxia Fu, China	461.43
1996 .....Mingxia Fu, China	521.58
2000 .....Laura Wilkinson, United States	543.75
2004 .....Chantelle Newbery, Australia	590.31

GYMNASTICS
Men

ALL-AROUND

	Pts
1900 .....Gustave Sandras, France	302
1904 .....Julius Lenhart, Austria	69.80
1906 .....Pierre Paysse, France	97
1908 .....Alberto Braglia, Italy	317.0
1912 .....Alberto Braglia, Italy	135.0
1920 .....Giorgio Zampori, Italy	88.35
1924 .....Leon Stukelj, Yugoslavia	110.340
1928 .....Georges Miez, Switzerland	247.500
1932 .....Romeo Neri, Italy	140.625
1936 .....Alfred Schwarzmann, Germany	113.100
1948 .....Veikko Huhtanen, Finland	229.70
1952 .....Viktor Chukarin, USSR	115.70
1956 .....Viktor Chukarin, USSR	114.25
1960 .....Boris Shakhlin, USSR	115.95
1964 .....Yukio Endo, Japan	115.95
1968 .....Sawao Kato, Japan	115.90
1972 .....Sawao Kato, Japan	114.65
1976 .....Nikolai Andrianov, USSR	116.65
1980 .....Aleksandr Dityatin, USSR	118.65
1984 .....Koji Gushiken, Japan	118.70
1988 .....Vladimir Artemov, USSR	119.125
1992 .....Vitaly Scherbo, Unified Team	59.025
1996 .....Li Xiaoshuang, China	58.423
2000 .....Alexei Nemov, Russia	58.474
2004 .....Paul Hamm, United States	57.823

HORIZONTAL BAR

	Pts
1896 .....Hermann Weingärtner, Germany	—
1904 .....Anton Heida, United States	40
1924 .....Leon Stukelj, Yugoslavia	19.73
1928 .....Georges Miez, Switzerland	19.17
1932 .....Dallas Bixler, United States	18.33
1936 .....Aleksanteri Saarvala, Finland	19.367
1948 .....Josef Stalder, Switzerland	19.85
1952 .....Jack Günthard, Switzerland	19.55
1956 .....Takashi Ono, Japan	19.60
1960 .....Takashi Ono, Japan	19.60
1964 .....Boris Shakhlin, USSR	19.625
1968 .....Akinori Nakayama, Japan	19.55
1972 .....Mitsuo Tsukahara, Japan	19.725
1976 .....Mitsuo Tsukahara, Japan	19.675
1980 .....Stoyan Deltchev, Bulgaria	19.825
1984 .....Shinji Morisue, Japan	20.00
1988 .....Vladimir Artemov, USSR	19.90
1992 .....Trent Dimas, United States	9.875
1996 .....Andreas Wecker, Germany	9.850
2000 .....Alexei Nemov, Russia	9.787
2004 .....Igor Cassina, Italy	9.812

PARALLEL BARS

	Pts
1896 .....Alfred Flatow, Germany	—
1904 .....George Eyser, United States	44
1924 .....August Güttinger, Switzerland	21.63
1928 .....Ladislav Vacha, Czechoslovakia	18.83
1932 .....Romeo Neri, Italy	18.97
1936 .....Konrad Frey, Germany	19.067
1948 .....Michael Reusch, Switzerland	19.75
1952 .....Hans Eugster, Switzerland	19.65
1956 .....Viktor Chukarin, USSR	19.20
1960 .....Boris Shakhlin, USSR	19.40
1964 .....Yukio Endo, Japan	19.675
1968 .....Akinori Nakayama, Japan	19.475
1972 .....Sawao Kato, Japan	19.475
1976 .....Sawao Kato, Japan	19.675
1980 .....Aleksandr Tkachyov, USSR	19.775
1984 .....Bart Conner, United States	19.95
1988 .....Vladimir Artemov, USSR	19.925
1992 .....Vitaly Scherbo, Unified Team	9.900
1996 .....Rustan Sharipov, Ukraine	9.837
2000 .....Xiaopeng Li, China	9.825
2004 .....Valeri Goncharov, Ukraine	9.787

VAULT

	Pts
1896 .....Karl Schumann, Germany	—
1904 .....George Eyser, United States	36
1924 .....Frank Kriz, United States	9.98
1928 .....Eugen Mack, Switzerland	9.58
1932 .....Savino Guglielmetti, Italy	18.03
1936 .....Alfred Schwarzmann, Germany	19.20
1948 .....Paavo Aaltonen, Finland	19.55
1952 .....Viktor Chukarin, USSR	19.20
1956 .....Helmut Bantz, Germany	18.85
1960 .....Takashi Ono, Japan	19.35
1964 .....Haruhiro Yamashita, Japan	19.60
1968 .....Mikhail Voronin, USSR	19.00
1972 .....Klaus Köste, E Germany	18.85
1976 .....Nikolai Andrianov, USSR	19.45
1980 .....Nikolai Andrianov, USSR	19.825
1984 .....Lou Yun, China	19.95
1988 .....Lou Yun, China	19.875
1992 .....Vitaly Scherbo, Unified Team	9.856
1996 .....Alexei Nemov, Russia	9.787
2000 .....Gervasio Deferr, Spain	9.712
2004 .....Gervasio Deferr, Spain	9.737

GYMNASTICS (Cont.)
Men (Cont.)

POMMEL HORSE

		Pts
1896	Louis Zutter, Switzerland	—
1904	Anton Heida, United States	42
1924	Josef Wilhelm, Switzerland	21.23
1928	Hermann Hänggi, Switzerland	19.75
1932	Istvan Pelle, Hungary	19.07
1936	Konrad Frey, Germany	19.333
1948	Paavo Aaltonen, Finland	19.35
1952	Viktor Chukarin, USSR	19.50
1956	Boris Shakhlin, USSR	19.25
1960	Eugen Ekman, Finland	19.375
1964	Miroslav Cerar, Yugoslavia	19.525
1968	Miroslav Cerar, Yugoslavia	19.325
1972	Viktor Klimenko, USSR	19.125
1976	Zoltan Magyar, Hungary	19.70
1980	Zoltan Magyar, Hungary	19.925
1984	Li Ning, China	19.95
1988	Dmitri Bilozerchev, USSR	19.95
1992	Vitaly Scherbo, Unified Team	9.925
1996	Donghua Li, Switzerland	9.875
2000	Marius Urzica, Romania	9.862
2004	Haibin Teng, China	9.837

RINGS

		Pts
1896	Ioannis Mitropoulos, Greece	—
1904	Hermann Glass, United States	45
1924	Francesco Martino, Italy	21.553
1928	Leon Stukelj, Yugoslavia	19.25
1932	George Gulack, United States	18.97
1936	Alois Hudec, Czechoslovakia	19.433
1948	Karl Frei, Switzerland	19.80
1952	Grant Shaginyan, USSR	19.75
1956	Albert Azaryan, USSR	19.35
1960	Albert Azaryan, USSR	19.725
1964	Takuji Haytta, Japan	19.475
1968	Akinori Nakayama, Japan	19.45
1972	Akinori Nakayama, Japan	19.35
1976	Nikolai Andrianov, USSR	19.65
1980	Aleksandr Dityatin, USSR	19.875
1984	Koji Gushiken, Japan	19.85
1988	Holger Behrendt, E Germany	19.925
1992	Vitaly Scherbo, Unified Team	9.937
1996	Yuri Chechi, Italy	9.887
2000	Szilveszter Csollany, Hungary	9.862
2004	Dimosthenis Tampakos, Greece	9.862

FLOOR EXERCISE

		Pts
1932	Istvan Pelle, Hungary	9.60
1936	Georges Miez, Switzerland	18.666

ALL-AROUND

		Pts
1952	Maria Gorokhovskaya, USSR	76.78
1956	Larissa Latynina, USSR	74.933
1960	Larissa Latynina, USSR	77.031
1964	Vera Caslavska, Czechoslovakia	77.564
1968	Vera Caslavska, Czechoslovakia	78.25
1972	Lyudmila Tousischeva, USSR	77.025
1976	Nadia Comaneci, Romania	79.275
1980	Yelena Davydova, USSR	79.15
1984	Mary Lou Retton, United States	79.175
1988	Yelena Shushunova, USSR	79.662
1992	Tatiana Gutsu, Unified Team	39.737
1996	Lilia Podkopayeva, Ukraine	39.255
2000	Simona Amanar, Romania	38.642
2004	Carly Patterson, United States	38.387

FLOOR EXERCISE (CONT.)

		Pts
1948	Ferenc Pataki, Hungary	19.35
1952	K. William Thoresson, Sweden	19.25
1956	Valentin Muratov, USSR	19.20
1960	Nobuyuki Aihara, Japan	19.45
1964	Franco Menichelli, Italy	19.45
1968	Sawao Kato, Japan	19.475
1972	Nikolai Andrianov, USSR	19.175
1976	Nikolai Andrianov, USSR	19.45
1980	Roland Brückner, E Germany	19.75
1984	Li Ning, China	19.925
1988	Sergei Kharkov, USSR	19.925
1992	Li Xiaoshuang, China	9.925
1996	Ioannis Melissanidis, Greece	9.850
2000	Igors Vihrovs, Latvia	9.812
2004	Kyle Shewfelt, Canada	9.787

TEAM COMBINED EXERCISES

		Pts
1904	Turngemeinde Philadelphia	374.43
1906	Norway	19.00
1908	Sweden	438
1912	Italy	265.75
1920	Italy	359.855
1924	Italy	839.058
1928	Switzerland	1718.625
1932	Italy	541.850
1936	Germany	657.430
1948	Finland	1358.30
1952	USSR	574.40
1956	USSR	568.25
1960	Japan	575.20
1964	Japan	577.95
1968	Japan	575.90
1972	Japan	571.25
1976	Japan	576.85
1980	USSR	598.60
1984	United States	591.40
1988	USSR	593.35
1992	Unified Team	585.45
1996	Russia	576.778
2000	China	231.919
2004	Japan	173.821

Women

VAULT

		Pts
1952	Yekaterina Kalinchuk, USSR	19.20
1956	Larissa Latynina, USSR	18.833
1960	Margarita Nikolayeva, USSR	19.316
1964	Vera Caslavska, Czechoslovakia	19.483
1968	Vera Caslavska, Czechoslovakia	19.775
1972	Karin Janz, E Germany	19.525
1976	Nelli Kim, USSR	19.80
1980	Natalya Shaposhnikova, USSR	19.725
1984	Ecaterina Szabo, Romania	19.875
1988	Svetlana Boginskaya, USSR	19.905
1992	Henrietta Oñodi, Hungary	9.925
	Lavinia Milosovici, Romania	9.925
1996	Simona Amanar, Romania	9.825
2000	Yelena Zamolodtchikova, Russia	9.731
2004	Monica Rosu, Romania	9.656

GYMNASTICS (Cont.)
Women (Cont.)

UNEVEN BARS

	Pts
1952 .....Margit Korondi, Hungary	19.40
1956 .....Agnes Keleti, Hungary	18.966
1960 ....Polina Astakhova, USSR	19.616
1964 ....Polina Astakhova, USSR	19.332
1968 ....Vera Caslavska, Czechoslovakia	19.65
1972 ....Karin Janz, E Germany	19.675
1976 ....Nadia Comaneci, Romania	20.00
1980 .....Maxi Gnauck, E Germany	19.875
1984 .....Ma Yanhong, China	19.95
1988 .....Daniela Silivas, Romania	20.00
1992 .....Lu Li, China	10.00
1996 .....Svetlana Khorkina, Russia	9.850
2000 .....Svetlana Khorkina, Russia	9.862
2004 .....Emilie Lepennec, France	9.687

BALANCE BEAM

	Pts
1952 .....Nina Bocharova, USSR	19.22
1956 .....Agnes Keleti, Hungary	18.80
1960 .....Eva Bosakova, Czechoslovakia	19.283
1964 .....Vera Caslavska, Czechoslovakia	19.449
1968 .....Natalya Kuchinskaya, USSR	19.65
1972 .....Olga Korbut, USSR	19.40
1976 .....Nadia Comaneci, Romania	19.95
1980 .....Nadia Comaneci, Romania	19.80
1984 .....Simona Pauca, Romania	19.80
1988 .....Daniela Silivas, Romania	19.924
1992 .....Tatiana Lisenko, Unified Team	9.975
1996 .....Shannon Miller, United States	9.862
2000 .....Xuan Li, China	9.825
2004 .....Catalina Ponor, Romania	9.787

FLOOR EXERCISE

	Pts
1952 .....Agnes Keleti, Hungary	19.36
1956 .....Agnes Keleti, Hungary	18.733
1960 .....Larissa Latynina, USSR	19.583
1964 .....Larissa Latynina, USSR	19.599
1968 .....Vera Caslavska, Czechoslovakia	19.675
1972 .....Olga Korbut, USSR	19.575
1976 .....Nelli Kim, USSR	19.85

FLOOR EXERCISE (Cont.)

	Pts
1980 .....Nadia Comaneci, Romania	19.875
1984 .....Ecaterina Szabo, Romania	19.975
1988 .....Daniela Silivas, Romania	19.937
1992 ....Lavinia Milosovici, Romania	10.00
1996 ....Lilia Podkopayeva, Ukraine	9.887
2000 ....Yelena Zamolodtchikova, Russia	9.850
2004 ....Catalina Ponor, Romania	9.750

TEAM COMBINED EXERCISES

	Pts
1928 ....The Netherlands	316.75
1932 ....Not held	
1936 ....Germany	506.50
1948 ....Czechoslovakia	445.45
1952 ....USSR	527.03
1956 ....USSR	444.800
1960 ....USSR	382.320
1964 ....USSR	280.890
1968 ....USSR	382.85
1972 ....USSR	380.50
1976 ....USSR	466.00
1980 ....USSR	394.90
1984 ....Romania	392.02
1988 ....USSR	395.475
1992 ....Unified Team	395.666
1996 ....United States	389.225
2000 ....Romania	154.608
2004 ....Romania	114.283

RHYTHMIC ALL-AROUND

	Pts
1984 .....Lori Fung, Canada	57.95
1988 .....Marina Lobach, USSR	60.00
1992 .....A. Timoshenko, Unified Team	59.037
1996 .....E. Serebrianskaya, Ukraine	39.683
2000 .....Yulia Barsukova, Russia	39.632
2004 .....Alina Kabaeva, Russia	108.400

RHYTHMIC TEAM COMBINED EXERCISES

	Pts
1996 .....Spain	38.933
2000 .....Russia	39.500
2004 .....China	249.750

SOCCER
Men

1900 .....Great Britain	1928 .....Uruguay	1964 .....Hungary	1988 .....Soviet Union
1904 .....Canada	1936 .....Italy	1968 .....Hungary	1992 .....Spain
1908 .....Great Britain	1948 .....Sweden	1972 .....Poland	1996 .....Nigeria
1912 .....Great Britain	1952 .....Hungary	1976 .....E Germany	2000 .....Cameroon
1920 .....Belgium	1956 .....Soviet Union	1980 .....Czechoslovakia	2004 .....Argentina
1924 .....Uruguay	1960 .....Yugoslavia	1984 .....France	

Women

1996 ....United States	
2000 ....Norway	
2004 ....United States	

BIATHLON
Men

10 KILOMETERS
1980	Frank Ullrich, E Germany	32:10.69
1984	Eirik Kvalfoss, Norway	30:53.8
1988	Frank-Peter Rötsch, W Germany	25:08.1
1992	Mark Kirchner, Germany	26:02.3
1994	Sergei Tchepikov, Russia	28:07.0
1998	Ole Einar Bjorndalen, Norway	27:16.2
2002	Ole Einar Bjorndalen, Norway	24:51.3

20 KILOMETERS
1960	Klas Lestander, Sweden	1:33:21.6
1964	Vladimir Melyanin, Soviet Union	1:20:26.8
1968	Magnar Solberg, Norway	1:13:45.9
1972	Magnar Solberg, Norway	1:15:55.5
1976	Nikolay Kruglov, Soviet Union	1:14:12.26
1980	Anatoliy Alyabiev, Soviet Union	1:08:16.31
1984	Peter Angerer, W Germany	1:11:52.7
1988	Frank-Peter Rötsch, W Germany	56:33.3

20 KILOMETERS *(Cont.)*
1992	Evgueni Redkine, Unified Team	57:34.4
1994	Sergei Tarasov, Russia	57:25.3
1998	Halvard Hanevold, Norway	56:16.4
2002	Ole Einar Bjordalen, Norway	51:03.3

4 X 7.5-KILOMETER RELAY
1968	Soviet Union	2:13:02.4
1972	Soviet Union	1:51:44.92
1976	Soviet Union	1:57:55.64
1980	Soviet Union	1:34:03.27
1984	Soviet Union	1:38:51.7
1988	Soviet Union	1:22:30.0
1992	Germany	1:24:43.5
1994	Germany	1:30:22.1
1998	Germany	1:19:43.3
2002	Norway	1:23:42.3

12.5 KILOMETERS PURSUIT
2002	Ole Einar Bjorndalen	1:23:42.3

Women

7.5 KILOMETERS
1992	Antissa Restzova, Unified Team	24:29.2
1994	Myriam Bedard, Canada	26:08.8
1998	Galina Koukleva, Russia	23:08.0
2002	Kati Wilhemn, Germany	20:41.4

10 KILOMETERS PURSUIT
2002	Olga Pyleva, Russia	31:07.7

15 KILOMETERS
1992	Antje Misersky, Germany	51:47.2
1994	Myriam Bedard, Canada	52:06.6
1998	Ekaterina Dofovska, Bulgaria	54:52.0
2002	Andrea Henkel, Germany	47:29.1

3 X 7.5-KILOMETER RELAY
1992	France	1:15:55.6
1994	Russia	1:47:19.5
1998	Germany	1:40:13.6
2002	Germany	1:27:55.0

BOBSLED

4-MAN
1924	Switzerland (Eduard Scherrer)	5:45.54
1928	United States (William Fiske) (5-man)	3:20.50
1932	United States (William Fiske)	7:53.68
1936	Switzerland (Pierre Musy)	5:19.85
1948	United States (Francis Tyler)	5:20.10
1952	Germany (Andreas Ostler)	5:07.84
1956	Switzerland (Franz Kapus)	5:10.44
1960	Not held	
1964	Canada (Victor Emery)	4:14.46
1968	Italy (Eugenio Monti) (2 runs)	2:17.39
1972	Switzerland (Jean Wicki)	4:43.07
1976	E Germany (Meinhard Nehmer)	3:40.43
1980	E Germany (Meinhard Nehmer)	3:59.92
1984	E Germany (Wolfgang Hoppe)	3:20.22
1988	Switzerland (Ekkehard Fasser)	3:47.51
1992	Austria (Ingo Appelt)	3:53.90
1994	Germany (Harold Czudaj)	3:27.78
1998	Germany (Christoph Langen)	2:39.41
2002	Germany (Andre Lange)	3:10.11

Note: Driver in parentheses.

2-MAN
1932	United States (Hubert Stevens)	8:14.74
1936	United States (Ivan Brown)	5:29.29
1948	Switzerland (Felix Endrich)	5:29.20
1952	Germany (Andreas Ostler)	5:24.54
1956	Italy (Lamberto Dalla Costa)	5:30.14
1960	Not held	
1964	Great Britain (Anthony Nash)	4:21.90
1968	Italy (Eugenio Monti)	4:41.54
1972	W Germany (Wolfgang Zimmerer)	4:57.07
1976	E Germany (Meinhard Nehmer)	3:44.42
1980	Switzerland (Erich Schärer)	4:09.36
1984	E Germany (Wolfgang Hoppe)	3:25.56
1988	USSR (Janis Kipours)	3:53.48
1992	Switzerland (Gustav Weder)	4:03.26
1994	Switzerland (Gustav Weder)	3:30.81
1998	Canada (Pierre Lueders)	3:37.24
	Italy (Guenther Huber)	3:37.24
2002	Germany (Martin Langen)	3:10:11

WOMEN
2-PERSON
2002	United States (Jill Bakken)	1:37:76

Note: Driver in parentheses.

CURLING

Men

1998 .....Switzerland, Canada, Norway
2002 .....Norway, Canada, Switzerland
Note: Gold, silver, and bronze medals.

Women

1998 .....Canada, Denmark, Sweden
2002 .....Britain, Switzerland, Canada
Note: Gold, silver, and bronze medals.

ICE HOCKEY

Men

1920* ....Canada, United States, Czechoslovakia
1924 .....Canada, United States, Great Britain
1928 .....Canada, Sweden, Switzerland
1932 .....Canada, United States, Germany
1936 .....Great Britain, Canada, United States
1948 .....Canada, Czechoslovakia, Switzerland
1952 .....Canada, United States, Sweden
1956 .....USSR, United States, Canada
1960 .....United States, Canada, USSR
1964 .....USSR, Sweden, Czechoslovakia
1968 .....USSR, Czechoslovakia, Canada

1972 .....USSR, United States, Czechoslovakia
1976 .....USSR, Czechoslovakia, W Germany
1980 .....United States, USSR, Sweden
1984 .....USSR, Czechoslovakia, Sweden
1988 .....USSR, Finland, Sweden
1992 .....Unified Team, Canada, Czechoslovakia
1994 .....Sweden, Canada, Finland
1998 .....Czech Republic, Russia, Finland
2002 .....Canada, United States, Russia
*Competition held at Summer Games in Antwerp.
Note: Gold, silver, and bronze medals.

Women

1998 .....United States, Canada, Finland
2002 .....Canada, United States, Sweden

Note: Gold, silver, and bronze medals.

LUGE

Men

SINGLES		DOUBLES	
1964 .....Thomas Köhler, East Germany	3:26.77	1964 ....Austria	1:41.62
1968 .....Manfred Schmid, Austria	2:52.48	1968 ....E Germany	1:35.85
1972 .....Wolfgang Scheidel, W Germany	3:27.58	1972 ....E Germany	1:28.35
1976 .....Detlef Guenther, W Germany	3:27.688	1976 ....E Germany	1:25.604
1980 .....Bernhard Glass, W Germany	2:54.796	1980 ....E Germany	1:19.331
1984 .....Paul Hildgartner, Italy	3:04.258	1984 ....W Germany	1:23.620
1988 .....Jens Müller, W Germany	3:05.548	1988 ....E Germany	1:31.940
1992 .....Georg Hackl, Germany	3:02.363	1992 ....Germany	1:32.053
1994 .....Georg Hackl, Germany	3:21.571	1994 ....Italy	1:36.720
1998 .....Georg Hackl, Germany	3:18.44	1998 ....Germany	1:41.105
2002 .....Armin Zoeggeler, Italy	2:57.941	2002 ....Germany	1:26.082

Women

SINGLES		SINGLES (Cont.)	
1964 .....Ortrun Enderlein, Germany	3:24.67	1984 .....Steffi Martin, E Germany	2:46.570
1968 .....Erica Lechner, Italy	2:28.66	1988 .....Steffi Walter (Martin) E Germany	3:03.973
1972 .....Anna-Maria Müller, E Germany	2:59.18	1992 .....Doris Neuner, Austria	3:06.696
1976 .....Margit Schumann, E Germany	2:50.621	1994 .....Gerda Weissensteiner, Italy	3:15.517
1980 .....Vera Zozulya, USSR	2:36.537	1998 .....Silke Kraushaar, Germany	3:23.779
		2002 .....Sylke Otto, Germany	2:52.464

YET ANOTHER SIGN OF THE APOCALYPSE

*The USOC said it would sue the organizers
of the Ferret Olympics unless they dropped the
word Olympics from their event.*

FIGURE SKATING

Men

1908* ....Ulrich Salchow, Sweden
1920† ....Gillis Grafström, Sweden
1924 ....Gillis Grafström, Sweden
1928 ....Gillis Grafström, Sweden
1932 ....Karl Schäfer, Austria
1936 ....Karl Schäfer, Austria
1948 ....Dick Button, United States
1952 ....Dick Button, United States
1956 ....Hayes Alan Jenkins, United States
1960 ....David Jenkins, United States
1964 ....Manfred Schnelldorfer, W Germany
1968 ....Wolfgang Schwarz, Austria
1972 ....Ondrej Nepela, Czechoslovakia
1976 ....John Curry, Great Britain
1980 ....Robin Cousins, Great Britain
1984 ....Scott Hamilton, United States
1988 ....Brian Boitano, United States
1992 ....Victor Petrenko, Unified Team
1994 ....Alexei Urmanov, Russia
1998 ....Ilia Kulik, Russia
2002 ....Alexei Yagudin, Russia

*Competition held at Summer Games in London.
†Competition held at Summer Games in Antwerp.

Women

1908* ....Madge Syers, Great Britain
1920† ....Magda Julin, Sweden
1924 ....Herma Szabo-Planck, Austria
1928 ....Sonja Henie, Norway
1932 ....Sonja Henie, Norway
1936 ....Sonja Henie, Norway
1948 ....Barbara Ann Scott, Canada
1952 ....Jeanette Altwegg, Great Britain
1956 ....Tenley Albright, United States
1960 ....Carol Heiss, United States
1964 ....Sjoukje Dijkstra, Netherlands
1968 ....Peggy Fleming, United States
1972 ....Beatrix Schuba, Austria
1976 ....Dorothy Hamill, United States
1980 ....Anett Pötzsch, E Germany
1984 ....Katarina Witt, E Germany
1988 ....Katarina Witt, E Germany
1992 ....Kristi Yamaguchi, United States
1994 ....Oksana Baiul, Ukraine
1998 ....Tara Lipinski, United States
2002 ....Sarah Hughes, United States

Mixed

PAIRS

1908* ..Anna Hübler & Heinrich Burger, Germany
1920†..Ludovika & Walter Jakobsson, Finland
1924 ....Helene Engelmann & Alfred Berger, Austria
1928 ....Andree Joly & Pierre Brunet, France
1932 ....Andree Brunet (Joly) & Pierre Brunet, France
1936 ....Maxi Herber & Ernst Baier, Germany
1948 ....Micheline Lannoy & Pierre Baugniet, Belgium
1952 ....Ria Falk and Paul Falk, W Germany
1956 ....Elisabeth Schwartz & Kurt Oppelt, Austria
1960 ....Barbara Wagner & Robert Paul, Canada
1964 ....Lyudmila Beloussova & Oleg Protopopov, USSR
1968 ....Lyudmila Beloussova & Oleg Protopopov, USSR
1972 ....Irina Rodnina & Alexei Ulanov, USSR
1976 ....Irina Rodnina & Aleksandr Zaitzev, USSR
1980 ....Irina Rodnina & Aleksandr Zaitzev, USSR
1984 ....Elena Valova & Oleg Vasiliev, USSR
1988 ....Ekaterina Gordeeva & Sergei Grinkov, USSR
1992 ....Natalia Michkouteniok & Artour Dmitriev, Unified Team
1994 ....Ekaterina Gordeeva & Sergei Grinkov, Russia
1998 ....Oksana Kazakova & Artur Dmitriev, Russia
2002 ....Elena Berezhnaya & Anton Sikharulidze, Russia/ Jamie Sale & David Pelletier, Canada

DANCE

1976 ....Lyudmila Pakhomova & Aleksandr Gorshkov, USSR
1980 ....Natalia Linichuk & Gennadi Karponosov, USSR
1984 ....Jayne Torvill & Christopher Dean, Great Britain
1988 ....Natalia Bestemianova & Andrei Bukin, USSR
1992 ....Marina Klimova & Sergei Ponomarenko, Unified Team
1994 ....Oksana Grishuk & Evgeny Platov, Russia
1998 ....Pasha Grishuk & Evgeny Platov, Russia
2002 ....Marina Anissina & Gwendal Peizeralt, France

*Competition held at Summer Games in London.
†Competition held at Summer Games in Antwerp.

SKELETON

Men

1928 .....Jennison Heaton, United States	3:01.8
1948 .....Nino Bibbia, Italy	5:23.2
2002 .....Jim Shea Jr., United States	1:41.96

Women

2002 .....Tristan Gale, United States	1:45.11

SPEED SKATING

Men

500 METERS

1924	Charles Jewtraw, United States	44.0
1928	Clas Thunberg, Finland	43.4 OR
	Bernt Evensen, Norway	43.4 OR
1932	John Shea, United States	43.4 EOR
1936	Ivar Ballangrud, Norway	43.4 EOR
1948	Finn Helgesen, Norway	43.1 OR
1952	Kenneth Henry, United States	43.2
1956	Yevgeny Grishin, USSR	40.2 EWR
1960	Yevgeny Grishin, USSR	40.2 EWR
1964	Terry McDermott, United States	40.1 OR
1968	Erhard Keller, W Germany	40.3
1972	Erhard Keller, W Germany	39.44 OR
1976	Yevgeny Kulikov, USSR	39.17 OR
1980	Eric Heiden, United States	38.03 OR
1984	Sergei Fokichev, USSR	38.19
1988	Uwe-Jens Mey, E Germany	36.45 WR
1992	Uwe-Jens Mey, E Germany	37.14
1994	Aleksandr Golubev, Russia	36.33
1998	Hiroyasu Shimizu, Japan (second run)	35.59 OR
2002	Casey FitzRandolph, U.S.	1:09.23*

1,000 METERS

1976	Peter Mueller, United States	1:19.32
1980	Eric Heiden, United States	1:15.18 OR
1984	Gaetan Boucher, Canada	1:15.80
1988	Nikolai Gulyaev, USSR	1:13.03 OR
1992	Olaf Zinke, Germany	1:14.85
1994	Dan Jansen, United States	1:12.43 WR
1998	Ids Postma, Netherlands	1:10.64 OR
2002	Gerard van Velde, Netherlands	1:07.18

1,500 METERS

1924	Clas Thunberg, Finland	2:20.8
1928	Clas Thunberg, Finland	2:21.1
1932	John Shea, United States	2:57.5
1936	Charles Mathisen, Norway	2:19.2 OR
1948	Sverre Farstad, Norway	2:17.6 OR
1952	Hjalmar Andersen, Norway	2:20.4
1956	Yevgeny Grishin, USSR	2:08.6 WR
	Yuri Mikhailov, USSR	2:08.6 WR
1960	Roald Aas, Norway	2:10.4
	Yevgeny Grishin, USSR	2:10.4
1964	Ants Anston, USSR	2:10.3
1968	Cornelis Verkerk, Netherlands	2:03.4 OR
1972	Ard Schenk, Netherlands	2:02.96 OR
1976	Jan Egil Storholt, Norway	1:59.38 OR
1980	Eric Heiden, United States	1:55.44 OR

1,500 METERS (Cont.)

1984	Gaetan Boucher, Canada	1:58.36
1988	Andre Hoffmann, E Germany	1:52.06 WR
1992	Johann Olav Koss, Norway	1:54.81
1994	Johann Olav Koss, Norway	1:51.29 WR
1998	Aadne Sondral, Norway	1:47.87 WR
2002	Derek Parra, United States	1:43.95

5,000 METERS

1924	Clas Thunberg, Finland	8:39.0
1928	Ivar Ballangrud, Norway	8:50.5
1932	Irving Jaffee, United States	9:40.8
1936	Ivar Ballangrud, Norway	8:19.6 OR
1948	Reidar Liaklev, Norway	8:29.4
1952	Hjalmar Andersen, Norway	8:10.6 OR
1956	Boris Shilkov, USSR	7:48.7 OR
1960	Viktor Kosichkin, USSR	7:51.3
1964	Knut Johannesen, Norway	7:38.4 OR
1968	Fred Anton Maier, Norway	7:22.4 WR
1972	Ard Schenk, Netherlands	7:23.61
1976	Sten Stensen, Norway	7:24.48
1980	Eric Heiden, United States	7:02.29 OR
1984	Sven Tomas Gustafson, Sweden	7:12.28
1988	Tomas Gustafson, Sweden	6:44.63 WR
1992	Geir Karlstad, Norway	6:59.97
1994	Johann Olav Koss, Norway	6:34.96 WR
1998	Gianni Romme, Netherlands	6:22.20 WR
2002	Jochem Uytdehaage, Net	6:41.66

10,000 METERS

1924	Julius Skutnabb, Finland	18:04.8
1928	Not held, thawing of ice	
1932	Irving Jaffee, United States	19:13.6
1936	Ivar Ballangrud, Norway	17:24.3 OR
1948	Ake Seyffarth, Sweden	17:26.3
1952	Hjalmar Andersen, Norway	16:45.8 OR
1956	Sigvard Ericsson, Sweden	16:35.9 OR
1960	Knut Johannesen, Norway	15:46.6 WR
1964	Jonny Nilsson, Sweden	15:50.1
1968	Johnny Höglin, Sweden	15:23.6 OR
1972	Ard Schenk, Netherlands	15:01.35 OR
1976	Piet Kleine, Netherlands	14:50.59 OR
1980	Eric Heiden, United States	14:28.13 WR
1984	Igor Malkov, USSR	14:39.90
1988	Tomas Gustafson, Sweden	13:48.20 WR
1992	Bart Veldkamp, Netherlands	14:12.12
1994	Johann Olav Koss, Norway	13:30.55 WR
1998	Gianni Romme, Netherlands	13:15.33 WR
2002	Jochem Uytdehaage, Neth	12:58.92 WR

Women

500 METERS

1960	Helga Haase, E Germany	45.9
1964	Lydia Skoblikova, USSR	45.0 OR
1968	Lyudmila Titova, USSR	46.1
1972	Anne Henning, United States	43.33 OR
1976	Sheila Young, United States	42.76 OR
1980	Karin Enke, E Germany	41.78 OR
1984	Christa Rothenburger, E Germany	41.02 OR

500 METERS (Cont.)

1988	Bonnie Blair, United States	39.10 WR
1992	Bonnie Blair, United States	40.33
1994	Bonnie Blair, United States	39.25
1998	Catriona LeMay Doan, Canada (second run)	38.21 OR
2002	Catriona LeMay, Canada	1:14.75*

Note: OR=Olympic Record; WR=World Record; EOR=Equals Olympic Record; EWR=Equals World Record; WB=World Best.

*Combined time.

SPEED SKATING (Cont.)

Women (Cont.)

1,000 METERS

1960	Klara Guseva, USSR	1:34.1
1964	Lydia Skoblikova, USSR	1:33.2 OR
1968	Carolina Geijssen, Netherlands	1:32.6 OR
1972	Monika Pflug, W Germany	1:31.40 OR
1976	Tatiana Averina, USSR	1:28.43 OR
1980	Natalya Petruseva, USSR	1:24.10 OR
1984	Karin Enke, E Germany	1:21.61 OR
1988	Christa Rothenburger, E Germany	1:17.65 WR
1992	Bonnie Blair, United States	1:21.90
1994	Bonnie Blair, United States	1:18.74
1998	Marianne Timmer, Netherlands	1:16.51 OR
2002	Chris Witty, United States	1:13.83

1,500 METERS

1960	Lydia Skoblikova, USSR	2:25.2 WR
1964	Lydia Skoblikova, USSR	2:22.6 OR
1968	Kaija Mustonen, Finland	2:22.4 OR
1972	Dianne Holum, United States	2:20.85 OR
1976	Galina Stepanskaya, USSR	2:16.58 OR
1980	Anne Borckink, Netherlands	2:10.95 OR
1984	Karin Enke, E Germany	2:03.42 WR
1988	Yvonne van Gennip, Netherlands	2:00.68 OR
1992	Jacqueline Boerner, Germany	2:05.87
1994	Emese Hunyady, Austria	2:02.19
1998	Marianne Timmer, Netherlands	1:57.58 WR

1,500 METERS (Cont.)

2002	Anni Friesinger, Germany	1:54.02

3,000 METERS

1960	Lydia Skoblikova, USSR	5:14.3
1964	Lydia Skoblikova, USSR	5:14.9
1968	Johanna Schut, Netherlands	4:56.2 OR
1972	Christina Baas-Kaiser, Netherlands	4:52.14 OR
1976	Tatiana Averina, USSR	4:45.19 OR
1980	Bjorg Eva Jensen, Norway	4:32.13 OR
1984	Andrea Schöne, E Germany	4:24.79 OR
1988	Yvonne van Gennip, Netherlands	4:11.94 WR
1992	Gunda Niemann, Germany	4:19.90
1994	Svetlana Bazhanova, Russia	4:17.43
1998	Gunda Niemann-Stirnemann, Germany	4:07.29 OR
2002	Claudia Pechstein, Germany	3:57.70

5,000 METERS

1988	Yvonne van Gennip, Netherlands	7:14.13 WR
1992	Gunda Niemann, Germany	7:31.57
1994	Claudia Pechstein, Germany	7:14.37
1998	Claudia Pechstein, Germany	6:59.61 WR
2002	Claudia Pechstein, Germany	6:46.91 WR

SHORT TRACK SPEED SKATING

Men

500 METERS

1994	Chae Ji-Hoon, S Korea	43.54
1998	Takafumi Nishitani, Japan	42.862
2002	Marc Gagnon, Canada	41.802 OR

1,000 METERS

1992	Kim Ki-Hoon, S Korea	1:30.76
1994	Kim Ki-Hoon, S Korea	1:34.57
1998	Kim Dong Sung, S Korea	1:32.375
2002	Steve Bradbury, Austrailia	1:29.109

1,500 METERS

2002	Apolo Anton Ohno, United States	2:18.541

5,000-METER RELAY

1992	Korea	7:14.02
1994	Italy	7:11.74
1998	Canada	7:06.075
2002	Canada	6:51.579

Women

500 METERS

1992	Cathy Turner, United States	47.04
1994	Cathy Turner, United States	45.98
1998	Annie Perreault, Canada	46.568
2002	Yang Yang, China	44.187

1,000 METERS

1994	Chun Lee Kyung, S Korea	1:36.87
1998	Chun Lee Kyung, S Korea	1:42.776
2002	Yang A. Yang, China	1:36.391

1,500 METERS

2002	Ko Gi-Hyun, Korea	2:31.581

3,000-METER RELAY

1992	Canada	4:36.62
1994	S Korea	4:26.64
1998	S Korea	4:16.260
2002	S Korea	4:12.793

ALPINE SKIING

Men

DOWNHILL

1948	Henri Oreiller, France	2:55.0
1952	Zeno Colo, Italy	2:30.8
1956	Anton Sailer, Austria	2:52.2
1960	Jean Vuarnet, France	2:06.0
1964	Egon Zimmermann, Austria	2:18.16
1968	Jean-Claude Killy, France	1:59.85
1972	Bernhard Russi, Switzerland	1:51.43
1976	Franz Klammer, Austria	1:45.73
1980	Leonhard Stock, Austria	1:45.50
1984	Bill Johnson, United States	1:45.59
1988	Pirmin Zurbriggen, Switzerland	1:59.63
1992	Patrick Ortlieb, Austria	1:50.37
1994	Tommy Moe, United States	1:45.75
1998	Jean-Luc Crétier, France	1:50.11
2002	Fritz Strobl, Austria	1:39.13

SLALOM

1948	Edi Reinalter, Switzerland	2:10.3
1952	Othmar Schneider, Austria	2:00.0
1956	Anton Sailer, Austria	3:14.7
1960	Ernst Hinterseer, Austria	2:08.9
1964	Josef Stiegler, Austria	2:11.13
1968	Jean-Claude Killy, France	1:39.73
1972	F. Fernandez Ochoa, Spain	1:49.27
1976	Piero Gros, Italy	2:03.29
1980	Ingemar Stenmark, Sweden	1:44.26
1984	Phil Mahre, United States	1:39.41
1988	Alberto Tomba, Italy	1:39.47
1992	Finn Christian Jagge, Norway	1:44.39
1994	Thomas Stangassinger, Austria	2:02.02
1998	Hans-Petter Buraas, Norway	1:49.31
2002	Jean-Pierre Vidal, France	1:41.06

ALPINE SKIING

Men (Cont.)

GIANT SLALOM		
1952	Stein Eriksen, Norway	2:25.0
1956	Anton Sailer, Austria	3:00.1
1960	Roger Staub, Switzerland	1:48.3
1964	Francois Bonlieu, France	1:46.71
1968	Jean-Claude Killy, France	3:29.28
1972	Gustav Thöni, Italy	3:09.62
1976	Heini Hemmi, Switzerland	3:26.97
1980	Ingemar Stenmark, Sweden	2:40.74
1984	Max Julen, Switzerland	2:41.18
1988	Alberto Tomba, Italy	2:06.37
1992	Alberto Tomba, Italy	2:06.98
1994	Markus Wasmeier, Germany	2:52.46
1998	Hermann Maier, Austria	2:38.51
2002	Stephan Eberharter, Austria	2:23.28

SUPER GIANT SLALOM		
1988	Franck Piccard, France	1:39.66
1992	Kjetil André Aamodt, Norway	1:13.04
1994	Markus Wasmeier, Germany	1:32.53
1998	Hermann Maier, Austria	1:34.82
2002	Kjetil André Aamodt, Norway	1:21.58

COMBINED*		
1936	Franz Pfnür, Germany	99.25
1948	Henri Oreiller, France	3.27
1988	Hubert Strolz, Austria	36.55
1992	Josef Polig, Italy	14.58
1994	Lasse Kjus, Norway	3:17.53
1998	Mario Reiter, Austria	3:08.06
2002	Kjetil André Aamodt, Norway	3:17.56

Women

DOWNHILL		
1948	Hedy Schlunegger, Switzerland	2:28.3
1952	Trude Jochum-Beiser, Austria	1:47.1
1956	Madeleine Berthod, Switzerland	1:40.7
1960	Heidi Biebl, W Germany	1:37.6
1964	Christl Haas, Austria	1:55.39
1968	Olga Pall, Austria	1:40.87
1972	Marie-Theres Nadig, Switzerland	1:36.68
1976	Rosi Mittermaier, W Germany	1:46.16
1980	Annemarie Moser-Pröll, Austria	1:37.52
1984	Michela Figini, Switzerland	1:13.36
1988	Marina Kiehl, W Germany	1:25.86
1992	Kerrin Lee-Gartner, Canada	1:52.55
1994	Katja Seizinger, Germany	1:35.93
1998	Katja Seizinger, Germany	1:28.89
2002	Carole Montillet, France	1:39.56

SLALOM		
1948	Gretchen Fraser, United States	1:57.2
1952	Andrea Mead Lawrence, United States	2:10.6
1956	Renee Colliard, Switzerland	1:52.3
1960	Anne Heggtveigt, Canada	1:49.6
1964	Christine Goitschel, France	1:29.86
1968	Marielle Goitschel, France	1:25.86
1972	Barbara Cochran, United States	1:31.24
1976	Rosi Mittermaier, W Germany	1:30.54
1980	Hanni Wenzel, Liechtenstein	1:25.09
1984	Paoletta Magoni, Italy	1:36.47
1988	Vreni Schneider, Switzerland	1:36.69
1992	Petra Kronberger, Austria	1:32.68
1994	Vreni Schneider, Switzerland	1:56.01
1998	Hilde Gerg, Germany	1:32.40
2002	Janica Kostelic, Croatia	1:46.10

GIANT SLALOM		
1952	Andrea Mead Lawrence, U.S.	2:06.8
1956	Ossi Reichert, W Germany	1:56.5
1960	Yvonne Rüegg, Switzerland	1:39.9
1964	Marielle Goitschel, France	1:52.24
1968	Nancy Greene, Canada	1:51.97
1972	Marie-Theres Nadig, Switzerland	1:29.90
1976	Kathy Kreiner, Canada	1:29.13
1980	Hanni Wenzel, Liechtenstein (2 runs)	2:41.66
1984	Debbie Armstrong, United States	2:20.98
1988	Vreni Schneider, Switzerland	2:06.49
1992	Pernilla Wiberg, Sweden	2:12.74
1994	Deborah Compagnoni, Italy	2:30.97
1998	Deborah Compagnoni, Italy	2:50.59
2002	Janica Kostelic, Croatia	2:30.01

SUPER GIANT SLALOM		
1988	Sigrid Wolf, Austria	1:19.03
1992	Deborah Compagnoni, Italy	1:21.22
1994	Diann Roffe-Steinrotter, U.S.	1:22.15
1998	Picabo Street, United States	1:18.02
2002	Daniela Ceccarelli, Italy	1:13.59

COMBINED*		
1988	Anita Wachter, Austria	29.25
1992	Petra Kronberger, Austria	2.55
1994	Pernilla Wiberg, Sweden	3:05.16
1998	Katja Seizinger, Germany	2:40.74
2002	Janica Kostelic, Croatia	2:43.28

*Beginning in 1994, scoring was based on time.

FREESTYLE SKIING

Men

MOGULS		Pts
1992	Edgar Grospiron, France	25.81
1994	Jean-Luc Brassard, Canada	27.24
1998	Jonny Moseley, United States	26.93
2002	Janne Lahtela, Finland	27.97

AERIALS		Pts
1994	Andreas Schoenbaechler, Switz.	234.67
1998	Eric Bergoust, United States	255.64
2002	Ales Valenta, Czech Republic	257.02

Women

MOGULS		Pts
1992	Donna Weinbrecht, United States	23.69
1994	Stine Lise Hattestad, Norway	25.97
1998	Tae Satoya, Japan	25.06
2002	Kari Traa, Norway	25.94

AERIALS		Pts
1994	Lina Cherjazova, Uzbekistan	166.84
1998	Nikki Stone, United States	193.00
2002	Alisa Camplin, Australia	193.47

NORDIC SKIING

Men

10 KILOMETERS CLASSICAL STYLE

1992	Vegard Ulvang, Norway	27:36.0
1994	Bjørn Dæhlie, Norway	24:20.1
1998	Bjørn Dæhlie, Norway	27:24.5

15 KILOMETERS CLASSICAL STYLE

1924	Thorlief Haug, Norway	1:14:31.0*
1928	Johan Gröttumsbraaten, Norway	1:37:01.0†
1932	Sven Utterström, Sweden	1:23:07.0‡
1936	Erik-August Larsson, Sweden	1:14:38.0*
1948	Martin Lundström, Sweden	1:13:50.0*
1952	Hallgeir Brenden, Norway	1:01:34.0*
1956	Hallgeir Brenden, Norway	49:39.0
1960	Haakon Brusveen, Norway	51:55.5
1964	Eero Mantyränta, Finland	50:54.1
1968	Harald Grönningen, Norway	47:54.2
1972	Sven-Ake Lundback, Sweden	45:28.24
1976	Nikolay Bajukov, Unified Team	43:58.47
1980	Thomas Wassberg, Sweden	41:57.63
1984	Gunde Swan, Sweden	41:25.6
1988	Michael Deviatyarov, USSR	41:18.9
2002	Andrus Veerpalu, Estonia	37:07.4

*Distance was 18 km. †Distance was 19.7 km.

‡Distance was 18.2 km.

15 KILOMETERS PURSUIT FREESTYLE

1992	Bjørn Dæhlie, Norway	1:05:37.9
1994	Bjørn Dæhlie, Norway	1:00:08.8
1998	Thomas Alsgaard, Norway	1:07:01.7

30 KILOMETERS CLASSICAL STYLE

1956	Veikko Hakulinen, Finland	1:44:06.0
1960	Sixten Jernberg, Sweden	1:51:03.9
1964	Eero Mantyränta, Finland	1:30:50.7
1968	Franco Nones, Italy	1:35:39.2
1972	Viaceslav Vedenine, USSR	1:36:31.2
1976	Sergei Savelyev, USSR	1:30:29.38
1980	Nikolai Simyatov, USSR	1:27:02.80
1984	Nikolai Simyatov, USSR	1:28:56.3
1988	Alexey Prokororov, USSR	1:24:26.3
1992	Vegard Ulvang, Norway	1:22:27.8
1994	Thomas Alsgaard, Norway	1:12:26.4
1998	Mika Myllylae, Finland	1:33:55.8

50 KILOMETERS FREESTYLE

1924	Thorleif Haug, Norway	3:44:32.0
1928	Per Erik Hedlund, Sweden	4:52:03.0
1932	Veli Saarinen, Finland	4:28:00.0
1936	Elis Wiklund, Sweden	3:30:11.0
1948	Nils Karlsson, Sweden	3:47:48.0
1952	Veikko Hakulinen, Finland	3:33:33.0
1956	Sixten Jernberg, Sweden	2:50:27.0
1960	Kalevi Hämäläinen, Finland	2:59:06.3
1964	Sixten Jernberg, Sweden	2:43:52.6
1968	Olle Ellefsaeter, Norway	2:28:45.8
1972	Paal Tyldrum, Norway	2:43:14.75
1976	Ivar Formo, Norway	2:37:30.50
1980	Nikolai Simyatov, USSR	2:27:24.60
1984	Thomas Wassberg, Sweden	2:15:55.8
1988	Gunde Svan, Sweden	2:04:30.9
1992	Bjørn Dæhlie, Norway	2:03:41.5
1994	Vladimir Smirnov, Kazakhstan	2:07:20.3
1998	Bjørn Dæhlie, Norway	2:05:08.2

4 X 10-KILOMETER RELAY MIXED STYLE

1936	Finland	2:41:33.0
1948	Sweden	2:32:80.0
1952	Finland	2:20:16.0
1956	USSR	2:15:30.0
1960	Finland	2:18:45.6
1964	Sweden	2:18:34.6
1968	Norway	2:08:33.5
1972	USSR	2:04:47.94
1976	Finland	2:07:59.72
1980	USSR	1:57:03.46
1984	Sweden	1:55:06.3
1988	Sweden	1:43:58.6
1992	Norway	1:39:26.0
1994	Italy	1:41:15.0
1998	Norway	1:40:55.7
2002	Norway	1:32:45.5

SKI JUMPING (NORMAL HILL)

		Pts
1964	Veikko Kankkonen, Finland	229.90
1968	Jiri Raska, Czechoslovakia	216.5
1972	Yukio Kasaya, Japan	244.2
1976	Hans-Georg Aschenbach, E Germany	252.0
1980	Toni Innauer, Austria	266.3
1984	Jens Weissflog, E Germany	215.2
1988	Matti Nykänen, Finland	229.1
1992	Ernst Vettori, Austria	222.8
1994	Espen Bredesen, Norway	282.0
1998	Jani Soininen, Finland	234.5
2002	Simon Ammann, Switzerland	269.0

SKI JUMPING (LARGE HILL)

		Pts
1924	Jacob Tullin Thams, Norway	18.960
1928	Alf Andersen, Norway	19.208
1932	Birger Ruud, Norway	228.1
1936	Birger Ruud, Norway	232.0
1948	Petter Hugsted, Norway	228.1
1952	Arnfinn Bergmann, Norway	226.0
1956	Antti Hyvärinen, Finland	227.0
1960	Helmut Recknagel, E Germany	227.2
1964	Toralf Engan, Norway	230.70
1968	Vladimir Beloussov, USSR	231.3
1972	Wojciech Fortuna, Poland	219.9
1976	Karl Schnabl, Austria	234.8
1980	Jouko Tormanen, Finland	271.0
1984	Matti Nykänen, Finland	231.2
1988	Matti Nykänen, Finland	224.0
1992	Toni Nieminen, Finland	239.5
1994	Jens Weissflog, Germany	274.5
1998	Kazuyoshi Funaki, Japan	272.3
2002	Simon Amman, Switzerland	281.4

TEAM SKI JUMPING

		Pts
1988	Finland	634.4
1992	Finland	644.4
1994	Germany	970.1
1998	Japan	933.0
2002	Germany	974.1

NORDIC SKIING *(Cont.)*
Men *(Cont.)*

NORDIC COMBINED	Pts
1924....Thorleif Haug, Norway	18.906*
1928....Johan Gröttumsbraaten, Norway	17.833*
1932....Johan Gröttumsbraaten, Norway	446.0
1936....Oddbjörn Hagen, Norway	430.30
1948....Heikki Hasu, Finland	448.80
1952....Simon Slattvik, Norway	451.621
1956....Sverre Stenersen, Norway	455.0
1960....Georg Thoma, W Germany	457.952
1964....Tormod Knutsen, Norway	469.28
1968....Frantz Keller, W Germany	449.04
1972....Ulrich Wehling, E Germany	413.34
1976....Ulrich Wehling, E Germany	423.39
1980....Ulrich Wehling, E Germany	432.20
1984....Tom Sandberg, Norway	422.595

NORDIC COMBINED *(Cont.)*	Pts
1988....Hippolyt Kempf, Switzerland	432.230
1992....Fabrice Guy, France	426.47
1994....Fred B. Lundberg, Norway	457.970
1998....Bjarte Engen Vik, Norway	41:21.1†
2002....Samppa Lajunen, Finland	38:18.7

TEAM NORDIC COMBINED	
1988....W Germany	
1992....Japan	
1994....Japan	
1998....Norway	
2002....Finland	

SPRINT NORDIC COMBINED	
2002....Samppa Lajunen, Finland	123.8

* Different scoring system; 1924–1952 distance was 18 km; 1952–present, 15 km.

† Times in the cross-country race were not converted into points. According to the Gundersen Method, used since 1988, starting times in the race are staggered in proportion to points earned in the ski jumping segment of the event.

Women

1.5 KILOMETERS SPRINT	
2002....Julija Tchepalova, Russia	3:10.6

5 KILOMETERS PURSUIT	
2002....Olga Danilova, Russia	24:52.1

5 KILOMETERS CLASSICAL STYLE	
1964....Klaudia Boyarskikh, USSR	17:50.5
1968....Toini Gustafsson, Sweden	16:45.2
1972....Galina Kulakova, USSR	17:00.50
1976....Helena Takalo, Finland	15:48.69
1980....Raisa Smetanina, USSR	15:06.92
1984....Marja-Liisa Hamalainen, Finland	17:04.0
1988....Marjo Matikainen, Finland	15:04.0
1992....Marjut Lukkarinen, Finland	14:13.8
1994....Lyubova Egorova, Russia	14:08.8
1998....Larissa Lazhutina, Russia	17:37.9

10 KILOMETERS CLASSICAL STYLE	
1952....Lydia Widemen, Finland	41:40.0
1956....Lyubov Kosyryeva, USSR	38:11.0
1960....Maria Gusakova, USSR	39:46.6
1964....Klaudia Boyarskikh, USSR	40:24.3
1968....Toini Gustafsson, Sweden	36:46.5
1972....Galina Kulakova, USSR	34:17.8
1976....Raisa Smetanina, USSR	30:13.41
1980....Barbara Petzold, E Germany	30:31.54
1984....Marja-Lissa Hamalainen, Finland	31:44.2
1988....Vida Ventsene, USSR	30:08.3
2002....Bante Skari, Norway	28:05.6

30 KILOMETERS CLASSICAL TYLE	
2002....Gabriela Paruzzi, Italy	1:30:57.1

10 KILOMETERS PURSUIT FREESTYLE	
1992....Lyubov Egorova, Unified Team	40:07.7
1994....Lyubov Egorova, Russia	41:38.1
1998....Larissa Lazhutina, Russia	46:06.9

15 KILOMETERS FREESTYLE	
2002....Stefania Belmondo, Italy	39:54.4

15 KILOMETERS CLASSICAL STYLE	
1992....Lyubov Egorova, Unified Team	42:20.8
1994....Manuela Di Centa, Italy	39:44.5
1998....Olga Danilova, Russia	46:55.04

20 KILOMETERS FREESTYLE	
1984....Marja-Liisa Hamalainen, Finland	1:01:45.0
1988....Tamara Tikhonova, USSR	55:53.6

30 KILOMETERS FREESTYLE	
1992....Stefania Belmondo, Italy	1:22:30.1
1994....Manuela Di Centa, Italy	1:25:41.6
1998....Julija Tchepalova, Russia	1:22:01.5

4 X 5-KILOMETER RELAY MIXED STYLE	
1956....Finland	1:9:01.0
1960....Sweden	1:4:21.4
1964....USSR	59:20.0
1968....Norway	57:30.0
1972....USSR	48:46.15
1976....USSR	1:07:49.75
1980....E Germany	1:02:11.10
1984....Norway	1:06:49.7
1988....USSR	59:51.1
1992....Unified Team	59:34.8
1994....Russia	57:12.5
1998....Russia	55:13.5
2002....Germany	49:30.6

SNOWBOARDING

Men

GIANT SLALOM	
1998....Ross Rebagliati, Canada	2:03.96

PARALLEL GIANT SLALOM	
2002....Philipp Schoch, Switzerland	

HALF-PIPE	Pts
1998....Gian Simmen, Switzerland	85.2
2002....Ross Powers, United States	46.1

Women

GIANT SLALOM	
1998....Karine Ruby, France	2:17.34

PARALLEL GIANT SLALOM	
2002....Isabella Blanc, France	

HALF-PIPE	Pts
1998....Nicola Thost, Germany	74.6
2002....Kelly Clark, United States	47.9

Track & Field

American Justin Gatlin, world-record holder in the 100m and 200m sprints.

Finn-tastic

Rising stars and well-known veterans broke new records and scaled new heights at Helsinki

BY MERRELL NODEN

FOR TRACK FANS, 2005 RESEMBLED one of those spring months that roll in all wintry gloom, but end with the sun shining and flowers blooming everywhere. By mid-August, when the track season reached its peak at the World Championships in Helsinki, one could only marvel at how resilient the sport is—how every year young athletes arrive to surpass their elders and fill us with wonder at the steady push of human excellence. In Helsinki, many of those blossoming talents were American, as the U.S. enjoyed its greatest medal haul ever at the Worlds, taking home 25 medals, 14 of them gold.

But the bad news first: That was the depressing spectacle of Marion Jones, winner of five medals in Sydney and the sport's one-time golden girl, struggling to keep up with sprinters she would have smoked in her sleep a few years ago. Jones opened her season with a last place finish in a 400, clocking a good-for-high school 55.03; she would end it with a seasonal 100 best of 11.28, slower than she ran in high school. Her poor performances may be attributable to the pressures of the BALCO investigation, in which she stands accused of using performance-enhancing drugs. But they did little to convince people she is telling the truth about her past drug use. Jones's husband, Tim Montgomery, had an even worse year. He lost not only his world 100 record, but also jeopardized his right to compete as the Court of Arbitration for Sport began deliberation about upholding the suspension imposed on him by the U.S. Anti-Doping Agency.

The season got a surprise kick-start on June 14, when Asafa Powell broke Montgomery's world record for the 100, clocking 9.77 in Athens. The 22-year-old Jamaican had two other marks faster than anyone else this year, but a groin tear meant that he was unable to face Olympic champion Justin Gatlin in Helsinki. There, Gatlin made history as the first man to win a 100-200 double at a world championship. He ran 9.88 to beat the 100 field by .17, the largest margin ever in a world championship 100, then returned to win the 200 (in 20.04), leading an American sweep of the first four places. Wallace Spearmon, who in June had led the Arkansas Razorbacks to their third straight NCAA outdoor title, finished second, in 20.20.

Just as impressive was quarter-miler Jeremy Wariner. The Olympic champ ran 43.93 to become the first person to break 44 seconds for the 400 since fellow Baylor sprinter Michael Johnson did so in 2000. Wariner also anchored an easy U.S. win in the 4 x 400. Still, it was 400-meter hurdler Bershawn Jackson who may have had the top single performance at the meet, running 47.30 in

Russian Yelena Isinbayeva set a new world record in the pole vault.

BOB MARTIN

the rain. Jackson's U.S. teammate Brian Clay also won the convincingly, beating Olympic Decathlon champ Roman Sebrle, 8,732 points to 8,521.

The U.S. women were just as impressive as the men. Sprinter Lauryn Williams moved up a spot from the silver medal she'd won in Athens, winning the 100 in 10.93, while Allyson Felix, 19, claimed the 200, in 22.16. Michelle Barber took the 100 hurdles (12.66), but the biggest surprise was long jumper Tianna Madison, who sailed 22' 71/4" to add a world championship to the gold medals she'd won at the indoor and outdoor NCAA's. She is only 19, and a junior at Tennessee.

One disappointment in Helsinki was American middle distance star Alan Webb. On July 29 Webb had run 3:48.92 for the mile at the Bislett Games in Oslo, making him the first American-born miler to break 3:50 since Jim Spivey back in 1991. Webb, who was thought to have a shot at a medal in Helsinki, finished ninth there. In Oslo, he'd finished fourth, two spots behind Kenyan-born Bernard Lagat, who seems now to be an American though it's all a little confusing. Late in August, Lagat ran a 3:29.30 1500 in Rieti and was given credit for breaking Sydney Maree's ancient U.S. record.

In many ways, what took getting used to this season was who wasn't competing: not only Montgomery and Jones, but also Hicham El Guerrouj, the world record holder in the mile, who was exhausted by public appearances and a virus in May, took the rest of the year off. The graceful Moroccan says he will compete in 2006 and then retire.

Two men rushed in to fill the vacuum left by El Guerrouj: Rashid Ramzi, a Moroccan now competing for Bahrain, did the "Peter Snell double," winning both the 800 and 1500 in Helsinki. Kenenisa Bekele of Ethiopia won the worlds 10,000 and later broke his own world record for the distance, clocking 26:17.53 in Brussels. For Bekele, it was a great finish to a

year that had begun tragically, with the sudden death in training of his fiancée, fellow distance runner Alem Techale, who was only 17.

There were women's world records set in three events: In the javelin, where Osleidys Menéndez of Cuba tossed the spear 71.70 meters to win in Helsinki, and in the relatively new event for women, the hammer, which Tatyana Kuzenkova of Russia tossed 77.06 meters.

Still it was hard not to name pole vaulter Yelena Isinbayeva the performer of the year. The 23-year-old Russian enjoyed a season that can only be described as "Bubkan," after the greatest male vaulter in history: Entering this season as the Olympic champion and world record holder, Isinbayeva set seven world records, four outdoors, three indoors. She is the only woman to have topped both 16 feet and the more significant mark of 5 meters. And while Isinbayeva has not quite shown Bubka's consummate skill at slicing the record as bologna-thin as possible for maximum bonuses—at one meet she went right from 4.95 meters to 5.00, thus costing herself four possible bonuses—she is only 23 and will learn. Watching her do so is sure to be a highlight of seasons to come.

U.S. Olympic Trials

Sacramento, July 9–18, 2004

Men

100 METERS
1. Maurice Green, adidas — 9.91
2. Justin Gatlin, Nike — 9.92
3. Shawn Crawford, Nike — 9.93

200 METERS
1. Shawn Crawford, Nike — 19.99
2. Justin Gatlin, Nike — 20.01
3. Bernard Williams, Nike — 20.30

400 METERS
1. Jeremy Wariner, Baylor — 44.37
2. Otis Harris, Nike — 44.67
3. Derrick Brew, Nike — 44.69

800 METERS
1. Jonathan Johnson, Texas Tech — 1:44.77
2. Khadevis Robinson, Nike — 1:44.91
3. Derrick Peterson, adidas — 1:45.08

1,500 METERS
1. Alan Webb, Nike — 3:36.13
2. Charlie Gruber, Nike — 3:38.45
3. Rob Myers, unattached — 3:38.93

3,000 M STEEPLECHASE
1. Daniel Lincoln, Nike — 8:15.02
2. Anthoney Famiglietti, adidas — 8:17.91
3. Robert Gary, adidas — 8:19.46

5,000 METERS
1. Tim Broe, adidas — 13:27.36
2. Jonathon Riley, Nike — 13:30.85
3. Bolota Asmerom, Nike — 13:32.77

10,000 METERS
1. Meb Keflezighi, Nike — 27:36.49
2. Abdi Abdirahman, Nike — 27:55.00
3. Daniel Browne, Nike — 28:07.47

110-METER HURDLES
1. Terrence Trammell, Mizuno — 13.09
2. Duane Ross, Nike — 13.21
3. Allen Johnson, Nike — 13.25

400-METER HURDLES
1. James Carter, Nike — 47.68
2. Angelo Taylor, Nike — 48.03
3. Bennie Brazell, Louisiana St — 48.05

20-KILOMETER RACE WALK
1. Tim Seaman, NYAC — 1:25:40
2. John Nunn, U.S. Army — 1:26:23
3. Kevin Eastler, U.S. Air Force — 1:28:49

HIGH JUMP
1. Jamie Nieto, Nike — 7 ft 7¾ in
2. Matt Hemingway, adidas — 7 ft 6½ in
3. Tora Harris, Nike — 7 ft 5¼ in

POLE VAULT
1. Timothy Mack, Nike — 19 ft 4¼ in
2. Toby Stevenson, Nike — 19 ft 2¼ in
3. Derek Miles, Nike — 19 ft ¼ in

LONG JUMP
1. Dwight Phillips, Nike — 27 ft 2 in
2. Tony Allmond, unattached — 26 ft 7 in
3. John Moffitt, Nike — 26 ft 5¾ in

TRIPLE JUMP
1. Melvin Lister, unattached — 58 ft 4 in
2. Walter Davis, Nike — 57 ft 10¼ in
3. Kenta Bell, Nike — 57 ft 8¼ in

SHOT PUT
1. Adam Nelson, Nike — 71 ft
2. Reese Hoffa, NYAC — 69 ft 4¼ in
3. John Godina, adidas — 69 ft 2 in

DISCUS THROW
1. Jarred Rome, unattached — 215 ft 9 in
2. Ian Waltz, unattached — 212 ft 3 in
3. Casey Malone, Nike — 211 ft 6 in

HAMMER THROW
1. James Parker, U.S. Air Force — 254 ft 6 in
2. A.G. Kruger, Ashland Elite — 249 ft 5 in
3. Travis Nutter, Pacific Bay TC — 237 ft 9 in

JAVELIN THROW
1. Breaux Greer, adidas — 270 ft 4 in
2. Brian Chaput, Penn — 261 ft 10 in
3. Leigh Smith, Tennessee — 250 ft 7 in

DECATHLON
1. Bryan Clay, Nike — 8660
2. Tom Pappas, Nike — 8517
3. Paul Terek, World's Greatest Ath. — 8312

MARATHON*
1. Alan Culpepper — 2:11:42
2. Meb Keflezighi — 2:11:47
3. Dan Browne — 2:12:02

*Held on Feb. 7 in Birmingham, AL

Women

100 METERS
1. LaTasha Colander, Nike — 10.97
2. Torri Edwards, adidas — 11.02
3. Lauryn Williams, Miami — 11.10

200 METERS
1. Allyson Felix, adidas — 22.28
2. Muna Lee, Nike — 22.36
3. Torri Edwards, adidas — 22.39

400 METERS
1. Monique Hennagan, unattached — 49.56
2. Sanya Richards, Nike — 49.89
3. DeeDee Trotter, Tennessee — 50.28

800 METERS
1. Jearl Miles-Clark, New Balance — 1:59.06
2. Nicole Teter, Nike — 2:00.25
3. Hazel Clark, Nike — 2:00.37

1,500 METERS
1. Carrie Tollefson, adidas — 4:08.32
2. Jennifer Toomey, Nike — 4:08.43
3. Amy Rudolph, adidas — 4:08.57

3,000 M STEEPLECHASE
1. Ann Gaffigan, Nebraska — 9:39.35AR
2. Kathryn Andersen, BYU — 9:45.52
3. Carrie Messner, Asics — 9:50.70

5,000 METERS
1. Shayne Culpepper, adidas — 15:07.41
2. Marla Runyan, Nike — 15:07.48
3. Shalane Flanagan, Nike — 15:10.52

10,000 METERS
1. Deena Kastor, Asics — 31:09.65
2. Elva Dryer, Nike — 31:58.14
3. Kate O'Neill, Nike — 32:07.25

Women (Cont.)

20-KILOMETER RACE WALK
1. Teresa Vaill, Walk U.S.A. — 1:35:57
2. Joanne Dow, adidas — 1:38:42
3. Bobbi Chapman, unattached — 1:39:01

100-METER HURDLES
1. Gail Devers, Nike — 12.55
2. Joanna Hayes, Nike — 12.55
3. Melissa Morrison, Adidas — 12.61

400-METER HURDLES
1. Sheena Johnson, Nike — 52.95
2. Brenda Taylor, Nike — 53.36
3. Lashinda Demus, S Carolina — 53.43

HIGH JUMP
1. Tisha Waller, Nike — 6 ft 6 in
2. Chaunte Howard, Georgia Tech — 6 ft 4¼ in
3. Amy Acuff, Asics — 6 ft 4¼ in

POLE VAULT
1. Stacy Dragila, Nike — 15 ft 7 in
2. Jillian Schwartz, Nike — 14 ft 11 in
3. Kellie Suttle, Nike — 14 ft 11 in

LONG JUMP
1. Marion Jones, Nike — 23 ft 4 in
2. Grace Upshaw, Nike — 22 ft 5 in
3. Akiba McKinney, unattached — 21 ft 6¾ in

TRIPLE JUMP
1. Tiombe Hurd, Nike — 47 ft 5 in
2. Shakeema Walker, unattached — 46 ft 1½ in
3. Vanitta Kinard, Nike — 45 ft ½ in

SHOT PUT
1. Laura Gerraughty, N Carolina — 60 ft 8½ in
2. Kristin Heaston, Nike — 59 ft 4¾ in
3. Jillian Camarena, Stanford — 58 ft 2 in

DISCUS THROW
1. Aretha Hill, Nike — 208 ft 6 in
2. Stephanie Brown, Moreno T. — 203 ft 1 in
3. Seilala Sua, Nike — 202 ft 1 in

HAMMER THROW
1. Erin Gilreath, NYAC — 231 ft
2. Anna Mahon, Nike — 227 ft 1 in
3. Amber Campbell, C Carolina — 216 ft 6 in

JAVELIN THROW
1. Kim Kreiner, Nike — 182 ft 7 in
2. Sarah Malone, Oregon — 177 ft 11 in
3. Denise O'Connell, unattached — 177 ft 4 in

HEPTAHLON
1. Shelia Burrell, Nike — 6194
2. Tiffany Lott-Hogan, unattached — 6159
3. Michelle Perry, Nike — 6126

MARATHON*
1. Colleen De Reuck — 2:28:25
2. Deena Kastor — 2:29:38
3. Jen Rhines — 2:29:57

*Held on April 3 in St. Louis.

2005 USATF Indoor Championships

Boston, Feb 25–27, 2005

Men

60 METERS
1. Mardy Scales, Nike — 6.61
2. Joshua Norman, unattached — 6.62
3. Aaron Armstrong, Nike — 6.64

200 METERS
1. Jimmie Hackley, unattached — 20.83
2. Coby M
3. Kevin Braunskill, unattached — 21.19

400 METERS
1. Bershawn Jackson, Nike — 46.05
2. James Davis, unattached — 46.75
3. Ashton Collins, unattached — 47.26

800 METERS
1. Kevin Hicks, Florida A&M — 1:48.73
2. Richard Smith, unattached — 1:48.80
3. Jesse O'Connell, unattached — 1:49.19

1,500 METERS
1. Scott McGowan, New Balance — 3:44.06
2. Rob Myers, Reebok — 3:45.18
3. Charlie Gruber, Nike — 3:46.11

3,000 METERS
1. Jonathon Riley, Nike — 7:53.73
2. Bolota Asmerom, Nike — 7:53.81
3. Luke Watson, Adidas — 7:57.23

5,000-METER RACE WALK
1. Tim Seaman, NYAC — 19:56.41
2. Curt Clausen, NYAC — 20:41.33
3. Benjamin Shorey, unattached — 21:48.56

60-METER HURDLES
1. Joel Brown, Nike — 7.64
2. Jermaine Cooper, unattached — 7.75
3. Derrick Williams, Central St — 7.87

HIGH JUMP
1. Tora Harris, Shore AC — 2.27m
2. Jamie Nieto, Niké — 2.24m
3. Adam Shunk, unattached — J2.24m

POLE VAULT
1. Brad Walker, Nike — 5.65m
2. Tommy Skipper, Oregon — 5.55m
3. Paul Litchfield, unattached — 5.45m

LONG JUMP
1. Brian Johnson, Holyfield I — 7.89m
2. Tony Allmond, Unattached — 7.76m
3. Juane Armon, Unattached — 7.73m

TRIPLE JUMP
1. Walter Davis, Nike — 17.31m
2. Kenta Bell, Nike — 16.86m
3. Chris Hercules, unattached — 16.83m

SHOT PUT
1. John Godina, Adidas — 21.83mM
1. Reese Hoffa, NYAC/Nike — 21.74mM
3. Adam Nelson, unattached — 21.59m

WEIGHT THROW
1. A.G. Kruger, Ashland Elite — 23.47m
2. Jake Freeman, unattached — 23.16m
3. Kibwe Johnson, unattached — 22.27m

HEPTAHLON*
1. Ryan Harlan, unattached — 3411
2. Paul Terek, unattached — 3323
3. Ryan Olkowski, unattached — 3265

* Held on March 5–6 in Chapel Hill, N Carolina.

Boston, Feb 25–27, 2005
Women

60 METERS
1. ....Angela Daigle, Nike — 7.09
2. ....Muna Lee, Nike — 7.11
3. ....Me'Lisa Barber — 7.18

200 METERS
1. ....Crystal Cox, unattached — 23.27
2. ....Rachelle Boone, Nike — 23.53
3. ....Debbie Dunn, unattached — 23.59

400 METERS
1. ....Dee Dee Trotter, adidas — 52.01
2. ....Mary Danner, unattached — 53.25
3. ....Maisha Pinkard, Hampton U. — 54.35

800 METERS
1. ....Hazel Clark, Nike — 2:01.98
2. ....Alice Schmidt, unattached — 2:02.32
3. ....Kameisha Bennett, Nike — 2:02.77

1,500 METERS
1. ....Jen Toomey, Nike — 4:13.25
2. ....Treniere Clement, Nike — 4:14.20
3. ....Christin Wurth, Nike — 4:14.74

3,000 METERS
1. ....Shayne Culpepper, Nike — 8:55.57
2. ....Amy Rudolph, adidas — 8:57.42
3. ....Lauren Fleshman, Nike — 8:59.93

3,000-METER RACE WALK
1. ....Amber Atonia, NYAC — 12:55.69
2. ....Joanne Dow, adidas — 13:09.62
3. ....Deborah Huberty, NYAC — 13:26.03

60-METER HURDLES
1. ....Gail Devers, Nike — 7.81
2. ....Joanna Hayes, Nike — 7.91
3. ....Anjanette Kirkland, Nike — 7.99

HIGH JUMP
1. ....Gwen Wentland, Nike — 1.88m
2. ....Kaylene Wagener, CP/SLO — 1.85m
3. ....Sharon Day, CP/SLO — 1.82m

POLE VAULT
1. ....Jennifer Stuczyski, Robert Wesl — 4.35m
2. ....Becky Holliday, unattached — 4.30m
3. ....Mary Sauer, Asics — J4.30m

LONG JUMP
1. ....Rose Richmond, unattached — 6.44m
2. ....Hyleas Fountain, Nike — 6.29m
3. ....Ola Sesay, unattached — 6.26m

TRIPLE JUMP
1. ....Shani Marks, unattached — 13.65m
2. ....Nicole Whitman, unattached — 13.23m
3. ....Simidele Adeagbo, Team XO — 13.19m

SHOT PUT
1. ....Jillian Camarena, unattached — 17.31m
2. ....Janae Stickland, unattached — 16.35m
3. ....Leann Boerema, unattached — 16.00m

WEIGHT THROW
1. ....Erin Gilreath, NYAC — 24.46mM
2. ....Amber Campblel Mjolnir TC — 23.99mM
3. ....LaQuanda Cotten, unattached — 21.42m

PENTATHLON*
1. ....Hyleas Fountain, Nike — 4417
2. ....Fiona Asigbee, unattached — 4347
3. ....Jackie Poulson, unattached — 4268

* Held on March 5–6 in Chapel Hill, N Carolina.

2005 IAAF World Cross-Country Championships

St. Etienne/St. Galmier

MEN (12,000 METERS; 7.5 MILES)
1. ....Kenenisa Bekele, Ethiopia — 35:06
2. ....Tadesse Zersenay, Eritrea — 35:20
3. ....Hassan Abdullah Ahma, Qatar — 35:34

WOMEN (8,000 METERS; 5 MILES)
1. ....Dibaba Tirunesh, Ethiopia — 26:34
2. ....Timbilili Alice, Kenya — 26:37
3. ....Kidane Werknesh, Ethiopia — 26:37

Chicago: October 10, 2004

MEN
1. ....Evans Rutto, Kenya — 2:06:16
2. ....Daniel Njenga, Kenya — 2:07:44
3. ....Toshinari Takaoka, Japan — 2:07:50

WOMEN
1. ....Constantina Tomescu-Dita, Romania — 2:23:45
2. ....Nuta Olaru, Romania — 2:24:33
3. ....Svetlana Zakharova, Russia — 2:25:01

New York City: November 7, 2004

MEN
1. ....Hendrik Ramaala, South Africa — 2:09:28
2. ....Meb Keflezighi, California, — 2:09:53
3. ....Timothy Cherigat, Kenya — 2:10:00

WOMEN
1. ....Paula Radcliffe, England — 2:23:10
2. ....Susan Chepkeme, Kenya — 2:23:13
3. ....Lyubov Denisova, Russia — 2:25:18

Tokyo: November 20, 2004

WOMEN ONLY
1. ....Bruna Genovese, Italy — 2:26:34
2. ....Kiyoko Shimahara, Japan — 2:26:43
3. ....Elfenesh Alemu, Ethopia — 2:26:58

Tokyo: February 13, 2005

MEN ONLY
1. ....Toshinari Takaoka, Japan — 2:07:41
2. ....Zebedayoo Bayo, Tanzania — 2:10:51
3. ....Vladimir Tsiamchyk, Belarus — 2:14:24

Rome: March 17, 2005

MEN
1. ....Alberico Di Cecco, Italy — 2:08:02
2. ....Philip Manyim, Kenya — 2:08:07
3. ....Daniel Yego, Kenya — 2:08:16

WOMEN
1. ....Silvia Skvortsova, Russia — 2:28:01
2. ....Tiziana Alagia, Italy — 2:31:46
3. ....Assale Tafa Magarsa, Ethiopia — 2:32:34

Paris: April 10, 2005

MEN
1. ....Salim Kipsang, Kenya — 2:08:02
2. ....Paul Biwott, Kenya — 2:08:15
3. ....Gashaw Melese, Ethiopia — 2:09:22

WOMEN
1. ....Lydiya Grigoryeva, Russia — 2:27:00
2. ....Florence Barsosio, Kenya — 2;27;18
3. ....Asha Gigi, Ethiopia — 2:27:37

Boston: April 18, 2005

MEN
1. ....Hailu Negussie, Ethiopia — 2:04:32
2. ....Wilson Onsare, Kenya — 2:05:04
3. ....Benson Cherono, Kenya — 2:05:20

WOMEN
1. ....Catherine Ndereba, Kenya — 2:17:38
2. ....Elfenesh Alemu, Ethiopia — 2:18:45
3. ....Bruna Genovese, Italy — 2:21:56

Rotterdam: April 10, 2005

MEN
1. ....Jimmy Muind, Kenya — 2:07:50
2. ....Jackson Koech, Kenya — 2:08;02
3. ....Felix Limo, Kenya — 2:09:01

WOMEN
1. ....Lornah Kiplagat, Netherlands — 2:28:36
2. ....Ana Dias, Portugal — 2:31:27
3. ....Isabel Eizmendi, Spain — 2:33:14

London: April 17, 2005

MEN
1. ....Martin Lel, Kenya — 2:07:26
2. ....Jaouad Gharib, Morocco — 2:07:49
3. ....Hendrick Ramaala, South Africa — 2:08:32

WOMEN
1. ....Paula Radcliffe, Britain — 2:17:42
2. ....Constantina Tomescu-Dita, Romania — 2:22:50
3. ....Susan Chepkemei, Kenya — 2:24:00

TRACK AND FIELD

World Records

As of October 1, 2005. World outdoor records are recognized by the International Amateur Athletics Federation (IAAF).

Men

Event	Mark	Record Holder	Date	Site
100 meters	9.77	Asafa Powell, Jamaica	6-14-05	Athens, Greece
200 meters	19.32	Michael Johnson, United States	8-1-96	Atlanta
400 meters	43.18	Michael Johnson, United States	8-26-99	Seville, Spain
800 meters	1:41.11	Wilson Kipketer, Denmark	8-24-97	Cologne
1,000 meters	2:11.96	Noah Ngeny, Kenya	9-5-99	Rieti, Italy
1,500 meters	3:26.00	Hicham El Guerrouj, Morocco	7-14-98	Rome
Mile	3:43.13	Hicham El Guerrouj, Morocco	7-7-99	Rome
2,000 meters	4:44.79	Hicham El Guerrouj, Morocco	9-7-99	Berlin
3,000 meters	7:20.67	Daniel Komen, Kenya	9-1-96	Rieti, Italy
Steeplechase	7:53.63*	Saif Saaeed Shaheen, Qatar	9-3-04	Brussels
5,000 meters	12:37.35	Kenenisa Bekele, Ethiopia	5-31-04	Hengelo, Netherlands
10,000 meters	26:17.53	Kenenisa Bekele, Ehtiopia	8-26-05	Brussels
20,000 meters	56:55.6	Arturo Barrios, Mexico	3-30-91	La Flâche, France
Hour	21,101 meters	Arturo Barrios, Mexico	3-30-91	La Flâche, France
25,000 meters	1:13:55.8	Toshihiko Seko, Japan	3-22-81	Christchurch, New Zealand
30,000 meters	1:29:18.8	Toshihiko Seko, Japan	3-22-81	Christchurch, New Zealand
Marathon	2:04:55	Paul Tergat, Kenya	9-28-03	Berlin
110-meter hurdles	12.91	Colin Jackson, Great Britain	8-20-93	Stuttgart, Germany
	12.91*	Xiang Liu, China	8-27-04	Athens
400-meter hurdles	46.78	Kevin Young, United States	8-6-92	Barcelona
20-kilometer walk	1:17:25	Bernardo Segura, Mexico	5-7-94	Bergen, Norway
30-kilometer walk	2:01:44.1	Maurizio Damilano, Italy	10-3-92	Cuneo, Italy
50-kilometer walk	3:40:57.9	Thierry Toutain, France	9-29-96	Héricourt, France
4 x 100-meter relay	37.40	United States (Mike Marsh, Leroy Burrell, Dennis Mitchell, Carl Lewis)	8-8-92	Barcelona
		United States (Jon Drummond, Andre Cason, Dennis Mitchell, Leroy Burrell)	8-21-93	Stuttgart, Germany
4 x 200-meter relay	1:18.68	Santa Monica TC (Mike Marsh, Leroy Burrell, Floyd Heard, Carl Lewis)	4-17-94	Walnut, CA
4 x 400-meter relay	2:54.20	United States (Jerome Young, Antonio Pettigrew, Tyree Washington, Michael Johnson)	7-22-98	New York City
4 x 800-meter relay	7:03.89	Great Britain (Peter Elliott, Garry Cook, Steve Cram, Sebastian Coe)	8-30-82	London
4 x 1,500-meter relay	14:38.8	W Germany (Thomas Wessinghage, Harald Hudak, Michael Lederer, Karl Fleschen)	8-17-77	Cologne, Germany
High jump	2.45m	Javier Sotomayor, Cuba	7-27-93	Salamanca, Spain
Pole vault	6.14m	Sergei Bubka, Ukraine	7-31-94	Sestriere, Italy
Long jump	8.95m	Mike Powell, United States	8-30-91	Tokyo
Triple jump	18.29m	Jonathan Edwards, Great Britain	8-7-95	Göteborg, Sweden
Shot put	23.12m	Randy Barnes, United States	5-20-90	Westwood, CA
Discus throw	74.08	Jürgen Schult, E Germany	6-6-86	Neubrandenburg, Germany
Hammer throw	86.74m	Yuri Syedikh, USSR	8-30-86	Stuttgart, Germany
Javelin throw	98.48m	Jan Zelezny, Czech Republic	5-25-96	Jena, Germany
Decathlon	9026 pts	Roman Sebrle, Czech Republic	5-27-01	Götzis, Austria

Note: The decathlon consists of 10 events: the 100 meters, long jump, shot put, high jump and 400 meters on the first day; the 110-meter hurdles, discus, pole vault, javelin and 1,500 meters on the second.

*Pending ratification.

Women

Event	Mark	Record Holder	Date	Site
100 meters	10.49	Florence Griffith Joyner, United States	7-16-88	Indianapolis
200 meters	21.34	Florence Griffith Joyner, United States	9-29-88	Seoul
400 meters	47.60	Marita Koch, E Germany	10-6-85	Canberra, Australia
800 meters	1:53.28	Jarmila Kratochvílová, Czechoslovakia	7-26-83	Munich
1,000 meters	2:28.98	Svetlana Masterkova, Russia	8-23-96	Brussels
1,500 meters	3:50.46	Qu Yunxia, China	9-11-93	Beijing
Mile	4:12.56	Svetlana Masterkova, Russia	8-14-96	Zurich
2,000 meters	5:25.36	Sonia O'Sullivan, Ireland	7-8-94	Edinburgh
3,000 meters	8:06.11	Wang Junxia, China	9-13-93	Beijing
Steeplechase	9:01.59	Gulnara Samitova, Russia	7-4-04	Iraklio, Greece
5,000 meters	14:24.68	Elvan Abeylegesse, Turkey	6-11-04	Bergen, Norway
10,000 meters	29:31.78	Wang Junxia, China	9-8-93	Beijing
Hour	18,340 meters	Tegla Loroupe, Kenya	8-8-98	Borgholzhausen, Germany
20,000 meters	1:05:26.6	Tegla Loroupe, Kenya	9-3-00	Borgholzhausen, Germany
25,000 meters	1:27:05.9	Tegla Loroupe, Kenya	9-21-02	Mengerskirchen
30,000 meters	1:38:29	Deena Kastor, U.S.A.	9-10-05	Chicago, IL
Marathon	2:15:25	Paula Radcliffe, Great Britain	4-13-03	London
100-meter hurdles	12.21	Yordanka Donkova, Bulgaria	8-20-88	Stara Zagora, Bulgaria
400-meter hurdles	52.34	Yuliya Pechonkina, Russia	8-8-03	Tula, Russia
5-kilometer walk	20:02.60	Gillian O'Sullivan, Ireland	7-13-02	Dublin
10-kilometer walk	41:56.23	Nadezhda Ryashkina, URS	7-24-90	Seattle
4 x 100-meter relay	41.37	East Germany (Silke Gladisch, Sabine Reiger, Ingrid Auerswald, Marlies Göhr)	10-6-85	Canberra, Australia
4 x 200-meter relay	1:27.46	United States (LaTasha Jenkins, LaTasha Colander-Richardson, Nanceen Perry, Marion Jones)	4-29-00	Philadelphia
4 x 400-meter relay	3:15.17	USSR (Tatyana Ledovskaya, Olga Nazarova, Maria Pinigina, Olga Bryzgina)	10-1-88	Seoul
4 x 800-meter relay	7:50.17	USSR (Nadezhda Olizarenko, Lyubov Gurina, Lyudmila Borisova, Irina Podyalovskaya)	8-5-84	Moscow
High jump	2.09m	Stefka Kostadinova, Bulgaria	8-30-87	Rome
Pole vault	5.01m	Yelena Isinbayeva, Russia	8-12-05	Brussels
Long jump	7.52m	Galina Chistyakova, USSR	6-11-88	Leningrad
Triple jump	15.50m	Inessa Kravets, Ukraine	8-10-95	Göteborg, Sweden
Shot put	22.63m	Natalya Lisovskaya, USSR	6-7-87	Moscow
Discus throw	76.80m	Gabriele Reinsch, E Germany	7-9-88	Neubrandenburg, Germany
Hammer throw	71.06m	Tatyana Lysenko, Russia	7-15-05	Tula, Russia
Javelin throw	71.70m	Osleidys Menéndez, Cuba	8-14-05	Helsinki, Finland
Heptathlon	7291 pts	Jackie Joyner-Kersee, United States	9-24-88	Seoul

Note: The heptathlon consists of 7 events: the 100-meter hurdles, high jump, shot put and 200 meters on the first day; the long jump, javelin and 800 meters on the second.

*Pending ratification.

American Records

As of October 1, 2005. American outdoor records are recognized by USA Track and Field (USATF). WR=world record. EWR=equals world record.

Men

Event	Mark	Record Holder	Date	Site
100 meters	9.78 WR	Tim Montgomery	9-14-02	Paris
200 meters	19.32 WR	Michael Johnson	8-1-96	Atlanta
400 meters	43.18 WR	Michael Johnson	8-26-99	Seville, Spain
800 meters	1:42.60	Johnny Gray	8-28-85	Koblenz, Germany
1,000 meters	2:13.9	Rick Wohlhuter	7-30-74	Oslo
1,500 meters	3:29.77	Sydney Maree	8-25-85	Cologne, Germany
Mile	3:47.69	Steve Scott	7-7-82	Oslo

Men (cont'd)

Event	Mark	Record Holder	Date	Site
2,000 meters	4:52.44	Jim Spivey	9-15-87	Lausanne, Switz.
3,000 meters	7:30.84	Bob Kennedy	8-8-98	Monte Carlo
Steeplechase	8:09.17	Henry Marsh	8-28-85	Koblenz, Germany
5,000 meters	12:58.21	Bob Kennedy	8-14-96	Zurich
10,000 meters	27:13.98	Mebrahtom Keflezighi	5-4-01	Palo Alto, California
20,000 meters	58:25.0	Bill Rodgers	8-9-77	Boston
Hour	20,547 meters	Bill Rodgers	8-9-77	Boston
25,000 meters	1:14:11.8	Bill Rodgers	2-21-79	Saratoga, CA
30,000 meters	1:31:49	Bill Rodgers	2-21-79	Saratoga, CA
Marathon	2:05:38	Khalid Khannouchi	4-14-02	London
110-meter hurdles	12.92	Roger Kingdom	8-16-89	Zurich
		Allen Johnson	6-23-96	Atlanta
		Allen Johnson	8-23-96	Brussels
400-meter hurdles	46.78 WR	Kevin Young	8-6-92	Barcelona
20-kilometer walk	1:23:40	Tim Seaman	8-14-00	La Jolla, CA
30-kilometer walk	2:14:31	Allen James	10-31-93	Atlanta
50-kilometer walk	3:59:41.1	Herman Nelson	6-9-96	Seattle
4x100-meter relay	37.40 WR	United States (Mike Marsh, Leroy Burrell, Dennis Mitchell, Carl Lewis)	8-8-92	Barcelona
		United States (Jon Drummond, Andre Cason, Dennis Mitchell, Leroy Burrell)	8-21-93	Stuttgart, Germany
4x200-meter relay	1:18.68 WR	Santa Monica Track Club (Mike Marsh, Leroy Burrell, Floyd Heard, Carl Lewis)	4-17-94	Walnut, CA
4x400-meter relay	2:54.20 WR	United States (Jerome Young, Antonio Pettigrew, Tyree Washington, Michael Johnson)	7-22-98	New York City
4x800-meter relay	7:06.5	Santa Monica Track Club (James Robinson, David Mack, Earl Jones, Johnny Gray)	4-26-86	Walnut, CA
4x1,500-meter relay	14:46.3	National Team (Dan Aldredge, Andy Clifford, Todd Harbour, Tom Duits)	6-24-79	Bourges, France
High jump	2.40m	Charles Austin	8-17-91	Zurich
Pole vault	6.03m	Jeff Hartwig	6-14-00	Jonesboro, AR
Long jump	8.95m	Mike Powell	8-30-91	Tokyo
Triple jump	18.09m	Kenny Harrison	7-27-96	Atlanta
Shot put	23.12m	Randy Barnes	5-20-90	Westwood, CA
Discus throw	72.34m	Ben Plucknett	7-7-81	Stockholm
Hammer throw	82.52m	Lance Deal	9-7-96	Milan
Javelin throw	87.68m	Breaux Greer	6-11-04	Bergen, Norway
Decathlon	8891 pts	Dan O'Brien	9-4/5-92	Talence, France

Women

Event	Mark	Record Holder	Date	Site
100 meters	10.49 WR	Florence Griffith Joyner	7-16-88	Indianapolis
200 meters	21.34 WR	Florence Griffith Joyner	9-29-88	Seoul
400 meters	48.83	Valerie Brisco-Hooks	8-6-84	Los Angeles
800 meters	1:56.40	Jearl Miles-Clark	8-11-99	Zurich
1,500 meters	3:57.12	Mary Slaney	7-26-83	Stockholm
Mile	4:16.71	Mary Slaney	8-21-85	Zurich
2,000 meters	5:32.7	Mary Slaney	8-3-84	Eugene, OR
3,000 meters	8:25.83	Mary Slaney	9-7-85	Rome
Steeplechase	9:41.94	Elizabeth Jackson	9-4-01	Brisbane, Australia
5,000 meters	14:45.38	Regina Jacobs	7-21-00	Sacramento, CA
10,000 meters	30:50.32	Deena Drossin	5-3-02	Palo Alto, CA
Marathon	2:21:21	Joan Samuelson	10-20-85	Chicago
100-meter hurdles	12.33	Gail Devers	7-23-00	Sacramento, CA
400-meter hurdles	52.61 WR	Kim Batten	8-11-95	Göteborg, Sweden
5,000-meter walk	20:56.88	Michelle Rohl	4-27-96	Philadelphia
10,000-meter walk	44:41.87	Michelle Rohl	7-26-94	St. Petersburg, Russia
4 x 100-meter relay	41.47	National Team (Chryste Gaines, Marion Jones, Inger Miller, Gail Devers)	8-9-97	Athens

Women (cont'd)

Event	Mark	Record Holder	Date	Site
4 x 200-meter relay	1:27.46 WR	USA Blue (LaTasha Jenkins, LaTasha Colander, Nanceen Perry, Marion Jones)	4-29-00	Philadelphia
4 x 400-meter relay	3:15.51	United States (Denean Howard, Diane Dixon, Valerie Brisco, Florence Griffith Joyner)	10-1-88	Seoul
4 x 800-meter relay	8:17.09	Athletics West (Sue Addison, Lee Arbogast, Mary Decker, Chris Mullen)	4-24-83	Walnut, CA
High jump	2.03m	Louise Ritter	7-9-88	Austin
		Louise Ritter	9-30-88	Seoul
Pole vault	4.83m	Stacy Dragila	6-9-01	Palo Alto, CA
Long jump	7.49m	Jackie Joyner-Kersee	5-22-94	New York City
			7-31-94	Sestriere, Italy
Triple jump	14.45m	Sheila Hudson	7-8-96	Stockholm
Shot put	20.18m	Ramona Pagel	6-25-88	San Diego
Discus throw	66.10m	Suzy Powell	4-27-02	La Jolla, CA
Hammer throw	73.87m	Erin Gilreath	6-25-05	Carson, CA
Javelin throw	60.86m	Kim Kreiner	8-7-03	Santo Domingo, D.R.
Heptathlon	7291 pts WR	Jackie Joyner-Kersee	9-23/24-88	Seoul

World and American Indoor Records

As of September 15, 2004. American indoor records are recognized by USA Track and Field. World Indoor records are recognized by the International Amateur Athletics Federation (IAAF).

Men

Event	Mark	Record Holder	Date	Site
50 meters	5.56	Donovan Bailey, Canada (W)	2-9-96	Reno
	5.56	Maurice Greene (A)	2-13-99	Los Angeles
55 meters*	5.99	Obadele Thompson, Barbados (W)	2-22-97	Colorado Springs
	6.00	Lee McRae (A)	3-14-86	Oklahoma City
60 meters	6.39	Maurice Greene (W, A)	3-1-98	Madrid
	6.39	Maurice Greene (W, A)	3-3-01	Atlanta
200 meters	19.92	Frankie Fredericks, Namibia (W)	2-18-96	Liévin, France
	20.26	Shawn Crawford (A)	3-11-00	Fayetteville, AR
	20.26	John Capel (A)	3-11-00	Fayetteville, AR
400 meters	44.63	Kerron Clement (A, W)	3-12-05	Fayetteville, AR
800 meters	1:42.67	Wilson Kipketer, Denmark (W)	3-9-97	Paris
	1:45.00	Johnny Gray (A)	3-8-92	Sindelfingen, Germany
1,000 meters	2:14.96	Wilson Kipketer, Denmark (W)	2-20-00	Birmingham, England
	2:17.85	David Krummenacker (A)	1-27-02	Boston
1,500 meters	3:31.18	Hicham El Guerrouj, Morocco (W)	2-02-97	Stuttgart, Germany
	3:38.12	Jeff Atkinson (A)	3-5-89	Budapest
Mile	3:48.45	Hicham El Guerrouj, Morocco (W)	2-12-97	Ghent, Belgium
	3:51.8	Steve Scott (A)	2-20-81	San Diego
3,000 meters	7:24.90	Daniel Komen, Kenya (W)	2-6-98	Budapest, Hungary
	7:39.23	Tim Broe (A)	1-27-02	Boston
5,000 meters	12:49.60	Kenenisa Bekele, Ethiopia (W)	2-20-04	Birmingham, England
	13:20.55	Doug Padilla (A)	2-12-82	New York City
50-meter hurdles	6.25	Mark McKoy, Canada (W)	3-5-86	Kobe, Japan
	6.35	Greg Foster (A)	1-27-85	Rosemont, Illinois
55-meter hurdles*	6.89	Renaldo Nehemiah (A)	1-20-79	New York City
60-meter hurdles	7.30	Colin Jackson, Great Britain (W)	3-6-94	Sindelfingen, Germany
	7.36	Greg Foster (A)	1-16-87	Los Angeles
	7.36	Allen Johnson (A)	3-6-04	Budapest, Hungary
5,000-meter walk	18:07.08	Mikhail Shchennikov, Russia (W)	2-14-95	Moscow
	19:18.40	Tim Lewis (A)	3-7-87	Indianapolis
4 x 200-meter relay	1:22.11	Great Britain (W) (Linford Christie, Darren Braithwaite, Ade Mafe, John Regis)	3-3-91	Glasgow
	1:22.71	National Team (A) (Thomas Jefferson, Raymond Pierre, Antonio McKay, Kevin Little)	3-3-91	Glasgow

Men (Cont.)

Event	Mark	Record Holder	Date	Site
4 x 400-meter relay	3:02.83	United States (W, A) (Andre Morris, Dameon Johnson, Deon Minor, Milt Campbell)	3-7-99	Maebashi, Japan
4 x 800-meter relay	7:13.94	Global Athletics & Marketing (W, A) (Rich Kenah, Joel Woody, Karl Paranya, David Krummenacker)†	2-6-00	Boston
High jump	7 ft 11½ in	Javier Sotomayor, Cuba (W)	3-4-89	Budapest, Hungary
	7 ft 10½ in	Hollis Conway (A)	3-10-91	Seville
Pole vault	20 ft 2 in	Sergei Bubka, Ukraine (W)	2-21-93	Donetsk, Ukraine
	19 ft 9½ in	Jeff Hartwig (A)	3-10-02	Sindelfingen, Germany
Long jump	28 ft 10¼ in	Carl Lewis (W, A)	1-27-84	New York City
Triple jump	58 ft 6 in	Alicier Urrutia, Cuba (W)	3-1-97	Sindelfingen, Germany
	58 ft 6 in	Christian Olsson, Sweden (W)	3-7-04	Budapest, Hungary
	58 ft 3¼ in	Mike Conley (A)	2-27-87	New York City
Shot put	74 ft 4¼ in	Randy Barnes (W, A)	1-20-89	Los Angeles
Weight throw*	84 ft 10¼ in	Lance Deal (W, A)	3-4-95	Atlanta
Pentathlon*	4478 pts	Steve Fritz, (W, A)	1-14-95	Lawrence, KS
Heptathlon	6476 pts	Dan O'Brien (W, A)	3-13/14-93	Toronto

*No recognized world record. †Pending ratification.

Women

Event	Mark	Record Holder	Date	Site
50 meters	5.96	Irina Privolova, Russia (W)	2-9-95	Madrid
	6.02	Gail Devers (A)	2-21-99	Liévin, France
55 meters*	6.54	Evelyn Ashford (A)	2-26-82	New York
		Jeanette Bolden (A)	2-21-86	Inglewood, CA
60 meters	6.92	Irina Privolova, Russia (W)	2-11-93	Madrid
	6.92	Irina Privolova, Russia (W)	2-9-95	Madrid
	6.95	Gail Devers (A)	3-12-93	Toronto
	6.95	Marion Jones (A)	3-7-98	Maebashi, Japan
200 meters	21.87	Merlene Ottey, Jamaica (W)	2-13-93	Liévin, France
	22.18	Michell Collins (A)	3-15-03	Birmingham, England
400 meters	49.59	Jarmila Kratochvílová, Czech. (W)	3-7-82	Milan
	50.64	Diane Dixon (A)	3-10-91	Seville
800 meters	1:55.82	Jolanda Ceplak, Slovenia (W)	3-3-02	Vienna
	1:58.71	Nicole Teter (A)	3-2-02	New York
1,000 meters	2:30.94	Maria Mutola, Mozambique (W)	2-25-99	Stockholm
	2:34.19	Jennifer Toomey (A)	2-20-04	Birmingham, England
1,500 meters	3:59.98	Regina Jacobs, United States (W, A)	2-1-03	Boston
Mile	4:17.14	Doina Melinte, Romania (W)	2-9-90	East Rutherford, NJ
	4:20.5	Mary Slaney (A)	2-19-82	San Diego
3,000 meters	8:29.15	Berhane Adere, Ethiopia (W)	2-3-02	Stuttgart
	8:39.14	Regina Jacobs (A)	3-7-99	Maebashi, Japan
5,000 meters	14:39.29	Berhane Adere, Ethiopia (W)	1-31-04	Stuttgart
	15:07.33	Marla Runyan (A)	2-18-01	New York
50-meter hurdles	6.58	Cornelia Oschkenat, E Germany (W)	2-20-88	Berlin
	6.67	Jackie Joyner-Kersee (A)	2-10-95	Reno, NV
55-meter hurdles*	7.30	Tiffany Lott (A)	2-20-97	Air Force Academy, CO
60-meter hurdles	7.69	Lyudmila Narozhilenko, Russia (W)	2-4-90	Chelyabinsk, Russia
	7.74	Gail Devers (A)	3-1-03	Boston
3,000-meter walk	11:40.33	Claudia Stef, Romania (W)	1-30-99	Bucharest, Romania
	12:20.79	Debbi Lawrence (A)	3-12-93	Toronto
4 x 200-meter relay	1:32.55	SC Eintracht Hamm, W Gemany (W)	2-20-88	Dortmund, W Germany
	1:32.55	LG Olympia Dortmund, Germany (W)	2-21-99	Karlsruhe, Germany
	1:33.24	National Team (A) (Flirtisha Harris, Chryste Gaines, Terri Dendy, Michele Collins)	2-12-94	Glasgow
4 x 400-meter relay	3:23.88	Russia (W)	3-7-04	Budapest, Hungary
	3:27.59	National Team (A) (Michelle Collins, Monique Hennagan, Zundra Feagin-Alexander, Shanelle Porter)	3-7-99	Maebashi, Japan

*No recognized world record. †Pending ratification.

Women (cont'd)

Event	Mark	Record Holder	Date	Site
4 x 800-meter relay	8:18.71	Russia (W) (Natalya Zaytseva, Olga Kuvnetsova, Yelena Afanasyeva, Yekaterina Podkopayeva)	2-4-94	Moscow
	8:25.50	Villanova (A) (Gina Procaccio, Debbie Grant, Michelle DiMuro, Celeste Halliday)	2-7-87	Gainesville, FL
High jump	6 ft 9½ in	Heike Henkel, Germany (W)	2-8-92	Karlsruhe, Germany
	6 ft 7 in	Tisha Waller (A)	2-28-98	Atlanta
Pole vault	15 ft 11¼ in	Yelena Isinbayeva, Russia (W)	3-6-04	Budapest, Hungary
	15 ft 9 ½ in	Stacy Dragila (A)	3-6-04	Budapest, Hungary
Long jump	24 ft 2¼ in	Heike Drechsler, E Germany (W)	2-13-88	Vienna
	23 ft 4¾ in	Jackie Joyner-Kersee (A)	3-5-94	Atlanta
Triple jump	50 ft 4¾ in	Tatyana Lebedeva, Russia (W)	3-6-04	Budapest, Hungary
	46 ft 8¼ in	Sheila Hudson-Strudwick (A)	3-4-95	Atlanta
Shot put	73 ft 10 in	Helena Fibingerová, Czech. (W)	2-19-77	Jablonec, Czech.
	65 ft ¾ in	Ramona Pagel (A)	2-20-87	Inglewood, CA
Weight throw*	78 ft 7 in	Erin Gilreath (A)	1-25-04	Gainesville, FL
Pentathlon	4991 pts	Irina Byelova, CIS (W)	2-14/15-92	Berlin
	4753	Le Shundra Nathan (A)	3-4/5-99	Maebashi, Japan

*No recognized world record. †Pending ratification.

World Track and Field Championships

Men

100 METERS

1983	Carl Lewis, United States	10.07
1987*	Carl Lewis, United States	9.93 WR
1991	Carl Lewis, United States	9.86 WR
1993	Linford Christie, Great Britain	9.87
1995	Donovan Bailey, Canada	9.97
1997	Maurice Greene, United States	9.86
1999	Maurice Greene, United States	9.80
2001	Maurice Greene, United States	9.82
2003	Kim Collins, St. Kitts & Nevis	10.07
2005	Justin Gatlin, United States	9.88

200 METERS

1983	Calvin Smith, United States	20.14
1987	Calvin Smith, United States	20.16
1991	Michael Johnson, United States	20.01
1993	Frank Fredericks, Namibia	19.85
1995	Michael Johnson, United States	19.79
1997	Ato Boldon, Trinidad and Tobago	20.04
1999	Maurice Greene, United States	19.90
2001	Konstadínos Kedéris, Greece	20.04
2003	John Capel, United States	20.30
2005	Justin Gatlin, United States	20.04

400 METERS

1983	Bert Cameron, Jamaica	45.05
1987	Thomas Schoenlebe, E Germany	44.33
1991	Antonio Pettigrew, United States	44.57
1993	Michael Johnson, United States	43.65
1995	Michael Johnson, United States	43.39
1997	Michael Johnson, United States	44.12
1999	Michael Johnson, United States	43.18 WR
2001	Avard Moncur, Bahamas	44.64
2003	Jerome Young, United States	44.50
2005	Jeremy Wariner, United States	43.93

800 METERS

1983	Willi Wulbeck, W Germany	1:43.65
1987	Billy Konchellah, Kenya	1:43.06

800 METERS (CONT.)

1991	Billy Konchellah, Kenya	1:43.99
1993	Paul Ruto, Kenya	1:44.71
1995	Wilson Kipketer, Denmark	1:45.08
1997	Wilson Kipketer, Denmark	1:43.38
1999	Wilson Kipketer, Denmark	1:43.30
2001	André Bucher, Switzerland	1:43.70
2003	Djabir Saïd-Guerni, Algeria	1:44.81
2005	Rashid Ramzi, Brunei	1:44.24

1,500 METERS

1983	Steve Cram, Great Britain	3:41.59
1987	Abdi Bile, Somalia	3:36.80
1991	Noureddine Morceli, Algeria	3:32.84
1993	Noureddine Morceli, Algeria	3:34.24
1995	Noureddine Morceli, Algeria	3:33.73
1997	Hicham El Guerrouj, Morocco	3:35.83
1999	Hicham El Guerrouj, Morocco	3:27.65
2001	Hicham El Guerrouj, Morocco	3:30.68
2003	Hicham El Guerrouj, Morocco	3:31.77
2005	Rashid Ramzi, Brunei	3:37.88

STEEPLECHASE

1983	Patriz Ilg, W Germany	8:15.06
1987	Francesco Panetta, Italy	8:08.57
1991	Moses Kiptanui, Kenya	8:12.59
1993	Moses Kiptanui, Kenya	8:06.36
1995	Moses Kiptanui, Kenya	8:04.16
1997	Wilson Boit Kipketer, Kenya	8:05.84
1999	Christopher Koskei, Kenya	8:11.76
2001	Reuben Kosgei, Kenya	8:15.16
2003	Saif Saaeed Shaheen, Qatar	8:04.39
2005	Saif Saaeed Shaheen, Qatar	8:13.31

5,000 METERS

1983	Eamonn Coghlan, Ireland	13:28.53
1987	Said Aouita, Morocco	13:26.44
1991	Yobes Ondieki, Kenya	13:14.45
1993	Ismael Kirui, Kenya	13:02.75

WR=World record. *Ben Johnson, Canada, disqualified.

Men *(Cont.)*

5,000 METERS (CONT.)

1995	Ismael Kirui, Kenya	13:16.77
1997	Daniel Komen, Kenya	13:07.38
1999	Salah Hissou, Morocco	12:58.13
2001	Richard Limo, Kenya	13:00.77
2003	Eliud Kipchoge, Kenya	12:52.79
2005	Benjamin Limo, Kenya	13:32.55

10,000 METERS

1983	Alberto Cova, Italy	28:01.04
1987	Paul Kipkoech, Kenya	27:38.63
1991	Moses Tanui, Kenya	27:38.74
1993	Haile Gebrselassie, Ethiopia	27:46.02
1995	Haile Gebrselassie, Ethiopia	27:12.95
1997	Haile Gebrselassie, Ethiopia	27:24.58
1999	Haile Gebrselassie, Ethiopia	27:57.27
2001	Charles Kamathi, Kenya	27:53.25
2003	Kenenisa Bekele, Ethiopia	26:49.57
2005	Kenenisa Bekele, Ethiopia	27:08.33

MARATHON

1983	Rob de Castella, Australia	2:10:03
1987	Douglas Wakiihuri, Kenya	2:11:48
1991	Hiromi Taniguchi, Japan	2:14:57
1993	Mark Plaatjes, United States	2:13:57
1995	Martín Fiz, Spain	2:11:41
1997	Abel Anton, Spain	2:13:16
1999	Abel Anton, Spain	2:13:36
2001	Gezahegne Abera, Ethiopia	2:12:42
2003	Jaouad Gharib, Morocco	2:08.31
2005	Jaouad Gharib, Morocco	2:10:10

110-METER HURDLES

1983	Greg Foster, United States	13.42
1987	Greg Foster, United States	13.21
1991	Greg Foster, United States	13.06
1993	Colin Jackson, Great Britain	12.91 WR
1995	Allen Johnson, United States	13.00
1997	Allen Johnson, United States	12.93
1999	Colin Jackson, Great Britain	13.04
2001	Allen Johnson, United States	13.04
2003	Allen Johnson, United States	13.12
2005	Ladji Doucoure, France	13:07

400-METER HURDLES

1983	Edwin Moses, United States	47.50
1987	Edwin Moses, United States	47.46
1991	Samuel Matete, Zambia	47.64
1993	Kevin Young, United States	47.18
1995	Derrick Adkins, United States	47.98
1997	Stéphane Diagana, France	47.70
1999	Fabrizio Mori, Italy	47.72
2001	Felix Sánchez, Dominican Rep.	47.49
2003	Felix Sánchez, Dominican Rep.	47.25
2005	Bershawn Jackson, United States	47.30

20-KILOMETER WALK

1983	Ernesto Canto, Mexico	1:20:49
1987	Maurizio Damilano, Italy	1:20:45
1991	Maurizio Damilano, Italy	1:19:37
1993	Valentin Massana, Spain	1:22:31
1995	Michele Didoni, Italy	1:19:59
1997	Daniel Garcia, Mexico	1:21:43
1999	Ilya Markov, Russia	1:23:34
2001	Roman Rasskazov, Russia	1:20:31
2003	Jefferson Pérez, Ecuador	1:17.21 WR
2005	Jefferson Perez, Ecuador	1:18:35

50-KILOMETER WALK

1983	Ronald Weigel, E Germany	3:43:08
1987	Hartwig Gauder, E Germany	3:40:53
1991	Aleksandr Potashov, USSR	3:53:09

50-KILOMETER WALK (CONT.)

1993	Jesus Angel Garcia, Spain	3:41:41
1995	Valentin Kononen, Finland	3:43:42
1997	Robert Korzeniowski, Poland	3:44:46
1999	German Skurygin, Russia	3:44:23
2001	Robert Korzeniowski, Poland	3:42:08
2003	R. Korzeniowski, Poland	3:36:03 WR
2005	S. Kirdyapkin, Russia	3:38:08

4 X 100-METER RELAY

1983	United States (Emmit King, Willie Gault, Calvin Smith, Carl Lewis)	37.86
1987	United States (Lee McRae, Lee McNeil, Harvey Glance, Carl Lewis)	37.90
1991	United States (A. Cason L. Burrell, D. Mitchell, C. Lewis)	37.50 WR
1993	United States (J. Drummond, A. Cason, D. Mitchell, L. Burrell)	37.48
1995	Canada (Robert Esmie, Glenroy Gilbert, Bruny Surin, Donovan Bailey)	38.31
1997	Canada (Robert Esmie, Glenroy Gilbert, Bruny Surin, Donovan Bailey)	37.86
1999	United States (Jon Drummond, Tim Montgomery, Brian Lewis, Maurice Greene)	37.59
2001	United States (Mickey Grimes, Bernard Williams, Dennis Mitchell, Tim Montgomery)	37.96
2003	United States (J. Capel, B. Williams D.Patton, J. Johnson)	38.06
2005	Trinidad and Tobago (L. Doucoure, R. Pognon, E. De Lepine, Dovy Lueyi)	38.08

4 X 400-METER RELAY

1983	USSR (S. Lovachev, A. Troschilo, N. Chernyetski, V. Markin)	3:00.79
1987	United States (Danny Everett, Rod Haley, Antonio McKay, Butch Reynolds)	2:57.29
1991	Great Britain (Roger Black Derek Redmond, John Regis, Kriss Akabusi)	2:57.53
1993	United States (Andrew Valmon, Quincy Watts, Butch Reynolds, Michael Johnson)	2:54.29 WR
1995	United States (Marlon Ramsey, Derek Mills, Butch Reynolds, Michael Johnson)	2:57.32
1997	United States (J. Young, A. Pettigrew, C. Jones, T. Washington)	2:56.47
1999	United States (Jerome Davis, Antonio Pettigrew, Angelo Taylor, Michael Johnson)	2:56.45
2001	United States (L. Byrd, A. Pettigrew, D. Brew, A. Taylor)	2:57.54
2003	United States (C. Harrison, T. Washington, D. Brew, J. Young)	2:58.88
2005	United States (D. Brew, R. Andrew D. Williamson, B. Wariner)	2:56.91

HIGH JUMP

1983	Gennadi Avdeyenko, USSR	7 ft 7¼ in
1987	Patrik Sjoberg, Sweden	7 ft 9¾ in
1991	Charles Austin, United States	7 ft 9¾ in
1993	Javier Sotomayor, Cuba	7 ft 10½ in
1995	Troy Kemp, Bahamas	7 ft 9¼ in
1997	Javier Sotomayor, Cuba	7 ft 9¼ in
1999	Vyacheslav Voronin, Russia	7 ft 9¼ in

Men (Cont.)

HIGH JUMP (CONT.)

2001	Martin Buss, Germany	7 ft 8¾ in
2003	Jacques Freitag, S Africa	7 ft 8½ in
2005	Yuriy Krymarenko, Ukraine	7ft¹⁄₃ in

POLE VAULT

1983	Sergei Bubka, USSR	18 ft 8¼ in
1987	Sergei Bubka, USSR	19 ft 2¼ in
1991	Sergei Bubka, USSR	19 ft 6¼ in
1993	Sergei Bubka, Ukraine	19 ft 8¼ in
1995	Sergei Bubka, Ukraine	19 ft 5 in

POLE VAULT (CONT.)

1997	Sergei Bubka, Ukraine	19 ft 8½ in
1999	Maksim Tarasov, Russia	19 ft 9 in
2001	Dmitri Markov, Australia	19 ft 10¼ in
2003	Guiseppe Gibilisco, Italy	19 ft 4¼ in
2005	Rens Blom, Netherlands	19 ft ¼ in

LONG JUMP

1983	Carl Lewis, United States	28 ft ¾ in
1987	Carl Lewis, United States	28 ft 5¼ in
1991	Mike Powell, U.S.	29 ft 4½ in WR
1993	Mike Powell, United States	28 ft 2¼ in
1995	Iván Pedroso, Cuba	28 ft 6½ in
1997	Iván Pedroso, Cuba	27 ft 7½ in
1999	Iván Pedroso, Cuba	28 ft 1 in
2001	Iván Pedroso, Cuba	27 ft 6¾ in
2003	Dwight Phillips, United States	27 ft 3½ in
2005	Dwight Phillips, United States	28 ft 2½ in

TRIPLE JUMP

1983	Zdzislaw Hoffmann, Poland	57 ft 2 in
1987	Khristo Markov, Bulgaria	58 ft 9½ in
1991	Kenny Harrison, United States	58 ft 4 in
1993	Mike Conley, United States	58 ft 7¼ in
1995	Jonathan Edwards, G.B.	60 ft ¼ in WR
1997	Yoelvis Quesada, Cuba	58 ft 6¾ in
1999	Charle Michael Friedek, Ger.	57 ft 8½ in
2001	Jonathan Edwards, G. Britain	58 ft 9½ in
2003	Christian Olsson, Sweden	58 ft 1¾ in
2005	Walter Davis, United States	57 ft 7¾ in

SHOT PUT

1983	Edward Sarul, Poland	70 ft 2¼ in
1987	Werner Günthör, Switz.	72 ft 11¼ in
1991	Werner Günthör, Switz.	71 ft 1¼ in
1993	Werner Günthör, Switz.	72 ft 1 in
1995	John Godina, United States	70 ft 5¼ in
1997	John Godina, United States	70 ft 4¼ in
1999	C.J. Hunter, United States	71 ft 6 in
2001	John Godina, United States	71 ft 9 in
2003	Andrei Mikahnevic, Bulgaria	71 ft 2 in
2005	Adam Nelson, United States	71ft 3½in

DISCUS THROW

1983	Imrich Bugar, Czechoslovakia	222 ft 2 in
1987	Juergen Schult, E Germany	225 ft 6 in
1991	Lars Riedel, Germany	217 ft 2 in
1993	Lars Riedel, Germany	222 ft 2 in
1995	Lars Riedel, Germany	225 ft 7 in
1997	Lars Riedel, Germany	224 ft 10 in
1999	Anthony Washington, U.S.	226 ft 8 in
2001	Lars Riedel, Germany	228 ft 9 in
2003	Virgilijus Alekna, Lithuania	228 ft 7¾ in
2005	Virgilijus Alekna, Lithuania	230ft 2¾in

HAMMER THROW

1983	Sergei Litvinov, USSR	271 ft 3 in
1987	Sergei Litvinov, USSR	272 ft 6 in
1991	Yuriy Sedykh, USSR	268 ft
1993	Andrey Abduvaliyev, Tajikistan	267 ft 10 in
1995	Andrey Abduvaliyev, Tajikistan	267 ft 7 in
1997	Heinz Weis, Germany	268 ft 4 in
1999	Karsten Kobs, Germany	263 ft 3 in
2001	Szymon Kiólkowski, Poland	273 ft 7 in
2003	Ivan Tikhon, Bulgaria	272 ft 5¾ in
2005	Ivan Tikhon	275 ft 2¾ in

JAVELIN

1983	Detlef Michel, E Germany	293 ft 7 in
1987	Seppo Räty, Finland	274 ft 1 in
1991	Kimmo Kinnunen, Finland	297 ft 11 in
1993	Jan Zelezny, Czech Republic	282 ft 1 in
1995	Jan Zelezny, Czech Republic	293 ft 11 in
1997	Marius Corbett, S Africa	290 ft 0 in
1999	Aki Parviainen, Finland	293 ft 8 in
2001	Jan Zelezny, Czech Republic	304 ft 5 in
2003	Sergey Makarov, Russia	280 ft 3¾ in
2005	Andrus Varnik,	285 ft 11¾ in

DECATHLON

1983	Daley Thompson, G. Britain	8666 pts
1987	Torsten Voss, E Germany	8680 pts
1991	Dan O'Brien, United States	8812 pts
1993	Dan O'Brien, United States	8817 pts
1995	Dan O'Brien, United States	8695 pts
1997	Tomás Dvorák, Czech Rep.	8837 pts
1999	Tomás Dvorák, Czech Rep.	8744 pts
2001	Tomás Dvorák, Czech Rep.	8902 pts
2003	Tom Pappas, United States	8750 pts
2005	Bryan Clay, United States	8732 pts

WR=World record.

Women

100 METERS

1983	Marlies Gohr, E Germany	10.97
1987	Silke Gladisch, E Germany	10.90
1991	Katrin Krabbe, Germany	10.99
1993	Gail Devers, United States	10.82
1995	Gwen Torrence, United States	10.85
1997	Marion Jones, United States	10.83
1999	Marion Jones, United States	10.70
2001	Zhanna Pintusevich-Block, Ukraine	10.82
2003	Kelli White, United States	10.85
2005	Lauryn Williams, United States	10.93

200 METERS

1983	Marita Koch, E Germany	22.13
1987	Silke Gladisch, E Germany	21.74
1991	Katrin Krabbe, Germany	22.09

200 METERS (CONT.)

1993	Merlene Ottey, Jamaica	21.98
1995	Merlene Ottey, Jamaica	22.12
1997	Zhanna Pintusevich, Ukraine	22.32
1999	Inger Miller, United States	21.77
2001	Marion Jones, United States	22.39
2003	Kelli White, United States	22.05
2005	Allyson Felix, United States	22.16

400 METERS

1983	Jarmila Kratochvilova, Czech.	47.99
1987	Olga Bryzgina, USSR	49.38
1991	Marie-José Pérec, France	49.13
1993	Jearl Miles, United States	49.82
1995	Marie-José Pérec, France	49.28
1997	Cathy Freeman, Australia	49.77

Women *(Cont.)*

400 METERS (CONT.)

1999	Cathy Freeman, Australia	49.67
2001	Amy Mbacke Thiam, Senegal	49.86
2003	Ana Guevara, Mexico	48.89
2005	Darling Williams, Bahamas	49.55

800 METERS

1983	Jarmila Kratochvilova, Czech.	1:54.68
1987	Sigrun Wodars, E Germany	1:55.26
1991	Lilia Nurutdinova, USSR	1:57.50
1993	Maria Mutola, Mozambique	1:55.43
1995	Ana Quirot, Cuba	1:56.11
1997	Ana Quirot, Cuba	1:57.14
1999	Ludmila Formanová, Czech Rep.	1:56.68
2001	Maria Mutola, Mozambique	1:57.17
2003	Maria Mutola, Mozambique	1:59.89
2005	Zulia Calatayud, Cuba	1:58.82

1,500 METERS

1983	Mary Slaney, United States	4:00.90
1987	Tatyana Samolenko, USSR	3:58.56
1991	Hassiba Boulmerka, Algeria	4:02.21
1993	Dong Liu, China	4:00.50
1995	Hassiba Boulmerka, Algeria	4:02.42
1997	Carla Sacramento, Portugal	4:04.24
1999	Svetlana Masterkova, Russia	3:59.53
2001	Gabriela Szabo, Romania	4:00.57
2003	Tatyana Tomashova, Russia	3:58.52
2005	Tatyana Tomashova, Russia	4:00.35

3,000 METERS

1983	Mary Slaney, United States	8:34.62
1987	Tatyana Samolenko, USSR	8:38.73
1991	Tatyana Dorovskikh, USSR	8:35.82
1993	Qu Yunxia, China	8:28.71

5,000 METERS

1995	Sonia O'Sullivan, Ireland	14:46.47
1997	Gabriela Szabo, Romania	14:57.68
1999	Gabriela Szabo, Romania	14:41.82
2001	Olga Yegorova, Russia	15:03.39
2003	Tirunesh Dibaba, Ethiopia	14:51.72
2005	Tirunesh Dibaba Ethiopia	14:38.59

10,000 METERS

1987	Ingrid Kristiansen, Norway	31:05.85
1991	Liz McColgan, Great Britain	31:14.31
1993	Wang Junxia, China	30:49:30
1995	Fernanda Ribeiro, Portugal	31:04.99
1997	Sally Barsosio, Kenya	31:32.92
1999	Gete Wami, Ethiopia	30:24.56
2001	Derartu Tulu, Ethiopia	31:48.81
2003	Berhane Adere, Ethiopia	30:04.18
2005	Tirunesha Dibaba, Ethiopia	30:24.02

MARATHON

1983	Grete Waitz, Norway	2:28:09
1987	Rosa Mota, Portugal	2:25:17
1991	Wanda Panfil, Poland	2:29:53
1993	Junko Asari, Japan	2:30:03
1995	Manuela Machado, Portugal	2:25:39*
1997	Hiromi Suzuki, Japan	2:29:48
1999	Jong Song-Ok, N Korea	2:26:59
2001	Lidia Simon, Romania	2:26.01
2003	Catherine Ndereba, Kenya	2:23:55
2005	Paula Radcliffe, Great Britain	2:20:57

100-METER HURDLES

1983	Bettine Jahn, E Germany	12.35
1987	Ginka Zagorcheva, Bulgaria	12.34

*400 meters short.

100-METER HURDLES (CONT.)

1991	Lyudmila Narozhilenko, USSR	12.59
1993	Gail Devers, United States	12.46
1995	Gail Devers, United States	12.68
1997	Ludmila Engquist, Sweden	12.50
1999	Gail Devers, United States	12.37
2001	Anjanette Kirkland, United States	12.42
2003	Perdita Felicien, Canada	12.53
2005	Michelle Perry, United States	12:66

400-METER HURDLES

1983	Yekaterina Fesenko, USSR	54.14
1987	Sabine Busch, E Germany	53.62
1991	Tatyana Ledovskaya, USSR	53.11
1993	Sally Gunnell, Great Britain	52.74 WR
1995	Kim Batten, United States	52.61
1997	Nezha Bidouane, Morocco	52.97
1999	Daimi Pernia, Cuba	52.89
2001	Nezha Bidouane, Morocco	53.34
2003	Jana Pittman, Australia	53.22
2005	Yuliya Pechonkina, Russia	52.90

10-KILOMETER WALK

1987	Irina Strakhova, USSR	44:12
1991	Alina Ivanova, USSR	42:57
1993	Sari Essayah, Finland	42:59
1995	Irina Stankina, Russia	42:13
1997	Annarita Sidoti, Italy	42:56

20-KILOMETER WALK

1999	Hongyu Liu, China	1:30:50
2001	Olimpiada Ivanova, Russia	1:27:48
2003	Yelena Nikolayeva, Russia	1:26:52
2005	Olimpiada Ivanova, Russia	1:25:41

4 X 100-METER RELAY

1983	E Germany (S. Gladisch, M. Koch, I. Auerswald, M. Gohr)	41.76
1987	United States (A. Brown, D. Williams, F. Griffith, P. Marshall)	41.58
1991	Jamaica (Dalia Duhaney, Juliet Cuthbert, Beverley McDonald, Merlene Ottey)	41.94
1993	Russia (Olga Bogoslovskaya, Galina Malchugina, Natalya Voronova, Irina Privalova)	41.49
1995	United States (Celena Mondie-Milner, Carlette Guidry, Chryste Gaines, Gwen Torrence)	42.12
1997	United States (C. Gaines, M. Jones, I. Miller, G.Devers)	41.47
1999	Bahamas (S. Fynes, C. Sturrup, P. Davis-Thompson, D. Ferguson)	41.92
2001	United States (Kelli White, Chryste Gaines, Inger Miller, Marion Jones)	41.71
2003	France (P. Girard, M. Hurtis S. Félix, C. Arron)	41.78
2005	Jamaica, (A. Daigie, M. Lee, M. B.L. Williams	41.78

4 X 400-METER RELAY

1983	E Germany (Kerstin Walther, Sabine Busch, Marita Koch, Dagmar Rubsam)	3:19.73
1987	E Germany (Dagmar Neubauer, Kirsten Emmelmann, Petra Müller, Sabine Busch)	3:18.63

Women (Cont.)

4 X 400-METER RELAY (CONT.)

1991	USSR (Tatyana Ledovskaya, Lyudmila Dzhigalova, Olga Nazarova, Olga Bryzgina)	3:18.43
1993	United States (Gwen Torrence, Maicel Malone, Natasha Kaiser-Brown, Jearl Miles)	3:16.71
1995	United States (Kim Graham, Rochelle Stevens, Camara Jones, Jearl Miles)	3:22.39
1997	Germany (A. Feller, U. Rohlander, A. Rucker, G. Breuer)	3:20.92
1999	Russia (Tatyana Chebykina, Svetlana Goncharenko, Olga Kotylarova, Natalya Nazarova)	3:21.98
2001	Jamaica (Sandie Richards, Catherine Scott, Debbie Ann Parris, Lorraine Fenton)	3:20.65
2003	United States (M. Barber, D. Washington, J. Miles-Clark, S. Richards)	3:22.63
2005	Russia, (Y. Pechonkina, O. Krasnomovets, N. Antyukh, S. Pospelova)	3:20.95

HIGH JUMP

1983	Tamara Bykova, USSR	6 ft 7 in
1987	Stefka Kostadinova, Bulgaria	6 ft 10¼ in
1991	Heike Henkel, Germany	6 ft 8¾ in
1993	Ioamnet Quintero, Cuba	6 ft 6¼ in
1995	Stefka Kostadinova, Bulgaria	6 ft 7 in
1997	Hanne Haugland, Norway	6 ft 6¼ in
1999	Inga Babakova, Ukraine	6 ft 6¼ in
2001	Hestrie Cloete, S Africa	6 ft 6¾ in
2003	Hestrie Cloete, S Africa	6 ft 9 in
2005	Kajsa Bergvist, Sweden	6 ft 7½ in

POLE VAULT

1999	Stacy Dragila, U.S.	15 ft 1 in EWR
2001	Stacy Dragila, United States	15 ft 7 in
2003	Svetlana Feofanova, Russia	15 ft 7 in
2005	Yelena Isinbayeva, Russia	16 ft 5¼ in

LONG JUMP

1983	Heike Daute, E Germany	23 ft 10¼ in
1987	Jackie Joyner-Kersee, U.S.	24 ft 1¾ in
1991	Jackie Joyner-Kersee, U.S.	24 ft ¼ in
1993	Heike Drechsler, Germany	23 ft 4 in
1995	Fiona May, Italy	22 ft 10¾ in
1997	Lyudmila Galkina, Russia	23 ft 1¾ in
1999	Niurka Montalvo, Spain	23 ft 2 in
2001	Fiona May, Italy	23 ft ½ in
2003	Eunice Barber, France	22 ft 11 in
2005	Tianna Madison, U.S.	22 ft 7¼ in

TRIPLE JUMP

1993	Ana Biryukova, Russia	49 ft 6 ¼ in WR
1995	Inessa Kravets, Ukraine	50 ft 10¼ in WR
1997	S. Kasparkova, Czech Rep.	49 ft 10½ in
1999	Paraskevi Tsiamíta, Greece	48 ft 10 in
2001	Tatyana Lebedeva, Russia	50 ft ½ in
2003	Tatyana Lebedeva, Russia	49 ft 9½ in
2005	Trecia Smith, Jamaica	49 ft 6¾ in

SHOT PUT

1983	Helena Fibingerova, Czech.	69 ft ¾ in
1987	Natalya Lisovskaya, USSR	69 ft 8¼ in
1991	Zhihong Huang, China	68 ft 4¼ in
1993	Zhihong Huang, China	67 ft 6 in
1995	Astrid Kumbernuss, Germany	69 ft 7½ in
1997	Astrid Kumbernuss, Germany	67 ft 11½ in
1999	Astrid Kumbernuss, Germany	65 ft 1½ in
2001	Yanina Korolchik, Belarus	67 ft 7½ in
2003	Svetlana Krivelyova, Russia	67 ft 8 in
2005	Nadezhda Ostapchuk, Russia	68 ft 3½ in

HAMMER THROW

1999	Mihaela Melinte, Romania	246 ft 9 in
2001	Yipsi Moreno, Cuba	231 ft 9 in
2003	Yipsi Moreno, Cuba	240 ft 7 in
2005	Olga Kuzenkova, Russia	246 ft 4¾ in

DISCUS THROW

1983	Martina Opitz, E Germany	226 ft 2 in
1987	Martina Hellmann, E Germany	235 ft
1991	Tsvetanka Khristova, Bulgaria	233 ft
1993	Olga Burova, Russia	221 ft 1 in
1995	Ellina Zvereva, Belarus	225 ft 2 in
1997	Beatrice Faumuina, New Zeal.	219 ft 3 in
1999	Franka Dietzsch, Germany	223 ft 7 in
2001	Natalya Sadova, Russia	224 ft 11 in
2003	Irina Yatchenko, Bulgaria	220 ft 10½ in
2005	Franka Dietzsch, Germany	218 ft 4½ in

JAVELIN

1983	Tiina Lillak, Finland	232 ft 4 in
1987	Fatima Whitbread, G.B.	251 ft 5 in
1991	Demei Xu, China	225 ft 8 in
1993	Trine Hattestad, Finland	227 ft
1995	Natalya Shikolenko, Belarus	221 ft 8 in
1997	Trine Hattestad, Norway	225 ft 8 in
1999	Miréla Manjani-Tzelili, Greece	220 ft 1 in
2001	Osleidys Menéndez, Cuba	228 ft 1 in
2003	Miréla Manjani, Greece	218 ft 3 in
2005	Osleidys Menendez, Cuba	235 ft 2¾ in

HEPTATHLON

1983	Ramona Neubert, E Germany	6714 pts
1987	Jackie Joyner-Kersee, U.S.	7128 pts
1991	Sabine Braun, Germany	6672 pts
1993	Jackie Joyner-Kersee, U.S.	6837 pts
1995	Ghada Shouaa, Syria	6651 pts
1997	Sabine Braun, Germany	6739 pts
1999	Eunice Barber, France	6861 pts
2001	Yelena Prokhorova, Russia	6694 pts
2003	Carolina Klüft, Sweden	7001 pts
2005	Carolina Kluft, Sweden	6887 pts

WR=World record. EWR=equals world record.

Track and Field News Athlete of the Year

Each year (since 1959 for men and 1974 for women) *Track and Field News* has chosen the outstanding athlete in the sport.

MEN

Year	Athlete	Event
1959	Martin Lauer, W Germany	110H/Decath
1960	Rafer Johnson, United States	Decathlon
1961	Ralph Boston, United States	Long jump
1962	Peter Snell, New Zealand	800/1,500
1963	C. K. Yang, Taiwan	Decath/PV
1964	Peter Snell, New Zealand	800/1,500
1965	Ron Clarke, Australia	5K/10K
1966	Jim Ryun, United States	800/1,500
1967	Jim Ryun, United States	1,500
1968	Bob Beamon, United States	Long jump
1969	Bill Toomey, United States	Decathlon
1970	Randy Matson, United States	Shot put
1971	Rod Milburn, United States	110H
1972	Lasse Viren, Finland	5K/10K
1973	Ben Jipcho, Kenya	1,500/5K/ST
1974	Rick Wohlhuter, United States	800/1,500
1975	John Walker, New Zealand	800/1,500
1976	Alberto Juantorena, Cuba	400/800
1977	Alberto Juantorena, Cuba	400/800
1978	Henry Rono, Kenya	5K/10K/ST
1979	Sebastian Coe, Great Britain	800/1,500
1980	Edwin Moses, United States	400H
1981	Sebastian Coe, Great Britain	800/1,500
1982	Carl Lewis, United States	100/200/LJ
1983	Carl Lewis, United States	100/200/LJ
1984	Carl Lewis, United States	100/200/LJ
1985	Said Aouita, Morocco	1,500/5000
1986	Yuri Syedikh, USSR	Hammer
1987	Ben Johnson, Canada	100
1988	Sergei Bubka, USSR	Pole vault
1989	Roger Kingdom, United States	110H
1990	Michael Johnson, United States	200/400
1991	Sergei Bubka, CIS	Pole vault
1992	Kevin Young, United States	400H
1993	Noureddine Morceli, Algeria	1,500/mile/3K
1994	Noureddine Morceli, Algeria	1,500/mile/3K
1995	Haile Gebrselassie, Ethiopia	5K/10K
1996	Michael Johnson, United States	200/400
1997	Wilson Kipketer, Denmark	800
1998	Haile Gebrselassie, Ethiopia	5K/10K
1999	Hicham El Guerrouj, Morocco	1,500/Mile
2000	Virgilijus Alekna, Lithuania	Discus
2001	Hicham El Guerrouj, Morocco	1,500/Mile
2002	Hicham El Guerrouj, Morocco	1,500/Mile
2003	Felix Sanchez, Dominican Rep.	400H
2004	Kenenisa Bekele, Ethiopia	5K/10K

WOMEN

Year	Athlete	Event
1974	Irena Szewinska, Poland	100/200/400
1975	Faina Melnik, USSR	Shot/Discus
1976	Tatyana Kazankina, USSR	800/1,500
1977	R. Ackermann, E Germany	High jump
1978	Marita Koch, E Germany	100/200/400
1979	Marita Koch, E Germany	100/200/400
1980	Ilona Briesenick, E Germany	Shot put
1981	Evelyn Ashford, United States	100/200
1982	Marita Koch, E Germany	100/200/400
1983	J. Kratochvilova, Czechoslovakia	200/400/800
1984	Evelyn Ashford, United States	100
1985	Marita Koch, E Germany	100/200/400
1986	Jackie Joyner-Kersee, U.S.	LJ/Hept
1987	Jackie Joyner-Kersee, U.S	100H/LJ/Hept
1988	Florence Griffith Joyner, U.S.	100/200
1989	Ana Quirot, Cuba	400/800
1990	Merlene Ottey, Jamaica	100/200
1991	Heike Henkel, Germany	High jump
1992	Heike Drechsler, Germany	Long Jump
1993	Wang Junxia, China	1.5K/3K/10K
1994	Jackie Joyner-Kersee, U.S.	100H/LJ/Hept
1995	Sonia O'Sullivan, Ireland	1,500/3K/5K
1996	Svetlana Masterkova, Russia	800/1,500
1997	Marion Jones, United States	100/200/LJ
1998	Marion Jones, United States	100/200/LJ
1999	Gabriela Szabo, Romania	1,500/5,000
2000	Marion Jones, United States	100/200/LJ
2001	Stacy Dragila, United States	Pole vault
2002	Paula Radcliffe, Great Britain	Marathon
2003	Maria Mutola, Mozambique	800
2004	Yelena Isinbayena, Russia	Pole vault

Marathon World Record Progression

Men

Record Holder	Time	Date	Site
John Hayes, United States	2:55:18.4	7-24-08	Shepherd's Bush, London
Robert Fowler, United States	2:52:45.4	1-1-09	Yonkers, NY
James Clark, United States	2:46:52.6	2-12-09	New York City
Albert Raines, United States	2:46:04.6	5-8-09	New York City
Frederick Barrett, Great Britain	2:42:31	5-26-09	Shepherd's Bush, London
Harry Green, Great Britain	2:38:16.2	5-12-13	Shepherd's Bush, London
Alexis Ahlgren, Sweden	2:36:06.6	5-31-13	Shepherd's Bush, London
Johannes Kolehmainen, Finland	2:32:35.8	8-22-20	Antwerp, Belgium
Albert Michelsen, United States	2:29:01.8	10-12-25	Port Chester, NY
Fusashige Suzuki, Japan	2:27:49	3-31-35	Tokyo
Yasuo Ikenaka, Japan	2:26:44	4-3-35	Tokyo
Kitei Son, Japan	2:26:42	11-3-35	Tokyo
Yun Bok Suh, Korea	2:25:39	4-19-47	Boston
James Peters, Great Britain	2:20:42.2	6-14-52	Chiswick, England
James Peters, Great Britain	2:18:40.2	6-13-53	Chiswick, England
James Peters, Great Britain	2:18:34.8	10-4-53	Turku, Finland
James Peters, Great Britain	2:17:39.4	6-26-54	Chiswick, England
Sergei Popov, USSR	2:15:17	8-24-58	Stockholm
Abebe Bikila, Ethiopia	2:15:16.2	9-10-60	Rome
Toru Terasawa, Japan	2:15:15.8	2-17-63	Beppu, Japan
Leonard Edelen, United States	2:14:28	6-15-63	Chiswick, England
Basil Heatley, Great Britain	2:13:55	6-13-64	Chiswick, England
Abebe Bikila, Ethiopia	2:12:11.2	6-21-64	Tokyo
Morio Shigematsu, Japan	2:12:00	6-12-65	Chiswick, England
Derek Clayton, Australia	2:09:36.4	12-3-67	Fukuoka, Japan
Derek Clayton, Australia	2:08:33.6	5-30-69	Antwerp, Belgium
Rob de Castella, Australia	2:08:18	12-6-81	Fukuoka, Japan
Steve Jones, Great Britain	2:08:05	10-21-84	Chicago
Carlos Lopes, Portugal	2:07:12	4-20-85	Rotterdam, Netherlands
Belayneh Dinsamo, Ethiopia	2:06:50	4-17-88	Rotterdam, Netherlands
Ronaldo Da Costa, Brazil	2:06:05	9-20-98	Berlin, Germany
Khalid Khannouchi, Morocco	2:05:42	10-24-99	Chicago
Khalid Khannouchi, United States	2:05:38	4-14-02	London
Paul Tergat, Kenya	2:04:55	9-28-03	Berlin

Women

Record Holder	Time	Date	Site
Dale Greig, Great Britain	3:27:45	5-23-64	Ryde, England
Mildred Simpson, New Zealand	3:19:33	7-21-64	Auckland, New Zealand
Maureen Wilton, Canada	3:15:22	5-6-67	Toronto
Anni Pede-Erdkamp, W Germany	3:07:26	9-16-67	Waldniel, W Germany
Caroline Walker, United States	3:02:53	2-28-70	Seaside, OR
Record Holder	Time	Date	Site
Elizabeth Bonner, United States	3:01:42	5-9-71	Philadelphia
Adrienne Beames, Australia	2:46:30	8-31-71	Werribee, Australia
Chantal Langlace, France	2:46:24	10-27-74	Neuf Brisach, France
Jacqueline Hansen, United States	2:43:54.5	12-1-74	Culver City, CA
Liane Winter, W Germany	2:42:24	4-21-75	Boston
Christa Vahlensieck, W Germany	2:40:15.8	5-3-75	Dülmen, W Germany
Jacqueline Hansen, United States	2:38:19	10-12-75	Eugene, OR
Chantal Langlace, France	2:35:15.4	5-1-77	Oyarzun, France
Christa Vahlensieck, W Germany	2:34:47.5	9-10-77	Berlin, W Germany
Grete Waitz, Norway	2:32:29.9	10-22-78	New York City
Grete Waitz, Norway	2:27:32.6	10-21-79	New York City
Grete Waitz, Norway	2:25:41.3	10-26-80	New York City
Grete Waitz, Norway	2:25:29	4-17-83	London
Joan Benoit Samuelson, United States	2:22:43	4-18-83	Boston
Ingrid Kristiansen, Norway	2:21:06	4-21-85	London
Tegla Loroupe, Kenya	2:20:47	4-19-98	Rotterdam, Netherlands
Tegla Loroupe, Kenya	2:20:43	9-26-99	Berlin
Naoko Takahashi, Japan	2:19:46	9-30-01	Berlin
Catherine Ndereba, Kenya	2:18:47	10-7-01	Chicago
Paula Radcliffe, Great Britain	2:17:18	10-13-02	Chicago
Paula Radcliffe, Great Britain	2:15:25	4-13-03	London

The Boston Marathon began in 1897 as a local Patriot's Day event. Run every year but 1918 since then, it has grown into one of the world's premier marathons.

Men

Year	Winner	Time	Year	Winner	Time
1897	John J. McDermott, United States	2:55:10	1952	Doroteo Flores, Guatemala	2:31:53
1898	Ronald J. McDonald, United States	2:42:00	1953	Keizo Yamada, Japan	2:18:51*
1899	Lawrence J. Brignolia, United States	2:54:38	1954	Veikko Karvonen, Finland	2:20:39
1900	James J. Caffrey, Canada	2:39:44	1955	Hideo Hamamura, Japan	2:18:22
1901	James J. Caffrey, Canada	2:29:23	1956	Antti Viskari, Finland	2:14:14
1902	Sammy Mellor, United States	2:43:12	1957	John J. Kelley, United States	2:20:05
1903	John C. Lorden, United States	2:41:29	1958	Franjo Mihalic, Yugoslavia	2:25:54
1904	Michael Spring, United States	2:38:04	1959	Eino Oksanen, Finland	2:22:42
1905	Fred Lorz, United States	2:38:25	1960	Paavo Kotila, Finland	2:20:54
1906	Timothy Ford, United States	2:45:45	1961	Eino Oksanen, Finland	2:23:39
1907	Tom Longboat, Canada	2:24:24	1962	Eino Oksanen, Finland	2:23:48
1908	Thomas Morrissey, United States	2:25:43	1963	Aurele Vandendriessche, Belgium	2:18:58
1909	Henri Renaud, United States	2:53:36	1964	Aurele Vandendriessche, Belgium	2:19:59
1910	Fred Cameron, Canada	2:28:52	1965	Morio Shigematsu, Japan	2:16:33
1911	Clarence H. DeMar, United States	2:21:39	1966	Kenji Kimihara, Japan	2:17:11
1912	Mike Ryan, United States	2:21:18	1967	David McKenzie, New Zealand	2:15:45
1913	Fritz Carlson, United States	2:25:14	1968	Amby Burfoot, United States	2:22:17
1914	James Duffy, Canada	2:25:01	1969	Yoshiaki Unetani, Japan	2:13:49
1915	Edouard Fabre, Canada	2:31:41	1970	Ron Hill, England	2:10:30
1916	Arthur Roth, United States	2:27:16	1971	Alvaro Mejia, Colombia	2:18:45
1917	Bill Kennedy, United States	2:28:37	1972	Olavi Suomalainen, Finland	2:15:39
1919	Carl Linder, United States	2:29:13	1973	Jon Anderson, United States	2:16:03
1920	Peter Trivoulidas, Greece	2:29:31	1974	Neil Cusack, Ireland	2:13:39
1921	Frank Zuna, United States	2:18:57	1975	Bill Rodgers, United States	2:09:55
1922	Clarence H. DeMar, United States	2:18:10	1976	Jack Fultz, United States	2:20:19
1923	Clarence H. DeMar, United States	2:23:37	1977	Jerome Drayton, Canada	2:14:46
1924	Clarence H. DeMar, United States	2:29:40	1978	Bill Rodgers, United States	2:10:13
1925	Chuck Mellor, United States	2:33:00	1979	Bill Rodgers, United States	2:09:27
1926	John C. Miles, Canada	2:25:40	1980	Bill Rodgers, United States	2:12:11
1927	Clarence H. DeMar, United States	2:40:22	1981	Toshihiko Seko, Japan	2:09:26
1928	Clarence H. DeMar, United States	2:37:07	1982	Alberto Salazar, United States	2:08:52
1929	John C. Miles, Canada	2:33:08	1983	Gregory A. Meyer, United States	2:09:00
1930	Clarence H. DeMar, United States	2:34:48	1984	Geoff Smith, England	2:10:34
1931	James (Hinky) Henigan, United States	2:46:45	1985	Geoff Smith, England	2:14:05
1932	Paul de Bruyn, Germany	2:33:36	1986	Rob de Castella, Australia	2:07:51
1933	Leslie Pawson, United States	2:31:01	1987	Toshihiko Seko, Japan	2:11:50
1934	Dave Komonen, Canada	2:32:53	1988	Ibrahim Hussein, Kenya	2:08:43
1935	John A. Kelley, United States	2:32:07	1989	Abebe Mekonnen, Ethiopia	2:09:06
1936	Ellison M. (Tarzan) Brown, United States	2:33:40	1990	Gelindo Bordin, Italy	2:08:19
1937	Walter Young, Canada	2:33:20	1991	Ibrahim Hussein, Kenya	2:11:06
1938	Leslie Pawson, United States	2:35:34	1992	Ibrahim Hussein, Kenya	2:08:14
1939	Ellison M. (Tarzan) Brown, United States	2:28:51	1993	Cosmas N'Deti, Kenya	2:09:33
1940	Gerard Cote, Canada	2:28:28	1994	Cosmas N'Deti, Kenya	2:07:15
1941	Leslie Pawson, United States	2:30:38	1995	Cosmas N'Deti, Kenya	2:09:22
1942	Bernard Joseph Smith, United States	2:26:51	1996	Moses Tanui, Kenya	2:09:16
1943	Gerard Cote, Canada	2:28:25	1997	Lameck Aguta, Kenya	2:10:34
1944	Gerard Cote, Canada	2:31:50	1998	Moses Tanui, Kenya	2:07:34
1945	John A. Kelley, United States	2:30:40	1999	Joseph Chebet, Kenya	2:09:52
1946	Stylianos Kyriakides, Greece	2:29:27	2000	Elijah Lagat, Kenya	2:09:47
1947	Yun Bok Suh, Korea	2:25:39	2001	Lee Bong-Ju, Korea	2:09:43
1948	Gerard Cote, Canada	2:31:02	2002	Rodgers Rop, Kenya	2:09:02
1949	Karl Gosta Leandersson, Sweden	2:31:50	2003	Robert Cheruiyot, Kenya	2:10:11
1950	Kee Yong Ham, Korea	2:32:39	2004	Timothy Cherigat, Kenya	2:10:37
1951	Shigeki Tanaka, Japan	2:27:45	2005	Hailu Negussie, Ethiopia	2:04.32

Note: Over the years the Boston course has varied in length. The distances have been 24 miles, 1,232 yards (1897–1923); 26 miles, 209 yards (1924–1926); 26 miles, 385 yards (1927–1952); and 25 miles, 958 yards (1953–1956). Since 1957, the course has been certified to be the standard marathon distance of 26 miles, 385 yards. (*Unofficial.)

Women

Year	Winner	Time	Year	Winner	Time
1966	Roberta Gibb, United States	3:21:40*	1986	Ingrid Kristiansen, Norway	2:24:55
1967	Roberta Gibb, United States	3:27:17*	1987	Rosa Mota, Portugal	2:25:21
1968	Roberta Gibb, United States	3:30:00*	1988	Rosa Mota, Portugal	2:24:30
1969	Sara Mae Berman, United States	3:22:46*	1989	Ingrid Kristiansen, Norway	2:24:33
1970	Sara Mae Berman, United States	3:05:07*	1990	Rosa Mota, Portugal	2:25:24
1971	Sara Mae Berman, United States	3:08:30*	1991	Wanda Panfil, Poland	2:24:18
1972	Nina Kuscsik, United States	3:10:36	1992	Olga Markova, Russia	2:23:43
1973	Jacqueline A. Hansen, United States	3:05:59	1993	Olga Markova, Russia	2:25:27
1974	Miki Gorman, United States	2:47:11	1994	Uta Pippig, Germany	2:21:45
1975	Liane Winter, W Germany	2:42:24	1995	Uta Pippig, Germany	2:25:11
1976	Kim Merritt, United States	2:47:10	1996	Uta Pippig, Germany	2:27:12
1977	Miki Gorman, United States	2:48:33	1997	Fatuma Roba, Ethiopia	2:26:23
1978	Gayle Barron, United States	2:44:52	1998	Fatuma Roba, Ethiopia	2:23:21
1979	Joan Benoit, United States	2:35:15	1999	Fatuma Roba, Ethiopia	2:23:25
1980	Jacqueline Gareau, Canada	2:34:28	2000	Catherine Ndereba, Kenya	2:26:11
1981	Allison Roe, New Zealand	2:26:46	2001	Catherine Ndereba, Kenya	2:23:53
1982	Charlotte Teske, W Germany	2:29:33	2002	Margaret Okayo, Kenya	2:20:43
1983	Joan Benoit, United States	2:22:43	2003	Svetlana Zakharova, Russia	2:25:20
1984	Lorraine Moller, New Zealand	2:29:28	2004	Catherine Ndereba, Kenya	2:24:27
1985	Lisa Larsen Weidenbach, United States	2:34:06	2005	Catherine Ndereba, Kenya	2:17:38

New York City Marathon

	MEN			WOMEN	
Year	Winner	Time	Year	Winner	Time
1970	Gary Muhrcke, United States	2:31:38	1970	No finisher	
1971	Norman Higgins, United States	2:22:54	1971	Beth Bonner, United States	2:55:22
1972	Sheldon Karlin, United States	2:27:52	1972	Nina Kuscsik, United States	3:08:41
1973	Tom Fleming, United States	2:21:54	1973	Nina Kuscsik, United States	2:57:07
1974	Norbert Sander, United States	2:26:30	1974	Katherine Switzer, United States	3:07:29
1975	Tom Fleming, United States	2:19:27	1975	Kim Merritt, United States	2:46:14
1976	Bill Rodgers, United States	2:10:10	1976	Miki Gorman, United States	2:39:11
1977	Bill Rodgers, United States	2:11:28	1977	Miki Gorman, United States	2:43:10
1978	Bill Rodgers, United States	2:12:12	1978	Grete Waitz, Norway	2:32:30
1979	Bill Rodgers, United States	2:11:42	1979	Grete Waitz, Norway	2:27:33
1980	Alberto Salazar, United States	2:09:41	1980	Grete Waitz, Norway	2:25:41
1981	Alberto Salazar, United States	2:08:13	1981	Allison Roe, New Zealand	2:25:29
1982	Alberto Salazar, United States	2:09:29	1982	Grete Waitz, Norway	2:27:14
1983	Rod Dixon, New Zealand	2:08:59	1983	Grete Waitz, Norway	2:27:00
1984	Orlando Pizzolato, Italy	2:14:53	1984	Grete Waitz, Norway	2:29:30
1985	Orlando Pizzolato, Italy	2:11:34	1985	Grete Waitz, Norway	2:28:34
1986	Gianni Poli, Italy	2:11:06	1986	Grete Waitz, Norway	2:28:06
1987	Ibrahim Hussein, Kenya	2:11:01	1987	Priscilla Welch, Great Britain	2:30:17
1988	Steve Jones, Great Britain	2:08:20	1988	Grete Waitz, Norway	2:28:07
1989	Juma Ikangaa, Tanzania	2:08:01	1989	Ingrid Kristiansen, Norway	2:25:30
1990	Douglas Wakiihuri, Kenya	2:12:39	1990	Wanda Panfiil, Poland	2:30:45
1991	Salvador Garcia, Mexico	2:09:28	1991	Liz McColgan, Scotland	2:27:23
1992	Willie Mtolo, S Africa	2:09:29	1992	Lisa Ondieki, Australia	2:24:40
1993	Andres Espinosa, Mexico	2:10:04	1993	Uta Pippig, Germany	2:26:24
1994	German Silva, Mexico	2:11:21	1994	Tegla Loroupe, Kenya	2:27:37
1995	German Silva, Mexico	2:11:00	1995	Tegla Loroupe, Kenya	2:28:06
1996	Giacomo Leone, Italy	2:09:54	1996	Anuta Catuna, Romania	2:28:18
1997	John Kagwe, Kenya	2:08:12	1997	Franziska Rochat-Moser, Switzerland	2:28:43
1998	John Kagwe, Kenya	2:08:45	1998	Franca Fiacconi, Italy	2:25:17
1999	Joseph Chebet, Kenya	2:09:14	1999	Adriana Fernandez, Mexico	2:25:06
2000	Abdelkhader El Mouaziz, Morocco	2:10:09	2000	Ludmila Petrova, Russia	2:25:45
2001	Tesfaye Jifar, Ethiopia	2:07:43	2001	Margaret Okayo, Kenya	2:24:21
2002	Rodgers Rop, Kenya	2:08:07	2002	Joyce Chepchumba, Kenya	2:25:56
2003	Martin Lel, Kenya	2:10:30	2003	Margaret Okayo, Kenya	2:22:31
2004	Hendrik Ramaala, South Africa	2:09:28	2004	Paula Radcliffe, England	2:23:10

World Cross-Country Championships

Men

Conducted by the International Amateur Athletic Federation (IAAF), this meet draws the best runners in the world at every distance from the mile to the marathon to compete in the same cross-country race.

Year	Winner	Winning Team	Year	Winner	Winning Team
1973	Pekka Paivarinta, Finland	Belgium	1990	Khalid Skah, Morocco	Kenya
1974	Eric DeBeck, Belgium	Belgium	1991	Khalid Skah, Morocco	Kenya
1975	Ian Stewart, Scotland	New Zealand	1992	John Ngugi, Kenya	Kenya
1976	Carlos Lopes, Portugal	England	1993	William Sigei, Kenya	Kenya
1977	Leon Schots, Belgium	Belgium	1994	William Sigei, Kenya	Kenya
1978	John Treacy, Ireland	France	1995	Paul Tergat, Kenya	Kenya
1979	John Treacy, Ireland	England	1996	Paul Tergat, Kenya	Kenya
1980	Craig Virgin, United States	England	1997	Paul Tergat, Kenya	Kenya
1981	Craig Virgin, United States	Ethiopia	1998	Paul Tergat, Kenya	Kenya
1982	Mohammed Kedir, Ethiopia	Ethiopia	1999	Paul Tergat, Kenya	Kenya
1983	Bekele Debele, Ethiopia	Ethiopia	2000	Mohammed Mourhit, Belgium	Kenya
1984	Carlos Lopes, Portugal	Ethiopia	2001	Mohammed Mourhit, Belgium	Kenya
1985	Carlos Lopes, Portugal	Ethiopia	2002	Kenenisa Bekele , Ethiopia	Kenya
1987	John Ngugi, Kenya	Kenya	2003	Kenenisa Bekele, Ethiopia	Kenya
1988	John Ngugi, Kenya	Kenya	2004	Kenenisa Bekele, Ethiopia	Ethiopia
1989	John Ngugi, Kenya	Kenya	2005	Kenenisa Bekele, Ethiopia	Ethiopia

Women

Year	Winner	Winning Team	Year	Winner	Winning Team
1973	Paola Cacchi, Italy	England	1990	Lynn Jennings, United States	USSR
1974	Paola Cacchi, Italy	England	1991	Lynn Jennings, United States	Kenya
1975	Julie Brown, United States	United States	1992	Lynn Jennings, United States	Kenya
1976	Carmen Valero, Spain	USSR	1993	Albertina Dias, Portugal	Kenya
1977	Carmen Valero, Spain	USSR	1994	Helen Chepngeno, Kenya	Portugal
1978	Grete Waitz, Norway	Romania	1995	Derartu Tulu, Ethiopia	Kenya
1979	Grete Waitz, Norway	United States	1996	Gete Wami, Ethiopia	Kenya
1980	Grete Waitz, Norway	USSR	1997	Derartu Tulu, Ethiopia	Ethiopia
1981	Grete Waitz, Norway	USSR	1998	Sonia O'Sullivan, Ireland	Kenya
1982	Maricica Puica, Romania	USSR	1999	Gete Wami, Ethiopia	Ethiopia
1983	Grete Waitz, Norway	United States	2000	Derartu Tulu, Ethiopia	Ethiopia
1984	Maricica Puica, Romania	United States	2001	Paula Radcliffe, Great Britain	Kenya
1985	Zola Budd, England	United States	2002	Paula Radcliffe, Great Britain	Ethiopia
1986	Zola Budd, England	England	2003	Werknesh Kidane, Ethiopia	Ethiopia
1987	Annette Sergent, France	United States	2004	Benita Johnson, Australia	Ethiopia
1988	Ingrid Kristiansen, Norway	USSR	2005	Dibaba Tirunesh, Ethiopia	Ethiopia
1989	Annette Sergent, France	USSR			

Notable Achievements

Longest Winning Streaks

MEN

Event	Name and Nationality	Streak	Years
100 meters	Bob Hayes, United States	49	1962–64
200 meters	Manfred Gemar, Germany	41	1956–60
400 meters	Michael Johnson, United States	58	1989–97

MEN (CONT)

Event	Name and Nationality	Streak	Years
800 meters	Mal Whitfield, United States	40	1951–54
1,500 meters	Hicham El Guerrouj, Morocco	23	1996–00
1,500 meters/mile	Steve Ovett, Great Britain	45	1977–80
Mile	Herb Elliott, Australia	35	1957–60
Steeplechase	Gaston Roelants, Belgium	45	1961–66
5,000 meters	Emil Zátopek, Czechoslovakia	48	1949–52
10,000 meters	Emil Zátopek, Czechoslovakia	38	1948–54
Marathon	Frank Shorter, United States	6	1971–73
110-meter hurdles	Jack Davis, United States	44	1952–55
400-meter hurdles	Edwin Moses, United States	107	1977–87
High jump	Ernie Shelton, United States	46	1953–55
Pole vault	Bob Richards, United States	50	1950–52
Long jump	Carl Lewis, United States	65	1981–91

Longest Winning Streaks *(Cont.)*

Triple jump	Adhemar da Silva, Brazil	60	1950–56
Shot put	Parry O'Brien, United States	116	1952–56
Discus throw	Ricky Bruch, Sweden	54	1972–73
Hammer throw	Imre Nemeth, Hungary	73	1946–50
Javelin throw	Janis Lusis, USSR	41	1967–70
Decathlon	Bob Mathias, United States	11	1948–56

WOMEN

Event	Name and Nationality	Streak	Years
100 meters	Merlene Ottey, Jamaica	56	1987–91
200 meters	Irena Szewinska, Poland	38	1973–75
400 meters	Irena Szewinska, Poland	36	1973–78
800 meters	Ana Fidelia Quirot, Cuba	36	1987–90
1,500 meters	Paula Ivan, Romania	15	1988–91
1,500 meters/mile	Paula Ivan, Romania	19	1988–90
3,000 meters	Mary Slaney, United States	10	1982–84
10,000 meters	Ingrid Kristiansen, Norway	5	1985–87
Marathon	Katrin Dörre, E Germany	10	1982–86
100-meter hurdles	Annelie Ernhardt, E Germany	44	1972–75
400-meter hurdles	Ann-Louise Skoglund, Sweden	18	1981–83
High jump	Iolanda Balas, Romania	140	1956–67
Long jump	Tatyana Shchelkanova, USSR	19	1964–66
Shot put	Nadezhda Chizhova, USSR	57	1969–73
Discus throw	Gisela Mauermeyer, Germany	65	1935–42
Javelin throw	Ruth Fuchs, E Germany	30	1972–73
Multi	Heide Rosendahl, W Germany	15	1969–72

Most Consecutive Years Ranked No. 1 in the World

MEN

No.	Name and Nationality	Event	Years
11	Sergei Bubka, Ukraine	Pole vault	1984–94
9	Viktor Saneyev, USSR	Triple jump	1968–76
8	Bob Richards, United States	Pole vault	1949–56
8	Ralph Boston, United States	Long jump	1960–67

WOMEN

No.	Name and Nationality	Event	Years
9	Iolanda Balas, Romania	High jump	1958–66
8	Ruth Fuchs, E Germany	Javelin	1972–79
7	Faina Melnick, USSR	Discus throw	1971–77

Major Barrier Breakers

MEN

Event	Mark	Name and Nationality	Date	Site
sub 10-second 100 meters	9.95	Jim Hines, United States	Oct. 14, 1968	Mexico City
sub 20-second 200 meters	19.83	Tommie Smith, United States	Oct. 16, 1968	Mexico City
sub 45-second 400 meters	44.9	Otis Davis, United States	Sept. 6, 1960	Rome
sub 1:45 800 meters	1:44.3	Peter Snell, New Zealand	Feb. 3, 1962	Christchurch, New Zealand
sub four minute mile	3:59.4	Roger Bannister, Great Britain	May 6, 1954	Oxford
sub 3:50 mile	3:49.4	John Walker, New Zealand	Aug. 12, 1975	Göteborg, Sweden
sub 13-minute 5,000 meters	12:58.39	Said Aouita, Morocco	July 22, 1986	Rome
sub 27:00 10,000 meters	26:58.38	Yobes Ondieki, Kenya	July 10, 1993	Oslo
sub 13-second 110-meter hurdles	12.93	Renaldo Nehemiah, United States	Aug. 19, 1981	Zurich
sub 50-second 400-meter hurdles	49.5	Glenn Davis, United States	June 29, 1956	Los Angeles
7 ft high jump	7 ft ⅝ in	Charles Dumas, United States	June 29, 1956	Los Angeles
8 ft high jump	8 ft	Javier Sotomayor, Cuba	July 29, 1989	San Juan
60 ft triple jump	60 ft ¼ in	Jonathan Edwards, Great Britain	Aug. 7, 1995	Göteborg, Sweden
20 ft pole vault	20 ft	Sergei Bubka, USSR	March 15, 1991	San Sebastian, Spain
70 ft shot put	70 ft 7¼ in	Randy Matson, United States	May 5, 1965	College Station, Texas
200 ft discus throw	200 ft 5 in	Al Oerter, United States	May 18, 1962	Los Angeles

Major Barrier Breakers *(Cont.)*

MEN (CONT)

Event	Mark	Name and Nationality	Date	Site
300 ft (new) javelin	300 ft 1 in	Steve Backley, Great Britain	Jan. 25, 1992	Auckland, New Zealand
9,000-pt decathlon	9026	Roman Sebrle, Czech Republic	May 27, 2001	Gotzis, Austria

WOMEN

Event	Mark	Name and Nationality	Date	Site
sub 11-second 100 meters	10.88	Marlies Oelsner, E Germany	July 1, 1977	Dresden
sub 22-second 200 meters	21.71	Marita Koch, E Germany	June 10, 1979	Karl Marxstadt, E Germany
sub 50-second 400 meters	49.9	Irena Szewinska, Poland	June 22, 1974	Warsaw
sub 2:00 800 meters	1:59.1	Shin Geum Dan, N Korea	Nov. 12, 1963	Djakarta
sub 4:00 1,500 meters	3:56.0	Tatyana Kazankina, USSR	June 28, 1976	Podolsk, USSR
sub 4:20 mile	4:17.55	Mary Decker, United States	Feb. 16, 1980	Houston
sub 15:00 5,000 meters	14:58.89	Ingrid Kristiansen, Norway	June 28, 1984	Oslo
sub 30:00 10,000 meters	29:31.78	Wang Junxia, China	Sept. 8, 1993	Beijing
sub 2:30 marathon	2:27:33	Grete Waitz, Norway	Oct. 21, 1979	New York City
sub 2:20 marathon	2:19:46	Naoko Takahashi, Japan	Sept. 30, 2001	Berlin
sub 13-second 100-meter hurdles	12.9	Karin Balzer, E Germany	Sept. 5, 1969	Berlin
6 ft high jump	6 ft	Iolanda Balas, Romania	Oct. 18, 1958	Budapest
15 ft pole vault	15 ft ½ in	Emma George, Australia	March 14, 1998	Melbourne
70 ft shot put	70 ft 4½ in	Nadyezhda Chizhova, USSR	Sept. 29, 1973	Varna, Bulgaria
200 ft discus throw	201 ft	Liesel Westermann, W Germany	Nov. 5, 1967	Sao Paulo
200 ft javelin throw	201 ft 4 in	Elvira Ozolina, USSR	Aug. 27, 1964	Kiev
first 7,000-point heptathlon	7,148	Jackie Joyner-Kersee, U.S.	July 6–7, 1986	Moscow

Olympic Accomplishments

Oldest Olympic gold medalist—Patrick (Babe) McDonald, United States, 42 years, 26 days, 56-pound weight throw, 1920.

Oldest Olympic medalist—Tebbs Lloyd Johnson, Great Britain, 48 years, 115 days, 1948 (bronze), 50K walk.

Youngest Olympic gold medalist—Barbara Jones, United States, 15 years 123 days, 1952, 4 x 100 relay.

Youngest gold medalist in individual event—Ulrike Meyfarth, W Germany, 16 years, 123 days, 1972, high jump.

World Record Accomplishments*

Most world records equaled or set in a day—6, Jesse Owens, United States, 5-25-35, (9.4 100 yards; 26' 8¼" long jump; 20.3 200 meters and 220 yards; and 22.6 220-yard hurdles and 200-meter hurdles.

Most records in a year—10, Gunder Hägg, Sweden, 1941–42, 1,500 to 5,000 meters.

Most records in a career—35, Sergei Bubka, 1983–94, pole vault indoors and out.

Longest span of record setting—11 years, 20 days, Irena Szewinska, Poland, 1965–76, 200 meters.

Youngest person to set a set world record—Carolina Gisolf, Holland, 15 years, 5 days, 1928, high jump, 5 ft 3⅜ in.

Youngest man to set a world record—John Thomas, United States, 17 years, 355 days, 1959, high jump, 7 ft 1¼ in.

Oldest person to set world record—Carlos Lopes, Portugal, 38 years, 59 days, marathon, 2:07:12.

Greatest percentage improvement—6.59, Bob Beamon, United States, 1968, long jump.

Longest lasting record—long jump, 26 ft 8¼ in, Jesse Owens, United States, 25 years, 79 days (1935–60).

Highest clearance over head, men—23¼ in, Franklin Jacobs, United States (5' 8"), 1978.

Highest clearance over head, woman—12¾ in, Yolanda Henry, United States (5' 6"), 1990.

*Marks sanctioned by the IAAF.

Swimming

**Michael Phelps
of the United States**

Young Americans

Michael Phelps and Katie Hoff steer toward the future at the World Championships

BY MARK BECHTEL

AFTER MICHAEL PHELPS' 2004 Olympic performance—he won seven medals, including six golds—he knew he was going to have a hard time repeating that haul at the 2005 World Championships in Montreal. So he didn't even try. Phelps gave up on two events he won in Athens, the 200-meter butterfly and the 400-meter individual medley, and replaced them with two new ones: the 100- and 400-meter freestyles. "I wanted a new challenge," said Phelps, who added 10 pounds to his 6'4" frame after returning from Athens. "I wanted to see how my body would react to something different."

Turns out, it didn't react well at all. In his 400 heat he started strongly but was gassed coming down the stretch. He touched the wall in 3:50.53—not fast enough to qualify for the final. It was the first time in his international career that he failed to qualify for a final, and it had him pondering his priorities; since becoming a celebrity in Athens, he's been inundated with sponsor obligations. "In the upcoming year, there needs to be more decisions that are going to help my swimming, not hurt my swimming," he said.

Phelps chose the 400 primarily because he wanted to go head-to-head with Australians Ian Thorpe and Grant Hackett. Thorpe, however, was a no-show. After Athens, the 22-year-old announced he was skipping the worlds to get in prime shape for the 2008 Olympics. "It is going to be a hard path for him to get himself back in shape, but it's not something he would do if he didn't think he was capable of coming back," said Tracey Menzies, Thorpe's coach. "It is good that he has had a bit of a break and time to grow as a person."

And Phelps's performance showed he's not anywhere near Hackett's class yet. The Aussie breezed to the gold in Montreal, and after the race he sought out his pal Phelps (the two trained together in 2003) to give him some encouraging words for that night's 4 x 100 freestyle relay. But after his showing in the 400, Phelps didn't need a pat on the back to get motivated for the race. "Straight off, knowing Michael, I felt sorry for my mates in the relay," said Hackett.

HEINZ KLUETMEIER

Katie Hoff led the American women with three golds at the World Championships.

Phelps led off for the U.S., swimming his leg in a brisk 49.17, which was good enough for a half-a-length lead. His teammates Neil Walker, Nate Dusing and Jason Lezak widened that, coming home in an American record of 3:13.77. It was the first time the U.S won the race at the worlds since 1998.

The relay gold was one of six medals Phelps won, a fine performance, but not what he was after (his goal was eight) and not as impressive as Hackett's. The 25-year-old took one fewer medal, but that ran his career world championship total to 18, the most ever. (Coming into the event he had been tied with Thorpe, Germany's Michael Gross and Jenny Thompson of the U.S. with 13.) Hackett stretched out the record with authority. In addition to his win in the 400 free, he won gold in the 800-meter freestyle, knocking half a second off Thorpe's world record. "Getting one of Ian's records is something to be very proud of," Hackett said. "He's one of the greatest swimmers in history, one the greatest athletes in fact." He also won the 1,500, becoming the first swimmer to win four world championships in the same event.

While the worlds weren't as kind to Phelps as he would have liked, they did prove him to be a prescient young man. Six

years ago, he was asked for his autograph by a 10-year-old girl at a swim meet. He obliged, but asked why she wanted it. "You'll be the best," she said. Phelps replied, "You too, someday." That girl was Katie Hoff, and in Montreal she showed that she's well on her way to fulfilling Phelps's prediction. Hoff qualified for the U.S. Olympic team in 2004 as its youngest member, but she failed to qualify for the final in her first event, the 400 IM, and threw up backstage after the race. She finished seventh in her other event, the 200 IM. "I had never felt pressure like that before," she said.

On Phelps's advice, she left Athens before the Games were over and started training with a vengeance. At the worlds, it paid off. She took three golds as part of an exciting up-and-coming U.S. women's team. (Kate Ziegler, 17, won the 800- and 1,500-meter freestyles, and Jessica Hardy, 18, broke the world record in the 100 breaststroke.) Hoff's most impressive performance was in the 4 x 200 freestyle relay; swimming second, she cut a second off of Australia's lead and sparked a U.S. comeback that led to gold and had Hoff and her teammates feeling sanguine about their future. "I definitely think the women's team stepped up more than everyone thought they would," said Hoff. "And hopefully that's going to carry over to Beijing."

2004–2005 Major Competitions

Men

U.S. OPEN
San Antonio, TX, December 2–4, 2004

50 free	Nick Brunelli, Ariz. Sun Devil	22.84
100 free	Nick Brunelli, Ariz. Sun Devil	50.35
200 free	Nick Brunelli, Ariz. Sun Devil	1:51.80
400 free	Ricardo Monasterio, Gator	3:54.23
1,500 free	Ricardo Monasterio, Gator	15:28.32
100 back	Ryan Lochte, Florida	56.14
200 back	Ryan Lochte, Florida	2:02.21
100 breast	Vladislav Polyakov, Alabama	1:01.94
200 breast	Vladislav Polyakov, Alabama	2:15.35
100 fly	Joe Bartoch, UNLV	54.68
200 fly	Daniel Madwed, Sharks	2:01.03
200 IM	Michael Alexandrov, Northwest.	2:03.57
400 IM	Ryan Lochte, Florida	4:29.95
400 m relay	Florida A	3:53.44
400 f relay	Alabama A	3:28.29
800 f relay	Florida A	7:43.20

U.S. NATIONAL CHAMPIONSHIPS (SPRING)
Irvine, Calif., August 3–7, 2005

50 free	Ben Wildman-Tobriner, Stanford	22.13
100 free	Roland Schoeman, Tucson	48.38
200 free	Michael Phelps, Wolverine	1:46.40
400 free	Klete Keller, Wolverine	3:46.20
800 free	Klete Keller, Wolverine	7:56.66
1,500 free	Charles Peterson, Carteret	15:24.64
100 back	Randall Bal, Stanford	54.09
200 back	Christian DeJong, Wolverines	1:58.25
100 breast	Daniel Velez, Rockville Mont.	1:03.70
200 breast	Matthew Weaner, Longhorn Aq.	2:14.40
100 fly	Roland Schoeman, .Tuscon	51.84†
200 fly	Michael Phelps, Wolverine	1:55.26
200 IM	U. Wisconsin	2:01.75
400 IM	Robert Margalis, St. Petersberg	4:18.66
400 m relay	Tucson Ford	3:42.23
400 f relay	Wolverine	3:19.38
800 f relay	Wolverine	7:12.35

DUEL IN THE POOL
Irvine, Calif., August 2–3, 2005

50 free	Nick Brunelli, United States	22.20
100 free	Jason Lezak, United States	48.96

U.S. OPEN
San Antonio, TX, December 2–4, 2005

50 free	Laura Nicholls, Pickering SC	26.14
100 free	Claudia Poll, Costa Rica	56.63
200 free	Claudia Poll, Costa Rica	2:00.34
400 free	Claudia Poll, Costa Rica	4:11.69
800 free	Brittany Reimer, S. Knights	8:38.16
100 back	Tricia Weaner, West Shore	1:03.59
200 back	Erica Meissner, Magnus Aqu.	2:14.15
100 breast	Alexandra Spann, Longhorn Aq.	1:11.14
200 breast	Vipa Bernhardt, Florida	2:31.56
100 fly	Amanda Sims, Santa Rosa	1:01.28
200 fly	Jessica Dickons, Great Britain	2:13.95
200 IM	Jennifer Forster, OH Sharks	2:16.87
400 IM	Jennifer Forster, OH Sharks	4:50.96

DUEL IN THE POOL *(CONT.)*

200 free	Peter Vanderkaay, U.S.	1:47.87
400 free	Grant Hackett, Australia	3:45.31
100 back	Aaron Peirsol, United States	54.04
200 back	Aaron Peirsol, United States	1:57.31
100 breast	Brendan Hansen, U.S.	59.21
200 breast	Brendan Hansen, U.S.	2:10.07
100 fly	Ian Crocker, United States	51.55
200 fly	Michael Phelps, United States	1:56.38
200 IM	Michael Phelps, United States	1:56.93
400 IM	Michael Phelps, United States	4:12.71
400 m relay	United States	3:36.39
400 f relay	United States	3:37.67

FINA WORLD CHAMPIONSHIPS
Montreal, Canada, July 24–31, 2005

50 free	Roland Schoeman, Russia	21.69
100 free	Filippo Magnini, Italy	48.12
200 free	Michael Phelps, United States	1:45.20
400 free	Grant Hackett, Australia	3:42.91
800 free	Grant Hackett, Australia*	7:38.65
1,500 free	Grant Hackett, Australia	14:42.58
50 back	Aristeidis Grigoriadis, Greece	24.95
100 back	Aaron Peirsol, United States	53.62
200 back	Aaron Peirsol, United States*	1:54.66
50 breast	Mark Warnecke, Germany	27.63
100 breast	Brendan Hansen, United States	59.37
200 breast	Brendan Hansen, United States	2:09.85
50 fly	Roland Schoeman, Russia*	22.96
100 fly	Ian Crocker, United States*	50.40
200 fly	Pawel Korzeniowski, Poland	1:55.02
200 IM	Ryan Lochte, United States	1:58.06
400 IM	Laszlo Cseh, Hungary	4:90.63
400 m relay	United States	3:31.85
400 f relay	United States	3:13.77
800 f relay	United States	7:06.58

FINA WORLD DIVING CHAMPIONSHIPS
Montreal, Canada, July 17–24, 2005

1-m spgbd	Alexandre Despatie, Canada	489.69
3-m spgbd	Alexandre Despatie, Canada	813.60
Platform	Jia Hu, China	698.01
3-m sync	He/Wang, China	384.42
10-m sync	Dobrosok/Galperin, Russia*	392.88

Women

U.S. OPEN *(CONT.)*

400 m relay	Florida A	4:20.16
400 f relay	Ontario A	3:50.16
800 f relay	Great Britain A	8:23.52

U.S. NATIONAL CHAMPIONSHIPS
Irvine, Calif., August 3–7, 2005

50 free	Amanda Weir, Swim Atlanta	25.45
100 free	Amanda Weir, Swim Atlanta	54.47
200 free	Brittany Reimer, Canada	1:59.73
400 free	Brittany Reimer, Canada	4:10.13
800 free	Kate Ziegler, The Fish	8:31.11
1,500 free	Kate Ziegler, The Fish	16:14.52
100 back	Helen Silver, Calif. Aquatic	1:02.64
200 back	Leah Retrum, Gator	2:11.00

Women (Cont.)

U.S. NATIONAL CHAMPIONSHIPS(CONT.)

100 breast ....Jessica Hardy, Irvine Novaq.	1:07.45
200 breast ...Rebecca Soni, Scarlet Aqua.	2:26.27
100 fly...........Elaine Breeden, Wildcat Aqua.	59.20
200 fly...........Elaine Breeden, Wildcat Aqua.	2:09.93
200 IM ....Ariana Kukors, King	2:14.57
400 IM ....Ariana Kukors, King	4:43.32
400 m relay...Stanford Palo Alto	4:10.00
400 f relay.....California Aquatic	3:44.43
800 f relay.....California Aquatic	8:13.29

DUEL IN THE POOL
Irvine, Calif., August 2-3, 2004

50 free..........Jodie Henry, Australia	. 25.06
100 free........Lisbeth Lenton, Australia	54.77
200 free........Lisbeth Lenton, Australia	1:59.49
400 free........Kate Ziegler, United States	4:08.97
100 back ......Natalie Coughlin, U.S.	1:00.67
200 back ......Hoelzer Margaret, U.S.	2:11.68
100 breast ....Leisel Jones, Australia	1:06.21
200 breast ....Leisel Jones, Australia	2:26.11
100 fly ....Jessicah Schipper, Australia	57.87
200 fly ....Jessicah Schipper, Australia	2:07.61
200 IM ....Katie Hoff, United States	2:15.75
400 IM ....United States	4:37.06
400 m relay ..Australia	3:58.93
400 f relay ....Australia	3:37.67

†Meet record. *American record. WR World record.

FINA WORLD CHAMPIONSHIPS
Montreal, Canada, July 24-31, 2005

50 free..........Lisbeth Lenton, Australia	24.59
100 free........Jodie Henry, Australia	54.18
200 free........Solenne Figues, France	11:58.60
400 free........Laure Manaudou, France	4:06.44
1,500 free.....Kate Ziegler, United States	16;00.41
50 back.........Giaan Rooney, Australia	28.63
100 back ......Kirsty Coventry, Zimbabwe	1:00.24
200 back ......Kirsty Coventry, Zimbabwe	2:08.52
50 breast ......Jade Edmistone, Australia*	30:45
100 breast ....Leisel Jones, Australia	1:06.25
200 breast ....Leisel Jones, Australia	2:21.72
50 fly ....Dani Miatke, Australia	26.11
100 fly ....Jessicah Schippers, Australia	57.23
200 fly ....Otylia Jedrzejczak, Poland*	2:05.61
200 IM ....Katie Hoff, United States	2:10.41
400 IM ....Katie Hoff, United States	4:36.07
400 m relay...Australia	3:57.47
400 f relay ....Australia	3:37.32
800 f relay.....United States	7:53.70

FINA WORLD DIVING CHAMPIONSHIPS
Montreal, Canada, July 17-24, 2005

1-m spgbd ...Blythe Hartley, Canada	325.65
3-m spgbd ...Jingjing Guo, China	645.54
Platform.......Laura Ann Wilkinson, U.S.A.	564.87
3-m sync ......Li/Guo, China	349.80
10-m sync ....Jia/Yuan. China	351.60

World and American Records Set in 2005

Men

Event	Mark	Record Holder	Date	Site
200 free	1:45.20	Michael Phelps, United States (A)	7-26-05	Montreal
800 free	7:38.65	Grant hackett, Australia (W)	7-27-05	Montreal
800 free	7:45.63	Larsen Jensen, United States (A)	7-27-05	Montreal
100 back	53.17	Aaron Peirsol, United States (W, A)	4-2-05	Indianapolis
200 back	1:54.66	Aaron Peirsol, United States (W, A)	7-29-05	Montreal
50 fly	22.96	Roland Schoeman, Russa (W)	7-25-05	Montreal
100 fly	50.40	Ian Crocker, United States (W, A)	7-30-05	Montreal
400 free relay	3:13.77	United States (A) (Michael Phelps, Neil Walker, Nate Dusing, Jason Lezak)	7-24-05	Montreal
800 free relay	7:06.58	United States (A) (Phelps, Lochte Vanderkaay, Keller)	7-29-05	Montreal

Women

Event	Mark	Record Holder	Date	Site
50 back	28.19	Janine Pietsch, Germany (W)	5-25-05	Berlin
50 breast	30:45	Jade Edmistone, Australia (W)	7-31-05	Montreal
50 breast	30.85	Jessica Hardy, United States (A)	7-31-05	Montreal
100 breast	1:06.20sf	Jessica Hardy, United States (W, A)	7-25-05	Montreal
200 breast	2:21.72	Leisel Jones, Australia (W)	7-29-05	Montreal
200 fly	2:05.61	Otylia Jedrejczak, Poland (W)	7-28-05	Montreal
200 IM	2:10.51	Katie Hoff, United States (W)	7-25-05	Montreal

World and American Records

MEN

Freestyle

Event	Time	Record Holder	Date	Site
50 meters	21.64	Alexander Popov, Russia (W)	6-16-00	Moscow
	21.76	Gary Hall Jr. (A)	8-15-00	Indianapolis
100 meters	47.84	Pieter van den Hoogenband, Netherlands (W)	9-19-00	Sydney
	48.17	Jason Lezak (A)	7-10-04	Long Beach, CA
200 meters	1:44.06	Ian Thorpe, Australia (W)	7-25-01	Fukuoka, Japan
	1:45.32	Michael Phelps (A)	8-16-04	Athens
400 meters	3:40.08	Ian Thorpe, Australia (W)	7-30-02	Manchester
	3:44.11	Klete Keller (A)	8-14-04	Athens
800 meters	7:38.65	Grant Hackett, Australia (W)	7-27-05	Montreal
	7:45.63	Larsen Jensen (A)	7-25-03	Montreal
1,500 meters	14:34.56	Grant Hackett, Australia (W)	7-30-01	Fukuoka, Japan
	14:45.29	Larsen Jensen (A)	8-21-04	Athens

Backstroke

Event	Time	Record Holder	Date	Site
50 meters	24.80	Thomas Rupprath, Germany (W)	7-27-03	Barcelona
	24.99	Lenny Krayzelburg (A)	8-28-99	Sydney
100 meters	53.17	Aaron Peirsol (W, A)	4-2-05	Indianapolis
200 meters	1:54.66	Aaron Peirsol (W, A)	7-29-05	Montreal

Breaststroke

Event	Time	Record Holder	Date	Site
50 meters	27.18	Oleg Lisogor, Ukraine (W)	8-1-02	Berlin
	27.39	Ed Moses (A)	3-31-01	Austin, TX
100 meters	59.30	Brendan Hansen (W, A)	7-8-04	Long Beach, CA
200 meters	2:09.04	Brendan Hansen (W, A)	7-11-04	Long Beach, CA

Butterfly

Event	Time	Record Holder	Date	Site
50 meters	22.96	Roland Schoeman, Russia (W)	7-25-05	Montreal
50 meters	23.30	Ian Crocker (W, A)	2-29-04	Austin, TX
100 meters	50.40	Ian Crocker (W, A)	7-30-05	Montreal
200 meters	1:53.93	Michael Phelps (W, A)	7-22-03	Barcelona

Individual Medley

Event	Time	Record Holder	Date	Site
200 meters	1:55.94	Michael Phelps (W, A)	8-9-03	College Park, MD
400 meters	4:08.26	Michael Phelps (W, A)	8-14-04	Athens

Relays

Event	Time	Record Holder	Date	Site
400-meter medley	3:30.68	United States (W,A) (Aaron Peirsol, Brendan Hansen Ian Crocker, Jason Lezak)	8-21-04	Athens
400-meter freestyle	3:13.17	S Africa (W) (Roland Schoeman, Lyndon Ferns, Darian Townsend Ryk Neethling)	8-15-04	Athens
	3:13.77	United States (A) (Michael Phelps, Neil Walker, Jason Lezak, Gary Hall Jr	7-24-05	Montreal
800-meter freestyle	7:04.66	Australia (W) (Ian Thorpe, Michael Klim, Bill Kirby, Grant Hackett)	7-27-01	Fukuoka, Japan
	7:06.58	United States (A) (Phelps, Lochte, Vanderkaay, Keller)	7-29-05	Montreal

Note: Records through Sept. 9, 2005.

WOMEN

Freestyle

Event	Time	Record Holder	Date	Site
50 meters	24.13	Inge de Bruijn, Netherlands (W)	9-22-00	Sydney
	24.63	Dara Torres (A)	9-23-00	Sydney
100 meters	53.52	Jodie Henry, Australia (W)	8-18-04	Athens
	53.99	Natalie Coughlin (A)	8-29-02	Yokohama, Japan
200 meters	1:56.64	Franziska van Almsick, Germany (W)	8-3-02	Berlin
	1:57.41	Lindsay Benko (A)	7-24-03	Barcelona
400 meters	4:03.85	Janet Evans (W, A)	9-22-88	Seoul
800 meters	8:16.22	Janet Evans (W, A)	8-20-89	Tokyo
1,500 meters	15:52.10	Janet Evans (W, A)	3-26-88	Orlando, FL

Backstroke

Event	Time	Record Holder	Date	Site
50 meters	28.19	Janine Pietsch, Germany (W)	5-25-05	Berlin
	28.49	Natalie Coughlin (A)	7-23-01	Fukuoka, Japan
100 meters	59.58	Natalie Coughlin (W, A)	8-13-02	Fort Lauderdale, FL
200 meters	2:06.62	Krisztina Egerszegi, Hungary (W)	8-25-91	Athens, Greece
	2:08.53	Natalie Coughlin (A)	8-16-02	Fort Lauderdale, FL

Breaststroke

Event	Time	Record Holder	Date	Site
50 meters	30.45	Jade Edmistone, Australia (W)	7-31-05	Montreal
	30.85	Jessica Hardy (A)	7-25-05	Montreal
100 meters	1:06.20	Jessica Hardy (W, A)	7-25-05	Montreal
200 meters	2:21.72	Leisel Jones, Australia (W)	7-29-05	Montreal
	2:22.44	Jessica Hardy (A)	7-12-04	Long Beach, CA

Butterfly

Event	Time	Record Holder	Date	Site
50 meters	25.57	Anna-Karin Kammerling, Sweden (W)	7-30-02	Berlin
	26.50	Dara Torres (A)	8-9-00	Indianapolis
100 meters	56.61	Inge de Bruijn, Netherlands (W)	9-17-00	Sydney
	57.58	Dara Torres (A)	8-9-00	Indianapolis
200 meters	2:05.61	Otylia Jedrejczak, Poland (W)	7-28-05	Montreal
	2:05.88	Misty Hyman (A)	9-20-00	Sydney

Individual Medley

Event	Time	Record Holder	Date	Site
200 meters	2:09.72	Yanyan Wu, China (W)	10-17-97	Shanghai
	2:10.41	Katie Hoff (A)	7-25-05	Montreal
400 meters	4:33.59	Yana Klochkova, Ukraine (W)	9-16-00	Sydney
	4:34.95	Kaitlin Sandeno (A)	8-14-04	Athens

Relays

Event	Time	Record Holder	Date	Site
400-meter medley	3:57.32	Australia (W) (Giaan Rooney, Leisel Jones, Petria Thomas, Jodie Henry)	8-21-04	Athens
	3:58.30	United States (A) (BJ Bedford, Megan Quann, Jenny Thompson, Dana Torres)	9-23-00	Sydney
400-meter freestyle	3:35.94	Australia (W) (Alice Mills, Lisbeth Lenton, Petria Thomas, Jodie Henry)	8-14-04	Athens
	3:36.39	United States (A) (Kara Lynn Joyce, Natalie Coughlin, Amanda Weir, Jenny Thompson)	8-14-04	Athens
800-meter freestyle	7:53.42	United States (W, A) (Natalie Coughlin, Carly Piper, Dana Vollmer, Kaitlin Sandeno)	8-18-04	Athens

MEN

50-meter Freestyle

1986	Tom Jager, United States	22.49‡
1991	Tom Jager, United States	22.16‡
1994	Alexander Popov, Russia	22.17
1998	Bill Pilczuk, United States	22.29
2001	Anthony Ervin, United States	22.09
2003	Alexander Popov, Russia	21.92‡
2005	Roland Schoeman, Russia	21.69

100-meter Freestyle

1973	Jim Montgomery, United States	51.70
1975	Andy Coan, United States	51.25
1978	David McCagg, United States	50.24
1982	Jorg Woithe, E Germany	50.18
1986	Matt Biondi, United States	48.94
1991	Matt Biondi, United States	49.18
1994	Alexander Popov, Russia	49.12
1998	Alexander Popov, Russia	48.93‡
2001	Anthony Ervin, United States	48.33‡
2003	Alexander Popov, Russia	48.42
2005	Filippo Magnini, Italy	48:12

200-meter Freestyle

1973	Jim Montgomery, United States	1:53.02
1975	Tim Shaw, United States	1:52.04‡
1978	Billy Forrester, United States	1:51.02‡
1982	Michael Gross, W Germany	1:49.84
1986	Michael Gross, W Germany	1:47.92
1991	Giorgio Lamberti, Italy	1:47.27‡
1994	Antti Kasvio, Finland	1:47.32
1998	Michael Klim, Australia	1:47.41
2001	Ian Thorpe, Australia	1:44.06*
2003	Ian Thorpe, Australia	1:45.14
2005	Michael Phelps, United States	1:45.20

400-meter Freestyle

1973	Rick DeMont, United States	3:58.18‡
1975	Tim Shaw, United States	3:54.88‡
1978	Vladimir Salnikov, USSR	3:51.94‡
1982	Vladimir Salnikov, USSR	3:51.30‡
1986	Rainer Henkel, W Germany	3:50.05
1991	Joerg Hoffman, Germany	3:48.04‡
1994	Kieran Perkins, Australia	3:43.80*
1998	Ian Thorpe, Australia	3:46.29
2001	Ian Thorpe, Australia	3:40.17*
2003	Ian Thorpe, Australia	3:42.58
2005	Grant Hackett, Australia	3:42.91

1,500-meter Freestyle

1973	Stephen Holland, Australia	15:31.85
1975	Tim Shaw, United States	15:28.92‡
1978	Vladimir Salnikov, USSR	15:03.99‡
1982	Vladimir Salnikov, USSR	15:01.77‡
1986	Rainer Henkel, W Germany	15:05.31
1991	Joerg Hoffman, Germany	14:50.36*
1994	Kieran Perkins, Australia	14:50.52
1998	Grant Hackett, Australia	14:51.70
2001	Grant Hackett, Australia	14:34.56*
2003	Grant Hackett, Australia	14:43.14
2005	Grant Hackett, Australia	14:42.58

100-meter Backstroke

1973	Roland Matthes, E Germany	57.47
1973	Roland Matthes, E Germany	58.15

100-meter Backstroke (Cont.)

1978	Bob Jackson, United States	56.36‡
1982	Dirk Richter, E Germany	55.95
1986	Igor Polianski, USSR	55.58‡
1991	Jeff Rouse, United States	55.23‡
1994	Martin Lopez Zubero, Spain	55.17‡
1998	Lenny Krayzelburg, United States	55.00‡
2001	Matt Welsh, Australia	54.31‡
2003	Aaron Peirsol, United States	53.61‡
2005	Aaron Peirsol, United States	53:62

200-meter Backstroke

1973	Roland Matthes, E Germany	2:01.87‡
1975	Zoltan Varraszto, Hungary	2:05.05
1978	Jesse Vassallo, United States	2:02.16
1982	Rick Carey, United States	2:00.82‡
1986	Igor Polianski, USSR	1:58.78‡
1991	Martin Zubero, Spain	1:59.52
1994	Vladimir Selkov, Russia	1:57.42‡
1998	Lenny Krayzelburg, United States	1:58.84
2001	Aaron Peirsol, United States	1:57.13‡
2003	Aaron Peirsol, United States	1:55.92
2005	Aaron Peirsol, United States	1:54.66*

100-meter Breaststroke

1973	John Hencken, United States	1:04.02‡
1975	David Wilkie, Great Britain	1:04.26‡
1978	Walter Kusch, W Germany	1:03.56‡
1982	Steve Lundquist, United States	1:02.75‡
1986	Victor Davis, Canada	1:02.71
1991	Norbert Rozsa, Hungary	1:01.45*
1994	Norbert Rozsa, Hungary	1:01.24‡
1998	Frederik Deburghgraeve, Belgium	1:01.34
2001	Roman Sloudnov, Russia	1:00.16
2003	Kosuke Kitajima, Japan	59.78*
2005	Brendan Hanson, United States	59:37

200-meter Breaststroke

1973	David Wilkie, Great Britain	2:19.28‡
1975	David Wilkie, Great Britain	2:18.23‡
1978	Nick Nevid, United States	2:18.37
1982	Victor Davis, Canada	2:14.77*
1986	Jozsef Szabo, Hungary	2:14.27‡
1991	Mike Barrowman, United States	2:11.23*
1994	Norbert Rozsa, Hungary	2:12.81
1998	Kurt Grote, United States	2:13.40
2001	Brendan Hansen, United States	2:10.69‡
2003	Kosuke Kitajima, Japan	2:09.42*
2005	Brendan Hansen, United States	2:09.85

100-meter Butterfly

1973	Bruce Robertson, Canada	55.69
1975	Greg Jagenburg, United States	55.63
1978	Joe Bottom, United States	54.30
1982	Matt Gribble, United States	53.88‡
1986	Pablo Morales, United States	53.54‡
1991	Anthony Nesty, Suriname	53.29‡
1994	Rafal Szukala, Poland	53.51
1998	Michael Klim, Australia	52.25‡
2001	Lars Frolander, Sweden	52.10‡
2003	Ian Crocker, United States	50.98*
2005	Ian Crocker, United States	50:40*

200-meter Butterfly

1973	Robin Backhaus, United States	2:03.32
1975	Bill Forrester, United States	2:01.95‡

* World record; ‡Meet record

MEN (Cont.)

200-meter Butterfly(Cont.)

1978	Mike Bruner, United States	1:59.38‡
1982	Michael Gross, E Germany	1:58.85‡
1986	Michael Gross, E Germany	1:56.53‡
1991	Melvin Stewart, United States	1:55.69*
1994	Denis Pankratov, Russia	1:56.54
1998	Denys Sylantyev, Ukraine	1:56.61
2001	Michael Phelps, United States	1:54.58*
2003	Michael Phelps, United States	1:54.35
2005	Pawel Korzeniowski, Poland	1:55.02

200-meter Individual Medley

1973	Gunnar Larsson, Sweden	2:08.36
1975	Andras Hargitay, Hungary	2:07.72
1978	Graham Smith, Canada	2:03.65*
1982	Aleksandr Sidorenko, USSR	2:03.30‡
1986	Tamás Darnyi, Hungary	2:01.57‡
1991	Tamás Darnyi, Hungary	1:59.36*
1994	Jani Sievin, Finland	1:58.16*
1998	Marcel Wouda, Netherlands	2:01.18
2001	Massimiliano Rosolino, Italy	1:59.71
2003	Michael Phelps, United States	1:56.04*
2005	Ryan Lochte, United States	1;58.06

400-meter Individual Medley

1975	Andras Hargitay, Hungary	4:32.57
1978	Jesse Vassallo, United States	4:20.05*
1982	Ricardo Prado, Brazil	4:19.78*
1986	Tamás Darnyi, Hungary	4:18.98‡
1991	Tamás Darnyi, Hungary	4:12.36*
1994	Tom Dolan, United States	4:12.30*
1998	Tom Dolan, United States	4:14.95
2001	Alessio Boggiatto, Italy	4:13.15
2003	Michael Phelps, United States	4:09.09*
2005	Laszlo Cseh, Hungary	4:09.63

400-meter Medley Relay

1973	United States (Mike Stamm, John Hencken, Joe Bottom, Jim Montgomery)	3:49.49
1975	United States (John Murphy, Rick Colella, Greg Jagenburg, Andy Coan)	3:49.00
1978	United States (Robert Jackson, Nick Nevid, Joe Bottom, David McCagg)	3:44.63
1982	United States (Rick Carey, Steve Lundquist, Matt Gribble, Rowdy Gaines)	3:40.84*
1986	United States (Dan Veatch, David Lundberg, Pablo Morales, Matt Biondi)	3:41.25
1991	United States (Jeff Rouse, Eric Wunderlich, Mark Henderson Matt Biondi)	3:39.66‡
1994	United States (Jeff Rouse, Eric Wunderlich, Mark Henderson, Gary Hall)	3:37.74‡
1998	Australia (Matt Welsh, Phil Rogers, Robin Backhaus, Rick Klatt, Jim Montgomery)	3:37.98
2001	Australia (Matt Welsh, Ian Thorpe, Geoff Huegill, Regan Harrison)	3:35.35
2003	United States (Aaron Peirsol Brendan Hansen,Ian Crocker, Jason Lezak)	3:31.54*
2005	United States (Aaron Peirsol Brendan Hansen,Ian Crocker, Jason Lezak)	3:31.85

400-meter Freestyle Relay

1973	United States (Mel Nash, Joe Bottom, Jim Montgomery, John Murphy)	3:27.18
1975	United States (Bruce Furniss, Jim Montgomery, Andy Coan, John Murphy)	3:24.85
1978	United States (Jack Babashoff, Rowdy Gaines, Jim Montgomery, David McCagg)	3:19.74
1982	United States (Chris Cavanaugh, Robin Leamy, David McCagg, Rowdy Gaines)	3:19.26*
1986	United States (Tom Jager, Mike Heath, Paul Wallace, Matt Biondi)	3:19.89
1991	United States (Tom Jager, Brent Lang, Doug Gjertsen, Matt Biondi)	3:17.15‡
1994	United States (Jon Olsen, Josh Davis, Ugur Taner, Gary Hall Jr.)	3:16.90‡
1998	United States (Bryan Jones, Jon Olsen, Bradley Schumacher, Gary Hall Jr.)	3:16.69‡
2001	Australia (Michael Klim, Ian Thorpe, Todd Pearson, Ashley Callus)	3:14.10‡
2003	Russia (Andrei Kapralov, Ivan Usov, Denis Pimankov Aleksander Popov)	3:14.06‡
2005	United States (Michael Phelps, Neil Walker, Nate Dusing, Jason Lezak)	3:13.77

800-meter Freestyle Relay

1973	United States (Kurt Krumpholz, Robin Backhaus, Rick Klatt, Jim Montgomery)	7:33.22*
1975	W Germany (Klaus Steinbach, Werner Lampe, Hans Joachim Geisler, Peter Nocke)	7:39.44
1978	United States (Bruce Furniss, Billy Forrester, Bobby Hackett, Rowdy Gaines)	7:20.82
1982	United States (Rich Saeger, Jeff Float, Kyle Miller, Rowdy Gaines)	7:21.09
1986	E Germany (Lars Hinneburg, Thomas Flemming, Dirk Richter, Sven Lodziewski)	7:15.91‡
1991	Germany (Peter Sitt, Steffan Zesner, Stefan Pfeiffer, Michael Gross)	7:13.50‡
1994	Sweden (Christer Waller, Tommy Werner, Lars Frolander, Anders Holmertz)	7:17.34
1998	Australia (Daniel Kowalski, Grant Hackett, Ian Thorpe, Anthony Rogis)	7:12.48‡
2001	Australia (Michael Klim, Ian Thorpe, William Kirby, Grant Hackett)	7:04.66*
2003	Australia (Grant Hackett, Craig, Stevens, N. Springer, Ian Thorpe)	7:08.58
2005	United States (Michael Phelps, Ryan Lochte, Peter Vanderkaay, Klete Keller)	7:06.58

WOMEN

50-meter Freestyle

1986....Tamara Costache, Romania	25.28*
1991....Zhuang Yong, China	25.47
1994....Le Jingyi, China	24.51*
1998....Amy Van Dyken, United States	25.15
2001....Inge de Bruijn, Netherlands	24.47
2003....Inge de Bruijn, Netherlands	24.47
2005....Lisbeth Lenton, Australia	24.59

100-meter Freestyle

1973....Kornelia Ender, E Germany	57.54
1975....Kornelia Ender, E Germany	56.50
1978....Barbara Krause, E Germany	55.68‡
1982....Birgit Meineke, E Germany	55.79
1986....Kristin Otto, E Germany	55.05‡
1991....Nicole Haislett, United States	55.17
1994....Le Jingyi, China	54.01*
1998....Jenny Thompson, United States	54.95
2001....Inge de Bruijn, Netherlands	54.18
2003....Hanna-Maria Seppälä, Finland	54.37
2005....Jodie Henry, Australia	54.18

200-meter Freestyle

1973.....Keena Rothhammer, United States	2:04.99
1975....Shirley Babashoff, United States	2:02.50
1978....Cynthia Woodhead, United States	1:58.53*
1982....Annemarie Verstappen, Netherlands	1:59.53‡
1986....Heike Friedrich, E Germany	1:58.26‡
1991....Hayley Lewis, Australia	2:00.48
1994....Franziska Van Almsick, Germany	1:56.78*
1998....Claudia Poll, Costa Rica	1:58.90
2001....Giaan Rooney, Australia	1:58.57
2003....Alena Popchanka, Bulgaria	1:58.32
2005....Solenne Figues, France	1:58.60

400-meter Freestyle

1973.....Heather Greenwood, United States	4:20.28
1975.....Shirley Babashoff, United States	4:22.70
1978....Tracey Wickham, Australia	4:06.28*
1982....Carmela Schmidt, E Germany	4:08.98
1986....Heike Friedrich, E Germany	4:07.45
1991....Janet Evans, United States	4:08.63
1994....Yang Aihua, China	4:09.64
1998....Chen Yan, China	4:06.72
2001....Yana Klochkova, Ukraine	4:07.30
2003....Hannah Stockbauer, Germany	4:06.75
2005....Laure Manaudou, France	4:06.44

800-meter Freestyle

1973....Novella Calligaris, Italy	8:52.97
1975....Jenny Turrall, Australia	8:44.75‡
1978....Tracey Wickham, Australia	8:24.94‡
1982....Kim Linehan, United States	8:27.48
1986....Astrid Strauss, E Germany	8:28.24
1991....Janet Evans, United States	8:24.05‡
1994....Janet Evans, United States	8:29.85
1998....Brooke Bennett, United States	8:28.71
2001....Hannah Stockbauer, Germany	8:24.66
2003....Hannah Stockbauer, Germany	8:23.66‡
2005....Kate Ziegler, United States	8:25.31

100-meter Backstroke

1973....Ulrike Richter, E Germany	1:05.42
1975....Ulrike Richter, E Germany	1:03.30‡

100-meter Backstroke (Cont.)

1978....Linda Jezek, United States	1:02.55‡
1982....Kristin Otto, E Germany	1:01.30‡
1986....Betsy Mitchell, United States	1:01.74
1991....Krisztina Egerszegi, Hungary	1:01.78
1994....He Cihong, China	1:00.57
1998....Lea Maurer, United States	1:01.16
2001....Natalie Coughlin, United States	1:00.37
2003....Antje Buschschulte, Germany	1:00.50
2005....Kirsty Coventry, Zimbabwe	1:00.24

200-meter Backstroke

1973....Melissa Belote, United States	2:20.52
1975....Birgit Treiber, E Germany	2:15.46*
1978....Linda Jezek, United States	2:11.93*
1982....Cornelia Sirch, E Germany	2:09.91*
1986....Cornelia Sirch, E Germany	2:11.37
1991....Krisztina Egerszegi, Hungary	2:09.15‡
1994....He Cihong, China	2:07.40
1998....Roxanna Maracineanu, France	2:11.26
2001....Diana Mocanu, Romania	2:09.94
2003....Katy Sexton, Great Britain	2:08.74
2005....Kirsty Coventry, Zimbabwe	2:08.52

100-meter Breaststroke

1973....Renate Vogel, E Germany	1:13.74
1975....Hannalore Anke, E Germany	1:12.72
1978....Julia Bogdanova, USSR	1:10.31*
1982....Ute Geweniger, E Germany	1:09.14‡
1986....Sylvia Gerasch, E Germany	1:08.11*
1991....Linley Frame, Australia	1:08.81
1994....Samantha Riley, Australia	1:07.96*
1998....Kristy Kowal, United States	1:08.42
2001....Xuejuan Luo, China	1:07.18‡
2003....Xuejuan Luo, China	1:06.80
2005....Leisel Jones, Australia	1:06.25

200-meter Breaststroke

1973 Renate Vogel, E Germany	2:40.01
1975....Hannalore Anke, E Germany	2:37.25‡
1978....Lina Kachushite, USSR	2:31.42*
1982....Svetlana Varganova, USSR	2:28.82‡
1986....Silke Hoerner, E Germany	2:27.40*
1991....Elena Volkova, USSR	2:29.53
1994....Samantha Riley, Australia	2:26.87‡
1998....Agnes Kovacs, Hungary	2:25.45‡
2001....Agnes Kovacs, Hungary	2:24.90
2003....Amanda Beard, United States	2:22.99*
2005....Leisel Jones, Australia	2:21.72*

100-meter Butterfly

1973....Kornelia Ender, E Germany	1:02.53
1975....Kornelia Ender, E Germany	1:01.24*
1978....Joan Pennington, United States	1:00.20‡
1982....Mary T. Meagher, United States	59.41‡
1986....Kornelia Gressler, E Germany	59.51
1991....Qian Hong, China	59.68
1994....Liu Limin, China	58.98‡
1998....Jenny Thompson, United States	58.46‡
2001....Petria Thomas, Australia	58:27
2003....Jenny Thompson, United States	57.96‡
2005....Jessicah Schipper, Australia	57.23‡

* World record; ‡Meet record.

WOMEN (Cont.)

200-meter Butterfly

1973	Rosemarie Kother, E Germany	2:13.76‡
1975	Rosemarie Kother, E Germany	2:15.92
1978	Tracy Caulkins, United States	2:09.87*
1982	Ines Geissler, E Germany	2:08.66‡
1986	Mary T. Meagher, United States	2:08.41‡
1991	Summer Sanders, United States	2:09.24
1994	Liu Limin, China	2:07.25‡
1998	Susie O'Neill, Australia	2:07.93‡
2001	Petria Thomas, Australia	2:06.73‡
2003	Otylia Jedrzejczak, Poland	2:07.56
2005	Otylia Jedrzejczak, Poland	2:05.61*

200-meter Individual Medley

1973	Andrea Huebner, E Germany	2:20.51
1975	Kathy Heddy, United States	2:19.80
1978	Tracy Caulkins, United States	2:14.07*
1982	Petra Schneider, E Germany	2:11.79
1986	Kristin Otto, E Germany	2:15.56
1991	Li Lin, China	2:13.40
1994	Lu Bin, China	2:12.34‡
1998	Wu Yanyan, China	2:10.88
2001	Martha Bowen, United States	2:11.93
2003	Yana Klochkova, Ukraine	2:10.75‡
2005	Katie Hoff, United States	2:10.41‡

400-meter Individual Medley

1973	Gudrun Wegner, E Germany	4:57.71
1975	Ulrike Tauber, E Germany	4:52.76‡
1978	Tracy Caulkins, United States	4:40.83*
1982	Petra Schneider, E Germany	4:36.10*
1986	Kathleen Nord, E Germany	4:43.75
1991	Lin Li, China	4:41.45
1994	Dai Guohong, China	4:39.14
1998	Chen Yan, China	4:36.66
2001	Yana Klochkova, Ukraine	4:36.98
2003	Yana Klochkova, Ukraine	4:36.74
2005	Katie Hoff, United States	4:36.07‡

400-meter Medley Relay

1973	E Germany (Ulrike Richter, Renate Vogel, Rosemarie Kother, Kornelia Ender)	4:16.84
1975	E Germany (Ulrike Richter, Hannelore Anke, Rosemarie Kother, Kornelia Ender)	4:14.74
1978	United States (Linda Jezek, Tracy Caulkins, Joan Pennington, Cynthia Woodhead)	4:08.21‡
1982	E Germany (Kristin Otto, Ute Gewinger, Ines Geissler, Birgit Meineke)	4:05.8*
1986	E Germany (Kathrin Zimmermann, Sylvia Gerasch, Kornelia Gressler, Kristin Otto)	4:04.82
1991	United States (Janie Wagstaff, Tracey McFarlane, Crissy Ahmann-Leighton, Nicole Haislett)	4:06.51
1994	China (He Cihong, Dai Guohong, Liu Limin, Lu Bin)	4:01.67*
1998	United States (Kristy Kowal, Lea Maurer, Jenny Thompson, Amy Van Dyken)	4:01.93
2001	Australia (Dyana Calub, Sarah Ryan, Petria Thomas, Leisel Jones)	4:07.30

400-meter Medley Relay (Cont.)

2003	China (Shu Xhan, Xuejuan Luo Yafei Zhou, Yu Yang)	3:59.89‡
2005	Australia (Sophie Edington, Leisel Jones, J. Schipper Lisbeth Lenton)	3:57.47‡

400-meter Freestyle Relay

1973	E Germany (Kornelia Ender, Andrea Eife, Andrea Huebner, Sylvia Eichner)	3:52.45
1975	E Germany (Kornelia Ender, Barbara Krause, Claudia Hempel, Ute Bruckner)	3:49.37
1978	United States (Tracy Caulkins, Stephanie Elkins, Joan Pennington, Cynthia Woodhead)	3:43.43*
1982	E Germany (Birgit Meineke, Susanne Link, Kristin Otto, Caren Metschuk)	3:43.97
1986	E Germany (Kristin Otto, Manuela Stellmach, Sabine Schulze, Heike Friedrich)	3:40.57*
1991	United States (Nicole Haislett, Julie Cooper, Whitney Hedgepeth, Jenny Thompson)	3:43.26
1994	China (Le Jingyi, Ying Shan, Le Ying, Lu Bin)	3:37.91*
1998	United States (Catherine Fox, Lindsey Farella, Melanie Valerio, B.J. Bedford)	3:42.11
2001	Germany (Petra Dallman, Antje Buschschulter, Katrin Meissner, Sandra Volkner)	3:39.58
2003	United States (Natalie Coughlin, Lindsay Benko, Rhiannon Jeffrey, Jenny Thompson)	3:38.09
2005	Australia (Jodie Henry, Alice Mills, Shayne Reese, Lisbeth Lenton)	3:37.32‡

800-meter Freestyle Relay

1986	E Germany (Manuela Stellmach, Astrid Strauss, Nadja Bergknecht, Heike Friedrich)	7:59.33*
1991	Germany (Kerstin Kielgass, Manuela Stellmach, Dagmar Hase, Stephanie Ortwig)	8:02.56
1994	China (Le Ying, Yang Alhua, Zhou Guabin, Lu Bin)	7:57.96
1998	Germany (Silvia Szalai, Antje Buschschulte, Janina Goetz, Franziska Van Almsick)	8:02.56
2001	Great Britain (Nicola Jackson, Janine Belton, Karen Legg, Karen Pickering)	7:58.69
2003	United States (Lindsay Benko, Rachel Komisarz, Rhiannon Jeffrey, Diana Munz)	7:55.70‡
2005	United States (Natalie Coughlin, Katie Hoff, Whitney Myers, Kaitlin Sandeno)	7:53.70‡

* World record; ‡Meet record.

World Diving Championships

MEN

1-meter Springboard

		Pts
1991	Edwin Jongejans, Netherlands	588.51
1994	Evan Stewart, Zimbabwe	382.14
1998	Yu Zhuocheng, China	417.54
2001	Wang Feng, China	444.03
2003	Xiang Xu, China	431.94
2005	Alexandre Despatie	489.69

3-meter Springboard

		Pts
1973	Phil Boggs, United States	618.57
1975	Phil Boggs, United States	597.12
1978	Phil Boggs, United States	913.95
1982	Greg Louganis, United States	752.67
1986	Greg Louganis, United States	750.06
1991	Kent Ferguson, United States	650.25
1994	Wu Zhuocheng, China	655.44
1998	Dmitry Sautin, Russia	746.79
2001	Dmitry Sautin, Russia	725.82
2003	Alexander Dobrosok, Russia	788.37
2005	Alexandre Despatie	813.60

Platform

		Pts
1973	Klaus Dibiasi, Italy	559.53
1975	Klaus Dibiasi, Italy	547.98
1978	Greg Louganis, United States	844.11
1982	Greg Louganis, United States	634.26
1986	Greg Louganis, United States	668.58
1991	Sun Shuwei, China	626.79
1994	Dmitry Sautin, Russia	634.71
1998	Dmitry Sautin, Russia	750.90
2001	Tian Lang, China	688.77
2003	Alexandre Despatie, Canada	716.91
2005	Jia Hu, China	698.01

3-meter Synchronized

		Pts
1998	China (Sun Shuwei, Tian Liang)	313.50
2001	China (Bo Peng, Kenan Wang)	342.63
2003	Russia (A. Dobrosok, D. Sautin)	369.18
2005	China (Chong He, Feng Wang)	384.42

10-meter Synchronized

		Pts
1998	China (Xu Hao, Yu Zhuocheng)	326.34
2001	China (Jian Tian, Jia Bu)	361.41
2003	Australia (M. Helm, R. Newbery)	384.6
2005	Russia (D. Dobroskok, G. Galperin)	392.88

WOMEN

1-meter Springboard

		Pts
1991	Gao Min, China	478.26
1994	Chen Lixia, China	279.30
1998	Irina Lashko, Russia	296.07
2001	Blythe Hartley, Canada	300.81
2003	Irina Lashko, Australia	299.97
2005	Blythe Hartley, Canada	325.65

3-meter Springboard

		Pts
1973	Christa Koehler, E Germany	442.17
1975	Irina Kalinina, USSR	489.81
1978	Irina Kalinina, USSR	691.43
1982	Megan Neyer, United States	501.03
1986	Gao Min, China	582.90
1991	Gao Min, China	539.01
1994	Tan Shuping, China	548.49
1998	Yulia Pakhalina, Russia	544.62
2001	Jingjing Guo, China	596.67
2003	Jingjing Guo, China	617.94
2005	Jingjing Guo, China	645.54

Platform

		Pts
1973	Ulrike Knape, Sweden	406.77
1975	Janet Ely, United States	403.89
1978	Irina Kalinina, USSR	412.71
1982	Wendy Wyland, United States	438.79
1986	Chen Lin, China	449.67
1991	Fu Mingxia, China	426.51
1994	Fu Mingxia, China	434.04
1998	Olena Zhupyna, Ukraine	550.41
2001	Mian Xu, China	532.65
2003	Emilie Heymans, Canada	597.45
2005	Laura Ann Wilkinson, United States	564.87

3-meter Synchronized

		Pts
1998	Russia (Irina Lashko, Yulia Pakhalina)	282.30
2001	China (Minxia Wu, Jingjing Guo)	347.31
2003	China (Minxia Wu, Jingjing Guo)	357.30
2005	China (Ting Li, Jingjing Guo)	349.80

10-meter Synchronized

		Pts
1998	Ukraine (O. Zhupyna, S. Serbina)	278.28
2001	China (Qing Duan, Xue Sang)	329.94
2003	China (Lishi Lao, Ting Li)	344.58
2005	China (Tong Jia, Pei Lin Yuan)	351.60

MEN

50-METER FREESTYLE

1988....Matt Biondi	22.14*
2000....Gary Hall Jr. and Anthony Ervin	21.98
2004....Gary Hall Jr.	21.93

100-METER FREESTLYE

1906....Charles Daniels	1:13.4
1908....Charles Daniels	1:05.6*
1912....Duke Kahanamoku	1:03.4
1920....Duke Kahanamoku	1:00.4
1924....John Weissmuller	59.0‡
1928....John Weissmuller	58.6‡
1948....Wally Ris	57.3‡
1952....Clarke Scholes	57.4
1964....Don Schollander	53.4‡
1972....Mark Spitz	51.22*
1976....Jim Montgomery	49.99*
1984....Rowdy Gaines	49.80‡
1988....Matt Biondi	48.63‡

200-METER FREESTYLE

1904....Charles Daniels	2:44.2
1906–1964 Not held	
1972....Mark Spitz	1:52.78*
1976....Bruce Furniss	1:50.29*

400-METER FREESTYLE

1904....Charles Daniels (440 yds)	6:16.2
1920....Norman Ross	5:26.8
1924....John Weissmuller	5:04.2‡
1932....Buster Crabbe	4:48.4‡
1936....Jack Medica	4:44.5‡
1948....William Smith	4:41.0‡
1964....Don Schollander	4:12.2*
1968....Mike Burton	4:09.0‡
1976....Brian Goodell	3:51.93*
1984....George DiCarlo	3:51.23‡

1,500-METER FREESTYLE

1920....Norman Ross	22:23.2
1948....James McLane	19:18.5
1952....Ford Konno	18:30.3‡
1968....Mike Burton	16:38.9‡
1972....Mike Burton	15:52.58‡
1976....Brian Goodell	15:02.40*
1984....Michael O'Brien	15:05.20

100-METER BACKSTROKE

1912....Harry Hebner	1:21.2
1920....Warren Kealoha	1:15.2
1924....Warren Kealoha	1:13.2‡
1928....George Kojac	1:08.2*
1936....Adolph Kiefer	1:05.9‡
1948....Allen Stack	1:06.4
1952....Yoshi Oyakawa	1:05.4‡
1976....John Naber	55.49*
1984....Rick Carey	55.79
1996....Jeff Rouse	54.10
2000....Lenny Krayzelburg	53.60‡
2004....Aaron Peirsol	54.06

200-METER BACKSTROKE

1964....Jed Graef	2:10.3*
1976....John Naber	1:59.19*
1984....Rick Carey	2:00.23
1996....Brad Bridgewater	1:58.54
2000....Lenny Krayzelburg	1:56.76‡
2004....Aaron Peirsol	1:54.95‡

100-METER BREASTROKE

1968....Donald McKenzie	1:07.7‡
1976....John Hencken	1:03.11*
1984....Steve Lundquist	1:01.65 *
1992....Nelson Diebel	1:01.50‡

200-METER BREASTROKE

1924....Robert Skelton	2:56.6
1948....Joseph Verdeur	2:39.3‡
1960....William Mulliken	2:37.4
1972....John Hencken	2:21.55
1992....Mike Barrowman	2:10.16*

100-METER BUTTERFLY

1968....Douglas Russell	55.9‡
1972....Mark Spitz	54.27*
1976....Matt Vogel	54.35
1992....Pablo Morales	53.32
2004....Michael Phelps	51.24‡

200-METER BUTTERFLY

1956....William Yorzyk	2:19.3‡
1960....Michael Troy	2:12.8*
1968....Carl Robie	2:08.7
1972....Mark Spitz	2:00.70*
1976....Mike Bruner	1:59.23*
1992....Melvin Stewart	1:56.26
2000....Tom Malchow	1:55.35‡
2004....Michael Phelps	1:54.04‡

200-METER INDIVIDUAL MEDLEY

1968....Charles Hickcox	2:12.0‡
2004....Michael Phelps	1:57.14‡

400-METER INDIVIDUAL MEDLEY

1964....Richard Roth	4:45.4*
1968....Charles Hickcox	4:48.4
1976....Rod Strachan	4:23.68*
1996....Tom Dolan	4:14.90
2000....Tom Dolan	4:11.76‡
2004....Michael Phelps	4:08.26*

* World record. ‡Meet (Olympic) record.

MEN (cont.)

3-METER SPRINGBOARD DIVING

1920	Louis Kuehn	675.4 points
1924	Albert White	696.4
1928	Pete Desjardins	185.04
1932	Michael Galitzen	161.38
1936	Richard Degener	163.57
1948	Bruce Harlan	163.64
1952	David Browning	205.29
1956	Robert Clotworthy	159.56
1960	Gary Tobian	170.00
1964	Kenneth Sitzberger	159.90
1968	Bernard Wrightson	170.15
1976	Philip Boggs	619.05
1984	Greg Louganis	754.41
1988	Greg Louganis	730.80

PLATFORM DIVING

1904	George Sheldon	12.66 points
1920	Clarence Pinkston	100.67
1924	Albert White	97.46
1928	Pete Desjardins	98.74
1932	Harold Smith	124.80
1936	Marshall Wayne	113.58
1948	Sammy Lee	130.05
1952	Sammy Lee	156.28
1960	Robert Webster	165.56
1964	Robert Webster	148.58
1984	Greg Louganis	576.99
1988	Greg Louganis	638.61

WOMEN

50-METER FREESTYLE

1996	Amy Van Dyken	24.87

100-METER FREESTLYE

1920	Ethelda Bleibtrey	1:13.6*
1924	Ethel Lackie	1:12.4
1928	Albina Osipowich	1:11.0‡
1932	Helene Madison	1:06.8‡
1968	Jan Henne	1:00.0
1972	Sandra Neilson	58.59‡
1984	Carrie Steinseifer	55.92
	Nancy Hogshead	55.92

200-METER FREESTYLE

1968	Debbie Meyer	2:10.5‡
1984	Mary Wayte	1:59.23
1992	Nicole Haislett	1:57.90

400-METER FREESTYLE

1924	Martha Norelius	6:02.2‡
1928	Martha Norelius	5:42.8*
1932	Helene Madison	5:28.5*
1948	Ann Curtis	5:17.8‡
1960	Chris von Saltza	4:50.6
1964	Virginia Duenkel	4:43.3‡
1968	Debbie Meyer	4:31.8‡
1984	Tiffany Cohen	4:07.10‡
1988	Janet Evans	4:03.85*

800-METER FREESTYLE

1968	Debbie Meyer	9:24.0‡
1972	Keena Rothhammer	8:53.86*
1984	Tiffany Cohen	8:24.95‡
1988	Janet Evans	8:20.20‡
1992	Janet Evans	8:25.52
1996	Brooke Bennett	8:27.89
2000	Brooke Bennett	8:19.67

100-METER BACKSTROKE

1924	Sybil Bauer	1:23.2‡
1932	Eleanor Holm	1:19.4
1960	Lynn Burke	1:09.3‡
1964	Cathy Ferguson	1:07.7*
1968	Kaye Hall	1:06.2*
1972	Melissa Belote	1:05.78‡
1984	Theresa Andrews	1:02.55
1996	Beth Botsford	1:01.19
2004	Natalie Coughlin	1:00.37

200-METER BACKSTROKE

1968	Pokey Watson	2:24.8‡
1972	Melissa Belote	2:19.19*

100-METER BREASTSTROKE

1972	Catherine Carr	1:13.58*
2000	Megan Quann	1:07.05

200-METER BREASTSTROKE

1968	Sharon Wichman	2:44.4‡
2004	Amanda Beard	2:23.37‡

100-METER BUTTERFLY

1956	Shelley Mann	1:11.0‡
1960	Carolyn Schuler	1:09.5‡
1964	Sharon Stouder	1:04.7*
1984	Mary T. Meagher	59.26
1996	Amy Van Dyken	59.13

200-METER BUTTERFLY

1972	Karen Moe	2:15.57*
1984	Mary T. Meagher	2:06.90‡
1992	Summer Sanders	2:08.67
2000	Misty Hyman	2:05.88‡

200-METER INDIVIDUAL MEDLEY

1968	Sharon Wichman	2:44.4‡
1984	Tracy Caulkins	2:12.64‡

400-METER INDIVIDUAL MEDLEY

1964	Donna De Varona	5:18.7‡
1968	Claudia Kolb	5:08.5‡
1984	Tracy Caulkins	4:39.24
1988	Janet Evans	4:37.76

* World record; ‡ Meet (Olympic) record.

WOMEN (cont.)

3-METER SPRINGBOARD DIVING

1920	Aileen Riggin	539.9 points
1924	Elizabeth Becker	474.5
1928	Helen Meany	78.62
1932	Georgia Coleman	87.52
1936	Marjorie Gestring	89.27
1948	Victoria Draves	108.74
1952	Patricia McCormick	147.30
1956	Patricia McCormick	142.36
1968	Sue Gossick	150.77
1972	Micki King	450.03
1976	Jennifer Chandler	506.19

PLATFORM DIVING

1924	Caroline Smith	33.2 points
1928	Elizabeth Becker Pinkston	31.6
1932	Dorothy Poynton	40.26
1936	Dorothy Poynton Hill	33.93
1948	Victoria Draves	68.87
1952	Patricia McCormick	79.37
1956	Patricia McCormick	84.85
1964	Lesley Bush	99.80
2000	Laura Wilkinson	543.75

* World record; ‡Meet (Olympic) record.

Notable Achievements

Barrier Breakers

MEN

Event	Barrier	Athlete and Nation	Time	Date
100 Freestyle	1:00	Johnny Weissmuller, United States	58.6	7-9-22
100 Freestyle	:50	James Montgomery, United States	49.99	7-25-76
200 Freestyle	2:00	Don Schollander, United States	1:58.8	7-27-63
200 Freestyle	1:50	Sergei Kopliakov, USSR	1:49.83	4-7-79
200 Freestyle	1:45	Ian Thorpe, Australia	1:44.06	7-25-01
400 Freestyle	4:00	Rick DeMont, United States	3:58.18	9-6-73
400 Freestyle	3:50	Vladimir Salnikov, USSR	3:49.57	3-12-82
800 Freestyle	8:00	Vladimir Salnikov, USSR	7:56.49	3-23-79
800 Freestyle	7:40	Ian Thorpe, Australia	7:39.16	7-24-01
1500 Freestyle	15:00	Vladimir Salnikov, USSR	14:58.27	7-22-80
1500 Freestyle	14:35	Grant Hackett, Australia	14:34.56	7-29-01
100 Backstroke	1:00	Thompson Mann, United States	59.6	10-16-64
200 Backstroke	2:00	John Naber, United States	1:59.19	7-24-76
100 Breaststroke	1:00	Roman Sloudnov, Russia	59.97	6-28-01
200 Breaststroke	2:30	Chester Jastremski, United States	2:29.6	8-19-61
200 Breaststroke	2:10	Kosuke Kitajima, Japan	2:09.42	7-24-03
100 Butterfly	1:00	Lance Larson, United States	59.0	6-29-60
200 Butterfly	2:00	Roger Pyttel, E Germany	1:59.63	6-3-76

WOMEN

Event	Barrier	Athlete and Nation	Time	Date
100 Freestyle	1:00	Dawn Fraser, Australia	59.9	10-27-62
200 Freestyle	2:00	Kornelia Ender, E Germany	1:59.78	6-2-76
400 Freestyle	4:30	Debbie Meyer, United States	4:29.0	8-18-67
800 Freestyle	10:00	Jane Cederqvist, Sweden	9:55.6	8-17-60
800 Freestyle	9:00	Ann Simmons, United States	8:59.4	9-10-71
1500 Freestyle	20:00	Ilsa Konrads, Australia	19:25.7	1-14-60
	16:00	Janet Evans, United States	15:52.10	3-26-88
100 Backstroke	1:00	Natalie Coughlin, United States	59.58	8-16-02
200 Backstroke	2:30	Satoko Tanaka, Japan	2:29.6	2-10-63
100 Butterfly	1:00	Christiane Knacke, E Germany	59.78	8-28-77
400 Individual Medley	5:00	Gudrun Wegner, E Germany	4:57.51	9-6-73

Olympic Achievements

MOST INDIVIDUAL GOLDS IN SINGLE OLYMPICS

MEN

No.	Athlete and Nation	Olympic Year	Events
4	Mark Spitz, United States	1972	100, 200 Free; 100, 200 Fly
4	Michael Phelps, United States	2004	100, 200 fly, 200 IM, 400 IM

WOMEN

No.	Athlete and Nation	Olympic Year	Events
4	Kristin Otto, E Germany	1988	50, 100 Free; 100 Back; 100 Fly
3	Debbie Meyer, United States	1968	200, 400, 800 Free
3	Shane Gould, Australia	1972	200, 400 Free; 200 IM
3	Kornelia Ender, E Germany	1976	100, 200 Free; 100 Fly
3	Janet Evans, United States	1988	400, 800 Free; 400 IM
3	Krisztina Egerszegi, Hungary	1992	100, 200 Back; 400 IM
3	Michelle Smith, Ireland	1996	400 Free; 200, 400 IM
3	Inge de Bruijn, Netherlands	2000	50, 100 Free; 100 Fly

MOST INDIVIDUAL OLYMPIC GOLD MEDALS, CAREER

MEN

No.	Athlete and Nation	Olympic Years and Events
4	Charles Meldrum Daniels, United States	1904 (220, 440 Free); 1906 (100 Free) 1908 (100 Free)
4	Roland Matthes, E Germany	1968 (100, 200 Back); 1972 (100, 200 Back)
4	Mark Spitz, United States	1972 (100, 200 Free; 100, 200 Fly)
4	Michael Phelps, United States	2004 (100, 200 fly; 200, 400 IM)

WOMEN

No.	Athlete and Nation	Olympic Years and Events
4	Kristin Otto, E Germany	1988 (50 Free; 100 Free, Back and Fly)
4	Janet Evans, United States	1988 (400, 800 Free; 400 IM); 1992 (800 Free)
4	Krisztina Egerszegi, Hungary	1992 (100, 200 Back; 400 IM); 1996 (200 Back)
4	Inge de Bruijn, Netherlands	2000 (50, 100 free; 100 fly); 2004 (50 free)
4	Yana Klochkova, Ukraine	2000 (200, 400 IM); 2004 (200, 400 IM)

Most Olympic Gold Medals in a Single Olympics, Men—7, Mark Spitz, United States, 1972: 100, 200 Free; 100, 200 Fly; 4 x 100, 4 x 200 Free Relays; 4 x 100 Medley Relay.

Most Olympic Gold Medals in a Single Olympics, Women—6, Kristin Otto, E Germany, 1988: 50, 100 Free; 100 Back; 100 Fly; 4 x 100 Free Relay; 4 x 100 Medley Relay.

Most Olympic Medals in a Single Olympics, Men—8, Michael Phelps, United States, 2004: (six gold, two bronze).

Most Olympic Medals in a Career, Men—11, Matt Biondi, United States: 1984 (one gold), '88 (five gold, one silver, one bronze), '92 (two gold, one silver); 11, Mark Spitz, United States: 1968 (two gold, one silver, one bronze), '72 (seven gold); 10, Gary Hall Jr., United States 1996 (one gold, three silver), 2000 (three gold, one bronze) 2004 (two gold).

Most Olympic Medals in a Career, Women—11, Jenny Thompson, United States: 1992 (two gold, one silver), 1996 (three gold), 2000 (three gold, one bronze); 2004 (one silver); 8, Dawn Fraser, Australia: 1956 (two gold, one silver), '60 (one gold, two silver), '64 (one gold, one silver); 8, Kornelia Ender, E Germany: 1972 (three silver), '76 (four gold, one silver); 8, Shirley Babashoff, United States: 1972 (one gold, two silver); '76 (one gold, four silver); 8, Inge de Bruijn, Netherlands: 2000 (three gold, one silver), 2004 (one gold, one silver, two bronze).

Winner, Same Event, Three Consecutive Olympics—Dawn Fraser, Australia, 100 Freestyle, 1956, '60, '64; Krisztina Egerszegi, Hungary, 200 Back, 1988, '92, '96.

Youngest Person to Win an Olympic Diving Gold—Marjorie Gestring, United States, 1936, 13 years, 9 months, springboard diving.

Youngest Person to Win an Olympic Swimming Gold—Krisztina Egerszegi, Hungary, 1988, 14 years, one month, 200 backstroke.

World Record Achievements

Most World Records, Career, Women—42, Ragnhild Hveger, Denmark, 1936–42.

Most World Records, Career, Men—32, Arne Borg, Sweden, 1921–29.

Most Freestyle Records Held Concurrently—5, Helene Madison, United States, 1931–33; 5, Shane Gould, Australia, 1972.

Most Consecutive Lowerings of a Record—10, Kornelia Ender, E Germany, 100 Freestyle, 7-13-73 to 7-19-76.

Longest Duration of World Record—19 years, 359 days, 1:04.6 in 100 Free, Willy den Ouden, Netherlands.

Skiing

World Cup champion Bode Miller of the United States

Bode's Well

Setting the stage for Olympic success in '06, American Bode Miller sizzled the slopes to World Cup glory, while an up-and-coming group of US women had breakout seasons

BY MARK BECHTEL

BODE MILLER WAS SO GOOD AT the Alpine World Ski Championships in Bormio, Italy, that even a run that resulted in a disqualification attracted scores of calls and emails from admirers. Fifteen seconds into his downhill run in the downhill-slalom combined event, Miller lost his left ski. Rules stipulate that once a skier passes a gate without two skis he's disqualified, but Miller refused to give up, continuing down the grueling, twisting Stelvio course on his right ski, lasting about 90 seconds before finally falling. "There aren't many skiers in the world who could do what he did today," said former U.S. Ski Team coach Bob Beattie. Race director Gunter Hujara was also impressed. He decided not to wave Miller off the course and said he would not have fined him for finishing, because, he said, "this little show ... was a good thing."

The performance was a hit with the Italian crowd as well as skiing fans back home, many of whom let Miller know how much they appreciated his one-legged act.

"One coach on the East Coast said, 'Bode, I'm having all my racers go up and ski on one ski this week, hoping that someday they can be just like you,'" Miller said, laughing. "I'm like, 'Guys, I DNF'd the race!'"

Miller's gutsy performance was noteworthy because it was one of the rare times all year that something didn't go his way. The 27-year-old ran away with the World Cup overall title, becoming just the second U.S. male to take skiing's top prize. And he bounced back at Stelvio to win the downhill by nearly a half-second over teammate Daron Rahlves. Miller's downhill run was a dominating display that underscored how Miller is not only the most gifted skier around, but one of the cagiest as well.

The starting order is determined by a skier's time in his final practice run; the top 30 are sent out in inverted order, followed in order by those whose times are outside the top 30. Miller decided to purposely put up a slow time on his run so he could start early, before the snow gets chopped up. It was a risky move. If he

Sweden's Anja Pärson won the women's World Cup for the second consecutive year.

added too much time to the run and finished outside the top 30, he'd start way back in the order. Before his run he activated the timing wand with his pole, then counted to two before embarking on a near-perfect run that left him 28th-fastest, meaning he'd start third. "I've been messing around with opening the wand for a while," Miller said. "It never worked as perfectly as it did here. I was right on the edge. That was as big a factor as anything I did in the race." On pristine snow, he blew away the field, finishing .44 seconds ahead of Rahlves, who was in turn .43 seconds faster than the bronze medalist, Austrian Michael Walchhofer. "It's no problem," said Rahlves of losing to his teammate. "This is all cool." Very cool, indeed: it was the first time American men ever finished one-two in a downhill world championship. "[That] is an awesome achievement," said Miller, who also won the Super G. "Never mind me, personally."

Easier said than done. Miller was impossible to ignore during the 2004–05 season. In addition to joining Phil Mahre (1984) as the only U.S. male world cup champ, Miller became just the second skier ever to win at least one race in all four disci-

plines—downhill, slalom, giant slalom and Super G—in the same season. After his win at Stelvio, British downhiller Finlay Mickel, who finished 11th, said, "Another stellar performance for the big man."

While the worlds served as a coronation of sorts for Miller and for Sweden's Anja Pärson, who won it for the second straight year, they were set to be a coming-out party for Lindsey Kildow. The 20-year-old American, who was sixth in the overall standings, was a breakout star, putting up six podium finishes and 15 top tens throughout the year, including a downhill win at Lake Louise, Alberta, in December. At Bremio, though, she couldn't find her way onto the podium, finishing fourth in both the combined and the downhill. "This race is going to be forever in my mind," Kildow said after the event. "I guess maybe my time is next year."

Miller time, on the other hand, was the present. He wrapped up the overall title with a week to spare, solidifying a legacy he'd like to burnish with an Olympic gold after narrowly missing out on a combined gold in 2002. After Miller clinched the overall title, U.S. men's coach Phil McNichol said, "Bode clearly showed us he's one of the greatest U.S. skiers ever—and one of the greatest skiers in the history of the sport."

FOR THE RECORD·2004–2005

World Cup Alpine Racing Season Results

Men

Date	Event	Site	Winner
10-24-04	Giant Slalom	Söelden, Austria	Bode Miller, United States
11-27-04	Downhill	Lake Louise, Alberta	Bode Miller, United States
11-28-04	Super G	Lake Louise, Alberta	Bode Miller, United States
12-2-04	Super G	Vail/Beaver Creek, Colorado	Stephan Goergl, Austria
12-3-04	Downhill	Vail/Beaver Creek, Colorado	Bode Miller, United States
12-4-04	Giant Slalom	Vail/Beaver Creek, Colorado	Lasse Kjus, Norway
12-5-04	Slalom	Vail/Beaver Creek, Colorado	Benjamin Raich, Austria
12-11-04	Downhill	Val d'Isere, France	Werner Franz, Austria
12-12-04	Giant Slalom	Val d'Isere, France	Bode Miller, United States
12-13-04	Slalom	Sestriere, Italy	Bode Miller, United States
12-17-04	Super G	Gardena, Italy	Michael Walchhofer, Austria
12-18-04	Downhill	Gardena, Italy	Max Rauffer, Germany
12-19-04	Giant Slalom	Alta Badia, Italy	Thomas Grandi, Canada
12-21-04	Giant Slalom	Flachau, Austria	Thomas Grandi, Canada
12-22-04	Slalom	Flachau, Austria	Giorgio Rocca, Italy
12-29-04	Downhill	Bormio, Italy	Johann Gruger, Austria
1-8-05	Downhill	Chamonix, France	Johann Gruger, Austria
1-9-05	Slalom	Chamonix, France	Giorgio Rocca, Italy
1-11-05	Giant Slalom	Adelboden, Switzerland	Masimiliano Blardone, Italy
1-14-05	Combined	Wengen, Switzerland	Benjamin Raich, Austria
1-15-05	Downhill	Wengen, Switzerland	Michael Walchhofer, Austria
1-16-05	Slalom	Wengen, Switzerland	Alois Vogl, Germany
1-23-05	Slalom	Kitzbüehel, Austria	Manfred Pranger, Austria
1-24-05	Super G	Kitzbüehel, Austria	Hermann Maier, Austria
1-25-05	Slalom	Schladming, Austria	Manfred Pranger, Austria
2-18-05	Downhill	Garmisch, Germany	Michael Walchhofer, Austria
2-19-05	Downhill	Garmisch, Germany	Michael Walchhofer, Austria
2-20-05	Super G	Garmisch, Germany	Christoph Gruber, Austria
2-26-05	Giant Slalom	Kranjska Gora, Slovenia	Benjamin Raich, Austria
2-27-05	Slalom	Kranjska Gora, Slovenia	Giorgio Rocca, Italy
3-5-05	Downhill	Kvitfjell, Norway	Hermann Maier, Austria
3-6-05	Super G	Kvitfjell, Norway	Hermann Maier, Austria
3-10-05	Downhill	Lenzerheide, Switzerland	Lasse Kjus, Norway
3-11-05	Super G	Lenzerheide, Switzerland	Bode Miller, United States
3-12-05	Giant Slalom	Lenzerheide, Switzerland	Daron Rahlves, United States Stephan Goergl, Austria
3-13-05	Slalom	Lenzerheide, Switzerland	Mario Matt, Austria

Women

Date	Event	Site	Winner
10-23-04	Giant Slalom	Söelden, Austria	Anja Pärson, Sweden
11-26-04	Giant Slalom	Aspen, Colorado	Tanja Poutiainen, Finland
11-27-04	Slalom	Aspen, Colorado	Janica Kostelic, Croatia
11-28-04	Slalom	Aspen, Colorado	Tanja Poutiainen, Finland
12-3-04	Downhill	Lake Louise, Alberta	Lindsey Kildow, United States
12-4-04	Downhill	Lake Louise, Alberta	Hilde Gerg, Germany
12-5-04	Super G	Lake Louise, Alberta	Michaela Dorfmeister, Austria
12-11-04	Super G	Altenmarkt, Austria	Alexandra Meissnitzer, Austria
12-12-04	Slalom	Altenmarkt, Austria	Tanja Poutiainen, Finland
12-21-04	Super G	St. Moritz, Switzerland	Hilde Gerg, Germany
12-22-04	Giant Slalom	St. Moritz, Switzerland	Tina Maze, Slovenia
12-28-04	Giant Slalom	Semmering, Austria	Marlies Schild, Austria
12-29-04	Slalom	Semmering, Austria	Marlies Schild, Austria
1-6-05	Downhill	Santa Caterina, Italy	Michaela Dorfmeister, Austria
1-7-05	Downhill	Santa Caterina, Italy	Ingrid Jacquemod, France
1-8-05	Giant Slalom	Santa Caterina, Italy	Tina Maze, Slovenia
1-9-05	Slalom	Santa Caterina, Italy	Marlies Schild, Austria
1-12-05	Super G	Cortina d'Ampezzo, Italy	Renate Götschl, Austria
1-14-05	Super G	Cortina d'Ampezzo, Italy	Renate Götschl, Austria
1-15-05	Downhill	Cortina d'Ampezzo, Italy	Renate Götschl, Austria
1-16-05	Downhill	Cortina d'Ampezzo, Italy	Michaela Dorfmeister, Austria
1-20-05	Slalom	Zagreb, Croatia	Tanja Poutiainen, Finland
1-22-05	Giant Slalom	Maribor, Slovenia	Tina Maze, Slovenia
1-23-05	Slalom	Maribor, Slovenia	Anja Pärson, Sweden

World Cup Alpine Racing Season Results (Cont.)

Women (Cont.)

Date	Event	Site	Winner
2-19-05	Super G	Aare, Sweden	Michaela Dorfmeister, Austria
2-20-05	Giant Slalom	Aare, Sweden	Maria Rienda Contreras, Spain
2-25-05	Super G	San Sicario, Italy	Anja Pärson, Sweden
2-26-05	Downhill	San Sicario, Italy	Anja Pärson, Sweden
2-27-05	Combined	San Sicario, Italy	Janica Kostelic, Croatia
3-10-05	Downhill	Lenzerheide, Switzerland	Renate Götschl, Austria
3-11-05	Super G	Lenzerheide, Switzerland	Michaela Dorfmeister, Austria
3-12-05	Slalom	Lenzerheide, Switzerland	Sarah Schleper, United States
3-13-05	Giant Slalom	Lenzerheide, Switzerland	Maria Rienda Contreras, Spain

World Cup Alpine Racing Final Standings

Men

OVERALL

	Pts
Bode Miller, United States	1,648
Benjamin Raich, Austria	1,454
Hermann Maier, Austria	1,295
Michael Walchhofer, Austria	1,012
Daron Rahlves, U.S.	984
Didier Defago, Switzerland	684
Lasse Kjus, Norway	580
Fritz Strobl, Austria	537
Kalle Palander, Finland	530
Johann Grugger, Austria	521

DOWNHILL

	Pts
Michael Walchhofer, Austria	681
Bode Miller, United States	618
Hermann Maier, Austria	451
Daron Rahlves, United States	444
Johann Grugger, Austria	418
Fritz Strobl, Austria	379
Werner Franz, Austria	254
Mario Scheiber, Austria	247
Christoph Gruber, Austria	242
Mario Buechel, Liechtenstein	237

SLALOM

	Pts
Benjamin Raich, Austria	552
Rainer Schoenfelder, Austria	408
Manfred Pranger, Austria	396
Giorgio Rocca, Italy	390
Alois Vogl, Germany	310
Mario Matt, Austria	294
Ivica Kostelic, Croatia	263
Manfred Mölgg, Austria	256
André Myhrer, Sweden	247
Kalle Palander, Finland	227

GIANT SLALOM

	Pts
Benjamin Raich, Austria	423
Bode Miller, United States	420
Thomas Grandi, Canada	366
Hermann Maier, Austria	362
Massimiliano Blardone, Italy	345
Kalle Palander, Finland	303
Lasse Kjus, Norway	258
Davide Simoncelli, Italy	207
Stephan Goergl, Austria	206
Fredrik Nyberg, Sweden	203

SUPER G

	Pts
Bode Miller, United States	470
Hermann Maier, Austria	453
Daron Rahlves, United States	362
Didier Defago, Switzerland	286
Michael Walchhofer, Austria	265
Benjamin Raich, Austria	262
Stephan Goergl, Austria	245
Mario Buechel, Liechtenstein	198
Mario Scheiber, Austria	166
Fritz Strobl, Austria	158

Women

OVERALL

	Pts
Anja Pärson, Sweden	1,359
Janica Kostelic, Croatia	1,356
Renate Götschl, Austria	1,164
Michaela Dorfmeister, Austria	1,122
Tanja Poutiainen, Finland	1,039
Lindsey Kildow, United States	914
Hilde Gerg, Germany	799
Marlies Schild, Austria	669
Julia Mancuso, United States	659
Tina Maze, Slovenia	650

DOWNHILL

	Pts
Renate Götschl, Austria	567
Hilde Gerg, Germany	495
Michaela Dorfmeister, Austria	432
Janica Kostelic, Croatia	387
Lindsey Kildow, United States	384
Ingrid Jacquemod, France	298
Carole Montillet, France	284
Anja Pärson, Sweden	209
Sylviane Berthod, Switzerland	207
Julia Mancuso, United States	170

SLALOM

	Pts
Tanja Poutiainen, Finland	570
Janica Kostelic, Croatia	400
Marlies Schild, Austria	376
Kristina Koznick, United States	355
Sarah Schleper, United States	337
Anja Pärson, Sweden	301
Nicole Hosp, Austria	204
M. B.-Schmuderer, Germany	194
Veronika Zuzulova, Slovakia	185
Nika Fleiss, Croatia	183

GIANT SLALOM

	Pts
Tanja Poutiainen, Finland	461
Anja Pärson, Sweden	410
M. J. Rienda Contreras, Spain	384
Tina Maze, Slovenia	366
Genevieve Simard, Canada	241
Nicole Hosp, Austria	238
Martina Ertl, Germany	230
Julia Mancuso, United States	230
Karen Putzer, Italy	226
Elisabeth Görgl, Austria	225

SUPER G

	Pts
Michael Dorfmeister, Austria	493
Renate Götschl, Austria	416
Lindsey Kildow, United States	396
Anja Pärson, Sweden	359
Hilde Gerg, Germany	296
Alexandra Meissnitzer, Austria	276
Janica Kostelic, Croatia	257
Lucia Recchia, Italy	240
Tina Maze, Slovenia	236
Martina Ertl, Germany	224

FOR THE RECORD·Year by Year

Event Descriptions

Downhill: A speed event entailing a single run on a course with a minimum vertical drop of 500 meters (800 for men's World Cup) and very few control gates.

Slalom: A technical event in which times for runs on two courses are totaled to determine the winner. Skiers must make many quick, short turns through a combination of gates (55–75 gates for men, 40–60 for women) over a short course (140–220-meter vertical drop for men, 120–180 for women).

Combined: An event in which scores from designated slalom and downhill races are combined to determine finish order.

Giant Slalom: A faster technical event with fewer, more broadly spaced gates than in the slalom. Times for runs on two courses with vertical drops of 250–400 meters for men and 250–300 meters for women are combined to determine the winner.

Super Giant Slalom: A speed event that is a cross between the downhill and the giant slalom.

Parallel Slalom: A technical event that combines slalom and giant slalom turns.

FIS World Championships

Sites

1931 ....Mürren, Switzerland	1936 ....Innsbruck, Austria
1932 ....Cortina d'Ampezzo, Italy	1937 ....Chamonix, France
1933 ....Innsbruck, Austria	1938 ....Engelberg, Switzerland
1934 ....St. Moritz, Switzerland	1939 ....Zakopane, Poland
1935 ....Mürren, Switzerland	

Men

DOWNHILL

1931 ....Walter Prager, Switzerland
1932 ....Gustav Lantschner, Austria
1933 ....Walter Prager, Switzerland
1934 ....David Zogg, Switzerland
1935 ....Franz Zingerle, Austria
1936 ....Rudolf Rominger, Switzerland
1937 ....Émile Allais, France
1938 ....James Couttet, France
1939 ....Hans Lantschner, Germany

SLALOM

1931 ....David Zogg, Switzerland
1932 ....Friedrich Dauber, Germany
1933 ....Anton Seelos, Austria
1934 ....Franz Pfnür, Germany
1935 ....Anton Seelos, Austria
1936 ....Rudi Matt, Austria
1937 ....Émile Allais, France
1938 ....Rudolf Rominger, Switzerland
1939 ....Rudolf Rominger, Switzerland

Women

DOWNHILL

1931 ....Esme Mackinnon, Great Britain
1932 ....Paola Wiesinger, Italy
1933 ....Inge Wersin-Lantschner, Austria
1934 ....Anni Rüegg, Switzerland
1935 ....Christel Cranz, Germany
1936 ....Evie Pinching, Great Britain
1937 ....Christel Cranz, Germany
1938 ....Lisa Resch, Germany
1939 ....Christel Cranz, Germany

SLALOM

1931 ....Esme Mackinnon, Great Britain
1932 ....Rösli Streiff, Switzerland
1933 ....Inge Wersin-Lantschner, Austria
1934 ....Christel Cranz, Germany
1935 ....Anni Rüegg, Switzerland
1936 ....Gerda Paumgarten, Austria
1937 ....Christel Cranz, Germany
1938 ....Christel Cranz, Germany
1939 ....Christel Cranz, Germany

FIS World Alpine Ski Championships

Sites

1950 ....Aspen, Colorado	1987 ....Crans-Montana, Switzerland
1954 ....Are, Sweden	1989 ....Vail, Colorado
1958 ....Badgastein, Austria	1991 ....Saalbach-Hinterglemm, Austria
1962 ....Chamonix, France	1993 ....Morioka-Shizukuishi, Japan
1966 ....Portillo, Chile	1996 ....Sierra Nevada, Spain
1970 ....Val Gardena, Italy	1997 ....Sestriere, Italy
1974 ....St. Moritz, Switzerland	1999 ....Vail, Colorado
1978 ....Garmisch-Partenkirchen, W Germany	2001 ....St. Anton, Switzerland
1982 ....Schladming, Austria	2003 ....St. Moritz, Switzerland
1985 ....Bormio, Italy	2005 ....Bormio, Italy

Men

DOWNHILL

1950.............Zeno Colo, Italy	1987.............Peter Müller, Switzerland
1954.............Christian Pravda, Austria	1989.............Hansjörg Tauscher, W Germany
1958.............Toni Sailer, Austria	1991.............Franz Heinzer, Switzerland
1962.............Karl Schranz, Austria	1993.............Urs Lehmann, Switzerland
1966.............Jean-Claude Killy, France	1996.............Patrick Ortlieb, Austria
1970.............Bernard Russi, Switzerland	1997.............Bruno Kernen, Switzerland
1974.............David Zwilling, Austria	1999.............Hermann Maier, Austria
1978.............Josef Walcher, Austria	2001.............Hannes Trinkl, Austria
1982.............Harti Weirather, Austria	2003.............Michael Walchhofer, Austria
1985.............Pirmin Zurbriggen, Switzerland	2005.............Bode Miller, United States

SLALOM

1950.............Zeno Colo, Italy	1987.............Peter Müller, Switzerland
1954.............Christian Pravda, Austria	1989.............Hansjörg Tauscher, W Germany
1958.............Toni Sailer, Austria	1991.............Franz Heinzer, Switzerland
1962.............Karl Schranz, Austria	1993.............Urs Lehmann, Switzerland
1966.............Jean-Claude Killy, France	1996.............Patrick Ortlieb, Austria
1970.............Bernard Russi, Switzerland	1997.............Bruno Kernen, Switzerland
1974.............David Zwilling, Austria	1999.............Hermann Maier, Austria
1978.............Josef Walcher, Austria	2001.............Hannes Trinkl, Austria
1982.............Harti Weirather, Austria	2003.............Ivica Kostelic, Croatia
1985.............Pirmin Zurbriggen, Switzerland	2005.............Benjamin Raich, Austria

GIANT SLALOM

1950.............Zeno Colo, Italy	1987.............Pirmin Zurbriggen, Switzerland
1954.............Stein Eriksen, Norway	1989.............Rudolf Nierlich, Austria
1958.............Toni Sailer, Austria	1991.............Rudolf Nierlich, Austria
1962.............Egon Zimmermann, Austria	1993.............Kjetil André Aamodt, Norway
1966.............Guy Périllat, France	1996.............Alberto Tomba, Italy
1970.............Karl Schranz, Austria	1997.............Michael von Grünigen, Switzerland
1974.............Gustavo Thoeni, Italy	1999.............Marco Büchel, Liechtenstein
1978.............Ingemar Stenmark, Sweden	2001.............Michael von Grünigen, Switzerland
1982.............Steve Mahre, United States	2003.............Bode Miller, United States
1985.............Markus Wasmaier, W Germany	2005.............Hermann Maier, Austria

COMBINED

1982.............Michel Vion, France	1996.............Marc Girardelli, Luxembourg
1985.............Pirmin Zurbriggen, Switzerland	1997.............Kjetil André Aamodt, Norway
1987.............Marc Girardelli, Luxembourg	1999.............Kjetil André Aamodt, Norway
1989.............Marc Girardelli, Luxembourg	2001.............Kjetil André Aamodt, Norway
1991.............Stefan Eberharter, Austria	2003.............Bode Miller, United States
1993.............Lasse Kjus, Norway	2005.............Benjamin Raich, Austria

SUPER G

1987.............Pirmin Zurbriggen, Switzerland	1999.............Hermann Maier, Austria
1989.............Martin Hangl, Switzerland	Lasse Kjus, Norway
1991.............Stefan Eberharter, Austria	2001.............Daron Rahlves, United States
1993.............Cancelled due to weather	2003.............Stephan Eberharter, Austria
1996.............Atle Skaardal, Norway	2005.............Bode Miller, United States
1997.............Atle Skaardal, Norway	

Women

DOWNHILL

1950.............Trude Beiser-Jochum, Austria	1987.............Maria Walliser, Switzerland
1954.............Ida Schopfer, Switzerland	1989.............Maria Walliser, Switzerland
1958.............Lucile Wheeler, Canada	1991.............Petra Kronberger, Austria
1962.............Christl Haas, Austria	1993.............Kate Pace, Canada
1966.............Erika Schinegger, Austria	1996.............Picabo Street, United States
1970.............Annerösli Zryd, Switzerland	1997.............Hilary Lindh, United States
1974.............Annemarie Moser-Pröll, Austria	1999.............Renate Göetschl, Austria
1978.............Annemarie Moser-Pröll, Austria	2001.............Michaela Dorfmeister, Austria
1982.............Gerry Sorensen, Canada	2003.............Melanie Turgeon, Canada
1985.............Michela Figini, Switzerland	2005.............Janica Kostelic, Croatia

Women (Cont.)

SLALOM

1950	Dagmar Rom, Austria	1987	Erika Hess, Switzerland
1954	Trude Klecker, Austria	1989	Mateja Svet, Yugoslavia
1958	Inger Bjornbakken, Norway	1991	Vreni Schneider, Switzerland
1962	Marianne Jahn, Austria	1993	Karin Buder, Austria
1966	Annie Famose, France	1996	Pernilla Wiberg, Sweden
1970	Ingrid Lafforgue, France	1997	Deborah Compagnoni, Italy
1974	Hanni Wenzel, Liechtenstein	1999	Trine Bakke, Norway
1978	Lea Sölkner, Austria	2001	Anja Pärson, Sweden
1982	Erika Hess, Switzerland	2003	Janica Kostelic, Croatia
1985	Perrine Pelen, France	2005	Janica Kostelic, Croatia

GIANT SLALOM

1950	Dagmar Rom, Austria	1987	Vreni Schneider, Switzerland
1954	Lucienne Schmith-Couttet, France	1989	Vreni Schneider, Switzerland
1958	Lucile Wheeler, Canada	1991	Pernilla Wiberg, Sweden
1962	Marianne Jahn, Austria	1993	Carole Merle, France
1966	Marielle Goitschel, France	1996	Deborah Compagnoni, Italy
1970	Betsy Clifford, Canada	1997	Deborah Compagnoni, Italy
1974	Fabienne Serrat, France	1999	Anita Wachter, Austria
1978	Maria Epple, W Germany	2001	Sonja Nef, Switzerland
1982	Erika Hess, Switzerland	2003	Anja Pärson, Sweden
1985	Diann Roffe, United States	2005	Anja Pärson, Sweden

COMBINED

1982	Erika Hess, Switzerland	1996	Pernilla Wiberg, Sweden
1985	Erika Hess, Switzerland	1997	Renate Göetschl, Austria
1987	Erika Hess, Switzerland	1999	Pernilla Wiberg, Sweden
1989	Tamara McKinney, United States	2001	Martina Ertl, Germany
1991	Chantal Bournissen, Switzerland	2003	Janica Kostelic, Croatia
1993	Miriam Vogt, Germany	2005	Janica Kostelic, Croatia

SUPER G

1987	Maria Walliser, Switzerland	1997	Isolde Kostner, Italy
1989	Ulrike Maier, Austria	1999	Alexandra Meissnitzer, Austria
1991	Ulrike Maier, Austria	2001	Regine Cavagnoud, France
1993	Katja Seizinger, Germany	2003	Michaela Dorfmeister, Austria
1996	Isolde Kostner, Italy	2005	Anja Pärson, Sweden

Note: The 1995 FIS World Alpine Ski Championships were postponed to 1996 due to lack of snow.

Breakthrough Bronze

Julia Mancuso is only 20, but by her precocious standards, the bronze medal she unexpectedly won in the women's Super G at the world championships in Bormio, Italy was overdue.

Mancuso was on skis at age two and enrolled in the Mighty Mites ski school in Squaw Valley, Calif., at three. "My parents would drop my sister and me off in the morning and pick us up at the big tree in the afternoon," she said on Sunday. "Always at the big tree." Mancuso skied a World Cup race at 15 (making her one of the youngest Americans ever to do so) and won a U.S.-record eight career medals at the world junior championships, including two in 2004.

On Sunday in early February, she started 16th among the top 30 racers in the world and upon finishing said bitingly, "I wasn't too pleased with my run." Scarcely half an hour later her time had held up for third place as some of the most accomplished racers in history (Renate Götschl and Michaela Dorfmeister of Austria and Hilde Gerg of Germany) as well as rising star Lindsey Kildow of the U.S. had either strayed off course or skied slowly on a challenging and deceptively slick run. "Kind of weird," Mancuso said later, reconsidering her analysis. "I always figured at the Olympics or world championships, you had to ski perfect to medal. I guess not."

Mancuso, who is in the middle of a breakout season and ranks 12th in the women's overall World Cup standings with seven top 10 finishes, formulated her race plan while watching videotape on Saturday night. "I was watching some of my good races in [giant slalom] from earlier this year," she said. "And I've been skiing really aggressively, taking a really straight line. So I said to myself, I'm going straight tomorrow." Straight to the medal stand, as it turned out. —*Tim Layden*

World Cup Season Title Holders

Men

OVERALL

1967 ....Jean-Claude Killy, France	1987 ....Pirmin Zurbriggen, Switzerland
1968 ....Jean-Claude Killy, France	1988 ....Pirmin Zurbriggen, Switzerland
1969 ....Karl Schranz, Austria	1989 ....Marc Girardelli, Luxembourg
1970 ....Karl Schranz, Austria	1990 ....Pirmin Zurbriggen, Switzerland
1971 ....Gustavo Thoeni, Italy	1991 ....Marc Girardelli, Luxembourg
1972 ....Gustavo Thoeni, Italy	1992 ....Paul Accola, Switzerland
1973 ....Gustavo Thoeni, Italy	1993 ....Marc Girardelli, Luxembourg
1974 ....Piero Gros, Italy	1994 ....Kjetil André Aamodt, Norway
1975 ....Gustavo Thoeni, Italy	1995 ....Alberto Tomba, Italy
1976 ....Ingemar Stenmark, Sweden	1996 ....Lasse Kjus, Norway
1977 ....Ingemar Stenmark, Sweden	1997 ....Luc Alphand, France
1978 ....Ingemar Stenmark, Sweden	1998 ....Hermann Maier, Austria
1979 ....Peter Lüscher, Switzerland	1999 ....Lasse Kjus, Norway
1980 ....Andreas Wenzel, Liechtenstein	2000 ....Hermann Maier, Austria
1981 ....Phil Mahre, United States	2001 ....Hermann Maier, Austria
1982 ....Phil Mahre, United States	2002 ....Stephan Eberharter, Austria
1983 ....Phil Mahre, United States	2003 ....Stephan Eberharter, Austria
1984 ....Pirmin Zurbriggen, Switzerland	2004 ....Hermann Maier, Austria
1985 ....Marc Girardelli, Luxembourg	2005 ....Bode Miller, United States
1986 ....Marc Girardelli, Luxembourg	

DOWNHILL

1967 ....Jean-Claude Killy, France	1986 ....Peter Wirnsberger, Austria
1968 ....Gerhard Nenning, Austria	1987 ....Pirmin Zurbriggen, Switzerland
1969 ....Karl Schranz, Austria	1988 ....Pirmin Zurbriggen, Switzerland
1970 ....Karl Schranz, Austria	1989 ....Marc Girardelli, Luxembourg
Karl Cordin, Austria	1990 ....Helmut Höflehner, Austria
1971 ....Bernhard Russi, Switzerland	1991 ....Franz Heinzer, Switzerland
1972 ....Bernhard Russi, Switzerland	1992 ....Franz Heinzer, Switzerland
1973 ....Roland Collumbin, Switzerland	1993 ....Franz Heinzer, Switzerland
1974 ....Roland Collumbin, Switzerland	1994 ....Marc Girardelli, Luxembourg
1975 ....Franz Klammer, Austria	1995 ....Luc Alphand, France
1976 ....Franz Klammer, Austria	1996 ....Luc Alphand, France
1977 ....Franz Klammer, Austria	1997 ....Luc Alphand, France
1978 ....Franz Klammer, Austria	1998 ....Andreas Schifferer, Austria
1979 ....Peter Müller, Switzerland	1999 ....Lasse Kjus, Norway
1980 ....Peter Müller, Switzerland	2000 ....Hermann Maier, Austria
1981 ....Harti Weirather, Austria	2001 ....Hermann Maier, Austria
1982 ....Steve Podborski, Canada	2002 ....Stephan Eberharter, Austria
Peter Müller, Switzerland	2003 ....Stephan Eberharter, Austria
1983 ....Franz Klammer, Austria	2004 ....Stephan Eberharter, Austria
1984 ....Urs Raber, Switzerland	2005 ....Michael Walchhofer, Austria
1985 ....Helmut Höflehner, Austria	

SLALOM

1967 ....Jean-Claude Killy, France	1987 ....Bojan Krizaj, Yugoslavia
1968 ....Domeng Giovanoli, Switzerland	1988 ....Alberto Tomba, Italy
1969 ....Jean-Noël Augert, France	1989 ....Armin Bittner, W Germany
1970 ....Patrick Russel, France	1990 ....Armin Bittner, W Germany
Alain Penz, France	1991 ....Marc Girardelli, Luxembourg
1971 ....Jean-Noël Augert, France	1992 ....Alberto Tomba, Italy
1972 ....Jean-Noël Augert, France	1993 ....Tomas Fogdof, Sweden
1973 ....Gustavo Thoeni, Italy	1994 ....Alberto Tomba, Italy
1974 ....Gustavo Thoeni, Italy	1995 ....Alberto Tomba, Italy
1975 ....Ingemar Stenmark, Sweden	1996 ....Sebastien Amiez, France
1976 ....Ingemar Stenmark, Sweden	1997 ....Thomas Sykora, Austria
1977 ....Ingemar Stenmark, Sweden	1998 ....Thomas Sykora, Austria
1978 ....Ingemar Stenmark, Sweden	1999 ....Thomas Stangassinger, Austria
1979 ....Ingemar Stenmark, Sweden	2000 ....Kjetil André Aamodt, Norway
1980 ....Ingemar Stenmark, Sweden	2001 ....Benjamin Raich, Austria
1981 ....Ingemar Stenmark, Sweden	2002 ....Ivica Kostelic, Croatia
1982 ....Phil Mahre, United States	2003 ....Kalle Palander, Finland
1983 ....Ingemar Stenmark, Sweden	2004 ....Rainer Schoenfelder, Austria
1984 ....Marc Girardelli, Luxembourg	2005 ....Benjamin Raich, Austria
1985 ....Marc Girardelli, Luxembourg	
1986 ....Rok Petrovic, Yugoslavia	

Men (Cont.)
GIANT SLALOM

1967	Jean-Claude Killy, France
1968	Jean-Claude Killy, France
1969	Karl Schranz, Austria
1970	Gustavo Thoeni, Italy
1971	Patrick Russel, France
1972	Gustavo Thoeni, Italy
1973	Hans Hinterseer, Austria
1974	Piero Gros, Italy
1975	Ingemar Stenmark, Sweden
1976	Ingemar Stenmark, Sweden
1977	Heini Hemmi, Switzerland
	Ingemar Stenmark, Sweden
1978	Ingemar Stenmark, Sweden
1979	Ingemar Stenmark, Sweden
1980	Ingemar Stenmark, Sweden
1981	Ingemar Stenmark, Sweden
1982	Phil Mahre, United States
1983	Phil Mahre, United States
1984	Ingemar Stenmark, Sweden
	Pirmin Zurbriggen, Switzerland
1985	Marc Girardelli, Luxembourg
1986	Joël Gaspoz, Switzerland
1987	Joël Gaspoz, Switzerland
	Pirmin Zurbriggen, Switzerland
1988	Alberto Tomba, Italy
1989	Pirmin Zurbriggen, Switzerland
1990	Ole-Cristian Furuseth, Norway
	Günther Mader, Austria
1991	Alberto Tomba, Italy
1992	Alberto Tomba, Italy
1993	Kjetil André Aamodt, Norway
1994	Christian Mayer, Austria
1995	Alberto Tomba, Italy
1996	Michael von Grünigen, Switzerland
1997	Michael von Grünigen, Switzerland
1998	Hermann Maier, Austria
1999	Michael von Grünigen, Switzerland
2000	Hermann Maier, Austria
2001	Hermann Maier, Austria
2002	Frederic Covili, France
2003	Michael von Grünigen, Switzerland
2004	Bode Miller, United States
2005	Benjamin Raich, Austria

SUPER G

1986	Markus Wasmeier, W Germany
1987	Pirmin Zurbriggen, Switzerland
1988	Pirmin Zurbriggen, Switzerland
1989	Pirmin Zurbriggen, Switzerland
1990	Pirmin Zurbriggen, Switzerland
1991	Franz Heinzer, Switzerland
1992	Paul Accola, Switzerland
1993	Kjetil André Aamodt, Norway
1994	Jan Einar Thorsen, Norway
1995	Peter Runggaldier, Italy
1996	Atle Skaardal, Norway
1997	Luc Alphand, France
1998	Hermann Maier, Austria
1999	Hermann Maier, Austria
2000	Hermann Maier, Austria
2001	Hermann Maier, Austria
2002	Stephan Eberharter, Austria
2003	Stephan Eberharter, Austria
2004	Hermann Maier, Austria
2005	Bode Miller, United States

COMBINED

1979	Andreas Wenzel, Liechtenstein
1980	Andreas Wenzel, Liechtenstein
1981	Phil Mahre, United States
1982	Phil Mahre, United States
1983	Phil Mahre, United States
1984	Andreas Wenzel, Liechtenstein
1985	Andreas Wenzel, Liechtenstein
1986	Markus Wasmeier, W Germany
1987	Pirmin Zurbriggen, Switzerland
1988	Hubert Strolz, Austria
1989	Marc Girardelli, Luxembourg
1990	Pirmin Zurbriggen, Switzerland
1991	Marc Girardelli, Luxembourg
1992	Paul Accola, Switzerland
1993	Marc Girardelli, Luxembourg
1994	Kjetil André Aamodt, Norway
1995	Marc Girardelli, Luxembourg
1996	Günther Mader, Austria
1997	Kjetil André Aamodt, Norway
1998	Werner Franz, Austria
1999	Kjetil André Aamodt, Norway
2000	Kjetil André Aamodt, Norway
	Lasse Kjus, Norway
2001	Lasse Kjus, Norway
2002	Kjetil André Aamodt, Norway
2003	Bode Miller, United States
2004	Bode Miller, United States
2005	Benjamin Raich, Austria

Women
OVERALL

1967	Nancy Greene, Canada
1968	Nancy Greene, Canada
1969	Gertrud Gabl, Austria
1970	Michèle Jacot, France
1971	Annemarie Pröll, Austria
1972	Annemarie Pröll, Austria
1973	Annemarie Pröll, Austria
1974	Annemarie Moser-Pröll, Austria
1975	Annemarie Moser-Pröll, Austria
1976	Rosi Mitermaier, W Germany
1977	Lise-Marie Morerod, Switzerland
1978	Hanni Wenzel, Liechtenstein
1979	Annemarie Moser-Pröll, Austria
1980	Hanni Wenzel, Liechtenstein
1981	Marie-Thérèse Nadig, Switzerland
1982	Erika Hess, Switzerland
1983	Tamara McKinney, United States
1984	Erika Hess, Switzerland
1985	Michela Figini, Switzerland
1986	Maria Walliser, Switzerland
1987	Maria Walliser, Switzerland
1988	Michela Figini, Switzerland
1989	Vreni Schneider, Switzerland
1990	Petra Kronberger, Austria
1991	Petra Kronberger, Austria
1992	Petra Kronberger, Austria
1993	Anita Wachter, Austria
1994	Vreni Schneider, Switzerland
1995	Vreni Schneider, Switzerland
1996	Katja Seizinger, Germany
1997	Pernilla Wiberg, Sweden
1998	Katja Seizinger, Germany
1999	Alexandra Meissnitzer, Austria
2000	Renate Götschl, Austria
2001	Janica Kostelic, Croatia
2002	Michaela Dorfmeister, Austria
2003	Janica Kostelic, Austria
2004	Anja Pärson, Sweden
2005	Anja Pärson, Sweden

Women (Cont.)
DOWNHILL

1967	Marielle Goitschel, France	1987	Michela Figini, Switzerland
1968	Isabelle Mir, France & Olga Pall, Austria	1988	Michela Figini, Switzerland
1969	Wiltrud Drexel, Austria	1989	Michela Figini, Switzerland
1970	Isabelle Mir, France	1990	Katrin Gutensohn-Knopf, Germany
1971	Annemarie Pröll, Austria	1991	Chantal Bournissen, Switzerland
1972	Annemarie Pröll, Austria	1992	Katja Seizinger, Germany
1973	Annemarie Pröll, Austria	1993	Katja Seizinger, Germany
1974	Annemarie Moser-Pröll, Austria	1994	Katja Seizinger, Germany
1975	Annemarie Moser-Pröll, Austria	1995	Picabo Street, United States
1976	Brigitte Totschnig, Austria	1996	Picabo Street, United States
1977	Brigitte Totschnig-Habersatter, Austria	1997	Renate Götschl, Austria
1978	Annemarie Moser-Pröll, Austria	1998	Katja Seizinger, Germany
1979	Annemarie Moser-Pröll, Austria	1999	Renate Götschl, Austria
1980	Marie-Thérèse Nadig, Switzerland	2000	Regina Haeusl, Germany
1981	Marie-Thérèse Nadig, Switzerland	2001	Isolde Kostner, Italy
1982	Marie-Cecile Gros-Gaudenier, France	2002	Isolde Kostner, Italy
1983	Doris De Agostini, Switzerland	2003	Michaela Dorfmeister, Austria
1984	Maria Walliser, Switzerland	2004	Renate Götschl, Austria
1985	Michela Figini, Switzerland	2005	Anja Pärson, Sweden
1986	Maria Walliser, Switzerland		

SLALOM

1967	Nancy Greene, Canada	1987	Maria Walliser, Switzerland
1968	Nancy Greene, Canada	1988	Michela Figini, Switzerland
1969	Gertrud Gabl, Austria	1989	Vreni Schneider, Switzerland
1970	Michèle Jacot, France	1990	Petra Kronberger, Austria
1971	Annemarie Pröll, Austria	1991	Petra Kronberger, Austria
1972	Annemarie Pröll, Austria	1992	Petra Kronberger, Austria
1973	Annemarie Pröll, Austria	1993	Anita Wachter, Austria
1974	Annemarie Moser-Pröll, Austria	1994	Vreni Schneider, Switzerland
1975	Annemarie Moser-Pröll, Austria	1995	Vreni Schneider, Switzerland
1976	Rosi Mitermaier, W Germany	1996	Katja Seizinger, Germany
1977	Lise-Marie Morerod, Switzerland	1997	Pernilla Wiberg, Sweden
1978	Hanni Wenzel, Liechtenstein	1998	Katja Seizinger, Germany
1979	Annemarie Moser-Pröll, Austria	1999	Alexandra Meissnitzer, Austria
1980	Hanni Wenzel, Liechtenstein	2000	Renate Götschl, Austria
1981	Marie-Thérèse Nadig, Switzerland	2001	Janica Kostelic, Croatia
1982	Erika Hess, Switzerland	2002	Laure Pequegnot, France
1983	Tamara McKinney, United States	2003	Janica Kostelic, Croatia
1984	Erika Hess, Switzerland	2004	Anja Pärson, Sweden
1985	Michela Figini, Switzerland	2005	Tanja Poutiainen, Finland
1986	Maria Walliser, Switzerland		

GIANT SLALOM

1967	Nancy Greene, Canada	1987	Vreni Schneider/ Maria Walliser, Switz
1968	Nancy Greene, Canada	1988	Mateja Svet, Yugoslavia
1969	Marilyn Cochran, United States	1989	Vreni Schneider, Switzerland
1970	Michèle Jacot/Françoise Macchi, France	1990	Anita Wachter, Austria
1971	Annemarie Pröll, Austria	1991	Vreni Schneider, Switzerland
1972	Annemarie Pröll, Austria	1992	Carole Merle, France
1973	Monika Kaserer, Austria	1993	Carole Merle, France
1974	Hanni Wenzel, Liechtenstein	1994	Anita Wachter, Austria
1975	Annemarie Moser-Pröll, Austria	1995	Vreni Schneider, Switzerland
1976	Lise-Marie Morerod, Switzerland	1996	Martina Ertl, Germany
1977	Lise-Marie Morerod, Switzerland	1997	Deborah Compagnoni, Italy
1978	Lise-Marie Morerod, Switzerland	1998	Martina Ertl, Germany
1979	Christa Kinshofer, W Germany	1999	Alexandra Meissnitzer, Austria
1980	Hanni Wenzel, Liechtenstein	2000	Michaela Dorfmeister, Austria
1981	Marie-Thérèse Nadig, Switzerland	2001	Sonja Nef, Switzerland
1982	Irene Epple, W Germany	2002	Sonja Nef, Switzerland
1983	Tamara McKinney, United States	2003	Anja Pärson, Sweden
1984	Erika Hess, Switzerland	2004	Anja Pärson, Sweden
1985	Maria Keihl, W Germany	2005	Tanja Poutiainen, Finland
	Michela Figini, Switzerland		
1986	Vreni Schneider, Switzerland		

SUPER G

1986	Maria Kiehl, W Germany	1992	Carole Merle, France
1987	Maria Walliser, Switzerland	1993	Katja Seizinger, Germany
1988	Michela Figini, Switzerland	1994	Katja Seizinger, Germany
1989	Carole Merle, France	1995	Katja Seizinger, Germany
1990	Carole Merle, France	1996	Katja Seizinger, Germany
1991	Carole Merle, France	1997	Hilde Gerg, Germany

Women (Cont.)
SUPER G (CONT.)

1998 ....Katja Seizinger, Germany	2002 ....Hilde Gerg, Germany
1999 ....Alexandra Meissnitzer, Austria	2003 ....Carole Montillet, France
2000 ....Renate Göetschl, Austria	2004 ....Renate Götschl, Austria
2001 ....Regine Cavagnoud, France	2005 ....Michaela Dorfmeister, Austria

COMBINED

1979 ....Annemarie Moser-Pröll, Austria	1992 ....Sabine Ginther, Austria
Hanni Wenzel, Liechtenstein	1993 ....Anita Wachter, Austria
1980 ....Hanni Wenzel, Liechtenstein	1994 ....Pernilla Wiberg, Sweden
1981 ....Marie-Thérèse Nadig, Switzerland	1995 ....Pernilla Wiberg, Sweden
1982 ....Irene Epple, W Germany	1996 ....Anita Wachter, Austria
1983 ....Hanni Wenzel, Liechtenstein	1997 ....Pernilla Wiberg, Sweden
1984 ....Erika Hess, Switzerland	1998 ....Hilde Gerg, Germany
1985 ....Brigitte Oertli, Switzerland	1999 ....Hilde Gerg, Germany
1986 ....Maria Walliser, Switzerland	2000 ....Renate Götschl, Austria
1987 ....Brigitte Oertli, Switzerland	2001 ....Janica Kostelic, Croatia
1988 ....Brigitte Oertli, Switzerland	2002 ....Renate Götschl, Austria
1989 ....Brigitte Oertli, Switzerland	2003 ....Janica Kostelic, Croatia
1990 ....Anita Wachter, Austria	2004 ....Anja Pärson, Sweden
1991 ....Sabine Ginther, Austria	2005 ....Janica Kostelic, Croatia

World Cup Career Victories

Men

DOWNHILL
25	Franz Klammer, Austria
19	Peter Müller, Switzerland
18	*Stephan Eberharder, Austria

SLALOM
40	Ingemar Stenmark, Sweden
35	Alberto Tomba, Italy
16	Marc Girardelli, Luxembourg

GIANT SLALOM
46	Ingemar Stenmark, Sweden
23	Michael Von Grünigen, Switz
15	Alberto Tomba, Italy

SUPER G
22	*Hermann Maier, Austria
10	Pirmin Zurbriggen, Switzerland
7	Marc Girardelli, Luxembourg

COMBINED
11	Phil Mahre, United States
	Pirmin Zurbriggen, Switzerland
	Marc Girardelli, Luxembourg

Women

DOWNHILL
36	Annemarie Moser-Pröell, Austria
19	*Renate Götschl, Austria
17	Michela Figini, Switzerland

SLALOM
34	Vreni Schneider, Switzerland
21	Erika Hess, Switzerland
16	*Janica Kostelic, Croatia

GIANT SLALOM
20	Vreni Schneider, Switzerland
16	Annemarie Moser-Pröell, Austria
14	Anita Wachter, Austria

SUPER G
16	Katja Seizinger, Germany
13	*Renate Götschl, Austria
12	Carole Merle, France

COMBINED
8	Hanni Wenzel, Liechtenstein
7	Annemarie Moser-Pröll, Austria
	Brigitte Oertli, Switzerland

*Active in 2004–05.

U.S. Olympic Gold Medalists

Men

Year	Winner	Event
1980 ....Phil Mahre		Combined
1984 ....Bill Johnson		Downhill
1984 ....Phil Mahre		Slalom
1994 ....Tommy Moe		Downhill

Women

Year	Winner	Event
1948 ....Gretchen Fraser		Slalom
1952 ....Andrea Mead Lawrence		Slalom
1952 ....Andrea Mead Lawrence		Giant Slalom
1972 ....Barbara Ann Cochran		Slalom
1984 ....Debbie Armstrong		Giant Slalom
1994 ....Diann Roffe-Steinrotter		Super G
1998 ....Picabo Street		Super G

Figure Skating

World champion
Irina Slutskaya
of Russia

FIGURE SKATING

Settling Old Scores

While a new point system confounded some veteran skaters, a crop of rising stars emerged

BY MERRELL NODEN

No one loves a good soap opera more than figure skating fans, especially when the opera ends with a smiling princess whose path to triumph had been thorny. This year's opera began when the International Skating Union awarded the world championships to Moscow, which happens to be the hometown of Irina Slutskaya. The 2002 world champion and Olympic silver medalist is now 26 years old, a veritable crone in a world of fresh-faced girls. Great as she's been in the past, Slutskaya recently has suffered a patch of bad fortune. She missed the 2003 world championships due to her mother's ongoing battle with kidney disease and finished an exhausted ninth at the 2004 championships due to her own struggle with vasculitis, a blood vessel disorder that makes her tire easily.

With the condition diagnosed and controlled through medication, Slutskaya returned to competition this winter, and in January won her sixth European skating title, tying her with Katarina Witt and Sonja Henie. For these hometown world championships, Slutskaya broke with the superstitious rule of her past and actually invited her mother to come watch her skate. It was a sign of either relief at a crisis weathered or her understanding that she doesn't have many such competitions left.

Slutskaya's return seemed to set up a showdown with Michelle Kwan of the U.S., whom she'd first faced at the world juniors in 1994. At the U.S. Figure Skating Championships, held January 9-16 at Portland's Rose Garden arena, Kwan had skated to Ravel's "Bolero", and while her routine was far from perfect, it was good enough to win her an eighth straight ladies' title (and ninth overall, tying the career record).

The U.S. championship was the last major competition to be contested under the old scoring system. "I'm going to be sad when the 6.0 system goes," said Kwan who, for the record, has earned 57 perfect 6.0's overall with 42 coming at nationals.

Indeed, the new system is expected to work against Kwan. Called the Code of Points, it requires judges to award a score for each technical element in a skater's program. The overall aim of the change is to reward difficulty and daring rather than the grace and expressiveness that have always been the hallmarks of Kwan's skating. Indeed, it favors skaters like Kimmie Meissner, who earned the greatest cheers at Nationals despite finishing third. A 15-year-old from Baltimore, Meissner became the first American skater to land a triple Axel in competition since Tonya Harding did so in 1991.

Meissner was too young to skate at the World Championships. That left Kwan and the young veteran Sasha Cohen as the U.S.'s two very legitimate gold medal contenders. But in Moscow, Kwan skated poorly, discombobulat-

American rising stars Evan Lysacek and Kimmie Meissner look to bring home some hardware from Turin.

ed, it seemed, by the new scoring system, which she had chosen not to test in competition all winter. Instead, Kwan gave herself a crash course by studying the men's qualifying round in Moscow and doing her practice skates with pad in hand in order to reckon up the new value of jumps and combinations.

Obviously, it wasn't enough. Kwan stood seventh after the preliminaries. In the free skate, she fell while attempting a triple Salchow and that, it turned out, cost her the bronze. She wound up fourth, just behind Carolina Kostner of Italy, making this the first worlds since 1995 in which Kwan has failed to medal. "I was terrible," she said honestly, leaving many to second guess her decision not to skate in Grand Prix events, where she would have gotten a taste of the new scoring system.

Cohen skated well at the end of a season that saw her move from New Jersey to California in order to reunite with coach John Nicks, but came up short. She took the new system as a challenge. "I have a lot of silver medals," she said with a wry smile. "But I'm happy with my skating and the new system."

That left Slutskaya to dazzle the crowd. Encouraged by her exuberant countrymen and women, who waved flags, blew airhorns and cheered lustily, she loaded her program with difficult elements, including seven triple jumps to emerge the winner with a strange-looking score of 222.21 points.

"This is probably the dearest medal of my collection," she said through tears. "I think nobody else at this world championships has gone through what I've been through, who has been sick and isn't completely recovered. And to win at home, where it is so hard to win."

The men's results were skewed by injury. Three-time world champion Evgengy Plushenko skated the prelims but withdrew with a sore groin before the free skate. That opened the door wide. Johnny Weir, the two-time U.S. champion, also came close to withdrawing, due to a foot injury, but hung in bravely, skating on a foot that was black and blue by competition's end. He finished a respectable fourth, passed for the bronze medal by surprising U.S. teammate Evan Lysacek, a 19-year-old from Naperville, Ill., who was making his world championship debut.

"I am a little bit shocked," allowed Lysacek. "It wasn't my best skate but I guess it was enough." Lysacek, gold medalist Stephane Labiel of Switzerland and silver medalist Jeffrey Buttle of Canada comprised perhaps the most surprising medal stand in recent memory, since not one had previously won a world medal. A healthy Plushenko surely will give all three a battle next February in Turin.

The women's free skate in Turin, scheduled for February 23, should be a doozy. Kostner will gain inspiration from skating before what will surely be a wildly partisan crowd, and Cohen sounds determined to prove she can finish better than second. Don't count out Emily Hughes, who placed third at this year's world juniors, and is the younger sister of Sarah Hughes, the defending Olympic champion, who's an intriguing possibility in her own right. Though she's flown well under the radar since winning in Salt Lake City, she might certainly return.

Of course, the sentimental pick will be Kwan, but it won't be easy. To win, she'll first have to make peace with the new scoring system and then beat her old rival, Slutskaya, who proved this year that a princess needn't be young to be much beloved.

FOR THE RECORD 2005

World Champions

Moscow, Russia, March 13–20

Women

1. ....Irína Slutskaya, Russia
2. ....Sasha Cohen, United States
3. ....Carolina Kostner, Italy

Men

1. ....Stephane Lambiel, Switzerland
1. ....Jeffrey Buttle, Canada
3. ....Evan Lysacek, United States

Pairs

1. ....Tatiana Totmianina/ Maxim Marinin, Russia
2. ....Maria Petrova/Alexei Tikhonov, Russia
3. ....Dan Zhang/Hao Zhang, China

Dance

1. ....Tatiana Navka/ Roman Kostomaro, Russia
2. ....Tanith Belin/Benjamin Agosto, United States
3. ....Elena Grushina/Rusian Gonccharov, Ukraine

World Figure Skating Championships Medal Table

Country	Gold	Silver	Bronze	Total
Russia	3	1	0	4
United States	0	2	1	3
Switzerland	1	0	0	1
Canada	0	1	0	1
China	0	0	1	1
Italy	0	0	1	1
Ukraine	0	0	1	1

Champions of the United States

Portland, Oregon, January 9–16

Women

1. ....Michelle Kwan, Los Angeles FSC
2. ....Sasha Cohen, Orange County FSC
3. ....Kimberly Meissner,
   Univ of Delaware FSC

Men

1. ....Johnny Weir, SC of New York
2. ....Timothy Goebel, Winterhurst FSC
3. ....Evan Lysacke, Dupage FSC

Pairs

1. ....Kathryn Orscher/Garrett Lucash,
   Charter Oak FSC
2. ....Rena Inoue/John Baldwin,
   All Year FSC
3. ....Marcy Hinzmann/Aaron Parchem,
   Detroit SC

Dance

1. ....Tanith Belbin/ Benjamin Agosto,
   Artic, FSC
2. ....Melissa Gregory/ Denis Petukhov,
   Broadmoor SC/ Skokie Valley SC
3. ....Lydia Manon/ Ryan O'Meara,
   Coyotes SC of Arizona

Skating Terminology*

Basic Skating Terms

Edges: The two sides of the skating blade, on either side of the grooved center. There is an inside edge, on the inner side of the leg; and an outside edge, on the outer side of the leg.

Free Foot, Hip, Knee, Side, etc.: The foot a skater is not skating on at any one time is the free foot; everything on that side of the body is then called "free." (See also "skating foot.")

Free Skating (Freestyle): A 4- or 5-minute competition program of free-skating components, choreographed to music, with no set elements. Skating moves include jumps, spins, steps and other linking movements.

Skating Foot, Hip, Knee, Side, etc.: Opposite of the free foot, hip, knee, side, etc. The foot a skater is skating on at any one time is the skating foot; everything on that side of the body is then called "skating."

Toe Picks (Toe Rakes): The teeth at the front of the skate blade, used primarily for certain jumps and spins.

Trace, Tracing: The line left on the ice by the skater's blade.

Jumps

Waltz: A beginner's jump, involving half a revolution in the air, taken from a forward outside edge and landed on the back outside edge of the other foot.

Toe Loop: A one-revolution jump taken off from and landed on the same back outside edge. This jump is similar to the loop jump except that the skater kicks the toe pick of the free leg into the ice upon takeoff, providing added power.

Toe Walley: A jump similar to the toe loop, except that the takeoff is from the inside edge.

Flip: A jump taken off with the toe pick of the free leg from a back inside edge and landed on a back outside edge, with one in-air revolution.

Lutz: A toe jump similar to the flip, taken off with the toe pick of the free leg from a backward outside edge. The skater enters the jump skating in one direction, and concludes the jump skating in the opposite direction. Usually performed in the corners of the rink. Named after inventor Alois Lutz, who first landed the jump in Vienna, 1918.

Salchow: A one-, two- or three-revolution jump. The skater takes off from the back inside edge of one foot and lands backwards on the outside edge of the right foot, the opposite foot from which the skater took off. Named for its originator and first Olympic champion (1908), Sweden's Ulrich Salchow.

Axel: A combination of the waltz and loop jumps, including one-and-a-half revolutions. The only jump begun from a forward outside edge, the Axel is landed on the back outside edge of the opposite foot. Named for its inventor, Norway's Axel Paulsen.

Spins

Spin: The rotation of the body in one place on the ice. Various spins are the back, fast or scratch, sit, camel, butterfly and layback.

Camel Spin: A spin with the skater in an arabesque position (the free leg at right angles to the leg on the ice).

Flying Camel Spin: A jump spin ending in the camel-spin position.

Flying Sit Spin: A jump spin in which the skater leaps off the ice, assumes a sitting position at the peak of the jump, lands and spins in a similar sitting position.

Pair Movements/Techniques

Death Spiral: One of the most dramatic moves in figure skating. The man, acting as the center of a circle, holds tightly to the hand of his partner and pulls her around him. The woman, gliding on one foot, achieves a position almost horizontal to the ice.

Lifts: The most spectacular moves in pairs skating. They involve any maneuver in which the man lifts the woman off the ice. The man often holds his partner above his head with one hand.

Throws: The man lifts the woman into the air and throws her away from him. She spins in the air and lands on one foot.

Twist: The man throws the woman into the air. She spins in the air (either a double- or triple-twist), and he catches her at the landing.

*Compiled by the United States Figure Skating Association.

World Champions

Women

1906	Madge Sayers-Cave, Great Britain
1907	Madge Sayers-Cave, Great Britain
1908	Lily Kronberger, Hungary
1909	Lily Kronberger, Hungary
1910	Lily Kronberger, Hungary
1911	Lily Kronberger, Hungary
1912	Opika von Meray Horvath, Hungary
1913	Opika von Meray Horvath, Hungary
1914	Opika von Meray Horvath, Hungary
1915–21	No competition
1922	Herma Plank-Szabo, Austria
1923	Herma Plank-Szabo, Austria
1924	Herma Plank-Szabo, Austria
1925	Herma Jaross-Szabo, Austria
1926	Herma Jaross-Szabo, Austria
1927	Sonja Henie, Norway
1928	Sonja Henie, Norway
1929	Sonja Henie, Norway
1930	Sonja Henie, Norway
1931	Sonja Henie, Norway
1932	Sonja Henie, Norway
1933	Sonja Henie, Norway
1934	Sonja Henie, Norway
1935	Sonja Henie, Norway
1936	Sonja Henie, Norway
1937	Cecilia Colledge, Great Britain
1938	Megan Taylor, Great Britain
1939	Megan Taylor, Great Britain
1940–46	No competition
1947	Barbara Ann Scott, Canada
1948	Barbara Ann Scott, Canada
1949	Alena Vrzanova, Czechoslovakia
1950	Alena Vrzanova, Czechoslovakia
1951	Jeannette Altwegg, Great Britain
1952	Jacqueline duBief, France
1953	Tenley Albright, United States
1954	Gundi Busch, W Germany
1955	Tenley Albright, United States
1956	Carol Heiss, United States
1957	Carol Heiss, United States

Women (Cont.)

1958	Carol Heiss, United States
1959	Carol Heiss, United States
1960	Carol Heiss, United States
1961	No competition
1962	Sjoukje Dijkstra, Netherlands
1963	Sjoukje Dijkstra, Netherlands
1964	Sjoukje Dijkstra, Netherlands
1965	Petra Burka, Canada
1966	Peggy Fleming, United States
1967	Peggy Fleming, United States
1968	Peggy Fleming, United States
1969	Gabriele Seyfert, E Germany
1970	Gabriele Seyfert, E Germany
1971	Beatrix Schuba, Austria
1972	Beatrix Schuba, Austria
1973	Karen Magnussen, Canada
1974	Christine Errath, E Germany
1975	Dianne DeLeeuw, Netherlands
1976	Dorothy Hamill, United States
1977	Linda Fratianne, United States
1978	Annett Poetzsch, E Germany
1979	Linda Fratianne, United States
1980	Annett Poetzsch, E Germany
1981	Denise Biellmann, Switzerland
1982	Elaine Zayak, United States
1983	Rosalynn Sumners, United States
1984	Katarina Witt, E Germany
1985	Katarina Witt, E Germany
1986	Debi Thomas, United States
1987	Katarina Witt, E Germany
1988	Katarina Witt, E Germany
1989	Midori Ito, Japan
1990	Jill Trenary, United States
1991	Kristi Yamaguchi, United States
1992	Kristi Yamaguchi, United States
1993	Oksana Baiul, Ukraine
1994	Yuka Sato, Japan
1995	Chen Lu, China
1996	Michelle Kwan, United States
1997	Tara Lipinski, United States
1998	Michelle Kwan, United States
1999	Maria Butyrskaya, Russia
2000	Michelle Kwan, United States
2001	Michelle Kwan, United States
2002	Irina Slutskaya, Russia
2003	Michelle Kwan, United States
2004	Shizuka Arakawa, Japan
2005	Irina Slutskaya, Russia

Men

1896	Gilbert Fuchs, Germany
1897	Gustav Hugel, Austria
1898	Henning Grenander, Sweden
1899	Gustav Hugel, Austria
1900	Gustav Hugel, Austria
1901	Ulrich Salchow, Sweden
1902	Ulrich Salchow, Sweden
1903	Ulrich Salchow, Sweden
1904	Ulrich Salchow, Sweden
1905	Ulrich Salchow, Sweden
1906	Gilbert Fuchs, Germany
1907	Ulrich Salchow, Sweden
1908	Ulrich Salchow, Sweden
1909	Ulrich Salchow, Sweden
1910	Ulrich Salchow, Sweden
1911	Ulrich Salchow, Sweden
1912	Fritz Kachler, Austria
1913	Fritz Kachler, Austria
1914	Gosta Sandhal, Sweden
1915–21	No competition
1922	Gillis Grafstrom, Sweden
1923	Fritz Kachler, Austria
1924	Gillis Grafstrom, Sweden
1925	Willy Bockl, Austria
1926	Willy Bockl, Austria
1927	Willy Bockl, Austria
1928	Willy Bockl, Austria
1929	Gillis Grafstrom, Sweden
1930	Karl Schafer, Austria
1931	Karl Schafer, Austria
1932	Karl Schafer, Austria
1933	Karl Schafer, Austria
1934	Karl Schafer, Austria
1935	Karl Schafer, Austria
1936	Karl Schafer, Austria
1937	Felix Kaspar, Austria
1938	Felix Kaspar, Austria
1939	Graham Sharp, Great Britain
1940–46	No competition
1947	Hans Gerschwiler, Switzerland
1948	Dick Button, United States
1949	Dick Button, United States
1950	Dick Button, United States
1951	Dick Button, United States
1952	Dick Button, United States
1953	Hayes Alan Jenkins, United States
1954	Hayes Alan Jenkins, United States
1955	Hayes Alan Jenkins, United States
1956	Hayes Alan Jenkins, United States
1957	David W. Jenkins, United States
1958	David W. Jenkins, United States
1959	David W. Jenkins, United States
1960	Alan Giletti, France
1961	No competition
1962	Donald Jackson, Canada
1963	Donald McPherson, Canada
1964	Manfred Schneldorfer, W Germany
1965	Alain Calmat, France
1966	Emmerich Danzer, Austria
1967	Emmerich Danzer, Austria
1968	Emmerich Danzer, Austria
1969	Tim Wood, United States
1970	Tim Wood, United States
1971	Andrej Nepela, Czechoslovakia
1972	Andrej Nepela, Czechoslovakia
1973	Andrej Nepela, Czechoslovakia
1974	Jan Hoffmann, E Germany
1975	Sergei Volkov, USSR
1976	John Curry, Great Britain
1977	Vladimir Kovalev, USSR
1978	Charles Tickner, United States
1979	Vladimir Kovalev, USSR
1980	Jan Hoffmann, E Germany
1981	Scott Hamilton, United States
1982	Scott Hamilton, United States
1983	Scott Hamilton, United States
1984	Scott Hamilton, United States
1985	Aleksandr Fadeev, USSR
1986	Brian Boitano, United States
1987	Brian Orser, Canada
1988	Brian Boitano, United States
1989	Kurt Browning, Canada
1990	Kurt Browning, Canada
1991	Kurt Browning, Canada
1992	Viktor Petrenko, CIS
1993	Kurt Browning, Canada
1994	Elvis Stojko, Canada
1995	Elvis Stojko, Canada
1996	Todd Eldredge, United States
1997	Elvis Stojko, Canada

Men (Cont.)

1998	Alexei Yagudin, Russia	2002	Alexei Yagudin, Russia
1999	Alexei Yagudin, Russia	2003	Evgeny Plushenko, Russia
2000	Alexei Yagudin, Russia	2004	Evgeny Plushenko, Russia
2001	Evgeny Plushenko, Russia	2005	Stephane Lambiell, Switzerland

Pairs

1908 ....Anna Hubler, Heinrich Burger, Germany
1909 ....Phyllis Johnson, James H. Johnson, Great Britain
1910 ....Anna Hubler, Heinrich Burger, Germany
1911 ....Ludowika Eilers, Walter Jakobsson, Germany/Finland
1912 ....Phyllis Johnson, James H. Johnson, Great Britain
1913 ....Helene Engelmann, Karl Majstrik, Germany
1914 ....Ludowika Jakobsson-Eilers, Walter Jakobsson-Eilers, Finland
1915–21 ......No competition
1922 ....Helene Engelmann, Alfred Berger, Germany
1923 ....Ludowika Jakobsson-Eilers, Walter Jakobsson-Eilers, Finland
1924 ....Helene Engelmann, Alfred Berger, Germany
1925 ....Herma Jaross-Szabo, Ludwig Wrede, Austria
1926 ....Andree Joly, Pierre Brunet, France
1927 ....Herma Jaross-Szabo, Ludwig Wrede, Austria
1928 ....Andree Joly, Pierre Brunet, France
1929 ....Lilly Scholz, Otto Kaiser, Austria
1930 ....Andree Brunet-Joly, Pierre Brunet-Joly, France
1931 ....Emilie Rotter, Laszlo Szollas, Hungary
1932 ....Andree Brunet-Joly, Pierre Brunet-Joly, France
1933 ....Emilie Rotter, Laszlo Szollas, Hungary
1934 ....Emilie Rotter, Laszlo Szollas, Hungary
1935 ....Emilie Rotter, Laszlo Szollas, Hungary
1936 ....Maxi Herber, Ernst Bajer, Germany
1937 ....Maxi Herber, Ernst Bajer, Germany
1938 ....Maxi Herber, Ernst Bajer, Germany
1939 ....Maxi Herber, Ernst Bajer, Germany
1940–46 ......No competition
1947 ....Micheline Lannoy, Pierre Baugniet, Belgium
1948 ....Micheline Lannoy, Pierre Baugniet, Belgium
1949 ....Andrea Kekessy, Ede Kiraly, Hungary
1950 ....Karol Kennedy, Peter Kennedy, United States
1951 ....Ria Baran, Paul Falk, W Germany
1952 ....Ria Baran Falk, Paul Falk, W Germany
1953 ....Jennifer Nicks, John Nicks, Great Britain
1954 ....Frances Dafoe, Norris Bowden, Canada
1955 ....Frances Dafoe, Norris Bowden, Canada
1956 ....Sissy Schwarz, Kurt Oppelt, Austria
1957 ....Barbara Wagner, Robert Paul, Canada
1958 ....Barbara Wagner, Robert Paul, Canada
1959 ....Barbara Wagner, Robert Paul, Canada
1960 ....Barbara Wagner, Robert Paul, Canada
1961 ....No competition
1962 ....Maria Jelinek, Otto Jelinek, Canada
1963 ....Marika Kilius, Hans-Jurgen Baumler, W Germany

1964 ....Marika Kilius, Hans-Jurgen Baumler, W Germany
1965 ....Ljudmila Protopopov, Oleg Protopopov, USSR
1966 ....Ljudmila Protopopov, Oleg Protopopov, USSR
1967 ....Ljudmila Protopopov, Oleg Protopopov, USSR
1968 ....Ljudmila Protopopov, Oleg Protopopov, USSR
1969 ....Irina Rodnina, Alexsei Ulanov, USSR
1970 ....Irina Rodnina, Alexsei Ulanov, USSR
1971 ....Irina Rodnina, Sergei Ulanov, USSR
1972 ....Irina Rodnina, Sergei Ulanov, USSR
1973 ....Irina Rodnina, Aleksandr Zaitsev, USSR
1974 ....Irina Rodnina, Aleksandr Zaitsev, USSR
1975 ....Irina Rodnina, Aleksandr Zaitsev, USSR
1976 ....Irina Rodnina, Aleksandr Zaitsev, USSR
1977 ....Irina Rodnina, Aleksandr Zaitsev, USSR
1978 ....Irina Rodnina, Aleksandr Zaitsev, USSR
1979 ....Tai Babilonia, Randy Gardner, United States
1980 ....Maria Cherkasova, Sergei Shakhrai, USSR
1981 ....Irina Vorobieva, Igor Lisovsky, USSR
1982 ....Sabine Baess, Tassilio Thierbach, E Germany
1983 ....Elena Valova, Oleg Vasiliev, USSR
1984 ....Barbara Underhill, Paul Martini, Canada
1985 ....Elena Valova, Oleg Vasiliev, USSR
1986 ....Ekaterina Gordeeva, Sergei Grinkov, USSR
1987 ....Ekaterina Gordeeva, Sergei Grinkov, USSR
1988 ....Elena Valova, Oleg Vasiliev, USSR
1989 ....Ekaterina Gordeeva, Sergei Grinkov, USSR
1990 ....Ekaterina Gordeeva, Sergei Grinkov, USSR
1991 ....Natalia Mishkutienok, Artur Dmitriev, USSR
1992 ....Natalia Mishkutienok, Artur Dmitriev, CIS
1993 ....Isabelle Brasseur, Lloyd Eisler, Canada
1994 ....Evgenia Shishkova, Vadim Naumov, Russia
1995 ....Radka Kovarikova, Rene Novotny, Czech Republic
1996 ....Marina Eltsova, Andrey Buskhov, Russia
1997 ....Mandy Wötzel, Ingo Steuer, Germany
1998 ....Jenni Meno, Todd Sand, United States
1999 ....Elena Berezhnaya, Anton Sikharulidze, Russia
2000 ....Maria Petrova and Aleksei Tikhonov, Russia
2001 ....Jamie Salé and David Pelletier, Canada
2002 ....Xue Shen and Hongbo Zhao, China
2003 ....Xue Shen and Hongbo Zhao, China
2004 ....Tatiana Totmianina and Maxim Marinin, Russia
2005 ....Tatiana Totmianina, Maxim Marinin, Russia

Dance

1950 ....Lois Waring, Michael McGean, United States	1973 ....Ljudmila Pakhomova, Aleksandr Gorshkov, USSR
1951 ....Jean Westwood, Lawrence Demmy, Great Britain	1974 ....Ljudmila Pakhomova, Aleksandr Gorshkov, USSR
1952 ....Jean Westwood, Lawrence Demmy, Great Britain	1975 ....Irina Moiseeva, Andreij Minenkov, USSR
1953 ....Jean Westwood, Lawrence Demmy, Great Britain	1976 ....Ljudmila Pakhomova, Aleksandr Gorshkov, USSR
1954 ....Jean Westwood, Lawrence Demmy, Great Britain	1977 ....Irina Moiseeva, Andreij Minenkov, USSR
1955 ....Jean Westwood, Lawrence Demmy, Great Britain	1978 ....Natalia Linichuk, Gennadi Karponosov, USSR
1956 ....Pamela Wieght, Paul Thomas, Great Britain	1979 ....Natalia Linichuk, Gennadi Karponosov,USSR
1957 ....June Markham, Courtney Jones, Great Britain	1980 ....Krisztina Regoeczy, Andras Sallai, Hungary
1958 ....June Markham, Courtney Jones, Great Britain	1981 ....Jayne Torvill, Christopher Dean, Great Britain
1959 ....Doreen D. Denny, Courtney Jones, Great Britain	1982 ....Jayne Torvill, Christopher Dean, Great Britain
1960 ....Doreen D. Denny, Courtney Jones, Great Britain	1983 ....Jayne Torvill, Christopher Dean, Great Britain
1961 ....No competition	1984 ....Jayne Torvill, Christopher Dean, Great Britain
1962 ....Eva Romanova, Pavel Roman, Czechoslovakia	1985..............Natalia Bestemianova/ Andrei Bukin, USSR
1963 ....Eva Romanova, Pavel Roman, Czechoslqvakia	1986..............Natalia Bestemianova/ Andrei Bukin, USSR
1964 ....Eva Romanova, Pavel Roman, Czechoslovakia	1987..............Natalia Bestemianova/ Andrei Bukin, USSR
1965 ....Eva Romanova, Pavel Roman, Czechoslovakia	1988..............Natalia Bestemianova/ Andrei Bukin, USSR
1966 ....Diane Towler, Bernard Ford, Great Britain	1989 ....Marina Klimova/ Sergei Ponomarenko, USSR
1967 ....Diane Towler, Bernard Ford, Great Britain	1990 ....Marina Klimova/ Sergei Ponomarenko, USSR
1968 ....Diane Towler, Bernard Ford, Great Britain	1991 ....Isabelle Duchesnay/ Paul Duchesnay, France
1969 ....Diane Towler, Bernard Ford, Great Britain	1992 ....Marina Klimova/ Sergei Ponomarenko, CIS
1970 ....Ljudmila Pakhomova, Aleksandr Gorshkov, USSR	1993 ....Renee Roca/ Gorsha Sur, United States
1971 ....Ljudmila Pakhomova, Aleksandr Gorshkov, USSR	1994 ....Oksana Grishuk/ Evgeny Platov, Russia
1972 ....Ljudmila Pakhomova, Aleksandr Gorshkov, USSR	1995 ....Oksana Grishuk/ Evgeny Platov, Russia
	1996 ....Oksana Grishuk/ Evgeny Platov, Russia
	1997 ....Oksana Grishuk/ Evgeny Platov, Russia
	1998 ....Anjelika Krylova/Oleg Ovsyannikov, Russia
	1999 ....Anjelika Krylova/Oleg Ovsyannikov, Russia
	2000...........Marina Anissina/ Gwendal Peizerat, France
	2001 ....Barbara Fusar-Poli/ Maurizio Margaglio, Italy
	2002 ....Irina Lobacheva/ Ilia Averbukh, Russia
	2003 ....Shae-Lynn Bourne/ Victor Kraatz, Canada
	2004 ....Tatiana Navka/Roman Kostomarov, Russia
	2005 ....Tatiana Navka/Roman Kostomarov, Russia

Champions of the United States

The championships held in 1914, 1918, 1920 and 1921 under the auspices of the International Skating Union of America were open to Canadians, although the competitions were considered to be United States championships. Beginning in 1922, the championships have been held under the auspices of the United States Figure Skating Association.

Women

1914 ....Theresa Weld, SC of Boston	1933 ....Maribel Y. Vinson, SC of Boston
1915–17 ......No competition	1934 ....Suzanne Davis, SC of Boston
1918 ....Rosemary S. Beresford, New York SC	1935 ....Maribel Y. Vinson, SC of Boston
1919 ....No competition	1936 ....Maribel Y. Vinson, SC of Boston
1920 ....Theresa Weld, SC of Boston	1937 ....Maribel Y. Vinson, SC of Boston
1921 ....Theresa Weld Blanchard, SC of Boston	1938 ....Joan Tozzer, SC of Boston
1922 ....Theresa Weld Blanchard, SC of Boston	1939 ....Joan Tozzer, SC of Boston
1923 ....Theresa Weld Blanchard, SC of Boston	1940 ....Joan Tozzer, SC of Boston
1924 ....Theresa Weld Blanchard, SC of Boston	1941 ....Jane Vaughn, Philadelphia SC & HS
1925 ....Beatrix Loughran, New York SC	1942 ....Jane Vaughn Sullivan, Philadelphia SC & HS
1926 ....Beatrix Loughran, New York SC	1943 ....Gretchen Van Zandt Merrill, SC of Boston
1927 ....Beatrix Loughran, New York SC	1944 ....Gretchen Van Zandt Merrill, SC of Boston
1928 ....Maribel Y. Vinson, SC of Boston	1945 ....Gretchen Van Zandt Merrill, SC of Boston
1929 ....Maribel Y. Vinson, SC of Boston	1946 ....Gretchen Van Zandt Merrill, SC of Boston
1930 ....Maribel Y. Vinson, SC of Boston	1947 ....Gretchen Van Zandt Merrill, SC of Boston
1931 ....Maribel Y. Vinson, SC of Boston	1948 ....Gretchen Van Zandt Merrill, SC of Boston
1932 ....Maribel Y. Vinson, SC of Boston	

Women *(Cont.)*

1949 ....Yvonne Claire Sherman, SC of New York	1978 ....Linda Fratianne, Los Angeles FSC
1950 ....Yvonne Claire Sherman, SC of New York	1979 ....Linda Fratianne, Los Angeles FSC
1951 ....Sonya Klopfer, Junior SC of New York	1980 ....Linda Fratianne, Los Angeles FSC
1952 ....Tenley E. Albright, SC of Boston	1981 ....Elaine Zayak, SC of New York
1953 ....Tenley E. Albright, SC of Boston	1982 ....Rosalynn Sumners, Seattle SC
1954 ....Tenley E. Albright, SC of Boston	1983 ....Rosalynn Sumners, Seattle SC
1955 ....Tenley E. Albright, SC of Boston	1984 ....Rosalynn Sumners, Seattle SC
1956 ....Tenley E. Albright, SC of Boston	1985 ....Tiffany Chin, San Diego FSC
1957 ....Carol E. Heiss, SC of New York	1986 ....Debi Thomas, Los Angeles FSC
1958 ....Carol E. Heiss, SC of New York	1987 ....Jill Trenary, Broadmoor SC
1959 ....Carol E. Heiss, SC of New York	1988 ....Debi Thomas, Los Angeles FSC
1960 ....Carol E. Heiss, SC of New York	1989 ....Jill Trenary, Broadmoor SC
1961 ....Laurence R. Owen, SC of Boston	1990 ....Jill Trenary, Broadmoor SC
1962 ....Barbara Roles Pursley, Arctic Blades FSC	1991 ....Tonya Harding, Carousel FSC
1963 ....Lorraine G. Hanlon, SC of Boston	1992 ....Kristi Yamaguchi, St Moritz ISC
1964 ....Peggy Fleming, Arctic Blades FSC	1993 ....Nancy Kerrigan, Colonial FSC
1965 ....Peggy Fleming, Arctic Blades FSC	1994 ....Tonya Harding, Portland FSC
1966 ....Peggy Fleming, City of Colorado Springs	1995 ....Nicole Bobek, Los Angeles FSC
1967 ....Peggy Fleming, Broadmoor SC	1996 ....Michelle Kwan, Los Angeles FSC
1968 ....Peggy Fleming, Broadmoor SC	1997 ....Tara Lipinski, Detroit SC
1969 ....Janet Lynn, Wagon Wheel FSC	1998 ....Michelle Kwan, Los Angeles FSC
1970 ....Janet Lynn, Wagon Wheel FSC	1999 ....Michelle Kwan, Los Angeles FSC
1971 ....Janet Lynn, Wagon Wheel FSC	2000 ....Michelle Kwan, Los Angeles FSC
1972 ....Janet Lynn, Wagon Wheel FSC	2001 ....Michelle Kwan, Los Angeles FSC
1973 ....Janet Lynn, Wagon Wheel FSC	2002 ....Michelle Kwan, Los Angeles FSC
1974 ....Dorothy Hamill, SC of New York	2003 ....Michelle Kwan, Los Angeles FSC
1975 ....Dorothy Hamill, SC of New York	2004 ....Michelle Kwan, Los Angeles FSC
1976 ....Dorothy Hamill, SC of New York	2005 ....Michelle Kwan, Los Angeles FSC
1977 ....Linda Fratianne, Los Angeles FSC	

Men

1914 ....Norman M. Scott, WC of Montreal	1954 ....Hayes Alan Jenkins, Broadmoor SC
1915–17 ......No competition	1955 ....Hayes Alan Jenkins, Broadmoor SC
1918 ....Nathaniel W. Niles, SC of Boston	1956 ....Hayes Alan Jenkins, Broadmoor SC
1919 ....No competition	1957 ....David Jenkins, Broadmoor SC
1920 ....Sherwin C. Badger, SC of Boston	1958 ....David Jenkins, Broadmoor SC
1921 ....Sherwin C. Badger, SC of Boston	1959 ....David Jenkins, Broadmoor SC
1922 ....Sherwin C. Badger, SC of Boston	1960 ....David Jenkins, Broadmoor SC
1923 ....Sherwin C. Badger, SC of Boston	1961 ....Bradley R. Lord, SC of Boston
1924 ....Sherwin C. Badger, SC of Boston	1962 ....Monty Hoyt, Broadmoor SC
1925 ....Nathaniel W. Niles, SC of Boston	1963 ....Thomas Litz, Hershey FSC
1926 ....Chris I. Christenson, Twin City FSC	1964 ....Scott Ethan Allen, SC of New York
1927 ....Nathaniel W. Niles, SC of Boston	1965 ....Gary C. Visconti, Detroit SC
1928 ....Roger F. Turner, SC of Boston	1966 ....Scott Ethan Allen, SC of New York
1929 ....Roger F. Turner, SC of Boston	1967 ....Gary C. Visconti, Detroit SC
1930 ....Roger F. Turner, SC of Boston	1968 ....Tim Wood, Detroit SC
1931 ....Roger F. Turner, SC of Boston	1969 ....Tim Wood, Detroit SC
1932 ....Roger F. Turner, SC of Boston	1970 ....Tim Wood, City of Colorado Springs
1933 ....Roger F. Turner, SC of Boston	1971 ....John Misha Petkevich, Great Falls FSC
1934 ....Roger F. Turner, SC of Boston	1972 ....Kenneth Shelley, Arctic Blades FSC
1935 ....Robin H. Lee, SC of New York	1973 ....Gordon McKellen Jr., SC of Lake Placid
1936 ....Robin H. Lee, SC of New York	1974 ....Gordon McKellen Jr., SC of Lake Placid
1937 ....Robin H. Lee, SC of New York	1975 ....Gordon McKellen Jr., SC of Lake Placid
1938 ....Robin H. Lee, Chicago FSC	1976 ....Terry Kubicka, Arctic Blades FSC
1939 ....Robin H. Lee, St Paul FSC	1977 ....Charles Tickner, Denver FSC
1940 ....Eugene Turner, Los Angeles FSC	1978 ....Charles Tickner, Denver FSC
1941 ....Eugene Turner, Los Angeles FSC	1979 ....Charles Tickner, Denver FSC
1942 ....Robert Specht, Chicago FSC	1980 ....Charles Tickner, Denver FSC
1943 ....Arthur R. Vaughn Jr., Phila. SC & HS	1981 ....Scott Hamilton, Philadelphia SC & HS
1944–45 ......No competition	1982 ....Scott Hamilton, Philadelphia SC & HS
1946 ....Dick Button, Philadelphia SC & HS	1983 ....Scott Hamilton, Philadelphia SC & HS
1947 ....Dick Button, Philadelphia SC & HS	1984 ....Scott Hamilton, Philadelphia SC & HS
1948 ....Dick Button, Philadelphia SC & HS	1985 ....Brian Boitano, Peninsula FSC
1949 ....Dick Button, Philadelphia SC & HS	1986 ....Brian Boitano, Peninsula FSC
1950 ....Dick Button, SC of Boston	1987 ....Brian Boitano, Peninsula FSC
1951 ....Dick Button, SC of Boston	1988 ....Brian Boitano, Peninsula FSC
1952 ....Dick Button, SC of Boston	1989 ....Christopher Bowman, Los Angeles FSC
1953 ....Hayes Alan Jenkins, Cleveland SC	1990 ....Todd Eldredge, Los Angeles FSC

Men (Cont.)

1991 ....Todd Eldredge, Los Angeles FSC
1992 ....Christopher Bowman, Los Angeles FSC
1993 ....Scott Davis, Broadmoor SC
1994 ....Scott Davis, Broadmoor SC
1995 ....Todd Eldredge, Detroit SC
1996 ....Rudy Galindo, St Moritz ISC
1997 ....Todd Eldredge, Detroit SC
1998 ....Todd Eldredge, Detroit SC
1999 ....Michael Weiss, Washington FSC
2000 ....Michael Weiss, Washington FSC
2001 ....Timothy Goebel, Winterhurst FSC
2002 ....Todd Eldredge, Los Angeles FSC
2003 ....Michael Weiss, Washington FSC
2004 ....Johnny Weir, SC of New York
2005 ....Johnny Weir, SC of New York

Pairs

1914.......Jeanne Chevalier, Norman M. Scott, WC of Montreal
1915–17..No competition
1918.......Theresa Weld, Nathaniel W. Niles, SC of Boston
1919.......No competition
1920.......Theresa Weld, Nathaniel W. Niles, SC of Boston
1921.......Theresa Weld Blanchard, Nathaniel W. Niles, SC of Boston
1922.......Theresa Weld Blanchard, Nathaniel W. Niles, SC of Boston
1923.......Theresa Weld Blanchard, Nathaniel W. Niles, SC of Boston
1924.......Theresa Weld Blanchard, Nathaniel W. Niles, SC of Boston
1925.......Theresa Weld Blanchard, Nathaniel W. Niles, SC of Boston
1926.......Theresa Weld Blanchard, Nathaniel W. Niles, SC of Boston
1927.......Theresa Weld Blanchard, Nathaniel W. Niles, SC of Boston
1928.......Maribel Y. Vinson, Thornton L. Coolidge, SC of Boston
1929.......Maribel Y. Vinson, Thornton L. Coolidge, SC of Boston
1930.......Beatrix Loughran, Sherwin C. Badger, SC of New York
1931.......Beatrix Loughran, Sherwin C. Badger, SC of New York
1932.......Beatrix Loughran, Sherwin C. Badger, SC of New York
1933.......Maribel Y. Vinson, George E. B. Hill, SC of Boston
1934.......Grace E. Madden, James L. Madden, SC of Boston
1935.......Maribel Y. Vinson, George E. B. Hill, SC of Boston
1936.......Maribel Y. Vinson, George E. B. Hill, SC of Boston
1937.......Maribel Y. Vinson, George E. B. Hill, SC of Boston
1938.......Joan Tozzer, M. Bernard Fox, SC of Boston
1939.......Joan Tozzer, M. Bernard Fox, SC of Boston
1940.......Joan Tozzer, M. Bernard Fox, SC of Boston
1941.......Donna Atwood, Eugene Turner, Mercury FSC/Los Angeles FSC
1942.......Doris Schubach, Walter Noffke, Springfield Ice Birds
1943.......Doris Schubach, Walter Noffke, Springfield Ice Birds
1944.......Doris Schubach, Walter Noffke, Springfield Ice Birds
1945.......Donna Jeanne Pospisil, Jean-Pierre Brunet, SC of New York
1946.......Donna Jeanne Pospisil, Jean-Pierre Brunet, SC of New York
1947.......Yvonne Claire Sherman, Robert J. Swenning, SC of New York
1948.......Karol Kennedy, Peter Kennedy, Seattle SC
1949.......Karol Kennedy, Peter Kennedy, Seattle SC
1950.......Karol Kennedy, Peter Kennedy, Broadmoor SC
1951.......Karol Kennedy, Peter Kennedy, Broadmoor SC
1952.......Karol Kennedy, Peter Kennedy, Broadmoor SC
1953.......Carole Ann Ormaca, Robin Greiner, SC of Fresno
1954.......Carole Ann Ormaca, Robin Greiner, SC of Fresno
1955.......Carole Ann Ormaca, Robin Greiner, St Moritz ISC
1956.......Carole Ann Ormaca, Robin Greiner, St Moritz ISC
1957.......Nancy Rouillard Ludington, Ronald Ludington, Commonwealth FSC/ SC of Boston
1958.......Nancy Rouillard Ludington, Ronald Ludington, Commonwealth FSC/ SC of Boston
1959.......Nancy Rouillard Ludington, Ronald Ludington, Commonwealth FSC
1960.......Nancy Rouillard Ludington, Ronald Ludington, Commonwealth FSC
1961.......Maribel Y. Owen, Dudley S. Richards, SC of Boston
1962.......Dorothyann Nelson, Pieter Kollen, Village of Lake Placid
1963.......Judianne Fotheringill, Jerry J. Fotheringill, Broadmoor SC
1964.......Judianne Fotheringill, Jerry J. Fotheringill, Broadmoor SC
1965.......Vivian Joseph, Ronald Joseph, Chicago FSC
1966.......Cynthia Kauffman, Ronald Kauffman, Seattle SC
1967.......Cynthia Kauffman, Ronald Kauffman, Seattle SC
1968.......Cynthia Kauffman, Ronald Kauffman, Seattle SC
1969.......Cynthia Kauffman, Ronald Kauffman, Seattle SC
1970.......Jo Jo Starbuck, Kenneth Shelley, Arctic Blades FSC
1971.......Jo Jo Starbuck, Kenneth Shelley, Arctic Blades FSC
1972.......Jo Jo Starbuck, Kenneth Shelley, Arctic Blades FSC
1973.......Melissa Militano, Mark Militano, SC of New York
1974.......Melissa Militano, Johnny Johns, SC of New York/Detroit SC
1975.......Melissa Militano, Johnny Johns, SC of NY/ Detroit SC

Pairs *(Cont.)*

1976.......Tai Babilonia, Randy Gardner,
Los Angeles FSC
1977.......Tai Babilonia, Randy Gardner, LA FSC
1978.......Tai Babilonia, Randy Gardner,
Los Angeles FSC/Santa Monica FSC
1979.......Tai Babilonia, Randy Gardner,
Los Angeles FSC/Santa Monica FSC
1980.......Tai Babilonia, Randy Gardner,
Los Angeles FSC/Santa Monica FSC
1981.......Caitlin Carruthers, Peter Carruthers,
SC of Wilmington
1982.......Caitlin Carruthers, Peter Carruthers,
SC of Wilmington
1983.......Caitlin Carruthers, Peter Carruthers,
SC of Wilmington
1984.......Caitlin Carruthers, Peter Carruthers,
SC of Wilmington
1985.......Jill Watson, Peter Oppegard, LA FSC
1986.......Gillian Wachsman, Todd Waggoner,
SC of Wilmington
1987.......Jill Watson, Peter Oppegard, Los Angeles FSC
1988.......Jill Watson, Peter Oppegard,
Los Angeles FSC
1989.......Kristi Yamaguchi/ Rudy Galindo, St Mortiz ISC
1990.......Kristi Yamaguchi/ Rudy Galindo, St Mortiz ISC

1991.......Natasha Kuchiki/ Todd Sand, LA FSC
1992.......Calla Urbanski/ Rocky Marval,
U of Delaware FSC/SC of New York
1993.......Calla Urbanski/ Rocky Marval,
U of Delaware FSC/SC of New York
1994.......Jenni Meno/ Todd Sand,
Winterhurst FSC/Los Angeles FSC
1995.......Jenni Meno/ Todd Sand,
Winterhurst FSC/Los Angeles FSC
1996.......Jenni Meno/ Todd Sand,
Winterhurst FSC/Los Angeles FSC
1997.......Kyoko Ina/ Jason Dungjen, SC of New York
1998.......Kyoko Ina/ Jason Dungjen, SC of New York
1999.......Danielle Hartsell/ Steve Hartsell, Detroit SC
2000.......Kyoko Ina/ John Zimmerman, SC of New
York/Birmingham FSC
2001.......Kyoko Ina/ John Zimmerman, SC of New
York/Birmingham FSC
2002.......Kyoko Ina/ John Zimmerman, SC of New
York/Birmingham FSC
2003.......Tiffany Scott/ Philip Dulebohn, Colonial FSC/
Univ of Delaware FSC
2004.......Rena Inoue/John Baldwin, All Year FSC
2005.......Kathryn Orscher/Garrett Lucash,
Charter Oak FSC

Dance

1914.......Waltz: Theresa Weld, Nathaniel W. Niles,
SC of Boston
1915–19 ..No competition
1920.......Waltz: Theresa Weld, Nathaniel W. Niles,
SC of Boston
Fourteenstep: Gertrude Cheever Porter,
Irving Brokaw, New York SC
1921.......Waltz and Fourteenstep: Theresa Weld
Blanchard, Nathaniel W. Niles, SC of Boston
1922.......Waltz: Beatrix Loughran, Edward M.
Howland, New York SC/SC of Boston
Fourteenstep: Theresa Weld Blanchard,
Nathaniel W. Niles, SC of Boston
1923.......Waltz: Mr. & Mrs. Henry W. Howe,
New York SC
Fourteenstep: Sydney Goode, James B.
Greene, New York SC
1924.......Waltz: Rosaline Dunn, Frederick Gabel,
New York SC
Fourteenstep: Sydney Goode, James B.
Greene, New York SC
1925.......Waltz and Fourteenstep: Virginia Slattery,
Ferrier T. Martin, New York SC
1926.......Waltz: Rosaline Dunn, Joseph K. Savage,
New York SC
Fourteenstep: Sydney Goode, James B.
Greene, New York SC
1927.......Waltz and Fourteenstep: Rosaline Dunn,
Joseph K. Savage, New York SC
1928.......Waltz: Rosaline Dunn, Joseph K. Savage,
New York SC
Fourteenstep: Ada Bauman Kelly, George T.
Braakman, New York SC
1929.......Waltz and Original Dance combined:
Edith C. Secord, Joseph K. Savage,
SC of New York
1930.......Waltz: Edith C. Secord, Joseph K. Savage,
SC of New York
Original: Clara Rotch Frothingham, George
E. B. Hill, SC of Boston
1931.......Waltz: Edith C. Secord, Ferrier T. Martin,
SC of New York
Original: Theresa Weld Blanchard, Nathaniel
W. Niles, SC of Boston

1932.......Waltz: Edith C. Secord, Joseph K. Savage,
SC of New York
Original: Clara Rotch Frothingham, George
E. B. Hill, SC of Boston
1933.......Waltz: Ilse Twaroschk, Frederick F.
Fleishmann, Brooklyn FSC
Original: Suzanne Davis, Frederick
Goodridge, SC of Boston
1934.......Waltz: Nettie C. Prantel, Roy Hunt, SC of
New York
Original: Suzanne Davis, Frederick
Goodridge, SC of Boston
1935.......Waltz: Nettie C. Prantel, Roy Hunt,
SC of New York
1936.......Marjorie Parker, Joseph K. Savage,
SC of New York
1937.......Nettie C. Prantel, Harold Hartshorne,
SC of New York
1938.......Nettie C. Prantel, Harold Hartshorne,
SC of New York
1939.......Sandy Macdonald, Harold Hartshorne,
SC of New York
1940.......Sandy Macdonald, Harold Hartshorne,
SC of New York
1941.......Sandy Macdonald, Harold Hartshorne, SCNY
1942.......Edith B. Whetstone, Alfred N. Richards, Jr,
Philadelphia SC & HS
1943.......Marcella May, James Lochead Jr., Skate & Ski Club
1944.......Marcella May, James Lochead Jr., Skate & Ski Club
1945.......Kathe Mehl Williams, Robert J. Swenning,
SC of New York
1946.......Anne Davies, Carleton C. Hoffner Jr.,
Washington FSC
1947.......Lois Waring, Walter H. Bainbridge Jr.,
Baltimore FSC/Washigton FSC
1948.......Lois Waring, Walter H. Bainbridge Jr.,
Baltimore FSC/Washington FSC
1949.......Lois Waring, Walter H. Bainbridge Jr.,
Baltimore FSC/Washington FSC
1950.......Lois Waring, Michael McGean, Baltimore FSC
1951.......Carmel Bodel, Edward L. Bodel, St. Moritz ISC
1952.......Lois Waring, Michael McGean,
Baltimore FSC

Dance (Cont.)

1953.......Carol Ann Peters, Daniel C. Ryan, Washington FSC
1954.......Carmel Bodel, Edward L. Bodel, St Moritz ISC
1955.......Carmel Bodel, Edward L. Bodel, St Moritz ISC
1956.......Joan Zamboni, Roland Junso, Arctic Blades FSC
1957.......Sharon McKenzie, Bert Wright, Los Angeles FSC
1958.......Andree Anderson, Donald Jacoby, Buffalo SC
1959.......Andree Anderson Jacoby, Donald Jacoby, Buffalo SC
1960.......Margie Ackles, Charles W. Phillips Jr., Los Angeles FSC/Arctic Blades FSC
1961.......Diane C. Sherbloom, Larry Pierce, Los Angeles FSC/WC of Indianapolis
1962.......Yvonne N. Littlefield, Peter F. Betts, Arctic Blades FSC/ Paramount, CA
1963.......Sally Schantz, Stanley Urban, SC of Boston/Buffalo SC
1964.......Darlene Streich, Charles D. Fetter Jr., WC of Indianapolis
1965.......Kristin Fortune, Dennis Sveum, Los Angeles FSC
1966.......Kristin Fortune, Dennis Sveum, Los Angeles FSC
1967.......Lorna Dyer, John Carrell, Broadmoor SC
1968.......Judy Schwomeyer, James Sladky, WC of Indianapolis/Genesee FSC
1969.......Judy Schwomeyer, James Sladky, WC of Indianapolis/Genesee FSC
1970.......Judy Schwomeyer, James Sladky, WC of Indianapolis/Genesee FSC
1971.......Judy Schwomeyer, James Sladky, WC of Indianapolis/Genesee FSC
1972.......Judy Schwomeyer, James Sladky, WC of Indianapolis/Genesee FSC
1973.......Mary Karen Campbell, Johnny Johns, Lansing SC/Detroit SC
1974.......Colleen O'Connor, Jim Millns, Broadmoor SC/ City of Colorado Springs
1975.......Colleen O'Connor, Jim Millns, Broadmoor SC
1976.......Colleen O'Connor, Jim Millns, Broadmoor SC
1977.......Judy Genovesi, Kent Weigle, SC of Hartford/Charter Oak FSC
1978.......Stacey Smith, John Summers, SC of Wilmington

1979.......Stacey Smith, John Summers, SC of Wilmington
1980.......Stacey Smith, John Summers, SC of Wilmington
1981.......Judy Blumberg, Michael Seibert, Broadmoor SC/ISC of Indianapolis
1982.......Judy Blumberg, Michael Seibert, Broadmoor SC/ISC of Indianapolis
1983.......Judy Blumberg, Michael Seibert, Pittsburgh FSC
1984.......Judy Blumberg, Michael Seibert, Pittsburgh FSC
1985.......Judy Blumberg, Michael Seibert, Pittsburgh FSC
1986.......Renee Roca, Donald Adair, Genesee FSC/Academy FSC
1987.......Suzanne Semanick, Scott Gregory, U of Delaware SC
1988.......Suzanne Semanick, Scott Gregory, U of Delaware SC
1989.......Susan Wynne, Joseph Druar, Broadmoor SC/Seattle SC
1990.......Susan Wynne, Joseph Druar, Broadmoor SC/Seattle SC
1991.......Elizabeth Punsalan/Jerod Swallow, Broadmoor SC
1992.......April Sargent, Russ Witherby, Ogdensburg FSC/U of Delaware FSC
1993.......Renee Roca, Gorsha Sur, Broadmoor SC
1994.......Elizabeth Punsalan, Jerod Swallow, Broadmoor SC/Detroit SC
1995.......Renee Roca, Gorsha Sur, Broadmoor SC
1996.......Elizabeth Punsalan, Jerod Swallow, Detroit SC
1997.......Elizabeth Punsalan, Jerod Swallow, Detroit SC
1998.......Elizabeth Punsalan, Jerod Swallow, Detroit SC
1999.......Naomi Lang, Peter Tchernyshev, Detroit SC
2000.......Naomi Lang, Peter Tchernyshev, Detroit SC
2001.......Naomi Lang, Peter Tchernyshev, Detroit SC
2002.......Naomi Lang, Peter Tchernyshev, American Academy FSC
2003.......Naomi Lang, Peter Tchernyshev, American Academy FSC
2004.......Tanith Belbin/Benjamin Agosto, Detroit SC
2005.......Tanith Belbin/Benjamin Agosto, Detroit SC

U.S. Olympic Gold Medalists

Women

1956	Tenley Albright
1960	Carol Heiss
1968	Peggy Fleming
1976	Dorothy Hamill
1992	Kristi Yamaguchi
1998	Tara Lipinski
2002	Sarah Hughes

Men

1948	Richard Button
1952	Richard Button
1956	Hayes Alan Jenkins
1960	David W. Jenkins
1984	Scott Hamilton
1988	Brian Boitano

Special Achievements

Women successfully landing a triple Axel in competition:
   Midori Ito, Japan, 1988 free-skating competition at Aichi, Japan.
   Tonya Harding, United States, 1991 U.S. Figure Skating Championship.
   Kimberly Meissner, United States, 2005 U.S. Figure Skating Championship
Men successfully landing three quadruple jumps in competition:
   Timothy Goebel, United States, 1999 Skate America, Colorado Springs (two Salchows and one toe loop).

Miscellaneous Sports

Seven-time Tour de France winner Lance Armstrong

Seventh Heaven

Lance Armstrong ended his cycling career on top, securing his place as the Tour's best-ever rider

BY MERRELL NODEN

U NLESS YOU'VE SPENT THE past year stranded on an island somewhere off the northern coast of Siberia, it won't exactly be news to you that on July 24th Lance Armstrong won his seventh straight Tour de France. Much as the mind boggles at that number—two more than anyone else has ever won—those seven are only part of why Armstrong is now a hero and inspiration to millions all over the world.

Just as historians agree that to rank as a great president, a man must have overcome truly extraordinary challenges (the Civil War in Lincoln's case, the Great Depression and World War II in FDR's), every so often, an athlete comes along whose inspiring performance transcends even the grand stage of a Super Bowl or Olympic final. If he triumphs, he taps into the deeper currents of history and culture and is transformed from a mere great athlete to a heroic symbol of humanity and its potential. It's an incredibly short list of athletes who have made that leap. There is Jesse Owens, whose four gold medals at the 1936 Olympics offered the perfect rebuttal to Hitler's claims of Aryan superiority, and Muhammad Ali, who chose to surrender his heavyweight crown rather than fight in what he considered an unjust war, becoming a potent symbol of the civil rights movement.

To that honored list, we must now add Armstrong, a man whose mother seemed to sense his potential for greatness 33 years earlier when she gave him a name befitting a storybook hero. Ever since he learned in the fall of 1996 that testicular cancer had spread throughout his body and that he had less than a 50% chance of surviving, Armstrong has fought and beaten the toughest of foes, thereby giving hope and inspiration to thousands of fans, not only cancer-sufferers, but others, as well.

"The bigger picture for Lance is not winning seven consecutive Tour de Frances," said former track star and American mile record-holder Steve Scott, who also overcame testicular cancer. "The bigger thing is what he has done for cancer patients worldwide with his foundation. Everybody's wearing the yellow wristbands. That gives awareness to people of cancer. The greater awareness brings more money for research. It's a cause for humanity as opposed to something that's for Lance."

Far from fleeing his responsibilities as a role model, he has welcomed them, offering himself up as a stirring model of courage and unyielding determination and raising more than $85 million for cancer research through his Lance Armstrong Foundation.

Of course, the world would be paying scant attention to Armstrong's suffering if he weren't a great cyclist. This year he wasted

Without Lance, next year's Tour de France promises to be a wide-open competition.

no time proving to the rest of the field that he meant business. On the very first stage, an 18.4-mile time trial, he blew past Jan Ullrich, who had started a minute ahead of him and who in the past has been the better time trial cyclist. Poor Ullrich: In 1997, at age 23, the German won the first of what he must have believed would be multiple Tours. But he has had the misfortune of having his career coincide with Armstrong's, much as Phil Mickelson must rue his having been born during the Tiger era of golf. The result: five second place finishes.

Competing this year for the new Discovery Channel team, Armstrong raced with ruthless, cold-blooded confidence, positioning himself exactly where he knew he needed to be on every stage. He took the yellow jersey for good on Stage 10, a 113-mile leg from Brignoud up to the mountaintop finish in Courchevel. Though beaten in a sprint finish by Spaniard Alejandro Valverde, he opened up considerable time on his major rivals, including Ullrich, Ivan Basso of Italy and Dane Michael Rasmussen, who would emerge as this year's top climber.

Some unforeseen disaster could have interrupted his unwavering race to the finish, but it never seemed likely—Armstrong looked calm and in control at all times. "Lance got a little more relaxed, a little nicer, every year," noted Spanish rider Carlos Sastre. Indeed, a kinder, gentler Armstrong seemed to take almost as much delight in the stage wins enjoyed by his teammates George Hincapie and Paolo Savoldelli. He would wait until the penultimate stage, a 34.5-mile individual time trial to claim his only stage win of his last Tour. In the end, he beat runner-up Basso by 4:40, with Ullrich third.

Armstrong left little doubt that he is serious about retirement, that is until late August, when the French sports newspaper *L'Equipe* ran a story claiming to have proof that a 1999 urine sample of Armstrong's tested positive for EPO, a blood-doping drug. Clearly incensed by the charge and suspicious of an attempt to smear his lega-

cy—*L'Equipe* has long been a skeptic of his—Armstrong briefly flirted with returning for an eighth Tour. Cycling greats Eddy Merckx and Miguel Indurain rallied to his defense, however, and Armstrong soon announced that he would retire after all.

Whatever Armstrong chooses to do in retirement, his departure will reinvigorate the Tour. "Next year more riders will have a chance to win," said Christian Prudhomme, the Tour's new director. "When he's in the peloton, he's the only rider who can win."

Among those who must surely assume they've got a chance of winning next year are Ullrich, Basso, Rasmussen and the unpredictable Alexander Vinokourov. Armstrong's retirement may have the opposite effect on American cycling, despite the encouraging finishes of Levi Leipheimer (6th) and Floyd Landis (9th). Dave Zabriskie wore the yellow jersey for three days during the 2005 Tour before crashing out of it. So the U.S. does have an immediate future in this still largely European sport, even though the Outdoor Life Network, which had broadcast the Tour daily, is already talking about cutting back on its coverage.

OLN executives know better than to bet on finding another Armstrong. When the peloton finally rolled into Paris, the consensus clearly was that he is one of a kind. "Vive la Tour!" said Armstrong, as he clutched the winner's trophy on the Champs Elysees. To which the whole world might well have answered, "Vive Lance! Et merci!"

Archery

National Men's Champions

1879...Will H. Thompson	1911...Dr. Robert Elmer	1949...Russ Reynolds	1981...Rick McKinney
1880...L.L. Pedinghaus	1912...George Bryant	1950...Stan Overby	1982...Rick McKinney
1881...F.H. Walworth	1913...George Bryant	1951...Russ Reynolds	1983...Rick McKinney
1882...D.H. Nash	1914...Dr. Robert Elmer	1952...Robert Larson	1984...Darrell Pace
1883...Col. Robert Williams	1915...Dr. Robert Elmer	1953...Bill Glackin	1985...Rick McKinney
1884...Col. Robert Williams	1916...Dr. Robert Elmer	1954...Robert Rhode	1986...Rick McKinney
1885...Col. Robert Williams	1919...Dr. Robert Elmer	1955...Joe Fries	1987...Rick McKinney
1886...W.A. Clark	1920...Dr. Robert Elmer	1956...Joe Fries	1988...Jay Barrs
1887...W.A. Clark	1921...James Jiles	1957...Joe Fries	1989...Ed Eliason
1888...Lewis Maxson	1922...Dr. Robert Elmer	1958...Robert Bitner	1990...Ed Eliason
1889...Lewis Maxson	1923...Bill Palmer	1959...Wilbert Vetrovsky	1991...Ed Eliason
1890...Lewis Maxson	1924...James Jiles	1960...Robert Kadlec	1992...Alan Rasor
1891...Lewis Maxson	1925...Dr. Paul Crouch	1961...Clayton Sherman	1993...Jay Barrs
1892...Lewis Maxson	1926...Stanley Spencer	1962...Charles Sandlin	1994...Jay Barrs
1893...Lewis Maxson	1927...Dr. Paul Crouch	1963...Dave Keaggy Jr.	1995...Justin Huish
1894...Lewis Maxson	1928...Bill Palmer	1964...Dave Keaggy Jr.	1996...Richard (Butch)
1895...W.B. Robinson	1929...Dr. E.K. Roberts	1965...George Slinzer	Johnson
1896...Lewis Maxson	1930...Russ Hoogerhyde	1966...Hardy Ward	1997...Richard (Butch)
1897...W.A. Clark	1931...Russ Hoogerhyde	1967...Ray Rogers	Johnson
1898...Lewis Maxson	1932...Russ Hoogerhyde	1968...Hardy Ward	1998...Victor Wunderle
1899...M.C. Howell	1933...Ralph Miller	1969...Ray Rogers	1999...Victor Wunderle
1900...A.R. Clark	1934...Russ Hoogerhyde	1970...Joe Thornton	2000...Richard (Butch)
1901...Will H. Thompson	1935...Gilman Keasey	1971...John Williams	Johnson
1902...Will H. Thompson	1936...Gilman Keasey	1972...Kevin Erlandson	2001...Richard (Butch)
1903...Will H. Thompson	1937...Russ Hoogerhyde	1973...Darrell Pace	Johnson
1904...George Bryant	1938...Pat Chambers	1974...Darrell Pace	2002...Victor Wunderle
1905...George Bryant	1939...Pat Chambers	1975...Darrell Pace	2003...Joseph Bailey
1906...Henry Richardson	1940...Russ Hoogerhyde	1976...Darrell Pace	2004...Sagar Mistry
1907...Henry Richardson	1941...Larry Hughes	1977...Rick McKinney	2005...Guy Krueger
1908...Will H. Thompson	1946...Wayne Thompson	1978...Darrell Pace	
1909...George Bryant	1947...Jack Wilson	1979...Rick McKinney	
1910...Henry Richardson	1948...Larry Hughes	1980...Rick McKinney	

National Women's Champions

1879...Mrs. S. Brown	1910...J.V. Sullivan	1947...Ann Weber	1977...Luann Ryon
1880...Mrs. T. Davies	1911...Mrs. J.S. Taylor	1948...Jean Lee	1978...Luann Ryon
1881...Mrs. A.H. Gibbes	1912...Mrs. Witwer Tayler	1949...Jean Lee	1979...Lynette Johnson
1882...Mrs. A.H. Gibbes	1913...Mrs. P. Fletcher	1950...Jean Lee	1980...Judi Adams
1883...Mrs. M.C. Howell	1914...Mrs. B.P. Gray	1951...Jean Lee	1981...Debra Metzger
1884...Mrs. H. Hall	1915...Cynthia Wesson	1952...Ann Weber	1982...Luann Ryon
1885...Mrs. M.C. Howell	1916...Cynthia Wesson	1953...Ann Weber	1983...Nancy Myrick
1886...Mrs. M.C. Howell	1919...Dorothy Smith	1954...Laurette Young	1984...Ruth Rowe
1887...Mrs. A.M. Phillips	1920...Cynthia Wesson	1955...Ann Clark	1985...Terri Pesho
1888...Mrs. A.M. Phillips	1921...Mrs. L.C. Smith	1956...Carole Meinhart	1986...Debra Ochs
1889...Mrs. A.M. Phillips	1922...Dorothy Smith	1957...Carole Meinhart	1987...Terry Quinn
1890...Mrs. M.C. Howell	1923...Norma Pierce	1958...Carole Meinhart	1988...Debra Ochs
1891...Mrs. M.C. Howell	1924...Dorothy Smith	1959...Carole Meinhart	1989...Debra Ochs
1892...Mrs. M.C. Howell	1925...Dorothy Smith	1960...Ann Clark	1990...Denise Parker
1893...Mrs. M.C. Howell	1926...Dorothy Smith	1961...Victoria Cook	1991...Denise Parker
1894...Mrs. Albert Kern	1927...Mrs. R. Johnson	1962...Nancy	1992...Sherry Block
1895...Mrs. M.C. Howell	1928...Beatrice Hodgson	Vonderheide	1993...Denise Parker
1896...Mrs. M.C. Howell	1929...Audrey Grubbs	1963...Nancy	1994...Judy Adams
1897...Mrs. J.S. Baker	1930...Audrey Grubbs	Vonderheide	1995...Jessica Carlson
1898...Mrs. M.C. Howell	1931...Dorothy	1964...Victoria Cook	1996...Janet Dykman
1899...Mrs. M.C. Howell	Cummings	1965...Nancy Pfeiffer	1997...Janet Dykman
1900...Mrs. M.C. Howell	1932...Ilda Hanchette	1966...Helen Thornton	1998...Janet Dykman
1901...Mrs. C.E.	1933...Madelaine Taylor	1967...Ardelle Mills	1999...Denise Parker
Woodruff	1934...Desales Mudd	1968...Victoria Cook	2000...Karen Scavatto
1902...Mrs. M.C. Howell	1935...Ruth Hodgert	1969...Doreen Wilber	2001...Kathie Loesch
1903...Mrs. M.C. Howell	1936...Gladys Hammer	1970...Nancy Myrick	2002...Jessica Peterson
1904...Mrs. M.C. Howell	1937...Gladys Hammer	1971...Doreen Wilber	2003...Samantha Marino
1905...Mrs. M.C. Howell	1938...Jean Tenney	1972...Ruth Rowe	2004...Khatuna Lorig
1906...Mrs. E.C. Cook	1939...Belvia Carter	1973...Doreen Wilber	2005...Khatuna Lorig
1907...Mrs. M.C. Howell	1940...Ann Weber	1974...Doreen Wilber	
1908...Harriet Case	1941...Ree Dillinger	1975...Irene Lorensen	
1909...Harriet Case	1946...Ann Weber	1976...Luann Ryon	

Chess

World Champions

FIDE

1866–94	Wilhelm Steinitz, Austria
1894–1921	Emanuel Lasker, Germany
1921–27	Jose Capablanca, Cuba
1927–35	Alexander Alekhine, France
1935–37	Max Euwe, Holland
1937–47	Alexander Alekhine, France
1948–57	Mikhail Botvinnik, USSR
1957–58	Vassily Smyslov, USSR
1958–59	Mikhail Botvinnik, USSR
1960–61	Mikhail Tal, USSR
1961–63	Mikhail Botvinnik, USSR
1963–69	Tigran Petrosian, USSR
1969–72	Boris Spassky, USSR

FIDE

1972–75	Bobby Fischer, United States
1975–85	Anatoly Karpov, USSR
1985–93	*Garry Kasparov, USSR
1994–98	Anatoly Karpov, Russia
1999–2000	Alexander Khalifman, Russia
2000–01	Anand Viswanathan, India
2002–04	Ruslan Ponomariov, Ukraine
2004–05	Rustam Kasimdzhanov, Uzbekistan
2005–	Veselin Topalov, Bulgaria

*Kasparov stripped of title by FIDE in 1993.

Professional Chess Association

1993–95	Garry Kasparov

United States Champions

1857–71	Paul Morphy	1961–62	Larry Evans	1989	R. Dzindzichashvili
1871–76	George Mackenzie	1962–68	Bobby Fischer		Stuart Rachels
1876–80	James Mason	1968–69	Larry Evans		Yasser Seirawan
1880–89	George Mackenzie	1969–72	Samuel Reshevsky	1990	Lev Alburt
1889–90	Samuel Lipschutz	1972–73	Robert Byrne	1991	Gata Kamski
1890	Jackson Showalter	1973–74	Lubomir Kavale	1992	Patrick Wolff
1890–91	Max Judd		John Grefe	1993	Alex Yermolinsky
1891–92	Jackson Showalter	1974–77	Walter Browne		A. Shabalov
1892–94	Samuel Lipschutz	1978–80	Lubomir Kavalek	1994	Boris Gulko
1894	Jackson Showalter	1980–81	Larry Evans	1995	Patrick Wolff
1894–95	Albert Hodges		Larry Christiansen		Nick DeFirmian
1895–97	Jackson Showalter		Walter Browne		Alexander Ivanov
1897–1906	Harry Pillsbury	1981–83	Walter Browne	1996	Alex Yermolinsky
1906–09	Vacant		Yasser Seirawan	1997	Alex Yermolinsky
1909–36	Frank Marshall	1983	R. Dzindzichashvili	1998	Alex Yermolinsky
1936–44	Samuel Reshevsky	1983	Larry Christiansen	1999	Boris Gulko
1944–46	Arnold Denker		Walter Browne	2000	Joel Benjamin
1946–48	Samuel Reshevsky	1984–85	Lev Alburt	2001	Joel Benjamin
1948–51	Herman Steiner	1986	Yasser Seirawan	2002	Larry Christiansen
1951–54	Larry Evans	1987	Joel Benjamin	2003	Alexander Shabalov
1954–57	Arthur Bisguier		Nick DeFirmian	2004	Hikaru Nakamura
1957–61	Bobby Fischer	1988	Michael Wilder		

Curling

World Men's Champions

Year	Country, Skip	Year	Country, Skip	Year	Country, Skip
1972	Canada, Crest Melesnuk	1984	Norway, Eigil Ramsfjell	1996	Canada, Jeff Stoughton
1973	Sweden, Kjell Oscarius	1985	Canada, Al Hackner	1997	Sweden, Peter Lindholm
1974	U.S., Bud Somerville	1986	Canada, Ed Luckowich	1998	Canada, Wayne Middaugh
1975	Switzerland, Otto Danieli	1987	Canada, Russ Howard	1999	Scotland, Hammy McMillan
1976	U.S., Bruce Roberts	1988	Norway, Eigil Ramsfjell	2000	Canada, Greg McAulay
1977	Sweden, Ragnar Kamp	1989	Canada, Pat Ryan	2001	Sweden, Peter Lindholm
1978	U.S., Bob Nichols	1990	Canada, Ed Werenich	2002	Canada, Randy Ferbey
1979	Norway, Kristian Soerum	1991	Scotland, David Smith	2003	Canada, Randy Ferbey
1980	Canada, Rich Folk	1992	Switzerland, Markus Eggler	2004	Sweden, Peja Lindholm
1981	Switzerland, Jurg Tanner	1993	Canada, Russ Howard	2005	Canada, David Nedohin
1982	Canada, Al Hackner	1994	Canada, Rick Folk		
1983	Canada, Ed Werenich	1995	Canada, Kerry Burtnyk		

World Women's Champions

Year	Country, Skip	Year	Country, Skip	Year	Country, Skip
1979	Switzerland, Gaby Casanova	1987	Canada, Pat Sanders	1998	Sweden, Elisabet Gustafson
1980	Canada, Marj Mitchell	1988	Germany, Andrea Schopp	1999	Sweden, Elisabet Gustafson
1981	Sweden, Elisabeth Hogstrom	1989	Canada, Heather Houston	2000	Canada, Kelley Law
1982	Denmark, Marianne Jorgenson	1990	Norway, Dordi Nordby	2001	Canada, Colleen Jones
		1991	Norway, Dordi Nordby	2002	Scotland, Jackie Lockhart
1983	Switzerland, Erika Mueller	1992	Sweden, Elisabet Johanssen	2003	United States, Debbie McCormick
1984	Canada, Connie Lallberte	1993	Canada, Sandra Peterson		
1985	Canada, Linda Moore	1994	Canada, Sandra Peterson	2004	Canada, Colleen Jones
1986	Canada, Marilyn Darte	1995	Sweden, Elisabet Gustafson	2005	Sweden, Anette Norberg
		1996	Canada, Marilyn Bodogh		
		1997	Canada, Sandra Schmirler		

U.S. Men's Champions

Year	Site	Winning Club	Skip
1957	Chicago, IL	Hibbing, MN	Harold Lauber
1958	Milwaukee, WI	Detroit, MI	Douglas Fisk
1959	Green Bay, WI	Hibbing, MN	Fran Kleffman
1960	Chicago, IL	Grafton, ND	Orvil Gilleshammer
1961	Grand Forks, ND	Seattle, WA	Frank Crealock
1962	Detroit, MI	Hibbing, MN	Fran Kleffman
1963	Duluth, MN	Detroit, MI	Mike Slyziuk
1964	Utica, NY	Duluth, MN	Robert Magle Jr.
1965	Seattle, WA	Superior, WI	Bud Somerville
1966	Hibbing, MN	Fargo, ND	Joe Zbacnik
1967	Winchester, MA	Seattle, WA	Bruce Roberts
1968	Madison, WI	Superior, WI	Bud Somerville
1969	Grand Forks, ND	Superior, WI	Bud Somerville
1970	Ardsley, NY	Grafton, ND	Art Tallackson
1971	Duluth, MN	Edmore, ND	Dale Dalziel
1972	Wilmette, IL	Grafton, ND	Robert Labonte
1973	Colorado Springs, CO	Winchester, MA	Charles Reeves
1974	Schenectady, NY	Superior, WI	Bud Somerville
1975	Detroit, MI	Seattle, WA	Ed Risling
1976	Wausau, WI	Hibbing, MN	Bruce Roberts
1977	Northbrook, IL	Hibbing, MN	Bruce Roberts
1978	Utica, NY	Superior, WI	Bob Nichols
1979	Superior, WI	Bemidji, MN	Scott Baird
1980	Bemidji, MN	Hibbing, MN	Paul Pustovar
1981	Fairbanks, AK	Superior, WI	Bob Nichols
1982	Brookline, MA	Madison, WI	Steve Brown
1983	Colorado Springs, CO	Colorado Springs, CO	Don Cooper
1984	Hibbing, MN	Hibbing, MN	Bruce Roberts
1985	Mequon, WI	Wilmette, IL	Tim Wright
1986	Seattle, WA	Madison, WI	Steve Brown
1987	Lake Placid, NY	Seattle, WA	Jim Vukich
1988	St. Paul, MN	Seattle, WA	Doug Jones
1989	Detroit, MI	Seattle, WA	Jim Vukich
1990	Superior, WI	Seattle, WA	Doug Jones
1991	Utica, NY	Madison, WI	Steve Brown
1992	Grafton, ND	Seattle, WA	Doug Jones
1993	St. Paul, MN	Bemidji, MN	Scott Baird
1994	Duluth, MN	Bemidji, MN	Scott Baird
1995	Appleton, WI	Superior, WI	Tim Somerville
1996	Bemidji, MN	Superior, WI	Tim Somerville
1997	Seattle,WA	Langdon, ND	Craig Disher
1998	Bismarck, SD	Stevens Pt., WI	Paul Pustovar
1999	Duluth, MN	Superior, WI	Tim Somerville
2000	Ogden, UT	Wisconsin3	Craig Brown
2001	Madison, WI	Washington	Jason Larway
2002	Virginia, MN	Wisconsin2	Paul Pustovar
2003	Utica, NY	Minnesota3	Pete Fenson
2004	Grand Forks, ND	Seattle, WA	Jason Larway
2005	Chicago, IL	Illinois	Russ Armstrong

U.S. Women's Champions

Year	Site	Winning Club	Skip
1977	Wilmette, IL	Hastings, NY	Margaret Smith
1978	Duluth, MN	Wausau, WI	Sandy Robarge
1979	Winchester, MA	Seattle, WA	Nancy Langley
1980	Seattle, WA	Seattle, WA	Sharon Kozal
1981	Kettle Moraine, WI	Seattle, WA	Nancy Langley
1982	Bowling Green, OH	Oak Park, IL	Ruth Schwenker
1983	Grafton, ND	Seattle, WA	Nancy Langley
1984	Wauwatosa, WI	Duluth, MN	Amy Hatten
1985	Hershey, PA	Fairbanks, AK	Bev Birklid
1986	Chicago, IL	St Paul, MN	Gerri Tilden
1987	St Paul, MN	Seattle, WA	Sharon Good
1988	Darien, CT	Seattle, WA	Nancy Langley
1989	Detroit, MI	Rolla, ND	Jan Lagasse
1990	Superior, WI	Denver, CO	Bev Behnke
1991	Utica, NY	Houston, TX	Maymar Gemmell
1992	Grafton, ND	Madison, WI	Lisa Schoeneberg
1993	St Paul, MN	Denver, CO	Bev Behnke
1994	Duluth, MN	Denver, CO	Bev Behnke
1995	Appleton, WI	Madison, WI	Lisa Schoeneberg
1996	Bemidji, MN	Madison, WI	Lisa Schoeneberg
1997	Seattle, WA	Arlington, WI	Patti Lank
1998	Bismarck, SD	Wilmette, IL	Kari Erickson
1999	Duluth, MN	Madison, WI	Patti Lank

U.S. Women's Champions (Cont.)

Year	Site	Winning Club	Skip
2000	Ogden, UT	Nebraska	Amy Wright
2001	Madison, WI	Illinois	Kari Erickson
2002	Virginia, MN	Madison, WI	Patti Lank
2003	Utica, NY	Illinois	Debbie McCormick
2004	Grand Forks, ND	Madison, WI	Patti Lank
2005	Chicago, IL	Massachusetts	Shelly Dropkin

Cycling

Professional Road Race World Champions

1927 ....Alfred Binda, Italy
1928 ....George Ronsse, Belgium
1929 ....George Ronsse, Belgium
1930 ....Alfred Binda, Italy
1931 ....Learco Guerra, Italy
1932 ....Alfred Binda, Italy
1933 ....George Speicher, France
1934 ....Karel Kaers, Belgium
1935 ....Jean Aerts, Belgium
1936 ....Antonio Magne, France
1937 ....Elio Meulenberg, Belgium
1938 ....Marcel Kint, Belgium
No competition 1939–45
1946 ....Hans Knecht, Switzerland
1947 ....Theo. Middelkamp, Holland
1948 ....Alberic Schotte, Belgium
1949 ....Henri Van Steenbergen, Belgium
1950 ....Alberic Schotte, Belgium
1951 ....Ferdinand Kubler, Switzerland
1952 ....Heinz Mueller, Germany
1953 ....Fausto Coppi, Italy
1954 ....Louison Bobet, France
1955 ....Stan Ockers, Belgium
1956 ....Rik Van Steenbergen, Belg.
1957 ....Rik Van Steenbergen,

Belgium
1958 ....Ercole Baldini, Italy
1959 ....Andre Darrigade, France
1960 ....Rik van Looy, Belgium
1961 ....Rik van Looy, Belgium
1962 ....Jean Stablenski, France
1963 ....Bennoni Beheyt, Belgium
1964 ....Jan Janssen, Holland
1965 ....Tommy Simpson, England
1966 ....Rudi Altig, West Germany
1967 ....Eddy Merckx, Belgium
1968 ....Vittorio Adorni, Italy
1969 ....Harm Ottenbros, Netherlands
1970 ....J.P. Monseré, Belgium
1971 ....Eddy Merckx, Belgium
1972 ....Marino Basso, Italy
1973 ....Felice Gimondi, Italy
1974 ....Eddy Merckx, Belgium
1975 ....Hennie Kuiper, Holland
1976 ....Freddy Maertens, Belgium
1977 ....Francesco Moser, Italy
1978 ....Gerri Knetemann, Holland
1979 ....Jan Raas, Holland
1980 ....Bernard Hinault, France
1981 ....Freddy Maertens, Belgium
1982 ....Giuseppe Saronni, Italy

1983 ....Greg LeMond, United States
1984 ....Claude Criquielion, Belgium
1985 ....Joop Zoetemelk, Holland
1986 ....Moreno Argentin, Italy
1987 ....Stephen Roche, Ireland
1988 ....Maurizio Fondriest, Italy
1989 ....Greg LeMond, United States
1990 ....Rudy Dhaenene, Belgium
1991 ....Gianni Bugno, Italy
1992 ....Gianni Bugno, Italy
1993 ....Lance Armstrong, United States
1994 ....Luc LeBlanc, France
1995 ....Abraham Olano, Spain
1996 ....Johan Museeuw, Belgium
1997 ....Laurent Brochard, France
1998 ....Oskar Camenzind, Switz
1999 ....Oscar Gomez Freire, Spain
2000 ....Romans Vainsteins, Latvia
2001 ....Oscar Gomez Freire, Spain
2002 ....Mario Cipollini, Italy
2003 ....Igor Astraloa, Spain
2004 ....Oscar Freire Gomez, Spain
2005 ....Tom Boonen, Belarus

Tour DuPont Winners

Year	Winner	Time
1989	Dag Otto Lauritzen, Norway	33 hrs, 28 min, 48 sec
1990	Raul Alcala, Mexico	45 hrs, 20 min, 9 sec
1991	Erik Breukink, Holland	48 hrs, 56 min, 53 sec
1992	Greg LeMond, United States	44 hrs, 27 min, 43 sec
1993	Raul Alcala, Mexico	46 hrs, 42 min, 52 sec
1994	Viatcheslav Ekimov, Russia	47 hrs, 14 min, 29 sec
1995	Lance Armstrong, United States	46 hrs, 31 min, 16 sec
1996	Lance Armstrong, United States	48 hrs, 20 min, 5 sec

Note: Race not held since 1996.

Tour de France Winners

Year	Winner	Time
1903	Maurice Garin, France	94 hrs, 33 min
1904	Henry Cornet, France	96 hrs, 5 min, 56 sec
1905	Louis Trousselier, France	110 hrs, 26 min, 58 sec
1906	Rene Pottier, France	Not available
1907	Lucien Petit-Breton, France	158 hrs, 54 min, 5 sec
1908	Lucien Petit-Breton, France	Not available
1909	Francois Faber, Luxembourg	157 hrs, 1 min, 22 sec
1910	Octave Lapize, France	162 hrs, 41 min, 30 sec
1911	Gustave Garrigou, France	195 hrs, 37 min
1912	Odile Defraye, Belgium	190 hrs, 30 min, 28 sec
1913	Philippe Thys, Belgium	197 hrs, 54 min
1914	Philippe Thys, Belgium	200 hrs, 28 min, 48 sec
1915–18	No race	
1919	Firmin Lambot, Belgium	231 hrs, 7 min, 15 sec
1920	Philippe Thys, Belgium	228 hrs, 36 min, 13 sec
1921	Leon Scieur, Belgium	221 hrs, 50 min, 26 sec
1922	Firmin Lambot, Belgium	222 hrs, 8 min, 6 sec
1923	Henri Pelissier, France	222 hrs, 15 min, 30 sec

Tour de France Winners (Cont.)

Year	Winner	Time
1924	Ottavio Bottechia, Italy	226 hrs, 18 min, 21 sec
1925	Ottavio Bottechia, Italy	219 hrs, 10 min, 18 sec
1926	Lucien Buysse, Belgium	238 hrs, 44 min, 25 sec
1927	Nicolas Frantz, Luxembourg	198 hrs, 16 min, 42 sec
1928	Nicolas Frantz, Luxembourg	192 hrs, 48 min, 58 sec
1929	Maurice Dewaele, Belgium	186 hrs, 39 min, 16 sec
1930	Andre Leducq, France	172 hrs, 12 min, 16 sec
1931	Antonin Magne, France	177 hrs, 10 min, 3 sec
1932	Andre Leducq, France	154 hrs, 12 min, 49 sec
1933	Georges Speicher, France	147 hrs, 51 min, 37 sec
1934	Antonin Magne, France	147 hrs, 13 min, 58 sec
1935	Romain Maes, Belgium	141 hrs, 32 min
1936	Sylvere Maes, Belgium	142 hrs, 47 min, 32 sec
1937	Roger Lapebie, France	138 hrs, 58 min, 31 sec
1938	Gino Bartali, Italy	148 hrs, 29 min, 12 sec
1939	Sylvere Maes, Belgium	132 hrs, 3 min, 17 sec
1940–46	No race	
1947	Jean Robic, France	148 hrs, 11 min, 25 sec
1948	Gino Bartali, Italy	147 hrs, 10 min, 36 sec
1949	Fausto Coppi, Italy	149 hrs, 40 min, 49 sec
1950	Ferdi Kubler, Switzerland	145 hrs, 36 min, 56 sec
1951	Hugo Koblet, Switzerland	142 hrs, 20 min, 14 sec
1952	Fausto Coppi, Italy	151 hrs, 57 min, 20 sec
1953	Louison Bobet, France	129 hrs, 23 min, 25 sec
1954	Louison Bobet, France	140 hrs, 6 min, 5 sec
1955	Louison Bobet, France	130 hrs, 29 min, 26 sec
1956	Roger Walkowiak, France	124 hrs, 1 min, 16 sec
1957	Jacques Anquetil, France	129 hrs, 46 min, 11 sec
1958	Charly Gaul, Luxembourg	116 hrs, 59 min, 5 sec
1959	Federico Bahamontes, Spain	123 hrs, 46 min, 45 sec
1960	Gastone Nencini, Italy	112 hrs, 8 min, 42 sec
1961	Jacques Anquetil, France	122 hrs, 1 min, 33 sec
1962	Jacques Anquetil, France	114 hrs, 31 min, 54 sec
1963	Jacques Anquetil, France	113 hrs, 30 min, 5 sec
1964	Jacques Anquetil, France	127 hrs, 9 min, 44 sec
1965	Felice Gimondi, Italy	116 hrs, 42 min, 6 sec
1966	Lucien Aimar, France	117 hrs, 34 min, 21 sec
1967	Roger Pingeon, France	136 hrs, 53 min, 50 sec
1968	Jan Janssen, Netherlands	133 hrs, 49 min, 32 sec
1969	Eddy Merckx, Belgium	116 hrs, 16 min, 2 sec
1970	Eddy Merckx, Belgium	119 hrs, 31 min, 49 sec
1971	Eddy Merckx, Belgium	96 hrs, 45 min, 14 sec
1972	Eddy Merckx, Belgium	108 hrs, 17 min, 18 sec
1973	Luis Ocana, Spain	122 hrs, 25 min, 34 sec
1974	Eddy Merckx, Belgium	116 hrs, 16 min, 58 sec
1975	Bernard Thevenet, France	114 hrs, 35 min, 31 sec
1976	Lucien Van Impe, Belgium	116 hrs, 22 min, 23 sec
1977	Bernard Thevenet, France	115 hrs, 38 min, 30 sec
1978	Bernard Hinault, France	108 hrs, 18 min
1979	Bernard Hinault, France	103 hrs, 6 min, 50 sec
1980	Joop Zoetemelk, Netherlands	109 hrs, 19 min, 14 sec
1981	Bernard Hinault, France	96 hrs, 19 min, 38 sec
1982	Bernard Hinault, France	92 hrs, 8 min, 46 sec
1983	Laurent Fignon, France	105 hrs, 7 min, 52 sec
1984	Laurent Fignon, France	112 hrs, 3 min, 40 sec
1985	Bernard Hinault, France	113 hrs, 24 min, 23 sec
1986	Greg LeMond, United States	110 hrs, 35 min, 19 sec
1987	Stephen Roche, Ireland	115 hrs, 27 min, 42 sec
1988	Pedro Delgado, Spain	84 hrs, 27 min, 53 sec
1989	Greg LeMond, United States	87 hrs, 38 min, 35 sec
1990	Greg LeMond, United States	90 hrs, 43 min, 20 sec
1991	Miguel Induráin, Spain	101 hrs, 1 min, 20 sec
1992	Miguel Induráin, Spain	100 hrs, 49 min, 30 sec
1993	Miguel Induráin, Spain	95 hrs, 57 min, 9 sec
1994	Miguel Induráin, Spain	103 hrs, 38 min, 38 sec
1995	Miguel Induráin, Spain	92 hrs, 44 min, 59 sec
1996	Bjarne Riis, Denmark	95 hrs, 57 min, 16 sec
1997	Jan Ullrich, Germany	100 hrs, 30 min, 35 sec

Cycling (Cont.)

Tour de France Winners (Cont.)

Year	Winner	Time
1998	Marco Pantani, Italy	92 hrs, 49 min, 46 sec
1999	Lance Armstrong, United States	91 hrs, 32 min, 16 sec
2000	Lance Armstrong, United States	92 hrs, 33 min, 8 sec
2001	Lance Armstrong, United States	86 hrs, 17 min, 28 sec
2002	Lance Armstrong, United States	82 hrs, 5 min, 12 sec
2003	Lance Armstrong, United States	83 hrs, 41 min, 12 sec
2004	Lance Armstrong, United States	83 hrs, 36 min, 2 sec
2005	Lance Armstrong, United States	82 hrs, 34 min, 5 sec

Sled Dog Racing

Iditarod

Year	Winner	Time	Year	Winner	Time
1973	Dick Wilmarth	20 days, 00:49:41	1990	Susan Butcher	11 days, 01:53:23
1974	Carl Huntington	20 days, 15:02:07	1991	Rick Swenson	12 days, 16:34:39
1975	Emmitt Peters	14 days, 14:43:45	1992	Martin Buser	10 days, 19:17:15
1976	Gerald Riley	18 days, 22:58:17	1993	Jeff King	10 days, 15:38:15
1977	Rick Swenson	16 days, 16:27:13	1994	Martin Buser	10 days, 13:02:39
1978	Dick Mackey	14 days, 18:52:24	1995	Doug Swingley	9 days, 02:42:19
1979	Rick Swenson	15 days, 10:37:47	1996	Jeff King	9 days, 05:43:13
1980	Joe May	14 days, 07:11:51	1997	Martin Buser	9 days, 08:30:45
1981	Rick Swenson	12 days, 08:45:02	1998	Jeff King	9 days, 05:52:26
1982	Rick Swenson	16 days, 04:40:10	1999	Doug Swingley	9 days, 14:31:19
1983	Dick Mackey	12 days, 14:10:44	2000	Doug Swingley	9 days, 00:58:06
1984	Dean Osmar	12 days, 15:07:33	2001	Doug Swingley	9 days, 19:55:50
1985	Libby Riddles	18 days, 00:20:17	2002	Martin Buser	8 days, 22:46:02
1986	Susan Butcher	11 days, 15:06:00	2003	Robert Sorlie	9 days, 15:47:36
1987	Susan Butcher	11 days, 02:05:13	2004	Mitch Seavey	9 days, 12:20:22
1988	Susan Butcher	11 days, 11:41:40	2005	Robert Sorlie	9 days, 18:39:31
1989	Joe Runyan	11 days, 05:24:34			

Fishing

Saltwater Fishing Records

Species	Weight	Where Caught	Date	Angler
Albacore	88 lb 2 oz	Gran Canaria, Canary Islands	Nov 19, 1977	Siegfried Dickemann
Amberjack, greater	155 lb 12 oz	Bermuda	Aug 16, 1992	Larry Trott
Amberjack, Pacific	104 lb	Baja California, Mexico	July 4, 1984	Richard Cresswell
Angler	126 lb 12 oz	Sognefjorden Hoyanger, Norway	July 4, 1996	Gunnar Thorsteinsen
Barracuda, great	85 lb	Christmas Island, Kiribati	April 11, 1992	John W. Helfrich
Barracuda, Mexican	21 lb	Phantom Isle, Costa Rica	Mar 27, 1987	E. Greg Kent
Barracuda, pickhandle	29 lb 12 oz	Malindi, Kenya	Nov 7, 2002	Paul Gerritsen
Bass, barred sand	13 lb 3 oz	Huntington Beach, California	Aug 29, 1988	Robert Halal
Bass, black sea	10 lb 4 oz	Virginia Beach, Virginia	Jan 1, 2000	Allan P. Paschall
Bass, European	20 lb 14 oz	Cap d'Agde, France	Sept. 8, 1999	Robert Mari
Bass, giant sea	563 lb 8 oz	Anacapa Island, California	Aug 20, 1968	James D. McAdam Jr.
Bass, striped	78 lb 8 oz	Atlantic City, New Jersey	Sept 21, 1982	Albert R. McReynolds
Bluefish	31 lb 12 oz	Hatteras Inlet, North Carolina	Jan 30, 1972	James M. Hussey
Bonefish	19 lb	Zululand, South Africa	May 26, 1962	Brian W. Batchelor
Bonito, Atlantic	18 lb 4 oz	Faial Island, Azores	July 8, 1953	D.G. Higgs
Bonito, Pacific	21 lb 3 oz	Malibu, California	July 30, 1978	Gino M. Picciolo
Cabezon	23 lb	Juan De Fuca Strait, Washington	Aug 4, 1990	Wesley S. Hunter
Cobia	135 lb 9 oz	Shark Bay, Australia	July 9, 1985	Peter W. Goulding
Cod, Atlantic	98 lb 12 oz	Isle of Shoals, New Hampshire	June 8, 1969	Alphonse Bielevich
Cod, Pacific	35 lb	Unalaska Bay, Alaska	June 16, 1999	Jim Johnson
Conger	133 lb 4 oz	South Devon, England	June 5, 1995	Vic Evans
Dolphinfish	87 lb	Papagallo Gulf, Costa Rica	Sept 25, 1976	Manuel Salazar
Drum, black	113 lb 1 oz	Lewes, Delaware	Sept 15, 1975	Gerald M. Townsend
Drum, red	94 lb 2 oz	Avon, North Carolina	Nov 7, 1984	David Deuel
Eel, American	9 lb 4 oz	Cape May, New Jersey	Nov 9, 1995	Jeff Pennick
Eel, marbled	36 lb 1 oz	Durban, South Africa	June 10, 1984	Ferdie van Nooten
Flounder, southern	20 lb 9 oz	Nassau Sound, Florida	Dec 23, 1983	Larenza W. Mungin
Flounder, summer	22 lb 7 oz	Montauk, New York	Sept 15, 1975	Charles Nappi
Grouper, Warsaw	436 lb 12 oz	Destin, Florida	Dec 22, 1985	Steve Haeusler
Halibut, Atlantic	355 lb 6 oz	Valevag, Norway	Oct 20, 1997	Odd Arve Gunderstad

Saltwater Fishing Records *(Cont.)*

Species	Weight	Where Caught	Date	Angler
Halibut, California	58 lb 9 oz	Santa Rosa Island, California	June 26, 1999	Roger W. Borrell
Halibut, Pacific	459 lb	Dutch Harbor, Alaska	June 11, 1996	Jack Tragis
Herring, Red	7 lb 7 oz	Sargasso Sea, Bahamas	Apr 1, 1965	Ward Bolster
Jack, crevalle	58 lb 6 oz	Barro do Kwanza, Angola	Dec 10, 2000	Nuno A. P. da Silva
Jack, horse-eye	29 lb 8 oz	Ascencion Island, S Atlantic Ocean	May 28, 1993	Mike Hanson
Jack, Pacific crevalle	39 lb	Playa Zancudo, Costa Rica	Mar 3, 1997	Ingrid Callaghan
Jewfish	680 lb	Fernandina Beach, Florida	May 20, 1961	Lynn Joyner
Kawakawa	29 lb	Isla Clarion, Mexico	Dec 17, 1986	Ronald Nakamura
Lingcod	76 lb 9 oz	Gulf of Alaska, Alaska	Aug 11, 2001	Antwan D. Tinsley
Mackerel, cero	17 lb 2 oz	Islamorada, Florida	Apr 5, 1986	G. Michael Mills
Mackerel, king	93 lb	San Juan, Puerto Rico	Apr 18, 1999	Steve Perez Graulau
Mackerel, narrowbarred	99 lb	Natal, South Africa	Mar 14, 1982	Michael J. Wilkinson
Mackerel, Spanish	13 lb	Ocracoke Inlet, North Carolina	Nov 4, 1987	Robert Cranton
Marlin, Atlantic blue	1,402 lb 2 oz	Vitoria, Brazil	Feb 29, 1992	Paulo R.A. Amorim
Marlin, black	1,560 lb	Cabo Blanco, Peru	Aug 4, 1953	Alfred C. Glassell Jr.
Marlin, Pacific blue	1,376 lb	Kaaiwi Point, Hawaii	May 31, 1982	J.W. de Beaubien
Marlin, striped	494 lb	Tutukaka, New Zealand	Jan 16, 1986	Bill Boniface
Marlin, white	181 lb 14 oz	Vitoria, Brazil	Dec 8, 1979	Evandro Luiz Coser
Permit	60 lb	Ilha do Mel Paranagua, Brazil	Dec 14, 2002	Renato P. Fiedler
Pollock	50 lb	Salstraumen, Norway	Nov 30, 1995	Thor Magnus-Lekang
Pompano, African	50 lb 8 oz	Daytona Beach, Florida	Apr 21, 1990	Tom Sargent
Roosterfish	114 lb	La Paz, Mexico	June 1, 1960	Abe Sackheim
Runner, blue	11 lb 2 oz	Dauphin Island, Alaska	June 28, 1997	Stacey M. Moiren
Runner, rainbow	37 lb 9 oz	Isla Clarion, Mexico	Nov 21, 1991	Tom Pfleger
Sailfish, Atlantic	141 lb 1 oz	Luanda, Angola	Feb 19, 1994	Alfredo de Sousa Neves
Sailfish, Pacific	221 lb	Santa Cruz Island, Ecuador	Feb 12, 1947	Carl W. Stewart
Seabass, white	83 lb 12 oz	San Felipe, Mexico	Mar 31, 1953	Lyal C. Baumgardner
Seatrout, spotted	17 lb 7 oz	Ft. Pierce, Florida	May 11, 1995	Craig F. Carson
Shark, bigeye thresher	802 lb	Tutukaka, New Zealand	Feb 8, 1981	Dianne North
Shark, blue	528 lb	Montauk Point, New York	Aug 9, 2001	Joe Seidel
Shark, grter hammrhd	991 lb	Sarasota, Florida	May 30, 1982	Allen Ogle
Shark, Greenland	1,708 lb 9 oz	Trondheimsfjord, Norway	Oct 18, 1987	Terje Nordtvedt
Shark, porbeagle	507 lb	Caithness, Scotland	Mar 9, 1993	Christopher Bennet
Shark, shortfin mako	1,221 lb	Chatham, Massachusetts	July 21, 2001	Luke Sweeney
Shark, tiger	1,780 lb	Cherry Grove, South Carolina	June 14, 1964	Walter Maxwell
Shark, tope	72 lb 12 oz	Parengarenga Harbor, N.Z.	Dec 19, 1986	Melanie B. Feldman
Shark, white	2,664 lb	Ceduna, Australia	Apr 21, 1959	Alfred Dean
Skipjack, black	26 lb	Baja California, Mexico	Oct 23, 1991	Clifford K. Hamaishi
Snapper, cubera	121 lb 8 oz	Cameron, Louisiana	July 5, 1982	Mike Hebert
Snook, common	53 lb 10 oz	Parismina Ranch, Costa Rica	Oct 18, 1978	Gilbert Ponzi
Spearfish, Mediterr.	90 lb 13 oz	Madeira Island, Portugal	June 2, 1980	Joseph Larkin
Spearfish, longbill	127 lb 13 oz	Puerto Rico, Gran Canaria, Spain	May 20, 1999	Paul Cashmore
Spearfish, shortbill	74 lb 8 oz	Bay of Islands, New Zealand	Mar 16, 1999	Leonie Kai Patterson
Swordfish	1,182 lb	Iquique, Chile	May 7, 1953	Louis Marron
Tarpon	286 lb 9 oz	Rubane, Guinea-Bissau	Mar 20, 2003	Max Domecq
Tautog	25 lb	Ocean City, New Jersey	Jan 20, 1998	Anthony Monica
Tilapia, Mozambique	6 lb 13 oz	Loskop Dam, S Africa	Apr 4, 2003	Eugene C. Kruger
Trevally, bigeye	31 lb 8 oz	Poivre Island, Seychelles	Apr 23, 1997	Les Sampson
Trevally, giant	145 lb 8 oz	Maui, Hawaii	Mar 28, 1991	Russell Mori
Tuna, Atlantic bigeye	392 lb 6 oz	Puerto Rico, Gran Canaria, Spain	July 25, 1996	Dieter Vogel
Tuna, blackfin	45 lb 8 oz	Key West, Florida	May 4, 1996	Sam J. Burnett
Tuna, bluefin	1,496 lb	Aulds Cove, Nova Scotia	Oct 26, 1979	Ken Fraser
Tuna, longtail	79 lb 2 oz	Montague Island, New South Wales, Australia	Apr 12, 1982	Tim Simpson
Tuna, Pacific bigeye	435 lb	Cabo Blanco, Peru	Apr 17, 1957	Russel Lee
Tuna, skipjack	45 lb 4 oz	Baja California, Mexico	Nov 16, 1996	Brian Evans
Tuna, southern bluefin	348 lb 5 oz	Whakatane, New Zealand	Jan 16, 1981	Rex Wood
Tuna, yellowfin	388 lb 12 oz	San Benedicto Is, Mexico	Apr 1, 1977	Curt Wiesenhutter
Tunny, little	35 lb 2 oz	Cape de Garde, Algeria	Dec 14, 1988	Jean Yves Chatard
Wahoo	158 lb 8 oz	Loreto, Baja California, Mexico	June 10, 1996	Keith Winter
Weakfish	19 lb 2 oz	Jones Beach Inlet, New York	Oct 11, 1984	Dennis Rooney
		Delaware Bay, Delaware	May 20, 1989	William E. Thomas
Yellowtail, California	88 lb 3 oz	Alijos Rocks, Baja Calif., Mexico	Jun 21, 2000	Ronald Fujii
Yellowtail, southern	114 lb 10 oz	Tauranga, New Zealand	Feb 5, 1984	Mike Godfrey

Freshwater Fishing Records

Species	Weight	Where Caught	Date	Angler
Barramundi	83 lb 7 oz	Lake Tinaroo, N Queensl'd, Aus.	Sept 23, 1999	David Powell
Bass, largemouth	22 lb 4 oz	Montgomery Lake, Georgia	June 2, 1932	George W. Perry
Bass, rock	3 lb	York River, Ontario	Aug 1, 1974	Peter Gulgin
Bass, shoal	8 lb 12 oz	Apalatchicola River, Florida	Jan 28, 1995	Carl W. Davis
Bass, smallmouth	10 lb 14 oz	Dale Hollow, Tennessee	April 24, 1969	John T. Gorman
Bass, Suwannee	3 lb 14 oz	Suwannee River, Florida	Mar 2, 1985	Ronnie Everett
Bass, white	6 lb 13 oz	Orange, Virginia	July 31, 1989	Ronald Sprouse
Bass, whiterock	27 lb 5 oz	Greers Ferry Lake, Arkansas	Apr 24, 1997	Jerald Shaum
Bass, yellow	2 lb 9 oz	Waverly, Tennessee	Feb 27, 1998	John Chappell
Bluegill	4 lb 12 oz	Ketona Lake, Alabama	Apr 9, 1950	T.S. Hudson
Bowfin	21 lb 8 oz	Florence, South Carolina	Jan 29, 1980	Robert Harmon
Buffalo, bigmouth	70 lb 5 oz	Bastrop, Louisiana	Apr 21, 1980	Delbert Sisk
Buffalo, black	63 lb 6 oz	Mississippi River, Iowa	Aug 14, 1999	Jim Winters
Buffalo, smallmouth	82 lb 3 oz	Athens Lake, Georgia	June 6, 1993	Randy Collins
Bullhead, brown	6 lb 5 oz	Lake Mahopac, New York	Sept 8, 2002	Ray Lawrence
Bullhead, yellow	4 lb 4 oz	Mormon Lake, Arizona	May 11, 1984	Emily Williams
Burbot	18 lb 11 oz	Angenmanalren, Sweden	Oct 22, 1996	Margit Agren
Carp, common	75 lb 11 oz	Lac de St. Cassien, France	May 21, 1987	Leo van der Gugten
Catfish, blue	116 lb 12 oz	Mississippi River, Arkansas	Aug 3, 2001	Charles Ashley Jr.
Catfish, channel	58 lb	Santee-Cooper Reservoir, SC	July 7, 1964	W.B. Whaley
Catfish, flathead	123 lb	Elk City Reservoir, Indep., KS	May 14, 1998	Ken Paulie
Catfish, white	21 lb 8 oz	Gorton Pond, East Lime, CT	Apr 22, 2001	Thomas Urquhart
Char, Arctic	32 lb 9 oz	Tree River, Canada	July 30, 1981	Jeffrey Ward
Crappie, white	5 lb 3 oz	Enid Dam, Mississippi	July 31, 1957	Fred L. Bright
Dolly Varden	20 lb 14 oz	Wulik River, Alaska	July 7, 2001	Raz Reid
Dorado	51 lb 5 oz	Corrièntes, Argentina	Sep 27, 1984	Armando Giudice
Drum, freshwater	54 lb 8 oz	Nickajack Lake, Tennessee	Apr 20, 1972	Benny E. Hull
Gar, alligator	279 lb	Rio Grande River, Texas	Dec 2, 1951	Bill Valverde
Gar, Florida	10 lb	Florida Everglades, Florida	Jan 28, 2002	Herbert Ratner Jr.
Gar, longnose	50 lb 5 oz	Trinity River, Texas	July 30, 1954	Townsend Miller
Gar, shortnose	5 lb 12 oz	Rend Lake, Illinois	July 16, 1995	Donna K. Willmert
Gar, spotted	9 lb 12 oz	Lake Mexia, Texas	Apr 7, 1994	Rick Rivard
Grayling, Arctic	5 lb 15 oz	Katseyedie River, Northwest Territories	Aug 16, 1967	Jeanne P. Branson
Inconnu	53 lb	Pah River, Alaska	Aug 20, 1986	Lawrence Hudnall
Kokanee	9 lb 6 oz	Okanagan Lake, Vernon, BC	June 18, 1988	Norm Kuhn
Muskellunge	67 lb 8 oz	Hayward, Wisconsin	July 24, 1949	Cal Johnson
Muskellunge, tiger	51 lb 3 oz	Lac Vieux-Desert, Michigan	July 16, 1919	John Knobla
Peacock, speckled	27 lb	Rio Negro, Brazil	Dec 4, 1994	Gerald (Doc) Lawson
Perch, Nile	230 lb	Lake Nasser, Egypt	Dec 20, 2000	William Toth
Perch, white	3 lb 1 oz	Forest Hill Park, NJ	May 6, 1989	Edward Tango
Perch, yellow	4 lb 3 oz	Bordentown, New Jersey	May 1865	C.C. Abbot
Pickerel, chain	9 lb 6 oz	Homerville, Georgia	Feb 17, 1961	Baxley McQuaig Jr.
Pike, northern	55 lb 1 oz	Lake of Grefeern, W Germany	Oct 16, 1986	Lothar Louis
Redhorse, greater	9 lb 3 oz	Salmon River, Pulaski, New York	May 11, 1985	Jason Wilson
Redhorse, silver	11 lb 7 oz	Plum Creek, Wisconsin	May 29, 1985	Neal Long
Salmon, Atlantic	79 lb 2 oz	Tana River, Norway	1928	Henrik Henriksen
Salmon, Chinook	97 lb 4 oz	Kenai River, Alaska	May 17, 1985	Les Anderson
Salmon, chum	35 lb	Edye Pass, Canada	July 11, 1995	Todd A. Johansson
Salmon, coho	33 lb 4 oz	Pulaski, New York	Sep 27, 1989	Jerry Lifton
Salmon, pink	14 lb 13 oz	Monroe, Washington	Sep 30, 2001	Alexander Minerich
Salmon, sockeye	15 lb 3 oz	Kenai River, Alaska	Aug 9, 1987	Stan Roach
Sauger	8 lb 12 oz	Lake Sakakawea, North Dakota	Oct 6, 1971	Mike Fischer
Shad, American	11 lb 4 oz	Connecticut River, Massachusetts	May 19, 1986	Bob Thibodo
Sturgeon, white	468 lb	Benicia, California	July 9, 1983	Joey Pallotta III
Sunfish, green	2 lb 2 oz	Stockton Lake, Missouri	June 18, 1971	Paul M. Dilley
Sunfish, redbreast	1 lb 12 oz	Suwannee River, Florida	May 29, 1984	Alvin Buchanan
Sunfish, redear	5 lb 7 oz	Diverson Canal, Georgia	Nov 6, 1998	Amos M. Gay
Tigerfish, giant	97 lb	Zaire River, Kinshasa, Zaire	July 9, 1988	Raymond Houtmans
Trout, Apache	5 lb 3 oz	Apache Reservation, Arizona	May 29, 1991	John Baldwin
Trout, brook	14 lb 8 oz	Nipigon River, Ontario	July 1916	W.J. Cook
Trout, brown	40 lb 4 oz	Heber Springs, Arkansas	May 9, 1992	Howard (Rip) Collins
Trout, bull	32 lb	Lake Pond Oreille, Idaho	Oct 27, 1949	N.L. Higgins
Trout, cutthroat	41 lb	Pyramid Lake, Nevada	Dec 1925	John Skimmerhorn
Trout, golden	11 lb	Cook's Lake, Wyoming	Aug 5, 1948	Charles S. Reed

Freshwater Fishing Records (Cont.)

Species	Weight	Where Caught	Date	Angler
Trout, lake	72 lb	Great Bear Lake, Northwest Territories	Aug 19, 1995	Lloyd Bull
Trout, rainbow	42 lb 2 oz	Bell Island, Alaska	June 22, 1970	David Robert White
Trout, tiger	20 lb 13 oz	Lake Michigan, Wisconsin	Aug 12, 1978	Pete M. Friedland
Walleye	25 lb	Old Hickory Lake, Tennessee	Aug 2, 1960	Mabry Harper
Warmouth	2 lb 7 oz	Yellow River, Holt, Florida	Oct 19, 1985	Tony D. Dempsey
Whitefish, lake	14 lb 6 oz	Meaford, Ontario	May 21, 1984	Dennis Laycock
Whitefish, mountain	5 lb 8 oz	Elbow River, Calgary, Alberta	Aug 1, 1995	Randy Woo
Whitefish, broad	9 lb	Tozitna River, Alaska	July 17, 1989	Al Mathews
Whitefish, round	6 lb	Putahow River, Manitoba	June 14, 1984	Allan J. Ristori
Zander	25 lb 2 oz	Trosa, Sweden	June 12, 1986	Harry Lee Tennison

Greyhound Racing

Annual Greyhound Race of Champions Winners*

Year	Winner (Sex)	Affiliation/Owner
1982	DD's Jackie (F)	Wonderland Park/ R.H. Walters Jr.
1983	Comin' Attraction (F)	Rocky Mt. Greyhound Park/ Bob Riggin
1984	Fallon (F)	Tampa Greyhound Track/ E.J. Alderson
1985	Lady Delight (F)	Lincoln Greyhound Park/ Julian A. Gay
1986	Ben G Speedboat (M)	Multnomah Kennel Club/ Louis Bennett
1987	ET's Pesky (F)	Supplemental (Flagler)/ Emil Tanis
1988	BB's Old Yellow (M)	Supplemental (Southland)/ Margie Bonita Hyers
1989	Osh Kosh Juliet (F)	Tampa Greyhound Track/ William F. Pollard
1990	Daring Don (M)	Interstate Kennel Club/ Perry Padrta
1991	Mo Kick (M)	Flagler Greyhound Track/ Eric M. Kennon
1992	Dicky Vallie (M)	Dairyland Greyhound Track/ George Benjamin
1993	Mega Morris (M)	Jacksonville Kennel Club/ Ferrell's Kennel

* The Greyhound Race of Champions has not been held since 1993.

Gymnastics

World Champions
MEN
All-Around

Year	Champion, Nation
1903	Joseph Martinez, France
1905	Marcel Lalue, France
1907	Joseph Czada, Czechoslovakia
1909	Marcos Torres, France
1911	Ferdinand Steiner, Czechoslovakia
1913	Marcos Torres, France
1922	Peter Sumi, Yugoslavia F. Pechacek, Czechoslovakia
1926	Peter Sumi, Yugoslavia
1930	Josip Primozic, Yugoslavia
1934	Eugene Mack, Switzerland
1938	Jan Gajdos, Czechoslovakia
1950	Walter Lehmann, Switzerland
1954	Valentin Mouratov, USSR Victor Chukarin, USSR
1958	Boris Shaklin, USSR
1962	Yuri Titov, USSR
1966	Mikhail Voronin, USSR
1970	Eizo Kenmotsu, Japan
1974	Shigeru Kasamatsu, Japan
1978	Nikolai Andrianov, USSR
1979	Alexander Ditiatin, USSR
1981	Yuri Korolev, USSR
1983	Dimitri Bilozertchev, USSR
1985	Yuri Korolev, USSR
1987	Dimitri Bilozertchev, USSR
1989	Igor Korobchinsky, USSR
1991	Grigori Misutin, CIS
1993	Vitaly Scherbo, Belarus
1994	Ivan Ivankov, Belarus
1995	Li Xiaoshuang, China
1997	Ivan Ivankov, Belarus
1999	Nicolae Krukov, Russia
2001	Feng Jing, China
2003	Paul Hamm, United States

Pommel Horse

Year	Champion, Nation
1930	Josip Primozic, Yugoslavia
1934	Eugene Mack, Switzerland
1938	Michael Reusch, Switzerland
1950	Josef Stalder, Switzerland
1954	Grant Chaguinjan, USSR
1958	Boris Shaklin, USSR
1962	Miroslav Cerar, Yugoslavia
1966	Miroslav Cerar, Yugoslavia
1970	Miroslav Cerar, Yugoslavia
1974	Zoltan Magyar, Hungary
1978	Zoltan Magyar, Hungary
1979	Zoltan Magyar, Hungary
1981	Michael Mikolai, East Germany
1983	Dmitri Bilozertchev, USSR
1985	Valentin Moguilny, USSR
1987	Zsolt Borkai, Hungary Dmitri Bilozertchev, USSR

World Champions (Cont.)

MEN (Cont.)

Pommel Horse (Cont.)

Year	Champion, Nation	Year	Champion, Nation	Year	Champion, Nation
1989	Valentin Moguilny, USSR	1993	Pae Gil Su, North Korea	1999	Alexei Nemov, Russia
1991	Valeri Belenki, USSR	1994	Marius Urzica, Romania	2001	Marius Urzica, Romania
1992	Pae Gil Su, North Korea	1995	Li Donghua, Switzerland	2003	Teng Haibin, China
	Vitaly Scherbo, CIS	1996	Pae Gil Su, North Korea		Takehiro Kashima, Japan
	Li Jing, China	1997	Valeri Belenki, Germany		

Floor Exercise

Year	Champion, Nation	Year	Champion, Nation	Year	Champion, Nation
1930	Josip Primozic, Yugoslavia	1974	Shigeru Kasamatsu, Japan	1993	Grigori Misutin, Ukraine
1934	Georges Miesz, Switzerland	1978	Kurt Thomas, United States	1994	Vitaly Scherbo, Belarus
1938	Jan Gajdos, Czechoslovakia	1979	Kurt Thomas, United States	1995	Vitaly Scherbo, Belarus
1950	Josef Stalder, Switzerland		Roland Brucker, GDR	1996	Vitaly Scherbo, Belarus
1954	Valentin Mouratov, USSR	1981	Yuri Korolev, USSR	1997	Alexei Nemov, Russia
	Masao Takemoto, Japan		Li Yuejui, Chi	1999	Alexei Nemov, Russia
1958	Masao Takemoto, Japan	1983	Tong Fei, China	2001	Marian Dragulescu, Rom
1962	Nobuyuki Aihara, Japan	1985	Tong Fei, China	2003	Paul Hamm, United States
	Yukio Endo, Japan	1987	Lou Yun, China		Jordan Jovtchev, Bulgaria
1966	Akinori Nakayama, Japan	1989	Igor Korobchinsky, USSR		
1970	Akinori Nakayama, Japan	1991	Igor Korobchinsky, USSR		

Rings

Year	Champion, Nation	Year	Champion, Nation	Year	Champion, Nation
1930	Emanuel Loffler, Czechoslovakia	1974	N. Andrianov, USSR	1992	Vitaly Scherbo, CIS
			D. Grecu, Rom.	1993	Yuri Chechi, Italy
1934	Alois Hudec, Czechoslovakia	1978	Nikolai Andrianov, USSR	1994	Yuri Chechi, Italy
1938	Alois Hudec, Czechoslovakia	1979	Alexander Ditiatin, USSR	1995	Yuri Chechi, Italy
1950	Walter Lehmann, Switzerland	1981	Alexander Ditiatin, USSR	1996	Yuri Chechi, Italy
		1983	Dimitri Bilozertchev, USSR	1997	Yuri Chechi, Italy
1954	Albert Azarian, USSR	1985	Li Ning, China	1999	Zhen Dong, China
1958	Albert Azarian, USSR		Yuri Korolev, USSR	2001	Jordan Jovtchev, Bulgaria
1962	Yuri Titov, USSR	1987	Yuri Korolev, USSR	2003	Jordan Jovtchev, Bulgaria
1966	Mikhail Voronin, USSR	1989	Andreas Aguilar, W Ger		Dimosthenis Tampakos, Greece
1970	Akinori Nakayama, Japan	1991	Grigory Misutin, USSR		

Parallel Bars

Year	Champion, Nation	Year	Champion, Nation	Year	Champion, Nation
1930	Josip Primozic, Yugoslavia	1979	Bart Conner, United States	1992	Li Jin, China
1934	Eugene Mack, Switzerland	1981	Koji Gushiken, Japan		Alexei Voropaev, CIS
1938	Michael Reusch, Switzerland		Alexandr Ditiatin, USSR	1993	Vitaly Scherbo, Belarus
1950	Hans Eugster, Switzerland	1983	Vladimir Artemov, USSR	1994	Huang Liping, China
1954	Victor Chukarin, USSR		Lou Yun, China	1995	Vitaly Scherbo, Belarus
1958	Boris Shaklin, USSR	1985	Sylvio Kroll, East Germany	1996	Rustam Sharipov, Ukraine
1962	Miroslav Cerar, Yugoslavia		Valentin Moguilny, USSR	1997	Zhang Jinjing, China
1966	Sergei Diamidov, USSR	1987	Vladimir Artemov, USSR	1999	Joo-Hyung Lee, S Korea
1970	Akinori Nakayama, Japan	1989	Li Jing, China	2001	Sean Townsend, U.S.
1974	Eizo Kenmotsu, Japan		Vladimir Artemov, USSR	2003	Li Xiao-Peng, China
1978	Eizo Kenmotsu, Japan	1991	Li Jing, China		

High Bar

Year	Champion, Nation	Year	Champion, Nation	Year	Champion, Nation
1930	Istvan Pelle, Hungary	1978	Shigeru Kasamatsu, Japan	1994	Vitaly Scherbo, Belarus
1934	Ernst Winter, Germany	1979	Kurt Thomas, United States	1995	Andreas Wecker, Germany
1938	Michael Reusch, Switzerland	1981	Alexander Takchev, USSR	1996	Jesús Carballo, Spain
1950	Paavo Aaltonen, Finland	1983	Dimitri Bilozertchev, USSR	1997	Jani Tanskanen, Finland
1954	Valentin Mouratov, USSR	1985	Tong Fei, China	1999	Jesus Carballo, Spain
1958	Boris Shaklin, USSR	1987	Dimitri Bilozertchev, USSR	2001	Vlasios Maras, Greece
1962	Takashi Ono, Japan	1989	Li Chunyang, China	2003	Takehiro Kashima, Japan
1966	Akinori Nakayama, Japan	1991	Li Chunyang, China		
1970	Eizo Kenmotsu, Japan		R. Buechner, Germ		
1974	Eberhard Gienger, West Germany	1992	Grigori Misutin, CIS		
		1993	Sergei Kharkov, Russia		

World Champions (Cont.)
MEN (Cont.)

Vault

Year	Champion, Nation	Year	Champion, Nation	Year	Champion, Nation
1934	Eugene Mack, Switzerland	1978	Junichi Shimizu, Japan	1992	Yoo Ok Youl, South Korea
1938	Eugene Mack, Switzerland	1979	Alexander Ditiatin, USSR	1993	Vitaly Scherbo, Belarus
1950	Ernst Gebendinger, Switzerland	1981	Ralf-Peter Hemmann, East Germany	1994	Vitaly Scherbo, Belarus
1954	Leo Sotornik, Czechoslovakia	1983	Arthur Akopian, USSR	1995	G. Misutin, Ukraine A. Nemov, Russia
1958	Yuri Titov, USSR	1985	Yuri Korolev, USSR	1996	Alexei Nemov, Russia
1962	Premysel Krbec, Czechoslovakia	1987	Lou Yun, China Sylvio Kroll, East Germany	1997	Sergei Fedorchenko, Kazakhstan
1966	Haruhiro Yamashita, Japan	1989	Joreg Behrend, East Germany	1999	Li Xiao-Peng, China
1970	Mitsuo Tsukahara, Japan			2001	Marian Dragulescu, Rom
1974	Shigeru Kasamatsu, Japan	1991	Yoo Ok Youl, South Korea	2003	Li Xiao-Peng, China

WOMEN

All-Around

Year	Champion, Nation	Year	Champion, Nation	Year	Champion, Nation
1934	Vlasta Dekanova, Czechoslovakia	1970	Ludmilla Tourischeva, USSR	1991	Kim Zmeskal, United States
1938	Vlasta Dekanova, Czechoslovakia	1974	Ludmilla Tourischeva, USSR	1993	Shannon Miller, United States
		1978	Elena Mukhina, USSR	1994	Shannon Miller, United States
1950	Helena Rakoczy, Poland	1979	Nelli Kim, USSR	1995	Lilia Podkopayeva, Ukraine
1954	Galina Roudiko, USSR	1981	Olga Bicherova, USSR	1997	Svetlana Khorkina, Russia
1958	Larissa Latynina, USSR	1983	Natalia Yurchenko, USSR	1999	Maria Olaru, Romania
1962	Larissa Latynina, USSR	1985	Elena Shoushounova, USSR Oksana Omeliantchik, USSR	2001	Svetlana Khorkina, Russia
1966	Vera Caslavska, Czechoslovakia	1987	Aurelia Dobre, Romania	2003	Svetlana Khorkina, Russia
		1989	Svetlana Bouguinskaia, USSR		

Floor Exercise

Year	Champion, Nation	Year	Champion, Nation	Year	Champion, Nation
1950	Helena Rakoczy, Poland	1979	Emilia Eberle, Romania	1992	Kim Zmeskal, United States
1954	Tamara Manina, USSR	1981	Natalia Ilenko, USSR	1993	Shannon Miller, United States
1958	Eva Bosakava, Czechoslovakia	1983	Ecaterina Szabo, Romania	1994	Dina Kochetkova, Russia
		1985	Oksana Omeliantchik, USSR	1995	Gina Gogean, Romania
1962	Larissa Latynina, USSR	1987	Elena Shoushounova, USSR Daniela Silivas, Romania	1996	Gina Gogean, Romania
1966	Natalia Kuchinskaya, USSR			1997	Gina Gogean, Romania
1970	Ludmilla Tourischeva, USSR	1989	Svetlana Bouguinskaia, USSR Daniela Silivas, Romania	1999	Andreea Raducan, Romania
1974	Ludmilla Tourischeva, USSR			2001	Andreea Raducan, Romania
1978	Nelli Kim, USSR Elena Mukhina, USSR	1991	Cristina Bontas, Romania Oksana Tchusovitina, USSR	2003	Daiane Dos Santos, Brazil

Uneven Bars

Year	Champion, Nation	Year	Champion, Nation	Year	Champion, Nation
1950	Gertchen Kolar, Austria Anna Pettersson, Sweden	1979	Ma Yanhong, China Maxi Gnauck, East Germany	1991	Gwang Suk Kim, North Korea
1954	Agnes Keleti, Hungary	1981	Maxi Gnauck, East Germany	1992	Lavinia Milosivici, Romania
1958	Larissa Latynina, USSR	1983	Maxi Gnauck, East Germany	1993	Shannon Miller, United States
1962	Irina Pervuschina, USSR	1985	Gabriele Fahrnich, East Germany	1994	Luo Li, China
1966	Natalia Kuchinskaya, USSR			1995	Svetlana Khorkina, Russia
1970	Karin Janz, East Germany	1987	Daniela Silivas, Romania Doerte Thuemmler, East Germany	1996	Svetlana Khorkina, Russia
1974	Annelore Zinke, East Germany			1997	Svetlana Khorkina, Russia
		1989	Fan Di, China Daniela Silivas, Romania	1999	Svetlana Khorkina, Russia
1978	Marcia Frederick, United States			2001	Svetlana Khorkina, Russia
				2003	Chellsie Memmel, U.S. Hollie Vise, United States

World Champions (Cont.)
WOMEN (Cont.)
Balance Beam

Year	Champion, Nation	Year	Champion, Nation	Year	Champion, Nation
1950	Helena Rakoczy, Poland	1981	Maxi Gnauck, East Germany	1995	Mo Huilan, China
1954	Keiko Tanaka, Japan	1983	Olga Mostepanova, USSR	1996	Dina Kochetkova, Russia
1958	Larissa Latynina, USSR	1985	Daniela Silivas, Romania	1997	Gina Gogean, Romania
1962	Eva Bosakova, Czech.	1987	Aurelia Dobre, Romania	1999	E. Zamolodchikova, Russia
1966	Natalia Kuchinskaya, USSR	1989	Daniela Silivas, Romania	2001	Andreea Raducan, Romania
1970	Erika Zuchold, East Germany	1991	Svetlana Boguinskaia, USSR	2003	Fan Ye, China
1974	Ludmilla Tourischeva, USSR	1992	Kim Zmeskal, United States		
1978	Nadia Comaneci, Romania	1993	Lavinia Milosovici, Romania		
1979	Vera Cerna, Czechoslovakia	1994	Shannon Miller, United States		

Vault

Year	Champion, Nation	Year	Champion, Nation	Year	Champion, Nation
1950	Helena Rakoczy, Poland	1981	Maxi Gnauck, East Germany	1995	L. Podkopayeva, Ukraine
1954	T. Manina, USSR	1983	Boriana Stoyanova, Bulgaria		Simona Amanar, Rom.
	Anna Pettersson, Sweden	1985	Elena Shoushounova, USSR	1996	Gina Gogean, Romania
1958	Larissa Latynina, USSR	1987	Elena Shoushounova, USSR	1997	Simona Amanar, Romania
1962	Vera Caslavska, Czech.	1989	Olesia Durnik, USSR	1999	Jie Ling, China
1966	Vera Caslavska, Czech.	1991	Lavinia Milosovici, Romania	2001	Svetlana Khorkina, Russia
1970	Erika Zuchold, East Germany	1992	Henrietta Onodi, Hungary	2003	Oksana Chusovitina,
1974	Olga Korbut, USSR	1993	Elena Piskun, Belarus		Uzbekistan
1978	Nelli Kim, USSR	1994	Gina Gogean, Romania		
1979	Dumitrita Turner, Romania				

National Champions
MEN
All-Around

Year	Champion	Year	Champion	Year	Champion
1963	Art Shurlock	1976	Kurt Thomas	1991	Chris Waller
1964	Rusty Mitchell	1977	Kurt Thomas	1992	John Roethlisberger
1965	Rusty Mitchell	1978	Kurt Thomas	1993	John Roethlisberger
1966	Rusty Mitchell	1979	Bart Conner	1994	Scott Keswick
1967	Katsuzoki Kanzaki	1980	Peter Vidmar	1995	John Roethlisberger
1968	Yoshi Hayasaki	1981	Jim Hartung	1996	Blaine Wilson
1969	Steve Hug	1982	Peter Vidmar	1997	Blaine Wilson
1970	Makoto Sakamoto	1983	Mitch Gaylord	1998	Blaine Wilson
	Mas Watanabe	1984	Mitch Gaylord	1999	Blaine Wilson
1971	Yoshi Takei	1985	Brian Babcock	2000	Blaine Wilson
1972	Yoshi Takei	1986	Tim Daggett	2001	Sean Townsend
1973	Marshall Avener	1987	Scott Johnson	2002	Paul Hamm
1974	John Crosby	1988	Dan Hayden	2003	Paul Hamm
1975	Tom Beach	1989	Tim Ryan	2004	Paul Hamm
	Bart Conner	1990	John Roethlisberger	2005	Todd Thornton

Floor Exercise

Year	Champion	Year	Champion	Year	Champion
1963	Tom Seward	1977	Ron Galimore	1991	Mike Racanelli
1964	Rusty Mitchell	1978	Kurt Thomas	1992	Gregg Curtis
1965	Rusty Mitchell	1979	Ron Galimore	1993	Kerry Huston
1966	Dan Millman	1980	Ron Galimore	1994	Jeremy Killen
1967	Katsuzoki Kanzaki	1981	Jim Hartung	1995	Daniel Stover
	Ron Aure	1982	Jim Hartung	1996	Jay Thornton
1968	Katsuzoki Kanzaki	1983	Mitch Gaylord	1997	Jason Gatson
1969	Steve Hug	1984	Peter Vidmar	1998	Jason Gatson
	Dave Thor	1985	Mark Oates	1999	Jason Gatson
1970	Makoto Sakamoto	1986	Robert Sundstrom	2000	Blaine Wilson
1971	John Crosby	1987	John Sweeney	2001	Sean Townsend
1972	Yoshi Takei	1988	Mark Oates	2002	Morgan Hamm
1973	John Crosby		Charles Lakes	2003	Morgan Hamm
1974	John Crosby	1989	Mike Racanelli	2004	Paul Hamm
1975	Peter Korman	1990	Bob Stelter	2005	Guillermo Alvarez

National Champions (Cont.)

MEN (Cont.)

Pommel Horse

Year	Champion	Year	Champion	Year	Champion
1963	Larry Spiegel	1978	Jim Hartung	1992	Chris Waller
1964	Sam Bailie	1979	Bart Conner	1993	Chris Waller
1965	Jack Ryan	1980	Jim Hartung	1994	Mihai Begiu
1966	Jack Ryan	1981	Jim Hartung	1995	Mark Sohn
1967	Paul Mayer/Dave Doty	1982	Jim Hartung	1996	Josh Stein
1968	Katsuoki Kanzaki	1983	Bart Conner	1997	John Roethlisberger
1969	Dave Thor	1984	Tim Daggett	1998	John Roethlisberger
1970	Mas Watanabe	1985	Phil Cahoy	1999	John Roethlisberger
1971	Leonard Caling	1986	Phil Cahoy	2000	John Roethlisberger
1972	Sadao Hamada	1987	Tim Daggett	2001	Brett McClure
1973	Marshall Avener	1988	Kevin Davis	2002	Paul Hamm
1974	Marshall Avener	1989	Kevin Davis	2003	Paul Hamm
1975	Bart Conner	1990	Patrick Kirksey	2004	Brett McClure
1977	Gene Whelan	1991	Chris Waller	2005	Yewki Tomita

Rings

Year	Champion	Year	Champion	Year	Champion
1963	Art Shurlock	1977	Kurt Thomas	1991	Scott Keswick
1964	Glen Gailis	1978	Mike Silverstein	1992	Tim Ryan
1965	Glen Gailis	1979	Bart Conner	1993	John Roethlisberger
1966	Glen Gailis	1980	Jim Hartung	1994	Scott Keswick
1967	Fred Dennis	1981	Jim Hartung	1995	Paul O'Neill
	Don Hatch	1982	Jim Hartung	1996	Kip Simons
1968	Yoshi Hayasaki		Peter Vidmar	1997	Blaine Wilson
1969	Fred Dennis	1983	Mitch Gaylord	1998	Jeff Johnson
	Bob Emery	1984	Jim Hartung	1999	Blaine Wilson
1970	Makoto Sakamoto	1985	Dan Hayden	2000	Blaine Wilson
1971	Yoshi Takei	1986	Dan Hayden	2001	Sean Townsend
1972	Yoshi Takei	1987	Scott Johnson	2002	Blaine Wilson
1973	Jim Ivicek	1988	Dan Hayden	2003	Blaine Wilson
1974	Tom Weeder	1989	Scott Keswick	2004	Raj Bhavsar
1975	Tom Beach	1990	Scott Keswick	2005	Sean Golden

Vault

Year	Champion	Year	Champion	Year	Champion
1963	Art Shurlock	1978	Jim Hartung	1991	Scott Keswick
1964	Gary Hery	1979	Ron Galimore	1992	Trent Dimas
1965	Brent Williams	1980	Ron Galimore	1993	Bill Roth
1966	Dan Millman	1981	Ron Galimore	1994	Keith Wiley
1967	Jack Kenan	1982	Jim Hartung/Jim Mikus	1995	David St. Pierre
	Sid Jensen	1983	Chris Reigel	1996	Blaine Wilson
1968	Rich Scorza	1984	Chris Reigel	1997	Blaine Wilson
1969	Dave Butzman	1985	Scott Johnson	1998	Brent Klaus
1970	Makoto Sakamoto		Mark Oates	1999	Guard Young
1971	Gary Morava	1986	Scott Wilbanks	2000	Blaine Wilson
1972	Mike Kelley	1987	John Sweeney	2001	Jason Furr
1973	Gary Morava	1988	John Sweeney/Bill Paul	2002	Paul Hamm
1974	John Crosby	1989	Bill Roth	2003	Raj Bhavsar
1975	Tom Beach	1990	Lance Ringnald	2004	David Sender
1977	Ron Galimore			2005	Sean Golden

Parallel Bars

Year	Champion	Year	Champion	Year	Champion
1963	Tom Seward	1971	Brent Simmons	1981	Bart Conner
1964	Rusty Mitchell	1972	Yoshi Takei	1982	Peter Vidmar
1965	Glen Gailis	1973	Marshall Avener	1983	Mitch Gaylord
1966	Ray Hadley	1974	Jim Ivicek	1984	Peter Vidmar
1967	Katsuzoki Kanzaki	1975	Bart Conner		Mitch Gaylord
	Tom Goldsborough	1977	Kurt Thomas		Tim Daggett
1968	Yoshi Hayasaki	1978	Bart Conner	1985	Tim Daggett
1969	Steve Hug	1979	Bart Conner	1986	Tim Daggett
1970	Makoto Sakamoto	1980	Phil Cahoy/Larry Gerard	1987	Scott Johnson

National Champions (Cont.)
MEN (Cont.)

Parallel Bars (Cont.)

Year	Champion	Year	Champion	Year	Champion
1988	D. Hayden/K. Davis	1994	Steve McCain	2000	Trent Wells
1989	Conrad Voorsanger	1995	John Roethlisberger	2001	Sean Townsend
1990	Trent Dimas	1996	Jair Lynch	2002	Sean Townsend
1991	Scott Keswick	1997	Blaine Wilson	2003	Jason Gatson
1992	Jair Lynch	1998	Blaine Wilson	2004	Alexander Artemev
1993	Chainey Umphrey	1999	Jason Gatson	2005	D.J. Bucher

High Bars

Year	Champion	Year	Champion	Year	Champion
1963	Art Shurlock	1979	Yoichi Tomita	1991	Lance Ringnald
1964	Glen Gailis	1980	Jim Hartung	1992	Jair Lynch
1965	Rusty Mitchell	1981	Bart Conner	1993	Steve McCain
1966	Katsuzoki Kanzaki	1982	Mitch Gaylord	1994	Scott Keswick
1967	Katsuzoki Kanzaki	1983	Mario McCutcheon	1995	John Roethlisberger
	Jerry Fontana	1984	Peter Vidmar	1996	Bill Roth
1968	Yoshi Hayasaki		Tim Daggett	1997	Douglas Stibel
1969	Rich Grisby		Mitch Gaylord	1998	Jason Gatson
1970	Makoto Sakamoto	1985	Dan Hayden	1999	Jamie Natalie
1971	Yoshi Takei	1986	D. Hayden/D. Moriel	2000	Trent Wells
1972	Tom Lindner	1987	David Moriel		Jamie Natalie
1973	John Crosby	1988	Dan Hayden	2001	Daniel Diaz-Luong
1974	Brent Simmons	1989	Tim Ryan	2002	Blaine Wilson
1975	Tom Beach	1990	Trent Dimas	2003	Paul Hamm
1977	Kurt Thomas		Lance Ringnald	2004	Paul Hamm
1978	Kurt Thomas			2005	D.J. Bucher

WOMEN

All-Around

Year	Champion	Year	Champion	Year	Champion
1963	Donna Schanezer	1977	Donna Turnbow	1993	Shannon Miller
1965	Gail Daley	1978	Kathy Johnson	1994	Dominique Dawes
1966	Donna Schanezer	1979	Leslie Pyfer	1995	Dominique Moceanu
1968	Linda Scott	1980	Julianne McNamara	1996	Shannon Miller
1969	Joyce Tanac	1981	Tracee Talavera	1997	V. Adler/ K. Powell
	Schroeder	1982	Tracee Talavera	1998	Kristen Maloney
1970	Cathy Rigby McCoy	1983	Dianne Durham	1999	Kristen Maloney
1971	Joan Moore Gnat	1984	Mary Lou Retton	2000	Elise Ray
	Linda Metheny	1985	Sabrina Mar	2001	Tasha Schwikert
	Mulvihill	1986	Jennifer Sey	2002	Tasha Schwikert
1972	Joan Moore Gnat	1987	Kristie Phillips	2003	Courtney Kupets
	Cathy Rigby McCoy	1988	Phoebe Mills	2004	Courtney Kupets/
1973	Joan Moore Gnat	1989	Brandy Johnson		Carly Patterson
1974	Joan Moore Gnat	1990	Kim Zmeskal	2005	Nastia Liukin
1975	Tammy Manville	1991	Kim Zmeskal		
1976	Denise Cheshire	1992	Kim Zmeskal		

Vault

Year	Champion	Year	Champion	Year	Champion
1963	Donna Schanezer	1976	Debbie Wilcox	1990	Brandy Johnson
1965	Gail Daley	1977	Lisa Cawthron	1991	Kerri Strug
1966	Donna Schanezer	1978	Rhonda Schwandt	1992	Kerri Strug
1968	Terry Spencer		Sharon Shapiro	1993	Dominique Dawes
1969	Joyce Tanac	1979	Christa Canary	1994	Dominique Dawes
	Schroeder	1980	J. McNamara/B. Kline	1995	Shannon Miller
	Cleo Carver	1981	Kim Neal	1996	Dominique Dawes
1970	Cathy Rigby McCoy	1982	Yumi Mordre	1997	Vanessa Atler
1971	Joan Moore Gnat	1983	Dianne Durham	1998	Dominique Moceanu
	Adele Gleaves	1984	Mary Lou Retton	1999	Vanessa Atler
1972	Cindy Eastwood	1985	Yolanda Mavity	2000	Kristen Maloney
1973	Roxanne Pierce	1986	Joyce Wilborn	2001	Mohini Bhardwaj
	Mancha	1987	Rhonda Faehn	2002	Elizabeth Tricase
1974	Dianne Dunbar	1988	Rhonda Faehn	2003	Annia Hatch
1975	Kolleen Casey	1989	Brandy Johnson	2004	Liz Tricase
				2005	Alicia Sacramone

National Champions (Cont.)

WOMEN (Cont.)

Uneven Bars

Year	Champion	Year	Champion	Year	Champion
1963	Donna Schanezer	1977	Donna Turnbow	1993	Shannon Miller
1965	Irene Haworth	1978	Marcia Frederick	1994	Dominique Dawes
1966	Donna Schanezer	1979	Marcia Frederick	1995	Dominique Dawes
1968	Linda Scott	1980	Marcia Frederick	1996	Dominique Dawes
1969	Joyce Tanac	1981	Julianne McNamara	1997	Kristy Powell
	Schroeder	1982	Marie Roethlisberger	1998	Elise Ray
	Lisa Nelson	1983	Julianne McNamara	1999	Jamie Dantzscher
1970	Roxanne Pierce	1984	Julianne McNamara		Jennie Thompson
	Mancha	1985	Sabrina Mar	2000	Elise Ray
1971	Joan Moore Gnat	1986	Marie Roethlisberger	2001	Katie Heenan
1972	Cathy Rigby McCoy	1987	Melissa Marlowe	2002	Tasha Schwikert
1973	Roxanne Pierce	1988	Chelle Stack	2003	Katie Heenan
	Mancha	1989	Chelle Stack	2004	Courtney Kupets
1974	Diane Dunbar	1990	Sandy Woolsey	2005	Nastia Liukin
1975	Leslie Wolfsberger	1991	Elisabeth Crandall		
1976	Leslie Wolfsberger	1992	Dominique Dawes		

Balance Beam

Year	Champion	Year	Champion	Year	Champion
1963	Leissa Krol	1979	Heidi Anderson	1993	Dominique Dawes
1965	Gail Daley	1980	Kelly Garrison-Steves	1994	Dominique Dawes
1966	Irene Haworth	1981	Tracee Talavera	1995	Doni Thompson
	Linda Scott	1982	Julianne McNamara		Monica Flammer
1968	Linda Scott	1983	Dianne Durham	1996	Dominique Dawes
1969	Lonna Woodward	1984	Pam Bileck	1997	Kendall Beck
1970	Joyce Tanac Schroeder		Tracee Talavera	1998	Dominique Moceanu
1971	Linda Metheny	1986	Angie Denkins	1999	Vanessa Atler
	Mulvihill	1987	Kristie Phillips	2000	Alyssa Beckerman
1972	Kim Chace	1985	Kelly Garrison-Steves		Amy Chow
1973	Nancy Thies Marshall	1988	Kelly Garrison-Steves	2001	Tasha Schwikert
1974	Joan Moore Gnat	1989	Brandy Johnson	2002	Tasha Schwikert
1975	Kyle Gayner	1990	Betty Okino	2003	Hollie Vise
1976	Carrie Englert	1991	Shannon Miller	2004	Courtney Kupets
1977	Donna Turnbow	1992	Kerri Strug	2005	Nastia Liukin
1978	Christa Canary		Kim Zmeskal		

Floor Exercise

Year	Champion	Year	Champion	Year	Champion
1963	Donna Schanezer	1979	Heidi Anderson	1993	Shannon Miller
1965	Gail Daley	1980	Beth Kline	1994	Dominique Dawes
1966	Donna Schanezer	1981	Michelle Goodwin	1995	Dominique Dawes
1968	Linda Scott	1982	Amy Koopman	1996	Dominique Dawes
1970	Cathy Rigby McCoy	1983	Dianne Durham	1997	Lindsay Wing
1971	Joan Moore Gnat	1984	Mary Lou Retton	1998	Vanessa Atler
	Linda Metheny	1985	Sabrina Mar	1999	Elise Ray
	Mulvihill	1986	Yolanda Mavity	2000	Kristen Maloney
1972	Joan Moore Gnat	1987	Kristie Phillips	2001	Tabitha Yim
1973	Joan Moore Gnat	1988	Phoebe Mills	2002	Tasha Schwikert
1974	Joan Moore Gnat	1989	Brandy Johnson	2003	Ashley Postell
1975	Kathy Howard	1990	Brandy Johnson	2004	Carly Patterson
1976	Carrie Englert	1991	Kim Zmeskal	2005	Alicia Sacramone
1977	Kathy Johnson		Dominique Dawes		
1978	Kathy Johnson	1992	Kim Zmeskal		

Handball

National Four-Wall Champions
MEN

1919.....Bill Ranft	1941.....Joe Platak	1963.....Oscar Obert	1985.....Naty Alvarado
1920.....Max Gold	1942.....Jack Clemente	1964.....Jimmy Jacobs	1986.....Naty Alvarado
1921.....Carl Haedge	1943.....Joe Platak	1965.....Jimmy Jacobs	1987.....Naty Alvarado
1922.....Art Shinners	1944.....Frank Coyle	1966.....Paul Haber	1988.....Naty Alvarado
1923.....Joe Murray	1945.....Joe Platak	1967.....Paul Haber	1989.....Poncho Monreal
1924.....Maynard Laswe	1946.....Angelo Trutio	1968.....Stuffy Singer	1990.....Naty Alvarado
1925.....Maynard Laswe	1947.....Gus Lewis	1969.....Paul Haber	1991.....John Bike
1926.....Maynard Laswe	1948.....Gus Lewis	1970.....Paul Haber	1992.....Octavio Silveyra
1927.....George Nelson	1949.....Vic Hershkowitz	1971.....Paul Haber	1993.....David Chapman
1928.....Joe Griffin	1950.....Ken Schneider	1972.....Fred Lewis	1994.....Octavio Silveyra
1929.....Al Banuet	1951.....Walter Plakan	1973.....Terry Muck	1995.....David Chapman
1930.....Al Banuet	1952.....Vic Hershkowitz	1974.....Fred Lewis	1996.....David Chapman
1931.....Al Banuet	1953.....Bob Brady	1975.....Fred Lewis	1997.....Octavio Silveyra
1932.....Angelo Trutio	1954.....Vic Hershkowitz	1976.....Fred Lewis	1998.....David Chapman
1933.....Sam Atcheson	1955.....Jimmy Jacobs	1977.....Naty Alvarado	1999.....David Chapman
1934.....Sam Atcheson	1956.....Jimmy Jacobs	1978.....Fred Lewis	2000.....David Chapman
1935.....Joe Platak	1957.....Jimmy Jacobs	1979.....Naty Alvarado	2001.....Vince Munoz
1936.....Joe Platak	1958.....John Sloan	1980.....Naty Alvarado	2002.....David Chapman
1937.....Joe Platak	1959.....John Sloan	1981.....Fred Lewis	2003.....John Bike
1938.....Joe Platak	1960.....Jimmy Jacobs	1982.....Naty Alvarado	2004.....David Chapman
1939.....Joe Platak	1961.....John Sloan	1983.....Naty Alvarado	2005.....Paul Brady
1940.....Joe Platak	1962.....Oscar Obert	1984.....Naty Alvarado	

WOMEN

1980.....Rosemary Bellini	1987.....Rosemary Bellini	1994.....Anna Engele	2000.....Priscilla Shumate
1981.....Rosemary Bellini	1988.....Rosemary Bellini	1995.....Anna Engele	2001.....Anna Christoff
1982.....Rosemary Bellini	1989.....Anna Engele	1996.....Anna Engele	2002.....Priscilla Shumate
1983.....Diane Harmon	1990.....Anna Engele	1997.....Lisa Fraser	2003.....Lisa Gilmore
1984.....Rosemary Bellini	1991.....Anna Engele	1998.....Lisa Fraser	2004.....Yvonne August
1985.....Peanut Motal	1992.....Lisa Fraser	1999.....Anna Christoff	2005.....Jennifer Schmitt
1986.....Peanut Motal	1993.....Anna Engele		

National Three-Wall Champions
MEN

1950.....Vic Hershkowitz	1964.....Marty Decatur	1978.....Fred Lewis	1992.....John Bike
1951.....Vic Hershkowitz	1965.....Carl Obert	1979.....Naty Alvarado	1993.....Eric Klarman
1952.....Vic Hershkowitz	1966.....Marty Decatur	1980.....Lou Russo	1994.....David Chapman
1953.....Vic Herskkowitz	1967.....Carl Obert	1981.....Naty Alvarado	1995.....David Chapman
1954.....Vic Hershkowitz	1968.....Marty Decatur	1982.....Naty Alvarado	1996.....Vince Munoz
1955.....Vic Hershkowitz	1969.....Marty Decatur	1983.....Naty Alvarado	1997.....Vince Munoz
1956.....Vic Hershkowitz	1970.....Steve August	1984.....Naty Alvarado	1998.....Vince Munoz
1957.....Vic Hershkowitz	1971.....Lou Russo	1985.....Vern Roberts	1999.....Vince Munoz
1958.....Vic Hershkowitz	1972.....Lou Russo	1986.....Vern Roberts	2000.....Vince Munoz
1959.....Jimmy Jacobs	1973.....Paul Haber	1987.....Vern Roberts	2001.....Vince Munoz
1960.....Jimmy Jacobs	1974.....Fred Lewis	1988.....Jon Kendler	2002.....Vince Munoz
1961.....Jimmy Jacobs	1975.....Lou Russo	1989.....John Bike	2003.....Vince Munoz
1962.....Oscar Obert	1976.....Lou Russo	1990.....Vince Munoz	2004.....Sean Lenning
1963.....Marty Decatur	1977.....Fred Lewis	1991.....John Bike	2005.....Vince Munoz

WOMEN

1981.....Allison Roberts	1988.....Rosemary Bellini	1995.....Allison Roberts	2002.....Priscilla Shumate
1982.....Allison Roberts	1989.....Rosemary Bellini	1996.....Anna Engele	2003.....Lisa Gilmore
1983.....Allison Roberts	1990.....Rosemary Bellini	1997.....Allison Roberts	2004.....Jennifer Schmitt
1984.....Rosemary Bellini	1991.....Rosemary Bellini	1998.....Anna Christoff	2005.....Megan Mehilos
1985.....Rosemary Bellini	1992.....Anna Engele	1999.....Allison Roberts	
1986.....Rosemary Bellini	1993.....Anna Engele	2000.....Priscilla Shumate	
1987.....Rosemary Bellini	1994.....Anna Engele	2001.....Anna Christoff	

World Four-Wall Champions

1984...................Merv Deckert, Canada		1994...................David Chapman, United States
1986...................Vern Roberts, United States		1997...................John Bike Jr., United States
1988...................Naty Alvarado, United States		2000...................David Chapman, United States
1991...................Pancho Monreal, United States		2003...................Paul Brady, Ireland

Lacrosse

United States Club Lacrosse Association Champions

1960 ......Mt. Washington Club	1976 ......Mt. Washington Club	1992 ......Maryland Lacrosse Club
1961 ......Baltimore Lacrosse Club	1977 ......Mt. Washington Club	1993 ......Mt. Washington Club
1962 ......Mt. Washington Club	1978 ......Long Island Athletic Club	1994 ......LI-Hofstra Lacrosse Club
1963 ......University Club	1979 ......Maryland Lacrosse Club	1995 ......Mt. Washington Club
1964 ......Mt. Washington Club	1980 ......Long Island Athletic Club	1996 ......LI-Hofstra Lacrosse Club
1965 ......Mt. Washington Club	1981 ......Long Island Athletic Club	1997 ......LI-Hofstra Lacrosse Club
1966 ......Mt. Washington Club	1982 ......Maryland Lacrosse Club	1998 ......LI-Hofstra Lacrosse Club
1967 ......Mt. Washington Club	1983 ......Maryland Lacrosse Club	1999 ......New York Athletic Club
1968 ......Long Island Athletic Club	1984 ......Maryland Lacrosse Club	2000 ......Team Toyota (Baltimore)
1969 ......Long Island Athletic Club	1985 ......LI-Hofstra Lacrosse Club	2001 ......LI Lacrosse Club
1970 ......Long Island Athletic Club	1986 ......LI-Hofstra Lacrosse Club	2002 ......Single Source Solutions
1971 ......Long Island Athletic Club	1987 ......LI-Hofstra Lacrosse Club	2003 ......Single Source Solutions
1972 ......Carling	1988 ......Maryland Lacrosse Club	2004 ......Single Source Solutions
1973 ......Long Island Athletic Club	1989 ......LI-Hofstra Lacrosse Club	2005 ......Team Source (Annapolis)
1974 ......Long Island Athletic Club	1990 ......Mt. Washington Club	
1975 ......Mt. Washington Club	1991 ......Mt. Washington Club	

National Lacrosse League Champions*

1987 ......Baltimore Thunder	1994 ......Philadelphia Wings	2001 ......Philadelphia Wings
1988 ......New Jersey Saints	1995 ......Philadelphia Wings	2002 ......Toronto Rock
1989 ......Philadelphia Wings	1996 ......Buffalo Bandits	2003 ......Toronto Rock
1990 ......Philadelphia Wings	1997 ......Rochester Knighthawks	2004 ......Calgary Roughnecks
1991 ......Detroit Turbos	1998 ......Philadelphia Wings	2005 ......Toronto Rock
1992 ......Buffalo Bandits	1999 ......Toronto Rock	
1993 ......Buffalo Bandits	2000 ......Toronto Rock	

*Indoor league formerly known as the Eagle Pro Box Lacrosse League, and the Major Indoor Lacrosse League.

Major League Lacrosse

2001 .....Long Island Lizards	2003 .....Long Island Lizards	2005 .....Baltimore Bayhawks
2002 .....Baltimore Bayhawks	2004 .....Philadelphia Barrage	

Little League Baseball

Little League World Series Champions

Year	Champion	Runner-Up	Score	Year	Champion	Runner-Up	Score
1947	Williamsport, PA	Lock Haven, PA	16–7	1977	Kao-Hsuing, Taiwan	El Cajun, CA	7–2
1948	Lock Haven, PA	St. Petersburg, FL	6–5	1978	Pin-Tung, Taiwan	Danville, CA	11–1
1949	Hammonton, NJ	Pensacola, FL	5–0	1979	Hsien, Taiwan	Campbell, CA	2–1
1950	Houston, TX	Bridgeport, CT	2–1	1980	Hua Lian, Taiwan	Tampa, FL	4–3
1951	Stamford, CT	Austin, TX	3–0	1981	Tai-Chung, Taiwan	Tampa, FL	4–2
1952	Norwalk, CT	Monongahela, PA	4–3	1982	Kirkland, WA	Hsien, Taiwan	6–0
1953	Birmingham, AL	Schenectady, NY	1–0	1983	Marietta, GA	Barahona, D.Rep.	3–1
1954	Schenectady, NY	Colton, CA	7–5	1984	Seoul, S. Korea	Altamonte Sgs, FL	6–2
1955	Morrisville, PA	Merchantville, NJ	4–3	1985	Seoul, S. Korea	Mexicali, Mex.	7–1
1956	Roswell, NM	Merchantville, NJ	3–1	1986	Tainan Park, Taiwan	Tucson, AZ	12–0
1957	Monterrey, Mex.	LaMesa, CA	4–0	1987	Hua Lian, Taiwan	Irvine, CA	21–1
1958	Monterrey, Mex.	Kankakee, IL	10–1	1988	Tai-Chung, Taiwan	Pearl City, HI	10–0
1959	Hamtramck, MI	Auburn, CA	12–0	1989	Trumbull, CT	Kaohsiung, Taiwan	5–2
1960	Levittown, PA	Ft. Worth, TX	5–0	1990	Taipei, Taiwan	Shippensburg, PA	9–0
1961	El Cajon, CA	El Campo, TX	4–2	1991	Tai-Chung, Taiwan	San Ramon Vly, CA	11–0
1962	San Jose, CA	Kankakee, IL	3–0	1992*	Long Beach, CA	Zamboanga, Phil.	6–0
1963	Granada Hills, CA	Stratford, CT	2–1	1993	Long Beach, CA	David Chiriqui, Pan.	3–2
1964	Staten Island, NY	Monterrey, Mex.	4–0	1994	Maracaibo, Venez.	Northridge, CA	4–3
1965	Windsor Locks, CT	Stoney Creek, Can.	3–1	1995	Tainan, Taiwan	Sprint, TX	17–3
1966	Houston, TX	W. New York, NJ	8–2	1996	Kao-Hsuing, Taiwan	Cranston, RI	13–3
1967	West Tokyo, Japan	Chicago, IL	4–1	1997	Guadalupe, Mex.	Mission Viejo, CA	5–4
1968	Osaka, Japan	Richmond, VA	1–0	1998	Toms River, NJ	Kashima, Japan	12–9
1969	Taipei, Taiwan	Santa Clara, CA	5–0	1999	Osaka, Japan	Phenix City, AL	5–0
1970	Wayne, NJ	Campbell, CA	2–0	2000	Maracaibo, Venez.	Bellaire, TX	3–2
1971	Tainan, Taiwan	Gary, IN	12–3	2001	Tokyo, Japan	Apopka, FL	2–1
1972	Taipei, Taiwan	Hammond, IN	6–0	2002	Louisville, KY	Sendai, Japan	1–0
1973	Tainan City, Taiwan	Tucson, AZ	12–0	2003	Tokyo, Japan	Boynton Beach, FL	10–1
1974	Kao-Hsuing, Taiwan	El Cajun, CA	7–2	2004	Willemstad, Curacao	Thousand Oaks, CA	5–2
1975	Lakewood, NJ	Tampa, FL	4–3	2005	West Oahu, Hawaii	Willemstad, Curacao	7-6
1976	Tokyo, Japan	Campbell, CA	10–3				

*Long Beach declared a 6–0 winner after the international tournament committee determined that Zamboanga City had used players that were not within its city limits.

Motor Boat Racing

American Boat Racing Association Gold Cup Champions

Year	Boat	Driver	Avg MPH	Year	Boat	Driver	Avg MPH
1904	Standard (June)	Carl Riotte	23.160	1956	Miss Thriftaway	Bill Muncey	96.552
1904	Vingt-et-Un II (Sep)	W. Sharpe Kilmer	24.900	1957	Miss Thriftaway	Bill Muncey	101.787
1905	Chip I	J. Wainwright	15.000	1958	Hawaii Kai III	Jack Regas	103.000
1906	Chip II	J. Wainwright	25.000	1959	Maverick	Bill Stead	104.481
1907	Chip II	J. Wainwright	23.903	1960	No race	—	—
1908	Dixie II	E.J. Schroeder	29.938	1961	Miss Century 21	Bill Muncey	99.678
1909	Dixie II	E.J. Schroeder	29.590	1962	Miss Century 21	Bill Muncey	100.710
1910	Dixie III	F.K. Burnham	32.473	1963	Miss Bardahl	Ron Musson	105.124
1911	MIT II	J.H. Hayden	37.000	1964	Miss Bardahl	Ron Musson	103.433
1912	P.D.Q. II	A.G. Miles	39.462	1965	Miss Bardahl	Ron Musson	103.132
1913	Ankle Deep	Cas Mankowski	42.779	1966	Tahoe Miss	Mira Slovak	93.019
1914	Baby Speed Demon II	Jim Blackton & Bob Edgren	48.458	1967	Miss Bardahl	Bill Shumacher	101.484
				1968	Miss Bardahl	Bill Shumacher	108.173
1915	Miss Detroit	Johnny Milot & Jack Beebe	37.656	1969	Miss Budweiser	Bill Sterett	98.504
				1970	Miss Budweiser	Dean Chenoweth	99.562
1916	Miss Minneapolis	Bernard Smith	48.860				
1917	Miss Detroit II	Gar Wood	54.410	1971	Miss Madison	Jim McCormick	98.043
1918	Miss Detroit II	Gar Wood	51.619	1972	Atlas Van Lines	Bill Muncey	104.277
1919	Miss Detroit III	Gar Wood	42.748	1973	Miss Budweiser	Dean Chenoweth	99.043
1920	Miss America I	Gar Wood	62.022				
1921	Miss America I	Gar Wood	52.825	1974	Pay 'n Pak	George Henley	104.428
1922	Packard Chriscraft	J.G. Vincent	40.253	1975	Pay 'n Pak	George Henley	108.921
1923	Packard Chriscraft	Caleb Bragg	43.867	1976	Miss U.S.	Tom D'Eath	100.412
1924	Baby Bootlegger	Caleb Bragg	45.302	1977	Atlas Van Lines	Bill Muncey	111.822
1925	Baby Bootlegger	Caleb Bragg	47.240	1978	Atlas Van Lines	Bill Muncey	111.412
1926	Greenwich Folly	George Townsend	47.984	1979	Atlas Van Lines	Bill Muncey	100.765
				1980	Miss Budweiser	Dean Chenoweth	106.932
1927	Greenwich Folly	George Townsend	47.662	1981	Miss Budweiser	Dean Chénoweth	116.932
1928	No race						
1929	Imp	Richard Hoyt	48.662	1982	Atlas Van Lines	Chip Hanauer	120.050
1930	Hotsy Totsy	Vic Kliesrath	52.673	1983	Atlas Van Lines	Chip Hanauer	118.507
1931	Hotsy Totsy	Vic Kliesrath	53.602	1984	Atlas Van Lines	Chip Hanauer	130.175
1932	Delphine IV	Bill Horn	57.775	1985	Miller American	Chip Hanauer	120.643
1933	El Lagarto	George Reis	56.260	1986	Miller American	Chip Hanauer	116.523
1934	El Lagarto	George Reis	55.000	1987	Miller American	Chip Hanauer	127.620
1935	El Lagarto	George Reis	55.056	1988	Miss Circus Circus	Chip Hanauer & Jim Prevost	123.756
1936	Impshi	Kaye Don	45.735				
1937	Notre Dame	Clell Perry	63.675	1989	Miss Budweiser	Tom D'Eath	131.209
1938	Alagi	Theo Rossi	64.340	1990	Miss Budweiser	Tom D'Eath	143.176
1939	My Sin	Z.G. Simmons Jr.	66.133	1991	Winston Eagle	Mark Tate	137.771
1940	Hotsy Totsy III	Sidney Allen	48.295	1992	Miss Budweiser	Chip Hanauer	136.282
1941	My Sin	Z.G. Simmons Jr.	52.509	1993	Miss Budweiser	Chip Hanauer	141.195
1942–45		No race	—	1994	Smokin' Joe Camel	Mark Tate	145.260
1946	Tempo VI	Guy Lombardo	68.132	1995	Miss Budweiser	Chip Hanauer	149.160
1947	Miss Peps V	Danny Foster	57.000	1996	PICO American Dream	Dave Villwock	149.328
1948	Miss Great Lakes	Danny Foster	46.845	1997	Miss Budweiser	Dave Villwock	129.366
1949	My Sweetie	Bill Cantrell	73.612	1998	Miss Budweiser	Dave Villwock	140.309
1950	Slo-Mo-Shun IV	Ted Jones	78.216	1999	Miss PICO	Chip Hanauer	152.591
1951	Slo-Mo-Shun V	Lou Fageol	90.871	2000	Miss Budweiser	Dave Villwock	162.850
1952	Slo-Mo-Shun IV	Stan Dollar	79.923	2001	Miss Tubby's Subs	Michael Hanson	140.519
1953	Slo-Mo-Shun IV	Joe Taggart & Lou Fageol	99.108	2002	Miss Budweiser	Dave Villwock	143.093
				2003	Miss Fox Hills	Mitch Evans	144.152
1954	Slo-Mo-Shun IV	Joe Taggart & Lou Fageol	92.613	2004	Miss Detroit Yacht Club	Nate Brown	141.195
1955	Gale V	Lee Schoenith	99.552	2005	Miss Al Deeby Dodge	Terry Troxell	142.448

Hydro-Prop* Annual Champion Drivers

Year	Driver	Boat	Wins	Year	Driver	Boat	Wins
1947	Danny Foster	Miss Peps V	6	1977	Mickey Remund	Miss Budweiser	3
1948	Dan Arena	Such Crust	2	1978	Bill Muncey	Atlas Van Lines	6
1949	Bill Cantrell	My Sweetie	7	1979	Bill Muncey	Atlas Van Lines	7
1950	Dan Foster	Such Crust/DaphneX	2	1980	Dean Chenoweth	Miss Budweiser	5
1951	Chuck Thompson	Miss Pepsi	5	1981	Dean Chenoweth	Miss Budweiser	6
1952	Chuck Thompson	Miss Pepsi	3	1982	Chip Hanauer	Atlas Van Lines	5
1953	Lee Schoenith	Gale II	1	1983	Chip Hanauer	Atlas Van Lines	3
1954	Lee Schoenith	Gale V	4	1984	Jim Kropfeld	Miss Budweiser	6
1955	Lee Schoenith	Gale V/Wha Hoppen	1	1985	Chip Hanauer	Miller American	5
1956	Russ Schleeh	Shanty I	3	1986	Jim Kropfeld	Miss Budweiser	3
1957	Jack Regas	Hawaii Kai III	5	1987	Jim Kropfeld	Miss Budweiser	5
1958	Mira Slovak	Bardah/Miss Buren	5	1988	Tom D'Eath	Miss Budweiser	4
1959	Bill Stead	Maverick	5	1989	Chip Hanauer	Miss Circus Circus	3
1960	Bill Muncey	Miss Thriftway	4	1990	Chip Hanauer	Miss Circus Circus	6
1961	Bill Muncey	Miss Century 21	4	1991	Mark Tate	Winston/Oberto	3
1962	Bill Muncey	Miss Century 21	5	1992	Chip Hanauer	Miss Budweiser	7
1963	Bill Cantrell	Gale V	0	1993	Chip Hanauer	Miss Budweiser	7
1964	Ron Musson	Miss Bardahl	4	1994	Mark Tate	Smokin' Joe Camel	5
1965	Ron Musson	Miss Bardahl	4	1995	Mark Tate	Smokin' Joe Camel	4
1966	Mira Slovak	Tahoe Miss	4	1996	Dave Villwock	PICO American Dream	6
1967	Bill Schumacher	Miss Bardahl	6	1997	Mark Tate	Close Call	1
1968	Bill Schumacher	Miss Bardahl	4	1998	Dave Villwock	Miss Budweiser	8
1969	Bill Sterett Sr.	Miss Budweiser	4	1999	Dave Villwock	Miss Budweiser	8
1970	Dean Chenoweth	Miss Budweiser	4	2000	Dave Villwock	Miss Budweiser	6
1971	Dean Chenoweth	Miss Budweiser	2	2001	Dave Villwock	Miss Budweiser	1
1972	Bill Muncey	Atlas Van Lines	6	2002	Dave Villwock	Miss Budweiser	3
1973	Mickey Remund	Pay 'n Pak	4	2003	Dave Villwock	Miss Budweiser	2
1974	George Henley	Pay 'n Pak	7	2004	Dave Villwock	Miss Budweiser	2
1975	Billy Schumacher	Weisfield's	2	2005	Steve David	Miss Madison	0
1976	Bill Muncey	Atlas Van Lines	5				

Hydro-Prop* Annual Champion Boats

Year	Boat	Owner	Wins	Year	Boat	Owner	Wins
1970	Miss Budweiser	Little-Friedkin	4	1988	Miss Budweiser	Bernie Little	4
1971	Miss Budweiser	Little-Friedkin	2	1989	Miss Budweiser	Bernie Little	4
1972	Atlas Van Lines	Joe Schoenith	6	1990	Miss Circus Circus	Bill Bennett	6
1973	Pay 'n Pak	Dave Heerensperger	4	1991	Miss Budweiser	Bernie Little	4
1974	Pay 'n Pak	Dave Heerensperger	7	1992	Miss Budweiser	Bernie Little	7
1975	Pay 'n Pak	Dave Heerensperger	5	1993	Miss Budweiser	Bernie Little	7
1976	Atlas Van Lines	Bill Muncey	5	1994	Miss Budweiser	Bernie Little	4
1977	Miss Budweiser	Bernie Little	3	1995	Miss Budweiser	Bernie Little	5
1978	Atlas Van Lines	Bill Muncey	6	1996	PICO Amer. Dream	Fred Leland	6
1979	Atlas Van Lines	Bill Muncey	7	1997	Miss Budweiser	Bernie Little	5
1980	Miss Budweiser	Bernie Little	5	1998	Miss Budweiser	Bernie Little	8
1981	Miss Budweiser	Bernie Little	6	1999	Miss Budweiser	Bernie Little	8
1982	Atlas Van Lines	Fran Muncey	5	2000	Miss Budweiser	Bernie Little	6
1983	Atlas Van Lines	Muncey-Lucero	3	2001	Miss Budweiser	Bernie Little	1
1984	Miss Budweiser	Bernie Little	6	2002	Miss Budweiser	Bernie Little	3
1985	Miller American	Muncey-Lucero	5	2003	Miss Budweiser	Joe Little	2
1986	Miss Budweiser	Bernie Little	3	2004	Miss Budweiser	Joe Little	2
1987	Miss Budweiser	Bernie Little	5	2005	Miss Elam	Erick Ellstrom	3

*Formerly known as Unlimited Hydroplane Racing Association.

Polo

United States Open Polo Champions

1904	Wanderers	1935	Greentree	1963	Tulsa	1986	Retama II
1905–09	Not contested	1936	Greentree	1964	Concar Oak Brook	1987	Aloha
1910	Ranelagh	1937	Old Westbury	1965	Oak Brook–Santa Barbara	1988	Les Diables Bleus
1911	Not contested	1938	Old Westbury	1966	Tulsa	1989	Les Diables Bleus
1912	Cooperstown	1939	Bostwick Field	1967	Bunntyco–Oak Brook	1990	Les Diables Bleus
1913	Cooperstown	1940	Aknusti	1968	Midland	1991	Grant's Farm Manor
1914	Meadow Brook Magpies	1941	Gulf Stream	1969	Tulsa Greenhill	1992	Hanalei Bay
1915	Not contested	1942–45	Not contested	1970	Tulsa Greenhill	1993	Gehache
1916	Meadow Brook	1946	Mexico	1971	Oak Brook	1994	Aspen
1917–18	Not contested	1947	Old Westbury	1972	Milwaukee	1995	Outback
1919	Meadow Brook	1948	Hurricanes	1973	Oak Brook	1996	Outback
1920	Meadow Brook	1949	Hurricanes	1974	Milwaukee	1997	Isla Carroll
1921	Great Neck	1950	Bostwick	1975	Milwaukee	1998	Esque
1922	Argentine	1951	Milwaukee	1976	Willow Bend	1999	Outback
1923	Meadow Brook	1952	Beverly Hills	1977	Retama	2000	Outback
1924	Midwick	1953	Meadow Brook	1978	Abercrombie & Kent	2001	Outback
1925	Orange County	1954	C.C.C.–Meadow Brook	1979	Retama	2002	Team Coca Cola
1926	Hurricanes	1955	C.C.C.	1980	Southern Hills	2003	C Spear
1927	Sands Point	1956	Brandywine	1981	Rolex A & K	2004	Isla Carroll
1928	Meadow Brook	1957	Detroit	1982	Retama	2005	White Birch
1929	Hurricanes	1958	Dallas	1983	Ft. Lauderdale		
1930	Hurricanes	1959	Circle F	1984	Retama		
1931	Santa Paula	1960	Oak Brook–C.C.C.	1985	Carter Ranch		
1932	Templeton	1961	Milwaukee				
1933	Aurora	1962	Santa Barbara				
1934	Templeton						

Top-Ranked Players

The United States Polo Association ranks its registered players from minus 2 to plus 10 goals, with 10-Goal players being the game's best. At present, the USPA recognizes eleven 10-Goal and twelve 9-Goal players:

10-GOAL	9-GOAL
Mariano Aguerre	Eduardo Novillo Astrada
Miguel Novillo Astrada	Francisco Bensadon
Javier Novillo Astrada	Lucas A. Criado
Michael Vincent Azzaro	Francisco de Narvaez
Adolfo Cambiaso	Melo E. Fernandez-Araujo
Carlos Gracida	Guillermo M. Gracida Jr.
Bautista Heguy	Eduardo Heguy
Marcos Heguy	Matias G. Magrini
Juan Ignacio Merlos	Agustin Merlos
Sebastian Merlos	Pablo MacDonough
Adam Snow	Facundo Pieres
	Gonzalo Pieres Jr.

YET ANOTHER SIGN OF THE APOCALYPSE

A Pennsylvania T-ball coach allegedly paid one of his players $25 to bean an autistic teammate to keep him out of a game.

Professional Rodeo Cowboys Association World Champions

All-Around

1929....Earl Thode	1950....Bill Linderman	1969....Larry Mahan	1988....Dave Appleton
1930....Clay Carr	1951....Casey Tibbs	1970....Larry Mahan	1989....Ty Murray
1931....John Schneider	1952....Harry Tompkins	1971....Phil Lyne	1990....Ty Murray
1932....Donald Nesbit	1953....Bill Linderman	1972....Phil Lyne	1991....Ty Murray
1933....Clay Carr	1954....Buck Rutherford	1973....Larry Mahan	1992....Ty Murray
1934....Leonard Ward	1955....Casey Tibbs	1974....Tom Ferguson	1993....Ty Murray
1935....Everett Bowman	1956....Jim Shoulders	1975....Tom Ferguson	1994....Ty Murray
1936....John Bowman	1957....Jim Shoulders	1976....Tom Ferguson	1995....Joe Beaver
1937....Everett Bowman	1958....Jim Shoulders	1977....Tom Ferguson	1996....Joe Beaver
1938....Burel Mulkey	1959....Jim Shoulders	1978....Tom Ferguson	1997....Dan Mortensen
1939....Paul Carney	1960....Harry Tompkins	1979....Tom Ferguson	1998....Ty Murray
1940....Fritz Truan	1961....Benny Reynolds	1980....Paul Tierney	1999....Fred Whitfield
1941....Homer Pettigrew	1962....Tom Nesmith	1981....Jimmie Cooper	2000....Joe Beaver
1942....Gerald Roberts	1963....Dean Oliver	1982....Chris Lybbert	2001....Cody Ohl
1943....Louis Brooks	1964....Dean Oliver	1983....Roy Cooper	2002....Trevor Brazile
1944....Louis Brooks	1965....Dean Oliver	1984....Dee Picket	2003....Trevor Brazile
1947....Todd Whatley	1966....Larry Mahan	1985....Lewis Feild	2004....Trevor Brazile
1948....Gerald Roberts	1967....Larry Mahan	1986....Lewis Feild	
1949....Jim Shoulders	1968....Larry Mahan	1987....Lewis Feild	

Saddle Bronc Riding

1929....Earl Thode	1950....Bill Linderman	1969....Bill Smith	1988....Clint Johnson
1930....Clay Carr	1951....Casey Tibbs	1970....Dennis Reiners	1989....Clint Johnson
1931....Earl Thode	1952....Casey Tibbs	1971....Bill Smith	1990....Robert Etbauer
1932....Peter Knight	1953....Casey Tibbs	1972....Mel Hyland	1991....Robert Etbauer
1933....Peter Knight	1954....Casey Tibbs	1973....Bill Smith	1992....Billy Etbauer
1934....Leonard Ward	1955....Deb Copenhaver	1974....John McBeth	1993....Dan Mortensen
1935....Peter Knight	1956....Deb Copenhaver	1975....Monty Henson	1994....Dan Mortensen
1936....Peter Knight	1957....Alvin Nelson	1976....Monty Henson	1995....Dan Mortensen
1937....Burel Mulkey	1958....Marty Wood	1977....Bobby Berger	1996....Billy Etbauer
1938....Burel Mulkey	1959....Casey Tibbs	1978....Joe Marvel	1997....Dan Mortensen
1939....Fritz Truan	1960....Enoch Walker	1979....Bobby Berger	1998....Dan Mortensen
1940....Fritz Truan	1961....Winston Bruce	1980....Clint Johnson	1999....Billy Etbauer
1941....Doff Aber	1962....Kenny McLean	1981....B. Gjermundson	2000....Billy Etbauer
1942....Doff Aber	1963....Guy Weeks	1982....Monty Henson	2001....Tom Reeves
1943....Louis Brooks	1964....Marty Wood	1983....B. Gjermundson	2002....Glen O'Neil
1944....Louis Brooks	1965....Shawn Davis	1984....B. Gjermundson	2003:...Dan Mortensen
1947....Carl Olson	1966....Marty Wood	1985....B. Gjermundson	2004....Billy Etbauer
1948....Gene Pruett	1967....Shawn Davis	1986....Bud Munroe	
1949....Casey Tibbs	1968....Shawn Davis	1987....Clint Johnson	

Bareback Riding

1932....Smoky Snyder	1953....Eddy Akridge	1972....Joe Alexander	1991....Clint Corey
1933....Nate Waldrum	1954....Eddy Akridge	1973....Joe Alexander	1992....Wayne Herman
1934....Leonard Ward	1955....Eddy Akridge	1974....Joe Alexander	1993....Deb Greenough
1935....Frank Schneider	1956....Jim Shoulders	1975....Joe Alexander	1994....Marvin Garrett
1936....Smoky Snyder	1957....Jim Shoulders	1976....Joe Alexander	1995....Marvin Garrett
1937....Paul Carney	1958....Jim Shoulders	1977....Joe Alexander	1996....Mark Garrett
1938....Pete Grubb	1959....Jack Buschbom	1978....Bruce Ford	1997....Eric Mouton
1939....Paul Carney	1960....Jack Buschbom	1979....Bruce Ford	1998....Mark Gomes
1940....Carl Dossey	1961....Eddy Akridge	1980....Bruce Ford	1999....Lan LaJeunesse
1941....George Mills	1962....Ralph Buell	1981....J.C. Trujillo	2000....Jeffrey Collins
1942....Louis Brooks	1963....John Hawkins	1982....Bruce Ford	2001....Lan LaJeunesse
1943....Bill Linderman	1964....Jim Houston	1983....Bruce Ford	2002....Bobby Mote
1944....Louis Brooks	1965....Jim Houston	1984....Larry Peabody	2003....Will Lowe
1947....Larry Finley	1966....Paul Mayo	1985....Lewis Feild	2004....Kelly Timberman
1948....Sonny Tureman	1967....Clyde Vamvoras	1986....Lewis Feild	
1949....Jack Buschbom	1968....Clyde Vamvoras	1987....Bruce Ford	
1950....Jim Shoulders	1969....Gary Tucker	1988....Marvin Garrett	
1951....Casey Tibbs	1970....Paul Mayo	1989....Marvin Garrett	
1952....Harry Tompkins	1971....Joe Alexander	1990....Chuck Logue	

Professional Rodeo Cowboys Association World Champions (Cont.)

Bull Riding

1929....John Schneider	1948....Harry Tompkins	1967....Larry Mahan	1986....Tuff Hedeman
1930....John Schneider	1949....Harry Tompkins	1968....George Paul	1987....Lane Frost
1931....Smokey Snyder	1950....Harry Tompkins	1969....Doug Brown	1988....Jim Sharp
1932....John Schneider	1951....Jim Shoulders	1970....Gary Leffew	1989....Tuff Hedeman
1932....Smokey Snyder	1952....Harry Tompkins	1971....Bill Nelson	1990....Jim Sharp
John Schneider	1953....Todd Whatley	1972....John Quintana	1991....Tuff Hedeman
1933....Frank Schneider	1954....Jim Shoulders	1973....Bobby Steiner	1992....Cody Custer
1934....Frank Schneider	1955....Jim Shoulders	1974....Don Gay	1993....Ty Murray
1935....Smokey Snyder	1956....Jim Shoulders	1975....Don Gay	1994....Daryl Mills
1936....Smokey Snyder	1957....Jim Shoulders	1976....Don Gay	1995....Jerome Davis
1937....Smokey Snyder	1958....Jim Shoulders	1977....Don Gay	1996....Terry West
1938....Kid Fletcher	1959....Jim Shoulders	1978....Don Gay	1997....Scott Mendes
1939....Dick Griffith	1960....Harry Tompkins	1979....Don Gay	1998....Ty Murray
1940....Dick Griffith	1961....Ronnie Rossen	1980....Don Gay	1999....Mike White
1941....Dick Griffith	1962....Freckles Brown	1981....Don Gay	2000....Cody Hancock
1942....Dick Griffith	1963....Bill Kornell	1982....Charles Sampson	2001....Blue Stone
1943....Ken Roberts	1964....Bob Wegner	1983....Cody Snyder	2002....Blue Stone
1944....Ken Roberts	1965....Larry Mahan	1984....Don Gay	2003....Terry West
1947....Wag Blessing	1966....Ronnie Rossen	1985....Ted Nuce	2004....Dustin Elliott

Calf Roping

1929....Everett Bowman	1950....Toots Mansfield	1969....Dean Oliver	1988....Joe Beaver
1930....Jake McClure	1951....Don McLaughlin	1970....Junior Garrison	1989....Rabe Rabon
1931....Herb Meyers	1952....Don McLaughlin	1971....Phil Lyne	1990....Troy Pruitt
1932....Richard Merchant	1953....Don McLaughlin	1972....Phil Lyne	1991....Fred Whitfield
1933....Bill McFarlane	1954....Don McLaughlin	1973....Ernie Taylor	1992....Joe Beaver
1934....Irby Mundy	1955....Dean Oliver	1974....Tom Ferguson	1993....Joe Beaver
1935....Everett Bowman	1956....Ray Wharton	1975....Jeff Copenhaver	1994....Herbert Theriot
1936....Clyde Burk	1957....Don McLaughlin	1976....Roy Cooper	1995....Fred Whitfield
1937....Everett Bowman	1958....Dean Oliver	1977....Roy Cooper	1996....Fred Whitfield
1938....Burel Mulkey	1959....Jim Bob Altizer	1978....Roy Cooper	1997....Cody Ohl
1939....Toots Mansfield	1960....Dean Oliver	1979....Paul Tierney	1998....Cody Ohl
1940....Toots Mansfield	1961....Dean Oliver	1980....Roy Cooper	1999....Fred Whitfield
1941....Toots Mansfield	1962....Dean Oliver	1981....Roy Cooper	2000....Fred Whitfield
1942....Clyde Burk	1963....Dean Oliver	1982....Roy Cooper	2001....Cody Ohl
1943....Toots Mansfield	1964....Dean Oliver	1983....Roy Cooper	2002....Fred Whitfield
1944....Clyde Burk	1965....Glen Franklin	1984....Roy Cooper	2003....Cody Ohl
1947....Troy Fort	1966....Junior Garrison	1985....Joe Beaver	2004....Monty Lewis
1948....Toots Mansfield	1967....Glen Franklin	1986....Chris Lybbert	
1949....Troy Fort	1968....Glen Franklin	1987....Joe Beaver	

Steer Wrestling

1929....Gene Ross	1950....Bill Linderman	1969....Roy Duvall	1988....John W. Jones
1930....Everett Bowman	1951....Dub Phillips	1970....John W. Jones	1989....John W. Jones
1931....Gene Ross	1952....Harley May	1971....Billy Hale	1990....Ote Berry
1932....Hugh Bennett	1953....Ross Dollarhide	1972....Roy Duvall	1991....Ote Berry
1933....Everett Bowman	1954....James Bynum	1973....Bob Marshall	1992....Mark Roy
1934....Shorty Ricker	1955....Benny Combs	1974....Tommy Puryear	1993....Steve Duhon
1935....Everett Bowman	1956....Harley May	1975....F. Shepperson	1994....Blaine Pederson
1936....Jack Kerschner	1957....Clark McEntire	1976....Tom Ferguson	1995....Ote Berry
1937....Gene Ross	1958....James Bynum	1977....Larry Ferguson	1996....Chad Bedell
1938....Everett Bowman	1959....Harry Charters	1978....Byron Walker	1997....Brad Gleason
1939....Harry Hart	1960....Bob A. Robinson	1979....Stan Williamson	1998....Mike Smith
1940....Homer Pettigrew	1961....Jim Bynum	1980....Butch Myers	1999....Mickey Gee
1941....Hub Whiteman	1962....Tom Nesmith	1981....Byron Walker	2000....Frank Thompson
1942....Homer Pettigrew	1963....Jim Bynum	1982....Stan Williamson	2001....Rope Myers
1943....Homer Pettigrew	1964....C.R. Boucher	1983....Joel Edmondson	2002....Sid Steiner
1944....Homer Pettigrew	1965....Harley May	1984....John W. Jones	2003....Teddy Johnson
1947....Todd Whatley	1966....Jack Roddy	1985....Ote Berry	2004....Luke Branquinho
1948....Homer Pettigrew	1967....Roy Duvall	1986....Steve Duhon	
1949....Bill McGuire	1968....Jack Roddy	1987....Steve Duhon	

Professional Rodeo Cowboys Association World Champions (Cont.)

Team Roping

1929....Charles.Maggini	1951....Olan Sims	1973....Leo Camarillo	1994....Jake Barnes
1930....Norman Cowan	1952....Asbury Schell	1974....H.P. Evetts	Clay O. Cooper
1931....Arthur Beloat	1953....Ben Johnson	1975....Leo Camarillo	1995....Bobby Hurley
1932....Ace Gardner	1954....Eddie Schell	1976....Leo Camarillo	Allen Bach
1933....Roy Adams	1955....Vern Castro	1977....Jerold Camarillo	1996....Steve Purcella
1934....Andy Jauregui	1956....Dale Smith	1978....Doyle Gellerman	Steve Northcott
1935....Lawrence Conltk	1957....Dale Smith	1979....Allen Bach	1997....Speed Williams
1936....John Rhodes	1958....Ted Ashworth	1980....Tee Woolman	Rich Skelton
1937....Asbury Schell	1959....Jim Rodriguez Jr.	1981....Walt Woodard	1998....Speed Williams
1938....John Rhodes	1960....Jim Rodriguez Jr.	1982....Tee Woolman	Rich Skelton
1939....Asbury Schell	1961....Al Hooper	1983....Leo Camarillo	1999....Speed Williams
1940....Pete Grubb	1962....Jim Rodriguez Jr.	1984....Dee Pickett	Rich Skelton
1941....Jim Hudson	1963....Les Hirdes	1985....Jake Barnes	2000....Speed Williams
1942....Verne Castro	1964....Bill Hamilton	1986....Clay O. Cooper	Rich Skelton
Vic Castro	1965....Jim Rodriguez Jr.	1987....Clay O. Cooper	2001....Speed Williams
1943....Mark Hull	1966....Ken Luman	1988....Jake Barnes	Rich Skelton
Leonard Block	1967....Joe Glenn	1989....Jake Barnes	2002....Speed Williams
1944....Murphy Chaney	1968....Art Arnold	1990....Allen Bach	Rich Skelton
1947....Jim Brister	1969....Jerold Camarillo	1991....Bob Harris	2003....Speed Williams
1948....Joe Glenn	1970....John Miller	1992....Clay O. Cooper	Rich Skelton
1949....Ed Yanez	1971....John Miller	1993....Bobby Hurley	2004 Speed Williams
1950....Buck Sorrels	1972....Leo Camarillo		Rich Skelton

Steer Roping

1929....Charles Maggini	1948....Everett Shaw	1967....Jim Bob Altizer	1986....Jim Davis
1930....Clay Carr	1949....Shoat Webster	1968....Sonny Davis	1987....Shaun Burchett
1931....Andy Jauregui	1950....Shoat Webster	1969....Walter Arnold	1988....Shaun Burchett
1932....George Weir	1951....Everett Shaw	1970....Don McLaughlin	1989....Guy Allen
1933....John Bowman	1952....Buddy Neal	1971....Olin Young	1990....Phil Lyne
1934....John McEntire	1953....Ike Rude	1972....Allen Keller	1991....Guy Allen
1935.....Richard Merchant	1954....Shoat Webster	1973....Roy Thompson	1992....Guy Allen
1936....John Bowman	1955....Shoat Webster	1974....Olin Young	1993....Guy Allen
1937....Everett Bowman	1956....Jim Snively	1975....Roy Thompson	1994....Guy Allen
1938....Hugh Bennett	1957....Clark McEntire	1976....Marvin Cantrell	1995....Guy Allen
1939....Dick Truitt	1958....Clark McEntire	1977....Buddy Cockrell	1996....Guy Allen
1940....Clay Carr	1959....Everett Shaw	1978....Sonny Worrell	1997....Guy Allen
1941....Ike Rude	1960....Don McLaughlin	1979....Gary Good	1998....Guy Allen
1942....King Merritt	1961....Clark McEntire	1980....Guy Allen	1999....Guy Allen
1943....Tom Rhodes	1962....Everett Shaw	1981....Arnold Felts	2000....Guy Allen
1944....Tom Rhodes	1963....Don McLaughlin	1982....Guy Allen	2001....Guy Allen
1945....Everett Shaw	1964....Sonny Davis	1983....Roy Cooper	2002....Buster Record
1946....Everett Shaw	1965....Sonney Wright	1984....Guy Allen	2003....Guy Allen
1947....Ike Rude	1966....Sonny Davis	1985....Jim Davis	2004....Guy Allen

Note: In 1945–46 champions were crowned only in Steer Roping.

Rowing

National Collegiate Rowing Champions

MEN

1985 ....Harvard	1992 ....Harvard	1999 ....California
1986 ....Wisconsin	1993 ....Brown	2000 ....California
1987 ....Harvard	1994 ....Brown	2001 ....California
1988 ....Harvard	1995 ....Brown	2002 ....California
1989 ....Harvard	1996 ....Princeton	2003 ....Harvard
1990 ....Wisconsin	1997 ....Washington	2004 ....Harvard
1991 ....Pennsylvania	1998 ....Princeton	2005 ....Harvard

WOMEN

1979 ....Yale	1988 ....Washington	1997 ....Washington
1980 ....California	1989 ....Cornell	1998 ....Washington
1981 ....Washington	1990 ....Princeton	1999 ....Brown
1982 ....Washington	1991 ....Boston University	2000 ....Brown
1983 ....Washington	1992 ....Boston University	2001 ....Washington
1984 ....Washington	1993 ....Princeton	2002 ....Brown
1985 ....Washington	1994 ....Princeton	2003 ....Harvard
1986 ....Wisconsin	1995 ....Princeton	2004 ....Brown
1987 ....Washington	1996 ....Brown	2005 ....California

Rugby Union

National Men's Club Championship

Year	Winner	Runner-Up	Year	Winner	Runner-Up
1979	Old Blues (CA)	St. Louis Falcons	1993	Old Mission Beach AC	Milwaukee
1980	Old Blues (CA)	St. Louis Falcons	1994	Old Mission Beach AC	Life College (GA)
1981	Old Blues (CA)	Old Blue (NY)	1995	Potomac Athletic Club	Old Mission Beach
1982	Old Blues (CA)	Denver Barbos	1996	Old Mission Beach AC	Old Blues (CA)
1983	Old Blues (CA)	Dallas Harlequins	1997	Gentlemen of Aspen	Old Blue (NY)
1984	Dallas Harlequins	Los Angeles	1998	Gentlemen of Aspen	Old Blue (NY)
1985	Milwaukee	Denver Barbos	1999	Gentlemen of Aspen	Golden Gate (CA)
1986	Old Blues (CA)	Old Blue (NY)	2000	Gentlemen of Aspen	Hayward Griffins
1987	Old Blues (CA)	Pittsburgh	2001	San Mateo	New York AC
1988	Old Mission Beach AC	Milwaukee	2002	San Mateo	Austin
1989	Old Mission Beach AC	Philly/Whitemarsh	2003	Boston Irish Wolfhounds	San Mateo
1990	Denver Barbos	Old Blues (CA)	2004	Boston Irish Wolfhounds	Austin
1991	Old Mission Beach AC	Washington	2005	Santa Monica	Back Bay
1992	Old Blues (CA)	Mystic River (MA)			

National Men's Collegiate Championship

Year	Winner	Runner-Up	Year	Winner	Runner-Up
1980	California	Air Force	1993	California	Air Force
1981	California	Harvard	1994	California	Navy
1982	California	Life College	1995	California	Air Force
1983	California	Air Force	1996	California	Penn St
1984	Harvard	Colorado	1997	California	Penn St
1985	California	Maryland	1998	California	Stanford
1986	California	Dartmouth	1999	California	Penn St
1987	San Diego State	Air Force	2000	California	Wyoming
1988	California	Dartmouth	2001	California	Penn St
1989	Air Force	Long Beach	2002	California	Utah
1990	Air Force	Army	2003	Air Force	Harvard
1991	California	Army	2004	California	Cal Poly SLO
1992	California	Army	2005	California	Utah

World Cup Championship

Year	Winner	Runner-Up	Year	Winner	Runner-Up
1987	New Zealand	France	1999	Australia	France
1991	Australia	England	2003	England	Australia
1995	South Africa	New Zealand			

Rugby League

American National Rugby League Champions

Year	Winner	Runner-Up
1998	Glen Mills Bulls	Philadelphia Bulldogs
1999	Glen Mills Bulls	New Jersey Sharks
2000	Glen Mills Bulls	Philadelphia Fight
2001	Glen Mills Bulls	Media Mantarays
2002	New York Knights	Glen Mills Bulls
2003	Connecticut Wildcats	Glen Mills Bulls
2004	Glen Mills Bulls	Connecticut Wildcats
2005	Glen Mills Bulls	Connecticut Wildcats

World Cup Championship

Year	Winner	Runner-Up	Host
1954	Great Britain	France	France
1957	Australia	International Team	Australia
1960	Great Britain	International Team	England
1968	Australia	France	Australia–New Zealand
1970	Great Britain	Australia	England
1972	Australia	Great Britain	France
1975	Australia	England	Worldwide
1977	Australia	Great Britain	Australia–New Zealand
1985–88	Australia	New Zealand	Worldwide
1989–92	Australia	Great Britain	Worldwide
1995	Australia	England	Great Britain
2000	Australia	New Zealand	G Britain-Ireland-France

Sailing

America's Cup Champions

SCHOONERS AND J-CLASS BOATS

Year	Winner	Skipper	Series	Loser	Skipper
1851	America	Richard Brown			
1870	Magic	Andrew Comstock	1–0	Cambria, Great Britain	J. Tannock
1871	Columbia (2–1)	Nelson Comstock	4–1	Livonia, Great Britain	J.R. Woods
	Sappho (2–0)	Sam Greenwood			
1876	Madeleine	Josephus Williams	2–0	Countess of Dufferin, Canada	J.E. Ellsworth
1881	Mischief	Nathanael Clock	2–0	Atalanta, Canada	Alexander Cuthbert
1885	Puritan	Aubrey Crocker	2–0	Genesta, Great Britain	John Carter
1886	Mayflower	Martin Stone	2–0	Galatea, Great Britain	Dan Bradford
1887	Volunteer	Henry Haff	2–0	Thistle, Great Britain	John Barr
1893	Vigilant	William Hansen	3–0	Valkyrie II, Great Britain	William Granfield
1895	Defender	Henry Haff	3–0	Valkyrie III, Great Britain	William Granfield
1899	Columbia	Charles Barr	3–0	Shamrock I, Great Britain	Archie Hogarth
1901	Columbia	Charles Barr	3–0	Shamrock II, Great Britain	E.A. Sycamore
1903	Reliance	Charles Barr	3–0	Shamrock III, Great Britain	Bob Wringe
1920	Resolute	Charles F. Adams	3–2	Shamrock IV, Great Britain	William Burton
1930	Enterprise	Harold Vanderbilt	4–0	Shamrock V, Great Britain	Ned Heard
1934	Rainbow	Harold Vanderbilt	4–2	Endeavour, Great Britain	T.O.M. Sopwith
1937	Ranger	Harold Vanderbilt	4–0	Endeavour II, Great Britain	T.O.M. Sopwith

12-METER BOATS

Year	Winner	Skipper	Series	Loser	Skipper
1958	Columbia	Briggs Cunningham	4–0	Sceptre, Great Britain	Graham Mann
1962	Weatherly	Bus Mosbacher	4–1	Gretel, Australia	Jock Sturrock
1964	Constellation	Bob Bavier & Eric Ridder	4–0	Sovereign, Australia	Peter Scott
1967	Intrepid	Bus Mosbacher	4–0	Dame Pattie, Australia	Jock Sturrock
1970	Intrepid	Bill Ficker	4–1	Gretel II, Australia	Jim Hardy
1974	Courageous	Ted Hood	4–0	Southern Cross, Australia	John Cuneo
1977	Courageous	Ted Turner	4–0	Australia	Noel Robins
1980	Freedom	Dennis Conner	4–1	Australia	Jim Hardy
1983	Australia II	John Bertrand	4–3	Liberty, United States	Dennis Conner
1987	Stars & Stripes	Dennis Conner	4–0	Kookaburra III, Australia	Iain Murray

60-FOOT CATAMARAN vs 133-FOOT MONOHULL

Year	Winner	Skipper	Series	Loser	Skipper
1988	Stars & Stripes	Dennis Conner	2–0	New Zealand	David Barnes

75-FOOT MONOHULL (IACC)

Year	Winner	Skipper	Series	Loser	Skipper
1992	America[3]	Bill Koch	4–1	Il Moro di Vinezia, Italy	Paul Cayard
1995	Black Magic I	Russell Coutts	5–0	Young America, United States	Dennis Conner
2000	New Zealand	Russell Coutts	5–0	Luna Rossa, Italy	Francesco de Angelis
2003	Swiss Alinghi	Russell Coutts	5–0	New Zealand	Dean Barker

Note: Winning entries have been from the United States every year but three: In 1983 an Australian vessel won, and in 1995 and 2000 a vessel from New Zealand won.

Men

50M FREE RIFLE PRONE

1947 .....O. Sannes, Norway
1949 .....A.C. Jackson, U.S.
1952 .....A.C. Jackson, U.S.
1954 .....G. Boa, Canada
1958 .....M. Nordquist
1962 .....K. Wenk, W Germany
1966 .....D. Boyd, U.S.
1970 .....M. Fiess, S. Africa
1974 .....K. Bulan, Czechoslovakia
1978 .....A. Allan, Great Britain
1982 .....V. Danilschenko, USSR
1986 .....S. Bereczky, Hungary
1990 .....V. Bochkarev, USSR
1994 .....Venjie Li, China
1998 .....Thomas Tamas, U.S.
1999 .....Thomas Tamas, U.S.
2000 .....Siarhei Martynau, Belarus
2001 .....Matthew Emmons, U.S.
2002 .....Matthew Emmons, U.S.

AIR RIFLE

1966 .....G. Kümmet, W Germany
1970 .....G. Kusterman, W Germ.
1974 .....E. Pedzisz, Poland
1978 .....O. Schlipf, W. Germany
1979 .....K. Hillenbrand
1981 .....F. Bessy, France
1982 .....F. Rettkowski, E Germ.
1983 .....P. Heberle, France
1985 .....P. Heberle, France
1986 .....H. Riederer, W Germany
1987 .....K. Ivanov, USSR
1989 .....J. P. Amet, France
1990 .....H. Riederer, W Germany
1994 .....Boris Polak, Israel
1998 .....Artem Khadjibekov, Russia
1999 .....Jozef Gonci, Slovakia
2000 .....Artem Khadjibekov, Russia
2001 .....Jason Parker, U.S.
2002 .....Jason Parker, U.S.

THREE POSITION RIFLE

1966 .....M. Thompson, U.S.
1970 .....M. Thompson Murdock, U.S.
1974 .....A. Pelova, Bulgaria
1978 .....W. Oliver, U.S.
1982 .....M. Helbig, E Germany
1986 .....V. Letcheva, Bulgaria
1990 .....V. Letcheva, Bulgaria
1994 .....A. Maloukhina, Russia
1998 .....Sonja Pfeilschifter, Germany
1999 .....Sonja Pfeilschifter, Germany
2000 .....Hong Shan, China
2001 .....Petra Horneber, Germany
2002 .....Petra Horneber, Germany

AIR RIFLE

1970 .....V. Cherkasque, USSR
1974 .....T. Ratkinova, USSR
1978 .....W. Oliver, U.S.
1979 .....K. Monez, U.S.
1981 .....S. Romaristova, USSR
1982 .....S. Lang, W Germany
1983 .....M. Helbig, E Germany
1985 .....E. Forian, Hungary
1986 .....V. Letcheva, Bulgaria
1987 .....V. Letcheva, Bulgaria
1989 .....V. Letcheva, Bulgaria

AIR RIFLE (CONT.)

MEN'S TRAP

1929 .....De Lumniczer, Hungary
1930 .....M. Arie, U.S.
1931 .....Kiszkurno, Poland
1933 .....De Lumniczer, Hungary
1934 .....A. Montagh, Hungary
1935 .....R. Sack, W Germany
1936 .....Kiszkurno, Poland
1937 .....K. Huber, Finland
1938 .....I. Strassburger, Hungary
1939 .....De Lumniczer, Hungary
1947 ....H. Liljedahl, Sweden
1949 .....F. Rocchi, Argentina
1950 .....C. Sala, Italy
1952 .....P.J. Grossi, Argentina
1954 .....C. Merlo, Italy
1958 .....F. Eisenlauer, U.S.
1959 .....H. Badravi, Egypt
1961 .....E. Mattarelli, Italy
1962 .....W. Zimenko, USSR
1965 .....J.E. Lire, Chile
1966 .....K. Jones, U.S.
1967 .....G. Rennard, Belgium
1969 .....E. Mattarelli, Italy
1970 .....M. Carrega, France
1971 .....M. Carrega, France
1973 .....A. Andrushkin, USSR
1974 .....M. Carrega, France
1975 .....J. Primrose, Canada
1977 .....E. Azkue, Spain
1978 .....E. Vallduvi, Spain
1979 .....M. Carrega, France
1981 .....A. Asanov, USSR
1982 .....L. Giovonnetti, Italy
1983 .....J. Primrose, Canada
1985 .....M. Bednarik,
           Czechoslovakia
1986 ....M. Bednarik,
           Czechoslovakia

Women

AIR RIFLE (Cont.)

1990 .....E. Joc, Hungary
1994 .....Sonja Pfeilschifter, Germany
1998 .....Sonja Pfeilschifter, Germany
1999.......Sonja Pfeilschifter, Germany
2000.......Sonja Pfeilschifter, Germany
2001.......Katerina Kurkova, Czech.
2002.......Katerina Kurkova, Czech.

SPORT PISTOL

1966 .....N. Rasskazova, USSR
1970 .....N. Stoljarova, USSR
1974 .....N. Stoljarova, USSR
1978 .....K. Dyer, U.S.
1982 .....P. Balogh, Hungary
1986 .....M. Dobrantcheva, USSR
1990 .....M. Logvinenko, USSR
1994 .....Soon Hee Boo, S Korea
1998 .....Yieqing Cai, China
1999 .....Soon Hee Boo, S Korea
2000 .....Lalita Vauhleuskaya,
           Belarus
2001 .....Munkhbayar Dorjsuren,
           Germany
2002 .....Munkhbayar Dorjsuren,
           Germany

MEN'S TRAP (Cont.)

1987 .....D. Monakov, USSR
1989 .....M. Venturini, Italy
1990 .....J. Damne, E Germany
1994 .....Dmitriy Monakov, Ukraine
1995 .....Giovanni Pellielo, Italy
1998 .....Giovanni Pellielo, Italy
1999 .....Joao Rebelo, Portugal
2000 .....Michael Diamond, Australia
2001 .....Michael Diamond, Australia
2002.......Khaled Almudhaf, Kuwait
2005.......Massimo Fabrizzi, Italy

THREE POSITION RIFLE

1929 .....O. Ericsson, Sweden
1930 .....Petersen, Denmark
1931 .....Amundson, Norway
1933 .....De Lisle, France
1935 .....Leskinnen, Finland
1937 .....Mazoyer, France
1939 .....Steigelmann, Germany
1947 .....I.H. Erben, Sweden
1949 .....P. Janhonen, Finland
1952 .....Kongshaug, Norway
1954 .....A. Bugdanov, USSR
1958 .....Itkis, USSR
1962 .....G. Anderson, U.S.
1966 .....G. Anderson, U.S.
1970 .....Parkhimovitch, USSR
1974 .....L. Wigger, U.S.
1978 .....E. Svensson, Sweden
1982 .....K. Ivanov, USSR
1986 .....P. Heinz, W Germany
1990 .....E. C. Lee, S Korea
1994 .....P. Kurka, Czech Republic
1998 .....Jozef Gonci, Slovakia
1999 .....Jozef Gonci, Slovakia
2000 .....Jozef Gonci, Slovakia
2001 .....Marcel Bürge, Switz
2002 .....Marcel Bürge, Switz

AIR PISTOL

1970 .....S. Carroll, U.S.
1974 .....Z. Simonian, USSR
1978 .....K. Hansson, Sweden
1979 .....R. Fox, U.S.
1981 .....N. Kalinina, USSR
1982 .....M. Dobrantcheva, USSR
1983 .....K. Bodin, Sweden
1985 .....M. Dobrantcheva, USSR
1986 .....A. Völker, E Germany
1987 .....J. Brajkovic, Yugoslavia
1989 .....N. Salukvadse, USSR
1990 .....Jasna Sekaric, Yugoslavia
1994 .....Jasna Sekaric, IOP
1998 .....Dorisuren Munkhbayar,
           Mongolia
1999 .....Nino Salukvadze,
           Georgia
2000 .....Luna Tao, China
2001 .....Olena Kostevych, Ukraine
2002 .....Olena Kostevych, Ukraine

U.S. Champions—Men

MAJOR FAST PITCH

1933 .........J.L. Gill Boosters, Chicago	1970 ....Raybestos Cardinals, Stratford, CT
1934 ....Ke-Nash-A, Kenosha, WI	1971 ....Welty Way, Cedar Rapids, IA
1935 ....Crimson Coaches, Toledo, OH	1972 ....Raybestos Cardinals, Stratford, CT
1936 ....Kodak Park, Rochester, NY	1973 ....Clearwater (FL) Bombers
1937 ....Briggs Body Team, Detroit	1974 ....Gianella Bros, Santa Rosa, CA
1938 ....The Pohlers, Cincinnati	1975 ....Rising Sun Hotel, Reading, PA
1939 ....Carr's Boosters, Covington, KY	1976 ....Raybestos Cardinals, Stratford, CT
1940 ....Kodak Park, Rochester, NY	1977 ....Billard Barbell, Reading, PA
1941 ....Bendix Brakes, South Bend, IN	1978 ....Billard Barbell, Reading, PA
1942 ....Deep Rock Oilers, Tulsa	1979 ....McArdle Pontiac/Cadillac, Midland, MI
1943 ....Hammer Air Field, Fresno	1980 ....Peterbilt Western, Seattle
1944 ....Hammer Air Field, Fresno	1981 ....Archer Daniels Midland, Decatur, IL
1945 ....Zollner Pistons, Fort Wayne, IN	1982 ....Peterbilt Western, Seattle
1946 ....Zollner Pistons, Fort Wayne, IN	1983 ....Franklin Cardinals, Stratford, CT
1947 ....Zollner Pistons, Fort Wayne, IN	1984 ....California Kings, Merced, CA
1948 ....Briggs Beautyware, Detroit	1985 ....Pay'n Pak, Seattle
1949 ....Tip Top Tailors, Toronto	1986 ....Pay'n Pak, Seattle
1950 ....Clearwater (FL) Bombers	1987 ....Pay'n Pak, Seattle
1951 ....Dow Chemical, Midland, MI	1988 ....TransAire, Elkhart, IN
1952 ....Briggs Beautyware, Detroit	1989 ....Penn Corp, Sioux City, IA
1953 ....Briggs Beautyware, Detroit	1990 ....Penn Corp, Sioux City, IA
1954 ....Clearwater (FL) Bombers	1991 ....Guanella Brothers, Rohnert Park, CA
1955 ....Raybestos Cardinals, Stratford, CT	1992 ....Natl Health Care Disc, Sioux City, IA
1956 ....Clearwater (FL) Bombers	1993 ....Natl Health Care Disc, Sioux City, IA
1957 ....Clearwater (FL) Bombers	1994 ....Decatur Pride, Decatur, IL
1958 ....Raybestos Cardinals, Stratford, CT	1995 ....Decatur Pride, Decatur, IL
1959 ....Sealmasters, Aurora, IL	1996 ....Green Bay All-Car, Green Bay, WI
1960 ....Clearwater (FL) Bombers	1997 ....Green Bay All-Car, Green Bay, WI
1961 ....Sealmasters, Aurora, IL	1998 ....Meierhoffer-Fleeman, St. Joseph, MO
1962 ....Clearwater (FL) Bombers	1999 ....Decatur Pride, Decatur, IL
1963 ....Clearwater (FL) Bombers	2000 ....Meierhoffer, St. Joseph, MO
1964 ....Burch Tool, Detroit	2001 ....Frontier Players Casino, St. Joseph, MO
1965 ....Sealmasters, Aurora, IL	2002 ....Frontier Players Casino, St. Joseph, MO
1966 ....Clearwater (FL) Bombers	2003 ....Farm Tavern, Madison, WI
1967 ....Sealmasters, Aurora, IL	2004 ....Farm Tavern, Madison, WI
1968 ....Clearwater (FL) Bombers	2005 ....Tampa Bay Smokers, Tampa Bay, FL
1969 ....Raybestos Cardinals, Stratford, CT	

SUPER SLOW PITCH

1981 ....Howard's/Western Steer, Denver, NC	1994 ....Bell Corp, Tampa, FL
1982 ....Jerry's Catering, Miami, FL	1995 ....Lighthouse/Worth, Stone Mt.., GA
1983 ....Howard's/Western Steer, Denver, NC	1996 ....Ritch's Superior, Windsor Locks, CT
1984 ....Howard's/Western Steer, Denver, NC	1997 ....Ritch's Superior, Windsor Locks, CT
1985 ....Steele's Sports, Grafton, OH	1998 ....Lighthouse/Worth, Stone Mt.., GA
1986 ....Steele's Sports, Grafton, OH	1999 ....Team Easton, Wilmington, NC
1987 ....Steele's Sports, Grafton, OH	2000 ....Team TPS, Louisville, KY
1988 ....Starpath, Monticello, KY	2002 ....Long Haul/Taylor Bros./Shen Corp./TPS,
1989 ....Ritch's Salvage, Harrisburg, NC	Albertville, MN
1990 ....Steele's Silver Bullets, Grafton, OH	2003 ....Resmondo/Hagae/Sunbelt/Taylor,
1991 ....Sunbelt/Worth, Centerville, GA	Canal Winchester, OH
1992 ....Ritch's Superior, Windsor Locks, CT	Note: Beginning in 2004 the Super Class Division
1993 ....Ritch's Superior, Windsor Locks, CT	was disbanded

YET ANOTHER SIGN OF THE APOCALYPSE

An Oklahoma state senator wants to legalize a form of cockfighting in which the birds wear tiny boxing gloves.

U.S. Champions—Men (Cont.)

MAJOR SLOW PITCH

1953..........Shields Construction, Newport, KY	1980..........Campbell Carpets, Concord, CA
1954..........Waldneck's Tavern, Cincinnati	1981..........Elite Coating, Gordon, CA
1955..........Lang Pet Shop, Covington, KY	1982..........Triangle Sports, Minneapolis
1956..........Gatliff Auto Sales, Newport, KY	1983..........No. 1 Electric & Heating, Gastonia, NC
1957..........Gatliff Auto Sales, Newport, KY	1984..........Lilly Air Systems, Chicago
1958..........East Side Sports, Detroit	1985..........Blanton's, Fayetteville, NC
1959..........Yorkshire Restaurant, Newport, KY	1986..........Non-Ferrous Metals, Cleveland
1960..........Hamilton Tailoring, Cincinnati	1987..........Starpath, Monticello, KY
1961..........Hamilton Tailoring, Cincinnati	1988..........Bell Corp/FAF, Tampa, FL
1962..........Skip Hogan A.C., Pittsburgh	1989..........Ritch's Salvage, Harrisburg, NC
1963..........Gatliff Auto Sales, Newport, KY	1990..........New Construction, Shelbyville, IN
1964..........Skip Hogan A.C., Pittsburgh	1991..........Riverside Paving, Louisville, KY
1965..........Skip Hogan A.C., Pittsburgh	1992..........Vernon's, Jacksonville, FL
1966..........Michael's Lounge, Detroit	1993..........Back Porch/Destin Roofing, Destin, FL
1967..........Jim's Sport Shop, Pittsburgh	1994..........Riverside RAM/Taylor Bros., Louisville, KY
1968..........County Sports, Levittown, NY	1995..........Riverside/RAM/Taylor/TPS, Louisville, KY
1969..........Copper Hearth, Milwaukee	1996..........Bell 2/Robert's/Easton, Orlando, FL
1970..........Little Caesar's, Southgate, MI	1997..........Long Haul/TPS, Albertville, MN
1971..........Pile Drivers, Virginia Beach, VA	1998..........Chase Mortgage/Easton, Wilmington, NC
1972..........Jiffy Club, Louisville, KY	1999..........Gasoline Heaven/Worth, Commack, NY
1973..........Howard's Furniture, Denver, NC	2000..........Long Haul/TPS, Albertville, MN
1974..........Howard's Furniture, Denver, NC	2001..........New Construction, Shelbyville, IN
1975..........Pyramid Cafe, Lakewood, OH	2002..........Twin States/Worth, Montgomery, AL
1976..........Warren Motors, Jacksonville, FL	2003..........New Construction/B&J/Snap-On,
1977..........Nelson Painting, Oklahoma City	Metamora, IL
1978..........Campbell Carpets, Concord, CA	2004..........U.S. Vinyl/ZWear, Lafayette, GA
1979..........Nelco Mfg Co., Oklahoma City	2005..........Vegas/Benfield/Easton, Manassas, VA

YET ANOTHER SIGN OF THE APOCALYPSE

In February, a Welsh rugby fan celebrated a win over England by cutting off his testicles.

U.S. Champions—Women

MAJOR FAST PITCH

1933.........Great Northerns, Chicago	1970.........Orange (CA) Lionettes
1934.........Hart Motors, Chicago	1971.........Raybestos Brakettes, Stratford, CT
1935.........Bloomer Girls, Cleveland	1972.........Raybestos Brakettes, Stratford, CT
1936.........Nat'l Screw & Mfg., Cleveland	1973.........Raybestos Brakettes, Stratford, CT
1937.........Nat'l Screw & Mfg., Cleveland	1974.........Raybestos Brakettes, Stratford, CT
1938.........J.J. Krieg's, Alameda, CA	1975.........Raybestos Brakettes, Stratford, CT
1939.........J.J. Krieg's, Alameda, CA	1976.........Raybestos Brakettes, Stratford, CT
1940.........Arizona Ramblers, Phoenix	1977.........Raybestos Brakettes, Stratford, CT
1941.........Higgins Midgets, Tulsa	1978.........Raybestos Brakettes, Stratford, CT
1942.........Jax Maids, New Orleans	1979.........Sun City (AZ) Saints
1943.........Jax Maids, New Orleans	1980.........Raybestos Brakettes, Stratford, CT
1944.........Lind & Pomeroy, Portland, OR	1981.........Orlando (FL) Rebels
1945.........Jax Maids, New Orleans	1982.........Raybestos Brakettes, Stratford, CT
1946.........Jax Maids, New Orleans	1983.........Raybestos Brakettes, Stratford, CT
1947.........Jax Maids, New Orleans	1984.........Los Angeles Diamonds
1948.........Arizona Ramblers, Phoenix	1985.........Hi-Ho Brakettes, Stratford, CT
1949.........Arizona Ramblers, Phoenix	1986.........Southern California Invasion, Los Angeles
1950.........Orange (CA) Lionettes	1987.........Orange County Majestics, Anaheim, CA
1951.........Orange (CA) Lionettes	1988.........Hi-Ho Brakettes, Stratford, CT
1952.........Orange (CA) Lionettes	1989.........Whittier (CA) Raiders
1953.........Betsy Ross Rockets, Fresno	1990.........Raybestos Brakettes, Stratford, CT
1954.........Leach Motor Rockets, Fresno	1991.........Raybestos Brakettes, Stratford, CT
1955.........Orange (CA) Lionettes	1992.........Raybestos Brakettes, Stratford, CT
1956.........Orange (CA) Lionettes	1993.........Redding Rebels, Redding, CA
1957.........Hacienda Rockets, Fresno	1994.........Redding Rebels, Redding, CA
1958.........Raybestos Brakettes, Stratford, CT	1995.........Redding Rebels, Redding, CA
1959.........Raybestos Brakettes, Stratford, CT	1996.........California Commotion, Woodland Hills, CA
1960.........Raybestos Brakettes, Stratford, CT	1997.........California Commotion, Woodland Hills, CA
1961.........Gold Sox, Whittier, CA	1998.........California Commotion, Woodland Hills, CA
1962.........Orange (CA) Lionettes	1999.........California Commotion, Woodland Hills, CA
1963.........Raybestos Brakettes, Stratford, CT	2000.........Phoenix Storm, Phoenix
1964.........Erv Lind Florists, Portland, OR	2001.........Phoenix Storm, Phoenix
1965.........Orange (CA) Lionettes	2002.........Stratford Brakettes, Stratford, CT
1966.........Raybestos Brakettes, Stratford, CT	2003.........Stratford Brakettes, Stratford, CT
1967.........Raybestos Brakettes, Stratford, CT	2004.........Stratford Brakettes, Stratford, CT
1968.........Raybestos Brakettes, Stratford, CT	2005.........Schutt Hurricanes, Burbank, CA
1969.........Orange (CA) Lionettes	

MAJOR SLOW PITCH

1959.........Pearl Laundry, Richmond, VA	1984.........Spooks, Anoka, MN
1960.........Carolina Rockets, High Pt, NC	1985.........Key Ford Mustangs, Pensacola, FL
1961.........Dairy Cottage, Covington, KY	1986.........Sur-Way Tomboys, Tifton, GA
1962.........Dana Gardens, Cincinnati	1987.........Key Ford Mustangs, Pensacola, FL
1963.........Dana Gardens, Cincinnati	1988.........Spooks, Anoka, MN
1964.........Dana Gardens, Cincinnati	1989.........Canaan's Illusions, Houston
1965.........Art's Acres, Omaha	1990.........Spooks, Anoka, MN
1966.........Dana Gardens, Cincinnati	1991.........Kannan's Illusions, San Antonio, TX
1967.........Ridge Maintenance, Cleveland	1992.........Universal Plastics, Cookeville, TN
1968.........Escue Pontiac, Cincinnati	1993.........Universal Plastics, Cookeville, TN
1969.........Converse Dots, Hialeah, FL	1994.........Universal Plastics, Cookeville, TN
1970.........Rutenschruder Floral, Cincinnati	1995.........Armed Forces, Sacramento, CA
1971.........Gators, Ft. Lauderdale, FL	1996.........Spooks, Anoka, MN
1972.........Riverside Ford, Cincinnati	1997.........Taylor's Major Slow Pitch, Glendale, MD
1973.........Sweeney Chevrolet, Cincinnati	1998.........Lakerettes, Conneaut Lake, PA
1974.........Marks Brothers Dots, Miami	1999.........Lakerettes, Conneaut Lake, PA
1975.........Marks Brothers Dots, Miami	2000.........Premier Motor Sports, Pittsboro, NC
1976.........Sorrento's Pizza, Cincinnati	2001.........Shooters/Nike, Orlando, FL
1977.........Fox Valley Lassies, St. Charles, IL	2002.........Diamond Queens, Nashville, TN
1978.........Bob Hoffman's Dots, Miami	2003.........Shooters/Worth, Orlando, FL
1979.........Bob Hoffman's Dots, Miami	2004.........Enough Said/Easton, Tallahassee, FL
1980.........Howard's Rubi-Otts, Graham, NC	2005.........Armed Forces, San Antonio, TX
1981.........Tifton (GA) Tomboys	
1982.........Richmond (VA) Stompers	Beginning in 2003, the ASA combined the Women's
1983.........Spooks, Anoka, MN	Class Major, Class-A and Class-B into 1 'open' class.

Speed Skating

All-Around World Champions

MEN

1891 .....Joseph F. Donoghue, U.S.	1936 .....Ivar Ballangrud, Norway	1975 .....Harm Kuipers, Netherlands
1893 .....Jaap Eden, Netherlands	1937 .....Michael Staksrud, Nor.	1976 .....Piet Kleine, Netherlands
1895 .....Jaap Eden, Netherlands	1938 .....Ivar Ballangrud, Norway	1977 .....Eric Heiden, U.S.
1896 .....Jaap Eden, Netherlands	1939 .....Birger Wasenius, Finland	1978 .....Eric Heiden, U.S.
1897 .....Jack K. McCulloch, Can.	1947 .....Lassi Parkkinen, Finland	1979 .....Eric Heiden, U.S.
1898 .....Peder Ostlund, Norway	1948 .....Odd Lundberg, Norway	1980 .....Hilbert van der Duin, Neth.
1899 .....Peder Ostlund, Norway	1949 .....Kornel Pajor, Hungary	1981 .....Amund Sjobrand, Norway
1900 .....Edvard Engelsaas, Nor.	1950 .....Hjalmar Andersen, Nor.	1982 .....Hilbert van der Duin, Neth.
1901 .....Franz F. Wathan, Finland	1951 .....Hjalmar Andersen, Nor.	1983 .....Rolf Falk-Larssen, Nor.
1904 .....Sigurd Mathisen, Norway	1952 .....Hjalmar Andersen, Nor.	1984 .....Oleg Bozhev, USSR
1905 .....C. Coen de Koning, Neth.	1953 .....Oleg Goncharenko, USSR	1985 .....Hein Vergeer, Netherlands
1908 .....Oscar Mathisen, Norway	1954 .....Boris Shilkov, USSR	1986 ......Hein Vergeer, Netherlands
1909 .....Oscar Mathisen, Norway	1955 .....Sigvard Ericsson, Swe.	1987 .....Nikolai Guliaev, USSR
1910 .....Nikolai Strunnikov, Russia	1956 .....Oleg Goncharenko, USSR	1988 .....Eric Flaim, U.S.
1911 .....Nikolai Strunnikov, Russia	1957 .....Knut Johannesen, Nor.	1989 .....Leo Visser, Netherlands
1912 .....Oscar Mathisen, Norway	1958 .....Oleg Goncharenko, USSR	1990 .....Johann Olav Koss, Nor.
1913 .....Oscar Mathisen, Norway	1959 .....Juhani Järvinen, Finland	1991 .....Johann Olav Koss, Nor.
1914 .....Oscar Mathisen, Norway	1960 .....Boris Stenin, USSR	1992 .....Roberto Sighel, Italy
1922 .....Harald Strom, Norway	1961 .....Henk van der Grift, Neth.	1993 .....Falko Zandstra, Neth.
1923 .....Klas Thunberg, Finland	1962 .....Viktor Kosichkin, USSR	1994 .....Johann Olav Koss, Nor.
1924 .....Roald Larsen, Norway	1963 .....Jonny Nilsson, Sweden	1995 .....Rintje Ritsma, Netherlands
1925 .....Klas Thunberg, Finland	1964 .....Knut Johannesen, Nor.	1996 .....Rintje Ritsma, Netherlands
1926 .....Ivar Ballangrud, Norway	1965 .....Per Ivar Moe, Norway	1997 .....Ids Postma, Netherlands
1927 .....Bernt Evensen, Norway	1966 .....Kees Verkerk, Neth.	1998 .....Ids Postma, Netherlands
1928 .....Klas Thunberg, Finland	1967 .....Kees Verkerk, Neth.	1999 .....Rintje Ritsma, Netherlands
1929 .....Klas Thunberg, Finland	1968 .....Fred Anton Maier, Nor.	2000 ....Gianni Romme, Netherlands
1930 .....Michael Staksrud, Nor.	1969 .....Dag Fornaes, Norway	2001 .....Rintje Ritsma, Netherlands
1931 .....Klas Thunberg, Finland	1970 .....Ard Schenk, Netherlands	2002 ....Jochem Uytdehaage, Neth.
1932 .....Ivar Ballangrud, Norway	1971 .....Ard Schenk, Netherlands	2003 ....Gianni Romme, Netherlands
1933 .....Hans Engnestangen, Nor.	1972 .....Ard Schenk, Netherlands	2004 .....Chad Hedrick, U.S.
1934 .....Bernt Evensen, Norway	1973 .....Göran Claeson, Sweden	2005 .....Shani Davis, U.S.
1935 .....Michael Staksrud, Nor.	1974 .....Sten Stensen, Norway	

WOMEN

1936 .....Kit Klein, U.S.	1965 .....Inga Artamonova, USSR	1987 .....Karin Kania, GDR
1937 .....Laila Schou Nilsen, Nor.	1966 .....Valentina Stenina, USSR	1988 .....Karin Kania, GDR
1938 .....Laila Schou Nilsen, Nor.	1967 .....Stien Kaiser, Netherlands	1989 .....Constanze Moser, GDR
1939 .....Verné Lesche, Finland	1968 .....Stien Kaiser, Netherlands	1990 .....Jacqueline Börner, GDR
1947 .....Verné Lesche, Finland	1969 .....Lasma Kauniste, USSR	1991 .....Gunda Kleemann, Ger.
1948 .....Maria Isakova, USSR	1970 .....Atje Keulen-Deelstra, Neth.	1992 .....Gunda Niemann-
1949 .....Maria Isakova, USSR	1971 .....Nina Statkevich, USSR	Kleemann, Germany
1950 .....Maria Isakova, USSR	1972 .....Atje Keulen-Deelstra, Neth.	1993 .....Gunda Niemann, Germany
1951 .....Eevi Huttunen, Finland	1973 .....Atje Keulen-Deelstra, Neth.	1994 .....Emese Hunyady, Austria
1952 .....Lidia Selikhova, USSR	1974 .....Atje Keulen-Deelstra, Neth.	1995 .....Gunda Niemann, Germany
1953 ....Khalida Shchegoleeva, USSR	1975 .....Karin Kessow, GDR	1996 ......Gunda Niemann, Germany
1954 .....Lidia Selikhova, USSR	1976 .....Sylvia Burka, Canada	1997 ......Gunda Niemann, Germany
1955 .....Rimma Zhukova, USSR	1977 .....Vera Bryndzej, USSR	1997 ......Gunda Niemann, Germany
1956 .....Sofia Kondakova, USSR	1978 .....Tatiana Averina, USSR	1998 .....Gunda Niemann, Germany
1957 .....Inga Artamonova, USSR	1979 .....Beth Heiden, U.S.	1999 .....Gunda Niemann, Germany
1958 .....Inga Artamonova, USSR	1980 .....Natalia Petruseva, USSR	2000 .....Claudia Pechstein, Ger.
1959 .....Tamara Rylova, USSR	1981 .....Natalia Petruseva, USSR	2001 .....Anni Friesinger, Germany
1960 .....Valentina Stenina, USSR	1982 .....Karin Busch, GDR	2002 .....Anni Friesinger, Germany
1961 .....Valentina Stenina, USSR	1983 .....Andrea Schöne, GDR	2003 .....Cindy Klassen, Canada
1962 .....Inga Artamonova, USSR	1984 .....Karin Enke-Busch, GDR	2004 .....Renate Groenewold, Neth
1963 .....Lidia Skoblikova, USSR	1985 .....Andrea Schöne, GDR	2005 .....Anni Friesinger, Germany
1964 .....Lidia Skoblikova, USSR	1986 .....Karin Kania-Enke, GDR	

Squash

National Men's Champions

National Women's Champions

HARD BALL		HARD BALL *(Cont.)*		SOFT BALL	
Year	Champion	Year	Champion	Year	Champion
1928	Eleanora Sears	1965	Joyce Davenport	1983	Alicia McConnell
1929	Margaret Howe	1966	Betty Meade	1984	Julie Harris
1930	Hazel Wightman	1967	Betty Meade	1985	Sue Clinch
1931	Ruth Banks	1968	Betty Meade	1986	Julie Harris
1932	Margaret Howe	1969	Joyce Davenport	1987	Diana Staley
1933	Susan Noel	1970	Nina Moyer	1988	Sara Luther
1934	Margaret Howe	1971	Carol Thesieres	1989	Nancy Gengler
1935	Margot Lumb	1972	Nina Moyer	1990	Joyce Maycock
1936	Anne Page	1973	Gretchen Spruance	1991	Ellie Pierce
1937	Anne Page	1974	Gretchen Spruance	1992	Demer Holleran
1938	Cecile Bowes	1975	Ginny Akabane	1993	Demer Holleran
1939	Anne Page	1976	Gretchen Spruance	1994	Demer Holleran
1940	Cecile Bowes	1977	Gretchen Spruance	1995	Ellie Pierce
1941	Cecile Bowes	1978	Gretchen Spruance	1996	Demer Holleran
1942–46	No tournament	1979	Heather McKay	1997	Demer Holleran
1947	Anne Page Homer	1980	Barbara Maltby	1998	Latasha Khan
1948	Cecile Bowes	1981	Barbara Maltby	1999	Demer Holleran
1949	Janet Morgan	1982	Alicia McConnell	2000	Latasha Khan
1950	Betty Howe	1983	Alicia McConnell	2001	Shabana Khan
1951	Jane Austin	1984	Alicia McConnell	2002	Latasha Khan
1952	Margaret Howe	1985	Alicia McConnell	2003	Latasha Khan
1953	Margaret Howe	1986	Alicia McConnell	2004	Latasha Khan
1954	Lois Dilks	1987	Alicia McConnell	2005	Latasha Khan
1955	Janet Morgan	1988	Alicia McConnell		
1956	Betty Howe Constable	1986	Alicia McConnell		
1957	Betty Howe Constable	1987	Alicia McConnell		
1958	Betty Howe Constable	1988	Alicia McConnell		
1959	Betty Howe Constable	1989	Demer Holleran		
1960	Margaret Varner	1990	Demer Holleran		
1961	Margaret Varner	1991	Demer Holleran		
1962	Margaret Varner	1992	Demer Holleran		
1963	Margaret Varner	1993	Demer Holleran		
1964	Ann Wetzel	1994	Demer Holleran		

Note: Tournament not held since 1994.

Triathlon

Ironman World Championship

	MEN				WOMEN	
Year	Winner	Time	Year		Winner	Time
1978	Gordon Haller	11:46	1978		No finishers	
1979	Tom Warren	11:15:56	1979		Lyn Lemaire	12:55
1980	Dave Scott	9:24:33	1980		Robin Beck	11:21:24
1981	John Howard	9:38:29	1981		Linda Sweeney	12:00:32
1982	Scott Tinley	9:19:41	1982		Kathleen McCartney	11:09:40
1982	Dave Scott	9:08:23	1982		Julie Leach	10:54:08
1983	Dave Scott	9:05:57	1983		Sylviane Puntous	10:43:36
1984	Dave Scott	8:54:20	1984		Sylviane Puntous	10:25:13
1985	Scott Tinley	8:50:54	1985		Joanne Ernst	10:25:22
1986	Dave Scott	8:28:37	1986		Paula Newby-Fraser	9:49:14
1987	Dave Scott	8:34:13	1987		Erin Baker	9:35:25
1988	Scott Molina	8:31:00	1988		Paula Newby-Fraser	9:01:01
1989	Mark Allen	8:09:15	1989		Paula Newby-Fraser	9:00:56
1990	Mark Allen	8:28:17	1990		Erin Baker	9:13:42
1991	Mark Allen	8:18:32	1991		Paula Newby-Fraser	9:07:52
1992	Mark Allen	8:09:09	1992		Paula Newby-Fraser	8:55:29
1993	Mark Allen	8:07:46	1993		Paula Newby-Fraser	8:58:23
1994	Greg Welch	8:20:27	1994		Paula Newby-Fraser	9:20:14
1995	Mark Allen	8:20:34	1995		Karen Smyers	9:16:46
1996	Luc Van Lierde	8:04:08	1996		Paula Newby-Fraser	9:06:49
1997	Thomas Hellriegel	8:33:01	1997		Heather Fuhr	9:31:43
1998	Peter Reid	8:24:20	1998		Natascha Badmann	9:24:16
1999	Luc Van Lierde	8:17:17	1999		Lori Bowden	9:13:02
2000	Peter Reid	8:21:01	2000		Natascha Badmann	9:26:17
2001	Tim DeBoom	8:31:18	2001		Natascha Badmann	9:28:37
2002	Tim DeBoom	8:29:56	2002		Natascha Badmann	9:07:54
2003	Peter Reid	8:22:35	2003		Lori Bowden	9:11:55
2004	Normann Stadler	8:33:20	2004		Natascha Buchman	9:50:04
2005	Faris Al-Sutan	8:14:17	2005		Natascha Buchman	9:09:30

Note: The Ironman Championship was contested twice in 1982.

Sites: Waikiki Beach (1978–79); Ala Moana Park (1980); Kailua-Kona (since 1981).

U.S. Triathlon National Champions*

	MEN		MEN		WOMEN		WOMEN (CONT.)
Year	Winner	Year	Winner	Year	Winner	Year	Winner
1984	Scott Molina	1995	Jeff Devlin	1984	Beth Mitchell	1996	Susan Latshaw
1985	Scott Molina	1996	Jeff Devlin	1985	L. Buchanan	1997	Sian Welch
1986	Scott Molina	1997	C. Wydoff	1986	K. Hanssen	1998	Siri Lindley
1987	Mike Pigg	1998	Hunter Kemper	1987	K. Hanssen	1999	Barb Lindquist
1988	Mike Pigg	1999	Hunter Kemper	1988	C. Kaushansky	2000	Joanna Zeiger
1989	Ken Glah	2000	Marcel Viffian	1989	Jan Ripple	2001	Karen Smyers
1990	Scott Molina	2001	Hunter Kemper	1990	Karen Smyers	2002	Barb Lindquist
1991	Mike Pigg	2002	Seth Wealing	1991	Karen Smyers	2003	Laura Reback
1992	Mike Pigg	2003	Hunter Kemper	1992	Karen Smyers	2004	Courtney
1993	Bill Braun	2004	Matt Reed	1993	Karen Smyers		Bennigson
1994	Scott Molina	2005	Hunter Kemper	1994	Karen Smyers	2005	Becky Lavelle
				1995	Karen Smyers		

*Olympic distances: 1.5 km swim, 40km bike, 10km run.

Volleyball

World Champions
MEN

Year	Winner	Runner-up	Site
1949	Soviet Union	Czechoslovakia	Prague
1952	Soviet Union	Czechoslovakia	Moscow
1956	Czechoslovakia	Soviet Union	Paris
1960	Soviet Union	Czechoslovakia	Rio de Janeiro
1962	Soviet Union	Czechoslovakia	Moscow
1966	Czechoslovakia	Romania	Prague
1970	East Germany	Bulgaria	Sofia, Bulgaria
1974	Poland	Soviet Union	Mexico City
1978	Soviet Union	Italy	Rome
1982	Soviet Union	Brazil	Buenos Aires
1986	United States	Soviet Union	Paris
1990	Italy	Cuba	Rio de Janeiro
1994	Italy	Netherlands	Athens
1998	Italy	Yugoslavia	Tokyo
2002	Brazil	Russia	Buenos Aires

World Champions (Cont.)

WOMEN

Year	Winner	Runner-up	Site
1952	Soviet Union	Poland	Moscow
1956	Soviet Union	Romania	Paris
1960	Soviet Union	Japan	Rio de Janeiro
1962	Japan	Soviet Union	Moscow
1966	Japan	United States	Prague
1970	Soviet Union	Japan	Sofia, Bulgaria
1974	Japan	Soviet Union	Mexico City
1978	Cuba	Japan	Rome
1982	China	Peru	Lima, Peru
1986	China	Cuba	Prague
1990	Soviet Union	China	Beijing
1994	Cuba	Brazil	Sao Paulo, Brazil
1998	Cuba	China	Osaka, Japan
2002	Italy	United States	Berlin

U.S. Men's Open Champions—Gold Division

Year	Site	Year	Site
1928	Germantown, PA YMCA	1968	Westside JCC, Los Angeles, CA
1929	Hyde Park YMCA, IL	1969	Los Angeles, CA YMCA
1930	Hyde Park YMCA, IL	1970	Chart House, San Diego
1931	San Antonio, TX YMCA	1971	Santa Monica, CA YMCA
1932	San Antonio, TX YMCA	1972	Chart House, San Diego
1933	Houston, TX YMCA	1973	Chuck's Steak, Los Angeles
1934	Houston, TX YMCA	1974	UC Santa Barbara, CA
1935	Houston, TX YMCA	1975	Chart House, San Diego
1936	Houston, TX YMCA	1976	Malibu, Los Angeles
1937	Duncan YMCA, IL	1977	Chuck's, Santa Barbara
1938	Houston, TX YMCA	1978	Chuck's, Los Angeles
1939	Houston, TX YMCA	1979	Nautilus, Long Beach CA
1940	Los Angeles AC, CA	1980	Olympic Club, San Francisco
1941	North Ave. YMCA, IL	1981	Nautilus, Long Beach CA
1942	North Ave. YMCA, IL	1982	Chuck's, Los Angeles
1943–44	No championships	1983	Nautilus Pacifica, CA
1945	North Ave. YMCA, IL	1984	Nautilus Pacifica, CA
1946	Pasadena, CA YMCA	1985	Molten/SSI Torrance, CA
1947	North Ave. YMCA, IL	1986	Molten, Torrance, CA
1948	Hollywood, CA YMCA	1987	Molten, Torrance, CA
1949	Downtown YMCA, CA	1988	Molten, Torrance, CA
1950	Long Beach, CA YMCA	1989	Not held
1951	Hollywood, CA YMCA	1990	Nike, Carson, CA
1952	Hollywood, CA YMCA	1991	Offshore, Woodland Hills, CA
1953	Hollywood, CA YMCA	1992	Creole Six Pack, Elmhurst, NY
1954	Stockton, CA YMCA	1993	Asics, Huntington Beach, CA
1955	Stockton, CA YMCA	1994	Asics/Paul Mitchell, Hunt. Beach, CA
1956	Hollywood, CA YMCA Stars	1995	Shakter, Belagarad, Ukraine
1957	Hollywood, CA YMCA Stars	1996	POL-AM-VBC, Brooklyn, NY
1958	Hollywood, CA YMCA Stars	1997	Canuck Stuff VBC, Calgary
1959	Hollywood, CA YMCA Stars	1998	T-Town, Tulsa, OK
1960	Westside JCC, CA	1999	Los Angeles Athletic Club,
1961	Hollywood, CA YMCA	2000	Paul Mitchell, Huntington Beach, CA
1962	Hollywood, CA YMCA	2001	Los Angeles Athletic Club,
1963	Hollywood, CA YMCA	2002	Paul Mitchell, Huntington Beach, CA
1964	Hollywood, CA YMCA Stars	2003	Paul Mitchell, Huntington Beach, CA
1965	Westside JCC, CA	2004	Bameso-I Dig, Dominican Republic
1966	Sand & Sea Club, CA	2005	Bameso-USA, Columbia, S.C.
1967	Fresno, CA VBC		

U.S. Women's Open Champions—Gold Division

1949	Eagles, Houston
1950	Voit #1, Santa Monica, CA
1951	Eagles, Houston
1952	Voit #1, Santa Monica, CA
1953	Voit #1, Los Angeles
1954	Houstonettes, Houston, TX
1955	Mariners, Santa Monica, CA
1956	Mariners, Santa Monica, CA
1957	Mariners, Santa Monica, CA
1958	Mariners, Santa Monica, CA
1959	Mariners, Santa Monica, CA
1960	Mariners, Santa Monica, CA
1961	Breakers, Long Beach, CA
1962	Shamrocks, Long Beach, CA
1963	Shamrocks, Long Beach, CA
1964	Shamrocks, Long Beach, CA
1965	Shamrocks, Long Beach, CA
1966	Renegades, Los Angeles
1967	Shamrocks, Long Beach, CA
1968	Shamrocks, Long Beach, CA
1969	Shamrocks, Long Beach, CA
1970	Shamrocks, Long Beach, CA
1971	Renegades, Los Angeles
1972	E Pluribus Unum, Houston
1973	E Pluribus Unum, Houston
1974	Renegades, Los Angeles
1975	Adidas, Norwalk, CA
1976	Pasadena, TX
1977	Spoilers, Hermosa, CA
1978	Nick's, Los Angeles
1979	Mavericks, Los Angeles
1980	NAVA, Fountain Valley, CA
1981	Utah State, Logan, UT
1982	Monarchs, Hilo, HI
1983	Syntex, Stockton, CA
1984	Chrysler, Palo Alto, CA
1985	Merrill Lynch, AZ
1986	Merrill Lynch, AZ
1987	Chrysler, Pleasanton, CA
1988	Chrysler, Hayward, CA
1989	Plymouth, Hayward, CA
1990	Plymouth, Hayward, CA
1991	Fitness, Champaign, IL
1992	Nick's Kronies, Chicago
1993	Nick's Fishmarket, Chicago
1994	Nick's Fishmarket, Chicago
1995	Kittleman/Branfield's/Nick's, Chi.
1996	Pure Texas Nuts, Austin, TX
1997	Kittleman/Branfield's/Nick's, Chi.
1998	The Exterminators, Barrington, IL
1999	Dominican Dream Team, Santo Domingo, D.R.
2000	Dominican Dream Team II, Santo Domingo, D.R.
2001	Dominican Dream Team III, Santo Domingo, D.R.
2002	Team Trim, Long Beach, CA
2003	The Exterminators, Barrington, IL
2004	U.S.A.-A2, Barrington, IL
2005	Bameso-USA, Columbia, S.C.

Wrestling

United States National Champions

1983

FREESTYLE		FREESTYLE *(Cont.)*		GRECO-ROMAN *(Cont.)*	
105.5	Rich Salamone	220	Greg Gibson	136.5	Dan Mello
114.5	Joe Gonzales	Hvy	Bruce Baumgartner	149.5	Jim Martinez
125.5	Joe Corso	Team	Sunkist Kids	163	James Andre
136.5	Rich Dellagatta*			180.5	Steve Goss
149.5	Bill Hugent	**GRECO-ROMAN**		198	Steve Fraser*
163	Lee Kemp	105.5	T.J. Jones	220	Dennis Koslowski
180.5	Chris Campbell	114.5	Mark Fuller	Hvy	No champion
198	Pete Bush	125.5	Rob Hermann	Team	Minn. Wrestling Club

1984

FREESTYLE		FREESTYLE *(Cont.)*		GRECO-ROMAN *(Cont.)*	
105.5	Rich Salamone	220	Harold Smith	149.5	Jim Martinez*
114.5	Charlie Heard	Hvy	Bruce Baumgartner	163	John Matthews
125.5	Joe Corso	Team	Sunkist Kids	180.5	Tom Press
136.5	Rich Dellagatta*			198	Mike Houck
149.5	Andre Metzger	**GRECO-ROMAN**		220	No champion
163	Dave Schultz*	105.5	T.J. Jones	Hvy	No champion
180.5	Mark Schultz	114.5	Mark Fuller	Team	Adirondack 3-Style, WA
198	Steve Fraser	136.5	Dan Mello		

1985

FREESTYLE		FREESTYLE *(Cont.)*		GRECO-ROMAN *(Cont.)*	
105.5	Tim Vanni	220	Greg Gibson	136.5	Buddy Lee
114.5	Jim Martin	286	Bruce Baumgartner	149.5	Jim Martinez
125.5	Charlie Heard	Team	Sunkist Kids	163	David Butler
136.5	Darryl Burley			180.5	Chris Catallo
149.5	Bill Nugent*	**GRECO-ROMAN**		198	Mike Houck
163	Kenny Monday	105.5	T.J. Jones	220	Greg Gibson
180.5	Mike Sheets	114.5	Mark Fuller	286	Dennis Koslowski
198	Mark Schultz	125.5	Eric Seward*	Team	U.S. Marine Corps

United States National Champions (Cont.)

1986

FREESTYLE

105.5	Rich Salamone
114.5	Joe Gonzales
125.5	Kevin Darkus
136.5	John Smith
149.5	Andre Metzger*
163	Dave Schultz
180.5	Mark Schultz
198	Jim Scherr
220	Dan Severn

FREESTYLE (Cont.)

286	Bruce Baumgartner
Team	Sunkist Kids (Div. I)
	Hawkeye Wrestling Club (Div. II)

GRECO-ROMAN

105.5	Eric Wetzel
114.5	Shawn Sheldon
125.5	Anthony Amado

GRECO-ROMAN (Cont.)

136.5	Frank Famiano
149.5	Jim Martinez
163	David Butler*
180.5	Darryl Gholar
198	Derrick Waldroup
220	Dennis Koslowski
286	Duane Koslowski
Team	U.S. Marine Corps (Div. I)
	U.S. Navy (Div. II)

1987

FREESTYLE

105.5	Takashi Irie
114.5	Mitsuru Sato
125.5	Barry Davis
136.5	Takumi Adachi
149.5	Andre Metzger
163	Dave Schultz*
180.5	Mark Schultz
198	Jim Scherr
220	Bill Scherr

FREESTYLE (Cont.)

286	Bruce Baumgartner
Team	Sunkist Kids (Div. I)
	Team Foxcatcher (Div. II)

GRECO-ROMAN

105.5	Eric Wetzel
114.5	Shawn Sheldon
125.5	Eric Seward
136.5	Frank Famiano

GRECO-ROMAN (Cont.)

149.5	Jim Martinez
163	David Butler
180.5	Chris Catallo
198	Derrick Waldroup*
220	Dennis Koslowski
286	Duane Koslowski
Team	U.S. Marine Corp (Div. I)
	U.S. Army (Div. II)

1988

FREESTYLE

105.5	Tim Vanni
114.5	Joe Gonzales
125.5	Kevin Darkus
136.5	John Smith*
149.5	Nate Carr
163	Kenny Monday
180.5	Dave Schultz
198	Melvin Douglas III
220	Bill Scherr

FREESTYLE (Cont.)

286	Bruce Baumgartner
Team	Sunkist Kids (Div. I)
	Team Foxcatcher (Div. II)

GRECO-ROMAN

105.5	T.J. Jones
114.5	Shawn Sheldon
125.5	Gogi Parseghian*
136.5	Dalen Wasmund

GRECO-ROMAN (Cont.)

149.5	Craig Pollard
163	Tony Thomas
180.5	Darryl Gholar
198	Mike Carolan
220	Dennis Koslowski
286	Duane Koslowski
Team	U.S. Marine Corps (Div. I)
	Sunkist Kids (Div. II)

1989

FREESTYLE

105.5	Tim Vanni
114.5	Zeke Jones
125.5	Brad Penrith
136.5	John Smith
149.5	Nate Carr
163	Rob Koll
180.5	Rico Chiapparelli
198	Jim Scherr*
220	Bill Scherr

FREESTYLE (Cont.)

286	Bruce Baumgartner
Team	Sunkist Kids (Div. I)
	Team Foxcatcher (Div. II)

GRECO-ROMAN

105.5	Lew Dorrance
114.5	Mark Fuller
125.5	Gogi Parseghian
136.5	Isaac Anderson

GRECO-ROMAN (Cont.)

149.5	Andy Seras*
163	David Butler
180.5	John Morgan
198	Michial Foy
220	Steve Lawson
286	Craig Pittman
Team	U.S. Marine Corps (Div. I)
	Jets USA (Div. II)

1990

FREESTYLE

105.5	Rob Eiter
114.5	Zeke Jones
125,5	Joe Melchiore
136.5	John Smith
149.5	Nate Carr
163	Rob Koll
180.5	Royce Alger
198	Chris Campbell*
220	Bill Scherr

FREESTYLE (Cont.)

286	Bruce Baumgartner
Team	Sunkist Kids (Div. I)
	Team Foxcatcher (Div. II)

GRECO-ROMAN

105.5	Lew Dorrance
114.5	Sam Henson
125.5	Mark Pustelnik
136.5	Isaac Anderson

GRECO-ROMAN (Cont.)

149.5	Andy Seras
163	David Butler
180.5	Derrick Waldroup
198	Randy Couture*
220	Chris Tironi
286	Matt Ghaffari
Team	Jets USA (Div. I)
	California Jets (Div. II)

*Outstanding wrestler.

United States National Champions (Cont.)

1991

FREESTYLE

105.5	Tim Vanni
114.5	Zeke Jones
125.5	Brad Penrith
136.5	John Smith*
149.5	Townsend Saunders
163	Kenny Monday
180.5	Kevin Jackson
198	Chris Campbell
220	Mark Coleman

FREESTYLE (Cont.)

286	Bruce Baumgartner
Team	Sunkist Kids (Div. I)
	Jets USA (Div. II)

GRECO-ROMAN

105.5	Eric Wetzel
114.5	Shawn Sheldon
125.5	Frank Famiano
136.5	Buddy Lee

GRECO-ROMAN (Cont.)

149.5	Andy Seras
163	Gordy Morgan
180.5	John Morgan*
198	Michial Foy
220	Dennis Koslowski
286	Craig Pittman
Team	Jets USA (Div. I)
	Sunkist Kids (Div. II)

1992

FREESTYLE

105.5	Rob Eiter
114.5	Jack Griffin
125.5	Kendall Cross*
136.5	John Fisher
149.5	Matt Demaray
163	Greg Elinsky
180.5	Royce Alger
198	Dan Chaid
220	Bill Scherr

FREESTYLE (Cont.)

286	Bruce Baumgartner
Team	Sunkist Kids (Div. I)
	Team Foxcatcher (Div. II)

GRECO-ROMAN

105.5	Eric Wetzel
114.5	Mark Fuller
125.5	Dennis Hall
136.5	Buddy Lee*

GRECO-ROMAN (Cont.)

149.5	Rodney Smith
163	Travis West
180.5	John Morgan
198	Michial Foy
220	Dennis Koslowski
286	Matt Ghaffari
Team	NY Athletic Club (Div. I)
	Sunkist Kids (Div. II)

1993

FREESTYLE

105.5	Rob Eiter
114.5	Zeke Jones
125.5	Brad Penrith
136.5	Tom Brands
149.5	Matt Demaray
163	Dave Schultz*
180.5	Kevin Jackson
198	Melvin Douglas
220	Kirk Trost

FREESTYLE (Cont.)

286	Bruce Baumgartner
Team	Sunkist Kids (Div. I)
	Team Foxcatcher (Div. II)

GRECO-ROMAN

105.5	Eric Wetzel
114.5	Shawn Sheldon
125.5	Dennis Hall*
136.5	Shon Lewis

GRECO-ROMAN (Cont.)

149.5	Andy Seras
163	Gordy Morgan
180.5	Dan Henderson
198	Randy Couture
220	James Johnson
286	Matt Ghaffari
Team	NY Athletic Club (Div. I)
	Sunkist Kids (Div. II)

1994

FREESTYLE

105.5	Tim Vanni
114.5	Zeke Jones
125.5	Terry Brands
136.5	Tom Brands
149.5	Matt Demaray
163	Dave Schultz
180.5	Royce Alger
198	Melvin Douglas
220	Mark Kerr

FREESTYLE (Cont.)

286	Bruce Baumgartner*
Team	Sunkist Kids (Div. I)
	Team Foxcatcher (Div. II)

GRECO-ROMAN

105.5	Isaac Ramaswamy
114.5	Shawn Sheldon
125.5	Dennis Hall
136.5	Shon Lewis

GRECO-ROMAN (Cont.)

149.5	Andy Seras*
163	Gordy Morgan
180.5	Dan Henderson
198	Derrick Waldroup

GRECO-ROMAN (Cont.)

220	James Johnson
286	Matt Ghaffari
Team	Armed Forces (Div. I)
	NY Athletic Club (Div. II)

1995

FREESTYLE

105.5	Rob Eiter
114.5	Lou Rosselli
125.5	Kendall Cross*
136.5	Tom Brands
149.5	Matt Demaray
163	Dave Schultz
180.5	Kevin Jackson
198	Melvin Douglas
220	Kurt Angle

FREESTYLE (Cont.)

286	Bruce Baumgartner
Team	Sunkist Kids (Div. I)
	Team Foxcatcher (Div. II)

GRECO-ROMAN

105.5	Isaac Ramaswamy
114.5	Shawn Sheldon
125.5	Dennis Hall*
136.5	Van Fronhofer

GRECO-ROMAN (Cont.)

149.5	Heath Sims
163	Matt Lindland
180.5	Marty Morgan
198	Michial Foy
220	James Johnson
286	Rulon Gardner
Team	Armed Forces (Div. I)
	Sunkist Kids (Div. II)

*Outstanding wrestler.

United States National Champions (Cont.)

1996

FREESTYLE

105.5	Rob Eiter
114.5	Lou Rosselli
125.5	Kendall Cross
136.5	Tom Brands
149.5	Townsend Saunders
163	Kenny Monday
180.5	Les Gutches*
198	Melvin Douglas
220	Kurt Angle

FREESTYLE (Cont.)

286	Bruce Baumgartner
Team	Sunkist Kids (Div. I)
	NY Athletic Club (Div. II)

GRECO-ROMAN

105.5	Mujaahid Maynard
114.5	Shawn Sheldon
125.5	Dennis Hall*
136.5	Shon Lewis

GRECO-ROMAN (Cont.)

149.5	Rodney Smith
163	Keith Sieracki
180.5	Marty Morgan
198	Michial Foy
220	John Oostendrop
286	Matt Ghaffari
Team	Armed Forces (Div. I)
	Sunkist Kids (Div. II)

1997

FREESTYLE

110	Kanamti Soloman
119	Zeke Jones
127.75	Terry Brands
138.75	Carl Kolat
152	Lincoln McIlravy*
167.5	Dan St. John
187.25	Les Gutches
213.75	Melvin Douglas

FREESTYLE (Cont.)

275.5	Tom Erikson
Team	Sunkist Kids (Div. I)
	NY Athletic Club (Div. II)

GRECO-ROMAN

110	Mark Yanagihara
119	Broderick Lee
127.75	Dennis Hall

GRECO-ROMAN (Cont.)

138.75	Kevin Bracken
152	Chris Saba
167.5	Miguel Spencer
187.25	Dan Henderson
213.75	Randy Couture*
275.5	Rulon Gardner
Team	Armed Forces (Div. I)
	NY Athletic Club (Div. II)

1998

FREESTYLE

119	Sam Henson
127.75	Tony Purler
138.75	Shawn Charles
152	Lincoln McIlravy
167.5	Steve Marianetti
187.25	Les Gutches*
213.75	Melvin Douglas

FREESTYLE (Cont.)

286	Tolly Thompson
Team	Sunkist Kids (Div. I)
	NY Athletic Club (Div. II)

GRECO-ROMAN

119	Shawn Sheldon
127.75	Dennis Hall
138.75	Shon Lewis

GRECO-ROMAN (Cont.)

152	Chris Saba
167.5	Matt Lindland
187.25	Dan Niebuhr*
213.75	Jason Klohs
286	Matt Ghaffari
Team	Armed Forces (Div. I)
	Sunkist Kids (Div. II)

1999

FREESTYLE

119	Lou Rosselli
127.75	Terry Brands
138.75	Cary Kolat
152	Lincoln McIlravy
167.5	Joe Williams
187.25	Les Gutches
213.75	Dominic Black

FREESTYLE (Cont.)

286	Stephen Neal*
Team	Sunkist Kids (Div. I)
	NY Athletic Club (Div. II)

GRECO-ROMAN

119	Steven Mays
127.75	Dennis Hall
138.75	Glen Nieradka

GRECO-ROMAN (Cont.)

152	David Zuniga
167.5	Matt Lindland
187.25	Quincey Clark
213.75	Randy Couture
286	Dremiel Byers*
Team	Minnesota Storm (Div. I)
	Sunkist Kids (Div. II)

2000

FREESTYLE

119	Sammie Henson
127.75	Keyy Boumans
138.75	Cary Kolat
152	Lincoln McIlravy
167.5	Brandon Slay*
187.25	Les Gutches
213.75	Melvin Douglas

FREESTYLE (Cont.)

286	Kerry McCoy
Team	Sunkist Kids (Div. I)
	NY Athletic Club (Div. II)

GRECO-ROMAN

119	Brandon Paulson
127.75	Dennis Hall
138.75	Kevin Bracken

GRECO-ROMAN (Cont.)

152	Heath Sims
167.5	Matt Lindland
187.25	Quincey Clark*
213.75	Jason Gleasman
286	Rulon Gardner
Team	Armed Forces (Div. I)
	Sunkist Kids (Div. II)

*Outstanding wrestler.

United States National Champions (Cont.)

2001

FREESTYLE		
119	Eric Akin	
127.75	Eric Guerrero	
138.75	Bill Zadick	
152	Ramico Blackmon	
167.5	Joe Williams	
187.25	Cael Sanderson*	
213.75	Dominic Black	

FREESTYLE *(Cont.)*

286	Kerry McCoy
Team	Sunkist Kids (Div. I)
	New York AC (Div. II)

GRECO-ROMAN

119	Jeff Cervone
127.75	Dennis Hall
138.75	Kevin Bracken

GRECO-ROMAN *(Cont.)*

152	Marcel Cooper
167.5	Keith Sieracki
187.25	Matt Lindland*
213.75	Garrett Lowney
286	Rulon Gardner
Team	Army (Div. I)
	Sunkist Kids (Div. II)

2002

FREESTYLE

121	Teague Moore
132	Eric Guerrero
145.5	Bill Zadick
163	Joe Williams*
185	Cael Sanderson
211.5	Tim Hartung
264.5	Kerry McCoy

FREESTYLE *(Cont.)*

Team	Sunkist Kids (Div. I)
	New York AC (Div. II)

GRECO-ROMAN

121	Brandon Paulson
132	Glenn Nieradka*
145.5	Kevin Bracken

GRECO-ROMAN *(Cont.)*

163	Keith Sieracki
185	Ethan Bosch
211.75	Garrett Lowney
264.5	Dremiel Byers
Team	Army (Div. I)
	New York AC (Div. II)

2003

FREESTYLE

121	Stephen Abas
132	Eric Guerrero*
145.5	Chris Bono
163	Joe Williams
185	Cael Sanderson
211.5	Daniel Cormier
264.5	Kerry McCoy

FREESTYLE *(Cont.)*

Team	Sunkist Kids (Div. I)
	Gator WC (Div. II)

GRECO-ROMAN

121	Brandon Paulson
132	James Gruenwald*
145.5	Kevin Bracken

GRECO-ROMAN *(Cont.)*

163	Keith Sieracki
185	Brad Vering
211.5	Garrett Lowney
264.5	Dremiel Byers
Team	Army (Div. I)
	Air Force (Div. II)

2004

FREESTYLE

121	Stephen Abbas
132	Eric Guerrero
145.5	Jamill Kelly
163	Joe Williams
185	Lee Fullhart*
211.5	Daniel Cormier
264.5	Kerry McCoy

FREESTYLE *(Cont.)*

Team	Sunkist Kids (Div. I)
	Gator WC (Div. II)

GRECO-ROMAN

121	Brandon Paulson
132	James Gruenwald
145.5	Faruk Sahin

GRECO-ROMAN *(Cont.)*

163	Darryl Christian
185	Brad Vering
211.5	Justin Ruiz
264.5	Dremiel Byers*
Team	New York AC (Div. I)
	Air Force (Div. II)

2005

FREESTYLE

121	Sam Henson
132	Michael Lightner*
145.5	Chris Bono
163	Joe Williams
185	Mo Lawal
211.5	Daniel Cormier
264.5	Tolly Thompson

FREESTYLE *(Cont.)*

Team	Sunkist Kids (Div. I)
	Gator WC (Div. II)

GRECO-ROMAN

121	Sam Hazewinkel
132	Joseph Warren
145.5	Harry Lester

GRECO-ROMAN *(Cont.)*

163	Darryl Christian
185	Brad Vering
211.5	Justin Ruiz
264.5	Dremiel Byers*
Team	New York AC (Div.I)
	Air Force (Div. II)

*Outstanding wrestler.

2004–05 was the NHL's Lost Season

The Sports Market

Lose Big, Win Big

While the NHL's lockout cost it an entire season, the NFL just kept rolling along, signing a mammoth TV-rights deal

BY MERRELL NODEN

THE ANNOUNCEMENT CAME ON February 16, on what would have been the 127th day of the 2004–05 National Hockey League season. "As I stand before you today," said NHL commissioner Gary Bettman, "it is my sad duty to announce that because [a] solution has not yet been attained, it no longer is practical to conduct even an abbreviated season." With those words, an entire major prosports season was lost to a labor dispute for the first time in U.S. history. There was talk, briefly, of the National Basketball Association following suit when its collective bargaining agreement expired, on June 30, but that didn't happen. That left Bettman and Bob Goodenow, the executive director of the NHL Players' Association, looking very much like villains to many hockey fans.

Despite this latest reminder of how much can go wrong in the world of big time sports, 2005 showed there was no shortage of rich men competing to buy teams, proud cities campaigning to build new stadiums and networks vying to pay astronomical broadcast rights. This was surprising since the year's biggest story in sports business screamed, "Caveat emptor!" Still, when you measure the risks against potential rewards like the NFL's colossal new television

contracts and the euphoria surrounding baseball's return to the nation's capital, you could begin to understand investors' hunger to buy a piece of the sports world. The NHL's example, while sad, was hardly a major deterrent.

The NHL's owners had been complaining for years about meager profits. Well, this year was different: They made none. The league's decision to lock out its players, which began on Sept. 15, when the league's six-year collective bargaining agreement expired, cost it not just revenue but fan goodwill, which, for a league that is at best No. 4 among North American pro sports leagues, is quite an important commodity.

At issue was a salary cap, which the league's owners wished to set at $42.5 million per team, $6.5 million less than $49 million the Players Association was proposing. Once the lockout became a reality, the players scattered to the four corners of the world, including 295 who took huge pay cuts to ply their trade in Europe, where the average salary is far below the NHL average of $1.8 million.

The two sides met throughout the fall and winter, but were unable to reach an agreement. In the midst of all this, some interesting ideas were floated. In what many dismissed as

Starting in 2006, the NFL will flip Monday Night Football to ESPN, while NBC will begin airing a Sunday night NFL game.

JOHN IACONO/SPORTS ILLUSTRATED

a stunt, buyout firm Bain Capital and Game Plan International, a sports consulting firm, offered to buy the entire league and its 30 teams for $3.5 billion. That went nowhere, perhaps because in 2004 Forbes magazine had valued the 30 teams at $4.9 billion.

When a new CBA was finally reached, after an all-night bargaining session on July 13, everybody said the right things. But it sure looked as if the owners had gotten the better deal. Among the features of the new CBA: a 24% rollback on all existing player contracts, a team-by-team salary cap of $39 million and a revenue sharing deal in which the top 10 money-making teams contribute to a fund shared by the bottom 15. On the plus side for the players—the minimum salary increased from $185,000 under the previous agreement to $450,000 this coming season.

Still, it was impossible not to see the new deal as a victory for the poor-mouthing owners. So, it came as no surprise when, on July 28, Goodenow resigned not long after helping negotiate an end to the 301-day lockout. Ted Saskin, who previously had been the Senior Director of the NHLPA, replaced him. But even with a deal in place, the strife continued, as a group of veteran players, led by Chris Chelios, questioned the way Saskin was hired and then accused the NHLPA of trying to obstruct their challenge.

Despite the uncertainty that surrounded the NHL, OLN, the Outdoor Life Network, announced on August 18 that it had reached a two-year, $135 million deal to televise at least 58 regular season NHL games, on Monday and Tuesday nights. OLN, which is owned by Comcast, reaches 65 million homes. The biggest previous event it broadcast was the Tour de France, but, with Lance Armstrong choosing to retire after winning his seventh straight Tour, there had been questions about what exactly the OLN would broadcast. OLN plans a number of innovations to make hockey more appealing to its mostly American target audience, including increased behind-the-scenes access, netcams and microphones on players and coaches.

Still, that deal was peanuts compared to the ones the NFL inked. In April, ESPN announced that, starting in 2006, it will take over broadcasting Monday Night Football, which had been on ABC since the show first aired in 1970. ESPN will pay $1.1 billion a year for the next eight years of MNF, more than twice what ABC had paid for broadcast rights. And the shakeup didn't stop there: NBC also paid $600 million a year to broadcast a weekly NFL game on Sunday night, a slot that NBC Sports chairman Dick Ebersol predicted would eventually draw higher ratings than MNF. Certainly, NBC has to be delighted that the NFL tossed in the Super Bowls for the 2008 and 2011 seasons.

Throw all that revenue, plus existing deals with Fox and CBS, into the NFL's vast coffers, and the league's revenues have suddenly jumped more than 50%, to an average of $3.735 billion a year. That's more than the total spending on Major League Baseball, NASCAR, the NBA, the PGA Tour, the NCAA basketball tournament, and the 2004 Summer Olympics combined! Despite having all that money to disburse, there were still rumblings of discontent within pro football, whose CBA expires after the 2007 season. "At the pace we're going," warned Gene Upshaw, executive director of the NFL Players Association, "we're not going to get there."

On the bright side, the NFL did get its first black owner. In February Reggie Fowler, a former University of Wyoming football player who built a supermarket supplies empire called Spiral Inc., purchased the Minnesota Vikings for a reported $625 million.

In other executive suite changes, Phil Knight, co-founder of Nike and the only chief executive officer the shoe giant has ever had, resigned in November 2004 and picked outsider William D. Perez to take his place. Perez had been the head of S.C. Johnson & Son, maker of Drano and Glade. And Ted Forstmann took over as head of sports management and marketing firm IMG last fall.

In September Ty Votaw announced his resignation as chairman of the LPGA. Votaw's tenure had lasted 6 1/2 years, during which he cut the number of tournaments, from 40 down to 31, but increased purses to an average of $1.4 million. In June, Carol Bivens, president of a large media services company, was named as his successor, making her the first woman to head the LPGA. Val Ackerman, the first and only president the WNBA has known, retired and quickly became President of USA Basketball for the next four years.

Meanwhile, virtually every pro sports team around New York City seemed to be angling for a new stadium. At the center of all the fuss was the Big Apple's bid to host the 2012 Olympics, the success of which, most everyone agreed, hinged on the building of a new stadium that would serve as an Olympic stadium and then become the home of some lucky local team. Plan A, which was in the works for several years,

was to build a stadium and convention center on the abandoned rail yards on the west side of Manhattan. The stadium would serve as the home of the New York Jets and then be converted to the Olympic stadium if the city were chosen to host the 2012 Games.

Mayor Michael Bloomberg was an enthusiastic supporter of the plan. From the start, though, community activists objected to what they described as a sweetheart deal. Under this plan, the city and state were each to pay $350 million to deck the rail yards and build a retractable roof, and the city by itself was to pay $700 million for open spaces and parking areas nearby. The Jets were to pay just $800 million of the projected $2.2 billion cost. Critics were quick to point out all sorts of ways the city might better spend public money, such as schools and affordable housing.

In early June a N.Y. state board failed to approve $300 million in funding for the stadium. With that, the deal collapsed, and New York deputy mayor Daniel Doctoroff, who was the New York Olympic bid leader, was forced to adopt a hasty plan B: a stadium in Queens that would become home to the New York Mets starting in 2009 and the Olympic Stadium in 2012. Doctoroff and his NYC2012 team were put in the awkward position of having to petition to make a major last-minute change in its Olympic bid plan, something the International Olympic Committee could not have been pleased with. Sure enough, New York was voted out of the running on just the second of four ballots. The Mets, however, are still to get their stadium, which is to stand just east of Shea Stadium and to cost an estimated $600 million.

In the end, the 2012 Summer Olympics were awarded, in something of an upset, to London, which becomes the first city to host the Games three times. Paris had long been thought to be the favorite this time, but the odds changed drastically when Olympic middle distance champion Sebastian Coe skillfully took over running London's bid in 2004. The centerpiece of their plan was a vast scheme to revitalize a forlorn and abandoned industrial section of East London.

The Jets, meanwhile, shifted their atten-

For the first time since the Kennedy administration, major leaguers played in D.C.

CHUCK SOLOMON

tion to the New Jersey Meadowlands, where for years they've played the role of lowly tenant with the New York Giants their landlord. The Giants have been planning to build an $800 million stadium as part of a huge $2 billion entertainment and retail development called Xanadu. After a brief dalliance with the idea of building their own stadium in Queens, the Jets finally decided against that idea in late September and instead joined the Giants as full partners in the new stadium complex.

The one stadium that seems sure to be built will be home to the MetroStars of Major League Soccer. Seating 20,000, it is to be the centerpiece of a new 250-acre entertainment waterfront complex in Harrison, N.J., just across from Newark. AEG, the MetroStars' parent company, agreed to pay the entire estimated $80 million cost of the stadium, which is expected to be ready for the 2007 season.

Of course the real money in soccer is elsewhere. The world's most valuable sports franchise, Manchester United, was taken over by American billionaire and Tampa Bay Buccaneers owner Malcolm Glazer. He bought an initial 2.9% stake in the club in March of 2003 and has steadily increased his share, now owning a total of 76.2% of the team. Hoping to corner 90% of the total shares, which would have enabled him to delist the team from the London stock exchange, Glazer offered to buy the remainder for 300 pence per share, a move that did nothing to make him popular round Manchester. When his three sons showed up for a game at Old Trafford, they had to be protected by police amid fan riots.

There were some feel-good developments in pro sports, however. It was hard not to be pleased by baseball's return to the nation's capital. After weathering some last minute obstacles, including a demand that half the stadium funding come from private sources, Washington, D.C., finally saw major-league baseball for the first time since the Senators decamped to Minnesota in 1960 (unless you count the 1969 All Star Game, which was played at Robert F. Kennedy Stadium). The Nationals did well both on the field and at the turnstiles, contending for a wildcard spot for most of the season and setting a franchise season attendance record on Sept. 7th, with 2,333,091, which beat a record set in 1983 by the Montreal Expos.

The NHL, meanwhile, spent the summer and fall using every ploy and stratagem to woo fans back. In addition to fiddling with the rules in an effort to promote scoring, franchises also lowered ticket prices and rolled out clever marketing campaigns to revitalize fan interest. The Florida Panthers placed 5,000 lawn signs throughout southeast Florida, while the Phoenix Coyotes went even further, offering a free pair of season tickets to any current season ticket holders who chose to renew.

The NHL's Brave New World season kicked off on Oct. 5, with OLN broadcasting its first game, between the New York Rangers and the Philadelphia Flyers. The players eagerly raced up and down the ice, which surely caused a lot of deep breathing. But don't be surprised if a lot of people, in the hockey world and beyond, are holding theirs instead.

Major League Baseball

Address: 75 Ninth Avenue, 5th Floor
New York, NY 10011 USA
Telephone: (866) 800-1275
Commissioner: Bud Selig
Chief Operating Officer: Robert DuPuy
Senior VP, Public Relations: Richard Levin
www.majorleaguebaseball.com

Major League Baseball Players Association

Address: 12 East 49th Street, 24th Floor
New York, NY 10017
Telephone: (212) 826-0808
Executive Director: Donald Fehr
Director of Communications: Greg Bouris
Director of Licensing: Judy Heeter
www.bigleaguers.com

Anaheim Angels

Address: P.O. Box 2000
Anaheim, CA 92803
Telephone: (714) 940-2000
Stadium (Capacity): Angel Stadium
of Anaheim (45,050)
Owner: Arturo Moreno
General Manager: Bill Stoneman
Manager: Mike Scioscia
Vice President of Communications: Tim Mead
www.angelsbaseball.com

Arizona Diamondbacks

Address: P.O. Box 2095
Phoenix, AZ 85001
Telephone: (602) 462-6500
Stadium (Capacity): Bank One Ballpark (49,033)
CEO: Jeff Moorad
Interim General Manager: Bob Gebhart
Manager: Bob Melvin
Director of Public Relations: Mike Swanson
www.azdiamondbacks.com

Atlanta Braves

Address: P.O. Box 4064
Atlanta, GA 30302
Telephone: (404) 522-7630
Stadium (Capacity): Turner Field (50,091)
Vice Chrmn./Sr. Advisor of Time Warner/AOL: Ted Turner
Executive VP & General Manager: John Schuerholz
Manager: Bobby Cox
Director of Public Relations: Jim Schultz
www.atlantabraves.com

Baltimore Orioles

Address: Oriole Park at Camden Yards
333 W Camden Street
Baltimore, MD 21201
Telephone: (410) 685-9800
Stadium (Capacity): Oriole Park at Camden Yards
(48,876)
Chairman of the Board/CEO: Peter G. Angelos
Vice Chairman/COO: Joseph E. Foss
Manager: Sam Perlozzo
Director of Public Relations: Bill Stetka
www.theorioles.com

Boston Red Sox

Address: 4 Yawkey Way
Fenway Park
Boston, MA 02215
Telephone: (617) 267-9440
Stadium (Capacity): Fenway Park (33,993)
Principal Owner: John W. Henry
Senior VP and General Manager: Theo Epstein
Manager: Terry Francona
VP of Public relations: Glenn Geffner
www.redsox.com

Chicago Cubs

Address: Wrigley Field
1060 West Addison
Chicago, IL 60613
Telephone: (773) 404-2827
Stadium (Capacity): Wrigley Field (39,538)
President and CEO: Andrew B. MacPhail
Vice President/GM: Jim Hendry
Manager: Dusty Baker
Director of Media Relations: Sharon Pannozzo
www.cubs.com

Chicago White Sox

Address: Comiskey Park
333 West 35th Street
Chicago, IL 60616
Telephone: (312) 674-1000
Stadium (Capacity): U.S. Cellular Field (40,615)
Chairman: Jerry Reinsdorf
General Manager: Kenny Williams
Manager: Ozzie Guillen
VP of Communications: Scott Reifert
www.whitesox.com

Cincinnati Reds

Address: 100 Main Street
Cincinnati, OH 45202
Telephone: (513) 765-7000
Stadium (Capacity): Great American Ball Park
(42,059)
CEO/General Partner: Carl Lindner
COO: John L. Allen
General Manager: Dan O'Brien
Managing Executive: John L. Allen
Manager: Jerry Narron
Director of Media Relations: Rob Butcher
www.cincinnatireds.com

Cleveland Indians

Address: Jacobs Field
2401 Ontario Street
Cleveland, OH 44115-4003
Telephone: (216) 420-4636
Stadium (Capacity): Jacobs Field (43,368)
President and CEO: Lawrence J. Dolan
Executive VP and General Manager: Mark Shapiro
Manager: Eric Wedge
Director of Media Relations: Bart Swain
www.indians.com

Colorado Rockies

Address: 2001 Blake Street
Denver, CO 80205
Telephone: (303) 292-0200
Stadium (Capacity): Coors Field (50,445)
Chairman and CEO: Charles K. Monfort
President: Keli McGregor
General Manager and Executive VP: Dan O'Dowd
Manager: Clint Hurdle
Vice President of Communications/PR: Jay Alves
www.coloradorockies.com

Detroit Tigers

Address: Comerica Park
2100 Woodward Avenue
Detroit, MI 48201
Telephone: (313) 962-4000
Stadium (Capacity): Comerica Park (40,120)
Owner: Mike Ilitch
President and GM: Dave Dombrowski
Manager: Jim Leyland
Manager of Media Relations: Brian Britten
www.detroittigers.com

Florida Marlins
Address: 2267 Dan Marino Boulevard
             Miami, FL 33056
Telephone: (305) 626-6100
Stadium (Capacity): Pro Player Stadium (36,331)
Owner: Jeffrey H. Loria
President: David Samson
Senior VP and General Manager: Larry Beinfest
Manager: TBA
VP of Communications/Broadcasting:P.J. Loyello
www.floridamarlins.com

Houston Astros
Address: P.O. Box 288
             Houston, TX 77001
Telephone: (713) 259-8000
Stadium (Capacity): Minute Maid Park (40,950)
Chairman: Drayton McLane
President of Baseball Operations: Tal Smith
Manager: Phil Garner
Director of Media Relations: Jimmy Stanton
www.astros.com

Kansas City Royals
Address: P.O. Box 419969
             Kansas City, MO 64141
Telephone: (816) 921-8000
Stadium (Capacity): Kauffman Stadium (40,785)
Owner and Chairman of the Board: David D. Glass
General Manager: Allard Baird
Manager: Buddy Bell
Vice President, Broadcasting/PR: David Witty
www.kcroyals.com

Los Angeles Dodgers
Address: 1000 Elysian Park Avenue
             Los Angeles, CA 90012-1199
Telephone: (323) 224-1500
Stadium (Capacity): Dodger Stadium (56,000)
Chairman: Frank McCourt
President and COO: Martin Greenspun
Executive VP/GM: Paul DePodesta
Manager: TBA
Director Public Relations: Josh Rawitch
www.dodgers.com

Milwaukee Brewers
Address: 1 Brewers Way
             Milwaukee, WI 53214
Telephone: (414) 902-4400
Stadium (Capacity): Miller Park (41,900)
Owner and Chairman: Mark Attanasio
General Manager: Doug Melvin
Manager: Ned Yost
Vice President of Communications: Tyler Barnes
www.milwaukeebrewers.com

Minnesota Twins
Address: 34 Kirby Puckett Place
             Minneapolis, MN 55415
Telephone: (612) 375-1366
Stadium (Capacity): Hubert H. Humphrey
  Metrodome (56,000)
Owner: Carl Pohlad
General Manager: Terry Ryan
Manager: Ron Gardenhire
Manager of Media Relations: Mike Herman
www.twinsbaseball.com

Washington Nationals
Address: 2400 East Capitol Street SE
             Washington, D.C., 20003
Telephone: (202) 675-9679
Stadium (Capacity): RFK Stadium (56,000)
President & CEO: Tony Tavares

Washington Nationals *(Cont.)*
Vice President and General Manager: Jim Bowden
Manager: Frank Robinson
Vice President of Communications: Chartese Berry
www.montrealexpos.com

New York Mets
Address: Shea Stadium
             123-01 Roosevelt Ave.
             Flushing, NY 11368
Telephone: (718) 507-6387
Stadium (Capacity): Shea Stadium (56,749)
Owner: Fred Wilpon
General Manager: Omar Minaya
Manager: Willie Randolph
VP of Media Relations: Jay Horwitz
www.mets.com

New York Yankees
Address: Yankee Stadium
             Bronx, NY 10451
Telephone: (718) 293-4300
Stadium (Capacity): Yankee Stadium (57,746)
Principal Owner: George Steinbrenner
Chief Operating Officer: Lonn Trost
VP/General Manager: Brian Cashman
Manager: Joe Torre
Director of Media Relations: Rick Cerone
www.yankees.com

Oakland Athletics
Address: 7000 Coliseum Way
             Oakland, CA 94621
Telephone: (510) 638-4900
Stadium (Capacity): Network Associates Coliseum
(50,000)
Co-Owner: Lewis Wolff
President: Michael Crowley
General Manager: Billy Beane
Manager: Ken Macha
Director of Public Relations: Jim Young
www.oaklandathletics.com

Philadelphia Phillies
Address: One Citizens Bank Way
             Philadelphia, PA 19101-7575
Telephone: (215) 463-6000
Stadium (Capacity): Citizens Bank Park (43,500)
Chairman: Bill Giles
President: David P. Montgomery
General Manager: TBA
Manager: Charlie Manuel
Vice President, Public Relations: Larry Shenk
www.phillies.com

Pittsburgh Pirates
Address: 115 Federal Street
             Pittsburgh, PA 15212
Telephone: (412) 323-5000
Stadium (Capacity): PNC Park (37,496)
CEO and Managing General Partner: Kevin McClatchy
Senior VP and General Manager: Dave Littlefield
Manager: Jim Tracy
Director of Media Relations: Jim Trdinich
www.pirateball.com

St. Louis Cardinals
Address: Busch Stadium/ 250 Stadium Plaza
             St. Louis, MO 63102
Telephone: (314) 421-3060
Stadium (Capacity): Busch Stadium (50,345)
President: Mark Lamping
Senior Vice President and GM: Walt Jocketty
Manager: Tony LaRussa
Director of Media Relations: Brian Bartow
www.stlcardinals.com

San Diego Padres
Address: P.O. Box 122000
San Diego, CA 92112
Telephone: (619) 795-5000
Stadium (Capacity): PETCO Park (42,445)
Chairman: John Moores
General Manager: Kevin Towers
Manager: Bruce Bochy
Director of Media Relations: Luis Garcia
www.padres.com

San Francisco Giants
Address: 24 Willie Mays Plaza
San Francisco, CA 94107
Telephone: (415) 972-2000
Stadium (Capacity): SBC Park (41,503)
President/Managing General Partner: Peter Magowan
General Manager: Brian Sabean
Manager: Felipe Alou
Director of Media Relations: Blake Rhodes
www.sfgiants.com

Seattle Mariners
Address: 1250 First Avenue South
Seattle, WA 98134
Telephone: (206) 346-4000
Stadium (Capacity): SAFECO Field (47,116)
Chairman and CEO: Howard Lincoln
General Manager: Bill Bavasi
Manager: Mike Hargrove
Director of Baseball Information: Tim Hevly
www.seattlemariners.com

Tampa Bay Devil Rays
Address: One Tropicana Drive
St. Petersburg, FL 33705
Telephone: (727) 825-3137
Stadium (Capacity): Tropicana Field (43,761)
President: Matthew Silverman
General Manager: TBA
Manager: Lou Piniella
Vice President, Public Relations: Rick Vaughn
www.devilrays.com

Texas Rangers
Address: 1000 Ballpark Way #400
Arlington, TX 76011
Telephone: (817) 273-5222
Stadium (Capacity): Ameriquest Field (49,115)
Owner: Thomas O. Hicks
General Manager: Jon Daniels
Manager: Buck Showalter
Manager of Media Relations: Rich Rice
www.texasrangers.com

Toronto Blue Jays
Address: SkyDome
1 Blue Jays Way, Suite 3200
Toronto, Ontario M5V 1J1 Canada
Telephone: (416) 341-1000
Stadium (Capacity): Rogers Centre (50,516)
President/CEO: Paul Godfrey
Senior Vice President/GM: J.P. Ricciardi
Manager: John Gibbons
Directo of Communications: Jay Stenhouse
www.bluejays.com

Pro Football Directory

National Football League
Address: 280 Park Avenue
New York, NY 10017
Telephone: (212) 450-2000
Commissioner: Paul Tagliabue
www.nfl.com

NFL Players Association
Address: 2021 L Street, N.W.
Washington, D.C. 20036
Telephone: (202) 463-2200
Executive Director: Gene Upshaw
Director of Communications: Carl Francis
www.nflpa.org

Arizona Cardinals
Address: P.O. Box 888
Phoenix, AZ 85001
Telephone: (602) 379-0101
Stadium (Capacity): Cardinals Stadium (73,000)
President and Owner: Bill Bidwill
VP of Football Operations: Rod Graves
Head Coach: Dennis Green
Director of Public Relations: Mark Dalton
www.azcardinals.com

Atlanta Falcons
Address: 4400 Falcon Park Way
Flowery Branch, GA 30542
Telephone: (770) 965-3115
Stadium (Capacity): Georgia Dome (71,149)
Owner and CEO: Arthur Blank
President and GM: Rich McKay
Coach: Jim Mora Jr.
Senior Director of Media Relations: Frank Kleha
www.atlantafalcons.com

Baltimore Ravens
Address: 11001 Owings Mills Blvd.
Owings Mills, MD 21117
Telephone: (410) 654-6200
Stadium (Capacity): M & T Bank Stadium (69,084)
Owner/CEO: Art Modell
President/COO: David Modell
Coach: Brian Billick
VP of Public Relations: Kevin Byrne
www.baltimoreravens.com

Buffalo Bills
Address: One Bills Drive
Orchard Park, NY 14127
Telephone: (716) 648-1800
Stadium (Capacity): Ralph Wilson Stadium (73,967)
Chairman: Ralph C. Wilson Jr.
President and General Manager: Tom Donohoe
Coach: Mike Mularkey
Vice President of Communications: Scott Berchtold
www.buffalobills.com

Carolina Panthers
Address: Ericsson Stadium
800 South Mint St.
Charlotte, NC 28202
Telephone: (704) 358-7000
Stadium (Capacity): Bank of America Stadium (73,298)
Founder and Owner: Jerry Richardson
President: Mark Richardson
General Manager: Marty Hurney
Coach: John Fox
Director of Communications: Charlie Dayton
www.panthers.com

Chicago Bears
Address:.   1000 Football Drive
          Lake Forest, IL 60045
Telephone: (847) 295-6600
Stadium (Capacity): Soldier Field (61,500)
President/CEO: Ted Phillips
General Manager: Jerry Angelo
Coach: Lovie Smith
Director of Public Relations: Scott Hagel
www.chicagobears.com

Cincinnati Bengals
Address: 100 Alfred Lerner Way
          Cincinnati, OH 44114
Telephone: (513) 621-3550
Stadium (Capacity): Paul Brown Stadium (65,327)
President: Mike Brown
Executive Vice President: Katherine Blackburn
Coach: Marvin Lewis
Director of Public Relations: Jack Brennan
www.bengals.com

Cleveland Browns
Address: 76 Lou Groza Boulevard
          Berea, OH 44017
Telephone: (440) 891-5000
Stadium (Capacity): Cleveland Browns Stadium (73,200)
Owner: Randy Lerner
Senior VP and General Manager: Phil Savage
Coach: Romeo Crennel
VP of Communications: Bill Bonsiewicz
www.clevelandbrowns.com

Dallas Cowboys
Address: One Cowboys Parkway
          Irving, TX 75063
Telephone: (972) 556-9900
Stadium (Capacity): Texas Stadium (65,639)
Owner, President and General Manager: Jerry Jones
Coach: Bill Parcells
Public Relations Director: Rich Dalrymple
www.dallascowboys.com

Denver Broncos
Address: 13655 Broncos Parkway
          Englewood, CO 80112
Telephone: (303) 649-9000
Stadium (Capacity): INVESCO Field at Mile High (76,125)
President and Chief Executive Officer: Pat Bowlen
General Manager: Ted Sundquist
Coach: Mike Shanahan
VP of Public Relations: Jim Saccomano
www.denverbroncos.com

Detroit Lions
Address: 222 Republic Drive
          Allen Park, MI 48101
Telephone: (313) 216-4000
Stadium (Capacity): Ford Field (65,000)
Owner/Chairman: William Clay Ford
President/CEO: Matt Millen
Coach: Steve Mariucci
Director of Media Relations: Matt Barnhart
www.detroitlions.com

Green Bay Packers
Address: 1265 Lombardi Avenue
          Green Bay, WI 54304
Telephone: (920) 569-7500
Stadium (Capacity): Lambeau Field (72,515)
President: Bob Harlan
Executive VP/GM/Coach: Mike Sherman
Executive Director of Public Relations: Jeff Blumb
www.packers.com

Houston Texans
Address: Two Reliant Park
          Houston, TX 77054
Telephone: (832) 667-2000
Stadium (Capacity): Reliant Stadium (71,054)
Chairman and CEO: Robert C. McNair
Senior VP and General Manager: Charley Casserly
Coach: Dom Capers
Media Realtions Manager: Rocky Harris
www.houstontexans.com

Indianapolis Colts
Address: 7001 West 56th Street
          Indianapolis, IN 46254
Telephone: (317) 297-2658
Stadium (Capacity): RCA Dome (56,127)
Owner and Chief Executive Officer: Jim Irsay
President: Bill Polian
Senior Executive Vice President: Pete Ward
Coach:Tony Dungy
Vice President of Public Relations: Craig Kelley
www.colts.com

Jacksonville Jaguars
Address: One Alltel Stadium Place
          Jacksonville, FL 32202
Telephone: (904) 633-6000
Stadium (Capacity): Alltel Stadium (73,000)
Owner: J. Wayne Weaver
Vice President and CFO: Bill Prescott
Senior VP of Football Operations: Paul Vance
Coach: Jack Del Rio
VP of Communications and Media: Dan Edwards
www.jaguars.com

Kansas City Chiefs
Address: One Arrowhead Drive
          Kansas City, MO 64129
Telephone: (816) 920-9300
Stadium (Capacity): Arrowhead Stadium (79,451)
Founder: Lamar Hunt
CEO, President and General Manager: Carl Peterson
Coach: Dick Vermeil
Public Relations Director: Bob Moore
www.kcchiefs.com

Miami Dolphins
Address: 7500 S.W. 30th Street
          Davie, FL 33314
Telephone: (954) 452-7000
Stadium (Capacity): Pro Player Stadium (75,540)
Chairman of the Board/Owner: H. Wayne Huizenga
General Manager: Randy Mueller
Head Coach: Nick Saban
Senior VP Media Relations: Harvey Greene
www.miamidolphins.com

Minnesota Vikings
Address: 9520 Viking Drive
          Eden Prairie, MN 55344
Telephone: (952) 828-6500
Stadium (Capacity): HHH Metrodome (64,121)
Owner: Zygi Wilf
President: Mark Wilf
Coach: Mike Tice
Public Relations Director: Bob Hagan
www.vikings.com

New England Patriots
Address: Gillette Stadium
          1 Patriot Place, Foxboro, MA 02035
Telephone: (508) 543-8200
Stadium (Capacity): Gillette Stadium (68,436)
Owner and Chairman: Robert K. Kraft
Vice Chairman: Jonathan Kraft
Coach: Bill Belichick
Director of Media Relations: Stacey James
www.patriots.com

New Orleans Saints
Address: 5800 Airline Drive
                Metairie, LA 70003
Telephone: (504) 733-0255
Stadium (Capacity): Louisiana Superdome (68,390)
Owner: Tom Benson
GM of Football Operations: Mickey Loomis
Head Coach: Jim Haslett
Director of Media Relations: Greg Bensel
www.neworleanssaints.com

New York Giants
Address: Giants Stadium
                East Rutherford, NJ 07073
Telephone: (201) 935-8111
Stadium (Capacity): Giants Stadium (80,242)
President and co-CEO: Wellington T. Mara
Chairman and co-CEO: Preston Robert Tisch
Senior VP and General Manager: Ernie Accorsi
Coach: Tom Coughlin
Vice President of Communications: Pat Hanlon
www.giants.com

New York Jets
Address: 1000 Fulton Avenue
                Hempstead, NY 11550
Telephone: (516) 560-8100
Stadium (Capacity): Giants Stadium (80,062)
Owner: Robert Wood Johnson IV
General Manager: Terry Bradway
Coach: Herman Edwards
VP of Public Relations: Ron Colangelo
www.newyorkjets.com

Oakland Raiders
Address: 1220 Harbor Bay Parkway
                Alameda, CA 94502
Telephone: (510) 864-5000
Stadium (Capacity): McAfee Coliseum (63,132)
Owner: Al Davis
Coach: Norv Turner
Director of Public Relations: Mike Taylor
www.raiders.com

Philadelphia Eagles
Address: NovaCare Complex
                1 NovaCare Way
                Philadelphia, PA 19145
Telephone: (215) 463-2500
Stadium (Capacity): Lincoln Financial Field (68,532)
Chairman: Jeffrey Lurie
Exec. VP of Football Operations/Coach: Andy Reid
Director of Football Media Services: Derek Boyko
www.philadelphiaeagles.com

Pittsburgh Steelers
Address: 3400 South Water Street
                Pittsburgh, PA 15203
Telephone: (412) 432-7800
Stadium (Capacity): Heinz Field (64,350)
Chairman: Dan Rooney
Director of Football Operations: Kevin Colbert
Coach: Bill Cowher
Manager of Public Relations: Burt Lauten
www.steelers.com

St. Louis Rams
Address: One Rams Way
                St. Louis, MO 63045
Telephone: (314) 982-7267
Stadium (Capacity): Edward Jones Dome (66,000)
Owner and Chairman: Georgia Frontiere
President: John Shaw
Coach: Mike Martz
Director of Public Relations: Duane Lewis
www.stlouisrams.com

San Diego Chargers
Address: Qualcomm Stadium
                4020 Murphy Canyon Road
                San Diego, CA 92123
Telephone: (858) 874-4500
Stadium (Capacity): Qualcomm Stadium (71,500)
Chairman: Alex G. Spanos
President and CEO: Dean A. Spanos
Executive VP and General Manager: A.J. Smith
Coach: Marty Schottenheimer
Director of Public Relations: Bill Johnston
www.chargers.com

San Francisco 49ers
Address: 4949 Centennial Boulevard
                Santa Clara, CA 95054
Telephone: (408) 562-4949
Stadium (Capacity): Monster Park (69,734)
Owner: Denise DeBartolo-York
Owner: John York
VP of Player Personnel: Scot McCloughan
Coach: Mike Nolan
Public Relations Director: Aaron Salkin
www.49ers.com

Seattle Seahawks
Address: 11220 N.E. 53rd Street
                Kirkland, WA 98033
Telephone: (425) 827-9777
Stadium (Capacity): Qwest Field (67,000)
Owner: Paul Allen
President: Jody Pratt
President of Football Operations: Tim Ruskell
Coach: Mike Holmgren
Director of Public Relations: Dave Pearson
www.seahawks.com

Tampa Bay Buccaneers
Address: One Buccaneer Place
                Tampa, FL 33607
Telephone: (813) 870-2700
Stadium (Capacity): Raymond James Stadium (66,321)
Owner: Malcolm Glazer
General Manager: Bruce Allen
Coach: Jon Gruden
Communications Manager: Jeff Kamis
www.buccaneers.com

Tennessee Titans
Address: 460 Great Circle Road
                Nashville, TN 37228
Telephone: (615) 565-4000
Stadium (Capacity): The Coliseum (68,798)
Owner: K.S. Adams Jr.
General Manager: Floyd Reese
Coach: Jeff Fisher
Director of Media Relations: Robbie Bohren
www.titansonline.com

Washington Redskins
Address: 21300 Redskins Park Drive
                Ashburn, VA 20147
Telephone: (703) 726-7000
Stadium (Capacity): Fedex Field (86,484)
Owner: Daniel M. Snyder
VP of Football Operations: Vinny Cerrato
Coach: Joe Gibbs
Director of Public Relations: Michelle Tessier
www.redskins.com

Other Leagues

Canadian Football League
Address: 50 Wellington Street East - 3rd Floor
              Toronto, Ontario M5E1C8 Canada
Telephone: (416) 322-9650
Commissioner:Tom E.S. Wright
Senior VP, Business Operations/Treasurer: James E. Grundy
Director of Football Media: Shawn Lackie
www.cfl.ca

NFL EUROPE
Address: 280 Park Avenue
              New York, NY 10017
Telephone: (212) 450-2000
Managing Directrors: John Beake and Jim Connolly
Chief Operating Officer: Dan Margoshes (London)
Director of Communications: David Tossel
www.nfleurope.com

Pro Basketball Directory

National Basketball Association

National Basketball Association
Address: 645 Fifth Avenue
              New York, NY 10022
Telephone: (212) 826-7000
Commissioner: David Stern
Deputy Commissioner: Russell Granik
Sr. VP of Communications: Brian McIntyre
www.nba.com

National Basketball Association Players Association
Address: 2 Penn Plaza
              Suite 2430
              New York, NY 10121
Telephone: (212) 655-0880
Executive Director: William Hunter
www.nbpa.com

Atlanta Hawks
Address: One CNN Center
              Atlanta, GA 30303
Telephone: (404) 827-3800
Arena (Capacity): Philips Arena (19,445)
Owner: Atlanta Spirit, LLC
President and CEO: Bernie Mullin
General Manager: Billy Knight
Coach: Mike Woodson
VP of Communications: Arthur Triche
www.hawks.com

Boston Celtics
Address: 151 Merrimac Street
              Boston, MA 02114
Telephone: (617) 523-6050
Arena (Capacity): FleetCenter (18,624)
CEO and Managing Partner: Wyc Grousbeck
Executive Dir. of Basketball Operations: Danny Ainge
Coach: Doc Rivers
Manager of Communications: Farra D'Orazio
www.celtics.com

Charlotte Bobcats
Address: 100 Hive Drive
              Charlotte, NC 28217
Telephone: (704) 424-4120
Arena (Capacity): Charlotte Coliseum (23,319)
Owner: Robert L. Johnson
General Manager and Coach: Bernie Bickerstaff
Director of Public Relations: Scott Leightman
www.bobcatsbasketball.com

Chicago Bulls
Address: 1901 W. Madison Street
              Chicago, IL 60612
Telephone: (312) 455-4000
Arena (Capacity): United Center (21,711)
Chairman: Jerry Reinsdorf
Executive VP of Basketball Operations: John Paxson
Coach: Scott Skiles
Senior Director of Media Services: Tim Hallam
www.bulls.com

Cleveland Cavaliers
Address: One Center Court
              Cleveland, OH 44115
Telephone: (216) 420-2000
Arena (Capacity): Gund Arena (20,562)
Chairman: Gordon Gund
President and GM: Jim Paxson
Coach: Mike Brown
Director of Public Relations: Amanda Mercado
www.cavs.com

Dallas Mavericks
Address: 2909 Taylor Street
              Dallas, TX 75224
Telephone: (214) 747-6287
Arena (Capacity): American Airlines Center (19,200)
Owner: Mark Cuban
General Manager: Don Nelson
Head Coach: Avery Johnson
Sr. VP of Marketing/Communications: Matt Fitzgerald
www.dallasmavericks.com

Denver Nuggets
Address: Pepsi Center
              1000 Chopper Circle
              Denver, CO 80204
Telephone: (303) 405-1100
Arena (Capacity): Pepsi Center (19,099)
Owner: E. Stanley Kroenke
General Manager: Kiki Vandeweghe
Coach: George Karl
Director of Media Relations: Eric Sebastian
www.nuggets.com

Detroit Pistons
Address: The Palace of Auburn Hills
              Four Championship Drive
              Auburn Hills, MI 48326
Telephone: (248) 377-0100
Arena (Capacity): The Palace of Auburn Hills (22,076)
Owner: William M. Davidson
President of Basketball Operations: Joe Dumars
Coach: Flip Saunders
VP of Public Relations: Matt Dobek
www.pistons.com

National Basketball Association (Cont.)

Golden State Warriors
Address: 1011 Broadway
             Oakland, CA 94607-4019
Telephone: (510) 986-2200
Arena (Capacity): The Arena in Oakland (19,596)
Owner and CEO: Christopher Cohan
Executive VP of Basketball Operations: Chris Mullin
Coach: Mike Montgomery
Director of Public Relations: Raymond Ridder
www.gs-warriors.com

Houston Rockets
Address: Two Greenway Plaza, Suite 400
             Houston, TX 77046
Telephone: (713) 627-3865
Arena (Capacity): Toyota Center (18,300)
Owner: Leslie Alexander
President and CEO: George Postolos
General Manager: Carroll Dawson
Coach: Jeff Van Gundy
Director of Team Communications: Nelson Luis
www.rockets.com

Indiana Pacers
Address: 125 S. Pennsylvania Street
             Indianapolis, IN 46204
Telephone: (317) 917-2500
Arena (Capacity): Conseco Fieldhouse (18,345)
Owners: Melvin Simon and Herbert Simon
CEO/President: Donnie Walsh
President of Basketball Operations: Larry Bird
Head Coach: Rick Carlisle
Media Relations Director: David Benner
www.pacers.com

Los Angeles Clippers
Address: The Staples Center
             1111 S. Figueroa Street - St. 1100
             Los Angeles, CA 90015
Telephone: (213) 742-7500
Arena (Capacity): The Staples Center (18,964)
Owner: Donald T. Sterling
Vice President of Basketball Operations: Elgin Baylor
Coach: Mike Dunleavy
Vice President of Communications: Joe Safety
www.clippers.com

Los Angeles Lakers
Address: 555 North Nash Street
             El Segundo, CA 90245
Telephone: (310) 426-6000
Arena (Capacity): The Staples Center (18,997)
Owner: Dr. Jerry Buss
General Manager: Mitch Kupchak
Coach: Phil Jackson
Director of Public Relations: John Black
www.lakers.com

Memphis Grizzlies
Address: 191 Beale Street
             Memphis TN 38103
Telephone: (901) 205-1235
Arena (Capacity): FedEx Forum (18,500)
Majority Owner: Michael E. Heisley
General Manager: Jerry West
Coach: Mike Fratello
Director of Media Relations: Kirk Clayborn
www.grizzlies.com

Miami Heat
Address: American Airlines Arena
             601 Biscayne Boulevard
             Miami, FL 33132
Telephone: (786) 777-1000
Arena (Capacity): American Airlines Arena (16,500)
Managing General Partner: Micky Arison
President of Basketball Operations: Pat Riley
General Manager: Randy Pfund
Coach: Stan Van Gundy
VP of Sports Media Relations: Tim Donovan
www.heat.com

Milwaukee Bucks
Address: The Bradley Center
             1001 N. Fourth Street
             Milwaukee, WI 53203
Telephone: (414) 227-0500
Arena (Capacity): The Bradley Center (18,717)
Owner: Herb Kohl
General Manager: Larry Harris
Coach: Terry Stotts
Public Relations Director: Cheri Hanson
www.bucks.com

Minnesota Timberwolves
Address: 600 First Avenue North
             Minneapolis, MN 55403
Telephone: (612) 673-1600
Arena (Capacity): Target Center (19,006)
Owner: Glen Taylor
VP of Basketball Operations: Kevin McHale
Coach: Dwone Casey
Director of Communications: Ted Johnson
www.timberwolves.com

New Jersey Nets
Address: 390 Murray Hill Parkway
             East Rutherford, NJ 07073
Telephone: (201) 935-8888
Arena (Capacity): Continental Airlines Arena (20,049)
Owner: Bruce Ratner
General Manager: Ed Stefanski
Coach: Lawrence Frank
Director of Public Relations: Gary Sussman
www.njnets.com

New Orleans Hornets
Address: 210 Park Avenue, Suite 1850
             Oklahoma, OK 73102
Telephone: (405) 208-4700
Arena (Capacity): New Orleans Arena (18,500)
Majority Owner: George Shinn
General Manager: Jeff Bower
Coach: Byron Scott
Manager of Sports Public Relations: Scott Hall
www.hornets.com

New York Knicks
Address: Madison Square Garden
             Two Pennsylvania Plaza
             New York, NY 10121
Telephone: (212) 465-6471
Arena (Capacity): Madison Square Garden (19,763)
Owner: ITT/Sheraton and Cablevision
Chairman: James Dolan
President of Basketball Operations: Isiah Thomas
Coach: Larry Brown
Vice President of Public Relations: Joe Favorito
www.nyknicks.com

National Basketball Association *(Cont.)*

Orlando Magic
Address: Two Magic Place
           8701 Maitland Summit Blvd.
           Orlando, FL 32810
Telephone: (407) 916-2400
Arena (Capacity): TD Waterhouse Centre (17,248)
Owner: Rich DeVos
Senior Executive Vice President: Pat Williams
Coach: Brian Hill
Director of Media Relations: Joel Glass
www.orlandomagic.com

Philadelphia 76ers
Address: First Union Center
           3601 South Broad Street
           Philadelphia, PA 19148
Telephone: (215) 339-7600
Arena (Capacity): Wachovia Center (20,444)
Chairman: Ed Snider
General Manager: Billy King
Coach: Maurice Cheeks
VP of Communications: Karen Frascona
www.sixers.com

Phoenix Suns
Address: 201 East Jeffreson Street
           Phoenix, AZ 85004
Telephone: (602) 379-7900
Arena (Capacity): America West Arena (19,023)
Chairman/CEO and Managing General Partner: Jerry Colangelo
President and General Manager: Bryan Colangelo
Coach: Mike D'Antoni
VP of Basketball Communications: Julie Fie
www.suns.com

Portland Trail Blazers
Address: One Center Court
           Suite 200
           Portland, OR 97227
Telephone: (503) 234-9291
Arena (Capacity): Rose Garden Arena (19,980)
Chairman of the Board: Paul Allen
President: Steve Patterson
General Manager: John Nash
Coach: Nate McMillan
Executive Director of Communications: Mike Hanson
www.blazers.com

Sacramento Kings
Address: One Sports Parkway
           Sacramento, CA 95834
Telephone: (916) 928-0000
Arena (Capacity): ARCO Arena (17,317)
Owners: Joe and Gavin Maloof
President of Basketball Operations: Geoff Petrie
Coach: Rick Adelman
Director of Media Relations: Troy Hanson
www.kings.com

San Antonio Spurs
Address: One SBC Center
           San Antonio, TX 78219
Telephone: (210) 444-5000
Arena (Capacity): SBC Center (18,500)
Chairman: Peter Holt
General Manager: R.C. Buford
Head Coach : Gregg Popovich
Director of Media Services: Tom James
www.spurs.com

Seattle SuperSonics
Address: 351 Elliott Avenue West
           Suite 500
           Seattle, WA 98119
Telephone: (206) 281-5800
Arena (Capacity): KeyArena (17,072)
Owner: The Basketball Club of Seattle, LLC
Chairman: Howard Schultz
President/CEO: Wally Walker
General Manager: Rick Sund
Coach: Bob Weiss
Director of Public Relations: Marc Moquin
www.supersonics.com

Toronto Raptors
Address: 40 Bay Street, Suite 400
           Toronto, Ontario M5J 2X2 Canada
Telephone: (416) 815-5600
Arena (Capacity): Air Canada Centre (19,800)
Owner: Maple Leaf Sports and Entertainment, Ltd.
General Manager: Rob Babcock
Coach: Sam Mitchell
Director of Media Relations: Jim Labumbard
www.raptors.com

Utah Jazz
Address: 301 West So. Temple
           Salt Lake City, UT 84101
Telephone: (801) 325-2500
Arena (Capacity): Delta Center (19,911)
Owner: Larry H. Miller
President: Dennis Haslam
VP of Basketball Operations: Kevin O'Connor
Coach: Jerry Sloan
Director of Media Relations: Kim Turner
www.utahjazz.com

Washington Wizards
Address: 601 F Street NW
           Washington D.C. 20004
Telephone: (202) 661-5000
Arena (Capacity): MCI Center (20,173)
Owner: Abe Pollin
President of Basketball Operations: Ernie Grunfeld
Coach: Eddie Jordan
Director of Public Relations: Nicole Hawkins
www.washingtonwizards.com

Women's National Basketball Association

Women's National Basketball Association
Address: 645 Fifth Avenue
             New York, NY 10022
Telephone: (212) 688-9622
President: Donna Orender
Senior Dir. of Communications: Sharon Robustelli
www.wnba.com

Charlotte Sting
Address: 129 West Trade Street, Suite 700
             Charlotte, NC 28202
Telephone: (704) 357-0252
Arena (Capacity): Charlotte Coliseum (12,843)
Owner Robert Johnson
Coach: Muggsy Bogues
VP of Public Relations: Scott Leightman
www.charlottesting.com

Connecticut Sun
Address: One Mohegan Sun Blvd.
             Uncasville, CT 06382
Telephone: (877) 786-8499
Arena (Capacity): Mohegan Sun Arena (9,341)
CEO: Mitchell Etess
General Manager: Chris Sienko
Coach: Mike Thibault
Media Relations Manager: Bill Tavares
www.connecticutsun.com

Detroit Shock
Address: 2 Championship Drive
             Auburn Hills, MI 48326
Telephone: (248) 377-0100
Arena (Capacity): The Palace of Auburn Hills (19,000)
Managing Partner: William Davidson
President: Tom Wilson
Head Coach: Bill Laimbeer
Director of Media Relations: Paul Hickey
www.detroitshock.com

Houston Comets
Address: Two Greenway Plaza, Suite 400
             Houston, TX. 77046-3865
Telephone: (713) 627-9622
Arena (Capacity): Toyota Center (18,500)
President: Leslie L. Alexander
Coach and General Manager: Van Chancellor
Director of Media Relations: Nelson Luis
www.houstoncomets.com

Indiana Fever
Address: 125 S. Pennsylvania Street
             Indianapolis, IN 46204
Telephone: (317) 917-2500
Arena (Capacity): Conseco Field House (18,345)
President: Donnie Walsh
Pres. of Basketball Operatons: Larry Bird
Coach: Rick Carlisle
VP of Communications: Quinn Buckner
www.wnba.com/fever

Los Angeles Sparks
Address: 555 Nash Street
             El Segundo, CA 90245
Telephone: (310) 330-2434
Arena (Capacity): Staples Center (19,282)
Chairman: Dr. Jerry Buss
General Manager: Virginia (Penny) Toler
Coach: Joe Bryant
Media Relations Director: Kristal Shipp
www.lasparks.com

Minnesota Lynx
Address: Target Center
             600 First Avenue North
             Minneapolis, MN 55403
Telephone: (612) 673-8400
Arena (Capacity): Target Center (19,006)
Owner: Glen Taylor
Coach: Suzie McConnell Serio
Public Relations Manager: Mike Cristaldi
www.wnba.com/lynx/

New York Liberty
Address: Two Penn Plaza
             New York, NY 10121
Telephone: (212) 465-5867
Arena (Capacity): Madison Square Garden (19,763)
GM and Vice President: Carol Blazejowski
Coach: Pat Coyle
VP of Marketing and Communications: Amy Scheer
www.nyliberty.com

Phoenix Mercury
Address: 201 East Jefferson Street
             Phoenix, AZ 85004
Telephone: (602) 514-8333
Arena (Capacity): America West Arena (10,746)
Chairman and CEO: Jerry Colangelo
General Manager: Seth Sulka
Coach: Carrie Graf
Media Relations Director: Tami Nealy
www.phoenixmercury.com

Sacramento Monarchs
Address: One Sports Parkway
             Sacramento, CA 95834
Telephone: (916) 928-0000
Arena (Capacity): ARCO Arena (17,317)
Owner: Maloof Family
President: John Thomas
GM and Coach: John Whisenant
Manager of Media Relations: Kimberly Williams
www.sacramentomonarchs.com

San Antonio Silver Stars
Address: One SBC Center
             San Antonio, TX 78219
Telephone: (210) 444-5050
Arena (Capacity): SBC Center (18,500)
Owner: Spurs Sports & Entertainment
COO: Clarissa Davis-Wrightsil
Coach: Dan Hughes
Media Services Manager: Kris Davis
www.sanantoniosilverstars.com

Women's National Basketball Association (Cont.)

Seattle Storm
Address: 351 Elliott Avenue West
           Suite 500
           Seattle, WA 98119
Telephone: (206) 281-5800
Arena (Capacity): Key Arena (12,000)
Owners: The Basketball Club of Seattle LLC
Chairman: Howard Schultz
Coach: Anne Donovan
Director, Public Relations: Valerie O'Neil
www.wnba.com/storm

Washington Mystics
Address: MCI Center
           401 9th Street NW
           Washington, DC 20004
Telephone: (202) 266-2361
Arena (Capacity): MCI Center (19,093)
President: Sheila Jackson
General Manager: Linda Hargrove
Coach: Ritchie Aderbato
Director, Public Relations: Nicole Boden
www.washingtonmystics.com

Hockey Directory

National Hockey League
Address: 1251 Avenue of the Americas
           47th floor
           New York, NY 10020-1198
Telephone: (212) 789-2000
Commissioner: Gary Bettman
President of NHL Enterprises: Ed Horne
Executive VP and Dir. of Hockey Operations: Colin Campbell
VP of Media Relations: Frank Brown
www.nhl.com

National Hockey League Players Association
Address: 777 Bay Street, Suite 2400
           Toronto, Ontario M5G 2C8 Canada
Telephone: (416) 313-2300
Executive Director: Ted Saskin
www.nhlpa.com

Mighty Ducks of Anaheim
Address: Arrowhead Pond of Anaheim
           2695 Katella Avenue
           Anaheim, CA 92806
Telephone: (877) 945-9464
Arena (Capacity): Arrowhead Pond of Anaheim (17,174)
CEO: Michael Schulman
Executive VP and General Manager: Brian Burke
Coach: Randy Carlyle
Director of Communications: Alex Gilchrist
www.mightyducks.com

Atlanta Thrashers
Address: 1 CNN Center
           P.O. Box 15538
           Atlanta, GA 30348
Telephone: (404) 827-5300
Arena (Capacity): Philips Arena (18,545)
Owner: Atlanta Spirit, LLC
Governor: Bruce Levenson
VP and General Manager: Don Waddell
Coach: Bob Hartley
Senior VP Communications: Tom Hughes
www.atlantathrashers.com

Boston Bruins
Address: One Fleet Center Place, Suite 250
           Boston, MA 02114-1303
Telephone: (617) 624-1900
Arena (Capacity): FleetCenter (17,565)
Owner and Governor: Jeremy M. Jacobs
Alternative Governor and President: Harry Sinden
VP/General Manager and Alt. Governor: Mike O'Connell
Coach: Mike Sullivan
Director of Media Relations: Heidi Holland
www.bostonbruins.com

Buffalo Sabres
Address: HSBC Arena
           One Seymour H. Knox III Plaza
           Buffalo, NY 14203
Telephone: (716) 855-4100
Arena (Capacity): HSBC Arena (18,690)
Owner: B. Thomas Golisano
General Manager: Darcy Regier
Coach: Lindy Ruff
VP of Communications: Michael Gilbert
www.sabres.com

Calgary Flames
Address: Pengrowth Saddledome
           555 Saddledome Rise, SE
           Calgary, Alberta T2G 2W1
Telephone: (403) 777-2177
Arena (Capacity): Pengrowth Saddledome (17,409)
Owners: Harley N. Hotchkiss, N. Murray Edwards, Alvin G. Libin, Allan P. Markin, J.R. "Bud" McCaig, Byron J.Seaman, Daryl K. Seaman, Clayton H. Riddell
President and CEO: Ken King
General Manager and Coach: Darryl Sutter
Director of Communications: Peter Hanlon
www.calgaryflames.com

Carolina Hurricanes

Address: 1400 Edwards Mill Road
Raleigh, NC 27607
Telephone: (919) 467-7825
Arena (Capacity): RBC Center (18,730)
Owner: Peter Karmanos
CEO and General Manager: Jim Rutherford
VP/Assistant General Manager: Jason Karmanos
Coach: Peter Laviolette
Director of Media Relations: Mike Sundheim
www.carolinahurricanes.com

Chicago Blackhawks

Address: United Center
1901 W. Madison Street
Chicago, IL 60612
Telephone: (312) 455-7000
Arena (Capacity): United Center (20,500)
President: William W. Wirtz
General Manager: Dave Tallon
Coach: Trent Yawney
Executive Director of Communications: Jim DeMaria
www.chicagoblackhawks.com

Colorado Avalanche

Address: Pepsi Center
1000 Chopper Circle
Denver, CO 80204
Telephone: (303) 405-1100
Arena (Capacity): Pepsi Center (18,007)
Owner and Governor: E. Stanley Kroenke
Alt. Governor, President and General Manager: Pierre
Lacroix
Coach: Joel Quenneville
VP of Communications and Team Services:
Jean Martineau
www.coloradoavalanche.com

Columbus Blue Jackets

Address: 200 West Nationwide Boulevard
Columbus, OH 43215
Telephone: (614) 246-4625
Arena (Capacity): Nationwide Arena (18,136)
Owner: John H. McConnell
President, GM and Coach: Doug MacLean
Coach: Dave King
Director of Communications: Rob Scichili
www.bluejackets.com

Dallas Stars

Address: 2601 Avenue of the Stars
Frisco, TX 75034
Telephone: (218) 387-5500
Arena (Capacity): American Airlines Center (18,532)
Owner: Thomas O. Hicks
General Manager: Doug Armstrong
Coach: Dave Tippett
Director of Media Relations: Mark Janko
www.dallasstars.com

Detroit Red Wings

Address: Joe Louis Arena
600 Civic Center Drive
Detroit, MI 48226
Telephone: (313) 396-7444
Arena (Capacity): Joe Louis Arena (20,056)
Owner and Governor: Mike Ilitch
Owner, Secretary and Treasurer: Marian Ilitch
Senior Vice President/Alt. Governor: Jim Devellano
General Manager: Ken Holland
Coach: Mike Babcock
Senior Director of Communications: John Hahn
www.detroitredwings.com

Edmonton Oilers

Address: 11230 110th Street
Edmonton, Alberta T5G 3H7
Telephone: (780) 414-4000
Arena (Capacity): Rexall Place (16,839)
Owner: Edmonton Investors Group
President and CEO: Patrick LaForge
General Manager: Kevin Lowe
Coach: Craig MacTavish
Manager of Communications: Justin Copertino
www.edmontonoilers.com

Florida Panthers

Address: 1 Panther Parkway
Sunrise, FL 33323
Telephone: (954) 835-7000
Arena (Capacity): Bank Atlantic Center (19,250)
Chairman of the Board/CEO: Alan Cohen
Alternate Governor: William A. Torrey
General Manager: Mike Keenan
Coach: Jaques Martin
VP of Communications: Randy Sieminski
www.floridapanthers.com

Los Angeles Kings

Address: The Staples Center
1111 South Figueroa Street
Los Angeles, CA 90015
Telephone: (213) 742-7100
Arena (Capacity): The Staples Center (18,118)
Owners: Philip Anschutz and Edward P. Roske Jr.
President and Governor: Tim Leiweke
Vice President and GM: Dave Taylor
Coach: Andy Murray
Director of Media Relations: Mike Altieri
www.lakings.com

Minnesota Wild

Address: 317 Washington Street
St. Paul, MN, 55102
Telephone: (651) 602-6000
Arena (Capacity): Excel Energy Center (18,064)
Chairman: Bob Naegele Jr.
General Manager: Doug Risebrough
Coach: Jacques Lemaire
VP of Communications/Broadcasting: Bill Robertson
www.wild.com

Montreal Canadiens

Address: Bell Centre
        1260 de la Gauchetiere West
        Montreal, Quebec H3B 5E8 Canada
Telephone: (514) 932-2582
Arena (Capacity): Bell Centre (21,273)
Owner: George N. Gillett Jr.
President and Governor: Pierre Boivin
Executive VP and General Manager: Bob Gainey
Coach: Claude Julien
Director of Communications: Donald Beauchamp
www.canadiens.com

Nashville Predators

Address: Gaylord Entertainment Center
        501 Broadway
        Nashville, TN 37203
Telephone: (615) 770-2300
Arena (Capacity): Gaylord Entertainment Center (17,113)
Owner, Chairman and Governor: Craig Leipold
President, COO: Jack Diller
Executive VP of Hockey Operations/GM: David Poile
Coach: Barry Trotz
Director of Communications: Ken Anderson
www.nashvillepredators.com

New Jersey Devils

Address: Continental Airlines Arena, PO Box 504
        East Rutherford, NJ 07073
Telephone: (201) 935-6050
Arena (Capacity): Continental Airlines Arena (19,040)
Owners: Ray Chambers, Louis Katz and George Steinbrenner
CEO, President and GM: Lou Lamoriello
Coach: Larry Robinson
Director of Public Relations: Jeff Altstadter
www.newjerseydevils.com

New York Islanders

Address: 1535 Old Country Road
        Plainview, NY 11803
Telephone: (516) 501-6700
Arena (Capacity): Nassau Coliseum (16,234)
Owners: Charles Wong and Sanjay Kumar
Senior VP of Operations and Alt. Governor: Michael J. Picker
General Manager/Alt. Governor: Mike Milbury
Coach: Steve Stirling
VP of Communications: Chris Botta
www.newyorkislanders.com

New York Rangers

Address: Madison Square Garden
        2 Pennsylvania Plaza
        New York, NY 10121
Telephone: (212) 465-6000
Arena (Capacity): Madison Square Garden (18,200)
Owner: Cablevision
President and General Manager: Glen Sather
Coach: Tom Renney
VP of Public Relations: John Rosasco
www.newyorkrangers.com

Ottawa Senators

Address: The Corel Centre
        1000 Palladium Drive
        Ottawa, Ontario K2V 1A5 Canada
Telephone: (613) 599-0250
Arena (Capacity): The Corel Centre (18,500)
Owner, Governor and Chairman: Eugene Melnyk

Ottawa Senators (Cont.)

President and Chief Executive Officer: Roy Mlakar
General Manager: John Muckler
Coach: Bryan Murray
VP of Communications: Phil Legault
www.ottawasenators.com

Philadelphia Flyers

Address: Wachovia Complex
        3601 South Broad Street
        Philadelphia, PA 19148
Telephone: (215) 465-4500
Arena (Capacity): Wachovia Center (19,523)
Majority Owner: Comcast-Spectacor
Chairman: Ed Snider
President: Ron Ryan
General Manager: Bob Clarke
Coach: Ken Hitchcock
Sr. Director of Communications: Zack Hill
www.philadelphiaflyers.com

Phoenix Coyotes

Address: Glendale Arena
        9400 W. Maryland Avenue
        Glendale, AZ 85305
Telephone: (623) 772-3200
Arena (Capacity): Glendale Arena (17,653)
Chairman and Governor: Steve Ellman
Managing Partner and Alt. Governor: Wayne Gretzky
VP and General Manager: Michael Barnett
Coach: Wayne Gretzky
VP of Media and Player Relations: Richard Nairn
www.phoenixcoyotes.com

Pittsburgh Penguins

Address: Mellon Arena
        66 Mario Lemieux Place
        Pittsburgh, PA 15219
Telephone: (412) 642-1300
Arena (Capacity): Mellon Arena (16,958)
Owner: Mario Lemieux (Lemieux Ownership Group)
General Manager: Craig Patrick
Coach: Eddie Olczyk
Director of Media Relations: Keith Wehner
www.pittsburghpenguins.com

St. Louis Blues

Address: Savvis Center
        1401 Clark Avenue
        St. Louis, MO 63103
Telephone: (314) 622-2500
Arena (Capacity): Savvis Center (20,022)
President and Chief Executive Officer: Mark Sauer
Senior VP and General Manager: Larry Pleau
Coach: Mike Kitchen
Director of Communications: Chuck Menke
www.stlouisblues.com

San Jose Sharks

Address: HP Pavillion at San Jose
        525 West Santa Clara Street
        San Jose, CA 95113
Telephone: (408) 287-7070
Arena (Capacity): HP Pavillion at San Jose (17,496)
Owner: San Jose Sports And Entertainment Enterprises
President and CEO: Greg Jamison
Executive VP and General Manager: Doug Wilson
Coach: Ron Wilson
Director of Media Relations: Ken Arnold
www.sjsharks.com

Tampa Bay Lightning

Address: 401 Channelside Drive
             Tampa, FL 33602
Telephone: (813) 301-6600
Arena (Capacity): St. Pete Times Forum (19,758)
Owner: Palace Sports & Entertainment/Bill Davidson
and David Hermelin
CEO and Governor: Tom Wilson
General Manager: Jay Feaster
Coach: John Tortorella
VP of Public Relations: Bill Wickett
www.tampabaylightning.com

Toronto Maple Leafs

Address: Air Canada Centre
             40 Bay Street - St. 400
             Toronto, Ontario M5J 2X2 Canada
Telephone: (416) 815-5500
Arena (Capacity): Air Canada Centre (18,819)
Chairman: Lawrence M. Tanenbaum
President and CEO: Richard Peddie
GM: John Ferguson
Coach: Pat Quinn
Director of Media Relations: Pat Park
www.mapleleafs.com

Vancouver Canucks

Address: General Motors Place/800 Griffiths Way
             Vancouver, B.C. V6B 6G1
Telephone: (604) 899-4600
Arena (Capacity): General Motors Place (18,422)
Chairman and Governor: John E. McCaw Jr.
President and CEO: Stanley McCammon
Chief Operating Officer: David Cobb
Senior VP/GM: David Nonis
Coach: Marc Crawford
Manager of Media Relations: Chris Brumwell
www.canucks.com

Washington Capitals

Address: 401 Ninth Street, NW
             Suite 750
             Washington, DC 20004
Telephone: (202) 266-2200
Arena (Capacity): MCI Center (18,672)
Majority Owner and Chairman: Ted Leonsis
Owner and President: Richard M. Patrick
VP and General Manager: George McPhee
Coach: Glen Hanlon
Director of Media Relations: Nate Ewell
www.washingtoncaps.com

Olympic Sports Directory

United States Olympic Committee

Address: Olympic House
             1 Olympic Plaza
             Colorado Springs, CO 80909
Telephone: (719) 632-5551
Acting CEO: Jim Scherr
Chief Communications Officer: Darryl Seibel
www.usolympicteam.com

U.S. Olympic Training Centers

Address: 1 Olympic Plaza
             Colorado Springs, CO 80909
Telephone: (719) 632-5551
Director: John Smith

Address: 421 Old Military Road
             Lake Placid, NY 12946
Telephone: (518) 523-2600
Director: Jack Favro

Address: 2800 Olympic Parkway
             Chula Vista, CA 91915
Telephone: (619) 656-1500
Director: Patrice Milkovich
www.olympic.org

International Olympic Committee

Address: Chateau de Vidy
             Case Postale 356
             CH-1007 Lausanne, Switzerland
Telephone: 41-21-621-6111
President: Jacques Rogge
Director General: Francois Carrard
www.olympic.org

Torino Olympic Organizing Committee for the 2006 Winter Games

Address: Via Nizza 262/58
             10126 Torino (Italy)
Telephone: 39 011 63 10 511
President: Valentino Castellani
Press Operations: Cristiano Carlutti
(XX Winter Games; Feb 10–26, 2006)
www.torino2006.org

Beijing Olympic Organizing Committee for the 2008 Summer Games

Address: 24 Dongsi Shitao Street
             Beijing, China 100007
Telephone: (8610) 65282009
(XXVIII Summer Games; Aug 8–24, 2008)
www.beijing-olympic.org.cn

U.S. Olympic Organizations

National Archery Association (NAA)

Address: 1 Olympic Plaza
             Colorado Springs, CO 80909
Telephone: (719) 866-4576
President: Darrell Pace
Executive Director: Brad Camp
Media Relations: Mary Beth Vorwerk
www.usarchery.org

USA Badminton (USAB)

Address: 1 Olympic Plaza
             Colorado Springs, CO 80909
Telephone: (719) 866-4808
President: Cliff Peters
Executive Director: Dan Cloppas
Media Contact: Barb Kissick
www.usabadminton.org

U.S. Olympic Organizations *(Cont.)*

USA Baseball
Address: P.O. Box 1131
             Durham, NC 27702
Telephone: (919) 474-8721
President: Mike Gaski
Executive Director/CEO: Paul V. Seiler
Director of Communications: David Fanucchi
www.usabaseball.com

USA Basketball
Address: 5465 Mark Dabling Blvd.
             Colorado Springs, CO 80918
Telephone: (719) 590-4800
President: Val Ackerman
Executive Director: Jim Tooley
Assistant Executive Director for Public Relations:
  Craig Miller
www.usabasketball.com

U.S. Biathlon Association (USBA)
Address: 29 Ethan Allen Avenue
             Colchester, VT 05446
Telephone: (802) 654-7833
President: Bob Pokelwaldt
Executive Director: Claire DelNegro
PR and Media Manager: Tom LaDue
www.usbiathlon.org

U.S. Bobsled and Skeleton Federation
Address: P.O. Box 828
             Lake Placid, NY 12946
Telephone: (518) 523-1842
President: James Shea, Sr.
Executive Director: Robie Vaughn
Media and PR Director Director: Julie Urbansky
www.usabobsledandskeleton.org

USA Boxing, Inc.
Address: 1 Olympic Plaza
             Colorado Springs, CO 80909
Telephone: (719) 866-4506
President: Sandy Martinez-Pino
Executive Director: Lamont Jones
Director of PR and Media: Julie Goldsticker
www.usaboxing.org

U.S. Canoe and Kayak Team
Address: 230 South Tryon Street - Suite 220
             Charlotte, NC 28202
Telephone: (704) 348-4330
President: Mike Sloan
Executive Director: David Yarborough
Media/Communications: Luke Dieker
www.usacanoekayak.org

USA Cycling
Address: 1 Olympic Plaza
             Colorado Springs, CO 80909
Telephone: (719) 866-4581
President: Jim Ochowicz
Chief Executive Officer: Gerard Bisceglia
Director of Communications: Andy Lee
www.usacycling.org

United States Diving, Inc. (USD)
Address: Pan American Plaza, Suite 430
             201 South Capitol Avenue
             Indianapolis, IN 46225
Telephone: (317) 237-5252
President: Dave Burgering
Executive Director: Todd Smith
Director of Communications: Kelli Servizzi
www.usdiving.org

U.S. Equestrian Team (USET)
Address: Pottersville Rd.
             Gladstone, NJ 07934
Telephone: (908) 234-1251
Executive Director: Lori Rawls
Director of Communications: Marty Bauman
www.uset.org

U.S. Fencing Association (USFA)
Address: 1 Olympic Plaza
             Colorado Springs, CO 80909
Telephone: (719) 866-4511
President: Nancy Anderson
Executive Director: Michael Massik
Media Relations Director: Cynthia Bent
www.usfencing.org

U.S. Field Hockey Association (USFHA)
Address: 1 Olympic Plaza
             Colorado Springs, CO 80909-5773
Telephone: (719) 866-4567
President: Sharon Taylor
Executive Director: Sheila Walker
Sport and Public Information Director:
  Howard Thomas
www.usfieldhockey.com

U.S. Figure Skating Association
Address: 20 First Street
             Colorado Springs, CO 80906
Telephone: (719) 635-5200
President: Chuck Foster
Director of Media Relations: Lindsay DeWall
www.usfsa.org

USA Gymnastics
Address: Pan American Plaza, Suite 300
             201 South Capitol Avenue
             Indianapolis, IN 46225
Telephone: (317) 237-5050
Chairman of the Board: Ron Froehlich
President: Robert Colarossi
Director of Public Relations: Steve Penny
www.usa-gymnastics.org

USA Hockey
Address: 1775 Bob Johnson Drive
             Colorado Springs, CO 80906
Telephone: (719) 576-8724
President: Ron DeGregorio
Executive Director: Doug Palazzari
Manager of Media and PR: TBA
www.usahockey.com

U.S. Olympic Organizations *(Cont.)*

United States Judo, Inc. (USJ)
Address: 1 Olympic Plaza Suite 202
Colorado Springs, CO 80909
Telephone: (719) 866-4730
President: Dr. Ronald Tripp
Executive Director: William Rosenberg
www.usjudo.org

U.S. Luge Association (USLA)
Address: 35 Church Street
Lake Placid, NY 12946
Telephone: (518) 523-2071
President: Doug Bateman
Executive Director: Ron Rossi
Public Relations Manager: Jon Lundin
www.usaluge.org

U.S. Modern Pentathlon Association
Address: 5407 Bandera Road - Suite 512
San Antonio, TX 78238
Telephone: (210) 229-2004
President: Steve Richards
Executive Director: Robert Marbut Jr.
www.usmpa.home.texas.net

U.S. Racquetball Association
Address: 1685 West Uintah
Colorado Springs, CO 80904
Telephone: (719) 635-5396
President: Randy Stafford
Executive Director: Jim Hiser
Public Relations Coordinator: Ryan John
www.usra.org

USA Roller Sports
Address: 4730 South Street
P.O. Box 6579
Lincoln, NE 68506
Telephone: (402) 483-7551
President: George Kolibaba
Communications Director: Bill Wolf
www.usarollersports.org

U.S. Rowing
Address: Pan American Plaza, Suite 400
201 South Capitol Avenue
Indianapolis, IN 46225
Telephone: (317) 237-5656/ 1 (800) 314-4769
Executive Director: Glenn Merry
Press Contact: Brett Johnson
www.usrowing.org

U.S. Sailing Association
Address: 15 Maritime Drive
P.O. Box 1260
Portsmouth, RI 02871
Telephone: (401) 683-0800
President: Janet C. Baxter
Executive Director: Charlie Leighton
Communications Manager: Marlieke de Lange Eaton
Olympic Yachting Director: Jonathan R. Harley
www.ussailing.org

USA Shooting
Address: 1 Olympic Plaza
Colorado Springs, CO 80909
Telephone: (719) 866-4670
Chairman of the Board: Dr. James Lally
CEO: Robert K. Mitchell
Media and Public Relations: Sara Greenlee
www.usashooting.com

U.S. Ski and Snowboard Association
Address: P.O. Box 100
Park City, UT 84060
Telephone: (435) 649-9090
Chairman: Chuck Ferries
President and CEO: Bill Marolt
V.P. of Communications and Media: Tom Kelly
www.usskiteam.com

U.S. Soccer Federation (USSF)
Address: 1801-1811 South Prairie Avenue
Chicago, IL 60616
Telephone: (312) 808-1300
President: Robert Contiguglia
Secretary General: Dan Flynn
Director of Communications: Jim Moorhouse
www.ussoccer.com

Amateur Softball Association (ASA)
Address: 2801 N.E. 50th Street
Oklahoma City, OK 73111
Telephone: (405) 424-5266
President: H. Franklin Taylor III
Executive Director: Ron Radigonda
Director of Communications: Brian McCall
www.softball.org

U.S. Speed Skating
Address: P.O. Box 450639
Westlake OH 44145
Telephone: (440) 899-0128
President: Fred Benjamin
Executive Director: Katie Marquard
Public Relations Director: Melissa Scott
www.usspeedskating.org

U.S. Swimming, Inc. (USS)
Address: 1 Olympic Plaza
Colorado Springs, CO 80909
Telephone: (719) 866-4578
President: Ron Van Pool
Executive Director: Chuck Wielgus
Public Relations Director: Mary Wagner
www.usa-swimming.org

U.S. Synchronized Swimming, Inc. (USSS)
Address: Pan American Plaza, Suite 901
201 South Capitol Avenue
Indianapolis, IN 46225
Telephone: (317) 237-5700
President: Virginia Jasontek
Executive Director: Terry Harper
Media Relations Director: Mandy Harlan
www.usasynchro.org

U.S. Table Tennis Association (USTTA)
Address: 1 Olympic Plaza
Colorado Springs, CO 80909
Telephone: (719) 866-4583
Executive Director: Teodor Gheorghe
President: Sheri Pittman
Director of Media and PR: Debbie Doney
www.usatt.org

U.S. Taekwondo Union (USTU)
Address: 1 Olympic Plaza, Suite 405
Colorado Springs, CO 80909
Telephone: (719) 866-4632
President: Sang Lee
Executive Director: R. Jay Warwick
Media and Communications Director: Chris Condron
www.ustu.org

U.S. Olympic Organizations (Cont.)

USA Team Handball
Address: 1 Olympic Plaza
Colrado Springs, CO 80909
Telephone: (719) 866-4036
President: Bob Djokovich
Executive Director: Mike Cavanaugh
www.usateamhandball.org

U.S. Tennis Association
Address: 70 West Red Oak Lane
White Plains, NY 10604
Telephone: (914) 696-7000
President: Alan G. Schwartz
Executive Director: Lee Hamilton
Director Marketing/Communications: David Newman
www.usta.com

USA Track & Field (formerly TAC)
Address: 1 RCA Dome, Suite 140
Indianapolis, IN 46225
Telephone: (317) 261-0500
President: Bill Roe
Chief Executive Officer: Craig A. Masback
Director of Communications: Jill Geer
www.usatf.org

USA Volleyball
Address: 715 South Circle Drive
Colorado Springs, CO 80910
Telephone: (719) 228-6800
President: Albert M. Monaco Jr.
Interim CEO: Howard Klostermann
Manager of Media Relations: Paul Soriano

www.usavolleyball.org

United States Water Polo (USWP)
Address: 1631 Mesa Avenue - Suite 1A
Colorado Springs, CO 80906
Telephone: (719) 634-0699
President: Rich Foster
Executive Director: Tom Seitz
Media Director: Eric Velazquez
www.usawaterpolo.com

USA Weightlifting
Address: 1 Olympic Plaza
Colorado Springs, CO 80909
Telephone: (719) 866-4508
President: Dennis Snethen
Executive Director and Media Contact: Wesley Barnett
www.usaweightlifting.org

USA Wrestling
Address: 6155 Lehman Drive
Colorado Springs, CO 80918
Telephone: (719) 598-8181
President: Bruce Baumgartner
Executive Director: Rich Bender
Director of Communications: Gary Abbott
www.usawrestling.org

Affiliated Sports Organizations

Amateur Athletic Union (AAU)
Address: Walt Disney World Resort; P.O. Box 22409
Lake Buena Vista, FL 32830-1000
Telephone: (407) 934-7200
President: Bobby Dodd
Media Contact: Melissa Wilson
www.aausports.org

U.S. Curling Association (USCA)
Address: 1100 Center Point Drive
P.O. Box 866
Stevens Point, WI 54481
Telephone: (715) 344-1199
President: Mark Swandby
Executive Director: David Garber
Communications Director: Rick Patzke
www.usacurl.org

USA Karate Federation
Address: 1300 Kenmore Boulevard
Akron, OH 44314
Telephone: (330) 753-3114
President: George Anderson
www.usakarate.org

U.S. Orienteering Federation
Address: P.O. Box 1444
Forest Park, GA 30298
Telephone: (404) 363-2110
President: Chuck Ferguson
Executive Director: Robin Shannonhouse
Marketing and Public Relations VP: Sherry Litasi
Publicity telephone: (303) 694-4914
www.us.orienteering.org

U.S. Squash Racquets Association
Address: 23 Cynwyd Road
P.O. Box 1216
Bala Cynwyd, PA 19004
Telephone: (610) 667-4006
President: Ken Stillman
Vice President: Charlie Johnson
www.us-squash.org

USA Triathlon
Address: 1365 Graden of the Gods Road
Colorado Springs, CO 80907
Telephone: (719) 597-9090
President: Brad Davison
Executive Director: TBA
Communications Director: B. J. Hoeptner Evans
www.usatriathlon.org

USA Waterski
Address: 1251 Holy Cow Road
Polk City, FL 33868
Telephone: (863) 324-4341
President: Andrea Plough
Executive Director: Steve McDermeit
Public Relations Manager: Scott Atkinson
www.usawaterski.org

Championship Auto Racing Teams (CART)
Address: 5350 Lakeview Parkway South Drive
Building 36 - Inner Park/Park 100
Indianapolis, IN 46268
Telephone: (317) 715-4100
President: Dick Eidswick
Director of Public Relations: Steve Shunck
www.cart.com

Indy Racing League
Address: 4565 West 16th Street
Indianapolis, IN 46222
Telephone: (317) 484-6526
President and Founder: Tony George
Director of Media Relations: Ron Green
www.indyracing.com

International Motor Sports Association
Address: 1394 Broadway Avenue
Braselton, GA 30517
Telephone: (706) 658-2120
COO: Tim Mayer
Executive Director: Doug Robinson
www.imsaracing.net

National Association for Stock Car Auto Racing (NASCAR)
Address: 1801 W International Speedway Blvd.
Daytona Beach, FL 32114-1243
Telephone: (386) 253-0611
CEO/Chairman: Brian France
President: Mike Helton
VP of Corporate Communications: Jim Hunter
www.nascar.com

National Hot Rod Association
Address: 2035 East Financial Way
Glendora, CA 91741
Telephone: (626) 914-4761
President: Tom Compton
VP of PR and Communications: Jerry Archambeault
www.nhra.com

Professional Bowlers Association LLC
Address: 719 Second Avenue - Suite 701
Seattle, WA 98104
Telephone: (206) 332-9688
Commissioner: Fred Schreyer
Director of Public Relations: Mitch Germann
www.pba.com

U.S. Chess Federation
Address: 65 East Street
Crossville, TN 38557
Telephone: (931) 787-1234
President: Bill Goichberg
Executive Director: Bill Hall
Director of Communications: Joan DuBois
www.uschess.org

International Game Fish Association
Address: 300 Gulf Stream Way
Dania Beach, FL 33004
Telephone: (954) 927-2628
President: Rob Kramer
www.igfa.org

Ladies Professional Golf Association
Address: 100 International Golf Drive
Daytona Beach, FL 32124
Telephone: (386) 274-6200
Commissioner: Carolyn Bivens
Director of Media Relations: Connie Wilson
www.lpga.com

PGA Tour
Address: 112 PGA Tour Boulevard
Ponte Vedra Beach, FL 32082
Telephone: (904) 285-3700
Commissioner: Tim Finchem
Senior VP of Communications: Bob Combs
www.pgatour.com

Professional Golfers' Association of America
Address: 100 Avenue of the Champions
Box 109601
Palm Beach Gardens, FL 33410-9601
Telephone: (561) 624-8400
President: Roger Warren
Director of Public Relations: Julius Mason
www.pgaonline.com

United States Golf Association
Address: P.O. Box 708, Golf House
Liberty Corner Road
Far Hills, NJ 07931-0708
Telephone: (908) 234-9687
President: Fred S. Ridley
Director of Media Relations: Craig Smith
www.usga.org

U.S. Handball Association
Address: 2333 North Tucson Boulevard
Tucson, AZ 85716
Telephone: (520) 795-0434
President: Bob Hickman
Executive Director: Vern Roberts
Director of Public Relations: Mark Carpenter
www.ushandball.org

Breeders' Cup Limited
Address: 2525 Harrodsburg Road
PO Box 4230
Lexington, KY 40504
Telephone: (859) 223-5444
President: D. G. Van Clief Jr.
Media Relations Director: James Gluckson
Director of Marketing: Damon Thayer
www.breederscup.com

The Jockeys' Guild, Inc.
Address: P.O. Box 150
Monrovia, CA 91017
Telephone: (866) 465-6257
Chairman of the Board: Dave Shepherd
www.jockeysguild.com

Thoroughbred Racing Associations of America
Address: 420 Fair Hill Drive, Suite 1
Elkton, MD 21921
Telephone: (410) 392-9200
Executive Vice President: Chris Scherf
www.tra-online.com

National Thoroughbred Racing Association
Address: 800 Third Avenue - Suite 901
New York, NY 10022
Telephone: (212) 230-9500
Senior VP/Mrkting & Industry Rels: Keith Chamblin
www.ntra.com

United States Trotting Association
Address: 750 Michigan Avenue
Columbus, OH 43215
Telephone: (614) 228-1385
President: F. Phillip Langley
Director of Publicity: John Pawlak
www.ustrotting.com

Iditarod Trail Committee
Address: P.O. Box 870800; Wasilla, AK 99687
Telephone: (907) 376-5155
Executive Director: Stan Hooley
Race Director: Joanne Potts
www.iditarod.com

U.S. Lacrosse
Address: 113 W University Parkway
Baltimore, MD 21210
Telephone: (410) 235-6882
Executive Director: Steven B. Stenersen
www.lacrosse.org

Little League Baseball, Inc.
Address: P.O. Box 3485
Williamsport, PA 17701
Telephone: (570) 326-1921
President & CEO: Stephen D. Keener
Senior Communications Executive: Lance Van Auken
www.littleleague.org

U.S. Polo Association
Address: 771 Corporate Drive, Suite 505
Lexington, KY 40503
Telephone: (859) 219-1000
Chairman: Jack Shelton
www.uspolo.org

American Powerboating Association
Address: 17640 Nine Mile Road
Eastpointe, MI 48021
Telephone: (586) 773-9700
Executive Administrator: Gloria Urbin
www.apba-racing.com

Professional Rodeo Cowboys Association
Address: 101 Pro Rodeo Drive
Colorado Springs, CO 80919
Telephone: (719) 593-8840
Commissioner: Troy Ellerman
Director of Communications: Leslie King
www.prorodeo.com

USA Rugby Football Union
Address: 1033 Walnut Street
Suite 200
Boulder, CO 80302
Telephone: (303) 539-0300
Chairman: Neal Brendel
CEO: Doug Arnot
Communications: Colleen Reilly Krueger
www.usarugby.org

The United Soccer Leagues
Address: 14497 North Dale Mabry Highway, Ste 201
Tampa, FL 33618
Telephone: (813) 963-3909
President and A-League Commissioner: Francisco Marcos
Director of Public Relations: Gerald Barnhart
www.uslsoccer.com

Major League Soccer
Address: 110 East 42nd Street, Suite 1000
New York, NY 10017
Telephone: (212) 687-1400
Commissioner: Don Garber
Director of Communications: Trey Fitzgerald
www.mlsnet.com

Major Indoor Soccer League
Address: 1175 Post Road East
Westport, CT 06880
Telephone: (203) 222-4900
Commissioner: Steve Ryan
Director of Communications: Jay Cavallo
www.misl.net

Women's United Soccer Association
Address: 6205 Peachtree Dunwoody Road
Atlanta, GA 30328
Telephone: (678) 645-0800
Commissioner: Tony DiCicco
Director of Public Relations: Shaun May
www.wusa.com

Association of Tennis Professionals Tour
Address: 201 ATP Tour Boulevard
Ponte Vedra Beach, FL 32082
Telephone: (904) 285-8000
Chief Executive Officer: Mark Miles
VP of Comm. and Media Relations: Greg Sharko
www.atptour.org

Sony Ericsson WTA Tour (Women's Tennis)
Address: One Progress Plaza - Suite 1500
St. Petersburg, FL 33701
Telephone: (727) 895-5000
Chief Executive Officer: Larry Scott
Director of Corporate Communications: Darrell Fry
www.wtatour.com

Association of Volleyball Professionals
Address: 6100 Center Drive - 9th Floor
Los Angeles, CA 90045
Telephone: (310) 426-8000
Commissioner: Leonard Armato
www.avp.com

MINOR LEAGUES
Baseball (AAA)

National Association of Professional Baseball Leagues
Address: 201 Bayshore Drive S.E. - P.O. Box A
St. Petersburg, FL 33731
Telephone: (727) 822-6937
President: Mike Moore
Director of Media Relations: Jim Ferguson
www.minorleaguebaseball.com

MINOR LEAGUES *(Cont.)*

Baseball (AAA) *(Cont.)*

International League
Address: 55 South High Street, Suite 202
             Dublin, OH 43017
Telephone: (614) 791-9300
President: Randy Mobley
www.ilbaseball.com

Pacific Coast League
Address: 1631 Mesa Avenue, Suite A
             Colorado Springs, CO 80906
Telephone: (719) 636-3399
President: Branch Rickey
www.pclbaseball.com

Hockey

American Hockey League
Address: 1 Monarch Place Suite 2400
             Springfield, MA 01144
Telephone: (413) 781-2030
President, CEO & Treasurer: David A. Andrews
VP of Hockey Operations: Jim Mill
VP of Communications: Jason Chaimovitch
www.theahl.com

Halls of Fame Directory

National Baseball Hall of Fame and Museum
Address: P.O. Box 590/25 Main Street
             Cooperstown, NY 13326
Telephone: (607) 547-7200
President: Dale Petroskey
Senior Vice President: Bill Haase
V.P. of Communications and Education: Jeff Idelson
www.baseballhalloffame.org

Naismith Memorial Basketball Hall of Fame
Address: 1000 West Columbus Avenue
             Springfield, MA 01105
Telephone: (413) 781-6500
President and CEO: John L. Doleva
VP of Marketing and Sales: Dan O'Keefe
www.hoophall.com

International Bowling Museum and Hall of Fame
Address: 111 Stadium Plaza
             St. Louis, MO 63102
Telephone: (314) 231-6340
Executive Director: Gerald Baltz
Marketing Director: Jim Baer
www.bowlingmuseum.com

National Boxing Hall of Fame
Address: 1 Hall of Fame Drive
             Canastota, NY 13032
Telephone: (315) 697-7095
President: Donald Ackerman
Executive Director: Edward Brophy
www.ibhof.com

Professional Football Hall of Fame
Address: 2121 George Halas Drive NW
             Canton, OH 44708
Telephone: (330) 456-8207
Executive Director: John Bankert
Vice President of Public Relations: Joe Horrigan
www.profootballhof.com

LPGA Hall of Fame
Address: 100 International Golf Drive
             Daytona Beach, FL 32124
Telephone: (386) 274-6200
Commissioner: Carolyn Bivens
Director of Media Relations: Connie Wilson
www.lpga.com

Hockey Hall of Fame
Address: 30 Yonge Street BCE Place
             Toronto, Ontario Canada M5E 1X8
Telephone: (416) 360-7735
Chairman: William Hay
President & COO: Jeff Denomme
VP of Marketing: Perter Jagla
www.hhof.com

National Museum of Racing and Hall of Fame
Address: 191 Union Avenue
             Saratoga Springs, NY 12866
Telephone: (518) 584-0400
Executive Director: Peter Hammell
Assistant Director: Catherine Maguire
Communications Officer: Mike Kane
www.racingmuseum.org

National Soccer Hall of Fame
Address: Wright Soccer Campus
             18 Stadium Circle
             Oneonta, NY 13820
Telephone: (607) 432-3351
President: Will Lunn
www.soccerhall.org

International Swimming Hall of Fame
Address: 1 Hall of Fame Drive
             Fort Lauderdale, FL 33316
Telephone: (954) 462-6536
President: Bruce Wigo
Media Contact: Preston Levi
www.ishof.org

International Tennis Hall of Fame
Address: 194 Bellevue Avenue
             Newport, RI 02840
Telephone: (401) 849-3990
CEO: Mark Stenning
Marketing Manager: Kat Anderson
www.tennisfame.com

National Track & Field Hall of Fame
Address: 216 Ft. Washington Avenue
             The Armory Foundation
             New York, NY 10032
Telephone: (317) 261-0500
Chief Executive Officer: Criag Masback
Director of Communications: Jill Geer
www.usatf.org

Sports Illustrated Trivia Quiz

We know how you are. We really do. A *Sports Illustrated*-type of sports fan is special. You're the type who nods knowingly when arcane names such as Wally Pipp or Tom Dempsey are mentioned, you can't help but smile when you reminisce about "Disco Demolition Night" (above), and you can probably recite the past ten Kentucky Derby winners, but not your home phone number. Hey, we're the same way. And because of this, we also know that not just any kind of trivia questions will cause you to stop and scratch that head of yours. So, here, for your perusal, are some of the weirdest, most detailed and, well, downright toughest trivia questions we could conjure up, many of them inspired by the record-breaking events from the past year. We'd ask, "Are you game?", but, like we said, we know you, so we'll just say "Good luck."

NBA

1. LeBron James, at 20 years, 80 days old, scored 56 points on March 20, 2005, becoming the youngest player ever to score 50 points in a single NBA game. Whose record for youngest to score 60 points did he break?

2. Name the only basketball player to lead the NCAA, ABA, and NBA in scoring average for a season during his career.

3. Reggie Miller, who retired from the Indiana Pacers at the end of the 2004–05 season, became the 13th NBA player to surpass 25,000 career points, but only the third such player to score all of his points with one team. Name the other two.

4. The San Antonio Spurs' Tim Duncan won his third NBA Finals MVP award in 2005, making him the fourth player in NBA history to win three. Name the most recent of the other three players who have won the Finals MVP award at least three times?

5. Current New York Knicks head coach Larry Brown holds the record for leading seven different NBA teams to the postseason. Which active head coach has the second-largest total of NBA teams taken to the playoffs and with how many teams?

6. In Game Two of the 2005 Eastern Conference semifinals against Washington, the Miami Heat's Dwyane Wade became only fifth player in NBA history with at least 30 points, 15 assists and five rebounds in a playoff game. Name two of the four others.

7. In 2005, a NBA team's leading scorer failed to get a field goal for the first time in league history. Name him and the team he played on.

HINT: Motor City Misses.

ANSWERS

NBA

Lebron James holds the NBA record for the youngest player in league history to score 30, 40, and 50 points in a game.

MANNY MILLAN

1. Rick Barry—who was 21 years, 261 days old when he scored 57 pts for the San Francisco Warriors against the New York Knicks during his rookie 1965–66 season.

2. Rick Barry—1964–65 (Univ. of Miami, Florida, NCAA); 1966–67 (San Francisco Warriors, NBA), 1968–69 (Oakland Oaks, ABA)

3. Jerry West (L.A. Lakers) and John Havlicek (Boston Celtics)

4. Shaquille O'Neal (1999–2000 through 2001–02) Michael Jordan (6) and Magic Johnson (3) are the other two players to win the Finals MVP award three or more times.

5. George Karl with five–Cleveland, Golden State, Seattle, Milwaukee, Denver. (Two retired coaches, Lenny Wilkens and Bill Fitch, are also tied for second all-time with Karl at five.)

6. Magic Johnson, Jerry West, Walt Frazier, and Oscar Robertson

7. Richard Hamilton–Detroit Pistons (Hamilton scored 14 points, but went 0-for-10 from the field during a January 6th, 2005 game against the Memphis Grizzlies).

NBA

8.

Only two players in NBA history have won both the league MVP award as well as the defensive player of the year award in the same year. Name them both.

9. Which NBA player holds the all-time playoff record for free throw attempts?

10. Both Michael Jordan and Kareem Abdul-Jabbar either lead or are in second place in seven all-time playoff statistical categories. Which player is just behind them with firsts or seconds in six playoff categories?

11. Which team has the best road playoff record in NBA history, based on winning percentage?

12. Of the NBA's all-time top ten scorers, two players were never part of a championship team. Name them

13. Eight NBA players have won both a Rookie of the Year award and a Finals MVP award during their career. Name six of them.

14. How many current NBA franchises have never reached the NBA Finals?

15. When was the last time an Eastern Conference team won a Game Seven in the NBA Finals?

16. Six times in league history consecutive NBA Finals have rematched the same two teams with a different team winning in the second year. Name four of these matchups.

17. Of the current NBA teams, which two would have to meet in the NBA Finals to match up the geographically closest Eastern and Western Conference franchises?

ANSWERS
NBA

8. Michael Jordan–1987–88 (Chicago Bulls); Hakeem Olajuwon–1993–94 (Houston Rockets)

9. Shaquille O'Neal–1,889 (Michael Jordan is second with 1,776).

10. Scottie Pippen–Steals-1st, 3-Point Attempts-2nd, 3-Points Made-2nd, Games Played-2nd, Minutes Played-2nd, Personal Fouls-2nd.

11. Los Angeles Lakers–.455 (128–155)

12. Karl Malone–2nd (36, 928 pts.) and Dominique Wilkins–9th (26,668 pts.)

13. Wilt Chamberlain, Willis Reed, Wes Unseld, Kareem Abdul-Jabbar, Larry Bird, Michael Jordan, Shaquille O'Neal, Tim Duncan

14. Twelve–Atlanta, Charlotte, Cleveland, Dallas, Denver, Memphis, Los Angeles Clippers, Miami, Minnesota, New Orleans, Sacramento, Toronto

15. 1984–Boston Celtics defeated the Los Angeles Lakers

In addition to holding the all-time NBA playoff record for free throw attempts, Shaquille O'Neal leads all active players with 978 playoff free throws made.

MANNY MILLAN

16. Lakers (1987–88) vs. Pistons (1988–89); Celtics (1983–84) vs. Lakers (1984–85); Lakers (1981–82) vs. 76ers (1982–83); Bullets (1977–78) vs. SuperSonics (1978–79); Lakers (1971--72) vs. Knicks (1972–73); Celtics (1956–57) vs. St. Louis Hawks (1957–58)

17. Minnesota (W) and Milwaukee (E) –roughly 320 miles apart.

COLLEGE BASKETBALL

18. Duke made it to the Sweet 16 for the 8th consecutive year in 2005, what is the record for the most consecutive Sweet 16 appearances?

19. Which College Football Hall of Fame coach is also enshrined in the Basketball Hall of Fame for his early contributions to college basketball?

20. Ohio State defeated Illinois 65–64 in the 2005 Big Ten Conference tournament final, preventing the Fighting Illini from going undefeated in the regular season. When was the last time a Division I college basketball team went undefeated in the regular season and which school did it?

21: Despite its Big Ten tourney loss, Illinois still tied the NCAA single-season record of 37 wins in 2005–05. Of the following six teams, which two have also reached that mark during one season?
a) UCLA b) UNLV c) Kentucky   d) Indiana e) Duke f) N. Carolina

22. Which active Division I college basketball head coach passed Dean Smith in March 2005 to become number one all-time in wins?

23. When was the last time no number one seeded teams made it to the NCAA Division I tournament's Final Four?
HINT: Denny's "Doctors of Dunk" defeated the Bruins for the title.

24. What is the lowest seeded team ever to advance to the Final Four?

25. What is the lowest seeded team ever to win the NCAA tournament?

26. What two future basketball Hall-of-Famers played together on the 1955–56 University of San Francisco Dons?

ANSWERS
COLLEGE BASKETBALL

DARREN CARROLL/SPORTS ILLUSTRATED

18. North Carolina–13

19. Amos Alonzo Stagg

20. 1975–76–Indiana

21. Duke–1985–86 and 1998–99; UNLV–1986–87

22. Pat Summitt–882 wins (Smith retired from the Univ. of North Carolina in 1997 with 879 career wins)

23. 1980–Louisville (#2), Iowa (#5), Purdue (#6), UCLA (#8)

Pat Summitt, head coach of the Univ. of Tennessee women's basketball team, begins the 2005–06 season with a career record of 882-172.

24. 11th–LSU (1986)

25. 8th–Villanova (1985)

26. K.C. Jones and Bill Russell

BASEBALL

27.

Randy Johnson made his 13th opening day start in 2005, good enough for third most all-time. Name the four pitchers who have made more opening day starts.

28.

Who is the only player in major league history to get at least 500 hits with four different teams?

29.

Since 1900, every player who has led a decade in hits is in the Hall of Fame except two. One is Pete Rose; the other, who led the major leagues in hits for the 1990's, is not yet eligible. Name this potential Hall of Famer.

HINT: He recently added a World Series ring to his resume.

30.

In 2005, New York Yankees' Alex Rodriguez, Gary Sheffield, and Hideki Matsui each drove in more than 100 R.B.I.'s for the second consecutive season, making them the first trio in more than 60 years to do so. Name the last set of three players to reach this feat and their team.

HINT: One of these three players briefly managed the same team years later.

31.

In Game Five of the Yankees-Angels ALDS series this year, Hideki Matsui went 0-for-5 and stranded eight runners on base. When was the last potentially series-clinching playoff game where a player went hitless with runners on base during every one of his at-bats and who was the player?

32.

This year Craig Biggio of the Houston Astros finally reached the World Series after having played 2,564 regular-season games. Whose record did he break for highest number of games played before a World Series appearance?

BASEBALL

TONY TRIOLO

27. Tom Seaver (16), Steve Carlton (14,) Jack Morris (14), Walter Johnson (14)

28. Rusty Staub (Houston–792, Montreal–531, Detroit–582, N.Y. Mets–720)

29. Mark Grace

30. Joe DiMaggio, Bill Dickey, and Lou Gehrig each had 100-R.B.I. seasons for the Yankees during the 1936–38 seasons. Dickey eventually came back to manage the Yankees for 105 games in 1946.

The "Le Grande Orange," Rusty Staub, swings at a pitch in a May 27, 1982 Mets–Yankees Mayor's Trophy game.

31. Game Six of the 1986 World Series–Boston's Bill Buckner went 0-for-5 stranding eight Red Sox runners. against the New York Mets.

32. Barry Bonds–2,439 games (San Francisco Giants in 2002 World Series)

BASEBALL

33.

Craig Biggio became the most plunked player in baseball history in 2005, ending the season with a career record of 273 at-bats where he was hit by a pitch. Whose record did he break?

34.
Name the only three players in major league history who had longer careers than Biggio without ever playing in a World Series.
HINT: All three spent time in the Windy City.

35.
In baseball, what does a player have to do to earn a "golden sombrero?"

36.
This season, Houston Astros' pitcher Roger Clemens started five games that his team eventually lost 1–0. Had he received the decision in all five losses, he would have tied the major league record for 1–0 losses, set by two different pitchers. Name them.

37.
In 2001, Barry Bond's 73 home runs broke the all-time professional baseball home run record, albeit by only one round-tripper. Whose record did he break?

38.
Name the only leadoff hitter in baseball's modern era to lead his team in both home runs and R.B.I.s for an entire season.

39.
Currently, there are four active pitchers who have struck out an entire side on just nine pitches. Name two of the four.

HINT: Two of them spent their early careers pitching in Stade Olympique.

40.
In 2005, Detroit Tiger second-basemen Placido Polanco finished the season batting .3313, .0005 better than Texas' Michael Young, yet Polanco was not named the American League batting champ because he spent part of the season with the NL's Philadelphia Phillies. Prior to this year, when was the last time a player lost the chance at a League title in a Triple Crown statistic because of a mid-year trade?

ANSWERS
BASEBALL

CHUCK SOLOMON

33. Don Baylor–267 career HBPs

34. Rafael Palmeiro (2,831 games), Andre Dawson (2,627 games) and Ernie Banks (2,528 games)

35. Strike out four times in one game.

36. Jim Bunning–1967 (Phillies), Ferguson Jenkins–1968 (Cubs)

37. Joe Bauman of the Class C Roswell (N.M.) Rockets hit 72 HR's during the 1954 Longhorn League season.

Pedro Martinez once struck out the side on nine pitches in a game in May 2002.

38. Bobby Bonds–1973 San Francisco Giants (39 HR's, 96 R.B.I.s)

39. Pedro Martinez, Ugueth Urbina, Andy Ashby, Byung-Hyun Kim

40. 1997–Mark McGwire led the majors with 58 home runs (34 with Oakland, then 24 with St. Louis), but did not win the National League home run title.

BASEBALL

41.

In 2005, for the first time in division-era major league baseball history, Atlanta Braves rookie rightfielder Jeff Francoeur managed to get his 10th career home run before doing what?

42.

Name the only player to score more than 100 runs, drive in more than 100 R.B.I.s and bat over .300 in each of his first five seasons.

43.

Who is the only player in major league history to have both a World Series-winning hit and World Series-ending final out?

44.

What year did Little League Baseball begin allowing co-ed teams?

45.

In 2005, Boston's Manny Ramirez and David Ortiz amassed more than 140 R.B.I.s each for the second season in a row. Name the last pair of teammates to accomplish this feat.
a) Lou Gehrig and Babe Ruth
b) Ted Williams and Jimmie Foxx
c) Mickey Mantle and Roger Maris
d) Ken Griffey, Jr. and Alex Rodriguez

46.

In which stadium did the most recent instance of a player hitting two inside-the-park home runs in the same game occur?

HINT: "Hefty Bag" outfield fences.

47.

In the 2005 ALCS, the Chicago White Sox's starting pitchers threw four consecutive complete games, a feat that was last accomplished in the 1956 World Series when one team's pitchers threw five straight complete games. Name three of those five pitchers.

48.

Devil Rays leftfielder Carl Crawford had amassed 565 hits, 157 steals and 46 triples by his 24th birthday in August 2005, making him only the third player since 1900 to reach 500 hits, 150 steals, and 40 triples that early in his career. Name one of the other two players.

DAVID E. KLUTHO

Through his first 5 seasons, Albert Pujols (r.) is batting .332 while averaging 41 HRs, and 127 R.B.I.s per season.

41. Drawing his first career walk.

42. Albert Pujols–2001–05 (St. Louis Cardinals)

43. Edgar Renteria–1997 World Series (Florida Marlins, Game Seven-winning hit against Cleveland Indians) and 2004 World Series (St. Louis Cardinals, Game Four final batted out against Boston Red Sox)

44. 1974

45. Lou Gehrig and Babe Ruth–1930–31

46. Hubert H. Humphrey Metrodome–Greg Gagne of the Twins hit two against Chicago White Sox on October 4, 1986.

47. Whitey Ford, Tom Sturdivant, Don Larsen, Bob Turley, and Johnny Kucks–New York Yankees (Larsen's outing was his infamous perfect game, but Turley ended up losing his complete game 1–0, when Brooklyn's Jackie Robinson hit a two-out RBI single in the 10th)

48. Ty Cobb (Tigers) and Sherry Magee (Phillies)

OTHER SPORTS

49.

When was the last year a Frenchmen won cycling's Tour de France?

50.
Who is the only woman ever named as *The Sporting News* "Man of the Year?"

51.
Where is soccer's World Cup kept?

52.
In 1960, what Olympic sport was not held because of adverse weather conditions and scheduling conflicts?

53.
In 2005, Danica Patrick became the first woman to lead an Indianapolis 500 and she eventually finished fourth in the race, the best-ever finish for a woman. What was the previous best-ever finish by a woman at Indy and who was the driver?

54.
The current 27-year drought since the last Triple Crown winner in horse racing is a record, name the second-longest period between Triple Crown winners and the horse that broke that streak?

55.
Since 1978, the year Affirmed won the last Triple Crown, how many horses have won both the Kentucky Derby and the Preakness Stakes, only to fall short at the Belmont Stakes?

56.
In the fall of 2004, swimmer Jenny Thompson, the most decorated US Olympian in history, retired. How many Olympic medals did she accumulate during her prolific career?

57.
Which college has won an NCAA-record 33 Division I team wrestling championships?

OTHER SPORTS

MANNY MILLAN

Jackie Joyner-Kersee won six medals over four different Olympics, including golds in the long jump and the heptathlon.

49. 1985–Bernard Hinault

50. Jackie Joyner-Kersee–1988

51. Zurich, Switzerland

52. Bobsledding

53. Janet Guthrie finished in 9th place at the 1978 Indianapolis 500.

54. 25 years (1948–73)–Secretariat

55. 10 (Spectacular Bid–1979, Pleasant Colony–1981, Alysheba–1987, Sunday Silence–1989, Silver Charm–1987, Real Quiet–1998, Charismatic–1999, War Emblem–2002, Funny Cide–2003, Smarty Jones–2004)

56. 12–During the 1992, 1996, 2000 and 2004 Olympics, Thompson won a cumulative total of 8 gold, 3 silver, and 1 bronze medals.

57. Oklahoma State

TENNIS

58. Who was the youngest player ever to win the U.S. Open?

59. In 2005, Roger Federer successfully defended both of his previous year's titles at Wimbledon and the U.S. Open. Who was the last tennis player to achieve this feat and in what year?

60. Roger Federer's win at the 2005 U.S. Open ran his record-setting streak of consecutive finals matches won up to 23. What two players are tied for second place all-time in consecutive finals won and how many in a row did they win? **HINT:** The two were fierce rivals in the late 1970s and early 1980s.

61. At 35, Andre Agassi's appearance in the 2005 U.S. Open final made him the oldest competitor to reach the final in 31 years. Who was the last player older than Agassi to play for the U.S. Open title?

62. Who is only tennis player in history to have achieved the "Golden Grand Slam" (winning all four Grand Slam events and an Olympic gold medal in the same calendar year)?

63. In 2005, Venus Williams' singles victory at Wimbledon set a record, marking the first time someone seeded so low won the All England Lawn Tennis Club Ladies Championship. Where was she seeded in the initial draw?

64. Which tennis player was ranked number one for a career total of 377 weeks, a record for both men's and women's tennis?

65. In 2005, Andre Agassi played in his 20th consecutive U.S. Open, setting an all-time Grand Slam appearance record. How many total Grand Slam tournaments has he played in during his career?

66. Which woman tennis player has the fastest-ever recorded serve?

SIMON BRUTY

58. Tracy Austin–16 years old (1979)

59. Don Budge–1938

60. Bjorn Borg and John McEnroe–12 finals matches won in a row

61. Ken Rosewall–At 39, he lost to Jimmy Connors in straight sets in the 1974 U.S. Open

62. Steffi Graf–1988

63. 14th

Venus Williams has won five career Grand Slam titles—two at the U.S. Open and three at Wimbledon .

64. Steffi Graf

65. 59

66. Venus Williams–127.4 mph (During the European Indoor Championships at Zürich, Switzerland, on October 16, 1998)

HOCKEY

67. Approximately what percentage of NHL players changed teams between the time the new collective bargaining agreement was signed in July and the start of 2005–06 season in October?

68. After the NHL's record 301-day lockout of 2004–05, what are the next four longest work stoppages in the modern era of professional sports?

69. In the 2005 NHL Draft, Sidney Crosby was chosen by Pittsburgh as the number one overall pick. Name the Penguins' last two overall number one draft picks.

BOXING

70. Who was the last unified heavyweight division champion?

71. Among boxing's three main sanctioning bodies (IBF, WBA, WBC), how many different heavyweight champions have held the title since January 1st, 2000?

72. According to the World Boxing Council, what is the maximum length of the bandages used to affix a boxer's gloves?

73. Which heavyweight champion holds both the record for longest reign as champion and most successful title defenses?

74.. Name the four different heavyweight champions who won Olympic boxing gold medals in weight divisions lower than heavyweight.

HINT: Between 1965 and 1978, three of the four fought against each other professionally.

ANSWERS
HOCKEY

67. 25%

68. 234 days (MLB, 1994–95); 191 days (NBA, 1998–99); 103 days (NHL, 1994–95); 57 days (NFL, 1982)

69. Marc André Fleury (2003); Mario Lemieux (1984)

ANSWERS
BOXING

JOHN IACONO/SPORTS ILLUSTRATED

Briton Lennox Lewis defeated Evander Holyfield in 1999 as part of his campaign to unify the heavyweight title.

when he fought Michael Grant instead of the then-number one WBA contender, John Ruiz.

71. Eight (Evander Holyfield, Hasim Rahman, Lennox Lewis, Roy Jones Jr., Chris Byrd, Vitali Klitschko, James Toney, and John Ruiz)

72. 2.5 meters (8 feet, 2½ inches)

73. Joe Louis–11 years, 7 months; 25 successful title defenses

74. Floyd Patterson (1952–middleweight); Muhammad Ali (1960–light heavyweight); Leon and Michael Spinks (1976–light heavyweight and middleweight, respectively)

70. Lennox Lewis, whose WBA title was withdrawn on April 29, 2000,

THE DRAFT

75. In 2005, for the first time, athletes from the same college were the overall number one picks in both the NFL and NBA drafts. Name the school.

HINT: BCS buster.

76. This past year, North Carolina became just the second school in history to have four players taken in the first round of the NBA draft. Name the other school and year.

77. North Carolina has now had multiple first-round NBA draft picks eight times. Excluding 2005, name three of the other seven sets of first-round draft picks and the years they were drafted.

78. In the 2005 NFL Draft, one college had four players chosen in the first round. Name the school and the added significance of the first two of the four players chosen from this school.

79. Name four first-round NFL draft picks who are currently in the Pro Football Hall of Fame.

80. What was the lowest overall position in an NFL draft where the first quarterback was chosen?

81. Which Heisman Trophy winner was the first African-American to be the overall number one pick in the NFL draft?

HINT: He was diagnosed with leukemia not long after being drafted and he died having never played in a single NFL game.

82. What future basketball Hall-of-Famer was chosen in the 7th round of the 1962 NFL draft by the Cleveland Browns, despite never having played a down of football during college?

THE DRAFT

75. Utah–Alex Smith (QB to NFL's San Francisco 49ers) and Andrew Bogut (C to NBA's Milwaukee Bucks)

76. Duke–1999 (Elton Brand, Trajan Langdon, Corey Maggette, and William Avery)

77. Walter Davis and Tommy LaGarde (1977), Michael Jordan and Sam Perkins (1984), Kenny Smith and Joe Wolf (1987), Rick Fox and Pete Chilcutt (1991), Jerry Stackhouse and Rasheed Wallace (1995), Antawn Jamison and Vince Carter (1998), Brendan Haywood and Joseph Forte (2001)

78. Auburn–By choosing RB Ronnie Brown second and RB Carnell (Cadillac) Williams in the fifth spot, it marked the highest-ever picks of two running backs from the same backfield and only the fourth time in NFL history two teammate-running backs were taken in the first round.

79. Eleven number one picks are in the Pro Football Hall of Fame–Bill Dudley

Despite Andrew Bogut's jersey number, he, along with Alex Smith, were both picked number one overall in the NBA and NFL Drafts, respectively.

(1942), Charley Trippi (1945), Chuck Bednarik (1949), Paul Hornung (1957), Buck Buchanan, (1963-AFL), Ron Yary (1968), O. J. Simpson (1969), Terry Bradshaw (1970), Lee Roy Selmon (1976), Earl Campbell (1978), John Elway (1983)

80. 76th–Chris Chandler (1988, Washington Redskins 3rd round)

81. Ernie Davis–In 1962, the Washington Redskins took Davis as the overall number one draft pick and then traded him to the Cleveland Browns. Davis was diagnosed with leukemia in July of 1962, eventually succumbing to the disease on May 18, 1963.

82. John Havlicek–A high school quarterback, Havlicek played baseball and basketball at Ohio State.

NFL

83. In 2004 Eagles coach Andy Reid became the third coach in NFL history to win a playoff game in five consecutive years. Name the other two coaches who accomplished this feat. **HINT:** Each of them did it with the same team all five years.

84. Who holds the record for most 300-yard passing games in the postseason (6)?

85. New England Patriots wide receiver Deion Branch was named the Super Bowl XXXIX MVP, only the fourth WR in NFL history to win this award. Name the other three.

86. Who is the only player in NFL history with 5 Super Bowl rings?

87. Name three of the four players in the Pro Football Hall of Fame who went by the first name of "Jack."

88. Name the only wide receiver with two 90+yard TD receptions in the same game

89. Who is the only running back in NFL history to gain over 200 yards in a game, but less than 1000 for his career.

90. Within a ½ inch, how long is a pro football?

91. Which future TV star was the only NFL player ever to score two safeties in the same game?

92. Prior to the New Orleans Saints relocating all of their 2005 home games because of damage to the Superdome caused by Hurricane Katrina, there have been two other instances in the past 20 years where a NFL team played a "home" game in a stadium other than its regular venue. Name them both and the reason for the move.

ANSWERS

NFL

ANDY HAYT

Joe Montana holds career playoff records for attempts, completions, touchdowns, and yards gained passing.

88. San Francisco 49ers WR John Taylor–Dec 11, 1989 (vs. Los Angeles Rams)

89A Arizona Cardinals RB LeShon Johnson had 214 yards and two TDs against the New Orleans Saints in Week Four of the 1996 season, but retired in 1999 with a career total of 955 yards and five TDs.

90. 11–11 1/4 inches, depending on temperature

91A Fred Dryer (of NBC's "Hunter")–Los Angeles Rams against Green Bay Packers, October 21, 1973

83. John Madden (Oakland Raiders) and Mike Holmgren (Green Bay Packers)

84. Joe Montana–San Francisco 49ers and Kansas City Chiefs

85. Jerry Rice–XXIII (San Francisco 49ers), Fred Biletnikoff–XI (Oakland Raiders), Lynn Swann–X (Pittsburgh Steelers)

86. Charles Haley (San Francisco 49ers–1989, 1990; Dallas Cowboys–1993, 1994, 1996)

87. Jack Ham (LB), Jack Lambert (LB), Jack Youngblood (DE), Jack Christiansen (S)

92. Oct 27, 2003– The San Diego Chargers Monday night game against the Miami Dolphins was moved to Sun Devil Stadium in Tempe, Arizona because San Diego's Qualcomm Stadium was being used as an evacuation center from local wild fires.

October 22,1989–The San Francisco 49ers Monday night game against the New England Patriots was relocated to Stanford Stadium in Palo Alto, Calif. because of damage sustained by Candlestick Park from the Loma Prieta earthquake.

NFL

93. Name the oldest rookie in NFL history to play in a season opener.
HINT: In 2004, he played for the Geelong Cats.

94. Who are the only two people in NFL history to win Super Bowls as players, assistant coaches, and head coaches?

95. Baltimore Colts quarterback Johnny Unitas holds a record of 47 consecutive games with a TD pass thrown. Which active player is second all-time with a mark of 36 straight games with a TD pass?

96. Which place kicker holds the all-time Super Bowl record for most field goals made?
a) Jason Elam
b) Jan Stenerud
c) Ray Wersching
d) Steve Christie

97. Before 1912, how many points was a touchdown worth?

98. Name the only person who has been a head coach of teams the NFL, WFL, USFL, CFL, as well as a NCAA Division I team.
HINT: During his career, he coached in Houston for three different football teams.

99. Since the NFL/AFL merger in 1970, how many expansion franchises have been added to the NFL?

100. Name the only head coaches in the Pro Football Hall of Fame whose teams never won a Super Bowl, NFL or AFL Championship?
a) Bud Grant
b) Sid Gillman
c) Weeb Ewbank
d) Marv Levy
HINT: His teams went 0-for-4 in Super Bowls.

JOHN BIEVER

Brett Favre moved into second place for career passing attempts and yards gained early on in the 2005–06 season, surpassing Broncos QB John Elway.

93. 31-year old Australian Ben Graham, started as the New York Jets' rookie punter for the 2005–06 season.

94. Tom Flores (Kansas City Chiefs backup quarterback–1969, Oakland Raiders assistant coach–1976, Oakland head coach 1981, 84) and Mike Ditka (Dallas Cowboys tight end–1971, Dallas assistant coach–1977, Chicago head coach–1986)

95. Brett Favre–36 (Green Bay Packers, 2002–04)

96. Ray Wersching–5 field goals for the San Francisco 49ers in Super Bowls XVI (4) and XIX (1)

97. 5 points

98. Jack Pardee–NFL (Bears, Redskins, Oilers), WFL (Florida Blazers), USFL (Houston Gamblers), CFL (Birmingham Barracudas), NCAA (University of Houston)

99. Six–Seattle Seahawks, Tampa Bay Buccaneers–1976; Carolina Panthers, Jacksonville Jaguars–1996; Cleveland Browns–1999; Houston Texans–2002. (All other new teams resulted from moves of existing franchises.)

100. Marv Levy (Buffalo Bills)

101. Name the last team to win an NFL championship without winning the Super Bowl?

102. There are five quarterbacks in the Pro Football Hall of Fame who had more interceptions than TD passes during their careers. Name three of them, including the most recent inductee.

HINT: Only one of them played football during the Super Bowl era.

103. Which player scored the NFL's first two-point conversion and against what team did he do it?

104. The 58–48 final score of the Rams-Bengals game on November 28, 2004 was the highest combined score for a NFL game since the 1970 merger with the AFL. What is the all-time record for the highest combined NFL game score?

105. Name the only two head coaches in NFL history who have taken teams from both the NFC and AFC Conference to the Super Bowl.

106. Which Pro Football Hall of Famer is the only player in NFL history to score six different ways during his career, including kicking field goals and extra points as well as scoring TDs from rushing, receiving, passing, and interception returns?

107. Which player holds the NFL single-season record for most combined yards gained rushing and receiving?

108. What was the crime and sentence being served by Mark Henderson, the infamous snow plow driver out on weekend furlough who cleared a spot on the Foxboro turf on December 12, 1982, enabling the Patriots to kick a winning field goal over the Miami Dolphins?

JOHN BIEVER

Bill Parcells coached Lawrence Taylor and the NFC's New York Giants to victories in Super Bowls XXI and XXV and led the AFC's Patriots to Super Bowl XXXI.

Tupa scored the NFL's first two-point coversion on Sept. 4, 1993 against the Cincinnati Bengals.

104. 113–On November 27, 1966, the Redskins beat the New York Giants, 72–41.

105. Bill Parcells (New England –AFC, New York Giants –NFC); Dan Reeves (Denver–AFC, Atlanta–NFC)

106. Don Hutson–Green Bay Packers 1935–45 (career TDs in passing (1), rushing (3), receiving (99), INT returns (30); career FGs (7), career XPs (172))

107. Marshall Faulk–2,429 yards (1,381 yards rushing, 1, 048 yards receiving–St. Louis Rams, 1999)

108. Henderson was serving a 15-year sentence at nearby Walpole State Penitentiary for robbery.

101. 1969 Minnesota Vikings–In the last game before the NFL/AFL merger, Super Bowl IV pitted the NFL champion Minnesota Vikings against the AFL champion Kansas City Chiefs.

102. Bobby Layne (196 TDs, 243 INTs); Y.A. Tittle (212 TDs, 221 INTs); Norm Van Brocklin (173 TDs, 178 INTs), Bob Waterfield (97 TDs, 128 INTs); most recent inductee Joe Namath (173 TDs, 220 INTs)

103. Cleveland Browns punter Tom

COLLEGE FOOTBALL

109. Prior to the Mount Union College Purple Raiders' 21–14 loss to the Ohio Northern Polar Bears on Oct. 22, 2005, how many consecutive regular-season games had the Raiders won in a row?

110. Who was the last offensive lineman to score a touchdown in a national championship game?

111. Which annual college football rivalry is also referred to as the Iron Bowl?

112. What was the only bowl game ever to feature opposing head coaches who were also brothers?

HINT: The dueling brothers headed up teams from the ACC and SEC.

113. Which Division I college football head coach was the fastest to reach 200 career victories?

114. On October 2, 2004, San Jose St. and Rice set a Division I record for most combined points scored in a regulation game. How many points did the two teams score?

115. Which school holds the NCAA record for most consecutive rushing yards gained without a loss?

116. Only one head coach in NCAA Division I history has taken five different schools to a bowl game. Name him and four of the colleges where he coached.

117. In 2004, Oklahoma running back Adrian Peterson set a NCAA record for freshman with 11 100-yard games in a season. Name the former Oklahoma running back who holds the all-time NCAA single-season record for most 100-yard games?

118. Name the most recent year in which a Division I football game ended in a tie.

COLLEGE FOOTBALL

JOSE NOGUENAS/OHIO NORTHERN UNIVERSITY

Mount Union's 11-year regular-season winning streak ended in 2005 vs. Ohio Northern.

109. 110–MUC's previous regular-season loss occurred on Oct. 15, 1994. Between those two losses, Mount Union posted a 144–5 record (including playoff games) and won six Division III national championships.

110. Mark Hutson–Number one-ranked Oklahoma executed a trick "fumblerooski" play in the 1988 Orange Bowl against the number two-ranked Miami Hurricanes, in which the 280-pound guard Hutson scooped up an intentionally fumbled center snap and carried the ball for a 29-yard TD with two minutes left in the game. Oklahoma lost the game and the championship, 20–14.

111. Auburn vs. Alabama

112. 1971 Gator Bowl–Vince Dooley (Georgia) vs. Bill Dooley (North Carolina). Georgia won 7–3.

113. Tom Osborne–Nebraska (21 full seasons plus 5 games)

114. 133–San Jose St. beat Rice, 70–63.

115. Nebraska–677 (against New Mexico St, Sept. 18, 1982)

116. Lou Holtz (William & Mary, North Carolina State, Arkansas, Notre Dame, South Carolina)

117. Quentin Griffin–12 100-yard games in 2002 for Oklahoma

118. 1995–Wisconsin and Illinois tied, 3–3, on November 25, 1995

GOLF

119. After seven years, Tiger Woods' record streak of 142 consecutive PGA Tour cuts made ended inMay 2005 at the EDS Byron Nelson Championship. What golfer holds the second-longest all-time cuts made streak?

120. Which player currently holds the PGA Tour's longest consecutive cuts made streak?

121. When Phil Mickelson won his second major at the 2005 PGA Championship, he joined the exclusive club of multiple-major winners. How many other male golfers, beside Phil, are in this club?

122. How many golfers have won just one of the PGA's four majors?

123. Since January 1st, 2000, which professional golfer has the best winning percentage in professional golf?

124. In 2006, the U.S. Open will return to Winged Foot Golf Club for only the second time since the infamous 1974 U.S. Open "Massacre," where Hale Irwin won with a score of 7-over. However, in the modern era, that mark is not the highest score, to par, to win one of golf's four major championships. Name the tournament and year that saw the highest-ever score, to par, to win one of golf's majors?

125. Who was the youngest-ever player to earn a PGA Tour card?

ANSWERS
GOLF

119: Byron Nelson–113

120: Ernie Els–24 (through October 2005)

121: 72 players have two or more majors

Annika Sorenstam won the LPGA's first two majors in 2005, the first time a player has done this since 1986.

122: 106 players have only won a single major.

123: Annika Sorenstam–won 37.4% of LPGA tournaments entered (Tiger Woods has win percentage of 26.5% in PGA Tour events over same period)

124: 9-over (293)–1963 U.S. Open at The Country Club at Brookline, Mass. (won by Julius Boros in a playoff)

125: Ty Tryon–16 years old (2001)

Awards

ROBERT BECK

SPORTS ILLUSTRATED'S
2004 Sportsmen of the Year
Boston Red Sox

Athlete Awards

Sports Illustrated Sportsman of the Year

1954	Roger Bannister, Track and Field
1955	Johnny Podres, Baseball
1956	Bobby Morrow, Track and Field
1957	Stan Musial, Baseball
1958	Rafer Johnson, Track and Field
1959	Ingemar Johansson, Boxing
1960	Arnold Palmer, Golf
1961	Jerry Lucas, Basketball
1962	Terry Baker, Football
1963	Pete Rozelle, Pro Football
1964	Ken Venturi, Golf
1965	Sandy Koufax, Baseball
1966	Jim Ryun, Track and Field
1967	Carl Yastrzemski, Baseball
1968	Bill Russell, Pro Basketball
1969	Tom Seaver, Baseball
1970	Bobby Orr, Hockey
1971	Lee Trevino, Golf
1972	B.J. King, Tennis/ J. Wooden, Bask
1973	Jackie Stewart, Auto Racing
1974	Muhammad Ali, Boxing
1975	Pete Rose, Baseball
1976	Chris Evert, Tennis
1977	Steve Cauthen, Horse Racing
1978	Jack Nicklaus, Golf
1979	Terry Bradshaw, Pro Football
	Willie Stargell, Baseball
1980	U.S. Olympic Hockey Team
1981	Sugar Ray Leonard, Boxing
1982	Wayne Gretzky, Hockey
1983	Mary Decker, Track and Field
1984	Mary Lou Retton, Gymnastics
	Edwin Moses, Track and Field
1985	Kareem Abdul-Jabbar, Pro Basketball
1986	Joe Paterno, Football
1987	Athletes Who Care:
	Bob Bourne, Hockey
	Kip Keino, Track and Field
	Judi Brown King, Track and Field
	Dale Murphy, Baseball
	Chip Rives, Football
	Patty Sheehan, Golf
	Rory Sparrow, Pro Basketball
	Reggie Williams, Pro Football
1988	Orel Hershiser, Baseball
1989	Greg LeMond, Cycling
1990	Joe Montana, Pro Football
1991	Michael Jordan, Pro Basketball
1992	Arthur Ashe, Tennis
1993	Don Shula, Pro Football
1994	Bonnie Blair, Speed Skating
	Johann Olav Koss, Speed Skating
1995	Cal Ripken Jr, Baseball
1996	Tiger Woods, Golf
1997	Dean Smith, College Basketball
1998	Mark McGwire, Sammy Sosa, Baseball
1999	U.S. Women's Soccer Team
2000	Tiger Woods, Golf
2001	C. Schilling/ R. Johnson, Baseball
2002	Lance Armstrong, Cycling
2003	Tim Duncan/David Robinson, Bask
2004	Boston Red Sox, Baseball

Associated Press Athletes of the Year

	MEN	WOMEN
1931	Pepper Martin, Baseball	Helene Madison, Swimming
1932	Gene Sarazen, Golf	Babe Didrikson, Track and Field
1933	Carl Hubbell, Baseball	Helen Jacobs, Tennis
1934	Dizzy Dean, Baseball	Virginia Van Wie, Golf
1935	Joe Louis, Boxing	Helen Wills Moody, Tennis
1936	Jesse Owens, Track and Field	Helen Stephens, Track and Field
1937	Don Budge, Tennis	Katherine Rawls, Swimming
1938	Don Budge, Tennis	Patty Berg, Golf
1939	Nile Kinnick, Football	Alice Marble, Tennis
1940	Tom Harmon, Football	Alice Marble, Tennis
1941	Joe DiMaggio, Baseball	Betty Hicks Newell, Golf
1942	Frank Sinkwich, Football	Gloria Callen, Swimming
1943	Gunder Haegg, Track and Field	Patty Berg, Golf
1944	Byron Nelson, Golf	Ann Curtis, Swimming
1945	Bryon Nelson, Golf	Babe Didrikson Zaharias, Golf
1946	Glenn Davis, Football	Babe Didrikson Zaharias, Golf
1947	Johnny Lujack, Football	Babe Didrikson Zaharias, Golf
1948	Lou Boudreau, Baseball	Fanny Blankers-Koen, Track and Field
1949	Leon Hart, Football	Marlene Bauer, Golf
1950	Jim Konstanty, Baseball	Babe Didrikson Zaharias, Golf
1951	Dick Kazmaier, Football	Maureen Connolly, Tennis
1952	Bob Mathias, Track and Field	Maureen Connolly, Tennis
1953	Ben Hogan, Golf	Maureen Connolly, Tennis
1954	Willie Mays, Baseball	Babe Didrikson Zaharias, Golf
1955	Hopalong Cassidy, Football	Patty Berg, Golf
1956	Mickey Mantle, Baseball	Pat McCormick, Diving
1957	Ted Williams, Baseball	Althea Gibson, Tennis
1958	Herb Elliott, Track and Field	Althea Gibson, Tennis
1959	Ingemar Johansson, Boxing	Maria Bueno, Tennis
1960	Rafer Johnson, Track and Field	Wilma Rudolph, Track and Field
1961	Roger Maris, Baseball	Wilma Rudolph, Track and Field
1962	Maury Wills, Baseball	Dawn Fraser, Swimming
1963	Sandy Koufax, Baseball	Mickey Wright, Golf
1964	Don Schollander, Swimming	Mickey Wright, Golf
1965	Sandy Koufax, Baseball	Kathy Whitworth, Golf
1966	Frank Robinson, Baseball	Kathy Whitworth, Golf
1967	Carl Yastrzemski, Baseball	Billie Jean King, Tennis
1968	Denny McLain, Baseball	Peggy Fleming, Skating
1969	Tom Seaver, Baseball	Debbie Meyer, Swimming

Associated Press Athletes of the Year (Cont.)

	MEN	WOMEN
1970	George Blanda, Pro Football	Chi Cheng, Track and Field
1971	Lee Trevino, Golf	Evonne Goolagong, Tennis
1972	Mark Spitz, Swimming	Olga Korbut, Gymnastics
1973	O.J. Simpson, Pro Football	Billie Jean King, Tennis
1974	Muhammad Ali, Boxing	Chris Evert, Tennis
1975	Fred Lynn, Baseball	Chris Evert, Tennis
1976	Bruce Jenner, Track and Field	Nadia Comaneci, Gymnastics
1977	Steve Cauthen, Horse Racing	Chris Evert, Tennis
1978	Ron Guidry, Baseball	Nancy Lopez, Golf
1979	Willie Stargell, Baseball	Tracy Austin, Tennis
1980	U.S. Olympic Hockey Team	Chris Evert Lloyd, Tennis
1981	John McEnroe, Tennis	Tracy Austin, Tennis
1982	Wayne Gretzky, Hockey	Mary Decker, Track and Field
1983	Carl Lewis, Track and Field	Martina Navratilova, Tennis
1984	Carl Lewis, Track and Field	Mary Lou Retton, Gymnastics
1985	Dwight Gooden, Baseball	Nancy Lopez, Golf
1986	Larry Bird, Pro Basketball	Martina Navratilova, Tennis
1987	Ben Johnson, Track and Field	Jackie Joyner-Kersee, Track and Field
1988	Orel Hershiser, Baseball	Florence Griffith Joyner, Track and Field
1989	Joe Montana, Pro Football	Steffi Graf, Tennis
1990	Joe Montana, Pro Football	Beth Daniel, Golf
1991	Michael Jordan, Pro Basketball	Monica Seles, Tennis
1992	Michael Jordan, Pro Basketball	Monica Seles, Tennis
1993	Michael Jordan, Pro Basketball	Sheryl Swoopes, Basketball
1994	George Foreman, Boxing	Bonnie Blair, Speed Skating
1995	Cal Ripken Jr, Baseball	Rebecca Lobo, Basketball
1996	Michael Johnson, Track and Field	Amy Van Dyken, Swimming
1997	Tiger Woods, Golf	Martina Hingis, Tennis
1998	Mark McGwire, Baseball	Se Ri Pak, Golf
1999	Tiger Woods, Golf	U.S. Women's Soccer Team
2000	Tiger Woods, Golf	Marion Jones, Track and Field
2001	Barry Bonds, Baseball	Jennifer Capriati, Tennis
2002	Lance Armstrong, Cycling	Serena Williams, Tennis
2003	Lance Armstrong, Cycling	Annika Sörenstam, Golf
2004	Lance Armstorng, Cycling	Annika Sorenstam, Golf

James E. Sullivan Award

Presented annually by the AAU to the athlete who "by his or her performance, example and influence as an amateur, has done the most during the year to advance the cause of sportsmanship."

1930	Bobby Jones, Golf	1963	John Pennel, Track and Field
1931	Barney Berlinger, Track and Field	1964	Don Schollander, Swimming
1932	Jim Bausch, Track and Field	1965	Bill Bradley, Basketball
1933	Glenn Cunningham, Track and Field	1966	Jim Ryun, Track and Field
1934	Bill Bonthron, Track and Field	1967	Randy Matson, Track and Field
1935	Lawson Little, Golf	1968	Debbie Meyer, Swimming
1936	Glenn Morris, Track and Field	1969	Bill Toomey, Track and Field
1937	Don Budge, Tennis	1970	John Kinsella, Swimming
1938	Don Lash, Track and Field	1971	Mark Spitz, Swimming
1939	Joe Burk, Rowing	1972	Frank Shorter, Track and Field
1940	Greg Rice, Track and Field	1973	Bill Walton, Basketball
1941	Leslie MacMitchell, Track and Field	1974	Rich Wohlhuter, Track and Field
1942	Cornelius Warmerdam, Track	1975	Tim Shaw, Swimming
1943	Gilbert Dodds, Track and Field	1976	Bruce Jenner, Track and Field
1944	Ann Curtis, Swimming	1977	John Naber, Swimming
1945	Doc Blanchard, Football	1978	Tracy Caulkins, Swimming
1946	Arnold Tucker, Football	1979	Kurt Thomas, Gymnastics
1947	John B. Kelly Jr, Rowing	1980	Eric Heiden, Speed Skating
1948	Bob Mathias, Track and Field	1981	Carl Lewis, Track and Field
1949	Dick Button, Skating	1982	Mary Decker, Track and Field
1950	Fred Wilt, Track and Field	1983	Edwin Moses, Track and Field
1951	Bob Richards, Track and Field	1984	Greg Louganis, Diving
1952	Horace Ashenfelter, Track and Field	1985	Joan B.-Samuelson, T & F
1953	Sammy Lee, Diving	1986	Jackie Joyner-Kersee, T & F
1954	Mal Whitfield, Track and Field	1987	Jim Abbott, Baseball
1955	Harrison Dillard, Track and Field	1988	Florence Griffith Joyner, Track
1956	Pat McCormick, Diving	1989	Janet Evans, Swimming
1957	Bobby Morrow, Track and Field	1990	John Smith, Wrestling
1958	Glenn Davis, Track and Field	1991	Mike Powell, Track and Field
1959	Parry O'Brien, Track and Field	1992	Bonnie Blair, Speed Skating
1960	Rafer Johnson, Track and Field	1993	Charlie Ward, Football, Basketball
1961	Wilma Rudolph, Track and Field	1994	Dan Jansen, Speed Skating
1962	Jim Beatty, Track and Field	1995	Bruce Baumgartner, Wrestling

James E. Sullivan Award (Cont.)

1997	Peyton Manning, Football
1998	Chamique Holdsclaw, Basketball
1999	Kelly and Coco Miller, Basketball
2000	Rulon Gardner, Wrestling
2001	Michelle Kwan, Figure Skating
2002	Sarah Hughes, Figure Skating
2003	Michael Phelps, Swimming
2004	Paul Hamm, Gymnastics

The Sporting News Sportsman of the Year

1996	Michael Johnson, Track and Field
1968	Denny McLain, Baseball
1969	Tom Seaver, Baseball
1970	John Wooden, Basketball
1971	Lee Trevino, Golf
1972	Charles O. Finley, Baseball
1973	O.J. Simpson, Pro Football
1974	Lou Brock, Baseball
1975	Archie Griffin, Football
1976	Larry O'Brien, Pro Basketball
1977	Steve Cauthen, Horse Racing
1978	Ron Guidry, Baseball
1979	Willie Stargell, Baseball
1980	George Brett, Baseball
1981	Wayne Gretzky, Hockey
1982	Whitey Herzog, Baseball
1983	Bowie Kuhn, Baseball
1984	Peter Ueberroth, LA Olympics
1985	Pete Rose, Baseball
1986	Larry Bird, Pro Basketball
1987	No award
1988	Jackie Joyner-Kersee, T & F
1989	Joe Montana, Pro Football
1990	Nolan Ryan, Baseball
1991	Michael Jordan, Pro Basketball
1992	Mike Krzyzewski, Basketball
1993	Pat Gillick/Cito Gaston, Baseball
1994	Emmitt Smith, Pro Football
1995	Cal Ripken Jr, Baseball
1996	Joe Torre, Baseball
1997	Michael Jordan, Basketball
1998	Mark McGwire, Baseball
1999	New York Yankees, Baseball
2000	Kurt Warner/ Marshall Faulk, Football
2001	Curt Schilling, Baseball
2002	Tyrone Willingham, Football
2003	Jack McKeon, Baseball Dick Vermeil, Football
2004	Tom Brady, Football

United Press International Male and Female Athlete of the Year

	MEN	WOMEN
1974	Muhammad Ali, Boxing	Irena Szewinska, Track and Field
1975	Joao Oliveira, Track and Field	Nadia Comaneci, Gymnastics
1976	Alberto Juantorena, Track and Field	Nadia Comaneci, Gymnastics
1977	Alberto Juantorena, Track and Field	Rosie Ackermann, Track and Field
1978	Henry Rono, Track and Field	Tracy Caulkins, Swimming
1979	Sebastian Coe, Track and Field	Marita Koch, Track and Field
1980	Eric Heiden, Speed Skating	Hanni Wenzel, Alpine Skiing
1981	Sebastian Coe, Track and Field	Chris Evert Lloyd, Tennis
1982	Daley Thompson, Track and Field	Marita Koch, Track and Field
1983	Carl Lewis, Track and Field	Jarmila Kratochvilova, Track and Field
1984	Carl Lewis, Track and Field	Martina Navratilova, Tennis
1985	Steve Cram, Track and Field	Mary Decker Slaney, Track and Field
1986	Diego Maradona, Soccer	Heike Drechsler, Track and Field
1987	Ben Johnson, Track and Field	Steffi Graf, Tennis
1988	Matt Biondi, Swimming	Florence Griffith Joyner, Track and Field
1989	Boris Becker, Tennis	Steffi Graf, Tennis
1990	Stefan Edberg, Tennis	Merlene Ottey, Track and Field
1991	Michael Jordan, Pro Basketball	Monica Seles, Tennis
1992	Mario Lemieux, Hockey	Monica Seles, Tennis
1993	Michael Jordan, Pro Basketball	Steffi Graf, Tennis
1994	Nick Price, Golf	Bonnie Blair, Speed Skating
1995	Cal Ripken Jr, Baseball	Steffi Graf, Tennis

Note: Award not given since 1995.
Presented by the Dial Corporation to the male and female national high school athlete/scholar of the year.

Dial Award

	BOYS	GIRLS
1979	Herschel Walker, Football	No award
1980	Bill Fralic, Football	Carol Lewis, Track and Field
1981	Kevin Willhite, Football	Cheryl Miller, Basketball
1982	Mike Smith, Basketball	Elaine Zayak, Skating
1983	Chris Spielman, Football	Melanie Buddemeyer, Swimming
1984	Hart Lee Dykes, Football	Nora Lewis, Basketball
1985	Jeff George, Football	Gea Johnson, Track and Field
1986	Scott Schaffner, Football	Mya Johnson, Track and Field
1987	Todd Marinovich, Football	Kristi Overton, Water Skiing
1988	Carlton Gray, Football	Courtney Cox, Basketball
1989	Robert Smith, Football	Lisa Leslie, Basketball
1990	Derrick Brooks, Football	Vicki Goetze, Golf
1991	Jeff Buckey, Football, Track and Field	Katie Smith, Basketball, Volleyball, Track
1992	Jacque Vaughn, Basketball	Amanda White, Track and Field, Swimming
1993	Tiger Woods, Golf	Kristin Folkl, Basketball
1994	Taymon Domzalski, Basketball	Shannon Miller, Gymnastics
1995	Brent Abernathy, Baseball	Shea Ralph, Basketball
1996	Grant Irons, Football	Grace Park, Golf
1997	Ronald Curry, Football	Michelle Kwan, Figure Skating

Note: Award not given since 1997.

Profiles

2005 Masters and British Open champion Tiger Woods

Henry Aaron (b. 2-5-34): Baseball OF. "Hammerin' Hank." Alltime leader in HR (755) and RBI (2,297); third in hits (3,771). 1957 MVP. Led league in HR and RBI four times each, runs scored three times, hits and batting average twice. No. 44, he had 44 homers four times. Had 40+ HR eight times; 100+ RBI 11 times; .300+ average 14 times. All-Star 24 times . Career span 1954–76; jersey number retired by Atlanta and Milwaukee.

Kareem Abdul-Jabbar (b. 4-16-47): Born Lew Alcindor. Basketball C. Alltime leader points scored (38,387), field goals attempted (28,307), field goals made (15,837); second alltime blocked shots (3,189); third alltime rebounds (17,440). Won six MVP awards (1971–72, 1974, 1976–77, 1980). Career scoring average was 24.6, rebounding average 11.2. Ten-time All-Star, All-Defensive team five times. 1970 Rookie of the Year. Played on six championship teams; was playoff MVP in 1971, 1985. Career span 1969–88 with Milwaukee, Los Angeles. Also played on three NCAA championship teams with UCLA; tournament MVP 1967–69; Player of the Year two times.

Affirmed (b. 2-21-75, d. 1-12-01): Thoroughbred race horse. Triple Crown winner in 1978 with jockey Steve Cauthen aboard. Trained by Laz Barrera.

Andre Agassi (b. 4-29-70): Tennis player. Won 1999 French Open to become fifth man in history to win all four Grand Slams. Won '92 Wimbledon, '94 and '99 U.S. Opens and '95, '00, '01 and '03 Australian Opens. Ranked No. 1 in 1995 and again in '99.

Troy Aikman (b. 11-21-66): Football QB. Quarterbacked Cowboys to three Super Bowl titles (XXVII, XXVIII, XXX). MVP of Super Bowl XXVII, in which he completed 22 of 30 passes for 273 yards and four TDs with no interceptions. Spent entire career (1989–2000) with Dallas Cowboys, passing for 32,942 yards and 171 TDs.

Michelle Akers (b. 2-1-66): Soccer player. Charter member of U.S. women's national team. Scored first goal ever for U.S. women's team on 8-21-85 against Denmark. Second alltime leading scorer in U.S. women's national team history (105 goals). Member of Women's World Cup champion team in 1991, '99, and third-place team in '95. Member of Olympic champion team in 1996. Battled chronic fatigue syndrome.

Tenley Albright (b. 7-18-35): Figure skater. Gold medalist at 1956 Olympics, silver medalist at 1952 Olympics. World champion two times (1953, 1955) and U.S. champion five consecutive years (1952–56).

Grover Cleveland Alexander (b. 2-26-1887, d. 11-4-50): Baseball RHP. Tied for third alltime in career wins (373), second in shutouts (90). Won 30+ games three times, 20+ games six other times. Set rookie record with 28 wins in 1911. Career span 1911–30 with Philadelphia (NL), Chicago (NL), St. Louis (NL).

Vasili Alexeyev (b. 1942): Soviet weightlifter. Gold medalist at two consecutive Olympics 1972, 1976. World champion eight times.

Muhammad Ali (b. 1-17-42): Born Cassius Clay. Boxer. Heavyweight champion three times (1964–67, 1974–78, 1978–79). Stripped of title in 1967 because he refused to serve in the Vietnam War. Career record 56–5 with 37 KOs. Defended title 19 times. Also light heavyweight gold medalist at 1960 Olympics. Battles Parkinson Syndrome.

Phog Allen (b. 11-18-1885, d. 9-16-74): College basketball coach. Ninth alltime in coaching wins (746); .739 career winning percentage. Won 1952 NCAA championship. Spent most of his career from 1920 to '56 with Kansas.

Bobby Allison (b. 12-3-37): Auto racer. Third alltime in NASCAR victories (84). Won Daytona 500 three times (1978, 1982, 1988). NASCAR champion in 1983.

Naty Alvarado (b. 7-25-55): Mexican-born handball player. "El Gato (The Cat)." Won a record 11 U.S. pro four-wall handball titles, starting in 1977.

Lance Alworth (b. 8-3-40): Football WR. "Bambi" led AFL in receiving in 1966, '68 and '69. 200+ yards in a game five times in career, a record. Gained 100+ yards in a game 41 times. In 1965 gained 1,602 yards receiving. Career span 1962–70 with San Diego and 1971–72 with Dallas. Elected to Pro Football Hall of Fame 1978.

Gary Anderson (b. 7-16-59): Football K. Four-time Pro Bowl kicker (1983, '85, '93, '98). NFL's alltime leading scorer (2,133 pts). Made league record 40 consecutive FGs in 1997–98 season. Made every field goal and extra point attempt during the 1998–99 season.

Sparky Anderson (b. 2-22-34): Baseball manager. Only manager to win World Series in both leagues (Cincinnati, 1975–76, Detroit, 1984); only manager to win 100 games in both leagues. Elected to Hall of Fame in 2000.

Willie Anderson (b. 1880, d. 1910): Scottish golfer. Won U.S. Open four times (1901 and an unmatched three straight, 1903–05). Also won four Western Opens between 1902 and 1909.

Mario Andretti (b. 2-28-40): Auto racer. The only driver in history to win the Daytona 500 (1967), the Indy 500 (1969) and a Formula One world championship (1978). Second alltime in CART victories (52). Twelve career Formula One victories. USAC/CART champion four times (consecutively 1965–66, 1969, 1984).

Earl Anthony (b. 4-27-38, d. 8-14-01): Bowler. Won PBA National Championship six times, more than any other bowler (consecutively 1973–75, 1981–83) and Tournament of Champions two times (1974, 1978). First bowler to top $1 million in career earnings. Bowler of the Year six times (consecutively 1974–76, 1981–83). Won 41 career PBA titles.

Said Aouita (b. 11-2-60): Track and field. Moroccan set world records in 2,000 meters (4:50.81 in 1987), and 5,000 meters (12:58.39 in 1987). 1984 Olympic champion in 5,000; 1988 Olympic third place in 800.

Al Arbour (b. 11-1-32): Hockey D-coach. Led NY Islanders to four consecutive Stanley Cup championships (1980–83). Also played on three Stanley Cup champions: Detroit, Chicago and Toronto, from 1953 to 1971.

Eddie Arcaro (b. 2-19-16, d. 11-14-97): Horse racing jockey. The only jockey to win the Triple Crown two times (aboard Whirlaway in 1941, Citation in 1948). Rode Preakness Stakes winner (1941, 1948, consecutively 1950–51, 1955, 1957) and Belmont Stakes winner (consecutively 1941–42, 1945, 1948, 1952, 1955) six times each and Kentucky Derby winner five times (1938, 1941, 1945, 1948, 1952). 4,779 career wins.

Nate Archibald (b. 9-2-48): Basketball player. "Tiny" only by NBA standards at 6' 1", 160 pounds. Six-time All-Star. Led NBA in scoring (34.0) and assists (11.4) in 1972–73. First team, all-NBA in 1973, '75 and '76. MVP of NBA All-Star Game in 1981. Career span 1970–84 with six teams.

Alexis Arguello (b. 4-19-52): Nicaraguan boxer. Won world titles in three weight classes: featherweight, super featherweight and lightweight. Won first title, WBA featherweight, on 11-23-74 when he KO'd Ruben Olivares in 13. Career record: 88–8, 64 KO.

Henry Armstrong (b. 12-12-12, d. 10-24-88): Boxer. Champion in three different weight classes: featherweight, welterweight, and lightweight. Career record 145-20-9 with 98 KOs (27 consecutively, 1937–38) from 1931 to 1945.

Lance Armstrong (b. 9-18-71): Cyclist. Recovered from testicular cancer to win seven straight Tour de France races (1999–05), a record. Two-time winner of Tour DuPont (1995, '96). Won 1993 world championships.

Arthur Ashe (b. 7-10-43, d. 2-6-93): Tennis player. First black man to win U.S. Open (1968, as an amateur), Australian Open (1970) and Wimbledon singles titles (1975). 33 career tournament victories. Member of Davis Cup team 1963–78; captain 1980–85. Stadium at the United States Tennis Center, home of the U.S. Open, named in his honor.

Assault (b. 1943, d. 1971): Thoroughbred race horse. Horse of the Year for 1946 when he won the Triple Crown. Won Kentucky Derby by eight lengths, Preakness by a neck, and the Belmont by three lengths. Trained by Max Hirsch.

Red Auerbach (b. 9-20-17): Basketball coach-executive. 938 career wins. Coached Boston from 1946 to 1965, winning nine championships, eight consecutively. Had .662 career winning percentage, with 50+ wins eight consecutive seasons. Also won seven championships as general manager.

Hobey Baker (b. 1-15-1892, d. 12-21-18): Sportsman. Member of both college football and hockey Halls of Fame. College hockey and football star at Princeton, 1911–14. Fighter pilot in World War I, died in plane crash. College hockey Player of the Year award named in his honor.

Seve Ballesteros (b. 4-9-57): Spanish golfer. Notorious scrambler. Won British Opens in 1979, '84 and '88. Won Masters in 1980 and '83.

Ernie Banks (b. 1-31-31): Baseball SS-1B. "Mr. Cub." Won two consecutive MVP awards, in 1958–59. 512 career HR. League leader in HR, RBI two times each; 40+ HR five times; 100+ RBI eight times; career batting average of .274. Career span 1953–71 with Chicago.

Roger Bannister (b. 3-23-29): Track and field. British runner broke the four-minute mile barrier, running 3:59.4 on 5-6-54.

Red Barber (b. 2-17-08, d. 10-22-92): Sportscaster. TV-radio baseball announcer was the voice of Cincinnati, Brooklyn and NY Yankees. His expressions, such as "sitting in the catbird seat," "pea patch" and "rhubarb," captivated audiences from 1934 to 1966.

Charles Barkley (b. 2-20-63): Basketball F. "The Round Mound of Rebound." Eleven-time All-Star. One of only four NBA players to amass 20,000 points, 10,000 rebounds, and 4,000 assists. Named one of NBA's greatest 50 players. Leading scorer on the 1992 Olympic team. League MVP for 1992–93 season. Played for Philadelphia, Phoenix, Houston. Career averages: 22.2 ppg, 11.7 rpg.

Rick Barry (b. 3-28-44): Basketball F. Only player in history to win scoring titles in NCAA (Miami (FL), 1965), NBA (San Francisco, 1967) and ABA (Oakland, 1969). Five-time first-team All-NBA. 1966 Rookie of the Year. 1975 playoff MVP with Golden State. Eight-time NBA All-Star. Career scoring average 23.2. Career span 1966–79.

Carmen Basilio (b. 4-2-27): Boxer. Won titles as a welterweight and middleweight. Won welterweight title by TKO of Tony DeMarco in 12 rounds on 6-10-55. Won and then lost middleweight title in two 15-round fights with Ray Robinson. Made three unsuccessful bids to regain middle title. *The Ring* Fighter of the Year for 1957. Career record: 56–16–7, 27 KOs.

Sammy Baugh (b. 3-17-14): Football QB-P. Led NFL in passing six times and punting four times, a record. Holds record for highest career punting average (45.1) and highest season average (51.0 in 1940). Career span 1937–52 with Washington, passing for 21,866 yards and 186 TDs.

Elgin Baylor (b. 9-16-34): Basketball F. Fourth alltime highest scoring average (27.4) in NBA history. Averaged 30+ points three consecutive seasons (1960-63). 1959 Rookie of the Year. 11-time All-Star. Played in eight NBA Finals without winning championship. Career span 1958–71 with Lakers. MVP of 1958 NCAA Tournament with Seattle.

Bob Beamon (b. 8-29-46): Track and field. Gold medalist in long jump at 1968 Olympics with world record leap of 29' 2½" that stood until 1991.

Franz Beckenbauer (b. 9-11-45): West German soccer player. Captain of 1974 World Cup champions and coach of 1990 champions. Also played for NY Cosmos from 1977 to 1980.

Boris Becker (b. 11-22-67): German tennis player. The youngest male player (17, in 1985) to win a Wimbledon singles title. Won three Wimbledon titles (1985–86, 1989), one U.S. Open (1989) and one Australian Open title (1991). Led West Germany to consecutive Davis Cup victories (1988–89).

Chuck Bednarik (b. 5-1-25): Football C-LB. Last of the great two-way players, was named All-Pro at both center and linebacker. Missed only three games in 14 seasons with Philadelphia from 1949–62. Seven-time All-NFL. Two-time All-America at Pennsylvania.

Clair Bee (b. 3-2-1896, d. 5-20-83): Basketball coach. Originated 1-3-1 defense, helped develop three-second rule, 24-second clock. Won 82.7 percent of games as coach for Rider College and Long Island University. Coach, Baltimore Bullets, 1952–54. Author, 23-volume Chip Hilton series for children, 21 nonfiction sports books.

Jean Beliveau (b. 8-31-31): Hockey C. Won MVP award twice (1956, 1964), playoff MVP in 1965. Led league in assists three times, goals two times and points once. 507 career goals, 712 assists. All-Star six times. Played on 10 Stanley Cup champions with Montreal from 1950 to 1971.

Bert Bell (b. 2-25-1895, d. 10-11-59): Football executive. Second NFL commissioner (1946–59). Also owner of Philadelphia (1933–40) and Pittsburgh (1941–46). Proposed the first NFL draft of college players, in 1936.

James (Cool Papa) Bell (b. 5-17-03, d. 3-7-91): Baseball OF. Legendary foot speed—according to Satchel Paige could flip light switch and be in bed before room was dark. Hit .392 in games against white major leaguers. Career span 1922–46 with many teams of the Negro Leagues, including the Pittsburgh Crawfords and the Homestead Grays. Inducted in the Hall of Fame in 1974.

Lyudmila Belousova/Oleg Protopov (no dates of birth available): Soviet figure skaters. Won Olympic gold medal in pairs competition in 1964 and 1968. Won four consecutive World and European championships (1965–68) and eight consecutive Soviet titles (1961–68).

Deane Beman (b. 4-22-38): Commissioner of the PGA Tour 1974–94. Won British Amateur title in 1959 and U.S. Amateur titles in 1960 and 1963.

Johnny Bench (b. 12-7-47): Baseball C. MVP in 1970, 1972; World Series MVP in 1976; Rookie of the Year in 1968. 389 career HR. League leader in HR two times, RBI three times. Career span 1967–83 with Cincinnati. Elected to Hall of Fame in 1989.

Patty Berg (b. 2-13-18): Golfer. Alltime women's leader in major championships (16), third alltime in career wins (57). Won Titleholders Championship and Western Open seven times each, the most of any golfer. Also won U.S. Women's Amateur (1938) and U.S. Women's Open (1946).

Yogi Berra (b. 5-12-25): Baseball C. Played on 10 World Series winners. Alltime Series leader in games, at-bats, hits and doubles. MVP in 1951 and consecutively 1954–55. 358 career HR. Career span 1946–63, '65. Managed pennant-winning Yankees (1964) and Mets (1973).

Jay Berwanger (b. 3-19-14, d. 6-26-02): College football RB. Won the first Heisman Trophy and named All-America with Chicago in 1935.

Raymond Berry (b. 2-27-33): Football WR. Led NFL in receiving 1958–60. In 13-season career, caught 631 passes, 68 for TDs. Career span 1955–67, all with Baltimore Colts. Coached New England Patriots from 1984–89 with 51–41 record.

George Best (b. 5-22-46): Northern Ireland soccer player. Led Manchester United to European Cup title in 1968. Named England's and Europe's Player of the Year in 1968. Played in North American Soccer League from 1976–81. Frequent troubles with alcohol and gambling shadowed career.

Abebe Bikila (b. 8-7-32, d. 10-25-73): Track and field. Ethiopian barefoot runner won consecutive gold medals in the marathon at Olympics, in 1960 and 1964.

Fred Biletnikoff (b. 2-23-43): Football WR. In 14 pro seasons caught 589 passes for 8,974 yards and 76 TDs. In 1971 led NFL receivers with 61 catches; in '72 led AFC with 58. Career span 1965–78, all with Raiders. Elected to Pro Football Hall of Fame in 1988.

Dmitri Bilozerchev (b. 12-22-66): Soviet gymnast. Won three gold medals at 1988 Olympics. Made comeback after shattering his left leg into 44 pieces in 1985. Two-time world champion (1983, '87). At 16, became youngest to win all-around world championship title in 1983.

Dave Bing (b. 11-24-43): Basketball G. NBA Rookie of Year in 1967. Led NBA in scoring (27.1) in 1968. MVP NBA All-Star game in 1976. In 12-year career from 1967–78, most of it with Detroit Pistons, averaged 20.3 points. Averaged 24.8 ppg in four years at Syracuse.

Matt Biondi (b. 10-8-65): Swimmer. Won five gold medals, one silver and one bronze at 1988 Olympics. Won one gold and one silver at 1992 Games.

Larry Bird (b. 12-7-56): Basketball F. Won three consecutive MVP awards (1984–86) and two playoff MVP awards (1984, 1986). Rookie of the Year (1980) and All-Star nine consecutive seasons. Led league in free throw percentage four times. Averaged 20+ points 10 times. Career span 1979–92 with Boston. Named College Player of the Year in 1979 with Indiana State. 1997–98 NBA Coach of the Year in first year as coach of Indiana Pacers.

Bonnie Blair (b. 3-18-64): Speed skater. Won gold medal in 500 meters and bronze medal in 1,000 meters at 1988 Olympics. Swept both Olympic events in 1992 and '94. 1989 World Sprint champion. Winner of 1992 Sullivan Award. *Sports Illustrated* 1994 Sportswoman of the Year.

Toe Blake (b. 8-21-12, d. 5-17-95): Hockey LW and coach. Second alltime highest winning percentage (.634) and eighth in wins (500). Led Montreal to eight Stanley Cup championships from 1955 to 1968 (consecutively 1956–60, 1965–66, '68). Also MVP and scoring leader in 1939. Played on two Stanley Cup champions with Montreal from 1932 to 1948.

Doc Blanchard (b. 12-11-24): College football FB. "Mr. Inside." Teamed with Glenn Davis to lead Army to three consecutive undefeated seasons (1944–46) and two consecutive national championships (1944–45). Won Heisman Trophy and Sullivan Award in 1945. All-America three times.

George Blanda (b. 9-17-27): Football QB-K. Alltime leader in seasons played (26), games played (340), and PAT's (943); third in points scored (2,002), kicked 335 field goals. Passed for 26,920 career yards and 236 touchdowns. Tied record with seven touchdown passes on Nov. 19, 1961. AFL Player of the Year (1961) when he threw 36 TDs. Played until age 48. Career span 1949–75 with Chicago, Houston, Oakland.

Fanny Blankers-Koen (b. 4-26-18, d. 1-25-04): Track and field. Dutch athlete won four gold medals at 1948 Olympics, in 100 meters; 200 meters; 80-meter hurdles; and 400-meter relay. She also set world records in high jump (5' 7¼" in 1943), long jump (20' 6" in 1943) and pentathlon (4,692 points in 1951).

Wade Boggs (b. 6-15-58): Baseball 3B. Won five batting titles (1983, consecutively 1985–88); had .350+ average five times, 200+ hits seven times. Won World Series with 1996 Yankees. Career span 1982–99 with Boston, New York Yankees, Tampa Bay; .328 career average, 3,010 hits.

Nick Bollettieri (b. 7-31-31): Tennis coach. Since 1976, has run Nick Bollettieri Tennis Academy in Bradenton, Fla. Former residents of the academy include Andre Agassi, Monica Seles and Jim Courier.

Barry Bonds (b. 7-24-64): Baseball OF. Baseball's single-season home run king, with 73 in 2001. Also produced .863 slugging percentage and 177 walks in 2001, breaking two of Babe Ruth's records, the first of which had stood since 1920. One of three players to top 40 homers (42) and 40 steals (40) in same season

(1996). Six-time National League MVP (1990, '92, '93, '01, '02, '03); Career span 1986–92 with Pittsburgh; 1993– with San Francisco.

Bjorn Borg (b. 6-6-56): Swedish tennis player. Third alltime in Grand Slam singles titles (11—tied with Rod Laver). Set modern record by winning five consecutive Wimbledon titles (1976–80). Won six French Open titles (1974–75, 1978–81). Reached U.S. Open final four times, but title eluded him. 65 career tournament victories. Led Sweden to Davis Cup win in 1975.

Julius Boros (b. 3-3-20, d. 5-28-94): Golfer. Won U.S. Opens in 1952 at Northwood CC in Dallas and in 1963 at The Country Club in Brookline, Mass. Won 1968 PGA Championship at Pecan Valley CC, San Antonio, when 48 years old, making him oldest winner of a major ever. Led PGA money list in 1952 and '55.

Mike Bossy (b. 1-22-57): Hockey RW. Set NHL rookie scoring record of 54 goals in 1978. Scored 50 or more each of first nine seasons. Totaled 573 goals and 1,126 points in 10 seasons (1977–87) with New York Islanders. Elected to Hall of Fame in 1991.

Ralph Boston (b. 5-9-39): Track and field. Long jumper won medals at three consecutive Olympics: gold in 1960, silver in '64, bronze in '68.

Ray Bourque (b. 12-28-60): Hockey D. Highest scoring defenseman in NHL history (1,579 pts). Won five Norris Trophies as NHL's top defenseman. Played in 19 consecutive All-Star games. No. 77. Won first and only Stanley Cup in 2001. Career span 1979–00 with Boston; 2000–01 with Colorado.

Scotty Bowman (b. 9-18-33): Retired in 2002 after leading Detroit to his ninth Stanley Cup title. Alltime leader in regular-season wins (1,244) and playoff wins (223). Coached Montreal, St. Louis, Buffalo, and Detroit. Won Jack Adams Award, Coach of the Year, 1976–77, 1995–96.

Bill Bradley (b. 7-28-43): Basketball F. Played on two NBA championship teams with New York from 1967 to '77. Player of the Year and NCAA tournament MVP in 1965 with Princeton; All-America three times; Sullivan Award winner in 1965. Rhodes scholar. U.S. Senator (D-NJ) 1979–96.

Terry Bradshaw (b. 9-2-48): Football QB. Played on four Super Bowl champions (1974, '75, '78, '79). Named Super Bowl MVP two consecutive seasons (1978–79). 212 career touchdown passes; 27,989 yards passing. Player of the Year in 1978. Career span 1970–83 with Pittsburgh.

Tom Brady (b. 8-3-77): Football QB. Led New England Patriots to Super Bowl victories in 2002 and '04, winning the Super Bowl MVP award in both games. Career span since 2000 with New England.

George Brett (b. 5-15-53): Baseball 3B-1B. Won batting titles in three different decades (1976, '80, '90). MVP in 1980 with .390 batting average. Hit .300+ 11 times. Led league in hits and triples three times. Career span 1973–93, with Kansas City. Career totals: 3,153 hits; 317 HR; 1,595 RBI; batting average .305. Elected to Hall of Fame in 1999.

Bret Hanover (b. 1962, d. 1993): Horse. Son of Adios. Won 62 of 68 harness races and earned $922,616. Undefeated as two-year-old. From total of 1,694 foals, he sired winners of $61 million and 511 horses that have recorded sub-2:00 performances.

Lou Brock (b. 6-18-39): Baseball OF. Second in career stolen bases (938); second highest single-season steals total (118) of modern era. Led league in steals eight times, with 50+ steals 12 consecutive seasons. Alltime World Series leader in steals (14—tied with Eddie Collins); hit .391 in World Series play. 3,023 career hits. Career span 1961–64 Chicago (NL), 1964–79 St. Louis.

Jim Brown (b. 2-17-36): Football FB. 126 career touchdowns; 12,312 career rushing yards. Led league in rushing record eight times. His 5.2 yards per carry average is the best ever. Player of the Year four times (1957, '58, '63, '65) and Rookie of the Year in 1957. Rushed for 1,000+ yards in seven seasons, 200+ yards in four games, 100+ yards in 54 other games. Career span 1957–65 with Cleveland; never missed a game. All-America in both football and lacrosse at Syracuse.

Larry Brown (b. 9-14-40): Basketball coach. Led Kansas University to the 1988 NCAA title, and the Detroit Pistons to the 2004 NBA championship. Played on gold-medal–winning 1964 U.S. Olympic team, coached 2004 Olympic team—only U.S. male to both play and coach in the Olympics. Peripatetic coaching career included stints at UCLA, and the NBA's Nuggets, Nets, Spurs, Clippers, Pacers, Sixers and Pistons. First coach in league history to guide seven different NBA franchises to the playoffs.

Paul Brown (b. 9-7-08, d. 8-5-91): Football coach. Led Cleveland to 10 consecutive championship games. Won four consecutive AAFC titles (1946–49) and three NFL titles (1950, '54, '55). Coached Cleveland from 1946 to 1962; became first coach of Cincinnati, 1968–75, and then general manager. Career coaching record 222-113-9. Also won national championship with Ohio State in 1942.

Avery Brundage (b. 9-28-1887, d. 5-5-75): Amateur sports executive. President of International Olympic Committee 1952–72. Served as president of U.S. Olympic Committee 1929–53. Also president of Amateur Athletic Union 1928–35. Member of 1912 U.S. Olympic track and field team.

Paul (Bear) Bryant (b. 9-11-13, d. 1-26-83): College football coach. Third in Division I-A football history with 323 wins. Won six national championships (1961, '64, '65, '73, '78, '79) with Alabama. Career record 323–85–17, including four undefeated seasons. Won 15 bowl games. Career span 1945–82 with Maryland, Kentucky, Texas A&M, Alabama.

Sergei Bubka (b. 12-4-63): Track and field. Ukrainian pole vaulter was gold medalist at 1988 Olympics. Only five-time world outdoor champion in any event (1983, '87, '91, '93, '95). First man to vault 20 feet, set world indoor record of 20' 2" on 2-21-93 and world outdoor record of 20' 1½" on 9-20-92.

Don Budge (b. 6-13-15, d. 1-26-00): Tennis player. First player to achieve the Grand Slam, in 1938. Won two consecutive Wimbledon and U.S. singles titles (1937, '38), one French and one Australian title (1938).

Dick Butkus (b. 12-9-42): Football LB. Regarded as greatest middle linebacker in NFL history. Selected to eight Pro Bowls. Career span 1965–73 with Chicago. All-America two times with Illinois. Award recognizing the outstanding college linebacker named in his honor.

Dick Button (b. 7-18-29): Figure skater. Gold medalist at 1948 and 1952 Olympics. World champion five consecutive years (1948–52) and U.S. champion seven consecutive years (1946–52). Sullivan Award winner in 1949.

Walter Byers (b. 3-13-22): Amateur sports executive. First director of NCAA, served from 1952 to 1987.

Frank Calder (b. 11-17-1877, d. 2-4-43): Hockey executive. First commissioner of NHL, served from 1917 to 1943. Rookie of the Year award named in his honor.

Walter Camp (b. 4-7-1859, d. 3-14-25): Football pioneer. Played for Yale in its first football game vs. Harvard on Nov. 17, 1876. Proposed rules such as 11 men per side, scrimmage line, center snap, yards and downs. Founded the All-America selections in 1889.

Roy Campanella (b. 11-19-21; d. 6-26-93): Baseball C. MVP in 1951, '53, '55. Played on five pennant winners; 1955 World Series winner with Brooklyn. Career span 1948–57, ended when paralyzed in car crash.

Earl Campbell (b. 3-29-55): Football RB. Led NFL in rushing three consecutive seasons. Rookie of the Year in 1978. Ran for 19 TDs in 1979 and 1,934 yards in 1980 when he was named league's Player of the Year twice. 9,407 career rushing yards. Career span 1978–85 with Houston, New Orleans. Won Heisman Trophy with Texas in 1977.

John Campbell (b. 4-8-55): Canadian harness racing driver. Alltime leading money winner with over $100 million in earnings. Leading money winner in 1986–90, 1992–95, '98, '00.

Billy Cannon (b. 2-8-37): Football RB. Led Louisiana State to national championship in 1958 and won Heisman Trophy in 1959. Signed contract with both NFL (Los Angeles) and AFL (Houston) teams. Houston won lawsuit for his services. Played in six AFL championship games with Houston, Oakland, Kansas City. Career span 1960–70. Served three-year jail term for 1983 conviction on counterfeiting charges.

Jose Canseco (b. 7-2-64): Baseball OF. One of three players to top 40 homers (42) and 40 steals (40) in same season (1988). Admitted steroid user during 1990s. AL MVP in 1988, when he also batted .307 with 124 RBI. AL Rookie of the Year in 1986. Career span 1985–01 with seven teams: 462 HRs, 1,407 RBIs, 1,942 K's.

Harry Caray (b. 3-1-17, d. 2-18-98): Sportscaster. TV-radio baseball announcer 1945–97 with St. Louis (NL), Oakland, Chicago (AL) Chicago (NL). Achieved celebrity status on Cubs' superstation WGN by singing "Take Me Out to the Ball Game" with Wrigley Field fans.

Rod Carew (b. 10-1-45): Baseball 2B-1B. Won seven batting titles (1969; '72–75, '77, '78). Had .328 career average, 3,053 career hits, and .300+ average 15 times. 1977 MVP; 1967 Rookie of the Year. Career span 1967–85; jersey number (29) retired by Minnesota and Anaheim.

Steve Carlton (b. 12-22-44): Baseball LHP. Four Cy Young awards (1972, '77, '80, '82). Second in career strikeouts (4,136). 329 career wins; won 20+ games six times. League leader in wins four times, innings pitched and strikeouts five times each. Struck out 19 batters in one game in 1969. Career span 1965–88 primarily with St. Louis and Philadelphia.

JoAnne Carner (b. 4-21-39): Golfer. Won 42 titles, including U.S. Women's Opens in 1971 and '76 and du Maurier Classic in 1975 and '78. LPGA top earner in 1974, '82, '83. LPGA Player of the Year in 1974, '81, '82. Won five Vare Trophies (1974, '75, '81–83).

Joe Carr (b. 10-22-1880; d. 5-20-39): Football administrator. Instrumental in forming American Professional Football Association in 1920. President of AAFA from 1922 to '39.

Don Carter (b. 7-29-26): Bowler. Won All-Star Tournament four times (1952, '54, '56, '58) and PBA National Championship in 1960. Voted Bowler of the Year six times (1953, '54, '57, '58, '60, '62).

Alexander Cartwright (b. 4-17-1820, d. 7-12-1892): Baseball pioneer. Credited with setting the basic rules of baseball: bases 90 feet apart, nine men per side, three strikes per out and three outs per inning. On June 19, 1846, in what is often cited as the first baseball game, his New York Knickerbockers lost to the New York Nine 23–1 at Elysian Fields in Hoboken, NJ.

Billy Casper (b. 6-24-31): Golfer. Famed putter. Won 51 PGA tournaments. PGA Player of Year in both 1966 and '70. Won Vardon Trophy in 1960, '63, '64, '65 and '68. Won the U.S. Open twice, in 1959 at Winged Foot in Mamaronek, New York, and in 1966 in 18-hole playoff over Arnold Palmer at Olympic Club, San Francisco. Beat Gene Littler in 18-hole playoff to win 1970 Masters.

Tracy Caulkins (b. 1-11-63): Swimmer. Won three gold medals at 1984 Olympics. Won 48 U.S. national titles, more than any other swimmer, from 1978 to 1984. Also won Sullivan Award in 1978.

Steve Cauthen (b. 5-1-60): Jockey. In 1978 became youngest jockey to win Triple Crown, aboard Affirmed. First jockey to top $6 million in season earnings (1977). Sports Illustrated Sportsman of Year for 1977. Moved to England in 1979; rode Epsom Derby winners Slip Anchor (1985) and Reference Point (1987).

Evonne Goolagong Cawley (b. 7-31-51): Tennis player. Won four Australian Open titles from 1974 through '77; won 1971 French Open; won Wimbledon in 1971 and '80. Runner-up four straight years at U.S. Open (1973–76), which she never won.

Bill Chadwick (b. 10-10-15): Hockey referee. Spent 16 years as a referee despite vision in only one eye. Developed hand signals to signify penalties. Also former television announcer for the New York Rangers.

Wilt Chamberlain (b. 8-21-36, d. 10-12-99): Basketball C. "The Big Dipper." "The Stilt." Scored 100 points in a single game in 1962. Alltime leader in rebounds (23,924) and rebounding average (22.9). Third in career points (31,419). Alltime single-season leader in points scored (4,029 in 1962), scoring average (50.4 in 1962), rebounding average (27.2 in 1961) and field goal percentage (.727 in 1973). Set record for most rebounds in a game in 1960 (55). Four MVP awards (1960, '66–68); playoff MVP in 1972 and 1960 Rookie of the Year. 13-time All-Star. 30.1 career scoring average. Career span 1959–72 with Philadelphia/Golden State Warriors, Philadelphia 76ers, Los Angeles.

Colin Chapman (b. 1928, d. 12-16-83): Auto racing engineer. Founded Lotus race and street cars, designing the first Lotus racer in 1948. Introduced the monocoque design for Formula One cars in 1962 and ground effects in 1978.

Julio Cesar Chavez (b. 7-12-62): Mexican boxer. Held titles as junior welterweight, lightweight and super featherweight. Career record: 103-6-2 (83 KOs).

Gerry Cheevers (b. 12-7-40): Hockey goalie. Goaltender for Stanley Cup-winning Boston Bruins teams of 1970 and 1972. In 12 seasons with Boston had 230-94-74 record with a goals against average of 2.89. Also coached Bruins from 1980–84, with 204-126-46 record. Elected to Hall of Fame 1985.

Cigar (b. 1990): Thoroughbred race horse. Tied Citation's American-record 16-race win-streak with a win on 7-13-96. Won $4 million Dubai World Cup on 3-27-96.

Citation (b. 4-11-45, d. 8-8-70): Thoroughbred race horse. Triple Crown winner in 1948 with jockey Eddie Arcaro aboard. Trained by Ben A. Jones.

King Clancy (b. 2-25-03, d. 11-6-86): Hockey D. Four-time All-Star. Coach, Montreal Maroons, Toronto. Also referee. Trophy named in his honor, recognizing leadership qualities and contribution to community.

Jim Clark (b. 3-4-36, d. 4-7-68): Scottish auto racer. Won 25 career Formula 1 races. Formula 1 champion two times (1963, 1965). Won Indy 500 in 1965. Named Indy 500 Rookie of the Year in 1963. Killed during competition in 1968 at age 32.

Bobby Clarke (b. 8-13-49): Hockey C. Won MVP award three times (1973, '75, '76). 358 career goals, 852 assists. Scored 100+ points three times. Played on two consecutive Stanley Cup champions (1974, '75) with Philadelphia. Career span 1969–84. Also general manager with Philadelphia 1984–90, Minnesota 1991–92, Florida 1993–94, and Philadelphia 1994–.

Roger Clemens (b. 8-4-62): Baseball RHP. Won seven Cy Young awards (1986, '87, '91, '97, '98, 2001, '04), most by any pitcher. Also 1986 MVP. Has struck out a record 20 batters in one game on two occasions. League leader in ERA six times, strikeouts four times, and wins four times. Won Triple Crown of pitching in 1997 and '98. Won 300th game on June 13, 2003. Career span 1984–96 with Boston; 1997–98 Toronto; 1999–03 NY Yankees; 2004– Houston.

Roberto Clemente (b. 8-18-34, d. 12-31-72): Baseball OF. Killed in plane crash while still an active player. Had 3,000 career hits and .317 career average. Won four batting titles; .300+ average 13 times. 1966 MVP; 1971 World Series MVP. Twelve consecutive Gold Gloves; led league in assists five times. Career span 1955–72 with Pittsburgh.

Ty Cobb (b. 12-18-1886, d. 7-17-61): Baseball OF. Alltime leader in batting average (.366), second in runs scored (2,245) and hits (4,189), fourth in stolen bases (892). 1911 MVP and 1909 Triple Crown winner. Twelve batting titles. Had .400+ average three times, .350+ average 13 other times; 200+ hits nine times. Led league in hits seven times, steals six times and runs scored five times. Career span 1905–28 with Detroit and Philadelphia.

Mickey Cochrane (b. 4-6-03, d. 6-28-62): Baseball C. Second highest career batting average among catchers (.320). MVP in 1928, '34. Had .300+ average eight times. Career span 1925–37 with Philadelphia and Detroit.

Sebastian Coe (b. 9-29-56): Track and field. Two-time Olympic gold medalist in the 1,500 meters (1980, '84). Also won two silver medals in 800 meters at same two Olympics. Set world record in 800 meters (1:41.73 in 1981) and 1,000 meters (2:12.18 in 1981). Served in British Parliament after his running career.

Eddie Collins (b. 5-2-1887, d. 3-25-51): Baseball 2B. 3,311 career hits; .333 career average; .330+ average 12 times. 743 career stolen bases; alltime co-leader in World Series steals (14—tied with Lou Brock); alltime leader in single-game steals (six, twice). 1914 MVP. Career span 1906–30 with Philadelphia (AL), Chicago (AL).

Nadia Comaneci (b. 11-12-61): Romanian gymnast. First ever to score a perfect 10 at Olympics (on uneven parallel bars in 1976). Won three gold, two silver and one bronze medal at 1976 Olympics. Also won two gold and two silver medals at 1980 Olympics.

Dennis Conner (b. 9-16-42): Sailing. Captain of three America's Cup winners (1980, '87,'88).

Maureen Connolly (b. 9-17-34, d. 6-21-69): Tennis player. "Little Mo." First woman to achieve the Grand Slam, in 1953. Won the U.S. singles title in 1951 at age 16. Thereafter lost only four matches before retiring in 1954 after breaking her leg in a riding accident. Was never beaten in singles at Wimbledon, winning three consecutive titles (1952–54). Won three consecutive U.S. singles titles (1951–53) and two consecutive French titles (1953–54). Also won Australian title (1953).

Jimmy Connors (b. 9-2-52): Tennis player. Alltime men's leader in tournament victories (109). Held men's No. 1 ranking in a record 160 consecutive weeks (7-29-74 through 8-16-77). Won five U.S. Open singles titles on three different surfaces (grass 1974, clay 1976, hard 1978, '82, '83). Won two Wimbledon singles titles (1974, '82) further apart than anyone since Bill Tilden. Also won 1974 Australian Open title. Reached Grand Slam final seven other times.

Jim Corbett (b. 9-1-1866; d. 2-18-33): Boxer. "Gentleman Jim." Invented jab. Won heavyweight title on 9-7-1892 with a KO of John Sullivan in 21 rounds; it was first heavyweight title fight using gloves. Lost title when KO'd by Bob Fitzsimmons in 14 on 3-17-1897, then lost two bids to regain it against Jim Jeffries. Career record: 11-4-2, 7 KOs, 2 ND.

Angel Cordero (b. 11-8-42): Jockey. Seventh alltime in wins (7,057) and earnings ($164,561,227). Led yearly earnings three times, in 1976, '82, '83, winning Eclipse Awards in the last two years.

Howard Cosell (b. 3-25-18, d. 4-23-95): Sports-caster. Lawyer–turned–TV-radio sports commentator. Best known for his work on "Monday Night Football." His nasal voice and "tell it like it is" approach made him a controversial figure.

James (Doc) Counsilman (b. 12-28-20, d. 1-4-04): Swimming coach. Coached Indiana from 1957 to 1990. Won six consecutive NCAA championships (1968–73). Career record 287-36-1. Coached U.S. men's team at Olympics in 1964, '76. Swam English Channel in 1979 at age 58.

Count Fleet (b. 3-24-40, d. 12-3-73): Thoroughbred race horse. Triple Crown winner in 1943 with jockey Johnny Longden aboard. Trained by Don Cameron.

Yvan Cournoyer (b. 11-22-43): Hockey RW. "The Roadrunner" had 428 goals and 435 assists during his 15-season career with the Montreal Canadiens. Had 25 or more goals in 12 straight seasons. Played on 10 Stanley Cup championship teams. Elected to Hall of Fame in 1982.

Margaret Smith Court (b. 7-16-42): Australian tennis player. Alltime leader in Grand Slam singles titles (24) and total Grand Slam titles (62). Achieved Grand Slam in 1970 and mixed doubles Grand Slam in 1963 with Ken Fletcher. Won 11 Australian singles titles (1960–66, 1969–71, '73), five French titles (1962, '64, '69, '70, '73), 5 U.S. titles (1962, '65, '69, '70, '73) and three Wimbledon titles (1963, '65, '70). Court also won 19 Grand Slam doubles titles and 19 mixed doubles titles.

Bob Cousy (b. 8-9-28): Basketball G. Led NBA in assists eight consecutive seasons. Averaged 18+ points and named to All-Star team 10 consecutive seasons. 1957 MVP. Played on six championship teams with Boston from 1950 to 1969. Finished career with 6,955 assists; in 1958 had 28 assists in a single game. Also played on 1947 NCAA title team with Holy Cross.

Dave Cowens (b. 10-25-48): Basketball C. NBA co-Rookie of Year in 1971. NBA MVP for 1973. All-Star game MVP in 1973. Career span 1970–71 through 1982–83, all but the last year with the Boston Celtics, averaging 17.6 points and 13.6 rebounds per game. Coached Charlotte 1996–99 and Golden State 2000–01. Elected to Hall of Fame in 1991.

Ben Crenshaw (b. 1-11-52): Golfer. Legendary putter. Won Masters in 1984 and '95. Captain of 1999 U.S. Ryder Cup team.

Johan Cruyff (b. 4-25-47): Dutch soccer player. Led Ajax Amsterdam to three European Cup titles, and guided the Netherlands to the 1974 World Cup final, a 2–1 loss to Germany.

Larry Csonka (b. 12-25-46): Football RB. In 11 seasons rushed for 8,081 yards and 64 TDs. MVP of Super Bowl VIII, when he rushed 33 times for a then Super Bowl–record 145 yards in Miami's 24–7 defeat of Minnesota. Career span 1968–74, '79 with Miami; 1976–78 with New York Giants. Elected to Hall of Fame in 1987.

Billy Cunningham (b. 6-3-43): Basketball player and coach. "Kangaroo Kid." In 11 pro seasons (1965–76) with Philadelphia 76ers and Carolina Cougars, averaged 21.2 points per game. Three-time first-team All-NBA selection (1969–71). 1973 ABA MVP. Coached 76ers to three NBA Finals and the 1983 NBA title. Elected to Hall of Fame in 1985.

Bjørn Dæhlie (b.6-19-67): Norwegian skier. Legendary cross-country skier won a Winter Olympics–record eight gold medals over three Games from 1992 to '98. Won a total of 12 Olympic medals and more than 40 World Cup races.

Chuck Daly (b. 7-20-30): Basketball coach. Coached the 1992 Olympic "Dream Team." Won two consecutive NBA titles with Detroit (1989, '90). Won 50+ games four consecutive seasons. Coached Detroit 1983–92, New Jersey 1992–94, and Orlando 1997–99.

Damascus (b. 1964, d. 1995): Thoroughbred race horse. After finishing third in 1967 Kentucky Derby, won the Preakness, the Belmont, the Dwyer, the American Derby, the Travers, the Woodward and others—12 of 16 starts. Unanimous Horse of the Year in 1967.

Stanley Dancer (b. 7-25-27, d. 9-9-05): Harness racing driver. Only driver to win the Trotting Triple Crown two times (Nevele Pride in 1968, Super Bowl in 1972). Also won Pacing Triple Crown driving Most Happy Fella in 1970. Won The Hambletonian four times (1968, '72, '75, '83). Driver of the Year in 1968.

Tamas Darnyi (b. 6-3-67): Hungarian swimmer. Gold medalist in 200-meter and 400-meter individual medleys at 1988 and '92 Olympics. Won both events at World Championships in 1986 and '91. Set world records in these events at 1991 Championships (1:59.36 and 4:12.36).

Al Davis (b. 7-4-29): Football executive. Owner and general manager of Raiders since 1963. Team has won three Super Bowl championships (1976, '80, '83). Served as AFL commissioner in 1966; helped negotiate AFL–NFL merger. Famously moved Raiders to Los Angeles in 1982 and back to Oakland in 1995.

Ernie Davis (b. 12-14-39, d. 5-18-63): Football RB. Won Heisman Trophy in 1961, the first black man to win the award. All-America three times at Syracuse. First selection in 1962 NFL draft, but became fatally ill with leukemia and never played professionally.

Glenn Davis (b. 12-26-24): College football HB. "Mr. Outside." Teamed with Doc Blanchard to lead Army to three consecutive undefeated seasons (1944–46) and two consecutive national championships (1944, '45). Won Heisman Trophy in 1946. Named All-America three times.

John Davis (b. 1-12-21, d. 7-13-84): Weightlifter. Gold medalist at two consecutive Olympics, 1948, '52. World champion six times.

Terrell Davis (b. 10-28-72): Football RB. One of only four players to rush for more than 2,000 yards in a season (2,008 in 1998). MVP of Super Bowl XXXII, rushing for 157 yards and three TDs for Denver. Forced to retire in 2002 after several knee injuries.

Pete Dawkins (b. 3-8-38): Football RB. 1958 Heisman Trophy winner while at Army. Never played pro football. Attended Oxford on Rhodes scholarship, won two Bronze Stars in Vietnam, rose to brigadier general before leaving Army to become investment banker. Made unsuccessful run for Senate from New Jersey in 1988.

Len Dawson (b. 6-20-35): Football QB. MVP of Super Bowl IV, a 23–7 victory against Minnesota. Threw 239 TDs in his career. Career span 1957–75, the last 13 seasons with Kansas City Chiefs. Elected to Hall of Fame in 1987.

Dizzy Dean (b. 1-16-11, d. 7-17-74): Baseball RHP. 1934 MVP with 30 wins. League leader in strikeouts, complete games four times each. 150 career wins. Arm trouble shortened career after 134 wins by age 26. Career span 1930–41 and 1947 with St. Louis and Chicago (NL).

Dave DeBusschere (b. 10-16-40, d. 5-14-03): Basketball F. NBA first-team All-Defensive Team six straight seasons, 1969–74. Member of NBA champion New York Knicks in 1970 and '73. Career span 1962–74 with Detroit and New York. Career stats: 16.1 ppg, 11.0 rpg. Youngest coach (24) in NBA history. Elected to NBA Hall of Fame in 1982.

Pierre de Coubertin (b. 1-1-1863, d. 9-2-37): Frenchman called the father of the Modern Olympics. President of International Olympic Committee from 1896 to 1925.

Oscar De La Hoya (b. 2-4-73): Boxer. Won title belts in five different weight classes between junior lightweight and junior middleweight divisions. 35–2 with 28 KOs. Won lightweight gold medal at 1992 Olympics in Barcelona.

Jack Dempsey (b. 6-24-1895, d. 5-31-83): Boxer. Heavyweight champ (1919–26), lost title to Gene Tunney and rematch in the famed "long count" bout in 1927. Career record 62-6-10 with 49 KOs from 1914–28.

Gail Devers (b. 11-19-66): Track and field sprinter-hurdler. Won 100 meters at 1992 and '96 Olympics. Successfully completed 100m/100h double at 1993 World Championships, winning 100 in 10.82 and 100 hurdles in American record 12.46. Also won '93 world indoor title in 60 (6.95). Battled Graves disease.

Klaus Dibiasi (b. 10-6-47): Italian diver. Gold medalist in platform at three consecutive Olympics (1968, '72, '76) and silver medalist at 1964 Olympics.

Eric Dickerson (b. 9-2-60): Football RB. Alltime single-season record holder in yards rushing (2,105 in 1984). Retired with 13,259 career rushing yards. Led league in rushing four times. Rushed for 1,000+ yards in seven consecutive seasons; 100+ yards in 61 games, including 12 times in 1984. Rookie of the Year in 1983. Career span 1983–93 with Los Angeles Rams, Indianapolis, Los Angeles Raiders and Atlanta.

Bill Dickey (b. 6-6-07 d. 11-12-93): Baseball C. Lifetime average .313. Hit 202 career home runs. Played on 11 AL All-Star teams. In eight World Series, hit five homers with 24 RBI. Career span 1928–43 and 1946, all with New York (AL). Inducted into Hall of Fame 1954.

Harrison Dillard (b. 7-8-23): Track and field. Only man to win Olympic gold medal in sprint (100 meters in 1948) and hurdles (110 meters in 1952). Sullivan Award winner in 1955.

Joe DiMaggio (b. 11-25-14 d. 3-8-99): Baseball OF. "The Yankee Clipper." Hit safely in record 56 straight games in 1941. MVP in 1939, '41, '47. Had .325 career batting average; .300+ average 11 times; 100+ RBI nine times. League leader in batting average, HR, and RBI two times each. Played on 10 World Series winners with New York (AL). Career span 1936–51.

Mike Ditka (b. 10-18-39): Football TE–Coach. First TE elected to Hall of Fame (1988). NFL Rookie of the Year in 1961. Named to five Pro Bowls. Made 427 catches for 5,812 yards and 43 TDs. Career span 1961–72 with Chicago, Philadelphia and Dallas. Coached Chicago to 46–10 win against New England in Super Bowl XX: Recorded 127–101 record as head coach of Chicago and New Orleans.

Tony Dorsett (b. 4-7-54): Football RB. Fifth leading rusher in NFL history (12,739 yards). Set record for longest run from scrimmage with 99-yard TD run on 1-3-83. Scored 91 career TDs. Rushed for 1,000+ yards in eight seasons. Named Rookie of the Year in 1977. Career span 1977–88 with Dallas, Denver. Graduated from Pittsburgh as alltime NCAA leader in yards rushing (6,082) and won 1976 Heisman Trophy.

Abner Doubleday (b. 6-26-1819, d. 1-26-1893): Civil War hero incorrectly credited as the inventor of baseball in Cooperstown, NY, in 1839.

Clyde Drexler (b. 6-22-62): Basketball G. Nicknamed "The Glide" for his smooth play. Member of U.S. "Dream Team" that won 1992 Olympic gold medal. Career span 1984–1994 with Portland and 1995–98 with Houston, with whom he won his first NBA title in 1995. Career stats: 20.4 ppg, 5.6 apg. Head coach at University of Houston from 1998–00.

Ken Dryden (b. 8-8-47): Hockey G. Goaltender of the Year five times (1973, 1976–79). Playoff MVP as a rookie in 1971, maintained rookie status and named Rookie of the Year in 1972. Led league in goals against average five times. Career record 258-57-74, including 46 shutouts. Career 2.24 goals against average is the modern record. Four playoff shutouts in 1977. Played on six Stanley Cup champions with Montreal from 1970 to 1979.

Don Drysdale (b. 7-23-36, d. 7-3-93): Baseball RHP. Set the major league record—broken in 1988 by Orel Hershiser—of 58 consecutive scoreless innings in 1968. Led NL three times in strikeouts (1959, '60, '62) and once in wins (1962). Won 1962 Cy Young Award with 25–9 mark. Career record of 209–166, with 2,484 K's and 2.95 ERA. Career span 1956–69, all with Dodgers. Inducted into Hall of Fame 1984.

Tim Duncan (b. 4-25-76): Basketball C. 2001 NBA MVP. First-team All-NBA every season in the league (1998–03). 1998 Rookie of the Year. 1999, 2003, 2005 NBA Finals MVP, when he led San Antonio to NBA titles. Also league MVP in '03 Career span 1997– with San Antonio.

Roberto Duran (b. 6-16-51): Panamanian boxer. Champion in three different weight classes: lightweight (1972–79), welterweight (1980, lost rematch to Sugar Ray Leonard in famous "no más" bout) and junior middleweight (1983–84). Career record: 104–15 (69 KOs).

Leo Durocher (b. 7-27-05, d. 10-7-91): Baseball manager. "Leo the Lip." Said "Nice guys finish last." Managed three pennant winners and 1954 World Series winner. Won 2,008 games in 24 years. Led Brooklyn 1939–48; New York (NL) 1948–55; Chicago (NL) 1966–72; and Houston 1972–73.

David Duval (b. 11-9-71): Golfer. Won 2001 British Open. Set record for tour earnings in a single season with $2.6 million in 1998, when he also won Vardon Trophy for lowest scoring average (69.13). Four-time all-America at Georgia Tech.

Tomás Dvorák (b. 5-11-72): Czech decathlete. Broke Dan O'Brien's seven-year-old decathlon world record by 103 points on 7-4-99 in Prague, amassing 8,994 points. Won decathlon bronze medal at Atlanta in '96.

Eddie Eagan (b. 4-26-1898, d. 6-14-67): Only American athlete to win gold medal at Summer and Winter Olympic Games (boxing 1920, bobsled '32).

Alan Eagleson (b. 4-24-33): Hockey labor leader. Founder of NHL Players' Association and its executive director from 1967–92. Resigned from Hall of Fame 3-25-98 and served six months of an 18-month jail sentence for three counts of fraud and theft involving players' insurance premiums.

Dale Earnhardt (b. 4-29-52, d. 2-18-01): Auto racer. "The Intimidator." NASCAR champion seven times (1980, 1986–87, 1990–91, 1993–94). Won 1998 Daytona 500 and 75 other NASCAR races. Died in crash on the final lap of the 2001 Daytona 500.

Stefan Edberg (b. 1-19-66): Swedish tennis player. Won two Wimbledon singles titles (1988, '90), two Australian Open titles (1985, '87) and two U.S. Open titles (1991, '92). Led Sweden to three Davis Cup titles (1984, '85, '87).

Gertrude Ederle (b. 10-23-06): Swimmer. First woman to swim the English Channel, in 1926. Swam 21 miles from France to England in 14:39. Also won three medals at the 1924 Olympics.

Hicham El Gerrouj (b. 9-14-74): Track and field. Morrocan runner broke world record in mile on 7-7-99, clocking 3:43.13 to trim 1.26 seconds from six-year-old previous record. Performance was his fourth world record, in addition to indoor mile, indoor 1,500 and outdoor 1,500. Won two gold medals at 2004 Games.

Herb Elliott (b. 2-25-38): Track and field. Australian runner was gold medalist in 1960 Olympic 1,500 meters in world record 3:35.6. Also set world mile record of 3:54.5 in 1958. Undefeated at 1,500 meters/mile in international competition. Retired at 22.

Ernie Els (b.10-17-69): South African golfer. Two-time U.S. Open winner (1994, '97); first foreign-born player to win the event twice since Alex Smith in 1910. 2002 British Open champion.

John Elway (b. 6-28-60): Football QB. First player taken in 1983 NFL draft. One of two NFL QBs with more than 50,000 passing yards (51,475). 300 career TD passes. Famous for last-minute drives. Won back-to-back Super Bowls (XXXII and XXXIII) after three previous Super Bowl losses. Career span 1983–99 with Denver.

Roy Emerson (b. 11-3-36): Australian tennis player. Second alltime in Grand Slam singles titles (12). Won six Australian titles, five consecutively (1961, 1963–67), two Wimbledon titles (1964, '65), two U.S. titles (1961, '64) and two French titles (1963, '67). Also won 13 Grand Slam doubles titles.

Kornelia Ender (b. 10-25-58): East German swimmer. Won four gold medals at 1976 Olympics and three silver medals at 1972 Olympics.

Julius Erving (b. 2-22-50): Basketball F. "Dr. J." His combined ABA and NBA career points (30,026) rank fifth alltime. Career scoring average of 24.2. Won four MVP awards (1974–76, '81); playoff MVP 1974, '76. All-Star 16 times. Led ABA in scoring three times. Played on three championship teams, with New York (ABA) and Philadelphia (NBA). Career span 1971–86. Elected to Hall of Fame in 1993.

Phil Esposito (b. 2-20-42): Hockey C. "Espo." First to break the 100-point barrier (126 in 1969). Led league in goals six consecutive seasons, points five times and assists three times. Won MVP award two times (1969, '74). 1,590 career points, 717 goals, and 873 assists. Scored 30+ goals 13 consecutive seasons and 100+ points six times. All-Star 10 times. Career span 1963–81 with Chicago, Boston, New York Rangers.

Tony Esposito (b. 4-23-43): Hockey goalie. Brother of Phil. A six-time All-Star during 16-season NHL career, almost all of it with the Chicago Blackhawks. Career GAA of 2.92. Won or shared Vezina Trophy three times. Elected to Hall of Fame in 1988.

Janet Evans (b. 8-28-71): Swimmer. Competed in 1988, '92 and '96 Olympics, winning three gold medals in '88 and one in '92. Set world record in 400-meter freestyle (4:03.85 in 1988), 800-meter freestyle (8:16.22 in 1989) and 1,500-meter freestyle (15:52.10 in 1988). Sullivan Award winner in 1989.

Lee Evans (b. 2-25-47): Track and field. Gold medalist in 400 meters at 1968 Olympics with world record time of 43.86, which stood until 1988.

Chris Evert (b. 12-21-54): Also Chris Evert Lloyd. Tennis player. Second alltime in tournament titles (157). Tied for fourth alltime in women's Grand Slam singles titles (18). Won at least one Grand Slam singles title every year from 1974–86. Won seven French Open titles (1974, '75, '79, '80, '83, '85, '86), six U.S. Open titles (1975–77, '78, '80, '82), three Wimbledon titles (1974, '76, '81) and two Australian Open titles (1982, '84). Reached Grand Slam finals 16 other times. Reached semifinals at 52 of her last 56 Grand Slams.

Weeb Ewbank (b. 5-6-07, d. 11-17-98): Football coach. Only coach to win titles in both the NFL and AFL. Coached Baltimore Colts to classic overtime defeat of New York Giants in 1958 and New York Jets to their stunning 16–7 win over Baltimore in Super Bowl III. Career record of 134-130-7. Career span 1954–62 with Colts and 1963–73 with Jets. Elected to Hall of Fame in 1978.

Patrick Ewing (b. 8-5-62): Basketball C. First NBA "lottery" pick. 1986 Rookie of the Year. A member of two gold-medal winning Olympic teams, including the 1992 "Dream Team." Career span 1985–02 with New York, Seattle, and Orlando; averaged 21.0 ppg, 9.8 rpg. Played in three NCAA title games with Georgetown (1982, '84, '85); tournament MVP in 1984.

Nick Faldo (b. 7-18-57): British golfer. Three-time winner of Masters (1989, '90, '96) and British Open (1987, '90, '92).

Juan Manuel Fangio (b. 6-24-11, d. 7-17-95): Argentine auto racer. 24 Formula 1 victories in just 51 starts. Formula 1 champion five times, the most of any driver (1951, '54–57). Retired in 1958.

Brett Favre (b.10-10-69): Football QB. Won NFL MVP award three years in a row (1995–97). Led Packers to victory in Super Bowl XXXI. Career span 1991– with Atlanta and Green Bay.

Bob Feller (b. 11-3-18): Baseball RHP. Pitched three no-hitters and 12 one-hitters. 266 career wins; 2,581 career strikeouts. Won 20+ games six times. League leader in wins six times, strikeouts seven times, innings pitched five times. Served four years in military during career. Career span 1936–41, 1945–56 with Cleveland.

Tom Ferguson (b. 12-20-50): Rodeo. First to top $1 million in career earnings. All-Around champion six consecutive years (1974–79).

Enzo Ferrari (b. 2-8-1898, d. 8-14-88): Auto racing engineer. Team owner since 1929, he built first Ferrari race car in Italy in 1947 and continued to preside over Ferrari race and street cars until his death. In 68 years of competition, Ferrari's cars have won over 5,000 races.

Herve Filion (b. 2-1-40): Harness racing driver. Alltime leader in career wins (more than 14,000). Driver of the Year 10 times, more than any other driver (consecutively 1969–74, '78, '81, '89).

Rollie Fingers (b. 8-25-46): Baseball RHP. Won 107 games in relief in his career; 341 career saves. 1981 Cy Young and MVP winner; 1974 World Series MVP. Saved six World Series games in his career. Career span 1968–85 with Oakland, San Diego, Milwaukee.

Bobby Fischer (b. 3-9-43): Chess. World champion from 1972 to 1975, the only American to hold title. Never played competitive chess during his reign. Forfeited title to Anatoly Karpov by refusing to play him.

Carlton Fisk (b. 12-26-47): Baseball C. Retired as alltime HR leader among catchers (352) and second in games caught (2,226). 376 career HR, including a record 75 after age 40. Rookie of the Year in 1972 and All-Star 11 times. Hit dramatic 12th-inning HR to win Game 6 of 1975 World Series. Career span 1969–93 with Boston, Chicago (AL). Elected to Hall of Fame in 2000.

Emerson Fittipaldi (b. 12-12-46): Brazilian auto racer. Won Indy 500 in 1989 and '93. Won CART championship in 1989. Formula 1 champion two times (1972, '74).

James Fitzsimmons (b. 7-23-1874, d. 3-11-66): Horse racing trainer. "Sunny Jim." Trained two Triple Crown winners (Gallant Fox in 1930, Omaha in 1935). Trained six Belmont Stakes winners (1930, '32, '35, '36, '39, '55), four Preakness Stakes winners (1930, '35, '55, '57) and three Kentucky Derby winners (1930, '35, '39).

Peggy Fleming (b. 7-27-48): Figure skater. Olympic champion 1968. World champion (1966–68) and U.S. champion (1964–68).

Curt Flood (b. 1-18-38, d. 1-20-97): Baseball OF. Challenged baseball's reserve clause by refusing to be traded after 1969 season. Supreme Court rejected his plea, but baseball was eventually forced to adopt free agency system. Won seven consecutive Gold Gloves from 1963 to 1969. Career batting average of .293. Career span 1956–69 with St. Louis.

Whitey Ford (b. 10-21-26): Baseball LHP. Alltime World Series leader in wins, losses, games started, innings pitched, hits allowed, walks and strikeouts. 236 career wins, 2.75 ERA. Led league in wins and winning percentage three times each; ERA, shutouts, innings pitched two times each. 1961 Cy Young winner and World Series MVP. Career span 1950, 1953–67 with New York Yankees.

Forego (b. 1970, d. 8-27-97): Thoroughbred race horse. Horse of the Year in 1974 (won 8 of 13 starts); '75 (won 6 of 9); and '76 (won 6 of 8). Finished fourth in 1973 Kentucky Derby. Over six years won 34 of 57 starts and $1,938,957.

George Foreman (b. 1-22-48): Boxer. Heavyweight champion (1973–74). Retired in 1977, but returned to the ring in 1987. At age 45, KO'd Michael Moorer to regain heavyweight title. Also heavyweight gold medalist at 1968 Olympics.

Dick Fosbury (b. 3-6-47): Track and field. Gold medalist in high jump at 1968 Olympics. Introduced back-to-the-bar style of high jumping, called the "Fosbury Flop."

Jimmie Foxx (b. 10-22-07, d. 7-21-67): Baseball 1B. Won three MVP awards (1932–33, '38). Fourth alltime highest slugging average (.609), with 534 career HR; hit 30+ HR 12 consecutive seasons, 100+ RBI 13 consecutive seasons. Won Triple Crown in 1933. Led league in HR four times, batting average two times. Career span 1925–45 with Philadelphia, Boston (AL).

A.J. Foyt (b. 1-16-35): Auto racer. Alltime leader in Indy Car victories (67). Won Indy 500 four times (1961, '64, '67, '77), Daytona 500 one time (1972), 24 Hours of Daytona two times (1983, '85) and 24 Hours of LeMans one time (1967). USAC champion seven times, more than any other driver (1960, '61, '63, '64, '67, '75, '79).

William H.G. France (b. 9-26-09, d. 6-7-92): Auto racing executive. Founder of NASCAR and president from 1948–72. Builder of Daytona and Talladega speedways.

Dawn Fraser (b. 9-4-37): Australian swimmer. First swimmer to win gold medal in same event at three consecutive Olympics (100-meter freestyle in 1956, '60, '64). First woman to break the one-minute barrier at 100 meters (59.9 in 1962).

Joe Frazier (b. 1-12-44): Boxer. "Smokin' Joe." Heavyweight champion (1970–73). Best known for his three epic bouts with Muhammad Ali. Career record 32-4-1 with 27 KOs from 1965 to 1976. Also heavyweight gold medalist at 1964 Olympics.

Walt Frazier (b. 3-29-45): Basketball G. "Clyde." Point guard on championship Knick teams of 1970 and '73. First team All-NBA in 1970, '72, '74 and '75. First team All-Defense every year from 1969–'75. Averaged 18.9 points per game in 13-season NBA career. Elected to Hall of Fame in 1986.

Frankie Frisch (b. 9-9-1898, d. 3-12-73): Baseball IF. "The Fordham Flash." Led NL in hits in 1923 (223). NL MVP in 1931. Hit over .300 13 seasons. Scored 100+ runs seven times. Drove in 100+ runs three times. Career .316 batting average. Career span 1919–37 with New York (NL) and St. Louis (NL). Elected to Hall of Fame in 1947.

Dan Gable (b. 10-25-48): Wrestler. Gold medalist in 149–pound division at 1972 Olympics. Twot-time NCAA champion (in 1968 at 130 pounds, in 1969 at 137 pounds). Coached Iowa to NCAA championship 15 times (1978–86, 1991–93 and 1995–97).

Clarence Gaines (b. 5-21-23): College basketball coach. "Bighouse." 828 career wins in 46 seasons at Division II Winston-Salem State from 1947–93.

John Galbreath (b. 8-10-1897, d. 7-20-88): Horse racing owner. Owner of Darby Dan Farms from 1935 until his death and of baseball's Pittsburgh Pirates from 1946 to 1985. Only man to breed and own winners of both the Kentucky Derby (Chateaugay in 1963 and Proud Clarion in 1967) and the Epsom Derby (Roberto in 1972).

Gallant Fox (b. 3-23-27, d. 11-13-54): Thoroughbred race horse. Triple Crown winner in 1930 with jockey Earle Sande aboard. Trained by James Fitzsimmons. The only Triple Crown winner to sire another Triple Crown winner (Omaha in 1935).

Don Garlits (b. 1-14-32): Auto racer. "Big Daddy." Has won 35 National Hot Rod Association Top Fuel events. Won three NHRA Top Fuel points titles (1975, 1985–86). First Top Fuel driver to surpass 190 mph (1963), 200 mph (1964), 240 mph (1973), 250 mph (1975) and 270 mph (1986). Credited with developing rear-engine dragster.

Haile Gebrselassie (b. 4-18-73): Track and field. Ethiopian distance runner has dominated long distance running since 1993. Holds world records in the 5,000 and 10,000 meters. Gold medalist in the 10,000 at the 1996 and 2000 Olympics.

Lou Gehrig (b. 6-19-03, d. 6-2-41): Baseball 1B. "The Iron Horse." Second alltime in consecutive games played (2,130), leader in grand slam HR (23), third in RBI (1,995) and slugging average (.632). MVP in 1927, '36; won Triple Crown in 1934. .340 career average; 493 career HR. 100+ RBI 13 consecutive seasons. Led league in RBI five times and HR three times. Played on seven World Series winners with New York (AL). Died of disease since named for him. Career span 1923–39.

Bernie Geoffrion (b. 2-16-31): Hockey RW. "Boom Boom" for his powerful slapshot. Won Hart Memorial Trophy for 1960–61. Scored 393 goals and 429 assists in 16 seasons (1950–68), the first 14 with Montreal, the final two with New York. Elected to Hall of Fame 1972.

Eddie Giacomin (b. 6-6-39): Hockey goalie. "Fast Eddie" led NHL goalies in wins for three straight seasons. Shared Vezina Trophy for 1970–71. Career GAA of 2.82. Career span 1965–78 with New York and Detroit.

Althea Gibson (b. 8-25-27, d. 9-28-03): Tennis player. Won two consecutive Wimbledon and U.S. singles titles (1957, '58), the first black player to win these tournaments. Also won the French Open in 1956.

Bob Gibson (b. 11-9-35): Baseball RHP. 1968 Cy Young and MVP award winner with modern National League–best ERA (1.12). Also 1970 Cy Young award winner. Pitched no-hitter in 1971. Record holder for most strikeouts in a World Series game (17); Series MVP in 1964, '67. Won 20+ games five times. 251 career wins; 3,117 strikeouts. Career span 1959–75 with St. Louis.

Josh Gibson (b. 12-21-11, d. 1-20-47): Baseball C. "The Black Babe Ruth." Couldn't play in major leagues because of racial barrier. Credited with 950 HR (75 in 1931, 69 in 1934) and .350 batting average. Had .400+ average two times. Career span 1930–46 with Homestead Grays, Pittsburgh Crawfords.

Kirk Gibson (b. 5-28-57): Baseball OF. Played on two World Series champions (Detroit in 1984 and Los Angeles in 1988). Hit dramatic pinch-hit HR to win Game 1 of 1988 series. MVP in 1988. Career span 1979–94 with Detroit, Los Angeles, Kansas City, Pittsburgh. Also starred in baseball and football at Michigan State.

Frank Gifford (b. 8-16-30): Football RB. NFL Player of Year in 1956 when he rushed for 819 yards and caught 51 passes. Played in seven Pro Bowls. Retired for one season after ferocious hit by Chuck Bednarik. Career span 1952–60 and 1962–64, all with New York (N). Elected to Hall of Fame in 1977.

Rod Gilbert (b. 7-1-41): Hockey RW. Played 16 seasons, all with the New York Rangers (1960–78), and had 406 goals and 615 assists. Elected to Hall of Fame 1982.

Sid Gillman (b. 10-26-11, d. 1-4-03): Football coach. Developed wide-open, pass-oriented style of offense, introduced techniques for situational player substitutions and the study of game films. Won AFL championship (1963) with San Diego Chargers. Career span 1955–59 Los Angeles; 1960–69 Los Angeles/San Diego Chargers; 1973–74 Houston. Lifetime record 123-104-7.

Pancho Gonzales (b. 5-9-28, d. 7-3-95): Tennis player. Won two consecutive U.S. singles titles (1948–49). In 1969, at age 41, beat Charlie Pasarell 22–24, 1–6, 16–14, 6–3, 11–9 in longest Wimbledon match ever (5:12).

Jeff Gordon (b. 8-4-71): Auto racer. NASCAR's alltime money winner. Four-time NASCAR Winston Cup champion (1995, '97, '98, '01). Youngest Winston Cup Series champion in the modern era, winning his first title at age 24. Won 1997 and '99 Daytona 500. Set NASCAR modern record with 13 wins in 1998.

Shane Gould (b. 11-23-56): Australian swimmer. Won three gold medals, one silver and one bronze at 1972 Olympics. Set 11 world records over 23-month period beginning in 1971. Held world record in five freestyle distances ranging from 100 meters to 1,500 meters in late 1971 and 1972. Retired at age 16.

Steffi Graf (b. 6-14-69): German tennis player. Achieved the Grand Slam in 1988. Won four Australian Open singles titles (1988–90, '94), seven Wimbledon titles (1988, '89, 1991–93, '95, '96), six French Open titles (1987, '88, '93, '95, '96, '99) and five U.S. Open titles (1988–89, '93, '95, '96). Held the No. 1 ranking a record 186 weeks. Gold medalist at 1988 Olympics. Second in alltime Grand Slam singles titles (22).

Otto Graham (b. 12-6-21): Football QB. Led Cleveland to 10 championship games in his 10-year career. Played on four consecutive AAFC champions (1946–49) and three NFL champions (1950, '54, '55). Combined league totals: 23,584 yards passing, 174 touchdown passes. Player of the Year two times (1953, '55). Led league in passing six times. Career span 1946–55.

Red Grange (b. 6-13-03, d. 1-28-91): Football HB. "The Galloping Ghost." All-America three consecutive seasons with Illinois (1923–25), scoring 31 touchdowns in 20-game collegiate career. Signed by George Halas of Chicago in 1925, attracted sellout crowds across the country. Established the first AFL with manager C.C. Pyle in 1926, but league folded after one year. Career span 1925–34 with Chicago, New York.

Rocky Graziano (b. 6-7-22, d. 5-22-90): Boxer. Middleweight champion from 1947–48. Career record 67–13. Endured three brutal title fights against Tony Zale, with Zale winning by KO in 1946 and 1948, and Graziano winning by KO in 1947.

Hank Greenberg (b. 1-1-11, d. 9-4-86): Baseball 1B. 331 career HR (58 in 1938). MVP in 1935, '40. League leader in HR and RBI four times each. Fifth alltime highest slugging average (.605). 100+ RBI seven times. Career span 1933-41, 1945-47 with Detroit, Pittsburgh.

Joe Greene (b. 9-24-46): Football DT. "Mean Joe." Anchored Pittsburgh's famed "Steel Curtain" defense. Selected for Pro Bowl 10 times. Played on four Super Bowl champions (1974, '75, '78, '79). Career span 1969–81 with Pittsburgh.

Maurice Greene (b. 7-23-74): Track and field. Won Olympic gold medals in Sydney in the 100 meters and the 4x100 relay. Held world record for 100 meters for three years after running 9.79 in Athens on 6-16-99.

Forrest Gregg (b. 10-18-33): Football OT/G. Played in then-record 188 straight games from 1956–71. Named all-NFL eight straight years starting in 1960. Career span 1956–71, most of it with Green Bay Packers. Played on winning Packer team in first two Super Bowls. Inducted into Hall of Fame in 1977.

Wayne Gretzky (b. 1-26-61): Hockey C. "The Great One." No. 99. Most dominant player in NHL history. Alltime scoring leader in points (2,795), assists (1,910), and goals (885). Alltime single-season scoring leader in points (215 in 1986), goals (92 in 1982) and assists (163 in 1986). Won nine MVP awards (1980-87, '89). Led league in assists 16 times, scoring 11 times, goals five times. Scored 200+ points four times, 100+ points 10 other times; 70+ goals four consecutive seasons; 50+ goals five other times; 100+ assists 11 consecutive seasons. Playoff MVP two times (1985, '88). Played on four Stanley Cup champions with Edmonton from 1978 to 1988. Career span 1978–99 with Edmonton, Los Angeles, St. Louis, and New York Rangers.

Bob Griese (b. 2-3-45): Football QB. Led Miami to three straight Super Bowls (1971–73), including the 1972 Miami team that went 17–0. Career span 1967–80 with Miami, passing for 25,092 yards and 192 TDs. Elected to Hall of Fame in 1990.

Florence Griffith Joyner (b. 12-21-59, d. 9-21-98): Track and field. Won three gold medals (100 meters, 200 meters, 4x100-meter relay) at 1988 Olympics; Set world record in 100 (10.49) in 1988 and in 200 (21.34) at the 1988 Olympics. Sullivan Award winner in 1988.

Ken Griffey Jr. (b. 11-21-69): Baseball OF. Hit 56 home runs in back-to-back seasons (1997–98). Became youngest man (31 years 261 day) to reach 450 HRs when he connected on 8-9-01. Won AL MVP award in 1997, when he hit .304 with 56 HRs and 147 RBI. 10 Gold Glove Awards. Father Ken Sr. starred with Cincinnati Reds in 1970s. Hit 500th HR in 2004.

Archie Griffin (b. 8-21-54): College football RB. Only player to win the Heisman Trophy two times

(1974–75), with Ohio State. Eighth alltime NCAA career yards rushing (5,177). Professional career span 1976–83 with Cincinnati; totaled 2,808 yards rushing and 192 receptions.

Lefty Grove (b. 3-6-00, d. 5-22-75): Baseball LHP. 300 career wins and fifth alltime highest winning percentage (.680). League leader in ERA nine times, strikeouts seven consecutive seasons. Won 20+ games eight times. 1931 MVP. Career span 1925–41 with Philadelphia (AL), Boston (AL).

Tony Gwynn (b. 5-9-60): Baseball OF. Won eight batting titles (1984, 1987–89, 1994–97). League leader in hits six times, with .300+ average 16 times, 200+ hits five times. Career span 1982–01 with San Diego: .338 average, 3,141 hits.

Walter Hagen (b. 12-21-1892, d. 10-5-69): Golfer. Third alltime leader in major championships (11). Won PGA Championship five times (1921, 1924–27), British Open four times (1922, '24, '28, '29) and U.S. Open two times (1914, '19). Won 40 career tournaments.

Marvin Hagler (b. 5-23-54): Boxer. "Marvelous." Middleweight champion (1980–87). Career record 62-3-2 with 52 KOs from 1973–87. Defended title 13 times.

George Halas (b. 2-2-1895, d. 10-31-83): Football owner and coach. "Papa Bear." Alltime leader in seasons coaching (40) and second in wins (324). Career record 324-151-31 intermittently from 1920–1967. Remained as owner until his death. Chicago won a record seven NFL championships during his tenure.

Glenn Hall (b. 10-3-31): Hockey goalie. "Mr. Goalie" was an All-Star in 11 of his 18 seasons. Set record for consecutive games played by a goaltender (502) and ended career with goals against average of 2.51. Won or shared Vezina Trophy three times. Career span 1952–71 with Detroit, Chicago and St. Louis.

Charles Haley (b. 1-6-64): Football DE. Only player in NFL history to be a member of five Super Bowl champions, two with San Francisco (1989, '90) and three with Dallas (1993, '94, '96). Career span 1986–99. Recorded 100.5 career sacks.

Mia Hamm (b. 3-17-72): Soccer player. Alltime leading scorer in U.S. women's national team history. Member of Women's World Cup champion team in 1991, '99, and third-place team in '95. Member of 1996 Olympic champion team. Debuted with national team against China on 8-3-87 as its youngest player ever, at age 15.

Arthur B. (Bull) Hancock (b. 1-24-10, d. 9-14-72): Horse racing owner. Owner of Claiborne Farm and arguably the greatest breeder in history. For 15 straight years, from 1955–69, a Claiborne stallion led the sire list. Foaled at Claiborne Farm were four Horses of the Year (Kelso, Round Table, Bold Ruler and Nashua).

Tom Harmon (b. 9-28-19, d. 3-17-90): Football RB. Won Heisman Trophy in 1940 with Michigan. Triple-threat back led nation in scoring and named All-America two consecutive seasons (1939, '40). Awarded Silver Star and Purple Heart in World War II. Played in NFL with Los Angeles (1946–47).

Franco Harris (b. 3-7-50): Football RB. Holds Super Bowl record for career rushing yards (354). Super Bowl MVP in 1974. Made the "Immaculate Reception" to win 1972 playoff game against Oakland. Played on four Super Bowl champions (1974, '75, '78, '79) with

Pittsburgh. Gained 1,000+ yards in nine seasons, 100+ yards in 47 games. Played in eight Pro Bowls. Rookie of the Year in 1972. Career span 1972–84 with Pittsburgh and Seattle. Rushed for 12,120 yards and scored 100 career touchdowns. Elected to the Hall of Fame in 1990.

Leon Hart (b. 11-2-28, d. 9-24-02): Football DE. Won Heisman Trophy in 1949, the last lineman to win the award. Played on three national champions with Notre Dame (1946, '47, '49), and the Irish went undefeated during his four years (36-0-2). Also played on three NFL champions with Detroit. Career span 1950–57.

Bill Hartack (b. 12-9-32): Horse racing jockey. Rode five Kentucky Derby winners (1957, '60, '62, '64, '69), three Preakness Stakes winners (1956, '64, '69) and one Belmont Stakes winner (1960).

Doug Harvey (b. 12-19-24, d. 12-26-90): Hockey D. Defensive Player of the Year seven times (1954–57, 1959–61). Led league in assists in 1954. All-Star 10 times. Played on six Stanley Cup champions with Montreal from 1947–68.

Dominik Hasek (b. 1-29-65): Czech hockey G. Two-time NHL MVP (1997, '98) with Buffalo; six-time Vezina Trophy winner (1994, '95, 1997–99, '01) as top goalie in league. Led NHL with a 1.95 goals-against average in 1993–94, the first sub-2.00 GAA since Bernie Parent in 1974. Topped that with 1.87 GAA in 1998–99. Guided Czech Republic to Olympic gold medal in 1998 at Nagano. Career span 1990–02 with Chicago, Buffalo and Detroit; 2003– Detroit.

Billy Haughton (b. 11-2-23, d. 7-15-86): Harness racing driver. Won the Pacing Triple Crown driving Rum Customer in 1968. Won The Hambletonian four times (1974, '76, '77, '80).

John Havlicek (b. 4-8-40): Basketball F/G. "Hondo" averaged 20.8 points per game over 16-season NBA career, all with Boston. First team All-NBA (1971–74). Member of eight NBA championship teams. Playoff MVP. Member of Ohio State team that won 1960 NCAA title. Elected to Hall of Fame in 1983.

Elvin Hayes (b. 11-17-45): Basketball C. Three-time first-team All-NBA selection (1975, '77, '79). 12-time All-Star (1969–80). Led NBA in scoring (1969) and in rebounding (1970, '74). Played from 1968–84 with San Diego/Houston Rockets and Baltimore/Washington Bullets, averaging 21.0 points and 12.5 rebounds per game. 1968 *Sporting News* College Player of Year as Houston senior. Elected to Hall of Fame in 1989.

Woody Hayes (b. 2-14-13, d. 3-12-87): College football coach. Won three national championship (1954, '57, '68) and four Rose Bowls. Career record 238-72-10, including four undefeated seasons, with Ohio State from 1951–1978. Forced to resign after striking an opposing player during 1978 Gator Bowl.

Marques Haynes (b. 10-3-26): Basketball G. Known as "The World's Greatest Dribbler." Beginning in 1946 barnstormed more than four million miles throughout 97 countries for the Harlem Globetrotters, Harlem Magicians, Meadowlark Lemon's Bucketeers, Harlem Wizards.

Thomas Hearns (b. 10-18-58): Boxer. "Hit Man." Champion in four weight classes: welterweight, super welterweight, middleweight and light heavyweight. Career record: 57–4–1 with 45 KOs.

Eric Heiden (b. 6-14-58): Speed skater. Won five gold medals at 1980 Olympics. World champion three consecutive years (1977–79). Won Sullivan Award in 1980.

Carol Heiss (b. 1-20-40): Figure skater. Gold medalist at 1960 Olympics, silver medalist at 1956 Olympics. World champion five consecutive years (1956–60) and U.S. champion four consecutive years (1957–60). Married 1956 gold medalist Hayes Jenkins.

Rickey Henderson (b. 12-25-57): Baseball OF. Career leader in stolen bases, walks and runs; modern single-season stolen base record holder (stole 130 bases in 1982). Led league in steals 11 times. 1990 MVP. Alltime leader in lead-off HRs. Career span 1979– with nine teams.

Sonja Henie (b. 4-8-12, d. 10-12-69): Norwegian figure skater. Gold medalist at three consecutive Olympics (1928, '32, '36). World champion 10 consecutive years (1927–36).

Orel Hershiser (b. 9-16-58): Baseball RHP. Alltime leader most consecutive scoreless innings pitched (59 in 1988). Cy Young Award winner in 1988 and World Series MVP. Career span 1983–00 with Los Angeles, Cleveland, San Francisco and New York (NL): 204–150, 3.48 ERA.

Foster Hewitt (b. 11-21-02, d. 4-22-85): Hockey sportscaster. In 1923, aired one of hockey's first radio broadcasts. Became the voice of hockey in Canada on radio and later television. Famous for the phrase, "He shoots ... he scores!"

Tommy Hitchcock (b. 2-11-00, d. 4-19-44): Polo. 10-goal rating 18 times in his 19-year career from 1922–40. Killed in plane crash in World War II.

Lew Hoad (b. 11-23-34): Australian tennis player. Won two Wimbledon singles titles (1956, '57). Also won French title and Australian title in 1956, but failed to achieve the Grand Slam when defeated at Forest Hills by countryman Ken Rosewall.

Ben Hogan (b. 8-13-12, d. 7-25-97): Golfer. Third alltime in career wins (63). Won U.S. Open four times (1948, '50, '51, '53), the Masters (1951, '53) and PGA Championship (1946, '48) two times each and British Open once (1953). PGA Player of the Year four times (1948, '50, '51, '53).

Marshall Holman (b. 9-29-54): Bowler. Won 21 PBA titles between 1975–88. Had leading average in 1987 (213.54) and was named PBA Bowler of the Year.

Nat Holman (b. 10-18-1896, d. 2-12-95): College basketball coach. Only coach in history to win NCAA and NIT championships in same season, in 1950 with CCNY; 423 career wins, a .689 winning percentage.

Larry Holmes (b. 11-3-49): Boxer. Heavyweight champion (1978–85). Career record 69–6 with 44 KOs from 1973–02. Defended title 21 times.

Lou Holtz (b. 1-6-37): Football coach. Has led four different programs to Top 20 seasons. Coached Notre Dame to national championship in 1988 and a 12–0 record with a 34–21 win over West Virginia in Fiesta Bowl. 12-8-2 career record in bowl games. Career span 1969–75 at William & Mary and N Carolina St; 1977–96 at Arkansas, Minnesota and Notre Dame; and 1999–2004 at S Carolina.

Evander Holyfield (b. 10-19-62): Boxer. Only man to win the heavyweight title four times. Won heavyweight belt for the first time on Oct. 25, 1990, when he KO'd James (Buster) Douglas in Las Vegas. Fought three epic bouts with Riddick Bowe and two memorable clashes with Mike Tyson (Tyson was disqualified in the rematch for biting Holyfield's ears, severing one of them.)

Red Holzman (b. 8-10-20; d. 11-13-98): Basketball coach. Led New York to NBA titles in 1970 and '73. NBA Coach of the Year in 1970. After two-year coaching stints with Milwaukee and St. Louis, coached New York from 1968–82. Career record: 696–604. Elected to Hall of Fame in 1985.

Harry Hopman (b. 8-12-06, d. 12-27-85): Australian tennis coach. As nonplaying captain, led Australia to 15 Davis Cup titles between 1950–69. Mentor to Lew Hoad, Ken Rosewall, Rod Laver and John Newcombe.

Willie Hoppe (b. 10-11-1887, d. 2-1-59): Billiards. Won 51 world championship matches from 1904–52.

Rogers Hornsby (b. 4-27-1896, d. 1-5-63): Baseball 2B. Second alltime in career batting average (.358), won seven batting titles, including with .424 average in 1924. Led league in slugging nine times. Triple Crown winner in 1922, '25; MVP award winner in 1925, '29. 2,930 hits and 1,584 RBI's from 1915–37 with five teams, including St. Louis (NL).

Paul Hornung (b. 12-23-35): Football RB-K. Led league in scoring three consecutive seasons, including a record 176 points in 1960 (15 touchdowns, 15 field goals, 41 extra points). Player of the Year in 1961. Career span 1957–66 with Green Bay. Suspended for 1963 season by Pete Rozelle for gambling. Also won Heisman Trophy in 1956 with Notre Dame.

Gordie Howe (b. 3-31-28): Hockey RW. Second alltime in goals (801), first in years played (26) and games (1,767). Finished career with 1,850 points and 1,049 assists. Won MVP award six times (1952, '53, '57, '58, '60, '63). Led league in scoring six times, goals five times and assists three times. All-Star 12 times. Played on four Stanley Cup champions with Detroit from 1946–71. Teamed with sons Mark and Marty in the WHA with Houston and New England from 1973–79, in NHL with Hartford in 1980.

Carl Hubbell (b. 6-22-03, d. 11-21-88): Baseball LHP. 253 career wins. MVP in 1933, '36. League leader in wins and ERA three times each. Won 24 consecutive games from 1936–37. Struck out Ruth, Gehrig, Foxx, Simmons and Cronin consecutively in 1934 All-Star game. Pitched no-hitter in 1929. Career span 1928–43 with New York (NL).

Sam Huff (b. 10-4-34): Football LB. Made 30 interceptions. MVP in 1959. Career span 1956–69 with New York Giants and Washington. Elected to Hall of Fame in 1982.

Bobby Hull (b. 1-3-39): Hockey LW. "The Golden Jet." Led league in goals seven times and points three times. 610 career goals. Won MVP award two consecutive seasons (1965, '66). Son Brett won MVP award in 1991, the only father and son to be so honored. All-Star 10 times. Career span 1957–72 with Chicago, 1973–80 with Winnipeg of WHA.

Brett Hull (b. 8-9-64): Hockey RW. Son of Bobby Hull. Won Hart Memorial Trophy for 1990–91 season. Scored Stanley Cup–winning goal for Dallas in third overtime of Game 6 against Buffalo in 1999. Career span 1986– with Calgary, St. Louis, Dallas and Detroit.

Jim (Catfish) Hunter (b. 4-8-46, d. 9-9-99): Baseball RHP. 1974 Cy Young award winner. Won 20+ games five consecutive seasons. Led league in wins and winning percentage two times each, ERA one time. 250+ innings pitched eight times. Pitched perfect game in 1968. Member of five World Series champions for Oakland and New York (AL). Career span 1965–79.

Don Hutson (b. 1-31-13, d. 6-26-97): Football WR. Finished his career as alltime leader in touchdown receptions (99). Led league in pass receptions eight times, receiving yards seven times and scoring five consecutive seasons. Caught at least one pass in 95 consecutive games. Player of the Year two consecutive seasons (1941, '42). Career span 1935–45 with Green Bay.

Hank Iba (b. 8-6-04; d. 1-15-93): College basketball coach. Coached Oklahoma A&M (which became Oklahoma State) from 1934–70. Team won NCAA titles in 1945 and '46. 767 career wins is seventh alltime.

Jackie Ickx (b. 1-1-45): Belgian auto racer. Won the 24 Hours of LeMans a record six times (1969, 1975–77, '81, '82) before retiring in 1985.

Punch Imlach (b. 3-15-18, d. 12-1-87): Hockey coach. 467 wins. With Toronto from 1958–69. Won four Stanley Cup championships (1962–64, 1967).

Miguel Induráin (b. 7-16-64): Cyclist. Won five consecutive Tours de France (1991–95), a feat unequaled until Lance Armstrong matched in 2003.

Juli Inkster (b.6-24-60): Golfer. 28 career victories. Became only the second woman ever to win all four of the LPGA's modern majors when she won the LPGA Championship on 6-27-99. Inducted to LPGA Hall of Fame in 1999.

Bo Jackson (b. 11-30-62): Baseball OF and Football RB. Only person in history to be named to baseball All-Star game and football Pro Bowl game. 1985 Heisman Trophy winner at Auburn. 1989 MLB All-Star game MVP. Signed with football's LA Raiders in 1988. Retired 1994 following hip replacement surgery.

Joe Jackson (b. 7-16-1889, d. 12-5-51): Baseball OF. "Shoeless Joe." Third alltime highest career batting average (.356), with .300+ average 11 times. One of the "Eight Men Out" banned from baseball for throwing 1919 World Series. Career span 1908–20 with Cleveland, Chicago (AL).

Phil Jackson (b. 9-17-45): Basketball F-Coach. Coached the Lakers to their third straight NBA Championship in 2002, his ninth title as coach. He returned to the Lakers in 2005 after one year retirement. Won six titles as coach of Chicago (1991–93, 1996–98). Best winning percentage in NBA history (726–258, .738). Spent 13 years as a scrappy forward in the NBA, winning an NBA title with New York in 1973.

Reggie Jackson (b. 5-18-46): Baseball OF. "Mr. October." Alltime leader in World Series slugging percentage (.755). 1977 Series MVP, hit three HR in final game on three consecutive pitches. 563 career HR total is eighth best alltime. Led league in HR four times. 1973 MVP. Alltime strikeout leader (2,597). In a 12-year period played on 10 first-place teams, five World Series winners. Career span 1967–87 with Oakland, Baltimore, New York (AL) and California. Inducted to Baseball Hall of Fame in 1993.

Bruce Jenner (b. 10-28-49): Track and Field. Set decathlon world record (8,634) in winning gold medal at 1976 Olympics. Sullivan Award winner in 1976.

John Henry (b. 1975): Thoroughbred race horse. Sold as yearling for $1,100, the gelding was Horse of the Year in 1981 and 1984 and retired with then-record $6,597,947 in winnings.

Ben Johnson (b. 12-30-61): Track and field. Canadian sprinter set world record in 100 meters (9.83 in 1987). Won event at 1988 Olympics in 9.79, but

gold medal revoked for failed drug test. Both world records revoked for steroid usage. Suspended for life after testing positive for elevated testosterone level at an indoor meet in Montreal on 1-17-93.

Earvin (Magic) Johnson (b. 8-14-59): Basketball G. Retired Nov. 7, 1991 after being diagnosed with HIV, the virus that causes AIDS. Returned to Lakers Feb '96 at age 36. Finished career second alltime in assists (10,141). MVP award three times (1987, '89, '90) and playoff MVP in 1980, '82 and '87. Played on five championship teams with Los Angeles. All-Star eight consecutive seasons. League leader in assists four times, steals two times, free throw percentage once. Career stats: 19.5 ppg, 11.2 apg, 7.2 rpg. Also won NCAA championship and named tournament MVP in 1979 with Michigan State.

Jack Johnson (b. 3-31-1878, d. 6-10-46): Boxer. First black heavyweight champion (1908–15). Career record 78-8-12 with 45 KOs from 1897–28.

Jimmy Johnson (b. 7-16-43): Football coach. Won two straight Super Bowls (1993, '94) as Dallas coach. Career record of 89–66 with Dallas and Miami. Led Miami (FL) to collegiate national championship in 1987. One of only three men to win college and NFL championships.

Michael Johnson (b. 9-13-67): Track and field. First man to win gold medals in both the 200 and 400 in the Olympics (1996). Broke 17-year-old 200-meter world record (19.66) at 1996 U.S. Olympic trials, then further lowered mark to 19.32 at Atlanta. Repeated in the 400 meters at the 2000 Sydney Games. Anchored U.S. 4x400 team at 1993 World Championship to world record of 2:54.29.

Randy Johnson (b. 9-10-63): Baseball LHP. Six-foot, 10-inch fireballer is tallest player in Major League history. Won Cy Young Award five times (1995, '99, 2000, '01, '02). Won "pitching triple crown" in 2002, leading league in wins, ERA and strikeouts. Led Arizona Diamondbacks to 2001 World Series victory, winning Series MVP award along with teammate Curt Schilling. Pitched no-hitter on 6-2-90 for Seattle against Oakland; pitched perfect game on 5-18-04 for Arizona against Atlanta. Career span 1988–89 with Montreal; 1989–98 Seattle; 1998 Houston; 1999–2004 Arizona; 2005– New York Yankees.

Walter Johnson (b. 11-6-1887, d. 12-10-46): Baseball RHP. "Big Train." Alltime leader in shutouts (110), second in wins (416), fourth in losses (279) and third in innings pitched (5,914). His record of 3,509 career strikeouts lasted for 56 years. 2.17 career ERA. MVP in 1913, '24. Won 20+ games 12 times. League leader in strikeouts 12 times, ERA five times, wins six times. Pitched no-hitter in 1920. Career span 1907–27 with Washington.

Ben A. Jones (b. 12-31-1882, d. 6-13-61): Horse racing trainer. Trained Triple Crown winner (Whirlaway in 1941). Trained six Kentucky Derby winners, more than any other trainer (1938, '41, '44, '48, '49, '52), two Preakness Stakes winners (1941, '44) and one Belmont Stakes winner (1941).

Bobby Jones (b. 3-17-02, d. 12-18-71): Golfer. Achieved golf's only recognized Grand Slam in 1930. Second alltime in major championships (13). Won U.S. Amateur five times, more than any golfer (1924, '25, '27, '28, '30), U.S. Open four times (1923, '26, '29, '30), British Open three times (1926, '27, '30) and British Amateur (1930). Also designed Augusta National course, site of the Masters, and founded the tournament. Winner of Sullivan Award in 1930.

K.C. Jones (b. 5-25-32): Basketball G-coach. Member of eight straight NBA-championship Boston teams in his nine season career from 1958–67. Averaged 7.4 points and 4.3 assists per game. Coached Celtics from 1983–88, with 308–102 regular season record and 65–37 playoff record with NBA titles in 1984 and '86.

Robert Trent Jones (b. 6-20-06, d. 6-14-00): English-born golf course architect designed or remodeled over 500 courses, including Baltusrol, Hazeltine, Oak Hill and Winged Foot. In the mid-60s five straight U.S. Opens were played on courses designed or remodeled by Jones.

Roy Jones Jr. (b.1-16-69): Boxer. Won titles as middleweight, super middleweight and light heavyweight. Career record: 49–2, 38 KOs. Won controversial silver medal at the 1988 Olympics in Seoul despite dominating his South Korean opponent in the final. Awarded Val Barker Trophy as outstanding boxer of '88 Games.

Sam Jones (b. 6-24-33): Basketball G. Played 12 seasons with Boston (1958–69), who won NBA title every year from 1959–66, plus 1968 and '69. Averaged 17.7 points per game. Elected to Hall of Fame in 1983.

Michael Jordan (b. 2-17-63): Basketball G. "Air." Arguably greatest player of all time. Led Bulls to six NBA titles (1991–93; 1996–98). Tied with Wilt Chamberlain for lead in career scoring average (30.1 ppg), and record holder for most points scored in a playoff game (63 in 1986). Guided Bulls to an NBA-record 72 wins in 1995–96. Led league in scoring a record 10 seasons, steals three times. League MVP in 1988, '91, '92, '96 and '98; Finals MVP in 1991–93 and 1996–98; Rookie of the Year in 1985. Career span 1984–93, 1995–98 with Chicago; 2001–03 with Washington. College Player of the Year in 1984. Played on NCAA title team with North Carolina in 1982. Member of gold medal-winning 1984 and '92 Olympic teams. Played minor league baseball in 1994.

Jackie Joyner-Kersee (b. 3-3-62): Track and field. Gold medalist in heptathlon and long jump at 1988 Olympics and in the former at the 1992 Olympics. Set heptathlon world record (7,291 points) at 1988 Olympics. Also won silver medal in heptathlon at 1984 Games and bronze in long jump at 1992 and '96 Olympics. Sullivan Award winner in 1986.

Alberto Juantorena (b. 3-12-51): Track and field. Cuban was gold medalist in 400 and 800 meters at 1976 Olympics.

Wang Junxia (b. 1963): Chinese distance runner. Broke four world records in six days in Sept. 1993. Broke 10,000 (29:31.78) on Sept 8; ran 1,500 in 3:51.92 in finishing second to countrywoman Qu Yunxia's world record of 3:50.46 on Sept 11; ran 3,000 record of 8:12.19 in heats on Sept 12 and lowered it to 8:06.11 on Sept 13. Won gold in 5,000 and silver in 10,000 at 1996 Olympics.

Sonny Jurgensen (b. 8-23-34): Football QB. In 18 seasons, passed for 32,224 yards and 255 TDs. Led NFL in passing both 1967 and '69. Career span 1957–74 with Philadelphia and Washington. Elected to Hall of Fame in 1983.

Duke Kahanamoku (b. 8-24-1890, d. 1-22-68): Swimmer. Won a total of five medals (3 gold and two silver) at three Olympics in 1912, '20, '24. Introduced the crawl stroke to America. Surfing pioneer and water polo player. Later sheriff of Honolulu.

Al Kaline (b. 12-19-34): Baseball OF. 3,007 career hits and 399 career HR. As a 20-year-old in 1955, became youngest player to win batting title, with .340 average. Had .300+ average nine times. Played in 18 All-Star games. Career span 1953–74 with Detroit.

Anatoly Karpov (b. 5-23-61): Soviet chess player. First world champion to receive title by default, in 1975, when Bobby Fischer chose not to defend his crown. Champion until 1985 when beaten by Garry Kasparov. Recognized by FIDE as champion in 1994.

Garry Kasparov (b. 4-13-63): Born Garik Weinstein. Chess player. World champion from 1985 to 1993 when stripped of title by FIDE. Won six-game series against IBM computer, Deep Blue, in 1996. Lost to improved version of Deep Blue in 1997.

Kip Keino (b. 1-17-40): Track and field. Kenyan was gold medalist in 1,500 meters at 1968 Olympics and in steeplechase at 1972 Olympics.

Jim Kelly (b. 2-14-60): Football QB. Led Buffalo to four straight Super Bowls—all losses. Career passer rating of 84.4. Led NFL in passing in 1990. In 11 NFL seasons passed for 35,467 yards and 237 TDs. Career span 1983–96 with Houston (USFL) and Buffalo Bills.

Kelso (b. 1957, d. 1983): Thoroughbred race horse. Gelding was Horse of the Year five straight years (1960–64). Finished in the money in 53 of 63 races. Career earnings $1,977,896.

Harmon Killebrew (b. 6-29-36): Baseball 3B-1B. 573 career HR total is seventh most alltime. 100+ RBI nine times, 40+ HR eight times. League leader in HR six times and RBI four times. 1969 MVP. 100+ walks and strikeouts seven times each. Career span 1954–75 with Washington and Minnesota.

Jean Claude Killy (b. 8-30-43): French skier. Won three gold medals at 1968 Olympics. World Cup overall champion two consecutive years (1967, '68).

Ralph Kiner (b. 10-27-22): Baseball OF. Led league in HR seven consecutive seasons. Third in alltime HR frequency (7.1 HR every 100 at bats). 369 career HR, with 50+ HR two times. 100+ RBI and runs scored in same season six times; 100+ walks six times. Career span 1946–55 with Pittsburgh, Chicago (NL), and Cleveland.

Billie Jean King (b. 11-22-43): Tennis player. Won a record 20 Wimbledon titles, including six singles titles (1966–68, '72, '73, '75). Won four U.S. singles titles (1967, '71, '72, '74), and singles titles at Australian Open (1968) and French Open (1972). Won 27 Grand Slam doubles titles—total of 39 Grand Slam titles is third alltime. Helped found the women's pro tour in 1970, serving as president of the Women's Tennis Association two times. Helped form Team Tennis.

Nile Kinnick (b. 7-9-18, d. 6-2-43): College football RB. Won the Heisman Trophy in 1939 with Iowa. Premier runner, passer and punter was killed in plane crash during routine Navy training flight. Stadium in Iowa City named in his honor.

Tom Kite (b. 12-9-49): Golfer. Winner of 19 career PGA Tour events, including the 1992 U.S. Open at Pebble Beach. Led PGA in scoring average in 1981 and '82. PGA Player of Year in 1989, when he won a then-record $1,395,278. Ryder Cup captain in 1997.

Franz Klammer (b. 12-3-54): Austrian alpine skier. Greatest downhiller ever. Gold medalist in downhill at 1976 Olympics. Also won four World Cup downhill titles (1975–78).

Bob Knight (b. 10-25-40): College basketball coach. Won three NCAA championships with Indiana in 1976, '81, '87. Coached U.S. Olympic team to gold medal in 1984. Fired by Indiana in 2000 after a series of disputes with the media, ex-players, students, and the university. Hired by Texas Tech in 2001, took team to 2003 NIT semifinals. Career span since 1966 with Army, Indiana and Texas Tech.

Olga Korbut (b. 5-16-55): Soviet gymnast. First ever to complete backward somersault on balance beam. Won three gold medals at 1972 Olympics.

Johann Olav Koss (b.10-29-68): Speed Skater. Norwegian won three gold medals at 1994 Olympics in Lillehammer, with world records in the 1,500, 5,000 and 10,000 meters. Won 1,500 meter gold medal and 10,000 meter silver medal in 1992 Games at Albertville.

Sandy Koufax (b. 12-30-35): Baseball LHP. Cy Young Award winner three times (1963, '65, '66); and MVP in 1963; World Series MVP in 1963, '65. Pitched four no-hitters, including one perfect game. League leader in ERA five consecutive seasons, strikeouts four times. Won 25+ games three times. Career record 165–87, with 2.76 ERA. Career span 1955–66 with Brooklyn/Los Angeles.

Jack Kramer (b. 8-1-21): Tennis player. Won two consecutive U.S. singles titles (1946, '47) and one Wimbledon title (1947). Also won six Grand Slam doubles titles. Served as executive director of Association of Tennis Professionals from 1972–75.

Ingrid Kristiansen (b. 3-21-56): Track and field. Norwegian runner is only person—male or female—to hold world records in 5,000 meters (14:37.33 set in 1986), 10,000 meters (30:13.74 set in 1986) and marathon (2:21:06 set in 1985). Also won Boston Marathon two times (1986, '89) and New York City Marathon once (1989).

Bob Kurland (b. 12-23-24): College basketball player. 6' 10¼" center on Oklahoma A&M teams that won NCAA titles in 1945 and '46. Consensus All-America and NCAA tournament MVP in both 1945 and '46. Led nation in scoring in 1946. His habit of swatting shots off rim led to creation of goaltending rule in 1945. Won gold medals in both 1948 and '52 Olympics. Turned down lucrative pro offers, playing instead for Phillips 66 Oilers AAU team.

Michelle Kwan (b. 7-7-80): Figure skater. Six-time U.S. champion (1996, 1998–02), four-time world champion (1996, '98, '00, '01); silver medalist in 1998 Olympics and bronze medalist in Salt Lake City in 2002.

Rene Lacoste (b. 7-2-05, d. 10-12-96): French tennis player. "The Crocodile." One of France's "Four Musketeers" of the 1920s. Won three French singles titles (1925, '27, '29), two consecutive U.S. titles (1926, '27) and two Wimbledon titles (1925, '28). Also designed casual shirt with embroidered crocodile that bears his name.

Marion Ladewig (b. 10-30-14): Bowler. Won All-Star Tournament eight times (1949–52, '54, '56, '59, '63) and WPBA National Championship once (1960). Also voted Bowler of the Year nine times (1950–54, 1957–59, '63).

Guy Lafleur (b. 9-20-51): Hockey RW. Won MVP award two consecutive seasons (1977, '78), playoff MVP in 1977. Scored 50+ goals and 100+ points six consecutive seasons. Led league in points scored three consecutive seasons, goals and assists one time

each. 560 career goals, 793 assists. Played on five Stanley Cup champions with Montreal from 1971–85.

Curly Lambeau (b. 4-9-1898; d. 6-1-65): Football QB and coach. Quarterback for Packers team in early 1920s. Record of 212-106-21 in his 29 seasons (1921–49) as Packer coach, winning three NFL titles in 1929–31.

Jack Lambert (b. 7-8-52): Football LB. Anchored Pittsburgh's famed "Steel Curtain" defense. Selected for Pro Bowl nine times. Played on four Super Bowl champions (1974, '75, '78, '79) with Pittsburgh from 1974–84. Elected to Hall of Fame 1990.

Jake LaMotta (b. 7-10-21): Boxer. "The Bronx Bull." Subject of *Raging Bull*, a film by Martin Scorsese, starring Robert DeNiro. Won middleweight title by knocking out Marcel Cerdan in 10 on 6-16-49. Lost title to Ray Robinson, who KO'd him in 13 on 2-13-51. Career record: 83–19–4, 30 KOs.

Kenesaw Mountain Landis (b. 11-20-1866, d. 11-25-44): Baseball's first and most powerful commissioner from 1920–44. By banning the eight "Black Sox" involved in the fixing of the 1919 World Series, he restored public confidence in the integrity of baseball.

Tom Landry (b. 9-11-24, d. 2-12-00): Football coach. Third alltime in wins (270). The first coach in Dallas history, from 1960–88. Led team to 13 division titles, seven championship games and five Super Bowls. Won two Super Bowl championships (1971, '77). Career record 270-178-6.

Dick (Night Train) Lane (b. 4-16-28, d. 1-29-02): Football DB. Third alltime in interceptions (68) and second in interception yardage (1,207). Set record with 14 interceptions as a rookie in 1952. Career span 1952–65 with Los Angeles, Chicago Cardinals, Detroit.

Joe Lapchick (b. 4-12-00, d. 8-10-70): Basketball C–coach. One of the first big men in basketball, member of New York's Original Celtics. Coached St. John's (1936–47, 1956–65) to four NIT titles. Coached New York Knicks, 1947–56.

Steve Largent (b. 9-28-54): Football WR. Retired as alltime leader in pass receptions (819), and TD receptions (100). 177 consecutive games with reception, 10 seasons with 50+ receptions and eight seasons with 1,000+ yards receiving. Career span 1976–89 with Seattle. Oklahoma congressman from 1994–01.

Don Larsen (b. 8-7-29): Baseball RHP. Pitched only perfect game in World Series history, for New York (AL) on 10-8-56, beating the Dodgers 2–0; named World Series MVP. Career span 1953–67 for many teams.

Tommy Lasorda (b. 9-22-27): Baseball manager. Spent nearly his entire minor and major league career in Dodgers organization as a pitcher, coach and manager. Managed Dodgers 1977–96, winning four pennants and two World Series (1981, '88). Only three men managed one baseball team longer. Coached U.S. Olympic baseball team to the gold medal at the 2000 Sydney Games.

Rod Laver (b. 8-9-38): Australian tennis player. "Rocket." Only player to achieve the Grand Slam twice (as an amateur in 1962 and as a pro in 1969). Third alltime in men's Grand Slam singles titles (11—tied with Bjorn Borg). Won four Wimbledon titles (1961, '62, '68, '69), three Australian titles (1960, '62, '69), two U.S. titles (1962, '69) and two French titles (1962, '69).

Also won eight Grand Slam doubles titles. First player to earn $1 million in prize money. 47 career tournament victories. Member of undefeated Australian Davis Cup team from 1959–62.

Andrea Mead Lawrence (b. 4-19-32): Skier. Gold medalist in slalom and giant slalom at 1952 Olympics.

Bobby Layne (b. 12-19-26; d. 12-1-86): Football QB. Led Detroit to NFL championships in both 1952 and '53. In 1952 led NFL in every passing category. Career span 1948–62, most with Detroit. Elected to Hall of Fame in 1967.

Sammy Lee (b. 8-1-20): Diver. Gold medalist at two consecutive Olympics (highboard in 1948, '52); bronze medalist in springboard at 1948 Olympics. Won the 1953 Sullivan Award. Also 1960 U.S. Olympic diving coach.

Jacques Lemaire (b. 9-7-45): Hockey C–Coach. As center for Montreal from 1967–79 was part of eight Stanley Cup winning teams. Over 12 seasons, all with Montreal, scored 366 goals and had 469 assists. Elected to Hall of Fame in 1984. Coached New Jersey to their first Stanley Cup in 1995.

Mario Lemieux (b. 10-5-65): Hockey C. Won MVP award in 1988, '93, '96. Playoff MVP in 1991. Led league in points five seasons and goals scored three seasons, assists one season. Rookie of the Year in 1985. Won 1992–93 scoring title despite sitting out six weeks to receive treatment for Hodgkin's disease, a form of cancer. Sat out 1994–95 season, returned in '95–96 to lead league in scoring and become second fastest player to score 500 career goals. Awarded ownership of Penguins in a settlement in 1999, and returned to the ice in 2001, when he scored 35 goals in 43 games. Career span 1984–94, 1995–97, 2001– with Pittsburgh.

Greg LeMond (b. 6-26-61): Cyclist. First American to win Tour de France; won event three times (1986, '89, '90). Recovered from hunting accident to win in 1989.

Ivan Lendl (b. 3-7-60): Tennis player. Second most alltime men's career tournament victories (94). Won three consecutive U.S. Open singles titles (1985–87) and three French Open titles (1984, '86, '87). Also won two Australian Open titles (1989, '90). Reached Grand Slam final nine other times.

Suzanne Lenglen (b. 5-24-1899, d. 7-4-38): French tennis player. Lost only one match from 1919–26. Won six Wimbledon singles and doubles titles (1919–23, '25). Won six French singles and doubles titles (1920–23, '25, '26).

Sugar Ray Leonard (b. 5-17-56): Boxer. Champion in five weight classes: welterweight, junior middleweight, middleweight, super middleweight and light heavyweight. Career record 36-3-1 with 25 KOs from 1977–97, including comeback loss to Hector Camacho at the age of 41. Also light welterweight gold medalist at 1976 Olympics.

Carl Lewis (b. 7-1-61): Track and field. Held world record for 100 meters (9.86), set at 1991 World Championships in Tokyo. Duplicated Jesse Owens's feat by winning four gold medals at 1984 Olympics (100 and 200 meters, 4x100-meter relay and long jump). Won 1996 Olympic long jump gold at age 35, giving him nine career gold medals and making him just the second track and field athlete (along with Al Oerter) to win four Olympic golds in a single event. Sullivan Award winner in 1981.

Nancy Lieberman-Cline (b. 7-1-58): Basketball G. Three-time All-America at Old Dominion. Player of the

Year (1979, '80). Olympian in 1976. Promoter of women's basketball: played in WPBL, WABA. First woman to play basketball in a men's professional league (USBL, 1986). Joined WNBA in 1997, retired in '98 to become GM/coach of the Detroit Shock.

Bob Lilly (b. 7-26-39): Football DT. Dallas Cowboys' first ever draft pick, first Pro Bowl player and first all-NFL choice. Made all-NFL eight times. Career span 1961–74, all with Dallas. Elected to Hall of Fame in 1980.

Tara Lipinski (b. 6-10-82): Figure skater. In 1998 at Nagano eclipsed Sonja Henie as the youngest individual Winter Olympic champion in history when, at 15, she won the women's figure skating gold medal. Also won U.S. and world championships in 1997.

Sonny Liston (b. 5-8-32, d. 12-30-70): Boxer. Heavyweight champion from 1962–64. Won title by KO of Floyd Patterson. Lost title when TKO'd by Cassius Clay (Muhammad Ali) and then lost rematch when KO'd in first round. Career record: 50–4, 39 KOs.

Vince Lombardi (b. 6-11-13, d. 9-3-70): Football coach. Highest alltime winning percentage (.740). Career record 105-35-6. Won five NFL championships and two consecutive Super Bowl titles with Green Bay from 1959–67. Coached Washington in 1969. Super Bowl trophy named in his honor.

Johnny Longden (b. 2-14-07, d. 2-14-03): Horse racing jockey. Rode Triple Crown winner Count Fleet in 1943. 6,032 career wins.

Nancy Lopez (b. 1-6-57): Golfer. 48 career LPGA Tour wins. LPGA Player of the Year four times (1978, '79, '85, '88). Winner of LPGA Championship three times (1978, '85, '89). Member of the LPGA Hall of Fame.

Greg Louganis (b. 1-29-60): Diver. Gold medalist in platform and springboard at two consecutive Olympics (1984, '88). World champion five times (platform in 1978, '82, '86; springboard in 1982, '86). Also Sullivan Award winner in 1984.

Joe Louis (b. 5-13-14, d. 4-12-81): Boxer. "The Brown Bomber." Longest title reign of any heavyweight champion (11 years, nine months) from 1937–49. Career record 63–3 with 49 KOs from 1934–51. Defended title 25 times.

Jerry Lucas (b. 3-30-40): Basketball F. Three-time first-team All-NBA (1965, '66, '68). Averaged 17.0 points and 15.6 rebounds per game from 1963–74 with Cincinnati, San Francisco and New York. Averaged over 20 points and 20 rebounds a game while at Ohio State. In 1960 member of both NCAA championship team and gold-medal winning U.S. Olympic team. Elected to Hall of Fame in 1979.

Sid Luckman (b. 11-21-16, d. 7-5-98): Football QB. Played on four NFL champions (1940, '41, '43, '46) with Chicago. Player of the Year in 1943. Tied record with seven touchdown passes in one game in 1943. All-Pro six times. 137 career touchdown passes. Career span 1939–50. Also All-America with Columbia.

Jon Lugbill (b. 5-27-61): Whitewater canoe racer. Won five world singles titles from 1979–89.

Hank Luisetti (b. 6-16-16, d. 12-17-02): Basketball F. The first player to use the one-handed shot. All-America at Stanford three consecutive years from 1936–38.

D. Wayne Lukas (b. 9-2-35): Horse racing trainer. Former college basketball coach and quarter horse trainer. Won six straight Triple Crown races from

1994–96, including all three Triple Crown races in 1995, the first trainer to accomplish that feat with multiple horses (Thunder Gulch and Timber County). Trained horses that have won 13 Triple Crown races—four Kentucky Derbys, five Preakness' and four Belmonts—and three Horses of the Year (Lady's Secret in 1986, Criminal Type in 1990, and Charismatic in 1999).

Connie Mack (b. 2-22-1862, d. 2-8-56): Born Cornelius McGillicuddy. Baseball manager. Managed Philadelphia for 50 years (1901–50) until age 87. Alltime leader in games (7,755), wins (3,731) and losses (3,948). Won nine pennants and five World Series (1910, '11, '13, '29, '30).

Greg Maddux (b. 4-14-66): Baseball P. Won 15 or more games in 15 straight seasons (1988–02). Fourtime Cy Young Award winner (1992–95). Led league in wins three times, ERA four times. 12 Gold Gloves. Won 300th game on 8-7-04. Career span 1986– with Chicago (NL) and Atlanta.

Larry Mahan (b. 11-21-43): Rodeo. All-around champion six times (1966–70, '73).

Frank Mahovlich (b. 1-10-38): Hockey LW. Winner of Calder Trophy for top rookie for 1957–58 season. In 18 NHL seasons with Toronto, Detroit and Montreal, had 533 goals and 570 assists. Played for six Stanley Cup winners. Elected to Hall of Fame 1981.

Phil Mahre (b. 5-10-57): Skier. Gold medalist in slalom at 1984 Olympics (twin brother Steve won silver medal). World Cup champion three consecutive years (1981–83).

Joe Malone (b. 2-28-1890, d. 5-15-69): Hockey F. "Phantom Joe." Led the NHL in its first season, 1917–18, with 44 goals in 20 games with Montreal. Led league in scoring two times (1918, '20). Holds NHL record with most goals scored, single game (7) in 1920.

Karl Malone (b. 7-24-63): Basketball F. "The Mailman." Finished 2003–04 season with 36,928 career points scored. Two-time NBA MVP (1997, '99). 11-time first-team All-NBA (1989–99). All-Star MVP, 1989, 1993 (shared with John Stockton). All-Rookie team, 1986. Member of 1992 and '96 Olympic teams. Career span 1985–2003 with Utah, 2003–04 with Los Angeles.

Moses Malone (b. 3-23-55): Basketball C. Threetime NBA MVP (1979, '82, '83). Playoff MVP in 1983, when he led Philadelphia to the NBA title. First-ballot Hall of Famer retired with 8,531 career free throws made, 16,212 rebounds and 27,409 points scored. Four-time first-team All-NBA. Led league in rebounding six times, five consecutively. Went directly to pros from high school. Career span 1974–95 with nine teams, including Houston and Philadelphia.

Hermann Maier (b.12-7-72): Austrian skier. Recovered from spectacular crash in the downhill to win two gold medals at 1998 Olympics in Nagano. Won 1998 Super G, Giant Slalom and overall World Cup season titles.

Man o' War (b. 1917, d. 1947): Thoroughbred race horse. Won 20 of 21 races 1919–20. Only loss was in 1919 in Sanford Stakes to Upset. Passed up Derby but won both Preakness and Belmont. Winner of $249,465. Sire of War Admiral, 1937 Triple Crown winner.

Mickey Mantle (b. 10-20-31, d. 8-13-95): Baseball OF. Won three MVP awards (1956, '57, '62); won Triple Crown in 1956. 536 career HR. Greatest switch hitter in history. Played in 20 All-Star games. Alltime World Series leader in HR (18), RBI (40) and runs scored (42). No. 7 was a member of seven World Series

winners with New York (AL). Career span 1951–68.

Diego Maradona (b. 10-30-60): Argentine soccer player. Led Argentina to 1986 World Cup victory and to 1990 World Cup finals. Led Naples to Italian League titles (1987, '90), Italian Cup (1987) and to UEFA Cup title (1989). Throughout 1980s often acknowledged as best player in the world. Tested positive for cocaine and suspended by FIFA and Italian Soccer Federation for 15 months in March 1991. Failed drug test in 1994 World Cup and suspended before second round.

Pete Maravich (b. 6-22-47, d. 1-5-88): Basketball G. "Pistol Pete." Alltime NCAA leader in points scored (3,667), scoring average (44.2) and games scoring 50+ points (28, including then Division I record 69 points in 1970). Alltime single-season leader in points scored (1,381) and scoring average (44.5) in 1970. NCAA scoring leader and All-America three consecutive seasons 1968–70 with Louisiana State. Averaged 20+ points eight times as a pro, leading the league in scoring in 1977. All-Star five times. Averaged 24.2 points per game from 1970–79 with Atlanta, New Orleans/Utah and Boston.

Gino Marchetti (b. 1-2-27): Football DE. Played in Pro Bowl every year from 1955–65, except 1958 when he broke right ankle tackling Frank Gifford in Colts' 23–17 win over the Giants. Career span 1952–66, almost all with Baltimore. Inducted into Hall of Fame in 1972.

Rocky Marciano (b. 9-1-23, d. 8-31-69): Boxer. Heavyweight champion (1952–56). Career record 49–0 with 43 KOs from 1947 to 1956. Only heavyweight to retire as undefeated champion.

Juan Marichal (b. 10-24-37): Baseball RHP. 243 career wins, 2.89 career ERA. Won 20+ games six times; 250+ innings pitched eight times; 200+ strikeouts six times. Pitched no-hitter in 1963. Career span 1960–75, mostly with San Francisco. Elected to Hall of Fame in 1983.

Dan Marino (b. 9-15-61): Football QB. Set alltime single-season record for yards passing (5,084) and touchdown passes (48) in 1984. Passed for 4,000+ yards five other seasons. Career totals: 61,361 yards passing, 420 touchdown passes, first alltime in both categories. Career span 1983–00 with Miami.

Roger Maris (b. 9-10-34, d. 12-14-85): Baseball OF. Broke Babe Ruth's alltime single-season HR record with 61 in 1961. Won consecutive MVP awards and led league in RBI 1960–61. Career span 1957–68 with Kansas City, New York (AL), St. Louis.

Billy Martin (b. 5-16-28, d. 12-25-89): Baseball 2B–manager. Volatile manager was hired and fired by Minnesota, Detroit, Texas, New York (AL) (five times!) and Oakland from 1969–88. Career record: 1253–1013. Won World Series with New York as manager in 1977 and as player four times.

Pedro Martinez (b. 10-25-71): Baseball P. Three Cy Young Awards (1997, '99, '00). Became second pitcher to win Cy Young Awards in both leagues in 1999. Became first pitcher in 25 years to have more than 300 Ks and ERA below 2.00 in 1997. Led league in ERA and strikeouts three times each. Started 1999 All-Star Game and was named MVP after striking out first four batters. Career span 1992– with Los Angeles, Montreal and Boston.

Eddie Mathews (b. 10-13-31, d. 2-18-01): Baseball 3B. 512 career HR and 30+ HR nine consecutive seasons. League leader in HR two times, walks four times. Career span 1952–68, mostly with Milwaukee.

Christy Mathewson (b. 8-12-1880, d. 10-7-25): Baseball RHP. Third alltime most wins (373, tied with Grover Alexander) and shutouts (79); career ERA 2.13. Led league in wins five times; won 30+ games four times and 20+ games nine other times. Led league in ERA and strikeouts five times each. Pitched two no-hitters. Pitched three shutouts in 1905 World Series. Career span 1900–16 with New York.

Bob Mathias (b. 11-17-30): Track and field. At age 17, youngest to win gold medal in decathlon at 1948 Olympics. First decathlete to win gold medal at consecutive Olympics (1948, '52). Also won Sullivan Award in 1948.

Ollie Matson (b. 5-1-30): Football RB. Versatile runner totalled 12,884 combined yards rushing, receiving and kick returning. Scored 73 career touchdowns, including a 105-yard kickoff return on 10-14-56, the second longest ever. Career span 1952–66 with Chicago Cardinals, Los Angeles, Detroit, Philadelphia. Also won bronze medal in 400 meters at 1952 Olympics. Elected to Hall of Fame in 1972.

Roland Matthes (b. 11-17-50): German swimmer. Gold medalist in 100-meter and 200-meter backstroke at two consecutive Olympics (1968, '72). Set 16 world records from 1967–73.

Don Maynard (b. 1-25-37): Football WR. Retired in 1973 as the NFL's alltime leading receiver. In 15 seasons, 10 with the New York Jets, caught 633 passes for 11,834 yards and 88 TDs. Averaged 18.7 yards per catch for career. Elected to Hall of Fame in 1987.

Willie Mays (b. 5-6-31): Baseball OF. "Say Hey Kid." MVP in 1954, '65; Rookie of the Year in 1951. Retired with third-most career HR (660); hit 50+ HR two times, 30+ HR nine other times. Led league in HR four times. 100+ RBI 10 times; 100+ runs scored 12 consecutive seasons. 3,283 career hits. Led league in stolen bases four consecutive seasons. 30 HR and 30 steals in same season two times and first man in history to hit 300+ HR and steal 300+ bases. Won 11 consecutive Gold Gloves; set record for career putouts by an outfielder and league record for total chances. His catch in the 1954 World Series off the bat of Vic Wertz called the greatest ever. Career span 1951–73 with New York/San Francisco and New York (NL).

Bill Mazeroski (b. 9-5-36): Baseball 2B. Hit dramatic ninth-inning home run in Game 7 to win 1960 World Series, first of only two Series' to end on a home run. Won eight Gold Gloves. Led league in assists nine times, double plays eight times and putouts five times. Inducted to Hall of Fame in 2001. Career 1956–72 with Pittsburgh; 2,016 hits, 138 HR, .260 avg.

Joe McCarthy (b. 4-21-1887, d. 1-3-78): Baseball manager. Alltime highest winning percentage among managers for regular season (.615). First manager to win pennants in both leagues (Chicago (NL), 1929, New York (AL), 1932). From 1926–50 his teams won seven World Series and nine pennants.

Mark McCormack (b. 11-6-30, d. 5-16-03): Sports marketing agent. Founded International Management Group in 1962. Also author of best-selling business advice books.

Pat McCormick (b. 5-12-30): Diver. Gold medalist in platform and springboard at two consecutive Olympics (1952, '56). Also won Sullivan Award in 1956.

Willie McCovey (b. 1-10-38): Baseball 1B. Led NL in HRs three times (1963, '68, '69) and in RBI twice

(1968, '69). 521 career homers. .270 career average. Hit 18 grand slams. Rookie of Year 1959. NL MVP in 1969. Career span 1959–80 with San Francisco, San Diego and Oakland. Elected to Hall of Fame in 1986.

John McEnroe (b. 2-26-59): Tennis player. Third alltime men's most career tournament victories (77). Won four U.S. Open singles titles (consecutively 1979–81, '84) and three Wimbledon titles (1981, '83, '84). Also won eight Grand Slam doubles titles. Led U.S. to five Davis Cup victories (1978, '79, '81, '82, '92).

John McGraw (b. 4-7-1873, d. 2-25-34): Baseball manager. Second alltime in games (4,801) and wins (2,784). Guided New York (NL) to three World Series titles and 10 pennants from 1902–32.

Mark McGwire (b. 10-1-63): Baseball 1B. Broke Roger Maris's 37-year-old single-season HR record with 70 in 1998. Rookie of the Year in 1987, when he hit rookie record 49 home runs. Hit 30+ HR 12 times, 40+ HR six times, 50+ HR four straight years (1996–99). Member of 1984 U.S. Olympic baseball team. Had 583 career HRs and 1,414 RBIs with Oakland and St. Louis from 1986–01.

Denny McLain (b. 3-29-44): Baseball RHP. Last pitcher to win 30+ games in a season (Detroit, 1968); won 20+ games two other times. Won two consecutive Cy Young Awards (1968 '69). Led league in innings pitched two times. Served 2½-year jail term for 1985 conviction of extortion, racketeering and drug possession. Re-entered prison in 1997 on fraud conviction. Career span 1963–72, mostly with Detroit.

Mary T. Meagher (b. 10-27-64): Swimmer. "Madame Butterfly." Won three gold medals at 1984 Olympics (100-meter butterfly, 200-meter butterfly and 400-medley relay). In 1981 set world records in 100-meter butterfly (57.93) and 200-meter butterfly (2:05.96).

Rick Mears (b. 12-3-51): Auto racer. Has won Indy 500 four times (1979, '84, '88, '91) and been CART champion three times (1979, '81, '82). Named Indy 500 Rookie of the Year in 1978.

Eddy Merckx (b. 1945): Belgian cyclist. Won five Tours de France, including four in a row (1969–72).

Mark Messier (b. 1-18-61): Hockey C. Two-time Hart Trophy (MVP) winner. Won Stanley Cups with Edmonton (1984, '85, '87, '88, '90) and New York Rangers (1994). Third alltime in scoring (1,804 pts), fourth in assists (1,146) and seventh in goals scored (658). Career span 1979– with Edmonton, New York Rangers and Vancouver.

Cary Middlecoff (b. 1-6-21, d. 9-1-98): Golfer. Won 40 PGA tournaments, including 1955 Masters and U.S. Opens in 1949 and '56. Won 1956 Vardon Trophy. Also a dentist.

George Mikan (b. 6-18-24): Basketball C. The first dominant big man in professional basketball. Averaged 20+ points per game and named to All-Star team six consecutive seasons. Led league (NBA and NBL) in scoring six times. Played on five championship teams in six years (1949–54) with Minneapolis. Also played on 1945 NIT championship team with DePaul. All-America three times. Served as ABA Commissioner from 1968–69.

Stan Mikita (b. 5-20-40): Hockey C. Won MVP award two consecutive seasons (1967, '68). 926 career assists, 1,467 career points. Led league in assists four straight seasons and points four times. 541 career goals. All-Star six times. Career span 1958–80 with Chicago.

Del Miller (b. 7-5-13; d. 8-19-96): Harness racing driver. Raced in eight decades, beginning in 1929; the longest career of any athlete. Won The Hambletonian in 1950.

Marvin Miller (b. 4-14-17): Labor negotiator. Union chief of MLB Players Association from 1966–84. Led strikes in 1972 and '81. Negotiated five labor contracts that increased minimum salary and pension fund, allowed for agents and arbitration, and brought about the end of the reserve clause and the start of free agency.

Art Monk (b. 12-5-57): Football WR. Caught 940 passed for 12,721 yards and 68 TDs during his career. Set NFL single season record with 106 catches in 1984. Career span 1980–95 with Washington, New York Jets and Philadelphia.

Earl Monroe (b. 11-21-44): Basketball G. "The Pearl" played 13 seasons (1967–80) with Baltimore and New York. NBA Rookie of Year in 1968. Four-time All-Star. Member of 1973 NBA championship Knicks team. Averaged 18.8 points a game. Elected to Basketball Hall of Fame 1989.

Joe Montana (b. 6-11-56): Football QB. Second alltime highest-rated passer (92.3); 40,551 career passing yards and 273 TD passes. Won four Super Bowl championships (1981, '84, '88, '89) with San Francisco. Named Super Bowl MVP three times (1981, '84, '89). Voted to eight Pro Bowls. Led his teams to 31 fourth-quarter comebacks. Also led Notre Dame to national championship in 1977. Career span 1979–94 with San Francisco and Kansas City. Elected to Hall of Fame in 2000.

Carlos Monzon (b. 8-7-42, d. 1-8-95): Argentine boxer. Longest title reign of any middleweight champion (6 years, nine months) from 1970–77. Career record 89-3-9 with 61 KOs from 1963–77. Won 82 consecutive bouts from 1964–77. Defended title 14 times. Retired as champion.

Helen Wills Moody (b. 10-6-05, d. 1-1-98): Tennis player. Third alltime in women's Grand Slam singles titles (19). Her eight Wimbledon titles are second most alltime (1927–30, '32, '33, '35, '38). Won seven U.S. titles (1923–25, 1927–29, '31) and four French titles (1928–30, '32). Also won 12 Grand Slam doubles titles.

Archie Moore (b. 12-13-16 d. 12-9-98): Boxer. "The Mongoose." Longest title reign of any light heavyweight champion (9 years, one month) from 1952–62. Career record 199-26-8 with an alltime record 145 KOs from 1935–65. Retired at age 52.

Davey Moore (b. 11-1-33; d. 3-23-63): Boxer. Won featherweight title by KO of Kid Bassey in 13 on 3-18-59. Five successful defenses of title, before losing it on 3-21-63 to Sugar Ramos who KO'd him in 10. Died two days after fight of brain damage suffered during fight. Career record: 58-7-1, 30 KOs.

Noureddine Morceli (b. 2-20-70). Algerian track and field middle distance runner. Set world record for mile (3:44.39) in Rieti, Italy, on 9-5-93. Set world record for 1,500 (3:28.86) on 9-5-92. World champion at 1,500 in 1991, '93 and '95. Won gold medal at 1996 Olympics in Atlanta. Only man ever to rank first in the world at 1,500/mile four straight years (1990–93).

Joe Morgan (b. 9-19-43): Baseball 2B. Sparkplug for Cincinnati's Big Red Machine in the 1970s. Won two MVP awards (1975, '76). 10-time All-Star. Amassed 1,865 career walks, 689 stolen bases. 100+ walks and runs scored eight times each; 40+ stolen bases nine times. Won five Gold Gloves. Retired at second alltime in games played by 2nd baseman (2,527). Career span 1963–84 with Houston, Cincinnati, San Francisco, Philadelphia and Oakland.

Willie Mosconi (b. 6-27-13; d. 9-16-93): Pocket billiards player. Won world title a record 15 straight times between 1941–57. Once pocketed 526 balls without a miss.

Edwin Moses (b. 8-31-55): Track and field. Gold medalist in the 400-meter hurdles at two Olympics (1976, '84); bronze medalist at 1988 Olympics. Won 122 consecutive races from 1977–87. Set four world records in 400-meter hurdles. Won the Sullivan Award in 1983.

Marion Motley (b. 6-5-20 d. 6-27-99): Football FB. All-time AAFC leader in yards rushing (3,024). Led NFL in rushing once. Combined league totals: 4,712 yards rushing, 39 touchdowns. Played for four consecutive AAFC champions (1946–49) and one NFL champion (1950). Career span with Cleveland 1946–1953.

Shirley Muldowney (b. 6-19-40): Drag racer. First woman to win the Top Fuel championship, which she won three times (1977, '80, '82).

Anthony Munoz (b. 8-19-58): Football OT. Probably the greatest offensive tackle ever. Made Pro Bowl a record-tying 11 times. Career span 1980–92 with Cincinnati. Elected to Hall of Fame 1998.

Isaac Murphy (b. 4-16-1861, d. 2-12-1896): Horse racing jockey. Top jockey of his era, Murphy, who was black, won three Kentucky Derbys (aboard Buchanan in 1884, Riley in 1890 and Kingman in 1891).

Eddie Murray (b. 2-24-56): Baseball 1B. One of greatest switch-hitters in baseball history. 100+ RBI six seasons and 30+ HRs five seasons. Retired with 3,255 hits, 504 HRs and 1,917 RBI—eighth alltime and most ever by switch hitter. Career span 1977–97 with Baltimore, Los Angeles, New York (NL), Cleveland and Anaheim. Inducted into Baseball Hall of Fame in 2003.

Jim Murray (b. 12-29-19; d. 8-16-98): Sportswriter. Won Pulitzer Prize in 1990. Named Sportswriter of the Year 14 times. Columnist for *Los Angeles Times* 1961–98.

Ty Murray (b. 10-11-69): Rodeo cowboy. All-around world champion, 1989–94, and '98. Set single-season earnings record in 1990 ($213,771). Rookie of the Year in 1988. At 20, became youngest man ever to win national all-around title in 1989.

Stan Musial (b. 11-21-20): Baseball OF–1B. "Stan the Man." Had .331 career batting average and 475 career HR. MVP award winner (1943, '46, '48). 3,630 career hits; 725 career doubles. Won seven batting titles. Led league in hits six times, slugging average five times, doubles eight times. Had .300+ batting average 17 times, 200+ hits six times, 100+ RBI 10 times, and 100+ runs scored 11 times. 24-time All-Star. Career span 1941–63 with St. Louis.

John Naber (b. 1-20-56): Swimmer. Won four gold medals and one silver medal at 1976 Olympics. Sullivan Award winner in 1977.

Bronko Nagurski (b. 11-3-08, d. 1-7-90): Football FB. Punishing runner played on three NFL champions (1932, '33, '43) with Bears. 2,778 career yards with Chicago from 1930–37 and 1943.

James Naismith (b. 11-6-1861, d. 11-28-39): Invented basketball in 1891 while an instructor at YMCA Training School in Springfield, Mass. Refined the game while a professor at Kansas from 1898–37. Hall of Fame is named in his honor.

Joe Namath (b. 5-31-43): Football QB. "Broadway Joe." Super Bowl MVP in 1968 after he guaranteed victory for New York. 173 career touchdown passes. Led league in yards passing three times, including 4,007 yards in 1967. Player of the Year, 1968; Rookie of the Year, 1965. Career span 1965–77 with New York Jets and Los Angeles.

Ilie Nastase (b. 7-19-46): Romanian tennis player. "Nasty" for his unruly deportment on court. Beat Arthur Ashe to win 1972 U.S. Open title. Won 1973 French Open. Twice Wimbledon runner-up (to Stan Smith in 1972 and Bjorn Borg in 1976).

Martina Navratilova (b. 10-18-56): Tennis player. Fourth in women's Grand Slam singles titles (18—tied with Chris Evert). Won a record nine Wimbledon titles, including six consecutively (1978, '79, 1982–87, '90). Won four U.S. Open titles (1983, '84, '86, '87), three Australian Open titles (1981, '83, '85) and two French Open titles (1982, '84). Reached Grand Slam final 13 other times. Also won 40 Grand Slam doubles titles. Her total of 58 Grand Slam titles is second alltime to Margaret Court. Set mark for longest winning streak with 74 matches in 1984. Also won the doubles Grand Slam in 1984 with Pam Shriver. Won 109 consecutive doubles matches with Shriver from 1983–85.

Byron Nelson (b. 2-14-12): Golfer. Won 52 career tournaments, including 11 consecutively in 1945. Won the Masters (1937, '42) and PGA Championship (1940, '45) two times each and U.S. Open once (1939).

Ernie Nevers (b. 6-11-03, d. 5-3-76): Football FB. Set alltime pro single game record for points scored (40) and touchdowns (six) on 11-28-29. Career span 1926–31 with Duluth and Chicago. Also a pitcher with St. Louis (AL), surrendered two of Babe Ruth's 60 home runs in 1927. All-America at Stanford, earned 11 letters in four sports.

John Newcombe (b. 5-23-44): Australian tennis player. Won three Wimbledon singles titles (1967, '70, '71), two U.S. titles (1967, '73) and two Australian Open titles (1973, '75). Also won 17 Grand Slam doubles titles.

Pete Newell (b. 8-31-15): College basketball coach. Despite coaching only 14 seasons, 1947–60, was first coach to win NIT, NCAA and Olympic crowns. Led San Francisco to 1949 NIT title, Cal to 1959 NCAA title, and the 1960 U.S. Olympic basketball team that included Jerry Lucas, Oscar Robertson and Jerry West to gold medal. Overall collegiate coaching record of 234–123.

Jack Nicklaus (b. 1-21-40): Golfer. "The Golden Bear." Alltime leader in major championships (20). Second alltime in career wins (70). Won Masters six times, more than any golfer (1963, '65, '66, '72, '75, '86—at age 46, the oldest player to win event), PGA Championship five times (1963, '71, '73, '75, '80), U.S. Open four times (1962, '67, '72, '80), British Open three times (1966, '70, '78) and U.S. Amateur twice (1959, '61). PGA Player of the Year five times (1967, '72, '73, '75, '76). Also NCAA champion with Ohio State in 1961.

Ray Nitschke (b. 12-29-36 d. 3-8-98): Football LB. Defensive signal-caller for the great Green Bay teams of the '60s. Voted Packer MVP by teammates after 1967 season. MVP of the 1962 NFL title game. Career span 1958–72 with Green Bay.

Chuck Noll (b. 1-5-32): Football coach. Only coach to win four Super Bowls (1975, '76, '79, '80). Coaching career 1969–91 with Pittsburgh; 209-156-1.

Greg Norman (b. 2-10-55): Golfer. "The Shark" led PGA in winnings in 1986, '90, '95, '96. Won Vardon Trophy twice, 1989, '90. Won two British Opens (1986, '93) but is more famous for his heartbreaking losses. PGA Player of the Year 1996.

James D. Norris (b. 11-6-06, d. 2-25-66): Hockey executive. Owner of the Detroit Red Wings from 1933–43 and Chicago from 1946–66. Teams won four Stanley Cup championships (1936, '37, '43, '61). Defensive Player of the Year award named in his honor. Also a boxing promoter, operated International Boxing Club from 1949–58.

Paavo Nurmi (b. 6-13-1897, d. 10-2-73): Track and field. Finnish middle- and long-distance runner won a total of nine gold medals at three Olympics in 1920, '24, '28.

Matti Nykänen (b. 7-17-63): Finnish ski jumper. Three-time Olympic gold medalist. Won 90-meter jump (1984, '88) and 70-meter jump (1988). World champion on 90-meter jump in 1982. Won four World Cups (1983, '85, '86, '88).

Dan O'Brien (b. 7-18-66): Track and field decathlete. Won world decathlon title in 1991, '93, '95. Set world decathlon record of 8,891 in Talence, France, on 9-4/5-92, that stood for seven years. Heavily favored to win 1992 Olympic decathlon but missed making U.S. team when he no-heighted in pole vault at U.S. Olympic Trials. Redeemed himself with gold medal at 1996 Olympics in Atlanta.

Parry O'Brien (b. 1-28-32): Track and field. Shot-putter who revolutionized the event with his "glide" technique and won Olympic gold medals in 1952 and '56, silver in '60. Set 10 world records from 1953–59, topped by a put of 63' 4" in 1959. Sullivan Award winner in 1959.

Al Oerter (b. 8-19-36): Track and field. Gold medalist in discus at four consecutive Olympics (1956, '60, '64, '68), setting Olympic record each time. First to break the 200-foot barrier, throwing 200' 5" in 1962.

Sadaharu Oh (b. 5-20-40): Baseball 1B in Japanese league. 868 career HR in 22 seasons for the Tokyo Giants. Led league in HR 15 times, RBI 13 times, batting five times and runs 13 consecutive seasons. Awarded MVP nine times; won two consecutive Triple Crowns and nine Gold Gloves.

Hakeem Olajuwon (b. 1-21-63): Basketball C. From Nigeria. Alltime NBA career leader in blocked shots (3,830). Became the first player to be named NBA MVP, NBA Defensive Player of the Year and NBA Finals MVP in the same season as Houston won its first NBA championship in 1994. Led NCAA in FG %, rebounding and blocked shots in 1984 at Houston. Member of 1996 U.S. Olympic team. Career span 1984–2002 with Houston and Toronto; 21.8 ppg, 11.1 rpg.

Merlin Olsen (b. 9-15-40): Fooball DT. Part of Los Angeles's "Fearsome Foursome" defensive line. Named to Pro Bowl 14 straight times. Career span 1962–76, all with the Los Angeles Rams. Elected to Hall of Fame 1982.

Omaha (b. 1932, d. 1959): Thoroughbred race horse. Won Triple Crown in 1935. Trained by Sunny Jim Fitzsimmons.

Mark O'Meara (b. 1-13-57): Golfer. Has 16 career PGA Tour victories, including the 1998 Masters and British Open, at age 41. Tour rookie of the year in 1981; won 1979 U.S. Amateur.

Shaquille O'Neal (b. 3-6-72): Basketball C. "Shaq." Three-time NBA Finals MVP after leading the Lakers to back-to-back-to-back NBA Finals victories (2000–02). Was named MVP of the regular season, All-Star game, and playoffs 1999–2000. Led league in scoring in 1995 and 2000, and in field goal percentage in 1994, 1998–02. Top pick of Orlando in 1992 NBA draft. NBA Rookie of the Year 1993. Member of 1996 U.S. Olympic team. Led NCAA in blocked shots in 1992 as an All-American at Louisiana State. Career span 1992–2004 with Orlando and Los Angeles Lakers. Signed with Miami in 2004.

Bobby Orr (b. 3-20-48): Hockey D. Defensive Player of the Year more than any other player, eight consecutive seasons (1968–75). Won MVP award three consecutive seasons (1970–72), playoff MVP two times (1970, '72). Also Rookie of the Year in 1967. Led league in assists five times and scoring two times. Career span 1966–77 with Boston.

Mel Ott (b. 3-2-09, d. 11-21-58): Baseball OF. 511 career HR, 1,861 RBI, .304 batting average. League leader in HR and walks six times each. 100+ RBI nine times and 100+ walks ten times. Career span 1926–47 with New York (NL).

Jim Otto (b. 1-5-38): Football C. Number 00 started every game (210) in his 15-year career (1960–74) with Oakland. Inducted to Hall of Fame in 1980.

Kristin Otto (b. 1966): German swimmer. Won six gold medals for East Germany at 1988 Olympics.

Jesse Owens (b. 9-12-13, d. 3-31-80): Track and field. Gold medalist in four events (100 meters and 200 meters; 4x100-meter relay and long jump) at 1936 Olympics. At the 1935 Big 10 championship set or equaled six world record in 70 minutes, including 100 yards, long jump, 220-yard low hurdles and 220 dash.

Alan Page (b. 8-7-45): Football DT. First defensive player to be named NFL Player of the Year, in 1972. Played in 236 straight games, including four Super Bowls. Four-time NFC Defensive Player of Year. Career span 1967–81 with Minnesota and Chicago. Now sits on Minnesota Supreme Court.

Satchel Paige (b. 7-7-06, d. 6-8-82): Baseball RHP. Alltime greatest black pitcher, didn't pitch in major leagues until 1948 at age 42 with Cleveland. Oldest pitcher in major league history at age 59 with Kansas City in 1965. Pitched in the Negro leagues from 1926–50 with Birmingham Black Barons, Pittsburgh Crawfords and Kansas City Monarchs. Estimated career record is 2,000 wins, 250 shutouts, 30,000 strikeouts, 45 no-hitters.

Se Ri Pak (b. 9-28-77): South Korean golfer. 16 career LPGA Tour victories. 1998 LPGA Rookie of the Year for winning the first two majors she ever entered, the LPGA Championship and the U.S. Open.

Arnold Palmer (b. 9-10-29): Golfer. Fourth alltime in career wins (60). Won the Masters four times (1958, '60, '62, '64), British Open two consecutive years (1961, '62) and U.S. Open (1960) and U.S. Amateur (1954) once each. PGA Player of the Year two times (1960, '62). First golfer to surpass $1 million in career earnings. Also won Seniors Championship two times (1980, '84) and U.S. Senior Open once (1981).

Jim Palmer (b. 10-15-45): Baseball RHP. 268 career wins, 2.86 ERA. Won three Cy Young Awards (1973, '75, '76). Won 20+ games eight times. Led league in wins three times, innings pitched four times, ERA two times. Never allowed a grand slam HR. Pitched on six World Series teams with Baltimore, including shutout at age 20. Pitched no-hitter in 1969. Career span 1965–84 with Baltimore.

Bernie Parent (b. 4-3-45): Hockey G. Alltime leader for wins in a season (47 in 1974). Goaltender of the Year, playoff MVP, league leader in wins, goals against average and shutouts two consecutive

seasons (1974–75). Career record 270-197-121, including 55 shutouts. Career 2.55 goals against average. Tied record of four playoff shutouts in 1975. Played on two consecutive Stanley Cup champions (1974–75). Career span 1965–79 with Philadelphia.

Brad Park (b. 7-6-48): Hockey D. Seven-time All-Star. In 17 seasons with the New York Rangers, Boston and Detroit (1968–85) scored 213 goals and had 683 assists. Elected to Hall of Fame 1988.

Jim Parker (b. 4-3-34): Football T/G. All-NFL four times at guard, four times at tackle. First full-time offensive lineman inducted to Hall of Fame, in 1973. Career span 1957–67, all with Baltimore. Winner of 1956 Outland Trophy as Ohio State senior.

Joe Paterno (b. 12-21-26): College football coach. Finished 2004 season with 339 career wins. Has won two national championships (1982, '86) with Penn State since 1966. Career record 339-109-3, including five undefeated seasons. Has also won 20 bowl games.

Lester Patrick (b. 12-30-1883, d. 6-1-60): Hockey coach. Led New York Rangers to three Stanley Cup championships (1928, '33, '40). Originated the NHL's farm system and developed playoff format.

Floyd Patterson (b. 1-4-35): Boxer. Heavyweight champion two times (1956–59, 1960–62). First heavyweight to regain title, in rematch with Ingemar Johansson. Career record 55-8-1 with 40 KOs from 1952–72. Also middleweight gold medalist at 1952 Olympics.

Walter Payton (b. 7-25-54, d. 11-1-99): Football RB. "Sweetness." Retired as alltime leader in yards rushing (16,726). Gained 1,000+ yards rushing in 10 seasons. 110 career rushing touchdowns (110). 125 career touchdowns. Seven-time All-Pro. Player of the Year two times (1977, '85). Led league in rushing five consecutive seasons. Career span 1975–87 with Chicago.

Pelé (b. 10-23-40): Born Edson Arantes do Nascimento. Brazilian soccer player. Soccer's great ambassador. Played on three World Cup winners with Brazil (1958, '62, '70). Helped promote soccer in U.S. by playing with New York Cosmos from 1975–77. Scored 1,281 goals in 22 years.

Willie Pep (b. 9-19-22): Boxer. Featherweight champion two times (1942–48, 1949–50). Lost title to Sandy Saddler, won it back in rematch, then lost it to Saddler again. Master tactician: legend has it he once won a round without throwing a punch. Career record 230-11-1 with 65 KOs from 1940–66. Won 73 consecutive bouts from 1940–43. Defended title nine times.

Gil Perreault (b. 11-13-50): Hockey C. NHL Rookie of the Year in 1970–71. Five-time All-Star. Scored 512 goals and had 814 assists in career from 1970–87 with Buffalo. Elected to Hall of Fame in 1990.

Fred Perry (b. 5-18-09, d. 2-2-95): British tennis player. Won three consecutive Wimbledon singles titles (1934–36), the last British man to win the tournament. Also won three U.S. titles (1933, '34, '36), one French title (1935) and one Australian title (1934).

Gaylord Perry (b. 9-15-38): Baseball RHP. First pitcher to win Cy Young Award in both leagues (Cleveland 1972, San Diego 1978). 314 career wins, 3,534 strikeouts. 20+ wins five times; 200+ strikeouts eight times; 250+ innings pitched 12 times. Pitched no-hitter in 1968. Admitted to throwing a spitter. Career span 1962–83 with eight teams.

Bob Pettit (b. 12-12-32): Basketball F. First player in history to break 20,000-point barrier (20,880 career points scored). 26.4 career scoring average; 16.2 rebound avg. MVP in 1956 and 1959; Rookie of the Year in 1955. All-Star 10 consecutive seasons. Led league in scoring two times, rebounding once. Career span 1954–64 with St. Louis.

Richard Petty (b. 7-2-37): Auto racer. Alltime leader in NASCAR victories (200). Seven-time Daytona 500 winner (1964, '66, '71, '73, '74, '79, '81) and NASCAR season points champion (1964, '67, '71, '72, '74, '75, '79), the most of any driver in both categories. First stock car racer to reach $1 million in earnings. Son of Lee Petty, three-time NASCAR champion. Retired after 1992 season.

Laffit Pincay Jr. (b. 12-29-46): Jockey. Only jockey with more than 9,000 career victories. Among the top money-winners of all time, with more than $215,000,000 in career earnings. Won five Eclipse Awards as outstanding jockey. Rode one Kentucky Derby winner (Swale), and three Belmont winners (Conquistador Cielo, Cavaet, Swale).

Scottie Pippen (b. 9-25-65): Basketball F. Won six NBA titles with Chicago (1991–93, 1996–98). Three-time first-team All-NBA (1994–96). Named to NBA's first-team All-Defensive team six times. Named MVP of the 1994 NBA All-Star Game. Member of 1992 and '96 gold medal-winning U.S. Olympic basketball teams. Career span 1987–2004 with Chicago, Houston and Portland.

Jacques Plante (b. 1-17-29, d. 2-27-86): Hockey G. First goalie to wear a mask. Third alltime in wins (435) and second lowest modern goals against average (2.38). Goaltender of the Year seven times, more than any other goalie (consecutively 1955–59, '61, '68). Won MVP award in 1961. Led league in goals against average eight times, wins six times and shutouts four times. Was on six Stanley Cup champions with Montreal from 1952–62 and played for four other teams until retirement in 1972.

Gary Player (b. 11-1-35): South African golfer. Won the Masters (1961, '74, '78) and British Open (1959, '68, '74) three times each, PGA Championship two times (1962, '72) and U.S. Open (1965). Also won Seniors Championship three times (1986, '88, '90) and U.S. Senior Open two consecutive years (1987, '88).

Sam Pollock (b. 12-15-25): Hockey executive. As general manager of Montreal from 1964–78 won nine Stanley Cup championships (1965, '66, '68, '69, '71, '73, '76, '78).

Denis Potvin (b. 10-29-53): Hockey D. Seven-time All-Star during 15-season career (1973–88), all with New York Islanders. Won Calder Trophy for 1973–74 season. Won Norris Trophy three times. Captained Islanders to four Stanley Cup championships. Elected to Hall of Fame in 1991.

Mike Powell (b. 11-10-63): Track and field. Long jumper broke Bob Beamon's 23-year-old world record at 1991 World Championships in Tokyo with a jump of 29' 4½". Won silver in 1992 Olympics.

Steve Prefontaine (b. 1-25-51, d. 5-30-75): Track and field. Distance runner killed in car accident at age 24. Held every American record from 2,000 meters to 10,000 meters at the time of his death. At age 21, finished fourth in the 5,000 meters at the 1972 Olympics in Munich after leading with less than 600 meters to go.

Annemarie Moser-Pröll (b. 3-27-53): Austrian skier. Gold medalist in downhill at 1980 Olympics. World Cup overall champion six times, more than any other skier (1971–75, '79).

Alain Prost (b. 2-24-55): French auto racer. Second alltime in Formula 1 victories (51). Formula 1 champion four times (1985–86, '89, '93).

Jack Ramsay (b. 2-21-25): Basketball coach. Coached 11 seasons at St. Joseph's University, with 234–72 record. Overall record of 864–783 as NBA coach. Coach of NBA champion 1977 Portland Trail Blazers. Elected to Hall of Fame 1992.

Jean Ratelle (b. 10-3-40): Hockey C. In 21-season career (1960–81) with the New York Rangers and Boston, scored 491 goals and had 776 assists. Twice won Lady Byng Trophy. Elected to Hockey Hall of Fame in 1985.

Willis Reed (b. 6-25-42): Basketball C. Most noted for his dramatic return to the court on 5-8-70, in the seventh and deciding game of the 1970 NBA Finals against Los Angeles. Playoff MVP of both New York championship teams, in 1970 and '73. NBA Rookie of Year in 1965. NBA MVP in 1970. Played 10 seasons (1965–74), all with New York. Career average of 18.7 points a game. Elected to Hall of Fame in 1981.

Harold Henry (Pee Wee) Reese (b. 7-23-18 d. 8-14-99): Baseball SS. Played for six pennant-winning Brooklyn teams. Led NL in runs scored in 1949, with 132. Career span 1940–58 with Brooklyn; .269 avg., 2,170 hits, 1,338 runs, 232 SB. Elected to Hall of Fame in 1984.

Mary Lou Retton (b. 1-24-68): Gymnast. Won all-around gold with a perfect 10 on her final vault at the 1984 Olympics in Los Angeles. Also won one silver and two bronze medals at those Games.

Grantland Rice (b. 11-1-1880, d. 7-13-54): Sportswriter. Legendary figure during sport's Golden Age of the 1920s. Wrote "For when the one great Scorer comes/ To write against your name/ He writes not that you won or lost/ But how you played the game." Also named the 1924–25 Notre Dame backfield the "Four Horsemen."

Jerry Rice (b. 10-13-62): Football WR. Alltime leader in touchdowns, touchdown receptions, receptions , receiving yards and in consecutive games with a TD reception (13 in 1988). Player of the Year in 1987 and led league in scoring (138 points on 23 touchdowns). Super Bowl MVP in 1989 with record 215 receiving yards on 11 catches. Also set Super Bowl record with three touchdown receptions in 1990 and in 1995. Career span 1985– 2004 with San Francisco and Oakland.

Henri Richard (b. 2-29-36): Hockey C. "The Pocket Rocket." Won 11 Stanley Cup championships with Montreal. Four-time All-Star. Career span 1955–75.

Maurice Richard (b. 8-4-21, d. 5-27-00): Hockey RW. "The Rocket." First player to score 50 goals in a season, in 1945. Led league in goals five times. 544 career goals. MVP in 1947. All-Star eight times. Tied playoff record for most goals in a game (five on March 23, 1944). Won eight Stanley Cups with Montreal 1942–59.

Bob Richards (b. 2-2-26): Track and field. The only pole vaulter to win gold medal at two consecutive Olympics (1952, '56). Also won Sullivan Award in 1951.

Branch Rickey (b. 12-20-1881, d. 12-9-65): Baseball executive. Integrated major league baseball in 1947 by signing Jackie Robinson to a contract with the Brooklyn Dodgers. Conceived of minor league farm system in 1919 at St. Louis; instituted batting cage and sliding pit.

Pat Riley (b. 3-20-45): Basketball coach. Coached Los Angeles to four NBA championships (1981, '85, '87, '88). Coach of the Year three times (1990, '93, '97) for three different teams. Led New York to NBA Finals in 1994. Coached teams to 50+ wins 13 years in a row. Coaching career 1984–2003 with Los Angeles, New York and Miami.

Cal Ripken Jr. (b. 8-24-60): Baseball SS–3B. Broke Lou Gehrig's record for most consecutive games played (2,131) on 9-5-95; streak ended at 2,632 games on 9-20-98. Two-time AL MVP (1983, '91). Rookie of the Year in 1982. 19-time All-Star. Set record for consecutive errorless games by a shortstop (95 in 1990). Hit 20+ HRs in 10 consecutive seasons. Career span 1981–01 with Baltimore; .276 avg., 431 HR, 1,695 RBI, 3,184 hits.

Glenn (Fireball) Roberts (b. 1-20-31, d. 7-2-64): Auto racer. Won 34 NASCAR races. Died as a result of a fiery accident in the World 600 at Charlotte Motor Speedway in May 1964. At the time of his death Roberts had won more major races than any other driver in NASCAR history.

Oscar Robertson (b. 11-24-38): Basketball G. "The Big O." Only player in NBA history to average a triple-double for an entire season (1962). Rookie of the Year in 1961, MVP in 1964, and nine-time first-team All-NBA (1961–69). Led league in assists eight times. Averaged 30+ points six times in seven seasons. MVP of NBA All-Star three times (1961, '64, '69). Career span 1960–74 with Cincinnati and Milwaukee; 9,887 career assists; 26,710 points, 25.7 ppg. Also College Player of the Year, All-America and NCAA scoring leader three consecutive seasons from 1958–60 with Cincinnati. Third all-time NCAA highest scoring average (33.8).

Brooks Robinson (b. 5-18-37): Baseball 3B. Alltime leader in assists, putouts, double plays and fielding average among 3rd basemen. Won 16 consecutive Gold Gloves. Led league in fielding average a record 11 times. MVP in 1964—led league in RBI—and MVP in 1970 World Series. Career span 1955–77 with Baltimore; .267 avg, 2,848 hits, 1,357 RBI.

David Robinson (b. 8-6-65): Basketball C. "The Admiral." Three-time Olympian (1988, '92, '96), and 1995 NBA MVP. One of only two players to win an NBA rebounding title (1991), a blocked shots title (1992) and a scoring title (1994). Four-time first-team All-NBA. All-American at Navy where he led the NCAA in both rebounding (13.0) and blocked shots (5.91) in 1986. 1990 NBA Rookie of the Year. Career span 1989–2003 with San Antonio.

Eddie Robinson (b. 2-13-19): College football coach. Retired with alltime college record 408 career wins through 1941–97 at Division I-AA Grambling State.

Frank Robinson (b. 8-31-35): Baseball OF–manager. Only player to win MVP awards in both leagues (Cincinnati, 1961, Baltimore, 1966). Won Triple Crown and World Series MVP in 1966. Rookie of the Year in 1956. Fifth in career HR (586). Became first black manager in major leagues, with Cleveland in 1975. Career span 1956–76 with Cincinnati, Baltimore, Los Angeles, California and Cleveland; .294 avg., 1,812 RBI, 2,943 hits, 1,829 runs.

Jackie Robinson (b. 1-13-19, d. 10-24-72): Baseball 2B. Broke the color barrier as first black player in major leagues in 1947 with Brooklyn. 1947 Rookie of the Year; 1949 MVP with league-leading .342 batting average. Led league in stolen bases two times; stole home 19 times. Played on six pennant winners with Brooklyn, 1947–56; .311 avg., 137 HR, 947 runs, 197 SB. Elected to Hall of Fame in 1962. No. 42 retired by every team in the major leagues.

Larry Robinson (b. 6-2-51): Hockey D. Twice won Norris Trophy as NHL's top defenseman. Member of six Montreal teams that won Stanley Cup. Awarded Conn Smythe Trophy as MVP of 1978 Stanley Cup. Career span 1972–92, all but the last three with Montreal. Coached New Jersey to Stanley Cup in 2000.

Sugar Ray Robinson (b. 5-3-21, d. 4-12-89): Born Walker Smith Jr. Boxer. Called best pound-for-pound boxer ever. Welterweight champ (1946–51) and middleweight champ five times. Career record: 174-19-6 with 109 KOs from 1940–65. Won 91 consecutive bouts from 1943–51. Fifteen losses came after age 35.

Knute Rockne (b. 3-4-1888, d. 3-31-31): College football coach. Won national championship three times (1924, '29, '30). Alltime highest winning percentage (.881). Career record 105-12-5, including five undefeated seasons, with Notre Dame from 1918–30.

Bill Rodgers (b. 12-23-47): Track and field. Won the Boston and New York City marathons four times each between 1975–80.

Dennis Rodman (b. 5-13-61): Basketball F. Won seven consecutive NBA rebounding titles (1992–98). Won two NBA titles with Detroit (1989, '90) and three with Chicago (1996–98). NBA Defensive Player of the Year (1990, '91). Career span 1986–00, mostly with Detroit and Chicago; 7.3 ppg, 13.1 rpg.

Chi Chi Rodriguez (b. 10-23-35): Golfer. Led senior money list for 1987 ($509,145). Won eight events during PGA career that began in 1960.

Art Rooney (b. 1-27-01; d. 8-25-88): Owner of Pittsburgh Steelers. Bought team in 1933 and ran it until his death in 1988. Elected to Hall of Fame in 1964.

Murray Rose (b. 1-6-39) Australian swimmer. Won three gold medals (including 400- and 1,500-meter freestyle) at 1956 Olympics. Also won one gold, one silver and one bronze medal at 1960 Olympics.

Pete Rose (b. 4-14-41): Baseball OF-IF. "Charlie Hustle." Baseball's alltime hits leader (4,256), who was banned from the game for life in 1989 for his gambling activities and, thus, is ineligible for the Hall of Fame. Had 44-game hitting streak in 1978. 1963 Rookie of the Year; 1973 MVP; 1975 World Series MVP. Won three batting titles, and led the league in hits seven times, runs scored four times and doubles five times. Alltime leader in games played (3,562) and at bats (14,053); second in doubles (746); fifth in runs scored (2,165). Career span 1963–86 with Cincinnati, Philadelphia and Montreal; .303 avg., 160 HR, 1,314 RBI. Manager of Cincinnati from 1984–89. Served five-month jail term for tax evasion in 1990.

Ken Rosewall (b. 11-2-34): Australian tennis player. Won Grand Slam singles titles at ages 18 and 35. Won four Australian titles (1953, '55, '71, '72), two French titles (1953, '68) and two U.S. titles (1956, '70). Reached four Wimbledon finals, but title eluded him.

Art Ross (b. 1-13-1886, d. 8-5-64): Hockey D–coach. Improved design of puck and goal net. Manager-coach of Boston, 1924–45, won Stanley Cup, 1938–39. The Art Ross Trophy is awarded to the NHL scoring champion.

Donald Ross (b. 1873, d. 4-26-48): Scottish-born golf course architect. Trained at St. Andrews under Old Tom Morris. Designed over 500 courses, including Pinehurst No. 2 course and Oakland Hills.

Patrick Roy (b. 10-5-65): Hockey G. Retired as alltime leader in career wins for a goalie (551). Won Vezina Trophy three times. Won Conn Smythe Trophy three times (1986, '93, '01). Career span 1984–2003 with Montreal and Colorado.

Pete Rozelle (b. 3-1-26, d. 12-6-96): Football executive. Fourth NFL commissioner, served from 1960–89. During his term, league expanded from 12 to 28 teams. Created Super Bowl in 1966 and negotiated merger with AFL. Devised plan for revenue sharing of lucrative TV monies among owners. Presided during players' strikes of 1982 and '87.

Wilma Rudolph (b. 6-23-40, d. 11-12-94): Track and field. Gold medalist in three events (100 , 200 and 4 x100-meter relay) at 1960 Olympics. Also won Sullivan Award in 1961.

Adolph Rupp (b. 9-2-01, d. 12-10-77): College basketball coach. Second alltime in NCAA wins (876) and winning percentage (.822). Won four NCAA championships (1948, '49, '51, '58). Career span 1930–72 with Kentucky.

Amos Rusie (b. 5-3-1871, d. 12-6-42): Baseball RHP. Fastball was so intimidating that in 1893 the pitching mound was moved back 5' 6" to its present distance of 60' 6". Led league in strikeouts and walks five times each. Career record 246–174, 3.07 ERA with New York (NL) from 1889–1901.

Bill Russell (b. 2-12-34): Basketball C. Won MVP award five times (1958, 1961–63, '65). Played on 11 championship teams, eight consecutively, with Boston (1957, 1959–66, '68, '69). Player-coach 1968–69 (league's first black coach). Second alltime in career rebounds (21,620) and rebounding average (22.5); second-highest single-game rebounding total (51 in 1960). Led league in rebounding four times. Career span 1956–69 with Boston; 15.1 ppg, 4.3 apg. Also played on two NCAA championship teams with San Francisco in 1955–56; tournament MVP in 1955. Member of gold medal-winning 1956 Olympic team.

Babe Ruth (b. 2-6-1895, d. 8-16-48): Born George Herman Ruth. Baseball P–OF. "The Bambino," "The Sultan of Swat." Most dominant player in history. Alltime leader in slugging average (.690), HR frequency (8.5 HR every 100 at bats); Hit 714 career HR, 2,211 RBI, and 2,056 walks. Hit 54 HR in 1920, more than any other team in the American League. 1923 MVP. 60 HR in 1927, a record that stood for 34 years. Second alltime in World Series HR (15), including his "called shot" off Charlie Root in 1932. Began career as a pitcher: 94 career wins and 2.28 ERA. Won 20+ games two times; ERA leader in 1916. Played on 10 pennant winners, seven World Series winners (three with Boston, four with New York (AL)). Sold to Yankees in 1920 (Boston hasn't won World Series since). Career span 1914–35 with Boston, New York (AL) and Boston (NL); .342 avg., 2,873 hits.

Nolan Ryan (b. 1-31-47): Baseball RHP. Pitched seven no-hitters. Alltime leader in career strikeouts (5,714) and walks (2,795). League leader in strikeouts

11 times, shutouts three times, ERA two times. 300+ strikeouts six times, including season record of 383 in 1973. Career span 1966–93 with New York (NL), California, Houston and Texas; 324–292, 3.19 ERA. Elected to Hall of Fame 1999.

Jim Ryun (b. 4-29-47): Track and field. Youngest ever to run sub-four-minute mile (3:59.0 at 17 years, 37 days). Set two world records in mile (3:51.3 in 1966 and 3:51.1 in 1967) and one in 1,500 (3:33.1 in 1967). Plagued by bad luck at Olympics: won silver medal in 1968 1,500 meters despite mononucleosis; was bumped and fell in 1972. Won Sullivan Award in 1967.

Toni Sailer (b. 11-17-35): Austrian skier. Won gold medals in 1956 Olympics in slalom, giant slalom and downhill, the first skier to accomplish the feat.

Juan Antonio Samaranch (b. 7-17-20): Amateur sports executive. From 1980–01, Spaniard served as president of International Olympic Committee.

Pete Sampras (b. 8-12-71): Tennis player. Alltime leader in men's Grand Slam singles titles (14). First player in ATP rankings history to hold No. 1 ranking for six consecutive years. Won 64 tournament titles.

Joan Benoit Samuelson (b. 5-16-57): Track and field. Gold medalist in first ever women's Olympic marathon (1984). Won Boston Marathon two times (1979, '83). Sullivan Award winner in 1985.

Barry Sanders (b. 7-16-68): Football RB. Third player in NFL history to rush for over 2,000 yards (2,053 in 1997). Led league in rushing four times (1990, '94, '96, '97). Rushed for 1,000+ yards in each of his 10 pro seasons. Retired abruptly in 1999, ranked second alltime in career rushing yards (15,269). NCAA single-season leader in yards rushing (2,628 in 1988), when he won the Heisman Trophy at Oklahoma State.

Gene Sarazen (b. 2-27-02 d. 5-13-99): Golfer. Won PGA Championship three times (1922, '23, '33), U.S. Open two times (1922, '32), British Open once (1932) and the Masters once (1935). His win at the Masters included golf's most famous shot, a double eagle on the 15th hole of the final round. Won 38 career tournaments. Also won Seniors Championship two times (1954, '58). Pioneered the sand wedge in 1930.

Glen Sather (b. 9-2-43): Hockey coach and general manager. 464 regular season wins. Led Edmonton to four Stanley Cup championships (1984, '85, '87, '88) from 1979–89 and 1993–94. Also played for six teams from 1966–76.

Terry Sawchuk (b. 12-28-29, d. 5-31-70): Hockey G. Alltime leader in shutouts (103); second in wins (447). Career 2.52 goals against average. Goaltender of the Year four times (1951–52, '54, '64). Led league in wins and shutouts three times and goals against average two times. Rookie of the Year in 1950. Tied record of four playoff shutouts in 1952. Played on four Stanley Cup champions with Detroit and Toronto from 1949–69.

Gale Sayers (b. 5-30-43): Football RB. Alltime leader in kickoff return average (30.6). Scored 56 career touchdowns, including a rookie record 22 in 1965. Tied record with six touchdowns in one game on 12-12-65. Led league in rushing and gained 1,000+ yards rushing two times. Rookie of the Year in 1965. Career span 1965–71 with Chicago cut short due to knee injury. Also All-America two times with Kansas.

Dolph Schayes (b. 5-19-28): Basketball player. Retired as NBA's all-time leading scorer (19,249 pts). First-team All-NBA six times. Over stretch of 10 years played in 706 consecutive games. Career span 1948–64 with Syracuse and Philadelphia; 18.2 ppg. College star at NYU. Elected to Hall of Fame 1972.

Bo Schembechler (b. 4-1-29): Football coach. In 21 seasons at Michigan from 1969–89, had a 194-48-5 record. Overall college coaching record 234-65-8.

Mike Schmidt (b. 9-27-49): Baseball 3B. Won three MVP awards (1980, '81, '86). 548 career home runs. Led league in HR eight times, slugging average five times, and RBI and walks four times each. Won 10 Gold Gloves. Career span 1972–89 with Philadelphia; .267 avg., 1,506 runs, 1,595 RBI. Elected to the Hall of Fame in 1995.

Don Schollander (b. 4-30-46): Swimmer. Won four gold medals (including 100- and 400-meter freestyle) at 1964 Olympics; won one gold and one silver medal at 1968 Olympics. Also won Sullivan Award in 1964.

Dick Schultz (b. 9-5-29): Amateur sports executive. Second executive director of the NCAA, served from 1987–93. Also served as athletic director at Cornell (1976–81) and Virginia (1981–87).

Seattle Slew (b. 1974; d. 5-7-02): Thoroughbred race horse. Horse of the Year for 1977, when he won the Triple Crown, winning the Kentucky Derby by 1¾ lengths; the Preakness by 1½; and the Belmont by 4. In three-year career from 1976–78, won 14 of 17 starts.

Tom Seaver (b. 11-17-44): Baseball RHP. "Tom Terrific." 311 career wins, 2.86 ERA. Cy Young Award winner three times (1969, '73, '75) and Rookie of the Year 1967. Struck out 3,640 batters in his career. Led league in strikeouts five times, winning percentage four times and wins and ERA three times each. Won 20+ games five times; 200+ strikeouts 10 times. Struck out 19 batters in one game in 1970, including the final 10 in succession. Pitched no-hitter in 1978. Career span 1967–86 with New York (NL), Cincinnati, Chicago (AL), Boston.

Secretariat (b. 3-30-70, d. 10-4-89): Thoroughbred race horse. Triple Crown winner in 1973 with jockey Ron Turcotte aboard. Ran fastest Kentucky Derby and Belmont Stakes ever. Trained by Lucien Laurin.

Katja Seizinger (b. 5-10-72): German skier. Won downhill gold medals in 1994 at Lillehammer and '98 at Nagano. Won Giant Slalom bronze medal at Nagano. 1998 World Cup champion in downhill, Super G and overall. 32 World Cup victories in downhill and Super G.

Monica Seles (b. 12-2-73): Tennis player. Won three consecutive French Open singles titles (1990–92), four Australian Open titles (1991–93, '96) and two U.S. Open titles (1991, '92). Seles's 1993 season ended on 4-30 when she was stabbed in the back by a deranged fan while seated during a changeover in a tournament in Hamburg, Germany; also missed 1994 season. Returned to tennis in 1995, reached U.S. Open final.

Bill Sharman (b. 5-25-26): Basketball G. First team All-Star four straight years 1956–59. Led NBA in free throw percentage every year from 1953–57, and in 1959 and '61. All-Star Game MVP in 1955. Career span 1950–61 with Washington and Boston; 17.8 ppg, 88.3 FT%. NBA Coach of the Year in 1972, when his Lakers won NBA title. Elected to Hall of Fame in 1974.

Wilbur Shaw (b. 10-31-02, d. 10-30-54): Auto racer. Won Indy 500 three times in four years (1937, '39, '40). AAA champion two times (1937, '39). Also pioneered the use of the crash helmet after suffering skull fracture in 1923 crash.

Patty Sheehan (b. 10-27-56): Golfer. Won back-to-back LPGA championships (1983, '84). Won 1992 and '94 U.S. Women's Opens, '93 LPGA title, '96 Nabisco. 1983 LPGA Player of Year. Vare Trophy winner in 1984. Qualified for Hall of Fame in 1993.

Fred Shero (b. 10-23-25, d. 11-24-90): Hockey coach. Fourth alltime highest winning percentage (.612). Led Philadelphia to two Stanley Cup championships (1974, '75). Former New York Rangers defender (1947–50) coached Philadelphia and New York from 1971–81; 390-225-119.

Bill Shoemaker (b. 8-19-31 d. 10-12-03): Horse racing jockey. Second alltime in wins (8,833). Rode Belmont Stakes winner five times (1957, '59, '62, '67, '75), Kentucky Derby winner four times (1955, '59, '65, '86—at age 54, the oldest jockey to win Derby) and Preakness Stakes winner two times (1963, '67). Also won Eclipse Award in 1981.

Eddie Shore (b. 11-25-02, d. 3-16-85): Hockey D. Won MVP award four times (1933, '35, '36, '38). All-Star seven times. Played on two Stanley Cup champions with Boston from 1926–40.

Frank Shorter (b. 10-31-47): Track and field. Gold medalist in marathon at 1972 Olympics, the first American to win the event since 1908. Olympic silver medalist in 1976 marathon. Sullivan Award winner in 1972.

Jim Shoulders (b. 5-13-28): Rodeo. 16 career titles. All-Around champion five times (1949, 1956–59).

Don Shula (b. 1-4-30): Football coach. Retired as alltime NFL leader in wins (347). Won two consecutive Super Bowl championships (1972, '73) with Miami, including NFL's only undefeated season in 1972. Also reached Super Bowl four other times. Career span 1963–95 with Baltimore and Miami.

Al Simmons (b. 5-22-02, d. 5-26-56): Baseball OF. "Bucketfoot Al" for hitting stance. Named AL MVP for 1929, when he led league with 157 RBI. Led league in batting average in 1930 (.381) and '31 (.390). Career span 1924–44 with several teams, including Philadelphia (AL); .334 avg., 307 HR. Elected to Hall of Fame in 1953.

O.J. Simpson (b. 7-9-47): Born Orenthal James. Football RB. "Juice." First man to be 2,000 yards rushing in one season (2,003 in 1973). 11,236 career yards rushing. Led league in rushing four times. Gained 1,000+ yards rushing five consecutive seasons. Player of the Year three times (1972, '73, '75). Gained 200+ yards rushing in a game a record six times. Scored 61 career touchdowns, including 23 in 1975. Also won Heisman Trophy with USC in 1968.

Sir Barton (b. 1916, d. 1937): Thoroughbred. In 1919, before they were linked as the Triple Crown, became first horse to win the Kentucky Derby, the Preakness and the Belmont. Won eight of 13 starts as 3-year-old.

George Sisler (b. 3-24-1893, d. 3-26-73): Baseball 1B. Set record in 1920 with 257 hits in one season. League leader in hits two times, banged out 200+ hits six times. Won two batting titles, including the 1922 crown with a .420 average; averaged .400+ two times and .300+ 11 other times. Career span 1915–30 with St. Louis (NL); .340 avg. and 2,812 hits.

Mary Decker Slaney (b. 8-4-58): Track and field. American record holder in five events ranging from 800 to 3,000 meters. Won 1,500 and 3,000 meters at World Championships in 1983. Lost chance for medal at 1984 Olympics when she tripped and fell after contact with Zola Budd. Won Sullivan Award in 1982. Competed in 1996 Olympics at age 37.

Bruce Smith (b. 6-18-63): Football DE. Alltime NFL leader in sacks (200). Played in four consecutive Super Bowls with Buffalo (1991–94), all losses. Career span 1985– with Buffalo and Washington.

Dean Smith (b. 2-28-31): College basketball coach. Alltime leader in wins (879); seventh alltime highest winning percentage (.776). Alltime most NCAA tournament appearances (27), reached Final Four 11 times. Won NCAA championship in 1982 and '93. Coached 1976 Olympic team to gold medal. Career span 1962–97 with North Carolina. 1997 *Sports Illustrated* Sportsman of the Year.

Emmitt Smith (b. 5-15-69): Football RB. Led NFL in rushing four times (1991, '92 , '93, '95). Set NFL record with 25 TDs in 1995. Named MVP of Super Bowl XXVIII, when he ran for 132 yards in a 30–13 Dallas victory over Buffalo. Career span 1990–2002 with Dallas, 2003–04 Arizona; in 2002, passed Walter Payton as the NFL's alltime leading rusher.

Ozzie Smith (b. 12-26-54): Baseball SS. "The Wizard of Oz." May be the best defensive shortstop in history. Holds alltime record for most assists in a season among shortstops (621 in 1980). Career double-play and assist leader among shortstops. 14-time All-Star. Won 13 consecutive Gold Gloves. Career span 1978–96 with San Diego and St. Louis; .262 avg., 2,460 hits, 580 SB.

Red Smith (b. 9-25-05, d. 1-15-82): Sportswriter. Won Pulitzer Prize in 1976. After Grantland Rice, the most widely syndicated sports columnist. His literary essays appeared in the *New York Herald Tribune* from 1945–71 and the *New York Times* from 1971–82.

Stan Smith (b. 12-14-46): Tennis. Won 39 tournaments in career, including 1972 Wimbledon in five sets over Ilie Nastase. Won 1971 U.S. Open over Jan Kodes and amateur version of U.S. Open in 1969. 1970 won inaugural Grand Prix Masters. Inducted to Tennis Hall of Fame in 1987.

Tommie Smith (b. 6-5-44): Track and field. Won 1968 Olympic 200 meters in world record of 19.83, then was expelled from Olympic Village, along with bronze medalist John Carlos, for raising black-gloved fist and bowing head during playing of national anthem to protest racism in U.S.

Conn Smythe (b. 2-1-1895, d. 11-18-80): Hockey executive. As general manager with Toronto from 1929–61 won seven Stanley Cup championships (1932, '42, '45, '47–49, '51). Award for playoff MVP named in his honor.

Sam Snead (b. 5-27-12, 5-23-02): Golfer. Alltime leader in career wins (81). Won the Masters (1949, '52, '54) and PGA Championship (1942, '49, '51) three times each and British Open (1946). Runner-up at U.S. Open four times, but title eluded him. PGA Player of the Year in 1949. Won Seniors Championship six times, more than any golfer (1964, '65, '67, '70, '72, '73).

Peter Snell (b. 12-17-38): Track and field. New Zealand runner was gold medalist in 800 meters at two consecutive Olympics (1960 and 1964). Also gold medalist in 1,500 meters at 1964 Olympics. Twice broke world mile record; broke world 800 record once.

Duke Snider (b. 9-19-26): Baseball OF. Holds NL record with 11 home runs and 26 RBI in World Series play. Played on six pennant winners with Brooklyn. Hit 40+ HR five consecutive seasons and 100+ RBI six times. Career span 1947–64 with Brooklyn/LA, New York (NL) and San Francisco; .295 average, 407 HR and 1,333 RBI.

Sammy Sosa (b. 11-12-68): Baseball RF. Followed Mark McGwire in eclipsing Roger Maris's single-season HR mark in 1998. Lost HR race to McGwire that season but won MVP with .308 average, 66 HR, 134 runs, 158 RBI. In 2001, became first man to hit 60+ home runs in three seasons. Career span 1989– with Texas, Chicago (AL) and Chicago (NL).

Javier Sotomayor (b. 10-13-67): Track and field. Cuban high jumper broke the 8-foot barrier with world record jump of 8' 0" in 1989. Set record of 8' ½" in 7-27-93 in Salamanca, Spain.

Warren Spahn (b. 4-23-21): Baseball LHP. Alltime leader in wins by a lefthander (363); 20+ wins 13 times. League leader in wins eight times, complete games nine times, strikeouts four consecutive seasons, innings pitched four times and ERA three times. 1957 Cy Young award. 63 career shutouts. Pitched two no-hitters after age 39. Career span 1942–65, all but last year with Boston/Milwaukee Braves.

Tris Speaker (b. 4-4-1888, d. 12-8-58): Baseball OF. Alltime leader in doubles (792), fifth in hits (3,514) and fifth in batting average (.345). One batting title (.386 in 1916), but .375+ average six times. League leader in doubles eight times, hits two times and HR and RBI one time each. 200+ hits four times, 40+ doubles 10 times and 100+ runs scored seven times. MVP in 1912. Career span 1907–28, mostly with Boston (AL) and Cleveland.

Michael Spinks (b. 7-13-56): Boxer. Defeated Larry Holmes for the heavyweight championship of the world on 9-22-85. Lost title to Mike Tyson in 91 seconds on 6-27-88. Won world light heavyweight title on 7-18-81 and defended it nine times before moving up to heavyweight division. 1976 Olympic middleweight champion.

Mark Spitz (b. 2-10-50): Swimmer. Won a record seven gold medals (two in freestyle, two in butterfly, three in relays) at 1972 Olympics, setting world record in each event. Also won two gold medals, one silver and one bronze medal at 1968 Olympics. Sullivan Award winner in 1971.

Amos Alonzo Stagg (b. 8-16-1862, d. 3-17-65): College football coach. 314 career wins. Won national title with Chicago in 1905. Coach of the Year with Pacific in 1943 at age 81. Five undefeated seasons. Career span 1892–46. Only person elected to both college football and basketball Halls of Fame. Played in the first basketball game in 1891.

Willie Stargell (b. 3-6-40, d. 4-9-01): Baseball OF–1B. "Pops" achieved a 1979 MVP triple crown, winning NL regular season, playoff and World Series MVP awards. Led NL in homers in 1971 and '73. Career span 1962–82 with Pittsburgh; .282 avg., 475 HR, 1,540 RBI. Elected to Hall of Fame in 1988.

Bart Starr (b. 1-9-34): Football QB. Played on three NFL champions (1961, '62, '65) and first two Super Bowl champions (1966, '67) with Green Bay. Also named MVP of first two Super Bowls. Player of the Year in 1966. Led league in passing three times. Career span 1956–71 with Green Bay; 24,718 passing yards, 152 TDs. Also coached Green Bay to 53-77-3 record from 1975–83.

Roger Staubach (b. 2-5-42): Football QB. Led Dallas to six NFC Championships, four Super Bowls and two Super Bowl titles (1971, '77). Player of the Year and Super Bowl MVP in 1971. Also led league in passing four times. Won Heisman Trophy with Navy as a junior in 1963. Served four-year military obligation before turning pro. Career span 1969–79 with Dallas; 22,700 passing yards, 153 TDs passing.

Jan Stenerud (b. 11-26-42): Football K. Scored 1,699 career NFL points. Converted 373 field goals in 558 attempts. Career span 1967–85 with Kansas City, Green Bay and Minnesota. First pure kicker inducted to Hall of Fame, 1991.

Casey Stengel (b. 7-30-1890, d. 9-29-75): Baseball manager. "The Ol' Perfesser." Managed New York (AL) to 10 pennants and seven World Series titles (five consecutively) in 12 years from 1949–60. Alltime leader in World Series games (63), wins (37) and losses (26). Platoon system was his trademark strategy, Stengelese his trademark language ("You could look it up."). Managed New York (NL) from 1962–65. Jersey number (37) retired by Yankees and Mets. Career mark: 1,905-1,842 (.508).

Ingemar Stenmark (b. 3-18-56): Swedish skier. Gold medalist in slalom and giant slalom at 1980 Olympics. World Cup overall champion three consecutive years (1976–78).

Woody Stephens (b. 9-1-13 d. 8-22-98): Horse racing trainer. Trained two Kentucky Derby winners (Cannonade, who won the 100th Derby in 1974 and Swale in 1984) and five straight Belmont winners from 1982–86, starting with 1982 Horse of the Year Conquistador Cielo.

David Stern (b. 9-22-42): Fourth NBA commissioner. Has served since 1984. Oversaw unprecedented growth of league. Owners rewarded him with five-year, $40-million contract extension in 1996.

Jackie Stewart (b. 6-11-39): Scottish auto racer. Fifth alltime in Formula 1 victories (27); Formula 1 champion three times (1969, '71, '73). Also Indy 500 Rookie of the Year in 1966. Retired in 1973.

Payne Stewart (b. 1-3-57, d. 10-25-99): Golfer. Two-time U.S. Open champion (1991, '99), also won 1989 PGA Championship. Killed in plane crash.

John Stockton (b. 3-26-62): Basketball G. Alltime leader in assists (15,177) and steals (3,128). Set single-season assist record (1,164) in 1990–91. Led NBA in assists a record nine consecutive seasons (1988–96). 10-time All-Star, consecutively 1989–97, 2000. Co-MVP (with Karl Malone) of 1993 All-Star Game. Member of 1992 and '96 Olympic teams. Career span 1984–2003 with Utah; 13.2 ppg, 10.7 rpg.

Picabo Street (b. 4-3-71): Skier. Won silver medal in downhill at 1994 Olympics in Lillehammer and gold in Super G at '98 Games in Nagano. World Cup downhill champion in 1995 and '96. Nine career World Cup victories.

John L. Sullivan (b. 10-15-1858, d. 2-2-18): Boxer. Last bareknuckle champion. Heavyweight title holder (1882–92), lost to Jim Corbett. Career record 38-1-3 with 33 KOs from 1878–92.

Paul Tagliabue (b. 11-24-40): Football executive. Fifth NFL commissioner, has served since 1989.

Anatoli Tarasov (b. 1918, d. 6-23-95): Hockey coach. Orchestrated Soviet Union's emergence as a hockey power. Won nine consecutive world amateur championships (1963–71) and three Olympic gold medals in 1964, '68, '72.

Fran Tarkenton (b. 2-3-40): Football QB. Hall of Famer retired with 342 touchdown passes, 47,003 yards passing, 6,467 pass attempts and 3,686 pass completions. Player of the Year in 1975. Career span 1961–78 with Minnesota, New York Giants.

Lawrence Taylor (b. 2-4-59): Football LB. Revolutionized the linebacker position. Retired as the alltime leader in sacks. Named to Pro Bowl a record 10 consecutive seasons. Player of the Year in 1986. Played on two Super Bowl champions with New York Giants (1986, '90). Career span 1981–93 with New York. Elected to Hall of Fame 1999.

Isiah Thomas (b. 4-30-61): Basketball G. Point guard for Detroit team that won NBA title in 1989 and '90. All-NBA First Team 1984–86. NBA All-Star Game MVP in 1984 and '86. Led NBA in assists (13.9) in 1984–85; finished career with 9,061 assists. Career span 1981–94 with Detroit; 19.2 ppg, 9.3 apg. GM of Toronto Raptors 1995–97. Coached Indiana Pacers 2000–03. Member of Indiana University team that won 1981 NCAA title.

Thurman Thomas (b. 5-15-66): Football RB. Rushed for 1,000+ yards eight years in a row (1989–96). Led AFC in rushing in 1990 and 1991. Career span 1988–01 with Buffalo and Miami; 12,074 yards, 88 TDs.

Daley Thompson (b. 7-30-58): Track and field. British decathlete was gold medalist at two consecutive Olympics in 1980 and '84. At 1984 Olympics set world record (8,847 points) that lasted eight years.

John Thompson (b. 9-2-41): College basketball coach. Former Boston Celtic coached at Georgetown (1973–99), where he mentored Patrick Ewing, Alonzo Mourning and Dikembe Mutombo. Won NCAA title in 1984, runner-up in '82 and '85. Career record: 596–239.

Bobby Thomson (b. 10-25-23): Baseball OF. Three-time All-Star who hit dramatic "shot heard 'round the world" off of Ralph Branca to win NL pennant for New York (NL) in 1951. The Giants had come from 13½ games behind to tie Brooklyn and force a three-game playoff. Career span 1946–60 with New York (NL), Milwaukee, Chicago (NL), Boston and Baltimore; .270, 264 HR, 1,026 RBI.

Ian Thorpe (b. 10-13-82): Australian swimmer. "Thorpedo." As a 17-year-old, won gold medal in the 400-meter freestyle and silver in the 200 free at 2000 Olympics in Sydney. World record holder in both events heading into 2004 games in Athens. Also won gold medals at Sydney in the 400- and 800-meter freestyle relays.

Jim Thorpe (b. 5-28-1888, d. 3-28-53): Sportsman. Gold medalist in decathlon and pentathlon at 1912 Olympics. Played pro baseball with New York (NL) and Cincinnati 1913–19, and pro football with several teams 1919–26. Stripped of gold medals when it was discovered he had played pro baseball, and they were restored only after his death. Also All-America two times with Carlisle.

Dick Tiger (b. 8-14-29; d. 12-14-71): Nigerian boxer. Born Richard Ihetu. Two-time middleweight champ, also won light heavyweight title. Fighter of the Year for 1962 and '65. Elected to Boxing Hall of Fame 1974.

Bill Tilden (b. 2-10-1893, d. 6-5-53): Tennis player. "Big Bill." Won seven U.S. singles titles, six consecutively (1920–25, '29) and three Wimbledon titles (1920, '21, '30). Also won six Grand Slam doubles titles. Led U.S. to seven consecutive Davis Cup victories (1920–26).

Ted Tinling (b. 6-23-10, d. 5-23-90): British tennis couturier. The premier source of women's tennis fashion, from Suzanne Lenglen to Steffi Graf—most notable creation: the frilled lace panties worn by Gorgeous Gussy Moran at Wimbledon in 1949.

Y.A. Tittle (b. 10-24-26): Football QB. Two-time NFL Most Valuable Player (1961, '63). Set NFL record with 36 TD passes in 1963. Career span 1948–64 with Baltimore, San Francisco and New York Giants; 33,070 yards, 242 TD. Inducted into Hall of Fame 1971.

Jayne Torvill/Christopher Dean (b. 10-7-57/ b. 7-27-58): British figure skaters. Won four consecutive ice dancing world championships (1981–84) and Olympic ice dancing gold medal (1984). Won world professional championships in 1985. Won Olympic ice dancing bronze in 1994.

Vladislav Tretiak (b. 4-25-52): Hockey G. Led USSR to gold medals at Olympics in 1972, '76, '84. Played on 13 world amateur champions from 1970–84.

Lee Trevino (b. 12-1-39): Golfer. Won U.S. Open (1968, '71), British Open (1971, '72) and PGA Championship (1974, '84) two times each. PGA Player of the Year in 1971. Also won U.S. Senior Open in 1990. First Senior $1 million season.

Emlen Tunnell (b. 3-29-25, d. 7-23-75): Football S. Alltime leader in interception return yardage with 1,282 and second in interceptions (79). All-Pro nine times. Career span 1948–61 with New York Giants and Green Bay.

Gene Tunney (b. 5-25-1897, d. 11-7-78): Boxer. Heavyweight champion (1926–28). Defeated Jack Dempsey two times, including famous "long count" bout. Career record 65-2-1 with 43 KOs from 1915–28. Retired as champion.

Ted Turner (b. 11-19-38): Sportsman. Skipper who successfully defended the America's Cup in 1977. Also owner of the Atlanta Braves since 1976 and Hawks since '77. Founded the Goodwill Games in 1986.

Mike Tyson (b. 6-30-66): Boxer. Became boxing's youngest heavyweight champion (20 years, 144 days) by knocking out Trevor Berbick in 1986. Lost crown in devastating upset to James (Buster) Douglas in 1990. Served three years in prison (1992–95) for rape. Regained piece of heavyweight title but lost it to Evander Holyfield in 1996. He "lost it" again in their rematch in 1997, when he was disqualified for biting Holyfield's ears. Retired in June 2005.

Johnny Unitas (b. 5-7-33, d. 9-11-02): Football QB. Set record by throwing TD passes in 47 consecutive games (1956–60). Three-time NFL MVP (1959, '64, '67). Led league in TD passes four consecutive seasons. Career span 1956–72 with Baltimore and San Diego; 290 TD passes, 40,239 passing yards.

Al Unser Sr. (b. 5-29-39): Auto racer. Won Indy 500 four times (1970, '71, '78, '87). Retired with 39 career CART victories. USAC/CART champion three times (1970, '83, '85). Brother of Bobby.

Bobby Unser (b. 2-20-34): Auto racer. Won Indianapolis 500 three times (1968, '75, '81). Retired with 35 career victories. USAC champion twice (1968, '74). Brother of Al Sr.

Harold S. Vanderbilt (b. 7-6-1884, d. 7-4-70): Sailor. Owner and skipper who successfully defended the America's Cup three consecutive times, in 1930, '34 and '37.

Glenna Collett Vare (b. 6-20-03, d. 2-2-89): Golfer. Won U.S. Women's Amateur six times, more than any golfer (1922, '25, '28–30, '35).

Bill Veeck (b. 2-9-14, d. 1-2-86): Baseball owner. From 1946–80, owned ballclubs in Cleveland, St. Louis (AL) and Chicago (AL). In 1948, Cleveland became baseball's first team to draw two million in attendance. That year Veeck integrated AL by signing Larry Doby and Satchel Paige. A brilliant promoter, Veeck sent midget Eddie Gaedel up to bat for St. Louis in 1951.

Guillermo Vilas (b. 8-17-52): Tennis. Argentine won 50 straight matches in 1977. In '77 won French Open, where he beat Brian Gottfried, and the U.S. Open, where he beat Jimmy Connors. Also won Australian Open twice, 1978–79.

Lasse Viren (b. 7-22-49): Track and field. Finnish runner was gold medalist in 5,000 and 10,000 meters at two consecutive Olympics (1972, '76).

Virginia Wade (b. 7-10-45): Tennis. Beloved in Britain, Wade won three major titles, most notably Wimbledon in 1977, its centenary year, where she triumphed over Betty Stove. Also won 1968 U.S. Open, '72 Australian Open, and doubles titles in '73 at the Australian, French and U.S. Opens, all with Margaret Smith Court.

Honus Wagner (b. 2-24-1874, d. 12-6-55): Baseball SS. Had .327 career batting average, 3,415 hits and eight batting titles. Averaged .300+ 15 consecutive seasons. Led league in RBI four times, with 100+ RBI nine times. Third alltime in triples (252) and league leader in doubles eight times. 703 career stolen bases, league leader in steals five times. Career span 1897–1917 with Pittsburgh.

Grete Waitz (b. 10-1-53): Track and field. Norwegian runner won New York City Marathon a record nine times (1978–80, '82–86, '88). Won the women's marathon at the 1983 World Championship.

Jersey Joe Walcott (b. 10-31-14, d. 2-25-94): Boxer. Heavyweight champion from 1951–52. Won title at age 37 on fifth attempt before surrendering it to Rocky Marciano. Later became sheriff of Camden, NJ.

Doak Walker (b. 1-1-27, d. 9-27-98): Football HB. Led NFL in scoring two times, his first and final seasons. All-Pro five times. Played on two consecutive NFL champions (1952–53) with Detroit. Career span 1950–55. Also won Heisman Trophy as a junior in 1948. All-America three consecutive seasons with SMU.

Herschel Walker (b. 3-3-62): Football RB. 1982 Heisman Trophy winner signed with the New Jersey Generals of the USFL in '83. Gained 5,562 rushing yards and scored 61 touchdowns in three seasons before league folded. Entered NFL in 1986 with Dallas and led league in rushing yards in 1988. Career span 1983–97 with New Jersey (USFL), Dallas, Minnesota, Philadelphia and New York Giants; 13,787 rushing yards and 143 TD (both leagues).

Bill Walsh (b. 11-30-31): Football coach. Led San Francisco to three Super Bowl wins, after the 1981, '84, '88 seasons. Career record with 49ers from 1979–88, 102-63-1. Perfected short-passing offense with quarterback Joe Montana.

Bill Walton (b. 11-5-52): Basketball C. College Player of the Year three consecutive seasons (1972–74). Played on two NCAA championship teams (1972, '73) with UCLA; tournament MVP twice (1972, '73). Sullivan Award winner in 1973. NBA MVP in 1978, playoff MVP in '77. Led league in rebounding and blocks in 1977. Career span 1974–86 with Portland, San Diego and Boston; 13.3 ppg, 10.5 rpg.

War Admiral (b. 1934, d. 1959): Thoroughbred race horse. A son of Man o' War, won Triple Crown and Horse of the Year honors in 1937.

Paul Warfield (b. 11-28-42): Football WR. Five-time All-NFL, averaged sensational 20.1 yards per catch during his career. Played on two Super Bowl–winning Miami teams. Career span 1964–77 with Cleveland and Miami; 427 receptions for 8,565 yards and 85 TDs. Inducted to Hall of Fame 1983.

Glenn (Pop) Warner (b. 4-5-1871, d. 9-7-54): College football coach. Fourth alltime in wins (319). Won three national championships with Pittsburgh (1916, '18) and Stanford (1926). Career record 319-106-32 with six teams from 1896–38.

Tom Watson (b. 9-4-49): Golfer. Winner of British Open five times (1975, '77, '80, '82, '83), the Masters two times (1977, '81) and U.S. Open once (1982). PGA Player of the Year six times, more than any golfer (1977–80, '82, '84).

Dick Weber (b. 12-23-29): Bowler. Won All-Star Tournament four times (1962, '63, '65, '66). Voted Bowler of the Year three times (1961, '63, '65). Won 31 career PBA titles.

Johnny Weismuller (b. 6-2-04, d. 1-21-84): Swimmer. Won three gold medals (including 100- and 400-meter freestyle) at 1924 Olympics and two gold medals at the 1928 Olympics. Also played Tarzan in the movies.

Jerry West (b. 5-28-38): Basketball G. "Mr. Clutch." 10 time first-team All-NBA; All-Defensive Team four times; 1969 playoff MVP. Led league in assists and scoring one time each. Career span 1960–72 with Los Angeles; 27.0 ppg, 6.7 apg. All-America two times with West Virginia. Played on 1960 gold medal-winning Olympic team. Guided the Lakers to seven NBA championships as either a general manager or a consultant from 1980 to 2001.

Whirlaway (b. 4-2-38, d. 4-6-53): Thoroughbred race horse. Triple Crown winner in 1941 with jockey Eddie Arcaro aboard. Trained by Ben A. Jones.

Byron (Whizzer) White (b. 6-8-17, d. 4-15-02): Football RB. Led NFL in rushing two times (Pittsburgh in 1938, Detroit in '40). Led NCAA in scoring and rushing with Colorado in 1937; named All-America. United States Supreme Court justice.

Reggie White (b. 12-19-62, d. 12-26-04): Football DE. "Minister of Defense." Retired as alltime NFL leader in sacks (198). Set a Super Bowl record with three sacks against New England in Super Bowl XXXI. He played in 13 Pro Bowls. Career span: 1984–05 with Memphis Showboats (USFL), Philadelphia, Green Bay and Carolina.

Charles Whittingham (b. 4-13-13 d. 4-20-99): Thoroughbred race horse trainer. Nicknamed "Bald Eagle" after losing his hair to tropical disease in World War II. Led yearly earnings list for trainers in 1970–73, '75, '81, '82. Won three Eclipse Awards and trained two Horses of the Year (Ack Ack in 1971 and Ferdinand in 1987).

Kathy Whitworth (b. 9-27-39): Golfer. Alltime LPGA leader with 88 tour victories, including six majors. Won LPGA Championship in 1967, '71 and '75. Won Titleholders Championship (extinct major) in 1965 and '66. Won Western Open (extinct major) in 1967. Won Vare Trophy every year from 1965–72, except '68. LPGA Player of Year from 1966–69 and 1971–73.

Hoyt Wilhelm (b. 7-26-23, d. 8-23-02): Baseball RHP. Hall of Famer. Threw knuckleball until age 48. Career 2.52 ERA, 227 saves. Hit home run in his first at bat (never hit another) and pitched no-hitter in 1958. Career span 1952–72 with nine teams.

Bud Wilkinson (b. 4-23-15 d. 2-9-94): Football coach. Coached Oklahoma to NCAA record 47 consecutive wins (1953–57). Won three national championships (1950, '55, '56) with Oklahoma, where he coached from 1947–1963. Won Orange Bowl four times and Sugar Bowl two times. Career record 145-29-4, including four undefeated seasons. Also coached St. Louis of NFL in 1978–79.

Billy Williams (b. 6-15-38): Baseball OF. "Sweet Swinging." Six-time All-Star and the 1961 NL Rookie of the Year. Career span 1959–76 with Chicago (NL) and Oakland; .290 avg., 426 HR, 1,475 RBI. Elected to Hall of Fame in 1987.

Ted Williams (b. 8-30-18, d. 7-5-02): Baseball OF. "The Splendid Splinter." Last player to hit .400 (.406 in 1941). MVP in 1946, '49 and Triple Crown winner in 1942, '47. Retired with career batting average of .344, along with 2,019 walks and a .634 slugging average. Won six AL batting titles, and led the league in HR and RBI four times each. Had .300+ average 15 consecutive seasons; 100+ RBI and runs scored nine times each; 30+ HR eight times; and 100+ walks 11 times. Lost nearly five seasons to military service. Career span 1939–42 and 1946–60 with Boston; 521 career HR.

Hack Wilson (b. 4-26-1900; d. 11-23-48): Baseball OF. Stood 5' 6" but weighed 210. Had five astounding seasons 1926–30, before alcohol ruined his career. Best was 1930 when he hit .356, scored 146 runs, hit a NL record 56 homers and drove in 190, which is still the major league record. Career span 1923–34 with several teams. Elected to Hall of Fame in 1979.

Dave Winfield (b. 10-3-51): Baseball OF. Drafted out of Univ. of Minnesota by baseball, basketball and football teams. Drove in 100+ runs eight times, and led the NL in 1979 with 118. Derided by George Steinbrenner as "Mr. May," but hit clutch double to win 1992 World Series for Toronto. Career span 1973–95 with San Diego, New York (AL), California, Toronto, Minnesota and Cleveland; .283 avg., 465 HR, 3,110 hits, 1,833 RBI and 1,669 runs. Inducted into Hall of Fame in 2001.

Major W.C. Wingfield (b. 10-16-1833, d. 4-18-12): British tennis pioneer. Credited with inventing the game of tennis, which he called "Sphairistike" or "sticky" and patented in February 1874.

Colonel Matt Winn (b. 6-30-1861, d. 10-6-49): General manager of Churchill Downs from 1904 until his death; made Kentucky Derby premier U.S. race.

Katarina Witt (b. 12-3-65): East German figure skater. Gold medalist at 1984 and '88 Olympics. Also world champion four times (1984, '85, '87, '88).

John Wooden (b. 10-14-10): College basketball coach. Coached UCLA to 10 NCAA championships in 12 years (1964, '65, '67–73, '75). Record winning streak of 88 games (1971–74). 664 career wins and fourth highest career winning percentage (.804). First member of basketball Hall of Fame as coach and player. Career span 1949–75 with UCLA. 1932 College Player of the Year at Purdue.

Tiger Woods (b. 12-30-75): Golfer. Produced the Tiger Slam in 2000–01, an unofficial Grand Slam during which he won four consecutive professional majors. Holds the tournament record for best scores at the Masters, the U.S. Open, the PGA Championship and the British Open. Became the youngest winner of the Masters in 1997, when he shot a record-270 to win by a record 12 strokes. Became the youngest player to win all four major tournaments ('99 PGA, '00 U.S. Open, '00 British Open). Also won three straight U.S. Junior Amateur titles (1991–93) and three straight U.S. Amateur titles (1994–96). Then took the PGA tour by storm, winning six of his first 21 tournaments. Already has 46 PGA Tour victories (including ten majors) and has won more money ($55,992,856) than any golfer in history. 1996 and 2000 *Sports Illustrated* Sportsman of the Year.

Mickey Wright (b. 2-14-35): Golfer. Second alltime in career wins (82) and major championships (13; tied with Louise Suggs). Won the U.S. Open four times (1958, '59, '61, '64), the LPGA Championship four times (1958, '60, '61, '63), and the Western Open three times (1962, '63, '66).

Kristi Yamaguchi (b.7-12-71): Figure skater. Olympic champion in 1992. Back-to-back world champion (1991, '92).

Cale Yarborough (b. 3-27-40): Auto racer. Won Daytona 500 four times (1968, '77, '83, '84). 83 career victories. NASCAR champion three consecutive years (1976–78).

Carl Yastrzemski (b. 8-22-39): Baseball OF. "Yaz." 1967 MVP and Triple Crown winner. Three batting titles. Second alltime in games played (3,308) and sixth in walks (1,845). Career span 1961–83 with Boston; .285 avg., 3,419 hits, 452 HR and 1,844 RBI.

Cy Young (b. 3-29-1867, d. 11-4-55): Baseball RHP. Alltime leader in wins (511), innings pitched (7,354⅔) and complete games (749); fourth in shutouts (76). Had 2.63 career ERA. Pitched three no-hitters, including a perfect game in 1904. Career span 1890–1911 with Cleveland and Boston (AL).

Steve Young (b. 10-11-61): Football QB. Career passer rating of 96.8. Led the league in passing six times. Led 49ers to victory in Super Bowl XXIX of which he was MVP for tossing a record six TD passes. Two-time NFL MVP (1992 and '94). Repeated concussions forced his retirement in 2000. Career span 1984–00 with Los Angeles Express (USFL), Tampa Bay and San Francisco; 33,124 yards, 232 TD passes; rushed for 43 TD.

Robin Yount (b. 9-16-55): Baseball OF–SS. Won AL MVP as a shortstop (1982) and a centerfielder (1989). Became Milwaukee's shortstop at 18. Career span 1974–93 with Milwaukee; .285 avg., 3,142 hits, 251 HR and 583 2B. Elected to Hall of Fame 1999.

Steve Yzerman (b. 5-9-65): Hockey C. Won three Stanley Cups with Red Wings (1997, '98, '02). Won Conn Smythe trophy in 1998. Scored 100+ points six consecutive seasons (1987–93). Career span 1983– with Detroit.

Babe Didrikson Zaharias (b. 6-26-14, d. 9-27-56): Sportswoman. Commonly called the greatest female athlete of all time, Zaharias was the Gold medalist in the 80-meter hurdles and javelin throw at the 1932 Olympics; she also won the silver medal in the high jump (her gold medal jump was disallowed for using the then-illegal western roll). Became a golfer in 1935 and won 12 major titles, including U.S. Open three times (1948, '50, '54—a year after cancer surgery). Also helped found the LPGA in 1949.

Tony Zale (b. 5-29-13, d. 3-20-97): Boxer. Born Anthony Zaleski. "The Man of Steel." Two-time middleweight champ. Fought Rocky Graziano for title three times in 21 months, winning twice. 67-18-2 with 44 KOs. Elected to Boxing Hall of Fame 1958.

Emil Zatopek (b. 9-19-22, d. 11-21-00): Track and field. Czech runner became only athlete to win gold medal in 5,000 and 10,000 meters and marathon, at 1952 Olympics. Also gold medalist in 10,000 meters at '48 Olympics.

Zinedine Zidane (b. 6-23-72): French soccer player. "Zizou." Led France to 1998 World Cup title; scored two goals in 3–0 win over Brazil in the final. Led Juventus to 1998 Italian League title and to '98 European Cup final. 1998 FIFA World Player of the Year. Led France to 2000 European Championship.

MORHY GASH/AP

Obituaries

Reggie White
1961-2004

Ted Atkinson, 88, jockey.

A native of Toronto, Atkinson didn't begin racing until the ripe old age – for a jockey – or 21. He became know for his skill with the whip (his nickname was the Slasher) and in 1946 he was the first rider to earn $1 million in purse winnings in one year. In 1953, he rode Horse of the Year Tom Fool to 21 wins in 30 starts, and by the time he retired in 1959, after 21 years in the saddle, he had won 3,795 races and purses of more than $17 million.

In Beaver Dam, Va., of natural causes, on May 5, 2005.

Bobby Avila, 80, baseball player and politician. *Bobby Avila became one of the first prominent Latin players in the major leagues, and a Mexican national hero, when he was picked up by the Cleveland Indians in 1949. SI writes:*

"He spent all but one of his 11 big league seasons with the Indians, playing in three All-Star games. In 1954, when the Indians went to the World Series, he led the American League with a .341 average and finished third in the MVP balloting despite playing most of the year with a broken thumb. During that season Hall of Fame pitcher Dizzy Dean predicted Avila would be the next player to bat .400. "If I ever did hit .400," Avila remarked, "they would make me president of Mexico. Actually, "Avila did have a second career in politics, getting elected to the Mexican national legislature in 1970 and serving as mayor of his hometown of Veracruz form 1976 until 1979.

Back in 1940, at age 16, he had signed with Puebla of the Mexican League and seven years later he signed with the Indians for a $17,500 bonus, no small sum at the time. Avila quickly became known as a dangerous hitter (he had a career average of .281) and a hard-nosed base runner. Indians manager Al Lopez once said Avila had "a find swing, a sharp eye … and a world of confidence in himself." He was also a trailblazing force as baseball slowly came to accept diversity in the decades after World War II. 'The greatest pride of my life,' Avila said in 1951, 'is to be a Mexican.'"

In Veracruz, Mexico, of complications from diabetes, on October 26, 2004.

Ray Boone, 81, baseball player.

Boone broke into the major leagues in 1948 and supplanted Hall of Famer Lou Boudreau as the Indians' shortstop that following year. He floundered in the role, but when traded to Detroit in 1953 and switched to third base, he focused on his hitting and led the AL with 116 RBIs in 1955 and twice made the All-Star team in 1954 and 1955. In 1972, his son Bob came up with the Phillies; Bob's boys Bret, the Mariners' second baseman, and Aaron, a third baseman with the Reds, were All-Stars on opposite sides in 2003 while their grandfather watched from the stands. 'Anybody that's not proud in this situation,' Ray said, 'there something wrong with them.'"

In San Diego, Calif., of undisclosed causes, on October 17, 2004.

Chico Carrasquel, 77 baseball player. *The first Latin-born player to appear in a major league All-Star Game. SI writes:*

"Carrasquel broke into the big leagues with the White Sox in 1950, taking the place of Hall of Fame shortstop Luke Appling. In his six yeas with Chicago, the slick fielding Venezuelan was an All-Star four times, including 1951, when he was voted the started and singled in his first at bat. He was traded to Cleveland before the 1956 season, but never enjoyed the same success, and his career was over by 1959. Carrasquel spent seven seasons doing Spanish-language broadcasts for the White Sox and worked in the team's community-relations department for years. He remained a hero in Venezuela and news of his was announced on television by Venezuela's president, Hugo Chavez, who shouted, 'Viva Carrasquel!'"

In Caracas, Venezuela, of cardiac arrest, on May 26, 2005.

Bob Casey, 79, broadcaster. *SI writes:*

"Beloved for his raspy baritone, Casey had worked Twins gams since the franchise arrived in Minnesota in 1961. He was planning to retire at the end of the season and reported to Fort Meyers, Fl, for his final spring training, but returned inn March 2005 after developing pneumonia. Shortly before he died, Yankees third baseman Alex Rodriguez – a longtime fan and friend – called him in the hospital to wish him well. Casey died the next morning. 'He's one of the great announcers of all time, and [we] grew very fond of each other,' said Rodriguez."

In Minneapolis, Minn., of complications from liver cancer and pneumonia, on March 27, 2005.

Eddie Crook Jr., 76, boxer. *Crook won a gold medal as a teammate of Muhammad Ali's at the 1960 Rome Olympics. SI writes:*

"Crook, who was the Army champ, won the middleweight gold medal in a narrow decision over Tadeusz Walasek of Poland. Walasek bloodied Crook's nose late in the final round, which swayed the crowd in his favor; Crook was booed when the decision was announced and as he received his medal. Crook, who was 31 at the time, decided not to turn pro. He served two tours in Vietnam and was awarded a Silver Star, a Bronze Star and two Purple Hearts. At his funeral in Columbus, Ga., the Reverend Debora Grant said, 'He was chosen to be a warrior, destined to be a soldier. And beloved, he fought ... for his country, for his family, for the gold and for his faith.'"

In Montgomery, Ala., of natural causes, on July 25, 2005.

Pete Cutino, 71, water polo player and coach.

Well-known for his bald plate, bushy mustache and fiery behavior, Pete Cutino coached at the University of California for 26 years, winning eight national championships and the NCAA's Coach of the Year Award four times. When he retired from Cal in 1988, Cutino had won 33 straight matches. In 1999 the NCAA established the Peter J. Cutino award, water polo's equivalent of the Heisman Trophy. A 1957 graduate of Cal Poly San Luis Obispo, Cutino received a master's degree in education from the school in 1959. He was named a three-time water polo all-conference selection while at Cal Poly.

In Monterey, Calif., of apparent heart failure, September 19, 2004.

Glenn Davis, 80, football player. *The halfback who led Army to three national championships and Glenn Davis won the Heisman Trophy in 1946. SI writes:*

"Half of football's most famous backfield – he was "Mr. Outside to fullback Doc Blanchard's "Mr. Inside" – Davis scored 59 touchdowns and averaged 8.3 yards per carry in his career, during which Army went 34-2-2. After his hitch in the service, Davis played two seasons for the Rams, but was slowed by injuries. 'Glenn was probably the fastest man in a football suit in 1945 and 1946," said Blanchard, the Heisman Trophy winner in '45. 'He was a complete back. He was strong and had great balance and quickness. He was just a terrific runner.'"

In La Quinta, Calif., of complications from prostate cancer, on March 9, 2005.

Rose Gacioch, 89, baseball player and bowler. *Voted to the All-American Girls Baseball League's All Star teams in 1952, '53 and '54, Rose Gacioch pitched a no-hitter in '53. SI writes:*

"It wasn't quite selling Babe Ruth to the Yankees to finance a play, but in the annals of baseball there aren't many worse moves than the South Bend Blue Sox selling Rose Gacioch to the Rockford Peaches in 1945 because the Sox's owner found her grammar unladylike. Gacioch was never particularly dainty – she was the basis for Rosie O'Donnell's character in the movie A Field of Their Own. Gacioch was a factory worker in Wheeling, W.Va., who had played one year of baseball and done some softball barnstorming when, at age 28, she tried out for the Sox of the newly formed All-American Girls Baseball League. After being sent to the Peaches, she became one of the league's top hitters, but it wasn't until the league allowed overhand pitching in 1948 that she became a star. Using the curveball that her brother, Steve, had taught her, she went on to become the league's only 20-game winner, going 20-7 in 1951. She retired when the AAGBL folded in 1954 – the same year she won the Women's International Bowling Congress classic division doubles championship. 'I made a nice life for myself,' she said. 'I didn't get paid much. I never got married; I didn't have the time. I got to see the world when I started playing ball.'"

In Clinton Township, Mich., of undisclosed causes, September 9, 2004.

Clarence Gaines, 81, basketball coach. *In the summer of 1945, 22 year-old Clarence Gaines took a job as the lone assistant coach on the Winston-Salem basketball team, figuring he'd spend a year or two there before moving on to dental school. But after the Rams' head coach resigned in '46, Gaines took his place on the bench. By the time he retired from the historically black school in '93, Big House (he stood 6'4" and weighed 275 pounds) had won more collegiate games (828) than anyone else but Adolph Rupp (876). SI writes:*

"Gaines could be strict – especially when it came to class work – but he was also a father figure to his players, staying in contact long after they left school. He enjoyed his finest season in 1967, coaching an unranked team led by future NBA Hall of Famer Earl Monroe to a 31-1 record and becoming the first black coach to win an NCAA title at any level. Gaines retired after the '92 – '93 season. Monroe was among the more than 2,000 who gathered in Winston-Salem to remember Gaines, who now ranks fifth on the wins list, after his death. Said former Georgetown coach John Thompson, 'He was one of the men who came before me who took a lot of stuff so I wouldn't have to.'"

In Winston-Salem, N.C., of complications from a stroke, on April 18, 2005.

Sue Gunter, 66, basketball coach. *Gunter coached women's basketball for 40 years including 22 seasons at LSU. Her 708 career wins rank third all time among women coaches behind Tennessee's Pat Summitt and Jody Conradt of Texas. Gunter had 20 or more wins in 14 seasons. In September 2005, she was inducted into the Naismith Basketball Hall of Fame. SI writes:*

"Gunter, who stopped coaching late in the 2003-04 season because of emphysema and bronchitis (her Tigers made it to the Final Four that spring), was the head coach of the 1980 U.S. Olympic women's basketball team, which won a qualifying tournament before the Olympics but did not compete because of the U.S. boycott of the Moscow Games 'I learned so much from Sue about the X's and O's of the game of basketball,' said Summitt, who was her assistant on the 1980 team. 'More importantly, she taught me about the delicate balance of coaching and teaching the game and the value of great player-coach relationships. She made playing basketball fun.'"

In Baton Rouge, La., of respiratory failure, on August 4, 2005.

Gunder Hagg, 85, runner. *Hagg set the world record in the mile in 1945 and held it until Roger Bannister broke the four-minute barrier in 1954. SI writes:*

"The son of a forest woodcutter, Hagg grew up in the Swedish countryside and said he competed from the age of 16 not to become a national hero but to 'make myself eligible for a decent job.' Without a coach or formal training regimen, Hagg rose to prominence in the summer of 1942, when he set world marks at seven distances and became the first person to run 5,000 meters in under 14 minutes. In all "Gunder the Wonder" set 15 middle-distance world records, and after a tour of he U.S. in 1943, he was named Male Athlete of the Year by the Associated Press. Two years later, Hagg ran the mile in 4:01.4, a mark that seemed unbreakable until Bannister's reknowned run."

In Malmo, Sweden, of undisclosed causes, on November 27, 2004.

Thomas Herrion, 23, football player. *The 49er's guard collapsed after coach Mike Nolan spoke to his team following the exhibition game against the Broncos on a relatively cool Saturday night. Medics administered CPR on the 6-foot-3, 310-pound player before an ambulance took him to a Denver hospital. SI writes:*

Herrion, who played in college at Utah, was on the field for San Francisco's 14-play, 91-yard drive that ended with a touchdown with 2 seconds left in the game. About three hours after he collapsed, the team confirmed his death.

Herrion, a first-year player with the 49ers, spent part of last season on the San Francisco and Dallas practice squads. He also played with the Hamburg Sea Devils of NFL Europe. Herrion played in junior college at Kilgore College in East Texas. Travis Fox, the offensive coordinator at Kilgore who shared an apartment with Herrion for two weeks this summer, said Herrion never struggled during intense drills in 97-degree heat. He added that the lineman had no injuries or health problems while playing at Kilgore. 'The young man was in shape,' he said. Herrion's nicknames at Kilgore were "Train" and "Big T." Fox said he was called "Thunder" in Germany because his head was too big for a regular helmet.

Fox said Herrion always talked about his niece, and family was a big motivation for playing. "When he got here," Fox recalled, "the first thing he told me was, 'I'm going to make this team and buy my mom a nice house.'"

In Denver, Colo., of a heart attack, August 20, 2005.

Bob Karstens, 89, basketball player. *Karstens became the first white player to sign a contract with the Harlem Globetrotters. SI writes:*

"He was discovered in the early 1940s when his Iowa club team played the Globetrotters. When star Reece (Goose) Tatum was drafted into the Army in 1942, team founder Abe Sapperstein hired Karstens to be the team's main showman. Karstens played the '42 and '43 seasons (he served as the team's manager until

1954) and is credited with devising signature Globetrotter routines like the Magic Ball pregame warmup and the yo-yo basketball. 'Being the only white guy was never a problem,' Karstens once said. 'I had the skills to fit in and do the tricks. Everyone respected that and that's all there was to it.'"

In Redlands, Calif., of natural causes, on December 31, 2004.

John "Johnny" Kelley, 97, runner. *Johnny Kelley ran the Boston Marathon a record 61 times, winning in 1935 and 1945, and finishing second seven times. SI writes:*
"He was as much a part of the race's landscape as Heartbreak Hill. In fact, the local climb became so-known in 1936 when Kelley passed Ellison (Tarzan) Brown on the incline (about 20 miles into the race) and tapped Brown on the shoulder as he went by. Though identified most with the Boston, Kelley competed all over the world – he was the only American to finish the 1936 Olympic marathon in Berlin – and was named Runner of the Century by Runner's World in 2000. He also worked a day job as an electrical maintenance man for 35 years (he retired in 1973). He was an avid painter, though he would abstain from his art three days before a race to conserve energy. Said four-time Boston winner Bill Rodgers, 'He was the Boston Marathon.'"

In South Yarmouth, Mass., of undisclosed causes, October 6, 2004.

Al Lucas, 26, football player. *The kickoff that followed the Los Angles Avengers' first touchdown in their Arena Football League game against the New York Dragons in April 2005 appeared to be a routine play – one of the thousands of moments of controlled chaos that Al Lucas had been part of in his peripatetic football career. But it ended in tragedy. SI writes:*
"Lucas, a 6'1", 300-pound lineman, rumbled down the Stadium Center field and zeroed in on Dragons kick returner Corey Johnson, who was closely shielded by a blocker, Mike Horacek. Lucas lowered his head, and as he crashed into the pair another Dragons player hurtled over his head. Replays appeared to show that Lucas's helmet collided with Horacek's knee. All three players crumpled to the turf. One didn't get up. For 10 minutes, as players prayed and the din gave way to silence, paramedics attended to Lucas on the field before strapping him to a stretcher. He was taken to a hospital and within the hour he was pronounced dead of a presumed spinal cord injury.

"Lucas is the first player in the AFL's 19-year history to die in a game. (Detroit's Chuck Hughes, who suffered a heart attack in 1971, is believed to be the only NFL player to die during a game.) The shock of Lucas's death was compounded by the sheer ordinariness of the play that caused it. Said coach Ed Hodgkiss, 'I had every confidence he was going to be O.K.'"

"For Lucas, who dreamed of returning to the NFL, the league became more than just a showcase. He spent his off-seasons in Macon, GA, where he lived with his wife De'Shonda, and daughter, Mariah, and did some coaching and substitute teaching at Northeast High, his alma mater. 'When he was laying on the ground,' said Avengers fullback Lonnie Ford, 'I was thinking that could be any one of us.'"

In Los Angeles, of a spinal cord injury, April 10, 2005.

Terry Long, 45, football player. *SI writes:*
"Once the NFL's smallest offensive lineman (he was 5'11" in height and weighed 272 pounds), Long had a troubled life since at least 1991, when he left the game after eight years with the Steelers. His career ended with a failed steroid test, a suspension by the NFL and a attempt to commit suicide by ingesting rat poison. In March 2005, Long, who was living in Franklin Park, PA, was indicted on federal charges of arson and mail fraud for allegedly setting fire to a Pittsburgh chicken procession plant he owned, in order to collect on an insurance policy. (He filed for bankruptcy on the day he was indicted.) He attempted suicide again after the indictments. In June 2005, paramedics found him unresponsive in his home and rushed him to a nearby hospital where he died hours later.

In Franklin Park, Penn., of undisclosed causes, on June 7, 2005.

Arthus Lydiard, 87, track coach.
Lydiard was credited with revolutionizing training and essentially inventing jogging. In the 1950s most runners used interval training (a series of short, fast runs), but Lydiard began preaching the benefits of running longer distances. The New Zealand native's ideas caught on when his runners won the gold in the 800 meters and the 5,000 meters at the 1960 Olympics. Lydiard's 1963 book, 'Run to the Top', remains one of the most influential book on distance training. John Walker, the 1976 1,500-meter gold medalist, called Lydiard a "coach of coaches," saying, 'His influence will live forever.'"

In Texas, of a heart attack, on December 11, 2004.

Gene Mauch, 79, baseball manager. *Dubbed "the little general," Gene Mauch won 1,901 games as a manager but became infamous for historic losses. A big league skipper for 26 years with California, Philadelphia, Montreal and Minnesota, Mauch was the National League manager of the year three times. He is sixth in baseball history with 3,938 games managed, and 11th on the career victories list. SI writes:*
"Mauch is forever linked to great collapses. He was manager of the Philadelphia Phillies in 1964 when they led the NL by 6 1/2 games with 12 games remaining, but lost 10 in a row -- and the pennant -- to the St. Louis Cardinals." "He also managed the California Angels in 1986 when they were within one out of advancing to the World Series before blowing a three-run lead to Boston in Game 5 of the ALCS. The Red Sox won that game and two more to win the series."

"Rod Carew, who played for Mauch in both Minnesota and Anaheim, said, '"He's always been a special guy to me. He's the best I've ever played for, well ahead of anyone else,' the Hall of Famer said."

"Bobby Wine, who played 12 seasons under Mauch in Philadelphia, said he taught a lot of people how to think ahead in baseball. "One time, Jim Bunning was having trouble with a baseball. The umpires wouldn't give him a new one,' Wine said. 'Gene came out to the mound, dropped the ball on the ground and spiked it with his shoes. Bunning got a new baseball."

"His first managing job was with the Phillies in 1960. and by 1962 Mauch was named NL manager of the year for\ leading the team to an 81-80 record . He won the award again in 1964, the year of the Phillies' great disappointment. Mauch guided Philadelphia to a record of 92-70, his best as a manager until 1982 when his Angels went 93-69. He left Philadelphia 54 games into the 1968 season.

"In 1969 he was hired as the manager of the Montreal Expos. Mauch stayed in Montreal for seven seasons and won his third and final manager of the year award in 1973 as he helped lift the lowly Expos to a 79-83 record and a fourth-place finish in the NL East. Mauch joined the

Minnesota Twins in 1976 and would spend the rest of his career in the AL. He was with the Twins until 1980, followed by two stints with the Angels, the first from 1981–82 and the second from 1985-87."

"One of Mauch's greatest collapses came at the end of his career, in the Angels' so-called "Donnie Moore" game." "With a 3-1 lead in games over the Boston Red Sox in the best-of-seven AL Championship series, the Angels held a 5-2 advantage going into the ninth inning of Game 5. After Mike Witt retired the first two batters, the Red Sox got a runner on before Don Baylor homered to make it 5-4. Mauch pulled Witt and brought in left-hander Gary Lucas to face the left-handed hitting Rich Gedman, who was 4-for-4 against Witt in the game. Lucas hit Gedman with a pitch—his first hit batter in four years—and Mauch brought in Moore, his closer. Henderson hit a two-run homer to put the Red Sox ahead 6-5. The managerial moves, though they made sense, still were questioned years later."

"The Angels tied the game again in the ninth but lost in 11 innings and then dropped the series when the Red Sox won two straight in Boston. Mauch was still following baseball closely when the Angels won the World Series in 2002, softening many of the team's ugly memories. 'I get so keyed up during these games,' Mauch said during the Angels' playoff series against the Minnesota Twins in 2002. 'All I did for 50 years was study the game day and night.'"

In Rancho Mirage, Calif., of cancer, on August 8, 2005.

Coley Wallace, 77, boxer and actor. *SI writes:*

"Wallace's career as a pro-heavyweight boxer didn't amount to much (he was 20-7-0), but as an amateur in 1948, he knocked out Rocky Marciano, handing the future champ the only loss of his career. Wallace was also known for his resemblance to Joe Louis. In 1953—with cotton stuffed in his cheeks to simulate Louis's puffy face—he played the Brown Bomber in 'The Joe Louis Story,' then reprised the role 27 years later in Martin Scorsese's 'Raging Bull.'"

In New York City, of heart failure, January 30, 2005.

Lennox Miller, 58, runner. *SI writes:*

"Throughout his sprinting career, Miller always seemed to be overshadowed just a bit. At the 1968 Olympics, running for his native Jamaica, he won silver in the 100 meters, finishing just behind Jim Hines, who set a world record. In 1972, Miller took the bronze. Even when he set a world record – as part of USC's 4x110-yard relay team in 1967 – he wasn't the one people remembered; the third leg was run by O.J. Simpson. But none of that mattered to Miller. 'We were college kids who ran in our spare time for the love of it,' he said in 2003."

"In 1996–22 years after he began practicing dentistry in Pasadena – Miller could finally say he had accomplished something truly distinctive. His daughter Inger won a gold medal as part of the U.S. 400-meter relay team, making the Millers the first father-daughter combination to win Olympic track and field medals. Before she received her gold, Inger said she was eager to get a look at the medal that would complete the family set. 'I've seen a silver and a bronze,' she said. 'I'll think we'll put them together with my dad's.'"

In Pasadena, Calif., of cancer, on November 8, 2004.

Coo Coo Marlin, 73, race car driver. *SI writes:*

"Coo Coo, the father of two-time Daytona 500 champ Sterling Marlin and one of stock car racing's early stars, got his nickname as a young boy because he had trouble pronouncing his given name, Clifton, never won a NASCAR race. But he was a four-time champ at the now-defunct Tennessee Fairgrounds, where the competition included future stars such as Bobby Allison and Red Farmer. In the 1974 Daytona 500, Marlin held a half-lap lead late in the race, but he was black-flagged by NASCAR officials, who told him they thought he had a loose lug nut. The car was fine--and Marlin, an independent driver without a sponsor, became convinced that NASCAR made the call so Richard Petty would win the race. 'I'm still mad,' he told SI in 2001. After he retired, Coo Coo continued to live on the 700-acre farm in Columbia, Tenn., where he grew up and where Sterling and his family live. 'My dad raced hard,' said Sterling. 'The lesson he taught me was to run every lap as if you were qualifying.'"

In Columbia, Tenn., of lung cancer, on August 14, 2005.

Sam Mills, 45, football coach. *SI writes:*

"An undersized (5'9", 225 pounds) linebacker, Mills played in the USFL for three seasons before having a successful 12-year career with the Saints and Carolina, during which he made the Pro Bowl five times. He started 173 of 181 games and recorded 1,319 tackles, 20.5 sacks, 11 interceptions and four touchdowns. He joined the Panthers' staff in 1998 and, after learning that he had cancer before the 2003 season, he continued to coach between chemotherapy treatments. "I'm around something I enjoy, and that is very important," Mills told the St. Paul Pioneer Press in February 2004. 'As long as I have the power in me to go ahead and coach, I will.'"

In Charlotte, N.C., of intestinal cancer, on April 18, 2005.

Houston Nutt, Sr., 74, basketball coach. *Patriarch of the first family of Arkansas sports. SI writes:*

"Born with a slight hearing deficiency hat worsened with age, Nutt coached basketball at the Arkansas School for the Deaf for 31 years. His four sons went on to become coaches: Houston Jr. is football coach at Arkansas, where his brother Danny coaches running backs; Dickey coaches basketball at Arkansas State; Dennis is the basketball coach at Texas State. 'I really love to go out on a field and watch kids play,' Nutt said in 1999. 'I always thought sports was the best thing you can have in life.'"

In Little Rock, Ark., of a stroke, on April 20, 2005.

Johnny Oates, 58, baseball player and manager. *Oates played 11 seasons as a light-hitting catcher for five teams, then managed Baltimore (1991-94) and Texas (1995-2001). SI writes:*

"There were times when Johnny Oates could be tense and tightly wound, no different from any other antacid-gobbling skipper. But the 750 people who gathered at his memorial in Virginia remembered a man of intense faith and preternatural inner peace. "He was more like a father figure than a manager," said former Rangers pitcher Jeff Zimmerman."

"He went 797-746 and led the Rangers to their only three postseason appearances but resigned early in a difficult 2001 season. Later that year he was diagnosed with brain cancer. Given less than a year to live, Oates survived to see his daughter Jenny get married in 2002 and see himself inducted into the Rangers' Hall of Fame in '03. 'My days are filled with faith, hope, spirit and the small pleasures many people take for granted,' he wrote in The Sporting News in April 2002. 'Whatever time I have left, I want it to mean something.'"

In Richmond, Va., of brain cancer, on December 24, 2004.

Al Onofrio, 83, college football coach. *SI writes:*

"After 12 years designing defenses for Missouri Tigers coach Dan Devine, Al Onofrio was given the head coaching job when Devine left for the NFL in 1971. In seven series his teams were just 38-41, but they were always dangerous, knocking off Nebraska twice as well as Ohio State, USC and Notre Dame. The win over the Irish in 1972 came a week after Nebraska routed the Tigers 62-0. Legendary Cornhuskers coach Bob Devaney was so impressed with the job Onofrio did to prepare his team for the eighth-ranked Irish in the wake of such a humiliating defeat that he sent a letter to Onofrio saying 'I sincerely believe that your preparation – mentally, physically and technically – was the best job done by any coach in the history of football.'"

In Tempe, Ariz., of non-Hodgkin's lymphoma, on November 5, 2004.

Mickey Owen, 89, baseball player. *SI writes:*

"One of the top backstops of the 1940s, Owen was a four-time All-Star, but he was best known as the goat who helped cost the Dodgers the '41 World Series. Owen dropped the third strike on what should have been the final out in Game 4, allowing the Yankees to rally for four runs and win 7-4. New York won the series the next day. Owen once said that he didn't feel his life had been ruined by the miscue: 'I would've been completely forgotten if I hadn't missed that pitch.'"

In Mount Vernon, Mo., of Alzheimer's disease, June 13, 2005.

Dick Radatz, 67, baseball player. *SI writes:*

"In the early 1960's, Dick (the Monster) Radatz used his size – he was 6'5" and weighed 235 pounds – snarling mound demeanor and an overpowering fastball to become first dominant closers for the Red Sox. (Radatz was given his nickname by Mickey Mantle, whom he struck out 12 times in 16 bats. Despite pitching for mostly inept teams, the two-time All-Star led the American League in saves in 1962, his rookie year, and again in '64; in his first three seasons in the majors he won or saved 118 of Boston's 224 victories. Said former Red Sox southpaw Bill Lee, 'He really was the model for scary relief pitchers to come.'"

In Easton, Mass., of head injuries sustained in a fall, on March 16, 2005.

Alexander Ragulin, 63, hockey player. *The fearsome face of Soviet hockey teams, Alexander Ragulin inspired fear on the ice, but refused to leave his homeland. SI writes:*

'I could have played in the NHL,' Alexander Ragulin, a pillar of Soviet Era teams that dominated international hockey in the 1960s and '70s, said a several years ago. 'But I never thought about leaving. That would have meant defecting, and that would have made me a traitor to my country.'"

One of the world's most intimidating defensemen, Ragulin stood 6'1" and weighed 225 pounds at a time when few players topped 200. Between 1962 and '73 he won three Olympic medals and 10 world titles. He is also in the International Ice Hockey Federation Hall of Fame."

"Ragulin became well-known in the West during the Summit series between Canada and the U.S.S.R. in 1972, which Canada won. After retiring in '73, he spent his life in Moscow, coaching and organizing teammate reunions. 'Perhaps some good came from our losing,' he once said. 'If we had won, then no one in Canada would want to remember our names.'"

In Moscow, Russia, of a heart attack, on November 17, 2004.

Gerald Roberts, 85, rodeo rider.

A native of Abilene, KS, Roberts was born into a rodeo family – his father held rodeos on the family ranch, and Roberts's brother and sister won world championships in bull riding and bronco riding. Roberts won two all-around rodeo world titles, in 1942 (at the age of 22) and '48. After retiring, he was inducted into the Professional Rodeo Cowboys Association Hall of Fame and the National Cowboy Hall of Fame. He then went on to Hollywood, consulting on westerns and serving as a stunt double for such actors as Jack Lemmon and Glen Ford.

In Salina, Kans., of undisclosed causes, on December 31, 2004.

James Stillman Rockefeller, 102, rower.

Nearly three decades before he became the chairman of Citigroup and sat on numerous boards, the Yale varsity oarsman rowed to a gold medal in the eights at the Paris Games in 1924. SI writes:

"A true Eli, Rockefeller was more proud of beating Harvard in the '24 regatta, which landed him on the July 7, 1924 cover of Time. Rockefeller, a grandnephew of John D. Rockefeller, hung his gold medal on a nail to the side of his fireplace in his Greenwich, CT, home. Miffed that his medal was really made of bronze, Rockefeller had it gold plated. 'My grandfather was painfully modest,' his grandson Stillman Rockefeller says. 'It was so out of character for him to gild something.'"

In Greenwich, Conn., of a stroke, August 10, 2004.

Charlie Saikley, 69, volleyball player.

Saikley was often described as the godfather of beach volleyball. In 1960 the Terre Haute, Ind., native moved to Manhattan Beach, Calif., where he became a high school math and special education teacher and worked part time for the parks and recreation department. Beach volleyball was then little more than a casual Southern California pastime; Saikley began running the Manhattan Beach Open in '65, turning it into the country's biggest tournament.

In Manhattan Beach, Calif., of multiple myeloma, on June 17, 2005.

Johnny Sample, 67, football player. *SI writes:*

"Sample played in two of the NFL's most important games. As a rookie he played on the Baltimore Colt's team that won the 1958 Championship Game over the Giants, the first pro game to go into overtime. And in his final game he intercepted a pass in Superbowl III, helping the Jets upset the Colts. Sample picked off 41 passes in his career. After retiring, Sample – who was always outspoken, especially when it came to the treatment of African-American players in the NFL – wrote a controversial autobiography, 'Confessions of a Dirty Ballplayer.'"

In Philadelphia, of heart disease, on April 26, 2005.

Alex Shibicky, 91, hockey player.

Shibicky was the first player to use the slap shot in the NHL. Shibicky, who scored 110 goals in his 11-year career, learned the shot from teammate Bun Cook in practice and unveiled it during a game in 1937. Three years later he helped the Rangers win the Stanley Cup. He spent his later years in South Surrey, B.C., where he continued to be a student of the slapper. "I'm 90 years old, and I'll still go out there and demonstrate," he said last year. "I had it down to a science."

In South Surrey, British Columbia, from natural causes, on July 9, 2005.

Max Schmeling, 99, boxer. *It is ironic that the last famous German who is associated with the Third Reich to die was not a Nazi. But Max Schmeling,* *powerful and handsome, who finally passed on last week just months shy of his 100th birthday, was at once "the Heil Hitler hero" who brought the greatest sports glory to the Führer and a very conflicted, very human citizen who wrestled with the devil as often as he boxed with the world's best fighters. SI writes:*

"Schmeling is, of course, best known for his two fights with Joe Louis. In 1936, when the German was already 30 and supposed to be a washed-up pug, he handed the Brown Bomber his first defeat. Then, in 1938, Louis brutally reduced Schmeling to a gory pulp in less than two minutes. The fights themselves, though, were on the undercard to ideology, as Schmeling and Louis were generally portrayed as stand-ins for fascism and democracy."

"Schmeling actually came to fame before Hitler took power in 1933. A mere laborer who built up his mind as well as his body, Schmeling not only became heavyweight champion but also part of the racy Berlin avant-garde set. He married a beautiful movie star, Anny Ondra. Candidly, Schmeling would later admit to having turned his head to the obvious horrors around him. He met Hitler on several occasions, but he would not accept Hitler's Nazi Dagger of Honor and he refused to fire his Jewish-American manager, Joe Jacobs. At the very risk of his life he also hid two Jewish boys in his apartment on Kristallnacht, the brutal Nazi pogrom of 1938. This was after Louis had annihilated him and Schmeling was no longer a useful figure to the Nazis. They paid him back for his renegade ways by drafting him into the army when he was 34."

"Schmeling was wounded in 1941 while parachuting into Crete, but he survived to become an extremely wealthy businessman -- largely thanks to his holdings in that most American of companies: Coca-Cola. He became friends with his old foe, Louis, and often gave the indigent old champ money. No athlete ever so faced the ambiguities and dissonance of life as did Max Schmeling."

In Hollenstedt, Germany, of natural causes, on February 2, 2005.

Hank Stram, 82, football coach. *Inducted into the Pro Football Hall of Fame in 2003, Stram coached the Kansas City Chiefs to two Superbowls. SI's Paul Zimmerman remembers Hank Stram:*

I've often wondered how Hank Stram would have fit into this modern world of the NFL, this era of the buttoned-up coaches who might see fit to hold two or three 20-minute press conferences a week, who put their assistants off-limits, who act like they're finding a cure for cancer. He probably would have laughed himself sick. 'Come over here, siddown, what you want to know?'"

"How well I remember Hank, with his toupee and flamboyant red vest under his dark blazer, as he patrolled the sidelines, giggling, snapping off his one-liners. He liked action. He liked crowds ... and writers around him, plenty of them. The media circus was meat and potatoes for him."

"'Have writers ever cost us a game?' he said. 'Does it matter what's written? Well, yeah, it means something to me, because it helps me get my ideas across. The dumbest thing you can do is get mad at the press.'"

"And his ideas came pouring out like a flood after that 23-7 victory in Super Bowl IV. It had really been a triumph of that great K.C. defense, the innovation of the stacked linebackers, the odd front that allowed 270-pound Curley Culp to manhandle Minnesota's undersized center, Mick Tingelhoff. But it was Stram's offense that got all the ink."

"Who can forget him, miked on the sidelines ... 'It's like stealing out there!' when one of his wideouts caught

still another square-out underneath the Vikings corners, playing back? Or the three Frank Pitts end-arounds K.C. ran ... oh no, not again, it can't work again ... each one for good yardage. Or the sucker trap that gave little Mike Garrett a five-yard TD, the ultimate in flim-flammery, designed for the great pursuit of DT Alan Page. And of course Page took himself out of the play, following the guard who was pulling out -- to nowhere -- as Garrett walked in."

"Stram football. Trick-'em football. He liked to hide little backs in the slot, behind his monster linemen, and sneak them downfield as pass catchers. When Dawson was hurt during the Super Bowl season, Stram designed a rollout attack for his big, mobile rookie -- Mike Livingston, who won five games with it. So the tactic stayed in the playbook, only now it bore the name, "Moving Pocket," which became the watchword for Stram's phrase that swept the football world during the offseason: Football of the Seventies."

In New Orleans, La., of complications from diabetes, on July 4, 2005.

Justin Strzelczyk, 36, football player

An 11th round draft pick in 1990, Justin Strzelczyk played for the Steelers for nine seasons, but suffered a season-ending knee injury in October 1998. After re-injuring his knee, the Steelers released him in 2000.

After leading New York state troopers on a high speed chase, the former Steelers offensive lineman was killed in a fiery car crash. Strzelczyk, who resided in McCandless, PA, fled from police after being involved in two minor automobile accidents near Syracuse, NY. He refused to pull over -- police say he tossed a beer bottle at them -- and after 40 miles his truck rammed an oil tanker at nearly 90 mph. (The other driver suffered only minor injuries.) Strezlczyk had been arrested in 1999 after slamming a loaded pistol onto a bar during a political argument. 'I had seen trouble with his mood disorders coming,' said his mother, Mary Joyce Strzelczyk."

In Herkimer, N.Y., of injuries sustained in an automobile accident, September 29, 2004.

Chuck Thompson, 83, broadcaster

A Hall of Fame radio play-by-play man, Thompson began his career calling Orioles games after the team moved to Baltimore in 1955 and continued to do so until his retirement in 2000. Thompson also called Baltimore Colts games for 30 years and was known for saying "Ain't the beer cold!" after big plays. Nationals manager Frank Robinson, whose 500th home run was called by Thompson, "He made [fans] feel like they were at the ballpark, and that's not easy to do on radio." Thompson received the Ford C. Frick Award in 1993, becoming the 17th announcer to enter the broadcast wing of the Baseball Hall of Fame.

In Towson, MD, of a stroke, March 6, 2005.

Hunter S. Thompson, 67, journalist. *Thompson committed suicide at his Colorado home. SI writes:*

"Over a raucous career that he began as sports editor of the Eglin Air Force Base newspaper in Florida in 1956, Thompson wrote about sports and politics with an unpredictably personal style that changed American culture. Intrigued by the NFL, heavyweight fights and big-game fishing as well as presidential campaigns, Thompson ripped across a hilarious landscape of his own invention peopled with friends and admirers from Muhammad Ali, Kenny Stabler and Jim Irsay to Bill Clinton and Johnny Depp. His first book, Hell's Angels (published in 1966), earned him the title "quintessential outlaw journalist" and an assignment to cover Nevada's

Mint 400 motorcycle race for SPORTS ILLUSTRATED, ultimately resulting in Fear and Loathing in Las Vegas (1971), his "gonzo" masterpiece, which Tom Wolfe pronounced "a scorching, epochal sensation." Thompson went on to write a dozen more books, hundreds of magazine pieces and a long-running column for ESPN.com.

In Woody Creek, CO, by self-inflicted gunshot, February 20, 2005.

Dick Weber, 75, bowler. *A three- time Bowler of the Year, Dick Weber was a member of both the ABC and PBA halls of fame. SI writes:*

"Weber won't be remembered as the best bowler ever – he ranks seventh on the PBA Tour's career victories list with 26, and his contemporaries Don Carter ad Earl Anthony were at least as accomplished as he was. But the gentleman roller, was a peerless ambassador for his sport. Former American Bowling Congress Hall of Fame executive director Steve James said, "He was probably the best-known bowler worldwide." The former Indianapolis postal worker began bowling with a Budweiser-sponsored touring team in 1955. Three years later he helped fund the PBA, and the skinny right hander was a fixture on Saturday afternoon bowling broadcasts throughout the '60s and '70s."

"Over the last two decades, while his son Pete cultivated an image as the sport's bad boy, Weber stayed active on the PBA's Senior Tour. He also appeared often on David Letterman's show and bowled in exhibitions around the U.S. 'My life is bowling,' he said at a clinic in Akron on December 2004. 'And it has always been.'

In St. Louis, Mo, of natural causes, on February 13, 2005.

Reggie White, 43, football player. *White played 15 NFL seasons for the Eagles, Packers and Panthers, made 13 straight Pro Bowls, twice was named the NFL's Defensive Player of the Year and won Super Bowl XXXI with Green Bay in 1997. He was also a Baptist minister who helped inner-city children but at times angered people with derogatory remarks about gays and women. SI writes:*

"Lions coach Steve Mariucci was Green Bay's quarterbacks coach from 1992 to '95 and invited Reggie and his wife, Sara, to dinner. 'My boys were three, five and seven, and they wanted to play football with Reggie,' Mariucci recalls. 'He was tired from practice, but he said, 'Of course. Let's go.' He told them to get their friends for a game in the yard. There must have been a dozen kids. Reggie played quarterback for both teams, and I asked him to throw one to my youngest, Stephen. Boom! The pass hit Stephen in the nose. Stephen was really crying, mad. Reggie tried to console him and picked him up. Whammo! Stephen smacked him in the face with his elbow. Then he got down and ran into the house. Reggie spent the entire evening trying to get Stephen back on board. All night long Reggie tried to tickle him and giggle with him and make amends. Finally, after a couple hours, they were wrestling on the floor and having a good old time. Reggie was a big kid.'"

"Former Cardinals running back Ron Wolfley recalls an exchange between Cardinals QB Neil Lomax and White: After sacking Lomax, White looked down at him and said, 'Neil, Jesus loves you.' Lomax replied, 'I know. But what's your problem?'"

"The first time I saw Reggie play, in 1985, I said, 'This guy will be in the Hall of Fame," says Packers offensive line coach Larry Beightol. 'He was a phenom. Bigger, stronger, faster. The guy who did the best job on him was a rookie I had in Green Bay [White was with Carolina]

named Mark Tauscher. After the game Reggie came into our locker room and congratulated Tausch on a fine job. Another time, when I was with the Chargers, he came across the field and said, 'Coach, I would highly recommend that your players stop cutting me. If they don't, I'm going to have to take it out on you.' I immediately told the boys, 'Do not touch Reggie's legs any longer.'"

"Former NFL safety Eugene Robinson played with White in Green Bay and Carolina and was a pallbearer at his funeral as were other NFLers, including Michael Perry, Brett Favre, and Adrian Murrell. 'He was always playing practical jokes with the hot and cold in the shower," said Robinson. 'Then he would take a big wad of soap and, after you'd dried off, slap you in the back. You'd have to go back and wash off again. That's Reggie White.'"

In Huntersville, N.C., of respiratory ailment, on December 26, 2004.

Stanley Dancer, 78, harness racing driver. *SI writes:*

"Dancer was the face of harness racing during the sport's golden era in the 1960's and '70s, becoming its most successful driver, trainer, and owner. Beginning his career in 1945 , Dancer won 3,781 races and more than $28 million in purses, taking the trotting Triple Crown twice and the Triple Crown for pacers once before retiring 10 years ago. His aggressive style and indestructibility—he survived 32 spills on the track, plus four auto accidents as well as a helicopter and a plane crash—brought his face beyond racing. He made SI's cover in 1968, was friends with Mickey Mantle and Whitey Ford, appeared on The Ed Sullivan Show and was name-checked by Paul Simon in the song 'Groundhog.' "It breaks my heart that harness racing is not as popular as it once was," he said in 1995.

In Pompano Beach, Fla., of pneumonia, on September 9, 2005.

Chris Schenkel, 82, broadcaster. *The voice of professional bowling for 36 years, Schenkel had covered nearly every sport during his six-decade career from the first televised Masters (1956) to the historic 1958 NFL Championship game to several Olympics. In all, 16 different sports inducted him into their Halls-of-Fame. SI writes:*

"Born in Bippus, Ind., a farm town of 275, Schenkel had a genial, upbeat manner, the kind that made people want to invite him into their living room. Schenkel's stock in trade—a smooth, soothing baritone often prompted questions, however. "People say, 'How did you develop your voice?'" he told SI in 2004 "I tell them I didn't. I've had it since I was 12."

Despite his prolific career, his fame never changed him. In in 1973 his best friend, a dairyman named Rodger Nelson, told SI, "When he doesn't point out a missed tackle, it's not because he's a Pollyanna or because he's a dummy. It's because he knows that player's family might be watching. That's old-fashioned courtesy. Chris is an Indiana farm boy in the best sense of that term."

In Fort Wayne, Ind., of emphysema, on September 11, 2005.

Joe Bauman, 83, baseball player. *SI writes:*

"Bauman hit 72 home runs in 1954 for the Roswell (N.M.) Rockets of the Class C Longhorn League, a professional baseball record that stood until Barry Bonds hit 73 in 2001. A 6'5" 225-pound first-baseman, Bauman played nine minor league seasons without reaching the majors. "Joe didn't just hit 'em over the fences," said Floyd Economides, who played against Bauman. "He hit them over the lights."

In Roswell, N.M., of pneumonia, on Sept. 20, 2005.

2 0 0 6 M a j o r   E v e n t s

JANUARY

Major College Bowl Games	Jan 1–3
Rose Bowl/National Championship	Jan 4
NFL Wild-Card Playoffs	Jan 7 & 8
U.S. Figure Skating Championships	Jan 7–15
NFL Divisional Playoffs	Jan 14 & 15
Australian Open Tennis	Jan 16–29
NFL Conference Championships	Jan 22
NHL All-Star Game	Jan. 29

FEBRUARY

Millrose Games	Feb 3
Super Bowl XL	Feb 5
Winter Olympics	Feb 10–26
AFC-NFC Pro Bowl	Feb 12
NBA All-Star Game	Feb 19
Daytona 500	Feb 19

MARCH

World Baseball Classic	March 3–20
March Madness Begins	March 16
The Players Championship	March 23–26
PBA World Championship	March 29–April 11

APRIL

Major League Soccer Season Begins	April 1*
NCAA Men's Basketball Final Four	April 1 & 3
NCAA Women's Basketball Final Four	April 2 & 4
Baseball Opening Day	April 2*
NCAA Men's Hockey Frozen Four	April 6–8
Masters Tournament	April 6–9
NHL Playoffs Begin	April 11*
Boston Marathon	April 17
NBA Playoffs Begin	April 22
NFL Draft	April 29-30

MAY

Kentucky Derby	May 6
Preakness Stakes	May 20
NASCAR All-Star Challenge	May 20
Stanley Cup Finals Begin	May 23*
Indianapolis 500	May 28

JUNE

French Open Tennis	May 29–June 11
NBA Finals Begin	June 8*
FIFA World Cup	June 7–July 9
Belmont Stakes	June 10
U.S. Open Golf	June 15–18
College World Series	June 16–26
NBA Draft	June 27

JULY

Wimbledon Tennis	June 26–July 9
Baseball All-Star Game	July 11
British Open Golf	July 20–23
Tour de France	July 1–23

AUGUST

Brickyard 400	Aug 6
PGA Championship	Aug 17–20
College Football Season Begins	Aug 26*

SEPTEMBER

U.S. Open Tennis	Aug 28–Sept 10
NFL Season Begins	Sept 7
NASCAR Chase for the Cup Begins	Sept 17
Ryder Cup	Sept 21–24

OCTOBER

NHL Season Begins	Oct 3*
World Series Begins	Oct 21*
Breeders Cup	Oct 28*
NBA Regular Season Begins	Oct 31*

NOVEMBER

Women's Tennis Tour Championships	Nov 6–12*
New York Marathon	Nov 5
MLS Cup 2006	Nov 12*
Tennis Masters Cup	Nov 9–19
NASCAR Chase for the Cup Ends	Nov 19

DECEMBER

Heisman Trophy Presentation	Dec 9
Major College Bowl Games Begin	Dec 19*

* Approximate date.

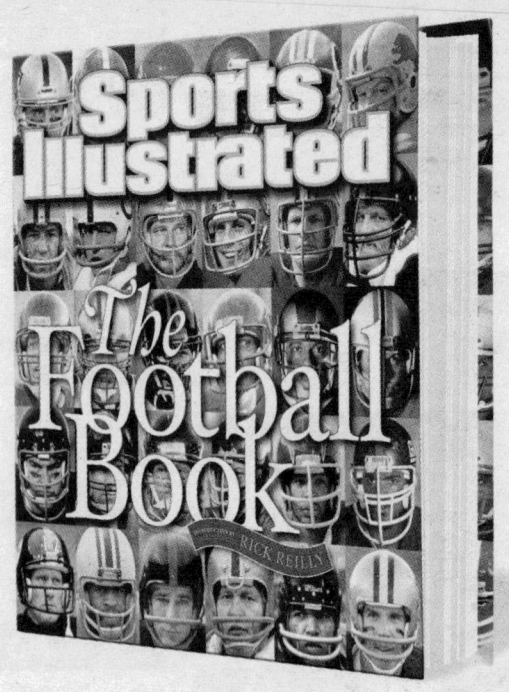